Your Starway to Love

An Astrological Guide to Relationships

Your Starway to Love

Easy Compatibility Analysis

Maritha Pottenger
Compiled and Programmed by
Rique Pottenger

International Standard Book Number 0-935127-22-4
Library of Congress Catalog Card Number 94-072199

Printed in the United States of America

Published by ACS Publications
P.O. Box 34487
San Diego, CA 92163-4487

Table of Contents

WHAT CAN YOU EXPECT FROM THIS BOOK?

Love assuredly makes the world go 'round. Few things are more important than the people to whom we give our hearts. A compatible romantic association helps make life rich, deep, exciting, and rewarding. A stressful relationship makes everything else more tense and uncomfortable.

Astrology can be a tool for understanding ourselves and the people we love. It can offer helpful hints for making the most of our relationships. Think of astrology as a mirror: a way to reflect back to us our strengths—and weaknesses—in terms of relating. Coming to terms with our conflicts, and learning to overcome them, is much easier if we can be a bit objective in that process. Astrology helps to provide that objective eye.

WHAT ASTROLOGY IS

Astrology is the art of examining the patterns in the heavens and how they correlate with patterns in people's lives and personalities. (If you wish more details about the specific tools of astrology—planets, houses, etc.—please see the Appendix.)

Astrology uses horoscopes: maps of the sky at the time and place of a person's birth. A complete horoscope would require your exact time (hour and minute), date (month, day and year) and place of birth. (Astrologers use the latitude and longitude of the birthplace in their calculations.) The patterns are so complex that they do not repeat for millions and millions of years. In order to have exactly the same horoscope as you, someone would have to be born the same minute, in the same place, as you were.

WHAT ASTROLOGY CAN (AND CANNOT) DO

Astrology can be a useful tool for understanding yourself better, for learning to make the most of your assets, and to compensate for your liabilities. It can offer similar insights into other people, and thus be useful in relationships. Astrology cannot find Prince or Princess Charming for you, but can help you see the strengths and potential weaknesses of someone you are considering. Astrology cannot give you "happily ever after," but can educate you about making the most of your opportunities, and learning to overcome possible challenges.

Astrology cannot guarantee perfection (or total unhappiness), but it can illustrate the highest (and lowest) potentials within a relationship. Each placement in astrology can be lived on the best (and on the worst) level. That choice is up to the person—free will. But knowing the possibilities can help you recognize them. Astrology often helps people to recognize—and use—talents and abilities which they had previously blocked. It is a way of validating your real self and what makes you special. It is a way of supporting the best in your partner, and helping to build on the best between you. Astrology cannot tell you everything you need to know about a potential relationship, but it can suggest areas which might be sensitive, where communication could be important, where conflicts might arise, and where you and a partner are most likely to support and affirm one another. It can point the way to greater love.

THIS BOOK USES ONLY PART OF A HOROSCOPE

Calculating an entire horoscope requires an exact birth time and extensive reference books (or a computer). It is not really feasible for a book such as this, where you need information quickly and easily. So, the astrology within this book is only a limited portion of your actual horoscope. (We hope that you will go further with the ancient wisdom of astrology. The Appendix offers some resources.) Although this limited portion of a horoscope will not give you the same degree of complexity and accuracy that your complete horoscope would, it can still give quite valuable information. It can reveal tendencies in terms of self-esteem, what nourishes you, where you seek security, how you attract others, what excites you, how you express yourself, and how you communicate. Naturally, the same information is available regarding potential partners.

DIVIDING UP THE TERRITORY

One important process that happens in lots of relationships requires a bit of discussion. Most people in relationships practice some kind of division of labor. For example, she cooks and he cleans up. Or, she fixes the car and he repairs the clothes. And so on. People also often divide up personality traits. For example, perhaps he tends to be a star, and she tends to be the audience. Perhaps he is the "strong, silent" type, and she likes to talk. And so on. If both people are content with such a division, and value the partner's contributions as much as their own, it can work very well. All too often, however, one partner feels that s/he is contributing much more than the other. Or, one partner feels that his/her personality trait is the "right" one and the other person should change to be like him/her. This is asking for trouble! Tolerance of each other's differences is vital in any healthy relationship.

Sometimes, such divisions are not really planned. They may even be unconscious. They might go back to childhood roots. Perhaps a woman was raised in a family that said women should not be assertive. Even though her personality style (and horoscope) are forceful, she may hold herself back. Instead, she may be attracted to a man who is very strong, aggressive, driving and demanding. He can live out (but in an excessive way) what she cannot (or will not) allow herself to express.

When people find themselves in relationships which involve **extremes** of personality or division of labor, it is often a sign that both partners are denying a part of themselves and living it out through the other. The person who consistently attracts selfish, self-centered, arrogant partners is probably inhibiting his/her own ability to put the self first, to be clear about what s/he wants and needs. The person who over and over again attracts partners who are unavailable or unwilling to commit, is probably suppressing his/her own fear of commitment, desire for freedom, urge to be separate—and instead, is letting a partner live it out. The person who attracts one dictatorial partner after another is probably denying his/her own desire for authority and control—and living it out through the partners.

YOU MAY NOT IDENTIFY WITH EVERYTHING YOU READ

Be aware as you read the interpretations in this book that people often do suppress parts of themselves in relationships—or choose partners to express something they deny within themselves. It is not uncommon for a couple to have a seesaw relationship—each doing an extreme opposite of the other's position. If they see themselves as two halves of a whole, and are happy, all is well. If they feel frustrated by the extremes, it is time to try a middle position! Sometimes you will identify with the descriptions you read in *Your Starway to Love*. Sometimes you will feel "We are just the reverse of that!" That is quite possible. But even if you have reversed the roles, the issue is still relevant for you. Finding the balance point—the golden mean between two extremes—is still a challenge in your relationship.

Sometimes your partner may be expressing qualities which your horoscope suggests are yours. Perhaps you have divided up the territory. If you admire those qualities, realize that you too have those abilities! Own your skills and begin to use them. If you are irritated with your partner's expression, perhaps you two have fallen into a seesaw relationship—between extremes. Each of you needs to find ways to move more to the middle, to each do a little bit (but in moderation—not in an extreme form) of what the other person is doing. The more you can compromise and meet in the middle, the more love will flourish and your relationship will grow.

"HIS" OR "HER" IN THIS BOOK

Writing an entire book about relationships without using pronouns (he or she, his or her, etc.) is very awkward. Writing "your partner" all the time gets old very fast! So, for convenience, the astrological descriptions in this book have been written from the point of view of a female reader who is reading about a male partner. **Please note** that the descriptions are accurate for each astrological combination discussed. **You can change any of the pronouns**. It does not matter whether you are a male or a female reader, whether your partner is male or female. If you are combining your placements with a female partner's, please just change all the male pronouns to female ones in your mind. Thanks!

HOW TO USE THIS BOOK

We know you're eager to get into the actual descriptions. Indeed, we're sure some readers have already leapt ahead and read some of the combinations between their planets and a partner's planets. That's great. We're happy you're eager for information.

To use this book and its companion volume most fully, we suggest you get out a worksheet from the back of the book and follow the instructions beginning on the next page. ***If you do not know the time of birth of yourself or your partner, or if you want a rapid analysis, use the Quick Compatibility Worksheet.*** If you want every single detail (and know both birth times), use the Comprehensive Compatibility Worksheet. This will take you through each step in order to ensure you get a complete picture.

May the insights within these volumes prove valuable for you and your partner. May your love life flourish, and happiness be a constant companion as you travel the Road of Life!

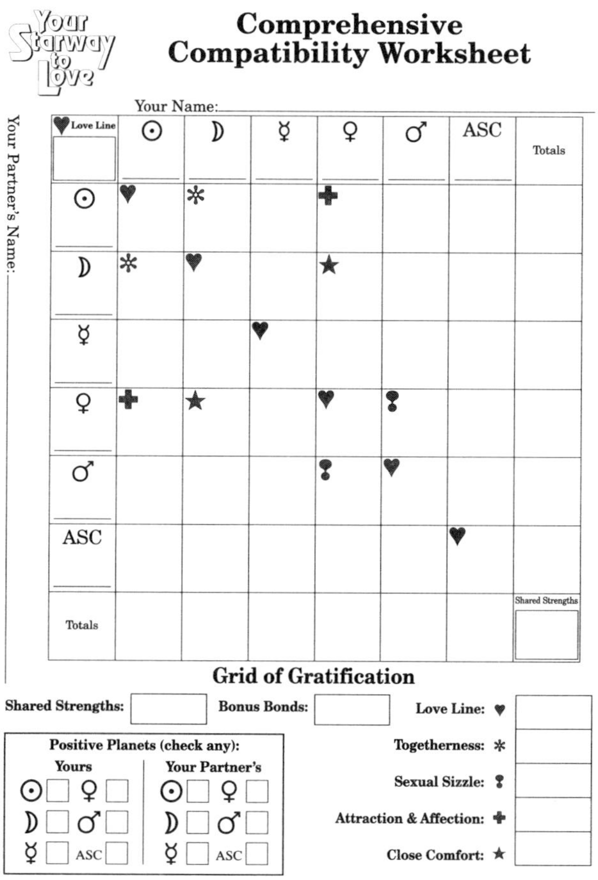

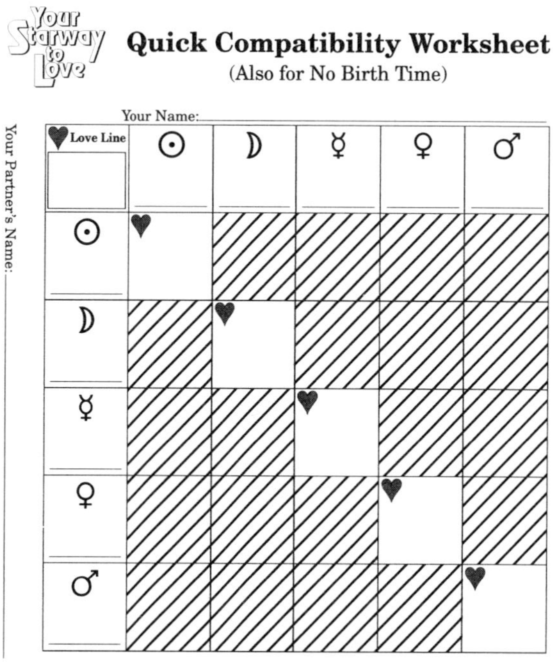

HOW TO FILL IN YOUR WORKSHEET

The instructions which follow use the example of Paul Newman and Joanne Woodward to help illustrate each step. Follow the procedures with your own birth information and that of your partner.

STEP ONE:

Write your name in the space provided at the top of the worksheet and your partner's name in the space along the left side. Open this book to the section titled **Planetary Positions** (pages 299–400). Find the page on which your year of birth appears. Then locate the month and the day on which you were born.

With the example of Paul Newman and Joanne Woodward, Joanne Woodward was born February 27, 1930. So, for her, we would turn to page 329 (the year 1930) and find the row for February 27. Paul Newman was born January 26,1925.

1930

February

Day	☉	☿	♀	♂
1	12♒	22♑	10♒	26♑
2	13♒	22♑	12♒	26♑
3	14♒	22♑	13♒	27♑
4	15♒	22♑	14♒	28♑
5	16♒	23♑	15♒	29♑
6	17♒	23♑	17♒	0♒
7	18♒	23♑	18♒	0♒
8	19♒	24♑	19♒	1♒
9	20♒	25♑	20♒	2♒
10	21♒	25♑	22♒	3♒
11	22♒	26♑	23♒	3♒
12	23♒	27♑	24♒	4♒
13	24♒	28♑	25♒	5♒
14	25♒	29♑	27♒	6♒
15	26♒	0♒	28♒	7♒
16	27♒	1♒	29♒	7♒
17	28♒	2♒	0♓	8♒
18	29♒	3♒	2♓	9♒
19	0♓	4♒	3♓	10♒
20	1♓	5♒	4♓	10♒
21	2♓	6♒	5♓	11♒
22	3♓	8♒	7♓	12♒
23	4♓	9♒	8♓	13♒
24	5♓	10♒	9♓	14♒
25	6♓	11♒	10♓	14♒
26	7♓	13♒	12♓	15♒
27	**8♓**	**14♒**	**13♓**	**16♒**
28	9♓	15♒	14♓	17♒

1925

January

Day	☉	☿	♀	♂
1	10♑	29♐	13♐	8♈
2	11♑	29♐	14♐	8♈
3	12♑	28♐	15♐	9♈
4	13♑	27♐	17♐	10♈
5	14♑	27♐	18♐	10♈
6	15♑	27♐	19♐	11♈
7	16♑	27♐	20♐	11♈
8	17♑	27♐	22♐	12♈
9	18♑	27♐	23♐	13♈
10	19♑	27♐	24♐	13♈
11	20♑	28♐	25♐	14♈
12	22♑	29♐	27♐	15♈
13	23♑	29♐	28♐	15♈
14	24♑	0♑	29♐	16♈
15	25♑	1♑	0♑	16♈
16	26♑	2♑	2♑	17♈
17	27♑	3♑	3♑	18♈
18	28♑	4♑	4♑	18♈
19	29♑	5♑	5♑	19♈
20	0♒	6♑	7♑	20♈
21	1♒	7♑	8♑	20♈
22	2♒	8♑	9♑	21♈
23	3♒	9♑	10♑	22♈
24	4♒	10♑	12♑	22♈
25	5♒	12♑	13♑	23♈
26	**6♒**	**13♑**	**14♑**	**23♈**
27	7♒	14♑	15♑	24♈
28	8♒	16♑	17♑	25♈
29	9♒	17♑	18♑	25♈
30	10♒	18♑	19♑	26♈
31	11♒	20♑	20♑	27♈

STEP TWO:

Note on the worksheet (across the top row) the symbol for the sign of the zodiac occupied by the Sun (☉), Mercury (☿), Venus (♀) and Mars (♂). A key for the symbols of the zodiac appears at the top of each set of facing pages. Also note down the number of degrees each planet occupies in its sign. Then follow the same procedure to note (down the leftmost column) the number of degrees and the signs of your partner's Sun, Mercury, Venus and Mars.

Joanne Woodward has her Sun at 8 degrees of the sign Pisces (♓), her Mercury at 14 degrees of the sign Aquarius (♒), her Venus at 13 degrees of the sign Pisces (♓), and her Mars at 16 degrees of the sign Aquarius (♒).

Paul Newman's Sun is at 6 degrees of the sign Aquarius (♒), his Mercury is at 13 degrees of the sign Capricorn (♑), his Venus is at 14 degrees of the sign Capricorn (♑), and his Mars is at 23 degrees of the sign Aries (♈).

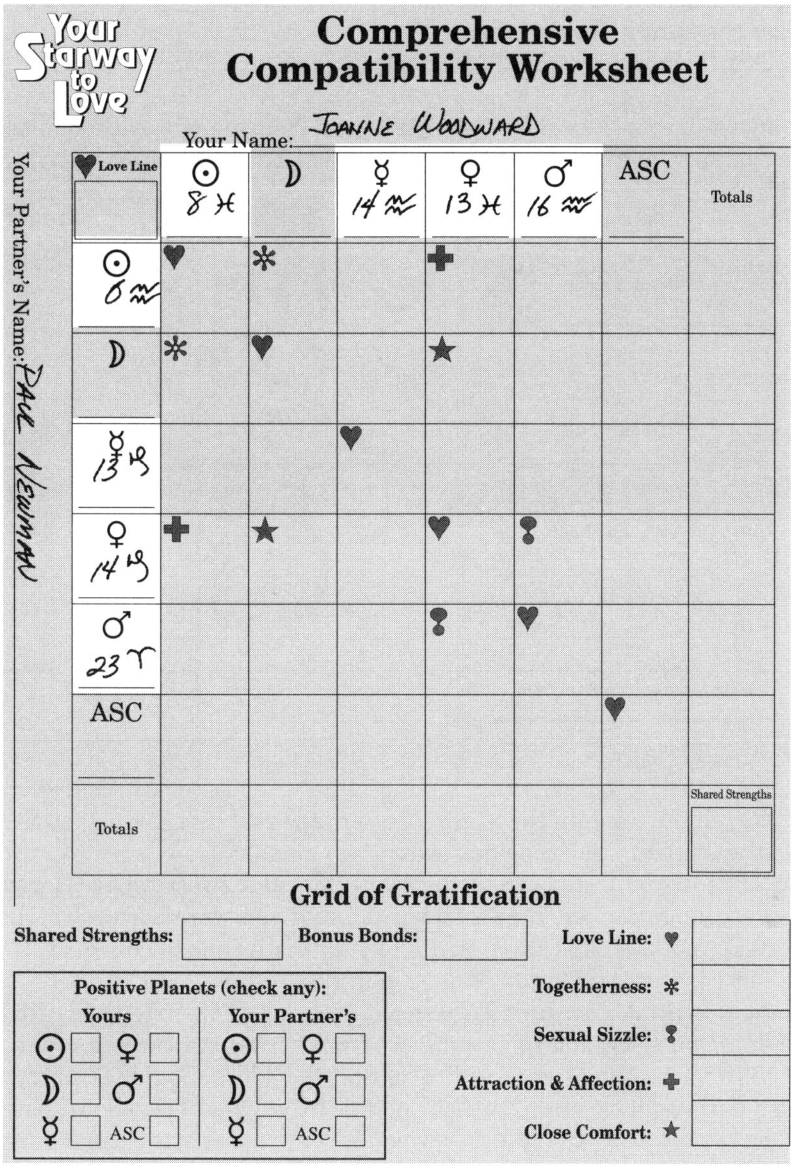
Your Starway to Love
Comprehensive Compatibility Worksheet
Your Name: JOANNE WOODWARD
Your Partner's Name: PAUL NEWMAN
Love Line
ASC
Totals
8 ♓
14 ♒
13 ♓
16 ♒
8 ♒
13 ♑
14 ♑
23 ♈
Shared Strengths
Grid of Gratification
Shared Strengths:
Bonus Bonds:
Love Line:
Togetherness:
Sexual Sizzle:
Attraction & Affection:
Close Comfort:
Positive Planets (check any):
Yours
Your Partner's

STEP THREE:

Turn to the section called **Moon Movements** (pages 401–504). Again, find your year, then your month, and then your day of birth. If only one sign is given that day, that sign is the sign of your Moon. Note it on the worksheet. If one sign appears on your birthday, but a time of day is printed with a second sign after it, then the Moon changed signs on your birthday. All times listed in this section are **Eastern Standard Time**. (See **Important Note** on the next page.) If you were born before the time listed, your Moon is in the first sign printed. Note that on the worksheet. If you were born after the time listed, your Moon is in the second sign printed. Note that on the worksheet. Repeat this procedure for your partner.

For the Quick Compatibility Worksheet, if the Moon changes sign on your birthday (or your partner's) and you don't have a known birth time, turn to pages 74-75. Read the

descriptions of the two Moon signs and choose the one which best fits you or your partner. Put that sign on the Quick Worksheet.

Joanne Woodward was born at 4:00 AM Eastern Standard Time in Georgia. Her Moon is in Aquarius.

Paul Newman was born 6:30 AM Eastern Standard Time in Ohio. Although the Moon started out in Aquarius that day, by the time Paul Newman was born, the Moon was in Pisces.

1930

February			
1	♓		
2	♓	7:23 pm	♈
3	♈		
4	♈		
5	♈	4:49 am	♉
6	♉		
7	♉	11:08 am	♊
8	♊		
9	♊	1:55 pm	♋
10	♋		
11	♋	2:00 pm	♌
12	♌		
13	♌	1:14 pm	♍
14	♍		
15	♍	1:50 pm	♎
16	♎		
17	♎	5:45 pm	♏
18	♏		
19	♏		
20	♏	1:49 am	♐
21	♐		
22	♐	1:13 pm	♑
23	♑		
24	♑		
25	♑	1:57 am	♒
26	♒		
27	**♒**	**2:13 pm**	**♓**
28	♓		

1925

January			
1	♈		
2	♈		
3	♈	6:31 am	♉
4	♉		
5	♉	5:52 pm	♊
6	♊		
7	♊		
8	♊	6:32 am	♋
9	♋		
10	♋	7:14 pm	♌
11	♌		
12	♌		
13	♌	6:55 am	♍
14	♍		
15	♍	4:33 pm	♎
16	♎		
17	♎	11:11 pm	♏
18	♏		
19	♏		
20	♏	2:34 am	♐
21	♐		
22	♐	3:22 am	♑
23	♑		
24	♑	3:09 am	♒
25	♒		
26	**♒**	**3:46 am**	**♓**
27	♓		
28	♓	6:59 am	♈
29	♈		
30	♈	1:58 pm	♉
31	♉		

IMPORTANT NOTE: the times in the **Moon Movements** tables are Eastern Standard Time. If you were born in the Central Time zone (midwest), you must add one hour to convert your time of birth to Eastern Time. If you were born in the Mountain zone (western area), you must add two hours to your birth time to convert it to Eastern Time. If you were born in the Pacific zone (the Pacific Coast states), you must add three hours to your birth time to convert it to Eastern Time.

If you were not born in the United States, you must adjust your birth time to its Eastern Standard equivalent. In the **Ascendant Tables** section (pages 542-567), the "→EST" column gives the number of hours you must add to or subtract from your birth time in order to convert it to Eastern Standard Time. A minus sign (-) indicates that the hours should be subtracted; otherwise, add the hours listed. If you have more hours to subtract than your birth hour, borrow one day (24 hours). You will have to identify the zone involved for some areas as we cannot list every possible city. The international tables are organized alphabetically by country, then by city within each country. The U.S. tables are alphabetical by state and then city.

Occasionally, by converting to Eastern Standard Time, birth times will actually shift to the next day (some American births) or to the previous day (some international births). **The day on which your birth time falls in Eastern Standard Time is the day that should be used when looking up your Moon sign.**

EXAMPLE: Phillis Schlafly was born in St. Louis, MO on August 15, 1924 at 11:25PM CST. We must **add** one hour to convert to Eastern Standard Time. Her converted birth time is 12:25AM on **August 16**. Therefore, we would look at August 16 to determine her Moon sign.

If you were born at a time when daylight savings was in effect (usually from late April to early October), you must subtract one hour to convert your time of birth to **standard** time. If you were born at a time when war time was in effect (around 1917-1918 and 1942-1945 in the United States), you must subtract one hour to convert your time of birth to **standard** time.

If you are unsure about your time of birth and two Moon signs are possible, read the descriptions of the two Moon signs involved (pages 86-87) and choose the one you feel is more likely yours.

STEP FOUR:

If you are using the Quick Compatibility Worksheet, skip Step Four.

Turn to the section called **What Was Rising?** (pages 505–540). First, convert your time of birth to the 24-hour clock. If you were born in the morning (AM), do nothing. If you were born in the PM, add 12 hours to your birth time. (For example, 2:00 PM becomes 14:00.) If Daylight Savings Time or War Time was in effect when you were born, subtract one hour to convert your time to standard time.

Next, look up your date of birth in the **Sidereal Time Tables** (pages 507–540) and note down the time listed for your date and year of birth. Add together your birth time and the sidereal time for your date of birth. Remember that you are adding hours and minutes to each other. (The number before the colon(:) is hours, the number after is minutes.) If the answer has more than 60 minutes, subtract 60 minutes and add one hour. For example: 10:57 (AM) + 6:41 (sidereal time) = 16:98 which is 17:38 (17 hours and 38 minutes into the day or 5:38 PM) If the sum is greater than 24 hours, subtract 24 hours. This is your **Star Time**.

For Joanne Woodward, we find February 27, 1930 in the **Sidereal Time Tables** and get: 10:24. She was born 4:00 AM, so her 24-hour time is also 4:00. She was born during Eastern Standard Time so no adjustment is necessary for Daylight or War Time. When we add together 4:00 (her birth time) and 10:24 (her sidereal time), we get 14:24 for her **Star Time**.

1930	Jan	Feb	Mar
1	6:40	8:42	10:32
2	6:44	8:46	10:36
3	6:48	8:50	10:40
4	6:52	8:54	10:44
5	6:55	8:58	10:48
6	6:59	9:02	10:52
7	7:03	9:06	10:56
8	7:07	9:10	11:00
9	7:11	9:13	11:04
10	7:15	9:17	11:08
11	7:19	9:21	11:12
12	7:23	9:25	11:16
13	7:27	9:29	11:20
14	7:31	9:33	11:24
15	7:35	9:37	11:27
16	7:39	9:41	11:31
17	7:43	9:45	11:35
18	7:47	9:49	11:39
19	7:51	9:53	11:43
20	7:55	9:57	11:47
21	7:59	10:01	11:51
22	8:02	10:05	11:55
23	8:06	10:09	11:59
24	8:10	10:13	12:03
25	8:14	10:17	12:07
26	8:18	10:20	12:11
27	8:22	10:24	12:15
28	8:26	10:28	12:19
29	8:30		12:23
30	8:34		12:27
31	8:38		12:31

1925	Jan	Feb	Mar
1	6:41	8:43	10:33
2	6:44	8:47	10:37
3	6:48	8:51	10:41
4	6:52	8:55	10:45
5	6:56	8:59	10:49
6	7:00	9:02	10:53
7	7:04	9:06	10:57
8	7:08	9:10	11:01
9	7:12	9:14	11:05
10	7:16	9:18	11:09
11	7:20	9:22	11:13
12	7:24	9:26	11:16
13	7:28	9:30	11:20
14	7:32	9:34	11:24
15	7:36	9:38	11:28
16	7:40	9:42	11:32
17	7:44	9:46	11:36
18	7:48	9:50	11:40
19	7:51	9:54	11:44
20	7:55	9:58	11:48
21	7:59	10:02	11:52
22	8:03	10:06	11:56
23	8:07	10:09	12:00
24	8:11	10:13	12:04
25	8:15	10:17	12:08
26	8:19	10:21	12:12
27	8:23	10:25	12:16
28	8:27	10:29	12:20
29	8:31		12:24
30	8:35		12:27
31	8:39		12:31

For Paul Newman, we find January 26, 1925 in the **Sidereal Time Tables** and get a sidereal time of 8:19. His birth time is 6:30 AM EST, so we make no changes for the 24-hour clock, Daylight Savings or War Time. Adding together his sidereal time and birth time, we get a **star time** for Paul Newman of 14:49.

Then, go to the **Ascendant Tables** (pages 543-567). Find the table which includes the country and then the city in which you were born. (These tables cover the United States first; then other countries are listed alphabetically. Within the United States, the states are listed alphabetically, with cities in alpha order within each state.)

Each sign (♈ through ♓) has a column of its own. In each column, the Star Time when that sign was rising is listed. Opposite your city of birth, find the Star Time just **before** your Star Time of birth (Confirm that the next time listed is **after** your Star Time.) The sign at the top of the column with the time **before** your birth time is your **Ascendant** (Rising Sign).

If your city of birth is not listed, look up the closest city. If you are unsure of your time, read the descriptions of Ascendants (pages 128-129) and choose the one which sounds most like you. Note your Ascendant sign and your partner's Ascendant sign, in the box marked ASC on the worksheet.

Joanne Woodward's **star time** is 14:24. Her city of birth (Thomasville, GA) is not large enough to be included in our list of Georgia cities. We note (by checking a map or calling our local library) that Thomasville is about halfway between the cities of Bainbridge and Valdosta.

Both of these cities show a **star time** just prior to Joanne's in the Capricorn (♑) column. (Capricorn rose at 13:39 in Bainbridge and at 13:33 in Valdosta.) To verify this, we check the next column (♒) and see that Aquarius did not rise until well after Joanne was born.

Therefore, Joanne Woodward has a Capricorn Ascendant.

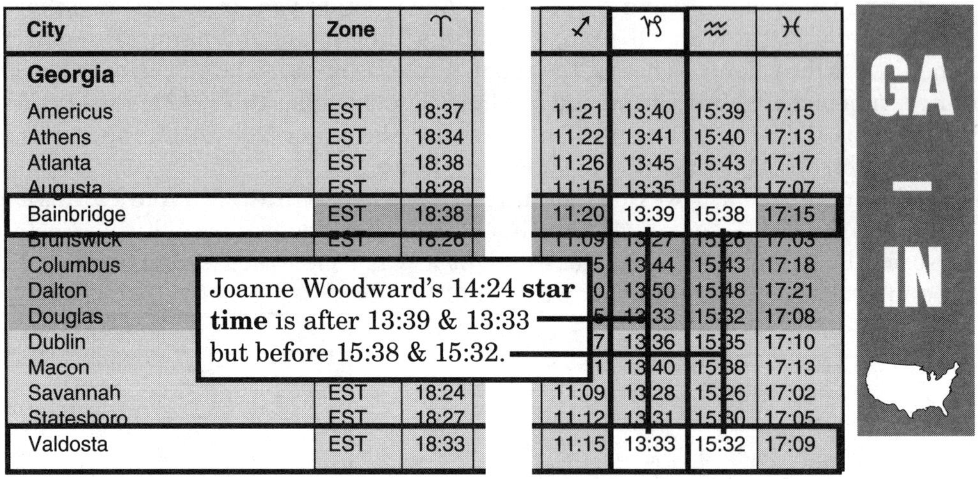
City | Zone | ♈ | ♐ | ♑ | ♒ | ♓
Georgia
Americus | EST | 18:37 | 11:21 | 13:40 | 15:39 | 17:15
Athens | EST | 18:34 | 11:22 | 13:41 | 15:40 | 17:13
Atlanta | EST | 18:38 | 11:26 | 13:45 | 15:43 | 17:17
Bainbridge | EST | 18:38 | 11:20 | 13:39 | 15:38 | 17:15
Columbus
Dalton
Douglas
Dublin
Macon
Savannah | EST | 18:24 | 11:09 | 13:28 | 15:26 | 17:02
Valdosta | EST | 18:33 | 11:15 | 13:33 | 15:32 | 17:09
Joanne Woodward's 14:24 star time is after 13:39 & 13:33 but before 15:38 & 15:32.
GA – IN

When we take Paul Newman's **star time** of 14:49 to the Ascendant Tables, along with Cleveland, Ohio (his birthplace), we find that at 14:49 **star time** on January 26, 1925 (in Cleveland), the sign of Capricorn was also rising (on his Ascendant).

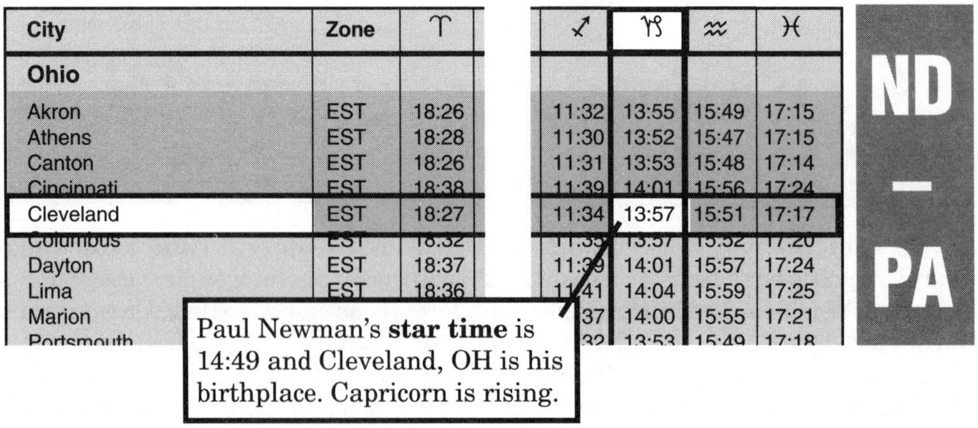
City | Zone | ♈ | ♐ | ♑ | ♒ | ♓
Ohio
Akron | EST | 18:26 | 11:32 | 13:55 | 15:49 | 17:15
Athens | EST | 18:28 | 11:30 | 13:52 | 15:47 | 17:15
Canton | EST | 18:26 | 11:31 | 13:53 | 15:48 | 17:14
Cleveland | EST | 18:27 | 11:34 | 13:57 | 15:51 | 17:17
Dayton | EST | 18:37 | 14:01 | 15:57 | 17:24
Lima | 14:04 | 15:59 | 17:25
Marion | 14:00 | 15:55 | 17:21
Paul Newman's star time is 14:49 and Cleveland, OH is his birthplace. Capricorn is rising.
ND – PA

At this point, you have recorded the signs and degrees for both your and your partner's Sun, Mercury, Venus, and Mars. You have recorded the sign of your Moon and Ascendant and of your partner's Moon and Ascendant (but no number of degrees for either the Moon or Ascendant).

You are ready to begin completing the **Grid of Gratification** on your **Compatibility Worksheet**.

STEP FIVE:

Below, you see a grid made up of a number of little boxes. By now, you have filled in the astrological symbols for each of your planetary placements, and for each of your partner's planetary placements (from positions given in **Planetary Positions**).

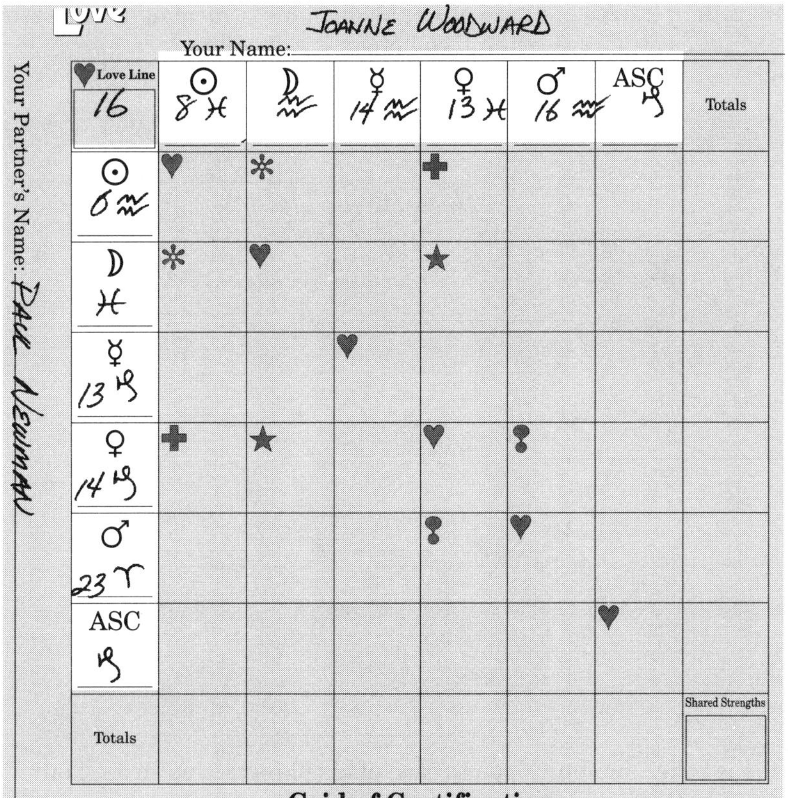

Grid of Gratification

STEP SIX:

Referring to the **Table of Compatibilities** on page 14, find the score which is given to your Sun Sign with his Sun Sign. Put that number in the box immediately below the symbol for your Sun and immediately to the right of the symbol of the Sun for him.

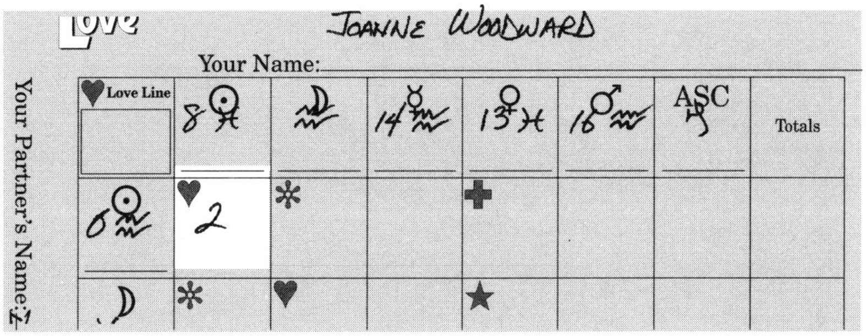

If you're using the Quick Compatibility Worksheet, also fill in the box below your Moon and to the right of your partner's Moon. Continue with your Mercury to your partner's Mercury; your Venus to your partner's Venus and your Mars to your partner's Mars. You will have a number in each of the five boxes marked with a heart. Skip to Step Seven.

Follow the same procedure for your Sun to his Moon (putting the number in the box below your Sun and to the right of the symbol for his Moon). Record the score for your Sun to his Mercury in the box below the symbol for your Sun and to the right of the symbol for his Mercury. Note the score for your Sun to his Venus in the box below your Sun and to the right of his Venus, etc. Once you have completed scoring your Sun with each of his "planets," the left-hand column is filled in. (For convenience, we are calling the Ascendant and the Moon planets, although the Ascendant is really a point where two great circles intersect and the Moon is a satellite.)

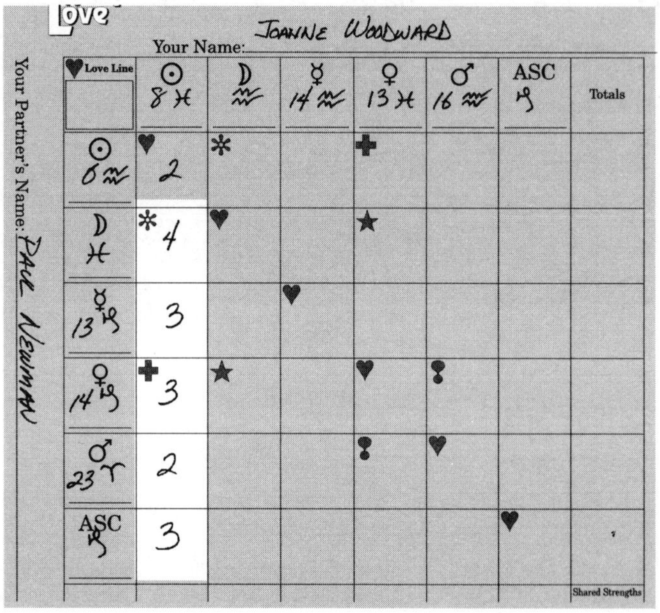
Love

Your Name: JOANNE WOODWARD

Your Partner's Name: PAUL NEWMAN

♥ Love Line	☉ 8♓	☽ ♒	☿ 14♒	♀ 13♓	♂ 16♒	ASC ♑	Totals
☉ 6♒	♥ 2	✱		✚			
☽ ♓	✱ 4	♥		★			
☿ 13♑	3		♥				
♀ 14♑	✚ 3	★		♥	❢		
♂ 23♈	2			❢	♥		
ASC ♑	3					♥	
							Shared Strengths

Next, complete the boxes for your Moon to each of his planets, and so on. Your Moon scores to each of his planets fill in the column which is second from the left.

When you have finished, you will have inserted 36 scores into the grid. (You do not have to look up his Sun to your Sun, because it is the same compatibility score, whether you look up yours first or his first.)

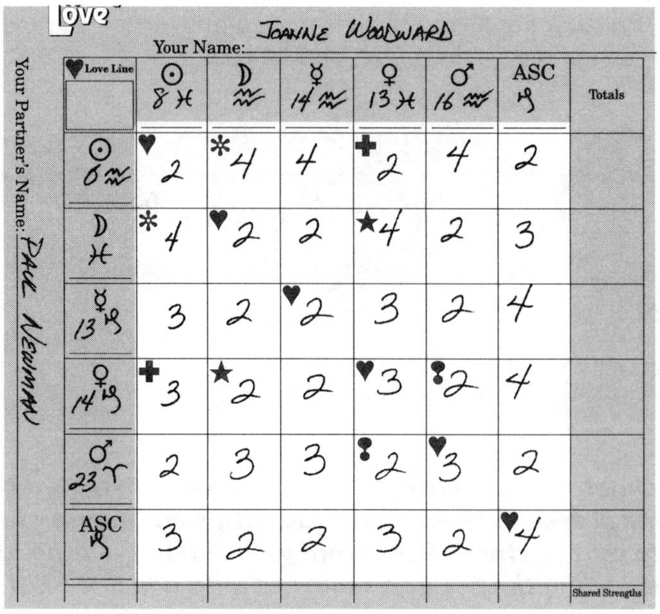
Love

Your Name: JOANNE WOODWARD

Your Partner's Name: PAUL NEWMAN

♥ Love Line	☉ 8♓	☽ ♒	☿ 14♒	♀ 13♓	♂ 16♒	ASC ♑	Totals
☉ 6♒	♥ 2	✱ 4	4	✚ 2	4	2	
☽ ♓	✱ 4	♥ 2	2	★ 4	2	3	
☿ 13♑	3	2	♥ 2	3	2	4	
♀ 14♑	✚ 3	★ 2	2	♥ 3	❢ 2	4	
♂ 23♈	2	3	3	❢ 2	♥ 3	2	
ASC ♑	3	2	2	3	2	♥ 4	
							Shared Strengths

STEP SEVEN:

Notice the boxes with hearts in them which run diagonally through the grid. These six scores (the Sun/Sun pairs; Moon/Moon pairs; Mercury/Mercury pairs; Venus/Venus pairs; Mars/Mars pairs; and Ascendant/Ascendant pairs) constitute your **Love Line**. Add them up. (If you hate math, now is the time to get out your calculator.) Note your score in the two boxes marked **Love Line**.

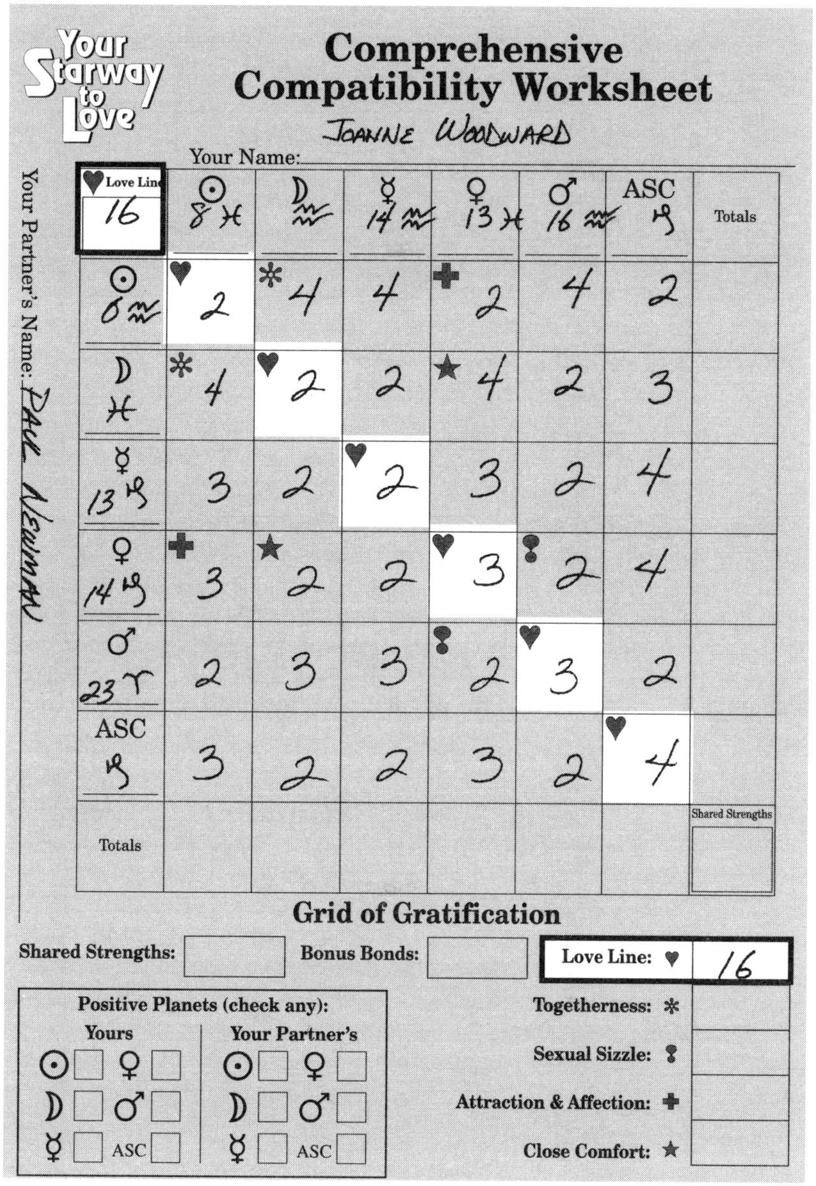

Your Starway to Love

Comprehensive Compatibility Worksheet

Your Name: JOANNE WOODWARD

Your Partner's Name: PAUL NEWMAN

♥ Love Line: 16	☉ 8 ♓	☽ ♒	☿ 14 ♒	♀ 13 ♓	♂ 16 ♒	ASC ♑	Totals
☉ 8 ♒	♥ 2	✻ 4	4	✚ 2	4	2	
☽ ♓	✻ 4	♥ 2	2	★ 4	2	3	
☿ 13 ♑	3	2	♥ 2	3	2	4	
♀ 14 ♑	✚ 3	★ 2	2	♥ 3	❢ 2	4	
♂ 23 ♈	2	3	3	❢ 2	♥ 3	2	
ASC ♑	3	2	2	3	2	♥ 4	
Totals							Shared Strengths

Grid of Gratification

Shared Strengths: [ ] Bonus Bonds: [ ] Love Line: ♥ 16

Positive Planets (check any):

Yours	Your Partner's
☉ ☐ ♀ ☐	☉ ☐ ♀ ☐
☽ ☐ ♂ ☐	☽ ☐ ♂ ☐
☿ ☐ ASC ☐	☿ ☐ ASC ☐

Togetherness: ✻

Sexual Sizzle: ❢

Attraction & Affection: ✚

Close Comfort: ★

If you are completing the Quick Compatibility Worksheet, you're done! Turn to page 16 to find out what it all means.

STEP EIGHT:

Add up each of the six rows and each of the six columns in the grid. Each row contains the scores of **one** of his planets to your six. Each column contains the scores for one of your planets to his six. When you are finished, you will have a total (the bottom of each column) for your Sun, your Moon, your Mercury, your Venus, your Mars, and your Ascendant.

Love

Your Name: Joanne Woodward

Your Partner's Name: Paul Newman

♥ Love Line 16	☉ 8 ♓	☽ ♒	☿ 14 ♒	♀ 13 ♓	♂ 16 ♒	ASC ♑	Totals
☉ 6 ♒	♥ 2	* 4	4	+ 2	4	2	
☽ ♓	* 4	♥ 2	2	★ 4	2	3	
☿ 13 ♑	3	2	♥ 2	3	2	4	
♀ 14 ♑	+ 3	★ 2	2	♥ 3	❢ 2	4	
♂ 23 ♈	2	3	3	❢ 2	♥ 3	2	
ASC ♑	3	2	2	3	2	♥ 4	
Totals	17	15	15	17	15	19	Shared Strengths

Grid of Gratification

You will also have a total (the far right of each row) for each of your partner's six planets.

Love

Your Name: Joanne Woodward

Your Partner's Name: Paul Newman

♥ Love Line 16	☉ 8 ♓	☽ ♒	☿ 14 ♒	♀ 13 ♓	♂ 16 ♒	ASC ♑	Totals
☉ 6 ♒	♥ 2	* 4	4	+ 2	4	2	18
☽ ♓	* 4	♥ 2	2	★ 4	2	3	17
☿ 13 ♑	3	2	♥ 2	3	2	4	16
♀ 14 ♑	+ 3	★ 2	2	♥ 3	❢ 2	4	16
♂ 23 ♈	2	3	3	❢ 2	♥ 3	2	15
ASC ♑	3	2	2	3	2	♥ 4	16
Totals	17	15	15	17	15	19	Shared Strengths 98

Grid of Gratification

STEP NINE:

Add together the six totals (for you) from Step Eight. Also add your partner's six totals together. You should come up with the same number. (If not, check your math.) That number is your **Shared Strengths**. Note your score in the boxes marked **Shared Strengths**.

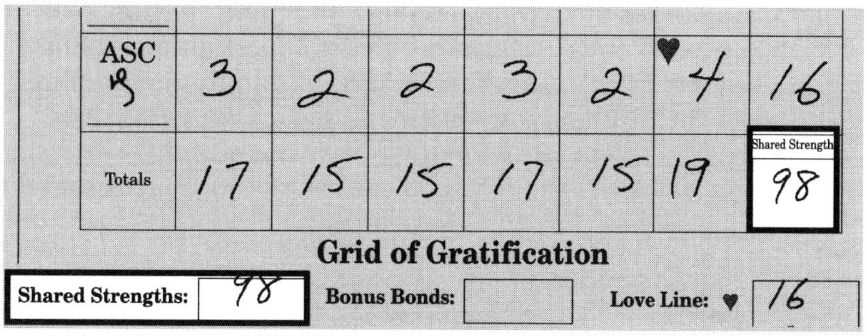

ASC ♑	3	2	2	3	2	♥ 4	16
Totals	17	15	15	17	15	19	Shared Strengths 98

Grid of Gratification

Shared Strengths: 98 Bonus Bonds: Love Line: ♥ 16

STEP TEN:

Check to see if any of the six totals (from Step Eight) are 15 or higher. If so, make a note on the worksheet of which planet (and for which person) had a score of 15 or above. Those planets are listed as **Positive Planets.**

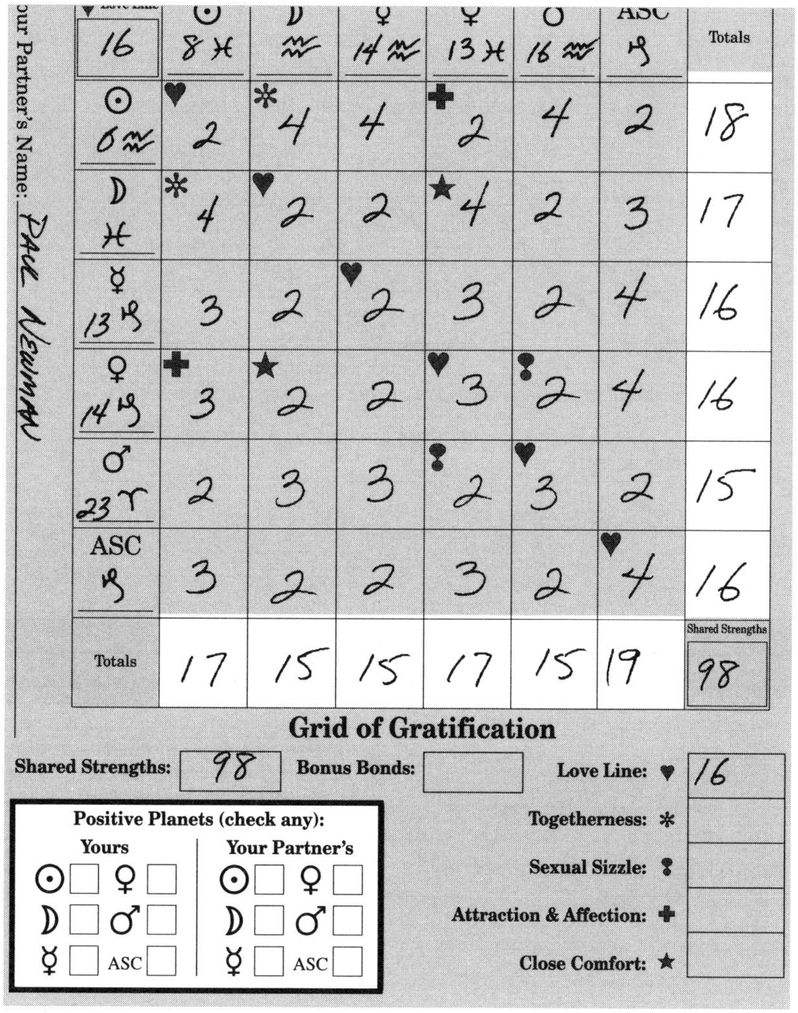

our Partner's Name: PAUL NEWMAN

♥ Love Line 16	☉ 8♓	☽ ♒	☿ 14♒	♀ 13♓	♂ 16♒	ASC ♑	Totals
☉ 6♒	♥ 2	✻ 4	4	✚ 2	4	2	18
☽ ♓	✻ 4	♥ 2	2	★ 4	2	3	17
☿ 13♑	3	2	♥ 2	3	2	4	16
♀ 14♑	✚ 3	★ 2	2	♥ 3	❢ 2	4	16
♂ 23♈	2	3	3	❢ 2	♥ 3	2	15
ASC ♑	3	2	2	3	2	♥ 4	16
Totals	17	15	15	17	15	19	Shared Strengths 98

Grid of Gratification

Shared Strengths: 98 Bonus Bonds: Love Line: ♥ 16

Positive Planets (check any):

Yours		Your Partner's	
☉ ☐	♀ ☐	☉ ☐	♀ ☐
☽ ☐	♂ ☐	☽ ☐	♂ ☐
☿ ☐	ASC ☐	☿ ☐	ASC ☐

Togetherness: ✻

Sexual Sizzle: ❢

Attraction & Affection: ✚

Close Comfort: ★

STEP ELEVEN:

Notice that several of the boxes in your grid have a little ✻, ✚, ★ or ❢ in the upper left.

Boxes with ✻ show the Sun/Moon cross pairs — very important for male/female compatibility. Add those two scores and write the result on the worksheet under **Togetherness.**

Boxes with ✚ show the Sun/Venus cross pairs — very important for feeling drawn together. Add those two scores and write the result on the worksheet under **Attraction and Affection.**

Boxes with a ★ show Moon/Venus cross pairs — very important for feeling at ease with one another and being able to share finances and living quarters. Family may be quite significant. Add those two scores and write the result on the worksheet under **Close Comfort.**

Boxes with ❢ show the Mars/Venus cross pairs — very important for excitement and sexual drive. Add those two scores and write the result on the worksheet under **Sexual Sizzle.**

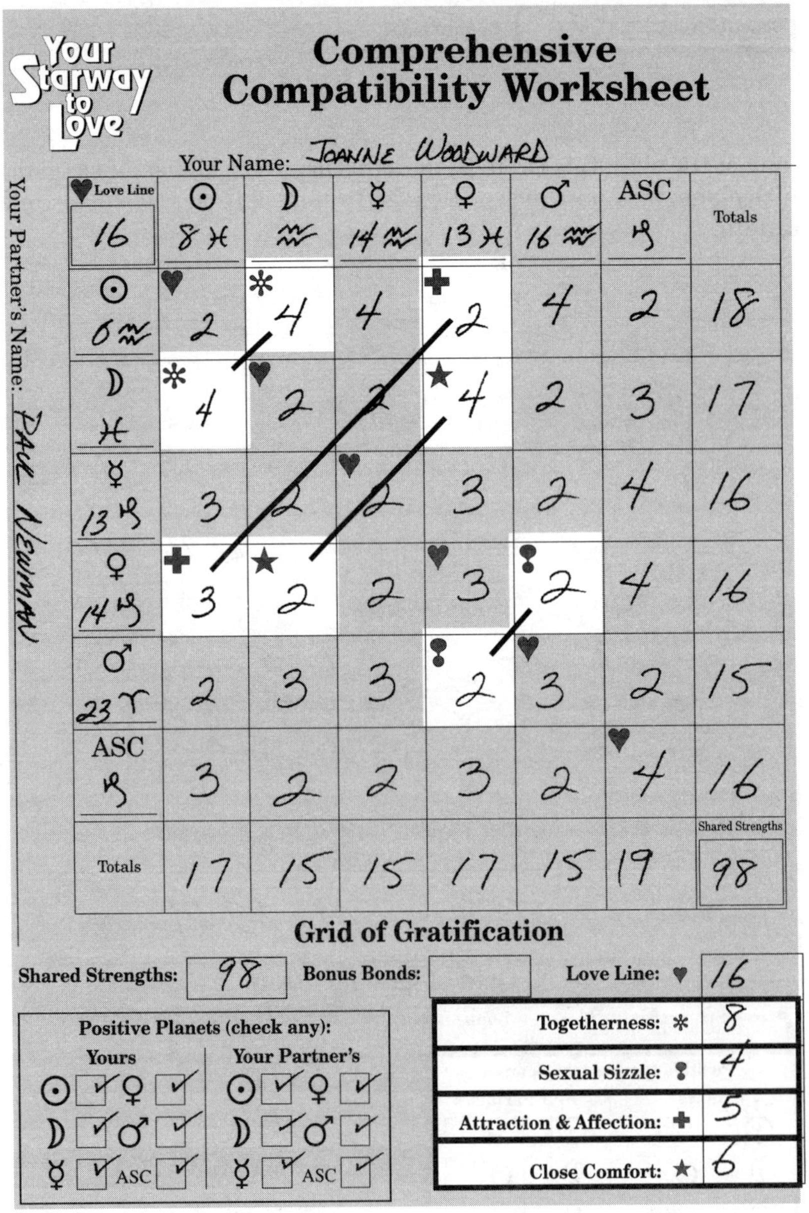

Your Starway to Love

Comprehensive Compatibility Worksheet

Your Name: JOANNE WOODWARD

Your Partner's Name: PAUL NEWMAN

♥ Love Line 16	☉ 8 ♓	☽ ♒	☿ 14 ♒	♀ 13 ♓	♂ 16 ♒	ASC ♑	Totals
☉ 6 ♒	♥ 2	✻ 4	4	✚ 2	4	2	18
☽ ♓	✻ 4	♥ 2	2	★ 4	2	3	17
☿ 13 ♑	3	2	♥ 2	3	2	4	16
♀ 14 ♑	✚ 3	★ 2	2	♥ 3	❢ 2	4	16
♂ 23 ♈	2	3	3	❢ 2	♥ 3	2	15
ASC ♑	3	2	2	3	2	♥ 4	16
Totals	17	15	15	17	15	19	Shared Strengths 98

Grid of Gratification

Shared Strengths: 98 **Bonus Bonds:** **Love Line:** ♥ 16

Positive Planets (check any):

Yours		Your Partner's	
☉ ✓	♀ ✓	☉ ✓	♀ ✓
☽ ✓	♂ ✓	☽ ✓	♂ ✓
☿ ✓	ASC ✓	☿ ✓	ASC ✓

Togetherness: ✻	8
Sexual Sizzle: ❢	4
Attraction & Affection: ✚	5
Close Comfort: ★	6

STEP TWELVE:

Look at the number you have written in for the degrees of your Sun sign. Compare it to the numbers for your partner's Sun, Mercury, Venus, and Mars. (You will not have a number for Ascendant or Moon degrees.) If your Sun is within five degrees (plus or minus) of any of your partner's numbers, put a check in the upper right of the box which is below your Sun and to the right of your partner's planet.

If you do not want to do any calculations, refer to the **Degree of Closeness** table on page 15. Just look up the number of your Sun and the table will tell you which numbers qualify for a check mark.

After you have compared the degree of your Sun to your partner's numbers, compare your Mercury degree, then your Venus degree, your Mars degree, etc. Count up the number of check marks you have made, and enter that number on the worksheet where it says: **Bonus Bonds**.

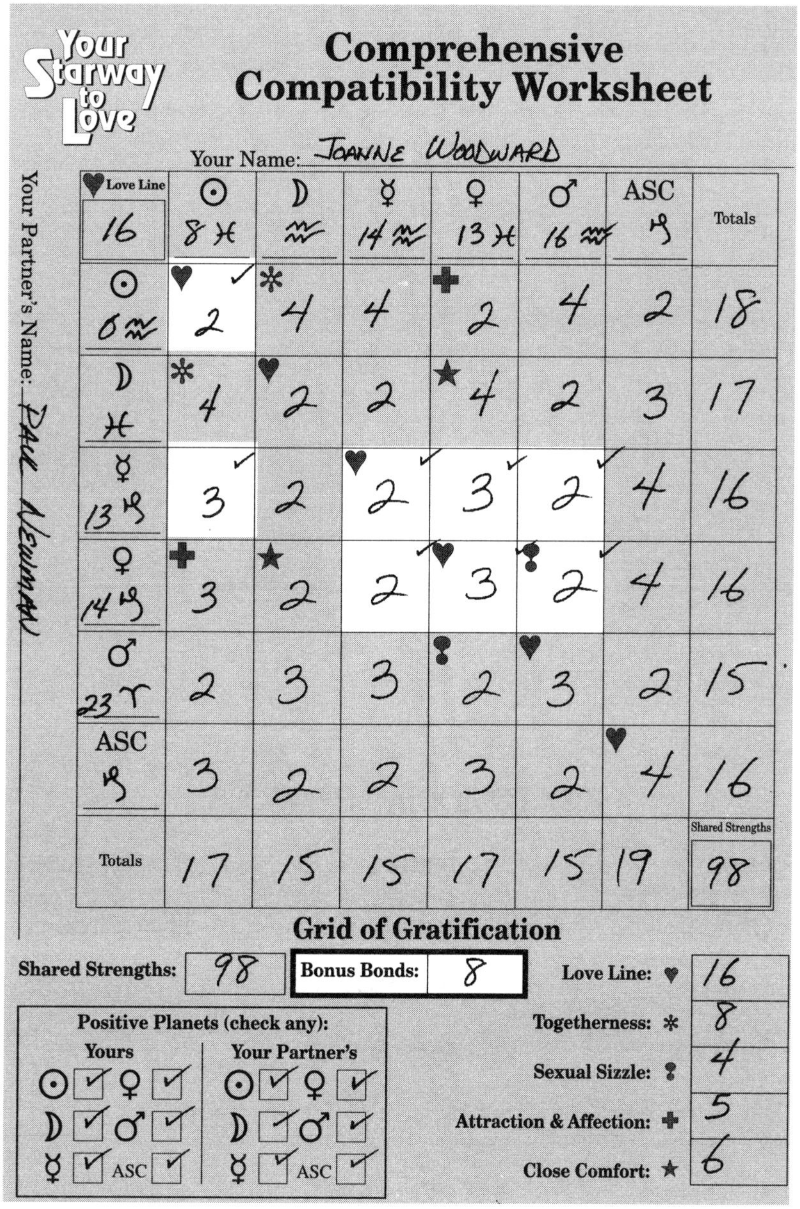

Your Starway to Love

Comprehensive Compatibility Worksheet

Your Name: JOANNE WOODWARD

Your Partner's Name: PAUL NEWMAN

♥ Love Line: 16	☉ 8♓	☽ ♒	☿ 14♒	♀ 13♓	♂ 16♒	ASC ♑	Totals
☉ 6♒	♥ ✓ 2	✻ 4	4	✚ 2	4	2	18
☽ ♓	✻ 4	♥ 2	2	★ 4	2	3	17
☿ 13♑	✓ 3	2	♥ ✓ 2	✓ 3	✓ 2	4	16
♀ 14♑	✚ 3	★ 2	✓ 2	♥ 3	❢ 2	✓ 4	16
♂ 23♈	2	3	3	❢ 2	♥ 3	2	15
ASC ♑	3	2	2	3	2	♥ 4	16
Totals	17	15	15	17	15	19	Shared Strengths: 98

Grid of Gratification

Shared Strengths: 98 **Bonus Bonds:** 8

Positive Planets (check any):

Yours		Your Partner's	
☉ ✓	♀ ✓	☉ ✓	♀ ✓
☽ ✓	♂ ✓	☽	♂ ✓
☿ ✓	ASC ✓	☿ ✓	ASC ✓

Love Line: ♥	16
Togetherness: ✻	8
Sexual Sizzle: ❢	4
Attraction & Affection: ✚	5
Close Comfort: ★	6

TABLE OF COMPATIBILITIES

	Your Planetary Placements											
Your Partner's Planetary Placements	♈	♉	♊	♋	♌	♍	♎	♏	♐	♑	♒	♓
♈	4	2	3	2	3	1	4	1	3	2	3	2
♉	2	4	2	3	2	3	1	4	1	3	2	3
♊	3	2	4	2	3	2	3	1	4	1	3	2
♋	2	3	2	4	2	3	2	3	1	4	1	3
♌	3	2	3	2	4	2	3	2	3	1	4	1
♍	1	3	2	3	2	4	2	3	2	3	1	4
♎	4	1	3	2	3	2	4	2	3	2	3	1
♏	1	4	1	3	2	3	2	4	2	3	2	3
♐	3	1	4	1	3	2	3	2	4	2	3	2
♑	2	3	1	4	1	3	2	3	2	4	2	3
♒	3	2	3	1	4	1	3	2	3	2	4	2
♓	2	3	2	3	1	4	1	3	2	3	2	4

KEY TO ZODIAC SYMBOLS

♈ = Aries	♉ = Taurus	♊ = Gemini
♋ = Cancer	♌ = Leo	♍ = Virgo
♎ = Libra	♏ = Scorpio	♐ = Sagittarius
♑ = Capricorn	♒ = Aquarius	♓ = Pisces

DEGREES OF CLOSENESS TABLE

Degrees Your Partner's Planet Can Be for Bonding

Degree of Your Planet

0	25	26	27	28	29	0	1	2	3	4	5
1	26	27	28	29	0	1	2	3	4	5	6
2	27	28	29	0	1	2	3	4	5	6	7
3	28	29	0	1	2	3	4	5	6	7	8
4	29	0	1	2	3	4	5	6	7	8	9
5	0	1	2	3	4	5	6	7	8	9	10
6	1	2	3	4	5	6	7	8	9	10	11
7	2	3	4	5	6	7	8	9	10	11	12
8	3	4	5	6	7	8	9	10	11	12	13
9	4	5	6	7	8	9	10	11	12	13	14
10	5	6	7	8	9	10	11	12	13	14	15
11	6	7	8	9	10	11	12	13	14	15	16
12	7	8	9	10	11	12	13	14	15	16	17
13	8	9	10	11	12	13	14	15	16	17	18
14	9	10	11	12	13	14	15	16	17	18	19
15	10	11	12	13	14	15	16	17	18	19	20
16	11	12	13	14	15	16	17	18	19	20	21
17	12	13	14	15	16	17	18	19	20	21	22
18	13	14	15	16	17	18	19	20	21	22	23
19	14	15	16	17	18	19	20	21	22	23	24
20	15	16	17	18	19	20	21	22	23	24	25
21	16	17	18	19	20	21	22	23	24	25	26
22	17	18	19	20	21	22	23	24	25	26	27
23	18	19	20	21	22	23	24	25	26	27	28
24	19	20	21	22	23	24	25	26	27	28	29
25	20	21	22	23	24	25	26	27	28	29	0
26	21	22	23	24	25	26	27	28	29	0	1
27	22	23	24	25	26	27	28	29	0	1	2
28	23	24	25	26	27	28	29	0	1	2	3
29	24	25	26	27	28	29	0	1	2	3	4

INTERPRETING YOUR COMPATIBILITY WORKSHEET

STEP ONE:

Be sure you have read the beginning of *Your Starway to Love* which describes vital issues in relationship analysis. Then, read the pages in *Your Starway to Love* which give keywords for your Sun sign, Moon sign, Mercury sign, Venus sign, Mars sign, and Ascendant sign. Consider whether you are expressing the best or the worst of your sign potentials. Then, read the key word descriptions for your partner's Sun, Moon, Mercury, Venus, Mars and Ascendant signs. Consider whether your partner is expressing the best or the worst of his sign potentials.

Next, read the paragraphs in *Your Starway to Love* describing the themes you are facing with this partner for each of your six pairs of planets which make up your **Love Line**: Sun to Sun (pages 38-83); Moon to Moon (pages 90-125); Mercury to Mercury (pages 174-209); Venus to Venus (pages 216-251); Mars to Mars (pages 258-293); and Ascendant to Ascendant (pages 132-167).

These descriptions are the most important part of your Compatibility Analysis. They are the foundation for everything else.

STEP TWO:

Find the category where your **Love Line** score falls on the table below, then read the meaning of your score. The **Love Line** is your most significant key to romantic attachments. It gives you an overall sense of your relationship, a basic rating.

Love Line Scores

Overall scores will fall into the following categories:

Comprehensive Worksheet		Quick Worksheet	
6-10 :	VERY CHALLENGING	5-8 :	VERY CHALLENGING
11-14 :	CHALLENGING	9-11 :	CHALLENGING
15-18 :	COMPATIBLE	12-15 :	COMPATIBLE
19-24 :	VERY COMPATIBLE	16-20 :	VERY COMPATIBLE

INTERPRETATIONS FOR LOVE LINE SCORES

VERY CHALLENGING LOVE LINE

There are some major differences in personality and style between the two of you. If you enjoy flowing in different directions, and can be tolerant of one another's different needs, your relationship can work well. If either of you tries to change the other — make your partner more like you — trouble is likely.

We are often attracted to people who have qualities far afield from our own. That "spark" of attraction needs a little clash in order to catch fire! The people who attract us initially are not always the best ones for us, however.

If you enjoy a bit of a challenge, if you are willing to work on your relationship and if you can appreciate and **enjoy** one another's differences (rather than trying to wipe them out), this can be a very rewarding relationship for you both. Each of you is likely to grow and change through exposure to other ideas, attitudes and ways of interacting.

CHALLENGING LOVE LINE

You know the old cliches — "Birds of a feather flock together" but "Opposites attract." People building an enduring relationship need enough in common to have some strong ties. But they need enough differences to build excitement and feed the flames of passion. The trick is managing the challenges that do exist in a positive manner.

You and your partner have some significant differences. Your challenge is to appreciate each other's points of view, without having to have agreement on everything. Be open to learning from each other (willing to change your minds). Learn where your clashes are — and what's worth fighting for — and what's **not**.

If you can reach a bottom-line agreement on issues that are bedrock for each of you, then the other differences will just add spice to your relationship. This is a relationship which could change you both — if you are willing to take the opportunity to transform yourselves. Don't expect a smooth, easy flow all the time, but do build on the commonalities you share and learn to take the differences as opportunities to expand your thinking and possibilities. Those differences also help to keep each of you interested in and attracted to each other!

COMPATIBLE LOVE LINE

Your relationship will have definite times of smooth, easy flow. You and your partner can tune into the same wavelength without much problem. This does not, of course, guarantee "happily ever after." You may egg each other on at times! Agreement (if you both want something unhealthy) may not be in the best interests of either of you or the relationship! But without some basic common ground, it's hard to build bridges to each other.

You have a lot going for each other. Your general personalities and styles of interacting are similar in many cases. Just as communication is easier if two people speak the same language, partnership is easier if two people have a compatible approach to relationships. The two of you have a good degree of compatibility.

Naturally, there will (and must) be some differences. You can cope most successfully in areas of stress or strain by using the strengths between you. If communication is a strong suit between you, talk about touchy areas. If your styles of expressing affection are compatible, be warm and supportive to one another before addressing difficult topics. Build on what is working well and the other areas will begin to flow more smoothly too! Reaching agreement is easier for you than for most couples.

VERY COMPATIBLE LOVE LINE

Your relationship has an amazingly high degree of compatibility and likeness. In fact, you two might seem like twin souls in some respects. Many times, you will be feeling similar feelings, finishing each other's sentences or otherwise tuning into one another.

Remember, however, the French phrase: *Vive la différence!* Successful relationships require both common ground and enough conflicts to strike some sparks between you. Too much harmony can seem boring at times; you need a bit of tension to enjoy its release! Also, people who have a high degree of compatibility will sometimes encourage each other to do things not in their best interests. Inner agreement may seem easier, but it also means you can agree to do something illegal, immoral or fattening. (Isn't everything?)

This is potentially a very positive, flowing, easy to harmonize association. Do be sure that when you both say "**go**" it is something healthy for you both to pursue! Most of the time, you should find it easy to cooperate and compromise. Empathy between you is likely to be high. It is easy for each of you to tap into good feelings about the other.

These first two steps are what matter most in analyzing compatibility. If you are doing a lot of analyses, or using the Quick Compatibility Worksheet, Steps One and Two are all you need. Use Step Two for a general rating of the relationship. Use Step One for specific ideas and suggestions of possible weak points, and ways to overcome them as well as strengths and talents to be shared. Reread the paragraphs describing your placements to really absorb the important concepts and helpful hints.

If you want more details and have completed the Comprehensive Compatibility Worksheet, see the **Optional Factors** (Steps Three through Six).

OPTIONAL FACTORS

STEP THREE:

If you have any **Positive Planets** checked, read the description of that planet in general (page 33 for Sun; 85 for Moon; 169 for Mercury; 211 for Venus; 253 for Mars and 127 for Ascendant in *Your Starway to Love*). Think in terms of building on the good connections indicated by **Positive Planets**. Focus on and enhance qualities in your relationship that relate to the **Positive Planets**.

A **positive Sun** shows a person who tends to shine, to be noticed, to be important in the relationship. The person with a positive Sun is usually vitalized and energized by the relationship. The positive Sun person can motivate others. Compliments and positive feedback work very well for that person.

Someone with a **positive Moon** finds it natural to build a home, to share feelings, to develop closeness. Such a person is probably supportive and feels nurtured by the relationship. Tenderness, caretaking, and compassion work very well for the positive Moon person.

The person with a **positive Venus** may find it easy to express affection, to be comfortable in the relationship. This person tends to be attractive to others. A positive Venus person can bring charm, grace, pleasure and comfort into the relationship.

The person with a **positive Mercury** finds communication rather smooth. A mentally stimulating or interesting relationship is likely. The person with a positive Mercury can teach as well as learn, and enjoys both with a partner.

A **positive Mars** shows excitement, enthusiasm and/or sexual desire within the relationship. The person with a positive Mars can energize others, stirring them up, feeding their excitement. Sexual charisma may be present.

A **positive Ascendant** indicates that the relationship feeds this person's individuality and encourages self-expression and self-development. Doing one's own thing constructively tends to make the relationship stronger and more durable.

Also reread the key words given for the placement of each **Positive Planet** in its sign (pages 34-36 for Sun; 86-87 for Moon; 170-171 for Mercury; 212-213 for Venus; 254-255 for Mars; and 128-129 for Ascendant). Encourage the traits which are constructive within your relationship.

STEP FOUR:

If your **Togetherness** score is 6 or greater, you stimulate his sense of manhood, and he stimulates your sense of womanhood. Your desire to maintain a relationship is increased. You may even feel like opposite halves of the same whole. You encourage one another to flourish.

If your **Sexual Sizzle** score is 6 or greater, your sexual excitement and interest can contribute to the growth of your relationship. You may add to each other's energy, enthusiasm and eagerness.

If your **Attraction and Affection** score is 6 or greater, you two feel very drawn together and may find it easy to be affectionate with one another. A magnetic pull could exist between you.

If your **Close Comfort** score is 6 or greater, you two naturally want to combine forces and share with one another. Building a nest together may appeal. Each of you wants to create a setting with strong mutual support.

STEP FIVE:

If your **Bonus Bonds** score is 8 or greater, there is a strong pull between the two of you. You tend to be drawn together (for good or ill). Feelings are likely to be more intense, but could be love or hate. Extremes are possible. This indicates extra cohesiveness, more of a tendency to bond with one another. People with high **Bonus Bonds** are more likely to be in each other's lives.

STEP SIX:

Look at your **Shared Strengths** score. If it is higher than 88, you have some additional compatibility to lean on. Your general orientation toward one another has some real common ground. Even if your **Love Line** score is relatively low, a high **Shared Strengths** means you have the potential of building a lasting, important, positive relationship. You want to pull together, to stay together. You find it rather easy to support one another. You seek compromises and increase the level of agreement between you.

Any of the above situations can help to compensate for a lower **Love Line** score. The more you focus on and develop your strengths, the better the relationship will work.

THE BOTTOM LINE

If you and your partner have a **Compatible Love Line** score, you are off to a good start. Do not assume, however, that all will be roses. (If you are **Very Compatible**, it is possible you might feel too much similarity — not enough spark between you.) Read the keywords for each of your placements, and each of your partner's placements. Read the paragraphs for your combined placements. Think about how to make the most of what you have in common. Notice where differences exist, and be accepting and tolerant of one another. Read the analysis for your **Love Line** score.

Also look to all the **Optional Factors** for clues to places you can build and expand on a base which is likely to be positive. The more you appreciate one another's good points, and strive to carry them further, the better you'll do together.

If you and your partner have a **Challenging** or **Very Challenging Love Line** score, recognize that there will be significant differences between you. If you find the thought of major differences with a partner threatening, you might want to consider looking for another person — someone with whom you already have a fair degree of compatibility. (If you are currently in a long-term marriage, the odds are you are already capitalizing on many of each other's strengths and emphasizing the best between you.)

If you find the thought of differences stimulating and exciting, you can build a very good relationship with this partner. You may have a good division of labor, each of you doing opposite qualities within the relationship. Appreciate each other's unique contributions. Use the **Optional Factors** to pinpoint areas you can easily reinforce in one another. Practice tolerance of each other's varied outlooks and strive to optimize the qualities in one another which you love, respect and admire. Build on the charisma, nurturing, communication, affection, sexual excitement, and self-development within your relationship. Accentuate the positive. Compliment, support and reaffirm one another.

We suggest that you read through the examples that follow. They illustrate how couples can compensate for a low **Love Line** score and also demonstrate that a high score is not a guarantee of "happily ever after." Each couple still has the power (and responsibility) to overcome their challenges and make the most of their strengths and positive connections.

FAMOUS EXAMPLES

Let's look at a few examples to illustrate how the compatibility worksheets relate to real life.

EXAMPLE ONE:
SONNY AND CHER

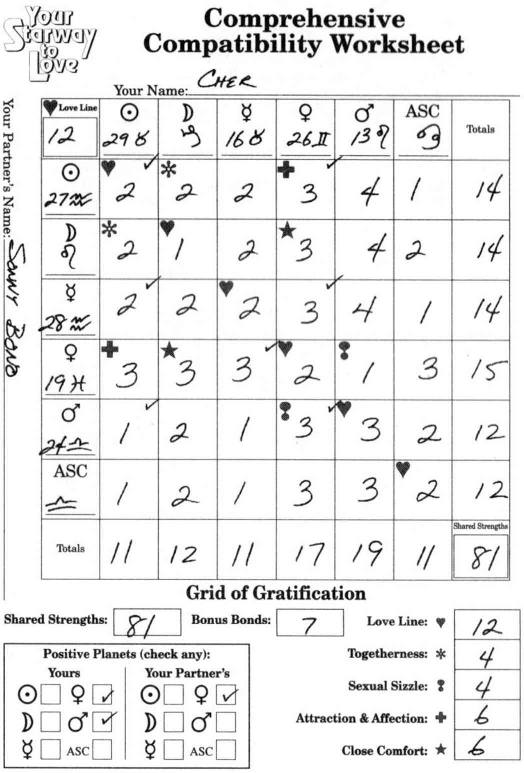

Comprehensive Compatibility Worksheet

Your Name: Cher

Your Partner's Name: Sonny Bono

Love Line 12	☉ 29♉	☽ ♑	☿ 16♉	♀ 26♊	♂ 13♌	ASC ♋	Totals
☉ 27♒	2	2	2	3	4	1	14
☽ ♌	2	1	2	3	4	2	14
☿ 28♒	2	2	2	3	4	1	14
♀ 19♓	3	3	3	2	1	3	15
♂ 24♎	1	2	1	3	3	2	12
ASC ♎	1	2	1	3	3	2	12
Totals	11	12	11	17	19	11	Shared Strengths 81

Grid of Gratification

Shared Strengths: 81 Bonus Bonds: 7

Positive Planets (check any): Yours	Your Partner's
☉ ☐ ♀ ☑	☉ ☐ ♀ ☑
☽ ☐ ♂ ☑	☽ ☐ ♂ ☐
☿ ☐ ASC ☐	☿ ☐ ASC ☐

Love Line: ♥	12
Togetherness: ✻	4
Sexual Sizzle:	4
Attraction & Affection: ✚	6
Close Comfort: ★	6

Sonny (Bono) and Cher's **Compatibility Worksheet** appears at right. Note that their **Love Line** score is 12—or **Challenging**. If you look at their **Love Line**, of the six pairs only the Mars/Mars combination was **Compatible** (score of 3 or 4). All five other pairs were **Challenging** (score of 2) or **Very Challenging** (score of 1).

The description for a **Love Line** score which is **Challenging** notes that the couple must be willing to compromise, to work positively with their differences. If we read each of the descriptions for the sign placements of Sonny and Cher's Sun, Moon, Mercury, etc. (in *Your Starway to Love*), we would get further information about how and where Sonny and Cher are (and are not) compatible. When we read the appropriate paragraphs (for their Sun/Sun combination, Moon/Moon combination, etc.), we get more information about the challenges between Sonny and Cher—and about ways they could have worked on overcoming those challenges.

These factors (the key words for each person's planetary placements, the paragraphs about the six pairs of "planets" and the **Love Line** score) give us the most important information about a possible relationship between Sonny and Cher. However, the **Optional Factors** can describe qualities which may compensate for a low **Love Line** score. **Optional Factors** point to special strengths we may be able to use in a relationship.

If we look at the **Optional Factors**, we notice that Sonny and Cher have scores of 6 or above for **Attraction** and **Close Comfort**, so we would expect strong attraction between them, despite the low **Love Line** score. We would also expect that they might wish to live together, even have a family perhaps, despite the challenges involved.

If we look at the totals for each planet, we see that the only planets registering as positive (a score of 15 or above) are Venus for Sonny and Mars and Venus for Cher. Since Venus and Mars are key factors in sexual attraction and excitement, we might assume that in the original involvement the attraction was mainly physical. However, for a couple wishing to maintain and improve their relationship, this gives a place to start. Focus on your assets! Build on sexual excitement (Mars/Venus). Feed one another's energy and enthusiasm (Mars). Be affectionate (Venus) with one another. By focusing on what is good and increasing it, other areas can become more positive as well. Start with what is best and work on spilling it out into other areas of your relationship!

EXAMPLE TWO:
PRINCESS DIANA & PRINCE CHARLES

The **Compatibility Worksheet** for Princess Diana and Prince Charles appears on the next page. Note that their **Love Line** score is 14—**Challenging** (like Sonny and Cher). Of their six pairs, however, three are quite compatible—their Suns, their Mercuries, and their Ascendants. This suggests that if they had only concentrated on shining in their own areas (the Sun), on communication (Mercury), and self-development (Ascendant), they could have accented the

Your Starway to Love

Comprehensive Compatibility Worksheet

Your Name: PRINCESS DIANA

Your Partner's Name: PRINCE CHARLES

♥ Love Line 14	☉ 10♋	☽ ♒	☿ 3♋	♀ 24♉	♂ 2♍	ASC ♐	Totals
☉ 22♏	♥ 3	✱ 2	3	✚ 4 ✓	3	2	17
☽ ♉	✱ 3	♥ 2	3	★ 4	3	1	16
☿ 9♏	3 ✓	2	♥ 3	4	3	2	17
♀ 16♎	✚ 2	★ 3	2	♥ 1	❢ 2	3	13
♂ 21♐	1	3	1	❢ 1 ✓	♥ 2	4	12
ASC ♌	2	4	2	2	2	♥ 3	15
Totals	14	16	14	16	15	15	Shared Strengths 90

Grid of Gratification

Shared Strengths: 90 Bonus Bonds: 3

Love Line: ♥	14
Togetherness: ✱	5
Sexual Sizzle: ❢	3
Attraction & Affection: ✚	6
Close Comfort: ★	7

Positive Planets (check any):

Yours				Your Partner's			
☉	☐	♀	☑	☉	☑	♀	☐
☽	☑	♂	☑	☽	☑	♂	☐
☿	☐	ASC	☑	☿	☑	ASC	☑

positive in their relationship. If we read the paragraphs for each **Love Line** pair, we get more details regarding strengths and weaknesses between them.

On page 49, we see that their Suns are compatible. (Hers is in Cancer; his is in Scorpio.) The paragraph notes both are sensitive to "hints, innuendoes, secrets and hidden messages." Princess Diana needs recognition for her devotion to "home, family, and loved ones." The combination warns that both people have "strong deep feelings that you tend to keep hidden" and "once you commit, you both value loyalty very highly." Unfortunately, it seems Prince Charles had committed years before to another woman (Camilla Parker Bowles whose Love Line with Charles is 17) and was as loyal to that other person as he could be under the circumstances. (The description of a Sun in Scorpio on page 35 also emphasizes the importance of loyalty!) On page 184, discussing Diana's and Charles' Mercuries, we again see a hint about secrecy or hidden matters: "Each of you can be like an iceberg—9/10 below the surface where communication is concerned.... You are likely to respect each other's needs for privacy and sensitivity." Princess Diana and Prince Charles took that to the extreme of leading separate lives!

In terms of **Optional Factors**, we note that Princess Di and Prince Charles have scores of 6 or above for **Attraction** and for **Close Comfort**. This emphasizes their initial attraction to one another and the possibility of building a home and/or family together. They managed the family but are far from the home their fairy-tale beginning promised.

We also note that the **Positive Planets** for Prince Charles are the Sun, Moon, Mercury and Ascendant—emphasizing his desire to shine, his nurturing side, his curiosity and interest in life, and his self-development as important resources within the relationship. Princess Diana's **Positive Planets** are the Moon, Venus, Mars, and Ascendant—emphasizing her mothering instincts, affection and desire for comfort, excitement and drive, and her self-development. Since both Diana and Charles have positive Moon and positive Ascendant contacts, their best bet would have been to divide their focus between self-expression and their individualistic interests (Ascendant) and family matters (Moon). Unfortunately, they've decide to take their individualistic interests to the extreme of living apart.

We further notice that the **Shared Strengths** score for Diana and Charles is 90. This implies that, despite a Challenging **Love Line** score, enough strength exists to build a lasting and positive relationship. If the two of them had faced their challenges and worked for constructive ways out of their conflicts, they could have made it. By focusing on the planets which **are** positive between them, they could have built bridges to one another. Instead they allowed their conflicts (and other people) to draw them further apart: a sad ending for a real-life Prince and Princess.

EXAMPLE THREE:

CORETTA SCOTT KING & MARTIN LUTHER KING, JR.

The **Love Line** score for the Kings was 15, giving their relationship a **Compatible** rating. Three of their pairs had a score of 3 or 4: their Suns (emphasizing the limelight and public attention), their Moons (emphasizing family connections and nurturing one another), their Mercuries (emphasizing communication). If we read the paragraphs describing each of the like pairs, we would get further information about potential strengths and weaknesses in their relationship.

Their compatible Suns were in Taurus and Capricorn (described on page 43). He needed admiration for his "strong sense of responsibility... conscientiousness, willingness to work, ambition." She needed to be admired for her "reliability, faithfulness, and desire to bring comfort and pleasure to others." They shared a Pisces Moon, noted for being idealistic, compassionate, mystical, spiritual, religious, etc. (page 89). Although her Mercury is in Aries and his is in Aquarius, they shared an independent approach to the mind: "You resist dogmas and other people's rules...You both tend to think for yourselves and to question authorities." (page 176) Although their Venus positions are challenging, his Venus in Pisces reaffirms his idealism, while her Venus in Gemini emphasizes her ability to stimulate him mentally. They certainly had their differences — his Mars in Gemini would seek constant stimulation from the world, ideas, and other people, while her Mars in Cancer is focused on home and family—but they were willing to compromise and worked very well together.

Your Starway to Love

Comprehensive Compatibility Worksheet

Your Name: Coretta Scott King

Your Partner's Name: Martin Luther King, Jr.

♥ Love Line: 15	☉ 7♉	☽ ♓	☿ 15♈	♀ 13♊	♂ 6♋	ASC ♎	Totals
☉ 25♑	♥ 3	✻ 3	2	✚ 1	4	2	15
☽ ♓	✻ 3	♥ 4	2	★ 2	3	1	15
☿ 12♒	2 ✓	2	♥ 3 ✓	3 ✓	1	3	14
♀ 11♓	✚ 3 ✓	★ 4	2 ✓	♥ 2 ✓	❢ 3 ✓	1	15
♂ 22♊	2	2	3	❢ 4	♥ 2	3	16
ASC ♉	4	3	2	2	3	♥ 1	15
Totals	17	18	14	14	16	11	Shared Strengths 90

Grid of Gratification

Shared Strengths: 90 Bonus Bonds: 7

Positive Planets (check any):

Yours		Your Partner's	
☉ ✓	♀	☉ ✓	♀ ✓
☽ ✓	♂ ✓	☽ ✓	♂ ✓
☿	ASC	☿	ASC ✓

Love Line: ♥	15
Togetherness: ✻	6
Sexual Sizzle: ❢	7
Attraction & Affection: ✚	4
Close Comfort: ★	6

Since their **Love Line** score was **Compatible**, we could rest here, but the **Optional Factors** can supply additional details and suggestions for improving even positive relationships.

The Kings had a high score for **Togetherness**, showing that they accentuated one another's masculinity and femininity. Their **Sexual Sizzle** was excellent (excitement and desire), and so was their **Close Comfort**, reflecting the family connection and a desire to share lives. All of this makes their good relationship look even better!

We also see that their **Shared Strengths** is 90—reflecting extra support for staying together, for making constructive connections. In addition, three of Coretta King's planets were positive: Sun (giving and receiving compliments and attention), Moon (nurturing and family life focus), and Mars (excitement, energy, and enthusiasm). Five of the planets were positive for Martin Luther King, Jr: Sun (being a star, recognizing others), Moon (building a home), Venus (affection, pleasure, comfort), Mars (excitement) and Ascendant (self-development).

Overall, we get a picture of a pair of people who had lots and lots going for their relationship!

EXAMPLE FOUR:
JOANNE WOODWARD AND PAUL NEWMAN

This long-term couple have beaten the odds, especially for people involved with Hollywood. If we examine their signs, we see that Joanne Woodward has placements in three signs: Pisces (her Sun and Venus), Aquarius (her Moon, Mercury and Mars) and Capricorn (her Ascendant). Paul Newman has four signs represented: Aquarius (his Sun), Pisces (his Moon), Capricorn (his Mercury, Venus, and Ascendant) and Aries (his Mars). These likenesses speak to the strengths of their relationship. They stimulate each other mentally, like breaking the rules, can be open and tolerant and appreciate each other's differences (Aquarius). They can be sensitive, tune into one another, and share ideals (Pisces). They are both willing to work hard, be conscientious,

Your Starway to Love

Comprehensive Compatibility Worksheet

Your Name: JOANNE WOODWARD

Your Partner's Name: PAUL NEWMAN

Love Line 16	☉ 8 ♓	☽ ♒	☿ 14 ♒	♀ 13 ♓	♂ 16 ♒	ASC ♑	Totals
☉ 6 ♒	2	4	4	2	4	2	18
☽ ♓	4	2	2	4	2	3	17
☿ 13 ♑	3	2	2	3	2	4	16
♀ 14 ♑	3	2	2	3	2	4	16
♂ 23 ♈	2	3	3	2	3	2	15
ASC ♑	3	2	2	3	2	4	16
Totals	17	15	15	17	15	19	Shared Strengths 98

Grid of Gratification

Shared Strengths: 98 **Bonus Bonds:** 8

Love Line: ♥	16
Togetherness: ✱	8
Sexual Sizzle:	4
Attraction & Affection: ✚	5
Close Comfort: ★	6

Positive Planets (check any):

Yours				Your Partner's			
☉	✓	♀	✓	☉	✓	♀	✓
☽	✓	♂	✓	☽	✓	♂	✓
☿	✓	ASC	✓	☿	✓	ASC	✓

responsible, and dedicated (Capricorn). In addition, he has his Mars in sexy, super-masculine Aries for more physical drive, energy, and need for excitement.

We see a **Love Line** score of 16—definitely **Compatible**. We note that affection and pleasure (Venus), sexual excitement and drive (Mars), and self-development and individualistic interests (Ascendant), are particular strengths in their **Love Line**. We would see further clues about their assets (and possible liabilities) in the paragraphs interpreting their planetary pairs (Sun/Sun, Moon/Moon, etc.).

Again, we have a positive vote, but we can get additional details with the **Optional Factors**. Paul Newman and Joanne Woodward have the highest possible score (an 8) for **Togetherness**. The classic male/female bond of Sun/Moon is doubly blessed in their case. This is a very cohesive connection! We also see a willingness to get close and personal with their **Close Comfort** score. Building a home together feels natural.

This constructive couple has the additional plus of a **Shared Strengths** score of 98—more tendency to pull together, to work things out. With such a high score, it is no surprise that, for Joanne and Paul, **every single planet** is a **Positive Planet**. They can use motivational skills and dramatic flair (Sun), nurturing capacities (Moon), communicative abilities (Mercury), affectionate tendencies (Venus), sexual charisma (Mars), and self-development (Ascendant) to contribute to their relationship. In other words, **anything and everything** can be an asset for them!

CASE STUDIES AND SPECIAL CASES

VERY LOW LOVE LINE

Even when the **Love Line** score is very low, a couple can build an excellent relationship. With a low score on the **Love Line**, strong differences will exist, so mutual tolerance and acceptance is vital. If either partner tries to make over, change or "improve" the other, trouble is in the wings. Both need to appreciate the partner's different style and personality, to love the partner as s/he is.

Also, it is essential that people build on whatever is strongly compatible in the relationship. The positive planetary scores and **Optional Factors** help you focus on where your strengths are.

EXAMPLE FIVE:

ANNE MORROW LINDBERGH AND CHARLES LINDBERGH

As you can see, the Lindberghs had an exceptionally low **Love Line** score, but managed a long and happy marriage. What was going on?

If we read the key words for their planetary placements, we see a very strong freedom focus for "Lindy." He has Sun in Aquarius, Moon in Sagittarius, Mars in Aquarius and Ascendant in Sag. This is a lot of need for space, independence and being able to do his own thing. Anne Morrow Lindbergh has a very strong domestic focus with Sun, Moon, Mercury and Mars all in Cancer!

Combining Cancer with Sagittarius or Aquarius is very challenging. It requires much tolerance (and recognition of each other's differences). The Lindberghs were able to appreciate each other's strong differences in personality and style, and enjoy them, instead of trying to make each other over.

Note that Venus (the planet of love and affection) is strongly positive for both of them. Mercury (the planet of communication) is also quite positive for Charles Lindbergh. Affection, acceptance, love, pleasure, and comfort (Venusian qualities) were probably emphasized by both of them in building a strong relationship.

We can also see, that although **Togetherness** was not strong for the Lindberghs, they scored very well for **Sexual Sizzle, Attraction and Affection** and **Close Comfort** (often associated with the desire to build a home together). Naturally, their very positive Venus (love/affection) scores contributed to the high scores for **Attraction and Affection** (the blend of the charismatic, magnetic Sun and loving Venus) and for **Close Comfort** (the blend of the nurturing, homefocused Moon and the affectionate, loving Venus).

By capitalizing on the best between them, and enjoying one another's differences, the Lindberghs built a long and happy marriage.

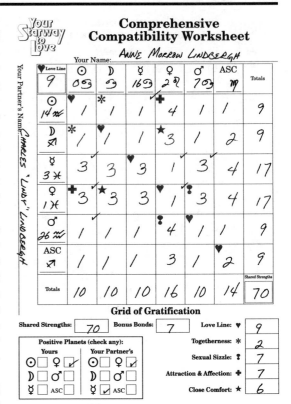

Your Starway to Love

Comprehensive Compatibility Worksheet

Your Name: Anne Morrow Lindbergh

Your Partner's Name: Charles "Lindy" Lindbergh

♥ Love Line 9	☉ 0♋	☽ ♋	☿ 16♋	♀ 2♌	♂ 7♋	ASC ♍	Totals
☉ 14♒	♥ 1	* 1	1	✚ 4	1	1	9
☽ ♐	* 1	♥ 1	1	★ 3	1	2	9
☿ 3♓	3	3	♥ 3	1	3	4	17
♀ 1♓	✚ 3	★ 3	3	♥ 1	❢ 3	4	17
♂ 26♒	1	1	1	❢ 4	♥ 1	1	9
ASC ♐	1	1	1	3	1	♥ 2	9
Totals	10	10	10	16	10	14	Shared Strengths 70

Grid of Gratification

Shared Strengths: 70 Bonus Bonds: 7

Positive Planets (check any):

Yours	Your Partner's
☉ ☐ ♀ ☑	☉ ☐ ♀ ☑
☽ ☐ ♂ ☐	☽ ☐ ♂ ☐
☿ ☐ ASC ☐	☿ ☑ ASC ☐

Love Line: ♥	9
Togetherness: *	2
Sexual Sizzle: ❢	7
Attraction & Affection: ✚	7
Close Comfort: ★	6

LOW LOVE LINE

EXAMPLE SIX: ROSALYN AND JIMMY CARTER

Your Starway to Love

Comprehensive Compatibility Worksheet

Your Name: Rosalyn Carter

Your Partner's Name: Jimmy Carter

♥ Love Line 14	☉ 25♌	☽ ♉	☿ 10♌	♀ 25♍	♂ 15♍	ASC ♍	Totals
☉ 8♎	♥ 3	* 1	3	✚ 2	2	2	13
☽ ♏	* 2	♥ 4	2	★ 3	3	3	17
☿ 21♍	2	3	♥ 2	4	4	4	19
♀ 23♌	✚ 4	★ 2	4	♥ 2	❢ 2	2	16
♂ 26♒	4	2	4	❢ 1	♥ 1	1	13
ASC ♎	3	1	3	2	2	♥ 2	13
Totals	18	13	18	14	14	14	Shared Strengths 90

Grid of Gratification

Shared Strengths: 90 Bonus Bonds: 7

Positive Planets (check any):

Yours	Your Partner's
☉ ☑ ♀ ☐	☉ ☐ ♀ ☑
☽ ☐ ♂ ☐	☽ ☑ ♂ ☐
☿ ☑ ASC ☐	☿ ☑ ASC ☐

Love Line: ♥	14
Togetherness: *	3
Sexual Sizzle: ❢	3
Attraction & Affection: ✚	6
Close Comfort: ★	5

The Carters have a low **Love Line** score, but are noteworthy (especially among political figures) for their good, equalitarian marriage.

Rosalyn has quite a few placements in Virgo (Venus, Mars, and Ascendant). Virgo is a wonderful sign if its analytical, flaw-finding skills are directed toward work, productivity, organization, and the real world. If directed toward people, criticism and nit-picking is a real danger. Rosalyn was a very hardworking spouse; she and Jimmy worked together successfully throughout their marriage. They continue to work (including physical labor) now with Habitat for Humanity: a charitable organization which builds homes for the very poor. Those receiving the homes in turn must work many hours (of "sweat equity") on their homes and the homes of others—encouraging the charity (and personal responsibility) to grow and expand. We suspect that Jimmy's Libra Sun and Ascendant (focus on people and compromise) contributes to his political focus and to his willingness to make the compromises necessary in any successful relationship. Jimmy's Virgo Mercury also shows that he thinks logically and follows much of Rosalyn's reasoning. His Venus in Leo indicates he is attracted by Leo qualities: the warmth, generosity, and charisma of Rosalyn's Leo Sun and Mercury. It appears the Carters are able to concentrate on their strengths and commonalities and do not allow their differences to damage their marriage.

To help compensate for the low **Love Line**, we see that the Carters have strong **Shared Strengths** indicating supportiveness of one another. Most dramatic, however, are the positive Mercury scores for Jimmy and Rosalyn Carter. Jimmy's Mercury score is 19, while Rosalyn's is 18. Most news reports and biographies have stressed the good communication between Jimmy and Rosalyn, how they discuss everything, the importance of talking with one another at the end of (and throughout) each day.

There are other positives (Jimmy's positive Venus; Rosalyn's positive Sun; their high score for **Attraction and Affection**), but everything in print about the Carters suggests that the highly positive Mercury fits their incredibly good communication and openness with one another.

COMPATIBLE LOVE LINE IS NO GUARANTEE

Although a **Love Line** score which is **Compatible** is very promising for shared efforts, it is **not** a guarantee! One (nonfamous) couple in our files, for example, has wonderful **Love Line** and other scores. But the man involved was an alcoholic, and the couple just could not maintain a marriage with that underlying problem!

Astrology shows us potentials—the best and the worst. Human beings choose, through their own actions (and inactions) whether to live out the most positive or least positive potentials of their horoscope.

Astrology is a wonderful tool, however, if we choose to use it to focus on our assets and to encourage and strengthen the best parts of ourselves and our relationships.

EXAMPLE SEVEN:

MARILYN MONROE AND JOE DIMAGGIO

Marilyn Monroe and Joe DiMaggio had a lot going for them. Their **Love Line** score was 15 (Compatible) and they had additional support from a **Shared Strengths** of 99. **Every single one** of Marilyn's "planets" was positive with Joe, while four of his six "planets" were positive with hers. They also had a good **Attraction and Affection** score. (He continued to send flowers to her grave regularly for many years after her death.)

Unfortunately, the pressures of living in a goldfish bowl (both famous personalities) were tremendous. Add in the scars Marilyn Monroe carried from her early life and the insecurity of being viewed as a sex symbol, plus whatever issues Joe DiMaggio brought to the relationship from his background—it was too much for them to handle.

Had Marilyn Monroe and Joe DiMaggio had less stress and early trauma to work through, they could have capitalized on their fine Sun (charisma, compliments and center stage), Venus (love and affection), Mars (sexual drive and energy), and Ascendant (self-development) scores. They could have trusted and relied on one another (**Shared Strengths**) and made the most of the **Attraction and Affection** between them.

Your Starway to Love

Comprehensive Compatibility Worksheet

Your Name: Marilyn Monroe

Your Partner's Name: Joe DiMaggio

♥ Love Line 15	☉ 10 ♊	☽ ♒	☿ 7 ♊	♀ 29 ♈	♂ 21 ♓	ASC ♌	Totals
☉ 2 ♐	4	3	4	3	2	3	19
☽ ♓	2	2	2	2	4	1	13
☿ 12 ♏	1	2	1	1	3	2	10
♀ 6 ♐	4	3	4	3	2	3	19
♂ 10 ♐	4	3	4	3	2	3	19
ASC ♐	4	3	4	3	2	3	19
Totals	19	16	19	15	15	15	Shared Strengths 99

Grid of Gratification

Shared Strengths: 99 **Bonus Bonds:** 8

Positive Planets (check any):

Yours			
☉	✓	♀	✓
☽	✓	♂	✓
☿	✓	ASC	✓

Your Partner's			
☉	✓	♀	✓
☽		♂	✓
☿		ASC	✓

Love Line: ♥	15
Togetherness: ✻	5
Sexual Sizzle:	5
Attraction & Affection: ✚	7
Close Comfort: ★	5

Comprehensive Compatibility Worksheet

Your Name: MIA FARROW

Your Partner's Name: WOODY ALLEN

♥ Love Line 18	☉ 21♒	☽ 12♑	☿ 7♒	♀ 7♈	♂ 26♑	ASC 10♉	Totals
☉ 9♐	♥ 3	✻ 2 ✓	3 ✓	✚ 3 ✓	2	1 ✓	14
☽ 24♒	✻ 4 ✓	♥ 2	4	★ 3	2 ✓	2	17
☿ 4♐	3	2	♥ 3 ✓	3 ✓	2	1	14
♀ 23♎	✚ 3 ✓	★ 2	3	♥ 3	❢ 2 ✓	1	14
♂ 26♑	2 ✓	4	2	❢ 2	♥ 4 ✓	3	17
ASC 2♍	1	3	1 ✓	1 ✓	3	♥ 3	12
Totals	16	15	16	15	15	11	Shared Strengths 88

Grid of Gratification

Shared Strengths:	88
Bonus Bonds:	14
Love Line: ♥	18
Togetherness: ✻	6
Sexual Sizzle: ❢	4
Attraction & Affection: ✚	6
Close Comfort: ★	5

Positive Planets (check any):

Yours				Your Partner's			
☉	☑	♀	☑	☉	☐	♀	☐
☽	☑	♂	☑	☽	☑	♂	☑
☿	☑	ASC	☐	☿	☐	ASC	☐

EXAMPLE EIGHT: MIA FARROW AND WOODY ALLEN

Mia Farrow and Woody Allen have a Love Line of 18—a strong compatible score—and they did manage a romantic partnership for many years. Even that score, however, could not survive Woody's attraction to an adopted daughter and the subsequent public battles which both Mia and Woody attempted to win by attacking the other in the media.

The low Ascendant scores (12 for him, 11 for her) suggest that each felt their relationship did not support self-development. Their Sexual Sizzle score was reasonable (4), but lower than Close Comfort, Attraction & Affection or Togethersness. Perhaps it was a warning signal. But other couples have average scores for Sexual Sizzle and manage to resist affairs.

In the end, each tried to build him/herself up (Ascendant) by tearing his/her partner down. This will not lead to healthy self-esteem.

EXAMPLE NINE: MADONNA AND SEAN PENN

Madonna and Sean Penn have a Love Line score of 15—compatible. But their brief and stormy marriage reflected the low scores each has for their Mars and Ascendant in the comparison. They couldn't handle their anger (a Martian issue) constructively. (A counselor probably would have recommended classes in techniques on "Fighting Fair.") The Ascendant shows where we need to personally call the shots. Each overdeveloped the Ascendant "self" side to the point that the compromises needed in a relationship were not considered. They did their own thing to the extreme of going their separate ways.

Madonna and Sean have a very high score for Bonus Bonds. This indicates lots of close connections between their horoscopes. Such a score is one key to intensity. It can point to love or hate, however. Madonna and Sean ended up living out both extremes.

Comprehensive Compatibility Worksheet

Your Name: MADONNA

Your Partner's Name: SEAN PENN

♥ Love Line 15	☉ 23♌	☽ 11♍	☿ 5♍	♀ 0♌	♂ 15♉	ASC 8♍	Totals
☉ 25♌	♥ 4 ✓	✻ 2	2	✚ 4 ✓	2	2	16
☽ 6♋	✻ 2	♥ 3 ✓	3 ✓	★ 2	3	3 ✓	16
☿ 12♌	4	2 ✓	♥ 2	4	2 ✓	2 ✓	16
♀ 10♍	✚ 2	★ 4 ✓	4 ✓	♥ 2	❢ 3 ✓	4 ✓	19
♂ 10♊	3	2 ✓	2 ✓	❢ 3	♥ 2 ✓	2 ✓	14
ASC 17♐	3	2	2	3	1 ✓	♥ 2	13
Totals	18	15	15	18	13	15	Shared Strengths 94

Grid of Gratification

Shared Strengths:	94
Bonus Bonds:	17
Love Line: ♥	15
Togetherness: ✻	4
Sexual Sizzle: ❢	6
Attraction & Affection: ✚	6
Close Comfort: ★	6

Positive Planets (check any):

Yours				Your Partner's			
☉	☑	♀	☑	☉	☑	♀	☑
☽	☑	♂	☐	☽	☑	♂	☐
☿	☑	ASC	☑	☿	☑	ASC	☐

Astrology points out the best and worst potentials we have to work with. It is still up to the people involved to live on the highest (or the lowest) level. Good compatibility scores indicate that the individuals involved have the ability to build on their commonalities and likenesses—but it is going to be their attitudes and actions which determine the final outcome!

Sign Combinations

SUN

Just as the Sun is the center and heart of our solar system, so is it the center of your horoscope. Where your Sun is, you want to shine, to be admired, to be appreciated, to be proud of yourself. You feel most radiant and alive when pouring energy into the activities of your Sun sign. The Sun also represents general personality traits, and the roles you most favor on the stage of life. Without the Sun, our solar system would have no life, and the Sun in your chart shows what is most important and vital to your existence.

Remember, for a full picture, you would also include the house of your Sun and its aspects, but we can still learn a great deal from sign placements only.

First read the shorthand description for the sign **your** Sun is in. Then, compare it with the shorthand description for the Sun sign of **your partner**. Next, read the paragraph which describes how the two of you may interact with one another. Each combination is also designated as either very compatible, compatible, challenging or very challenging. (These rate as 4-3-2-1 on our **Compatibility Scale**.)

> Your partner's Sun sign is a major key to his heart. Notice, admire and appreciate his Sun sign qualities and he'll feel that you truly value him. Praise his Sun sign characteristics and he'll adore you. Feed his self-esteem and vitality through Sun sign activities and he'll recognize how good you are for him.

SUN IN ARIES: THE LEADER, EXPLORER, WARRIOR, RISK-TAKER, THRILL-SEEKER

Want to be proud of: what you do and who you are
Shine through: courage, physical skills, drive, pioneering spirit, integrity
Want appreciation for: valor, directness, energy, independence, enterprise
Feel radiant, alive when: active, independent, assertive, moving quickly
Pour energy into: competition, being first, everything you are
General personality: forceful, confident, can be self-centered, adventurous
Favorite roles: leader, explorer, warrior, risk-taker, thrill-seeker
Most important to you: excitement, beginnings, acts of courage and will

SUN IN TAURUS: THE SENSUALIST, NATURE LOVER, INDULGER, ARTIST, TYCOON

Want to be proud of: what you own or enjoy, what you earn
Shine through: dependability, stability, easygoingness, artistic skills
Want appreciation for: possessions, financial matters, comfort, relaxed attitude
Feel radiant, alive when: involved in sensual pleasures or creating beauty
Pour energy into: earning money, collecting possessions, enjoying nature
General personality: persistent, dependable, can be stubborn, loyal, determined
Favorite roles: artist, tycoon, sensualist, nature lover, indulger
Most important to you: material security, beauty, nature, pleasure

SUN IN GEMINI: THE STUDENT, TEACHER, FLIRT, SOCIALITE, JOURNALIST, FAIR WITNESS

Want to be proud of: what you learn and/or communicate; your dexterity
Shine through: flexibility, versatility, wide range of interests, knowledge
Want appreciation for: fluency, multiple talents, mental alertness
Feel radiant, alive when: talking, using hands, gaining knowledge or information
Pour energy into: thinking, contrasting, comparing, perceiving, socializing
General personality: chatty, restless, adaptable, lighthearted, youthful
Favorite roles: student, teacher, flirt, socialite, journalist, fair witness
Most important to you: communication, social interchanges, variety in life

SUN IN CANCER: THE PARENT, PATRIOT, BABY, HOST(ESS), CARETAKER

Want to be proud of: your roots, family, ancestry, caring nature
Shine through: nurturing, protectiveness, vulnerability, warmth
Want appreciation for: sympathy, compassion, emotions, home, nest
Feel radiant, alive when: emotionally secure, nurturing others or being taken care of
Pour energy into: family, home, past, cooking, preservation, safety
General personality: sensitive, supportive, focused on home,
Favorite roles: parent, patriot, baby, host(ess), caretaker
Most important to you: emotional security, a nest, traditions, and sentiment

SUN IN LEO: THE STAR, KING OR QUEEN, ENTERTAINER, CHILD, PROMOTER, LOVER

Want to be proud of: charisma, creativity, generosity, confidence, dramatic instincts
Shine through: risk-taking, zest, enthusiasm, creative acts
Want appreciation for: promotional skills, leadership ability, persuasiveness
Feel radiant, alive when: noticed, onstage, gaining love, attention, applause
Pour energy into: procreation, love, speculation, gaining positive regard
General personality: ardent, magnetic, may be arrogant, generous, seeks attention
Favorite roles: the "star", king or queen, entertainer, child, clown, lover
Most important to you: pouring out emotionally/financially and garnering a positive return (love, admiration, money, applause)

SUN IN VIRGO: THE TECHNICIAN, SERVANT, ANALYST, EFFICIENCY EXPERT

Want to be proud of: competence, careful attention to detail, discretion
Shine through: work, health, common sense, "fix-it" talents
Want appreciation for: analytical abilities, pragmatism, helpfulness
Feel radiant, alive when: improving, repairing, finding flaws and fixing them
Pour energy into: efficiency in the body and on the job, doing things right
General personality: conscientious, well-organized, efficient, dedicated
Favorite roles: the technician, the servant, the analyst, efficiency expert
Most important to you: good health and doing things **right**

SUN IN LIBRA: THE PEACEMAKER, ARTIST, DIPLOMAT, PARTNER, BALANCER, STRATEGIST

Want to be proud of: your balance, sense of fair play, grace, good taste
Shine through: diplomacy, partnership, aesthetics, cooperation or competition
Want appreciation for: beauty instincts, relationships skills, evenhandedness
Feel radiant, alive when: harmonizing, weighing, involved with beauty/teamwork
Pour energy into: arts, interpersonal relations, justice
General personality: charming, sociable, companionable, gracious, friendly
Favorite roles: peacemaker, artist, diplomat, partner, balancer, strategist
Most important to you: interactions with others, fairness, equality, niceness

SUN IN SCORPIO: THE SEDUCER, DETECTIVE, HYPNOTIST, THERAPIST, CATALYST, TRANSFORMER

Want to be proud of: passion, resourcefulness, loyalty, emotional strength/courage
Shine through: confrontations, penetration, focus, concentration
Want appreciation for: sharing of joint resources, perseverance, depth insight
Feel radiant, alive when: mastering addictions, probing hidden matters, making intimate connections
Pour energy into: intimacy, sex, appetite mastery, delving into secrets
General personality: willful, insightful, private, power-oriented, passionate
Favorite roles: seducer, detective, hypnotist, therapist, catalyst, transformer
Most important to you: control, mastery, completion, depth understanding

SUN IN SAGITTARIUS: THE PROFESSOR, WHEELER-DEALER, PHILOSOPHER, GYPSY, PREACHER

Want to be proud of: what you know, benevolence, generosity, moral principles
Shine through: sense of fun, optimism, lavish approach, trust in life
Want appreciation for: humor, free spirit, ideals, ethics, gregariousness
Feel radiant, alive when: adventuring, exploring, seeking Truth, having fun
Pour energy into: philosophy, travel, education, religion, good times
General personality: fun-loving, extravagant, restless, glib, optimistic
Favorite roles: professor, wheeler-dealer, philosopher, gypsy
Most important to you: expanding mind and/or horizons, truth, good times

SUN IN CAPRICORN: THE PRESIDENT, EXECUTOR, FATHER FIGURE, WISE OLD ONE

Want to be proud of: status, contribution to the world, sense of responsibility
Shine through: career, grasp of tradition, formal settings
Want appreciation for: being serious, hardworking, dedicated, parental
Feel radiant, alive when: wielding power, accomplishing, providing structure
Pour energy into: profession, practical judgments, duties, reaching the top
General personality: responsible, practical, conservative, diligent, orderly
Favorite roles: president, executor, father figure, Wise Old Man (Woman)
Most important to you: status, power, authority, expertise, structure

SUN IN AQUARIUS: THE INVENTOR, REBEL, ALIEN, GENIUS, SCIENTIST, CASUAL FRIEND

Want to be proud of: uniqueness, individuality, unconventionality, unusual nature
Shine through: being progressive or different, humanitarian causes, mind
Want appreciation for: independence, tolerance, eccentricity, originality
Feel radiant, alive when: logical, objective, futuristic, rebellious
Pour energy into: new ideas, groups, providing options, networking
General personality: innovative, offbeat, freedom-loving, experimental
Favorite roles: inventor, rebel, alien, genius, scientist, casual friend
Most important to you: tolerance, choices, the new (future), variety and change

SUN IN PISCES: THE ARTIST, RESCUER, VICTIM, DREAMER, MYSTIC, IDEALIST

Want to be proud of: compassion, feeling for beauty, sensitivity
Shine through: spiritual, artistic, mystical, idealistic, visionary activities
Want appreciation for: tenderness, unifying spirit, psychic skills, beauty instincts
Feel radiant, alive when: involved with a dream, transcending, inspiring
Pour energy into: beauty, art, nature, escapism, helping/healing activities
General personality: emotional (may be shy), sympathetic, intuitive, romantic
Favorite roles: artist, rescuer, victim, dreamer, mystic, idealist
Most important to you: helping and healing; making world better or more beautiful

SUN PAIRS

ARIES/ARIES

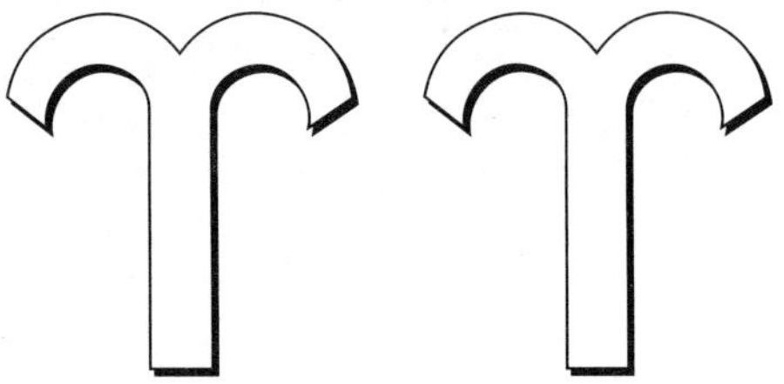

PIONEERING PARTNERS

Admiring one another comes easily. Each of you can appreciate the other's integrity and courage. Direct and forthright, you let one another know what you like. You can both shine through being open, eager, and willing to pioneer. You feed each other's energy and passion. Praise for your honesty, vitality, and independence means much to you both. Excitement energizes you both. You may enjoy pushing the limits or living a bit on the edge. Feeling vital, alive, and passionate is important to each of you. Others probably see you as an active, assertive, and adventurous couple.

VERY COMPATIBLE—4

ARIES/TAURUS

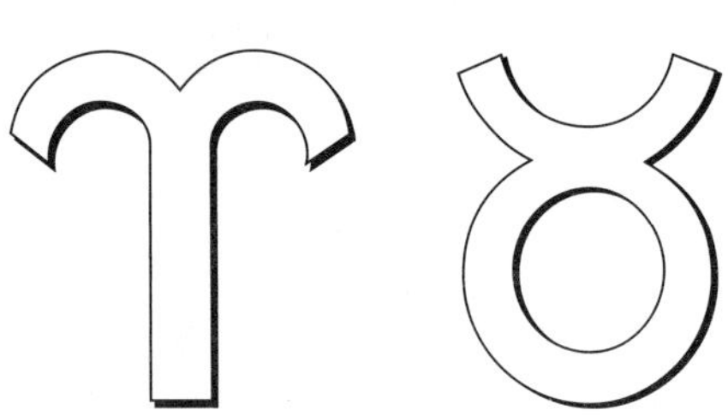

COURAGE AND COMMON SENSE

He needs recognition for his dependability. His self-esteem may be tied to what he earns, owns, and enjoys. Perhaps you can admire him as a good provider, a lover of beauty, or someone who makes your senses sing. To get to his heart, praise his good sense, financial skills, artistic ability, or sensual expertise. You need praise and recognition from him for your courage, honesty, and liveliness. You can energize him, and he can help to ground you.

CHALLENGING—2

ARIES/GEMINI

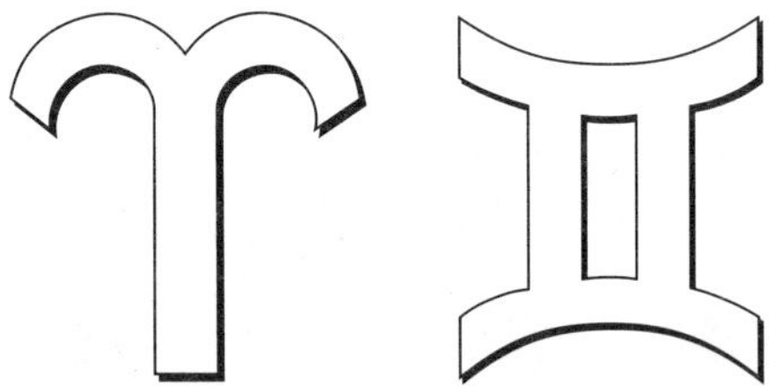

QUICK WITS

You both enjoy being noted for your youthful spirits, so shared fun and games are likely. Praise his quick wits, perception, or way with words and he'll adore you. To reach his heart, admire his mind. He is likely to admire your energy, enthusiasm, and eagerness for experience. Encourage him to recognize your passion, courage, and honesty. Give him opportunities to appreciate your open, spontaneous, and active nature.

COMPATIBLE—3

ARIES/CANCER

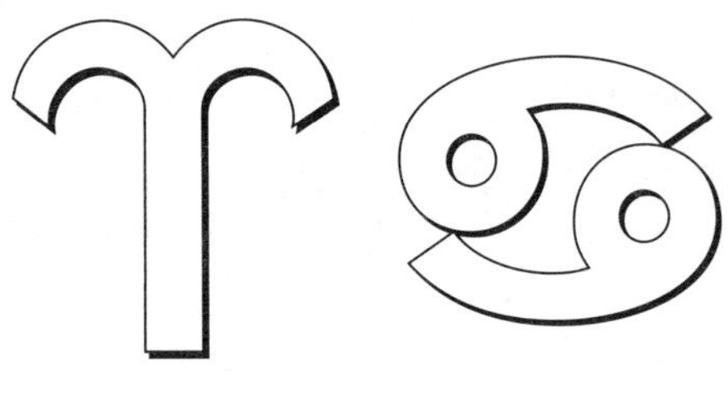

IMMEDIATE INSIGHT

Different strokes feed your self-esteem than his, so the two of you must be open to varying styles. You need him to recognize and admire your direct, eager, courageous nature. He may occasionally feel you come on too strong. He needs you to appreciate and praise his sensitivity, protective instincts, and concern for the home. Don't expect him to be as open as you; he doesn't wear his heart on his sleeve. He can be quite loving, but his style is more subtle (indirect) than yours. You push straight ahead in life. He goes around or under obstacles.

CHALLENGING—2

THRILL-SEEKERS

ARIES/LEO

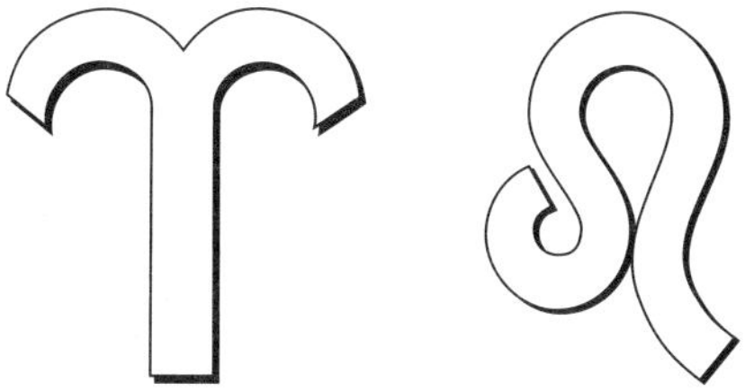

You can stir each other up in all sorts of exciting ways! Each of you can appreciate your partner's enthusiasm, passion, and love of life. You need him to admire your integrity and free spirit. He wants you to recognize his generosity, dramatic skills and ability to create excitement. Praise is as vital to him as his daily bread! Practice positive feedback regularly (no negative!) and he'll be ready to follow you anywhere. If you make him feel like a King, he'll happily make you his Queen.

COMPATIBLE—3

EFFICIENT EXPLORERS

ARIES/VIRGO

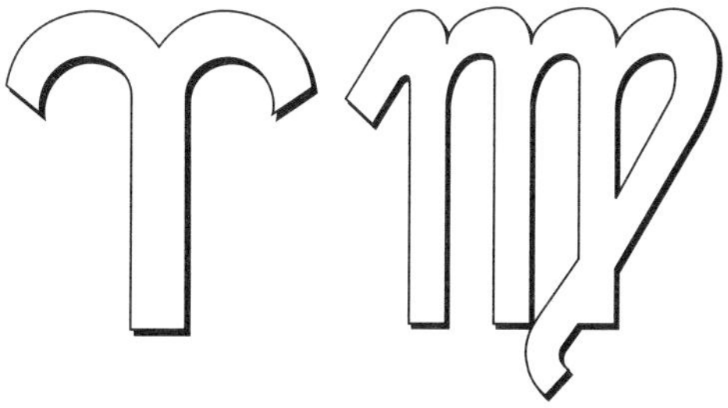

Your ego needs vary considerably from his, so mutual tolerance is essential. He wants admiration for his competence, dedication and skill with details. Praise his expertise, the way he handles his job, and he'll work hard for you. Don't expect him to be as spontaneous as you are. You need him to acknowledge your independence, courage, and energy. He may strike you as critical or nit-picking. You may seem impulsive or rash to him. Appreciate and admire each other's strengths and you can build a solid bond.

VERY CHALLENGING—1

BALANCING ACT

ARIES/LIBRA

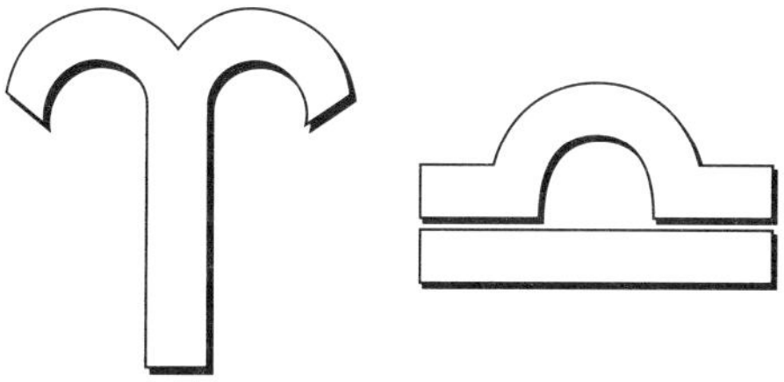

Attraction comes naturally to you two, although you are opposites in some ways. You need him to admire your honesty, free spirit, and eager thrust into life. He needs you to admire his eye for beauty, social skills, and desire for balance. Praise his diplomacy, negotiating abilities, or artistic instincts. You may fall into the role of initiator more often, but he picks up on your cues very well. Together you can create a lovely dance of give-and-take.

VERY COMPATIBLE—4

DIRECT DETECTION

ARIES/SCORPIO

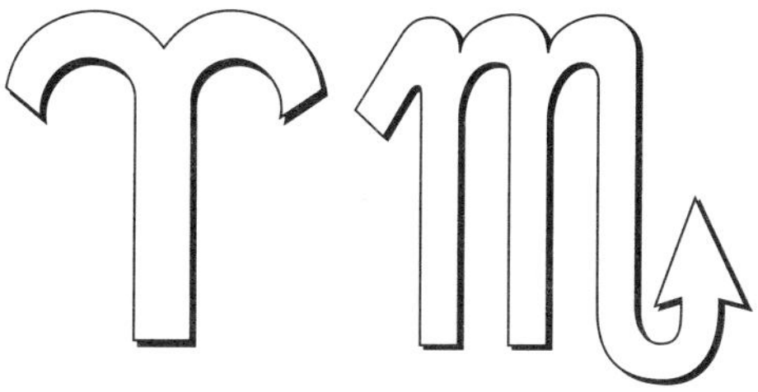

You both must believe in "Viva la difference!" for your relationship to function optimally. He wants admiration for his intensity, resourcefulness, depth, and ability to cope with secrets and hidden matters. You need recognition for your honesty and openness. You appreciate simplicity; he thrives on complexities. You go straight ahead, full speed, in life. He moves cautiously, seeking back-door routes and escape hatches. Sexual attraction could be a shared bond. Passion comes easily to you both. It is essential for you to praise his subtle strategies, and for him to admire your active openness.

VERY CHALLENGING—1

ARIES/SAGITTARIUS

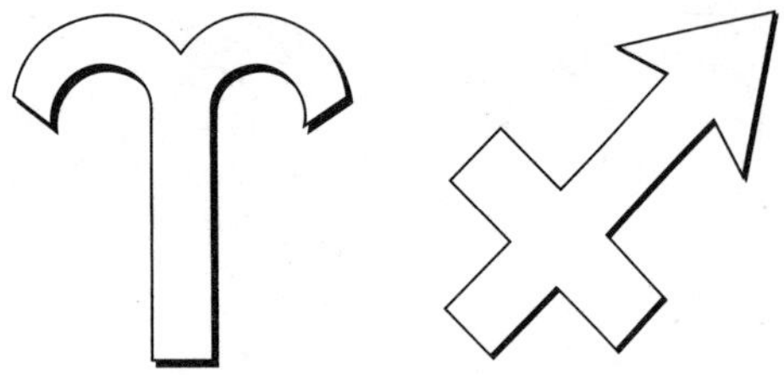

HIGH ON LIFE

The two of you just naturally feed each other's fire. You'll admire his adventurous spirit, love of freedom, and enthusiastic pursuit of **more** in life. He'll appreciate your daring, directness, and devotion to action. Praise his generosity, expansive mind, and exploring instincts, and he'll eagerly pioneer and share excitement with you. You can pep each other up, and both of you tend to be optimistic—ready for anything in life and in love.

COMPATIBLE—3

ARIES/CAPRICORN

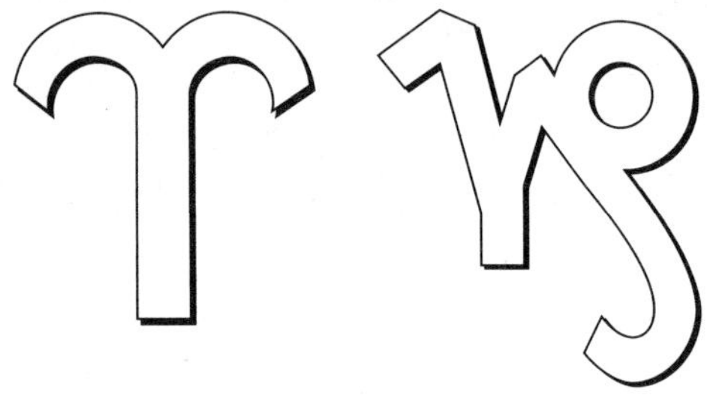

RISK-TAKER AND RULE-MAKER

The two of you tend to take pride in different areas, but sharing may be easier if you stroke each other's egos (as well as bodies) properly. He wants respect—to be admired as an achiever. Praise him for his success in his work (or any endeavors for which he is responsible). You need him to appreciate and acknowledge your independence, honesty and forthright approach. Since you are both strong individuals, beware of fighting for control. You can shine in areas calling for spontaneity and optimism. He can shine in situations demanding caution, planning ahead, and hard work. Divide up the territory and you'll do well.

CHALLENGING—2

ARIES/AQUARIUS

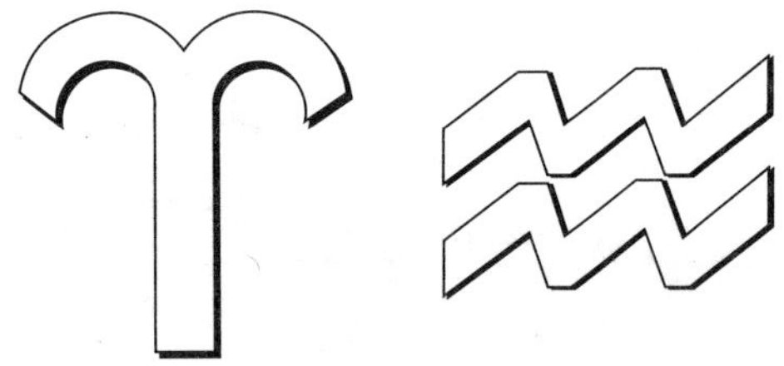

RISK-TAKING REBELS

Each of you wants to be admired for your free spirit and interest in the new. The way to his heart is to praise his passion for justice, ability to relate to anyone, or interest in technology. He could be somewhat unconventional, futuristic, or independent. He needs to acknowledge your energy, courage, and integrity. You shine through honesty, openness, and direct action. Recognize his uniqueness. Allow his individuality to shine, and he is likely to respond with affection and support for your special gifts.

COMPATIBLE—3

ARIES/PISCES

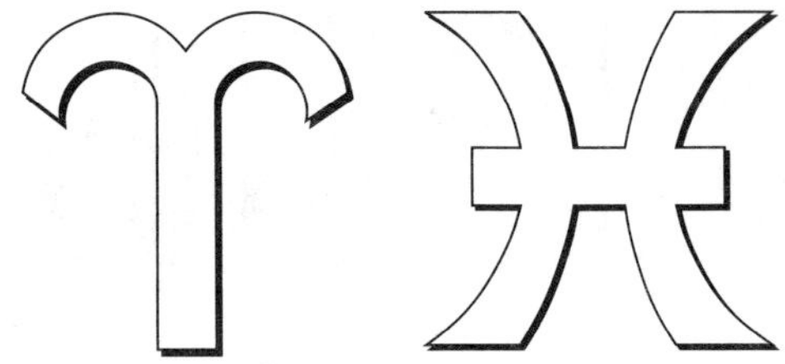

MYSTICAL WARRIORS

Although your basic personalities differ, if you genuinely appreciate each other's special qualities, all will be well. Recognize and admire his idealism, sensitivity, poetic nature, or wonderful imagination. Praise his capacity to visualize. Even though he may be more retiring or private, he needs to appreciate your openness, drive for action and free spirit. His whimsy, artistic yearnings, romantic instincts and intuition can be gifts to you. Your courage, spontaneity and honesty can be gifts to him.

CHALLENGING—2

COMMON SENSE AND COURAGE

TAURUS/ARIES

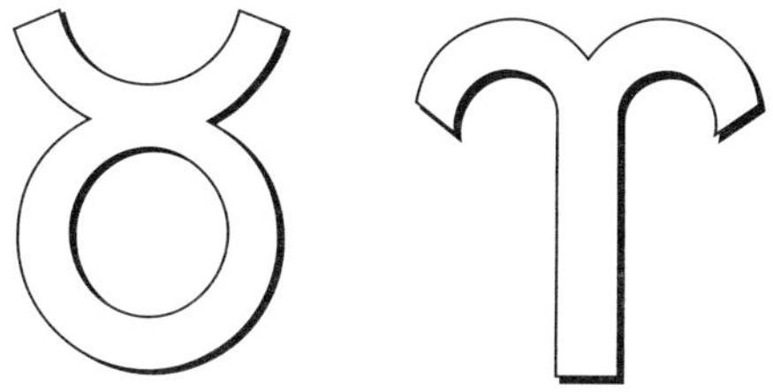

He needs recognition for his courage, directness, and willingness to act. Praise his honesty, spontaneity, and energy. Acknowledge his eagerness to live and love. Admire his passion and integrity—and he is yours! He needs to appreciate your reliability and good sense. He may admire your sensual skills, artistic eye, or financial abilities. You're a bit more relaxed; he can be a real go-getter. You can help ground him, and he can energize you.

CHALLENGING—2

LOVE OF LUXURY

TAURUS/TAURUS

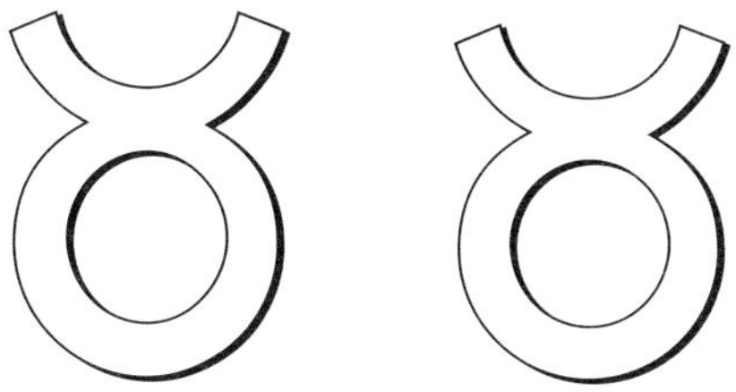

The finer things in life appeal to you both. What you earn, what you own, and what you enjoy in life are sources of pride. Either of you may tie self-esteem to your salary, your possessions, your sensuality, or your feeling for beauty. Praise him for exactly those qualities you seek recognition of: dependability, simplicity, love of beauty and nature, financial instincts and the ability to indulge the physical senses. Together, you can eat, drink, and enjoy great massages.

VERY COMPATIBLE—4

SENSUAL SOCIALITES

TAURUS/GEMINI

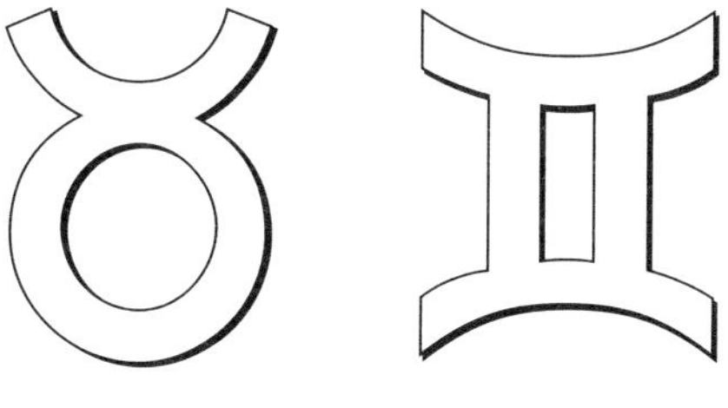

Your sources of pride differ, but can be complementary to one another. Recognize his mind. Praise his versatility, perceptiveness, and fluency. Admire his way with words, vast collection of knowledge, or curiosity about everything. He'll adore you for appreciating what matters most to him. He needs to appreciate and acknowledge your steadiness, reliability, and skill at creating beauty and comfort (even when he's more scattered). He may admire or praise your sensuality, financial instincts, or love of nature. He can expose you to new ideas, and you can encourage him to persevere.

CHALLENGING—2

PAMPERED PATRIOTS

TAURUS/CANCER

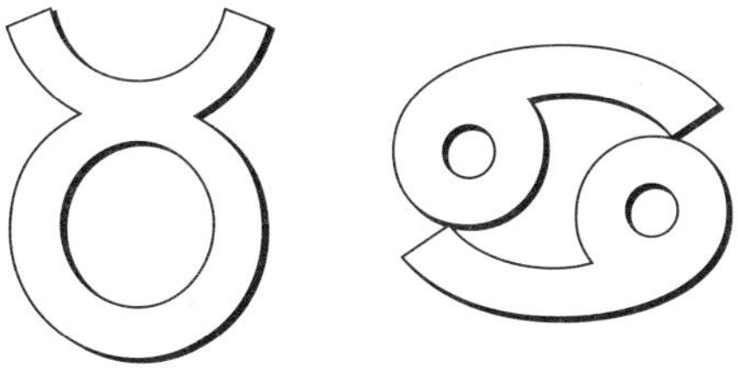

The two of you can really spoil each other! Praise his culinary abilities, assisting (helpful) instincts, patriotism, family feelings, or skill at taking care of things. His self-esteem is tied to protecting and preserving. You both may enjoy good food, drink and fine possessions. He can appreciate your sensuality, financial acumen, and ability to make people comfortable. Shared pleasures come easily to you both and physical demonstrations of affection are second nature.

COMPATIBLE—3

TAURUS/LEO

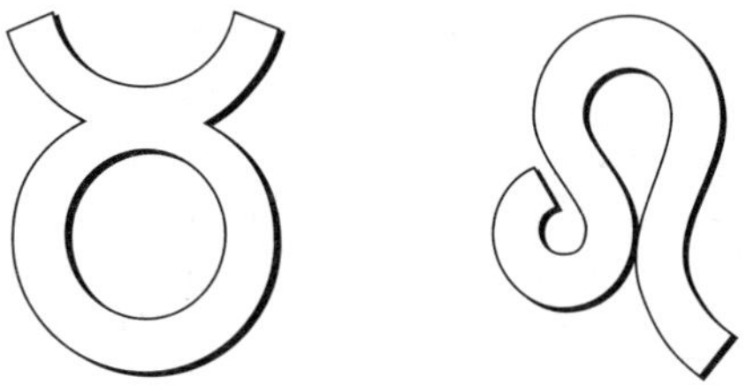

DIGNIFIED AND DEPENDABLE

Praise and sincere compliments are definitely the way to his heart! Show your respect. Admire his dramatic skills, natural dignity, leadership, creativity, or sense of fun. Positive feedback will get you what you want. Avoid criticism—period! He can value your stability, good sense and sensual appreciation of life's pleasures. He's more of a risk-taker; you prefer to consolidate your gains. Since you are both quite strong-willed, don't fall into power struggles. Each of you must be willing to take turns. You can both enjoy fine possessions and indulging in food, drink, or satisfying sensual/sexual experiences.

CHALLENGING—2

TAURUS/VIRGO

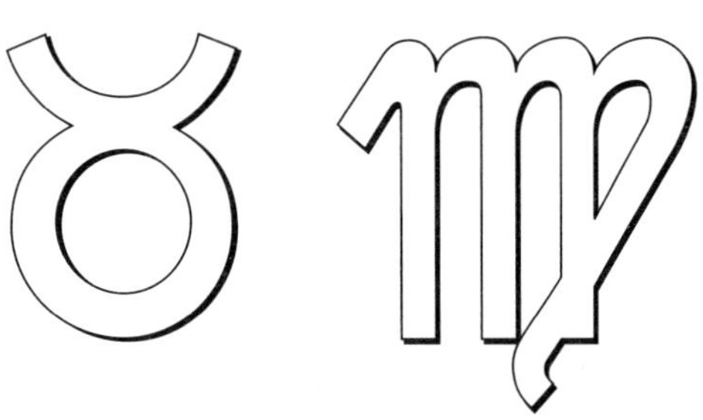

EARTHY EFFICIENCY

It is easy for you to appreciate each other's common sense. You both take pride in your accomplishments. You may both enjoy nature, the Earth, or any activity with measurable results. You two could share tasks, taking satisfaction in a job well done. Admire his competence, discipline, efficiency, and productivity, and he will see you as worthy of commitment. Praise his dedication to excellence, his achievements at work, or his understanding of health and nutrition. He can appreciate your practicality, comfortable nature, and skill at enjoying life.

COMPATIBLE—3

TAURUS/LIBRA

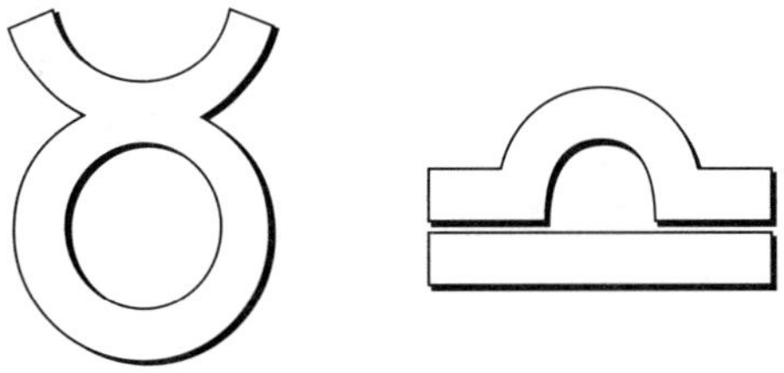

ARTISTIC

You take pride in different areas, but can mix well if you respect each other's talents. Praise his skills with people—diplomacy, empathy, negotiating (or competitive) skills. Admire his instinct for balance, harmony, and equality. You both have artistic impulses, though his may be more visual and yours more tactile. Give him opportunities to appreciate your sensuality, feeling for finances, and desire to create comfort. You both enjoy ease and keeping life pleasant.

VERY CHALLENGING—1

TAURUS/SCORPIO

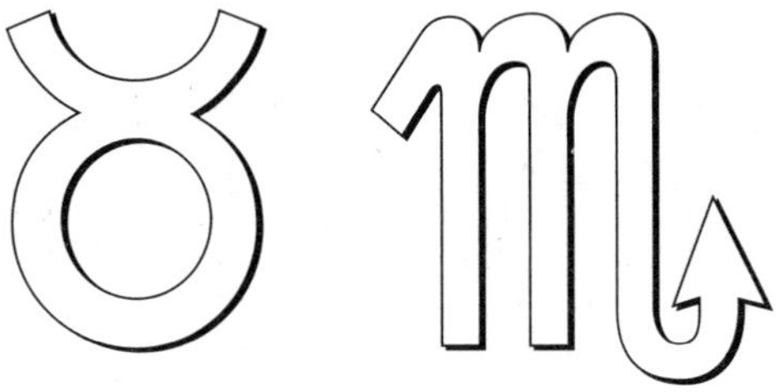

POSSESSIONS AND PLEASURES

Indulgence is the name of the game! Both of you have heightened sensuality. You may tune into one another sexually and are likely to enjoy good food, drink, massages, hot tubs, or other forms of physical pleasure. You may admire each other's fine possessions. Praise his intensity, sexual magnetism, and desire to look beneath the surface in life. He is proud of his depths and self-control. He can appreciate your practicality, perseverance, and pleasure-loving nature.

VERY COMPATIBLE—4

GROUNDED GYPSY?

TAURUS/SAGITTARIUS

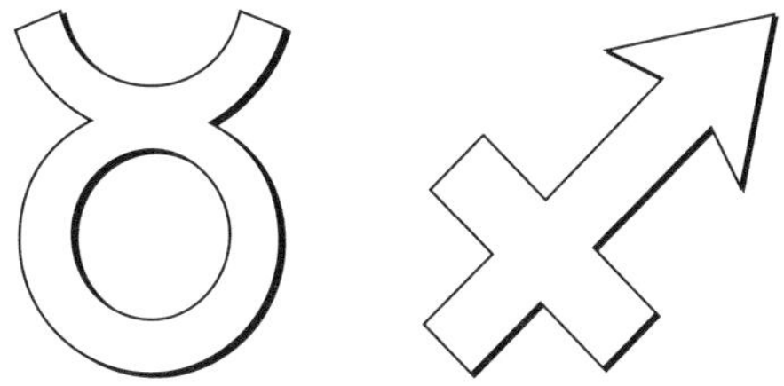

Self-esteem comes from very different sources for each of you, so openness and compromise are essential. He wants to be admired for his mind, his adventurous spirit, his ethics or moral principles, his beliefs, his humor, or a readiness to travel on an instant's notice. You need recognition for your practicality, groundedness, sensuality, and skill with the material world. Don't polarize over mental versus physical, or safety versus adventure. Do appreciate one another for your best qualities.

VERY CHALLENGING—1

RELIABLE RULES

TAURUS/CAPRICORN

Each of you appreciates dependability in the other. The way to his heart is to admire his status, his professional accomplishments, his expertise, his handling of power, or his strong sense of responsibility. Praise his self-discipline, conscientiousness, willingness to work, ambition, and pragmatism. He can admire and appreciate your good sense, skill with finances, reliability, faithfulness, and desire to bring comfort and pleasure to others. You both demonstrate love by doing things for people.

COMPATIBLE—3

INDIVIDUALISTIC INDULGENCE

TAURUS/AQUARIUS

You tend to pride yourselves on different qualities, so open-mindedness is vital. He wants to be admired for being unique, unusual, bright, progressive, humanitarian, or objective. He is proud of his ability to handle change and variety. You need recognition for your steadiness and reliability. You are skilled at creating material comforts and pleasures. Together, you two need to blend the mental and physical, the new and familiar, the exciting and the comfortable.

CHALLENGING—2

EASY DOES IT

TAURUS/PISCES

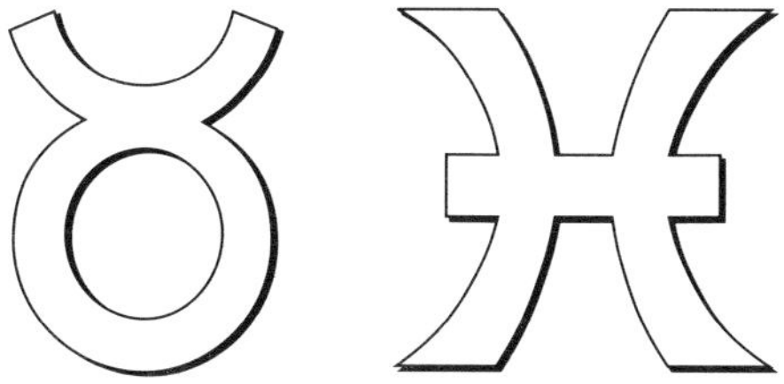

You both have artistic, creative talent, and the ability to please others. He needs to be recognized for his imagination, sensitivity, dramatic flair, romantic ideals, persuasive abilities, and love of beauty and ease. You need to be admired for your good sense, dependability, skill with the material and financial worlds, and ability to create comfort. An appreciation of art, nature, or a smooth, easy flow in life can be a shared bond between you.

COMPATIBLE—3

GEMINI/ARIES

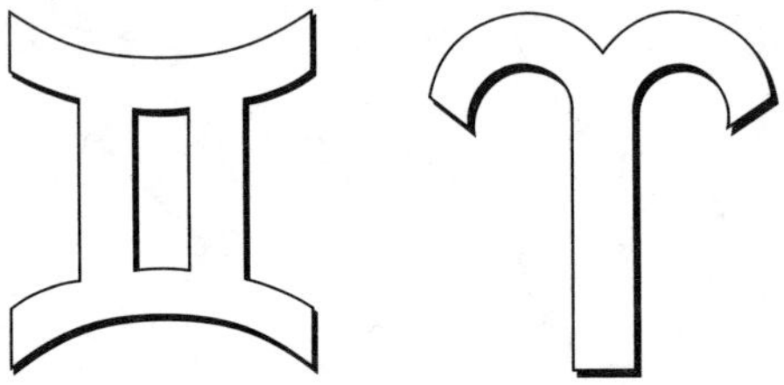

QUICK WITS

You two share a lively, youthful attitude. Ever-ready to laugh and enjoy life, you may participate in many varieties of fun and games. He wants recognition for his energy, pioneering spirit, integrity, and openness. Praise him for being first, for his courage, honesty, and directness. You feel loved when he admires your mind, communication skills, alertness, versatility, and interest in everything. You refresh and enliven one another.

COMPATIBLE—3

GEMINI/TAURUS

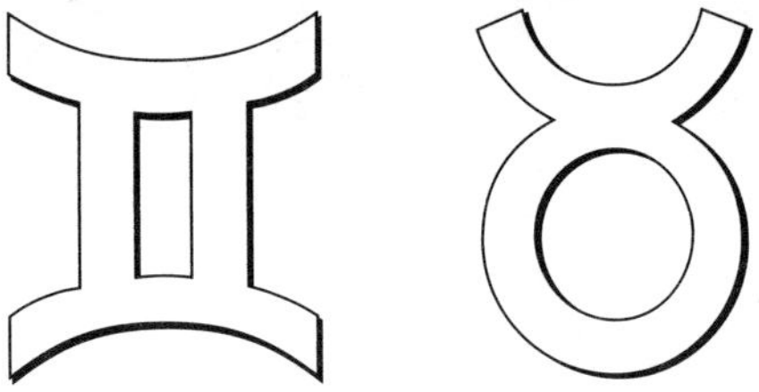

SENSUAL SOCIALITES

"Different strokes for different folks" applies here. Admire his reliability, financial skills, or sensual expertise, and he will value you greatly. He feels loved when you do things for him, or appreciate his simplicity, ability to create comfort, eye for beauty, or practical, common sense. Give him opportunities to admire your verbal, mental, or perceptual skills. You shine through your mind and need praise for your curiosity, versatility, flexibility, and eagerness to learn. You can expose him to new experiences, and he can help you be more focused and grounded.

CHALLENGING—2

GEMINI/GEMINI

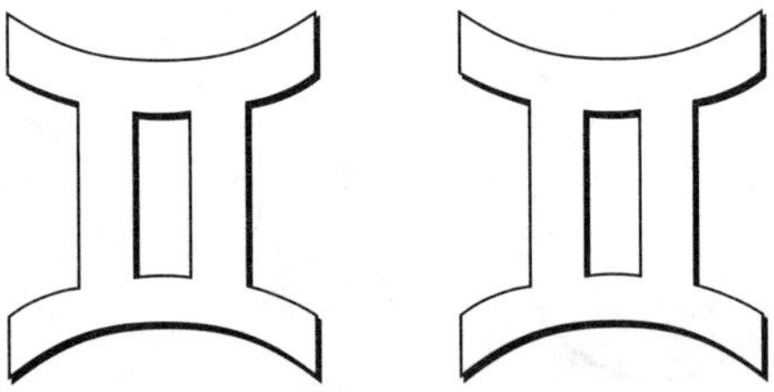

JOKING JOURNALISTS

Love goes with laughter and lightness for the two of you! The way to his heart is to praise and admire in him those qualities you wish to be recognized and appreciated within you: a quick wit, good verbal skills, an excellent mind, curiosity and interest in everything, adaptability, and an eagerness for fresh, new experiences. Together, you never stop learning (and discussing)!

VERY COMPATIBLE—4

GEMINI/CANCER

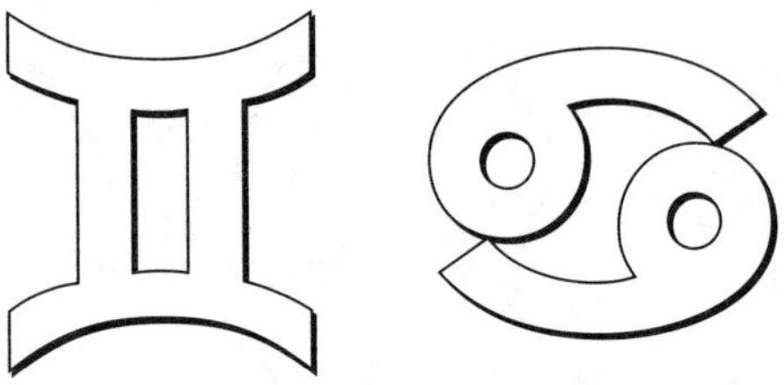

DEVOTED DILETTANTES

You seek applause through different channels so must understand that recognition means one thing to you and another to him. He wants to be admired for his caretaking capabilities, patriotic fervor, family feelings, sensitivity, emotional warmth, or protective, preserving instincts. You need to be praised for your mind, way with words, multiple talents and interests, or adaptability. You shine in communication; he shines in silent caring. Be understanding of one another.

CHALLENGING—2

YOUTHFUL

GEMINI/LEO

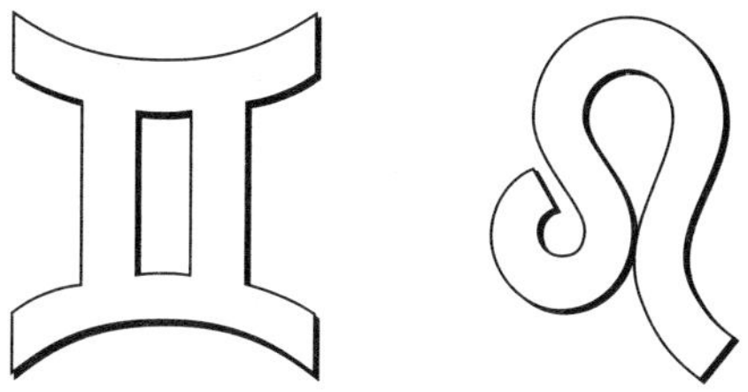

You spark the inner child in each other, easily stimulating each other's humor and love of life. Tell your Leo (sincerely!) how great he is and he'll adore you. Admire his regal air, his dramatic flair, his savoir-faire. Praise his dignity, generosity, and creativity. Give him opportunities to admire your mind, your ability to talk, and your enthusiasm for learning anything and everything. He brings sparkle and enthusiasm to your life. You bring interesting ideas and fresh perceptions to him.

COMPATIBLE—3

KNOWLEDGE OVER ALL

GEMINI/VIRGO

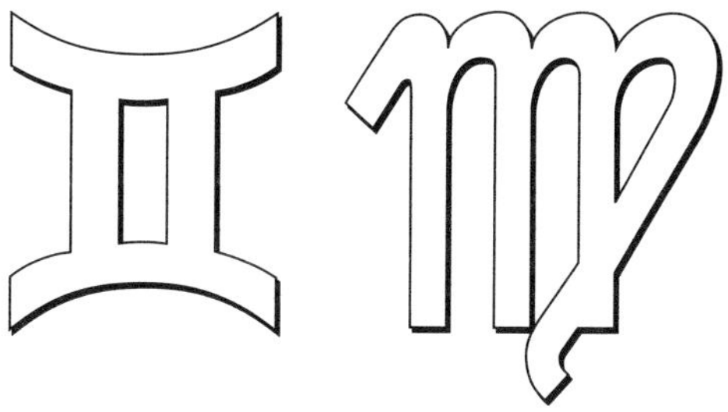

You both can shine mentally, but in different ways. He is proud of his common sense and ability to focus. Praise him for his competence, dedication, skill with details, work accomplishments, efficiency, and productivity. Quality is vital to him. You thrive on quantities of information—curious about anything and everything. It is essential that he appreciate and admire your versatility, adaptability and verbal skills. You may be more scattered and he more organized, but you can be more flexible when he gets obsessed with details. Both of you value learning. Love each other for your minds (as well as bodies).

CHALLENGING—2

OBJECTIVE AND OPEN

GEMINI/LIBRA

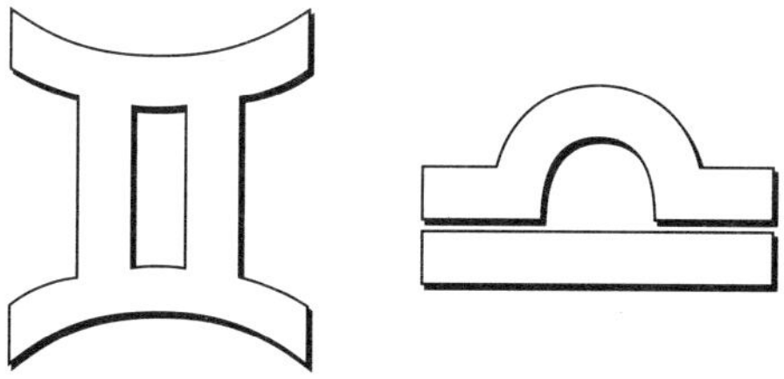

You both feel loved when you can communicate and be truly heard and understood by the other. Praise his social skills, artistic eye, negotiating ability, drive for balance, ear for harmony, or instinct for equality and justice. He'll see you as a person of rare discernment. You need him to recognize and admire your quick wits, lively curiosity, flexibility, interest in everything, desire to communicate, and eagerness to learn. Together, you can share information, ideas, and intimacy.

COMPATIBLE—3

THERAPEUTIC TEACHER

GEMINI/SCORPIO

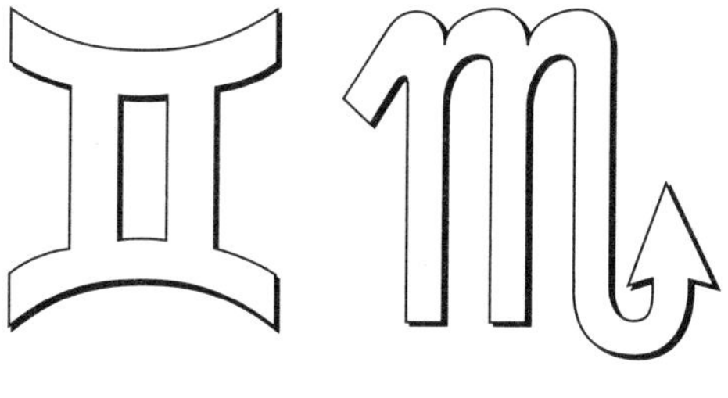

Your self-esteem needs differ considerably, so tolerance is essential on both sides. He seeks recognition for his depth, subtlety, passion, and intensity. Praise his sexual charisma, ability to uncover hidden information, or powerful drive. You need recognition for your breadth of interests, lighthearted, friendly spirit, and ability to be detached. Flirting may come easily to you, but he could be jealous or possessive, so tread carefully. You take pride in your words, wit, and sense of wonder. He can help you get to the bottom of things. You can help him to lighten up.

VERY CHALLENGING—1

GEMINI/SAGITTARIUS

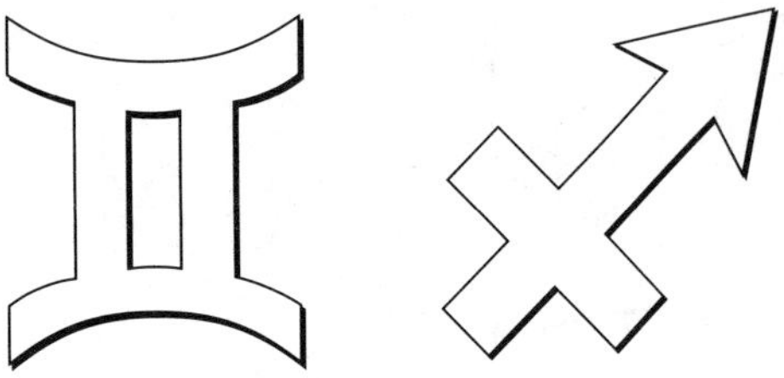

STUDENT AND TEACHER

You two make a fun, friendly, frolicking twosome, both eager to explore life. Praise his intellectual breadth, athletic skills, spirit of adventure, or sense of humor. Admire his ethics, religion, love of travel, or desire to explore. He needs to appreciate your alertness, quick perceptions, and interest in anything and everything. Your self-esteem is tied to your mind, verbal skills and flexibility. Both of you enjoy discussing things, so communication and constant learning should be shared bonds between you.

VERY COMPATIBLE—4

GEMINI/CAPRICORN

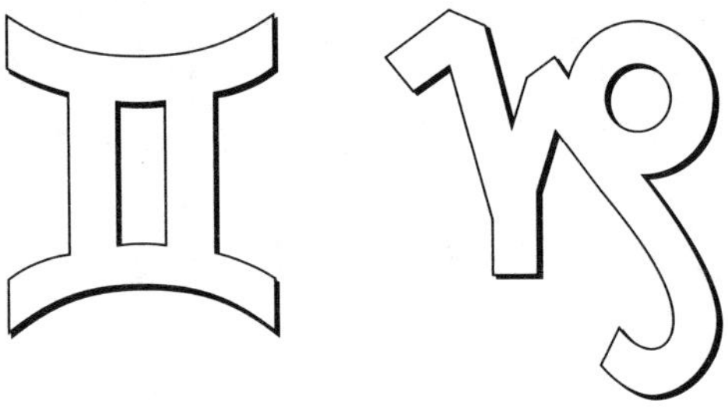

LEARNING LIMITS

For this relationship to flourish, you each must admire and praise in the other, qualities different from those you prize within yourselves. You pride yourself on being lighthearted, friendly, versatile, and multitalented. He prides himself on being serious, cautious, responsible, and hardworking. Compliment him on his career accomplishments. Notice how others respect him. Admire his expertise, skill with the power structure, and practical focus. You need him to appreciate your flippancy, sense of fun, and flexibility. He may admire your way with words. He can contribute to stability in your life, and you can contribute to flux and adaptability in his.

VERY CHALLENGING—1

GEMINI/AQUARIUS

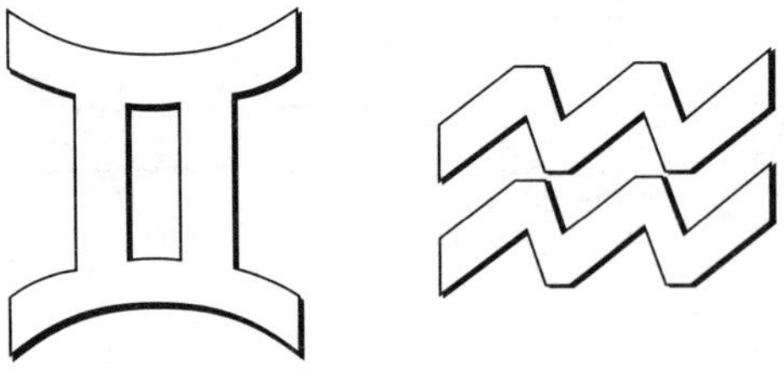

STUDENTS OF SCIENCE

Both of you pride yourselves on your ability to think, communicate, and to be fair and impartial, so common ground should be easy to find. The way to his heart is through his mind. Admire his uniqueness. Praise his originality and he'll respond wonderfully. Since you both seek mental stimulation, this can be a lively relationship. He will appreciate your quick wit and perceptiveness. You will enjoy his open mind, futuristic ideas, and enthusiasm for the new and different. You each take pride in the other's alertness and eagerness to learn.

COMPATIBLE—3

VARIED VISIONS

GEMINI/PISCES

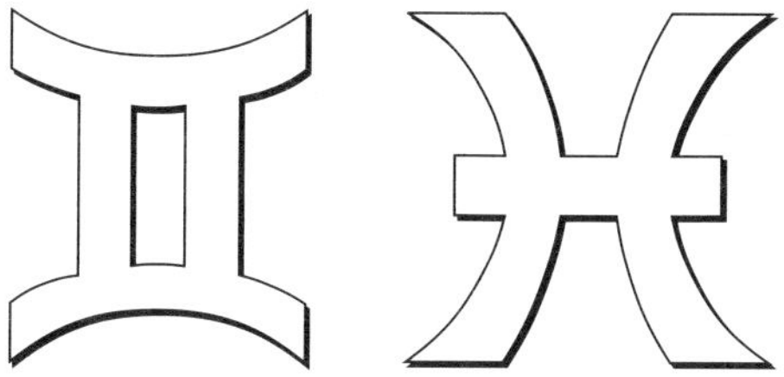

A multiplicity of interests may draw you together, but your areas of pride and self-esteem do differ. He needs praise for his sensitivity, intuition, eye for beauty, or ability to assess life and see the big picture. You need praise for your liveliness, logic, and laughter. You figure things out by talking them over; he figures things out by mulling them over. He seeks recognition for his compassion, inwardness, imagination, romantic ideals, or feeling for beauty and nature. You seek recognition for your mind, your enthusiasm for fresh experiences, and your eagerness to learn from everyone and everything. You can teach him to open up more, and he can educate you regarding the joys of contemplation.

CHALLENGING—2

IMMEDIATE INSIGHT

CANCER/ARIES

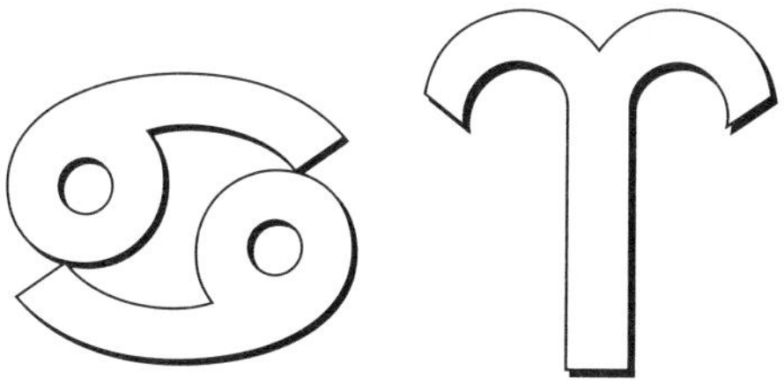

You're looking for love in different ways, so tolerance and understanding are vital. Praise him for courage, leadership, integrity and openness. Admire his straightforward style, independent nature, and energy and enthusiasm for life. He may have to learn to appreciate your gentleness, empathy, and nurturing spirit. You need recognition for your domestic skills, warmth, caring, and desire to help others. Don't polarize over freedom versus closeness needs, or adventures versus the nest. Do value each other's strong points, and achieve a middle ground which pleases you both.

CHALLENGING—2

PAMPERED PATRIOTS

CANCER/TAURUS

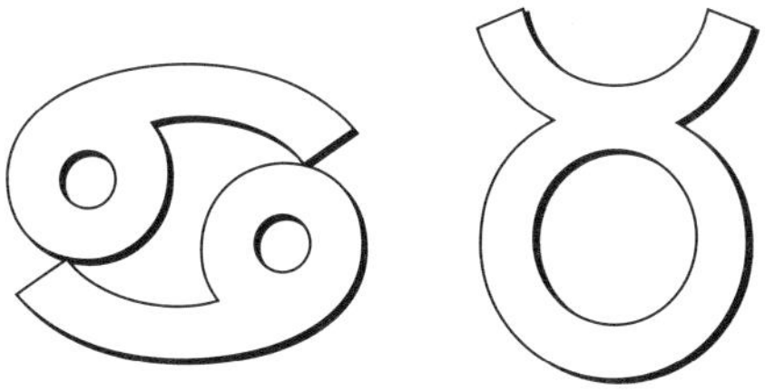

The two of you can really spoil each other! Praise his money-making abilities, skill at putting people at ease, sensuality, or lovely things. Appreciate how easy it is to feel comfortable with him. Admire his simple, relaxed, easygoing attitudes. Give him opportunities to praise your cooking, nurturing instincts, patriotism, family feelings, or skill at taking care of things. Your self-esteem is tied to protecting and preserving. You both may enjoy good food, drink, and fine possessions. Shared pleasures come easily to you both and physical demonstrations of affection are natural.

COMPATIBLE—3

CANCER/GEMINI

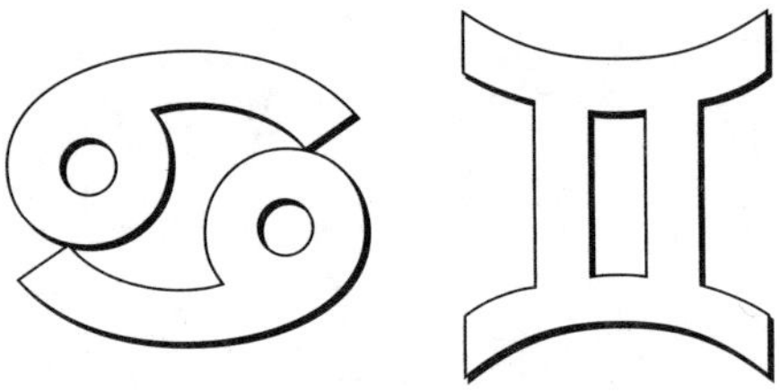

DEVOTED DILETTANTES

You seek applause through different channels so must understand that recognition means one thing to you and another to him. You want to be admired for your caretaking capabilities, patriotic fervor, family feelings, sensitivity, emotional warmth, or protective, preserving instincts. He needs to be praised for his mind, way with words, multiple talents and interests, or adaptability. He shines in thinking, speaking, or conveying information. You shine in nurturing, assisting, and silent caring. Be understanding of one another.

CHALLENGING—2

CANCER/CANCER

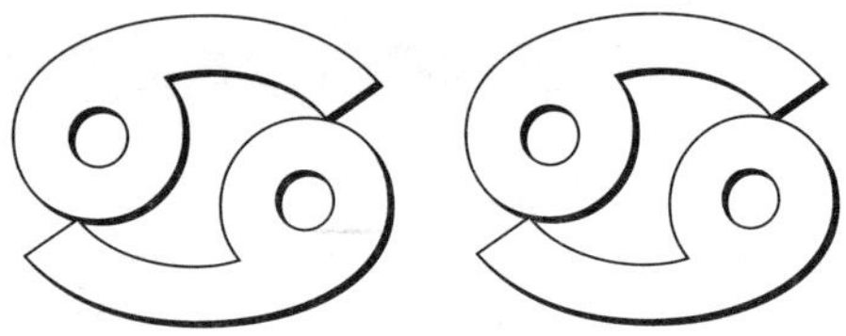

COMPASSIONATE CARETAKERS

Hearth and home or caring and compassion can be a strong bond between you. Each of you is capable of great emotional warmth. Praise him for those qualities you wish others to admire in you: protective instincts, nurturing abilities, culinary skills, an attachment to family, roots, and/or country. Admire his home, his possessions, his loved ones, and his caring nature. Take turns caring for, pampering, and looking after one another, and you'll build a good emotional connection.

VERY COMPATIBLE—4

CANCER/LEO

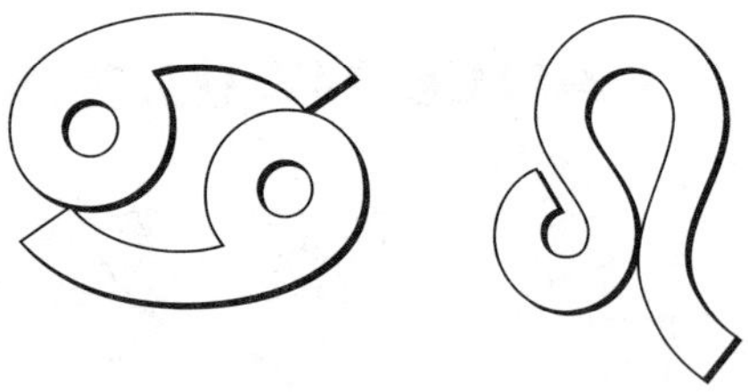

HOST(ESS) WITH THE MOST(ESS)

Make your Leo feel like King of the Castle and he'll be ready for you to be Queen of Hearth and Home. Praise him lavishly. Leos thrive on positive attention. Sincerely admire his dignity, generosity, or creativity. Let him take center stage, be dramatic, and impressive. Applaud him whenever possible and he'll view you as exciting and attractive. He needs to learn to appreciate your sensitive, more retiring nature, and to admire your empathy, caring, and devotion to loved ones. If you can keep a balance between introversion and extroversion, between public and private lives, you can build a warm, loving connection with one another.

CHALLENGING—2

ASSISTING ANALYSIS

CANCER/VIRGO

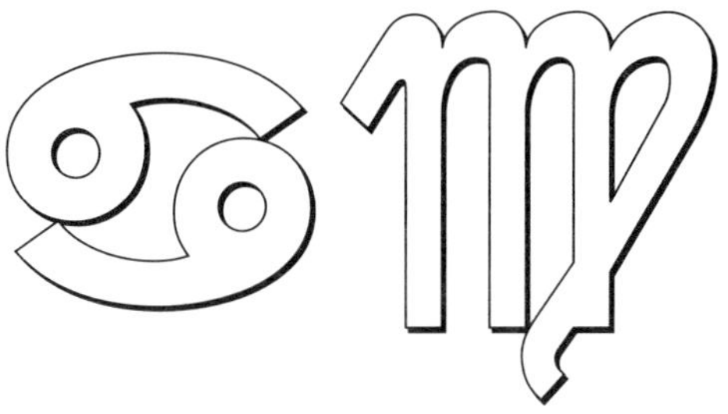

You both are natural caretakers, eager to assist others. Your focus tends to be more on people and emotional needs, while his tends to be more on things and work duties. Admire his competence, efficiency, and ability to figure out what is wrong and fix it. He has an eye for flaws (can be critical) and loves to improve or repair things. (If he tries to improve people, gently steer him toward objects instead.) He needs recognition for his health, productivity, work achievements, and common sense. You need appreciation for your emotional warmth, nurturing abilities, devotion to family and loved ones. You each demonstrate love partly through service—doing for others.

COMPATIBLE—3

PARENTAL PARTNERS

CANCER/LIBRA

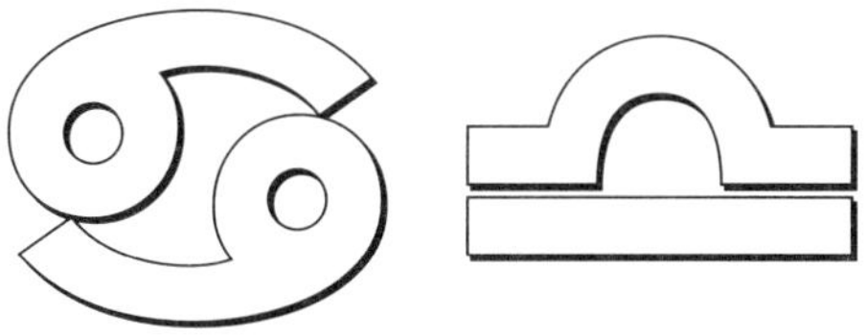

Emotional attachments are important to each of you, though you may vary in the degree of closeness desired. He thrives on face-to-face interactions and finds other people fun and stimulating. You prefer a small, private circle. He can be a good negotiator, diplomat, or consultant. You tend to keep some things inside, not wearing your heart on your sleeve. Praise his eye for beauty, instinct for balance and harmony, social skills, or friendly nature. Admire his cooperative and competitive spirit. You need him to appreciate your caring, sensitivity, faithfulness, and willingness to build a home full of love and warmth. Commitment to shared feelings can make a strong bond between you.

CHALLENGING—2

CARING CATALYSTS

CANCER/SCORPIO

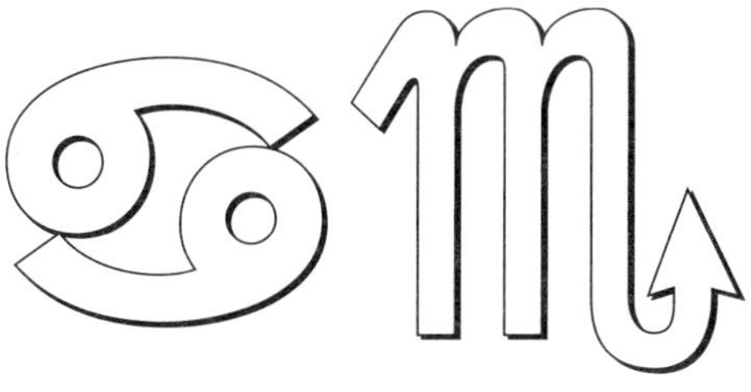

You both appreciate the subtle dance of love and are sensitive to hints, innuendoes, secrets, and hidden messages. Admire his passion, intensity, forcefulness, and resourcefulness. Praise his animal magnetism, strength of will, and "do or die" determination. He must voice appreciation of your sensitivity, warmth, caring, and compassion. You need recognition for your devotion to home, family, and loved ones, your nurturing instincts, and your desire to protect and preserve. You both have strong, deep feelings that you tend to keep hidden. Don't bury too much! Once you commit, you both value loyalty very highly.

COMPATIBLE—3

CANCER/SAGITTARIUS RESTLESS ROOTS

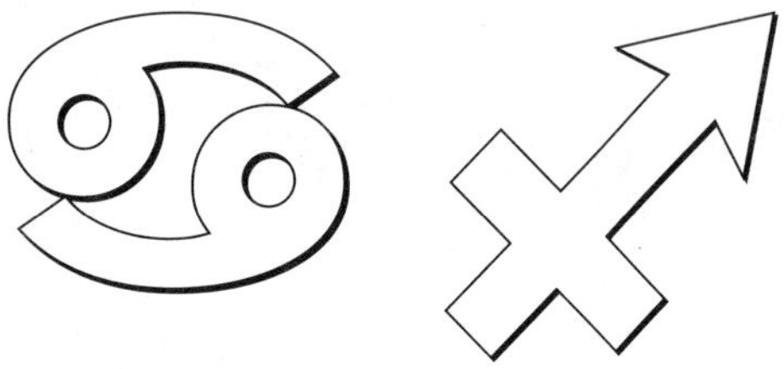

You thrive on different kinds of activity, so must respect each other's uniqueness. He wants admiration for his adventurous spirit, sense of humor, or philosophical bent. Praise his mind, ethics, ideals, optimism, or ready wit. You need him to recognize and appreciate your loyalty, family ties, nurturing instincts, and desire to protect and save. Travel, movement, and exploration energize him. Security, safety, and a homey atmosphere energize you. With compromise, each of you can enrich the other's life. Be willing to take turns so that each of you can do what you love.

VERY CHALLENGING—1

CANCER/CAPRICORN FAMILY FOCUS

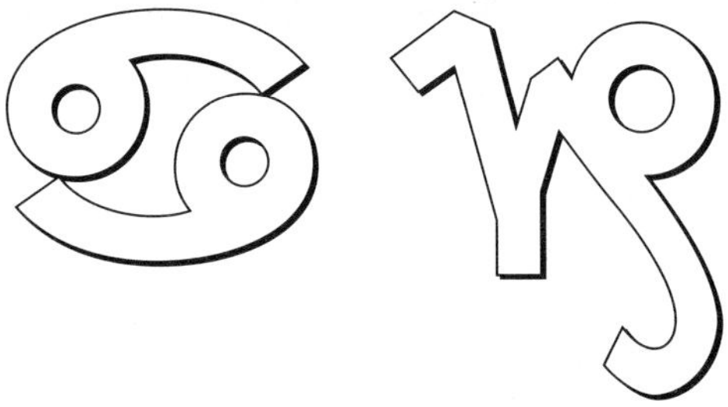

Both of you take pride in your loyalty and carrying through on your responsibilities. Family ties may matter a lot to you both. Each of you tends to be a caretaker—someone who looks after others. He takes pride in his realism and productive accomplishments. Praise his career, status, sense of responsibility, dedication, or practicality. He should find it easy to admire your caring nature, compassion, and protective, preserving instincts. Each of you appreciates security and stability. Together, you build for the long haul.

VERY COMPATIBLE—4

CANCER/AQUARIUS REBEL ROOTS

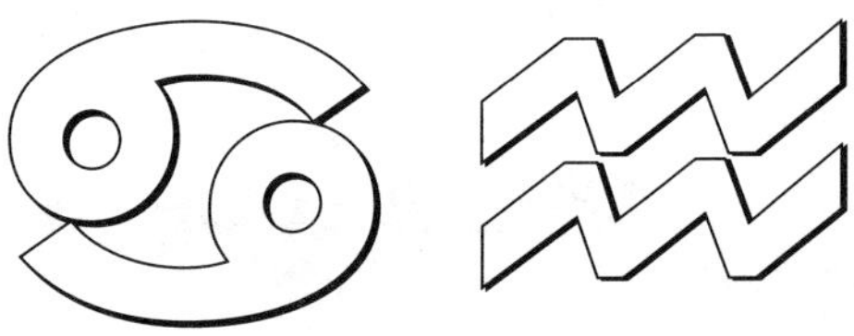

Pride and self-esteem are tied to different areas for each of you, so mutual tolerance is essential. Praise his individuality, inventiveness, and independent spirit. Tell him he's not like anyone else! Admire his skill with technology, future focus, networking abilities, or unusual interests and talents. You want him to appreciate your caring, compassion and concern. He must be able to admire your sentimental attachments, feeling for hearth and home, and desire for emotional safety and security. Don't polarize between freedom needs versus a desire for closeness, or feel torn between stability versus change. Do be open to what you can learn from one another.

VERY CHALLENGING—1

MOTHERING MYSTICISM — CANCER/PISCES

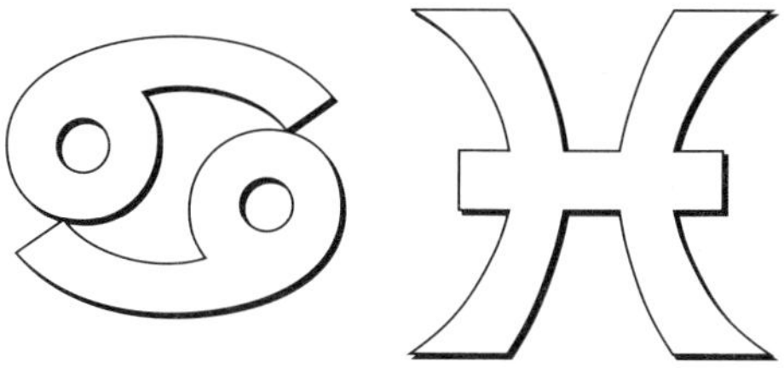

Both of you tend to admire sensitivity, empathy, and concern for others. You can praise his skill with imagination, fantasy, or visualizing. Recognize his poetic, mystical, tender, or romantic side. Appreciate that many of his feelings are hidden. He can applaud your willingness to help others. You both have strong rescuing instincts. He can admire your roots, family connections, emotional loyalty, feeling for the helpless, and urge to build a warm, loving home environment. You both keep your emotions somewhat under cover, being protective (of self and others). Be sure you share what matters. Sometimes you understand each other without words.

COMPATIBLE—3

THRILL-SEEKERS — LEO/ARIES

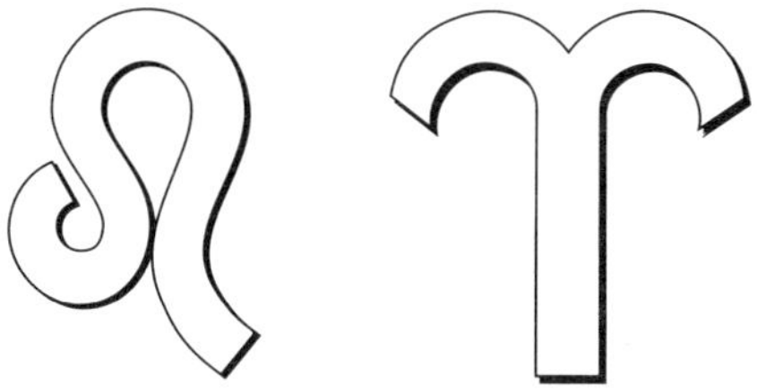

You can stir each other up in all sorts of exciting ways! Each of you can appreciate your partner's enthusiasm, passion, and love of life. You need to admire his integrity and free spirit. You want him to recognize your generosity, dramatic skills and ability to create excitement. Praise is as vital to you as your daily bread! Remember that he wants life to be an adventure. Demonstrate your courage; let him know you're eager for thrills. You can encourage one another to live life to the hilt—always ready for action and adventure.

COMPATIBLE—3

DIGNIFIED AND DEPENDABLE — LEO/TAURUS

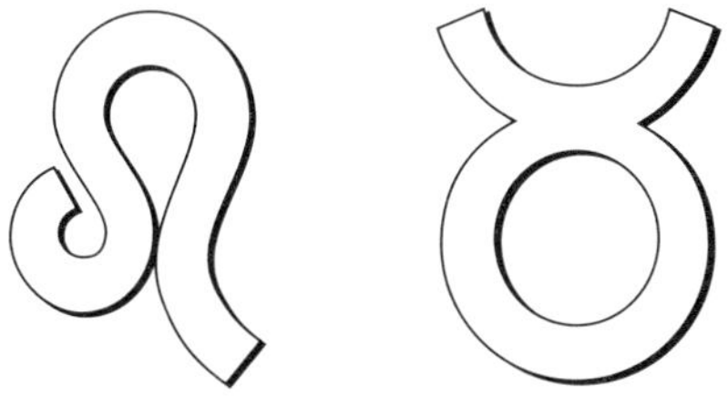

Demonstrate your appreciation of your partner's stability, good sense, sensual appreciation, or skill with earning and owning things. He can excel at creating comfort. Physical gratification could be a way of life. He needs to understand that praise and sincere compliments are definitely the way to your heart! You need respect. You are more of a risk-taker; he prefers to consolidate his gains. Since you are both quite strong-willed, don't fall into power struggles. Each of you must be willing to take turns. You can both enjoy fine possessions and indulging in food, drink, or satisfying sensual/sexual experiences.

CHALLENGING—2

LEO/GEMINI

YOUTHFUL

You spark the inner child in each other, easily stimulating each other's humor and love of life. Praise your Gemini's wit, wisdom, and sense of wonder, and he'll adore you. Admire his youthful attitude, flexibility, multiple talents, and way with words. Praise his curiosity and eagerness to learn. Give him opportunities to admire your creativity, enthusiasm, generosity, and dramatic abilities. He needs to notice that you can be a star. You bring sparkle and enthusiasm to his life. He brings interesting ideas and fresh perceptions to you.

COMPATIBLE—3

LEO/CANCER

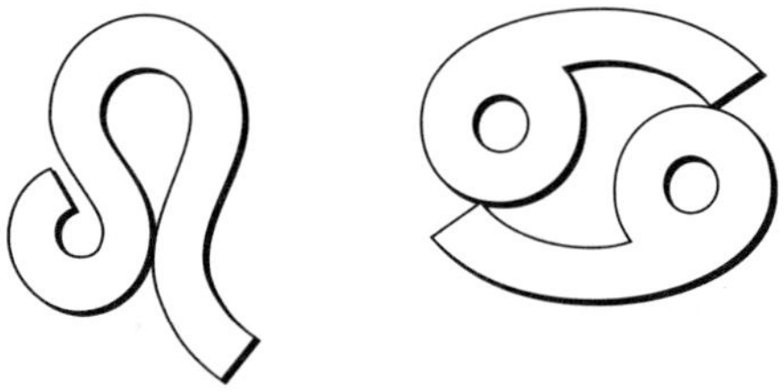

HOST(ESS) WITH THE MOST(ESS)

Appreciate your partner's needs for privacy, his periodic urge to go inside and mull things over. Praise his sensitivity, caring for hearth and home, and devotion to loved ones. Notice his collections (he probably hangs on to things and to people). Admire his deep feelings. He needs to recognize your flair, to allow you a place to shine and be admired, to support and acknowledge your generosity, creativity, and ability to excite others. If you two can keep a balance between introversion and extroversion, between public and private lives, you can build a warm, loving connection with one another.

CHALLENGING—2

LEO/LEO

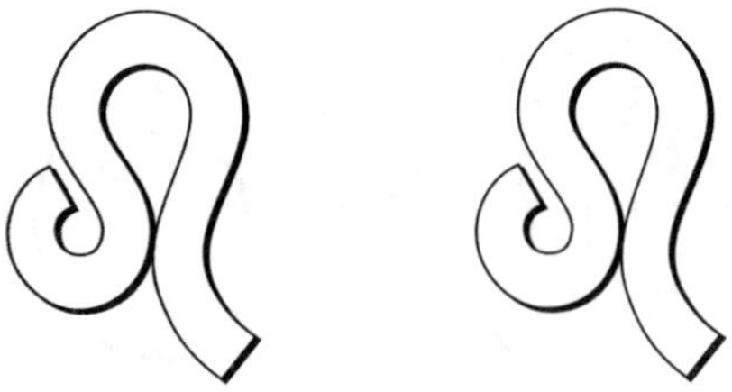

KING AND QUEEN OF LOVE

You were both born to rule! Acknowledge each other's royalty and all will be well. Each of you can be a great leader, motivator, and cheerleader. You both find it easy to focus on the positive, praising and complimenting others. But attention, admiration, and applause are the breath of life for each of you. The partner must respect, admire, and praise you. Lavish appreciation is rarely out of line. Don't compete for the limelight with one another; therein lie power plays and discomfort. Do make sure that each of you has an area to shine, to be center stage, to be noticed, to be a star. Treat him like a King, and encourage him to treat you like a Queen.

VERY COMPATIBLE: 4

THE QUEEN AND THE SERVANT

LEO/VIRGO

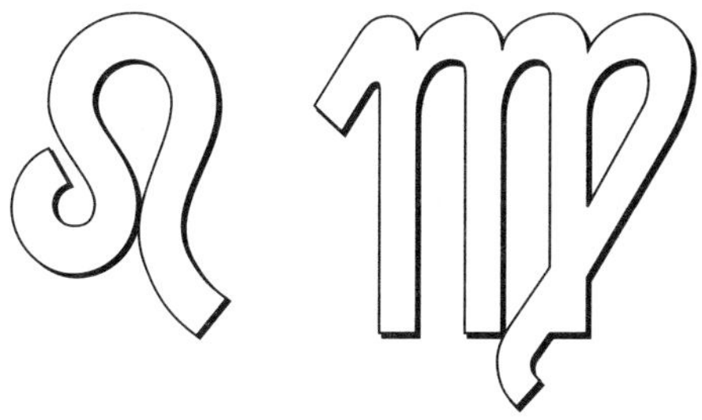

To understand one another, you have to realize that he prefers praise and admiration in a discreet manner, whereas you have a streak of flamboyance. Recognize his competence, skill with repairs, nutrition, or details. Compliment his expertise, and ability to accomplish in quiet, unassuming ways. He needs to appreciate your dramatic flair. Compliments to you can even be a bit exaggerated. He has to understand that being a star comes naturally to you. You instinctively seek the limelight and it is vital that your partner praise and applaud your exciting, dynamic, magnetic nature. You enliven his life, and he helps you be more sensible and productive.

CHALLENGING—2

PEOPLE PLEASERS

LEO/LIBRA

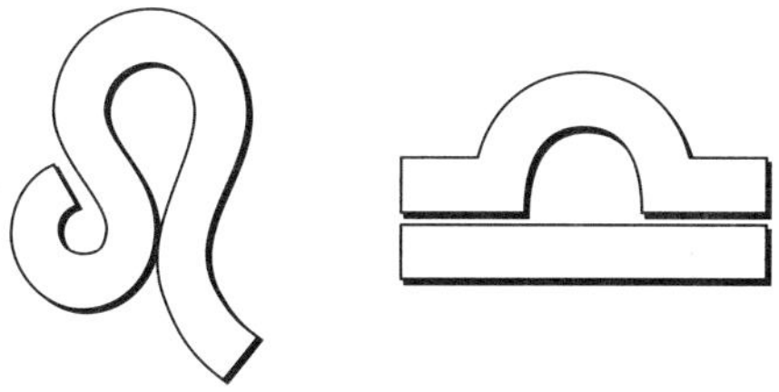

Both of you can really enjoy people. You must recognize and applaud his negotiating skills, interpersonal abilities, and artistic eye, or feeling for balance and harmony. Praise him as a competitor and as a peacemaker. Notice his sociability and willingness to relate to others. He needs to understand your craving for excitement. You thrive on applause, attention, and admiration from others. He must be willing to feed your dramatic instincts and value your ability to motivate other people. Each of you can enjoy fun, games, and the stimulation of others. Activity, excitement, and social interactions energize you both and generate enthusiasm.

COMPATIBLE—3

STAR SEDUCERS

LEO/SCORPIO

Both of you are strong personalities, so tread gently with each other's egos. Dominance games won't work very well. You need to admire his subtlety, his grasp of hidden meanings, his ability to look below the surface in life. Praise his power, potency, and perseverance. Notice his resourcefulness and magnetism. Either of you could be quite sexually alluring, so avoid the traps of jealousy and possessiveness. He needs to appreciate your dramatic flair and desire for excitement. Respect and recognition feed your vitality. You are energized by admiration, attention, and applause. Your association is likely to be very good **or** very bad. Each of you lives and loves to the hilt!

CHALLENGING—2

LEO/SAGITTARIUS

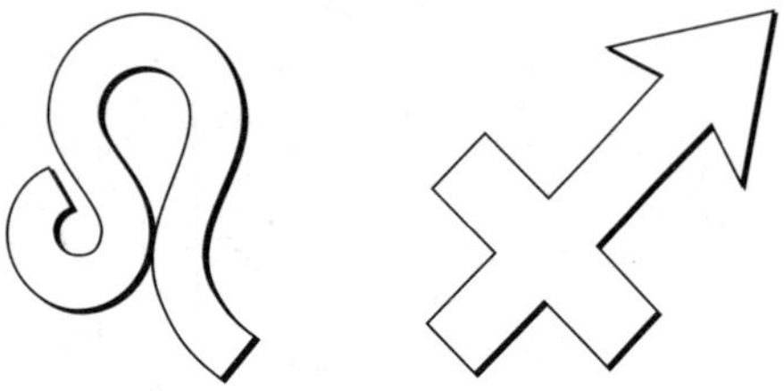

ADRENALINE ADDICTS

High-energy people, you both thrive on action and adventure. Fun-loving, you may share lots of games, parties, or eager exploration of life. You can appreciate his free spirit, optimism, broad mindedness, sense of humor and urge to seek truth, justice and more stimulation from life. He could be quite a risk-taker, promoter, seller, gambler, or explorer of life's many possibilities. You need praise and attention from him. Your dramatic talent, generosity, motivational skills, and expressive, exciting nature need to be respected and admired. Both of you love the rush of adrenaline, the sense of living and loving to the **max**.

COMPATIBLE—3

LEO/CAPRICORN

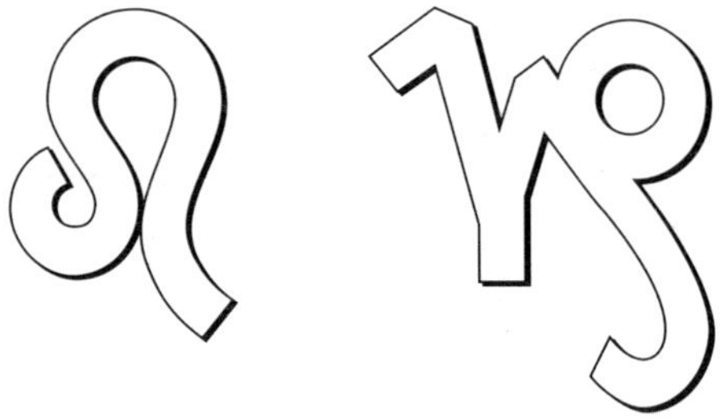

PERSUASIVE AND POWERFUL

Both of you definitely want respect, but you each seek recognition through different paths. He wants to work his way to the top, to make it on society's terms, to be admired for his career, sense of responsibility, stability, and skill at dealing with structure and authorities. His patience may be noteworthy. He may excel at doing things well. You feel a sense of urgency and prefer immediate action. You want power right away, and may use dramatic skills, persuasiveness, magnetism, or leadership to sway other people. Exciting and full of zest, you're willing to take chances for greater gain. He needs to recognize and appreciate your charisma, generosity, and enthusiasm. You can learn more patience and perseverance from him. He can learn from you to raise the ante in life.

VERY CHALLENGING—1

LEO/AQUARIUS

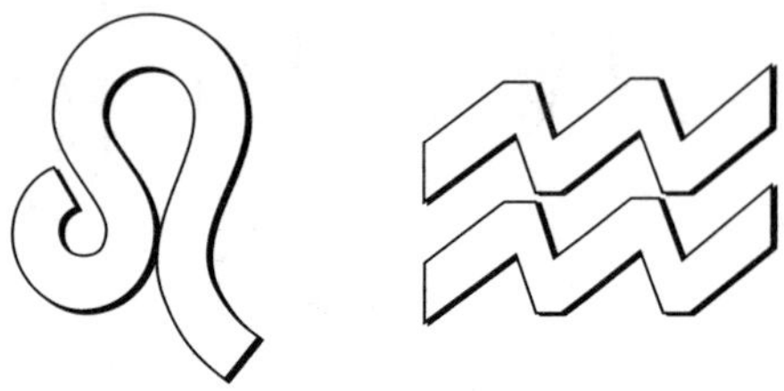

EXTRAORDINARY

Each of you needs very much to be seen as special by the other. He needs to be admired as unique, individualistic, inventive, and independent. Praise his unusual perspective, progressive viewpoints, feeling for technology, or stimulating mind. He must appreciate your ability to shine, to take center stage, to persuade and motivate others. He could admire and applaud your dramatic flair, promotional skills, fun-loving spirit, or generosity. Warm and enthusiastic, loving and being loved come naturally to you. You touch the inner child in everyone and keep life exciting. Together, you can feed each other's originality and creativity.

VERY COMPATIBLE—4

SHOWY OR SUBTLE?

LEO/PISCES

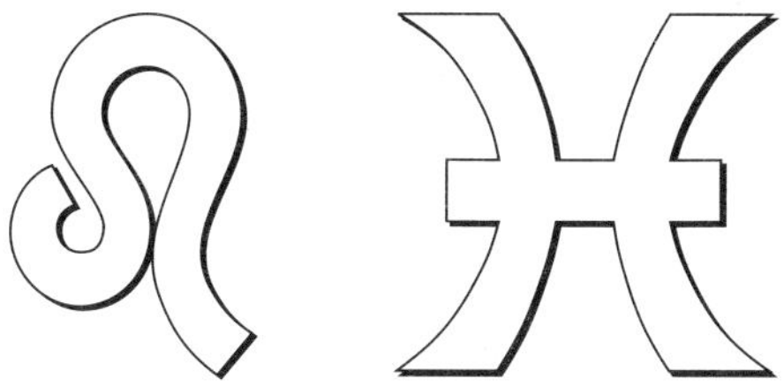

Each of you has dramatic flair and an instinct for showmanship. He seeks admiration for his magical, mystical, mysterious side. He may be noteworthy for being subtle, sensitive, or inward. His imagination is marked, and he could inspire and excite others with his visions. You need direct, open admiration. You can be quite expressive, sometimes coming across as larger than life. Your partner must applaud and appreciate you. Both of you can be romantics, in love with love. Be sensible in what you demand from each other. Remember that you need to show off, and he needs to explore his inner realms. You can draw him out; he can draw you in.

VERY CHALLENGING—1

EFFICIENT EXPLORERS

VIRGO/ARIES

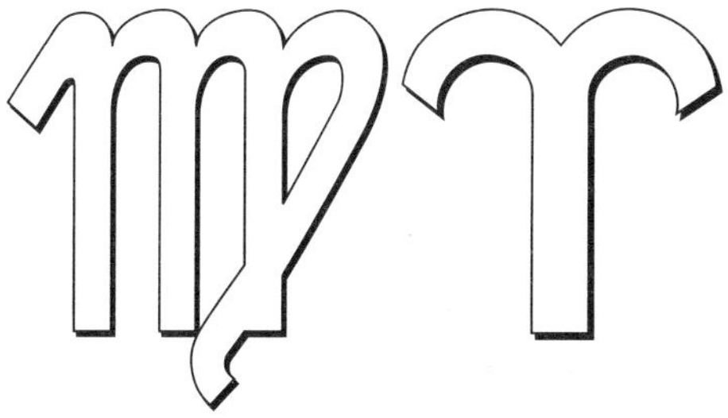

Your ego needs vary considerably from his, so mutual tolerance is essential. He wants admiration for his courage, pioneering spirit, sense of adventure, and willingness to act. Praise his quick responses, eager enthusiasm, and desire to be in the forefront of life. Don't expect him to be as detail-oriented as you are. You need him to acknowledge your competence, dedication, and willingness to work. It is important that he recognize your achievements. He needs you to note his independence, courage, and energy. He may seem rash or impulsive to you. You might seem critical or nit-picking to him. Appreciate and admire each other's strengths and you can build a solid bond.

VERY CHALLENGING—1

EARTHY EFFICIENCY

VIRGO/TAURUS

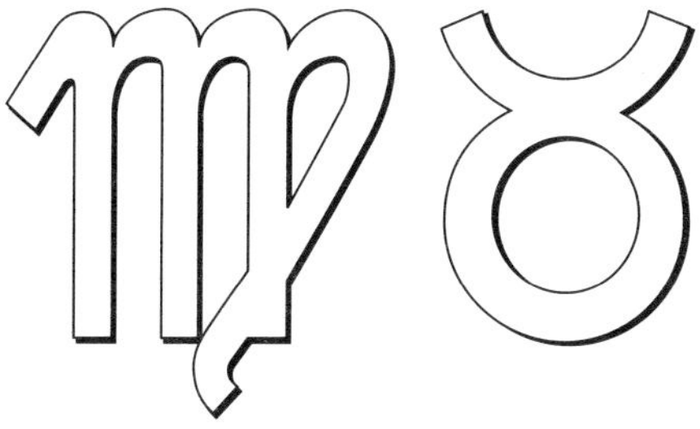

It is easy for you to appreciate each other's common sense. You both take pride in your accomplishments. You may both enjoy nature, the Earth, or any activity with measurable results. You two could share tasks, taking satisfaction in a job well done. Admire what he earns and owns. Recognize his skill at creating comfort, his sensual expertise, and ability to enjoy the material world. He needs to acknowledge your competence, discipline, efficiency and productivity. You may be quite involved with health, nutrition, or anything focused on improving, enhancing or repairing. Together, you two can accomplish and relax, working in the world, but also gaining and giving much pleasure through material indulgences.

COMPATIBLE—3

VIRGO/GEMINI

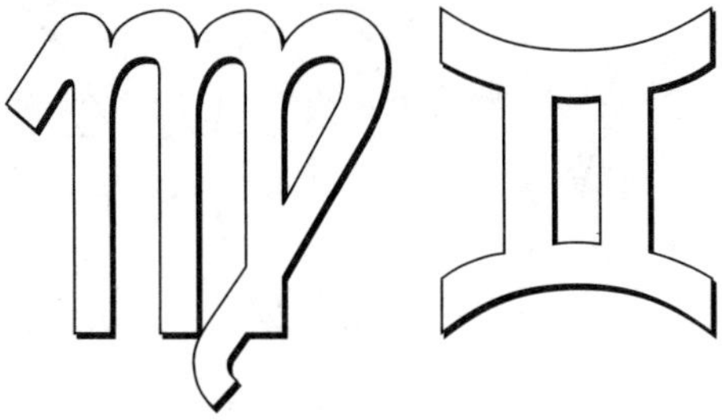

KNOWLEDGE OVER ALL

You both can shine mentally, but in different ways. You are proud of your common sense and ability to focus. You need praise for your competence, dedication, skill with details, work accomplishments, efficiency, and productivity. Quality is vital to you. He, however, thrives on quantities of information—curious about anything and everything. It is essential that you appreciate and admire his versatility, adaptability and verbal skills. His youthful attitude and openness to new experiences can enrich your life. You can help him focus; he can help broaden your interests. Both of you value learning. Love each other for your minds (as well as bodies).

CHALLENGING—2

VIRGO/CANCER

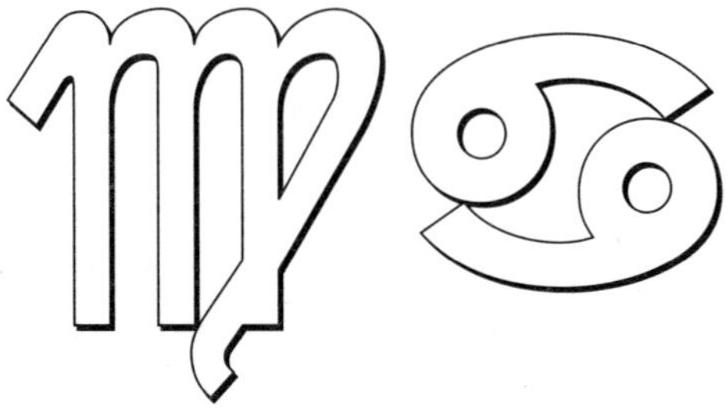

ASSISTING ANALYSIS

You both are natural caretakers, eager to assist others. He may focus more on personal issues, emotional reactions, or security needs. You tend to focus more on necessities and work duties. He needs to be recognized for his ability to accumulate (money or things), his empathy or compassion, and his attachments (to people, to country, to possessions). Appreciate his feeling for hearth and home, his devotion to loved ones. He needs to admire your competence, efficiency, and ability to figure out what is wrong and fix it. You each demonstrate love partly through service—doing for others. Assisting one another can help draw you closer.

COMPATIBLE—3

VIRGO/LEO

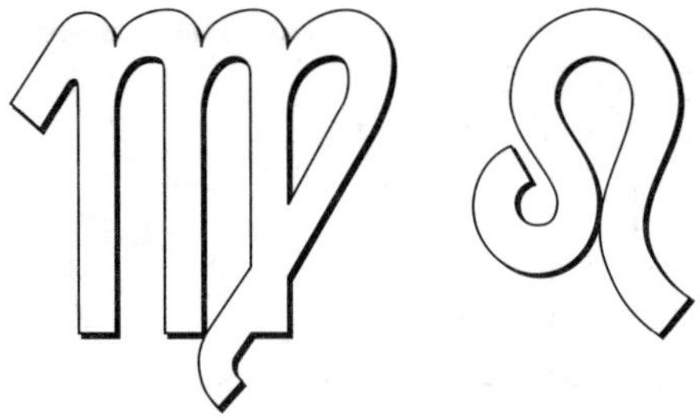

THE SERVANT AND THE KING

To understand one another, you have to realize that you prefer praise and admiration in a discreet manner, whereas he has a streak of flamboyance. Compliments to him can be a bit exaggerated. Being a star comes naturally. He instinctively seeks the limelight, and needs to be praised and applauded for his exciting, dynamic, and magnetic nature. He can come across with quite a royal manner. He needs to recognize your competence, skill with repairs, nutrition, or details. He should compliment your expertise, and ability to accomplish in quiet, unassuming ways. Don't fall into the servant role (taking care of business) while he is the king. Make sure you both play as well as work. He can enliven your life, and you can help him be a bit more sensible and productive.

CHALLENGING—2

PRACTICAL AND PRODUCTIVE

VIRGO/VIRGO

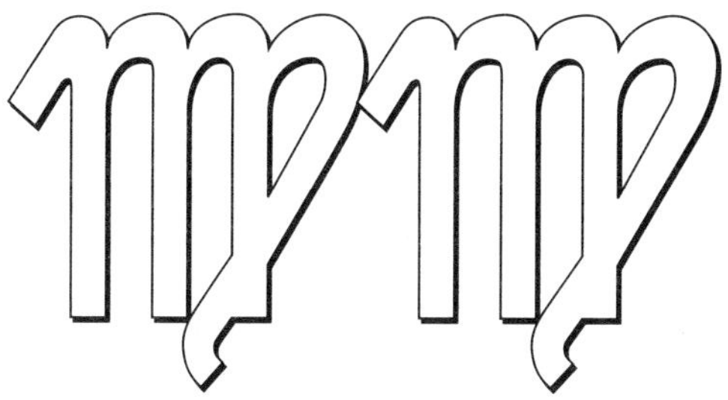

Each of you tends to show your love by doing things for your partner, so this could be a very service-oriented relationship. Praise and admire in him exactly what you are proud of within yourself: competence, discipline, craftsmanship skills, good with details, nutritional interest, or a willingness to work. You both find self-esteem partly through your productive efforts. Getting the job done well is a source of pride. Achievement energizes you both. You could even share tasks as well as love. You both shine as efficiency experts.

VERY COMPATIBLE—4

ANALYST AND ARTIST

VIRGO/LIBRA

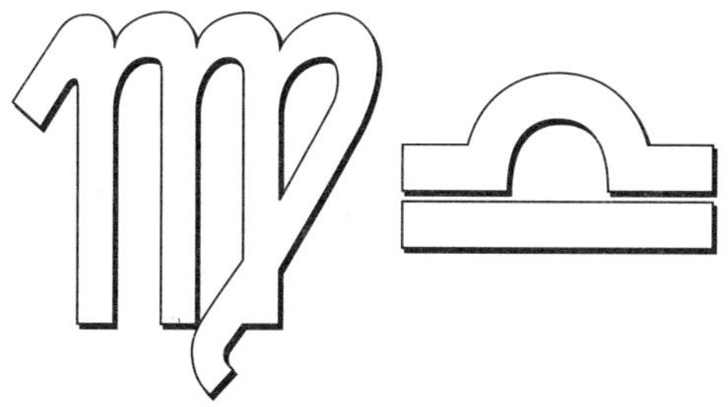

Your self-esteem is mainly tied to work, productivity, and getting the job done. His self-esteem is largely tied to people, beauty, and creating balance or harmony. Praise him for his sense of fair play, passion for justice, artistic creativity, or ability to deal well with people. Admire his negotiating skills, competitive instincts, eye for equality or interests in relationships. What energizes you is for him to respect your work, admire your competence, appreciate your skill with details, or notice your interest in health, nutrition, efficiency, handicrafts, or any productive efforts. Together, you can balance love and work, ease and effort. Give priority to both practical and emotional needs.

CHALLENGING—2

FINELY FOCUSED

VIRGO/SCORPIO

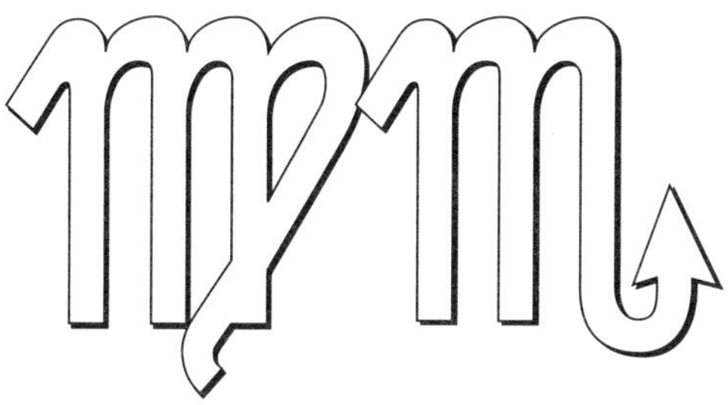

You both appreciate commitment, perseverance and follow-through. Admire his tenacity, financial acumen, sexual charisma, resourcefulness, intense emotions, or instinctive understanding of life's subtle cues. Praise his insight into people's motivations, his strength of will, and his interest in hidden matters. He must recognize and respect your diligence, productivity, skill with details, or general efficiency. You need acknowledgment for your achievements, your ability to get things done, your practicality, and your ability to concentrate. You both can be extremely loyal and capable of focusing intensely on what you want to accomplish. You finish what you start!

COMPATIBLE—3

VIRGO/SAGITTARIUS

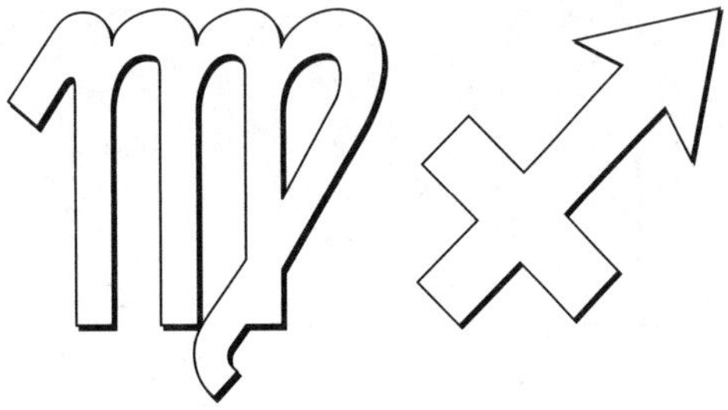

CAREFUL AND CAREFREE

You like things right, can handle details, focus, and be organized. He thinks big and may overextend or commit to too much. For the relationship to flourish, you each must appreciate the very different talents of the other. Praise him for his optimism, his adventurous spirit, his broad perspective, and confident independence. Appreciate his freewheeling extroversion and eager, impulsive pursuit of fun. He must learn to recognize and respect your desire for tangible results, your skill with details and your caution which prepares for worst-case scenarios. He can grow to admire your more modest, unassuming demeanor, and value you as a very capable person. He enlarges your world and brings in excitement. You help him ground his dreams and be more practical about big ideas.

CHALLENGING—2

VIRGO/CAPRICORN

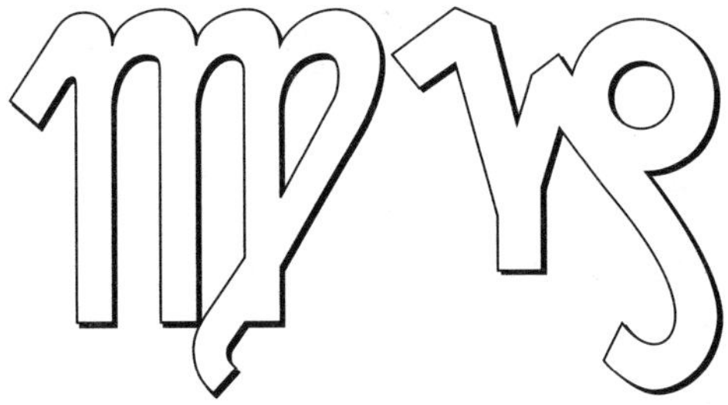

RELIABLY RESPONSIBLE

Both of you appreciate the value of productive work and responsible action. Each of you can demonstrate love by doing tasks for the other. Admire his career achievements, status, dedication, power, expertise, air of authority, or conscientiousness. Notice and applaud his skill at getting down to business and getting things done. He should find it easy to praise your diligence, skill with details, craftsmanship, focus, concentration, and practicality. You two could share tasks, or a business as well as an emotional bond, but both of you must guard against letting flaw-finding attitudes slip over from work into the emotional side of your relationship. By all means work on improving your relationship, but do **not** turn your partner into a chore!

COMPATIBLE—3

VIRGO/AQUARIUS

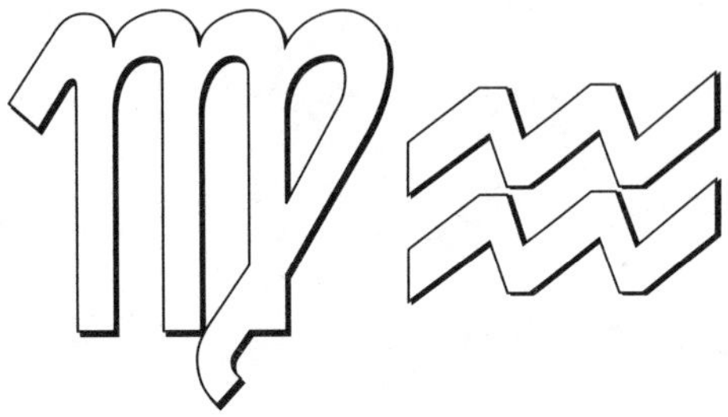

CONSCIENTIOUS VERSUS CASUAL

Different strokes for different folks definitely applies here. Applaud his uniqueness. Admire his independence, inventiveness, and individuality. He needs to be recognized as a free spirit. He may be proud of his humanitarian principles, feel for the future, grasp of new technology, skill at brainstorming, or ability to relate to anyone about anything. You need him to appreciate your quiet, modest style. He must be able to admire your skill with details, diligence, dedication, and passion for achievement. He envisions possibilities and potentials. You deal with practicalities and get real, measurable results. Together, you can turn theory into practice.

VERY CHALLENGING—1

INDISPENSABLE IMAGINATION

VIRGO/PISCES

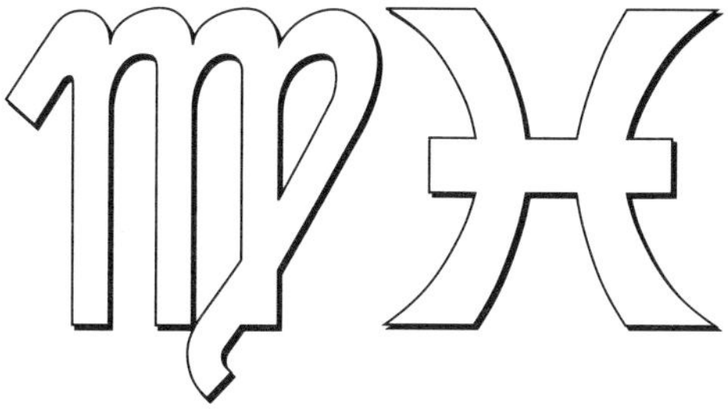

Although opposites in some ways, there is a natural attraction between you. He deals with dreams, images, and idealized desires. You deal with practicalities, tasks, and the necessary details of reality. Together, you can be chronically dissatisfied (never perfect enough) or bring dreams to earth and make visions real. Appreciate and applaud his imagination, empathy, and imagery. Admire his whimsical, magical, romantic, mysterious, fantasy side. Praise his intuition and understanding of ideals. It is vital that he appreciate your common sense, willingness to work, productivity, and modesty. He needs to praise your diligence, detail-orientation, and determination to get the job **done**. When you combine forces, you can make ideal images a reality, bringing dreams into form.

VERY COMPATIBLE—4

BALANCING ACT

LIBRA/ARIES

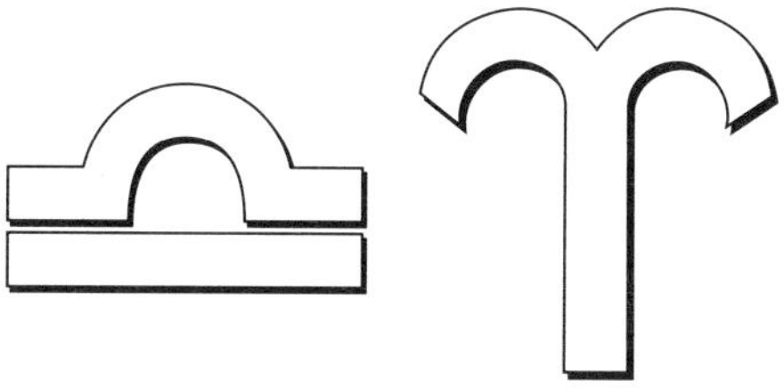

Attraction comes naturally to you two, although you are opposites in some ways. You need to admire his honesty, free spirit and eager thrust into life. He needs to admire your feeling for beauty, social skills, and desire for balance. Recognize his courage, adventurous nature, and eager thrust into life and love. Praise his integrity, enthusiasm, spontaneity, and directness. It is important for him to acknowledge your diplomacy, negotiating abilities, and artistic instincts. You may find that he acts often, while you tend to react. He can be the initiator, while you easily become the responder. Be willing to alternate a bit. Together, the two of you can create a lovely dance of give-and-take.

VERY COMPATIBLE—4

ARTISTIC

LIBRA/TAURUS

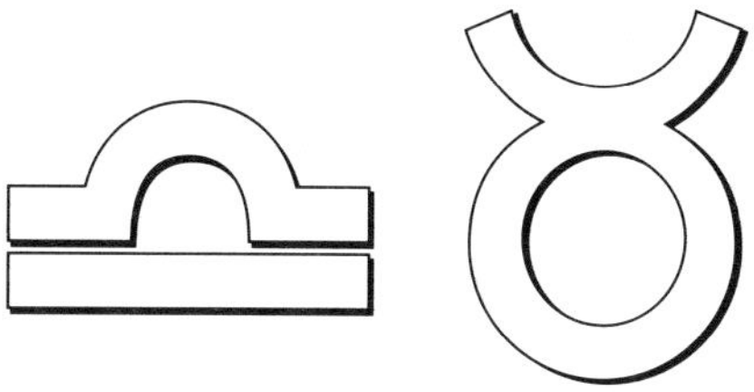

You take pride in different areas, but can mix well if you respect each other's talents. Praise his sensuality, eye for beauty, love of comfort, and easygoing nature. Admire what he earns and owns. He needs to recognize your talent for handling people—diplomatic, empathic, and skilled at competition or negotiation. You gravitate toward balance, harmony, and equality. Both of you have artistic impulses, though yours may be more visual and his more tactile. You each enjoy ease, and keeping life pleasant.

VERY CHALLENGING—1

LIBRA/GEMINI

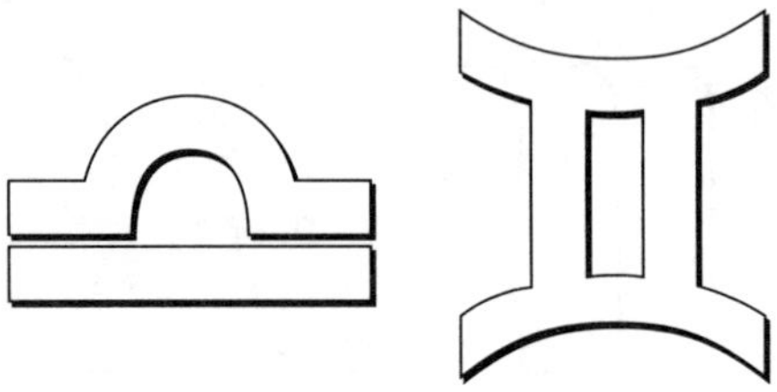

OBJECTIVE AND OPEN

You both feel loved when you can communicate and be truly heard and understood by the other. Praise his quick wits, lively curiosity, way with words, interest in everything, and eagerness to learn. Admire his mind and he'll see you as a person of great discernment. He needs to appreciate your social skills, artistic eye, negotiating ability, drive for balance, ear for harmony, and instinct for equality and justice. Each of you can enjoy people, concepts, and the exercising of your logical, observing sides. Together, you can share information, ideas, and intimacy.

COMPATIBLE—3

LIBRA/CANCER

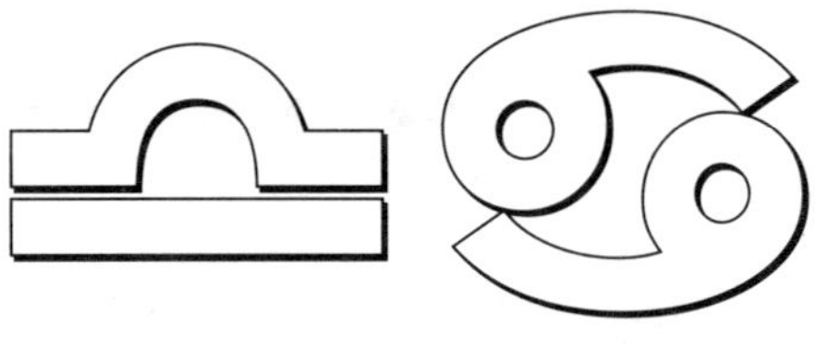

PARENTAL PARTNERS

Emotional attachments are important to each of you, though you may vary in the degree of closeness desired. You thrive on face-to-face interactions and find other people fun and stimulating. He may prefer a small, private circle. You can be a good negotiator, diplomat, or consultant. He tends to keep some things inside, not wearing his heart on his sleeve. Praise his caring, sensitivity, faithfulness, ability to amass money or possessions, and loyalty to kin and country. Respect what brings him security and safety in life, or assists his collecting efforts. He needs to acknowledge your feeling for beauty, instinct for balance and harmony, social skills, and friendly nature. Commitment to shared feelings can make a strong bond between you.

CHALLENGING—2

LIBRA/LEO

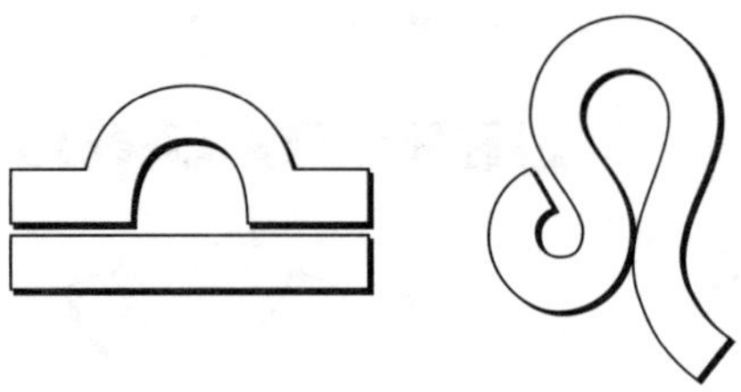

PEOPLE PLEASERS

Both of you can really enjoy people. He must recognize and applaud your negotiating skills, interpersonal abilities, and artistic eye, or feeling for balance and harmony. You need praise as a competitor or as a peacemaker. Notice his dramatic instincts and ability to excite and motivate others. Appreciate his persuasiveness. He thrives on applause, attention and admiration from others. Always praise; never criticize. Positive feedback works wonders with him. Each of you can enjoy fun, games, and the stimulation of others. Activity, excitement, and social interactions energize you both and generate enthusiasm.

COMPATIBLE—3

ARTIST AND ANALYST

LIBRA/VIRGO

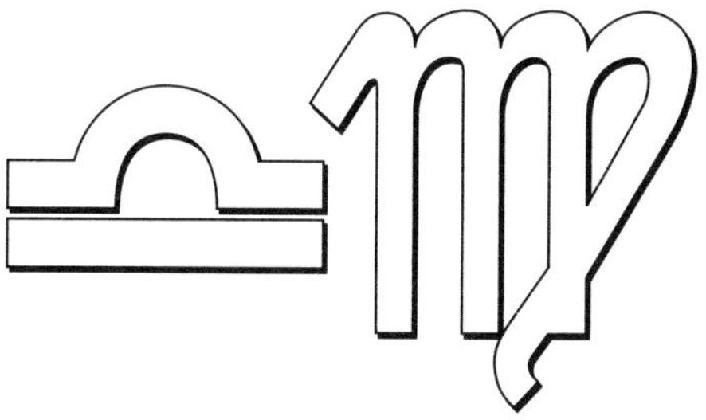

His self-esteem is mainly tied to work, productivity, and getting the job done. Your self-esteem is largely tied to people, beauty, and creating balance or harmony. Praise him for his competence, dedication, skill with details and ability to figure out what is wrong and fix it. He may be quite capable in areas of health, nutrition, handicrafts, or any form of efficiency expertise. You need appreciation for your negotiating skills, equality instincts, or interpersonal abilities. Do not polarize between love and work, ease and effort, or tact and criticism. He can learn from you to give people more of a priority. You can learn from him to give projects appropriate attention. Together, you can meet each other's practical **and** emotional needs.

CHALLENGING—2

PLEASANT PARTNERS

LIBRA/LIBRA

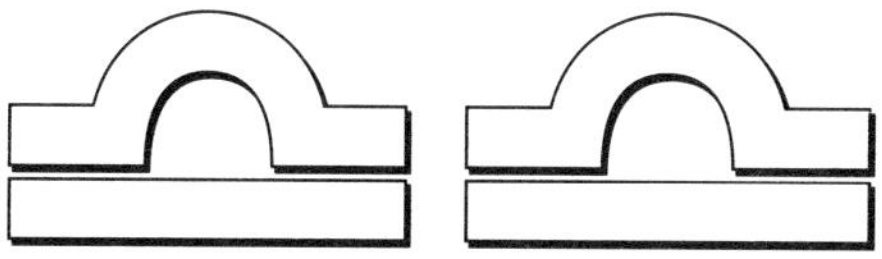

Relationships are the natural environment for both of you. Each of you is energized by one-on-one encounters. You have skills at cooperation, but also competition. Face-to-face interactions provide a fruitful learning ground. Praise and recognize within him exactly what builds your own self-esteem: social skills, artistic creativity, a desire for balance and harmony, a passion for equality and fair play, and a natural grace and charm or poise. Admiration from others is essential to you both, so some flirtatiousness is possible. Both of you need to be understanding when your partner basks in the limelight of another admirer. Each of you would prefer to feel liked and appreciated by everyone around. Togetherness (shared activities) energize you both.

VERY COMPATIBLE—4

SWEET SEDUCTION

LIBRA/SCORPIO

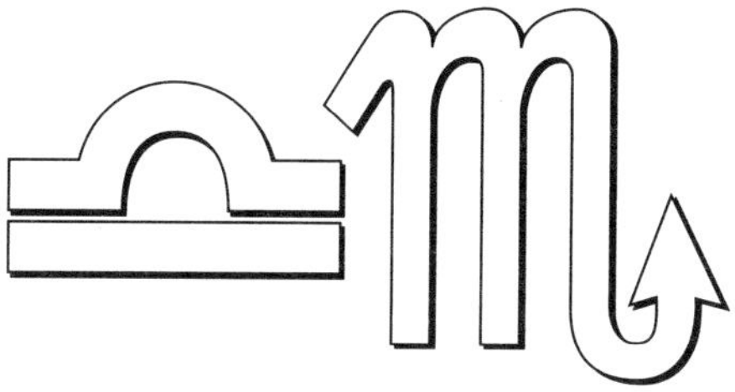

You both flower in the context of partnership. Each of you is energized from making an intimate connection. He needs praise and admiration for his emotional intensity, sexuality, strength of will, ability to uncover secrets, or commitment and thoroughness. You require recognition for your balance and poise, grace, charm, diplomatic skills, or eye for color and harmony. You focus more on sharing, taking turns, and communication in relationships. He focuses more on issues of money, sensuality, sexuality, and joint resources and pleasures. You tend to be more lighthearted and sociable. He tends to be more serious and secretive. Each of you can enrich the world of the other.

CHALLENGING—2

LIBRA/SAGITTARIUS

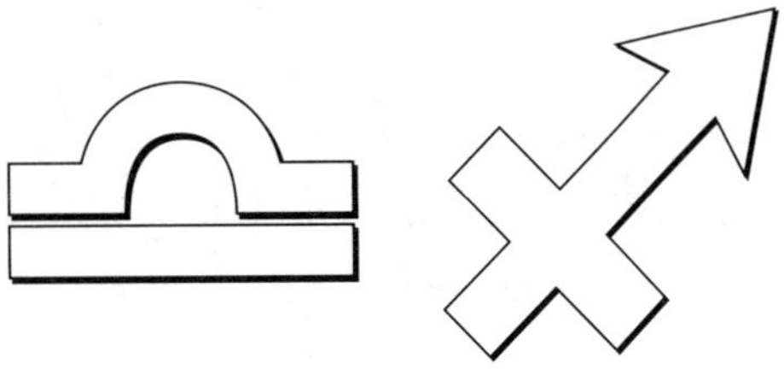

PLEASANTLY PLAYFUL

You are both naturally friendly sorts, so usually do well in social settings. Involvement with people and/or ideas and ideals stimulates each of you. He wants people to notice his adventurous spirit, his wide-ranging mind, his optimistic attitude, or his sense of humor. He may shine in sports, travel, knowledge, or ethical principles. Restless and independent, he cherishes compliments on his many experiences, interesting ideas, quick wit, or outgoing nature. You need appreciation from him for your grace, charm, beauty, balance, and skill at pleasing people. He may admire your artistic eye, instinct for fairness, or love of harmony. Your relationship is fed by social interaction, communication, and play.

COMPATIBLE—3

LIBRA/CAPRICORN

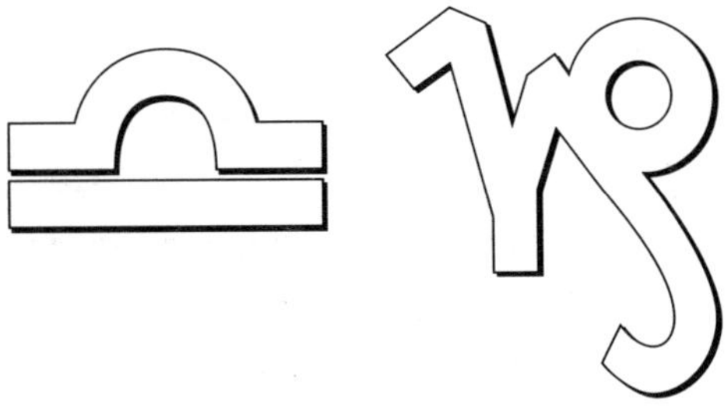

FAIR AND FIRM

He tends to admire power, authority and control. You may have to teach him to appreciate equality, fairness, and sharing. Praise him for his vocational attainments, position in society, expertise, air of authority, or self-discipline. Recognize his conscientiousness, hard work, and drive. Give him opportunities to praise your grace, poise, tact, and charm. He can learn to applaud your desire for harmony, feeling for beauty, and passion for balance (justice). Don't polarize as dictator and diplomat, or power player and peacemaker. You can help him to relax, ease up, and enjoy sharing more. He can help you to focus, pursue ambitions, and be more disciplined.

CHALLENGING—2

LIBRA/AQUARIUS

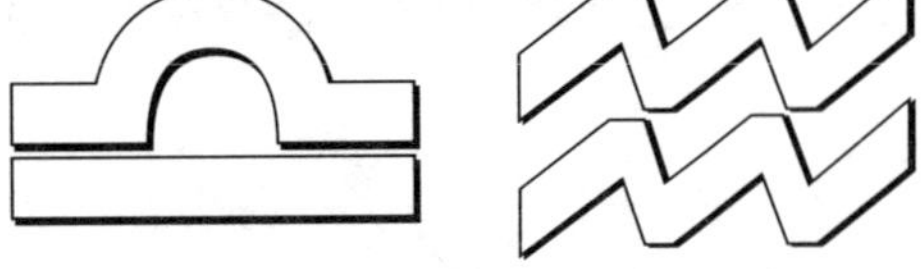

JUSTICE FOR ALL

Both of you shine with ideas and people. Passionate discussions may appeal, or the stimulation of varied people and diverse concepts. Praise his uniqueness. Recognize his unconventional streak, inventive spirit, intuitive grasp of technology, or feeling for the future. Appreciate his wide-ranging mind and independent attitudes. Social settings give you a chance to shine. He can admire your skill with people, your grace, charm, and tact. You need recognition for your feeling for justice, balance, and harmony. Communication can draw you together. A shared sense of equality and fair play strengthens the bond between you.

COMPATIBLE—3

LOVE IN TECHNICOLOR

LIBRA/PISCES

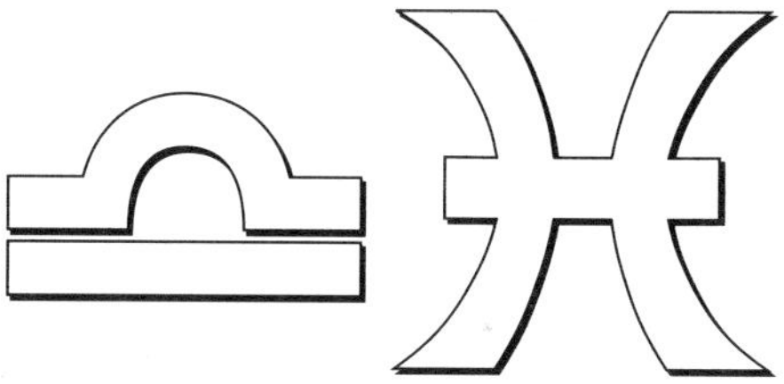

You shine in the public world of people. He shines in the private world of imagination. Sharing will require compromises from you both. He needs recognition for his visualizing skills, "what if?" potentials, or creative imagination. Admire his sensitivity, compassion for the underdog, or ability to understand the feelings of others. He might create through poetry, music, science, dance, art, or any form of beauty or love of nature and patterns. You need one-on-one interaction. You shine in the company of others—through charm, poise, empathy, and tact. Loving relationships are natural for you. Pleasing people is your forte. A shared feeling for beauty can draw you together. He can show you fantastic inner realms, and you can draw him out to enjoy the world of people more.

VERY CHALLENGING—1

DIRECT DETECTION

SCORPIO/ARIES

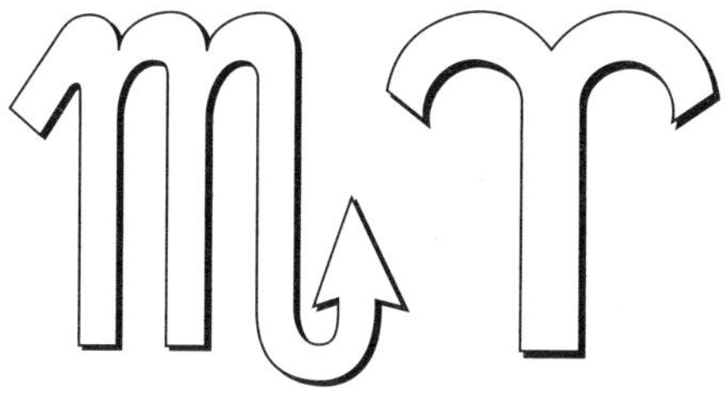

You both must believe in "Viva la difference!" for your relationship to function optimally. You want admiration for your intensity, resourcefulness, depth and ability to cope with secrets and hidden matters. He needs recognition for his honesty, energy, courage, and eager enthusiasm for life. He appreciates simplicity. You thrive on complexities. He goes straight ahead, full speed, in life. You move cautiously, seeking indirect routes and escape hatches. Sexual attraction could be a shared bond. Passion comes easily to you both. It is essential for him to praise your subtle strategies, and for you to admire his active openness.

VERY CHALLENGING—1

POSSESSIONS AND PLEASURES

SCORPIO/TAURUS

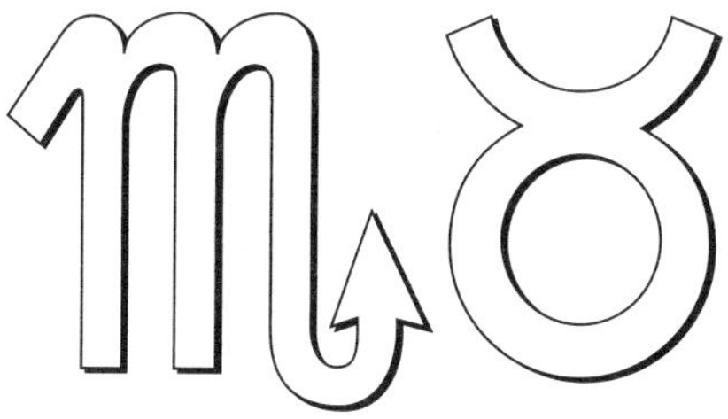

Indulgence is the name of the game! Both of you have heightened sensuality. You may tune into one another sexually and are likely to enjoy good food, drink, massages, hot tubs, or other forms of physical pleasures. You may admire each other's fine possessions. Praise his practicality, perseverance, and pleasure-loving nature. Appreciate his ability to create comfort, to garner possessions, and to enjoy the material world. He needs to acknowledge your intensity, sexual magnetism, and desire to look beneath the surface in life. You are proud of your depths and self-control. Together, you can combine comfort and confrontation, intensity and ease, with a shared desire to gratify each other's senses.

VERY COMPATIBLE—4

SCORPIO/GEMINI

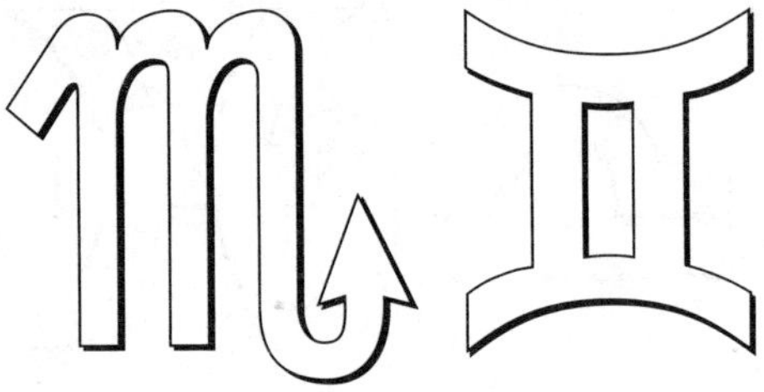

THERAPEUTIC TEACHER

Your self-esteem needs differ considerably, so tolerance is essential on both sides. He seeks recognition for his breadth of interests, lighthearted attitude, way with words, objectivity, and logic. He wants to be admired for his mind, communication skills, or multiple interests and talents. You want recognition for your depth, subtlety, passion, and intensity. He should praise your sexual allure, ability to uncover hidden information, and resourcefulness. Flirting may come easily to him, so do not let your tendency toward jealousy get out of hand. You tend to be more serious than he. He takes pride in his words, wit, and sense of wonder. You can help him get to the bottom of things. He can help you to lighten up.

VERY CHALLENGING—1

SCORPIO/CANCER

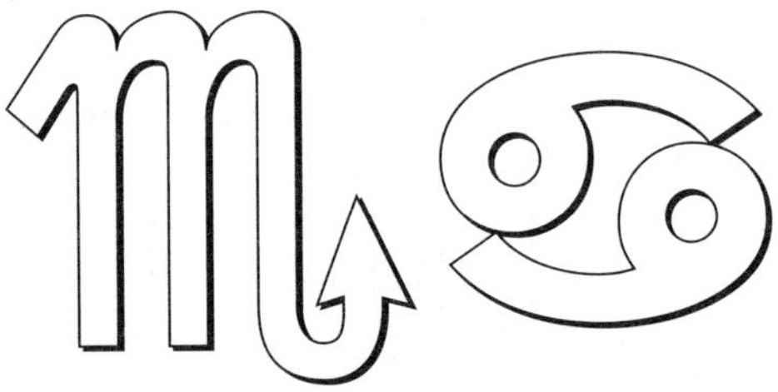

CARING CATALYSTS

You both appreciate the subtle dance of love and are sensitive to hints, innuendoes, secrets, and hidden messages. Admire his devotion to home, family, or country. Notice his nurturing instincts or desire to protect and preserve. He may collect things, or enjoy amassing money. Security and safety are important to him. You need recognition for your passion, intensity, and resourcefulness. He should praise your animal magnetism, strength of will, and "do or die" determination. You both have strong, deep feelings that you tend to keep hidden. Don't bury too much! Bring what matters out into the open and discuss it. Once you two commit, you both value loyalty very highly.

COMPATIBLE—3

SCORPIO/LEO

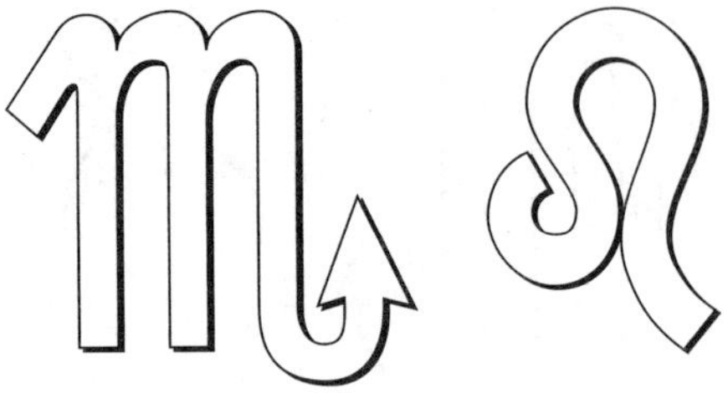

STAR SEDUCERS

Both of you are strong personalities, so tread gently with each other's egos. Dominance games won't work very well. You need to admire his dramatic flair and ability to excite and motivate others. Respect and recognition feed his vitality. He is energized by admiration, attention, and applause. He needs to admire your subtlety, grasp of hidden meanings, and ability to look below the surface in life. You want your perseverance, resourcefulness, and magnetism to be noticed. Either of you could be quite sexually alluring, so avoid the traps of jealousy and possessiveness. Your association is likely to be very good **or** very bad. Each of you lives and loves to the hilt!

CHALLENGING—2

FINELY FOCUSED

SCORPIO/VIRGO

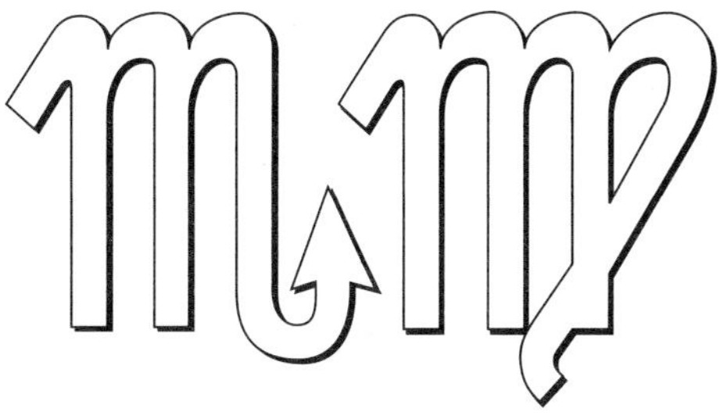

You both appreciate commitment, perseverance, and follow-through. Admire his achievements, ability to get things done, practicality and ability to concentrate. He wants recognition for his diligence, productivity, skill with details, and general efficiency. You need appreciation for your tenacity, financial acumen, sexual charisma, resourcefulness, intense emotions, and instinctive understanding of life's subtle cues. He should praise your insight into people's motivations, strength of will, and interest in hidden matters. You both can be extremely loyal and capable of focusing intensely on what you want to accomplish. You finish what you start!

COMPATIBLE—3

SWEET SEDUCTION

SCORPIO/LIBRA

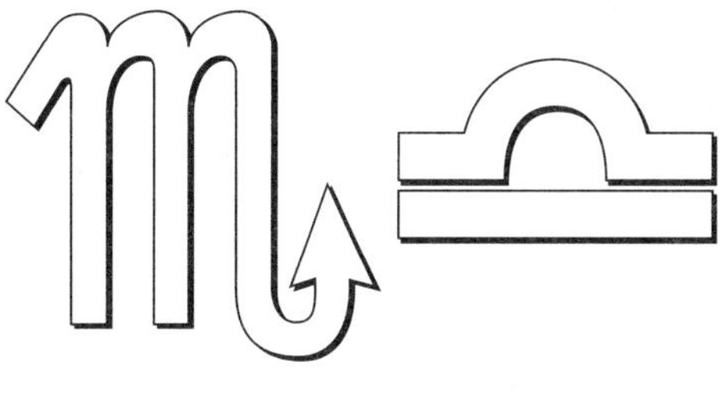

You both flower in the context of partnership. Each of you is energized from making an intimate connection. You need praise and admiration for your emotional intensity, sexual allure, strength of will, ability to uncover secrets, commitment, and thoroughness. He requires recognition for his balance and poise, attractiveness, charm, diplomatic skills, or eye for color and harmony. Both of you are concerned with sharing, taking turns, and communication in relationships as well as issues of money, sensuality, sexuality, and joint resources and pleasures. He tends to be more lighthearted and sociable. You tend to be more serious and secretive. Each of you can enrich the world of the other.

CHALLENGING—2

INTENSE INTIMACY

SCORPIO/SCORPIO

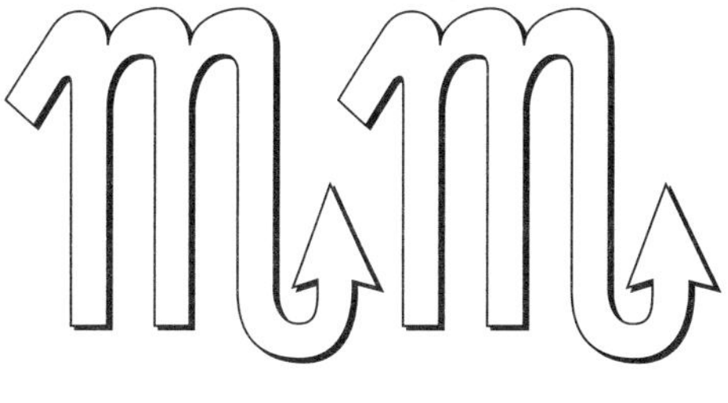

Few people can approach the depth and intensity which are just natural to you both. Recognize and admire in him exactly what you want him to notice in you. Acknowledge each other's passionate nature, strong will, resourcefulness, and desire to get to the bottom of things in life. Don't slip into jealousy, possessiveness, or power plays with each other. Do praise one another's tenacity, interest in mysteries, ability to uncover secrets or hidden knowledge, and willingness to look at the dark side of life. You can energize each other sexually and sensually. You can encourage one another to explore tough psychological issues, gaining a rare and deep bond of intimacy.

VERY COMPATIBLE—4

SCORPIO/SAGITTARIUS

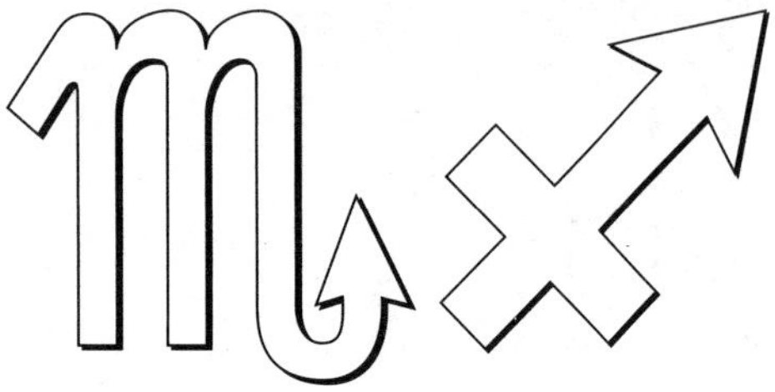

CASUALLY CAPTIVATING

You need recognition for your depth and intensity. He needs recognition for his breadth and humor. Understanding each other can build bridges. Praise his independence, eager, exploring spirit, adventurousness, optimism, or lively wit. Notice his quick mind, broad range of interests, or love of travel, learning and fun. Give him opportunities to compliment your passion, perseverance, and powerful nature. You need praise for your intensity, capacity for intimacy, and desire to look beneath the surface in life. Don't struggle between being separate versus committed, or between many lighthearted activities versus a few serious ones. Open up your worlds to one another, and you'll both be richer for the experience.

CHALLENGING—2

SCORPIO/CAPRICORN

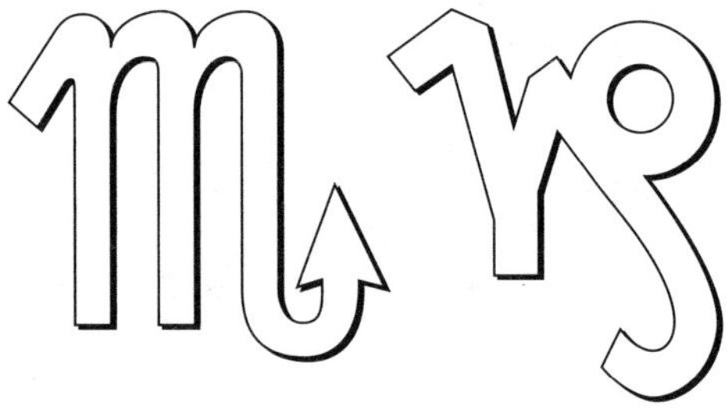

POWERFUL PERSEVERANCE

You both have a serious streak and a strong drive to carry through on your commitments. Be sure you each can forgive and forget when necessary. Admire his ambitions, diligence, sense of responsibility, and practicality. Recognize his understanding of rules, regulations, and power structures. He needs to shine by gaining power, mastery, expertise and status. He can certainly appreciate your depth, perseverance, self-control, and intense emotional nature. You each need a measure of control, so take charge in your own careers or tasks. Don't try to rule one another. Both of you can be very loyal, once committed.

COMPATIBLE—3

SCORPIO/AQUARIUS

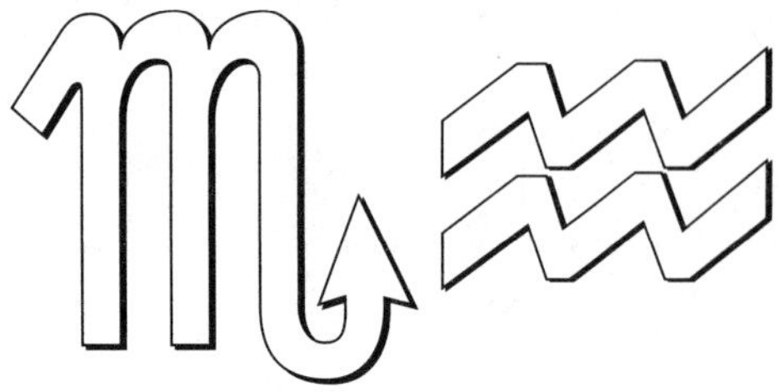

INTENSE OR INDEPENDENT?

You each need to shine in different areas, so respect for one another is vital. Admire his independence, inventiveness, and inquiring mind. Appreciate his uniqueness, originality, and unconventional ideas. Perhaps his humanitarian ideals, networking skills, or feel for technology and the future, are noteworthy. He needs to appreciate your emotional intensity, passionate commitment, and strong will. You shine more privately and in intimate settings. He can shine more publicly or in groups. You thrive on emotional bonds. He is energized by freedom and detachment. Don't turn your association into a battle between intensity and space, or depth versus breadth. Do allow each other to be true to your inner natures.

CHALLENGING—2

BONDED

SCORPIO/PISCES

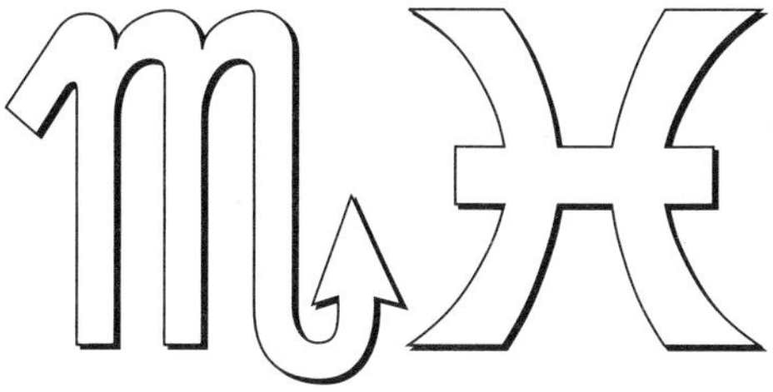

Emotional depths beckon to you both. Each of you can shine in the realm of empathy and feelings. Admire his sensitivity, artistic inclinations, compassion, or skill at visualizing possibilities. Compliment his imagination, idealism, or intuition. He can easily appreciate your ability to look beneath the surface of life, to examine intense emotional issues, and to make a strong, intimate connection with a mate. Both of you may feel torn between expressing openly versus holding back and holding feelings in. Don't let excessive secrecy interfere in your association. Share what really matters, and tread gently and carefully in each other's tender spots.

COMPATIBLE—3

HIGH ON LIFE

SAGITTARIUS/ARIES

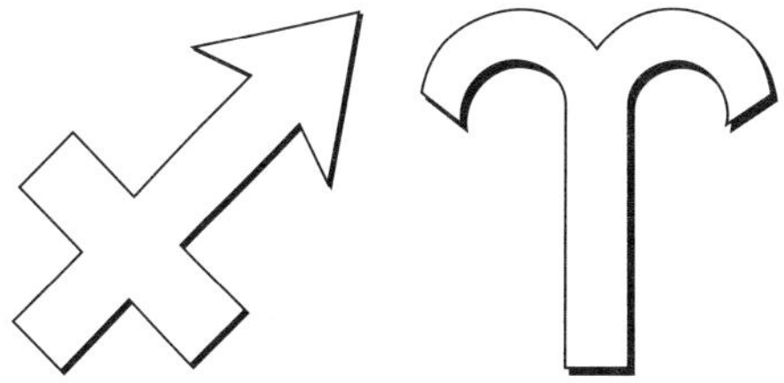

The two of you just naturally feed each other's fire! You'll admire his adventurous spirit, daring, directness, and devotion to action. He'll appreciate your sense of humor, love of freedom, and enthusiastic pursuit of **more** in life. Both of you adore feeling vital and alive. Taking risks is something you do naturally. Pioneers and explorers, you go for the gusto in life. Praise his courage, spontaneity, willingness to be on the forefront, and he'll eagerly share your quests for expanded horizons and more excitement. You can pep each other up, and both tend to be optimistic—ready for anything in life and in love.

COMPATIBLE—3

GROUNDED GYPSY?

SAGITTARIUS/TAURUS

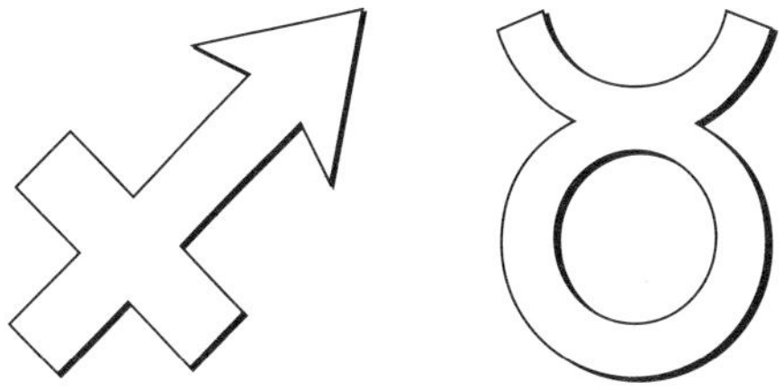

Self-esteem comes from very different sources for each of you, so openness and compromise are essential. You want to be admired for your mind, your adventurous spirit, your ethics and moral principles, your beliefs, your humor, or a readiness to travel on an instant's notice. He needs recognition for his practicality, groundedness, sensuality, and skill with the material world. His self-esteem is tied to what he earns and what he owns. He needs applause for his material possessions, ability to create comfort, or love of nature. Don't polarize over mental versus physical, or safety versus adventure. Do appreciate one another for your best qualities.

VERY CHALLENGING—1

SAGITTARIUS/GEMINI

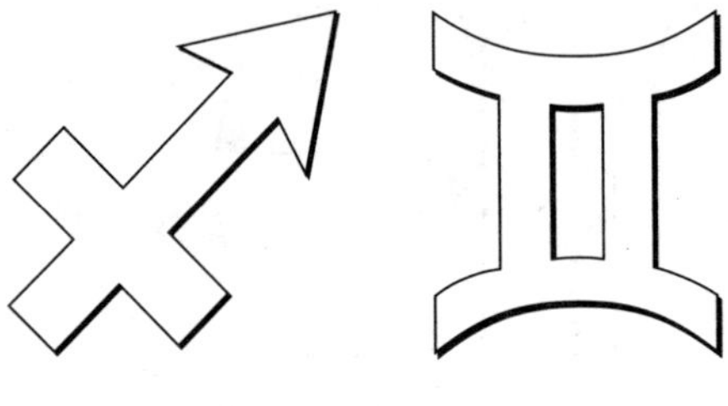

STUDENT AND TEACHER

You two make a fun, friendly, frolicking twosome, both eager to explore life. Praise his bright mind, ever-present curiosity, alertness, or interest in anything and everything. His self-esteem is tied to his mind, verbal or writing skills, and flexibility; he needs recognition in these areas. You need to be appreciated for your intellectual breadth, spiritual aspirations, spirit of adventure, and sense of humor. Your ethics, religion, love of travel, or desire to explore are important sources of vitality. Both of you enjoy discussing things, so communication and constant learning should be shared bonds between you.

VERY COMPATIBLE—4

SAGITTARIUS/CANCER

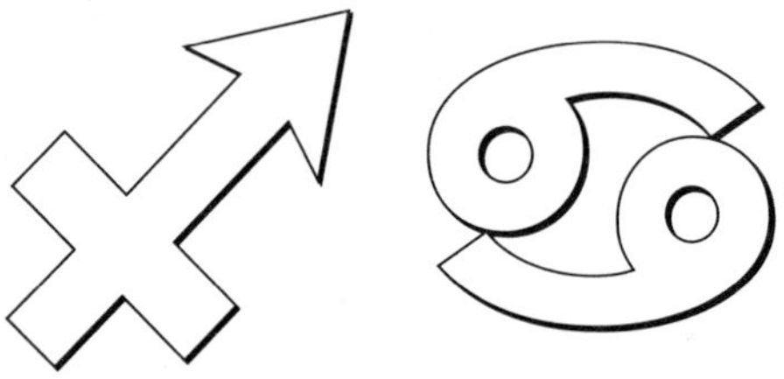

RESTLESS ROOTS

You thrive on different kinds of activity, so must respect each other's uniqueness. You want admiration for your adventurous spirit, sense of humor, or philosophical bent. The way to your heart is to praise your mind, ethics, ideals, optimism, or ready wit. He needs you to recognize and appreciate his loyalty, family ties, caretaking instincts and desire to protect and save. Home, hearth, country, financial security and the familiar matter to him. Travel, movement, and exploration energize you. Security, safety, and a homey atmosphere energize him. With compromise, each of you can enrich the other's life. Be willing to take turns so that each of you can do what you love.

VERY CHALLENGING—1

SAGITTARIUS/LEO

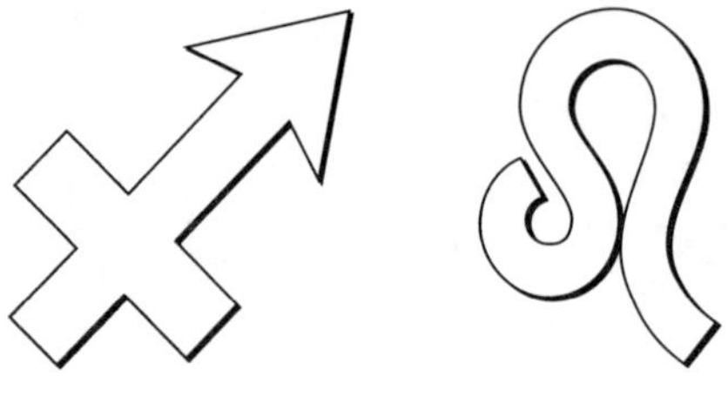

ADRENALINE ADDICTS

High-energy people, you both thrive on action and adventure. Fun-loving, you may share lots of games, parties, or eager exploration of life. He can appreciate your free spirit, optimism, broad-mindedness, sense of humor, and urge to seek truth, justice, and more stimulation from life. He needs praise and attention from you. Positive feedback is the way to go. Applaud his generosity, dramatic talent, motivational skills, and ability to create excitement. Treat him royally. Admire him wholeheartedly, and he will see you in the best possible light. You both could be risk-takers, promoters, sellers, gamblers, or explorers of life's many possibilities. Both of you love the rush of adrenaline, the sense of living and loving to the **max**.

COMPATIBLE—3

CAREFREE AND CAREFUL

SAGITTARIUS/VIRGO

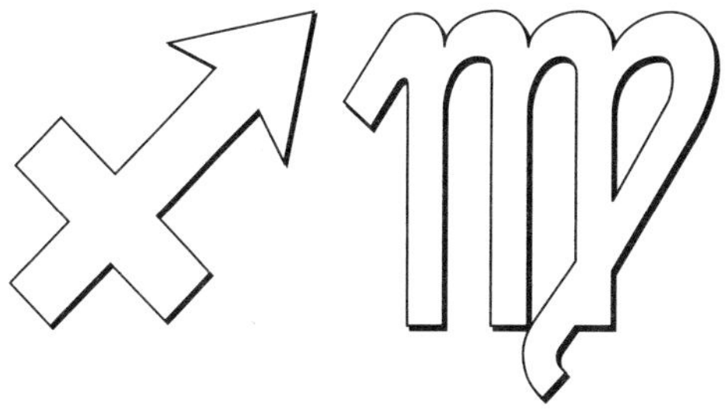

He likes things right, can handle details, focus, and be organized. You think big and may overextend or commit to too much. For the relationship to flourish, you each must appreciate the very different talents of the other. Recognize and respect his desire for tangible results, skill with details, and tendency to consider "worst case" scenarios. He tends to be more a worrier or pessimist, while you can be quite the optimist. He needs to appreciate your adventurous spirit, broad perspective, interest in philosophical or spiritual issues, and desire for independence. You can be quite extroverted, eager, impulsive, and fun-loving. He is more modest, introverted and serious. You enlarge his world and bring in excitement. He helps you to ground your dreams, and to be more practical about big ideas.

CHALLENGING—2

PLEASANTLY PLAYFUL

SAGITTARIUS/LIBRA

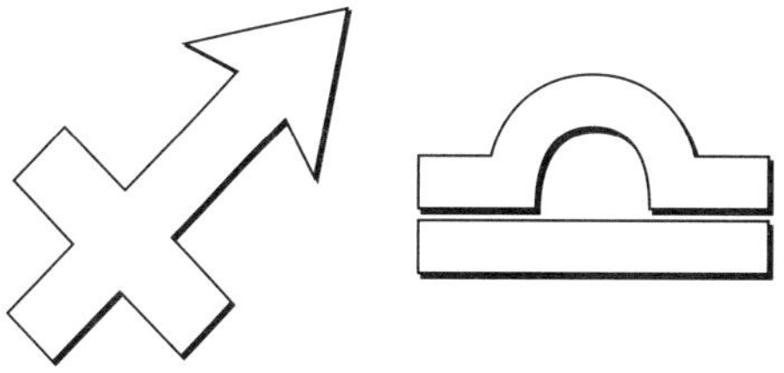

You are both naturally friendly sorts, so usually do well in social settings. Involvement with people and/or ideas and ideals stimulates each of you. He wants people to notice his charm, attractiveness, diplomacy, artistic eye, or love of harmony. He craves admiration for his interpersonal skills, empathy, or drive for justice and equality. You need recognition for your adventurous spirit, wide-ranging mind, optimistic attitude, and sense of humor. You may shine in travel, knowledge, or ethical principles. You are likely to have many experiences, interesting ideas, quick wit, or an outgoing nature. Both of you find other people stimulating and can be energized by social interactions. Your relationship is fed by people contact, communication, and play.

COMPATIBLE—3

CASUALLY CAPTIVATING

SAGITTARIUS/SCORPIO

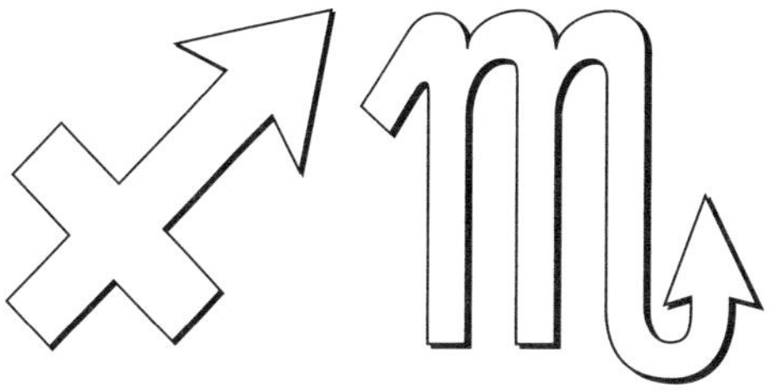

He needs recognition for his depth and intensity. You need recognition for your breadth and humor. Understanding each other can build bridges. Praise his penetrating insights, passion, perseverance, and powerful nature. Notice his skill at looking beneath the surface, unearthing secrets, and dealing with subtle messages. He needs to appreciate your independence, eager, exploring spirit, adventurousness, optimism, and lively wit. You shine through your quick mind, broad range of interests, and love of travel, learning, and fun. Don't struggle between being separate versus committed, or between many lighthearted activities versus a few serious ones. Open up your worlds to one another, and you'll both be richer for the experience.

CHALLENGING—2

SAGITTARIUS/SAGITTARIUS "THE SKY'S THE LIMIT"

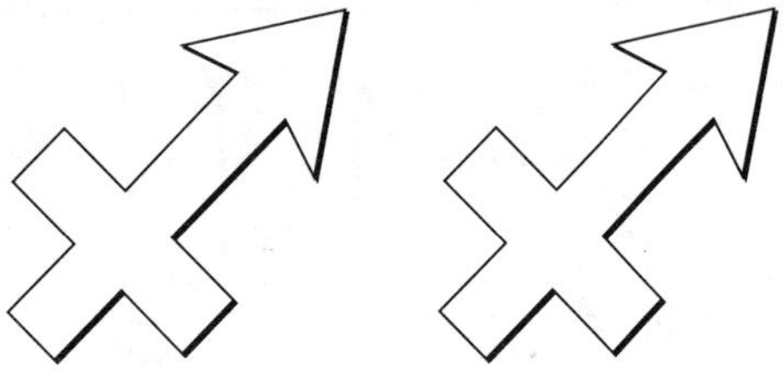

Fellow travellers in life's great adventure, you can easily rouse one another to greater heights. Praise in him exactly the qualities you wish to be admired in you: an urge to explore, an eager mind, a yen for adventure (including travel), a need to search for truth and to seek moral, ethical, religious, or spiritual principles. You can notice one another's quick wits, fun-loving attitudes, and optimism. You both thrive in an atmosphere of freedom, mental stimulation, and fun. Anything which expands your horizons energizes you both.

VERY COMPATIBLE—4

SAGITTARIUS/CAPRICORN ADVENTUROUS ACHIEVERS

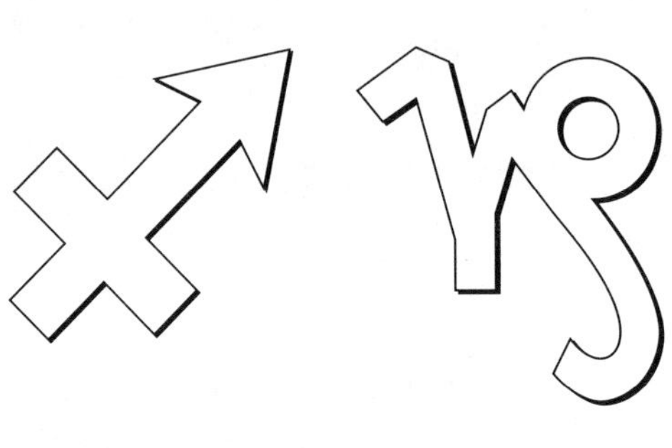

Although you seek recognition in different areas, mutual respect allows you to share lives and love. Praise his diligence, expertise, and sense of responsibility. Admire his achievements, ambition, and arduous efforts. He needs recognition for his executive skills, dedication to excellence, and eagerness to rise to high status and authority. His talents lie in formal, traditional paths to power. You need appreciation for your free spirit, your sense of adventure, and your quest for inspiration in life. You may shine through education, science, or spiritual endeavors. You feel energized when broadening your physical and/or mental horizons. He may be more formal or reserved where you are casual or carefree. He may cope with rules better than you. He can help you work within established structures. You can help him stretch beyond current boundaries.

CHALLENGING—2

SAGITTARIUS/AQUARIUS EAGER EXPERIMENTERS

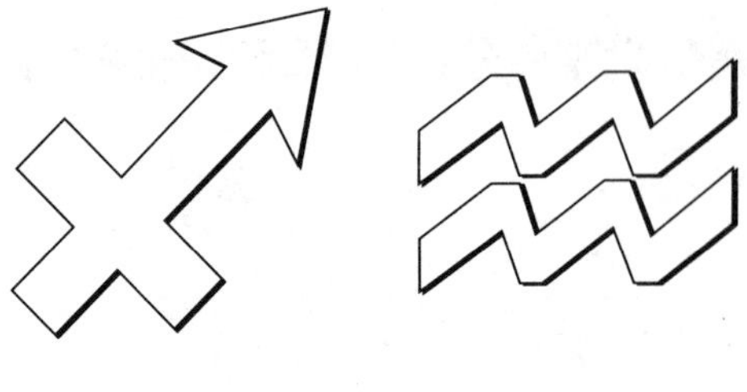

You share a thirst for experience, and a streak of independence. Each of you is energized by adventure, new people or new discoveries, and mental stimulation. Admire his unusual perspective, flashes of genius, humanitarian ideals, progressive concepts, or scientific bent. Praise his ability to go beyond ordinary limits, to understand technology, and to envision the future. He should find it easy to admire your sense of fun, your eagerness to learn, your love of new possibilities. He can appreciate your drive for freedom, insight, inspiration, and idealism. You both need a bit of space in a relationship, and are willing to break the "rules" when appropriate. You thrive on challenges and rise to the occasion.

COMPATIBLE—3

EXTENDED EXPECTATIONS

SAGITTARIUS/PISCES

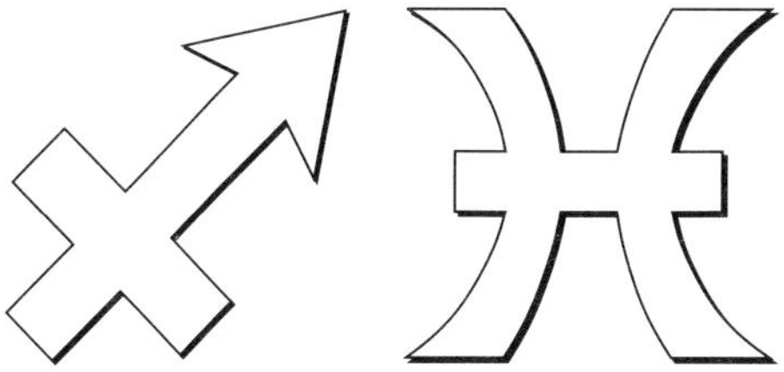

Fellow idealists where love is concerned, either of you may want a bit more than is possible. Either of you could seek an ideal relationship (that doesn't exist), expect your partner to be perfect, or hold yourself to a more-than-human standard. Shared ideals work best. Each of you needs to feel uplifted by love. Romantic scenes can be staged. The two of you could share an interest in helping the less fortunate, or in a religious or spiritual focus, or be moved by the grandeur of nature. He's more internal; you're more expressive. Don't polarize between being blunt and being tactful. Do understand each other's viewpoints and you can build a relationship which is positive and assists or inspires others (but is not perfect).

CHALLENGING—2

RULE-MAKER AND RISK-TAKER

CAPRICORN/ARIES

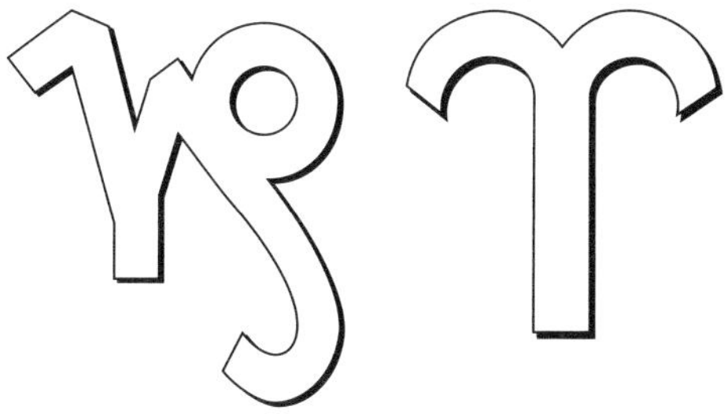

The two of you tend to take pride in different areas, but sharing may be easier if you stroke each other's egos (as well as bodies) properly. He wants to be appreciated and acknowledged for his independence, pioneering spirit, honesty, and ability to be direct and open. His courage, energy, or ability to act may be noteworthy. You want respect—to be admired as an achiever. He needs to praise your successes in your work (or any endeavors for which you are responsible). Since you are both strong individuals, beware of fighting for control. He can shine in areas calling for spontaneity and optimism. You can shine in situations demanding caution, planning ahead, and hard work. Divide up the territory and you'll do well.

CHALLENGING—2

RELIABLE RULES

CAPRICORN/TAURUS

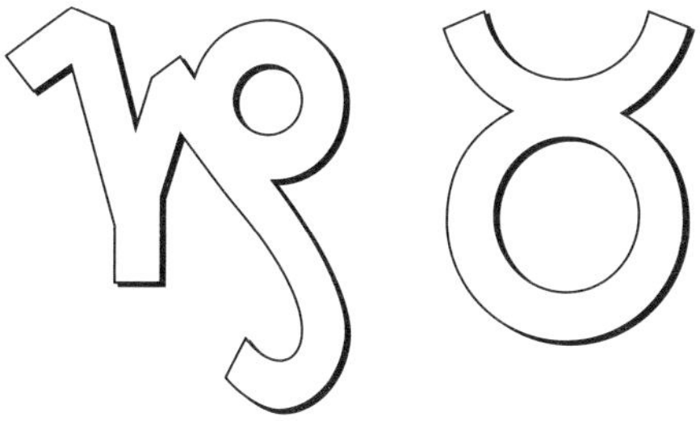

Each of you appreciates dependability in the other. The way to his heart is to admire his good sense, skill with finances, reliability, or desire to bring comfort and pleasure to others as well as himself. He needs praise and applause for what he earns and what he owns. Notice his sensuality, possessions, love of nature, appreciation of simplicity, or pleasant nature. He needs to appreciate your professional accomplishments, expertise, and strong sense of responsibility. You shine through self-discipline, conscientiousness, willingness to work, ambition, and pragmatism. You both demonstrate love by doing things for people. You could share tasks (or even a business) as well as a romantic connection.

COMPATIBLE—3

CAPRICORN/GEMINI

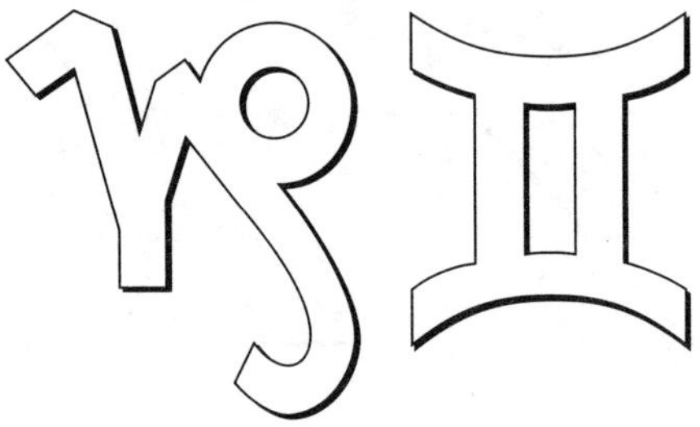

LEARNING LIMITS

For this relationship to flourish, you each must admire and praise in the other qualities different from those you prize within yourselves. He prides himself on being lighthearted, friendly, versatile, and multi-talented. You pride yourself on being serious, cautious, responsible, and hardworking. Compliment him on his sense of fun, flexibility, or flippancy. Notice his way with words, alertness, curiosity and eagerness to learn. He needs to respect you, admire your expertise, and notice your career accomplishments. You can contribute to stability in his life, and he can contribute to flux and adaptability in yours.

VERY CHALLENGING—1

CAPRICORN/CANCER

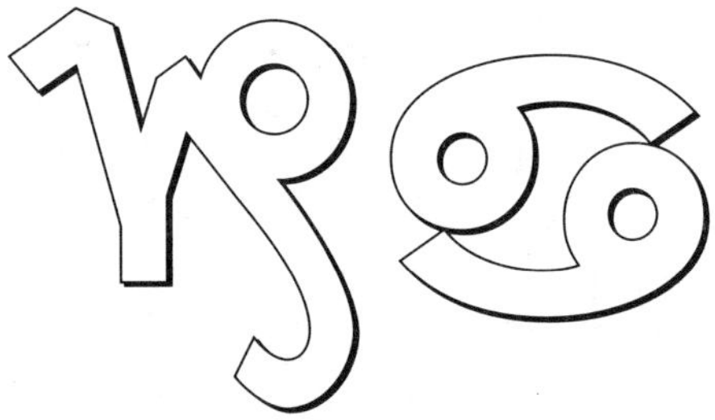

FAMILY FOCUS

Both of you take pride in your loyalty and carrying through on your responsibilities. Family ties may matter a lot to you both. Each of you tends to be a caretaker—someone who looks after others. He takes pride in his family, country, possessions, or ability to protect and preserve. Praise his caring nature, compassion, appreciation of food, or devotion to loved ones. He needs to notice and admire your realism and productive accomplishments, and to appreciate your career, status, responsibility, dedication, and practicality. Each of you appreciates security and stability. Together, you build for the long haul.

VERY COMPATIBLE—4

CAPRICORN/LEO

POWERFUL AND PERSUASIVE

Both of you definitely want respect, but you each seek recognition through different paths. You want to work your way to the top, to make it on society's terms, to be admired for your career, sense of responsibility, stability, and determination to do things well, to deal in excellence. Your patience may be noteworthy. He feels a sense of urgency and prefers immediate action. He wants power right away and may use dramatic skills, persuasiveness, magnetism, or leadership to sway other people. Exciting and full of zest, he is willing to take chances for greater gain. You need to recognize and appreciate his charisma, generosity, and enthusiasm. Praise works wonders with him, but avoid criticism as much as possible! He can learn more patience and perseverance from you. He can help bring more drama and dynamism into your life.

VERY CHALLENGING—1

RELIABLY RESPONSIBLE

CAPRICORN/VIRGO

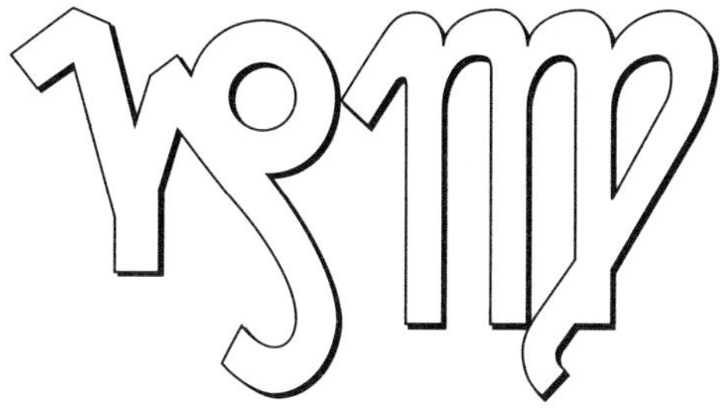

Both of you appreciate the value of productive work and responsible action. Each of you can demonstrate love by doing tasks for the other. Admire his diligence, skill with details, craftsmanship, focus, concentration, and practicality. He needs to recognize and appreciate your career achievements, status, dedication, expertise, air of authority, and conscientiousness. Both of you are good at getting down to business and getting things done. You two could share tasks, or a business as well as an emotional bond, but both of you must guard against letting flaw-finding attitudes slip over from work into the emotional side of your relationship. By all means work on improving your relationship, but do **not** turn your partner into a chore!

COMPATIBLE—3

FIRM AND FAIR

CAPRICORN/LIBRA

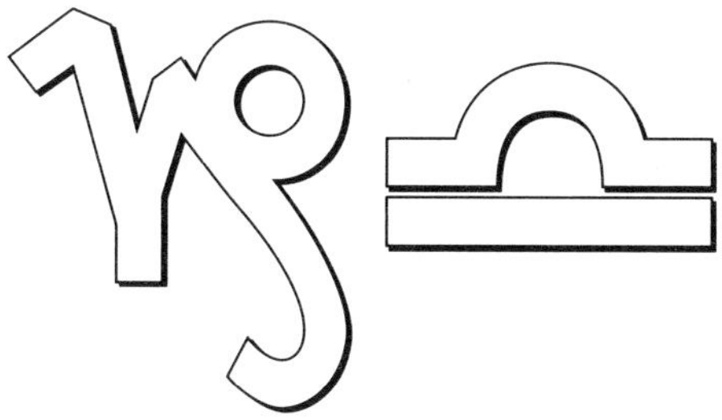

He needs respect and admiration in the interpersonal and aesthetic realms. Praise his skill with others, negotiating instincts, tact, empathy, desire for balance and fair play, or eye for beauty. You need him to recognize and appreciate your vocational attainments, dedication to excellence, air of authority, and self-discipline. You shine through hard work, taking responsibility, and being thorough. Don't polarize between ease and effort, or power player and peacemaker. Compromise with one another between love and work, as well as between work and play. Together, you can have a full life of outer world accomplishments as well as strong emotional connections.

CHALLENGING—2

POWERFUL PERSEVERANCE

CAPRICORN/SCORPIO

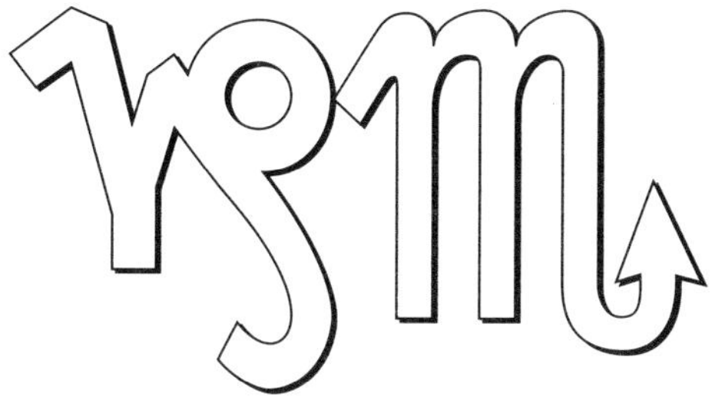

You both have a serious streak and a strong drive to carry through on your commitments. Be sure you each can forgive and forget when necessary. Admire his depth, perseverance, self-control, and ability to get to the bottom of things. Recognize his need for power and his intense approach to life. Applaud his resourcefulness and determination. He needs to appreciate your ambitions, diligence, sense of responsibility, and practicality. You easily understand rules, regulations, and power structures, and can shine by gaining mastery, expertise, or status. You each need a measure of control, so take charge in your own careers or tasks. Don't try to rule one another. Both of you can be very loyal, once committed.

COMPATIBLE—3

CAPRICORN/SAGITTARIUS ADVENTUROUS ACHIEVERS

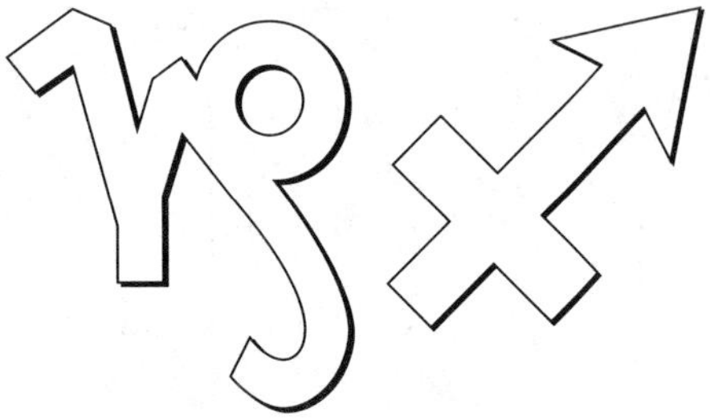

Although you seek recognition in different areas, mutual respect allows you to share lives and love. Praise his free spirit, sense of adventure, humor, and quest for inspiration in life. He may shine through education, science, philosophy, the intellect, or anything which broadens mental or physical horizons. He is energized by exploration. You need recognition and respect for your diligence, expertise, and sense of responsibility. He needs to admire your achievements, hard work, executive skills, dedication to excellence, and eagerness to rise higher in life. You may be more formal or reserved, while he is casual or carefree. You may cope with rules better than he does. You can help him work within established structures. He can help you stretch beyond current boundaries.

CHALLENGING—2

CAPRICORN/CAPRICORN EXCELLENT EXPERTISE

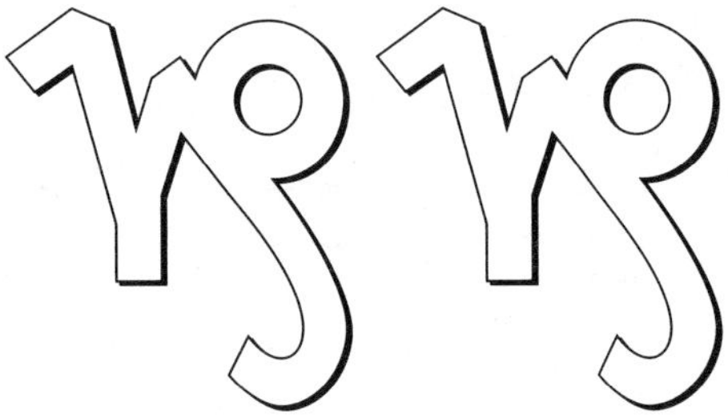

You two understand each other well which is good because you both tend to keep your hearts private, and love hidden from view. Admire in him exactly those qualities for which you would like to receive recognition: ambition, a drive for excellence, a strong sense of responsibility, and skill at dealing with power players and power issues. Praise one another's hard work, career accomplishments, status advancements, and dedication to doing what needs to be done. You are both practical and capable people. Sometimes duties might compete with love, or either of you might fear being vulnerable to another person. You may avoid relationships for fear of being hurt, rejected, or criticized. You both may need to practice making courtship a priority. Just about whatever task you set yourselves to do, you **can** do!

VERY COMPATIBLE—4

CAPRICORN/AQUARIUS RULE-MAKER OR RULE-BREAKER?

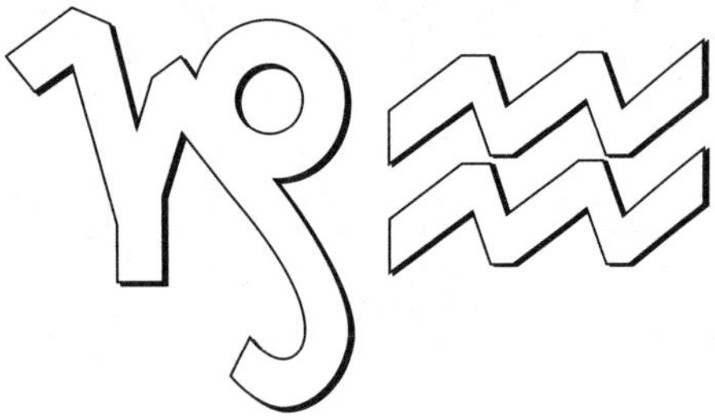

What energizes each of you is quite different, so lots of tolerance and understanding is vital. He wants to be admired as a free soul— unconventional, unpredictable, uncommitted, and unlimited. You thrive on commitment, regularity, and fitting into societal demands and expectations. He is willing to be the rebel, the questioner, the revolutionary. You are a natural executive—someone who understands and can rise in the power structure. He may seem a bit irresponsible, irreverent, or shocking to you. You might seem too formal, traditional or disciplined (dutiful) to him. You can help him become more skilled at knowing which rules in life and love really need to be followed. He can help you learn which rules can be broken!

CHALLENGING—2

EMPATHIC EXPERTISE

CAPRICORN/PISCES

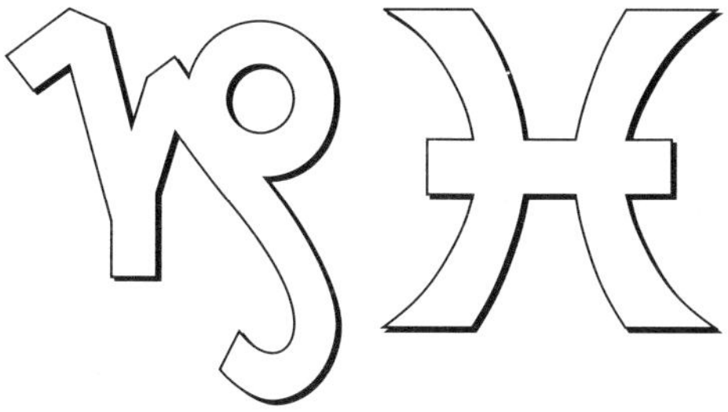

Admire his imagination, compassion, sensitivity, or sympathy for the underdog. Praise his eye for beauty, empathic understanding of others, intuition, idealism, or global grasp of the big picture. He needs to recognize your dedication, sense of responsibility, good sense, and need to achieve. Getting your tasks done—and done well—energizes you. You take pride in being an expert, being realistic, and able to do what's necessary to accomplish your goals. The two of you might sometimes feel like the idealist and the realist, but are generally compatible. Each of you appreciates security. He helps feed your tender side. You help vitalize his practical side.

COMPATIBLE—3

RISK-TAKING REBELS

AQUARIUS/ARIES

Each of you wants to be admired for your free spirit and interest in the new. The way to his heart is to praise his courage, energy, enthusiasm, pioneering spirit, and open nature. Admire his directness and spontaneity. Recognize his need to move, his urge to be in the forefront, and his willingness to try almost anything. He needs to appreciate your passion for justice, ability to relate to anyone, or interest in technology. You shine as an individual; he must acknowledge your uniqueness. Each of you can energize the other, encouraging one another's adventurousness.

COMPATIBLE—3

INDIVIDUALISTIC INDULGENCE

AQUARIUS/TAURUS

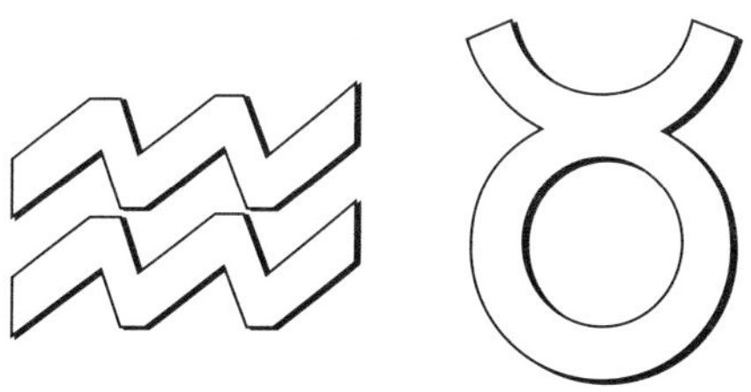

You tend to pride yourselves on different qualities, so open-mindedness is vital. You want to be admired for being unique, unusual, bright, progressive, humanitarian, or objective. You are proud of your ability to handle change and variety. He needs recognition for his steadiness and reliability. He is skilled at creating material comforts and pleasures. He tends to focus on the now. You tend to look ahead and envision future possibilities. He prefers the known; you are drawn toward the unknown. Together, you two need to blend the mental and physical, the new and familiar, the exciting and the comfortable. A middle ground brings you the best of both.

CHALLENGING—2

AQUARIUS/GEMINI

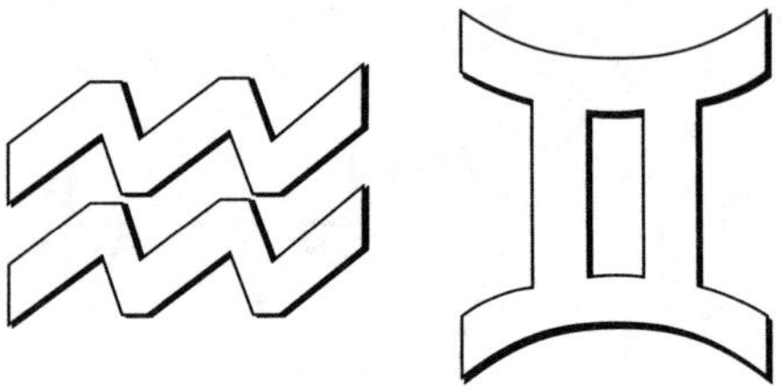

STUDENTS OF SCIENCE

Both of you pride yourselves on your ability to think, communicate, and be fair and impartial, so common ground should be easy to find. The way to his heart is through his mind. Admire his quick wit, curiosity, perceptiveness, and flexibility. Appreciate his interest in everything, enthusiasm for knowledge, or ability to communicate. He should find it easy to enjoy your originality, open mind, futuristic ideas, and enthusiasm for the new and different. Since you both seek mental stimulation, this can be a lively relationship. You will each take pride in the other's alertness and eagerness to learn.

COMPATIBLE—3

AQUARIUS/CANCER

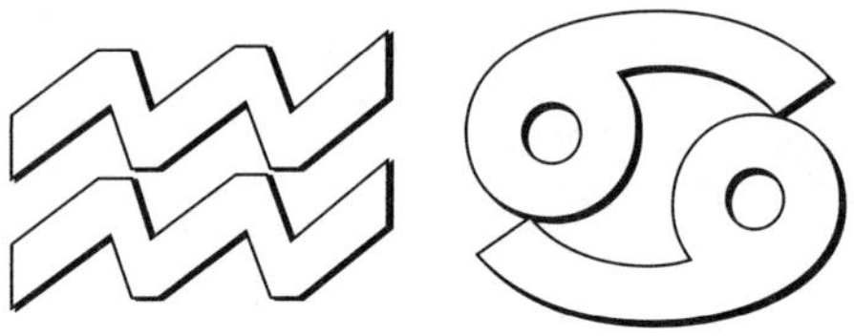

REBEL ROOTS

Pride and self-esteem are tied to different areas for each of you, so mutual tolerance is essential. Praise his feeling for hearth and home, and desire for emotional safety and security. Respect his sentimental attachments (to people, things, memories, country). Notice his caring, compassion, and concerns. He may have to learn to value your individuality, inventiveness, and independent spirit. You're not like anyone else! He can grow to appreciate your skill with technology, friends, networking abilities, or unusual interests and talents. Don't polarize between freedom needs versus a desire for closeness, or feel torn between stability versus change. Do be open to what you can learn from one another.

VERY CHALLENGING—1

AQUARIUS/LEO

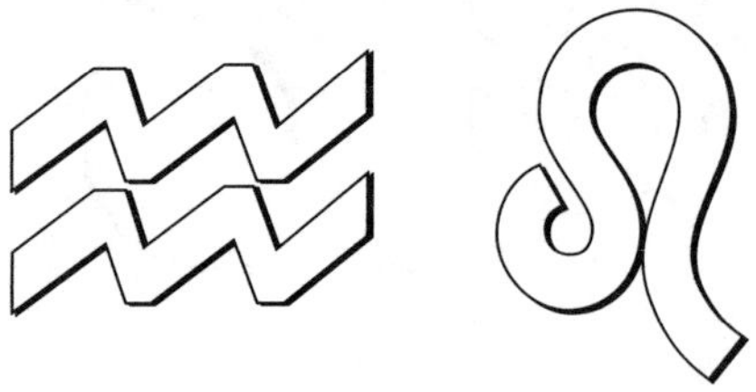

EXTRAORDINARY

Each of you needs very much to be seen as special by the other. He needs to be admired and applauded. Let him take center stage; he could have considerable dramatic skill. Recognize his promotional skills, generosity, or fun-loving spirit. He can be quite warm and enthusiastic. Eager to love and be loved, he can be good at giving compliments and **loves** to be adored. Praise him! He needs to admire you as unique, individualistic, inventive, and independent. You shine through unusual perspectives, progressive viewpoints, a feeling for technology, and a stimulating mind. You both can be quite creative and original.

VERY COMPATIBLE—4

CASUAL VS. CONSCIENTIOUS

AQUARIUS/VIRGO

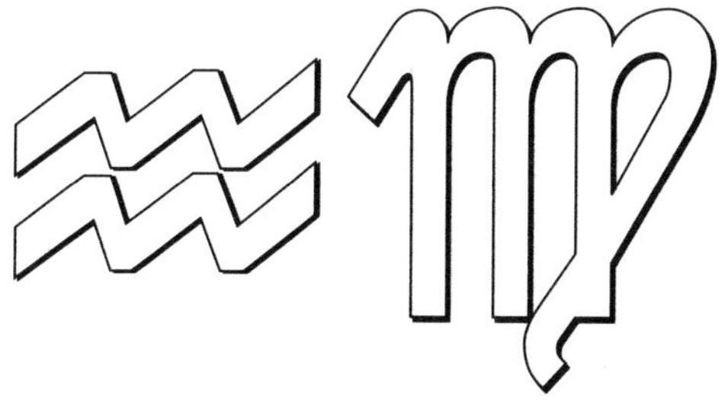

Different strokes for different folks definitely applies here. You need to appreciate and admire his skill with details, his diligence, dedication, and desire for tangible results. He needs to get things done, to make them real. You are skilled at envisioning potentials and possibilities. It is vital that he applaud your uniqueness, inventiveness, and individuality. You are a free spirit, and may be proud of your humanitarian principles or ability to relate to anyone about anything. You could shine as a brainstormer. You invent and imagine. He brings things down to earth, dealing with practicalities and getting results. He may be more picky or critical, while you are more tolerant, but compromise finds a middle ground. Together, you can turn theory into practice.

VERY CHALLENGING—1

JUSTICE FOR ALL

AQUARIUS/LIBRA

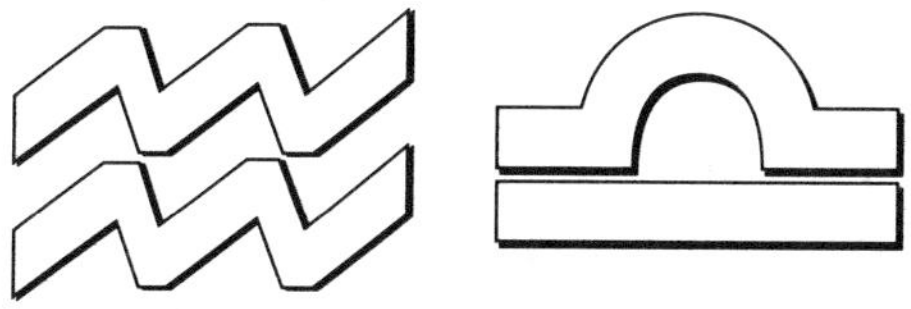

Both of you shine with ideas and people. Passionate discussions may appeal, or the stimulation of varied people and diverse concepts. Praise his skill with people, attractiveness, tact, or charm. Admire his feeling for justice, balance and harmony, or eye for beauty. He needs to understand your unconventional streak, and appreciate your inventive spirit, intuitive grasp of technology, and feeling for the future. You both enjoy meeting people on the same level, relating as peers. You learn much through interaction with others. Communication can draw you together. A shared sense of equality and fair play strengthens the bond between you.

COMPATIBLE—3

INDEPENDENT OR INTENSE?

AQUARIUS/SCORPIO

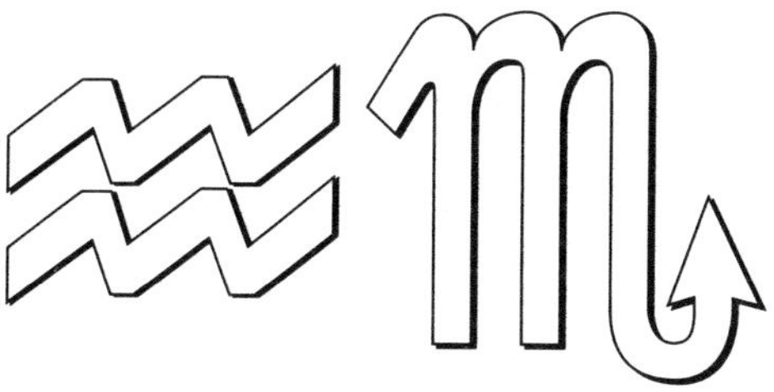

You each need to shine in different areas, so respect for one another is vital. Admire his passionate intensity, sexual drive, strong will, resourcefulness or self-control. He thrives on intimate encounters and emotional confrontations. All-or-nothing is his style. Your independence, inventiveness and inquiring mind must be recognized. He has to appreciate and applaud your uniqueness, originality, and unconventional ideas. Your humanitarian ideals, networking skills, or feel for technology and the future may be noteworthy. He is energized by intimate connections and intense one-on-one interactions. You thrive on friendship and may share feelings with a number of other people. Don't turn your association into a battle between intensity and space, or depth versus breadth. Do allow each other to be true to your inner natures.

CHALLENGING—2

AQUARIUS/SAGITTARIUS — EAGER EXPERIMENTERS

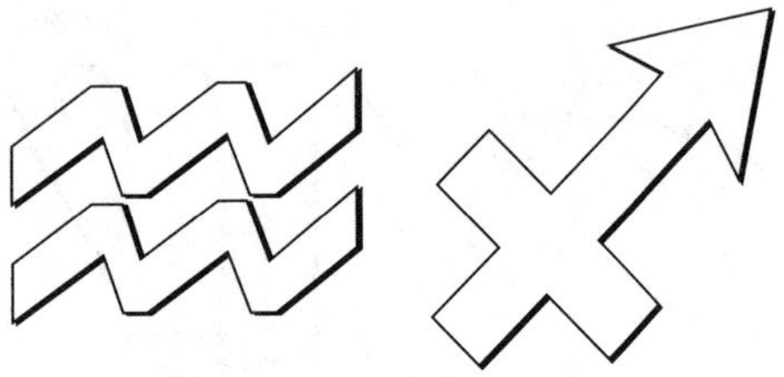

You share a thirst for experience, and a streak of independence. Each of you is energized by adventure, new people or new discoveries, and mental stimulation. Admire his sense of fun, eagerness to learn, and love of new possibilities. Appreciate his drive for freedom, insight, inspiration, and idealism. He should find it easy to value your unusual perspectives, flashes of genius, humanitarian ideals, progressive concepts, or scientific bent. You need praise for going beyond ordinary limits, understanding technology, and envisioning the future. You both need a bit of space in a relationship, and are willing to break the "rules" when appropriate. You thrive on challenges and rise to the occasion.

COMPATIBLE—3

AQUARIUS/CAPRICORN — RULE-BREAKER OR RULE-MAKER?

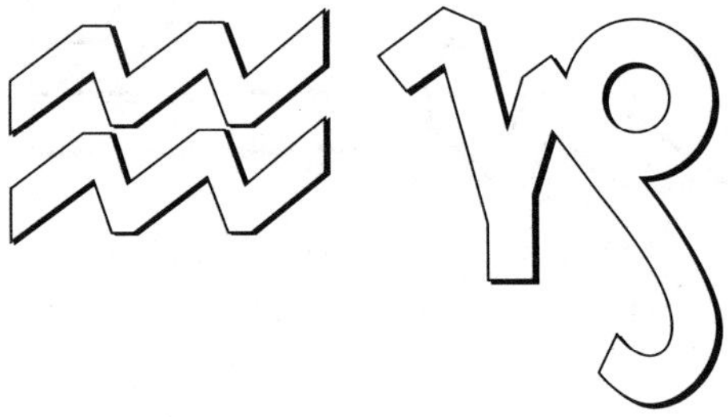

What energizes each of you is quite different, so lots of tolerance and understanding is vital. You want to be admired as a free soul— unconventional, unpredictable, unusual, and unlimited. He thrives on responsibility, regularity, and fitting into societal demands and expectations. You are willing to be the rebel, the questioner, the revolutionary. He is a natural executive—someone who understands and can rise in the power structure. You may seem a bit irresponsible, irreverent, or shocking to him. He might seem too formal, traditional, or dictatorial (restrictive) to you. He can help you become more skilled at knowing which rules in life and love really need to be followed. You can help him learn which rules can be broken!

CHALLENGING—2

AQUARIUS/AQUARIUS — PROGRESSIVE PARTNERS

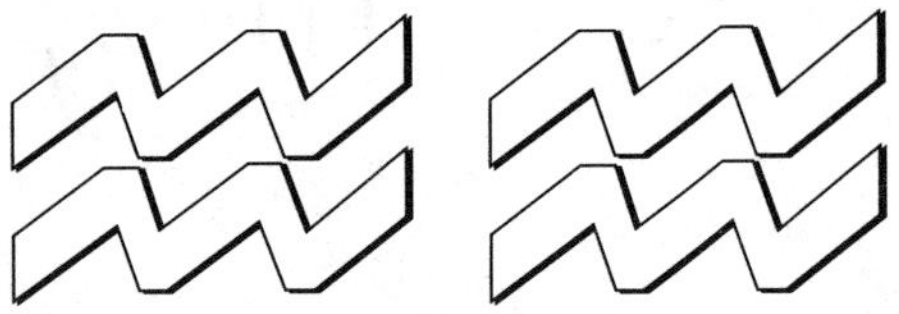

Fellow free souls, you have much in common. Admire in him the independence, inventiveness, and individuality which you also exhibit. Each of you thrives in an atmosphere of openness, newness, and choices. Give each other some breathing space. The bonds of love have to be quite loose in your cases. Recognize his flair for future trends, progressive ideas, unconventional concepts, and he can acknowledge yours. You two may share a zest for friends, social causes, equality, justice, networking, technology, groups, or anything unusual or different. Changes energize you both. Love for each of you is electric, a bit unpredictable, and exciting.

VERY COMPATIBLE—4

UNUSUAL UNDERSTANDING

AQUARIUS/PISCES

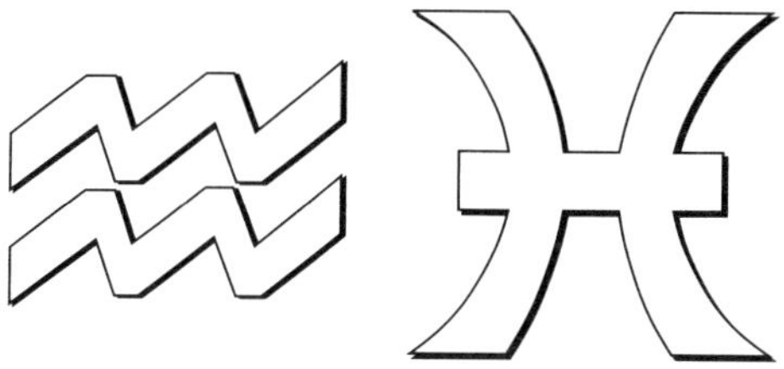

Although you both can tune into the larger world, concerned about wider issues, differences do exist. Admire his compassion for the underdog, creative imagination, mystical instincts, eye for beauty, or idealistic nature. Praise his willingness to help, heal, inspire, and uplift others. His inner world is rich and full. He needs to acknowledge and appreciate your independence, passion for justice and equality, skill as a friend and networker, and interest in what is unusual. Humanitarian activities might draw you together—or an interest in the future. You may be a bit more objective and he more emotional, but you both want to leave the world a better place for your having lived here.

CHALLENGING—2

MYSTICAL WARRIORS

PISCES/ARIES

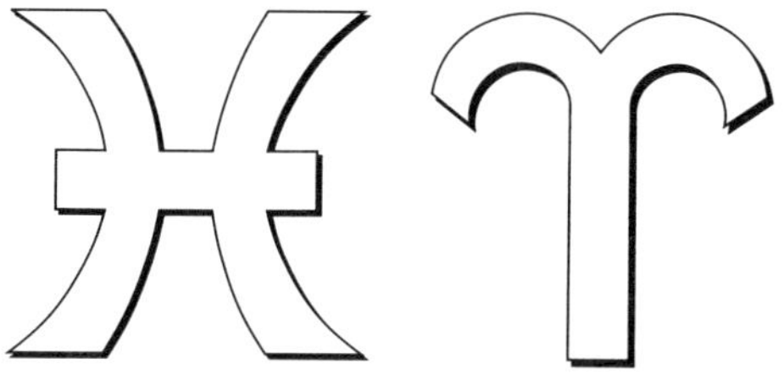

Although your basic personalities differ, if you genuinely appreciate each other's special qualities, all will be well. Recognize and admire his courage, spontaneity, and honesty. Praise his pioneering spirit, ability to be in the forefront, energy, and enthusiasm. He could be quite active, direct, and eager to conquer any obstacles. He needs to appreciate your idealism, sensitivity, poetic nature, and wonderful imagination. Your capacity to visualize is noteworthy. Although you may be more shy or retiring, he can help draw you out. You can help him be more compassionate and contemplative.

CHALLENGING—2

EASY DOES IT

PISCES/TAURUS

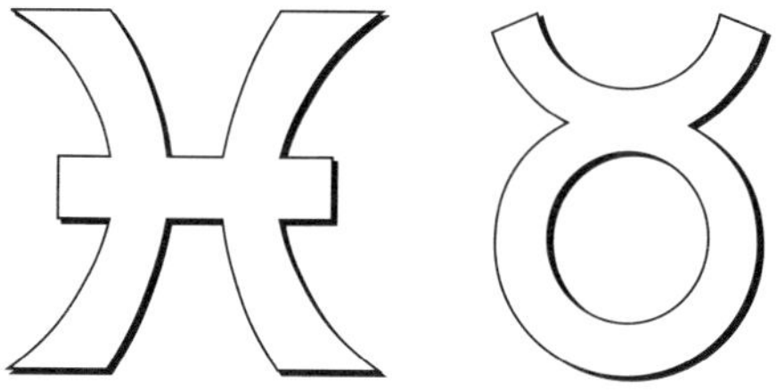

You both have artistic, creative talent, and the ability to please others. He needs to be recognized for his good sense, dependability, skill with the material or financial world, or ability to create comfort. He can be energized by nature, sensual pleasures, making money, or anything which is physically gratifying. You need to be appreciated for your imagination, sensitivity, dramatic flair, romantic ideals, persuasive abilities, and love of beauty and ease. An appreciation of art, nature, or a smooth, easy flow in life can be a shared bond between you. You both want to keep life and love pleasant.

COMPATIBLE—3

PISCES/GEMINI

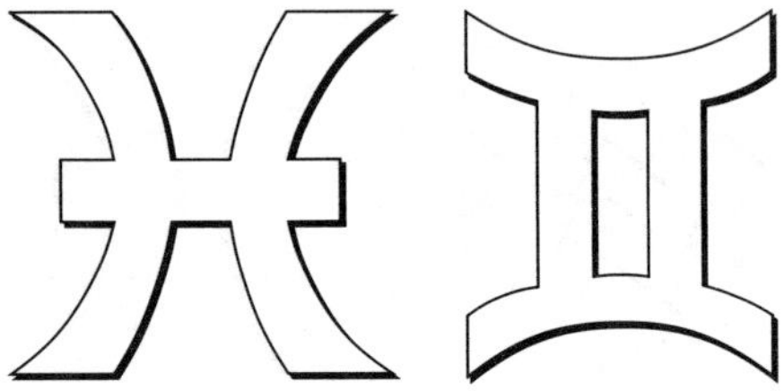

VARIED VISIONS

A multiplicity of interests may draw you together, but your areas of pride and self-esteem do differ. You need praise for your sensitivity, intuition, eye for beauty, or ability to assess life and see the big picture. He needs praise for his liveliness, logic, and laughter. He could be quite quick-witted, curious, and eager to gain and give information. He tends to figure things out by telling people about it (talking them out). You figure things out by mulling them over. You seek recognition for your compassion, inwardness, imagination, romantic ideals, or feeling for beauty and nature. He seeks recognition for his mind, his enthusiasm for fresh experiences, and his eagerness to learn from everyone and everything. He can teach you to open up more, and you can educate him regarding the joys of contemplation.

CHALLENGING—2

PISCES/CANCER

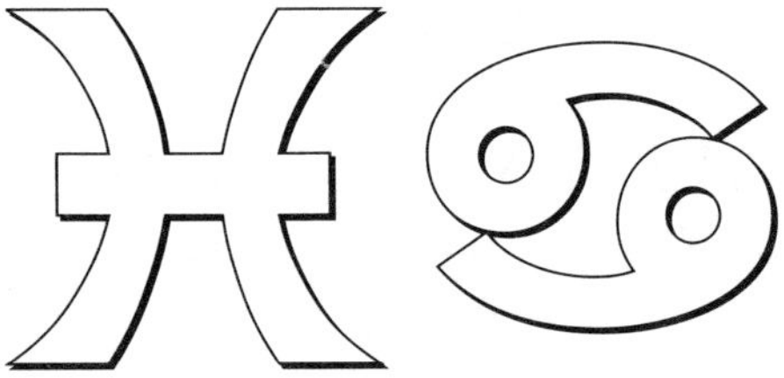

MOTHERING MYSTICISM

Both of you tend to admire sensitivity, empathy, and concern for others. Praise his roots, family connections, emotional loyalty, feeling for the helpless, and urge to build a warm home environment. He may be very attached to possessions, money, country, or loved ones. It is vital that he admire your imagination, feeling for fantasy, or visualizing skills. Your poetic, mystical, tender, and romantic side must be recognized. You each have strong rescuing instincts. You both keep your emotions somewhat under cover, being protective (of self and others). Be sure you share what matters. Don't suppress important issues or feelings. Sometimes you understand each other without words.

COMPATIBLE—3

PISCES/LEO

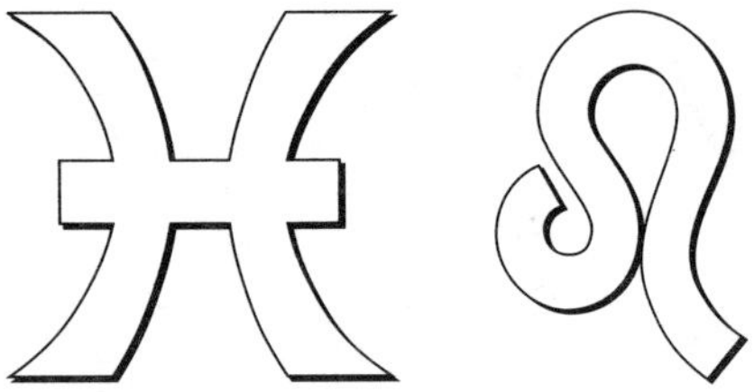

SUBTLE OR SHOWY?

Each of you has dramatic flair and an instinct for showmanship. You seek admiration for your magical, mystical, mysterious side, but tend to be subtle, sensitive, and somewhat inward. He needs direct, open admiration. He can be quite expressive, dramatic, and even larger than life. He needs a stage to perform upon. Applause is vital. He is energized by recognition. Compliment him and he's convinced you are the wisest of partners. Both of you can be romantics, in love with love. Be sensible in what you demand from each other. Remember that he needs to show off, and you need to explore your inner realms. He can draw you out; you can draw him in.

VERY CHALLENGING—1

INDISPENSABLE IMAGINATION

PISCES/VIRGO

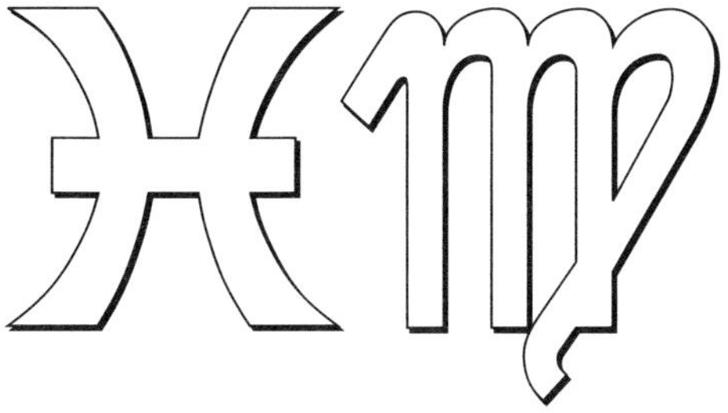

Although opposites in some ways, there is a natural attraction between you. You deal with dreams, images, and idealized desires. He deals with practicalities, work, and the necessary details of reality. Together, you can be chronically dissatisfied (never perfect enough), or bring dreams to earth and make visions real. Appreciate and applaud his common sense, willingness to work, productivity and efficiency. Praise his diligence, detail-orientation, and determination to get the job **done**. He needs to appreciate your imagination, empathy, and imagery. He can learn to value your whimsical, magical, romantic, mysterious, fantasy side as well as your intuition and understanding of ideals. Don't polarize between facts and fancy. When you combine forces, you can make ideal images a reality, bringing dreams into form.

VERY COMPATIBLE—4

LOVE IN TECHNICOLOR

PISCES/LIBRA

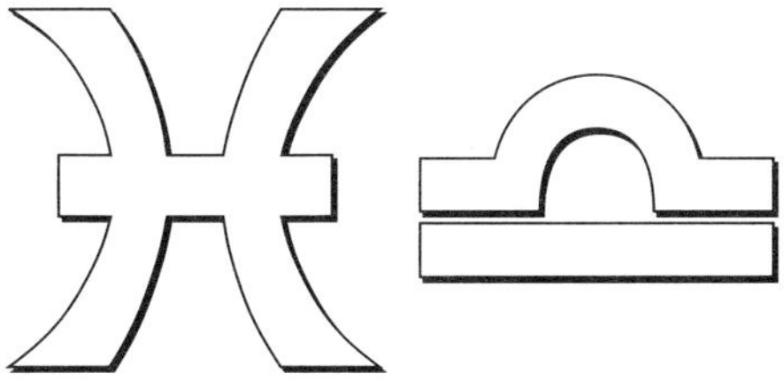

He shines in the public world of people. You shine in the private world of imagination. Sharing will require compromises from you both. You need recognition for your visualizing skills, "what if?" potentials, and creative imagination. He must admire your sensitivity, compassion for the underdog, and ability to understand the feelings of others. You might create through poetry, music, science, dance, art, or any form of beauty, or love of nature and patterns. He needs one-on-one interaction. He shines in the company of others—through charm, poise, empathy, and tact. He can be a skilled negotiator or competitor as well as an instinctive diplomat. Loving relationships are natural for you both. Pleasing people is your forte. A shared feeling for beauty can draw you together. You can show him fantastic inner realms, and he can draw you out to enjoy a wider world of contacts.

VERY CHALLENGING—1

BONDED

PISCES/SCORPIO

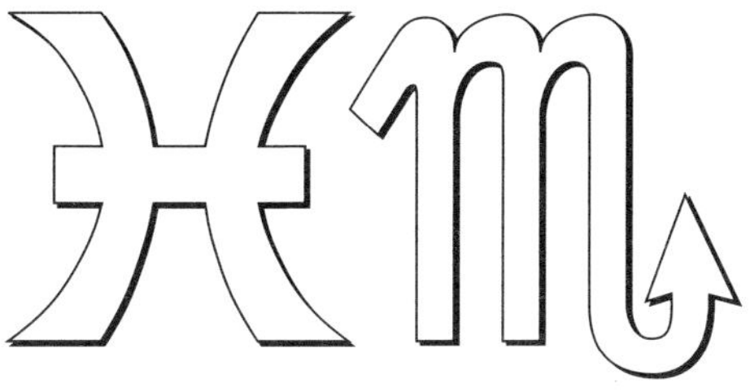

Emotional depths beckon to you both. Each of you can shine in the realm of empathy and feelings. Admire his willingness to look beneath the surface, sensitivity to secrets, sexual drive, and desire for a strong, intimate connection with a mate. He may shine through resourcefulness, a drive for power, an instinctive understanding of nonverbal cues and innuendoes, or through dogged determination. He needs to appreciate your sensitivity, artistic inclinations, compassion, and skill at visualizing possibilities. He should compliment your imagination, idealism, and intuition. Both of you may feel torn between expressing openly versus holding feelings in. Don't let excessive withholding interfere in your association. Share what really matters, and tread gently and carefully in each other's tender spots.

COMPATIBLE—3

PISCES/SAGITTARIUS

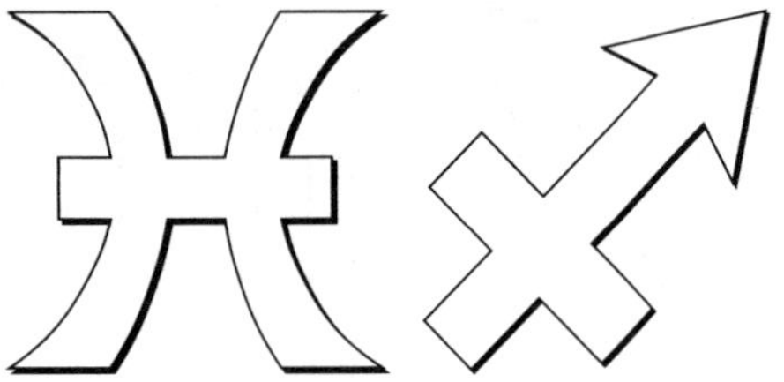

EXTENDED EXPECTATIONS

Fellow idealists where love is concerned, either of you may want a bit more than is possible. Either of you could seek an ideal relationship (that doesn't exist), expect your partner to be perfect, or hold yourself to a more-than-human standard. Shared ideals work best. Each of you needs to feel uplifted by love. Romantic scenes can be staged. The two of you could share an interest in helping the less fortunate, or in a religious or spiritual focus, or be moved by the grandeur of nature. You're more internal; he is more expressive. Don't polarize between being blunt and being tactful. Do understand each other's viewpoints and you can build a relationship which is positive, and assists or inspires others (but is not perfect).

CHALLENGING—2

PISCES/CAPRICORN

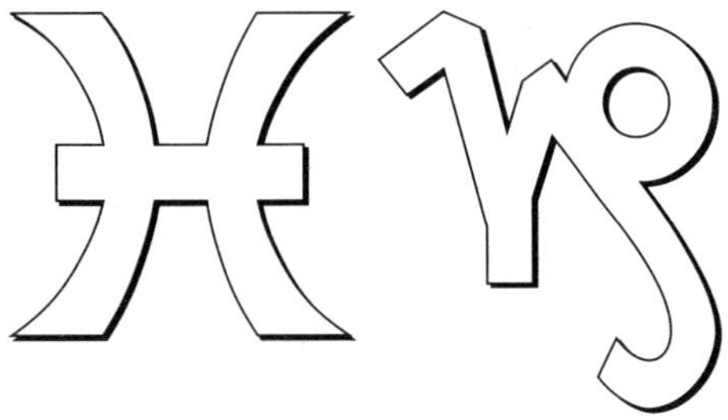

EMPATHIC EXPERTISE

Admire his dedication, sense of responsibility, drive for status, handling of power and need to achieve. Recognize his formal, traditional side which wants to play by the rules and **win**. Compliment his expertise, realism, and quest for excellence. Getting the job done well energizes him. He needs to appreciate your imagination, compassion, sensitivity, and sympathy for the underdog. You have an eye for beauty, empathic understanding of others, intuition, idealism, and a global grasp of the big picture. The two of you might sometimes feel like the idealist and the realist, or Pollyanna and the pessimist, but are generally compatible. Each of you appreciates security. You help feed his tender side. He helps vitalize your practical side.

COMPATIBLE—3

PISCES/AQUARIUS

UNUSUAL UNDERSTANDING

Although you both can tune into the larger world, concerned about wider issues, differences do exist. Admire his independence, passion for justice and equality, skill as a friend or networker, and interest in what is new and different. He wants to be acknowledged as unique, inventive, and unusual. Although he goes off the beaten path, what he brings back is often fascinating. He needs to understand and appreciate your compassion for the underdog, creative imagination, mystical instincts, eye for beauty, and idealistic nature. He should praise your willingness to help, heal, inspire, and uplift others. Your inner world is rich and full. Humanitarian activities might draw you together—or an interest in the future. He may be a bit more objective or logical, and you a bit more emotional and intuitive, but you both want to leave the world a better place for your having lived here.

CHALLENGING—2

INTUITIVE IDEALISTS

PISCES/PISCES

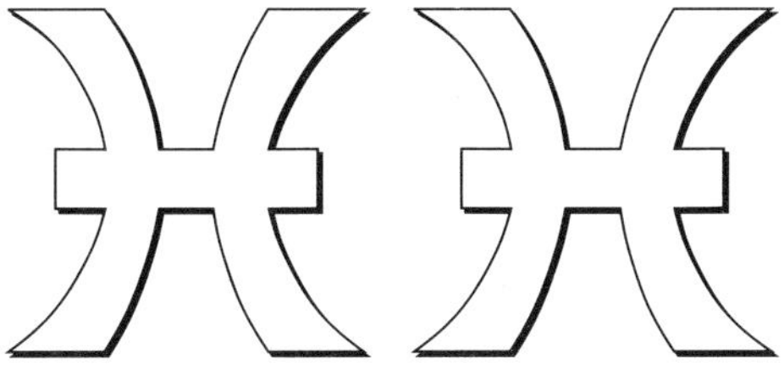

Romance appeals to you both. Each of you has a sensitive, magical side, with a gift for instinctively attracting love. Admire his imagination, idealism, and intuition. He can do likewise, appreciating yours. Each of you needs to be recognized for your compassion, visualizing skills, utopian dreams, and emotional nature. You both have a flair for drama, persuasion, for casting a spell on others. An aura of mysterious allure clings to you both. Praise and share with one another a feeling for beauty, nature, mysticism, religion, or anything inspirational and transcendent.

VERY COMPATIBLE—4

MOON

The Moon is a key to your emotional nature. The Moon represents both our dependencies and vulnerabilities (where we look for support and safety) and the way we tend to nurture others. The Moon is a key to our moods and our feelings. It is also a key to our home—both the physical home and the emotional environment we wish to create in our nest.

Remember, for a full picture, you would also include the house of your Moon and its aspects, but we can still learn a great deal from sign placements only.

First read the shorthand description for the sign **your** Moon is in. Then, compare it with the shorthand description for the Moon sign of your partner. Next, read the paragraph which discusses how the two of you might interact with one another. Each combination is also designated as either very compatible, compatible, challenging or very challenging. (These rate as 4-3-2-1 on our **Compatibility Scale**.)

> Your partner's Moon sign gives you clues regarding the kind of support he values. Moon sign characteristics indicate how your partner needs to be nurtured and what makes him feel safe and secure. Feed your partner's Moon and he'll feel at home with you.

MOON IN ARIES: FEELINGS—FAST & FURIOUS

Emotional Reactions: rapid, immediate, lively
Feel Safest When: being courageous, self-reliant, assertive
Nurture: through actions, in own way, when and how **you** want
Moods: shift rapidly (could have quick temper), usually upbeat
Home: lots of activity, people do own thing, excitement, set up on **your** terms
Other: high spirits, spontaneous, eager, enthusiastic, youthful

MOON IN TAURUS: MELLOW MOODS

Emotional Reactions: slow, steady, predictable
Feel Safest When: involved with money, possessions, beauty or nature
Nurture: in practical ways—through doing for others, being dependable
Moods: regular, even-tempered, placid, rarely moody
Home: comfortable, nice things, stable, pleasant (without clashes)
Other: touchy-feely, may be materialistic, faithful, affectionate, loyal

MOON IN GEMINI: MERCURIAL MOODS

Emotional Reactions: flexible, adaptable, may be rationalized, perceptive
Feel Safest When: thinking, communicating, interacting with people
Nurture: through explaining, making sense of things, teaching
Moods: restless, more intellectual than emotional, naturally curious
Home: mentally stimulating, changeable, lots of people coming and going
Other: good observer, rational, logical, rapid insights, may talk with hands

MOON IN CANCER: STRONGLY SENTIMENTAL

Emotional Reactions: deep, strong, hidden, vulnerable, caring
Feel Safest When: protecting or being protected, emotionally attached
Nurture: through being emotionally supportive, preserving, hanging on
Moods: varied, much internal, may swing between vulnerability and caretaking
Home: cozy, good food, protective, private, family-centered
Other: strong impact from mother, very warm, caring, home/family important

MOON IN LEO: EXTRAVAGANTLY EXPRESSIVE

Emotional Reactions: fiery, dramatic, charismatic, egocentric, impressive
Feel Safest When: onstage, getting admiration, attention, applause, love
Nurture: through generosity, compliments, encouragement, motivation
Moods: exuberant, lively, magnetic, extroverted, occasional mood swings (up/down)
Home: large, impressive, a source of pride, exciting, lots of recreation
Other: strong family impulse, sense of inner child, zestful, enthusiastic

MOON IN VIRGO: CALM AND COMPETENT

Emotional Reactions: studied, meticulous, sometimes critical, analytical
Feel Safest When: doing a good job, repairing, fixing, improving
Nurture: "doing for," serving, may seem indispensable, finding flaws and fixing them
Moods: more practical than emotional, can nitpick, serious, helpful
Home: neat, orderly, may work from the home or have family business
Other: can be self-critical, retiring, needs to be needed, competent

MOON IN LIBRA: EVEN-TEMPERED EMOTIONS

Emotional Reactions: affectionate, charming, graceful, good natured
Feel Safest When: everything is pleasant, attractive, agreeable and fair
Nurture: teamwork, sharing, joint efforts, peacemaking (diplomacy)
Moods: adapts to people (may be two-faced or chameleon-like), unruffled
Home: lovely, good taste, pleasing, sociable, pleasant (no arguments)
Other: wants people around (may dislike being alone), agreeable, serene, poised

MOON IN SCORPIO: POTENT PASSIONS

Emotional Reactions: intense, volcanic, much kept secret, powerful
Feel Safest When: in control, facing intense emotions, probing hidden depths
Nurture: intuition or manipulation, facing challenges or taking control
Moods: hidden, learning to let go emotionally/financially (may be jealous or possessive), very loyal
Home: very private, rousing intense emotions, a place to build inner strength
Other: skill with innuendoes, nonverbal messages, resourceful, a survivor

MOON IN SAGITTARIUS: JOVIAL JESTER

Emotional Reactions: idealistic, expressive, gregarious, confident
Feel Safest When: adventuring, exploring, expanding knowledge, traveling, having fun
Nurture: stimulating mind, generosity, promoting best potentials
Moods: optimistic, may be self-righteous, extroverted, outgoing
Home: trailer, traveller, bringing philosophy, foreigners, ideas into home
Other: can inspire others with faith, trust, goals, values, humor

MOON IN CAPRICORN: SERIOUS AND STABLE

Emotional Reactions: serious, cautious, inhibited, grounded, practical
Feel Safest When: in charge, dealing with facts, working hard, in position of power or status
Nurture: through being responsible, teaching limits, providing reality checks
Moods: pessimistic, careful, practical, businesslike, formal
Home: status symbol, well-planned, orderly, a place of work or accomplishment
Other: may face reality young ("old when young and young when old"), business skills

MOON IN AQUARIUS: UNIQUELY UNCONVENTIONAL

Emotional Reactions: rational/intellectual more than emotional, eccentric, unpredictable
Feel Safest When: being unconventional, unique, involved with the new, different
Nurture: freedom, choices, alternative, by offering objectivity, openness
Moods: cool (can be aloof), casually friendly, may resist emotional ties
Home: unusual, eclectic, open to friends, change, variety, mind in focus
Other: can treat family like friends (equalitarian/tolerant or cool) and friends like family (warm, supportive)

MOON IN PISCES: IDEALIZED IMPRESSIONS

Emotional Reactions: sensitive, empathic, compassionate, romantic, idealistic
Feel Safest When: creating beauty, involved with mystical, spiritual, religious, healing
Nurture: by rescuing others, making life better or more beautiful
Moods: impressionable, gullible, softhearted, tender, influenced by moods of those around
Home: a sanctuary, retreat, confused, spiritual center, artistic, idealized
Other: may fool self or be deceived, wants to see the best in others, visualizing skills

MOON PAIRS

ARIES/ARIES

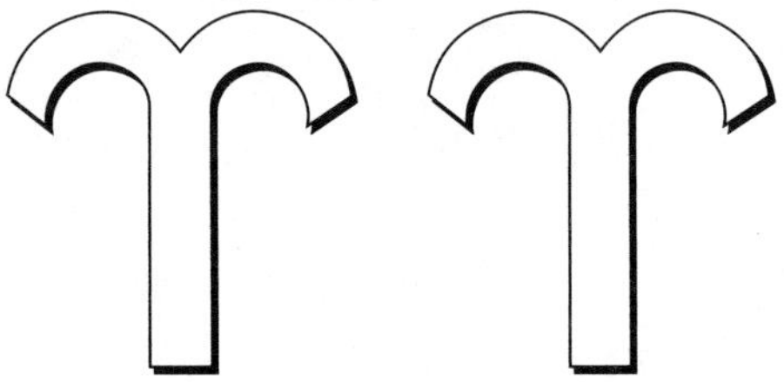

EAGER EMOTIONS

You both feel your home is a great place to drop into occasionally. Active and on the go, you never settle in too much. Housework may consist of "a lick and a promise" as there is always something more exciting to pursue. Other people are drawn to your positive, youthful attitudes.

VERY COMPATIBLE—4

ARIES/TAURUS

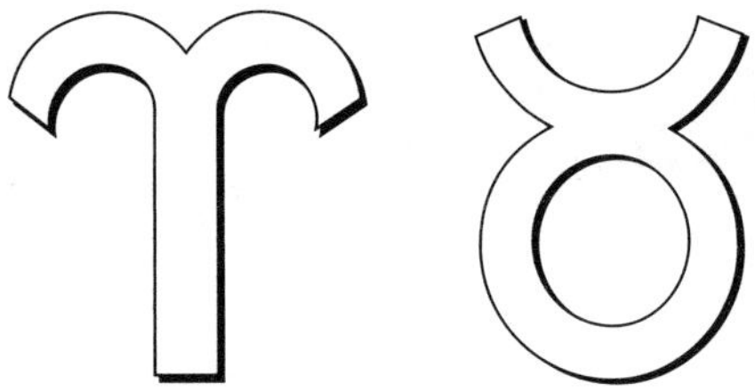

RESTLESS RELAXATION

You like a home full of action and excitement, while he wants comfort and stability in the nest. Your moods shift momentarily, while he is reliable for his steadiness. Don't rock his boat too much, but do contribute more fun, frolic and movement to his life. He brings you skills with the material world.

CHALLENGING—2

ARIES/GEMINI

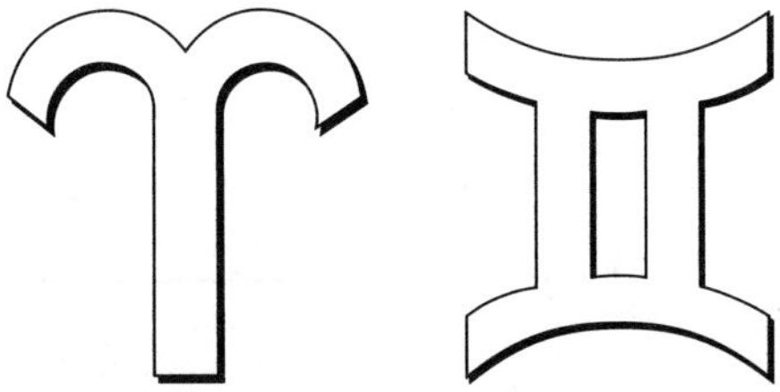

GO GETTERS

You both enjoy a home full of variety and movement. Lots of people coming and going is just fine. Physical and mental stimulation are important. Restless and eager, each of you gets bored easily so both need to be involved with many interests and activities. You find it easy to cheer one another up.

COMPATIBLE—3

ARIES/CANCER

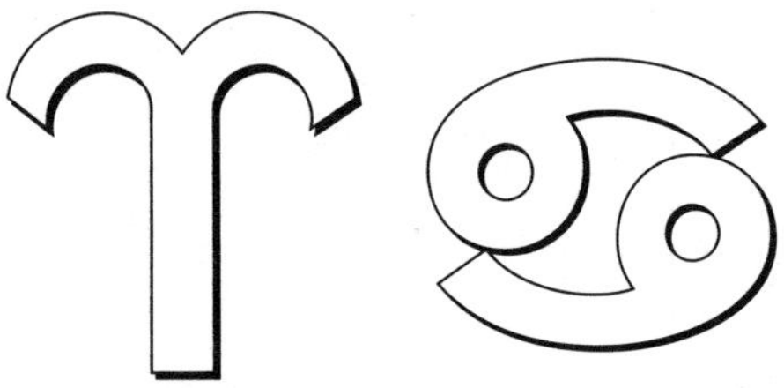

DOMESTIC DIFFERENCES

You're open and direct about what you feel; he tends to keep things hidden inside. You like movement, action and excitement in the home. He sees the nest as a place to protect and be private. If you get irritated, you quickly forgive and forget; he can brood over hurts. He can help you appreciate what's worth saving and you can encourage him to let go more emotionally.

CHALLENGING—2

FAMILY FUN

ARIES/LEO

Each of you has a childlike, fun-loving spirit with a wonderful sense of humor. You tend to stir each other up, inciting one another to take chances, seek excitement, and keep active. Extravagant moods are possible, but none last very long. A home where people can play and be spontaneous appeals to you both.

COMPATIBLE—3

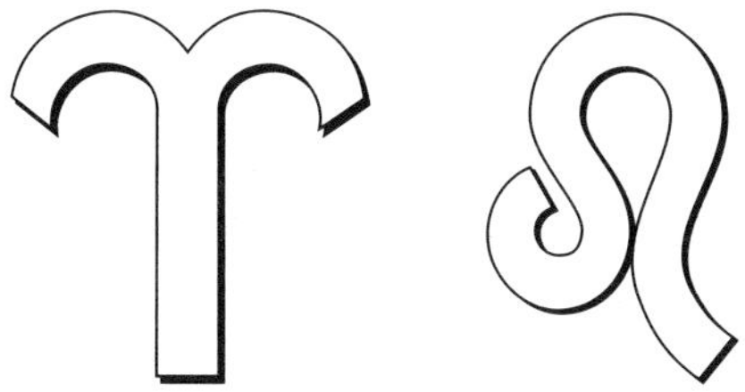

AMBIVALENT ATTITUDES

ARIES/VIRGO

Your emotional styles are quite different. You react quickly; he analyzes (and then reanalyzes). You tend to be upbeat and prefer to believe the best of life; he can be critical, looking for flaws. You may want to play when he wants to work. He can help you be more serious and you can help him be more relaxed.

VERY CHALLENGING—1

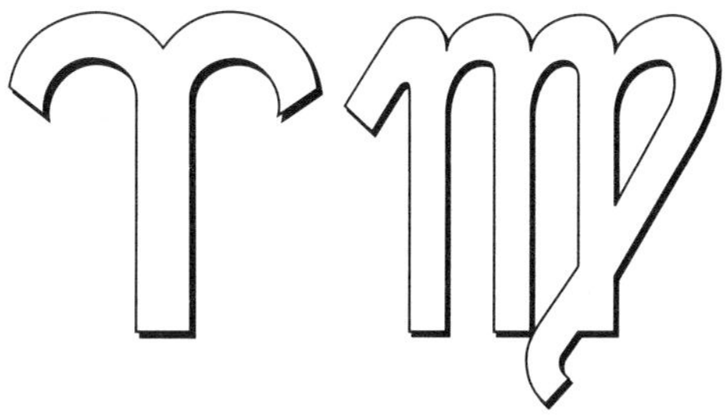

GIVE AND TAKE

ARIES/LIBRA

The two of you may experience the attraction of opposites. Your courage, optimism and freshness feed his charm and desire to share. His diplomacy complements your directness. He may care more about appearances than you; you're probably more expressive than he.

VERY COMPATIBLE—4

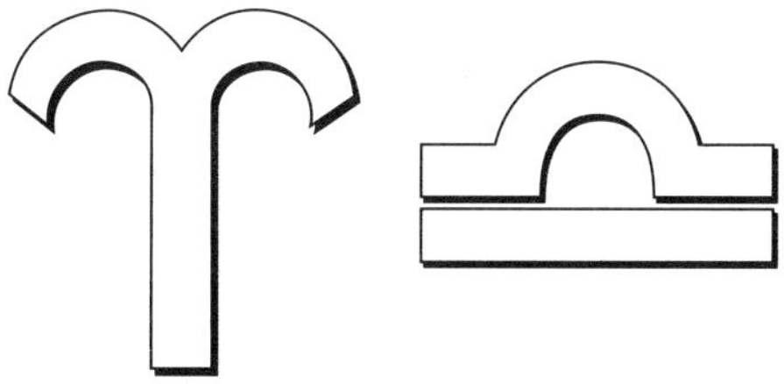

DIRECT OR DEVIOUS?

ARIES/SCORPIO

The two of you handle feelings very differently. You tend to react quickly, perhaps even rashly at times. He mulls things over and holds back on showing feelings. He values emotional control; you value openness. You take the straight line approach; he uses the back door or indirect routes. Shared passion, however, could be a strong bond.

VERY CHALLENGING—1

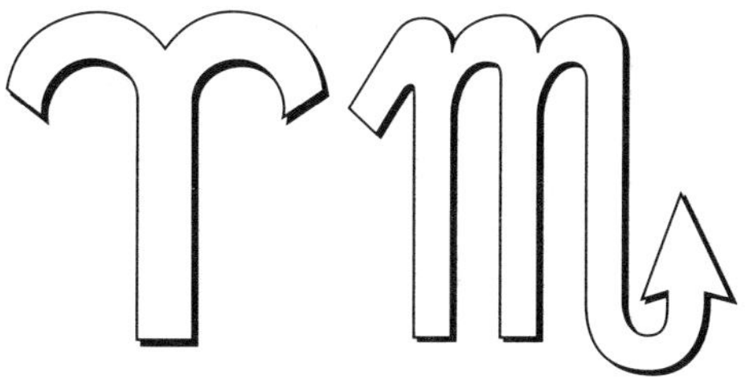

ARIES/SAGITTARIUS

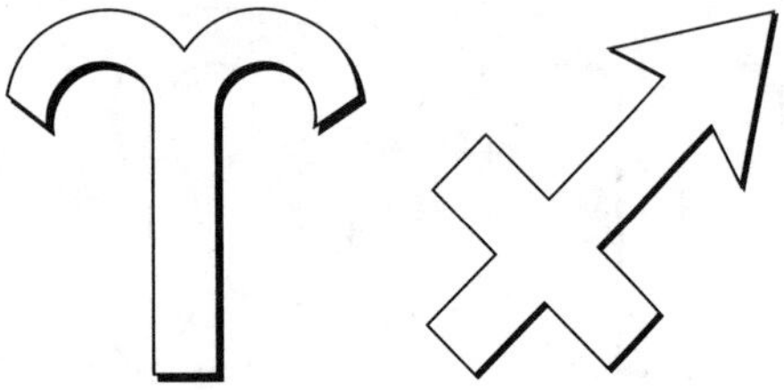

EMOTIONAL ENTHUSIASM

Both of you find security in adventure. You may enjoy exploring the world together, traveling, or simply having lots of action, movement and excitement on the home front. Fellow optimists, you easily look on the bright side in situations. You nurture each other's confidence.

COMPATIBLE—3

ARIES/CAPRICORN

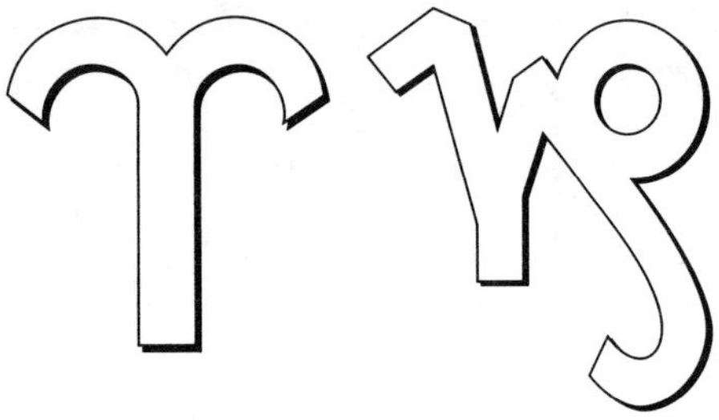

OPTIMIST AND PESSIMIST

Your emotions are right out there in the open, whereas he has mastered the stiff upper lip technique. You believe in being honest and direct; he believes in maintaining control and decorum. Your feeling nature is upbeat and optimistic; he tends to be a worrier. Learn from one another and you both will grow.

CHALLENGING—2

ARIES/AQUARIUS

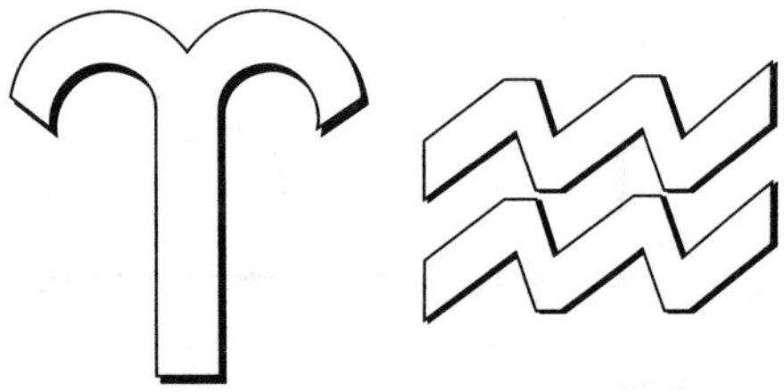

FREE FOLKS

You both have a streak of independence. You like home, but don't want to feel tied down by it. Either of you can be warm and nurturing—but on your own terms, in your own way. Too much clinging turns you off. You feed each other's attraction toward the new, the different, the fresh and exciting.

COMPATIBLE—3

ARIES/PISCES

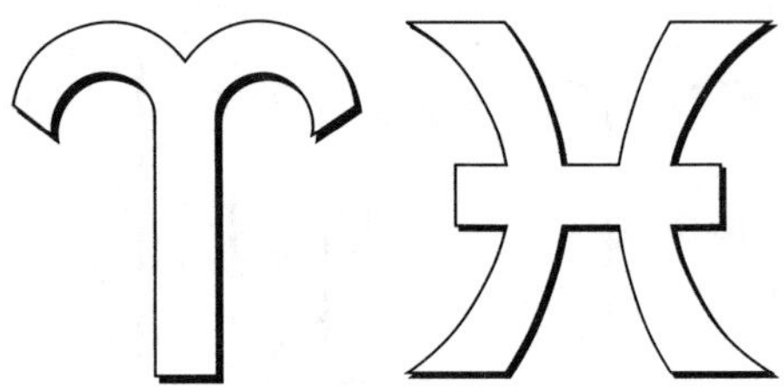

DIRECTING DREAMS

Neither of you may be overly fond of housework. You're too busy running around and he's too busy visualizing and imagining possibilities. You could seem a bit volatile to him, while he may seem a bit too inward to you. Your courage, directness and eagerness can inspire him; his empathy and idealism can nurture you.

CHALLENGING—2

RELAXING RESTLESSNESS

TAURUS/ARIES

You like a comfortable, stable home, while he is eager for action and excitement. You are easygoing and rarely moody; he might have temper flashes (but also gets over them quickly). His free spirit could enliven your life. Your dependability and skill with material resources can bring more security into his world.

CHALLENGING—2

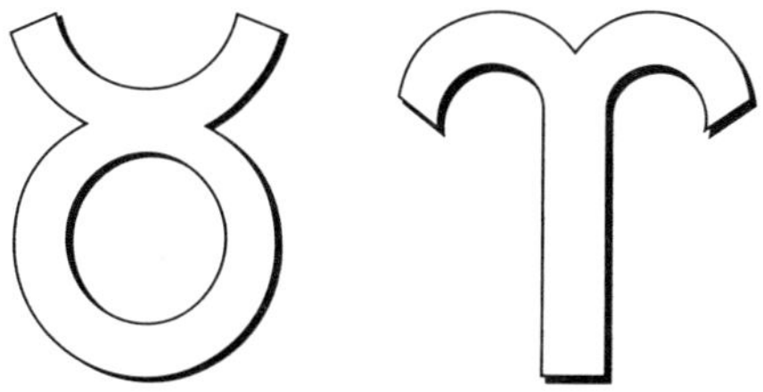

SECURELY SENSUAL

TAURUS/TAURUS

You are likely to be very comfortable with one another, both appreciating regularity in your lives and domestic routines, both enjoying good food and sensual pleasures of all kinds. Each of you tends to be easy to get along with as you are good-natured. You both appreciate (and can create) material security.

VERY COMPATIBLE—4

BODY AND MIND

TAURUS/GEMINI

You find it easy to relax, be comfortable, and be silent. He is restless and needs to be thinking or talking most of the time. You take care of people in very practical ways; he nurtures others mentally. You experience emotions in your body and need physical contact and support; he is more objective and detached.

CHALLENGING—2

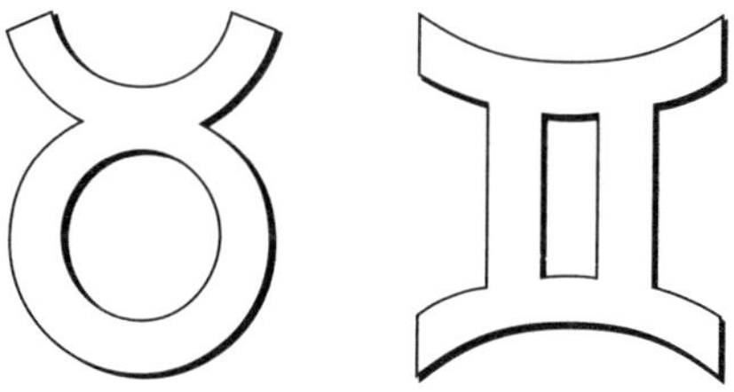

NICE AND EASY

TAURUS/CANCER

Each of you values comfort and security. Commitment to family is important. You both know how to make a house a home. You have a real talent for putting people at ease and he has a strong protective, caretaking streak. Emotionally, you both seek safety and dependability.

COMPATIBLE—3

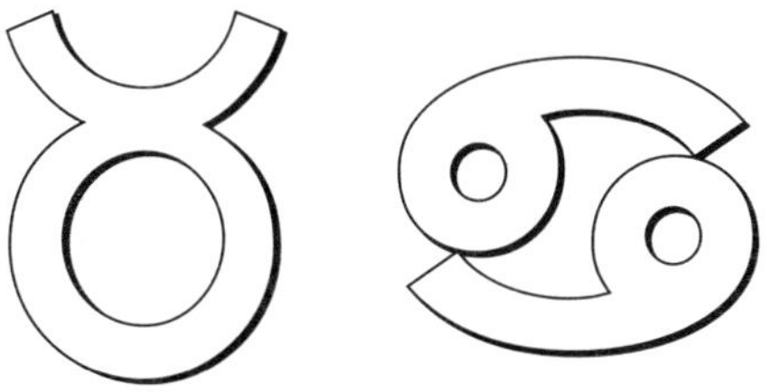

TAURUS/LEO

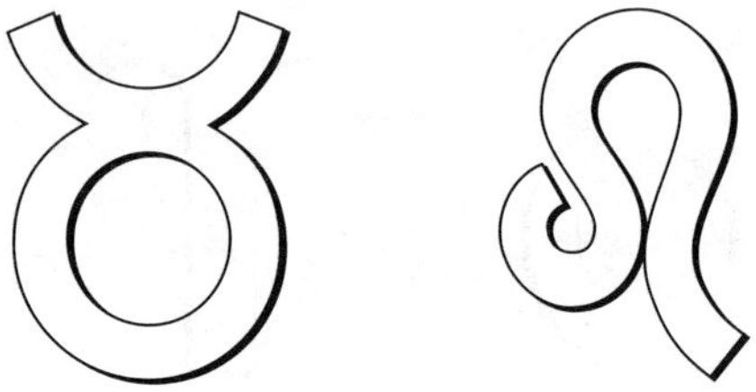

MELLOW MAGNETISM

You're mellow, affectionate and easygoing. His emotions are volatile, dramatic and larger-than-life. You want a comfortable home; he wants a home he can show off to others. You can help him relax. He can bring more fun and excitement into your life.

CHALLENGING—2

TAURUS/VIRGO

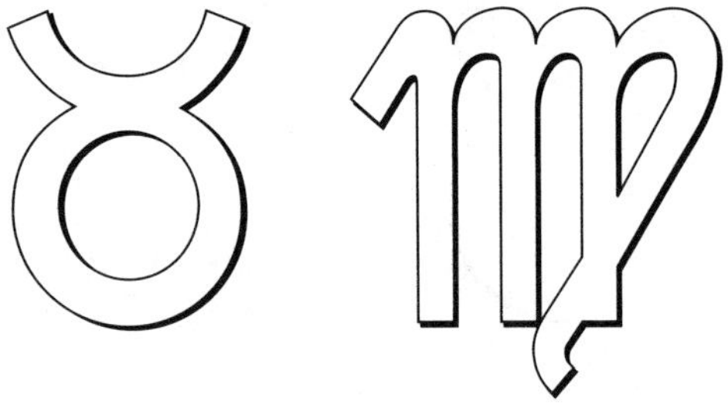

DOMESTIC DILIGENCE

You both tend to be practical, focused on serving people's physical needs. Each of you wants a home that works, and he may even be willing to do minor repairs. He might be a bit picky, but has skill at keeping the domestic arena organized. You can encourage his sensual side.

COMPATIBLE—3

TAURUS/LIBRA

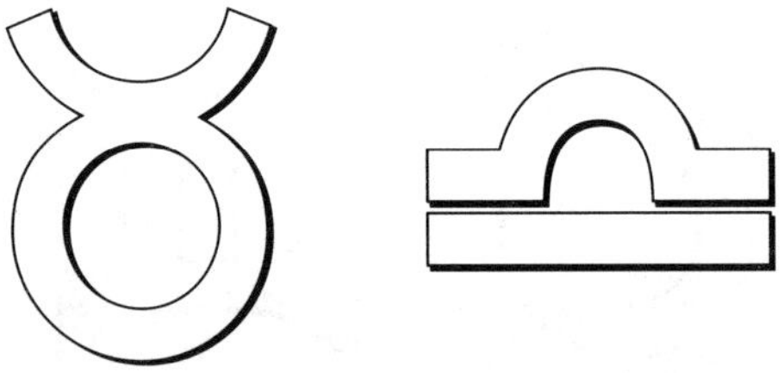

ARTISTIC ABODE

Both of you appreciate a beautiful home, but you are more oriented toward physical comfort and possessions and he is more focused on social interactions. You are probably more stable and predictable emotionally; his moods may shift with the people he is around.

VERY CHALLENGING—1

TAURUS/SCORPIO

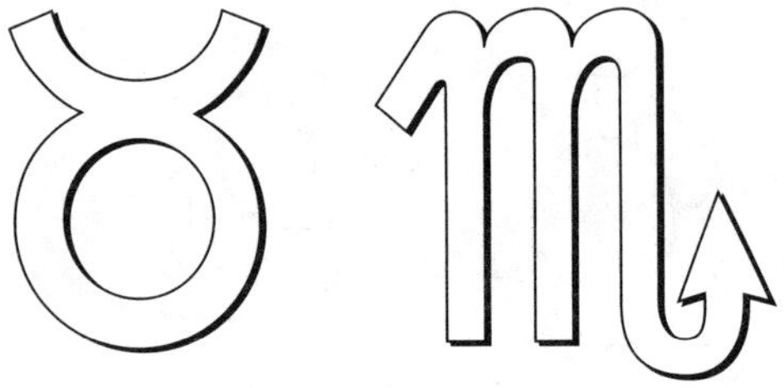

FEELING FINE

Possessions and pleasures could be a strong bond between you. Each of you appreciates good food and other physical indulgences. Your homes may be full of interesting textures, feature a waterbed, jacuzzi, soft rugs, art or other forms of gratifying the senses.

VERY COMPATIBLE—4

RESTLESS ROOTS

TAURUS/SAGITTARIUS

You want comfort, stability and some familiarity or predictability in the home. He wants adventures. You are comfortable staying in one place; he may prefer to wander the world. He wants more, better, higher, faster, whereas your emotions center on what is possible in the real world.

VERY CHALLENGING—1

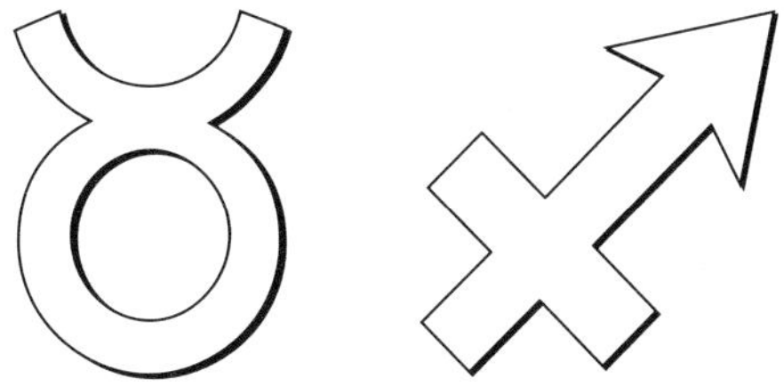

RELIABLE ROOMMATES

TAURUS/CAPRICORN

Both of you appreciate tangible results. You nurture people by doing things for them. Support, for you both, demands reliability. Each of you may have good instincts for hanging on to possessions and material goods. Business skills are likely. You two may look to a home partly as an investment.

COMPATIBLE—3

SURPRISING SECURITY

TAURUS/AQUARIUS

You want a domestic routine which is comfortable and stable. He detests routine and wants change, variety and surprises. You nurture people by being reliable and doing things for them. He nurtures people by being eccentric and stimulating them mentally. He can encourage your flexibility and you can feed his practical side.

CHALLENGING—2

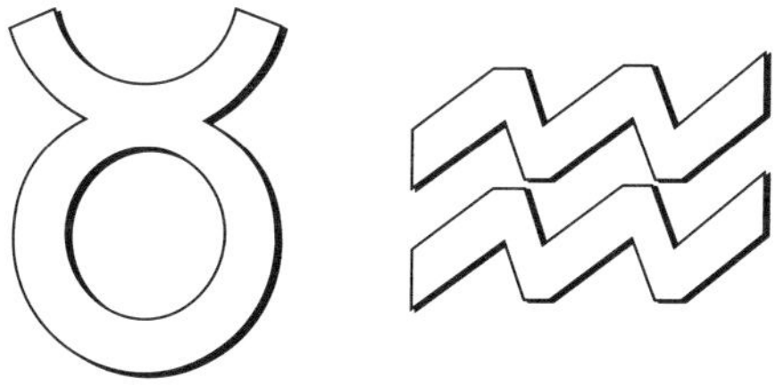

EASY DOES IT

TAURUS/PISCES

You want a home which is attractive and comfortable. He wants a home which is beautiful and can be a retreat from the world. Both of you prefer to avoid conflict in the domestic arena. You strive to encourage a smooth, easy flow, emotionally and physically.

COMPATIBLE—3

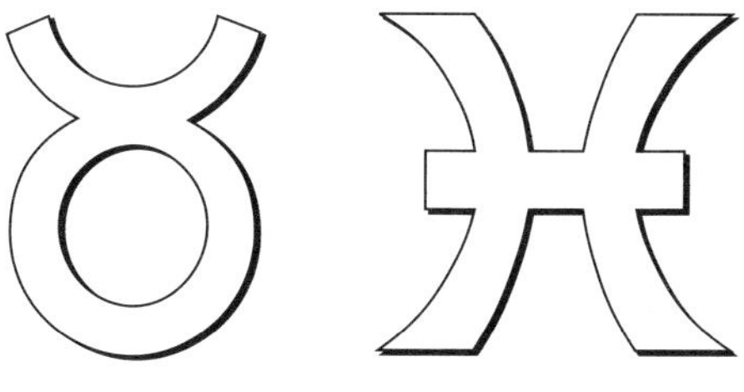

GEMINI/ARIES

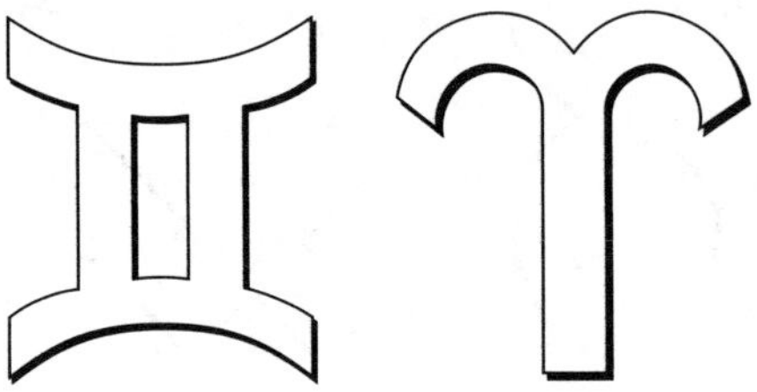

GO GETTERS

You both enjoy a home full of variety and movement. Lots of people coming and going is just fine. Physical and mental stimulation are important. Restless and eager, each of you gets bored easily so both need to be involved with many interests and activities. You find it easy to cheer one another up.

COMPATIBLE—3

GEMINI/TAURUS

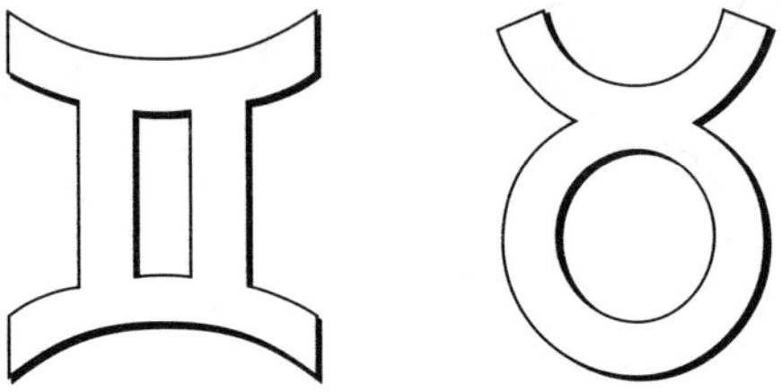

MIND AND BODY

You thrive on social activity and interactions with others. He finds it easy to relax, be comfortable, and be silent. You are restless, versatile and nurture people's minds. He takes care of people in very practical ways. You expose him to new experiences and he helps you appreciate the familiar.

CHALLENGING—2

GEMINI/GEMINI

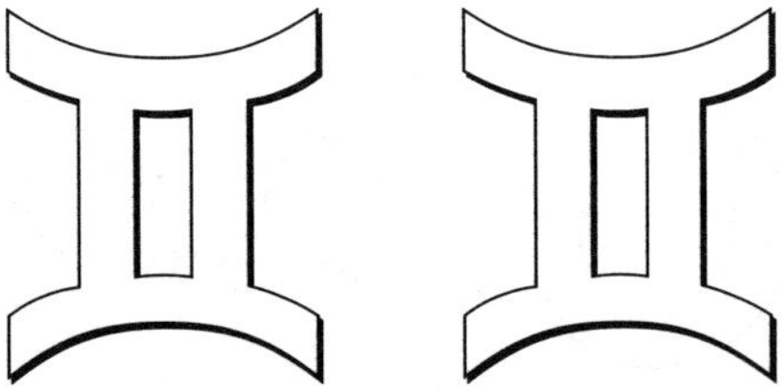

LOTS OF LEARNING

You both appreciate learning and communicating, so tend toward a lively home with many people coming and going, and/or lots of conversation. You nurture people's minds and objectivity. Lighthearted, you two probably share a good sense of humor.

VERY COMPATIBLE—4

GEMINI/CANCER

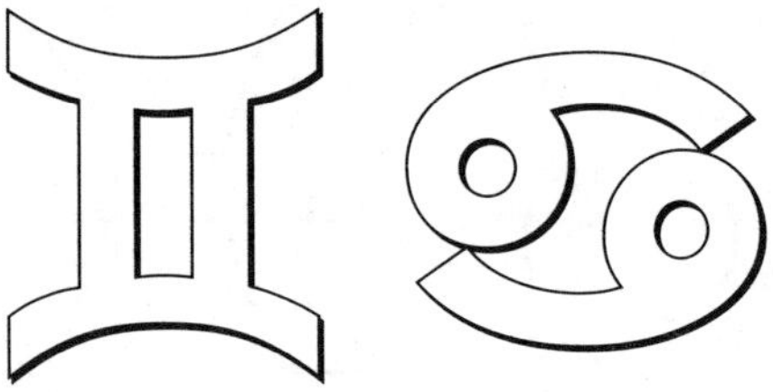

ABSENT OR ATTACHED?

Home may be a real place for him, whereas it is more a state of mind for you. He could be quite attached to a particular house or certain possessions. A tendency to save things is likely. You are more interested in people and discussions and ever ready to move on to the next topic. Be understanding of one another.

CHALLENGING—2

PARTY PEOPLE

GEMINI/LEO

People are a central focus in your emotional lives. You thrive on intellectual stimulation and a wide variety of conversations. He thrives on admiration, attention and positive feedback from others. He can be quite a motivator of others; you help people learn and laugh.

COMPATIBLE—3

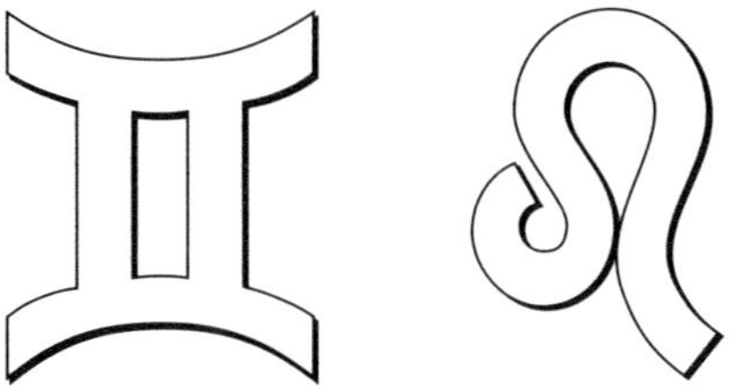

FLEXIBLE FOCUS

GEMINI/VIRGO

Although you both nurture thinking and observing, your style is varied and all over the map. He tends to be focused, concerned with precise details and follow-through. He needs to fix things; you need to change the subject. He can nurture your concentration; you can nurture his curiosity.

CHALLENGING—2

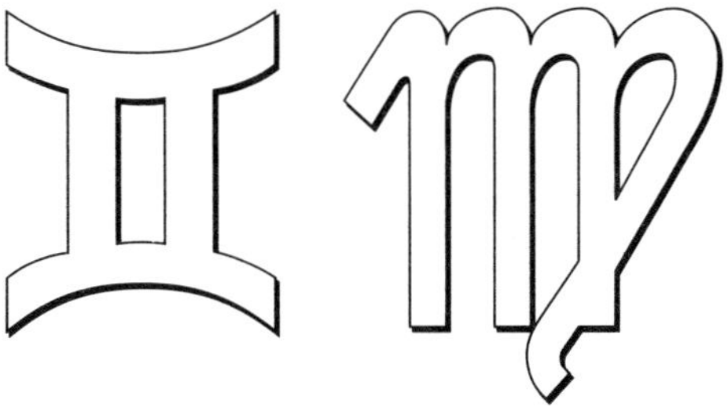

FLUENT FOLKS

GEMINI/LIBRA

You both want a home full of people and ideas. Sociability is ranked high. Each of you can nurture concepts and communications. You encourage people to learn, discuss and to explore the world of the mind. He may be more diplomatic and you more casual and fun-loving.

COMPATIBLE—3

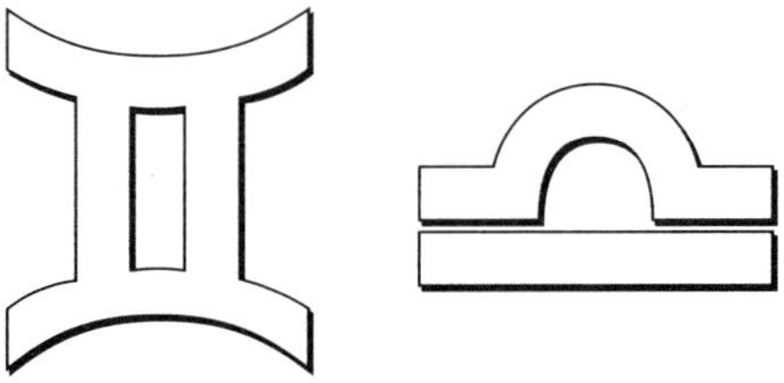

LIGHT VERSUS HEAVY

GEMINI/SCORPIO

You can be objective about emotional matters; he tends to feel very intensely (and might brood or sulk). You view home as a place to fill with conversation and social interactions; he values privacy very highly. You can help him to be more casual and lighthearted. He can help you to look more deeply into issues.

VERY CHALLENGING—1

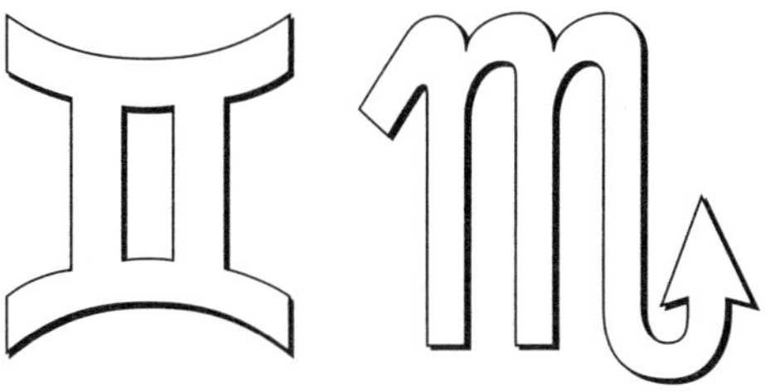

GEMINI/SAGITTARIUS

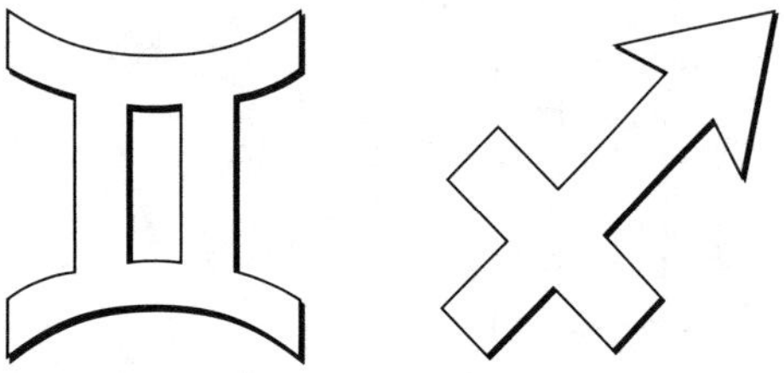

AT HOME IN THE WORLD

Both of you can feel at home almost anywhere in the world, and enjoy bringing the world—books, foreigners, discussions, ideas—into your home. You value a home full of laughter. Each of you is inclined to look for the silver lining if things go wrong. You cheer each other up.

VERY COMPATIBLE—4

GEMINI/CAPRICORN

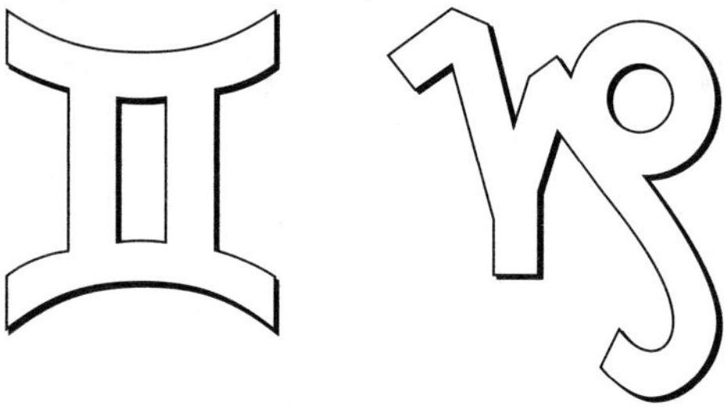

ADAPTABLE ACHIEVEMENT

You can live in cheerful chaos—as long as it's interesting. He would prefer a place for everything and everything in its place. You can crack jokes about emotional matters; he tends to be serious (sometimes inhibited). He encourages you to be more focused; you can help him to lighten up.

VERY CHALLENGING—1

GEMINI/AQUARIUS

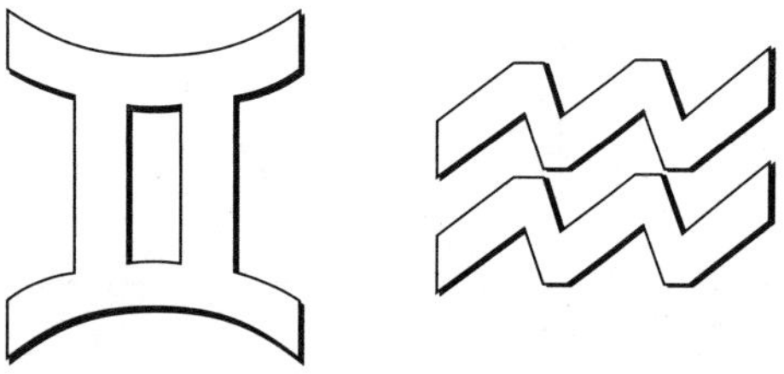

YOUNG AT HEART

Both of you nurture freshness. You two are eager to experience many different things and seek out mentally stimulating people and ideas. What is said and learned may matter more than ordinary physical details (like housework). The lure of the new is strong. You can each be quite objective

COMPATIBLE—3

GEMINI/PISCES

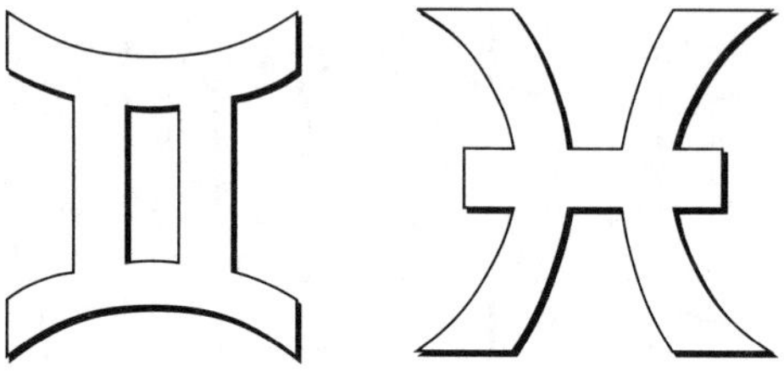

VARIED VISIONS

You are eager to share your home with others, particularly if they have interesting ideas or conversation. He wants a private retreat, a sanctuary from the world. You nurture by talking; he nurtures by remaining silent. If you are willing to share styles and accommodate one another, you can create the best of both your worlds.

CHALLENGING—2

DOMESTIC DIFFERENCES

CANCER/ARIES

He's open, direct and lets it all hang out emotionally. You are more sensitive and inward. He wants a home full of movement, action, and excitement. You want a nest which is private and and protected. You can help him appreciate what's worth saving, and he can encourage you to take more risks emotionally.

CHALLENGING—2

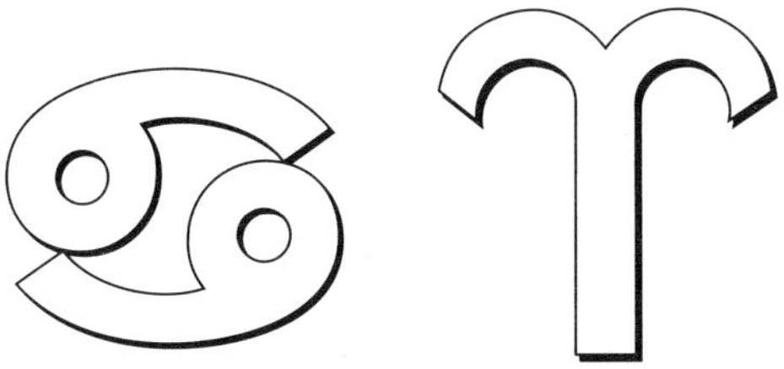

NICE AND EASY

CANCER/TAURUS

Each of you values comfort and security. Commitment to family is important. You both know how to make a house a home. You have a strong nurturing, caretaking streak, and he has talent for putting people at ease. Emotionally, you both seek safety and dependability.

COMPATIBLE—3

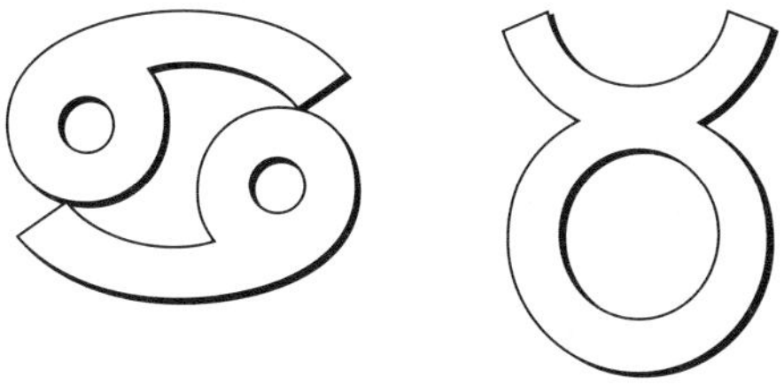

ATTACHED OR ABSENT?

CANCER/GEMINI

Home may be a real place for you, whereas it is more a state of mind for him. You could be quite attached to a particular house or certain possessions. A tendency to save things is likely. He is more interested in people and discussions and ever ready to move on to the next topic. Be understanding of one another.

CHALLENGING—2

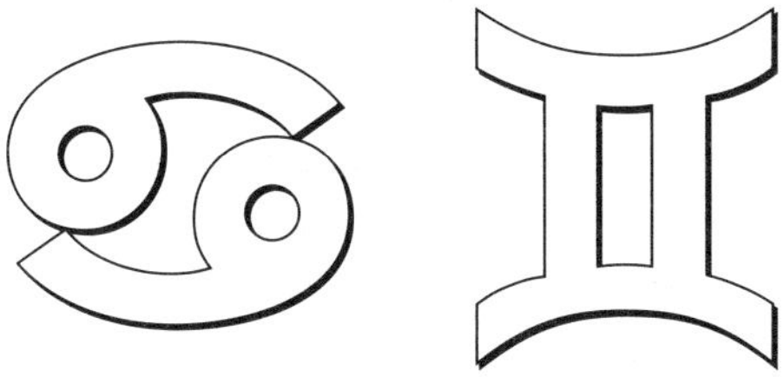

HOME, SWEET HOME

CANCER/CANCER

You both are instinctively nurturing and value roots, home, family and emotional attachments. Each of you seeks safety, security and reassurance within the nest. You want to depend upon your mate. Either of you (or both) could be good cooks and you probably both enjoy eating.

VERY COMPATIBLE—4

CANCER/LEO

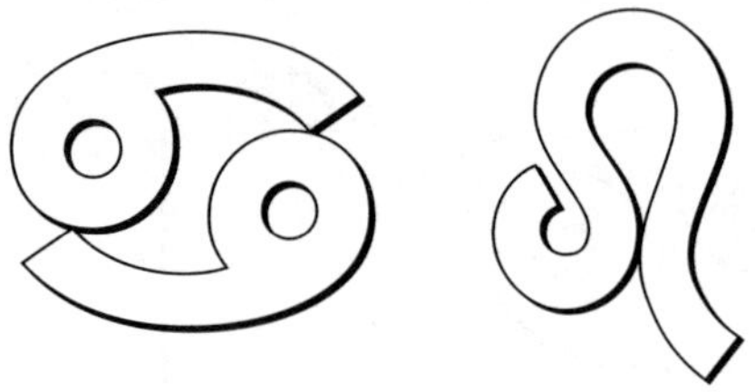

WARM AND WONDERFUL

Home is a warm, cosy nest for you where everyone feels safe and secure. Home is a showplace for him—where he can be noticed and applauded. You both yearn for emotional attachments, but his moods are fiery and dramatic while you keep much inside. Family matters to you both.

CHALLENGING—2

CANCER/VIRGO

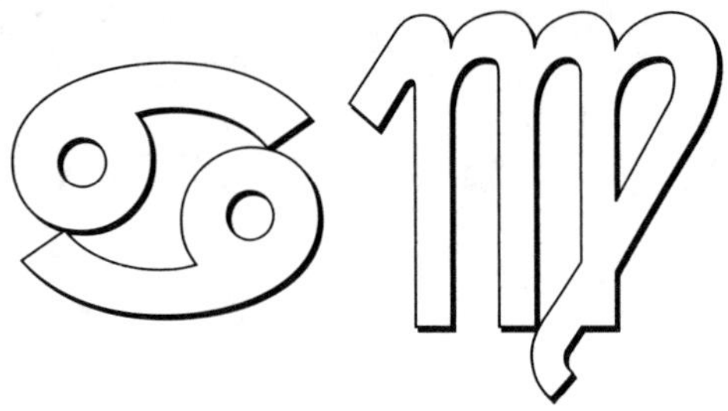

SENSIBLY SUPPORTIVE

You are both natural caretakers. Your focus is more on looking after emotional hurts and his is more on fixing the physical world. You both practice reliability in emotional matters. He may be a bit more picky than you. You can nurture him, and he can do practical things for you.

COMPATIBLE—3

CANCER/LIBRA

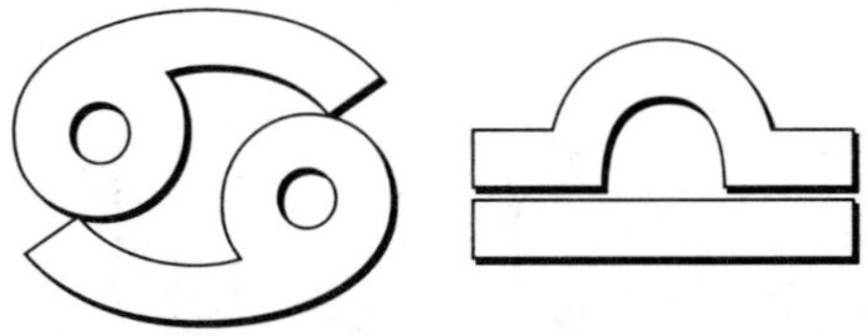

SHARED SPACE

Each of you wants emotional connections, but you may want more reassurance and security while he wants a bit more detachment and space. You tend to be home-focused. He tends to be people-focused (especially peer relationships). You can help him be more vulnerable emotionally; he can help you be more objective.

CHALLENGING—2

CANCER/SCORPIO

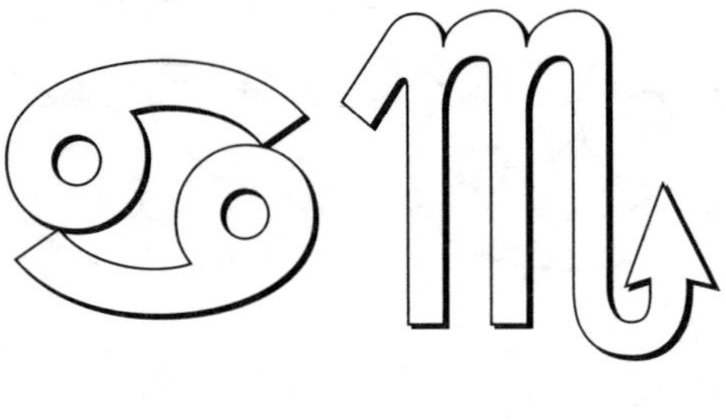

PRIVATE PEOPLE

Both of you have deep, strong feelings which you tend to hold in rather than reveal. His nurturing style is apt to be more controlling than yours, but each of you is capable of creating an intense connection. You both want a home which is very private, letting a select few in.

COMPATIBLE—3

FARAWAY FAMILY?

CANCER/SAGITTARIUS

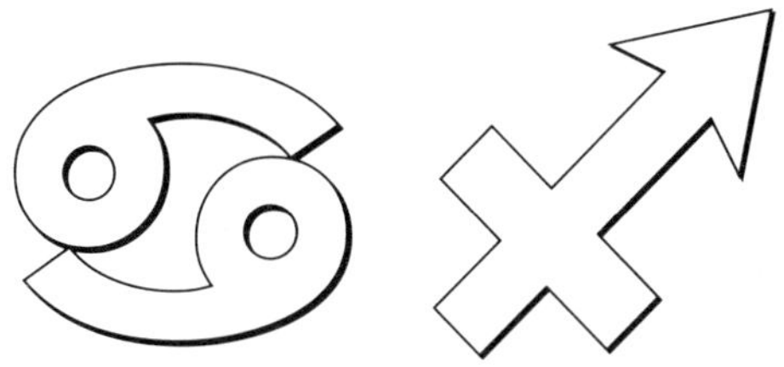

You are very connected to home, family and security. He has a natural wanderlust—a restlessness that has a hard time staying put. His moods tend to be upbeat and optimistic, while you are more cautious and protective. He can expose you to new adventures, and you can help him put down a few roots.

VERY CHALLENGING—1

DOMESTIC DEPENDABILITY

CANCER/CAPRICORN

Each of you has a strong parental streak. You find it natural to look after others, or tell them what they should do (for their own good). If you play parent with one another, just be sure to take turns being in charge. Emotionally, you both seek commitment and safety.

VERY COMPATIBLE—4

DIFFERENT DOMICILES

CANCER/AQUARIUS

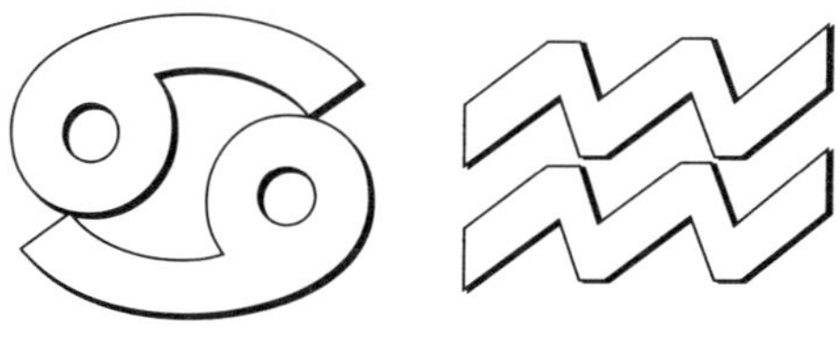

You are settling in—cooking, making a nest, collecting possessions and he's off with friends or unpredictably absent. You need more emotional security while he needs more variety and change. Compromise will allow you to experiment a bit, and him to appreciate some domesticity.

VERY CHALLENGING—1

PRIVATE PLACES

CANCER/PISCES

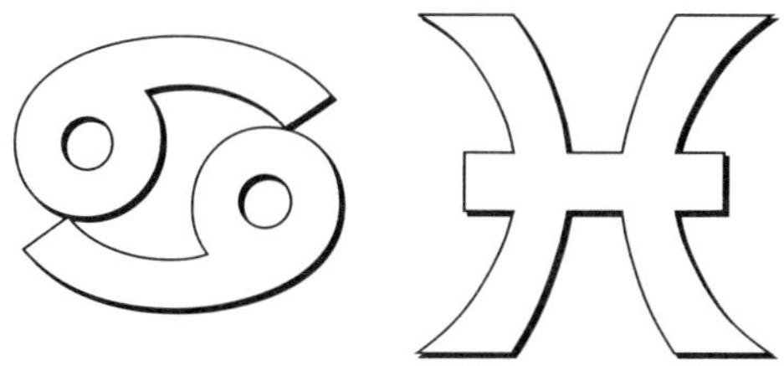

Each of you has a very sensitive, empathic side. You may be able to tune into one another (without words). You both want a home which is a sanctuary (retreat) from the outside world—your own, special, private place. You both tend to hold feelings inside, so work to bring up what's important.

COMPATIBLE—3

LEO/ARIES

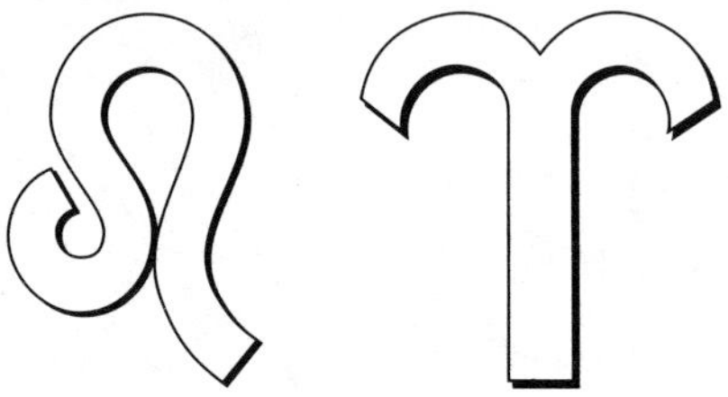

FAMILY FUN

Each of you has a childlike, fun-loving spirit with a wonderful sense of humor. You tend to stir each other up, inciting one another to take chances, seek excitement and keep active. Extravagant moods are possible, but none last very long. A home where people can play and be spontaneous appeals to you both.

COMPATIBLE—3

LEO/TAURUS

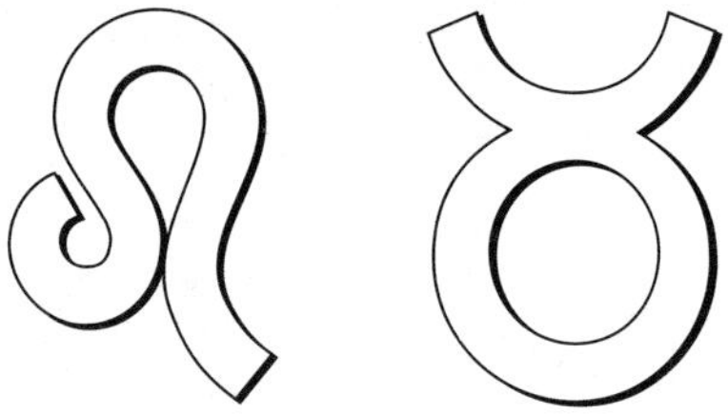

MELLOW MAGNETISM

You have dramatic flair and know how to make an emotional impact; he tends to be mellow, laid-back and easygoing. He wants a comfortable home where he can just relax, while you want a place you can be proud of—a showcase. You can bring a little more fun and excitement to him; he can help you kick back and enjoy.

CHALLENGING—2

LEO/GEMINI

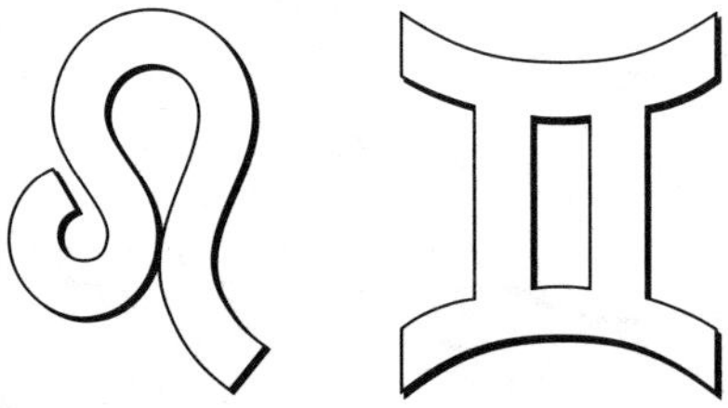

PARTY PEOPLE

People are a central focus in your emotional lives. He thrives on intellectual stimulation and a wide variety of conversations. You thrive on admiration, attention and positive feedback from others. You are a wonderful cheerleader, appreciating others and encouraging them to do more; he helps people learn and collect information.

COMPATIBLE—3

LEO/CANCER

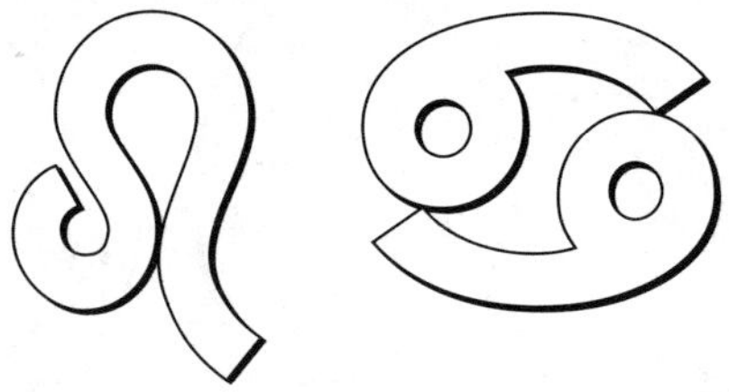

WARM AND WONDERFUL

Loving and being loved is central in your emotional life, but you need drama and excitement. He wants emotional attachments, but with safety and predictability. You express your feelings; he tends to hold them inside. Because family is usually important to you both, it can be a strong bond between you.

CHALLENGING—2

LAVISH LIVING

LEO/LEO

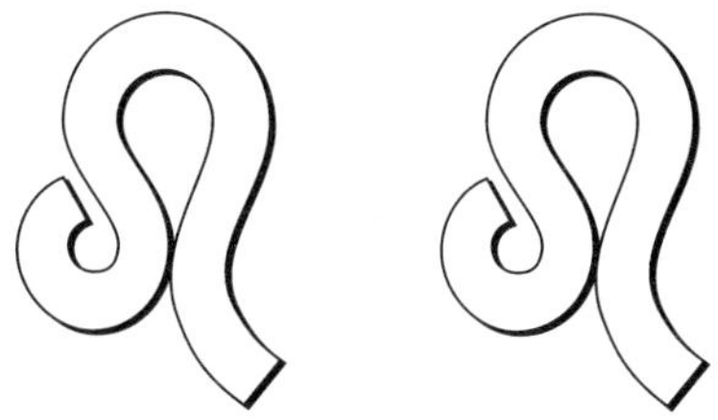

Excitement is the name of the game for you both. You thrive on fun, drama and larger-than-life involvements. Your home may be a showplace admired by others, or you both may be at home onstage, teaching, promoting, or involved in any creative, expressive, risk-taking activities. You light up people's lives.

VERY COMPATIBLE—4

ORNATE OR ORGANIZED?

LEO/VIRGO

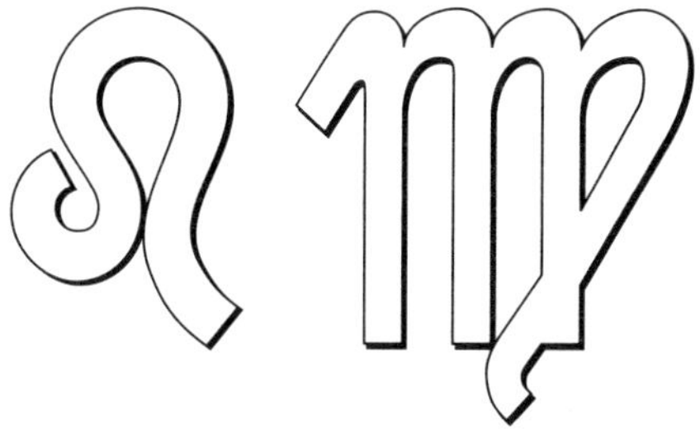

You nurture people by encouraging them, exciting them and believing in them. He nurtures people by telling them what is wrong and how to improve or fix it (or themselves). You want a grand, exciting, impressive home. He wants an orderly, organized home. Find a middle ground for mutual satisfaction.

CHALLENGING—2

EMOTIONAL EXTROVERTS

LEO/LIBRA

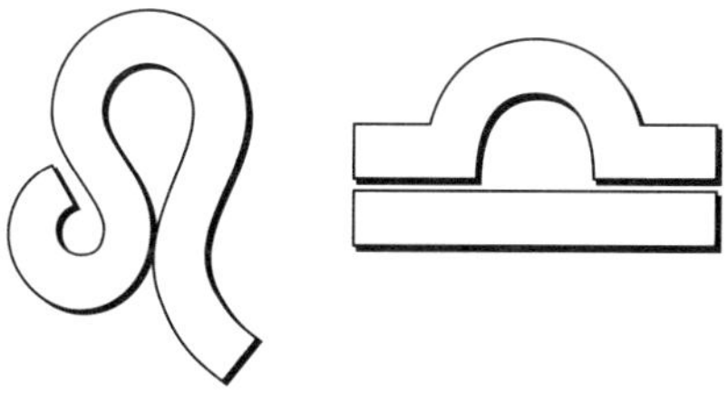

Both of you are sociable and appreciate a home with fun activities and interesting people to chat with. You may be a bit more dramatic emotionally, while he is more diplomatic. Each of you has natural charisma which can attract others. Lively times are likely.

COMPATIBLE—3

EXPLOSIVE EMOTIONS

LEO/SCORPIO

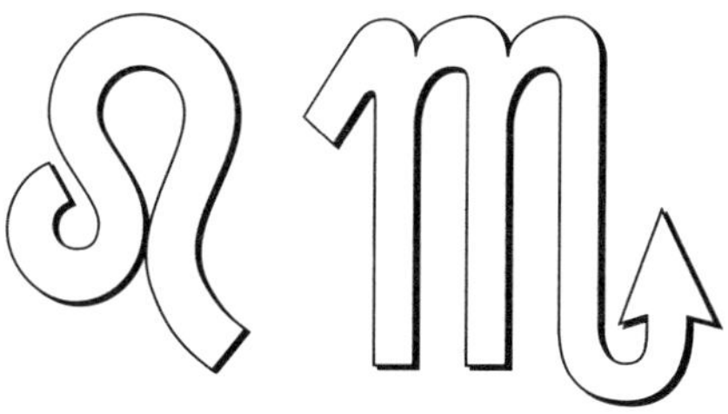

Emotional intensity is the focus here! Each of you has very strong emotional reactions, but you let it all hang out and he may hold and hold (perhaps until it blows). You tend to be up-front; he tends to be indirect. Each of you needs to feel in charge, so compromising will demand a lot from both of you. Bonds built between you go very deep.

CHALLENGING—2

LEO/SAGITTARIUS

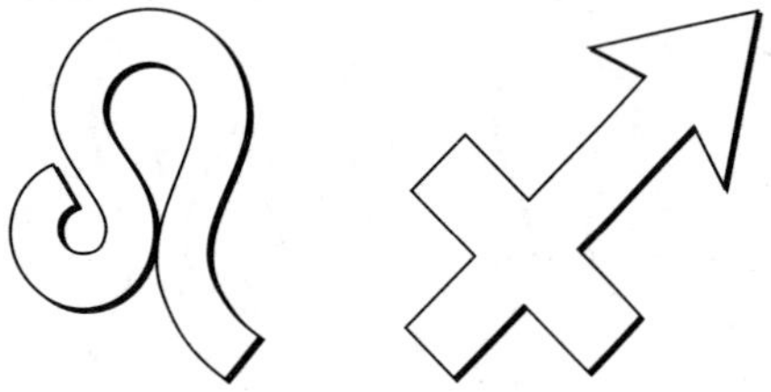

FUN FIRST!

You both want a home full of laughter, excitement and adventures. (Or, you'll take a road trip for the fun and frolic.) Upbeat and optimistic, you encourage one another to do more, feel more and constantly expand your domestic horizons. Dull is not in your vocabularies.

COMPATIBLE—3

LEO/CAPRICORN

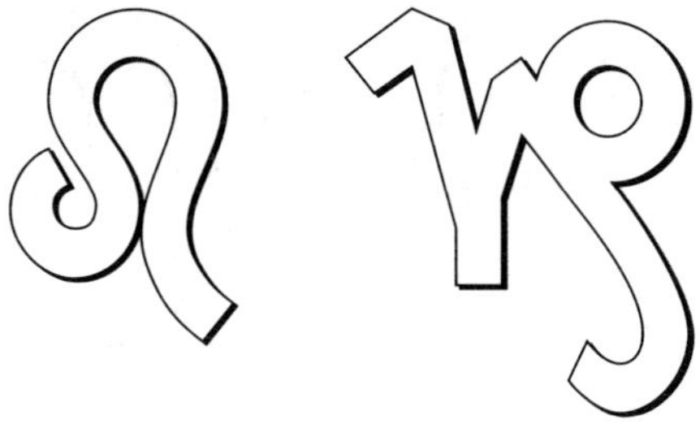

WHO'S ON TOP?

You want to be Queen of the Castle, but he wants to be President at home, so power issues are likely. Perhaps you can each have an area where you call the shots! Your emotional nature is fiery, exciting and enthusiastic. He tends to be serious, cautious and guarded.

VERY CHALLENGING—1

LEO/AQUARIUS

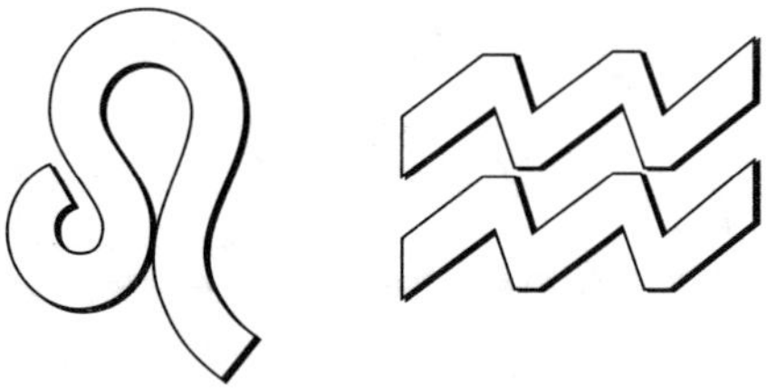

HEART AND HEAD

Although opposites in some ways, there is a natural attraction between you. Your feelings are fiery, expressive and exciting. He tends to be more detached, objective and cool. You can bring more fun, excitement and drama into the home. He can bring unusual ideas, intellectual stimulation and new technology.

VERY COMPATIBLE—4

LEO/PISCES

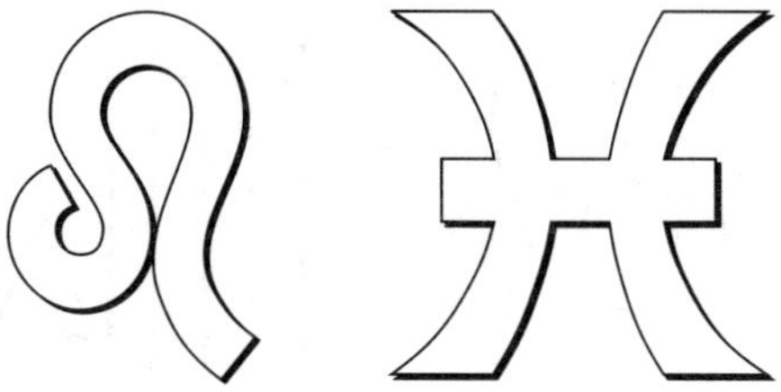

ENLARGED EMOTIONS

You want a home you can be proud of, one you can show to the world. He wants a home which is shut away from the world—a private sanctuary. For you, dramatic gestures and intense emotions are natural; you are expressive. He feels deeply and can be empathic, but keeps much inside. You both, however, have a romantic streak.

VERY CHALLENGING—1

AMBIVALENT ATTITUDES

VIRGO/ARIES

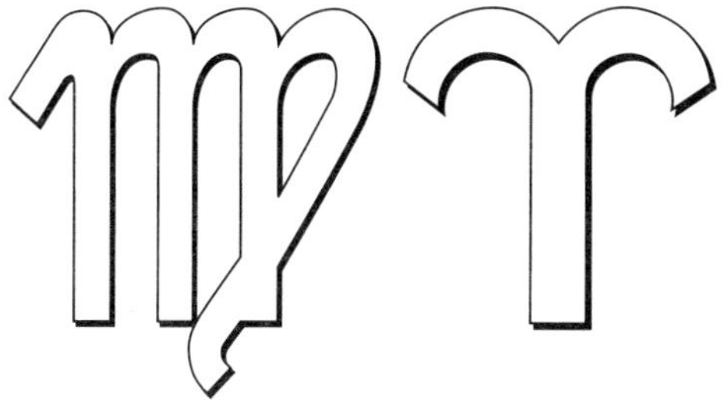

Your emotional styles are quite different. He reacts quickly, perhaps impulsively. You are more cautious and tend to analyze situations. He is optimistic and eager; you can be a worrier and try to plan for what might go wrong. He may want to play when you want to work. You can help him organize and he can help you loosen up.

VERY CHALLENGING—1

DOMESTIC DILIGENCE

VIRGO/TAURUS

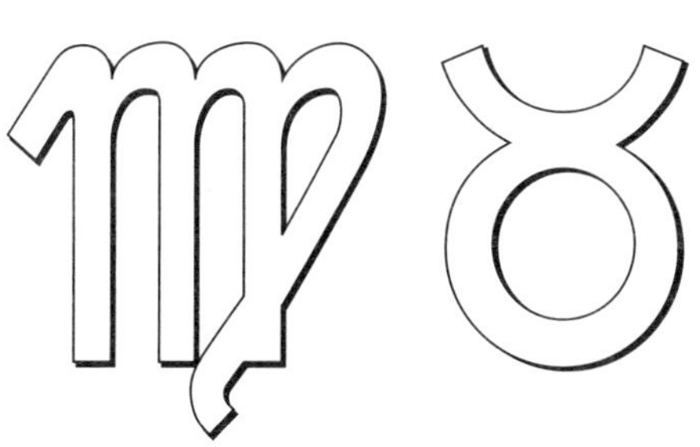

You both tend to be practical, focused on serving people's physical needs. Each of you wants a home that works, and you may even be willing to do minor repairs. He can be quite sensual, so you may enjoy sharing massages or other caresses. You are good at organizing the domestic arena.

COMPATIBLE—3

FLEXIBLE FOCUS

VIRGO/GEMINI

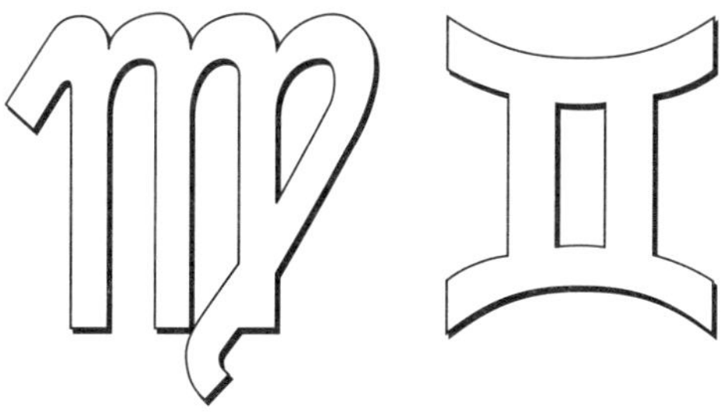

Although you both nurture thinking and observing, his style is varied and all over the map. You tend to be focused, concerned with precise details and follow-through. It is enough for him to **know** something; you need to **do** something or **improve** something. He can nurture your curiosity; you can nurture his concentration.

CHALLENGING—2

SENSIBLY SUPPORTIVE

VIRGO/CANCER

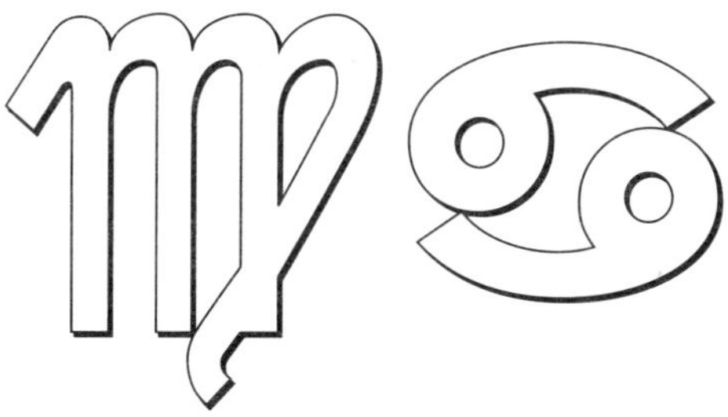

You are both natural caretakers. You tend to be supportive and look for ways to assist others. You may be more inclined to see the flaws (in the home and in other people). He is more inclined to keep feelings inside. You both want a stable home life with reliable people to share it.

COMPATIBLE—3

VIRGO/LEO

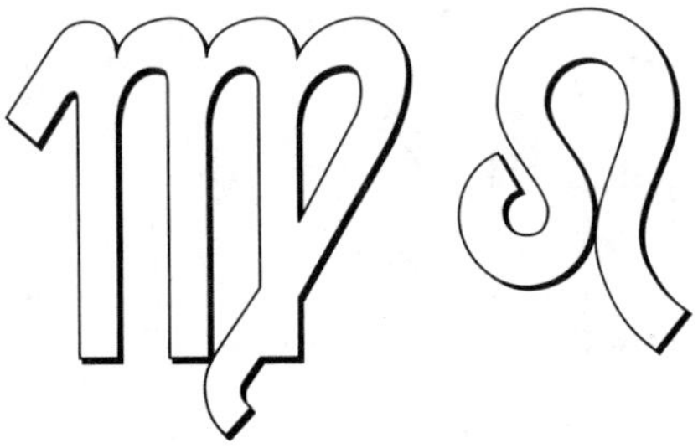

ORGANIZED OR ORNATE?

You nurture people by serving them, doing things for them, and trying to improve their lives. He nurtures people by encouraging them, exciting them, and believing in them. You want an orderly, organized home, while he wants a place that is grand and impressive. With compromises, you can both be satisfied.

CHALLENGING—2

VIRGO/VIRGO

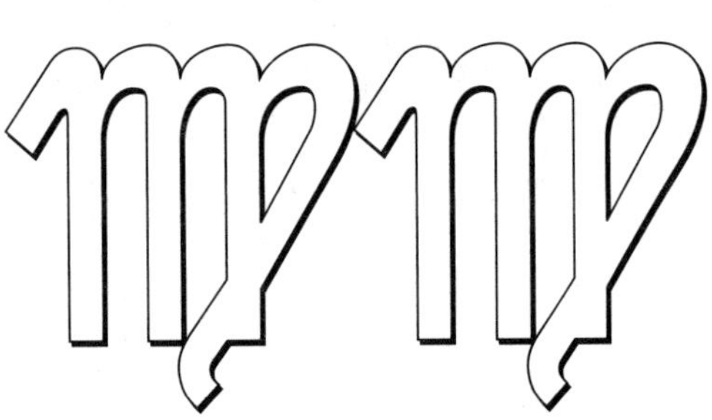

PRECISE PEOPLE

Both of you are cautious emotionally—not inclined to "get serious" until you're sure it's not a mistake. You could work together around the house, have a career from the home, or be very dedicated to organizing the house to be as efficient and orderly as possible. Both of you tend to take care of people by doing things for them.

VERY COMPATIBLE—4

VIRGO/LIBRA

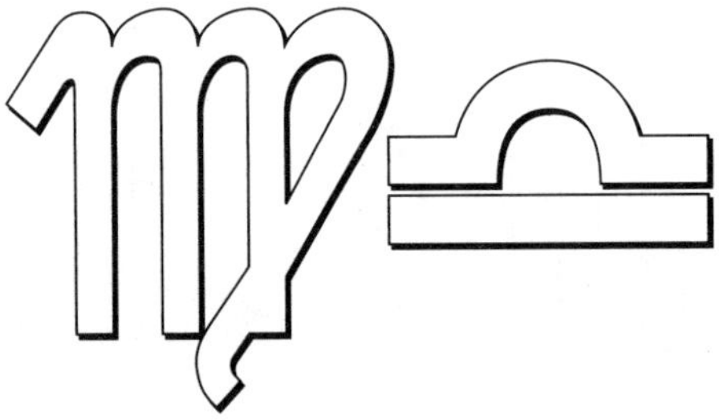

PLEASANT PRAGMATISM

You tend to focus on the degree of order and efficiency in the home. You can work very hard at it. He tends to focus on the people in the home, seeking social interactions. His nurturing style is graceful and charming. You are more cautious, concerned with what might go wrong, and determined not to make a mistake. Learn from one another.

CHALLENGING—2

VIRGO/SCORPIO

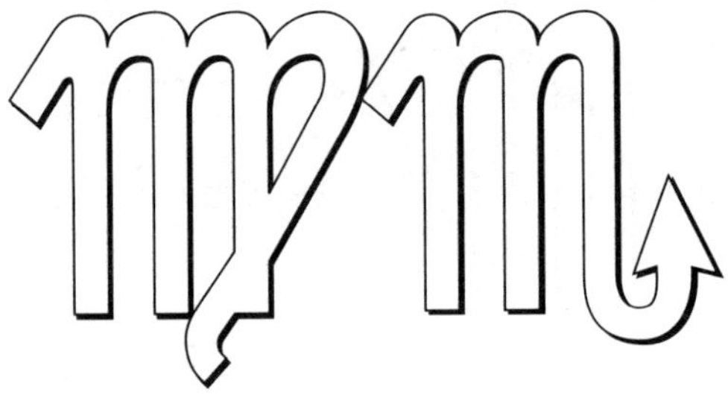

COMPLETE CONTROL

Each of you has good organizational skills you can put to work in the home. (The down side is controlling your emotions—overdoing the "stiff upper lip" approach.) You nurture people by finding flaws and indicating how to fix them. He nurtures by uncovering (digging up) negativity and learning how to transform it to a positive. Be gentle! You are both very dedicated and loyal.

COMPATIBLE—3

THE ODD COUPLE

VIRGO/SAGITTARIUS

You like a home which is orderly and organized. He tends to run from here to there and rarely pays attention to details (such as housework). You're emotionally focused; he is scattered. You tend to be cautious and plan ahead; he tends to be optimistic (even rash) and spontaneous. You'll have to work within your differences to blend domestic lives.

CHALLENGING—2

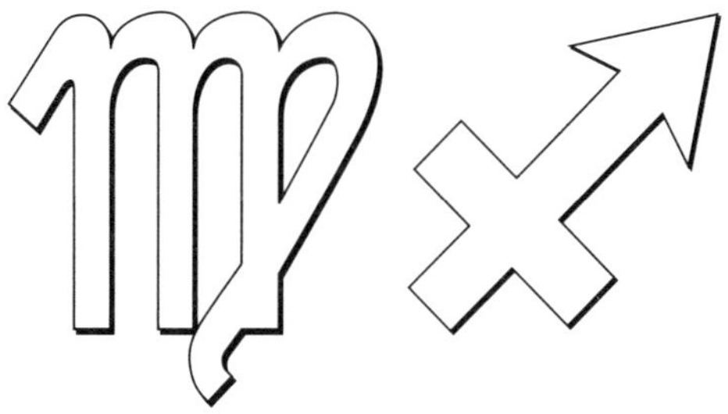

ORDERLY ABODE

VIRGO/CAPRICORN

Both of you like neat homes with a sense of order and predictability. Each of you is willing to work on the home, or from the home. You tend to take emotional matters seriously and move cautiously to avoid making a mistake. You both may fear being hurt, but would do almost anything for those you love.

COMPATIBLE—3

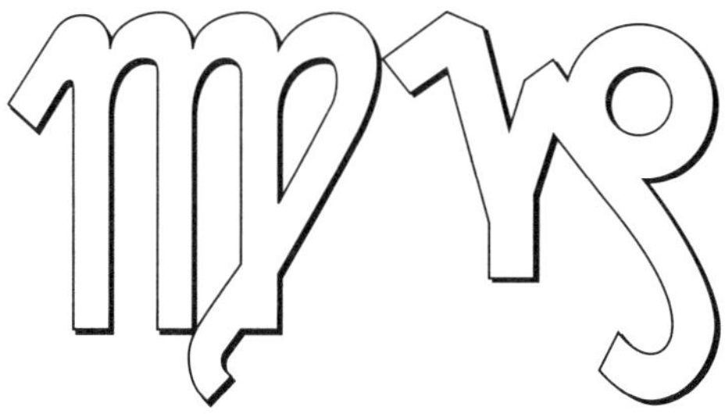

LIVELY LOGIC

VIRGO/AQUARIUS

You want a home which is sensible and orderly. He operates well in the midst of chaos. Your emotional approach is practical and step-by-step. He leaps from here to there and skips around. You nurture people by serving them and being helpful. He nurtures by surprising people and exposing them to new ideas. Can you accept each other's different styles?

VERY CHALLENGING—1

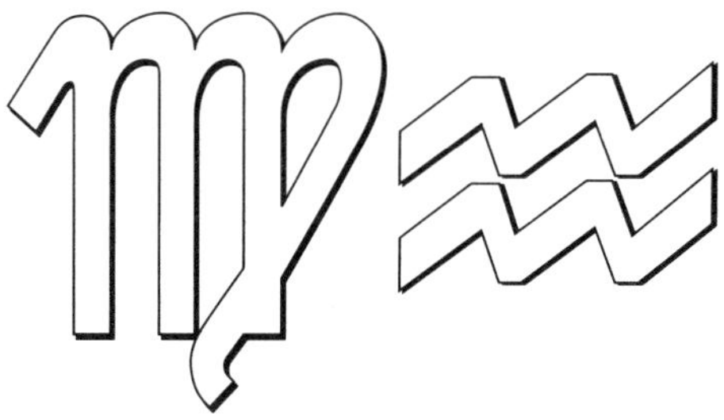

DREAMER AND DOER

VIRGO/PISCES

The two of you could be great partners in terms of home and emotional matters. He is the dreamer, the artist and you are the craftsperson, who makes dreams real. You can help bring his fantasies to earth and manifest them. You help ground him. He helps to inspire you.

VERY COMPATIBLE—4

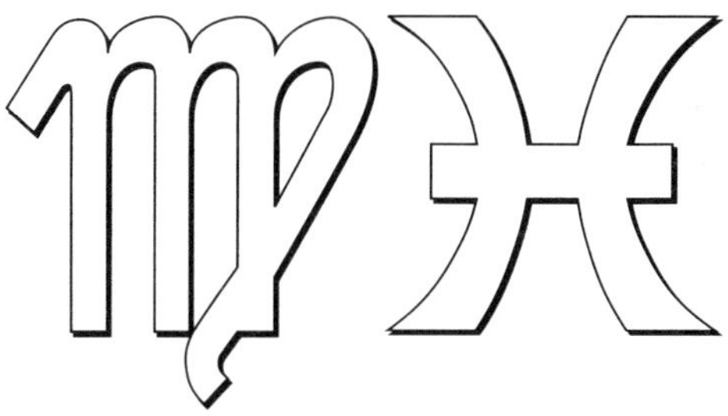

LIBRA/ARIES

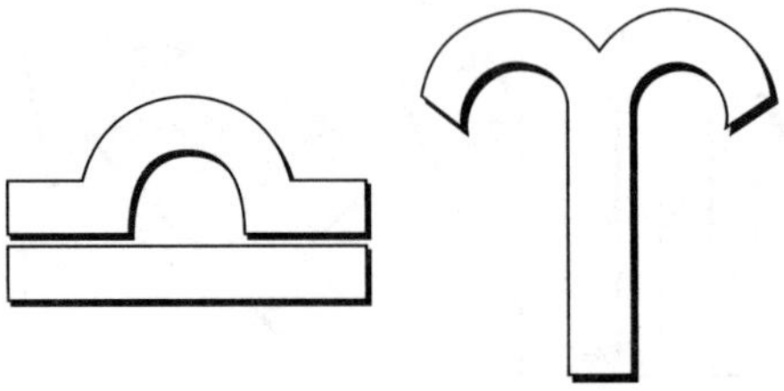

GIVE AND TAKE

The two of you may experience the attraction of opposites. His courage, optimism and freshness feed your beauty, charm and desire to share. Your diplomacy complements his directness. You may care more about art, culture or tact than he; he is probably more active and restless than you.

VERY COMPATIBLE—4

LIBRA/TAURUS

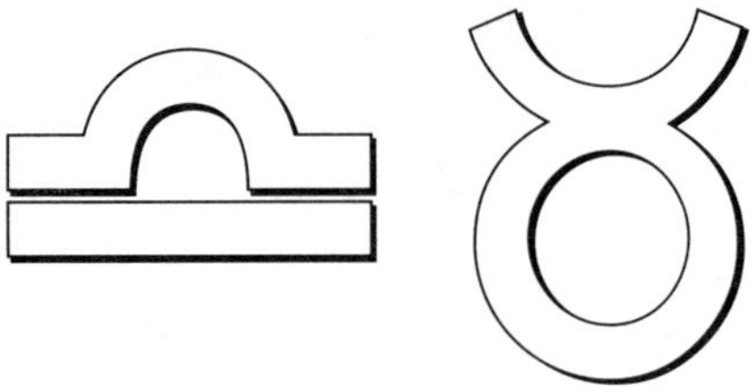

ARTISTIC ABODE

Both of you appreciate a beautiful home, but he is more oriented toward physical comfort and possessions and you are more focused on social interactions. He is probably more stable and predictable emotionally; your moods may shift with the people around you.

VERY CHALLENGING—1

LIBRA/GEMINI

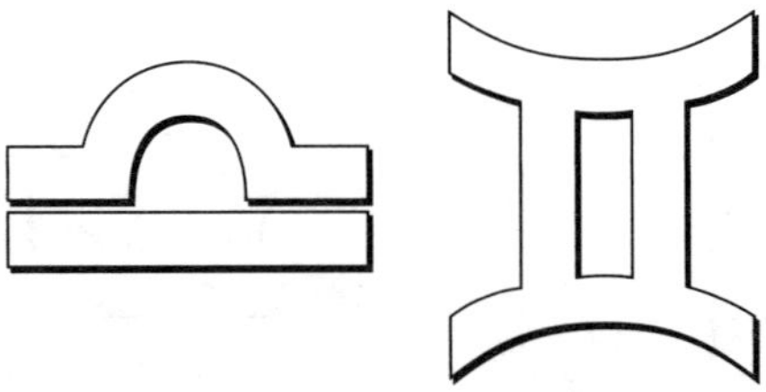

FLUENT FOLKS

You both want a home full of people and ideas. Sociability is ranked high. Each of you can nurture concepts and communications. You encourage people to learn, discuss and to explore the world of the mind. You may be more diplomatic and he more casual and fun-loving.

COMPATIBLE—3

LIBRA/CANCER

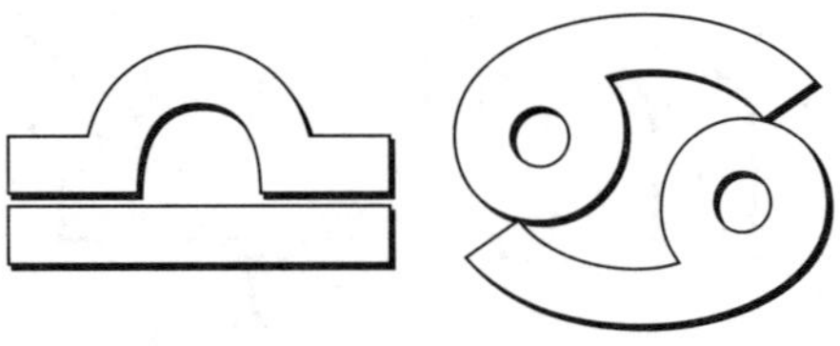

SHARED SPACE

Each of you wants emotional connections, but you may want more equality and sharing while he might be a bit possessive of the people he cares about—or come across as somewhat parental. You need the stimulation of other people; he can be very private. Love must be the tie that binds.

CHALLENGING—2

EMOTIONAL EXTROVERTS

LIBRA/LEO

Both of you are sociable and appreciate a home with fun activities and interesting people to chat with. He may be a bit more dramatic emotionally, while you are more diplomatic. Each of you has natural charisma which can attract others. Lively times are likely.

COMPATIBLE—3

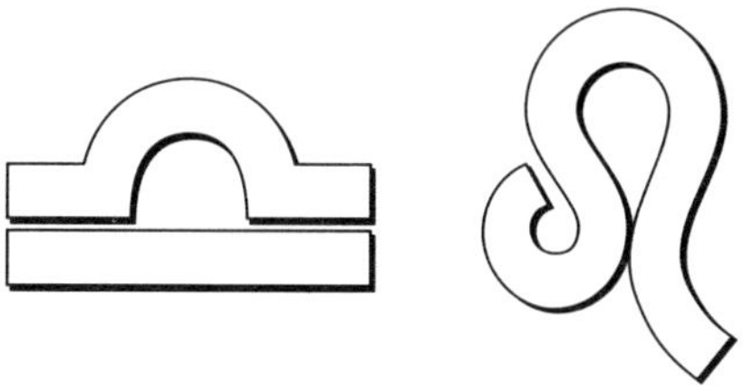

PLEASANT PRAGMATISM

LIBRA/VIRGO

He tends to focus on the degree of order and efficiency in the home. He may be quite a hard worker. You tend to focus on the people in the home, seeking social interactions. Your nurturing style is graceful and charming. He is more cautious, concerned with what might go wrong, and determined not to make a mistake. Learn from one another.

CHALLENGING—2

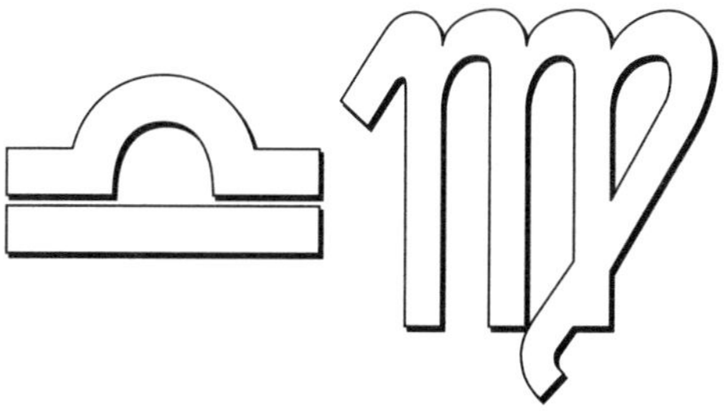

A PRETTY PLACE

LIBRA/LIBRA

You both can be very graceful, charming and sociable. You are likely to desire a lovely home and entertaining (or at least having people over to chat with) probably appeals. Each of you tends to smooth over trouble; don't hide too much dirt under the carpet emotionally. You can both be very loving and supportive.

VERY COMPATIBLE—4

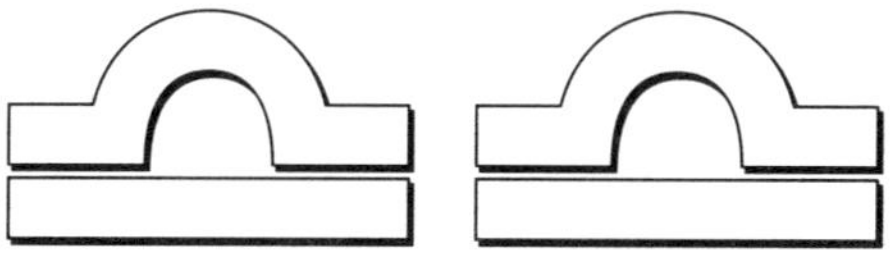

JOINT VENTURES

LIBRA/SCORPIO

Each of you has a strong emotional desire for partnership. Your style, however, is more pleasant and charming. His emotional tendency is toward intensity (and sometimes possessiveness or jealousy). You can encourage him to be more objective; he can encourage you to look more deeply into life.

CHALLENGING—2

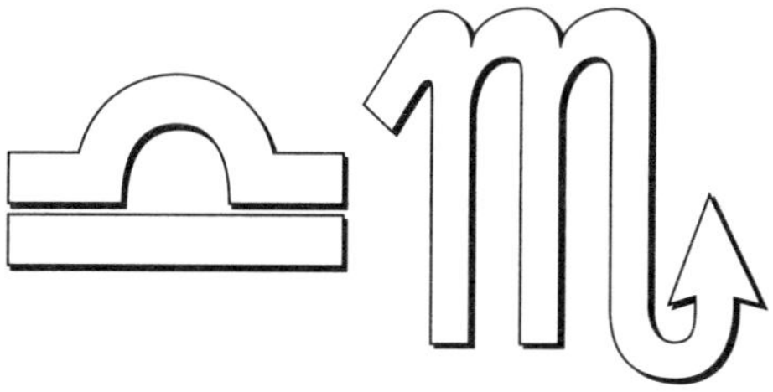

LIBRA/SAGITTARIUS

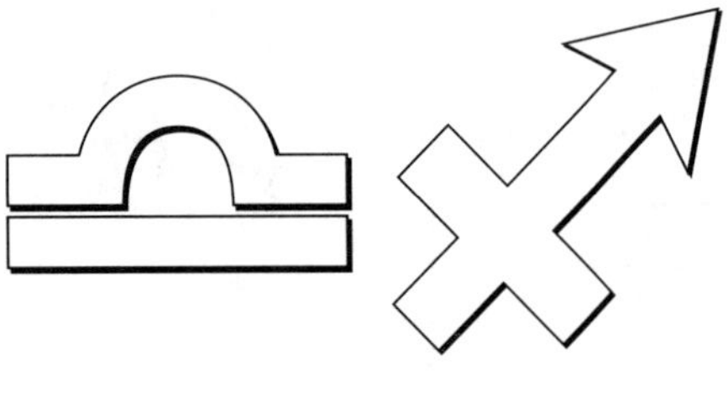

SOCIAL SHARING

Each of you is fed by sociability and fun activities. You are a natural diplomat and he can be friends with anyone. Outgoing and eager to share, you both enjoy a home full of conversation, beauty and interesting people. You are very supportive and he is quite encouraging—able to see the best in anything.

COMPATIBLE—3

LIBRA/CAPRICORN

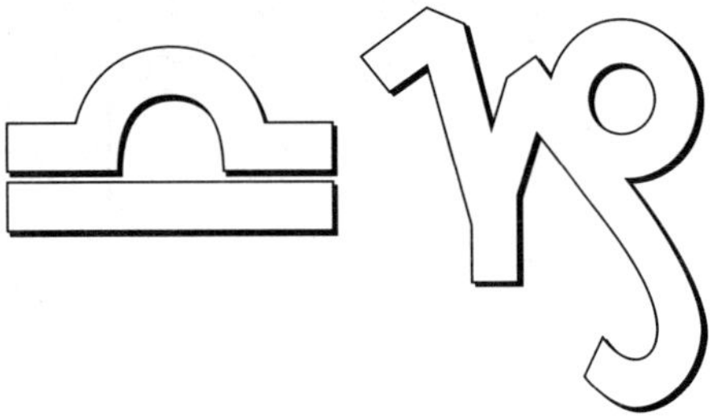

TOUGH TEAMWORK

You want a home between equals, whereas he can come across as "Big Daddy" who expects to be in charge. You are diplomatic; he can be dogmatic. If you appeal to his need for emotional safety and security, you can help him learn to share and to compromise. He can help you be stronger and hold firm to your positions.

CHALLENGING—2

LIBRA/AQUARIUS

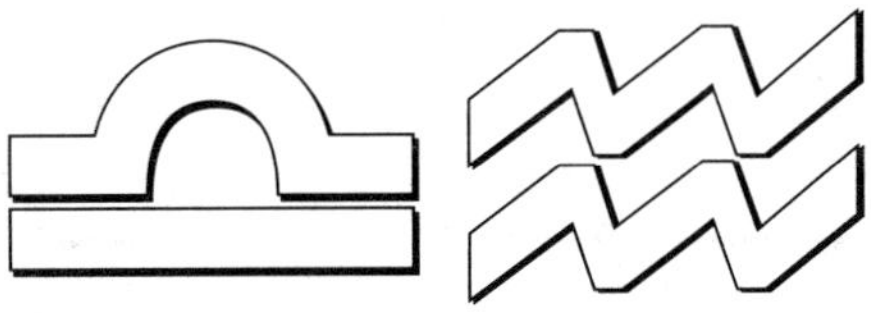

SHARED STIMULATION

Both of you can nurture people mentally, being drawn to interesting conversations and a variety of people. A home which is full of new ideas, friends and intellectual stimulation is best for both of you. You take care of people by explaining things to them and by networking.

COMPATIBLE—3

LIBRA/PISCES

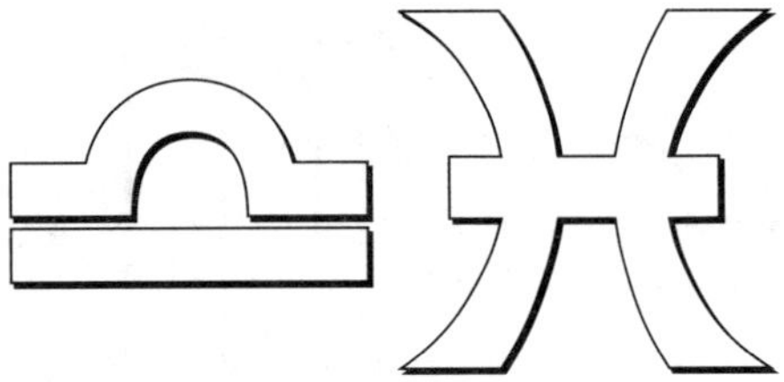

ATTRACTIVE ABODE

Both of you have an emotional need for beauty and could express it in your home. You, however, want a home where you can have people and lots of social interaction. He values domestic privacy and may be quite silent at times. You both tend to avoid unpleasantness, so must strive to acknowledge your differences and work through them.

VERY CHALLENGING—1

DEVIOUS OR DIRECT?

SCORPIO/ARIES

The two of you handle feelings very differently. He tends to react quickly, perhaps even rashly at times. You mull things over before revealing any feelings. You value emotional privacy; he values openness. He takes the straight line approach; You use back door or indirect routes. Shared passion, however, could be a strong bond.

VERY CHALLENGING—1

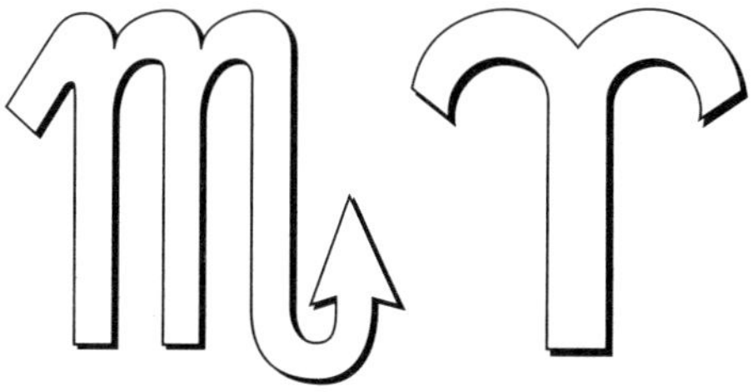

FEELING FINE

SCORPIO/TAURUS

Possessions and pleasures could be a strong bond between you. Each of you appreciates good food and other physical indulgences. Your homes may be full of interesting textures, feature a waterbed, jacuzzi, soft rugs, art or other forms of gratifying the senses.

VERY COMPATIBLE—4

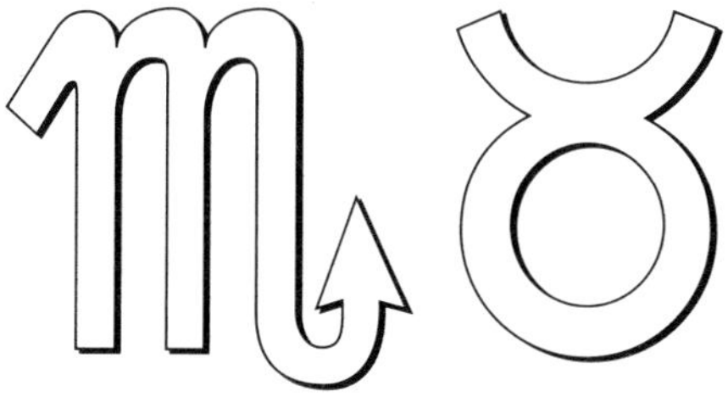

HEAVY VERSUS LIGHT

SCORPIO/GEMINI

You are intensely emotional; he tends to be more casual and detached. He may talk about thinking when you are asking about feelings. Your privacy at home is vital to you, while he likes to bring in new ideas and new people. You can help him look more deeply into people and life. He can help you be more casual and lighthearted.

VERY CHALLENGING—1

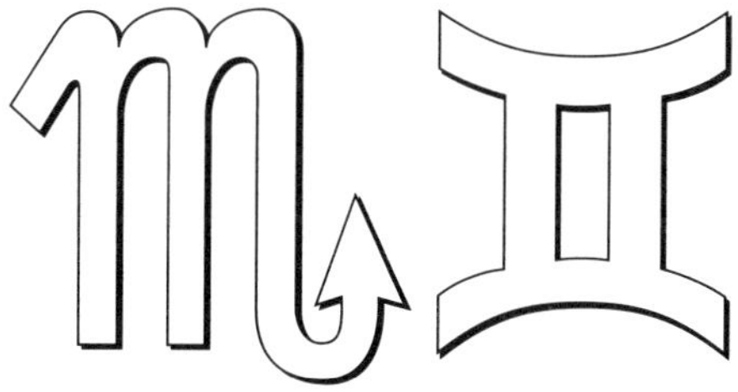

PRIVATE PEOPLE

SCORPIO/CANCER

Both of you have deep, strong feelings which you tend to hold in rather than reveal. You may both have to work on bringing up important issues rather than brooding about or avoiding them. Each of you is is capable of creating an intense emotional connection. You both want a home which is very private, letting only a select few in.

COMPATIBLE—3

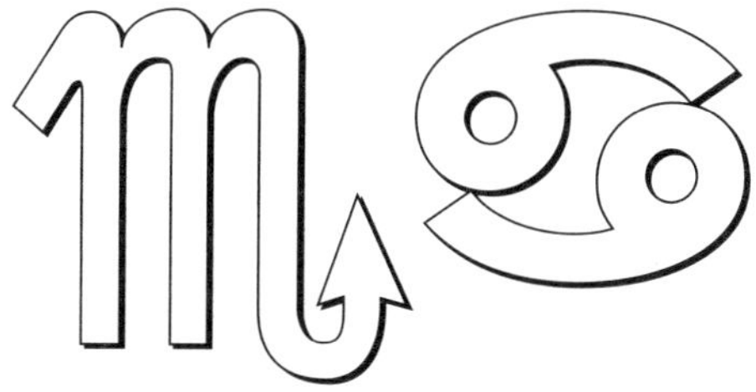

SCORPIO/LEO

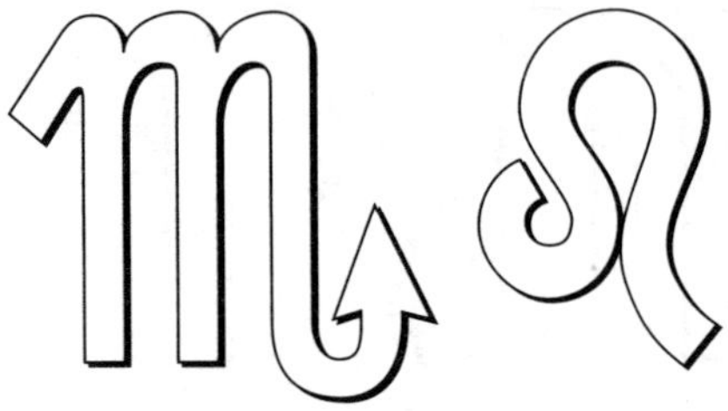

EXPLOSIVE EMOTIONS

Emotional intensity is the focus here! Each of you has very strong emotional reactions, but he lets it all hang out and you may hold back and hold in your feelings. He tends to be up-front; you may feel you have to be indirect (even manipulative). Each of you wants to be in charge, so compromising will demand a lot from both of you. Bonds built between you go very deep.

CHALLENGING—2

SCORPIO/VIRGO

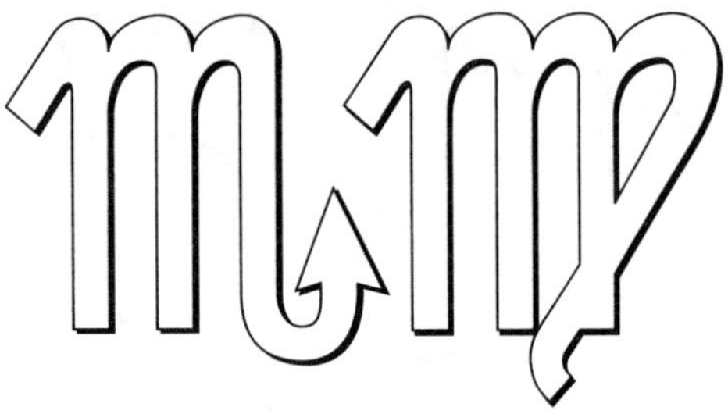

COMPLETE CONTROL

Each of you has good organizational skills you can put to work in the home. (The down side is controlling your emotions—overdoing the "stiff upper lip" approach.) He nurtures people by finding flaws and indicating how to fix them. You nurture by uncovering (digging up) deep emotional issues (obsessions, compulsions). Be gentle! You are both very dedicated and loyal.

COMPATIBLE—3

SCORPIO/LIBRA

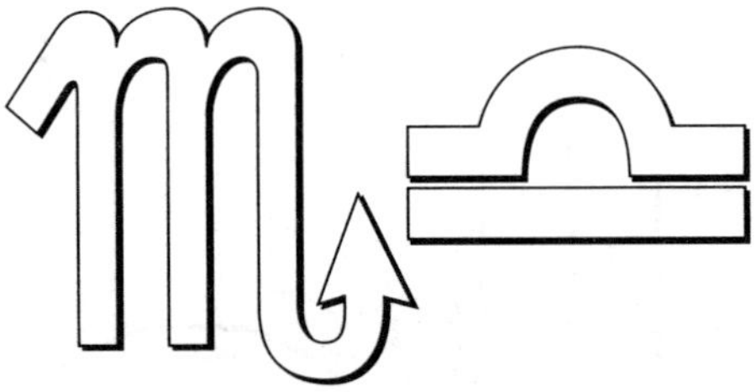

JOINT VENTURES

Each of you has a strong emotional desire for partnership. You may feel the need on a more intense, deep level, while he can be a bit more casual about it. He finds other people stimulating; you like to have a total one-on-one focus. He can encourage you to be more objective and you can encourage him to look more deeply into life.

CHALLENGING—2

SCORPIO/SCORPIO

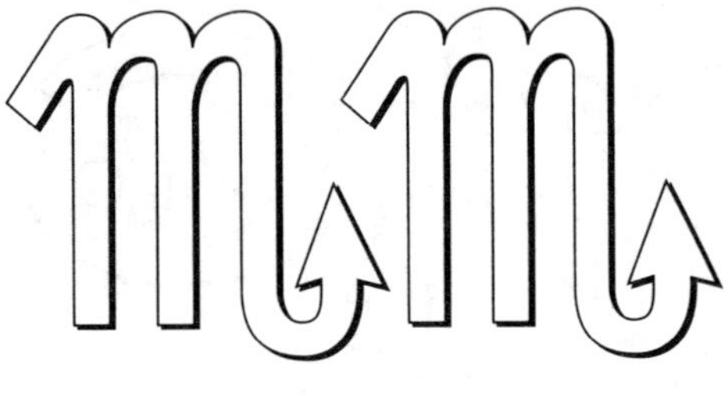

ULTIMATE EMOTIONS

No lightweights here! You both feel very deeply and intensely about home and emotional matters. Each of you tends to keep much inside and may sometimes manipulate rather than attempt direct confrontation. You are both capable of incredible commitment and will go to the limit for the ones you love!

VERY COMPATIBLE—4

IN HERE VERSUS OUT THERE

SCORPIO/SAGITTARIUS

Fireworks are likely. Strong emotions reign, but you keep much inside while he can be larger-than-life in his expressions. You want privacy and an intense one-on-one focus. He likes to wander the world and relate to a wide circle of people. He can expand your horizons and you can help him focus on vital, intimate exchanges.

CHALLENGING—2

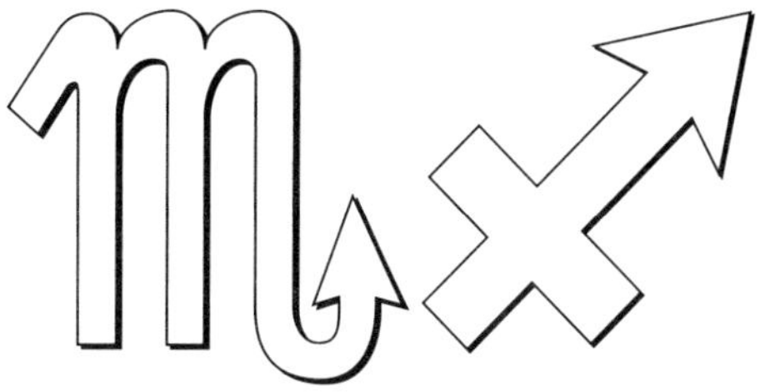

SERIOUS SUPPORT

SCORPIO/CAPRICORN

Both of you take emotional matters very seriously. You—because you feel so very deeply. He—because he is cautious and does not want to be hurt. Being dependable is your best gift to one another. Each of you appreciates order in the home and commitment in a partner.

COMPATIBLE—3

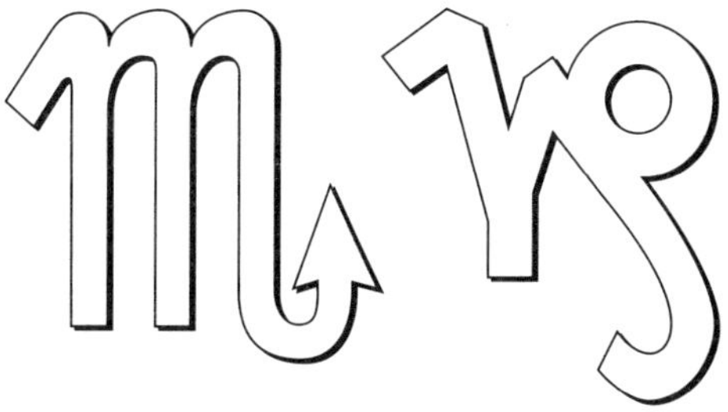

HOT/COLD

SCORPIO/AQUARIUS

You are dealing with an attachment/separation conflict in terms of home and emotional matters. When you want commitment and total focus, he wants detachment and stimulation from the outside world. You must find a way to allow some of each in your lives. He can expose you to new interests; you can help him get into emotional depths.

CHALLENGING—2

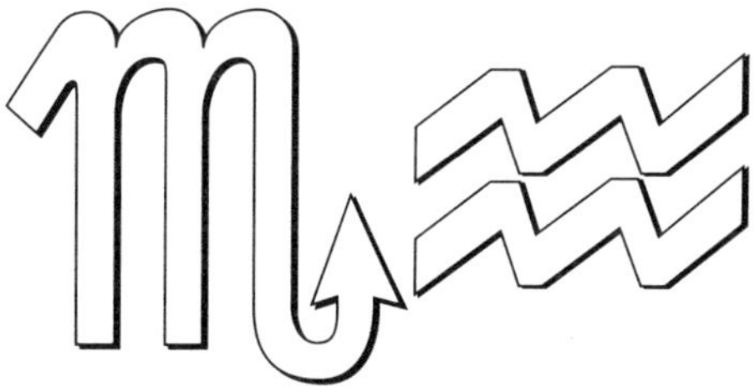

RETIRING ROOMIE

SCORPIO/PISCES

You are both emotionally tuned into the home environment, and sensitive to people's feelings there. Shared empathy can be a strong bond, but don't let your tendencies to keep much inside get out of hand. Do discuss issues! Guard each other's need for privacy. You both appreciate a housemate who is sensitive.

COMPATIBLE—3

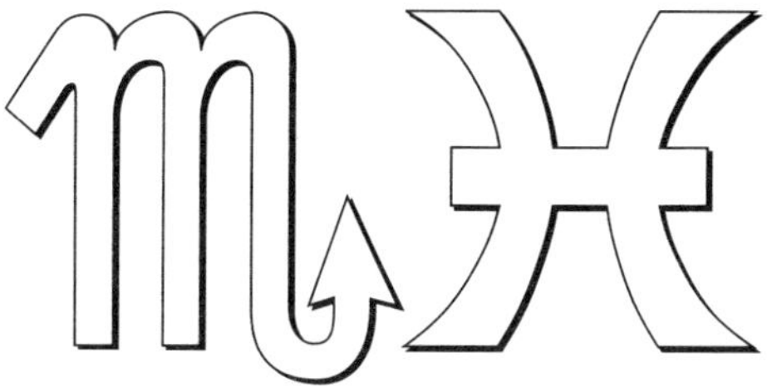

SAGITTARIUS/ARIES — EMOTIONAL ENTHUSIASM

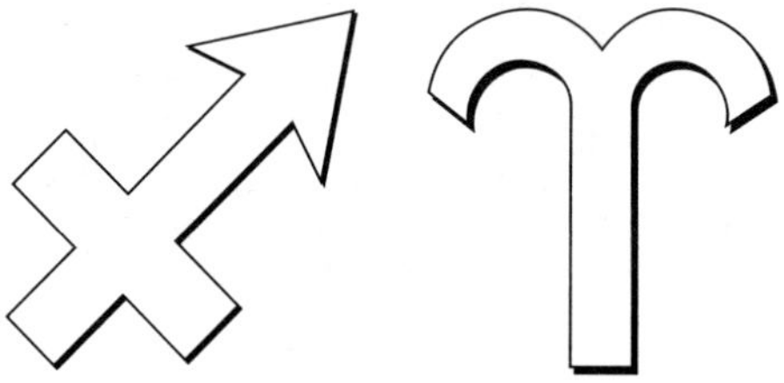

Both of you find security in adventure. You may enjoy exploring the world together, traveling, or simply having lots of action, movement and excitement on the home front. Fellow optimists, you easily look on the bright side in situations. You nurture each other's confidence.

COMPATIBLE—3

SAGITTARIUS/TAURUS — RESTLESS ROOTS

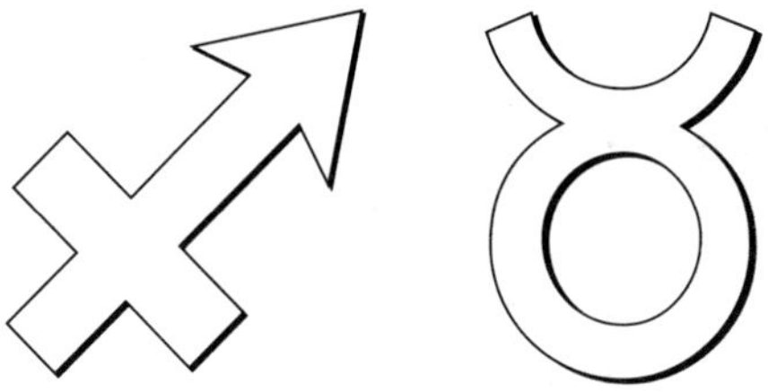

You want an adventurous home full of books, fascinating people or exciting experiences. He wants comfort, stability and predictability in the home. He enjoys staying in one place; you can have fun wandering the world. You are ready for more, better, higher, faster, while his emotions center on what is possible in the real world.

VERY CHALLENGING—1

SAGITTARIUS/GEMINI — AT HOME IN THE WORLD

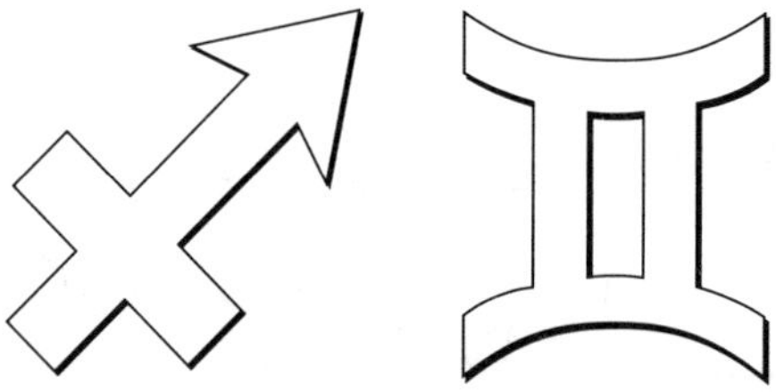

Both of you can feel at home almost anywhere in the world, and enjoy bringing the world—books, foreigners, discussions, ideas—into your home. You value a home full of laughter. Each of you is inclined to look for the silver lining if things go wrong. You cheer each other up.

VERY COMPATIBLE—4

SAGITTARIUS/CANCER — FARAWAY FAMILY?

You tend to be upbeat and optimistic, while his moods are more cautious and protective. You have a bit of wanderlust—or an urge to keep the home exciting, active, and on the go. He values security and safety in the domestic arena. You can expose him to new adventures and he can help you put down a few roots.

VERY CHALLENGING—1

FUN FIRST! — SAGITTARIUS/LEO

You both want a home full of laughter, excitement and adventures. (Or, you'll take a road trip for the fun and frolic.) Upbeat and optimistic, you encourage one another to do more, feel more and constantly expand your domestic horizons. Dull is not in your vocabularies.

COMPATIBLE—3

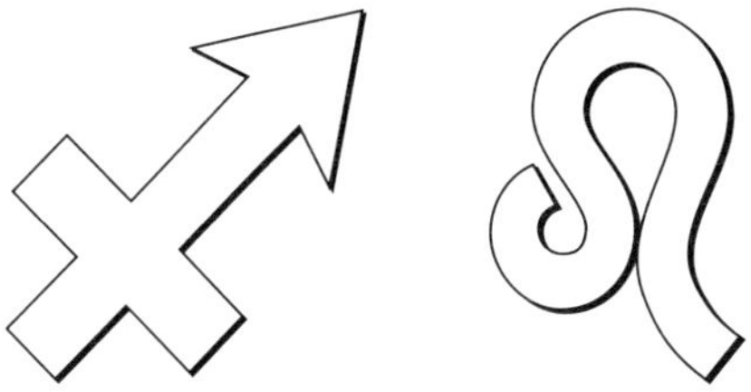

THE ODD COUPLE — SAGITTARIUS/VIRGO

You like a home full of movement, adventures and fun. He likes a home which is orderly and organized. You can be emotionally scattered and rash; he is emotionally focused and cautious. You're spontaneous; he's into planning (and worrying) ahead. The two of you will have to work within your differences to blend domestic lives.

CHALLENGING—2

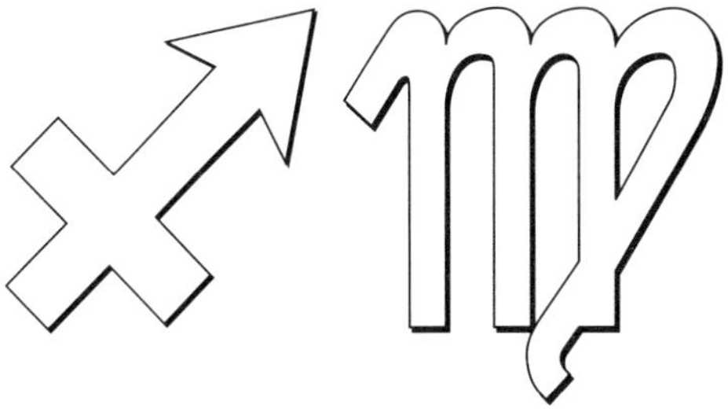

SOCIAL SHARING — SAGITTARIUS/LIBRA

Each of you is fed by sociability and fun activities. He is a natural diplomat and you can be friends with anyone. Outgoing and eager to share, you both can enjoy a home full of conversation, beauty and interesting people. He can be a good partner and you are an excellent motivator— encouraging others and seeing the best in everything.

COMPATIBLE—3

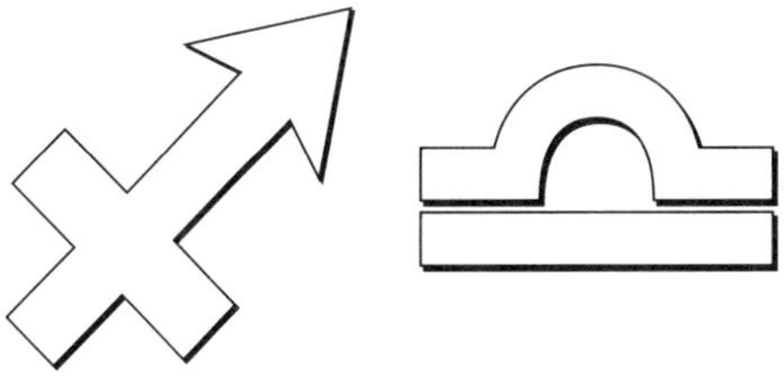

OUT THERE VERSUS IN HERE — SAGITTARIUS/SCORPIO

Fireworks are likely. Strong emotions reign, but you are open, spontaneous and optimistic, while he keeps much inside (and might even be secretive). You may like to travel and relate to many people, while he tends to be somewhat possessive (or wants to focus intensely one at a time). You can expand his horizons, and he can encourage your intimate connections.

CHALLENGING—2

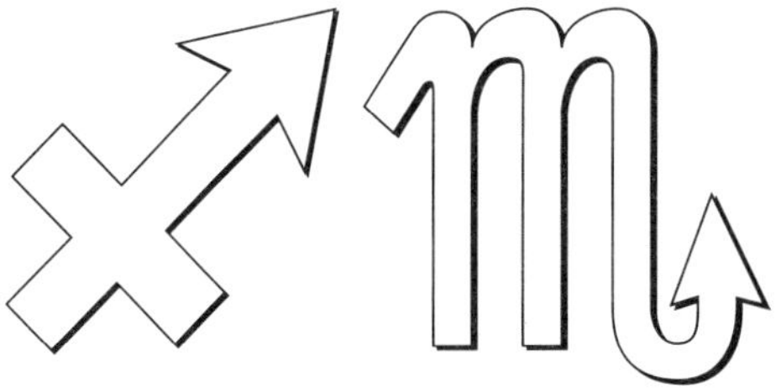

SAGITTARIUS/SAGITTARIUS WANDERLUST!

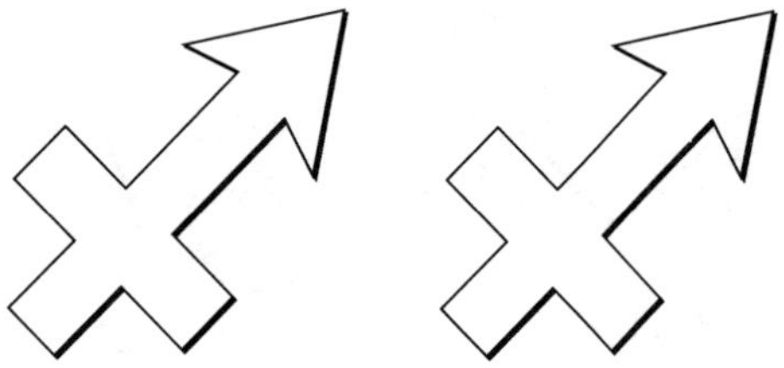

Both of you can be a lot of fun! You may enjoy traveling together, or bringing fun and frolic into the household. Lively, witty, and optimistic, you tend to nurture people by entertaining them and cheering them up. Friendly and outgoing, you both easily relate to others. Life is never dull around you two.

VERY COMPATIBLE—4

SAGITTARIUS/CAPRICORN UP AND DOWN

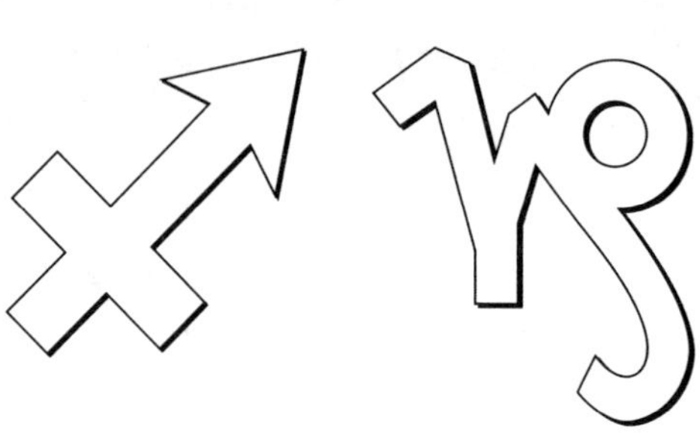

You may fall into the roles of the optimist and pessimist around emotional matters. You can always see the silver lining and he is quite aware of all the dark clouds. You may want more fun and spontaneity in the home, while he prefers more order. You can help him laugh more; he can help you look ahead.

CHALLENGING—2

SAGITTARIUS/AQUARIUS ON THE MOVE

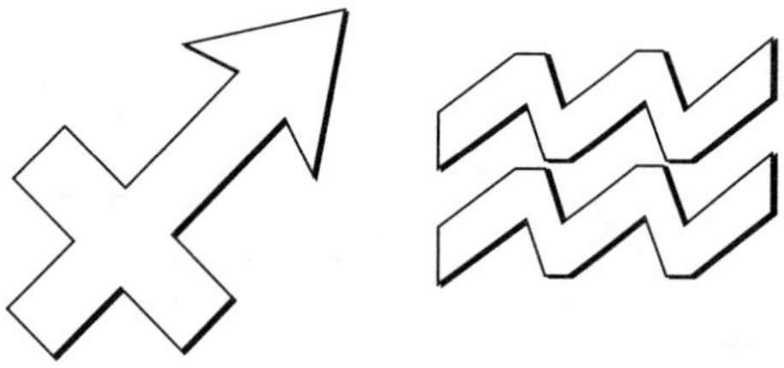

You both can feel at home in the world, and don't have to have a nest per se. You are fed by interactions with people—the more interesting, unusual, and entertaining, the better. Lively and sociable, you keep each other active. Your home is likely to have lots of people coming and going (including both of you).

COMPATIBLE—3

SAGITTARIUS/PISCES NATURE MYSTICS

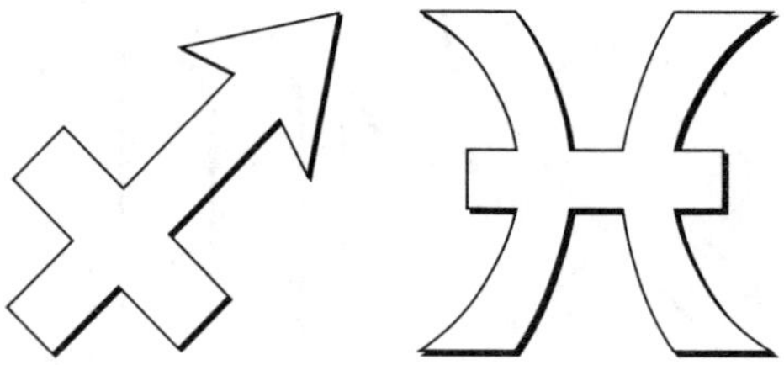

Although you both can idealize home and nurturing, you may expect more than is possible of family or of your nest. You may want more fun and sociability, while he looks more for privacy and a place to withdraw and refresh. A shared feeling for nature could enrich your domestic life. You can both see the best in those you love.

CHALLENGING—2

PESSIMIST AND OPTIMIST

CAPRICORN/ARIES

He knows what he wants and he wants it right now, whereas you are cautious about asking, for fear of rejection. He believes in being honest and direct; you believe in maintaining control and safety. His feeling nature is upbeat and optimistic; you tend to be a worrier. Learn from one another and you both will grow.

CHALLENGING—2

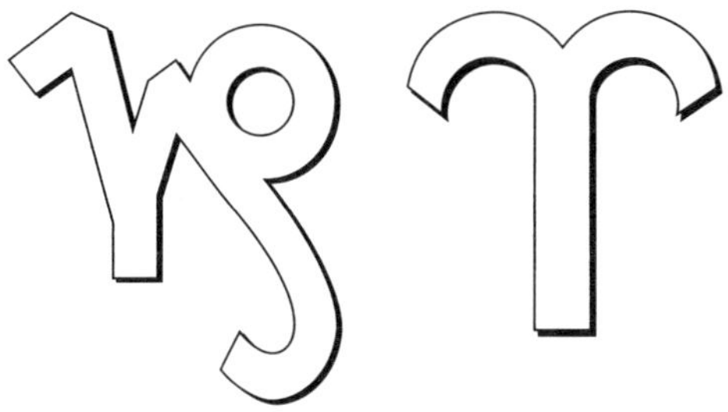

RELIABLE ROOMMATES

CAPRICORN/TAURUS

Both of you appreciate tangible results. You both nurture people by doing things for them. Support, for you two, demands reliability. Each of you may have good instincts for hanging on to possessions and material goods. Business skills are likely. You may look to a home partly as an investment.

COMPATIBLE—3

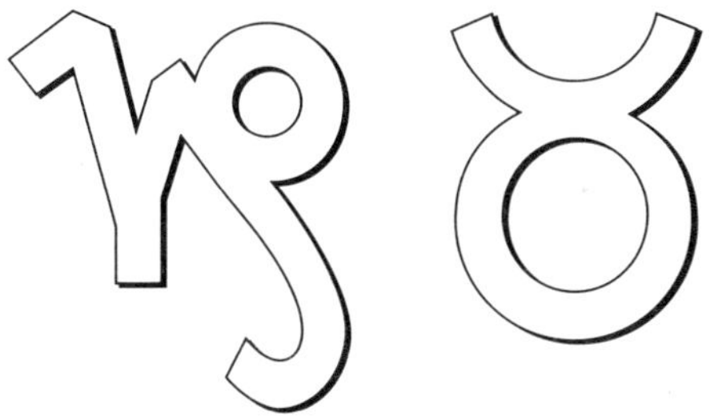

ADAPTABLE ACHIEVEMENT

CAPRICORN/GEMINI

You would prefer an orderly home and are willing to work for it. He can cheerfully live in chaos—as long as it's interesting. He can crack jokes about emotional matters; you tend to be serious (sometimes inhibited). You encourage him to be more focused; he can help you to lighten up.

VERY CHALLENGING—1

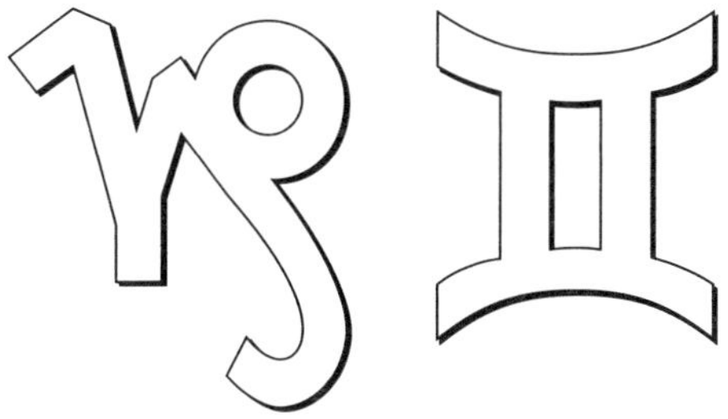

DOMESTIC DEPENDABILITY

CAPRICORN/CANCER

Each of you has a strong parental streak. You find it natural to look after others, or tell them what they should do (for their own good). If you play parent with one another, just be sure to take turns being in charge. Emotionally, you both seek commitment and safety.

VERY COMPATIBLE—4

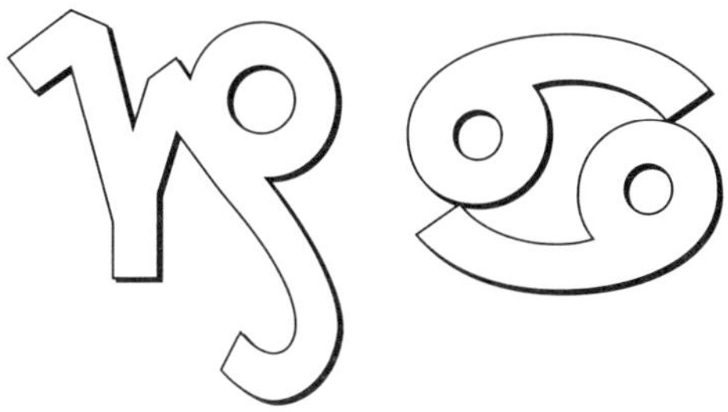

CAPRICORN/LEO

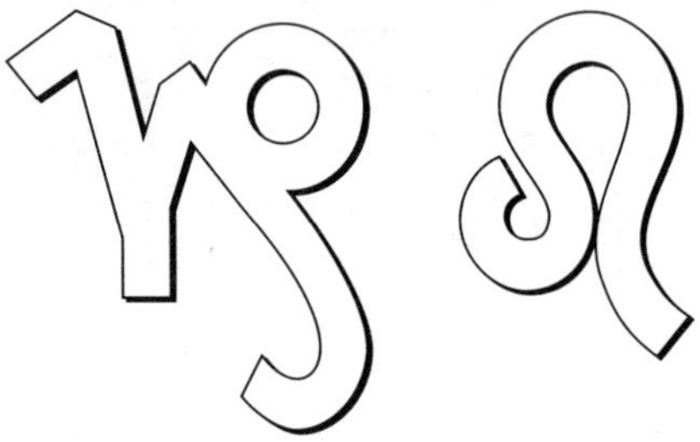

WHO'S ON TOP?

He wants to be King of the Castle, but you want to be President at home, so power issues are likely. Perhaps you can each have an area where you call the shots! His emotional nature is fiery, dramatic, exciting and enthusiastic. You tend to be serious, cautious and guarded.

VERY CHALLENGING—1

CAPRICORN/VIRGO

ORDERLY ABODE

Both of you like neat homes with a sense of order and predictability. Each of you is willing to work on the home, or from the home. You two tend to take emotional matters seriously and move cautiously to avoid making a mistake. You both may fear being hurt, but would do almost anything for those you love.

COMPATIBLE—3

CAPRICORN/LIBRA

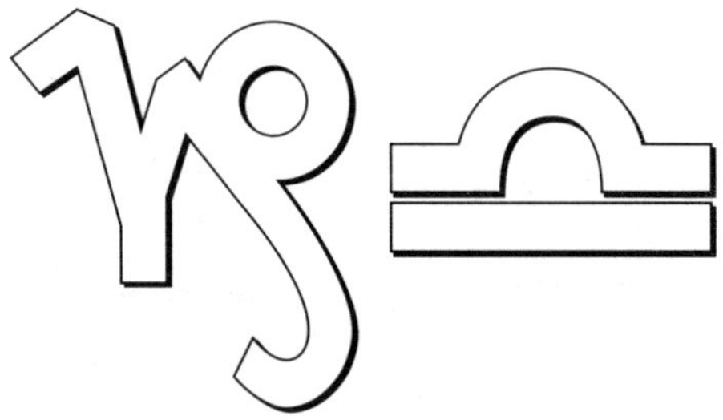

TOUGH TEAMWORK

You feel most comfortable with an orderly home. He is more focused on the people in the home. He tends to be friendly and people easily respond to him, whereas you are more guarded emotionally (for fear of being hurt). He can encourage you to trust more, and you can encourage him to be more grounded and practical.

CHALLENGING—2

CAPRICORN/SCORPIO

SERIOUS SUPPORT

Both of you take emotional matters very seriously. He—because his feelings are so intense. You—because you are cautious and do not want to be hurt. Being dependable is your best gift to one another. Each of you appreciates order in the home and commitment in a partner.

COMPATIBLE—3

UP AND DOWN — CAPRICORN/SAGITTARIUS

You may fall into the roles of the optimist and pessimist around emotional matters. He can always see the silver lining and you are quite aware of all the dark clouds. He may want more fun and spontaneity in the home, while you prefer more order. He can help you laugh more; you can help him to look ahead and plan.

CHALLENGING—2

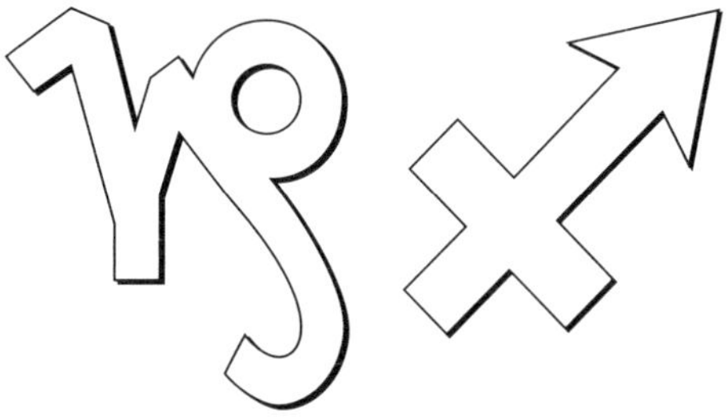

TAKE IT SLOW — CAPRICORN/CAPRICORN

You may have both been hurt emotionally in the past, so tend to be cautious now. Neither of you wants to take chances with your feelings, so move slowly and earn each other's trust. You both want a home which is orderly and a responsible partner you can depend on to always be there when needed.

VERY COMPATIBLE—4

A NORMAL NEST? — CAPRICORN/AQUARIUS

The two of you may polarize as the conventional person and the rebel. You like the known, predictable and safe, in emotions and home life. He is drawn to the unusual, the different, and the eccentric. If you are both willing to compromise, he can expose you to new alternatives and you can help him appreciate the familiar and secure.

CHALLENGING—2

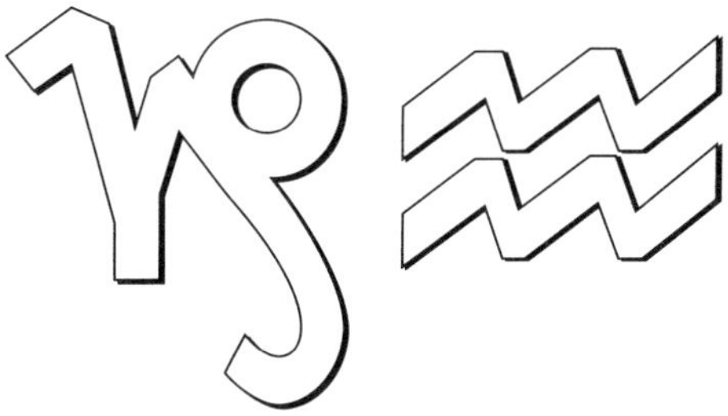

EFFECTIVE EMOTIONS — CAPRICORN/PISCES

You will work hard to create a safe, secure emotional setting. He is a bit of a dreamer, but can be sensitive and empathic. You may put in more effort, while he puts in more imagination, but the end result can be a home which is lovely and romantic, but also practical and efficient.

COMPATIBLE—3

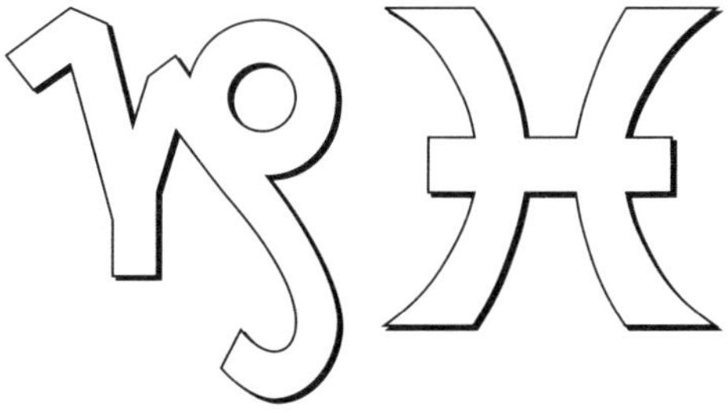

AQUARIUS/ARIES

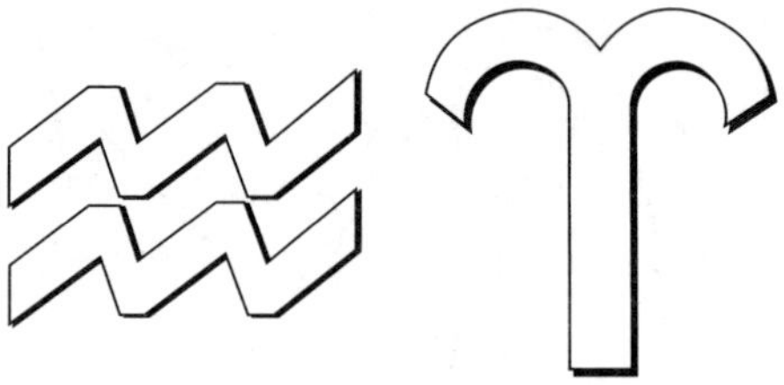

FREE FOLKS

You both have a streak of independence. You like home, but don't want to feel tied down by it. Either of you can be warm and nurturing—but on your own terms, in your own way. Too much clinging turns you off. You feed each other's attraction toward the new, the different, the fresh and exciting.

COMPATIBLE—3

AQUARIUS/TAURUS

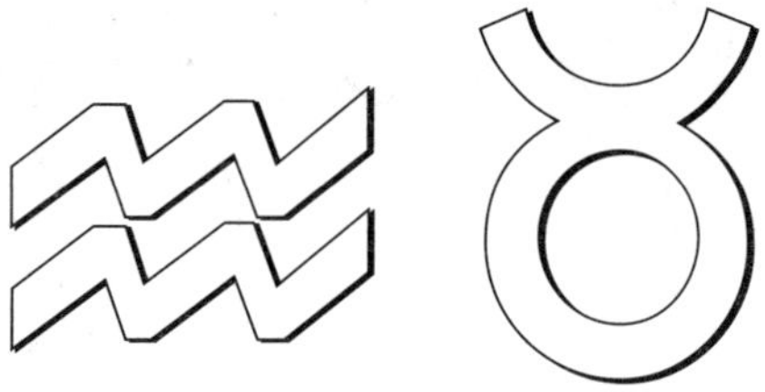

SURPRISING SECURITY

He wants a domestic routine which is comfortable and stable. You detest routine and want change, variety and surprises. He nurtures people by being reliable and doing things for them. You nurture people by being eccentric and stimulating them mentally. You can encourage his flexibility, and he can feed your practical side.

CHALLENGING—2

AQUARIUS/GEMINI

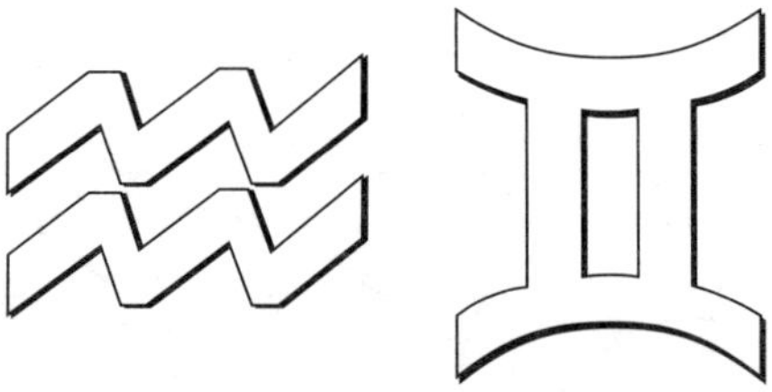

YOUNG AT HEART

Both of you nurture freshness. You are eager to experience many different things and seek out mentally stimulating people and ideas. What is said and learned may matter more than ordinary physical details (like housework). The lure of the new is strong. You can each be quite objective

COMPATIBLE—3

AQUARIUS/CANCER

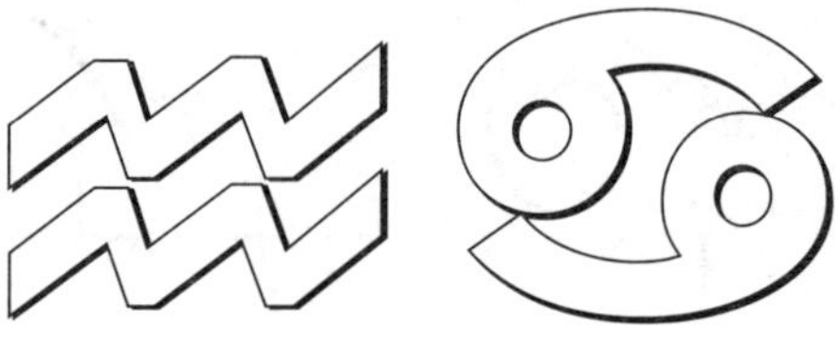

DIFFERENT DOMICILES

You're ready to take a new class, see a fascinating friend, or explore an interesting idea, and he wants to settle into the nest, be private, collect possessions, and just be a homebody. He needs emotional security, while you need more variety and change. Compromise will allow him to experiment a bit and you to appreciate some domesticity.

VERY CHALLENGING—1

HEAD AND HEART

AQUARIUS/LEO

Although opposites in some ways, there is a natural attraction between you. His feelings are fiery, expressive and dramatic (sometimes arrogant). You are more detached and objective. He can bring more fun, excitement and drama into the home. You can bring unusual ideas, intellectual stimulation and new technology.

VERY COMPATIBLE—4

LIVELY LOGIC

AQUARIUS/VIRGO

He wants a home which is sensible and orderly. You operate well in the midst of chaos. His emotional approach is practical and step-by-step. You leap from feeling to feeling, skipping steps. He nurtures people by fixing things and being helpful. You nurture by surprising people and exposing them to new ideas. Can you accept each other's different styles?

VERY CHALLENGING—1

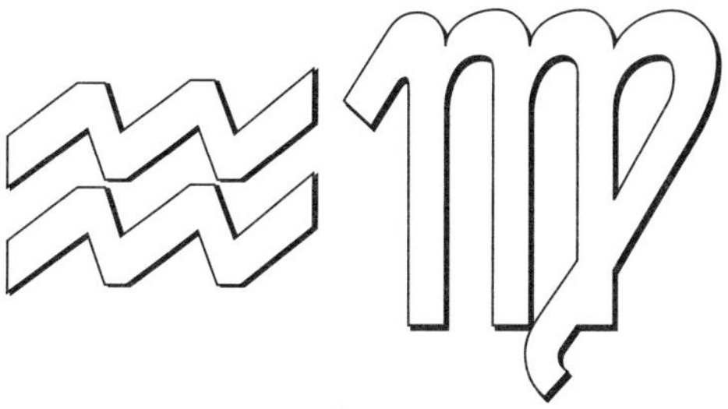

SHARED STIMULATION

AQUARIUS/LIBRA

Both of you can nurture people mentally, being drawn to interesting conversations and a variety of people. A home which is full of new ideas, friends and intellectual stimulation is best for both of you. You take care of people by explaining things to them and by networking.

COMPATIBLE—3

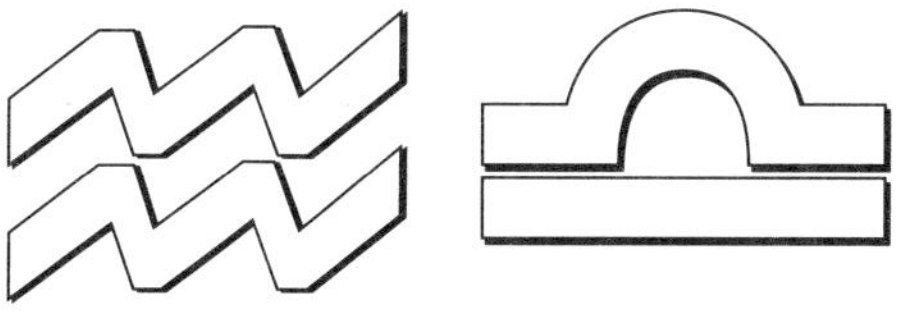

HOT/COLD

AQUARIUS/SCORPIO

You are dealing with an attachment/separation conflict in terms of home and emotional matters. When you want some space or to be with friends, he wants an intense, intimate or sexual connection. You must balance freedom and closeness within both of your lives. You can expose him to new interests; he can help you get to deeper emotional and sexual levels.

CHALLENGING—2

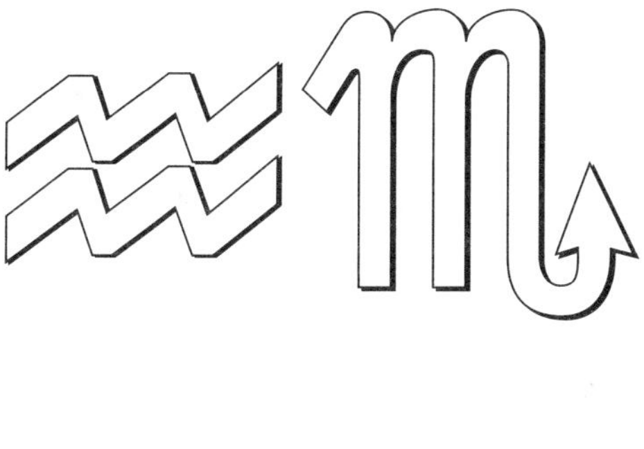

AQUARIUS/SAGITTARIUS

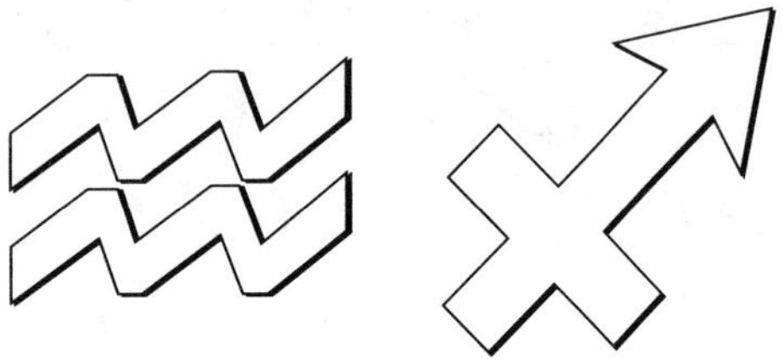

ON THE MOVE

You both can feel at home in the world, and don't have to have a nest per se. You are fed by interactions with people—the more interesting, unusual and entertaining, the better. Lively and sociable, you keep each other active. Your home is likely to have lots of people coming and going (including both of you).

COMPATIBLE—3

AQUARIUS/CAPRICORN

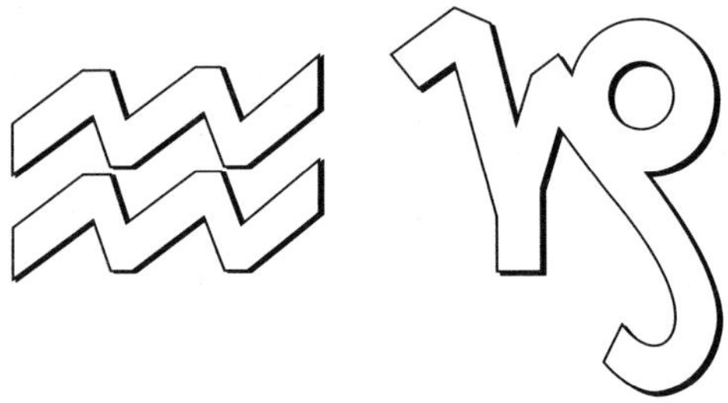

A NORMAL NEST?

The two of you may polarize as the conventional person and the rebel. He likes the known, predictable and safe in emotions and home life. You are drawn to the unusual, the different and the eccentric. If you two are willing to compromise, you can expose him to new alternatives and he can help you appreciate the familiar and secure.

CHALLENGING—2

AQUARIUS/AQUARIUS

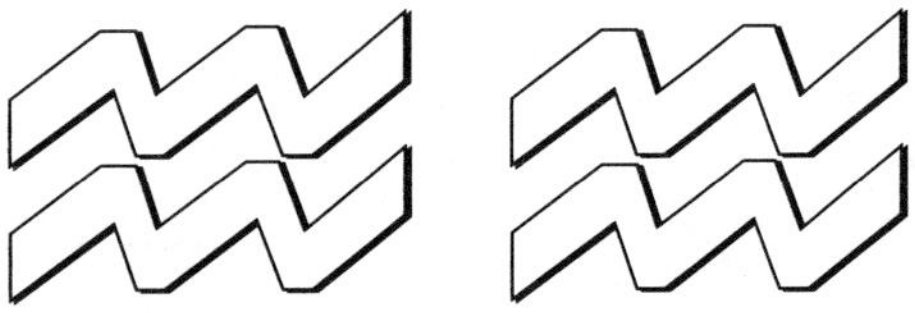

UNIQUE URGES

You both are likely to have a unique approach to the home and emotional matters. You may be more objective than most, or fill your home with unusual objects, new ideas, fascinating people, or anything progressive or eccentric. You both nurture people mentally and are fed by the new, the different, and the unconventional.

VERY COMPATIBLE—4

AQUARIUS/PISCES

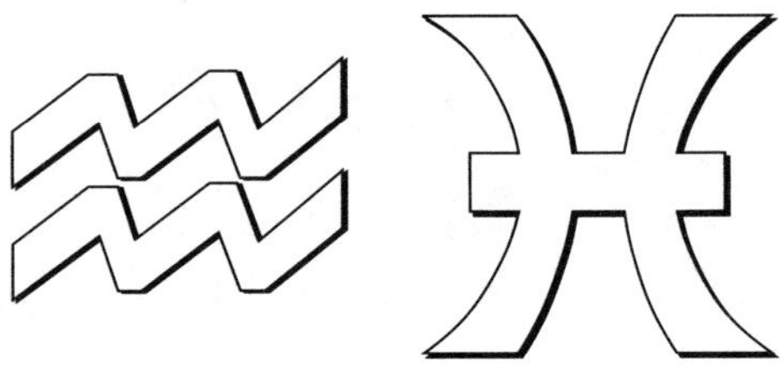

HUMANITARIAN HOUSEHOLD

You both have instincts to care for more than just your personal family, so might be involved with humanitarian or charitable concerns. You may be a bit more objective and he a bit more sensitive emotionally. You can be chaotic or unconventional in regard to the house; he wants to create a beautiful, ideal environment.

CHALLENGING—2

DIRECTING DREAMS

PISCES/ARIES

Neither of you may be overly fond of housework. He is too busy running around and you're too busy visualizing and imagining possibilities. He could seem a bit volatile to you, while you may seem a bit too inward to him. His courage, directness and eagerness can inspire you; your empathy and idealism can nurture him.

CHALLENGING—2

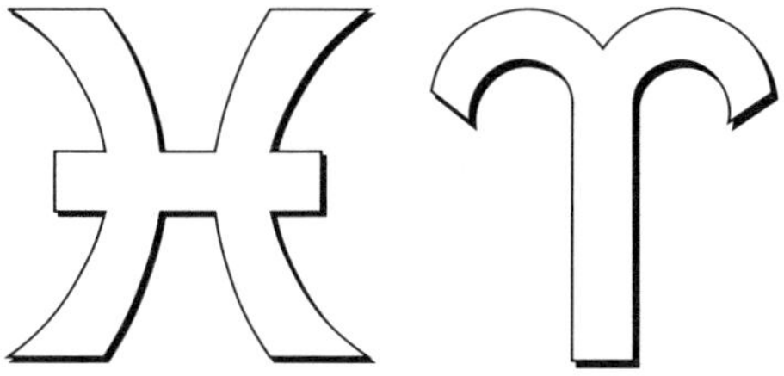

EASY DOES IT

PISCES/TAURUS

He wants a home which is attractive and comfortable. You want a home which is beautiful and can be a retreat from the world. Both of you prefer to avoid conflict in the domestic arena. You strive to encourage a smooth, easy flow emotionally and physically.

COMPATIBLE—3

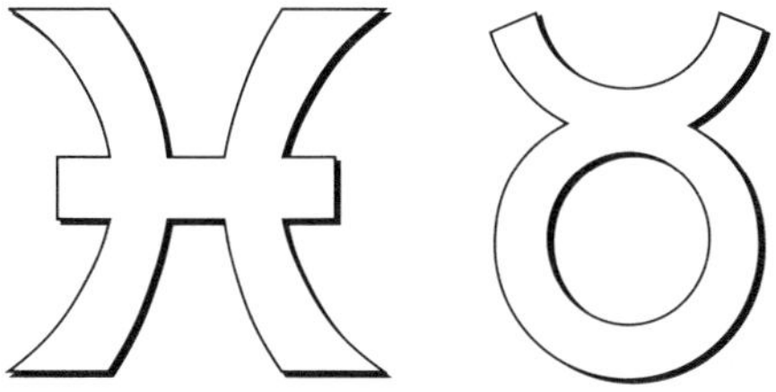

VARIED VISIONS

PISCES/GEMINI

You want a home which is a sanctuary—a private retreat from the world. He is eager to share your home with others, particularly if they have interesting ideas or conversation. You nurture by remaining silent; he nurtures by talking. If you are willing to share styles and accommodate one another, you can create the best of both your worlds.

CHALLENGING—2

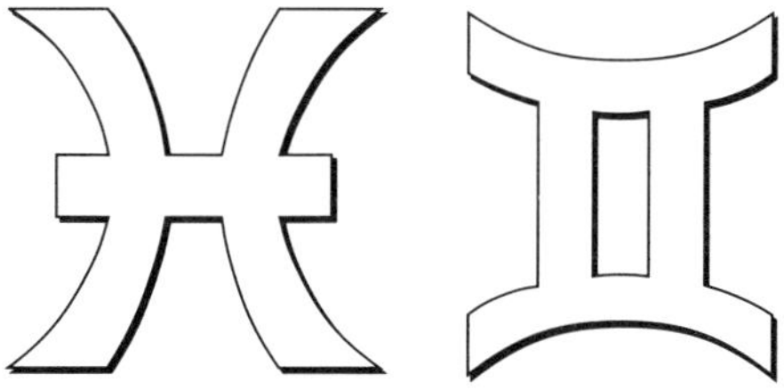

PRIVATE PLACES

PISCES/CANCER

Each of you has a very sensitive, empathic side. You may be able to tune into one another (without words). You both want a home which is a sanctuary (retreat) from the outside world—your own, special, private place. The two of you tend to hold feelings inside, so work to bring up what's important.

COMPATIBLE—3

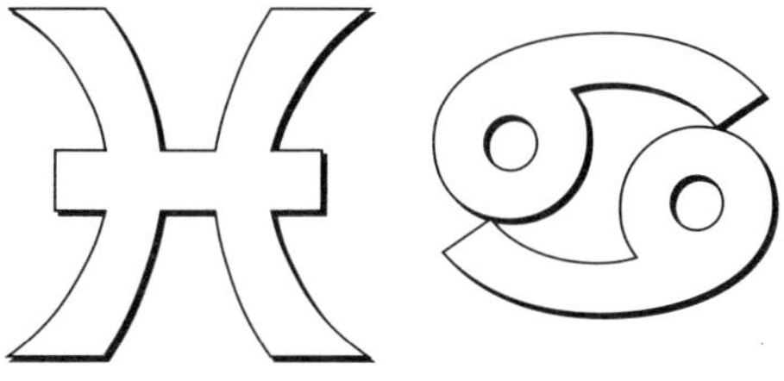

PISCES/LEO

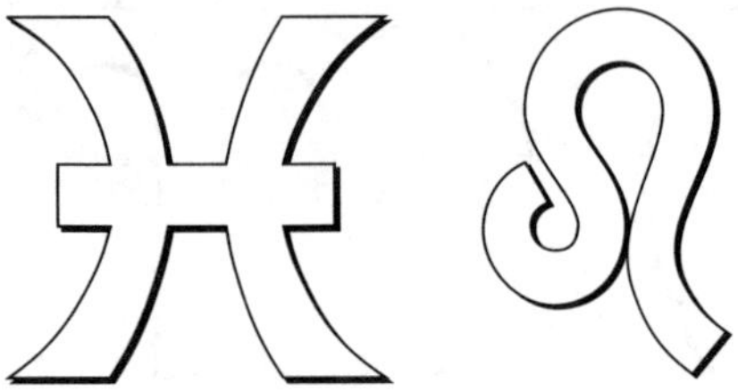

ENLARGED EMOTIONS

You want a private, special home which has almost a holy feeling. He wants a home he can be proud of, one he can show to the world. For him, dramatic gestures and intense emotions are natural; he is quite expressive. You feel deeply and are very empathic, but keeps much inside. You both, however, have a romantic streak.

VERY CHALLENGING—1

PISCES/VIRGO

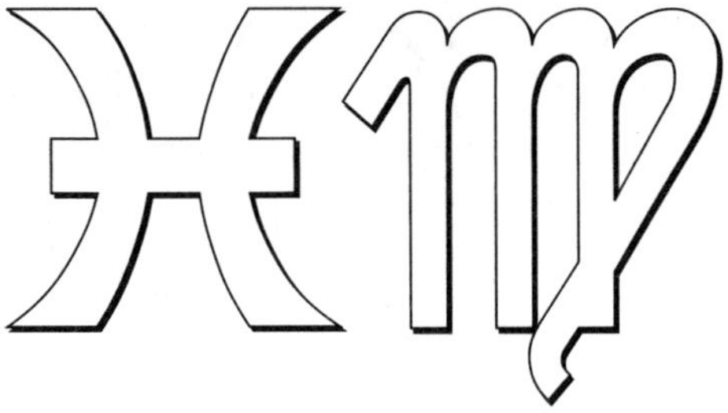

DREAMER AND DOER

The two of you could be great partners in terms of home and emotional matters. You are the dreamer, the artist, and he is the craftsperson, who makes dreams real. He can help bring your fantasies to earth and manifest them. He helps ground you. You help to inspire him.

VERY COMPATIBLE—4

PISCES/LIBRA

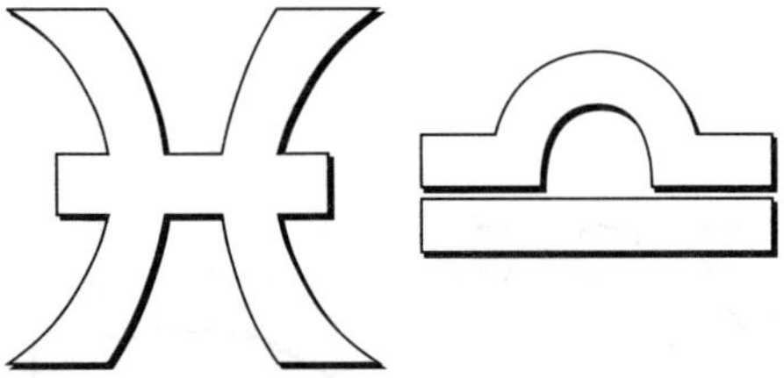

ATTRACTIVE ABODE

Both of you have an emotional need for beauty and could express it in your home. He, however, wants a home where you can have people and lots of social interaction. You value domestic privacy and may be quite silent at times. You both tend to avoid unpleasantness, so must strive to acknowledge your differences and work through them.

VERY CHALLENGING—1

PISCES/SCORPIO

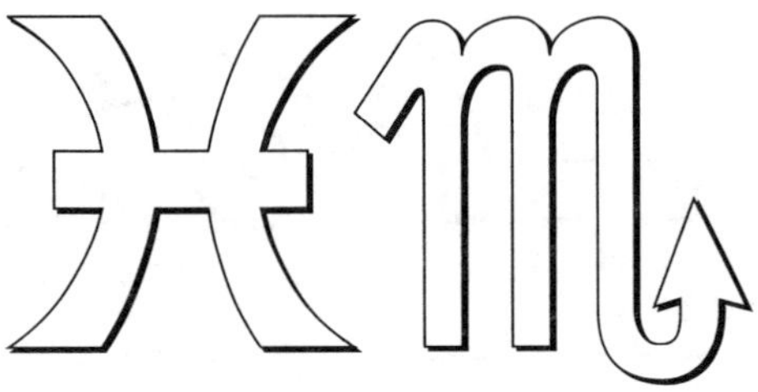

RETIRING ROOMIE

You are both emotionally tuned into the home environment, and sensitive to people's feelings there. Shared empathy can be a strong bond, but don't let your tendencies to keep much inside get out of hand. Do discuss issues! Guard each other's need for privacy. You both appreciate a housemate who is sensitive.

COMPATIBLE—3

NATURE MYSTICS

PISCES/SAGITTARIUS

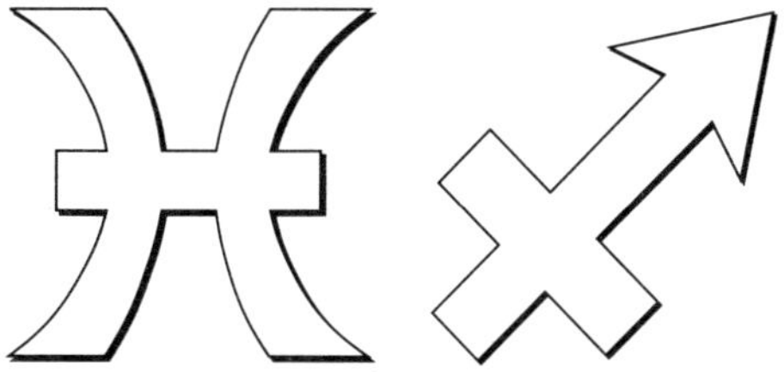

Although you both can idealize home and nurturing, you may expect more than is possible of family or of your nest. He may want more fun and sociability, while you look more for privacy and a place to withdraw and refresh. A shared feeling for nature could enrich your domestic life. You can both see the best in those you love.

CHALLENGING—2

EFFECTIVE EMOTIONS

PISCES/CAPRICORN

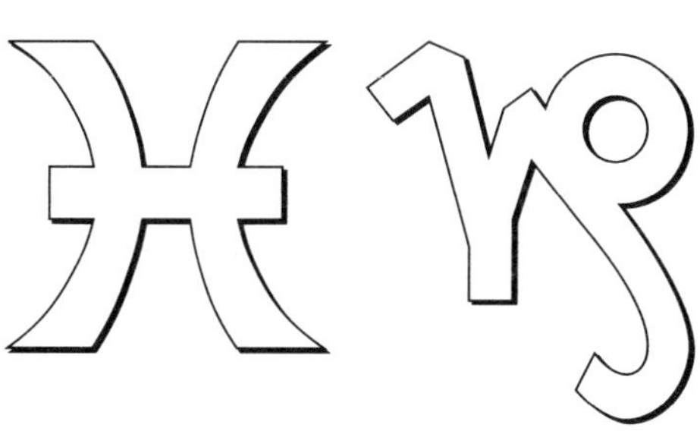

He may have been hurt before, so wants very much a safe, secure emotional attachment. Your empathy and sensitivity can be very reassuring to him. He may be more practical than you; you are quite imaginative. By combining forces, you could create a home which is lovely and romantic, but also practical and efficient.

COMPATIBLE—3

HUMANITARIAN HOUSEHOLD

PISCES/AQUARIUS

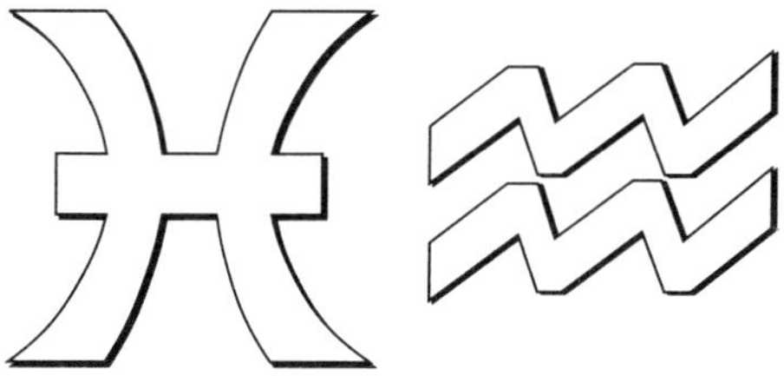

You both have instincts to care for more than just your personal family, so might be involved with humanitarian or charitable concerns. He may be a bit more objective and you a bit more emotionally sensitive. He can be chaotic or unconventional in regard to the house, while you want to create a beautiful, ideal environment.

CHALLENGING—2

TENDER TRIUMPH

PISCES/PISCES

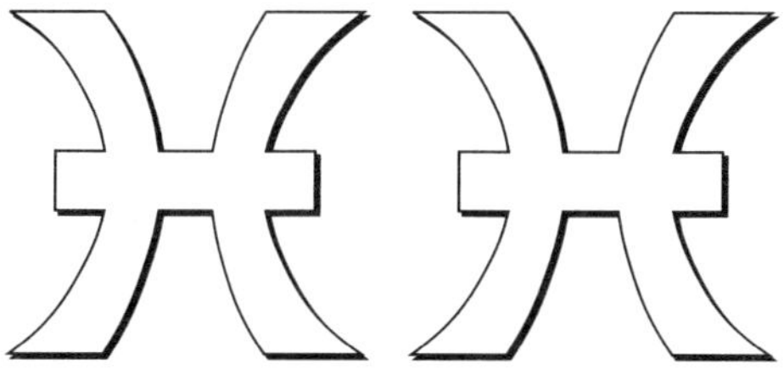

You are both very sensitive and empathic, so can be aware of each other's emotionally tender areas. You both yearn for a home which is beautiful, romantic, near nature, and/or very private. Blessed with wonderful imaginations, you can encourage each other's romantic sides and indulge each other's fantasies.

VERY COMPATIBLE—4

THE ASCENDANT

Your Ascendant is the degree of the zodiac which was rising at your birthplace, at the moment of your birth. Technically, the Ascendant is the intersection of the horizon and the eliptic (the Earth's path around the Sun) in the east. On a horoscope, the Ascendant is the horizontal line to the left, which designates the beginning of the first house. The sign of the zodiac on your Ascendant is also called your "rising sign."

The Ascendant represents our instinctive identity and early sense of self. This early self always remains, even though we grow more and more into our Sun sign as we go through life. The Ascendant symbolizes what we do naturally, spontaneously—our instinctive actions. The Ascendant is also a key to one's personal style and to the areas in life in which **you** want to call the shots; you want to do it **your** way.

Remember, for a full picture, you would also include the aspects to your Ascendant, but we can still learn a great deal from sign placements only. The tables in this book can give you a rough idea only for your Ascendant. It could be the sign before or the sign after the one you choose. To be truly sure, you would need to know your exact birth time and have a skilled astrologer or astrological company (see back of book) calculate your horoscope.

First read the shorthand description for the sign **your** Ascendant is in. Then, compare it with the shorthand description for the Ascendant sign of your partner. Next, read the paragraph which discusses how the two of you might interact with one another. Each combination is also designated as either very compatible, compatible, challenging or very challenging. (These rate as 4-3-2-1 on our **Compatibility Scale**.)

Look to your partner's Ascendant sign for clues to what he does instinctively, his initial reactions. Respect your partner's desire to do things **his** way where activities of the Ascendant are concerned. Encourage him to express the qualities of his Ascendant and he will feel that you truly understand and recognize his special nature.

ARIES ASCENDANT: "I am ME."

Early Identity: loner instincts, desire to be first, pioneering spirit
Instinctive Actions: movement, courage, self-expression, very direct
Personal Style: restless, spontaneous, impulsive, adventurous, good at beginning
Personally Call Shots: everything you do

TAURUS ASCENDANT: "I enjoy the physical, sensual and financial world."

Early Identity: earthy, comfortable, artistic, nature-loving, sensuous
Instinctive Actions: enjoy beauty, collect possessions, indulge appetites
Personal Style: sensible, stable, grounded, persistent, skilled with resources
Personally Call Shots: material resources, finances, art, sensual indulgence

GEMINI ASCENDANT: "I think, conceptualize and communicate."

Early Identity: mental, curious, interested in everything, restless, seeks variety
Instinctive Actions: thinking, talking, using hands, learning, gathering information
Personal Style: varied, restless, distractible, sociable, alert
Personally Call Shots: learning, teaching, thinking, speaking, reading, mental pursuits

CANCER ASCENDANT: "I care for and am cared for."

Early Identity: warm, caring, shy, inward, mother influence (pro or con) strong
Instinctive Actions: seek protection or take care of others, feel, safeguard
Personal Style: protective, intuitive, tenacious, family-focused
Personally Call Shots: emotional matters, within the nest, where security is involved

LEO ASCENDANT: "I draw excitement, drama and applause through my creative efforts."

Early Identity: energetic, exciting, childlike, zestful, enthusiastic
Instinctive Actions: seek limelight, gain attention or applause, love, praise
Personal Style: dramatic, magnetic, fun-loving, generous, larger than life
Personally Call Shots: creativity, love relationships, gambling, risk-taking

VIRGO ASCENDANT: "I function efficiently in my work and health."

Early Identity: retiring, helpful, modest, self-critical, practical
Instinctive Actions: to find flaws and fix them, to work, to criticize, to enhance
Personal Style: pragmatic, painstaking, detail-oriented, considerate
Personally Call Shots: work, health, and any form of improvement or repairs

LIBRA ASCENDANT: "I interact with others and seek balance."

Early Identity: feeling for beauty, design; desire to fit in with others
Instinctive Actions: to relate, react, join, confront, meet others; to balance
Personal Style: graceful, charming, diplomatic, in good taste
Personally Call Shots: partnerships, competition, aesthetic involvements

SCORPIO ASCENDANT: "I pursue a deeper understanding of myself and life."

Early Identity: secretive, relentless, hermit tendencies, determined, intense
Instinctive Actions: to probe beneath surface, to gain power, to rouse intense emotions
Personal Style: incisive, powerful, emotionally demanding, resourceful
Personally Call Shots: sex, money, self-understanding, appetite mastery

SAGITTARIUS ASCENDANT: "I seek constant expansion."

Early Identity: fun-loving, upbeat, peppy, self-confident, outgoing
Instinctive Actions: to travel, expand mind or ideals, have fun, enlarge world
Personal Style: overextended, optimistic, gregarious, independent, adventurous
Personally Call Shots: philosophy/religion, values, goals, beliefs

CAPRICORN ASCENDANT: "I work with what is possible in the world."

Early Identity: frustrated and blocked OR strong, dependable, achieving
Instinctive Actions: take responsibility, assess limitations, figure out rules
Personal Style: practical, responsible, formal, hardworking, dedicated
Personally Call Shots: profession, status matters, being an authority/expert

AQUARIUS ASCENDANT: "I am an individualist."

Early Identity: unique, equalitarian, independent, intellectual, tolerant
Instinctive Actions: break loose, open up, break free, shock people, change
Personal Style: unconventional, tolerant, futuristic, intellectual
Personally Call Shots: groups, friends, future trends, free self-expression

PISCES ASCENDANT: "I seek infinite love and beauty."

Early Identity: shy, mystical, mysterious, self-sacrificing, artistic, healing
Instinctive Actions: to dream, to rescue, to escape, to imagine, to visualize
Personal Style: grace in action; beauty in motion, intuitive, sensitive
Personally Call Shots: beauty, utopias, spiritual or idealistic pursuits

ASCENDANT PAIRS

ARIES/ARIES

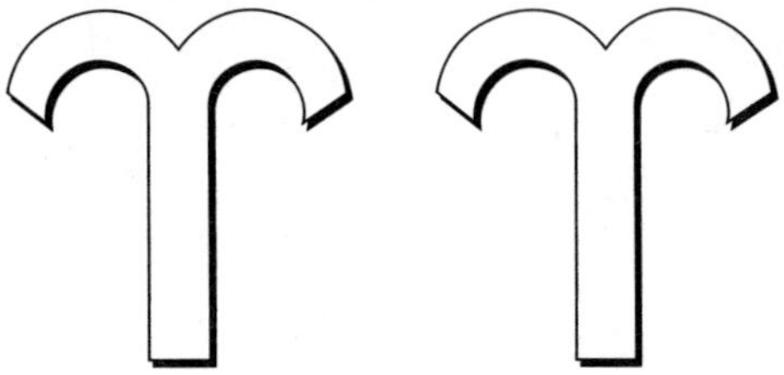

RAPID ROMANCE

Love (or lust) at first sight is a real possibility. Both of you tend to be direct, full-speed-ahead with no-holds-barred individuals. Sexual desire is a natural focus. Either of you can move quickly, so affairs may begin (and may end) rapidly. Each of you wants what you want and you want it now! Either of you can be impulsive and occasionally self-centered, but you can stir each other's blood and have lots of excitement together!

VERY COMPATIBLE—4

ARIES/TAURUS

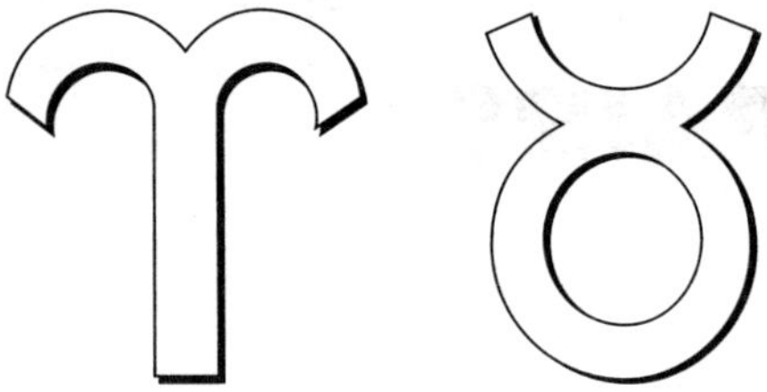

LIVELY OR LAID-BACK?

You tend to react quickly and spontaneously, while he is more cautious and deliberate. You're ready for action, but slow savoring is more his style. He may feel you are a bit impulsive or blunt, and you may feel he is somewhat stubborn or stuck-in-the-mud. You can bring fire and excitement into his life and he can bring stability and comfort into yours.

CHALLENGING—2

ARIES/GEMINI

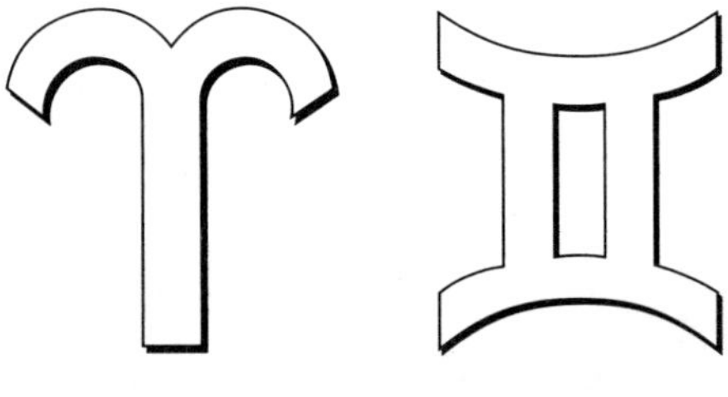

PLAYFUL PARTNERS

Both of you appreciate activity and variety. You probably feed each other's energy and sense of fun. You may be more fiery and emotional, while he is more casual and lighthearted. Play is something you both do well. You each have a fresh, youthful spirit. Activity and variety keep you both interested and involved. Stimulate each other's minds and bodies and all will be well.

COMPATIBLE—3

ARIES/CANCER

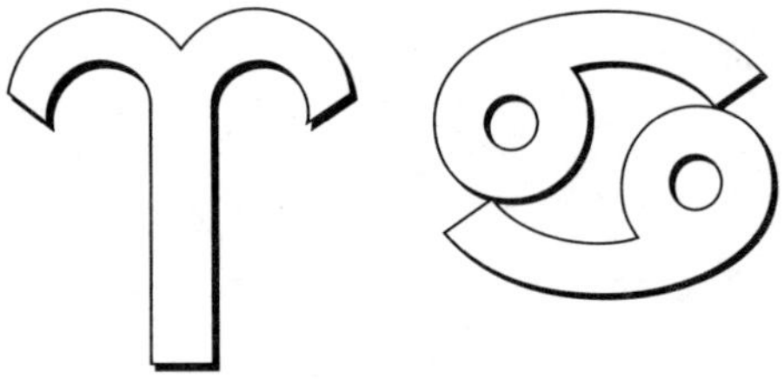

STEAMY SCENES

The two of you are mixing fire and water, so the resultant steam can be intense and warming—or abrupt and scalding. You may need to cultivate patience when he is too cautious or possessive. He may have to learn that you are a free soul who needs to maintain some independence within a relationship. With mutual tolerance, both the heat of passion and the light of understanding can be generated.

CHALLENGING—2

JOYFUL JOINING

ARIES/LEO

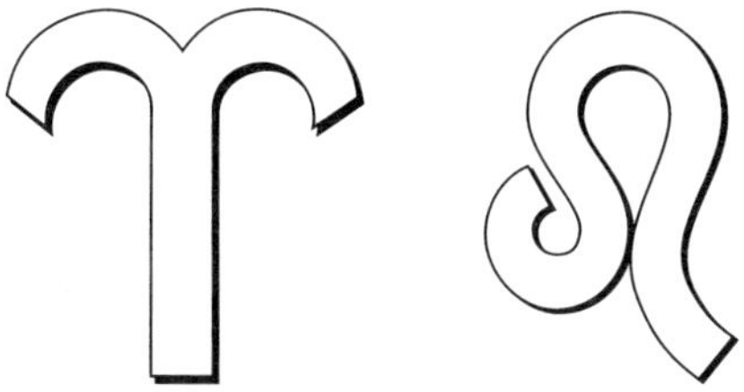

Both of you can be real balls of fire! You enjoy the thrill of pursuit and the rush of adrenaline. Each of you seeks excitement, passion and thrills. You may need more space than he does. He may need more attention and admiration than you. When sparks fly, tempers could flash, and stupendous scenes are possible. But you both usually forgive rapidly too. Each of you is capable of great emotional response and can build a relationship full of joy, verve and liveliness.

COMPATIBLE—3

DIRECT OR DISCREET?

ARIES/VIRGO

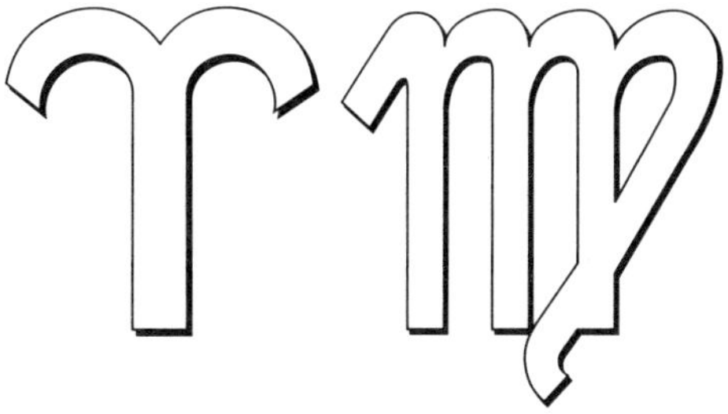

Personal styles will vary here. You can react quickly, perhaps even rushing into love. He tends to mull things over, pick at them, and analyze the flaws before doing something. Your passionate style is more spontaneous; he may fall into criticism or excessive analysis. Stimulate his mind in order to stimulate his body. You can teach him the joys of direct, courageous action, and he can teach you the value of discretion.

VERY CHALLENGING—1

TEMPTING TEAMWORK

ARIES/LIBRA

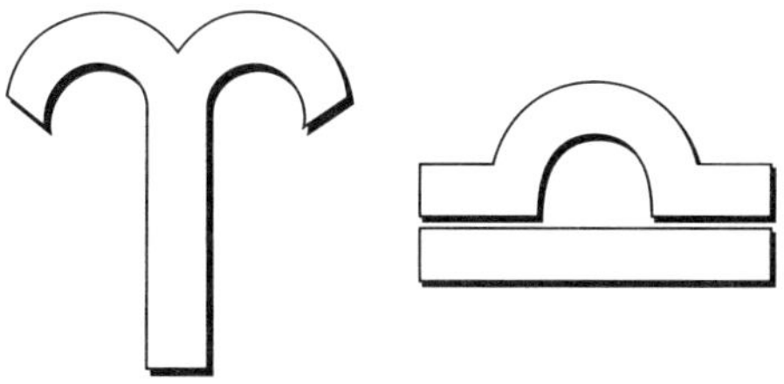

You two make a polarity package and opposites often attract. You can bring enthusiasm and passion to the relationship, while he brings tact and sympathy. You're eager to be swept away, and he responds well to your excitement. You may need a bit more independence, and he may need more ease (no arguments). However, the two of you make a natural team.

VERY COMPATIBLE—4

POWERFUL PASSIONS

ARIES/SCORPIO

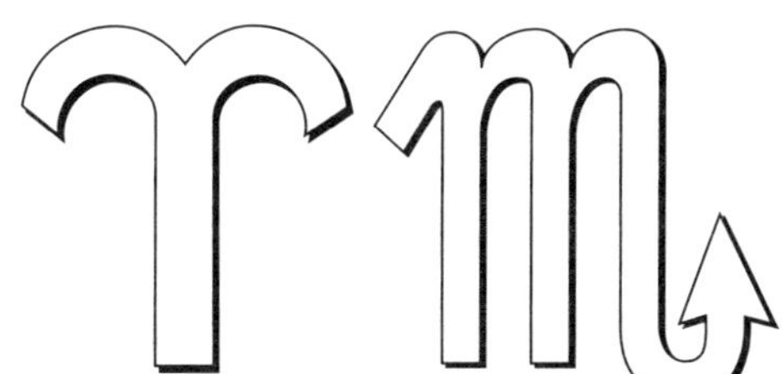

Passion, sex and intense emotions are likely on both sides. Because you are both strong personalities, the compromises of a relationship may prove challenging. You could blow hot and cold with one another—ready to go all out one moment and withdrawing totally the next. If you respect each other and get your timetables in sync, this can be a very powerful bond.

VERY CHALLENGING—1

ARIES/SAGITTARIUS

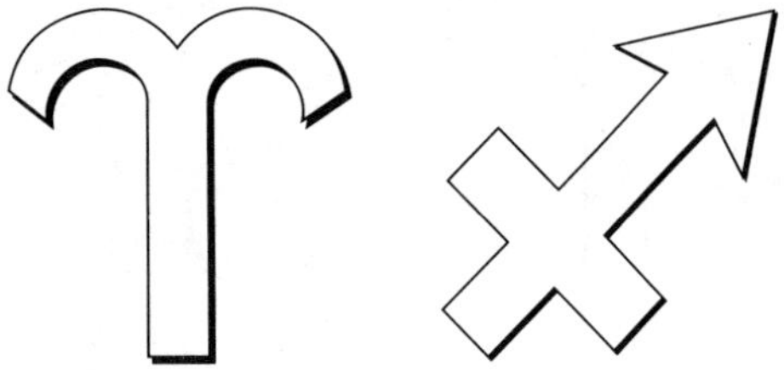

AMOROUS ADVENTURES

Adventure beckons to you both! High energy types, you can have lots of fun together. Each of you needs a good measure of freedom, so don't try to be a "do everything together" couple. You just naturally stir each other up. Your relationship can be full of thrills, fun, games and action. Seek out activities which help you feel excited and alive; you both thrive on it!

COMPATIBLE—3

ARIES/CAPRICORN

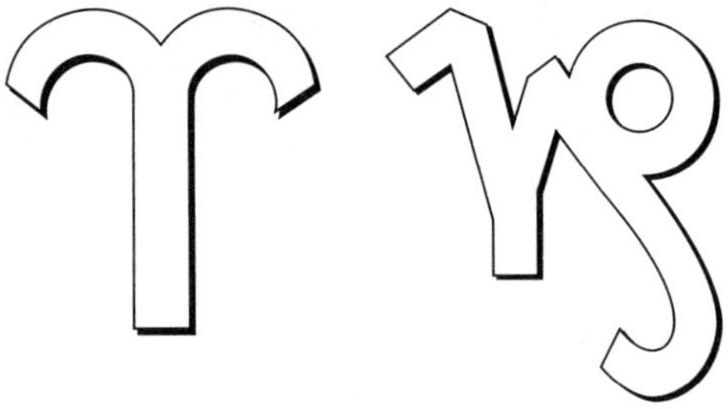

SPARKLING STEADILY

Your styles may clash at first. You want action, excitement, courage and fun. He wants stability, responsibility, and a slow, gradual growth of love. You go all out. He waits, is cautious and needs to plan things. You may seem impulsive to him. He may seem pessimistic or controlling to you. With compromise, you can bring more sparkle into his life, and he can bring more steadiness into yours.

CHALLENGING—2

ARIES/AQUARIUS

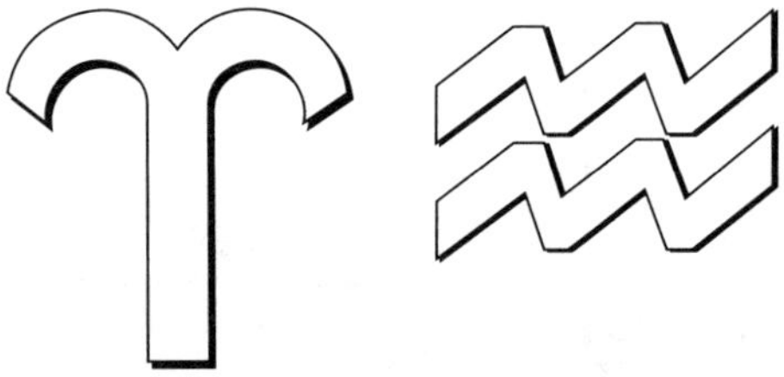

EAGER EXPERIMENTERS

Freedom is a watchword for you both. Commitment can occur, but no leashes and no possessiveness allowed! You may encourage each other's venturesome spirits and expose yourselves to a wide variety of experiences. Eager and experimental, either of you might proclaim: "I'll try anything once." You can bring him back to a personal level if he gets lost theorizing and thinking about the big picture. He can help tone down your immediate, impulsive urges with some objectivity and detachment. Both of you are individualists and willing to tread a new or unconventional path.

COMPATIBLE—3

ARIES/PISCES

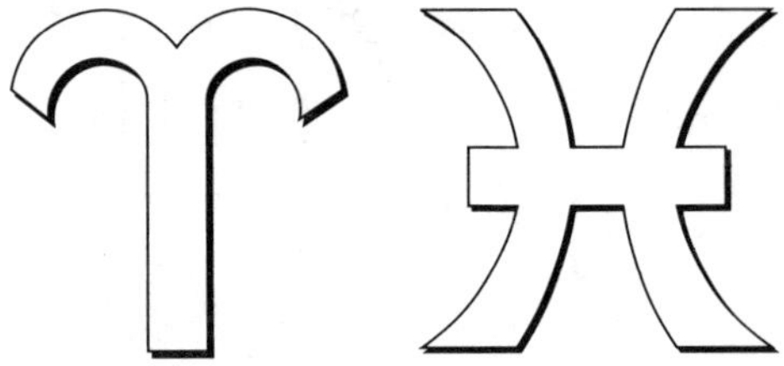

IMPULSIVE IMAGINATION

A strong difference in personal styles is implied. You go after what (or who) you want openly, directly and eagerly. You can move swiftly into action. He mulls things over, keeps feelings hidden inside and may seem confused or overly idealistic at times. You can encourage action and a straightforward focus within him. He can encourage more imagination and sensitivity in you.

CHALLENGING—2

STEADY SURPRISES

TAURUS/ARIES

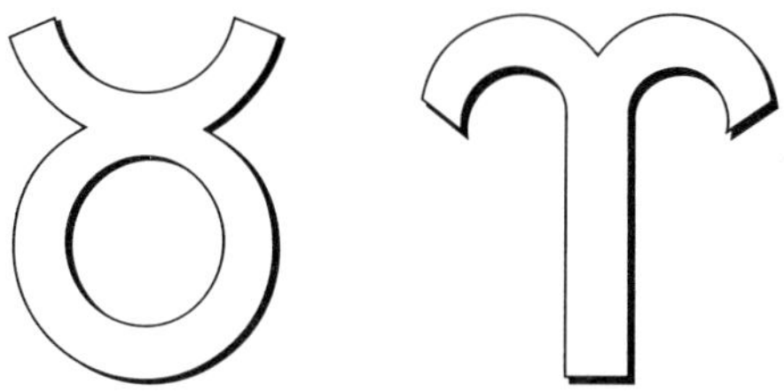

You may be more sensual, while he is more sexual. He tends to react quickly, while you'd rather take your time. He wants flash, dash and excitement. You want stability, security and safety. His style features immediacy, courage and direct action. Your style features pleasure, comfort and sweetness. If you join forces, you can have the confidence to begin and the perseverance to carry on in life and love.

CHALLENGING—2

DUAL DEPENDABILITY

TAURUS/TAURUS

Both of you appreciate love, pleasure and the physical senses. You may enjoy sharing fine meals, a hot tub or a lovely massage. You may both indulge the other or be a bit stubborn or possessive. You might both value beauty and/or material security. Dependable, you also each want a partner who will be there when needed. Accepting and affectionate, you can be very comfortable just being together.

VERY COMPATIBLE—4

FAMILIAR FLIRTATIONS

TAURUS/GEMINI

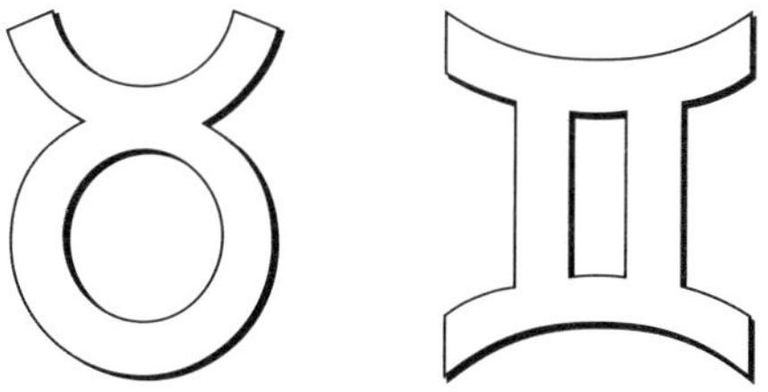

Your style is more even, regular and stable, while his is changeable and restless. You know what you enjoy and you like to indulge over and over with familiar pleasures. He appreciates variety, so is more willing to experiment. You may be ready for commitment before he is. Gemini can be like a butterfly, rarely stopping in one spot for long. He can bring new experiences into your life and you may be more lighthearted and casual around him. You can help him develop more follow-through and patience.

CHALLENGING—2

CUDDLING COUPLE

TAURUS/CANCER

Together, you can create a veritable feast for your senses. You two are the most "touchy feely" of the signs (although the placements of the Moon and Venus are also important), so hugs, caresses, hand-holding and massage can help you make a deep connection. You may both value fine food, wine or lovely possessions. You are likely to become attached to things and may find it difficult to throw them away. Commitment appeals to each of you and loyalty is central.

COMPATIBLE—3

TAURUS/LEO

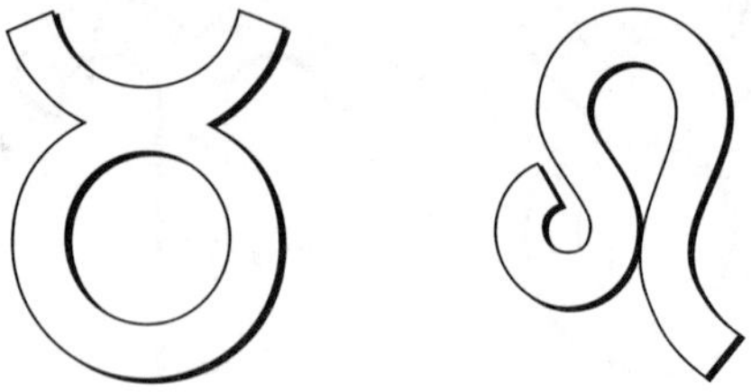

POWER PLAY

You each have a strong core of willpower, so any attempts to rule the other will degenerate into power struggles. Your approaches to finances may differ widely; compromise is called for. Consider having "mine, his, and ours" in terms of bank accounts. You can bring loyalty, steadiness and affection into his life, while he adds drama, excitement and a fun-loving spirit to yours.

CHALLENGING—2

TAURUS/VIRGO

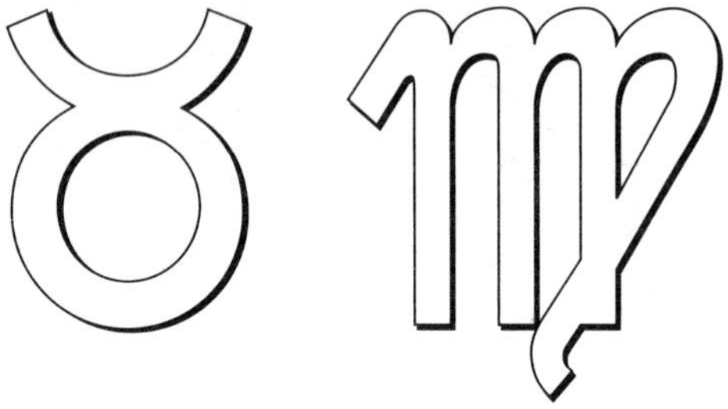

PRACTICAL PARTNERS

You both tend to be practical with good common sense. What you do (and what your partner does) matter more than pretty phrases. You appreciate results and dependability. He might be a bit critical or picky in relationships, but is usually helpful and a good worker. You can be a bit stubborn, but are very loyal and affectionate. You can bring more sensuality into his life, and he can bring more organization into yours.

COMPATIBLE—3

TAURUS/LIBRA

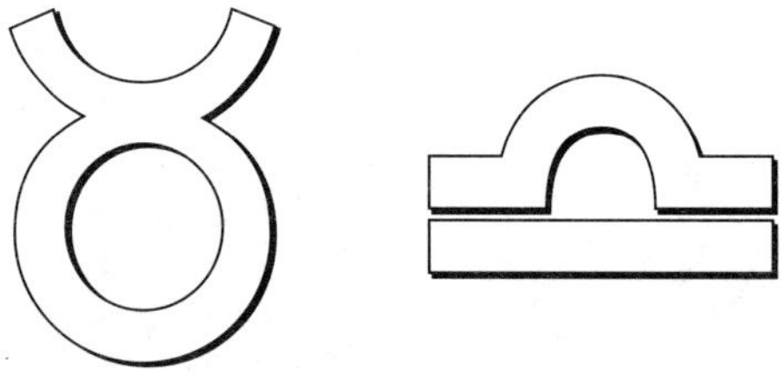

LOVELY LOVING

You both appreciate pleasure and beauty. You, however, know your own mind and can be very set on your course. He tends to be more reactive and may appear to vacillate—responding to others rather than choosing for himself. You both can be quite affectionate and loving. He needs to understand your desire for material security and sensual indulgence. You have to understand that he needs to bounce ideas and conversation back and forth with other people.

VERY CHALLENGING—1

TAURUS/SCORPIO

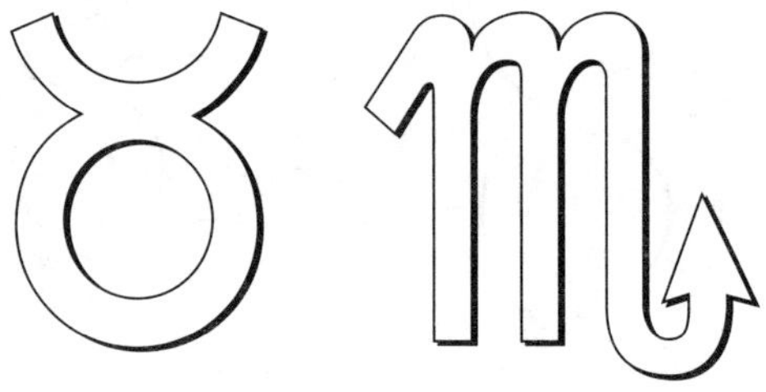

SATISFYING SENSUALITY

You both are very strong-willed and can be quite possessive and stubborn. Respecting each other's boundaries will be vital. The two of you are working on balancing self-indulgence and self-mastery. Since opposites attract, you could easily polarize around finances, possessions or pleasures. One could nag the other about weight or smoking or drinking or spending money. If you each control yourselves, you won't need to try to control your partner. Then, you can be incredibly loyal, deeply sensual, and satisfyingly intimate with one another.

VERY COMPATIBLE—4

SAFETY VS. SPECULATION

TAURUS/SAGITTARIUS

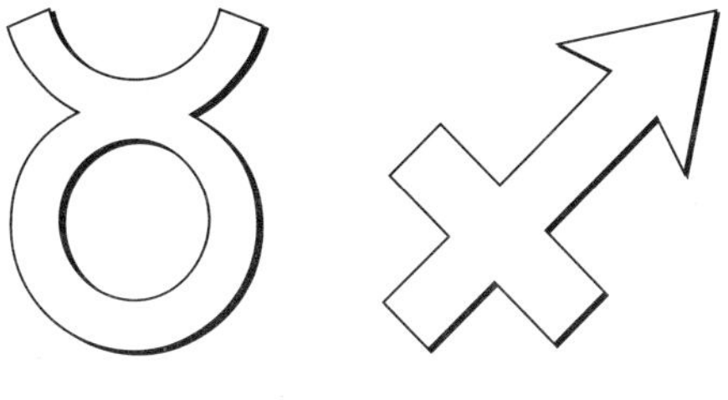

The two of you have some major differences. You want more stability and commitment, while he wants more adventure and freedom. You prefer to focus on tangibles and money in the bank, while he is willing to take a chance, a flyer, to speculate or gamble. You are dependable and he tends to try to do too much, so he may promise more than he can deliver. If you are tolerant and open to one another, he broadens your horizons and you help him settle down a bit.

VERY CHALLENGING—1

COMMITTED COUPLE

TAURUS/CAPRICORN

Both of you tend to be practical, grounded people. In relationships, you each are willing to **do** things for your partner (and can expect the same in return). You might even work together (in an actual career or just enjoying shared tasks or joint pleasures). You can help him relax and be more sensual. He can help you focus and be more organized. Both of you are capable of great loyalty and prefer a definite commitment.

COMPATIBLE—3

MATTER OVER MIND?

TAURUS/AQUARIUS

Although you two can have a clash of wills, you could learn much from one another. You are apt to seek stability, while he is attracted to change and freedom. You may be more physical and grounded, while he is more intellectualized and detached. He can help you develop more objectivity and appreciation of the new. You can help him "come down to earth" and melt any airy detachment with your sensual expertise.

CHALLENGING—2

ARTISTIC ARDOR?

TAURUS/PISCES

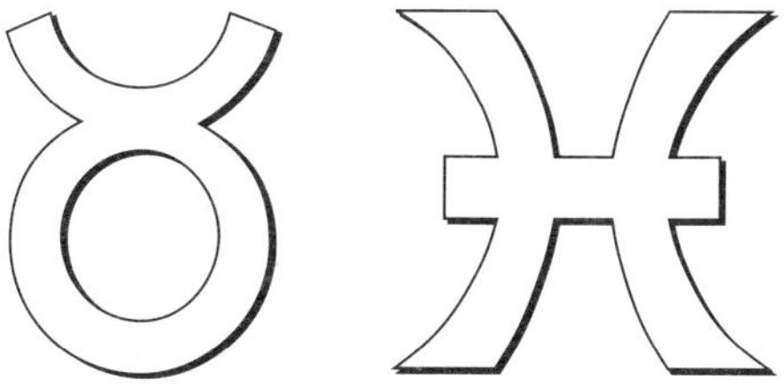

You are likely to feed each other's appreciation of beauty, pleasure and ease. An artistic bond is possible. You are apt to be more practical and grounded in the "real" world, while he is more idealistic (and may "space out" at times). You can help him connect physically and sensually, and he can add some mystery, magic and romance to your life.

COMPATIBLE—3

GEMINI/ARIES

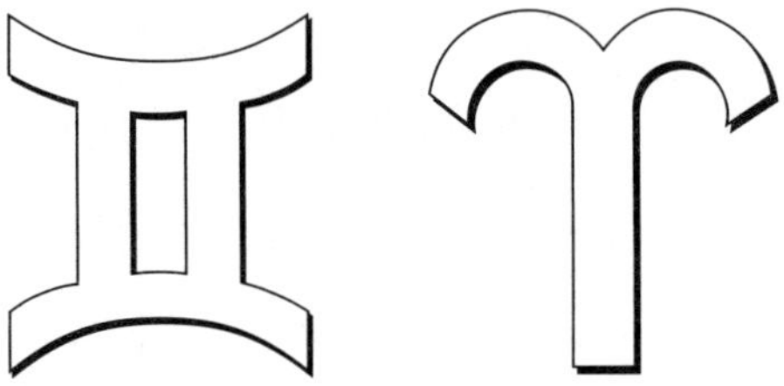

KINDRED KIDS

Energy, variety, movement and restlessness are highlighted. Both of you know how to laugh and play. He may be more assertive, courageous or impulsive, while you emphasize communicating, thinking it over and looking at a situation from several points of view. You both have a youthful spirit that enjoys life and constantly seeks fresh, new experiences.

COMPATIBLE—3

GEMINI/TAURUS

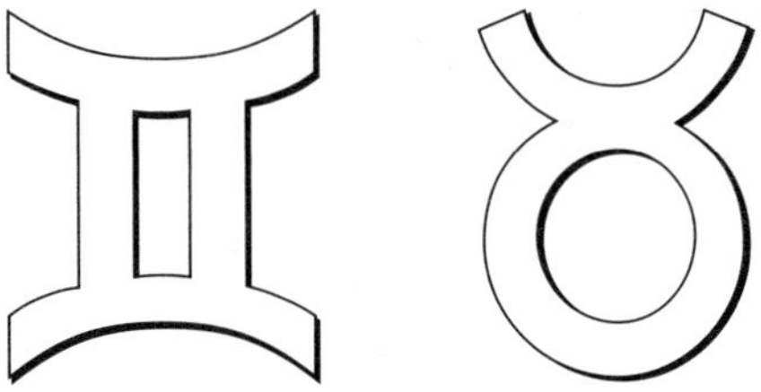

LIGHT OR LASTING?

You can flit from topic to topic or person to person, while he is as solid as a rock. You prefer variety; he seeks the known and familiar. You emphasize talking (discussing); he emphasizes being and enjoying (without words). You can help him lighten up and laugh more. He can help you accept more security and appreciate dependability.

CHALLENGING—2

GEMINI/GEMINI

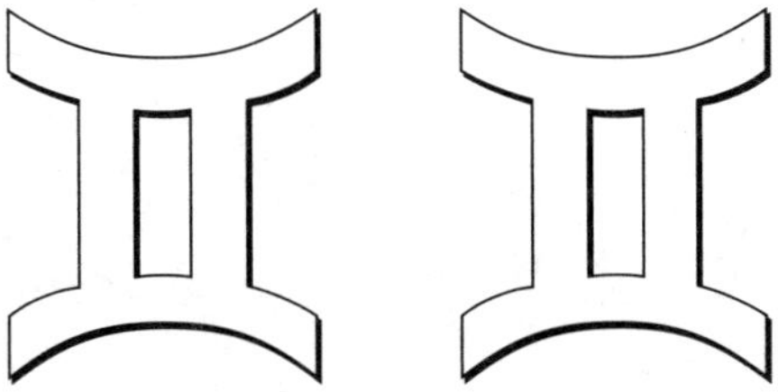

LOVE OF LEARNING

Communication reigns supreme! The two of you know that if you can talk it over, you can work it out. Learning is a way of life for you both. Quick, alert, perceptive, bright, you appreciate a partner who stimulates your mind. (You may fall in love mentally before physically.) You both may also flirt, but understand that it is just a game. You are fellow comrades (buddies) in life. You enjoy fun, games, conversation and learning more together.

VERY COMPATIBLE—4

GEMINI/CANCER

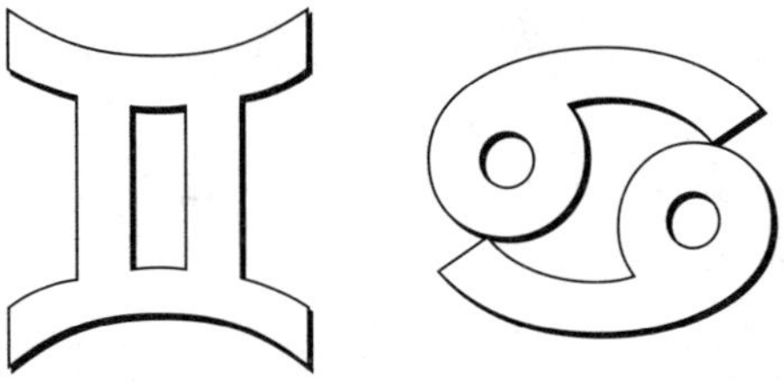

MIND YOUR MOODS

You may be mental when he's emotional. You're looking for space, variety and fun when he's feeling possessive or insecure. You'll discuss anything and everything, and he clams up on a moment's notice. You can remain frustrated with each other's styles of being or learn to appreciate a different approach. He can add depth and empathy to your observations, and you can add lightness and a bit of detachment to his moods and emotional storms.

CHALLENGING—2

LOVE AND LAUGHTER

GEMINI/LEO

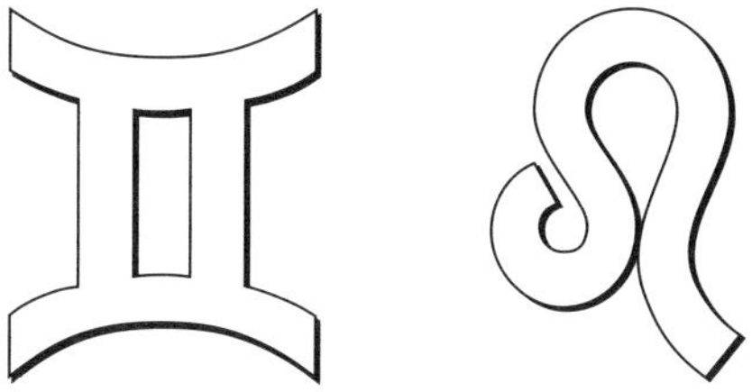

Frivolity is something you can agree upon! Laughter, sociability and fun with friends appeal to both of you. He has a bit of that "lordly air" wanting to be king, but you can probably tease him out of it if he slips from dramatic and generous toward arrogant and pompous. You relate to a **lot** of people, which may sometimes hurt his ego, but he also takes pride in showing you off. A playful spirit is your best gift to each other.

COMPATIBLE—3

QUANTITY VS. QUALITY

GEMINI/VIRGO

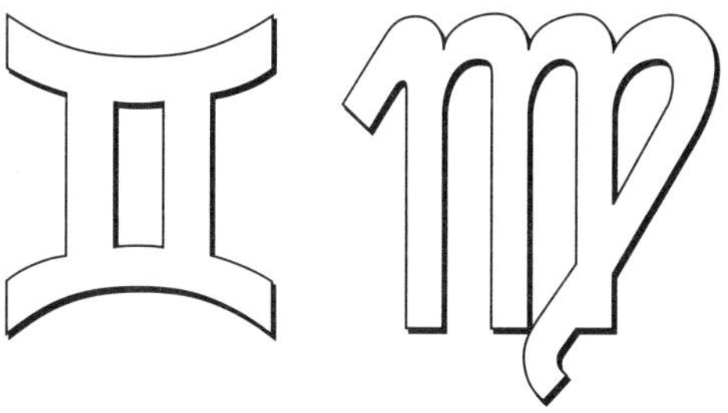

Communication comes instinctively to you both. So, naturally, you might sometimes talk an issue to death. You can be more casual (even flippant), while he can be more serious (and sometimes critical). A love of learning links you both. Sharing ideas, teaching, taking classes, disseminating information, or any kind of constructive communication deepens the connections between you. Your focus is quantity (learning about everything) and his is quality (focusing and doing it completely), but you can each add to the other's fund of knowledge and information.

CHALLENGING—2

CLEAR COMMUNICATORS

GEMINI/LIBRA

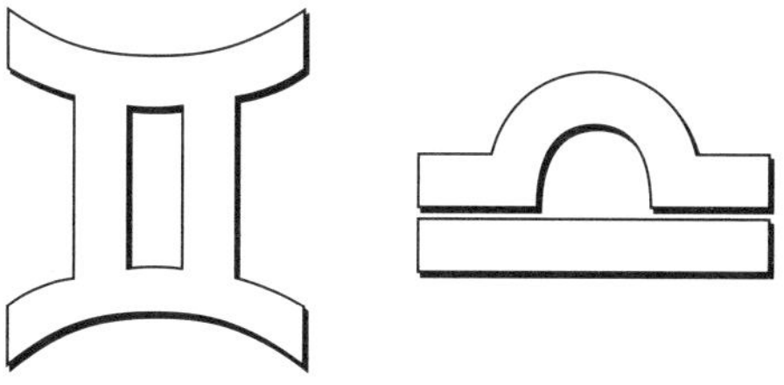

Each of you is instinctively equalitarian, so you're off to a good start in building a relationship. You both value communication and probably strive to be open and clear with one another. He may want more affection or one-on-one than you're used to giving. You may want more social variety (even the occasional flirtation). As long as you talk with and understand each other, the relationship will flourish.

COMPATIBLE—3

RESTLESS OR RELENTLESS?

GEMINI/SCORPIO

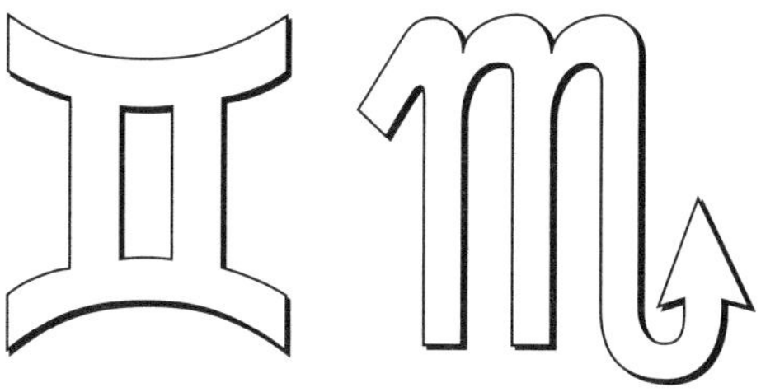

Your approaches are different enough that a meeting of the minds is challenging. You're open and communicative (perhaps **too** talkative in his eyes). He is intense, inward and can be secretive. You're lighthearted and like to laugh. His emotions are deep, strong and sometimes overwhelming. You are sociable and like a variety of people. His focus is narrow (and he could be jealous or possessive). If you learn from one another, you can teach him to lighten up and he can expose you to incredible, passionate depths.

VERY CHALLENGING—1

GEMINI/SAGITTARIUS

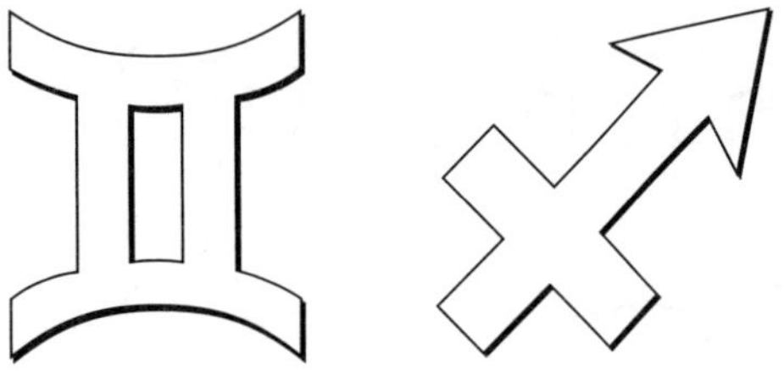

MENTAL MASTERS

There may be a natural attraction between you. A shared love of variety, mental stimulation, communication and new experiences is likely. The two of you may trade back and forth between the roles of wise professor and wide-eyed student. You probably encourage each other to learn, to travel, and to expand your horizons. Humor could be an important bond between you.

VERY COMPATIBLE—4

GEMINI/CAPRICORN

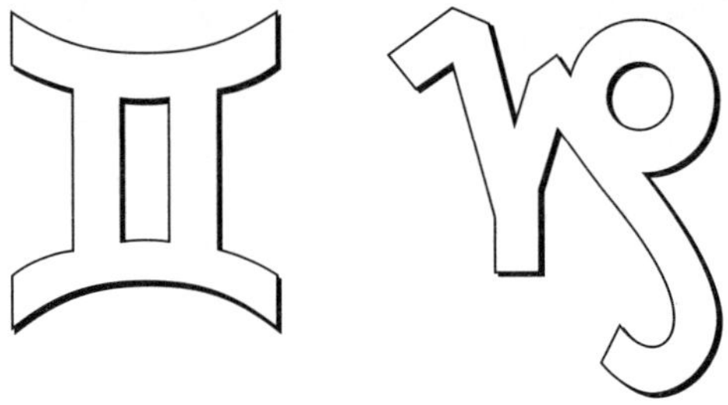

FLIPPANT OR FOCUSED?

Different approaches challenge you both to make a strong connection. You are quick, perceptive, restless and communicative. He is cautious, responsible, stable and more reticent. You can be quite flip, and he can be deadly serious. You are people-oriented. He is work- or power-oriented. If you are tolerant and willing to grow with one another, you can help him lighten up and he can help you carry things through (finish up).

VERY CHALLENGING—1

GEMINI/AQUARIUS

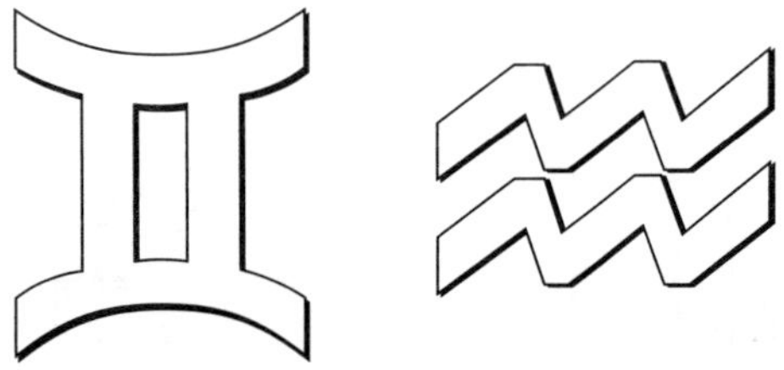

FRIENDS AND LOVERS

You both can be quite curious, observant, sociable and objective. Mental and communicative skills are likely. This placement emphasizes the mind more than the emotions. Either of you could rationalize feelings away or "shine them on." Naturally friendly, the two of you find it easy to share. Equalitarian, you both want a relationship that is a true partnership.

COMPATIBLE—3

GEMINI/PISCES

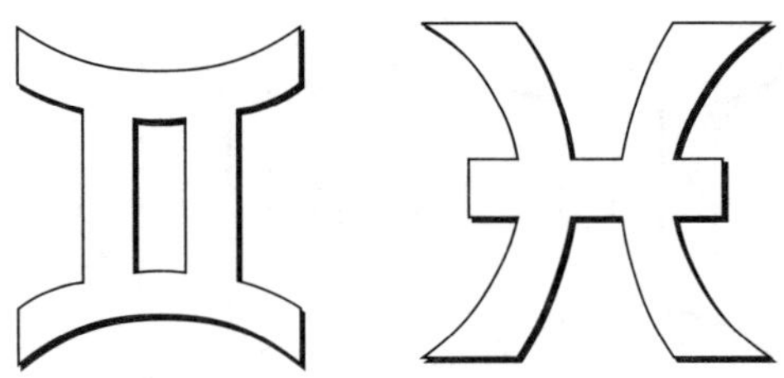

ROMANTIC RADAR

You can both be restless and like sponges that pick up on or react to everything going on around you. Your style is to discuss everything; talking helps you to understand. His style is to absorb impressions and mull them over inside. You can both succumb to "information overload." He may be more romantic or idealistic than you. You can be more objective and lighthearted than he. Both of you could be multitalented with lots to learn, give and share with one another.

CHALLENGING—2

HOT AND HEAVY

CANCER/ARIES

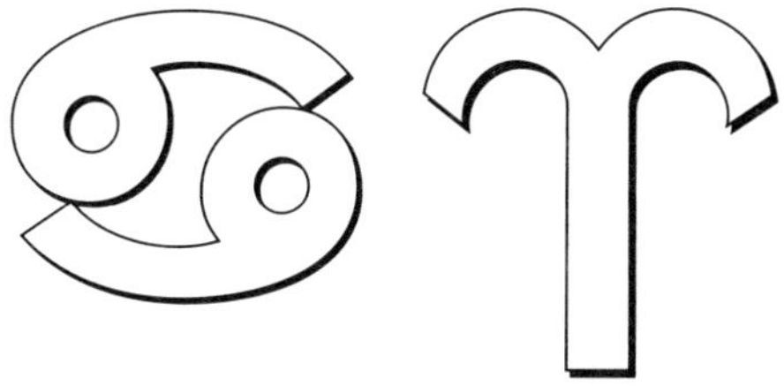

The two of you may be a really "hot" number. Your water and his fire make steam—warming and intense or volatile and scalding. He will probably want more space than you, and you may need more reassurance and emotional support than he. If you are mutually tolerant, you can build both passion and understanding. He can encourage you to take more chances and you can encourage him to build lasting emotional commitments.

CHALLENGING—2

CUDDLY COUPLE

CANCER/TAURUS

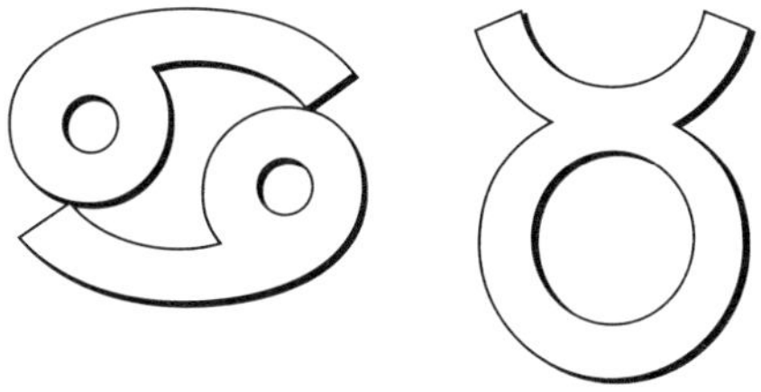

Indulge each other! Natural sensualists, both of you can enjoy good food, soft carpets, soothing massages, a jacuzzi or myriad forms of physical gratification. Hugs, loving touches, hand-holding and any affectionate contact help you to build your connection. You may share a love of beauty, comfort, possessions or security. You are both willing to commit yourselves to love.

COMPATIBLE—3

MIND YOUR MOODS

CANCER/GEMINI

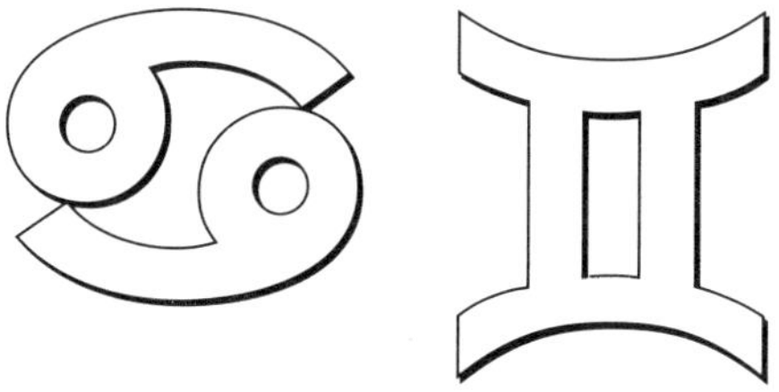

You may be more sensitive and emotional, while he's more mental or detached. You like to settle in and put down roots, while he may flit from flower to flower. If he likes to flirt, it could arouse your insecurities. You may need to cater to his yen for new experiences, and he may need to learn to give you more reassurance, emotional support and commitment. You can bring more depth and understanding of emotional matters to his perceptions, and he can help you detach from moodiness and lighten up a bit.

CHALLENGING—2

SENTIMENTAL SWEETHEARTS

CANCER/CANCER

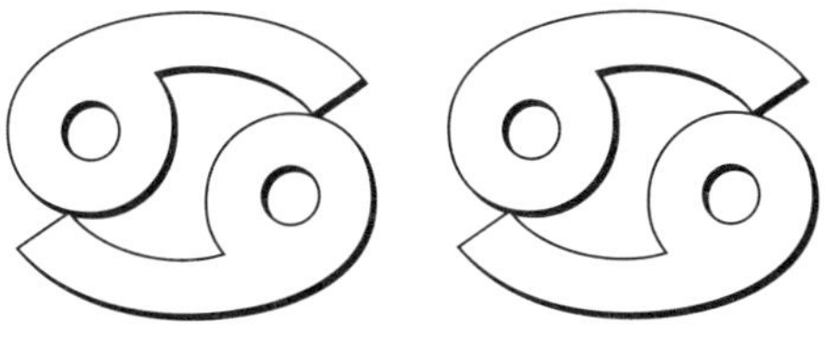

You both understand the meaning of commitment. Family ties could have been quite influential in each of your lives. You both have a nurturing streak which sometimes might mean you carry more than your fair share of any emotional burdens in a relationship. The two of you may enjoy food a great deal, love pets, be attached to plants, or have sentimental possessions you just cannot bear to part with. Sensitive and caring, each of you can be quite supportive in a relationship. You are likely to find it easy to tune into each other's moods.

VERY COMPATIBLE—4

CANCER/LEO

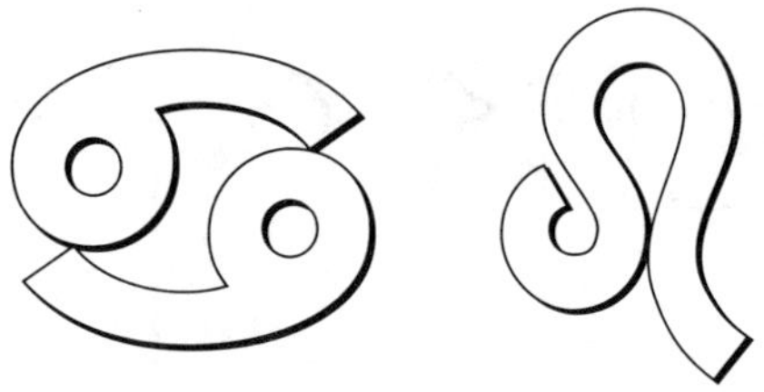

WARM WOOERS

This combination can indicate a very warm, caring couple. Cancer is nurturing and emotionally supportive, while Leo is passionate and eager to love and be loved. Both of you may appreciate family and value the loyalty of your mate a great deal. Each of you tends to be emotional, although you can be shy, sensitive and inward, while he thrives on limelight, attention and admiration. When you truly connect, there is a depth of feeling few couples can match.

CHALLENGING—2

CANCER/VIRGO

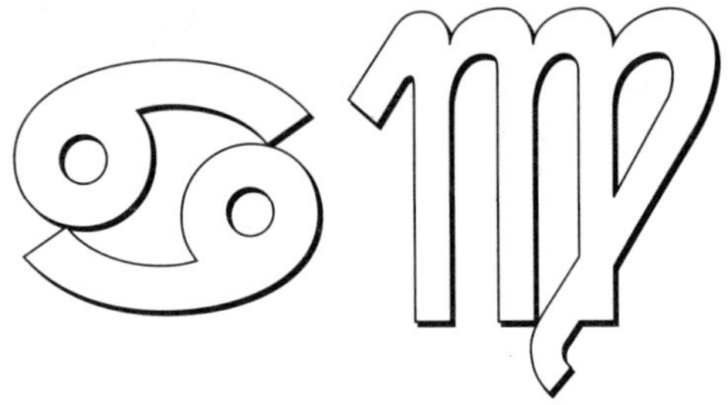

SUPPORTIVE SWEETHEARTS

Fulfilling your commitments is important to each of you. He may be a bit more work-oriented or practical, while you are more focused on emotional matters. He can be critical on occasion and may have to learn to take care as you can be quite sensitive. You may be more focused on domestic issues, but he values efficiency, so he can learn to share your concerns. Either of you may worry a bit too much, but he is ready to fix any practical or physical flaws, and you're eager to heal any emotional wounds. Mutual support and some division of labor can work well between you.

COMPATIBLE—3

CANCER/LIBRA

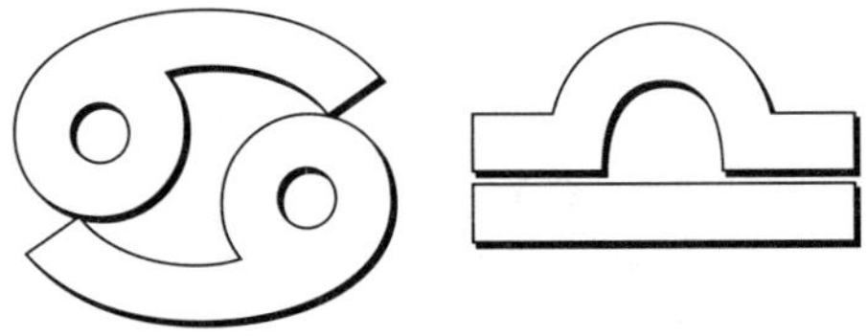

TOO CLOSE FOR COMFORT?

Each of you values emotional closeness, but your styles may differ. You tend to operate gently and subtly and don't reveal all your feelings. He tends to discuss matters and may adopt both sides of an argument to "try them on for size." He may enjoy competition on occasion, while you prefer a sense of safety and reassurance. You need some time alone, while he prefers having another person around to bat ideas back and forth. When you both focus on love, caring and commitment, your commonalities become more obvious.

CHALLENGING—2

CANCER/SCORPIO

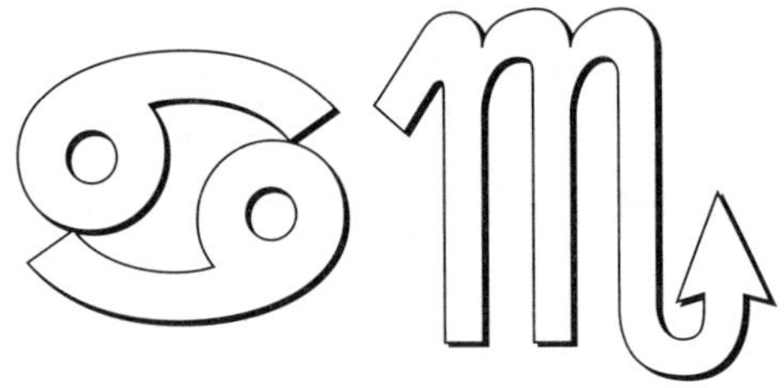

TOTAL TOGETHERNESS

You are both capable of an intense emotional commitment. When you give yourselves, it is heart and soul. Each of you is quite sensitive, so you are more apt to tread softly near your partner's tender areas. If threatened or feeling insecure, either of you may withdraw (even sulk). Or, either of you could succumb to jealousy or possessiveness when feeling down. On its best level, this can be a relationship with someone who connects bone-deep, with whom you can share all the corners of your psyche.

COMPATIBLE—3

CAUTIOUS OR CAREFREE?

CANCER/SAGITTARIUS

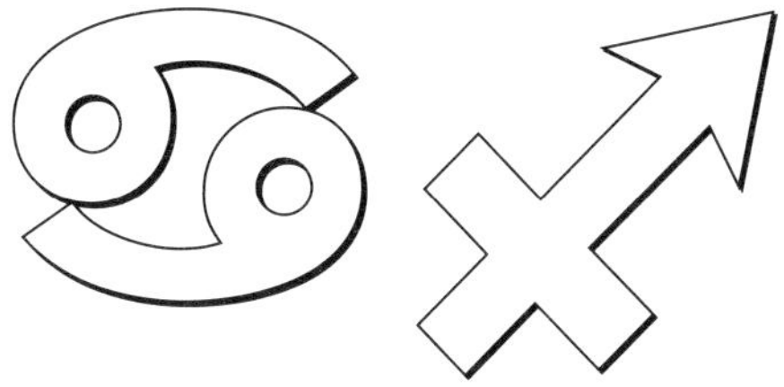

Although attraction is quite possible, compromise is vital if you are to live together. Your style is more emotional, sensitive, cautious or home-centered. His style is more brash, extroverted and ready to wander to the ends of the Earth. You may see him as incapable of commitment (strong freedom needs) and he may see you as a clinging vine. If both of you are tolerant, he can broaden your horizons and you can increase his sensitivity to emotional concerns.

VERY CHALLENGING—1

PARENTAL PARTNERS

CANCER/CAPRICORN

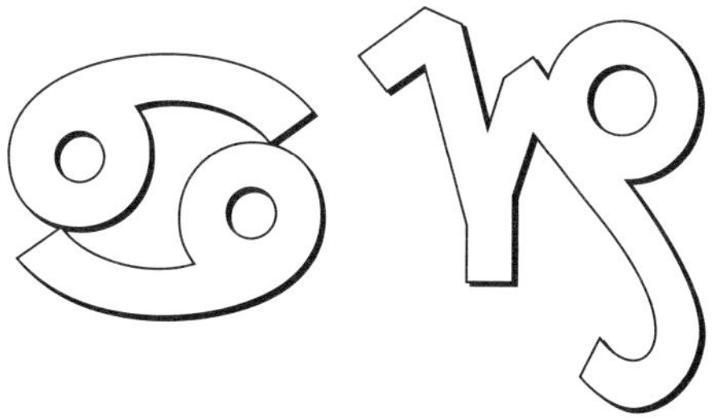

Loyalty and commitment are probably important to both of you. Each of you looks for security, wanting to create something lasting. You both can be somewhat parental in your styles—you warm and nurturing, he solid and responsible. Sometimes old feelings either of you has about Mom or Dad slip in and affect the current relationship. If you share concerns (home and career) and tasks (emotional and physical) rather than polarizing and feeling like opposites, you can definitely build for the long haul.

VERY COMPATIBLE—4

COMPROMISING COUPLE

CANCER/AQUARIUS

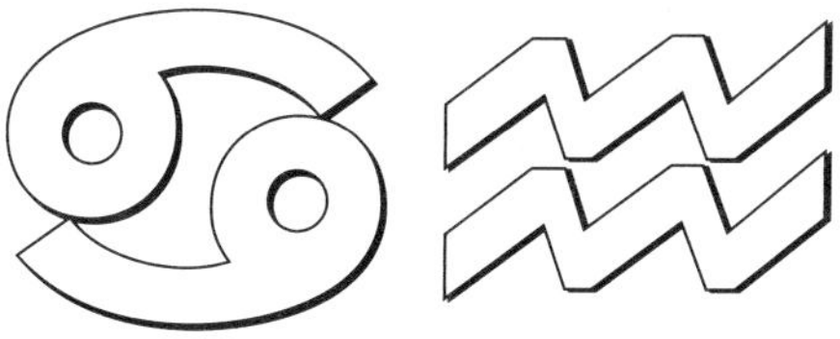

Your needs may be quite different, so compromise will be essential. You yearn for the home fires, emotional commitment and a secure base. He thrives on innovation, stimulation from the outer world, variety and personal freedom. You may value family while he values social causes, intellectual stimulation or being with friends. By loving without possessiveness, you can share a feeling connection **and** interesting experiences in the wider world.

VERY CHALLENGING—1

SENSITIVE SWEETHEARTS

CANCER/PISCES

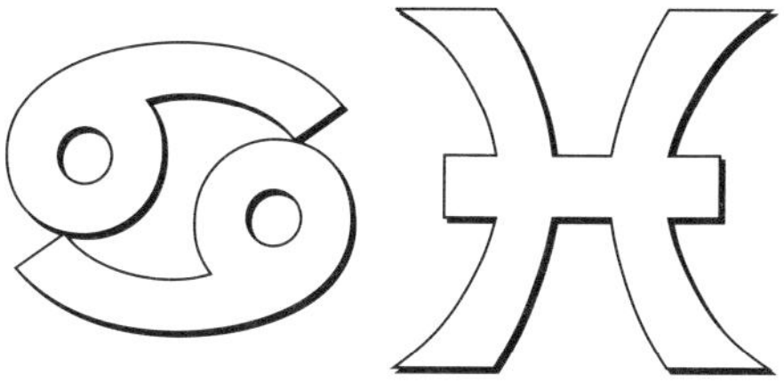

Your personal styles are very compatible as each of you is far more sensitive than the average person. You both can be shy and tend to withdraw or clam up when hurt. You may both need to learn to speak up and discuss things on occasion. Because you each can be intuitive, you may tune into each other often without words. Practicalities are not a favored subject with either of you, so you might be tempted to retreat into your own, private, little world. You can both be very kind and empathic.

COMPATIBLE—3

LEO/ARIES

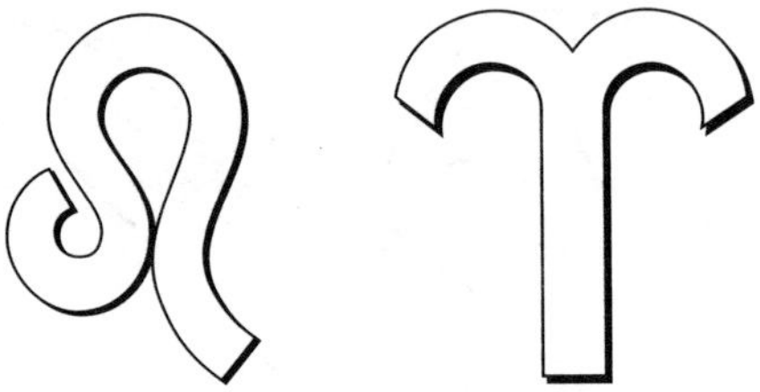

JOYFUL JOINING

The flames of passion may burn very brightly between you. Each of you enjoys the rush of adrenaline and the challenge of pursuit. Together, excitement and thrills rate high on your list of experiences to seek. He may need more space and independence (occasionally the loner) than you. You may need more attention, admiration and applause than he. Either of you could spark the quick trigger of the other's temper. Yet you can also bring much joy, love, vitality and **fun** to one another.

COMPATIBLE—3

LEO/TAURUS

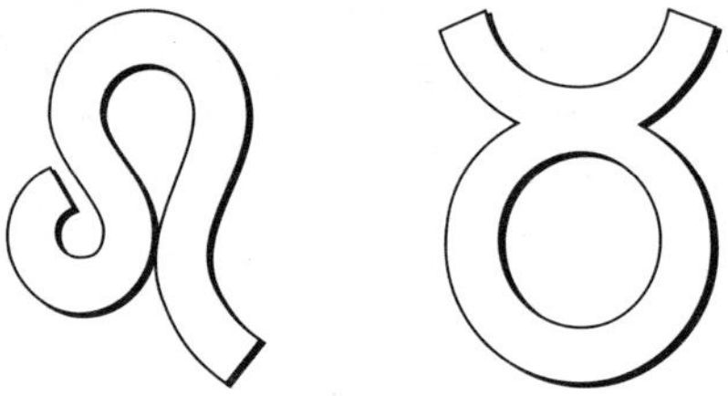

POWER PLAY

No wimps here! Each of you has incredible willpower. Attempts by either of you to play lord or lady of the manor and hold sway over the other are doomed to failure. Compromise is vital. Trying to push each other around or pressuring and persuading just encourages stubborn resistance. Your financial habits may vary widely; be tolerant. You both are capable of great loyalty and tremendous pleasure in sensual and sexual arenas.

CHALLENGING—2

LEO/GEMINI

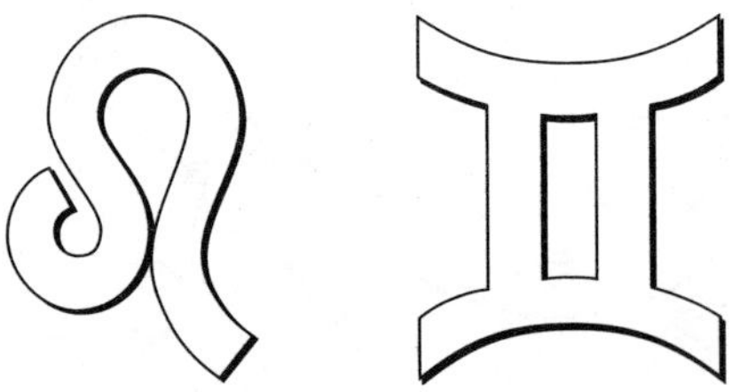

LOVE AND LAUGHTER

Love and laughter are key ingredients for you both. Sociable and fun-loving activities with friends and lots of recreation help sustain your relationship. You may be more dramatic and expressive while he is more casual and detached, but you share a youthful attitude which can enjoy almost anything. You may bring more excitement into his life, while he widens your circle of acquaintances or contributes many fascinating tidbits of information.

COMPATIBLE—3

LEO/CANCER

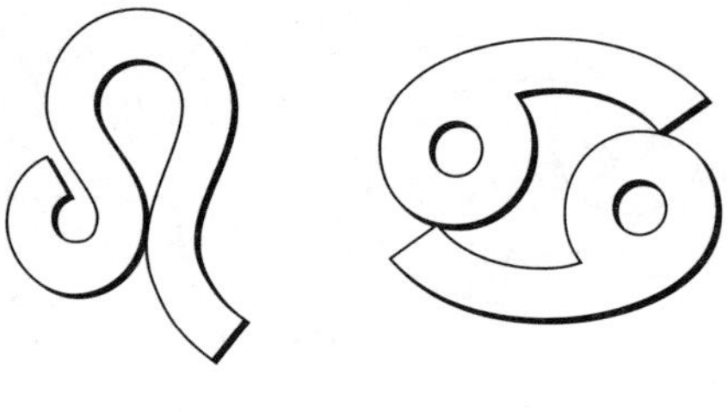

WARM WOOERS

This combination is potentially one of the warmest, most loving possible. You are eager to love, to share your appreciation of one another. You can be a wonderful cheerleader (encourager) of your partner. He may value family, emotional closeness, roots or security. Children might be important to you both. You are probably more expressive; he may keep a lot inside, not discussing it. Each of you can be intensely loyal, taking real joy in sharing.

CHALLENGING—2

A NATURAL HIGH

LEO/LEO

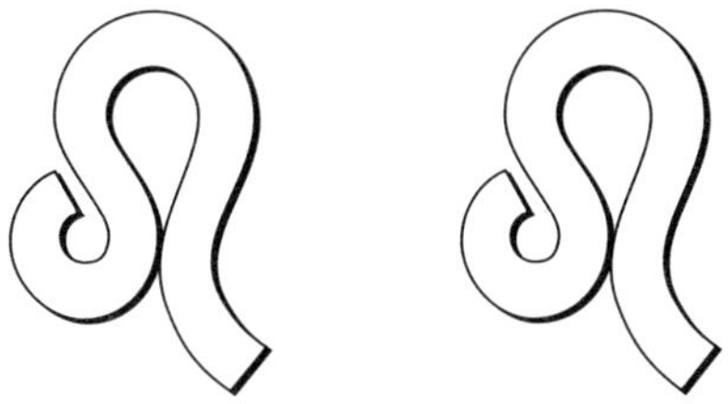

The natural generosity, dramatic flair, creativity, passion and urge to love may be doubled with the two of you. Sex appeal is likely on both sides. Leos make great trainers and motivators so you can be each other's best fans—encouraging, admiring and applauding one another's efforts. Ego clashes are possible if you compete for center stage. It is vital for each of you to have an area to shine—to be the king or queen. If you take turns being the main attraction, you can share much passion, joy, excitement and love.

VERY COMPATIBLE—4

EXCITING OR EXACTING?

LEO/VIRGO

Your personal styles may be very different. You tend to have natural flair with dramatic instincts that ensure people notice when you walk into a room. He tends to be reserved, perhaps even inhibited. You learned young how to play, to enjoy life; he learned how to work. You may exaggerate when you get excited; he can be a stickler for details. If you listen and learn from one another, he can help you be more practical, and you can add excitement and thrills to his life.

CHALLENGING—2

SOCIAL BUTTERFLIES

LEO/LIBRA

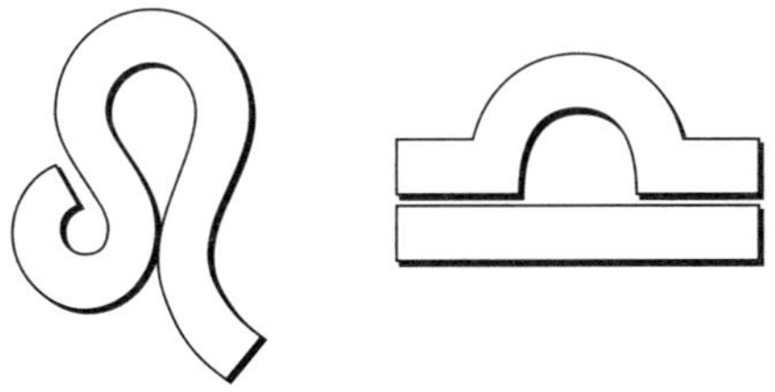

An active social life probably appeals to both of you. He needs lots of one-on-one encounters, as his instinctive pattern is to react, to share the world with others. He figures out what he wants partly by discussing it with someone else. You need an audience to appreciate your flair, creativity, passion and the love you have to give. He needs to learn that positive feedback works ten times better than negative with you. Each of you can be quite romantic and you thrive when involved in a loving partnership.

COMPATIBLE—3

FIREWORKS!

LEO/SCORPIO

Sparks can really fly in this relationship! Sex appeal, magnetism and charisma are likely on both sides. But each of you is very strong-willed and the two of you may battle royally. Your generosity may be extravagant in his eyes. His emotional caution may feel like withholding from your perspective. You naturally sparkle when others are around, and he could be jealous or possessive. You tend to be open and expressive. He tends to be private and secretive. If the two of you can master the intricacies of compromise, this relationship is likely to be deep, transformative and passionate.

CHALLENGING—2

LEO/SAGITTARIUS

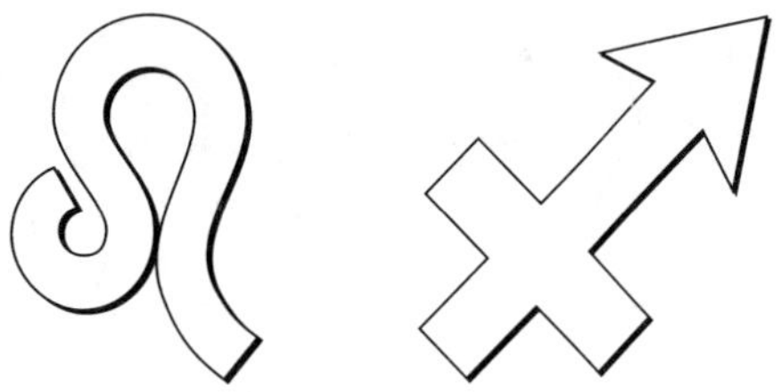

FUN AND FROLIC

Excitement and activity are the name of the game for the two of you. Playful, generous, enthusiastic, you could egg each other on for more and more fun (or take bigger and bigger chances or gambles). Naturally expressive, you can appreciate each other's directness. What you see is what you get. He may need a bit more freedom to roam than you, and you may need more drama and positive attention. Generally, you are likely to feed each other's confidence, optimism and zest for life.

COMPATIBLE—3

LEO/CAPRICORN

PLAY OR WORK?

Your personal styles are quite different. You are generous, charismatic and seek excitement. He is cautious, reserved and prefers not to take chances. You remain young-at-heart with a playful spirit. He was old when young and can be quite parental—inclined to work hard and feel responsible. (But he often seems younger with age.) If the two of you are open to growth, you can learn more control and practicality from him and he can learn to relax, play and find more joy in life through you.

VERY CHALLENGING—1

LEO/AQUARIUS

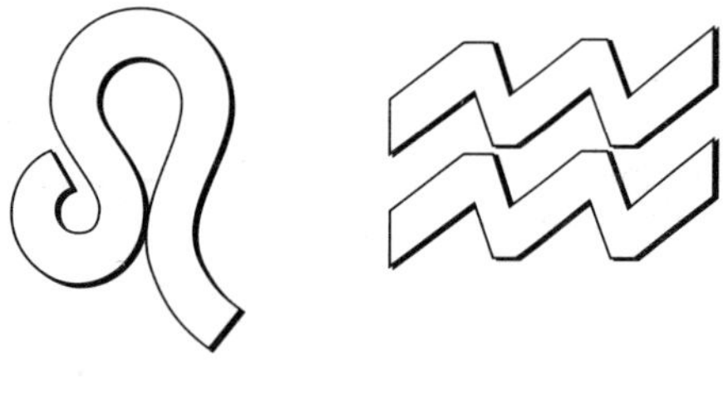

CLOSENESS VS. FREEDOM

Yours is the natural attraction of opposites. You tend to be warm and expressive; he tends to be cool and detached. You want emotional response; he wants intellectual stimulation. You're eager to love and to be loved. He values freedom. Yet each of you has a kernel of those opposing qualities or you wouldn't be drawn together. If you can share a middle ground, the two of you can love with openness, making room for both the heart and the head within your relationship.

VERY COMPATIBLE—4

LEO/PISCES

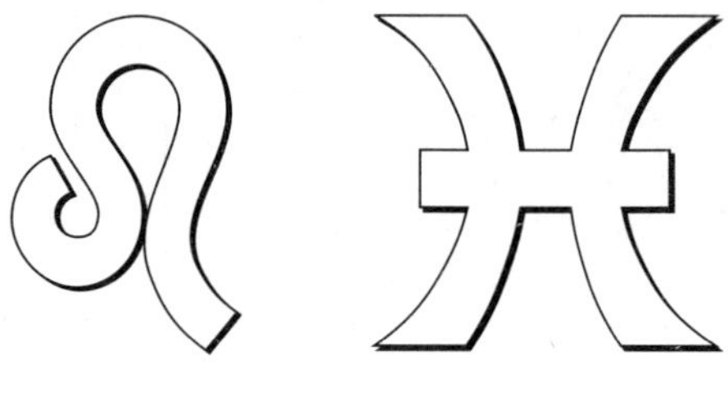

PUBLIC OR PRIVATE?

Although both of you have a romantic streak, your personal styles could vary widely. You tend to be outgoing, exuberant and eager to shine in the world. He tends to be protective, sensitive, or shy and inward. You need the stimulation of play, fun and the admiration of others. He needs privacy and an artistic or inspirational outlet. Combining forces will enrich both your lives if the two of you are understanding and willing to adapt to each other's needs.

VERY CHALLENGING—1

DISCREET OR DIRECT?

VIRGO/ARIES

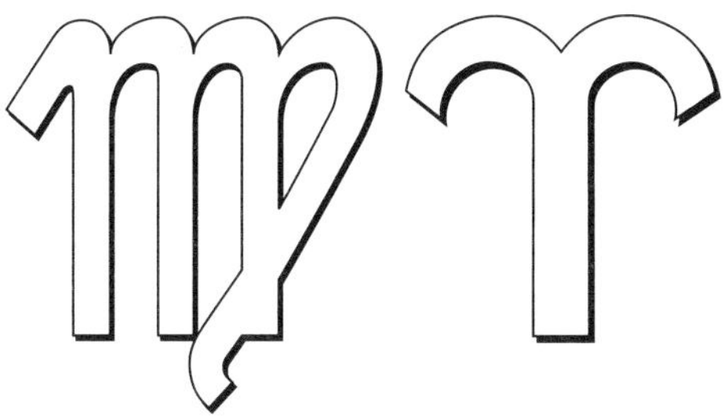

Personal styles will vary here. He can react quickly, perhaps even rushing into love. You tend to mull things over, pick at them, and worry about what might go wrong before doing something. His passionate style is more spontaneous; you may fall into self-doubts or excessive analysis. He needs to recognize that stimulating your mind is as vital as stimulating your body. You can teach him the value of discretion and he can teach you the joy of direct, courageous action.

VERY CHALLENGING—1

PRACTICAL PARTNERS

VIRGO/TAURUS

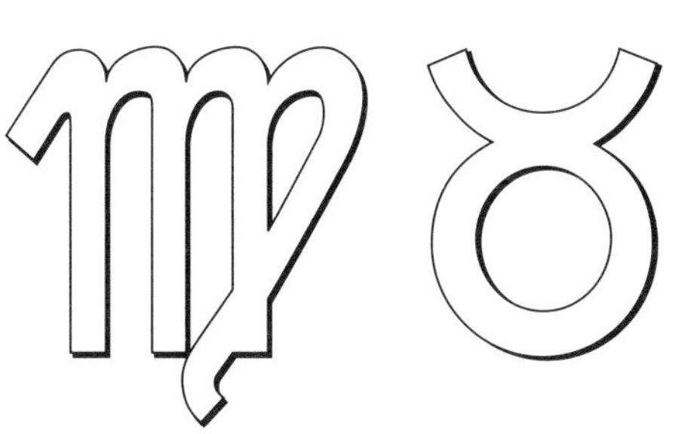

You both tend to be practical with good common sense. What you do (and what your partner does) matters more than pretty phrases. You both appreciate results and dependability. You might be a bit critical (of yourself or others), but are very helpful and a good worker. He can be a bit stubborn, but is very loyal and affectionate. He can bring more sensuality into your life and you can bring more organization into his.

COMPATIBLE—3

QUALITY VS. QUANTITY

VIRGO/GEMINI

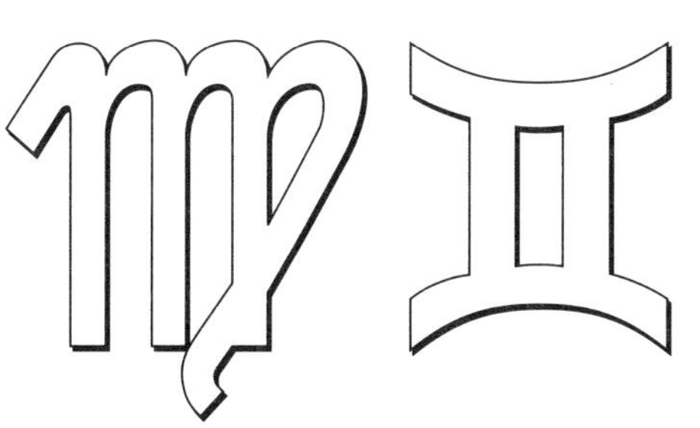

Communication comes instinctively to you both. So naturally, you might sometimes talk an issue to death. He can be more casual (even flippant) while you are probably more serious (and sometimes critical). A love of learning links you both. Sharing ideas, teaching, taking classes, disseminating information, or any kind of constructive communication deepens the connections between you. His focus is on quantity (learning about everything) and yours is on quality (focusing and doing it completely), but you can each add to the other's fund of knowledge and information.

CHALLENGING—2

SUPPORTIVE SWEETHEARTS

VIRGO/CANCER

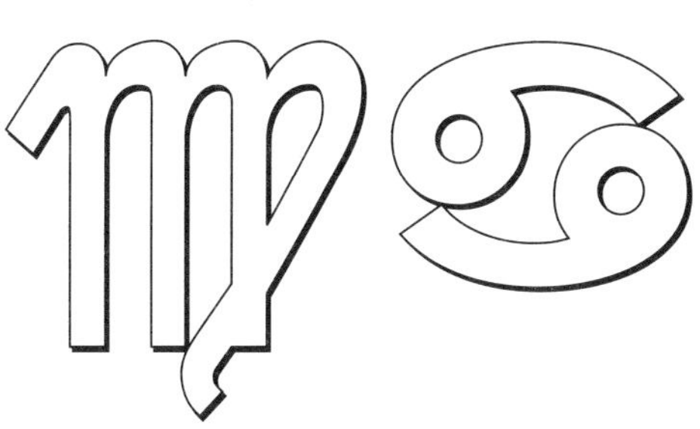

Fulfilling your commitments is important to each of you. You may be a bit more work or task-oriented, while he focuses more on matters of safety or protection. Although he does not wear his heart on his sleeve, he is quite sensitive, so tread gently, especially when feeling critical. He values warmth and being there for each other. Either of you may worry a bit too much, but you are ready to fix any practical or physical flaws and he is eager to heal any emotional wounds. Mutual support and some division of labor can work well between you.

COMPATIBLE—3

VIRGO/LEO

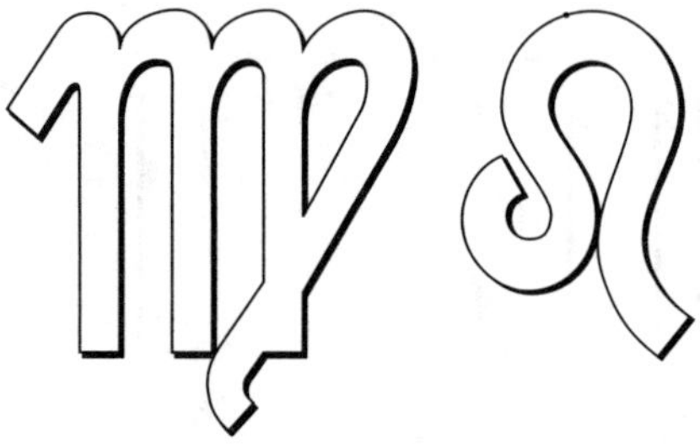

EXACTING OR EXCITING

Your personal styles may be very different. He tends to have natural flair with dramatic instincts that insure people notice when he walks into a room. You tend to be reserved, perhaps even inhibited. He learned young how to play, to enjoy life; you learned how to work. He may exaggerate when he gets excited; you can be a stickler for details. If you listen and learn from one another, you can help him be more practical and he can add excitement and thrills to your life.

CHALLENGING—2

VIRGO/VIRGO

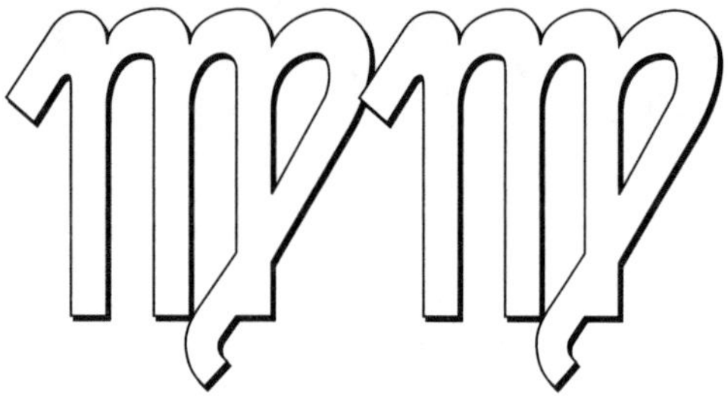

HARDWORKING HONEYS

Unlike some romantic, idealistic or impulsive combinations, the two of you expect love to grow slowly. Each of you is practical, hardworking and sensible. You can be critical (of yourself and of others) as you both instinctively seek flaws so that you can repair them. Since you will analyze one another extensively, you know a commitment is real once it is made. You may work together, or at least share tasks, as well as an emotional bond. Dependability and a willingness to be of service are among your gifts to one another.

VERY COMPATIBLE—4

VIRGO/LIBRA

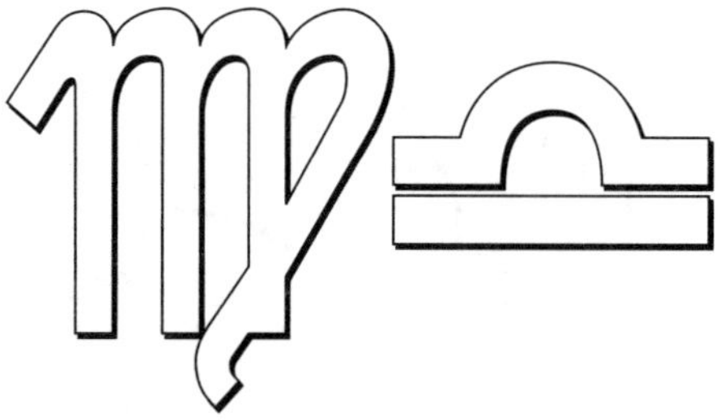

PLEASINGLY PRECISE

Each of you can contribute something which enlarges the other's experience. You are apt to be reserved, practical, analytical, and perhaps self-critical. He is apt to be more relaxed, charming and perhaps a bit lazy, indulgent or pleasure-seeking. You can be quite focused on work, duty and service. He understands the value of relationships and being able to relax. You can teach him to focus more and he can encourage you to take it easy and like yourself more.

CHALLENGING—2

VIRGO/SCORPIO

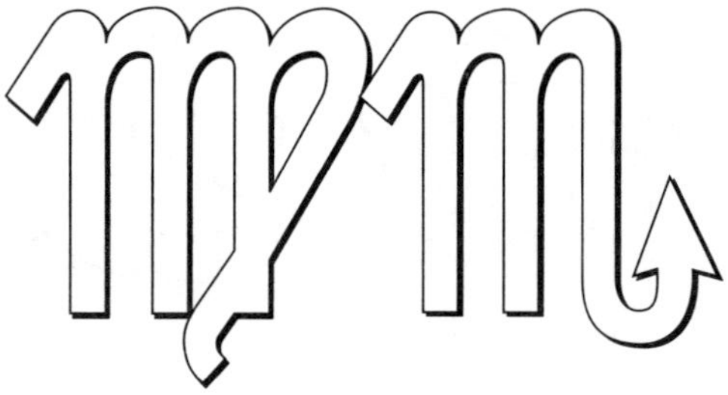

PRACTICAL PASSION

You both may have organizational skills and a love of solving problems. So, when difficulties occur, you easily rise to the challenge. You may be more practical, while he can be intense and brooding. He may feel a bit possessive or perhaps that your focus on efficiency is overdone. Either of you can sometimes overanalyze or get obsessive about a topic. If you learn from one another, he brings more passion, intensity and emotional depth to your life and you can encourage his pragmatic, helpful and service-oriented side. Once committed, you both are inclined to hang on and hang in until the very end.

COMPATIBLE—3

DASHING DETAILS

VIRGO/SAGITTARIUS

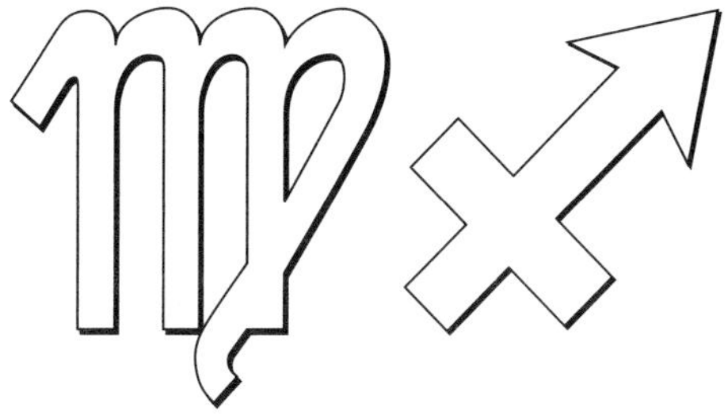

If you combine talents, you can be a dynamite duo. He tends to be enthusiastic, gregarious, ready for adventure and looking at the big picture. You are probably reserved, a bit shy, and skilled with details. He could seem disorganized, scattered and overextended compared to you. You could seem too meticulous or critical to him. If you blend your styles, you can ground his enthusiasms and help make his dreams real. He can lift you from the everyday world to exciting, inspiring realms.

CHALLENGING—2

CONSCIENTIOUS COUPLE

VIRGO/CAPRICORN

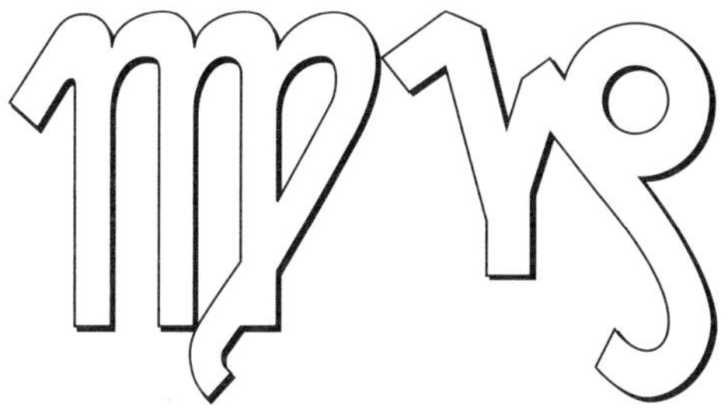

Both of you are likely to be conscientious, hardworking, practical and responsible. Doing a good job matters to the two of you. Because your identity is found partially through a job, either one of you could occasionally neglect the relationship by focusing so much on productivity and competence at your tasks or duties. You tend more toward service and humility, while he needs authority and control. Keep a balance of power between you. When you make a commitment, each of you will put your whole effort toward success.

COMPATIBLE—3

RATIONAL ROMANTICS

VIRGO/AQUARIUS

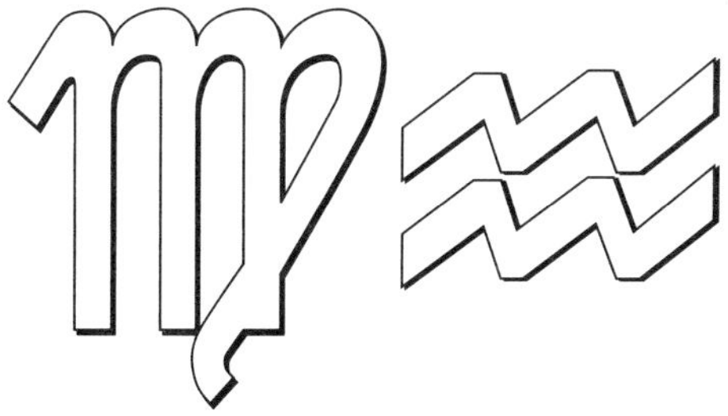

Communication and an openness to learning could be strong links between you. Your style is more practical, sensible, step-by-step and oriented toward obtaining results (getting the job done). His style is more theoretical, erratic, unconventional and oriented toward maintaining freedom and many choices. He can be the experimenter, while you are the technician. You may see him as chaotic, and he may see you as hung up on petty details. If you learn from one another, you can help him to focus and test some of his wild ideas (or flashes of insight). He can widen your perspective and help you do mental headstands.

VERY CHALLENGING—1

FOCUS OR FANTASY?

VIRGO/PISCES

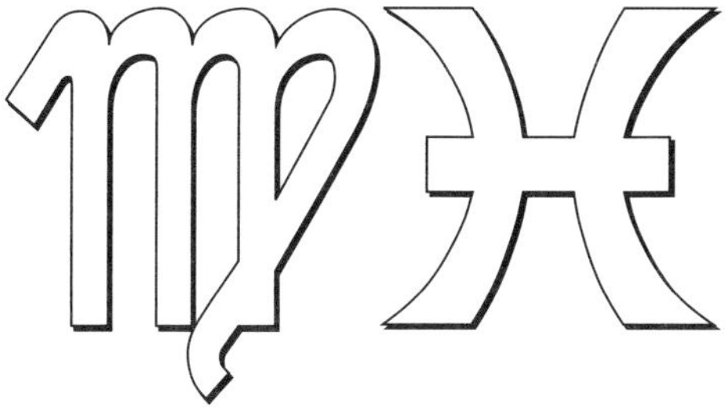

Yours is a natural attraction of opposites. Each of you is dealing with the polarity of the real versus the ideal. You tend to be more practical, grounded and sensible. He tends to be more imaginative, romantic and idealistic. (But you may sometimes switch ends on this seesaw.) You probably learn step-by-step, while he absorbs information in whole concepts. You can bring in more logic, order, and common sense and he can bring in more magic, mystery and imagination. Together, you can turn visions into reality.

VERY COMPATIBLE—4

LIBRA/ARIES

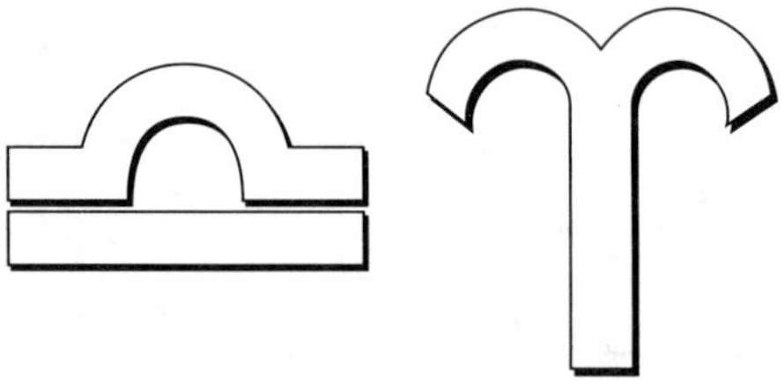

COURAGEOUS COMPROMISING

You two can prove the old proverb that opposites attract. He can bring enthusiasm and passion to the relationship, while you bring tact and sympathy. He may seem more self-centered, while you tend to think first of the other person. He can teach you to go after what you want, while you expose him to the joys of compromise. He may prefer a bit more space and independence, while you want to be a couple who shares lots of things. Respect his need to be on his own at times, and he can go the extra mile for social activities that are important to you. With mutual caring, you make a great team.

VERY COMPATIBLE—4

LIBRA/TAURUS

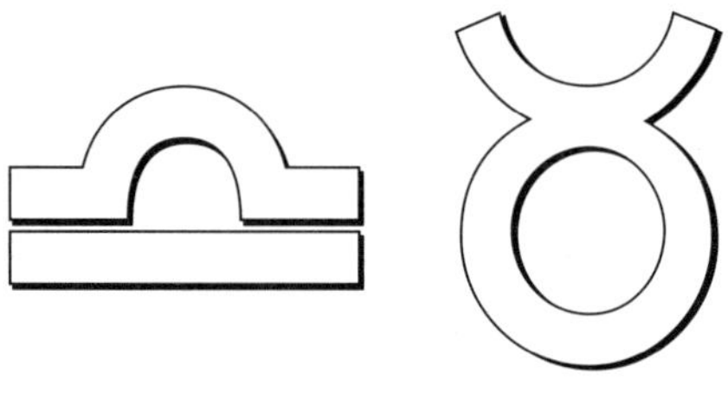

LOVELY LOVING

You both appreciate pleasure and beauty. He, however, knows his own mind and can be very set on his course. You tend to react to others rather than acting directly, so you may vacillate, trying to figure out what other people want. You both can be quite affectionate and loving. You need to understand his desire for material security and sensual indulgence. He has to understand your need for other people to bounce ideas and conversation back and forth.

VERY CHALLENGING—1

LIBRA/GEMINI

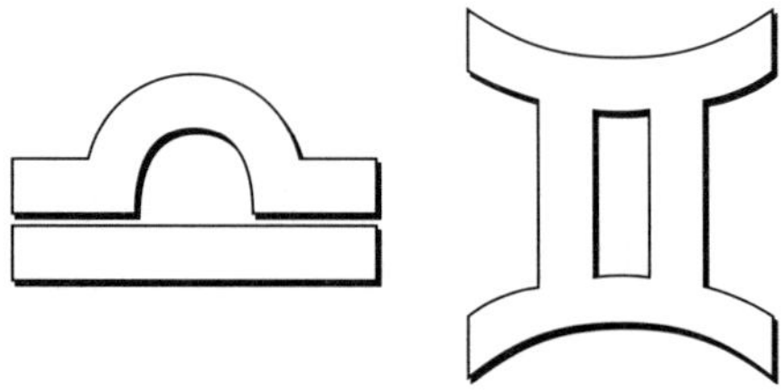

CLEAR COMMUNICATION

Each of you is instinctively equalitarian, so you're off to a good start in building a relationship. You both value communication and probably strive to be open and clear with one another. You may want more affection or one-on-one than he is used to giving. He may want more social variety (even the occasional flirtation). Your style is a bit more warm and emotional, while his is a bit more cool and casual. As long as you talk with and understand each other, the relationship will flourish.

COMPATIBLE—3

LIBRA/CANCER

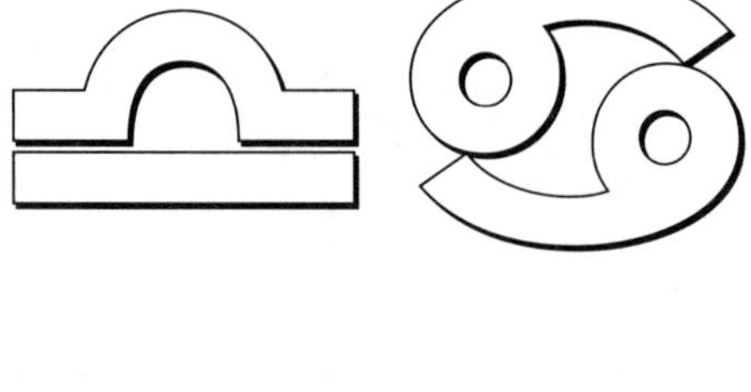

TOO CLOSE FOR COMFORT?

Each of you values emotional closeness, but your styles may differ. He tends to operate cautiously and subtly and does not reveal all his feelings. You tend to discuss matters and may adopt both sides of an argument in order to figure out what you really believe. You may enjoy competition on occasion or lots of one-on-one encounters, while he enjoys silence and a sense of safety. He needs some time alone, while you prefer having another person around to bat ideas back and forth. When you both focus on love, caring, and commitment, your commonalities become more obvious.

CHALLENGING—2

SOCIAL BUTTERFLIES

LIBRA/LEO

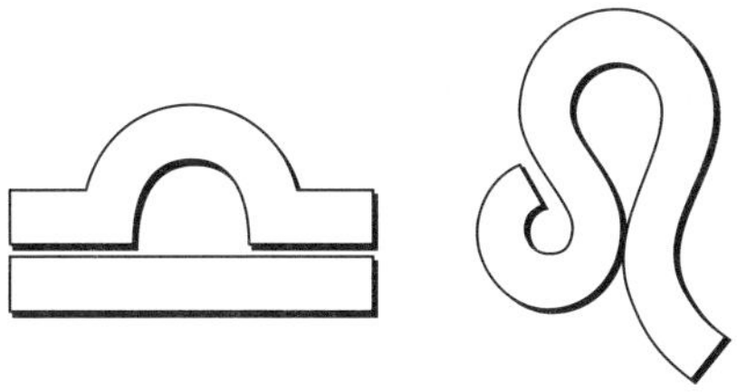

An active social life probably appeals to both of you. You need lots of one-on-one, as your instinctive pattern is to react, to share the world with others. Sometimes, you may be too dependent on the opinions of others, swayed by what they want. He needs an audience to appreciate his flair, creativity, and passion. He needs to be noticed and applauded by others. Praise will work wonders when you want an impact! Each of you can be quite romantic, and you thrive when involved in a loving partnership.

COMPATIBLE—3

PLEASINGLY PRECISE

LIBRA/VIRGO

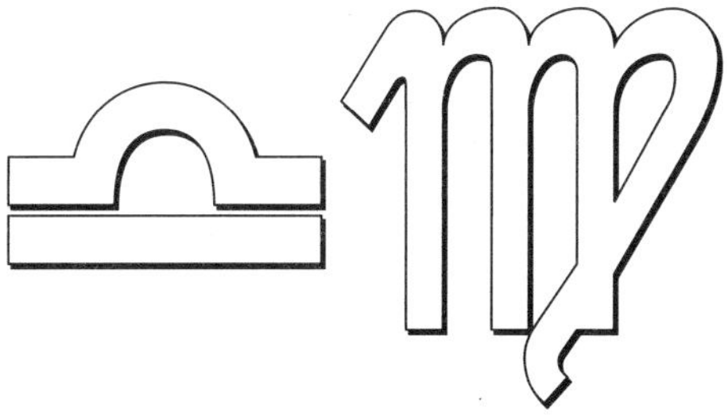

Each of you can enlarge the other's experience. He is apt to be reserved, practical, analytical, and perhaps critical (of himself and/or other people). His work may be very important to him; he gains a sense of worth through competence and getting the job done. You are apt to be more relaxed, charming and perhaps a bit indulgent. You may accentuate relationship issues while he emphasizes work, duty and service. He can teach you how to focus and get more done. You can encourage him to take it easy and like himself more.

CHALLENGING—2

CHARMING COUPLE

LIBRA/LIBRA

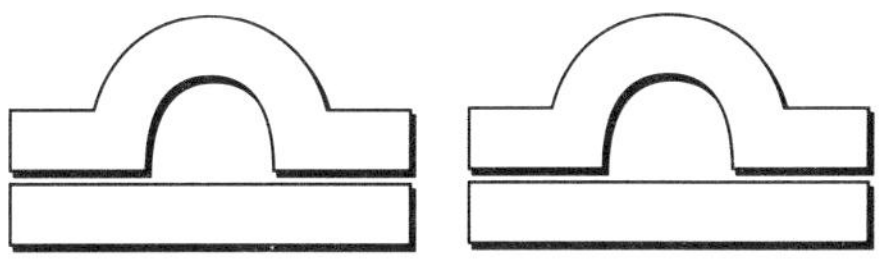

Since both of you prefer togetherness to solitude, a partnership is a real possibility. Each of you can encourage the grace, charm and love of beauty in the other. The two of you may slip into competitive interactions on occasion. If you keep track of who wins and who loses in your association, interactions could get tense. You both may be skilled negotiators and strategists, but are also quite capable of empathy and compromise. Seek win/win solutions and all will be well.

VERY COMPATIBLE—4

TENDER AND TOUGH

LIBRA/SCORPIO

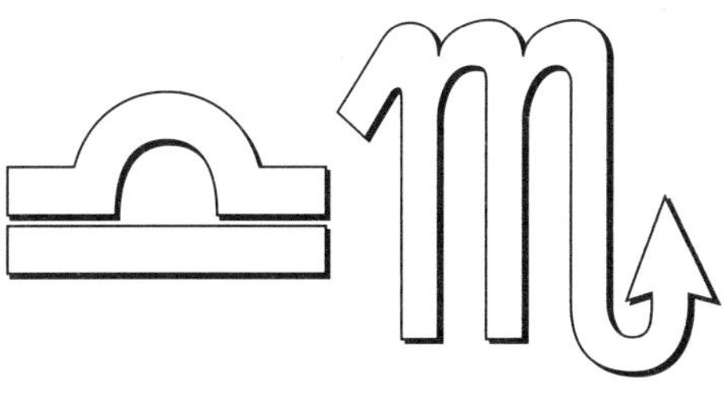

Partnership is an important need for both of you, but your styles may vary. You're probably more diplomatic, balanced and sociable. He's more likely to be intense, all-or-nothing and private. You can waver and be indecisive, while he tends to be immovable once he's set his mind on something. You can help him relax, kick back, and enjoy people and beauty. He can help you look beneath the surface, focus and plumb the depths of passion.

CHALLENGING—2

LIBRA/SAGITTARIUS

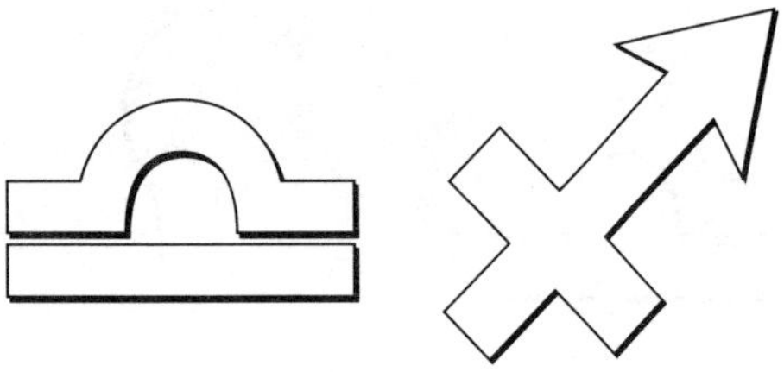

SOCIABLE SWEETHEARTS

Both of you enjoy activity and people. Sociable and outgoing, you not only enjoy yourselves but also light up your circle of friends. You may be a bit more diplomatic and tactful, while he is a bit more blunt. However, you share a passion for justice and fair play. Competitive games, trips, outings with friends or elegant evenings with stimulating conversation might appeal. He could be more energetic, outdoorsy or freedom-loving, while you excel at culture, beauty, grace and pleasure. Generally, though, you each know how to enjoy life and other people.

COMPATIBLE—3

LIBRA/CAPRICORN

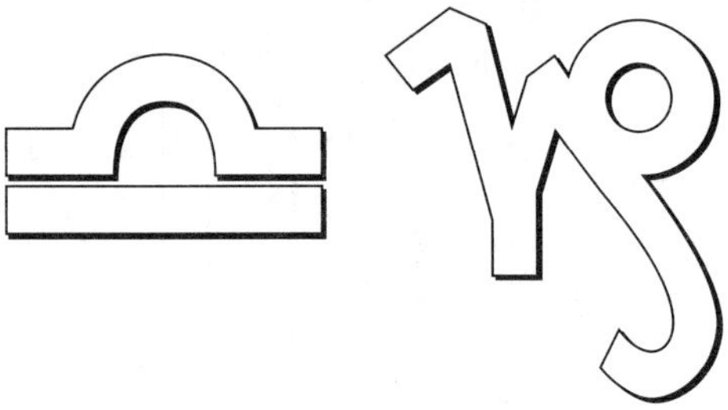

EASE VS. EFFORT

Contrasting needs and styles will challenge you both to create a meeting in the middle. You tend to be relaxed, gracious and people-oriented. He tends to be reserved, formal and work-oriented. You are a team player; he seeks authority and power. You will need to support his ambitions in a career lest he play dictator at home. He can learn from you how to relax and be more easygoing. The two of you will need to keep a balance between love (relationship needs) and work (career or status demands). You each value the goodwill and respect of others.

CHALLENGING—2

LIBRA/AQUARIUS

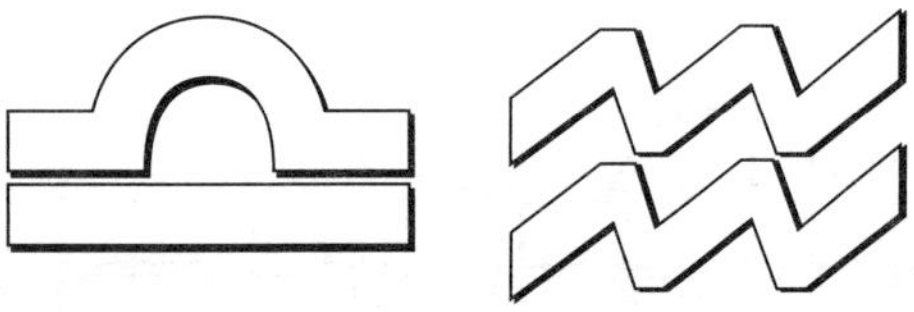

FOND FRIENDS

Both of you appreciate the worth of learning and good communication. You probably find it easy to talk to each other, although you are more diplomatic and tactful, while he is more unconventional (even outrageous). He may need more independence and space than you, while you need more grace, beauty and smooth flow in your life. Each of you can stimulate the other mentally. You are both equalitarian, so you find it easy to cooperate without dominance games. You both are naturally friendly.

COMPATIBLE—3

LIBRA/PISCES

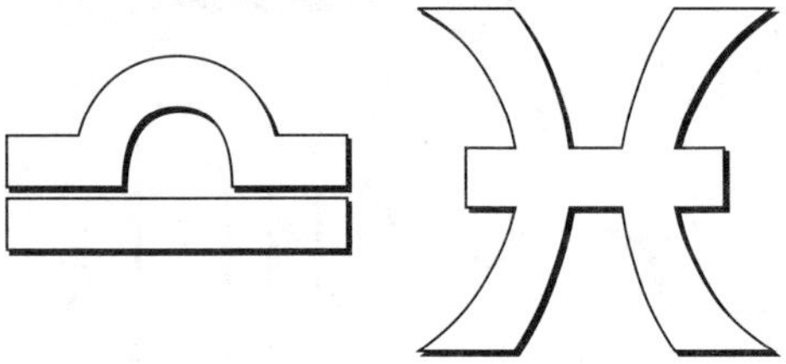

SOFT-FOCUS SENTIMENT

Both of you are likely to value beauty and harmony. Consequently, you might encourage one another to avoid unpleasantness or confrontations of any sort. You prefer to be sweet, kind and diplomatic, while he can easily don rose-colored glasses and pretend everything is perfect even when it is not. You may share a love of beauty, and you are both capable of the sacrifices and compromises necessary to combine your life with someone else's. You can feed each other's romantic streaks.

VERY CHALLENGING—1

POWERFUL PASSIONS

SCORPIO/ARIES

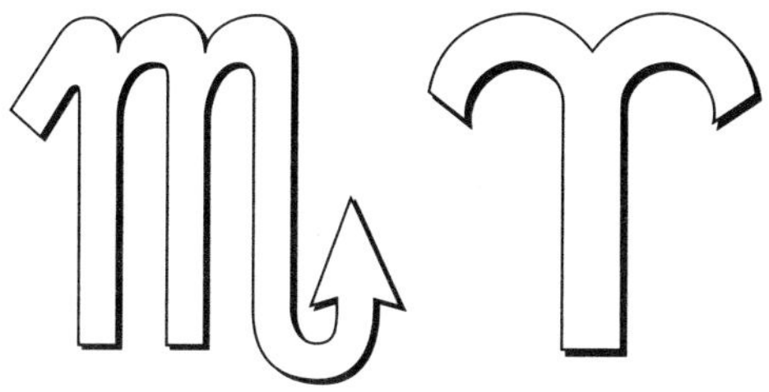

Passion, sex and intense emotions are likely on both sides. Because you are both strong personalities, the compromises of a relationship may prove challenging. You could blow hot and cold with one another—ready to go all-out one moment and withdrawing totally the next. The two of you may bounce between wanting to be free and wanting to get close. If you respect each other and get your time tables in sync, this can be a very powerful bond.

VERY CHALLENGING—1

SATISFYING SENSUALITY

SCORPIO/TAURUS

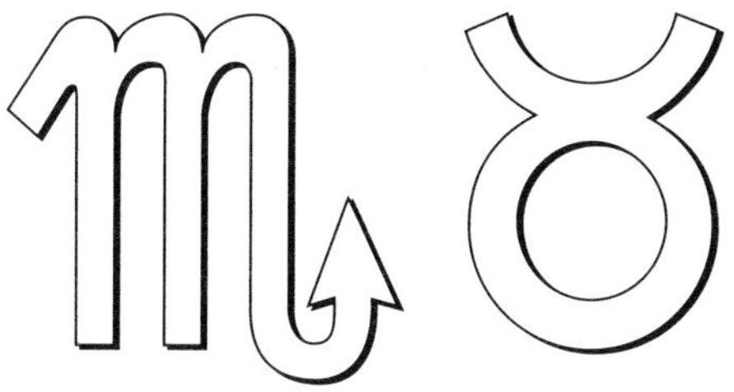

You both are very strong-willed and can be quite possessive and stubborn. Respecting each other's boundaries will be vital. The two of you are working on balancing self-indulgence and self-mastery. Since opposites attract you could easily polarize around finances, possessions or pleasures. One could nag the other about weight or smoking or drinking or spending money. If you each control yourselves, you won't need to try to control your partner. Then you can be incredibly loyal, deeply sensual, and satisfyingly intimate with one another.

VERY COMPATIBLE—4

RELENTLESS OR RESTLESS?

SCORPIO/GEMINI

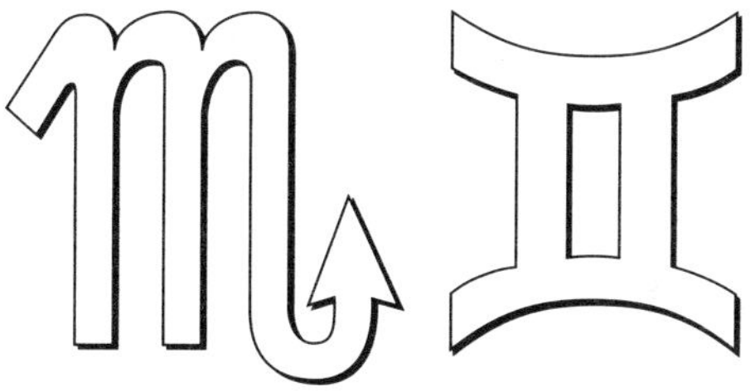

Your approaches are different enough that a meeting of the minds is challenging. He's open and communicative (perhaps **too** talkative in your eyes). You are intense, inward and can be secretive. He is lighthearted and likes to laugh. Your emotions are deep, strong and sometimes overwhelming. He is sociable and likes a variety of people. You prefer to focus closely on one person at a time, and discuss issues deeply and thoroughly. (Superficialities bore you.) If you learn from one another, he can teach you to lighten up and you can expose him to incredible, passionate depths.

VERY CHALLENGING—1

TOTAL TOGETHERNESS

SCORPIO/CANCER

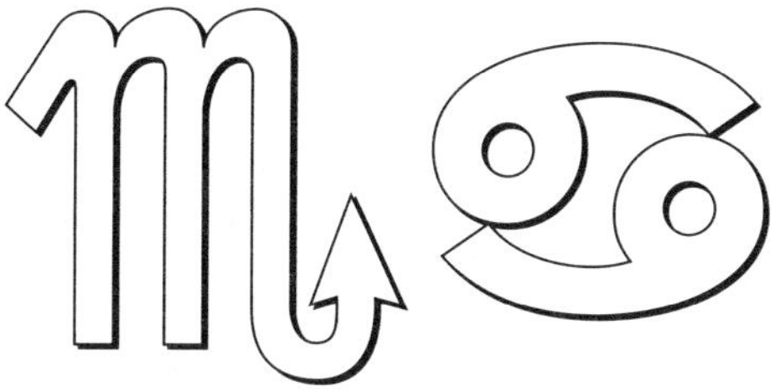

You are both capable of an intense emotional commitment. When you give yourselves, it is heart and soul. Each of you is quite sensitive, so you are more apt to tread softly near your partner's tender areas. If threatened or feeling insecure, either of you may withdraw (even sulk). Or, either of you could succumb to jealousy or possessiveness when feeling down. On its best level, this can be a relationship with someone who connects bone-deep, with whom you can share all the corners of your psyche.

COMPATIBLE—3

SCORPIO/LEO

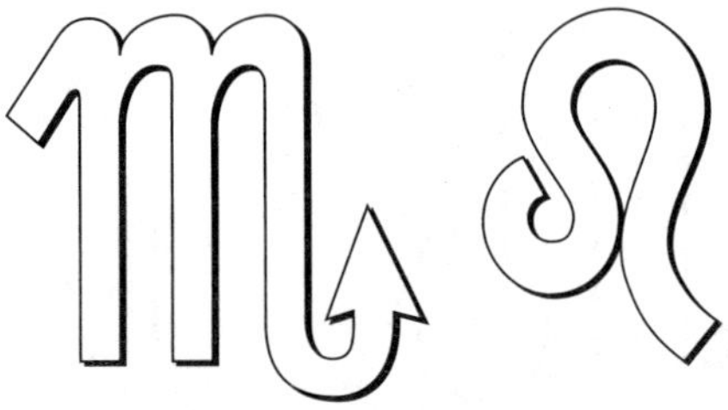

FIREWORKS!

Sparks can really fly in this relationship! Sex appeal, magnetism and allure are likely on both sides. But each of you is very strong-willed and the two of you may butt heads. His generosity may be extravagant in your eyes. Your caution may be withholding from his perspective. His sparkle, charisma and need to shine when others are around could arouse your jealousy or insecurity. He tends to be open and expressive. You tend to be more private. **If** the two of you can master the intricacies of compromise, this relationship is likely to be deep, transformative and passionate.

CHALLENGING—2

SCORPIO/VIRGO

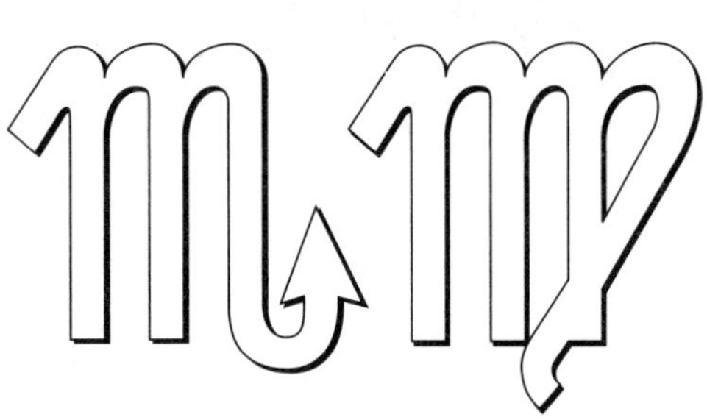

PRACTICAL PASSION

You both may have organizational skills and a love of solving problems. So, when difficulties occur, you rise to the challenge. He may be more practical or work-oriented, while you are more concerned with getting to the bottom of things, facing emotional challenges. You might feel that his need to work is overdone. Either of you can sometimes overanalyze or get obsessive about a topic. If you learn from one another, you bring more passion, intensity and emotional depth to his life and he can encourage your pragmatic common sense. Once committed, you both are inclined to hang on and hang in until the very end.

COMPATIBLE—3

SCORPIO/LIBRA

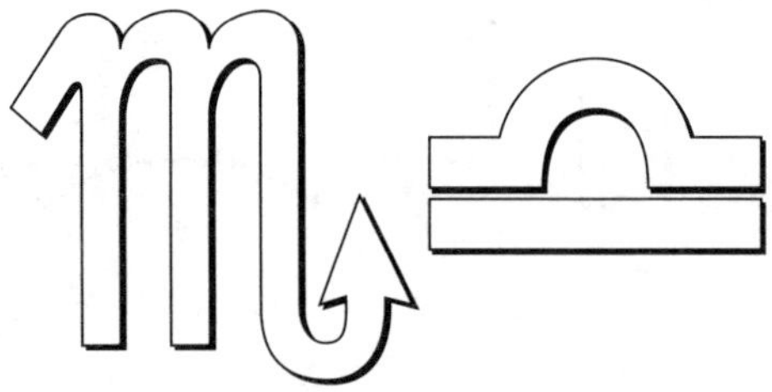

TOUGH AND TENDER

Partnership is an important need for both of you, but your styles may vary. He is probably more diplomatic, balanced and sociable. You are more likely to be intense, all-or-nothing and private. He can waver and be indecisive, while you tend to be stubborn once you've set your mind on something. He can help you relax, kick back, and enjoy people and beauty. You can help him look beneath the surface, focus, and plumb the depths of passion.

CHALLENGING—2

SCORPIO/SCORPIO

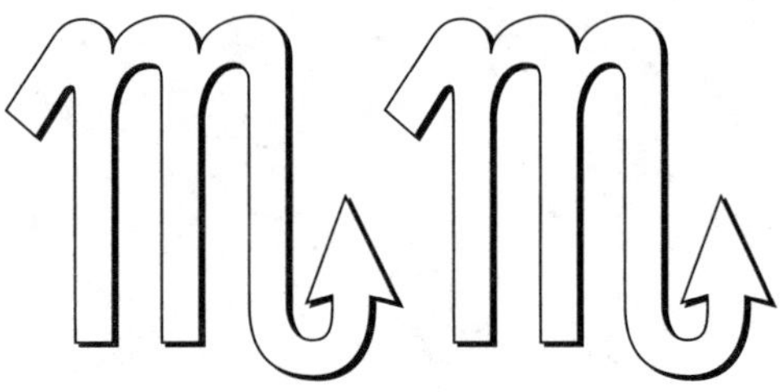

EMOTIONAL EXTREMES

More than most pairs, you two have the potential of an intense, powerful connection. A love relationship between you is apt to be very, very good or downright awful. A Scorpio rising person can be the most loyal and committed of lovers, or the most relentless of adversaries. Jealousy, possessiveness or being too suspicious are potential dangers. Trust in one another is vital. The two of you may enjoy investigating hidden areas, probing each other's psyches, or plumbing the depths of passion together.

VERY COMPATIBLE—4

SUBTLE VS. SCATTERED

SCORPIO/SAGITTARIUS

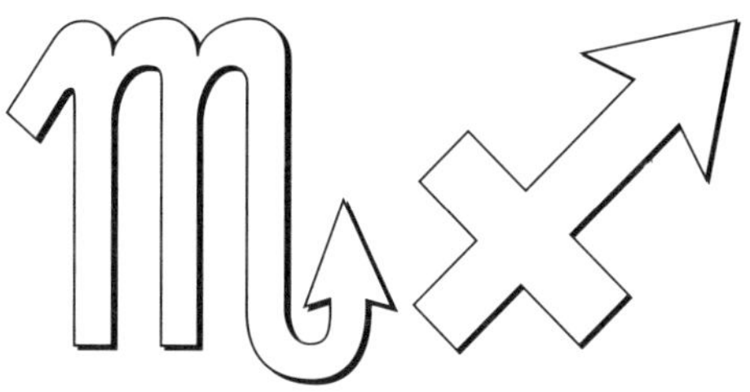

Mutual tolerance and adaptability to each other's styles will be necessary for this relationship to flourish. You tend to be somewhat private and may feel emotional hurts very deeply. He tends to be blunt (sometimes tactless) and expresses so much he does not hang on to any feeling long. You value commitment; he values freedom. You can learn more openness, confidence and independence from him. He can learn discretion, self-control and to appreciate emotional nuances through you.

CHALLENGING—2

PERSEVERING PARTNERS

SCORPIO/CAPRICORN

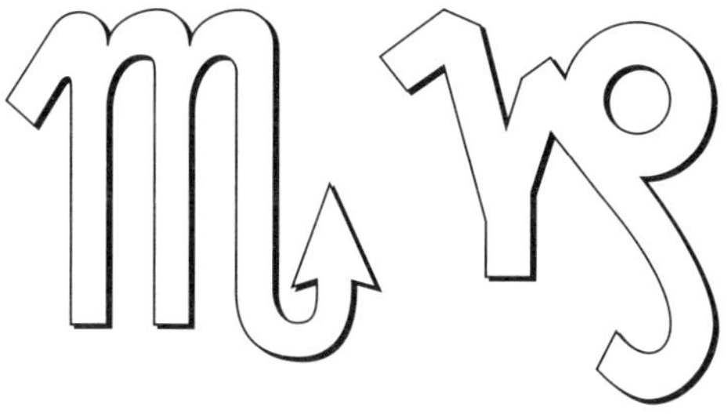

Both of you can be ambitious, dedicated and serious. When you make a commitment, you do carry through. Either of you could be cynical, or feel disdainful of most of humanity. The two of you tend to mistrust romance of too much "sweetness and light." Yet you will work through heavy challenges to the relationship if necessary. You may focus on what the relationship needs, while he focuses more on what his career needs, but you both are grounded and can be highly effective people at whatever you decide to do.

COMPATIBLE—3

CHALLENGING CLOSENESS

SCORPIO/AQUARIUS

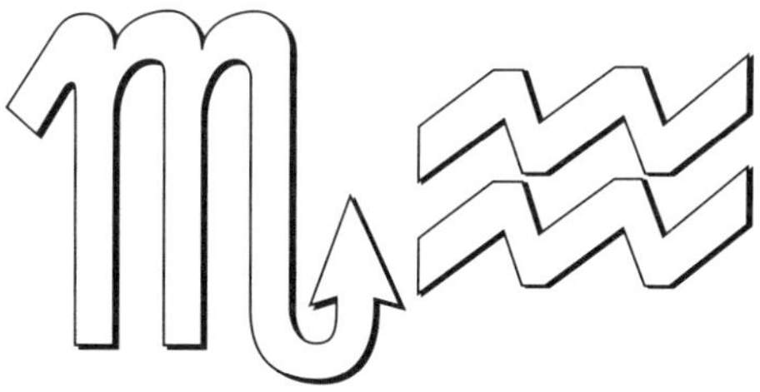

The two of you will be facing the challenge of keeping a balance between freedom and closeness or security versus change in your lives. You may want a closer emotional bond, while he plays it cool (and vice versa). Getting your time tables in sync is important. You may seek safety and commitment, while he enjoys the new, unusual and ever-changing. Rather than polarizing on different sides, each of you needs to appreciate the other's point of view and strive for a moderate, in-between position.

CHALLENGING—2

INTUITIVE INTIMACY

SCORPIO/PISCES

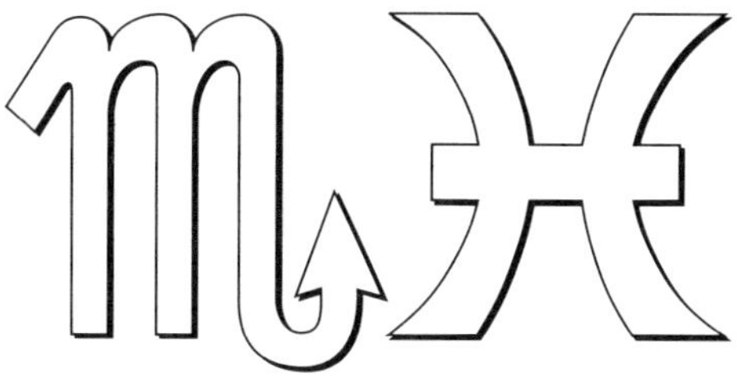

Each of you may easily tune into the feelings of the other. Intuitive, you can enjoy just being together, without having to make conversation. Neither of you is likely to wear your heart on your sleeve. Sometimes this can mean one of you sulks, stays resentful or keeps secret feelings or issues that should be aired. When using your empathy, each of you may feel no one understands you as well as your partner.

COMPATIBLE—3

SAGITTARIUS/ARIES AMOROUS ADVENTURES

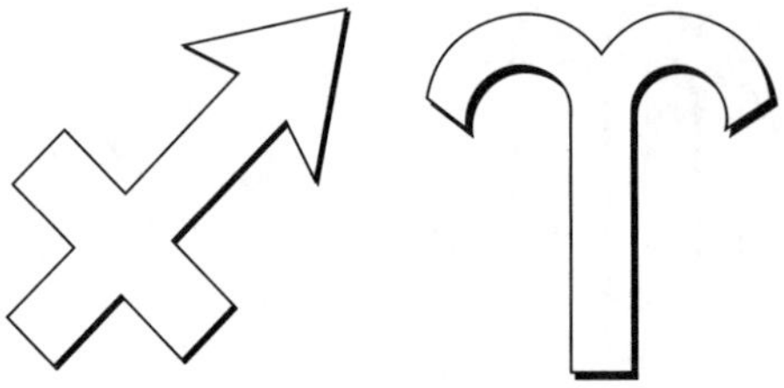

Adventure beckons to you both! High energy types, you can have lots of fun together. Each of you needs a good measure of freedom, so don't try to be a "do everything together" couple. You just naturally stir each other up. Your relationship can be full of thrills, fun, games and activity. You both are energized by excitement and enjoy being on the go, feeling vital and alive.

COMPATIBLE—3

SAGITTARIUS/TAURUS SPECULATION VS. SAFETY

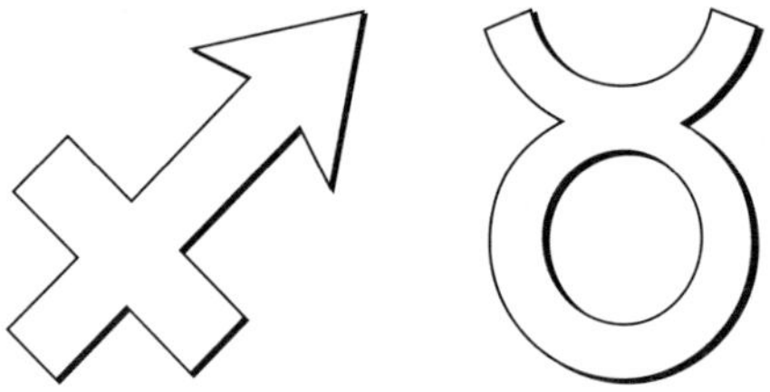

The two of you have some major differences. You like to be out in the world, exploring, having fun, and trying things, while he likes the known, familiar and comfortable. He tends to focus on tangibles and money in the bank, while you are willing to take a chance or gamble for a greater gain. He may seem too stable or stolid to you at times; you may seem too flighty or overextended to him. If you are tolerant and open to one another, you broaden his horizons and he helps you to settle down a bit.

VERY CHALLENGING—1

SAGITTARIUS/GEMINI MENTAL MASTERS

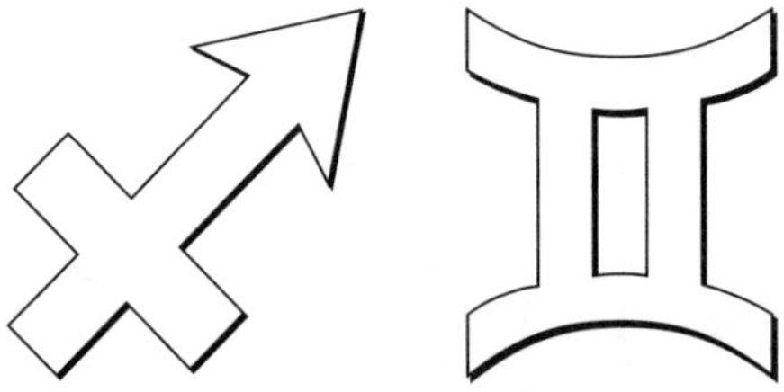

There may be a natural attraction between you. A shared love of variety, mental stimulation, communication and new experiences is likely. The two of you may trade back and forth between the roles of wise professor and wide-eyed student. You probably encourage each other to learn, to travel, to expand your horizons. Humor could be an important bond between you.

VERY COMPATIBLE—4

SAGITTARIUS/CANCER CAREFREE OR CAUTIOUS?

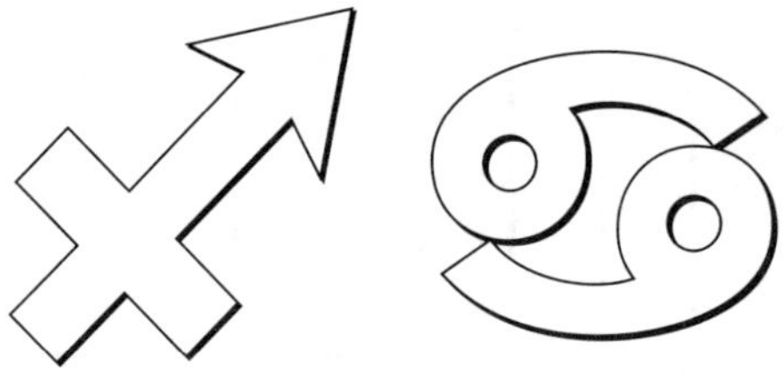

Although attraction is quite possible, compromise is vital if you are to live together. He will tend to be more conservative, centered in the home, or seeking safety. You tend to be more adventurous, outgoing and eager to be active in the outer world. He may see you as flighty and flirtatious; you may see him as possessive and needy. If both of you are tolerant, you can broaden his horizons and he can increase your sensitivity to emotional nuances and security issues.

VERY CHALLENGING—1

FUN AND FROLIC

SAGITTARIUS/LEO

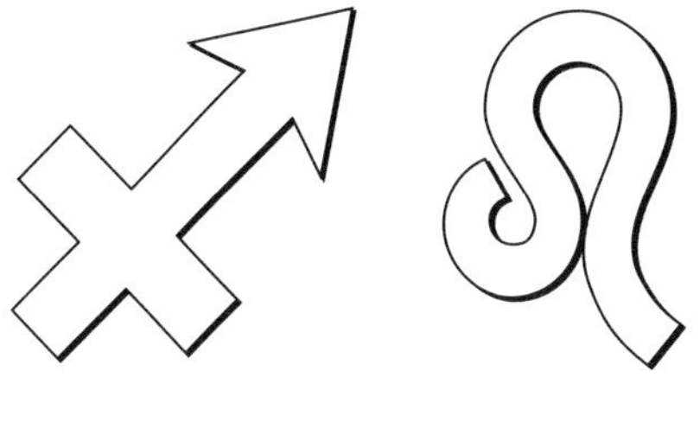

Excitement and activity are the name of the game for the two of you. Playful, generous, enthusiastic, you could egg each other on for more and more fun (or take bigger and bigger chances or gambles). Naturally expressive, you can appreciate each other's directness. What you see is what you get. You may need a bit more freedom, adventure, or intellectual stimulation, and he may need more drama, recognition and to be center stage for people to admire. Generally, you are likely to feed each other's confidence, optimism and zest for life.

COMPATIBLE—3

DASHING DETAILS

SAGITTARIUS/VIRGO

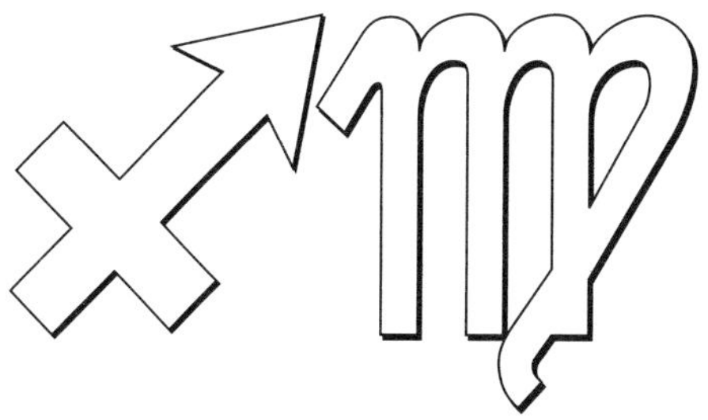

If you combine talents, you can be a dynamite duo. You tend to be enthusiastic, friendly, ready for new experiences, and looking at the big picture. He is probably reserved, a bit shy, and skilled with details. You could seem disorganized, scattered and overextended compared to him. He could seem too meticulous or critical to you. If you blend your styles, he can ground your enthusiasms and help make your dreams real. You can lift him from the everyday world to exciting, inspiring realms.

CHALLENGING—2

SOCIABLE SWEETHEARTS

SAGITTARIUS/LIBRA

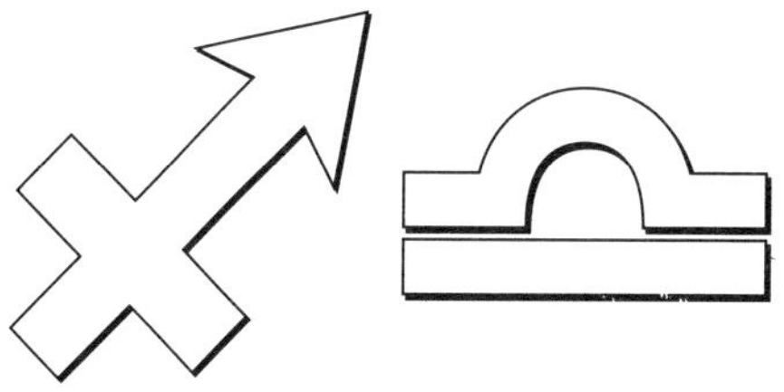

Both of you thrive on activity and people. Sociable and outgoing, you not only enjoy yourselves, but also light up your circle of friends. He may be a bit more diplomatic and tactful, while you can be a bit more blunt, but you share a passion for justice and fair play. Competitive games, trips, outings with friends or elegant evenings with stimulating conversation might appeal. You could be more energetic, outdoorsy or philosophical, while he excels at culture, charm, grace and pleasure. You each know how to enjoy life and other people.

COMPATIBLE—3

SCATTERED VS. SUBTLE

SAGITTARIUS/SCORPIO

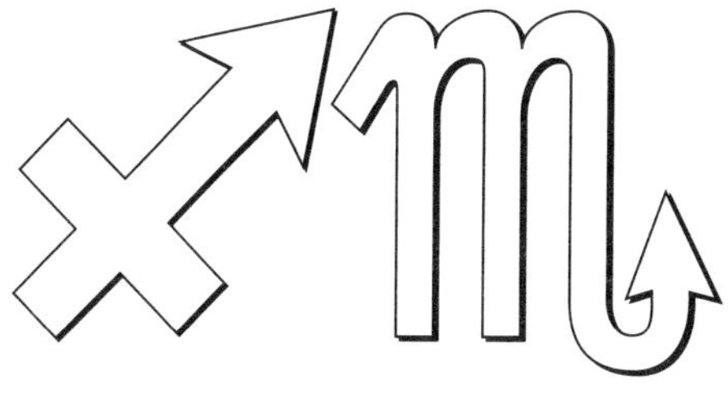

Mutual tolerance and adaptability to each other's styles will be necessary for this relationship to flourish. He tends to be somewhat private and may feel emotional hurts very deeply (but would never show it). You tend to be blunt and express impulsively. You value freedom; he might seem a bit possessive to you. He values thoroughness and follow-through; you might seem scattered to him. He could learn more openness, humor, and independence from you. You can learn discretion, self-control and to appreciate emotional nuances through him.

CHALLENGING—2

SAGITTARIUS/SAGITTARIUS FUN FOREVER!

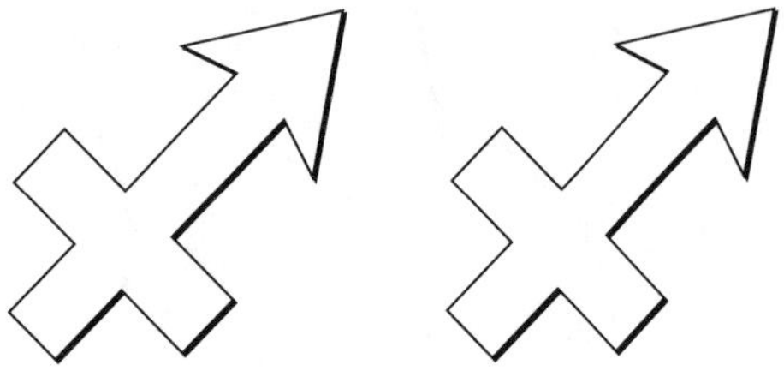

Each of you enjoys adventure and broadening your horizons. You may travel together; study; discuss philosophy, ethics or religion; or simply laugh a lot and enjoy good friends. Gregarious, you may have a broad social circle and can usually talk to anyone about almost anything. You each have a strong sense of personal freedom, so possessiveness is a no-no. You don't get into the intense, emotional depths of some other signs, but can have a great deal of fun. Humor may be a strong bond between you.

VERY COMPATIBLE—4

SAGITTARIUS/CAPRICORN UP AND DOWN

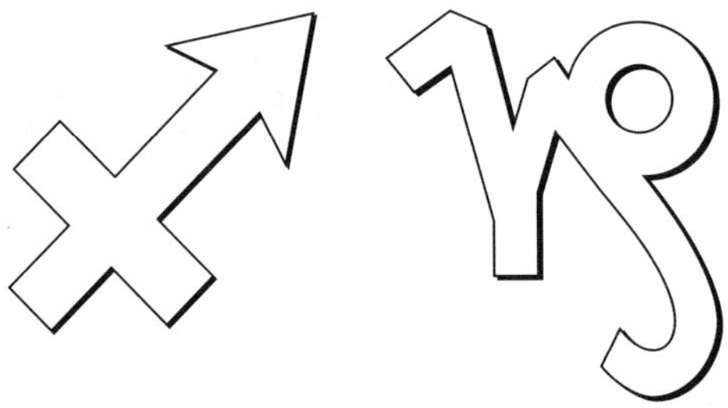

Although your personal styles are quite different, the two of you can do well if you combine forces. You are more an optimist; he is more a pessimist. You are naturally friendly and outgoing; he is more reserved. You are casual (what he might call messy and chaotic) while he is organized (what you might call compulsive). You can bring more laughter and zest to his life, but don't expect him to get excited by all your enthusiasms. He can bring more stability and planning to your life as long as he avoids excessive criticism or control. Together, you can envision the best and work hard to create it.

CHALLENGING—2

SAGITTARIUS/AQUARIUS FOREVER FREE

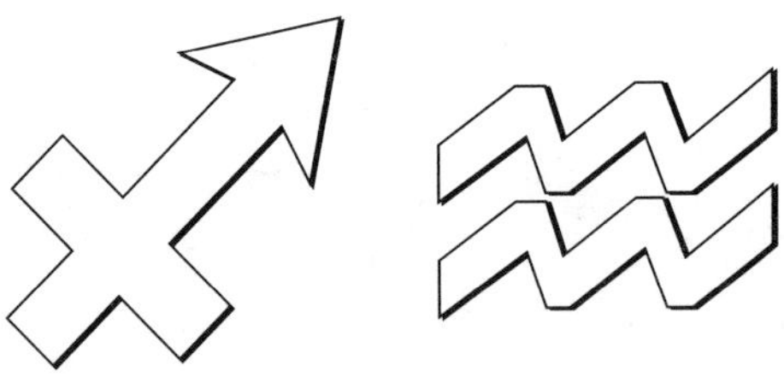

Each of you needs personal freedom, so a "no strings" relationship works best. Commitment is quite possible, but either of you might run at the thought of being "trapped" or tied down in a relationship. You are likely to stimulate each other mentally, enjoy social activities, relate to a wide variety of people and may share an interest in politics, fighting for justice or some kind of activist role in life. Encouraging each other's individuality is your strongest bond.

COMPATIBLE—3

SAGITTARIUS/PISCES MYSTICAL MATES

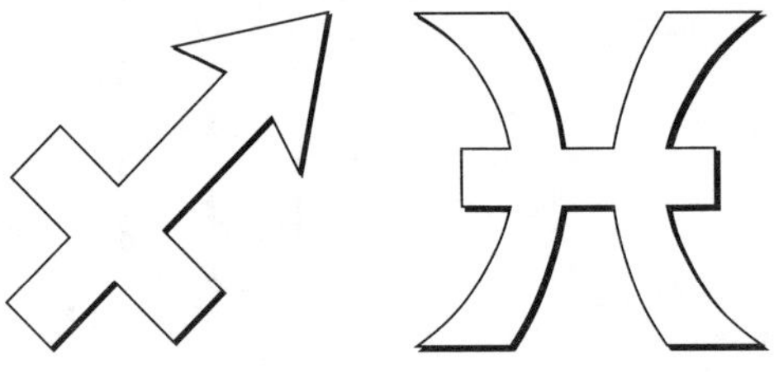

Since both of you are idealists, you have a lot in common. You might share a mystical connection, an interest in religious or spiritual matters, an urge to make the world better—or simply a drive to be the most moral, ethical, **best** person possible. You tend to be more direct and he more circumspect, so you could clash over issues of truth versus compassion or honesty versus tact. Find a middle ground. A shared love of nature or quest for transcendence can be a strong bond between you.

CHALLENGING—2

STEADYING SPARKLE

CAPRICORN/ARIES

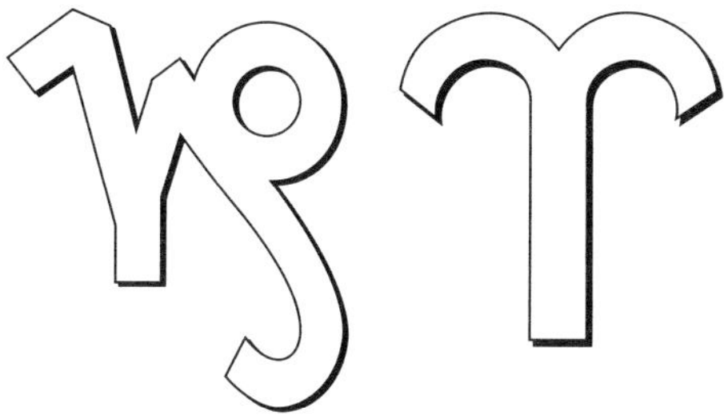

Your styles may clash at first. He wants action, excitement, courage and fun. You want stability, responsibility, and a slow, gradual growth of love. He goes all-out. You wait, are cautious and need to plan things. You may seem too pessimistic to him. He may seem impulsive or rash to you. With compromise, he can bring more sparkle into your life and you can bring more steadiness into his.

CHALLENGING—2

COMMITTED COUPLE

CAPRICORN/TAURUS

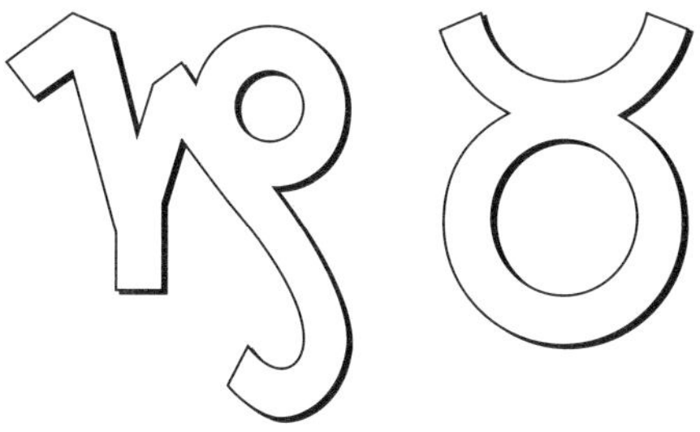

Both of you tend to be practical, grounded people. In relationships, you each are willing to DO things for your partner (and can expect the same in return). You might even work together (in a career or enjoying shared tasks or joint pleasures). He can help you relax and be more sensual. You can help him focus and be more organized. Both of you are capable of great loyalty and prefer a definite commitment.

COMPATIBLE—3

FOCUSED VS. FLIPPANT

CAPRICORN/GEMINI

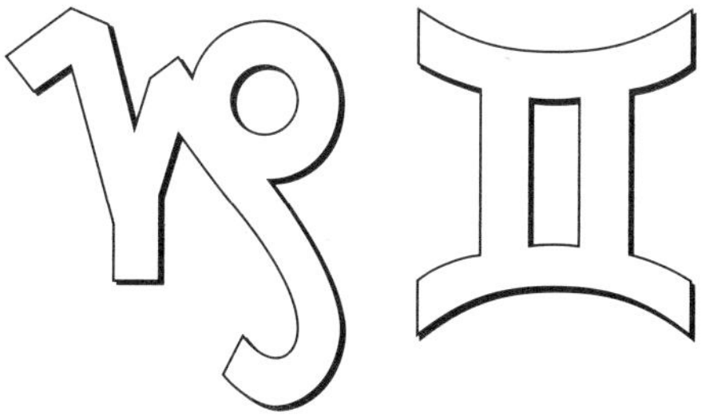

Different approaches challenge you both to make a strong connection. He is quick, perceptive, restless and communicative. You are cautious, responsible, stable and more reticent. He can be quite flippant when you are trying to be serious. He is more concerned with ideas or people; you are more concerned with tasks and results. You may see him as hopelessly scattered or superficial and he might see you as too judgmental or controlling. If you are tolerant and willing to grow with one another, he can help you lighten up and you can help him finish up.

VERY CHALLENGING—1

PARENTAL PARTNERS

CAPRICORN/CANCER

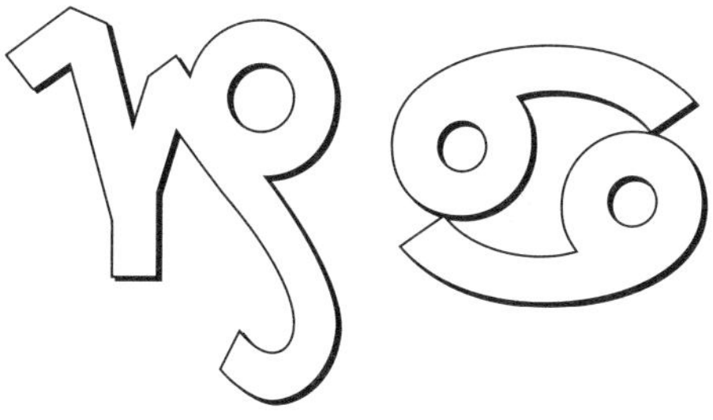

Loyalty and commitment are probably important to both of you. Each of you looks for security, wanting to create something lasting. You both can be somewhat parental in your styles—he nurturing and protective, you solid and responsible. Sometimes old feelings either of you has about Mom or Dad slip in and affect the current relationship. If you share concerns (home and career) and tasks (emotional and physical) rather than polarizing and feeling like opposites, you can definitely build for the long haul.

VERY COMPATIBLE—4

CAPRICORN/LEO

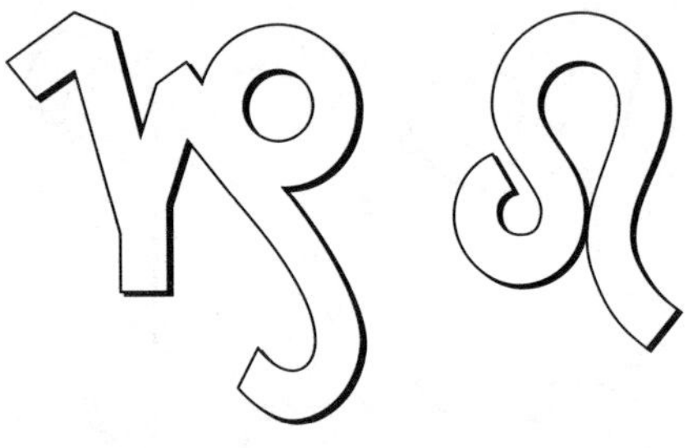

WORK OR PLAY?

Your personal styles are quite different. He is dramatic, charismatic, exciting and can be extravagant. You tend to be cautious, reserved and prefer not to take chances. He remains young at heart, ever ready to play (like a child). You easily take on the role of parent, feeling responsible and wanting to make sure duties are done. If the two of you are open to growth, he can learn more control and practicality from you and you can learn to relax, play and find more joy in life through him.

VERY CHALLENGING—1

CAPRICORN/VIRGO

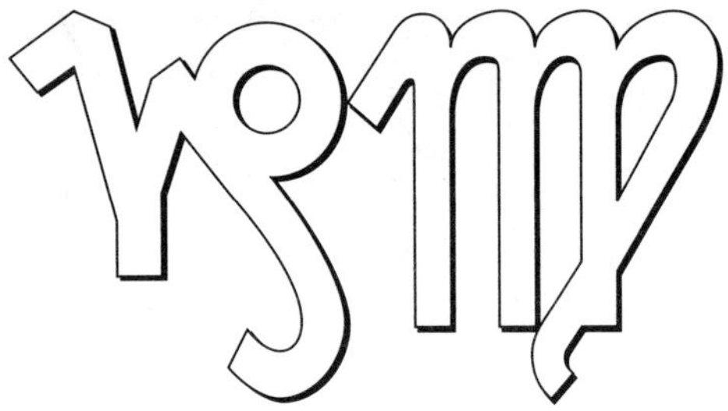

CONSCIENTIOUS COUPLE

Both of you are likely to be conscientious, hardworking, practical and responsible. Doing a good job matters to the two of you. Because your identity is found partially through a job, either one of you could occasionally neglect the relationship by focusing too much on productivity, and competence at your tasks or duties. You may share tasks, or even a profession as well as a romantic bond. Each of you shows your love by **doing** things for the partner. When you make a commitment, each of you will put your whole effort toward success.

COMPATIBLE—3

CAPRICORN/LIBRA

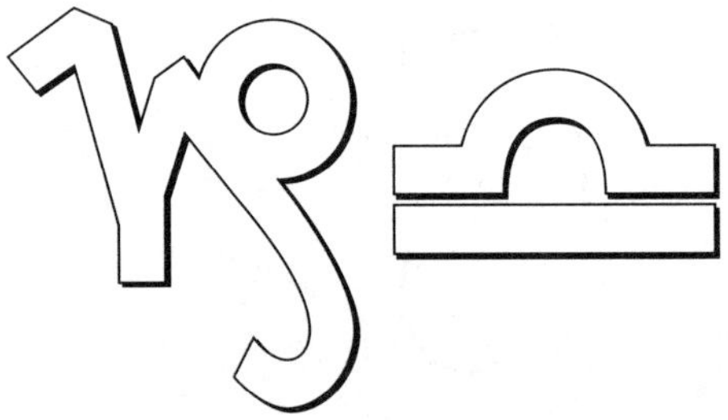

EFFORT VS. EASE

Contrasting needs and styles will challenge you both to create a meeting in the middle. He tends to be gracious, charming and relaxed. You tend to be more reserved, shy and cautious. He can be a fence-sitter, torn between many choices. You like definite answers and clear decisions. He needs to support you in any job you want as your work is important to your self-esteem. You can learn from him how to relax and be more easygoing. The two of you will need to keep a balance between love (relationship needs) and work (career or status demands). You each value the good will and respect of others.

CHALLENGING—2

CAPRICORN/SCORPIO

PERSEVERING PARTNERS

Both of you can be ambitious, dedicated and serious. When you make a commitment, you carry through. Either of you could be cynical, or feel disdainful of most of humanity. The two of you tend to mistrust romance of too much "sweetness and light." Yet you will work through heavy challenges to the relationship if necessary. You may be more concerned with tasks, and he more with sexuality, but you are both grounded and highly effective at whatever you decide to accomplish.

COMPATIBLE—3

UP AND DOWN — CAPRICORN/SAGITTARIUS

Although your personal styles are quite different, the two of you can do well if you combine forces. He is more an optimist; you are more a pessimist. He is naturally friendly and outgoing; you are more reserved. He is casual (what you might call messy and chaotic) while you are organized (what he might call picky). He can bring more laughter and zest to your life, but must recognize you won't get excited by all his varied enthusiasms. You can bring more stability and planning to his life as long as you avoid excessive criticism or trying to control too much. Together, you both can envision the best and work hard to create it.

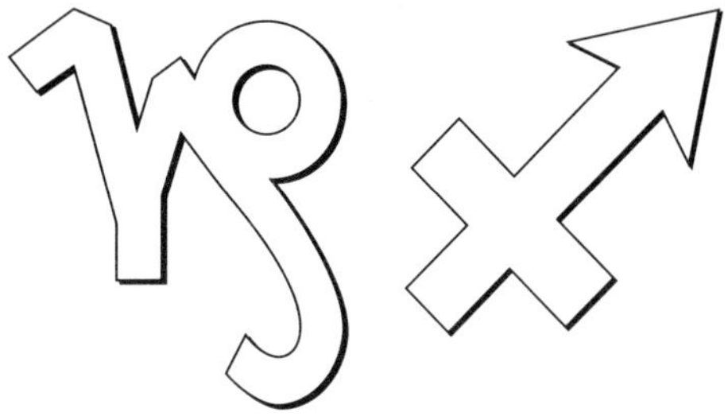

CHALLENGING—2

RESPONSIBLE ROMANCE — CAPRICORN/CAPRICORN

Fellow realists, both of you tend to be more practical than most people about relationships. You each value responsibility, ambition and dependability. You must know that you can trust your partner to carry through on promises. Since each of you needs to achieve and to rise to a position of authority and expertise, it is best to choose separate areas. If you don't try to dominate one another, you can celebrate each other's successes.

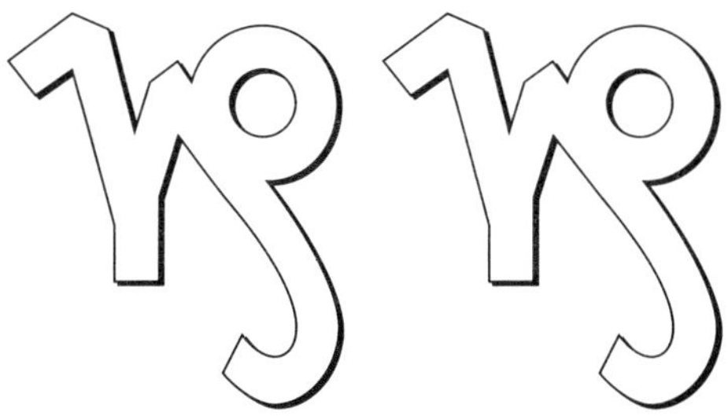

VERY COMPATIBLE—4

DIFFERENT DARLINGS — CAPRICORN/AQUARIUS

Diverse styles are highlighted here, but you have much to offer each other. You appreciate order, responsibility and structure. He values change, the freedom to rebel and going outside the rules. You can help him recognize essential limits and work within them. He can help you know when to thumb your nose at the world and do your own thing. Don't try to tie him too closely to a schedule. He needs to recognize, despite freedom urges, that any commitments he makes must be carried through responsibly. You can improve his practical coping skills and he can loosen you up, and encourage your individuality.

CHALLENGING—2

WHIMSICAL, WORKING WOOERS — CAPRICORN/PISCES

With a shared desire to accomplish something worthwhile, you may work well together. You are quite responsible, hardworking and dependable. He tends to be more dreamy and imaginative. You can help him to be more sensible and pragmatic. He can help you to be more whimsical and intuitive. He may open you up to romantic, magical realms, while you show him ways to make his dreams into reality. You both may enjoy quiet time—just being together.

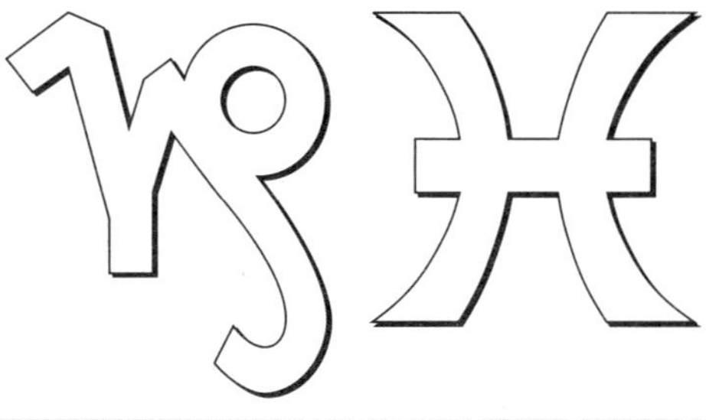

COMPATIBLE—3

AQUARIUS/ARIES

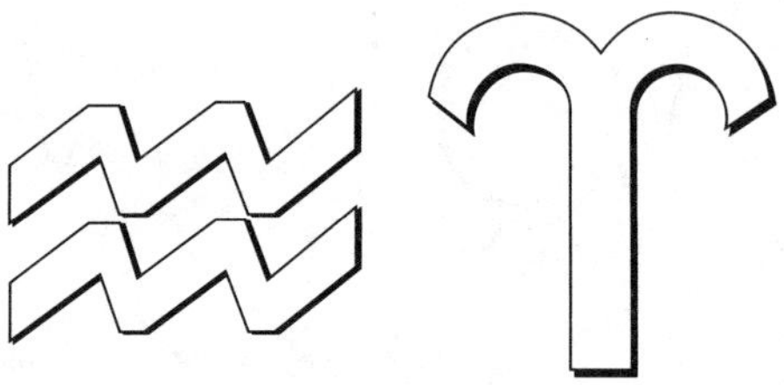

EAGER EXPERIMENTERS

Freedom is a watchword for you both. Commitment can occur, but no leashes, and no possessiveness allowed! You may encourage each other's venturesome spirits and expose yourselves to a wide variety of experiences. Eager and experimental, either of you might proclaim: "I'll try anything once." He can bring you back to a personal level if you get lost theorizing and thinking about the big picture. You can help him moderate his immediate, impulsive urges with some objectivity and detachment. Both of you are individualists and willing to tread a new or unconventional path.

COMPATIBLE—3

AQUARIUS/TAURUS

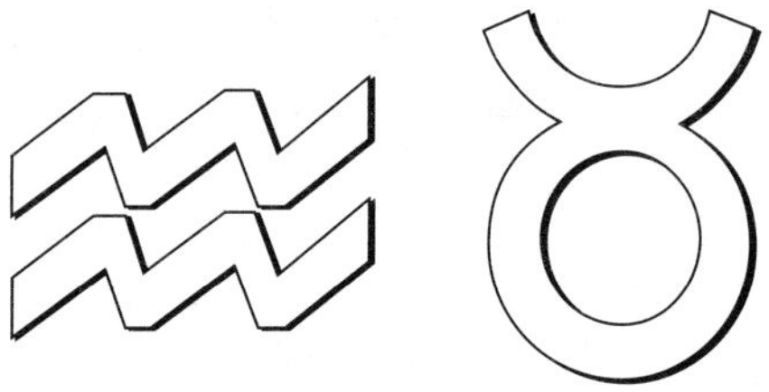

MIND OVER MATTER?

Although you two can have a clash of wills, you could learn much from one another. He is apt to seek the stable and familiar, while you are attracted to the new and unusual. He may be more physical and grounded, while you are more curious and unconventional. You can help him develop more objectivity and appreciation of progress. He can help you "come down to earth" and put some of your "wild" ideas to work in the world.

CHALLENGING—2

AQUARIUS/GEMINI

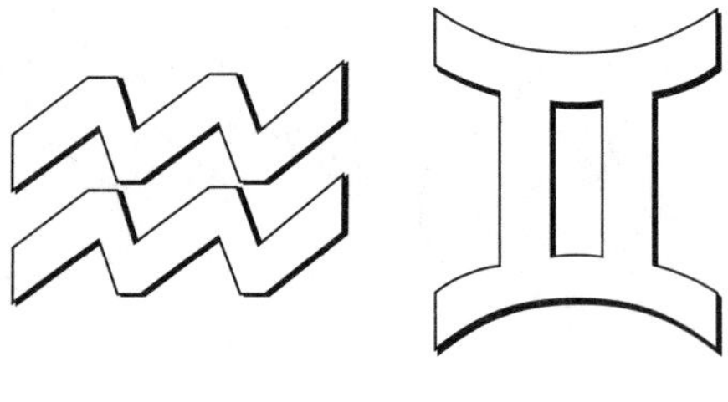

FRIENDS AND LOVERS

You both can be quite curious, observant, sociable and objective. Mental and communicative skills are likely. This placement emphasizes the mind more than emotions. Either of you could rationalize feelings away or "shine them on." Naturally friendly, the two of you find it easy to share. Equalitarian, you both want a relationship that is a true partnership.

COMPATIBLE—3

AQUARIUS/CANCER

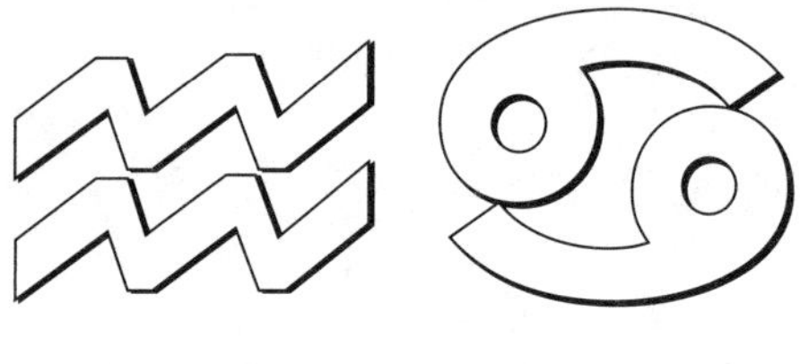

COMPROMISING COUPLE

Your needs may be quite different, so compromise will be essential. He yearns for the home fires, emotional commitment and a secure base. You thrive on innovation, stimulation from the outer world, variety and personal freedom. He may value family, while you value social causes, intellectual stimulation or being with friends. By loving without possessiveness, you can share a feeling connection **and** interesting experiences in the wider world.

VERY CHALLENGING—1

FREEDOM VS. CLOSENESS

AQUARIUS/LEO

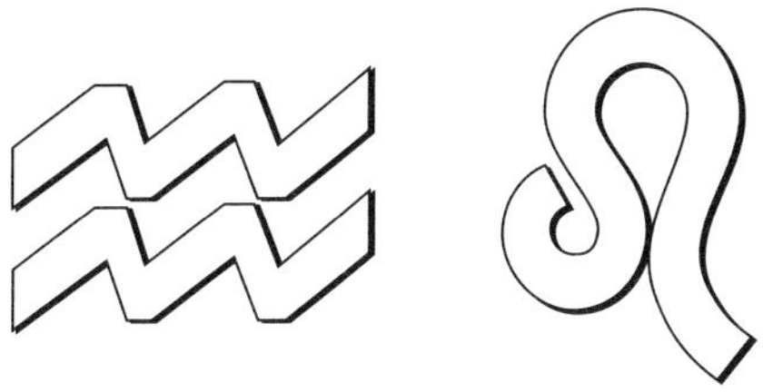

Yours is the natural attraction of opposites. The two of you can balance head and heart issues. One of you may be warm, expressive and open, when the other is cooler and detached. One could emphasize emotional response, while the other emphasizes intellectual stimulation. One seeks love; the other seeks freedom. Each of you have some of these opposing qualities, or you would not be drawn together. If you can share a middle ground, the two of you can love with openness. Each of you can be highly original and creative.

VERY COMPATIBLE—4

RATIONAL ROMANTICS

AQUARIUS/VIRGO

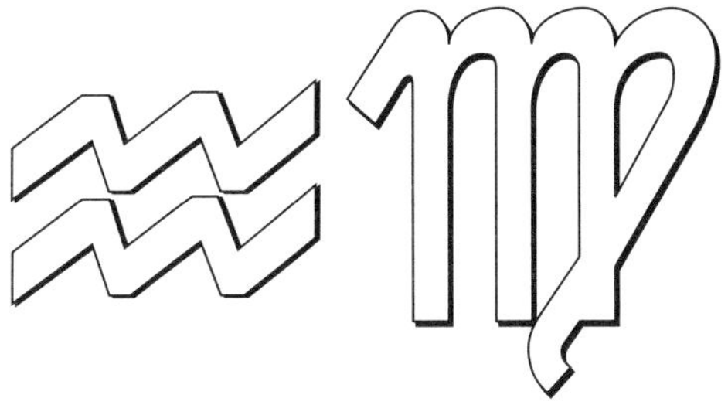

Communication and an openness to learning could be strong links between you. His style is more practical, sensible, step-by-step and oriented toward obtaining results (getting the job done). His work may be very important to him. Your style is more unconventional; you may be concerned with maintaining freedom, or just having lots of choices. You can be the experimenter while he is the technician. He may see you as chaotic and you may see him as hung up on petty details. If you learn from one another, he can help you to focus and test some of your wild ideas (or flashes of insight). You can widen his perspective and help him to consider alternatives.

VERY CHALLENGING—1

FOND FRIENDS

AQUARIUS/LIBRA

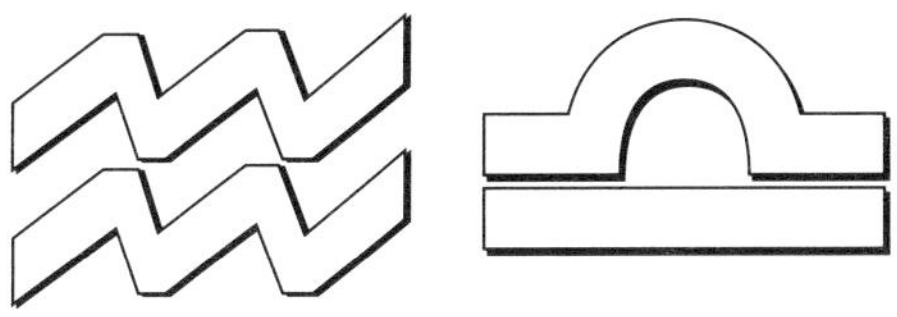

Both of you appreciate the worth of learning and good communication. You probably find it easy to talk to each other, although he may be more diplomatic and tactful (or wishy-washy), while you are more original and unconventional (or outrageous). You need a wider circle of friends or involvement in the outer world than he. He may need more grace, beauty and smooth flow in his life. Each of you can stimulate the other mentally, and you are both equalitarian, so find it easy to cooperate without dominance games. You both are naturally friendly.

COMPATIBLE—3

CHALLENGING CLOSENESS

AQUARIUS/SCORPIO

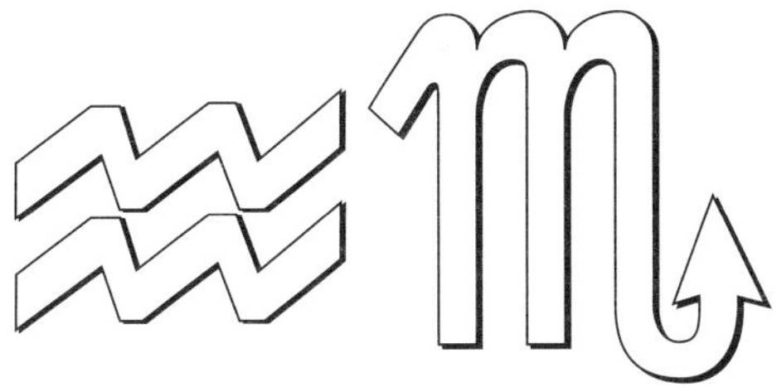

The two of you will be facing the challenge of keeping a balance between freedom and closeness or security versus change in your lives. He may want a closer emotional bond, while you play it cool (and vice versa). Getting your time tables in sync is important. He may seek safety and commitment, while you enjoy the new, unusual and ever-changing. Rather than polarizing on different sides, each of you needs to appreciate the other's point of view.

CHALLENGING—2

AQUARIUS/SAGITTARIUS FOREVER FREE

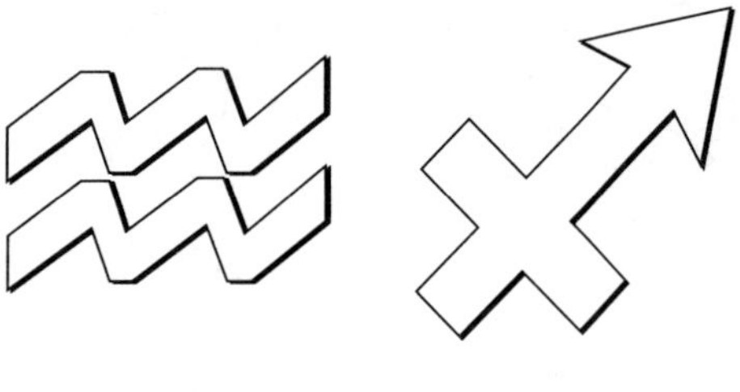

Each of you needs personal freedom, so a "no strings" relationship works best. Commitment is quite possible, but either of you might run at the thought of being "trapped" or tied down in a relationship. You are likely to stimulate each other mentally, enjoy social activities, relate to a wide variety of people and may share an interest in politics, fighting for justice or some kind of activist role in life. Encouraging each other's individuality is your strongest bond.

COMPATIBLE—3

AQUARIUS/CAPRICORN DIFFERENT DARLINGS

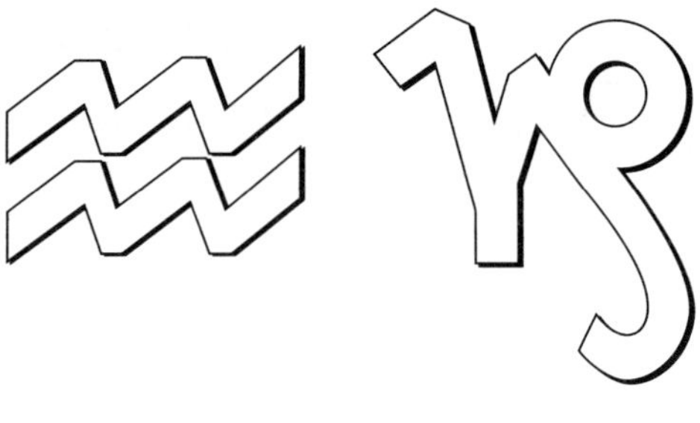

Diverse styles are highlighted here, but you have much to offer each other. He appreciates order, responsibility and structure. You value change, the freedom of many choices and being able to alter the rules. He can help you recognize essential limits and work within them. You can help him know when to thumb his nose at the world and do his own thing. He needs to realize you cannot be tied to a schedule. You need to recognize, despite your restlessness, that any commitments to him must be carried through responsibly. He can improve your practical coping skills and you can loosen him up.

CHALLENGING—2

AQUARIUS/AQUARIUS BOSOM BUDDIES

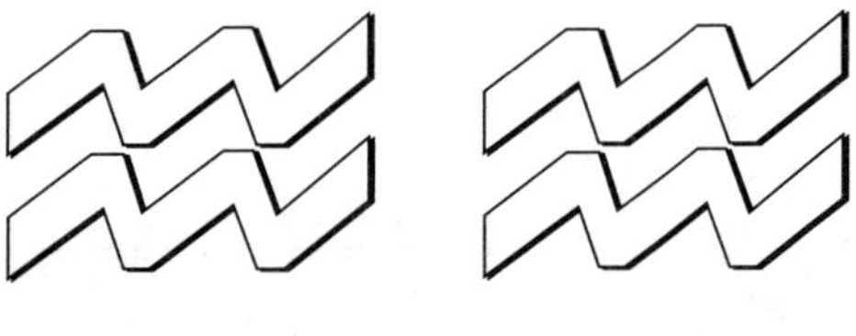

Each of you can recognize and appreciate the free spirit in the other. Open and perhaps a bit unconventional, you may opt for a relationship that is unusual, long-distance, individualistic, concerned with causes or very social. Breaking the usual rules is quite possible. You are likely to find each other very mentally stimulating. Others may see you as cool or impersonal, but each of you cherishes your uniqueness and that of your partner. Ideally, the two of you are best of friends.

VERY COMPATIBLE—4

AQUARIUS/PISCES IDEALISTIC INTIMATES

Different personal styles are likely, but you may share a dream of a better world. You tend to look ahead, and may have definite ideas about what the best possible world would be. He is likely to be imaginative, perhaps artistic, with a yen to make a more ideal world. If carried to an extreme, you both could be unrealistic. You may be more open and eager to talk, while he tends toward silence and holding things inside. You can help him be more objective when he dons those rose-colored glasses. He can help you spot subtle emotional cues.

CHALLENGING—2

IMAGINATIVE IMPULSES

PISCES/ARIES

A strong difference in personal styles is implied. He goes after what (or who) he wants openly, directly and eagerly. He can move swiftly into action. You are much more sensitive, shy, and disinclined to act until you are sure no one will be hurt. He can encourage action and a straightforward focus within you. You can encourage more imagination and sensitivity in him.

CHALLENGING—2

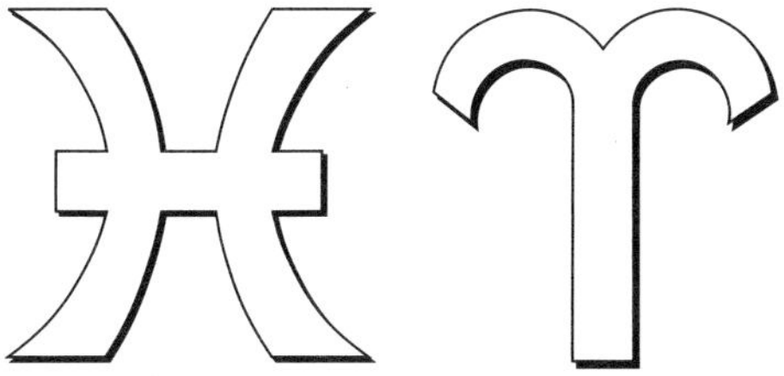

ARTISTIC ARDOR

PISCES/TAURUS

You are likely to feed each other's appreciation of beauty, pleasure and ease. An artistic bond is possible. He is apt to be more practical and grounded in the "real" world while you are more idealistic, imaginative and sensitive. He can help you connect physically and monetarily, and you can add some mystery, magic and romance to his life. You can feed his imagination; he can feed your senses.

COMPATIBLE—3

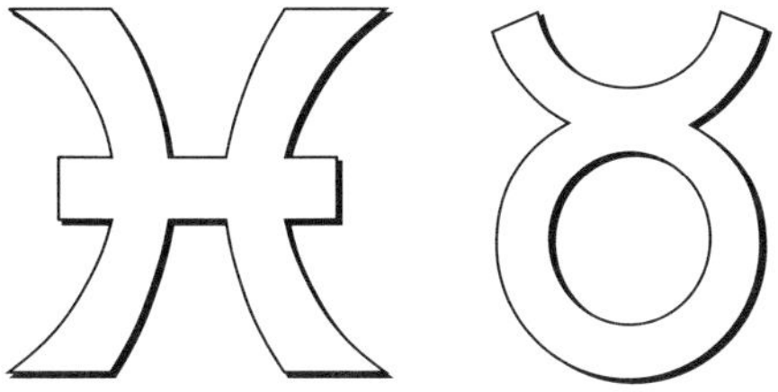

ROMANTIC RADAR

PISCES/GEMINI

You can both be restless and like sponges that pick up on or react to everything going on around you. His style is to discuss everything; talking helps him to understand. Your style is to absorb impressions and mull them over inside. You can both succumb to "information overload." You may be more romantic or idealistic than he. He can be more objective and lighthearted than you. Both of you could be multitalented with lots to learn, give and share with one another.

CHALLENGING—2

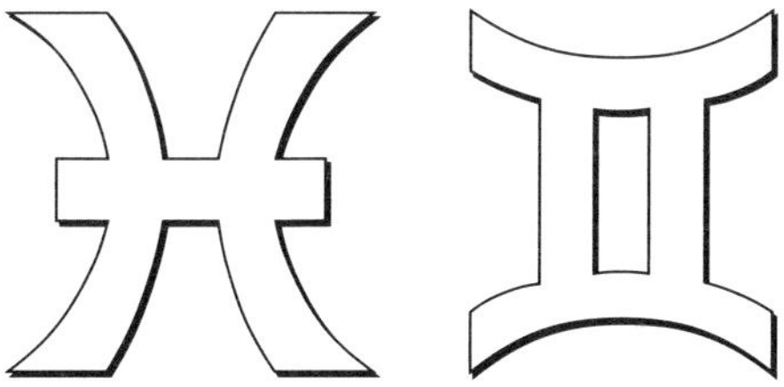

SENSITIVE SWEETHEARTS

PISCES/CANCER

Your personal styles are very compatible as each of you is far more sensitive than the average person. You both can be shy and tend to withdraw or clam up when hurt. You may both need to learn to speak up and discuss things on occasion. Because you can each be intuitive, you may tune into each other often without words. Practicalities are not a favored subject with either of you, so you might be tempted to retreat into your own, private, little world. You can both be very kind and empathic.

COMPATIBLE—3

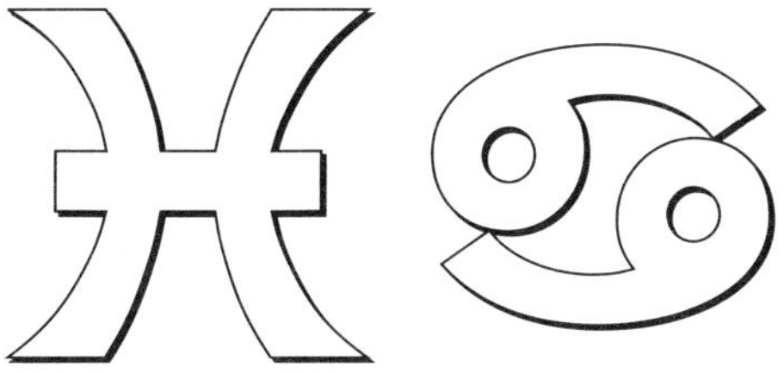

PISCES/LEO

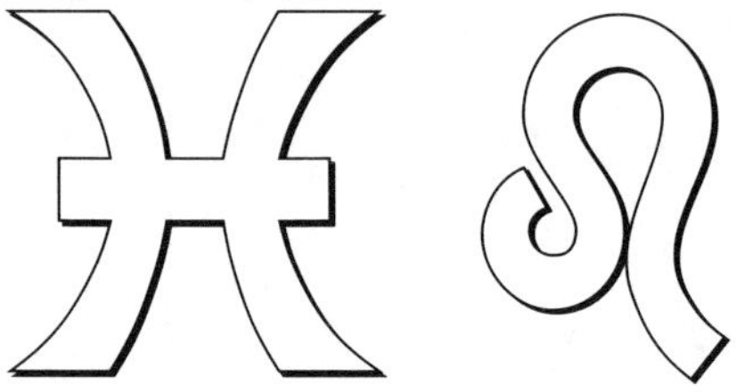

PRIVATE OR PUBLIC?

Although both of you have a romantic streak, your personal styles could vary widely. He tends to be outgoing, exuberant and eager to shine in the world. You tend to be sensitive, imaginative, shy, and inward. He needs the stimulation of play, fun and the admiration of others. You need privacy and an artistic or inspirational outlet. Combining forces will enrich both your lives if the two of you are understanding and willing to adapt to each other's needs.

VERY CHALLENGING—1

PISCES/VIRGO

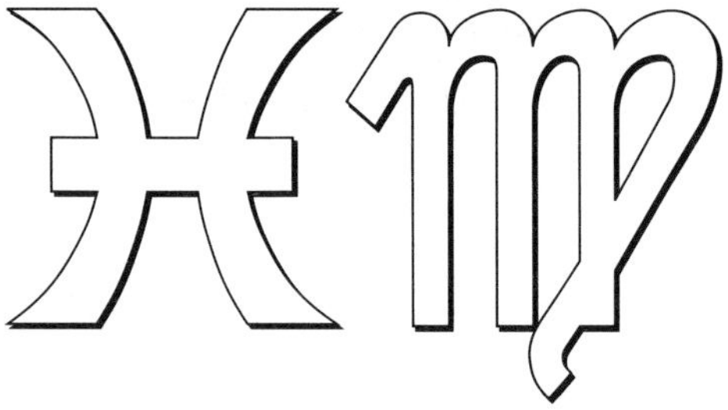

FANTASY OR FOCUS?

Yours is a natural attraction of opposites. Each of you is dealing with the polarity of the real versus the ideal. He tends to be more practical, grounded and sensible. You tend to be more imaginative, romantic and idealistic. (But you can switch ends at times on the seesaw.) He probably learns step-by-step, while you absorb information in whole concepts. He can bring more logic, order, and common sense into your life and you can bring more magic, mystery and imagination into his. Together, you can ground your dreams, turning visions into reality.

VERY COMPATIBLE—4

PISCES/LIBRA

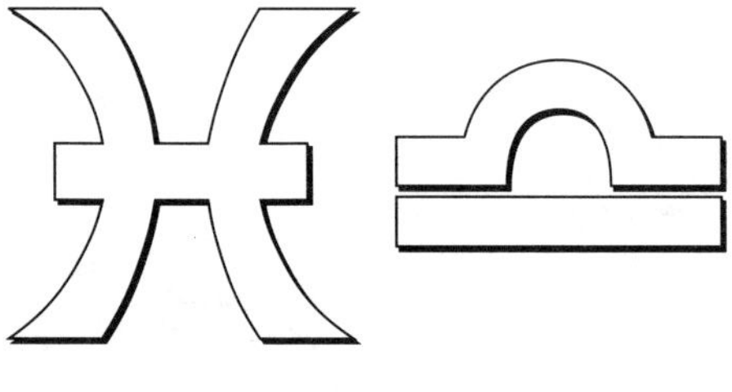

SOFT-FOCUS SENTIMENT

Both of you are likely to value beauty and harmony. Consequently, you might encourage one another to avoid unpleasantness or confrontations of any sort. He prefers to be kind, tactful, and diplomatic, while you can easily done rose-colored glasses and pretend everything is perfect even when it is not. The two of you may share a love of beauty and are both capable of the sacrifices and compromises necessary to share your life with someone else. You can feed each other's romantic streaks.

VERY CHALLENGING—1

PISCES/SCORPIO

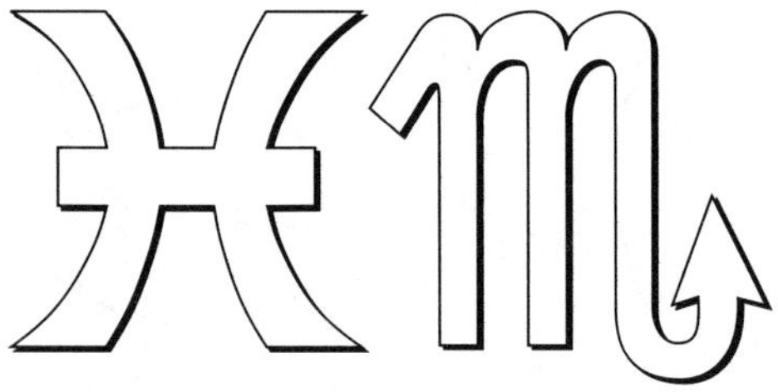

INTIMATE INTUITION

Each of you may easily tune into the feelings of the other. Intuitive, you can enjoy just being together, without having to make conversation. Neither of you is likely to wear your heart on your sleeve. Sometimes this can mean one of you sulks, stays resentful or keeps secret feelings or issues that should be aired. When using your empathy, each of you may feel no one understands you as well as your partner.

COMPATIBLE—3

MYSTICAL MATES

PISCES/SAGITTARIUS

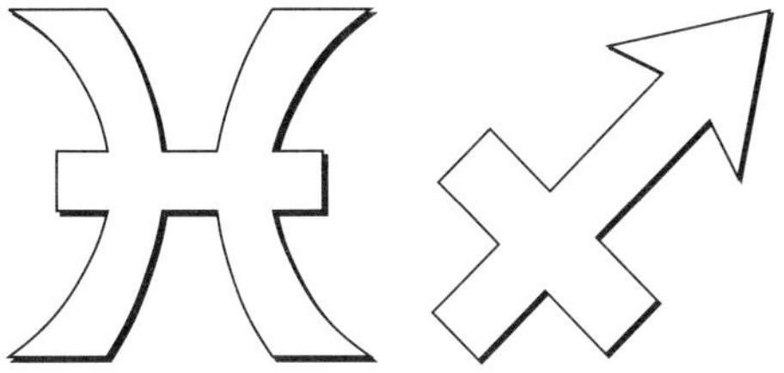

Since both of you are idealists, you have a lot in common. You might share a mystical connection, an interest in religious or spiritual matters, an urge to make the world better, or simply a drive to be the most moral, ethical, **best** person possible. He tends to be more direct and you more circumspect, so you could clash over issues of truth versus compassion or honesty versus tact. Find a middle ground. A shared love of nature or quest for transcendence can be a strong bond between you.

CHALLENGING—2

WHIMSICAL, WORKING WOOERS

PISCES/CAPRICORN

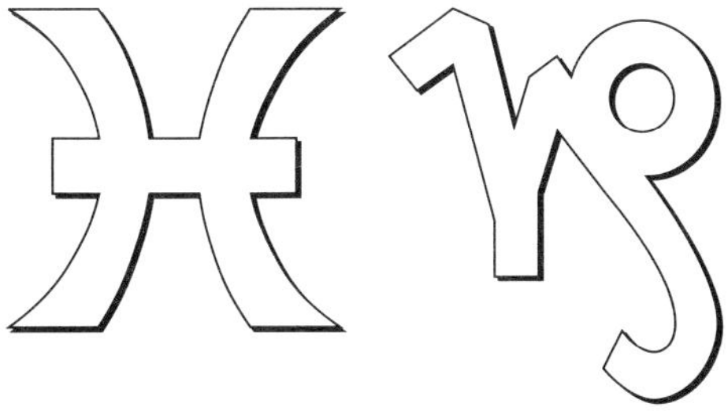

With a shared desire to accomplish something worthwhile, you may work well together. He can be quite responsible, hardworking and dependable. You have wonderful imaginative and visualizing capacities. He can help you to be more sensible and pragmatic. You can help him to be more whimsical and intuitive. You may open him up to romantic, magical realms, while he shows you ways to make your dreams into reality. You both may enjoy quiet time—just being together.

COMPATIBLE—3

IDEALISTIC INTIMATES

PISCES/AQUARIUS

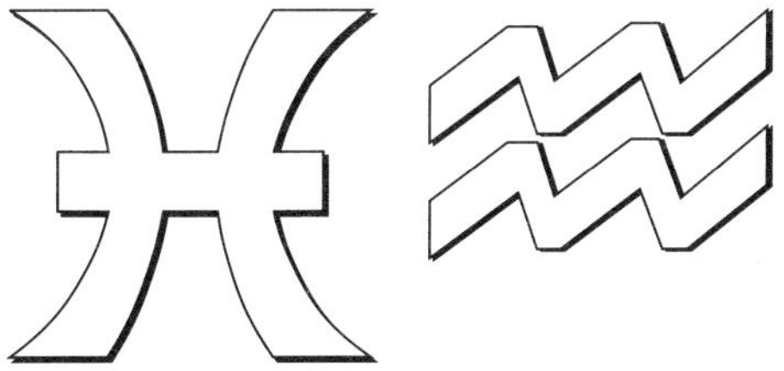

Different personal styles are likely, but you may share a dream of a better world. You both tend to look ahead, and may have definite ideas about what the best possible world would be. You are likely to be imaginative, perhaps artistic, with a yen to make a more ideal world. He is a reformer at heart, with a passion for justice and fair play. If carried to an extreme, you both could be unrealistic. He may be more unconventional or rebellious, while you tend more toward shyness and holding back. He can help you be more objective. You can help him spot subtle emotional cues.

CHALLENGING—2

MAGICAL MATES

PISCES/PISCES

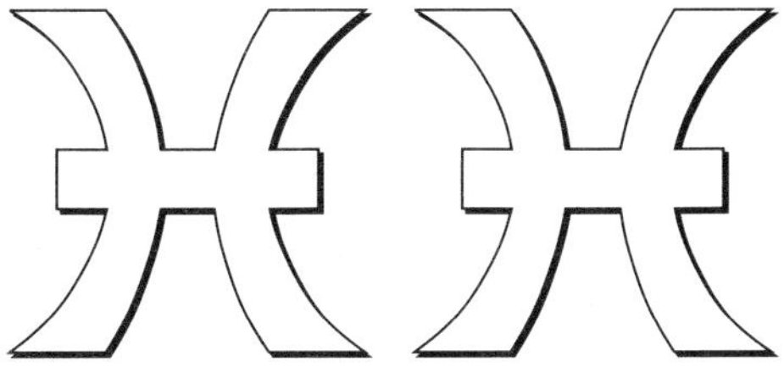

You may feel that you have found your soul mate! More than any pair, you can be sensitive to each other's feelings. Quiet time together can be very soothing. You might also share a love of art, beauty, nature, fantasy, fiction, or compassionate or imaginative activities. Because you are attuned to another, you might also feed each other's anxieties, insecurities, depression or escapism (into drugs, alcohol, fantasy, etc.). Naturally romantic, you would like to guard your partner against any hard wind from life. You believe in perfect love.

VERY COMPATIBLE—4

MERCURY

Mercury is the primary planet of the reasoning mind, so is one of the keys to communication, our voice and the way we tend to express (or not) our ideas. Mercury also rules the hands so has something to say about our dexterity. Mercury is a key to how we think, how we learn and what interests us.

Remember, for a full picture, you would also include the house of your Mercury and its aspects, but we can still learn a great deal from sign placements only.

First read the shorthand description for the sign **your** Mercury is in. Then, compare it with the shorthand description for the Mercury sign of your partner. Next, read the paragraph which describes a bit about how you two might interact with one another. Each combination is also designated as either very compatible, compatible, challenging or very challenging. (These rate as 4-3-2-1 on our **Compatibility Scale**.)

> Your partner's Mercury sign offers clues about how to talk to him and what is most likely to be "heard." The more each of you tunes in to your partner's Mercury, the better you will understand each other.

MERCURY IN ARIES: THE VERBAL DUELIST

Communication Style: rapid, direct (honest), impulsive, aggressive (biting, ironic, sarcastic), may interrupt
Voice: powerful, might be loud, forceful, could be skilled orator or debater
Dexterity: may have mechanical skills, manual strength or be quick with hands
Interests: anything personal, courage, the new, freedom, self-reliance, self-expression
Thinking: original, questions authorities, seeks new ideas, takes mental risks
Learn Best: by direct experience, when challenged, in short spurts, when active

MERCURY IN TAURUS: THE COMFORTABLE COMMUNICATOR

Communication Style: often silent, deliberate, slow, comfortable
Voice: pleasant (may have musical talent), relaxing; silent unless something worth saying
Dexterity: very sensuous, may communicate through touch
Interests: money, sensuality, physical comforts and possessions
Thinking: grounded, practical, good memory, business/financial skills
Learn Best: slowly, regularly, comfortably; dealing with facts, figures, tangible world.

MERCURY IN GEMINI: THE INQUISITIVE INVESTIGATOR

Communication Style: talkative, may use hands to communicate, clever, quick-witted
Voice: can be a good mimic, talent for accents & foreign languages, light
Dexterity: lots of dexterity, agility; good hand-eye coordination
Interests: anything and everything; may enjoy word games, travel, socializing
Thinking: rapid, insatiably curious, logical, may be superficial, never stops figuring things out
Learn Best: flitting from topic to topic, quick perceptions, varied experiences

MERCURY IN CANCER: THE FEELING THINKER

Communication Style: talk when feeling safe (otherwise silent), sensitive
Voice: soothing, protective (or insecure and whining), arouses emotions
Dexterity: may be very skilled at cooking, carpentry or home-centered arts
Interests: family, food, home, land, public, security, homeland, feelings
Thinking: emotional, uses intuition, good memory
Learn Best: by absorbing information and experiences, in protected setting

MERCURY IN LEO: THE ENTERTAINER

Communication Style: dramatic, exaggerative, humorous, persuasive, gives compliments
Voice: can be loud, excited, tends to stir others up, natural salesperson
Dexterity: flamboyant gestures likely, may move too quickly
Interests: love, power, children, fame, creativity, positive attention
Thinking: with the heart, self-focused, drawn to exciting possibilities
Learn Best: through self-expression, with an adrenaline rush, when admired

MERCURY IN VIRGO: THE WORDSMITH

Communication Style: exacting, precise, professional, meticulous analysis
Voice: cool, rational ("Mr. Spock"), may be critical or dryly humorous
Dexterity: technical or mechanical skills possible, may be good with models, miniatures or fine, detail work
Interests: health, improving/repairing, science, math, job or career
Thinking: cool, logical, impersonal, skeptical, good common sense
Learn Best: step-by-step, with organized presentation, through finding flaws and fixing them

MERCURY IN LIBRA: THE DIPLOMAT

Communication Style: graceful, charming, but can be cool, dispassionate, objective
Voice: refined, pleasant, knack for expressing what people want to hear
Dexterity: may create beauty through hands or tongue; delicate touch
Interests: relationships, fair play, aesthetic matters, love, harmony, the law
Thinking: compares and contrasts; balances opposites; natural strategist
Learn Best: seeking both sides, in pleasant surroundings, through teamwork or competition

MERCURY IN SCORPIO: THE RELENTLESS RESEARCHER

Communication Style: can be manipulative or sarcastic but also passionate, intense
Voice: hypnotic, persuasive, can be confrontive and willful or powerfully convincing
Dexterity: controlled; suspicious (may expect worst of people) but knows the "sexy moves"
Interests: anything hidden (occult, psychology, mysteries) or involving power
Thinking: incisive, penetrating, intuitive, shrewd, thorough; research talent
Learn Best: by getting to the bottom/the end; ferreting out secrets; transforming concepts

MERCURY IN SAGITTARIUS: THE SAGE (PHILOSOPHER)

Communication Style: blunt, honest, talkative, intellectual, natural storyteller
Voice: may be pompous (know-it-all) tone, but can be skilled comic and mimic
Dexterity: moving too fast can lead to stumbling or stubbed toes, grand gestures
Interests: law, travel, writing, philosophy, Higher Truth, anything fun
Thinking: optimistic, may overgeneralize or leap to conclusions, natural student
Learn Best: if able to discuss anything, go anywhere, ask any questions

MERCURY IN CAPRICORN: THE CAREFUL COMMUNICATOR

Communication Style: reticent, careful with words, formal, earnest, polite
Voice: inhibited and blocked OR aura of authority and expertise
Dexterity: careful, rarely spontaneous gestures, every move is pre-planned
Interests: status, control, authority, career, traditions, success
Thinking: cautious (may doubt mental ability til proven); practical, businesslike
Learn Best: in structured setting, with organization, concentration, thoroughness

MERCURY IN AQUARIUS: THE UNCONVENTIONAL THINKER

Communication Style: quirky, unconventional, irreverent, outspoken, talkative
Voice: cool & dispassionate usually; colorful/exciting when politics or humanitarian principles are involved
Dexterity: more in head than body; mind may race ahead of hands (and other people)
Interests: the new, science, organizations, reading, progress, the unusual
Thinking: original, inventive, unconventional, sudden insights, rapid perception
Learn Best: on your own, by questioning authorities, through quick flashes of brilliance

MERCURY IN PISCES: INTUITIVE UNDERSTANDING

Communication Style: poetic, vague, imaginative, evasive, idealistic, nonverbal
Voice: soft (may be hard to hear); often silent; speaks much when feeling safe
Dexterity: talent for mimicry, musical instruments, songwriting, singing
Interests: the mystical, arts, downtrodden, spiritual or unseen realms, romance
Thinking: intuitive, impressionable, symbolic (may be hard to put into words), great creative imagination, visualizing skills
Learn Best: absorbing, globally, holistically, psychically, through emotions

MERCURY PAIRS

ARIES/ARIES

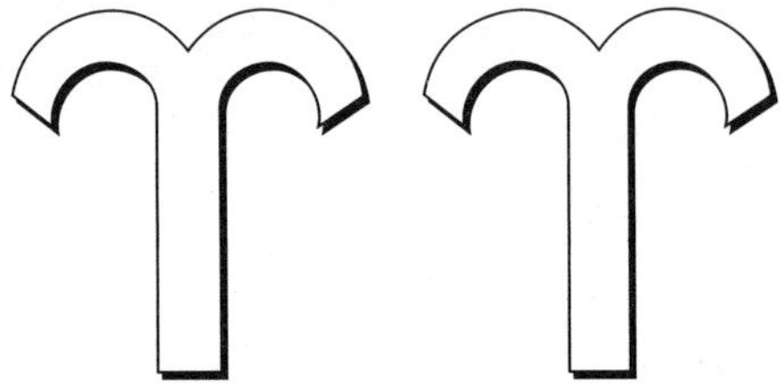

TONGUES LIKE SWORDS

You both can think and speak quickly, and may use words as weapons (sarcastic, argumentative, biting). When your partner's impulsive communication embarrasses or annoys either of you, remember it could as easily be you blurting things out. Communication is vital to your association and you both can find ideas exciting. You learn well through personal experience, excite each other mentally and may both enjoy verbal fireworks.

VERY COMPATIBLE—4

ARIES/TAURUS

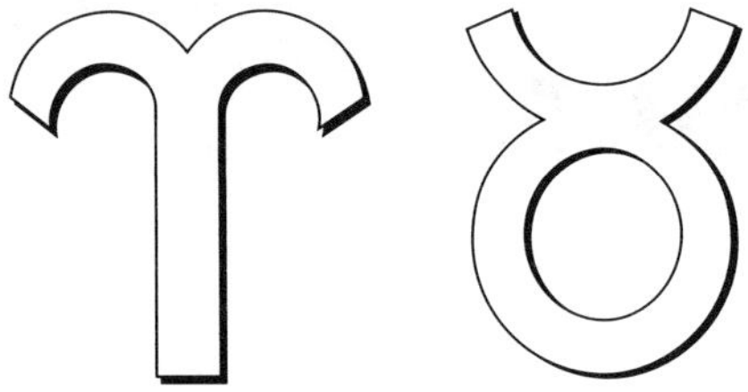

THE HARE AND THE TORTOISE

You're tempted to finish his sentences sometimes when he gets so deliberate and slow. Don't play tortoise and hare. If you slow down a bit, he'll teach you about savoring and enjoying communication. Some of your independent thinking can rub off on him and some of his pragmatism can rub off on you. You can sometimes provide the initiating spark, while he supplies patience and follow-through.

CHALLENGING—2

ARIES/GEMINI

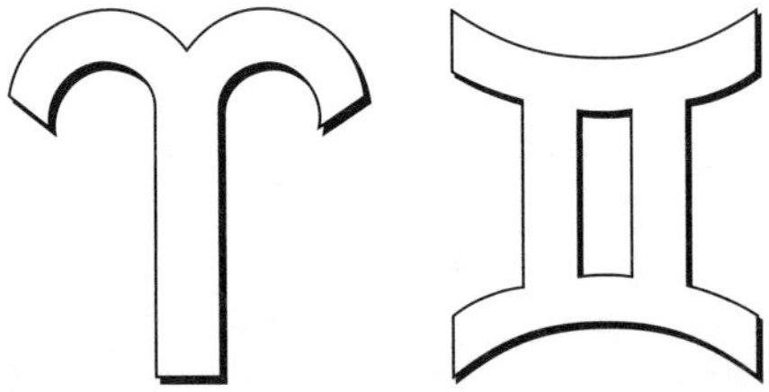

QUICK TONGUE & QUICK WITS

You find it easy to keep up with one another mentally. Your speech can be a bit more cutting (ironic, sarcastic), but his quick-wittedness is strong. Repartee and humor come easily in your association. You stimulate each other's curiosity and eagerness to learn. Word play and shared fun with games are possible. Each of you brings out expressiveness in the other. You are both quite perceptive.

COMPATIBLE—3

ARIES/CANCER

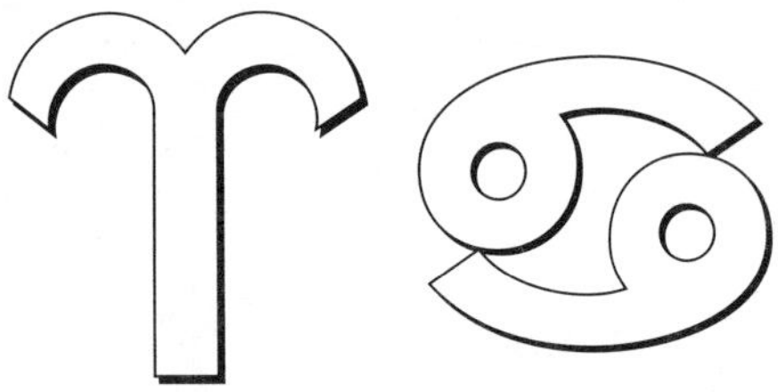

TONGUE LIKE A SWORD AND CARING COMMUNICATOR

You're ready to let it all hang out and he's worried that someone's feelings will be hurt. Bluntness and honesty come naturally to you, while he may approach topics sideways (like a crab). Try to appreciate each other's different styles without needing to change them. With compromise, each of you can think independently and be very direct with your ideas, but still choose words which bring people closer.

CHALLENGING—2

EAGER BEAVER AND SUPER SALESPERSON

ARIES/LEO

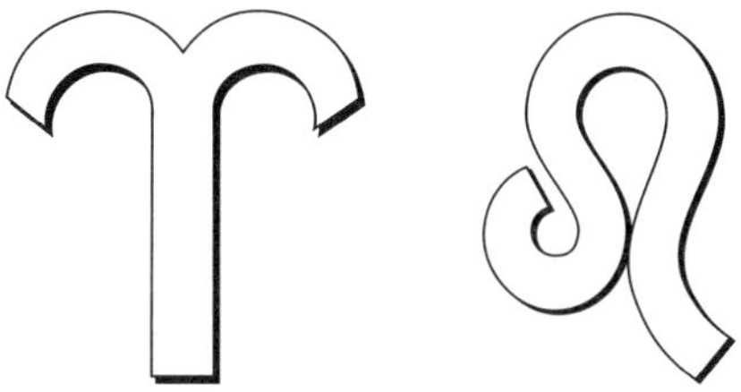

You find lots to discuss with one another. Communication is exciting when you are together. You tend to stimulate each other and both may have to practice listening as well as talking. Spontaneity and lots of dramatic conversations are likely. You can quickly exhaust topics and tend to move on rapidly in conversations. Although each of you may find your mind or tongue works faster than that of other acquaintances, the two of you easily keep up with one another.

COMPATIBLE—3

UTTERLY UNCHECKED AND PERFECTLY PRECISE

ARIES/VIRGO

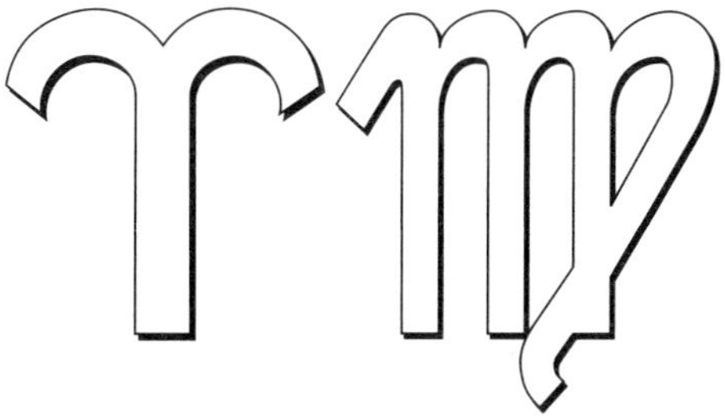

You shoot from the hip verbally and don't want to waste time, while he strives for flawless grammar, correct pronunciation and just the **right** phrase for the occasion. Don't criticize or antagonize one another. You can learn more precision from him and he can learn more spontaneity from you. He can appreciate the excitement you bring to topics, and you can appreciate his common sense and practicality.

VERY CHALLENGING—1

OPPOSITES ATTRACT

ARIES/LIBRA

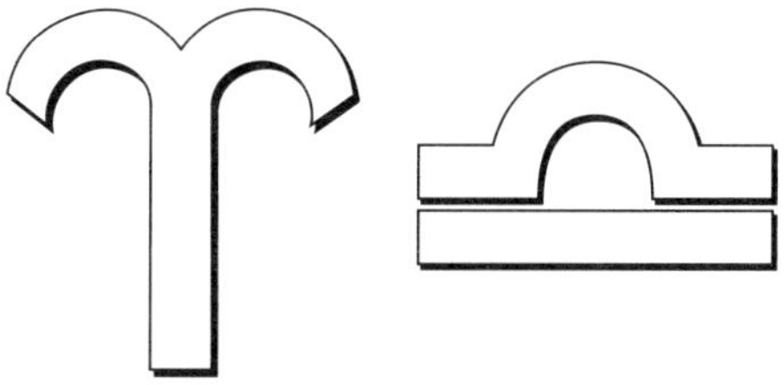

Does it seem you're on opposite sides of lots of issues? Does he sometimes argue both sides of an issue (just for fun)? Are you more blunt while he believes in "little white lies"? There is a middle ground if you only seek it. Balancing conversational give-and-take may be a bit challenging, but the rewards are great. Even though your styles are sometimes opposite, you are drawn together mentally—like each other's missing halves.

VERY COMPATIBLE—4

NO-HOLDS-BARRED VS. SUBTLE AND SECRETIVE

ARIES/SCORPIO

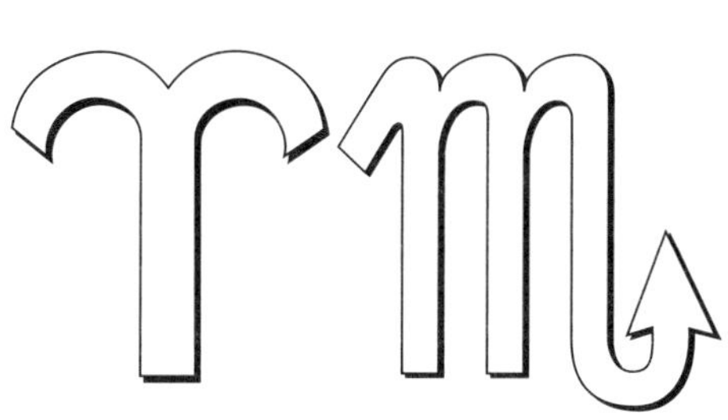

You like to deal with subjects rapidly and move on to something new. He can be like a bulldog—chewing ideas to death. You are both capable of aggressing with words, but he'll remember what was said much longer than you. Don't say things to one another that you'll regret later. You can learn verbal subtlety from him, and he can learn more directness and forthright expression from you.

VERY CHALLENGING—1

ARIES/SAGITTARIUS

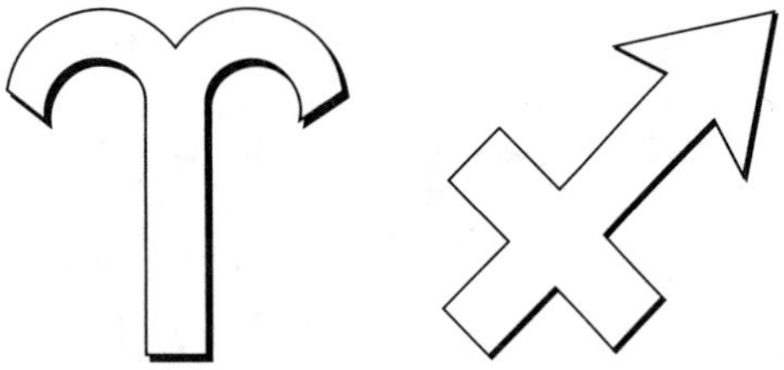

IMPULSIVELY HONEST

The two of you can raise foot-in-mouth to a new art form. You stimulate each other to impulsive speech and may jump to conclusions or trip over words sometimes in your hurry to "get it out." You both think quickly and may be impatient waiting for others to "catch up"—but you've met your match here! You can spark humor and an adventurous spirit in each other.

COMPATIBLE—3

ARIES/CAPRICORN

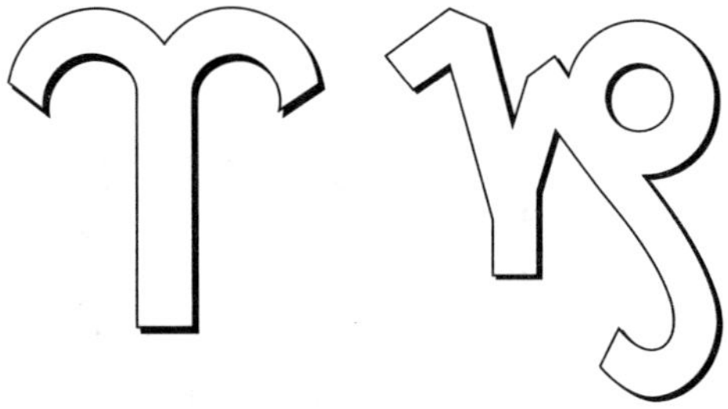

RAPID RESPONSE AND CAREFULLY CORRECT

You're confident and expressive with the mind and tongue. He's cautious, responsible and concerned with his place in society. You are verbally open and direct. He's formal and may even be inhibited (worried about making a mistake). Don't let him squash your spontaneity with a need for control, but do learn from him to consider the consequences of what you say.

CHALLENGING—2

ARIES/AQUARIUS

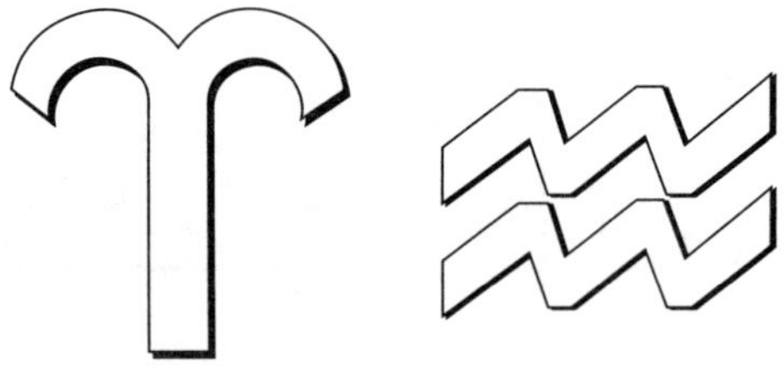

THE PIONEER AND THE FREE SPIRIT

Fellow rebels! Both of you are independent thinkers and may sometimes say things purely for the shock value. You two resist dogmas and other people's rules. You are attracted to new ideas and insights. You stimulate one another to be free and individualistic in your thoughts and speech. You both tend to think for yourselves and to question authorities. You enjoy exposing one another to new ideas.

COMPATIBLE—3

ARIES/PISCES

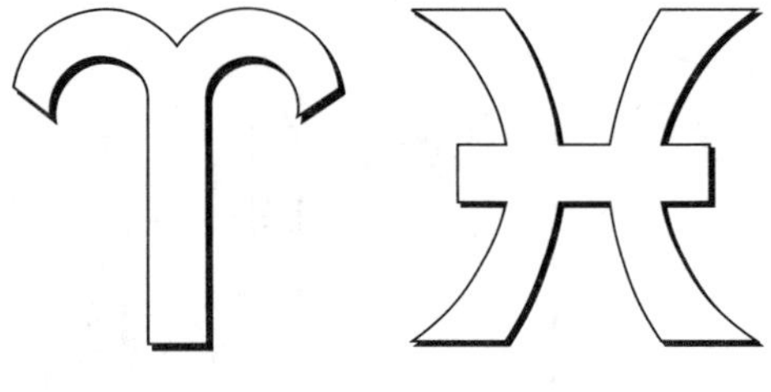

DEFINITELY DIRECT AND SENSITIVELY SUBTLE

You trust personal experience, while he trusts "vibes." You say what you mean and mean what you say. He can be poetic (and unclear). He may even lie sometimes to protect someone's feelings (including his own). Honesty is admirable, but tact has its place. Try to learn from one another's different styles of thought and speech. He can become a bit more forthright and forthcoming, and you can become more subtle and sensitive.

CHALLENGING—2

THE TORTOISE AND THE HARE

TAURUS/ARIES

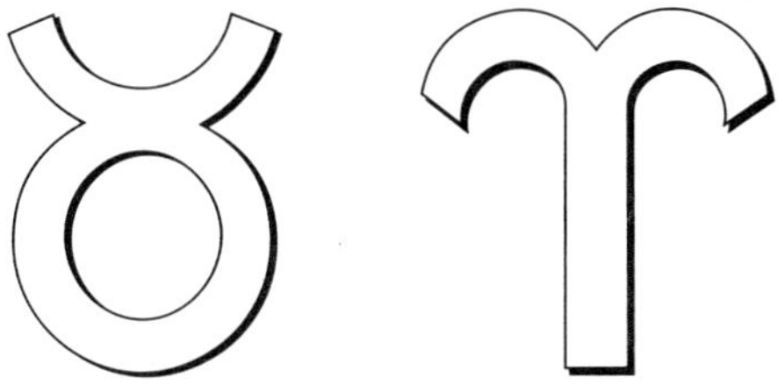

Your communication style is rather deliberate. He may try to rush you along. Impulsive speech is a potential for him. He reacts quickly, thinks on his feet, and sometimes speaks before thinking. You follow familiar mental pathways, want learning to be effortless and can be a bit too attached to the solid or already known. You can learn a little expressiveness and risk-taking from him, and he can learn a bit of patience and fortitude from you.

CHALLENGING—2

COMFORTABLE COMMUNICATORS

TAURUS/TAURUS

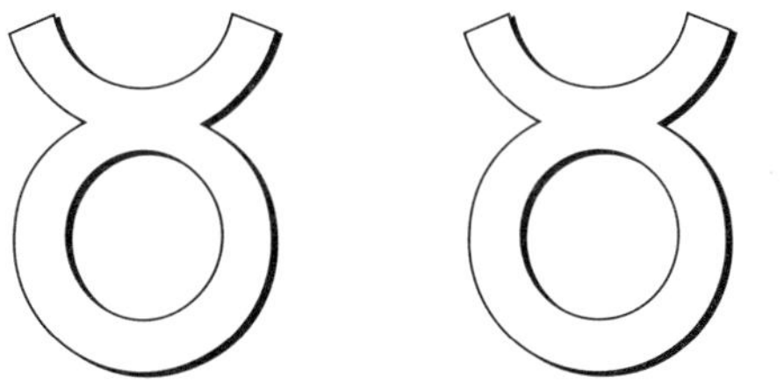

You both enjoy being laid-back and comfortable in the communication realm. A relaxed attitude appeals. Mental exertion does not. You can be verbally affectionate and prefer pleasant interactions. You may both enjoy thinking, talking about, or creating beauty with your hands. You learn through doing and may share business skills, or a good, practical mind. You can be skilled at giving and receiving massages.

VERY COMPATIBLE—4

DELIBERATE VS. DILETTANTE

TAURUS/GEMINI

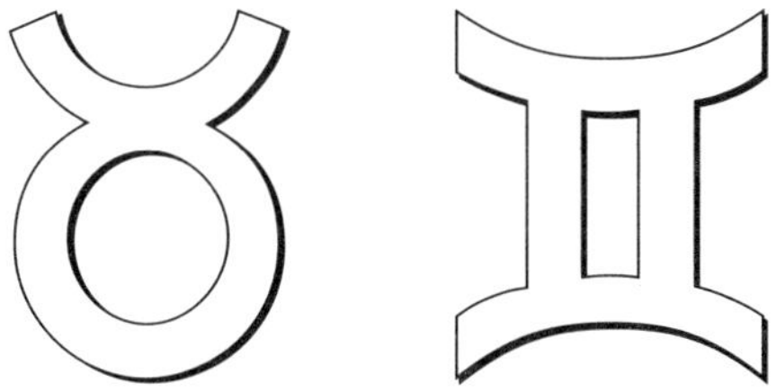

You like to learn steadily in a systematic fashion and he picks things up in bits and starts. You tend to speak only when you feel you have something relevant to say, while he may enjoy talking for the sheer joy of it. You can learn a bit of lightheartedness from him and he may adopt some practicality from you. He could expose you to new ideas, while you could teach him something about follow-through and commitment.

CHALLENGING—2

QUIET, UNASSUMING

TAURUS/CANCER

You both know when to remain silent. You want conversations to be pleasant and agreeable, while he wants to protect everyone's feelings (including his own). You both may have business skills and can easily apply your minds (and conversations) to handling possessions or amassing security. Each of you could enjoy touching a lot, although you may require a bit of drawing out verbally. (You tend not to push your viewpoints.)

COMPATIBLE—3

TAURUS/LEO

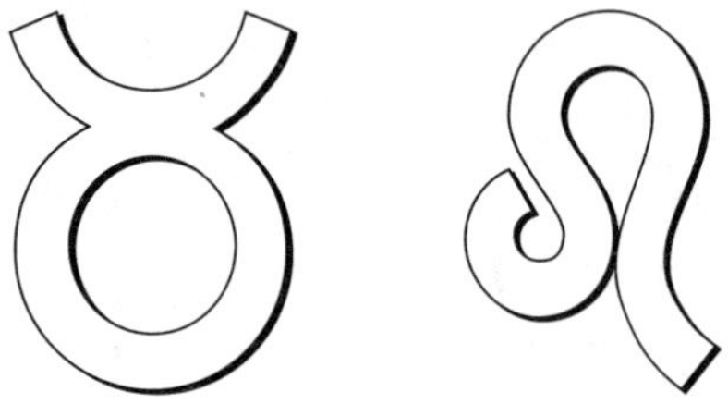

STRONG OPINIONS

You both may feel that **your** way of thinking is the **only** way. Firm opinions are likely. His verbal style is more dramatic and persuasive (sometimes arrogant). Yours is more step-by-step. His exaggerations may drive you crazy at times, while your "literal" mind can annoy him greatly (especially if you miss his jokes). You can learn from him to add some zip and zest to your speech, while he can learn from you to be more sensible and grounded.

CHALLENGING—2

TAURUS/VIRGO

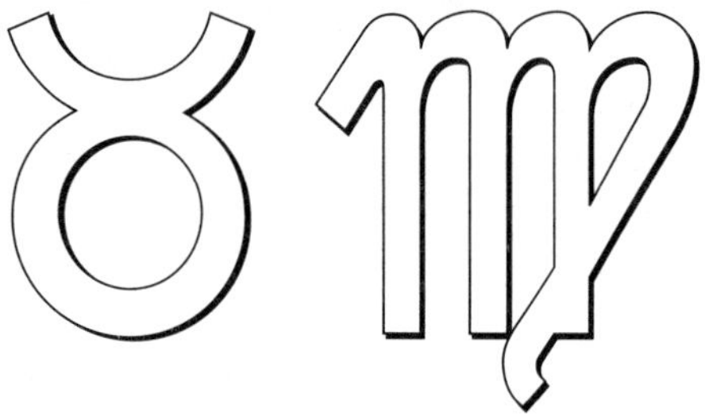

PRAGMATISTS

Both of you have a practical, sensible bent. You may even put your minds to work earning money through writing, speaking, mental or physical dexterity, etc. Each of you communicates well in professional environments (where something relevant needs to be conveyed), but is probably not keen on social chitchat. You both tend toward common sense and prefer to think about real issues and basic needs.

COMPATIBLE—3

TAURUS/LIBRA

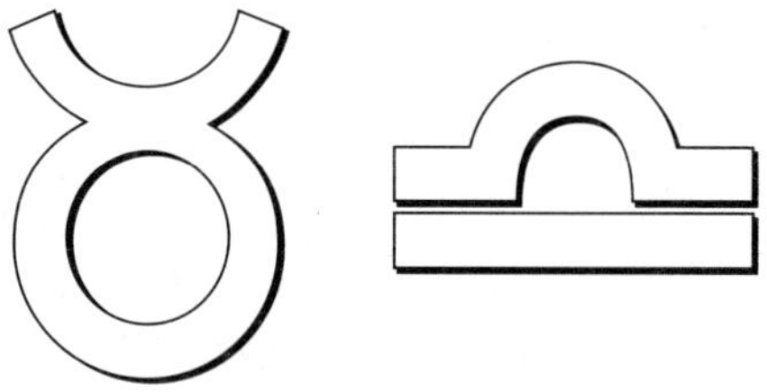

LOVELY LANGUAGE

Each of you may have talent for flowing conversations, poetic language or creating beauty with words (singing, song writing, etc.). Or you could simply be masters at avoiding unpleasant thoughts or words. You may seek more understanding of practical matters, while he pursues abstract concepts. Money, possessions and material security are of interest to you, while he prefers to discuss relationships, competition or face-to-face encounters. Each of you could bring a new perspective to the other.

VERY CHALLENGING—1

TAURUS/SCORPIO

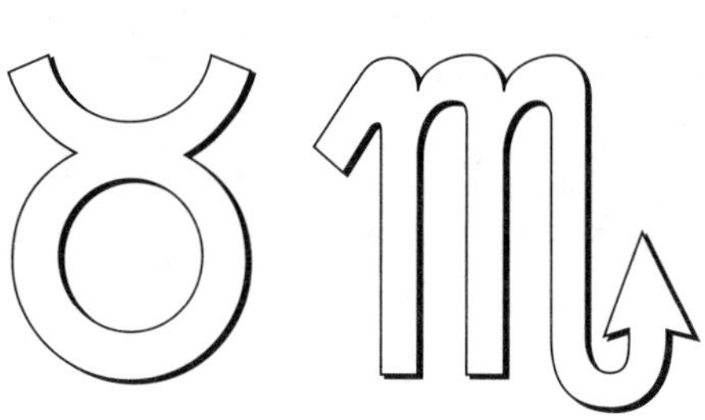

COMFORT VS. CONFRONTATION

You'd just as soon keep conversations pleasant and affectionate, while he is sometimes drawn to the dark side. You want to discuss love and pleasure while he wants to dig up disagreeable issues. Life should be big enough for intense emotional confrontations **and** good feelings. If things get too heavy, a massage (you both have sensually skilled fingers) will bring back positive vibes. Although opposites, you have a natural attraction and can help each other find the golden mean.

VERY COMPATIBLE—4

MATERIAL VS. SPIRITUAL

TAURUS/SAGITTARIUS

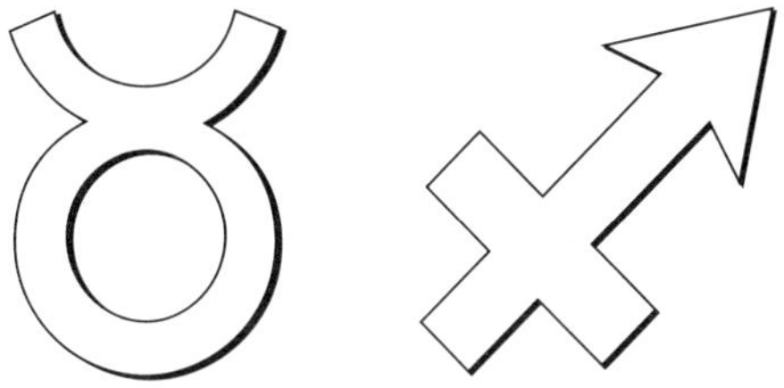

You want to focus on current, practical issues and he wants to discuss his dreams and schemes for the future. He has grand plans and you want to know where the money is coming from. It is important to have aspirations to reach for, but we also need the common sense to figure out the necessary steps toward our vision. Each of you can supply something the other has less developed if you learn together rather than trying to make the other over.

VERY CHALLENGING—1

BUSINESSLIKE

TAURUS/CAPRICORN

You both have good, common sense. You can easily apply your minds to the "real world" so material success or business ventures could be significant topics of conversations. You encourage each other to put your minds to work and prefer ideas and exchanges that generate results. You may use your minds, tongues, or hands in your professions. You both think in terms of facts and what is possible.

COMPATIBLE—3

SECURITY VS. RISK

TAURUS/AQUARIUS

You're more cautious, stable and grounded in your thinking and speech. You tend toward familiar pathways. He is more rebellious, independent and concerned with abstractions. The two of you could polarize around the known versus the unknown, or the tried and true versus the new and different. A bit of both works best. He may shock you sometimes just to show you alternatives and options, but you can help him come "down to earth" and get results rather than just theorizing.

CHALLENGING—2

PRETTY PRETENSE

TAURUS/PISCES

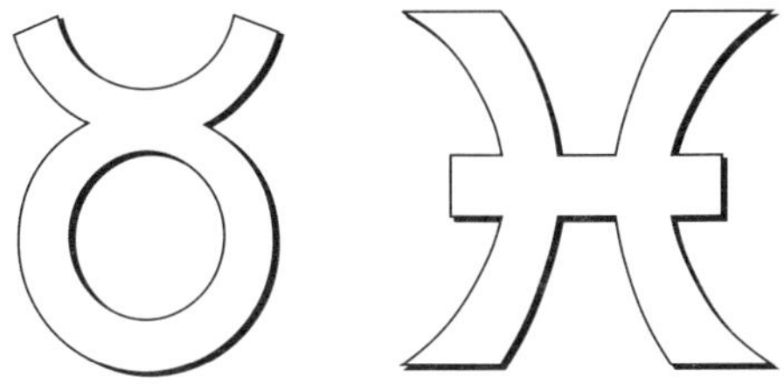

You both could have an artistic bent with your minds or tongues (feeling for music, poetry, songwriting, playing an instrument, etc.). Each of you prefers to keep conversations pleasant and avoid arguments or strife. You can provide a bit more pragmatism and he a bit more imagination, but you easily combine forces. Your thinking and speech with one another tend to be complementary (and complimentary).

COMPATIBLE—3

GEMINI/ARIES

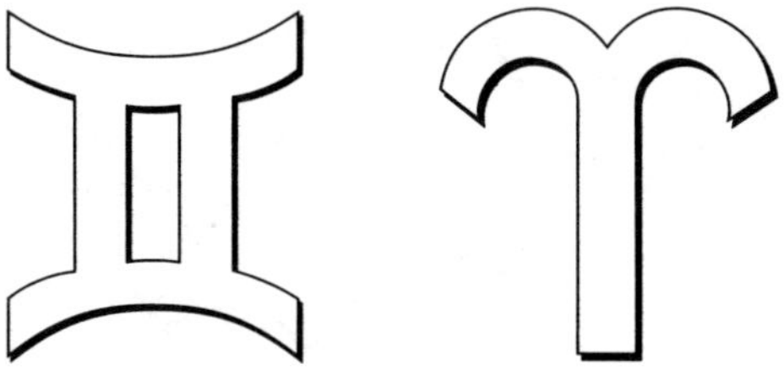

QUICK WITS & QUICK TONGUE

He may stimulate you mentally as you both can be quite quick-witted. But pure curiosity is more your style where he has been known to use words as weapons (ironic, argumentative). You both perceive rapidly, speak easily and get bored quickly! You tend to keep each other "up," laugh easily and spark new ideas in one another. Word play may appeal. Each of you thrives on conversation, mental stimulation and fun.

COMPATIBLE—3

GEMINI/TAURUS

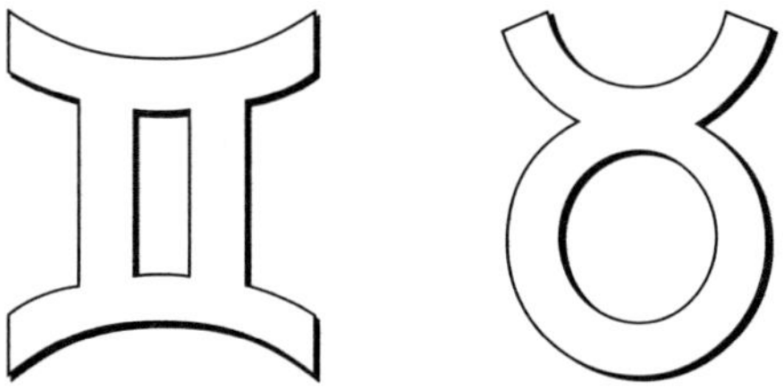

THE DILETTANTE VS. THE DELIBERATOR

You want to flit like a butterfly from topic to topic, while he plods along, learning slowly and steadily. You can discuss almost anything, while he prefers to have a practical focus before opening his mouth. You can learn more mental patience and steadiness from him. He can learn more versatility and flexibility from you. He can help ground you, and you can help him diversify his interests.

CHALLENGING—2

GEMINI/GEMINI

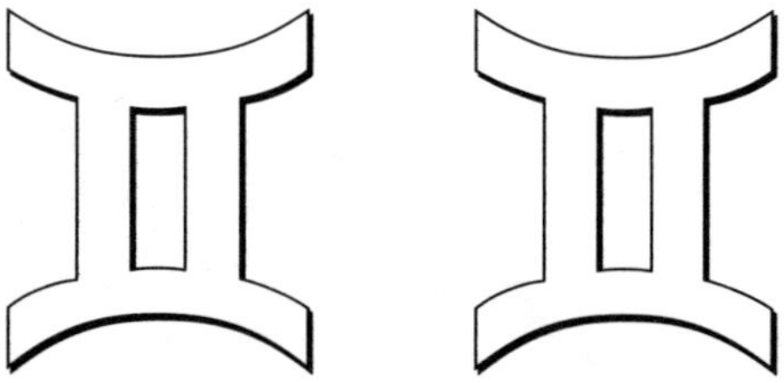

CASUAL CONVERSATION

The mental world is your oyster. You both love to learn about anything and everything, so tend to stimulate each other's endless curiosity. You also both love to communicate, so each may need to practice listening more than talking. You stimulate a fresh, youthful, open, flexible attitude in one another. Each of you can enjoy socializing, traveling, learning, teaching and new experiences of all sorts.

VERY COMPATIBLE—4

GEMINI/CANCER

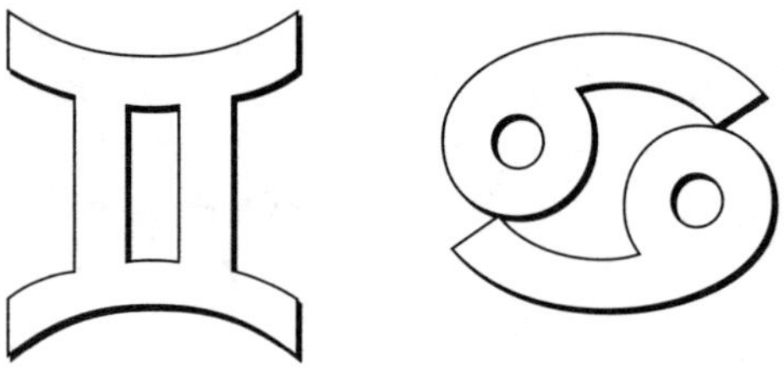

THINKING VS. FEELING

You are naturally quick, logical and detached in your thinking. He is swayed by moods and protective instincts. You may need to learn to listen more and he may need to learn to share (especially feelings) rather than holding back and holding in. You can enhance detachment and he can aid nonverbal perceptions and intuitive insights. Together you can blend the rational and the emotional within each of you.

CHALLENGING—2

WORD PLAY

GEMINI/LEO

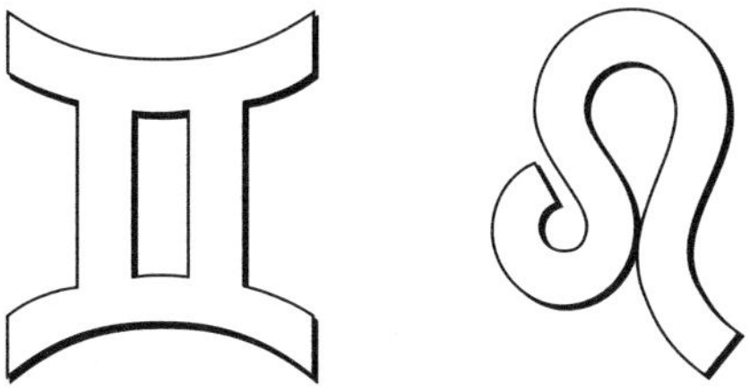

Words can be fun for both of you. You are a natural communicator who instinctively seeks and shares information. He is a natural entertainer with wit, charisma and dramatic emphasis in his verbal style. Your thinking is a bit more objective; his is more colored by a need for excitement and drama. (He may exaggerate.) Mental playfulness is likely for both of you. You each have a youthful, fun-loving spirit.

COMPATIBLE—3

MENTAL MASTERS

GEMINI/VIRGO

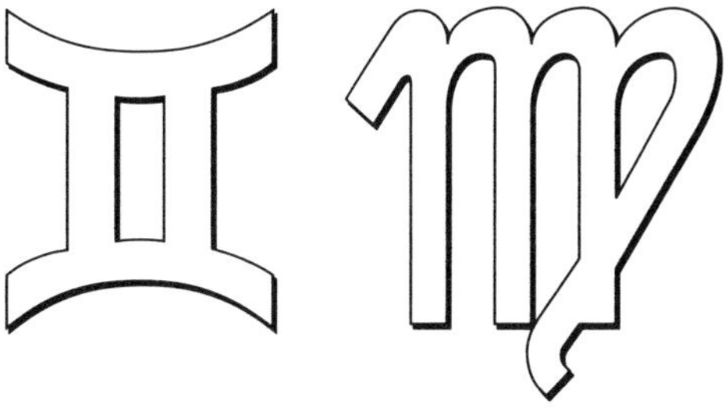

Quantity versus quality may emerge in your communications. You adore learning about anything and everything, while he needs to be thorough and gets the details **just right**. You may want to scatter just when he wants to focus. He can learn lightheartedness from you and you can learn follow-through from him. You both may use communication skills, writing, finger dexterity or your hands in your work.

CHALLENGING—2

SOCIABILITY

GEMINI/LIBRA

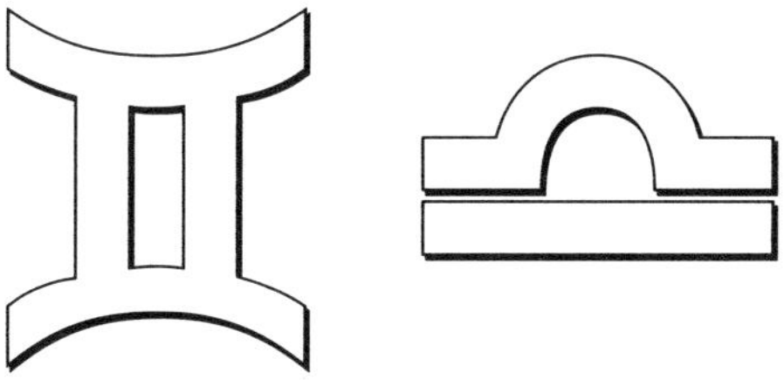

Communication tends to flow between you. Each of you is capable of being quite logical, rational and objective. You both tend to be equalitarian, with good instincts for cooperating. You can stimulate each other mentally and enjoy shared social activities. Contact with others adds to your association with each other. Both of you have a knack for putting others at their ease.

COMPATIBLE—3

SURFACE AND SECRETS

GEMINI/SCORPIO

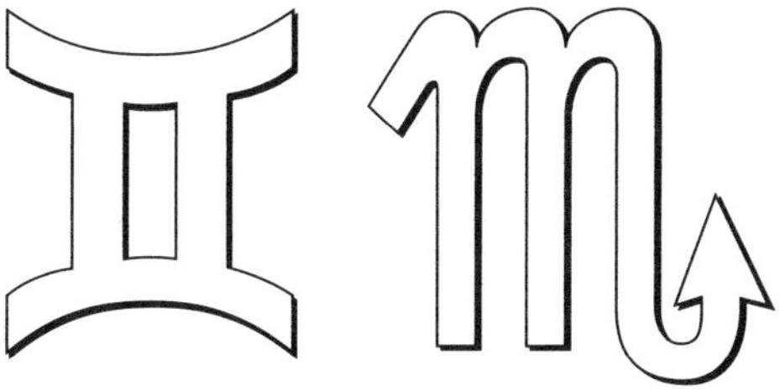

You want to learn anything and everything, and can be drawn to many different interests. He loves to probe deeply, intently, completely. You chat easily and naturally. He can clam up and even be quite secretive. You can learn discretion and perseverance from him. He can learn flexibility and the ability to be casual about life from you. Together, you have both breadth and depth.

VERY CHALLENGING—1

GEMINI/SAGITTARIUS

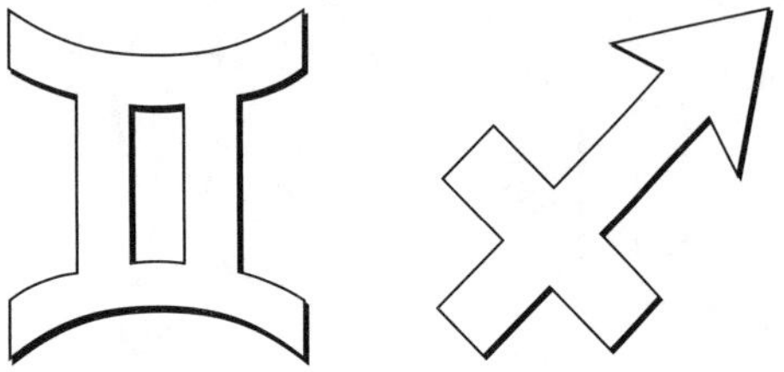

LIFELONG LEARNING

You are both natural students and teachers, and can easily stimulate one another to more learning and discovering. You may enjoy traveling together, finding new vistas exciting. Your curiosity tends more toward the here-and-how—people and situations right around you. He could be a mite more concerned with issues of long-range goals, plans, values or ethical and moral principles. You spark each other's humor and hunger for knowledge.

VERY COMPATIBLE—4

GEMINI/CAPRICORN

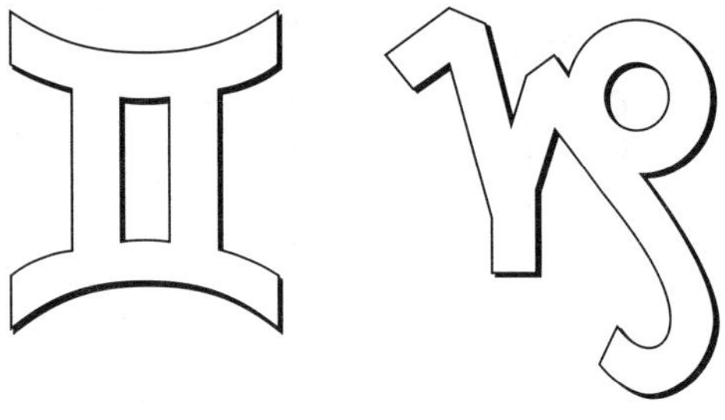

CASUAL VS. CORRECT

You love to learn, to move in many directions mentally. He tends to be more stable, concerned with what is "right." You believe in more than one possibility; he believes in one "correct" way. He may be formal or inhibited (afraid of making a mistake) in his thinking or communicating— or forcing his view on others. You flow naturally into verbal expression. You can learn focus and control from him. He can learn flexibility and detachment from you.

VERY CHALLENGING—1

GEMINI/AQUARIUS

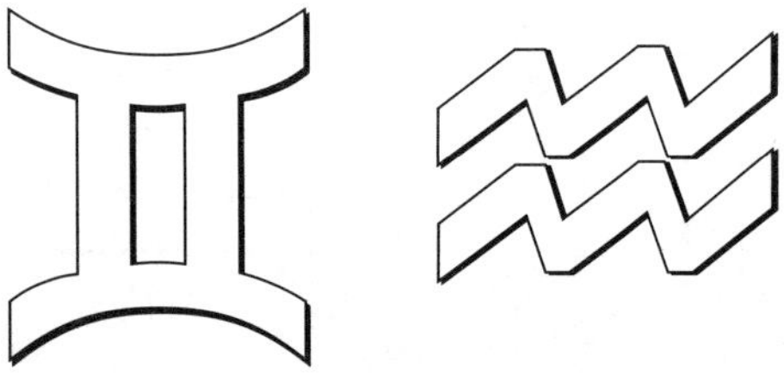

INQUISITIVE INQUIRERS

You both are skilled at logic, detachment and being part of a team. Cooperating and sharing ideas flow naturally. You stimulate one another mentally. He may be a bit more outrageous in some statements. You may have a quicker sense of fun, but each of you tends to be rational, good with words, and gregarious. Social contacts or networking could be important in your relationship. You both have inquiring minds.

COMPATIBLE—3

GEMINI/PISCES

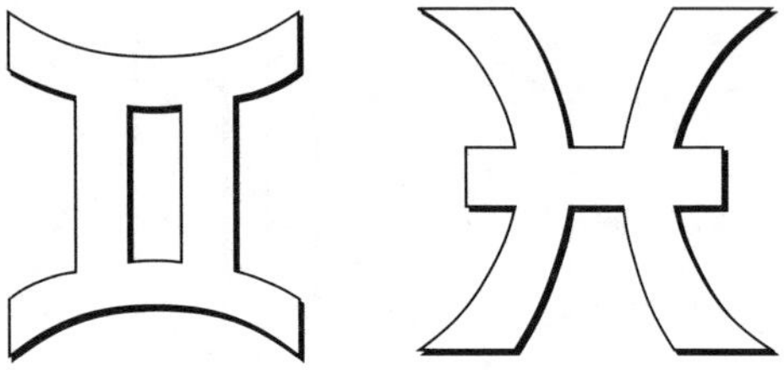

INSATIABLY CURIOUS

You both can overextend yourselves trying to learn or absorb too much at one time. Your style is more linear, rational and objective, while his is more global, inclusive and holistic. Together you can learn to blend the rational and intuitive; the verbal and the nonverbal. You can teach him more humor and lightness. He can teach you sensitivity to nonverbal cues and enhance your capacity to see connections or patterns in life.

CHALLENGING—2

CARING COMMUNICATOR & TONGUE LIKE A SWORD

CANCER/ARIES

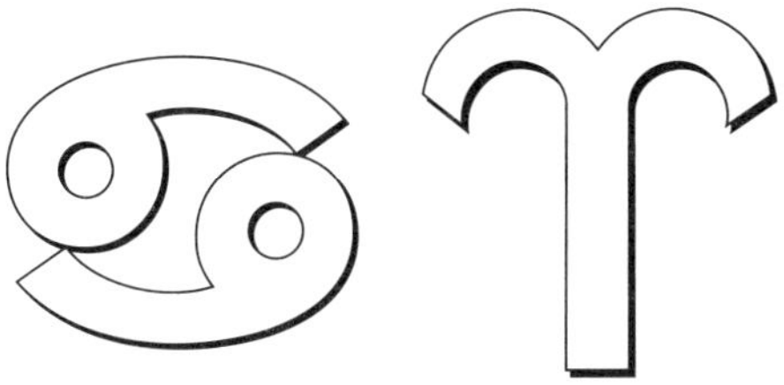

You tend to be more cautious in expressing yourself, sensitive to the feelings of everyone involved. He tends to be direct, forthright— even cutting if the impulse strikes him. He can make up his mind quite quickly, while you're mulling over the pros and cons. You can learn spontaneity from him, and he can learn sensitivity from you. Together, you can blend honesty with caring and compassion.

CHALLENGING—2

QUIET, UNASSUMING

CANCER/TAURUS

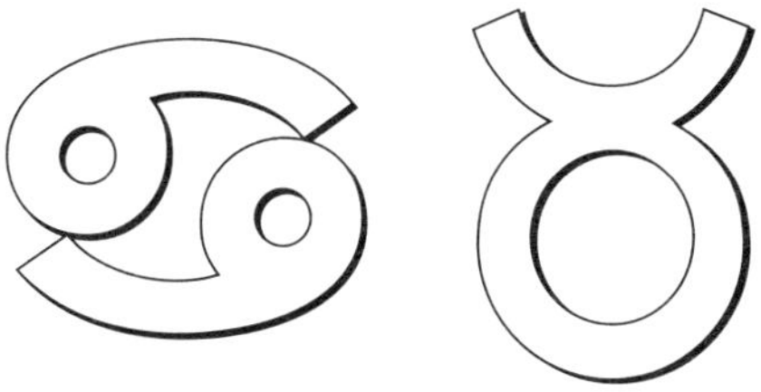

You both prefer learning and communication which flows smoothly. You tend to think in terms of feelings and impressions and may be protective (of yourself and/or others) in what you say and when and how you speak. He tends to be relaxed and easygoing, preferring to avoid unpleasantness (but sometimes quite fixed in his opinions). You both appreciate silence and the comfort of a loving touch.

COMPATIBLE—3

FEELING VS. THINKING

CANCER/GEMINI

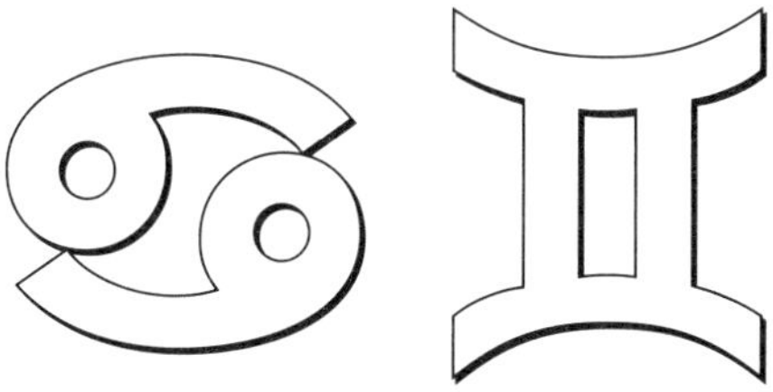

You tend to lead with the heart, while he emphasizes the head. Some of your learning is intuitive; he trusts logic more. You want to absorb fully while he finds it easy to flit from topic to topic. You are careful with what you say, not wanting to hurt anyone's feelings. He tends to be quite expressive, sometimes talking for the pure pleasure of it. The two of you are learning to blend thinking with feeling.

CHALLENGING—2

CARING, CLOSE COMMUNICATORS

CANCER/CANCER

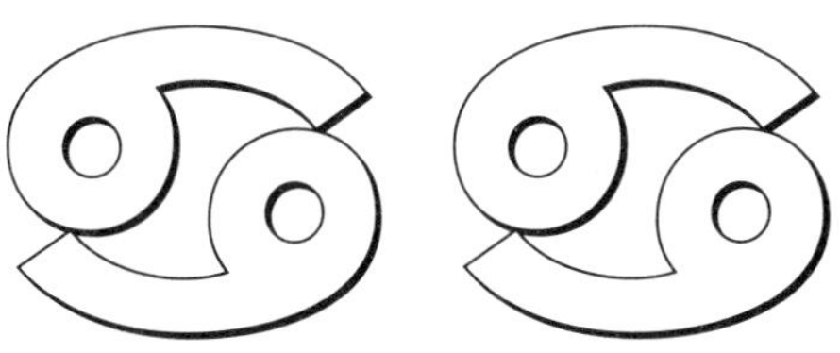

You may have a close, nonverbal bond with one another. You both have intuitive skills, with the capacity to tune into one another. Each of you is likely to be protective, sensitive to everyone's feelings in your verbal style. You may nurture thinking and communicating— enjoying feeding the mind. You can blend emotions and logic and the two of you communicate on many levels. You understand one another.

VERY COMPATIBLE—4

CANCER/LEO

SUBDUED AND SUPERCHARGED

You are likely to think before speaking, to consider whether anyone's feelings could be hurt. He tends to let it all hang out (and could seem egocentric or arrogant at times). He **needs** admiration from others for his thinking, communicating or use of hands or mind. He might be a natural entertainer, raconteur and salesperson. You can both be quite warm and caring, so may enjoy talking about family and loved ones.

CHALLENGING—2

CANCER/VIRGO

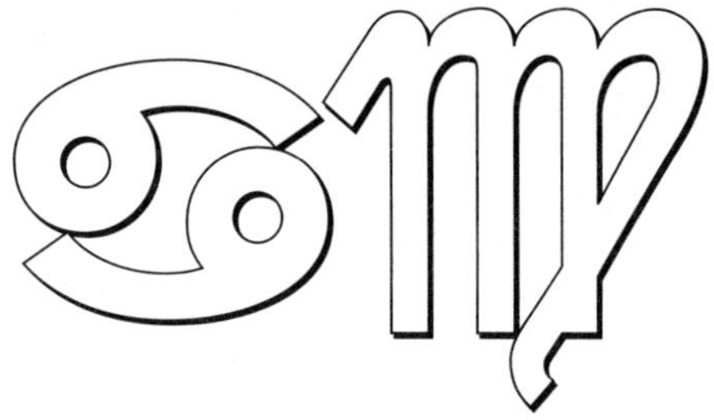

HELPFUL HINTS

Both of you can be cautious communicators. You want to avoid hurting anyone's feelings and he wants to avoid making any mistakes! Your mental focus tends to center on feelings and issues of caring, while he often focuses on work and productivity. You bring compassion to his critical eye and he brings precision to your soft heart. Both of you may enjoy thinking and talking about sensible ways to amass more security in life.

COMPATIBLE—3

CANCER/LIBRA

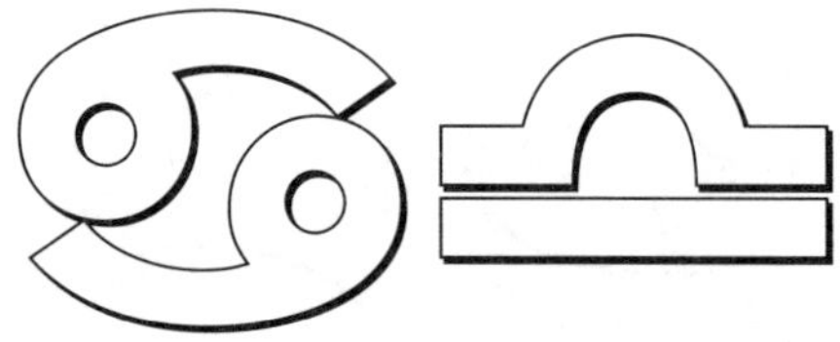

CONCERNED COMMUNICATORS

Each of you tempers objectivity with caring and concern. You tend to hold more inside, afraid of hurting others (or being hurt). He tends to rely on diplomacy (or "little white lies") to protect his interests in conversation. Your mental focus may center a bit more on home and family, while his is on cooperation, competition or beauty. Both of you appreciate the value of balancing rationality with feelings.

CHALLENGING—2

CANCER/SCORPIO

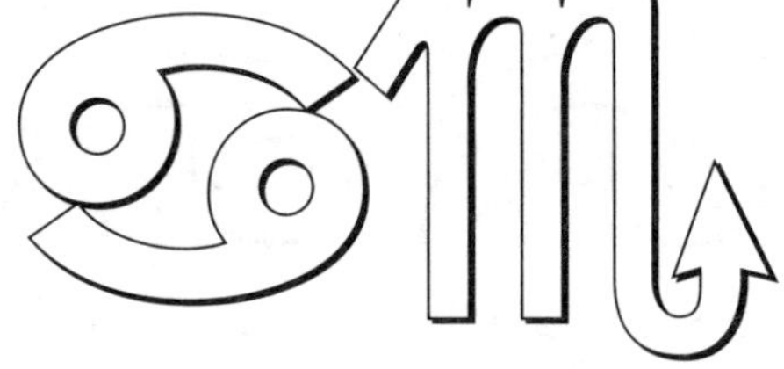

NONVERBAL EXPERTS

Each of you can be like an iceberg—9/10 below the surface where communication is concerned. Neither of you cares to wear your heart on your sleeve (unless you are convinced it is totally safe). Despite possible periods of silence, brooding or moodiness, you are quite sensitive to one another and easily pick up on the "vibes" going out. You are likely to respect each other's needs for privacy and sensitivity.

COMPATIBLE—3

KIND AND KINETIC

CANCER/SAGITTARIUS

You tend toward caring conversations, remaining silent rather than risking hurt (to yourself or others), while he is the original "foot in mouth" individual. Bluntness may be his middle name or a marked concern with honesty. You can learn more openness, humor and directness from him. He can learn compassion, sensitivity and gentleness from you. Appreciate each other's styles without trying to change them.

VERY CHALLENGING—1

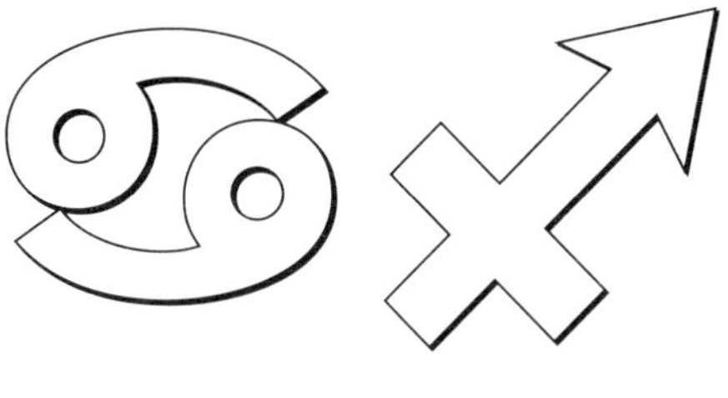

DEPENDENT OR DOMINANT?

CANCER/CAPRICORN

In some ways you can seem like opposites. He may want to maintain control of conversations and have firm ideas of "right" and "wrong" thinking, while you are more concerned with emotional reactions and people's feelings. Yet you both can feel drawn together and may share a talent for understanding business concepts, family matters and the practical survival demands of everyday life.

VERY COMPATIBLE—4

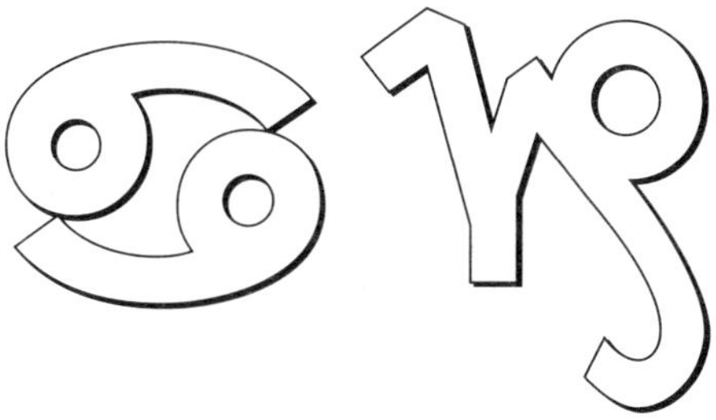

SOFT VS. SUDDEN

CANCER/AQUARIUS

You think about what will protect people, while he thinks about what will shock people. You believe in remaining silent rather than hurting someone's feelings and he believes in questioning authority and pursuing rebellious concepts. He can converse for hours, while you appreciate quiet moments. With mutual tolerance, you can learn objectivity and openness from him, and he can learn sensitivity from you.

VERY CHALLENGING—1

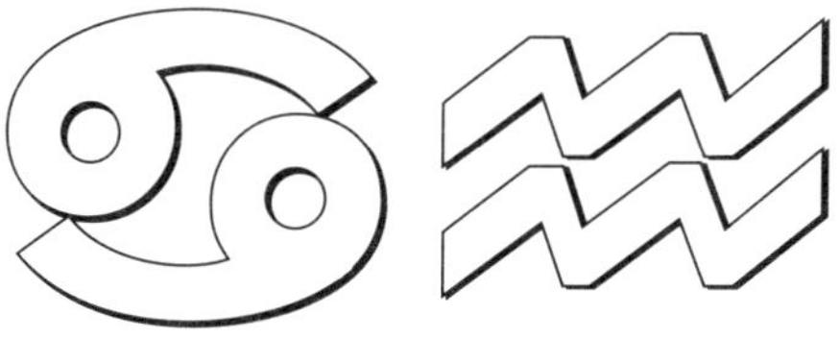

PROTECTION REIGNS SUPREME

CANCER/PISCES

Each of you may prefer to avoid verbal unpleasantness, so could use silence, evasion or "polite lies" to try to keep things flowing smoothly. Either of you might clam up when threatened. When your feelings are engaged, you speak easily. Each of you may tune in nonverbally, and easily understand the other. You both learn well globally, holistically, and when your emotions are involved.

COMPATIBLE—3

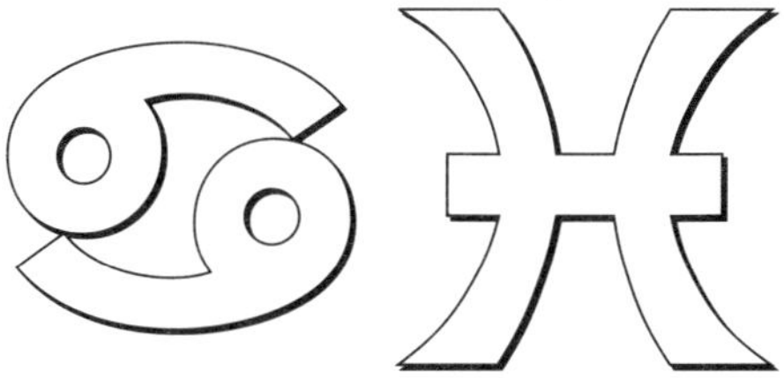

LEO/ARIES

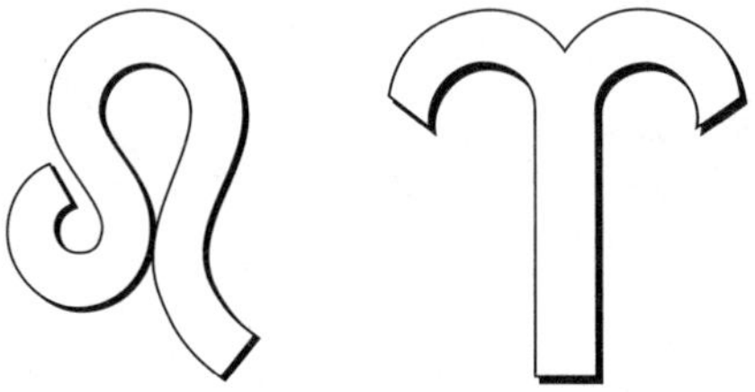

SUPER SALESPERSON AND EAGER BEAVER

You find lots to discuss with one another. Communication is exciting when you are together. You tend to stimulate each other and may both have to practice listening rather than talking. Spontaneity and lots of dramatic conversations are likely. You can quickly exhaust topics and tend to move on rapidly in conversations. Although each of you may find your mind or tongue is faster than those of other acquaintances, the two of you easily keep up with one another.

COMPATIBLE—3

LEO/TAURUS

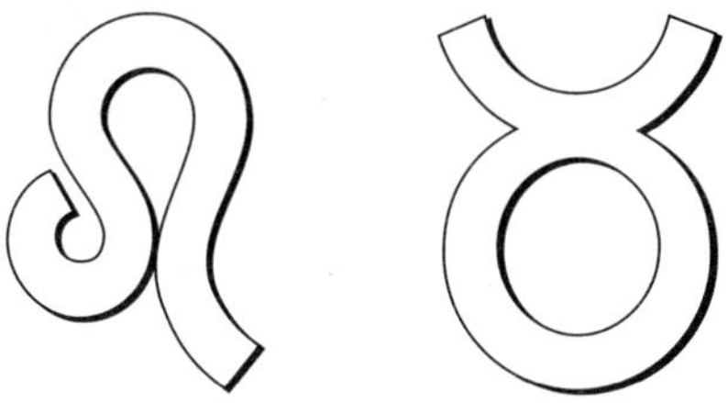

STRONG OPINIONS

You each may feel that **your** way of thinking is the **only** way. Firm opinions are likely. Your verbal style is more dramatic and persuasive (sometimes arrogant). His is more step-by-step. His deliberateness may drive you crazy at times as you may think or speak more quickly, but your exaggerations can annoy him greatly. He can learn from you to add some zip and zest to his speech, while you can learn from him to be more sensible and grounded.

CHALLENGING—2

LEO/GEMINI

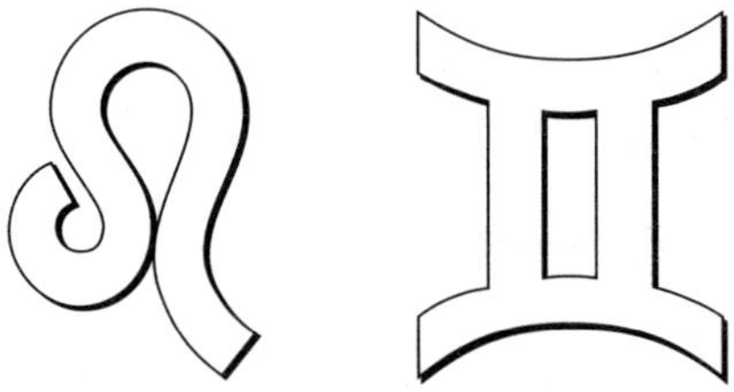

WORD PLAY

Words can be fun for both of you. You are a natural entertainer, with wit, charisma and dramatic emphasis in your verbal style. He is a natural communicator who instinctively seeks and shares information. His thinking is a bit more objective; yours is more colored by a need for excitement and drama. (You may exaggerate.) Mental playfulness is likely for both of you. You each have a youthful, fun-loving spirit.

COMPATIBLE—3

LEO/CANCER

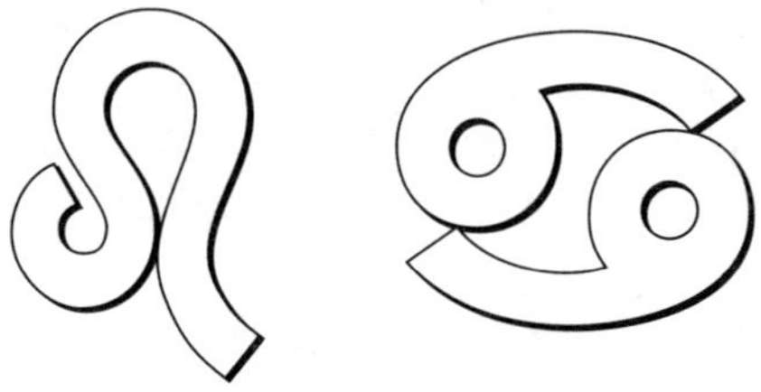

SUBDUED AND SUPERCHARGED

You tend to let it all hang out verbally—with a flair for drama and entertainment. You **want** to be admired for your thinking, communication or use of hands. He tends to think before speaking, to consider whether anyone's feelings could be hurt. You might be a natural raconteur or salesperson, while he has more need to keep his ideas private. Both of you can be quite warm and caring, so may enjoy talking about family and loved ones.

CHALLENGING—2

ENTERTAINMENT TONIGHT

LEO/LEO

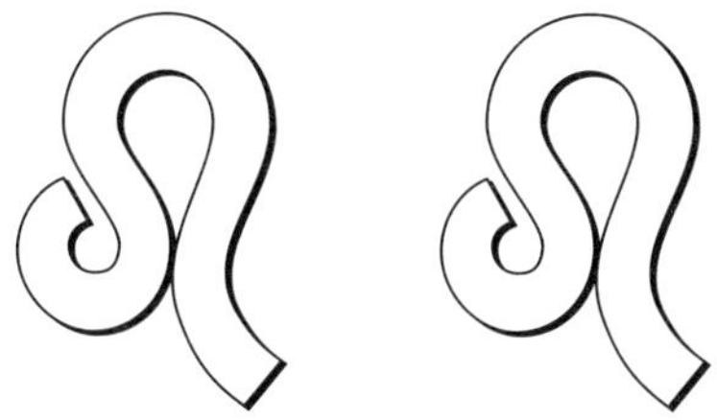

You two are both great motivators. You love giving (and getting) compliments and can be great coaches, trainers or cheerleaders. Blessed with a keen sense of humor, you easily share laughs with others. Each of you may find it easy to dramatize and could exaggerate at times or promise a bit more than you deliver, but in general you make great salespeople, raconteurs and actors and actresses.

VERY COMPATIBLE—4

THE DRAMATIST MEETS THE CRITIC

LEO/VIRGO

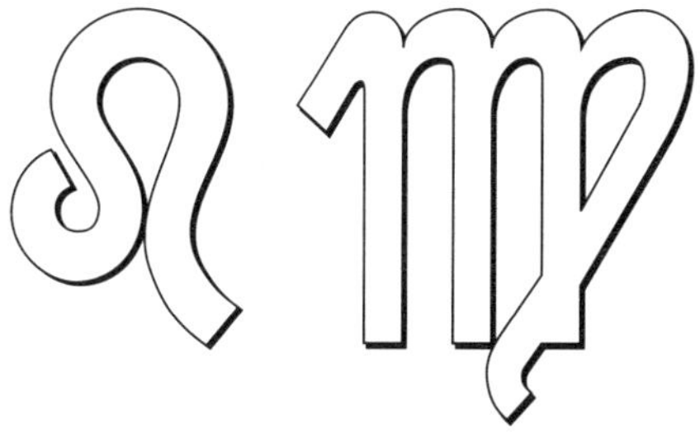

You are instinctively dramatic and expressive in speaking. You tend to stir others up, thrive on excitement in conversations and have been known to exaggerate. He seeks exactness, technical expertise and precision in speech. His nit-picking might burst your bubbles of optimism, unless you learn some practicality from him. You can teach him some of your creative flair with words and sense of fun.

CHALLENGING—2

LIVELY AND LIKABLE

LEO/LIBRA

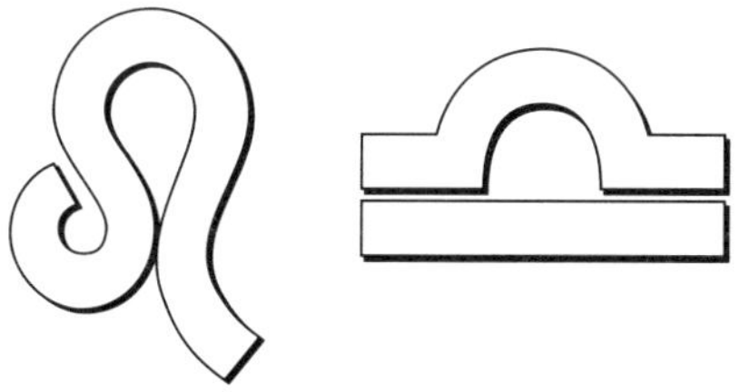

Each of you can be quite sociable. You tend a bit more toward drama, and he a bit more toward diplomacy, but you both enjoy people and good conversation. Communication with those you love is natural for you two, so family or close associates are often topics of interest. He can be more of a strategist in his thinking, while you're more spontaneous, but you both enjoy bringing more pleasure and ease to others.

COMPATIBLE—3

PROMOTION VS. PRIVACY

LEO/SCORPIO

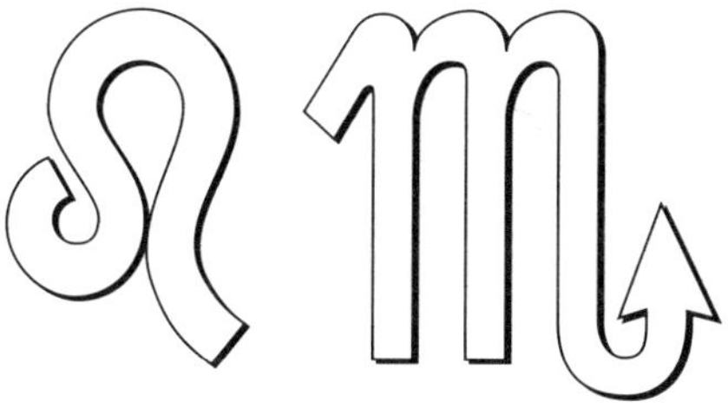

You want people to admire your thinking, speaking or mental skills. You may impress people with your flair, charisma, dramatic instincts or spellbinding conversational abilities. His thinking tends toward back-door routes and some manipulative instincts are possible. If either of you tries to control or influence the other's thinking or speaking, rocky times lie ahead. You can learn subtlety and to read nonverbal cues from him. He can learn directness and the joy of compliments from you.

CHALLENGING—2

LEO/SAGITTARIUS

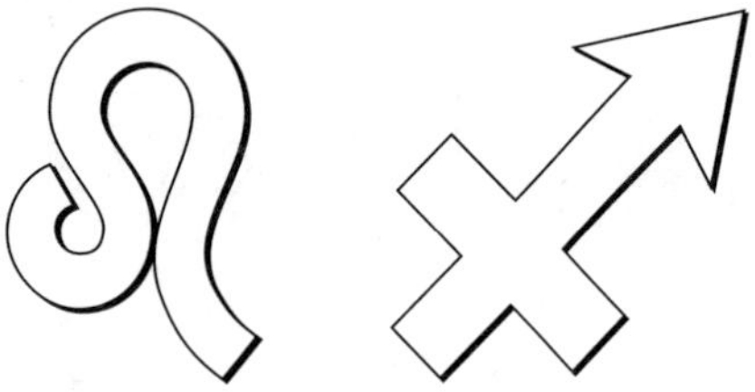

LARGER THAN LIFE

Both of you know how to win friends and influence people! You can each be quite persuasive and impressive in your thinking and speaking. You both can also grandstand, exaggerate and jump to conclusions. Your thinking is oriented toward excitement. You want thrills and fun in your conversations. Each of you enjoys lively exchanges. You both think optimistically and can cheer others up and onward.

COMPATIBLE—3

LEO/CAPRICORN

WHO IS IN CHARGE?

Each of you thinks like a leader, so don't get in each other's way! You tend to be more expressive, dynamic and eager to make an impression on others. He tends to be more guarded, cautious, planning carefully for a successful outcome. You can teach him confidence and enthusiasm. He can teach you practicality and concentrated focus. Don't step on each other's conversational toes. Do keep room for both work and play.

VERY CHALLENGING—1

LEO/AQUARIUS

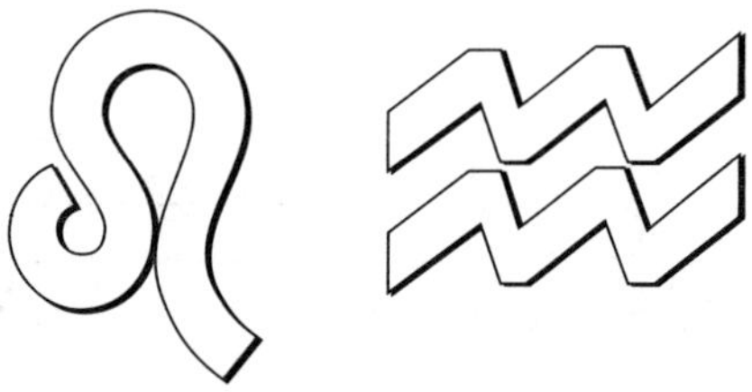

PASSION VS. DETACHMENT

You think with your heart—pouring into speech, motivating others, inspiring them, egging them onward. He thinks with his head—objective, rational and somewhat detached. You want people to like and admire what you say; he can sometimes say things for their shock value. Despite being opposite in some respects, you are naturally drawn together and share much creativity and originality. The way you think and communicate excites each other.

VERY COMPATIBLE—4

LEO/PISCES

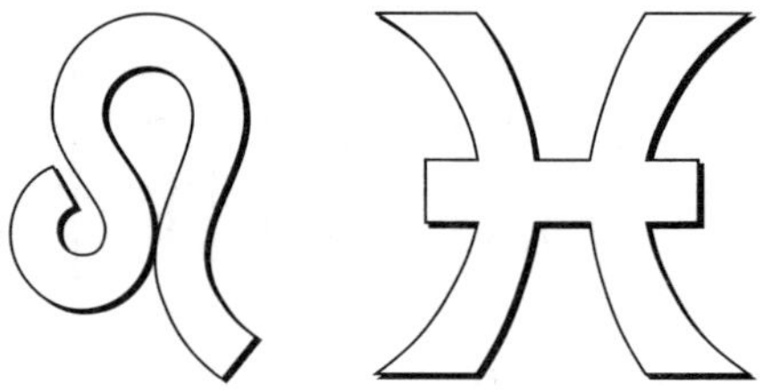

MAGICAL, MYSTICAL MINDS

You tend to think and speak quickly, while he will mull things over and may not reveal what's going on inside. You want excitement, drama and fun in conversations. He wants mystery, poetry, and inspiration. You can share a magical touch, each having skills at persuasion. You can encourage him to be more open and forthcoming. He can encourage you to be more patient and keep some feelings within rather than immediately revealing them.

VERY CHALLENGING—1

PERFECTLY PRECISE AND UTTERLY UNCHECKED

VIRGO/ARIES

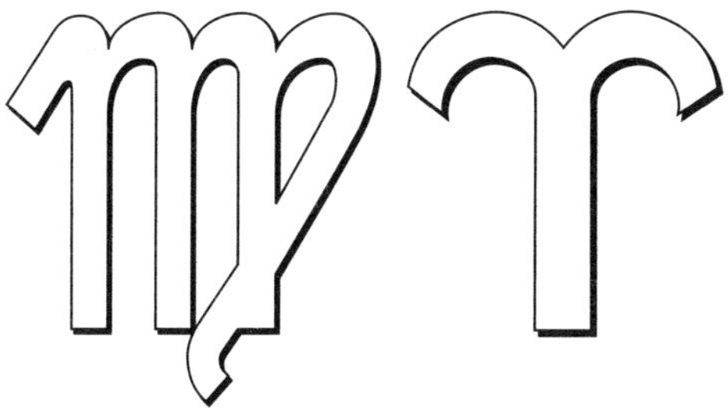

You strive to organize your thinking, speak well and use words correctly, while he tends to shoot from the hip verbally and doesn't want to waste time. You may search for just the **right** phrase and could sometimes feel critical of his careless language or quick temper. You can learn more spontaneity from him, and he can learn more precision from you. You can appreciate the excitement he brings to topics, and he can appreciate your common sense and practicality.

VERY CHALLENGING—1

PRAGMATISTS

VIRGO/TAURUS

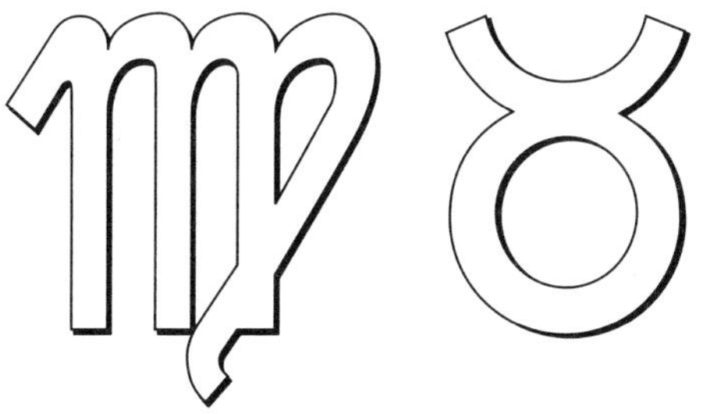

Both of you have a practical, sensible bent. You may even put your minds to work earning money through writing, speaking, mental or physical dexterity, etc. Each of you communicates well in professional environments (where something relevant needs to be conveyed), but is probably not keen on social chitchat. You both tend toward common sense and prefer to think about real issues and basic needs.

COMPATIBLE—3

MENTAL MASTERS

VIRGO/GEMINI

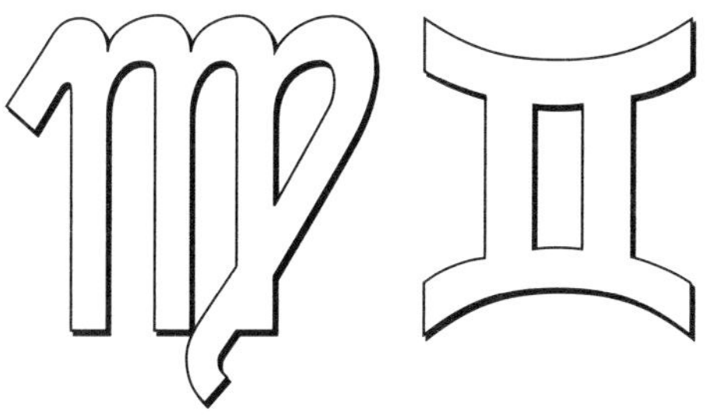

Quantity versus quality may emerge in your communications. He adores learning about anything and everything, while you need to be thorough and get the details **just right**. He may want to scatter just when you want to focus. You can learn lightheartedness from him, and he can learn follow-through from you. You both may use communication skills, writing, finger dexterity or your hands in your work.

CHALLENGING—2

HELPFUL HINTS

VIRGO/CANCER

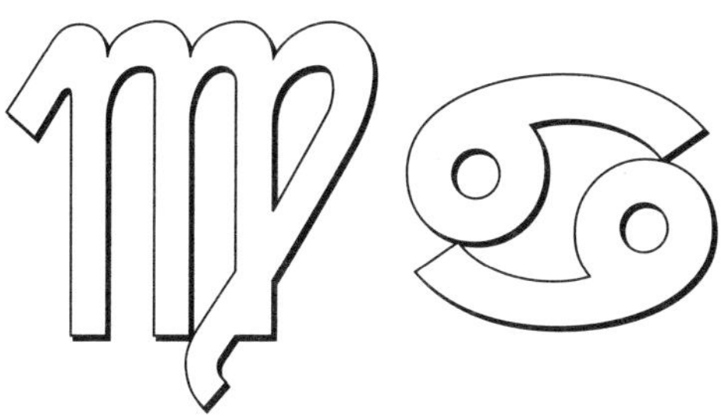

Both of you can be cautious communicators. He wants to avoid hurting anyone's feelings and you want to avoid making any mistakes! His mental focus tends to center on feelings and issues of caring, while yours often focuses on work and productivity. You help to ground his intuitive perceptions and he helps soften your judgments. Both of you may enjoy thinking and talking about sensible ways to amass more security in life.

COMPATIBLE—3

VIRGO/LEO

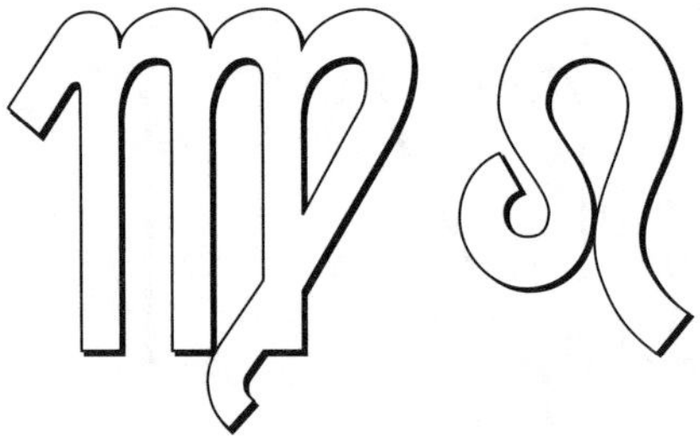

THE CRITIC MEETS THE DRAMATIST

He is instinctively dramatic and expressive in speaking. He tends to stir others up, thrive on excitement in conversations and has been known to exaggerate. You seek exactness, technical expertise and precision in speech. You're inclined to correct his exaggerations, which is not always appreciated. You can enhance his reality-testing. He can enliven your sense of fun and add to your creative flair with words.

CHALLENGING—2

VIRGO/VIRGO

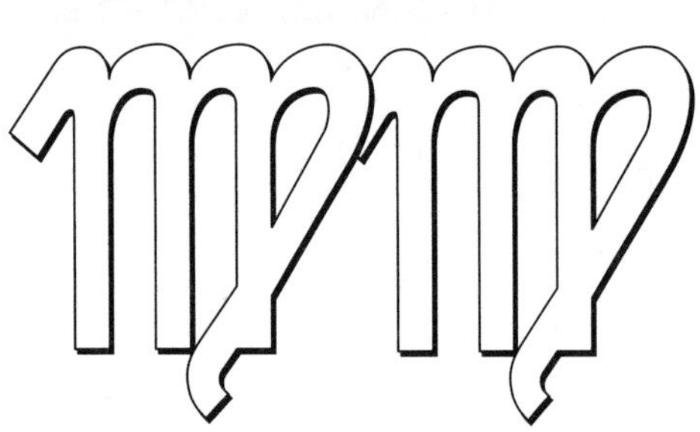

EFFICIENCY EXPERTS

Both of you can be rational, logical, organized and thorough in your thinking. Your speech tends to be precise, exact and very realistic. (You may abhor exaggeration.) The two of you might share an interest in health, work, repairs or any form of finding flaws and fixing them. Each of you may work with your mind, hands, or tongue or have fine technical skills. You both are blessed with good common sense.

VERY COMPATIBLE—4

VIRGO/LIBRA

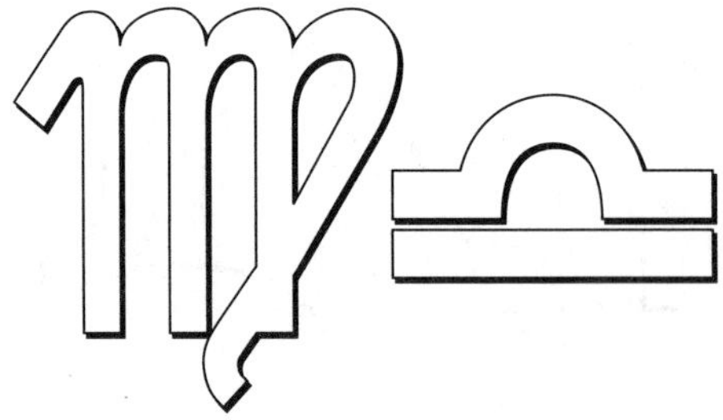

THE TECHNICIAN AND THE DIPLOMAT

You want to figure everything out, and do and say it just **right** (so may be silent if afraid of making a mistake). He wants everything to be fair and balanced, so may fence-sit while gathering more data. You're a bit more focused on practicalities while he's a bit more focused on people, but you can learn from one another. Together, you can be sociable as well as competent, charming as well as accurate.

CHALLENGING—2

VIRGO/SCORPIO

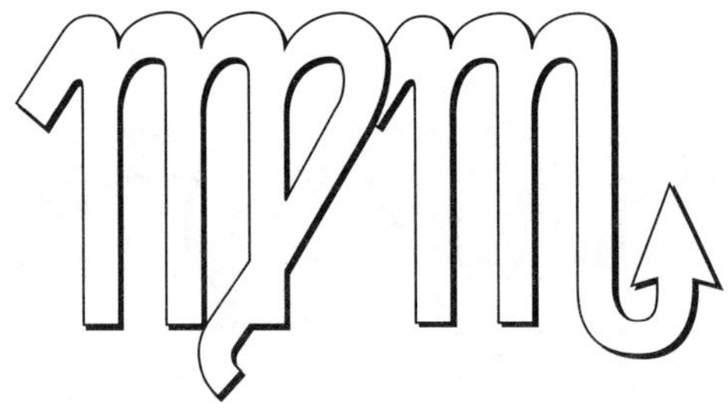

ORGANIZATION UNLIMITED

The two of you can turn organization into a fine art! Each of you may have a mind like a filing cabinet. You know how to figure things out and keep everything in its place. Research and business skills are likely. You both have a penchant for efficiency in thinking and in speaking (no wasted words). Don't nitpick each other, but do enjoy your shared skills at being practical, thorough and sensible.

COMPATIBLE—3

ACCURACY AND EXAGGERATION

VIRGO/SAGITTARIUS

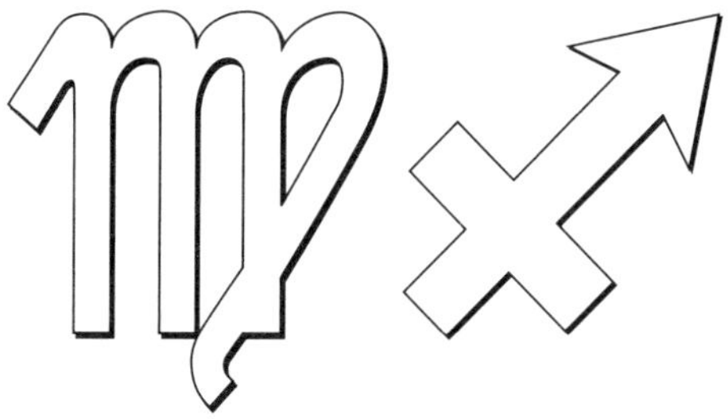

You tend to be precise in your thinking and speech, while he tends to speak quickly and may exaggerate or jump to conclusions. He can easily get overextended with multiple interests, while you prefer to finish up, one thing at a time. If each of you is open, some of his optimism and humor will rub off on you, and some of your careful attention to detail and desire to be correct will rub off on him.

CHALLENGING—2

REALISTIC

VIRGO/CAPRICORN

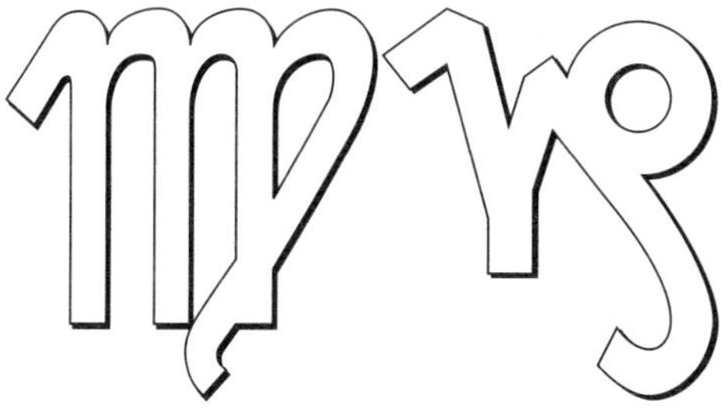

Both of you can be quite sensible, practical and skilled at dealing with real-world questions. Each of you may have business abilities and is good at facing facts and doing what is necessary. You may put your minds to work and conversations could center more around accomplishments or tasks, rather than social banter. You each possess a dry wit, but are primarily focused on thinking and speaking accurately and well.

COMPATIBLE—3

THE TECHNICIAN AND THE SCIENTIST

VIRGO/AQUARIUS

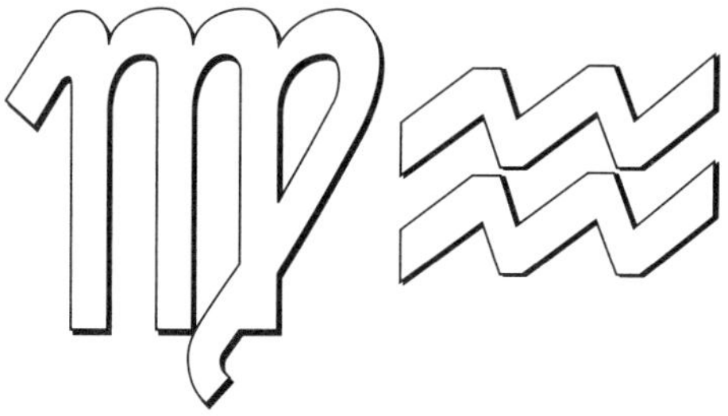

You are good with details and have an organized mind. He is good with theories and prefers the overview to details. You tend to look for one "right" answer, while he tends to assume that many possibilities exist. You prefer to be modest, correct and unassuming in your speech. He likes to shock people and challenge their beliefs. You can help him be more grounded, and he can help you to envision more possibilities.

VERY CHALLENGING—1

BRINGING DREAMS TO EARTH

VIRGO/PISCES

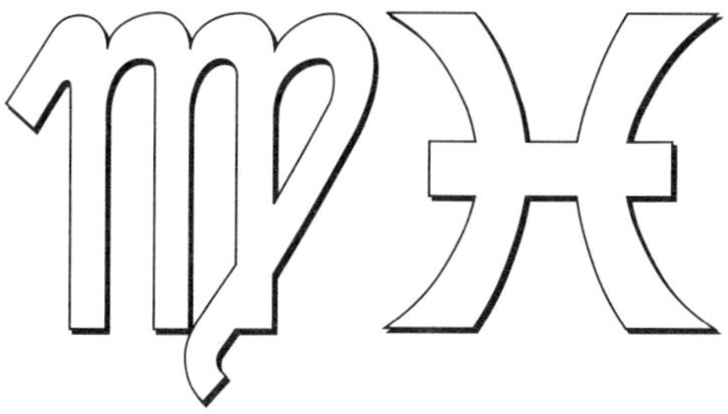

You tend to be the realist and he the idealist in your thinking and speech. You may be concerned with work, survival issues or basic needs while he dreams about infinite love, beauty, grace or escapism. You look at the details; he looks at the whole. Each of you supplies something the other needs to develop. Even though opposite in some respects, you are drawn together and tend to complete one another.

VERY COMPATIBLE—4

LIBRA/ARIES

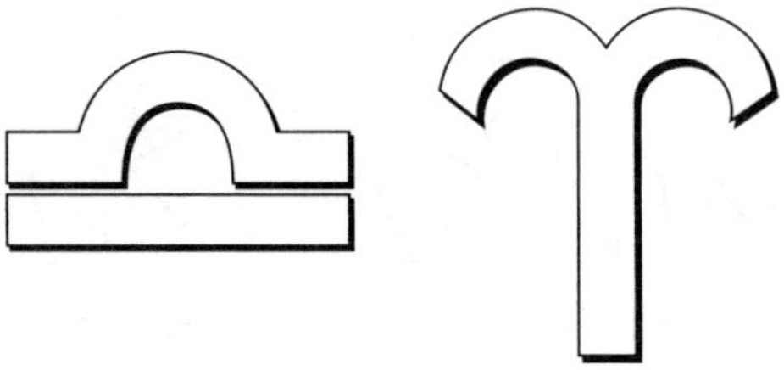

OPPOSITES ATTRACT

Does it seem you're on opposite sides of lots of issues? Are you diplomatic and tactful while he just blurts out exactly what he's thinking? Do you sit on the fence while he leaps ahead? There is a middle ground if you only seek it. Balancing conversational give-and-take may be a bit challenging, but the rewards are great. Even though your styles are sometimes opposite, you are drawn together mentally—like each other's missing halves.

VERY COMPATIBLE—4

LIBRA/TAURUS

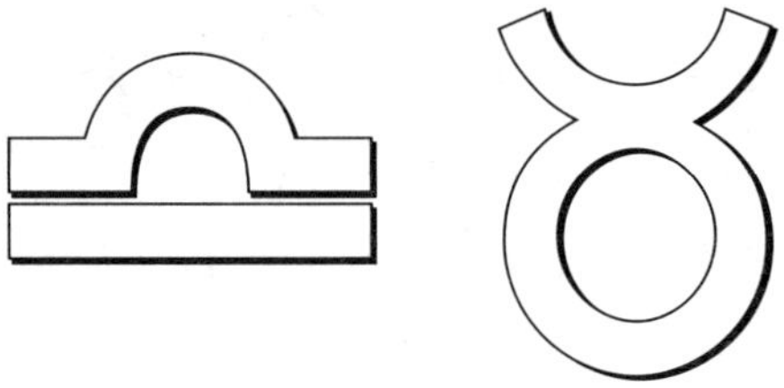

LOVELY LANGUAGE

Each of you may have talent for flowing conversations, poetic language or creating beauty with words (singing, song writing, etc.). Or you could simply be masters at avoiding unpleasant thoughts or words. You might be more skilled at abstractions and he at practicalities. You may seek more understanding of relationships, while he is more focused on money, possessions or material security. Each of you could bring a new perspective to the other.

VERY CHALLENGING—1

LIBRA/GEMINI

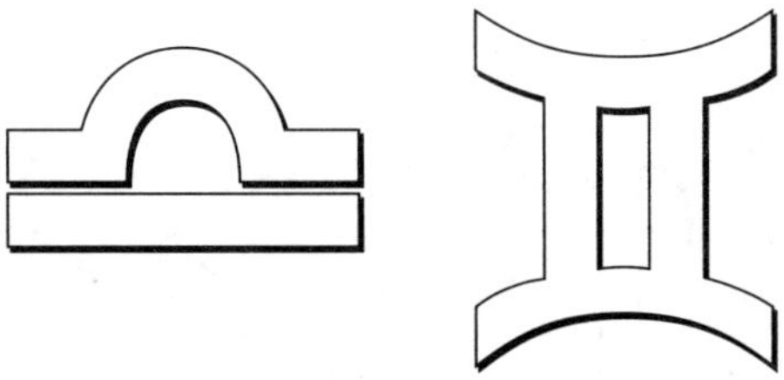

SOCIABILITY

Communication tends to flow between you. Each of you is capable of being quite logical, rational and objective. You both tend to be equalitarian, with good instincts for cooperating. You can stimulate each other mentally and enjoy shared social activities. Contact with other people adds to your association with one another. Both of you have a knack for putting others at ease.

COMPATIBLE—3

LIBRA/CANCER

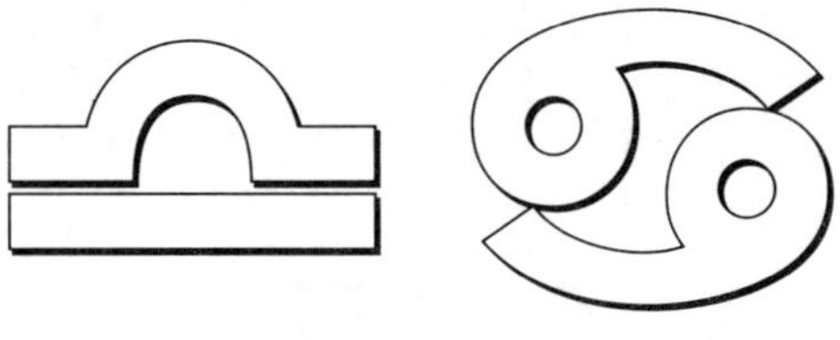

CONCERNED COMMUNICATORS

Each of you tempers objectivity with caring and concern. He tends to hold more inside, afraid of hurting others (or being hurt). You tend to rely on tact, diplomacy (or "little white lies") to protect your interests in conversation. Your mental focus may center a bit more on beauty, relationships or aesthetics, and his on home, food, country and roots. Both of you appreciate the value of balancing rationality with feelings.

CHALLENGING—2

LIKABLE AND LIVELY

LIBRA/LEO

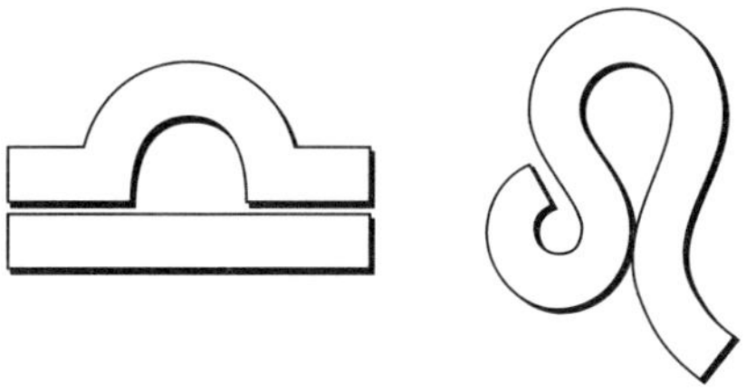

Each of you can be quite sociable. He tends a bit more toward drama, and you a bit more toward diplomacy, but you both enjoy people and good conversation. Communication with those you love is natural for you two, so family or close associates are often topics of interest. You can be more of a strategist in your thinking, while he is more spontaneous, but you both enjoy bringing more pleasure and ease to others.

COMPATIBLE—3

THE DIPLOMAT AND THE TECHNICIAN

LIBRA/VIRGO

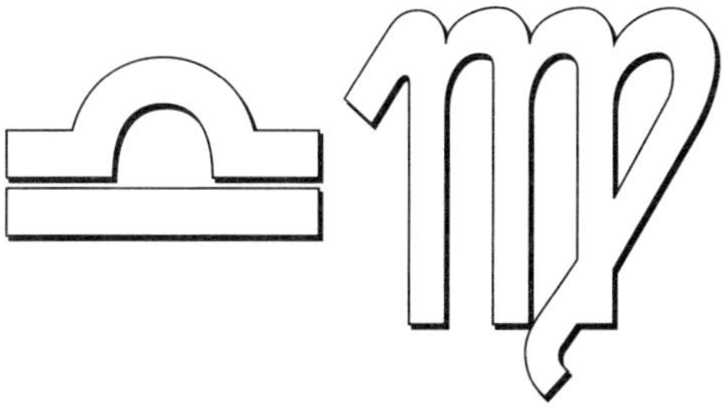

He wants to figure everything out and do and say it just **right** (so may be silent if afraid of making a mistake). You want everything to be fair and balanced, so may vacillate while gathering more data. He's a bit more focused on practicalities while you're a bit more focused on people, but you can learn from one another. Together, you can be sociable as well as competent, charming as well as accurate.

CHALLENGING—2

CHARMING COMMUNICATORS

LIBRA/LIBRA

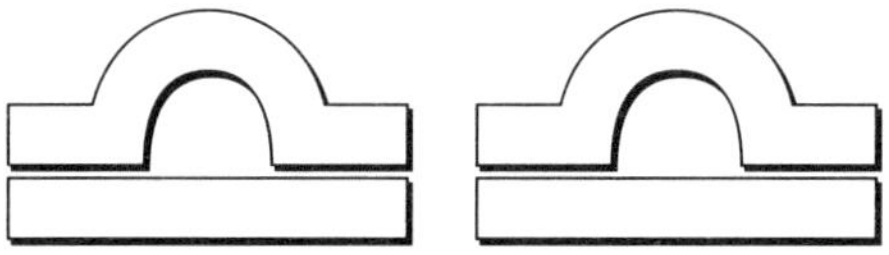

You both can be quite charming and diplomatic when you choose, knowing how to win friends and influence people. Reasonably objective and fair, you each prefer to keep things pleasant. Often curious about people, the two of you may enjoy discussing relationships or issues of equality, justice and fair play. Both of you are skilled at comparing and contrasting, so may sometimes have trouble making up your minds or deciding from among several choices.

VERY COMPATIBLE—4

THE TOASTMASTER & THE SPY

LIBRA/SCORPIO

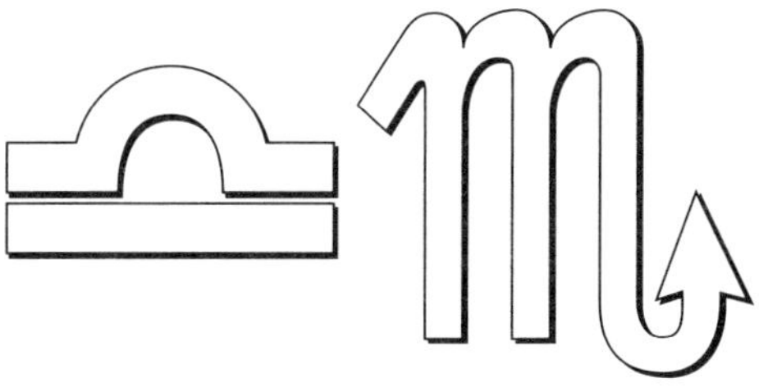

You like to keep the conversational ball rolling smoothly and comfortably, whereas he is willing to play "I've got a secret." You prefer to focus on people, pleasure and beauty, while he is concerned with what lies beneath the surface and who controls avenues of thinking and communicating. He can help you look deeper and be more aware of manipulations. You can help him relax and enjoy people as they are.

CHALLENGING—2

LIBRA/SAGITTARIUS

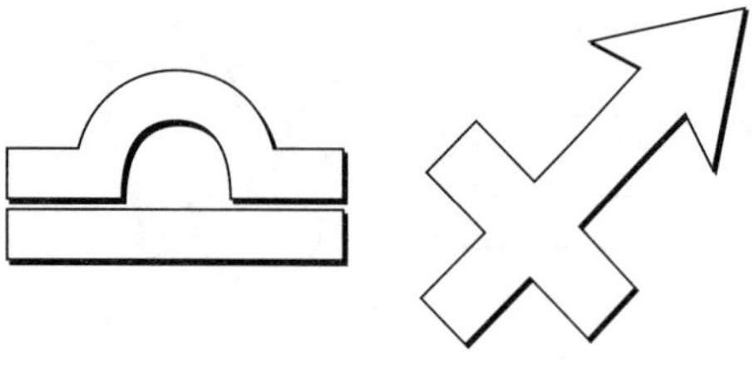

FRIENDLY FACES

Each of you has a natural charm and probably verbal skills. You may be a bit more diplomatic, and he a bit more blunt (direct). You both are likely to be interested in people, intrigued by ideas and active in exchanging information with others. You have more of an aesthetic sense; he may be more philosophical or concerned with ultimate meaning. You both are probably sociable and fun people to be around.

COMPATIBLE—3

LIBRA/CAPRICORN

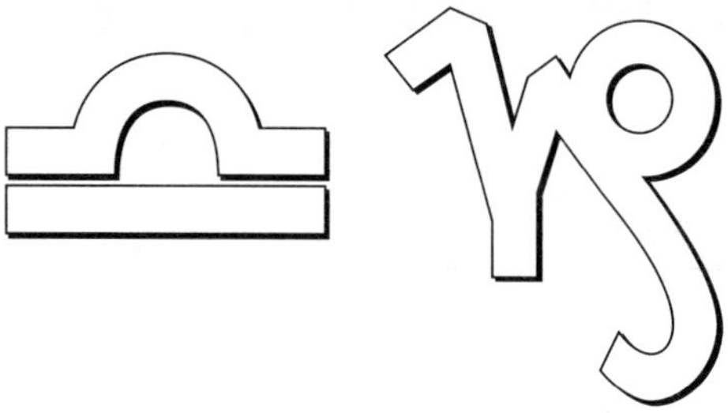

AFFABLE ACCOMPLISHMENT

You tend to view words as bridges to people, ways to make connections and share. He tends to view words as tools for accomplishment. You may be naturally graceful or poetic in your thinking and speech. He is likely to be more cautious, responsible and wanting to get it right. The two of you might clash over focusing more on professional (career) demands or relationship issues. You two both need love and work to be fully happy.

CHALLENGING—2

LIBRA/AQUARIUS

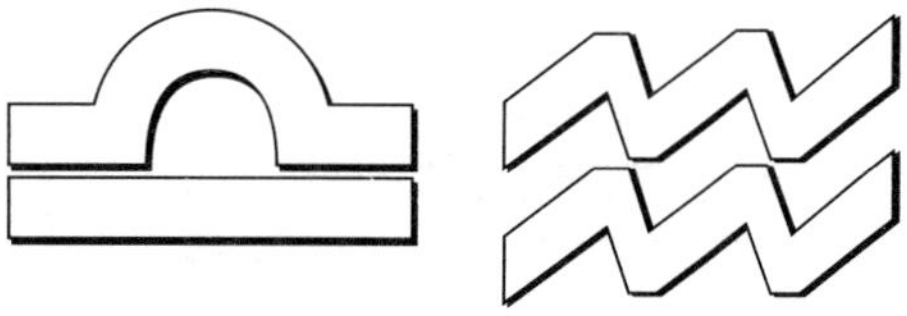

FAIR AND FRIENDLY

Each of you finds it easy to talk to people. Blessed with equalitarian instincts and natural verbal fluency, you can meet everyone on their own level. Both of you are eager to learn in any context. You may share a passion for justice or fair play. You might focus more on aesthetics or relationships while he looks more at technology or the future, but each of you can be logical, objective and open to whatever the world offers.

COMPATIBLE—3

LIBRA/PISCES

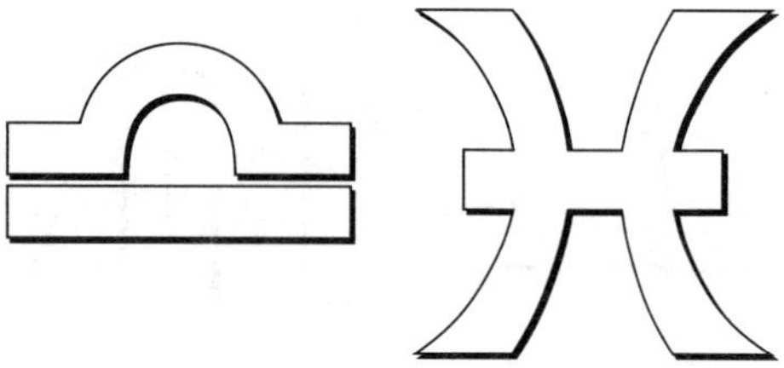

HAVE A NICE DAY!

Either of you may exhibit a strong interest in beauty—perhaps even to the extent of poetry, singing, songwriting or creating beauty with your hands. You both may evade unpleasantness by ignoring it or using "little white lies." You tend to say the "nice" expected thing, where he may retreat to dreaming or fantasies. Your thinking tends to be more step-by-step where his may be more global or holistic. Each of you can learn from the other.

VERY CHALLENGING—1

SUBTLE AND SECRETIVE VS. NO-HOLDS-BARRED

SCORPIO/ARIES

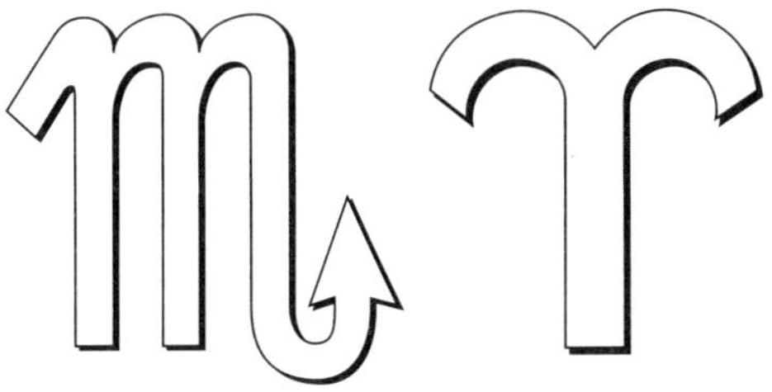

He likes to deal with subjects rapidly and move on to something new. You like to be thorough, sticking with ideas until finished. You are both capable of aggressing with words, but you'll remember what was said much longer than he does. Don't brood over his off-the-cuff remarks. He can learn verbal subtlety and perseverance of thought from you, and you can learn more directness and forthright expression from him.

VERY CHALLENGING—1

CONFRONTATION VS. COMFORT

SCORPIO/TAURUS

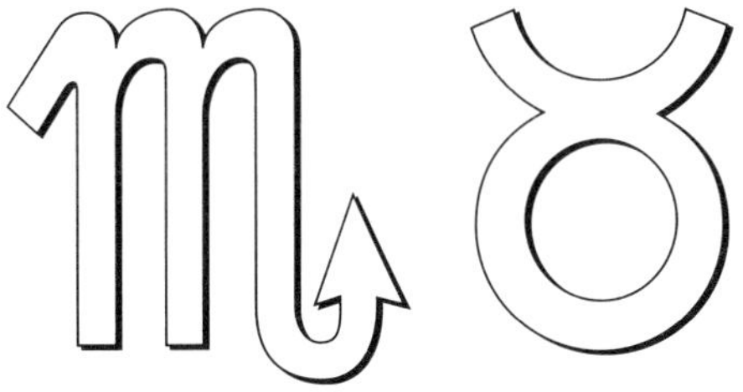

He'd just as soon keep conversations pleasant and affectionate, while you are drawn to confront and resolve problems. You're willing to face tough issues, while he'd prefer to keep things easy. Life should be big enough for intense emotional confrontations **and** good feelings. If things get too heavy, a massage (you both have sensually skilled fingers) will bring back positive vibes. Although opposites, you have a natural attraction and can help each other find the golden mean.

VERY COMPATIBLE—4

SURFACE AND SECRETS

SCORPIO/GEMINI

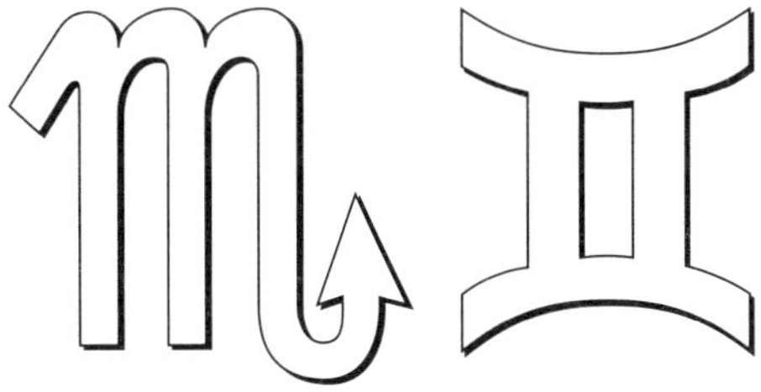

He wants to learn anything and everything, and can be drawn to many different interests. You love to probe deeply, intently, completely. He chats easily and naturally, while you have stronger needs for privacy. He can learn discretion and perseverance from you, and you can learn flexibility and the ability to be casual about life from him. Together, you have both breadth and depth.

VERY CHALLENGING—1

NONVERBAL EXPERTS

SCORPIO/CANCER

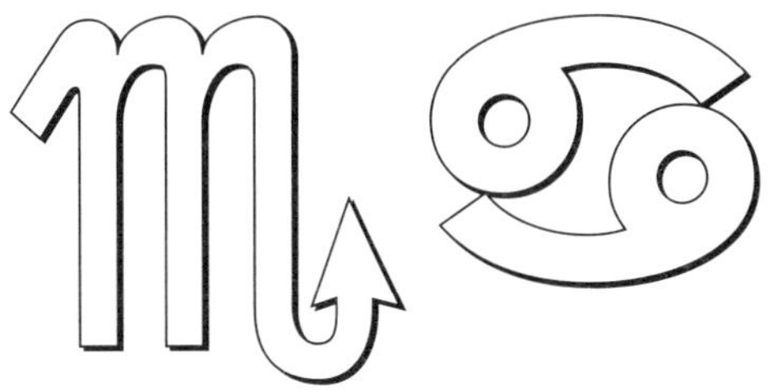

Each of you can be like an iceberg — 9/10ths below the surface where communication is concerned. Neither of you cares to wear your heart on your sleeve (unless you are convinced it is totally safe). Despite possible periods of silence, brooding or moodiness, you are quite sensitive to one another and easily pick up on the "vibes" going out. You are likely to respect each other's needs for privacy and sensitivity.

COMPATIBLE—3

SCORPIO/LEO

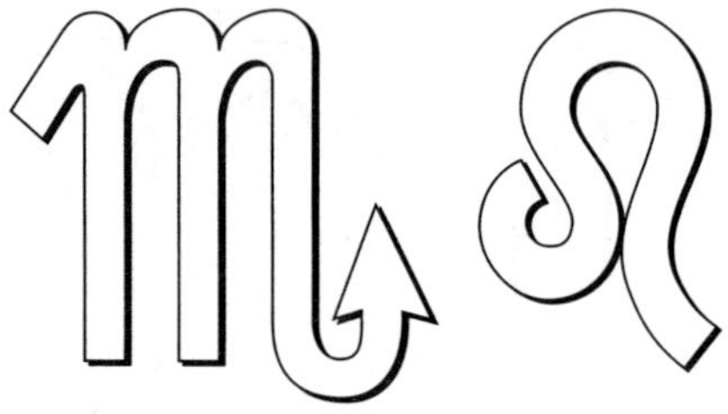

PRIVACY VS. PROMOTION

He wants people to admire his mind and may impress people with his flair, charisma, dramatic instincts or spellbinding abilities. Your thinking tends to be more complex and subtle (with manipulation a possibility). If either of you tries to control or influence the other's thinking or speaking, rocky times lie ahead. You can learn directness and the joy of compliments from him, while he learns from you to read nonverbal cues and look below the surface.

CHALLENGING—2

SCORPIO/VIRGO

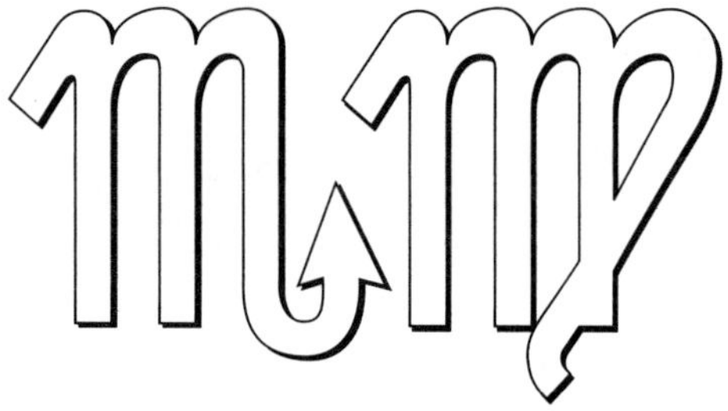

ORGANIZATION UNLIMITED

The two of you can turn organization into a fine art! Each of you may have a mind like a filing cabinet. You know how to figure things out and keep everything in its place. Research and business skills are likely. You both have a penchant for efficiency in thinking and in speaking (no wasted words). Don't nitpick each other, but do enjoy your shared skills at being practical, thorough and sensible.

COMPATIBLE—3

SCORPIO/LIBRA

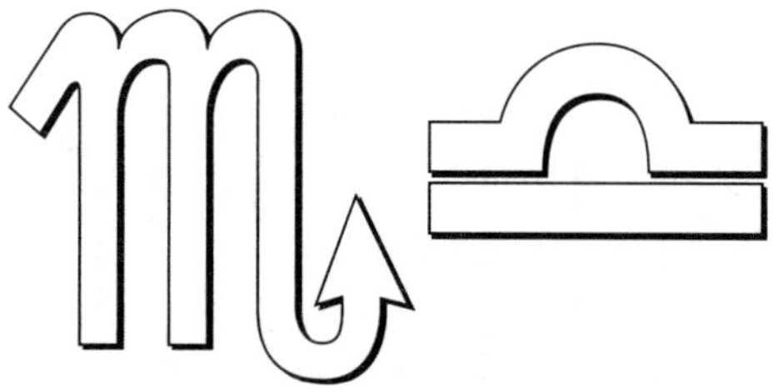

THE SPY & THE TOASTMASTER

He likes to keep the conversational ball rolling smoothly and comfortably, whereas you are willing to play "I've got a secret." He may prefer to look on the surface, while you tend to probe beneath and be concerned with what is unsaid. You're probably more willing to confront uncomfortable issues in your relationship. You can help him appreciate complexities and recognize manipulations. He can help you relax and enjoy people as they are.

CHALLENGING—2

SCORPIO/SCORPIO

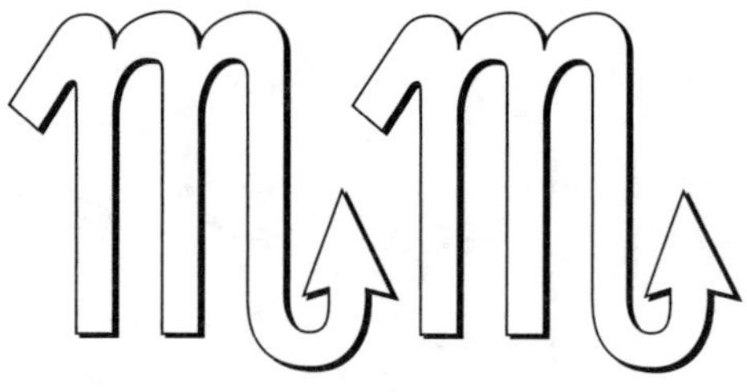

INCISIVE INTELLECTS

Each of you has met your match! No other Mercury placement is so intense; can push so hard in conversations or manipulate so deftly. Each of you naturally understands complexities and sees many layers in life. Each of you can be utterly tenacious with an idea, refusing to release until thoroughly understood. Both of you can be passionate about learning, may strive to control knowledge or communication, yet you seek a deeper understanding of yourselves and the world.

VERY COMPATIBLE—4

CYNICAL VS. CAREFREE — SCORPIO/SAGITTARIUS

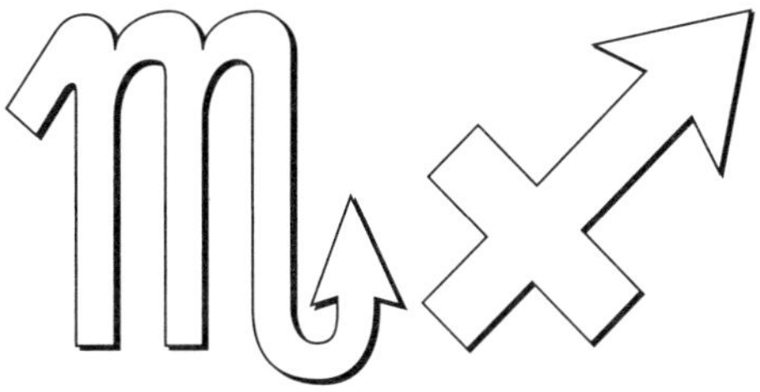

You believe that certain thoughts are meant to stay private. He believes in letting it all hang out! Bluntness may be a way of life for him, while you are willing to look for subtle ways to express yourself. His thinking tends to be optimistic (sometimes overly so), whereas you are apt to be a bit cynical or suspicious—knowing that there are bad guys as well as good guys out there! Appreciate each other's viewpoints and choose the best position as each moment occurs.

CHALLENGING—2

DISCERNING AND DISCIPLINED — SCORPIO/CAPRICORN

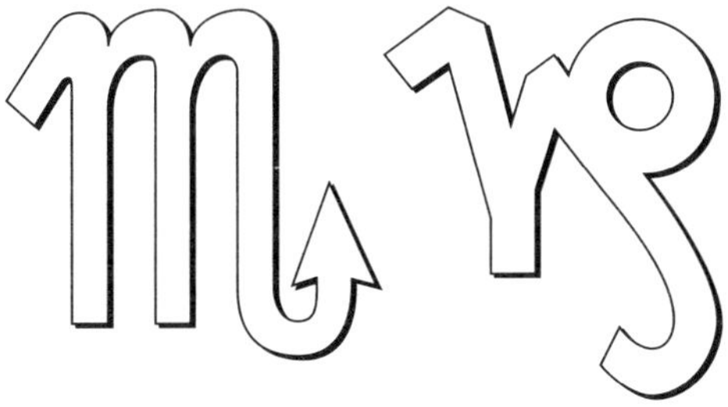

Each of you knows that knowledge is power and **might** be tempted to control the channels of information or communication. You both have a natural shrewdness which could be an asset in the business world. Your minds are quite organized and thorough, with excellent skills for research or anything requiring systematic attention. As long as neither of you tries to dominate the other intellectually, you will challenge one another to rise to your highest potentials.

COMPATIBLE—3

THE PAST AND THE FUTURE — SCORPIO/AQUARIUS

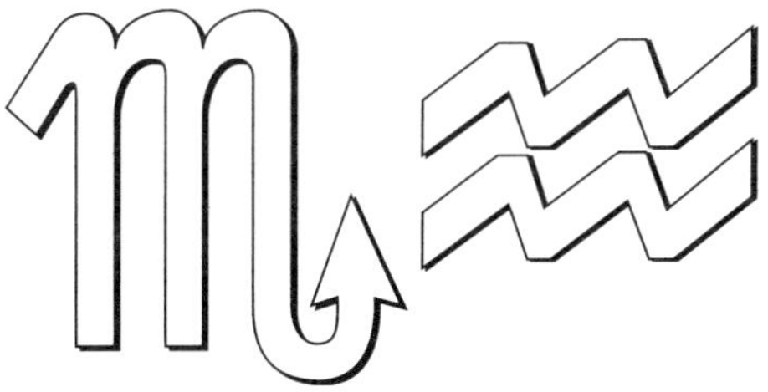

Your mental approach is very thorough; you don't like to let go of any ideas until you have completely worked them out. He tends to be constantly pushing ahead, looking toward the future and discussing possibilities. You are controlled (and somewhat private) in what you say. He is quirky, unconventional and may shock people with some comments. Each of you learns best doing things your own way and challenging others who tell you what you should think.

CHALLENGING—2

MAGIC AND MIRRORS — SCORPIO/PISCES

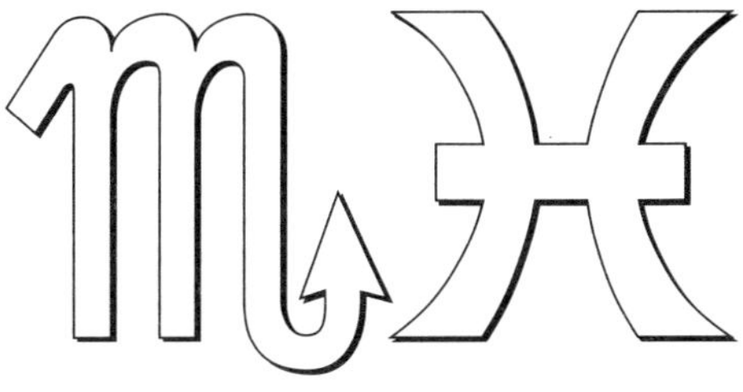

Each of you is sensitive to what lies beneath the surface of words. You both understand nonverbal cues and can be quite persuasive or even hypnotic in your communications. The two of you naturally work with emotions as well as intellect, blending thinking and feeling. Manipulation could come easily to either of you; don't get sucked into that temptation. Do share your wonderful imaginations with each other.

COMPATIBLE—3

SAGITTARIUS/ARIES

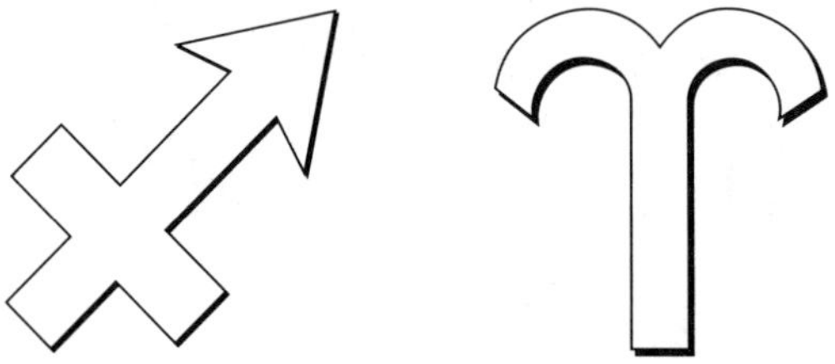

IMPULSIVELY HONEST

The two of you can raise foot-in-mouth to a new art form. You stimulate each other to impulsive speech and may jump to conclusions or trip over words sometimes in your hurry to "get it out." You both think quickly and may be impatient waiting for others to "catch up"—but you've met your match here! You can spark humor and an adventurous spirit in each other.

COMPATIBLE—3

SAGITTARIUS/TAURUS

SPIRITUAL VS. MATERIAL

You want to discuss your dreams and visions for the future, while he wants to focus on current, practical issues. You have grand plans and he wants to know where the money is coming from. It is important to have aspirations to reach for, but we also need the common sense to figure out the necessary steps toward our goals. Each of you can supply something the other has less developed if you learn together rather than trying to make the other over.

VERY CHALLENGING—1

SAGITTARIUS/GEMINI

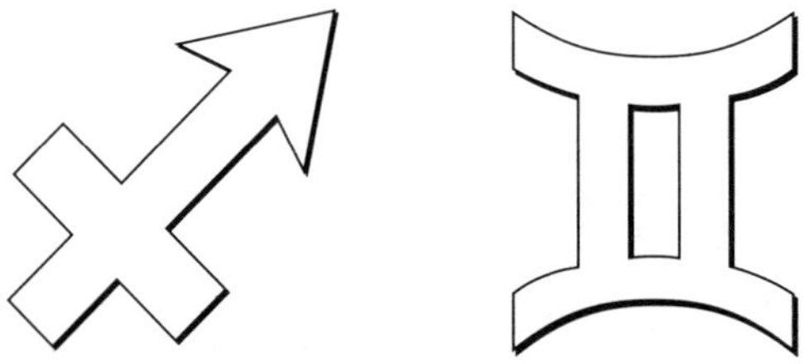

LIFELONG LEARNING

You are both natural students and teachers, and can easily stimulate one another to more learning and discovering. You may enjoy traveling together, finding new vistas exciting. His curiosity tends more toward the here-and-now—people and situations right around him. You could be a mite more concerned with issues of long-range goals, philosophy, beliefs, values or moral principles. You spark each other's humor and hunger for knowledge.

VERY COMPATIBLE—4

SAGITTARIUS/CANCER

KINETIC AND KIND

You believe that "honesty is the best policy" while he believes it is better to be silent than risk hurting someone (or yourself). His primary focus is on those closest, while you are drawn to the wider world. He can learn more openness, humor and directness from you, while you can learn the value of silence and protecting feelings through him. Appreciate each other's styles without trying to change them.

VERY CHALLENGING—1

LARGER THAN LIFE

SAGITTARIUS/LEO

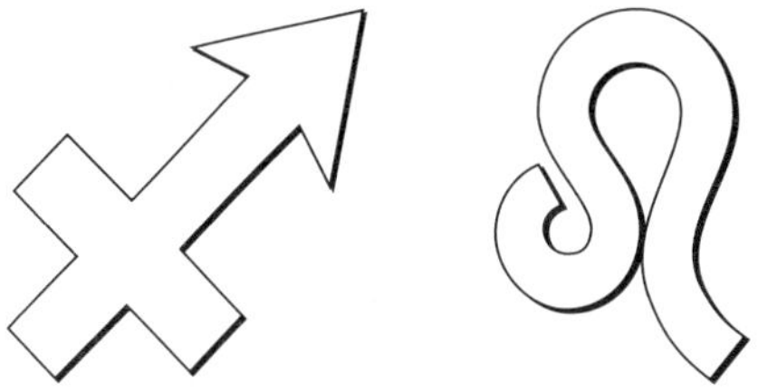

Both of you know how to win friends and influence people! You can each be quite persuasive and impressive in your thinking and speaking. You both can also grandstand, exaggerate and jump to conclusions. Your thinking is oriented toward excitement. You want thrills and fun in your conversations. Each of you enjoys lively exchanges. You both think optimistically and can cheer others up and onward.

COMPATIBLE—3

EXAGGERATION AND ACCURACY

SAGITTARIUS/VIRGO

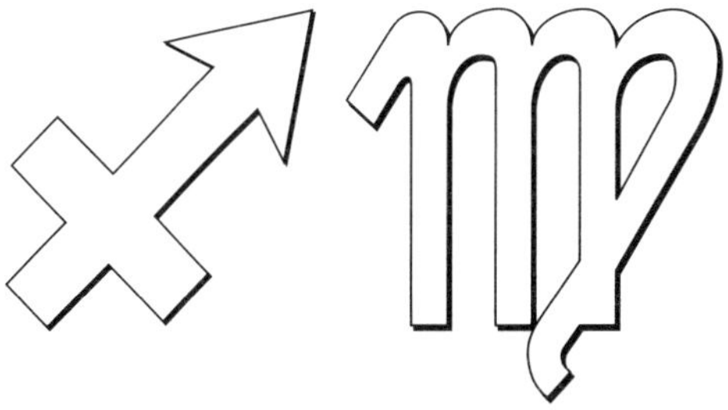

You tend to think and speak quickly, while he searches for just the **right** concept or word. Your optimism may seem overdone to him and he could nitpick or criticize some of your rosy assumptions. You love multiple interests, while he prefers to focus and complete projects a step at a time. If each of you is open, some of your optimism and humor will rub off on him and some of his careful attention to detail and desire to be correct will rub off on you.

CHALLENGING—2

FRIENDLY FACES

SAGITTARIUS/LIBRA

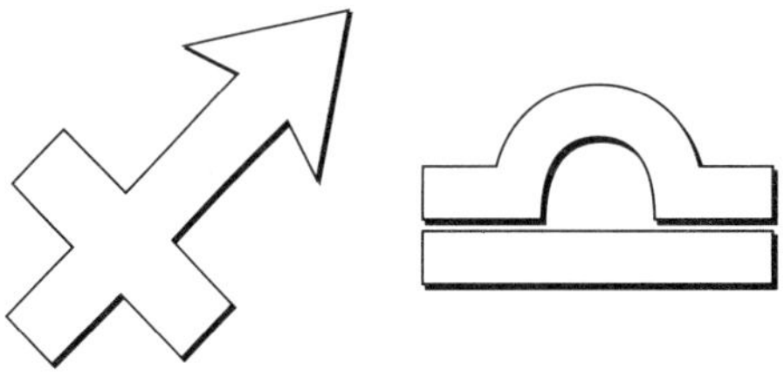

Each of you has a natural charm and probably verbal skills. He may be a bit more diplomatic, and you a bit more direct (blunt). You both are likely to be interested in people, intrigued by ideas, and active in exchanging information with others. He could have more of an aesthetic sense; you may be more philosophical or concerned with ultimate meaning. You both are probably sociable and fun people to be around.

COMPATIBLE—3

CAREFREE VS. CYNICAL

SAGITTARIUS/SCORPIO

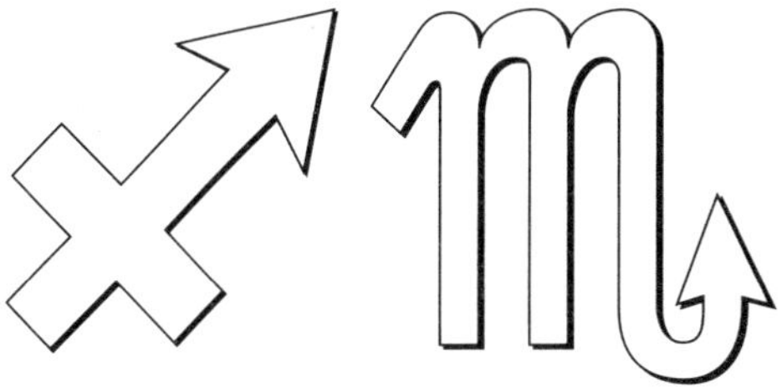

You believe that honesty is the best policy. He believes that certain thoughts are meant to stay private. You want people to be up-front and say what's going on, while he tends to seek subtle ways to express himself. Your thinking tends to be optimistic (sometimes Pollyanna), whereas he is apt to be a bit cynical or suspicious—believing in evil equal to good. Appreciate each other's viewpoints and choose the best position as each moment occurs.

CHALLENGING—2

SAGITTARIUS/SAGITTARIUS FAST TALKERS!

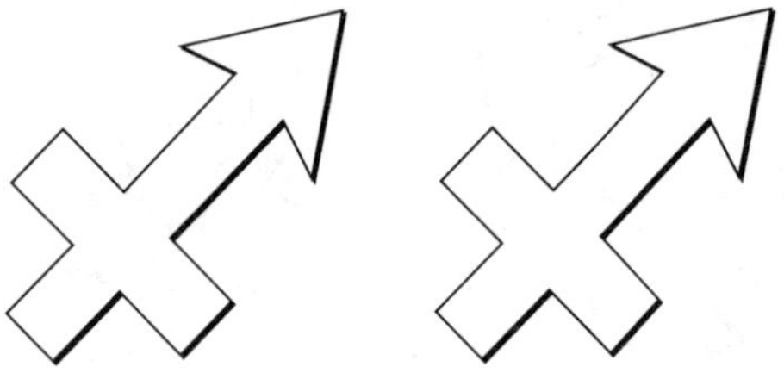

No other Mercury placement can keep up with you two! Natural storytellers, comedians, and promoters—you can talk to anyone, at any time, about anything. Never at a loss for words, if you're not sure of your facts, you'll chime in with an assumption or opinion. Honesty is important to both of you. Each of you has an inner faith that helps you spot the silver linings in dark clouds. Most people enjoy your company, as you are quite magnetic.

VERY COMPATIBLE—4

SAGITTARIUS/CAPRICORN CAREFREE VS. CAUTIOUS

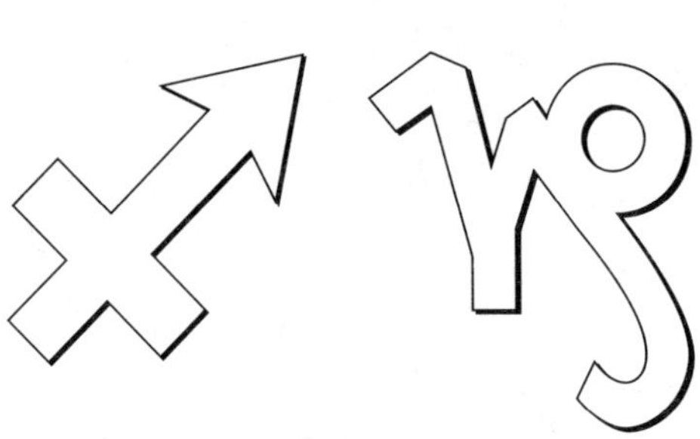

You tend to look at the bright side; he tends to consider what could go wrong. You are casual, friendly and talkative. He is careful, more formal and reserved. Sometimes you just want to have fun, while he's concerned about finishing tasks. You can help him appreciate positive potentials, and he can help you plan better and be prepared if you listen rather than trying to change each other.

CHALLENGING—2

SAGITTARIUS/AQUARIUS INFORMED & INTELLECTUAL

Communication could be a middle name for either of you! Naturally friendly and eager to discuss ideas, you tend to be at home with anyone. Seldom at a loss for words, you will cheerfully talk about almost anything. The two of you may particularly enjoy theorizing about the future, justice, or the nature of humanity. You appreciate new ideas and stir each other to greater heights mentally and verbally.

COMPATIBLE—3

SAGITTARIUS/PISCES TRUTH VS. COMPASSION

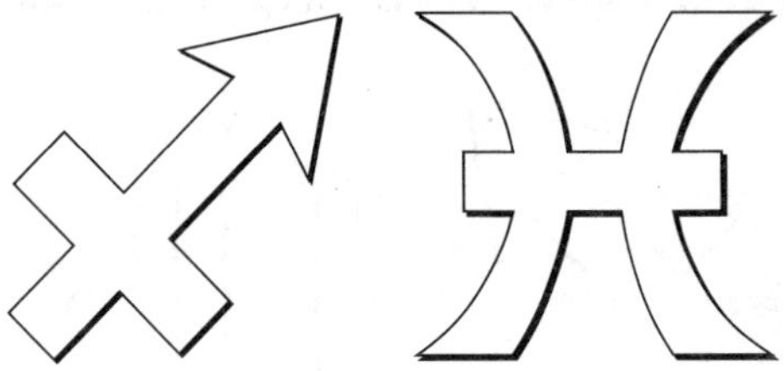

You believe in the truth, the whole truth, and nothing but the truth. He believes in protecting people's feelings and kindhearted deception. You tend to think and speak quickly (sometimes impulsively), while he tends to meditate before speaking—and remain silent if someone is at risk. Each of you is quite idealistic, so can find a compromise which allows for different kinds of truth and different viewpoints among people.

CHALLENGING—2

CAREFULLY CORRECT AND RAPID RESPONSE

CAPRICORN/ARIES

He's confident and expressive with the mind and tongue. You're cautious, responsible and concerned with your place in society. He's verbally open and direct. You're formal and may even be inhibited (worried about making a mistake). He may aggress with words, while you prefer to think first. Together, you can blend independent thinking with a recognition that we live in a society with certain rules and expectations.

CHALLENGING—2

BUSINESSLIKE

CAPRICORN/TAURUS

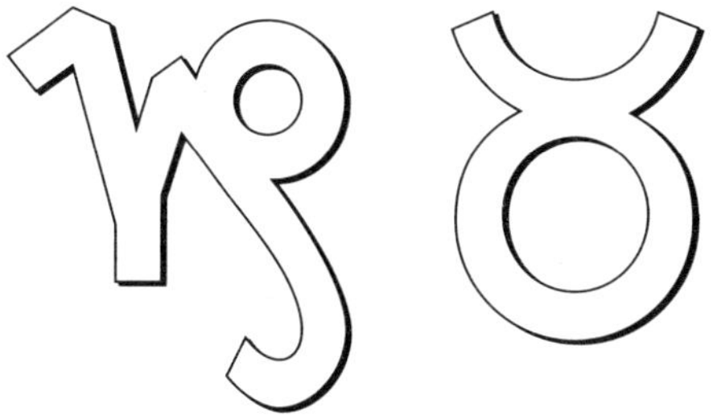

You both have good, common sense. You can easily apply your minds to the "real world" and material success or business ventures could be significant topics of conversations. You encourage each other to put your minds to work and prefer ideas and exchanges that generate results. You may use your minds, tongues, or hands in your professions. You both think in terms of facts and what is possible.

COMPATIBLE—3

CORRECT VS. CASUAL

CAPRICORN/GEMINI

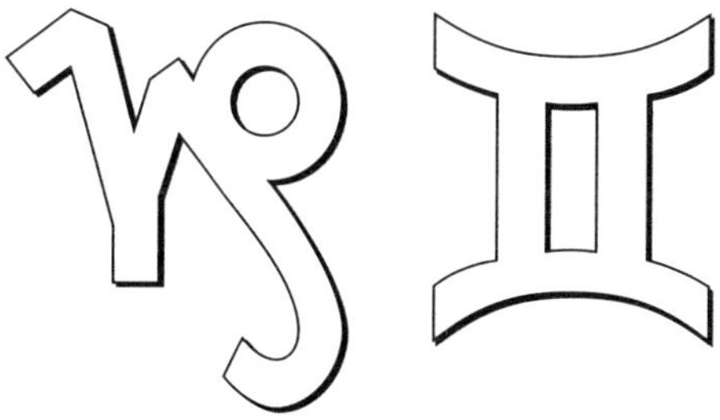

He loves to learn, to move in many directions mentally. You tend to be more stable, concerned with what is "right." You believe in rules and structure; he believes in unfettered curiosity. You might be formal or concerned about making a mistake in your thinking or communicating. He tends to be flippant, lighthearted and extremely articulate. He can learn focus and control from you. You can learn flexibility and detachment from him.

VERY CHALLENGING—1

DEPENDENT OR DOMINANT?

CAPRICORN/CANCER

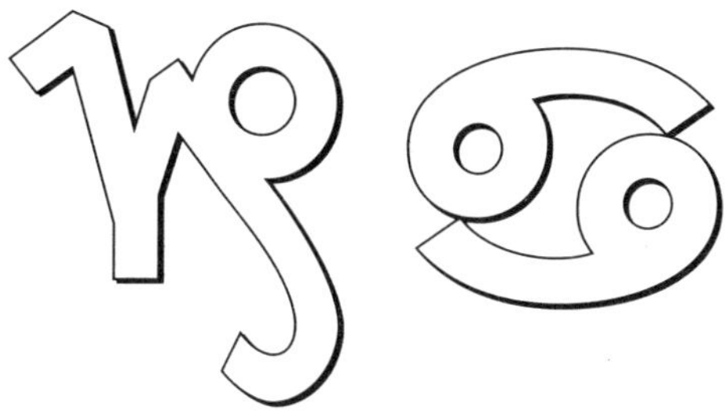

In some ways you can seem like opposites. You both value security, but you are more concerned with what the world thinks and outer standards of right and wrong, while he is more focused on family and personal demands and feelings. Yet you both can feel drawn together and may share a talent for understanding business concepts, family matters and the practical survival demands of everyday life.

VERY COMPATIBLE—4

CAPRICORN/LEO

WHO'S IN CHARGE?

Each of you thinks like a leader, so don't get in each other's way! He tends to be more expressive, dynamic and eager to make an impression on others. You tend to be more guarded, cautious, planning carefully for a successful outcome. He can teach you confidence and enthusiasm. You can teach him concentration and mental follow-through. Don't step on each other's conversational toes. Do keep room for both work and play.

VERY CHALLENGING—1

CAPRICORN/VIRGO

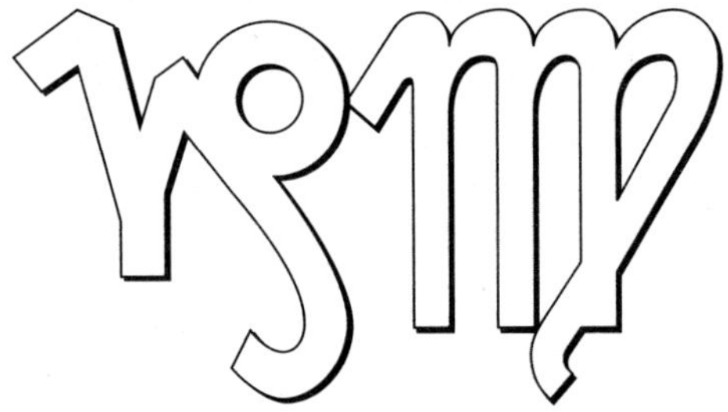

REALISTIC

Both of you can be quite sensible, practical and skilled at dealing with real-world questions. Each of you may have business abilities and is good at facing facts and doing what is necessary. You may put your minds to work and conversations could center more around accomplishments or tasks than social banter. You each possess a dry wit, but are primarily focused on thinking and speaking accurately and well.

COMPATIBLE—3

CAPRICORN/LIBRA

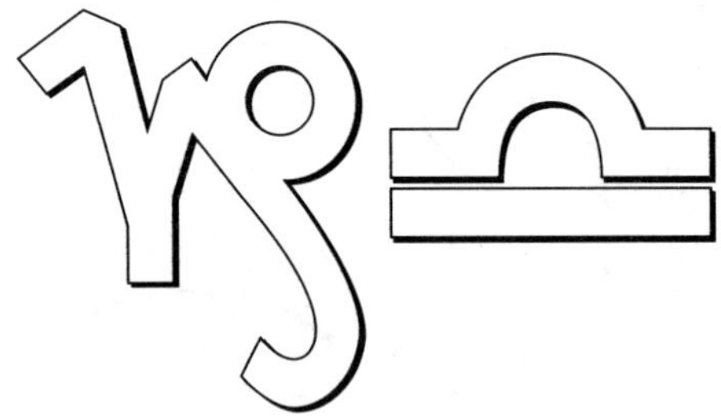

AFFABLE ACCOMPLISHMENT

He tends to view words as bridges to people, ways to make connections. You tend to view words as tools for practical use and getting things done. You may put your mind to work or be concerned about making mistakes, while he could have a more aesthetic, artistic, or relaxed attitude. The two of your might clash over focusing more on professional (work) demands or relationship issues. You need both to be fully happy.

CHALLENGING—2

CAPRICORN/SCORPIO

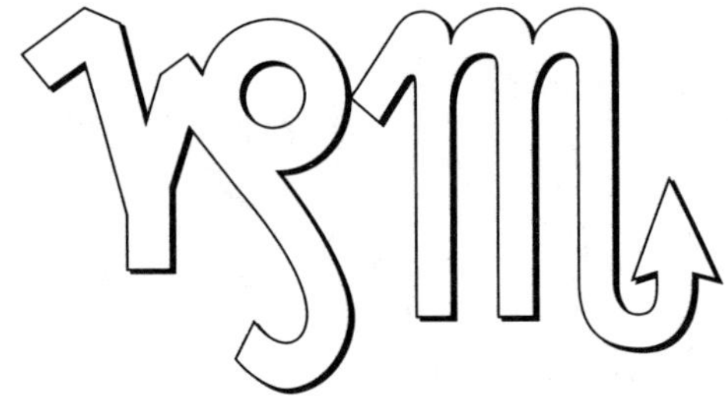

DISCIPLINED AND DISCERNING

Each of you knows that knowledge is power and **might** be tempted to control the channels of information or communication. You both have a natural shrewdness which could be an asset in the business world. Your minds are quite organized and thorough, with excellent skills for research or anything requiring systematic attention. As long as neither of you tries to dominate the other intellectually, you will challenge one another to rise to your highest potentials.

COMPATIBLE—3

CAUTIOUS VS. CAREFREE

CAPRICORN/SAGITTARIUS

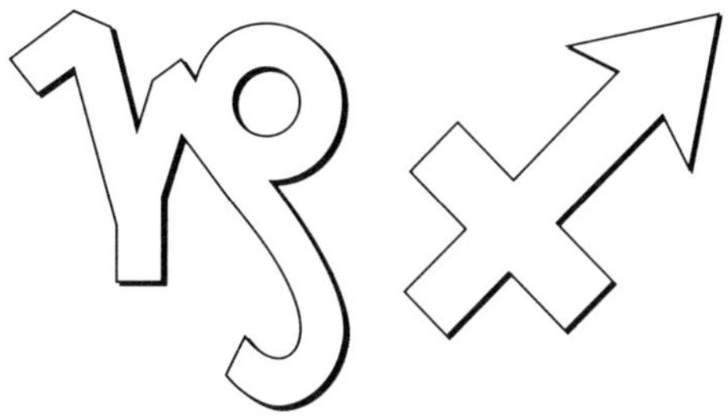

You tend to be cautious and wonder what might go wrong; he looks on the bright side and believes all will be fine. You are somewhat reserved and do not want to make a mistake in your thinking or speaking. He is casual, friendly and words just flow (sometimes too much). You can help him plan ahead and exercise a little control of his bluntness or impulsive speech. He can help you appreciate positive potentials.

CHALLENGING—2

CAREFUL COMMUNICATORS

CAPRICORN/CAPRICORN

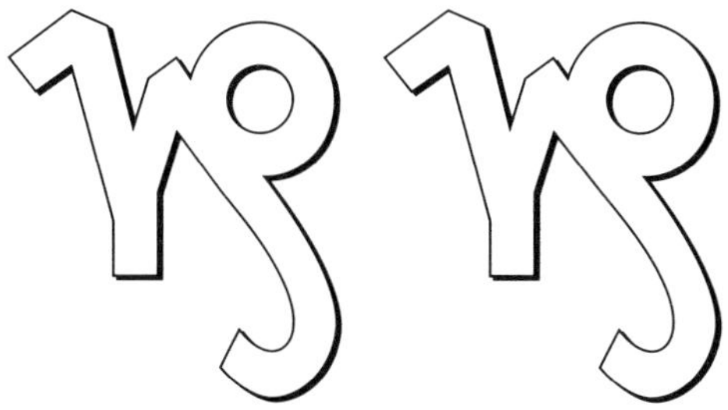

Both of you tend to be serious in your thinking and speech. You are responsible in how you express yourselves and really dislike making mistakes. Each of you may put your minds to work or use articulate or manual skills on the job. You may be quite verbal in a professional setting, but tend to be more reserved in a purely social setting. The two of you are likely to have business skills and good common sense.

VERY COMPATIBLE—4

CONVENTIONAL VS. UNCONVENTIONAL THINKING

CAPRICORN/AQUARIUS

You tend to think and speak in socially-accepted ways. He may enjoy shocking people or challenging authorities. You believe in caution and planning. He can be impulsive and leap ahead with ideas. Your thinking tends to be linear (step-by-step) while he jumps to conclusions which can be either brilliant or off the wall. A bit of both approaches is healthiest if the two of you will compromise.

CHALLENGING—2

PRACTICAL AND POETIC

CAPRICORN/PISCES

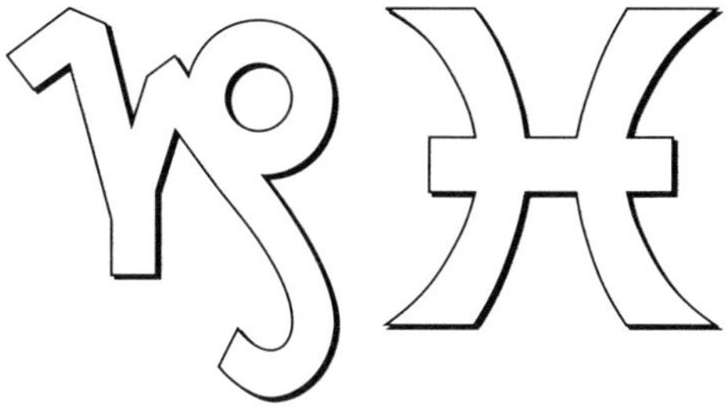

You can be the realist when he is the idealist. Your thinking tends to be cautious. You prefer to get it right and may remain silent rather than risking an error. He tends to be imaginative, creative and (perhaps) inclined toward fantasy. He'd prefer that life and people be beautiful and might even avoid reality on occasion. If you combine forces, you can help ground his dreams, and he can help inspire your thinking, bringing in magic and romance.

COMPATIBLE—3

AQUARIUS/ARIES

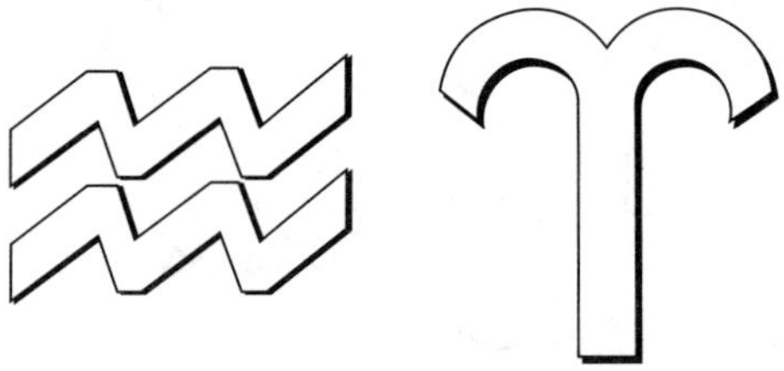

THE FREE SPIRIT AND THE PIONEER

Fellow rebels! Both of you are independent thinkers and may sometimes say things purely for the shock value. You two resist dogmas and other people's rules. You are attracted to new ideas and insights. You stimulate one another to be free and individualistic in your thoughts and speech. You both tend to think for yourselves and to question authorities. You enjoy exposing one another to new ideas.

COMPATIBLE—3

AQUARIUS/TAURUS

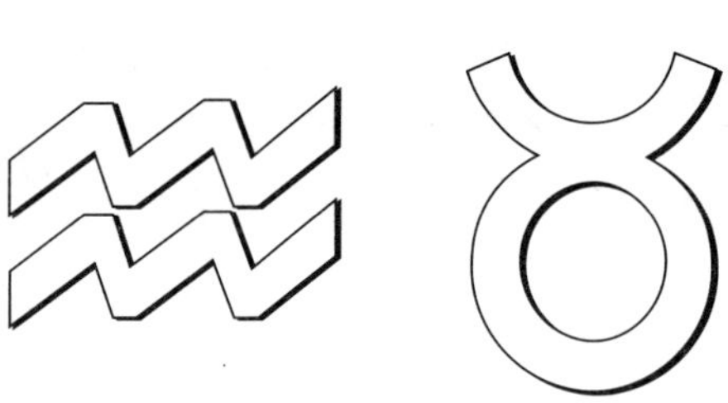

RISK VS. SECURITY

He's more cautious, stable and grounded in his thinking and speech, tending toward familiar pathways. You are more independent, original and concerned with equality. The two of you could polarize around the known versus the unknown, or the tried and true versus the new and different. A bit of both works best. You may shock him sometimes with unusual interests or activities, but he can help you come "down to earth" and get results rather than just theorizing.

CHALLENGING—2

AQUARIUS/GEMINI

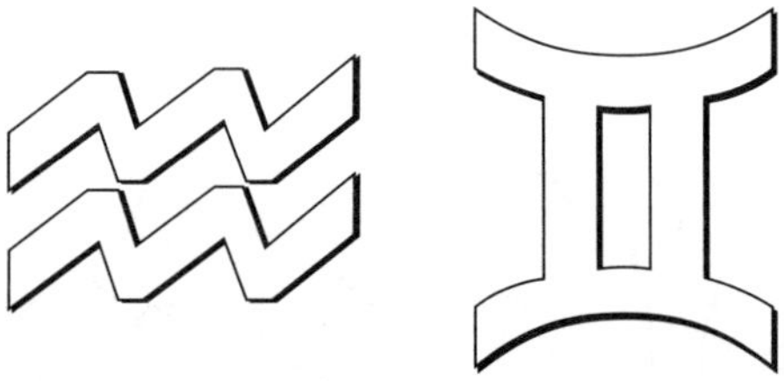

INQUISITIVE INQUIRERS

You both are skilled at logic, detachment and being part of a team. Cooperating and sharing ideas flow naturally. You stimulate one another mentally. You may have more unusual interests or involvements. He may have a quicker sense of fun, but each of you tends to be rational, good with words, and gregarious. Social contacts or networking could be important in your relationship. You both have inquiring minds.

COMPATIBLE—3

AQUARIUS/CANCER

SUDDEN VS. SOFT

He thinks about the familiar, the secure and people close to him, while you consider the unusual, the different and the new. You are willing to question authority, while he would prefer to remain silent rather than getting into unpleasant emotions. You can probably converse for hours, while he appreciates quiet moments. With mutual tolerance, you can learn to wait for his input and he can develop a mind more open to the unconventional.

VERY CHALLENGING—1

DETACHMENT VS. PASSION

AQUARIUS/LEO

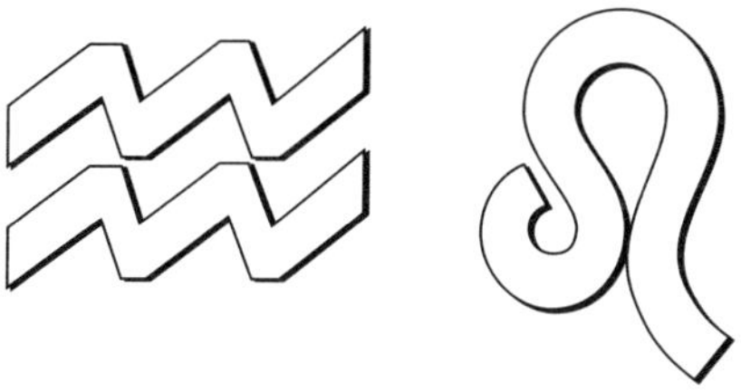

He can be quite dramatic, magnetic, persuasive (and sometimes arrogant) in thinking and speech. You tend to be more cool and objective (sometimes detached). He **needs** to be admired for his mind; you **need** to be unique in your approach to the world of the mind. Despite being opposites in some respects, you are naturally drawn together and share much creativity and originality. The way you think and communicate excites each other.

VERY COMPATIBLE—4

THE SCIENTIST AND THE TECHNICIAN

AQUARIUS/VIRGO

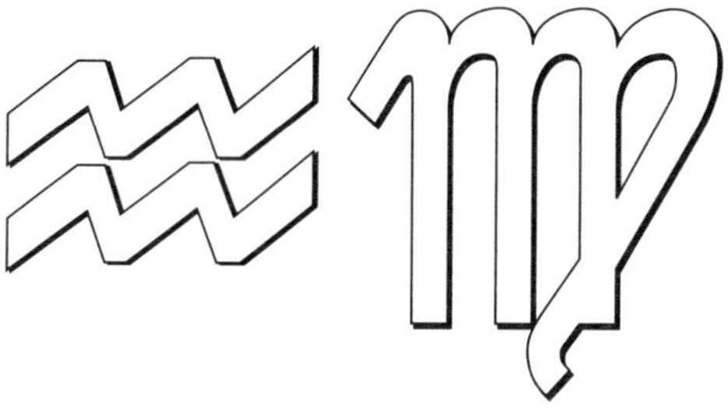

He is probably good with details and has an organized mind. You are good with theories and may prefer the overview to details. He tends to look for one "right" answer, while you tend to assume many possibilities exist. Your thinking and speech can be unusual or unconventional, while he needs to be correct, efficient and practical. He can help you be more grounded, and you can help him to envision more possibilities.

VERY CHALLENGING—1

FRIENDLY AND FAIR

AQUARIUS/LIBRA

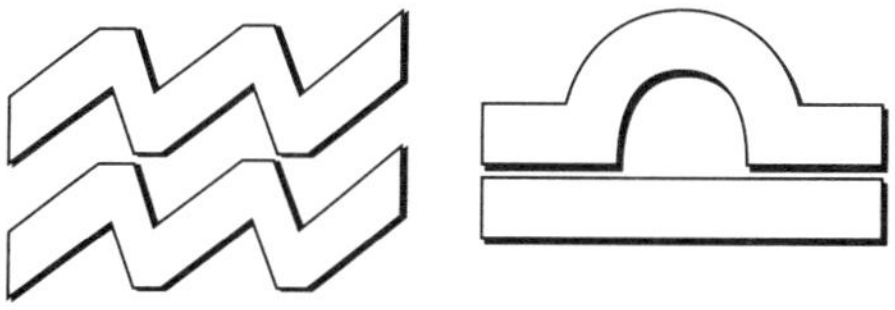

Each of you finds it easy to talk to people. Blessed with equalitarian instincts and natural verbal fluency, you can meet everyone on their own level. Both of you are eager to learn in any context. You may share a passion for justice or fair play. He might focus more on aesthetics or competitive issues, while you look toward the future or the unusual, but each of you can be logical, objective and open to whatever the world offers.

COMPATIBLE—3

THE FUTURE AND THE PAST

AQUARIUS/SCORPIO

His mental approach is very thorough; he doesn't like to let go of any ideas until he has completely worked them out. You tend to be constantly pushing ahead, looking toward the future and discussing possibilities. He is controlled (and somewhat private) in what he says. You are quirky, unconventional, and may shock people with some comments. Each of you learns best doing things your own way and challenging others who tell you what you should think.

CHALLENGING—2

AQUARIUS/SAGITTARIUS

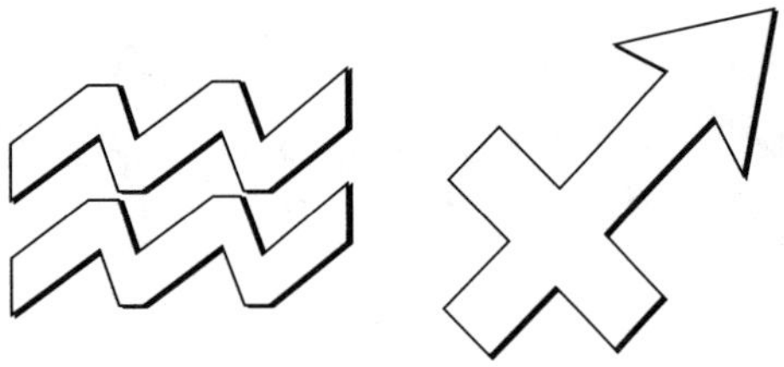

INFORMED & INTELLECTUAL

Communication could be a middle name for either of you! Naturally friendly and eager to discuss ideas, you tend to be at home with anyone. Seldom at a loss for words, you will cheerfully talk about almost anything. The two of you may particularly enjoy theorizing about the future, justice, or the nature of humanity. You appreciate new ideas and stir each other to greater heights mentally and verbally.

COMPATIBLE—3

AQUARIUS/CAPRICORN

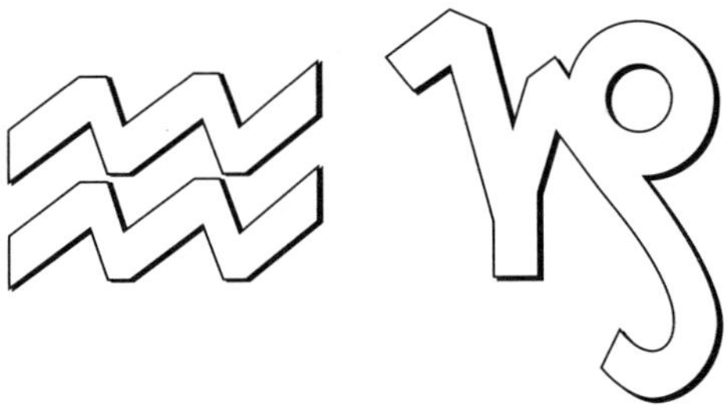

UNCONVENTIONAL VS. CONVENTIONAL THINKING

He tends to think and speak in socially-accepted ways. You may enjoy shocking people or challenging authorities. He believes in caution and planning. You can be impulsive and leap ahead with ideas. His thinking tends to be linear (step-by-step) while you can jump to conclusions which are either brilliant or off the wall. A bit of both approaches is healthiest if the two of you will compromise.

CHALLENGING—2

AQUARIUS/AQUARIUS

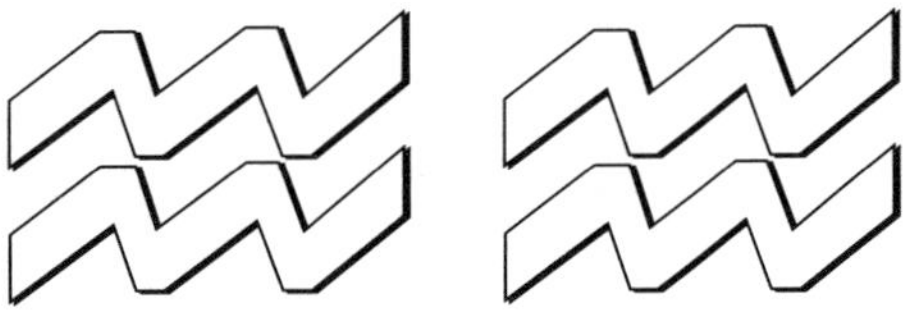

FREE THINKERS!

No dogmas for either of you! Both of you are intellectual rebels, eager to question authorities, break the rules, and find new answers. Each of you can be skilled at networking, brainstorming, creative answers, and seeing multiple possibilities. Naturally friendly, you find it easy to talk to almost anyone. Fair play and equality may matter to you both. You could also share an interest in the future.

VERY COMPATIBLE—4

AQUARIUS/PISCES

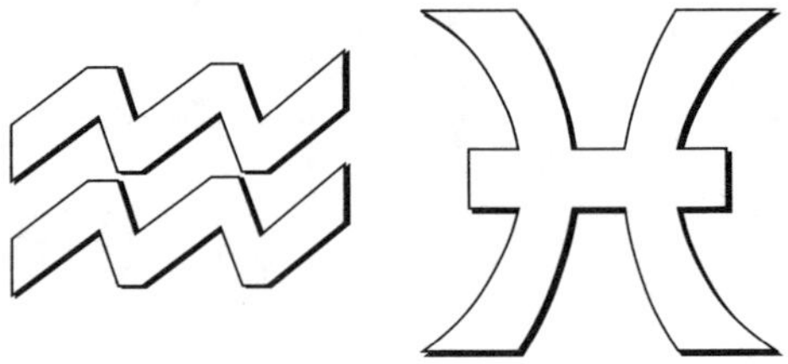

COSMIC CONSCIOUSNESS

Each of you is good at seeing the broad perspective. You have a sense of vision, an ability to get beyond the parts and see the whole. He may be a bit more imaginative, and you a bit more rational. You can be mentally rebellious and verbally unconventional, while he tends to be more intuitive, vague or graceful with his use of language. You may find humanitarian instincts, unusual interests, or networking a bond between you.

CHALLENGING—2

SENSITIVELY SUBTLE AND DEFINITELY DIRECT

PISCES/ARIES

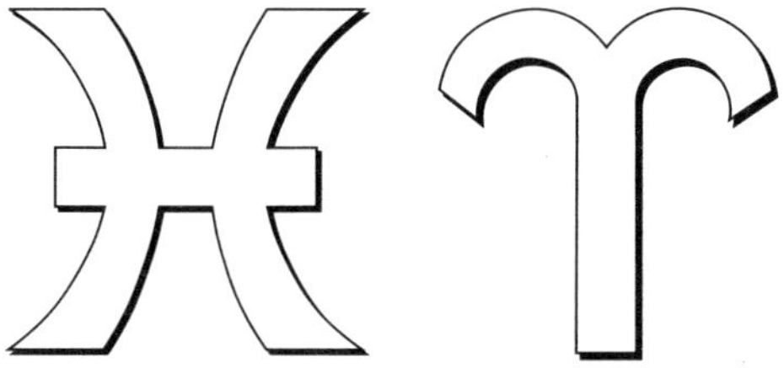

You trust "vibes" and intuition, while he trusts personal experience and what he believes. He says what he means and means what he says, while you can be poetic, metaphorical, symbolic, and may fall into rose-colored glasses in your thinking and speech (or lie to protect someone). Honesty is admirable, but tact has its place. Try to learn from one another's different styles of thought and speech.

CHALLENGING—2

PRETTY PRETENSE

PISCES/TAURUS

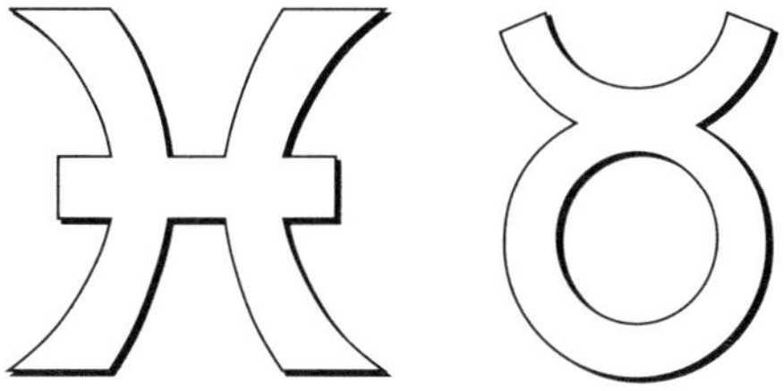

You both could have an artistic bent with your minds or tongues (feeling for music, poetry, songwriting, playing an instrument, etc.). Each of you prefers to keep conversations pleasant and avoid arguments or strife. He can provide a bit more pragmatism and you a bit more imagination, but the two of you can easily combine forces. Your thinking and speech with one another tend to be complementary (and complimentary).

COMPATIBLE—3

INSATIABLY CURIOUS

PISCES/GEMINI

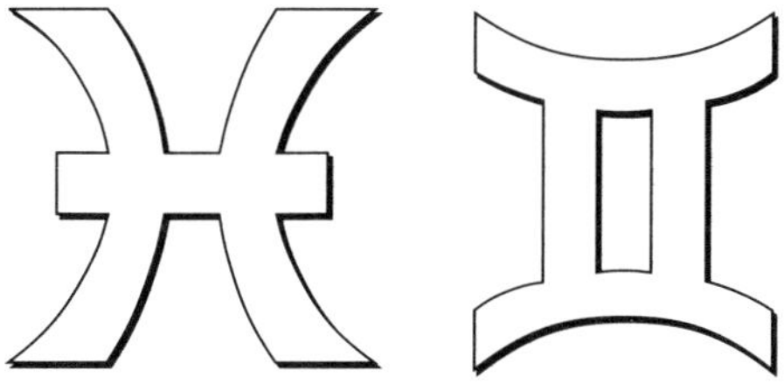

You both can overextend yourselves trying to learn or absorb too much at one time. His style is more linear, rational and objective, while yours is more global, inclusive and holistic. Together you can learn to blend the rational and intuitive; the verbal and the nonverbal. He can teach you more humor and lightness. You can teach him sensitivity to nonverbal cues and enhance his capacity to see connections, patterns, and transcendent meaning in life.

CHALLENGING—2

PROTECTION REIGNS SUPREME

PISCES/CANCER

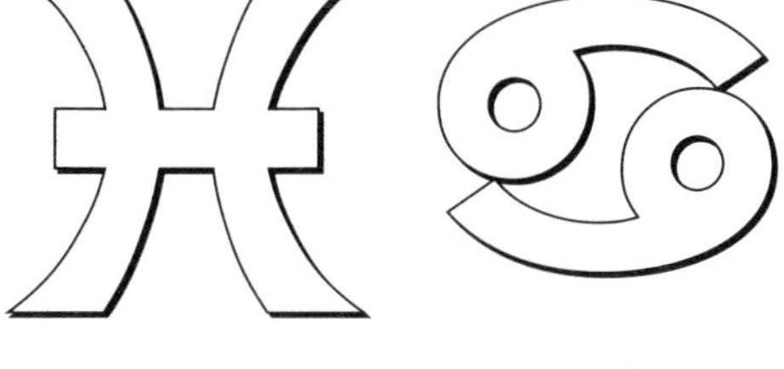

Each of you may prefer to avoid verbal unpleasantness, so could use silence, evasion or "polite lies" to try to keep things flowing smoothly. Either of you might clam up when threatened. When your feelings are engaged, you speak easily. Each of you may tune in nonverbally, and easily understand the other. You both learn well globally, holistically, and when your emotions are involved.

COMPATIBLE—3

PISCES/LEO

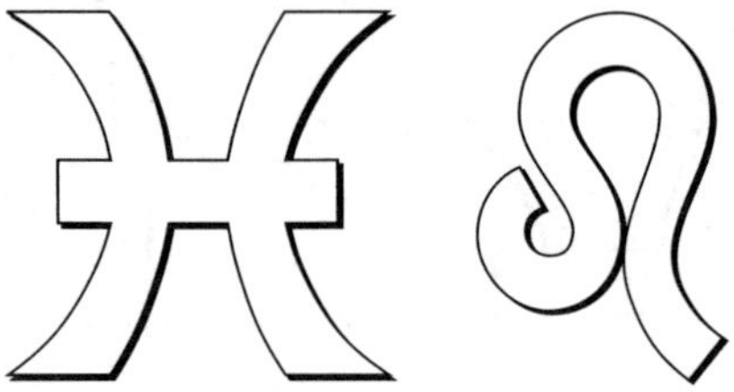

MAGICAL, MYSTICAL MINDS

He tends to think and speak quickly, while you will mull things over and may not reveal what's going on inside. He wants excitement, drama and fun in conversations. You want sensitivity, romance and inspiration. You can share a magical touch, each having skills at persuasion. He can encourage you to be more open and forthcoming. You can encourage him to be more patient and keep some feelings within rather than immediately revealing them.

VERY CHALLENGING—1

PISCES/VIRGO

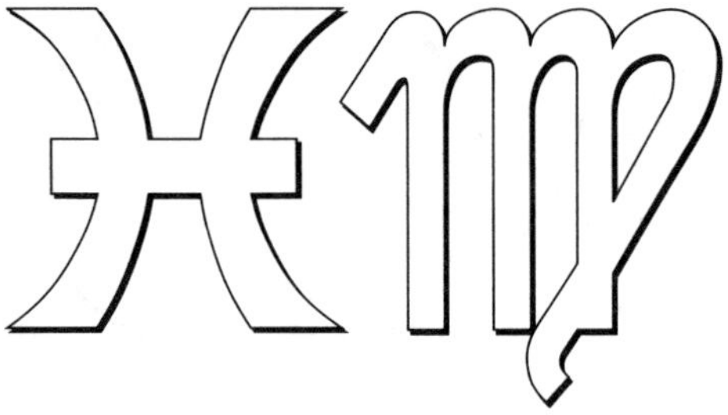

BRINGING DREAMS TO EARTH

He tends to be the realist and you the idealist in your thinking and speech. He may be concerned with work, survival issues or basic needs while you dream about infinite love, beauty, grace, or escapism. He looks at the details; you looks at the whole. Each of you supplies something the other needs to develop. Even though opposite in some respects, you are drawn together and tend to complete one another.

VERY COMPATIBLE—4

PISCES/LIBRA

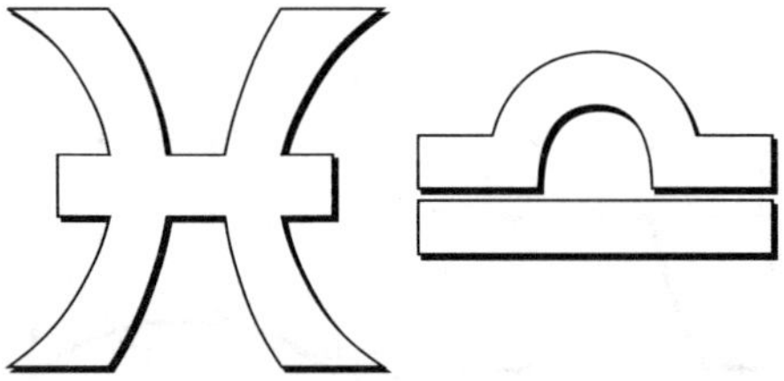

"HAVE A NICE DAY!"

Either of you may exhibit a strong interest in beauty—perhaps even to the extent of poetry, singing, songwriting or creating beauty with your hands. You both may evade unpleasantness by ignoring it or by using "little white lies." He tends to say the "nice" expected thing, where you may retreat to dreaming or fantasies. His thinking tends to be more step-by-step where yours may be more global or holistic. Each of you can learn from the other.

VERY CHALLENGING—1

PISCES/SCORPIO

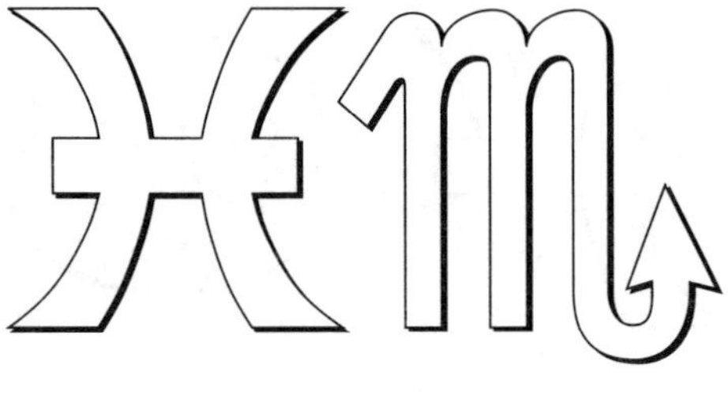

MAGIC AND MIRRORS

Each of you is sensitive to what lies beneath the surface of words. You both understand nonverbal cues and can be quite persuasive or even hypnotic in your communications. The two of you naturally work with emotions as well as intellect, blending thinking and feeling. Manipulation could come easily to either of you; don't get sucked into that temptation. Do share your wonderful imaginations with each other.

COMPATIBLE—3

PISCES/SAGITTARIUS

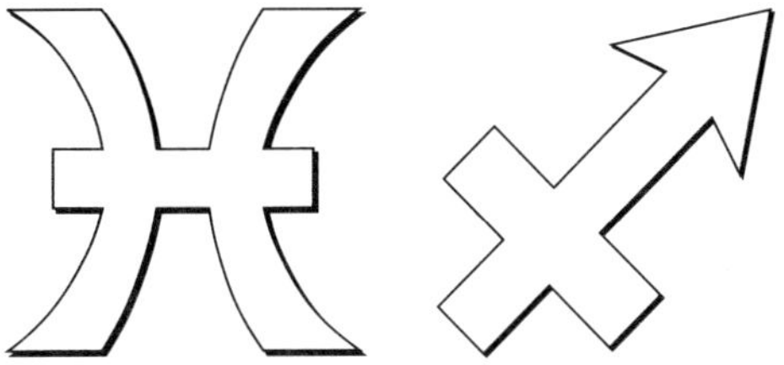

COMPASSION VS. TRUTH

He believes in the truth, the whole truth, and nothing but the truth. You believe in protecting people's feelings and kindhearted deception. He tends to think and speak quickly (sometimes impulsively), while you tend to meditate before speaking—and remain silent if someone is at risk. Each of you is quite idealistic, so can find a compromise which allows for different kinds of truth and different viewpoints among people.

CHALLENGING—2

PISCES/CAPRICORN

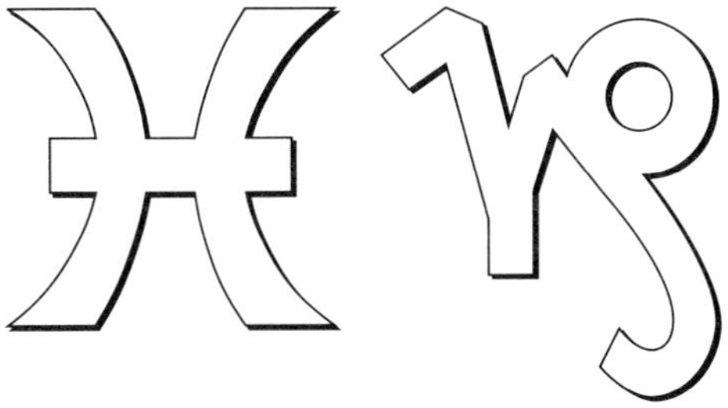

POETIC AND PRACTICAL

He can be the realist when you are the idealist. His thinking tends to be cautious. He prefers to get it right and may remain silent rather than risking an error. You tend to be imaginative, creative and (perhaps) inclined toward fantasy. You'd prefer that life and people be beautiful and might even avoid reality on occasion. If you both combine forces, he can help ground your dreams and you can help inspire his thinking, bringing in magic and romance.

COMPATIBLE—3

PISCES/AQUARIUS

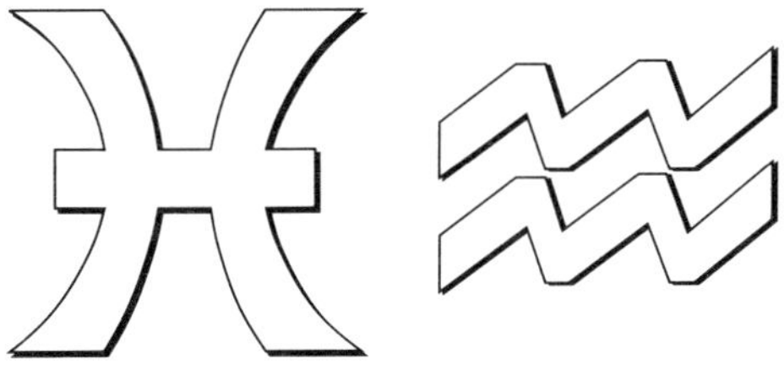

COSMIC CONSCIOUSNESS

Each of you is good at seeing the broad perspective. You have a sense of vision, an ability to get beyond the parts and see the whole. You may be a bit more imaginative, and he a bit more rational. He can be mentally rebellious and verbally unconventional, while you tend to be more intuitive, romantic, or poetic with your use of language. Humanitarian instincts, unusual interests, or networking might be a bond between the two of you.

CHALLENGING—2

PISCES/PISCES

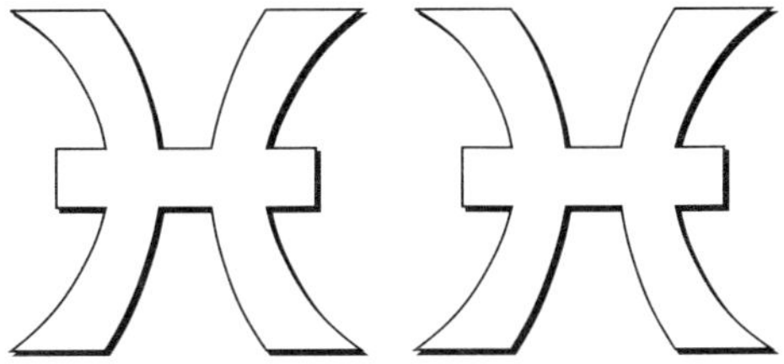

MYSTERIOUS MAGIC

The two of you may communicate more in the realm of the heart than the head. Naturally intuitive, romantic, idealistic, and imaginative in your thinking, each of you can use language with grace and beauty. You may occasionally fall into confusion, rose-colored glasses or fantasies of wish fulfillment. Generally, you both can bring a vital element of allure, insight, and visualizing skills to your relationship.

VERY COMPATIBLE—4

VENUS

The primary key word for Venus is "pleasure." Venus represents what we enjoy and where we find pleasure. This includes pleasure from the material world of art and beauty as well as pleasure through our sensual nature. It also includes pleasure from people. Venus symbolizes many sides of relationships—what we seek in partnerships, how we tend to attract love and how we express affection to others. Venus also represents our vision of the feminine—what women see as feminine in other women (as well as themselves) and what men see as feminine and are attracted to in women.

Remember, for a full picture, you would also include the house of your Venus and its aspects, but we can still learn a great deal from sign placements only.

First read the shorthand description for the sign **your** Venus is in. Then, compare it with the shorthand description for the Venus sign of your partner. Next, read the paragraph which discusses how the two of you might interact with one another. Each combination is also designated as either very compatible, compatible, challenging or very challenging. (These rate as 4-3-2-1 on our **Compatibility Scale**.)

Your partner's Venus sign offers important clues about what he enjoys and how he defines love. Indulge him with Venusian pleasures and he'll believe you're more fun than anyone else. Pay attention to the characteristics of his Venus sign and you'll know how to please him.

VENUS IN ARIES: "LOVE IS AN ADVENTURE!"

Enjoy: independence, activity, competition, being first, doing things **once**
Seek in Partnership: fireworks (even strife), conquests, freedom, excitement
Attract Love by: being honest, spontaneous, confident, outgoing
Express Affection: swiftly, spontaneously, roughly, impulsively, directly
Sensual Nature: strong, ardent, quick to fall in (and out) of love (and lust)
Vision of the Feminine: initiating, energetic, feisty, athletic, free-spirited

VENUS IN TAURUS: "THERE ARE NO ROCKS IN THE RIVER OF LOVE."

Enjoy: art, nature, money, physical pleasures, possessions, comfort
Seek in Partnership: dependability, financial security, pleasure, beauty
Attract Love by: being relaxed, attractive, skilled with finances
Express Affection: touching, stroking, providing for, being reliable
Sensual Nature: very strong, loves good food, drink, back rubs, massages
Vision of the Feminine: sensual, loyal, soft, easygoing, rounded, sweet-tempered

VENUS IN GEMINI: A MENTAL RELATIONSHIP

Enjoy: learning, talking, variety, wit, ideas, new experiences
Seek in Partnership: mental stimulation, conversation, understanding
Attract Love by: being versatile, multitalented, good communicator
Express Affection: verbally, flirtatiously, irregularly, teasingly, with humor
Sensual Nature: more mental or visual, could be cool, playful
Vision of the Feminine: bright, expressive, sociable, lighthearted, entertaining

VENUS IN CANCER: SHARING THE MOTHERING

Enjoy: security, food, home, family, emotional closeness, commitment
Seek in Partnership: fidelity, permanence, receptivity, caretaking
Attract Love by: being nurturing, dependent, supportive, caring, warm
Express Affection: protectively, tenaciously, kindly, sensitively
Sensual Nature: strong, appreciates food, physical contact and caresses
Vision of the Feminine: motherly and childlike, emotional, rounded, family-oriented

VENUS IN LEO: WISH UPON A STAR!

Enjoy: excitement, creativity, drama, love, attention, applause
Seek in Partnership: adrenaline rush, zest, enthusiasm, confidence
Attract Love by: being generous, fun-loving, exuberant and expressive
Express Affection: wholeheartedly, extravagantly, passionately
Sensual Nature: strong, natural magnetism and sex appeal
Vision of the Feminine: sexy, glamorous, admired by others, full of compliments

VENUS IN VIRGO: WORKING AT RELATIONSHIPS

Enjoy: competence, doing a good job, finding flaws and fixing them
Seek in Partnership: common sense, a good worker; dependability
Attract Love by: serving others, being practical, helpful
Express Affection: cautiously, modestly, by doing things for partner
Sensual Nature: may be puritanical **or** very earthy
Vision of the Feminine: neat, clean, well-organized, efficient, sensible, modest

VENUS IN LIBRA: "EVEN-STEVEN," PLEASE

Enjoy: harmony, relationships, ease, beauty, art, justice and balance
Seek in Partnership: equality, affection, beauty, peace, niceness
Attract Love by: being gracious, polite, kind, good-natured, attractive
Express Affection: gracefully, charmingly, with consideration
Sensual Nature: tend to adapt to partner's needs
Vision of the Feminine: sweet, loving, beautiful, refined, delicate

VENUS IN SCORPIO: INTENSE INTIMACY

Enjoy: mastery, challenges, secrets, emotional confrontations, power
Seek in Partnership: intimate bonding, deep connections, to be "swept away"
Attract Love by: being fascinating, seductive, mysterious, enthralling
Express Affection: intensely (jealousy is possible), totally, completely
Sensual Nature: strong, passionate, can be all-or-nothing tendencies
Vision of the Feminine: sexy, tough, femme fatale, enticing, powerful, challenging

VENUS IN SAGITTARIUS: "EXCESS IS NOT NEARLY ENOUGH."

Enjoy: fun, outdoors, sports, travel, gambling, Higher Truths, learning
Seek in Partnership: adventure, good times, excitement, expanded horizons
Attract Love by: being witty, a risk-taker, honest, sociable
Express Affection: generously, grandly, extravagantly, idealistically
Sensual Nature: loves all good things in life (but can overdo)
Vision of the Feminine: friendly, outgoing, independent, active, eager, optimistic

VENUS IN CAPRICORN: "MARRIAGE IS FOREVER (SO BE SURE BEFORE COMMITTING)."

Enjoy: responsibility, power, control, authority, success, competence
Seek in Partnership: stability, increased status, safety, permanence
Attract Love by: being capable, careful, achievement-oriented, building career
Express Affection: cautiously, seriously (sometimes dutifully), responsibly
Sensual Nature: can be repressed **or** extremely earthy with excellent stamina
Vision of the Feminine: sensible, fits well into society, mature, ambitious, faithful

VENUS IN AQUARIUS: PALS IN PARTNERSHIP

Enjoy: uniqueness, mental stimulation, the new, progress, friends, change
Seek in Partnership: freedom, the unusual, tolerance, variety, excitement
Attract Love by: being fair, intellectual, open to anything, original
Express Affection: unconventionally, freely, experimentally, verbally
Sensual Nature: can be cool, intellectual or very open (try anything)
Vision of the Feminine: intelligent, independent, unorthodox, free-wheeling, equalitarian

VENUS IN PISCES: DREAMY DESIRE

Enjoy: compassion, beauty, nature, mystical experiences, fantasy, imagination
Seek in Partnership: romance, magic, a soul mate, a transcendent union
Attract Love by: rescuing others (or seeking rescue), being attractive, kind
Express Affection: gently, sensitively, evasively, idealistically, sweetly
Sensual Nature: can be more fantasy than reality **or** real magic—love flows
Vision of the Feminine: submissive, giving, graceful, pretty, delicate, devoted, ethereal

VENUS PAIRS

ARIES/ARIES

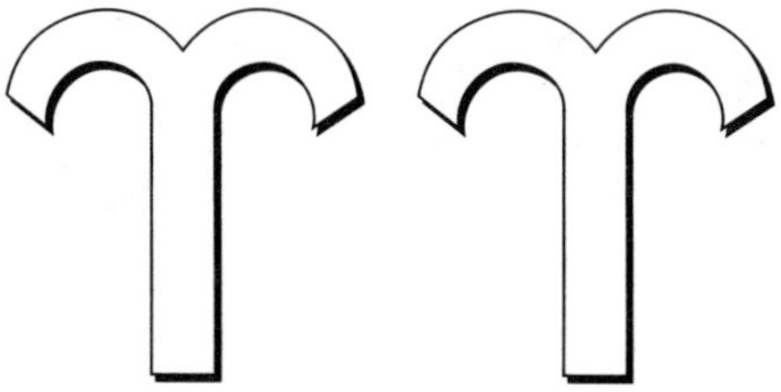

ACTIVE AND ARDENT

You both enjoy initiative, action and doing things **once**. You attract people through courage, confidence and independence. You can feed one another's energy, sexual drive and excitement from life, but you can also feed each other's impulsiveness, competitive instincts or desire to call the shots. Respect each other's freedom needs and you can keep your association vital, alive and on the move.

VERY COMPATIBLE—4

ARIES/TAURUS

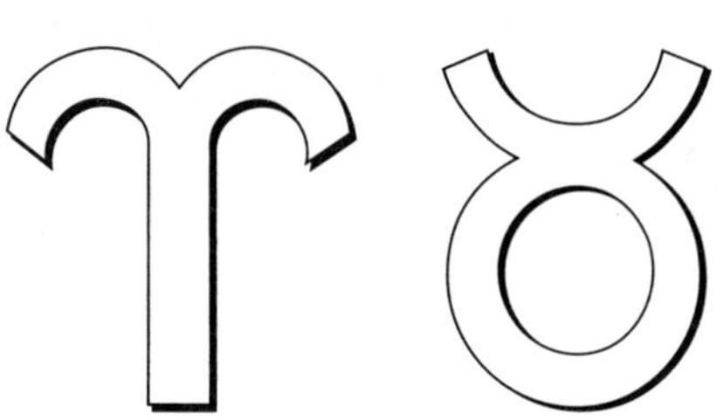

COMFORTABLE COURAGE

You enjoy adventure, action and spontaneity. Courage, strength and directness attract others to you. He enjoys relaxation, physical indulgences and comfort. Dependability, sensuality and easygoingness attract others to him. You can encourage him to be more than a couch potato, but only by playing to what he loves. Gratify his desire for back rubs, beauty, or material goodies and he'll be more amenable to doing some of the activities you find exciting. He can encourage and deepen your sensual appreciation.

CHALLENGING—2

ARIES/GEMINI

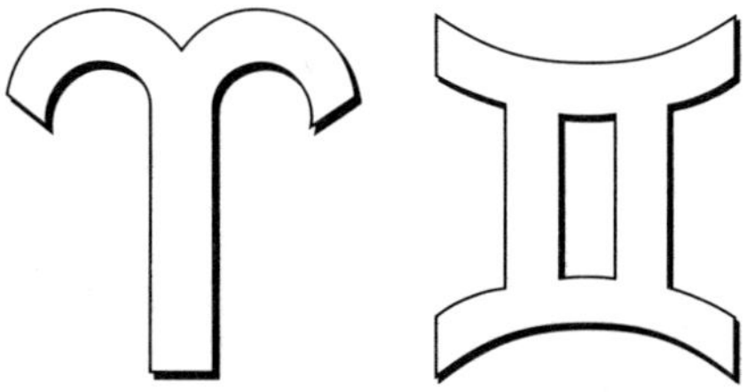

LIGHT AND LIVELY

You love to move, to master challenges, to test your strength and to be yourself. He loves to learn, to experience new things and to test his wits. Your honesty, confidence and initiative attract people. Flexibility, alertness and intelligence attract others to him. You can do lots of fun, exciting things together. Each of you encourages a youthful spirit in the other. You feed each other's needs for variety. You both bore quickly with the same amusements, so keep recreation lively and diverse.

COMPATIBLE—3

ARIES/CANCER

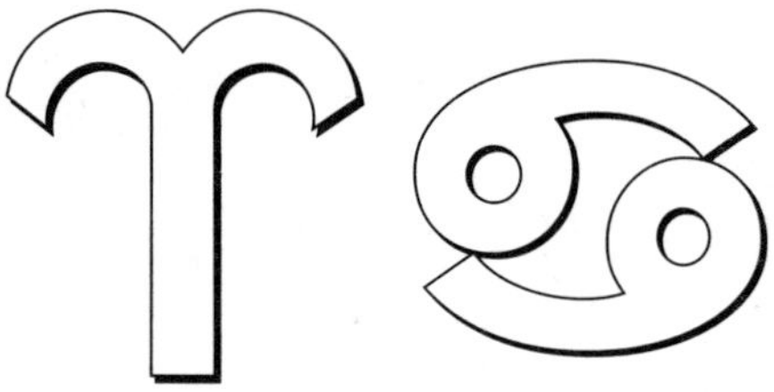

NURTURE NOW!

You enjoy excitement, immediate action and independence. You attract by speed, self-assertion and knowing what you want. He enjoys safety, making emotional connections and home-centered activities. He attracts by warmth, supportiveness and security. Your relationship will have to balance independence and commitment; freedom and closeness; adventure and domestic matters. Compromise allows the two of you to take turns getting what you need.

CHALLENGING—2

DYNAMIC DUO

ARIES/LEO

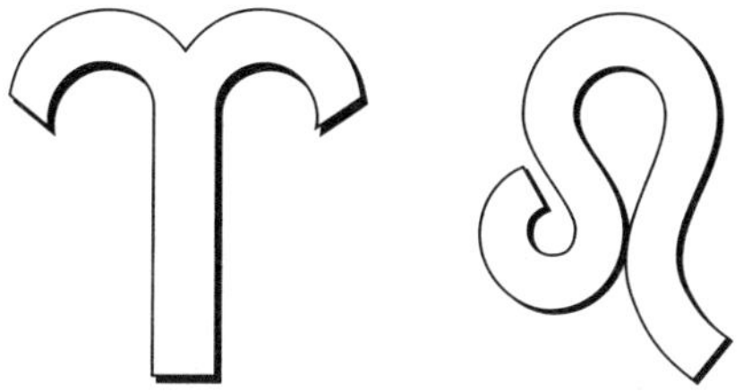

You love courage, directness and assertion. He loves confidence, zest and dynamism. You attract by action, "chemistry," and independence. He attracts by charisma, creativity and generosity. You easily feed each other's needs for excitement and can have lots of fun together. You find each other stimulating. (This can include strong sexual attraction.) You may egg each other on to rash, impulsive or foolhardy acts, but usually accentuate one another's faith and zest for life.

COMPATIBLE—3

EAGER ENTERPRISE

ARIES/VIRGO

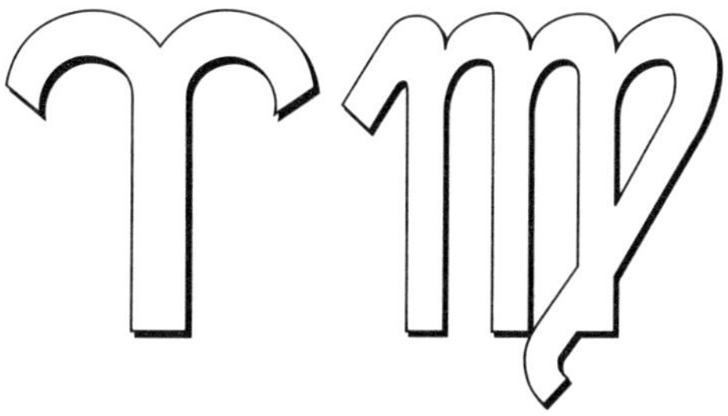

You love immediacy, doing things once and acts of courage. He loves getting the details right, competent achievements and repairing (people, things or situations). You attract by challenges, being forthright and your sense of adventure. He attracts by orderliness, precise work and a willingness to be of service. If you don't want anger, impatience, criticism, nit-picking or feeling trapped to pervade your association, try working together. Share tasks. Improve the world—not each other!

VERY CHALLENGING—1

TO AND FRO

ARIES/LIBRA

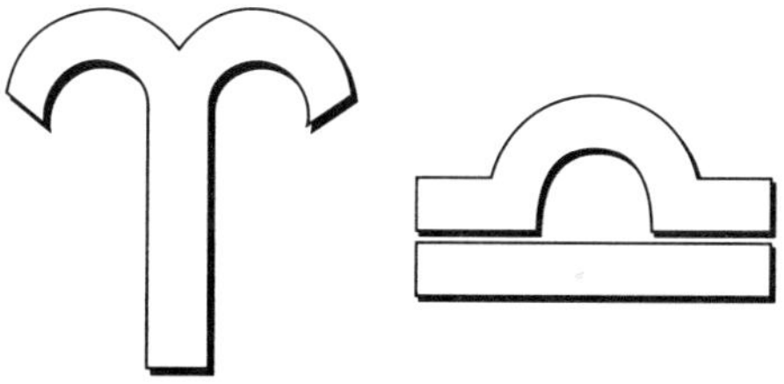

You love doing your own thing, keeping active and acts of daring or honesty. He loves teamwork, appreciating beauty and acts of diplomacy or tact. You enjoy strength, courage and confidence. He enjoys diplomacy, empathy and a cooperative spirit. Opposites attract and you two may be quite drawn to one another. Like a seesaw, the two of you are learning to balance assertion and accommodation in this relationship. Each of you must compromise to be sure you both get what you want and need.

VERY COMPATIBLE—4

POTENT PASSIONS

ARIES/SCORPIO

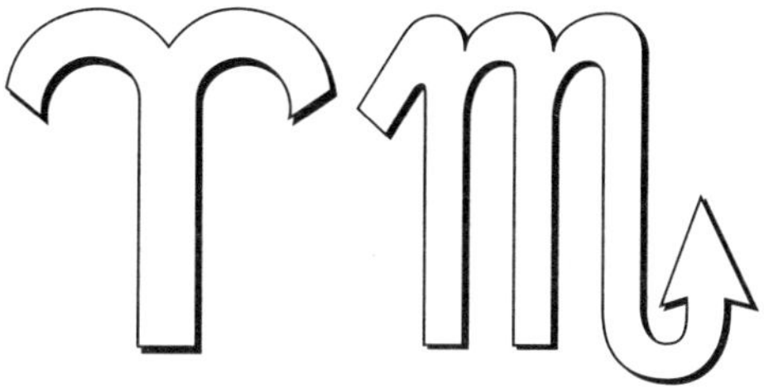

You love independence, immediate responses and "what you see is what you get." He loves intense interactions, mulling things over and secrets. You attract through openness, courage and confidence. He attracts through mystery, seductions (or obsessions) and power. If either of you tries to control the other—watch out! You both have strong wills and might slip into competing with each other. Seek ways to cooperate as a team. Excitement (including sexual) could be high. Challenges can bring out the best in you both.

VERY CHALLENGING—1

ARIES/SAGITTARIUS

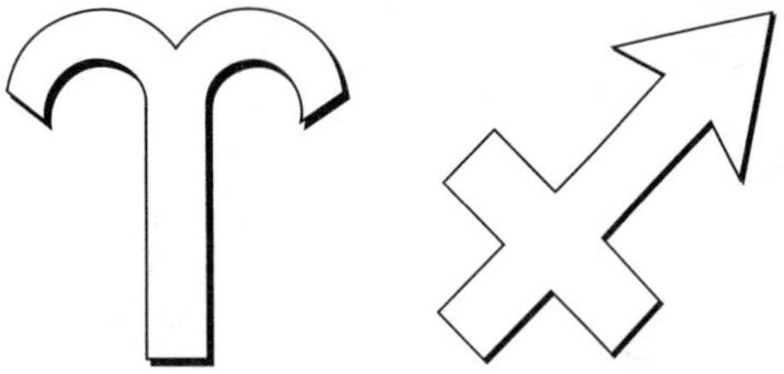

FIERY FUN

You love courage, directness and confidence. He loves adventure, honesty and faith. You attract by excitement, independence and strength. He attracts through risk-taking, philosophizing and exploring. You tend to energize each other and encourage further expansion, chances, and pioneering activities. You may feed each other's impatience, impulsivity, or foolhardiness. You can build one another's strength, honesty and ability to act. Together, you feel vital, alive and willing to try anything.

COMPATIBLE—3

ARIES/CAPRICORN

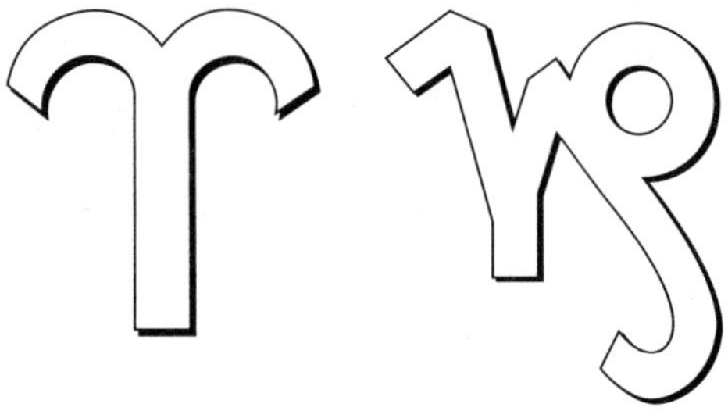

EAGER EXPERTISE

You love immediacy, fiery passions and personal initiative. He loves careful campaigns, practicality and ambition. You attract by eagerness, courage and being up front. He attracts through status, responsibility and power/success. A battle of wills is possible unless you clearly mark "his" territory and "yours." Your spontaneity may upset his desire to maintain control. Learn to combine sensible planning and a no-holds-barred thrust for fun and excitement.

CHALLENGING—2

ARIES/AQUARIUS

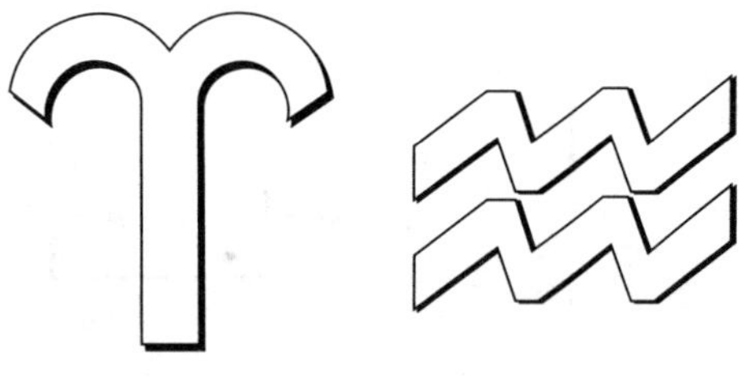

FRIENDLY FREEDOM

You love spontaneity, self-expression and doing things **once**. He loves individuality, progress and anything on the cutting edge of change. You attract by courage, directness and self-confidence. He attracts by uniqueness, tolerance and openness. You may stimulate each other's needs for freedom. If you allow one another space, you will each bring more excitement and interest back to the relationship. Seek out the new and varied. You both thrive on challenges and new possibilities.

COMPATIBLE—3

ARIES/PISCES

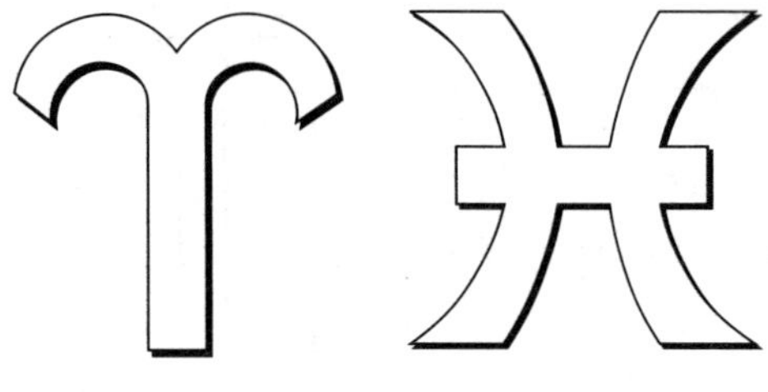

IMMEDIATE INSPIRATION

You love strength, immediacy and exciting activities. He loves compassion, magic and inspirational activities. You attract through movement, courage and independence. He attracts through empathy, idealism and artistic leanings. You two might polarize between self-assertion and self-sacrifice. You are learning to blend pleasure from personal gratification with pleasure from helping, healing or creating beauty. Optimally, you encourage each other's personal power as well as caring concern.

CHALLENGING—2

COMFORTABLE COURAGE

TAURUS/ARIES

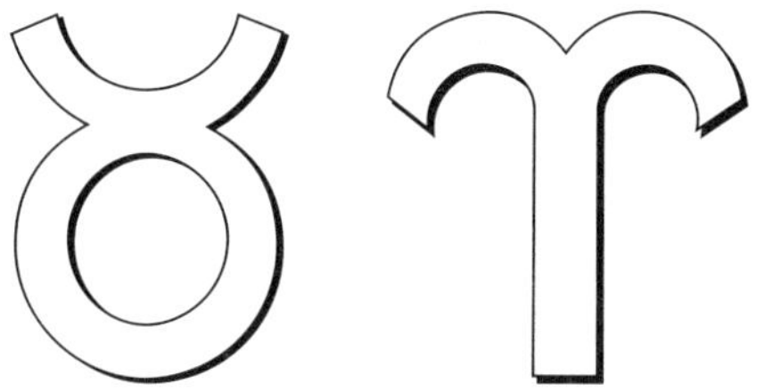

You enjoy relaxation, physical indulgences and comfort. He enjoys adventure, action and spontaneity. Sensuality, an easygoing nature and financial skills attract others to you. Courage, directness and an active nature attract others to him. You can teach him the joys of massage and slow, sensual savoring. He can encourage you to be more than a couch potato—by joining in with what he finds exciting. Together, you can balance relaxation and the adrenaline rush.

CHALLENGING—2

SENSUAL SATISFACTION

TAURUS/TAURUS

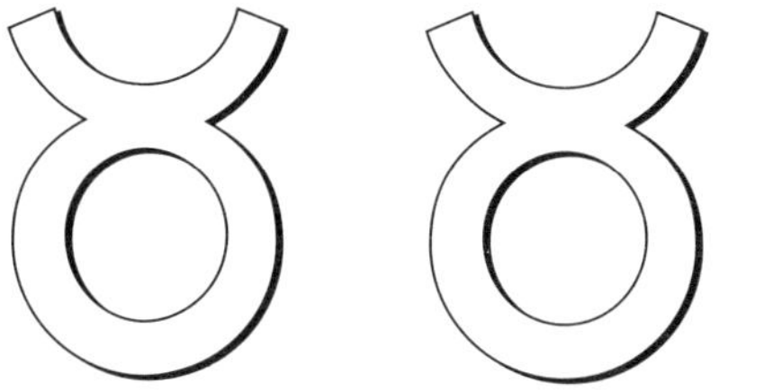

You both love beautiful things, sensual pleasures (eating, drinking, back rubs, etc.) and financial security. You are attracted to one another's dependability, easygoingness and affectionate natures. Together, you may overdo relaxation, material indulgence, or stubbornness, but you really do like one another. You can encourage each other financially and artistically, and enjoy pleasing and pampering one another.

VERY COMPATIBLE—4

SENSUAL AND SOCIAL

TAURUS/GEMINI

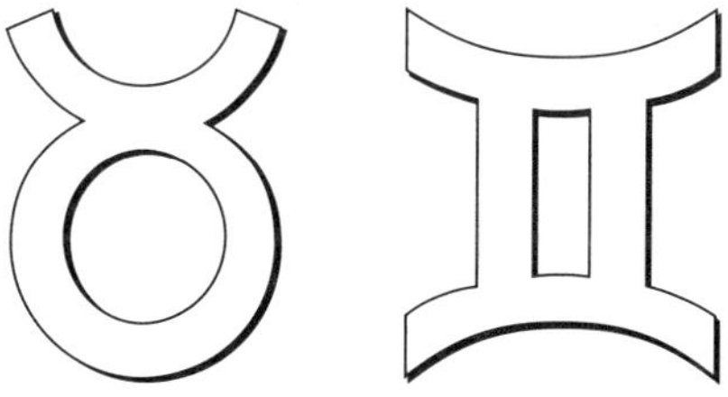

You enjoy material gratification, monetary security and the world of nature. He enjoys mental challenges, conversation and picking up fascinating bits of information. You attract through security, and a sensual and affectionate nature. He attracts through quick wits, social interactions and flexibility. You can help him appreciate patience and follow-through. He can help you appreciate adaptability. Together, you seek pleasure in mind and in body.

CHALLENGING—2

SATISFYING SAFETY

TAURUS/CANCER

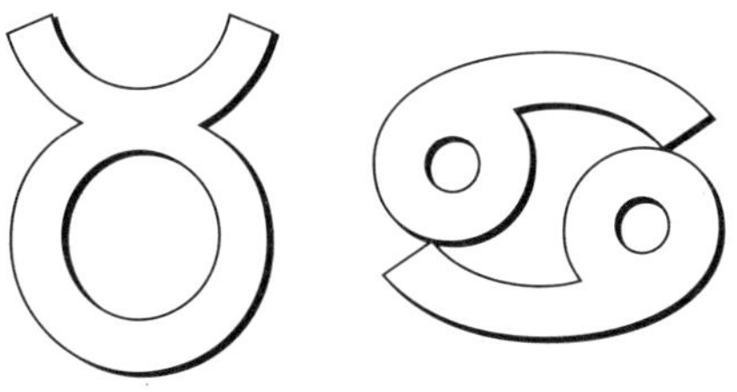

You enjoy financial safety, physical pleasures and peace and calm. He enjoys emotional security, nurturing activities and a happy home. The two of you can reassure one another and may be excellent at building a nest egg or establishing a firm domestic foundation. You both appreciate cuddling and may have a strong sensual connection. You both are attracted by loyalty, perseverance and dependability.

COMPATIBLE—3

TAURUS/LEO

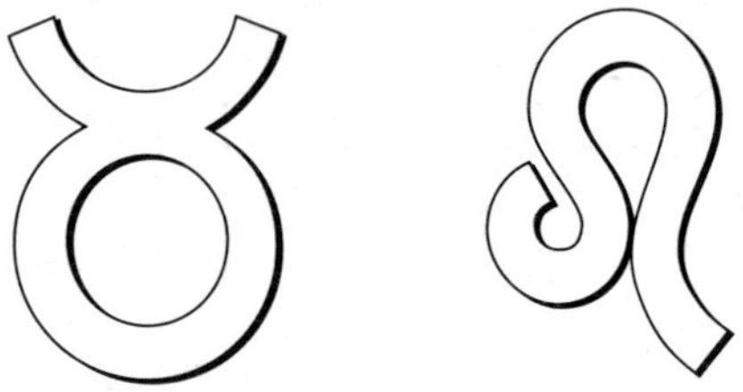

COMFORTABLE CHARISMA

You love financial security, familiar pleasures and a relaxed atmosphere. He loves speculation, new and creative activities, and an atmosphere of excitement. You attract through being known, practical and predictable. He attracts through charisma, excitement and exaggeration (larger than life). If you can compromise between security and risk, the relationship can work. You both appreciate loyalty and sensual gratifications.

CHALLENGING—2

TAURUS/VIRGO

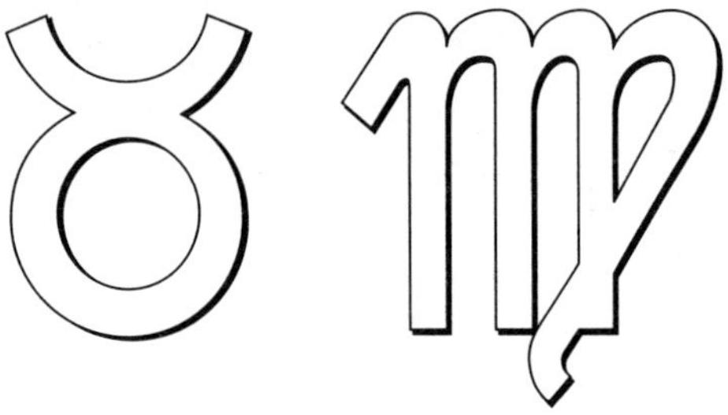

DEDICATED DEARS

You enjoy nature, physical pleasures and a sense of calmness. He enjoys measurable results, practicality and a sense of service. You attract through financial skills and comfort. He attracts through common sense and a willingness to work. Both of you may have business skills and each of you can be quite pragmatic. You may share an appreciation of the physical world and a good understanding of reality.

COMPATIBLE—3

TAURUS/LIBRA

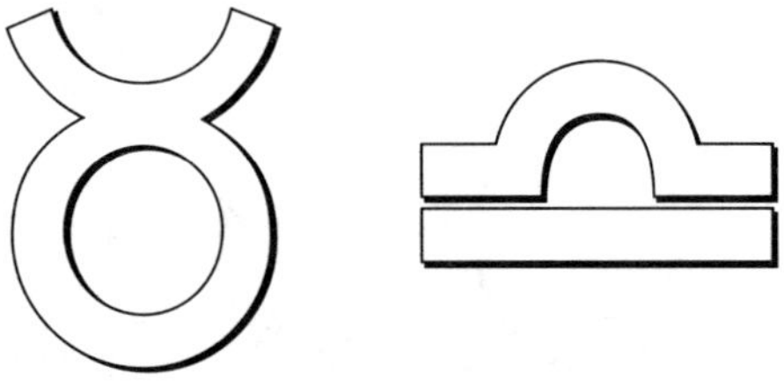

BEAUTY AND BALANCE

You love monetary safety, the world of nature and sensual gratifications. He loves aesthetics, the world of people and serenity, grace or balance. You attract by being practical and affectionate. He draws people in by being physically attractive and/or socially poised. Both of you have a feeling for beauty and can enjoy just kicking back and relaxing. Although your interests may differ considerably, each of you is capable of being quite affectionate and loving.

VERY CHALLENGING—1

TAURUS/SCORPIO

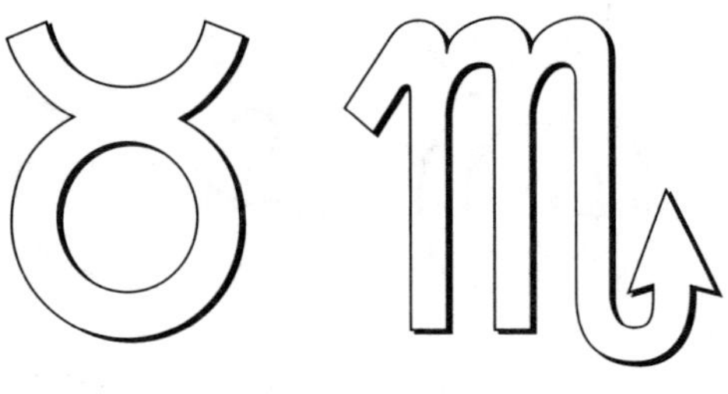

SENSUAL AND SEXY

You love sensual indulgence and a smooth, easy flow in life. He loves a sense of control (appetite mastery) and to confront challenges. You attract by being practical, sensible and easy to get along with. He attracts by being intense and emotional. Although opposites, you tend to be drawn together. You share an appreciation of financial security and talent for enjoying the physical (and sexual) world.

VERY COMPATIBLE—4

FAMILIAR OR FARAWAY?

TAURUS/SAGITTARIUS

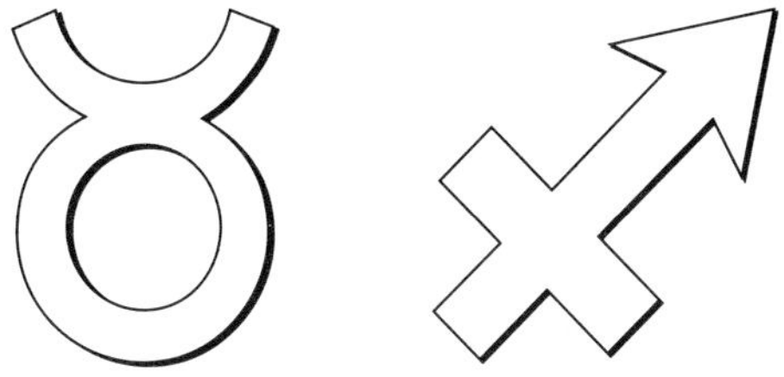

You love back rubs, financial security and a familiar, comfortable routine. He loves philosophical discussions, grand dreams and schemes, and going exploring. You may feel he is wildly impractical, while he sees you as incredibly hidebound. You attract by dependability; he attracts through adventure. He can expand your horizons, bringing more excitement to your life. You can encourage him to see the value of some practicality and common sense.

VERY CHALLENGING—1

PRACTICAL POWER

TAURUS/CAPRICORN

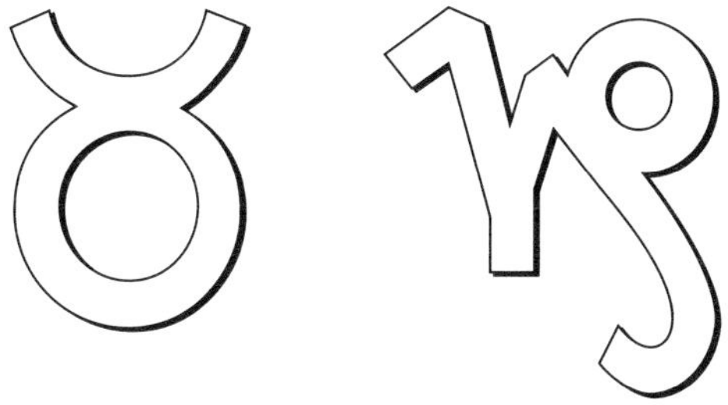

You love monetary dependability, an easygoing nature and sensual pleasures. He loves success, status and a position of power and authority. You attract through physical indulgences and practicality. He attracts through being ambitious and hardworking. Both of you are likely to have business skills and understand reality well. Each of you may measure love more in deeds than in words; you do things for the people you care about.

COMPATIBLE—3

FAMILIAR OR FAR-OUT?

TAURUS/AQUARIUS

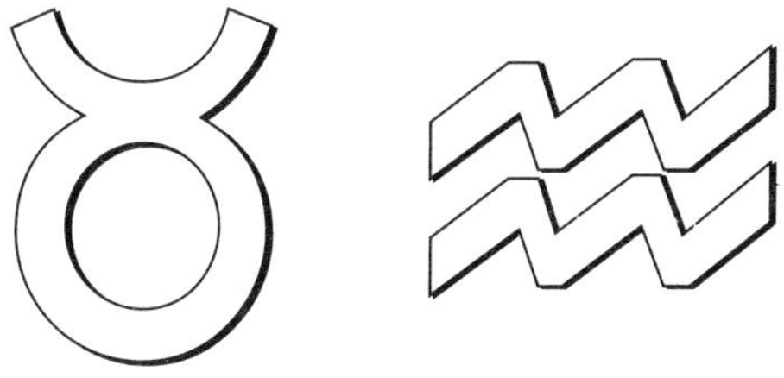

You enjoy dependability, familiar routines and physical pleasures. He enjoys change, the new and different, and mental pleasures. You attract by being sensible, loyal, comfortable and affectionate. He attracts by being unique, unusual, exciting and unpredictable. You might battle over security vs. risk or stability vs. change until you can appreciate, tolerate and learn from each other's viewpoints.

CHALLENGING—2

DEPENDABLE DREAMS

TAURUS/PISCES

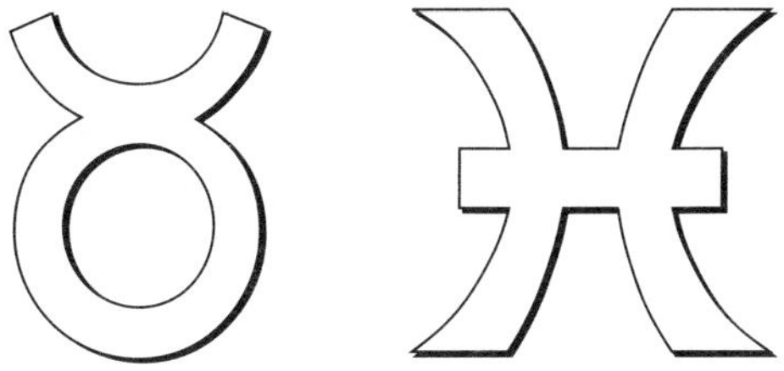

You enjoy practicality, tangible beauty, and the world of nature. He enjoys inspiration, beauty in any form and the world of the imagination. You attract through dependability, sensuality and financial security. He attracts through mystery, compassion, sensitivity, fantasies, or his inner visions of perfection. You can make beautiful music together if you keep a balance between realism and idealism.

COMPATIBLE—3

GEMINI/ARIES

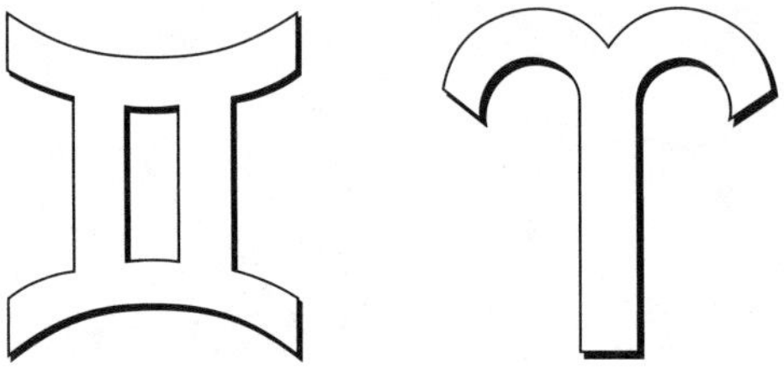

LIGHT AND LIVELY

You love to learn, to experience new things and to test your wits. He loves to move, to master challenges, to test his strength and to be himself. Intelligence, flexibility and alertness attract others to you. Honesty, confidence and a lively spirit attract others to him. You can do lots of fun, exciting things together. Each of you encourages a youthful spirit in the other. You feed each other's needs for variety. You both bore quickly with the same amusements, so keep recreation lively and diverse.

COMPATIBLE—3

GEMINI/TAURUS

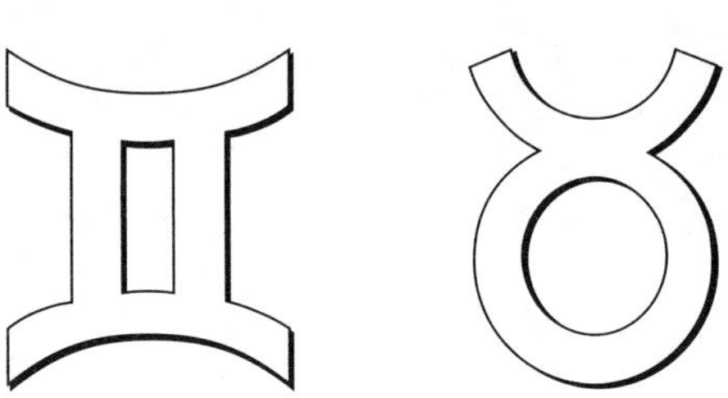

SOCIAL AND SENSUAL

You enjoy mental challenges, communication and picking up fascinating bits of information. He enjoys material gratification, monetary security and the world of nature. He attracts through security, and a sensual and affectionate nature. You attract through quick wits, sociability and flexibility. He can help you appreciate patience and follow-through. You can help him appreciate adaptability. Together, you seek pleasure in mind and in body.

CHALLENGING—2

GEMINI/GEMINI

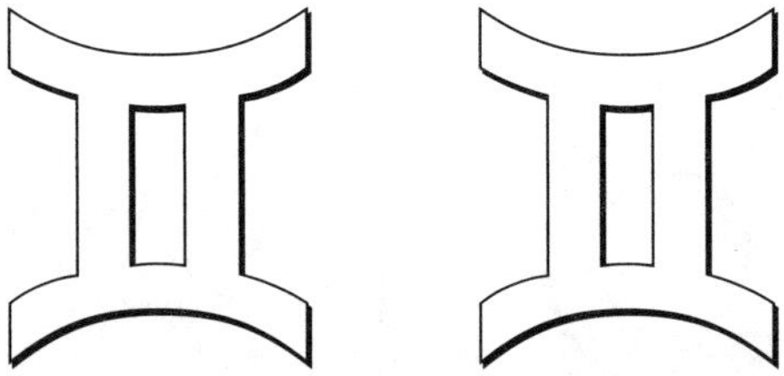

WITTY WISDOM

You both enjoy the world of the mind and tongue and may find it easy to discuss anything and everything. You are each attracted by the other's intelligence, multiple interests and flexibility. Either of you can get into the art of flirtation or verbal teasing. You appreciate variety in your sensual experiences—and a light touch. Humor may come easily. You can encourage and appreciate one another's social skills, youthful spirit and capacity to enjoy learning.

VERY COMPATIBLE—4

GEMINI/CANCER

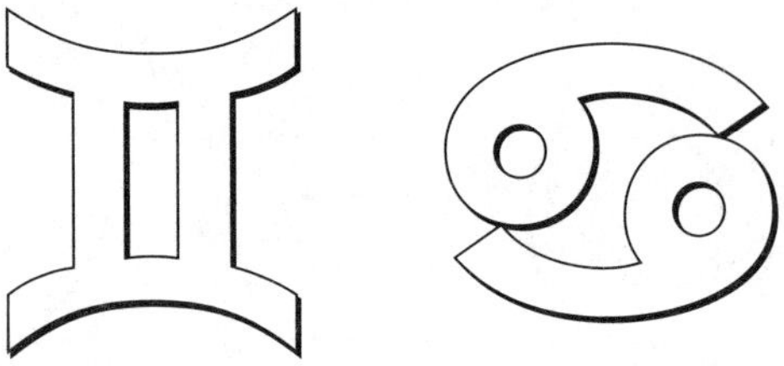

CASUAL COMPASSION

You enjoy communication, being casual and carefree. He enjoys security, food and family. You attract through openness, lightheartedness and brains. He attracts through nurturing, warmth and receptivity. You're apt to be more expressive while he is more silent. You can help him appreciate flexibility and new experiences. He can help you appreciate safety, permanence and protection.

CHALLENGING—2

GLIB GENEROSITY

GEMINI/LEO

You enjoy learning, communicating and laughing. He enjoys attention, drama and excitement. You attract people through wit, versatility and varied experiences. He attracts by charisma, enthusiasm and generosity. You are likely to feed each other's optimism and fun-loving spirits. You both enjoy the stimulation of social activities. You may be more lighthearted (sometimes a flirt) while he is more intense. His exuberance feeds your playful side. You frolic together easily.

COMPATIBLE—3

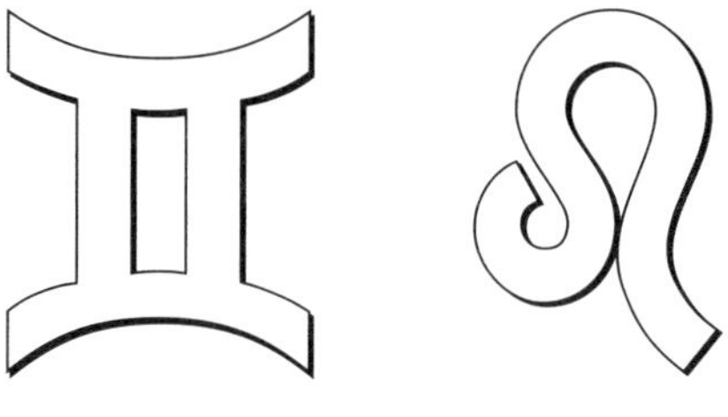

FLEXIBLE FOCUS

GEMINI/VIRGO

Both of you enjoy learning and communicating, but your approach tends to be more casual and his more serious or studied. You attract others by intelligence, lightheartedness and versatility. He attracts through competence, dedication and practicality. You love flitting from flower to flower (and may flirt as well). He likes to finish up projects. You can help him to lighten up and he can help you to persevere when appropriate. Together, you both learn and experience much.

CHALLENGING—2

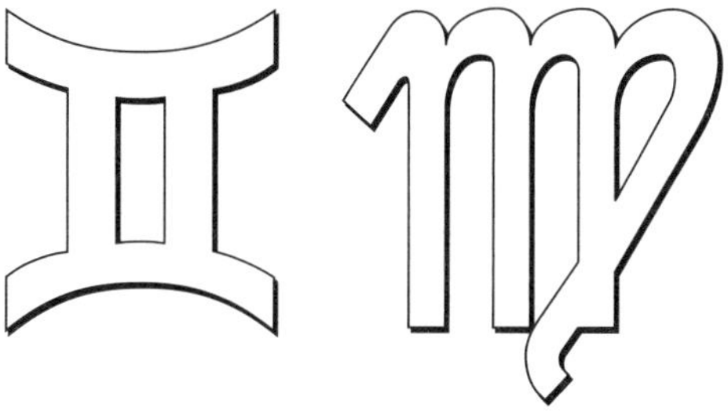

OPEN AND OBJECTIVE

GEMINI/LIBRA

You both enjoy communicating ideas. Your focus tends to be more fun-loving and casual, while he may be more concerned with balance and harmony. You both have social flair and a talent for getting along with people. You attract people through versatility, new experiences and quick wits. He attracts others through kindness, charm and aesthetic skills. Each of you can stimulate the other mentally and expand your circle of interpersonal relations.

COMPATIBLE—3

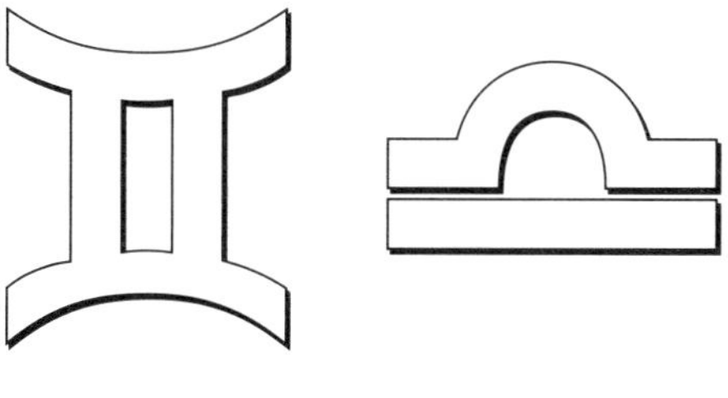

FLIT (AWAY) OR FOCUS?

GEMINI/SCORPIO

You enjoy lightness, open discussions and variety. He enjoys intensity, some secrets and finishing up what he starts. You attract people through intelligence, a sense of fun and multiple talents. He attracts through sexuality, mystery and power. He can bring in many layers to your relationship and you can help him to lighten up and laugh. Don't try to change each other completely, but do be open to learning from your different styles. Together, you can achieve depth and breadth in love.

VERY CHALLENGING—1

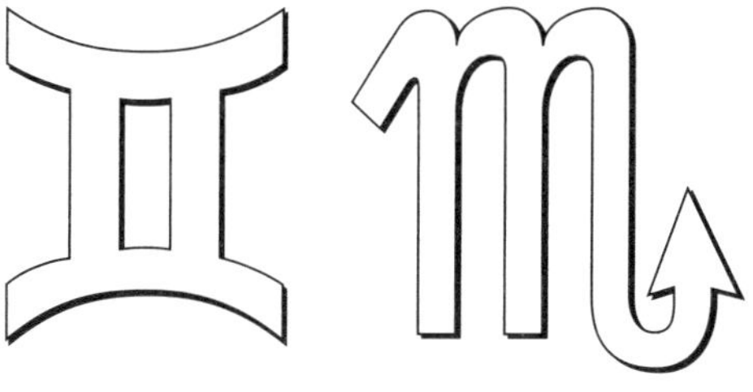

GEMINI/SAGITTARIUS

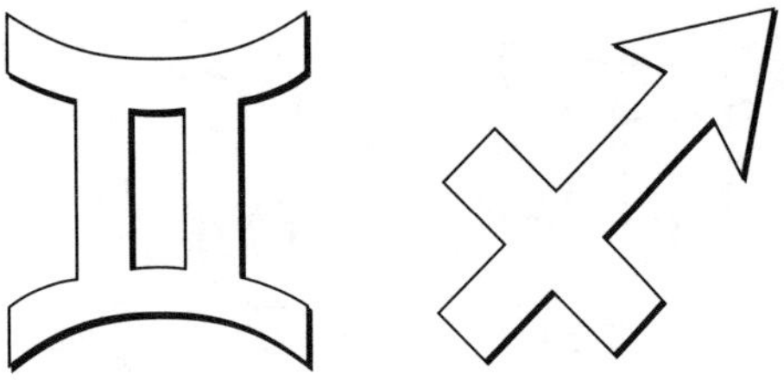

LOVE OF LAUGHTER

You both probably love to talk, so be sure each of you makes room to listen as well. Mental and social stimulation are important for each of you and you probably share a keen sense of humor. You can help him appreciate the here and now and people right around. He can help you envision far horizons, consider philosophical principles and look for adventures. There is a natural attraction between you, but each of you can also easily flirt. Be open and honest and things flow smoothly.

VERY COMPATIBLE—4

GEMINI/CAPRICORN

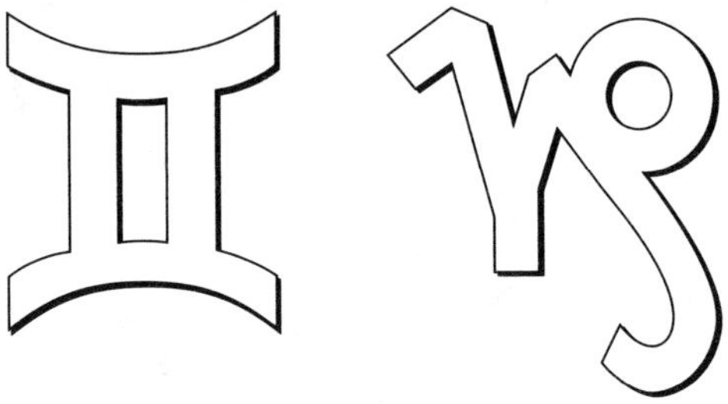

ADAPTABLE ACHIEVEMENT

You enjoy the world of the mind and tongue. He enjoys the world of success, ambition and making it to the top. You attract people through your sense of fun, versatility and quick wits. He attracts through being responsible, strong and competent. You are apt to be more lighthearted, while he is more serious. He is apt to focus (perhaps too much at times) where you prefer to scatter. If you can each move a bit more toward the middle, this relationship can work well. Each of you broadens the other.

VERY CHALLENGING—1

GEMINI/AQUARIUS

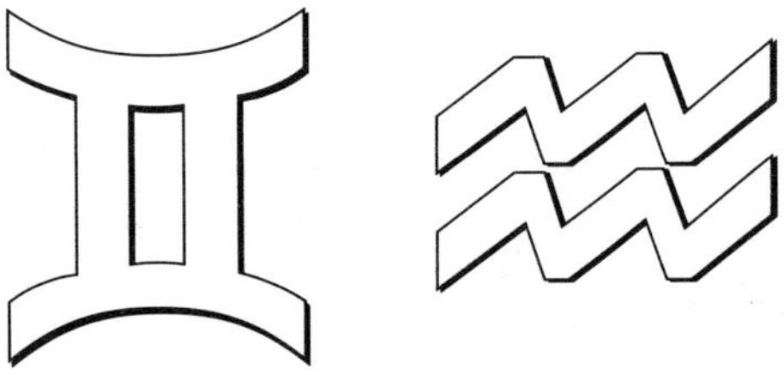

SOCIALLY STIMULATING

You both enjoy the world of thinking, talking and learning. Your focus tends to be more on people and places right around, while he is drawn to the unusual, different and new. You attract love by being expressive, fun-loving and flexible. He attracts love by being progressive, original and free-wheeling. Each of you is likely to stimulate the other to new ideas and new experiences. You can enjoy social activities together, encouraging one another to expand your intellectual horizons.

COMPATIBLE—3

GEMINI/PISCES

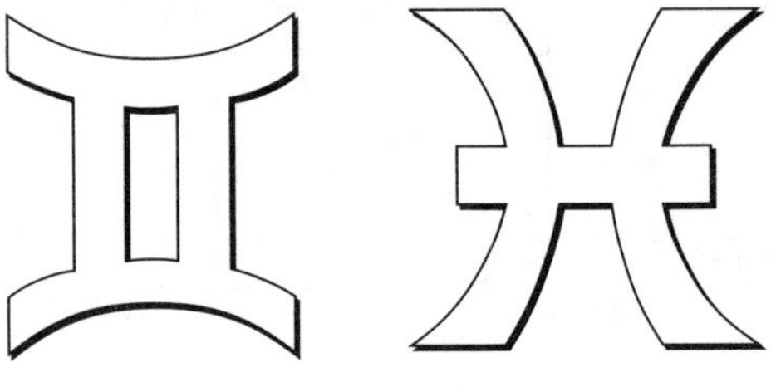

INTELLECTUAL IDEALISM

You enjoy the world of thinking and communicating. He enjoys the world of visualizing and imagining. You attract people through being open, flexible, and eager to learn and experience. He attracts people through being compassionate, idealistic, romantic and mysterious. You tend to be more fun-loving, flirtatious and casual. He tends to be more sensitive, (sometimes evasive) and mystical. You can help him see reality; he can help you envision higher potentials.

CHALLENGING—2

NURTURE NOW!

CANCER/ARIES

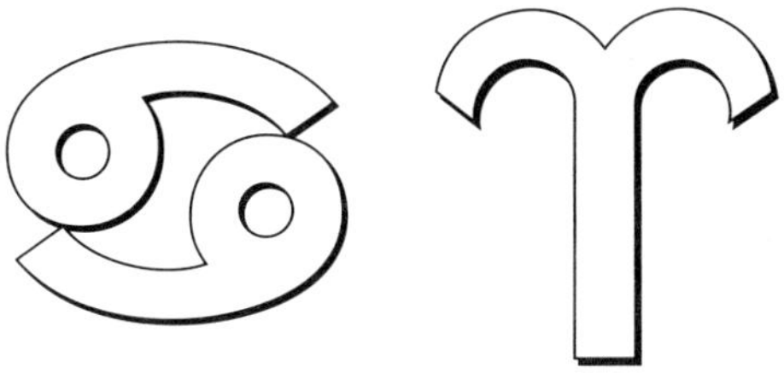

You enjoy security, emotional commitments and home-centered activities. He enjoys excitement, independence and immediacy. You attract others through your warmth, supportiveness and helpfulness. He attracts others through his confidence, assertion and spontaneity. Your relationship will have to balance freedom and closeness, being alone and being together, adventures and domesticity. With compromise, each of you can take turns getting what you want (and adapt a few of the qualities of your partner).

CHALLENGING—2

SATISFYING SAFETY

CANCER/TAURUS

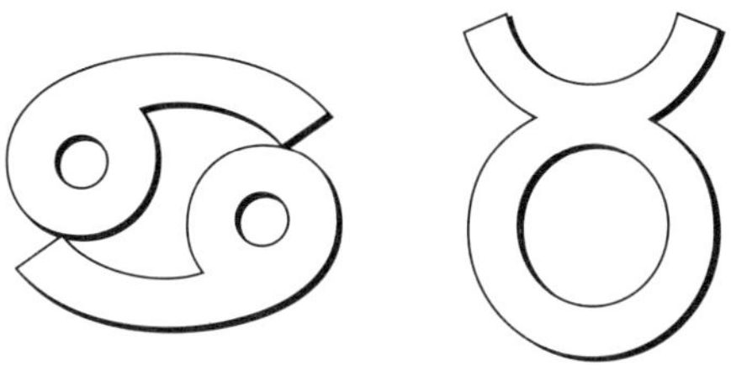

You enjoy nurturing, making emotional commitments and creating a happy home. He enjoys building financial safety, indulging in physical pleasures and a sense of peace and calm. Each of you may be skilled at reassuring the other and good at building up a nest egg or material foundation. You are both likely to find cuddling gratifying and may have a strong sensual bond. You are attracted by each other's loyalty, perseverance and dependability.

COMPATIBLE—3

CASUAL COMPASSION

CANCER/GEMINI

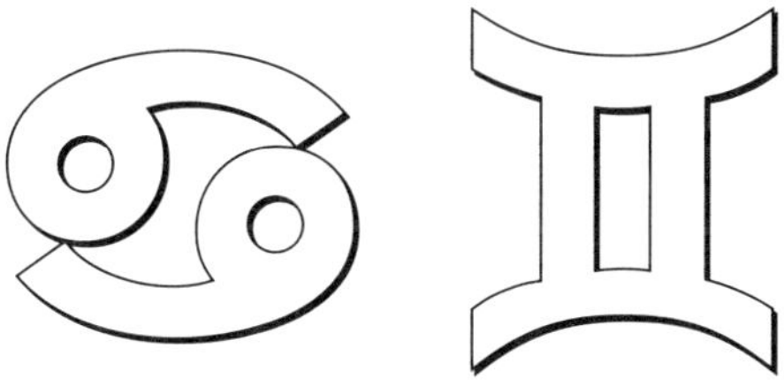

You probably enjoy nurturing, protecting and family-centered activities. He tends to enjoy communication, lightness and learning new things. You attract through being warm, helpful and building a nest. He attracts through being lighthearted, quick-witted and fun-loving. You may be more inward, while he is more outgoing. He can help you enjoy new experiences and gain flexibility, while you can help him develop more commitment, and appreciate permanence.

CHALLENGING—2

COMPASSIONATE CARESSES

CANCER/CANCER

Both of you enjoy safety, food, and emotional closeness. Each of you can attract others through being supportive, caring, family-oriented and protective. You may tend to collect things and can be good at hanging on to what you have financially and materially. With strong sensual natures, both of you can enjoy caresses and physical indulgences of all kinds. Fidelity is important; it is essential that you trust one another. Tread gingerly in each other's sensitive areas.

VERY COMPATIBLE—4

CANCER/LEO

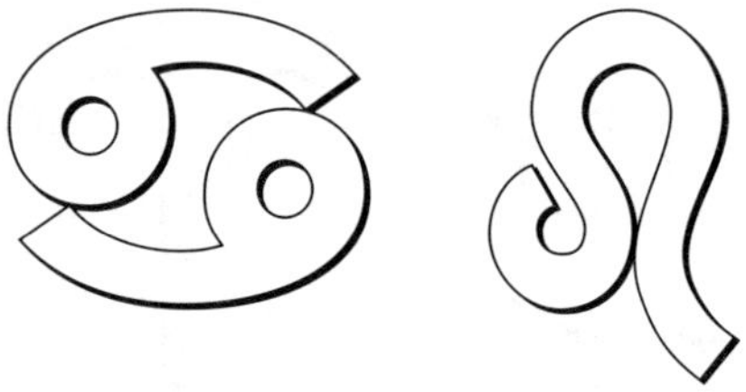

WONDERFULLY WARM

You enjoy warmth, emotional commitment and homey feelings. He enjoys drama, excitement and recognition. You tend to attract people through your nurturing, caretaking and sensitivity. He tends to attract people through his charisma, exuberance and fun-loving spirit. His pleasures are apt to be more extroverted than yours. He can draw you out, encouraging your expressive side, and you can help him to stop, think and develop his sensitive side.

CHALLENGING—2

CANCER/VIRGO

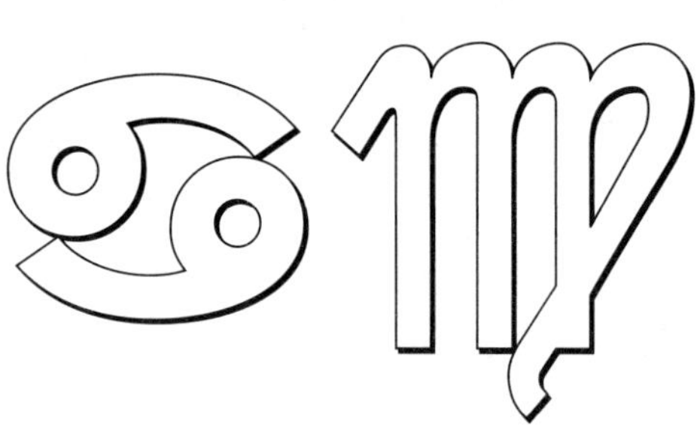

PRACTICAL PROTECTION

You appreciate warmth, protection and family feelings. He appreciates competence, helpfulness and common sense. You tend to attract people through your caring, compassion and receptivity. He tends to attract through his practicality, skill with details and dependability. Each of you values fidelity and being there for those you love. You are apt to be more cuddly and affectionate and could expand his sensual horizons. He can help bring logic to your emotions.

COMPATIBLE—3

CANCER/LIBRA

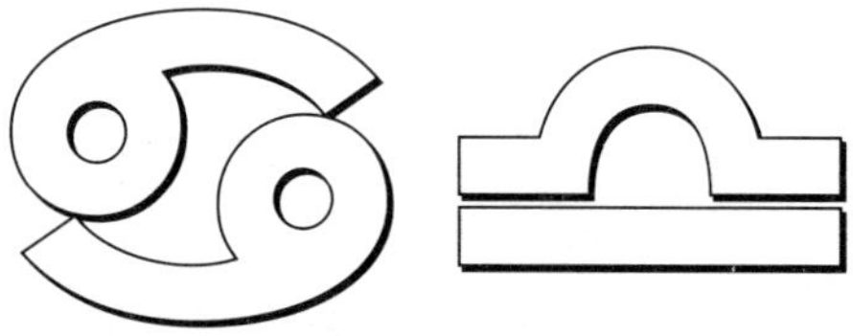

CLOSE CONTACT

You enjoy home-centered activities, emotional commitments and security. He enjoys relationships, beauty and harmonizing. You attract people through your warmth, caring and protectiveness. He attracts people through his kindness, charm and sense of justice. Each of you needs relationships, but you tend to seek more emotional closeness, while he can be a bit detached. You can help deepen his feelings and he can strengthen your connection to beauty.

CHALLENGING—2

CANCER/SCORPIO

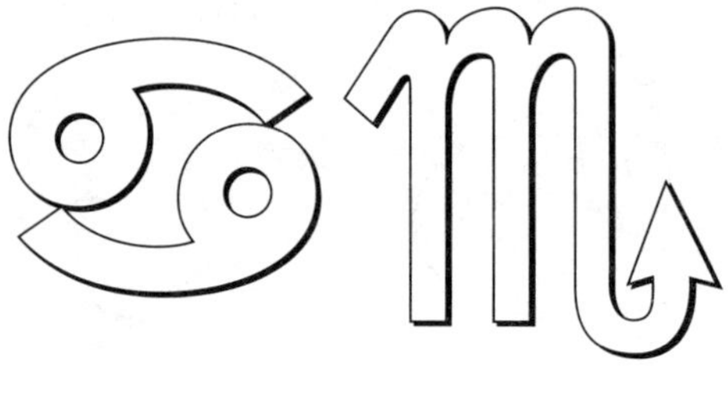

EMOTIONAL EMPHASIS

You enjoy food, feelings, and family. He enjoys being "swept away" in intimate, passionate bonds. You attract people through warmth, protection and/or dependency. He attracts people through intensity, fascination, passion and a sense of power. You both are likely to be very emotional people, but keeping much inside (not wearing your hearts on your sleeves). You may intuitively tune into each other. Tread gently and kindly with one another's hidden sensitivities.

COMPATIBLE—3

INTROVERT OR EXTROVERT?

CANCER/SAGITTARIUS

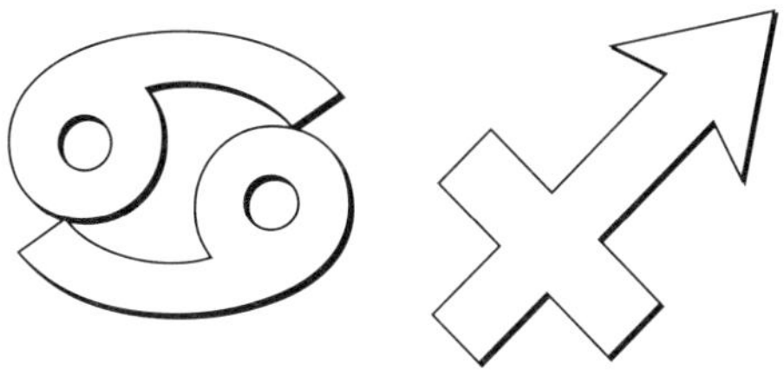

You enjoy closeness, security and a family focus. He enjoys independence, taking risks and the open road. You attract people with your warmth, childlike qualities and kindness. He attracts people with his humor, excitement and extravagant approach to life. If you each learn from the other—rather than trying to change him/her—you help him become more settled, nurturing and home-centered. He can help you become more adventurous, confident and fun-loving.

VERY CHALLENGING—1

PROTECTIVE AND PARENTAL

CANCER/CAPRICORN

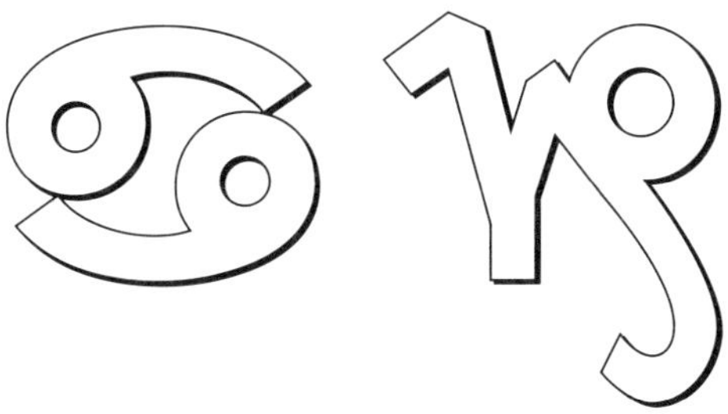

You both share a strong focus on parental archetypes—stable, appreciating security, concerned with family. Your style tends to be more motherly—warm, supportive and nurturing, while his style tends to be more fatherly—ambitious, responsible and cautious. Don't set up your interactions as a pull between dominance and dependency or work and home. Do appreciate each other's dependability.

VERY COMPATIBLE—4

ERRATIC EMPATHY

CANCER/AQUARIUS

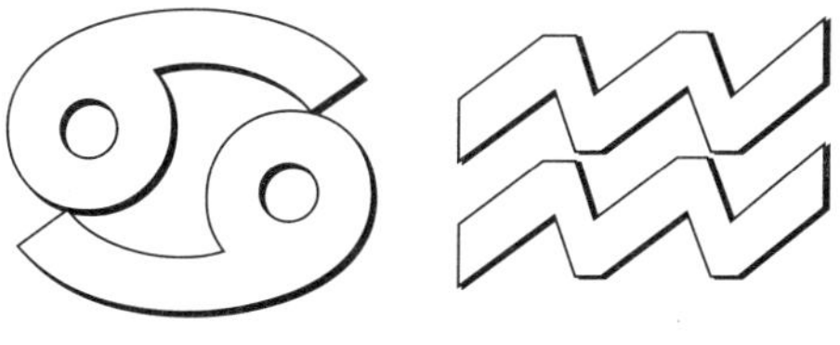

You enjoy emotional commitments, food, and feeling safe and secure. He enjoys detachment, friends and being on the cutting edge of change. You attract people with warmth, protectiveness and fidelity. He attracts people by being original, intellectual and/or equalitarian. The two of you could feel torn between stability and risk-taking or family and the wider world, unless you learn to compromise. You can help him be more sensitive; he can help you add logic to your emotions.

VERY CHALLENGING—1

COMPASSIONATE CARETAKERS

CANCER/PISCES

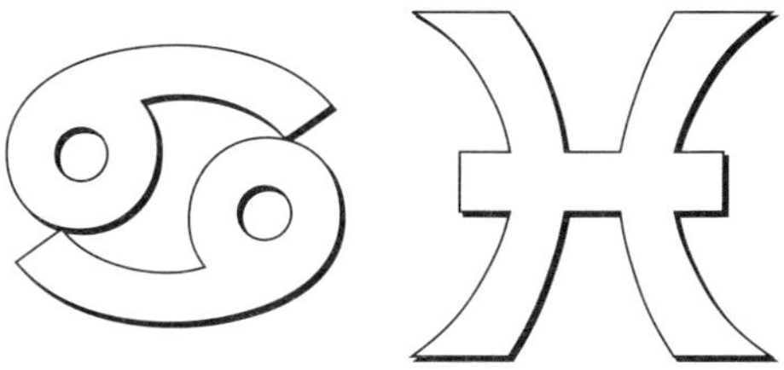

Both of you tend to be deeply feeling people, but will not reveal your emotions to the world. You may be able to sense what is going on inside the other. Each of you can enjoy compassion and may be a natural caretaker. Sometimes either of you might sacrifice or give too much in relationships. If you create trust in one another, you can make a deep commitment. Taking turns taking care of each other is the best bet.

COMPATIBLE—3

LEO/ARIES

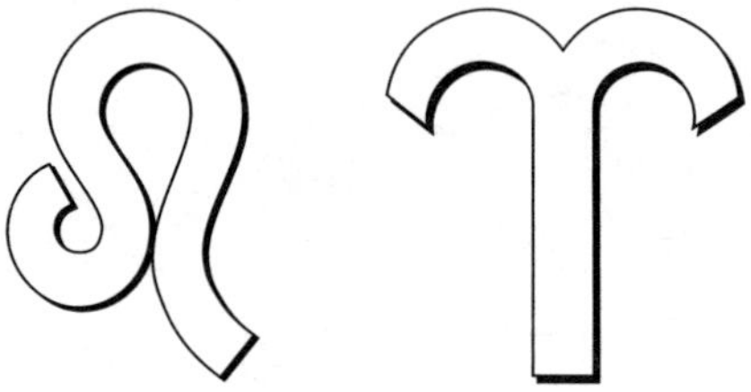

DYNAMIC DUO

You enjoy drama, promotion, attention and applause. He enjoys being direct, courageous and assertive. You attract through creativity, generosity and sex appeal. He attracts through being energetic, independent and active. You easily feed one another's needs for excitement, and are likely to have lots of fun together. You probably find each other stimulating (sexually as well). You may incite each other to rash, impulsive, or foolish actions, but also strengthen one another's faith and zest for life.

COMPATIBLE—3

LEO/TAURUS

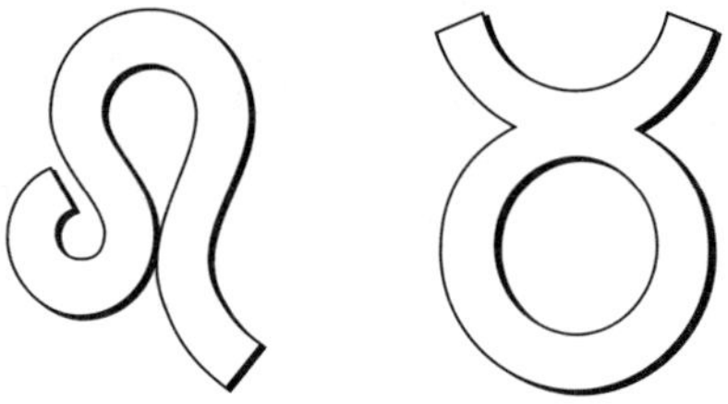

COMFORTABLE CHARISMA

You enjoy excitement, attention and being center stage. He enjoys comfort, physical pleasures and possessions. You attract through sex appeal, charisma and an exuberant, fun-loving spirit. He attracts through dependability, financial skills and a relaxed attitude. He may seem stubborn or stolid to you and you may seem hysteric or exaggerative to him unless you adopt a bit of his pragmatism and he adopts a little of your enthusiasm. You may feed each other's sensuality.

CHALLENGING—2

LEO/GEMINI

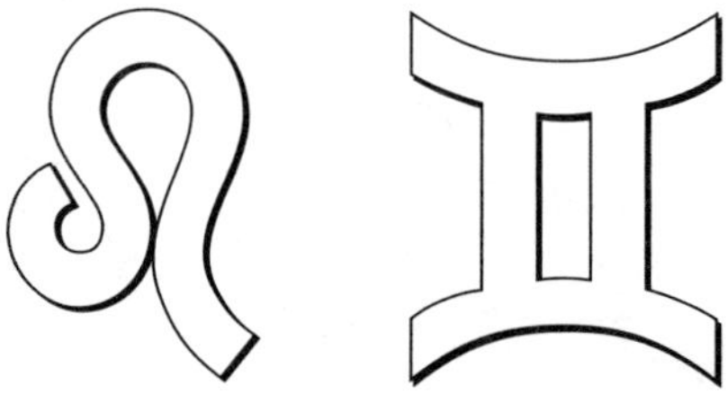

GLIB GENEROSITY

You enjoy attention, excitement, drama and the adrenaline rush. He enjoys laughter, learning and lighthearted teasing. You attract people through charisma, sex appeal and enthusiasm. He attracts people with wit, versatility and varied experiences. You both tend to be optimistic and feed each other's search for fun and frolic. He may be attracted to a variety of people, while you are more focused. Your exuberance feeds his playful side. You can enjoy socializing together.

COMPATIBLE—3

LEO/CANCER

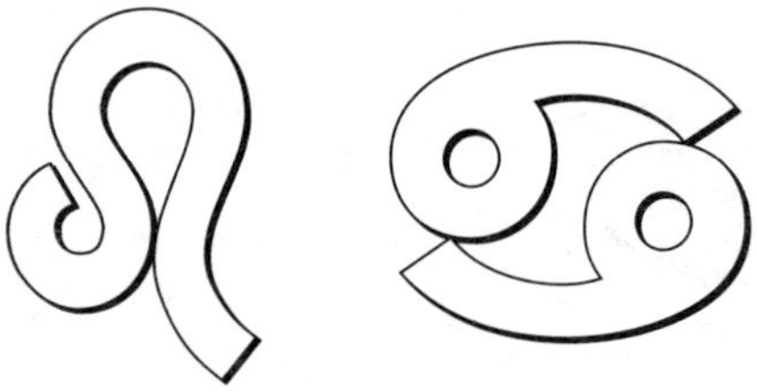

WONDERFULLY WARM

You can both be extremely warm and loving people, and family or emotional commitments matter to you both. You, however, tend to be more expressive, while he can hold more inside. You attract people with your vibrant, expressive, fun-loving spirit. He attracts people by being kind, helpful and protective. His more guarded approach to love can help tone down your wholehearted (sometimes rash) enthusiasm. Your confidence and rush for romance can enliven his life.

CHALLENGING—2

LARGER THAN LIFE

LEO/LEO

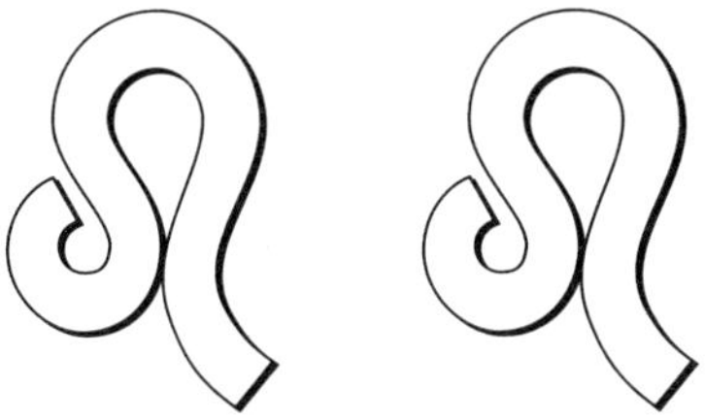

Crown you King and Queen of Romance! You both enjoy drama, gaining attention, being applauded and the adrenaline rush of being loved. Each of you has innate sex appeal, charisma and a contagious enthusiasm that sweeps others along in your quest for excitement. Both of you can be generous, extravagant, passionate, rash, foolhardy, creative and full of zest for living and loving. You feed the fire in one another which can sometimes burn too brightly, but adds the spark of desire and highlights emotions.

VERY COMPATIBLE—4

POPULAR AND PRAGMATIC

LEO/VIRGO

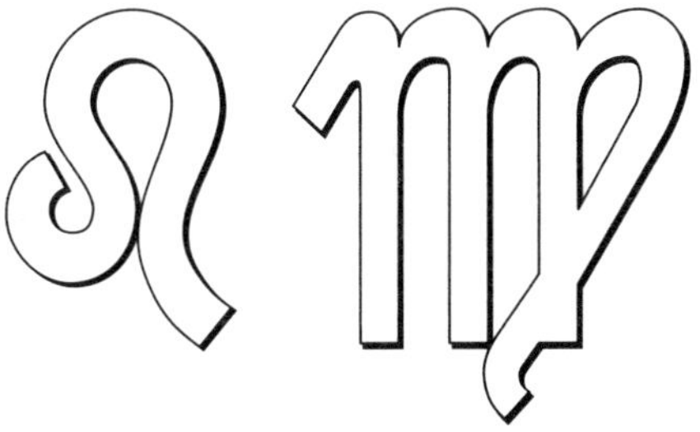

You enjoy fun, frolic, love, attention and anything exciting. He enjoys accomplishment, repairs, doing things well and being helpful. You attract people through charisma, confidence and creativity. He attracts people through competence, common sense and careful attention. The two of you could conflict over work versus play or having the limelight versus humble service. Learn from each other and you will become more practical while he becomes more outgoing and enthusiastic.

CHALLENGING—2

CHARISMATIC CHARM

LEO/LIBRA

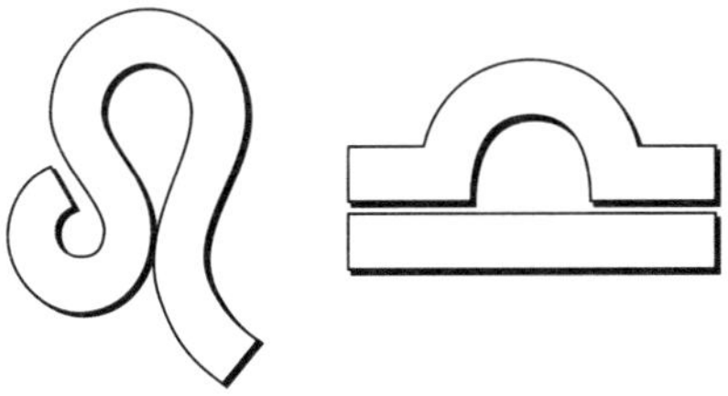

Both of you enjoy interactions with others. Your style tends to be more dramatic and noteworthy. His may be more diplomatic and charming, but you both enjoy sharing the social arena. Your charisma, sex appeal and flair tend to attract people, while his feeling for beauty, justice, harmony and balance draws others in. Your fun-loving spirit can add zest and excitement to his life, while his aesthetic skills and charm can bring added grace and beauty to your life.

COMPATIBLE—3

POWERFUL PASSIONS

LEO/SCORPIO

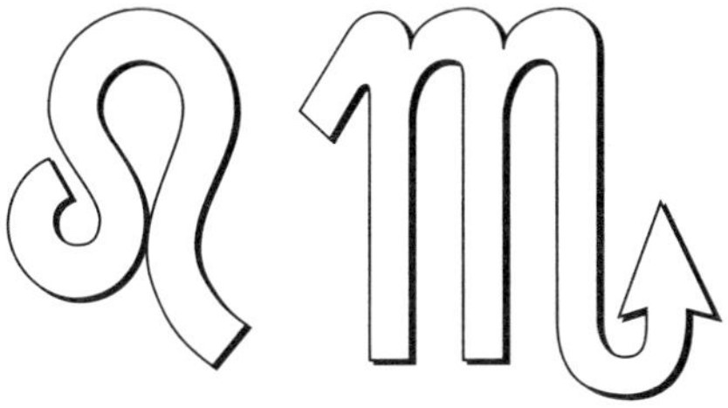

You enjoy excitement, drama and being the center of attention. He enjoys power, challenges and intense emotional interactions. You attract others through open, direct, charismatic allure. He attracts through seductive, mysterious, somewhat hidden sex appeal. Both of you want your own way, so don't fall into struggles for control. Be willing to compromise with one another. You can help him be more open and expressive. He can show you greater depths.

CHALLENGING—2

LEO/SAGITTARIUS

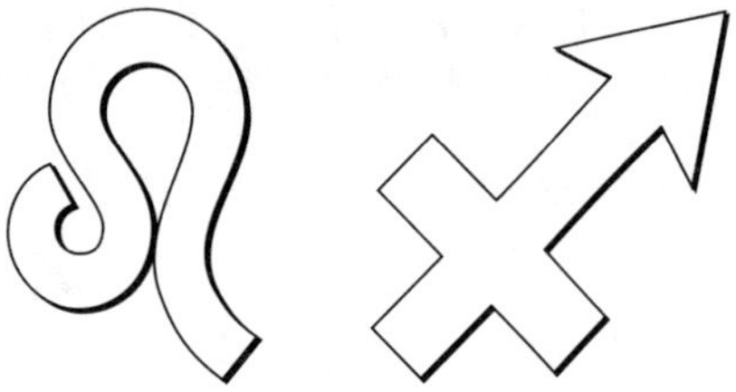

ENTHUSIASTIC AND EXTRAVAGANT

Love could be a ball of fire with you two around! Both of you enjoy excitement, activity and are willing to take risks in love. You both have natural charisma and magnetism. You have more dramatic instincts, where he may lean more to philosophy (or plain fun and frolic). You can both be quite generous, extravagant (and wholeheartedly foolish at times) around love and money. Rather than feeding each other's craziness (and excesses), strive to bring out the best in one another.

COMPATIBLE—3

LEO/CAPRICORN

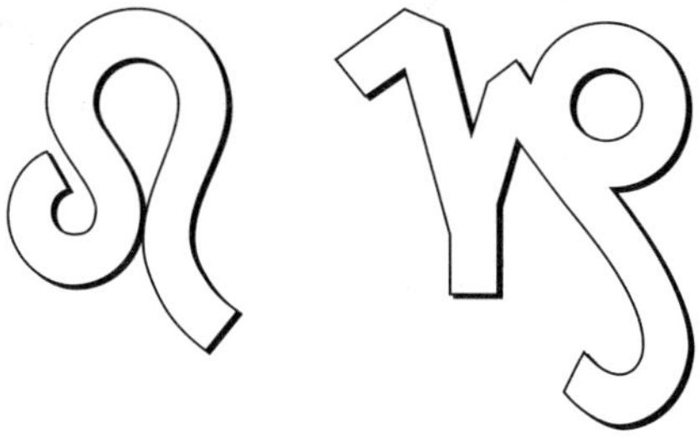

AMBITIOUS ACHIEVERS

Making it to the top is important to you both—enjoying recognition, respect and power. He may enjoy more slow and steady progress, while you prefer flash and dash, but status appeals to both of you. You can spark the initial attraction, the passion and the fire, but he has the capacity for staying power, for endurance and creating a lasting result. Together, you can finish as well as start in love and in life. He helps ground you; you help inspire his confidence.

VERY CHALLENGING—1

LEO/AQUARIUS

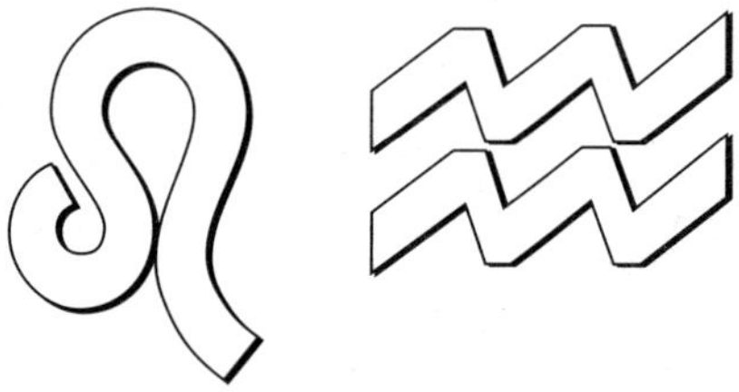

DYNAMIC AND DETACHED

You enjoy dramatic emotions, romance and excitement of all kinds. He enjoys the world of the mind, new possibilities and freedom. You attract through magnetism, sex appeal and exuberance. He attracts through independence, originality and a sense of fair play. Opposites in many ways, you probably feel a natural attraction. Don't play Mr. Spock versus the Hysteric. Do allow your sense of fun to enliven his logic and his rationality to moderate your enthusiasms.

VERY COMPATIBLE—4

LEO/PISCES

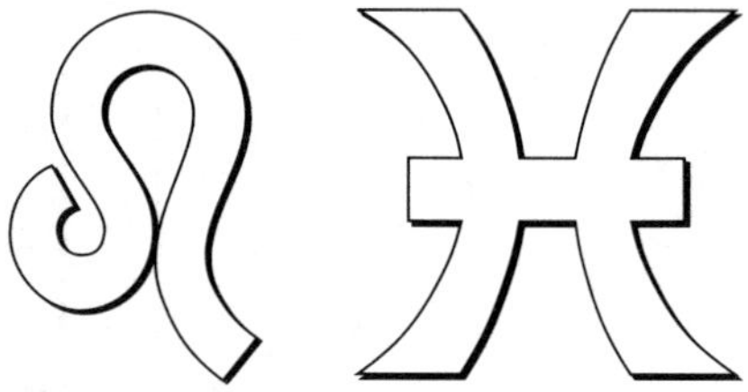

ROYAL ROMANCE

Both of you have a strong streak of romance in your souls, but yours tends to be open, expressive and eager, while his tends to be more inward and hidden. You attract through direct charisma, stage presence and enthusiasm. He attracts through mystery, imagination, fantasies and (perhaps) rescuing or being rescued. You can help him to become more outgoing and sociable. He can aid you in moderating your impulses, and toning down your larger-than-life tendencies. You can be magical together.

VERY CHALLENGING—1

EAGER ENTERPRISE

VIRGO/ARIES

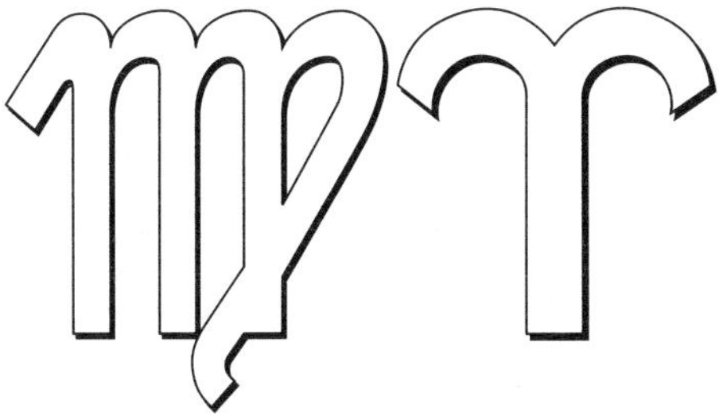

You enjoy putting things right, being competent and aiding healthy functioning. He enjoys courage, action, and immediate responses. You attract people by being orderly, helpful and careful in your work. He attracts people by being forthright, adventurous, and seeking challenges. Critical judgment or a pull between spontaneity and caution could affect your relationship. Share tasks and be harder on any problems than on each other.

VERY CHALLENGING—1

DEDICATED DEARS

VIRGO/TAURUS

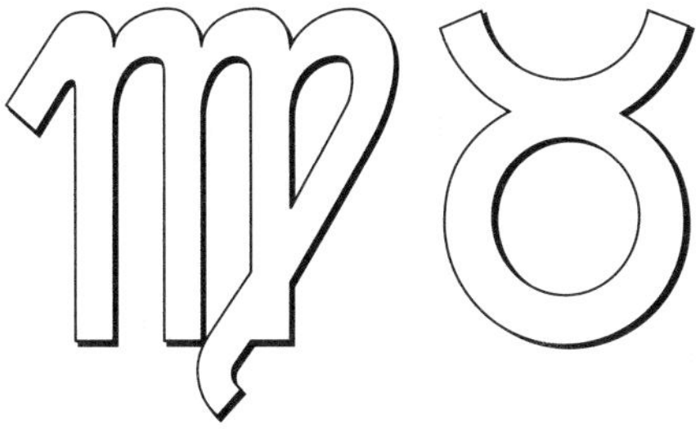

Both of you have an earthy attachment to practicality and common sense and may enjoy the world of nature. You appreciate competence, service and attention to detail. He appreciates dependability, physical possessions and comfort. He may attract others through financial skills or an easygoing attitude. You can attract through a modest but hardworking outlook. Both of you may have business skills, but you might be better with details. He could encourage you to be more sensual.

COMPATIBLE—3

FLEXIBLE FOCUS

VIRGO/GEMINI

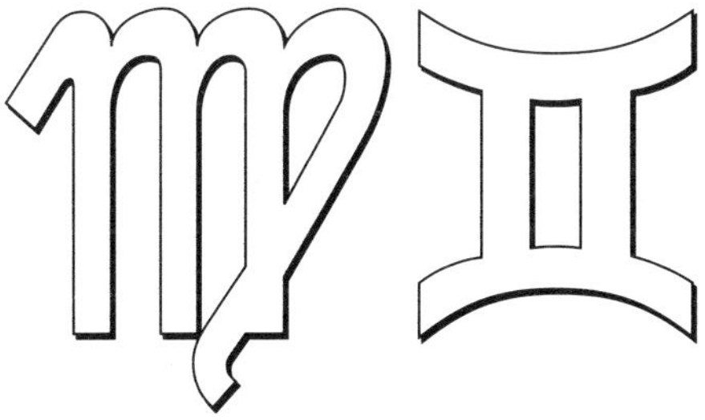

Both of you could enjoy the world of the mind—thinking, communicating and learning. Your social approach tends to be more focused and serious, while his tends to be more scattered and casual. He appreciates variety and might be a bit of a flirt, whereas you tend to be more cautious and committed in relationships. You can help him be more practical about love, and he can help you to lighten up and know when to laugh. You are likely to stimulate each other mentally.

CHALLENGING—2

PRACTICAL PROTECTION

VIRGO/CANCER

You enjoy competence, common sense and being helpful. He enjoys warmth, family feelings and protecting others. Your practicality, skill with details and dependability appeal to others. His caring, compassion and helpfulness appeal. Both of you are likely to value fidelity and being there for the ones you love. You can help him be more pragmatic and grounded. He can help you be more empathic and tuned into what others are feeling.

COMPATIBLE—3

VIRGO/LEO

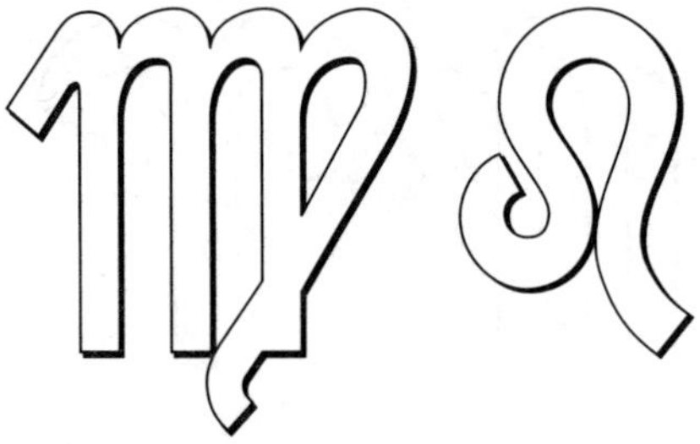

PRAGMATIC AND POPULAR

You are likely to be attracted by his flash and dash—his dramatic flair, magnetic personality and fun-loving social skills. He is likely to be attracted by your helpfulness, your competence, your desire to be of service and do things well. Don't divide this relationship into the playboy and the worker, or the "star" and the little gray mouse. Do learn and share roles with each other. He can learn a little humility from you and you can learn a bit more confidence from him.

CHALLENGING—2

VIRGO/VIRGO

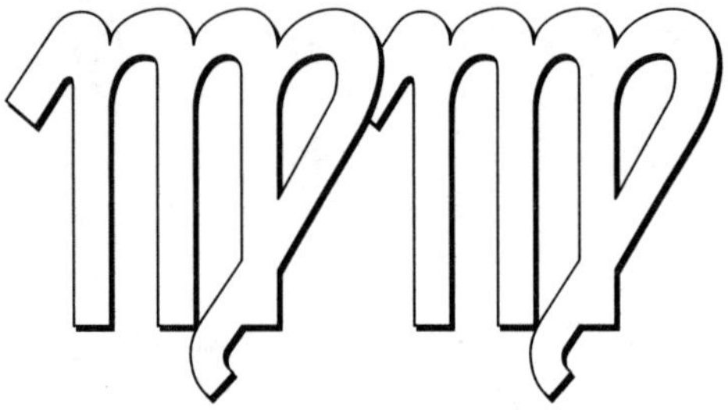

CAPABLE AND COMPETENT

Both of you tend to take relationships seriously—wanting to do it right, and worried about making a mistake. This could lead to holding back, inhibiting your responses or being critical of one another (trying to get everything "just so"). Your best bet is to work together—either a dual career or sharing tasks which focus your serious, nit-picking sides onto the job rather than each other. Once you commit, each of you will put much effort into making a relationship work **well**.

VERY COMPATIBLE—4

VIRGO/LIBRA

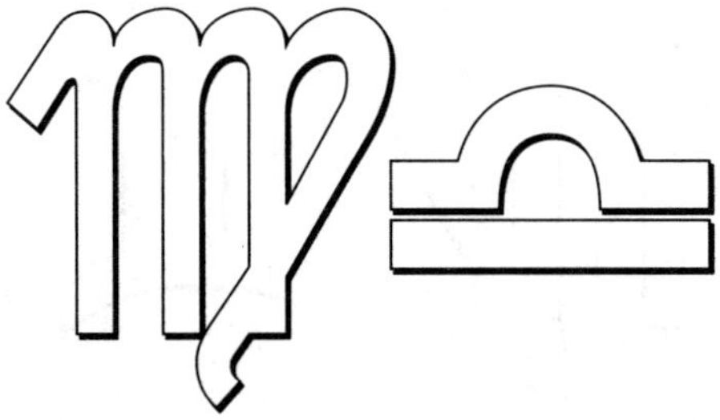

CHARMINGLY COMPETENT

You enjoy learning, productive accomplishment and improving things. He enjoys people, beauty and balance. You attract others through being practical and helpful. He attracts with charm, affection, and social skills. Your relationship could polarize over time and energy for work versus time and energy for love and sharing. Or, you may be more focused on duty, while he's more focused on pleasure. By taking turns and keeping room for both sides, you satisfy everyone.

CHALLENGING—2

VIRGO/SCORPIO

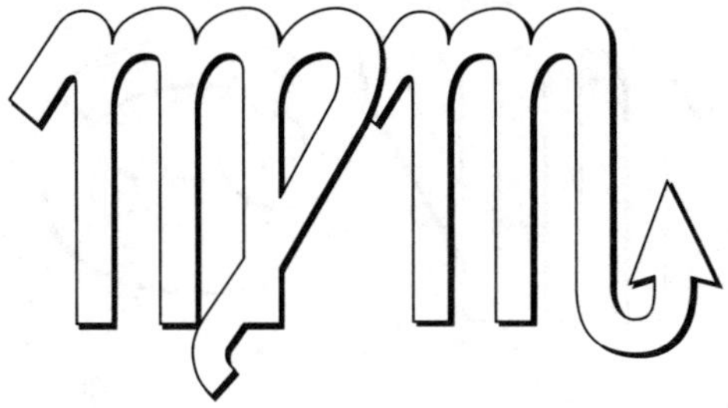

SERIOUS SEDUCTION

Both of you tend to take love seriously. You each appreciate loyalty and carrying through on promises. You may attract through perseverance, practicality and patience. He may attract through seduction, deep feelings, or an aura of power (or mystery). You could be a bit more grounded and he a bit more intense (possibly even possessive) and inward (nonrevealing) about feelings. You are likely to encourage each other's organizational skills and willingness to make a commitment.

COMPATIBLE—3

SENSIBLE SEEKING

VIRGO/SAGITTARIUS

You appreciate focus, common sense, and doing a good job. He loves adventure, exploration and going for the big time. You attract through competence and a willingness to be of service. He attracts through humor, friendliness and a zest for life. You may feel he takes too many chances or promises and then doesn't deliver. He might feel you are too critical or too serious. With tolerance, you can help him ground his dreams and he can help you laugh and lighten your load.

CHALLENGING—2

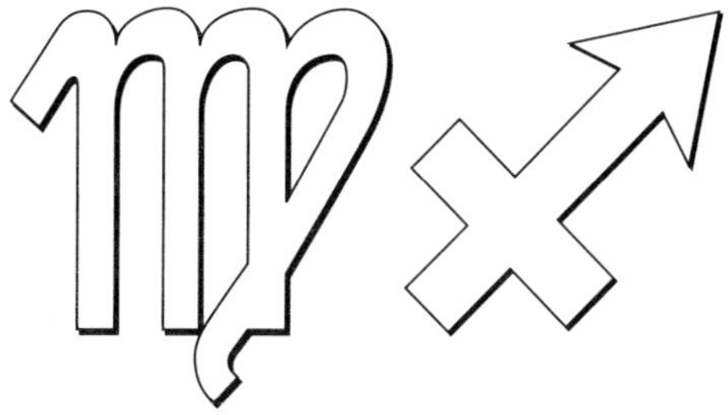

CAREFUL CONTROL

VIRGO/CAPRICORN

You both tend to be serious and cautious where love is concerned. The two of you may fear being hurt, controlled, rejected or criticized. Each of you is apt to have definite standards in relationships and could be picky. You can both be very responsible, hardworking and dedicated as a way of attracting a partner. You are likely to prefer a relationship with someone who is sensible, competent and willing to improve. Either of you could delay relationships (through fear), but once you commit, you will both do almost anything to make the relationship work.

COMPATIBLE—3

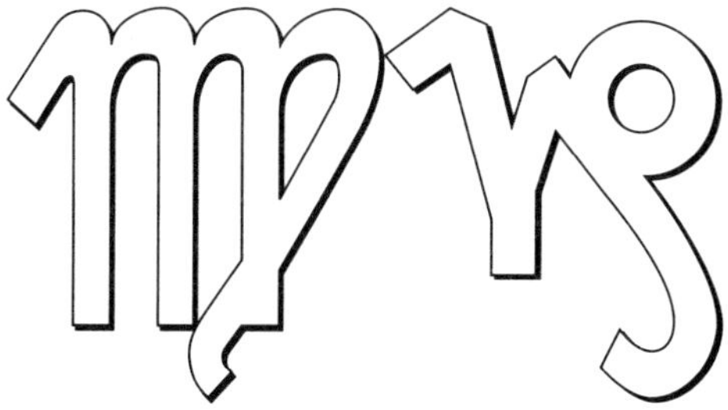

ORGANIZED ORIGINALITY

VIRGO/AQUARIUS

You enjoy precision, doing a good job, and organizing things. He enjoys independence, being different, and exploring the unusual. You may attract through dependability, helpfulness, and a practical attitude. He attracts through originality, mental stimulation and a free-wheeling attitude. He may seem rash, cool or flaky to you. You might seem critical, too serious or nit-picky to him. You are likely to learn much from one another and can stimulate each other's thinking.

VERY CHALLENGING—1

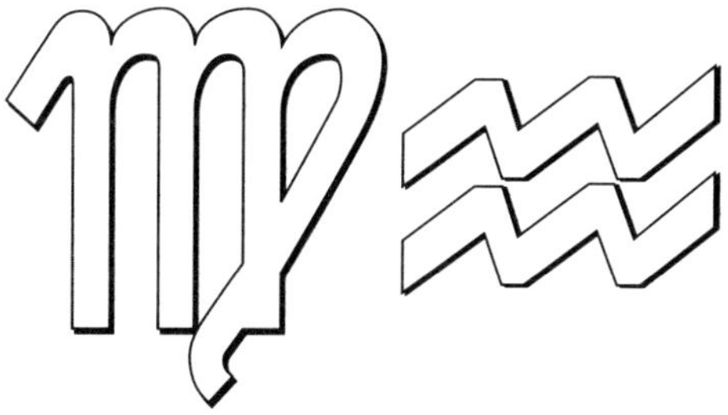

PRACTICALLY POETIC

VIRGO/PISCES

The two of you are facing a polarity: the real versus the ideal. You both may feel torn between love of fantasy, magic, illusion, beauty and idealism versus love of practicality, critical judgment, focused attention, productive work and an awareness of the way life (and love) really are. Don't take opposite sides and fight. Do combine your dreams. Share a mystical, rose-colored glasses vision and find ways to make your dreams come true together.

VERY COMPATIBLE—4

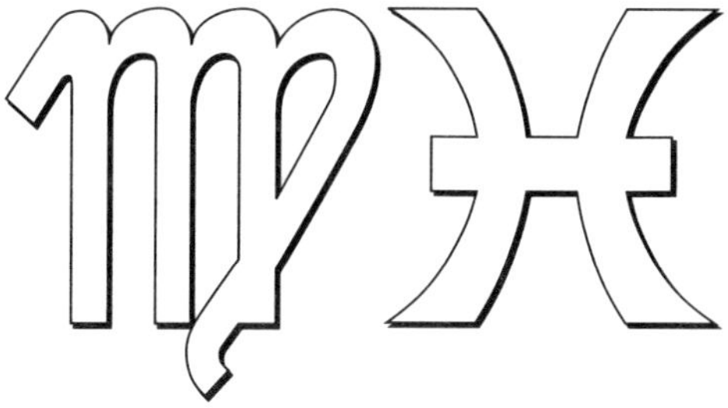

LIBRA/ARIES

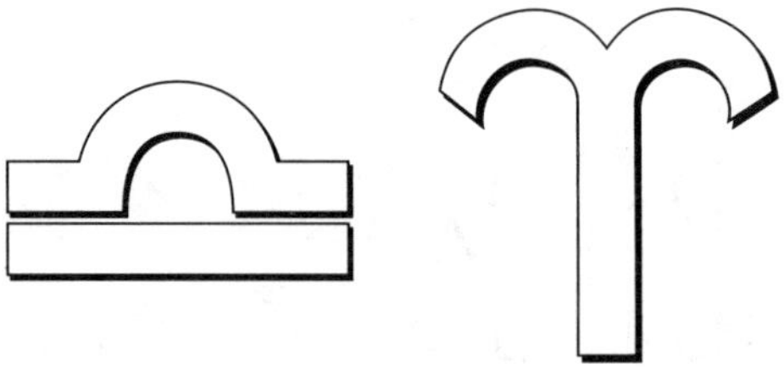

TO AND FRO

The two of you fall easily into a dance between self and other, between freedom and closeness, between independence and assertion. You probably attract people through grace, charm, beauty and kindness. He tends to attract through courage, directness and a free spirit. You may feel things always go **his** way and he may feel you vacillate a lot or try to please everyone. Keep a balance between who is calling the shots and who is compromising, and your natural attraction to one another can flow smoothly.

VERY COMPATIBLE—4

LIBRA/TAURUS

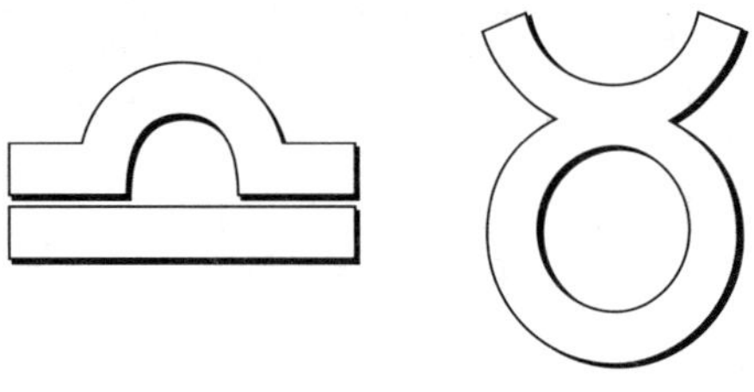

BEAUTY AND BALANCE

You appreciate the world of people, grace, beauty and justice. He enjoys the world of the senses, money and nature. You can both be pleasant and charming, although he may be a bit more practical and you a bit more social. You could enjoy art, beauty or simply relaxing together. Either of you might find it easier to avoid conflict than bring up problems that need to be faced. Despite some different pleasures, you both can be quite affectionate and loving.

VERY CHALLENGING—1

LIBRA/GEMINI

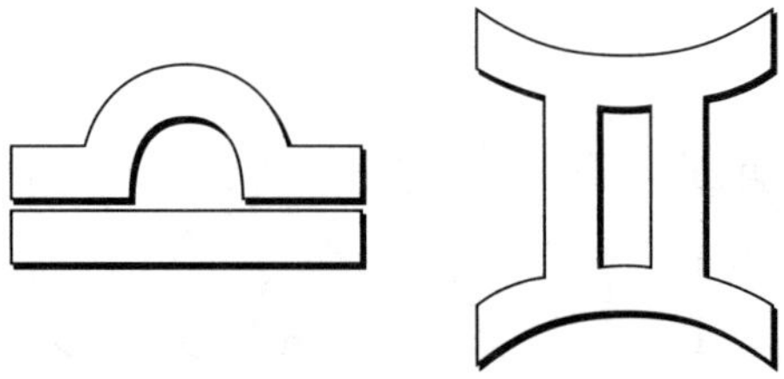

OPEN AND OBJECTIVE

Ideas and people bring pleasure to you both. You may be a bit more socially poised and able to make everyone feel comfortable. He may be a bit more versatile, with a good sense of humor. Communication is something you can both enjoy. Each of you tends to treat other people fairly, and be willing to take turns in a relationship. A social network and lots of contact with friends can help to support your relationship.

COMPATIBLE—3

LIBRA/CANCER

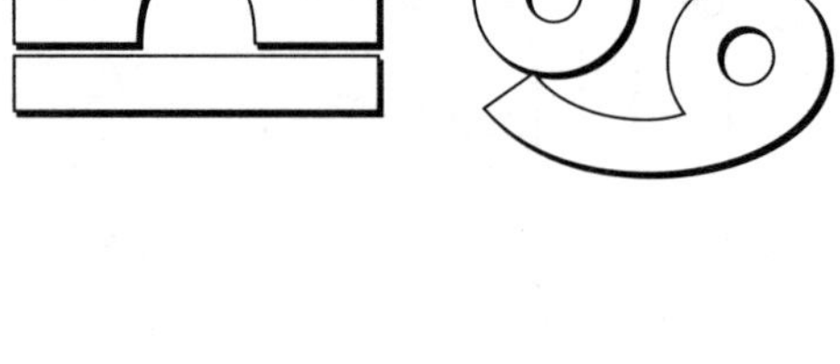

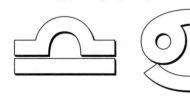

CLOSE CONTACT

Both of you can enjoy emotional closeness and sharing. You may be a bit more equalitarian and he a bit more possessive. Your style in love is more toward teamwork; he might come across as somewhat parental in a partnership. You can bring more beauty and balance into his life. He can bring more warmth and nurturing into yours.

CHALLENGING—2

CHARISMATIC CHARM

LIBRA/LEO

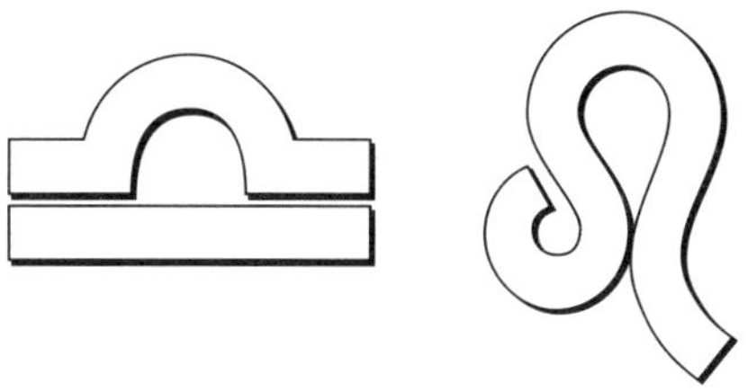

Both of you enjoy people. You may be more diplomatic and sweet, while he is more dramatic and could gravitate toward center stage. His charisma, sex appeal, confidence or generosity may attract people. You attract through beauty, grace, charm and a natural empathy for others. You can help him see two sides to any issue and he can add more zest, enthusiasm and fun to your life.

COMPATIBLE—3

CHARMINGLY COMPETENT

LIBRA/VIRGO

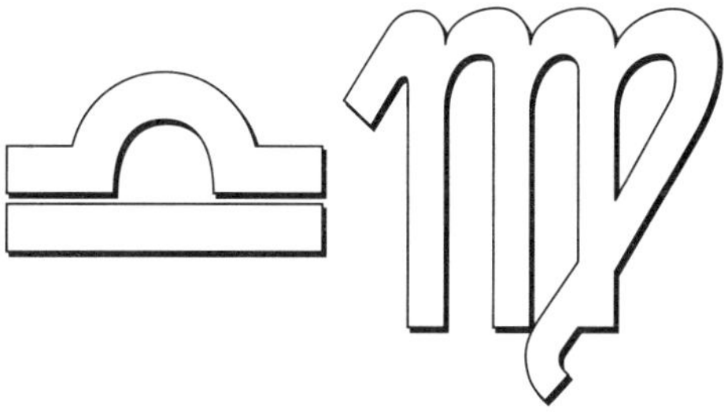

You enjoy people, beauty and balance. He enjoys work, fixing things and getting the details right. You attract through charm, affection and a graceful attitude. He attracts through being productive, practical and penny-wise. You might feel he is too critical or serious, and he might feel that you are too relaxed or concerned with what other people think. The two of you might polarize over issues of love versus work, or duty versus pleasure. Keep room for both and your lives (and relationship) will be more satisfying.

CHALLENGING—2

POISED PARTNERS

LIBRA/LIBRA

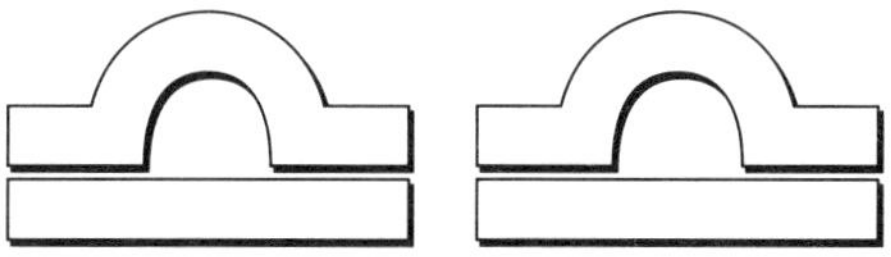

You both enjoy people, one-on-one encounters, art or aesthetics, balance, justice and harmony. You attract through grace, charm, and an ability to put others at ease. Each of you can be somewhat other-directed, tending to react rather than initiate. Compromises and negotiations are natural. You both have talent for identifying win/win solutions. Either of you could be inclined to avoid unpleasantness, sweeping emotional "dirt" under the carpet (ignoring it). With a desire to share equally, you two should find it easy to combine desires and lives.

VERY COMPATIBLE—4

SHARED SECRETS

LIBRA/SCORPIO

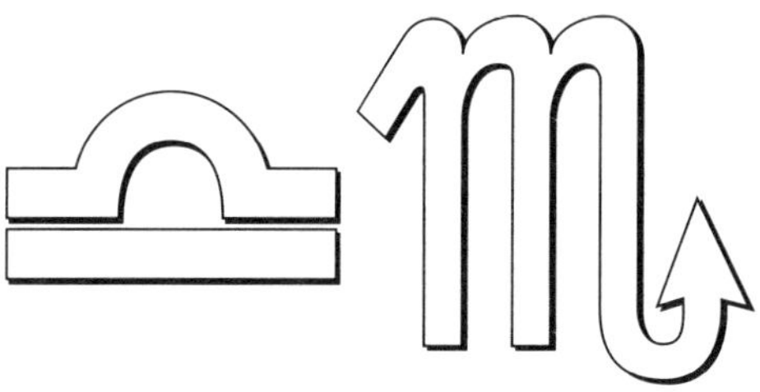

You both enjoy partnership and relationships can be a real source of pleasure. You are likely to be more sociable, while he is a bit more inward and really needs private time. You attract people through kindness, empathy and grace. He attracts through intensity, sex appeal, or a commanding, masterful presence. You are fairly open and can enjoy interacting (perhaps even flirting) with other people; he might be a bit possessive. Be aware of each other's needs for reassurance and support. Togetherness feeds both your psyches.

CHALLENGING—2

LIBRA/SAGITTARIUS

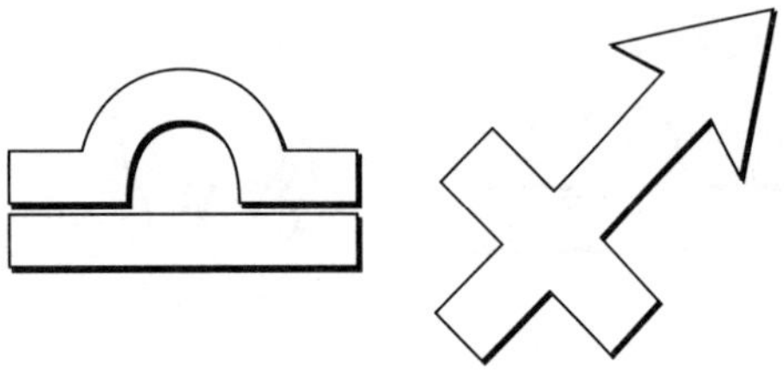

ATTRACTIVE AND AFFABLE

Fun and frolic appeal to you both! Each of you loves laughter, enjoys people and is likely to be socially skilled. You attract more through grace, beauty, charm and an instinct for pleasing people. He attracts more through wit, wisdom and wonder. You may bring more art, aesthetics or balance into his life. He may add adventure, speculation, travel or anything expansive to your life. The accent is on good times—having fun—when you are together.

COMPATIBLE—3

LIBRA/CAPRICORN

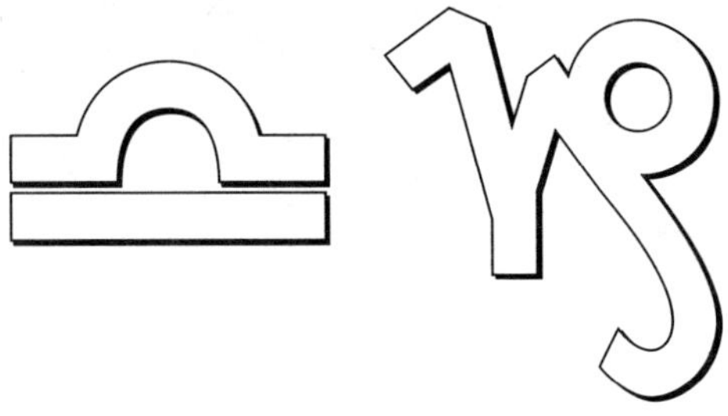

COOPERATIVE CONTROL?

You enjoy people, beauty, sharing and teamwork. He enjoys responsibility, ambition, control and authority. You attract people through kindness, empathy and grace. He attracts through power, withdrawal or dependability. You both are challenged to balance time and energy devoted to love and to work. You may also be torn between parenting (dominating) versus partnership (sharing) instincts. A complete life allows a little of all of them.

CHALLENGING—2

LIBRA/AQUARIUS

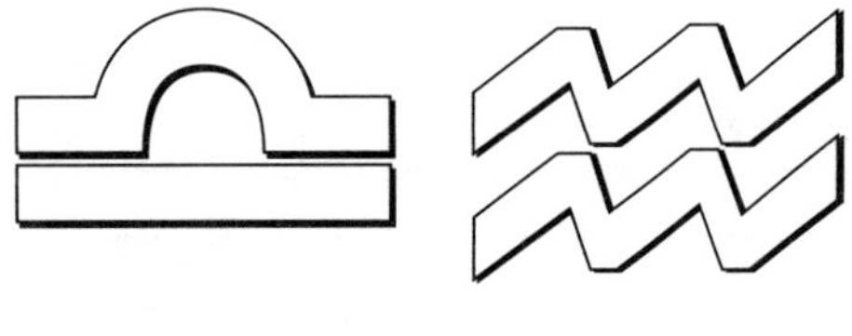

NATURAL NETWORKERS

The world of the mind can be a real common ground between the two of you. You both probably enjoy getting stimulating ideas from another person. You attract through listening, sharing and cooperating. He attracts through an independent spirit, openness and a quick mind. You may be ready for partnership, while he is still on a "friends" basis. The more you communicate and find common ground, the better your relationship flows.

COMPATIBLE—3

LIBRA/PISCES

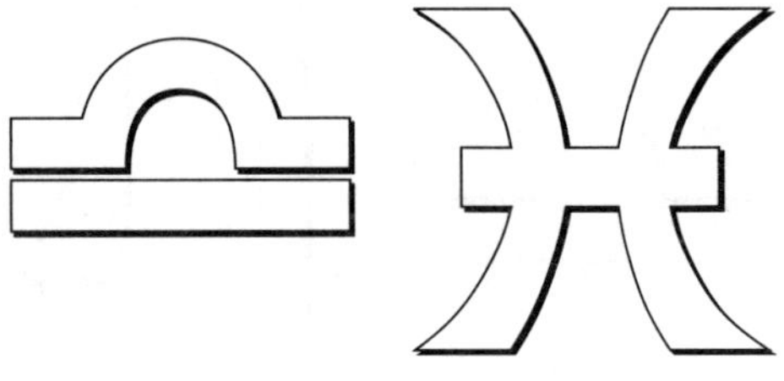

BLISSFUL BEAUTY

Beauty or love of harmony might draw the two of you together. You love balance, justice, and pretty things. He loves grace, sensitivity, and rescuing or protecting others. You may be more sociable, while he enjoys privacy more. You both are motivated to create a flowing, pleasant relationship. Don't avoid facing unpleasant facts, but do find ways to bring more love, caring and compassion into the world and into your relationship.

VERY CHALLENGING—1

POTENT PASSIONS

SCORPIO/ARIES

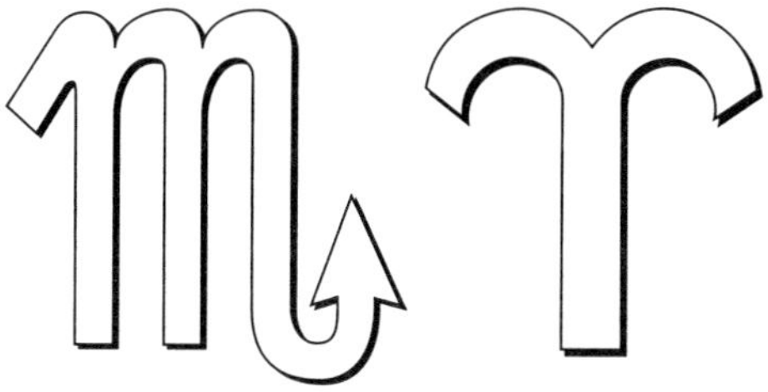

You love intensity, looking beneath the surface and deep commitments. He loves independence, directness and open action. You attract through mystery, sexual allure and emotional fascination. He attracts through courage, confidence and telling it like it is. Compromise is essential, as neither of you reacts well to someone else trying to take control in a relationship. Sexual tension and excitement, however, could be very strong. Both of you tend to rise to a challenge and can do well by seeking out win/win opportunities.

VERY CHALLENGING—1

SEXY AND SENSUAL

SCORPIO/TAURUS

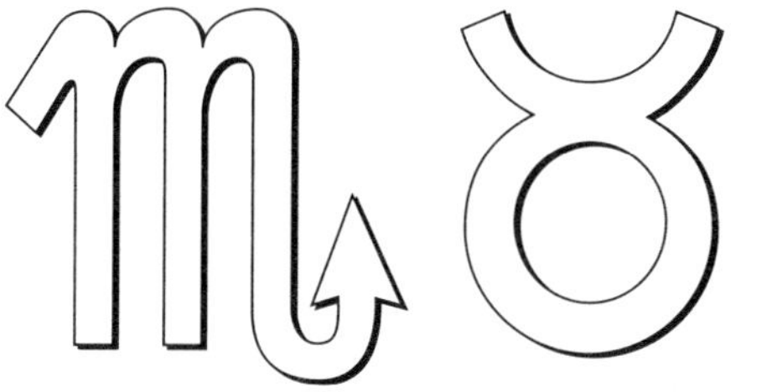

Both of you have a strong, sensual streak and may enjoy lots of physical contact. He loves indulgence and a smooth, easy flow. You're more apt to confront troubling issues and be concerned about appetite mastery (e.g., dieting, not smoking, etc.). You fascinate with your intensity, emotionality and sexual allure. He appeals through his practical, easygoing nature. There is a natural attraction between you. Financial security probably matters to you both, and you share an appreciation of life's pleasures.

VERY COMPATIBLE—4

FOCUS OR FLIT (AWAY)?

SCORPIO/GEMINI

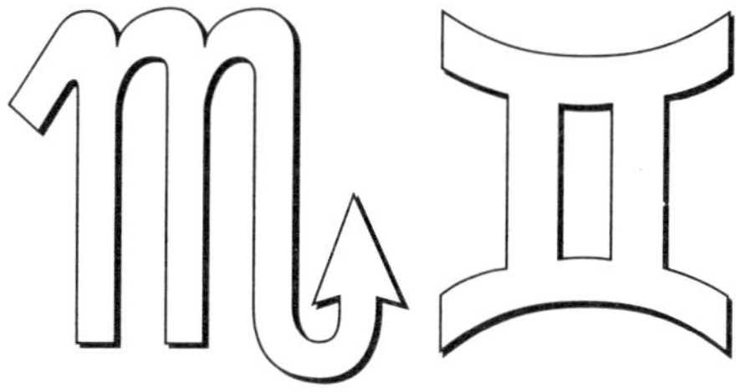

You enjoy intensity, privacy and completing projects. He enjoys variety, lightness and the ability to discuss anything under the sun. You attract people through sexual magnetism, emotional depth and a bit of mystery. He attracts through lightheartedness, a sense of fun and multiple interests. You can bring in many layers to your relationship and he can help you lighten up and laugh. With mutual tolerance and adaptability, you can achieve both breadth and depth in love.

VERY CHALLENGING—1

EMOTIONAL EMPHASIS

SCORPIO/CANCER

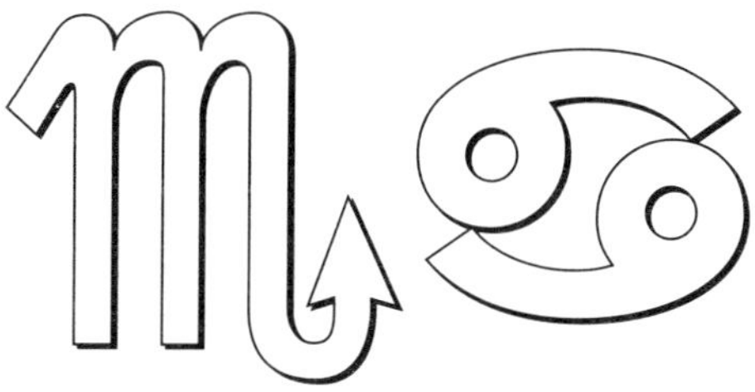

You enjoy being enthralled, seduced and caught up in a passionate bond. He enjoys food, family and feeling safe. You attract via sexual fascination, intensity and a wholehearted commitment. He attracts through warmth, caring and protectiveness. Each of you can be quite sensitive, easily tuning into the other person's feelings. You each also need some time alone and you must respect each other's urges for privacy (not revealing everything). You can be quite supportive of one another.

COMPATIBLE—3

SCORPIO/LEO

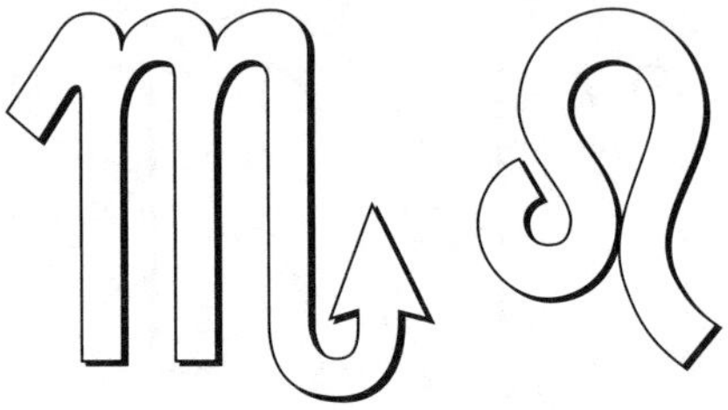

POWERFUL PASSIONS

You enjoy challenges, intense emotional interactions and passionate connections. He enjoys excitement, drama and being the center of attention. You attract through mystery, allure and staying power. He attracts through charisma, confidence and a fun-loving attitude. Each of you can be quite willful. If you jockey for control, the power struggles will look like the irresistible force meeting the immovable object. Look for encounters in which you both end up winning. He can encourage you to be more open and less serious. You can encourage him to share the stage and achieve more depth in relating.

CHALLENGING—2

SCORPIO/VIRGO

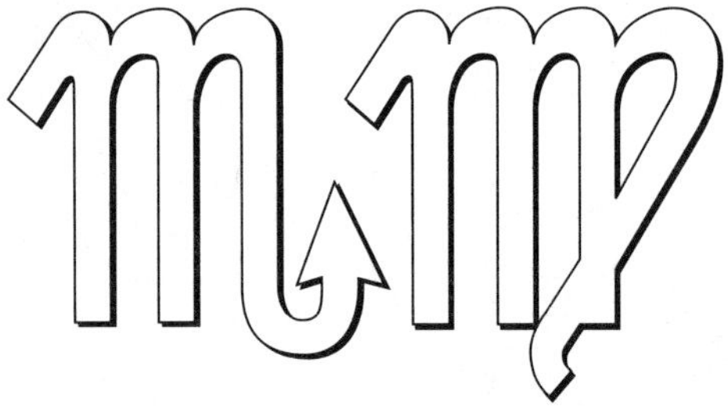

SERIOUS SEDUCTION

Love is a serious matter for you both. Each of you is seeking loyalty and someone you can depend upon to carry through on commitments. You may draw others in through a fascinating, alluring, or mysterious manner. He may attract through being competent, helpful and patient. You may be a bit more emotional, and he a bit more practical. Both of you have excellent organizational skills and a determination to finish what you start. You share a degree of reserve, but once you both "warm up," the connection can be quite strong.

COMPATIBLE—3

SCORPIO/LIBRA

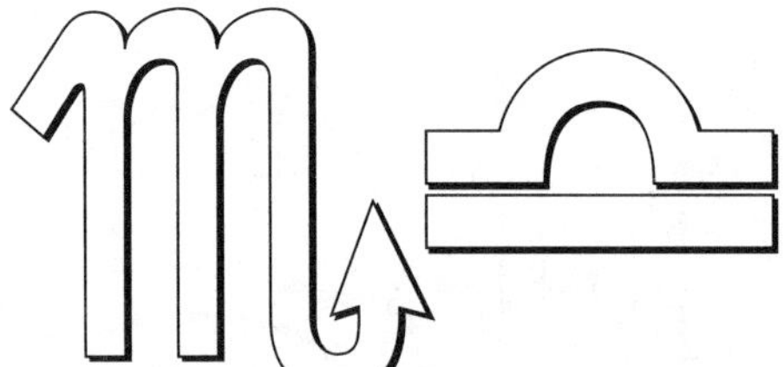

SHARED SECRETS

Relationships are important to each of you. You discover yourselves partly through interactions with others. Your focus tends to be more one-centered and intense. His focus tends to be more sociable, relating to a wider range of people. You attract through fascination, sexual allure and loyalty. He attracts through charm, empathy and an interest in people. Togetherness is important to both of you. Each of you has an instinctive drive for partnership.

CHALLENGING—2

SCORPIO/SCORPIO

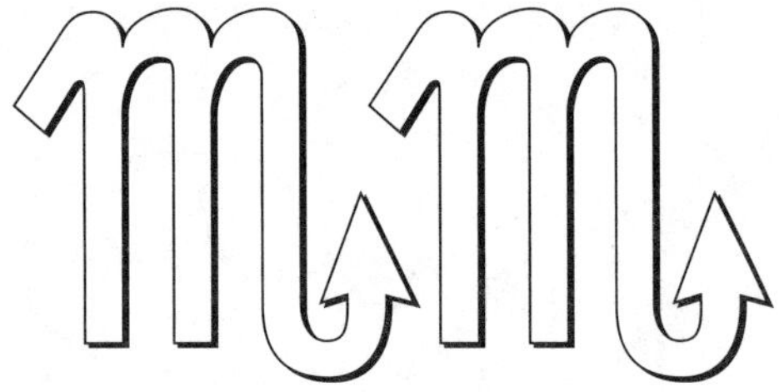

EXTREMELY ENTHRALLING

Both of you enjoy a sense of mastery, personal control, and passionate encounters. You may exude a sensual/sexual allure which fascinates others. The two of you seek a bond so deep, so intense, so enthralling that you feel "swept away." You want to merge psyches and souls so must tread carefully lest jealousy, possessiveness or power games poison your interactions. You two can understand each other better than almost anyone else if you use your intuition wisely. Your relationship might powerfully transform you both.

VERY COMPATIBLE—4

ALLURING ADVENTURES

SCORPIO/SAGITTARIUS

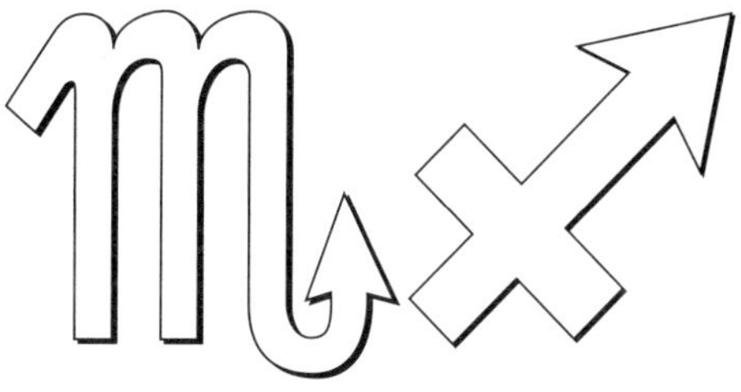

You love depth, commitment and emotionally powerful experiences. He loves breadth, freedom and fun and games. You attract through magnetic allure and understanding people's hidden agendas. He attracts through humor and an adventurous spirit. His expansive urges may infringe on your need for privacy, and your desire for loyalty may cramp his style and joy at wandering the world. With understanding and tolerance of your differences, he can widen your world and you can deepen his perceptions.

CHALLENGING—2

COMPLETE COMMITMENT

SCORPIO/CAPRICORN

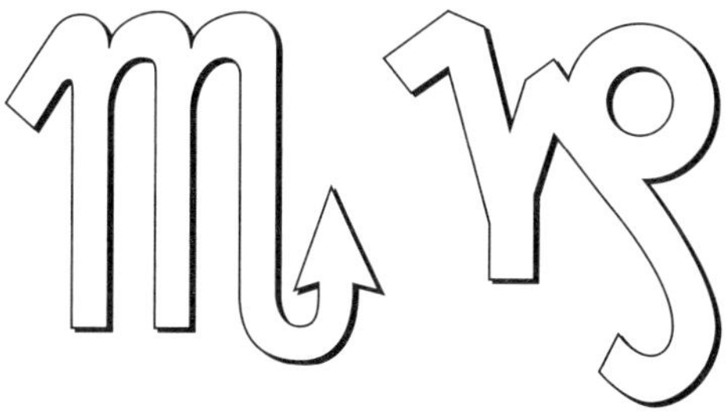

Both of you appreciate loyalty and commitment. You love intense emotional experiences and uncovering secrets or hidden information. He loves control, success and the role of the expert. You attract emotionally—with a fascinating allure and seductive presence. He attracts practically—with responsibility, dedication and hard work. Each of you tend to be serious about love and will think well (and often long) before committing.

COMPATIBLE—3

SECRETIVE OR SOCIABLE?

SCORPIO/AQUARIUS

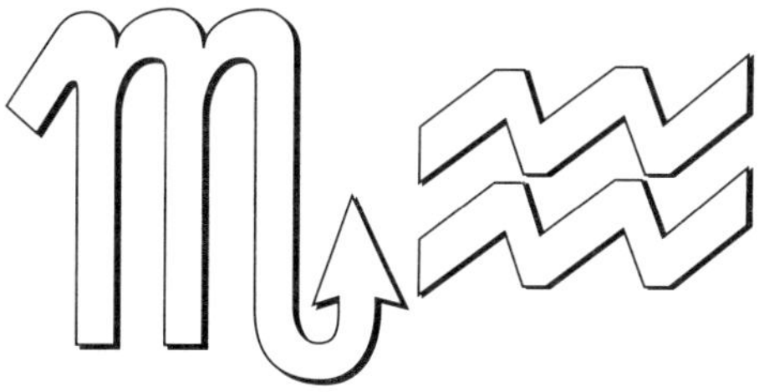

You enjoy intense emotional encounters where you can share deep, profound feelings with a partner. He enjoys discussions and social situations where he can theorize about what's new, the future or anything unusual. You attract through being fascinating and perhaps a bit mysterious. He attracts through being original and perhaps a bit unconventional. His love of freedom could clash with your love of a total, emotional bond. Compromise allows you to balance intensity and a need for space. Practice loving with an open hand, creating intimacy within an atmosphere of freedom.

CHALLENGING—2

PRIVATE POETRY

SCORPIO/PISCES

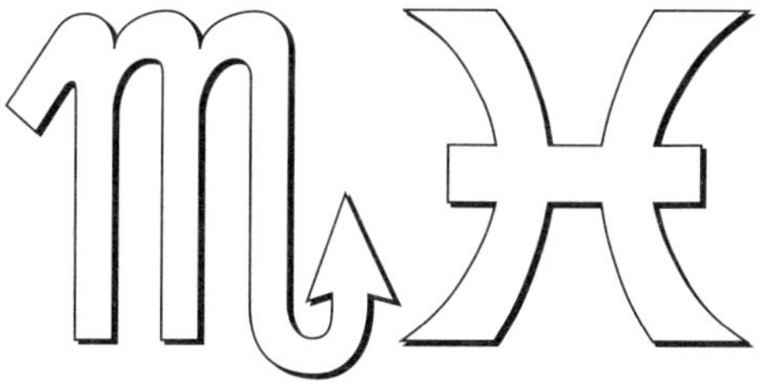

You both can be empathic and tune into those you love. You enjoy challenges, secrets and emotional depths. He enjoys beauty, nature and the world of the imagination. You attract through being sensual and seductive. He attracts through being kind, eager to rescue (or needing assistance). The two of you are likely to respect each other's needs for privacy and some time alone. You will, at times, understand each other without any words.

COMPATIBLE—3

SAGITTARIUS/ARIES

FIERY FUN

You love honesty, confidence and a good sense of humor. He loves courage, directness and an eagerness for life. You attract through being bright, fun-loving and friendly. He attracts through excitement, independence and assertiveness. You tend to energize each other and encourage each other to try more, take chances and do new, pioneering things. You may feed each other's impatience, impulsivity, or foolhardiness. You can build one another's strength, candor, and ability to act. Together, you feel vital, alive and willing to try anything.

COMPATIBLE—3

SAGITTARIUS/TAURUS

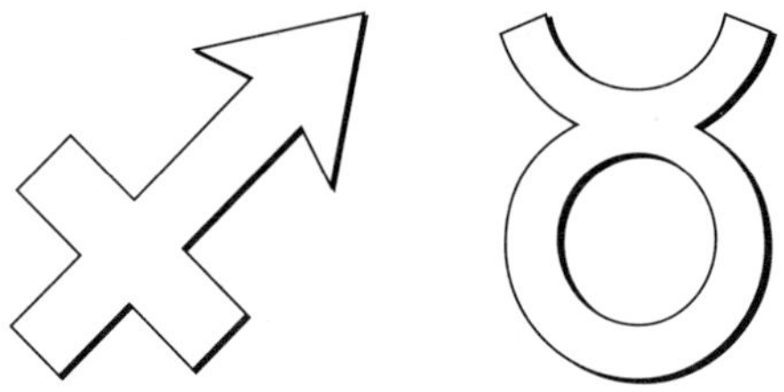

FAMILIAR OR FARAWAY?

You love travel, fun and games, seeking the meaning of life and laughter. He loves back rubs, financial security and a familiar, comfortable routine. You may feel he is a stick-in-the-mud, while he sees you as impractical and much too optimistic. You attract through a friendly, outgoing attitude; he attracts through dependability. You can expand his horizons, and bring more excitement into his life, encourage him to explore new ideas and new experiences. He can help you be more grounded and practical, feeding your common sense.

VERY CHALLENGING—1

SAGITTARIUS/GEMINI

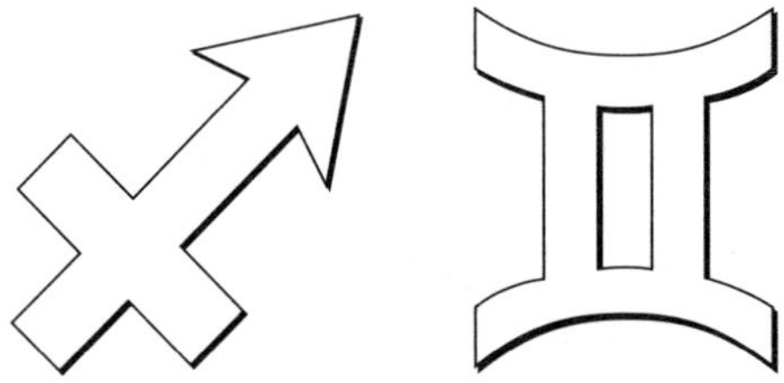

LOVE OF LAUGHTER

You both probably love to talk, so be sure each of you makes room to listen as well. Mental and social stimulation are important for each of you and you probably share a keen sense of humor. He can help you appreciate the here and now and people right around. You can help him envision far horizons, consider philosophical principles and look for life's meaning. There is a natural attraction between you, but each of you can also easily flirt. Be open and honest and things flow smoothly.

VERY COMPATIBLE—4

SAGITTARIUS/CANCER

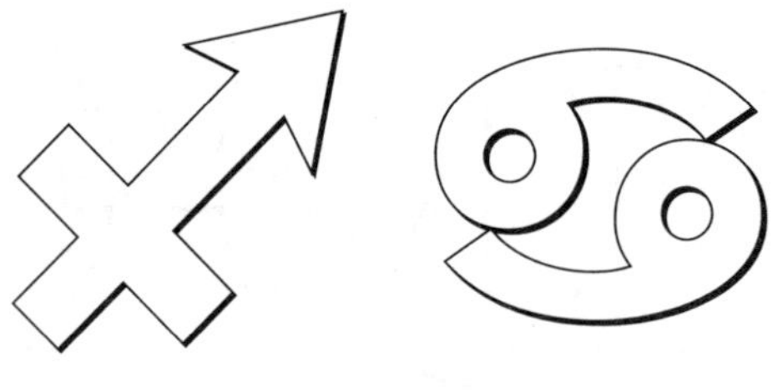

EXTROVERT OR INTROVERT?

You enjoy independence, travel, laughter and the thrill of going for the gusto or the big time in life. He enjoys safety, support, and a family or personal focus. You attract people with humor, excitement, generosity and a natural friendliness. He attracts through being warm, kind, protective and reliable. If you each learn from the other—rather than trying to change him/her—you can help him broaden his perspectives and he can help you build a safe, secure foundation. Your optimism can balance his caution.

VERY CHALLENGING—1

ENTHUSIASTIC & EXTRAVAGANT

SAGITTARIUS/LEO

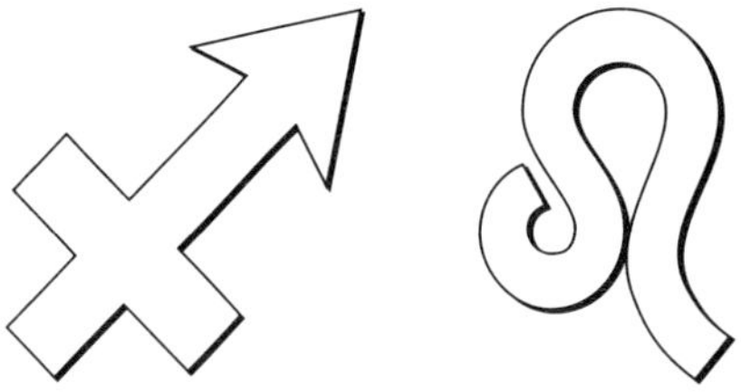

Love could be a ball of fire with you two around. Both of you enjoy excitement, activity and are willing to take risks in love. You both have natural charisma and magnetism. He may have more dramatic instincts, where you may lean more to philosophy (or plain fun and frolic). You can both be quite generous, extravagant (and wholeheartedly foolish at times) around love and money. Rather than feeding each other's craziness (and excesses), strive to bring out the best in one another.

COMPATIBLE—3

SENSIBLE SEEKING

SAGITTARIUS/VIRGO

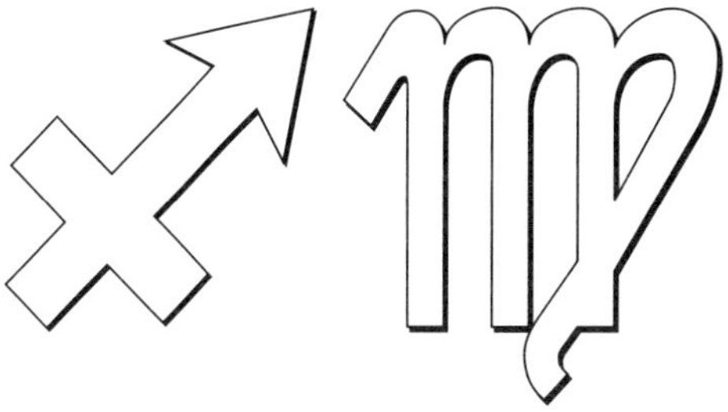

You love laughter, travel, learning and finding the silver lining in any of life's clouds. He appreciates focus, follow-through, common sense, and doing a good job. You attract through humor, friendliness and a zest for life. He attracts through competence and a willingness to be of service. He may feel you are scattered, late, or promise and then don't deliver. You might feel he is too critical or too serious. With tolerance, he can help you to ground your dreams and you can help him to laugh and lighten his load.

CHALLENGING—2

ATTRACTIVE AND AFFABLE

SAGITTARIUS/LIBRA

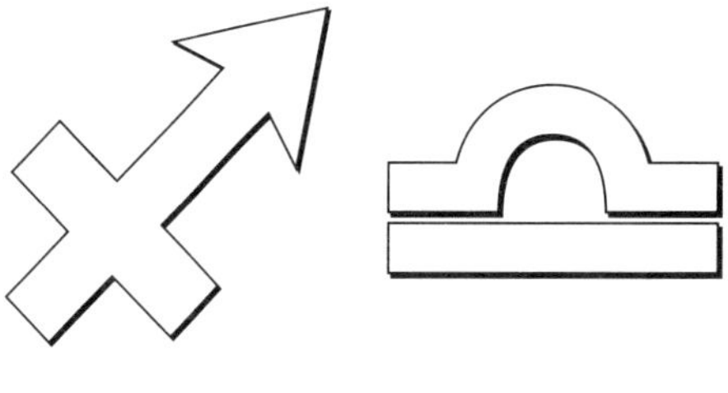

Fun and frolic appeal to you both! Each of you loves laughter, enjoys people and is likely to be socially skilled. He attracts more through charm, tact, and an instinct for pleasing people. You attract more through wit, wisdom and wonder. He may bring more art, aesthetics or balance into your life. You may add learning, speculation, travel or anything expansive to his life. The accent is on good times—having fun—when you are together.

COMPATIBLE—3

ADVENTUROUS ALLURE

SAGITTARIUS/SCORPIO

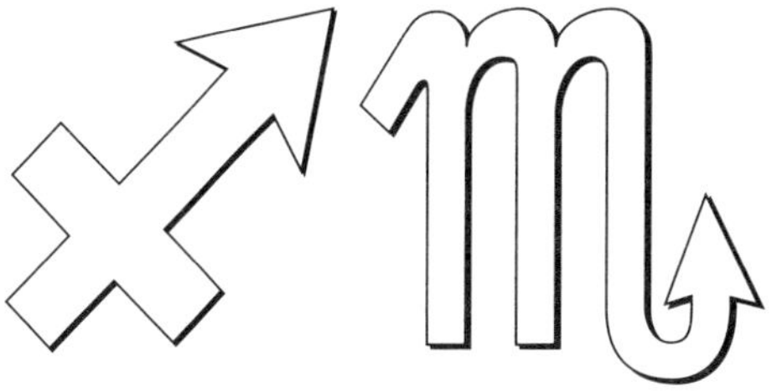

You love breadth, freedom, fun, games and laughter in life. He loves depth, sexual tension, and emotionally powerful experiences. You attract through optimism, humor and a willingness to be anybody's friend. He attracts through intensity, a magnetic allure, looking deeper and understanding people's hidden agendas. Your expansive urges may infringe on his need for privacy, and his desire for loyalty may turn into possessiveness or jealousy if you wander the world or socialize with many different people. With understanding and tolerance of your differences, you can widen his world and he can deepen your perceptions.

CHALLENGING—2

SAGITTARIUS/SAGITTARIUS EXTRAVAGANTLY EXCITING

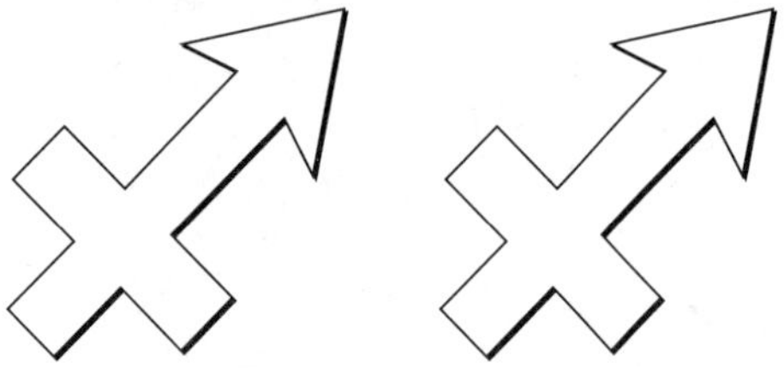

You both love fun, travel, learning, and anything which expands your horizons—mentally, physically, emotionally or spiritually. Often restless, you could appreciate sports, the outdoors or just keeping active. Both of you attract people through your humor, optimism, friendliness and generosity. You may sometimes egg each other on (rash, impulsive or extravagant), but you two can do pleasure in a **big** way, indulging one another to the hilt.

VERY COMPATIBLE—4

SAGITTARIUS/CAPRICORN ADVENTUROUS AUTHORITY

You enjoy fun, risking for greater gain, activity and expanding your horizons. He enjoys being the authority, gaining power and career accomplishments. You attract through generosity, openness and a friendly spirit. He attracts through caution, a respectful attitude and hard work. You tend to be optimistic in love; he tends to be a pessimist. You jump wholeheartedly into pleasure; he plays it cool, not wanting to risk being hurt or disappointed. He can help you be more sensible and you can help him be more spontaneous.

CHALLENGING—2

SAGITTARIUS/AQUARIUS INTELLIGENTLY INDEPENDENT

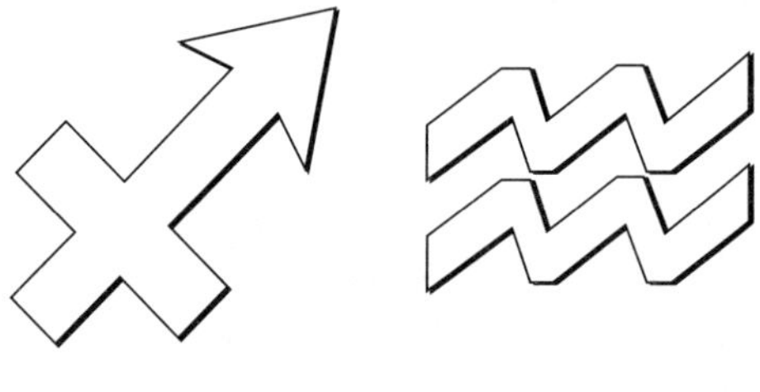

You both enjoy people, independence and new experiences. You may be a bit more emotional, expressive and impulsive in terms of love, while he is a bit more calm, cool and collected. But you both appreciate each other's individuality. You attract through generosity, being friendly, optimistic and witty. He attracts through being unconventional, tolerant, progressive and intelligent. You both need a bit of space in your love relationships, so would not be a "do everything together" couple. You can enjoy sharing new ideas, people and experiences with each other.

COMPATIBLE—3

SAGITTARIUS/PISCES SEEKING THE SUBLIME

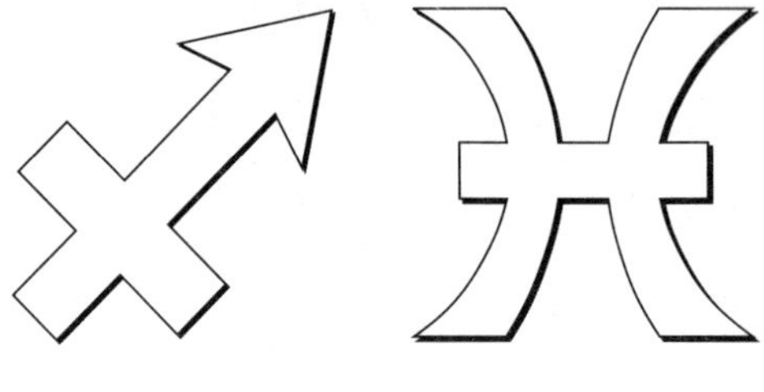

You are both idealistic about love and may yearn for more than is possible. You tend to seek someone bright, fun-loving, adventurous, generous and outgoing. He tends to seek someone sensitive, intuitive, attractive, artistic and compassionate. Either of you can be in love with love. You both easily appreciate the best in one another, but must guard against rose-colored glasses or feeling hurt when your partner turns out to be only human. Nature or any activities which help, uplift, inspire or assist people could bond you.

CHALLENGING—2

EAGER EXPERTISE

CAPRICORN/ARIES

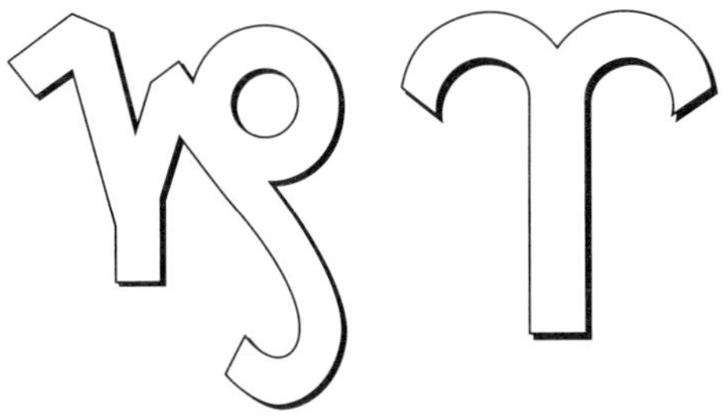

You tend to play it safe in love, looking for dependability and someone who is responsible and ambitious. He is more impulsive and falls quickly into fiery passions. You attract through being cautious, practical and conscientious. He attracts through eagerness, courage and assertion. Since you both feel strongly about love, a battle of wills is possible unless each of you compromises. You may see him as rash or self-centered and he may see you as controlling or inhibited. Combine sensible planning and an all-out thrust for fun and excitement.

CHALLENGING—2

PRACTICAL POWER

CAPRICORN/TAURUS

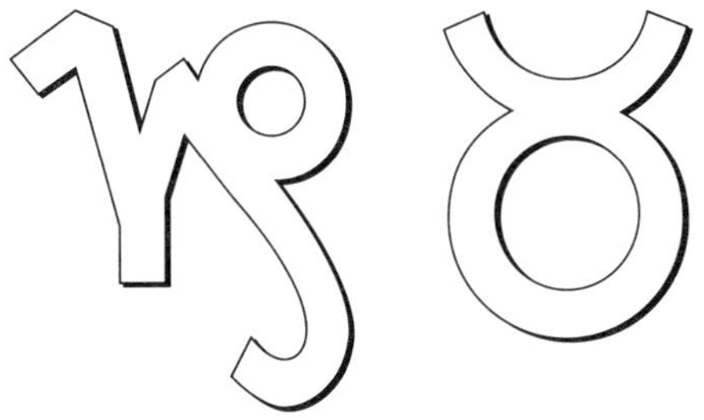

You both appreciate tangible results and may show your love through doing things for each other. Deeds matter much more than words! You appreciate success, status, power and authority. He appreciates monetary dependability, and an easygoing and sensual nature. He attracts through physical indulgences and practicality. You attract through being ambitious and hardworking. Both of you may have business skills and understand reality well. Each of you can be very solid and loyal in love; once committed, you carry through.

COMPATIBLE—3

ADAPTABLE ACHIEVEMENT

CAPRICORN/GEMINI

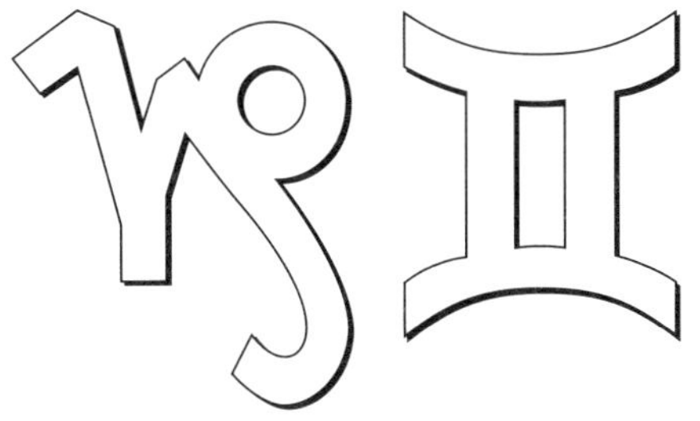

You tend to be cautious, careful and responsible in love. He enjoys a playful (even flirtatious) approach. You attract people through being responsible, dedicated and competent. He attracts people through a sense of fun, versatility and quick wits. You are probably more serious (perhaps inhibited), while he is more lighthearted. He can scatter; you know how to focus. If you can both move toward the middle, this relationship can work well. Each of you broadens the other.

VERY CHALLENGING—1

PROTECTIVE AND PARENTAL

CAPRICORN/CANCER

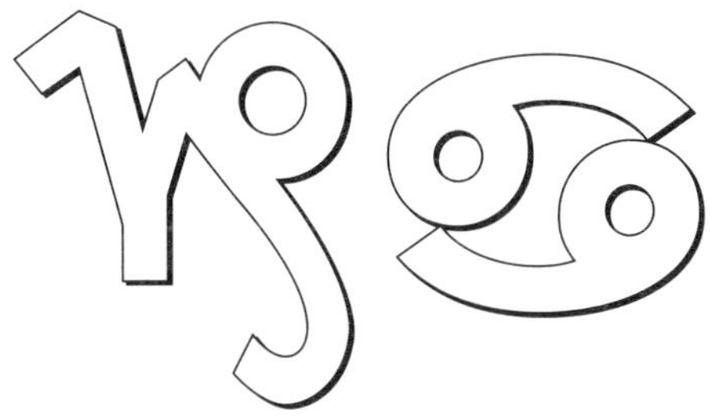

You both share a strong focus on parental archetypes — stable, appreciating security, concerned with family. Each of you is learning to balance the polarity pull between home (and family) versus work (career). Either of you may feel torn in terms of time and energy demands for the domestic scene versus the outer world. Or, you could be trying to harmonize emotional needs and practical demands. Don't set up your interactions as a pull between dominance and dependency or work and home. Do appreciate each other's dependability.

VERY COMPATIBLE—4

CAPRICORN/LEO

AMBITIOUS ACHIEVERS

Making it to the top is important to you both—enjoying recognition, respect and power. You may enjoy more slow and steady progress, while he prefers flash and dash, but status appeals to both of you. He can spark the initial attraction, the passion and the fire, but you have the capacity for staying power, for endurance and creating a lasting result. Together, you can finish as well as start in love and in life. You help to ground him; he helps to inspire your confidence.

VERY CHALLENGING—1

CAPRICORN/VIRGO

CAREFUL CONTROL

You both tend to be serious and cautious where love is concerned. The two of you may fear being hurt, controlled, rejected or criticized. Each of you is apt to have definite standards in relationships and could be picky. You can both be very responsible, hardworking and dedicated as a way of attracting a partner. You are likely to prefer a relationship with someone who is sensible, competent and willing to improve. Either of you could delay relationships (through fear), but once you commit, you will both do almost anything to make the relationship work.

COMPATIBLE—3

CAPRICORN/LIBRA

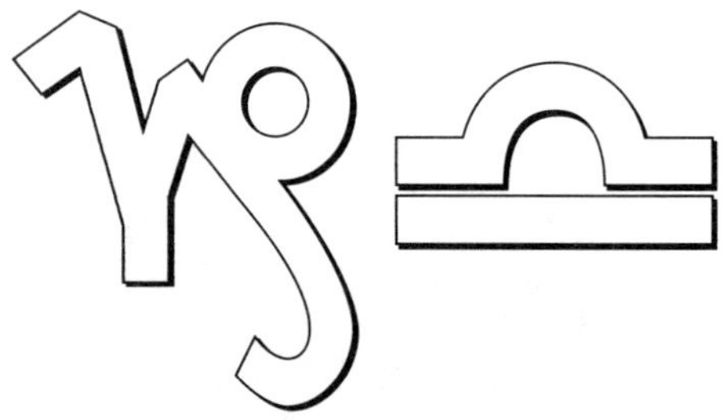

COOPERATIVE CONTROL?

You enjoy safety, predictability and stability in love. He enjoys people, beauty, sharing and teamwork. You attract through being dependable, responsible and in control. He attracts people through kindness, empathy and charm. You both are challenged to balance time and energy devoted to love and to work. You may also be torn between parenting (dominating) versus partnership (sharing) instincts. A complete life allows a little of all of them.

CHALLENGING—2

CAPRICORN/SCORPIO

COMPLETE COMMITMENT

Both of you appreciate loyalty and commitment. He seeks intense emotional experiences and uncovering secrets or hidden information in his love relationships. You seek control, safety and success, but may delay or hold back until you're sure you're not making a mistake. He may attract through a fascinating allure or seductive presence. You attract practically—with responsibility, dedication and hard work. Each of you tends to be serious about love and will think well (and often long) before committing.

COMPATIBLE—3

AUTHORITATIVE ADVENTURE

CAPRICORN/SAGITTARIUS

You tend to be serious, careful and responsible about love. He tends to be fun-loving, generous and perhaps overconfident. You don't want to make a mistake and he doesn't want less than the best. You attract through planning, respect and hard work. He attracts through generosity, openness, and a friendly spirit. He is apt to be optimistic in love; you are apt to be a pessimist. He jumps wholeheartedly into pleasure; you play it cool, not wanting to risk being hurt or disappointed. You can help him be more sensible and he can help you be more spontaneous.

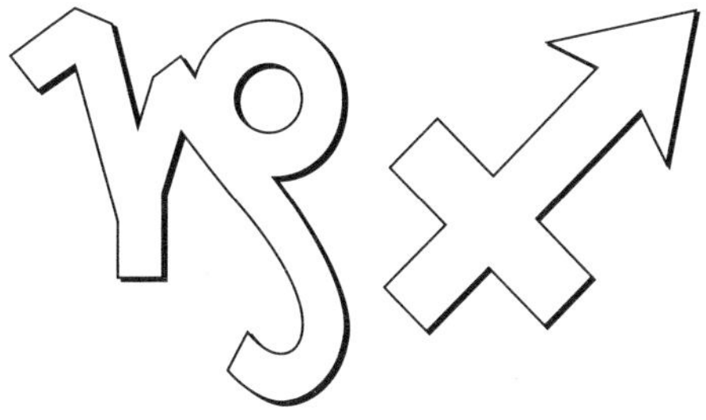

CHALLENGING—2

SERIOUS AND SENSIBLE

CAPRICORN/CAPRICORN

You both take love seriously, so may delay a bit to be sure you aren't making a mistake. Each of you appreciates a partner who is responsible, hardworking, dependable and wants to amount to something. Shared ambitions may be a bond between you. Each of you can show your love by doing practical things for your partner. Either of you might sometimes doubt, criticize, or hold back on feelings for fear of being hurt, put down, rejected or disappointed. Once you have committed, however, you both do whatever is necessary to make the relationship work.

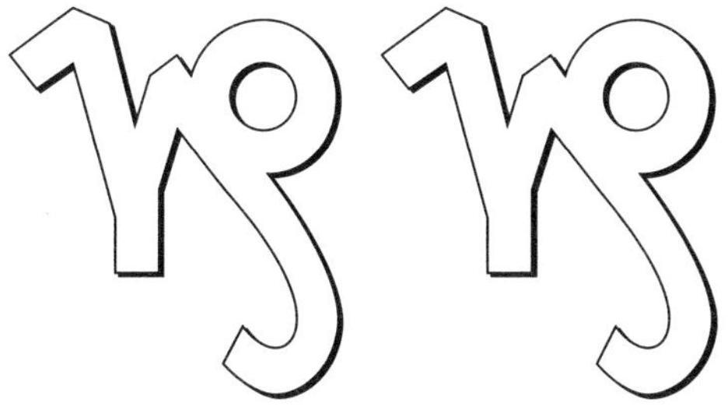

VERY COMPATIBLE—4

CONVENTIONAL OR UNCONVENTIONAL?

CAPRICORN/AQUARIUS

You enjoy safety and dependability in love, looking for a responsible, hardworking partner. He enjoys experimenting, trying new and different experiences and seeks a partner who is unusual. You attract through being dedicated and practical. He attracts through being different and original. You may view his affection as strange or offbeat and he might see you as too conventional or cautious. You can help him be more sensible about pleasure and relationships, and he can help you break the rules when needed.

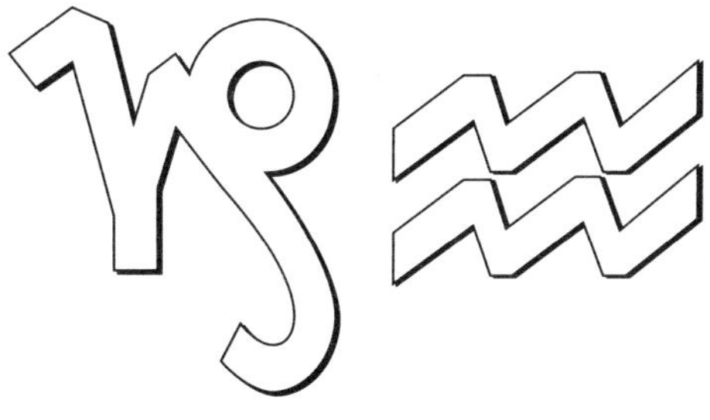

CHALLENGING—2

MASTERFUL MAGIC

CAPRICORN/PISCES

You enjoy safety, responsibility, power and success in the outer world. He enjoys the imagination, fantasy, beauty, and helping or inspiring activities. You attract others through careful planning, common sense and being a good worker. He attracts others through a magical, mysterious allure, romantic imagery or compassion and sensitivity. He can bring more dreams into your life and you can bring more practicality into his. Together, you can turn visions into reality.

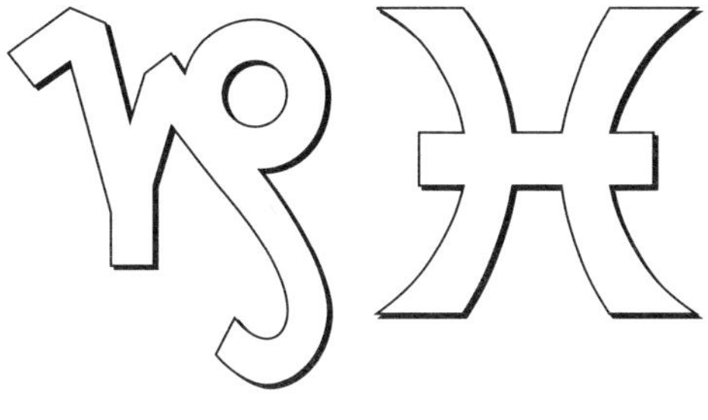

COMPATIBLE—3

AQUARIUS/ARIES

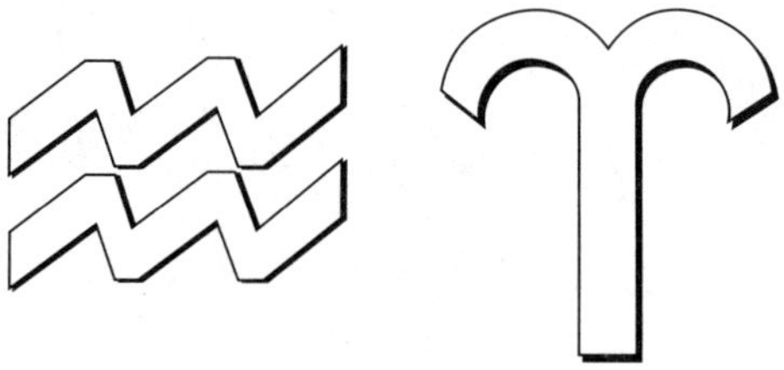

FRIENDLY FREEDOM

You love individuality, progress, and anything on the cutting edge of change. He loves spontaneity, self-expression and doing things **once**. You attract by openness, uniqueness and tolerance of any differences. He attracts by courage, directness and self-confidence. You may stimulate each other's needs for freedom. If you allow one another space, you will each bring more excitement and interest back to the relationship. Seek out the new and varied. You both thrive on challenges and new possibilities.

COMPATIBLE—3

AQUARIUS/TAURUS

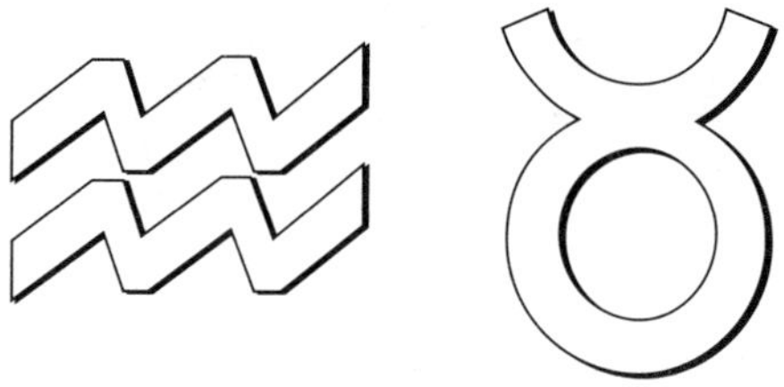

FAR-OUT OR FAMILIAR?

He enjoys dependability, familiar routines and physical pleasures, while you enjoy change, the new and different, and mental pleasures. He attracts by being sensible, loyal, comfortable and affectionate. You attract by being unique, unusual, exciting and unpredictable. The two of you might battle over security vs. risk or stability vs. change until you come to appreciate, tolerate and learn from each other's viewpoints.

CHALLENGING—2

AQUARIUS/GEMINI

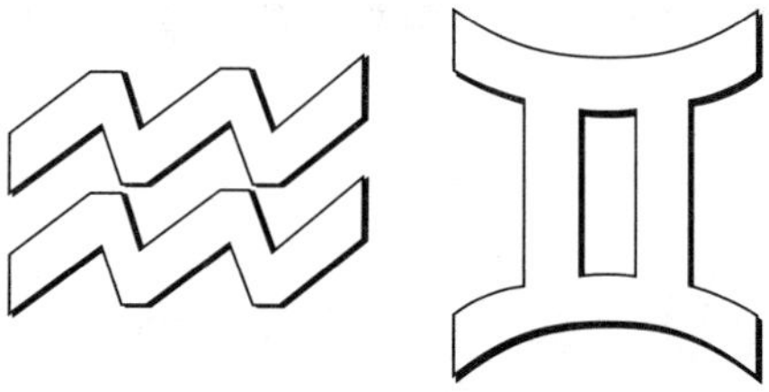

SOCIALLY STIMULATING

You both enjoy the world of thinking, talking and learning. His focus tends to be more on people and places right around, while you are drawn to the unusual, different and new. He attracts love by being expressive, fun-loving and flexible. You attract love by being progressive, original and a free thinker. Each of you is likely to stimulate the other to new ideas and new experiences. You can enjoy social activities together, encouraging one another to expand your intellectual horizons.

COMPATIBLE—3

AQUARIUS/CANCER

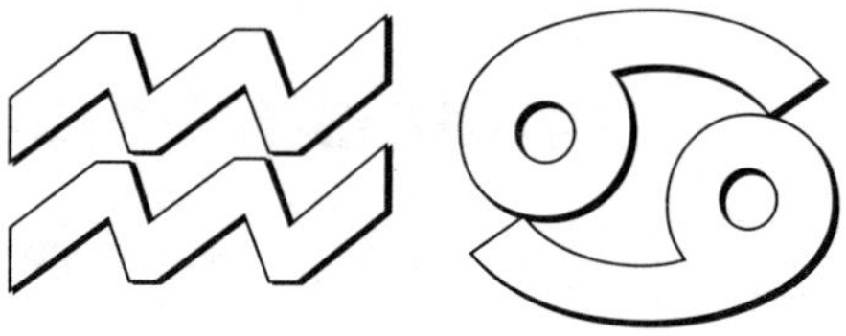

ERRATIC EMPATHY

He enjoys food, family and feeling safe and secure. You enjoy friends, new experiences and anything unusual or a bit different. You attract by being open-minded, bright, original and equalitarian. He attracts people with warmth, protectiveness and fidelity. The two of you could feel torn between stability and risk-taking or family and the wider world, unless you learn to compromise. Together, you can work on balancing logic and emotions, sensitivity and detachment.

VERY CHALLENGING—1

DETACHED AND DYNAMIC

AQUARIUS/LEO

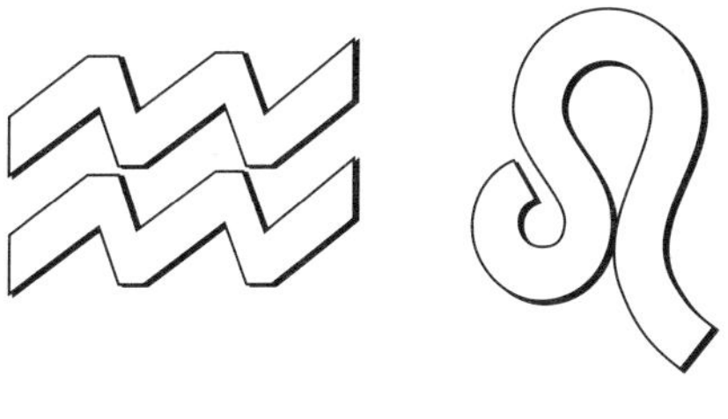

You enjoy the world of the mind, new possibilities and freedom. He enjoys drama, being noticed, and excitement of all kinds. You attract through originality, being fair and opening people up to new ideas and new experiences. He attracts through magnetism, sex appeal and exuberance. Opposites in many ways, you probably feel a natural pull toward one another. Don't get pulled between logic and emotion. Do allow your objectivity to moderate his extravagance and his sense of fun to enliven your rationality.

VERY COMPATIBLE—4

ORGANIZED ORIGINALITY

AQUARIUS/VIRGO

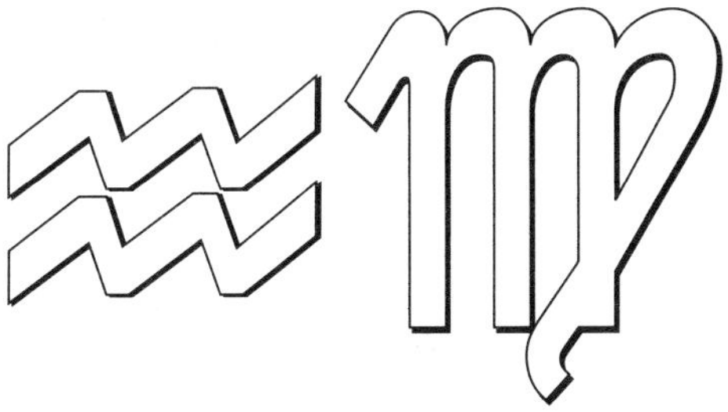

You enjoy mental stimulation, open-mindedness and exploring the unusual. He enjoys precision, doing a good job, and organizing things. You attract others because you are tolerant and willing to be friends with anyone. He attracts through dependability, helpfulness, and a practical attitude. He may seem a bit picky, cool, or serious to you. You might seem a bit too independent or unconventional to him. You see more the overview, while he focuses more on details. You are likely to learn much from one another and can stimulate each other's thinking.

VERY CHALLENGING—1

NATURAL NETWORKERS

AQUARIUS/LIBRA

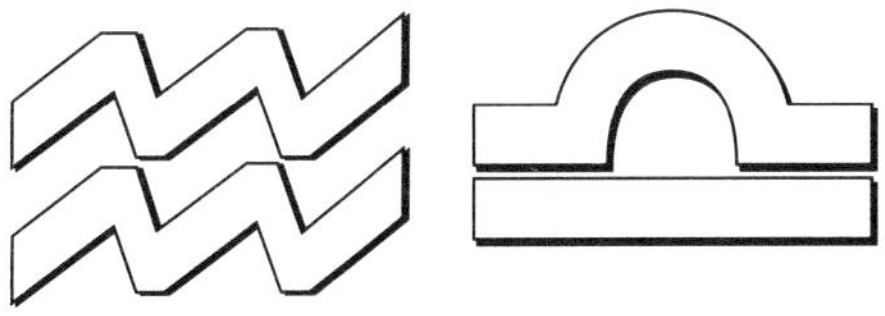

The mind can be a real common ground between the two of you. You both probably enjoy getting stimulating ideas from another person. He attracts through being charming, sharing and cooperative. You attract through an independent spirit, openness and a quick mind. He may want more of a commitment, while you are still on a "friends" basis. The more you communicate and find common ground, the better your relationship flows.

COMPATIBLE—3

SOCIABLE OR SECRETIVE?

AQUARIUS/SCORPIO

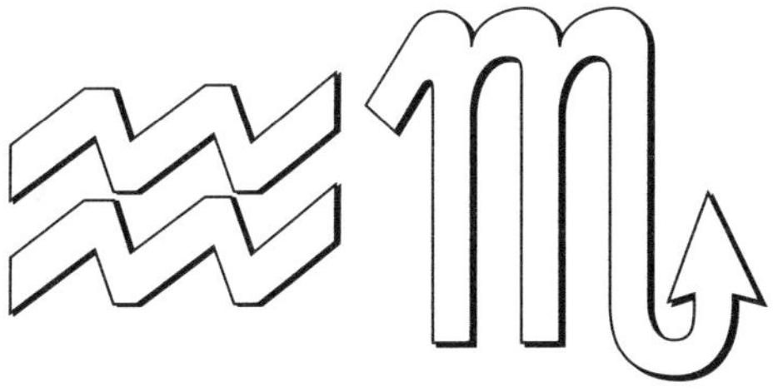

You enjoy discussions, friends, new experiences and anything unusual. He enjoys intense (often sexual) encounters and privacy. You attract through being original and a bit unconventional. He attracts through being fascinating, seductive and powerful. He could be more jealous or possessive than you, and you may need more friends and social contact than he. Compromise allows you to balance intensity and a need for space. Practice creating intimacy within an atmosphere of freedom.

CHALLENGING—2

AQUARIUS/SAGITTARIUS

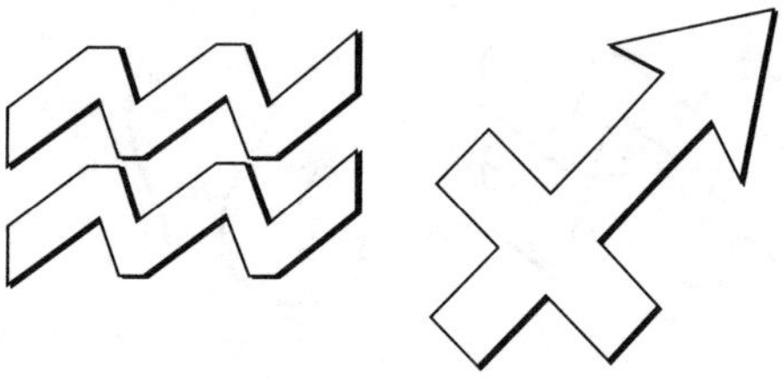

INTELLIGENTLY INDEPENDENT

You both enjoy people, independence and new experiences. He might be a bit more expressive or impulsive in terms of love, while you can be more objective and calm. But you appreciate each other's individuality and enjoy being with someone who is a bit unusual. He attracts through generosity, being friendly, optimistic and witty. You attract through being unconventional, tolerant, progressive and intelligent. You both need space in your love relationships, so would not be a "do-everything-together" couple. You enjoy sharing new ideas, people and experiences.

COMPATIBLE—3

AQUARIUS/CAPRICORN

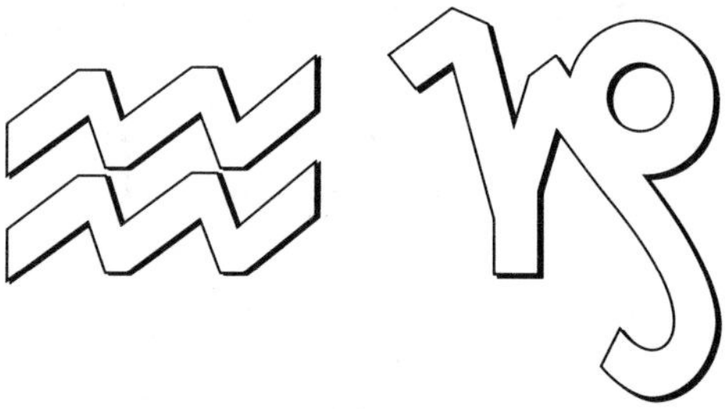

CONVENTIONAL/ UNCONVENTIONAL?

You enjoy experimenting, trying new and different experiences and need a partner who is unique and perhaps a bit unusual. He enjoys safety and dependability in love, looking for a responsible, hardworking partner. You attract through being different, open-minded and friendly. He attracts through being dedicated, responsible and practical. You may feel he is controlling, inhibited or too cautious about affection, while he views you as too independent or offbeat. He can help you be more sensible about relationships and you can help him break the rules when needed.

CHALLENGING—2

AQUARIUS/AQUARIUS

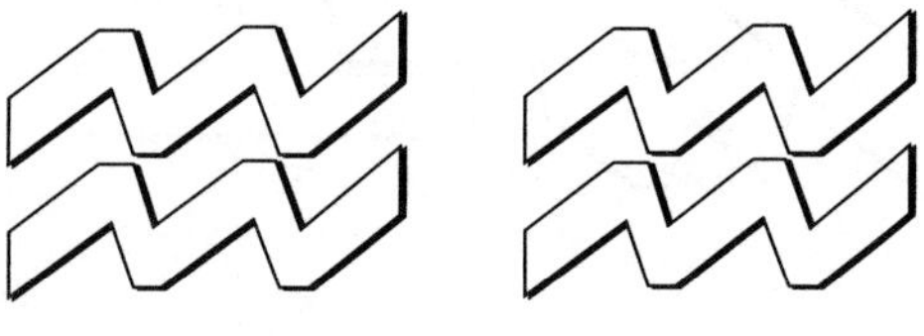

UNUSUAL & UNCONVENTIONAL

Both of you enjoy unusual associations. You appreciate a partner who is bright, friendly, open-minded and different in some way. Each of you needs some space in love relationships, so don't expect to share everything. You attract through experimenting, talking, bringing new ideas and new experiences to one another. You may share humanitarian causes, groups, networking activities, an interest in technology, or anything progressive, futuristic or unconventional. You can broaden each other's perspectives, stimulate each other's thinking.

VERY COMPATIBLE—4

AQUARIUS/PISCES

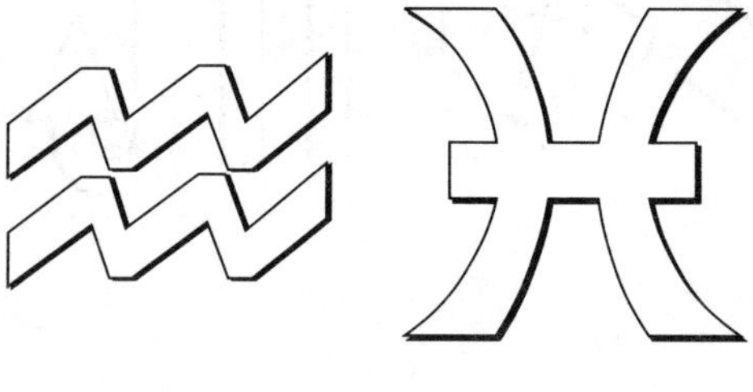

FREE AND FANCIFUL

You enjoy openness, friends, mental stimulation and new experiences. He enjoys privacy, the imagination and fantasy, and anything artistic, idealistic or compassionate. You attract through being tolerant, unusual, and interesting. He attracts through being mysterious, sensitive, and willing to help or inspire. You may share an appreciation for humanitarian or idealistic causes.

CHALLENGING—2

IMMEDIATE INSPIRATION

PISCES/ARIES

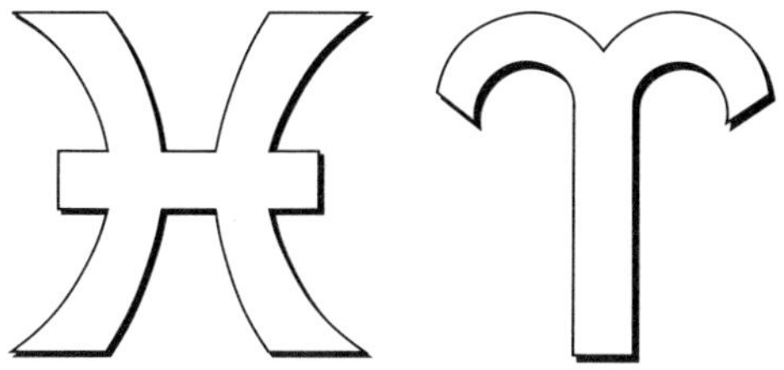

You love compassion, romance and inspirational activities. He loves strength, immediacy and exciting activities. You attract through empathy, idealism, artistic leanings or a desire to heal and rescue others. He attracts through courage, independence, assertion and directness. You two might polarize between self-assertion and self-sacrifice. You are learning to blend pleasure from personal gratification with pleasure from helping, healing or creating beauty. Optimally, you encourage each other's personal power as well as caring concern.

CHALLENGING—2

DEPENDABLE DREAMS

PISCES/TAURUS

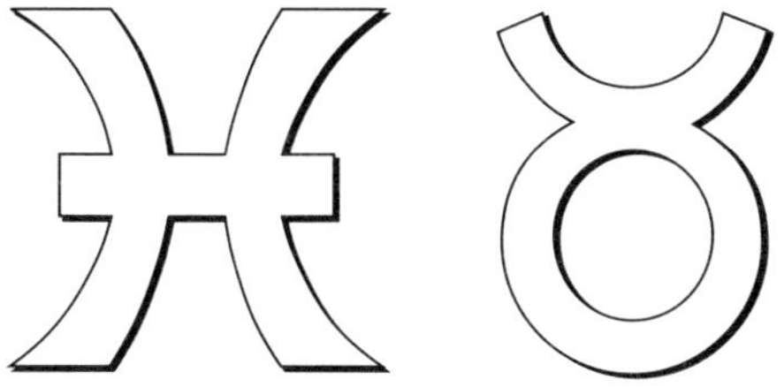

You enjoy inspiration, beauty in any form, and the world of the spirit and imagination. He enjoys practicality, tangible beauty and monetary success. You attract through sensitivity, mystery, compassion, or a vivid imagination. He attracts through dependability, sensuality and financial security. You may be more romantic, while he is more pragmatic in terms of pleasures. The two of you can make beautiful music together if you keep a balance between realism and idealism. You may share a love of nature.

COMPATIBLE—3

INTELLECTUAL IDEALISM

PISCES/GEMINI

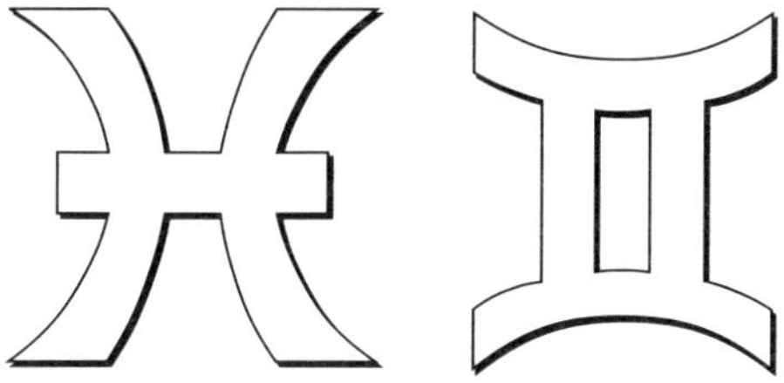

You enjoy the inner world of imagination, romance, fantasy and spiritual ideas. He enjoys the outer world of concepts, rationality and logic. You attract people through being compassionate, idealistic and magical. He attracts people through being open, flexible and eager to learn and experience. He can be quite fun-loving, flirtatious and casual. You tend to be more sensitive, (sometimes easily hurt) and mystical. He can help you face reality; you can help him envision higher potentials and seek the best.

CHALLENGING—2

COMPASSIONATE CARETAKERS

PISCES/CANCER

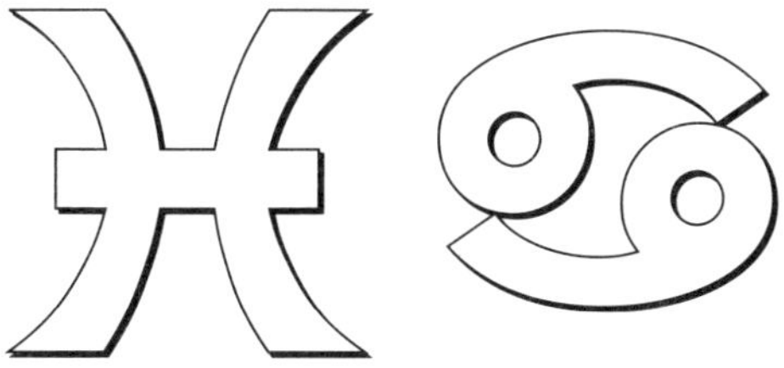

Both of you tend to be deeply feeling people, but will not reveal your emotions to the world. You may be able to sense what is going on inside the other. Each of you can enjoy compassion and may be a natural caretaker. Sometimes either of you might sacrifice or give too much in relationships. If you create trust in one another, you can make a deep commitment. Taking turns taking care of each other is the best bet.

COMPATIBLE—3

PISCES/LEO

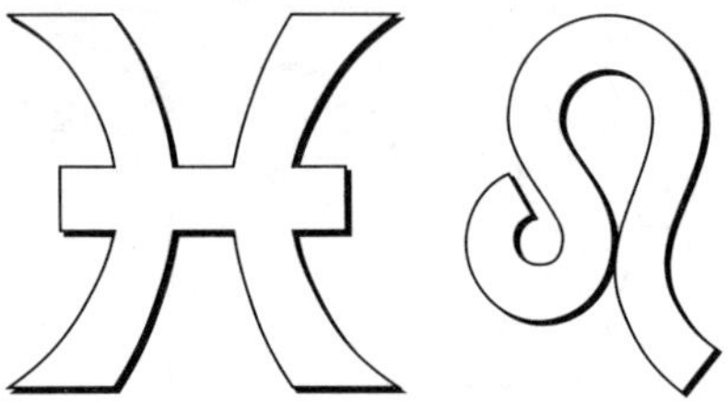

ROYAL ROMANCE

Both of you have a strong streak of romance in your souls, but he tends to be open, expressive and eager, while you tend to be more inward and hidden. He attracts through direct charisma, stage presence and enthusiasm. You attract through mystery, imagination, fantasies and (perhaps) rescuing or being rescued. He can help you to become more outgoing and sociable. You can aid him in moderating his impulses, and toning down his larger-than-life tendencies. You two can be magical together.

VERY CHALLENGING—1

PISCES/VIRGO

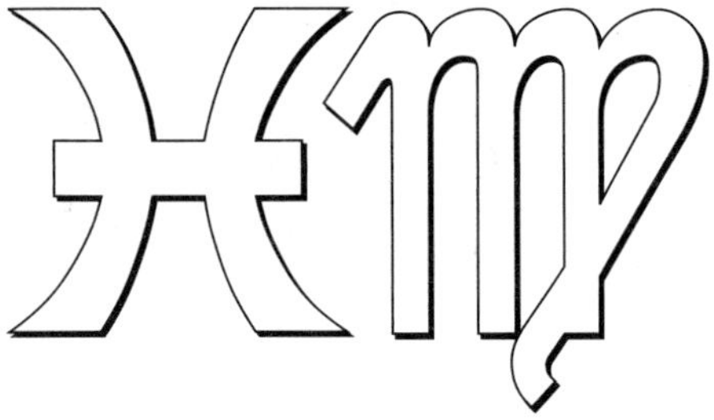

POETICALLY PRACTICAL

The two of you are facing a polarity: the real versus the ideal. You both may feel torn between love of fantasy, magic, illusion, beauty and idealism versus love of practicality, critical judgment, focused attention, productive work and an awareness of the way life (and love) really are. Don't take opposite sides and fight. Do combine your dreams. Share a mystical, rose-colored glasses vision and find ways to make your dreams come true together.

VERY COMPATIBLE—4

PISCES/LIBRA

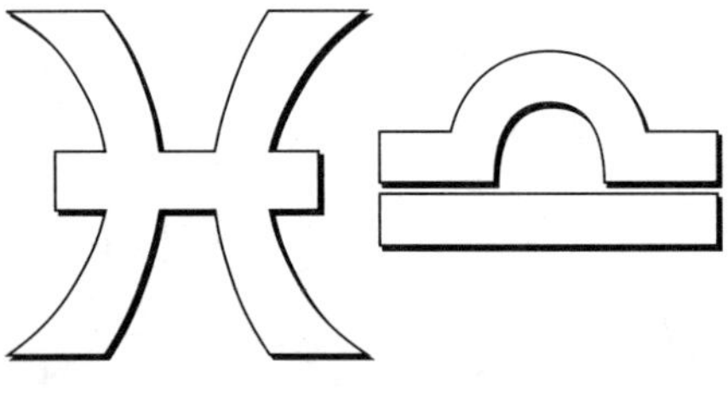

BLISSFUL BEAUTY

Beauty or love of harmony might draw the two of you together. You love grace, sensitivity, and have a desire to rescue or protect others. He loves balance, justice, and beauty in things and people. He may prefer a wider social circle, while you enjoy a bit more privacy. You both are motivated to create a flowing, pleasant relationship. Don't avoid facing unpleasant facts, but do find ways to bring more love, caring and compassion into the world and into your relationship.

VERY CHALLENGING—1

PISCES/SCORPIO

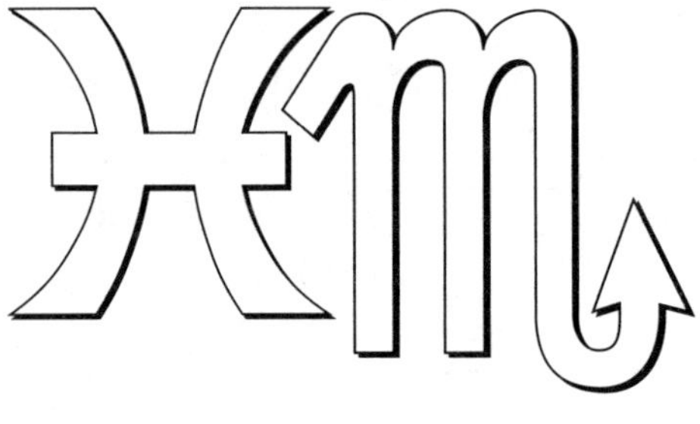

PRIVATE POETRY

You both can be empathic and tune into those you love. He enjoys challenges, secrets and emotional depths. You enjoy beauty, nature and the world of the imagination. He attracts by being sensual, powerful and seductive. You attract through being kind, eager to rescue (or needing assistance), and idealistic. The two of you are likely to respect each other's needs for privacy and some time alone. You will, at times, understand each other without any words.

COMPATIBLE—3

SEEKING THE SUBLIME

PISCES/SAGITTARIUS

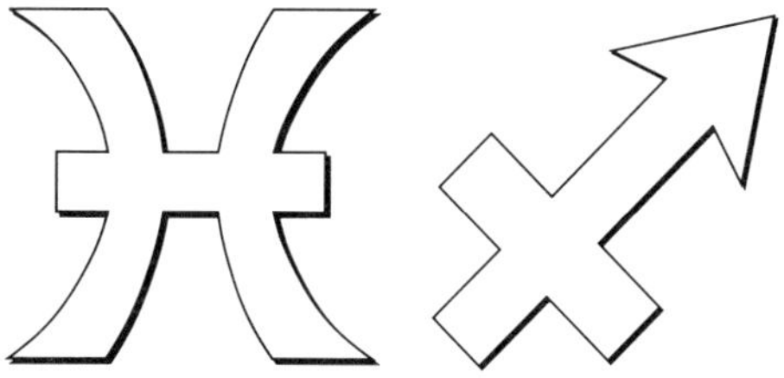

You are both a bit idealistic about love and may yearn for more than is possible. You tend to seek someone sensitive, intuitive, artistic, imaginative or compassionate. He tends to seek someone bright, fun-loving, adventurous, generous and outgoing. Either of you can be a bit in love with love, expecting a lot of a partner. You both find it easy to appreciate the best in one another, but must guard against donning rose-colored glasses or feeling hurt and disappointed when your partner turns out to be only human. A love of nature or any activities which help, uplift, inspire or assist people could be a strong bond between you.

CHALLENGING—2

MAGICAL MASTERY

PISCES/CAPRICORN

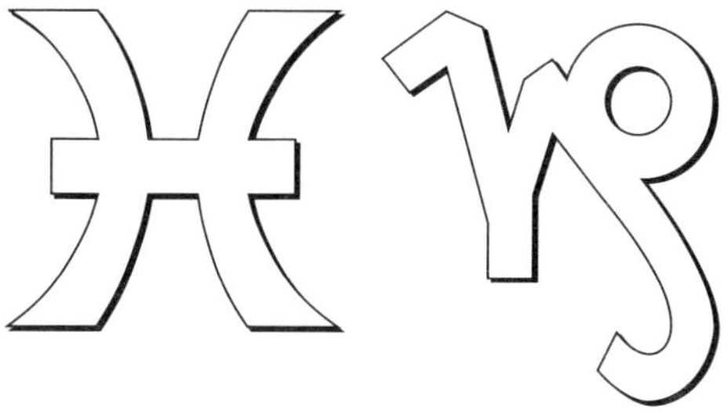

You enjoy the imagination, fantasy, romance, beauty and helping or inspiring activities. He enjoys safety, responsibility, power, and success in the outer world. You attract others through a magical, mysterious air, compassion or a healing spirit. He attracts others through careful planning, common sense and being a good worker. You can bring more dreams and romance into his life and he can bring more practicality and common sense into yours. Together, you can turn visions into reality.

COMPATIBLE—3

FANCIFUL AND FREE

PISCES/AQUARIUS

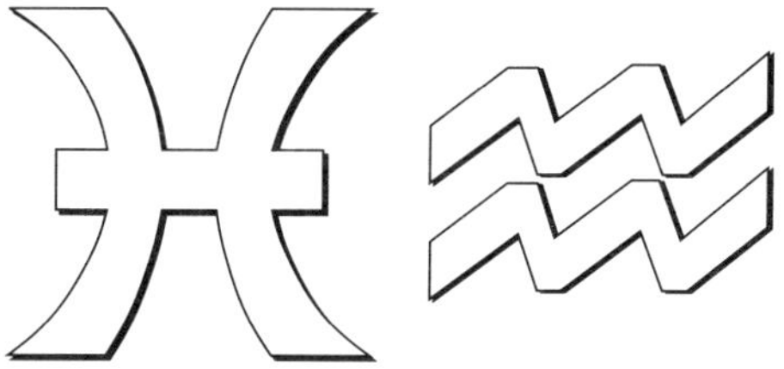

You enjoy art, beauty, mystery, nature, spiritual ideals, romance or idealistic images. He enjoys openness, friends, mental stimulation and new experiences. You attract through being sensitive, imaginative, and willing to help and assist others. He attracts through being tolerant, unusual, and interesting. He may be out in the world more, with you preferring more private time. You might share an appreciation for humanitarian causes and enjoy activities which contribute to society.

CHALLENGING—2

INSPIRED INTIMACY

PISCES/PISCES

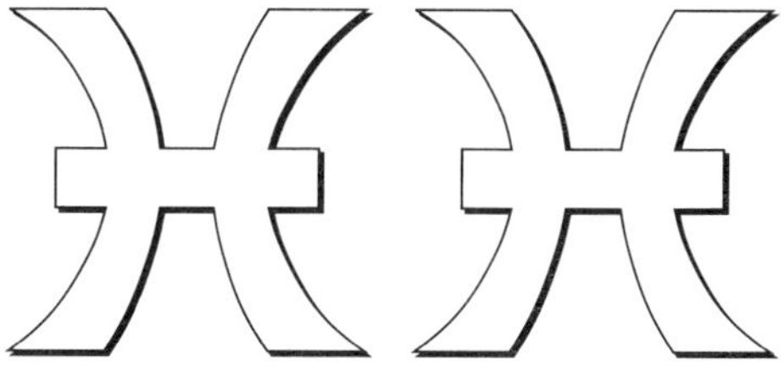

Fellow romantics, each of you is capable of being in love with love or seeking that "perfect" ideal partner who does not exist! Either of you could don rose-colored glasses and be hurt or disappointed when you see your partner more clearly later. Or, you might prefer fantasy to reality in terms of love relationships. If you share your quest for something inspirational, you may enjoy sharing beauty, nature, healing or helping activities with one another. You might find it easy to see each other's highest potentials.

VERY COMPATIBLE—4

MARS

Mars represents our basic instincts, the qualities we express naturally, without thinking. Mars is also a key to one's sexual drive and the way we tend to handle anger—along with likely targets of our anger. Mars symbolizes our definition of masculinity—both what men see admirable or masculine in other men and what women tend to see as masculine (and be attracted by) in a man. (Because certain placements of Mars do not fit traditional stereotypes about masculinity, it may be harder for men with those placements to express the sensitive, tender, romantic or emotional sides of their nature. They may tend to deny those qualities and be extra-macho trying to overcome a basic part of themselves. However, they can come to accept a different perspective on their maleness and learn to take pride in their more inward, feeling tendencies.) Mars is also a key to where we tend to put our energy.

First read the shorthand description for the sign **your** Mars is in. Then, compare it with the shorthand description for the Mars sign of your partner. Next, read the paragraph which discusses how the two of you might interact with one another. Each combination is also designated as either very compatible, compatible, challenging or very challenging. (These rate as 4-3-2-1 on our **Compatibility Scale**.)

> Look to your partner's Mars sign to discover what will turn him on. Play to the qualities of his Mars sign and he'll be energized and excited.

MARS IN ARIES: THE ACTIVE LOVER

Basic Instincts: firm, active, direct, competitive, vigorous
Sex Drive: immediate, quick response, "conquest" appeals, ardent
Handling of Anger: quick to anger, quick to forget
Targets (Irritation): anything, but particularly limits to personal freedom
Energy Directed toward: personal action, excitement, challenges, competition
Image of Masculinity: "macho," strong, aggressive, forceful, confident, self-reliant

MARS IN TAURUS: THE SENSUALIST

Basic Instincts: steady, stubborn, deliberate, determined
Sex Drive: sensual, savoring, slow to build but enduring
Handling of Anger: slow to anger, generally easygoing
Targets (Irritation): money, possessions, sensuality
Energy Directed toward: gratification, earning and owning, comfort
Image of Masculinity: financially secure, stable, sexual stamina, dependable

MARS IN GEMINI: MIND GAMES

Basic Instincts: flexible, clever, adaptable, intellectual
Sex Drive: visuals important, mind must be turned on, flirtatious
Handling of Anger: may aggress with words (biting, ironic, sarcastic), arguments or rationalize anger away
Targets (Irritation): language, ideas, relatives
Energy Directed toward: communication, eyes, hands, tongue, mental activity
Image of Masculinity: intelligent, versatile, articulate, tall, agile, quick-witted

MARS IN CANCER: THE CARING LOVER

Basic Instincts: indirect (may be passive-aggressive), shy, sensitive
Sex Drive: affected by insecurities, may mix sex and nurturing, prefers commitment
Handling of Anger: temper outbursts, may hold back feelings, then blow
Targets (Irritation): home, family, vulnerabilities
Energy Directed toward: domestic matters, preservation, emotional safety
Image of Masculinity: protective, patriotic, dedicated to family, good provider

MARS IN LEO: THE EXCITING LOVER

Basic Instincts: majestic, pushy, arrogant, royal, dynamic, charismatic
Sex Drive: joyful, exciting, enthusiastic (occasionally self-centered), zestful
Handling of Anger: quick to respond, quick to forgive
Targets (Irritation): lovers, children, creative products, speculation
Energy Directed toward: gaining attention, limelight, and positive feedback
Image of Masculinity: flamboyant, exciting, respected, famous, sexy, admired

MARS IN VIRGO: THE SENSIBLE LOVER

Basic Instincts: analytical, modest, helpful, critical, hardworking
Sex Drive: performance focus may inhibit, want to do it "right", dedicated
Handling of Anger: nit-pick, criticize, fix things, work rather than confront
Targets (Irritation): duties, service, colleagues, health matters
Energy Directed toward: repairs, competence, efficiency, productivity
Image of Masculinity: organized, practical, hardworking, sensible, reliable.

MARS IN LIBRA: THE LOVER OF BEAUTY

Basic Instincts: sociable, cooperative, indecisive, competitive
Sex Drive: teamwork focus, may be too refined, can be quite loving
Handling of Anger: "smiling" anger, tact covers anger, attracts anger in others
Targets (Irritation): partners (other people in general), litigation
Energy Directed toward: relationships, beauty, balancing, equalizing
Image of Masculinity: sociable, well-dressed, civilized, refined, courtly

MARS IN SCORPIO: THE PASSIONATE POSSESSOR

Basic Instincts: compulsive, back-door strategies, willful, intense
Sex Drive: passionate, intense, all-or-nothing extremes, seductive
Handling of Anger: may brood or be explosive, slow to forgive/forget
Targets (Irritation): mates, handling of joint resources and shared pleasures
Energy Directed toward: joint possessions and pleasures, gaining power and mastery
Image of Masculinity: powerful, sexy, tough, much below the surface, forceful

MARS IN SAGITTARIUS: THE WORLD'S GREATEST LOVER

Basic Instincts: rash, headstrong, self-confident, "God is on my side"
Sex Drive: eager, great expectations, athletic, gusto, exuberant
Handling of Anger: quick to respond, quick to forget
Targets (Irritation): ideas, ideals, ethical/moral issues
Energy Directed toward: exploration, seeking enlightenment, understanding, good times
Image of Masculinity: witty, playful, upbeat, generous, eager to go places and do things

MARS IN CAPRICORN: THE RESPONSIBLE LOVER

Basic Instincts: either anxious and insecure OR in charge, dominant, successful
Sex Drive: performance anxiety possible, great endurance, prefers to be in control
Handling of Anger: slow to anger, practical about expression (can do "stiff upper lip" very well)
Targets (Irritation): authority figures, bureaucracies, profession
Energy Directed toward: ambition, career, contribution to society or status
Image of Masculinity: responsible, successful, mature, dignified, authoritative

MARS IN AQUARIUS: THE FREEWHEELING LOVER

Basic Instincts: eccentric, nonconforming, expressed mentally/verbally
Sex Drive: quirky, individualistic, fed by the unusual, experimental
Handling of Anger: detached, intellectualized, rationalized
Targets (Irritation): progress, the new, equal opportunity issues, friends
Energy Directed toward: anything on the cutting edge of change
Image of Masculinity: intelligent, progressive, unusual, independent, forthright

MARS IN PISCES: THE DREAM LOVER

Basic Instincts: empathic, compassionate, tender, kind, tends to rescue
Sex Drive: magical, illusory, escapist or inspirational, romantic
Handling of Anger: may repress anger, more likely to hurt self than others
Targets (Irritation): dreams, visions, fantasies, ideals, faith (or lack of)
Energy Directed toward: quest for ideal love, beauty, transcendence ("happily ever after")
Image of Masculinity: creative, artistic, humanitarian, spiritual, romantic, peaceful

MARS PAIRS

ARIES/ARIES

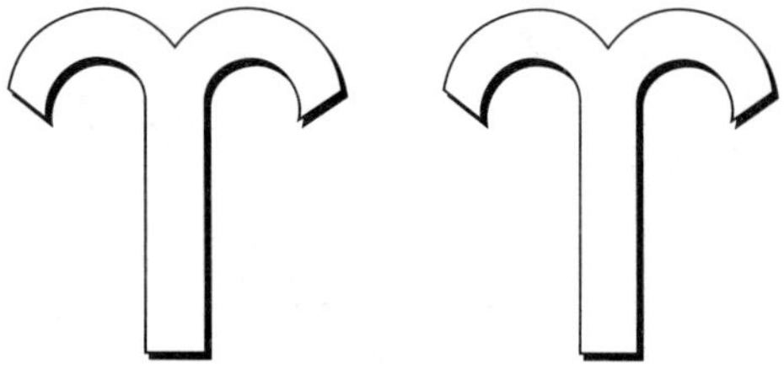

HELLO, I LOVE YOU. (WON'T YOU TELL ME YOUR NAME?)

Both of you fall in lust quickly. Responsive and ready for excitement, you may enjoy the thrill of pursuit. Since freedom is also important, either of you might lose interest once you've made a conquest. Eager and enthusiastic, you easily fan the flames of desire in one another.
VERY COMPATIBLE—4

ARIES/TAURUS

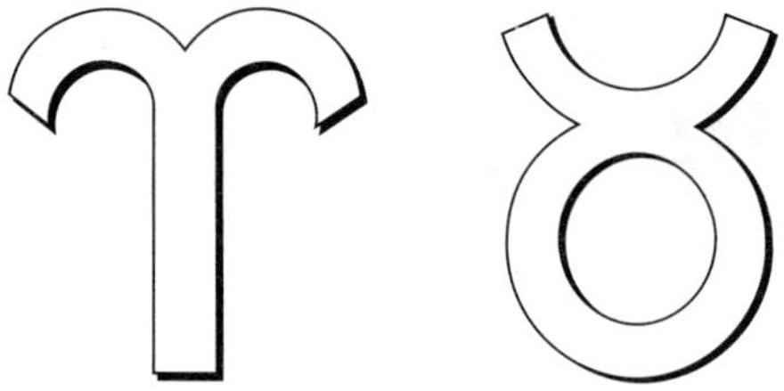

I WANT YOUR HANDS ON ME

You know what you want and can respond quickly. He tends to be more deliberate. You can act on impulse, while he waits to be sure. His desire for comfort and the familiar may clash with your quest for excitement and new experiences, but your passion feeds his sensuality.
CHALLENGING—2

ARIES/GEMINI

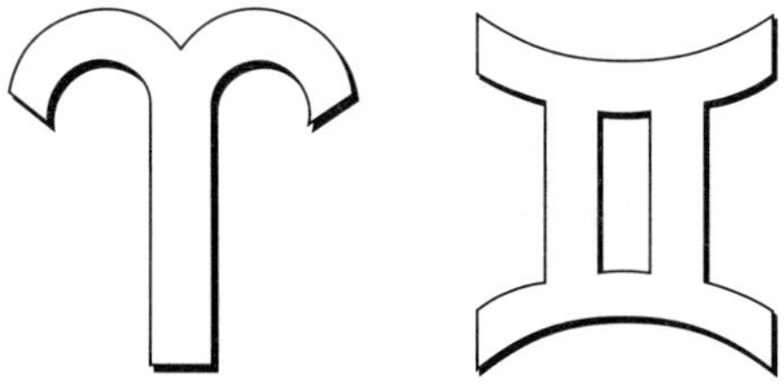

FLY ME TO THE MOON

You both can react rapidly, but you tend to be more direct and immediate, while he may prefer to think or talk. Newness and variety appeal to you both, so you can share excitement when trying out alternatives. You bring adventures to him; he brings ideas to you.
COMPATIBLE—3

ARIES/CANCER

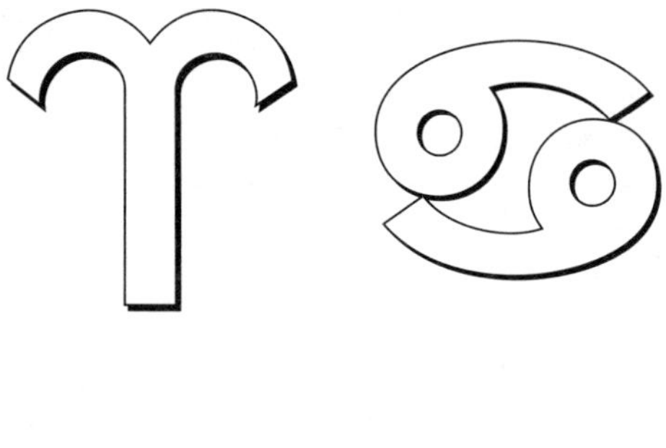

STRANGERS IN THE NIGHT

You are ready to go, and he's carefully checking to make sure this is a safe step. You're direct and open, he's more inward. Your irritations are quickly aired and quickly forgotten; he may brood over hurts. Your passion can fuel his protectiveness; his nurturing feeds your excitement.
CHALLENGING—2

MAXIMUM OVERDRIVE

ARIES/LEO

Both of you enjoy excitement, thrills and the rush of adrenaline. Eager to move, explore and enjoy, you can really turn each other on. You feed each other's fire, with an urge to try, to risk, to adventure. His charisma energizes you; your openness excites him.

COMPATIBLE—3

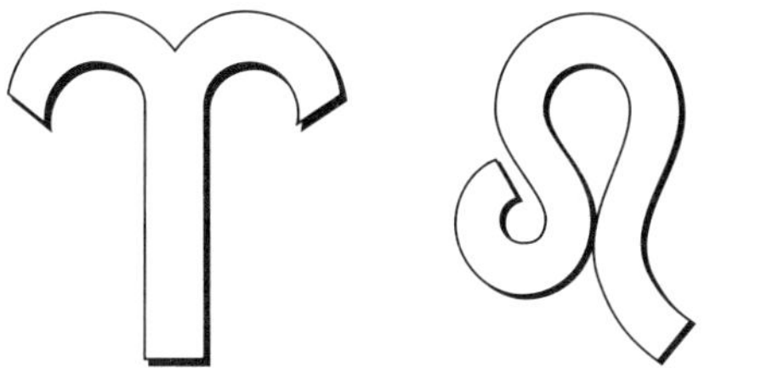

MORNING HAS BROKEN

ARIES/VIRGO

You are more eager, impulsive and spontaneous, while he is more careful, checking every little detail. You prefer once over lightly, while he wants everything just so. His expertise and regard for doing things well can enhance your excitement, and you can help him let go more.

VERY CHALLENGING—1

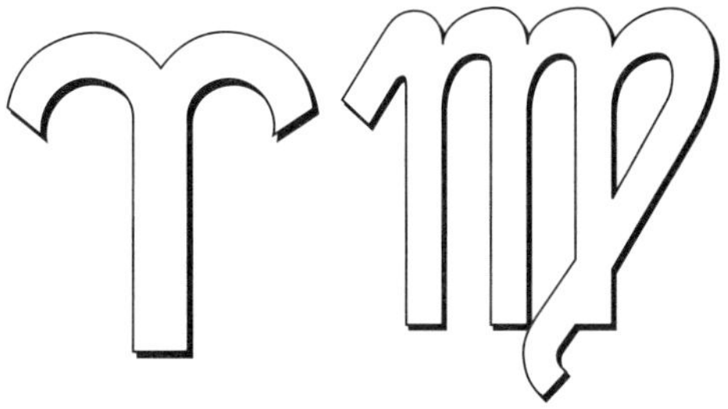

CHEEK TO CHEEK

ARIES/LIBRA

You two have the natural attraction of opposites: one who acts and one who reacts; one who is direct and blunt and one who is tactful and diplomatic. Think of your relationship as a dance where each can have a turn at leading (and following). Balance brings harmony and sexual satisfaction to you both.

VERY COMPATIBLE—4

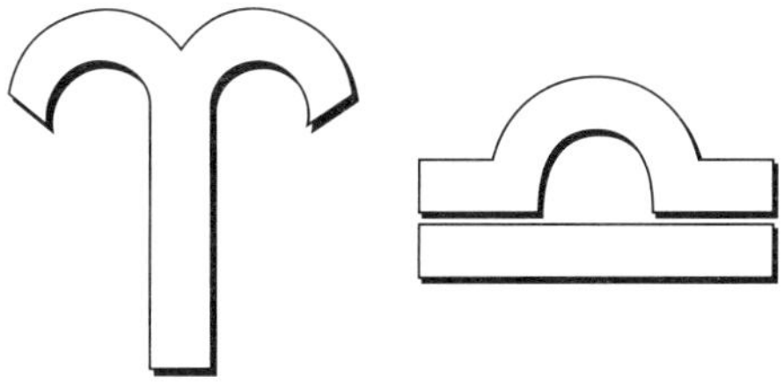

YOU SEND ME

ARIES/SCORPIO

You are open, honest and direct. He takes back door routes and underground ways to get what he wants. You are spontaneous (sometimes impulsive). He is controlled (sometimes secretive). Yet you both have a high level of passion. Each of you can feed the intense desire of the other.

VERY CHALLENGING—1

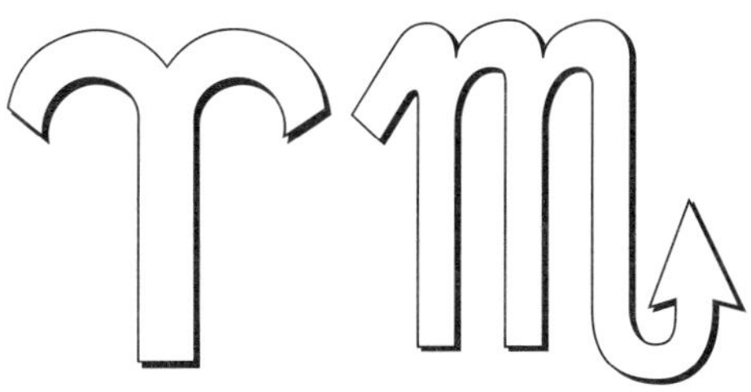

ARIES/SAGITTARIUS

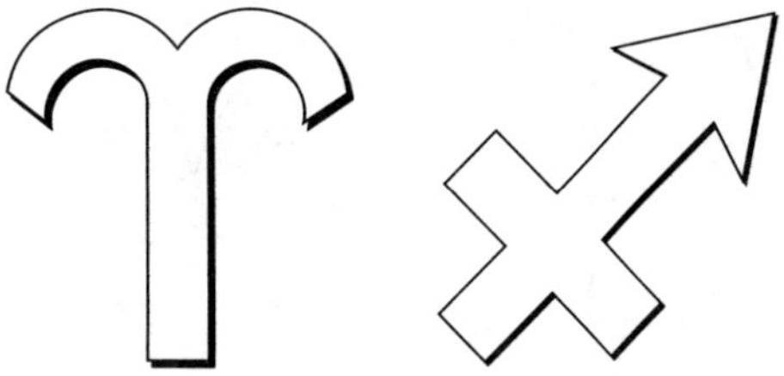

LOVE IS A MANY SPLENDORED THING

Both of you have an adventurous, freedom-loving streak. You need to go places and do things. Activity feeds your excitement. You may also encourage each other's impulsivity and tendency to take on too much. You keep desire alive with fresh, new and exciting experiences.

COMPATIBLE—3

ARIES/CAPRICORN

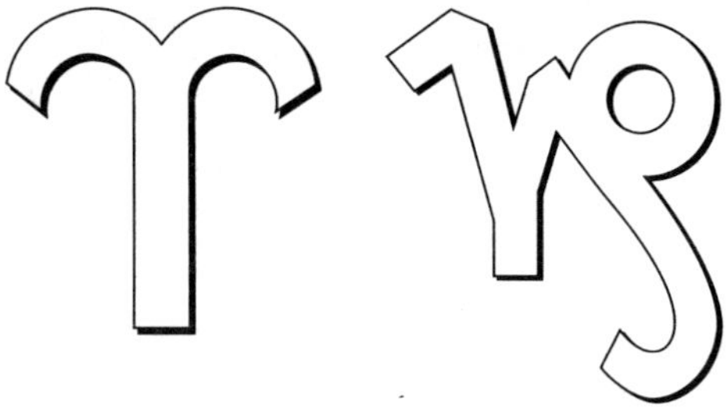

LET'S CALL THE WHOLE THING OFF

You are spontaneous and eager. He is cautious and controlled. You want to do your own thing. He wants authority and control. You can help him to cut loose occasionally, and he can help you to plan ahead when advisable. You may fan the initial spark of desire, but he has great staying power.

CHALLENGING—2

ARIES/AQUARIUS

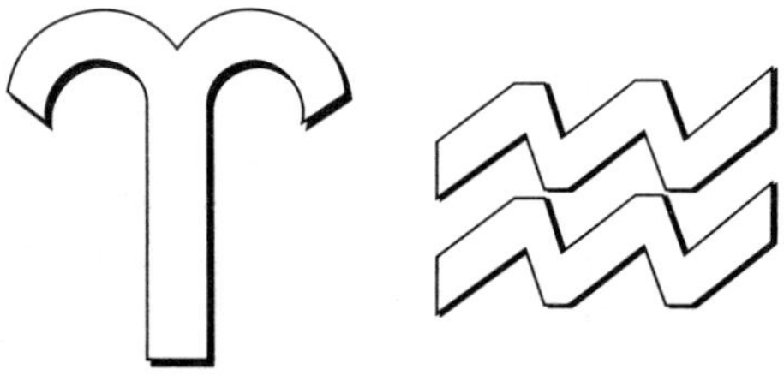

IF EVER I WOULD LEAVE YOU

Each of you tends to be an independent operator, so respect each other's need for space. You both enjoy new experiences, and get bored with repetition. You can encourage him to get into his body and out of his head, and he can help you to sometimes think first and act later.

COMPATIBLE—3

ARIES/PISCES

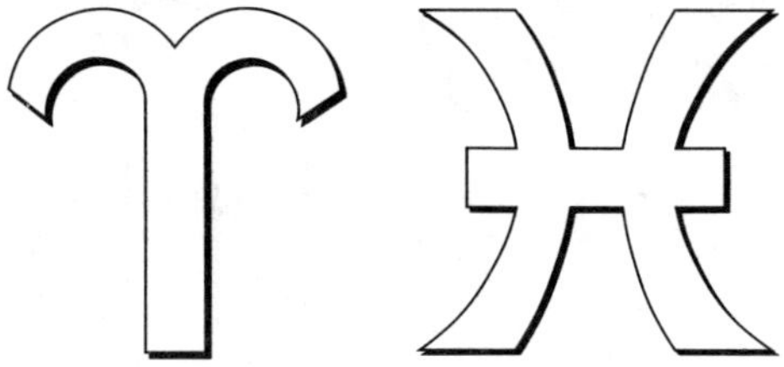

LOVE IS A ROSE

You're eager to march into action and he's admiring the colors of the sunset. You're direct and open; he's sensitive and doesn't share everything he's feeling. You can turn him on and help him find more excitement in life. He can help you stop and smell the flowers.

CHALLENGING—2

I WANT YOUR HANDS ON ME

TAURUS/ARIES

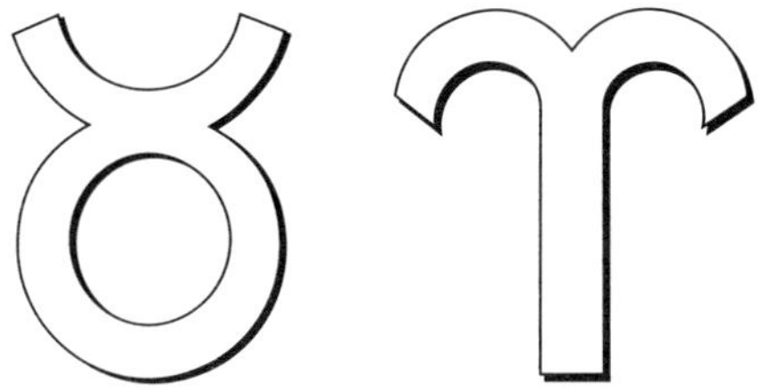

He knows what he wants and can respond quickly. You may want more time to warm up. He can act on impulse, while you wait to be sure. Your desire for comfort and the familiar may clash with his quest for excitement and new experiences, but your sensuality feeds his passion.

CHALLENGING—2

I WANT A LOVER WITH A SLOW HAND

TAURUS/TAURUS

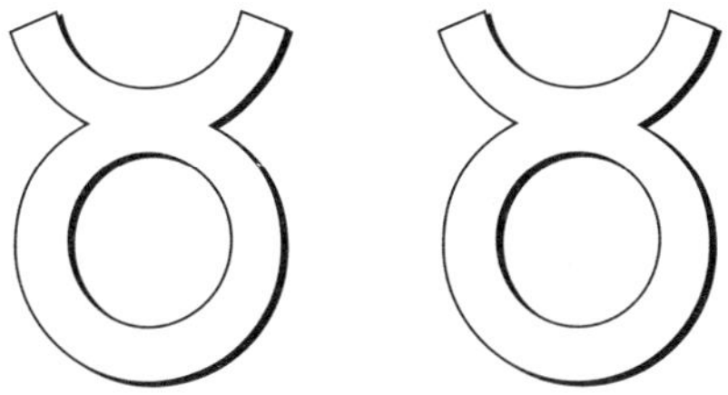

Since you both appreciate textures and how things feel, you can give great hugs, back rubs and caresses. Naturally affectionate, you want to keep each other comfortable and satisfied. You probably enjoy sharing pleasure from food, drink, possessions or any form of sensuality.

VERY COMPATIBLE—4

PEOPLE WILL SAY WE'RE IN LOVE

TAURUS/GEMINI

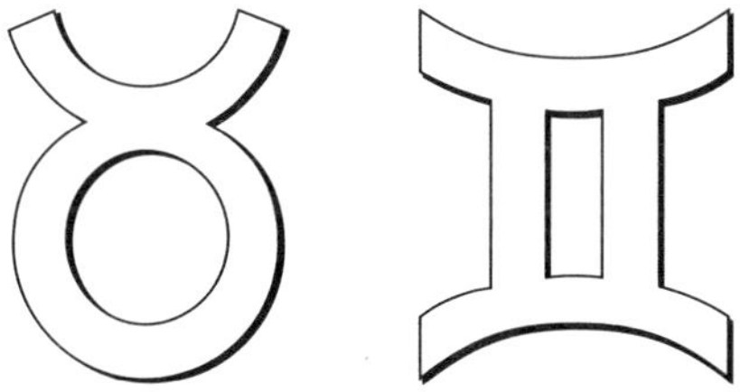

Your sexual style is slow, sensual and savoring. His responses are quicker and more flexible. Words and visual stimulation turn him on. Hugs and caresses are vital for you. He can encourage you to try new experiences and you can nourish his appreciation of comfort and familiarity.

CHALLENGING—2

I WANNA HOLD YOUR HAND

TAURUS/CANCER

Both of you appreciate security and stability. His sensitivity feeds your sensuality and your easygoing nature encourages him to open up a bit emotionally. Hugs, caresses, and kisses could be a major focus. Loyalty is vital to both of you. Carrying through on commitments comes naturally. You find it easy to reassure each other.

COMPATIBLE—3

TAURUS/LEO

SOMETIMES WHEN WE TOUCH

You both have strong physical needs and powerful wills. Compromise may be a bit challenging. His sexual style has considerable flash, dash and flair, while you focus more on comfort and a sensual build-up. He can help you feel more vital and alive. You can help him appreciate stability.

CHALLENGING—2

TAURUS/VIRGO

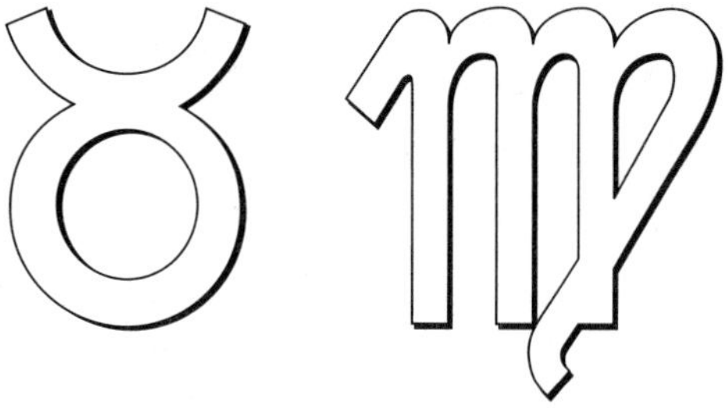

LET'S GET PHYSICAL

Patience is a virtue familiar to you both. He may be a bit more critical, while you tend to be easygoing. But both of you are practical and willing to hang in there to make things work better. Well grounded, the two of you enjoy sharing physical connections.

COMPATIBLE—3

TAURUS/LIBRA

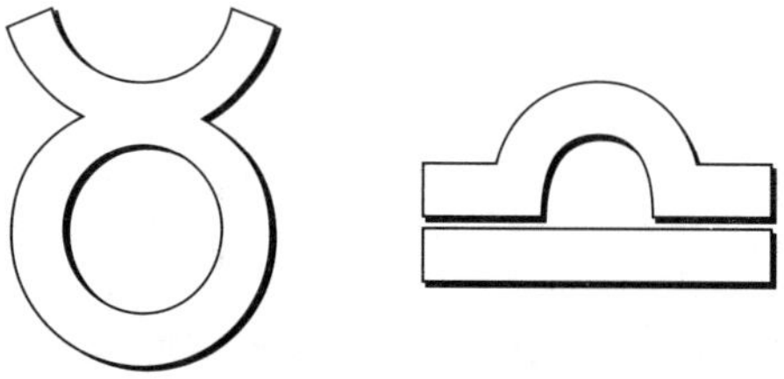

DANCE WITH ME

Beauty and pleasure could be a shared bond. Each of you appreciates grace and harmony, although you may be drawn more to tactile experiences while visual beauty strongly appeals to him. He can help you see both sides to issues. You can help him stand firm and persevere.

VERY CHALLENGING—1

TAURUS/SCORPIO

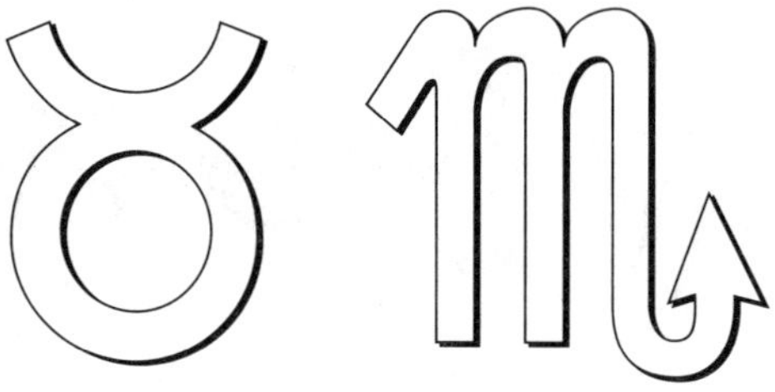

BEAUTY AND THE BEAST

Sexual magnetism is likely. You two may feel the pull of chemistry. Extremes are possible. The two of you might swing between feast and famine around food, sex, or other pleasures. Expect to arouse strong emotions (negative and positive) in one another. A deep bond can occur.

VERY COMPATIBLE—4

SOMEWHERE OUT THERE

TAURUS/SAGITTARIUS

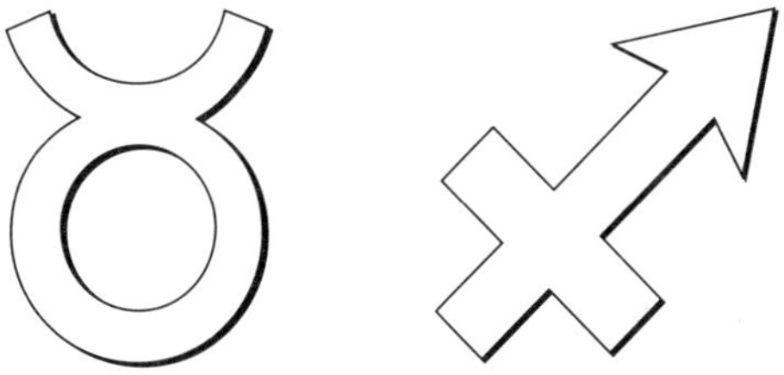

You want the known, safe and familiar. He wants the unknown, risks, and the new. You're solid and dependable; he sometimes promises more than he can deliver. With mutual understanding, you can help him to be more grounded and reliable and he can teach you to be more adventurous.

VERY CHALLENGING—1

SOMEONE TO WATCH OVER ME

TAURUS/CAPRICORN

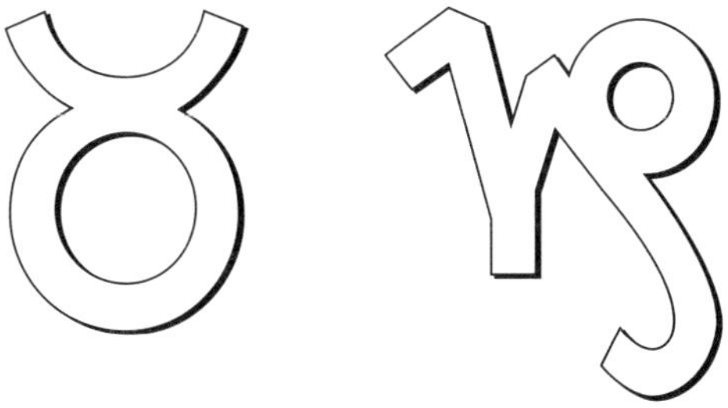

Safety and familiarity rank high with each of you. Practical and grounded, you are not into a high-risk love life. Dependability and practicality turn you both on. You get excited by physical contact and by competence. He may take an authority role more often than you, but you nourish each other's attraction to known pleasures.

COMPATIBLE—3

DESPERADO

TAURUS/AQUARIUS

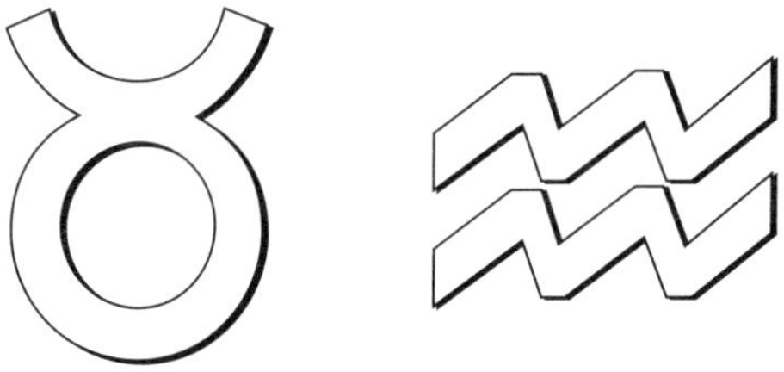

Although you share a strong sensual streak, you could polarize around issues of security versus risk. You may feel safest treading the usual paths of pleasure, while he wants to experiment with the new (or even strange). He can help you loosen up and you can help him appreciate familiar favorites.

CHALLENGING—2

THE COLOR OF LOVE

TAURUS/PISCES

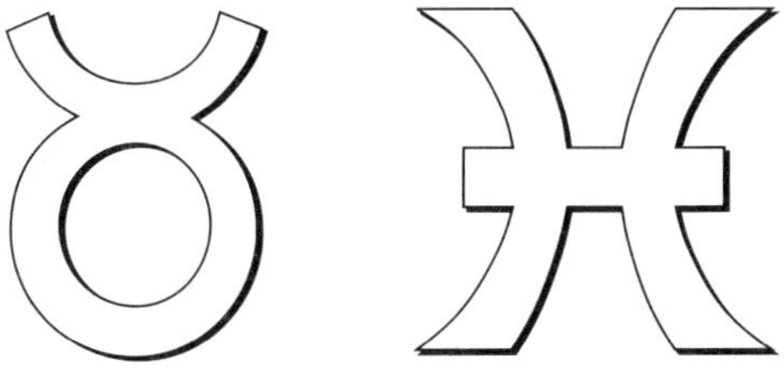

Beauty turns you both on. You, however, need physical contact and caresses, while he can operate from pure imagination. He may be a bit more romantic or idealistic, while you are more practical. Nature and aesthetic experiences feed your libidos.

COMPATIBLE—3

GEMINI/ARIES

FLY ME TO THE MOON

Rapid reactions are likely for both of you. You each can be quite alert and responsive. He tends to prefer immediate action, while you may want to talk things over. You both enjoy variety and seek out new experiences. You stimulate each other mentally and physically.

COMPATIBLE—3

GEMINI/TAURUS

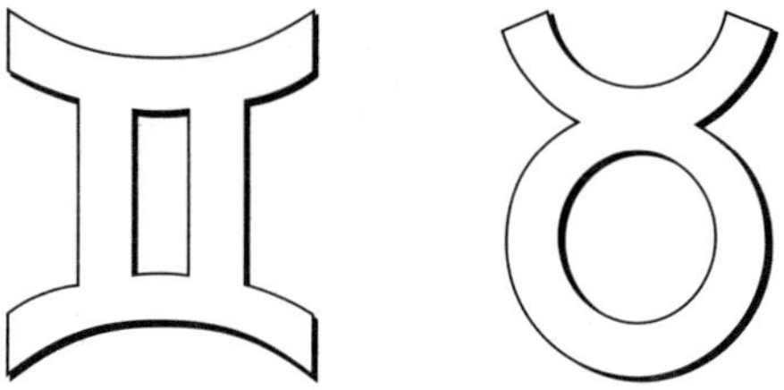

PEOPLE WILL SAY WE'RE IN LOVE

You need mental as well as physical stimulation and respond well to the lure of new experiences. He enjoys the familiar (perhaps even the conventional), but can be very sensually gratifying. Appetite indulgence comes easily to him. Learning more is natural for you. Be open to each other's viewpoints.

CHALLENGING—2

GEMINI/GEMINI

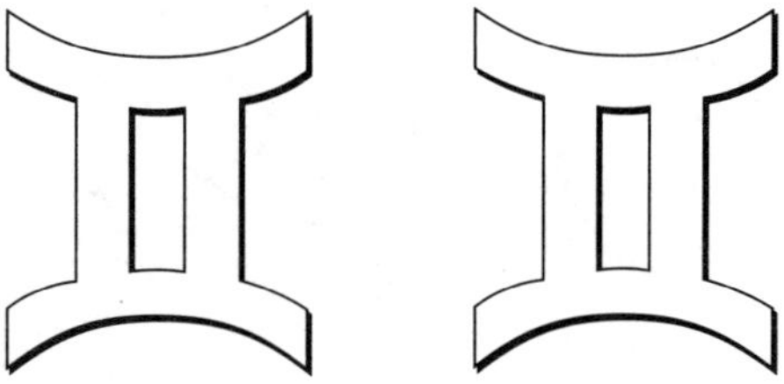

I'LL HAVE TO SAY I LOVE YOU IN A SONG

Variety is the spice of life and love for you both. Word games could add excitement to your sexual encounters and you might have a fresh perspective on oral sex. Although you both can flirt, usually the roving eye is just looking. Eager to learn more, the two of you may continually expand your sensual horizons.

VERY COMPATIBLE—4

GEMINI/CANCER

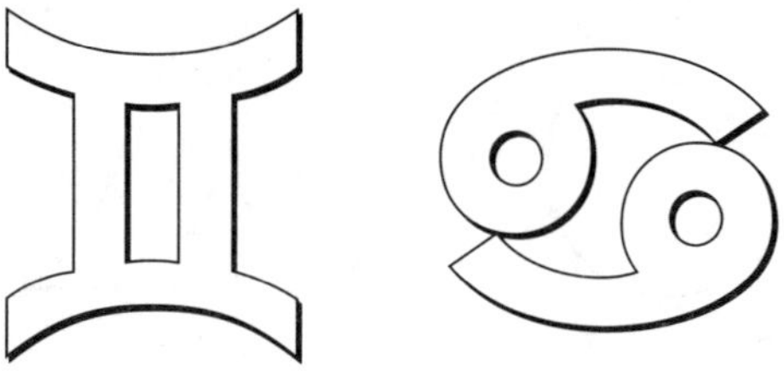

STILL THE ONE

Lighthearted, flexible and insatiably curious, you get turned on by learning more. Sensitive and somewhat inward, he needs a safe environment or the role of protector. You can help him to be more playful and he can encourage you to explore your feelings more deeply.

CHALLENGING—2

HAPPY TOGETHER

GEMINI/LEO

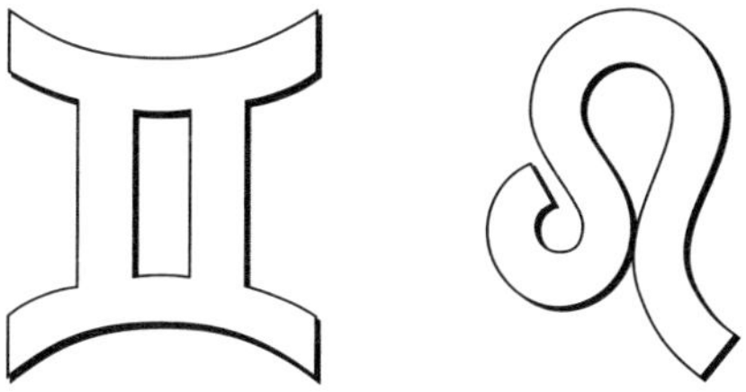

You both can be playful in your enjoyment of desire. A sense of fun fans your passions. Laughing together can be a turn-on. You may want a bit more mental stimulation, while he needs drama and excitement, but generally you each feed the other's inner child and zest for life, love, and learning.

COMPATIBLE—3

WHAT IS THIS THING CALLED LOVE?

GEMINI/VIRGO

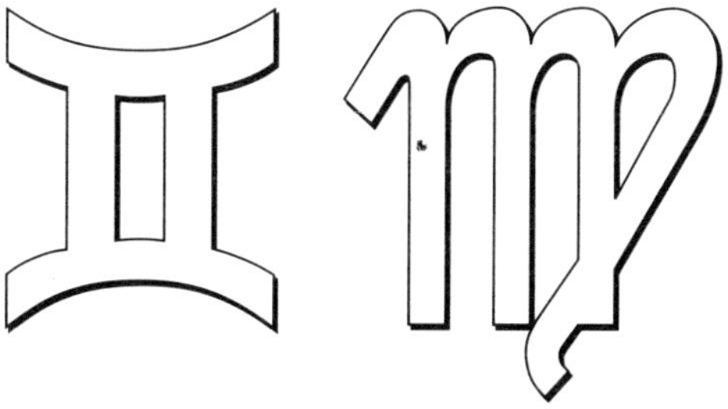

You each respond best sexually when your mind as well as body is involved. Learning excites both of you, although you might explore more diverse areas, while he tends to be thorough and focused on just a few. Reading sex manuals, novels or other mental stimulation could lead to gratifying physical encounters.

CHALLENGING—2

WORDS OF LOVE

GEMINI/LIBRA

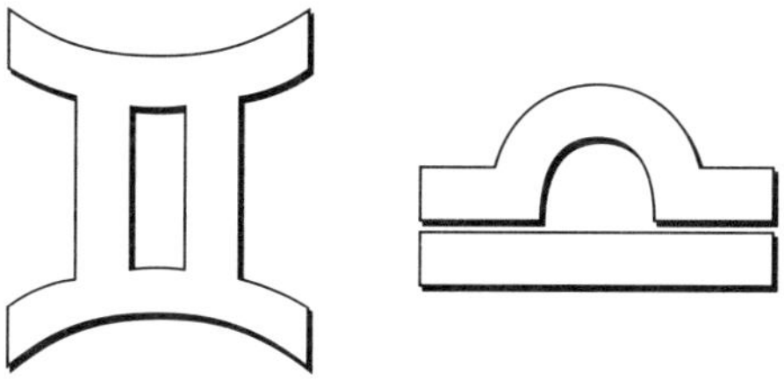

Good conversation could be a warm-up for both of you. Social give-and-take has its appeal. Sexually, a light touch is probably preferred. Good communication is likely between you. Tell each other what you enjoy most. Each of you can be flexible and adapt to what the other wants, so pleasing one another comes easily.

COMPATIBLE—3

SHADOW OF YOUR SMILE

GEMINI/SCORPIO

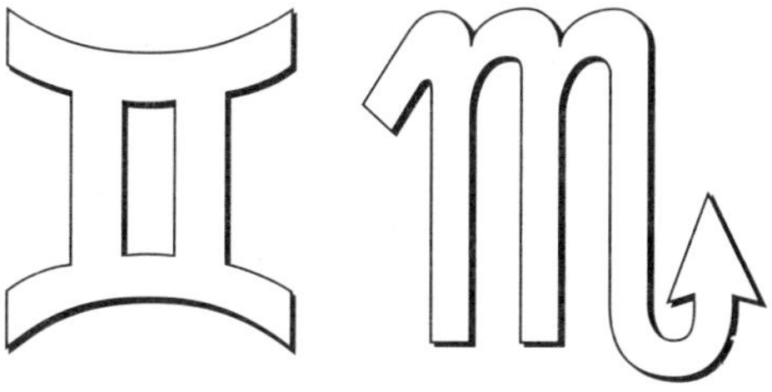

You may feel light and playful just when he's feeling hot and heavy. You might want conversation when he wants silence. Although your sexual styles could differ, you can encourage him to share more, and he can encourage you to plumb the depths of your passions to an incredible degree.

VERY CHALLENGING—1

GEMINI/SAGITTARIUS

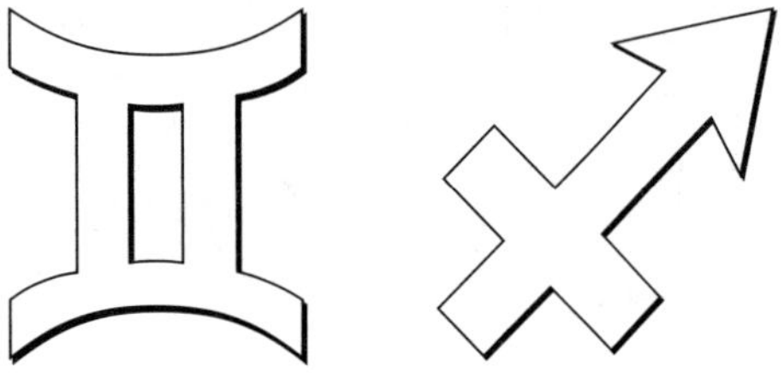

ISN'T IT ROMANTIC?

You two will never run out of topics of conversation! Each of you finds people and communication stimulating and may enjoy talking about sexual matters almost as much as doing them! Somewhat flirtatious, you must be able to trust one another. Mental stimulation turns both of you on.

VERY COMPATIBLE—4

GEMINI/CAPRICORN

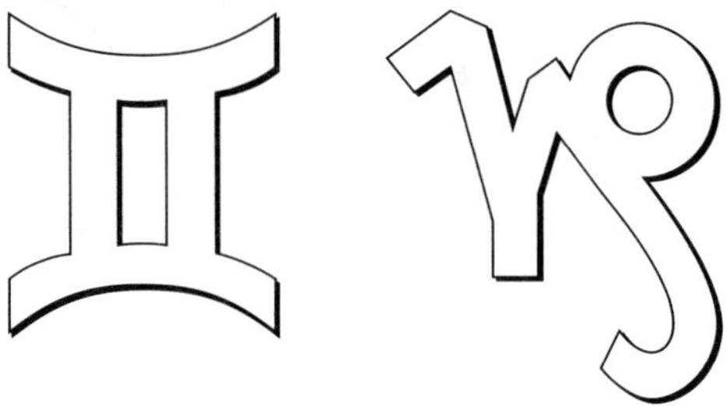

IT'S NOT FOR ME TO SAY

You tend to be lighthearted, flippant and casual about desire. He tends to be serious, cautious and work hard for excellence. You want communication; he wants control. Compromise is essential for you both. He can help you be more practical and stable, and you can help him laugh more and take life (and love) more lightly.

VERY CHALLENGING—1

GEMINI/AQUARIUS

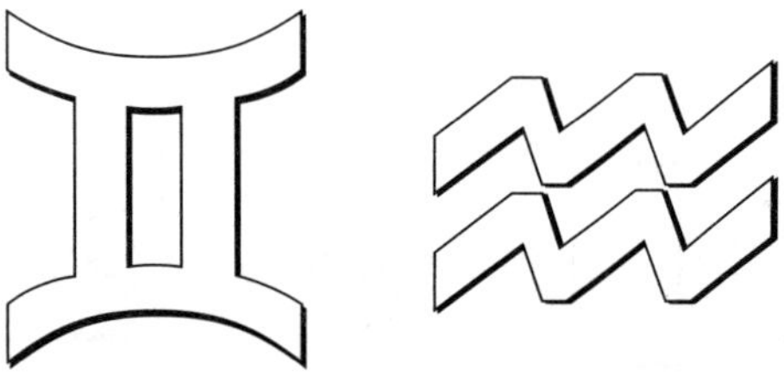

NOT A DAY GOES BY

Freshness appeals to you both. New experiences feed your sense of excitement. Mental stimulation may intensify your desire. Discussions could enhance your shared pleasure as communication is vital to you both. Open and curious, you may be willing to experiment with one another.

COMPATIBLE—3

GEMINI/PISCES

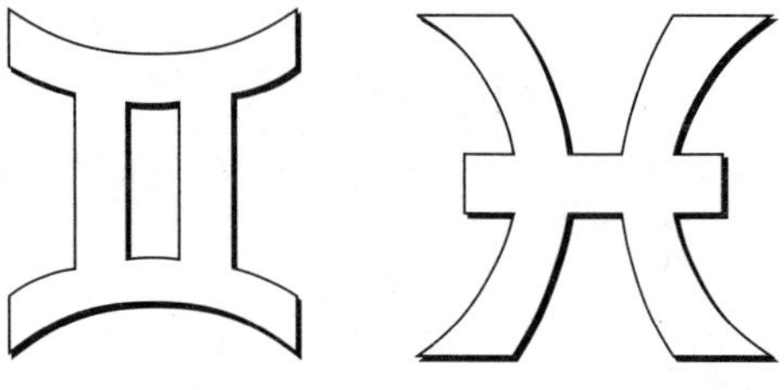

TWELFTH OF NEVER

Getting your timing together may be a challenge. You may want to talk when he wants silence. You focus on thoughts while he's concerned about feelings. You like to flirt and he tends to withdraw. Yet you can be quite tuned into one another. He can increase your sensitivity and you can encourage his curiosity and openness.

CHALLENGING—2

STRANGERS IN THE NIGHT

CANCER/ARIES

He's off and running, and you want him to take it slow, to build gradually to a peak of desire. You're sensitive; he's impulsive. He tends to immediately express any anger or frustration, whereas you hesitate for fear of hurting him, or being hurt yourself. Yet his passion can stimulate your nurturing spirit, and your gentleness can fuel his excitement.

CHALLENGING—2

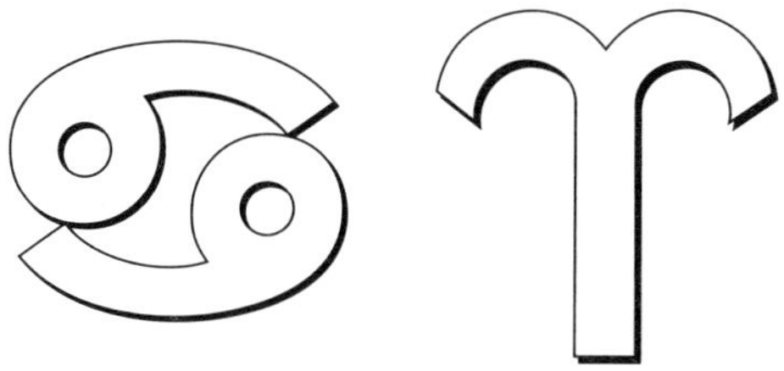

I WANNA HOLD YOUR HAND

CANCER/TAURUS

Both of you appreciate security and stability. Your sensitivity encourages his sensuality, and his affectionate nature encourages you to open up and feel safer emotionally. Hugs, caresses and kisses could be a major focus. Loyalty is vital to both of you. Carrying through on commitments comes naturally. You find it easy to reassure each other.

COMPATIBLE—3

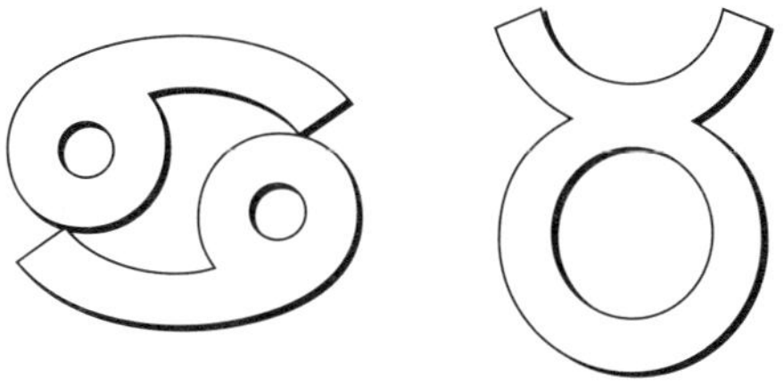

STILL THE ONE

CANCER/GEMINI

Sensitive and somewhat inward, you need someone to help you feel safe and protected. Lighthearted, flexible and insatiably curious, he gets turned on by learning, visual stimuli, or conversation. He can help you be more playful and casual, and you can encourage him to explore his feelings more deeply.

CHALLENGING—2

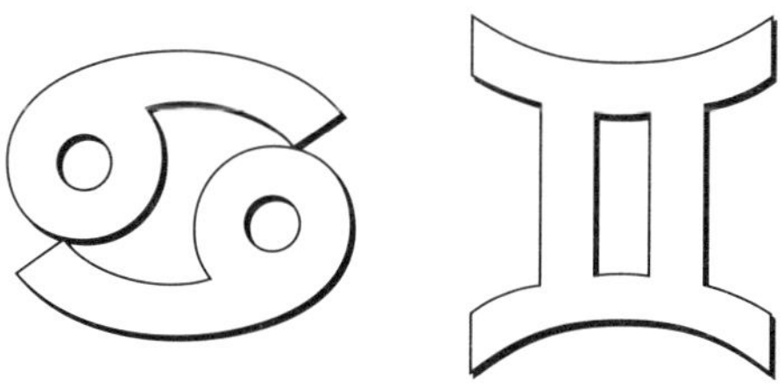

LOVE WILL KEEP US TOGETHER

CANCER/CANCER

Each of you flourishes in an atmosphere of emotional support and deep caring. You may take turns nurturing one another, each protecting in your areas of strength. Perhaps you feel like family to one another. Don't brood over hurts or hold back on sharing feeling with each other. Do enjoy your joint capacity to make commitments and give feelings priority.

VERY COMPATIBLE—4

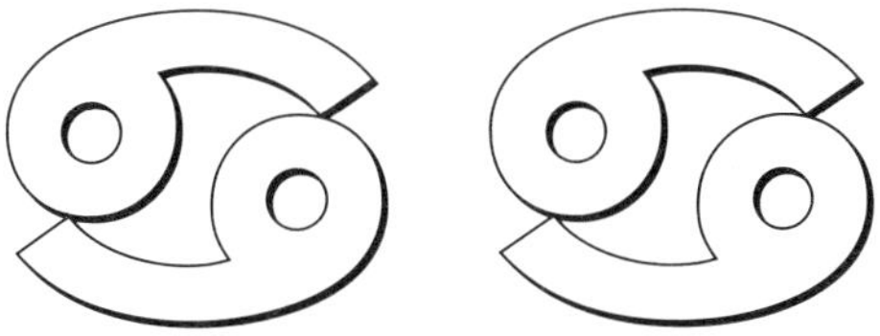

CANCER/LEO

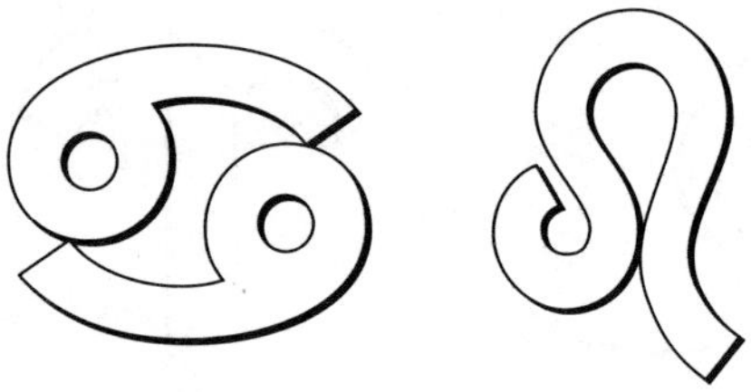

LOVE ME WITH A FEELING

You are somewhat sensitive and are energized by a sense of safety and commitment He is expressive, exuberant and eager. With dramatic flair, he is ready for anything, while you need a bit more time to warm up and be sure this is what you want. You can encourage him to be more tender, and he can encourage you to take more risks.

CHALLENGING—2

CANCER/VIRGO

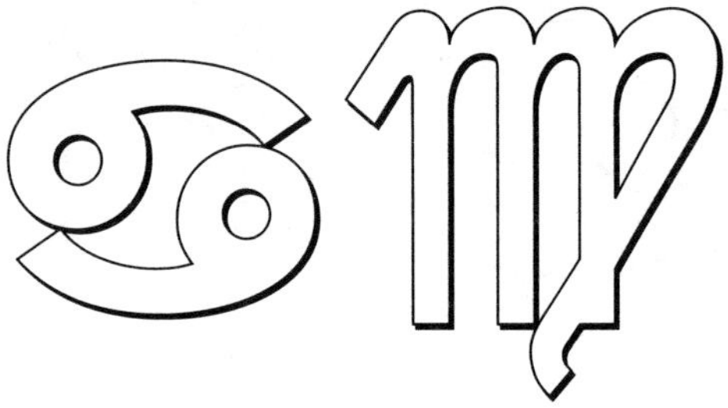

(YOU'RE THE) WIND BENEATH MY WINGS

Each of you has good caretaking instincts. Your focus is more on emotional matters, while he is more centered on practical concerns, such as work or repairs. You tend to be more supportive, while he can be somewhat critical. He really wants to do passion **right**. You both appreciate dependability and knowing that you can rely on one another.

COMPATIBLE—3

CANCER/LIBRA

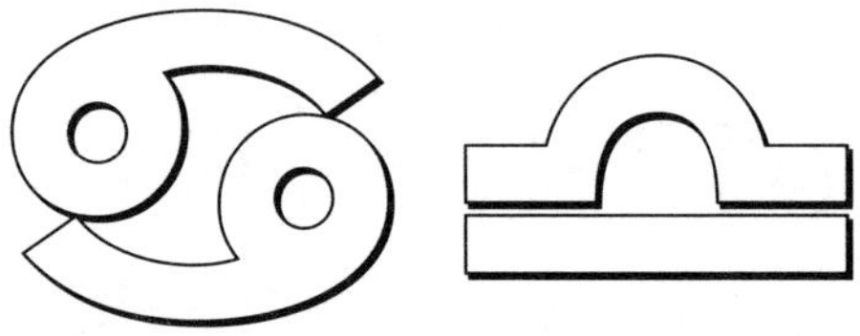

OUR DAY WILL COME

Although you agree on a desire for closeness, you may disagree regarding the question of how much. He tends to be more social, diplomatic, charming and lighthearted, while you seek an emotional commitment. He may see you as possessive; you may see him as flirtatious. Compromise allows you to enjoy his social network and him to enjoy your domestic skills.

CHALLENGING—2

CANCER/SCORPIO

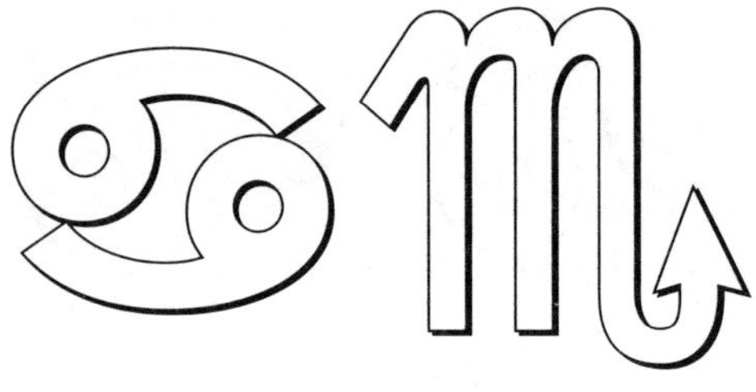

I'LL BE WATCHING YOU

Both of you have strong, intense feelings and tend to take things to heart. Thus, you can each hold back a bit, protecting yourselves until you are sure it is safe to care. Temper explosions could occur if either of you holds too much inside. Generally, though, you can be quite sensitive to one another.

COMPATIBLE—3

SEND IN THE CLOWNS — CANCER/SAGITTARIUS

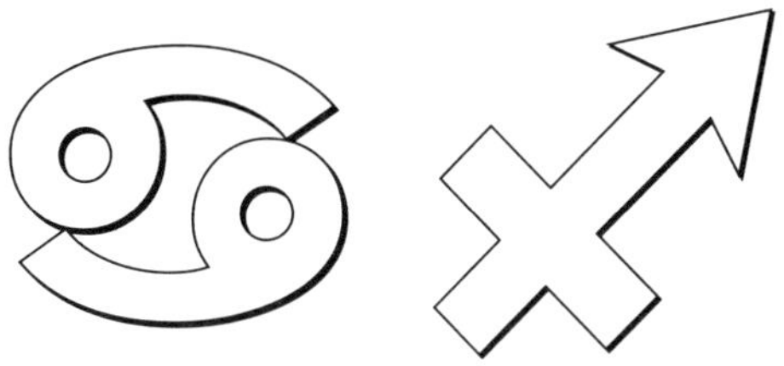

The two of you are apt to be working on a classic "freedom vs. closeness" struggle. When one of you wants commitment, the other wants independence. When one of you is ready to go adventuring, the other wants to keep the home fires burning. You both will have to work hard at taking turns between independence and attachment.

VERY CHALLENGING—1

I'M OLD-FASHIONED — CANCER/CAPRICORN

Each of you has a parental streak within, so being supportive, solid and dependable comes naturally. Don't try to turn your partner into a child, but do take turns taking care of one another. You both value fidelity, dependability, family, roots and an appreciation of the past. You are naturally drawn together.

VERY COMPATIBLE—4

WILD HEART — CANCER/AQUARIUS

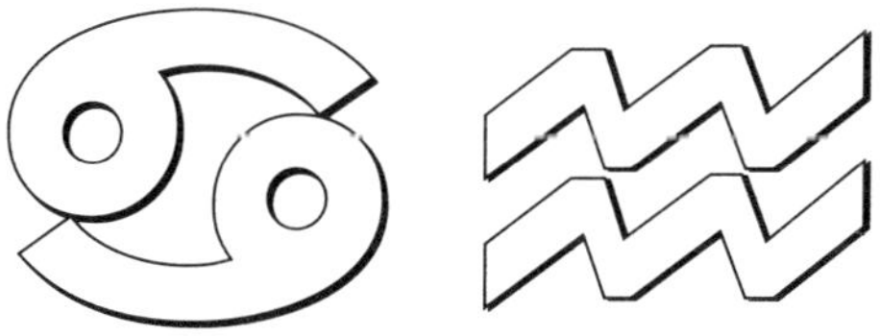

Your sexual styles may be quite different—one more open, experimental and free-wheeling; the other more cautious, conservative and oriented toward safety. You can learn from one another if neither of you tries to totally change the other to your way. The two of you may feel torn between risk and security, but life demands some of each.

VERY CHALLENGING—1

LOVE ME TENDER — CANCER/PISCES

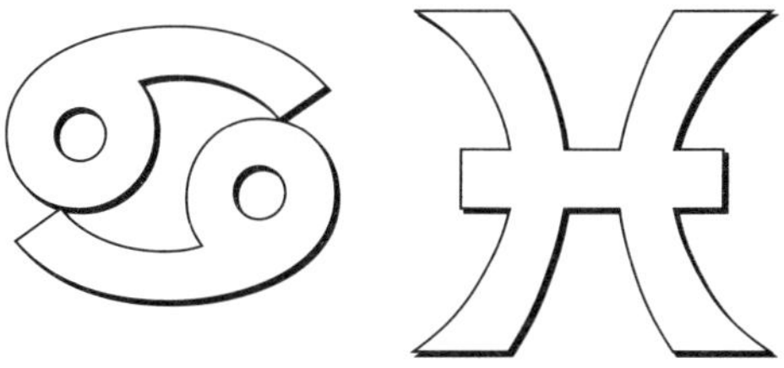

Each of you has a very gentle, sensitive, empathic side, and you may even tune into each other's feelings without words. With deep, strong emotions, either of you can be swept away but would tend to hold back initially for fear of being hurt. Tenderness is your best connection.

COMPATIBLE—3

LEO/ARIES

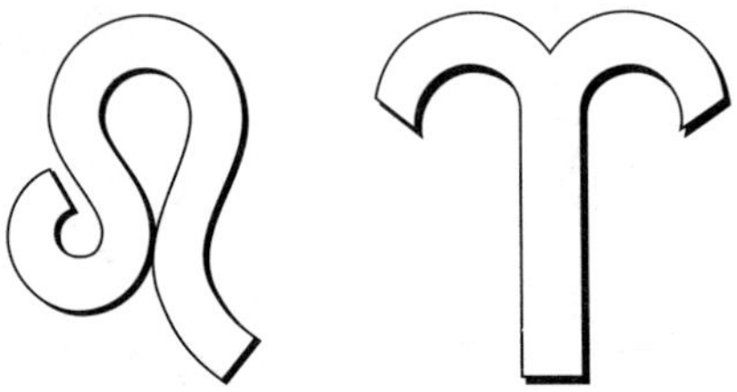

MAXIMUM OVERDRIVE

Both of you enjoy excitement, thrills and the rush of adrenaline. Eager to move, explore, and enjoy, you can really turn each other on. You feed each other's fire, with an urge to try, to risk, to adventure. Your charisma energizes him; his courage excites you.

COMPATIBLE—3

LEO/TAURUS

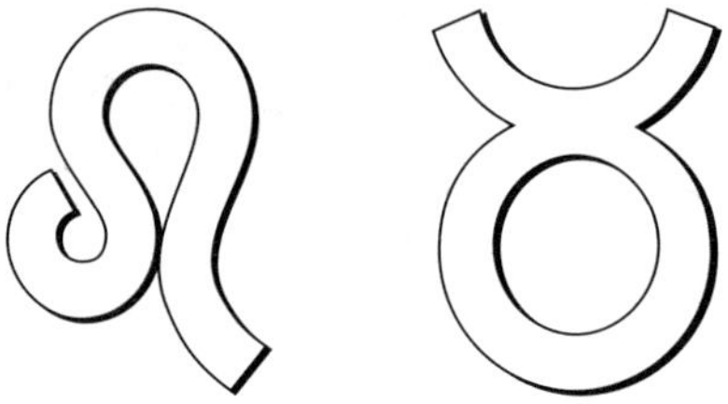

SOMETIMES WHEN WE TOUCH

You both have strong physical needs and powerful wills. Compromise may be a bit challenging. Your sexual style is exciting, dramatic and eager, while he may focus more on comfort or physical contact. You can help him feel more vital and alive. He can help you appreciate stability.

CHALLENGING—2

LEO/GEMINI

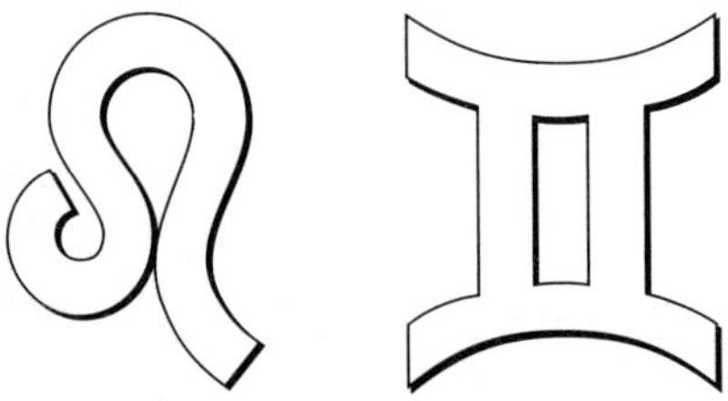

HAPPY TOGETHER

You both can be playful in your enjoyment of desire. A sense of fun fans your passions. Laughing together can be a turn-on. He may want a bit more mental stimulation, while you need drama and excitement, but generally you each feed the other's inner child and zest for life and learning.

COMPATIBLE—3

LEO/CANCER

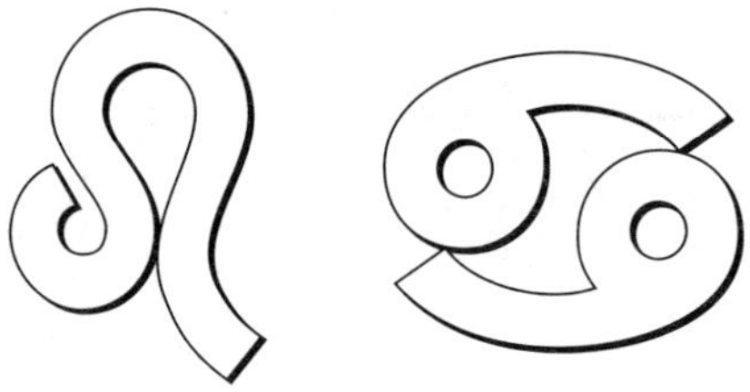

LOVE ME WITH A FEELING

You can be quite expressive, exuberant, and eager, while he may be more cautious, holding back to protect himself or others. With dramatic flair, you are ready for anything, while he needs a bit more time to be sure this is what he wants. You can encourage him to take more risks, and he may encourage you to look within more.

CHALLENGING—2

LIGHT MY FIRE!

LEO/LEO

Both of you are blessed with above average sex appeal and charisma. With a sense of drama and a need for excitement, turning each other on comes easily. You may also feed each other's rashness or extravagance, but generally you bring out one another's fun-loving spirit and ability to play.

VERY COMPATIBLE—4

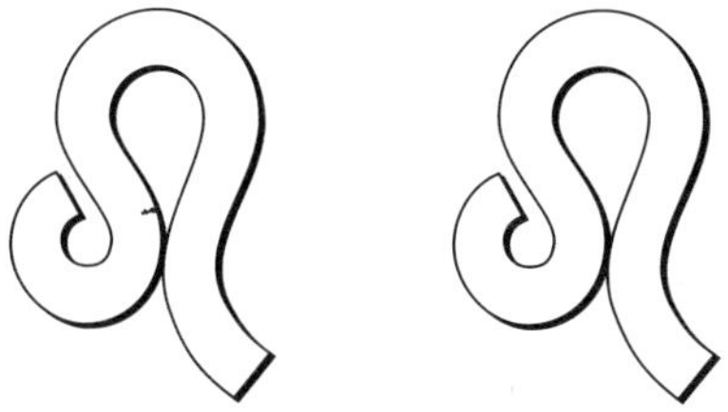

BLUE MOON

LEO/VIRGO

Your sexual styles may differ a bit. You seek excitement and drama. He is concerned with competence and performance. You may find him critical or inhibited; he may feel you exaggerate or overdo. With caring, you can liven up his experiences and he can help you appreciate practical necessities.

CHALLENGING—2

LOVE THE ONE YOU'RE WITH

LEO/LIBRA

Both of you can be quite attractive to the opposite sex when you choose. You can be magnetic, sexy and exciting. He can be charming, flirtatious and diplomatic. You both enjoy social interaction as well, so other people are important. You may find it easy to be with one another.

COMPATIBLE—3

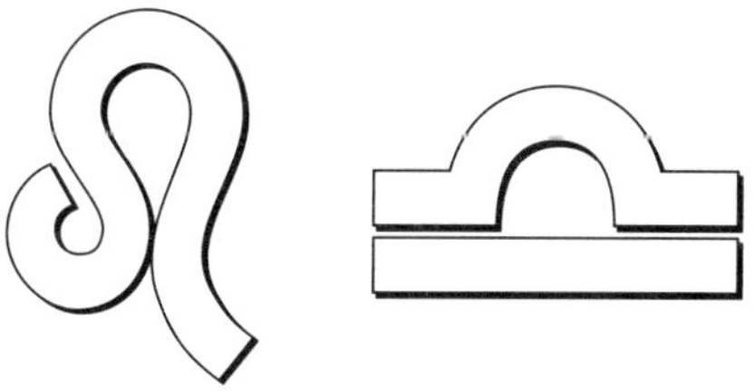

GETTING SO EXCITED

LEO/SCORPIO

You both know what you want; you want things **your** way. Compromising will be challenging for each of you—but quite rewarding. Both of you can be intensely sexual and together you may rise to heights neither of you has reached before. He can help you look deeper into life, and you can help him open up and express more.

CHALLENGING—2

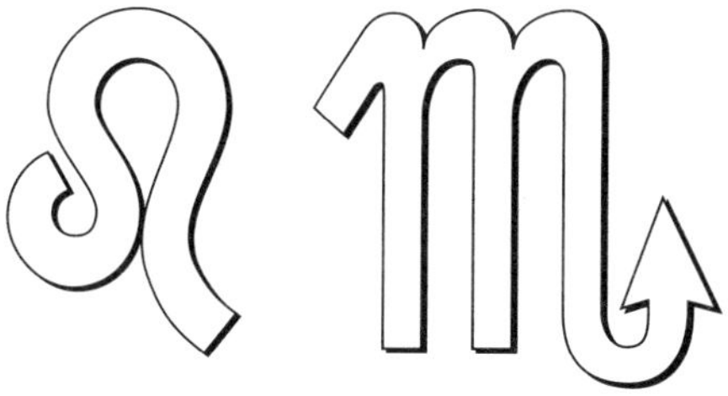

LEO/SAGITTARIUS

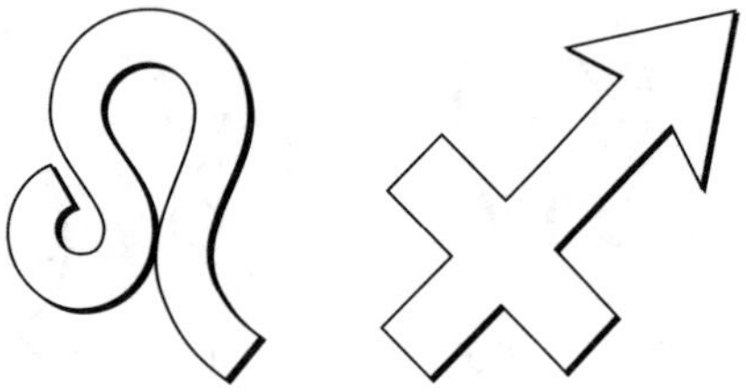

ANTICIPATION

Two fellow adventurers, you can easily feed the fire and passion within each other. Willing to risk, to try new things, to seek that adrenaline high, you light up each other's lives! You may also encourage foolhardiness or excessive confidence, but generally you feel more alive and have more fun when together.

COMPATIBLE—3

LEO/CAPRICORN

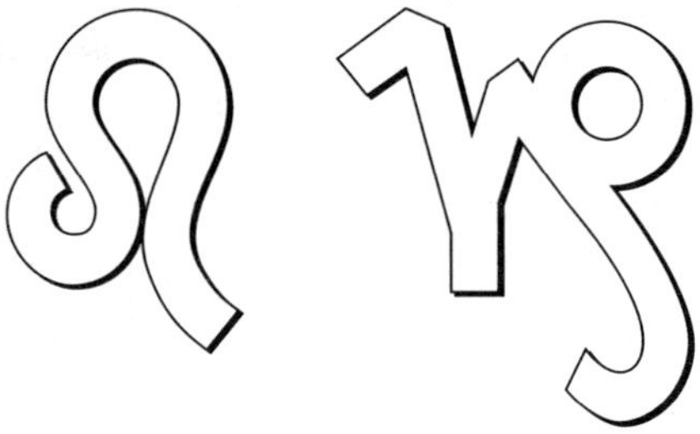

UNDER MY THUMB?

You want to be Queen and he wants to be Executive, so who will rule the roost? Don't fall into power struggles. Let each other hold sway in the areas you do best. You bring life, excitement and sexual magnetism in your shared activities. He brings practicality, responsibility and good planning.

VERY CHALLENGING—1

LEO/AQUARIUS

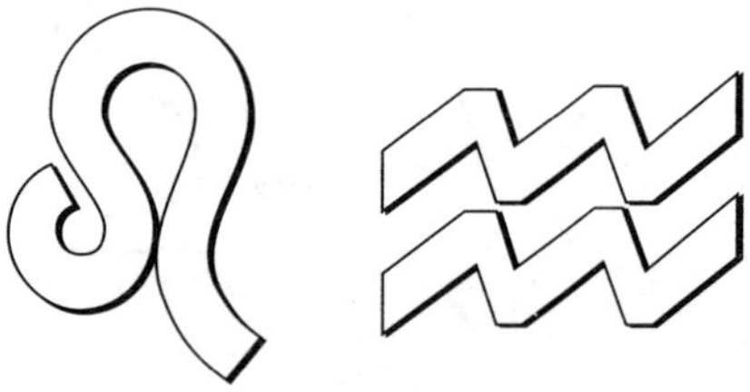

CAN'T HELP LOVING THAT (WO)MAN

The two of you are naturally attracted, but will have to work out the polarity of head versus heart. You could feel pulled between passion and detachment; between what logic says versus what you feel. Don't take opposite ends and fight. Do have a bit of each in your relationship. Lively interchanges work best for you both.

VERY COMPATIBLE—4

LEO/PISCES

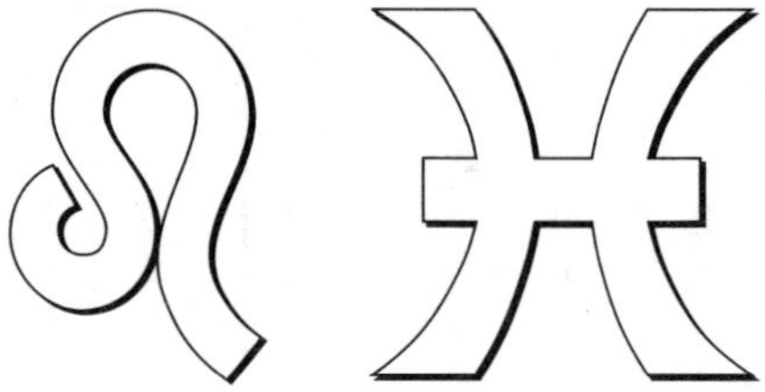

DO YOU BELIEVE IN MAGIC?

Although you both can be quite romantic, your style is more dramatic and outward, while his is more inward and reserved. He may feel you come on too strong at times; you may feel he is too sensitive, or keeps too much inside. Learn to appreciate each other's different viewpoints and you will both grow.

VERY CHALLENGING—1

MORNING HAS BROKEN

VIRGO/ARIES

You take awhile to warm up, and want everything just so, while he is eager, impulsive and spontaneous (and sometimes in a hurry). You may feel he's careless and he may feel you're picky. He can help you relax and enjoy the moment. You can help him plan ahead when appropriate.

VERY CHALLENGING—1

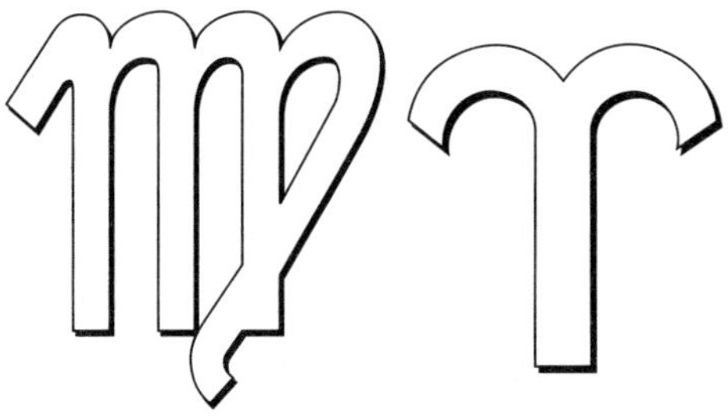

LET'S GET PHYSICAL

VIRGO/TAURUS

Patience is a virtue familiar to you both. You can be a bit of a perfectionist, while he tends to be relaxed. But both of you are practical and willing to hang in there to make things work better. Well grounded, the two of you enjoy sharing physical connections.

COMPATIBLE—3

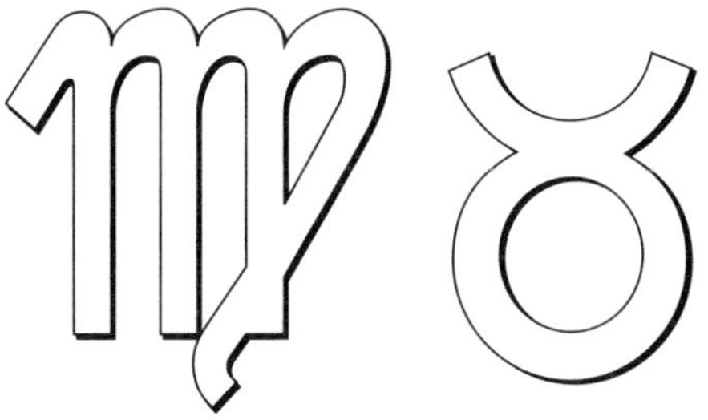

WHAT IS THIS THING CALLED LOVE?

VIRGO/GEMINI

You each respond best sexually when your mind as well as body is involved. Learning excites both of you, although he might jump all over the map, exploring many areas, while you tend to focus on just a few. Reading sex manuals, novels, watching exciting movies, or other mental stimulation could lead to gratifying physical encounters.

CHALLENGING—2

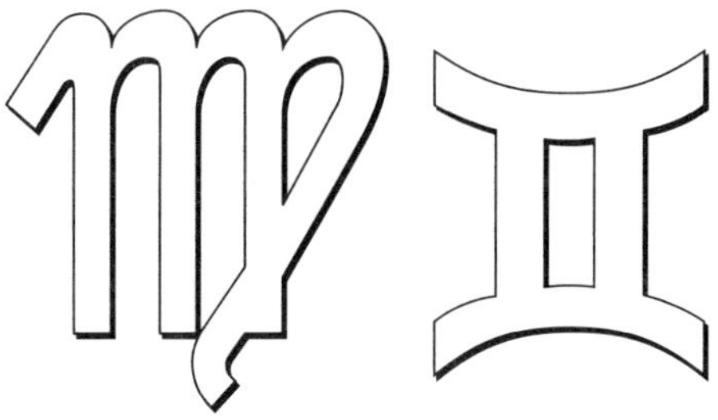

(YOU'RE THE) WIND BENEATH MY WINGS

VIRGO/CANCER

Each of you has good caretaking instincts. You may focus more on service in practical, physical ways, while he may center more on protection or loyalty issues. Neatness may matter more to you. Feeling you're on his side turns him on. You both appreciate dependability and knowing that you can rely on one another.

COMPATIBLE—3

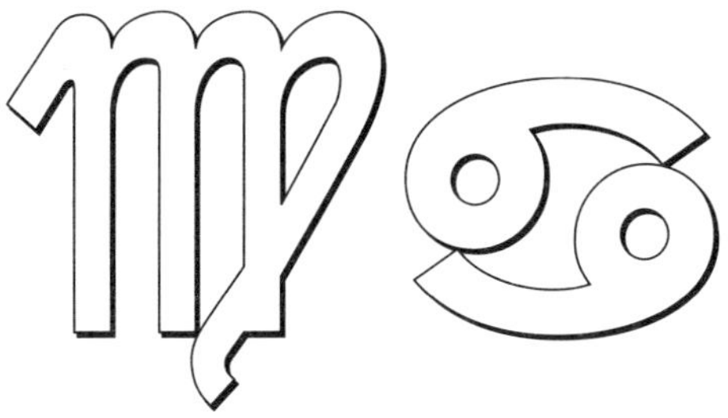

VIRGO/LEO

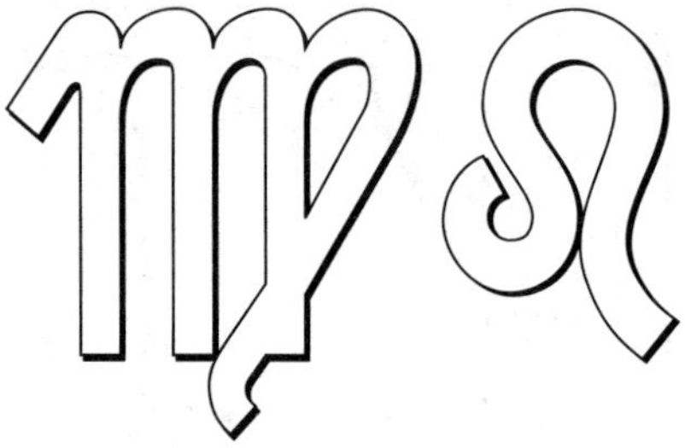

BLUE MOON

Your sexual styles may differ a bit. He seeks excitement and drama. You are more practical and concerned with doing things right. He may feel you are critical or inhibited. You may feel he exaggerates or can be arrogant. With caring, you can help him be more sensible, and he can liven up your life.

CHALLENGING—2

VIRGO/VIRGO

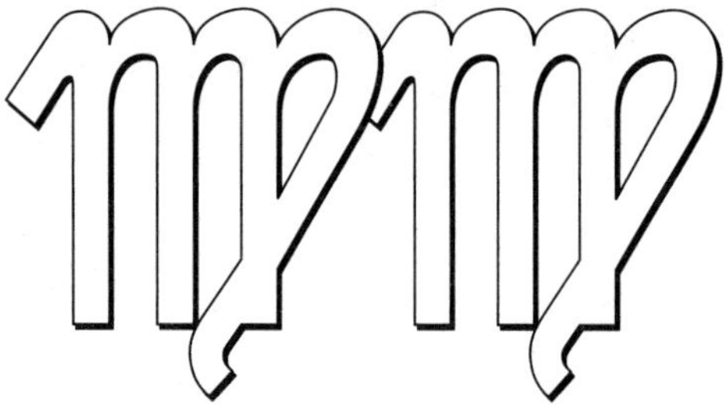

DEDICATED TO THE ONE I LOVE

Once the two of you get past early doubts, you are determined to do a **good** job sexually. Although both of you may be cautious initially, once committed, you'll do everything possible to serve and satisfy one another. Either of you might overdo criticism from a need to improve, but you can build a strong physical bond together.

VERY COMPATIBLE—4

VIRGO/LIBRA

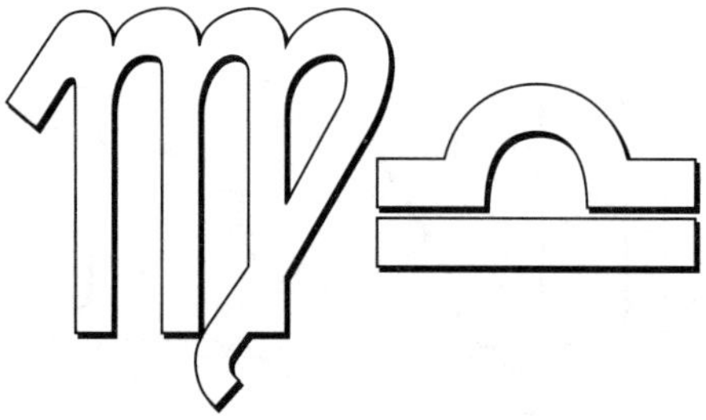

HE'S THE KIND OF MAN A WOMAN NEEDS

You have a need to serve, and he has a need to be social and interact with others. You may be more focused on work, when he is focused on people. You take sex seriously, while he can be more lighthearted about it. Your style is earnest and dedicated; his is gracious and charming. He can help you relax and enjoy life and love more.

CHALLENGING—2

VIRGO/SCORPIO

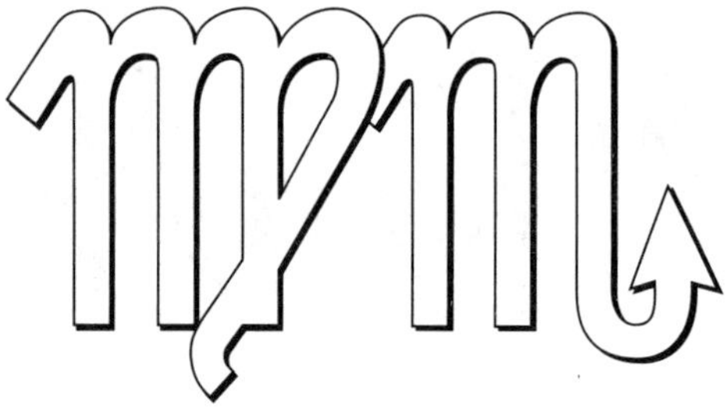

UNFORGETTABLE

Either of you can get obsessed by certain details and forget the larger picture. His passions run very deeply, but he keeps much beneath the surface. You take time to warm up, but have great endurance once you get going. Either of you could use your organizational skills to set just the right scene for love.

COMPATIBLE—3

DANCING IN THE DARK

VIRGO/SAGITTARIUS

You take sex seriously, while he sees it more as an adventure. You want planning, care, and a slow build-up. He wants excitement, immediacy, and a sense of exploration. If you are open to learning from one another, all can be well. You can enjoy his enthusiasm and he can learn to appreciate your practicality.

CHALLENGING—2

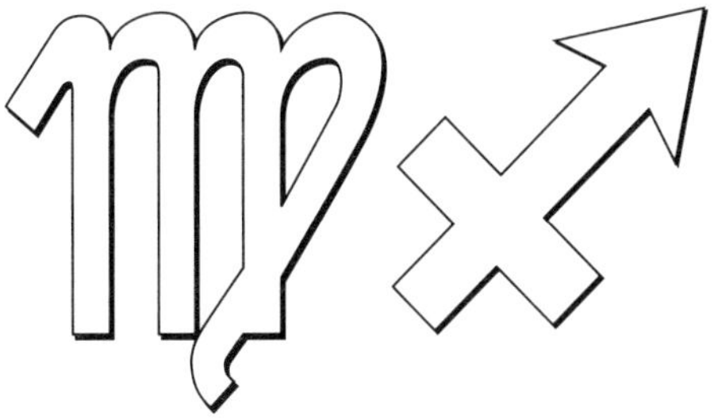

IF I LOVED YOU

VIRGO/CAPRICORN

You both share a desire for safety and a tendency to take your time in getting involved. Neither of you wants to make a mistake in love! You can, however, fall into the servant role, and he is a take-charge type. Make sure you both get what you need. Lots of physical contact works well for you both.

COMPATIBLE—3

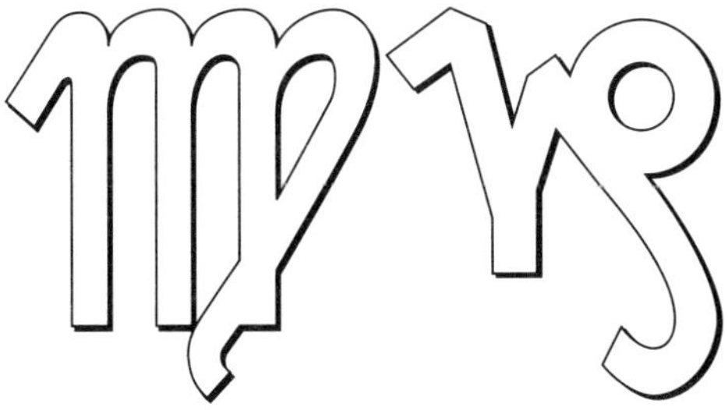

MAKE BELIEVE

VIRGO/AQUARIUS

Each of you will have to adapt to the other's style. He may see you as sexually inhibited, conventional or critical, while you could see him as eccentric, too experimental or aloof. He can help you see other options and you can help him stay grounded. A relationship which starts in the mind (and then the body follows) works best.

VERY CHALLENGING—1

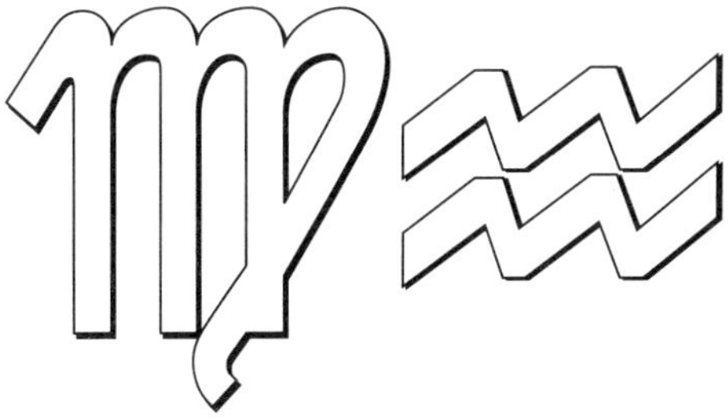

YOU WERE MEANT FOR ME

VIRGO/PISCES

The two of you could literally make beautiful music together! You are blending lovely, artistic, idealistic images with the common sense to create something better here on Earth. If you don't polarize into the space cadet and super critic, your natural attraction can lead to poetry in motion when you make love.

VERY COMPATIBLE—4

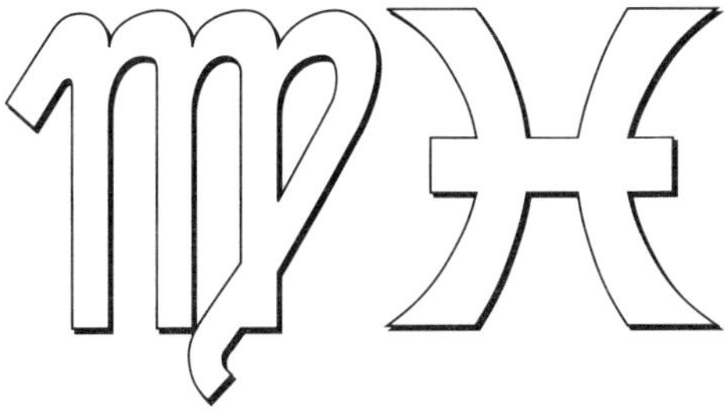

LIBRA/ARIES

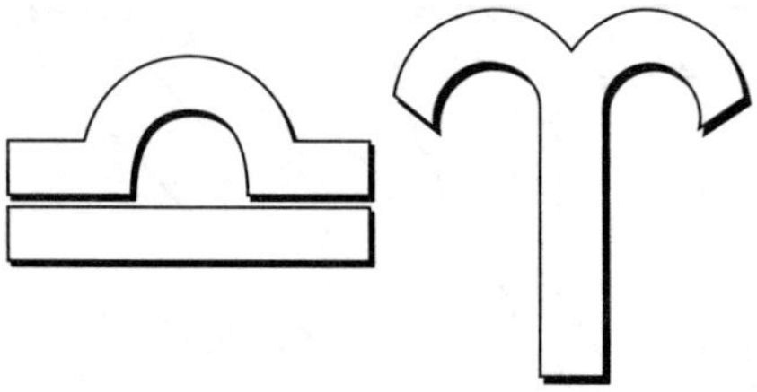

CHEEK TO CHEEK

You two have the natural attraction of opposites: one who acts and one who reacts; one who is direct and blunt and one who is tactful and diplomatic. Think of your relationship as a dance where each can have a turn at leading (and following). Balance brings harmony and sexual satisfaction to you both.

VERY COMPATIBLE—4

LIBRA/TAURUS

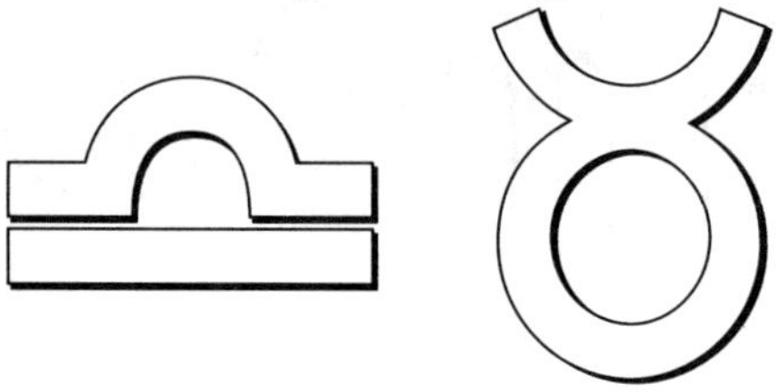

DANCE WITH ME

Beauty and pleasure could be a shared bond. Each of you appreciates grace and harmony although he may be drawn more to tactile experiences, while visual beauty strongly appeals to you. You can help him see both sides to any issue. He can help you stand firm and persevere.

VERY CHALLENGING—1

LIBRA/GEMINI

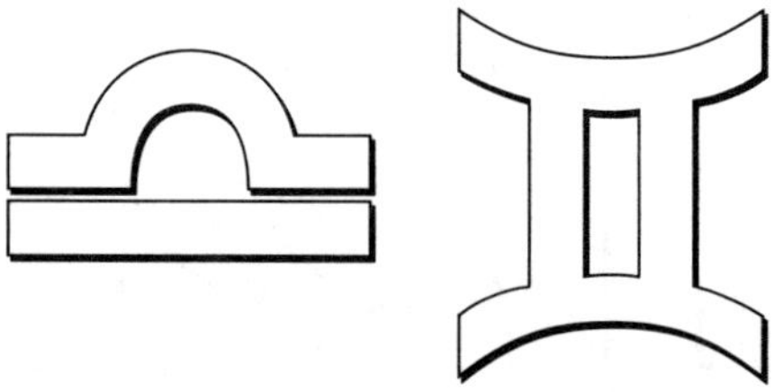

WORDS OF LOVE

Good conversation could be a warm-up for both of you. Social give-and-take has its appeal. Sexually, a light touch is probably preferred. Good communication is likely between you. Tell each other what you enjoy most. Each of you can be flexible and adapt to what the other wants, so pleasing one another comes easily.

COMPATIBLE—3

LIBRA/CANCER

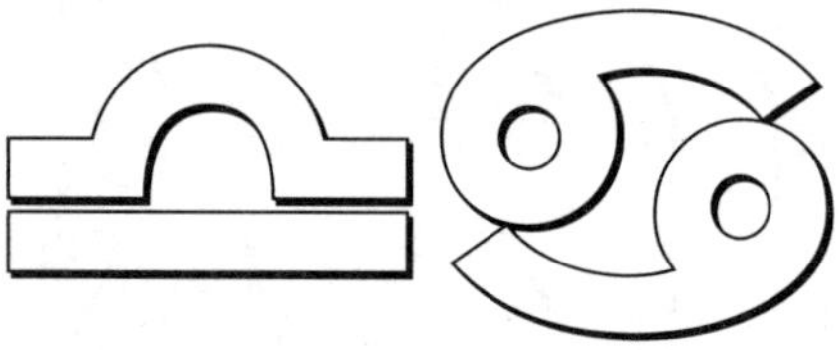

OUR DAY WILL COME

Although you agree on a desire for closeness, you may disagree regarding the question of how much. You tend to be more social, diplomatic, charming and lighthearted, while he is concerned with safety and protection. You may see him as possessive; he might view you as flirtatious. Compromise allows him to enjoy your social network, and you to appreciate his intense feelings and desire to safeguard others.

CHALLENGING—2

LOVE THE ONE YOU'RE WITH

LIBRA/LEO

Both of you can be quite attractive to the opposite sex when you choose. He can be magnetic, sexy and exciting. You can be charming, flirtatious and diplomatic. You both enjoy social interaction as well, so other people are important. You may find it easy to be with one another.

COMPATIBLE—3

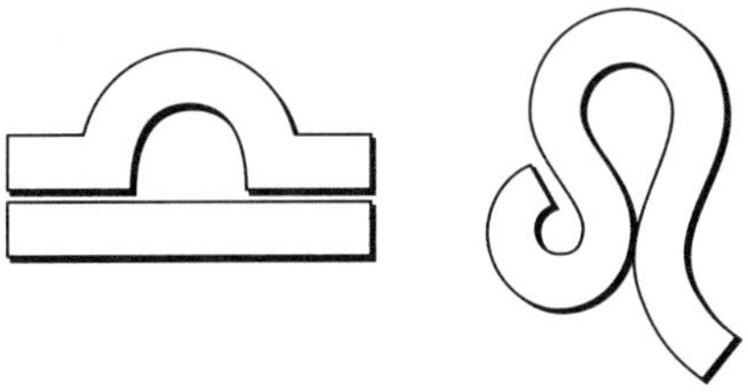

YOU'RE THE KIND OF WOMAN A MAN NEEDS

LIBRA/VIRGO

Your sexual styles are somewhat different. People and interactions are very important to you. He easily focuses on work, or on performance and doing things right. He can be quite serious and dedicated; you tend to be more lighthearted. A pleasant atmosphere is essential for you; a sense of accomplishment is vital for him.

CHALLENGING—2

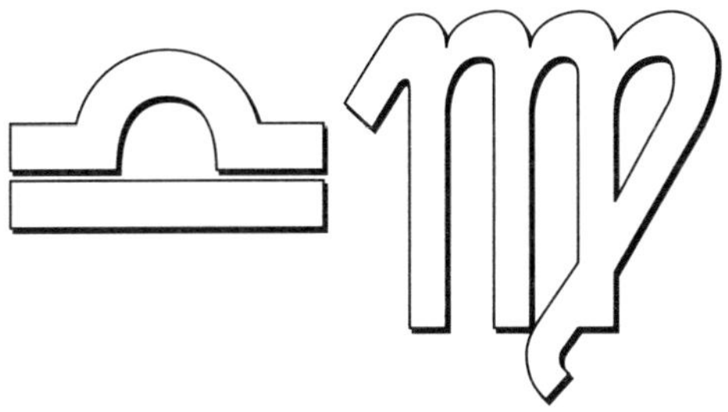

A TASTE OF HONEY

LIBRA/LIBRA

Since both of you naturally think about other people, it may be difficult to decide who leads and who follows. Naturally charming, sociable and gracious, you are easy people to be with. You both appreciate and respond well to beauty and grace. Pleasing one another is important to each of you.

VERY COMPATIBLE—4

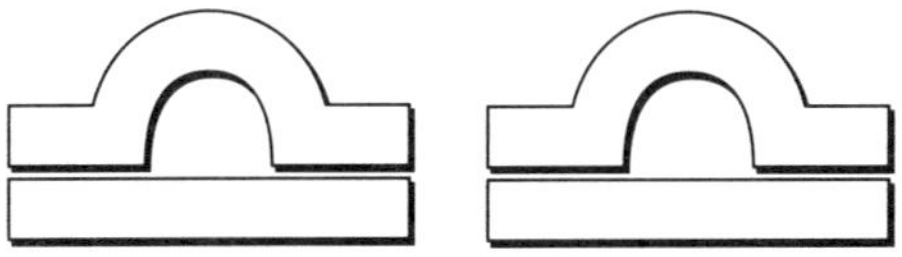

LOVING YOU

LIBRA/SCORPIO

You share a focus on partnership, but he is apt to be more intense and inward, while you are more charming and sociable. He can be quite sexual, but might be a bit possessive. You need beauty, grace and consideration to be turned on. You can help him be more objective and he can help you reach more intense depths.

CHALLENGING—2

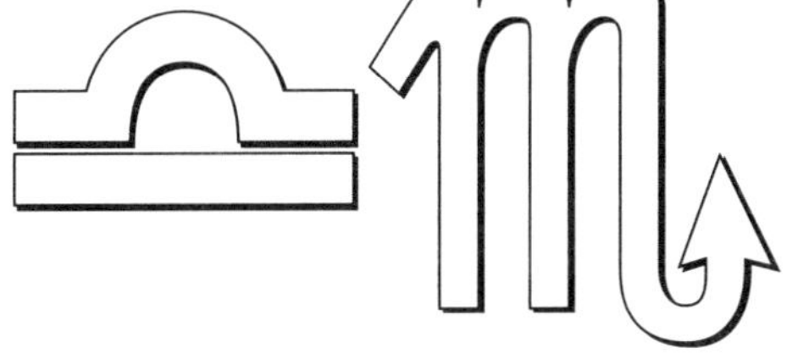

LIBRA/SAGITTARIUS

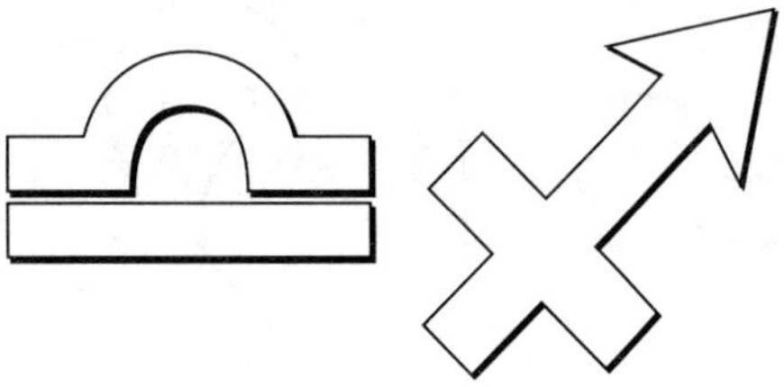

S'WONDERFUL

You both can have fun with people and sexually. Outgoing and friendly, you enjoy social give-and-take as well as having a good time in bed. You may focus more on creating a beautiful environment, while he can be adventurous and enthusiastic. He brings excitement to you, and you bring grace and charm to him.

COMPATIBLE—3

LIBRA/CAPRICORN

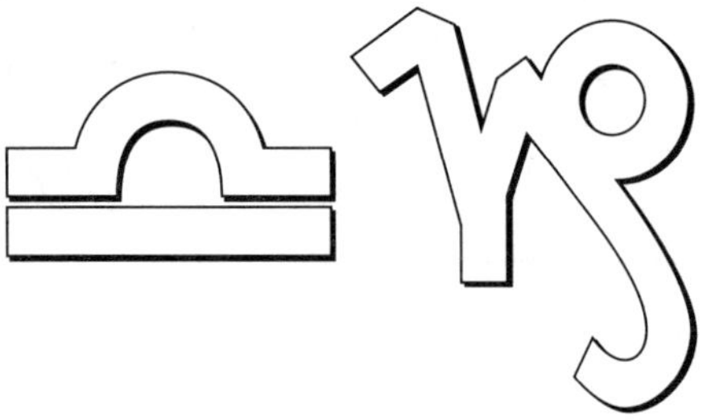

TIL THERE WAS YOU

Your sexual style is a give-and-take, a dance between equals. He is accustomed to being in charge. Compromise is called for. He is apt to be more cautious (fearful of giving up control), but can appreciate your grace and charm. You may respond well to his competence, sense of responsibility and dedication.

CHALLENGING—2

LIBRA/AQUARIUS

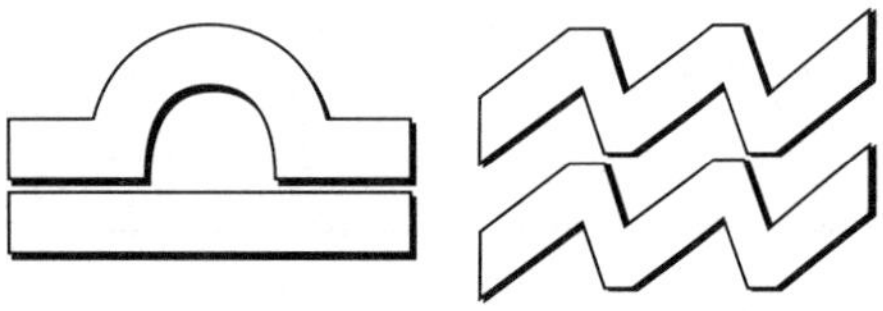

PILLOW TALK

There's a good chance you both enjoy talking in bed! Mental stimulation is important, so tell each other what you enjoy and what's good can get even better. Sharing and an equalitarian attitude are natural for you both, so pleasing one another should flow easily. You may widen his social circle and he may expose you to new (even unusual) ideas.

COMPATIBLE—3

LIBRA/PISCES

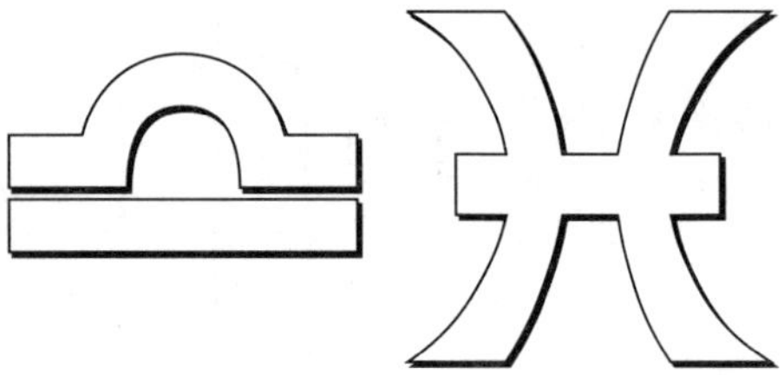

KISSES SWEETER THAN WINE

You get turned on by interacting with someone, talking and building a sense of closeness. He responds strongly to fantasies and imagery. A shared appreciation of beauty could help you get together. Create an attractive environment to share when making love. You can help him let more feelings out; he can encourage your imagination.

VERY CHALLENGING—1

YOU SEND ME

SCORPIO/ARIES

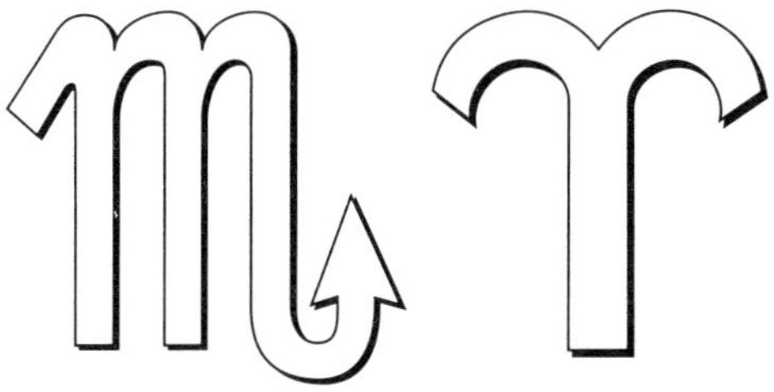

You are intense, inward, passionate and need intimacy on a deep level. He is open, honest, impulsive and sometimes rash. You don't wear your heart on your sleeve; what you see is what you get with him. Yet you both have a high level of passion. Each of you can feed the flames of desire in the other.

VERY CHALLENGING—1

BEAUTY AND THE BEAST

SCORPIO/TAURUS

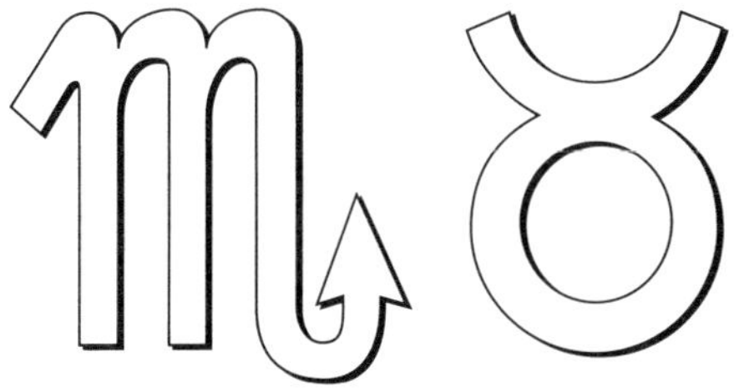

Sexual magnetism is likely. You two may feel the pull of chemistry. Extremes are possible. The two of you might swing between feast and famine around food, sex, or other pleasures. Expect to arouse strong emotions (negative and positive) in one another. A deep bond can occur.

VERY COMPATIBLE—4

THE SHADOW OF YOUR SMILE

SCORPIO/GEMINI

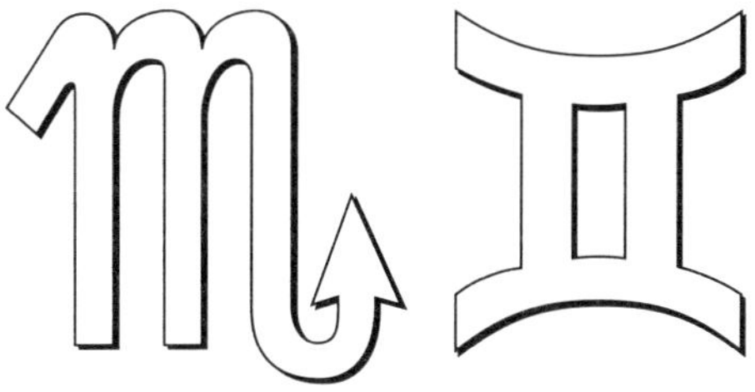

You may want deep, meaningful interactions when he just wants to laugh or take things lightly. You might want one-on-one when he wants variety. You could look for an intense commitment when he's feeling casual. You can encourage him to take the time and caring to get to a deeper level of intimacy, and he can encourage you to sometimes lighten up.

VERY CHALLENGING—1

I'LL BE WATCHING YOU

SCORPIO/CANCER

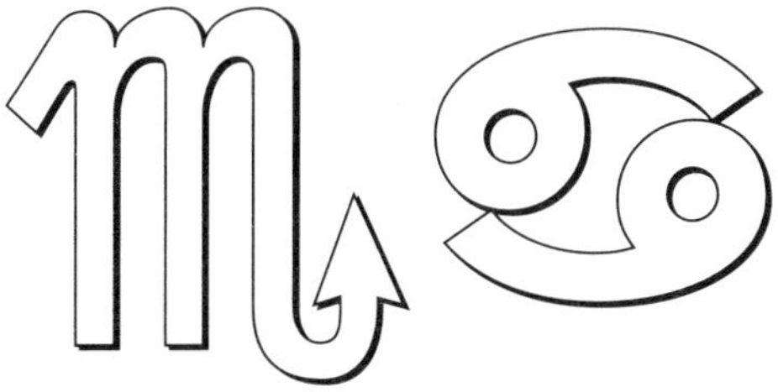

Both of you have strong, intense feelings and tend to take things to heart. Thus, you can each hold back a bit, protecting yourselves until you are sure it is safe to care. Temper explosions could occur if either of you holds too much inside. Generally, though, you can be quite sensitive to one another.

COMPATIBLE—3

SCORPIO/LEO

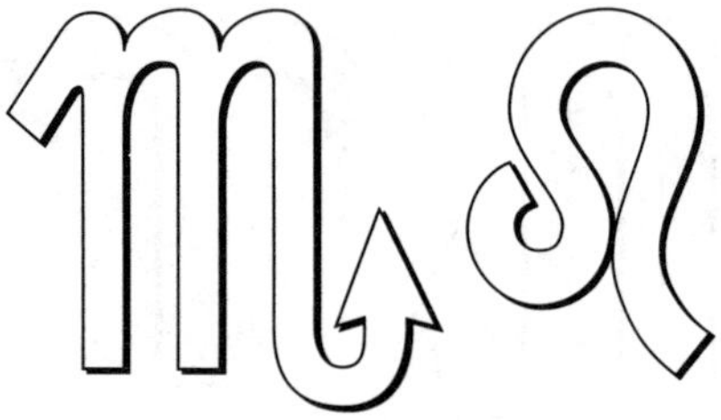

GETTING SO EXCITED

You both know what you want; you want things **your** way. Compromising will be challenging for each of you—but quite rewarding. Both of you can be intensely sexual, and together you may rise to heights neither of you has reached before. You can help him look deeper into life, and he can help you be more dramatic and expressive.

CHALLENGING—2

SCORPIO/VIRGO

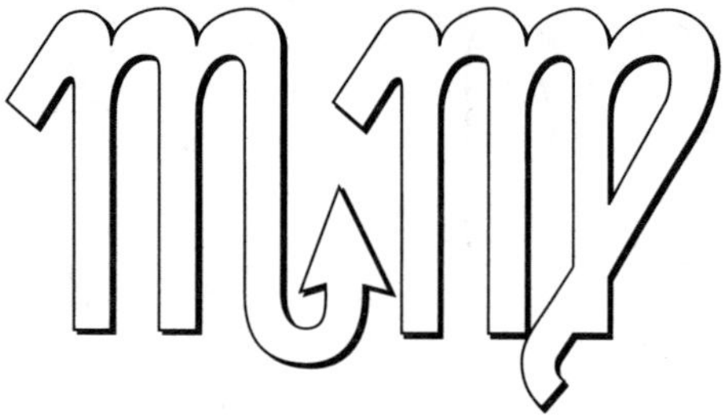

UNFORGETTABLE

Either of you can get obsessed by certain details and forget the larger picture. Your passions run very deeply, but once you make a commitment, it is forever. He is cautious initially, but has great endurance once he gets going. Either of you could use your organizational skills to set just the right scene for love.

COMPATIBLE—3

SCORPIO/LIBRA

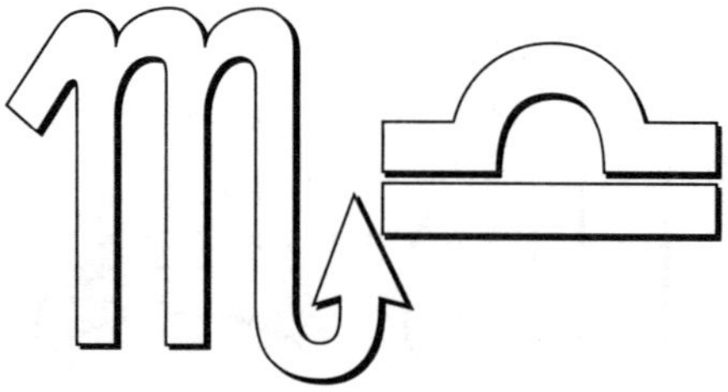

LOVIN' YOU

You two share a focus on partnership, but you are apt to be more intense and inward, while he is more charming and sociable. You require an intense, one-on-one encounter, while he enjoys talking to (and thinking about) many different people. He can help you be more objective, and you can help him reach more passionate, committed depths.

CHALLENGING—2

SCORPIO/SCORPIO

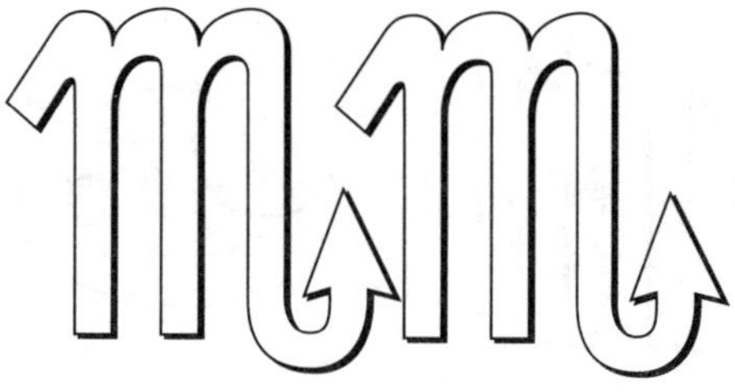

FEVER!

You two can be intensely passionate, sexual and capable of a great, intimate connection. Either of you can also withdraw periodically, to recharge and recover. Jealousy or possessiveness are possible downsides. A commitment that is absolute is the up side. You can care and share more deeply than with anyone else.

VERY COMPATIBLE—4

WHAT'LL I DO?

SCORPIO/SAGITTARIUS

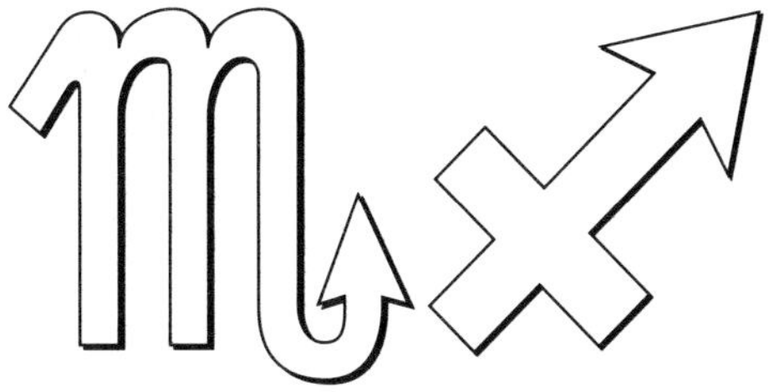

You want depth and he wants breadth. You are totally focused on one person at a time; he likes to at least think about variety. You want security in love; he wants adventures. If you learn from one another, you will add to each other's pleasures and enlarge your lives. Appreciate your different styles.

CHALLENGING—2

TWO HEARTS

SCORPIO/CAPRICORN

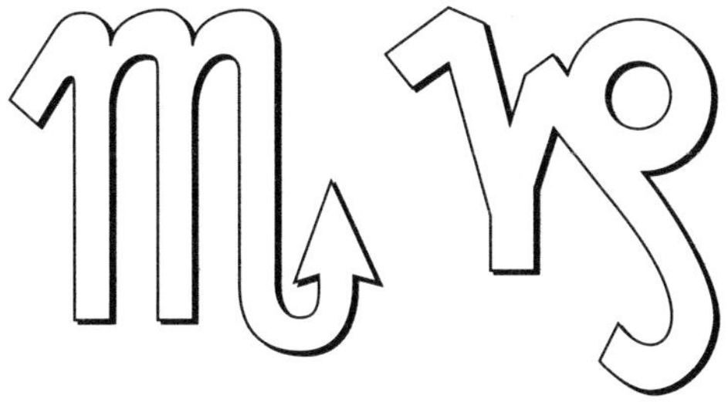

Sex can be pretty serious for both of you! He doesn't want to make any mistakes, and once you commit, you are totally focused on that other person. Although he may take a while to warm up, his endurance could be incredible. The two of you may enjoy marathon sessions of lovemaking.

COMPATIBLE—3

MY FIRST LOVE SONG

SCORPIO/AQUARIUS

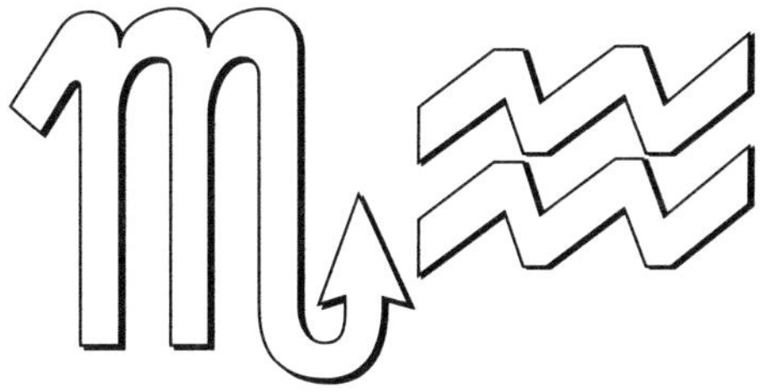

You are looking for a passionate, total commitment. He is looking for variety, excitement, and the new and the different. He may feel you are possessive. You may feel he is undependable. If you are willing to compromise, he can learn from you to look deeper, and you can learn from him to consider more possibilities in life and love.

CHALLENGING—2

LOVE MAKES THE WORLD GO 'ROUND

SCORPIO/PISCES

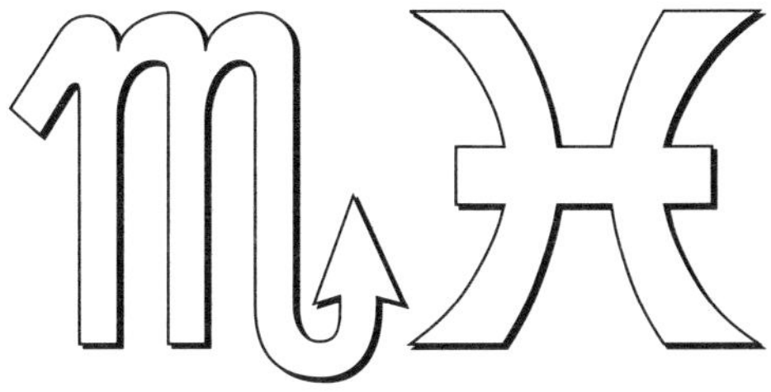

Both of you get very emotionally involved in your sexuality. When you make love, it is total. When he makes love, his whole mind and imagination are involved. You both tend to be inward, so be sure to share enough that you please each other easily. Don't hold on to old hurts. Do use your sensitivity to tune into one another.

COMPATIBLE—3

SAGITTARIUS/ARIES — LOVE IS A MANY SPLENDORED THING

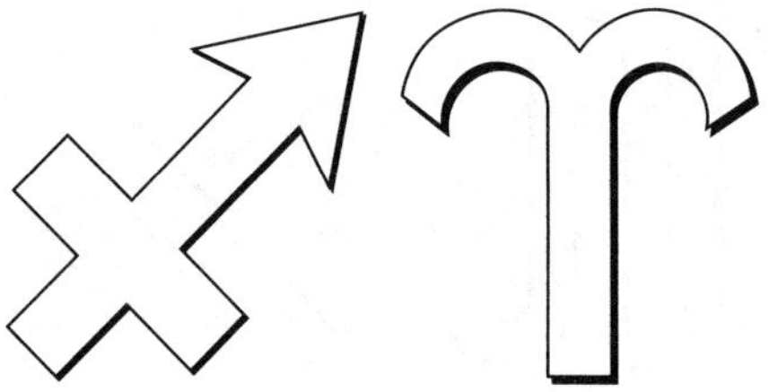

Both of you have an adventurous, freedom-loving streak. You need to go places and do things. Activity feeds your excitement. You may also encourage each other's impulsivity and tendency to take on too much. You keep desire alive with fresh, new and exciting experiences.

COMPATIBLE—3

SAGITTARIUS/TAURUS — SOMEWHERE OUT THERE

You want amorous adventures, excitement, liveliness and fun. He wants the known, safe and familiar. You get turned on by humor, learning and exploring. He gets turned on by comfort, physical caresses and beauty. With mutual understanding, he can help you to be more grounded and you can teach him to be more adventurous.

VERY CHALLENGING—1

SAGITTARIUS/GEMINI — ISN'T IT ROMANTIC?

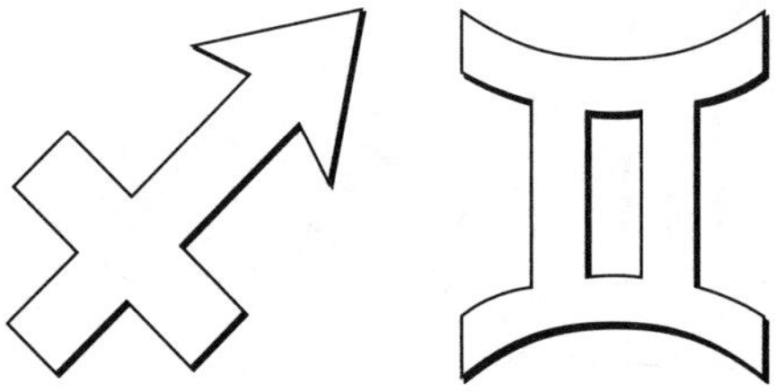

You two will never run out of topics of conversation! Each of you finds people and communication stimulating and may enjoy talking about sexual matters almost as much as doing them! Somewhat flirtatious, you must be able to trust one another. Mental stimulation turns both of you on.

VERY COMPATIBLE—4

SAGITTARIUS/CANCER — SEND IN THE CLOWNS

The two of you are apt to be working on a classic freedom versus closeness struggle. When one of you wants commitment, the other wants independence. When one of you is ready to go adventuring, the other wants to keep the home fires burning. You both will have to work hard at taking turns between independence and attachment.

VERY CHALLENGING—1

ANTICIPATION

SAGITTARIUS/LEO

Two fellow adventurers, you can easily feed the fire and passion within each other. Willing to risk, to try new things, to seek that adrenaline high, you light up each other's lives! You may also encourage foolhardiness or excessive confidence, but generally you feel more alive and have more fun when together.

COMPATIBLE—3

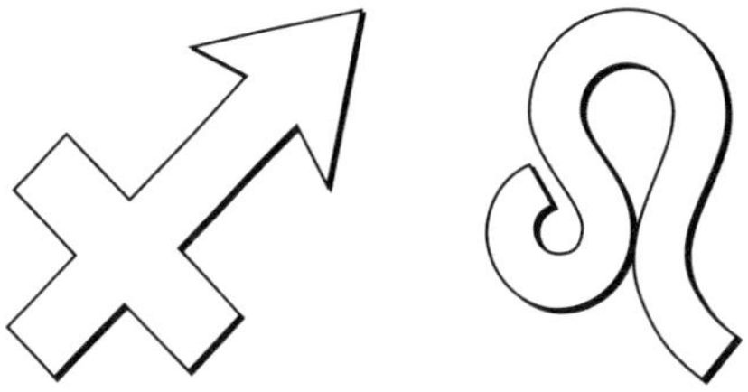

DANCING IN THE DARK

SAGITTARIUS/VIRGO

You may be more open-minded and he more conservative about sex. You enjoy exploring, trying new things and reading new ideas. He tends to be more serious, planning things slowly and carefully. If you appreciate one another, all will be well. You can enjoy his practicality, and he can be excited by your enthusiasm.

CHALLENGING—2

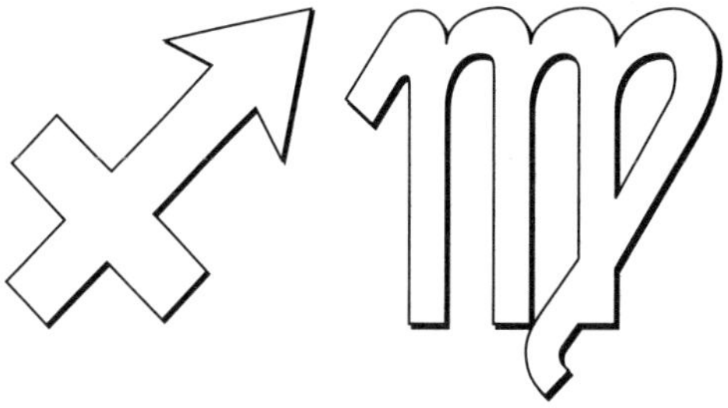

S'WONDERFUL

SAGITTARIUS/LIBRA

You both can have fun with people and sexuality. Outgoing and friendly, you enjoy social give-and-take as well as having a good time in bed. He may focus more on beauty and visual cues, while you may be more turned on mentally. His grace and charm can feed your passion, and your sense of humor and enthusiasm revs his motor.

COMPATIBLE—3

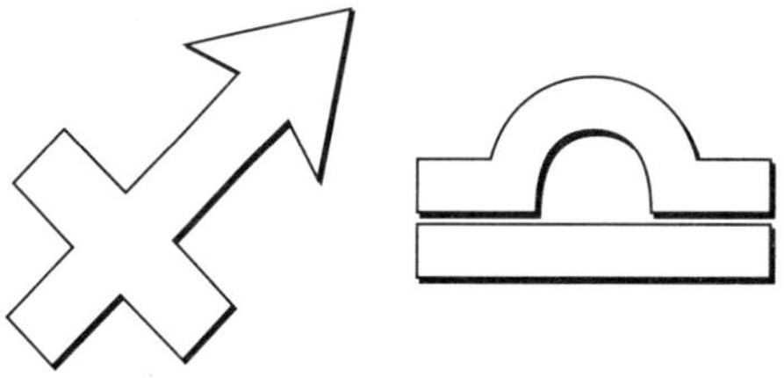

WHAT'LL I DO?

SAGITTARIUS/SCORPIO

You want breadth and he wants depth. He tends to be totally focused and could be possessive; you have to feel free. He prefers security; you want some adventures. If you learn from one another, you will add to each other's pleasures and enlarge your lives. Appreciate your different styles.

CHALLENGING—2

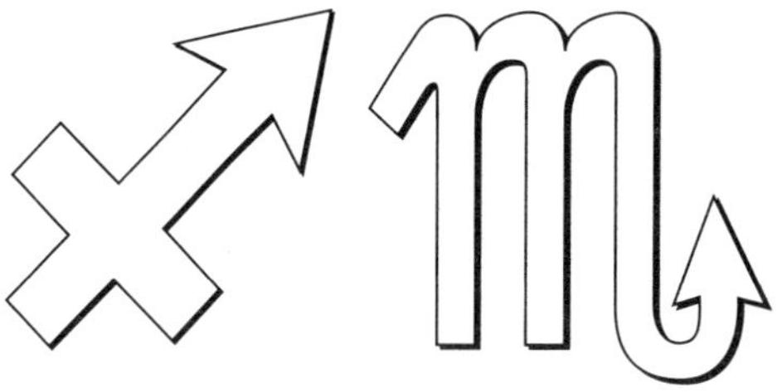

SAGITTARIUS/SAGITTARIUS WILDFIRE

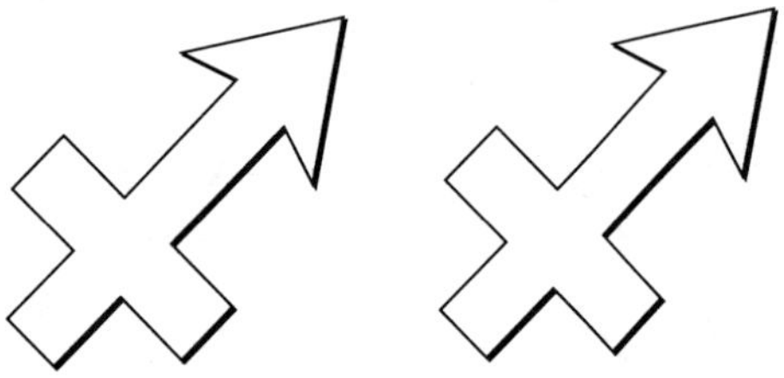

Having a good time—in bed and out of it—is something you both just do naturally. Laughter, fun, excitement and adventures appeal to you both. You may be athletic, intellectual, varied or just full of gusto in your sexual styles. Each of you can do passion in a big way.

VERY COMPATIBLE—4

SAGITTARIUS/CAPRICORN I'M ON FIRE

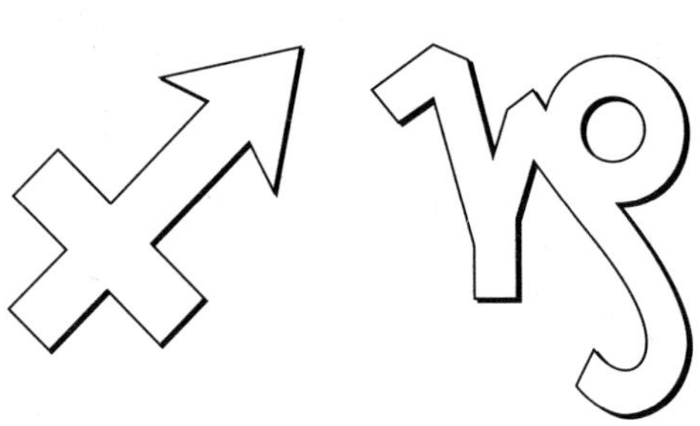

You can easily provide the initial spark, but he has good staying power. Your forte is fun, laughter and beginnings. His forte is dedication, planning and completion. If you don't try to make each other over, but cooperate, your styles will complement one another.

CHALLENGING—2

SAGITTARIUS/AQUARIUS THE SWEET TABOO

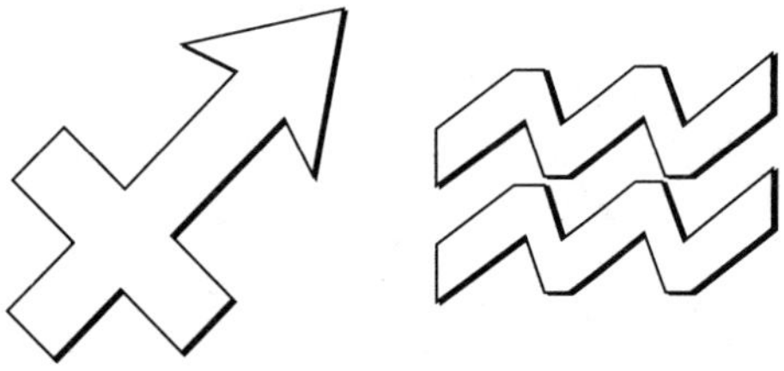

Both of you need to feel free, so don't try to tie each other down too much. Adventurous and willing to try the new, you may expand each other's horizons mentally as well as physically and sexually. Intellectual stimulation can feed your passions. Movement and variety stimulate you both. Try new places and positions.

COMPATIBLE—3

SAGITTARIUS/PISCES OVER THE RAINBOW

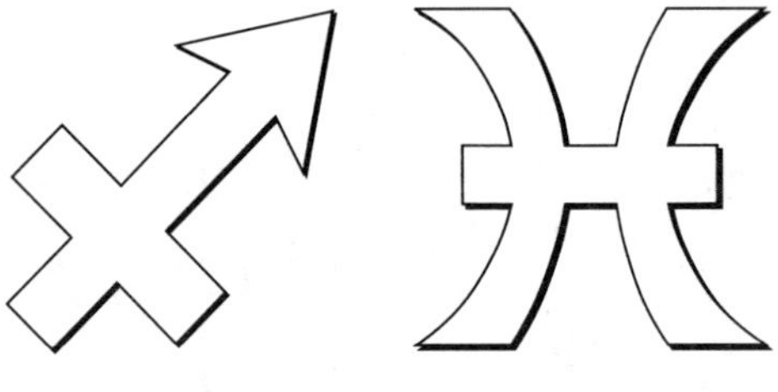

You are both idealists, but you tend to seek your image of perfection in the outer world—exploring, reading or traveling. He tends to seek perfection inside—through art, creative imagination, meditation or some inner work. With communication, insight and understanding, you can each become that ideal love for the other.

CHALLENGING—2

LET'S CALL THE WHOLE THING OFF

CAPRICORN/ARIES

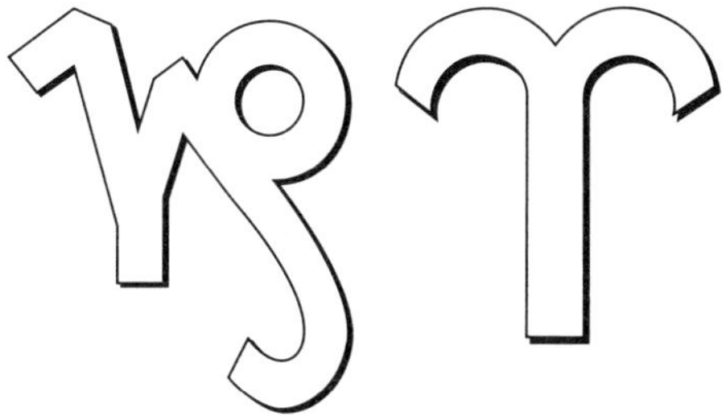

You are cautious, wary of making a mistake and want to be sexually responsible. He is eager, enthusiastic, impulsive, and hates to wait. You want safety; he wants adventures. You take it slow; he wants it fast. He can help you to cut loose occasionally, and you can help him to plan ahead when advisable.

CHALLENGING—2

SOMEONE TO WATCH OVER ME

CAPRICORN/TAURUS

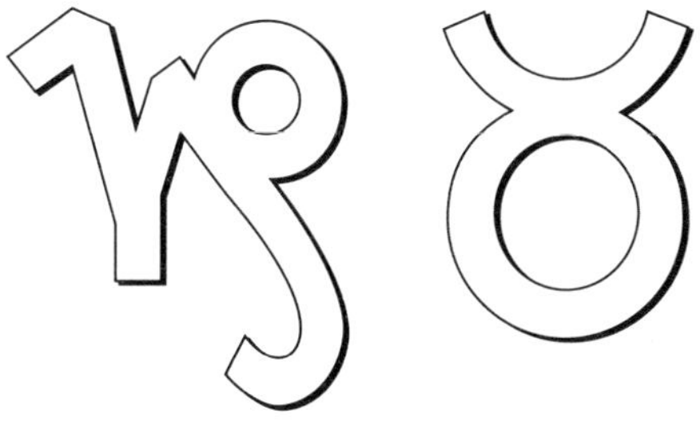

Safety and familiarity rank high with each of you. Practical and grounded, you are not into a high-risk love life. Dependability and practicality turn you both on. You each get excited by physical contact and by competence. You may focus more on effort and he more upon ease, but you nourish one another's attraction to known pleasures.

COMPATIBLE—3

IT'S NOT FOR ME TO SAY

CAPRICORN/GEMINI

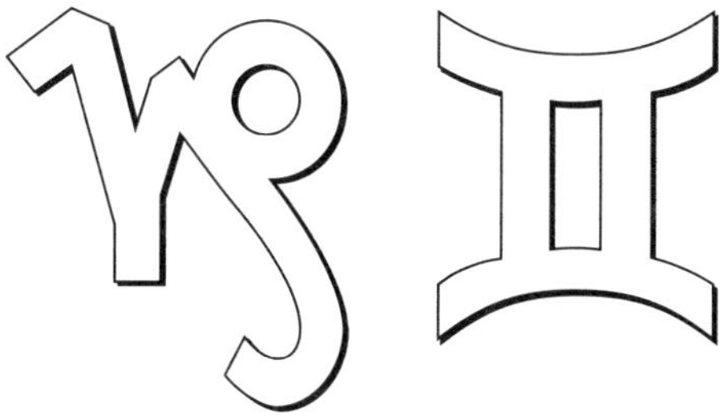

You tend to be serious about sexuality, not wanting to make a mistake. He can be more lighthearted, flippant and casual about desire. You want to feel safe; he enjoys variety (perhaps flirting) and fun. Compromise is essential for you both. He can help you laugh more and take life more lightly. You can help him be more practical and stable.

VERY CHALLENGING—1

I'M OLD-FASHIONED

CAPRICORN/CANCER

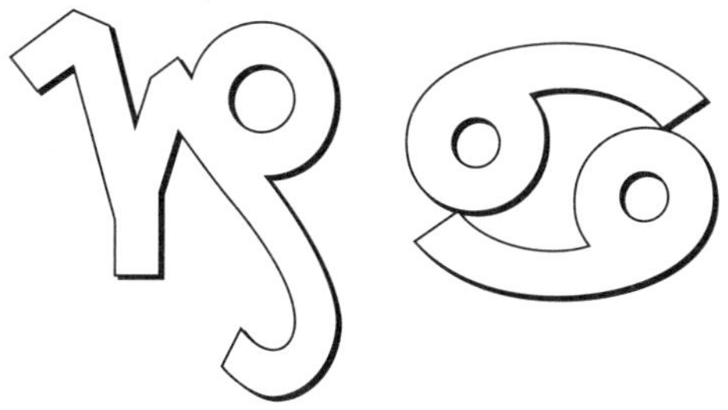

Each of you has a parental streak within, so being supportive, solid and dependable comes naturally. Don't try to turn your partner into a child, but do take turns taking care of one another. You both value fidelity, dependability, family, roots, and an appreciation of the past. You are naturally drawn together.

VERY COMPATIBLE—4

CAPRICORN/LEO

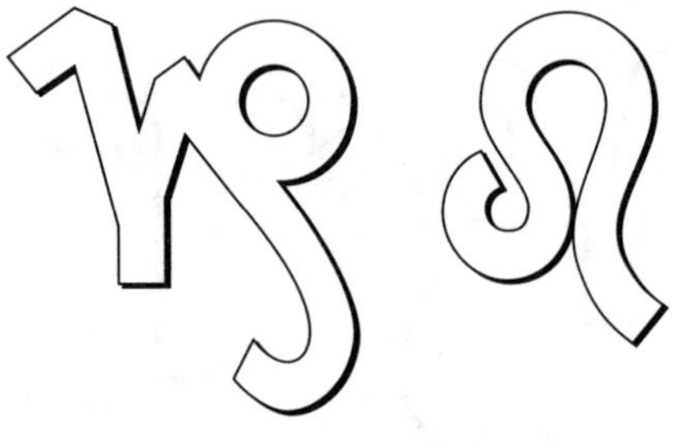

UNDER MY THUMB?

You want to be the Executive and he wants to be the King, so who will rule the roost? Don't fall into power struggles. Let each other hold sway in the areas you do best. He brings life, excitement and sexual magnetism to your shared activities. You bring practicality, responsibility and good planning.

VERY CHALLENGING—1

CAPRICORN/VIRGO

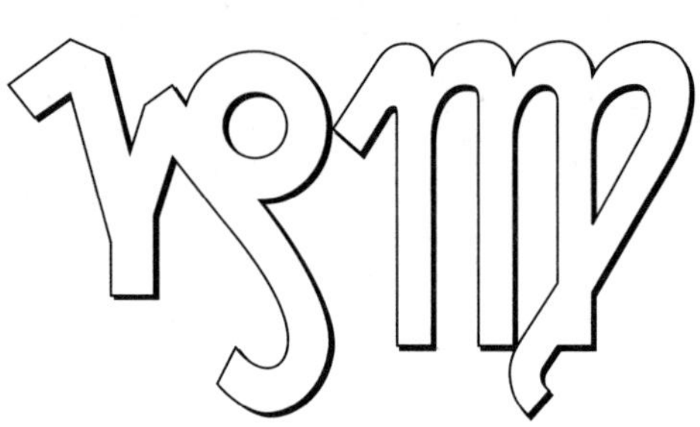

IF I LOVED YOU

You both share a desire for safety and a tendency to take your time in getting involved. Neither of you wants to make a mistake in love! Either of you could inhibit yourself (or your partner) through criticism, or a performance focus. Lots of physical contact works well for you both. Relax and enjoy!

COMPATIBLE—3

CAPRICORN/LIBRA

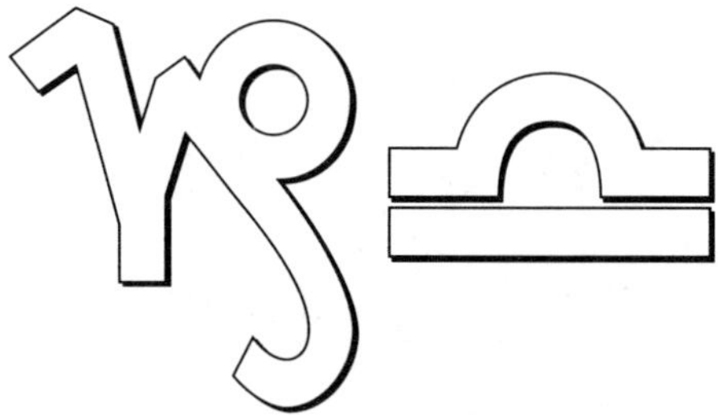

TIL THERE WAS YOU

You may be more cautious sexually, while he is more ready to get involved and interact. You want to avoid any mistakes, whereas he finds people stimulating. Compromise is called for. He can appreciate your sense of responsibility and competence. You can appreciate his charm, poise, and ability to put you at ease.

CHALLENGING—2

CAPRICORN/SCORPIO

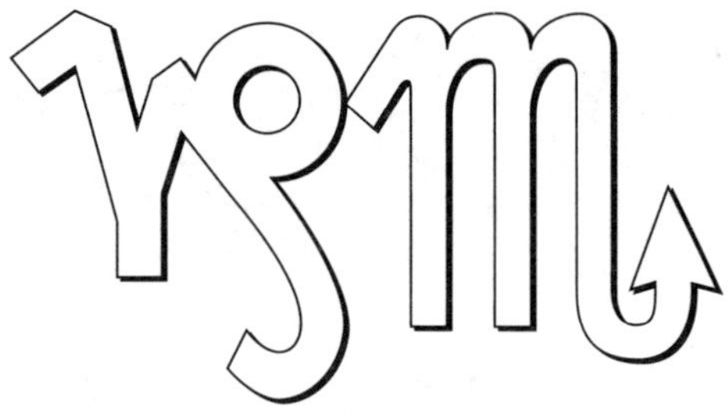

TWO HEARTS

Sex can be pretty serious for both of you! You don't want to make any mistakes, and once he commits, he is totally focused on his partner. You both believe in finishing what you start and with good endurance, may enjoy marathon sessions of lovemaking. You can plan and organize well to create optimum environments for each other.

COMPATIBLE—3

I'M ON FIRE — CAPRICORN/SAGITTARIUS

He may provide the initial spark and action to come together, but you have good staying power. His forte is fun, laughter and beginnings. Your forte is dedication, planning and completion. If you don't try to make each other over, but cooperate, your sexual styles will complement one another.

CHALLENGING—2

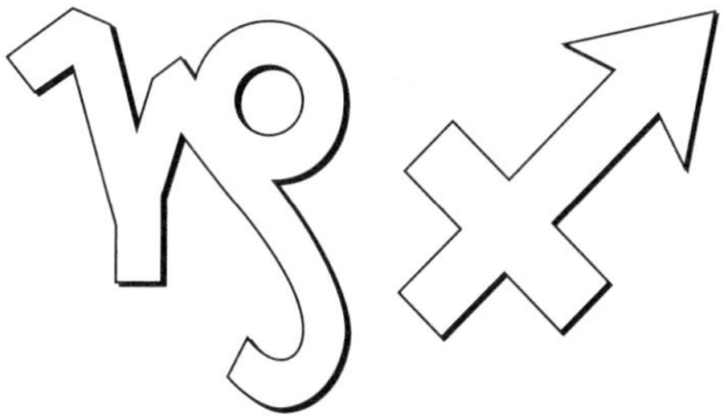

ALWAYS — CAPRICORN/CAPRICORN

You both tend to take sex seriously and want to avoid a mistake at all costs. Responsible, you definitely look before leaping. Although you both need time to warm up, once hot, you can last a **long** time. You appreciate each other's achievements outside the bedroom as well, valuing a partner who is competent and capable.

VERY COMPATIBLE—4

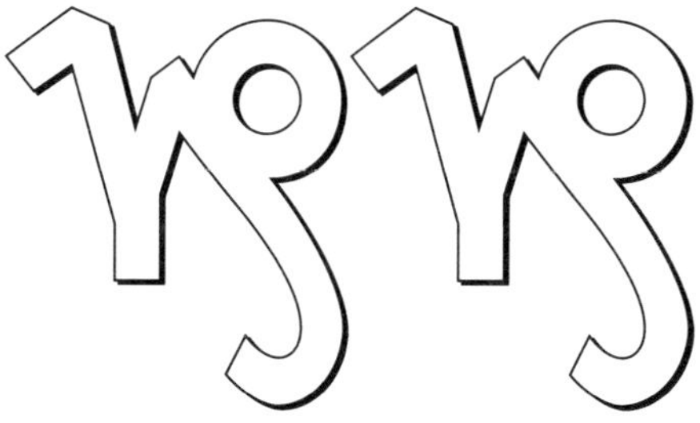

THAT'S THE WAY I'VE ALWAYS HEARD IT SHOULD BE — CAPRICORN/AQUARIUS

You tend to be more conventional and cautious, where he is more sexually adventurous. You like the known and familiar; he likes to at least consider the new and different. Find a compromise which allows a bit of both for fullest satisfaction. He can enlarge your options, and you can help him appreciate security.

CHALLENGING—2

IF I LOVED YOU — CAPRICORN/PISCES

Neither of you is inclined to rush, sexually. You need time to feel safe, to be sure it's right, and to warm up. He needs time to tune into feelings, exercise his imagination and fantasies, and be willing to act. Your dedication and his empathy can make a good combination for learning how to please each other.

COMPATIBLE—3

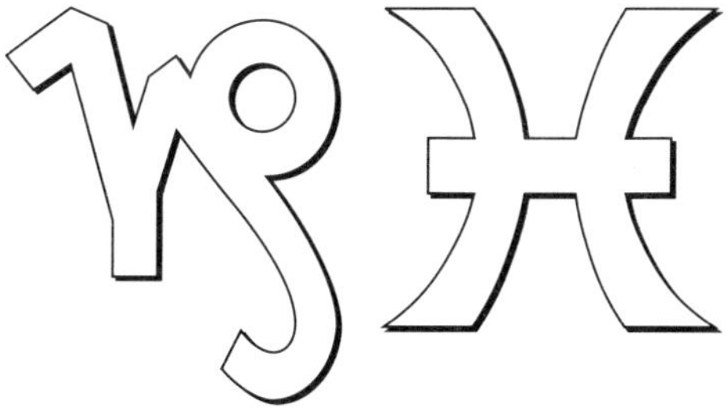

AQUARIUS/ARIES

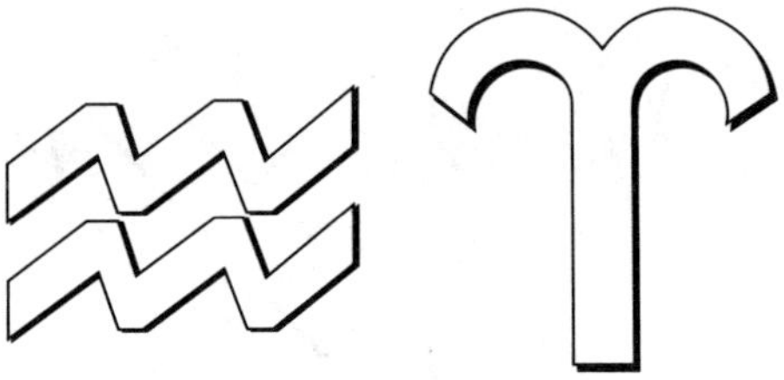

IF EVER I WOULD LEAVE YOU

Each of you tends to be an independent operator, so respect each other's need for space. You both enjoy new experiences, and get bored with repetition. He can encourage you to get into your body and out of your head, and you can help him to sometimes think first and act later.

COMPATIBLE—3

AQUARIUS/TAURUS

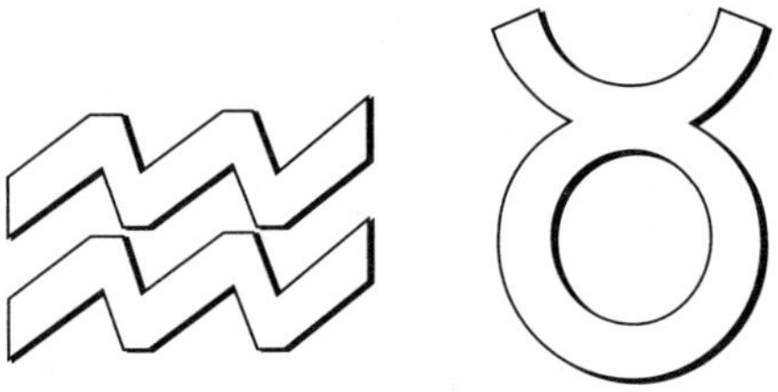

DESPERADO

Although you share a strong sensual streak, you could polarize around issues of security versus risk. He may feel safest treading the usual paths of pleasure, while you want to experiment with the new (or unusual). You can help him loosen up and he can help you appreciate familiar favorites.

CHALLENGING—2

AQUARIUS/GEMINI

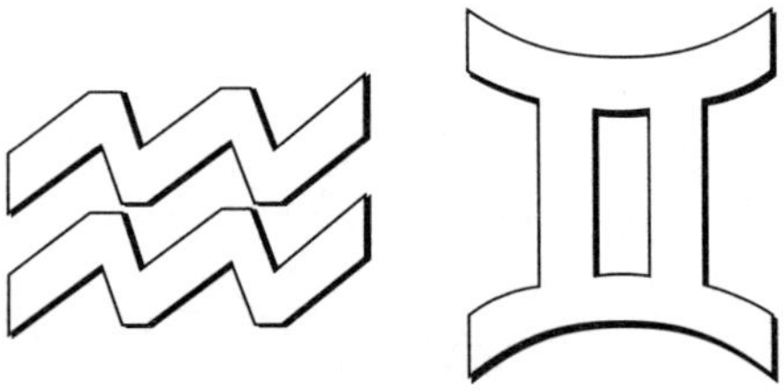

NOT A DAY GOES BY

Freshness appeals to you both. New experiences feed your sense of excitement. Mental stimulation may intensify your desire. Discussions could enhance your shared pleasure as communication is vital to you both. Open and curious, you may be willing to experiment with one another.

COMPATIBLE—3

AQUARIUS/CANCER

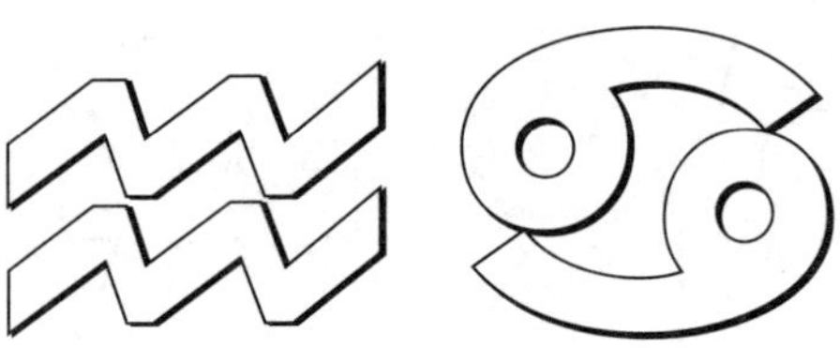

WILD HEART

Your sexual styles may be quite different—one more open, experimental and free-wheeling; the other more cautious, conservative and oriented toward safety. You can learn from one another if neither of you tries to totally change the other to your way. The two of you may feel torn between risk and security, but life demands some of each.

VERY CHALLENGING—1

CAN'T HELP LOVIN' THAT (WO)MAN

AQUARIUS/LEO

The two of you are naturally attracted, but will have to work out the polarity of head versus heart. You could feel pulled between passion and detachment; between what logic says versus what you feel. Don't take opposite ends and fight. Do have a bit of each in your relationship. Lively interchanges work best for you both.

VERY COMPATIBLE—4

MAKE BELIEVE

AQUARIUS/VIRGO

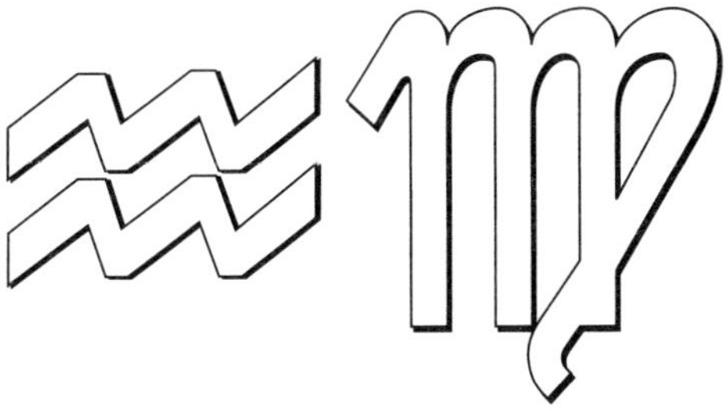

Each of you will have to adapt to the other's style. You may see him as sexually inhibited, conventional or critical, while he could see you as eccentric, too experimental or aloof. You can help him see other options and he can help you stay grounded. A relationship which starts in the mind (and then the body follows) works best.

VERY CHALLENGING—1

PILLOW TALK

AQUARIUS/LIBRA

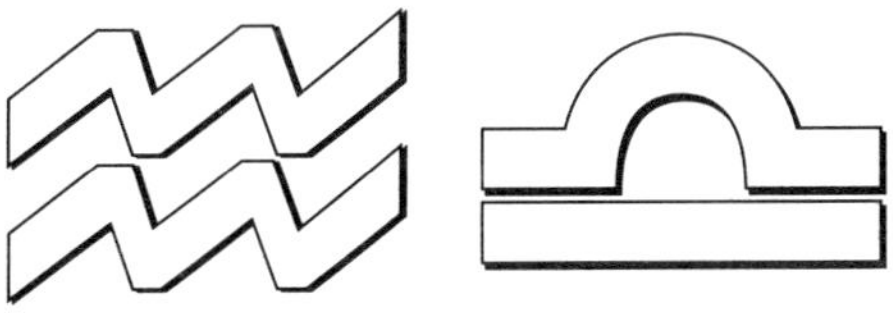

There's a good chance you both enjoy talking in bed! Mental stimulation is important, so tell each other what you enjoy and what's good can get even better. Sharing and an equalitarian attitude are natural for you both, so pleasing one another should flow easily. He may share beauty or competitive interests with you, and you may expose him to new (even unusual) ideas.

COMPATIBLE—3

MY FIRST LOVE SONG

AQUARIUS/SCORPIO

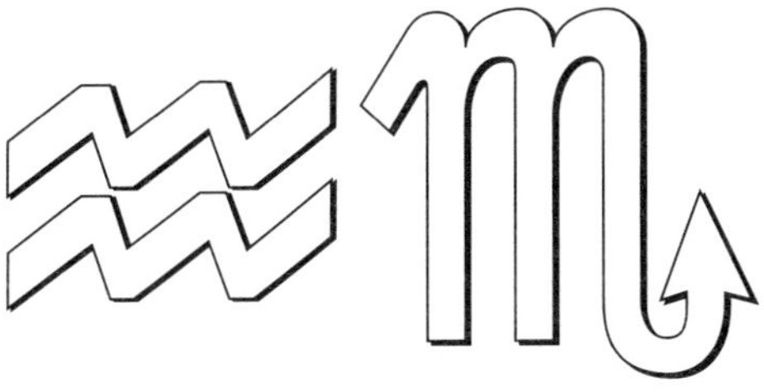

He is looking for a passionate, intense encounter. You want to keep a sense of independence and enjoy exploring the new and the different. You may feel that he is possessive. He may feel you are eccentric. If you are willing to compromise, you can learn from him to look deeper, and he can learn from you to consider more possibilities in life.

CHALLENGING—2

AQUARIUS/SAGITTARIUS

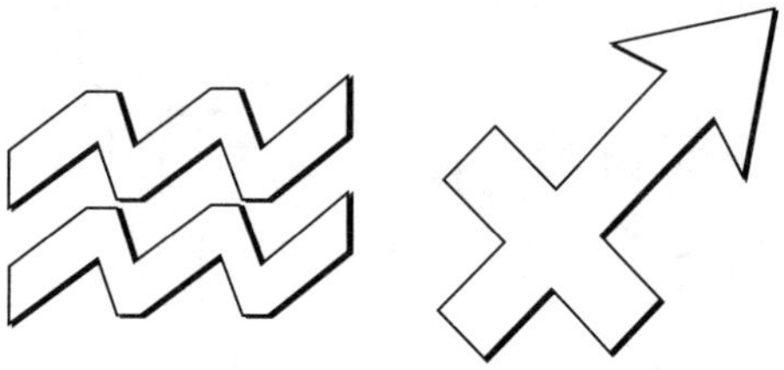

THE SWEET TABOO

Both of you need to feel free, so don't try to tie each other down too much. Adventurous and willing to try the new, you may expand each other's horizons mentally as well as physically and sexually. Intellectual stimulation can feed your passions. Movement and variety stimulate you both. Try new places and positions.

COMPATIBLE—3

AQUARIUS/CAPRICORN

THAT'S THE WAY I'VE ALWAYS HEARD IT SHOULD BE

You cherish your independence, while he is used to being in charge and in control. He prefers the known and familiar; you like to at least consider the new and different. Find a compromise which allows a bit of both for fullest satisfaction. You can enlarge his options, and he can help you appreciate security.

CHALLENGING—2

AQUARIUS/AQUARIUS

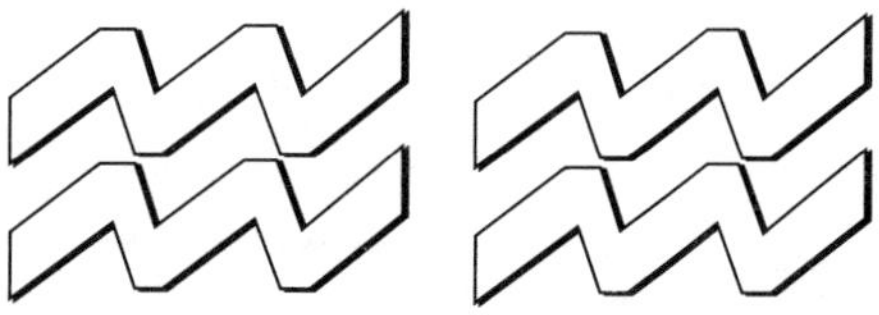

WILD THING

Fellow individualists, you will make love in your own unique fashions! Open and experimental, you're willing to at least think about almost anything. New positions and places may turn you both on. Somewhat independent, you need to allow each other some space. Mental stimulation soon turns to physical with each of you.

VERY COMPATIBLE—4

AQUARIUS/PISCES

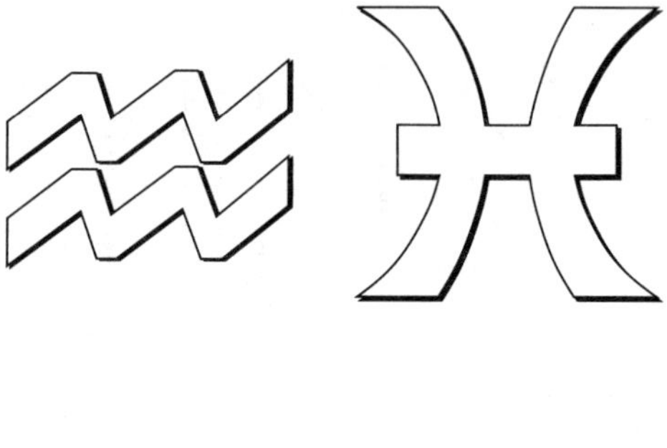

OPEN YOUR HEART

A rich inner life could contribute to your sexual experiences. You are willing to seek the new and consider alternatives. He is imaginative and easily turned on by fantasy. You may want to discuss everything, whereas he keeps much inside. Your open-mindedness and his empathy can aid mutual pleasure.

CHALLENGING—2

LOVE IS A ROSE

PISCES/ARIES

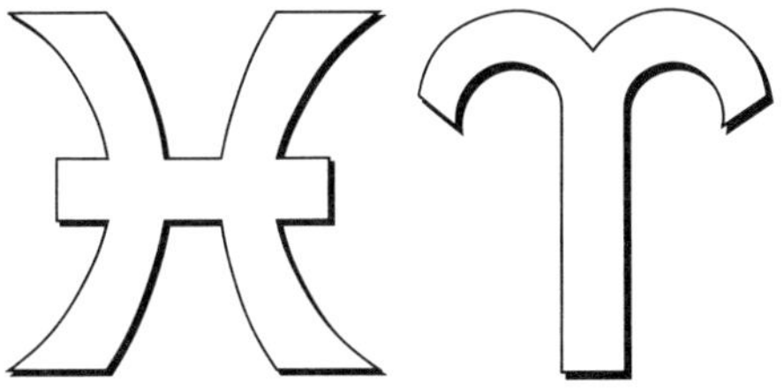

You're admiring the colors of the sunset, and he's eager to march into action! You're sensitive and don't reveal everything you are feeling. He is direct and open. He gets turned on quickly; you need to ease into it. He can help you find more excitement in life. You can help him stop and smell the flowers.

CHALLENGING—2

THE COLOR OF LOVE

PISCES/TAURUS

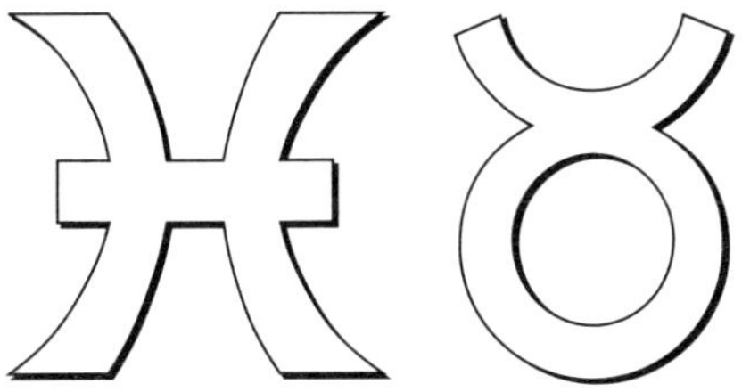

Beauty turns you both on. He, however, needs physical contact, while you can operate from pure imagination. You may be more romantic or idealistic, while he is more practical. He can help ground you; you can help sensitize him. Nature and aesthetic experiences feed your libidos.

COMPATIBLE—3

TWELFTH OF NEVER

PISCES/GEMINI

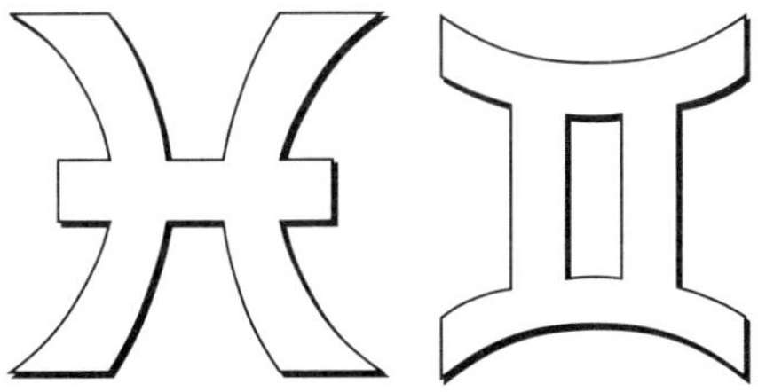

Getting your timing together may be a challenge. You may want to talk when he wants silence, and vice versa. You are concerned about feelings, and he is focused on logic. You withdraw while he is more of an extravert. You can increase his empathy and sensitivity, and he can encourage your curiosity and openness.

CHALLENGING—2

LOVE ME TENDER

PISCES/CANCER

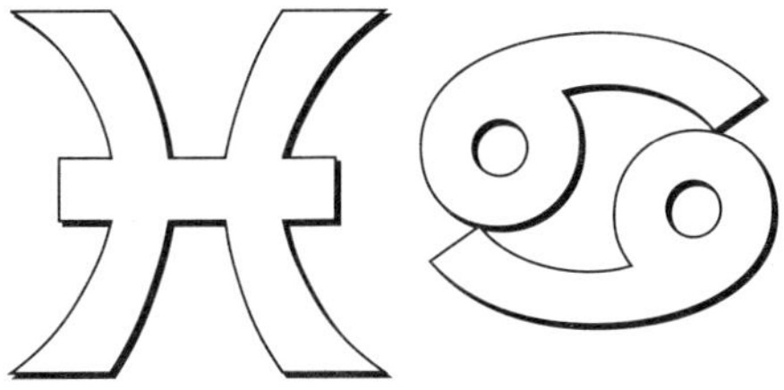

Each of you has a very gentle, sensitive, empathic side, and you may even tune into each other's feelings without words. With deep, strong emotions, either of you can be swept away but would tend to hold back initially for fear of being hurt. Tenderness is your best connection.

COMPATIBLE—3

PISCES/LEO

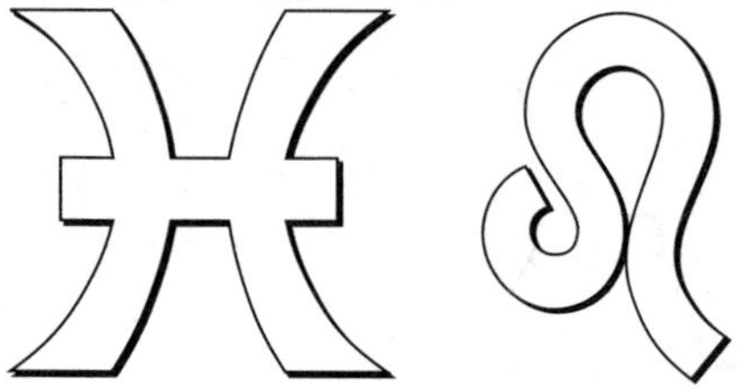

DO YOU BELIEVE IN MAGIC?

Although you both can be quite romantic, his sexual style is more dramatic and flamboyant, while yours is more inward and reserved. You may feel he comes on too strong at times; he may feel you are too sensitive or keep too much hidden. Learn to appreciate each other's different viewpoints and you will both grow.

VERY CHALLENGING—1

PISCES/VIRGO

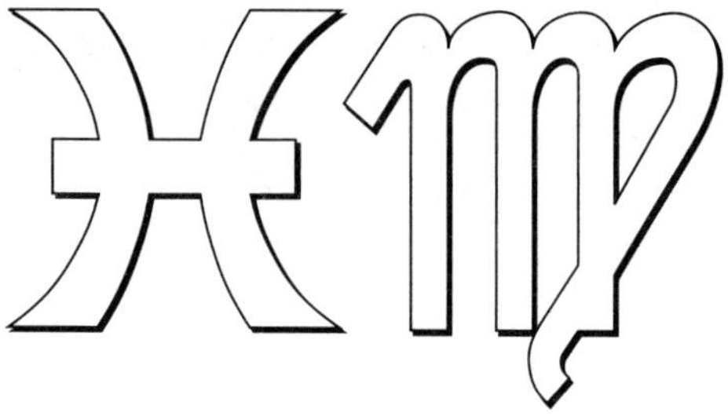

YOU WERE MEANT FOR ME

The two of you could literally make beautiful music together! You are blending lovely, artistic, idealistic images with the common sense to create something better here on Earth. If you don't polarize into the space cadet and super critic, your natural attraction can lead to poetry in motion when you make love.

VERY COMPATIBLE—4

PISCES/LIBRA

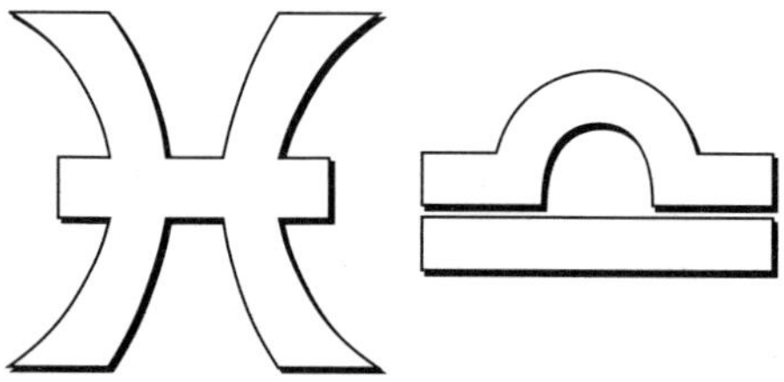

KISSES SWEETER THAN WINE

He gets turned on by interacting with someone, talking and perhaps even competing. You respond strongly to sensitivity and shared emotions. A shared appreciation of beauty could help you get together. Create an attractive environment to share when making love. He can help you be more expressive; you can encourage his imagination and empathy.

VERY CHALLENGING—1

PISCES/SCORPIO

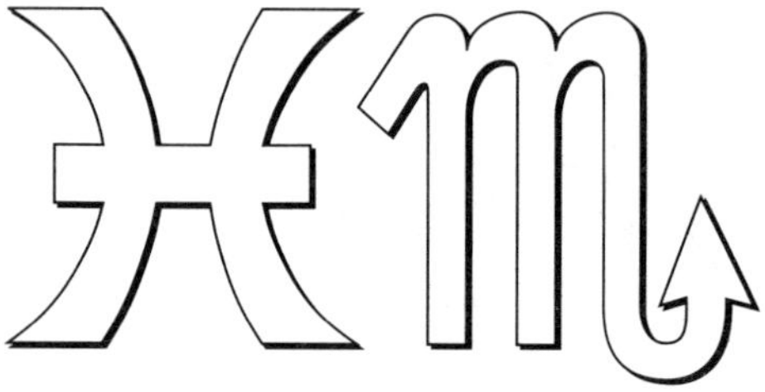

LOVE MAKES THE WORLD GO 'ROUND

Both of you get very emotionally involved in your sexuality. When he makes love, it is total. When you make love, your whole heart and soul are involved. You both tend to be inward, so be sure to share enough that you please each other easily. Don't hold on to old hurts. Do use your sensitivity to tune into one another.

COMPATIBLE—3

OVER THE RAINBOW

PISCES/SAGITTARIUS

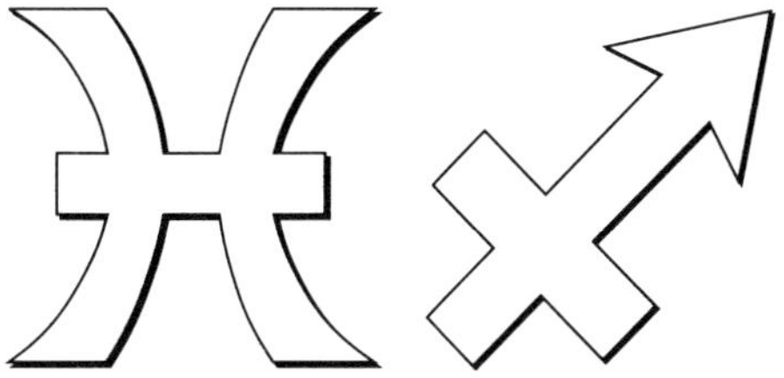

You are both idealists, but he tends to seek his image of perfection in the outer world—exploring, reading or traveling. You tend to seek perfection inside—through art, creative imagination, meditation or some inner work. With communication, insight and understanding, you can each become that ideal love for the other.

CHALLENGING—2

IF I LOVED YOU

PISCES/CAPRICORN

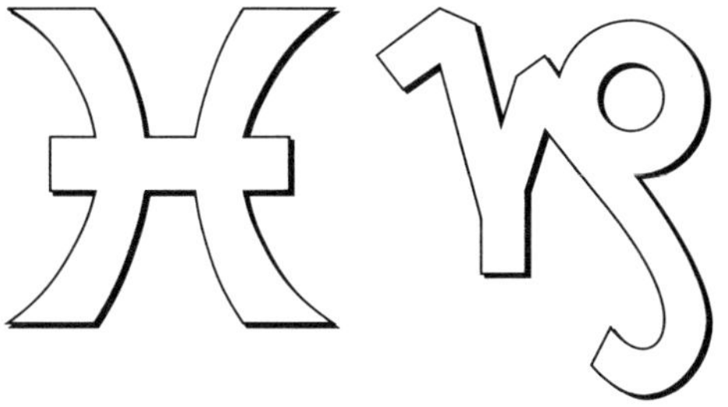

Neither of you is inclined to rush, sexually. He needs time to feel in control and to be sure it's right (not a mistake). You need time to tune into feelings, exercise your imagination, and be willing to act. His dedication and your empathy can make a good combination for learning how to please each other.

COMPATIBLE—3

OPEN YOUR HEART

PISCES/AQUARIUS

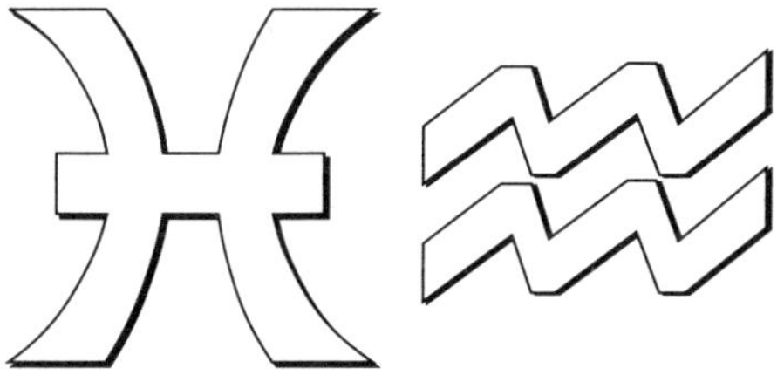

A rich inner life could contribute to your sexual experiences. He is willing to seek the new and consider alternatives. You are imaginative and easily turned on by romance. He may want to try and discuss everything, whereas you could be more timid. His open-mindedness and your empathy can aid mutual pleasure.

CHALLENGING—2

IF

PISCES/PISCES

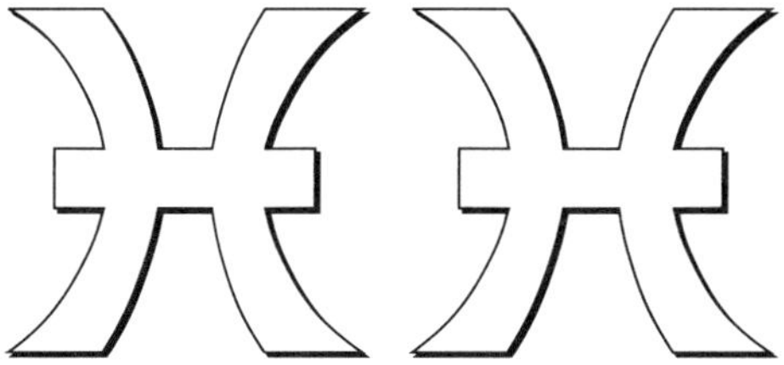

Making love can be like a beautiful dream between you (or either of you could decide fantasy beats reality). Empathic, tender and sensitive, you find it easy to tune into a partner's desires. You can turn sex into a work of art, a graceful dance that inspires each of you to greater heights.

VERY COMPATIBLE—4

Your Starway to Love
Book of Planetary Positions

Planetary Positions

1909

Your Starway to Love

☉ =Sun ☿ = Mercury ♀ = Venus ♂ = Mars ♈ = Aries ♉ = Taurus ♊ = Gemini ♋ = Cancer

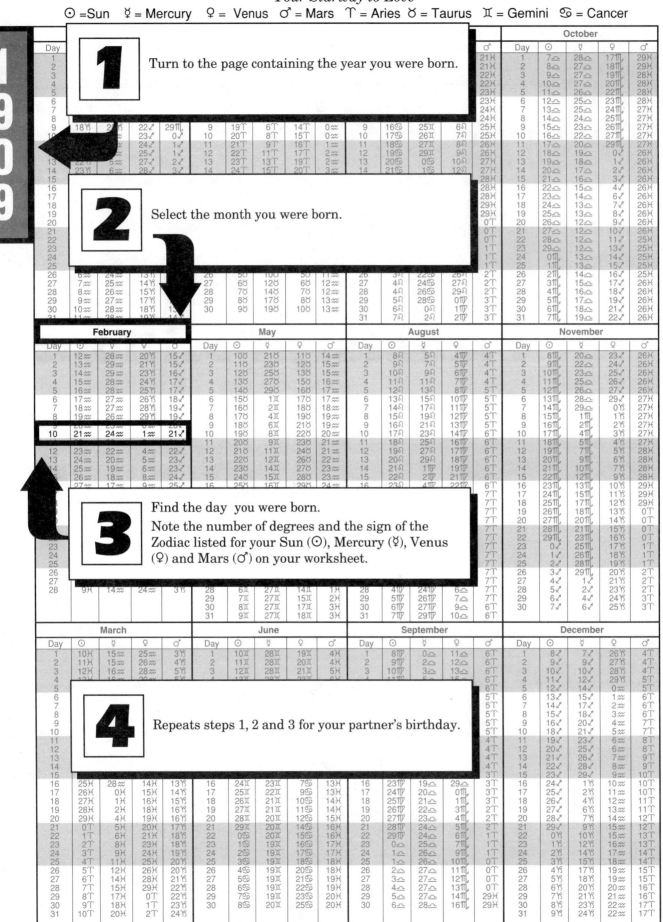

1 Turn to the page containing the year you were born.

2 Select the month you were born.

3 Find the day you were born.
Note the number of degrees and the sign of the Zodiac listed for your Sun (☉), Mercury (☿), Venus (♀) and Mars (♂) on your worksheet.

4 Repeats steps 1, 2 and 3 for your partner's birthday.

January

Day	☉	☿	♀	♂
1				
2				
3				
4				
5				
6				
7				
8				
9	18♑	[illegible]	22♐	29♏
10			23♐	0♐
11			24♐	1♐
12			25♐	1♐
13	22♑	5♒	27♐	2♐
14	23♑	6♒	28♐	3♐
15				
16				
17				
18				
19				
20				
21				
22				
23				
24				
25				
26	6♒	24♒	13♑	
27	7♒	25♒	14♑	
28	8♒	26♒	15♑	
29	9♒	27♒	17♑	
30	10♒	28♒	18♑	13♐

February

Day	☉	☿	♀	♂
1	12♒	28♒	20♑	15♐
2	13♒	29♒	21♑	15♐
3	14♒	29♒	23♑	16♐
4	15♒	28♒	24♑	17♐
5	16♒	28♒	25♑	17♐
6	17♒	27♒	26♑	18♐
7	18♒	27♒	28♑	19♐
8	19♒	26♒	29♑	19♐
10	21♒	24♒	1♒	21♐
12	23♒	22♒	4♒	22♐
13	24♒	20♒	5♒	23♐
14	25♒	19♒	6♒	23♐
15	26♒	18♒	8♒	24♐
16	27♒	17♒	9♒	25♐
23				
24				
25				
26				
27				
28	9♓	14♒	24♒	3♑

March

Day	☉	☿	♀	♂
1	10♓	15♒	25♒	3♑
2	11♓	15♒	26♒	4♑
3	12♓	16♒	28♒	5♑
4				
5				
6				
7				
8				
9				
10				
11				
12				
13				
14				
15				
16	25♓	28♒	14♓	13♑
17	26♓	0♓	15♓	14♑
18	27♓	1♓	16♓	15♑
19	28♓	2♓	18♓	16♑
20	29♓	4♓	19♓	16♑
21	0♈	5♓	20♓	17♑
22	1♈	6♓	21♓	18♑
23	2♈	8♓	23♓	18♑
24	3♈	9♓	24♓	19♑
25	4♈	11♓	25♓	20♑
26	5♈	12♓	26♓	20♑
27	6♈	14♓	28♓	21♑
28	7♈	15♓	29♓	22♑
29	8♈	17♓	0♈	22♑
30	9♈	18♓	1♈	23♑
31	10♈	20♓	2♈	24♑

April

Day	☉	☿	♀	♂
9	19♈	6♈	14♈	0♒
10	20♈	8♈	15♈	0♒
11	21♈	9♈	16♈	1♒
12	22♈	11♈	17♈	2♒
13	23♈	13♈	19♈	2♒
14	24♈	15♈	20♈	3♒
26	5♉	10♉	5♉	11♒
27	6♉	12♉	6♉	12♒
28	7♉	14♉	7♉	12♒
29	8♉	17♉	8♉	13♒
30	9♉	19♉	10♉	13♒

May

Day	☉	☿	♀	♂
1	10♉	21♉	11♉	14♒
2	11♉	23♉	12♉	15♒
3	12♉	25♉	13♉	15♒
4	13♉	27♉	15♉	16♒
5	14♉	29♉	16♉	17♒
6	15♉	1♊	17♉	17♒
7	16♉	2♊	18♉	18♒
8	17♉	4♊	19♉	19♒
9	18♉	6♊	21♉	19♒
10	19♉	8♊	22♉	20♒
11	20♉	9♊	23♉	21♒
12	21♉	11♊	24♉	21♒
13	22♉	12♊	26♉	22♒
14	23♉	14♊	27♉	23♒
15	24♉	15♊	28♉	23♒
16	25♉	16♊	29♉	24♒
28	6♊	27♊	14♊	1♓
29	7♊	27♊	15♊	2♓
30	8♊	27♊	17♊	3♓
31	9♊	27♊	18♊	3♓

June

Day	☉	☿	♀	♂
1	10♊	28♊	19♊	4♓
2	11♊	28♊	20♊	4♓
3	12♊	28♊	21♊	5♓
16	24♊	23♊	7♋	13♓
17	25♊	22♊	9♋	13♓
18	26♊	21♊	10♋	14♓
19	27♊	21♊	11♋	14♓
20	28♊	20♊	12♋	15♓
21	29♊	20♊	14♋	16♓
22	0♋	20♊	15♋	16♓
23	1♋	19♊	16♋	17♓
24	2♋	19♊	17♋	17♓
25	3♋	19♊	18♋	18♓
26	4♋	19♊	20♋	18♓
27	5♋	19♊	21♋	19♓
28	6♋	19♊	22♋	19♓
29	7♋	19♊	23♋	20♓
30	8♋	20♊	25♋	20♓

July

Day	☉	☿	♀	♂
1				21♓
2				21♓
3				22♓
4				22♓
5				23♓
6				23♓
7				24♓
8				24♓
9	16♋	25♊	6♌	25♓
10	17♋	26♊	7♌	25♓
11	18♋	27♊	8♌	26♓
12	19♋	29♊	9♌	26♓
13	20♋	0♋	10♌	27♓
14	21♋	1♋	12♌	27♓
15				28♓
16				28♓
17				28♓
18				29♓
19				29♓
20				0♈
21				0♈
22				0♈
23				1♈
24				1♈
25				1♈
26	3♌	22♋	26♌	2♈
27	4♌	24♋	27♌	2♈
28	4♌	26♋	29♌	2♈
29	5♌	28♋	0♍	3♈
30	6♌	0♌	1♍	3♈
31	7♌	2♌	2♍	3♈

August

Day	☉	☿	♀	♂
1	8♌	5♌	4♍	4♈
2	9♌	7♌	5♍	4♈
3	10♌	9♌	6♍	4♈
4	11♌	11♌	7♍	4♈
5	12♌	13♌	8♍	5♈
6	13♌	15♌	10♍	5♈
7	14♌	17♌	11♍	5♈
8	15♌	19♌	12♍	5♈
9	16♌	21♌	13♍	5♈
10	17♌	23♌	14♍	6♈
11	18♌	25♌	16♍	6♈
12	19♌	27♌	17♍	6♈
13	20♌	29♌	18♍	6♈
14	21♌	1♍	19♍	6♈
15	22♌	2♍	21♍	6♈
16	23♌	4♍	22♍	6♈
17				7♈
18				7♈
19				7♈
20				7♈
21				7♈
22				7♈
23				7♈
24				7♈
25				7♈
26				7♈
27				7♈
28	4♍	24♍	6♎	7♈
29	5♍	26♍	7♎	7♈
30	6♍	27♍	9♎	6♈
31	7♍	29♍	10♎	6♈

September

Day	☉	☿	♀	♂
1	8♍	0♎	11♎	6♈
2	9♍	2♎	12♎	6♈
3	10♍	3♎	13♎	6♈
4				6♈
5				6♈
6				5♈
7				5♈
8				5♈
9				5♈
10				5♈
11				4♈
12				4♈
13				4♈
14				4♈
15				3♈
16	23♍	19♎	29♎	3♈
17	24♍	20♎	0♏	3♈
18	25♍	21♎	1♏	3♈
19	26♍	22♎	3♏	2♈
20	27♍	23♎	4♏	2♈
21	28♍	24♎	5♏	2♈
22	29♍	24♎	6♏	1♈
23	0♎	25♎	7♏	1♈
24	1♎	26♎	9♏	1♈
25	1♎	26♎	10♏	0♈
26	2♎	27♎	11♏	0♈
27	3♎	27♎	12♏	0♈
28	4♎	27♎	13♏	0♈
29	5♎	27♎	14♏	29♓
30	6♎	28♎	16♏	29♓

October

Day	☉	☿	♀	♂
1	7♎	28♎	17♏	29♓
2	8♎	27♎	18♏	29♓
3	9♎	27♎	19♏	28♓
4	10♎	27♎	20♏	28♓
5	11♎	26♎	22♏	28♓
6	12♎	25♎	23♏	28♓
7	13♎	25♎	24♏	27♓
8	14♎	24♎	25♏	27♓
9	15♎	23♎	26♏	27♓
10	16♎	22♎	27♏	27♓
11	17♎	20♎	29♏	27♓
12	18♎	19♎	0♐	26♓
13	19♎	18♎	1♐	26♓
14	20♎	17♎	2♐	26♓
15	21♎	16♎	3♐	26♓
16	22♎	15♎	4♐	26♓
17	23♎	14♎	6♐	26♓
18	24♎	13♎	7♐	26♓
19	25♎	13♎	8♐	26♓
20	26♎	12♎	9♐	26♓
21	27♎	12♎	10♐	26♓
22	28♎	12♎	11♐	25♓
23	29♎	12♎	13♐	25♓
24	0♏	13♎	14♐	25♓
25	1♏	13♎	15♐	25♓
26	2♏	14♎	16♐	25♓
27	3♏	15♎	17♐	26♓
28	4♏	16♎	18♐	26♓
29	5♏	17♎	19♐	26♓
30	6♏	18♎	21♐	26♓
31	7♏	19♎	22♐	26♓

November

Day	☉	☿	♀	♂
1	8♏	20♎	23♐	26♓
2	9♏	22♎	24♐	26♓
3	10♏	23♎	25♐	26♓
4	11♏	25♎	26♐	26♓
5	12♏	26♎	27♐	26♓
6	13♏	28♎	29♐	27♓
7	14♏	29♎	0♑	27♓
8	15♏	1♏	1♑	27♓
9	16♏	2♏	2♑	27♓
10	17♏	4♏	3♑	27♓
11	18♏	5♏	4♑	27♓
12	19♏	7♏	5♑	28♓
13	20♏	9♏	6♑	28♓
14	21♏	10♏	7♑	28♓
15	22♏	12♏	9♑	28♓
16	23♏	13♏	10♑	29♓
17	24♏	15♏	11♑	29♓
18	25♏	17♏	12♑	29♓
19	26♏	18♏	13♑	0♈
20	27♏	20♏	14♑	0♈
21	28♏	21♏	15♑	0♈
22	29♏	23♏	16♑	0♈
23	0♐	25♏	17♑	1♈
24	1♐	26♏	18♑	1♈
25	2♐	28♏	19♑	1♈
26	3♐	29♏	20♑	2♈
27	4♐	1♐	21♑	2♈
28	5♐	2♐	23♑	2♈
29	6♐	4♐	24♑	3♈
30	7♐	6♐	25♑	3♈

December

Day	☉	☿	♀	♂
1	8♐	7♐	26♑	4♈
2	9♐	9♐	27♑	4♈
3	10♐	10♐	28♑	4♈
4	11♐	12♐	29♑	5♈
5	12♐	14♐	0♒	5♈
6	13♐	15♐	1♒	6♈
7	14♐	17♐	2♒	6♈
8	15♐	18♐	3♒	6♈
9	16♐	20♐	4♒	7♈
10	18♐	21♐	5♒	7♈
11	19♐	23♐	6♒	8♈
12	20♐	25♐	6♒	8♈
13	21♐	26♐	7♒	9♈
14	22♐	28♐	8♒	9♈
15	23♐	29♐	9♒	10♈
16	24♐	1♑	10♒	10♈
17	25♐	2♑	11♒	10♈
18	26♐	4♑	12♒	11♈
19	27♐	6♑	13♒	11♈
20	28♐	7♑	14♒	12♈
21	29♐	9♑	15♒	12♈
22	0♑	10♑	15♒	13♈
23	1♑	12♑	16♒	13♈
24	2♑	14♑	17♒	14♈
25	3♑	15♑	18♒	14♈
26	4♑	17♑	19♒	15♈
27	5♑	18♑	19♒	15♈
28	6♑	20♑	20♒	16♈
29	7♑	21♑	21♒	16♈
30	8♑	23♑	22♒	17♈
31	9♑	24♑	22♒	17♈

Planetary Positions

♌ = Leo ♍ = Virgo ♎ = Libra ♏ = Scorpio ♐ = Sagittarius ♑ = Capricorn ♒ = Aquarius ♓ = Pisces

1900

January

Day	☉	☿	♀	♂
1	10♑	19♐	7♒	14♑
2	11♑	21♐	8♒	15♑
3	12♑	22♐	9♒	16♑
4	13♑	23♐	10♒	16♑
5	14♑	25♐	12♒	17♑
6	15♑	26♐	13♒	18♑
7	16♑	27♐	14♒	19♑
8	18♑	29♐	15♒	19♑
9	19♑	0♑	17♒	20♑
10	20♑	2♑	18♒	21♑
11	21♑	3♑	19♒	22♑
12	22♑	5♑	20♒	23♑
13	23♑	6♑	22♒	23♑
14	24♑	7♑	23♒	24♑
15	25♑	9♑	24♒	25♑
16	26♑	10♑	25♒	26♑
17	27♑	12♑	26♒	26♑
18	28♑	13♑	28♒	27♑
19	29♑	15♑	29♒	28♑
20	0♒	17♑	0♓	29♑
21	1♒	18♑	1♓	0♒
22	2♒	20♑	3♓	0♒
23	3♒	21♑	4♓	1♒
24	4♒	23♑	5♓	2♒
25	5♒	24♑	6♓	3♒
26	6♒	26♑	8♓	3♒
27	7♒	28♑	9♓	4♒
28	8♒	29♑	10♓	5♒
29	9♒	1♒	11♓	6♒
30	10♒	2♒	12♓	7♒
31	11♒	4♒	14♓	7♒

February

Day	☉	☿	♀	♂
1	12♒	6♒	15♓	8♒
2	13♒	7♒	16♓	9♒
3	14♒	9♒	17♓	10♒
4	15♒	11♒	19♓	11♒
5	16♒	13♒	20♓	11♒
6	17♒	14♒	21♓	12♒
7	18♒	16♒	22♓	13♒
8	19♒	18♒	23♓	14♒
9	20♒	20♒	25♓	14♒
10	21♒	21♒	26♓	15♒
11	22♒	23♒	27♓	16♒
12	23♒	25♒	28♓	17♒
13	24♒	27♒	0♈	18♒
14	25♒	29♒	1♈	18♒
15	26♒	0♓	2♈	19♒
16	27♒	2♓	3♈	20♒
17	28♒	4♓	4♈	21♒
18	29♒	6♓	6♈	22♒
19	0♓	8♓	7♈	22♒
20	1♓	10♓	8♈	23♒
21	2♓	12♓	9♈	24♒
22	3♓	13♓	10♈	25♒
23	4♓	15♓	12♈	25♒
24	5♓	17♓	13♈	26♒
25	6♓	19♓	14♈	27♒
26	7♓	21♓	15♈	28♒
27	8♓	22♓	16♈	29♒
28	9♓	24♓	18♈	29♒

March

Day	☉	☿	♀	♂
1	10♓	26♓	19♈	0♓
2	11♓	27♓	20♈	1♓
3	12♓	29♓	21♈	2♓
4	13♓	0♈	22♈	3♓
5	14♓	2♈	23♈	3♓
6	15♓	3♈	25♈	4♓
7	16♓	4♈	26♈	5♓
8	17♓	5♈	27♈	6♓
9	18♓	6♈	28♈	7♓
10	19♓	7♈	29♈	7♓
11	20♓	8♈	1♉	8♓
12	21♓	8♈	2♉	9♓
13	22♓	9♈	3♉	10♓
14	23♓	9♈	4♉	10♓
15	24♓	9♈	5♉	11♓
16	25♓	9♈	6♉	12♓
17	26♓	9♈	8♉	13♓
18	27♓	9♈	9♉	14♓
19	28♓	8♈	10♉	14♓
20	29♓	8♈	11♉	15♓
21	0♈	7♈	12♉	16♓
22	1♈	6♈	13♉	17♓
23	2♈	6♈	14♉	18♓
24	3♈	5♈	16♉	18♓
25	4♈	4♈	17♉	19♓
26	5♈	3♈	18♉	20♓
27	6♈	2♈	19♉	21♓
28	7♈	1♈	20♉	21♓
29	8♈	1♈	21♉	22♓
30	9♈	0♈	22♉	23♓
31	10♈	29♓	23♉	24♓

April

Day	☉	☿	♀	♂
1	11♈	28♓	25♉	25♓
2	12♈	28♓	26♉	25♓
3	13♈	27♓	27♉	26♓
4	14♈	27♓	28♉	27♓
5	15♈	27♓	29♉	28♓
6	16♈	27♓	0♊	28♓
7	17♈	27♓	1♊	29♓
8	18♈	27♓	2♊	0♈
9	19♈	27♓	3♊	1♈
10	20♈	27♓	4♊	2♈
11	21♈	27♓	5♊	2♈
12	22♈	27♓	7♊	3♈
13	23♈	28♓	8♊	4♈
14	24♈	28♓	9♊	5♈
15	25♈	29♓	10♊	5♈
16	26♈	29♓	11♊	6♈
17	27♈	0♈	12♊	7♈
18	28♈	1♈	13♊	8♈
19	29♈	2♈	14♊	9♈
20	0♉	3♈	15♊	9♈
21	1♉	3♈	16♊	10♈
22	2♉	4♈	17♊	11♈
23	3♉	5♈	18♊	12♈
24	4♉	6♈	19♊	12♈
25	5♉	8♈	20♊	13♈
26	6♉	9♈	21♊	14♈
27	6♉	10♈	22♊	15♈
28	7♉	11♈	23♊	15♈
29	8♉	12♈	24♊	16♈
30	9♉	14♈	25♊	17♈

May

Day	☉	☿	♀	♂
1	10♉	15♈	26♊	18♈
2	11♉	16♈	27♊	19♈
3	12♉	18♈	28♊	19♈
4	13♉	19♈	29♊	20♈
5	14♉	21♈	0♋	21♈
6	15♉	22♈	1♋	22♈
7	16♉	24♈	1♋	22♈
8	17♉	25♈	2♋	23♈
9	18♉	27♈	3♋	24♈
10	19♉	29♈	4♋	25♈
11	20♉	0♉	5♋	25♈
12	21♉	2♉	6♋	26♈
13	22♉	4♉	7♋	27♈
14	23♉	6♉	7♋	28♈
15	24♉	7♉	8♋	28♈
16	25♉	9♉	9♋	29♈
17	26♉	11♉	10♋	0♉
18	27♉	13♉	11♋	1♉
19	28♉	15♉	11♋	1♉
20	29♉	17♉	12♋	2♉
21	0♊	19♉	13♋	3♉
22	1♊	21♉	14♋	4♉
23	2♊	23♉	14♋	4♉
24	3♊	25♉	15♋	5♉
25	4♊	27♉	16♋	6♉
26	4♊	29♉	16♋	7♉
27	5♊	2♊	17♋	7♉
28	6♊	4♊	18♋	8♉
29	7♊	6♊	18♋	9♉
30	8♊	8♊	19♋	10♉
31	9♊	10♊	19♋	10♉

June

Day	☉	☿	♀	♂
1	10♊	13♊	20♋	11♉
2	11♊	15♊	20♋	12♉
3	12♊	17♊	21♋	13♉
4	13♊	19♊	21♋	13♉
5	14♊	21♊	22♋	14♉
6	15♊	23♊	22♋	15♉
7	16♊	26♊	22♋	15♉
8	17♊	28♊	23♋	16♉
9	18♊	0♋	23♋	17♉
10	19♊	2♋	23♋	18♉
11	20♊	4♋	23♋	18♉
12	21♊	6♋	24♋	19♉
13	22♊	7♋	24♋	20♉
14	23♊	9♋	24♋	21♉
15	24♊	11♋	24♋	21♉
16	25♊	13♋	24♋	22♉
17	26♊	15♋	24♋	23♉
18	26♊	16♋	24♋	23♉
19	27♊	18♋	24♋	24♉
20	28♊	20♋	24♋	25♉
21	29♊	21♋	24♋	26♉
22	0♋	23♋	23♋	26♉
23	1♋	24♋	23♋	27♉
24	2♋	26♋	23♋	28♉
25	3♋	27♋	23♋	28♉
26	4♋	28♋	22♋	29♉
27	5♋	0♌	22♋	0♊
28	6♋	1♌	22♋	1♊
29	7♋	2♌	21♋	1♊
30	8♋	3♌	21♋	2♊

July

Day	☉	☿	♀	♂
1	9♋	5♌	20♋	3♊
2	10♋	6♌	20♋	3♊
3	11♋	7♌	19♋	4♊
4	12♋	8♌	18♋	5♊
5	13♋	9♌	18♋	6♊
6	14♋	10♌	17♋	6♊
7	15♋	10♌	17♋	7♊
8	16♋	11♌	16♋	8♊
9	17♋	12♌	15♋	8♊
10	17♋	13♌	15♋	9♊
11	18♋	13♌	14♋	10♊
12	19♋	14♌	13♋	10♊
13	20♋	14♌	13♋	11♊
14	21♋	15♌	12♋	12♊
15	22♋	15♌	12♋	13♊
16	23♋	15♌	11♋	13♊
17	24♋	15♌	11♋	14♊
18	25♋	15♌	10♋	15♊
19	26♋	15♌	10♋	15♊
20	27♋	15♌	9♋	16♊
21	28♋	15♌	9♋	17♊
22	29♋	15♌	9♋	17♊
23	0♌	14♌	8♋	18♊
24	1♌	14♌	8♋	19♊
25	2♌	13♌	8♋	19♊
26	3♌	13♌	8♋	20♊
27	4♌	12♌	8♋	21♊
28	5♌	12♌	8♋	21♊
29	6♌	11♌	8♋	22♊
30	7♌	10♌	8♋	23♊
31	8♌	9♌	8♋	23♊

August

Day	☉	☿	♀	♂
1	8♌	9♌	8♋	24♊
2	9♌	8♌	8♋	25♊
3	10♌	7♌	8♋	25♊
4	11♌	7♌	8♋	26♊
5	12♌	6♌	8♋	27♊
6	13♌	5♌	8♋	27♊
7	14♌	5♌	9♋	28♊
8	15♌	4♌	9♋	29♊
9	16♌	4♌	9♋	29♊
10	17♌	4♌	10♋	0♋
11	18♌	4♌	10♋	1♋
12	19♌	4♌	11♋	1♋
13	20♌	4♌	11♋	2♋
14	21♌	4♌	11♋	3♋
15	22♌	5♌	12♋	3♋
16	23♌	5♌	12♋	4♋
17	24♌	6♌	13♋	5♋
18	25♌	6♌	14♋	5♋
19	26♌	7♌	14♋	6♋
20	27♌	8♌	15♋	7♋
21	28♌	9♌	15♋	7♋
22	29♌	10♌	16♋	8♋
23	0♍	12♌	17♋	9♋
24	1♍	13♌	17♋	9♋
25	2♍	15♌	18♋	10♋
26	2♍	16♌	19♋	11♋
27	3♍	18♌	20♋	11♋
28	4♍	19♌	20♋	12♋
29	5♍	21♌	21♋	12♋
30	6♍	23♌	22♋	13♋
31	7♍	25♌	23♋	14♋

September

Day	☉	☿	♀	♂
1	8♍	27♌	23♋	14♋
2	9♍	28♌	24♋	15♋
3	10♍	0♍	25♋	16♋
4	11♍	2♍	26♋	16♋
5	12♍	4♍	27♋	17♋
6	13♍	6♍	28♋	17♋
7	14♍	8♍	29♋	18♋
8	15♍	10♍	29♋	19♋
9	16♍	12♍	0♌	19♋
10	17♍	14♍	1♌	20♋
11	18♍	16♍	2♌	21♋
12	19♍	18♍	3♌	21♋
13	20♍	19♍	4♌	22♋
14	21♍	21♍	5♌	22♋
15	22♍	23♍	6♌	23♋
16	23♍	25♍	7♌	24♋
17	24♍	27♍	8♌	24♋
18	25♍	29♍	9♌	25♋
19	26♍	0♎	10♌	25♋
20	27♍	2♎	11♌	26♋
21	28♍	4♎	12♌	27♋
22	29♍	6♎	13♌	27♋
23	0♎	7♎	14♌	28♋
24	1♎	9♎	15♌	28♋
25	2♎	11♎	16♌	29♋
26	3♎	12♎	17♌	0♌
27	4♎	14♎	18♌	0♌
28	5♎	16♎	19♌	1♌
29	6♎	17♎	20♌	1♌
30	7♎	19♎	21♌	2♌

October

Day	☉	☿	♀	♂
1	8♎	21♎	22♌	3♌
2	9♎	22♎	23♌	3♌
3	10♎	24♎	24♌	4♌
4	11♎	25♎	25♌	4♌
5	11♎	27♎	26♌	5♌
6	12♎	28♎	27♌	6♌
7	13♎	0♏	29♌	6♌
8	14♎	1♏	0♍	7♌
9	15♎	3♏	1♍	7♌
10	16♎	4♏	2♍	8♌
11	17♎	6♏	3♍	8♌
12	18♎	7♏	4♍	9♌
13	19♎	9♏	5♍	9♌
14	20♎	10♏	6♍	10♌
15	21♎	11♏	7♍	11♌
16	22♎	13♏	8♍	11♌
17	23♎	14♏	10♍	12♌
18	24♎	16♏	11♍	12♌
19	25♎	17♏	12♍	13♌
20	26♎	18♏	13♍	13♌
21	27♎	19♏	14♍	14♌
22	28♎	21♏	15♍	14♌
23	29♎	22♏	16♍	15♌
24	0♏	23♏	18♍	15♌
25	1♏	24♏	19♍	16♌
26	2♏	26♏	20♍	17♌
27	3♏	27♏	21♍	17♌
28	4♏	28♏	22♍	18♌
29	5♏	29♏	23♍	18♌
30	6♏	0♐	25♍	19♌
31	7♏	1♐	26♍	19♌

November

Day	☉	☿	♀	♂
1	8♏	2♐	27♍	20♌
2	9♏	3♐	28♍	20♌
3	10♏	3♐	29♍	21♌
4	11♏	4♐	0♎	21♌
5	12♏	5♐	2♎	22♌
6	13♏	5♐	3♎	22♌
7	14♏	6♐	4♎	23♌
8	15♏	6♐	5♎	23♌
9	16♏	6♐	6♎	24♌
10	17♏	6♐	7♎	24♌
11	18♏	6♐	9♎	25♌
12	19♏	6♐	10♎	25♌
13	20♏	5♐	11♎	25♌
14	21♏	5♐	12♎	26♌
15	22♏	4♐	13♎	26♌
16	23♏	3♐	15♎	27♌
17	24♏	2♐	16♎	27♌
18	25♏	1♐	17♎	28♌
19	26♏	0♐	18♎	28♌
20	27♏	28♏	19♎	29♌
21	28♏	27♏	21♎	29♌
22	29♏	26♏	22♎	0♍
23	0♐	24♏	23♎	0♍
24	1♐	23♏	24♎	0♍
25	2♐	22♏	25♎	1♍
26	4♐	21♏	27♎	1♍
27	5♐	21♏	28♎	2♍
28	6♐	20♏	29♎	2♍
29	7♐	20♏	0♏	2♍
30	8♐	20♏	2♏	3♍

December

Day	☉	☿	♀	♂
1	9♐	20♏	3♏	3♍
2	10♐	21♏	4♏	4♍
3	11♐	21♏	5♏	4♍
4	12♐	22♏	6♏	4♍
5	13♐	22♏	8♏	5♍
6	14♐	23♏	9♏	5♍
7	15♐	24♏	10♏	5♍
8	16♐	25♏	11♏	6♍
9	17♐	26♏	13♏	6♍
10	18♐	27♏	14♏	6♍
11	19♐	28♏	15♏	7♍
12	20♐	29♏	16♏	7♍
13	21♐	1♐	18♏	7♍
14	22♐	2♐	19♏	8♍
15	23♐	3♐	20♏	8♍
16	24♐	5♐	21♏	8♍
17	25♐	6♐	22♏	8♍
18	26♐	7♐	24♏	9♍
19	27♐	9♐	25♏	9♍
20	28♐	10♐	26♏	9♍
21	29♐	12♐	27♏	10♍
22	0♑	13♐	29♏	10♍
23	1♑	15♐	0♐	10♍
24	2♑	16♐	1♐	10♍
25	3♑	17♐	2♐	10♍
26	4♑	19♐	4♐	11♍
27	5♑	20♐	5♐	11♍
28	6♑	22♐	6♐	11♍
29	7♑	23♐	7♐	11♍
30	8♑	25♐	9♐	11♍
31	9♑	26♐	10♐	12♍

☉ = Sun ☿ = Mercury ♀ = Venus ♂ = Mars ♈ = Aries ♉ = Taurus ♊ = Gemini ♋ = Cancer

1901

January

Day	☉	☿	♀	♂
1	10♑	28♐	11♐	12♍
2	11♑	0♑	12♐	12♍
3	12♑	1♑	13♐	12♍
4	13♑	3♑	15♐	12♍
5	14♑	4♑	16♐	12♍
6	15♑	6♑	17♐	12♍
7	16♑	7♑	18♐	12♍
8	17♑	9♑	20♐	12♍
9	18♑	10♑	21♐	12♍
10	19♑	12♑	22♐	12♍
11	20♑	14♑	23♐	13♍
12	21♑	15♑	25♐	13♍
13	22♑	17♑	26♐	13♍
14	23♑	18♑	27♐	13♍
15	24♑	20♑	28♐	13♍
16	25♑	22♑	0♑	12♍
17	26♑	23♑	1♑	12♍
18	27♑	25♑	2♑	12♍
19	28♑	27♑	3♑	12♍
20	29♑	28♑	5♑	12♍
21	0♒	0♒	6♑	12♍
22	2♒	2♒	7♑	12♍
23	3♒	3♒	8♑	12♍
24	4♒	5♒	10♑	12♍
25	5♒	7♒	11♑	12♍
26	6♒	8♒	12♑	11♍
27	7♒	10♒	13♑	11♍
28	8♒	12♒	15♑	11♍
29	9♒	14♒	16♑	11♍
30	10♒	15♒	17♑	11♍
31	11♒	17♒	18♑	10♍

February

Day	☉	☿	♀	♂
1	12♒	19♒	20♑	10♍
2	13♒	21♒	21♑	10♍
3	14♒	22♒	22♑	10♍
4	15♒	24♒	23♑	9♍
5	16♒	26♒	25♑	9♍
6	17♒	28♒	26♑	9♍
7	18♒	0♓	27♑	9♍
8	19♒	1♓	28♑	8♍
9	20♒	3♓	0♒	8♍
10	21♒	5♓	1♒	8♍
11	22♒	6♓	2♒	7♍
12	23♒	8♓	3♒	7♍
13	24♒	10♓	5♒	6♍
14	25♒	11♓	6♒	6♍
15	26♒	13♓	7♒	6♍
16	27♒	14♓	8♒	5♍
17	28♒	16♓	10♒	5♍
18	29♒	17♓	11♒	5♍
19	0♓	18♓	12♒	4♍
20	1♓	19♓	13♒	4♍
21	2♓	20♓	15♒	3♍
22	3♓	21♓	16♒	3♍
23	4♓	21♓	17♒	3♍
24	5♓	22♓	18♒	2♍
25	6♓	22♓	20♒	2♍
26	7♓	22♓	21♒	1♍
27	8♓	22♓	22♒	1♍
28	9♓	22♓	23♒	1♍

March

Day	☉	☿	♀	♂
1	10♓	22♓	25♒	0♍
2	11♓	21♓	26♒	0♍
3	12♓	20♓	27♒	29♌
4	13♓	20♓	28♒	29♌
5	14♓	19♓	29♒	29♌
6	15♓	18♓	1♓	28♌
7	16♓	17♓	2♓	28♌
8	17♓	16♓	3♓	28♌
9	18♓	15♓	4♓	27♌
10	19♓	14♓	6♓	27♌
11	20♓	13♓	7♓	27♌
12	21♓	12♓	8♓	26♌
13	22♓	11♓	9♓	26♌
14	23♓	11♓	11♓	26♌
15	24♓	10♓	12♓	26♌
16	25♓	9♓	13♓	25♌
17	26♓	9♓	14♓	25♌
18	27♓	9♓	16♓	25♌
19	28♓	8♓	17♓	25♌
20	29♓	8♓	18♓	25♌
21	0♈	8♓	19♓	24♌
22	1♈	8♓	21♓	24♌
23	2♈	8♓	22♓	24♌
24	3♈	9♓	23♓	24♌
25	4♈	9♓	24♓	24♌
26	5♈	9♓	26♓	24♌
27	6♈	10♓	27♓	23♌
28	7♈	10♓	28♓	23♌
29	8♈	11♓	29♓	23♌
30	9♈	12♓	1♈	23♌
31	10♈	12♓	2♈	23♌

April

Day	☉	☿	♀	♂
1	11♈	13♓	3♈	23♌
2	12♈	14♓	4♈	23♌
3	13♈	15♓	6♈	23♌
4	14♈	16♓	7♈	23♌
5	15♈	17♓	8♈	23♌
6	16♈	18♓	9♈	23♌
7	17♈	19♓	10♈	23♌
8	18♈	20♓	12♈	23♌
9	19♈	21♓	13♈	23♌
10	20♈	23♓	14♈	23♌
11	21♈	24♓	15♈	23♌
12	22♈	25♓	17♈	23♌
13	23♈	27♓	18♈	24♌
14	24♈	28♓	19♈	24♌
15	25♈	29♓	20♈	24♌
16	26♈	1♈	22♈	24♌
17	26♈	2♈	23♈	24♌
18	27♈	4♈	24♈	24♌
19	28♈	5♈	25♈	24♌
20	29♈	7♈	27♈	25♌
21	0♉	8♈	28♈	25♌
22	1♉	10♈	29♈	25♌
23	2♉	11♈	0♉	25♌
24	3♉	13♈	2♉	25♌
25	4♉	15♈	3♉	25♌
26	5♉	16♈	4♉	26♌
27	6♉	18♈	5♉	26♌
28	7♉	20♈	6♉	26♌
29	8♉	22♈	8♉	26♌
30	9♉	24♈	9♉	27♌

May

Day	☉	☿	♀	♂
1	10♉	25♈	10♉	27♌
2	11♉	27♈	11♉	27♌
3	12♉	29♈	13♉	28♌
4	13♉	1♉	14♉	28♌
5	14♉	3♉	15♉	28♌
6	15♉	5♉	16♉	28♌
7	16♉	7♉	18♉	29♌
8	17♉	9♉	19♉	29♌
9	18♉	11♉	20♉	29♌
10	19♉	13♉	21♉	0♍
11	20♉	16♉	22♉	0♍
12	21♉	18♉	24♉	0♍
13	22♉	20♉	25♉	1♍
14	23♉	22♉	26♉	1♍
15	24♉	24♉	27♉	1♍
16	25♉	26♉	29♉	2♍
17	26♉	29♉	0♊	2♍
18	27♉	1♊	1♊	2♍
19	28♉	3♊	2♊	3♍
20	28♉	5♊	4♊	3♍
21	29♉	7♊	5♊	4♍
22	0♊	9♊	6♊	4♍
23	1♊	11♊	7♊	4♍
24	2♊	14♊	8♊	5♍
25	3♊	16♊	10♊	5♍
26	4♊	18♊	11♊	6♍
27	5♊	20♊	12♊	6♍
28	6♊	21♊	13♊	6♍
29	7♊	23♊	15♊	7♍
30	8♊	25♊	16♊	7♍
31	9♊	27♊	17♊	8♍

June

Day	☉	☿	♀	♂
1	10♊	29♊	18♊	8♍
2	11♊	0♋	20♊	9♍
3	12♊	2♋	21♊	9♍
4	13♊	4♋	22♊	10♍
5	14♊	5♋	23♊	10♍
6	15♊	7♋	24♊	10♍
7	16♊	8♋	26♊	11♍
8	17♊	10♋	27♊	11♍
9	18♊	11♋	28♊	12♍
10	19♊	12♋	29♊	12♍
11	20♊	13♋	1♋	13♍
12	21♊	15♋	2♋	13♍
13	21♊	16♋	3♋	14♍
14	22♊	17♋	4♋	14♍
15	23♊	18♋	5♋	15♍
16	24♊	19♋	7♋	15♍
17	25♊	20♋	8♋	16♍
18	26♊	21♋	9♋	16♍
19	27♊	22♋	10♋	17♍
20	28♊	22♋	12♋	17♍
21	29♊	23♋	13♋	18♍
22	0♋	24♋	14♋	18♍
23	1♋	24♋	15♋	19♍
24	2♋	25♋	17♋	19♍
25	3♋	25♋	18♋	20♍
26	4♋	25♋	19♋	20♍
27	5♋	26♋	20♋	21♍
28	6♋	26♋	21♋	21♍
29	7♋	26♋	23♋	22♍
30	8♋	26♋	24♋	22♍

July

Day	☉	☿	♀	♂
1	9♋	26♋	25♋	23♍
2	10♋	26♋	26♋	24♍
3	11♋	26♋	28♋	24♍
4	12♋	25♋	29♋	25♍
5	12♋	25♋	0♌	25♍
6	13♋	25♋	1♌	26♍
7	14♋	24♋	2♌	26♍
8	15♋	24♋	4♌	27♍
9	16♋	23♋	5♌	27♍
10	17♋	22♋	6♌	28♍
11	18♋	22♋	7♌	29♍
12	19♋	21♋	9♌	29♍
13	20♋	21♋	10♌	0♎
14	21♋	20♋	11♌	0♎
15	22♋	19♋	12♌	1♎
16	23♋	19♋	13♌	1♎
17	24♋	18♋	15♌	2♎
18	25♋	18♋	16♌	3♎
19	26♋	17♋	17♌	3♎
20	27♋	17♋	18♌	4♎
21	28♋	16♋	20♌	4♎
22	29♋	16♋	21♌	5♎
23	0♌	16♋	22♌	5♎
24	1♌	16♋	23♌	6♎
25	2♌	16♋	24♌	7♎
26	2♌	16♋	26♌	7♎
27	3♌	16♋	27♌	8♎
28	4♌	17♋	28♌	8♎
29	5♌	17♋	29♌	9♎
30	6♌	18♋	0♍	10♎
31	7♌	18♋	2♍	10♎

August

Day	☉	☿	♀	♂
1	8♌	19♋	3♍	11♎
2	9♌	20♋	4♍	11♎
3	10♌	21♋	5♍	12♎
4	11♌	22♋	7♍	13♎
5	12♌	23♋	8♍	13♎
6	13♌	24♋	9♍	14♎
7	14♌	26♋	10♍	14♎
8	15♌	27♋	11♍	15♎
9	16♌	28♋	13♍	16♎
10	17♌	0♌	14♍	16♎
11	18♌	2♌	15♍	17♎
12	19♌	3♌	16♍	18♎
13	20♌	5♌	18♍	18♎
14	21♌	7♌	19♍	19♎
15	22♌	9♌	20♍	19♎
16	23♌	11♌	21♍	20♎
17	24♌	13♌	22♍	21♎
18	25♌	15♌	24♍	21♎
19	25♌	17♌	25♍	22♎
20	26♌	19♌	26♍	23♎
21	27♌	21♌	27♍	23♎
22	28♌	23♌	28♍	24♎
23	29♌	25♌	0♎	24♎
24	0♍	27♌	1♎	25♎
25	1♍	29♌	2♎	26♎
26	2♍	1♍	3♎	26♎
27	3♍	3♍	4♎	27♎
28	4♍	4♍	6♎	28♎
29	5♍	6♍	7♎	28♎
30	6♍	8♍	8♎	29♎
31	7♍	10♍	9♎	0♏

September

Day	☉	☿	♀	♂
1	8♍	12♍	10♎	0♏
2	9♍	14♍	12♎	1♏
3	10♍	16♍	13♎	2♏
4	11♍	18♍	14♎	2♏
5	12♍	19♍	15♎	3♏
6	13♍	21♍	16♎	4♏
7	14♍	23♍	18♎	4♏
8	15♍	25♍	19♎	5♏
9	16♍	27♍	20♎	6♏
10	17♍	28♍	21♎	6♏
11	18♍	0♎	22♎	7♏
12	19♍	2♎	24♎	8♏
13	20♍	3♎	25♎	8♏
14	21♍	5♎	26♎	9♏
15	22♍	6♎	27♎	10♏
16	23♍	8♎	28♎	10♏
17	24♍	10♎	0♏	11♏
18	25♍	11♎	1♏	12♏
19	26♍	13♎	2♏	12♏
20	27♍	14♎	3♏	13♏
21	28♍	16♎	4♏	14♏
22	28♍	17♎	6♏	14♏
23	29♍	19♎	7♏	15♏
24	0♎	20♎	8♏	16♏
25	1♎	22♎	9♏	16♏
26	2♎	23♎	10♏	17♏
27	3♎	25♎	12♏	18♏
28	4♎	26♎	13♏	19♏
29	5♎	27♎	14♏	19♏
30	6♎	29♎	15♏	20♏

October

Day	☉	☿	♀	♂
1	7♎	0♏	16♏	21♏
2	8♎	1♏	18♏	21♏
3	9♎	3♏	19♏	22♏
4	10♎	4♏	20♏	23♏
5	11♎	5♏	21♏	23♏
6	12♎	6♏	22♏	24♏
7	13♎	8♏	23♏	25♏
8	14♎	9♏	25♏	26♏
9	15♎	10♏	26♏	26♏
10	16♎	11♏	27♏	27♏
11	17♎	12♏	28♏	28♏
12	18♎	13♏	29♏	28♏
13	19♎	14♏	0♐	29♏
14	20♎	15♏	2♐	0♐
15	21♎	16♏	3♐	0♐
16	22♎	17♏	4♐	1♐
17	23♎	17♏	5♐	2♐
18	24♎	18♏	6♐	3♐
19	25♎	19♏	7♐	3♐
20	26♎	19♏	9♐	4♐
21	27♎	20♏	10♐	5♐
22	28♎	20♏	11♐	6♐
23	29♎	20♏	12♐	6♐
24	0♏	20♏	13♐	7♐
25	1♏	20♏	14♐	8♐
26	2♏	20♏	16♐	8♐
27	3♏	20♏	17♐	9♐
28	4♏	19♏	18♐	10♐
29	5♏	19♏	19♐	11♐
30	6♏	18♏	20♐	11♐
31	7♏	17♏	21♐	12♐

November

Day	☉	☿	♀	♂
1	8♏	16♏	23♐	13♐
2	9♏	15♏	24♐	14♐
3	10♏	14♏	25♐	14♐
4	11♏	12♏	26♐	15♐
5	12♏	11♏	27♐	16♐
6	13♏	10♏	28♐	17♐
7	14♏	9♏	29♐	17♐
8	15♏	7♏	0♑	18♐
9	16♏	6♏	2♑	19♐
10	17♏	6♏	3♑	19♐
11	18♏	5♏	4♑	20♐
12	19♏	5♏	5♑	21♐
13	20♏	4♏	6♑	22♐
14	21♏	4♏	7♑	22♐
15	22♏	5♏	8♑	23♐
16	23♏	5♏	9♑	24♐
17	24♏	5♏	10♑	25♐
18	25♏	6♏	12♑	25♐
19	26♏	7♏	13♑	26♐
20	27♏	8♏	14♑	27♐
21	28♏	9♏	15♑	28♐
22	29♏	10♏	16♑	28♐
23	0♐	11♏	17♑	29♐
24	1♐	12♏	18♑	0♑
25	2♐	13♏	19♑	1♑
26	3♐	15♏	20♑	2♑
27	4♐	16♏	21♑	2♑
28	5♐	17♏	22♑	3♑
29	6♐	19♏	23♑	4♑
30	7♐	20♏	24♑	5♑

December

Day	☉	☿	♀	♂
1	8♐	21♏	26♑	5♑
2	9♐	23♏	27♑	6♑
3	10♐	24♏	28♑	7♑
4	11♐	26♏	29♑	8♑
5	12♐	27♏	0♒	8♑
6	13♐	29♏	1♒	9♑
7	14♐	0♐	2♒	10♑
8	15♐	2♐	3♒	11♑
9	16♐	3♐	4♒	11♑
10	17♐	5♐	5♒	12♑
11	18♐	6♐	6♒	13♑
12	19♐	8♐	7♒	14♑
13	21♐	9♐	8♒	15♑
14	22♐	11♐	9♒	15♑
15	23♐	13♐	9♒	16♑
16	24♐	14♐	10♒	17♑
17	25♐	16♐	11♒	18♑
18	26♐	17♐	12♒	18♑
19	27♐	19♐	13♒	19♑
20	28♐	20♐	14♒	20♑
21	29♐	22♐	15♒	21♑
22	0♑	23♐	16♒	22♑
23	1♑	25♐	17♒	22♑
24	2♑	27♐	17♒	23♑
25	3♑	28♐	18♒	24♑
26	4♑	0♑	19♒	25♑
27	5♑	1♑	20♒	25♑
28	6♑	3♑	21♒	26♑
29	7♑	4♑	21♒	27♑
30	8♑	6♑	22♒	28♑
31	9♑	8♑	23♒	29♑

Planetary Positions

♌ = Leo ♍ = Virgo ♎ = Libra ♏ = Scorpio ♐ = Sagittarius ♑ = Capricorn ♒ = Aquarius ♓ = Pisces

1902

January

Day	☉	☿	♀	♂
1	10♑	9♑	24♒	29♑
2	11♑	11♑	24♒	0♒
3	12♑	12♑	25♒	1♒
4	13♑	14♑	26♒	2♒
5	14♑	16♑	26♒	3♒
6	15♑	17♑	27♒	3♒
7	16♑	19♑	28♒	4♒
8	17♑	21♑	28♒	5♒
9	18♑	22♑	29♒	6♒
10	19♑	24♑	29♒	6♒
11	20♑	26♑	0♓	7♒
12	21♑	27♑	0♓	8♒
13	22♑	29♑	1♓	9♒
14	23♑	1♒	1♓	10♒
15	24♑	2♒	1♓	10♒
16	25♑	4♒	2♓	11♒
17	26♑	6♒	2♓	12♒
18	27♑	7♒	2♓	13♒
19	28♑	9♒	3♓	14♒
20	29♑	11♒	3♓	14♒
21	0♒	13♒	3♓	15♒
22	1♒	14♒	3♓	16♒
23	2♒	16♒	3♓	17♒
24	3♒	18♒	3♓	18♒
25	4♒	19♒	3♓	18♒
26	5♒	21♒	3♓	19♒
27	6♒	22♒	3♓	20♒
28	7♒	24♒	3♓	21♒
29	8♒	25♒	3♓	21♒
30	9♒	27♒	3♓	22♒
31	10♒	28♒	3♓	23♒

February

Day	☉	☿	♀	♂
1	11♒	29♒	2♓	24♒
2	12♒	1♓	2♓	25♒
3	13♒	2♓	2♓	25♒
4	14♒	3♓	1♓	26♒
5	15♒	4♓	1♓	27♒
6	16♒	4♓	0♓	28♒
7	18♒	5♓	0♓	29♒
8	19♒	5♓	29♒	29♒
9	20♒	5♓	29♒	0♓
10	21♒	5♓	28♒	1♓
11	22♒	5♓	28♒	2♓
12	23♒	5♓	27♒	3♓
13	24♒	5♓	26♒	3♓
14	25♒	4♓	26♒	4♓
15	26♒	3♓	25♒	5♓
16	27♒	2♓	25♒	6♓
17	28♒	1♓	24♒	6♓
18	29♒	0♓	23♒	7♓
19	0♓	29♒	23♒	8♓
20	1♓	28♒	22♒	9♓
21	2♓	27♒	22♒	10♓
22	3♓	26♒	21♒	10♓
23	4♓	25♒	21♒	11♓
24	5♓	24♒	20♒	12♓
25	6♓	23♒	20♒	13♓
26	7♓	22♒	19♒	14♓
27	8♓	22♒	19♒	14♓
28	9♓	21♒	19♒	15♓

March

Day	☉	☿	♀	♂
1	10♓	21♒	18♒	16♓
2	11♓	21♒	18♒	17♓
3	12♓	21♒	18♒	18♓
4	13♓	20♒	18♒	18♓
5	14♓	21♒	18♒	19♓
6	15♓	21♒	18♒	20♓
7	16♓	21♒	18♒	21♓
8	17♓	21♒	18♒	21♓
9	18♓	22♒	18♒	22♓
10	19♓	22♒	18♒	23♓
11	20♓	23♒	18♒	24♓
12	21♓	24♒	18♒	25♓
13	22♓	25♒	18♒	25♓
14	23♓	25♒	18♒	26♓
15	24♓	26♒	19♒	27♓
16	25♓	27♒	19♒	28♓
17	26♓	28♒	19♒	28♓
18	27♓	29♒	20♒	29♓
19	28♓	0♓	20♒	0♈
20	29♓	1♓	20♒	1♈
21	0♈	2♓	21♒	2♈
22	1♈	3♓	21♒	2♈
23	2♈	5♓	22♒	3♈
24	3♈	6♓	22♒	4♈
25	4♈	7♓	23♒	5♈
26	5♈	8♓	24♒	5♈
27	6♈	10♓	24♒	6♈
28	7♈	11♓	25♒	7♈
29	8♈	13♓	25♒	8♈
30	9♈	14♓	26♒	9♈
31	10♈	15♓	27♒	9♈

April

Day	☉	☿	♀	♂
1	11♈	17♓	27♒	10♈
2	12♈	18♓	28♒	11♈
3	13♈	20♓	29♒	12♈
4	13♈	21♓	0♓	12♈
5	14♈	23♓	0♓	13♈
6	15♈	25♓	1♓	14♈
7	16♈	26♓	2♓	15♈
8	17♈	28♓	3♓	15♈
9	18♈	29♓	3♓	16♈
10	19♈	1♈	4♓	17♈
11	20♈	3♈	5♓	18♈
12	21♈	5♈	6♓	18♈
13	22♈	6♈	7♓	19♈
14	23♈	8♈	8♓	20♈
15	24♈	10♈	9♓	21♈
16	25♈	12♈	9♓	22♈
17	26♈	14♈	10♓	22♈
18	27♈	16♈	11♓	23♈
19	28♈	18♈	12♓	24♈
20	29♈	20♈	13♓	25♈
21	0♉	22♈	14♓	25♈
22	1♉	24♈	15♓	26♈
23	2♉	26♈	16♓	27♈
24	3♉	28♈	17♓	28♈
25	4♉	0♉	18♓	28♈
26	5♉	2♉	19♓	29♈
27	6♉	4♉	20♓	0♉
28	7♉	6♉	21♓	1♉
29	8♉	8♉	22♓	1♉
30	9♉	10♉	23♓	2♉

May

Day	☉	☿	♀	♂
1	10♉	12♉	24♓	3♉
2	11♉	15♉	25♓	4♉
3	12♉	17♉	26♓	4♉
4	13♉	19♉	27♓	5♉
5	14♉	21♉	28♓	6♉
6	15♉	23♉	29♓	7♉
7	16♉	25♉	0♈	7♉
8	17♉	27♉	1♈	8♉
9	18♉	29♉	2♈	9♉
10	19♉	1♊	3♈	9♉
11	20♉	3♊	4♈	10♉
12	21♉	5♊	5♈	11♉
13	21♉	7♊	6♈	12♉
14	22♉	9♊	7♈	12♉
15	23♉	11♊	8♈	13♉
16	24♉	13♊	9♈	14♉
17	25♉	14♊	10♈	15♉
18	26♉	16♊	12♈	15♉
19	27♉	17♊	13♈	16♉
20	28♉	19♊	14♈	17♉
21	29♉	20♊	15♈	18♉
22	0♊	22♊	16♈	18♉
23	1♊	23♊	17♈	19♉
24	2♊	24♊	18♈	20♉
25	3♊	26♊	19♈	20♉
26	4♊	27♊	20♈	21♉
27	5♊	28♊	21♈	22♉
28	6♊	29♊	22♈	23♉
29	7♊	0♋	24♈	23♉
30	8♊	1♋	25♈	24♉
31	9♊	2♋	26♈	25♉

June

Day	☉	☿	♀	♂
1	10♊	2♋	27♈	26♉
2	11♊	3♋	28♈	26♉
3	12♊	4♋	29♈	27♉
4	13♊	4♋	0♉	28♉
5	14♊	5♋	1♉	28♉
6	15♊	5♋	2♉	29♉
7	16♊	6♋	4♉	0♊
8	16♊	6♋	5♉	1♊
9	17♊	6♋	6♉	1♊
10	18♊	6♋	7♉	2♊
11	19♊	6♋	8♉	3♊
12	20♊	6♋	9♉	3♊
13	21♊	6♋	10♉	4♊
14	22♊	6♋	12♉	5♊
15	23♊	6♋	13♉	5♊
16	24♊	5♋	14♉	6♊
17	25♊	5♋	15♉	7♊
18	26♊	4♋	16♉	8♊
19	27♊	4♋	17♉	8♊
20	28♊	3♋	18♉	9♊
21	29♊	3♋	20♉	10♊
22	0♋	2♋	21♉	10♊
23	1♋	2♋	22♉	11♊
24	2♋	1♋	23♉	12♊
25	3♋	1♋	24♉	13♊
26	4♋	0♋	25♉	13♊
27	5♋	0♋	26♉	14♊
28	6♋	29♊	28♉	15♊
29	7♋	29♊	29♉	15♊
30	7♋	28♊	0♊	16♊

July

Day	☉	☿	♀	♂
1	8♋	28♊	1♊	17♊
2	9♋	28♊	2♊	17♊
3	10♋	27♊	3♊	18♊
4	11♋	27♊	5♊	19♊
5	12♋	27♊	6♊	19♊
6	13♋	27♊	7♊	20♊
7	14♋	27♊	8♊	21♊
8	15♋	28♊	9♊	21♊
9	16♋	28♊	10♊	22♊
10	17♋	28♊	12♊	23♊
11	18♋	29♊	13♊	24♊
12	19♋	29♊	14♊	24♊
13	20♋	0♋	15♊	25♊
14	21♋	1♋	16♊	26♊
15	22♋	1♋	17♊	26♊
16	23♋	2♋	19♊	27♊
17	24♋	3♋	20♊	28♊
18	25♋	4♋	21♊	28♊
19	26♋	5♋	22♊	29♊
20	27♋	7♋	23♊	0♋
21	27♋	8♋	25♊	0♋
22	28♋	9♋	26♊	1♋
23	29♋	11♋	27♊	2♋
24	0♌	12♋	28♊	2♋
25	1♌	14♋	29♊	3♋
26	2♌	16♋	0♋	4♋
27	3♌	17♋	2♋	4♋
28	4♌	19♋	3♋	5♋
29	5♌	21♋	4♋	6♋
30	6♌	23♋	5♋	6♋
31	7♌	25♋	6♋	7♋

August

Day	☉	☿	♀	♂
1	8♌	27♋	8♋	8♋
2	9♌	29♋	9♋	8♋
3	10♌	1♌	10♋	9♋
4	11♌	3♌	11♋	10♋
5	12♌	5♌	12♋	10♋
6	13♌	7♌	14♋	11♋
7	14♌	9♌	15♋	12♋
8	15♌	11♌	16♋	12♋
9	16♌	13♌	17♋	13♋
10	17♌	15♌	18♋	14♋
11	18♌	17♌	20♋	14♋
12	19♌	19♌	21♋	15♋
13	20♌	21♌	22♋	16♋
14	20♌	23♌	23♋	16♋
15	21♌	25♌	24♋	17♋
16	22♌	27♌	26♋	18♋
17	23♌	29♌	27♋	18♋
18	24♌	1♍	28♋	19♋
19	25♌	3♍	29♋	19♋
20	26♌	5♍	1♌	20♋
21	27♌	7♍	2♌	21♋
22	28♌	8♍	3♌	21♋
23	29♌	10♍	4♌	22♋
24	0♍	12♍	5♌	23♋
25	1♍	14♍	7♌	23♋
26	2♍	16♍	8♌	24♋
27	3♍	17♍	9♌	25♋
28	4♍	19♍	10♌	25♋
29	5♍	21♍	11♌	26♋
30	6♍	22♍	13♌	27♋
31	7♍	24♍	14♌	27♋

September

Day	☉	☿	♀	♂
1	8♍	25♍	15♌	28♋
2	9♍	27♍	16♌	28♋
3	10♍	29♍	18♌	29♋
4	11♍	0♎	19♌	0♌
5	12♍	2♎	20♌	0♌
6	13♍	3♎	21♌	1♌
7	14♍	5♎	23♌	2♌
8	15♍	6♎	24♌	2♌
9	16♍	8♎	25♌	3♌
10	17♍	9♎	26♌	4♌
11	18♍	10♎	27♌	4♌
12	18♍	12♎	29♌	5♌
13	19♍	13♎	0♍	5♌
14	20♍	14♎	1♍	6♌
15	21♍	16♎	2♍	7♌
16	22♍	17♎	4♍	7♌
17	23♍	18♎	5♍	8♌
18	24♍	20♎	6♍	9♌
19	25♍	21♎	7♍	9♌
20	26♍	22♎	9♍	10♌
21	27♍	23♎	10♍	10♌
22	28♍	24♎	11♍	11♌
23	29♍	25♎	12♍	12♌
24	0♎	26♎	13♍	12♌
25	1♎	27♎	15♍	13♌
26	2♎	28♎	16♍	13♌
27	3♎	29♎	17♍	14♌
28	4♎	0♏	18♍	15♌
29	5♎	1♏	20♍	15♌
30	6♎	1♏	21♍	16♌

October

Day	☉	☿	♀	♂
1	7♎	2♏	22♍	17♌
2	8♎	3♏	23♍	17♌
3	9♎	3♏	25♍	18♌
4	10♎	4♏	26♍	18♌
5	11♎	4♏	27♍	19♌
6	12♎	4♏	28♍	20♌
7	13♎	4♏	0♎	20♌
8	14♎	4♏	1♎	21♌
9	15♎	4♏	2♎	21♌
10	16♎	4♏	3♎	22♌
11	17♎	4♏	5♎	23♌
12	18♎	3♏	6♎	23♌
13	19♎	2♏	7♎	24♌
14	20♎	2♏	8♎	24♌
15	21♎	1♏	10♎	25♌
16	22♎	0♏	11♎	25♌
17	23♎	29♎	12♎	26♌
18	24♎	27♎	13♎	27♌
19	25♎	26♎	15♎	27♌
20	26♎	25♎	16♎	28♌
21	27♎	24♎	17♎	28♌
22	28♎	23♎	18♎	29♌
23	29♎	22♎	20♎	0♍
24	0♏	21♎	21♎	0♍
25	1♏	20♎	22♎	1♍
26	2♏	19♎	23♎	1♍
27	3♏	19♎	25♎	2♍
28	4♏	19♎	26♎	2♍
29	5♏	19♎	27♎	3♍
30	6♏	19♎	28♎	4♍
31	7♏	19♎	0♏	4♍

November

Day	☉	☿	♀	♂
1	8♏	20♎	1♏	5♍
2	9♏	20♎	2♏	5♍
3	10♏	21♎	3♏	6♍
4	11♏	22♎	5♏	6♍
5	12♏	23♎	6♏	7♍
6	13♏	24♎	7♏	8♍
7	14♏	25♎	8♏	8♍
8	15♏	27♎	10♏	9♍
9	16♏	28♎	11♏	9♍
10	17♏	29♎	12♏	10♍
11	18♏	1♏	13♏	10♍
12	19♏	2♏	15♏	11♍
13	20♏	4♏	16♏	11♍
14	21♏	5♏	17♏	12♍
15	22♏	7♏	18♏	13♍
16	23♏	8♏	20♏	13♍
17	24♏	10♏	21♏	14♍
18	25♏	11♏	22♏	14♍
19	26♏	13♏	23♏	15♍
20	27♏	14♏	25♏	15♍
21	28♏	16♏	26♏	16♍
22	29♏	18♏	27♏	16♍
23	0♐	19♏	29♏	17♍
24	1♐	21♏	0♐	17♍
25	2♐	22♏	1♐	18♍
26	3♐	24♏	2♐	18♍
27	4♐	26♏	4♐	19♍
28	5♐	27♏	5♐	19♍
29	6♐	29♏	6♐	20♍
30	7♐	0♐	7♐	20♍

December

Day	☉	☿	♀	♂
1	8♐	2♐	9♐	21♍
2	9♐	3♐	10♐	21♍
3	10♐	5♐	11♐	22♍
4	11♐	7♐	12♐	22♍
5	12♐	8♐	14♐	23♍
6	13♐	10♐	15♐	23♍
7	14♐	11♐	16♐	24♍
8	15♐	13♐	17♐	24♍
9	16♐	14♐	19♐	25♍
10	17♐	16♐	20♐	25♍
11	18♐	18♐	21♐	26♍
12	19♐	19♐	22♐	26♍
13	20♐	21♐	24♐	27♍
14	21♐	22♐	25♐	27♍
15	22♐	24♐	26♐	28♍
16	23♐	25♐	27♐	28♍
17	24♐	27♐	29♐	29♍
18	25♐	29♐	0♑	29♍
19	26♐	0♑	1♑	0♎
20	27♐	2♑	2♑	0♎
21	28♐	3♑	4♑	0♎
22	29♐	5♑	5♑	1♎
23	0♑	7♑	6♑	1♎
24	1♑	8♑	8♑	2♎
25	2♑	10♑	9♑	2♎
26	3♑	11♑	10♑	3♎
27	5♑	13♑	11♑	3♎
28	6♑	15♑	13♑	3♎
29	7♑	16♑	14♑	4♎
30	8♑	18♑	15♑	4♎
31	9♑	19♑	16♑	5♎

☉ = Sun ☿ = Mercury ♀ = Venus ♂ = Mars ♈ = Aries ♉ = Taurus ♊ = Gemini ♋ = Cancer

1903

January

Day	☉	☿	♀	♂
1	10♑	21♑	18♑	5♎
2	11♑	23♑	19♑	6♎
3	12♑	24♑	20♑	6♎
4	13♑	26♑	21♑	6♎
5	14♑	27♑	23♑	7♎
6	15♑	29♑	24♑	7♎
7	16♑	1♒	25♑	7♎
8	17♑	2♒	26♑	8♎
9	18♑	4♒	28♑	8♎
10	19♑	5♒	29♑	8♎
11	20♑	7♒	0♒	9♎
12	21♑	8♒	1♒	9♎
13	22♑	10♒	3♒	10♎
14	23♑	11♒	4♒	10♎
15	24♑	12♒	5♒	10♎
16	25♑	14♒	6♒	10♎
17	26♑	15♒	8♒	11♎
18	27♑	16♒	9♒	11♎
19	28♑	17♒	10♒	11♎
20	29♑	17♒	11♒	12♎
21	0♒	18♒	13♒	12♎
22	1♒	19♒	14♒	12♎
23	2♒	19♒	15♒	13♎
24	3♒	19♒	16♒	13♎
25	4♒	19♒	18♒	13♎
26	5♒	19♒	19♒	13♎
27	6♒	19♒	20♒	14♎
28	7♒	18♒	21♒	14♎
29	8♒	17♒	23♒	14♎
30	9♒	16♒	24♒	14♎
31	10♒	15♒	25♒	14♎

April

Day	☉	☿	♀	♂
1	10♈	29♓	9♉	6♎
2	11♈	0♈	11♉	6♎
3	12♈	2♈	12♉	6♎
4	13♈	4♈	13♉	5♎
5	14♈	6♈	14♉	5♎
6	15♈	8♈	15♉	4♎
7	16♈	10♈	17♉	4♎
8	17♈	12♈	18♉	4♎
9	18♈	14♈	19♉	3♎
10	19♈	16♈	20♉	3♎
11	20♈	18♈	22♉	3♎
12	21♈	20♈	23♉	2♎
13	22♈	22♈	24♉	2♎
14	23♈	24♈	25♉	2♎
15	24♈	26♈	26♉	1♎
16	25♈	29♈	28♉	1♎
17	26♈	1♉	29♉	1♎
18	27♈	3♉	0♊	0♎
19	28♈	5♉	1♊	0♎
20	29♈	7♉	2♊	0♎
21	0♉	9♉	4♊	0♎
22	1♉	11♉	5♊	29♍
23	2♉	13♉	6♊	29♍
24	3♉	15♉	7♊	29♍
25	4♉	17♉	8♊	29♍
26	5♉	19♉	9♊	29♍
27	6♉	21♉	11♊	28♍
28	7♉	23♉	12♊	28♍
29	8♉	24♉	13♊	28♍
30	9♉	26♉	14♊	28♍

July

Day	☉	☿	♀	♂
1	8♋	17♊	23♌	11♎
2	9♋	18♊	24♌	11♎
3	10♋	19♊	25♌	12♎
4	11♋	20♊	26♌	12♎
5	12♋	22♊	27♌	13♎
6	13♋	23♊	28♌	13♎
7	14♋	25♊	29♌	14♎
8	15♋	26♊	0♍	14♎
9	16♋	28♊	1♍	15♎
10	17♋	29♊	2♍	15♎
11	18♋	1♋	3♍	16♎
12	19♋	3♋	4♍	16♎
13	20♋	5♋	5♍	17♎
14	21♋	7♋	6♍	17♎
15	22♋	9♋	7♍	18♎
16	22♋	11♋	8♍	18♎
17	23♋	13♋	9♍	19♎
18	24♋	15♋	10♍	19♎
19	25♋	17♋	11♍	20♎
20	26♋	19♋	11♍	20♎
21	27♋	21♋	12♍	21♎
22	28♋	23♋	13♍	21♎
23	29♋	25♋	14♍	22♎
24	0♌	27♋	15♍	22♎
25	1♌	29♋	16♍	23♎
26	2♌	1♌	16♍	24♎
27	3♌	4♌	17♍	24♎
28	4♌	6♌	18♍	25♎
29	5♌	8♌	19♍	25♎
30	6♌	10♌	19♍	26♎
31	7♌	12♌	20♍	26♎

October

Day	☉	☿	♀	♂
1	7♎	12♎	17♍	6♐
2	8♎	11♎	17♍	7♐
3	9♎	10♎	16♍	7♐
4	10♎	9♎	16♍	8♐
5	11♎	7♎	16♍	9♐
6	12♎	6♎	16♍	10♐
7	13♎	5♎	16♍	10♐
8	14♎	5♎	16♍	11♐
9	15♎	4♎	16♍	12♐
10	16♎	3♎	16♍	12♐
11	17♎	3♎	16♍	13♐
12	18♎	3♎	16♍	14♐
13	19♎	3♎	16♍	15♐
14	20♎	3♎	16♍	15♐
15	21♎	3♎	16♍	16♐
16	22♎	4♎	17♍	17♐
17	23♎	5♎	17♍	17♐
18	24♎	6♎	17♍	18♐
19	25♎	6♎	18♍	19♐
20	26♎	8♎	18♍	20♐
21	27♎	9♎	18♍	20♐
22	28♎	10♎	19♍	21♐
23	29♎	11♎	19♍	22♐
24	0♏	13♎	20♍	23♐
25	1♏	14♎	20♍	23♐
26	2♏	16♎	21♍	24♐
27	3♏	17♎	21♍	25♐
28	4♏	19♎	22♍	26♐
29	5♏	20♎	23♍	26♐
30	6♏	22♎	23♍	27♐
31	7♏	23♎	24♍	28♐

February

Day	☉	☿	♀	♂
1	11♒	14♒	26♒	15♎
2	12♒	13♒	28♒	15♎
3	13♒	12♒	29♒	15♎
4	14♒	10♒	0♓	15♎
5	15♒	9♒	1♓	15♎
6	16♒	8♒	3♓	15♎
7	17♒	7♒	4♓	16♎
8	18♒	6♒	5♓	16♎
9	19♒	5♒	6♓	16♎
10	20♒	5♒	8♓	16♎
11	21♒	4♒	9♓	16♎
12	22♒	4♒	10♓	16♎
13	23♒	4♒	11♓	16♎
14	24♒	4♒	13♓	16♎
15	25♒	4♒	14♓	16♎
16	26♒	4♒	15♓	16♎
17	27♒	4♒	16♓	16♎
18	28♒	4♒	18♓	16♎
19	29♒	5♒	19♓	16♎
20	0♓	5♒	20♓	16♎
21	1♓	6♒	21♓	16♎
22	2♓	6♒	23♓	16♎
23	3♓	7♒	24♓	16♎
24	4♓	8♒	25♓	16♎
25	5♓	9♒	26♓	16♎
26	6♓	10♒	28♓	16♎
27	7♓	10♒	29♓	16♎
28	8♓	11♒	0♈	16♎

May

Day	☉	☿	♀	♂
1	10♉	28♉	15♊	28♍
2	11♉	29♉	17♊	28♍
3	12♉	1♊	18♊	28♍
4	13♉	2♊	19♊	28♍
5	14♉	4♊	20♊	28♍
6	14♉	5♊	21♊	28♍
7	15♉	6♊	22♊	27♍
8	16♉	8♊	24♊	27♍
9	17♉	9♊	25♊	27♍
10	18♉	10♊	26♊	27♍
11	19♉	11♊	27♊	27♍
12	20♉	12♊	28♊	27♍
13	21♉	12♊	29♊	28♍
14	22♉	13♊	1♋	28♍
15	23♉	14♊	2♋	28♍
16	24♉	14♊	3♋	28♍
17	25♉	15♊	4♋	28♍
18	26♉	15♊	5♋	28♍
19	27♉	16♊	6♋	28♍
20	28♉	16♊	8♋	28♍
21	29♉	16♊	9♋	28♍
22	0♊	16♊	10♋	28♍
23	1♊	16♊	11♋	29♍
24	2♊	16♊	12♋	29♍
25	3♊	16♊	13♋	29♍
26	4♊	16♊	14♋	29♍
27	5♊	15♊	16♋	29♍
28	6♊	15♊	17♋	29♍
29	7♊	15♊	18♋	0♎
30	8♊	14♊	19♋	0♎
31	9♊	14♊	20♋	0♎

August

Day	☉	☿	♀	♂
1	8♌	14♌	21♍	27♎
2	9♌	16♌	22♍	27♎
3	10♌	18♌	22♍	28♎
4	11♌	20♌	23♍	29♎
5	12♌	22♌	24♍	29♎
6	13♌	24♌	24♍	0♏
7	14♌	25♌	25♍	0♏
8	14♌	27♌	25♍	1♏
9	15♌	29♌	26♍	1♏
10	16♌	1♍	27♍	2♏
11	17♌	3♍	27♍	3♏
12	18♌	4♍	28♍	3♏
13	19♌	6♍	28♍	4♏
14	20♌	8♍	29♍	4♏
15	21♌	9♍	29♍	5♏
16	22♌	11♍	29♍	6♏
17	23♌	13♍	0♎	6♏
18	24♌	14♍	0♎	7♏
19	25♌	16♍	0♎	8♏
20	26♌	17♍	1♎	8♏
21	27♌	19♍	1♎	9♏
22	28♌	20♍	1♎	9♏
23	29♌	22♍	1♎	10♏
24	0♍	23♍	1♎	11♏
25	1♍	25♍	2♎	11♏
26	2♍	26♍	2♎	12♏
27	3♍	27♍	2♎	13♏
28	4♍	29♍	2♎	13♏
29	5♍	0♎	2♎	14♏
30	6♍	1♎	2♎	14♏
31	7♍	2♎	1♎	15♏

November

Day	☉	☿	♀	♂
1	8♏	25♎	24♍	28♐
2	9♏	27♎	25♍	29♐
3	10♏	28♎	26♍	0♑
4	11♏	0♏	27♍	1♑
5	12♏	2♏	27♍	1♑
6	13♏	3♏	28♍	2♑
7	14♏	5♏	29♍	3♑
8	15♏	7♏	0♎	4♑
9	16♏	8♏	0♎	4♑
10	17♏	10♏	1♎	5♑
11	18♏	11♏	2♎	6♑
12	19♏	13♏	3♎	7♑
13	20♏	15♏	4♎	8♑
14	21♏	16♏	5♎	8♑
15	22♏	18♏	6♎	9♑
16	23♏	20♏	7♎	10♑
17	24♏	21♏	7♎	11♑
18	25♏	23♏	8♎	11♑
19	26♏	24♏	9♎	12♑
20	27♏	26♏	10♎	13♑
21	28♏	27♏	11♎	14♑
22	29♏	29♏	12♎	14♑
23	0♐	1♐	13♎	15♑
24	1♐	2♐	14♎	16♑
25	2♐	4♐	15♎	17♑
26	3♐	5♐	16♎	17♑
27	4♐	7♐	17♎	18♑
28	5♐	8♐	18♎	19♑
29	6♐	10♐	19♎	20♑
30	7♐	12♐	20♎	21♑

March

Day	☉	☿	♀	♂
1	9♓	13♒	1♈	16♎
2	10♓	14♒	3♈	15♎
3	11♓	15♒	4♈	15♎
4	12♓	16♒	5♈	15♎
5	13♓	17♒	6♈	15♎
6	14♓	18♒	8♈	15♎
7	15♓	19♒	9♈	15♎
8	16♓	21♒	10♈	14♎
9	17♓	22♒	11♈	14♎
10	18♓	23♒	12♈	14♎
11	19♓	25♒	14♈	14♎
12	20♓	26♒	15♈	13♎
13	21♓	28♒	16♈	13♎
14	22♓	29♒	17♈	13♎
15	23♓	0♓	19♈	12♎
16	24♓	2♓	20♈	12♎
17	25♓	3♓	21♈	12♎
18	26♓	5♓	22♈	12♎
19	27♓	6♓	24♈	11♎
20	28♓	8♓	25♈	11♎
21	29♓	10♓	26♈	10♎
22	0♈	11♓	27♈	10♎
23	1♈	13♓	28♈	10♎
24	2♈	15♓	0♉	9♎
25	3♈	16♓	1♉	9♎
26	4♈	18♓	2♉	9♎
27	5♈	20♓	3♉	8♎
28	6♈	21♓	5♉	8♎
29	7♈	23♓	6♉	7♎
30	8♈	25♓	7♉	7♎
31	9♈	27♓	8♉	7♎

June

Day	☉	☿	♀	♂
1	10♊	13♊	21♋	0♎
2	10♊	13♊	22♋	1♎
3	11♊	12♊	23♋	1♎
4	12♊	12♊	25♋	1♎
5	13♊	11♊	26♋	1♎
6	14♊	10♊	27♋	2♎
7	15♊	10♊	28♋	2♎
8	16♊	9♊	29♋	2♎
9	17♊	9♊	0♌	3♎
10	18♊	9♊	1♌	3♎
11	19♊	8♊	2♌	3♎
12	20♊	8♊	3♌	4♎
13	21♊	8♊	4♌	4♎
14	22♊	8♊	6♌	4♎
15	23♊	8♊	7♌	5♎
16	24♊	8♊	8♌	5♎
17	25♊	8♊	9♌	5♎
18	26♊	8♊	10♌	6♎
19	27♊	8♊	11♌	6♎
20	28♊	8♊	12♌	6♎
21	29♊	9♊	13♌	7♎
22	0♋	9♊	14♌	7♎
23	1♋	10♊	15♌	8♎
24	2♋	10♊	16♌	8♎
25	2♋	11♊	17♌	8♎
26	3♋	12♊	18♌	9♎
27	4♋	13♊	19♌	9♎
28	5♋	13♊	20♌	10♎
29	6♋	14♊	21♌	10♎
30	7♋	15♊	22♌	11♎

September

Day	☉	☿	♀	♂
1	8♍	4♎	1♎	16♏
2	9♍	5♎	1♎	16♏
3	10♍	6♎	1♎	17♏
4	10♍	7♎	1♎	18♏
5	11♍	8♎	0♎	18♏
6	12♍	9♎	0♎	19♏
7	13♍	10♎	0♎	20♏
8	14♍	11♎	29♍	20♏
9	15♍	12♎	29♍	21♏
10	16♍	13♎	28♍	22♏
11	17♍	14♎	28♍	22♏
12	18♍	15♎	27♍	23♏
13	19♍	15♎	27♍	24♏
14	20♍	16♎	26♍	24♏
15	21♍	16♎	25♍	25♏
16	22♍	17♎	25♍	26♏
17	23♍	17♎	24♍	26♏
18	24♍	18♎	24♍	27♏
19	25♍	18♎	23♍	28♏
20	26♍	18♎	22♍	28♏
21	27♍	18♎	22♍	29♏
22	28♍	18♎	21♍	0♐
23	29♍	18♎	21♍	0♐
24	0♎	17♎	20♍	1♐
25	1♎	17♎	20♍	2♐
26	2♎	16♎	19♍	3♐
27	3♎	16♎	19♍	3♐
28	4♎	15♎	18♍	4♐
29	5♎	14♎	18♍	5♐
30	6♎	13♎	17♍	5♐

December

Day	☉	☿	♀	♂
1	8♐	13♐	21♎	21♑
2	9♐	15♐	22♎	22♑
3	10♐	16♐	23♎	23♑
4	11♐	18♐	24♎	24♑
5	12♐	19♐	25♎	24♑
6	13♐	21♐	26♎	25♑
7	14♐	23♐	27♎	26♑
8	15♐	24♐	28♎	27♑
9	16♐	26♐	0♏	28♑
10	17♐	27♐	1♏	28♑
11	18♐	29♐	2♏	29♑
12	19♐	0♑	3♏	0♒
13	20♐	2♑	4♏	1♒
14	21♐	3♑	5♏	1♒
15	22♐	5♑	6♏	2♒
16	23♐	7♑	7♏	3♒
17	24♐	8♑	8♏	4♒
18	25♐	10♑	9♏	5♒
19	26♐	11♑	11♏	5♒
20	27♐	13♑	12♏	6♒
21	28♐	14♑	13♏	7♒
22	29♐	16♑	14♏	8♒
23	0♑	17♑	15♏	8♒
24	1♑	19♑	16♏	9♒
25	2♑	20♑	17♏	10♒
26	3♑	21♑	19♏	11♒
27	4♑	23♑	20♏	12♒
28	5♑	24♑	21♏	13♒
29	6♑	25♑	22♏	13♒
30	7♑	27♑	23♏	14♒
31	8♑	28♑	24♏	15♒

Planetary Positions

♌ = Leo ♍ = Virgo ♎ = Libra ♏ = Scorpio ♐ = Sagittarius ♑ = Capricorn ♒ = Aquarius ♓ = Pisces

1904

January

Day	☉	☿	♀	♂
1	9♑	29♑	25♏	15♒
2	10♑	0♒	27♏	16♒
3	11♑	1♒	28♏	17♒
4	12♑	1♒	29♏	18♒
5	13♑	2♒	0♐	19♒
6	14♑	3♒	1♐	19♒
7	15♑	3♒	2♐	20♒
8	17♑	3♒	4♐	21♒
9	18♑	3♒	5♐	22♒
10	19♑	3♒	6♐	23♒
11	20♑	2♒	7♐	23♒
12	21♑	2♒	8♐	24♒
13	22♑	1♒	9♐	25♒
14	23♑	0♒	11♐	26♒
15	24♑	29♑	12♐	27♒
16	25♑	28♑	13♐	27♒
17	26♑	26♑	14♐	28♒
18	27♑	25♑	15♐	29♒
19	28♑	24♑	17♐	0♓
20	29♑	23♑	18♐	0♓
21	0♒	21♑	19♐	1♓
22	1♒	20♑	20♐	2♓
23	2♒	19♑	21♐	3♓
24	3♒	19♑	23♐	4♓
25	4♒	18♑	24♐	4♓
26	5♒	18♑	25♐	5♓
27	6♒	17♑	26♐	6♓
28	7♒	17♑	27♐	7♓
29	8♒	17♑	29♐	7♓
30	9♒	17♑	0♑	8♓
31	10♒	17♑	1♑	9♓

April

Day	☉	☿	♀	♂
1	11♈	17♈	15♓	26♈
2	12♈	19♈	17♓	27♈
3	13♈	21♈	18♓	27♈
4	14♈	23♈	19♓	28♈
5	15♈	25♈	20♓	29♈
6	16♈	27♈	21♓	0♉
7	17♈	29♈	23♓	0♉
8	18♈	1♉	24♓	1♉
9	19♈	3♉	25♓	2♉
10	20♈	5♉	26♓	3♉
11	21♈	6♉	28♓	3♉
12	22♈	8♉	29♓	4♉
13	23♈	10♉	0♈	5♉
14	24♈	11♉	1♈	6♉
15	25♈	13♉	3♈	6♉
16	26♈	14♉	4♈	7♉
17	27♈	16♉	5♈	8♉
18	28♈	17♉	6♈	8♉
19	29♈	18♉	7♈	9♉
20	0♉	20♉	9♈	10♉
21	1♉	21♉	10♈	11♉
22	2♉	22♉	11♈	11♉
23	3♉	23♉	12♈	12♉
24	4♉	23♉	14♈	13♉
25	5♉	24♉	15♈	14♉
26	6♉	25♉	16♈	14♉
27	7♉	25♉	17♈	15♉
28	7♉	26♉	18♈	16♉
29	8♉	26♉	20♈	16♉
30	9♉	26♉	21♈	17♉

July

Day	☉	☿	♀	♂
1	9♋	29♊	7♋	0♋
2	10♋	1♋	8♋	1♋
3	11♋	3♋	9♋	2♋
4	12♋	5♋	11♋	2♋
5	13♋	7♋	12♋	3♋
6	14♋	9♋	13♋	4♋
7	15♋	11♋	14♋	4♋
8	16♋	13♋	16♋	5♋
9	17♋	16♋	17♋	6♋
10	17♋	18♋	18♋	6♋
11	18♋	20♋	19♋	7♋
12	19♋	22♋	20♋	8♋
13	20♋	24♋	22♋	8♋
14	21♋	26♋	23♋	9♋
15	22♋	28♋	24♋	10♋
16	23♋	0♌	25♋	10♋
17	24♋	2♌	27♋	11♋
18	25♋	4♌	28♋	12♋
19	26♋	6♌	29♋	12♋
20	27♋	8♌	0♌	13♋
21	28♋	10♌	2♌	14♋
22	29♋	12♌	3♌	14♋
23	0♌	14♌	4♌	15♋
24	1♌	16♌	5♌	16♋
25	2♌	18♌	6♌	16♋
26	3♌	19♌	8♌	17♋
27	4♌	21♌	9♌	18♋
28	5♌	23♌	10♌	18♋
29	6♌	25♌	11♌	19♋
30	7♌	26♌	13♌	20♋
31	8♌	28♌	14♌	20♋

October

Day	☉	☿	♀	♂
1	8♎	20♍	0♏	0♍
2	9♎	21♍	2♏	0♍
3	10♎	22♍	3♏	1♍
4	11♎	23♍	4♏	2♍
5	12♎	24♍	5♏	2♍
6	13♎	26♍	7♏	3♍
7	13♎	27♍	8♏	3♍
8	14♎	29♍	9♏	4♍
9	15♎	0♎	10♏	5♍
10	16♎	2♎	12♏	5♍
11	17♎	3♎	13♏	6♍
12	18♎	5♎	14♏	7♍
13	19♎	7♎	15♏	7♍
14	20♎	8♎	16♏	8♍
15	21♎	10♎	18♏	8♍
16	22♎	12♎	19♏	9♍
17	23♎	14♎	20♏	10♍
18	24♎	15♎	21♏	10♍
19	25♎	17♎	23♏	11♍
20	26♎	19♎	24♏	11♍
21	27♎	20♎	25♏	12♍
22	28♎	22♎	26♏	13♍
23	29♎	24♎	28♏	13♍
24	0♏	26♎	29♏	14♍
25	1♏	27♎	0♐	14♍
26	2♏	29♎	1♐	15♍
27	3♏	1♏	2♐	16♍
28	4♏	2♏	4♐	16♍
29	5♏	4♏	5♐	17♍
30	6♏	6♏	6♐	17♍
31	7♏	7♏	7♐	18♍

February

Day	☉	☿	♀	♂
1	11♒	18♑	2♑	10♓
2	12♒	18♑	3♑	11♓
3	13♒	19♑	5♑	11♓
4	14♒	19♑	6♑	12♓
5	15♒	20♑	7♑	13♓
6	16♒	21♑	8♑	14♓
7	17♒	21♑	9♑	15♓
8	18♒	22♑	11♑	15♓
9	19♒	23♑	12♑	16♓
10	20♒	24♑	13♑	17♓
11	21♒	25♑	14♑	18♓
12	22♒	26♑	15♑	18♓
13	23♒	27♑	17♑	19♓
14	24♒	29♑	18♑	20♓
15	25♒	0♒	19♑	21♓
16	26♒	1♒	20♑	22♓
17	27♒	2♒	22♑	22♓
18	28♒	3♒	23♑	23♓
19	29♒	5♒	24♑	24♓
20	0♓	6♒	25♑	25♓
21	1♓	7♒	26♑	25♓
22	2♓	9♒	28♑	26♓
23	3♓	10♒	29♑	27♓
24	4♓	11♒	0♒	28♓
25	5♓	13♒	1♒	29♓
26	6♓	14♒	3♒	29♓
27	7♓	16♒	4♒	0♈
28	8♓	17♒	5♒	1♈
29	9♓	19♒	6♒	2♈

May

Day	☉	☿	♀	♂
1	10♉	26♉	22♈	18♉
2	11♉	26♉	23♈	19♉
3	12♉	26♉	25♈	19♉
4	13♉	26♉	26♈	20♉
5	14♉	26♉	27♈	21♉
6	15♉	26♉	28♈	21♉
7	16♉	25♉	29♈	22♉
8	17♉	25♉	1♉	23♉
9	18♉	25♉	2♉	24♉
10	19♉	24♉	3♉	24♉
11	20♉	24♉	4♉	25♉
12	21♉	23♉	6♉	26♉
13	22♉	22♉	7♉	26♉
14	23♉	22♉	8♉	27♉
15	24♉	21♉	9♉	28♉
16	25♉	21♉	11♉	29♉
17	26♉	20♉	12♉	29♉
18	27♉	20♉	13♉	0♊
19	28♉	19♉	14♉	1♊
20	29♉	19♉	15♉	1♊
21	0♊	18♉	17♉	2♊
22	1♊	18♉	18♉	3♊
23	2♊	18♉	19♉	4♊
24	3♊	18♉	20♉	4♊
25	4♊	17♉	22♉	5♊
26	5♊	17♉	23♉	6♊
27	5♊	17♉	24♉	6♊
28	6♊	18♉	25♉	7♊
29	7♊	18♉	26♉	8♊
30	8♊	18♉	28♉	8♊
31	9♊	18♉	29♉	9♊

August

Day	☉	☿	♀	♂
1	8♌	29♌	15♌	21♋
2	9♌	1♍	16♌	22♋
3	10♌	3♍	18♌	22♋
4	11♌	4♍	19♌	23♋
5	12♌	6♍	20♌	24♋
6	13♌	7♍	21♌	24♋
7	14♌	8♍	22♌	25♋
8	15♌	10♍	24♌	26♋
9	16♌	11♍	25♌	26♋
10	17♌	13♍	26♌	27♋
11	18♌	14♍	27♌	27♋
12	19♌	15♍	29♌	28♋
13	20♌	16♍	0♍	29♋
14	21♌	18♍	1♍	29♋
15	22♌	19♍	2♍	0♌
16	23♌	20♍	4♍	1♌
17	24♌	21♍	5♍	1♌
18	25♌	22♍	6♍	2♌
19	26♌	23♍	7♍	3♌
20	27♌	24♍	9♍	3♌
21	28♌	25♍	10♍	4♌
22	29♌	26♍	11♍	5♌
23	0♍	27♍	12♍	5♌
24	1♍	27♍	13♍	6♌
25	2♍	28♍	15♍	6♌
26	3♍	29♍	16♍	7♌
27	3♍	29♍	17♍	8♌
28	4♍	0♎	18♍	8♌
29	5♍	0♎	20♍	9♌
30	6♍	1♎	21♍	10♌
31	7♍	1♎	22♍	10♌

November

Day	☉	☿	♀	♂
1	8♏	9♏	9♐	19♍
2	9♏	10♏	10♐	19♍
3	10♏	12♏	11♐	20♍
4	11♏	14♏	12♐	20♍
5	12♏	15♏	13♐	21♍
6	13♏	17♏	15♐	22♍
7	14♏	18♏	16♐	22♍
8	15♏	20♏	17♐	23♍
9	16♏	22♏	18♐	23♍
10	17♏	23♏	20♐	24♍
11	18♏	25♏	21♐	25♍
12	19♏	26♏	22♐	25♍
13	20♏	28♏	23♐	26♍
14	21♏	29♏	25♐	26♍
15	22♏	1♐	26♐	27♍
16	23♏	3♐	27♐	28♍
17	24♏	4♐	28♐	28♍
18	25♏	6♐	29♐	29♍
19	26♏	7♐	1♑	29♍
20	27♏	9♐	2♑	0♎
21	28♏	10♐	3♑	1♎
22	29♏	12♐	4♑	1♎
23	0♐	13♐	6♑	2♎
24	2♐	15♐	7♑	2♎
25	3♐	16♐	8♑	3♎
26	4♐	18♐	9♑	3♎
27	5♐	19♐	10♑	4♎
28	6♐	21♐	12♑	5♎
29	7♐	22♐	13♑	5♎
30	8♐	24♐	14♑	6♎

March

Day	☉	☿	♀	♂
1	10♓	20♒	7♒	2♈
2	11♓	22♒	9♒	3♈
3	12♓	23♒	10♒	4♈
4	13♓	25♒	11♒	5♈
5	14♓	27♒	12♒	5♈
6	15♓	28♒	14♒	6♈
7	16♓	0♓	15♒	7♈
8	17♓	1♓	16♒	8♈
9	18♓	3♓	17♒	8♈
10	19♓	5♓	18♒	9♈
11	20♓	6♓	20♒	10♈
12	21♓	8♓	21♒	11♈
13	22♓	10♓	22♒	12♈
14	23♓	12♓	23♒	12♈
15	24♓	13♓	25♒	13♈
16	25♓	15♓	26♒	14♈
17	26♓	17♓	27♒	15♈
18	27♓	19♓	28♒	15♈
19	28♓	21♓	29♒	16♈
20	29♓	23♓	1♓	17♈
21	0♈	25♓	2♓	18♈
22	1♈	27♓	3♓	18♈
23	2♈	28♓	4♓	19♈
24	3♈	0♈	6♓	20♈
25	4♈	2♈	7♓	21♈
26	5♈	4♈	8♓	21♈
27	6♈	6♈	9♓	22♈
28	7♈	8♈	10♓	23♈
29	8♈	11♈	12♓	24♈
30	9♈	13♈	13♓	24♈
31	10♈	15♈	14♓	25♈

June

Day	☉	☿	♀	♂
1	10♊	19♉	0♊	10♊
2	11♊	19♉	1♊	11♊
3	12♊	20♉	3♊	11♊
4	13♊	20♉	4♊	12♊
5	14♊	21♉	5♊	13♊
6	15♊	22♉	6♊	13♊
7	16♊	23♉	7♊	14♊
8	17♊	23♉	9♊	15♊
9	18♊	24♉	10♊	15♊
10	19♊	25♉	11♊	16♊
11	20♊	26♉	12♊	17♊
12	21♊	28♉	14♊	17♊
13	22♊	29♉	15♊	18♊
14	23♊	0♊	16♊	19♊
15	24♊	1♊	17♊	20♊
16	25♊	3♊	19♊	20♊
17	26♊	4♊	20♊	21♊
18	27♊	5♊	21♊	22♊
19	27♊	7♊	22♊	22♊
20	28♊	8♊	23♊	23♊
21	29♊	10♊	25♊	24♊
22	0♋	12♊	26♊	24♊
23	1♋	13♊	27♊	25♊
24	2♋	15♊	28♊	26♊
25	3♋	17♊	0♋	26♊
26	4♋	19♊	1♋	27♊
27	5♋	21♊	2♋	28♊
28	6♋	22♊	3♋	28♊
29	7♋	24♊	4♋	29♊
30	8♋	26♊	6♋	0♋

September

Day	☉	☿	♀	♂
1	8♍	1♎	23♍	11♌
2	9♍	1♎	25♍	12♌
3	10♍	1♎	26♍	12♌
4	11♍	1♎	27♍	13♌
5	12♍	1♎	28♍	13♌
6	13♍	1♎	0♎	14♌
7	14♍	0♎	1♎	15♌
8	15♍	0♎	2♎	15♌
9	16♍	29♍	3♎	16♌
10	17♍	28♍	4♎	17♌
11	18♍	28♍	6♎	17♌
12	19♍	27♍	7♎	18♌
13	20♍	26♍	8♎	19♌
14	21♍	25♍	9♎	19♌
15	22♍	24♍	11♎	20♌
16	23♍	23♍	12♎	20♌
17	24♍	22♍	13♎	21♌
18	25♍	21♍	14♎	22♌
19	26♍	20♍	16♎	22♌
20	27♍	19♍	17♎	23♌
21	28♍	18♍	18♎	24♌
22	29♍	18♍	19♎	24♌
23	0♎	17♍	21♎	25♌
24	1♎	17♍	22♎	25♌
25	2♎	17♍	23♎	26♌
26	3♎	17♍	24♎	27♌
27	4♎	17♍	25♎	27♌
28	5♎	18♍	27♎	28♌
29	6♎	18♍	28♎	29♌
30	7♎	19♍	29♎	29♌

December

Day	☉	☿	♀	♂
1	9♐	25♐	15♑	6♎
2	10♐	27♐	16♑	7♎
3	11♐	28♐	18♑	7♎
4	12♐	29♐	19♑	8♎
5	13♐	1♑	20♑	9♎
6	14♐	2♑	21♑	9♎
7	15♐	4♑	23♑	10♎
8	16♐	5♑	24♑	10♎
9	17♐	6♑	25♑	11♎
10	18♐	8♑	26♑	11♎
11	19♐	9♑	27♑	12♎
12	20♐	10♑	29♑	13♎
13	21♐	11♑	0♒	13♎
14	22♐	12♑	1♒	14♎
15	23♐	13♑	2♒	14♎
16	24♐	14♑	3♒	15♎
17	25♐	15♑	5♒	15♎
18	26♐	16♑	6♒	16♎
19	27♐	16♑	7♒	16♎
20	28♐	17♑	8♒	17♎
21	29♐	17♑	9♒	18♎
22	0♑	17♑	11♒	18♎
23	1♑	17♑	12♒	19♎
24	2♑	17♑	13♒	19♎
25	3♑	16♑	14♒	20♎
26	4♑	16♑	15♒	20♎
27	5♑	15♑	17♒	21♎
28	6♑	14♑	18♒	21♎
29	7♑	13♑	19♒	22♎
30	8♑	12♑	20♒	22♎
31	9♑	10♑	21♒	23♎

1905

Your Starway to Love

☉ =Sun ☿ = Mercury ♀ = Venus ♂ = Mars ♈ = Aries ♉ = Taurus ♊ = Gemini ♋ = Cancer

January

Day	☉	☿	♀	♂
1	10♑	9♑	22♒	23♎
2	11♑	7♑	24♒	24♎
3	12♑	6♑	25♒	25♎
4	13♑	5♑	26♒	25♎
5	14♑	4♑	27♒	26♎
6	15♑	3♑	28♒	26♎
7	16♑	2♑	0♓	27♎
8	17♑	2♑	1♓	27♎
9	18♑	1♑	2♓	28♎
10	19♑	1♑	3♓	28♎
11	20♑	1♑	4♓	29♎
12	21♑	1♑	5♓	29♎
13	22♑	1♑	7♓	0♏
14	23♑	2♑	8♓	0♏
15	24♑	2♑	9♓	1♏
16	25♑	2♑	10♓	1♏
17	26♑	3♑	11♓	2♏
18	27♑	4♑	12♓	2♏
19	28♑	4♑	13♓	3♏
20	29♑	5♑	15♓	3♏
21	1♒	6♑	16♓	4♏
22	2♒	7♑	17♓	4♏
23	3♒	8♑	18♓	5♏
24	4♒	9♑	19♓	5♏
25	5♒	10♑	20♓	6♏
26	6♒	11♑	21♓	6♏
27	7♒	13♑	22♓	6♏
28	8♒	14♑	23♓	7♏
29	9♒	15♑	25♓	7♏
30	10♒	16♑	26♓	8♏
31	11♒	18♑	27♓	8♏

April

Day	☉	☿	♀	♂
1	11♈	29♈	14♉	25♏
2	12♈	1♉	14♉	25♏
3	13♈	2♉	15♉	25♏
4	14♈	3♉	15♉	25♏
5	15♈	4♉	15♉	25♏
6	16♈	5♉	15♉	25♏
7	17♈	5♉	15♉	25♏
8	18♈	6♉	15♉	25♏
9	19♈	6♉	15♉	25♏
10	20♈	7♉	14♉	25♏
11	21♈	7♉	14♉	25♏
12	22♈	7♉	14♉	25♏
13	23♈	7♉	14♉	24♏
14	24♈	7♉	13♉	24♏
15	25♈	7♉	13♉	24♏
16	26♈	7♉	13♉	24♏
17	27♈	7♉	12♉	24♏
18	27♈	6♉	12♉	24♏
19	28♈	6♉	11♉	23♏
20	29♈	5♉	11♉	23♏
21	0♉	5♉	10♉	23♏
22	1♉	4♉	10♉	23♏
23	2♉	3♉	9♉	23♏
24	3♉	3♉	8♉	22♏
25	4♉	2♉	8♉	22♏
26	5♉	1♉	7♉	22♏
27	6♉	1♉	7♉	21♏
28	7♉	0♉	6♉	21♏
29	8♉	0♉	5♉	21♏
30	9♉	29♈	5♉	21♏

July

Day	☉	☿	♀	♂
1	9♋	17♋	23♉	10♏
2	10♋	19♋	24♉	10♏
3	11♋	21♋	25♉	10♏
4	12♋	23♋	26♉	10♏
5	12♋	25♋	27♉	10♏
6	13♋	27♋	28♉	11♏
7	14♋	29♋	29♉	11♏
8	15♋	1♌	0♊	11♏
9	16♋	2♌	1♊	11♏
10	17♋	4♌	2♊	12♏
11	18♋	6♌	3♊	12♏
12	19♋	8♌	4♊	12♏
13	20♋	9♌	5♊	12♏
14	21♋	11♌	6♊	13♏
15	22♋	13♌	7♊	13♏
16	23♋	14♌	8♊	13♏
17	24♋	16♌	9♊	14♏
18	25♋	17♌	10♊	14♏
19	26♋	19♌	11♊	14♏
20	27♋	20♌	12♊	15♏
21	28♋	22♌	13♊	15♏
22	29♋	23♌	14♊	15♏
23	0♌	25♌	15♊	16♏
24	1♌	26♌	16♊	16♏
25	2♌	27♌	17♊	17♏
26	3♌	29♌	18♊	17♏
27	3♌	0♍	19♊	17♏
28	4♌	1♍	20♊	18♏
29	5♌	2♍	21♊	18♏
30	6♌	3♍	22♊	19♏
31	7♌	4♍	23♊	19♏

October

Day	☉	☿	♀	♂
1	7♎	29♍	5♍	25♐
2	8♎	0♎	6♍	26♐
3	9♎	2♎	7♍	27♐
4	10♎	4♎	9♍	27♐
5	11♎	6♎	10♍	28♐
6	12♎	8♎	11♍	29♐
7	13♎	9♎	12♍	29♐
8	14♎	11♎	13♍	0♑
9	15♎	13♎	15♍	1♑
10	16♎	15♎	16♍	2♑
11	17♎	16♎	17♍	2♑
12	18♎	18♎	18♍	3♑
13	19♎	20♎	19♍	4♑
14	20♎	21♎	21♍	4♑
15	21♎	23♎	22♍	5♑
16	22♎	25♎	23♍	6♑
17	23♎	27♎	24♍	6♑
18	24♎	28♎	26♍	7♑
19	25♎	0♏	27♍	8♑
20	26♎	1♏	28♍	9♑
21	27♎	3♏	29♍	9♑
22	28♎	5♏	1♎	10♑
23	29♎	6♏	2♎	11♑
24	0♏	8♏	3♎	12♑
25	1♏	9♏	4♎	12♑
26	2♏	11♏	5♎	13♑
27	3♏	13♏	7♎	14♑
28	4♏	14♏	8♎	14♑
29	5♏	16♏	9♎	15♑
30	6♏	17♏	10♎	16♑
31	7♏	19♏	12♎	17♑

February

Day	☉	☿	♀	♂
1	12♒	19♑	28♓	9♏
2	13♒	20♑	29♓	9♏
3	14♒	21♑	0♈	10♏
4	15♒	23♑	1♈	10♏
5	16♒	24♑	2♈	11♏
6	17♒	26♑	3♈	11♏
7	18♒	27♑	4♈	11♏
8	19♒	29♑	5♈	12♏
9	20♒	0♒	6♈	12♏
10	21♒	1♒	7♈	13♏
11	22♒	3♒	8♈	13♏
12	23♒	4♒	9♈	13♏
13	24♒	6♒	11♈	14♏
14	25♒	7♒	12♈	14♏
15	26♒	9♒	13♈	15♏
16	27♒	11♒	14♈	15♏
17	28♒	12♒	15♈	15♏
18	29♒	14♒	16♈	16♏
19	0♓	15♒	16♈	16♏
20	1♓	17♒	17♈	17♏
21	2♓	19♒	18♈	17♏
22	3♓	20♒	19♈	17♏
23	4♓	22♒	20♈	18♏
24	5♓	24♒	21♈	18♏
25	6♓	25♒	22♈	18♏
26	7♓	27♒	23♈	19♏
27	8♓	29♒	24♈	19♏
28	9♓	1♓	25♈	19♏

May

Day	☉	☿	♀	♂
1	10♉	29♈	4♉	20♏
2	11♉	28♈	4♉	20♏
3	12♉	28♈	3♉	20♏
4	13♉	28♈	2♉	19♏
5	14♉	27♈	2♉	19♏
6	15♉	27♈	1♉	18♏
7	16♉	27♈	1♉	18♏
8	17♉	27♈	0♉	18♏
9	18♉	27♈	0♉	17♏
10	19♉	28♈	0♉	17♏
11	20♉	28♈	29♈	17♏
12	21♉	28♈	29♈	16♏
13	22♉	29♈	29♈	16♏
14	23♉	29♈	29♈	16♏
15	24♉	0♉	29♈	15♏
16	25♉	0♉	28♈	15♏
17	26♉	1♉	28♈	15♏
18	27♉	2♉	28♈	14♏
19	28♉	2♉	28♈	14♏
20	28♉	3♉	28♈	13♏
21	29♉	4♉	28♈	13♏
22	0♊	5♉	29♈	13♏
23	1♊	6♉	29♈	13♏
24	2♊	7♉	29♈	12♏
25	3♊	8♉	29♈	12♏
26	4♊	10♉	29♈	12♏
27	5♊	11♉	0♉	11♏
28	6♊	12♉	0♉	11♏
29	7♊	13♉	0♉	11♏
30	8♊	15♉	1♉	11♏
31	9♊	16♉	1♉	10♏

August

Day	☉	☿	♀	♂
1	8♌	5♍	24♊	20♏
2	9♌	6♍	25♊	20♏
3	10♌	7♍	27♊	21♏
4	11♌	8♍	28♊	21♏
5	12♌	9♍	29♊	21♏
6	13♌	10♍	0♋	22♏
7	14♌	11♍	1♋	22♏
8	15♌	11♍	2♋	23♏
9	16♌	12♍	3♋	23♏
10	17♌	12♍	4♋	24♏
11	18♌	13♍	5♋	24♏
12	19♌	13♍	6♋	25♏
13	20♌	14♍	8♋	25♏
14	21♌	14♍	9♋	26♏
15	22♌	14♍	10♋	26♏
16	23♌	14♍	11♋	27♏
17	24♌	14♍	12♋	27♏
18	25♌	14♍	13♋	28♏
19	26♌	14♍	14♋	29♏
20	26♌	13♍	15♋	29♏
21	27♌	13♍	17♋	0♐
22	28♌	12♍	18♋	0♐
23	29♌	12♍	19♋	1♐
24	0♍	11♍	20♋	1♐
25	1♍	10♍	21♋	2♐
26	2♍	10♍	22♋	2♐
27	3♍	9♍	23♋	3♐
28	4♍	8♍	25♋	4♐
29	5♍	7♍	26♋	4♐
30	6♍	6♍	27♋	5♐
31	7♍	5♍	28♋	5♐

November

Day	☉	☿	♀	♂
1	8♏	20♏	13♎	17♑
2	9♏	22♏	14♎	18♑
3	10♏	23♏	15♎	19♑
4	11♏	25♏	17♎	20♑
5	12♏	26♏	18♎	20♑
6	13♏	28♏	19♎	21♑
7	14♏	29♏	20♎	22♑
8	15♏	1♐	22♎	23♑
9	16♏	2♐	23♎	23♑
10	17♏	4♐	24♎	24♑
11	18♏	5♐	25♎	25♑
12	19♏	7♐	27♎	26♑
13	20♏	8♐	28♎	26♑
14	21♏	9♐	29♎	27♑
15	22♏	11♐	0♏	28♑
16	23♏	12♐	2♏	29♑
17	24♏	14♐	3♏	29♑
18	25♏	15♐	4♏	0♒
19	26♏	16♐	5♏	1♒
20	27♏	18♐	7♏	2♒
21	28♏	19♐	8♏	2♒
22	29♏	20♐	9♏	3♒
23	0♐	21♐	10♏	4♒
24	1♐	23♐	12♏	5♒
25	2♐	24♐	13♏	5♒
26	3♐	25♐	14♏	6♒
27	4♐	26♐	15♏	7♒
28	5♐	27♐	17♏	8♒
29	6♐	28♐	18♏	8♒
30	7♐	29♐	19♏	9♒

March

Day	☉	☿	♀	♂
1	10♓	2♓	26♈	20♏
2	11♓	4♓	27♈	20♏
3	12♓	6♓	27♈	20♏
4	13♓	8♓	28♈	20♏
5	14♓	10♓	29♈	21♏
6	15♓	11♓	0♉	21♏
7	16♓	13♓	1♉	21♏
8	17♓	15♓	2♉	22♏
9	18♓	17♓	2♉	22♏
10	19♓	19♓	3♉	22♏
11	20♓	21♓	4♉	22♏
12	21♓	23♓	5♉	23♏
13	22♓	25♓	5♉	23♏
14	23♓	27♓	6♉	23♏
15	24♓	29♓	7♉	23♏
16	25♓	1♈	7♉	23♏
17	26♓	3♈	8♉	24♏
18	27♓	5♈	9♉	24♏
19	28♓	7♈	9♉	24♏
20	29♓	9♈	10♉	24♏
21	0♈	11♈	10♉	24♏
22	1♈	13♈	11♉	24♏
23	2♈	15♈	11♉	24♏
24	3♈	16♈	12♉	25♏
25	4♈	18♈	12♉	25♏
26	5♈	20♈	12♉	25♏
27	6♈	22♈	13♉	25♏
28	7♈	23♈	13♉	25♏
29	8♈	25♈	14♉	25♏
30	9♈	27♈	14♉	25♏
31	10♈	28♈	14♉	25♏

June

Day	☉	☿	♀	♂
1	10♊	18♉	1♉	10♏
2	11♊	19♉	2♉	10♏
3	12♊	21♉	2♉	10♏
4	13♊	22♉	3♉	10♏
5	14♊	24♉	3♉	9♏
6	15♊	26♉	4♉	9♏
7	16♊	27♉	5♉	9♏
8	17♊	29♉	5♉	9♏
9	18♊	1♊	6♉	9♏
10	19♊	3♊	6♉	9♏
11	20♊	5♊	7♉	9♏
12	21♊	6♊	8♉	9♏
13	21♊	8♊	8♉	8♏
14	22♊	10♊	9♉	8♏
15	23♊	12♊	10♉	8♏
16	24♊	14♊	11♉	8♏
17	25♊	17♊	11♉	8♏
18	26♊	19♊	12♉	8♏
19	27♊	21♊	13♉	8♏
20	28♊	23♊	14♉	8♏
21	29♊	25♊	14♉	8♏
22	0♋	27♊	15♉	8♏
23	1♋	0♋	16♉	9♏
24	2♋	2♋	17♉	9♏
25	3♋	4♋	18♉	9♏
26	4♋	6♋	19♉	9♏
27	5♋	8♋	20♉	9♏
28	6♋	10♋	20♉	9♏
29	7♋	13♋	21♉	9♏
30	8♋	15♋	22♉	9♏

September

Day	☉	☿	♀	♂
1	8♍	4♍	29♋	6♐
2	9♍	3♍	0♌	7♐
3	10♍	3♍	2♌	7♐
4	11♍	2♍	3♌	8♐
5	12♍	1♍	4♌	8♐
6	13♍	1♍	5♌	9♐
7	14♍	1♍	6♌	10♐
8	15♍	1♍	7♌	10♐
9	16♍	1♍	9♌	11♐
10	17♍	1♍	10♌	12♐
11	18♍	1♍	11♌	12♐
12	19♍	2♍	12♌	13♐
13	20♍	2♍	13♌	13♐
14	21♍	3♍	15♌	14♐
15	22♍	4♍	16♌	15♐
16	23♍	5♍	17♌	15♐
17	24♍	6♍	18♌	16♐
18	25♍	7♍	19♌	17♐
19	26♍	9♍	20♌	17♐
20	27♍	10♍	22♌	18♐
21	28♍	11♍	23♌	19♐
22	29♍	13♍	24♌	19♐
23	29♍	15♍	25♌	20♐
24	0♎	16♍	26♌	21♐
25	1♎	18♍	28♌	21♐
26	2♎	20♍	29♌	22♐
27	3♎	21♍	0♍	23♐
28	4♎	23♍	1♍	23♐
29	5♎	25♍	2♍	24♐
30	6♎	27♍	4♍	25♐

December

Day	☉	☿	♀	♂
1	8♐	29♐	20♏	10♒
2	9♐	0♑	22♏	11♒
3	10♐	1♑	23♏	11♒
4	11♐	1♑	24♏	12♒
5	12♐	1♑	25♏	13♒
6	13♐	1♑	27♏	14♒
7	14♐	1♑	28♏	14♒
8	15♐	1♑	29♏	15♒
9	16♐	1♑	0♐	16♒
10	17♐	0♑	2♐	17♒
11	19♐	29♐	3♐	17♒
12	20♐	28♐	4♐	18♒
13	21♐	27♐	5♐	19♒
14	22♐	26♐	7♐	20♒
15	23♐	24♐	8♐	21♒
16	24♐	23♐	9♐	21♒
17	25♐	22♐	10♐	22♒
18	26♐	20♐	12♐	23♒
19	27♐	19♐	13♐	24♒
20	28♐	18♐	14♐	24♒
21	29♐	17♐	15♐	25♒
22	0♑	16♐	17♐	26♒
23	1♑	16♐	18♐	27♒
24	2♑	15♐	19♐	27♒
25	3♑	15♐	20♐	28♒
26	4♑	15♐	22♐	29♒
27	5♑	15♐	23♐	0♓
28	6♑	15♐	24♐	0♓
29	7♑	16♐	26♐	1♓
30	8♑	16♐	27♐	2♓
31	9♑	17♐	28♐	3♓

Planetary Positions

♌ = Leo ♍ = Virgo ♎ = Libra ♏ = Scorpio ♐ = Sagittarius ♑ = Capricorn ♒ = Aquarius ♓ = Pisces

1906

January

Day	☉	☿	♀	♂
1	10♑	17♐	29♐	4♓
2	11♑	18♐	1♑	4♓
3	12♑	19♐	2♑	5♓
4	13♑	20♐	3♑	6♓
5	14♑	21♐	4♑	7♓
6	15♑	22♐	6♑	7♓
7	16♑	23♐	7♑	8♓
8	17♑	24♐	8♑	9♓
9	18♑	25♐	9♑	10♓
10	19♑	27♐	11♑	10♓
11	20♑	28♐	12♑	11♓
12	21♑	29♐	13♑	12♓
13	22♑	0♑	14♑	13♓
14	23♑	2♑	16♑	13♓
15	24♑	3♑	17♑	14♓
16	25♑	4♑	18♑	15♓
17	26♑	6♑	19♑	16♓
18	27♑	7♑	21♑	17♓
19	28♑	9♑	22♑	17♓
20	29♑	10♑	23♑	18♓
21	0♒	11♑	24♑	19♓
22	1♒	13♑	26♑	20♓
23	2♒	14♑	27♑	20♓
24	3♒	16♑	28♑	21♓
25	4♒	17♑	29♑	22♓
26	5♒	19♑	1♒	23♓
27	6♒	20♑	2♒	23♓
28	7♒	22♑	3♒	24♓
29	8♒	23♑	4♒	25♓
30	9♒	25♑	6♒	26♓
31	10♒	26♑	7♒	26♓

February

Day	☉	☿	♀	♂
1	11♒	28♑	8♒	27♓
2	12♒	0♒	10♒	28♓
3	13♒	1♒	11♒	29♓
4	14♒	3♒	12♒	29♓
5	16♒	4♒	13♒	0♈
6	17♒	6♒	15♒	1♈
7	18♒	8♒	16♒	2♈
8	19♒	9♒	17♒	2♈
9	20♒	11♒	18♒	3♈
10	21♒	13♒	20♒	4♈
11	22♒	14♒	21♒	5♈
12	23♒	16♒	22♒	5♈
13	24♒	18♒	23♒	6♈
14	25♒	19♒	25♒	7♈
15	26♒	21♒	26♒	8♈
16	27♒	23♒	27♒	8♈
17	28♒	25♒	28♒	9♈
18	29♒	26♒	0♓	10♈
19	0♓	28♒	1♓	11♈
20	1♓	0♓	2♓	11♈
21	2♓	2♓	3♓	12♈
22	3♓	4♓	5♓	13♈
23	4♓	6♓	6♓	14♈
24	5♓	8♓	7♓	14♈
25	6♓	9♓	8♓	15♈
26	7♓	11♓	10♓	16♈
27	8♓	13♓	11♓	17♈
28	9♓	15♓	12♓	17♈

March

Day	☉	☿	♀	♂
1	10♓	17♓	13♓	18♈
2	11♓	19♓	15♓	19♈
3	12♓	21♓	16♓	20♈
4	13♓	23♓	17♓	20♈
5	14♓	25♓	18♓	21♈
6	15♓	27♓	20♓	22♈
7	16♓	28♓	21♓	22♈
8	17♓	0♈	22♓	23♈
9	18♓	2♈	23♓	24♈
10	19♓	4♈	25♓	25♈
11	20♓	5♈	26♓	25♈
12	21♓	7♈	27♓	26♈
13	22♓	9♈	28♓	27♈
14	23♓	10♈	0♈	28♈
15	24♓	11♈	1♈	28♈
16	25♓	13♈	2♈	29♈
17	26♓	14♈	3♈	0♉
18	27♓	15♈	5♈	1♉
19	28♓	16♈	6♈	1♉
20	29♓	17♈	7♈	2♉
21	0♈	18♈	8♈	3♉
22	1♈	19♈	10♈	3♉
23	2♈	19♈	11♈	4♉
24	3♈	19♈	12♈	5♉
25	4♈	19♈	13♈	6♉
26	5♈	19♈	14♈	6♉
27	6♈	19♈	16♈	7♉
28	7♈	19♈	17♈	8♉
29	8♈	19♈	18♈	8♉
30	9♈	18♈	19♈	9♉
31	10♈	18♈	21♈	10♉

April

Day	☉	☿	♀	♂
1	11♈	17♈	22♈	11♉
2	12♈	17♈	23♈	11♉
3	13♈	16♈	24♈	12♉
4	14♈	15♈	26♈	13♉
5	15♈	14♈	27♈	13♉
6	15♈	14♈	28♈	14♉
7	16♈	13♈	29♈	15♉
8	17♈	12♈	1♉	16♉
9	18♈	11♈	2♉	16♉
10	19♈	11♈	3♉	17♉
11	20♈	10♈	4♉	18♉
12	21♈	9♈	6♉	18♉
13	22♈	9♈	7♉	19♉
14	23♈	8♈	8♉	20♉
15	24♈	8♈	9♉	21♉
16	25♈	8♈	10♉	21♉
17	26♈	8♈	12♉	22♉
18	27♈	8♈	13♉	23♉
19	28♈	8♈	14♉	23♉
20	29♈	8♈	15♉	24♉
21	0♉	8♈	17♉	25♉
22	1♉	8♈	18♉	25♉
23	2♉	8♈	19♉	26♉
24	3♉	9♈	20♉	27♉
25	4♉	9♈	22♉	28♉
26	5♉	10♈	23♉	28♉
27	6♉	10♈	24♉	29♉
28	7♉	11♈	25♉	0♊
29	8♉	12♈	26♉	0♊
30	9♉	13♈	28♉	1♊

May

Day	☉	☿	♀	♂
1	10♉	13♈	29♉	2♊
2	11♉	14♈	0♊	2♊
3	12♉	15♈	1♊	3♊
4	13♉	16♈	3♊	4♊
5	14♉	17♈	4♊	5♊
6	15♉	18♈	5♊	5♊
7	16♉	20♈	6♊	6♊
8	17♉	21♈	7♊	7♊
9	18♉	22♈	9♊	7♊
10	19♉	23♈	10♊	8♊
11	20♉	24♈	11♊	9♊
12	21♉	26♈	12♊	9♊
13	22♉	27♈	14♊	10♊
14	22♉	29♈	15♊	11♊
15	23♉	0♉	16♊	11♊
16	24♉	2♉	17♊	12♊
17	25♉	3♉	18♊	13♊
18	26♉	5♉	20♊	13♊
19	27♉	6♉	21♊	14♊
20	28♉	8♉	22♊	15♊
21	29♉	10♉	23♊	15♊
22	0♊	11♉	24♊	16♊
23	1♊	13♉	26♊	17♊
24	2♊	15♉	27♊	17♊
25	3♊	17♉	28♊	18♊
26	4♊	19♉	29♊	19♊
27	5♊	21♉	1♋	20♊
28	6♊	22♉	2♋	20♊
29	7♊	24♉	3♋	21♊
30	8♊	26♉	4♋	22♊
31	9♊	28♉	5♋	22♊

June

Day	☉	☿	♀	♂
1	10♊	1♊	7♋	23♊
2	11♊	3♊	8♋	24♊
3	12♊	5♊	9♋	24♊
4	13♊	7♊	10♋	25♊
5	14♊	9♊	11♋	26♊
6	15♊	11♊	13♋	26♊
7	16♊	13♊	14♋	27♊
8	16♊	16♊	15♋	28♊
9	17♊	18♊	16♋	28♊
10	18♊	20♊	17♋	29♊
11	19♊	22♊	19♋	0♋
12	20♊	24♊	20♋	0♋
13	21♊	27♊	21♋	1♋
14	22♊	29♊	22♋	2♋
15	23♊	1♋	23♋	2♋
16	24♊	3♋	25♋	3♋
17	25♊	5♋	26♋	4♋
18	26♊	7♋	27♋	4♋
19	27♊	9♋	28♋	5♋
20	28♊	11♋	29♋	6♋
21	29♊	13♋	1♌	6♋
22	0♋	15♋	2♌	7♋
23	1♋	17♋	3♌	8♋
24	2♋	19♋	4♌	8♋
25	3♋	20♋	5♌	9♋
26	4♋	22♋	7♌	10♋
27	5♋	24♋	8♌	10♋
28	6♋	26♋	9♌	11♋
29	7♋	27♋	10♌	12♋
30	7♋	29♋	11♌	12♋

July

Day	☉	☿	♀	♂
1	8♋	0♌	13♌	13♋
2	9♋	2♌	14♌	13♋
3	10♋	4♌	15♌	14♋
4	11♋	5♌	16♌	15♋
5	12♋	6♌	17♌	15♋
6	13♋	8♌	18♌	16♋
7	14♋	9♌	20♌	17♋
8	15♋	10♌	21♌	17♋
9	16♋	12♌	22♌	18♋
10	17♋	13♌	23♌	19♋
11	18♋	14♌	24♌	19♋
12	19♋	15♌	25♌	20♋
13	20♋	16♌	27♌	21♋
14	21♋	17♌	28♌	21♋
15	22♋	18♌	29♌	22♋
16	23♋	19♌	0♍	23♋
17	24♋	20♌	1♍	23♋
18	25♋	21♌	3♍	24♋
19	26♋	22♌	4♍	25♋
20	27♋	23♌	5♍	25♋
21	28♋	23♌	6♍	26♋
22	28♋	24♌	7♍	27♋
23	29♋	24♌	8♍	27♋
24	0♌	25♌	9♍	28♋
25	1♌	25♌	11♍	28♋
26	2♌	26♌	12♍	29♋
27	3♌	26♌	13♍	0♌
28	4♌	26♌	14♍	0♌
29	5♌	26♌	15♍	1♌
30	6♌	26♌	16♍	2♌
31	7♌	26♌	18♍	2♌

August

Day	☉	☿	♀	♂
1	8♌	26♌	19♍	3♌
2	9♌	26♌	20♍	4♌
3	10♌	25♌	21♍	4♌
4	11♌	25♌	22♍	5♌
5	12♌	24♌	23♍	6♌
6	13♌	24♌	24♍	6♌
7	14♌	23♌	26♍	7♌
8	15♌	22♌	27♍	7♌
9	16♌	21♌	28♍	8♌
10	17♌	21♌	29♍	9♌
11	18♌	20♌	0♎	9♌
12	19♌	19♌	1♎	10♌
13	20♌	18♌	2♎	11♌
14	20♌	17♌	3♎	11♌
15	21♌	17♌	5♎	12♌
16	22♌	16♌	6♎	13♌
17	23♌	15♌	7♎	13♌
18	24♌	15♌	8♎	14♌
19	25♌	14♌	9♎	15♌
20	26♌	14♌	10♎	15♌
21	27♌	14♌	11♎	16♌
22	28♌	14♌	12♎	16♌
23	29♌	14♌	13♎	17♌
24	0♍	14♌	15♎	18♌
25	1♍	14♌	16♎	18♌
26	2♍	15♌	17♎	19♌
27	3♍	15♌	18♎	20♌
28	4♍	16♌	19♎	20♌
29	5♍	17♌	20♎	21♌
30	6♍	18♌	21♎	22♌
31	7♍	19♌	22♎	22♌

September

Day	☉	☿	♀	♂
1	8♍	20♌	23♎	23♌
2	9♍	21♌	24♎	23♌
3	10♍	23♌	25♎	24♌
4	11♍	24♌	26♎	25♌
5	12♍	26♌	27♎	25♌
6	13♍	27♌	28♎	26♌
7	14♍	29♌	0♏	27♌
8	15♍	1♍	1♏	27♌
9	16♍	2♍	2♏	28♌
10	17♍	4♍	3♏	29♌
11	18♍	6♍	4♏	29♌
12	19♍	8♍	5♏	0♍
13	19♍	10♍	6♏	0♍
14	20♍	11♍	7♏	1♍
15	21♍	13♍	8♏	2♍
16	22♍	15♍	9♏	2♍
17	23♍	17♍	10♏	3♍
18	24♍	19♍	11♏	4♍
19	25♍	21♍	12♏	4♍
20	26♍	23♍	13♏	5♍
21	27♍	25♍	14♏	5♍
22	28♍	26♍	15♏	6♍
23	29♍	28♍	16♏	7♍
24	0♎	0♎	17♏	7♍
25	1♎	2♎	18♏	8♍
26	2♎	4♎	18♏	9♍
27	3♎	5♎	19♏	9♍
28	4♎	7♎	20♏	10♍
29	5♎	9♎	21♏	11♍
30	6♎	11♎	22♏	11♍

October

Day	☉	☿	♀	♂
1	7♎	12♎	23♏	12♍
2	8♎	14♎	24♏	12♍
3	9♎	16♎	25♏	13♍
4	10♎	17♎	26♏	14♍
5	11♎	19♎	27♏	14♍
6	12♎	21♎	27♏	15♍
7	13♎	22♎	28♏	16♍
8	14♎	24♎	29♏	16♍
9	15♎	26♎	0♐	17♍
10	16♎	27♎	1♐	17♍
11	17♎	29♎	1♐	18♍
12	18♎	0♏	2♐	19♍
13	19♎	2♏	3♐	19♍
14	20♎	3♏	4♐	20♍
15	21♎	5♏	4♐	21♍
16	22♎	7♏	5♐	21♍
17	23♎	8♏	6♐	22♍
18	24♎	10♏	6♐	22♍
19	25♎	11♏	7♐	23♍
20	26♎	12♏	8♐	24♍
21	27♎	14♏	8♐	24♍
22	28♎	15♏	9♐	25♍
23	29♎	17♏	9♐	26♍
24	0♏	18♏	10♐	26♍
25	1♏	20♏	11♐	27♍
26	2♏	21♏	11♐	28♍
27	3♏	22♏	11♐	28♍
28	4♏	24♏	12♐	29♍
29	5♏	25♏	12♐	29♍
30	6♏	27♏	13♐	0♎
31	7♏	28♏	13♐	1♎

November

Day	☉	☿	♀	♂
1	8♏	29♏	13♐	1♎
2	9♏	1♐	14♐	2♎
3	10♏	2♐	14♐	3♎
4	11♏	3♐	14♐	3♎
5	12♏	4♐	14♐	4♎
6	13♏	5♐	15♐	4♎
7	14♏	7♐	15♐	5♎
8	15♏	8♐	15♐	6♎
9	16♏	9♐	15♐	6♎
10	17♏	10♐	15♐	7♎
11	18♏	11♐	15♐	8♎
12	19♏	12♐	15♐	8♎
13	20♏	12♐	14♐	9♎
14	21♏	13♐	14♐	9♎
15	22♏	14♐	14♐	10♎
16	23♏	14♐	14♐	11♎
17	24♏	15♐	14♐	11♎
18	25♏	15♐	13♐	12♎
19	26♏	15♐	13♐	12♎
20	27♏	15♐	13♐	13♎
21	28♏	15♐	12♐	14♎
22	29♏	15♐	12♐	14♎
23	0♐	15♐	11♐	15♎
24	1♐	14♐	11♐	16♎
25	2♐	13♐	10♐	16♎
26	3♐	12♐	9♐	17♎
27	4♐	11♐	9♐	17♎
28	5♐	10♐	8♐	18♎
29	6♐	9♐	8♐	19♎
30	7♐	7♐	7♐	19♎

December

Day	☉	☿	♀	♂
1	8♐	6♐	7♐	20♎
2	9♐	4♐	6♐	21♎
3	10♐	3♐	5♐	21♎
4	11♐	2♐	5♐	22♎
5	12♐	1♐	4♐	22♎
6	13♐	0♐	4♐	23♎
7	14♐	0♐	3♐	24♎
8	15♐	29♏	3♐	24♎
9	16♐	29♏	2♐	25♎
10	17♐	29♏	2♐	26♎
11	18♐	29♏	1♐	26♎
12	19♐	0♐	1♐	27♎
13	20♐	0♐	1♐	27♎
14	21♐	1♐	0♐	28♎
15	22♐	1♐	0♐	29♎
16	23♐	2♐	0♐	29♎
17	24♐	3♐	0♐	0♏
18	25♐	4♐	0♐	0♏
19	26♐	5♐	29♏	1♏
20	27♐	6♐	29♏	2♏
21	28♐	7♐	29♏	2♏
22	29♐	8♐	29♏	3♏
23	0♑	9♐	0♐	3♏
24	1♑	11♐	0♐	4♏
25	3♑	12♐	0♐	5♏
26	4♑	13♐	0♐	5♏
27	5♑	15♐	0♐	6♏
28	6♑	16♐	1♐	7♏
29	7♑	17♐	1♐	7♏
30	8♑	19♐	1♐	8♏
31	9♑	20♐	2♐	8♏

1907

Your Starway to Love

☉ =Sun ☿ = Mercury ♀ = Venus ♂ = Mars ♈ = Aries ♉ = Taurus ♊ = Gemini ♋ = Cancer

January

Day	☉	☿	♀	♂
1	10♑	22♐	2♐	9♏
2	11♑	23♐	2♐	10♏
3	12♑	24♐	3♐	10♏
4	13♑	26♐	3♐	11♏
5	14♑	27♐	4♐	11♏
6	15♑	29♐	4♐	12♏
7	16♑	0♑	5♐	13♏
8	17♑	2♑	5♐	13♏
9	18♑	3♑	6♐	14♏
10	19♑	5♑	7♐	14♏
11	20♑	6♑	7♐	15♏
12	21♑	8♑	8♐	16♏
13	22♑	9♑	9♐	16♏
14	23♑	11♑	9♐	17♏
15	24♑	12♑	10♐	17♏
16	25♑	14♑	11♐	18♏
17	26♑	16♑	12♐	19♏
18	27♑	17♑	12♐	19♏
19	28♑	19♑	13♐	20♏
20	29♑	20♑	14♐	20♏
21	0♒	22♑	15♐	21♏
22	1♒	23♑	16♐	22♏
23	2♒	25♑	17♐	22♏
24	3♒	27♑	17♐	23♏
25	4♒	28♑	18♐	23♏
26	5♒	0♒	19♐	24♏
27	6♒	2♒	20♐	25♏
28	7♒	3♒	21♐	25♏
29	8♒	5♒	22♐	26♏
30	9♒	7♒	23♐	26♏
31	10♒	8♒	24♐	27♏

February

Day	☉	☿	♀	♂
1	11♒	10♒	25♐	28♏
2	12♒	12♒	26♐	28♏
3	13♒	14♒	27♐	29♏
4	14♒	15♒	28♐	29♏
5	15♒	17♒	29♐	0♐
6	16♒	19♒	0♑	0♐
7	17♒	21♒	1♑	1♐
8	18♒	22♒	2♑	2♐
9	19♒	24♒	3♑	2♐
10	20♒	26♒	4♑	3♐
11	21♒	28♒	5♑	3♐
12	22♒	0♓	6♑	4♐
13	23♒	2♓	7♑	5♐
14	24♒	3♓	8♑	5♐
15	25♒	5♓	9♑	6♐
16	26♒	7♓	10♑	6♐
17	27♒	9♓	11♑	7♐
18	28♒	11♓	12♑	7♐
19	29♒	12♓	13♑	8♐
20	0♓	14♓	14♑	9♐
21	1♓	16♓	15♑	9♐
22	2♓	18♓	16♑	10♐
23	3♓	19♓	17♑	10♐
24	4♓	21♓	18♑	11♐
25	5♓	22♓	19♑	11♐
26	6♓	24♓	20♑	12♐
27	7♓	25♓	22♑	12♐
28	8♓	26♓	23♑	13♐

March

Day	☉	☿	♀	♂
1	9♓	28♓	24♑	14♐
2	10♓	29♓	25♑	14♐
3	11♓	29♓	26♑	15♐
4	12♓	0♈	27♑	15♐
5	13♓	1♈	28♑	16♐
6	14♓	1♈	29♑	16♐
7	15♓	2♈	0♒	17♐
8	16♓	2♈	2♒	17♐
9	17♓	2♈	3♒	18♐
10	18♓	2♈	4♒	18♐
11	19♓	2♈	5♒	19♐
12	20♓	1♈	6♒	20♐
13	21♓	1♈	7♒	20♐
14	22♓	0♈	8♒	21♐
15	23♓	29♓	9♒	21♐
16	24♓	28♓	11♒	22♐
17	25♓	28♓	12♒	22♐
18	26♓	27♓	13♒	23♐
19	27♓	26♓	14♒	23♐
20	28♓	25♓	15♒	24♐
21	29♓	24♓	16♒	24♐
22	0♈	23♓	17♒	25♐
23	1♈	22♓	19♒	25♐
24	2♈	22♓	20♒	26♐
25	3♈	21♓	21♒	26♐
26	4♈	20♓	22♒	27♐
27	5♈	20♓	23♒	27♐
28	6♈	19♓	24♒	28♐
29	7♈	19♓	26♒	28♐
30	8♈	19♓	27♒	29♐
31	9♈	19♓	28♒	29♐

April

Day	☉	☿	♀	♂
1	10♈	19♓	29♒	0♑
2	11♈	19♓	0♓	0♑
3	12♈	19♓	1♓	1♑
4	13♈	19♓	3♓	1♑
5	14♈	20♓	4♓	2♑
6	15♈	20♓	5♓	2♑
7	16♈	20♓	6♓	3♑
8	17♈	21♓	7♓	3♑
9	18♈	22♓	8♓	3♑
10	19♈	22♓	10♓	4♑
11	20♈	23♓	11♓	4♑
12	21♈	24♓	12♓	5♑
13	22♈	25♓	13♓	5♑
14	23♈	26♓	14♓	6♑
15	24♈	27♓	15♓	6♑
16	25♈	28♓	17♓	7♑
17	26♈	29♓	18♓	7♑
18	27♈	0♈	19♓	7♑
19	28♈	1♈	20♓	8♑
20	29♈	2♈	21♓	8♑
21	0♉	3♈	23♓	9♑
22	1♉	5♈	24♓	9♑
23	2♉	6♈	25♓	9♑
24	3♉	7♈	26♓	10♑
25	4♉	9♈	27♓	10♑
26	5♉	10♈	28♓	11♑
27	6♉	11♈	0♈	11♑
28	7♉	13♈	1♈	11♑
29	8♉	14♈	2♈	12♑
30	9♉	16♈	3♈	12♑

May

Day	☉	☿	♀	♂
1	10♉	17♈	4♈	12♑
2	11♉	19♈	6♈	13♑
3	12♉	21♈	7♈	13♑
4	13♉	22♈	8♈	13♑
5	14♉	24♈	9♈	14♑
6	15♉	26♈	10♈	14♑
7	15♉	27♈	12♈	14♑
8	16♉	29♈	13♈	15♑
9	17♉	1♉	14♈	15♑
10	18♉	3♉	15♈	15♑
11	19♉	5♉	16♈	15♑
12	20♉	7♉	18♈	16♑
13	21♉	9♉	19♈	16♑
14	22♉	11♉	20♈	16♑
15	23♉	13♉	21♈	16♑
16	24♉	15♉	22♈	17♑
17	25♉	17♉	23♈	17♑
18	26♉	19♉	25♈	17♑
19	27♉	21♉	26♈	17♑
20	28♉	23♉	27♈	17♑
21	29♉	25♉	28♈	18♑
22	0♊	27♉	29♈	18♑
23	1♊	29♉	1♉	18♑
24	2♊	2♊	2♉	18♑
25	3♊	4♊	3♉	18♑
26	4♊	6♊	4♉	18♑
27	5♊	8♊	5♉	18♑
28	6♊	10♊	7♉	18♑
29	7♊	13♊	8♉	19♑
30	8♊	15♊	9♉	19♑
31	9♊	17♊	10♉	19♑

June

Day	☉	☿	♀	♂
1	10♊	19♊	11♉	19♑
2	11♊	21♊	13♉	19♑
3	11♊	23♊	14♉	19♑
4	12♊	25♊	15♉	19♑
5	13♊	27♊	16♉	19♑
6	14♊	29♊	18♉	19♑
7	15♊	1♋	19♉	19♑
8	16♊	3♋	20♉	19♑
9	17♊	5♋	21♉	19♑
10	18♊	6♋	22♉	19♑
11	19♊	8♋	24♉	19♑
12	20♊	10♋	25♉	19♑
13	21♊	12♋	26♉	19♑
14	22♊	13♋	27♉	18♑
15	23♊	15♋	28♉	18♑
16	24♊	16♋	0♊	18♑
17	25♊	18♋	1♊	18♑
18	26♊	19♋	2♊	18♑
19	27♊	20♋	3♊	18♑
20	28♊	22♋	4♊	18♑
21	29♊	23♋	6♊	17♑
22	0♋	24♋	7♊	17♑
23	1♋	26♋	8♊	17♑
24	2♋	27♋	9♊	17♑
25	2♋	28♋	10♊	16♑
26	3♋	29♋	12♊	16♑
27	4♋	0♌	13♊	16♑
28	5♋	1♌	14♊	16♑
29	6♋	2♌	15♊	15♑
30	7♋	3♌	17♊	15♑

July

Day	☉	☿	♀	♂
1	8♋	3♌	18♊	15♑
2	9♋	4♌	19♊	15♑
3	10♋	5♌	20♊	14♑
4	11♋	5♌	21♊	14♑
5	12♋	6♌	23♊	14♑
6	13♋	6♌	24♊	14♑
7	14♋	7♌	25♊	13♑
8	15♋	7♌	26♊	13♑
9	16♋	7♌	27♊	13♑
10	17♋	7♌	29♊	12♑
11	18♋	7♌	0♋	12♑
12	19♋	7♌	1♋	12♑
13	20♋	7♌	2♋	11♑
14	21♋	7♌	4♋	11♑
15	22♋	7♌	5♋	11♑
16	23♋	6♌	6♋	11♑
17	23♋	6♌	7♋	10♑
18	24♋	5♌	8♋	10♑
19	25♋	5♌	10♋	10♑
20	26♋	4♌	11♋	10♑
21	27♋	4♌	12♋	9♑
22	28♋	3♌	13♋	9♑
23	29♋	2♌	15♋	9♑
24	0♌	2♌	16♋	9♑
25	1♌	1♌	17♋	8♑
26	2♌	0♌	18♋	8♑
27	3♌	0♌	19♋	8♑
28	4♌	29♋	21♋	8♑
29	5♌	28♋	22♋	8♑
30	6♌	28♋	23♋	8♑
31	7♌	27♋	24♋	8♑

August

Day	☉	☿	♀	♂
1	8♌	27♋	26♋	7♑
2	9♌	27♋	27♋	7♑
3	10♌	27♋	28♋	7♑
4	11♌	26♋	29♋	7♑
5	12♌	26♋	1♌	7♑
6	13♌	27♋	2♌	7♑
7	14♌	27♋	3♌	7♑
8	14♌	27♋	4♌	7♑
9	15♌	28♋	5♌	7♑
10	16♌	28♋	7♌	7♑
11	17♌	29♋	8♌	7♑
12	18♌	0♌	9♌	7♑
13	19♌	0♌	10♌	7♑
14	20♌	1♌	12♌	7♑
15	21♌	3♌	13♌	7♑
16	22♌	4♌	14♌	7♑
17	23♌	5♌	15♌	7♑
18	24♌	7♌	17♌	8♑
19	25♌	8♌	18♌	8♑
20	26♌	10♌	19♌	8♑
21	27♌	11♌	20♌	8♑
22	28♌	13♌	21♌	8♑
23	29♌	15♌	23♌	8♑
24	0♍	16♌	24♌	9♑
25	1♍	18♌	25♌	9♑
26	2♍	20♌	26♌	9♑
27	3♍	22♌	28♌	9♑
28	4♍	24♌	29♌	9♑
29	5♍	26♌	0♍	10♑
30	6♍	28♌	1♍	10♑
31	7♍	0♍	3♍	10♑

September

Day	☉	☿	♀	♂
1	8♍	2♍	4♍	11♑
2	9♍	4♍	5♍	11♑
3	10♍	6♍	6♍	11♑
4	11♍	8♍	8♍	11♑
5	11♍	10♍	9♍	12♑
6	12♍	12♍	10♍	12♑
7	13♍	13♍	11♍	12♑
8	14♍	15♍	13♍	13♑
9	15♍	17♍	14♍	13♑
10	16♍	19♍	15♍	14♑
11	17♍	21♍	16♍	14♑
12	18♍	23♍	18♍	14♑
13	19♍	25♍	19♍	15♑
14	20♍	26♍	20♍	15♑
15	21♍	28♍	21♍	15♑
16	22♍	0♎	22♍	16♑
17	23♍	2♎	24♍	16♑
18	24♍	3♎	25♍	17♑
19	25♍	5♎	26♍	17♑
20	26♍	7♎	27♍	18♑
21	27♍	8♎	29♍	18♑
22	28♍	10♎	0♎	19♑
23	29♍	12♎	1♎	19♑
24	0♎	13♎	2♎	20♑
25	1♎	15♎	4♎	20♑
26	2♎	16♎	5♎	21♑
27	3♎	18♎	6♎	21♑
28	4♎	20♎	7♎	22♑
29	5♎	21♎	9♎	22♑
30	6♎	23♎	10♎	23♑

October

Day	☉	☿	♀	♂
1	7♎	24♎	11♎	23♑
2	8♎	26♎	12♎	24♑
3	9♎	27♎	14♎	24♑
4	10♎	29♎	15♎	25♑
5	11♎	0♏	16♎	25♑
6	12♎	1♏	17♎	26♑
7	13♎	3♏	19♎	26♑
8	14♎	4♏	20♎	27♑
9	15♎	6♏	21♎	27♑
10	16♎	7♏	22♎	28♑
11	17♎	8♏	24♎	29♑
12	18♎	10♏	25♎	29♑
13	19♎	11♏	26♎	0♒
14	20♎	12♏	27♎	0♒
15	21♎	14♏	29♎	1♒
16	22♎	15♏	0♏	2♒
17	23♎	16♏	1♏	2♒
18	24♎	17♏	2♏	3♒
19	25♎	18♏	4♏	3♒
20	26♎	20♏	5♏	4♒
21	27♎	21♏	6♏	5♒
22	28♎	22♏	7♏	5♒
23	29♎	23♏	9♏	6♒
24	0♏	24♏	10♏	6♒
25	1♏	25♏	11♏	7♒
26	2♏	26♏	12♏	8♒
27	3♏	26♏	14♏	8♒
28	4♏	27♏	15♏	9♒
29	5♏	28♏	16♏	9♒
30	6♏	28♏	17♏	10♒
31	7♏	29♏	19♏	11♒

November

Day	☉	☿	♀	♂
1	8♏	29♏	20♏	11♒
2	9♏	29♏	21♏	12♒
3	10♏	0♐	22♏	13♒
4	11♏	0♐	24♏	13♒
5	12♏	29♏	25♏	14♒
6	13♏	29♏	26♏	15♒
7	14♏	29♏	27♏	15♒
8	15♏	28♏	29♏	16♒
9	16♏	27♏	0♐	17♒
10	17♏	26♏	1♐	17♒
11	18♏	25♏	2♐	18♒
12	19♏	24♏	4♐	19♒
13	20♏	23♏	5♐	19♒
14	21♏	21♏	6♐	20♒
15	22♏	20♏	7♐	21♒
16	23♏	19♏	9♐	21♒
17	24♏	18♏	10♐	22♒
18	25♏	16♏	11♐	23♒
19	26♏	15♏	12♐	23♒
20	27♏	15♏	14♐	24♒
21	28♏	14♏	15♐	25♒
22	29♏	14♏	16♐	25♒
23	0♐	14♏	17♐	26♒
24	1♐	14♏	19♐	27♒
25	2♐	14♏	20♐	27♒
26	3♐	14♏	21♐	28♒
27	4♐	15♏	22♐	29♒
28	5♐	15♏	24♐	29♒
29	6♐	16♏	25♐	0♓
30	7♐	17♏	26♐	1♓

December

Day	☉	☿	♀	♂
1	8♐	18♏	27♐	1♓
2	9♐	19♏	29♐	2♓
3	10♐	20♏	0♑	3♓
4	11♐	21♏	1♑	3♓
5	12♐	22♏	2♑	4♓
6	13♐	23♏	4♑	5♓
7	14♐	25♏	5♑	6♓
8	15♐	26♏	6♑	6♓
9	16♐	27♏	7♑	7♓
10	17♐	29♏	9♑	8♓
11	18♐	0♐	10♑	8♓
12	19♐	1♐	11♑	9♓
13	20♐	3♐	12♑	10♓
14	21♐	4♐	14♑	10♓
15	22♐	6♐	15♑	11♓
16	23♐	7♐	16♑	12♓
17	24♐	9♐	17♑	12♓
18	25♐	10♐	19♑	13♓
19	26♐	12♐	20♑	14♓
20	27♐	13♐	21♑	15♓
21	28♐	15♐	22♑	15♓
22	29♐	16♐	24♑	16♓
23	0♑	18♐	25♑	17♓
24	1♑	19♐	26♑	17♓
25	2♑	21♐	27♑	18♓
26	3♑	22♐	29♑	19♓
27	4♑	24♐	0♒	19♓
28	5♑	25♐	1♒	20♓
29	6♑	27♐	2♒	21♓
30	7♑	29♐	4♒	22♓
31	8♑	0♑	5♒	22♓

Planetary Positions

♌ = Leo ♍ = Virgo ♎ = Libra ♏ = Scorpio ♐ = Sagittarius ♑ = Capricorn ♒ = Aquarius ♓ = Pisces

1908

January

Day	☉	☿	♀	♂
1	9♑	2♑	6♒	23♓
2	10♑	3♑	7♒	24♓
3	11♑	5♑	9♒	24♓
4	12♑	6♑	10♒	25♓
5	13♑	8♑	11♒	26♓
6	14♑	10♑	12♒	26♓
7	16♑	11♑	13♒	27♓
8	17♑	13♑	15♒	28♓
9	18♑	14♑	16♒	29♓
10	19♑	16♑	17♒	29♓
11	20♑	18♑	18♒	0♈
12	21♑	19♑	20♒	1♈
13	22♑	21♑	21♒	1♈
14	23♑	22♑	22♒	2♈
15	24♑	24♑	23♒	3♈
16	25♑	26♑	25♒	4♈
17	26♑	27♑	26♒	4♈
18	27♑	29♑	27♒	5♈
19	28♑	1♒	28♒	6♈
20	29♑	3♒	0♓	6♈
21	0♒	4♒	1♓	7♈
22	1♒	6♒	2♓	8♈
23	2♒	8♒	3♓	8♈
24	3♒	9♒	4♓	9♈
25	4♒	11♒	6♓	10♈
26	5♒	13♒	7♓	11♈
27	6♒	15♒	8♓	11♈
28	7♒	16♒	9♓	12♈
29	8♒	18♒	11♓	13♈
30	9♒	20♒	12♓	13♈
31	10♒	22♒	13♓	14♈

February

Day	☉	☿	♀	♂
1	11♒	23♒	14♓	15♈
2	12♒	25♒	16♓	15♈
3	13♒	27♒	17♓	16♈
4	14♒	28♒	18♓	17♈
5	15♒	0♓	19♓	18♈
6	16♒	2♓	20♓	18♈
7	17♒	3♓	22♓	19♈
8	18♒	5♓	23♓	20♈
9	19♒	6♓	24♓	20♈
10	20♒	8♓	25♓	21♈
11	21♒	9♓	26♓	22♈
12	22♒	10♓	28♓	22♈
13	23♒	11♓	29♓	23♈
14	24♒	12♓	0♈	24♈
15	25♒	13♓	1♈	25♈
16	26♒	14♓	3♈	25♈
17	27♒	14♓	4♈	26♈
18	28♒	15♓	5♈	27♈
19	29♒	15♓	6♈	27♈
20	0♓	15♓	7♈	28♈
21	1♓	15♓	9♈	29♈
22	2♓	15♓	10♈	29♈
23	3♓	14♓	11♈	0♉
24	4♓	14♓	12♈	1♉
25	5♓	13♓	13♈	1♉
26	6♓	12♓	15♈	2♉
27	7♓	11♓	16♈	3♉
28	8♓	10♓	17♈	3♉
29	9♓	9♓	18♈	4♉

March

Day	☉	☿	♀	♂
1	10♓	8♓	19♈	5♉
2	11♓	7♓	20♈	6♉
3	12♓	6♓	22♈	6♉
4	13♓	5♓	23♈	7♉
5	14♓	4♓	24♈	8♉
6	15♓	3♓	25♈	8♉
7	16♓	3♓	26♈	9♉
8	17♓	2♓	28♈	10♉
9	18♓	2♓	29♈	10♉
10	19♓	1♓	0♉	11♉
11	20♓	1♓	1♉	12♉
12	21♓	1♓	2♉	12♉
13	22♓	1♓	3♉	13♉
14	23♓	1♓	4♉	14♉
15	24♓	1♓	6♉	14♉
16	25♓	1♓	7♉	15♉
17	26♓	1♓	8♉	16♉
18	27♓	2♓	9♉	17♉
19	28♓	2♓	10♉	17♉
20	29♓	3♓	11♉	18♉
21	0♈	3♓	13♉	19♉
22	1♈	4♓	14♉	19♉
23	2♈	5♓	15♉	20♉
24	3♈	6♓	16♉	21♉
25	4♈	6♓	17♉	21♉
26	5♈	7♓	18♉	22♉
27	6♈	8♓	19♉	23♉
28	7♈	9♓	20♉	23♉
29	8♈	10♓	22♉	24♉
30	9♈	12♓	23♉	25♉
31	10♈	13♓	24♉	25♉

April

Day	☉	☿	♀	♂
1	11♈	14♓	25♉	26♉
2	12♈	15♓	26♉	27♉
3	13♈	16♓	27♉	27♉
4	14♈	18♓	28♉	28♉
5	15♈	19♓	29♉	29♉
6	16♈	20♓	0♊	29♉
7	17♈	22♓	1♊	0♊
8	18♈	23♓	3♊	1♊
9	19♈	24♓	4♊	1♊
10	20♈	26♓	5♊	2♊
11	21♈	27♓	6♊	3♊
12	22♈	29♓	7♊	3♊
13	23♈	0♈	8♊	4♊
14	24♈	2♈	9♊	5♊
15	25♈	4♈	10♊	5♊
16	26♈	5♈	11♊	6♊
17	27♈	7♈	12♊	7♊
18	28♈	9♈	13♊	7♊
19	29♈	10♈	14♊	8♊
20	0♉	12♈	15♊	9♊
21	1♉	14♈	16♊	9♊
22	2♉	16♈	17♊	10♊
23	3♉	17♈	18♊	11♊
24	4♉	19♈	19♊	11♊
25	5♉	21♈	20♊	12♊
26	6♉	23♈	21♊	13♊
27	7♉	25♈	22♊	13♊
28	7♉	27♈	23♊	14♊
29	8♉	29♈	24♊	15♊
30	9♉	1♉	25♊	15♊

May

Day	☉	☿	♀	♂
1	10♉	3♉	26♊	16♊
2	11♉	5♉	27♊	17♊
3	12♉	7♉	28♊	17♊
4	13♉	9♉	29♊	18♊
5	14♉	11♉	0♋	19♊
6	15♉	13♉	0♋	19♊
7	16♉	16♉	1♋	20♊
8	17♉	18♉	2♋	21♊
9	18♉	20♉	3♋	21♊
10	19♉	22♉	4♋	22♊
11	20♉	24♉	5♋	23♊
12	21♉	26♉	6♋	23♊
13	22♉	29♉	6♋	24♊
14	23♉	1♊	7♋	25♊
15	24♉	3♊	8♋	25♊
16	25♉	5♊	9♋	26♊
17	26♉	7♊	9♋	26♊
18	27♉	9♊	10♋	27♊
19	28♉	11♊	11♋	28♊
20	29♉	13♊	12♋	28♊
21	0♊	15♊	12♋	29♊
22	1♊	17♊	13♋	0♋
23	2♊	19♊	14♋	0♋
24	3♊	20♊	14♋	1♋
25	4♊	22♊	15♋	2♋
26	5♊	24♊	16♋	2♋
27	5♊	25♊	16♋	3♋
28	6♊	27♊	17♋	4♋
29	7♊	29♊	17♋	4♋
30	8♊	0♋	18♋	5♋
31	9♊	1♋	18♋	6♋

June

Day	☉	☿	♀	♂
1	10♊	3♋	19♋	6♋
2	11♊	4♋	19♋	7♋
3	12♊	5♋	20♋	8♋
4	13♊	7♋	20♋	8♋
5	14♊	8♋	20♋	9♋
6	15♊	9♋	21♋	9♋
7	16♊	10♋	21♋	10♋
8	17♊	11♋	21♋	11♋
9	18♊	12♋	21♋	11♋
10	19♊	13♋	21♋	12♋
11	20♊	14♋	22♋	13♋
12	21♊	14♋	22♋	13♋
13	22♊	15♋	22♋	14♋
14	23♊	16♋	22♋	15♋
15	24♊	16♋	22♋	15♋
16	25♊	16♋	22♋	16♋
17	26♊	17♋	22♋	17♋
18	27♊	17♋	22♋	17♋
19	27♊	17♋	21♋	18♋
20	28♊	18♋	21♋	18♋
21	29♊	18♋	21♋	19♋
22	0♋	18♋	21♋	20♋
23	1♋	18♋	20♋	20♋
24	2♋	17♋	20♋	21♋
25	3♋	17♋	20♋	22♋
26	4♋	17♋	19♋	22♋
27	5♋	17♋	19♋	23♋
28	6♋	16♋	18♋	24♋
29	7♋	16♋	18♋	24♋
30	8♋	15♋	17♋	25♋

July

Day	☉	☿	♀	♂
1	9♋	15♋	17♋	26♋
2	10♋	14♋	16♋	26♋
3	11♋	14♋	15♋	27♋
4	12♋	13♋	15♋	27♋
5	13♋	12♋	14♋	28♋
6	14♋	12♋	14♋	29♋
7	15♋	11♋	13♋	29♋
8	16♋	11♋	12♋	0♌
9	17♋	10♋	12♋	1♌
10	18♋	10♋	11♋	1♌
11	18♋	9♋	11♋	2♌
12	19♋	9♋	10♋	3♌
13	20♋	9♋	9♋	3♌
14	21♋	8♋	9♋	4♌
15	22♋	8♋	8♋	4♌
16	23♋	8♋	8♋	5♌
17	24♋	8♋	8♋	6♌
18	25♋	8♋	7♋	6♌
19	26♋	9♋	7♋	7♌
20	27♋	9♋	6♋	8♌
21	28♋	9♋	6♋	8♌
22	29♋	10♋	6♋	9♌
23	0♌	11♋	6♋	10♌
24	1♌	11♋	6♋	10♌
25	2♌	12♋	5♋	11♌
26	3♌	13♋	5♋	12♌
27	4♌	14♋	5♋	12♌
28	5♌	15♋	5♋	13♌
29	6♌	16♋	5♋	13♌
30	7♌	18♋	5♋	14♌
31	8♌	19♋	6♋	15♌

August

Day	☉	☿	♀	♂
1	9♌	20♋	6♋	15♌
2	9♌	22♋	6♋	16♌
3	10♌	23♋	6♋	17♌
4	11♌	25♋	6♋	17♌
5	12♌	27♋	7♋	18♌
6	13♌	29♋	7♋	19♌
7	14♌	0♌	7♋	19♌
8	15♌	2♌	8♋	20♌
9	16♌	4♌	8♋	20♌
10	17♌	6♌	8♋	21♌
11	18♌	8♌	9♋	22♌
12	19♌	10♌	9♋	22♌
13	20♌	12♌	10♋	23♌
14	21♌	14♌	10♋	24♌
15	22♌	16♌	11♋	24♌
16	23♌	18♌	12♋	25♌
17	24♌	20♌	12♋	26♌
18	25♌	22♌	13♋	26♌
19	26♌	24♌	13♋	27♌
20	27♌	26♌	14♋	27♌
21	28♌	28♌	15♋	28♌
22	29♌	0♍	15♋	29♌
23	0♍	2♍	16♋	29♌
24	1♍	4♍	17♋	0♍
25	2♍	6♍	18♋	1♍
26	3♍	8♍	18♋	1♍
27	4♍	10♍	19♋	2♍
28	4♍	12♍	20♋	2♍
29	5♍	14♍	21♋	3♍
30	6♍	15♍	22♋	4♍
31	7♍	17♍	22♋	4♍

September

Day	☉	☿	♀	♂
1	8♍	19♍	23♋	5♍
2	9♍	21♍	24♋	6♍
3	10♍	22♍	25♋	6♍
4	11♍	24♍	26♋	7♍
5	12♍	26♍	27♋	8♍
6	13♍	27♍	28♋	8♍
7	14♍	29♍	28♋	9♍
8	15♍	1♎	29♋	10♍
9	16♍	2♎	0♌	10♍
10	17♍	4♎	1♌	11♍
11	18♍	5♎	2♌	11♍
12	19♍	7♎	3♌	12♍
13	20♍	9♎	4♌	13♍
14	21♍	10♎	5♌	13♍
15	22♍	12♎	6♌	14♍
16	23♍	13♎	7♌	15♍
17	24♍	15♎	8♌	15♍
18	25♍	16♎	9♌	16♍
19	26♍	17♎	10♌	17♍
20	27♍	19♎	11♌	17♍
21	28♍	20♎	12♌	18♍
22	29♍	22♎	13♌	18♍
23	0♎	23♎	14♌	19♍
24	1♎	24♎	15♌	20♍
25	2♎	26♎	16♌	20♍
26	3♎	27♎	17♌	21♍
27	4♎	28♎	18♌	22♍
28	5♎	29♎	19♌	22♍
29	6♎	0♏	20♌	23♍
30	7♎	2♏	21♌	24♍

October

Day	☉	☿	♀	♂
1	8♎	3♏	22♌	24♍
2	9♎	4♏	23♌	25♍
3	10♎	5♏	24♌	25♍
4	11♎	6♏	26♌	26♍
5	12♎	7♏	27♌	27♍
6	13♎	8♏	28♌	27♍
7	14♎	9♏	29♌	28♍
8	15♎	10♏	0♍	29♍
9	16♎	10♏	1♍	29♍
10	16♎	11♏	2♍	0♎
11	17♎	12♏	3♍	1♎
12	18♎	12♏	4♍	1♎
13	19♎	13♏	5♍	2♎
14	20♎	13♏	7♍	3♎
15	21♎	13♏	8♍	3♎
16	22♎	14♏	9♍	4♎
17	23♎	14♏	10♍	4♎
18	24♎	14♏	11♍	5♎
19	25♎	13♏	12♍	6♎
20	26♎	13♏	13♍	6♎
21	27♎	13♏	15♍	7♎
22	28♎	12♏	16♍	8♎
23	29♎	11♏	17♍	8♎
24	0♏	10♏	18♍	9♎
25	1♏	9♏	19♍	10♎
26	2♏	8♏	20♍	10♎
27	3♏	7♏	21♍	11♎
28	4♏	5♏	23♍	12♎
29	5♏	4♏	24♍	12♎
30	6♏	3♏	25♍	13♎
31	7♏	2♏	26♍	14♎

November

Day	☉	☿	♀	♂
1	8♏	1♏	27♍	14♎
2	9♏	0♏	29♍	15♎
3	10♏	29♎	0♎	15♎
4	11♏	28♎	1♎	16♎
5	12♏	28♎	2♎	17♎
6	13♏	28♎	3♎	17♎
7	14♏	28♎	4♎	18♎
8	15♏	28♎	6♎	19♎
9	16♏	28♎	7♎	19♎
10	17♏	29♎	8♎	20♎
11	18♏	0♏	9♎	21♎
12	19♏	0♏	10♎	21♎
13	20♏	1♏	12♎	22♎
14	21♏	2♏	13♎	23♎
15	22♏	3♏	14♎	23♎
16	23♏	5♏	15♎	24♎
17	24♏	6♏	16♎	25♎
18	25♏	7♏	18♎	25♎
19	26♏	8♏	19♎	26♎
20	27♏	10♏	20♎	26♎
21	29♏	11♏	21♎	27♎
22	0♐	13♏	22♎	28♎
23	1♐	14♏	24♎	28♎
24	2♐	15♏	25♎	29♎
25	3♐	17♏	26♎	0♏
26	4♐	18♏	27♎	0♏
27	5♐	20♏	28♎	1♏
28	6♐	21♏	0♏	2♏
29	7♐	23♏	1♏	2♏
30	8♐	25♏	2♏	3♏

December

Day	☉	☿	♀	♂
1	9♐	26♏	3♏	4♏
2	10♐	28♏	5♏	4♏
3	11♐	29♏	6♏	5♏
4	12♐	1♐	7♏	6♏
5	13♐	2♐	8♏	6♏
6	14♐	4♐	9♏	7♏
7	15♐	5♐	11♏	8♏
8	16♐	7♐	12♏	8♏
9	17♐	8♐	13♏	9♏
10	18♐	10♐	14♏	10♏
11	19♐	12♐	16♏	10♏
12	20♐	13♐	17♏	11♏
13	21♐	15♐	18♏	12♏
14	22♐	16♐	19♏	12♏
15	23♐	18♐	21♏	13♏
16	24♐	19♐	22♏	14♏
17	25♐	21♐	23♏	14♏
18	26♐	23♐	24♏	15♏
19	27♐	24♐	26♏	15♏
20	28♐	26♐	27♏	16♏
21	29♐	27♐	28♏	17♏
22	0♑	29♐	29♏	17♏
23	1♑	0♑	0♐	18♏
24	2♑	2♑	2♐	19♏
25	3♑	4♑	3♐	19♏
26	4♑	5♑	4♐	20♏
27	5♑	7♑	5♐	21♏
28	6♑	8♑	7♐	21♏
29	7♑	10♑	8♐	22♏
30	8♑	12♑	9♐	23♏
31	9♑	13♑	10♐	23♏

☉ =Sun ☿ = Mercury ♀ = Venus ♂ = Mars ♈ = Aries ♉ = Taurus ♊ = Gemini ♋ = Cancer

1909

January

Day	☉	☿	♀	♂
1	10♑	15♑	12♐	24♏
2	11♑	17♑	13♐	25♏
3	12♑	18♑	14♐	25♏
4	13♑	20♑	15♐	26♏
5	14♑	21♑	17♐	27♏
6	15♑	23♑	18♐	27♏
7	16♑	25♑	19♐	28♏
8	17♑	26♑	20♐	29♏
9	18♑	28♑	22♐	29♏
10	19♑	0♒	23♐	0♐
11	20♑	1♒	24♐	1♐
12	21♑	3♒	25♐	1♐
13	22♑	5♒	27♐	2♐
14	23♑	6♒	28♐	3♐
15	24♑	8♒	29♐	3♐
16	25♑	10♒	0♑	4♐
17	26♑	11♒	2♑	5♐
18	27♑	13♒	3♑	5♐
19	29♑	14♒	4♑	6♐
20	0♒	16♒	5♑	7♐
21	1♒	17♒	7♑	7♐
22	2♒	19♒	8♑	8♐
23	3♒	20♒	9♑	9♐
24	4♒	22♒	10♑	9♐
25	5♒	23♒	12♑	10♐
26	6♒	24♒	13♑	11♐
27	7♒	25♒	14♑	11♐
28	8♒	26♒	15♑	12♐
29	9♒	27♒	17♑	13♐
30	10♒	28♒	18♑	13♐
31	11♒	28♒	19♑	14♐

February

Day	☉	☿	♀	♂
1	12♒	28♒	20♑	15♐
2	13♒	29♒	21♑	15♐
3	14♒	29♒	23♑	16♐
4	15♒	28♒	24♑	17♐
5	16♒	28♒	25♑	17♐
6	17♒	27♒	26♑	18♐
7	18♒	27♒	28♑	19♐
8	19♒	26♒	29♑	19♐
9	20♒	25♒	0♒	20♐
10	21♒	24♒	1♒	21♐
11	22♒	23♒	3♒	21♐
12	23♒	22♒	4♒	22♐
13	24♒	20♒	5♒	23♐
14	25♒	19♒	6♒	23♐
15	26♒	18♒	8♒	24♐
16	27♒	17♒	9♒	25♐
17	28♒	16♒	10♒	25♐
18	29♒	15♒	11♒	26♐
19	0♓	15♒	13♒	27♐
20	1♓	14♒	14♒	27♐
21	2♓	14♒	15♒	28♐
22	3♓	14♒	16♒	29♐
23	4♓	13♒	18♒	29♐
24	5♓	13♒	19♒	0♑
25	6♓	13♒	20♒	1♑
26	7♓	14♒	21♒	1♑
27	8♓	14♒	23♒	2♑
28	9♓	14♒	24♒	3♑

March

Day	☉	☿	♀	♂
1	10♓	15♒	25♒	3♑
2	11♓	15♒	26♒	4♑
3	12♓	16♒	28♒	5♑
4	13♓	16♒	29♒	5♑
5	14♓	17♒	0♓	6♑
6	15♓	18♒	1♓	7♑
7	16♓	19♒	3♓	7♑
8	17♓	20♒	4♓	8♑
9	18♓	21♒	5♓	9♑
10	19♓	22♒	6♓	9♑
11	20♓	23♒	8♓	10♑
12	21♓	24♒	9♓	11♑
13	22♓	25♒	10♓	11♑
14	23♓	26♒	11♓	12♑
15	24♓	27♒	13♓	13♑
16	25♓	28♒	14♓	13♑
17	26♓	0♓	15♓	14♑
18	27♓	1♓	16♓	15♑
19	28♓	2♓	18♓	16♑
20	29♓	4♓	19♓	16♑
21	0♈	5♓	20♓	17♑
22	1♈	6♓	21♓	18♑
23	2♈	8♓	23♓	18♑
24	3♈	9♓	24♓	19♑
25	4♈	11♓	25♓	20♑
26	5♈	12♓	26♓	20♑
27	6♈	14♓	28♓	21♑
28	7♈	15♓	29♓	22♑
29	8♈	17♓	0♈	22♑
30	9♈	18♓	1♈	23♑
31	10♈	20♓	2♈	24♑

April

Day	☉	☿	♀	♂
1	11♈	22♓	4♈	24♑
2	12♈	23♓	5♈	25♑
3	13♈	25♓	6♈	26♑
4	14♈	27♓	7♈	26♑
5	15♈	29♓	9♈	27♑
6	16♈	0♈	10♈	28♑
7	17♈	2♈	11♈	28♑
8	18♈	4♈	12♈	29♑
9	19♈	6♈	14♈	0♒
10	20♈	8♈	15♈	0♒
11	21♈	9♈	16♈	1♒
12	22♈	11♈	17♈	2♒
13	23♈	13♈	19♈	2♒
14	24♈	15♈	20♈	3♒
15	25♈	17♈	21♈	4♒
16	26♈	19♈	22♈	4♒
17	27♈	21♈	24♈	5♒
18	28♈	23♈	25♈	6♒
19	28♈	25♈	26♈	6♒
20	29♈	27♈	27♈	7♒
21	0♉	0♉	28♈	8♒
22	1♉	2♉	0♉	8♒
23	2♉	4♉	1♉	9♒
24	3♉	6♉	2♉	10♒
25	4♉	8♉	3♉	10♒
26	5♉	10♉	5♉	11♒
27	6♉	12♉	6♉	12♒
28	7♉	14♉	7♉	12♒
29	8♉	17♉	8♉	13♒
30	9♉	19♉	10♉	13♒

May

Day	☉	☿	♀	♂
1	10♉	21♉	11♉	14♒
2	11♉	23♉	12♉	15♒
3	12♉	25♉	13♉	15♒
4	13♉	27♉	15♉	16♒
5	14♉	29♉	16♉	17♒
6	15♉	1♊	17♉	17♒
7	16♉	2♊	18♉	18♒
8	17♉	4♊	19♉	19♒
9	18♉	6♊	21♉	19♒
10	19♉	8♊	22♉	20♒
11	20♉	9♊	23♉	21♒
12	21♉	11♊	24♉	21♒
13	22♉	12♊	26♉	22♒
14	23♉	14♊	27♉	23♒
15	24♉	15♊	28♉	23♒
16	25♉	16♊	29♉	24♒
17	26♉	17♊	1♊	24♒
18	27♉	19♊	2♊	25♒
19	28♉	20♊	3♊	26♒
20	29♉	21♊	4♊	26♒
21	29♉	22♊	5♊	27♒
22	0♊	23♊	7♊	28♒
23	1♊	23♊	8♊	28♒
24	2♊	24♊	9♊	29♒
25	3♊	25♊	10♊	0♓
26	4♊	26♊	12♊	0♓
27	5♊	26♊	13♊	1♓
28	6♊	27♊	14♊	1♓
29	7♊	27♊	15♊	2♓
30	8♊	27♊	17♊	3♓
31	9♊	27♊	18♊	3♓

June

Day	☉	☿	♀	♂
1	10♊	28♊	19♊	4♓
2	11♊	28♊	20♊	4♓
3	12♊	28♊	21♊	5♓
4	13♊	28♊	23♊	6♓
5	14♊	27♊	24♊	6♓
6	15♊	27♊	25♊	7♓
7	16♊	27♊	26♊	7♓
8	17♊	27♊	28♊	8♓
9	18♊	26♊	29♊	9♓
10	19♊	26♊	0♋	9♓
11	20♊	25♊	1♋	10♓
12	21♊	25♊	2♋	10♓
13	22♊	24♊	4♋	11♓
14	22♊	24♊	5♋	12♓
15	23♊	23♊	6♋	12♓
16	24♊	23♊	7♋	13♓
17	25♊	22♊	9♋	13♓
18	26♊	21♊	10♋	14♓
19	27♊	21♊	11♋	14♓
20	28♊	20♊	12♋	15♓
21	29♊	20♊	14♋	16♓
22	0♋	20♊	15♋	16♓
23	1♋	19♊	16♋	17♓
24	2♋	19♊	17♋	17♓
25	3♋	19♊	18♋	18♓
26	4♋	19♊	20♋	18♓
27	5♋	19♊	21♋	19♓
28	6♋	19♊	22♋	19♓
29	7♋	19♊	23♋	20♓
30	8♋	20♊	25♋	20♓

July

Day	☉	☿	♀	♂
1	9♋	20♊	26♋	21♓
2	10♋	20♊	27♋	21♓
3	11♋	21♊	28♋	22♓
4	12♋	21♊	29♋	22♓
5	13♋	22♊	1♌	23♓
6	13♋	23♊	2♌	23♓
7	14♋	23♊	3♌	24♓
8	15♋	24♊	4♌	24♓
9	16♋	25♊	6♌	25♓
10	17♋	26♊	7♌	25♓
11	18♋	27♊	8♌	26♓
12	19♋	29♊	9♌	26♓
13	20♋	0♋	10♌	27♓
14	21♋	1♋	12♌	27♓
15	22♋	3♋	13♌	28♓
16	23♋	4♋	14♌	28♓
17	24♋	6♋	15♌	28♓
18	25♋	7♋	17♌	29♓
19	26♋	9♋	18♌	29♓
20	27♋	11♋	19♌	0♈
21	28♋	12♋	20♌	0♈
22	29♋	14♋	21♌	0♈
23	0♌	16♋	23♌	1♈
24	1♌	18♋	24♌	1♈
25	2♌	20♋	25♌	1♈
26	3♌	22♋	26♌	2♈
27	4♌	24♋	27♌	2♈
28	4♌	26♋	29♌	2♈
29	5♌	28♋	0♍	3♈
30	6♌	0♌	1♍	3♈
31	7♌	2♌	2♍	3♈

August

Day	☉	☿	♀	♂
1	8♌	5♌	4♍	4♈
2	9♌	7♌	5♍	4♈
3	10♌	9♌	6♍	4♈
4	11♌	11♌	7♍	4♈
5	12♌	13♌	8♍	5♈
6	13♌	15♌	10♍	5♈
7	14♌	17♌	11♍	5♈
8	15♌	19♌	12♍	5♈
9	16♌	21♌	13♍	5♈
10	17♌	23♌	14♍	6♈
11	18♌	25♌	16♍	6♈
12	19♌	27♌	17♍	6♈
13	20♌	29♌	18♍	6♈
14	21♌	1♍	19♍	6♈
15	22♌	2♍	21♍	6♈
16	23♌	4♍	22♍	6♈
17	24♌	6♍	23♍	7♈
18	25♌	8♍	24♍	7♈
19	26♌	10♍	25♍	7♈
20	27♌	11♍	27♍	7♈
21	27♌	13♍	28♍	7♈
22	28♌	15♍	29♍	7♈
23	29♌	16♍	0♎	7♈
24	0♍	18♍	1♎	7♈
25	1♍	20♍	3♎	7♈
26	2♍	21♍	4♎	7♈
27	3♍	23♍	5♎	7♈
28	4♍	24♍	6♎	7♈
29	5♍	26♍	7♎	7♈
30	6♍	27♍	9♎	6♈
31	7♍	29♍	10♎	6♈

September

Day	☉	☿	♀	♂
1	8♍	0♎	11♎	6♈
2	9♍	2♎	12♎	6♈
3	10♍	3♎	13♎	6♈
4	11♍	5♎	15♎	6♈
5	12♍	6♎	16♎	6♈
6	13♍	7♎	17♎	5♈
7	14♍	9♎	18♎	5♈
8	15♍	10♎	19♎	5♈
9	16♍	11♎	21♎	5♈
10	17♍	12♎	22♎	5♈
11	18♍	14♎	23♎	4♈
12	19♍	15♎	24♎	4♈
13	20♍	16♎	25♎	4♈
14	21♍	17♎	27♎	4♈
15	22♍	18♎	28♎	3♈
16	23♍	19♎	29♎	3♈
17	24♍	20♎	0♏	3♈
18	25♍	21♎	1♏	3♈
19	26♍	22♎	3♏	2♈
20	27♍	23♎	4♏	2♈
21	28♍	24♎	5♏	2♈
22	29♍	24♎	6♏	1♈
23	0♎	25♎	7♏	1♈
24	1♎	26♎	9♏	1♈
25	1♎	26♎	10♏	0♈
26	2♎	27♎	11♏	0♈
27	3♎	27♎	12♏	0♈
28	4♎	27♎	13♏	0♈
29	5♎	27♎	14♏	29♓
30	6♎	28♎	16♏	29♓

October

Day	☉	☿	♀	♂
1	7♎	28♎	17♏	29♓
2	8♎	27♎	18♏	29♓
3	9♎	27♎	19♏	28♓
4	10♎	27♎	20♏	28♓
5	11♎	26♎	22♏	28♓
6	12♎	25♎	23♏	28♓
7	13♎	25♎	24♏	27♓
8	14♎	24♎	25♏	27♓
9	15♎	23♎	26♏	27♓
10	16♎	22♎	27♏	27♓
11	17♎	20♎	29♏	27♓
12	18♎	19♎	0♐	26♓
13	19♎	18♎	1♐	26♓
14	20♎	17♎	2♐	26♓
15	21♎	16♎	3♐	26♓
16	22♎	15♎	4♐	26♓
17	23♎	14♎	6♐	26♓
18	24♎	13♎	7♐	26♓
19	25♎	13♎	8♐	26♓
20	26♎	12♎	9♐	26♓
21	27♎	12♎	10♐	26♓
22	28♎	12♎	11♐	25♓
23	29♎	12♎	13♐	25♓
24	0♏	13♎	14♐	25♓
25	1♏	13♎	15♐	25♓
26	2♏	14♎	16♐	25♓
27	3♏	15♎	17♐	26♓
28	4♏	16♎	18♐	26♓
29	5♏	17♎	19♐	26♓
30	6♏	18♎	21♐	26♓
31	7♏	19♎	22♐	26♓

November

Day	☉	☿	♀	♂
1	8♏	20♎	23♐	26♓
2	9♏	22♎	24♐	26♓
3	10♏	23♎	25♐	26♓
4	11♏	25♎	26♐	26♓
5	12♏	26♎	27♐	26♓
6	13♏	28♎	29♐	27♓
7	14♏	29♎	0♑	27♓
8	15♏	1♏	1♑	27♓
9	16♏	2♏	2♑	27♓
10	17♏	4♏	3♑	27♓
11	18♏	5♏	4♑	27♓
12	19♏	7♏	5♑	28♓
13	20♏	9♏	6♑	28♓
14	21♏	10♏	7♑	28♓
15	22♏	12♏	9♑	28♓
16	23♏	13♏	10♑	29♓
17	24♏	15♏	11♑	29♓
18	25♏	17♏	12♑	29♓
19	26♏	18♏	13♑	0♈
20	27♏	20♏	14♑	0♈
21	28♏	21♏	15♑	0♈
22	29♏	23♏	16♑	0♈
23	0♐	25♏	17♑	1♈
24	1♐	26♏	18♑	1♈
25	2♐	28♏	19♑	1♈
26	3♐	29♏	20♑	2♈
27	4♐	1♐	21♑	2♈
28	5♐	2♐	23♑	2♈
29	6♐	4♐	24♑	3♈
30	7♐	6♐	25♑	3♈

December

Day	☉	☿	♀	♂
1	8♐	7♐	26♑	4♈
2	9♐	9♐	27♑	4♈
3	10♐	10♐	28♑	4♈
4	11♐	12♐	29♑	5♈
5	12♐	14♐	0♒	5♈
6	13♐	15♐	1♒	6♈
7	14♐	17♐	2♒	6♈
8	15♐	18♐	3♒	6♈
9	16♐	20♐	4♒	7♈
10	18♐	21♐	5♒	7♈
11	19♐	23♐	6♒	8♈
12	20♐	25♐	6♒	8♈
13	21♐	26♐	7♒	9♈
14	22♐	28♐	8♒	9♈
15	23♐	29♐	9♒	10♈
16	24♐	1♑	10♒	10♈
17	25♐	2♑	11♒	10♈
18	26♐	4♑	12♒	11♈
19	27♐	6♑	13♒	11♈
20	28♐	7♑	14♒	12♈
21	29♐	9♑	15♒	12♈
22	0♑	10♑	15♒	13♈
23	1♑	12♑	16♒	13♈
24	2♑	14♑	17♒	14♈
25	3♑	15♑	18♒	14♈
26	4♑	17♑	19♒	15♈
27	5♑	18♑	19♒	15♈
28	6♑	20♑	20♒	16♈
29	7♑	21♑	21♒	16♈
30	8♑	23♑	22♒	17♈
31	9♑	24♑	22♒	17♈

Planetary Positions

♌ = Leo ♍ = Virgo ♎ = Libra ♏ = Scorpio ♐ = Sagittarius ♑ = Capricorn ♒ = Aquarius ♓ = Pisces

1910

January

Day	☉	☿	♀	♂
1	10♑	26♑	23♒	18♈
2	11♑	28♑	24♒	18♈
3	12♑	29♑	24♒	19♈
4	13♑	0♒	25♒	20♈
5	14♑	2♒	25♒	20♈
6	15♑	3♒	26♒	21♈
7	16♑	5♒	27♒	21♈
8	17♑	6♒	27♒	22♈
9	18♑	7♒	28♒	22♈
10	19♑	8♒	28♒	23♈
11	20♑	9♒	28♒	23♈
12	21♑	10♒	29♒	24♈
13	22♑	11♒	29♒	24♈
14	23♑	11♒	0♓	25♈
15	24♑	12♒	0♓	26♈
16	25♑	12♒	0♓	26♈
17	26♑	12♒	0♓	27♈
18	27♑	12♒	1♓	27♈
19	28♑	12♒	1♓	28♈
20	29♑	12♒	1♓	28♈
21	0♒	11♒	1♓	29♈
22	1♒	10♒	1♓	0♉
23	2♒	9♒	1♓	0♉
24	3♒	8♒	1♓	1♉
25	4♒	7♒	1♓	1♉
26	5♒	6♒	1♓	2♉
27	6♒	5♒	1♓	2♉
28	7♒	3♒	0♓	3♉
29	8♒	2♒	0♓	4♉
30	9♒	1♒	0♓	4♉
31	10♒	0♒	29♒	5♉

February

Day	☉	☿	♀	♂
1	11♒	29♑	29♒	5♉
2	12♒	28♑	29♒	6♉
3	14♒	28♑	28♒	6♉
4	15♒	27♑	28♒	7♉
5	16♒	27♑	27♒	8♉
6	17♒	27♑	27♒	8♉
7	18♒	27♑	26♒	9♉
8	19♒	27♑	26♒	9♉
9	20♒	27♑	25♒	10♉
10	21♒	27♑	24♒	11♉
11	22♒	27♑	24♒	11♉
12	23♒	28♑	23♒	12♉
13	24♒	28♑	22♒	12♉
14	25♒	29♑	22♒	13♉
15	26♒	0♒	21♒	14♉
16	27♒	1♒	21♒	14♉
17	28♒	1♒	20♒	15♉
18	29♒	2♒	20♒	15♉
19	0♓	3♒	19♒	16♉
20	1♓	4♒	18♒	17♉
21	2♓	5♒	18♒	17♉
22	3♓	6♒	18♒	18♉
23	4♓	7♒	17♒	18♉
24	5♓	9♒	17♒	19♉
25	6♓	10♒	16♒	20♉
26	7♓	11♒	16♒	20♉
27	8♓	12♒	16♒	21♉
28	9♓	13♒	16♒	21♉

March

Day	☉	☿	♀	♂
1	10♓	15♒	15♒	22♉
2	11♓	16♒	15♒	23♉
3	12♓	17♒	15♒	23♉
4	13♓	19♒	15♒	24♉
5	14♓	20♒	15♒	24♉
6	15♓	22♒	15♒	25♉
7	16♓	23♒	15♒	26♉
8	17♓	24♒	15♒	26♉
9	18♓	26♒	15♒	27♉
10	19♓	27♒	16♒	27♉
11	20♓	29♒	16♒	28♉
12	21♓	0♓	16♒	29♉
13	22♓	2♓	16♒	29♉
14	23♓	4♓	17♒	0♊
15	24♓	5♓	17♒	1♊
16	25♓	7♓	17♒	1♊
17	26♓	8♓	18♒	2♊
18	27♓	10♓	18♒	2♊
19	28♓	12♓	19♒	3♊
20	29♓	14♓	19♒	4♊
21	0♈	15♓	20♒	4♊
22	1♈	17♓	20♒	5♊
23	2♈	19♓	21♒	5♊
24	3♈	21♓	21♒	6♊
25	4♈	22♓	22♒	7♊
26	5♈	24♓	23♒	7♊
27	6♈	26♓	23♒	8♊
28	7♈	28♓	24♒	9♊
29	8♈	0♈	25♒	9♊
30	9♈	2♈	25♒	10♊
31	10♈	4♈	26♒	10♊

April

Day	☉	☿	♀	♂
1	11♈	6♈	27♒	11♊
2	12♈	8♈	28♒	12♊
3	13♈	10♈	28♒	12♊
4	14♈	12♈	29♒	13♊
5	15♈	14♈	0♓	13♊
6	16♈	16♈	1♓	14♊
7	17♈	18♈	1♓	15♊
8	17♈	20♈	2♓	15♊
9	18♈	22♈	3♓	16♊
10	19♈	24♈	4♓	17♊
11	20♈	26♈	5♓	17♊
12	21♈	28♈	6♓	18♊
13	22♈	0♉	7♓	18♊
14	23♈	2♉	8♓	19♊
15	24♈	5♉	8♓	20♊
16	25♈	7♉	9♓	20♊
17	26♈	9♉	10♓	21♊
18	27♈	10♉	11♓	22♊
19	28♈	12♉	12♓	22♊
20	29♈	14♉	13♓	23♊
21	0♉	16♉	14♓	23♊
22	1♉	18♉	15♓	24♊
23	2♉	20♉	16♓	25♊
24	3♉	21♉	17♓	25♊
25	4♉	23♉	18♓	26♊
26	5♉	24♉	19♓	26♊
27	6♉	26♉	20♓	27♊
28	7♉	27♉	21♓	28♊
29	8♉	28♉	22♓	28♊
30	9♉	29♉	23♓	29♊

May

Day	☉	☿	♀	♂
1	10♉	1♊	24♓	0♋
2	11♉	2♊	25♓	0♋
3	12♉	3♊	26♓	1♋
4	13♉	4♊	27♓	1♋
5	14♉	4♊	28♓	2♋
6	15♉	5♊	29♓	3♋
7	16♉	6♊	0♈	3♋
8	17♉	6♊	1♈	4♋
9	18♉	7♊	2♈	5♋
10	19♉	7♊	3♈	5♋
11	20♉	7♊	4♈	6♋
12	21♉	8♊	5♈	6♋
13	22♉	8♊	6♈	7♋
14	23♉	8♊	8♈	8♋
15	23♉	8♊	9♈	8♋
16	24♉	8♊	10♈	9♋
17	25♉	7♊	11♈	10♋
18	26♉	7♊	12♈	10♋
19	27♉	7♊	13♈	11♋
20	28♉	6♊	14♈	11♋
21	29♉	6♊	15♈	12♋
22	0♊	5♊	16♈	13♋
23	1♊	5♊	17♈	13♋
24	2♊	4♊	18♈	14♋
25	3♊	4♊	20♈	14♋
26	4♊	3♊	21♈	15♋
27	5♊	3♊	22♈	16♋
28	6♊	2♊	23♈	16♋
29	7♊	2♊	24♈	17♋
30	8♊	1♊	25♈	18♋
31	9♊	1♊	26♈	18♋

June

Day	☉	☿	♀	♂
1	10♊	0♊	27♈	19♋
2	11♊	0♊	28♈	19♋
3	12♊	0♊	0♉	20♋
4	13♊	29♉	1♉	21♋
5	14♊	29♉	2♉	21♋
6	15♊	29♉	3♉	22♋
7	16♊	29♉	4♉	23♋
8	17♊	29♉	5♉	23♋
9	17♊	29♉	6♉	24♋
10	18♊	29♉	7♉	24♋
11	19♊	0♊	9♉	25♋
12	20♊	0♊	10♉	26♋
13	21♊	0♊	11♉	26♋
14	22♊	1♊	12♉	27♋
15	23♊	2♊	13♉	28♋
16	24♊	2♊	14♉	28♋
17	25♊	3♊	15♉	29♋
18	26♊	4♊	17♉	29♋
19	27♊	5♊	18♉	0♌
20	28♊	5♊	19♉	1♌
21	29♊	6♊	20♉	1♌
22	0♋	7♊	21♉	2♌
23	1♋	9♊	22♉	3♌
24	2♋	10♊	23♉	3♌
25	3♋	11♊	25♉	4♌
26	4♋	12♊	26♉	4♌
27	5♋	14♊	27♉	5♌
28	6♋	15♊	28♉	6♌
29	7♋	16♊	29♉	6♌
30	8♋	18♊	0♊	7♌

July

Day	☉	☿	♀	♂
1	8♋	20♊	2♊	8♌
2	9♋	21♊	3♊	8♌
3	10♋	23♊	4♊	9♌
4	11♋	25♊	5♊	9♌
5	12♋	26♊	6♊	10♌
6	13♋	28♊	7♊	11♌
7	14♋	0♋	9♊	11♌
8	15♋	2♋	10♊	12♌
9	16♋	4♋	11♊	13♌
10	17♋	6♋	12♊	13♌
11	18♋	8♋	13♊	14♌
12	19♋	10♋	15♊	14♌
13	20♋	12♋	16♊	15♌
14	21♋	14♋	17♊	16♌
15	22♋	17♋	18♊	16♌
16	23♋	19♋	19♊	17♌
17	24♋	21♋	20♊	18♌
18	25♋	23♋	22♊	18♌
19	26♋	25♋	23♊	19♌
20	27♋	27♋	24♊	19♌
21	28♋	29♋	25♊	20♌
22	28♋	1♌	26♊	21♌
23	29♋	4♌	28♊	21♌
24	0♌	6♌	29♊	22♌
25	1♌	8♌	0♋	23♌
26	2♌	10♌	1♋	23♌
27	3♌	12♌	2♋	24♌
28	4♌	14♌	3♋	24♌
29	5♌	16♌	5♋	25♌
30	6♌	17♌	6♋	26♌
31	7♌	19♌	7♋	26♌

August

Day	☉	☿	♀	♂
1	8♌	21♌	8♋	27♌
2	9♌	23♌	9♋	28♌
3	10♌	25♌	11♋	28♌
4	11♌	27♌	12♋	29♌
5	12♌	28♌	13♋	29♌
6	13♌	0♍	14♋	0♍
7	14♌	2♍	15♋	1♍
8	15♌	3♍	17♋	1♍
9	16♌	5♍	18♋	2♍
10	17♌	7♍	19♋	3♍
11	18♌	8♍	20♋	3♍
12	19♌	10♍	21♋	4♍
13	20♌	11♍	23♋	5♍
14	21♌	13♍	24♋	5♍
15	21♌	14♍	25♋	6♍
16	22♌	16♍	26♋	6♍
17	23♌	17♍	28♋	7♍
18	24♌	19♍	29♋	8♍
19	25♌	20♍	0♌	8♍
20	26♌	21♍	1♌	9♍
21	27♌	23♍	2♌	10♍
22	28♌	24♍	4♌	10♍
23	29♌	25♍	5♌	11♍
24	0♍	26♍	6♌	12♍
25	1♍	28♍	7♌	12♍
26	2♍	29♍	8♌	13♍
27	3♍	0♎	10♌	13♍
28	4♍	1♎	11♌	14♍
29	5♍	2♎	12♌	15♍
30	6♍	3♎	13♌	15♍
31	7♍	4♎	15♌	16♍

September

Day	☉	☿	♀	♂
1	8♍	5♎	16♌	17♍
2	9♍	6♎	17♌	17♍
3	10♍	7♎	18♌	18♍
4	11♍	7♎	19♌	19♍
5	12♍	8♎	21♌	19♍
6	13♍	9♎	22♌	20♍
7	14♍	9♎	23♌	20♍
8	15♍	10♎	24♌	21♍
9	16♍	10♎	26♌	22♍
10	17♍	11♎	27♌	22♍
11	18♍	11♎	28♌	23♍
12	19♍	11♎	29♌	24♍
13	20♍	11♎	1♍	24♍
14	20♍	11♎	2♍	25♍
15	21♍	11♎	3♍	26♍
16	22♍	11♎	4♍	26♍
17	23♍	10♎	5♍	27♍
18	24♍	10♎	7♍	28♍
19	25♍	9♎	8♍	28♍
20	26♍	8♎	9♍	29♍
21	27♍	8♎	10♍	29♍
22	28♍	7♎	12♍	0♎
23	29♍	6♎	13♍	1♎
24	0♎	5♎	14♍	1♎
25	1♎	4♎	15♍	2♎
26	2♎	2♎	17♍	3♎
27	3♎	1♎	18♍	3♎
28	4♎	0♎	19♍	4♎
29	5♎	29♍	20♍	5♎
30	6♎	28♍	22♍	5♎

October

Day	☉	☿	♀	♂
1	7♎	28♍	23♍	6♎
2	8♎	27♍	24♍	7♎
3	9♎	27♍	25♍	7♎
4	10♎	26♍	27♍	8♎
5	11♎	26♍	28♍	9♎
6	12♎	26♍	29♍	9♎
7	13♎	27♍	0♎	10♎
8	14♎	27♍	2♎	11♎
9	15♎	27♍	3♎	11♎
10	16♎	28♍	4♎	12♎
11	17♎	29♍	5♎	13♎
12	18♎	0♎	7♎	13♎
13	19♎	1♎	8♎	14♎
14	20♎	2♎	9♎	14♎
15	21♎	4♎	10♎	15♎
16	22♎	5♎	12♎	16♎
17	23♎	6♎	13♎	16♎
18	24♎	8♎	14♎	17♎
19	25♎	9♎	15♎	18♎
20	26♎	11♎	17♎	18♎
21	27♎	13♎	18♎	19♎
22	28♎	14♎	19♎	20♎
23	29♎	16♎	20♎	20♎
24	0♏	17♎	22♎	21♎
25	1♏	19♎	23♎	22♎
26	2♏	21♎	24♎	22♎
27	3♏	22♎	25♎	23♎
28	4♏	24♎	27♎	24♎
29	5♏	26♎	28♎	24♎
30	6♏	27♎	29♎	25♎
31	7♏	29♎	0♏	26♎

November

Day	☉	☿	♀	♂
1	8♏	1♏	2♏	26♎
2	9♏	2♏	3♏	27♎
3	10♏	4♏	4♏	28♎
4	11♏	6♏	5♏	28♎
5	12♏	7♏	7♏	29♎
6	13♏	9♏	8♏	0♏
7	14♏	11♏	9♏	0♏
8	15♏	12♏	10♏	1♏
9	16♏	14♏	12♏	2♏
10	17♏	15♏	13♏	2♏
11	18♏	17♏	14♏	3♏
12	19♏	19♏	15♏	4♏
13	20♏	20♏	17♏	4♏
14	21♏	22♏	18♏	5♏
15	22♏	23♏	19♏	6♏
16	23♏	25♏	20♏	6♏
17	24♏	27♏	22♏	7♏
18	25♏	28♏	23♏	8♏
19	26♏	0♐	24♏	9♏
20	27♏	1♐	25♏	9♏
21	28♏	3♐	27♏	10♏
22	29♏	4♐	28♏	11♏
23	0♐	6♐	29♏	11♏
24	1♐	8♐	0♐	12♏
25	2♐	9♐	2♐	13♏
26	3♐	11♐	3♐	13♏
27	4♐	12♐	4♐	14♏
28	5♐	14♐	5♐	15♏
29	6♐	15♐	7♐	15♏
30	7♐	17♐	8♐	16♏

December

Day	☉	☿	♀	♂
1	8♐	18♐	9♐	17♏
2	9♐	20♐	11♐	17♏
3	10♐	22♐	12♐	18♏
4	11♐	23♐	13♐	19♏
5	12♐	25♐	14♐	19♏
6	13♐	26♐	16♐	20♏
7	14♐	28♐	17♐	21♏
8	15♐	29♐	18♐	21♏
9	16♐	1♑	19♐	22♏
10	17♐	2♑	21♐	23♏
11	18♐	4♑	22♐	24♏
12	19♐	5♑	23♐	24♏
13	20♐	7♑	24♐	25♏
14	21♐	8♑	26♐	26♏
15	22♐	10♑	27♐	26♏
16	23♐	11♑	28♐	27♏
17	24♐	12♑	29♐	28♏
18	25♐	14♑	1♑	28♏
19	26♐	15♑	2♑	29♏
20	27♐	17♑	3♑	0♐
21	28♐	18♑	4♑	0♐
22	29♐	19♑	6♑	1♐
23	1♑	20♑	7♑	2♐
24	2♑	21♑	8♑	3♐
25	3♑	22♑	9♑	3♐
26	4♑	23♑	11♑	4♐
27	5♑	24♑	12♑	5♐
28	6♑	25♑	13♑	5♐
29	7♑	26♑	14♑	6♐
30	8♑	26♑	16♑	7♐
31	9♑	26♑	17♑	7♐

1911

Your Starway to Love

☉ =Sun ☿ = Mercury ♀ = Venus ♂ = Mars ♈ = Aries ♉ = Taurus ♊ = Gemini ♋ = Cancer

January

Day	☉	☿	♀	♂
1	10♑	26♑	18♑	8♐
2	11♑	26♑	20♑	9♐
3	12♑	26♑	21♑	10♐
4	13♑	26♑	22♑	10♐
5	14♑	25♑	23♑	11♐
6	15♑	24♑	25♑	12♐
7	16♑	23♑	26♑	12♐
8	17♑	22♑	27♑	13♐
9	18♑	21♑	28♑	14♐
10	19♑	19♑	0♒	15♐
11	20♑	18♑	1♒	15♐
12	21♑	17♑	2♒	16♐
13	22♑	15♑	3♒	17♐
14	23♑	14♑	5♒	17♐
15	24♑	13♑	6♒	18♐
16	25♑	12♑	7♒	19♐
17	26♑	12♑	8♒	19♐
18	27♑	11♑	10♒	20♐
19	28♑	11♑	11♒	21♐
20	29♑	10♑	12♒	22♐
21	0♒	10♑	13♒	22♐
22	1♒	10♑	15♒	23♐
23	2♒	10♑	16♒	24♐
24	3♒	11♑	17♒	24♐
25	4♒	11♑	18♒	25♐
26	5♒	11♑	20♒	26♐
27	6♒	12♑	21♒	27♐
28	7♒	13♑	22♒	27♐
29	8♒	13♑	23♒	28♐
30	9♒	14♑	25♒	29♐
31	10♒	15♑	26♒	0♑

April

Day	☉	☿	♀	♂
1	10♈	22♈	10♉	13♒
2	11♈	24♈	11♉	14♒
3	12♈	26♈	12♉	15♒
4	13♈	28♈	14♉	16♒
5	14♈	0♉	15♉	16♒
6	15♈	1♉	16♉	17♒
7	16♈	3♉	17♉	18♒
8	17♈	5♉	18♉	19♒
9	18♈	6♉	20♉	19♒
10	19♈	8♉	21♉	20♒
11	20♈	9♉	22♉	21♒
12	21♈	10♉	23♉	22♒
13	22♈	12♉	25♉	22♒
14	23♈	13♉	26♉	23♒
15	24♈	14♉	27♉	24♒
16	25♈	15♉	28♉	25♒
17	26♈	15♉	29♉	25♒
18	27♈	16♉	1♊	26♒
19	28♈	17♉	2♊	27♒
20	29♈	17♉	3♊	28♒
21	0♉	18♉	4♊	28♒
22	1♉	18♉	5♊	29♒
23	2♉	18♉	6♊	0♓
24	3♉	18♉	8♊	1♓
25	4♉	18♉	9♊	1♓
26	5♉	18♉	10♊	2♓
27	6♉	18♉	11♊	3♓
28	7♉	18♉	12♊	4♓
29	8♉	18♉	14♊	4♓
30	9♉	17♉	15♊	5♓

July

Day	☉	☿	♀	♂
1	8♋	5♋	24♌	20♈
2	9♋	7♋	25♌	21♈
3	10♋	9♋	26♌	22♈
4	11♋	11♋	27♌	22♈
5	12♋	13♋	28♌	23♈
6	13♋	16♋	28♌	24♈
7	14♋	18♋	29♌	24♈
8	15♋	20♋	0♍	25♈
9	16♋	22♋	1♍	26♈
10	17♋	24♋	2♍	26♈
11	18♋	26♋	3♍	27♈
12	19♋	28♋	4♍	28♈
13	20♋	0♌	5♍	28♈
14	21♋	2♌	6♍	29♈
15	22♋	4♌	7♍	0♉
16	23♋	6♌	8♍	0♉
17	23♋	8♌	9♍	1♉
18	24♋	10♌	9♍	2♉
19	25♋	11♌	10♍	2♉
20	26♋	13♌	11♍	3♉
21	27♋	15♌	12♍	4♉
22	28♋	17♌	13♍	4♉
23	29♋	18♌	14♍	5♉
24	0♌	20♌	14♍	6♉
25	1♌	22♌	15♍	6♉
26	2♌	23♌	16♍	7♉
27	3♌	25♌	17♍	8♉
28	4♌	26♌	18♍	8♉
29	5♌	28♌	18♍	9♉
30	6♌	29♌	19♍	9♉
31	7♌	1♍	20♍	10♉

October

Day	☉	☿	♀	♂
1	7♎	21♍	14♍	9♊
2	8♎	22♍	14♍	9♊
3	9♎	24♍	14♍	9♊
4	10♎	26♍	14♍	10♊
5	11♎	27♍	13♍	10♊
6	12♎	29♍	13♍	10♊
7	13♎	1♎	13♍	10♊
8	14♎	2♎	13♍	10♊
9	15♎	4♎	13♍	10♊
10	16♎	6♎	14♍	10♊
11	17♎	8♎	14♍	11♊
12	18♎	9♎	14♍	11♊
13	19♎	11♎	14♍	11♊
14	20♎	13♎	14♍	11♊
15	21♎	15♎	15♍	11♊
16	22♎	16♎	15♍	11♊
17	23♎	18♎	15♍	11♊
18	24♎	20♎	16♍	11♊
19	25♎	21♎	16♍	11♊
20	26♎	23♎	17♍	11♊
21	27♎	25♎	17♍	11♊
22	28♎	27♎	18♍	11♊
23	29♎	28♎	18♍	11♊
24	0♏	0♏	19♍	11♊
25	1♏	2♏	19♍	11♊
26	2♏	3♏	20♍	11♊
27	3♏	5♏	20♍	10♊
28	4♏	6♏	21♍	10♊
29	5♏	8♏	22♍	10♊
30	6♏	10♏	22♍	10♊
31	7♏	11♏	23♍	10♊

February

Day	☉	☿	♀	♂
1	11♒	16♑	27♒	0♑
2	12♒	17♑	28♒	1♑
3	13♒	18♑	0♓	2♑
4	14♒	19♑	1♓	2♑
5	15♒	20♑	2♓	3♑
6	16♒	21♑	3♓	4♑
7	17♒	22♑	5♓	5♑
8	18♒	24♑	6♓	5♑
9	19♒	25♑	7♓	6♑
10	20♒	26♑	8♓	7♑
11	21♒	27♑	10♓	7♑
12	22♒	29♑	11♓	8♑
13	23♒	0♒	12♓	9♑
14	24♒	1♒	13♓	10♑
15	25♒	3♒	15♓	10♑
16	26♒	4♒	16♓	11♑
17	27♒	6♒	17♓	12♑
18	28♒	7♒	18♓	13♑
19	29♒	8♒	20♓	13♑
20	0♓	10♒	21♓	14♑
21	1♓	11♒	22♓	15♑
22	2♓	13♒	23♓	15♑
23	3♓	14♒	25♓	16♑
24	4♓	16♒	26♓	17♑
25	5♓	18♒	27♓	18♑
26	6♓	19♒	28♓	18♑
27	7♓	21♒	0♈	19♑
28	8♓	22♒	1♈	20♑

May

Day	☉	☿	♀	♂
1	10♉	17♉	16♊	6♓
2	11♉	16♉	17♊	7♓
3	12♉	16♉	18♊	7♓
4	13♉	15♉	19♊	8♓
5	14♉	14♉	21♊	9♓
6	15♉	14♉	22♊	10♓
7	16♉	13♉	23♊	10♓
8	16♉	13♉	24♊	11♓
9	17♉	12♉	25♊	12♓
10	18♉	11♉	26♊	13♓
11	19♉	11♉	28♊	13♓
12	20♉	10♉	29♊	14♓
13	21♉	10♉	0♋	15♓
14	22♉	10♉	1♋	16♓
15	23♉	9♉	2♋	16♓
16	24♉	9♉	3♋	17♓
17	25♉	9♉	5♋	18♓
18	26♉	9♉	6♋	18♓
19	27♉	9♉	7♋	19♓
20	28♉	9♉	8♋	20♓
21	29♉	9♉	9♋	21♓
22	0♊	9♉	10♋	21♓
23	1♊	10♉	11♋	22♓
24	2♊	10♉	13♋	23♓
25	3♊	10♉	14♋	24♓
26	4♊	11♉	15♋	24♓
27	5♊	11♉	16♋	25♓
28	6♊	12♉	17♋	26♓
29	7♊	13♉	18♋	27♓
30	8♊	14♉	19♋	27♓
31	9♊	14♉	20♋	28♓

August

Day	☉	☿	♀	♂
1	8♌	2♍	20♍	11♉
2	9♌	4♍	21♍	11♉
3	10♌	5♍	22♍	12♉
4	11♌	6♍	22♍	12♉
5	12♌	8♍	23♍	13♉
6	13♌	9♍	23♍	14♉
7	14♌	10♍	24♍	14♉
8	15♌	11♍	25♍	15♉
9	15♌	13♍	25♍	15♉
10	16♌	14♍	26♍	16♉
11	17♌	15♍	26♍	17♉
12	18♌	16♍	26♍	17♉
13	19♌	17♍	27♍	18♉
14	20♌	18♍	27♍	18♉
15	21♌	19♍	28♍	19♉
16	22♌	19♍	28♍	20♉
17	23♌	20♍	28♍	20♉
18	24♌	21♍	29♍	21♉
19	25♌	22♍	29♍	21♉
20	26♌	22♍	29♍	22♉
21	27♌	23♍	29♍	22♉
22	28♌	23♍	29♍	23♉
23	29♌	23♍	29♍	23♉
24	0♍	24♍	29♍	24♉
25	1♍	24♍	29♍	24♉
26	2♍	24♍	29♍	25♉
27	3♍	24♍	29♍	25♉
28	4♍	24♍	29♍	26♉
29	5♍	24♍	29♍	26♉
30	6♍	24♍	29♍	27♉
31	7♍	23♍	29♍	27♉

November

Day	☉	☿	♀	♂
1	8♏	13♏	24♍	10♊
2	9♏	14♏	25♍	9♊
3	10♏	16♏	25♍	9♊
4	11♏	18♏	26♍	9♊
5	12♏	19♏	27♍	9♊
6	13♏	21♏	28♍	8♊
7	14♏	22♏	28♍	8♊
8	15♏	24♏	29♍	8♊
9	16♏	25♏	0♎	8♊
10	17♏	27♏	1♎	7♊
11	18♏	28♏	2♎	7♊
12	19♏	0♐	3♎	7♊
13	20♏	2♐	4♎	6♊
14	21♏	3♐	5♎	6♊
15	22♏	5♐	6♎	6♊
16	23♏	6♐	6♎	5♊
17	24♏	8♐	7♎	5♊
18	25♏	9♐	8♎	4♊
19	26♏	11♐	9♎	4♊
20	27♏	12♐	10♎	4♊
21	28♏	13♐	11♎	3♊
22	29♏	15♐	12♎	3♊
23	0♐	16♐	13♎	3♊
24	1♐	18♐	14♎	2♊
25	2♐	19♐	15♎	2♊
26	3♐	21♐	16♎	1♊
27	4♐	22♐	17♎	1♊
28	5♐	24♐	18♎	1♊
29	6♐	25♐	19♎	0♊
30	7♐	26♐	20♎	0♊

March

Day	☉	☿	♀	♂
1	10♓	24♒	2♈	21♑
2	11♓	26♒	3♈	21♑
3	12♓	27♒	4♈	22♑
4	13♓	29♒	6♈	23♑
5	14♓	1♓	7♈	24♑
6	15♓	2♓	8♈	24♑
7	16♓	4♓	9♈	25♑
8	17♓	6♓	11♈	26♑
9	18♓	7♓	12♈	26♑
10	19♓	9♓	13♈	27♑
11	20♓	11♓	14♈	28♑
12	21♓	13♓	16♈	29♑
13	22♓	15♓	17♈	29♑
14	23♓	17♓	18♈	0♒
15	24♓	18♓	19♈	1♒
16	24♓	20♓	20♈	2♒
17	25♓	22♓	22♈	2♒
18	26♓	24♓	23♈	3♒
19	27♓	26♓	24♈	4♒
20	28♓	28♓	25♈	5♒
21	29♓	0♈	27♈	5♒
22	0♈	2♈	28♈	6♒
23	1♈	4♈	29♈	7♒
24	2♈	6♈	0♉	8♒
25	3♈	8♈	1♉	8♒
26	4♈	10♈	3♉	9♒
27	5♈	12♈	4♉	10♒
28	6♈	14♈	5♉	11♒
29	7♈	16♈	6♉	11♒
30	8♈	18♈	8♉	12♒
31	9♈	20♈	9♉	13♒

June

Day	☉	☿	♀	♂
1	10♊	15♉	22♋	29♓
2	11♊	16♉	23♋	29♓
3	12♊	17♉	24♋	0♈
4	12♊	18♉	25♋	1♈
5	13♊	19♉	26♋	2♈
6	14♊	21♉	27♋	2♈
7	15♊	22♉	28♋	3♈
8	16♊	23♉	29♋	4♈
9	17♊	24♉	0♌	5♈
10	18♊	26♉	2♌	5♈
11	19♊	27♉	3♌	6♈
12	20♊	29♉	4♌	7♈
13	21♊	0♊	5♌	7♈
14	22♊	2♊	6♌	8♈
15	23♊	3♊	7♌	9♈
16	24♊	5♊	8♌	10♈
17	25♊	7♊	9♌	10♈
18	26♊	9♊	10♌	11♈
19	27♊	10♊	11♌	12♈
20	28♊	12♊	12♌	12♈
21	29♊	14♊	13♌	13♈
22	0♋	16♊	14♌	14♈
23	1♋	18♊	15♌	15♈
24	2♋	20♊	16♌	15♈
25	3♋	22♊	17♌	16♈
26	3♋	24♊	19♌	17♈
27	4♋	26♊	20♌	17♈
28	5♋	28♊	21♌	18♈
29	6♋	0♋	22♌	19♈
30	7♋	3♋	23♌	19♈

September

Day	☉	☿	♀	♂
1	8♍	23♍	29♍	28♉
2	9♍	22♍	28♍	28♉
3	10♍	22♍	28♍	29♉
4	11♍	21♍	28♍	29♉
5	12♍	20♍	27♍	0♊
6	12♍	19♍	27♍	0♊
7	13♍	18♍	26♍	1♊
8	14♍	17♍	26♍	1♊
9	15♍	16♍	25♍	2♊
10	16♍	15♍	25♍	2♊
11	17♍	14♍	24♍	2♊
12	18♍	13♍	24♍	3♊
13	19♍	13♍	23♍	3♊
14	20♍	12♍	22♍	4♊
15	21♍	11♍	22♍	4♊
16	22♍	11♍	21♍	4♊
17	23♍	10♍	20♍	5♊
18	24♍	10♍	20♍	5♊
19	25♍	10♍	19♍	5♊
20	26♍	10♍	19♍	6♊
21	27♍	11♍	18♍	6♊
22	28♍	11♍	18♍	6♊
23	29♍	12♍	17♍	7♊
24	0♎	12♍	17♍	7♊
25	1♎	13♍	16♍	7♊
26	2♎	14♍	16♍	8♊
27	3♎	15♍	15♍	8♊
28	4♎	17♍	15♍	8♊
29	5♎	18♍	15♍	8♊
30	6♎	19♍	14♍	9♊

December

Day	☉	☿	♀	♂
1	8♐	28♐	21♎	0♊
2	9♐	29♐	22♎	29♉
3	10♐	0♑	23♎	29♉
4	11♐	1♑	24♎	29♉
5	12♐	3♑	25♎	28♉
6	13♐	4♑	27♎	28♉
7	14♐	5♑	28♎	28♉
8	15♐	6♑	29♎	27♉
9	16♐	7♑	0♏	27♉
10	17♐	8♑	1♏	27♉
11	18♐	8♑	2♏	27♉
12	19♐	9♑	3♏	26♉
13	20♐	10♑	4♏	26♉
14	21♐	10♑	5♏	26♉
15	22♐	10♑	6♏	26♉
16	23♐	10♑	8♏	26♉
17	24♐	10♑	9♏	25♉
18	25♐	10♑	10♏	25♉
19	26♐	10♑	11♏	25♉
20	27♐	9♑	12♏	25♉
21	28♐	8♑	13♏	25♉
22	29♐	7♑	14♏	25♉
23	0♑	6♑	15♏	25♉
24	1♑	5♑	17♏	25♉
25	2♑	3♑	18♏	24♉
26	3♑	2♑	19♏	24♉
27	4♑	1♑	20♏	24♉
28	5♑	29♐	21♏	24♉
29	6♑	28♐	22♏	24♉
30	7♑	27♐	24♏	24♉
31	8♑	26♐	25♏	24♉

Planetary Positions

♌ = Leo ♍ = Virgo ♎ = Libra ♏ = Scorpio ♐ = Sagittarius ♑ = Capricorn ♒ = Aquarius ♓ = Pisces

1912

January

Day	☉	☿	♀	♂
1	9♑	25♐	26♏	24♉
2	10♑	25♐	27♏	24♉
3	11♑	24♐	28♏	24♉
4	12♑	24♐	29♏	24♉
5	14♑	24♐	1♐	25♉
6	15♑	24♐	2♐	25♉
7	16♑	24♐	3♐	25♉
8	17♑	25♐	4♐	25♉
9	18♑	25♐	5♐	25♉
10	19♑	26♐	6♐	25♉
11	20♑	27♐	8♐	25♉
12	21♑	27♐	9♐	25♉
13	22♑	28♐	10♐	26♉
14	23♑	29♐	11♐	26♉
15	24♑	0♑	12♐	26♉
16	25♑	1♑	14♐	26♉
17	26♑	2♑	15♐	26♉
18	27♑	3♑	16♐	27♉
19	28♑	4♑	17♐	27♉
20	29♑	5♑	18♐	27♉
21	0♒	7♑	19♐	27♉
22	1♒	8♑	21♐	28♉
23	2♒	9♑	22♐	28♉
24	3♒	10♑	23♐	28♉
25	4♒	12♑	24♐	28♉
26	5♒	13♑	25♐	29♉
27	6♒	14♑	27♐	29♉
28	7♒	16♑	28♐	29♉
29	8♒	17♑	29♐	29♉
30	9♒	18♑	0♑	0♊
31	10♒	20♑	2♑	0♊

April

Day	☉	☿	♀	♂
1	11♈	29♈	16♓	28♊
2	12♈	29♈	17♓	28♊
3	13♈	29♈	18♓	29♊
4	14♈	0♉	20♓	29♊
5	15♈	0♉	21♓	0♋
6	16♈	0♉	22♓	0♋
7	17♈	0♉	23♓	1♋
8	18♈	29♈	25♓	1♋
9	19♈	29♈	26♓	2♋
10	20♈	29♈	27♓	3♋
11	21♈	28♈	28♓	3♋
12	22♈	27♈	29♓	4♋
13	23♈	27♈	1♈	4♋
14	24♈	26♈	2♈	5♋
15	25♈	25♈	3♈	5♋
16	26♈	25♈	4♈	6♋
17	27♈	24♈	6♈	6♋
18	28♈	23♈	7♈	7♋
19	29♈	23♈	8♈	8♋
20	0♉	22♈	9♈	8♋
21	1♉	21♈	11♈	9♋
22	2♉	21♈	12♈	9♋
23	3♉	20♈	13♈	10♋
24	4♉	20♈	14♈	10♋
25	5♉	19♈	15♈	11♋
26	6♉	19♈	17♈	11♋
27	7♉	19♈	18♈	12♋
28	8♉	19♈	19♈	13♋
29	9♉	19♈	20♈	13♋
30	9♉	19♈	22♈	14♋

July

Day	☉	☿	♀	♂
1	9♋	24♋	8♋	20♌
2	10♋	26♋	9♋	21♌
3	11♋	28♋	10♋	21♌
4	12♋	0♌	11♋	22♌
5	13♋	1♌	13♋	23♌
6	14♋	3♌	14♋	23♌
7	15♋	5♌	15♋	24♌
8	16♋	7♌	16♋	25♌
9	17♋	8♌	17♋	25♌
10	18♋	10♌	19♋	26♌
11	18♋	11♌	20♋	26♌
12	19♋	13♌	21♋	27♌
13	20♋	14♌	22♋	28♌
14	21♋	16♌	24♋	28♌
15	22♋	17♌	25♋	29♌
16	23♋	18♌	26♋	29♌
17	24♋	20♌	27♋	0♍
18	25♋	21♌	29♋	1♍
19	26♋	22♌	0♌	1♍
20	27♋	24♌	1♌	2♍
21	28♋	25♌	2♌	3♍
22	29♋	26♌	3♌	3♍
23	0♌	27♌	5♌	4♍
24	1♌	28♌	6♌	4♍
25	2♌	29♌	7♌	5♍
26	3♌	0♍	8♌	6♍
27	4♌	1♍	10♌	6♍
28	5♌	2♍	11♌	7♍
29	6♌	2♍	12♌	7♍
30	7♌	3♍	13♌	8♍
31	8♌	4♍	15♌	9♍

October

Day	☉	☿	♀	♂
1	8♎	5♎	1♏	19♎
2	9♎	7♎	2♏	19♎
3	10♎	9♎	4♏	20♎
4	11♎	11♎	5♏	21♎
5	12♎	12♎	6♏	21♎
6	13♎	14♎	7♏	22♎
7	14♎	16♎	8♏	23♎
8	15♎	17♎	10♏	23♎
9	16♎	19♎	11♏	24♎
10	17♎	21♎	12♏	25♎
11	18♎	23♎	13♏	25♎
12	18♎	24♎	15♏	26♎
13	19♎	26♎	16♏	27♎
14	20♎	27♎	17♏	27♎
15	21♎	29♎	18♏	28♎
16	22♎	1♏	20♏	29♎
17	23♎	2♏	21♏	29♎
18	24♎	4♏	22♏	0♏
19	25♎	5♏	23♏	1♏
20	26♎	7♏	24♏	1♏
21	27♎	9♏	26♏	2♏
22	28♎	10♏	27♏	3♏
23	29♎	12♏	28♏	3♏
24	0♏	13♏	29♏	4♏
25	1♏	15♏	1♐	5♏
26	2♏	16♏	2♐	6♏
27	3♏	18♏	3♐	6♏
28	4♏	19♏	4♐	7♏
29	5♏	21♏	6♐	8♏
30	6♏	22♏	7♐	8♏
31	7♏	24♏	8♐	9♏

February

Day	☉	☿	♀	♂
1	11♒	21♑	3♑	0♊
2	12♒	23♑	4♑	1♊
3	13♒	24♑	5♑	1♊
4	14♒	26♑	6♑	1♊
5	15♒	27♑	8♑	2♊
6	16♒	29♑	9♑	2♊
7	17♒	0♒	10♑	3♊
8	18♒	2♒	11♑	3♊
9	19♒	3♒	12♑	3♊
10	20♒	5♒	14♑	4♊
11	21♒	6♒	15♑	4♊
12	22♒	8♒	16♑	4♊
13	23♒	10♒	17♑	5♊
14	24♒	11♒	18♑	5♊
15	25♒	13♒	20♑	6♊
16	26♒	14♒	21♑	6♊
17	27♒	16♒	22♑	6♊
18	28♒	18♒	23♑	7♊
19	29♒	19♒	25♑	7♊
20	0♓	21♒	26♑	8♊
21	1♓	23♒	27♑	8♊
22	2♓	25♒	28♑	9♊
23	3♓	26♒	29♑	9♊
24	4♓	28♒	1♒	9♊
25	5♓	0♓	2♒	10♊
26	6♓	2♓	3♒	10♊
27	7♓	3♓	4♒	11♊
28	8♓	5♓	6♒	11♊
29	9♓	7♓	7♒	12♊

May

Day	☉	☿	♀	♂
1	10♉	19♈	23♈	14♋
2	11♉	19♈	24♈	15♋
3	12♉	20♈	25♈	15♋
4	13♉	20♈	26♈	16♋
5	14♉	20♈	28♈	17♋
6	15♉	21♈	29♈	17♋
7	16♉	21♈	0♉	18♋
8	17♉	22♈	1♉	18♋
9	18♉	23♈	3♉	19♋
10	19♉	24♈	4♉	19♋
11	20♉	24♈	5♉	20♋
12	21♉	25♈	6♉	21♋
13	22♉	26♈	8♉	21♋
14	23♉	27♈	9♉	22♋
15	24♉	28♈	10♉	22♋
16	25♉	29♈	11♉	23♋
17	26♉	0♉	12♉	23♋
18	27♉	2♉	14♉	24♋
19	28♉	3♉	15♉	25♋
20	29♉	4♉	16♉	25♋
21	0♊	5♉	17♉	26♋
22	1♊	7♉	19♉	26♋
23	2♊	8♉	20♉	27♋
24	3♊	10♉	21♉	28♋
25	4♊	11♉	22♉	28♋
26	5♊	13♉	23♉	29♋
27	6♊	14♉	25♉	29♋
28	6♊	16♉	26♉	0♌
29	7♊	17♉	27♉	1♌
30	8♊	19♉	28♉	1♌
31	9♊	21♉	0♊	2♌

August

Day	☉	☿	♀	♂
1	9♌	4♍	16♌	9♍
2	10♌	5♍	17♌	10♍
3	10♌	5♍	18♌	11♍
4	11♌	6♍	19♌	11♍
5	12♌	6♍	21♌	12♍
6	13♌	6♍	22♌	13♍
7	14♌	7♍	23♌	13♍
8	15♌	7♍	24♌	14♍
9	16♌	7♍	26♌	14♍
10	17♌	6♍	27♌	15♍
11	18♌	6♍	28♌	16♍
12	19♌	6♍	29♌	16♍
13	20♌	6♍	1♍	17♍
14	21♌	5♍	2♍	18♍
15	22♌	5♍	3♍	18♍
16	23♌	4♍	4♍	19♍
17	24♌	3♍	6♍	19♍
18	25♌	2♍	7♍	20♍
19	26♌	2♍	8♍	21♍
20	27♌	1♍	9♍	21♍
21	28♌	0♍	10♍	22♍
22	29♌	29♌	12♍	23♍
23	0♍	28♌	13♍	23♍
24	1♍	27♌	14♍	24♍
25	2♍	27♌	15♍	25♍
26	3♍	26♌	17♍	25♍
27	4♍	25♌	18♍	26♍
28	5♍	25♌	19♍	26♍
29	5♍	24♌	20♍	27♍
30	6♍	24♌	22♍	28♍
31	7♍	24♌	23♍	28♍

November

Day	☉	☿	♀	♂
1	8♏	25♏	9♐	10♏
2	9♏	27♏	10♐	10♏
3	10♏	28♏	12♐	11♏
4	11♏	29♏	13♐	12♏
5	12♏	1♐	14♐	12♏
6	13♏	2♐	15♐	13♏
7	14♏	4♐	17♐	14♏
8	15♏	5♐	18♐	14♏
9	16♏	6♐	19♐	15♏
10	17♏	8♐	20♐	16♏
11	18♏	9♐	21♐	17♏
12	19♏	10♐	23♐	17♏
13	20♏	12♐	24♐	18♏
14	21♏	13♐	25♐	19♏
15	22♏	14♐	26♐	19♏
16	23♏	15♐	28♐	20♏
17	24♏	16♐	29♐	21♏
18	26♏	18♐	0♑	21♏
19	27♏	19♐	1♑	22♏
20	28♏	20♐	2♑	23♏
21	29♏	21♐	4♑	24♏
22	0♐	21♐	5♑	24♏
23	1♐	22♐	6♑	25♏
24	2♐	23♐	7♑	26♏
25	3♐	24♐	9♑	26♏
26	4♐	24♐	10♑	27♏
27	5♐	24♐	11♑	28♏
28	6♐	25♐	12♑	28♏
29	7♐	25♐	13♑	29♏
30	8♐	25♐	15♑	0♐

March

Day	☉	☿	♀	♂
1	10♓	9♓	8♒	12♊
2	11♓	11♓	9♒	13♊
3	12♓	13♓	10♒	13♊
4	13♓	15♓	12♒	14♊
5	14♓	17♓	13♒	14♊
6	15♓	19♓	14♒	14♊
7	16♓	21♓	15♒	15♊
8	17♓	22♓	17♒	15♊
9	18♓	24♓	18♒	16♊
10	19♓	26♓	19♒	16♊
11	20♓	28♓	20♒	17♊
12	21♓	0♈	21♒	17♊
13	22♓	2♈	23♒	18♊
14	23♓	4♈	24♒	18♊
15	24♓	6♈	25♒	19♊
16	25♓	8♈	26♒	19♊
17	26♓	10♈	28♒	20♊
18	27♓	12♈	29♒	20♊
19	28♓	13♈	0♓	21♊
20	29♓	15♈	1♓	21♊
21	0♈	17♈	3♓	22♊
22	1♈	18♈	4♓	22♊
23	2♈	20♈	5♓	23♊
24	3♈	21♈	6♓	23♊
25	4♈	23♈	7♓	24♊
26	5♈	24♈	9♓	25♊
27	6♈	25♈	10♓	25♊
28	7♈	26♈	11♓	26♊
29	8♈	27♈	12♓	26♊
30	9♈	28♈	14♓	27♊
31	10♈	28♈	15♓	27♊

June

Day	☉	☿	♀	♂
1	10♊	23♉	1♊	2♌
2	11♊	24♉	2♊	3♌
3	12♊	26♉	3♊	3♌
4	13♊	28♉	4♊	4♌
5	14♊	0♊	6♊	5♌
6	15♊	2♊	7♊	5♌
7	16♊	4♊	8♊	6♌
8	17♊	6♊	9♊	6♌
9	18♊	8♊	11♊	7♌
10	19♊	10♊	12♊	8♌
11	20♊	12♊	13♊	8♌
12	21♊	14♊	14♊	9♌
13	22♊	16♊	16♊	9♌
14	23♊	19♊	17♊	10♌
15	24♊	21♊	18♊	11♌
16	25♊	23♊	19♊	11♌
17	26♊	25♊	20♊	12♌
18	27♊	27♊	22♊	12♌
19	28♊	0♋	23♊	13♌
20	28♊	2♋	24♊	14♌
21	29♊	4♋	25♊	14♌
22	0♋	6♋	27♊	15♌
23	1♋	8♋	28♊	15♌
24	2♋	10♋	29♊	16♌
25	3♋	12♋	0♋	17♌
26	4♋	14♋	1♋	17♌
27	5♋	16♋	3♋	18♌
28	6♋	18♋	4♋	18♌
29	7♋	20♋	5♋	19♌
30	8♋	22♋	6♋	20♌

September

Day	☉	☿	♀	♂
1	8♍	24♌	24♍	29♍
2	9♍	24♌	25♍	0♎
3	10♍	24♌	27♍	0♎
4	11♍	24♌	28♍	1♎
5	12♍	25♌	29♍	2♎
6	13♍	25♌	0♎	2♎
7	14♍	26♌	1♎	3♎
8	15♍	27♌	3♎	4♎
9	16♍	28♌	4♎	4♎
10	17♍	29♌	5♎	5♎
11	18♍	1♍	6♎	6♎
12	19♍	2♍	8♎	6♎
13	20♍	3♍	9♎	7♎
14	21♍	5♍	10♎	7♎
15	22♍	7♍	11♎	8♎
16	23♍	8♍	13♎	9♎
17	24♍	10♍	14♎	9♎
18	25♍	12♍	15♎	10♎
19	26♍	13♍	16♎	11♎
20	27♍	15♍	17♎	11♎
21	28♍	17♍	19♎	12♎
22	29♍	19♍	20♎	13♎
23	0♎	21♍	21♎	13♎
24	1♎	22♍	22♎	14♎
25	2♎	24♍	24♎	15♎
26	3♎	26♍	25♎	15♎
27	4♎	28♍	26♎	16♎
28	5♎	0♎	27♎	17♎
29	6♎	2♎	29♎	17♎
30	7♎	3♎	0♏	18♎

December

Day	☉	☿	♀	♂
1	9♐	24♐	16♑	1♐
2	10♐	24♐	17♑	1♐
3	11♐	23♐	18♑	2♐
4	12♐	22♐	19♑	3♐
5	13♐	21♐	21♑	3♐
6	14♐	20♐	22♑	4♐
7	15♐	19♐	23♑	5♐
8	16♐	18♐	24♑	6♐
9	17♐	16♐	26♑	6♐
10	18♐	15♐	27♑	7♐
11	19♐	13♐	28♑	8♐
12	20♐	12♐	29♑	9♐
13	21♐	11♐	0♒	9♐
14	22♐	10♐	2♒	10♐
15	23♐	10♐	3♒	11♐
16	24♐	9♐	4♒	11♐
17	25♐	9♐	5♒	12♐
18	26♐	8♐	6♒	13♐
19	27♐	8♐	8♒	14♐
20	28♐	9♐	9♒	14♐
21	29♐	9♐	10♒	15♐
22	0♑	9♐	11♒	16♐
23	1♑	10♐	12♒	16♐
24	2♑	10♐	13♒	17♐
25	3♑	11♐	15♒	18♐
26	4♑	12♐	16♒	19♐
27	5♑	13♐	17♒	19♐
28	6♑	14♐	18♒	20♐
29	7♑	15♐	19♒	21♐
30	8♑	16♐	21♒	22♐
31	9♑	17♐	22♒	22♐

Your Starway to Love

☉ = Sun ☿ = Mercury ♀ = Venus ♂ = Mars ♈ = Aries ♉ = Taurus ♊ = Gemini ♋ = Cancer

January

Day	☉	☿	♀	♂
1	10♑	18♐	23♒	23♐
2	11♑	19♐	24♒	24♐
3	12♑	21♐	25♒	25♐
4	13♑	22♐	26♒	25♐
5	14♑	23♐	28♒	26♐
6	15♑	25♐	29♒	27♐
7	16♑	26♐	0♓	28♐
8	17♑	27♐	1♓	28♐
9	18♑	29♐	2♓	29♐
10	19♑	0♑	3♓	0♑
11	20♑	1♑	5♓	0♑
12	21♑	3♑	6♓	1♑
13	22♑	4♑	7♓	2♑
14	23♑	6♑	8♓	3♑
15	24♑	7♑	9♓	3♑
16	25♑	9♑	10♓	4♑
17	27♑	10♑	11♓	5♑
18	28♑	12♑	13♓	6♑
19	29♑	13♑	14♓	6♑
20	0♒	15♑	15♓	7♑
21	1♒	16♑	16♓	8♑
22	2♒	18♑	17♓	9♑
23	3♒	19♑	18♓	9♑
24	4♒	21♑	19♓	10♑
25	5♒	22♑	20♓	11♑
26	6♒	24♑	22♓	12♑
27	7♒	25♑	23♓	12♑
28	8♒	27♑	24♓	13♑
29	9♒	29♑	25♓	14♑
30	10♒	0♒	26♓	15♑
31	11♒	2♒	27♓	15♑

February

Day	☉	☿	♀	♂
1	12♒	3♒	28♓	16♑
2	13♒	5♒	29♓	17♑
3	14♒	7♒	0♈	18♑
4	15♒	8♒	1♈	18♑
5	16♒	10♒	2♈	19♑
6	17♒	12♒	3♈	20♑
7	18♒	14♒	4♈	21♑
8	19♒	15♒	6♈	22♑
9	20♒	17♒	7♈	22♑
10	21♒	19♒	8♈	23♑
11	22♒	21♒	9♈	24♑
12	23♒	22♒	10♈	25♑
13	24♒	24♒	11♈	25♑
14	25♒	26♒	12♈	26♑
15	26♒	28♒	13♈	27♑
16	27♒	0♓	14♈	28♑
17	28♒	1♓	15♈	28♑
18	29♒	3♓	16♈	29♑
19	0♓	5♓	17♈	0♒
20	1♓	7♓	17♈	1♒
21	2♓	9♓	18♈	1♒
22	3♓	11♓	19♈	2♒
23	4♓	13♓	20♈	3♒
24	5♓	14♓	21♈	4♒
25	6♓	16♓	22♈	5♒
26	7♓	18♓	23♈	5♒
27	8♓	20♓	24♈	6♒
28	9♓	22♓	25♈	7♒

March

Day	☉	☿	♀	♂
1	10♓	24♓	26♈	8♒
2	11♓	25♓	26♈	8♒
3	12♓	27♓	27♈	9♒
4	13♓	29♓	28♈	10♒
5	14♓	0♈	29♈	11♒
6	15♓	2♈	0♉	11♒
7	16♓	3♈	0♉	12♒
8	17♓	5♈	1♉	13♒
9	18♓	6♈	2♉	14♒
10	19♓	7♈	3♉	15♒
11	20♓	8♈	3♉	15♒
12	21♓	9♈	4♉	16♒
13	22♓	10♈	5♉	17♒
14	23♓	11♈	5♉	18♒
15	24♓	11♈	6♉	18♒
16	25♓	12♈	7♉	19♒
17	26♓	12♈	7♉	20♒
18	27♓	12♈	8♉	21♒
19	28♓	12♈	8♉	21♒
20	29♓	12♈	9♉	22♒
21	0♈	11♈	9♉	23♒
22	1♈	11♈	10♉	24♒
23	2♈	11♈	10♉	25♒
24	3♈	10♈	10♉	25♒
25	4♈	9♈	11♉	26♒
26	5♈	9♈	11♉	27♒
27	6♈	8♈	11♉	28♒
28	7♈	7♈	12♉	28♒
29	8♈	6♈	12♉	29♒
30	9♈	5♈	12♉	0♓
31	10♈	4♈	12♉	1♓

April

Day	☉	☿	♀	♂
1	11♈	4♈	12♉	2♓
2	12♈	3♈	12♉	2♓
3	13♈	2♈	12♉	3♓
4	14♈	1♈	12♉	4♓
5	15♈	1♈	12♉	5♓
6	16♈	1♈	12♉	5♓
7	17♈	0♈	12♉	6♓
8	18♈	0♈	12♉	7♓
9	19♈	0♈	12♉	8♓
10	20♈	0♈	12♉	8♓
11	21♈	0♈	11♉	9♓
12	22♈	0♈	11♉	10♓
13	23♈	0♈	11♉	11♓
14	24♈	0♈	10♉	12♓
15	25♈	0♈	10♉	12♓
16	26♈	1♈	9♉	13♓
17	27♈	1♈	9♉	14♓
18	28♈	2♈	8♉	15♓
19	29♈	2♈	8♉	15♓
20	0♉	3♈	7♉	16♓
21	0♉	4♈	7♉	17♓
22	1♉	5♈	6♉	18♓
23	2♉	5♈	5♉	19♓
24	3♉	6♈	5♉	19♓
25	4♉	7♈	4♉	20♓
26	5♉	8♈	4♉	21♓
27	6♉	9♈	3♉	22♓
28	7♉	10♈	2♉	22♓
29	8♉	12♈	2♉	23♓
30	9♉	13♈	1♉	24♓

May

Day	☉	☿	♀	♂
1	10♉	14♈	1♉	25♓
2	11♉	15♈	0♉	25♓
3	12♉	17♈	29♈	26♓
4	13♉	18♈	29♈	27♓
5	14♉	19♈	29♈	28♓
6	15♉	21♈	28♈	29♓
7	16♉	22♈	28♈	29♓
8	17♉	24♈	27♈	0♈
9	18♉	25♈	27♈	1♈
10	19♉	27♈	27♈	2♈
11	20♉	28♈	27♈	2♈
12	21♉	0♉	26♈	3♈
13	22♉	2♉	26♈	4♈
14	23♉	3♉	26♈	5♈
15	24♉	5♉	26♈	5♈
16	25♉	7♉	26♈	6♈
17	26♉	9♉	26♈	7♈
18	27♉	10♉	26♈	8♈
19	28♉	12♉	26♈	8♈
20	29♉	14♉	26♈	9♈
21	0♊	16♉	27♈	10♈
22	0♊	18♉	27♈	11♈
23	1♊	20♉	27♈	11♈
24	2♊	22♉	27♈	12♈
25	3♊	24♉	28♈	13♈
26	4♊	26♉	28♈	14♈
27	5♊	28♉	28♈	15♈
28	6♊	0♊	29♈	15♈
29	7♊	3♊	29♈	16♈
30	8♊	5♊	29♈	17♈
31	9♊	7♊	0♉	18♈

June

Day	☉	☿	♀	♂
1	10♊	9♊	0♉	18♈
2	11♊	11♊	1♉	19♈
3	12♊	14♊	1♉	20♈
4	13♊	16♊	2♉	21♈
5	14♊	18♊	3♉	21♈
6	15♊	20♊	3♉	22♈
7	16♊	22♊	4♉	23♈
8	17♊	24♊	4♉	23♈
9	18♊	26♊	5♉	24♈
10	19♊	29♊	6♉	25♈
11	20♊	1♋	7♉	26♈
12	21♊	3♋	7♉	26♈
13	22♊	5♋	8♉	27♈
14	23♊	7♋	9♉	28♈
15	23♊	9♋	9♉	29♈
16	24♊	10♋	10♉	29♈
17	25♊	12♋	11♉	0♉
18	26♊	14♋	12♉	1♉
19	27♊	16♋	13♉	2♉
20	28♊	18♋	13♉	2♉
21	29♊	19♋	14♉	3♉
22	0♋	21♋	15♉	4♉
23	1♋	23♋	16♉	5♉
24	2♋	24♋	17♉	5♉
25	3♋	26♋	18♉	6♉
26	4♋	27♋	19♉	7♉
27	5♋	29♋	19♉	7♉
28	6♋	0♌	20♉	8♉
29	7♋	1♌	21♉	9♉
30	8♋	3♌	22♉	10♉

July

Day	☉	☿	♀	♂
1	9♋	4♌	23♉	10♉
2	10♋	5♌	24♉	11♉
3	11♋	6♌	25♉	12♉
4	12♋	8♌	26♉	12♉
5	13♋	9♌	27♉	13♉
6	14♋	10♌	28♉	14♉
7	14♋	11♌	29♉	15♉
8	15♋	12♌	0♊	15♉
9	16♋	13♌	1♊	16♉
10	17♋	13♌	2♊	17♉
11	18♋	14♌	3♊	17♉
12	19♋	15♌	4♊	18♉
13	20♋	16♌	5♊	19♉
14	21♋	16♌	6♊	20♉
15	22♋	17♌	7♊	20♉
16	23♋	17♌	8♊	21♉
17	24♋	17♌	9♊	22♉
18	25♋	18♌	10♊	22♉
19	26♋	18♌	11♊	23♉
20	27♋	18♌	12♊	24♉
21	28♋	18♌	13♊	24♉
22	29♋	18♌	14♊	25♉
23	0♌	18♌	15♊	26♉
24	1♌	18♌	16♊	26♉
25	2♌	18♌	17♊	27♉
26	3♌	17♌	18♊	28♉
27	4♌	17♌	19♊	28♉
28	4♌	16♌	20♊	29♉
29	5♌	16♌	22♊	0♊
30	6♌	15♌	23♊	1♊
31	7♌	15♌	24♊	1♊

August

Day	☉	☿	♀	♂
1	8♌	14♌	25♊	2♊
2	9♌	13♌	26♊	3♊
3	10♌	12♌	27♊	3♊
4	11♌	12♌	28♊	4♊
5	12♌	11♌	29♊	5♊
6	13♌	10♌	0♋	5♊
7	14♌	9♌	1♋	6♊
8	15♌	9♌	2♋	7♊
9	16♌	8♌	4♋	7♊
10	17♌	8♌	5♋	8♊
11	18♌	7♌	6♋	8♊
12	19♌	7♌	7♋	9♊
13	20♌	7♌	8♋	10♊
14	21♌	7♌	9♋	10♊
15	22♌	7♌	10♋	11♊
16	23♌	7♌	11♋	12♊
17	24♌	7♌	13♋	12♊
18	25♌	7♌	14♋	13♊
19	26♌	8♌	15♋	14♊
20	27♌	8♌	16♋	14♊
21	28♌	9♌	17♋	15♊
22	28♌	10♌	18♋	15♊
23	29♌	11♌	19♋	16♊
24	0♍	12♌	21♋	17♊
25	1♍	13♌	22♋	17♊
26	2♍	15♌	23♋	18♊
27	3♍	16♌	24♋	19♊
28	4♍	17♌	25♋	19♊
29	5♍	19♌	26♋	20♊
30	6♍	21♌	27♋	20♊
31	7♍	22♌	29♋	21♊

September

Day	☉	☿	♀	♂
1	8♍	24♌	0♌	22♊
2	9♍	26♌	1♌	22♊
3	10♍	28♌	2♌	23♊
4	11♍	0♍	3♌	23♊
5	12♍	1♍	4♌	24♊
6	13♍	3♍	6♌	25♊
7	14♍	5♍	7♌	25♊
8	15♍	7♍	8♌	26♊
9	16♍	9♍	9♌	26♊
10	17♍	11♍	10♌	27♊
11	18♍	13♍	12♌	27♊
12	19♍	15♍	13♌	28♊
13	20♍	17♍	14♌	29♊
14	21♍	19♍	15♌	29♊
15	22♍	20♍	16♌	0♋
16	23♍	22♍	17♌	0♋
17	24♍	24♍	19♌	1♋
18	25♍	26♍	20♌	1♋
19	26♍	28♍	21♌	2♋
20	27♍	0♎	22♌	2♋
21	28♍	1♎	23♌	3♋
22	29♍	3♎	25♌	4♋
23	0♎	5♎	26♌	4♋
24	1♎	7♎	27♌	5♋
25	2♎	8♎	28♌	5♋
26	2♎	10♎	29♌	6♋
27	3♎	12♎	1♍	6♋
28	4♎	13♎	2♍	7♋
29	5♎	15♎	3♍	7♋
30	6♎	17♎	4♍	8♋

October

Day	☉	☿	♀	♂
1	7♎	18♎	5♍	8♋
2	8♎	20♎	7♍	9♋
3	9♎	22♎	8♍	9♋
4	10♎	23♎	9♍	10♋
5	11♎	25♎	10♍	10♋
6	12♎	26♎	12♍	11♋
7	13♎	28♎	13♍	11♋
8	14♎	29♎	14♍	11♋
9	15♎	1♏	15♍	12♋
10	16♎	2♏	16♍	12♋
11	17♎	4♏	18♍	13♋
12	18♎	5♏	19♍	13♋
13	19♎	7♏	20♍	14♋
14	20♎	8♏	21♍	14♋
15	21♎	10♏	23♍	14♋
16	22♎	11♏	24♍	15♋
17	23♎	13♏	25♍	15♋
18	24♎	14♏	26♍	16♋
19	25♎	15♏	27♍	16♋
20	26♎	17♏	29♍	16♋
21	27♎	18♏	0♎	17♋
22	28♎	19♏	1♎	17♋
23	29♎	21♏	2♎	18♋
24	0♏	22♏	4♎	18♋
25	1♏	23♏	5♎	18♋
26	2♏	25♏	6♎	19♋
27	3♏	26♏	7♎	19♋
28	4♏	27♏	9♎	19♋
29	5♏	28♏	10♎	20♋
30	6♏	29♏	11♎	20♋
31	7♏	0♐	12♎	20♋

November

Day	☉	☿	♀	♂
1	8♏	2♐	14♎	21♋
2	9♏	3♐	15♎	21♋
3	10♏	4♐	16♎	21♋
4	11♏	4♐	17♎	21♋
5	12♏	5♐	19♎	22♋
6	13♏	6♐	20♎	22♋
7	14♏	7♐	21♎	22♋
8	15♏	7♐	22♎	22♋
9	16♏	8♐	24♎	23♋
10	17♏	8♐	25♎	23♋
11	18♏	9♐	26♎	23♋
12	19♏	9♐	27♎	23♋
13	20♏	9♐	28♎	23♋
14	21♏	9♐	0♏	24♋
15	22♏	8♐	1♏	24♋
16	23♏	8♐	2♏	24♋
17	24♏	7♐	3♏	24♋
18	25♏	6♐	5♏	24♋
19	26♏	5♐	6♏	24♋
20	27♏	4♐	7♏	24♋
21	28♏	3♐	8♏	24♋
22	29♏	2♐	10♏	24♋
23	0♐	0♐	11♏	24♋
24	1♐	29♏	12♏	25♋
25	2♐	28♏	14♏	25♋
26	3♐	27♏	15♏	25♋
27	4♐	25♏	16♏	25♋
28	5♐	25♏	17♏	25♋
29	6♐	24♏	19♏	25♋
30	7♐	23♏	20♏	24♋

December

Day	☉	☿	♀	♂
1	8♐	23♏	21♏	24♋
2	9♐	23♏	22♏	24♋
3	10♐	23♏	24♏	24♋
4	11♐	23♏	25♏	24♋
5	12♐	23♏	26♏	24♋
6	13♐	24♏	27♏	24♋
7	15♐	24♏	29♏	24♋
8	16♐	25♏	0♐	24♋
9	17♐	26♏	1♐	23♋
10	18♐	27♏	2♐	23♋
11	19♐	28♏	4♐	23♋
12	20♐	29♏	5♐	23♋
13	21♐	0♐	6♐	23♋
14	22♐	1♐	7♐	22♋
15	23♐	2♐	9♐	22♋
16	24♐	3♐	10♐	22♋
17	25♐	5♐	11♐	22♋
18	26♐	6♐	12♐	21♋
19	27♐	7♐	14♐	21♋
20	28♐	9♐	15♐	21♋
21	29♐	10♐	16♐	20♋
22	0♑	11♐	17♐	20♋
23	1♑	13♐	19♐	20♋
24	2♑	14♐	20♐	19♋
25	3♑	16♐	21♐	19♋
26	4♑	17♐	22♐	19♋
27	5♑	19♐	24♐	18♋
28	6♑	20♐	25♐	18♋
29	7♑	22♐	26♐	18♋
30	8♑	23♐	27♐	17♋
31	9♑	25♐	29♐	17♋

Planetary Positions

♌ = Leo ♍ = Virgo ♎ = Libra ♏ = Scorpio ♐ = Sagittarius ♑ = Capricorn ♒ = Aquarius ♓ = Pisces

1914

January

Day	☉	☿	♀	♂
1	10♑	26♐	0♑	16♋
2	11♑	28♐	1♑	16♋
3	12♑	29♐	2♑	16♋
4	13♑	1♑	4♑	15♋
5	14♑	2♑	5♑	15♋
6	15♑	4♑	6♑	14♋
7	16♑	5♑	8♑	14♋
8	17♑	7♑	9♑	14♋
9	18♑	8♑	10♑	13♋
10	19♑	10♑	11♑	13♋
11	20♑	11♑	13♑	12♋
12	21♑	13♑	14♑	12♋
13	22♑	15♑	15♑	12♋
14	23♑	16♑	16♑	11♋
15	24♑	18♑	18♑	11♋
16	25♑	19♑	19♑	11♋
17	26♑	21♑	20♑	10♋
18	27♑	23♑	21♑	10♋
19	28♑	24♑	23♑	10♋
20	29♑	26♑	24♑	9♋
21	0♒	28♑	25♑	9♋
22	1♒	29♑	26♑	9♋
23	2♒	1♒	28♑	9♋
24	3♒	3♒	29♑	8♋
25	4♒	4♒	0♒	8♋
26	5♒	6♒	1♒	8♋
27	6♒	8♒	3♒	8♋
28	7♒	9♒	4♒	7♋
29	8♒	11♒	5♒	7♋
30	9♒	13♒	6♒	7♋
31	10♒	15♒	8♒	7♋

February

Day	☉	☿	♀	♂
1	12♒	16♒	9♒	7♋
2	13♒	18♒	10♒	6♋
3	14♒	20♒	11♒	6♋
4	15♒	22♒	13♒	6♋
5	16♒	24♒	14♒	6♋
6	17♒	25♒	15♒	6♋
7	18♒	27♒	16♒	6♋
8	19♒	29♒	18♒	6♋
9	20♒	1♓	19♒	6♋
10	21♒	3♓	20♒	6♋
11	22♒	4♓	21♒	6♋
12	23♒	6♓	23♒	6♋
13	24♒	8♓	24♒	6♋
14	25♒	9♓	25♒	6♋
15	26♒	11♓	26♒	6♋
16	27♒	13♓	28♒	6♋
17	28♒	14♓	29♒	6♋
18	29♒	16♓	0♓	6♋
19	0♓	17♓	2♓	6♋
20	1♓	18♓	3♓	6♋
21	2♓	20♓	4♓	6♋
22	3♓	21♓	5♓	6♋
23	4♓	22♓	7♓	6♋
24	5♓	23♓	8♓	6♋
25	6♓	23♓	9♓	7♋
26	7♓	24♓	10♓	7♋
27	8♓	24♓	12♓	7♋
28	9♓	25♓	13♓	7♋

March

Day	☉	☿	♀	♂
1	10♓	25♓	14♓	7♋
2	11♓	25♓	15♓	7♋
3	12♓	25♓	17♓	8♋
4	13♓	24♓	18♓	8♋
5	14♓	24♓	19♓	8♋
6	15♓	23♓	20♓	8♋
7	16♓	22♓	22♓	8♋
8	17♓	22♓	23♓	9♋
9	18♓	21♓	24♓	9♋
10	19♓	20♓	25♓	9♋
11	20♓	19♓	26♓	9♋
12	21♓	18♓	28♓	10♋
13	22♓	17♓	29♓	10♋
14	23♓	16♓	0♈	10♋
15	24♓	15♓	1♈	11♋
16	25♓	14♓	3♈	11♋
17	26♓	13♓	4♈	11♋
18	27♓	13♓	5♈	11♋
19	28♓	12♓	6♈	12♋
20	29♓	12♓	8♈	12♋
21	0♈	11♓	9♈	12♋
22	1♈	11♓	10♈	13♋
23	2♈	11♓	11♈	13♋
24	3♈	11♓	13♈	13♋
25	4♈	11♓	14♈	14♋
26	5♈	11♓	15♈	14♋
27	6♈	11♓	16♈	14♋
28	7♈	12♓	18♈	15♋
29	8♈	12♓	19♈	15♋
30	9♈	13♓	20♈	16♋
31	10♈	13♓	21♈	16♋

April

Day	☉	☿	♀	♂
1	11♈	14♓	23♈	16♋
2	12♈	15♓	24♈	17♋
3	13♈	15♓	25♈	17♋
4	14♈	16♓	26♈	18♋
5	15♈	17♓	28♈	18♋
6	16♈	18♓	29♈	18♋
7	17♈	19♓	0♉	19♋
8	18♈	20♓	1♉	19♋
9	19♈	21♓	2♉	20♋
10	19♈	22♓	4♉	20♋
11	20♈	23♓	5♉	20♋
12	21♈	24♓	6♉	21♋
13	22♈	26♓	7♉	21♋
14	23♈	27♓	9♉	22♋
15	24♈	28♓	10♉	22♋
16	25♈	29♓	11♉	23♋
17	26♈	1♈	12♉	23♋
18	27♈	2♈	14♉	24♋
19	28♈	4♈	15♉	24♋
20	29♈	5♈	16♉	24♋
21	0♉	6♈	17♉	25♋
22	1♉	8♈	18♉	25♋
23	2♉	10♈	20♉	26♋
24	3♉	11♈	21♉	26♋
25	4♉	13♈	22♉	27♋
26	5♉	14♈	23♉	27♋
27	6♉	16♈	25♉	28♋
28	7♉	18♈	26♉	28♋
29	8♉	19♈	27♉	29♋
30	9♉	21♈	28♉	29♋

May

Day	☉	☿	♀	♂
1	10♉	23♈	0♊	0♌
2	11♉	25♈	1♊	0♌
3	12♉	27♈	2♊	1♌
4	13♉	28♈	3♊	1♌
5	14♉	0♉	4♊	2♌
6	15♉	2♉	6♊	2♌
7	16♉	4♉	7♊	3♌
8	17♉	6♉	8♊	3♌
9	18♉	8♉	9♊	4♌
10	19♉	10♉	11♊	4♌
11	20♉	12♉	12♊	5♌
12	21♉	14♉	13♊	5♌
13	22♉	17♉	14♊	6♌
14	23♉	19♉	15♊	6♌
15	24♉	21♉	17♊	7♌
16	24♉	23♉	18♊	7♌
17	25♉	25♉	19♊	8♌
18	26♉	27♉	20♊	8♌
19	27♉	0♊	21♊	9♌
20	28♉	2♊	23♊	9♌
21	29♉	4♊	24♊	10♌
22	0♊	6♊	25♊	10♌
23	1♊	8♊	26♊	11♌
24	2♊	10♊	28♊	12♌
25	3♊	12♊	29♊	12♌
26	4♊	15♊	0♋	13♌
27	5♊	17♊	1♋	13♌
28	6♊	19♊	2♋	14♌
29	7♊	21♊	4♋	14♌
30	8♊	23♊	5♋	15♌
31	9♊	24♊	6♋	15♌

June

Day	☉	☿	♀	♂
1	10♊	26♊	7♋	16♌
2	11♊	28♊	8♋	16♌
3	12♊	0♋	10♋	17♌
4	13♊	2♋	11♋	18♌
5	14♊	3♋	12♋	18♌
6	15♊	5♋	13♋	19♌
7	16♊	7♋	14♋	19♌
8	17♊	8♋	16♋	20♌
9	18♊	10♋	17♋	20♌
10	18♊	11♋	18♋	21♌
11	19♊	12♋	19♋	21♌
12	20♊	14♋	20♋	22♌
13	21♊	15♋	22♋	23♌
14	22♊	16♋	23♋	23♌
15	23♊	18♋	24♋	24♌
16	24♊	19♋	25♋	24♌
17	25♊	20♋	26♋	25♌
18	26♊	21♋	28♋	25♌
19	27♊	22♋	29♋	26♌
20	28♊	23♋	0♌	27♌
21	29♊	24♋	1♌	27♌
22	0♋	25♋	2♌	28♌
23	1♋	25♋	4♌	28♌
24	2♋	26♋	5♌	29♌
25	3♋	27♋	6♌	29♌
26	4♋	27♋	7♌	0♍
27	5♋	28♋	8♌	1♍
28	6♋	28♋	10♌	1♍
29	7♋	28♋	11♌	2♍
30	8♋	29♋	12♌	2♍

July

Day	☉	☿	♀	♂
1	9♋	29♋	13♌	3♍
2	9♋	29♋	14♌	4♍
3	10♋	29♋	15♌	4♍
4	11♋	29♋	17♌	5♍
5	12♋	29♋	18♌	5♍
6	13♋	29♋	19♌	6♍
7	14♋	29♋	20♌	6♍
8	15♋	28♋	21♌	7♍
9	16♋	28♋	23♌	8♍
10	17♋	27♋	24♌	8♍
11	18♋	27♋	25♌	9♍
12	19♋	26♋	26♌	9♍
13	20♋	26♋	27♌	10♍
14	21♋	25♋	28♌	11♍
15	22♋	24♋	0♍	11♍
16	23♋	24♋	1♍	12♍
17	24♋	23♋	2♍	12♍
18	25♋	22♋	3♍	13♍
19	26♋	22♋	4♍	14♍
20	27♋	21♋	5♍	14♍
21	28♋	21♋	7♍	15♍
22	29♋	20♋	8♍	15♍
23	29♋	20♋	9♍	16♍
24	0♌	19♋	10♍	17♍
25	1♌	19♋	11♍	17♍
26	2♌	19♋	12♍	18♍
27	3♌	19♋	13♍	19♍
28	4♌	19♋	15♍	19♍
29	5♌	19♋	16♍	20♍
30	6♌	19♋	17♍	20♍
31	7♌	20♋	18♍	21♍

August

Day	☉	☿	♀	♂
1	8♌	20♋	19♍	22♍
2	9♌	21♋	20♍	22♍
3	10♌	21♋	21♍	23♍
4	11♌	22♋	23♍	23♍
5	12♌	23♋	24♍	24♍
6	13♌	24♋	25♍	25♍
7	14♌	25♋	26♍	25♍
8	15♌	26♋	27♍	26♍
9	16♌	27♋	28♍	27♍
10	17♌	28♋	29♍	27♍
11	18♌	0♌	1♎	28♍
12	19♌	1♌	2♎	28♍
13	20♌	3♌	3♎	29♍
14	21♌	5♌	4♎	0♎
15	22♌	6♌	5♎	0♎
16	22♌	8♌	6♎	1♎
17	23♌	10♌	7♎	2♎
18	24♌	12♌	8♎	2♎
19	25♌	14♌	9♎	3♎
20	26♌	16♌	10♎	4♎
21	27♌	18♌	12♎	4♎
22	28♌	20♌	13♎	5♎
23	29♌	22♌	14♎	5♎
24	0♍	24♌	15♎	6♎
25	1♍	26♌	16♎	7♎
26	2♍	28♌	17♎	7♎
27	3♍	0♍	18♎	8♎
28	4♍	2♍	19♎	9♎
29	5♍	3♍	20♎	9♎
30	6♍	5♍	21♎	10♎
31	7♍	7♍	22♎	11♎

September

Day	☉	☿	♀	♂
1	8♍	9♍	23♎	11♎
2	9♍	11♍	25♎	12♎
3	10♍	13♍	26♎	13♎
4	11♍	15♍	27♎	13♎
5	12♍	17♍	28♎	14♎
6	13♍	19♍	29♎	15♎
7	14♍	20♍	0♏	15♎
8	15♍	22♍	1♏	16♎
9	16♍	24♍	2♏	17♎
10	17♍	26♍	3♏	17♎
11	18♍	28♍	4♏	18♎
12	19♍	29♍	5♏	18♎
13	20♍	1♎	6♏	19♎
14	21♍	3♎	7♏	20♎
15	22♍	4♎	8♏	20♎
16	22♍	6♎	9♏	21♎
17	23♍	8♎	10♏	22♎
18	24♍	9♎	11♏	22♎
19	25♍	11♎	12♏	23♎
20	26♍	12♎	13♏	24♎
21	27♍	14♎	14♏	24♎
22	28♍	15♎	15♏	25♎
23	29♍	17♎	16♏	26♎
24	0♎	18♎	17♏	26♎
25	1♎	20♎	17♏	27♎
26	2♎	21♎	18♏	28♎
27	3♎	23♎	19♏	28♎
28	4♎	24♎	20♏	29♎
29	5♎	26♎	21♏	0♏
30	6♎	27♎	22♏	1♏

October

Day	☉	☿	♀	♂
1	7♎	29♎	23♏	1♏
2	8♎	0♏	24♏	2♏
3	9♎	1♏	25♏	3♏
4	10♎	3♏	25♏	3♏
5	11♎	4♏	26♏	4♏
6	12♎	5♏	27♏	5♏
7	13♎	7♏	28♏	5♏
8	14♎	8♏	29♏	6♏
9	15♎	9♏	29♏	7♏
10	16♎	10♏	0♐	7♏
11	17♎	11♏	1♐	8♏
12	18♎	13♏	2♐	9♏
13	19♎	14♏	2♐	9♏
14	20♎	15♏	3♐	10♏
15	21♎	16♏	4♐	11♏
16	22♎	17♏	4♐	11♏
17	23♎	18♏	5♐	12♏
18	24♎	19♏	6♐	13♏
19	25♎	19♏	6♐	14♏
20	26♎	20♏	7♐	14♏
21	27♎	21♏	7♐	15♏
22	28♎	21♏	8♐	16♏
23	29♎	22♏	8♐	16♏
24	0♏	22♏	9♐	17♏
25	1♏	23♏	9♐	18♏
26	2♏	23♏	10♐	18♏
27	3♏	23♏	10♐	19♏
28	4♏	23♏	10♐	20♏
29	5♏	23♏	11♐	21♏
30	6♏	22♏	11♐	21♏
31	7♏	22♏	11♐	22♏

November

Day	☉	☿	♀	♂
1	8♏	21♏	12♐	23♏
2	9♏	20♏	12♐	23♏
3	10♏	19♏	12♐	24♏
4	11♏	18♏	12♐	25♏
5	12♏	17♏	12♐	26♏
6	13♏	16♏	12♐	26♏
7	14♏	15♏	12♐	27♏
8	15♏	13♏	12♐	28♏
9	16♏	12♏	12♐	28♏
10	17♏	11♏	12♐	29♏
11	18♏	10♏	12♐	0♐
12	19♏	9♏	12♐	1♐
13	20♏	8♏	12♐	1♐
14	21♏	8♏	11♐	2♐
15	22♏	7♏	11♐	3♐
16	23♏	7♏	11♐	3♐
17	24♏	7♏	10♐	4♐
18	25♏	7♏	10♐	5♐
19	26♏	8♏	9♐	6♐
20	27♏	8♏	9♐	6♐
21	28♏	9♏	8♐	7♐
22	29♏	10♏	8♐	8♐
23	0♐	10♏	7♐	9♐
24	1♐	11♏	7♐	9♐
25	2♐	12♏	6♐	10♐
26	3♐	14♏	6♐	11♐
27	4♐	15♏	5♐	11♐
28	5♐	16♏	4♐	12♐
29	6♐	17♏	4♐	13♐
30	7♐	19♏	3♐	14♐

December

Day	☉	☿	♀	♂
1	8♐	20♏	3♐	14♐
2	9♐	21♏	2♐	15♐
3	10♐	23♏	1♐	16♐
4	11♐	24♏	1♐	17♐
5	12♐	26♏	0♐	17♐
6	13♐	27♏	0♐	18♐
7	14♐	29♏	29♏	19♐
8	15♐	0♐	29♏	20♐
9	16♐	1♐	29♏	20♐
10	17♐	3♐	28♏	21♐
11	18♐	5♐	28♏	22♐
12	19♐	6♐	28♏	23♐
13	20♐	8♐	27♏	23♐
14	21♐	9♐	27♏	24♐
15	22♐	11♐	27♏	25♐
16	23♐	12♐	27♏	26♐
17	24♐	14♐	27♏	26♐
18	25♐	15♐	27♏	27♐
19	26♐	17♐	27♏	28♐
20	27♐	18♐	27♏	29♐
21	28♐	20♐	27♏	29♐
22	0♑	21♐	27♏	0♑
23	1♑	23♐	27♏	1♑
24	2♑	24♐	28♏	2♑
25	3♑	26♐	28♏	2♑
26	4♑	28♐	28♏	3♑
27	5♑	29♐	29♏	4♑
28	6♑	1♑	29♏	5♑
29	7♑	2♑	29♏	5♑
30	8♑	4♑	0♐	6♑
31	9♑	5♑	0♐	7♑

☉ =Sun ☿ = Mercury ♀ = Venus ♂ = Mars ♈ = Aries ♉ = Taurus ♊ = Gemini ♋ = Cancer

January

Day	☉	☿	♀	♂
1	10♑	7♑	1♐	8♑
2	11♑	9♑	1♐	8♑
3	12♑	10♑	2♐	9♑
4	13♑	12♑	2♐	10♑
5	14♑	14♑	3♐	11♑
6	15♑	15♑	3♐	11♑
7	16♑	17♑	4♐	12♑
8	17♑	18♑	5♐	13♑
9	18♑	20♑	5♐	14♑
10	19♑	22♑	6♐	14♑
11	20♑	23♑	7♐	15♑
12	21♑	25♑	7♐	16♑
13	22♑	27♑	8♐	17♑
14	23♑	28♑	9♐	18♑
15	24♑	0♒	10♐	18♑
16	25♑	2♒	10♐	19♑
17	26♑	3♒	11♐	20♑
18	27♑	5♒	12♐	21♑
19	28♑	7♒	13♐	21♑
20	29♑	9♒	14♐	22♑
21	0♒	10♒	15♐	23♑
22	1♒	12♒	15♐	24♑
23	2♒	14♒	16♐	25♑
24	3♒	15♒	17♐	25♑
25	4♒	17♒	18♐	26♑
26	5♒	19♒	19♐	27♑
27	6♒	20♒	20♐	28♑
28	7♒	22♒	21♐	28♑
29	8♒	24♒	22♐	29♑
30	9♒	25♒	23♐	0♒
31	10♒	27♒	24♐	1♒

April

Day	☉	☿	♀	♂
1	10♈	15♓	29♒	18♓
2	11♈	17♓	1♓	19♓
3	12♈	18♓	2♓	19♓
4	13♈	20♓	3♓	20♓
5	14♈	21♓	4♓	21♓
6	15♈	23♓	5♓	22♓
7	16♈	24♓	7♓	22♓
8	17♈	26♓	8♓	23♓
9	18♈	27♓	9♓	24♓
10	19♈	29♓	10♓	25♓
11	20♈	1♈	11♓	26♓
12	21♈	2♈	12♓	26♓
13	22♈	4♈	14♓	27♓
14	23♈	6♈	15♓	28♓
15	24♈	8♈	16♓	29♓
16	25♈	9♈	17♓	29♓
17	26♈	11♈	18♓	0♈
18	27♈	13♈	20♓	1♈
19	28♈	15♈	21♓	2♈
20	29♈	17♈	22♓	3♈
21	0♉	19♈	23♓	3♈
22	1♉	21♈	24♓	4♈
23	2♉	23♈	25♓	5♈
24	3♉	25♈	27♓	6♈
25	4♉	27♈	28♓	6♈
26	5♉	29♈	29♓	7♈
27	6♉	1♉	0♈	8♈
28	7♉	3♉	1♈	9♈
29	8♉	5♉	3♈	10♈
30	9♉	7♉	4♈	10♈

July

Day	☉	☿	♀	♂
1	8♋	2♋	18♊	26♉
2	9♋	2♋	20♊	27♉
3	10♋	1♋	21♊	28♉
4	11♋	1♋	22♊	29♉
5	12♋	1♋	23♊	29♉
6	13♋	0♋	24♊	0♊
7	14♋	0♋	26♊	1♊
8	15♋	0♋	27♊	1♊
9	16♋	0♋	28♊	2♊
10	17♋	0♋	29♊	3♊
11	18♋	1♋	1♋	3♊
12	19♋	1♋	2♋	4♊
13	20♋	1♋	3♋	5♊
14	21♋	2♋	4♋	6♊
15	22♋	2♋	5♋	6♊
16	23♋	3♋	7♋	7♊
17	24♋	4♋	8♋	8♊
18	24♋	4♋	9♋	8♊
19	25♋	5♋	10♋	9♊
20	26♋	6♋	12♋	10♊
21	27♋	7♋	13♋	10♊
22	28♋	8♋	14♋	11♊
23	29♋	10♋	15♋	12♊
24	0♌	11♋	16♋	13♊
25	1♌	12♋	18♋	13♊
26	2♌	14♋	19♋	14♊
27	3♌	15♋	20♋	15♊
28	4♌	17♋	21♋	15♊
29	5♌	19♋	23♋	16♊
30	6♌	20♋	24♋	17♊
31	7♌	22♋	25♋	17♊

October

Day	☉	☿	♀	♂
1	7♎	3♏	12♎	26♋
2	8♎	3♏	13♎	27♋
3	9♎	4♏	14♎	27♋
4	10♎	5♏	16♎	28♋
5	11♎	5♏	17♎	29♋
6	12♎	6♏	18♎	29♋
7	13♎	6♏	19♎	0♌
8	14♎	7♏	21♎	0♌
9	15♎	7♏	22♎	1♌
10	16♎	7♏	23♎	1♌
11	17♎	7♏	24♎	2♌
12	18♎	7♏	26♎	2♌
13	19♎	7♏	27♎	3♌
14	20♎	6♏	28♎	3♌
15	21♎	6♏	29♎	4♌
16	22♎	5♏	1♏	5♌
17	23♎	4♏	2♏	5♌
18	24♎	3♏	3♏	6♌
19	25♎	2♏	4♏	6♌
20	26♎	1♏	6♏	7♌
21	27♎	0♏	7♏	7♌
22	28♎	29♎	8♏	8♌
23	29♎	27♎	9♏	8♌
24	0♏	26♎	11♏	9♌
25	1♏	25♎	12♏	9♌
26	2♏	24♎	13♏	10♌
27	3♏	23♎	14♏	10♌
28	4♏	22♎	16♏	11♌
29	5♏	22♎	17♏	11♌
30	6♏	21♎	18♏	12♌
31	7♏	21♎	19♏	12♌

February

Day	☉	☿	♀	♂
1	11♒	28♒	25♐	2♒
2	12♒	0♓	26♐	2♒
3	13♒	1♓	27♐	3♒
4	14♒	2♓	28♐	4♒
5	15♒	3♓	29♐	5♒
6	16♒	5♓	0♑	5♒
7	17♒	6♓	1♑	6♒
8	18♒	6♓	2♑	7♒
9	19♒	7♓	3♑	8♒
10	20♒	8♓	4♑	9♒
11	21♒	8♓	5♑	9♒
12	22♒	8♓	6♑	10♒
13	23♒	8♓	7♑	11♒
14	24♒	8♓	8♑	12♒
15	25♒	8♓	9♑	12♒
16	26♒	7♓	10♑	13♒
17	27♒	6♓	11♑	14♒
18	28♒	6♓	12♑	15♒
19	29♒	5♓	13♑	16♒
20	0♓	4♓	14♑	16♒
21	1♓	3♓	15♑	17♒
22	3♓	2♓	16♑	18♒
23	4♓	0♓	17♑	19♒
24	5♓	29♒	19♑	20♒
25	6♓	28♒	20♑	20♒
26	7♓	27♒	21♑	21♒
27	8♓	26♒	22♑	22♒
28	9♓	26♒	23♑	23♒

May

Day	☉	☿	♀	♂
1	10♉	9♉	5♈	11♈
2	11♉	11♉	6♈	12♈
3	12♉	13♉	7♈	13♈
4	13♉	16♉	9♈	13♈
5	14♉	18♉	10♈	14♈
6	15♉	20♉	11♈	15♈
7	16♉	22♉	12♈	16♈
8	17♉	24♉	13♈	16♈
9	17♉	26♉	15♈	17♈
10	18♉	28♉	16♈	18♈
11	19♉	0♊	17♈	19♈
12	20♉	2♊	18♈	19♈
13	21♉	4♊	19♈	20♈
14	22♉	6♊	21♈	21♈
15	23♉	8♊	22♈	22♈
16	24♉	10♊	23♈	23♈
17	25♉	12♊	24♈	23♈
18	26♉	14♊	25♈	24♈
19	27♉	16♊	27♈	25♈
20	28♉	17♊	28♈	26♈
21	29♉	19♊	29♈	26♈
22	0♊	20♊	0♉	27♈
23	1♊	22♊	1♉	28♈
24	2♊	23♊	3♉	29♈
25	3♊	25♊	4♉	29♈
26	4♊	26♊	5♉	0♉
27	5♊	27♊	6♉	1♉
28	6♊	29♊	7♉	2♉
29	7♊	0♋	9♉	2♉
30	8♊	1♋	10♉	3♉
31	9♊	2♋	11♉	4♉

August

Day	☉	☿	♀	♂
1	8♌	24♋	26♋	18♊
2	9♌	26♋	28♋	19♊
3	10♌	28♋	29♋	19♊
4	11♌	0♌	0♌	20♊
5	12♌	2♌	1♌	21♊
6	13♌	4♌	2♌	21♊
7	14♌	6♌	4♌	22♊
8	15♌	8♌	5♌	23♊
9	16♌	10♌	6♌	23♊
10	16♌	12♌	7♌	24♊
11	17♌	14♌	9♌	25♊
12	18♌	16♌	10♌	25♊
13	19♌	18♌	11♌	26♊
14	20♌	20♌	12♌	27♊
15	21♌	22♌	14♌	27♊
16	22♌	24♌	15♌	28♊
17	23♌	26♌	16♌	29♊
18	24♌	28♌	17♌	29♊
19	25♌	0♍	18♌	0♋
20	26♌	2♍	20♌	1♋
21	27♌	4♍	21♌	1♋
22	28♌	6♍	22♌	2♋
23	29♌	8♍	23♌	2♋
24	0♍	9♍	25♌	3♋
25	1♍	11♍	26♌	4♋
26	2♍	13♍	27♌	4♋
27	3♍	15♍	28♌	5♋
28	4♍	17♍	0♍	6♋
29	5♍	18♍	1♍	6♋
30	6♍	20♍	2♍	7♋
31	7♍	22♍	3♍	8♋

November

Day	☉	☿	♀	♂
1	8♏	21♎	21♏	13♌
2	9♏	22♎	22♏	13♌
3	10♏	22♎	23♏	14♌
4	11♏	22♎	24♏	14♌
5	12♏	23♎	26♏	14♌
6	13♏	24♎	27♏	15♌
7	14♏	25♎	28♏	15♌
8	15♏	26♎	29♏	16♌
9	16♏	27♎	1♐	16♌
10	17♏	28♎	2♐	17♌
11	18♏	0♏	3♐	17♌
12	19♏	1♏	4♐	18♌
13	20♏	2♏	6♐	18♌
14	21♏	4♏	7♐	18♌
15	22♏	5♏	8♐	19♌
16	23♏	6♏	9♐	19♌
17	24♏	8♏	11♐	20♌
18	25♏	9♏	12♐	20♌
19	26♏	11♏	13♐	20♌
20	27♏	13♏	14♐	21♌
21	28♏	14♏	16♐	21♌
22	29♏	16♏	17♐	22♌
23	0♐	17♏	18♐	22♌
24	1♐	19♏	19♐	22♌
25	2♐	20♏	21♐	23♌
26	3♐	22♏	22♐	23♌
27	4♐	23♏	23♐	23♌
28	5♐	25♏	24♐	24♌
29	6♐	27♏	26♐	24♌
30	7♐	28♏	27♐	24♌

March

Day	☉	☿	♀	♂
1	10♓	25♒	24♑	23♒
2	11♓	24♒	25♑	24♒
3	12♓	24♒	26♑	25♒
4	13♓	24♒	27♑	26♒
5	14♓	23♒	28♑	27♒
6	15♓	23♒	0♒	27♒
7	16♓	23♒	1♒	28♒
8	17♓	23♒	2♒	29♒
9	18♓	24♒	3♒	0♓
10	19♓	24♒	4♒	1♓
11	20♓	24♒	5♒	1♓
12	21♓	25♒	6♒	2♓
13	22♓	25♒	8♒	3♓
14	23♓	26♒	9♒	4♓
15	24♓	27♒	10♒	4♓
16	25♓	27♒	11♒	5♓
17	26♓	28♒	12♒	6♓
18	27♓	29♒	13♒	7♓
19	28♓	0♓	14♒	8♓
20	29♓	1♓	16♒	8♓
21	0♈	2♓	17♒	9♓
22	1♈	3♓	18♒	10♓
23	1♈	4♓	19♒	11♓
24	2♈	5♓	20♒	12♓
25	3♈	6♓	21♒	13♓
26	4♈	7♓	23♒	13♓
27	5♈	9♓	24♒	14♓
28	6♈	10♓	25♒	15♓
29	7♈	11♓	26♒	15♓
30	8♈	13♓	27♒	16♓
31	9♈	14♓	28♒	17♓

June

Day	☉	☿	♀	♂
1	10♊	3♋	12♉	5♉
2	11♊	4♋	13♉	5♉
3	12♊	5♋	15♉	6♉
4	13♊	5♋	16♉	7♉
5	13♊	6♋	17♉	8♉
6	14♊	7♋	18♉	8♉
7	15♊	7♋	19♉	9♉
8	16♊	8♋	21♉	10♉
9	17♊	8♋	22♉	10♉
10	18♊	9♋	23♉	11♉
11	19♊	9♋	24♉	12♉
12	20♊	9♋	25♉	13♉
13	21♊	9♋	27♉	13♉
14	22♊	9♋	28♉	14♉
15	23♊	9♋	29♉	15♉
16	24♊	9♋	0♊	16♉
17	25♊	9♋	1♊	16♉
18	26♊	9♋	3♊	17♉
19	27♊	9♋	4♊	18♉
20	28♊	8♋	5♊	18♉
21	29♊	8♋	6♊	19♉
22	0♋	7♋	7♊	20♉
23	1♋	7♋	9♊	21♉
24	2♋	6♋	10♊	21♉
25	3♋	6♋	11♊	22♉
26	4♋	5♋	12♊	23♉
27	4♋	4♋	14♊	24♉
28	5♋	4♋	15♊	24♉
29	6♋	3♋	16♊	25♉
30	7♋	3♋	17♊	26♉

September

Day	☉	☿	♀	♂
1	8♍	23♍	5♍	8♋
2	9♍	25♍	6♍	9♋
3	10♍	27♍	7♍	9♋
4	11♍	28♍	8♍	10♋
5	12♍	0♎	10♍	11♋
6	13♍	1♎	11♍	11♋
7	13♍	3♎	12♍	12♋
8	14♍	4♎	13♍	13♋
9	15♍	6♎	14♍	13♋
10	16♍	7♎	16♍	14♋
11	17♍	9♎	17♍	14♋
12	18♍	10♎	18♍	15♋
13	19♍	12♎	19♍	16♋
14	20♍	13♎	21♍	16♋
15	21♍	14♎	22♍	17♋
16	22♍	16♎	23♍	17♋
17	23♍	17♎	24♍	18♋
18	24♍	18♎	26♍	19♋
19	25♍	20♎	27♍	19♋
20	26♍	21♎	28♍	20♋
21	27♍	22♎	29♍	20♋
22	28♍	23♎	1♎	21♋
23	29♍	25♎	2♎	22♋
24	0♎	26♎	3♎	22♋
25	1♎	27♎	4♎	23♋
26	2♎	28♎	6♎	23♋
27	3♎	29♎	7♎	24♋
28	4♎	0♏	8♎	25♋
29	5♎	1♏	9♎	25♋
30	6♎	2♏	11♎	26♋

December

Day	☉	☿	♀	♂
1	8♐	0♐	28♐	25♌
2	9♐	1♐	29♐	25♌
3	10♐	3♐	1♑	25♌
4	11♐	4♐	2♑	26♌
5	12♐	6♐	3♑	26♌
6	13♐	8♐	4♑	26♌
7	14♐	9♐	6♑	26♌
8	15♐	11♐	7♑	27♌
9	16♐	12♐	8♑	27♌
10	17♐	14♐	9♑	27♌
11	18♐	15♐	11♑	27♌
12	19♐	17♐	12♑	28♌
13	20♐	19♐	13♑	28♌
14	21♐	20♐	14♑	28♌
15	22♐	22♐	16♑	28♌
16	23♐	23♐	17♑	28♌
17	24♐	25♐	18♑	29♌
18	25♐	26♐	19♑	29♌
19	26♐	28♐	20♑	29♌
20	27♐	0♑	22♑	29♌
21	28♐	1♑	23♑	29♌
22	29♐	3♑	24♑	29♌
23	0♑	4♑	25♑	29♌
24	1♑	6♑	27♑	29♌
25	2♑	8♑	28♑	0♍
26	3♑	9♑	29♑	0♍
27	4♑	11♑	0♒	0♍
28	5♑	12♑	2♒	0♍
29	6♑	14♑	3♒	0♍
30	7♑	16♑	4♒	0♍
31	8♑	17♑	5♒	0♍

Planetary Positions

♌ = Leo ♍ = Virgo ♎ = Libra ♏ = Scorpio ♐ = Sagittarius ♑ = Capricorn ♒ = Aquarius ♓ = Pisces

1916

January

Day	☉	☿	♀	♂
1	9♑	19♑	7♒	0♍
2	10♑	21♑	8♒	0♍
3	11♑	22♑	9♒	0♍
4	13♑	24♑	10♒	0♍
5	14♑	25♑	12♒	0♍
6	15♑	27♑	13♒	0♍
7	16♑	29♑	14♒	0♍
8	17♑	0♒	15♒	29♌
9	18♑	2♒	17♒	29♌
10	19♑	3♒	18♒	29♌
11	20♑	5♒	19♒	29♌
12	21♑	7♒	20♒	29♌
13	22♑	8♒	22♒	29♌
14	23♑	10♒	23♒	29♌
15	24♑	11♒	24♒	28♌
16	25♑	12♒	25♒	28♌
17	26♑	14♒	26♒	28♌
18	27♑	15♒	28♒	28♌
19	28♑	16♒	29♒	28♌
20	29♑	17♒	0♓	27♌
21	0♒	18♒	1♓	27♌
22	1♒	19♒	3♓	27♌
23	2♒	20♒	4♓	27♌
24	3♒	21♒	5♓	26♌
25	4♒	21♒	6♓	26♌
26	5♒	22♒	8♓	26♌
27	6♒	22♒	9♓	25♌
28	7♒	22♒	10♓	25♌
29	8♒	21♒	11♓	25♌
30	9♒	21♒	12♓	24♌
31	10♒	20♒	14♓	24♌

February

Day	☉	☿	♀	♂
1	11♒	20♒	15♓	24♌
2	12♒	19♒	16♓	23♌
3	13♒	18♒	17♓	23♌
4	14♒	17♒	19♓	22♌
5	15♒	15♒	20♓	22♌
6	16♒	14♒	21♓	22♌
7	17♒	13♒	22♓	21♌
8	18♒	12♒	23♓	21♌
9	19♒	11♒	25♓	20♌
10	20♒	10♒	26♓	20♌
11	21♒	9♒	27♓	20♌
12	22♒	8♒	28♓	19♌
13	23♒	7♒	29♓	19♌
14	24♒	7♒	1♈	18♌
15	25♒	7♒	2♈	18♌
16	26♒	6♒	3♈	18♌
17	27♒	6♒	4♈	17♌
18	28♒	6♒	5♈	17♌
19	29♒	6♒	7♈	17♌
20	0♓	7♒	8♈	16♌
21	1♓	7♒	9♈	16♌
22	2♓	7♒	10♈	15♌
23	3♓	8♒	11♈	15♌
24	4♓	8♒	13♈	15♌
25	5♓	9♒	14♈	14♌
26	6♓	10♒	15♈	14♌
27	7♓	11♒	16♈	14♌
28	8♓	11♒	17♈	14♌
29	9♓	12♒	19♈	13♌

March

Day	☉	☿	♀	♂
1	10♓	13♒	20♈	13♌
2	11♓	14♒	21♈	13♌
3	12♓	15♒	22♈	12♌
4	13♓	16♒	23♈	12♌
5	14♓	17♒	25♈	12♌
6	15♓	19♒	26♈	12♌
7	16♓	20♒	27♈	12♌
8	17♓	21♒	28♈	11♌
9	18♓	22♒	29♈	11♌
10	19♓	23♒	0♉	11♌
11	20♓	25♒	2♉	11♌
12	21♓	26♒	3♉	11♌
13	22♓	27♒	4♉	11♌
14	23♓	29♒	5♉	11♌
15	24♓	0♓	6♉	11♌
16	25♓	2♓	7♉	11♌
17	26♓	3♓	8♉	10♌
18	27♓	5♓	10♉	10♌
19	28♓	6♓	11♉	10♌
20	29♓	8♓	12♉	10♌
21	0♈	9♓	13♉	10♌
22	1♈	11♓	14♉	10♌
23	2♈	12♓	15♉	10♌
24	3♈	14♓	16♉	10♌
25	4♈	16♓	17♉	10♌
26	5♈	17♓	19♉	10♌
27	6♈	19♓	20♉	11♌
28	7♈	21♓	21♉	11♌
29	8♈	22♓	22♉	11♌
30	9♈	24♓	23♉	11♌
31	10♈	26♓	24♉	11♌

April

Day	☉	☿	♀	♂
1	11♈	28♓	25♉	11♌
2	12♈	0♈	26♉	11♌
3	13♈	1♈	27♉	11♌
4	14♈	3♈	29♉	11♌
5	15♈	5♈	0♊	12♌
6	16♈	7♈	1♊	12♌
7	17♈	9♈	2♊	12♌
8	18♈	11♈	3♊	12♌
9	19♈	13♈	4♊	12♌
10	20♈	15♈	5♊	12♌
11	21♈	17♈	6♊	13♌
12	22♈	19♈	7♊	13♌
13	23♈	21♈	8♊	13♌
14	24♈	23♈	9♊	13♌
15	25♈	25♈	10♊	14♌
16	26♈	27♈	11♊	14♌
17	27♈	29♈	12♊	14♌
18	28♈	2♉	13♊	14♌
19	29♈	4♉	14♊	15♌
20	0♉	6♉	15♊	15♌
21	1♉	8♉	16♊	15♌
22	2♉	10♉	17♊	16♌
23	3♉	12♉	18♊	16♌
24	4♉	14♉	19♊	16♌
25	5♉	16♉	20♊	16♌
26	6♉	18♉	21♊	17♌
27	7♉	20♉	22♊	17♌
28	8♉	22♉	23♊	17♌
29	9♉	24♉	24♊	18♌
30	10♉	26♉	25♊	18♌

May

Day	☉	☿	♀	♂
1	10♉	28♉	26♊	18♌
2	11♉	29♉	27♊	19♌
3	12♉	1♊	28♊	19♌
4	13♉	2♊	29♊	20♌
5	14♉	4♊	29♊	20♌
6	15♉	5♊	0♋	20♌
7	16♉	7♊	1♋	21♌
8	17♉	8♊	2♋	21♌
9	18♉	9♊	3♋	21♌
10	19♉	11♊	4♋	22♌
11	20♉	12♊	4♋	22♌
12	21♉	13♊	5♋	23♌
13	22♉	14♊	6♋	23♌
14	23♉	15♊	7♋	24♌
15	24♉	15♊	8♋	24♌
16	25♉	16♊	8♋	24♌
17	26♉	17♊	9♋	25♌
18	27♉	17♊	10♋	25♌
19	28♉	18♊	10♋	26♌
20	29♉	18♊	11♋	26♌
21	0♊	19♊	12♋	27♌
22	1♊	19♊	12♋	27♌
23	2♊	19♊	13♋	27♌
24	3♊	19♊	14♋	28♌
25	4♊	19♊	14♋	28♌
26	5♊	19♊	15♋	29♌
27	6♊	19♊	15♋	29♌
28	7♊	19♊	16♋	0♍
29	7♊	19♊	16♋	0♍
30	8♊	18♊	17♋	1♍
31	9♊	18♊	17♋	1♍

June

Day	☉	☿	♀	♂
1	10♊	18♊	17♋	2♍
2	11♊	17♊	18♋	2♍
3	12♊	17♊	18♋	3♍
4	13♊	16♊	19♋	3♍
5	14♊	15♊	19♋	4♍
6	15♊	15♊	19♋	4♍
7	16♊	14♊	19♋	5♍
8	17♊	14♊	19♋	5♍
9	18♊	13♊	20♋	6♍
10	19♊	13♊	20♋	6♍
11	20♊	12♊	20♋	7♍
12	21♊	12♊	20♋	7♍
13	22♊	12♊	20♋	8♍
14	23♊	11♊	20♋	8♍
15	24♊	11♊	20♋	9♍
16	25♊	11♊	19♋	9♍
17	26♊	11♊	19♋	10♍
18	27♊	11♊	19♋	10♍
19	28♊	11♊	19♋	11♍
20	29♊	11♊	18♋	11♍
21	29♊	11♊	18♋	12♍
22	0♋	11♊	18♋	12♍
23	1♋	12♊	17♋	13♍
24	2♋	12♊	17♋	13♍
25	3♋	13♊	16♋	14♍
26	4♋	13♊	16♋	15♍
27	5♋	14♊	15♋	15♍
28	6♋	15♊	15♋	16♍
29	7♋	16♊	14♋	16♍
30	8♋	16♊	14♋	17♍

July

Day	☉	☿	♀	♂
1	9♋	17♊	13♋	17♍
2	10♋	18♊	13♋	18♍
3	11♋	20♊	12♋	18♍
4	12♋	21♊	11♋	19♍
5	13♋	22♊	11♋	20♍
6	14♋	23♊	10♋	20♍
7	15♋	25♊	9♋	21♍
8	16♋	26♊	9♋	21♍
9	17♋	28♊	8♋	22♍
10	18♋	29♊	8♋	22♍
11	19♋	1♋	7♋	23♍
12	19♋	2♋	7♋	24♍
13	20♋	4♋	6♋	24♍
14	21♋	6♋	6♋	25♍
15	22♋	8♋	5♋	25♍
16	23♋	10♋	5♋	26♍
17	24♋	12♋	5♋	26♍
18	25♋	14♋	4♋	27♍
19	26♋	16♋	4♋	28♍
20	27♋	18♋	4♋	28♍
21	28♋	20♋	4♋	29♍
22	29♋	22♋	3♋	29♍
23	0♌	24♋	3♋	0♎
24	1♌	26♋	3♋	1♎
25	2♌	28♋	3♋	1♎
26	3♌	0♌	3♋	2♎
27	4♌	2♌	3♋	2♎
28	5♌	5♌	3♋	3♎
29	6♌	7♌	3♋	4♎
30	7♌	9♌	4♋	4♎
31	8♌	11♌	4♋	5♎

August

Day	☉	☿	♀	♂
1	9♌	13♌	4♋	5♎
2	10♌	15♌	4♋	6♎
3	11♌	17♌	5♋	7♎
4	11♌	19♌	5♋	7♎
5	12♌	21♌	5♋	8♎
6	13♌	23♌	6♋	8♎
7	14♌	25♌	6♋	9♎
8	15♌	26♌	7♋	10♎
9	16♌	28♌	7♋	10♎
10	17♌	0♍	7♋	11♎
11	18♌	2♍	8♋	12♎
12	19♌	4♍	8♋	12♎
13	20♌	5♍	9♋	13♎
14	21♌	7♍	10♋	13♎
15	22♌	9♍	10♋	14♎
16	23♌	10♍	11♋	15♎
17	24♌	12♍	11♋	15♎
18	25♌	14♍	12♋	16♎
19	26♌	15♍	13♋	17♎
20	27♌	17♍	14♋	17♎
21	28♌	18♍	14♋	18♎
22	29♌	20♍	15♋	19♎
23	0♍	21♍	16♋	19♎
24	1♍	23♍	16♋	20♎
25	2♍	24♍	17♋	20♎
26	3♍	26♍	18♋	21♎
27	4♍	27♍	19♋	22♎
28	5♍	29♍	20♋	22♎
29	6♍	0♎	20♋	23♎
30	6♍	1♎	21♋	24♎
31	7♍	3♎	22♋	24♎

September

Day	☉	☿	♀	♂
1	8♍	4♎	23♋	25♎
2	9♍	5♎	24♋	26♎
3	10♍	6♎	25♋	26♎
4	11♍	8♎	26♋	27♎
5	12♍	9♎	27♋	28♎
6	13♍	10♎	27♋	28♎
7	14♍	11♎	28♋	29♎
8	15♍	12♎	29♋	0♏
9	16♍	13♎	0♌	0♏
10	17♍	14♎	1♌	1♏
11	18♍	15♎	2♌	2♏
12	19♍	16♎	3♌	2♏
13	20♍	17♎	4♌	3♏
14	21♍	17♎	5♌	4♏
15	22♍	18♎	6♌	4♏
16	23♍	19♎	7♌	5♏
17	24♍	19♎	8♌	6♏
18	25♍	20♎	9♌	6♏
19	26♍	20♎	10♌	7♏
20	27♍	20♎	11♌	8♏
21	28♍	21♎	12♌	8♏
22	29♍	21♎	13♌	9♏
23	0♎	21♎	14♌	10♏
24	1♎	21♎	15♌	10♏
25	2♎	20♎	16♌	11♏
26	3♎	20♎	17♌	11♏
27	4♎	20♎	18♌	12♏
28	5♎	19♎	19♌	13♏
29	6♎	18♎	21♌	14♏
30	7♎	17♎	22♌	15♏

October

Day	☉	☿	♀	♂
1	8♎	17♎	23♌	15♏
2	9♎	16♎	24♌	16♏
3	10♎	14♎	25♌	17♏
4	11♎	13♎	26♌	17♏
5	12♎	12♎	27♌	18♏
6	13♎	11♎	28♌	19♏
7	14♎	10♎	29♌	19♏
8	15♎	9♎	0♍	20♏
9	16♎	8♎	1♍	21♏
10	17♎	7♎	3♍	22♏
11	18♎	6♎	4♍	22♏
12	19♎	6♎	5♍	23♏
13	20♎	6♎	6♍	24♏
14	21♎	5♎	7♍	24♏
15	22♎	6♎	8♍	25♏
16	23♎	6♎	9♍	26♏
17	23♎	6♎	10♍	26♏
18	24♎	7♎	12♍	27♏
19	25♎	7♎	13♍	28♏
20	26♎	8♎	14♍	29♏
21	27♎	9♎	15♍	29♏
22	28♎	10♎	16♍	0♐
23	29♎	12♎	17♍	1♐
24	0♏	13♎	18♍	1♐
25	1♏	14♎	20♍	2♐
26	2♏	16♎	21♍	3♐
27	3♏	17♎	22♍	4♐
28	4♏	18♎	23♍	4♐
29	5♏	20♎	24♍	5♐
30	6♏	22♎	25♍	6♐
31	7♏	23♎	27♍	7♐

November

Day	☉	☿	♀	♂
1	8♏	25♎	28♍	7♐
2	9♏	26♎	29♍	8♐
3	10♏	28♎	0♎	9♐
4	11♏	29♎	2♎	9♐
5	12♏	1♏	3♎	10♐
6	13♏	3♏	4♎	11♐
7	14♏	4♏	5♎	12♐
8	15♏	6♏	6♎	12♐
9	16♏	8♏	7♎	13♐
10	17♏	9♏	9♎	14♐
11	18♏	11♏	10♎	15♐
12	19♏	13♏	11♎	15♐
13	20♏	14♏	12♎	16♐
14	22♏	16♏	13♎	17♐
15	23♏	17♏	15♎	18♐
16	24♏	19♏	16♎	18♐
17	25♏	21♏	17♎	19♐
18	26♏	22♏	18♎	20♐
19	27♏	24♏	19♎	21♐
20	28♏	25♏	21♎	21♐
21	29♏	27♏	22♎	22♐
22	0♐	29♏	23♎	23♐
23	1♐	0♐	24♎	24♐
24	2♐	2♐	25♎	24♐
25	3♐	3♐	27♎	25♐
26	4♐	5♐	28♎	26♐
27	5♐	6♐	29♎	27♐
28	6♐	8♐	0♏	27♐
29	7♐	10♐	2♏	28♐
30	8♐	11♐	3♏	29♐

December

Day	☉	☿	♀	♂
1	9♐	13♐	4♏	0♑
2	10♐	14♐	5♏	0♑
3	11♐	16♐	6♏	1♑
4	12♐	17♐	8♏	2♑
5	13♐	19♐	9♏	3♑
6	14♐	20♐	10♏	3♑
7	15♐	22♐	11♏	4♑
8	16♐	24♐	13♏	5♑
9	17♐	25♐	14♏	6♑
10	18♐	27♐	15♏	6♑
11	19♐	28♐	16♏	7♑
12	20♐	0♑	17♏	8♑
13	21♐	1♑	19♏	9♑
14	22♐	3♑	20♏	10♑
15	23♐	5♑	21♏	10♑
16	24♐	6♑	22♏	11♑
17	25♐	8♑	24♏	12♑
18	26♐	9♑	25♏	13♑
19	27♐	11♑	26♏	13♑
20	28♐	12♑	27♏	14♑
21	29♐	14♑	29♏	15♑
22	0♑	15♑	0♐	16♑
23	1♑	17♑	1♐	16♑
24	2♑	18♑	2♐	17♑
25	3♑	20♑	4♐	18♑
26	4♑	21♑	5♐	19♑
27	5♑	23♑	6♐	20♑
28	6♑	24♑	7♐	20♑
29	7♑	26♑	9♐	21♑
30	8♑	27♑	10♐	22♑
31	9♑	28♑	11♐	23♑

1917

Your Starway to Love

☉ =Sun ☿ = Mercury ♀ = Venus ♂ = Mars ♈ = Aries ♉ = Taurus ♊ = Gemini ♋ = Cancer

January

Day	☉	☿	♀	♂
1	10♑	29♑	12♐	23♑
2	11♑	1♒	14♐	24♑
3	12♑	2♒	15♐	25♑
4	13♑	3♒	16♐	26♑
5	14♑	3♒	17♐	27♑
6	15♑	4♒	18♐	27♑
7	16♑	5♒	20♐	28♑
8	17♑	5♒	21♐	29♑
9	18♑	6♒	22♐	0♒
10	19♑	6♒	23♐	1♒
11	20♑	6♒	25♐	1♒
12	21♑	5♒	26♐	2♒
13	22♑	5♒	27♐	3♒
14	23♑	4♒	28♐	4♒
15	25♑	3♒	0♑	4♒
16	26♑	2♒	1♑	5♒
17	27♑	1♒	2♑	6♒
18	28♑	0♒	3♑	7♒
19	29♑	29♑	5♑	8♒
20	0♒	27♑	6♑	8♒
21	1♒	26♑	7♑	9♒
22	2♒	25♑	8♑	10♒
23	3♒	24♑	10♑	11♒
24	4♒	23♑	11♑	12♒
25	5♒	22♑	12♑	12♒
26	6♒	21♑	13♑	13♒
27	7♒	21♑	15♑	14♒
28	8♒	20♑	16♑	15♒
29	9♒	20♑	17♑	15♒
30	10♒	20♑	18♑	16♒
31	11♒	20♑	20♑	17♒

February

Day	☉	☿	♀	♂
1	12♒	20♑	21♑	18♒
2	13♒	20♑	22♑	19♒
3	14♒	20♑	23♑	19♒
4	15♒	21♑	25♑	20♒
5	16♒	21♑	26♑	21♒
6	17♒	22♑	27♑	22♒
7	18♒	23♑	28♑	23♒
8	19♒	23♑	0♒	23♒
9	20♒	24♑	1♒	24♒
10	21♒	25♑	2♒	25♒
11	22♒	26♑	3♒	26♒
12	23♒	27♑	5♒	27♒
13	24♒	28♑	6♒	27♒
14	25♒	29♑	7♒	28♒
15	26♒	0♒	8♒	29♒
16	27♒	1♒	10♒	0♓
17	28♒	2♒	11♒	1♓
18	29♒	4♒	12♒	1♓
19	0♓	5♒	13♒	2♓
20	1♓	6♒	15♒	3♓
21	2♓	7♒	16♒	4♓
22	3♓	9♒	17♒	4♓
23	4♓	10♒	18♒	5♓
24	5♓	11♒	20♒	6♓
25	6♓	13♒	21♒	7♓
26	7♓	14♒	22♒	8♓
27	8♓	16♒	23♒	8♓
28	9♓	17♒	25♒	9♓

March

Day	☉	☿	♀	♂
1	10♓	19♒	26♒	10♓
2	11♓	20♒	27♒	11♓
3	12♓	21♒	28♒	12♓
4	13♓	23♒	0♓	12♓
5	14♓	25♒	1♓	13♓
6	15♓	26♒	2♓	14♓
7	16♓	28♒	3♓	15♓
8	17♓	29♒	5♓	15♓
9	18♓	1♓	6♓	16♓
10	19♓	3♓	7♓	17♓
11	20♓	4♓	8♓	18♓
12	21♓	6♓	10♓	19♓
13	22♓	8♓	11♓	19♓
14	23♓	9♓	12♓	20♓
15	24♓	11♓	13♓	21♓
16	25♓	13♓	15♓	22♓
17	26♓	15♓	16♓	23♓
18	27♓	16♓	17♓	23♓
19	28♓	18♓	18♓	24♓
20	29♓	20♓	19♓	25♓
21	0♈	22♓	21♓	26♓
22	1♈	24♓	22♓	26♓
23	2♈	26♓	23♓	27♓
24	3♈	28♓	24♓	28♓
25	4♈	29♓	26♓	29♓
26	5♈	1♈	27♓	0♈
27	6♈	3♈	28♓	0♈
28	7♈	5♈	29♓	1♈
29	8♈	7♈	1♈	2♈
30	9♈	9♈	2♈	3♈
31	10♈	11♈	3♈	3♈

April

Day	☉	☿	♀	♂
1	11♈	14♈	4♈	4♈
2	12♈	16♈	6♈	5♈
3	13♈	18♈	7♈	6♈
4	14♈	20♈	8♈	7♈
5	15♈	22♈	9♈	7♈
6	16♈	24♈	11♈	8♈
7	17♈	26♈	12♈	9♈
8	18♈	28♈	13♈	10♈
9	19♈	0♉	14♈	10♈
10	20♈	2♉	16♈	11♈
11	21♈	4♉	17♈	12♈
12	22♈	6♉	18♈	13♈
13	23♈	8♉	19♈	14♈
14	24♈	9♉	21♈	14♈
15	25♈	11♉	22♈	15♈
16	26♈	13♉	23♈	16♈
17	27♈	14♉	24♈	17♈
18	28♈	16♉	25♈	17♈
19	29♈	17♉	27♈	18♈
20	0♉	19♉	28♈	19♈
21	1♉	20♉	29♈	20♈
22	1♉	21♉	0♉	20♈
23	2♉	23♉	2♉	21♈
24	3♉	24♉	3♉	22♈
25	4♉	25♉	4♉	23♈
26	5♉	25♉	5♉	23♈
27	6♉	26♉	7♉	24♈
28	7♉	27♉	8♉	25♈
29	8♉	28♉	9♉	26♈
30	9♉	28♉	10♉	26♈

May

Day	☉	☿	♀	♂
1	10♉	29♉	12♉	27♈
2	11♉	29♉	13♉	28♈
3	12♉	29♉	14♉	29♈
4	13♉	29♉	15♉	29♈
5	14♉	29♉	16♉	0♉
6	15♉	29♉	18♉	1♉
7	16♉	29♉	19♉	2♉
8	17♉	29♉	20♉	2♉
9	18♉	29♉	21♉	3♉
10	19♉	29♉	23♉	4♉
11	20♉	28♉	24♉	5♉
12	21♉	28♉	25♉	5♉
13	22♉	27♉	26♉	6♉
14	23♉	27♉	28♉	7♉
15	24♉	26♉	29♉	8♉
16	25♉	26♉	0♊	8♉
17	26♉	25♉	1♊	9♉
18	27♉	25♉	2♊	10♉
19	28♉	24♉	4♊	11♉
20	29♉	23♉	5♊	11♉
21	0♊	23♉	6♊	12♉
22	1♊	22♉	7♊	13♉
23	1♊	22♉	9♊	14♉
24	2♊	22♉	10♊	14♉
25	3♊	21♉	11♊	15♉
26	4♊	21♉	12♊	16♉
27	5♊	21♉	14♊	17♉
28	6♊	21♉	15♊	17♉
29	7♊	21♉	16♊	18♉
30	8♊	21♉	17♊	19♉
31	9♊	21♉	18♊	19♉

June

Day	☉	☿	♀	♂
1	10♊	21♉	20♊	20♉
2	11♊	21♉	21♊	21♉
3	12♊	21♉	22♊	22♉
4	13♊	22♉	23♊	22♉
5	14♊	22♉	25♊	23♉
6	15♊	23♉	26♊	24♉
7	16♊	23♉	27♊	25♉
8	17♊	24♉	28♊	25♉
9	18♊	25♉	29♊	26♉
10	19♊	26♉	1♋	27♉
11	20♊	26♉	2♋	27♉
12	21♊	27♉	3♋	28♉
13	22♊	28♉	4♋	29♉
14	23♊	29♉	6♋	0♊
15	24♊	1♊	7♋	0♊
16	24♊	2♊	8♋	1♊
17	25♊	3♊	9♋	2♊
18	26♊	4♊	11♋	2♊
19	27♊	5♊	12♋	3♊
20	28♊	7♊	13♋	4♊
21	29♊	8♊	14♋	5♊
22	0♋	10♊	15♋	5♊
23	1♋	11♊	17♋	6♊
24	2♋	13♊	18♋	7♊
25	3♋	15♊	19♋	7♊
26	4♋	16♊	20♋	8♊
27	5♋	18♊	22♋	9♊
28	6♋	20♊	23♋	9♊
29	7♋	22♊	24♋	10♊
30	8♋	24♊	25♋	11♊

July

Day	☉	☿	♀	♂
1	9♋	26♊	26♋	12♊
2	10♋	28♊	28♋	12♊
3	11♋	0♋	29♋	13♊
4	12♋	2♋	0♌	14♊
5	13♋	4♋	1♌	14♊
6	14♋	6♋	3♌	15♊
7	14♋	8♋	4♌	16♊
8	15♋	10♋	5♌	16♊
9	16♋	12♋	6♌	17♊
10	17♋	14♋	7♌	18♊
11	18♋	17♋	9♌	18♊
12	19♋	19♋	10♌	19♊
13	20♋	21♋	11♌	20♊
14	21♋	23♋	12♌	21♊
15	22♋	25♋	14♌	21♊
16	23♋	27♋	15♌	22♊
17	24♋	29♋	16♌	23♊
18	25♋	1♌	17♌	23♊
19	26♋	3♌	18♌	24♊
20	27♋	5♌	20♌	25♊
21	28♋	7♌	21♌	25♊
22	29♋	9♌	22♌	26♊
23	0♌	11♌	23♌	27♊
24	1♌	13♌	24♌	27♊
25	2♌	15♌	26♌	28♊
26	3♌	17♌	27♌	29♊
27	4♌	19♌	28♌	29♊
28	5♌	20♌	29♌	0♋
29	5♌	22♌	1♍	1♋
30	6♌	24♌	2♍	1♋
31	7♌	26♌	3♍	2♋

August

Day	☉	☿	♀	♂
1	8♌	27♌	4♍	3♋
2	9♌	29♌	5♍	3♋
3	10♌	1♍	7♍	4♋
4	11♌	2♍	8♍	5♋
5	12♌	4♍	9♍	5♋
6	13♌	5♍	10♍	6♋
7	14♌	7♍	11♍	7♋
8	15♌	8♍	13♍	7♋
9	16♌	10♍	14♍	8♋
10	17♌	11♍	15♍	9♋
11	18♌	13♍	16♍	9♋
12	19♌	14♍	18♍	10♋
13	20♌	15♍	19♍	11♋
14	21♌	17♍	20♍	11♋
15	22♌	18♍	21♍	12♋
16	23♌	19♍	22♍	13♋
17	24♌	20♍	24♍	13♋
18	25♌	21♍	25♍	14♋
19	26♌	23♍	26♍	15♋
20	27♌	24♍	27♍	15♋
21	28♌	25♍	28♍	16♋
22	29♌	26♍	0♎	17♋
23	29♌	27♍	1♎	17♋
24	0♍	28♍	2♎	18♋
25	1♍	29♍	3♎	18♋
26	2♍	29♍	4♎	19♋
27	3♍	0♎	6♎	20♋
28	4♍	1♎	7♎	20♋
29	5♍	2♎	8♎	21♋
30	6♍	2♎	9♎	22♋
31	7♍	3♎	10♎	22♋

September

Day	☉	☿	♀	♂
1	8♍	3♎	12♎	23♋
2	9♍	3♎	13♎	24♋
3	10♍	4♎	14♎	24♋
4	11♍	4♎	15♎	25♋
5	12♍	4♎	16♎	25♋
6	13♍	4♎	18♎	26♋
7	14♍	4♎	19♎	27♋
8	15♍	4♎	20♎	27♋
9	16♍	3♎	21♎	28♋
10	17♍	3♎	22♎	29♋
11	18♍	2♎	24♎	29♋
12	19♍	2♎	25♎	0♌
13	20♍	1♎	26♎	0♌
14	21♍	0♎	27♎	1♌
15	22♍	29♍	28♎	2♌
16	23♍	28♍	0♏	2♌
17	24♍	27♍	1♏	3♌
18	25♍	26♍	2♏	4♌
19	26♍	25♍	3♏	4♌
20	27♍	24♍	4♏	5♌
21	28♍	23♍	6♏	5♌
22	29♍	22♍	7♏	6♌
23	0♎	21♍	8♏	7♌
24	1♎	21♍	9♏	7♌
25	2♎	20♍	10♏	8♌
26	3♎	20♍	11♏	8♌
27	4♎	20♍	13♏	9♌
28	4♎	19♍	14♏	10♌
29	5♎	20♍	15♏	10♌
30	6♎	20♍	16♏	11♌

October

Day	☉	☿	♀	♂
1	7♎	20♍	17♏	11♌
2	8♎	21♍	19♏	12♌
3	9♎	22♍	20♏	13♌
4	10♎	23♍	21♏	13♌
5	11♎	24♍	22♏	14♌
6	12♎	25♍	23♏	14♌
7	13♎	26♍	24♏	15♌
8	14♎	27♍	26♏	16♌
9	15♎	29♍	27♏	16♌
10	16♎	0♎	28♏	17♌
11	17♎	2♎	29♏	17♌
12	18♎	3♎	0♐	18♌
13	19♎	5♎	1♐	19♌
14	20♎	6♎	3♐	19♌
15	21♎	8♎	4♐	20♌
16	22♎	10♎	5♐	20♌
17	23♎	11♎	6♐	21♌
18	24♎	13♎	7♐	21♌
19	25♎	15♎	8♐	22♌
20	26♎	16♎	10♐	23♌
21	27♎	18♎	11♐	23♌
22	28♎	20♎	12♐	24♌
23	29♎	22♎	13♐	24♌
24	0♏	23♎	14♐	25♌
25	1♏	25♎	15♐	25♌
26	2♏	27♎	16♐	26♌
27	3♏	28♎	18♐	27♌
28	4♏	0♏	19♐	27♌
29	5♏	2♏	20♐	28♌
30	6♏	3♏	21♐	28♌
31	7♏	5♏	22♐	29♌

November

Day	☉	☿	♀	♂
1	8♏	7♏	23♐	29♌
2	9♏	8♏	24♐	0♍
3	10♏	10♏	26♐	0♍
4	11♏	11♏	27♐	1♍
5	12♏	13♏	28♐	1♍
6	13♏	15♏	29♐	2♍
7	14♏	16♏	0♑	3♍
8	15♏	18♏	1♑	3♍
9	16♏	20♏	2♑	4♍
10	17♏	21♏	3♑	4♍
11	18♏	23♏	4♑	5♍
12	19♏	24♏	6♑	5♍
13	20♏	26♏	7♑	6♍
14	21♏	27♏	8♑	6♍
15	22♏	29♏	9♑	7♍
16	23♏	0♐	10♑	7♍
17	24♏	2♐	11♑	8♍
18	25♏	4♐	12♑	8♍
19	26♏	5♐	13♑	9♍
20	27♏	7♐	14♑	9♍
21	28♏	8♐	15♑	10♍
22	29♏	10♐	16♑	10♍
23	0♐	11♐	17♑	11♍
24	1♐	13♐	18♑	11♍
25	2♐	14♐	20♑	12♍
26	3♐	16♐	21♑	12♍
27	4♐	17♐	22♑	13♍
28	5♐	19♐	23♑	13♍
29	6♐	20♐	24♑	14♍
30	7♐	22♐	25♑	14♍

December

Day	☉	☿	♀	♂
1	8♐	23♐	26♑	15♍
2	9♐	25♐	27♑	15♍
3	10♐	26♐	28♑	16♍
4	11♐	28♐	29♑	16♍
5	13♐	29♐	0♒	17♍
6	14♐	1♑	1♒	17♍
7	15♐	2♑	2♒	17♍
8	16♐	4♑	3♒	18♍
9	17♐	5♑	4♒	18♍
10	18♐	6♑	4♒	19♍
11	19♐	8♑	5♒	19♍
12	20♐	9♑	6♒	20♍
13	21♐	10♑	7♒	20♍
14	22♐	12♑	8♒	20♍
15	23♐	13♑	9♒	21♍
16	24♐	14♑	10♒	21♍
17	25♐	15♑	11♒	22♍
18	26♐	16♑	12♒	22♍
19	27♐	17♑	13♒	22♍
20	28♐	18♑	13♒	23♍
21	29♐	18♑	14♒	23♍
22	0♑	19♑	15♒	23♍
23	1♑	19♑	16♒	24♍
24	2♑	20♑	17♒	24♍
25	3♑	20♑	17♒	25♍
26	4♑	20♑	18♒	25♍
27	5♑	19♑	19♒	25♍
28	6♑	19♑	19♒	26♍
29	7♑	18♑	20♒	26♍
30	8♑	17♑	21♒	26♍
31	9♑	16♑	21♒	27♍

Planetary Positions

♌ = Leo ♍ = Virgo ♎ = Libra ♏ = Scorpio ♐ = Sagittarius ♑ = Capricorn ♒ = Aquarius ♓ = Pisces

1918

January

Day	☉	☿	♀	♂
1	10♑	15♑	22♒	27♍
2	11♑	14♑	23♒	27♍
3	12♑	12♑	23♒	28♍
4	13♑	11♑	24♒	28♍
5	14♑	10♑	24♒	28♍
6	15♑	9♑	25♒	29♍
7	16♑	7♑	25♒	29♍
8	17♑	6♑	26♒	29♍
9	18♑	5♑	26♒	29♍
10	19♑	5♑	27♒	0♎
11	20♑	4♑	27♒	0♎
12	21♑	4♑	27♒	0♎
13	22♑	4♑	28♒	0♎
14	23♑	3♑	28♒	1♎
15	24♑	4♑	28♒	1♎
16	25♑	4♑	28♒	1♎
17	26♑	4♑	28♒	1♎
18	27♑	4♑	28♒	1♎
19	28♑	5♑	28♒	2♎
20	29♑	6♑	29♒	2♎
21	0♒	6♑	28♒	2♎
22	1♒	7♑	28♒	2♎
23	2♒	8♑	28♒	2♎
24	3♒	9♑	28♒	2♎
25	4♒	10♑	28♒	3♎
26	5♒	11♑	28♒	3♎
27	6♒	12♑	28♒	3♎
28	7♒	13♑	27♒	3♎
29	8♒	14♑	27♒	3♎
30	10♒	15♑	26♒	3♎
31	11♒	16♑	26♒	3♎

February

Day	☉	☿	♀	♂
1	12♒	18♑	26♒	3♎
2	13♒	19♑	25♒	3♎
3	14♒	20♑	25♒	3♎
4	15♒	21♑	24♒	3♎
5	16♒	23♑	23♒	3♎
6	17♒	24♑	23♒	3♎
7	18♒	26♑	22♒	3♎
8	19♒	27♑	22♒	3♎
9	20♒	28♑	21♒	3♎
10	21♒	0♒	20♒	3♎
11	22♒	1♒	20♒	3♎
12	23♒	3♒	19♒	3♎
13	24♒	4♒	19♒	3♎
14	25♒	6♒	18♒	2♎
15	26♒	7♒	17♒	2♎
16	27♒	9♒	17♒	2♎
17	28♒	10♒	16♒	2♎
18	29♒	12♒	16♒	2♎
19	0♓	13♒	15♒	2♎
20	1♓	15♒	15♒	1♎
21	2♓	16♒	15♒	1♎
22	3♓	18♒	14♒	1♎
23	4♓	20♒	14♒	1♎
24	5♓	21♒	14♒	0♎
25	6♓	23♒	13♒	0♎
26	7♓	25♒	13♒	0♎
27	8♓	26♒	13♒	0♎
28	9♓	28♒	13♒	29♍

March

Day	☉	☿	♀	♂
1	10♓	0♓	13♒	29♍
2	11♓	2♓	13♒	29♍
3	12♓	3♓	13♒	28♍
4	13♓	5♓	13♒	28♍
5	14♓	7♓	13♒	28♍
6	15♓	9♓	13♒	27♍
7	16♓	11♓	13♒	27♍
8	17♓	12♓	13♒	27♍
9	18♓	14♓	14♒	26♍
10	19♓	16♓	14♒	26♍
11	20♓	18♓	14♒	25♍
12	21♓	20♓	14♒	25♍
13	22♓	22♓	15♒	25♍
14	23♓	24♓	15♒	24♍
15	24♓	26♓	16♒	24♍
16	25♓	28♓	16♒	24♍
17	26♓	0♈	17♒	23♍
18	27♓	2♈	17♒	23♍
19	28♓	4♈	18♒	22♍
20	29♓	6♈	18♒	22♍
21	0♈	8♈	19♒	22♍
22	1♈	10♈	19♒	21♍
23	2♈	12♈	20♒	21♍
24	3♈	14♈	21♒	20♍
25	4♈	16♈	21♒	20♍
26	5♈	18♈	22♒	20♍
27	6♈	19♈	23♒	19♍
28	7♈	21♈	23♒	19♍
29	8♈	23♈	24♒	19♍
30	9♈	25♈	25♒	18♍
31	10♈	26♈	25♒	18♍

April

Day	☉	☿	♀	♂
1	11♈	28♈	26♒	18♍
2	12♈	0♉	27♒	17♍
3	13♈	1♉	28♒	17♍
4	14♈	2♉	29♒	17♍
5	15♈	4♉	29♒	17♍
6	16♈	5♉	0♓	16♍
7	17♈	6♉	1♓	16♍
8	18♈	7♉	2♓	16♍
9	19♈	7♉	3♓	16♍
10	20♈	8♉	4♓	15♍
11	20♈	9♉	5♓	15♍
12	21♈	9♉	6♓	15♍
13	22♈	10♉	6♓	15♍
14	23♈	10♉	7♓	15♍
15	24♈	10♉	8♓	15♍
16	25♈	10♉	9♓	14♍
17	26♈	10♉	10♓	14♍
18	27♈	10♉	11♓	14♍
19	28♈	10♉	12♓	14♍
20	29♈	10♉	13♓	14♍
21	0♉	9♉	14♓	14♍
22	1♉	9♉	15♓	14♍
23	2♉	8♉	16♓	14♍
24	3♉	8♉	17♓	14♍
25	4♉	7♉	18♓	14♍
26	5♉	7♉	19♓	14♍
27	6♉	6♉	20♓	14♍
28	7♉	5♉	21♓	14♍
29	8♉	5♉	22♓	14♍
30	9♉	4♉	23♓	14♍

May

Day	☉	☿	♀	♂
1	10♉	3♉	24♓	14♍
2	11♉	3♉	25♓	14♍
3	12♉	2♉	26♓	14♍
4	13♉	2♉	27♓	14♍
5	14♉	1♉	28♓	14♍
6	15♉	1♉	29♓	15♍
7	16♉	1♉	0♈	15♍
8	17♉	1♉	1♈	15♍
9	18♉	0♉	2♈	15♍
10	19♉	0♉	4♈	15♍
11	20♉	0♉	5♈	15♍
12	21♉	1♉	6♈	15♍
13	22♉	1♉	7♈	16♍
14	23♉	1♉	8♈	16♍
15	24♉	1♉	9♈	16♍
16	25♉	2♉	10♈	16♍
17	25♉	2♉	11♈	16♍
18	26♉	3♉	12♈	17♍
19	27♉	3♉	13♈	17♍
20	28♉	4♉	14♈	17♍
21	29♉	5♉	15♈	17♍
22	0♊	5♉	17♈	18♍
23	1♊	6♉	18♈	18♍
24	2♊	7♉	19♈	18♍
25	3♊	8♉	20♈	19♍
26	4♊	9♉	21♈	19♍
27	5♊	10♉	22♈	19♍
28	6♊	11♉	23♈	19♍
29	7♊	13♉	24♈	20♍
30	8♊	14♉	25♈	20♍
31	9♊	15♉	27♈	20♍

June

Day	☉	☿	♀	♂
1	10♊	16♉	28♈	21♍
2	11♊	18♉	29♈	21♍
3	12♊	19♉	0♉	21♍
4	13♊	21♉	1♉	22♍
5	14♊	22♉	2♉	22♍
6	15♊	24♉	3♉	23♍
7	16♊	25♉	5♉	23♍
8	17♊	27♉	6♉	23♍
9	18♊	29♉	7♉	24♍
10	19♊	0♊	8♉	24♍
11	19♊	2♊	9♉	25♍
12	20♊	4♊	10♉	25♍
13	21♊	6♊	11♉	25♍
14	22♊	8♊	12♉	26♍
15	23♊	9♊	14♉	26♍
16	24♊	11♊	15♉	27♍
17	25♊	13♊	16♉	27♍
18	26♊	16♊	17♉	27♍
19	27♊	18♊	18♉	28♍
20	28♊	20♊	19♉	28♍
21	29♊	22♊	21♉	29♍
22	0♋	24♊	22♉	29♍
23	1♋	26♊	23♉	0♎
24	2♋	28♊	24♉	0♎
25	3♋	0♋	25♉	1♎
26	4♋	3♋	26♉	1♎
27	5♋	5♋	28♉	2♎
28	6♋	7♋	29♉	2♎
29	7♋	9♋	0♊	3♎
30	8♋	11♋	1♊	3♎

July

Day	☉	☿	♀	♂
1	9♋	13♋	2♊	4♎
2	9♋	16♋	3♊	4♎
3	10♋	18♋	5♊	5♎
4	11♋	20♋	6♊	5♎
5	12♋	22♋	7♊	6♎
6	13♋	24♋	8♊	6♎
7	14♋	26♋	9♊	7♎
8	15♋	28♋	10♊	7♎
9	16♋	0♌	12♊	8♎
10	17♋	2♌	13♊	8♎
11	18♋	3♌	14♊	9♎
12	19♋	5♌	15♊	9♎
13	20♋	7♌	16♊	10♎
14	21♋	9♌	17♊	11♎
15	22♋	11♌	19♊	11♎
16	23♋	12♌	20♊	11♎
17	24♋	14♌	21♊	12♎
18	25♋	16♌	22♊	12♎
19	26♋	17♌	23♊	13♎
20	27♋	19♌	25♊	14♎
21	28♋	20♌	26♊	14♎
22	29♋	22♌	27♊	15♎
23	0♌	23♌	28♊	15♎
24	0♌	25♌	29♊	16♎
25	1♌	26♌	1♋	16♎
26	2♌	28♌	2♋	17♎
27	3♌	29♌	3♋	17♎
28	4♌	0♍	4♋	18♎
29	5♌	1♍	5♋	19♎
30	6♌	3♍	6♋	19♎
31	7♌	4♍	8♋	20♎

August

Day	☉	☿	♀	♂
1	8♌	5♍	9♋	20♎
2	9♌	6♍	10♋	21♎
3	10♌	7♍	11♋	22♎
4	11♌	8♍	12♋	22♎
5	12♌	9♍	14♋	23♎
6	13♌	10♍	15♋	23♎
7	14♌	11♍	16♋	24♎
8	15♌	12♍	17♋	25♎
9	16♌	13♍	19♋	25♎
10	17♌	13♍	20♋	26♎
11	18♌	14♍	21♋	26♎
12	19♌	15♍	22♋	27♎
13	20♌	15♍	23♋	28♎
14	21♌	16♍	25♋	28♎
15	22♌	16♍	26♋	29♎
16	23♌	16♍	27♋	29♎
17	23♌	17♍	28♋	0♏
18	24♌	17♍	29♋	1♏
19	25♌	17♍	1♌	1♏
20	26♌	17♍	2♌	2♏
21	27♌	17♍	3♌	3♏
22	28♌	17♍	4♌	3♏
23	29♌	16♍	5♌	4♏
24	0♍	16♍	7♌	4♏
25	1♍	15♍	8♌	5♏
26	2♍	15♍	9♌	6♏
27	3♍	14♍	10♌	6♏
28	4♍	13♍	12♌	7♏
29	5♍	12♍	13♌	8♏
30	6♍	11♍	14♌	8♏
31	7♍	11♍	15♌	9♏

September

Day	☉	☿	♀	♂
1	8♍	10♍	16♌	10♏
2	9♍	9♍	18♌	10♏
3	10♍	8♍	19♌	11♏
4	11♍	7♍	20♌	12♏
5	12♍	6♍	21♌	12♏
6	13♍	5♍	23♌	13♏
7	14♍	5♍	24♌	14♏
8	15♍	4♍	25♌	14♏
9	16♍	4♍	26♌	15♏
10	17♍	3♍	28♌	16♏
11	18♍	3♍	29♌	16♏
12	19♍	3♍	0♍	17♏
13	20♍	3♍	1♍	18♏
14	21♍	4♍	2♍	18♏
15	22♍	4♍	4♍	19♏
16	23♍	5♍	5♍	20♏
17	23♍	6♍	6♍	20♏
18	24♍	7♍	7♍	21♏
19	25♍	8♍	9♍	22♏
20	26♍	9♍	10♍	22♏
21	27♍	10♍	11♍	23♏
22	28♍	11♍	12♍	24♏
23	29♍	13♍	14♍	24♏
24	0♎	14♍	15♍	25♏
25	1♎	16♍	16♍	26♏
26	2♎	18♍	17♍	26♏
27	3♎	19♍	19♍	27♏
28	4♎	21♍	20♍	28♏
29	5♎	23♍	21♍	29♏
30	6♎	24♍	22♍	29♏

October

Day	☉	☿	♀	♂
1	7♎	26♍	24♍	0♐
2	8♎	28♍	25♍	1♐
3	9♎	0♎	26♍	1♐
4	10♎	1♎	27♍	2♐
5	11♎	3♎	28♍	3♐
6	12♎	5♎	0♎	3♐
7	13♎	7♎	1♎	4♐
8	14♎	9♎	2♎	5♐
9	15♎	10♎	3♎	6♐
10	16♎	12♎	5♎	6♐
11	17♎	14♎	6♎	7♐
12	18♎	16♎	7♎	8♐
13	19♎	17♎	8♎	8♐
14	20♎	19♎	10♎	9♐
15	21♎	21♎	11♎	10♐
16	22♎	23♎	12♎	11♐
17	23♎	24♎	13♎	11♐
18	24♎	26♎	15♎	12♐
19	25♎	28♎	16♎	13♐
20	26♎	29♎	17♎	14♐
21	27♎	1♏	18♎	14♐
22	28♎	2♏	20♎	15♐
23	29♎	4♏	21♎	16♐
24	0♏	6♏	22♎	16♐
25	1♏	7♏	23♎	17♐
26	2♏	9♏	25♎	18♐
27	3♏	10♏	26♎	19♐
28	4♏	12♏	27♎	19♐
29	5♏	14♏	28♎	20♐
30	6♏	15♏	0♏	21♐
31	7♏	17♏	1♏	22♐

November

Day	☉	☿	♀	♂
1	8♏	18♏	2♏	22♐
2	9♏	20♏	4♏	23♐
3	10♏	21♏	5♏	24♐
4	11♏	23♏	6♏	25♐
5	12♏	24♏	7♏	25♐
6	13♏	26♏	9♏	26♐
7	14♏	27♏	10♏	27♐
8	15♏	29♏	11♏	28♐
9	16♏	0♐	12♏	28♐
10	17♏	2♐	14♏	29♐
11	18♏	3♐	15♏	0♑
12	19♏	5♐	16♏	1♑
13	20♏	6♐	17♏	1♑
14	21♏	8♐	19♏	2♑
15	22♏	9♐	20♏	3♑
16	23♏	11♐	21♏	4♑
17	24♏	12♐	22♏	4♑
18	25♏	13♐	24♏	5♑
19	26♏	15♐	25♏	6♑
20	27♏	16♐	26♏	7♑
21	28♏	18♐	27♏	7♑
22	29♏	19♐	29♏	8♑
23	0♐	20♐	0♐	9♑
24	1♐	22♐	1♐	10♑
25	2♐	23♐	2♐	10♑
26	3♐	24♐	4♐	11♑
27	4♐	25♐	5♐	12♑
28	5♐	26♐	6♐	13♑
29	6♐	28♐	7♐	14♑
30	7♐	29♐	9♐	14♑

December

Day	☉	☿	♀	♂
1	8♐	0♑	10♐	15♑
2	9♐	0♑	11♐	16♑
3	10♐	1♑	12♐	17♑
4	11♐	2♑	14♐	17♑
5	12♐	3♑	15♐	18♑
6	13♐	3♑	16♐	19♑
7	14♐	4♑	17♐	20♑
8	15♐	4♑	19♐	21♑
9	16♐	4♑	20♐	21♑
10	17♐	4♑	21♐	22♑
11	18♐	3♑	23♐	23♑
12	19♐	3♑	24♐	24♑
13	20♐	2♑	25♐	24♑
14	21♐	1♑	26♐	25♑
15	22♐	0♑	28♐	26♑
16	23♐	29♐	29♐	27♑
17	24♐	28♐	0♑	28♑
18	25♐	27♐	1♑	28♑
19	26♐	25♐	3♑	29♑
20	28♐	24♐	4♑	0♒
21	29♐	23♐	5♑	1♒
22	0♑	21♐	6♑	1♒
23	1♑	20♐	8♑	2♒
24	2♑	19♐	9♑	3♒
25	3♑	19♐	10♑	4♒
26	4♑	18♐	11♑	5♒
27	5♑	18♐	13♑	5♒
28	6♑	18♐	14♑	6♒
29	7♑	18♐	15♑	7♒
30	8♑	18♐	16♑	8♒
31	9♑	18♐	18♑	8♒

1919

Your Starway to Love

☉ =Sun ☿ = Mercury ♀ = Venus ♂ = Mars ♈ = Aries ♉ = Taurus ♊ = Gemini ♋ = Cancer

January

Day	☉	☿	♀	♂
1	10♑	18♐	19♑	9♒
2	11♑	19♐	20♑	10♒
3	12♑	19♐	21♑	11♒
4	13♑	20♐	23♑	12♒
5	14♑	21♐	24♑	12♒
6	15♑	22♐	25♑	13♒
7	16♑	23♐	26♑	14♒
8	17♑	24♐	28♑	15♒
9	18♑	25♐	29♑	16♒
10	19♑	26♐	0♒	16♒
11	20♑	27♐	1♒	17♒
12	21♑	28♐	3♒	18♒
13	22♑	29♐	4♒	19♒
14	23♑	1♑	5♒	20♒
15	24♑	2♑	7♒	20♒
16	25♑	3♑	8♒	21♒
17	26♑	4♑	9♒	22♒
18	27♑	6♑	10♒	23♒
19	28♑	7♑	12♒	23♒
20	29♑	8♑	13♒	24♒
21	0♒	10♑	14♒	25♒
22	1♒	11♑	15♒	26♒
23	2♒	13♑	17♒	27♒
24	3♒	14♑	18♒	27♒
25	4♒	16♑	19♒	28♒
26	5♒	17♑	20♒	29♒
27	6♒	18♑	22♒	0♓
28	7♒	20♑	23♒	1♓
29	8♒	21♑	24♒	1♓
30	9♒	23♑	25♒	2♓
31	10♒	24♑	27♒	3♓

April

Day	☉	☿	♀	♂
1	10♈	22♈	11♉	19♈
2	11♈	21♈	12♉	20♈
3	12♈	21♈	13♉	21♈
4	13♈	20♈	14♉	22♈
5	14♈	20♈	15♉	23♈
6	15♈	19♈	17♉	23♈
7	16♈	18♈	18♉	24♈
8	17♈	17♈	19♉	25♈
9	18♈	17♈	20♉	26♈
10	19♈	16♈	22♉	26♈
11	20♈	15♈	23♉	27♈
12	21♈	14♈	24♉	28♈
13	22♈	14♈	25♉	29♈
14	23♈	13♈	26♉	29♈
15	24♈	13♈	28♉	0♉
16	25♈	12♈	29♉	1♉
17	26♈	12♈	0♊	1♉
18	27♈	11♈	1♊	2♉
19	28♈	11♈	2♊	3♉
20	29♈	11♈	3♊	4♉
21	0♉	11♈	5♊	4♉
22	1♉	11♈	6♊	5♉
23	2♉	11♈	7♊	6♉
24	3♉	11♈	8♊	7♉
25	4♉	11♈	9♊	7♉
26	5♉	11♈	11♊	8♉
27	6♉	12♈	12♊	9♉
28	7♉	12♈	13♊	10♉
29	8♉	13♈	14♊	10♉
30	9♉	13♈	15♊	11♉

July

Day	☉	☿	♀	♂
1	8♋	29♋	24♌	25♊
2	9♋	0♌	25♌	26♊
3	10♋	2♌	26♌	26♊
4	11♋	3♌	27♌	27♊
5	12♋	5♌	28♌	28♊
6	13♋	6♌	29♌	28♊
7	14♋	8♌	29♌	29♊
8	15♋	9♌	0♍	0♋
9	16♋	11♌	1♍	0♋
10	17♋	12♌	2♍	1♋
11	18♋	13♌	3♍	2♋
12	19♋	15♌	4♍	2♋
13	20♋	16♌	5♍	3♋
14	21♋	17♌	6♍	4♋
15	22♋	18♌	7♍	4♋
16	23♋	19♌	8♍	5♋
17	24♋	20♌	8♍	6♋
18	25♋	21♌	9♍	6♋
19	25♋	22♌	10♍	7♋
20	26♋	23♌	11♍	8♋
21	27♋	24♌	12♍	8♋
22	28♋	25♌	13♍	9♋
23	29♋	25♌	13♍	10♋
24	0♌	26♌	14♍	10♋
25	1♌	27♌	15♍	11♋
26	2♌	27♌	16♍	12♋
27	3♌	28♌	16♍	12♋
28	4♌	28♌	17♍	13♋
29	5♌	29♌	18♍	14♋
30	6♌	29♌	18♍	14♋
31	7♌	29♌	19♍	15♋

October

Day	☉	☿	♀	♂
1	7♎	10♎	11♍	25♌
2	8♎	12♎	11♍	25♌
3	9♎	13♎	11♍	26♌
4	10♎	15♎	11♍	26♌
5	11♎	17♎	11♍	27♌
6	12♎	18♎	11♍	28♌
7	13♎	20♎	11♍	28♌
8	14♎	22♎	11♍	29♌
9	15♎	23♎	12♍	29♌
10	16♎	25♎	12♍	0♍
11	17♎	27♎	12♍	1♍
12	18♎	28♎	12♍	1♍
13	19♎	0♏	13♍	2♍
14	20♎	1♏	13♍	2♍
15	21♎	3♏	13♍	3♍
16	22♎	5♏	14♍	4♍
17	23♎	6♏	14♍	4♍
18	24♎	8♏	15♍	5♍
19	25♎	9♏	15♍	5♍
20	26♎	11♏	16♍	6♍
21	27♎	12♏	16♍	7♍
22	28♎	14♏	17♍	7♍
23	29♎	15♏	17♍	8♍
24	0♏	17♏	18♍	8♍
25	1♏	18♏	18♍	9♍
26	2♏	19♏	19♍	10♍
27	3♏	21♏	20♍	10♍
28	4♏	22♏	20♍	11♍
29	5♏	24♏	21♍	11♍
30	6♏	25♏	22♍	12♍
31	7♏	26♏	23♍	13♍

February

Day	☉	☿	♀	♂
1	11♒	26♑	28♒	4♓
2	12♒	28♑	29♒	5♓
3	13♒	29♑	0♓	5♓
4	14♒	1♒	2♓	6♓
5	15♒	2♒	3♓	7♓
6	16♒	4♒	4♓	8♓
7	17♒	5♒	5♓	8♓
8	18♒	7♒	7♓	9♓
9	19♒	9♒	8♓	10♓
10	20♒	10♒	9♓	11♓
11	21♒	12♒	10♓	12♓
12	22♒	14♒	12♓	12♓
13	23♒	15♒	13♓	13♓
14	24♒	17♒	14♓	14♓
15	25♒	19♒	15♓	15♓
16	26♒	20♒	17♓	16♓
17	27♒	22♒	18♓	16♓
18	28♒	24♒	19♓	17♓
19	0♓	26♒	20♓	18♓
20	1♓	28♒	21♓	19♓
21	2♓	29♒	23♓	19♓
22	3♓	1♓	24♓	20♓
23	4♓	3♓	25♓	21♓
24	5♓	5♓	26♓	22♓
25	6♓	7♓	28♓	23♓
26	7♓	9♓	29♓	23♓
27	8♓	10♓	0♈	24♓
28	9♓	12♓	1♈	25♓

May

Day	☉	☿	♀	♂
1	10♉	14♈	16♊	12♉
2	11♉	15♈	18♊	13♉
3	12♉	16♈	19♊	13♉
4	13♉	16♈	20♊	14♉
5	14♉	17♈	21♊	15♉
6	15♉	18♈	22♊	15♉
7	16♉	19♈	24♊	16♉
8	17♉	20♈	25♊	17♉
9	18♉	21♈	26♊	18♉
10	18♉	22♈	27♊	18♉
11	19♉	24♈	28♊	19♉
12	20♉	25♈	29♊	20♉
13	21♉	26♈	0♋	21♉
14	22♉	27♈	2♋	21♉
15	23♉	29♈	3♋	22♉
16	24♉	0♉	4♋	23♉
17	25♉	2♉	5♋	23♉
18	26♉	3♉	6♋	24♉
19	27♉	5♉	7♋	25♉
20	28♉	6♉	9♋	26♉
21	29♉	8♉	10♋	26♉
22	0♊	9♉	11♋	27♉
23	1♊	11♉	12♋	28♉
24	2♊	13♉	13♋	28♉
25	3♊	14♉	14♋	29♉
26	4♊	16♉	15♋	0♊
27	5♊	18♉	16♋	1♊
28	6♊	20♉	18♋	1♊
29	7♊	22♉	19♋	2♊
30	8♊	24♉	20♋	3♊
31	9♊	25♉	21♋	3♊

August

Day	☉	☿	♀	♂
1	8♌	29♌	20♍	16♋
2	9♌	29♌	20♍	16♋
3	10♌	29♌	21♍	17♋
4	11♌	29♌	21♍	18♋
5	12♌	28♌	22♍	18♋
6	13♌	28♌	23♍	19♋
7	14♌	28♌	23♍	20♋
8	15♌	27♌	24♍	20♋
9	16♌	27♌	24♍	21♋
10	17♌	26♌	24♍	22♋
11	17♌	25♌	25♍	22♋
12	18♌	24♌	25♍	23♋
13	19♌	24♌	26♍	24♋
14	20♌	23♌	26♍	24♋
15	21♌	22♌	26♍	25♋
16	22♌	21♌	26♍	25♋
17	23♌	20♌	27♍	26♋
18	24♌	20♌	27♍	27♋
19	25♌	19♌	27♍	27♋
20	26♌	18♌	27♍	28♋
21	27♌	18♌	27♍	29♋
22	28♌	17♌	27♍	29♋
23	29♌	17♌	27♍	0♌
24	0♍	17♌	27♍	1♌
25	1♍	17♌	27♍	1♌
26	2♍	17♌	27♍	2♌
27	3♍	17♌	27♍	3♌
28	4♍	17♌	27♍	3♌
29	5♍	17♌	26♍	4♌
30	6♍	18♌	26♍	4♌
31	7♍	19♌	26♍	5♌

November

Day	☉	☿	♀	♂
1	8♏	28♏	23♍	13♍
2	9♏	29♏	24♍	14♍
3	10♏	1♐	25♍	14♍
4	11♏	2♐	26♍	15♍
5	12♏	3♐	26♍	16♍
6	13♏	4♐	27♍	16♍
7	14♏	6♐	28♍	17♍
8	15♏	7♐	29♍	17♍
9	16♏	8♐	0♎	18♍
10	17♏	9♐	1♎	18♍
11	18♏	10♐	2♎	19♍
12	19♏	11♐	3♎	20♍
13	20♏	12♐	3♎	20♍
14	21♏	13♐	4♎	21♍
15	22♏	14♐	5♎	21♍
16	23♏	15♐	6♎	22♍
17	24♏	16♐	7♎	23♍
18	25♏	17♐	8♎	23♍
19	26♏	17♐	9♎	24♍
20	27♏	18♐	10♎	24♍
21	28♏	18♐	11♎	25♍
22	29♏	18♐	12♎	25♍
23	0♐	18♐	13♎	26♍
24	1♐	18♐	14♎	26♍
25	2♐	18♐	15♎	27♍
26	3♐	17♐	16♎	28♍
27	4♐	16♐	17♎	28♍
28	5♐	16♐	18♎	29♍
29	6♐	15♐	19♎	29♍
30	7♐	13♐	20♎	0♎

March

Day	☉	☿	♀	♂
1	10♓	14♓	3♈	26♓
2	11♓	16♓	4♈	26♓
3	12♓	18♓	5♈	27♓
4	13♓	20♓	6♈	28♓
5	14♓	22♓	8♈	29♓
6	15♓	24♓	9♈	0♈
7	16♓	26♓	10♈	0♈
8	17♓	28♓	11♈	1♈
9	18♓	0♈	13♈	2♈
10	19♓	1♈	14♈	3♈
11	20♓	3♈	15♈	3♈
12	21♓	5♈	16♈	4♈
13	22♓	7♈	17♈	5♈
14	23♓	8♈	19♈	6♈
15	24♓	10♈	20♈	7♈
16	25♓	12♈	21♈	7♈
17	26♓	13♈	22♈	8♈
18	27♓	14♈	24♈	9♈
19	28♓	16♈	25♈	10♈
20	29♓	17♈	26♈	10♈
21	0♈	18♈	27♈	11♈
22	1♈	19♈	28♈	12♈
23	2♈	20♈	0♉	13♈
24	3♈	20♈	1♉	13♈
25	3♈	21♈	2♉	14♈
26	4♈	22♈	3♉	15♈
27	5♈	22♈	5♉	16♈
28	6♈	22♈	6♉	16♈
29	7♈	22♈	7♉	17♈
30	8♈	22♈	8♉	18♈
31	9♈	22♈	9♉	19♈

June

Day	☉	☿	♀	♂
1	10♊	27♉	22♋	4♊
2	11♊	29♉	23♋	5♊
3	12♊	2♊	24♋	6♊
4	13♊	4♊	25♋	6♊
5	13♊	6♊	26♋	7♊
6	14♊	8♊	28♋	8♊
7	15♊	10♊	29♋	8♊
8	16♊	12♊	0♌	9♊
9	17♊	14♊	1♌	10♊
10	18♊	17♊	2♌	10♊
11	19♊	19♊	3♌	11♊
12	20♊	21♊	4♌	12♊
13	21♊	23♊	5♌	13♊
14	22♊	25♊	6♌	13♊
15	23♊	28♊	7♌	14♊
16	24♊	0♋	8♌	15♊
17	25♊	2♋	9♌	15♊
18	26♊	4♋	10♌	16♊
19	27♊	6♋	12♌	17♊
20	28♊	8♋	13♌	17♊
21	29♊	10♋	14♌	18♊
22	0♋	12♋	15♌	19♊
23	1♋	14♋	16♌	19♊
24	2♋	16♋	17♌	20♊
25	3♋	18♋	18♌	21♊
26	4♋	20♋	19♌	21♊
27	4♋	22♋	20♌	22♊
28	5♋	23♋	21♌	23♊
29	6♋	25♋	22♌	24♊
30	7♋	27♋	23♌	24♊

September

Day	☉	☿	♀	♂
1	8♍	20♌	26♍	6♌
2	9♍	21♌	25♍	6♌
3	10♍	22♌	25♍	7♌
4	11♍	23♌	24♍	8♌
5	12♍	24♌	24♍	8♌
6	13♍	25♌	23♍	9♌
7	14♍	27♌	23♍	10♌
8	14♍	28♌	22♍	10♌
9	15♍	0♍	22♍	11♌
10	16♍	2♍	21♍	11♌
11	17♍	3♍	20♍	12♌
12	18♍	5♍	20♍	13♌
13	19♍	7♍	19♍	13♌
14	20♍	9♍	19♍	14♌
15	21♍	11♍	18♍	15♌
16	22♍	13♍	17♍	15♌
17	23♍	14♍	17♍	16♌
18	24♍	16♍	16♍	16♌
19	25♍	18♍	16♍	17♌
20	26♍	20♍	15♍	18♌
21	27♍	22♍	15♍	18♌
22	28♍	24♍	14♍	19♌
23	29♍	26♍	14♍	20♌
24	0♎	27♍	13♍	20♌
25	1♎	29♍	13♍	21♌
26	2♎	1♎	12♍	21♌
27	3♎	3♎	12♍	22♌
28	4♎	5♎	12♍	23♌
29	5♎	6♎	12♍	23♌
30	6♎	8♎	11♍	24♌

December

Day	☉	☿	♀	♂
1	8♐	12♐	21♎	0♎
2	9♐	11♐	22♎	1♎
3	10♐	9♐	24♎	1♎
4	11♐	8♐	25♎	2♎
5	12♐	7♐	26♎	3♎
6	13♐	6♐	27♎	3♎
7	14♐	4♐	28♎	4♎
8	15♐	4♐	29♎	4♎
9	16♐	3♐	0♏	5♎
10	17♐	2♐	1♏	5♎
11	18♐	2♐	2♏	6♎
12	19♐	2♐	3♏	6♎
13	20♐	2♐	5♏	7♎
14	21♐	2♐	6♏	7♎
15	22♐	2♐	7♏	8♎
16	23♐	3♐	8♏	8♎
17	24♐	3♐	9♏	9♎
18	25♐	4♐	10♏	10♎
19	26♐	5♐	11♏	10♎
20	27♐	6♐	12♏	11♎
21	28♐	7♐	14♏	11♎
22	29♐	8♐	15♏	12♎
23	0♑	9♐	16♏	12♎
24	1♑	10♐	17♏	13♎
25	2♑	11♐	18♏	13♎
26	3♑	12♐	19♏	14♎
27	4♑	13♐	20♏	14♎
28	5♑	15♐	22♏	15♎
29	6♑	16♐	23♏	15♎
30	7♑	17♐	24♏	16♎
31	8♑	19♐	25♏	16♎

Planetary Positions

♌ = Leo ♍ = Virgo ♎ = Libra ♏ = Scorpio ♐ = Sagittarius ♑ = Capricorn ♒ = Aquarius ♓ = Pisces

1920

January

Day	☉	☿	♀	♂
1	9♑	20♐	26♏	17♎
2	11♑	21♐	27♏	17♎
3	12♑	23♐	29♏	18♎
4	13♑	24♐	0♐	18♎
5	14♑	26♐	1♐	19♎
6	15♑	27♐	2♐	19♎
7	16♑	28♐	3♐	19♎
8	17♑	0♑	5♐	20♎
9	18♑	1♑	6♐	20♎
10	19♑	3♑	7♐	21♎
11	20♑	4♑	8♐	21♎
12	21♑	6♑	9♐	22♎
13	22♑	7♑	10♐	22♎
14	23♑	9♑	12♐	23♎
15	24♑	10♑	13♐	23♎
16	25♑	12♑	14♐	24♎
17	26♑	13♑	15♐	24♎
18	27♑	15♑	16♐	24♎
19	28♑	17♑	18♐	25♎
20	29♑	18♑	19♐	25♎
21	0♒	20♑	20♐	26♎
22	1♒	21♑	21♐	26♎
23	2♒	23♑	22♐	27♎
24	3♒	25♑	24♐	27♎
25	4♒	26♑	25♐	27♎
26	5♒	28♑	26♐	28♎
27	6♒	29♑	27♐	28♎
28	7♒	1♒	28♐	29♎
29	8♒	3♒	0♑	29♎
30	9♒	4♒	1♑	29♎
31	10♒	6♒	2♑	0♏

February

Day	☉	☿	♀	♂
1	11♒	8♒	3♑	0♏
2	12♒	9♒	4♑	0♏
3	13♒	11♒	6♑	1♏
4	14♒	13♒	7♑	1♏
5	15♒	15♒	8♑	2♏
6	16♒	16♒	9♑	2♏
7	17♒	18♒	11♑	2♏
8	18♒	20♒	12♑	3♏
9	19♒	22♒	13♑	3♏
10	20♒	24♒	14♑	3♏
11	21♒	25♒	15♑	3♏
12	22♒	27♒	17♑	4♏
13	23♒	29♒	18♑	4♏
14	24♒	1♓	19♑	4♏
15	25♒	3♓	20♑	5♏
16	26♒	4♓	22♑	5♏
17	27♒	6♓	23♑	5♏
18	28♒	8♓	24♑	6♏
19	29♒	10♓	25♑	6♏
20	0♓	12♓	26♑	6♏
21	1♓	14♓	28♑	6♏
22	2♓	15♓	29♑	6♏
23	3♓	17♓	0♒	7♏
24	4♓	19♓	1♒	7♏
25	5♓	21♓	3♒	7♏
26	6♓	22♓	4♒	7♏
27	7♓	24♓	5♒	7♏
28	8♓	25♓	6♒	8♏
29	9♓	27♓	7♒	8♏

March

Day	☉	☿	♀	♂
1	10♓	28♓	9♒	8♏
2	11♓	29♓	10♒	8♏
3	12♓	0♈	11♒	8♏
4	13♓	1♈	12♒	8♏
5	14♓	2♈	14♒	9♏
6	15♓	3♈	15♒	9♏
7	16♓	4♈	16♒	9♏
8	17♓	4♈	17♒	9♏
9	18♓	4♈	18♒	9♏
10	19♓	5♈	20♒	9♏
11	20♓	5♈	21♒	9♏
12	21♓	5♈	22♒	9♏
13	22♓	4♈	23♒	9♏
14	23♓	4♈	25♒	9♏
15	24♓	3♈	26♒	9♏
16	25♓	3♈	27♒	9♏
17	26♓	2♈	28♒	9♏
18	27♓	1♈	29♒	9♏
19	28♓	0♈	1♓	9♏
20	29♓	0♈	2♓	9♏
21	0♈	29♓	3♓	9♏
22	1♈	28♓	4♓	9♏
23	2♈	27♓	6♓	9♏
24	3♈	26♓	7♓	9♏
25	4♈	25♓	8♓	9♏
26	5♈	24♓	9♓	8♏
27	6♈	24♓	11♓	8♏
28	7♈	23♓	12♓	8♏
29	8♈	23♓	13♓	8♏
30	9♈	22♓	14♓	8♏
31	10♈	22♓	15♓	7♏

April

Day	☉	☿	♀	♂
1	11♈	22♓	17♓	7♏
2	12♈	22♓	18♓	7♏
3	13♈	22♓	19♓	7♏
4	14♈	22♓	20♓	7♏
5	15♈	22♓	22♓	6♏
6	16♈	22♓	23♓	6♏
7	17♈	22♓	24♓	6♏
8	18♈	23♓	25♓	5♏
9	19♈	23♓	26♓	5♏
10	20♈	24♓	28♓	5♏
11	21♈	25♓	29♓	5♏
12	22♈	25♓	0♈	4♏
13	23♈	26♓	1♈	4♏
14	24♈	27♓	3♈	4♏
15	25♈	28♓	4♈	3♏
16	26♈	28♓	5♈	3♏
17	27♈	29♓	6♈	2♏
18	28♈	0♈	8♈	2♏
19	29♈	2♈	9♈	2♏
20	0♉	3♈	10♈	1♏
21	1♉	4♈	11♈	1♏
22	2♉	5♈	12♈	1♏
23	3♉	6♈	14♈	0♏
24	4♉	7♈	15♈	0♏
25	5♉	9♈	16♈	29♎
26	6♉	10♈	17♈	29♎
27	7♉	11♈	19♈	29♎
28	8♉	13♈	20♈	28♎
29	9♉	14♈	21♈	28♎
30	10♉	16♈	22♈	28♎

May

Day	☉	☿	♀	♂
1	11♉	17♈	23♈	27♎
2	11♉	19♈	25♈	27♎
3	12♉	20♈	26♈	27♎
4	13♉	22♈	27♈	26♎
5	14♉	24♈	28♈	26♎
6	15♉	25♈	0♉	26♎
7	16♉	27♈	1♉	25♎
8	17♉	29♈	2♉	25♎
9	18♉	0♉	3♉	25♎
10	19♉	2♉	5♉	24♎
11	20♉	4♉	6♉	24♎
12	21♉	6♉	7♉	24♎
13	22♉	8♉	8♉	24♎
14	23♉	10♉	9♉	23♎
15	24♉	12♉	11♉	23♎
16	25♉	14♉	12♉	23♎
17	26♉	16♉	13♉	23♎
18	27♉	18♉	14♉	23♎
19	28♉	20♉	16♉	22♎
20	29♉	22♉	17♉	22♎
21	0♊	24♉	18♉	22♎
22	1♊	26♉	19♉	22♎
23	2♊	28♉	20♉	22♎
24	3♊	0♊	22♉	22♎
25	4♊	3♊	23♉	22♎
26	5♊	5♊	24♉	21♎
27	6♊	7♊	25♉	21♎
28	7♊	9♊	27♉	21♎
29	8♊	11♊	28♉	21♎
30	8♊	14♊	29♉	21♎
31	9♊	16♊	0♊	21♎

June

Day	☉	☿	♀	♂
1	10♊	18♊	1♊	21♎
2	11♊	20♊	3♊	21♎
3	12♊	22♊	4♊	21♎
4	13♊	24♊	5♊	21♎
5	14♊	26♊	6♊	21♎
6	15♊	28♊	8♊	21♎
7	16♊	0♋	9♊	21♎
8	17♊	2♋	10♊	22♎
9	18♊	4♋	11♊	22♎
10	19♊	6♋	13♊	22♎
11	20♊	8♋	14♊	22♎
12	21♊	9♋	15♊	22♎
13	22♊	11♋	16♊	22♎
14	23♊	13♋	17♊	22♎
15	24♊	14♋	19♊	23♎
16	25♊	16♋	20♊	23♎
17	26♊	18♋	21♊	23♎
18	27♊	19♋	22♊	23♎
19	28♊	21♋	24♊	23♎
20	29♊	22♋	25♊	24♎
21	29♊	23♋	26♊	24♎
22	0♋	25♋	27♊	24♎
23	1♋	26♋	28♊	24♎
24	2♋	27♋	0♋	24♎
25	3♋	28♋	1♋	25♎
26	4♋	0♌	2♋	25♎
27	5♋	1♌	3♋	25♎
28	6♋	2♌	5♋	26♎
29	7♋	3♌	6♋	26♎
30	8♋	4♌	7♋	26♎

July

Day	☉	☿	♀	♂
1	9♋	5♌	8♋	27♎
2	10♋	5♌	10♋	27♎
3	11♋	6♌	11♋	27♎
4	12♋	7♌	12♋	28♎
5	13♋	8♌	13♋	28♎
6	14♋	8♌	14♋	28♎
7	15♋	9♌	16♋	29♎
8	16♋	9♌	17♋	29♎
9	17♋	10♌	18♋	29♎
10	18♋	10♌	19♋	0♏
11	19♋	10♌	21♋	0♏
12	20♋	10♌	22♋	1♏
13	20♋	10♌	23♋	1♏
14	21♋	10♌	24♋	1♏
15	22♋	10♌	26♋	2♏
16	23♋	10♌	27♋	2♏
17	24♋	10♌	28♋	3♏
18	25♋	9♌	29♋	3♏
19	26♋	9♌	0♌	4♏
20	27♋	9♌	2♌	4♏
21	28♋	8♌	3♌	4♏
22	29♋	7♌	4♌	5♏
23	0♌	7♌	5♌	5♏
24	1♌	6♌	7♌	6♏
25	2♌	5♌	8♌	6♏
26	3♌	5♌	9♌	7♏
27	4♌	4♌	10♌	7♏
28	5♌	3♌	12♌	8♏
29	6♌	3♌	13♌	8♏
30	7♌	2♌	14♌	9♏
31	8♌	1♌	15♌	9♏

August

Day	☉	☿	♀	♂
1	9♌	1♌	16♌	10♏
2	10♌	0♌	18♌	10♏
3	11♌	0♌	19♌	11♏
4	11♌	0♌	20♌	11♏
5	12♌	29♋	21♌	12♏
6	13♌	29♋	23♌	12♏
7	14♌	29♋	24♌	13♏
8	15♌	29♋	25♌	14♏
9	16♌	0♌	26♌	14♏
10	17♌	0♌	28♌	15♏
11	18♌	0♌	29♌	15♏
12	19♌	1♌	0♍	16♏
13	20♌	2♌	1♍	16♏
14	21♌	2♌	2♍	17♏
15	22♌	3♌	4♍	17♏
16	23♌	4♌	5♍	18♏
17	24♌	5♌	6♍	19♏
18	25♌	7♌	7♍	19♏
19	26♌	8♌	9♍	20♏
20	27♌	9♌	10♍	20♏
21	28♌	11♌	11♍	21♏
22	29♌	12♌	12♍	22♏
23	0♍	14♌	14♍	22♏
24	1♍	16♌	15♍	23♏
25	2♍	18♌	16♍	23♏
26	3♍	19♌	17♍	24♏
27	4♍	21♌	19♍	25♏
28	5♍	23♌	20♍	25♏
29	6♍	25♌	21♍	26♏
30	7♍	27♌	22♍	26♏
31	7♍	29♌	23♍	27♏

September

Day	☉	☿	♀	♂
1	8♍	1♍	25♍	28♏
2	9♍	3♍	26♍	28♏
3	10♍	5♍	27♍	29♏
4	11♍	7♍	28♍	0♐
5	12♍	9♍	0♎	0♐
6	13♍	11♍	1♎	1♐
7	14♍	13♍	2♎	2♐
8	15♍	14♍	3♎	2♐
9	16♍	16♍	5♎	3♐
10	17♍	18♍	6♎	3♐
11	18♍	20♍	7♎	4♐
12	19♍	22♍	8♎	5♐
13	20♍	24♍	10♎	5♐
14	21♍	26♍	11♎	6♐
15	22♍	27♍	12♎	7♐
16	23♍	29♍	13♎	7♐
17	24♍	1♎	14♎	8♐
18	25♍	3♎	16♎	9♐
19	26♍	4♎	17♎	9♐
20	27♍	6♎	18♎	10♐
21	28♍	8♎	19♎	11♐
22	29♍	9♎	21♎	11♐
23	0♎	11♎	22♎	12♐
24	1♎	13♎	23♎	13♐
25	2♎	14♎	24♎	13♐
26	3♎	16♎	26♎	14♐
27	4♎	18♎	27♎	15♐
28	5♎	19♎	28♎	16♐
29	6♎	21♎	29♎	16♐
30	7♎	22♎	0♏	17♐

October

Day	☉	☿	♀	♂
1	8♎	24♎	2♏	18♐
2	9♎	25♎	3♏	18♐
3	10♎	27♎	4♏	19♐
4	11♎	28♎	5♏	20♐
5	12♎	0♏	7♏	20♐
6	13♎	1♏	8♏	21♐
7	14♎	3♏	9♏	22♐
8	15♎	4♏	10♏	23♐
9	16♎	5♏	12♏	23♐
10	17♎	7♏	13♏	24♐
11	18♎	8♏	14♏	25♐
12	19♎	10♏	15♏	25♐
13	20♎	11♏	16♏	26♐
14	21♎	12♏	18♏	27♐
15	22♎	14♏	19♏	28♐
16	23♎	15♏	20♏	28♐
17	24♎	16♏	21♏	29♐
18	25♎	18♏	23♏	0♑
19	26♎	19♏	24♏	0♑
20	27♎	20♏	25♏	1♑
21	28♎	21♏	26♏	2♑
22	28♎	22♏	28♏	3♑
23	29♎	23♏	29♏	3♑
24	0♏	24♏	0♐	4♑
25	1♏	25♏	1♐	5♑
26	2♏	26♏	2♐	6♑
27	3♏	27♏	4♐	6♑
28	4♏	28♏	5♐	7♑
29	5♏	29♏	6♐	8♑
30	6♏	0♐	7♐	9♑
31	7♏	0♐	9♐	9♑

November

Day	☉	☿	♀	♂
1	8♏	1♐	10♐	10♑
2	9♏	1♐	11♐	11♑
3	10♏	2♐	12♐	12♑
4	11♏	2♐	13♐	12♑
5	12♏	2♐	15♐	13♑
6	13♏	2♐	16♐	14♑
7	14♏	2♐	17♐	15♑
8	15♏	2♐	18♐	15♑
9	17♏	1♐	20♐	16♑
10	18♏	0♐	21♐	17♑
11	19♏	0♐	22♐	18♑
12	20♏	29♏	23♐	18♑
13	21♏	28♏	24♐	19♑
14	22♏	26♏	26♐	20♑
15	23♏	25♏	27♐	21♑
16	24♏	24♏	28♐	21♑
17	25♏	22♏	29♐	22♑
18	26♏	21♏	1♑	23♑
19	27♏	20♏	2♑	24♑
20	28♏	19♏	3♑	24♑
21	29♏	18♏	4♑	25♑
22	0♐	17♏	5♑	26♑
23	1♐	17♏	7♑	27♑
24	2♐	16♏	8♑	27♑
25	3♐	16♏	9♑	28♑
26	4♐	16♏	10♑	29♑
27	5♐	16♏	12♑	0♒
28	6♐	17♏	13♑	0♒
29	7♐	17♏	14♑	1♒
30	8♐	18♏	15♑	2♒

December

Day	☉	☿	♀	♂
1	9♐	19♏	16♑	3♒
2	10♐	19♏	18♑	4♒
3	11♐	20♏	19♑	4♒
4	12♐	21♏	20♑	5♒
5	13♐	22♏	21♑	6♒
6	14♐	24♏	22♑	7♒
7	15♐	25♏	24♑	7♒
8	16♐	26♏	25♑	8♒
9	17♐	27♏	26♑	9♒
10	18♐	29♏	27♑	10♒
11	19♐	0♐	28♑	11♒
12	20♐	1♐	0♒	11♒
13	21♐	3♐	1♒	12♒
14	22♐	4♐	2♒	13♒
15	23♐	6♐	3♒	14♒
16	24♐	7♐	4♒	14♒
17	25♐	8♐	6♒	15♒
18	26♐	10♐	7♒	16♒
19	27♐	11♐	8♒	17♒
20	28♐	13♐	9♒	17♒
21	29♐	14♐	10♒	18♒
22	0♑	16♐	12♒	19♒
23	1♑	17♐	13♒	20♒
24	2♑	19♐	14♒	21♒
25	3♑	20♐	15♒	21♒
26	4♑	22♐	16♒	22♒
27	5♑	23♐	18♒	23♒
28	6♑	25♐	19♒	24♒
29	7♑	27♐	20♒	24♒
30	8♑	28♐	21♒	25♒
31	9♑	0♑	22♒	26♒

☉ =Sun ☿ = Mercury ♀ = Venus ♂ = Mars ♈ = Aries ♉ = Taurus ♊ = Gemini ♋ = Cancer

1921

January

Day	☉	☿	♀	♂
1	10♑	1♑	23♒	27♒
2	11♑	3♑	25♒	28♒
3	12♑	4♑	26♒	28♒
4	13♑	6♑	27♒	29♒
5	14♑	7♑	28♒	0♓
6	15♑	9♑	29♒	1♓
7	16♑	11♑	0♓	1♓
8	17♑	12♑	2♓	2♓
9	18♑	14♑	3♓	3♓
10	19♑	15♑	4♓	4♓
11	20♑	17♑	5♓	5♓
12	21♑	19♑	6♓	5♓
13	22♑	20♑	7♓	6♓
14	24♑	22♑	8♓	7♓
15	25♑	24♑	10♓	8♓
16	26♑	25♑	11♓	8♓
17	27♑	27♑	12♓	9♓
18	28♑	28♑	13♓	10♓
19	29♑	0♒	14♓	11♓
20	0♒	2♒	15♓	12♓
21	1♒	4♒	16♓	12♓
22	2♒	5♒	17♓	13♓
23	3♒	7♒	19♓	14♓
24	4♒	9♒	20♓	15♓
25	5♒	10♒	21♓	15♓
26	6♒	12♒	22♓	16♓
27	7♒	14♒	23♓	17♓
28	8♒	16♒	24♓	18♓
29	9♒	17♒	25♓	18♓
30	10♒	19♒	26♓	19♓
31	11♒	21♒	27♓	20♓

April

Day	☉	☿	♀	♂
1	11♈	13♓	10♉	5♉
2	12♈	14♓	10♉	6♉
3	13♈	15♓	10♉	7♉
4	14♈	17♓	10♉	7♉
5	15♈	18♓	10♉	8♉
6	16♈	19♓	10♉	9♉
7	17♈	20♓	10♉	9♉
8	18♈	22♓	9♉	10♉
9	19♈	23♓	9♉	11♉
10	20♈	24♓	9♉	12♉
11	21♈	26♓	8♉	12♉
12	22♈	27♓	8♉	13♉
13	23♈	29♓	7♉	14♉
14	24♈	0♈	7♉	14♉
15	25♈	2♈	7♉	15♉
16	26♈	3♈	6♉	16♉
17	27♈	5♈	5♉	17♉
18	28♈	6♈	5♉	17♉
19	29♈	8♈	4♉	18♉
20	0♉	10♈	4♉	19♉
21	1♉	11♈	3♉	19♉
22	2♉	13♈	2♉	20♉
23	2♉	15♈	2♉	21♉
24	3♉	17♈	1♉	22♉
25	4♉	18♈	0♉	22♉
26	5♉	20♈	0♉	23♉
27	6♉	22♈	29♈	24♉
28	7♉	24♈	29♈	24♉
29	8♉	26♈	28♈	25♉
30	9♉	28♈	28♈	26♉

July

Day	☉	☿	♀	♂
1	9♋	19♋	23♉	8♋
2	10♋	19♋	24♉	9♋
3	11♋	18♋	25♉	10♋
4	12♋	18♋	26♉	10♋
5	13♋	17♋	27♉	11♋
6	14♋	17♋	28♉	12♋
7	15♋	16♋	29♉	12♋
8	15♋	15♋	0♊	13♋
9	16♋	15♋	1♊	14♋
10	17♋	14♋	2♊	14♋
11	18♋	14♋	3♊	15♋
12	19♋	13♋	4♊	15♋
13	20♋	13♋	5♊	16♋
14	21♋	12♋	6♊	17♋
15	22♋	12♋	7♊	17♋
16	23♋	12♋	8♊	18♋
17	24♋	11♋	9♊	19♋
18	25♋	11♋	10♊	19♋
19	26♋	11♋	11♊	20♋
20	27♋	11♋	12♊	21♋
21	28♋	11♋	13♊	21♋
22	29♋	12♋	14♊	22♋
23	0♌	12♋	15♊	23♋
24	1♌	12♋	16♊	23♋
25	2♌	13♋	18♊	24♋
26	3♌	13♋	19♊	25♋
27	4♌	14♋	20♊	25♋
28	5♌	15♋	21♊	26♋
29	6♌	16♋	22♊	27♋
30	6♌	17♋	23♊	27♋
31	7♌	18♋	24♊	28♋

October

Day	☉	☿	♀	♂
1	7♎	2♏	6♍	7♍
2	8♎	3♏	7♍	8♍
3	9♎	4♏	9♍	9♍
4	10♎	5♏	10♍	9♍
5	11♎	7♏	11♍	10♍
6	12♎	8♏	12♍	10♍
7	13♎	9♏	13♍	11♍
8	14♎	10♏	15♍	12♍
9	15♎	11♏	16♍	12♍
10	16♎	11♏	17♍	13♍
11	17♎	12♏	18♍	14♍
12	18♎	13♏	20♍	14♍
13	19♎	14♏	21♍	15♍
14	20♎	14♏	22♍	15♍
15	21♎	15♏	23♍	16♍
16	22♎	15♏	24♍	17♍
17	23♎	16♏	26♍	17♍
18	24♎	16♏	27♍	18♍
19	25♎	16♏	28♍	19♍
20	26♎	16♏	29♍	19♍
21	27♎	16♏	1♎	20♍
22	28♎	16♏	2♎	20♍
23	29♎	16♏	3♎	21♍
24	0♏	15♏	4♎	22♍
25	1♏	14♏	6♎	22♍
26	2♏	14♏	7♎	23♍
27	3♏	13♏	8♎	24♍
28	4♏	12♏	9♎	24♍
29	5♏	10♏	10♎	25♍
30	6♏	9♏	12♎	25♍
31	7♏	8♏	13♎	26♍

February

Day	☉	☿	♀	♂
1	12♒	23♒	28♓	21♓
2	13♒	24♒	29♓	22♓
3	14♒	26♒	0♈	22♓
4	15♒	28♒	2♈	23♓
5	16♒	0♓	3♈	24♓
6	17♒	1♓	4♈	25♓
7	18♒	3♓	5♈	25♓
8	19♒	5♓	6♈	26♓
9	20♒	6♓	7♈	27♓
10	21♒	8♓	8♈	28♓
11	22♒	9♓	9♈	28♓
12	23♒	11♓	10♈	29♓
13	24♒	12♓	11♈	0♈
14	25♒	13♓	12♈	1♈
15	26♒	14♓	13♈	2♈
16	27♒	15♓	14♈	2♈
17	28♒	16♓	15♈	3♈
18	29♒	17♓	16♈	4♈
19	0♓	17♓	16♈	5♈
20	1♓	17♓	17♈	5♈
21	2♓	18♓	18♈	6♈
22	3♓	18♓	19♈	7♈
23	4♓	18♓	20♈	8♈
24	5♓	17♓	21♈	8♈
25	6♓	17♓	22♈	9♈
26	7♓	16♓	23♈	10♈
27	8♓	16♓	24♈	11♈
28	9♓	15♓	24♈	11♈

May

Day	☉	☿	♀	♂
1	10♉	0♉	27♈	27♉
2	11♉	2♉	27♈	27♉
3	12♉	4♉	26♈	28♉
4	13♉	6♉	26♈	29♉
5	14♉	8♉	25♈	29♉
6	15♉	10♉	25♈	0♊
7	16♉	12♉	25♈	1♊
8	17♉	14♉	25♈	1♊
9	18♉	16♉	24♈	2♊
10	19♉	19♉	24♈	3♊
11	20♉	21♉	24♈	4♊
12	21♉	23♉	24♈	4♊
13	22♉	25♉	24♈	5♊
14	23♉	27♉	24♈	6♊
15	24♉	0♊	24♈	6♊
16	25♉	2♊	24♈	7♊
17	26♉	4♊	24♈	8♊
18	27♉	6♊	24♈	8♊
19	28♉	8♊	24♈	9♊
20	29♉	10♊	25♈	10♊
21	0♊	12♊	25♈	11♊
22	1♊	14♊	25♈	11♊
23	2♊	16♊	25♈	12♊
24	2♊	18♊	26♈	13♊
25	3♊	20♊	26♈	13♊
26	4♊	22♊	27♈	14♊
27	5♊	23♊	27♈	15♊
28	6♊	25♊	27♈	15♊
29	7♊	27♊	28♈	16♊
30	8♊	28♊	28♈	17♊
31	9♊	0♋	29♈	17♊

August

Day	☉	☿	♀	♂
1	8♌	19♋	25♊	29♋
2	9♌	21♋	26♊	29♋
3	10♌	22♋	27♊	0♌
4	11♌	23♋	28♊	0♌
5	12♌	25♋	0♋	1♌
6	13♌	26♋	1♋	2♌
7	14♌	28♋	2♋	2♌
8	15♌	0♌	3♋	3♌
9	16♌	2♌	4♋	4♌
10	17♌	3♌	5♋	4♌
11	18♌	5♌	6♋	5♌
12	19♌	7♌	7♋	6♌
13	20♌	9♌	8♋	6♌
14	21♌	11♌	10♋	7♌
15	22♌	13♌	11♋	8♌
16	23♌	15♌	12♋	8♌
17	24♌	17♌	13♋	9♌
18	25♌	19♌	14♋	9♌
19	26♌	21♌	15♋	10♌
20	27♌	23♌	16♋	11♌
21	28♌	25♌	18♋	11♌
22	29♌	27♌	19♋	12♌
23	0♍	29♌	20♋	13♌
24	0♍	1♍	21♋	13♌
25	1♍	3♍	22♋	14♌
26	2♍	5♍	23♋	15♌
27	3♍	7♍	25♋	15♌
28	4♍	9♍	26♋	16♌
29	5♍	11♍	27♋	17♌
30	6♍	13♍	28♋	17♌
31	7♍	15♍	29♋	18♌

November

Day	☉	☿	♀	♂
1	8♏	6♏	14♎	27♍
2	9♏	5♏	15♎	27♍
3	10♏	4♏	17♎	28♍
4	11♏	3♏	18♎	28♍
5	12♏	2♏	19♎	29♍
6	13♏	1♏	20♎	0♎
7	14♏	1♏	22♎	0♎
8	15♏	1♏	23♎	1♎
9	16♏	0♏	24♎	2♎
10	17♏	0♏	25♎	2♎
11	18♏	1♏	27♎	3♎
12	19♏	1♏	28♎	3♎
13	20♏	1♏	29♎	4♎
14	21♏	2♏	0♏	5♎
15	22♏	3♏	2♏	5♎
16	23♏	4♏	3♏	6♎
17	24♏	5♏	4♏	6♎
18	25♏	6♏	5♏	7♎
19	26♏	7♏	7♏	8♎
20	27♏	9♏	8♏	8♎
21	28♏	10♏	9♏	9♎
22	29♏	11♏	10♏	9♎
23	0♐	12♏	12♏	10♎
24	1♐	14♏	13♏	11♎
25	2♐	15♏	14♏	11♎
26	3♐	17♏	15♏	12♎
27	4♐	18♏	17♏	13♎
28	5♐	20♏	18♏	13♎
29	6♐	21♏	19♏	14♎
30	7♐	23♏	20♏	14♎

March

Day	☉	☿	♀	♂
1	10♓	14♓	25♈	12♈
2	11♓	13♓	26♈	13♈
3	12♓	12♓	27♈	14♈
4	13♓	11♓	28♈	14♈
5	14♓	10♓	28♈	15♈
6	15♓	9♓	29♈	16♈
7	16♓	8♓	0♉	17♈
8	17♓	7♓	1♉	17♈
9	18♓	6♓	1♉	18♈
10	19♓	5♓	2♉	19♈
11	20♓	5♓	3♉	20♈
12	21♓	4♓	3♉	20♈
13	22♓	4♓	4♉	21♈
14	23♓	4♓	4♉	22♈
15	24♓	4♓	5♉	23♈
16	25♓	3♓	6♉	23♈
17	26♓	4♓	6♉	24♈
18	27♓	4♓	7♉	25♈
19	28♓	4♓	7♉	26♈
20	29♓	4♓	8♉	26♈
21	0♈	5♓	8♉	27♈
22	1♈	5♓	8♉	28♈
23	2♈	6♓	9♉	28♈
24	3♈	6♓	9♉	29♈
25	4♈	7♓	9♉	0♉
26	5♈	8♓	10♉	1♉
27	6♈	8♓	10♉	1♉
28	7♈	9♓	10♉	2♉
29	8♈	10♓	10♉	3♉
30	9♈	11♓	10♉	4♉
31	10♈	12♓	10♉	4♉

June

Day	☉	☿	♀	♂
1	10♊	2♋	29♈	18♊
2	11♊	3♋	0♉	19♊
3	12♊	4♋	1♉	19♊
4	13♊	6♋	1♉	20♊
5	14♊	7♋	2♉	21♊
6	15♊	8♋	3♉	21♊
7	16♊	10♋	3♉	22♊
8	17♊	11♋	4♉	23♊
9	18♊	12♋	5♉	24♊
10	19♊	13♋	5♉	24♊
11	20♊	14♋	6♉	25♊
12	21♊	15♋	7♉	26♊
13	22♊	16♋	8♉	26♊
14	23♊	17♋	8♉	27♊
15	24♊	17♋	9♉	28♊
16	24♊	18♋	10♉	28♊
17	25♊	19♋	11♉	29♊
18	26♊	19♋	12♉	0♋
19	27♊	20♋	12♉	0♋
20	28♊	20♋	13♉	1♋
21	29♊	20♋	14♉	2♋
22	0♋	21♋	15♉	2♋
23	1♋	21♋	16♉	3♋
24	2♋	21♋	17♉	3♋
25	3♋	21♋	18♉	4♋
26	4♋	21♋	18♉	5♋
27	5♋	21♋	19♉	6♋
28	6♋	20♋	20♉	6♋
29	7♋	20♋	21♉	7♋
30	8♋	20♋	22♉	8♋

September

Day	☉	☿	♀	♂
1	8♍	16♍	0♌	18♌
2	9♍	18♍	1♌	19♌
3	10♍	20♍	3♌	20♌
4	11♍	22♍	4♌	20♌
5	12♍	23♍	5♌	21♌
6	13♍	25♍	6♌	22♌
7	14♍	27♍	7♌	22♌
8	15♍	29♍	9♌	23♌
9	16♍	0♎	10♌	24♌
10	17♍	2♎	11♌	24♌
11	18♍	3♎	12♌	25♌
12	19♍	5♎	13♌	25♌
13	20♍	7♎	14♌	26♌
14	21♍	8♎	16♌	27♌
15	22♍	10♎	17♌	27♌
16	23♍	11♎	18♌	28♌
17	24♍	13♎	19♌	29♌
18	25♍	14♎	20♌	29♌
19	26♍	16♎	22♌	0♍
20	27♍	17♎	23♌	0♍
21	28♍	19♎	24♌	1♍
22	29♍	20♎	25♌	2♍
23	0♎	21♎	26♌	2♍
24	1♎	23♎	28♌	3♍
25	2♎	24♎	29♌	4♍
26	3♎	26♎	0♍	4♍
27	4♎	27♎	1♍	5♍
28	5♎	28♎	2♍	5♍
29	6♎	29♎	4♍	6♍
30	6♎	1♏	5♍	7♍

December

Day	☉	☿	♀	♂
1	8♐	24♏	22♏	15♎
2	9♐	26♏	23♏	16♎
3	11♐	27♏	24♏	16♎
4	12♐	29♏	25♏	17♎
5	13♐	0♐	27♏	17♎
6	14♐	2♐	28♏	18♎
7	15♐	3♐	29♏	19♎
8	16♐	5♐	0♐	19♎
9	17♐	6♐	2♐	20♎
10	18♐	8♐	3♐	20♎
11	19♐	10♐	4♐	21♎
12	20♐	11♐	6♐	22♎
13	21♐	13♐	7♐	22♎
14	22♐	14♐	8♐	23♎
15	23♐	16♐	9♐	23♎
16	24♐	17♐	11♐	24♎
17	25♐	19♐	12♐	25♎
18	26♐	20♐	13♐	25♎
19	27♐	22♐	14♐	26♎
20	28♐	24♐	16♐	26♎
21	29♐	25♐	17♐	27♎
22	0♑	27♐	18♐	27♎
23	1♑	28♐	19♐	28♎
24	2♑	0♑	21♐	29♎
25	3♑	1♑	22♐	29♎
26	4♑	3♑	23♐	0♏
27	5♑	5♑	24♐	0♏
28	6♑	6♑	26♐	1♏
29	7♑	8♑	27♐	2♏
30	8♑	9♑	28♐	2♏
31	9♑	11♑	29♐	3♏

Planetary Positions

♌ = Leo ♍ = Virgo ♎ = Libra ♏ = Scorpio ♐ = Sagittarius ♑ = Capricorn ♒ = Aquarius ♓ = Pisces

January

Day	☉	☿	♀	♂
1	10♑	13♑	1♑	3♏
2	11♑	14♑	2♑	4♏
3	12♑	16♑	3♑	4♏
4	13♑	18♑	4♑	5♏
5	14♑	19♑	6♑	6♏
6	15♑	21♑	7♑	6♏
7	16♑	23♑	8♑	7♏
8	17♑	24♑	9♑	7♏
9	18♑	26♑	11♑	8♏
10	19♑	27♑	12♑	9♏
11	20♑	29♑	13♑	9♏
12	21♑	1♒	14♑	10♏
13	22♑	3♒	16♑	10♏
14	23♑	4♒	17♑	11♏
15	24♑	6♒	18♑	11♏
16	25♑	8♒	20♑	12♏
17	26♑	9♒	21♑	13♏
18	27♑	11♒	22♑	13♏
19	28♑	12♒	23♑	14♏
20	29♑	14♒	25♑	14♏
21	0♒	16♒	26♑	15♏
22	1♒	17♒	27♑	15♏
23	2♒	19♒	28♑	16♏
24	3♒	20♒	0♒	16♏
25	4♒	22♒	1♒	17♏
26	5♒	23♒	2♒	18♏
27	6♒	24♒	3♒	18♏
28	8♒	26♒	5♒	19♏
29	9♒	27♒	6♒	19♏
30	10♒	28♒	7♒	20♏
31	11♒	29♒	8♒	20♏

February

Day	☉	☿	♀	♂
1	12♒	0♓	10♒	21♏
2	13♒	0♓	11♒	21♏
3	14♒	1♓	12♒	22♏
4	15♒	1♓	13♒	22♏
5	16♒	1♓	15♒	23♏
6	17♒	1♓	16♒	24♏
7	18♒	1♓	17♒	24♏
8	19♒	1♓	18♒	25♏
9	20♒	0♓	20♒	25♏
10	21♒	29♒	21♒	26♏
11	22♒	28♒	22♒	26♏
12	23♒	27♒	23♒	27♏
13	24♒	26♒	25♒	27♏
14	25♒	25♒	26♒	28♏
15	26♒	24♒	27♒	28♏
16	27♒	23♒	28♒	29♏
17	28♒	22♒	0♓	29♏
18	29♒	21♒	1♓	0♐
19	0♓	20♒	2♓	0♐
20	1♓	19♒	3♓	1♐
21	2♓	18♒	5♓	1♐
22	3♓	17♒	6♓	2♐
23	4♓	17♒	7♓	2♐
24	5♓	17♒	8♓	3♐
25	6♓	16♒	10♓	3♐
26	7♓	16♒	11♓	4♐
27	8♓	16♒	12♓	4♐
28	9♓	16♒	13♓	5♐

March

Day	☉	☿	♀	♂
1	10♓	16♒	15♓	5♐
2	11♓	17♒	16♓	6♐
3	12♓	17♒	17♓	6♐
4	13♓	17♒	18♓	7♐
5	14♓	18♒	20♓	7♐
6	15♓	18♒	21♓	8♐
7	16♓	19♒	22♓	8♐
8	17♓	20♒	23♓	8♐
9	18♓	21♒	25♓	9♐
10	19♓	21♒	26♓	9♐
11	20♓	22♒	27♓	10♐
12	21♓	23♒	28♓	10♐
13	22♓	24♒	0♈	11♐
14	23♓	25♒	1♈	11♐
15	24♓	26♒	2♈	12♐
16	25♓	28♒	3♈	12♐
17	26♓	29♒	5♈	12♐
18	27♓	0♓	6♈	13♐
19	28♓	1♓	7♈	13♐
20	29♓	2♓	8♈	14♐
21	0♈	4♓	10♈	14♐
22	1♈	5♓	11♈	14♐
23	2♈	6♓	12♈	15♐
24	3♈	8♓	13♈	15♐
25	4♈	9♓	15♈	16♐
26	5♈	11♓	16♈	16♐
27	6♈	12♓	17♈	16♐
28	7♈	13♓	18♈	17♐
29	8♈	15♓	20♈	17♐
30	9♈	17♓	21♈	17♐
31	10♈	18♓	22♈	18♐

April

Day	☉	☿	♀	♂
1	11♈	20♓	23♈	18♐
2	12♈	21♓	24♈	19♐
3	13♈	23♓	26♈	19♐
4	14♈	25♓	27♈	19♐
5	15♈	26♓	28♈	20♐
6	16♈	28♓	29♈	20♐
7	17♈	0♈	1♉	20♐
8	18♈	1♈	2♉	20♐
9	19♈	3♈	3♉	21♐
10	20♈	5♈	4♉	21♐
11	21♈	7♈	6♉	21♐
12	22♈	9♈	7♉	22♐
13	22♈	10♈	8♉	22♐
14	23♈	12♈	9♉	22♐
15	24♈	14♈	11♉	22♐
16	25♈	16♈	12♉	23♐
17	26♈	18♈	13♉	23♐
18	27♈	20♈	14♉	23♐
19	28♈	22♈	15♉	23♐
20	29♈	24♈	17♉	23♐
21	0♉	26♈	18♉	24♐
22	1♉	28♈	19♉	24♐
23	2♉	0♉	20♉	24♐
24	3♉	3♉	22♉	24♐
25	4♉	5♉	23♉	24♐
26	5♉	7♉	24♉	24♐
27	6♉	9♉	25♉	25♐
28	7♉	11♉	27♉	25♐
29	8♉	13♉	28♉	25♐
30	9♉	15♉	29♉	25♐

May

Day	☉	☿	♀	♂
1	10♉	18♉	0♊	25♐
2	11♉	20♉	1♊	25♐
3	12♉	22♉	3♊	25♐
4	13♉	24♉	4♊	25♐
5	14♉	26♉	5♊	25♐
6	15♉	28♉	6♊	25♐
7	16♉	0♊	8♊	25♐
8	17♉	2♊	9♊	25♐
9	18♉	4♊	10♊	25♐
10	19♉	5♊	11♊	25♐
11	20♉	7♊	12♊	25♐
12	21♉	9♊	14♊	25♐
13	22♉	11♊	15♊	25♐
14	23♉	12♊	16♊	25♐
15	24♉	14♊	17♊	25♐
16	25♉	15♊	18♊	25♐
17	26♉	17♊	20♊	25♐
18	26♉	18♊	21♊	25♐
19	27♉	19♊	22♊	25♐
20	28♉	20♊	23♊	24♐
21	29♉	22♊	25♊	24♐
22	0♊	23♊	26♊	24♐
23	1♊	24♊	27♊	24♐
24	2♊	25♊	28♊	24♐
25	3♊	26♊	29♊	23♐
26	4♊	27♊	1♋	23♐
27	5♊	27♊	2♋	23♐
28	6♊	28♊	3♋	23♐
29	7♊	29♊	4♋	23♐
30	8♊	29♊	5♋	22♐
31	9♊	0♋	7♋	22♐

June

Day	☉	☿	♀	♂
1	10♊	0♋	8♋	22♐
2	11♊	0♋	9♋	21♐
3	12♊	1♋	10♋	21♐
4	13♊	1♋	11♋	21♐
5	14♊	1♋	13♋	21♐
6	15♊	1♋	14♋	20♐
7	16♊	1♋	15♋	20♐
8	17♊	1♋	16♋	20♐
9	18♊	0♋	17♋	19♐
10	19♊	0♋	19♋	19♐
11	19♊	0♋	20♋	19♐
12	20♊	0♋	21♋	18♐
13	21♊	29♊	22♋	18♐
14	22♊	29♊	23♋	18♐
15	23♊	28♊	25♋	17♐
16	24♊	28♊	26♋	17♐
17	25♊	27♊	27♋	17♐
18	26♊	26♊	28♋	16♐
19	27♊	26♊	29♋	16♐
20	28♊	25♊	1♌	16♐
21	29♊	25♊	2♌	15♐
22	0♋	24♊	3♌	15♐
23	1♋	24♊	4♌	15♐
24	2♋	23♊	5♌	15♐
25	3♋	23♊	7♌	14♐
26	4♋	23♊	8♌	14♐
27	5♋	22♊	9♌	14♐
28	6♋	22♊	10♌	14♐
29	7♋	22♊	11♌	13♐
30	8♋	22♊	12♌	13♐

July

Day	☉	☿	♀	♂
1	9♋	22♊	14♌	13♐
2	10♋	22♊	15♌	13♐
3	10♋	23♊	16♌	12♐
4	11♋	23♊	17♌	12♐
5	12♋	23♊	18♌	12♐
6	13♋	24♊	20♌	12♐
7	14♋	24♊	21♌	12♐
8	15♋	25♊	22♌	12♐
9	16♋	26♊	23♌	12♐
10	17♋	26♊	24♌	11♐
11	18♋	27♊	25♌	11♐
12	19♋	28♊	27♌	11♐
13	20♋	29♊	28♌	11♐
14	21♋	0♋	29♌	11♐
15	22♋	2♋	0♍	11♐
16	23♋	3♋	1♍	11♐
17	24♋	4♋	2♍	11♐
18	25♋	6♋	4♍	11♐
19	26♋	7♋	5♍	11♐
20	27♋	9♋	6♍	11♐
21	28♋	10♋	7♍	11♐
22	29♋	12♋	8♍	11♐
23	0♌	14♋	9♍	11♐
24	1♌	16♋	10♍	11♐
25	1♌	17♋	12♍	12♐
26	2♌	19♋	13♍	12♐
27	3♌	21♋	14♍	12♐
28	4♌	23♋	15♍	12♐
29	5♌	25♋	16♍	12♐
30	6♌	27♋	17♍	12♐
31	7♌	29♋	19♍	12♐

August

Day	☉	☿	♀	♂
1	8♌	1♌	20♍	13♐
2	9♌	3♌	21♍	13♐
3	10♌	6♌	22♍	13♐
4	11♌	8♌	23♍	13♐
5	12♌	10♌	24♍	14♐
6	13♌	12♌	25♍	14♐
7	14♌	14♌	26♍	14♐
8	15♌	16♌	28♍	14♐
9	16♌	18♌	29♍	15♐
10	17♌	20♌	0♎	15♐
11	18♌	22♌	1♎	15♐
12	19♌	24♌	2♎	16♐
13	20♌	26♌	3♎	16♐
14	21♌	28♌	4♎	16♐
15	22♌	0♍	5♎	17♐
16	23♌	2♍	6♎	17♐
17	23♌	3♍	8♎	17♐
18	24♌	5♍	9♎	18♐
19	25♌	7♍	10♎	18♐
20	26♌	9♍	11♎	18♐
21	27♌	11♍	12♎	19♐
22	28♌	12♍	13♎	19♐
23	29♌	14♍	14♎	20♐
24	0♍	16♍	15♎	20♐
25	1♍	17♍	16♎	20♐
26	2♍	19♍	17♎	21♐
27	3♍	21♍	18♎	21♐
28	4♍	22♍	19♎	22♐
29	5♍	24♍	21♎	22♐
30	6♍	25♍	22♎	23♐
31	7♍	27♍	23♎	23♐

September

Day	☉	☿	♀	♂
1	8♍	29♍	24♎	24♐
2	9♍	0♎	25♎	24♐
3	10♍	2♎	26♎	25♐
4	11♍	3♎	27♎	25♐
5	12♍	4♎	28♎	26♐
6	13♍	6♎	29♎	26♐
7	14♍	7♎	0♏	27♐
8	15♍	9♎	1♏	27♐
9	16♍	10♎	2♏	28♐
10	17♍	11♎	3♏	28♐
11	18♍	13♎	4♏	29♐
12	19♍	14♎	5♏	29♐
13	20♍	15♎	6♏	0♑
14	21♍	16♎	7♏	0♑
15	22♍	17♎	8♏	1♑
16	23♍	19♎	9♏	1♑
17	24♍	20♎	10♏	2♑
18	24♍	21♎	11♏	3♑
19	25♍	22♎	12♏	3♑
20	26♍	23♎	13♏	4♑
21	27♍	24♎	14♏	4♑
22	28♍	25♎	15♏	5♑
23	29♍	25♎	15♏	6♑
24	0♎	26♎	16♏	6♑
25	1♎	27♎	17♏	7♑
26	2♎	28♎	18♏	7♑
27	3♎	29♎	19♏	8♑
28	4♎	29♎	20♏	9♑
29	5♎	29♎	21♏	9♑
30	6♎	0♏	22♏	10♑

October

Day	☉	☿	♀	♂
1	7♎	0♏	23♏	10♑
2	8♎	0♏	23♏	11♑
3	9♎	0♏	24♏	12♑
4	10♎	0♏	25♏	12♑
5	11♎	0♏	26♏	13♑
6	12♎	0♏	27♏	14♑
7	13♎	29♎	27♏	14♑
8	14♎	29♎	28♏	15♑
9	15♎	28♎	29♏	15♑
10	16♎	27♎	29♏	16♑
11	17♎	26♎	0♐	17♑
12	18♎	25♎	1♐	17♑
13	19♎	24♎	2♐	18♑
14	20♎	23♎	2♐	19♑
15	21♎	22♎	3♐	19♑
16	22♎	20♎	3♐	20♑
17	23♎	19♎	4♐	21♑
18	24♎	18♎	5♐	21♑
19	25♎	17♎	5♐	22♑
20	26♎	16♎	6♐	23♑
21	27♎	16♎	6♐	23♑
22	28♎	15♎	7♐	24♑
23	29♎	15♎	7♐	25♑
24	0♏	15♎	7♐	25♑
25	1♏	15♎	8♐	26♑
26	2♏	15♎	8♐	27♑
27	3♏	15♎	8♐	28♑
28	4♏	16♎	9♐	28♑
29	5♏	17♎	9♐	29♑
30	6♏	18♎	9♐	0♒
31	7♏	18♎	9♐	0♒

November

Day	☉	☿	♀	♂
1	8♏	20♎	10♐	1♒
2	9♏	21♎	10♐	2♒
3	10♏	22♎	10♐	2♒
4	11♏	23♎	10♐	3♒
5	12♏	25♎	10♐	4♒
6	13♏	26♎	10♐	4♒
7	14♏	27♎	10♐	5♒
8	15♏	29♎	10♐	6♒
9	16♏	0♏	9♐	7♒
10	17♏	2♏	9♐	7♒
11	18♏	3♏	9♐	8♒
12	19♏	5♏	9♐	9♒
13	20♏	7♏	8♐	9♒
14	21♏	8♏	8♐	10♒
15	22♏	10♏	8♐	11♒
16	23♏	11♏	7♐	12♒
17	24♏	13♏	7♐	12♒
18	25♏	15♏	6♐	13♒
19	26♏	16♏	6♐	14♒
20	27♏	18♏	5♐	14♒
21	28♏	19♏	5♐	15♒
22	29♏	21♏	4♐	16♒
23	0♐	22♏	3♐	17♒
24	1♐	24♏	3♐	17♒
25	2♐	26♏	2♐	18♒
26	3♐	27♏	2♐	19♒
27	4♐	29♏	1♐	20♒
28	5♐	0♐	0♐	20♒
29	6♐	2♐	0♐	21♒
30	7♐	4♐	29♏	22♒

December

Day	☉	☿	♀	♂
1	8♐	5♐	29♏	22♒
2	9♐	7♐	28♏	23♒
3	10♐	8♐	28♏	24♒
4	11♐	10♐	27♏	25♒
5	12♐	11♐	27♏	25♒
6	13♐	13♐	26♏	26♒
7	14♐	15♐	26♏	27♒
8	15♐	16♐	26♏	28♒
9	16♐	18♐	25♏	28♒
10	17♐	19♐	25♏	29♒
11	18♐	21♐	25♏	0♓
12	19♐	22♐	25♏	0♓
13	20♐	24♐	25♏	1♓
14	21♐	26♐	25♏	2♓
15	22♐	27♐	25♏	3♓
16	23♐	29♐	25♏	3♓
17	24♐	0♑	25♏	4♓
18	26♐	2♑	25♏	5♓
19	27♐	3♑	25♏	6♓
20	28♐	5♑	25♏	6♓
21	29♐	7♑	25♏	7♓
22	0♑	8♑	25♏	8♓
23	1♑	10♑	26♏	9♓
24	2♑	11♑	26♏	9♓
25	3♑	13♑	26♏	10♓
26	4♑	15♑	27♏	11♓
27	5♑	16♑	27♏	12♓
28	6♑	18♑	27♏	12♓
29	7♑	19♑	28♏	13♓
30	8♑	21♑	28♏	14♓
31	9♑	23♑	29♏	14♓

Your Starway to Love

☉ =Sun ☿ = Mercury ♀ = Venus ♂ = Mars ♈ = Aries ♉ = Taurus ♊ = Gemini ♋ = Cancer

January

Day	☉	☿	♀	♂
1	10♑	24♑	29♏	15♓
2	11♑	26♑	0♐	16♓
3	12♑	27♑	1♐	17♓
4	13♑	29♑	1♐	17♓
5	14♑	0♒	2♐	18♓
6	15♑	2♒	2♐	19♓
7	16♑	3♒	3♐	20♓
8	17♑	5♒	4♐	20♓
9	18♑	6♒	4♐	21♓
10	19♑	7♒	5♐	22♓
11	20♑	9♒	6♐	23♓
12	21♑	10♒	7♐	23♓
13	22♑	11♒	7♐	24♓
14	23♑	12♒	8♐	25♓
15	24♑	13♒	9♐	25♓
16	25♑	14♒	10♐	26♓
17	26♑	14♒	11♐	27♓
18	27♑	15♒	12♐	28♓
19	28♑	15♒	12♐	28♓
20	29♑	15♒	13♐	29♓
21	0♒	15♒	14♐	0♈
22	1♒	15♒	15♐	1♈
23	2♒	14♒	16♐	1♈
24	3♒	13♒	17♐	2♈
25	4♒	13♒	18♐	3♈
26	5♒	12♒	19♐	3♈
27	6♒	11♒	20♐	4♈
28	7♒	9♒	21♐	5♈
29	8♒	8♒	22♐	6♈
30	9♒	7♒	23♐	6♈
31	10♒	6♒	24♐	7♈

February

Day	☉	☿	♀	♂
1	11♒	5♒	25♐	8♈
2	12♒	3♒	26♐	9♈
3	13♒	2♒	27♐	9♈
4	14♒	2♒	28♐	10♈
5	15♒	1♒	29♐	11♈
6	16♒	0♒	0♑	11♈
7	17♒	0♒	1♑	12♈
8	18♒	29♑	2♑	13♈
9	19♒	29♑	3♑	14♈
10	20♒	29♑	4♑	14♈
11	21♒	29♑	5♑	15♈
12	22♒	29♑	6♑	16♈
13	23♒	0♒	7♑	17♈
14	24♒	0♒	8♑	17♈
15	26♒	1♒	9♑	18♈
16	27♒	1♒	10♑	19♈
17	28♒	2♒	11♑	19♈
18	29♒	2♒	12♑	20♈
19	0♓	3♒	13♑	21♈
20	1♓	4♒	14♑	22♈
21	2♓	5♒	16♑	22♈
22	3♓	6♒	17♑	23♈
23	4♓	7♒	18♑	24♈
24	5♓	8♒	19♑	24♈
25	6♓	9♒	20♑	25♈
26	7♓	10♒	21♑	26♈
27	8♓	11♒	22♑	27♈
28	9♓	12♒	23♑	27♈

March

Day	☉	☿	♀	♂
1	10♓	14♒	24♑	28♈
2	11♓	15♒	25♑	29♈
3	12♓	16♒	27♑	29♈
4	13♓	17♒	28♑	0♉
5	14♓	19♒	29♑	1♉
6	15♓	20♒	0♒	2♉
7	16♓	21♒	1♒	2♉
8	17♓	23♒	2♒	3♉
9	18♓	24♒	3♒	4♉
10	19♓	26♒	5♒	4♉
11	20♓	27♒	6♒	5♉
12	21♓	29♒	7♒	6♉
13	22♓	0♓	8♒	6♉
14	23♓	2♓	9♒	7♉
15	24♓	3♓	10♒	8♉
16	25♓	5♓	11♒	9♉
17	26♓	6♓	13♒	9♉
18	27♓	8♓	14♒	10♉
19	28♓	10♓	15♒	11♉
20	29♓	11♓	16♒	11♉
21	0♈	13♓	17♒	12♉
22	1♈	15♓	18♒	13♉
23	2♈	16♓	19♒	13♉
24	3♈	18♓	21♒	14♉
25	4♈	20♓	22♒	15♉
26	5♈	22♓	23♒	16♉
27	6♈	23♓	24♒	16♉
28	7♈	25♓	25♒	17♉
29	7♈	27♓	26♒	18♉
30	8♈	29♓	28♒	18♉
31	9♈	1♈	29♒	19♉

April

Day	☉	☿	♀	♂
1	10♈	3♈	0♓	20♉
2	11♈	5♈	1♓	20♉
3	12♈	7♈	2♓	21♉
4	13♈	9♈	4♓	22♉
5	14♈	11♈	5♓	23♉
6	15♈	13♈	6♓	23♉
7	16♈	15♈	7♓	24♉
8	17♈	17♈	8♓	25♉
9	18♈	19♈	9♓	25♉
10	19♈	21♈	11♓	26♉
11	20♈	23♈	12♓	27♉
12	21♈	25♈	13♓	27♉
13	22♈	27♈	14♓	28♉
14	23♈	29♈	15♓	29♉
15	24♈	1♉	16♓	29♉
16	25♈	3♉	18♓	0♊
17	26♈	6♉	19♓	1♊
18	27♈	8♉	20♓	1♊
19	28♈	10♉	21♓	2♊
20	29♈	12♉	22♓	3♊
21	0♉	14♉	24♓	3♊
22	1♉	15♉	25♓	4♊
23	2♉	17♉	26♓	5♊
24	3♉	19♉	27♓	6♊
25	4♉	21♉	28♓	6♊
26	5♉	23♉	0♈	7♊
27	6♉	24♉	1♈	8♊
28	7♉	26♉	2♈	8♊
29	8♉	27♉	3♈	9♊
30	9♉	29♉	4♈	10♊

May

Day	☉	☿	♀	♂
1	10♉	0♊	6♈	10♊
2	11♉	1♊	7♈	11♊
3	12♉	2♊	8♈	12♊
4	13♉	4♊	9♈	12♊
5	14♉	5♊	10♈	13♊
6	15♉	6♊	12♈	14♊
7	16♉	6♊	13♈	14♊
8	17♉	7♊	14♈	15♊
9	18♉	8♊	15♈	16♊
10	19♉	9♊	16♈	16♊
11	19♉	9♊	18♈	17♊
12	20♉	10♊	19♈	18♊
13	21♉	10♊	20♈	18♊
14	22♉	10♊	21♈	19♊
15	23♉	11♊	22♈	20♊
16	24♉	11♊	24♈	20♊
17	25♉	11♊	25♈	21♊
18	26♉	11♊	26♈	22♊
19	27♉	11♊	27♈	22♊
20	28♉	11♊	28♈	23♊
21	29♉	10♊	0♉	24♊
22	0♊	10♊	1♉	24♊
23	1♊	10♊	2♉	25♊
24	2♊	9♊	3♉	26♊
25	3♊	9♊	4♉	26♊
26	4♊	8♊	6♉	27♊
27	5♊	8♊	7♉	28♊
28	6♊	7♊	8♉	28♊
29	7♊	7♊	9♉	29♊
30	8♊	6♊	10♉	0♋
31	9♊	6♊	12♉	0♋

June

Day	☉	☿	♀	♂
1	10♊	5♊	13♉	1♋
2	11♊	5♊	14♉	2♋
3	12♊	4♊	15♉	2♋
4	13♊	4♊	16♉	3♋
5	14♊	3♊	18♉	3♋
6	14♊	3♊	19♉	4♋
7	15♊	3♊	20♉	5♋
8	16♊	2♊	21♉	5♋
9	17♊	2♊	22♉	6♋
10	18♊	2♊	24♉	7♋
11	19♊	2♊	25♉	7♋
12	20♊	2♊	26♉	8♋
13	21♊	3♊	27♉	9♋
14	22♊	3♊	28♉	9♋
15	23♊	3♊	0♊	10♋
16	24♊	4♊	1♊	11♋
17	25♊	4♊	2♊	11♋
18	26♊	5♊	3♊	12♋
19	27♊	5♊	5♊	13♋
20	28♊	6♊	6♊	13♋
21	29♊	7♊	7♊	14♋
22	0♋	8♊	8♊	15♋
23	1♋	8♊	9♊	15♋
24	2♋	9♊	11♊	16♋
25	3♋	10♊	12♊	17♋
26	4♋	12♊	13♊	17♋
27	5♋	13♊	14♊	18♋
28	5♋	14♊	15♊	18♋
29	6♋	15♊	17♊	19♋
30	7♋	17♊	18♊	20♋

July

Day	☉	☿	♀	♂
1	8♋	18♊	19♊	20♋
2	9♋	19♊	20♊	21♋
3	10♋	21♊	21♊	22♋
4	11♋	23♊	23♊	22♋
5	12♋	24♊	24♊	23♋
6	13♋	26♊	25♊	24♋
7	14♋	28♊	26♊	24♋
8	15♋	29♊	28♊	25♋
9	16♋	1♋	29♊	26♋
10	17♋	3♋	0♋	26♋
11	18♋	5♋	1♋	27♋
12	19♋	7♋	2♋	28♋
13	20♋	9♋	4♋	28♋
14	21♋	11♋	5♋	29♋
15	22♋	13♋	6♋	29♋
16	23♋	15♋	7♋	0♌
17	24♋	17♋	9♋	1♌
18	25♋	20♋	10♋	1♌
19	26♋	22♋	11♋	2♌
20	26♋	24♋	12♋	3♌
21	27♋	26♋	13♋	3♌
22	28♋	28♋	15♋	4♌
23	29♋	0♌	16♋	5♌
24	0♌	2♌	17♋	5♌
25	1♌	4♌	18♋	6♌
26	2♌	7♌	20♋	7♌
27	3♌	9♌	21♋	7♌
28	4♌	11♌	22♋	8♌
29	5♌	13♌	23♋	8♌
30	6♌	15♌	24♋	9♌
31	7♌	16♌	26♋	10♌

August

Day	☉	☿	♀	♂
1	8♌	18♌	27♋	10♌
2	9♌	20♌	28♋	11♌
3	10♌	22♌	29♋	12♌
4	11♌	24♌	1♌	12♌
5	12♌	26♌	2♌	13♌
6	13♌	28♌	3♌	14♌
7	14♌	29♌	4♌	14♌
8	15♌	1♍	6♌	15♌
9	16♌	3♍	7♌	15♌
10	17♌	5♍	8♌	16♌
11	18♌	6♍	9♌	17♌
12	18♌	8♍	10♌	17♌
13	19♌	9♍	12♌	18♌
14	20♌	11♍	13♌	19♌
15	21♌	13♍	14♌	19♌
16	22♌	14♍	15♌	20♌
17	23♌	16♍	17♌	21♌
18	24♌	17♍	18♌	21♌
19	25♌	18♍	19♌	22♌
20	26♌	20♍	20♌	22♌
21	27♌	21♍	22♌	23♌
22	28♌	23♍	23♌	24♌
23	29♌	24♍	24♌	24♌
24	0♍	25♍	25♌	25♌
25	1♍	27♍	27♌	26♌
26	2♍	28♍	28♌	26♌
27	3♍	29♍	29♌	27♌
28	4♍	0♎	0♍	28♌
29	5♍	1♎	1♍	28♌
30	6♍	3♎	3♍	29♌
31	7♍	4♎	4♍	29♌

September

Day	☉	☿	♀	♂
1	8♍	5♎	5♍	0♍
2	9♍	6♎	6♍	1♍
3	10♍	7♎	8♍	1♍
4	11♍	8♎	9♍	2♍
5	12♍	9♎	10♍	3♍
6	13♍	9♎	11♍	3♍
7	14♍	10♎	13♍	4♍
8	15♍	11♎	14♍	5♍
9	15♍	11♎	15♍	5♍
10	16♍	12♎	16♍	6♍
11	17♍	13♎	18♍	6♍
12	18♍	13♎	19♍	7♍
13	19♍	13♎	20♍	8♍
14	20♍	14♎	21♍	8♍
15	21♍	14♎	23♍	9♍
16	22♍	14♎	24♍	10♍
17	23♍	14♎	25♍	10♍
18	24♍	14♎	26♍	11♍
19	25♍	13♎	28♍	12♍
20	26♍	13♎	29♍	12♍
21	27♍	12♎	0♎	13♍
22	28♍	12♎	1♎	13♍
23	29♍	11♎	3♎	14♍
24	0♎	10♎	4♎	15♍
25	1♎	9♎	5♎	15♍
26	2♎	8♎	6♎	16♍
27	3♎	7♎	8♎	17♍
28	4♎	6♎	9♎	17♍
29	5♎	5♎	10♎	18♍
30	6♎	4♎	11♎	19♍

October

Day	☉	☿	♀	♂
1	7♎	3♎	13♎	19♍
2	8♎	2♎	14♎	20♍
3	9♎	1♎	15♎	20♍
4	10♎	0♎	16♎	21♍
5	11♎	0♎	18♎	22♍
6	12♎	29♍	19♎	22♍
7	13♎	29♍	20♎	23♍
8	14♎	29♍	21♎	24♍
9	15♎	29♍	23♎	24♍
10	16♎	29♍	24♎	25♍
11	17♎	0♎	25♎	26♍
12	18♎	0♎	26♎	26♍
13	19♎	1♎	28♎	27♍
14	20♎	2♎	29♎	27♍
15	21♎	3♎	0♏	28♍
16	22♎	4♎	1♏	29♍
17	23♎	5♎	3♏	29♍
18	24♎	6♎	4♏	0♎
19	25♎	8♎	5♏	1♎
20	26♎	9♎	6♏	1♎
21	27♎	11♎	8♏	2♎
22	28♎	12♎	9♏	3♎
23	29♎	14♎	10♏	3♎
24	0♏	15♎	11♏	4♎
25	1♏	17♎	12♏	4♎
26	2♏	19♎	14♏	5♎
27	3♏	20♎	15♏	6♎
28	4♏	22♎	16♏	6♎
29	5♏	24♎	17♏	7♎
30	6♏	25♎	19♏	8♎
31	7♏	27♎	20♏	8♎

November

Day	☉	☿	♀	♂
1	8♏	28♎	21♏	9♎
2	9♏	0♏	22♏	10♎
3	10♏	2♏	24♏	10♎
4	11♏	3♏	25♏	11♎
5	12♏	5♏	26♏	12♎
6	13♏	7♏	27♏	12♎
7	14♏	8♏	29♏	13♎
8	15♏	10♏	0♐	13♎
9	16♏	12♏	1♐	14♎
10	17♏	13♏	2♐	15♎
11	18♏	15♏	4♐	15♎
12	19♏	17♏	5♐	16♎
13	20♏	18♏	6♐	17♎
14	21♏	20♏	7♐	17♎
15	22♏	21♏	9♐	18♎
16	23♏	23♏	10♐	19♎
17	24♏	25♏	11♐	19♎
18	25♏	26♏	12♐	20♎
19	26♏	28♏	14♐	20♎
20	27♏	29♏	15♐	21♎
21	28♏	1♐	16♐	22♎
22	29♏	2♐	17♐	22♎
23	0♐	4♐	19♐	23♎
24	1♐	6♐	20♐	24♎
25	2♐	7♐	21♐	24♎
26	3♐	9♐	22♐	25♎
27	4♐	10♐	24♐	26♎
28	5♐	12♐	25♐	26♎
29	6♐	13♐	26♐	27♎
30	7♐	15♐	27♐	28♎

December

Day	☉	☿	♀	♂
1	8♐	16♐	29♐	28♎
2	9♐	18♐	0♑	29♎
3	10♐	20♐	1♑	29♎
4	11♐	21♐	2♑	0♏
5	12♐	23♐	4♑	1♏
6	13♐	24♐	5♑	1♏
7	14♐	26♐	6♑	2♏
8	15♐	27♐	7♑	3♏
9	16♐	29♐	9♑	3♏
10	17♐	0♑	10♑	4♏
11	18♐	2♑	11♑	5♏
12	19♐	3♑	12♑	5♏
13	20♐	5♑	14♑	6♏
14	21♐	6♑	15♑	6♏
15	22♐	8♑	16♑	7♏
16	23♐	9♑	17♑	8♏
17	24♐	11♑	19♑	8♏
18	25♐	12♑	20♑	9♏
19	26♐	14♑	21♑	10♏
20	27♐	15♑	22♑	10♏
21	28♐	17♑	24♑	11♏
22	29♐	18♑	25♑	12♏
23	0♑	19♑	26♑	12♏
24	1♑	21♑	27♑	13♏
25	2♑	22♑	29♑	14♏
26	3♑	23♑	0♒	14♏
27	4♑	24♑	1♒	15♏
28	5♑	25♑	2♒	15♏
29	6♑	26♑	4♒	16♏
30	7♑	27♑	5♒	17♏
31	8♑	28♑	6♒	17♏

Planetary Positions

♌ = Leo ♍ = Virgo ♎ = Libra ♏ = Scorpio ♐ = Sagittarius ♑ = Capricorn ♒ = Aquarius ♓ = Pisces

1924

January

Day	☉	☿	♀	♂
1	10♑	28♑	7♒	18♏
2	11♑	29♑	9♒	19♏
3	12♑	29♑	10♒	19♏
4	13♑	29♑	11♒	20♏
5	14♑	29♑	12♒	21♏
6	15♑	29♑	13♒	21♏
7	16♑	28♑	15♒	22♏
8	17♑	27♑	16♒	23♏
9	18♑	26♑	17♒	23♏
10	19♑	25♑	18♒	24♏
11	20♑	24♑	20♒	24♏
12	21♑	23♑	21♒	25♏
13	22♑	22♑	22♒	26♏
14	23♑	20♑	23♒	26♏
15	24♑	19♑	25♒	27♏
16	25♑	18♑	26♒	28♏
17	26♑	17♑	27♒	28♏
18	27♑	16♑	28♒	29♏
19	28♑	15♑	0♓	0♐
20	29♑	14♑	1♓	0♐
21	0♒	14♑	2♓	1♐
22	1♒	13♑	3♓	2♐
23	2♒	13♑	4♓	2♐
24	3♒	13♑	6♓	3♐
25	4♒	13♑	7♓	3♐
26	5♒	13♑	8♓	4♐
27	6♒	13♑	9♓	5♐
28	7♒	14♑	11♓	5♐
29	8♒	14♑	12♓	6♐
30	9♒	15♑	13♓	7♐
31	10♒	15♑	14♓	7♐

April

Day	☉	☿	♀	♂
1	11♈	21♈	26♉	16♑
2	12♈	23♈	27♉	16♑
3	13♈	25♈	28♉	17♑
4	14♈	27♈	29♉	18♑
5	15♈	29♈	0♊	18♑
6	16♈	1♉	1♊	19♑
7	17♈	3♉	2♊	20♑
8	18♈	4♉	3♊	20♑
9	19♈	6♉	4♊	21♑
10	20♈	8♉	5♊	21♑
11	21♈	9♉	6♊	22♑
12	22♈	11♉	7♊	23♑
13	23♈	12♉	8♊	23♑
14	24♈	13♉	9♊	24♑
15	25♈	15♉	10♊	24♑
16	26♈	16♉	11♊	25♑
17	27♈	17♉	12♊	26♑
18	28♈	17♉	13♊	26♑
19	29♈	18♉	14♊	27♑
20	0♉	19♉	15♊	27♑
21	1♉	20♉	16♊	28♑
22	2♉	20♉	17♊	29♑
23	3♉	21♉	18♊	29♑
24	4♉	21♉	19♊	0♒
25	5♉	21♉	20♊	0♒
26	6♉	21♉	21♊	1♒
27	7♉	21♉	22♊	1♒
28	8♉	21♉	23♊	2♒
29	9♉	21♉	24♊	3♒
30	10♉	21♉	25♊	3♒

July

Day	☉	☿	♀	♂
1	9♋	4♋	10♋	2♓
2	10♋	6♋	9♋	2♓
3	11♋	8♋	8♋	3♓
4	12♋	10♋	8♋	3♓
5	13♋	12♋	7♋	3♓
6	14♋	14♋	6♋	3♓
7	15♋	17♋	6♋	3♓
8	16♋	19♋	5♋	4♓
9	17♋	21♋	5♋	4♓
10	18♋	23♋	4♋	4♓
11	19♋	25♋	4♋	4♓
12	20♋	27♋	3♋	4♓
13	21♋	29♋	3♋	4♓
14	21♋	1♌	3♋	5♓
15	22♋	3♌	2♋	5♓
16	23♋	5♌	2♋	5♓
17	24♋	7♌	2♋	5♓
18	25♋	9♌	2♋	5♓
19	26♋	11♌	1♋	5♓
20	27♋	13♌	1♋	5♓
21	28♋	14♌	1♋	5♓
22	29♋	16♌	1♋	5♓
23	0♌	18♌	1♋	5♓
24	1♌	20♌	1♋	5♓
25	2♌	21♌	1♋	5♓
26	3♌	23♌	1♋	5♓
27	4♌	25♌	1♋	5♓
28	5♌	26♌	2♋	5♓
29	6♌	28♌	2♋	5♓
30	7♌	29♌	2♋	5♓
31	8♌	1♍	2♋	5♓

October

Day	☉	☿	♀	♂
1	8♎	21♍	23♌	26♒
2	9♎	22♍	24♌	26♒
3	10♎	24♍	25♌	26♒
4	11♎	25♍	26♌	26♒
5	12♎	27♍	27♌	26♒
6	13♎	28♍	28♌	27♒
7	14♎	0♎	0♍	27♒
8	15♎	2♎	1♍	27♒
9	16♎	3♎	2♍	27♒
10	17♎	5♎	3♍	27♒
11	18♎	7♎	4♍	28♒
12	19♎	9♎	5♍	28♒
13	20♎	10♎	6♍	28♒
14	21♎	12♎	7♍	28♒
15	22♎	14♎	9♍	29♒
16	23♎	16♎	10♍	29♒
17	24♎	17♎	11♍	29♒
18	25♎	19♎	12♍	0♓
19	26♎	21♎	13♍	0♓
20	27♎	22♎	14♍	0♓
21	28♎	24♎	15♍	0♓
22	29♎	26♎	17♍	1♓
23	0♏	28♎	18♍	1♓
24	1♏	29♎	19♍	1♓
25	2♏	1♏	20♍	2♓
26	3♏	3♏	21♍	2♓
27	4♏	4♏	22♍	3♓
28	5♏	6♏	24♍	3♓
29	6♏	7♏	25♍	3♓
30	7♏	9♏	26♍	4♓
31	8♏	11♏	27♍	4♓

February

Day	☉	☿	♀	♂
1	11♒	16♑	15♓	8♐
2	12♒	17♑	17♓	9♐
3	13♒	18♑	18♓	9♐
4	14♒	19♑	19♓	10♐
5	15♒	20♑	20♓	11♐
6	16♒	21♑	22♓	11♐
7	17♒	22♑	23♓	12♐
8	18♒	23♑	24♓	12♐
9	19♒	24♑	25♓	13♐
10	20♒	25♑	26♓	14♐
11	21♒	26♑	28♓	14♐
12	22♒	28♑	29♓	15♐
13	23♒	29♑	0♈	16♐
14	24♒	0♒	1♈	16♐
15	25♒	1♒	2♈	17♐
16	26♒	3♒	4♈	18♐
17	27♒	4♒	5♈	18♐
18	28♒	5♒	6♈	19♐
19	29♒	7♒	7♈	19♐
20	0♓	8♒	8♈	20♐
21	1♓	10♒	10♈	21♐
22	2♓	11♒	11♈	21♐
23	3♓	13♒	12♈	22♐
24	4♓	14♒	13♈	23♐
25	5♓	16♒	14♈	23♐
26	6♓	17♒	16♈	24♐
27	7♓	19♒	17♈	25♐
28	8♓	20♒	18♈	25♐
29	9♓	22♒	19♈	26♐

May

Day	☉	☿	♀	♂
1	11♉	21♉	26♊	4♒
2	12♉	20♉	27♊	4♒
3	12♉	20♉	28♊	5♒
4	13♉	19♉	28♊	6♒
5	14♉	19♉	29♊	6♒
6	15♉	18♉	0♋	7♒
7	16♉	18♉	1♋	7♒
8	17♉	17♉	2♋	8♒
9	18♉	16♉	3♋	8♒
10	19♉	16♉	3♋	9♒
11	20♉	15♉	4♋	9♒
12	21♉	15♉	5♋	10♒
13	22♉	14♉	6♋	11♒
14	23♉	14♉	6♋	11♒
15	24♉	13♉	7♋	12♒
16	25♉	13♉	8♋	12♒
17	26♉	13♉	9♋	13♒
18	27♉	12♉	9♋	13♒
19	28♉	12♉	10♋	14♒
20	29♉	12♉	10♋	14♒
21	0♊	12♉	11♋	15♒
22	1♊	12♉	12♋	15♒
23	2♊	12♉	12♋	16♒
24	3♊	12♉	13♋	16♒
25	4♊	13♉	13♋	17♒
26	5♊	13♉	14♋	17♒
27	6♊	14♉	14♋	18♒
28	7♊	14♉	15♋	18♒
29	8♊	15♉	15♋	19♒
30	8♊	15♉	15♋	19♒
31	9♊	16♉	16♋	20♒

August

Day	☉	☿	♀	♂
1	9♌	2♍	3♋	5♓
2	10♌	4♍	3♋	5♓
3	11♌	5♍	3♋	5♓
4	12♌	6♍	4♋	5♓
5	12♌	8♍	4♋	4♓
6	13♌	9♍	4♋	4♓
7	14♌	10♍	5♋	4♓
8	15♌	12♍	5♋	4♓
9	16♌	13♍	6♋	4♓
10	17♌	14♍	7♋	4♓
11	18♌	15♍	7♋	3♓
12	19♌	16♍	8♋	3♓
13	20♌	17♍	8♋	3♓
14	21♌	18♍	9♋	3♓
15	22♌	19♍	10♋	2♓
16	23♌	20♍	10♋	2♓
17	24♌	21♍	11♋	2♓
18	25♌	22♍	12♋	2♓
19	26♌	23♍	12♋	1♓
20	27♌	24♍	13♋	1♓
21	28♌	24♍	14♋	1♓
22	29♌	25♍	15♋	1♓
23	0♍	25♍	15♋	0♓
24	1♍	26♍	16♋	0♓
25	2♍	26♍	17♋	0♓
26	3♍	27♍	18♋	0♓
27	4♍	27♍	19♋	29♒
28	5♍	27♍	19♋	29♒
29	6♍	27♍	20♋	29♒
30	7♍	27♍	21♋	29♒
31	7♍	27♍	22♋	28♒

November

Day	☉	☿	♀	♂
1	9♏	12♏	28♍	5♓
2	10♏	14♏	0♎	5♓
3	11♏	16♏	1♎	5♓
4	12♏	17♏	2♎	6♓
5	13♏	19♏	3♎	6♓
6	14♏	20♏	4♎	7♓
7	15♏	22♏	5♎	7♓
8	16♏	23♏	7♎	8♓
9	17♏	25♏	8♎	8♓
10	18♏	26♏	9♎	9♓
11	19♏	28♏	10♎	9♓
12	20♏	0♐	11♎	10♓
13	21♏	1♐	13♎	10♓
14	22♏	3♐	14♎	11♓
15	23♏	4♐	15♎	11♓
16	24♏	6♐	16♎	12♓
17	25♏	7♐	17♎	12♓
18	26♏	9♐	19♎	13♓
19	27♏	10♐	20♎	13♓
20	28♏	12♐	21♎	14♓
21	29♏	13♐	22♎	14♓
22	0♐	15♐	24♎	15♓
23	1♐	16♐	25♎	15♓
24	2♐	18♐	26♎	16♓
25	3♐	19♐	27♎	16♓
26	4♐	21♐	28♎	17♓
27	5♐	22♐	0♏	17♓
28	6♐	23♐	1♏	18♓
29	7♐	25♐	2♏	18♓
30	8♐	26♐	3♏	19♓

March

Day	☉	☿	♀	♂
1	10♓	23♒	20♈	26♐
2	11♓	25♒	21♈	27♐
3	12♓	27♒	23♈	28♐
4	13♓	28♒	24♈	28♐
5	14♓	0♓	25♈	29♐
6	15♓	2♓	26♈	0♑
7	16♓	3♓	27♈	0♑
8	17♓	5♓	29♈	1♑
9	18♓	7♓	0♉	2♑
10	19♓	9♓	1♉	2♑
11	20♓	10♓	2♉	3♑
12	21♓	12♓	3♉	3♑
13	22♓	14♓	4♉	4♑
14	23♓	16♓	5♉	5♑
15	24♓	18♓	7♉	5♑
16	25♓	19♓	8♉	6♑
17	26♓	21♓	9♉	7♑
18	27♓	23♓	10♉	7♑
19	28♓	25♓	11♉	8♑
20	29♓	27♓	12♉	8♑
21	0♈	29♓	13♉	9♑
22	1♈	1♈	15♉	10♑
23	2♈	3♈	16♉	10♑
24	3♈	5♈	17♉	11♑
25	4♈	7♈	18♉	12♑
26	5♈	9♈	19♉	12♑
27	6♈	11♈	20♉	13♑
28	7♈	13♈	21♉	13♑
29	8♈	15♈	22♉	14♑
30	9♈	17♈	23♉	15♑
31	10♈	19♈	25♉	15♑

June

Day	☉	☿	♀	♂
1	10♊	17♉	16♋	20♒
2	11♊	17♉	16♋	21♒
3	12♊	18♉	17♋	21♒
4	13♊	19♉	17♋	22♒
5	14♊	20♉	17♋	22♒
6	15♊	21♉	17♋	23♒
7	16♊	22♉	17♋	23♒
8	17♊	24♉	18♋	24♒
9	18♊	25♉	18♋	24♒
10	19♊	26♉	18♋	24♒
11	20♊	27♉	18♋	25♒
12	21♊	29♉	17♋	25♒
13	22♊	0♊	17♋	26♒
14	23♊	2♊	17♋	26♒
15	24♊	3♊	17♋	27♒
16	25♊	5♊	17♋	27♒
17	26♊	6♊	17♋	27♒
18	27♊	8♊	16♋	28♒
19	28♊	10♊	16♋	28♒
20	29♊	12♊	16♋	28♒
21	0♋	13♊	15♋	29♒
22	0♋	15♊	15♋	29♒
23	1♋	17♊	14♋	0♓
24	2♋	19♊	14♋	0♓
25	3♋	21♊	13♋	0♓
26	4♋	23♊	13♋	0♓
27	5♋	25♊	12♋	1♓
28	6♋	27♊	11♋	1♓
29	7♋	29♊	11♋	1♓
30	8♋	1♋	10♋	2♓

September

Day	☉	☿	♀	♂
1	8♍	26♍	23♋	28♒
2	9♍	26♍	24♋	28♒
3	10♍	26♍	25♋	28♒
4	11♍	25♍	26♋	27♒
5	12♍	24♍	27♋	27♒
6	13♍	24♍	27♋	27♒
7	14♍	23♍	28♋	27♒
8	15♍	22♍	29♋	27♒
9	16♍	21♍	0♌	26♒
10	17♍	20♍	1♌	26♒
11	18♍	19♍	2♌	26♒
12	19♍	18♍	3♌	26♒
13	20♍	17♍	4♌	26♒
14	21♍	16♍	5♌	26♒
15	22♍	15♍	6♌	26♒
16	23♍	14♍	7♌	26♒
17	24♍	14♍	8♌	26♒
18	25♍	13♍	9♌	25♒
19	26♍	13♍	10♌	25♒
20	27♍	13♍	11♌	25♒
21	28♍	13♍	12♌	25♒
22	29♍	13♍	13♌	25♒
23	0♎	13♍	14♌	25♒
24	1♎	14♍	15♌	25♒
25	2♎	14♍	17♌	25♒
26	3♎	15♍	18♌	25♒
27	4♎	16♍	19♌	25♒
28	5♎	17♍	20♌	26♒
29	6♎	18♍	21♌	26♒
30	7♎	19♍	22♌	26♒

December

Day	☉	☿	♀	♂
1	9♐	28♐	5♏	19♓
2	10♐	29♐	6♏	20♓
3	11♐	0♑	7♏	21♓
4	12♐	2♑	8♏	21♓
5	13♐	3♑	9♏	22♓
6	14♐	4♑	11♏	22♓
7	15♐	5♑	12♏	23♓
8	16♐	6♑	13♏	23♓
9	17♐	8♑	14♏	24♓
10	18♐	9♑	16♏	25♓
11	19♐	10♑	17♏	25♓
12	20♐	10♑	18♏	26♓
13	21♐	11♑	19♏	26♓
14	22♐	12♑	21♏	27♓
15	23♐	12♑	22♏	27♓
16	24♐	13♑	23♏	28♓
17	25♐	13♑	24♏	29♓
18	26♐	13♑	26♏	29♓
19	27♐	13♑	27♏	0♈
20	28♐	13♑	28♏	0♈
21	29♐	12♑	29♏	1♈
22	0♑	11♑	0♐	2♈
23	1♑	11♑	2♐	2♈
24	2♑	9♑	3♐	3♈
25	3♑	8♑	4♐	3♈
26	4♑	7♑	5♐	4♈
27	5♑	6♑	7♐	5♈
28	6♑	4♑	8♐	5♈
29	7♑	3♑	9♐	6♈
30	8♑	2♑	10♐	7♈
31	9♑	0♑	12♐	7♈

1925

Your Starway to Love

☉ = Sun ☿ = Mercury ♀ = Venus ♂ = Mars ♈ = Aries ♉ = Taurus ♊ = Gemini ♋ = Cancer

January

Day	☉	☿	♀	♂
1	10♑	29♐	13♐	8♈
2	11♑	29♐	14♐	8♈
3	12♑	28♐	15♐	9♈
4	13♑	27♐	17♐	10♈
5	14♑	27♐	18♐	10♈
6	15♑	27♐	19♐	11♈
7	16♑	27♐	20♐	11♈
8	17♑	27♐	22♐	12♈
9	18♑	27♐	23♐	13♈
10	19♑	27♐	24♐	13♈
11	20♑	28♐	25♐	14♈
12	22♑	29♐	27♐	15♈
13	23♑	29♐	28♐	15♈
14	24♑	0♑	29♐	16♈
15	25♑	1♑	0♑	16♈
16	26♑	2♑	2♑	17♈
17	27♑	3♑	3♑	18♈
18	28♑	4♑	4♑	18♈
19	29♑	5♑	5♑	19♈
20	0♒	6♑	7♑	20♈
21	1♒	7♑	8♑	20♈
22	2♒	8♑	9♑	21♈
23	3♒	9♑	10♑	22♈
24	4♒	10♑	12♑	22♈
25	5♒	12♑	13♑	23♈
26	6♒	13♑	14♑	23♈
27	7♒	14♑	15♑	24♈
28	8♒	16♑	17♑	25♈
29	9♒	17♑	18♑	25♈
30	10♒	18♑	19♑	26♈
31	11♒	20♑	20♑	27♈

April

Day	☉	☿	♀	♂
1	11♈	0♉	5♈	5♊
2	12♈	0♉	6♈	6♊
3	13♈	1♉	8♈	7♊
4	14♈	2♉	9♈	7♊
5	15♈	2♉	10♈	8♊
6	16♈	2♉	11♈	8♊
7	17♈	3♉	13♈	9♊
8	18♈	3♉	14♈	10♊
9	19♈	3♉	15♈	10♊
10	20♈	2♉	16♈	11♊
11	21♈	2♉	17♈	12♊
12	22♈	2♉	19♈	12♊
13	23♈	2♉	20♈	13♊
14	24♈	1♉	21♈	14♊
15	25♈	0♉	22♈	14♊
16	26♈	0♉	24♈	15♊
17	27♈	29♈	25♈	16♊
18	28♈	28♈	26♈	16♊
19	29♈	28♈	27♈	17♊
20	0♉	27♈	29♈	17♊
21	1♉	26♈	0♉	18♊
22	2♉	26♈	1♉	19♊
23	3♉	25♈	2♉	19♊
24	3♉	24♈	4♉	20♊
25	4♉	24♈	5♉	21♊
26	5♉	23♈	6♉	21♊
27	6♉	23♈	7♉	22♊
28	7♉	23♈	8♉	23♊
29	8♉	22♈	10♉	23♊
30	9♉	22♈	11♉	24♊

July

Day	☉	☿	♀	♂
1	9♋	21♋	27♋	3♌
2	10♋	23♋	28♋	4♌
3	11♋	25♋	0♌	4♌
4	12♋	27♋	1♌	5♌
5	13♋	29♋	2♌	6♌
6	14♋	1♌	3♌	6♌
7	15♋	3♌	4♌	7♌
8	15♋	4♌	6♌	7♌
9	16♋	6♌	7♌	8♌
10	17♋	8♌	8♌	9♌
11	18♋	9♌	9♌	9♌
12	19♋	11♌	10♌	10♌
13	20♋	13♌	12♌	11♌
14	21♋	14♌	13♌	11♌
15	22♋	16♌	14♌	12♌
16	23♋	17♌	15♌	13♌
17	24♋	18♌	17♌	13♌
18	25♋	20♌	18♌	14♌
19	26♋	21♌	19♌	14♌
20	27♋	23♌	20♌	15♌
21	28♋	24♌	21♌	16♌
22	29♋	25♌	23♌	16♌
23	0♌	26♌	24♌	17♌
24	1♌	27♌	25♌	18♌
25	2♌	29♌	26♌	18♌
26	3♌	0♍	28♌	19♌
27	4♌	1♍	29♌	19♌
28	5♌	2♍	0♍	20♌
29	6♌	3♍	1♍	21♌
30	7♌	4♍	2♍	21♌
31	7♌	4♍	4♍	22♌

October

Day	☉	☿	♀	♂
1	7♎	3♎	18♏	2♎
2	8♎	4♎	19♏	2♎
3	9♎	6♎	20♏	3♎
4	10♎	8♎	21♏	4♎
5	11♎	10♎	23♏	4♎
6	12♎	12♎	24♏	5♎
7	13♎	13♎	25♏	5♎
8	14♎	15♎	26♏	6♎
9	15♎	17♎	27♏	7♎
10	16♎	18♎	28♏	7♎
11	17♎	20♎	0♐	8♎
12	18♎	22♎	1♐	9♎
13	19♎	24♎	2♐	9♎
14	20♎	25♎	3♐	10♎
15	21♎	27♎	4♐	11♎
16	22♎	28♎	5♐	11♎
17	23♎	0♏	7♐	12♎
18	24♎	2♏	8♐	13♎
19	25♎	3♏	9♐	13♎
20	26♎	5♏	10♐	14♎
21	27♎	6♏	11♐	15♎
22	28♎	8♏	12♐	15♎
23	29♎	10♏	13♐	16♎
24	0♏	11♏	15♐	17♎
25	1♏	13♏	16♐	17♎
26	2♏	14♏	17♐	18♎
27	3♏	16♏	18♐	19♎
28	4♏	17♏	19♐	19♎
29	5♏	19♏	20♐	20♎
30	6♏	20♏	21♐	20♎
31	7♏	22♏	22♐	21♎

February

Day	☉	☿	♀	♂
1	12♒	21♑	22♑	27♈
2	13♒	22♑	23♑	28♈
3	14♒	24♑	24♑	29♈
4	15♒	25♑	25♑	29♈
5	16♒	27♑	27♑	0♉
6	17♒	28♑	28♑	1♉
7	18♒	0♒	29♑	1♉
8	19♒	1♒	0♒	2♉
9	20♒	3♒	2♒	2♉
10	21♒	4♒	3♒	3♉
11	22♒	6♒	4♒	4♉
12	23♒	7♒	5♒	4♉
13	24♒	9♒	7♒	5♉
14	25♒	11♒	8♒	6♉
15	26♒	12♒	9♒	6♉
16	27♒	14♒	10♒	7♉
17	28♒	15♒	12♒	8♉
18	29♒	17♒	13♒	8♉
19	0♓	19♒	14♒	9♉
20	1♓	20♒	15♒	10♉
21	2♓	22♒	17♒	10♉
22	3♓	24♒	18♒	11♉
23	4♓	26♒	19♒	11♉
24	5♓	27♒	20♒	12♉
25	6♓	29♒	22♒	13♉
26	7♓	1♓	23♒	13♉
27	8♓	3♓	24♒	14♉
28	9♓	5♓	25♒	15♉

May

Day	☉	☿	♀	♂
1	10♉	22♈	12♉	24♊
2	11♉	22♈	13♉	25♊
3	12♉	22♈	15♉	26♊
4	13♉	22♈	16♉	26♊
5	14♉	22♈	17♉	27♊
6	15♉	23♈	18♉	28♊
7	16♉	23♈	20♉	28♊
8	17♉	23♈	21♉	29♊
9	18♉	24♈	22♉	0♋
10	19♉	24♈	23♉	0♋
11	20♉	25♈	25♉	1♋
12	21♉	26♈	26♉	1♋
13	22♉	27♈	27♉	2♋
14	23♉	27♈	28♉	3♋
15	24♉	28♈	29♉	3♋
16	25♉	29♈	1♊	4♋
17	26♉	0♉	2♊	5♋
18	27♉	1♉	3♊	5♋
19	28♉	2♉	4♊	6♋
20	29♉	3♉	6♊	7♋
21	0♊	5♉	7♊	7♋
22	1♊	6♉	8♊	8♋
23	2♊	7♉	9♊	8♋
24	3♊	8♉	11♊	9♋
25	3♊	10♉	12♊	10♋
26	4♊	11♉	13♊	10♋
27	5♊	13♉	14♊	11♋
28	6♊	14♉	15♊	12♋
29	7♊	16♉	17♊	12♋
30	8♊	17♉	18♊	13♋
31	9♊	19♉	19♊	13♋

August

Day	☉	☿	♀	♂
1	8♌	5♍	5♍	23♌
2	9♌	6♍	6♍	23♌
3	10♌	7♍	7♍	24♌
4	11♌	7♍	8♍	25♌
5	12♌	8♍	10♍	25♌
6	13♌	8♍	11♍	26♌
7	14♌	9♍	12♍	26♌
8	15♌	9♍	13♍	27♌
9	16♌	9♍	15♍	28♌
10	17♌	9♍	16♍	28♌
11	18♌	9♍	17♍	29♌
12	19♌	9♍	18♍	0♍
13	20♌	9♍	19♍	0♍
14	21♌	9♍	21♍	1♍
15	22♌	9♍	22♍	1♍
16	23♌	8♍	23♍	2♍
17	24♌	8♍	24♍	3♍
18	25♌	7♍	25♍	3♍
19	26♌	7♍	27♍	4♍
20	27♌	6♍	28♍	5♍
21	28♌	5♍	29♍	5♍
22	29♌	4♍	0♎	6♍
23	0♍	4♍	1♎	7♍
24	1♍	3♍	3♎	7♍
25	1♍	2♍	4♎	8♍
26	2♍	1♍	5♎	8♍
27	3♍	0♍	6♎	9♍
28	4♍	29♌	7♎	10♍
29	5♍	28♌	9♎	10♍
30	6♍	28♌	10♎	11♍
31	7♍	27♌	11♎	12♍

November

Day	☉	☿	♀	♂
1	8♏	23♏	24♐	22♎
2	9♏	25♏	25♐	22♎
3	10♏	26♏	26♐	23♎
4	11♏	28♏	27♐	24♎
5	12♏	29♏	28♐	24♎
6	13♏	1♐	29♐	25♎
7	14♏	2♐	0♑	26♎
8	15♏	3♐	1♑	26♎
9	16♏	5♐	3♑	27♎
10	17♏	6♐	4♑	28♎
11	18♏	8♐	5♑	28♎
12	19♏	9♐	6♑	29♎
13	20♏	10♐	7♑	0♏
14	21♏	12♐	8♑	0♏
15	22♏	13♐	9♑	1♏
16	23♏	14♐	10♑	2♏
17	24♏	16♐	11♑	2♏
18	25♏	17♐	12♑	3♏
19	26♏	18♐	13♑	4♏
20	27♏	19♐	14♑	4♏
21	28♏	20♐	15♑	5♏
22	29♏	21♐	16♑	6♏
23	0♐	22♐	18♑	6♏
24	1♐	23♐	19♑	7♏
25	2♐	24♐	20♑	8♏
26	3♐	25♐	21♑	8♏
27	4♐	26♐	22♑	9♏
28	5♐	26♐	23♑	10♏
29	6♐	27♐	24♑	10♏
30	7♐	27♐	25♑	11♏

March

Day	☉	☿	♀	♂
1	10♓	6♓	27♒	15♉
2	11♓	8♓	28♒	16♉
3	12♓	10♓	29♒	17♉
4	13♓	12♓	0♓	17♉
5	14♓	14♓	1♓	18♉
6	15♓	16♓	3♓	19♉
7	16♓	18♓	4♓	19♉
8	17♓	20♓	5♓	20♉
9	18♓	22♓	6♓	20♉
10	19♓	23♓	8♓	21♉
11	20♓	25♓	9♓	22♉
12	21♓	27♓	10♓	22♉
13	22♓	29♓	11♓	23♉
14	23♓	1♈	13♓	24♉
15	24♓	3♈	14♓	24♉
16	25♓	5♈	15♓	25♉
17	26♓	7♈	16♓	26♉
18	27♓	9♈	18♓	26♉
19	28♓	11♈	19♓	27♉
20	29♓	13♈	20♓	28♉
21	0♈	15♈	21♓	28♉
22	1♈	16♈	23♓	29♉
23	2♈	18♈	24♓	29♉
24	3♈	20♈	25♓	0♊
25	4♈	21♈	26♓	1♊
26	5♈	23♈	28♓	1♊
27	6♈	24♈	29♓	2♊
28	7♈	25♈	0♈	3♊
29	8♈	27♈	1♈	3♊
30	9♈	28♈	3♈	4♊
31	10♈	29♈	4♈	5♊

June

Day	☉	☿	♀	♂
1	10♊	20♉	20♊	14♋
2	11♊	22♉	22♊	15♋
3	12♊	24♉	23♊	15♋
4	13♊	26♉	24♊	16♋
5	14♊	27♉	25♊	17♋
6	15♊	29♉	26♊	17♋
7	16♊	1♊	28♊	18♋
8	17♊	3♊	29♊	19♋
9	18♊	5♊	0♋	19♋
10	19♊	7♊	1♋	20♋
11	20♊	9♊	3♋	20♋
12	21♊	11♊	4♋	21♋
13	22♊	13♊	5♋	22♋
14	23♊	15♊	6♋	22♋
15	24♊	17♊	7♋	23♋
16	25♊	20♊	9♋	24♋
17	25♊	22♊	10♋	24♋
18	26♊	24♊	11♋	25♋
19	27♊	26♊	12♋	25♋
20	28♊	28♊	14♋	26♋
21	29♊	1♋	15♋	27♋
22	0♋	3♋	16♋	27♋
23	1♋	5♋	17♋	28♋
24	2♋	7♋	19♋	29♋
25	3♋	9♋	20♋	29♋
26	4♋	11♋	21♋	0♌
27	5♋	13♋	22♋	1♌
28	6♋	15♋	23♋	1♌
29	7♋	17♋	25♋	2♌
30	8♋	19♋	26♋	2♌

September

Day	☉	☿	♀	♂
1	8♍	27♌	12♎	12♍
2	9♍	27♌	13♎	13♍
3	10♍	26♌	15♎	14♍
4	11♍	26♌	16♎	14♍
5	12♍	26♌	17♎	15♍
6	13♍	27♌	18♎	15♍
7	14♍	27♌	19♎	16♍
8	15♍	28♌	21♎	17♍
9	16♍	28♌	22♎	17♍
10	17♍	29♌	23♎	18♍
11	18♍	0♍	24♎	19♍
12	19♍	1♍	25♎	19♍
13	20♍	2♍	27♎	20♍
14	21♍	4♍	28♎	21♍
15	22♍	5♍	29♎	21♍
16	23♍	6♍	0♏	22♍
17	24♍	8♍	1♏	23♍
18	25♍	9♍	3♏	23♍
19	26♍	11♍	4♏	24♍
20	27♍	13♍	5♏	24♍
21	28♍	15♍	6♏	25♍
22	29♍	16♍	7♏	26♍
23	0♎	18♍	8♏	26♍
24	1♎	20♍	10♏	27♍
25	2♎	22♍	11♏	28♍
26	3♎	24♍	12♏	28♍
27	4♎	25♍	13♏	29♍
28	5♎	27♍	14♏	0♎
29	6♎	29♍	16♏	0♎
30	7♎	1♎	17♏	1♎

December

Day	☉	☿	♀	♂
1	8♐	27♐	26♑	12♏
2	10♐	27♐	27♑	12♏
3	11♐	27♐	28♑	13♏
4	12♐	27♐	29♑	14♏
5	13♐	26♐	0♒	14♏
6	14♐	26♐	1♒	15♏
7	15♐	25♐	1♒	16♏
8	16♐	24♐	2♒	17♏
9	17♐	22♐	3♒	17♏
10	18♐	21♐	4♒	18♏
11	19♐	20♐	5♒	19♏
12	20♐	18♐	6♒	19♏
13	21♐	17♐	7♒	20♏
14	22♐	16♐	8♒	21♏
15	23♐	15♐	9♒	21♏
16	24♐	14♐	10♒	22♏
17	25♐	13♐	10♒	23♏
18	26♐	12♐	11♒	23♏
19	27♐	11♐	12♒	24♏
20	28♐	11♐	13♒	25♏
21	29♐	11♐	14♒	25♏
22	0♑	11♐	14♒	26♏
23	1♑	11♐	15♒	27♏
24	2♑	11♐	16♒	27♏
25	3♑	12♐	17♒	28♏
26	4♑	12♐	17♒	29♏
27	5♑	13♐	18♒	29♏
28	6♑	14♐	19♒	0♐
29	7♑	15♐	19♒	1♐
30	8♑	16♐	20♒	1♐
31	9♑	16♐	20♒	2♐

Planetary Positions

♌ = Leo ♍ = Virgo ♎ = Libra ♏ = Scorpio ♐ = Sagittarius ♑ = Capricorn ♒ = Aquarius ♓ = Pisces

1926

January

Day	☉	☿	♀	♂
1	10♑	18♐	21♒	3♐
2	11♑	19♐	22♒	4♐
3	12♑	20♐	22♒	4♐
4	13♑	21♐	23♒	5♐
5	14♑	22♐	23♒	6♐
6	15♑	23♐	23♒	6♐
7	16♑	25♐	24♒	7♐
8	17♑	26♐	24♒	8♐
9	18♑	27♐	25♒	8♐
10	19♑	29♐	25♒	9♐
11	20♑	0♑	25♒	10♐
12	21♑	1♑	25♒	10♐
13	22♑	3♑	26♒	11♐
14	23♑	4♑	26♒	12♐
15	24♑	5♑	26♒	13♐
16	25♑	7♑	26♒	13♐
17	26♑	8♑	26♒	14♐
18	27♑	10♑	26♒	15♐
19	28♑	11♑	26♒	15♐
20	29♑	13♑	26♒	16♐
21	0♒	14♑	26♒	17♐
22	1♒	16♑	26♒	17♐
23	2♒	17♑	25♒	18♐
24	3♒	19♑	25♒	19♐
25	4♒	20♑	25♒	20♐
26	5♒	22♑	25♒	20♐
27	7♒	23♑	24♒	21♐
28	8♒	25♑	24♒	22♐
29	9♒	26♑	23♒	22♐
30	10♒	28♑	23♒	23♐
31	11♒	0♒	22♒	24♐

April

Day	☉	☿	♀	♂
1	11♈	9♈	26♒	7♒
2	12♈	8♈	27♒	7♒
3	13♈	7♈	27♒	8♒
4	14♈	7♈	28♒	9♒
5	15♈	6♈	29♒	9♒
6	16♈	5♈	0♓	10♒
7	17♈	5♈	1♓	11♒
8	18♈	4♈	2♓	12♒
9	19♈	4♈	3♓	12♒
10	20♈	3♈	4♓	13♒
11	21♈	3♈	5♓	14♒
12	22♈	3♈	5♓	14♒
13	23♈	3♈	6♓	15♒
14	23♈	3♈	7♓	16♒
15	24♈	3♈	8♓	17♒
16	25♈	3♈	9♓	17♒
17	26♈	3♈	10♓	18♒
18	27♈	3♈	11♓	19♒
19	28♈	4♈	12♓	20♒
20	29♈	4♈	13♓	20♒
21	0♉	5♈	14♓	21♒
22	1♉	5♈	15♓	22♒
23	2♉	6♈	16♓	22♒
24	3♉	7♈	17♓	23♒
25	4♉	8♈	18♓	24♒
26	5♉	8♈	19♓	25♒
27	6♉	9♈	20♓	25♒
28	7♉	10♈	21♓	26♒
29	8♉	11♈	22♓	27♒
30	9♉	12♈	23♓	27♒

July

Day	☉	☿	♀	♂
1	9♋	3♌	3♊	11♈
2	10♋	4♌	4♊	12♈
3	11♋	6♌	5♊	12♈
4	11♋	7♌	6♊	13♈
5	12♋	8♌	7♊	14♈
6	13♋	9♌	9♊	14♈
7	14♋	10♌	10♊	15♈
8	15♋	11♌	11♊	15♈
9	16♋	13♌	12♊	16♈
10	17♋	14♌	13♊	17♈
11	18♋	14♌	14♊	17♈
12	19♋	15♌	16♊	18♈
13	20♋	16♌	17♊	19♈
14	21♋	17♌	18♊	19♈
15	22♋	18♌	19♊	20♈
16	23♋	18♌	20♊	20♈
17	24♋	19♌	22♊	21♈
18	25♋	20♌	23♊	22♈
19	26♋	20♌	24♊	22♈
20	27♋	20♌	25♊	23♈
21	28♋	21♌	26♊	24♈
22	29♋	21♌	28♊	24♈
23	0♌	21♌	29♊	25♈
24	1♌	21♌	0♋	25♈
25	1♌	21♌	1♋	26♈
26	2♌	21♌	2♋	26♈
27	3♌	21♌	3♋	27♈
28	4♌	21♌	5♋	28♈
29	5♌	20♌	6♋	28♈
30	6♌	20♌	7♋	29♈
31	7♌	19♌	8♋	29♈

October

Day	☉	☿	♀	♂
1	7♎	16♎	24♍	19♉
2	8♎	18♎	25♍	19♉
3	9♎	19♎	27♍	19♉
4	10♎	21♎	28♍	19♉
5	11♎	23♎	29♍	19♉
6	12♎	24♎	0♎	19♉
7	13♎	26♎	2♎	19♉
8	14♎	27♎	3♎	19♉
9	15♎	29♎	4♎	19♉
10	16♎	0♏	5♎	19♉
11	17♎	2♏	7♎	18♉
12	18♎	3♏	8♎	18♉
13	19♎	5♏	9♎	18♉
14	20♎	6♏	10♎	18♉
15	21♎	8♏	12♎	18♉
16	22♎	9♏	13♎	17♉
17	23♎	11♏	14♎	17♉
18	24♎	12♏	15♎	17♉
19	25♎	14♏	17♎	17♉
20	26♎	15♏	18♎	16♉
21	27♎	17♏	19♎	16♉
22	28♎	18♏	20♎	16♉
23	29♎	19♏	22♎	15♉
24	0♏	21♏	23♎	15♉
25	1♏	22♏	24♎	15♉
26	2♏	23♏	25♎	14♉
27	3♏	25♏	27♎	14♉
28	4♏	26♏	28♎	14♉
29	5♏	27♏	29♎	13♉
30	6♏	28♏	0♏	13♉
31	7♏	0♐	2♏	13♉

February

Day	☉	☿	♀	♂
1	12♒	1♒	22♒	24♐
2	13♒	3♒	21♒	25♐
3	14♒	5♒	21♒	26♐
4	15♒	6♒	20♒	27♐
5	16♒	8♒	20♒	27♐
6	17♒	9♒	19♒	28♐
7	18♒	11♒	18♒	29♐
8	19♒	13♒	18♒	29♐
9	20♒	15♒	17♒	0♑
10	21♒	16♒	17♒	1♑
11	22♒	18♒	16♒	1♑
12	23♒	20♒	15♒	2♑
13	24♒	22♒	15♒	3♑
14	25♒	23♒	14♒	4♑
15	26♒	25♒	14♒	4♑
16	27♒	27♒	13♒	5♑
17	28♒	29♒	13♒	6♑
18	29♒	1♓	12♒	6♑
19	0♓	2♓	12♒	7♑
20	1♓	4♓	12♒	8♑
21	2♓	6♓	11♒	9♑
22	3♓	8♓	11♒	9♑
23	4♓	10♓	11♒	10♑
24	5♓	12♓	11♒	11♑
25	6♓	14♓	11♒	11♑
26	7♓	16♓	10♒	12♑
27	8♓	17♓	10♒	13♑
28	9♓	19♓	10♒	14♑

May

Day	☉	☿	♀	♂
1	10♉	13♈	24♓	28♒
2	11♉	15♈	25♓	29♒
3	12♉	16♈	26♓	0♓
4	13♉	17♈	27♓	0♓
5	14♉	18♈	28♓	1♓
6	15♉	19♈	0♈	2♓
7	16♉	21♈	1♈	3♓
8	17♉	22♈	2♈	3♓
9	18♉	24♈	3♈	4♓
10	19♉	25♈	4♈	5♓
11	20♉	27♈	5♈	5♓
12	21♉	28♈	6♈	6♓
13	22♉	0♉	7♈	7♓
14	23♉	1♉	8♈	8♓
15	24♉	3♉	9♈	8♓
16	25♉	4♉	10♈	9♓
17	26♉	6♉	11♈	10♓
18	27♉	8♉	13♈	10♓
19	27♉	10♉	14♈	11♓
20	28♉	11♉	15♈	12♓
21	29♉	13♉	16♈	13♓
22	0♊	15♉	17♈	13♓
23	1♊	17♉	18♈	14♓
24	2♊	19♉	19♈	15♓
25	3♊	21♉	20♈	15♓
26	4♊	23♉	21♈	16♓
27	5♊	25♉	23♈	17♓
28	6♊	27♉	24♈	18♓
29	7♊	29♉	25♈	18♓
30	8♊	1♊	26♈	19♓
31	9♊	3♊	27♈	20♓

August

Day	☉	☿	♀	♂
1	8♌	19♌	9♋	0♉
2	9♌	18♌	11♋	0♉
3	10♌	18♌	12♋	1♉
4	11♌	17♌	13♋	2♉
5	12♌	16♌	14♋	2♉
6	13♌	15♌	16♋	3♉
7	14♌	15♌	17♋	3♉
8	15♌	14♌	18♋	4♉
9	16♌	13♌	19♋	4♉
10	17♌	12♌	20♋	5♉
11	18♌	12♌	22♋	5♉
12	19♌	11♌	23♋	6♉
13	20♌	11♌	24♋	6♉
14	21♌	10♌	25♋	7♉
15	22♌	10♌	26♋	7♉
16	23♌	10♌	28♋	8♉
17	24♌	9♌	29♋	8♉
18	24♌	9♌	0♌	9♉
19	25♌	10♌	1♌	9♉
20	26♌	10♌	2♌	9♉
21	27♌	10♌	4♌	10♉
22	28♌	11♌	5♌	10♉
23	29♌	11♌	6♌	11♉
24	0♍	12♌	7♌	11♉
25	1♍	13♌	9♌	12♉
26	2♍	14♌	10♌	12♉
27	3♍	15♌	11♌	12♉
28	4♍	16♌	12♌	13♉
29	5♍	18♌	13♌	13♉
30	6♍	19♌	15♌	14♉
31	7♍	20♌	16♌	14♉

November

Day	☉	☿	♀	♂
1	8♏	1♐	3♏	12♉
2	9♏	2♐	4♏	12♉
3	10♏	3♐	5♏	12♉
4	11♏	4♐	7♏	11♉
5	12♏	5♐	8♏	11♉
6	13♏	6♐	9♏	11♉
7	14♏	7♐	10♏	10♉
8	15♏	8♐	12♏	10♉
9	16♏	9♐	13♏	10♉
10	17♏	9♐	14♏	9♉
11	18♏	10♐	15♏	9♉
12	19♏	11♐	17♏	9♉
13	20♏	11♐	18♏	8♉
14	21♏	11♐	19♏	8♉
15	22♏	11♐	21♏	8♉
16	23♏	11♐	22♏	7♉
17	24♏	11♐	23♏	7♉
18	25♏	11♐	24♏	7♉
19	26♏	10♐	26♏	7♉
20	27♏	10♐	27♏	6♉
21	28♏	9♐	28♏	6♉
22	29♏	8♐	29♏	6♉
23	0♐	7♐	1♐	6♉
24	1♐	5♐	2♐	6♉
25	2♐	4♐	3♐	5♉
26	3♐	3♐	4♐	5♉
27	4♐	1♐	6♐	5♉
28	5♐	0♐	7♐	5♉
29	6♐	29♏	8♐	5♉
30	7♐	28♏	9♐	5♉

March

Day	☉	☿	♀	♂
1	10♓	21♓	10♒	14♑
2	11♓	23♓	10♒	15♑
3	12♓	25♓	11♒	16♑
4	13♓	27♓	11♒	16♑
5	14♓	28♓	11♒	17♑
6	15♓	0♈	11♒	18♑
7	16♓	2♈	11♒	19♑
8	17♓	3♈	12♒	19♑
9	18♓	5♈	12♒	20♑
10	19♓	6♈	12♒	21♑
11	20♓	8♈	13♒	21♑
12	21♓	9♈	13♒	22♑
13	22♓	10♈	13♒	23♑
14	23♓	11♈	14♒	24♑
15	24♓	12♈	14♒	24♑
16	25♓	13♈	15♒	25♑
17	26♓	13♈	15♒	26♑
18	27♓	14♈	16♒	26♑
19	28♓	14♈	17♒	27♑
20	29♓	15♈	17♒	28♑
21	0♈	15♈	18♒	29♑
22	1♈	15♈	18♒	29♑
23	2♈	15♈	19♒	0♒
24	3♈	14♈	20♒	1♒
25	4♈	14♈	20♒	1♒
26	5♈	13♈	21♒	2♒
27	6♈	13♈	22♒	3♒
28	7♈	12♈	23♒	4♒
29	8♈	11♈	23♒	4♒
30	9♈	11♈	24♒	5♒
31	10♈	10♈	25♒	6♒

June

Day	☉	☿	♀	♂
1	10♊	6♊	28♈	20♓
2	11♊	8♊	29♈	21♓
3	12♊	10♊	0♉	22♓
4	13♊	12♊	2♉	22♓
5	14♊	14♊	3♉	23♓
6	15♊	17♊	4♉	24♓
7	16♊	19♊	5♉	25♓
8	17♊	21♊	6♉	25♓
9	18♊	23♊	7♉	26♓
10	19♊	25♊	8♉	27♓
11	20♊	27♊	10♉	27♓
12	20♊	0♋	11♉	28♓
13	21♊	2♋	12♉	29♓
14	22♊	4♋	13♉	29♓
15	23♊	6♋	14♉	0♈
16	24♊	8♋	15♉	1♈
17	25♊	10♋	16♉	1♈
18	26♊	12♋	18♉	2♈
19	27♊	13♋	19♉	3♈
20	28♊	15♋	20♉	4♈
21	29♊	17♋	21♉	4♈
22	0♋	19♋	22♉	5♈
23	1♋	21♋	23♉	6♈
24	2♋	22♋	25♉	6♈
25	3♋	24♋	26♉	7♈
26	4♋	25♋	27♉	8♈
27	5♋	27♋	28♉	8♈
28	6♋	29♋	29♉	9♈
29	7♋	0♌	0♊	10♈
30	8♋	1♌	2♊	10♈

September

Day	☉	☿	♀	♂
1	8♍	22♌	17♌	14♉
2	9♍	24♌	18♌	15♉
3	10♍	25♌	20♌	15♉
4	11♍	27♌	21♌	15♉
5	12♍	29♌	22♌	16♉
6	13♍	1♍	23♌	16♉
7	14♍	2♍	24♌	16♉
8	15♍	4♍	26♌	16♉
9	16♍	6♍	27♌	17♉
10	17♍	8♍	28♌	17♉
11	18♍	10♍	29♌	17♉
12	19♍	12♍	1♍	17♉
13	20♍	14♍	2♍	18♉
14	21♍	16♍	3♍	18♉
15	22♍	18♍	4♍	18♉
16	23♍	20♍	6♍	18♉
17	24♍	21♍	7♍	18♉
18	25♍	23♍	8♍	19♉
19	26♍	25♍	9♍	19♉
20	26♍	27♍	11♍	19♉
21	27♍	29♍	12♍	19♉
22	28♍	1♎	13♍	19♉
23	29♍	2♎	14♍	19♉
24	0♎	4♎	15♍	19♉
25	1♎	6♎	17♍	19♉
26	2♎	8♎	18♍	19♉
27	3♎	9♎	19♍	19♉
28	4♎	11♎	20♍	19♉
29	5♎	13♎	22♍	19♉
30	6♎	14♎	23♍	19♉

December

Day	☉	☿	♀	♂
1	8♐	27♏	11♐	5♉
2	9♐	26♏	12♐	5♉
3	10♐	26♏	13♐	5♉
4	11♐	25♏	14♐	5♉
5	12♐	25♏	16♐	5♉
6	13♐	25♏	17♐	5♉
7	14♐	25♏	18♐	5♉
8	15♐	26♏	19♐	5♉
9	16♐	26♏	21♐	5♉
10	17♐	27♏	22♐	5♉
11	18♐	28♏	23♐	5♉
12	19♐	28♏	24♐	5♉
13	20♐	29♏	26♐	5♉
14	21♐	0♐	27♐	5♉
15	22♐	1♐	28♐	5♉
16	23♐	3♐	29♐	5♉
17	25♐	4♐	1♑	5♉
18	26♐	5♐	2♑	5♉
19	27♐	6♐	3♑	5♉
20	28♐	7♐	5♑	6♉
21	29♐	9♐	6♑	6♉
22	0♑	10♐	7♑	6♉
23	1♑	11♐	8♑	6♉
24	2♑	13♐	10♑	6♉
25	3♑	14♐	11♑	7♉
26	4♑	16♐	12♑	7♉
27	5♑	17♐	13♑	7♉
28	6♑	18♐	15♑	7♉
29	7♑	20♐	16♑	7♉
30	8♑	21♐	17♑	8♉
31	9♑	23♐	18♑	8♉

☉ =Sun ☿ = Mercury ♀ = Venus ♂ = Mars ♈ = Aries ♉ = Taurus ♊ = Gemini ♋ = Cancer

1927

January

Day	☉	☿	♀	♂
1	10♑	24♐	20♑	8♉
2	11♑	26♐	21♑	9♉
3	12♑	27♐	22♑	9♉
4	13♑	29♐	23♑	9♉
5	14♑	0♑	25♑	9♉
6	15♑	2♑	26♑	10♉
7	16♑	3♑	27♑	10♉
8	17♑	5♑	28♑	10♉
9	18♑	6♑	0♒	11♉
10	19♑	8♑	1♒	11♉
11	20♑	9♑	2♒	11♉
12	21♑	11♑	3♒	12♉
13	22♑	12♑	5♒	12♉
14	23♑	14♑	6♒	12♉
15	24♑	16♑	7♒	13♉
16	25♑	17♑	8♒	13♉
17	26♑	19♑	10♒	14♉
18	27♑	20♑	11♒	14♉
19	28♑	22♑	12♒	14♉
20	29♑	24♑	13♒	15♉
21	0♒	25♑	15♒	15♉
22	1♒	27♑	16♒	16♉
23	2♒	29♑	17♒	16♉
24	3♒	0♒	18♒	16♉
25	4♒	2♒	20♒	17♉
26	5♒	4♒	21♒	17♉
27	6♒	5♒	22♒	18♉
28	7♒	7♒	23♒	18♉
29	8♒	9♒	25♒	19♉
30	9♒	10♒	26♒	19♉
31	10♒	12♒	27♒	19♉

February

Day	☉	☿	♀	♂
1	11♒	14♒	28♒	20♉
2	12♒	16♒	0♓	20♉
3	13♒	17♒	1♓	21♉
4	14♒	19♒	2♓	21♉
5	15♒	21♒	3♓	22♉
6	16♒	23♒	5♓	22♉
7	17♒	25♒	6♓	23♉
8	18♒	26♒	7♓	23♉
9	19♒	28♒	8♓	24♉
10	20♒	0♓	10♓	24♉
11	21♒	2♓	11♓	25♉
12	22♒	4♓	12♓	25♉
13	24♒	5♓	13♓	26♉
14	25♒	7♓	15♓	26♉
15	26♒	9♓	16♓	27♉
16	27♒	11♓	17♓	27♉
17	28♒	12♓	18♓	28♉
18	29♒	14♓	20♓	28♉
19	0♓	16♓	21♓	29♉
20	1♓	17♓	22♓	29♉
21	2♓	19♓	23♓	0♊
22	3♓	20♓	25♓	0♊
23	4♓	21♓	26♓	1♊
24	5♓	23♓	27♓	1♊
25	6♓	24♓	28♓	2♊
26	7♓	25♓	0♈	2♊
27	8♓	25♓	1♈	3♊
28	9♓	26♓	2♈	3♊

March

Day	☉	☿	♀	♂
1	10♓	27♓	3♈	4♊
2	11♓	27♓	5♈	4♊
3	12♓	27♓	6♈	5♊
4	13♓	28♓	7♈	5♊
5	14♓	27♓	8♈	6♊
6	15♓	27♓	9♈	6♊
7	16♓	27♓	11♈	7♊
8	17♓	26♓	12♈	7♊
9	18♓	26♓	13♈	8♊
10	19♓	25♓	14♈	9♊
11	20♓	24♓	16♈	9♊
12	21♓	23♓	17♈	10♊
13	22♓	22♓	18♈	10♊
14	23♓	21♓	19♈	11♊
15	24♓	20♓	21♈	11♊
16	25♓	20♓	22♈	12♊
17	26♓	19♓	23♈	12♊
18	27♓	18♓	24♈	13♊
19	28♓	17♓	25♈	14♊
20	29♓	16♓	27♈	14♊
21	0♈	16♓	28♈	15♊
22	1♈	15♓	29♈	15♊
23	2♈	15♓	0♉	16♊
24	3♈	14♓	2♉	16♊
25	4♈	14♓	3♉	17♊
26	5♈	14♓	4♉	17♊
27	6♈	14♓	5♉	18♊
28	7♈	14♓	6♉	19♊
29	8♈	14♓	8♉	19♊
30	9♈	14♓	9♉	20♊
31	9♈	15♓	10♉	20♊

April

Day	☉	☿	♀	♂
1	10♈	15♓	11♉	21♊
2	11♈	16♓	12♉	21♊
3	12♈	16♓	14♉	22♊
4	13♈	17♓	15♉	23♊
5	14♈	17♓	16♉	23♊
6	15♈	18♓	17♉	24♊
7	16♈	19♓	18♉	24♊
8	17♈	20♓	20♉	25♊
9	18♈	21♓	21♉	25♊
10	19♈	22♓	22♉	26♊
11	20♈	23♓	23♉	27♊
12	21♈	24♓	24♉	27♊
13	22♈	25♓	26♉	28♊
14	23♈	26♓	27♉	28♊
15	24♈	27♓	28♉	29♊
16	25♈	28♓	29♉	0♋
17	26♈	0♈	0♊	0♋
18	27♈	1♈	2♊	1♋
19	28♈	2♈	3♊	1♋
20	29♈	4♈	4♊	2♋
21	0♉	5♈	5♊	2♋
22	1♉	6♈	6♊	3♋
23	2♉	8♈	8♊	4♋
24	3♉	9♈	9♊	4♋
25	4♉	11♈	10♊	5♋
26	5♉	12♈	11♊	5♋
27	6♉	14♈	12♊	6♋
28	7♉	16♈	14♊	7♋
29	8♉	17♈	15♊	7♋
30	9♉	19♈	16♊	8♋

May

Day	☉	☿	♀	♂
1	10♉	21♈	17♊	8♋
2	11♉	22♈	18♊	9♋
3	12♉	24♈	19♊	9♋
4	13♉	26♈	21♊	10♋
5	14♉	28♈	22♊	11♋
6	15♉	29♈	23♊	11♋
7	16♉	1♉	24♊	12♋
8	17♉	3♉	25♊	12♋
9	18♉	5♉	26♊	13♋
10	19♉	7♉	28♊	14♋
11	20♉	9♉	29♊	14♋
12	20♉	11♉	0♋	15♋
13	21♉	13♉	1♋	15♋
14	22♉	15♉	2♋	16♋
15	23♉	17♉	3♋	17♋
16	24♉	20♉	4♋	17♋
17	25♉	22♉	6♋	18♋
18	26♉	24♉	7♋	18♋
19	27♉	26♉	8♋	19♋
20	28♉	28♉	9♋	20♋
21	29♉	0♊	10♋	20♋
22	0♊	3♊	11♋	21♋
23	1♊	5♊	12♋	21♋
24	2♊	7♊	14♋	22♋
25	3♊	9♊	15♋	23♋
26	4♊	11♊	16♋	23♋
27	5♊	13♊	17♋	24♋
28	6♊	16♊	18♋	24♋
29	7♊	18♊	19♋	25♋
30	8♊	20♊	20♋	26♋
31	9♊	22♊	21♋	26♋

June

Day	☉	☿	♀	♂
1	10♊	24♊	22♋	27♋
2	11♊	26♊	24♋	27♋
3	12♊	27♊	25♋	28♋
4	13♊	29♊	26♋	29♋
5	14♊	1♋	27♋	29♋
6	15♊	3♋	28♋	0♌
7	15♊	5♋	29♋	0♌
8	16♊	6♋	0♌	1♌
9	17♊	8♋	1♌	2♌
10	18♊	10♋	2♌	2♌
11	19♊	11♋	3♌	3♌
12	20♊	13♋	4♌	3♌
13	21♊	14♋	5♌	4♌
14	22♊	15♋	7♌	5♌
15	23♊	17♋	8♌	5♌
16	24♊	18♋	9♌	6♌
17	25♊	19♋	10♌	7♌
18	26♊	21♋	11♌	7♌
19	27♊	22♋	12♌	8♌
20	28♊	23♋	13♌	8♌
21	29♊	24♋	14♌	9♌
22	0♋	25♋	15♌	10♌
23	1♋	26♋	16♌	10♌
24	2♋	27♋	17♌	11♌
25	3♋	28♋	18♌	11♌
26	4♋	28♋	19♌	12♌
27	5♋	29♋	20♌	13♌
28	6♋	0♌	21♌	13♌
29	6♋	0♌	22♌	14♌
30	7♋	1♌	23♌	14♌

July

Day	☉	☿	♀	♂
1	8♋	1♌	24♌	15♌
2	9♋	2♌	25♌	16♌
3	10♋	2♌	26♌	16♌
4	11♋	2♌	27♌	17♌
5	12♋	2♌	28♌	18♌
6	13♋	2♌	29♌	18♌
7	14♋	2♌	29♌	19♌
8	15♋	2♌	0♍	19♌
9	16♋	2♌	1♍	20♌
10	17♋	2♌	2♍	21♌
11	18♋	1♌	3♍	21♌
12	19♋	1♌	4♍	22♌
13	20♋	0♌	5♍	22♌
14	21♋	0♌	6♍	23♌
15	22♋	29♋	7♍	24♌
16	23♋	29♋	7♍	24♌
17	24♋	28♋	8♍	25♌
18	25♋	27♋	9♍	26♌
19	26♋	27♋	10♍	26♌
20	26♋	26♋	11♍	27♌
21	27♋	25♋	11♍	27♌
22	28♋	25♋	12♍	28♌
23	29♋	24♋	13♍	29♌
24	0♌	24♋	14♍	29♌
25	1♌	23♋	14♍	0♍
26	2♌	23♋	15♍	1♍
27	3♌	22♋	16♍	1♍
28	4♌	22♋	16♍	2♍
29	5♌	22♋	17♍	2♍
30	6♌	22♋	18♍	3♍
31	7♌	22♋	18♍	4♍

August

Day	☉	☿	♀	♂
1	8♌	22♋	19♍	4♍
2	9♌	22♋	19♍	5♍
3	10♌	22♋	20♍	6♍
4	11♌	23♋	20♍	6♍
5	12♌	23♋	21♍	7♍
6	13♌	24♋	21♍	7♍
7	14♌	25♋	22♍	8♍
8	15♌	26♋	22♍	9♍
9	16♌	27♋	23♍	9♍
10	17♌	28♋	23♍	10♍
11	18♌	29♋	23♍	11♍
12	18♌	0♌	24♍	11♍
13	19♌	1♌	24♍	12♍
14	20♌	3♌	24♍	12♍
15	21♌	4♌	24♍	13♍
16	22♌	6♌	25♍	14♍
17	23♌	8♌	25♍	14♍
18	24♌	9♌	25♍	15♍
19	25♌	11♌	25♍	16♍
20	26♌	13♌	25♍	16♍
21	27♌	15♌	25♍	17♍
22	28♌	17♌	25♍	18♍
23	29♌	19♌	25♍	18♍
24	0♍	21♌	25♍	19♍
25	1♍	23♌	25♍	19♍
26	2♍	25♌	24♍	20♍
27	3♍	27♌	24♍	21♍
28	4♍	29♌	24♍	21♍
29	5♍	0♍	24♍	22♍
30	6♍	2♍	23♍	23♍
31	7♍	4♍	23♍	23♍

September

Day	☉	☿	♀	♂
1	8♍	6♍	22♍	24♍
2	9♍	8♍	22♍	25♍
3	10♍	10♍	21♍	25♍
4	11♍	12♍	21♍	26♍
5	12♍	14♍	20♍	27♍
6	13♍	16♍	20♍	27♍
7	14♍	18♍	19♍	28♍
8	15♍	20♍	19♍	28♍
9	16♍	21♍	18♍	29♍
10	16♍	23♍	17♍	0♎
11	17♍	25♍	17♍	0♎
12	18♍	27♍	16♍	1♎
13	19♍	29♍	15♍	2♎
14	20♍	0♎	15♍	2♎
15	21♍	2♎	14♍	3♎
16	22♍	4♎	14♍	4♎
17	23♍	5♎	13♍	4♎
18	24♍	7♎	13♍	5♎
19	25♍	9♎	12♍	6♎
20	26♍	10♎	12♍	6♎
21	27♍	12♎	11♍	7♎
22	28♍	13♎	11♍	8♎
23	29♍	15♎	10♍	8♎
24	0♎	17♎	10♍	9♎
25	1♎	18♎	10♍	10♎
26	2♎	20♎	10♍	10♎
27	3♎	21♎	9♍	11♎
28	4♎	23♎	9♍	11♎
29	5♎	24♎	9♍	12♎
30	6♎	26♎	9♍	13♎

October

Day	☉	☿	♀	♂
1	7♎	27♎	9♍	13♎
2	8♎	28♎	9♍	14♎
3	9♎	0♏	9♍	15♎
4	10♎	1♏	9♍	15♎
5	11♎	3♏	9♍	16♎
6	12♎	4♏	9♍	17♎
7	13♎	5♏	9♍	17♎
8	14♎	7♏	10♍	18♎
9	15♎	8♏	10♍	19♎
10	16♎	9♏	10♍	19♎
11	17♎	10♏	10♍	20♎
12	18♎	12♏	11♍	21♎
13	19♎	13♏	11♍	21♎
14	20♎	14♏	12♍	22♎
15	21♎	15♏	12♍	23♎
16	22♎	16♏	12♍	23♎
17	23♎	17♏	13♍	24♎
18	24♎	18♏	13♍	25♎
19	25♎	19♏	14♍	25♎
20	26♎	20♏	15♍	26♎
21	27♎	21♏	15♍	27♎
22	28♎	22♏	16♍	27♎
23	29♎	23♏	16♍	28♎
24	0♏	23♏	17♍	29♎
25	1♏	24♏	18♍	29♎
26	2♏	25♏	18♍	0♏
27	3♏	25♏	19♍	1♏
28	4♏	25♏	20♍	1♏
29	5♏	25♏	21♍	2♏
30	6♏	26♏	21♍	3♏
31	7♏	25♏	22♍	4♏

November

Day	☉	☿	♀	♂
1	8♏	25♏	23♍	4♏
2	9♏	25♏	24♍	5♏
3	10♏	24♏	24♍	6♏
4	11♏	24♏	25♍	6♏
5	12♏	23♏	26♍	7♏
6	13♏	22♏	27♍	8♏
7	14♏	21♏	28♍	8♏
8	15♏	19♏	29♍	9♏
9	16♏	18♏	0♎	10♏
10	17♏	17♏	1♎	10♏
11	18♏	16♏	2♎	11♏
12	19♏	14♏	2♎	12♏
13	20♏	13♏	3♎	12♏
14	21♏	12♏	4♎	13♏
15	22♏	11♏	5♎	14♏
16	23♏	10♏	6♎	14♏
17	24♏	10♏	7♎	15♏
18	25♏	10♏	8♎	16♏
19	26♏	10♏	9♎	17♏
20	27♏	10♏	10♎	17♏
21	28♏	10♏	11♎	18♏
22	29♏	10♏	12♎	19♏
23	0♐	11♏	13♎	19♏
24	1♐	11♏	14♎	20♏
25	2♐	12♏	15♎	21♏
26	3♐	13♏	16♎	21♏
27	4♐	14♏	17♎	22♏
28	5♐	15♏	18♎	23♏
29	6♐	16♏	19♎	24♏
30	7♐	17♏	21♎	24♏

December

Day	☉	☿	♀	♂
1	8♐	19♏	22♎	25♏
2	9♐	20♏	23♎	26♏
3	10♐	21♏	24♎	26♏
4	11♐	23♏	25♎	27♏
5	12♐	24♏	26♎	28♏
6	13♐	25♏	27♎	28♏
7	14♐	27♏	28♎	29♏
8	15♐	28♏	29♎	0♐
9	16♐	0♐	0♏	1♐
10	17♐	1♐	1♏	1♐
11	18♐	3♐	3♏	2♐
12	19♐	4♐	4♏	3♐
13	20♐	6♐	5♏	3♐
14	21♐	7♐	6♏	4♐
15	22♐	9♐	7♏	5♐
16	23♐	10♐	8♏	5♐
17	24♐	12♐	9♏	6♐
18	25♐	13♐	10♏	7♐
19	26♐	15♐	12♏	8♐
20	27♐	16♐	13♏	8♐
21	28♐	18♐	14♏	9♐
22	29♐	19♐	15♏	10♐
23	0♑	21♐	16♏	10♐
24	1♑	22♐	17♏	11♐
25	2♑	24♐	19♏	12♐
26	3♑	26♐	20♏	13♐
27	4♑	27♐	21♏	13♐
28	5♑	29♐	22♏	14♐
29	6♑	0♑	23♏	15♐
30	8♑	2♑	24♏	16♐
31	9♑	3♑	26♏	16♐

Planetary Positions

♌ = Leo ♍ = Virgo ♎ = Libra ♏ = Scorpio ♐ = Sagittarius ♑ = Capricorn ♒ = Aquarius ♓ = Pisces

1928

January

Day	☉	☿	♀	♂
1	10♑	5♑	27♏	17♐
2	11♑	7♑	28♏	18♐
3	12♑	8♑	29♏	18♐
4	13♑	10♑	0♐	19♐
5	14♑	11♑	1♐	20♐
6	15♑	13♑	3♐	21♐
7	16♑	15♑	4♐	21♐
8	17♑	16♑	5♐	22♐
9	18♑	18♑	6♐	23♐
10	19♑	19♑	7♐	24♐
11	20♑	21♑	9♐	24♐
12	21♑	23♑	10♐	25♐
13	22♑	24♑	11♐	26♐
14	23♑	26♑	12♐	26♐
15	24♑	28♑	13♐	27♐
16	25♑	29♑	15♐	28♐
17	26♑	1♒	16♐	29♐
18	27♑	3♒	17♐	29♐
19	28♑	4♒	18♐	0♑
20	29♑	6♒	19♐	1♑
21	0♒	8♒	21♐	2♑
22	1♒	10♒	22♐	2♑
23	2♒	11♒	23♐	3♑
24	3♒	13♒	24♐	4♑
25	4♒	15♒	25♐	5♑
26	5♒	16♒	27♐	5♑
27	6♒	18♒	28♐	6♑
28	7♒	20♒	29♐	7♑
29	8♒	22♒	0♑	7♑
30	9♒	23♒	1♑	8♑
31	10♒	25♒	3♑	9♑

April

Day	☉	☿	♀	♂
1	11♈	15♓	17♓	25♒
2	12♈	17♓	19♓	26♒
3	13♈	18♓	20♓	27♒
4	14♈	20♓	21♓	27♒
5	15♈	21♓	22♓	28♒
6	16♈	22♓	23♓	29♒
7	17♈	24♓	25♓	0♓
8	18♈	25♓	26♓	0♓
9	19♈	27♓	27♓	1♓
10	20♈	29♓	28♓	2♓
11	21♈	0♈	0♈	3♓
12	22♈	2♈	1♈	4♓
13	23♈	4♈	2♈	4♓
14	24♈	5♈	3♈	5♓
15	25♈	7♈	4♈	6♓
16	26♈	9♈	6♈	7♓
17	27♈	10♈	7♈	7♓
18	28♈	12♈	8♈	8♓
19	29♈	14♈	9♈	9♓
20	0♉	16♈	11♈	10♓
21	1♉	18♈	12♈	10♓
22	2♉	20♈	13♈	11♓
23	3♉	22♈	14♈	12♓
24	4♉	24♈	16♈	13♓
25	5♉	25♈	17♈	13♓
26	6♉	27♈	18♈	14♓
27	7♉	0♉	19♈	15♓
28	8♉	2♉	20♈	16♓
29	9♉	4♉	22♈	17♓
30	10♉	6♉	23♈	17♓

July

Day	☉	☿	♀	♂
1	9♋	7♋	9♋	3♉
2	10♋	6♋	10♋	4♉
3	11♋	5♋	11♋	5♉
4	12♋	5♋	13♋	6♉
5	13♋	5♋	14♋	6♉
6	14♋	4♋	15♋	7♉
7	15♋	4♋	16♋	8♉
8	16♋	4♋	18♋	8♉
9	17♋	3♋	19♋	9♉
10	18♋	3♋	20♋	10♉
11	19♋	3♋	21♋	11♉
12	20♋	3♋	22♋	11♉
13	21♋	4♋	24♋	12♉
14	21♋	4♋	25♋	13♉
15	22♋	4♋	26♋	13♉
16	23♋	5♋	27♋	14♉
17	24♋	5♋	29♋	15♉
18	25♋	6♋	0♌	15♉
19	26♋	6♋	1♌	16♉
20	27♋	7♋	2♌	17♉
21	28♋	8♋	4♌	17♉
22	29♋	9♋	5♌	18♉
23	0♌	10♋	6♌	19♉
24	1♌	11♋	7♌	19♉
25	2♌	13♋	9♌	20♉
26	3♌	14♋	10♌	21♉
27	4♌	15♋	11♌	21♉
28	5♌	17♋	12♌	22♉
29	6♌	18♋	13♌	23♉
30	7♌	20♋	15♌	23♉
31	8♌	22♋	16♌	24♉

October

Day	☉	☿	♀	♂
1	8♎	3♏	2♏	29♊
2	9♎	4♏	4♏	0♋
3	10♎	5♏	5♏	0♋
4	11♎	6♏	6♏	0♋
5	12♎	7♏	7♏	1♋
6	13♎	7♏	8♏	1♋
7	14♎	8♏	10♏	2♋
8	15♎	8♏	11♏	2♋
9	16♎	9♏	12♏	2♋
10	17♎	9♏	13♏	3♋
11	18♎	9♏	15♏	3♋
12	19♎	10♏	16♏	3♋
13	20♎	10♏	17♏	4♋
14	21♎	9♏	18♏	4♋
15	22♎	9♏	20♏	4♋
16	23♎	9♏	21♏	5♋
17	24♎	8♏	22♏	5♋
18	25♎	7♏	23♏	5♋
19	26♎	7♏	24♏	6♋
20	27♎	6♏	26♏	6♋
21	28♎	5♏	27♏	6♋
22	29♎	3♏	28♏	6♋
23	0♏	2♏	29♏	7♋
24	1♏	1♏	1♐	7♋
25	2♏	0♏	2♐	7♋
26	3♏	28♎	3♐	7♋
27	4♏	27♎	4♐	8♋
28	5♏	26♎	6♐	8♋
29	6♏	25♎	7♐	8♋
30	7♏	25♎	8♐	8♋
31	8♏	24♎	9♐	8♋

February

Day	☉	☿	♀	♂
1	11♒	27♒	4♑	10♑
2	12♒	28♒	5♑	10♑
3	13♒	0♓	6♑	11♑
4	14♒	1♓	7♑	12♑
5	15♒	3♓	9♑	13♑
6	16♒	4♓	10♑	13♑
7	17♒	5♓	11♑	14♑
8	18♒	6♓	12♑	15♑
9	19♒	7♓	14♑	16♑
10	20♒	8♓	15♑	16♑
11	21♒	9♓	16♑	17♑
12	22♒	10♓	17♑	18♑
13	23♒	10♓	18♑	19♑
14	24♒	11♓	20♑	19♑
15	25♒	11♓	21♑	20♑
16	26♒	11♓	22♑	21♑
17	27♒	11♓	23♑	22♑
18	28♒	10♓	25♑	22♑
19	29♒	10♓	26♑	23♑
20	0♓	9♓	27♑	24♑
21	1♓	8♓	28♑	25♑
22	2♓	7♓	29♑	25♑
23	3♓	6♓	1♒	26♑
24	4♓	5♓	2♒	27♑
25	5♓	4♓	3♒	28♑
26	6♓	3♓	4♒	28♑
27	7♓	2♓	6♒	29♑
28	8♓	1♓	7♒	0♒
29	9♓	0♓	8♒	1♒

May

Day	☉	☿	♀	♂
1	11♉	8♉	24♈	18♓
2	12♉	10♉	25♈	19♓
3	13♉	12♉	27♈	20♓
4	13♉	14♉	28♈	20♓
5	14♉	16♉	29♈	21♓
6	15♉	19♉	0♉	22♓
7	16♉	21♉	1♉	23♓
8	17♉	23♉	3♉	23♓
9	18♉	25♉	4♉	24♓
10	19♉	27♉	5♉	25♓
11	20♉	29♉	6♉	26♓
12	21♉	1♊	8♉	26♓
13	22♉	4♊	9♉	27♓
14	23♉	6♊	10♉	28♓
15	24♉	8♊	11♉	29♓
16	25♉	9♊	13♉	29♓
17	26♉	11♊	14♉	0♈
18	27♉	13♊	15♉	1♈
19	28♉	15♊	16♉	2♈
20	29♉	17♊	17♉	3♈
21	0♊	19♊	19♉	3♈
22	1♊	20♊	20♉	4♈
23	2♊	22♊	21♉	5♈
24	3♊	23♊	22♉	6♈
25	4♊	25♊	24♉	6♈
26	5♊	26♊	25♉	7♈
27	6♊	28♊	26♉	8♈
28	7♊	29♊	27♉	9♈
29	8♊	0♋	28♉	9♈
30	9♊	2♋	0♊	10♈
31	9♊	3♋	1♊	11♈

August

Day	☉	☿	♀	♂
1	9♌	23♋	17♌	25♉
2	10♌	25♋	18♌	25♉
3	11♌	27♋	20♌	26♉
4	12♌	29♋	21♌	27♉
5	13♌	1♌	22♌	27♉
6	13♌	3♌	23♌	28♉
7	14♌	5♌	25♌	29♉
8	15♌	7♌	26♌	29♉
9	16♌	9♌	27♌	0♊
10	17♌	11♌	28♌	1♊
11	18♌	13♌	29♌	1♊
12	19♌	15♌	1♍	2♊
13	20♌	17♌	2♍	3♊
14	21♌	19♌	3♍	3♊
15	22♌	21♌	4♍	4♊
16	23♌	23♌	6♍	4♊
17	24♌	25♌	7♍	5♊
18	25♌	27♌	8♍	6♊
19	26♌	29♌	9♍	6♊
20	27♌	1♍	11♍	7♊
21	28♌	3♍	12♍	8♊
22	29♌	5♍	13♍	8♊
23	0♍	7♍	14♍	9♊
24	1♍	9♍	16♍	9♊
25	2♍	10♍	17♍	10♊
26	3♍	12♍	18♍	11♊
27	4♍	14♍	19♍	11♊
28	5♍	16♍	20♍	12♊
29	6♍	18♍	22♍	12♊
30	7♍	19♍	23♍	13♊
31	8♍	21♍	24♍	13♊

November

Day	☉	☿	♀	♂
1	9♏	24♎	10♐	8♋
2	10♏	24♎	12♐	9♋
3	11♏	24♎	13♐	9♋
4	12♏	24♎	14♐	9♋
5	13♏	25♎	15♐	9♋
6	14♏	25♎	17♐	9♋
7	15♏	26♎	18♐	9♋
8	16♏	27♎	19♐	9♋
9	17♏	28♎	20♐	9♋
10	18♏	29♎	21♐	9♋
11	19♏	0♏	23♐	9♋
12	20♏	1♏	24♐	9♋
13	21♏	2♏	25♐	9♋
14	22♏	4♏	26♐	9♋
15	23♏	5♏	28♐	9♋
16	24♏	6♏	29♐	9♋
17	25♏	8♏	0♑	9♋
18	26♏	9♏	1♑	9♋
19	27♏	11♏	2♑	9♋
20	28♏	12♏	4♑	9♋
21	29♏	14♏	5♑	9♋
22	0♐	15♏	6♑	9♋
23	1♐	17♏	7♑	8♋
24	2♐	18♏	8♑	8♋
25	3♐	20♏	10♑	8♋
26	4♐	21♏	11♑	8♋
27	5♐	23♏	12♑	8♋
28	6♐	25♏	13♑	7♋
29	7♐	26♏	15♑	7♋
30	8♐	28♏	16♑	7♋

March

Day	☉	☿	♀	♂
1	10♓	29♒	9♒	1♒
2	11♓	28♒	10♒	2♒
3	12♓	28♒	12♒	3♒
4	13♓	27♒	13♒	4♒
5	14♓	27♒	14♒	4♒
6	15♓	26♒	15♒	5♒
7	16♓	26♒	17♒	6♒
8	17♓	26♒	18♒	7♒
9	18♓	26♒	19♒	8♒
10	19♓	26♒	20♒	8♒
11	20♓	26♒	21♒	9♒
12	21♓	27♒	23♒	10♒
13	22♓	27♒	24♒	11♒
14	23♓	28♒	25♒	11♒
15	24♓	28♒	26♒	12♒
16	25♓	29♒	28♒	13♒
17	26♓	29♒	29♒	14♒
18	27♓	0♓	0♓	14♒
19	28♓	1♓	1♓	15♒
20	29♓	2♓	3♓	16♒
21	0♈	3♓	4♓	17♒
22	1♈	4♓	5♓	17♒
23	2♈	5♓	6♓	18♒
24	3♈	6♓	7♓	19♒
25	4♈	7♓	9♓	20♒
26	5♈	8♓	10♓	21♒
27	6♈	9♓	11♓	21♒
28	7♈	10♓	12♓	22♒
29	8♈	11♓	14♓	23♒
30	9♈	13♓	15♓	24♒
31	10♈	14♓	16♓	24♒

June

Day	☉	☿	♀	♂
1	10♊	4♋	2♊	12♈
2	11♊	5♋	3♊	12♈
3	12♊	6♋	5♊	13♈
4	13♊	7♋	6♊	14♈
5	14♊	8♋	7♊	14♈
6	15♊	8♋	8♊	15♈
7	16♊	9♋	10♊	16♈
8	17♊	10♋	11♊	17♈
9	18♊	10♋	12♊	17♈
10	19♊	11♋	13♊	18♈
11	20♊	11♋	14♊	19♈
12	21♊	12♋	16♊	20♈
13	22♊	12♋	17♊	20♈
14	23♊	12♋	18♊	21♈
15	24♊	12♋	19♊	22♈
16	25♊	12♋	21♊	23♈
17	26♊	12♋	22♊	23♈
18	27♊	12♋	23♊	24♈
19	28♊	12♋	24♊	25♈
20	29♊	12♋	25♊	26♈
21	0♋	12♋	27♊	26♈
22	1♋	11♋	28♊	27♈
23	1♋	11♋	29♊	28♈
24	2♋	11♋	0♋	28♈
25	3♋	10♋	2♋	29♈
26	4♋	9♋	3♋	0♉
27	5♋	9♋	4♋	1♉
28	6♋	8♋	5♋	1♉
29	7♋	8♋	7♋	2♉
30	8♋	7♋	8♋	3♉

September

Day	☉	☿	♀	♂
1	8♍	23♍	25♍	14♊
2	9♍	24♍	27♍	15♊
3	10♍	26♍	28♍	15♊
4	11♍	28♍	29♍	16♊
5	12♍	29♍	0♎	16♊
6	13♍	1♎	2♎	17♊
7	14♍	2♎	3♎	17♊
8	15♍	4♎	4♎	18♊
9	16♍	5♎	5♎	18♊
10	17♍	7♎	6♎	19♊
11	18♍	8♎	8♎	20♊
12	19♍	10♎	9♎	20♊
13	20♍	11♎	10♎	21♊
14	21♍	13♎	11♎	21♊
15	22♍	14♎	13♎	22♊
16	23♍	16♎	14♎	22♊
17	24♍	17♎	15♎	23♊
18	25♍	18♎	16♎	23♊
19	26♍	20♎	18♎	24♊
20	27♍	21♎	19♎	24♊
21	28♍	22♎	20♎	25♊
22	29♍	24♎	21♎	25♊
23	0♎	25♎	22♎	26♊
24	1♎	26♎	24♎	26♊
25	2♎	27♎	25♎	27♊
26	3♎	28♎	26♎	27♊
27	4♎	29♎	27♎	27♊
28	5♎	0♏	29♎	28♊
29	6♎	2♏	0♏	28♊
30	7♎	3♏	1♏	29♊

December

Day	☉	☿	♀	♂
1	9♐	29♏	17♑	7♋
2	10♐	1♐	18♑	6♋
3	11♐	2♐	19♑	6♋
4	12♐	4♐	21♑	6♋
5	13♐	5♐	22♑	6♋
6	14♐	7♐	23♑	5♋
7	15♐	9♐	24♑	5♋
8	16♐	10♐	25♑	5♋
9	17♐	12♐	27♑	4♋
10	18♐	13♐	28♑	4♋
11	19♐	15♐	29♑	3♋
12	20♐	16♐	0♒	3♋
13	21♐	18♐	1♒	3♋
14	22♐	20♐	3♒	2♋
15	23♐	21♐	4♒	2♋
16	24♐	23♐	5♒	2♋
17	25♐	24♐	6♒	1♋
18	26♐	26♐	7♒	1♋
19	27♐	27♐	9♒	0♋
20	28♐	29♐	10♒	0♋
21	29♐	1♑	11♒	0♋
22	0♑	2♑	12♒	29♊
23	1♑	4♑	13♒	29♊
24	2♑	5♑	14♒	28♊
25	3♑	7♑	16♒	28♊
26	4♑	9♑	17♒	28♊
27	5♑	10♑	18♒	27♊
28	6♑	12♑	19♒	27♊
29	7♑	13♑	20♒	27♊
30	8♑	15♑	22♒	26♊
31	9♑	17♑	23♒	26♊

☉ =Sun ☿ = Mercury ♀ = Venus ♂ = Mars ♈ = Aries ♉ = Taurus ♊ = Gemini ♋ = Cancer

1929

January

Day	☉	☿	♀	♂
1	10♑	18♑	24♒	26♊
2	11♑	20♑	25♒	25♊
3	12♑	22♑	26♒	25♊
4	13♑	23♑	27♒	25♊
5	14♑	25♑	29♒	24♊
6	15♑	27♑	0♓	24♊
7	16♑	28♑	1♓	24♊
8	17♑	0♒	2♓	23♊
9	18♑	1♒	3♓	23♊
10	19♑	3♒	4♓	23♊
11	21♑	5♒	5♓	23♊
12	22♑	6♒	7♓	23♊
13	23♑	8♒	8♓	22♊
14	24♑	9♒	9♓	22♊
15	25♑	11♒	10♓	22♊
16	26♑	12♒	11♓	22♊
17	27♑	14♒	12♓	22♊
18	28♑	15♒	13♓	22♊
19	29♑	17♒	14♓	21♊
20	0♒	18♒	16♓	21♊
21	1♒	19♒	17♓	21♊
22	2♒	20♒	18♓	21♊
23	3♒	21♒	19♓	21♊
24	4♒	22♒	20♓	21♊
25	5♒	23♒	21♓	21♊
26	6♒	24♒	22♓	21♊
27	7♒	24♒	23♓	21♊
28	8♒	24♒	24♓	21♊
29	9♒	24♒	25♓	21♊
30	10♒	24♒	26♓	21♊
31	11♒	24♒	27♓	21♊

April

Day	☉	☿	♀	♂
1	11♈	25♓	8♉	9♋
2	12♈	27♓	8♉	9♋
3	13♈	29♓	8♉	10♋
4	14♈	1♈	8♉	10♋
5	15♈	2♈	7♉	11♋
6	16♈	4♈	7♉	11♋
7	17♈	6♈	7♉	12♋
8	18♈	8♈	6♉	12♋
9	19♈	10♈	6♉	13♋
10	20♈	12♈	6♉	13♋
11	21♈	14♈	5♉	14♋
12	22♈	16♈	5♉	14♋
13	23♈	18♈	4♉	14♋
14	24♈	20♈	4♉	15♋
15	25♈	22♈	3♉	15♋
16	26♈	24♈	2♉	16♋
17	27♈	26♈	2♉	16♋
18	28♈	28♈	1♉	17♋
19	29♈	0♉	1♉	17♋
20	0♉	3♉	0♉	18♋
21	1♉	5♉	29♈	18♋
22	2♉	7♉	29♈	19♋
23	3♉	9♉	28♈	19♋
24	4♉	11♉	27♈	20♋
25	4♉	13♉	27♈	21♋
26	5♉	15♉	26♈	21♋
27	6♉	17♉	26♈	22♋
28	7♉	19♉	25♈	22♋
29	8♉	21♉	25♈	23♋
30	9♉	23♉	24♈	23♋

July

Day	☉	☿	♀	♂
1	9♋	18♊	23♉	28♌
2	10♋	18♊	24♉	29♌
3	11♋	19♊	25♉	29♌
4	12♋	20♊	26♉	0♍
5	13♋	21♊	27♉	0♍
6	14♋	22♊	28♉	1♍
7	15♋	24♊	29♉	2♍
8	16♋	25♊	0♊	2♍
9	16♋	26♊	1♊	3♍
10	17♋	28♊	2♊	3♍
11	18♋	29♊	3♊	4♍
12	19♋	1♋	4♊	5♍
13	20♋	2♋	5♊	5♍
14	21♋	4♋	6♊	6♍
15	22♋	5♋	7♊	7♍
16	23♋	7♋	8♊	7♍
17	24♋	9♋	9♊	8♍
18	25♋	11♋	10♊	8♍
19	26♋	13♋	11♊	9♍
20	27♋	15♋	13♊	10♍
21	28♋	17♋	14♊	10♍
22	29♋	19♋	15♊	11♍
23	0♌	21♋	16♊	11♍
24	1♌	23♋	17♊	12♍
25	2♌	25♋	18♊	13♍
26	3♌	27♋	19♊	13♍
27	4♌	29♋	20♊	14♍
28	5♌	1♌	21♊	14♍
29	6♌	3♌	22♊	15♍
30	7♌	5♌	23♊	16♍
31	7♌	8♌	24♊	16♍

October

Day	☉	☿	♀	♂
1	8♎	22♎	7♍	26♎
2	9♎	21♎	8♍	27♎
3	10♎	20♎	9♍	28♎
4	10♎	19♎	10♍	28♎
5	11♎	18♎	12♍	29♎
6	12♎	17♎	13♍	0♏
7	13♎	16♎	14♍	0♏
8	14♎	15♎	15♍	1♏
9	15♎	13♎	16♍	2♏
10	16♎	12♎	18♍	3♏
11	17♎	11♎	19♍	3♏
12	18♎	10♎	20♍	4♏
13	19♎	10♎	21♍	5♏
14	20♎	9♎	23♍	5♏
15	21♎	8♎	24♍	6♏
16	22♎	8♎	25♍	7♏
17	23♎	8♎	26♍	7♏
18	24♎	8♎	28♍	8♏
19	25♎	8♎	29♍	9♏
20	26♎	9♎	0♎	9♏
21	27♎	9♎	1♎	10♏
22	28♎	10♎	2♎	11♏
23	29♎	11♎	4♎	11♏
24	0♏	12♎	5♎	12♏
25	1♏	13♎	6♎	13♏
26	2♏	14♎	7♎	14♏
27	3♏	16♎	9♎	14♏
28	4♏	17♎	10♎	15♏
29	5♏	18♎	11♎	16♏
30	6♏	20♎	12♎	16♏
31	7♏	21♎	14♎	17♏

February

Day	☉	☿	♀	♂
1	12♒	24♒	29♓	21♊
2	13♒	23♒	0♈	21♊
3	14♒	22♒	1♈	21♊
4	15♒	21♒	2♈	21♊
5	16♒	20♒	3♈	21♊
6	17♒	19♒	4♈	22♊
7	18♒	18♒	5♈	22♊
8	19♒	17♒	6♈	22♊
9	20♒	15♒	7♈	22♊
10	21♒	14♒	8♈	22♊
11	22♒	13♒	9♈	22♊
12	23♒	12♒	10♈	22♊
13	24♒	11♒	11♈	23♊
14	25♒	11♒	12♈	23♊
15	26♒	10♒	13♈	23♊
16	27♒	10♒	14♈	23♊
17	28♒	9♒	15♈	23♊
18	29♒	9♒	15♈	24♊
19	0♓	9♒	16♈	24♊
20	1♓	9♒	17♈	24♊
21	2♓	9♒	18♈	24♊
22	3♓	9♒	19♈	25♊
23	4♓	10♒	20♈	25♊
24	5♓	10♒	21♈	25♊
25	6♓	11♒	22♈	25♊
26	7♓	11♒	22♈	26♊
27	8♓	12♒	23♈	26♊
28	9♓	12♒	24♈	26♊

May

Day	☉	☿	♀	♂
1	10♉	25♉	24♈	24♋
2	11♉	27♉	23♈	24♋
3	12♉	29♉	23♈	25♋
4	13♉	1♊	23♈	25♋
5	14♉	2♊	22♈	26♋
6	15♉	4♊	22♈	26♋
7	16♉	5♊	22♈	27♋
8	17♉	7♊	22♈	27♋
9	18♉	8♊	22♈	28♋
10	19♉	10♊	22♈	28♋
11	20♉	11♊	22♈	29♋
12	21♉	12♊	22♈	0♌
13	22♉	14♊	22♈	0♌
14	23♉	15♊	22♈	1♌
15	24♉	16♊	22♈	1♌
16	25♉	17♊	22♈	2♌
17	26♉	18♊	22♈	2♌
18	27♉	18♊	22♈	3♌
19	28♉	19♊	23♈	3♌
20	29♉	20♊	23♈	4♌
21	0♊	20♊	23♈	4♌
22	1♊	21♊	24♈	5♌
23	2♊	21♊	24♈	6♌
24	3♊	22♊	24♈	6♌
25	3♊	22♊	25♈	7♌
26	4♊	22♊	25♈	7♌
27	5♊	22♊	26♈	8♌
28	6♊	22♊	26♈	8♌
29	7♊	22♊	27♈	9♌
30	8♊	22♊	27♈	9♌
31	9♊	22♊	28♈	10♌

August

Day	☉	☿	♀	♂
1	8♌	10♌	26♊	17♍
2	9♌	12♌	27♊	18♍
3	10♌	14♌	28♊	18♍
4	11♌	16♌	29♊	19♍
5	12♌	18♌	0♋	19♍
6	13♌	20♌	1♋	20♍
7	14♌	22♌	2♋	21♍
8	15♌	24♌	3♋	21♍
9	16♌	26♌	4♋	22♍
10	17♌	27♌	6♋	23♍
11	18♌	29♌	7♋	23♍
12	19♌	1♍	8♋	24♍
13	20♌	3♍	9♋	24♍
14	21♌	5♍	10♋	25♍
15	22♌	6♍	11♋	26♍
16	23♌	8♍	12♋	26♍
17	24♌	10♍	14♋	27♍
18	25♌	12♍	15♋	28♍
19	26♌	13♍	16♋	28♍
20	27♌	15♍	17♋	29♍
21	28♌	16♍	18♋	0♎
22	29♌	18♍	19♋	0♎
23	0♍	20♍	20♋	1♎
24	1♍	21♍	22♋	1♎
25	1♍	23♍	23♋	2♎
26	2♍	24♍	24♋	3♎
27	3♍	26♍	25♋	3♎
28	4♍	27♍	26♋	4♎
29	5♍	29♍	27♋	5♎
30	6♍	0♎	29♋	5♎
31	7♍	1♎	0♌	6♎

November

Day	☉	☿	♀	♂
1	8♏	23♎	15♎	18♏
2	9♏	24♎	16♎	18♏
3	10♏	26♎	17♎	19♏
4	11♏	27♎	19♎	20♏
5	12♏	29♎	20♎	21♏
6	13♏	1♏	21♎	21♏
7	14♏	2♏	22♎	22♏
8	15♏	4♏	24♎	23♏
9	16♏	5♏	25♎	23♏
10	17♏	7♏	26♎	24♏
11	18♏	9♏	27♎	25♏
12	19♏	10♏	29♎	25♏
13	20♏	12♏	0♏	26♏
14	21♏	14♏	1♏	27♏
15	22♏	15♏	2♏	28♏
16	23♏	17♏	4♏	28♏
17	24♏	18♏	5♏	29♏
18	25♏	20♏	6♏	0♐
19	26♏	22♏	7♏	0♐
20	27♏	23♏	9♏	1♐
21	28♏	25♏	10♏	2♐
22	29♏	26♏	11♏	3♐
23	0♐	28♏	12♏	3♐
24	1♐	0♐	14♏	4♐
25	2♐	1♐	15♏	5♐
26	3♐	3♐	16♏	6♐
27	4♐	4♐	17♏	6♐
28	5♐	6♐	19♏	7♐
29	7♐	7♐	20♏	8♐
30	8♐	9♐	21♏	8♐

March

Day	☉	☿	♀	♂
1	10♓	13♒	25♈	27♊
2	11♓	14♒	26♈	27♊
3	12♓	15♒	26♈	27♊
4	13♓	16♒	27♈	28♊
5	14♓	17♒	28♈	28♊
6	15♓	18♒	29♈	28♊
7	16♓	19♒	29♈	29♊
8	17♓	20♒	0♉	29♊
9	18♓	21♒	1♉	29♊
10	19♓	22♒	1♉	0♋
11	20♓	24♒	2♉	0♋
12	21♓	25♒	2♉	0♋
13	22♓	26♒	3♉	1♋
14	23♓	28♒	4♉	1♋
15	24♓	29♒	4♉	2♋
16	25♓	0♓	5♉	2♋
17	26♓	2♓	5♉	2♋
18	27♓	3♓	5♉	3♋
19	28♓	4♓	6♉	3♋
20	29♓	6♓	6♉	4♋
21	0♈	7♓	7♉	4♋
22	1♈	9♓	7♉	4♋
23	2♈	10♓	7♉	5♋
24	3♈	12♓	7♉	5♋
25	4♈	14♓	8♉	6♋
26	5♈	15♓	8♉	6♋
27	6♈	17♓	8♉	7♋
28	7♈	18♓	8♉	7♋
29	8♈	20♓	8♉	7♋
30	9♈	22♓	8♉	8♋
31	10♈	23♓	8♉	8♋

June

Day	☉	☿	♀	♂
1	10♊	22♊	29♈	11♌
2	11♊	22♊	29♈	11♌
3	12♊	21♊	0♉	12♌
4	13♊	21♊	1♉	12♌
5	14♊	20♊	1♉	13♌
6	15♊	20♊	2♉	13♌
7	16♊	19♊	3♉	14♌
8	17♊	19♊	3♉	15♌
9	18♊	18♊	4♉	15♌
10	19♊	18♊	5♉	16♌
11	20♊	17♊	6♉	16♌
12	21♊	17♊	6♉	17♌
13	22♊	16♊	7♉	18♌
14	23♊	16♊	8♉	18♌
15	24♊	15♊	9♉	19♌
16	25♊	15♊	10♉	19♌
17	26♊	14♊	10♉	20♌
18	26♊	14♊	11♉	20♌
19	27♊	14♊	12♉	21♌
20	28♊	14♊	13♉	22♌
21	29♊	14♊	14♉	22♌
22	0♋	14♊	15♉	23♌
23	1♋	14♊	16♉	23♌
24	2♋	14♊	17♉	24♌
25	3♋	14♊	18♉	25♌
26	4♋	15♊	18♉	25♌
27	5♋	15♊	19♉	26♌
28	6♋	16♊	20♉	26♌
29	7♋	16♊	21♉	27♌
30	8♋	17♊	22♉	27♌

September

Day	☉	☿	♀	♂
1	8♍	3♎	1♌	7♎
2	9♍	4♎	2♌	7♎
3	10♍	5♎	3♌	8♎
4	11♍	7♎	4♌	9♎
5	12♍	8♎	6♌	9♎
6	13♍	9♎	7♌	10♎
7	14♍	10♎	8♌	11♎
8	15♍	11♎	9♌	11♎
9	16♍	12♎	10♌	12♎
10	17♍	14♎	11♌	12♎
11	18♍	15♎	13♌	13♎
12	19♍	16♎	14♌	14♎
13	20♍	17♎	15♌	14♎
14	21♍	17♎	16♌	15♎
15	22♍	18♎	17♌	16♎
16	23♍	19♎	19♌	16♎
17	24♍	20♎	20♌	17♎
18	25♍	21♎	21♌	18♎
19	26♍	21♎	22♌	18♎
20	27♍	22♎	23♌	19♎
21	28♍	22♎	25♌	20♎
22	29♍	23♎	26♌	20♎
23	0♎	23♎	27♌	21♎
24	1♎	23♎	28♌	22♎
25	2♎	23♎	29♌	22♎
26	3♎	23♎	1♍	23♎
27	4♎	23♎	2♍	24♎
28	5♎	23♎	3♍	24♎
29	6♎	23♎	4♍	25♎
30	7♎	22♎	5♍	26♎

December

Day	☉	☿	♀	♂
1	9♐	11♐	22♏	9♐
2	10♐	12♐	24♏	10♐
3	11♐	14♐	25♏	11♐
4	12♐	15♐	26♏	11♐
5	13♐	17♐	27♏	12♐
6	14♐	18♐	29♏	13♐
7	15♐	20♐	0♐	14♐
8	16♐	22♐	1♐	14♐
9	17♐	23♐	2♐	15♐
10	18♐	25♐	4♐	16♐
11	19♐	26♐	5♐	16♐
12	20♐	28♐	6♐	17♐
13	21♐	29♐	7♐	18♐
14	22♐	1♑	9♐	19♐
15	23♐	3♑	10♐	19♐
16	24♐	4♑	11♐	20♐
17	25♐	6♑	12♐	21♐
18	26♐	7♑	14♐	22♐
19	27♐	9♑	15♐	22♐
20	28♐	10♑	16♐	23♐
21	29♐	12♑	17♐	24♐
22	0♑	13♑	19♐	25♐
23	1♑	15♑	20♐	25♐
24	2♑	17♑	21♐	26♐
25	3♑	18♑	23♐	27♐
26	4♑	20♑	24♐	27♐
27	5♑	21♑	25♐	28♐
28	6♑	23♑	26♐	29♐
29	7♑	24♑	28♐	0♑
30	8♑	26♑	29♐	1♑
31	9♑	27♑	0♑	1♑

Planetary Positions

♌ = Leo ♍ = Virgo ♎ = Libra ♏ = Scorpio ♐ = Sagittarius ♑ = Capricorn ♒ = Aquarius ♓ = Pisces

1930

January

Day	☉	☿	♀	♂
1	10♑	28♑	1♑	2♑
2	11♑	0♒	3♑	3♑
3	12♑	1♒	4♑	4♑
4	13♑	2♒	5♑	4♑
5	14♑	3♒	6♑	5♑
6	15♑	4♒	8♑	6♑
7	16♑	5♒	9♑	7♑
8	17♑	6♒	10♑	7♑
9	18♑	7♒	11♑	8♑
10	19♑	8♒	13♑	9♑
11	20♑	8♒	14♑	10♑
12	21♑	8♒	15♑	10♑
13	22♑	8♒	16♑	11♑
14	23♑	8♒	18♑	12♑
15	24♑	8♒	19♑	13♑
16	25♑	7♒	20♑	13♑
17	26♑	7♒	21♑	14♑
18	27♑	6♒	23♑	15♑
19	28♑	5♒	24♑	16♑
20	29♑	4♒	25♑	16♑
21	0♒	2♒	26♑	17♑
22	1♒	1♒	28♑	18♑
23	2♒	0♒	29♑	19♑
24	3♒	29♑	0♒	20♑
25	5♒	27♑	1♒	20♑
26	6♒	26♑	3♒	21♑
27	7♒	25♑	4♒	22♑
28	8♒	24♑	5♒	23♑
29	9♒	24♑	7♒	23♑
30	10♒	23♑	8♒	24♑
31	11♒	23♑	9♒	25♑

April

Day	☉	☿	♀	♂
1	11♈	10♈	24♈	12♓
2	12♈	12♈	25♈	12♓
3	13♈	14♈	26♈	13♓
4	14♈	17♈	28♈	14♓
5	15♈	19♈	29♈	15♓
6	16♈	21♈	0♉	16♓
7	17♈	23♈	1♉	16♓
8	18♈	25♈	3♉	17♓
9	19♈	27♈	4♉	18♓
10	20♈	29♈	5♉	19♓
11	21♈	1♉	6♉	20♓
12	22♈	3♉	8♉	20♓
13	23♈	5♉	9♉	21♓
14	24♈	7♉	10♉	22♓
15	25♈	9♉	11♉	23♓
16	25♈	11♉	12♉	23♓
17	26♈	12♉	14♉	24♓
18	27♈	14♉	15♉	25♓
19	28♈	16♉	16♉	26♓
20	29♈	17♉	17♉	26♓
21	0♉	19♉	19♉	27♓
22	1♉	20♉	20♉	28♓
23	2♉	22♉	21♉	29♓
24	3♉	23♉	22♉	0♈
25	4♉	24♉	23♉	0♈
26	5♉	26♉	25♉	1♈
27	6♉	27♉	26♉	2♈
28	7♉	28♉	27♉	3♈
29	8♉	28♉	28♉	3♈
30	9♉	29♉	0♊	4♈

July

Day	☉	☿	♀	♂
1	9♋	23♊	14♌	21♉
2	10♋	25♊	15♌	21♉
3	11♋	27♊	17♌	22♉
4	11♋	29♊	18♌	23♉
5	12♋	1♋	19♌	23♉
6	13♋	3♋	20♌	24♉
7	14♋	5♋	21♌	25♉
8	15♋	7♋	22♌	26♉
9	16♋	9♋	24♌	26♉
10	17♋	11♋	25♌	27♉
11	18♋	13♋	26♌	28♉
12	19♋	15♋	27♌	28♉
13	20♋	17♋	28♌	29♉
14	21♋	20♋	29♌	0♊
15	22♋	22♋	1♍	0♊
16	23♋	24♋	2♍	1♊
17	24♋	26♋	3♍	2♊
18	25♋	28♋	4♍	3♊
19	26♋	0♌	5♍	3♊
20	27♋	2♌	6♍	4♊
21	28♋	4♌	8♍	5♊
22	29♋	6♌	9♍	5♊
23	0♌	8♌	10♍	6♊
24	1♌	10♌	11♍	7♊
25	2♌	12♌	12♍	7♊
26	2♌	14♌	13♍	8♊
27	3♌	16♌	14♍	9♊
28	4♌	18♌	16♍	9♊
29	5♌	20♌	17♍	10♊
30	6♌	22♌	18♍	11♊
31	7♌	23♌	19♍	11♊

October

Day	☉	☿	♀	♂
1	7♎	22♍	22♏	20♋
2	8♎	22♍	23♏	21♋
3	9♎	23♍	24♏	21♋
4	10♎	23♍	24♏	22♋
5	11♎	24♍	25♏	22♋
6	12♎	24♍	26♏	23♋
7	13♎	25♍	27♏	23♋
8	14♎	26♍	27♏	24♋
9	15♎	27♍	28♏	24♋
10	16♎	29♍	29♏	25♋
11	17♎	0♎	29♏	25♋
12	18♎	1♎	0♐	26♋
13	19♎	3♎	1♐	26♋
14	20♎	4♎	1♐	27♋
15	21♎	6♎	2♐	27♋
16	22♎	8♎	2♐	28♋
17	23♎	9♎	3♐	28♋
18	24♎	11♎	3♐	29♋
19	25♎	12♎	4♐	29♋
20	26♎	14♎	4♐	0♌
21	27♎	16♎	5♐	0♌
22	28♎	18♎	5♐	1♌
23	29♎	19♎	6♐	1♌
24	0♏	21♎	6♐	2♌
25	1♏	23♎	6♐	2♌
26	2♏	24♎	6♐	3♌
27	3♏	26♎	7♐	3♌
28	4♏	28♎	7♐	4♌
29	5♏	29♎	7♐	4♌
30	6♏	1♏	7♐	4♌
31	7♏	3♏	7♐	5♌

February

Day	☉	☿	♀	♂
1	12♒	22♑	10♒	26♑
2	13♒	22♑	12♒	26♑
3	14♒	22♑	13♒	27♑
4	15♒	22♑	14♒	28♑
5	16♒	23♑	15♒	29♑
6	17♒	23♑	17♒	0♒
7	18♒	23♑	18♒	0♒
8	19♒	24♑	19♒	1♒
9	20♒	25♑	20♒	2♒
10	21♒	25♑	22♒	3♒
11	22♒	26♑	23♒	3♒
12	23♒	27♑	24♒	4♒
13	24♒	28♑	25♒	5♒
14	25♒	29♑	27♒	6♒
15	26♒	0♒	28♒	7♒
16	27♒	1♒	29♒	7♒
17	28♒	2♒	0♓	8♒
18	29♒	3♒	2♓	9♒
19	0♓	4♒	3♓	10♒
20	1♓	5♒	4♓	10♒
21	2♓	6♒	5♓	11♒
22	3♓	8♒	7♓	12♒
23	4♓	9♒	8♓	13♒
24	5♓	10♒	9♓	14♒
25	6♓	11♒	10♓	14♒
26	7♓	13♒	12♓	15♒
27	8♓	14♒	13♓	16♒
28	9♓	15♒	14♓	17♒

May

Day	☉	☿	♀	♂
1	10♉	0♊	1♊	5♈
2	11♉	1♊	2♊	6♈
3	12♉	1♊	3♊	7♈
4	13♉	2♊	5♊	7♈
5	14♉	2♊	6♊	8♈
6	15♉	2♊	7♊	9♈
7	16♉	2♊	8♊	10♈
8	17♉	3♊	9♊	10♈
9	18♉	3♊	11♊	11♈
10	19♉	3♊	12♊	12♈
11	20♉	2♊	13♊	13♈
12	21♉	2♊	14♊	13♈
13	22♉	2♊	15♊	14♈
14	23♉	2♊	17♊	15♈
15	24♉	1♊	18♊	16♈
16	25♉	1♊	19♊	16♈
17	26♉	0♊	20♊	17♈
18	27♉	0♊	22♊	18♈
19	27♉	29♉	23♊	19♈
20	28♉	28♉	24♊	20♈
21	29♉	28♉	25♊	20♈
22	0♊	27♉	26♊	21♈
23	1♊	27♉	28♊	22♈
24	2♊	26♉	29♊	23♈
25	3♊	26♉	0♋	23♈
26	4♊	25♉	1♋	24♈
27	5♊	25♉	2♋	25♈
28	6♊	25♉	4♋	26♈
29	7♊	24♉	5♋	26♈
30	8♊	24♉	6♋	27♈
31	9♊	24♉	7♋	28♈

August

Day	☉	☿	♀	♂
1	8♌	25♌	20♍	12♊
2	9♌	27♌	21♍	13♊
3	10♌	28♌	22♍	14♊
4	11♌	0♍	23♍	14♊
5	12♌	2♍	25♍	15♊
6	13♌	3♍	26♍	16♊
7	14♌	5♍	27♍	16♊
8	15♌	7♍	28♍	17♊
9	16♌	8♍	29♍	18♊
10	17♌	10♍	0♎	18♊
11	18♌	11♍	1♎	19♊
12	19♌	13♍	2♎	20♊
13	20♌	14♍	4♎	20♊
14	21♌	15♍	5♎	21♊
15	22♌	17♍	6♎	21♊
16	23♌	18♍	7♎	22♊
17	24♌	19♍	8♎	23♊
18	25♌	21♍	9♎	23♊
19	25♌	22♍	10♎	24♊
20	26♌	23♍	11♎	25♊
21	27♌	24♍	12♎	25♊
22	28♌	25♍	13♎	26♊
23	29♌	26♍	14♎	27♊
24	0♍	27♍	15♎	27♊
25	1♍	28♍	17♎	28♊
26	2♍	29♍	18♎	29♊
27	3♍	0♎	19♎	29♊
28	4♍	1♎	20♎	0♋
29	5♍	2♎	21♎	0♋
30	6♍	3♎	22♎	1♋
31	7♍	4♎	23♎	2♋

November

Day	☉	☿	♀	♂
1	8♏	4♏	7♐	5♌
2	9♏	6♏	7♐	6♌
3	10♏	8♏	7♐	6♌
4	11♏	9♏	7♐	6♌
5	12♏	11♏	7♐	7♌
6	13♏	13♏	7♐	7♌
7	14♏	14♏	7♐	8♌
8	15♏	16♏	7♐	8♌
9	16♏	17♏	6♐	8♌
10	17♏	19♏	6♐	9♌
11	18♏	21♏	6♐	9♌
12	19♏	22♏	5♐	10♌
13	20♏	24♏	5♐	10♌
14	21♏	25♏	4♐	10♌
15	22♏	27♏	4♐	11♌
16	23♏	28♏	4♐	11♌
17	24♏	0♐	3♐	11♌
18	25♏	2♐	2♐	12♌
19	26♏	3♐	2♐	12♌
20	27♏	5♐	1♐	12♌
21	28♏	6♐	1♐	12♌
22	29♏	8♐	0♐	13♌
23	0♐	9♐	29♏	13♌
24	1♐	11♐	29♏	13♌
25	2♐	12♐	28♏	14♌
26	3♐	14♐	28♏	14♌
27	4♐	15♐	27♏	14♌
28	5♐	17♐	27♏	14♌
29	6♐	18♐	26♏	15♌
30	7♐	20♐	25♏	15♌

March

Day	☉	☿	♀	♂
1	10♓	17♒	15♓	17♒
2	11♓	18♒	17♓	18♒
3	12♓	20♒	18♓	19♒
4	13♓	21♒	19♓	20♒
5	14♓	23♒	20♓	21♒
6	15♓	24♒	22♓	21♒
7	16♓	26♒	23♓	22♒
8	17♓	27♒	24♓	23♒
9	18♓	29♒	25♓	24♒
10	19♓	0♓	27♓	24♒
11	20♓	2♓	28♓	25♒
12	21♓	4♓	29♓	26♒
13	22♓	5♓	0♈	27♒
14	23♓	7♓	2♈	28♒
15	24♓	9♓	3♈	28♒
16	25♓	10♓	4♈	29♒
17	26♓	12♓	5♈	0♓
18	27♓	14♓	7♈	1♓
19	28♓	16♓	8♈	2♓
20	29♓	17♓	9♈	2♓
21	0♈	19♓	10♈	3♓
22	1♈	21♓	12♈	4♓
23	2♈	23♓	13♈	5♓
24	3♈	25♓	14♈	5♓
25	4♈	27♓	15♈	6♓
26	5♈	29♓	16♈	7♓
27	6♈	0♈	18♈	8♓
28	7♈	2♈	19♈	9♓
29	8♈	4♈	20♈	9♓
30	9♈	6♈	21♈	10♓
31	10♈	8♈	23♈	11♓

June

Day	☉	☿	♀	♂
1	10♊	24♉	8♋	29♈
2	11♊	24♉	10♋	29♈
3	12♊	24♉	11♋	0♉
4	13♊	24♉	12♋	1♉
5	14♊	24♉	13♋	2♉
6	15♊	25♉	14♋	2♉
7	16♊	25♉	16♋	3♉
8	17♊	25♉	17♋	4♉
9	18♊	26♉	18♋	5♉
10	19♊	26♉	19♋	5♉
11	20♊	27♉	20♋	6♉
12	20♊	28♉	22♋	7♉
13	21♊	29♉	23♋	7♉
14	22♊	29♉	24♋	8♉
15	23♊	0♊	25♋	9♉
16	24♊	1♊	26♋	10♉
17	25♊	2♊	28♋	10♉
18	26♊	3♊	29♋	11♉
19	27♊	5♊	0♌	12♉
20	28♊	6♊	1♌	13♉
21	29♊	7♊	2♌	13♉
22	0♋	8♊	4♌	14♉
23	1♋	10♊	5♌	15♉
24	2♋	11♊	6♌	16♉
25	3♋	13♊	7♌	16♉
26	4♋	14♊	8♌	17♉
27	5♋	16♊	10♌	18♉
28	6♋	18♊	11♌	18♉
29	7♋	19♊	12♌	19♉
30	8♋	21♊	13♌	20♉

September

Day	☉	☿	♀	♂
1	8♍	4♎	24♎	2♋
2	9♍	5♎	25♎	3♋
3	10♍	5♎	26♎	4♋
4	11♍	6♎	27♎	4♋
5	12♍	6♎	28♎	5♋
6	13♍	6♎	29♎	5♋
7	14♍	7♎	0♏	6♋
8	15♍	7♎	1♏	7♋
9	16♍	7♎	2♏	7♋
10	17♍	7♎	3♏	8♋
11	18♍	6♎	4♏	8♋
12	19♍	6♎	5♏	9♋
13	20♍	6♎	6♏	10♋
14	21♍	5♎	7♏	10♋
15	22♍	4♎	8♏	11♋
16	23♍	4♎	9♏	11♋
17	24♍	3♎	10♏	12♋
18	25♍	2♎	11♏	13♋
19	26♍	1♎	12♏	13♋
20	27♍	0♎	13♏	14♋
21	27♍	29♍	14♏	14♋
22	28♍	28♍	14♏	15♋
23	29♍	27♍	15♏	16♋
24	0♎	26♍	16♏	16♋
25	1♎	25♍	17♏	17♋
26	2♎	24♍	18♏	17♋
27	3♎	23♍	19♏	18♋
28	4♎	23♍	20♏	18♋
29	5♎	22♍	20♏	19♋
30	6♎	22♍	21♏	19♋

December

Day	☉	☿	♀	♂
1	8♐	22♐	25♏	15♌
2	9♐	23♐	25♏	15♌
3	10♐	25♐	24♏	15♌
4	11♐	26♐	24♏	16♌
5	12♐	28♐	23♏	16♌
6	13♐	29♐	23♏	16♌
7	14♐	0♑	23♏	16♌
8	15♐	2♑	23♏	16♌
9	16♐	3♑	22♏	16♌
10	17♐	5♑	22♏	16♌
11	18♐	6♑	22♏	16♌
12	19♐	8♑	22♏	17♌
13	20♐	9♑	22♏	17♌
14	21♐	10♑	22♏	17♌
15	23♐	12♑	22♏	17♌
16	24♐	13♑	22♏	17♌
17	25♐	14♑	22♏	17♌
18	26♐	16♑	23♏	17♌
19	27♐	17♑	23♏	17♌
20	28♐	18♑	23♏	17♌
21	29♐	19♑	23♏	17♌
22	0♑	20♑	24♏	17♌
23	1♑	20♑	24♏	17♌
24	2♑	21♑	24♏	17♌
25	3♑	22♑	25♏	17♌
26	4♑	22♑	25♏	16♌
27	5♑	22♑	26♏	16♌
28	6♑	22♑	26♏	16♌
29	7♑	22♑	27♏	16♌
30	8♑	22♑	27♏	16♌
31	9♑	21♑	28♏	16♌

1931

Your Starway to Love

☉ =Sun ☿ = Mercury ♀ = Venus ♂ = Mars ♈ = Aries ♉ = Taurus ♊ = Gemini ♋ = Cancer

January

Day	☉	☿	♀	♂
1	10♑	21♑	28♏	16♌
2	11♑	20♑	29♏	15♌
3	12♑	19♑	0♐	15♌
4	13♑	17♑	0♐	15♌
5	14♑	16♑	1♐	15♌
6	15♑	15♑	2♐	14♌
7	16♑	13♑	2♐	14♌
8	17♑	12♑	3♐	14♌
9	18♑	11♑	4♐	14♌
10	19♑	10♑	5♐	13♌
11	20♑	9♑	5♐	13♌
12	21♑	8♑	6♐	13♌
13	22♑	7♑	7♐	12♌
14	23♑	7♑	8♐	12♌
15	24♑	6♑	9♐	12♌
16	25♑	6♑	10♐	11♌
17	26♑	6♑	10♐	11♌
18	27♑	6♑	11♐	11♌
19	28♑	6♑	12♐	10♌
20	29♑	7♑	13♐	10♌
21	0♒	7♑	14♐	10♌
22	1♒	8♑	15♐	9♌
23	2♒	8♑	16♐	9♌
24	3♒	9♑	17♐	8♌
25	4♒	10♑	18♐	8♌
26	5♒	11♑	19♐	8♌
27	6♒	11♑	20♐	7♌
28	7♒	12♑	21♐	7♌
29	8♒	13♑	22♐	6♌
30	9♒	15♑	23♐	6♌
31	10♒	16♑	24♐	6♌

April

Day	☉	☿	♀	♂
1	11♈	26♈	0♓	0♌
2	11♈	28♈	2♓	1♌
3	12♈	29♈	3♓	1♌
4	13♈	1♉	4♓	1♌
5	14♈	2♉	5♓	1♌
6	15♈	4♉	6♓	2♌
7	16♈	5♉	8♓	2♌
8	17♈	6♉	9♓	2♌
9	18♈	8♉	10♓	3♌
10	19♈	9♉	11♓	3♌
11	20♈	10♉	12♓	3♌
12	21♈	10♉	13♓	4♌
13	22♈	11♉	15♓	4♌
14	23♈	12♉	16♓	4♌
15	24♈	12♉	17♓	5♌
16	25♈	13♉	18♓	5♌
17	26♈	13♉	19♓	5♌
18	27♈	13♉	21♓	6♌
19	28♈	13♉	22♓	6♌
20	29♈	13♉	23♓	6♌
21	0♉	13♉	24♓	7♌
22	1♉	13♉	25♓	7♌
23	2♉	13♉	27♓	7♌
24	3♉	13♉	28♓	8♌
25	4♉	12♉	29♓	8♌
26	5♉	12♉	0♈	9♌
27	6♉	11♉	1♈	9♌
28	7♉	11♉	3♈	9♌
29	8♉	10♉	4♈	10♌
30	9♉	9♉	5♈	10♌

July

Day	☉	☿	♀	♂
1	8♋	10♋	20♊	11♍
2	9♋	12♋	21♊	12♍
3	10♋	14♋	22♊	12♍
4	11♋	17♋	23♊	13♍
5	12♋	19♋	25♊	14♍
6	13♋	21♋	26♊	14♍
7	14♋	23♋	27♊	15♍
8	15♋	25♋	28♊	15♍
9	16♋	27♋	29♊	16♍
10	17♋	29♋	1♋	17♍
11	18♋	1♌	2♋	17♍
12	19♋	3♌	3♋	18♍
13	20♋	5♌	4♋	18♍
14	21♋	6♌	6♋	19♍
15	22♋	8♌	7♋	19♍
16	23♋	10♌	8♋	20♍
17	24♋	12♌	9♋	21♍
18	25♋	13♌	10♋	21♍
19	26♋	15♌	12♋	22♍
20	27♋	17♌	13♋	22♍
21	27♋	18♌	14♋	23♍
22	28♋	20♌	15♋	24♍
23	29♋	22♌	17♋	24♍
24	0♌	23♌	18♋	25♍
25	1♌	25♌	19♋	25♍
26	2♌	26♌	20♋	26♍
27	3♌	28♌	21♋	27♍
28	4♌	29♌	23♋	27♍
29	5♌	0♍	24♋	28♍
30	6♌	2♍	25♋	28♍
31	7♌	3♍	26♋	29♍

October

Day	☉	☿	♀	♂
1	7♎	24♍	13♎	9♏
2	8♎	26♍	14♎	10♏
3	9♎	27♍	16♎	11♏
4	10♎	29♍	17♎	11♏
5	11♎	1♎	18♎	12♏
6	12♎	3♎	19♎	13♏
7	13♎	4♎	21♎	14♏
8	14♎	6♎	22♎	14♏
9	15♎	8♎	23♎	15♏
10	16♎	10♎	24♎	16♏
11	17♎	11♎	26♎	16♏
12	18♎	13♎	27♎	17♏
13	19♎	15♎	28♎	18♏
14	20♎	17♎	29♎	18♏
15	21♎	18♎	1♏	19♏
16	22♎	20♎	2♏	20♏
17	23♎	22♎	3♏	21♏
18	24♎	24♎	4♏	21♏
19	25♎	25♎	6♏	22♏
20	26♎	27♎	7♏	23♏
21	27♎	29♎	8♏	23♏
22	28♎	0♏	9♏	24♏
23	29♎	2♏	11♏	25♏
24	0♏	3♏	12♏	25♏
25	1♏	5♏	13♏	26♏
26	2♏	7♏	14♏	27♏
27	3♏	8♏	16♏	28♏
28	4♏	10♏	17♏	28♏
29	5♏	12♏	18♏	29♏
30	6♏	13♏	19♏	0♐
31	7♏	15♏	21♏	0♐

February

Day	☉	☿	♀	♂
1	11♒	17♑	25♐	5♌
2	12♒	18♑	26♐	5♌
3	13♒	19♑	27♐	4♌
4	14♒	20♑	28♐	4♌
5	15♒	22♑	29♐	4♌
6	16♒	23♑	0♑	3♌
7	17♒	24♑	1♑	3♌
8	18♒	25♑	2♑	3♌
9	19♒	27♑	3♑	2♌
10	20♒	28♑	4♑	2♌
11	22♒	0♒	5♑	2♌
12	23♒	1♒	6♑	1♌
13	24♒	2♒	7♑	1♌
14	25♒	4♒	8♑	1♌
15	26♒	5♒	9♑	0♌
16	27♒	7♒	10♑	0♌
17	28♒	8♒	11♑	0♌
18	29♒	10♒	12♑	0♌
19	0♓	11♒	14♑	29♋
20	1♓	13♒	15♑	29♋
21	2♓	14♒	16♑	29♋
22	3♓	16♒	17♑	29♋
23	4♓	18♒	18♑	29♋
24	5♓	19♒	19♑	28♋
25	6♓	21♒	20♑	28♋
26	7♓	22♒	21♑	28♋
27	8♓	24♒	22♑	28♋
28	9♓	26♒	24♑	28♋

May

Day	☉	☿	♀	♂
1	10♉	9♉	6♈	11♌
2	11♉	8♉	7♈	11♌
3	12♉	7♉	9♈	11♌
4	13♉	7♉	10♈	12♌
5	14♉	6♉	11♈	12♌
6	15♉	6♉	12♈	13♌
7	16♉	5♉	13♈	13♌
8	17♉	5♉	14♈	14♌
9	18♉	4♉	16♈	14♌
10	19♉	4♉	17♈	14♌
11	20♉	4♉	18♈	15♌
12	21♉	4♉	19♈	15♌
13	21♉	4♉	20♈	16♌
14	22♉	4♉	22♈	16♌
15	23♉	4♉	23♈	17♌
16	24♉	4♉	24♈	17♌
17	25♉	4♉	25♈	18♌
18	26♉	4♉	27♈	18♌
19	27♉	5♉	28♈	19♌
20	28♉	5♉	29♈	19♌
21	29♉	6♉	0♉	20♌
22	0♊	6♉	1♉	20♌
23	1♊	7♉	3♉	21♌
24	2♊	8♉	4♉	21♌
25	3♊	9♉	5♉	22♌
26	4♊	9♉	6♉	22♌
27	5♊	10♉	7♉	23♌
28	6♊	11♉	9♉	23♌
29	7♊	12♉	10♉	24♌
30	8♊	13♉	11♉	24♌
31	9♊	14♉	12♉	25♌

August

Day	☉	☿	♀	♂
1	8♌	4♍	28♋	0♎
2	9♌	5♍	29♋	0♎
3	10♌	7♍	0♌	1♎
4	11♌	8♍	1♌	2♎
5	12♌	9♍	3♌	2♎
6	13♌	10♍	4♌	3♎
7	14♌	11♍	5♌	3♎
8	15♌	12♍	6♌	4♎
9	16♌	13♍	7♌	5♎
10	17♌	14♍	9♌	5♎
11	18♌	15♍	10♌	6♎
12	19♌	16♍	11♌	7♎
13	19♌	16♍	12♌	7♎
14	20♌	17♍	14♌	8♎
15	21♌	18♍	15♌	8♎
16	22♌	18♍	16♌	9♎
17	23♌	19♍	17♌	10♎
18	24♌	19♍	19♌	10♎
19	25♌	19♍	20♌	11♎
20	26♌	19♍	21♌	12♎
21	27♌	20♍	22♌	12♎
22	28♌	20♍	24♌	13♎
23	29♌	20♍	25♌	14♎
24	0♍	20♍	26♌	14♎
25	1♍	19♍	27♌	15♎
26	2♍	19♍	28♌	15♎
27	3♍	19♍	0♍	16♎
28	4♍	18♍	1♍	17♎
29	5♍	17♍	2♍	17♎
30	6♍	17♍	3♍	18♎
31	7♍	16♍	5♍	19♎

November

Day	☉	☿	♀	♂
1	8♏	16♏	22♏	1♐
2	9♏	18♏	23♏	2♐
3	10♏	19♏	24♏	3♐
4	11♏	21♏	26♏	3♐
5	12♏	22♏	27♏	4♐
6	13♏	24♏	28♏	5♐
7	14♏	25♏	29♏	6♐
8	15♏	27♏	1♐	6♐
9	16♏	29♏	2♐	7♐
10	17♏	0♐	3♐	8♐
11	18♏	2♐	4♐	8♐
12	19♏	3♐	6♐	9♐
13	20♏	5♐	7♐	10♐
14	21♏	6♐	8♐	11♐
15	22♏	7♐	9♐	11♐
16	23♏	9♐	11♐	12♐
17	24♏	10♐	12♐	13♐
18	25♏	12♐	13♐	14♐
19	26♏	13♐	14♐	14♐
20	27♏	15♐	16♐	15♐
21	28♏	16♐	17♐	16♐
22	29♏	18♐	18♐	17♐
23	0♐	19♐	19♐	17♐
24	1♐	20♐	21♐	18♐
25	2♐	22♐	22♐	19♐
26	3♐	23♐	23♐	20♐
27	4♐	24♐	24♐	20♐
28	5♐	26♐	26♐	21♐
29	6♐	27♐	27♐	22♐
30	7♐	28♐	28♐	23♐

March

Day	☉	☿	♀	♂
1	10♓	27♒	25♑	28♋
2	11♓	29♒	26♑	28♋
3	12♓	1♓	27♑	28♋
4	13♓	3♓	28♑	28♋
5	14♓	4♓	29♑	28♋
6	15♓	6♓	0♒	27♋
7	16♓	8♓	1♒	27♋
8	17♓	10♓	3♒	27♋
9	18♓	12♓	4♒	27♋
10	19♓	13♓	5♒	27♋
11	20♓	15♓	6♒	27♋
12	21♓	17♓	7♒	28♋
13	22♓	19♓	8♒	28♋
14	23♓	21♓	10♒	28♋
15	24♓	23♓	11♒	28♋
16	25♓	25♓	12♒	28♋
17	26♓	27♓	13♒	28♋
18	27♓	29♓	14♒	28♋
19	28♓	1♈	15♒	28♋
20	29♓	3♈	16♒	28♋
21	0♈	5♈	18♒	28♋
22	1♈	7♈	19♒	28♋
23	2♈	9♈	20♒	29♋
24	3♈	11♈	21♒	29♋
25	4♈	13♈	22♒	29♋
26	5♈	15♈	23♒	29♋
27	6♈	17♈	25♒	29♋
28	7♈	19♈	26♒	0♌
29	8♈	21♈	27♒	0♌
30	9♈	22♈	28♒	0♌
31	10♈	24♈	29♒	0♌

June

Day	☉	☿	♀	♂
1	10♊	16♉	13♉	25♌
2	11♊	17♉	15♉	26♌
3	12♊	18♉	16♉	26♌
4	13♊	19♉	17♉	27♌
5	14♊	21♉	18♉	27♌
6	15♊	22♉	19♉	28♌
7	15♊	24♉	21♉	28♌
8	16♊	25♉	22♉	29♌
9	17♊	27♉	23♉	29♌
10	18♊	28♉	24♉	0♍
11	19♊	0♊	25♉	0♍
12	20♊	2♊	27♉	1♍
13	21♊	3♊	28♉	1♍
14	22♊	5♊	29♉	2♍
15	23♊	7♊	0♊	2♍
16	24♊	9♊	2♊	3♍
17	25♊	11♊	3♊	4♍
18	26♊	13♊	4♊	4♍
19	27♊	14♊	5♊	5♍
20	28♊	17♊	6♊	5♍
21	29♊	19♊	8♊	6♍
22	0♋	21♊	9♊	6♍
23	1♋	23♊	10♊	7♍
24	2♋	25♊	11♊	7♍
25	3♋	27♊	12♊	8♍
26	4♋	29♊	14♊	9♍
27	5♋	1♋	15♊	9♍
28	6♋	4♋	16♊	10♍
29	6♋	6♋	17♊	10♍
30	7♋	8♋	19♊	11♍

September

Day	☉	☿	♀	♂
1	8♍	15♍	6♍	19♎
2	9♍	14♍	7♍	20♎
3	10♍	13♍	8♍	21♎
4	11♍	12♍	10♍	21♎
5	12♍	11♍	11♍	22♎
6	13♍	10♍	12♍	23♎
7	14♍	9♍	13♍	23♎
8	15♍	9♍	15♍	24♎
9	16♍	8♍	16♍	25♎
10	17♍	7♍	17♍	25♎
11	17♍	7♍	18♍	26♎
12	18♍	6♍	20♍	27♎
13	19♍	6♍	21♍	27♎
14	20♍	6♍	22♍	28♎
15	21♍	6♍	23♍	29♎
16	22♍	6♍	25♍	29♎
17	23♍	6♍	26♍	0♏
18	24♍	7♍	27♍	1♏
19	25♍	8♍	28♍	1♏
20	26♍	8♍	0♎	2♏
21	27♍	9♍	1♎	3♏
22	28♍	10♍	2♎	3♏
23	29♍	12♍	3♎	4♏
24	0♎	13♍	5♎	5♏
25	1♎	14♍	6♎	5♏
26	2♎	16♍	7♎	6♏
27	3♎	17♍	8♎	7♏
28	4♎	19♍	9♎	7♏
29	5♎	20♍	11♎	8♏
30	6♎	22♍	12♎	9♏

December

Day	☉	☿	♀	♂
1	8♐	29♐	29♐	23♐
2	9♐	0♑	1♑	24♐
3	10♐	1♑	2♑	25♐
4	11♐	2♑	3♑	26♐
5	12♐	3♑	4♑	26♐
6	13♐	4♑	6♑	27♐
7	14♐	5♑	7♑	28♐
8	15♐	5♑	8♑	29♐
9	16♐	6♑	9♑	29♐
10	17♐	6♑	11♑	0♑
11	18♐	6♑	12♑	1♑
12	19♐	6♑	13♑	2♑
13	20♐	6♑	14♑	2♑
14	21♐	6♑	16♑	3♑
15	22♐	5♑	17♑	4♑
16	23♐	5♑	18♑	5♑
17	24♐	4♑	19♑	5♑
18	25♐	3♑	21♑	6♑
19	26♐	1♑	22♑	7♑
20	27♐	0♑	23♑	8♑
21	28♐	29♐	24♑	8♑
22	29♐	27♐	26♑	9♑
23	0♑	26♐	27♑	10♑
24	1♑	25♐	28♑	11♑
25	2♑	24♐	29♑	12♑
26	3♑	23♐	0♒	12♑
27	4♑	22♐	2♒	13♑
28	5♑	21♐	3♒	14♑
29	7♑	21♐	4♒	15♑
30	8♑	20♐	5♒	15♑
31	9♑	20♐	7♒	16♑

Planetary Positions

♌ = Leo ♍ = Virgo ♎ = Libra ♏ = Scorpio ♐ = Sagittarius ♑ = Capricorn ♒ = Aquarius ♓ = Pisces

1932

January

Day	☉	☿	♀	♂
1	10♑	20♐	8♒	17♑
2	11♑	20♐	9♒	18♑
3	12♑	21♐	10♒	18♑
4	13♑	21♐	12♒	19♑
5	14♑	21♐	13♒	20♑
6	15♑	22♐	14♒	21♑
7	16♑	23♐	15♒	22♑
8	17♑	24♐	17♒	22♑
9	18♑	24♐	18♒	23♑
10	19♑	25♐	19♒	24♑
11	20♑	26♐	20♒	25♑
12	21♑	27♐	22♒	25♑
13	22♑	29♐	23♒	26♑
14	23♑	0♑	24♒	27♑
15	24♑	1♑	25♒	28♑
16	25♑	2♑	26♒	29♑
17	26♑	3♑	28♒	29♑
18	27♑	4♑	29♒	0♒
19	28♑	6♑	0♓	1♒
20	29♑	7♑	1♓	2♒
21	0♒	8♑	3♓	2♒
22	1♒	10♑	4♓	3♒
23	2♒	11♑	5♓	4♒
24	3♒	12♑	6♓	5♒
25	4♒	14♑	8♓	6♒
26	5♒	15♑	9♓	6♒
27	6♒	17♑	10♓	7♒
28	7♒	18♑	11♓	8♒
29	8♒	20♑	12♓	9♒
30	9♒	21♑	14♓	10♒
31	10♒	23♑	15♓	10♒

February

Day	☉	☿	♀	♂
1	11♒	24♑	16♓	11♒
2	12♒	26♑	17♓	12♒
3	13♒	27♑	19♓	13♒
4	14♒	29♑	20♓	14♒
5	15♒	0♒	21♓	14♒
6	16♒	2♒	22♓	15♒
7	17♒	3♒	23♓	16♒
8	18♒	5♒	25♓	17♒
9	19♒	6♒	26♓	17♒
10	20♒	8♒	27♓	18♒
11	21♒	10♒	28♓	19♒
12	22♒	11♒	29♓	20♒
13	23♒	13♒	1♈	21♒
14	24♒	15♒	2♈	21♒
15	25♒	16♒	3♈	22♒
16	26♒	18♒	4♈	23♒
17	27♒	20♒	5♈	24♒
18	28♒	21♒	7♈	25♒
19	29♒	23♒	8♈	25♒
20	0♓	25♒	9♈	26♒
21	1♓	27♒	10♈	27♒
22	2♓	29♒	11♈	28♒
23	3♓	0♓	13♈	28♒
24	4♓	2♓	14♈	29♒
25	5♓	4♓	15♈	0♓
26	6♓	6♓	16♈	1♓
27	7♓	8♓	17♈	2♓
28	8♓	10♓	18♈	2♓
29	9♓	11♓	20♈	3♓

March

Day	☉	☿	♀	♂
1	10♓	13♓	21♈	4♓
2	11♓	15♓	22♈	5♓
3	12♓	17♓	23♈	6♓
4	13♓	19♓	24♈	6♓
5	14♓	21♓	25♈	7♓
6	15♓	23♓	27♈	8♓
7	16♓	25♓	28♈	9♓
8	17♓	27♓	29♈	10♓
9	18♓	29♓	0♉	10♓
10	19♓	1♈	1♉	11♓
11	20♓	3♈	2♉	12♓
12	21♓	4♈	4♉	13♓
13	22♓	6♈	5♉	13♓
14	23♓	8♈	6♉	14♓
15	24♓	10♈	7♉	15♓
16	25♓	11♈	8♉	16♓
17	26♓	13♈	9♉	17♓
18	27♓	15♈	10♉	17♓
19	28♓	16♈	12♉	18♓
20	29♓	17♈	13♉	19♓
21	0♈	19♈	14♉	20♓
22	1♈	20♈	15♉	21♓
23	2♈	21♈	16♉	21♓
24	3♈	22♈	17♉	22♓
25	4♈	23♈	18♉	23♓
26	5♈	23♈	19♉	24♓
27	6♈	24♈	20♉	24♓
28	7♈	24♈	22♉	25♓
29	8♈	25♈	23♉	26♓
30	9♈	25♈	24♉	27♓
31	10♈	25♈	25♉	28♓

April

Day	☉	☿	♀	♂
1	11♈	25♈	26♉	28♓
2	12♈	25♈	27♉	29♓
3	13♈	25♈	28♉	0♈
4	14♈	24♈	29♉	1♈
5	15♈	24♈	0♊	1♈
6	16♈	23♈	1♊	2♈
7	17♈	23♈	2♊	3♈
8	18♈	22♈	3♊	4♈
9	19♈	21♈	4♊	5♈
10	20♈	21♈	5♊	5♈
11	21♈	20♈	6♊	6♈
12	22♈	19♈	8♊	7♈
13	23♈	18♈	9♊	8♈
14	24♈	18♈	10♊	8♈
15	25♈	17♈	11♊	9♈
16	26♈	16♈	12♊	10♈
17	27♈	16♈	13♊	11♈
18	28♈	15♈	14♊	12♈
19	29♈	15♈	15♊	12♈
20	0♉	14♈	16♊	13♈
21	1♉	14♈	16♊	14♈
22	2♉	14♈	17♊	15♈
23	3♉	14♈	18♊	15♈
24	4♉	14♈	19♊	16♈
25	5♉	14♈	20♊	17♈
26	6♉	14♈	21♊	18♈
27	7♉	14♈	22♊	18♈
28	8♉	14♈	23♊	19♈
29	9♉	15♈	24♊	20♈
30	10♉	15♈	25♊	21♈

May

Day	☉	☿	♀	♂
1	11♉	16♈	26♊	21♈
2	12♉	16♈	27♊	22♈
3	13♉	17♈	27♊	23♈
4	14♉	18♈	28♊	24♈
5	14♉	18♈	29♊	25♈
6	15♉	19♈	0♋	25♈
7	16♉	20♈	1♋	26♈
8	17♉	21♈	1♋	27♈
9	18♉	22♈	2♋	28♈
10	19♉	23♈	3♋	28♈
11	20♉	24♈	4♋	29♈
12	21♉	25♈	4♋	0♉
13	22♉	27♈	5♋	1♉
14	23♉	28♈	6♋	1♉
15	24♉	29♈	7♋	2♉
16	25♉	0♉	7♋	3♉
17	26♉	2♉	8♋	4♉
18	27♉	3♉	8♋	4♉
19	28♉	4♉	9♋	5♉
20	29♉	6♉	10♋	6♉
21	0♊	7♉	10♋	7♉
22	1♊	9♉	11♋	7♉
23	2♊	11♉	11♋	8♉
24	3♊	12♉	12♋	9♉
25	4♊	14♉	12♋	10♉
26	5♊	16♉	13♋	10♉
27	6♊	17♉	13♋	11♉
28	7♊	19♉	13♋	12♉
29	8♊	21♉	14♋	12♉
30	9♊	23♉	14♋	13♉
31	10♊	25♉	14♋	14♉

June

Day	☉	☿	♀	♂
1	10♊	27♉	15♋	15♉
2	11♊	29♉	15♋	15♉
3	12♊	0♊	15♋	16♉
4	13♊	3♊	15♋	17♉
5	14♊	5♊	15♋	18♉
6	15♊	7♊	15♋	18♉
7	16♊	9♊	15♋	19♉
8	17♊	11♊	15♋	20♉
9	18♊	13♊	15♋	21♉
10	19♊	15♊	15♋	21♉
11	20♊	17♊	15♋	22♉
12	21♊	20♊	15♋	23♉
13	22♊	22♊	15♋	23♉
14	23♊	24♊	15♋	24♉
15	24♊	26♊	14♋	25♉
16	25♊	28♊	14♋	26♉
17	26♊	1♋	14♋	26♉
18	27♊	3♋	13♋	27♉
19	28♊	5♋	13♋	28♉
20	29♊	7♋	12♋	28♉
21	0♋	9♋	12♋	29♉
22	1♋	11♋	11♋	0♊
23	1♋	13♋	11♋	1♊
24	2♋	15♋	10♋	1♊
25	3♋	17♋	10♋	2♊
26	4♋	19♋	9♋	3♊
27	5♋	21♋	8♋	3♊
28	6♋	23♋	8♋	4♊
29	7♋	25♋	7♋	5♊
30	8♋	26♋	7♋	6♊

July

Day	☉	☿	♀	♂
1	9♋	28♋	6♋	6♊
2	10♋	0♌	5♋	7♊
3	11♋	1♌	5♋	8♊
4	12♋	3♌	4♋	8♊
5	13♋	5♌	4♋	9♊
6	14♋	6♌	3♋	10♊
7	15♋	8♌	3♋	10♊
8	16♋	9♌	2♋	11♊
9	17♋	11♌	2♋	12♊
10	18♋	12♌	1♋	13♊
11	19♋	14♌	1♋	13♊
12	20♋	15♌	0♋	14♊
13	21♋	16♌	0♋	15♊
14	22♋	17♌	0♋	15♊
15	22♋	19♌	0♋	16♊
16	23♋	20♌	29♊	17♊
17	24♋	21♌	29♊	17♊
18	25♋	22♌	29♊	18♊
19	26♋	23♌	29♊	19♊
20	27♋	24♌	29♊	19♊
21	28♋	25♌	29♊	20♊
22	29♋	26♌	29♊	21♊
23	0♌	27♌	29♊	21♊
24	1♌	28♌	29♊	22♊
25	2♌	28♌	29♊	23♊
26	3♌	29♌	29♊	24♊
27	4♌	0♍	0♋	24♊
28	5♌	0♍	0♋	25♊
29	6♌	1♍	0♋	26♊
30	7♌	1♍	1♋	26♊
31	8♌	1♍	1♋	27♊

August

Day	☉	☿	♀	♂
1	9♌	2♍	1♋	28♊
2	10♌	2♍	2♋	28♊
3	11♌	2♍	2♋	29♊
4	12♌	2♍	2♋	0♋
5	13♌	2♍	3♋	0♋
6	14♌	2♍	3♋	1♋
7	14♌	1♍	4♋	2♋
8	15♌	1♍	5♋	2♋
9	16♌	1♍	5♋	3♋
10	17♌	0♍	6♋	4♋
11	18♌	29♌	6♋	4♋
12	19♌	29♌	7♋	5♋
13	20♌	28♌	8♋	6♋
14	21♌	27♌	8♋	6♋
15	22♌	26♌	9♋	7♋
16	23♌	26♌	10♋	8♋
17	24♌	25♌	10♋	8♋
18	25♌	24♌	11♋	9♋
19	26♌	23♌	12♋	9♋
20	27♌	22♌	13♋	10♋
21	28♌	22♌	13♋	11♋
22	29♌	21♌	14♋	11♋
23	0♍	20♌	15♋	12♋
24	1♍	20♌	16♋	13♋
25	2♍	20♌	17♋	13♋
26	3♍	19♌	18♋	14♋
27	4♍	19♌	18♋	15♋
28	5♍	19♌	19♋	15♋
29	6♍	19♌	20♋	16♋
30	7♍	20♌	21♋	17♋
31	8♍	20♌	22♋	17♋

September

Day	☉	☿	♀	♂
1	9♍	21♌	23♋	18♋
2	10♍	22♌	24♋	18♋
3	10♍	22♌	25♋	19♋
4	11♍	23♌	26♋	20♋
5	12♍	24♌	27♋	20♋
6	13♍	26♌	27♋	21♋
7	14♍	27♌	28♋	22♋
8	15♍	28♌	29♋	22♋
9	16♍	0♍	0♌	23♋
10	17♍	1♍	1♌	23♋
11	18♍	3♍	2♌	24♋
12	19♍	5♍	3♌	25♋
13	20♍	6♍	4♌	25♋
14	21♍	8♍	5♌	26♋
15	22♍	10♍	6♌	27♋
16	23♍	12♍	7♌	27♋
17	24♍	14♍	8♌	28♋
18	25♍	15♍	9♌	28♋
19	26♍	17♍	10♌	29♋
20	27♍	19♍	12♌	0♌
21	28♍	21♍	13♌	0♌
22	29♍	23♍	14♌	1♌
23	0♎	25♍	15♌	1♌
24	1♎	27♍	16♌	2♌
25	2♎	28♍	17♌	3♌
26	3♎	0♎	18♌	3♌
27	4♎	2♎	19♌	4♌
28	5♎	4♎	20♌	4♌
29	6♎	6♎	21♌	5♌
30	7♎	7♎	22♌	6♌

October

Day	☉	☿	♀	♂
1	8♎	9♎	23♌	6♌
2	9♎	11♎	24♌	7♌
3	10♎	13♎	26♌	7♌
4	11♎	14♎	27♌	8♌
5	12♎	16♎	28♌	9♌
6	13♎	18♎	29♌	9♌
7	14♎	19♎	0♍	10♌
8	15♎	21♎	1♍	10♌
9	16♎	23♎	2♍	11♌
10	17♎	24♎	3♍	11♌
11	18♎	26♎	4♍	12♌
12	19♎	28♎	6♍	13♌
13	20♎	29♎	7♍	13♌
14	21♎	1♏	8♍	14♌
15	22♎	2♏	9♍	14♌
16	23♎	4♏	10♍	15♌
17	24♎	6♏	11♍	15♌
18	25♎	7♏	12♍	16♌
19	26♎	9♏	14♍	17♌
20	27♎	10♏	15♍	17♌
21	28♎	12♏	16♍	18♌
22	29♎	13♏	17♍	18♌
23	0♏	15♏	18♍	19♌
24	1♏	16♏	19♍	19♌
25	2♏	18♏	21♍	20♌
26	3♏	19♏	22♍	20♌
27	4♏	21♏	23♍	21♌
28	5♏	22♏	24♍	21♌
29	6♏	23♏	25♍	22♌
30	7♏	25♏	26♍	23♌
31	8♏	26♏	28♍	23♌

November

Day	☉	☿	♀	♂
1	9♏	28♏	29♍	24♌
2	10♏	29♏	0♎	24♌
3	11♏	0♐	1♎	25♌
4	12♏	2♐	2♎	25♌
5	13♏	3♐	4♎	26♌
6	14♏	4♐	5♎	26♌
7	15♏	6♐	6♎	27♌
8	16♏	7♐	7♎	27♌
9	17♏	8♐	8♎	28♌
10	18♏	10♐	10♎	28♌
11	19♏	11♐	11♎	29♌
12	20♏	12♐	12♎	29♌
13	21♏	13♐	13♎	0♍
14	22♏	14♐	14♎	0♍
15	23♏	15♐	16♎	1♍
16	24♏	16♐	17♎	1♍
17	25♏	17♐	18♎	2♍
18	26♏	18♐	19♎	2♍
19	27♏	19♐	20♎	3♍
20	28♏	19♐	22♎	3♍
21	29♏	20♐	23♎	3♍
22	0♐	20♐	24♎	4♍
23	1♐	20♐	25♎	4♍
24	2♐	21♐	27♎	5♍
25	3♐	21♐	28♎	5♍
26	4♐	20♐	29♎	6♍
27	5♐	20♐	0♏	6♍
28	6♐	20♐	1♏	7♍
29	7♐	19♐	3♏	7♍
30	8♐	18♐	4♏	7♍

December

Day	☉	☿	♀	♂
1	9♐	17♐	5♏	8♍
2	10♐	16♐	6♏	8♍
3	11♐	14♐	8♏	9♍
4	12♐	13♐	9♏	9♍
5	13♐	12♐	10♏	10♍
6	14♐	10♐	11♏	10♍
7	15♐	9♐	13♏	10♍
8	16♐	8♐	14♏	11♍
9	17♐	7♐	15♏	11♍
10	18♐	6♐	16♏	11♍
11	19♐	5♐	17♏	12♍
12	20♐	5♐	19♏	12♍
13	21♐	4♐	20♏	13♍
14	22♐	4♐	21♏	13♍
15	23♐	4♐	22♏	13♍
16	24♐	5♐	24♏	14♍
17	25♐	5♐	25♏	14♍
18	26♐	5♐	26♏	14♍
19	27♐	6♐	27♏	15♍
20	28♐	7♐	29♏	15♍
21	29♐	7♐	0♐	15♍
22	0♑	8♐	1♐	15♍
23	1♑	9♐	2♐	16♍
24	2♑	10♐	4♐	16♍
25	3♑	11♐	5♐	16♍
26	4♑	12♐	6♐	17♍
27	5♑	14♐	7♐	17♍
28	6♑	15♐	9♐	17♍
29	7♑	16♐	10♐	17♍
30	8♑	17♐	11♐	18♍
31	9♑	19♐	12♐	18♍

☉ = Sun ☿ = Mercury ♀ = Venus ♂ = Mars ♈ = Aries ♉ = Taurus ♊ = Gemini ♋ = Cancer

1933

January

Day	☉	☿	♀	♂
1	10♑	20♐	14♐	18♍
2	11♑	21♐	15♐	18♍
3	12♑	23♐	16♐	18♍
4	13♑	24♐	17♐	19♍
5	14♑	25♐	19♐	19♍
6	15♑	27♐	20♐	19♍
7	16♑	28♐	21♐	19♍
8	17♑	0♑	22♐	19♍
9	19♑	1♑	24♐	19♍
10	20♑	3♑	25♐	20♍
11	21♑	4♑	26♐	20♍
12	22♑	6♑	27♐	20♍
13	23♑	7♑	28♐	20♍
14	24♑	8♑	0♑	20♍
15	25♑	10♑	1♑	20♍
16	26♑	12♑	2♑	20♍
17	27♑	13♑	3♑	20♍
18	28♑	15♑	5♑	20♍
19	29♑	16♑	6♑	20♍
20	0♒	18♑	7♑	20♍
21	1♒	19♑	8♑	20♍
22	2♒	21♑	10♑	20♍
23	3♒	22♑	11♑	20♍
24	4♒	24♑	12♑	20♍
25	5♒	26♑	13♑	20♍
26	6♒	27♑	15♑	20♍
27	7♒	29♑	16♑	20♍
28	8♒	0♒	17♑	20♍
29	9♒	2♒	18♑	20♍
30	10♒	4♒	20♑	20♍
31	11♒	5♒	21♑	20♍

April

Day	☉	☿	♀	♂
1	11♈	26♓	6♈	2♍
2	12♈	25♓	7♈	1♍
3	13♈	25♓	8♈	1♍
4	14♈	25♓	9♈	1♍
5	15♈	25♓	11♈	1♍
6	16♈	25♓	12♈	1♍
7	17♈	25♓	13♈	1♍
8	18♈	25♓	14♈	1♍
9	19♈	25♓	16♈	1♍
10	20♈	25♓	17♈	1♍
11	21♈	26♓	18♈	1♍
12	22♈	26♓	19♈	1♍
13	23♈	27♓	21♈	1♍
14	24♈	27♓	22♈	1♍
15	25♈	28♓	23♈	1♍
16	26♈	29♓	24♈	1♍
17	27♈	0♈	26♈	1♍
18	28♈	0♈	27♈	1♍
19	29♈	1♈	28♈	1♍
20	0♉	2♈	29♈	1♍
21	1♉	3♈	1♉	1♍
22	2♉	4♈	2♉	1♍
23	3♉	5♈	3♉	2♍
24	4♉	7♈	4♉	2♍
25	5♉	8♈	5♉	2♍
26	6♉	9♈	7♉	2♍
27	6♉	10♈	8♉	2♍
28	7♉	12♈	9♉	2♍
29	8♉	13♈	10♉	3♍
30	9♉	14♈	12♉	3♍

July

Day	☉	☿	♀	♂
1	9♋	5♌	28♋	27♍
2	10♋	6♌	29♋	27♍
3	11♋	7♌	0♌	28♍
4	12♋	8♌	1♌	29♍
5	13♋	8♌	3♌	29♍
6	14♋	9♌	4♌	0♎
7	15♋	10♌	5♌	0♎
8	16♋	11♌	6♌	1♎
9	17♋	11♌	7♌	1♎
10	17♋	12♌	9♌	2♎
11	18♋	12♌	10♌	2♎
12	19♋	13♌	11♌	3♎
13	20♋	13♌	12♌	3♎
14	21♋	13♌	14♌	4♎
15	22♋	13♌	15♌	5♎
16	23♋	13♌	16♌	5♎
17	24♋	13♌	17♌	6♎
18	25♋	13♌	18♌	6♎
19	26♋	13♌	20♌	7♎
20	27♋	13♌	21♌	7♎
21	28♋	13♌	22♌	8♎
22	29♋	12♌	23♌	9♎
23	0♌	12♌	25♌	9♎
24	1♌	11♌	26♌	10♎
25	2♌	11♌	27♌	10♎
26	3♌	10♌	28♌	11♎
27	4♌	9♌	29♌	11♎
28	5♌	8♌	1♍	12♎
29	6♌	8♌	2♍	13♎
30	7♌	7♌	3♍	13♎
31	8♌	6♌	4♍	14♎

October

Day	☉	☿	♀	♂
1	8♎	22♎	18♏	24♏
2	9♎	23♎	20♏	25♏
3	10♎	25♎	21♏	26♏
4	11♎	26♎	22♏	26♏
5	12♎	28♎	23♏	27♏
6	12♎	29♎	24♏	28♏
7	13♎	1♏	25♏	28♏
8	14♎	2♏	27♏	29♏
9	15♎	4♏	28♏	0♐
10	16♎	5♏	29♏	1♐
11	17♎	7♏	0♐	1♐
12	18♎	8♏	1♐	2♐
13	19♎	10♏	2♐	3♐
14	20♎	11♏	3♐	3♐
15	21♎	12♏	5♐	4♐
16	22♎	14♏	6♐	5♐
17	23♎	15♏	7♐	6♐
18	24♎	16♏	8♐	6♐
19	25♎	18♏	9♐	7♐
20	26♎	19♏	10♐	8♐
21	27♎	20♏	12♐	8♐
22	28♎	21♏	13♐	9♐
23	29♎	23♏	14♐	10♐
24	0♏	24♏	15♐	11♐
25	1♏	25♏	16♐	11♐
26	2♏	26♏	17♐	12♐
27	3♏	27♏	18♐	13♐
28	4♏	28♏	19♐	14♐
29	5♏	29♏	21♐	14♐
30	6♏	0♐	22♐	15♐
31	7♏	1♐	23♐	16♐

February

Day	☉	☿	♀	♂
1	12♒	7♒	22♑	19♍
2	13♒	9♒	23♑	19♍
3	14♒	10♒	25♑	19♍
4	15♒	12♒	26♑	19♍
5	16♒	14♒	27♑	19♍
6	17♒	16♒	28♑	19♍
7	18♒	17♒	0♒	18♍
8	19♒	19♒	1♒	18♍
9	20♒	21♒	2♒	18♍
10	21♒	23♒	3♒	18♍
11	22♒	25♒	5♒	17♍
12	23♒	26♒	6♒	17♍
13	24♒	28♒	7♒	17♍
14	25♒	0♓	8♒	17♍
15	26♒	2♓	10♒	16♍
16	27♒	4♓	11♒	16♍
17	28♒	6♓	12♒	16♍
18	29♒	7♓	13♒	15♍
19	0♓	9♓	15♒	15♍
20	1♓	11♓	16♒	15♍
21	2♓	13♓	17♒	14♍
22	3♓	15♓	18♒	14♍
23	4♓	17♓	20♒	13♍
24	5♓	18♓	21♒	13♍
25	6♓	20♓	22♒	13♍
26	7♓	22♓	23♒	12♍
27	8♓	24♓	25♒	12♍
28	9♓	25♓	26♒	11♍

May

Day	☉	☿	♀	♂
1	10♉	16♈	13♉	3♍
2	11♉	17♈	14♉	3♍
3	12♉	19♈	15♉	3♍
4	13♉	20♈	17♉	4♍
5	14♉	22♈	18♉	4♍
6	15♉	23♈	19♉	4♍
7	16♉	25♈	20♉	4♍
8	17♉	26♈	21♉	5♍
9	18♉	28♈	23♉	5♍
10	19♉	0♉	24♉	5♍
11	20♉	2♉	25♉	5♍
12	21♉	3♉	26♉	6♍
13	22♉	5♉	28♉	6♍
14	23♉	7♉	29♉	6♍
15	24♉	9♉	0♊	7♍
16	25♉	11♉	1♊	7♍
17	26♉	13♉	3♊	7♍
18	27♉	15♉	4♊	8♍
19	28♉	17♉	5♊	8♍
20	29♉	19♉	6♊	8♍
21	0♊	21♉	7♊	9♍
22	1♊	23♉	9♊	9♍
23	2♊	25♉	10♊	9♍
24	3♊	27♉	11♊	10♍
25	4♊	29♉	12♊	10♍
26	4♊	1♊	14♊	10♍
27	5♊	4♊	15♊	11♍
28	6♊	6♊	16♊	11♍
29	7♊	8♊	17♊	12♍
30	8♊	10♊	19♊	12♍
31	9♊	12♊	20♊	12♍

August

Day	☉	☿	♀	♂
1	8♌	6♌	5♍	14♎
2	9♌	5♌	7♍	15♎
3	10♌	4♌	8♍	16♎
4	11♌	4♌	9♍	16♎
5	12♌	3♌	10♍	17♎
6	13♌	3♌	12♍	17♎
7	14♌	2♌	13♍	18♎
8	15♌	2♌	14♍	19♎
9	16♌	2♌	15♍	19♎
10	17♌	2♌	16♍	20♎
11	18♌	2♌	18♍	20♎
12	19♌	2♌	19♍	21♎
13	20♌	3♌	20♍	22♎
14	21♌	3♌	21♍	22♎
15	22♌	4♌	22♍	23♎
16	23♌	4♌	24♍	24♎
17	24♌	5♌	25♍	24♎
18	25♌	6♌	26♍	25♎
19	26♌	7♌	27♍	25♎
20	27♌	8♌	28♍	26♎
21	28♌	10♌	0♎	27♎
22	29♌	11♌	1♎	27♎
23	0♍	12♌	2♎	28♎
24	1♍	14♌	3♎	29♎
25	2♍	15♌	4♎	29♎
26	2♍	17♌	6♎	0♏
27	3♍	19♌	7♎	1♏
28	4♍	21♌	8♎	1♏
29	5♍	22♌	9♎	2♏
30	6♍	24♌	10♎	3♏
31	7♍	26♌	12♎	3♏

November

Day	☉	☿	♀	♂
1	8♏	2♐	24♐	16♐
2	9♏	2♐	25♐	17♐
3	10♏	3♐	26♐	18♐
4	11♏	4♐	27♐	19♐
5	12♏	4♐	28♐	19♐
6	13♏	4♐	29♐	20♐
7	14♏	5♐	1♑	21♐
8	15♏	5♐	2♑	22♐
9	16♏	5♐	3♑	22♐
10	17♏	5♐	4♑	23♐
11	18♏	4♐	5♑	24♐
12	19♏	4♐	6♑	25♐
13	20♏	3♐	7♑	25♐
14	21♏	2♐	8♑	26♐
15	22♏	1♐	9♑	27♐
16	23♏	0♐	10♑	28♐
17	24♏	29♏	11♑	28♐
18	25♏	27♏	12♑	29♐
19	26♏	26♏	13♑	0♑
20	27♏	25♏	15♑	1♑
21	28♏	23♏	16♑	1♑
22	29♏	22♏	17♑	2♑
23	0♐	21♏	18♑	3♑
24	1♐	20♏	19♑	4♑
25	2♐	20♏	20♑	4♑
26	4♐	19♏	21♑	5♑
27	5♐	19♏	22♑	6♑
28	6♐	19♏	23♑	7♑
29	7♐	19♏	24♑	8♑
30	8♐	19♏	25♑	8♑

March

Day	☉	☿	♀	♂
1	10♓	27♓	27♒	11♍
2	11♓	28♓	28♒	11♍
3	12♓	0♈	0♓	10♍
4	13♓	1♈	1♓	10♍
5	14♓	2♈	2♓	9♍
6	15♓	3♈	3♓	9♍
7	16♓	4♈	5♓	9♍
8	17♓	5♈	6♓	8♍
9	18♓	6♈	7♓	8♍
10	19♓	7♈	8♓	8♍
11	20♓	7♈	10♓	7♍
12	21♓	7♈	11♓	7♍
13	22♓	7♈	12♓	6♍
14	23♓	7♈	13♓	6♍
15	24♓	7♈	15♓	6♍
16	25♓	7♈	16♓	5♍
17	26♓	7♈	17♓	5♍
18	27♓	6♈	18♓	5♍
19	28♓	6♈	20♓	5♍
20	29♓	5♈	21♓	4♍
21	0♈	4♈	22♓	4♍
22	1♈	3♈	23♓	4♍
23	2♈	2♈	25♓	3♍
24	3♈	1♈	26♓	3♍
25	4♈	1♈	27♓	3♍
26	5♈	0♈	28♓	3♍
27	6♈	29♓	0♈	2♍
28	7♈	28♓	1♈	2♍
29	8♈	27♓	2♈	2♍
30	9♈	27♓	3♈	2♍
31	10♈	26♓	5♈	2♍

June

Day	☉	☿	♀	♂
1	10♊	14♊	21♊	13♍
2	11♊	17♊	22♊	13♍
3	12♊	19♊	23♊	14♍
4	13♊	21♊	25♊	14♍
5	14♊	23♊	26♊	14♍
6	15♊	25♊	27♊	15♍
7	16♊	27♊	28♊	15♍
8	17♊	29♊	0♋	16♍
9	18♊	1♋	1♋	16♍
10	19♊	3♋	2♋	17♍
11	20♊	5♋	3♋	17♍
12	21♊	7♋	4♋	18♍
13	22♊	9♋	6♋	18♍
14	23♊	11♋	7♋	19♍
15	24♊	12♋	8♋	19♍
16	25♊	14♋	9♋	19♍
17	26♊	16♋	11♋	20♍
18	26♊	17♋	12♋	20♍
19	27♊	19♋	13♋	21♍
20	28♊	21♋	14♋	21♍
21	29♊	22♋	16♋	22♍
22	0♋	24♋	17♋	22♍
23	1♋	25♋	18♋	23♍
24	2♋	26♋	19♋	23♍
25	3♋	28♋	20♋	24♍
26	4♋	29♋	22♋	24♍
27	5♋	0♌	23♋	25♍
28	6♋	1♌	24♋	25♍
29	7♋	3♌	25♋	26♍
30	8♋	4♌	27♋	26♍

September

Day	☉	☿	♀	♂
1	8♍	28♌	13♎	4♏
2	9♍	0♍	14♎	5♏
3	10♍	2♍	15♎	5♏
4	11♍	4♍	16♎	6♏
5	12♍	6♍	18♎	6♏
6	13♍	8♍	19♎	7♏
7	14♍	10♍	20♎	8♏
8	15♍	12♍	21♎	8♏
9	16♍	13♍	22♎	9♏
10	17♍	15♍	24♎	10♏
11	18♍	17♍	25♎	10♏
12	19♍	19♍	26♎	11♏
13	20♍	21♍	27♎	12♏
14	21♍	23♍	28♎	12♏
15	22♍	25♍	0♏	13♏
16	23♍	27♍	1♏	14♏
17	24♍	28♍	2♏	15♏
18	25♍	0♎	3♏	15♏
19	26♍	2♎	4♏	16♏
20	27♍	4♎	5♏	17♏
21	28♍	5♎	7♏	17♏
22	29♍	7♎	8♏	18♏
23	0♎	9♎	9♏	19♏
24	1♎	10♎	10♏	19♏
25	2♎	12♎	11♏	20♏
26	3♎	14♎	13♏	21♏
27	4♎	15♎	14♏	21♏
28	5♎	17♎	15♏	22♏
29	6♎	19♎	16♏	23♏
30	7♎	20♎	17♏	23♏

December

Day	☉	☿	♀	♂
1	9♐	19♏	26♑	9♑
2	10♐	20♏	27♑	10♑
3	11♐	21♏	28♑	11♑
4	12♐	21♏	29♑	11♑
5	13♐	22♏	29♑	12♑
6	14♐	23♏	0♒	13♑
7	15♐	24♏	1♒	14♑
8	16♐	25♏	2♒	14♑
9	17♐	26♏	3♒	15♑
10	18♐	28♏	4♒	16♑
11	19♐	29♏	5♒	17♑
12	20♐	0♐	6♒	18♑
13	21♐	1♐	7♒	18♑
14	22♐	3♐	8♒	19♑
15	23♐	4♐	8♒	20♑
16	24♐	5♐	9♒	21♑
17	25♐	7♐	10♒	21♑
18	26♐	8♐	11♒	22♑
19	27♐	10♐	12♒	23♑
20	28♐	11♐	12♒	24♑
21	29♐	13♐	13♒	25♑
22	0♑	14♐	14♒	25♑
23	1♑	16♐	14♒	26♑
24	2♑	17♐	15♒	27♑
25	3♑	19♐	16♒	28♑
26	4♑	20♐	16♒	28♑
27	5♑	22♐	17♒	29♑
28	6♑	23♐	18♒	0♒
29	7♑	25♐	18♒	1♒
30	8♑	26♐	19♒	2♒
31	9♑	28♐	19♒	2♒

1934

Planetary Positions

♌ = Leo ♍ = Virgo ♎ = Libra ♏ = Scorpio ♐ = Sagittarius ♑ = Capricorn ♒ = Aquarius ♓ = Pisces

January

Day	☉	☿	♀	♂
1	10♑	29♐	20♒	3♒
2	11♑	1♑	20♒	4♒
3	12♑	2♑	21♒	5♒
4	13♑	4♑	21♒	6♒
5	14♑	5♑	22♒	6♒
6	15♑	7♑	22♒	7♒
7	16♑	8♑	22♒	8♒
8	17♑	10♑	23♒	9♒
9	18♑	12♑	23♒	9♒
10	19♑	13♑	23♒	10♒
11	20♑	15♑	23♒	11♒
12	21♑	16♑	23♒	12♒
13	22♑	18♑	24♒	13♒
14	23♑	20♑	24♒	13♒
15	24♑	21♑	24♒	14♒
16	25♑	23♑	24♒	15♒
17	26♑	25♑	24♒	16♒
18	27♑	26♑	23♒	17♒
19	28♑	28♑	23♒	17♒
20	29♑	0♒	23♒	18♒
21	0♒	1♒	23♒	19♒
22	2♒	3♒	23♒	20♒
23	3♒	5♒	22♒	21♒
24	4♒	6♒	22♒	21♒
25	5♒	8♒	22♒	22♒
26	6♒	10♒	21♒	23♒
27	7♒	11♒	21♒	24♒
28	8♒	13♒	20♒	24♒
29	9♒	15♒	20♒	25♒
30	10♒	17♒	19♒	26♒
31	11♒	19♒	19♒	27♒

April

Day	☉	☿	♀	♂
1	11♈	13♓	25♒	14♈
2	12♈	14♓	26♒	15♈
3	13♈	15♓	27♒	15♈
4	14♈	16♓	28♒	16♈
5	15♈	17♓	29♒	17♈
6	16♈	18♓	0♓	18♈
7	17♈	19♓	1♓	18♈
8	18♈	21♓	2♓	19♈
9	19♈	22♓	3♓	20♈
10	20♈	23♓	3♓	21♈
11	21♈	24♓	4♓	21♈
12	22♈	26♓	5♓	22♈
13	23♈	27♓	6♓	23♈
14	24♈	29♓	7♓	24♈
15	25♈	0♈	8♓	24♈
16	26♈	2♈	9♓	25♈
17	26♈	3♈	10♓	26♈
18	27♈	5♈	11♓	27♈
19	28♈	6♈	12♓	27♈
20	29♈	8♈	13♓	28♈
21	0♉	9♈	14♓	29♈
22	1♉	11♈	15♓	0♉
23	2♉	13♈	16♓	0♉
24	3♉	14♈	17♓	1♉
25	4♉	16♈	18♓	2♉
26	5♉	18♈	19♓	3♉
27	6♉	20♈	20♓	3♉
28	7♉	21♈	21♓	4♉
29	8♉	23♈	22♓	5♉
30	9♉	25♈	23♓	6♉

July

Day	☉	☿	♀	♂
1	9♋	24♋	3♊	20♊
2	10♋	23♋	4♊	21♊
3	11♋	23♋	6♊	21♊
4	12♋	23♋	7♊	22♊
5	12♋	22♋	8♊	23♊
6	13♋	22♋	9♊	23♊
7	14♋	21♋	10♊	24♊
8	15♋	21♋	12♊	25♊
9	16♋	20♋	13♊	25♊
10	17♋	19♋	14♊	26♊
11	18♋	19♋	15♊	27♊
12	19♋	18♋	16♊	28♊
13	20♋	17♋	17♊	28♊
14	21♋	17♋	19♊	29♊
15	22♋	16♋	20♊	0♋
16	23♋	16♋	21♊	0♋
17	24♋	15♋	22♊	1♋
18	25♋	15♋	23♊	2♋
19	26♋	15♋	25♊	2♋
20	27♋	14♋	26♊	3♋
21	28♋	14♋	27♊	4♋
22	29♋	14♋	28♊	4♋
23	0♌	14♋	29♊	5♋
24	1♌	14♋	1♋	6♋
25	2♌	14♋	2♋	6♋
26	3♌	15♋	3♋	7♋
27	3♌	15♋	4♋	8♋
28	4♌	16♋	5♋	8♋
29	5♌	16♋	7♋	9♋
30	6♌	17♋	8♋	10♋
31	7♌	18♋	9♋	10♋

October

Day	☉	☿	♀	♂
1	7♎	1♏	25♍	20♌
2	8♎	2♏	26♍	20♌
3	9♎	3♏	27♍	21♌
4	10♎	5♏	29♍	22♌
5	11♎	6♏	0♎	22♌
6	12♎	7♏	1♎	23♌
7	13♎	8♏	2♎	23♌
8	14♎	9♏	4♎	24♌
9	15♎	10♏	5♎	25♌
10	16♎	11♏	6♎	25♌
11	17♎	12♏	7♎	26♌
12	18♎	13♏	9♎	26♌
13	19♎	14♏	10♎	27♌
14	20♎	15♏	11♎	28♌
15	21♎	16♏	12♎	28♌
16	22♎	16♏	14♎	29♌
17	23♎	17♏	15♎	29♌
18	24♎	18♏	16♎	0♍
19	25♎	18♏	17♎	1♍
20	26♎	18♏	19♎	1♍
21	27♎	19♏	20♎	2♍
22	28♎	19♏	21♎	2♍
23	29♎	19♏	22♎	3♍
24	0♏	19♏	24♎	4♍
25	1♏	19♏	25♎	4♍
26	2♏	18♏	26♎	5♍
27	3♏	18♏	27♎	5♍
28	4♏	17♏	29♎	6♍
29	5♏	16♏	0♏	6♍
30	6♏	15♏	1♏	7♍
31	7♏	14♏	2♏	8♍

February

Day	☉	☿	♀	♂
1	12♒	20♒	18♒	28♒
2	13♒	22♒	18♒	28♒
3	14♒	24♒	17♒	29♒
4	15♒	26♒	16♒	0♓
5	16♒	27♒	16♒	1♓
6	17♒	29♒	15♒	2♓
7	18♒	1♓	14♒	2♓
8	19♒	3♓	14♒	3♓
9	20♒	4♓	13♒	4♓
10	21♒	6♓	13♒	5♓
11	22♒	8♓	12♒	6♓
12	23♒	9♓	12♒	6♓
13	24♒	11♓	11♒	7♓
14	25♒	12♓	11♒	8♓
15	26♒	13♓	10♒	9♓
16	27♒	15♓	10♒	10♓
17	28♒	16♓	9♒	10♓
18	29♒	17♓	9♒	11♓
19	0♓	18♓	9♒	12♓
20	1♓	19♓	9♒	13♓
21	2♓	19♓	8♒	13♓
22	3♓	20♓	8♒	14♓
23	4♓	20♓	8♒	15♓
24	5♓	20♓	8♒	16♓
25	6♓	20♓	8♒	17♓
26	7♓	20♓	8♒	17♓
27	8♓	20♓	8♒	18♓
28	9♓	20♓	8♒	19♓

May

Day	☉	☿	♀	♂
1	10♉	27♈	25♓	6♉
2	11♉	29♈	26♓	7♉
3	12♉	1♉	27♓	8♉
4	13♉	3♉	28♓	9♉
5	14♉	5♉	29♓	9♉
6	15♉	7♉	0♈	10♉
7	16♉	9♉	1♈	11♉
8	17♉	11♉	2♈	12♉
9	18♉	13♉	3♈	12♉
10	19♉	15♉	4♈	13♉
11	20♉	17♉	5♈	14♉
12	21♉	20♉	6♈	14♉
13	22♉	22♉	7♈	15♉
14	23♉	24♉	9♈	16♉
15	24♉	26♉	10♈	17♉
16	25♉	28♉	11♈	17♉
17	26♉	0♊	12♈	18♉
18	27♉	3♊	13♈	19♉
19	28♉	5♊	14♈	20♉
20	28♉	7♊	15♈	20♉
21	29♉	9♊	16♈	21♉
22	0♊	11♊	17♈	22♉
23	1♊	13♊	18♈	22♉
24	2♊	15♊	20♈	23♉
25	3♊	17♊	21♈	24♉
26	4♊	19♊	22♈	25♉
27	5♊	21♊	23♈	25♉
28	6♊	23♊	24♈	26♉
29	7♊	25♊	25♈	27♉
30	8♊	26♊	26♈	28♉
31	9♊	28♊	27♈	28♉

August

Day	☉	☿	♀	♂
1	8♌	19♋	10♋	11♋
2	9♌	20♋	11♋	12♋
3	10♌	21♋	13♋	12♋
4	11♌	22♋	14♋	13♋
5	12♌	23♋	15♋	14♋
6	13♌	25♋	16♋	14♋
7	14♌	26♋	17♋	15♋
8	15♌	28♋	19♋	16♋
9	16♌	29♋	20♋	16♋
10	17♌	1♌	21♋	17♋
11	18♌	3♌	22♋	17♋
12	19♌	5♌	23♋	18♋
13	20♌	6♌	25♋	19♋
14	21♌	8♌	26♋	19♋
15	22♌	10♌	27♋	20♋
16	23♌	12♌	28♋	21♋
17	24♌	14♌	29♋	21♋
18	25♌	16♌	1♌	22♋
19	26♌	18♌	2♌	23♋
20	26♌	20♌	3♌	23♋
21	27♌	22♌	4♌	24♋
22	28♌	24♌	6♌	25♋
23	29♌	26♌	7♌	25♋
24	0♍	28♌	8♌	26♋
25	1♍	0♍	9♌	27♋
26	2♍	2♍	10♌	27♋
27	3♍	4♍	12♌	28♋
28	4♍	6♍	13♌	28♋
29	5♍	8♍	14♌	29♋
30	6♍	10♍	15♌	0♌
31	7♍	12♍	17♌	0♌

November

Day	☉	☿	♀	♂
1	8♏	13♏	4♏	8♍
2	9♏	11♏	5♏	9♍
3	10♏	10♏	6♏	9♍
4	11♏	9♏	7♏	10♍
5	12♏	8♏	9♏	10♍
6	13♏	6♏	10♏	11♍
7	14♏	5♏	11♏	12♍
8	15♏	5♏	12♏	12♍
9	16♏	4♏	14♏	13♍
10	17♏	3♏	15♏	13♍
11	18♏	3♏	16♏	14♍
12	19♏	3♏	17♏	14♍
13	20♏	3♏	19♏	15♍
14	21♏	3♏	20♏	16♍
15	22♏	4♏	21♏	16♍
16	23♏	4♏	22♏	17♍
17	24♏	5♏	24♏	17♍
18	25♏	6♏	25♏	18♍
19	26♏	7♏	26♏	18♍
20	27♏	8♏	27♏	19♍
21	28♏	9♏	29♏	19♍
22	29♏	10♏	0♐	20♍
23	0♐	11♏	1♐	20♍
24	1♐	13♏	3♐	21♍
25	2♐	14♏	4♐	22♍
26	3♐	15♏	5♐	22♍
27	4♐	17♏	6♐	23♍
28	5♐	18♏	8♐	23♍
29	6♐	19♏	9♐	24♍
30	7♐	21♏	10♐	24♍

March

Day	☉	☿	♀	♂
1	10♓	19♓	8♒	20♓
2	11♓	18♓	8♒	21♓
3	12♓	17♓	9♒	21♓
4	13♓	17♓	9♒	22♓
5	14♓	16♓	9♒	23♓
6	15♓	15♓	9♒	24♓
7	16♓	14♓	10♒	24♓
8	17♓	13♓	10♒	25♓
9	18♓	12♓	10♒	26♓
10	19♓	11♓	11♒	27♓
11	20♓	10♓	11♒	28♓
12	21♓	9♓	12♒	28♓
13	22♓	8♓	12♒	29♓
14	23♓	8♓	13♒	0♈
15	24♓	7♓	13♒	1♈
16	25♓	7♓	14♒	1♈
17	26♓	7♓	15♒	2♈
18	27♓	6♓	15♒	3♈
19	28♓	6♓	16♒	4♈
20	29♓	6♓	17♒	5♈
21	0♈	6♓	17♒	5♈
22	1♈	7♓	18♒	6♈
23	2♈	7♓	19♒	7♈
24	3♈	7♓	19♒	8♈
25	4♈	8♓	20♒	8♈
26	5♈	8♓	21♒	9♈
27	6♈	9♓	21♒	10♈
28	7♈	10♓	22♒	11♈
29	8♈	10♓	23♒	11♈
30	9♈	11♓	24♒	12♈
31	10♈	12♓	25♒	13♈

June

Day	☉	☿	♀	♂
1	10♊	0♋	29♈	29♉
2	11♊	1♋	0♉	0♊
3	12♊	3♋	1♉	0♊
4	13♊	4♋	2♉	1♊
5	14♊	6♋	3♉	2♊
6	15♊	7♋	4♉	3♊
7	16♊	9♋	5♉	3♊
8	17♊	10♋	7♉	4♊
9	18♊	11♋	8♉	5♊
10	19♊	13♋	9♉	5♊
11	20♊	14♋	10♉	6♊
12	21♊	15♋	11♉	7♊
13	21♊	16♋	12♉	7♊
14	22♊	17♋	14♉	8♊
15	23♊	18♋	15♉	9♊
16	24♊	19♋	16♉	10♊
17	25♊	20♋	17♉	10♊
18	26♊	20♋	18♉	11♊
19	27♊	21♋	19♉	12♊
20	28♊	22♋	20♉	12♊
21	29♊	22♋	22♉	13♊
22	0♋	23♋	23♉	14♊
23	1♋	23♋	24♉	14♊
24	2♋	23♋	25♉	15♊
25	3♋	24♋	26♉	16♊
26	4♋	24♋	27♉	17♊
27	5♋	24♋	29♉	17♊
28	6♋	24♋	0♊	18♊
29	7♋	24♋	1♊	19♊
30	8♋	24♋	2♊	19♊

September

Day	☉	☿	♀	♂
1	8♍	14♍	18♌	1♌
2	9♍	16♍	19♌	2♌
3	10♍	17♍	20♌	2♌
4	11♍	19♍	21♌	3♌
5	12♍	21♍	23♌	4♌
6	13♍	23♍	24♌	4♌
7	14♍	24♍	25♌	5♌
8	15♍	26♍	26♌	5♌
9	16♍	28♍	28♌	6♌
10	17♍	0♎	29♌	7♌
11	18♍	1♎	0♍	7♌
12	19♍	3♎	1♍	8♌
13	20♍	4♎	3♍	9♌
14	21♍	6♎	4♍	9♌
15	22♍	8♎	5♍	10♌
16	23♍	9♎	6♍	11♌
17	24♍	11♎	7♍	11♌
18	25♍	12♎	9♍	12♌
19	26♍	14♎	10♍	12♌
20	27♍	15♎	11♍	13♌
21	28♍	17♎	12♍	14♌
22	29♍	18♎	14♍	14♌
23	29♍	20♎	15♍	15♌
24	0♎	21♎	16♍	15♌
25	1♎	23♎	17♍	16♌
26	2♎	24♎	19♍	17♌
27	3♎	25♎	20♍	17♌
28	4♎	27♎	21♍	18♌
29	5♎	28♎	22♍	19♌
30	6♎	29♎	24♍	19♌

December

Day	☉	☿	♀	♂
1	8♐	22♏	11♐	25♍
2	9♐	24♏	13♐	25♍
3	10♐	25♏	14♐	26♍
4	11♐	27♏	15♐	26♍
5	12♐	28♏	16♐	27♍
6	13♐	0♐	18♐	27♍
7	14♐	1♐	19♐	28♍
8	15♐	3♐	20♐	28♍
9	16♐	4♐	21♐	29♍
10	17♐	6♐	23♐	29♍
11	18♐	8♐	24♐	0♎
12	19♐	9♐	25♐	0♎
13	21♐	11♐	26♐	1♎
14	22♐	12♐	28♐	1♎
15	23♐	14♐	29♐	2♎
16	24♐	15♐	0♑	2♎
17	25♐	17♐	1♑	3♎
18	26♐	18♐	3♑	3♎
19	27♐	20♐	4♑	4♎
20	28♐	21♐	5♑	4♎
21	29♐	23♐	6♑	5♎
22	0♑	25♐	8♑	5♎
23	1♑	26♐	9♑	6♎
24	2♑	28♐	10♑	6♎
25	3♑	29♐	11♑	7♎
26	4♑	1♑	13♑	7♎
27	5♑	3♑	14♑	8♎
28	6♑	4♑	15♑	8♎
29	7♑	6♑	17♑	8♎
30	8♑	7♑	18♑	9♎
31	9♑	9♑	19♑	9♎

1935

Your Starway to Love

☉ = Sun ☿ = Mercury ♀ = Venus ♂ = Mars ♈ = Aries ♉ = Taurus ♊ = Gemini ♋ = Cancer

January

Day	☉	☿	♀	♂
1	10♑	10♑	20♑	10♎
2	11♑	12♑	22♑	10♎
3	12♑	14♑	23♑	11♎
4	13♑	15♑	24♑	11♎
5	14♑	17♑	25♑	12♎
6	15♑	19♑	27♑	12♎
7	16♑	20♑	28♑	12♎
8	17♑	22♑	29♑	13♎
9	18♑	24♑	0♒	13♎
10	19♑	25♑	2♒	14♎
11	20♑	27♑	3♒	14♎
12	21♑	29♑	4♒	14♎
13	22♑	0♒	5♒	15♎
14	23♑	2♒	7♒	15♎
15	24♑	4♒	8♒	15♎
16	25♑	5♒	9♒	16♎
17	26♑	7♒	10♒	16♎
18	27♑	9♒	12♒	17♎
19	28♑	10♒	13♒	17♎
20	29♑	12♒	14♒	17♎
21	0♒	14♒	15♒	18♎
22	1♒	15♒	17♒	18♎
23	2♒	17♒	18♒	18♎
24	3♒	19♒	19♒	19♎
25	4♒	20♒	20♒	19♎
26	5♒	22♒	22♒	19♎
27	6♒	23♒	23♒	19♎
28	7♒	25♒	24♒	20♎
29	8♒	26♒	25♒	20♎
30	9♒	27♒	27♒	20♎
31	10♒	29♒	28♒	21♎

February

Day	☉	☿	♀	♂
1	11♒	0♓	29♒	21♎
2	12♒	1♓	0♓	21♎
3	13♒	2♓	2♓	21♎
4	14♒	2♓	3♓	22♎
5	15♒	3♓	4♓	22♎
6	16♒	3♓	5♓	22♎
7	18♒	4♓	7♓	22♎
8	19♒	4♓	8♓	23♎
9	20♒	4♓	9♓	23♎
10	21♒	4♓	10♓	23♎
11	22♒	3♓	12♓	23♎
12	23♒	3♓	13♓	23♎
13	24♒	2♓	14♓	23♎
14	25♒	1♓	15♓	24♎
15	26♒	0♓	17♓	24♎
16	27♒	29♒	18♓	24♎
17	28♒	28♒	19♓	24♎
18	29♒	27♒	20♓	24♎
19	0♓	25♒	22♓	24♎
20	1♓	24♒	23♓	24♎
21	2♓	23♒	24♓	24♎
22	3♓	22♒	25♓	24♎
23	4♓	22♒	27♓	25♎
24	5♓	21♒	28♓	25♎
25	6♓	20♒	29♓	25♎
26	7♓	20♒	0♈	25♎
27	8♓	19♒	1♈	25♎
28	9♓	19♒	3♈	25♎

March

Day	☉	☿	♀	♂
1	10♓	19♒	4♈	25♎
2	11♓	19♒	5♈	25♎
3	12♓	19♒	6♈	25♎
4	13♓	19♒	8♈	24♎
5	14♓	19♒	9♈	24♎
6	15♓	20♒	10♈	24♎
7	16♓	20♒	11♈	24♎
8	17♓	21♒	13♈	24♎
9	18♓	21♒	14♈	24♎
10	19♓	22♒	15♈	24♎
11	20♓	23♒	16♈	24♎
12	21♓	23♒	17♈	24♎
13	22♓	24♒	19♈	23♎
14	23♓	25♒	20♈	23♎
15	24♓	26♒	21♈	23♎
16	25♓	27♒	22♈	23♎
17	26♓	28♒	24♈	23♎
18	27♓	29♒	25♈	22♎
19	28♓	0♓	26♈	22♎
20	29♓	1♓	27♈	22♎
21	0♈	3♓	29♈	22♎
22	1♈	4♓	0♉	21♎
23	2♈	5♓	1♉	21♎
24	3♈	6♓	2♉	21♎
25	4♈	8♓	3♉	20♎
26	5♈	9♓	5♉	20♎
27	6♈	11♓	6♉	20♎
28	7♈	12♓	7♉	19♎
29	8♈	13♓	8♉	19♎
30	9♈	15♓	9♉	19♎
31	10♈	16♓	11♉	18♎

April

Day	☉	☿	♀	♂
1	11♈	18♓	12♉	18♎
2	12♈	19♓	13♉	18♎
3	13♈	21♓	14♉	17♎
4	14♈	22♓	15♉	17♎
5	14♈	24♓	17♉	17♎
6	15♈	26♓	18♉	16♎
7	16♈	27♓	19♉	16♎
8	17♈	29♓	20♉	15♎
9	18♈	1♈	21♉	15♎
10	19♈	2♈	23♉	15♎
11	20♈	4♈	24♉	14♎
12	21♈	6♈	25♉	14♎
13	22♈	8♈	26♉	14♎
14	23♈	10♈	27♉	13♎
15	24♈	12♈	29♉	13♎
16	25♈	13♈	0♊	12♎
17	26♈	15♈	1♊	12♎
18	27♈	17♈	2♊	12♎
19	28♈	19♈	3♊	11♎
20	29♈	21♈	5♊	11♎
21	0♉	23♈	6♊	11♎
22	1♉	25♈	7♊	10♎
23	2♉	27♈	8♊	10♎
24	3♉	29♈	9♊	10♎
25	4♉	1♉	11♊	9♎
26	5♉	4♉	12♊	9♎
27	6♉	6♉	13♊	9♎
28	7♉	8♉	14♊	9♎
29	8♉	10♉	15♊	8♎
30	9♉	12♉	16♊	8♎

May

Day	☉	☿	♀	♂
1	10♉	14♉	18♊	8♎
2	11♉	16♉	19♊	8♎
3	12♉	19♉	20♊	7♎
4	13♉	21♉	21♊	7♎
5	14♉	23♉	22♊	7♎
6	15♉	25♉	23♊	7♎
7	16♉	27♉	25♊	7♎
8	17♉	29♉	26♊	7♎
9	18♉	1♊	27♊	7♎
10	19♉	3♊	28♊	6♎
11	20♉	5♊	29♊	6♎
12	21♉	7♊	0♋	6♎
13	22♉	8♊	1♋	6♎
14	22♉	10♊	3♋	6♎
15	23♉	12♊	4♋	6♎
16	24♉	14♊	5♋	6♎
17	25♉	15♊	6♋	6♎
18	26♉	17♊	7♋	6♎
19	27♉	18♊	8♋	6♎
20	28♉	20♊	9♋	6♎
21	29♉	21♊	11♋	6♎
22	0♊	22♊	12♋	6♎
23	1♊	23♊	13♋	6♎
24	2♊	25♊	14♋	6♎
25	3♊	26♊	15♋	6♎
26	4♊	27♊	16♋	6♎
27	5♊	28♊	17♋	7♎
28	6♊	29♊	18♋	7♎
29	7♊	0♋	20♋	7♎
30	8♊	0♋	21♋	7♎
31	9♊	1♋	22♋	7♎

June

Day	☉	☿	♀	♂
1	10♊	2♋	23♋	7♎
2	11♊	2♋	24♋	7♎
3	12♊	3♋	25♋	8♎
4	13♊	3♋	26♋	8♎
5	14♊	3♋	27♋	8♎
6	15♊	4♋	28♋	8♎
7	16♊	4♋	29♋	8♎
8	16♊	4♋	0♌	9♎
9	17♊	4♋	2♌	9♎
10	18♊	4♋	3♌	9♎
11	19♊	4♋	4♌	9♎
12	20♊	4♋	5♌	10♎
13	21♊	4♋	6♌	10♎
14	22♊	3♋	7♌	10♎
15	23♊	3♋	8♌	11♎
16	24♊	2♋	9♌	11♎
17	25♊	2♋	10♌	11♎
18	26♊	1♋	11♌	12♎
19	27♊	1♋	12♌	12♎
20	28♊	0♋	13♌	12♎
21	29♊	0♋	14♌	13♎
22	0♋	29♊	15♌	13♎
23	1♋	29♊	16♌	13♎
24	2♋	28♊	17♌	14♎
25	3♋	28♊	18♌	14♎
26	4♋	27♊	19♌	14♎
27	5♋	27♊	20♌	15♎
28	6♋	26♊	21♌	15♎
29	7♋	26♊	22♌	15♎
30	7♋	26♊	23♌	16♎

July

Day	☉	☿	♀	♂
1	8♋	25♊	24♌	16♎
2	9♋	25♊	25♌	17♎
3	10♋	25♊	26♌	17♎
4	11♋	25♊	27♌	18♎
5	12♋	25♊	28♌	18♎
6	13♋	26♊	29♌	18♎
7	14♋	26♊	29♌	19♎
8	15♋	26♊	0♍	19♎
9	16♋	27♊	1♍	20♎
10	17♋	27♊	2♍	20♎
11	18♋	28♊	3♍	21♎
12	19♋	29♊	4♍	21♎
13	20♋	29♊	5♍	22♎
14	21♋	0♋	5♍	22♎
15	22♋	1♋	6♍	23♎
16	23♋	2♋	7♍	23♎
17	24♋	3♋	8♍	24♎
18	25♋	5♋	9♍	24♎
19	26♋	6♋	9♍	25♎
20	27♋	7♋	10♍	25♎
21	28♋	9♋	11♍	26♎
22	28♋	10♋	12♍	26♎
23	29♋	12♋	12♍	27♎
24	0♌	13♋	13♍	27♎
25	1♌	15♋	14♍	28♎
26	2♌	17♋	14♍	28♎
27	3♌	19♋	15♍	29♎
28	4♌	20♋	16♍	29♎
29	5♌	22♋	16♍	0♏
30	6♌	24♋	17♍	0♏
31	7♌	26♋	17♍	1♏

August

Day	☉	☿	♀	♂
1	8♌	28♋	18♍	1♏
2	9♌	0♌	18♍	2♏
3	10♌	2♌	19♍	2♏
4	11♌	4♌	19♍	3♏
5	12♌	6♌	20♍	4♏
6	13♌	9♌	20♍	4♏
7	14♌	11♌	21♍	5♏
8	15♌	13♌	21♍	5♏
9	16♌	15♌	21♍	6♏
10	17♌	17♌	22♍	6♏
11	18♌	19♌	22♍	7♏
12	19♌	21♌	22♍	8♏
13	20♌	23♌	22♍	8♏
14	20♌	25♌	22♍	9♏
15	21♌	27♌	23♍	9♏
16	22♌	29♌	23♍	10♏
17	23♌	1♍	23♍	11♏
18	24♌	3♍	23♍	11♏
19	25♌	4♍	23♍	12♏
20	26♌	6♍	23♍	12♏
21	27♌	8♍	23♍	13♏
22	28♌	10♍	22♍	14♏
23	29♌	12♍	22♍	14♏
24	0♍	13♍	22♍	15♏
25	1♍	15♍	22♍	15♏
26	2♍	17♍	21♍	16♏
27	3♍	19♍	21♍	17♏
28	4♍	20♍	21♍	17♏
29	5♍	22♍	20♍	18♏
30	6♍	23♍	20♍	19♏
31	7♍	25♍	19♍	19♏

September

Day	☉	☿	♀	♂
1	8♍	27♍	19♍	20♏
2	9♍	28♍	18♍	21♏
3	10♍	0♎	18♍	21♏
4	11♍	1♎	17♍	22♏
5	12♍	3♎	17♍	22♏
6	13♍	4♎	16♍	23♏
7	14♍	6♎	15♍	24♏
8	15♍	7♎	15♍	24♏
9	16♍	8♎	14♍	25♏
10	17♍	10♎	14♍	26♏
11	18♍	11♎	13♍	26♏
12	19♍	13♎	12♍	27♏
13	19♍	14♎	12♍	28♏
14	20♍	15♎	11♍	28♏
15	21♍	16♎	11♍	29♏
16	22♍	18♎	10♍	0♐
17	23♍	19♎	10♍	0♐
18	24♍	20♎	9♍	1♐
19	25♍	21♎	9♍	2♐
20	26♍	22♎	8♍	2♐
21	27♍	23♎	8♍	3♐
22	28♍	24♎	8♍	4♐
23	29♍	25♎	7♍	5♐
24	0♎	26♎	7♍	5♐
25	1♎	27♎	7♍	6♐
26	2♎	28♎	7♍	7♐
27	3♎	29♎	7♍	7♐
28	4♎	0♏	7♍	8♐
29	5♎	0♏	7♍	9♐
30	6♎	1♏	7♍	9♐

October

Day	☉	☿	♀	♂
1	7♎	2♏	7♍	10♐
2	8♎	2♏	7♍	11♐
3	9♎	2♏	7♍	11♐
4	10♎	3♏	7♍	12♐
5	11♎	3♏	7♍	13♐
6	12♎	3♏	7♍	14♐
7	13♎	3♏	8♍	14♐
8	14♎	3♏	8♍	15♐
9	15♎	2♏	8♍	16♐
10	16♎	2♏	9♍	16♐
11	17♎	1♏	9♍	17♐
12	18♎	0♏	9♍	18♐
13	19♎	0♏	10♍	19♐
14	20♎	29♎	10♍	19♐
15	21♎	28♎	11♍	20♐
16	22♎	26♎	11♍	21♐
17	23♎	25♎	12♍	22♐
18	24♎	24♎	12♍	22♐
19	25♎	23♎	13♍	23♐
20	26♎	22♎	14♍	24♐
21	27♎	20♎	14♍	24♐
22	28♎	20♎	15♍	25♐
23	29♎	19♎	16♍	26♐
24	0♏	18♎	16♍	27♐
25	1♏	18♎	17♍	27♐
26	2♏	17♎	18♍	28♐
27	3♏	17♎	19♍	29♐
28	4♏	17♎	19♍	0♑
29	5♏	18♎	20♍	0♑
30	6♏	18♎	21♍	1♑
31	7♏	19♎	22♍	2♑

November

Day	☉	☿	♀	♂
1	8♏	19♎	23♍	3♑
2	9♏	20♎	23♍	3♑
3	10♏	21♎	24♍	4♑
4	11♏	22♎	25♍	5♑
5	12♏	23♎	26♍	6♑
6	13♏	25♎	27♍	6♑
7	14♏	26♎	28♍	7♑
8	15♏	27♎	29♍	8♑
9	16♏	29♎	0♎	9♑
10	17♏	0♏	0♎	9♑
11	18♏	2♏	1♎	10♑
12	19♏	3♏	2♎	11♑
13	20♏	5♏	3♎	12♑
14	21♏	6♏	4♎	12♑
15	22♏	8♏	5♎	13♑
16	23♏	9♏	6♎	14♑
17	24♏	11♏	7♎	15♑
18	25♏	12♏	8♎	15♑
19	26♏	14♏	9♎	16♑
20	27♏	16♏	10♎	17♑
21	28♏	17♏	11♎	18♑
22	29♏	19♏	12♎	18♑
23	0♐	20♏	13♎	19♑
24	1♐	22♏	14♎	20♑
25	2♐	24♏	15♎	21♑
26	3♐	25♏	17♎	22♑
27	4♐	27♏	18♎	22♑
28	5♐	28♏	19♎	23♑
29	6♐	0♐	20♎	24♑
30	7♐	1♐	21♎	25♑

December

Day	☉	☿	♀	♂
1	8♐	3♐	22♎	25♑
2	9♐	5♐	23♎	26♑
3	10♐	6♐	24♎	27♑
4	11♐	8♐	25♎	28♑
5	12♐	9♐	26♎	28♑
6	13♐	11♐	27♎	29♑
7	14♐	12♐	28♎	0♒
8	15♐	14♐	0♏	1♒
9	16♐	16♐	1♏	2♒
10	17♐	17♐	2♏	2♒
11	18♐	19♐	3♏	3♒
12	19♐	20♐	4♏	4♒
13	20♐	22♐	5♏	5♒
14	21♐	23♐	6♏	5♒
15	22♐	25♐	7♏	6♒
16	23♐	27♐	9♏	7♒
17	24♐	28♐	10♏	8♒
18	25♐	0♑	11♏	9♒
19	26♐	1♑	12♏	9♒
20	27♐	3♑	13♏	10♒
21	28♐	5♑	14♏	11♒
22	29♐	6♑	15♏	12♒
23	0♑	8♑	17♏	12♒
24	1♑	9♑	18♏	13♒
25	2♑	11♑	19♏	14♒
26	3♑	13♑	20♏	15♒
27	5♑	14♑	21♏	16♒
28	6♑	16♑	22♏	16♒
29	7♑	17♑	24♏	17♒
30	8♑	19♑	25♏	18♒
31	9♑	21♑	26♏	19♒

Planetary Positions

♌ = Leo ♍ = Virgo ♎ = Libra ♏ = Scorpio ♐ = Sagittarius ♑ = Capricorn ♒ = Aquarius ♓ = Pisces

1936

January

Day	☉	☿	♀	♂
1	10♑	22♑	27♏	20♒
2	11♑	24♑	28♏	20♒
3	12♑	25♑	0♐	21♒
4	13♑	27♑	1♐	22♒
5	14♑	29♑	2♐	23♒
6	15♑	0♒	3♐	23♒
7	16♑	2♒	4♐	24♒
8	17♑	3♒	5♐	25♒
9	18♑	5♒	7♐	26♒
10	19♑	6♒	8♐	27♒
11	20♑	8♒	9♐	27♒
12	21♑	9♒	10♐	28♒
13	22♑	10♒	11♐	29♒
14	23♑	11♒	13♐	0♓
15	24♑	13♒	14♐	0♓
16	25♑	14♒	15♐	1♓
17	26♑	15♒	16♐	2♓
18	27♑	16♒	17♐	3♓
19	28♑	16♒	19♐	4♓
20	29♑	17♒	20♐	4♓
21	0♒	17♒	21♐	5♓
22	1♒	18♒	22♐	6♓
23	2♒	18♒	23♐	7♓
24	3♒	17♒	25♐	8♓
25	4♒	17♒	26♐	8♓
26	5♒	17♒	27♐	9♓
27	6♒	16♒	28♐	10♓
28	7♒	15♒	0♑	11♓
29	8♒	14♒	1♑	11♓
30	9♒	13♒	2♑	12♓
31	10♒	12♒	3♑	13♓

February

Day	☉	☿	♀	♂
1	11♒	11♒	4♑	14♓
2	12♒	9♒	6♑	15♓
3	13♒	8♒	7♑	15♓
4	14♒	7♒	8♑	16♓
5	15♒	6♒	9♑	17♓
6	16♒	5♒	10♑	18♓
7	17♒	4♒	12♑	18♓
8	18♒	3♒	13♑	19♓
9	19♒	3♒	14♑	20♓
10	20♒	2♒	15♑	21♓
11	21♒	2♒	17♑	22♓
12	22♒	2♒	18♑	22♓
13	23♒	2♒	19♑	23♓
14	24♒	2♒	20♑	24♓
15	25♒	2♒	21♑	25♓
16	26♒	2♒	23♑	25♓
17	27♒	3♒	24♑	26♓
18	28♒	3♒	25♑	27♓
19	29♒	4♒	26♑	28♓
20	0♓	4♒	28♑	28♓
21	1♓	5♒	29♑	29♓
22	2♓	6♒	0♒	0♈
23	3♓	7♒	1♒	1♈
24	4♓	8♒	2♒	2♈
25	5♓	9♒	4♒	2♈
26	6♓	10♒	5♒	3♈
27	7♓	11♒	6♒	4♈
28	8♓	12♒	7♒	5♈
29	9♓	13♒	9♒	5♈

March

Day	☉	☿	♀	♂
1	10♓	14♒	10♒	6♈
2	11♓	15♒	11♒	7♈
3	12♓	16♒	12♒	8♈
4	13♓	18♒	14♒	8♈
5	14♓	19♒	15♒	9♈
6	15♓	20♒	16♒	10♈
7	16♓	21♒	17♒	11♈
8	17♓	23♒	18♒	11♈
9	18♓	24♒	20♒	12♈
10	19♓	26♒	21♒	13♈
11	20♓	27♒	22♒	14♈
12	21♓	28♒	23♒	15♈
13	22♓	0♓	25♒	15♈
14	23♓	1♓	26♒	16♈
15	24♓	3♓	27♒	17♈
16	25♓	4♓	28♒	18♈
17	26♓	6♓	29♒	18♈
18	27♓	8♓	1♓	19♈
19	28♓	9♓	2♓	20♈
20	29♓	11♓	3♓	21♈
21	0♈	12♓	4♓	21♈
22	1♈	14♓	6♓	22♈
23	2♈	16♓	7♓	23♈
24	3♈	17♓	8♓	24♈
25	4♈	19♓	9♓	24♈
26	5♈	21♓	11♓	25♈
27	6♈	23♓	12♓	26♈
28	7♈	24♓	13♓	27♈
29	8♈	26♓	14♓	27♈
30	9♈	28♓	15♓	28♈
31	10♈	0♈	17♓	29♈

April

Day	☉	☿	♀	♂
1	11♈	2♈	18♓	29♈
2	12♈	4♈	19♓	0♉
3	13♈	6♈	20♓	1♉
4	14♈	8♈	22♓	2♉
5	15♈	10♈	23♓	2♉
6	16♈	12♈	24♓	3♉
7	17♈	14♈	25♓	4♉
8	18♈	16♈	27♓	5♉
9	19♈	18♈	28♓	5♉
10	20♈	20♈	29♓	6♉
11	21♈	22♈	0♈	7♉
12	22♈	24♈	1♈	8♉
13	23♈	26♈	3♈	8♉
14	24♈	28♈	4♈	9♉
15	25♈	0♉	5♈	10♉
16	26♈	2♉	6♈	11♉
17	27♈	4♉	8♈	11♉
18	28♈	7♉	9♈	12♉
19	29♈	9♉	10♈	13♉
20	0♉	11♉	11♈	13♉
21	1♉	13♉	13♈	14♉
22	2♉	15♉	14♈	15♉
23	3♉	17♉	15♈	16♉
24	4♉	19♉	16♈	16♉
25	5♉	20♉	17♈	17♉
26	6♉	22♉	19♈	18♉
27	7♉	24♉	20♈	18♉
28	8♉	26♉	21♈	19♉
29	9♉	27♉	22♈	20♉
30	10♉	29♉	24♈	21♉

May

Day	☉	☿	♀	♂
1	11♉	0♊	25♈	21♉
2	12♉	2♊	26♈	22♉
3	13♉	3♊	27♈	23♉
4	14♉	4♊	28♈	23♉
5	15♉	5♊	0♉	24♉
6	15♉	7♊	1♉	25♉
7	16♉	8♊	2♉	26♉
8	17♉	9♊	3♉	26♉
9	18♉	9♊	5♉	27♉
10	19♉	10♊	6♉	28♉
11	20♉	11♊	7♉	28♉
12	21♉	12♊	8♉	29♉
13	22♉	12♊	10♉	0♊
14	23♉	13♊	11♉	1♊
15	24♉	13♊	12♉	1♊
16	25♉	14♊	13♉	2♊
17	26♉	14♊	14♉	3♊
18	27♉	14♊	16♉	3♊
19	28♉	14♊	17♉	4♊
20	29♉	14♊	18♉	5♊
21	0♊	14♊	19♉	5♊
22	1♊	14♊	21♉	6♊
23	2♊	14♊	22♉	7♊
24	3♊	13♊	23♉	8♊
25	4♊	13♊	24♉	8♊
26	5♊	13♊	25♉	9♊
27	6♊	12♊	27♉	10♊
28	7♊	12♊	28♉	10♊
29	8♊	11♊	29♉	11♊
30	9♊	11♊	0♊	12♊
31	10♊	10♊	2♊	12♊

June

Day	☉	☿	♀	♂
1	11♊	9♊	3♊	13♊
2	11♊	9♊	4♊	14♊
3	12♊	8♊	5♊	15♊
4	13♊	8♊	7♊	15♊
5	14♊	7♊	8♊	16♊
6	15♊	7♊	9♊	17♊
7	16♊	7♊	10♊	17♊
8	17♊	6♊	11♊	18♊
9	18♊	6♊	13♊	19♊
10	19♊	6♊	14♊	19♊
11	20♊	6♊	15♊	20♊
12	21♊	6♊	16♊	21♊
13	22♊	6♊	18♊	21♊
14	23♊	6♊	19♊	22♊
15	24♊	6♊	20♊	23♊
16	25♊	6♊	21♊	23♊
17	26♊	6♊	22♊	24♊
18	27♊	7♊	24♊	25♊
19	28♊	7♊	25♊	25♊
20	29♊	8♊	26♊	26♊
21	0♋	8♊	27♊	27♊
22	1♋	9♊	29♊	28♊
23	2♋	10♊	0♋	28♊
24	2♋	10♊	1♋	29♊
25	3♋	11♊	2♋	0♋
26	4♋	12♊	4♋	0♋
27	5♋	13♊	5♋	1♋
28	6♋	14♊	6♋	2♋
29	7♋	16♊	7♋	2♋
30	8♋	17♊	8♋	3♋

July

Day	☉	☿	♀	♂
1	9♋	18♊	10♋	4♋
2	10♋	19♊	11♋	4♋
3	11♋	21♊	12♋	5♋
4	12♋	22♊	13♋	6♋
5	13♋	24♊	15♋	6♋
6	14♋	25♊	16♋	7♋
7	15♋	27♊	17♋	8♋
8	16♋	29♊	18♋	8♋
9	17♋	1♋	19♋	9♋
10	18♋	2♋	21♋	10♋
11	19♋	4♋	22♋	10♋
12	20♋	6♋	23♋	11♋
13	21♋	8♋	24♋	12♋
14	22♋	10♋	26♋	12♋
15	23♋	12♋	27♋	13♋
16	23♋	14♋	28♋	14♋
17	24♋	16♋	29♋	14♋
18	25♋	18♋	1♌	15♋
19	26♋	21♋	2♌	16♋
20	27♋	23♋	3♌	16♋
21	28♋	25♋	4♌	17♋
22	29♋	27♋	5♌	17♋
23	0♌	29♋	7♌	18♋
24	1♌	1♌	8♌	19♋
25	2♌	3♌	9♌	19♋
26	3♌	5♌	10♌	20♋
27	4♌	7♌	12♌	21♋
28	5♌	9♌	13♌	21♋
29	6♌	12♌	14♌	22♋
30	7♌	14♌	15♌	23♋
31	8♌	16♌	17♌	23♋

August

Day	☉	☿	♀	♂
1	9♌	17♌	18♌	24♋
2	10♌	19♌	19♌	25♋
3	11♌	21♌	20♌	25♋
4	12♌	23♌	22♌	26♋
5	13♌	25♌	23♌	27♋
6	14♌	27♌	24♌	27♋
7	14♌	29♌	25♌	28♋
8	15♌	0♍	26♌	29♋
9	16♌	2♍	28♌	29♋
10	17♌	4♍	29♌	0♌
11	18♌	6♍	0♍	1♌
12	19♌	7♍	1♍	1♌
13	20♌	9♍	3♍	2♌
14	21♌	11♍	4♍	2♌
15	22♌	12♍	5♍	3♌
16	23♌	14♍	6♍	4♌
17	24♌	15♍	8♍	4♌
18	25♌	17♍	9♍	5♌
19	26♌	18♍	10♍	6♌
20	27♌	20♍	11♍	6♌
21	28♌	21♍	12♍	7♌
22	29♌	23♍	14♍	8♌
23	0♍	24♍	15♍	8♌
24	1♍	25♍	16♍	9♌
25	2♍	27♍	17♍	10♌
26	3♍	28♍	19♍	10♌
27	4♍	29♍	20♍	11♌
28	5♍	1♎	21♍	11♌
29	6♍	2♎	22♍	12♌
30	7♍	3♎	24♍	13♌
31	8♍	4♎	25♍	13♌

September

Day	☉	☿	♀	♂
1	9♍	5♎	26♍	14♌
2	10♍	6♎	27♍	15♌
3	11♍	7♎	29♍	15♌
4	11♍	8♎	0♎	16♌
5	12♍	9♎	1♎	17♌
6	13♍	10♎	2♎	17♌
7	14♍	11♎	3♎	18♌
8	15♍	12♎	5♎	18♌
9	16♍	13♎	6♎	19♌
10	17♍	14♎	7♎	20♌
11	18♍	14♎	8♎	20♌
12	19♍	15♎	10♎	21♌
13	20♍	15♎	11♎	22♌
14	21♍	16♎	12♎	22♌
15	22♍	16♎	13♎	23♌
16	23♍	16♎	15♎	23♌
17	24♍	16♎	16♎	24♌
18	25♍	16♎	17♎	25♌
19	26♍	16♎	18♎	25♌
20	27♍	16♎	19♎	26♌
21	28♍	16♎	21♎	27♌
22	29♍	16♎	22♎	27♌
23	0♎	15♎	23♎	28♌
24	1♎	14♎	24♎	28♌
25	2♎	14♎	26♎	29♌
26	3♎	13♎	27♎	0♍
27	4♎	12♎	28♎	0♍
28	5♎	11♎	29♎	1♍
29	6♎	10♎	1♏	2♍
30	7♎	9♎	2♏	2♍

October

Day	☉	☿	♀	♂
1	8♎	7♎	3♏	3♍
2	9♎	6♎	4♏	3♍
3	10♎	5♎	5♏	4♍
4	11♎	4♎	7♏	5♍
5	12♎	3♎	8♏	5♍
6	13♎	3♎	9♏	6♍
7	14♎	2♎	10♏	7♍
8	15♎	2♎	12♏	7♍
9	16♎	1♎	13♏	8♍
10	17♎	1♎	14♏	8♍
11	18♎	2♎	15♏	9♍
12	19♎	2♎	17♏	10♍
13	20♎	2♎	18♏	10♍
14	21♎	3♎	19♏	11♍
15	22♎	4♎	20♏	12♍
16	23♎	5♎	21♏	12♍
17	24♎	6♎	23♏	13♍
18	25♎	7♎	24♏	13♍
19	26♎	8♎	25♏	14♍
20	27♎	9♎	26♏	15♍
21	28♎	11♎	28♏	15♍
22	29♎	12♎	29♏	16♍
23	0♏	14♎	0♐	16♍
24	1♏	15♎	1♐	17♍
25	2♏	17♎	2♐	18♍
26	3♏	18♎	4♐	18♍
27	4♏	20♎	5♐	19♍
28	5♏	21♎	6♐	19♍
29	6♏	23♎	7♐	20♍
30	7♏	25♎	9♐	21♍
31	8♏	26♎	10♐	21♍

November

Day	☉	☿	♀	♂
1	9♏	28♎	11♐	22♍
2	10♏	0♏	12♐	23♍
3	11♏	1♏	13♐	23♍
4	12♏	3♏	15♐	24♍
5	13♏	5♏	16♐	24♍
6	14♏	6♏	17♐	25♍
7	15♏	8♏	18♐	26♍
8	16♏	9♏	20♐	26♍
9	17♏	11♏	21♐	27♍
10	18♏	13♏	22♐	27♍
11	19♏	14♏	23♐	28♍
12	20♏	16♏	24♐	29♍
13	21♏	18♏	26♐	29♍
14	22♏	19♏	27♐	0♎
15	23♏	21♏	28♐	0♎
16	24♏	22♏	29♐	1♎
17	25♏	24♏	1♑	2♎
18	26♏	26♏	2♑	2♎
19	27♏	27♏	3♑	3♎
20	28♏	29♏	4♑	3♎
21	29♏	0♐	5♑	4♎
22	0♐	2♐	7♑	5♎
23	1♐	3♐	8♑	5♎
24	2♐	5♐	9♑	6♎
25	3♐	7♐	10♑	6♎
26	4♐	8♐	11♑	7♎
27	5♐	10♐	13♑	7♎
28	6♐	11♐	14♑	8♎
29	7♐	13♐	15♑	9♎
30	8♐	14♐	16♑	9♎

December

Day	☉	☿	♀	♂
1	9♐	16♐	17♑	10♎
2	10♐	17♐	19♑	10♎
3	11♐	19♐	20♑	11♎
4	12♐	21♐	21♑	12♎
5	13♐	22♐	22♑	12♎
6	14♐	24♐	24♑	13♎
7	15♐	25♐	25♑	13♎
8	16♐	27♐	26♑	14♎
9	17♐	28♐	27♑	14♎
10	18♐	0♑	28♑	15♎
11	19♐	1♑	0♒	16♎
12	20♐	3♑	1♒	16♎
13	21♐	5♑	2♒	17♎
14	22♐	6♑	3♒	17♎
15	23♐	8♑	4♒	18♎
16	24♐	9♑	5♒	18♎
17	25♐	11♑	7♒	19♎
18	26♐	12♑	8♒	20♎
19	27♐	14♑	9♒	20♎
20	28♐	15♑	10♒	21♎
21	29♐	17♑	11♒	21♎
22	0♑	18♑	13♒	22♎
23	1♑	19♑	14♒	22♎
24	2♑	21♑	15♒	23♎
25	3♑	22♑	16♒	24♎
26	4♑	23♑	17♒	24♎
27	5♑	25♑	18♒	25♎
28	6♑	26♑	20♒	25♎
29	7♑	27♑	21♒	26♎
30	8♑	28♑	22♒	26♎
31	9♑	29♑	23♒	27♎

☉ = Sun ☿ = Mercury ♀ = Venus ♂ = Mars ♈ = Aries ♉ = Taurus ♊ = Gemini ♋ = Cancer

1937

January

Day	☉	☿	♀	♂
1	10♑	0♒	24♒	27♎
2	11♑	0♒	25♒	28♎
3	12♑	1♒	27♒	29♎
4	13♑	1♒	28♒	29♎
5	14♑	1♒	29♒	0♏
6	15♑	2♒	0♓	0♏
7	16♑	1♒	1♓	1♏
8	18♑	1♒	2♓	1♏
9	19♑	0♒	4♓	2♏
10	20♑	0♒	5♓	2♏
11	21♑	29♑	6♓	3♏
12	22♑	28♑	7♓	3♏
13	23♑	27♑	8♓	4♏
14	24♑	25♑	9♓	4♏
15	25♑	24♑	10♓	5♏
16	26♑	23♑	11♓	6♏
17	27♑	21♑	13♓	6♏
18	28♑	20♑	14♓	7♏
19	29♑	19♑	15♓	7♏
20	0♒	18♑	16♓	8♏
21	1♒	17♑	17♓	8♏
22	2♒	17♑	18♓	9♏
23	3♒	16♑	19♓	9♏
24	4♒	16♑	20♓	10♏
25	5♒	16♑	21♓	10♏
26	6♒	15♑	22♓	11♏
27	7♒	15♑	23♓	11♏
28	8♒	16♑	25♓	12♏
29	9♒	16♑	26♓	12♏
30	10♒	16♑	27♓	13♏
31	11♒	17♑	28♓	13♏

April

Day	☉	☿	♀	♂
1	11♈	18♈	5♉	4♐
2	12♈	20♈	5♉	5♐
3	13♈	22♈	5♉	5♐
4	14♈	24♈	5♉	5♐
5	15♈	26♈	4♉	5♐
6	16♈	28♈	4♉	5♐
7	17♈	0♉	4♉	5♐
8	18♈	2♉	3♉	5♐
9	19♈	4♉	3♉	5♐
10	20♈	6♉	2♉	5♐
11	21♈	8♉	2♉	5♐
12	22♈	9♉	1♉	5♐
13	23♈	11♉	1♉	6♐
14	24♈	12♉	0♉	6♐
15	25♈	14♉	29♈	6♐
16	26♈	15♉	29♈	6♐
17	27♈	16♉	28♈	5♐
18	28♈	17♉	27♈	5♐
19	29♈	19♉	27♈	5♐
20	0♉	20♉	26♈	5♐
21	1♉	20♉	26♈	5♐
22	2♉	21♉	25♈	5♐
23	3♉	22♉	24♈	5♐
24	4♉	23♉	24♈	5♐
25	5♉	23♉	23♈	5♐
26	6♉	24♉	23♈	5♐
27	7♉	24♉	22♈	5♐
28	7♉	24♉	22♈	4♐
29	8♉	24♉	21♈	4♐
30	9♉	24♉	21♈	4♐

July

Day	☉	☿	♀	♂
1	9♋	0♋	23♉	20♏
2	10♋	2♋	24♉	20♏
3	11♋	4♋	25♉	20♏
4	12♋	7♋	26♉	20♏
5	13♋	9♋	27♉	20♏
6	14♋	11♋	28♉	20♏
7	15♋	13♋	29♉	20♏
8	16♋	15♋	0♊	20♏
9	17♋	17♋	1♊	20♏
10	18♋	20♋	2♊	21♏
11	18♋	22♋	3♊	21♏
12	19♋	24♋	4♊	21♏
13	20♋	26♋	5♊	21♏
14	21♋	28♋	7♊	21♏
15	22♋	0♌	8♊	22♏
16	23♋	2♌	9♊	22♏
17	24♋	4♌	10♊	22♏
18	25♋	6♌	11♊	22♏
19	26♋	8♌	12♊	23♏
20	27♋	10♌	13♊	23♏
21	28♋	12♌	14♊	23♏
22	29♋	14♌	15♊	23♏
23	0♌	15♌	16♊	24♏
24	1♌	17♌	17♊	24♏
25	2♌	19♌	18♊	24♏
26	3♌	21♌	19♊	25♏
27	4♌	22♌	20♊	25♏
28	5♌	24♌	22♊	25♏
29	6♌	26♌	23♊	26♏
30	7♌	27♌	24♊	26♏
31	8♌	29♌	25♊	26♏

October

Day	☉	☿	♀	♂
1	8♎	20♍	7♍	1♑
2	9♎	21♍	9♍	1♑
3	10♎	22♍	10♍	2♑
4	11♎	24♍	11♍	3♑
5	12♎	25♍	12♍	3♑
6	13♎	27♍	13♍	4♑
7	14♎	28♍	15♍	5♑
8	14♎	0♎	16♍	5♑
9	15♎	1♎	17♍	6♑
10	16♎	3♎	18♍	7♑
11	17♎	5♎	20♍	7♑
12	18♎	6♎	21♍	8♑
13	19♎	8♎	22♍	9♑
14	20♎	10♎	23♍	9♑
15	21♎	11♎	24♍	10♑
16	22♎	13♎	26♍	11♑
17	23♎	15♎	27♍	12♑
18	24♎	17♎	28♍	12♑
19	25♎	18♎	29♍	13♑
20	26♎	20♎	1♎	14♑
21	27♎	22♎	2♎	14♑
22	28♎	24♎	3♎	15♑
23	29♎	25♎	4♎	16♑
24	0♏	27♎	6♎	17♑
25	1♏	29♎	7♎	17♑
26	2♏	0♏	8♎	18♑
27	3♏	2♏	9♎	19♑
28	4♏	4♏	11♎	19♑
29	5♏	5♏	12♎	20♑
30	6♏	7♏	13♎	21♑
31	7♏	9♏	14♎	22♑

February

Day	☉	☿	♀	♂
1	12♒	17♑	29♓	14♏
2	13♒	18♑	0♈	14♏
3	14♒	19♑	1♈	15♏
4	15♒	20♑	2♈	15♏
5	16♒	20♑	3♈	16♏
6	17♒	21♑	4♈	16♏
7	18♒	22♑	5♈	16♏
8	19♒	23♑	6♈	17♏
9	20♒	24♑	7♈	17♏
10	21♒	26♑	8♈	18♏
11	22♒	27♑	9♈	18♏
12	23♒	28♑	10♈	19♏
13	24♒	29♑	11♈	19♏
14	25♒	0♒	12♈	20♏
15	26♒	1♒	13♈	20♏
16	27♒	3♒	13♈	21♏
17	28♒	4♒	14♈	21♏
18	29♒	5♒	15♈	21♏
19	0♓	7♒	16♈	22♏
20	1♓	8♒	17♈	22♏
21	2♓	10♒	18♈	23♏
22	3♓	11♒	19♈	23♏
23	4♓	12♒	20♈	24♏
24	5♓	14♒	20♈	24♏
25	6♓	15♒	21♈	24♏
26	7♓	17♒	22♈	25♏
27	8♓	18♒	23♈	25♏
28	9♓	20♒	24♈	25♏

May

Day	☉	☿	♀	♂
1	10♉	24♉	21♈	4♐
2	11♉	24♉	20♈	4♐
3	12♉	24♉	20♈	3♐
4	13♉	24♉	20♈	3♐
5	14♉	23♉	20♈	3♐
6	15♉	23♉	20♈	3♐
7	16♉	23♉	20♈	2♐
8	17♉	22♉	19♈	2♐
9	18♉	22♉	19♈	2♐
10	19♉	21♉	19♈	2♐
11	20♉	20♉	20♈	1♐
12	21♉	20♉	20♈	1♐
13	22♉	19♉	20♈	1♐
14	23♉	19♉	20♈	0♐
15	24♉	18♉	20♈	0♐
16	25♉	18♉	20♈	0♐
17	26♉	17♉	21♈	29♏
18	27♉	17♉	21♈	29♏
19	28♉	16♉	21♈	29♏
20	29♉	16♉	22♈	28♏
21	0♊	16♉	22♈	28♏
22	1♊	15♉	22♈	27♏
23	2♊	15♉	23♈	27♏
24	3♊	15♉	23♈	27♏
25	4♊	15♉	24♈	26♏
26	5♊	15♉	24♈	26♏
27	5♊	16♉	25♈	26♏
28	6♊	16♉	25♈	25♏
29	7♊	16♉	26♈	25♏
30	8♊	17♉	27♈	25♏
31	9♊	17♉	27♈	24♏

August

Day	☉	☿	♀	♂
1	9♌	1♍	26♊	27♏
2	9♌	2♍	27♊	27♏
3	10♌	4♍	28♊	28♏
4	11♌	5♍	29♊	28♏
5	12♌	6♍	0♋	28♏
6	13♌	8♍	2♋	29♏
7	14♌	9♍	3♋	29♏
8	15♌	11♍	4♋	0♐
9	16♌	12♍	5♋	0♐
10	17♌	13♍	6♋	1♐
11	18♌	14♍	7♋	1♐
12	19♌	16♍	8♋	1♐
13	20♌	17♍	9♋	2♐
14	21♌	18♍	11♋	2♐
15	22♌	19♍	12♋	3♐
16	23♌	20♍	13♋	3♐
17	24♌	21♍	14♋	4♐
18	25♌	22♍	15♋	4♐
19	26♌	23♍	16♋	5♐
20	27♌	24♍	17♋	5♐
21	28♌	25♍	19♋	6♐
22	29♌	26♍	20♋	6♐
23	0♍	26♍	21♋	7♐
24	1♍	27♍	22♋	7♐
25	2♍	28♍	23♋	8♐
26	3♍	28♍	24♋	9♐
27	3♍	29♍	26♋	9♐
28	4♍	29♍	27♋	10♐
29	5♍	29♍	28♋	10♐
30	6♍	0♎	29♋	11♐
31	7♍	0♎	0♌	11♐

November

Day	☉	☿	♀	♂
1	8♏	10♏	16♎	22♑
2	9♏	12♏	17♎	23♑
3	10♏	13♏	18♎	24♑
4	11♏	15♏	19♎	24♑
5	12♏	17♏	20♎	25♑
6	13♏	18♏	22♎	26♑
7	14♏	20♏	23♎	27♑
8	15♏	21♏	24♎	27♑
9	16♏	23♏	25♎	28♑
10	17♏	24♏	27♎	29♑
11	18♏	26♏	28♎	0♒
12	19♏	28♏	29♎	1♒
13	20♏	29♏	0♏	1♒
14	21♏	1♐	2♏	2♒
15	22♏	2♐	3♏	3♒
16	23♏	4♐	4♏	3♒
17	24♏	5♐	5♏	4♒
18	25♏	7♐	7♏	5♒
19	26♏	8♐	8♏	6♒
20	27♏	10♐	9♏	6♒
21	28♏	11♐	10♏	7♒
22	29♏	13♐	12♏	8♒
23	0♐	14♐	13♏	8♒
24	2♐	16♐	14♏	9♒
25	3♐	17♐	16♏	10♒
26	4♐	19♐	17♏	11♒
27	5♐	20♐	18♏	11♒
28	6♐	22♐	19♏	12♒
29	7♐	23♐	21♏	13♒
30	8♐	25♐	22♏	14♒

March

Day	☉	☿	♀	♂
1	10♓	21♒	24♈	26♏
2	11♓	23♒	25♈	26♏
3	12♓	25♒	26♈	27♏
4	13♓	26♒	27♈	27♏
5	14♓	28♒	27♈	27♏
6	15♓	29♒	28♈	28♏
7	16♓	1♓	29♈	28♏
8	17♓	3♓	29♈	28♏
9	18♓	4♓	0♉	29♏
10	19♓	6♓	0♉	29♏
11	20♓	8♓	1♉	29♏
12	21♓	10♓	1♉	0♐
13	22♓	11♓	2♉	0♐
14	23♓	13♓	2♉	0♐
15	24♓	15♓	3♉	1♐
16	25♓	17♓	3♉	1♐
17	26♓	19♓	4♉	1♐
18	27♓	20♓	4♉	1♐
19	28♓	22♓	4♉	2♐
20	29♓	24♓	5♉	2♐
21	0♈	26♓	5♉	2♐
22	1♈	28♓	5♉	3♐
23	2♈	0♈	5♉	3♐
24	3♈	2♈	6♉	3♐
25	4♈	4♈	6♉	3♐
26	5♈	6♈	6♉	3♐
27	6♈	8♈	6♉	4♐
28	7♈	10♈	6♉	4♐
29	8♈	12♈	6♉	4♐
30	9♈	14♈	6♉	4♐
31	10♈	16♈	6♉	4♐

June

Day	☉	☿	♀	♂
1	10♊	18♉	28♈	24♏
2	11♊	18♉	29♈	24♏
3	12♊	19♉	29♈	23♏
4	13♊	20♉	0♉	23♏
5	14♊	20♉	1♉	23♏
6	15♊	21♉	1♉	23♏
7	16♊	22♉	2♉	22♏
8	17♊	23♉	3♉	22♏
9	18♊	24♉	4♉	22♏
10	19♊	25♉	4♉	22♏
11	20♊	27♉	5♉	21♏
12	21♊	28♉	6♉	21♏
13	22♊	29♉	7♉	21♏
14	23♊	0♊	8♉	21♏
15	24♊	2♊	9♉	21♏
16	25♊	3♊	9♉	20♏
17	26♊	5♊	10♉	20♏
18	27♊	6♊	11♉	20♏
19	27♊	8♊	12♉	20♏
20	28♊	9♊	13♉	20♏
21	29♊	11♊	14♉	20♏
22	0♋	13♊	15♉	20♏
23	1♋	15♊	16♉	20♏
24	2♋	16♊	17♉	20♏
25	3♋	18♊	18♉	20♏
26	4♋	20♊	18♉	20♏
27	5♋	22♊	19♉	20♏
28	6♋	24♊	20♉	20♏
29	7♋	26♊	21♉	20♏
30	8♋	28♊	22♉	20♏

September

Day	☉	☿	♀	♂
1	8♍	0♎	1♌	12♐
2	9♍	0♎	3♌	12♐
3	10♍	29♍	4♌	13♐
4	11♍	29♍	5♌	14♐
5	12♍	29♍	6♌	14♐
6	13♍	28♍	7♌	15♐
7	14♍	28♍	8♌	15♐
8	15♍	27♍	10♌	16♐
9	16♍	26♍	11♌	17♐
10	17♍	25♍	12♌	17♐
11	18♍	24♍	13♌	18♐
12	19♍	23♍	14♌	18♐
13	20♍	22♍	16♌	19♐
14	21♍	21♍	17♌	20♐
15	22♍	20♍	18♌	20♐
16	23♍	19♍	19♌	21♐
17	24♍	18♍	20♌	21♐
18	25♍	18♍	22♌	22♐
19	26♍	17♍	23♌	23♐
20	27♍	16♍	24♌	23♐
21	28♍	16♍	25♌	24♐
22	29♍	16♍	26♌	25♐
23	0♎	15♍	28♌	25♐
24	1♎	15♍	29♌	26♐
25	2♎	16♍	0♍	27♐
26	3♎	16♍	1♍	27♐
27	4♎	16♍	2♍	28♐
28	5♎	17♍	4♍	29♐
29	6♎	18♍	5♍	29♐
30	7♎	19♍	6♍	0♑

December

Day	☉	☿	♀	♂
1	9♐	26♐	23♏	14♒
2	10♐	27♐	24♏	15♒
3	11♐	29♐	26♏	16♒
4	12♐	0♑	27♏	17♒
5	13♐	2♑	28♏	18♒
6	14♐	3♑	29♏	18♒
7	15♐	4♑	1♐	19♒
8	16♐	6♑	2♐	20♒
9	17♐	7♑	3♐	21♒
10	18♐	8♑	4♐	21♒
11	19♐	9♑	6♐	22♒
12	20♐	10♑	7♐	23♒
13	21♐	11♑	8♐	24♒
14	22♐	12♑	9♐	24♒
15	23♐	13♑	11♐	25♒
16	24♐	14♑	12♐	26♒
17	25♐	15♑	13♐	27♒
18	26♐	15♑	14♐	27♒
19	27♐	15♑	16♐	28♒
20	28♐	16♑	17♐	29♒
21	29♐	16♑	18♐	0♓
22	0♑	15♑	19♐	0♓
23	1♑	15♑	21♐	1♓
24	2♑	15♑	22♐	2♓
25	3♑	14♑	23♐	3♓
26	4♑	13♑	24♐	3♓
27	5♑	12♑	26♐	4♓
28	6♑	11♑	27♐	5♓
29	7♑	9♑	28♐	6♓
30	8♑	8♑	29♐	6♓
31	9♑	7♑	1♑	7♓

1938

Planetary Positions

∞ = Leo ♍ = Virgo ♎ = Libra ♏ = Scorpio ♐ = Sagittarius ♑ = Capricorn ♒ = Aquarius ≠ = Pisces

January

Day	☉	☿	♀	♂
1	10♑	5♑	2♑	8≠
2	11♑	4♑	3♑	9≠
3	12♑	3♑	5♑	9≠
4	13♑	2♑	6♑	10≠
5	14♑	1♑	7♑	11≠
6	15♑	0♑	8♑	12≠
7	16♑	0♑	10♑	12≠
8	17♑	0♑	11♑	13≠
9	18♑	29♐	12♑	14≠
10	19♑	29♐	13♑	15≠
11	20♑	29♐	15♑	15≠
12	21♑	0♑	16♑	16≠
13	22♑	0♑	17♑	17≠
14	23♑	1♑	18♑	18≠
15	24♑	1♑	20♑	19≠
16	25♑	2♑	21♑	19≠
17	26♑	3♑	22♑	20≠
18	27♑	3♑	23♑	21≠
19	28♑	4♑	25♑	22≠
20	29♑	5♑	26♑	22≠
21	1♒	6♑	27♑	23≠
22	2♒	7♑	28♑	24≠
23	3♒	8♑	0♒	25≠
24	4♒	10♑	1♒	25≠
25	5♒	11♑	2♒	26≠
26	6♒	12♑	3♒	27≠
27	7♒	13♑	5♒	28≠
28	8♒	14♑	6♒	28≠
29	9♒	16♑	7♒	29≠
30	10♒	17♑	8♒	0♈
31	11♒	18♑	10♒	1♈

February

Day	☉	☿	♀	♂
1	12♒	20♑	11♒	1♈
2	13♒	21♑	12♒	2♈
3	14♒	22♑	13♒	3♈
4	15♒	24♑	15♒	3♈
5	16♒	25♑	16♒	4♈
6	17♒	27♑	17♒	5♈
7	18♒	28♑	19♒	6♈
8	19♒	29♑	20♒	6♈
9	20♒	1♒	21♒	7♈
10	21♒	2♒	22♒	8♈
11	22♒	4♒	24♒	9♈
12	23♒	5♒	25♒	9♈
13	24♒	7♒	26♒	10♈
14	25♒	9♒	27♒	11♈
15	26♒	10♒	29♒	12♈
16	27♒	12♒	0≠	12♈
17	28♒	13♒	1≠	13♈
18	29♒	15♒	2≠	14♈
19	0≠	17♒	4≠	15♈
20	1≠	18♒	5≠	15♈
21	2≠	20♒	6≠	16♈
22	3≠	22♒	7≠	17♈
23	4≠	23♒	9≠	18♈
24	5≠	25♒	10≠	18♈
25	6≠	27♒	11≠	19♈
26	7≠	28♒	12≠	20♈
27	8≠	0≠	14≠	20♈
28	9≠	2≠	15≠	21♈

March

Day	☉	☿	♀	♂
1	10≠	4≠	16≠	22♈
2	11≠	6≠	17≠	23♈
3	12≠	7≠	19≠	23♈
4	13≠	9≠	20≠	24♈
5	14≠	11≠	21≠	25♈
6	15≠	13≠	22≠	26♈
7	16≠	15≠	24≠	26♈
8	17≠	17≠	25≠	27♈
9	18≠	19≠	26≠	28♈
10	19≠	21≠	27≠	28♈
11	20≠	23≠	29≠	29♈
12	21≠	24≠	0♈	0♉
13	22≠	26≠	1♈	1♉
14	23≠	28≠	2♈	1♉
15	24≠	0♈	4♈	2♉
16	25≠	2♈	5♈	3♉
17	26≠	4♈	6♈	4♉
18	27≠	6♈	7♈	4♉
19	28≠	8♈	8♈	5♉
20	29≠	10♈	10♈	6♉
21	0♈	12♈	11♈	6♉
22	1♈	14♈	12♈	7♉
23	2♈	16♈	13♈	8♉
24	3♈	18♈	15♈	9♉
25	4♈	19♈	16♈	9♉
26	5♈	21♈	17♈	10♉
27	6♈	23♈	18♈	11♉
28	7♈	24♈	20♈	11♉
29	8♈	26♈	21♈	12♉
30	9♈	27♈	22♈	13♉
31	10♈	28♈	23♈	14♉

April

Day	☉	☿	♀	♂
1	11♈	0♉	25♈	14♉
2	12♈	1♉	26♈	15♉
3	13♈	2♉	27♈	16♉
4	14♈	3♉	28♈	16♉
5	15♈	3♉	0♉	17♉
6	16♈	4♉	1♉	18♉
7	17♈	5♉	2♉	18♉
8	18♈	5♉	3♉	19♉
9	19♈	5♉	4♉	20♉
10	20♈	6♉	6♉	21♉
11	21♈	6♉	7♉	21♉
12	22♈	6♉	8♉	22♉
13	23♈	5♉	9♉	23♉
14	24♈	5♉	11♉	23♉
15	25♈	5♉	12♉	24♉
16	26♈	5♉	13♉	25♉
17	27♈	4♉	14♉	25♉
18	28♈	4♉	16♉	26♉
19	28♈	3♉	17♉	27♉
20	29♈	2♉	18♉	28♉
21	0♉	2♉	19♉	28♉
22	1♉	1♉	20♉	29♉
23	2♉	0♉	22♉	0♊
24	3♉	0♉	23♉	0♊
25	4♉	29♈	24♉	1♊
26	5♉	28♈	25♉	2♊
27	6♉	28♈	27♉	2♊
28	7♉	27♈	28♉	3♊
29	8♉	27♈	29♉	4♊
30	9♉	26♈	0♊	4♊

May

Day	☉	☿	♀	♂
1	10♉	26♈	1♊	5♊
2	11♉	26♈	3♊	6♊
3	12♉	25♈	4♊	6♊
4	13♉	25♈	5♊	7♊
5	14♉	25♈	6♊	8♊
6	15♉	25♈	8♊	9♊
7	16♉	25♈	9♊	9♊
8	17♉	26♈	10♊	10♊
9	18♉	26♈	11♊	11♊
10	19♉	26♈	12♊	11♊
11	20♉	27♈	14♊	12♊
12	21♉	27♈	15♊	13♊
13	22♉	28♈	16♊	13♊
14	23♉	28♈	17♊	14♊
15	24♉	29♈	19♊	15♊
16	25♉	0♉	20♊	15♊
17	26♉	0♉	21♊	16♊
18	27♉	1♉	22♊	17♊
19	28♉	2♉	23♊	17♊
20	29♉	3♉	25♊	18♊
21	29♉	4♉	26♊	19♊
22	0♊	5♉	27♊	19♊
23	1♊	6♉	28♊	20♊
24	2♊	8♉	29♊	21♊
25	3♊	9♉	1♋	21♊
26	4♊	10♉	2♋	22♊
27	5♊	11♉	3♋	23♊
28	6♊	13♉	4♋	23♊
29	7♊	14♉	5♋	24♊
30	8♊	15♉	7♋	25♊
31	9♊	17♉	8♋	25♊

June

Day	☉	☿	♀	♂
1	10♊	18♉	9♋	26♊
2	11♊	20♉	10♋	27♊
3	12♊	22♉	11♋	27♊
4	13♊	23♉	13♋	28♊
5	14♊	25♉	14♋	29♊
6	15♊	27♉	15♋	29♊
7	16♊	29♉	16♋	0♋
8	17♊	0♊	17♋	1♋
9	18♊	2♊	19♋	1♋
10	19♊	4♊	20♋	2♋
11	20♊	6♊	21♋	3♋
12	21♊	8♊	22♋	3♋
13	22♊	10♊	23♋	4♋
14	22♊	12♊	25♋	5♋
15	23♊	14♊	26♋	5♋
16	24♊	16♊	27♋	6♋
17	25♊	18♊	28♋	7♋
18	26♊	21♊	29♋	7♋
19	27♊	23♊	1∞	8♋
20	28♊	25♊	2∞	9♋
21	29♊	27♊	3∞	9♋
22	0♋	29♊	4∞	10♋
23	1♋	1♋	5∞	11♋
24	2♋	4♋	7∞	11♋
25	3♋	6♋	8∞	12♋
26	4♋	8♋	9∞	13♋
27	5♋	10♋	10∞	13♋
28	6♋	12♋	11∞	14♋
29	7♋	14♋	12∞	15♋
30	8♋	16♋	14∞	15♋

July

Day	☉	☿	♀	♂
1	9♋	18♋	15∞	16♋
2	10♋	20♋	16∞	17♋
3	11♋	22♋	17∞	17♋
4	12♋	24♋	18∞	18♋
5	13♋	26♋	19∞	19♋
6	13♋	28♋	21∞	19♋
7	14♋	0∞	22∞	20♋
8	15♋	2∞	23∞	20♋
9	16♋	4∞	24∞	21♋
10	17♋	6∞	25∞	22♋
11	18♋	7∞	26∞	22♋
12	19♋	9∞	28∞	23♋
13	20♋	11∞	29∞	24♋
14	21♋	12∞	0♍	24♋
15	22♋	14∞	1♍	25♋
16	23♋	15∞	2♍	26♋
17	24♋	17∞	3♍	26♋
18	25♋	18∞	5♍	27♋
19	26♋	20∞	6♍	28♋
20	27♋	21∞	7♍	28♋
21	28♋	23∞	8♍	29♋
22	29♋	24∞	9♍	0∞
23	0∞	25∞	10♍	0∞
24	1∞	27∞	11♍	1∞
25	2∞	28∞	13♍	1∞
26	3∞	29∞	14♍	2∞
27	4∞	0♍	15♍	3∞
28	4∞	1♍	16♍	3∞
29	5∞	3♍	17♍	4∞
30	6∞	4♍	18♍	5∞
31	7∞	5♍	19♍	5∞

August

Day	☉	☿	♀	♂
1	8∞	6♍	21♍	6∞
2	9∞	6♍	22♍	7∞
3	10∞	7♍	23♍	7∞
4	11∞	8♍	24♍	8∞
5	12∞	9♍	25♍	9∞
6	13∞	9♍	26♍	9∞
7	14∞	10♍	27♍	10∞
8	15∞	11♍	28♍	10∞
9	16∞	11♍	29♍	11∞
10	17∞	11♍	1♎	12∞
11	18∞	12♍	2♎	12∞
12	19∞	12♍	3♎	13∞
13	20∞	12♍	4♎	14∞
14	21∞	12♍	5♎	14∞
15	22∞	12♍	6♎	15∞
16	23∞	12♍	7♎	16∞
17	24∞	12♍	8♎	16∞
18	25∞	12♍	9♎	17∞
19	26∞	11♍	10♎	17∞
20	27∞	11♍	11♎	18∞
21	27∞	10♍	13♎	19∞
22	28∞	10♍	14♎	19∞
23	29∞	9♍	15♎	20∞
24	0♍	8♍	16♎	21∞
25	1♍	7♍	17♎	21∞
26	2♍	6♍	18♎	22∞
27	3♍	5♍	19♎	23∞
28	4♍	5♍	20♎	23∞
29	5♍	4♍	21♎	24∞
30	6♍	3♍	22♎	25∞
31	7♍	2♍	23♎	25∞

September

Day	☉	☿	♀	♂
1	8♍	1♍	24♎	26∞
2	9♍	1♍	25♎	26∞
3	10♍	0♍	26♎	27∞
4	11♍	0♍	27♎	28∞
5	12♍	29∞	28♎	28∞
6	13♍	29∞	29♎	29∞
7	14♍	29∞	0♏	0♍
8	15♍	29∞	1♏	0♍
9	16♍	29∞	2♏	1♍
10	17♍	0♍	3♏	1♍
11	18♍	0♍	4♏	2♍
12	19♍	1♍	5♏	3♍
13	20♍	2♍	6♏	3♍
14	21♍	3♍	7♏	4♍
15	22♍	4♍	8♏	5♍
16	23♍	5♍	9♏	5♍
17	24♍	6♍	10♏	6♍
18	25♍	8♍	11♏	7♍
19	26♍	9♍	12♏	7♍
20	27♍	11♍	12♏	8♍
21	28♍	12♍	13♏	8♍
22	29♍	14♍	14♏	9♍
23	0♎	16♍	15♏	10♍
24	0♎	17♍	16♏	10♍
25	1♎	19♍	17♏	11♍
26	2♎	21♍	18♏	12♍
27	3♎	23♍	18♏	12♍
28	4♎	25♍	19♏	13♍
29	5♎	26♍	20♏	14♍
30	6♎	28♍	21♏	14♍

October

Day	☉	☿	♀	♂
1	7♎	0♎	22♏	15♍
2	8♎	2♎	22♏	15♍
3	9♎	4♎	23♏	16♍
4	10♎	5♎	24♏	17♍
5	11♎	7♎	25♏	17♍
6	12♎	9♎	25♏	18♍
7	13♎	11♎	26♏	19♍
8	14♎	13♎	27♏	19♍
9	15♎	14♎	27♏	20♍
10	16♎	16♎	28♏	20♍
11	17♎	18♎	29♏	21♍
12	18♎	19♎	29♏	22♍
13	19♎	21♎	0♐	22♍
14	20♎	23♎	0♐	23♍
15	21♎	25♎	1♐	24♍
16	22♎	26♎	1♐	24♍
17	23♎	28♎	2♐	25♍
18	24♎	29♎	2♐	26♍
19	25♎	1♏	3♐	26♍
20	26♎	3♏	3♐	27♍
21	27♎	4♏	3♐	27♍
22	28♎	6♏	4♐	28♍
23	29♎	8♏	4♐	29♍
24	0♏	9♏	4♐	29♍
25	1♏	11♏	4♐	0♎
26	2♏	12♏	5♐	1♎
27	3♏	14♏	5♐	1♎
28	4♏	15♏	5♐	2♎
29	5♏	17♏	5♐	2♎
30	6♏	18♏	5♐	3♎
31	7♏	20♏	5♐	4♎

November

Day	☉	☿	♀	♂
1	8♏	21♏	5♐	4♎
2	9♏	23♏	5♐	5♎
3	10♏	24♏	5♐	6♎
4	11♏	26♏	5♐	6♎
5	12♏	27♏	4♐	7♎
6	13♏	29♏	4♐	8♎
7	14♏	0♐	4♐	8♎
8	15♏	2♐	3♐	9♎
9	16♏	3♐	3♐	9♎
10	17♏	5♐	3♐	10♎
11	18♏	6♐	2♐	11♎
12	19♏	8♐	2♐	11♎
13	20♏	9♐	1♐	12♎
14	21♏	10♐	1♐	13♎
15	22♏	12♐	0♐	13♎
16	23♏	13♐	0♐	14♎
17	24♏	14♐	29♏	14♎
18	25♏	16♐	29♏	15♎
19	26♏	17♐	28♏	16♎
20	27♏	18♐	27♏	16♎
21	28♏	19♐	27♏	17♎
22	29♏	21♐	26♏	18♎
23	0♐	22♐	26♏	18♎
24	1♐	23♐	25♏	19♎
25	2♐	24♐	24♏	19♎
26	3♐	25♐	24♏	20♎
27	4♐	26♐	23♏	21♎
28	5♐	27♐	23♏	21♎
29	6♐	28♐	22♏	22♎
30	7♐	28♐	22♏	23♎

December

Day	☉	☿	♀	♂
1	8♐	29♐	21♏	23♎
2	9♐	29♐	21♏	24♎
3	10♐	0♑	21♏	25♎
4	11♐	0♑	20♏	25♎
5	12♐	0♑	20♏	26♎
6	13♐	0♑	20♏	26♎
7	14♐	29♐	20♏	27♎
8	15♐	29♐	20♏	28♎
9	16♐	28♐	20♏	28♎
10	17♐	27♐	20♏	29♎
11	18♐	26♐	20♏	0♏
12	20♐	25♐	20♏	0♏
13	21♐	23♐	20♏	1♏
14	22♐	22♐	20♏	1♏
15	23♐	21♐	20♏	2♏
16	24♐	19♐	20♏	3♏
17	25♐	18♐	20♏	3♏
18	26♐	17♐	21♏	4♏
19	27♐	16♐	21♏	5♏
20	28♐	15♐	21♏	5♏
21	29♐	14♐	22♏	6♏
22	0♑	14♐	22♏	6♏
23	1♑	14♐	22♏	7♏
24	2♑	13♐	23♏	8♏
25	3♑	14♐	23♏	8♏
26	4♑	14♐	24♏	9♏
27	5♑	14♐	24♏	10♏
28	6♑	14♐	25♏	10♏
29	7♑	15♐	26♏	11♏
30	8♑	16♐	26♏	11♏
31	9♑	16♐	27♏	12♏

1939

Your Starway to Love

☉ =Sun ☿ = Mercury ♀ = Venus ♂ = Mars ♈ = Aries ♉ = Taurus ♊ = Gemini ♋ = Cancer

January

Day	☉	☿	♀	♂
1	10♑	17♐	27♏	13♏
2	11♑	18♐	28♏	13♏
3	12♑	19♐	29♏	14♏
4	13♑	20♐	29♏	14♏
5	14♑	21♐	0♐	15♏
6	15♑	22♐	1♐	16♏
7	16♑	24♐	2♐	16♏
8	17♑	25♐	2♐	17♏
9	18♑	26♐	3♐	18♏
10	19♑	27♐	4♐	18♏
11	20♑	29♐	5♐	19♏
12	21♑	0♑	6♐	19♏
13	22♑	1♑	7♐	20♏
14	23♑	3♑	7♐	21♏
15	24♑	4♑	8♐	21♏
16	25♑	5♑	9♐	22♏
17	26♑	7♑	10♐	23♏
18	27♑	8♑	11♐	23♏
19	28♑	10♑	12♐	24♏
20	29♑	11♑	13♐	24♏
21	0♒	12♑	14♐	25♏
22	1♒	14♑	15♐	26♏
23	2♒	15♑	16♐	26♏
24	3♒	17♑	17♐	27♏
25	4♒	18♑	18♐	27♏
26	5♒	20♑	19♐	28♏
27	6♒	21♑	20♐	29♏
28	7♒	23♑	21♐	29♏
29	8♒	24♑	22♐	0♐
30	9♒	26♑	23♐	0♐
31	10♒	28♑	24♐	1♐

February

Day	☉	☿	♀	♂
1	11♒	29♑	25♐	2♐
2	12♒	1♒	26♐	2♐
3	13♒	2♒	27♐	3♐
4	14♒	4♒	28♐	4♐
5	15♒	6♒	29♐	4♐
6	17♒	7♒	0♑	5♐
7	18♒	9♒	1♑	5♐
8	19♒	11♒	2♑	6♐
9	20♒	12♒	3♑	7♐
10	21♒	14♒	4♑	7♐
11	22♒	16♒	5♑	8♐
12	23♒	17♒	6♑	8♐
13	24♒	19♒	7♑	9♐
14	25♒	21♒	8♑	10♐
15	26♒	23♒	9♑	10♐
16	27♒	24♒	11♑	11♐
17	28♒	26♒	12♑	11♐
18	29♒	28♒	13♑	12♐
19	0♓	0♓	14♑	13♐
20	1♓	2♓	15♑	13♐
21	2♓	3♓	16♑	14♐
22	3♓	5♓	17♑	14♐
23	4♓	7♓	18♑	15♐
24	5♓	9♓	19♑	16♐
25	6♓	11♓	21♑	16♐
26	7♓	13♓	22♑	17♐
27	8♓	15♓	23♑	17♐
28	9♓	17♓	24♑	18♐

March

Day	☉	☿	♀	♂
1	10♓	19♓	25♑	18♐
2	11♓	20♓	26♑	19♐
3	12♓	22♓	27♑	20♐
4	13♓	24♓	28♑	20♐
5	14♓	26♓	0♒	21♐
6	15♓	28♓	1♒	21♐
7	16♓	0♈	2♒	22♐
8	17♓	1♈	3♒	23♐
9	18♓	3♈	4♒	23♐
10	19♓	5♈	5♒	24♐
11	20♓	6♈	6♒	24♐
12	21♓	8♈	8♒	25♐
13	22♓	9♈	9♒	25♐
14	23♓	11♈	10♒	26♐
15	24♓	12♈	11♒	27♐
16	25♓	13♈	12♒	27♐
17	26♓	14♈	13♒	28♐
18	27♓	15♈	15♒	28♐
19	28♓	16♈	16♒	29♐
20	29♓	16♈	17♒	29♐
21	0♈	17♈	18♒	0♑
22	1♈	17♈	19♒	1♑
23	2♈	17♈	20♒	1♑
24	3♈	18♈	22♒	2♑
25	4♈	18♈	23♒	2♑
26	5♈	17♈	24♒	3♑
27	6♈	17♈	25♒	3♑
28	7♈	17♈	26♒	4♑
29	8♈	16♈	27♒	4♑
30	9♈	16♈	29♒	5♑
31	10♈	15♈	0♓	5♑

April

Day	☉	☿	♀	♂
1	11♈	14♈	1♓	6♑
2	12♈	14♈	2♓	7♑
3	13♈	13♈	3♓	7♑
4	14♈	12♈	5♓	8♑
5	15♈	11♈	6♓	8♑
6	16♈	10♈	7♓	9♑
7	16♈	10♈	8♓	9♑
8	17♈	9♈	9♓	10♑
9	18♈	8♈	10♓	10♑
10	19♈	8♈	12♓	11♑
11	20♈	7♈	13♓	11♑
12	21♈	7♈	14♓	12♑
13	22♈	6♈	15♓	12♑
14	23♈	6♈	16♓	13♑
15	24♈	6♈	18♓	13♑
16	25♈	6♈	19♓	14♑
17	26♈	6♈	20♓	14♑
18	27♈	6♈	21♓	15♑
19	28♈	6♈	22♓	15♑
20	29♈	6♈	24♓	16♑
21	0♉	6♈	25♓	16♑
22	1♉	7♈	26♓	17♑
23	2♉	7♈	27♓	17♑
24	3♉	8♈	28♓	18♑
25	4♉	8♈	0♈	18♑
26	5♉	9♈	1♈	19♑
27	6♉	10♈	2♈	19♑
28	7♉	10♈	3♈	20♑
29	8♉	11♈	4♈	20♑
30	9♉	12♈	6♈	20♑

May

Day	☉	☿	♀	♂
1	10♉	13♈	7♈	21♑
2	11♉	14♈	8♈	21♑
3	12♉	15♈	9♈	22♑
4	13♉	16♈	10♈	22♑
5	14♉	17♈	12♈	23♑
6	15♉	19♈	13♈	23♑
7	16♉	20♈	14♈	24♑
8	17♉	21♈	15♈	24♑
9	18♉	22♈	16♈	24♑
10	19♉	24♈	18♈	25♑
11	20♉	25♈	19♈	25♑
12	21♉	27♈	20♈	26♑
13	22♉	28♈	21♈	26♑
14	23♉	29♈	22♈	26♑
15	23♉	1♉	24♈	27♑
16	24♉	3♉	25♈	27♑
17	25♉	4♉	26♈	27♑
18	26♉	6♉	27♈	28♑
19	27♉	7♉	28♈	28♑
20	28♉	9♉	0♉	28♑
21	29♉	11♉	1♉	29♑
22	0♊	13♉	2♉	29♑
23	1♊	14♉	3♉	29♑
24	2♊	16♉	4♉	0♒
25	3♊	18♉	6♉	0♒
26	4♊	20♉	7♉	0♒
27	5♊	22♉	8♉	1♒
28	6♊	24♉	9♉	1♒
29	7♊	26♉	10♉	1♒
30	8♊	28♉	12♉	1♒
31	9♊	0♊	13♉	2♒

June

Day	☉	☿	♀	♂
1	10♊	2♊	14♉	2♒
2	11♊	4♊	15♉	2♒
3	12♊	7♊	16♉	2♒
4	13♊	9♊	18♉	3♒
5	14♊	11♊	19♉	3♒
6	15♊	13♊	20♉	3♒
7	16♊	15♊	21♉	3♒
8	17♊	18♊	22♉	3♒
9	17♊	20♊	24♉	4♒
10	18♊	22♊	25♉	4♒
11	19♊	24♊	26♉	4♒
12	20♊	26♊	27♉	4♒
13	21♊	28♊	29♉	4♒
14	22♊	1♋	0♊	4♒
15	23♊	3♋	1♊	4♒
16	24♊	5♋	2♊	4♒
17	25♊	7♋	3♊	5♒
18	26♊	9♋	5♊	5♒
19	27♊	11♋	6♊	5♒
20	28♊	13♋	7♊	5♒
21	29♊	15♋	8♊	5♒
22	0♋	16♋	9♊	5♒
23	1♋	18♋	11♊	5♒
24	2♋	20♋	12♊	5♒
25	3♋	22♋	13♊	5♒
26	4♋	23♋	14♊	5♒
27	5♋	25♋	16♊	5♒
28	6♋	27♋	17♊	5♒
29	7♋	28♋	18♊	4♒
30	8♋	0♌	19♊	4♒

July

Day	☉	☿	♀	♂
1	8♋	1♌	20♊	4♒
2	9♋	3♌	22♊	4♒
3	10♋	4♌	23♊	4♒
4	11♋	6♌	24♊	4♒
5	12♋	7♌	25♊	4♒
6	13♋	8♌	26♊	4♒
7	14♋	10♌	28♊	3♒
8	15♋	11♌	29♊	3♒
9	16♋	12♌	0♋	3♒
10	17♋	13♌	1♋	3♒
11	18♋	14♌	3♋	3♒
12	19♋	15♌	4♋	2♒
13	20♋	16♌	5♋	2♒
14	21♋	17♌	6♋	2♒
15	22♋	18♌	7♋	2♒
16	23♋	19♌	9♋	1♒
17	24♋	20♌	10♋	1♒
18	25♋	21♌	11♋	1♒
19	26♋	21♌	12♋	1♒
20	27♋	22♌	14♋	0♒
21	28♋	22♌	15♋	0♒
22	29♋	23♌	16♋	0♒
23	29♋	23♌	17♋	0♒
24	0♌	24♌	18♋	29♑
25	1♌	24♌	20♋	29♑
26	2♌	24♌	21♋	29♑
27	3♌	24♌	22♋	29♑
28	4♌	24♌	23♋	28♑
29	5♌	24♌	25♋	28♑
30	6♌	24♌	26♋	28♑
31	7♌	24♌	27♋	27♑

August

Day	☉	☿	♀	♂
1	8♌	23♌	28♋	27♑
2	9♌	23♌	0♌	27♑
3	10♌	22♌	1♌	27♑
4	11♌	22♌	2♌	26♑
5	12♌	21♌	3♌	26♑
6	13♌	21♌	4♌	26♑
7	14♌	20♌	6♌	26♑
8	15♌	19♌	7♌	26♑
9	16♌	18♌	8♌	25♑
10	17♌	17♌	9♌	25♑
11	18♌	17♌	11♌	25♑
12	19♌	16♌	12♌	25♑
13	20♌	15♌	13♌	25♑
14	21♌	14♌	14♌	25♑
15	21♌	14♌	16♌	24♑
16	22♌	13♌	17♌	24♑
17	23♌	13♌	18♌	24♑
18	24♌	13♌	19♌	24♑
19	25♌	12♌	20♌	24♑
20	26♌	12♌	22♌	24♑
21	27♌	12♌	23♌	24♑
22	28♌	12♌	24♌	24♑
23	29♌	13♌	25♌	24♑
24	0♍	13♌	27♌	24♑
25	1♍	13♌	28♌	24♑
26	2♍	14♌	29♌	24♑
27	3♍	15♌	0♍	24♑
28	4♍	16♌	2♍	24♑
29	5♍	17♌	3♍	24♑
30	6♍	18♌	4♍	24♑
31	7♍	19♌	5♍	24♑

September

Day	☉	☿	♀	♂
1	8♍	20♌	7♍	24♑
2	9♍	22♌	8♍	24♑
3	10♍	23♌	9♍	25♑
4	11♍	25♌	10♍	25♑
5	12♍	27♌	12♍	25♑
6	13♍	28♌	13♍	25♑
7	14♍	0♍	14♍	25♑
8	15♍	2♍	15♍	25♑
9	16♍	4♍	17♍	26♑
10	17♍	5♍	18♍	26♑
11	18♍	7♍	19♍	26♑
12	19♍	9♍	20♍	26♑
13	20♍	11♍	21♍	27♑
14	20♍	13♍	23♍	27♑
15	21♍	15♍	24♍	27♑
16	22♍	17♍	25♍	27♑
17	23♍	19♍	26♍	28♑
18	24♍	21♍	28♍	28♑
19	25♍	22♍	29♍	28♑
20	26♍	24♍	0♎	29♑
21	27♍	26♍	1♎	29♑
22	28♍	28♍	3♎	29♑
23	29♍	0♎	4♎	0♒
24	0♎	2♎	5♎	0♒
25	1♎	3♎	6♎	0♒
26	2♎	5♎	8♎	1♒
27	3♎	7♎	9♎	1♒
28	4♎	9♎	10♎	2♒
29	5♎	10♎	11♎	2♒
30	6♎	12♎	13♎	2♒

October

Day	☉	☿	♀	♂
1	7♎	14♎	14♎	3♒
2	8♎	15♎	15♎	3♒
3	9♎	17♎	16♎	4♒
4	10♎	19♎	18♎	4♒
5	11♎	20♎	19♎	5♒
6	12♎	22♎	20♎	5♒
7	13♎	24♎	21♎	5♒
8	14♎	25♎	23♎	6♒
9	15♎	27♎	24♎	6♒
10	16♎	28♎	25♎	7♒
11	17♎	0♏	26♎	7♒
12	18♎	2♏	28♎	8♒
13	19♎	3♏	29♎	8♒
14	20♎	5♏	0♏	9♒
15	21♎	6♏	1♏	9♒
16	22♎	8♏	3♏	10♒
17	23♎	9♏	4♏	10♒
18	24♎	11♏	5♏	11♒
19	25♎	12♏	6♏	11♒
20	26♎	14♏	8♏	12♒
21	27♎	15♏	9♏	13♒
22	28♎	16♏	10♏	13♒
23	29♎	18♏	11♏	14♒
24	0♏	19♏	13♏	14♒
25	1♏	21♏	14♏	15♒
26	2♏	22♏	15♏	15♒
27	3♏	23♏	16♏	16♒
28	4♏	25♏	18♏	16♒
29	5♏	26♏	19♏	17♒
30	6♏	27♏	20♏	18♒
31	7♏	29♏	21♏	18♒

November

Day	☉	☿	♀	♂
1	8♏	0♐	23♏	19♒
2	9♏	1♐	24♏	19♒
3	10♏	2♐	25♏	20♒
4	11♏	4♐	26♏	21♒
5	12♏	5♐	28♏	21♒
6	13♏	6♐	29♏	22♒
7	14♏	7♐	0♐	22♒
8	15♏	8♐	1♐	23♒
9	16♏	9♐	3♐	24♒
10	17♏	10♐	4♐	24♒
11	18♏	11♐	5♐	25♒
12	19♏	11♐	6♐	25♒
13	20♏	12♐	8♐	26♒
14	21♏	13♐	9♐	27♒
15	22♏	13♐	10♐	27♒
16	23♏	14♐	11♐	28♒
17	24♏	14♐	13♐	28♒
18	25♏	14♐	14♐	29♒
19	26♏	14♐	15♐	0♓
20	27♏	14♐	16♐	0♓
21	28♏	13♐	18♐	1♓
22	29♏	13♐	19♐	2♓
23	0♐	12♐	20♐	2♓
24	1♐	11♐	21♐	3♓
25	2♐	10♐	23♐	4♓
26	3♐	9♐	24♐	4♓
27	4♐	8♐	25♐	5♓
28	5♐	6♐	26♐	5♓
29	6♐	5♐	28♐	6♓
30	7♐	4♐	29♐	7♓

December

Day	☉	☿	♀	♂
1	8♐	2♐	0♑	7♓
2	9♐	1♐	1♑	8♓
3	10♐	0♐	2♑	9♓
4	11♐	29♏	4♑	9♓
5	12♐	29♏	5♑	10♓
6	13♐	28♏	6♑	11♓
7	14♐	28♏	7♑	11♓
8	15♐	28♏	9♑	12♓
9	16♐	28♏	10♑	13♓
10	17♐	28♏	11♑	13♓
11	18♐	28♏	12♑	14♓
12	19♐	29♏	14♑	15♓
13	20♐	0♐	15♑	15♓
14	21♐	0♐	16♑	16♓
15	22♐	1♐	17♑	17♓
16	23♐	2♐	19♑	17♓
17	24♐	3♐	20♑	18♓
18	25♐	4♐	21♑	19♓
19	26♐	5♐	22♑	19♓
20	27♐	6♐	24♑	20♓
21	28♐	8♐	25♑	21♓
22	29♐	9♐	26♑	21♓
23	0♑	10♐	27♑	22♓
24	1♑	11♐	29♑	23♓
25	2♑	13♐	0♒	23♓
26	4♑	14♐	1♒	24♓
27	5♑	15♐	2♒	25♓
28	6♑	17♐	4♒	25♓
29	7♑	18♐	5♒	26♓
30	8♑	20♐	6♒	27♓
31	9♑	21♐	7♒	27♓

Planetary Positions

♌ = Leo ♍ = Virgo ♎ = Libra ♏ = Scorpio ♐ = Sagittarius ♑ = Capricorn ♒ = Aquarius ♓ = Pisces

1940

January

Day	☉	☿	♀	♂
1	10♑	22♐	9♒	28♓
2	11♑	24♐	10♒	29♓
3	12♑	25♐	11♒	29♓
4	13♑	27♐	12♒	0♈
5	14♑	28♐	14♒	1♈
6	15♑	0♑	15♒	1♈
7	16♑	1♑	16♒	2♈
8	17♑	3♑	17♒	3♈
9	18♑	4♑	18♒	4♈
10	19♑	6♑	20♒	4♈
11	20♑	7♑	21♒	5♈
12	21♑	9♑	22♒	6♈
13	22♑	10♑	23♒	6♈
14	23♑	12♑	25♒	7♈
15	24♑	14♑	26♒	8♈
16	25♑	15♑	27♒	8♈
17	26♑	17♑	28♒	9♈
18	27♑	18♑	0♓	10♈
19	28♑	20♑	1♓	10♈
20	29♑	21♑	2♓	11♈
21	0♒	23♑	3♓	12♈
22	1♒	25♑	4♓	12♈
23	2♒	26♑	6♓	13♈
24	3♒	28♑	7♓	14♈
25	4♒	0♒	8♓	14♈
26	5♒	1♒	9♓	15♈
27	6♒	3♒	11♓	16♈
28	7♒	5♒	12♓	16♈
29	8♒	6♒	13♓	17♈
30	9♒	8♒	14♓	18♈
31	10♒	10♒	15♓	19♈

April

Day	☉	☿	♀	♂
1	11♈	17♓	26♉	0♊
2	12♈	18♓	27♉	0♊
3	13♈	18♓	28♉	1♊
4	14♈	18♓	29♉	2♊
5	15♈	19♓	0♊	2♊
6	16♈	20♓	2♊	3♊
7	17♈	20♓	3♊	4♊
8	18♈	21♓	4♊	4♊
9	19♈	22♓	5♊	5♊
10	20♈	23♓	6♊	6♊
11	21♈	24♓	7♊	6♊
12	22♈	25♓	8♊	7♊
13	23♈	26♓	9♊	8♊
14	24♈	27♓	10♊	8♊
15	25♈	28♓	11♊	9♊
16	26♈	29♓	12♊	10♊
17	27♈	0♈	13♊	10♊
18	28♈	1♈	14♊	11♊
19	29♈	2♈	15♊	11♊
20	0♉	4♈	16♊	12♊
21	1♉	5♈	17♊	13♊
22	2♉	6♈	17♊	13♊
23	3♉	8♈	18♊	14♊
24	4♉	9♈	19♊	15♊
25	5♉	11♈	20♊	15♊
26	6♉	12♈	21♊	16♊
27	7♉	14♈	22♊	17♊
28	8♉	15♈	23♊	17♊
29	9♉	17♈	24♊	18♊
30	10♉	18♈	25♊	19♊

July

Day	☉	☿	♀	♂
1	9♋	3♌	2♋	29♋
2	10♋	4♌	2♋	29♋
3	11♋	4♌	1♋	0♌
4	12♋	5♌	1♋	0♌
5	13♋	5♌	0♋	1♌
6	14♋	5♌	0♋	2♌
7	15♋	5♌	29♊	2♌
8	16♋	5♌	29♊	3♌
9	17♋	5♌	29♊	4♌
10	18♋	5♌	28♊	4♌
11	19♋	5♌	28♊	5♌
12	20♋	5♌	28♊	6♌
13	21♋	4♌	27♊	6♌
14	22♋	4♌	27♊	7♌
15	23♋	4♌	27♊	7♌
16	23♋	3♌	27♊	8♌
17	24♋	3♌	27♊	9♌
18	25♋	2♌	27♊	9♌
19	26♋	1♌	27♊	10♌
20	27♋	1♌	27♊	11♌
21	28♋	0♌	27♊	11♌
22	29♋	29♋	27♊	12♌
23	0♌	29♋	27♊	13♌
24	1♌	28♋	27♊	13♌
25	2♌	27♋	28♊	14♌
26	3♌	27♋	28♊	14♌
27	4♌	26♋	28♊	15♌
28	5♌	26♋	28♊	16♌
29	6♌	25♋	29♊	16♌
30	7♌	25♋	29♊	17♌
31	8♌	25♋	0♋	18♌

October

Day	☉	☿	♀	♂
1	8♎	27♎	24♌	27♍
2	9♎	28♎	25♌	28♍
3	10♎	0♏	26♌	28♍
4	11♎	1♏	27♌	29♍
5	12♎	2♏	28♌	0♎
6	13♎	4♏	29♌	0♎
7	14♎	5♏	0♍	1♎
8	15♎	7♏	1♍	2♎
9	16♎	8♏	3♍	2♎
10	17♎	9♏	4♍	3♎
11	18♎	10♏	5♍	4♎
12	19♎	12♏	6♍	4♎
13	20♎	13♏	7♍	5♎
14	21♎	14♏	8♍	6♎
15	22♎	15♏	9♍	6♎
16	23♎	17♏	11♍	7♎
17	24♎	18♏	12♍	7♎
18	25♎	19♏	13♍	8♎
19	26♎	20♏	14♍	9♎
20	27♎	21♏	15♍	9♎
21	28♎	22♏	16♍	10♎
22	29♎	23♏	18♍	11♎
23	0♏	24♏	19♍	11♎
24	1♏	25♏	20♍	12♎
25	2♏	25♏	21♍	13♎
26	3♏	26♏	22♍	13♎
27	4♏	27♏	23♍	14♎
28	5♏	27♏	25♍	15♎
29	6♏	28♏	26♍	15♎
30	7♏	28♏	27♍	16♎
31	8♏	28♏	28♍	17♎

February

Day	☉	☿	♀	♂
1	11♒	11♒	17♓	19♈
2	12♒	13♒	18♓	20♈
3	13♒	15♒	19♓	21♈
4	14♒	17♒	20♓	21♈
5	15♒	19♒	22♓	22♈
6	16♒	20♒	23♓	23♈
7	17♒	22♒	24♓	23♈
8	18♒	24♒	25♓	24♈
9	19♒	26♒	26♓	25♈
10	20♒	27♒	28♓	25♈
11	21♒	29♒	29♓	26♈
12	22♒	1♓	0♈	27♈
13	23♒	3♓	1♈	27♈
14	24♒	5♓	2♈	28♈
15	25♒	7♓	4♈	29♈
16	26♒	8♓	5♈	29♈
17	27♒	10♓	6♈	0♉
18	28♒	12♓	7♈	1♉
19	29♒	14♓	8♈	1♉
20	0♓	15♓	10♈	2♉
21	1♓	17♓	11♈	3♉
22	2♓	19♓	12♈	3♉
23	3♓	20♓	13♈	4♉
24	4♓	22♓	14♈	5♉
25	5♓	23♓	15♈	6♉
26	6♓	24♓	17♈	6♉
27	7♓	25♓	18♈	7♉
28	8♓	27♓	19♈	8♉
29	9♓	28♓	20♈	8♉

May

Day	☉	☿	♀	♂
1	11♉	20♈	25♊	19♊
2	12♉	22♈	26♊	20♊
3	13♉	23♈	27♊	21♊
4	14♉	25♈	28♊	21♊
5	15♉	27♈	29♊	22♊
6	16♉	29♈	0♋	23♊
7	16♉	1♉	0♋	23♊
8	17♉	2♉	1♋	24♊
9	18♉	4♉	2♋	25♊
10	19♉	6♉	3♋	25♊
11	20♉	8♉	3♋	26♊
12	21♉	10♉	4♋	26♊
13	22♉	12♉	5♋	27♊
14	23♉	14♉	5♋	28♊
15	24♉	16♉	6♋	28♊
16	25♉	18♉	7♋	29♊
17	26♉	21♉	7♋	0♋
18	27♉	23♉	8♋	0♋
19	28♉	25♉	8♋	1♋
20	29♉	27♉	9♋	2♋
21	0♊	29♉	9♋	2♋
22	1♊	1♊	10♋	3♋
23	2♊	4♊	10♋	4♋
24	3♊	6♊	11♋	4♋
25	4♊	8♊	11♋	5♋
26	5♊	10♊	11♋	6♋
27	6♊	12♊	12♋	6♋
28	7♊	14♊	12♋	7♋
29	8♊	17♊	12♋	7♋
30	9♊	19♊	13♋	8♋
31	10♊	21♊	13♋	9♋

August

Day	☉	☿	♀	♂
1	9♌	25♋	0♋	18♌
2	10♌	25♋	1♋	19♌
3	11♌	25♋	1♋	20♌
4	12♌	25♋	2♋	20♌
5	13♌	25♋	2♋	21♌
6	14♌	26♋	3♋	21♌
7	15♌	26♋	3♋	22♌
8	15♌	27♋	4♋	23♌
9	16♌	28♋	4♋	23♌
10	17♌	29♋	5♋	24♌
11	18♌	29♋	6♋	25♌
12	19♌	1♌	6♋	25♌
13	20♌	2♌	7♋	26♌
14	21♌	3♌	8♋	27♌
15	22♌	4♌	8♋	27♌
16	23♌	6♌	9♋	28♌
17	24♌	7♌	10♋	28♌
18	25♌	9♌	11♋	29♌
19	26♌	11♌	12♋	0♍
20	27♌	12♌	12♋	0♍
21	28♌	14♌	13♋	1♍
22	29♌	16♌	14♋	2♍
23	0♍	18♌	15♋	2♍
24	1♍	20♌	16♋	3♍
25	2♍	22♌	17♋	4♍
26	3♍	24♌	17♋	4♍
27	4♍	26♌	18♋	5♍
28	5♍	28♌	19♋	5♍
29	6♍	29♌	20♋	6♍
30	7♍	1♍	21♋	7♍
31	8♍	3♍	22♋	7♍

November

Day	☉	☿	♀	♂
1	9♏	28♏	29♍	17♎
2	10♏	28♏	1♎	18♎
3	11♏	28♏	2♎	19♎
4	12♏	27♏	3♎	19♎
5	13♏	27♏	4♎	20♎
6	14♏	26♏	5♎	20♎
7	15♏	25♏	7♎	21♎
8	16♏	24♏	8♎	22♎
9	17♏	23♏	9♎	22♎
10	18♏	22♏	10♎	23♎
11	19♏	20♏	11♎	24♎
12	20♏	19♏	13♎	24♎
13	21♏	18♏	14♎	25♎
14	22♏	17♏	15♎	26♎
15	23♏	15♏	16♎	26♎
16	24♏	14♏	17♎	27♎
17	25♏	14♏	19♎	28♎
18	26♏	13♏	20♎	28♎
19	27♏	12♏	21♎	29♎
20	28♏	12♏	22♎	0♏
21	29♏	12♏	24♎	0♏
22	0♐	12♏	25♎	1♏
23	1♐	12♏	26♎	2♏
24	2♐	13♏	27♎	2♏
25	3♐	13♏	28♎	3♏
26	4♐	14♏	0♏	4♏
27	5♐	15♏	1♏	4♏
28	6♐	16♏	2♏	5♏
29	7♐	17♏	3♏	6♏
30	8♐	18♏	5♏	6♏

March

Day	☉	☿	♀	♂
1	10♓	28♓	21♈	9♉
2	11♓	29♓	22♈	10♉
3	12♓	0♈	24♈	10♉
4	13♓	0♈	25♈	11♉
5	14♓	0♈	26♈	12♉
6	15♓	0♈	27♈	12♉
7	16♓	0♈	28♈	13♉
8	17♓	0♈	29♈	14♉
9	18♓	0♈	1♉	14♉
10	19♓	29♓	2♉	15♉
11	20♓	28♓	3♉	16♉
12	21♓	28♓	4♉	16♉
13	22♓	27♓	5♉	17♉
14	23♓	26♓	6♉	18♉
15	24♓	25♓	7♉	18♉
16	25♓	24♓	9♉	19♉
17	26♓	23♓	10♉	20♉
18	27♓	22♓	11♉	20♉
19	28♓	21♓	12♉	21♉
20	29♓	21♓	13♉	22♉
21	0♈	20♓	14♉	22♉
22	1♈	19♓	15♉	23♉
23	2♈	19♓	16♉	24♉
24	3♈	18♓	18♉	24♉
25	4♈	18♓	19♉	25♉
26	5♈	17♓	20♉	26♉
27	6♈	17♓	21♉	26♉
28	7♈	17♓	22♉	27♉
29	8♈	17♓	23♉	28♉
30	9♈	17♓	24♉	28♉
31	10♈	17♓	25♉	29♉

June

Day	☉	☿	♀	♂
1	11♊	23♊	13♋	9♋
2	11♊	25♊	13♋	10♋
3	12♊	27♊	13♋	11♋
4	13♊	29♊	13♋	11♋
5	14♊	1♋	13♋	12♋
6	15♊	2♋	13♋	13♋
7	16♊	4♋	13♋	13♋
8	17♊	6♋	13♋	14♋
9	18♊	8♋	13♋	15♋
10	19♊	9♋	13♋	15♋
11	20♊	11♋	13♋	16♋
12	21♊	12♋	12♋	16♋
13	22♊	14♋	12♋	17♋
14	23♊	16♋	12♋	18♋
15	24♊	17♋	11♋	18♋
16	25♊	18♋	11♋	19♋
17	26♊	20♋	11♋	20♋
18	27♊	21♋	10♋	20♋
19	28♊	22♋	10♋	21♋
20	29♊	23♋	9♋	22♋
21	0♋	25♋	9♋	22♋
22	1♋	26♋	8♋	23♋
23	2♋	27♋	7♋	23♋
24	3♋	28♋	7♋	24♋
25	3♋	29♋	6♋	25♋
26	4♋	0♌	5♋	25♋
27	5♋	0♌	5♋	26♋
28	6♋	1♌	4♋	27♋
29	7♋	2♌	4♋	27♋
30	8♋	3♌	3♋	28♋

September

Day	☉	☿	♀	♂
1	9♍	5♍	23♋	8♍
2	10♍	7♍	24♋	9♍
3	11♍	9♍	25♋	9♍
4	12♍	11♍	26♋	10♍
5	12♍	13♍	27♋	11♍
6	13♍	15♍	28♋	11♍
7	14♍	17♍	29♋	12♍
8	15♍	19♍	0♌	12♍
9	16♍	21♍	0♌	13♍
10	17♍	22♍	1♌	14♍
11	18♍	24♍	2♌	14♍
12	19♍	26♍	4♌	15♍
13	20♍	28♍	5♌	16♍
14	21♍	0♎	6♌	16♍
15	22♍	1♎	7♌	17♍
16	23♍	3♎	8♌	18♍
17	24♍	5♎	9♌	18♍
18	25♍	6♎	10♌	19♍
19	26♍	8♎	11♌	19♍
20	27♍	10♎	12♌	20♍
21	28♍	11♎	13♌	21♍
22	29♍	13♎	14♌	21♍
23	0♎	14♎	15♌	22♍
24	1♎	16♎	16♌	23♍
25	2♎	18♎	17♌	23♍
26	3♎	19♎	18♌	24♍
27	4♎	21♎	19♌	25♍
28	5♎	22♎	20♌	25♍
29	6♎	24♎	21♌	26♍
30	7♎	25♎	23♌	27♍

December

Day	☉	☿	♀	♂
1	9♐	19♏	6♏	7♏
2	10♐	20♏	7♏	8♏
3	11♐	21♏	8♏	8♏
4	12♐	23♏	9♏	9♏
5	13♐	24♏	11♏	10♏
6	14♐	25♏	12♏	10♏
7	15♐	27♏	13♏	11♏
8	16♐	28♏	14♏	12♏
9	17♐	0♐	16♏	12♏
10	18♐	1♐	17♏	13♏
11	19♐	2♐	18♏	14♏
12	20♐	4♐	19♏	14♏
13	21♐	5♐	21♏	15♏
14	22♐	7♐	22♏	16♏
15	23♐	8♐	23♏	16♏
16	24♐	10♐	24♏	17♏
17	25♐	11♐	26♏	18♏
18	26♐	13♐	27♏	18♏
19	27♐	14♐	28♏	19♏
20	28♐	16♐	29♏	20♏
21	29♐	17♐	0♐	20♏
22	0♑	19♐	2♐	21♏
23	1♑	20♐	3♐	22♏
24	2♑	22♐	4♐	22♏
25	3♑	23♐	5♐	23♏
26	4♑	25♐	7♐	24♏
27	5♑	27♐	8♐	24♏
28	6♑	28♐	9♐	25♏
29	7♑	0♑	10♐	26♏
30	8♑	1♑	12♐	26♏
31	9♑	3♑	13♐	27♏

1941

Your Starway to Love

☉ =Sun ☿ = Mercury ♀ = Venus ♂ = Mars ♈ = Aries ♉ = Taurus ♊ = Gemini ♋ = Cancer

January

Day	☉	☿	♀	♂
1	10♑	4♑	14♐	28♏
2	11♑	6♑	15♐	28♏
3	12♑	8♑	17♐	29♏
4	13♑	9♑	18♐	0♐
5	14♑	11♑	19♐	0♐
6	16♑	12♑	20♐	1♐
7	17♑	14♑	22♐	2♐
8	18♑	16♑	23♐	2♐
9	19♑	17♑	24♐	3♐
10	20♑	19♑	25♐	4♐
11	21♑	20♑	27♐	4♐
12	22♑	22♑	28♐	5♐
13	23♑	24♑	29♐	6♐
14	24♑	25♑	0♑	6♐
15	25♑	27♑	2♑	7♐
16	26♑	29♑	3♑	8♐
17	27♑	0♒	4♑	8♐
18	28♑	2♒	5♑	9♐
19	29♑	4♒	7♑	10♐
20	0♒	6♒	8♑	10♐
21	1♒	7♒	9♑	11♐
22	2♒	9♒	10♑	12♐
23	3♒	11♒	12♑	12♐
24	4♒	12♒	13♑	13♐
25	5♒	14♒	14♑	14♐
26	6♒	16♒	15♑	14♐
27	7♒	18♒	17♑	15♐
28	8♒	19♒	18♑	16♐
29	9♒	21♒	19♑	16♐
30	10♒	23♒	20♑	17♐
31	11♒	25♒	22♑	18♐

February

Day	☉	☿	♀	♂
1	12♒	26♒	23♑	19♐
2	13♒	28♒	24♑	19♐
3	14♒	29♒	25♑	20♐
4	15♒	1♓	27♑	21♐
5	16♒	3♓	28♑	21♐
6	17♒	4♓	29♑	22♐
7	18♒	5♓	0♒	23♐
8	19♒	7♓	2♒	23♐
9	20♒	8♓	3♒	24♐
10	21♒	9♓	4♒	25♐
11	22♒	10♓	5♒	25♐
12	23♒	11♓	7♒	26♐
13	24♒	12♓	8♒	27♐
14	25♒	13♓	9♒	27♐
15	26♒	13♓	10♒	28♐
16	27♒	13♓	12♒	29♐
17	28♒	13♓	13♒	29♐
18	29♒	13♓	14♒	0♑
19	0♓	13♓	15♒	1♑
20	1♓	13♓	17♒	2♑
21	2♓	12♓	18♒	2♑
22	3♓	12♓	19♒	3♑
23	4♓	11♓	20♒	4♑
24	5♓	10♓	22♒	4♑
25	6♓	9♓	23♒	5♑
26	7♓	8♓	24♒	6♑
27	8♓	7♓	25♒	6♑
28	9♓	6♓	27♒	7♑

March

Day	☉	☿	♀	♂
1	10♓	5♓	28♒	8♑
2	11♓	4♓	29♒	8♑
3	12♓	3♓	0♓	9♑
4	13♓	2♓	2♓	10♑
5	14♓	1♓	3♓	10♑
6	15♓	0♓	4♓	11♑
7	16♓	0♓	5♓	12♑
8	17♓	0♓	7♓	13♑
9	18♓	29♒	8♓	13♑
10	19♓	29♒	9♓	14♑
11	20♓	29♒	10♓	15♑
12	21♓	29♒	12♓	15♑
13	22♓	29♒	13♓	16♑
14	23♓	29♒	14♓	17♑
15	24♓	29♒	15♓	17♑
16	25♓	0♓	17♓	18♑
17	26♓	0♓	18♓	19♑
18	27♓	1♓	19♓	19♑
19	28♓	1♓	20♓	20♑
20	29♓	2♓	22♓	21♑
21	0♈	3♓	23♓	22♑
22	1♈	4♓	24♓	22♑
23	2♈	5♓	25♓	23♑
24	3♈	5♓	26♓	24♑
25	4♈	6♓	28♓	24♑
26	5♈	7♓	29♓	25♑
27	6♈	8♓	0♈	26♑
28	7♈	10♓	1♈	26♑
29	8♈	11♓	3♈	27♑
30	9♈	12♓	4♈	28♑
31	10♈	13♓	5♈	28♑

April

Day	☉	☿	♀	♂
1	11♈	14♓	6♈	29♑
2	12♈	16♓	8♈	0♒
3	13♈	17♓	9♈	0♒
4	14♈	18♓	10♈	1♒
5	15♈	20♓	11♈	2♒
6	16♈	21♓	13♈	3♒
7	17♈	22♓	14♈	3♒
8	18♈	24♓	15♈	4♒
9	19♈	25♓	16♈	5♒
10	20♈	27♓	18♈	5♒
11	21♈	28♓	19♈	6♒
12	22♈	0♈	20♈	7♒
13	23♈	1♈	21♈	7♒
14	24♈	3♈	23♈	8♒
15	25♈	5♈	24♈	9♒
16	26♈	6♈	25♈	9♒
17	27♈	8♈	26♈	10♒
18	28♈	10♈	27♈	11♒
19	29♈	12♈	29♈	12♒
20	0♉	13♈	0♉	12♒
21	1♉	15♈	1♉	13♒
22	2♉	17♈	2♉	14♒
23	3♉	19♈	4♉	14♒
24	4♉	21♈	5♉	15♒
25	5♉	23♈	6♉	16♒
26	6♉	25♈	7♉	16♒
27	7♉	26♈	9♉	17♒
28	8♉	28♈	10♉	18♒
29	8♉	0♉	11♉	18♒
30	9♉	3♉	12♉	19♒

May

Day	☉	☿	♀	♂
1	10♉	5♉	14♉	20♒
2	11♉	7♉	15♉	20♒
3	12♉	9♉	16♉	21♒
4	13♉	11♉	17♉	22♒
5	14♉	13♉	18♉	23♒
6	15♉	15♉	20♉	23♒
7	16♉	17♉	21♉	24♒
8	17♉	20♉	22♉	25♒
9	18♉	22♉	23♉	25♒
10	19♉	24♉	25♉	26♒
11	20♉	26♉	26♉	27♒
12	21♉	28♉	27♉	27♒
13	22♉	0♊	28♉	28♒
14	23♉	2♊	0♊	29♒
15	24♉	5♊	1♊	29♒
16	25♉	7♊	2♊	0♓
17	26♉	9♊	3♊	1♓
18	27♉	11♊	4♊	1♓
19	28♉	13♊	6♊	2♓
20	29♉	14♊	7♊	3♓
21	0♊	16♊	8♊	3♓
22	1♊	18♊	9♊	4♓
23	2♊	20♊	11♊	5♓
24	3♊	22♊	12♊	5♓
25	4♊	23♊	13♊	6♓
26	5♊	25♊	14♊	7♓
27	6♊	26♊	16♊	7♓
28	6♊	28♊	17♊	8♓
29	7♊	29♊	18♊	9♓
30	8♊	1♋	19♊	9♓
31	9♊	2♋	20♊	10♓

June

Day	☉	☿	♀	♂
1	10♊	3♋	22♊	11♓
2	11♊	5♋	23♊	11♓
3	12♊	6♋	24♊	12♓
4	13♊	7♋	25♊	13♓
5	14♊	8♋	27♊	13♓
6	15♊	9♋	28♊	14♓
7	16♊	10♋	29♊	15♓
8	17♊	11♋	0♋	15♓
9	18♊	11♋	1♋	16♓
10	19♊	12♋	3♋	16♓
11	20♊	13♋	4♋	17♓
12	21♊	13♋	5♋	18♓
13	22♊	14♋	6♋	18♓
14	23♊	14♋	8♋	19♓
15	24♊	15♋	9♋	20♓
16	25♊	15♋	10♋	20♓
17	26♊	15♋	11♋	21♓
18	27♊	16♋	13♋	22♓
19	28♊	16♋	14♋	22♓
20	28♊	16♋	15♋	23♓
21	29♊	16♋	16♋	23♓
22	0♋	15♋	17♋	24♓
23	1♋	15♋	19♋	25♓
24	2♋	15♋	20♋	25♓
25	3♋	15♋	21♋	26♓
26	4♋	14♋	22♋	26♓
27	5♋	14♋	24♋	27♓
28	6♋	13♋	25♋	28♓
29	7♋	13♋	26♋	28♓
30	8♋	12♋	27♋	29♓

July

Day	☉	☿	♀	♂
1	9♋	12♋	28♋	29♓
2	10♋	11♋	0♌	0♈
3	11♋	10♋	1♌	1♈
4	12♋	10♋	2♌	1♈
5	13♋	9♋	3♌	2♈
6	14♋	9♋	4♌	2♈
7	15♋	8♋	6♌	3♈
8	16♋	8♋	7♌	3♈
9	17♋	7♋	8♌	4♈
10	18♋	7♋	9♌	5♈
11	18♋	7♋	11♌	5♈
12	19♋	6♋	12♌	6♈
13	20♋	6♋	13♌	6♈
14	21♋	6♋	14♌	7♈
15	22♋	6♋	15♌	7♈
16	23♋	6♋	17♌	8♈
17	24♋	7♋	18♌	8♈
18	25♋	7♋	19♌	9♈
19	26♋	7♋	20♌	9♈
20	27♋	8♋	22♌	10♈
21	28♋	9♋	23♌	10♈
22	29♋	9♋	24♌	11♈
23	0♌	10♋	25♌	11♈
24	1♌	11♋	26♌	12♈
25	2♌	12♋	28♌	12♈
26	3♌	13♋	29♌	13♈
27	4♌	14♋	0♍	13♈
28	5♌	15♋	1♍	14♈
29	6♌	17♋	2♍	14♈
30	7♌	18♋	4♍	14♈
31	8♌	20♋	5♍	15♈

August

Day	☉	☿	♀	♂
1	9♌	21♋	6♍	15♈
2	10♌	23♋	7♍	16♈
3	10♌	25♋	9♍	16♈
4	11♌	26♋	10♍	16♈
5	12♌	28♋	11♍	17♈
6	13♌	0♌	12♍	17♈
7	14♌	2♌	13♍	18♈
8	15♌	4♌	15♍	18♈
9	16♌	6♌	16♍	18♈
10	17♌	8♌	17♍	19♈
11	18♌	10♌	18♍	19♈
12	19♌	12♌	19♍	19♈
13	20♌	14♌	21♍	20♈
14	21♌	16♌	22♍	20♈
15	22♌	18♌	23♍	20♈
16	23♌	20♌	24♍	21♈
17	24♌	22♌	25♍	21♈
18	25♌	24♌	27♍	21♈
19	26♌	26♌	28♍	21♈
20	27♌	28♌	29♍	22♈
21	28♌	0♍	0♎	22♈
22	29♌	2♍	1♎	22♈
23	0♍	4♍	3♎	22♈
24	1♍	6♍	4♎	22♈
25	2♍	8♍	5♎	23♈
26	3♍	10♍	6♎	23♈
27	4♍	11♍	7♎	23♈
28	4♍	13♍	9♎	23♈
29	5♍	15♍	10♎	23♈
30	6♍	17♍	11♎	23♈
31	7♍	19♍	12♎	23♈

September

Day	☉	☿	♀	♂
1	8♍	20♍	13♎	23♈
2	9♍	22♍	15♎	24♈
3	10♍	24♍	16♎	24♈
4	11♍	25♍	17♎	24♈
5	12♍	27♍	18♎	24♈
6	13♍	29♍	19♎	24♈
7	14♍	0♎	21♎	24♈
8	15♍	2♎	22♎	24♈
9	16♍	4♎	23♎	24♈
10	17♍	5♎	24♎	24♈
11	18♍	7♎	25♎	24♈
12	19♍	8♎	26♎	24♈
13	20♍	10♎	28♎	23♈
14	21♍	11♎	29♎	23♈
15	22♍	13♎	0♏	23♈
16	23♍	14♎	1♏	23♈
17	24♍	15♎	2♏	23♈
18	25♍	17♎	4♏	23♈
19	26♍	18♎	5♏	23♈
20	27♍	20♎	6♏	22♈
21	28♍	21♎	7♏	22♈
22	29♍	22♎	8♏	22♈
23	0♎	24♎	9♏	22♈
24	1♎	25♎	11♏	22♈
25	2♎	26♎	12♏	21♈
26	3♎	27♎	13♏	21♈
27	4♎	29♎	14♏	21♈
28	5♎	0♏	15♏	21♈
29	6♎	1♏	17♏	20♈
30	7♎	2♏	18♏	20♈

October

Day	☉	☿	♀	♂
1	8♎	3♏	19♏	20♈
2	9♎	4♏	20♏	19♈
3	10♎	5♏	21♏	19♈
4	11♎	6♏	22♏	19♈
5	12♎	7♏	24♏	18♈
6	13♎	8♏	25♏	18♈
7	14♎	9♏	26♏	18♈
8	15♎	9♏	27♏	18♈
9	16♎	10♏	28♏	17♈
10	16♎	11♏	29♏	17♈
11	17♎	11♏	0♐	17♈
12	18♎	12♏	2♐	16♈
13	19♎	12♏	3♐	16♈
14	20♎	12♏	4♐	16♈
15	21♎	12♏	5♐	15♈
16	22♎	12♏	6♐	15♈
17	23♎	12♏	7♐	15♈
18	24♎	12♏	8♐	15♈
19	25♎	11♏	10♐	14♈
20	26♎	11♏	11♐	14♈
21	27♎	10♏	12♐	14♈
22	28♎	9♏	13♐	13♈
23	29♎	8♏	14♐	13♈
24	0♏	7♏	15♐	13♈
25	1♏	6♏	16♐	13♈
26	2♏	4♏	18♐	13♈
27	3♏	3♏	19♐	12♈
28	4♏	2♏	20♐	12♈
29	5♏	1♏	21♐	12♈
30	6♏	0♏	22♐	12♈
31	7♏	29♎	23♐	12♈

November

Day	☉	☿	♀	♂
1	8♏	28♎	24♐	12♈
2	9♏	27♎	25♐	12♈
3	10♏	27♎	26♐	11♈
4	11♏	26♎	28♐	11♈
5	12♏	26♎	29♐	11♈
6	13♏	26♎	0♑	11♈
7	14♏	27♎	1♑	11♈
8	15♏	27♎	2♑	11♈
9	16♏	28♎	3♑	11♈
10	17♏	29♎	4♑	11♈
11	18♏	29♎	5♑	11♈
12	19♏	0♏	6♑	11♈
13	20♏	1♏	7♑	11♈
14	21♏	3♏	8♑	11♈
15	22♏	4♏	9♑	11♈
16	23♏	5♏	10♑	11♈
17	24♏	6♏	12♑	11♈
18	25♏	8♏	13♑	11♈
19	26♏	9♏	14♑	12♈
20	27♏	11♏	15♑	12♈
21	28♏	12♏	16♑	12♈
22	0♐	13♏	17♑	12♈
23	1♐	15♏	18♑	12♈
24	2♐	16♏	19♑	12♈
25	3♐	18♏	20♑	12♈
26	4♐	19♏	21♑	13♈
27	5♐	21♏	22♑	13♈
28	6♐	23♏	23♑	13♈
29	7♐	24♏	24♑	13♈
30	8♐	26♏	25♑	14♈

December

Day	☉	☿	♀	♂
1	9♐	27♏	26♑	14♈
2	10♐	29♏	27♑	14♈
3	11♐	0♐	27♑	14♈
4	12♐	2♐	28♑	15♈
5	13♐	3♐	29♑	15♈
6	14♐	5♐	0♒	15♈
7	15♐	7♐	1♒	15♈
8	16♐	8♐	2♒	16♈
9	17♐	10♐	3♒	16♈
10	18♐	11♐	4♒	16♈
11	19♐	13♐	5♒	17♈
12	20♐	14♐	5♒	17♈
13	21♐	16♐	6♒	17♈
14	22♐	17♐	7♒	18♈
15	23♐	19♐	8♒	18♈
16	24♐	21♐	9♒	18♈
17	25♐	22♐	9♒	19♈
18	26♐	24♐	10♒	19♈
19	27♐	25♐	11♒	19♈
20	28♐	27♐	12♒	20♈
21	29♐	28♐	12♒	20♈
22	0♑	0♑	13♒	21♈
23	1♑	2♑	14♒	21♈
24	2♑	3♑	14♒	21♈
25	3♑	5♑	15♒	22♈
26	4♑	6♑	16♒	22♈
27	5♑	8♑	16♒	23♈
28	6♑	10♑	17♒	23♈
29	7♑	11♑	17♒	24♈
30	8♑	13♑	18♒	24♈
31	9♑	15♑	18♒	24♈

Planetary Positions

♌ = Leo ♍ = Virgo ♎ = Libra ♏ = Scorpio ♐ = Sagittarius ♑ = Capricorn ♒ = Aquarius ♓ = Pisces

1942

January

Day	☉	☿	♀	♂
1	10♑	16♑	19♒	25♈
2	11♑	18♑	19♒	25♈
3	12♑	19♑	19♒	26♈
4	13♑	21♑	20♒	26♈
5	14♑	23♑	20♒	27♈
6	15♑	24♑	20♒	27♈
7	16♑	26♑	21♒	28♈
8	17♑	28♑	21♒	28♈
9	18♑	29♑	21♒	29♈
10	19♑	1♒	21♒	29♈
11	20♑	3♒	21♒	0♉
12	21♑	4♒	21♒	0♉
13	22♑	6♒	21♒	1♉
14	23♑	7♒	21♒	1♉
15	24♑	9♒	21♒	2♉
16	25♑	11♒	21♒	2♉
17	26♑	12♒	21♒	3♉
18	27♑	14♒	21♒	3♉
19	28♑	15♒	20♒	4♉
20	0♒	17♒	20♒	4♉
21	1♒	18♒	20♒	5♉
22	2♒	20♒	19♒	5♉
23	3♒	21♒	19♒	6♉
24	4♒	22♒	19♒	6♉
25	5♒	23♒	18♒	7♉
26	6♒	24♒	18♒	7♉
27	7♒	25♒	17♒	8♉
28	8♒	26♒	17♒	8♉
29	9♒	26♒	16♒	9♉
30	10♒	27♒	15♒	9♉
31	11♒	27♒	15♒	10♉

April

Day	☉	☿	♀	♂
1	11♈	23♓	25♒	15♊
2	12♈	25♓	26♒	15♊
3	13♈	26♓	27♒	16♊
4	14♈	28♓	28♒	17♊
5	15♈	0♈	29♒	17♊
6	16♈	2♈	0♓	18♊
7	17♈	3♈	1♓	18♊
8	18♈	5♈	2♓	19♊
9	19♈	7♈	2♓	20♊
10	20♈	9♈	3♓	20♊
11	21♈	11♈	4♓	21♊
12	22♈	13♈	5♓	21♊
13	23♈	15♈	6♓	22♊
14	24♈	17♈	7♓	23♊
15	25♈	19♈	8♓	23♊
16	26♈	21♈	9♓	24♊
17	27♈	23♈	10♓	24♊
18	28♈	25♈	11♓	25♊
19	29♈	27♈	12♓	26♊
20	29♈	29♈	13♓	26♊
21	0♉	1♉	14♓	27♊
22	1♉	3♉	15♓	28♊
23	2♉	6♉	16♓	28♊
24	3♉	8♉	17♓	29♊
25	4♉	10♉	18♓	29♊
26	5♉	12♉	19♓	0♋
27	6♉	14♉	21♓	1♋
28	7♉	16♉	22♓	1♋
29	8♉	18♉	23♓	2♋
30	9♉	20♉	24♓	2♋

July

Day	☉	☿	♀	♂
1	9♋	19♊	4♊	11♌
2	10♋	19♊	5♊	11♌
3	11♋	20♊	6♊	12♌
4	12♋	21♊	7♊	12♌
5	13♋	21♊	9♊	13♌
6	13♋	22♊	10♊	14♌
7	14♋	23♊	11♊	14♌
8	15♋	24♊	12♊	15♌
9	16♋	25♊	13♊	16♌
10	17♋	27♊	14♊	16♌
11	18♋	28♊	16♊	17♌
12	19♋	29♊	17♊	17♌
13	20♋	1♋	18♊	18♌
14	21♋	2♋	19♊	19♌
15	22♋	3♋	20♊	19♌
16	23♋	5♋	22♊	20♌
17	24♋	7♋	23♊	21♌
18	25♋	8♋	24♊	21♌
19	26♋	10♋	25♊	22♌
20	27♋	12♋	26♊	22♌
21	28♋	14♋	28♊	23♌
22	29♋	16♋	29♊	24♌
23	0♌	18♋	0♋	24♌
24	1♌	20♋	1♋	25♌
25	2♌	22♋	2♋	26♌
26	3♌	24♋	4♋	26♌
27	4♌	26♋	5♋	27♌
28	4♌	28♋	6♋	27♌
29	5♌	0♌	7♋	28♌
30	6♌	2♌	8♋	29♌
31	7♌	4♌	10♋	29♌

October

Day	☉	☿	♀	♂
1	7♎	26♎	26♍	9♎
2	8♎	25♎	27♍	10♎
3	9♎	25♎	28♍	10♎
4	10♎	24♎	29♍	11♎
5	11♎	23♎	1♎	12♎
6	12♎	22♎	2♎	12♎
7	13♎	22♎	3♎	13♎
8	14♎	20♎	4♎	14♎
9	15♎	19♎	6♎	14♎
10	16♎	18♎	7♎	15♎
11	17♎	17♎	8♎	16♎
12	18♎	16♎	9♎	16♎
13	19♎	15♎	11♎	17♎
14	20♎	14♎	12♎	18♎
15	21♎	13♎	13♎	18♎
16	22♎	12♎	14♎	19♎
17	23♎	11♎	16♎	20♎
18	24♎	11♎	17♎	20♎
19	25♎	11♎	18♎	21♎
20	26♎	11♎	19♎	21♎
21	27♎	11♎	21♎	22♎
22	28♎	11♎	22♎	23♎
23	29♎	12♎	23♎	23♎
24	0♏	12♎	24♎	24♎
25	1♏	13♎	26♎	25♎
26	2♏	14♎	27♎	25♎
27	3♏	15♎	28♎	26♎
28	4♏	16♎	29♎	27♎
29	5♏	17♎	1♏	27♎
30	6♏	18♎	2♏	28♎
31	7♏	20♎	3♏	29♎

February

Day	☉	☿	♀	♂
1	12♒	27♒	14♒	11♉
2	13♒	27♒	14♒	11♉
3	14♒	27♒	13♒	12♉
4	15♒	26♒	12♒	12♉
5	16♒	25♒	12♒	13♉
6	17♒	25♒	11♒	13♉
7	18♒	24♒	11♒	14♉
8	19♒	23♒	10♒	14♉
9	20♒	21♒	9♒	15♉
10	21♒	20♒	9♒	16♉
11	22♒	19♒	8♒	16♉
12	23♒	18♒	8♒	17♉
13	24♒	17♒	8♒	17♉
14	25♒	16♒	7♒	18♉
15	26♒	15♒	7♒	18♉
16	27♒	14♒	7♒	19♉
17	28♒	13♒	6♒	19♉
18	29♒	13♒	6♒	20♉
19	0♓	12♒	6♒	21♉
20	1♓	12♒	6♒	21♉
21	2♓	12♒	6♒	22♉
22	3♓	12♒	6♒	22♉
23	4♓	12♒	6♒	23♉
24	5♓	12♒	6♒	24♉
25	6♓	12♒	6♒	24♉
26	7♓	12♒	6♒	25♉
27	8♓	13♒	6♒	25♉
28	9♓	13♒	6♒	26♉

May

Day	☉	☿	♀	♂
1	10♉	22♉	25♓	3♋
2	11♉	24♉	26♓	4♋
3	12♉	26♉	27♓	4♋
4	13♉	28♉	28♓	5♋
5	14♉	0♊	29♓	5♋
6	15♉	2♊	0♈	6♋
7	16♉	4♊	1♈	7♋
8	17♉	5♊	2♈	7♋
9	18♉	7♊	3♈	8♋
10	19♉	8♊	4♈	9♋
11	20♉	10♊	6♈	9♋
12	21♉	11♊	7♈	10♋
13	22♉	13♊	8♈	10♋
14	23♉	14♊	9♈	11♋
15	24♉	15♊	10♈	12♋
16	25♉	17♊	11♈	12♋
17	26♉	18♊	12♈	13♋
18	27♉	19♊	13♈	13♋
19	28♉	20♊	14♈	14♋
20	29♉	21♊	16♈	15♋
21	0♊	21♊	17♈	15♋
22	0♊	22♊	18♈	16♋
23	1♊	23♊	19♈	16♋
24	2♊	23♊	20♈	17♋
25	3♊	24♊	21♈	18♋
26	4♊	24♊	22♈	18♋
27	5♊	25♊	23♈	19♋
28	6♊	25♊	25♈	20♋
29	7♊	25♊	26♈	20♋
30	8♊	26♊	27♈	21♋
31	9♊	26♊	28♈	21♋

August

Day	☉	☿	♀	♂
1	8♌	6♌	11♋	0♍
2	9♌	8♌	12♋	1♍
3	10♌	11♌	13♋	1♍
4	11♌	13♌	14♋	2♍
5	12♌	15♌	16♋	2♍
6	13♌	17♌	17♋	3♍
7	14♌	19♌	18♋	4♍
8	15♌	21♌	19♋	4♍
9	16♌	23♌	20♋	5♍
10	17♌	25♌	22♋	6♍
11	18♌	26♌	23♋	6♍
12	19♌	28♌	24♋	7♍
13	20♌	0♍	25♋	7♍
14	21♌	2♍	26♋	8♍
15	22♌	4♍	28♋	9♍
16	23♌	6♍	29♋	9♍
17	24♌	7♍	0♌	10♍
18	25♌	9♍	1♌	11♍
19	26♌	11♍	3♌	11♍
20	27♌	13♍	4♌	12♍
21	28♌	14♍	5♌	13♍
22	28♌	16♍	6♌	13♍
23	29♌	18♍	7♌	14♍
24	0♍	19♍	9♌	14♍
25	1♍	21♍	10♌	15♍
26	2♍	22♍	11♌	16♍
27	3♍	24♍	12♌	16♍
28	4♍	25♍	14♌	17♍
29	5♍	27♍	15♌	18♍
30	6♍	28♍	16♌	18♍
31	7♍	0♎	17♌	19♍

November

Day	☉	☿	♀	♂
1	8♏	21♎	4♏	0♏
2	9♏	23♎	6♏	0♏
3	10♏	24♎	7♏	1♏
4	11♏	26♎	8♏	2♏
5	12♏	27♎	9♏	2♏
6	13♏	29♎	11♏	3♏
7	14♏	0♏	12♏	4♏
8	15♏	2♏	13♏	4♏
9	16♏	3♏	14♏	5♏
10	17♏	5♏	16♏	6♏
11	18♏	7♏	17♏	6♏
12	19♏	8♏	18♏	7♏
13	20♏	10♏	19♏	8♏
14	21♏	11♏	21♏	8♏
15	22♏	13♏	22♏	9♏
16	23♏	15♏	23♏	10♏
17	24♏	16♏	24♏	10♏
18	25♏	18♏	26♏	11♏
19	26♏	19♏	27♏	12♏
20	27♏	21♏	28♏	12♏
21	28♏	23♏	29♏	13♏
22	29♏	24♏	1♐	14♏
23	0♐	26♏	2♐	14♏
24	1♐	27♏	3♐	15♏
25	2♐	29♏	4♐	16♏
26	3♐	1♐	6♐	16♏
27	4♐	2♐	7♐	17♏
28	5♐	4♐	8♐	18♏
29	6♐	5♐	9♐	19♏
30	7♐	7♐	11♐	19♏

March

Day	☉	☿	♀	♂
1	10♓	14♒	6♒	26♉
2	11♓	14♒	6♒	27♉
3	12♓	15♒	7♒	28♉
4	13♓	16♒	7♒	28♉
5	14♓	17♒	7♒	29♉
6	15♓	18♒	8♒	29♉
7	16♓	19♒	8♒	0♊
8	17♓	20♒	9♒	1♊
9	18♓	21♒	9♒	1♊
10	19♓	22♒	10♒	2♊
11	20♓	23♒	10♒	2♊
12	21♓	24♒	11♒	3♊
13	22♓	25♒	11♒	3♊
14	23♓	26♒	12♒	4♊
15	24♓	28♒	12♒	5♊
16	25♓	29♒	13♒	5♊
17	26♓	0♓	14♒	6♊
18	27♓	2♓	14♒	6♊
19	28♓	3♓	15♒	7♊
20	29♓	4♓	16♒	8♊
21	0♈	6♓	16♒	8♊
22	1♈	7♓	17♒	9♊
23	2♈	9♓	18♒	9♊
24	3♈	10♓	19♒	10♊
25	4♈	12♓	19♒	11♊
26	5♈	13♓	20♒	11♊
27	6♈	15♓	21♒	12♊
28	7♈	16♓	22♒	12♊
29	8♈	18♓	23♒	13♊
30	9♈	20♓	23♒	14♊
31	10♈	21♓	24♒	14♊

June

Day	☉	☿	♀	♂
1	10♊	26♊	29♈	22♋
2	11♊	26♊	0♉	23♋
3	12♊	25♊	1♉	23♋
4	13♊	25♊	3♉	24♋
5	14♊	25♊	4♉	24♋
6	15♊	25♊	5♉	25♋
7	16♊	24♊	6♉	26♋
8	17♊	24♊	7♉	26♋
9	18♊	23♊	8♉	27♋
10	19♊	23♊	9♉	28♋
11	20♊	22♊	11♉	28♋
12	21♊	22♊	12♉	29♋
13	22♊	21♊	13♉	29♋
14	23♊	20♊	14♉	0♌
15	23♊	20♊	15♉	1♌
16	24♊	19♊	16♉	1♌
17	25♊	19♊	17♉	2♌
18	26♊	18♊	19♉	2♌
19	27♊	18♊	20♉	3♌
20	28♊	18♊	21♉	4♌
21	29♊	17♊	22♉	4♌
22	0♋	17♊	23♉	5♌
23	1♋	17♊	24♉	6♌
24	2♋	17♊	26♉	6♌
25	3♋	17♊	27♉	7♌
26	4♋	17♊	28♉	7♌
27	5♋	17♊	29♉	8♌
28	6♋	18♊	0♊	9♌
29	7♋	18♊	2♊	9♌
30	8♋	18♊	3♊	10♌

September

Day	☉	☿	♀	♂
1	8♍	1♎	18♌	20♍
2	9♍	3♎	20♌	20♍
3	10♍	4♎	21♌	21♍
4	11♍	5♎	22♌	21♍
5	12♍	7♎	23♌	22♍
6	13♍	8♎	25♌	23♍
7	14♍	9♎	26♌	23♍
8	15♍	10♎	27♌	24♍
9	16♍	12♎	28♌	25♍
10	17♍	13♎	0♍	25♍
11	18♍	14♎	1♍	26♍
12	19♍	15♎	2♍	27♍
13	20♍	16♎	3♍	27♍
14	21♍	17♎	4♍	28♍
15	22♍	18♎	6♍	29♍
16	23♍	19♎	7♍	29♍
17	24♍	20♎	8♍	0♎
18	25♍	21♎	9♍	1♎
19	26♍	22♎	11♍	1♎
20	27♍	23♎	12♍	2♎
21	28♍	23♎	13♍	2♎
22	29♍	24♎	14♍	3♎
23	0♎	24♎	16♍	4♎
24	1♎	25♎	17♍	4♎
25	1♎	25♎	18♍	5♎
26	2♎	26♎	19♍	6♎
27	3♎	26♎	21♍	6♎
28	4♎	26♎	22♍	7♎
29	5♎	26♎	23♍	8♎
30	6♎	26♎	24♍	8♎

December

Day	☉	☿	♀	♂
1	8♐	8♐	12♐	20♏
2	9♐	10♐	13♐	21♏
3	10♐	12♐	14♐	21♏
4	11♐	13♐	16♐	22♏
5	12♐	15♐	17♐	23♏
6	13♐	16♐	18♐	23♏
7	14♐	18♐	20♐	24♏
8	15♐	19♐	21♐	25♏
9	16♐	21♐	22♐	25♏
10	18♐	23♐	23♐	26♏
11	19♐	24♐	25♐	27♏
12	20♐	26♐	26♐	28♏
13	21♐	27♐	27♐	28♏
14	22♐	29♐	28♐	29♏
15	23♐	0♑	0♑	0♐
16	24♐	2♑	1♑	0♐
17	25♐	4♑	2♑	1♐
18	26♐	5♑	3♑	2♐
19	27♐	7♑	5♑	2♐
20	28♐	8♑	6♑	3♐
21	29♐	10♑	7♑	4♐
22	0♑	11♑	8♑	5♐
23	1♑	13♑	10♑	5♐
24	2♑	15♑	11♑	6♐
25	3♑	16♑	12♑	7♐
26	4♑	18♑	13♑	7♐
27	5♑	19♑	15♑	8♐
28	6♑	21♑	16♑	9♐
29	7♑	22♑	17♑	10♐
30	8♑	24♑	18♑	10♐
31	9♑	25♑	20♑	11♐

1943

Your Starway to Love

☉ =Sun ☿ = Mercury ♀ = Venus ♂ = Mars ♈ = Aries ♉ = Taurus ♊ = Gemini ♋ = Cancer

January

Day	☉	☿	♀	♂
1	10♑	27♑	21♑	12♐
2	11♑	28♑	22♑	12♐
3	12♑	0♒	23♑	13♐
4	13♑	1♒	25♑	14♐
5	14♑	3♒	26♑	14♐
6	15♑	4♒	27♑	15♐
7	16♑	5♒	28♑	16♐
8	17♑	6♒	0♒	17♐
9	18♑	7♒	1♒	17♐
10	19♑	8♒	2♒	18♐
11	20♑	9♒	4♒	19♐
12	21♑	10♒	5♒	19♐
13	22♑	10♒	6♒	20♐
14	23♑	11♒	7♒	21♐
15	24♑	11♒	9♒	22♐
16	25♑	11♒	10♒	22♐
17	26♑	11♒	11♒	23♐
18	27♑	10♒	12♒	24♐
19	28♑	10♒	14♒	25♐
20	29♑	9♒	15♒	25♐
21	0♒	8♒	16♒	26♐
22	1♒	7♒	17♒	27♐
23	2♒	6♒	19♒	27♐
24	3♒	5♒	20♒	28♐
25	4♒	3♒	21♒	29♐
26	5♒	2♒	22♒	0♑
27	6♒	1♒	24♒	0♑
28	7♒	0♒	25♒	1♑
29	8♒	29♑	26♒	2♑
30	9♒	28♑	27♒	2♑
31	10♒	27♑	29♒	3♑

April

Day	☉	☿	♀	♂
1	11♈	7♈	12♉	18♒
2	12♈	9♈	14♉	19♒
3	13♈	11♈	15♉	19♒
4	14♈	13♈	16♉	20♒
5	15♈	15♈	17♉	21♒
6	16♈	18♈	18♉	22♒
7	17♈	20♈	20♉	22♒
8	17♈	22♈	21♉	23♒
9	18♈	24♈	22♉	24♒
10	19♈	26♈	23♉	25♒
11	20♈	28♈	24♉	25♒
12	21♈	0♉	26♉	26♒
13	22♈	2♉	27♉	27♒
14	23♈	4♉	28♉	28♒
15	24♈	6♉	29♉	28♒
16	25♈	8♉	0♊	29♒
17	26♈	10♉	2♊	0♓
18	27♈	12♉	3♊	1♓
19	28♈	14♉	4♊	1♓
20	29♈	15♉	5♊	2♓
21	0♉	17♉	6♊	3♓
22	1♉	19♉	8♊	4♓
23	2♉	20♉	9♊	4♓
24	3♉	22♉	10♊	5♓
25	4♉	23♉	11♊	6♓
26	5♉	25♉	12♊	7♓
27	6♉	26♉	13♊	7♓
28	7♉	27♉	15♊	8♓
29	8♉	28♉	16♊	9♓
30	9♉	0♊	17♊	10♓

July

Day	☉	☿	♀	♂
1	8♋	21♊	24♌	25♈
2	9♋	22♊	25♌	26♈
3	10♋	24♊	26♌	27♈
4	11♋	26♊	27♌	27♈
5	12♋	28♊	28♌	28♈
6	13♋	0♋	28♌	29♈
7	14♋	2♋	29♌	29♈
8	15♋	4♋	0♍	0♉
9	16♋	6♋	1♍	1♉
10	17♋	8♋	2♍	2♉
11	18♋	10♋	3♍	2♉
12	19♋	12♋	4♍	3♉
13	20♋	14♋	4♍	4♉
14	21♋	16♋	5♍	4♉
15	22♋	18♋	6♍	5♉
16	23♋	20♋	7♍	6♉
17	24♋	23♋	8♍	6♉
18	25♋	25♋	8♍	7♉
19	26♋	27♋	9♍	8♉
20	27♋	29♋	10♍	8♉
21	28♋	1♌	10♍	9♉
22	29♋	3♌	11♍	10♉
23	29♋	5♌	12♍	10♉
24	0♌	7♌	12♍	11♉
25	1♌	9♌	13♍	12♉
26	2♌	11♌	14♍	12♉
27	3♌	13♌	14♍	13♉
28	4♌	15♌	15♍	14♉
29	5♌	17♌	15♍	14♉
30	6♌	19♌	16♍	15♉
31	7♌	21♌	16♍	16♉

October

Day	☉	☿	♀	♂
1	7♎	25♍	5♍	18♊
2	8♎	25♍	5♍	18♊
3	9♎	25♍	5♍	18♊
4	10♎	25♍	5♍	18♊
5	11♎	25♍	5♍	19♊
6	12♎	25♍	6♍	19♊
7	13♎	26♍	6♍	19♊
8	14♎	26♍	6♍	20♊
9	15♎	27♍	7♍	20♊
10	16♎	28♍	7♍	20♊
11	17♎	29♍	8♍	20♊
12	18♎	0♎	8♍	20♊
13	19♎	2♎	9♍	21♊
14	20♎	3♎	9♍	21♊
15	21♎	4♎	10♍	21♊
16	22♎	6♎	10♍	21♊
17	23♎	7♎	11♍	21♊
18	24♎	9♎	12♍	22♊
19	25♎	10♎	12♍	22♊
20	26♎	12♎	13♍	22♊
21	27♎	14♎	14♍	22♊
22	28♎	15♎	14♍	22♊
23	29♎	17♎	15♍	22♊
24	0♏	19♎	16♍	22♊
25	1♏	20♎	17♍	22♊
26	2♏	22♎	17♍	22♊
27	3♏	24♎	18♍	22♊
28	4♏	25♎	19♍	22♊
29	5♏	27♎	20♍	22♊
30	6♏	29♎	21♍	22♊
31	7♏	0♏	21♍	22♊

February

Day	☉	☿	♀	♂
1	11♒	26♑	0♓	4♑
2	12♒	26♑	1♓	5♑
3	13♒	25♑	2♓	5♑
4	15♒	25♑	4♓	6♑
5	16♒	25♑	5♓	7♑
6	17♒	25♑	6♓	8♑
7	18♒	25♑	7♓	8♑
8	19♒	25♑	9♓	9♑
9	20♒	26♑	10♓	10♑
10	21♒	26♑	11♓	11♑
11	22♒	27♑	12♓	11♑
12	23♒	27♑	14♓	12♑
13	24♒	28♑	15♓	13♑
14	25♒	29♑	16♓	13♑
15	26♒	29♑	17♓	14♑
16	27♒	0♒	18♓	15♑
17	28♒	1♒	20♓	16♑
18	29♒	2♒	21♓	16♑
19	0♓	3♒	22♓	17♑
20	1♓	4♒	23♓	18♑
21	2♓	5♒	25♓	19♑
22	3♓	7♒	26♓	19♑
23	4♓	8♒	27♓	20♑
24	5♓	9♒	28♓	21♑
25	6♓	10♒	0♈	22♑
26	7♓	11♒	1♈	22♑
27	8♓	13♒	2♈	23♑
28	9♓	14♒	3♈	24♑

May

Day	☉	☿	♀	♂
1	10♉	1♊	18♊	10♓
2	11♉	1♊	19♊	11♓
3	12♉	2♊	20♊	12♓
4	13♉	3♊	22♊	13♓
5	14♉	4♊	23♊	13♓
6	15♉	4♊	24♊	14♓
7	16♉	5♊	25♊	15♓
8	17♉	5♊	26♊	16♓
9	18♉	5♊	27♊	16♓
10	19♉	6♊	29♊	17♓
11	20♉	6♊	0♋	18♓
12	21♉	6♊	1♋	19♓
13	22♉	6♊	2♋	19♓
14	23♉	6♊	3♋	20♓
15	24♉	5♊	4♋	21♓
16	24♉	5♊	5♋	22♓
17	25♉	5♊	7♋	22♓
18	26♉	4♊	8♋	23♓
19	27♉	4♊	9♋	24♓
20	28♉	3♊	10♋	25♓
21	29♉	3♊	11♋	25♓
22	0♊	2♊	12♋	26♓
23	1♊	2♊	13♋	27♓
24	2♊	1♊	14♋	28♓
25	3♊	1♊	15♋	28♓
26	4♊	0♊	17♋	29♓
27	5♊	0♊	18♋	0♈
28	6♊	29♉	19♋	1♈
29	7♊	29♉	20♋	1♈
30	8♊	28♉	21♋	2♈
31	9♊	28♉	22♋	3♈

August

Day	☉	☿	♀	♂
1	8♌	23♌	17♍	16♉
2	9♌	24♌	17♍	17♉
3	10♌	26♌	18♍	17♉
4	11♌	28♌	18♍	18♉
5	12♌	0♍	19♍	19♉
6	13♌	1♍	19♍	19♉
7	14♌	3♍	19♍	20♉
8	15♌	5♍	20♍	21♉
9	16♌	6♍	20♍	21♉
10	17♌	8♍	20♍	22♉
11	18♌	9♍	20♍	22♉
12	19♌	11♍	20♍	23♉
13	20♌	12♍	20♍	24♉
14	21♌	14♍	21♍	24♉
15	22♌	15♍	21♍	25♉
16	22♌	17♍	21♍	25♉
17	23♌	18♍	21♍	26♉
18	24♌	19♍	20♍	27♉
19	25♌	21♍	20♍	27♉
20	26♌	22♍	20♍	28♉
21	27♌	23♍	20♍	28♉
22	28♌	25♍	20♍	29♉
23	29♌	26♍	19♍	0♊
24	0♍	27♍	19♍	0♊
25	1♍	28♍	19♍	1♊
26	2♍	29♍	18♍	1♊
27	3♍	0♎	18♍	2♊
28	4♍	1♎	18♍	2♊
29	5♍	2♎	17♍	3♊
30	6♍	3♎	17♍	3♊
31	7♍	4♎	16♍	4♊

November

Day	☉	☿	♀	♂
1	8♏	2♏	22♍	22♊
2	9♏	4♏	23♍	22♊
3	10♏	5♏	24♍	22♊
4	11♏	7♏	25♍	22♊
5	12♏	9♏	26♍	22♊
6	13♏	10♏	27♍	22♊
7	14♏	12♏	28♍	21♊
8	15♏	14♏	29♍	21♊
9	16♏	15♏	29♍	21♊
10	17♏	17♏	0♎	21♊
11	18♏	18♏	1♎	21♊
12	19♏	20♏	2♎	21♊
13	20♏	22♏	3♎	20♊
14	21♏	23♏	4♎	20♊
15	22♏	25♏	5♎	20♊
16	23♏	26♏	6♎	20♊
17	24♏	28♏	7♎	19♊
18	25♏	29♏	8♎	19♊
19	26♏	1♐	9♎	19♊
20	27♏	3♐	10♎	18♊
21	28♏	4♐	11♎	18♊
22	29♏	6♐	12♎	18♊
23	0♐	7♐	14♎	17♊
24	1♐	9♐	15♎	17♊
25	2♐	10♐	16♎	17♊
26	3♐	12♐	17♎	16♊
27	4♐	13♐	18♎	16♊
28	5♐	15♐	19♎	16♊
29	6♐	16♐	20♎	15♊
30	7♐	18♐	21♎	15♊

March

Day	☉	☿	♀	♂
1	10♓	15♒	5♈	25♑
2	11♓	17♒	6♈	25♑
3	12♓	18♒	7♈	26♑
4	13♓	20♒	8♈	27♑
5	14♓	21♒	10♈	28♑
6	15♓	22♒	11♈	28♑
7	16♓	24♒	12♈	29♑
8	17♓	25♒	13♈	0♒
9	18♓	27♒	14♈	1♒
10	19♓	28♒	16♈	1♒
11	20♓	0♓	17♈	2♒
12	21♓	2♓	18♈	3♒
13	22♓	3♓	19♈	3♒
14	23♓	5♓	21♈	4♒
15	24♓	6♓	22♈	5♒
16	25♓	8♓	23♈	6♒
17	26♓	10♓	24♈	6♒
18	27♓	11♓	25♈	7♒
19	28♓	13♓	27♈	8♒
20	29♓	15♓	28♈	9♒
21	0♈	17♓	29♈	9♒
22	1♈	18♓	0♉	10♒
23	2♈	20♓	2♉	11♒
24	3♈	22♓	3♉	12♒
25	4♈	24♓	4♉	12♒
26	5♈	26♓	5♉	13♒
27	6♈	28♓	6♉	14♒
28	7♈	29♓	8♉	15♒
29	8♈	1♈	9♉	16♒
30	9♈	3♈	10♉	16♒
31	10♈	5♈	11♉	17♒

June

Day	☉	☿	♀	♂
1	10♊	28♉	23♋	4♈
2	11♊	27♉	24♋	4♈
3	12♊	27♉	25♋	5♈
4	13♊	27♉	26♋	6♈
5	14♊	27♉	28♋	7♈
6	15♊	27♉	29♋	7♈
7	16♊	27♉	0♌	8♈
8	17♊	27♉	1♌	9♈
9	17♊	28♉	2♌	9♈
10	18♊	28♉	3♌	10♈
11	19♊	28♉	4♌	11♈
12	20♊	29♉	5♌	12♈
13	21♊	29♉	6♌	12♈
14	22♊	0♊	7♌	13♈
15	23♊	1♊	8♌	14♈
16	24♊	2♊	9♌	15♈
17	25♊	2♊	10♌	15♈
18	26♊	3♊	11♌	16♈
19	27♊	4♊	12♌	17♈
20	28♊	5♊	13♌	17♈
21	29♊	6♊	14♌	18♈
22	0♋	8♊	15♌	19♈
23	1♋	9♊	16♌	20♈
24	2♋	10♊	17♌	20♈
25	3♋	11♊	18♌	21♈
26	4♋	13♊	19♌	22♈
27	5♋	14♊	20♌	22♈
28	6♋	16♊	21♌	23♈
29	7♋	17♊	22♌	24♈
30	8♋	19♊	23♌	25♈

September

Day	☉	☿	♀	♂
1	8♍	5♎	15♍	4♊
2	9♍	6♎	15♍	5♊
3	10♍	6♎	14♍	6♊
4	11♍	7♎	14♍	6♊
5	12♍	8♎	13♍	7♊
6	13♍	8♎	12♍	7♊
7	14♍	9♎	12♍	8♊
8	15♍	9♎	11♍	8♊
9	16♍	9♎	11♍	9♊
10	17♍	9♎	10♍	9♊
11	18♍	9♎	9♍	9♊
12	19♍	9♎	9♍	10♊
13	20♍	9♎	8♍	10♊
14	21♍	9♎	8♍	11♊
15	21♍	9♎	7♍	11♊
16	22♍	8♎	7♍	12♊
17	23♍	8♎	6♍	12♊
18	24♍	7♎	6♍	13♊
19	25♍	6♎	6♍	13♊
20	26♍	5♎	5♍	13♊
21	27♍	4♎	5♍	14♊
22	28♍	3♎	5♍	14♊
23	29♍	2♎	5♍	15♊
24	0♎	1♎	5♍	15♊
25	1♎	0♎	4♍	15♊
26	2♎	29♍	4♍	16♊
27	3♎	28♍	4♍	16♊
28	4♎	27♍	4♍	17♊
29	5♎	26♍	4♍	17♊
30	6♎	26♍	5♍	17♊

December

Day	☉	☿	♀	♂
1	8♐	20♐	22♎	15♊
2	9♐	21♐	23♎	14♊
3	10♐	23♐	24♎	14♊
4	11♐	24♐	25♎	13♊
5	12♐	26♐	27♎	13♊
6	13♐	27♐	28♎	13♊
7	14♐	29♐	29♎	12♊
8	15♐	0♑	0♏	12♊
9	16♐	2♑	1♏	11♊
10	17♐	3♑	2♏	11♊
11	18♐	5♑	3♏	11♊
12	19♐	6♑	4♏	10♊
13	20♐	8♑	6♏	10♊
14	21♐	9♑	7♏	10♊
15	22♐	10♑	8♏	9♊
16	23♐	12♑	9♏	9♊
17	24♐	13♑	10♏	9♊
18	25♐	15♑	11♏	8♊
19	26♐	16♑	12♏	8♊
20	27♐	17♑	14♏	8♊
21	28♐	18♑	15♏	8♊
22	29♐	19♑	16♏	7♊
23	0♑	20♑	17♏	7♊
24	2♑	21♑	18♏	7♊
25	3♑	22♑	19♏	7♊
26	4♑	23♑	21♏	6♊
27	5♑	24♑	22♏	6♊
28	6♑	24♑	23♏	6♊
29	7♑	25♑	24♏	6♊
30	8♑	25♑	25♏	6♊
31	9♑	25♑	26♏	6♊

1944

Planetary Positions

♌ = Leo ♍ = Virgo ♎ = Libra ♏ = Scorpio ♐ = Sagittarius ♑ = Capricorn ♒ = Aquarius ♓ = Pisces

January

Day	☉	☿	♀	♂
1	10♑	25♑	28♏	5♊
2	11♑	24♑	29♏	5♊
3	12♑	24♑	0♐	5♊
4	13♑	23♑	1♐	5♊
5	14♑	22♑	2♐	5♊
6	15♑	21♑	4♐	5♊
7	16♑	20♑	5♐	5♊
8	17♑	18♑	6♐	5♊
9	18♑	17♑	7♐	5♊
10	19♑	16♑	8♐	5♊
11	20♑	14♑	10♐	5♊
12	21♑	13♑	11♐	5♊
13	22♑	12♑	12♐	5♊
14	23♑	11♑	13♐	5♊
15	24♑	10♑	14♐	5♊
16	25♑	10♑	16♐	5♊
17	26♑	9♑	17♐	5♊
18	27♑	9♑	18♐	5♊
19	28♑	9♑	19♐	5♊
20	29♑	9♑	20♐	5♊
21	0♒	9♑	22♐	6♊
22	1♒	9♑	23♐	6♊
23	2♒	9♑	24♐	6♊
24	3♒	10♑	25♐	6♊
25	4♒	10♑	26♐	6♊
26	5♒	11♑	28♐	6♊
27	6♒	12♑	29♐	7♊
28	7♒	12♑	0♑	7♊
29	8♒	13♑	1♑	7♊
30	9♒	14♑	3♑	7♊
31	10♒	15♑	4♑	7♊

February

Day	☉	☿	♀	♂
1	11♒	16♑	5♑	8♊
2	12♒	17♑	6♑	8♊
3	13♒	18♑	7♑	8♊
4	14♒	19♑	9♑	8♊
5	15♒	21♑	10♑	9♊
6	16♒	22♑	11♑	9♊
7	17♒	23♑	12♑	9♊
8	18♒	24♑	13♑	10♊
9	19♒	26♑	15♑	10♊
10	20♒	27♑	16♑	10♊
11	21♒	28♑	17♑	10♊
12	22♒	29♑	18♑	11♊
13	23♒	1♒	20♑	11♊
14	24♒	2♒	21♑	11♊
15	25♒	4♒	22♑	12♊
16	26♒	5♒	23♑	12♊
17	27♒	6♒	25♑	12♊
18	28♒	8♒	26♑	13♊
19	29♒	9♒	27♑	13♊
20	0♓	11♒	28♑	13♊
21	1♓	12♒	29♑	14♊
22	2♓	14♒	1♒	14♊
23	3♓	16♒	2♒	15♊
24	4♓	17♒	3♒	15♊
25	5♓	19♒	4♒	15♊
26	6♓	20♒	6♒	16♊
27	7♓	22♒	7♒	16♊
28	8♓	23♒	8♒	17♊
29	10♓	25♒	9♒	17♊

March

Day	☉	☿	♀	♂
1	11♓	27♒	10♒	17♊
2	12♓	28♒	12♒	18♊
3	13♓	0♓	13♒	18♊
4	14♓	2♓	14♒	19♊
5	15♓	4♓	15♒	19♊
6	16♓	5♓	17♒	20♊
7	17♓	7♓	18♒	20♊
8	18♓	9♓	19♒	20♊
9	19♓	11♓	20♒	21♊
10	20♓	13♓	22♒	21♊
11	21♓	14♓	23♒	22♊
12	22♓	16♓	24♒	22♊
13	23♓	18♓	25♒	23♊
14	24♓	20♓	26♒	23♊
15	24♓	22♓	28♒	24♊
16	25♓	24♓	29♒	24♊
17	26♓	26♓	0♓	25♊
18	27♓	28♓	1♓	25♊
19	28♓	0♈	3♓	25♊
20	29♓	2♈	4♓	26♊
21	0♈	4♈	5♓	26♊
22	1♈	6♈	6♓	27♊
23	2♈	8♈	7♓	27♊
24	3♈	10♈	9♓	28♊
25	4♈	12♈	10♓	28♊
26	5♈	14♈	11♓	29♊
27	6♈	16♈	12♓	29♊
28	7♈	18♈	14♓	0♋
29	8♈	20♈	15♓	0♋
30	9♈	22♈	16♓	1♋
31	10♈	24♈	17♓	1♋

April

Day	☉	☿	♀	♂
1	11♈	26♈	19♓	2♋
2	12♈	27♈	20♓	2♋
3	13♈	29♈	21♓	3♋
4	14♈	1♉	22♓	3♋
5	15♈	2♉	23♓	4♋
6	16♈	4♉	25♓	4♋
7	17♈	5♉	26♓	5♋
8	18♈	7♉	27♓	6♋
9	19♈	8♉	28♓	6♋
10	20♈	9♉	0♈	7♋
11	21♈	11♉	1♈	7♋
12	22♈	12♉	2♈	8♋
13	23♈	13♉	3♈	8♋
14	24♈	13♉	5♈	9♋
15	25♈	14♉	6♈	9♋
16	26♈	15♉	7♈	10♋
17	27♈	15♉	8♈	10♋
18	28♈	16♉	9♈	11♋
19	29♈	16♉	11♈	11♋
20	0♉	16♉	12♈	12♋
21	1♉	16♉	13♈	12♋
22	2♉	16♉	14♈	13♋
23	3♉	16♉	16♈	14♋
24	4♉	16♉	17♈	14♋
25	5♉	16♉	18♈	15♋
26	6♉	16♉	19♈	15♋
27	7♉	15♉	21♈	16♋
28	8♉	15♉	22♈	16♋
29	9♉	14♉	23♈	17♋
30	10♉	14♉	24♈	17♋

May

Day	☉	☿	♀	♂
1	11♉	13♉	25♈	18♋
2	12♉	12♉	27♈	18♋
3	13♉	12♉	28♈	19♋
4	14♉	11♉	29♈	20♋
5	15♉	11♉	0♉	20♋
6	16♉	10♉	2♉	21♋
7	17♉	9♉	3♉	21♋
8	17♉	9♉	4♉	22♋
9	18♉	8♉	5♉	22♋
10	19♉	8♉	6♉	23♋
11	20♉	8♉	8♉	24♋
12	21♉	7♉	9♉	24♋
13	22♉	7♉	10♉	25♋
14	23♉	7♉	11♉	25♋
15	24♉	7♉	13♉	26♋
16	25♉	7♉	14♉	26♋
17	26♉	7♉	15♉	27♋
18	27♉	7♉	16♉	27♋
19	28♉	7♉	18♉	28♋
20	29♉	8♉	19♉	29♋
21	0♊	8♉	20♉	29♋
22	1♊	8♉	21♉	0♌
23	2♊	9♉	22♉	0♌
24	3♊	9♉	24♉	1♌
25	4♊	10♉	25♉	2♌
26	5♊	11♉	26♉	2♌
27	6♊	12♉	27♉	3♌
28	7♊	12♉	29♉	3♌
29	8♊	13♉	0♊	4♌
30	9♊	14♉	1♊	4♌
31	10♊	15♉	2♊	5♌

June

Day	☉	☿	♀	♂
1	11♊	16♉	3♊	6♌
2	12♊	17♉	5♊	6♌
3	12♊	18♉	6♊	7♌
4	13♊	20♉	7♊	7♌
5	14♊	21♉	8♊	8♌
6	15♊	22♉	10♊	8♌
7	16♊	24♉	11♊	9♌
8	17♊	25♉	12♊	10♌
9	18♊	27♉	13♊	10♌
10	19♊	28♉	15♊	11♌
11	20♊	0♊	16♊	11♌
12	21♊	1♊	17♊	12♌
13	22♊	3♊	18♊	13♌
14	23♊	4♊	19♊	13♌
15	24♊	6♊	21♊	14♌
16	25♊	8♊	22♊	14♌
17	26♊	10♊	23♊	15♌
18	27♊	12♊	24♊	16♌
19	28♊	14♊	26♊	16♌
20	29♊	16♊	27♊	17♌
21	0♋	18♊	28♊	17♌
22	1♋	20♊	29♊	18♌
23	2♋	22♊	1♋	19♌
24	3♋	24♊	2♋	19♌
25	3♋	26♊	3♋	20♌
26	4♋	28♊	4♋	20♌
27	5♋	0♋	5♋	21♌
28	6♋	2♋	7♋	22♌
29	7♋	4♋	8♋	22♌
30	8♋	7♋	9♋	23♌

July

Day	☉	☿	♀	♂
1	9♋	9♋	10♋	23♌
2	10♋	11♋	12♋	24♌
3	11♋	13♋	13♋	25♌
4	12♋	15♋	14♋	25♌
5	13♋	17♋	15♋	26♌
6	14♋	20♋	16♋	26♌
7	15♋	22♋	18♋	27♌
8	16♋	24♋	19♋	28♌
9	17♋	26♋	20♋	28♌
10	18♋	28♋	21♋	29♌
11	19♋	0♌	23♋	29♌
12	20♋	2♌	24♋	0♍
13	21♋	4♌	25♋	1♍
14	22♋	6♌	26♋	1♍
15	23♋	7♌	28♋	2♍
16	24♋	9♌	29♋	3♍
17	24♋	11♌	0♌	3♍
18	25♋	13♌	1♌	4♍
19	26♋	15♌	2♌	4♍
20	27♋	16♌	4♌	5♍
21	28♋	18♌	5♌	6♍
22	29♋	20♌	6♌	6♍
23	0♌	21♌	7♌	7♍
24	1♌	23♌	9♌	7♍
25	2♌	24♌	10♌	8♍
26	3♌	26♌	11♌	9♍
27	4♌	27♌	12♌	9♍
28	5♌	29♌	14♌	10♍
29	6♌	0♍	15♌	11♍
30	7♌	2♍	16♌	11♍
31	8♌	3♍	17♌	12♍

August

Day	☉	☿	♀	♂
1	9♌	4♍	18♌	12♍
2	10♌	6♍	20♌	13♍
3	11♌	7♍	21♌	14♍
4	12♌	8♍	22♌	14♍
5	13♌	9♍	23♌	15♍
6	14♌	11♍	25♌	16♍
7	15♌	12♍	26♌	16♍
8	16♌	13♍	27♌	17♍
9	16♌	14♍	28♌	17♍
10	17♌	15♍	0♍	18♍
11	18♌	16♍	1♍	19♍
12	19♌	17♍	2♍	19♍
13	20♌	17♍	3♍	20♍
14	21♌	18♍	5♍	21♍
15	22♌	19♍	6♍	21♍
16	23♌	20♍	7♍	22♍
17	24♌	20♍	8♍	22♍
18	25♌	21♍	9♍	23♍
19	26♌	21♍	11♍	24♍
20	27♌	22♍	12♍	24♍
21	28♌	22♍	13♍	25♍
22	29♌	22♍	14♍	26♍
23	0♍	22♍	16♍	26♍
24	1♍	22♍	17♍	27♍
25	2♍	22♍	18♍	28♍
26	3♍	22♍	19♍	28♍
27	4♍	22♍	21♍	29♍
28	5♍	22♍	22♍	29♍
29	6♍	21♍	23♍	0♎
30	7♍	21♍	24♍	1♎
31	8♍	20♍	25♍	1♎

September

Day	☉	☿	♀	♂
1	9♍	19♍	27♍	2♎
2	10♍	19♍	28♍	3♎
3	11♍	18♍	29♍	3♎
4	12♍	17♍	0♎	4♎
5	12♍	16♍	2♎	5♎
6	13♍	15♍	3♎	5♎
7	14♍	14♍	4♎	6♎
8	15♍	13♍	5♎	7♎
9	16♍	12♍	7♎	7♎
10	17♍	11♍	8♎	8♎
11	18♍	10♍	9♎	9♎
12	19♍	10♍	10♎	9♎
13	20♍	9♍	11♎	10♎
14	21♍	9♍	13♎	10♎
15	22♍	9♍	14♎	11♎
16	23♍	9♍	15♎	12♎
17	24♍	9♍	16♎	12♎
18	25♍	9♍	18♎	13♎
19	26♍	9♍	19♎	14♎
20	27♍	10♍	20♎	14♎
21	28♍	10♍	21♎	15♎
22	29♍	11♍	23♎	16♎
23	0♎	12♍	24♎	16♎
24	1♎	13♍	25♎	17♎
25	2♎	14♍	26♎	18♎
26	3♎	16♍	27♎	18♎
27	4♎	17♍	29♎	19♎
28	5♎	19♍	0♏	20♎
29	6♎	20♍	1♏	20♎
30	7♎	22♍	2♏	21♎

October

Day	☉	☿	♀	♂
1	8♎	23♍	4♏	22♎
2	9♎	25♍	5♏	22♎
3	10♎	27♍	6♏	23♎
4	11♎	28♍	7♏	24♎
5	12♎	0♎	9♏	24♎
6	13♎	2♎	10♏	25♎
7	14♎	4♎	11♏	26♎
8	15♎	5♎	12♏	26♎
9	16♎	7♎	13♏	27♎
10	17♎	9♎	15♏	28♎
11	18♎	11♎	16♏	28♎
12	19♎	12♎	17♏	29♎
13	20♎	14♎	18♏	0♏
14	21♎	16♎	20♏	0♏
15	22♎	18♎	21♏	1♏
16	23♎	19♎	22♏	2♏
17	24♎	21♎	23♏	3♏
18	25♎	23♎	24♏	3♏
19	26♎	25♎	26♏	4♏
20	27♎	26♎	27♏	5♏
21	28♎	28♎	28♏	5♏
22	29♎	0♏	29♏	6♏
23	0♏	1♏	1♐	7♏
24	1♏	3♏	2♐	7♏
25	2♏	4♏	3♐	8♏
26	3♏	6♏	4♐	9♏
27	4♏	8♏	5♐	9♏
28	5♏	9♏	7♐	10♏
29	6♏	11♏	8♐	11♏
30	7♏	13♏	9♐	11♏
31	8♏	14♏	10♐	12♏

November

Day	☉	☿	♀	♂
1	9♏	16♏	12♐	13♏
2	10♏	17♏	13♐	14♏
3	11♏	19♏	14♐	14♏
4	12♏	20♏	15♐	15♏
5	13♏	22♏	16♐	16♏
6	14♏	23♏	18♐	16♏
7	15♏	25♏	19♐	17♏
8	16♏	27♏	20♐	18♏
9	17♏	28♏	21♐	18♏
10	18♏	0♐	23♐	19♏
11	19♏	1♐	24♐	20♏
12	20♏	3♐	25♐	20♏
13	21♏	4♐	26♐	21♏
14	22♏	6♐	27♐	22♏
15	23♏	7♐	29♐	23♏
16	24♏	9♐	0♑	23♏
17	25♏	10♐	1♑	24♏
18	26♏	12♐	2♑	25♏
19	27♏	13♐	4♑	25♏
20	28♏	14♐	5♑	26♏
21	29♏	16♐	6♑	27♏
22	0♐	17♐	7♑	28♏
23	1♐	19♐	8♑	28♏
24	2♐	20♐	10♑	29♏
25	3♐	22♐	11♑	0♐
26	4♐	23♐	12♑	0♐
27	5♐	24♐	13♑	1♐
28	6♐	26♐	14♑	2♐
29	7♐	27♐	16♑	3♐
30	8♐	28♐	17♑	3♐

December

Day	☉	☿	♀	♂
1	9♐	29♐	18♑	4♐
2	10♐	1♑	19♑	5♐
3	11♐	2♑	20♑	5♐
4	12♐	3♑	22♑	6♐
5	13♐	4♑	23♑	7♐
6	14♐	5♑	24♑	8♐
7	15♐	6♑	25♑	8♐
8	16♐	7♑	26♑	9♐
9	17♐	7♑	28♑	10♐
10	18♐	8♑	29♑	10♐
11	19♐	8♑	0♒	11♐
12	20♐	9♑	1♒	12♐
13	21♐	9♑	2♒	13♐
14	22♐	9♑	4♒	13♐
15	23♐	9♑	5♒	14♐
16	24♐	8♑	6♒	15♐
17	25♐	8♑	7♒	16♐
18	26♐	7♑	8♒	16♐
19	27♐	6♑	10♒	17♐
20	28♐	5♑	11♒	18♐
21	29♐	4♑	12♒	18♐
22	0♑	2♑	13♒	19♐
23	1♑	1♑	14♒	20♐
24	2♑	0♑	15♒	21♐
25	3♑	28♐	17♒	21♐
26	4♑	27♐	18♒	22♐
27	5♑	26♐	19♒	23♐
28	6♑	25♐	20♒	24♐
29	7♑	24♐	21♒	24♐
30	8♑	24♐	22♒	25♐
31	9♑	23♐	24♒	26♐

1945

Your Starway to Love

☉ =Sun ☿ = Mercury ♀ = Venus ♂ = Mars ♈ = Aries ♉ = Taurus ♊ = Gemini ♋ = Cancer

January

Day	☉	☿	♀	♂
1	10♑	23♐	25♒	27♐
2	11♑	23♐	26♒	27♐
3	12♑	23♐	27♒	28♐
4	13♑	23♐	28♒	29♐
5	15♑	23♐	29♒	0♑
6	16♑	24♐	0♓	0♑
7	17♑	24♐	2♓	1♑
8	18♑	25♐	3♓	2♑
9	19♑	25♐	4♓	3♑
10	20♑	26♐	5♓	3♑
11	21♑	27♐	6♓	4♑
12	22♑	28♐	7♓	5♑
13	23♑	29♐	8♓	6♑
14	24♑	0♑	9♓	6♑
15	25♑	1♑	11♓	7♑
16	26♑	2♑	12♓	8♑
17	27♑	3♑	13♓	9♑
18	28♑	5♑	14♓	9♑
19	29♑	6♑	15♓	10♑
20	0♒	7♑	16♓	11♑
21	1♒	8♑	17♓	12♑
22	2♒	10♑	18♓	12♑
23	3♒	11♑	19♓	13♑
24	4♒	12♑	20♓	14♑
25	5♒	14♑	22♓	15♑
26	6♒	15♑	23♓	15♑
27	7♒	16♑	24♓	16♑
28	8♒	18♑	25♓	17♑
29	9♒	19♑	26♓	18♑
30	10♒	21♑	27♓	18♑
31	11♒	22♑	28♓	19♑

February

Day	☉	☿	♀	♂
1	12♒	24♑	29♓	20♑
2	13♒	25♑	0♈	21♑
3	14♒	27♑	1♈	21♑
4	15♒	28♑	2♈	22♑
5	16♒	0♒	3♈	23♑
6	17♒	1♒	4♈	24♑
7	18♒	3♒	5♈	24♑
8	19♒	4♒	6♈	25♑
9	20♒	6♒	7♈	26♑
10	21♒	8♒	8♈	27♑
11	22♒	9♒	9♈	28♑
12	23♒	11♒	10♈	28♑
13	24♒	12♒	11♈	29♑
14	25♒	14♒	12♈	0♒
15	26♒	16♒	12♈	1♒
16	27♒	17♒	13♈	1♒
17	28♒	19♒	14♈	2♒
18	29♒	21♒	15♈	3♒
19	0♓	22♒	16♈	4♒
20	1♓	24♒	17♈	4♒
21	2♓	26♒	18♈	5♒
22	3♓	28♒	18♈	6♒
23	4♓	0♓	19♈	7♒
24	5♓	1♓	20♈	8♒
25	6♓	3♓	21♈	8♒
26	7♓	5♓	22♈	9♒
27	8♓	7♓	22♈	10♒
28	9♓	9♓	23♈	11♒

March

Day	☉	☿	♀	♂
1	10♓	11♓	24♈	11♒
2	11♓	12♓	25♈	12♒
3	12♓	14♓	25♈	13♒
4	13♓	16♓	26♈	14♒
5	14♓	18♓	27♈	15♒
6	15♓	20♓	27♈	15♒
7	16♓	22♓	28♈	16♒
8	17♓	24♓	28♈	17♒
9	18♓	26♓	29♈	18♒
10	19♓	28♓	29♈	18♒
11	20♓	0♈	0♉	19♒
12	21♓	2♈	0♉	20♒
13	22♓	4♈	1♉	21♒
14	23♓	6♈	1♉	21♒
15	24♓	7♈	2♉	22♒
16	25♓	9♈	2♉	23♒
17	26♓	11♈	2♉	24♒
18	27♓	13♈	3♉	25♒
19	28♓	14♈	3♉	25♒
20	29♓	16♈	3♉	26♒
21	0♈	18♈	3♉	27♒
22	1♈	19♈	3♉	28♒
23	2♈	20♈	3♉	28♒
24	3♈	22♈	4♉	29♒
25	4♈	23♈	4♉	0♓
26	5♈	24♈	4♉	1♓
27	6♈	25♈	4♉	2♓
28	7♈	26♈	3♉	2♓
29	8♈	26♈	3♉	3♓
30	9♈	27♈	3♉	4♓
31	10♈	27♈	3♉	5♓

April

Day	☉	☿	♀	♂
1	11♈	28♈	3♉	5♓
2	12♈	28♈	2♉	6♓
3	13♈	28♈	2♉	7♓
4	14♈	28♈	2♉	8♓
5	15♈	28♈	1♉	9♓
6	16♈	28♈	1♉	9♓
7	17♈	27♈	0♉	10♓
8	18♈	27♈	0♉	11♓
9	19♈	26♈	29♈	12♓
10	20♈	26♈	29♈	12♓
11	21♈	25♈	28♈	13♓
12	22♈	24♈	28♈	14♓
13	23♈	24♈	27♈	15♓
14	24♈	23♈	26♈	16♓
15	25♈	22♈	26♈	16♓
16	26♈	21♈	25♈	17♓
17	27♈	21♈	24♈	18♓
18	28♈	20♈	24♈	19♓
19	29♈	19♈	23♈	19♓
20	0♉	19♈	23♈	20♓
21	1♉	18♈	22♈	21♓
22	2♉	18♈	21♈	22♓
23	3♉	17♈	21♈	23♓
24	4♉	17♈	20♈	23♓
25	5♉	17♈	20♈	24♓
26	6♉	17♈	19♈	25♓
27	7♉	17♈	19♈	26♓
28	8♉	17♈	19♈	26♓
29	9♉	17♈	18♈	27♓
30	9♉	17♈	18♈	28♓

May

Day	☉	☿	♀	♂
1	10♉	18♈	18♈	29♓
2	11♉	18♈	18♈	0♈
3	12♉	18♈	17♈	0♈
4	13♉	19♈	17♈	1♈
5	14♉	19♈	17♈	2♈
6	15♉	20♈	17♈	3♈
7	16♉	21♈	17♈	3♈
8	17♉	21♈	17♈	4♈
9	18♉	22♈	17♈	5♈
10	19♉	23♈	17♈	6♈
11	20♉	24♈	18♈	6♈
12	21♉	25♈	18♈	7♈
13	22♉	26♈	18♈	8♈
14	23♉	27♈	18♈	9♈
15	24♉	28♈	18♈	9♈
16	25♉	29♈	19♈	10♈
17	26♉	1♉	19♈	11♈
18	27♉	2♉	20♈	12♈
19	28♉	3♉	20♈	13♈
20	29♉	5♉	20♈	13♈
21	0♊	6♉	21♈	14♈
22	1♊	7♉	21♈	15♈
23	2♊	9♉	22♈	16♈
24	3♊	10♉	22♈	16♈
25	4♊	12♉	23♈	17♈
26	5♊	14♉	23♈	18♈
27	6♊	15♉	24♈	19♈
28	6♊	17♉	25♈	19♈
29	7♊	19♉	25♈	20♈
30	8♊	20♉	26♈	21♈
31	9♊	22♉	27♈	22♈

June

Day	☉	☿	♀	♂
1	10♊	24♉	27♈	22♈
2	11♊	26♉	28♈	23♈
3	12♊	28♉	29♈	24♈
4	13♊	0♊	29♈	25♈
5	14♊	2♊	0♉	25♈
6	15♊	4♊	1♉	26♈
7	16♊	6♊	2♉	27♈
8	17♊	8♊	3♉	28♈
9	18♊	10♊	3♉	28♈
10	19♊	12♊	4♉	29♈
11	20♊	14♊	5♉	0♉
12	21♊	16♊	6♉	1♉
13	22♊	18♊	7♉	1♉
14	23♊	21♊	8♉	2♉
15	24♊	23♊	8♉	3♉
16	25♊	25♊	9♉	3♉
17	26♊	27♊	10♉	4♉
18	27♊	29♊	11♉	5♉
19	28♊	1♋	12♉	6♉
20	28♊	4♋	13♉	6♉
21	29♊	6♋	14♉	7♉
22	0♋	8♋	15♉	8♉
23	1♋	10♋	16♉	9♉
24	2♋	12♋	17♉	9♉
25	3♋	14♋	18♉	10♉
26	4♋	16♋	19♉	11♉
27	5♋	18♋	20♉	12♉
28	6♋	20♋	20♉	12♉
29	7♋	22♋	21♉	13♉
30	8♋	24♋	22♉	14♉

July

Day	☉	☿	♀	♂
1	9♋	26♋	23♉	14♉
2	10♋	27♋	24♉	15♉
3	11♋	29♋	25♉	16♉
4	12♋	1♌	26♉	17♉
5	13♋	3♌	27♉	17♉
6	14♋	4♌	28♉	18♉
7	15♋	6♌	0♊	19♉
8	16♋	8♌	1♊	19♉
9	17♋	9♌	2♊	20♉
10	18♋	11♌	3♊	21♉
11	19♋	12♌	4♊	22♉
12	19♋	14♌	5♊	22♉
13	20♋	15♌	6♊	23♉
14	21♋	16♌	7♊	24♉
15	22♋	18♌	8♊	24♉
16	23♋	19♌	9♊	25♉
17	24♋	20♌	10♊	26♉
18	25♋	21♌	11♊	26♉
19	26♋	23♌	12♊	27♉
20	27♋	24♌	13♊	28♉
21	28♋	25♌	14♊	29♉
22	29♋	26♌	15♊	29♉
23	0♌	27♌	16♊	0♊
24	1♌	28♌	18♊	1♊
25	2♌	29♌	19♊	1♊
26	3♌	0♍	20♊	2♊
27	4♌	0♍	21♊	3♊
28	5♌	1♍	22♊	3♊
29	6♌	2♍	23♊	4♊
30	7♌	2♍	24♊	5♊
31	8♌	3♍	25♊	5♊

August

Day	☉	☿	♀	♂
1	9♌	4♍	26♊	6♊
2	10♌	4♍	27♊	7♊
3	10♌	4♍	29♊	7♊
4	11♌	5♍	0♋	8♊
5	12♌	5♍	1♋	9♊
6	13♌	5♍	2♋	9♊
7	14♌	5♍	3♋	10♊
8	15♌	5♍	4♋	11♊
9	16♌	5♍	5♋	11♊
10	17♌	4♍	6♋	12♊
11	18♌	4♍	8♋	13♊
12	19♌	3♍	9♋	13♊
13	20♌	3♍	10♋	14♊
14	21♌	2♍	11♋	15♊
15	22♌	2♍	12♋	15♊
16	23♌	1♍	13♋	16♊
17	24♌	0♍	14♋	17♊
18	25♌	29♌	16♋	17♊
19	26♌	28♌	17♋	18♊
20	27♌	28♌	18♋	18♊
21	28♌	27♌	19♋	19♊
22	29♌	26♌	20♋	20♊
23	0♍	25♌	21♋	20♊
24	1♍	24♌	23♋	21♊
25	2♍	24♌	24♋	22♊
26	3♍	23♌	25♋	22♊
27	4♍	23♌	26♋	23♊
28	5♍	22♌	27♋	24♊
29	5♍	22♌	28♋	24♊
30	6♍	22♌	0♌	25♊
31	7♍	22♌	1♌	25♊

September

Day	☉	☿	♀	♂
1	8♍	22♌	2♌	26♊
2	9♍	23♌	3♌	27♊
3	10♍	23♌	4♌	27♊
4	11♍	24♌	5♌	28♊
5	12♍	24♌	7♌	28♊
6	13♍	25♌	8♌	29♊
7	14♍	26♌	9♌	0♋
8	15♍	27♌	10♌	0♋
9	16♍	29♌	11♌	1♋
10	17♍	0♍	13♌	1♋
11	18♍	1♍	14♌	2♋
12	19♍	3♍	15♌	3♋
13	20♍	4♍	16♌	3♋
14	21♍	6♍	17♌	4♋
15	22♍	8♍	19♌	4♋
16	23♍	9♍	20♌	5♋
17	24♍	11♍	21♌	5♋
18	25♍	13♍	22♌	6♋
19	26♍	15♍	23♌	7♋
20	27♍	17♍	25♌	7♋
21	28♍	18♍	26♌	8♋
22	29♍	20♍	27♌	8♋
23	0♎	22♍	28♌	9♋
24	1♎	24♍	29♌	9♋
25	2♎	26♍	1♍	10♋
26	3♎	28♍	2♍	10♋
27	4♎	29♍	3♍	11♋
28	5♎	1♎	4♍	11♋
29	6♎	3♎	6♍	12♋
30	7♎	5♎	7♍	12♋

October

Day	☉	☿	♀	♂
1	8♎	7♎	8♍	13♋
2	9♎	8♎	9♍	14♋
3	10♎	10♎	10♍	14♋
4	11♎	12♎	12♍	15♋
5	12♎	14♎	13♍	15♋
6	13♎	15♎	14♍	16♋
7	14♎	17♎	15♍	16♋
8	15♎	19♎	17♍	17♋
9	16♎	20♎	18♍	17♋
10	17♎	22♎	19♍	18♋
11	18♎	24♎	20♍	18♋
12	19♎	25♎	21♍	18♋
13	20♎	27♎	23♍	19♋
14	20♎	29♎	24♍	19♋
15	21♎	0♏	25♍	20♋
16	22♎	2♏	26♍	20♋
17	23♎	4♏	28♍	21♋
18	24♎	5♏	29♍	21♋
19	25♎	7♏	0♎	22♋
20	26♎	8♏	1♎	22♋
21	27♎	10♏	3♎	22♋
22	28♎	11♏	4♎	23♋
23	29♎	13♏	5♎	23♋
24	0♏	14♏	6♎	24♋
25	1♏	16♏	7♎	24♋
26	2♏	17♏	9♎	24♋
27	3♏	19♏	10♎	25♋
28	4♏	20♏	11♎	25♋
29	5♏	22♏	12♎	26♋
30	6♏	23♏	14♎	26♋
31	7♏	25♏	15♎	26♋

November

Day	☉	☿	♀	♂
1	8♏	26♏	16♎	27♋
2	9♏	28♏	17♎	27♋
3	10♏	29♏	19♎	27♋
4	11♏	0♐	20♎	28♋
5	12♏	2♐	21♎	28♋
6	13♏	3♐	22♎	28♋
7	14♏	4♐	24♎	29♋
8	15♏	6♐	25♎	29♋
9	16♏	7♐	26♎	29♋
10	17♏	8♐	27♎	0♌
11	18♏	10♐	29♎	0♌
12	19♏	11♐	0♏	0♌
13	20♏	12♐	1♏	0♌
14	21♏	13♐	2♏	1♌
15	22♏	15♐	4♏	1♌
16	23♏	16♐	5♏	1♌
17	24♏	17♐	6♏	1♌
18	26♏	18♐	7♏	1♌
19	27♏	19♐	9♏	2♌
20	28♏	20♐	10♏	2♌
21	29♏	20♐	11♏	2♌
22	0♐	21♐	12♏	2♌
23	1♐	22♐	14♏	2♌
24	2♐	22♐	15♏	2♌
25	3♐	23♐	16♏	3♌
26	4♐	23♐	17♏	3♌
27	5♐	23♐	19♏	3♌
28	6♐	23♐	20♏	3♌
29	7♐	23♐	21♏	3♌
30	8♐	23♐	22♏	3♌

December

Day	☉	☿	♀	♂
1	9♐	22♐	24♏	3♌
2	10♐	21♐	25♏	3♌
3	11♐	20♐	26♏	3♌
4	12♐	19♐	27♏	3♌
5	13♐	18♐	29♏	3♌
6	14♐	17♐	0♐	3♌
7	15♐	15♐	1♐	3♌
8	16♐	14♐	2♐	3♌
9	17♐	13♐	4♐	3♌
10	18♐	11♐	5♐	3♌
11	19♐	10♐	6♐	3♌
12	20♐	9♐	8♐	3♌
13	21♐	8♐	9♐	3♌
14	22♐	8♐	10♐	3♌
15	23♐	7♐	11♐	3♌
16	24♐	7♐	13♐	2♌
17	25♐	7♐	14♐	2♌
18	26♐	7♐	15♐	2♌
19	27♐	7♐	16♐	2♌
20	28♐	8♐	18♐	2♌
21	29♐	8♐	19♐	1♌
22	0♑	9♐	20♐	1♌
23	1♑	9♐	21♐	1♌
24	2♑	10♐	23♐	1♌
25	3♑	11♐	24♐	0♌
26	4♑	12♐	25♐	0♌
27	5♑	13♐	26♐	0♌
28	6♑	14♐	28♐	0♌
29	7♑	15♐	29♐	29♋
30	8♑	16♐	0♑	29♋
31	9♑	18♐	1♑	29♋

Planetary Positions

♌ = Leo ♍ = Virgo ♎ = Libra ♏ = Scorpio ♐ = Sagittarius ♑ = Capricorn ♒ = Aquarius ♓ = Pisces

1946

January

Day	☉	☿	♀	♂
1	10♑	19♐	3♑	28♋
2	11♑	20♐	4♑	28♋
3	12♑	21♐	5♑	27♋
4	13♑	23♐	6♑	27♋
5	14♑	24♐	8♑	27♋
6	15♑	25♐	9♑	26♋
7	16♑	27♐	10♑	26♋
8	17♑	28♐	11♑	26♋
9	18♑	29♐	13♑	25♋
10	19♑	1♑	14♑	25♋
11	20♑	2♑	15♑	24♋
12	21♑	4♑	17♑	24♋
13	22♑	5♑	18♑	24♋
14	23♑	7♑	19♑	23♋
15	24♑	8♑	20♑	23♋
16	25♑	10♑	22♑	22♋
17	26♑	11♑	23♑	22♋
18	28♑	13♑	24♑	22♋
19	29♑	14♑	25♑	21♋
20	0♒	16♑	27♑	21♋
21	1♒	17♑	28♑	20♋
22	2♒	19♑	29♑	20♋
23	3♒	20♑	0♒	20♋
24	4♒	22♑	2♒	19♋
25	5♒	23♑	3♒	19♋
26	6♒	25♑	4♒	19♋
27	7♒	27♑	5♒	18♋
28	8♒	28♑	7♒	18♋
29	9♒	0♒	8♒	18♋
30	10♒	1♒	9♒	17♋
31	11♒	3♒	10♒	17♋

April

Day	☉	☿	♀	♂
1	11♈	0♈	25♈	21♋
2	12♈	0♈	26♈	22♋
3	13♈	29♓	28♈	22♋
4	14♈	29♓	29♈	23♋
5	15♈	28♓	0♉	23♋
6	16♈	28♓	1♉	23♋
7	17♈	28♓	3♉	24♋
8	18♈	28♓	4♉	24♋
9	19♈	28♓	5♉	24♋
10	20♈	28♓	6♉	25♋
11	21♈	28♓	8♉	25♋
12	22♈	28♓	9♉	26♋
13	23♈	28♓	10♉	26♋
14	24♈	29♓	11♉	26♋
15	25♈	29♓	13♉	27♋
16	26♈	0♈	14♉	27♋
17	27♈	0♈	15♉	28♋
18	28♈	1♈	16♉	28♋
19	29♈	2♈	17♉	28♋
20	0♉	3♈	19♉	29♋
21	0♉	3♈	20♉	29♋
22	1♉	4♈	21♉	0♌
23	2♉	5♈	22♉	0♌
24	3♉	6♈	24♉	1♌
25	4♉	7♈	25♉	1♌
26	5♉	8♈	26♉	2♌
27	6♉	10♈	27♉	2♌
28	7♉	11♈	28♉	2♌
29	8♉	12♈	0♊	3♌
30	9♉	13♈	1♊	3♌

July

Day	☉	☿	♀	♂
1	9♋	4♌	15♌	6♍
2	10♋	5♌	17♌	7♍
3	11♋	7♌	18♌	7♍
4	12♋	8♌	19♌	8♍
5	13♋	9♌	20♌	9♍
6	14♋	10♌	21♌	9♍
7	14♋	10♌	22♌	10♍
8	15♋	11♌	24♌	10♍
9	16♋	12♌	25♌	11♍
10	17♋	13♌	26♌	12♍
11	18♋	14♌	27♌	12♍
12	19♋	14♌	28♌	13♍
13	20♋	15♌	29♌	13♍
14	21♋	15♌	0♍	14♍
15	22♋	16♌	2♍	14♍
16	23♋	16♌	3♍	15♍
17	24♋	16♌	4♍	16♍
18	25♋	16♌	5♍	16♍
19	26♋	16♌	6♍	17♍
20	27♋	16♌	7♍	17♍
21	28♋	16♌	9♍	18♍
22	29♋	16♌	10♍	19♍
23	0♌	16♌	11♍	19♍
24	1♌	16♌	12♍	20♍
25	2♌	15♌	13♍	21♍
26	3♌	15♌	14♍	21♍
27	4♌	14♌	15♍	22♍
28	5♌	14♌	16♍	22♍
29	5♌	13♌	18♍	23♍
30	6♌	12♌	19♍	24♍
31	7♌	11♌	20♍	24♍

October

Day	☉	☿	♀	♂
1	7♎	20♎	21♏	4♏
2	8♎	21♎	22♏	5♏
3	9♎	23♎	23♏	6♏
4	10♎	24♎	23♏	6♏
5	11♎	26♎	24♏	7♏
6	12♎	27♎	25♏	8♏
7	13♎	29♎	25♏	9♏
8	14♎	0♏	26♏	9♏
9	15♎	2♏	26♏	10♏
10	16♎	3♏	27♏	11♏
11	17♎	5♏	28♏	11♏
12	18♎	6♏	28♏	12♏
13	19♎	8♏	29♏	13♏
14	20♎	9♏	29♏	13♏
15	21♎	11♏	29♏	14♏
16	22♎	12♏	0♐	15♏
17	23♎	14♏	0♐	15♏
18	24♎	15♏	1♐	16♏
19	25♎	16♏	1♐	17♏
20	26♎	18♏	1♐	18♏
21	27♎	19♏	2♐	18♏
22	28♎	20♏	2♐	19♏
23	29♎	21♏	2♐	20♏
24	0♏	23♏	2♐	20♏
25	1♏	24♏	2♐	21♏
26	2♏	25♏	2♐	22♏
27	3♏	26♏	2♐	22♏
28	4♏	28♏	2♐	23♏
29	5♏	29♏	2♐	24♏
30	6♏	0♐	2♐	25♏
31	7♏	1♐	2♐	25♏

February

Day	☉	☿	♀	♂
1	12♒	5♒	12♒	17♋
2	13♒	6♒	13♒	17♋
3	14♒	8♒	14♒	16♋
4	15♒	10♒	15♒	16♋
5	16♒	11♒	17♒	16♋
6	17♒	13♒	18♒	16♋
7	18♒	15♒	19♒	15♋
8	19♒	17♒	20♒	15♋
9	20♒	18♒	22♒	15♋
10	21♒	20♒	23♒	15♋
11	22♒	22♒	24♒	15♋
12	23♒	24♒	25♒	15♋
13	24♒	26♒	27♒	15♋
14	25♒	27♒	28♒	14♋
15	26♒	29♒	29♒	14♋
16	27♒	1♓	0♓	14♋
17	28♒	3♓	2♓	14♋
18	29♒	5♓	3♓	14♋
19	0♓	7♓	4♓	14♋
20	1♓	8♓	5♓	14♋
21	2♓	10♓	7♓	14♋
22	3♓	12♓	8♓	14♋
23	4♓	14♓	9♓	14♋
24	5♓	16♓	10♓	14♋
25	6♓	18♓	12♓	14♋
26	7♓	20♓	13♓	14♋
27	8♓	21♓	14♓	14♋
28	9♓	23♓	15♓	14♋

May

Day	☉	☿	♀	♂
1	10♉	14♈	2♊	4♌
2	11♉	16♈	3♊	4♌
3	12♉	17♈	5♊	5♌
4	13♉	19♈	6♊	5♌
5	14♉	20♈	7♊	6♌
6	15♉	21♈	8♊	6♌
7	16♉	23♈	9♊	7♌
8	17♉	25♈	11♊	7♌
9	18♉	26♈	12♊	8♌
10	19♉	28♈	13♊	8♌
11	20♉	29♈	14♊	9♌
12	21♉	1♉	16♊	9♌
13	22♉	3♉	17♊	10♌
14	23♉	4♉	18♊	10♌
15	24♉	6♉	19♊	11♌
16	25♉	8♉	20♊	11♌
17	26♉	10♉	22♊	12♌
18	27♉	12♉	23♊	12♌
19	28♉	14♉	24♊	13♌
20	29♉	16♉	25♊	13♌
21	0♊	18♉	26♊	14♌
22	0♊	20♉	28♊	14♌
23	1♊	22♉	29♊	15♌
24	2♊	24♉	0♋	15♌
25	3♊	26♉	1♋	16♌
26	4♊	28♉	2♋	16♌
27	5♊	0♊	4♋	17♌
28	6♊	2♊	5♋	17♌
29	7♊	4♊	6♋	18♌
30	8♊	7♊	7♋	18♌
31	9♊	9♊	8♋	19♌

August

Day	☉	☿	♀	♂
1	8♌	11♌	21♍	25♍
2	9♌	10♌	22♍	25♍
3	10♌	9♌	23♍	26♍
4	11♌	9♌	24♍	27♍
5	12♌	8♌	25♍	27♍
6	13♌	7♌	27♍	28♍
7	14♌	7♌	28♍	29♍
8	15♌	6♌	29♍	29♍
9	16♌	6♌	0♎	0♎
10	17♌	5♌	1♎	0♎
11	18♌	5♌	2♎	1♎
12	19♌	5♌	3♎	2♎
13	20♌	5♌	4♎	2♎
14	21♌	5♌	5♎	3♎
15	22♌	5♌	6♎	4♎
16	23♌	6♌	7♎	4♎
17	24♌	6♌	9♎	5♎
18	25♌	7♌	10♎	5♎
19	26♌	7♌	11♎	6♎
20	27♌	8♌	12♎	7♎
21	28♌	9♌	13♎	7♎
22	28♌	10♌	14♎	8♎
23	29♌	11♌	15♎	9♎
24	0♍	12♌	16♎	9♎
25	1♍	14♌	17♎	10♎
26	2♍	15♌	18♎	11♎
27	3♍	17♌	19♎	11♎
28	4♍	18♌	20♎	12♎
29	5♍	20♌	21♎	13♎
30	6♍	22♌	22♎	13♎
31	7♍	24♌	23♎	14♎

November

Day	☉	☿	♀	♂
1	8♏	2♐	2♐	26♏
2	9♏	3♐	2♐	27♏
3	10♏	4♐	2♐	27♏
4	11♏	4♐	2♐	28♏
5	12♏	5♐	1♐	29♏
6	13♏	6♐	1♐	0♐
7	14♏	6♐	0♐	0♐
8	15♏	7♐	0♐	1♐
9	16♏	7♐	0♐	2♐
10	17♏	7♐	29♏	2♐
11	18♏	7♐	29♏	3♐
12	19♏	7♐	28♏	4♐
13	20♏	7♐	28♏	5♐
14	21♏	7♐	27♏	5♐
15	22♏	6♐	26♏	6♐
16	23♏	5♐	26♏	7♐
17	24♏	4♐	25♏	8♐
18	25♏	3♐	25♏	8♐
19	26♏	2♐	24♏	9♐
20	27♏	1♐	23♏	10♐
21	28♏	0♐	23♏	10♐
22	29♏	28♏	22♏	11♐
23	0♐	27♏	22♏	12♐
24	1♐	26♏	21♏	13♐
25	2♐	24♏	21♏	13♐
26	3♐	23♏	20♏	14♐
27	4♐	23♏	20♏	15♐
28	5♐	22♏	19♏	16♐
29	6♐	21♏	19♏	16♐
30	7♐	21♏	18♏	17♐

March

Day	☉	☿	♀	♂
1	10♓	25♓	17♓	14♋
2	11♓	27♓	18♓	15♋
3	12♓	28♓	19♓	15♋
4	13♓	0♈	20♓	15♋
5	14♓	1♈	22♓	15♋
6	15♓	3♈	23♓	15♋
7	16♓	4♈	24♓	15♋
8	17♓	5♈	25♓	15♋
9	18♓	6♈	27♓	15♋
10	19♓	7♈	28♓	16♋
11	20♓	8♈	29♓	16♋
12	21♓	9♈	0♈	16♋
13	22♓	9♈	2♈	16♋
14	23♓	10♈	3♈	16♋
15	24♓	10♈	4♈	17♋
16	25♓	10♈	5♈	17♋
17	26♓	10♈	7♈	17♋
18	27♓	10♈	8♈	17♋
19	28♓	10♈	9♈	18♋
20	29♓	9♈	10♈	18♋
21	0♈	9♈	12♈	18♋
22	1♈	8♈	13♈	18♋
23	2♈	8♈	14♈	19♋
24	3♈	7♈	15♈	19♋
25	4♈	6♈	17♈	19♋
26	5♈	5♈	18♈	20♋
27	6♈	4♈	19♈	20♋
28	7♈	4♈	20♈	20♋
29	8♈	3♈	22♈	20♋
30	9♈	2♈	23♈	21♋
31	10♈	1♈	24♈	21♋

June

Day	☉	☿	♀	♂
1	10♊	11♊	10♋	19♌
2	11♊	13♊	11♋	20♌
3	12♊	15♊	12♋	21♌
4	13♊	18♊	13♋	21♌
5	14♊	20♊	14♋	22♌
6	15♊	22♊	16♋	22♌
7	16♊	24♊	17♋	23♌
8	17♊	26♊	18♋	23♌
9	18♊	28♊	19♋	24♌
10	19♊	0♋	20♋	24♌
11	20♊	2♋	22♋	25♌
12	21♊	4♋	23♋	25♌
13	22♊	6♋	24♋	26♌
14	23♊	8♋	25♋	27♌
15	23♊	10♋	26♋	27♌
16	24♊	12♋	28♋	28♌
17	25♊	14♋	29♋	28♌
18	26♊	15♋	0♌	29♌
19	27♊	17♋	1♌	29♌
20	28♊	19♋	2♌	0♍
21	29♊	20♋	4♌	0♍
22	0♋	22♋	5♌	1♍
23	1♋	23♋	6♌	2♍
24	2♋	25♋	7♌	2♍
25	3♋	26♋	8♌	3♍
26	4♋	28♋	9♌	3♍
27	5♋	29♋	11♌	4♍
28	6♋	1♌	12♌	4♍
29	7♋	2♌	13♌	5♍
30	8♋	3♌	14♌	6♍

September

Day	☉	☿	♀	♂
1	8♍	25♌	24♎	14♎
2	9♍	27♌	25♎	15♎
3	10♍	29♌	26♎	16♎
4	11♍	1♍	27♎	16♎
5	12♍	3♍	28♎	17♎
6	13♍	5♍	29♎	18♎
7	14♍	7♍	0♏	18♎
8	15♍	9♍	1♏	19♎
9	16♍	11♍	2♏	20♎
10	17♍	13♍	3♏	20♎
11	18♍	14♍	4♏	21♎
12	19♍	16♍	5♏	22♎
13	20♍	18♍	6♏	22♎
14	21♍	20♍	7♏	23♎
15	22♍	22♍	8♏	24♎
16	23♍	24♍	9♏	24♎
17	24♍	26♍	10♏	25♎
18	25♍	27♍	10♏	26♎
19	26♍	29♍	11♏	26♎
20	27♍	1♎	12♏	27♎
21	28♍	3♎	13♏	28♎
22	29♍	5♎	14♏	28♎
23	0♎	6♎	15♏	29♎
24	1♎	8♎	16♏	0♏
25	2♎	10♎	16♏	0♏
26	3♎	11♎	17♏	1♏
27	3♎	13♎	18♏	2♏
28	4♎	15♎	19♏	2♏
29	5♎	16♎	20♏	3♏
30	6♎	18♎	20♏	4♏

December

Day	☉	☿	♀	♂
1	8♐	21♏	18♏	18♐
2	9♐	21♏	18♏	19♐
3	10♐	22♏	18♏	19♐
4	11♐	22♏	17♏	20♐
5	12♐	22♏	17♏	21♐
6	13♐	23♏	17♏	22♐
7	14♐	24♏	17♏	22♐
8	16♐	25♏	17♏	23♐
9	17♐	26♏	17♏	24♐
10	18♐	27♏	17♏	25♐
11	19♐	28♏	17♏	25♐
12	20♐	29♏	17♏	26♐
13	21♐	0♐	18♏	27♐
14	22♐	1♐	18♏	28♐
15	23♐	3♐	18♏	28♐
16	24♐	4♐	18♏	29♐
17	25♐	5♐	19♏	0♑
18	26♐	7♐	19♏	1♑
19	27♐	8♐	19♏	1♑
20	28♐	10♐	20♏	2♑
21	29♐	11♐	20♏	3♑
22	0♑	12♐	21♏	4♑
23	1♑	14♐	21♏	4♑
24	2♑	15♐	22♏	5♑
25	3♑	17♐	22♏	6♑
26	4♑	18♐	23♏	7♑
27	5♑	20♐	23♏	7♑
28	6♑	21♐	24♏	8♑
29	7♑	23♐	25♏	9♑
30	8♑	24♐	25♏	10♑
31	9♑	26♐	26♏	10♑

1947

Your Starway to Love

☉ =Sun ☿ = Mercury ♀ = Venus ♂ = Mars ♈ = Aries ♉ = Taurus ♊ = Gemini ♋ = Cancer

January

Day	☉	☿	♀	♂
1	10♑	27♐	27♏	11♑
2	11♑	29♐	27♏	12♑
3	12♑	0♑	28♏	13♑
4	13♑	2♑	29♏	14♑
5	14♑	3♑	0♐	14♑
6	15♑	5♑	0♐	15♑
7	16♑	6♑	1♐	16♑
8	17♑	8♑	2♐	17♑
9	18♑	9♑	3♐	17♑
10	19♑	11♑	4♐	18♑
11	20♑	13♑	5♐	19♑
12	21♑	14♑	5♐	20♑
13	22♑	16♑	6♐	20♑
14	23♑	17♑	7♐	21♑
15	24♑	19♑	8♐	22♑
16	25♑	21♑	9♐	23♑
17	26♑	22♑	10♐	24♑
18	27♑	24♑	11♐	24♑
19	28♑	26♑	12♐	25♑
20	29♑	27♑	13♐	26♑
21	0♒	29♑	14♐	27♑
22	1♒	1♒	15♐	27♑
23	2♒	2♒	16♐	28♑
24	3♒	4♒	17♐	29♑
25	4♒	6♒	18♐	0♒
26	5♒	7♒	19♐	1♒
27	6♒	9♒	20♐	1♒
28	7♒	11♒	21♐	2♒
29	8♒	13♒	22♐	3♒
30	9♒	14♒	23♐	4♒
31	10♒	16♒	24♐	4♒

April

Day	☉	☿	♀	♂
1	11♈	13♓	2♓	22♓
2	12♈	14♓	3♓	22♓
3	13♈	15♓	4♓	23♓
4	14♈	16♓	5♓	24♓
5	15♈	17♓	6♓	25♓
6	16♈	18♓	7♓	26♓
7	17♈	19♓	9♓	26♓
8	18♈	20♓	10♓	27♓
9	19♈	21♓	11♓	28♓
10	19♈	22♓	12♓	29♓
11	20♈	23♓	13♓	29♓
12	21♈	25♓	15♓	0♈
13	22♈	26♓	16♓	1♈
14	23♈	27♓	17♓	2♈
15	24♈	29♓	18♓	3♈
16	25♈	0♈	19♓	3♈
17	26♈	1♈	21♓	4♈
18	27♈	3♈	22♓	5♈
19	28♈	4♈	23♓	6♈
20	29♈	6♈	24♓	6♈
21	0♉	7♈	25♓	7♈
22	1♉	9♈	27♓	8♈
23	2♉	11♈	28♓	9♈
24	3♉	12♈	29♓	9♈
25	4♉	14♈	0♈	10♈
26	5♉	15♈	1♈	11♈
27	6♉	17♈	2♈	12♈
28	7♉	19♈	4♈	13♈
29	8♉	21♈	5♈	13♈
30	9♉	22♈	6♈	14♈

July

Day	☉	☿	♀	♂
1	9♋	27♋	21♊	0♊
2	9♋	27♋	22♊	1♊
3	10♋	27♋	23♊	1♊
4	11♋	27♋	25♊	2♊
5	12♋	27♋	26♊	3♊
6	13♋	26♋	27♊	4♊
7	14♋	26♋	28♊	4♊
8	15♋	25♋	0♋	5♊
9	16♋	25♋	1♋	6♊
10	17♋	24♋	2♋	6♊
11	18♋	24♋	3♋	7♊
12	19♋	23♋	4♋	8♊
13	20♋	22♋	6♋	8♊
14	21♋	22♋	7♋	9♊
15	22♋	21♋	8♋	10♊
16	23♋	21♋	9♋	11♊
17	24♋	20♋	11♋	11♊
18	25♋	19♋	12♋	12♊
19	26♋	19♋	13♋	13♊
20	27♋	18♋	14♋	13♊
21	28♋	18♋	15♋	14♊
22	29♋	18♋	17♋	15♊
23	0♌	17♋	18♋	15♊
24	0♌	17♋	19♋	16♊
25	1♌	17♋	20♋	17♊
26	2♌	17♋	22♋	17♊
27	3♌	17♋	23♋	18♊
28	4♌	17♋	24♋	19♊
29	5♌	18♋	25♋	20♊
30	6♌	18♋	27♋	20♊
31	7♌	19♋	28♋	21♊

October

Day	☉	☿	♀	♂
1	7♎	29♎	15♎	0♌
2	8♎	1♏	16♎	1♌
3	9♎	2♏	17♎	1♌
4	10♎	3♏	18♎	2♌
5	11♎	5♏	20♎	2♌
6	12♎	6♏	21♎	3♌
7	13♎	7♏	22♎	4♌
8	14♎	8♏	23♎	4♌
9	15♎	10♏	25♎	5♌
10	16♎	11♏	26♎	5♌
11	17♎	12♏	27♎	6♌
12	18♎	13♏	28♎	6♌
13	19♎	14♏	0♏	7♌
14	20♎	15♏	1♏	7♌
15	21♎	16♏	2♏	8♌
16	22♎	17♏	3♏	9♌
17	23♎	18♏	5♏	9♌
18	24♎	18♏	6♏	10♌
19	25♎	19♏	7♏	10♌
20	26♎	20♏	8♏	11♌
21	27♎	20♏	10♏	11♌
22	28♎	21♏	11♏	12♌
23	29♎	21♏	12♏	12♌
24	0♏	21♏	13♏	13♌
25	1♏	21♏	15♏	13♌
26	2♏	21♏	16♏	14♌
27	3♏	21♏	17♏	14♌
28	4♏	21♏	18♏	15♌
29	5♏	21♏	20♏	15♌
30	6♏	20♏	21♏	16♌
31	7♏	19♏	22♏	16♌

February

Day	☉	☿	♀	♂
1	11♒	18♒	25♐	5♒
2	13♒	20♒	26♐	6♒
3	14♒	21♒	27♐	7♒
4	15♒	23♒	28♐	8♒
5	16♒	25♒	29♐	8♒
6	17♒	27♒	0♑	9♒
7	18♒	28♒	1♑	10♒
8	19♒	0♓	2♑	11♒
9	20♒	2♓	3♑	12♒
10	21♒	4♓	4♑	12♒
11	22♒	5♓	5♑	13♒
12	23♒	7♓	6♑	14♒
13	24♒	9♓	8♑	15♒
14	25♒	10♓	9♑	15♒
15	26♒	12♓	10♑	16♒
16	27♒	14♓	11♑	17♒
17	28♒	15♓	12♑	18♒
18	29♒	16♓	13♑	19♒
19	0♓	18♓	14♑	19♒
20	1♓	19♓	15♑	20♒
21	2♓	20♓	16♑	21♒
22	3♓	21♓	18♑	22♒
23	4♓	22♓	19♑	23♒
24	5♓	22♓	20♑	23♒
25	6♓	23♓	21♑	24♒
26	7♓	23♓	22♑	25♒
27	8♓	23♓	23♑	26♒
28	9♓	23♓	24♑	26♒

May

Day	☉	☿	♀	♂
1	10♉	24♈	7♈	15♈
2	11♉	26♈	8♈	16♈
3	12♉	28♈	10♈	16♈
4	13♉	0♉	11♈	17♈
5	14♉	2♉	12♈	18♈
6	15♉	4♉	13♈	19♈
7	16♉	6♉	14♈	19♈
8	17♉	8♉	16♈	20♈
9	18♉	10♉	17♈	21♈
10	19♉	12♉	18♈	22♈
11	20♉	14♉	19♈	22♈
12	21♉	16♉	21♈	23♈
13	22♉	18♉	22♈	24♈
14	23♉	20♉	23♈	25♈
15	24♉	23♉	24♈	26♈
16	24♉	25♉	25♈	26♈
17	25♉	27♉	27♈	27♈
18	26♉	29♉	28♈	28♈
19	27♉	1♊	29♈	29♈
20	28♉	4♊	0♉	29♈
21	29♉	6♊	1♉	0♉
22	0♊	8♊	3♉	1♉
23	1♊	10♊	4♉	2♉
24	2♊	12♊	5♉	2♉
25	3♊	14♊	6♉	3♉
26	4♊	16♊	7♉	4♉
27	5♊	18♊	9♉	5♉
28	6♊	20♊	10♉	5♉
29	7♊	22♊	11♉	6♉
30	8♊	24♊	12♉	7♉
31	9♊	26♊	13♉	8♉

August

Day	☉	☿	♀	♂
1	8♌	19♋	29♋	22♊
2	9♌	20♋	0♌	22♊
3	10♌	21♋	1♌	23♊
4	11♌	22♋	3♌	24♊
5	12♌	23♋	4♌	24♊
6	13♌	24♋	5♌	25♊
7	14♌	25♋	6♌	26♊
8	15♌	26♋	8♌	26♊
9	16♌	28♋	9♌	27♊
10	17♌	29♋	10♌	28♊
11	18♌	1♌	11♌	28♊
12	19♌	2♌	13♌	29♊
13	20♌	4♌	14♌	0♋
14	21♌	6♌	15♌	0♋
15	22♌	8♌	16♌	1♋
16	22♌	9♌	17♌	2♋
17	23♌	11♌	19♌	2♋
18	24♌	13♌	20♌	3♋
19	25♌	15♌	21♌	3♋
20	26♌	17♌	22♌	4♋
21	27♌	19♌	24♌	5♋
22	28♌	21♌	25♌	5♋
23	29♌	23♌	26♌	6♋
24	0♍	25♌	27♌	7♋
25	1♍	27♌	29♌	7♋
26	2♍	29♌	0♍	8♋
27	3♍	1♍	1♍	9♋
28	4♍	3♍	2♍	9♋
29	5♍	5♍	4♍	10♋
30	6♍	7♍	5♍	11♋
31	7♍	9♍	6♍	11♋

November

Day	☉	☿	♀	♂
1	8♏	18♏	23♏	17♌
2	9♏	17♏	24♏	17♌
3	10♏	16♏	26♏	18♌
4	11♏	15♏	27♏	18♌
5	12♏	14♏	28♏	19♌
6	13♏	12♏	29♏	19♌
7	14♏	11♏	1♐	20♌
8	15♏	10♏	2♐	20♌
9	16♏	9♏	3♐	21♌
10	17♏	8♏	4♐	21♌
11	18♏	7♏	6♐	22♌
12	19♏	6♏	7♐	22♌
13	20♏	6♏	8♐	23♌
14	21♏	6♏	9♐	23♌
15	22♏	5♏	11♐	23♌
16	23♏	6♏	12♐	24♌
17	24♏	6♏	13♐	24♌
18	25♏	6♏	14♐	25♌
19	26♏	7♏	16♐	25♌
20	27♏	8♏	17♐	26♌
21	28♏	9♏	18♐	26♌
22	29♏	9♏	19♐	26♌
23	0♐	10♏	21♐	27♌
24	1♐	12♏	22♐	27♌
25	2♐	13♏	23♐	28♌
26	3♐	14♏	24♐	28♌
27	4♐	15♏	26♐	28♌
28	5♐	17♏	27♐	29♌
29	6♐	18♏	28♐	29♌
30	7♐	19♏	29♐	0♍

March

Day	☉	☿	♀	♂
1	10♓	23♓	25♑	27♒
2	11♓	23♓	27♑	28♒
3	12♓	22♓	28♑	29♒
4	13♓	22♓	29♑	0♓
5	14♓	21♓	0♒	0♓
6	15♓	20♓	1♒	1♓
7	16♓	19♓	2♒	2♓
8	17♓	18♓	3♒	3♓
9	18♓	17♓	5♒	4♓
10	19♓	16♓	6♒	4♓
11	20♓	15♓	7♒	5♓
12	21♓	14♓	8♒	6♓
13	22♓	13♓	9♒	7♓
14	23♓	13♓	10♒	7♓
15	24♓	12♓	12♒	8♓
16	25♓	11♓	13♒	9♓
17	26♓	11♓	14♒	10♓
18	27♓	10♓	15♒	11♓
19	28♓	10♓	16♒	11♓
20	29♓	9♓	17♒	12♓
21	0♈	9♓	19♒	13♓
22	1♈	9♓	20♒	14♓
23	2♈	9♓	21♒	15♓
24	3♈	9♓	22♒	15♓
25	4♈	10♓	23♒	16♓
26	5♈	10♓	24♒	17♓
27	6♈	10♓	26♒	18♓
28	7♈	11♓	27♒	18♓
29	8♈	11♓	28♒	19♓
30	9♈	12♓	29♒	20♓
31	10♈	13♓	0♓	21♓

June

Day	☉	☿	♀	♂
1	10♊	28♊	15♉	8♉
2	11♊	29♊	16♉	9♉
3	12♊	1♋	17♉	10♉
4	13♊	3♋	18♉	10♉
5	14♊	4♋	19♉	11♉
6	15♊	6♋	21♉	12♉
7	16♊	7♋	22♉	13♉
8	17♊	9♋	23♉	13♉
9	18♊	10♋	24♉	14♉
10	18♊	12♋	26♉	15♉
11	19♊	13♋	27♉	16♉
12	20♊	14♋	28♉	16♉
13	21♊	15♋	29♉	17♉
14	22♊	17♋	0♊	18♉
15	23♊	18♋	2♊	19♉
16	24♊	19♋	3♊	19♉
17	25♊	20♋	4♊	20♉
18	26♊	21♋	5♊	21♉
19	27♊	22♋	6♊	21♉
20	28♊	22♋	8♊	22♉
21	29♊	23♋	9♊	23♉
22	0♋	24♋	10♊	24♉
23	1♋	25♋	11♊	24♉
24	2♋	25♋	13♊	25♉
25	3♋	26♋	14♊	26♉
26	4♋	26♋	15♊	26♉
27	5♋	26♋	16♊	27♉
28	6♋	27♋	17♊	28♉
29	7♋	27♋	19♊	29♉
30	8♋	27♋	20♊	29♉

September

Day	☉	☿	♀	♂
1	8♍	11♍	7♍	12♋
2	9♍	13♍	9♍	12♋
3	10♍	15♍	10♍	13♋
4	11♍	16♍	11♍	14♋
5	12♍	18♍	12♍	14♋
6	13♍	20♍	13♍	15♋
7	14♍	22♍	15♍	16♋
8	15♍	24♍	16♍	16♋
9	16♍	25♍	17♍	17♋
10	17♍	27♍	18♍	17♋
11	18♍	29♍	20♍	18♋
12	19♍	1♎	21♍	19♋
13	20♍	2♎	22♍	19♋
14	21♍	4♎	23♍	20♋
15	22♍	6♎	25♍	21♋
16	22♍	7♎	26♍	21♋
17	23♍	9♎	27♍	22♋
18	24♍	10♎	28♍	22♋
19	25♍	12♎	0♎	23♋
20	26♍	13♎	1♎	24♋
21	27♍	15♎	2♎	24♋
22	28♍	17♎	3♎	25♋
23	29♍	18♎	5♎	25♋
24	0♎	20♎	6♎	26♋
25	1♎	21♎	7♎	27♋
26	2♎	22♎	8♎	27♋
27	3♎	24♎	10♎	28♋
28	4♎	25♎	11♎	28♋
29	5♎	27♎	12♎	29♋
30	6♎	28♎	13♎	29♋

December

Day	☉	☿	♀	♂
1	8♐	21♏	1♑	0♍
2	9♐	22♏	2♑	0♍
3	10♐	24♏	3♑	1♍
4	11♐	25♏	4♑	1♍
5	12♐	27♏	6♑	1♍
6	13♐	28♏	7♑	2♍
7	14♐	0♐	8♑	2♍
8	15♐	1♐	9♑	2♍
9	16♐	3♐	11♑	3♍
10	17♐	4♐	12♑	3♍
11	18♐	6♐	13♑	3♍
12	19♐	7♐	14♑	3♍
13	20♐	9♐	16♑	4♍
14	21♐	10♐	17♑	4♍
15	22♐	12♐	18♑	4♍
16	23♐	13♐	19♑	5♍
17	24♐	15♐	21♑	5♍
18	25♐	16♐	22♑	5♍
19	26♐	18♐	23♑	5♍
20	27♐	19♐	24♑	5♍
21	28♐	21♐	26♑	6♍
22	0♑	23♐	27♑	6♍
23	1♑	24♐	28♑	6♍
24	2♑	26♐	29♑	6♍
25	3♑	27♐	1♒	6♍
26	4♑	29♐	2♒	7♍
27	5♑	0♑	3♒	7♍
28	6♑	2♑	4♒	7♍
29	7♑	4♑	5♒	7♍
30	8♑	5♑	7♒	7♍
31	9♑	7♑	8♒	7♍

1948

Planetary Positions

♌ = Leo ♍ = Virgo ♎ = Libra ♏ = Scorpio ♐ = Sagittarius ♑ = Capricorn ♒ = Aquarius ♓ = Pisces

January

Day	☉	☿	♀	♂
1	10♑	8♑	9♒	7♍
2	11♑	10♑	10♒	7♍
3	12♑	12♑	12♒	7♍
4	13♑	13♑	13♒	7♍
5	14♑	15♑	14♒	8♍
6	15♑	16♑	15♒	8♍
7	16♑	18♑	17♒	8♍
8	17♑	20♑	18♒	8♍
9	18♑	21♑	19♒	8♍
10	19♑	23♑	20♒	8♍
11	20♑	25♑	22♒	8♍
12	21♑	26♑	23♒	8♍
13	22♑	28♑	24♒	7♍
14	23♑	0♒	25♒	7♍
15	24♑	1♒	26♒	7♍
16	25♑	3♒	28♒	7♍
17	26♑	5♒	29♒	7♍
18	27♑	6♒	0♓	7♍
19	28♑	8♒	1♓	7♍
20	29♑	10♒	3♓	7♍
21	0♒	11♒	4♓	7♍
22	1♒	13♒	5♓	6♍
23	2♒	15♒	6♓	6♍
24	3♒	17♒	7♓	6♍
25	4♒	18♒	9♓	6♍
26	5♒	20♒	10♓	6♍
27	6♒	21♒	11♓	5♍
28	7♒	23♒	12♓	5♍
29	8♒	25♒	14♓	5♍
30	9♒	26♒	15♓	5♍
31	10♒	28♒	16♓	4♍

February

Day	☉	☿	♀	♂
1	11♒	29♒	17♓	4♍
2	12♒	0♓	18♓	4♍
3	13♒	1♓	20♓	3♍
4	14♒	3♓	21♓	3♍
5	15♒	4♓	22♓	3♍
6	16♒	4♓	23♓	2♍
7	17♒	5♓	24♓	2♍
8	18♒	6♓	26♓	2♍
9	19♒	6♓	27♓	1♍
10	20♒	6♓	28♓	1♍
11	21♒	7♓	29♓	0♍
12	22♒	6♓	1♈	0♍
13	23♒	6♓	2♈	0♍
14	24♒	6♓	3♈	29♌
15	25♒	5♓	4♈	29♌
16	26♒	4♓	5♈	29♌
17	27♒	3♓	6♈	28♌
18	28♒	2♓	8♈	28♌
19	29♒	1♓	9♈	27♌
20	0♓	0♓	10♈	27♌
21	1♓	29♒	11♈	27♌
22	2♓	28♒	12♈	26♌
23	3♓	27♒	14♈	26♌
24	5♓	26♒	15♈	25♌
25	6♓	25♒	16♈	25♌
26	7♓	24♒	17♈	25♌
27	8♓	23♒	18♈	24♌
28	9♓	23♒	19♈	24♌
29	10♓	22♒	21♈	24♌

March

Day	☉	☿	♀	♂
1	11♓	22♒	22♈	23♌
2	12♓	22♒	23♈	23♌
3	13♓	22♒	24♈	23♌
4	14♓	22♒	25♈	22♌
5	15♓	22♒	26♈	22♌
6	16♓	22♒	28♈	22♌
7	17♓	22♒	29♈	21♌
8	18♓	22♒	0♉	21♌
9	19♓	23♒	1♉	21♌
10	20♓	23♒	2♉	20♌
11	21♓	24♒	3♉	20♌
12	22♓	25♒	4♉	20♌
13	23♓	25♒	6♉	20♌
14	24♓	26♒	7♉	20♌
15	25♓	27♒	8♉	19♌
16	26♓	28♒	9♉	19♌
17	27♓	29♒	10♉	19♌
18	28♓	0♓	11♉	19♌
19	29♓	1♓	12♉	19♌
20	0♈	2♓	13♉	19♌
21	0♈	3♓	15♉	19♌
22	1♈	4♓	16♉	18♌
23	2♈	5♓	17♉	18♌
24	3♈	7♓	18♉	18♌
25	4♈	8♓	19♉	18♌
26	5♈	9♓	20♉	18♌
27	6♈	11♓	21♉	18♌
28	7♈	12♓	22♉	18♌
29	8♈	13♓	23♉	18♌
30	9♈	15♓	24♉	18♌
31	10♈	16♓	25♉	18♌

April

Day	☉	☿	♀	♂
1	11♈	18♓	27♉	18♌
2	12♈	19♓	28♉	18♌
3	13♈	21♓	29♉	18♌
4	14♈	22♓	0♊	18♌
5	15♈	24♓	1♊	18♌
6	16♈	25♓	2♊	18♌
7	17♈	27♓	3♊	19♌
8	18♈	29♓	4♊	19♌
9	19♈	0♈	5♊	19♌
10	20♈	2♈	6♊	19♌
11	21♈	4♈	7♊	19♌
12	22♈	5♈	8♊	19♌
13	23♈	7♈	9♊	19♌
14	24♈	9♈	10♊	20♌
15	25♈	11♈	11♊	20♌
16	26♈	13♈	12♊	20♌
17	27♈	14♈	13♊	20♌
18	28♈	16♈	14♊	20♌
19	29♈	18♈	15♊	20♌
20	0♉	20♈	16♊	21♌
21	1♉	22♈	17♊	21♌
22	2♉	24♈	17♊	21♌
23	3♉	26♈	18♊	21♌
24	4♉	28♈	19♊	22♌
25	5♉	0♉	20♊	22♌
26	6♉	2♉	21♊	22♌
27	7♉	4♉	22♊	22♌
28	8♉	7♉	23♊	23♌
29	9♉	9♉	24♊	23♌
30	10♉	11♉	24♊	23♌

May

Day	☉	☿	♀	♂
1	11♉	13♉	25♊	24♌
2	12♉	15♉	26♊	24♌
3	13♉	17♉	27♊	24♌
4	14♉	20♉	28♊	25♌
5	15♉	22♉	28♊	25♌
6	16♉	24♉	29♊	25♌
7	17♉	26♉	0♋	26♌
8	18♉	28♉	1♋	26♌
9	18♉	0♊	1♋	26♌
10	19♉	2♊	2♋	27♌
11	20♉	4♊	3♋	27♌
12	21♉	6♊	3♋	27♌
13	22♉	8♊	4♋	28♌
14	23♉	10♊	5♋	28♌
15	24♉	11♊	5♋	29♌
16	25♉	13♊	6♋	29♌
17	26♉	15♊	6♋	29♌
18	27♉	17♊	7♋	0♍
19	28♉	18♊	7♋	0♍
20	29♉	20♊	8♋	1♍
21	0♊	21♊	8♋	1♍
22	1♊	23♊	9♋	1♍
23	2♊	24♊	9♋	2♍
24	3♊	25♊	9♋	2♍
25	4♊	26♊	10♋	3♍
26	5♊	28♊	10♋	3♍
27	6♊	29♊	10♋	4♍
28	7♊	0♋	11♋	4♍
29	8♊	1♋	11♋	4♍
30	9♊	2♋	11♋	5♍
31	10♊	3♋	11♋	5♍

June

Day	☉	☿	♀	♂
1	11♊	3♋	11♋	6♍
2	12♊	4♋	11♋	6♍
3	13♊	5♋	11♋	7♍
4	13♊	5♋	11♋	7♍
5	14♊	6♋	11♋	8♍
6	15♊	6♋	11♋	8♍
7	16♊	7♋	11♋	9♍
8	17♊	7♋	11♋	9♍
9	18♊	7♋	10♋	10♍
10	19♊	7♋	10♋	10♍
11	20♊	7♋	10♋	11♍
12	21♊	7♋	10♋	11♍
13	22♊	7♋	9♋	12♍
14	23♊	7♋	9♋	12♍
15	24♊	7♋	8♋	13♍
16	25♊	6♋	8♋	13♍
17	26♊	6♋	7♋	14♍
18	27♊	6♋	7♋	14♍
19	28♊	5♋	6♋	15♍
20	29♊	5♋	6♋	15♍
21	0♋	4♋	5♋	16♍
22	1♋	4♋	4♋	16♍
23	2♋	3♋	4♋	17♍
24	3♋	2♋	3♋	17♍
25	4♋	2♋	3♋	18♍
26	4♋	1♋	2♋	18♍
27	5♋	1♋	1♋	19♍
28	6♋	0♋	1♋	19♍
29	7♋	0♋	0♋	20♍
30	8♋	29♊	29♊	20♍

July

Day	☉	☿	♀	♂
1	9♋	29♊	29♊	21♍
2	10♋	29♊	28♊	22♍
3	11♋	29♊	28♊	22♍
4	12♋	28♊	27♊	23♍
5	13♋	28♊	27♊	23♍
6	14♋	28♊	27♊	24♍
7	15♋	28♊	26♊	24♍
8	16♋	29♊	26♊	25♍
9	17♋	29♊	26♊	25♍
10	18♋	29♊	25♊	26♍
11	19♋	0♋	25♊	27♍
12	20♋	0♋	25♊	27♍
13	21♋	1♋	25♊	28♍
14	22♋	2♋	25♊	28♍
15	23♋	2♋	25♊	29♍
16	24♋	3♋	25♊	29♍
17	25♋	4♋	25♊	0♎
18	25♋	5♋	25♊	1♎
19	26♋	6♋	25♊	1♎
20	27♋	7♋	25♊	2♎
21	28♋	9♋	25♊	2♎
22	29♋	10♋	25♊	3♎
23	0♌	12♋	26♊	3♎
24	1♌	13♋	26♊	4♎
25	2♌	15♋	26♊	5♎
26	3♌	16♋	26♊	5♎
27	4♌	18♋	27♊	6♎
28	5♌	20♋	27♊	6♎
29	6♌	22♋	28♊	7♎
30	7♌	23♋	28♊	8♎
31	8♌	25♋	29♊	8♎

August

Day	☉	☿	♀	♂
1	9♌	27♋	29♊	9♎
2	10♌	29♋	0♋	9♎
3	11♌	1♌	0♋	10♎
4	12♌	3♌	1♋	11♎
5	13♌	5♌	1♋	11♎
6	14♌	7♌	2♋	12♎
7	15♌	9♌	2♋	13♎
8	16♌	12♌	3♋	13♎
9	17♌	14♌	4♋	14♎
10	17♌	16♌	4♋	14♎
11	18♌	18♌	5♋	15♎
12	19♌	20♌	6♋	16♎
13	20♌	22♌	7♋	16♎
14	21♌	24♌	7♋	17♎
15	22♌	26♌	8♋	18♎
16	23♌	28♌	9♋	18♎
17	24♌	0♍	10♋	19♎
18	25♌	2♍	10♋	19♎
19	26♌	4♍	11♋	20♎
20	27♌	5♍	12♋	21♎
21	28♌	7♍	13♋	21♎
22	29♌	9♍	14♋	22♎
23	0♍	11♍	15♋	23♎
24	1♍	13♍	15♋	23♎
25	2♍	14♍	16♋	24♎
26	3♍	16♍	17♋	25♎
27	4♍	18♍	18♋	25♎
28	5♍	20♍	19♋	26♎
29	6♍	21♍	20♋	26♎
30	7♍	23♍	21♋	27♎
31	8♍	25♍	22♋	28♎

September

Day	☉	☿	♀	♂
1	9♍	26♍	23♋	28♎
2	10♍	28♍	24♋	29♎
3	11♍	29♍	25♋	0♏
4	12♍	1♎	26♋	0♏
5	13♍	2♎	27♋	1♏
6	13♍	4♎	28♋	2♏
7	14♍	5♎	29♋	2♏
8	15♍	7♎	0♌	3♏
9	16♍	8♎	1♌	4♏
10	17♍	10♎	2♌	4♏
11	18♍	11♎	3♌	5♏
12	19♍	12♎	4♌	6♏
13	20♍	14♎	5♌	6♏
14	21♍	15♎	6♌	7♏
15	22♍	16♎	7♌	8♏
16	23♍	18♎	8♌	8♏
17	24♍	19♎	9♌	9♏
18	25♍	20♎	10♌	10♏
19	26♍	21♎	11♌	10♏
20	27♍	23♎	12♌	11♏
21	28♍	24♎	13♌	12♏
22	29♍	25♎	14♌	12♏
23	0♎	26♎	15♌	13♏
24	1♎	27♎	16♌	14♏
25	2♎	28♎	17♌	15♏
26	3♎	29♎	19♌	15♏
27	4♎	0♏	20♌	16♏
28	5♎	1♏	21♌	17♏
29	6♎	2♏	22♌	17♏
30	7♎	2♏	23♌	18♏

October

Day	☉	☿	♀	♂
1	8♎	3♏	24♌	19♏
2	9♎	4♏	25♌	19♏
3	10♎	4♏	26♌	20♏
4	11♎	5♏	27♌	21♏
5	12♎	5♏	29♌	21♏
6	13♎	5♏	0♍	22♏
7	14♎	5♏	1♍	23♏
8	15♎	5♏	2♍	24♏
9	16♎	5♏	3♍	24♏
10	17♎	5♏	4♍	25♏
11	18♎	5♏	5♍	26♏
12	19♎	4♏	6♍	26♏
13	20♎	4♏	8♍	27♏
14	21♎	3♏	9♍	28♏
15	22♎	2♏	10♍	29♏
16	23♎	1♏	11♍	29♏
17	24♎	0♏	12♍	0♐
18	25♎	29♎	13♍	1♐
19	26♎	28♎	15♍	1♐
20	27♎	26♎	16♍	2♐
21	28♎	25♎	17♍	3♐
22	29♎	24♎	18♍	4♐
23	0♏	23♎	19♍	4♐
24	1♏	22♎	20♍	5♐
25	2♏	21♎	22♍	6♐
26	3♏	20♎	23♍	6♐
27	4♏	20♎	24♍	7♐
28	5♏	20♎	25♍	8♐
29	6♏	20♎	26♍	9♐
30	7♏	20♎	28♍	9♐
31	8♏	20♎	29♍	10♐

November

Day	☉	☿	♀	♂
1	9♏	21♎	0♎	11♐
2	10♏	21♎	1♎	12♐
3	11♏	22♎	2♎	12♐
4	12♏	23♎	4♎	13♐
5	13♏	24♎	5♎	14♐
6	14♏	25♎	6♎	15♐
7	15♏	26♎	7♎	15♐
8	16♏	27♎	8♎	16♐
9	17♏	29♎	10♎	17♐
10	18♏	0♏	11♎	17♐
11	19♏	2♏	12♎	18♐
12	20♏	3♏	13♎	19♐
13	21♏	4♏	14♎	20♐
14	22♏	6♏	16♎	20♐
15	23♏	7♏	17♎	21♐
16	24♏	9♏	18♎	22♐
17	25♏	11♏	19♎	23♐
18	26♏	12♏	20♎	23♐
19	27♏	14♏	22♎	24♐
20	28♏	15♏	23♎	25♐
21	29♏	17♏	24♎	26♐
22	0♐	18♏	25♎	26♐
23	1♐	20♏	27♎	27♐
24	2♐	21♏	28♎	28♐
25	3♐	23♏	29♎	29♐
26	4♐	25♏	0♏	29♐
27	5♐	26♏	1♏	0♑
28	6♐	28♏	3♏	1♑
29	7♐	29♏	4♏	2♑
30	8♐	1♐	5♏	3♑

December

Day	☉	☿	♀	♂
1	9♐	2♐	6♏	3♑
2	10♐	4♐	8♏	4♑
3	11♐	6♐	9♏	5♑
4	12♐	7♐	10♏	6♑
5	13♐	9♐	11♏	6♑
6	14♐	10♐	13♏	7♑
7	15♐	12♐	14♏	8♑
8	16♐	13♐	15♏	9♑
9	17♐	15♐	16♏	9♑
10	18♐	17♐	17♏	10♑
11	19♐	18♐	19♏	11♑
12	20♐	20♐	20♏	12♑
13	21♐	21♐	21♏	12♑
14	22♐	23♐	22♏	13♑
15	23♐	24♐	24♏	14♑
16	24♐	26♐	25♏	15♑
17	25♐	28♐	26♏	16♑
18	26♐	29♐	27♏	16♑
19	27♐	1♑	29♏	17♑
20	28♐	2♑	0♐	18♑
21	29♐	4♑	1♐	19♑
22	0♑	6♑	2♐	19♑
23	1♑	7♑	4♐	20♑
24	2♑	9♑	5♐	21♑
25	3♑	10♑	6♐	22♑
26	4♑	12♑	7♐	23♑
27	5♑	14♑	9♐	23♑
28	6♑	15♑	10♐	24♑
29	7♑	17♑	11♐	25♑
30	8♑	18♑	12♐	26♑
31	9♑	20♑	14♐	26♑

1949

Your Starway to Love

☉ =Sun ☿ = Mercury ♀ = Venus ♂ = Mars ♈ = Aries ♉ = Taurus ♊ = Gemini ♋ = Cancer

January

Day	☉	☿	♀	♂
1	10♑	22♑	15♐	27♑
2	11♑	23♑	16♐	28♑
3	13♑	25♑	17♐	29♑
4	14♑	27♑	19♐	0♒
5	15♑	28♑	20♐	0♒
6	16♑	0♒	21♐	1♒
7	17♑	1♒	22♐	2♒
8	18♑	3♒	24♐	3♒
9	19♑	4♒	25♐	4♒
10	20♑	6♒	26♐	4♒
11	21♑	7♒	27♐	5♒
12	22♑	9♒	29♐	6♒
13	23♑	10♒	0♑	7♒
14	24♑	12♒	1♑	7♒
15	25♑	13♒	2♑	8♒
16	26♑	14♒	4♑	9♒
17	27♑	15♒	5♑	10♒
18	28♑	17♒	6♑	11♒
19	29♑	17♒	7♑	11♒
20	0♒	18♒	9♑	12♒
21	1♒	19♒	10♑	13♒
22	2♒	20♒	11♑	14♒
23	3♒	20♒	12♑	15♒
24	4♒	20♒	14♑	15♒
25	5♒	20♒	15♑	16♒
26	6♒	20♒	16♑	17♒
27	7♒	20♒	17♑	18♒
28	8♒	19♒	19♑	18♒
29	9♒	18♒	20♑	19♒
30	10♒	18♒	21♑	20♒
31	11♒	17♒	22♑	21♒

April

Day	☉	☿	♀	♂
1	11♈	29♓	7♈	8♈
2	12♈	1♈	8♈	9♈
3	13♈	3♈	10♈	10♈
4	14♈	5♈	11♈	10♈
5	15♈	7♈	12♈	11♈
6	16♈	9♈	13♈	12♈
7	17♈	11♈	15♈	13♈
8	18♈	13♈	16♈	13♈
9	19♈	15♈	17♈	14♈
10	20♈	17♈	18♈	15♈
11	21♈	19♈	19♈	16♈
12	22♈	21♈	21♈	16♈
13	23♈	23♈	22♈	17♈
14	24♈	25♈	23♈	18♈
15	25♈	27♈	24♈	19♈
16	26♈	29♈	26♈	19♈
17	27♈	1♉	27♈	20♈
18	28♈	3♉	28♈	21♈
19	29♈	5♉	29♈	22♈
20	0♉	8♉	1♉	23♈
21	1♉	10♉	2♉	23♈
22	2♉	12♉	3♉	24♈
23	3♉	14♉	4♉	25♈
24	4♉	16♉	6♉	26♈
25	5♉	18♉	7♉	26♈
26	6♉	20♉	8♉	27♈
27	7♉	22♉	9♉	28♈
28	8♉	23♉	11♉	29♈
29	9♉	25♉	12♉	29♈
30	10♉	27♉	13♉	0♉

July

Day	☉	☿	♀	♂
1	9♋	17♊	29♋	15♊
2	10♋	19♊	0♌	16♊
3	11♋	20♊	1♌	16♊
4	12♋	21♊	3♌	17♊
5	13♋	22♊	4♌	18♊
6	14♋	24♊	5♌	18♊
7	15♋	25♊	6♌	19♊
8	16♋	27♊	8♌	20♊
9	17♋	28♊	9♌	20♊
10	18♋	0♋	10♌	21♊
11	19♋	2♋	11♌	22♊
12	20♋	4♋	12♌	23♊
13	20♋	5♋	14♌	23♊
14	21♋	7♋	15♌	24♊
15	22♋	9♋	16♌	25♊
16	23♋	11♋	17♌	25♊
17	24♋	13♋	19♌	26♊
18	25♋	15♋	20♌	27♊
19	26♋	17♋	21♌	27♊
20	27♋	19♋	22♌	28♊
21	28♋	21♋	23♌	29♊
22	29♋	24♋	25♌	29♊
23	0♌	26♋	26♌	0♋
24	1♌	28♋	27♌	1♋
25	2♌	0♌	28♌	1♋
26	3♌	2♌	29♌	2♋
27	4♌	4♌	1♍	3♋
28	5♌	6♌	2♍	3♋
29	6♌	8♌	3♍	4♋
30	7♌	10♌	4♍	5♋
31	8♌	12♌	6♍	5♋

October

Day	☉	☿	♀	♂
1	8♎	13♎	19♏	15♌
2	9♎	12♎	21♏	15♌
3	10♎	11♎	22♏	16♌
4	11♎	10♎	23♏	17♌
5	12♎	9♎	24♏	17♌
6	13♎	8♎	25♏	18♌
7	14♎	7♎	26♏	18♌
8	15♎	6♎	27♏	19♌
9	16♎	5♎	29♏	20♌
10	17♎	5♎	0♐	20♌
11	18♎	4♎	1♐	21♌
12	19♎	4♎	2♐	21♌
13	20♎	4♎	3♐	22♌
14	21♎	4♎	4♐	23♌
15	22♎	4♎	5♐	23♌
16	22♎	5♎	7♐	24♌
17	23♎	6♎	8♐	24♌
18	24♎	6♎	9♐	25♌
19	25♎	7♎	10♐	26♌
20	26♎	8♎	11♐	26♌
21	27♎	10♎	12♐	27♌
22	28♎	11♎	13♐	27♌
23	29♎	12♎	15♐	28♌
24	0♏	13♎	16♐	28♌
25	1♏	15♎	17♐	29♌
26	2♏	16♎	18♐	0♍
27	3♏	18♎	19♐	0♍
28	4♏	19♎	20♐	1♍
29	5♏	21♎	21♐	1♍
30	6♏	23♎	22♐	2♍
31	7♏	24♎	23♐	2♍

February

Day	☉	☿	♀	♂
1	12♒	15♒	24♑	22♒
2	13♒	14♒	25♑	22♒
3	14♒	13♒	26♑	23♒
4	15♒	12♒	27♑	24♒
5	16♒	11♒	29♑	25♒
6	17♒	9♒	0♒	26♒
7	18♒	8♒	1♒	26♒
8	19♒	8♒	2♒	27♒
9	20♒	7♒	4♒	28♒
10	21♒	6♒	5♒	29♒
11	22♒	5♒	6♒	0♓
12	23♒	5♒	7♒	0♓
13	24♒	5♒	9♒	1♓
14	25♒	5♒	10♒	2♓
15	26♒	5♒	11♒	3♓
16	27♒	5♒	12♒	4♓
17	28♒	5♒	14♒	4♓
18	29♒	5♒	15♒	5♓
19	0♓	6♒	16♒	6♓
20	1♓	6♒	17♒	7♓
21	2♓	7♒	19♒	7♓
22	3♓	7♒	20♒	8♓
23	4♓	8♒	21♒	9♓
24	5♓	9♒	22♒	10♓
25	6♓	9♒	24♒	11♓
26	7♓	10♒	25♒	11♓
27	8♓	11♒	26♒	12♓
28	9♓	12♒	27♒	13♓

May

Day	☉	☿	♀	♂
1	10♉	29♉	14♉	1♉
2	11♉	0♊	15♉	2♉
3	12♉	2♊	17♉	2♉
4	13♉	3♊	18♉	3♉
5	14♉	5♊	19♉	4♉
6	15♉	6♊	20♉	5♉
7	16♉	7♊	22♉	5♉
8	17♉	8♊	23♉	6♉
9	18♉	10♊	24♉	7♉
10	19♉	11♊	25♉	8♉
11	20♉	12♊	27♉	8♉
12	21♉	12♊	28♉	9♉
13	22♉	13♊	29♉	10♉
14	23♉	14♊	0♊	11♉
15	24♉	15♊	1♊	11♉
16	25♉	15♊	3♊	12♉
17	26♉	16♊	4♊	13♉
18	27♉	16♊	5♊	13♉
19	28♉	17♊	6♊	14♉
20	29♉	17♊	8♊	15♉
21	0♊	17♊	9♊	16♉
22	1♊	17♊	10♊	16♉
23	2♊	17♊	11♊	17♉
24	3♊	17♊	13♊	18♉
25	4♊	17♊	14♊	19♉
26	5♊	17♊	15♊	19♉
27	6♊	17♊	16♊	20♉
28	7♊	16♊	17♊	21♉
29	7♊	16♊	19♊	21♉
30	8♊	15♊	20♊	22♉
31	9♊	15♊	21♊	23♉

August

Day	☉	☿	♀	♂
1	9♌	14♌	7♍	6♋
2	10♌	16♌	8♍	7♋
3	11♌	18♌	9♍	7♋
4	11♌	20♌	10♍	8♋
5	12♌	22♌	12♍	9♋
6	13♌	24♌	13♍	9♋
7	14♌	26♌	14♍	10♋
8	15♌	28♌	15♍	11♋
9	16♌	0♍	16♍	11♋
10	17♌	1♍	18♍	12♋
11	18♌	3♍	19♍	13♋
12	19♌	5♍	20♍	13♋
13	20♌	7♍	21♍	14♋
14	21♌	8♍	22♍	15♋
15	22♌	10♍	24♍	15♋
16	23♌	12♍	25♍	16♋
17	24♌	13♍	26♍	17♋
18	25♌	15♍	27♍	17♋
19	26♌	16♍	28♍	18♋
20	27♌	18♍	0♎	18♋
21	28♌	19♍	1♎	19♋
22	29♌	21♍	2♎	20♋
23	0♍	22♍	3♎	20♋
24	1♍	24♍	4♎	21♋
25	2♍	25♍	6♎	22♋
26	3♍	27♍	7♎	22♋
27	4♍	28♍	8♎	23♋
28	5♍	29♍	9♎	24♋
29	6♍	1♎	10♎	24♋
30	6♍	2♎	12♎	25♋
31	7♍	3♎	13♎	26♋

November

Day	☉	☿	♀	♂
1	8♏	26♎	25♐	3♍
2	9♏	27♎	26♐	3♍
3	10♏	29♎	27♐	4♍
4	11♏	1♏	28♐	5♍
5	12♏	2♏	29♐	5♍
6	13♏	4♏	0♑	6♍
7	14♏	6♏	1♑	6♍
8	15♏	7♏	2♑	7♍
9	16♏	9♏	3♑	7♍
10	17♏	10♏	4♑	8♍
11	18♏	12♏	5♑	8♍
12	19♏	14♏	6♑	9♍
13	20♏	15♏	7♑	9♍
14	21♏	17♏	9♑	10♍
15	23♏	19♏	10♑	11♍
16	24♏	20♏	11♑	11♍
17	25♏	22♏	12♑	12♍
18	26♏	23♏	13♑	12♍
19	27♏	25♏	14♑	13♍
20	28♏	27♏	15♑	13♍
21	29♏	28♏	16♑	14♍
22	0♐	0♐	17♑	14♍
23	1♐	1♐	18♑	15♍
24	2♐	3♐	19♑	15♍
25	3♐	4♐	20♑	16♍
26	4♐	6♐	21♑	16♍
27	5♐	8♐	22♑	17♍
28	6♐	9♐	23♑	17♍
29	7♐	11♐	24♑	18♍
30	8♐	12♐	25♑	18♍

March

Day	☉	☿	♀	♂
1	10♓	13♒	29♒	14♓
2	11♓	14♒	0♓	15♓
3	12♓	15♒	1♓	15♓
4	13♓	17♒	2♓	16♓
5	14♓	18♒	4♓	17♓
6	15♓	19♒	5♓	18♓
7	16♓	20♒	6♓	18♓
8	17♓	22♒	7♓	19♓
9	18♓	23♒	8♓	20♓
10	19♓	24♒	10♓	21♓
11	20♓	26♒	11♓	22♓
12	21♓	27♒	12♓	22♓
13	22♓	28♒	13♓	23♓
14	23♓	0♓	15♓	24♓
15	24♓	1♓	16♓	25♓
16	25♓	3♓	17♓	26♓
17	26♓	4♓	18♓	26♓
18	27♓	6♓	20♓	27♓
19	28♓	7♓	21♓	28♓
20	29♓	9♓	22♓	29♓
21	0♈	10♓	23♓	29♓
22	1♈	12♓	25♓	0♈
23	2♈	14♓	26♓	1♈
24	3♈	15♓	27♓	2♈
25	4♈	17♓	28♓	3♈
26	5♈	19♓	0♈	3♈
27	6♈	20♓	1♈	4♈
28	7♈	22♓	2♈	5♈
29	8♈	24♓	3♈	6♈
30	9♈	26♓	5♈	6♈
31	10♈	27♓	6♈	7♈

June

Day	☉	☿	♀	♂
1	10♊	14♊	22♊	24♉
2	11♊	14♊	24♊	24♉
3	12♊	13♊	25♊	25♉
4	13♊	13♊	26♊	26♉
5	14♊	12♊	27♊	27♉
6	15♊	12♊	28♊	27♉
7	16♊	11♊	0♋	28♉
8	17♊	11♊	1♋	29♉
9	18♊	10♊	2♋	29♉
10	19♊	10♊	3♋	0♊
11	20♊	9♊	5♋	1♊
12	21♊	9♊	6♋	2♊
13	22♊	9♊	7♋	2♊
14	23♊	9♊	8♋	3♊
15	24♊	9♊	9♋	4♊
16	25♊	9♊	11♋	4♊
17	26♊	9♊	12♋	5♊
18	27♊	9♊	13♋	6♊
19	28♊	9♊	14♋	7♊
20	29♊	9♊	16♋	7♊
21	29♊	10♊	17♋	8♊
22	0♋	10♊	18♋	9♊
23	1♋	11♊	19♋	9♊
24	2♋	11♊	21♋	10♊
25	3♋	12♊	22♋	11♊
26	4♋	13♊	23♋	11♊
27	5♋	13♊	24♋	12♊
28	6♋	14♊	25♋	13♊
29	7♋	15♊	27♋	14♊
30	8♋	16♊	28♋	14♊

September

Day	☉	☿	♀	♂
1	8♍	4♎	14♎	26♋
2	9♍	6♎	15♎	27♋
3	10♍	7♎	16♎	27♋
4	11♍	8♎	18♎	28♋
5	12♍	9♎	19♎	29♋
6	13♍	10♎	20♎	29♋
7	14♍	11♎	21♎	0♌
8	15♍	12♎	22♎	1♌
9	16♍	13♎	23♎	1♌
10	17♍	14♎	25♎	2♌
11	18♍	15♎	26♎	3♌
12	19♍	15♎	27♎	3♌
13	20♍	16♎	28♎	4♌
14	21♍	17♎	29♎	4♌
15	22♍	17♎	1♏	5♌
16	23♍	18♎	2♏	6♌
17	24♍	18♎	3♏	6♌
18	25♍	19♎	4♏	7♌
19	26♍	19♎	5♏	7♌
20	27♍	19♎	6♏	8♌
21	28♍	19♎	8♏	9♌
22	29♍	19♎	9♏	9♌
23	0♎	19♎	10♏	10♌
24	1♎	19♎	11♏	11♌
25	2♎	18♎	12♏	11♌
26	3♎	18♎	14♏	12♌
27	4♎	17♎	15♏	12♌
28	5♎	16♎	16♏	13♌
29	6♎	15♎	17♏	14♌
30	7♎	14♎	18♏	14♌

December

Day	☉	☿	♀	♂
1	9♐	14♐	25♑	19♍
2	10♐	15♐	26♑	19♍
3	11♐	17♐	27♑	20♍
4	12♐	19♐	28♑	20♍
5	13♐	20♐	29♑	21♍
6	14♐	22♐	0♒	21♍
7	15♐	23♐	1♒	22♍
8	16♐	25♐	2♒	22♍
9	17♐	26♐	3♒	23♍
10	18♐	28♐	3♒	23♍
11	19♐	29♐	4♒	24♍
12	20♐	1♑	5♒	24♍
13	21♐	3♑	6♒	24♍
14	22♐	4♑	7♒	25♍
15	23♐	6♑	7♒	25♍
16	24♐	7♑	8♒	26♍
17	25♐	9♑	9♒	26♍
18	26♐	10♑	9♒	27♍
19	27♐	12♑	10♒	27♍
20	28♐	13♑	11♒	28♍
21	29♐	15♑	12♒	28♍
22	0♑	16♑	12♒	28♍
23	1♑	18♑	13♒	29♍
24	2♑	19♑	13♒	29♍
25	3♑	21♑	14♒	0♎
26	4♑	22♑	14♒	0♎
27	5♑	24♑	15♒	0♎
28	6♑	25♑	15♒	1♎
29	7♑	26♑	16♒	1♎
30	8♑	27♑	16♒	2♎
31	9♑	29♑	17♒	2♎

Planetary Positions

♌ = Leo ♍ = Virgo ♎ = Libra ♏ = Scorpio ♐ = Sagittarius ♑ = Capricorn ♒ = Aquarius ♓ = Pisces

1950

January

Day	☉	☿	♀	♂
1	10♑	0♒	17♒	2♎
2	11♑	1♒	17♒	3♎
3	12♑	2♒	18♒	3♎
4	13♑	2♒	18♒	3♎
5	14♑	3♒	18♒	4♎
6	15♑	4♒	18♒	4♎
7	16♑	4♒	19♒	4♎
8	17♑	4♒	19♒	5♎
9	18♑	4♒	19♒	5♎
10	19♑	4♒	19♒	5♎
11	20♑	4♒	19♒	6♎
12	21♑	3♒	19♒	6♎
13	22♑	2♒	19♒	6♎
14	23♑	1♒	18♒	7♎
15	24♑	0♒	18♒	7♎
16	26♑	29♑	18♒	7♎
17	27♑	28♑	18♒	7♎
18	28♑	26♑	18♒	8♎
19	29♑	25♑	17♒	8♎
20	0♒	24♑	17♒	8♎
21	1♒	23♑	16♒	8♎
22	2♒	22♑	16♒	9♎
23	3♒	21♑	15♒	9♎
24	4♒	20♑	15♒	9♎
25	5♒	19♑	14♒	9♎
26	6♒	19♑	14♒	9♎
27	7♒	18♑	13♒	10♎
28	8♒	18♑	13♒	10♎
29	9♒	18♑	12♒	10♎
30	10♒	18♑	11♒	10♎
31	11♒	18♑	11♒	10♎

April

Day	☉	☿	♀	♂
1	11♈	15♈	25♒	29♍
2	12♈	17♈	26♒	28♍
3	13♈	19♈	27♒	28♍
4	14♈	21♈	28♒	28♍
5	15♈	23♈	29♒	27♍
6	16♈	25♈	0♓	27♍
7	17♈	28♈	1♓	26♍
8	18♈	29♈	1♓	26♍
9	19♈	1♉	2♓	26♍
10	20♈	3♉	3♓	26♍
11	21♈	5♉	4♓	25♍
12	22♈	7♉	5♓	25♍
13	23♈	9♉	6♓	25♍
14	24♈	11♉	7♓	24♍
15	25♈	12♉	8♓	24♍
16	26♈	14♉	9♓	24♍
17	27♈	15♉	10♓	24♍
18	28♈	17♉	11♓	24♍
19	29♈	18♉	12♓	23♍
20	0♉	19♉	13♓	23♍
21	1♉	20♉	14♓	23♍
22	2♉	22♉	16♓	23♍
23	2♉	23♉	17♓	23♍
24	3♉	23♉	18♓	23♍
25	4♉	24♉	19♓	22♍
26	5♉	25♉	20♓	22♍
27	6♉	26♉	21♓	22♍
28	7♉	26♉	22♓	22♍
29	8♉	27♉	23♓	22♍
30	9♉	27♉	24♓	22♍

July

Day	☉	☿	♀	♂
1	9♋	27♊	4♊	8♎
2	10♋	29♊	6♊	9♎
3	11♋	1♋	7♊	9♎
4	12♋	3♋	8♊	10♎
5	13♋	5♋	9♊	10♎
6	14♋	8♋	10♊	11♎
7	15♋	10♋	12♊	11♎
8	15♋	12♋	13♊	11♎
9	16♋	14♋	14♊	12♎
10	17♋	16♋	15♊	12♎
11	18♋	18♋	16♊	13♎
12	19♋	21♋	17♊	14♎
13	20♋	23♋	19♊	14♎
14	21♋	25♋	20♊	15♎
15	22♋	27♋	21♊	15♎
16	23♋	29♋	22♊	16♎
17	24♋	1♌	23♊	16♎
18	25♋	3♌	25♊	17♎
19	26♋	5♌	26♊	17♎
20	27♋	7♌	27♊	18♎
21	28♋	9♌	28♊	18♎
22	29♋	11♌	29♊	19♎
23	0♌	13♌	1♋	19♎
24	1♌	15♌	2♋	20♎
25	2♌	16♌	3♋	20♎
26	3♌	18♌	4♋	21♎
27	4♌	20♌	5♋	22♎
28	5♌	22♌	7♋	22♎
29	6♌	24♌	8♋	23♎
30	6♌	25♌	9♋	23♎
31	7♌	27♌	10♋	24♎

October

Day	☉	☿	♀	♂
1	7♎	20♍	26♍	4♐
2	8♎	21♍	27♍	4♐
3	9♎	22♍	29♍	5♐
4	10♎	23♍	0♎	6♐
5	11♎	24♍	1♎	7♐
6	12♎	25♍	2♎	7♐
7	13♎	26♍	4♎	8♐
8	14♎	28♍	5♎	9♐
9	15♎	29♍	6♎	9♐
10	16♎	1♎	7♎	10♐
11	17♎	3♎	9♎	11♐
12	18♎	4♎	10♎	12♐
13	19♎	6♎	11♎	12♐
14	20♎	7♎	12♎	13♐
15	21♎	9♎	14♎	14♐
16	22♎	11♎	15♎	14♐
17	23♎	13♎	16♎	15♐
18	24♎	14♎	17♎	16♐
19	25♎	16♎	19♎	17♐
20	26♎	18♎	20♎	17♐
21	27♎	19♎	21♎	18♐
22	28♎	21♎	22♎	19♐
23	29♎	23♎	24♎	20♐
24	0♏	25♎	25♎	20♐
25	1♏	26♎	26♎	21♐
26	2♏	28♎	27♎	22♐
27	3♏	0♏	29♎	23♐
28	4♏	1♏	0♏	23♐
29	5♏	3♏	1♏	24♐
30	6♏	5♏	2♏	25♐
31	7♏	6♏	4♏	25♐

February

Day	☉	☿	♀	♂
1	12♒	19♑	10♒	10♎
2	13♒	19♑	10♒	10♎
3	14♒	19♑	9♒	11♎
4	15♒	20♑	8♒	11♎
5	16♒	21♑	8♒	11♎
6	17♒	21♑	7♒	11♎
7	18♒	22♑	7♒	11♎
8	19♒	23♑	6♒	11♎
9	20♒	24♑	6♒	11♎
10	21♒	25♑	5♒	11♎
11	22♒	26♑	5♒	11♎
12	23♒	27♑	5♒	11♎
13	24♒	28♑	4♒	11♎
14	25♒	29♑	4♒	11♎
15	26♒	0♒	4♒	11♎
16	27♒	2♒	4♒	11♎
17	28♒	3♒	3♒	11♎
18	29♒	4♒	3♒	11♎
19	0♓	5♒	3♒	11♎
20	1♓	7♒	3♒	11♎
21	2♓	8♒	3♒	11♎
22	3♓	9♒	3♒	10♎
23	4♓	11♒	3♒	10♎
24	5♓	12♒	3♒	10♎
25	6♓	14♒	3♒	10♎
26	7♓	15♒	4♒	10♎
27	8♓	17♒	4♒	10♎
28	9♓	18♒	4♒	9♎

May

Day	☉	☿	♀	♂
1	10♉	27♉	25♓	22♍
2	11♉	27♉	26♓	22♍
3	12♉	28♉	27♓	22♍
4	13♉	28♉	28♓	22♍
5	14♉	27♉	29♓	22♍
6	15♉	27♉	0♈	22♍
7	16♉	27♉	2♈	22♍
8	17♉	27♉	3♈	22♍
9	18♉	26♉	4♈	22♍
10	19♉	26♉	5♈	22♍
11	20♉	25♉	6♈	22♍
12	21♉	25♉	7♈	22♍
13	22♉	24♉	8♈	23♍
14	23♉	24♉	9♈	23♍
15	24♉	23♉	10♈	23♍
16	25♉	23♉	11♈	23♍
17	26♉	22♉	13♈	23♍
18	27♉	21♉	14♈	23♍
19	28♉	21♉	15♈	23♍
20	29♉	20♉	16♈	24♍
21	0♊	20♉	17♈	24♍
22	1♊	20♉	18♈	24♍
23	2♊	19♉	19♈	24♍
24	2♊	19♉	20♈	24♍
25	3♊	19♉	22♈	25♍
26	4♊	19♉	23♈	25♍
27	5♊	19♉	24♈	25♍
28	6♊	19♉	25♈	25♍
29	7♊	19♉	26♈	26♍
30	8♊	19♉	27♈	26♍
31	9♊	19♉	28♈	26♍

August

Day	☉	☿	♀	♂
1	8♌	29♌	11♋	24♎
2	9♌	0♍	13♋	25♎
3	10♌	2♍	14♋	26♎
4	11♌	3♍	15♋	26♎
5	12♌	5♍	16♋	27♎
6	13♌	6♍	17♋	27♎
7	14♌	8♍	19♋	28♎
8	15♌	9♍	20♋	29♎
9	16♌	11♍	21♋	29♎
10	17♌	12♍	22♋	0♏
11	18♌	13♍	23♋	0♏
12	19♌	15♍	25♋	1♏
13	20♌	16♍	26♋	2♏
14	21♌	17♍	27♋	2♏
15	22♌	18♍	28♋	3♏
16	23♌	20♍	0♌	3♏
17	24♌	21♍	1♌	4♏
18	25♌	22♍	2♌	5♏
19	26♌	23♍	3♌	5♏
20	27♌	24♍	4♌	6♏
21	28♌	25♍	6♌	6♏
22	29♌	26♍	7♌	7♏
23	0♍	27♍	8♌	8♏
24	0♍	28♍	9♌	8♏
25	1♍	28♍	11♌	9♏
26	2♍	29♍	12♌	10♏
27	3♍	0♎	13♌	10♏
28	4♍	0♎	14♌	11♏
29	5♍	1♎	15♌	12♏
30	6♍	1♎	17♌	12♏
31	7♍	2♎	18♌	13♏

November

Day	☉	☿	♀	♂
1	8♏	8♏	5♏	26♐
2	9♏	10♏	6♏	27♐
3	10♏	11♏	7♏	28♐
4	11♏	13♏	9♏	28♐
5	12♏	14♏	10♏	29♐
6	13♏	16♏	11♏	0♑
7	14♏	18♏	13♏	1♑
8	15♏	19♏	14♏	1♑
9	16♏	21♏	15♏	2♑
10	17♏	22♏	16♏	3♑
11	18♏	24♏	18♏	4♑
12	19♏	25♏	19♏	4♑
13	20♏	27♏	20♏	5♑
14	21♏	29♏	21♏	6♑
15	22♏	0♐	23♏	7♑
16	23♏	2♐	24♏	8♑
17	24♏	3♐	25♏	8♑
18	25♏	5♐	26♏	9♑
19	26♏	6♐	28♏	10♑
20	27♏	8♐	29♏	11♑
21	28♏	9♐	0♐	11♑
22	29♏	11♐	1♐	12♑
23	0♐	12♐	3♐	13♑
24	1♐	14♐	4♐	14♑
25	2♐	15♐	5♐	14♑
26	3♐	17♐	6♐	15♑
27	4♐	18♐	8♐	16♑
28	5♐	20♐	9♐	17♑
29	6♐	21♐	10♐	17♑
30	7♐	23♐	11♐	18♑

March

Day	☉	☿	♀	♂
1	10♓	19♒	4♒	9♎
2	11♓	21♒	5♒	9♎
3	12♓	23♒	5♒	9♎
4	13♓	24♒	6♒	8♎
5	14♓	26♒	6♒	8♎
6	15♓	27♒	6♒	8♎
7	16♓	29♒	7♒	8♎
8	17♓	0♓	7♒	7♎
9	18♓	2♓	8♒	7♎
10	19♓	4♓	8♒	7♎
11	20♓	5♓	9♒	6♎
12	21♓	7♓	10♒	6♎
13	22♓	9♓	10♒	6♎
14	23♓	11♓	11♒	5♎
15	24♓	12♓	11♒	5♎
16	25♓	14♓	12♒	5♎
17	26♓	16♓	13♒	4♎
18	27♓	18♓	14♒	4♎
19	28♓	20♓	14♒	4♎
20	29♓	21♓	15♒	3♎
21	0♈	23♓	16♒	3♎
22	1♈	25♓	17♒	2♎
23	2♈	27♓	17♒	2♎
24	3♈	29♓	18♒	2♎
25	4♈	1♈	19♒	1♎
26	5♈	3♈	20♒	1♎
27	6♈	5♈	21♒	0♎
28	7♈	7♈	21♒	0♎
29	8♈	9♈	22♒	0♎
30	9♈	11♈	23♒	29♍
31	10♈	13♈	24♒	29♍

June

Day	☉	☿	♀	♂
1	10♊	19♉	0♉	26♍
2	11♊	20♉	1♉	27♍
3	12♊	20♉	2♉	27♍
4	13♊	21♉	3♉	27♍
5	14♊	21♉	4♉	28♍
6	15♊	22♉	5♉	28♍
7	16♊	23♉	6♉	28♍
8	17♊	23♉	8♉	29♍
9	18♊	24♉	9♉	29♍
10	19♊	25♉	10♉	29♍
11	20♊	26♉	11♉	0♎
12	21♊	27♉	12♉	0♎
13	22♊	28♉	13♉	1♎
14	23♊	0♊	15♉	1♎
15	24♊	1♊	16♉	1♎
16	24♊	2♊	17♉	2♎
17	25♊	3♊	18♉	2♎
18	26♊	5♊	19♉	2♎
19	27♊	6♊	20♉	3♎
20	28♊	8♊	22♉	3♎
21	29♊	9♊	23♉	4♎
22	0♋	11♊	24♉	4♎
23	1♋	12♊	25♉	5♎
24	2♋	14♊	26♉	5♎
25	3♋	16♊	27♉	5♎
26	4♋	18♊	29♉	6♎
27	5♋	19♊	0♊	6♎
28	6♋	21♊	1♊	7♎
29	7♋	23♊	2♊	7♎
30	8♋	25♊	3♊	8♎

September

Day	☉	☿	♀	♂
1	8♍	2♎	19♌	13♏
2	9♍	2♎	20♌	14♏
3	10♍	2♎	22♌	15♏
4	11♍	2♎	23♌	15♏
5	12♍	2♎	24♌	16♏
6	13♍	2♎	25♌	17♏
7	14♍	2♎	26♌	17♏
8	15♍	2♎	28♌	18♏
9	16♍	1♎	29♌	19♏
10	17♍	0♎	0♍	19♏
11	18♍	0♎	1♍	20♏
12	19♍	29♍	3♍	21♏
13	20♍	28♍	4♍	21♏
14	21♍	27♍	5♍	22♏
15	22♍	26♍	6♍	23♏
16	23♍	25♍	8♍	23♏
17	24♍	24♍	9♍	24♏
18	25♍	23♍	10♍	25♏
19	26♍	22♍	11♍	25♏
20	27♍	21♍	13♍	26♏
21	28♍	20♍	14♍	27♏
22	29♍	19♍	15♍	28♏
23	0♎	19♍	16♍	28♏
24	1♎	18♍	18♍	29♏
25	2♎	18♍	19♍	0♐
26	3♎	18♍	20♍	0♐
27	4♎	18♍	21♍	1♐
28	5♎	18♍	22♍	2♐
29	5♎	19♍	24♍	2♐
30	6♎	19♍	25♍	3♐

December

Day	☉	☿	♀	♂
1	8♐	24♐	13♐	19♑
2	9♐	26♐	14♐	20♑
3	10♐	27♐	15♐	21♑
4	11♐	29♐	16♐	21♑
5	12♐	0♑	18♐	22♑
6	14♐	2♑	19♐	23♑
7	15♐	3♑	20♐	24♑
8	16♐	4♑	21♐	24♑
9	17♐	6♑	23♐	25♑
10	18♐	7♑	24♐	26♑
11	19♐	8♑	25♐	27♑
12	20♐	10♑	26♐	28♑
13	21♐	11♑	28♐	28♑
14	22♐	12♑	29♐	29♑
15	23♐	13♑	0♑	0♒
16	24♐	14♑	2♑	1♒
17	25♐	15♑	3♑	1♒
18	26♐	16♑	4♑	2♒
19	27♐	17♑	5♑	3♒
20	28♐	17♑	7♑	4♒
21	29♐	18♑	8♑	5♒
22	0♑	18♑	9♑	5♒
23	1♑	18♑	10♑	6♒
24	2♑	18♑	12♑	7♒
25	3♑	18♑	13♑	8♒
26	4♑	18♑	14♑	8♒
27	5♑	17♑	15♑	9♒
28	6♑	16♑	17♑	10♒
29	7♑	15♑	18♑	11♒
30	8♑	14♑	19♑	12♒
31	9♑	13♑	20♑	12♒

1951

Your Starway to Love

☉ =Sun ☿ = Mercury ♀ = Venus ♂ = Mars ♈ = Aries ♉ = Taurus ♊ = Gemini ♋ = Cancer

January

Day	☉	☿	♀	♂
1	10♑	12♑	22♑	13♒
2	11♑	10♑	23♑	14♒
3	12♑	9♑	24♑	15♒
4	13♑	7♑	25♑	16♒
5	14♑	6♑	27♑	16♒
6	15♑	5♑	28♑	17♒
7	16♑	4♑	29♑	18♒
8	17♑	3♑	0♒	19♒
9	18♑	3♑	2♒	19♒
10	19♑	2♑	3♒	20♒
11	20♑	2♑	4♒	21♒
12	21♑	2♑	5♒	22♒
13	22♑	2♑	7♒	23♒
14	23♑	2♑	8♒	23♒
15	24♑	2♑	9♒	24♒
16	25♑	3♑	10♒	25♒
17	26♑	3♑	12♒	26♒
18	27♑	4♑	13♒	27♒
19	28♑	5♑	14♒	27♒
20	29♑	5♑	15♒	28♒
21	0♒	6♑	17♒	29♒
22	1♒	7♑	18♒	0♓
23	2♒	8♑	19♒	1♓
24	3♒	9♑	20♒	1♓
25	4♒	10♑	22♒	2♓
26	5♒	11♑	23♒	3♓
27	6♒	12♑	24♒	4♓
28	7♒	13♑	25♒	4♓
29	8♒	15♑	27♒	5♓
30	9♒	16♑	28♒	6♓
31	11♒	17♑	29♒	7♓

February

Day	☉	☿	♀	♂
1	12♒	18♑	0♓	8♓
2	13♒	20♑	2♓	8♓
3	14♒	21♑	3♓	9♓
4	15♒	22♑	4♓	10♓
5	16♒	24♑	5♓	11♓
6	17♒	25♑	7♓	12♓
7	18♒	26♑	8♓	12♓
8	19♒	28♑	9♓	13♓
9	20♒	29♑	10♓	14♓
10	21♒	1♒	12♓	15♓
11	22♒	2♒	13♓	15♓
12	23♒	4♒	14♓	16♓
13	24♒	5♒	15♓	17♓
14	25♒	7♒	17♓	18♓
15	26♒	8♒	18♓	19♓
16	27♒	10♒	19♓	19♓
17	28♒	11♒	20♓	20♓
18	29♒	13♒	22♓	21♓
19	0♓	14♒	23♓	22♓
20	1♓	16♒	24♓	22♓
21	2♓	18♒	25♓	23♓
22	3♓	19♒	27♓	24♓
23	4♓	21♒	28♓	25♓
24	5♓	23♒	29♓	26♓
25	6♓	24♒	0♈	26♓
26	7♓	26♒	2♈	27♓
27	8♓	28♒	3♈	28♓
28	9♓	29♒	4♈	29♓

March

Day	☉	☿	♀	♂
1	10♓	1♓	5♈	29♓
2	11♓	3♓	6♈	0♈
3	12♓	5♓	8♈	1♈
4	13♓	7♓	9♈	2♈
5	14♓	8♓	10♈	3♈
6	15♓	10♓	11♈	3♈
7	16♓	12♓	13♈	4♈
8	17♓	14♓	14♈	5♈
9	18♓	16♓	15♈	6♈
10	19♓	18♓	16♈	6♈
11	20♓	20♓	18♈	7♈
12	21♓	22♓	19♈	8♈
13	22♓	24♓	20♈	9♈
14	23♓	25♓	21♈	10♈
15	24♓	27♓	22♈	10♈
16	25♓	29♓	24♈	11♈
17	26♓	1♈	25♈	12♈
18	27♓	3♈	26♈	13♈
19	28♓	5♈	27♈	13♈
20	29♓	7♈	29♈	14♈
21	0♈	9♈	0♉	15♈
22	1♈	11♈	1♉	16♈
23	2♈	13♈	2♉	16♈
24	3♈	15♈	3♉	17♈
25	4♈	17♈	5♉	18♈
26	5♈	19♈	6♉	19♈
27	6♈	21♈	7♉	19♈
28	7♈	22♈	8♉	20♈
29	8♈	24♈	9♉	21♈
30	9♈	26♈	11♉	22♈
31	10♈	27♈	12♉	22♈

April

Day	☉	☿	♀	♂
1	11♈	29♈	13♉	23♈
2	12♈	0♉	14♉	24♈
3	13♈	1♉	15♉	25♈
4	14♈	3♉	17♉	25♈
5	15♈	4♉	18♉	26♈
6	16♈	5♉	19♉	27♈
7	17♈	5♉	20♉	28♈
8	18♈	6♉	21♉	28♈
9	19♈	7♉	23♉	29♈
10	20♈	7♉	24♉	0♉
11	21♈	8♉	25♉	1♉
12	21♈	8♉	26♉	1♉
13	22♈	8♉	27♉	2♉
14	23♈	9♉	29♉	3♉
15	24♈	9♉	0♊	4♉
16	25♈	8♉	1♊	4♉
17	26♈	8♉	2♊	5♉
18	27♈	8♉	3♊	6♉
19	28♈	8♉	5♊	7♉
20	29♈	7♉	6♊	7♉
21	0♉	7♉	7♊	8♉
22	1♉	6♉	8♊	9♉
23	2♉	5♉	9♊	9♉
24	3♉	5♉	10♊	10♉
25	4♉	4♉	12♊	11♉
26	5♉	3♉	13♊	12♉
27	6♉	3♉	14♊	12♉
28	7♉	2♉	15♊	13♉
29	8♉	1♉	16♊	14♉
30	9♉	1♉	17♊	15♉

May

Day	☉	☿	♀	♂
1	10♉	0♉	19♊	15♉
2	11♉	0♉	20♊	16♉
3	12♉	29♈	21♊	17♉
4	13♉	29♈	22♊	17♉
5	14♉	29♈	23♊	18♉
6	15♉	29♈	24♊	19♉
7	16♉	28♈	26♊	20♉
8	17♉	28♈	27♊	20♉
9	18♉	28♈	28♊	21♉
10	19♉	28♈	29♊	22♉
11	20♉	29♈	0♋	23♉
12	21♉	29♈	1♋	23♉
13	22♉	29♈	2♋	24♉
14	23♉	0♉	4♋	25♉
15	24♉	0♉	5♋	25♉
16	25♉	1♉	6♋	26♉
17	25♉	1♉	7♋	27♉
18	26♉	2♉	8♋	28♉
19	27♉	3♉	9♋	28♉
20	28♉	3♉	10♋	29♉
21	29♉	4♉	11♋	0♊
22	0♊	5♉	13♋	0♊
23	1♊	6♉	14♋	1♊
24	2♊	7♉	15♋	2♊
25	3♊	8♉	16♋	3♊
26	4♊	9♉	17♋	3♊
27	5♊	10♉	18♋	4♊
28	6♊	12♉	19♋	5♊
29	7♊	13♉	20♋	5♊
30	8♊	14♉	21♋	6♊
31	9♊	16♉	22♋	7♊

June

Day	☉	☿	♀	♂
1	10♊	17♉	24♋	7♊
2	11♊	18♉	25♋	8♊
3	12♊	20♉	26♋	9♊
4	13♊	21♉	27♋	10♊
5	14♊	23♉	28♋	10♊
6	15♊	25♉	29♋	11♊
7	16♊	26♉	0♌	12♊
8	17♊	28♉	1♌	12♊
9	18♊	0♊	2♌	13♊
10	19♊	2♊	3♌	14♊
11	19♊	3♊	4♌	14♊
12	20♊	5♊	5♌	15♊
13	21♊	7♊	6♌	16♊
14	22♊	9♊	7♌	16♊
15	23♊	11♊	8♌	17♊
16	24♊	13♊	9♌	18♊
17	25♊	15♊	10♌	19♊
18	26♊	17♊	11♌	19♊
19	27♊	19♊	12♌	20♊
20	28♊	21♊	13♌	21♊
21	29♊	24♊	14♌	21♊
22	0♋	26♊	15♌	22♊
23	1♋	28♊	16♌	23♊
24	2♋	0♋	17♌	23♊
25	3♋	2♋	18♌	24♊
26	4♋	5♋	19♌	25♊
27	5♋	7♋	20♌	25♊
28	6♋	9♋	21♌	26♊
29	7♋	11♋	22♌	27♊
30	8♋	13♋	23♌	27♊

July

Day	☉	☿	♀	♂
1	9♋	15♋	24♌	28♊
2	10♋	17♋	25♌	29♊
3	10♋	19♋	26♌	29♊
4	11♋	21♋	27♌	0♋
5	12♋	23♋	27♌	1♋
6	13♋	25♋	28♌	1♋
7	14♋	27♋	29♌	2♋
8	15♋	29♋	0♍	3♋
9	16♋	1♌	1♍	4♋
10	17♋	3♌	2♍	4♋
11	18♋	5♌	2♍	5♋
12	19♋	7♌	3♍	6♋
13	20♋	8♌	4♍	6♋
14	21♋	10♌	5♍	7♋
15	22♋	12♌	6♍	8♋
16	23♋	13♌	6♍	8♋
17	24♋	15♌	7♍	9♋
18	25♋	17♌	8♍	10♋
19	26♋	18♌	8♍	10♋
20	27♋	20♌	9♍	11♋
21	28♋	21♌	10♍	12♋
22	29♋	23♌	10♍	12♋
23	0♌	24♌	11♍	13♋
24	1♌	25♌	12♍	14♋
25	1♌	27♌	12♍	14♋
26	2♌	28♌	13♍	15♋
27	3♌	29♌	13♍	15♋
28	4♌	1♍	14♍	16♋
29	5♌	2♍	14♍	17♋
30	6♌	3♍	15♍	17♋
31	7♌	4♍	15♍	18♋

August

Day	☉	☿	♀	♂
1	8♌	5♍	16♍	19♋
2	9♌	6♍	16♍	19♋
3	10♌	7♍	16♍	20♋
4	11♌	8♍	17♍	21♋
5	12♌	9♍	17♍	21♋
6	13♌	10♍	17♍	22♋
7	14♌	11♍	18♍	23♋
8	15♌	12♍	18♍	23♋
9	16♌	12♍	18♍	24♋
10	17♌	13♍	18♍	25♋
11	18♌	13♍	18♍	25♋
12	19♌	14♍	18♍	26♋
13	20♌	14♍	18♍	27♋
14	21♌	15♍	18♍	27♋
15	22♌	15♍	18♍	28♋
16	23♌	15♍	18♍	29♋
17	23♌	15♍	18♍	29♋
18	24♌	15♍	18♍	0♌
19	25♌	15♍	18♍	0♌
20	26♌	15♍	17♍	1♌
21	27♌	15♍	17♍	2♌
22	28♌	14♍	17♍	2♌
23	29♌	14♍	16♍	3♌
24	0♍	13♍	16♍	4♌
25	1♍	12♍	16♍	4♌
26	2♍	12♍	15♍	5♌
27	3♍	11♍	15♍	6♌
28	4♍	10♍	14♍	6♌
29	5♍	9♍	14♍	7♌
30	6♍	8♍	13♍	8♌
31	7♍	7♍	12♍	8♌

September

Day	☉	☿	♀	♂
1	8♍	6♍	12♍	9♌
2	9♍	5♍	11♍	9♌
3	10♍	5♍	11♍	10♌
4	11♍	4♍	10♍	11♌
5	12♍	3♍	9♍	11♌
6	13♍	3♍	9♍	12♌
7	14♍	2♍	8♍	13♌
8	15♍	2♍	8♍	13♌
9	16♍	2♍	7♍	14♌
10	17♍	2♍	6♍	15♌
11	18♍	2♍	6♍	15♌
12	19♍	2♍	5♍	16♌
13	20♍	2♍	5♍	16♌
14	21♍	3♍	4♍	17♌
15	22♍	4♍	4♍	18♌
16	23♍	5♍	4♍	18♌
17	24♍	6♍	3♍	19♌
18	24♍	7♍	3♍	20♌
19	25♍	8♍	3♍	20♌
20	26♍	9♍	3♍	21♌
21	27♍	11♍	2♍	21♌
22	28♍	12♍	2♍	22♌
23	29♍	14♍	2♍	23♌
24	0♎	15♍	2♍	23♌
25	1♎	17♍	2♍	24♌
26	2♎	19♍	2♍	25♌
27	3♎	20♍	2♍	25♌
28	4♎	22♍	2♍	26♌
29	5♎	24♍	2♍	26♌
30	6♎	26♍	3♍	27♌

October

Day	☉	☿	♀	♂
1	7♎	27♍	3♍	28♌
2	8♎	29♍	3♍	28♌
3	9♎	1♎	3♍	29♌
4	10♎	3♎	4♍	0♍
5	11♎	5♎	4♍	0♍
6	12♎	6♎	4♍	1♍
7	13♎	8♎	5♍	1♍
8	14♎	10♎	5♍	2♍
9	15♎	12♎	6♍	3♍
10	16♎	14♎	6♍	3♍
11	17♎	15♎	7♍	4♍
12	18♎	17♎	7♍	4♍
13	19♎	19♎	8♍	5♍
14	20♎	20♎	8♍	6♍
15	21♎	22♎	9♍	6♍
16	22♎	24♎	10♍	7♍
17	23♎	26♎	10♍	7♍
18	24♎	27♎	11♍	8♍
19	25♎	29♎	12♍	9♍
20	26♎	0♏	12♍	9♍
21	27♎	2♏	13♍	10♍
22	28♎	4♏	14♍	10♍
23	29♎	5♏	15♍	11♍
24	0♏	7♏	15♍	12♍
25	1♏	9♏	16♍	12♍
26	2♏	10♏	17♍	13♍
27	3♏	12♏	18♍	14♍
28	4♏	13♏	19♍	14♍
29	5♏	15♏	19♍	15♍
30	6♏	16♏	20♍	15♍
31	7♏	18♏	21♍	16♍

November

Day	☉	☿	♀	♂
1	8♏	19♏	22♍	16♍
2	9♏	21♏	23♍	17♍
3	10♏	23♏	24♍	18♍
4	11♏	24♏	25♍	18♍
5	12♏	26♏	26♍	19♍
6	13♏	27♏	27♍	19♍
7	14♏	29♏	28♍	20♍
8	15♏	0♐	28♍	21♍
9	16♏	1♐	29♍	21♍
10	17♏	3♐	0♎	22♍
11	18♏	4♐	1♎	22♍
12	19♏	6♐	2♎	23♍
13	20♏	7♐	3♎	24♍
14	21♏	9♐	4♎	24♍
15	22♏	10♐	5♎	25♍
16	23♏	12♐	6♎	25♍
17	24♏	13♐	7♎	26♍
18	25♏	14♐	8♎	27♍
19	26♏	16♐	10♎	27♍
20	27♏	17♐	11♎	28♍
21	28♏	18♐	12♎	28♍
22	29♏	20♐	13♎	29♍
23	0♐	21♐	14♎	29♍
24	1♐	22♐	15♎	0♎
25	2♐	23♐	16♎	1♎
26	3♐	25♐	17♎	1♎
27	4♐	26♐	18♎	2♎
28	5♐	27♐	19♎	2♎
29	6♐	28♐	20♎	3♎
30	7♐	29♐	21♎	3♎

December

Day	☉	☿	♀	♂
1	8♐	29♐	22♎	4♎
2	9♐	0♑	24♎	5♎
3	10♐	1♑	25♎	5♎
4	11♐	1♑	26♎	6♎
5	12♐	2♑	27♎	6♎
6	13♐	2♑	28♎	7♎
7	14♐	2♑	29♎	7♎
8	15♐	2♑	0♏	8♎
9	16♐	2♑	1♏	8♎
10	17♐	2♑	2♏	9♎
11	18♐	1♑	4♏	10♎
12	19♐	0♑	5♏	10♎
13	20♐	29♐	6♏	11♎
14	21♐	28♐	7♏	11♎
15	22♐	27♐	8♏	12♎
16	23♐	26♐	9♏	12♎
17	24♐	24♐	11♏	13♎
18	25♐	23♐	12♏	13♎
19	26♐	22♐	13♏	14♎
20	27♐	20♐	14♏	15♎
21	29♐	19♐	15♏	15♎
22	0♑	18♐	16♏	16♎
23	1♑	17♐	18♏	16♎
24	2♑	17♐	19♏	17♎
25	3♑	16♐	20♏	17♎
26	4♑	16♐	21♏	18♎
27	5♑	16♐	22♏	18♎
28	6♑	16♐	23♏	19♎
29	7♑	16♐	25♏	19♎
30	8♑	17♐	26♏	20♎
31	9♑	17♐	27♏	20♎

Planetary Positions

♌ = Leo ♍ = Virgo ♎ = Libra ♏ = Scorpio ♐ = Sagittarius ♑ = Capricorn ♒ = Aquarius ♓ = Pisces

1952

January

Day	☉	☿	♀	♂
1	10♑	18♐	28♏	21♎
2	11♑	18♐	29♏	21♎
3	12♑	19♐	1♐	22♎
4	13♑	20♐	2♐	22♎
5	14♑	21♐	3♐	23♎
6	15♑	22♐	4♐	23♎
7	16♑	23♐	5♐	24♎
8	17♑	24♐	6♐	24♎
9	18♑	25♐	8♐	25♎
10	19♑	26♐	9♐	25♎
11	20♑	27♐	10♐	26♎
12	21♑	29♐	11♐	26♎
13	22♑	0♑	12♐	27♎
14	23♑	1♑	14♐	27♎
15	24♑	2♑	15♐	28♎
16	25♑	4♑	16♐	28♎
17	26♑	5♑	17♐	29♎
18	27♑	7♑	19♐	29♎
19	28♑	8♑	20♐	0♏
20	29♑	9♑	21♐	0♏
21	0♒	11♑	22♐	1♏
22	1♒	12♑	23♐	1♏
23	2♒	14♑	25♐	1♏
24	3♒	15♑	26♐	2♏
25	4♒	16♑	27♐	2♏
26	5♒	18♑	28♐	3♏
27	6♒	19♑	29♐	3♏
28	7♒	21♑	1♑	4♏
29	8♒	22♑	2♑	4♏
30	9♒	24♑	3♑	5♏
31	10♒	26♑	4♑	5♏

February

Day	☉	☿	♀	♂
1	11♒	27♑	6♑	5♏
2	12♒	29♑	7♑	6♏
3	13♒	0♒	8♑	6♏
4	14♒	2♒	9♑	7♏
5	15♒	3♒	10♑	7♏
6	16♒	5♒	12♑	7♏
7	17♒	7♒	13♑	8♏
8	18♒	8♒	14♑	8♏
9	19♒	10♒	15♑	9♏
10	20♒	12♒	17♑	9♏
11	21♒	13♒	18♑	9♏
12	22♒	15♒	19♑	10♏
13	23♒	17♒	20♑	10♏
14	24♒	18♒	21♑	10♏
15	25♒	20♒	23♑	11♏
16	26♒	22♒	24♑	11♏
17	27♒	24♒	25♑	11♏
18	28♒	25♒	26♑	12♏
19	29♒	27♒	28♑	12♏
20	1♓	29♒	29♑	12♏
21	2♓	1♓	0♒	13♏
22	3♓	3♓	1♒	13♏
23	4♓	4♓	2♒	13♏
24	5♓	6♓	4♒	14♏
25	6♓	8♓	5♒	14♏
26	7♓	10♓	6♒	14♏
27	8♓	12♓	7♒	14♏
28	9♓	14♓	9♒	15♏
29	10♓	16♓	10♒	15♏

March

Day	☉	☿	♀	♂
1	11♓	18♓	11♒	15♏
2	12♓	20♓	12♒	16♏
3	13♓	22♓	14♒	16♏
4	14♓	23♓	15♒	16♏
5	15♓	25♓	16♒	16♏
6	16♓	27♓	17♒	16♏
7	17♓	29♓	18♒	17♏
8	18♓	1♈	20♒	17♏
9	19♓	3♈	21♒	17♏
10	20♓	4♈	22♒	17♏
11	21♓	6♈	23♒	17♏
12	22♓	8♈	25♒	17♏
13	23♓	9♈	26♒	18♏
14	24♓	11♈	27♒	18♏
15	25♓	12♈	28♒	18♏
16	26♓	14♈	0♓	18♏
17	27♓	15♈	1♓	18♏
18	28♓	16♈	2♓	18♏
19	29♓	17♈	3♓	18♏
20	0♈	18♈	4♓	18♏
21	1♈	19♈	6♓	18♏
22	2♈	19♈	7♓	18♏
23	3♈	20♈	8♓	18♏
24	4♈	20♈	9♓	18♏
25	4♈	20♈	11♓	18♏
26	5♈	20♈	12♓	18♏
27	6♈	20♈	13♓	18♏
28	7♈	20♈	14♓	18♏
29	8♈	20♈	16♓	18♏
30	9♈	20♈	17♓	18♏
31	10♈	19♈	18♓	18♏

April

Day	☉	☿	♀	♂
1	11♈	19♈	19♓	18♏
2	12♈	18♈	20♓	18♏
3	13♈	17♈	22♓	18♏
4	14♈	17♈	23♓	18♏
5	15♈	16♈	24♓	18♏
6	16♈	15♈	25♓	18♏
7	17♈	14♈	27♓	17♏
8	18♈	13♈	28♓	17♏
9	19♈	13♈	29♓	17♏
10	20♈	12♈	0♈	17♏
11	21♈	11♈	2♈	17♏
12	22♈	11♈	3♈	16♏
13	23♈	10♈	4♈	16♏
14	24♈	10♈	5♈	16♏
15	25♈	9♈	6♈	16♏
16	26♈	9♈	8♈	16♏
17	27♈	9♈	9♈	15♏
18	28♈	9♈	10♈	15♏
19	29♈	9♈	11♈	15♏
20	0♉	9♈	13♈	14♏
21	1♉	9♈	14♈	14♏
22	2♉	9♈	15♈	14♏
23	3♉	9♈	16♈	13♏
24	4♉	10♈	18♈	13♏
25	5♉	10♈	19♈	13♏
26	6♉	11♈	20♈	12♏
27	7♉	11♈	21♈	12♏
28	8♉	12♈	22♈	12♏
29	9♉	13♈	24♈	11♏
30	10♉	13♈	25♈	11♏

May

Day	☉	☿	♀	♂
1	11♉	14♈	26♈	11♏
2	12♉	15♈	27♈	10♏
3	13♉	16♈	29♈	10♏
4	14♉	17♈	0♉	9♏
5	15♉	18♈	1♉	9♏
6	16♉	19♈	2♉	9♏
7	17♉	20♈	3♉	8♏
8	18♉	22♈	5♉	8♏
9	19♉	23♈	6♉	8♏
10	19♉	24♈	7♉	7♏
11	20♉	25♈	8♉	7♏
12	21♉	27♈	10♉	7♏
13	22♉	28♈	11♉	6♏
14	23♉	29♈	12♉	6♏
15	24♉	1♉	13♉	6♏
16	25♉	2♉	15♉	5♏
17	26♉	4♉	16♉	5♏
18	27♉	5♉	17♉	5♏
19	28♉	7♉	18♉	4♏
20	29♉	9♉	19♉	4♏
21	0♊	10♉	21♉	4♏
22	1♊	12♉	22♉	4♏
23	2♊	14♉	23♉	3♏
24	3♊	16♉	24♉	3♏
25	4♊	17♉	26♉	3♏
26	5♊	19♉	27♉	3♏
27	6♊	21♉	28♉	2♏
28	7♊	23♉	29♉	2♏
29	8♊	25♉	0♊	2♏
30	9♊	27♉	2♊	2♏
31	10♊	29♉	3♊	2♏

June

Day	☉	☿	♀	♂
1	11♊	1♊	4♊	2♏
2	12♊	3♊	5♊	2♏
3	13♊	5♊	7♊	1♏
4	14♊	8♊	8♊	1♏
5	14♊	10♊	9♊	1♏
6	15♊	12♊	10♊	1♏
7	16♊	14♊	11♊	1♏
8	17♊	16♊	13♊	1♏
9	18♊	18♊	14♊	1♏
10	19♊	21♊	15♊	1♏
11	20♊	23♊	16♊	1♏
12	21♊	25♊	18♊	1♏
13	22♊	27♊	19♊	1♏
14	23♊	29♊	20♊	1♏
15	24♊	1♋	21♊	1♏
16	25♊	4♋	23♊	1♏
17	26♊	6♋	24♊	1♏
18	27♊	8♋	25♊	2♏
19	28♊	10♋	26♊	2♏
20	29♊	12♋	28♊	2♏
21	0♋	14♋	29♊	2♏
22	1♋	16♋	0♋	2♏
23	2♋	17♋	1♋	2♏
24	3♋	19♋	2♋	2♏
25	4♋	21♋	4♋	3♏
26	5♋	23♋	5♋	3♏
27	5♋	25♋	6♋	3♏
28	6♋	26♋	7♋	3♏
29	7♋	28♋	9♋	3♏
30	8♋	0♌	10♋	4♏

July

Day	☉	☿	♀	♂
1	9♋	1♌	11♋	4♏
2	10♋	3♌	12♋	4♏
3	11♋	4♌	13♋	4♏
4	12♋	6♌	15♋	5♏
5	13♋	7♌	16♋	5♏
6	14♋	9♌	17♋	5♏
7	15♋	10♌	18♋	6♏
8	16♋	11♌	20♋	6♏
9	17♋	13♌	21♋	6♏
10	18♋	14♌	22♋	7♏
11	19♋	15♌	23♋	7♏
12	20♋	16♌	25♋	7♏
13	21♋	17♌	26♋	8♏
14	22♋	18♌	27♋	8♏
15	23♋	19♌	28♋	8♏
16	24♋	20♌	29♋	9♏
17	25♋	21♌	1♌	9♏
18	25♋	22♌	2♌	9♏
19	26♋	23♌	3♌	10♏
20	27♋	24♌	4♌	10♏
21	28♋	24♌	6♌	11♏
22	29♋	25♌	7♌	11♏
23	0♌	25♌	8♌	11♏
24	1♌	26♌	9♌	12♏
25	2♌	26♌	11♌	12♏
26	3♌	27♌	12♌	13♏
27	4♌	27♌	13♌	13♏
28	5♌	27♌	14♌	14♏
29	6♌	27♌	15♌	14♏
30	7♌	27♌	17♌	15♏
31	8♌	27♌	18♌	15♏

August

Day	☉	☿	♀	♂
1	9♌	27♌	19♌	16♏
2	10♌	27♌	20♌	16♏
3	11♌	26♌	22♌	17♏
4	12♌	26♌	23♌	17♏
5	13♌	25♌	24♌	18♏
6	14♌	25♌	25♌	18♏
7	15♌	24♌	27♌	19♏
8	16♌	24♌	28♌	19♏
9	17♌	23♌	29♌	20♏
10	17♌	22♌	0♍	20♏
11	18♌	21♌	1♍	21♏
12	19♌	20♌	3♍	21♏
13	20♌	20♌	4♍	22♏
14	21♌	19♌	5♍	22♏
15	22♌	18♌	6♍	23♏
16	23♌	17♌	8♍	23♏
17	24♌	17♌	9♍	24♏
18	25♌	16♌	10♍	24♏
19	26♌	16♌	11♍	25♏
20	27♌	15♌	13♍	26♏
21	28♌	15♌	14♍	26♏
22	29♌	15♌	15♍	27♏
23	0♍	15♌	16♍	27♏
24	1♍	15♌	18♍	28♏
25	2♍	15♌	19♍	28♏
26	3♍	16♌	20♍	29♏
27	4♍	16♌	21♍	0♐
28	5♍	17♌	22♍	0♐
29	6♍	18♌	24♍	1♐
30	7♍	19♌	25♍	1♐
31	8♍	20♌	26♍	2♐

September

Day	☉	☿	♀	♂
1	9♍	21♌	27♍	3♐
2	10♍	22♌	29♍	3♐
3	11♍	23♌	0♎	4♐
4	12♍	25♌	1♎	5♐
5	13♍	26♌	2♎	5♐
6	14♍	28♌	4♎	6♐
7	15♍	0♍	5♎	6♐
8	15♍	1♍	6♎	7♐
9	16♍	3♍	7♎	8♐
10	17♍	5♍	8♎	8♐
11	18♍	7♍	10♎	9♐
12	19♍	8♍	11♎	10♐
13	20♍	10♍	12♎	10♐
14	21♍	12♍	13♎	11♐
15	22♍	14♍	15♎	12♐
16	23♍	16♍	16♎	12♐
17	24♍	18♍	17♎	13♐
18	25♍	20♍	18♎	14♐
19	26♍	22♍	20♎	14♐
20	27♍	23♍	21♎	15♐
21	28♍	25♍	22♎	16♐
22	29♍	27♍	23♎	16♐
23	0♎	29♍	24♎	17♐
24	1♎	1♎	26♎	18♐
25	2♎	3♎	27♎	18♐
26	3♎	4♎	28♎	19♐
27	4♎	6♎	29♎	20♐
28	5♎	8♎	1♏	20♐
29	6♎	10♎	2♏	21♐
30	7♎	11♎	3♏	22♐

October

Day	☉	☿	♀	♂
1	8♎	13♎	4♏	22♐
2	9♎	15♎	5♏	23♐
3	10♎	16♎	7♏	24♐
4	11♎	18♎	8♏	24♐
5	12♎	20♎	9♏	25♐
6	13♎	21♎	10♏	26♐
7	14♎	23♎	12♏	26♐
8	15♎	25♎	13♏	27♐
9	16♎	26♎	14♏	28♐
10	17♎	28♎	15♏	29♐
11	18♎	29♎	17♏	29♐
12	19♎	1♏	18♏	0♑
13	20♎	3♏	19♏	1♑
14	21♎	4♏	20♏	1♑
15	22♎	6♏	21♏	2♑
16	23♎	7♏	23♏	3♑
17	24♎	9♏	24♏	4♑
18	25♎	10♏	25♏	4♑
19	26♎	12♏	26♏	5♑
20	27♎	13♏	28♏	6♑
21	28♎	15♏	29♏	6♑
22	29♎	16♏	0♐	7♑
23	0♏	18♏	1♐	8♑
24	1♏	19♏	2♐	9♑
25	2♏	20♏	4♐	9♑
26	3♏	22♏	5♐	10♑
27	4♏	23♏	6♐	11♑
28	5♏	25♏	7♐	12♑
29	6♏	26♏	9♐	12♑
30	7♏	27♏	10♐	13♑
31	8♏	29♏	11♐	14♑

November

Day	☉	☿	♀	♂
1	9♏	0♐	12♐	15♑
2	10♏	1♐	13♐	15♑
3	11♏	3♐	15♐	16♑
4	12♏	4♐	16♐	17♑
5	13♏	5♐	17♐	18♑
6	14♏	6♐	18♐	18♑
7	15♏	7♐	20♐	19♑
8	16♏	8♐	21♐	20♑
9	17♏	10♐	22♐	20♑
10	18♏	11♐	23♐	21♑
11	19♏	12♐	24♐	22♑
12	20♏	12♐	26♐	23♑
13	21♏	13♐	27♐	23♑
14	22♏	14♐	28♐	24♑
15	23♏	15♐	29♐	25♑
16	24♏	15♐	0♑	26♑
17	25♏	16♐	2♑	27♑
18	26♏	16♐	3♑	27♑
19	27♏	16♐	4♑	28♑
20	28♏	17♐	5♑	29♑
21	29♏	16♐	7♑	0♒
22	0♐	16♐	8♑	0♒
23	1♐	16♐	9♑	1♒
24	2♐	15♐	10♑	2♒
25	3♐	14♐	11♑	3♒
26	4♐	14♐	13♑	3♒
27	5♐	12♐	14♑	4♒
28	6♐	11♐	15♑	5♒
29	7♐	10♐	16♑	6♒
30	8♐	9♐	17♑	6♒

December

Day	☉	☿	♀	♂
1	9♐	7♐	19♑	7♒
2	10♐	6♐	20♑	8♒
3	11♐	5♐	21♑	9♒
4	12♐	3♐	22♑	9♒
5	13♐	2♐	23♑	10♒
6	14♐	2♐	25♑	11♒
7	15♐	1♐	26♑	12♒
8	16♐	1♐	27♑	13♒
9	17♐	0♐	28♑	13♒
10	18♐	0♐	29♑	14♒
11	19♐	0♐	1♒	15♒
12	20♐	1♐	2♒	16♒
13	21♐	1♐	3♒	16♒
14	22♐	2♐	4♒	17♒
15	23♐	2♐	5♒	18♒
16	24♐	3♐	6♒	19♒
17	25♐	4♐	8♒	19♒
18	26♐	5♐	9♒	20♒
19	27♐	6♐	10♒	21♒
20	28♐	7♐	11♒	22♒
21	29♐	8♐	12♒	23♒
22	0♑	9♐	14♒	23♒
23	1♑	10♐	15♒	24♒
24	2♑	11♐	16♒	25♒
25	3♑	13♐	17♒	26♒
26	4♑	14♐	18♒	26♒
27	5♑	15♐	19♒	27♒
28	6♑	17♐	21♒	28♒
29	7♑	18♐	22♒	29♒
30	8♑	19♐	23♒	29♒
31	9♑	21♐	24♒	0♓

1953

Your Starway to Love

☉ =Sun ☿ = Mercury ♀ = Venus ♂ = Mars ♈ = Aries ♉ = Taurus ♊ = Gemini ♋ = Cancer

January

Day	☉	☿	♀	♂
1	10♑	22♐	25♒	1♓
2	12♑	24♐	26♒	2♓
3	13♑	25♐	27♒	3♓
4	14♑	27♐	29♒	3♓
5	15♑	28♐	0♓	4♓
6	16♑	29♐	1♓	5♓
7	17♑	1♑	2♓	6♓
8	18♑	2♑	3♓	6♓
9	19♑	4♑	4♓	7♓
10	20♑	5♑	5♓	8♓
11	21♑	7♑	6♓	9♓
12	22♑	8♑	8♓	9♓
13	23♑	10♑	9♓	10♓
14	24♑	12♑	10♓	11♓
15	25♑	13♑	11♓	12♓
16	26♑	15♑	12♓	13♓
17	27♑	16♑	13♓	13♓
18	28♑	18♑	14♓	14♓
19	29♑	19♑	15♓	15♓
20	0♒	21♑	16♓	16♓
21	1♒	23♑	17♓	16♓
22	2♒	24♑	19♓	17♓
23	3♒	26♑	20♓	18♓
24	4♒	27♑	21♓	19♓
25	5♒	29♑	22♓	19♓
26	6♒	1♒	23♓	20♓
27	7♒	2♒	24♓	21♓
28	8♒	4♒	25♓	22♓
29	9♒	6♒	26♓	23♓
30	10♒	7♒	27♓	23♓
31	11♒	9♒	28♓	24♓

February

Day	☉	☿	♀	♂
1	12♒	11♒	29♓	25♓
2	13♒	13♒	0♈	26♓
3	14♒	14♒	1♈	26♓
4	15♒	16♒	2♈	27♓
5	16♒	18♒	3♈	28♓
6	17♒	20♒	4♈	29♓
7	18♒	21♒	5♈	29♓
8	19♒	23♒	6♈	0♈
9	20♒	25♒	7♈	1♈
10	21♒	27♒	8♈	2♈
11	22♒	29♒	9♈	2♈
12	23♒	0♓	10♈	3♈
13	24♒	2♓	10♈	4♈
14	25♒	4♓	11♈	5♈
15	26♒	6♓	12♈	5♈
16	27♒	8♓	13♈	6♈
17	28♒	10♓	14♈	7♈
18	29♒	11♓	15♈	8♈
19	0♓	13♓	16♈	8♈
20	1♓	15♓	17♈	9♈
21	2♓	17♓	17♈	10♈
22	3♓	18♓	18♈	11♈
23	4♓	20♓	19♈	11♈
24	5♓	22♓	20♈	12♈
25	6♓	23♓	20♈	13♈
26	7♓	25♓	21♈	14♈
27	8♓	26♓	22♈	14♈
28	9♓	27♓	23♈	15♈

March

Day	☉	☿	♀	♂
1	10♓	28♓	23♈	16♈
2	11♓	29♓	24♈	17♈
3	12♓	0♈	24♈	17♈
4	13♓	1♈	25♈	18♈
5	14♓	2♈	26♈	19♈
6	15♓	2♈	26♈	20♈
7	16♓	3♈	27♈	20♈
8	17♓	3♈	27♈	21♈
9	18♓	3♈	28♈	22♈
10	19♓	3♈	28♈	23♈
11	20♓	3♈	29♈	23♈
12	21♓	2♈	29♈	24♈
13	22♓	2♈	29♈	25♈
14	23♓	1♈	0♉	26♈
15	24♓	1♈	0♉	26♈
16	25♓	0♈	0♉	27♈
17	26♓	29♓	1♉	28♈
18	27♓	28♓	1♉	28♈
19	28♓	27♓	1♉	29♈
20	29♓	26♓	1♉	0♉
21	0♈	25♓	1♉	1♉
22	1♈	24♓	1♉	1♉
23	2♈	24♓	1♉	2♉
24	3♈	23♓	1♉	3♉
25	4♈	22♓	1♉	4♉
26	5♈	21♓	1♉	4♉
27	6♈	21♓	1♉	5♉
28	7♈	21♓	1♉	6♉
29	8♈	20♓	1♉	6♉
30	9♈	20♓	0♉	7♉
31	10♈	20♓	0♉	8♉

April

Day	☉	☿	♀	♂
1	11♈	20♓	0♉	9♉
2	12♈	20♓	29♈	9♉
3	13♈	20♓	29♈	10♉
4	14♈	20♓	28♈	11♉
5	15♈	21♓	28♈	12♉
6	16♈	21♓	27♈	12♉
7	17♈	21♓	27♈	13♉
8	18♈	22♓	26♈	14♉
9	19♈	23♓	26♈	14♉
10	20♈	23♓	25♈	15♉
11	21♈	24♓	24♈	16♉
12	22♈	25♓	24♈	17♉
13	23♈	26♓	23♈	17♉
14	24♈	26♓	23♈	18♉
15	25♈	27♓	22♈	19♉
16	26♈	28♓	21♈	19♉
17	27♈	29♓	21♈	20♉
18	28♈	1♈	20♈	21♉
19	29♈	2♈	20♈	22♉
20	0♉	3♈	19♈	22♉
21	1♉	4♈	18♈	23♉
22	2♉	5♈	18♈	24♉
23	3♉	7♈	18♈	24♉
24	4♉	8♈	17♈	25♉
25	5♉	9♈	17♈	26♉
26	6♉	11♈	16♈	26♉
27	7♉	12♈	16♈	27♉
28	8♉	14♈	16♈	28♉
29	9♉	15♈	16♈	29♉
30	10♉	17♈	15♈	29♉

May

Day	☉	☿	♀	♂
1	11♉	18♈	15♈	0♊
2	11♉	20♈	15♈	1♊
3	12♉	21♈	15♈	1♊
4	13♉	23♈	15♈	2♊
5	14♉	25♈	15♈	3♊
6	15♉	26♈	15♈	3♊
7	16♉	28♈	15♈	4♊
8	17♉	0♉	15♈	5♊
9	18♉	2♉	15♈	6♊
10	19♉	4♉	16♈	6♊
11	20♉	5♉	16♈	7♊
12	21♉	7♉	16♈	8♊
13	22♉	9♉	16♈	8♊
14	23♉	11♉	17♈	9♊
15	24♉	13♉	17♈	10♊
16	25♉	15♉	17♈	10♊
17	26♉	17♉	18♈	11♊
18	27♉	19♉	18♈	12♊
19	28♉	21♉	19♈	12♊
20	29♉	24♉	19♈	13♊
21	0♊	26♉	20♈	14♊
22	1♊	28♉	20♈	14♊
23	2♊	0♊	21♈	15♊
24	3♊	2♊	21♈	16♊
25	4♊	4♊	22♈	17♊
26	5♊	7♊	23♈	17♊
27	6♊	9♊	23♈	18♊
28	7♊	11♊	24♈	19♊
29	8♊	13♊	25♈	19♊
30	8♊	15♊	25♈	20♊
31	9♊	18♊	26♈	21♊

June

Day	☉	☿	♀	♂
1	10♊	20♊	27♈	21♊
2	11♊	22♊	28♈	22♊
3	12♊	24♊	28♈	23♊
4	13♊	26♊	29♈	23♊
5	14♊	28♊	0♉	24♊
6	15♊	0♋	1♉	25♊
7	16♊	2♋	1♉	25♊
8	17♊	4♋	2♉	26♊
9	18♊	5♋	3♉	27♊
10	19♊	7♋	4♉	27♊
11	20♊	9♋	5♉	28♊
12	21♊	11♋	6♉	29♊
13	22♊	12♋	7♉	29♊
14	23♊	14♋	7♉	0♋
15	24♊	15♋	8♉	1♋
16	25♊	17♋	9♉	1♋
17	26♊	18♋	10♉	2♋
18	27♊	20♋	11♉	3♋
19	28♊	21♋	12♉	3♋
20	29♊	23♋	13♉	4♋
21	0♋	24♋	14♉	5♋
22	0♋	25♋	15♉	5♋
23	1♋	26♋	16♉	6♋
24	2♋	28♋	17♉	7♋
25	3♋	29♋	18♉	7♋
26	4♋	0♌	19♉	8♋
27	5♋	1♌	20♉	9♋
28	6♋	2♌	21♉	9♋
29	7♋	3♌	22♉	10♋
30	8♋	3♌	23♉	11♋

July

Day	☉	☿	♀	♂
1	9♋	4♌	24♉	11♋
2	10♋	5♌	25♉	12♋
3	11♋	6♌	26♉	13♋
4	12♋	6♌	27♉	13♋
5	13♋	7♌	28♉	14♋
6	14♋	7♌	29♉	15♋
7	15♋	8♌	0♊	15♋
8	16♋	8♌	1♊	16♋
9	17♋	8♌	2♊	17♋
10	18♋	8♌	3♊	17♋
11	19♋	8♌	4♊	18♋
12	20♋	8♌	5♊	19♋
13	21♋	8♌	6♊	19♋
14	21♋	8♌	7♊	20♋
15	22♋	8♌	8♊	21♋
16	23♋	8♌	9♊	21♋
17	24♋	7♌	10♊	22♋
18	25♋	7♌	11♊	22♋
19	26♋	6♌	12♊	23♋
20	27♋	6♌	14♊	24♋
21	28♋	5♌	15♊	24♋
22	29♋	4♌	16♊	25♋
23	0♌	4♌	17♊	26♋
24	1♌	3♌	18♊	26♋
25	2♌	2♌	19♊	27♋
26	3♌	2♌	20♊	28♋
27	4♌	1♌	21♊	28♋
28	5♌	0♌	22♊	29♋
29	6♌	0♌	23♊	0♌
30	7♌	29♋	25♊	0♌
31	8♌	29♋	26♊	1♌

August

Day	☉	☿	♀	♂
1	9♌	28♋	27♊	2♌
2	10♌	28♋	28♊	2♌
3	11♌	28♋	29♊	3♌
4	12♌	28♋	0♋	3♌
5	12♌	28♋	1♋	4♌
6	13♌	28♋	2♋	5♌
7	14♌	28♋	4♋	5♌
8	15♌	28♋	5♋	6♌
9	16♌	29♋	6♋	7♌
10	17♌	29♋	7♋	7♌
11	18♌	0♌	8♋	8♌
12	19♌	0♌	9♋	9♌
13	20♌	1♌	10♋	9♌
14	21♌	2♌	12♋	10♌
15	22♌	3♌	13♋	11♌
16	23♌	5♌	14♋	11♌
17	24♌	6♌	15♋	12♌
18	25♌	7♌	16♋	12♌
19	26♌	9♌	17♋	13♌
20	27♌	10♌	18♋	14♌
21	28♌	12♌	20♋	14♌
22	29♌	14♌	21♋	15♌
23	0♍	15♌	22♋	16♌
24	1♍	17♌	23♋	16♌
25	2♍	19♌	24♋	17♌
26	3♍	21♌	25♋	18♌
27	4♍	23♌	27♋	18♌
28	5♍	25♌	28♋	19♌
29	6♍	27♌	29♋	20♌
30	7♍	29♌	0♌	20♌
31	7♍	0♍	1♌	21♌

September

Day	☉	☿	♀	♂
1	8♍	2♍	3♌	21♌
2	9♍	4♍	4♌	22♌
3	10♍	6♍	5♌	23♌
4	11♍	8♍	6♌	23♌
5	12♍	10♍	7♌	24♌
6	13♍	12♍	8♌	25♌
7	14♍	14♍	10♌	25♌
8	15♍	16♍	11♌	26♌
9	16♍	18♍	12♌	26♌
10	17♍	20♍	13♌	27♌
11	18♍	22♍	14♌	28♌
12	19♍	23♍	16♌	28♌
13	20♍	25♍	17♌	29♌
14	21♍	27♍	18♌	0♍
15	22♍	29♍	19♌	0♍
16	23♍	1♎	20♌	1♍
17	24♍	2♎	22♌	2♍
18	25♍	4♎	23♌	2♍
19	26♍	6♎	24♌	3♍
20	27♍	7♎	25♌	3♍
21	28♍	9♎	26♌	4♍
22	29♍	11♎	28♌	5♍
23	0♎	12♎	29♌	5♍
24	1♎	14♎	0♍	6♍
25	2♎	16♎	1♍	7♍
26	3♎	17♎	2♍	7♍
27	4♎	19♎	4♍	8♍
28	5♎	20♎	5♍	8♍
29	6♎	22♎	6♍	9♍
30	7♎	23♎	7♍	10♍

October

Day	☉	☿	♀	♂
1	8♎	25♎	9♍	10♍
2	9♎	26♎	10♍	11♍
3	10♎	28♎	11♍	12♍
4	11♎	29♎	12♍	12♍
5	12♎	1♏	13♍	13♍
6	13♎	2♏	15♍	14♍
7	14♎	4♏	16♍	14♍
8	15♎	5♏	17♍	15♍
9	16♎	6♏	18♍	15♍
10	17♎	8♏	20♍	16♍
11	18♎	9♏	21♍	17♍
12	19♎	10♏	22♍	17♍
13	20♎	12♏	23♍	18♍
14	21♎	13♏	25♍	19♍
15	22♎	14♏	26♍	19♍
16	23♎	16♏	27♍	20♍
17	24♎	17♏	28♍	20♍
18	25♎	18♏	29♍	21♍
19	26♎	19♏	1♎	22♍
20	27♎	20♏	2♎	22♍
21	28♎	22♏	3♎	23♍
22	29♎	23♏	4♎	24♍
23	29♎	24♏	6♎	24♍
24	0♏	25♏	7♎	25♍
25	1♏	26♏	8♎	25♍
26	2♏	26♏	9♎	26♍
27	3♏	27♏	11♎	27♍
28	4♏	28♏	12♎	27♍
29	5♏	29♏	13♎	28♍
30	6♏	29♏	14♎	29♍
31	7♏	0♐	16♎	29♍

November

Day	☉	☿	♀	♂
1	8♏	0♐	17♎	0♎
2	9♏	0♐	18♎	0♎
3	10♏	1♐	19♎	1♎
4	11♏	1♐	21♎	2♎
5	12♏	1♐	22♎	2♎
6	13♏	0♐	23♎	3♎
7	14♏	0♐	24♎	3♎
8	16♏	29♏	26♎	4♎
9	17♏	29♏	27♎	5♎
10	18♏	28♏	28♎	5♎
11	19♏	27♏	29♎	6♎
12	20♏	25♏	1♏	7♎
13	21♏	24♏	2♏	7♎
14	22♏	23♏	3♏	8♎
15	23♏	21♏	4♏	8♎
16	24♏	20♏	6♏	9♎
17	25♏	19♏	7♏	10♎
18	26♏	18♏	8♏	10♎
19	27♏	17♏	9♏	11♎
20	28♏	16♏	11♏	12♎
21	29♏	15♏	12♏	12♎
22	0♐	15♏	13♏	13♎
23	1♐	15♏	14♏	13♎
24	2♐	15♏	16♏	14♎
25	3♐	15♏	17♏	15♎
26	4♐	15♏	18♏	15♎
27	5♐	15♏	19♏	16♎
28	6♐	16♏	21♏	16♎
29	7♐	17♏	22♏	17♎
30	8♐	18♏	23♏	18♎

December

Day	☉	☿	♀	♂
1	9♐	19♏	24♏	18♎
2	10♐	20♏	26♏	19♎
3	11♐	21♏	27♏	20♎
4	12♐	22♏	28♏	20♎
5	13♐	23♏	29♏	21♎
6	14♐	24♏	1♐	21♎
7	15♐	25♏	2♐	22♎
8	16♐	27♏	3♐	23♎
9	17♐	28♏	4♐	23♎
10	18♐	29♏	6♐	24♎
11	19♐	1♐	7♐	24♎
12	20♐	2♐	8♐	25♎
13	21♐	4♐	9♐	26♎
14	22♐	5♐	11♐	26♎
15	23♐	7♐	12♐	27♎
16	24♐	8♐	13♐	27♎
17	25♐	9♐	14♐	28♎
18	26♐	11♐	16♐	29♎
19	27♐	12♐	17♐	29♎
20	28♐	14♐	18♐	0♏
21	29♐	15♐	20♐	0♏
22	0♑	17♐	21♐	1♏
23	1♑	18♐	22♐	2♏
24	2♑	20♐	23♐	2♏
25	3♑	22♐	25♐	3♏
26	4♑	23♐	26♐	3♏
27	5♑	25♐	27♐	4♏
28	6♑	26♐	28♐	5♏
29	7♑	28♐	0♑	5♏
30	8♑	29♐	1♑	6♏
31	9♑	1♑	2♑	6♏

Planetary Positions

♌ = Leo ♍ = Virgo ♎ = Libra ♏ = Scorpio ♐ = Sagittarius ♑ = Capricorn ♒ = Aquarius ♓ = Pisces

1954

January

Day	☉	☿	♀	♂
1	10♑	2♑	3♑	7♏
2	11♑	4♑	5♑	8♏
3	12♑	5♑	6♑	8♏
4	13♑	7♑	7♑	9♏
5	14♑	9♑	8♑	9♏
6	15♑	10♑	10♑	10♏
7	16♑	12♑	11♑	11♏
8	17♑	13♑	12♑	11♏
9	18♑	15♑	13♑	12♏
10	19♑	17♑	15♑	12♏
11	20♑	18♑	16♑	13♏
12	21♑	20♑	17♑	14♏
13	22♑	22♑	18♑	14♏
14	24♑	23♑	20♑	15♏
15	25♑	25♑	21♑	15♏
16	26♑	26♑	22♑	16♏
17	27♑	28♑	23♑	17♏
18	28♑	0♒	25♑	17♏
19	29♑	1♒	26♑	18♏
20	0♒	3♒	27♑	18♏
21	1♒	5♒	29♑	19♏
22	2♒	7♒	0♒	19♏
23	3♒	8♒	1♒	20♏
24	4♒	10♒	2♒	21♏
25	5♒	12♒	4♒	21♏
26	6♒	14♒	5♒	22♏
27	7♒	15♒	6♒	22♏
28	8♒	17♒	7♒	23♏
29	9♒	19♒	9♒	23♏
30	10♒	21♒	10♒	24♏
31	11♒	22♒	11♒	25♏

April

Day	☉	☿	♀	♂
1	11♈	13♓	26♈	25♐
2	12♈	15♓	27♈	26♐
3	13♈	16♓	28♈	26♐
4	14♈	17♓	0♉	27♐
5	15♈	18♓	1♉	27♐
6	16♈	20♓	2♉	27♐
7	17♈	21♓	3♉	28♐
8	18♈	22♓	5♉	28♐
9	19♈	24♓	6♉	29♐
10	20♈	25♓	7♉	29♐
11	21♈	27♓	8♉	29♐
12	22♈	28♓	10♉	0♑
13	23♈	0♈	11♉	0♑
14	24♈	1♈	12♉	1♑
15	25♈	3♈	13♉	1♑
16	26♈	4♈	14♉	1♑
17	27♈	6♈	16♉	2♑
18	28♈	8♈	17♉	2♑
19	29♈	9♈	18♉	2♑
20	0♉	11♈	19♉	3♑
21	1♉	13♈	21♉	3♑
22	2♉	14♈	22♉	3♑
23	3♉	16♈	23♉	4♑
24	3♉	18♈	24♉	4♑
25	4♉	20♈	25♉	4♑
26	5♉	22♈	27♉	4♑
27	6♉	24♈	28♉	5♑
28	7♉	26♈	29♉	5♑
29	8♉	27♈	0♊	5♑
30	9♉	29♈	2♊	5♑

July

Day	☉	☿	♀	♂
1	9♋	17♋	16♌	1♑
2	10♋	16♋	17♌	0♑
3	11♋	15♋	18♌	0♑
4	12♋	15♋	19♌	0♑
5	13♋	14♋	21♌	29♐
6	14♋	14♋	22♌	29♐
7	15♋	13♋	23♌	29♐
8	16♋	12♋	24♌	29♐
9	16♋	12♋	25♌	28♐
10	17♋	11♋	26♌	28♐
11	18♋	11♋	28♌	28♐
12	19♋	10♋	29♌	28♐
13	20♋	10♋	0♍	27♐
14	21♋	10♋	1♍	27♐
15	22♋	9♋	2♍	27♐
16	23♋	9♋	3♍	27♐
17	24♋	9♋	4♍	27♐
18	25♋	9♋	6♍	26♐
19	26♋	9♋	7♍	26♐
20	27♋	10♋	8♍	26♐
21	28♋	10♋	9♍	26♐
22	29♋	10♋	10♍	26♐
23	0♌	11♋	11♍	26♐
24	1♌	12♋	12♍	26♐
25	2♌	12♋	14♍	26♐
26	3♌	13♋	15♍	26♐
27	4♌	14♋	16♍	26♐
28	5♌	15♋	17♍	26♐
29	6♌	16♋	18♍	26♐
30	7♌	17♋	19♍	26♐
31	7♌	18♋	20♍	26♐

October

Day	☉	☿	♀	♂
1	7♎	2♏	20♏	18♑
2	8♎	4♏	21♏	18♑
3	9♎	5♏	22♏	19♑
4	10♎	6♏	22♏	19♑
5	11♎	7♏	23♏	20♑
6	12♎	8♏	24♏	20♑
7	13♎	9♏	24♏	21♑
8	14♎	10♏	25♏	22♑
9	15♎	11♏	25♏	22♑
10	16♎	11♏	26♏	23♑
11	17♎	12♏	26♏	24♑
12	18♎	13♏	27♏	24♑
13	19♎	13♏	27♏	25♑
14	20♎	14♏	28♏	25♑
15	21♎	14♏	28♏	26♑
16	22♎	14♏	28♏	27♑
17	23♎	15♏	29♏	27♑
18	24♎	15♏	29♏	28♑
19	25♎	15♏	29♏	29♑
20	26♎	15♏	29♏	29♑
21	27♎	14♏	0♐	0♒
22	28♎	14♏	0♐	0♒
23	29♎	13♏	0♐	1♒
24	0♏	12♏	0♐	2♒
25	1♏	11♏	0♐	2♒
26	2♏	10♏	0♐	3♒
27	3♏	9♏	0♐	4♒
28	4♏	8♏	0♐	4♒
29	5♏	7♏	0♐	5♒
30	6♏	6♏	0♐	6♒
31	7♏	4♏	29♏	6♒

February

Day	☉	☿	♀	♂
1	12♒	24♒	12♒	25♏
2	13♒	26♒	14♒	26♏
3	14♒	27♒	15♒	26♏
4	15♒	29♒	16♒	27♏
5	16♒	1♓	17♒	27♏
6	17♒	2♓	19♒	28♏
7	18♒	4♓	20♒	29♏
8	19♒	6♓	21♒	29♏
9	20♒	7♓	22♒	0♐
10	21♒	8♓	24♒	0♐
11	22♒	10♓	25♒	1♐
12	23♒	11♓	26♒	1♐
13	24♒	12♓	27♒	2♐
14	25♒	13♓	29♒	2♐
15	26♒	14♓	0♓	3♐
16	27♒	15♓	1♓	4♐
17	28♒	15♓	2♓	4♐
18	29♒	16♓	4♓	5♐
19	0♓	16♓	5♓	5♐
20	1♓	16♓	6♓	6♐
21	2♓	16♓	7♓	6♐
22	3♓	16♓	9♓	7♐
23	4♓	15♓	10♓	7♐
24	5♓	15♓	11♓	8♐
25	6♓	14♓	12♓	8♐
26	7♓	13♓	14♓	9♐
27	8♓	12♓	15♓	9♐
28	9♓	12♓	16♓	10♐

May

Day	☉	☿	♀	♂
1	10♉	1♉	3♊	6♑
2	11♉	4♉	4♊	6♑
3	12♉	6♉	5♊	6♑
4	13♉	8♉	6♊	6♑
5	14♉	10♉	8♊	7♑
6	15♉	12♉	9♊	7♑
7	16♉	14♉	10♊	7♑
8	17♉	16♉	11♊	7♑
9	18♉	18♉	13♊	7♑
10	19♉	21♉	14♊	7♑
11	20♉	23♉	15♊	8♑
12	21♉	25♉	16♊	8♑
13	22♉	27♉	17♊	8♑
14	23♉	29♉	19♊	8♑
15	24♉	1♊	20♊	8♑
16	25♉	3♊	21♊	8♑
17	26♉	6♊	22♊	8♑
18	27♉	8♊	23♊	8♑
19	28♉	10♊	25♊	8♑
20	29♉	12♊	26♊	8♑
21	0♊	14♊	27♊	8♑
22	1♊	16♊	28♊	9♑
23	2♊	17♊	29♊	9♑
24	2♊	19♊	1♋	9♑
25	3♊	21♊	2♋	9♑
26	4♊	23♊	3♋	8♑
27	5♊	25♊	4♋	8♑
28	6♊	26♊	6♋	8♑
29	7♊	28♊	7♋	8♑
30	8♊	29♊	8♋	8♑
31	9♊	1♋	9♋	8♑

August

Day	☉	☿	♀	♂
1	8♌	20♋	21♍	26♐
2	9♌	21♋	22♍	26♐
3	10♌	23♋	24♍	26♐
4	11♌	24♋	25♍	26♐
5	12♌	26♋	26♍	26♐
6	13♌	28♋	27♍	26♐
7	14♌	29♋	28♍	26♐
8	15♌	1♌	29♍	26♐
9	16♌	3♌	0♎	26♐
10	17♌	5♌	1♎	27♐
11	18♌	7♌	2♎	27♐
12	19♌	9♌	3♎	27♐
13	20♌	11♌	5♎	27♐
14	21♌	13♌	6♎	27♐
15	22♌	15♌	7♎	27♐
16	23♌	17♌	8♎	28♐
17	24♌	19♌	9♎	28♐
18	25♌	21♌	10♎	28♐
19	26♌	23♌	11♎	28♐
20	27♌	25♌	12♎	29♐
21	28♌	27♌	13♎	29♐
22	29♌	29♌	14♎	29♐
23	0♍	1♍	15♎	0♑
24	0♍	3♍	16♎	0♑
25	1♍	5♍	17♎	0♑
26	2♍	7♍	18♎	1♑
27	3♍	9♍	19♎	1♑
28	4♍	11♍	20♎	1♑
29	5♍	12♍	21♎	2♑
30	6♍	14♍	22♎	2♑
31	7♍	16♍	23♎	2♑

November

Day	☉	☿	♀	♂
1	8♏	3♏	29♏	7♒
2	9♏	2♏	29♏	8♒
3	10♏	1♏	29♏	8♒
4	11♏	0♏	28♏	9♒
5	12♏	0♏	28♏	10♒
6	13♏	29♎	27♏	10♒
7	14♏	29♎	27♏	11♒
8	15♏	29♎	26♏	12♒
9	16♏	29♎	26♏	12♒
10	17♏	29♎	25♏	13♒
11	18♏	0♏	25♏	14♒
12	19♏	0♏	24♏	15♒
13	20♏	1♏	24♏	15♒
14	21♏	2♏	23♏	16♒
15	22♏	3♏	22♏	17♒
16	23♏	4♏	22♏	17♒
17	24♏	5♏	21♏	18♒
18	25♏	7♏	21♏	19♒
19	26♏	8♏	20♏	19♒
20	27♏	9♏	19♏	20♒
21	28♏	10♏	19♏	21♒
22	29♏	12♏	18♏	21♒
23	0♐	13♏	18♏	22♒
24	1♐	15♏	17♏	23♒
25	2♐	16♏	17♏	24♒
26	3♐	18♏	17♏	24♒
27	4♐	19♏	16♏	25♒
28	5♐	21♏	16♏	26♒
29	6♐	22♏	16♏	26♒
30	7♐	24♏	15♏	27♒

March

Day	☉	☿	♀	♂
1	10♓	10♓	17♓	11♐
2	11♓	9♓	19♓	11♐
3	12♓	8♓	20♓	12♐
4	13♓	7♓	21♓	12♐
5	14♓	6♓	22♓	13♐
6	15♓	5♓	24♓	13♐
7	16♓	5♓	25♓	14♐
8	17♓	4♓	26♓	14♐
9	18♓	3♓	27♓	15♐
10	19♓	3♓	29♓	15♐
11	20♓	2♓	0♈	16♐
12	21♓	2♓	1♈	16♐
13	22♓	2♓	2♈	17♐
14	23♓	2♓	4♈	17♐
15	24♓	2♓	5♈	18♐
16	25♓	2♓	6♈	18♐
17	26♓	2♓	7♈	19♐
18	27♓	2♓	9♈	19♐
19	28♓	3♓	10♈	20♐
20	29♓	3♓	11♈	20♐
21	0♈	4♓	12♈	20♐
22	1♈	4♓	14♈	21♐
23	2♈	5♓	15♈	21♐
24	3♈	6♓	16♈	22♐
25	4♈	6♓	17♈	22♐
26	5♈	7♓	19♈	23♐
27	6♈	8♓	20♈	23♐
28	7♈	9♓	21♈	24♐
29	8♈	10♓	22♈	24♐
30	9♈	11♓	23♈	25♐
31	10♈	12♓	25♈	25♐

June

Day	☉	☿	♀	♂
1	10♊	2♋	10♋	8♑
2	11♊	4♋	12♋	8♑
3	12♊	5♋	13♋	8♑
4	13♊	6♋	14♋	8♑
5	14♊	7♋	15♋	8♑
6	15♊	9♋	16♋	7♑
7	16♊	10♋	18♋	7♑
8	17♊	11♋	19♋	7♑
9	18♊	12♋	20♋	7♑
10	19♊	13♋	21♋	7♑
11	20♊	14♋	22♋	6♑
12	21♊	14♋	23♋	6♑
13	22♊	15♋	25♋	6♑
14	23♊	16♋	26♋	6♑
15	24♊	16♋	27♋	5♑
16	25♊	17♋	28♋	5♑
17	25♊	18♋	29♋	5♑
18	26♊	18♋	1♌	5♑
19	27♊	18♋	2♌	4♑
20	28♊	19♋	3♌	4♑
21	29♊	19♋	4♌	4♑
22	0♋	19♋	5♌	3♑
23	1♋	19♋	6♌	3♑
24	2♋	19♋	8♌	3♑
25	3♋	19♋	9♌	2♑
26	4♋	18♋	10♌	2♑
27	5♋	18♋	11♌	2♑
28	6♋	18♋	12♌	2♑
29	7♋	17♋	14♌	1♑
30	8♋	17♋	15♌	1♑

September

Day	☉	☿	♀	♂
1	8♍	18♍	24♎	3♑
2	9♍	20♍	25♎	3♑
3	10♍	21♍	26♎	4♑
4	11♍	23♍	27♎	4♑
5	12♍	25♍	28♎	4♑
6	13♍	26♍	29♎	5♑
7	14♍	28♍	0♏	5♑
8	15♍	0♎	1♏	6♑
9	16♍	1♎	2♏	6♑
10	17♍	3♎	3♏	7♑
11	18♍	5♎	4♏	7♑
12	19♍	6♎	5♏	8♑
13	20♍	8♎	6♏	8♑
14	21♍	9♎	7♏	8♑
15	22♍	11♎	8♏	9♑
16	23♍	12♎	9♏	9♑
17	24♍	14♎	9♏	10♑
18	25♍	15♎	10♏	10♑
19	26♍	17♎	11♏	11♑
20	27♍	18♎	12♏	11♑
21	28♍	20♎	13♏	12♑
22	29♍	21♎	14♏	13♑
23	0♎	22♎	14♏	13♑
24	1♎	24♎	15♏	14♑
25	2♎	25♎	16♏	14♑
26	3♎	26♎	17♏	15♑
27	4♎	28♎	18♏	15♑
28	5♎	29♎	18♏	16♑
29	6♎	0♏	19♏	16♑
30	7♎	1♏	20♏	17♑

December

Day	☉	☿	♀	♂
1	8♐	25♏	15♏	28♒
2	9♐	27♏	15♏	29♒
3	10♐	28♏	15♏	29♒
4	12♐	0♐	15♏	0♓
5	13♐	1♐	15♏	1♓
6	14♐	3♐	15♏	1♓
7	15♐	5♐	15♏	2♓
8	16♐	6♐	15♏	3♓
9	17♐	8♐	15♏	3♓
10	18♐	9♐	15♏	4♓
11	19♐	11♐	15♏	5♓
12	20♐	12♐	15♏	6♓
13	21♐	14♐	16♏	6♓
14	22♐	15♐	16♏	7♓
15	23♐	17♐	16♏	8♓
16	24♐	19♐	17♏	8♓
17	25♐	20♐	17♏	9♓
18	26♐	22♐	17♏	10♓
19	27♐	23♐	18♏	11♓
20	28♐	25♐	18♏	11♓
21	29♐	26♐	19♏	12♓
22	0♑	28♐	19♏	13♓
23	1♑	0♑	20♏	13♓
24	2♑	1♑	21♏	14♓
25	3♑	3♑	21♏	15♓
26	4♑	4♑	22♏	16♓
27	5♑	6♑	22♏	16♓
28	6♑	7♑	23♏	17♓
29	7♑	9♑	24♏	18♓
30	8♑	11♑	25♏	19♓
31	9♑	12♑	25♏	19♓

Your Starway to Love

☉ =Sun ☿ = Mercury ♀ = Venus ♂ = Mars ♈ = Aries ♉ = Taurus ♊ = Gemini ♋ = Cancer

1955

January

Day	☉	☿	♀	♂
1	10♑	14♑	26♏	20♓
2	11♑	16♑	27♏	21♓
3	12♑	17♑	28♏	21♓
4	13♑	19♑	28♏	22♓
5	14♑	20♑	29♏	23♓
6	15♑	22♑	0♐	24♓
7	16♑	24♑	1♐	24♓
8	17♑	25♑	2♐	25♓
9	18♑	27♑	2♐	26♓
10	19♑	29♑	3♐	26♓
11	20♑	0♒	4♐	27♓
12	21♑	2♒	5♐	28♓
13	22♑	4♒	6♐	29♓
14	23♑	5♒	7♐	29♓
15	24♑	7♒	8♐	0♈
16	25♑	9♒	9♐	1♈
17	26♑	10♒	10♐	1♈
18	27♑	12♒	11♐	2♈
19	28♑	14♒	12♐	3♈
20	29♑	15♒	13♐	4♈
21	0♒	17♒	14♐	4♈
22	1♒	18♒	15♐	5♈
23	2♒	20♒	16♐	6♈
24	3♒	21♒	17♐	6♈
25	4♒	22♒	18♐	7♈
26	5♒	24♒	19♐	8♈
27	6♒	25♒	20♐	9♈
28	8♒	26♒	21♐	9♈
29	9♒	27♒	22♐	10♈
30	10♒	28♒	23♐	11♈
31	11♒	28♒	24♐	11♈

February

Day	☉	☿	♀	♂
1	12♒	29♒	25♐	12♈
2	13♒	29♒	26♐	13♈
3	14♒	0♓	27♐	14♈
4	15♒	0♓	28♐	14♈
5	16♒	29♒	29♐	15♈
6	17♒	29♒	0♑	16♈
7	18♒	29♒	1♑	16♈
8	19♒	28♒	2♑	17♈
9	20♒	27♒	3♑	18♈
10	21♒	26♒	5♑	19♈
11	22♒	25♒	6♑	19♈
12	23♒	24♒	7♑	20♈
13	24♒	23♒	8♑	21♈
14	25♒	22♒	9♑	21♈
15	26♒	21♒	10♑	22♈
16	27♒	19♒	11♑	23♈
17	28♒	18♒	12♑	24♈
18	29♒	17♒	13♑	24♈
19	0♓	17♒	14♑	25♈
20	1♓	16♒	16♑	26♈
21	2♓	15♒	17♑	26♈
22	3♓	15♒	18♑	27♈
23	4♓	15♒	19♑	28♈
24	5♓	14♒	20♑	28♈
25	6♓	14♒	21♑	29♈
26	7♓	14♒	22♑	0♉
27	8♓	15♒	24♑	1♉
28	9♓	15♒	25♑	1♉

March

Day	☉	☿	♀	♂
1	10♓	15♒	26♑	2♉
2	11♓	16♒	27♑	3♉
3	12♓	16♒	28♑	3♉
4	13♓	17♒	29♑	4♉
5	14♓	17♒	0♒	5♉
6	15♓	18♒	2♒	5♉
7	16♓	19♒	3♒	6♉
8	17♓	20♒	4♒	7♉
9	18♓	20♒	5♒	8♉
10	19♓	21♒	6♒	8♉
11	20♓	22♒	7♒	9♉
12	21♓	23♒	9♒	10♉
13	22♓	25♒	10♒	10♉
14	23♓	26♒	11♒	11♉
15	24♓	27♒	12♒	12♉
16	25♓	28♒	13♒	12♉
17	26♓	29♒	14♒	13♉
18	27♓	0♓	16♒	14♉
19	28♓	2♓	17♒	14♉
20	29♓	3♓	18♒	15♉
21	0♈	4♓	19♒	16♉
22	1♈	6♓	20♒	17♉
23	2♈	7♓	21♒	17♉
24	3♈	9♓	23♒	18♉
25	4♈	10♓	24♒	19♉
26	5♈	11♓	25♒	19♉
27	6♈	13♓	26♒	20♉
28	7♈	14♓	27♒	21♉
29	8♈	16♓	28♒	21♉
30	9♈	18♓	0♓	22♉
31	10♈	19♓	1♓	23♉

April

Day	☉	☿	♀	♂
1	11♈	21♓	2♓	23♉
2	12♈	22♓	3♓	24♉
3	13♈	24♓	4♓	25♉
4	14♈	26♓	6♓	25♉
5	15♈	27♓	7♓	26♉
6	16♈	29♓	8♓	27♉
7	17♈	1♈	9♓	27♉
8	18♈	3♈	10♓	28♉
9	19♈	5♈	12♓	29♉
10	20♈	6♈	13♓	29♉
11	21♈	8♈	14♓	0♊
12	22♈	10♈	15♓	1♊
13	23♈	12♈	16♓	2♊
14	23♈	14♈	18♓	2♊
15	24♈	16♈	19♓	3♊
16	25♈	18♈	20♓	4♊
17	26♈	20♈	21♓	4♊
18	27♈	22♈	22♓	5♊
19	28♈	24♈	23♓	6♊
20	29♈	26♈	25♓	6♊
21	0♉	28♈	26♓	7♊
22	1♉	0♉	27♓	8♊
23	2♉	2♉	28♓	8♊
24	3♉	4♉	29♓	9♊
25	4♉	7♉	1♈	10♊
26	5♉	9♉	2♈	10♊
27	6♉	11♉	3♈	11♊
28	7♉	13♉	4♈	12♊
29	8♉	15♉	5♈	12♊
30	9♉	17♉	7♈	13♊

May

Day	☉	☿	♀	♂
1	10♉	19♉	8♈	14♊
2	11♉	21♉	9♈	14♊
3	12♉	23♉	10♈	15♊
4	13♉	25♉	11♈	16♊
5	14♉	27♉	13♈	16♊
6	15♉	29♉	14♈	17♊
7	16♉	1♊	15♈	18♊
8	17♉	3♊	16♈	18♊
9	18♉	5♊	18♈	19♊
10	19♉	7♊	19♈	20♊
11	20♉	8♊	20♈	20♊
12	21♉	10♊	21♈	21♊
13	22♉	11♊	22♈	22♊
14	23♉	13♊	24♈	22♊
15	24♉	14♊	25♈	23♊
16	25♉	16♊	26♈	24♊
17	26♉	17♊	27♈	24♊
18	26♉	18♊	28♈	25♊
19	27♉	19♊	0♉	26♊
20	28♉	21♊	1♉	26♊
21	29♉	22♊	2♉	27♊
22	0♊	23♊	3♉	27♊
23	1♊	24♊	4♉	28♊
24	2♊	24♊	6♉	29♊
25	3♊	25♊	7♉	29♊
26	4♊	26♊	8♉	0♋
27	5♊	27♊	9♉	1♋
28	6♊	27♊	10♉	1♋
29	7♊	28♊	12♉	2♋
30	8♊	28♊	13♉	3♋
31	9♊	28♊	14♉	3♋

June

Day	☉	☿	♀	♂
1	10♊	29♊	15♉	4♋
2	11♊	29♊	16♉	5♋
3	12♊	29♊	18♉	5♋
4	13♊	29♊	19♉	6♋
5	14♊	29♊	20♉	7♋
6	15♊	29♊	21♉	7♋
7	16♊	28♊	23♉	8♋
8	17♊	28♊	24♉	9♋
9	18♊	28♊	25♉	9♋
10	19♊	27♊	26♉	10♋
11	20♊	27♊	27♉	11♋
12	20♊	27♊	29♉	11♋
13	21♊	26♊	0♊	12♋
14	22♊	26♊	1♊	12♋
15	23♊	25♊	2♊	13♋
16	24♊	24♊	3♊	14♋
17	25♊	24♊	5♊	14♋
18	26♊	23♊	6♊	15♋
19	27♊	23♊	7♊	16♋
20	28♊	22♊	8♊	16♋
21	29♊	22♊	10♊	17♋
22	0♋	21♊	11♊	18♋
23	1♋	21♊	12♊	18♋
24	2♋	21♊	13♊	19♋
25	3♋	20♊	14♊	20♋
26	4♋	20♊	16♊	20♋
27	5♋	20♊	17♊	21♋
28	6♋	20♊	18♊	22♋
29	7♋	20♊	19♊	22♋
30	8♋	20♊	20♊	23♋

July

Day	☉	☿	♀	♂
1	9♋	21♊	22♊	23♋
2	10♋	21♊	23♊	24♋
3	11♋	21♊	24♊	25♋
4	11♋	22♊	25♊	25♋
5	12♋	22♊	27♊	26♋
6	13♋	23♊	28♊	27♋
7	14♋	24♊	29♊	27♋
8	15♋	24♊	0♋	28♋
9	16♋	25♊	1♋	29♋
10	17♋	26♊	3♋	29♋
11	18♋	27♊	4♋	0♌
12	19♋	28♊	5♋	1♌
13	20♋	0♋	6♋	1♌
14	21♋	1♋	8♋	2♌
15	22♋	2♋	9♋	2♌
16	23♋	3♋	10♋	3♌
17	24♋	5♋	11♋	4♌
18	25♋	6♋	12♋	4♌
19	26♋	8♋	14♋	5♌
20	27♋	10♋	15♋	6♌
21	28♋	11♋	16♋	6♌
22	29♋	13♋	17♋	7♌
23	0♌	15♋	19♋	8♌
24	1♌	17♋	20♋	8♌
25	1♌	19♋	21♋	9♌
26	2♌	21♋	22♋	9♌
27	3♌	23♋	24♋	10♌
28	4♌	25♋	25♋	11♌
29	5♌	27♋	26♋	11♌
30	6♌	29♋	27♋	12♌
31	7♌	1♌	28♋	13♌

August

Day	☉	☿	♀	♂
1	8♌	3♌	0♌	13♌
2	9♌	5♌	1♌	14♌
3	10♌	7♌	2♌	15♌
4	11♌	9♌	3♌	15♌
5	12♌	11♌	5♌	16♌
6	13♌	14♌	6♌	16♌
7	14♌	16♌	7♌	17♌
8	15♌	18♌	8♌	18♌
9	16♌	20♌	10♌	18♌
10	17♌	22♌	11♌	19♌
11	18♌	24♌	12♌	20♌
12	19♌	26♌	13♌	20♌
13	20♌	27♌	14♌	21♌
14	21♌	29♌	16♌	22♌
15	22♌	1♍	17♌	22♌
16	23♌	3♍	18♌	23♌
17	24♌	5♍	19♌	23♌
18	24♌	7♍	21♌	24♌
19	25♌	9♍	22♌	25♌
20	26♌	10♍	23♌	25♌
21	27♌	12♍	24♌	26♌
22	28♌	14♍	26♌	27♌
23	29♌	15♍	27♌	27♌
24	0♍	17♍	28♌	28♌
25	1♍	19♍	29♌	29♌
26	2♍	20♍	1♍	29♌
27	3♍	22♍	2♍	0♍
28	4♍	23♍	3♍	0♍
29	5♍	25♍	4♍	1♍
30	6♍	27♍	5♍	2♍
31	7♍	28♍	7♍	2♍

September

Day	☉	☿	♀	♂
1	8♍	0♎	8♍	3♍
2	9♍	1♎	9♍	4♍
3	10♍	2♎	10♍	4♍
4	11♍	4♎	12♍	5♍
5	12♍	5♎	13♍	6♍
6	13♍	7♎	14♍	6♍
7	14♍	8♎	15♍	7♍
8	15♍	9♎	17♍	7♍
9	16♍	11♎	18♍	8♍
10	17♍	12♎	19♍	9♍
11	18♍	13♎	20♍	9♍
12	19♍	14♎	22♍	10♍
13	20♍	16♎	23♍	11♍
14	21♍	17♎	24♍	11♍
15	22♍	18♎	25♍	12♍
16	23♍	19♎	27♍	13♍
17	24♍	20♎	28♍	13♍
18	25♍	21♎	29♍	14♍
19	25♍	22♎	0♎	15♍
20	26♍	23♎	2♎	15♍
21	27♍	24♎	3♎	16♍
22	28♍	25♎	4♎	16♍
23	29♍	25♎	5♎	17♍
24	0♎	26♎	7♎	18♍
25	1♎	27♎	8♎	18♍
26	2♎	27♎	9♎	19♍
27	3♎	28♎	10♎	20♍
28	4♎	28♎	12♎	20♍
29	5♎	28♎	13♎	21♍
30	6♎	29♎	14♎	22♍

October

Day	☉	☿	♀	♂
1	7♎	29♎	15♎	22♍
2	8♎	29♎	17♎	23♍
3	9♎	28♎	18♎	23♍
4	10♎	28♎	19♎	24♍
5	11♎	28♎	20♎	25♍
6	12♎	27♎	21♎	25♍
7	13♎	27♎	23♎	26♍
8	14♎	26♎	24♎	27♍
9	15♎	25♎	25♎	27♍
10	16♎	24♎	26♎	28♍
11	17♎	23♎	28♎	29♍
12	18♎	22♎	29♎	29♍
13	19♎	21♎	0♏	0♎
14	20♎	19♎	1♏	0♎
15	21♎	18♎	3♏	1♎
16	22♎	17♎	4♏	2♎
17	23♎	16♎	5♏	2♎
18	24♎	15♎	6♏	3♎
19	25♎	14♎	8♏	4♎
20	26♎	14♎	9♏	4♎
21	27♎	13♎	10♏	5♎
22	28♎	13♎	11♏	6♎
23	29♎	13♎	13♏	6♎
24	0♏	13♎	14♏	7♎
25	1♏	14♎	15♏	8♎
26	2♏	14♎	16♏	8♎
27	3♏	15♎	18♏	9♎
28	4♏	16♎	19♏	9♎
29	5♏	17♎	20♏	10♎
30	6♏	18♎	21♏	11♎
31	7♏	19♎	23♏	11♎

November

Day	☉	☿	♀	♂
1	8♏	20♎	24♏	12♎
2	9♏	21♎	25♏	13♎
3	10♏	23♎	26♏	13♎
4	11♏	24♎	28♏	14♎
5	12♏	25♎	29♏	15♎
6	13♏	27♎	0♐	15♎
7	14♏	28♎	1♐	16♎
8	15♏	0♏	3♐	17♎
9	16♏	1♏	4♐	17♎
10	17♏	3♏	5♐	18♎
11	18♏	5♏	6♐	18♎
12	19♏	6♏	8♐	19♎
13	20♏	8♏	9♐	20♎
14	21♏	9♏	10♐	20♎
15	22♏	11♏	11♐	21♎
16	23♏	13♏	13♐	22♎
17	24♏	14♏	14♐	22♎
18	25♏	16♏	15♐	23♎
19	26♏	17♏	16♐	24♎
20	27♏	19♏	18♐	24♎
21	28♏	21♏	19♐	25♎
22	29♏	22♏	20♐	26♎
23	0♐	24♏	21♐	26♎
24	1♐	25♏	23♐	27♎
25	2♐	27♏	24♐	28♎
26	3♐	28♏	25♐	28♎
27	4♐	0♐	26♐	29♎
28	5♐	2♐	28♐	29♎
29	6♐	3♐	29♐	0♏
30	7♐	5♐	0♑	1♏

December

Day	☉	☿	♀	♂
1	8♐	6♐	1♑	1♏
2	9♐	8♐	3♑	2♏
3	10♐	9♐	4♑	3♏
4	11♐	11♐	5♑	3♏
5	12♐	13♐	6♑	4♏
6	13♐	14♐	8♑	5♏
7	14♐	16♐	9♑	5♏
8	15♐	17♐	10♑	6♏
9	16♐	19♐	11♑	7♏
10	17♐	20♐	13♑	7♏
11	18♐	22♐	14♑	8♏
12	19♐	24♐	15♑	9♏
13	20♐	25♐	16♑	9♏
14	21♐	27♐	17♑	10♏
15	22♐	28♐	19♑	10♏
16	23♐	0♑	20♑	11♏
17	24♐	2♑	21♑	12♏
18	25♐	3♑	22♑	12♏
19	27♐	5♑	24♑	13♏
20	28♐	6♑	25♑	14♏
21	29♐	8♑	26♑	14♏
22	0♑	9♑	27♑	15♏
23	1♑	11♑	29♑	16♏
24	2♑	13♑	0♒	16♏
25	3♑	14♑	1♒	17♏
26	4♑	16♑	2♒	18♏
27	5♑	17♑	4♒	18♏
28	6♑	19♑	5♒	19♏
29	7♑	21♑	6♒	20♏
30	8♑	22♑	7♒	20♏
31	9♑	24♑	9♒	21♏

Planetary Positions

♌ = Leo ♍ = Virgo ♎ = Libra ♏ = Scorpio ♐ = Sagittarius ♑ = Capricorn ♒ = Aquarius ♓ = Pisces

1956

January

Day	☉	☿	♀	♂
1	10♑	25♑	10♒	22♏
2	11♑	27♑	11♒	22♏
3	12♑	28♑	12♒	23♏
4	13♑	0♒	14♒	24♏
5	14♑	1♒	15♒	24♏
6	15♑	3♒	16♒	25♏
7	16♑	4♒	17♒	25♏
8	17♑	5♒	18♒	26♏
9	18♑	7♒	20♒	27♏
10	19♑	8♒	21♒	27♏
11	20♑	9♒	22♒	28♏
12	21♑	10♒	23♒	29♏
13	22♑	11♒	25♒	29♏
14	23♑	12♒	26♒	0♐
15	24♑	12♒	27♒	1♐
16	25♑	13♒	28♒	1♐
17	26♑	13♒	0♓	2♐
18	27♑	13♒	1♓	3♐
19	28♑	13♒	2♓	3♐
20	29♑	13♒	3♓	4♐
21	0♒	13♒	4♓	5♐
22	1♒	12♒	6♓	5♐
23	2♒	11♒	7♓	6♐
24	3♒	11♒	8♓	7♐
25	4♒	9♒	9♓	7♐
26	5♒	8♒	11♓	8♐
27	6♒	7♒	12♓	9♐
28	7♒	6♒	13♓	9♐
29	8♒	5♒	14♓	10♐
30	9♒	3♒	15♓	11♐
31	10♒	2♒	17♓	11♐

April

Day	☉	☿	♀	♂
1	11♈	6♈	27♉	21♑
2	12♈	8♈	28♉	22♑
3	13♈	10♈	29♉	22♑
4	14♈	12♈	0♊	23♑
5	15♈	14♈	1♊	24♑
6	16♈	16♈	2♊	24♑
7	17♈	18♈	3♊	25♑
8	18♈	21♈	4♊	26♑
9	19♈	23♈	5♊	26♑
10	20♈	25♈	6♊	27♑
11	21♈	27♈	7♊	28♑
12	22♈	29♈	8♊	28♑
13	23♈	1♉	9♊	29♑
14	24♈	3♉	10♊	0♒
15	25♈	5♉	11♊	0♒
16	26♈	7♉	12♊	1♒
17	27♈	9♉	13♊	1♒
18	28♈	11♉	14♊	2♒
19	29♈	13♉	15♊	3♒
20	0♉	15♉	16♊	3♒
21	1♉	17♉	16♊	4♒
22	2♉	19♉	17♊	5♒
23	3♉	20♉	18♊	5♒
24	4♉	22♉	19♊	6♒
25	5♉	23♉	20♊	6♒
26	6♉	25♉	21♊	7♒
27	7♉	26♉	22♊	8♒
28	8♉	28♉	23♊	8♒
29	9♉	29♉	23♊	9♒
30	10♉	0♊	24♊	10♒

July

Day	☉	☿	♀	♂
1	9♋	20♊	26♊	14♓
2	10♋	22♊	25♊	14♓
3	11♋	24♊	25♊	15♓
4	12♋	25♊	24♊	15♓
5	13♋	27♊	24♊	16♓
6	14♋	29♊	24♊	16♓
7	15♋	1♋	23♊	16♓
8	16♋	3♋	23♊	17♓
9	17♋	5♋	23♊	17♓
10	18♋	7♋	23♊	17♓
11	19♋	9♋	23♊	18♓
12	20♋	11♋	23♊	18♓
13	21♋	13♋	23♊	19♓
14	22♋	15♋	23♊	19♓
15	23♋	17♋	23♊	19♓
16	24♋	19♋	23♊	19♓
17	25♋	21♋	23♊	20♓
18	26♋	24♋	23♊	20♓
19	26♋	26♋	23♊	20♓
20	27♋	28♋	23♊	21♓
21	28♋	0♌	23♊	21♓
22	29♋	2♌	24♊	21♓
23	0♌	4♌	24♊	21♓
24	1♌	6♌	24♊	22♓
25	2♌	8♌	25♊	22♓
26	3♌	10♌	25♊	22♓
27	4♌	12♌	26♊	22♓
28	5♌	14♌	26♊	22♓
29	6♌	16♌	27♊	23♓
30	7♌	18♌	27♊	23♓
31	8♌	20♌	28♊	23♓

October

Day	☉	☿	♀	♂
1	8♎	29♍	24♌	14♓
2	9♎	28♍	26♌	14♓
3	10♎	28♍	27♌	14♓
4	11♎	27♍	28♌	13♓
5	12♎	27♍	29♌	13♓
6	13♎	27♍	0♍	13♓
7	14♎	28♍	1♍	13♓
8	15♎	28♍	2♍	13♓
9	16♎	28♍	4♍	13♓
10	17♎	29♍	5♍	13♓
11	18♎	0♎	6♍	13♓
12	19♎	1♎	7♍	13♓
13	20♎	2♎	8♍	13♓
14	21♎	3♎	9♍	13♓
15	22♎	4♎	10♍	13♓
16	23♎	6♎	12♍	13♓
17	24♎	7♎	13♍	13♓
18	25♎	9♎	14♍	14♓
19	26♎	10♎	15♍	14♓
20	27♎	12♎	16♍	14♓
21	28♎	13♎	17♍	14♓
22	29♎	15♎	19♍	14♓
23	0♏	16♎	20♍	14♓
24	1♏	18♎	21♍	14♓
25	2♏	20♎	22♍	15♓
26	3♏	21♎	23♍	15♓
27	4♏	23♎	25♍	15♓
28	5♏	25♎	26♍	15♓
29	6♏	26♎	27♍	15♓
30	7♏	28♎	28♍	16♓
31	8♏	0♏	29♍	16♓

February

Day	☉	☿	♀	♂
1	11♒	1♒	18♓	12♐
2	12♒	0♒	19♓	13♐
3	13♒	29♑	20♓	13♐
4	14♒	29♑	21♓	14♐
5	15♒	28♑	23♓	14♐
6	16♒	28♑	24♓	15♐
7	17♒	28♑	25♓	16♐
8	18♒	28♑	26♓	16♐
9	19♒	28♑	27♓	17♐
10	20♒	28♑	29♓	18♐
11	21♒	28♑	0♈	18♐
12	22♒	28♑	1♈	19♐
13	23♒	29♑	2♈	20♐
14	24♒	29♑	3♈	20♐
15	25♒	0♒	5♈	21♐
16	27♒	1♒	6♈	22♐
17	28♒	1♒	7♈	22♐
18	29♒	2♒	8♈	23♐
19	0♓	3♒	9♈	24♐
20	1♓	4♒	11♈	24♐
21	2♓	5♒	12♈	25♐
22	3♓	6♒	13♈	26♐
23	4♓	7♒	14♈	26♐
24	5♓	8♒	15♈	27♐
25	6♓	9♒	16♈	28♐
26	7♓	10♒	18♈	28♐
27	8♓	12♒	19♈	29♐
28	9♓	13♒	20♈	0♑
29	10♓	14♒	21♈	0♑

May

Day	☉	☿	♀	♂
1	11♉	1♊	25♊	10♒
2	12♉	3♊	26♊	11♒
3	13♉	4♊	26♊	12♒
4	14♉	4♊	27♊	12♒
5	15♉	5♊	28♊	13♒
6	16♉	6♊	29♊	13♒
7	17♉	7♊	29♊	14♒
8	18♉	7♊	0♋	15♒
9	19♉	8♊	1♋	15♒
10	20♉	8♊	1♋	16♒
11	20♉	8♊	2♋	16♒
12	21♉	9♊	3♋	17♒
13	22♉	9♊	3♋	18♒
14	23♉	9♊	4♋	18♒
15	24♉	9♊	4♋	19♒
16	25♉	9♊	5♋	19♒
17	26♉	9♊	5♋	20♒
18	27♉	8♊	6♋	21♒
19	28♉	8♊	6♋	21♒
20	29♉	8♊	7♋	22♒
21	0♊	7♊	7♋	22♒
22	1♊	7♊	7♋	23♒
23	2♊	6♊	8♋	24♒
24	3♊	6♊	8♋	24♒
25	4♊	5♊	8♋	25♒
26	5♊	5♊	8♋	25♒
27	6♊	4♊	9♋	26♒
28	7♊	3♊	9♋	27♒
29	8♊	3♊	9♋	27♒
30	9♊	2♊	9♋	28♒
31	10♊	2♊	9♋	28♒

August

Day	☉	☿	♀	♂
1	9♌	22♌	28♊	23♓
2	10♌	24♌	29♊	23♓
3	11♌	25♌	29♊	23♓
4	12♌	27♌	0♋	23♓
5	13♌	29♌	1♋	23♓
6	14♌	1♍	1♋	24♓
7	15♌	2♍	2♋	24♓
8	16♌	4♍	3♋	24♓
9	17♌	6♍	3♋	24♓
10	18♌	7♍	4♋	24♓
11	18♌	9♍	5♋	24♓
12	19♌	11♍	5♋	24♓
13	20♌	12♍	6♋	24♓
14	21♌	14♍	7♋	24♓
15	22♌	15♍	8♋	24♓
16	23♌	17♍	9♋	23♓
17	24♌	18♍	9♋	23♓
18	25♌	19♍	10♋	23♓
19	26♌	21♍	11♋	23♓
20	27♌	22♍	12♋	23♓
21	28♌	23♍	13♋	23♓
22	29♌	25♍	14♋	23♓
23	0♍	26♍	15♋	23♓
24	1♍	27♍	15♋	22♓
25	2♍	28♍	16♋	22♓
26	3♍	0♎	17♋	22♓
27	4♍	1♎	18♋	22♓
28	5♍	2♎	19♋	22♓
29	6♍	3♎	20♋	21♓
30	7♍	4♎	21♋	21♓
31	8♍	5♎	22♋	21♓

November

Day	☉	☿	♀	♂
1	9♏	1♏	0♎	16♓
2	10♏	3♏	2♎	16♓
3	11♏	5♏	3♎	17♓
4	12♏	6♏	4♎	17♓
5	13♏	8♏	5♎	17♓
6	14♏	10♏	6♎	18♓
7	15♏	11♏	8♎	18♓
8	16♏	13♏	9♎	18♓
9	17♏	15♏	10♎	18♓
10	18♏	16♏	11♎	19♓
11	19♏	18♏	13♎	19♓
12	20♏	19♏	14♎	20♓
13	21♏	21♏	15♎	20♓
14	22♏	23♏	16♎	20♓
15	23♏	24♏	17♎	21♓
16	24♏	26♏	19♎	21♓
17	25♏	27♏	20♎	21♓
18	26♏	29♏	21♎	22♓
19	27♏	0♐	22♎	22♓
20	28♏	2♐	23♎	23♓
21	29♏	4♐	25♎	23♓
22	0♐	5♐	26♎	23♓
23	1♐	7♐	27♎	24♓
24	2♐	8♐	28♎	24♓
25	3♐	10♐	0♏	25♓
26	4♐	11♐	1♏	25♓
27	5♐	13♐	2♏	26♓
28	6♐	14♐	3♏	26♓
29	7♐	16♐	5♏	27♓
30	8♐	18♐	6♏	27♓

March

Day	☉	☿	♀	♂
1	11♓	15♒	22♈	1♑
2	12♓	17♒	23♈	2♑
3	13♓	18♒	25♈	2♑
4	14♓	19♒	26♈	3♑
5	15♓	21♒	27♈	4♑
6	16♓	22♒	28♈	4♑
7	17♓	24♒	29♈	5♑
8	18♓	25♒	0♉	5♑
9	19♓	27♒	1♉	6♑
10	20♓	28♒	3♉	7♑
11	21♓	0♓	4♉	7♑
12	22♓	1♓	5♉	8♑
13	23♓	3♓	6♉	9♑
14	24♓	4♓	7♉	9♑
15	25♓	6♓	8♉	10♑
16	26♓	8♓	9♉	11♑
17	27♓	9♓	11♉	11♑
18	28♓	11♓	12♉	12♑
19	29♓	13♓	13♉	13♑
20	0♈	14♓	14♉	13♑
21	1♈	16♓	15♉	14♑
22	2♈	18♓	16♉	15♑
23	3♈	19♓	17♉	15♑
24	4♈	21♓	18♉	16♑
25	5♈	23♓	19♉	17♑
26	6♈	25♓	20♉	17♑
27	7♈	27♓	21♉	18♑
28	7♈	29♓	23♉	19♑
29	8♈	1♈	24♉	19♑
30	9♈	2♈	25♉	20♑
31	10♈	4♈	26♉	20♑

June

Day	☉	☿	♀	♂
1	11♊	2♊	9♋	29♒
2	12♊	1♊	9♋	29♒
3	13♊	1♊	9♋	0♓
4	14♊	1♊	9♋	0♓
5	14♊	0♊	9♋	1♓
6	15♊	0♊	8♋	2♓
7	16♊	0♊	8♋	2♓
8	17♊	0♊	8♋	3♓
9	18♊	0♊	8♋	3♓
10	19♊	1♊	7♋	4♓
11	20♊	1♊	7♋	4♓
12	21♊	1♊	6♋	5♓
13	22♊	2♊	6♋	5♓
14	23♊	2♊	5♋	6♓
15	24♊	3♊	5♋	6♓
16	25♊	3♊	4♋	7♓
17	26♊	4♊	4♋	7♓
18	27♊	5♊	3♋	8♓
19	28♊	5♊	3♋	8♓
20	29♊	6♊	2♋	9♓
21	0♋	7♊	1♋	9♓
22	1♋	8♊	1♋	10♓
23	2♋	9♊	0♋	10♓
24	3♋	11♊	0♋	11♓
25	4♋	12♊	29♊	11♓
26	5♋	13♊	28♊	12♓
27	6♋	14♊	28♊	12♓
28	6♋	16♊	27♊	13♓
29	7♋	17♊	27♊	13♓
30	8♋	19♊	26♊	14♓

September

Day	☉	☿	♀	♂
1	9♍	6♎	23♋	21♓
2	10♍	7♎	24♋	20♓
3	11♍	8♎	25♋	20♓
4	12♍	8♎	26♋	20♓
5	13♍	9♎	27♋	20♓
6	14♍	10♎	28♋	19♓
7	15♍	10♎	29♋	19♓
8	16♍	11♎	0♌	19♓
9	16♍	11♎	1♌	19♓
10	17♍	12♎	2♌	18♓
11	18♍	12♎	3♌	18♓
12	19♍	12♎	4♌	18♓
13	20♍	12♎	5♌	18♓
14	21♍	12♎	6♌	17♓
15	22♍	12♎	7♌	17♓
16	23♍	12♎	8♌	17♓
17	24♍	11♎	9♌	16♓
18	25♍	11♎	10♌	16♓
19	26♍	10♎	11♌	16♓
20	27♍	10♎	12♌	16♓
21	28♍	9♎	13♌	15♓
22	29♍	8♎	15♌	15♓
23	0♎	7♎	16♌	15♓
24	1♎	6♎	17♌	15♓
25	2♎	5♎	18♌	15♓
26	3♎	4♎	19♌	14♓
27	4♎	3♎	20♌	14♓
28	5♎	2♎	21♌	14♓
29	6♎	1♎	22♌	14♓
30	7♎	0♎	23♌	14♓

December

Day	☉	☿	♀	♂
1	9♐	19♐	7♏	27♓
2	10♐	21♐	8♏	28♓
3	11♐	22♐	9♏	28♓
4	12♐	24♐	11♏	29♓
5	13♐	25♐	12♏	29♓
6	14♐	27♐	13♏	0♈
7	15♐	28♐	14♏	0♈
8	16♐	0♑	16♏	1♈
9	17♐	1♑	17♏	1♈
10	18♐	3♑	18♏	2♈
11	19♐	4♑	19♏	2♈
12	20♐	6♑	21♏	3♈
13	21♐	7♑	22♏	3♈
14	22♐	9♑	23♏	4♈
15	23♐	10♑	24♏	4♈
16	24♐	12♑	26♏	5♈
17	25♐	13♑	27♏	6♈
18	26♐	15♑	28♏	6♈
19	27♐	16♑	29♏	7♈
20	28♐	17♑	1♐	7♈
21	29♐	19♑	2♐	8♈
22	0♑	20♑	3♐	8♈
23	1♑	21♑	4♐	9♈
24	2♑	22♑	5♐	9♈
25	3♑	23♑	7♐	10♈
26	4♑	24♑	8♐	10♈
27	5♑	25♑	9♐	11♈
28	6♑	26♑	10♐	12♈
29	7♑	26♑	12♐	12♈
30	8♑	27♑	13♐	13♈
31	10♑	27♑	14♐	13♈

☉ = Sun ☿ = Mercury ♀ = Venus ♂ = Mars ♈ = Aries ♉ = Taurus ♊ = Gemini ♋ = Cancer

1957

January

Day	☉	☿	♀	♂
1	11♑	27♑	15♐	14♈
2	12♑	27♑	17♐	14♈
3	13♑	27♑	18♐	15♈
4	14♑	27♑	19♐	16♈
5	15♑	26♑	20♐	16♈
6	16♑	25♑	22♐	17♈
7	17♑	24♑	23♐	17♈
8	18♑	23♑	24♐	18♈
9	19♑	22♑	25♐	18♈
10	20♑	21♑	27♐	19♈
11	21♑	19♑	28♐	20♈
12	22♑	18♑	29♐	20♈
13	23♑	17♑	0♑	21♈
14	24♑	16♑	2♑	21♈
15	25♑	15♑	3♑	22♈
16	26♑	14♑	4♑	23♈
17	27♑	13♑	5♑	23♈
18	28♑	12♑	7♑	24♈
19	29♑	12♑	8♑	24♈
20	0♒	11♑	9♑	25♈
21	1♒	11♑	10♑	26♈
22	2♒	11♑	12♑	26♈
23	3♒	11♑	13♑	27♈
24	4♒	12♑	14♑	27♈
25	5♒	12♑	15♑	28♈
26	6♒	12♑	17♑	29♈
27	7♒	13♑	18♑	29♈
28	8♒	14♑	19♑	0♉
29	9♒	14♑	20♑	0♉
30	10♒	15♑	22♑	1♉
31	11♒	16♑	23♑	2♉

February

Day	☉	☿	♀	♂
1	12♒	17♑	24♑	2♉
2	13♒	18♑	25♑	3♉
3	14♒	19♑	27♑	3♉
4	15♒	20♑	28♑	4♉
5	16♒	21♑	29♑	5♉
6	17♒	22♑	0♒	5♉
7	18♒	23♑	2♒	6♉
8	19♒	24♑	3♒	6♉
9	20♒	26♑	4♒	7♉
10	21♒	27♑	5♒	8♉
11	22♒	28♑	7♒	8♉
12	23♒	29♑	8♒	9♉
13	24♒	1♒	9♒	10♉
14	25♒	2♒	10♒	10♉
15	26♒	4♒	12♒	11♉
16	27♒	5♒	13♒	11♉
17	28♒	6♒	14♒	12♉
18	29♒	8♒	15♒	13♉
19	0♓	9♒	17♒	13♉
20	1♓	11♒	18♒	14♉
21	2♓	12♒	19♒	15♉
22	3♓	14♒	20♒	15♉
23	4♓	15♒	22♒	16♉
24	5♓	17♒	23♒	16♉
25	6♓	18♒	24♒	17♉
26	7♓	20♒	25♒	18♉
27	8♓	21♒	27♒	18♉
28	9♓	23♒	28♒	19♉

March

Day	☉	☿	♀	♂
1	10♓	25♒	29♒	20♉
2	11♓	26♒	0♓	20♉
3	12♓	28♒	2♓	21♉
4	13♓	0♓	3♓	21♉
5	14♓	1♓	4♓	22♉
6	15♓	3♓	5♓	23♉
7	16♓	5♓	7♓	23♉
8	17♓	6♓	8♓	24♉
9	18♓	8♓	9♓	25♉
10	19♓	10♓	10♓	25♉
11	20♓	12♓	12♓	26♉
12	21♓	14♓	13♓	26♉
13	22♓	15♓	14♓	27♉
14	23♓	17♓	15♓	28♉
15	24♓	19♓	17♓	28♉
16	25♓	21♓	18♓	29♉
17	26♓	23♓	19♓	0♊
18	27♓	25♓	20♓	0♊
19	28♓	27♓	22♓	1♊
20	29♓	29♓	23♓	1♊
21	0♈	1♈	24♓	2♊
22	1♈	3♈	25♓	3♊
23	2♈	5♈	27♓	3♊
24	3♈	7♈	28♓	4♊
25	4♈	9♈	29♓	5♊
26	5♈	11♈	0♈	5♊
27	6♈	13♈	2♈	6♊
28	7♈	15♈	3♈	6♊
29	8♈	17♈	4♈	7♊
30	9♈	19♈	5♈	8♊
31	10♈	21♈	7♈	8♊

April

Day	☉	☿	♀	♂
1	11♈	23♈	8♈	9♊
2	12♈	25♈	9♈	10♊
3	13♈	27♈	10♈	10♊
4	14♈	29♈	12♈	11♊
5	15♈	0♉	13♈	12♊
6	16♈	2♉	14♈	12♊
7	17♈	4♉	15♈	13♊
8	18♈	5♉	16♈	13♊
9	19♈	7♉	18♈	14♊
10	20♈	8♉	19♈	15♊
11	21♈	10♉	20♈	15♊
12	22♈	11♉	21♈	16♊
13	23♈	12♉	23♈	17♊
14	24♈	13♉	24♈	17♊
15	25♈	15♉	25♈	18♊
16	26♈	15♉	26♈	18♊
17	27♈	16♉	28♈	19♊
18	28♈	17♉	29♈	20♊
19	29♈	18♉	0♉	20♊
20	0♉	18♉	1♉	21♊
21	1♉	19♉	3♉	22♊
22	2♉	19♉	4♉	22♊
23	3♉	19♉	5♉	23♊
24	4♉	19♉	6♉	23♊
25	5♉	19♉	7♉	24♊
26	6♉	19♉	9♉	25♊
27	7♉	19♉	10♉	25♊
28	8♉	19♉	11♉	26♊
29	9♉	19♉	12♉	27♊
30	10♉	18♉	14♉	27♊

May

Day	☉	☿	♀	♂
1	11♉	18♉	15♉	28♊
2	12♉	17♉	16♉	28♊
3	12♉	17♉	17♉	29♊
4	13♉	16♉	19♉	0♋
5	14♉	16♉	20♉	0♋
6	15♉	15♉	21♉	1♋
7	16♉	14♉	22♉	2♋
8	17♉	14♉	24♉	2♋
9	18♉	13♉	25♉	3♋
10	19♉	13♉	26♉	3♋
11	20♉	12♉	27♉	4♋
12	21♉	12♉	28♉	5♋
13	22♉	11♉	0♊	5♋
14	23♉	11♉	1♊	6♋
15	24♉	11♉	2♊	7♋
16	25♉	10♉	3♊	7♋
17	26♉	10♉	5♊	8♋
18	27♉	10♉	6♊	9♋
19	28♉	10♉	7♊	9♋
20	29♉	10♉	8♊	10♋
21	0♊	10♉	10♊	10♋
22	1♊	10♉	11♊	11♋
23	2♊	11♉	12♊	12♋
24	3♊	11♉	13♊	12♋
25	4♊	11♉	14♊	13♋
26	5♊	12♉	16♊	14♋
27	6♊	12♉	17♊	14♋
28	7♊	13♉	18♊	15♋
29	8♊	14♉	19♊	15♋
30	9♊	15♉	21♊	16♋
31	9♊	15♉	22♊	17♋

June

Day	☉	☿	♀	♂
1	10♊	16♉	23♊	17♋
2	11♊	17♉	24♊	18♋
3	12♊	18♉	25♊	19♋
4	13♊	19♉	27♊	19♋
5	14♊	20♉	28♊	20♋
6	15♊	21♉	29♊	20♋
7	16♊	23♉	0♋	21♋
8	17♊	24♉	2♋	22♋
9	18♊	25♉	3♋	22♋
10	19♊	27♉	4♋	23♋
11	20♊	28♉	5♋	24♋
12	21♊	29♉	6♋	24♋
13	22♊	1♊	8♋	25♋
14	23♊	3♊	9♋	25♋
15	24♊	4♊	10♋	26♋
16	25♊	6♊	11♋	27♋
17	26♊	7♊	13♋	27♋
18	27♊	9♊	14♋	28♋
19	28♊	11♊	15♋	29♋
20	29♊	13♊	16♋	29♋
21	0♋	15♊	18♋	0♌
22	1♋	17♊	19♋	0♌
23	1♋	19♊	20♋	1♌
24	2♋	21♊	21♋	2♌
25	3♋	23♊	22♋	2♌
26	4♋	25♊	24♋	3♌
27	5♋	27♊	25♋	4♌
28	6♋	29♊	26♋	4♌
29	7♋	1♋	27♋	5♌
30	8♋	3♋	28♋	5♌

July

Day	☉	☿	♀	♂
1	9♋	5♋	0♌	6♌
2	10♋	8♋	1♌	7♌
3	11♋	10♋	2♌	7♌
4	12♋	12♋	3♌	8♌
5	13♋	14♋	5♌	9♌
6	14♋	16♋	6♌	9♌
7	15♋	18♋	7♌	10♌
8	16♋	21♋	8♌	10♌
9	17♋	23♋	9♌	11♌
10	18♋	25♋	11♌	12♌
11	19♋	27♋	12♌	12♌
12	20♋	29♋	13♌	13♌
13	21♋	1♌	14♌	14♌
14	21♋	3♌	16♌	14♌
15	22♋	5♌	17♌	15♌
16	23♋	7♌	18♌	15♌
17	24♋	8♌	19♌	16♌
18	25♋	10♌	20♌	17♌
19	26♋	12♌	22♌	17♌
20	27♋	14♌	23♌	18♌
21	28♋	16♌	24♌	19♌
22	29♋	17♌	25♌	19♌
23	0♌	19♌	26♌	20♌
24	1♌	21♌	28♌	21♌
25	2♌	22♌	29♌	21♌
26	3♌	24♌	0♍	22♌
27	4♌	26♌	1♍	22♌
28	5♌	27♌	3♍	23♌
29	6♌	29♌	4♍	24♌
30	7♌	0♍	5♍	24♌
31	8♌	2♍	6♍	25♌

August

Day	☉	☿	♀	♂
1	9♌	3♍	7♍	26♌
2	10♌	4♍	9♍	26♌
3	11♌	6♍	10♍	27♌
4	12♌	7♍	11♍	27♌
5	13♌	8♍	12♍	28♌
6	13♌	10♍	13♍	29♌
7	14♌	11♍	15♍	29♌
8	15♌	12♍	16♍	0♍
9	16♌	13♍	17♍	1♍
10	17♌	14♍	18♍	1♍
11	18♌	16♍	19♍	2♍
12	19♌	17♍	21♍	3♍
13	20♌	18♍	22♍	3♍
14	21♌	18♍	23♍	4♍
15	22♌	19♍	24♍	4♍
16	23♌	20♍	25♍	5♍
17	24♌	21♍	27♍	6♍
18	25♌	22♍	28♍	6♍
19	26♌	22♍	29♍	7♍
20	27♌	23♍	0♎	8♍
21	28♌	24♍	1♎	8♍
22	29♌	24♍	3♎	9♍
23	0♍	24♍	4♎	9♍
24	1♍	25♍	5♎	10♍
25	2♍	25♍	6♎	11♍
26	3♍	25♍	7♎	11♍
27	4♍	25♍	9♎	12♍
28	5♍	25♍	10♎	13♍
29	6♍	25♍	11♎	13♍
30	7♍	25♍	12♎	14♍
31	8♍	25♍	13♎	15♍

September

Day	☉	☿	♀	♂
1	8♍	24♍	15♎	15♍
2	9♍	24♍	16♎	16♍
3	10♍	23♍	17♎	17♍
4	11♍	22♍	18♎	17♍
5	12♍	21♍	19♎	18♍
6	13♍	20♍	20♎	18♍
7	14♍	20♍	22♎	19♍
8	15♍	19♍	23♎	20♍
9	16♍	18♍	24♎	20♍
10	17♍	17♍	25♎	21♍
11	18♍	16♍	26♎	22♍
12	19♍	15♍	28♎	22♍
13	20♍	14♍	29♎	23♍
14	21♍	13♍	0♏	24♍
15	22♍	12♍	1♏	24♍
16	23♍	12♍	2♏	25♍
17	24♍	11♍	3♏	25♍
18	25♍	11♍	5♏	26♍
19	26♍	11♍	6♏	27♍
20	27♍	11♍	7♏	27♍
21	28♍	11♍	8♏	28♍
22	29♍	12♍	9♏	29♍
23	0♎	12♍	10♏	29♍
24	1♎	13♍	12♏	0♎
25	2♎	14♍	13♏	1♎
26	3♎	15♍	14♏	1♎
27	4♎	16♍	15♏	2♎
28	5♎	17♍	16♏	3♎
29	6♎	19♍	17♏	3♎
30	7♎	20♍	19♏	4♎

October

Day	☉	☿	♀	♂
1	8♎	21♍	20♏	5♎
2	9♎	23♍	21♏	5♎
3	10♎	25♍	22♏	6♎
4	11♎	26♍	23♏	7♎
5	12♎	28♍	24♏	7♎
6	13♎	0♎	26♏	8♎
7	14♎	1♎	27♏	8♎
8	15♎	3♎	28♏	9♎
9	16♎	5♎	29♏	10♎
10	17♎	6♎	0♐	10♎
11	18♎	8♎	1♐	11♎
12	19♎	10♎	2♐	12♎
13	20♎	12♎	4♐	12♎
14	21♎	13♎	5♐	13♎
15	22♎	15♎	6♐	14♎
16	23♎	17♎	7♐	14♎
17	24♎	19♎	8♐	15♎
18	25♎	20♎	9♐	16♎
19	26♎	22♎	10♐	16♎
20	27♎	24♎	12♐	17♎
21	28♎	26♎	13♐	18♎
22	29♎	27♎	14♐	18♎
23	0♏	29♎	15♐	19♎
24	1♏	1♏	16♐	20♎
25	2♏	2♏	17♐	20♎
26	3♏	4♏	18♐	21♎
27	4♏	6♏	19♐	22♎
28	5♏	7♏	20♐	22♎
29	6♏	9♏	22♐	23♎
30	7♏	10♏	23♐	24♎
31	8♏	12♏	24♐	24♎

November

Day	☉	☿	♀	♂
1	9♏	14♏	25♐	25♎
2	10♏	15♏	26♐	26♎
3	11♏	17♏	27♐	26♎
4	12♏	18♏	28♐	27♎
5	13♏	20♏	29♐	28♎
6	14♏	21♏	0♑	28♎
7	15♏	23♏	1♑	29♎
8	16♏	25♏	2♑	0♏
9	17♏	26♏	3♑	0♏
10	18♏	28♏	4♑	1♏
11	19♏	29♏	6♑	2♏
12	20♏	1♐	7♑	2♏
13	21♏	2♐	8♑	3♏
14	22♏	4♐	9♑	4♏
15	23♏	5♐	10♑	4♏
16	24♏	7♐	11♑	5♏
17	25♏	8♐	12♑	6♏
18	26♏	10♐	13♑	6♏
19	27♏	11♐	14♑	7♏
20	28♏	13♐	15♑	8♏
21	29♏	14♐	16♑	8♏
22	0♐	16♐	17♑	9♏
23	1♐	17♐	18♑	10♏
24	2♐	19♐	19♑	10♏
25	3♐	20♐	20♑	11♏
26	4♐	21♐	21♑	12♏
27	5♐	23♐	22♑	12♏
28	6♐	24♐	22♑	13♏
29	7♐	26♐	23♑	14♏
30	8♐	27♐	24♑	14♏

December

Day	☉	☿	♀	♂
1	9♐	28♐	25♑	15♏
2	10♐	0♑	26♑	16♏
3	11♐	1♑	27♑	16♏
4	12♐	2♑	28♑	17♏
5	13♐	3♑	29♑	18♏
6	14♐	5♑	0♒	18♏
7	15♐	6♑	0♒	19♏
8	16♐	7♑	1♒	20♏
9	17♐	8♑	2♒	20♏
10	18♐	9♑	3♒	21♏
11	19♐	9♑	4♒	22♏
12	20♐	10♑	4♒	23♏
13	21♐	11♑	5♒	23♏
14	22♐	11♑	6♒	24♏
15	23♐	11♑	7♒	25♏
16	24♐	12♑	7♒	25♏
17	25♐	11♑	8♒	26♏
18	26♐	11♑	9♒	27♏
19	27♐	11♑	9♒	27♏
20	28♐	10♑	10♒	28♏
21	29♐	9♑	11♒	29♏
22	0♑	8♑	11♒	29♏
23	1♑	7♑	12♒	0♐
24	2♑	6♑	12♒	1♐
25	3♑	5♑	13♒	1♐
26	4♑	3♑	13♒	2♐
27	5♑	2♑	14♒	3♐
28	6♑	1♑	14♒	4♐
29	7♑	29♐	14♒	4♐
30	8♑	28♐	15♒	5♐
31	9♑	27♐	15♒	6♐

Planetary Positions

♌ = Leo ♍ = Virgo ♎ = Libra ♏ = Scorpio ♐ = Sagittarius ♑ = Capricorn ♒ = Aquarius ♓ = Pisces

1958

January

Day	☉	☿	♀	♂
1	10♑	27♐	15♒	6♐
2	11♑	26♐	16♒	7♐
3	12♑	26♐	16♒	8♐
4	13♑	25♐	16♒	8♐
5	14♑	25♐	16♒	9♐
6	15♑	25♐	16♒	10♐
7	16♑	25♐	16♒	11♐
8	17♑	26♐	16♒	11♐
9	18♑	26♐	16♒	12♐
10	19♑	27♐	16♒	13♐
11	20♑	27♐	16♒	13♐
12	21♑	28♐	16♒	14♐
13	23♑	29♐	16♒	15♐
14	24♑	0♑	16♒	15♐
15	25♑	1♑	15♒	16♐
16	26♑	2♑	15♒	17♐
17	27♑	3♑	15♒	18♐
18	28♑	4♑	14♒	18♐
19	29♑	5♑	14♒	19♐
20	0♒	6♑	13♒	20♐
21	1♒	7♑	13♒	20♐
22	2♒	9♑	12♒	21♐
23	3♒	10♑	12♒	22♐
24	4♒	11♑	11♒	22♐
25	5♒	12♑	11♒	23♐
26	6♒	14♑	10♒	24♐
27	7♒	15♑	9♒	25♐
28	8♒	16♑	9♒	25♐
29	9♒	18♑	8♒	26♐
30	10♒	19♑	8♒	27♐
31	11♒	21♑	7♒	27♐

February

Day	☉	☿	♀	♂
1	12♒	22♑	6♒	28♐
2	13♒	23♑	6♒	29♐
3	14♒	25♑	5♒	0♑
4	15♒	26♑	5♒	0♑
5	16♒	28♑	4♒	1♑
6	17♒	29♑	4♒	2♑
7	18♒	1♒	3♒	2♑
8	19♒	2♒	3♒	3♑
9	20♒	4♒	2♒	4♑
10	21♒	5♒	2♒	5♑
11	22♒	7♒	2♒	5♑
12	23♒	9♒	1♒	6♑
13	24♒	10♒	1♒	7♑
14	25♒	12♒	1♒	7♑
15	26♒	13♒	1♒	8♑
16	27♒	15♒	1♒	9♑
17	28♒	17♒	1♒	10♑
18	29♒	18♒	1♒	10♑
19	0♓	20♒	1♒	11♑
20	1♓	22♒	1♒	12♑
21	2♓	24♒	1♒	12♑
22	3♓	25♒	1♒	13♑
23	4♓	27♒	1♒	14♑
24	5♓	29♒	1♒	15♑
25	6♓	1♓	2♒	15♑
26	7♓	2♓	2♒	16♑
27	8♓	4♓	2♒	17♑
28	9♓	6♓	3♒	18♑

March

Day	☉	☿	♀	♂
1	10♓	8♓	3♒	18♑
2	11♓	10♓	3♒	19♑
3	12♓	12♓	4♒	20♑
4	13♓	13♓	4♒	20♑
5	14♓	15♓	5♒	21♑
6	15♓	17♓	5♒	22♑
7	16♓	19♓	6♒	23♑
8	17♓	21♓	6♒	23♑
9	18♓	23♓	7♒	24♑
10	19♓	25♓	7♒	25♑
11	20♓	27♓	8♒	26♑
12	21♓	29♓	9♒	26♑
13	22♓	1♈	9♒	27♑
14	23♓	3♈	10♒	28♑
15	24♓	5♈	11♒	28♑
16	25♓	7♈	12♒	29♑
17	26♓	9♈	12♒	0♒
18	27♓	10♈	13♒	1♒
19	28♓	12♈	14♒	1♒
20	29♓	14♈	15♒	2♒
21	0♈	16♈	15♒	3♒
22	1♈	17♈	16♒	4♒
23	2♈	19♈	17♒	4♒
24	3♈	21♈	18♒	5♒
25	4♈	22♈	19♒	6♒
26	5♈	23♈	19♒	7♒
27	6♈	25♈	20♒	7♒
28	7♈	26♈	21♒	8♒
29	8♈	27♈	22♒	9♒
30	9♈	28♈	23♒	9♒
31	10♈	28♈	24♒	10♒

April

Day	☉	☿	♀	♂
1	11♈	29♈	25♒	11♒
2	12♈	0♉	26♒	12♒
3	13♈	0♉	27♒	12♒
4	14♈	1♉	28♒	13♒
5	15♈	1♉	29♒	14♒
6	16♈	1♉	0♓	15♒
7	17♈	1♉	1♓	15♒
8	18♈	1♉	1♓	16♒
9	19♈	0♉	2♓	17♒
10	20♈	0♉	3♓	18♒
11	21♈	0♉	4♓	18♒
12	22♈	29♈	5♓	19♒
13	23♈	29♈	6♓	20♒
14	24♈	28♈	7♓	20♒
15	25♈	27♈	8♓	21♒
16	26♈	27♈	9♓	22♒
17	27♈	26♈	11♓	23♒
18	28♈	25♈	12♓	23♒
19	29♈	25♈	13♓	24♒
20	0♉	24♈	14♓	25♒
21	1♉	23♈	15♓	26♒
22	2♉	23♈	16♓	26♒
23	3♉	22♈	17♓	27♒
24	4♉	21♈	18♓	28♒
25	4♉	21♈	19♓	29♒
26	5♉	21♈	20♓	29♒
27	6♉	20♈	21♓	0♓
28	7♉	20♈	22♓	1♓
29	8♉	20♈	23♓	2♓
30	9♉	20♈	24♓	2♓

May

Day	☉	☿	♀	♂
1	10♉	20♈	25♓	3♓
2	11♉	20♈	26♓	4♓
3	12♉	20♈	27♓	4♓
4	13♉	21♈	29♓	5♓
5	14♉	21♈	0♈	6♓
6	15♉	21♈	1♈	7♓
7	16♉	22♈	2♈	7♓
8	17♉	22♈	3♈	8♓
9	18♉	23♈	4♈	9♓
10	19♉	24♈	5♈	10♓
11	20♉	24♈	6♈	10♓
12	21♉	25♈	7♈	11♓
13	22♉	26♈	9♈	12♓
14	23♉	27♈	10♈	13♓
15	24♉	28♈	11♈	13♓
16	25♉	29♈	12♈	14♓
17	26♉	0♉	13♈	15♓
18	27♉	1♉	14♈	15♓
19	28♉	2♉	15♈	16♓
20	29♉	4♉	16♈	17♓
21	0♊	5♉	18♈	18♓
22	1♊	6♉	19♈	18♓
23	2♊	8♉	20♈	19♓
24	3♊	9♉	21♈	20♓
25	3♊	10♉	22♈	21♓
26	4♊	12♉	23♈	21♓
27	5♊	13♉	24♈	22♓
28	6♊	15♉	25♈	23♓
29	7♊	16♉	27♈	23♓
30	8♊	18♉	28♈	24♓
31	9♊	20♉	29♈	25♓

June

Day	☉	☿	♀	♂
1	10♊	21♉	0♉	26♓
2	11♊	23♉	1♉	26♓
3	12♊	25♉	2♉	27♓
4	13♊	27♉	3♉	28♓
5	14♊	29♉	5♉	29♓
6	15♊	1♊	6♉	29♓
7	16♊	3♊	7♉	0♈
8	17♊	5♊	8♉	1♈
9	18♊	7♊	9♉	1♈
10	19♊	9♊	10♉	2♈
11	20♊	11♊	12♉	3♈
12	21♊	13♊	13♉	4♈
13	22♊	15♊	14♉	4♈
14	23♊	17♊	15♉	5♈
15	24♊	19♊	16♉	6♈
16	25♊	21♊	17♉	6♈
17	26♊	24♊	19♉	7♈
18	26♊	26♊	20♉	8♈
19	27♊	28♊	21♉	8♈
20	28♊	0♋	22♉	9♈
21	29♊	2♋	23♉	10♈
22	0♋	5♋	24♉	11♈
23	1♋	7♋	26♉	11♈
24	2♋	9♋	27♉	12♈
25	3♋	11♋	28♉	13♈
26	4♋	13♋	29♉	13♈
27	5♋	15♋	0♊	14♈
28	6♋	17♋	1♊	15♈
29	7♋	19♋	3♊	15♈
30	8♋	21♋	4♊	16♈

July

Day	☉	☿	♀	♂
1	9♋	23♋	5♊	17♈
2	10♋	25♋	6♊	17♈
3	11♋	27♋	7♊	18♈
4	12♋	29♋	9♊	19♈
5	13♋	0♌	10♊	19♈
6	14♋	2♌	11♊	20♈
7	15♋	4♌	12♊	21♈
8	16♋	6♌	13♊	21♈
9	16♋	7♌	14♊	22♈
10	17♋	9♌	16♊	23♈
11	18♋	10♌	17♊	23♈
12	19♋	12♌	18♊	24♈
13	20♋	13♌	19♊	25♈
14	21♋	15♌	20♊	25♈
15	22♋	16♌	22♊	26♈
16	23♋	18♌	23♊	27♈
17	24♋	19♌	24♊	27♈
18	25♋	21♌	25♊	28♈
19	26♋	22♌	26♊	29♈
20	27♋	23♌	28♊	29♈
21	28♋	24♌	29♊	0♉
22	29♋	25♌	0♋	1♉
23	0♌	27♌	1♋	1♉
24	1♌	28♌	2♋	2♉
25	2♌	29♌	4♋	2♉
26	3♌	0♍	5♋	3♉
27	4♌	1♍	6♋	4♉
28	5♌	2♍	7♋	4♉
29	6♌	3♍	8♋	5♉
30	7♌	3♍	10♋	6♉
31	7♌	4♍	11♋	6♉

August

Day	☉	☿	♀	♂
1	8♌	5♍	12♋	7♉
2	9♌	5♍	13♋	7♉
3	10♌	6♍	14♋	8♉
4	11♌	6♍	16♋	9♉
5	12♌	7♍	17♋	9♉
6	13♌	7♍	18♋	10♉
7	14♌	7♍	19♋	10♉
8	15♌	8♍	20♋	11♉
9	16♌	8♍	22♋	11♉
10	17♌	8♍	23♋	12♉
11	18♌	8♍	24♋	13♉
12	19♌	7♍	25♋	13♉
13	20♌	7♍	27♋	14♉
14	21♌	7♍	28♋	14♉
15	22♌	6♍	29♋	15♉
16	23♌	6♍	0♌	15♉
17	24♌	5♍	1♌	16♉
18	25♌	5♍	3♌	16♉
19	26♌	4♍	4♌	17♉
20	27♌	3♍	5♌	17♉
21	28♌	2♍	6♌	18♉
22	29♌	1♍	7♌	18♉
23	0♍	0♍	9♌	19♉
24	1♍	29♌	10♌	19♉
25	1♍	29♌	11♌	20♉
26	2♍	28♌	12♌	20♉
27	3♍	27♌	14♌	21♉
28	4♍	26♌	15♌	21♉
29	5♍	26♌	16♌	22♉
30	6♍	25♌	17♌	22♉
31	7♍	25♌	19♌	23♉

September

Day	☉	☿	♀	♂
1	8♍	25♌	20♌	23♉
2	9♍	25♌	21♌	23♉
3	10♍	25♌	22♌	24♉
4	11♍	25♌	23♌	24♉
5	12♍	25♌	25♌	25♉
6	13♍	26♌	26♌	25♉
7	14♍	26♌	27♌	25♉
8	15♍	27♌	28♌	26♉
9	16♍	28♌	0♍	26♉
10	17♍	29♌	1♍	27♉
11	18♍	0♍	2♍	27♉
12	19♍	1♍	3♍	27♉
13	20♍	3♍	5♍	28♉
14	21♍	4♍	6♍	28♉
15	22♍	6♍	7♍	28♉
16	23♍	7♍	8♍	29♉
17	24♍	9♍	10♍	29♉
18	25♍	11♍	11♍	29♉
19	26♍	12♍	12♍	29♉
20	27♍	14♍	13♍	0♊
21	28♍	16♍	14♍	0♊
22	29♍	18♍	16♍	0♊
23	0♎	19♍	17♍	0♊
24	1♎	21♍	18♍	1♊
25	2♎	23♍	19♍	1♊
26	3♎	25♍	21♍	1♊
27	4♎	27♍	22♍	1♊
28	5♎	29♍	23♍	1♊
29	6♎	0♎	24♍	2♊
30	7♎	2♎	26♍	2♊

October

Day	☉	☿	♀	♂
1	8♎	4♎	27♍	2♊
2	8♎	6♎	28♍	2♊
3	9♎	8♎	29♍	2♊
4	10♎	9♎	1♎	2♊
5	11♎	11♎	2♎	2♊
6	12♎	13♎	3♎	2♊
7	13♎	15♎	4♎	2♊
8	14♎	16♎	6♎	2♊
9	15♎	18♎	7♎	3♊
10	16♎	20♎	8♎	3♊
11	17♎	22♎	9♎	3♊
12	18♎	23♎	11♎	3♊
13	19♎	25♎	12♎	2♊
14	20♎	26♎	13♎	2♊
15	21♎	28♎	14♎	2♊
16	22♎	0♏	16♎	2♊
17	23♎	1♏	17♎	2♊
18	24♎	3♏	18♎	2♊
19	25♎	5♏	19♎	2♊
20	26♎	6♏	21♎	2♊
21	27♎	8♏	22♎	2♊
22	28♎	9♏	23♎	1♊
23	29♎	11♏	24♎	1♊
24	0♏	12♏	26♎	1♊
25	1♏	14♏	27♎	1♊
26	2♏	15♏	28♎	1♊
27	3♏	17♏	29♎	0♊
28	4♏	18♏	1♏	0♊
29	5♏	20♏	2♏	0♊
30	6♏	21♏	3♏	0♊
31	7♏	23♏	4♏	29♉

November

Day	☉	☿	♀	♂
1	8♏	24♏	6♏	29♉
2	9♏	26♏	7♏	29♉
3	10♏	27♏	8♏	28♉
4	11♏	29♏	9♏	28♉
5	12♏	0♐	11♏	28♉
6	13♏	2♐	12♏	27♉
7	14♏	3♐	13♏	27♉
8	15♏	4♐	14♏	27♉
9	16♏	6♐	16♏	26♉
10	17♏	7♐	17♏	26♉
11	18♏	8♐	18♏	26♉
12	19♏	10♐	19♏	25♉
13	20♏	11♐	21♏	25♉
14	21♏	12♐	22♏	25♉
15	22♏	14♐	23♏	24♉
16	23♏	15♐	25♏	24♉
17	24♏	16♐	26♏	24♉
18	25♏	17♐	27♏	23♉
19	26♏	18♐	28♏	23♉
20	27♏	19♐	0♐	22♉
21	28♏	20♐	1♐	22♉
22	29♏	21♐	2♐	22♉
23	0♐	22♐	3♐	21♉
24	1♐	23♐	5♐	21♉
25	2♐	24♐	6♐	21♉
26	3♐	24♐	7♐	20♉
27	4♐	25♐	8♐	20♉
28	5♐	25♐	10♐	20♉
29	6♐	26♐	11♐	20♉
30	7♐	26♐	12♐	19♉

December

Day	☉	☿	♀	♂
1	8♐	26♐	13♐	19♉
2	10♐	25♐	15♐	19♉
3	11♐	25♐	16♐	19♉
4	12♐	24♐	17♐	18♉
5	13♐	24♐	18♐	18♉
6	14♐	23♐	20♐	18♉
7	15♐	21♐	21♐	18♉
8	16♐	20♐	22♐	18♉
9	17♐	19♐	23♐	17♉
10	18♐	17♐	25♐	17♉
11	19♐	16♐	26♐	17♉
12	20♐	15♐	27♐	17♉
13	21♐	14♐	28♐	17♉
14	22♐	12♐	0♑	17♉
15	23♐	11♐	1♑	17♉
16	24♐	11♐	2♑	17♉
17	25♐	10♐	3♑	17♉
18	26♐	10♐	5♑	17♉
19	27♐	9♐	6♑	17♉
20	28♐	9♐	7♑	17♉
21	29♐	10♐	8♑	17♉
22	0♑	10♐	10♑	17♉
23	1♑	10♐	11♑	17♉
24	2♑	11♐	12♑	17♉
25	3♑	11♐	14♑	17♉
26	4♑	12♐	15♑	17♉
27	5♑	13♐	16♑	17♉
28	6♑	14♐	17♑	17♉
29	7♑	15♐	19♑	17♉
30	8♑	16♐	20♑	17♉
31	9♑	17♐	21♑	17♉

1959

Your Starway to Love

☉ =Sun ☿ = Mercury ♀ = Venus ♂ = Mars ♈ = Aries ♉ = Taurus ♊ = Gemini ♋ = Cancer

January

Day	☉	☿	♀	♂
1	10♑	18♐	22♑	17♉
2	11♑	19♐	24♑	18♉
3	12♑	20♐	25♑	18♉
4	13♑	21♐	26♑	18♉
5	14♑	23♐	27♑	18♉
6	15♑	24♐	29♑	18♉
7	16♑	25♐	0♒	19♉
8	17♑	27♐	1♒	19♉
9	18♑	28♐	2♒	19♉
10	19♑	29♐	4♒	19♉
11	20♑	1♑	5♒	19♉
12	21♑	2♑	6♒	20♉
13	22♑	4♑	7♒	20♉
14	23♑	5♑	9♒	20♉
15	24♑	6♑	10♒	20♉
16	25♑	8♑	11♒	21♉
17	26♑	9♑	12♒	21♉
18	27♑	11♑	14♒	21♉
19	28♑	12♑	15♒	22♉
20	29♑	14♑	16♒	22♉
21	0♒	15♑	17♒	22♉
22	1♒	17♑	19♒	23♉
23	2♒	18♑	20♒	23♉
24	3♒	20♑	21♒	23♉
25	4♒	21♑	22♒	24♉
26	5♒	23♑	24♒	24♉
27	7♒	25♑	25♒	24♉
28	8♒	26♑	26♒	25♉
29	9♒	28♑	27♒	25♉
30	10♒	29♑	29♒	25♉
31	11♒	1♒	0♓	26♉

April

Day	☉	☿	♀	♂
1	11♈	6♈	14♉	25♊
2	12♈	5♈	15♉	25♊
3	13♈	4♈	16♉	26♊
4	14♈	3♈	17♉	27♊
5	15♈	3♈	18♉	27♊
6	16♈	2♈	20♉	28♊
7	17♈	2♈	21♉	28♊
8	18♈	1♈	22♉	29♊
9	19♈	1♈	23♉	29♊
10	20♈	1♈	24♉	0♋
11	21♈	1♈	26♉	0♋
12	22♈	1♈	27♉	1♋
13	23♈	1♈	28♉	2♋
14	24♈	1♈	29♉	2♋
15	24♈	1♈	0♊	3♋
16	25♈	1♈	2♊	3♋
17	26♈	2♈	3♊	4♋
18	27♈	2♈	4♊	4♋
19	28♈	3♈	5♊	5♋
20	29♈	3♈	6♊	6♋
21	0♉	4♈	7♊	6♋
22	1♉	5♈	9♊	7♋
23	2♉	5♈	10♊	7♋
24	3♉	6♈	11♊	8♋
25	4♉	7♈	12♊	8♋
26	5♉	8♈	13♊	9♋
27	6♉	9♈	14♊	10♋
28	7♉	10♈	16♊	10♋
29	8♉	11♈	17♊	11♋
30	9♉	12♈	18♊	11♋

July

Day	☉	☿	♀	♂
1	9♋	3♌	24♌	18♌
2	10♋	5♌	25♌	19♌
3	11♋	6♌	26♌	19♌
4	11♋	7♌	26♌	20♌
5	12♋	8♌	27♌	21♌
6	13♋	9♌	28♌	21♌
7	14♋	11♌	29♌	22♌
8	15♋	12♌	0♍	22♌
9	16♋	12♌	1♍	23♌
10	17♋	13♌	1♍	24♌
11	18♋	14♌	2♍	24♌
12	19♋	15♌	3♍	25♌
13	20♋	16♌	4♍	26♌
14	21♋	16♌	4♍	26♌
15	22♋	17♌	5♍	27♌
16	23♋	18♌	6♍	27♌
17	24♋	18♌	7♍	28♌
18	25♋	18♌	7♍	29♌
19	26♋	19♌	8♍	29♌
20	27♋	19♌	8♍	0♍
21	28♋	19♌	9♍	0♍
22	29♋	19♌	10♍	1♍
23	0♌	19♌	10♍	2♍
24	1♌	19♌	11♍	2♍
25	2♌	19♌	11♍	3♍
26	2♌	19♌	12♍	4♍
27	3♌	19♌	12♍	4♍
28	4♌	18♌	13♍	5♍
29	5♌	18♌	13♍	5♍
30	6♌	17♌	14♍	6♍
31	7♌	17♌	14♍	7♍

October

Day	☉	☿	♀	♂
1	7♎	17♎	1♍	16♎
2	8♎	19♎	2♍	17♎
3	9♎	21♎	2♍	18♎
4	10♎	22♎	2♍	18♎
5	11♎	24♎	3♍	19♎
6	12♎	25♎	3♍	20♎
7	13♎	27♎	4♍	20♎
8	14♎	29♎	4♍	21♎
9	15♎	0♏	5♍	22♎
10	16♎	2♏	5♍	22♎
11	17♎	3♏	6♍	23♎
12	18♎	5♏	6♍	24♎
13	19♎	6♏	7♍	24♎
14	20♎	8♏	8♍	25♎
15	21♎	9♏	8♍	26♎
16	22♎	10♏	9♍	27♎
17	23♎	12♏	10♍	27♎
18	24♎	13♏	10♍	28♎
19	25♎	15♏	11♍	29♎
20	26♎	16♏	12♍	29♎
21	27♎	17♏	13♍	0♏
22	28♎	19♏	13♍	1♏
23	29♎	20♏	14♍	1♏
24	0♏	22♏	15♍	2♏
25	1♏	23♏	16♍	3♏
26	2♏	24♏	17♍	3♏
27	3♏	25♏	17♍	4♏
28	4♏	27♏	18♍	5♏
29	5♏	28♏	19♍	5♏
30	6♏	29♏	20♍	6♏
31	7♏	0♐	21♍	7♏

February

Day	☉	☿	♀	♂
1	12♒	3♒	1♓	26♉
2	13♒	4♒	2♓	27♉
3	14♒	6♒	4♓	27♉
4	15♒	7♒	5♓	27♉
5	16♒	9♒	6♓	28♉
6	17♒	11♒	7♓	28♉
7	18♒	13♒	9♓	29♉
8	19♒	14♒	10♓	29♉
9	20♒	16♒	11♓	29♉
10	21♒	18♒	12♓	0♊
11	22♒	19♒	14♓	0♊
12	23♒	21♒	15♓	1♊
13	24♒	23♒	16♓	1♊
14	25♒	25♒	17♓	2♊
15	26♒	27♒	19♓	2♊
16	27♒	28♒	20♓	2♊
17	28♒	0♓	21♓	3♊
18	29♒	2♓	22♓	3♊
19	0♓	4♓	24♓	4♊
20	1♓	6♓	25♓	4♊
21	2♓	8♓	26♓	5♊
22	3♓	10♓	27♓	5♊
23	4♓	11♓	28♓	6♊
24	5♓	13♓	0♈	6♊
25	6♓	15♓	1♈	7♊
26	7♓	17♓	2♈	7♊
27	8♓	19♓	3♈	8♊
28	9♓	21♓	5♈	8♊

May

Day	☉	☿	♀	♂
1	10♉	14♈	19♊	12♋
2	11♉	15♈	20♊	12♋
3	12♉	16♈	21♊	13♋
4	13♉	17♈	23♊	14♋
5	14♉	19♈	24♊	14♋
6	15♉	20♈	25♊	15♋
7	16♉	21♈	26♊	15♋
8	17♉	23♈	27♊	16♋
9	18♉	24♈	28♊	16♋
10	19♉	26♈	29♊	17♋
11	20♉	27♈	1♋	18♋
12	21♉	29♈	2♋	18♋
13	22♉	1♉	3♋	19♋
14	23♉	2♉	4♋	19♋
15	24♉	4♉	5♋	20♋
16	25♉	6♉	6♋	21♋
17	26♉	7♉	7♋	21♋
18	27♉	9♉	9♋	22♋
19	27♉	11♉	10♋	22♋
20	28♉	13♉	11♋	23♋
21	29♉	15♉	12♋	24♋
22	0♊	17♉	13♋	24♋
23	1♊	19♉	14♋	25♋
24	2♊	21♉	15♋	25♋
25	3♊	23♉	16♋	26♋
26	4♊	25♉	17♋	26♋
27	5♊	27♉	18♋	27♋
28	6♊	29♉	20♋	28♋
29	7♊	1♊	21♋	28♋
30	8♊	3♊	22♋	29♋
31	9♊	5♊	23♋	29♋

August

Day	☉	☿	♀	♂
1	8♌	16♌	14♍	7♍
2	9♌	15♌	15♍	8♍
3	10♌	14♌	15♍	9♍
4	11♌	14♌	15♍	9♍
5	12♌	13♌	16♍	10♍
6	13♌	12♌	16♍	10♍
7	14♌	11♌	16♍	11♍
8	15♌	11♌	16♍	12♍
9	16♌	10♌	16♍	12♍
10	17♌	9♌	16♍	13♍
11	18♌	9♌	16♍	14♍
12	19♌	8♌	16♍	14♍
13	20♌	8♌	16♍	15♍
14	21♌	8♌	16♍	15♍
15	22♌	8♌	16♍	16♍
16	23♌	8♌	16♍	17♍
17	24♌	8♌	15♍	17♍
18	25♌	8♌	15♍	18♍
19	25♌	8♌	15♍	19♍
20	26♌	9♌	14♍	19♍
21	27♌	9♌	14♍	20♍
22	28♌	10♌	14♍	21♍
23	29♌	11♌	13♍	21♍
24	0♍	12♌	13♍	22♍
25	1♍	13♌	12♍	22♍
26	2♍	14♌	12♍	23♍
27	3♍	15♌	11♍	24♍
28	4♍	17♌	11♍	24♍
29	5♍	18♌	10♍	25♍
30	6♍	20♌	9♍	26♍
31	7♍	21♌	9♍	26♍

November

Day	☉	☿	♀	♂
1	8♏	1♐	22♍	7♏
2	9♏	2♐	23♍	8♏
3	10♏	3♐	24♍	9♏
4	11♏	4♐	25♍	9♏
5	12♏	5♐	26♍	10♏
6	13♏	6♐	27♍	11♏
7	14♏	7♐	28♍	11♏
8	15♏	8♐	28♍	12♏
9	16♏	8♐	29♍	13♏
10	17♏	9♐	0♎	14♏
11	18♏	9♐	1♎	14♏
12	19♏	10♐	2♎	15♏
13	20♏	10♐	3♎	16♏
14	21♏	10♐	4♎	16♏
15	22♏	10♐	6♎	17♏
16	23♏	10♐	7♎	18♏
17	24♏	9♐	8♎	18♏
18	25♏	8♐	9♎	19♏
19	26♏	8♐	10♎	20♏
20	27♏	7♐	11♎	20♏
21	28♏	6♐	12♎	21♏
22	29♏	4♐	13♎	22♏
23	0♐	3♐	14♎	23♏
24	1♐	2♐	15♎	23♏
25	2♐	0♐	16♎	24♏
26	3♐	29♏	17♎	25♏
27	4♐	28♏	18♎	25♏
28	5♐	27♏	19♎	26♏
29	6♐	26♏	20♎	27♏
30	7♐	25♏	22♎	27♏

March

Day	☉	☿	♀	♂
1	10♓	23♓	6♈	9♊
2	11♓	24♓	7♈	9♊
3	12♓	26♓	8♈	10♊
4	13♓	28♓	10♈	10♊
5	14♓	0♈	11♈	11♊
6	15♓	1♈	12♈	11♊
7	16♓	3♈	13♈	12♊
8	17♓	4♈	14♈	12♊
9	18♓	6♈	16♈	13♊
10	19♓	7♈	17♈	13♊
11	20♓	8♈	18♈	14♊
12	21♓	9♈	19♈	14♊
13	22♓	10♈	21♈	15♊
14	23♓	11♈	22♈	15♊
15	24♓	12♈	23♈	16♊
16	25♓	12♈	24♈	16♊
17	26♓	13♈	25♈	17♊
18	27♓	13♈	27♈	17♊
19	28♓	13♈	28♈	18♊
20	29♓	13♈	29♈	18♊
21	0♈	13♈	0♉	19♊
22	1♈	13♈	2♉	19♊
23	2♈	12♈	3♉	20♊
24	3♈	12♈	4♉	21♊
25	4♈	11♈	5♉	21♊
26	5♈	11♈	6♉	22♊
27	6♈	10♈	8♉	22♊
28	7♈	9♈	9♉	23♊
29	8♈	8♈	10♉	23♊
30	9♈	7♈	11♉	24♊
31	10♈	6♈	12♉	24♊

June

Day	☉	☿	♀	♂
1	10♊	8♊	24♋	0♌
2	11♊	10♊	25♋	1♌
3	12♊	12♊	26♋	1♌
4	13♊	14♊	27♋	2♌
5	14♊	16♊	28♋	2♌
6	15♊	19♊	29♋	3♌
7	16♊	21♊	0♌	4♌
8	17♊	23♊	1♌	4♌
9	18♊	25♊	2♌	5♌
10	19♊	27♊	3♌	5♌
11	20♊	29♊	4♌	6♌
12	21♊	1♋	5♌	7♌
13	21♊	3♋	6♌	7♌
14	22♊	5♋	8♌	8♌
15	23♊	7♋	9♌	8♌
16	24♊	9♋	10♌	9♌
17	25♊	11♋	11♌	10♌
18	26♊	13♋	12♌	10♌
19	27♊	15♋	13♌	11♌
20	28♊	17♋	13♌	11♌
21	29♊	18♋	14♌	12♌
22	0♋	20♋	15♌	13♌
23	1♋	22♋	16♌	13♌
24	2♋	23♋	17♌	14♌
25	3♋	25♋	18♌	15♌
26	4♋	26♋	19♌	15♌
27	5♋	28♋	20♌	16♌
28	6♋	29♋	21♌	16♌
29	7♋	1♌	22♌	17♌
30	8♋	2♌	23♌	18♌

September

Day	☉	☿	♀	♂
1	8♍	23♌	8♍	27♍
2	9♍	25♌	7♍	28♍
3	10♍	27♌	7♍	28♍
4	11♍	28♌	6♍	29♍
5	12♍	0♍	6♍	0♎
6	13♍	2♍	5♍	0♎
7	14♍	4♍	5♍	1♎
8	15♍	6♍	4♍	1♎
9	16♍	8♍	3♍	2♎
10	17♍	10♍	3♍	3♎
11	18♍	12♍	3♍	3♎
12	19♍	14♍	2♍	4♎
13	20♍	15♍	2♍	5♎
14	21♍	17♍	1♍	5♎
15	22♍	19♍	1♍	6♎
16	23♍	21♍	1♍	7♎
17	24♍	23♍	0♍	7♎
18	25♍	25♍	0♍	8♎
19	26♍	27♍	0♍	9♎
20	26♍	28♍	0♍	9♎
21	27♍	0♎	0♍	10♎
22	28♍	2♎	0♍	11♎
23	29♍	4♎	0♍	11♎
24	0♎	6♎	0♍	12♎
25	1♎	7♎	0♍	13♎
26	2♎	9♎	0♍	13♎
27	3♎	11♎	0♍	14♎
28	4♎	12♎	0♍	15♎
29	5♎	14♎	1♍	15♎
30	6♎	16♎	1♍	16♎

December

Day	☉	☿	♀	♂
1	8♐	24♏	23♎	28♏
2	9♐	24♏	24♎	29♏
3	10♐	24♏	25♎	0♐
4	11♐	24♏	26♎	0♐
5	12♐	24♏	27♎	1♐
6	13♐	24♏	28♎	2♐
7	14♐	25♏	29♎	2♐
8	15♐	25♏	1♏	3♐
9	16♐	26♏	2♏	4♐
10	17♐	27♏	3♏	5♐
11	18♐	28♏	4♏	5♐
12	19♐	28♏	5♏	6♐
13	20♐	0♐	6♏	7♐
14	21♐	1♐	7♏	7♐
15	22♐	2♐	9♏	8♐
16	23♐	3♐	10♏	9♐
17	25♐	4♐	11♏	10♐
18	26♐	5♐	12♏	10♐
19	27♐	7♐	13♏	11♐
20	28♐	8♐	14♏	12♐
21	29♐	9♐	16♏	12♐
22	0♑	11♐	17♏	13♐
23	1♑	12♐	18♏	14♐
24	2♑	14♐	19♏	15♐
25	3♑	15♐	20♏	15♐
26	4♑	16♐	21♏	16♐
27	5♑	18♐	23♏	17♐
28	6♑	19♐	24♏	18♐
29	7♑	21♐	25♏	18♐
30	8♑	22♐	26♏	19♐
31	9♑	24♐	27♏	20♐

Planetary Positions

♌ = Leo ♍ = Virgo ♎ = Libra ♏ = Scorpio ♐ = Sagittarius ♑ = Capricorn ♒ = Aquarius ♓ = Pisces

January

Day	☉	☿	♀	♂
1	10♑	25♐	29♏	20♐
2	11♑	27♐	0♐	21♐
3	12♑	28♐	1♐	22♐
4	13♑	0♑	2♐	23♐
5	14♑	1♑	3♐	23♐
6	15♑	3♑	5♐	24♐
7	16♑	4♑	6♐	25♐
8	17♑	6♑	7♐	26♐
9	18♑	7♑	8♐	26♐
10	19♑	9♑	9♐	27♐
11	20♑	11♑	11♐	28♐
12	21♑	12♑	12♐	29♐
13	22♑	14♑	13♐	29♐
14	23♑	15♑	14♐	0♑
15	24♑	17♑	15♐	1♑
16	25♑	18♑	17♐	1♑
17	26♑	20♑	18♐	2♑
18	27♑	22♑	19♐	3♑
19	28♑	23♑	20♐	4♑
20	29♑	25♑	21♐	4♑
21	0♒	27♑	23♐	5♑
22	1♒	28♑	24♐	6♑
23	2♒	0♒	25♐	7♑
24	3♒	2♒	26♐	7♑
25	4♒	3♒	28♐	8♑
26	5♒	5♒	29♐	9♑
27	6♒	7♒	0♑	10♑
28	7♒	8♒	1♑	10♑
29	8♒	10♒	2♑	11♑
30	9♒	12♒	4♑	12♑
31	10♒	14♒	5♑	13♑

February

Day	☉	☿	♀	♂
1	11♒	15♒	6♑	13♑
2	12♒	17♒	7♑	14♑
3	13♒	19♒	9♑	15♑
4	14♒	21♒	10♑	16♑
5	15♒	22♒	11♑	16♑
6	16♒	24♒	12♑	17♑
7	17♒	26♒	13♑	18♑
8	18♒	28♒	15♑	19♑
9	19♒	0♓	16♑	19♑
10	20♒	1♓	17♑	20♑
11	21♒	3♓	18♑	21♑
12	22♒	5♓	20♑	22♑
13	24♒	7♓	21♑	22♑
14	25♒	8♓	22♑	23♑
15	26♒	10♓	23♑	24♑
16	27♒	12♓	24♑	25♑
17	28♒	13♓	26♑	25♑
18	29♒	15♓	27♑	26♑
19	0♓	16♓	28♑	27♑
20	1♓	18♓	29♑	28♑
21	2♓	19♓	1♒	29♑
22	3♓	21♓	2♒	29♑
23	4♓	22♓	3♒	0♒
24	5♓	23♓	4♒	1♒
25	6♓	24♓	6♒	2♒
26	7♓	24♓	7♒	2♒
27	8♓	25♓	8♒	3♒
28	9♓	25♓	9♒	4♒
29	10♓	26♓	10♒	5♒

March

Day	☉	☿	♀	♂
1	11♓	26♓	12♒	5♒
2	12♓	26♓	13♒	6♒
3	13♓	26♓	14♒	7♒
4	14♓	25♓	15♒	8♒
5	15♓	25♓	17♒	8♒
6	16♓	24♓	18♒	9♒
7	17♓	24♓	19♒	10♒
8	18♓	23♓	20♒	11♒
9	19♓	22♓	22♒	11♒
10	20♓	21♓	23♒	12♒
11	21♓	20♓	24♒	13♒
12	22♓	19♓	25♒	14♒
13	23♓	18♓	26♒	15♒
14	24♓	17♓	28♒	15♒
15	25♓	16♓	29♒	16♒
16	26♓	15♓	0♓	17♒
17	27♓	15♓	1♓	18♒
18	28♓	14♓	3♓	18♒
19	29♓	13♓	4♓	19♒
20	0♈	13♓	5♓	20♒
21	1♈	13♓	6♓	21♒
22	2♈	12♓	8♓	21♒
23	3♈	12♓	9♓	22♒
24	4♈	12♓	10♓	23♒
25	5♈	12♓	11♓	24♒
26	6♈	12♓	12♓	25♒
27	7♈	12♓	14♓	25♒
28	8♈	13♓	15♓	26♒
29	9♈	13♓	16♓	27♒
30	10♈	14♓	17♓	28♒
31	10♈	14♓	19♓	28♒

April

Day	☉	☿	♀	♂
1	11♈	15♓	20♓	29♒
2	12♈	15♓	21♓	0♓
3	13♈	16♓	22♓	1♓
4	14♈	17♓	24♓	1♓
5	15♈	18♓	25♓	2♓
6	16♈	19♓	26♓	3♓
7	17♈	20♓	27♓	4♓
8	18♈	21♓	28♓	5♓
9	19♈	22♓	0♈	5♓
10	20♈	23♓	1♈	6♓
11	21♈	24♓	2♈	7♓
12	22♈	25♓	3♈	8♓
13	23♈	26♓	5♈	8♓
14	24♈	28♓	6♈	9♓
15	25♈	29♓	7♈	10♓
16	26♈	0♈	8♈	11♓
17	27♈	1♈	10♈	12♓
18	28♈	3♈	11♈	12♓
19	29♈	4♈	12♈	13♓
20	0♉	6♈	13♈	14♓
21	1♉	7♈	14♈	15♓
22	2♉	9♈	16♈	15♓
23	3♉	10♈	17♈	16♓
24	4♉	12♈	18♈	17♓
25	5♉	13♈	19♈	18♓
26	6♉	15♈	21♈	18♓
27	7♉	17♈	22♈	19♓
28	8♉	18♈	23♈	20♓
29	9♉	20♈	24♈	21♓
30	10♉	22♈	26♈	22♓

May

Day	☉	☿	♀	♂
1	11♉	24♈	27♈	22♓
2	12♉	25♈	28♈	23♓
3	13♉	27♈	29♈	24♓
4	14♉	29♈	0♉	25♓
5	15♉	1♉	2♉	25♓
6	16♉	3♉	3♉	26♓
7	17♉	5♉	4♉	27♓
8	18♉	7♉	5♉	28♓
9	19♉	9♉	7♉	28♓
10	20♉	11♉	8♉	29♓
11	21♉	13♉	9♉	0♈
12	21♉	15♉	10♉	1♈
13	22♉	17♉	12♉	1♈
14	23♉	19♉	13♉	2♈
15	24♉	21♉	14♉	3♈
16	25♉	24♉	15♉	4♈
17	26♉	26♉	16♉	4♈
18	27♉	28♉	18♉	5♈
19	28♉	0♊	19♉	6♈
20	29♉	2♊	20♉	7♈
21	0♊	5♊	21♉	8♈
22	1♊	7♊	23♉	8♈
23	2♊	9♊	24♉	9♈
24	3♊	11♊	25♉	10♈
25	4♊	13♊	26♉	11♈
26	5♊	15♊	27♉	11♈
27	6♊	17♊	29♉	12♈
28	7♊	19♊	0♊	13♈
29	8♊	21♊	1♊	14♈
30	9♊	23♊	2♊	14♈
31	10♊	25♊	4♊	15♈

June

Day	☉	☿	♀	♂
1	11♊	27♊	5♊	16♈
2	12♊	29♊	6♊	17♈
3	13♊	1♋	7♊	17♈
4	14♊	2♋	9♊	18♈
5	15♊	4♋	10♊	19♈
6	15♊	6♋	11♊	20♈
7	16♊	7♋	12♊	20♈
8	17♊	9♋	13♊	21♈
9	18♊	10♋	15♊	22♈
10	19♊	12♋	16♊	23♈
11	20♊	13♋	17♊	23♈
12	21♊	15♋	18♊	24♈
13	22♊	16♋	20♊	25♈
14	23♊	17♋	21♊	25♈
15	24♊	18♋	22♊	26♈
16	25♊	20♋	23♊	27♈
17	26♊	21♋	24♊	28♈
18	27♊	22♋	26♊	28♈
19	28♊	23♋	27♊	29♈
20	29♊	24♋	28♊	0♉
21	0♋	25♋	29♊	1♉
22	1♋	25♋	1♋	1♉
23	2♋	26♋	2♋	2♉
24	3♋	27♋	3♋	3♉
25	4♋	28♋	4♋	4♉
26	5♋	28♋	6♋	4♉
27	6♋	29♋	7♋	5♉
28	6♋	29♋	8♋	6♉
29	7♋	0♌	9♋	6♉
30	8♋	0♌	10♋	7♉

July

Day	☉	☿	♀	♂
1	9♋	0♌	12♋	8♉
2	10♋	0♌	13♋	9♉
3	11♋	0♌	14♋	9♉
4	12♋	0♌	15♋	10♉
5	13♋	0♌	17♋	11♉
6	14♋	0♌	18♋	11♉
7	15♋	0♌	19♋	12♉
8	16♋	29♋	20♋	13♉
9	17♋	29♋	22♋	14♉
10	18♋	29♋	23♋	14♉
11	19♋	28♋	24♋	15♉
12	20♋	28♋	25♋	16♉
13	21♋	27♋	26♋	16♉
14	22♋	26♋	28♋	17♉
15	23♋	26♋	29♋	18♉
16	24♋	25♋	0♌	18♉
17	25♋	24♋	1♌	19♉
18	26♋	24♋	3♌	20♉
19	27♋	23♋	4♌	21♉
20	27♋	22♋	5♌	21♉
21	28♋	22♋	6♌	22♉
22	29♋	21♋	8♌	23♉
23	0♌	21♋	9♌	23♉
24	1♌	21♋	10♌	24♉
25	2♌	20♋	11♌	25♉
26	3♌	20♋	12♌	25♉
27	4♌	20♋	14♌	26♉
28	5♌	20♋	15♌	27♉
29	6♌	20♋	16♌	27♉
30	7♌	20♋	17♌	28♉
31	8♌	21♋	19♌	29♉

August

Day	☉	☿	♀	♂
1	9♌	21♋	20♌	29♉
2	10♌	21♋	21♌	0♊
3	11♌	22♋	22♌	1♊
4	12♌	23♋	24♌	1♊
5	13♌	24♋	25♌	2♊
6	14♌	25♋	26♌	3♊
7	15♌	26♋	27♌	3♊
8	16♌	27♋	28♌	4♊
9	17♌	28♋	0♍	5♊
10	18♌	29♋	1♍	5♊
11	19♌	1♌	2♍	6♊
12	19♌	2♌	3♍	7♊
13	20♌	4♌	5♍	7♊
14	21♌	5♌	6♍	8♊
15	22♌	7♌	7♍	8♊
16	23♌	9♌	8♍	9♊
17	24♌	11♌	10♍	10♊
18	25♌	12♌	11♍	10♊
19	26♌	14♌	12♍	11♊
20	27♌	16♌	13♍	12♊
21	28♌	18♌	14♍	12♊
22	29♌	20♌	16♍	13♊
23	0♍	22♌	17♍	13♊
24	1♍	24♌	18♍	14♊
25	2♍	26♌	19♍	15♊
26	3♍	28♌	21♍	15♊
27	4♍	0♍	22♍	16♊
28	5♍	2♍	23♍	17♊
29	6♍	4♍	24♍	17♊
30	7♍	6♍	26♍	18♊
31	8♍	8♍	27♍	18♊

September

Day	☉	☿	♀	♂
1	9♍	10♍	28♍	19♊
2	10♍	12♍	29♍	20♊
3	11♍	14♍	0♎	20♊
4	12♍	16♍	2♎	21♊
5	13♍	17♍	3♎	21♊
6	14♍	19♍	4♎	22♊
7	15♍	21♍	5♎	22♊
8	16♍	23♍	7♎	23♊
9	17♍	25♍	8♎	24♊
10	17♍	26♍	9♎	24♊
11	18♍	28♍	10♎	25♊
12	19♍	0♎	12♎	25♊
13	20♍	2♎	13♎	26♊
14	21♍	3♎	14♎	26♊
15	22♍	5♎	15♎	27♊
16	23♍	7♎	16♎	27♊
17	24♍	8♎	18♎	28♊
18	25♍	10♎	19♎	28♊
19	26♍	11♎	20♎	29♊
20	27♍	13♎	21♎	0♋
21	28♍	15♎	23♎	0♋
22	29♍	16♎	24♎	1♋
23	0♎	18♎	25♎	1♋
24	1♎	19♎	26♎	2♋
25	2♎	21♎	28♎	2♋
26	3♎	22♎	29♎	3♋
27	4♎	24♎	0♏	3♋
28	5♎	25♎	1♏	4♋
29	6♎	26♎	2♏	4♋
30	7♎	28♎	4♏	4♋

October

Day	☉	☿	♀	♂
1	8♎	29♎	5♏	5♋
2	9♎	1♏	6♏	5♋
3	10♎	2♏	7♏	6♋
4	11♎	3♏	9♏	6♋
5	12♎	5♏	10♏	7♋
6	13♎	6♏	11♏	7♋
7	14♎	7♏	12♏	8♋
8	15♎	9♏	13♏	8♋
9	16♎	10♏	15♏	9♋
10	17♎	11♏	16♏	9♋
11	18♎	12♏	17♏	9♋
12	19♎	13♏	18♏	10♋
13	20♎	14♏	20♏	10♋
14	21♎	15♏	21♏	11♋
15	22♎	17♏	22♏	11♋
16	23♎	18♏	23♏	11♋
17	24♎	18♏	24♏	12♋
18	25♎	19♏	26♏	12♋
19	26♎	20♏	27♏	12♋
20	27♎	21♏	28♏	13♋
21	28♎	22♏	29♏	13♋
22	29♎	22♏	1♐	13♋
23	0♏	23♏	2♐	14♋
24	1♏	23♏	3♐	14♋
25	2♏	24♏	4♐	14♋
26	3♏	24♏	5♐	15♋
27	4♏	24♏	7♐	15♋
28	5♏	24♏	8♐	15♋
29	6♏	24♏	9♐	15♋
30	7♏	24♏	10♐	16♋
31	8♏	23♏	12♐	16♋

November

Day	☉	☿	♀	♂
1	9♏	22♏	13♐	16♋
2	10♏	22♏	14♐	16♋
3	11♏	21♏	15♐	17♋
4	12♏	20♏	16♐	17♋
5	13♏	18♏	18♐	17♋
6	14♏	17♏	19♐	17♋
7	15♏	16♏	20♐	17♋
8	16♏	15♏	21♐	18♋
9	17♏	13♏	23♐	18♋
10	18♏	12♏	24♐	18♋
11	19♏	11♏	25♐	18♋
12	20♏	10♏	26♐	18♋
13	21♏	9♏	27♐	18♋
14	22♏	9♏	29♐	18♋
15	23♏	8♏	0♑	18♋
16	24♏	8♏	1♑	19♋
17	25♏	8♏	2♑	19♋
18	26♏	8♏	3♑	19♋
19	27♏	9♏	5♑	19♋
20	28♏	9♏	6♑	19♋
21	29♏	10♏	7♑	19♋
22	0♐	10♏	8♑	19♋
23	1♐	11♏	9♑	19♋
24	2♐	12♏	11♑	19♋
25	3♐	13♏	12♑	19♋
26	4♐	14♏	13♑	18♋
27	5♐	16♏	14♑	18♋
28	6♐	17♏	15♑	18♋
29	7♐	18♏	17♑	18♋
30	8♐	19♏	18♑	18♋

December

Day	☉	☿	♀	♂
1	9♐	21♏	19♑	18♋
2	10♐	22♏	20♑	18♋
3	11♐	23♏	21♑	18♋
4	12♐	25♏	23♑	17♋
5	13♐	26♏	24♑	17♋
6	14♐	28♏	25♑	17♋
7	15♐	29♏	26♑	17♋
8	16♐	1♐	27♑	16♋
9	17♐	2♐	29♑	16♋
10	18♐	4♐	0♒	16♋
11	19♐	5♐	1♒	16♋
12	20♐	7♐	2♒	15♋
13	21♐	8♐	3♒	15♋
14	22♐	10♐	5♒	15♋
15	23♐	11♐	6♒	14♋
16	24♐	13♐	7♒	14♋
17	25♐	14♐	8♒	14♋
18	26♐	16♐	9♒	13♋
19	27♐	17♐	10♒	13♋
20	28♐	19♐	12♒	13♋
21	29♐	20♐	13♒	12♋
22	0♑	22♐	14♒	12♋
23	1♑	24♐	15♒	12♋
24	2♑	25♐	16♒	11♋
25	3♑	27♐	17♒	11♋
26	4♑	28♐	19♒	10♋
27	5♑	0♑	20♒	10♋
28	6♑	1♑	21♒	10♋
29	7♑	3♑	22♒	9♋
30	9♑	5♑	23♒	9♋
31	10♑	6♑	24♒	8♋

1961

Your Starway to Love

☉ =Sun ☿ = Mercury ♀ = Venus ♂ = Mars ♈ = Aries ♉ = Taurus ♊ = Gemini ♋ = Cancer

January

Day	☉	☿	♀	♂
1	11♑	8♑	26♒	8♋
2	12♑	9♑	27♒	8♋
3	13♑	11♑	28♒	7♋
4	14♑	13♑	29♒	7♋
5	15♑	14♑	0♓	7♋
6	16♑	16♑	1♓	6♋
7	17♑	17♑	2♓	6♋
8	18♑	19♑	3♓	5♋
9	19♑	21♑	5♓	5♋
10	20♑	22♑	6♓	5♋
11	21♑	24♑	7♓	4♋
12	22♑	26♑	8♓	4♋
13	23♑	27♑	9♓	4♋
14	24♑	29♑	10♓	3♋
15	25♑	1♒	11♓	3♋
16	26♑	2♒	12♓	3♋
17	27♑	4♒	13♓	3♋
18	28♑	6♒	14♓	2♋
19	29♑	7♒	16♓	2♋
20	0♒	9♒	17♓	2♋
21	1♒	11♒	18♓	2♋
22	2♒	13♒	19♓	1♋
23	3♒	14♒	20♓	1♋
24	4♒	16♒	21♓	1♋
25	5♒	18♒	22♓	1♋
26	6♒	19♒	23♓	1♋
27	7♒	21♒	24♓	1♋
28	8♒	23♒	25♓	1♋
29	9♒	24♒	26♓	0♋
30	10♒	26♒	27♓	0♋
31	11♒	27♒	28♓	0♋

February

Day	☉	☿	♀	♂
1	12♒	29♒	29♓	0♋
2	13♒	0♓	0♈	0♋
3	14♒	2♓	1♈	0♋
4	15♒	3♓	2♈	0♋
5	16♒	4♓	3♈	0♋
6	17♒	5♓	4♈	0♋
7	18♒	6♓	5♈	0♋
8	19♒	7♓	6♈	0♋
9	20♒	8♓	7♈	0♋
10	21♒	9♓	8♈	0♋
11	22♒	9♓	9♈	0♋
12	23♒	9♓	9♈	0♋
13	24♒	9♓	10♈	0♋
14	25♒	9♓	11♈	0♋
15	26♒	9♓	12♈	0♋
16	27♒	8♓	13♈	1♋
17	28♒	8♓	14♈	1♋
18	29♒	7♓	15♈	1♋
19	0♓	6♓	15♈	1♋
20	1♓	5♓	16♈	1♋
21	2♓	4♓	17♈	1♋
22	3♓	3♓	18♈	1♋
23	4♓	2♓	18♈	2♋
24	5♓	1♓	19♈	2♋
25	6♓	0♓	20♈	2♋
26	7♓	29♒	21♈	2♋
27	8♓	28♒	21♈	3♋
28	9♓	27♒	22♈	3♋

March

Day	☉	☿	♀	♂
1	10♓	26♒	22♈	3♋
2	11♓	26♒	23♈	3♋
3	12♓	25♒	24♈	3♋
4	13♓	25♒	24♈	4♋
5	14♓	25♒	25♈	4♋
6	15♓	24♒	25♈	4♋
7	16♓	24♒	26♈	5♋
8	17♓	24♒	26♈	5♋
9	18♓	25♒	27♈	5♋
10	19♓	25♒	27♈	5♋
11	20♓	25♒	27♈	6♋
12	21♓	26♒	28♈	6♋
13	22♓	26♒	28♈	6♋
14	23♓	27♒	28♈	7♋
15	24♓	27♒	28♈	7♋
16	25♓	28♒	29♈	7♋
17	26♓	29♒	29♈	8♋
18	27♓	0♓	29♈	8♋
19	28♓	1♓	29♈	8♋
20	29♓	2♓	29♈	9♋
21	0♈	3♓	29♈	9♋
22	1♈	4♓	29♈	10♋
23	2♈	5♓	29♈	10♋
24	3♈	6♓	29♈	10♋
25	4♈	7♓	29♈	11♋
26	5♈	8♓	29♈	11♋
27	6♈	9♓	28♈	11♋
28	7♈	11♓	28♈	12♋
29	8♈	12♓	28♈	12♋
30	9♈	13♓	27♈	13♋
31	10♈	15♓	27♈	13♋

April

Day	☉	☿	♀	♂
1	11♈	16♓	26♈	14♋
2	12♈	17♓	26♈	14♋
3	13♈	19♓	25♈	14♋
4	14♈	20♓	25♈	15♋
5	15♈	22♓	24♈	15♋
6	16♈	23♓	24♈	16♋
7	17♈	25♓	23♈	16♋
8	18♈	26♓	23♈	17♋
9	19♈	28♓	22♈	17♋
10	20♈	0♈	21♈	17♋
11	21♈	1♈	21♈	18♋
12	22♈	3♈	20♈	18♋
13	23♈	5♈	19♈	19♋
14	24♈	6♈	19♈	19♋
15	25♈	8♈	18♈	20♋
16	26♈	10♈	18♈	20♋
17	27♈	12♈	17♈	21♋
18	28♈	14♈	17♈	21♋
19	29♈	15♈	16♈	22♋
20	0♉	17♈	16♈	22♋
21	1♉	19♈	15♈	23♋
22	2♉	21♈	15♈	23♋
23	3♉	23♈	14♈	24♋
24	4♉	25♈	14♈	24♋
25	5♉	27♈	14♈	25♋
26	6♉	29♈	13♈	25♋
27	7♉	1♉	13♈	26♋
28	8♉	3♉	13♈	26♋
29	9♉	5♉	13♈	27♋
30	10♉	8♉	13♈	27♋

May

Day	☉	☿	♀	♂
1	11♉	10♉	13♈	28♋
2	12♉	12♉	13♈	28♋
3	13♉	14♉	13♈	29♋
4	13♉	16♉	13♈	29♋
5	14♉	18♉	13♈	0♌
6	15♉	20♉	13♈	0♌
7	16♉	23♉	13♈	1♌
8	17♉	25♉	13♈	1♌
9	18♉	27♉	14♈	2♌
10	19♉	29♉	14♈	2♌
11	20♉	1♊	14♈	3♌
12	21♉	3♊	15♈	3♌
13	22♉	5♊	15♈	4♌
14	23♉	7♊	15♈	4♌
15	24♉	9♊	16♈	5♌
16	25♉	11♊	16♈	5♌
17	26♉	13♊	17♈	6♌
18	27♉	14♊	17♈	6♌
19	28♉	16♊	18♈	7♌
20	29♉	18♊	18♈	7♌
21	0♊	20♊	19♈	8♌
22	1♊	21♊	19♈	9♌
23	2♊	23♊	20♈	9♌
24	3♊	24♊	21♈	10♌
25	4♊	26♊	21♈	10♌
26	5♊	27♊	22♈	11♌
27	6♊	28♊	23♈	11♌
28	7♊	29♊	23♈	12♌
29	8♊	1♋	24♈	12♌
30	9♊	2♋	25♈	13♌
31	10♊	3♋	26♈	14♌

June

Day	☉	☿	♀	♂
1	10♊	4♋	26♈	14♌
2	11♊	5♋	27♈	15♌
3	12♊	6♋	28♈	15♌
4	13♊	6♋	29♈	16♌
5	14♊	7♋	0♉	16♌
6	15♊	8♋	0♉	17♌
7	16♊	8♋	1♉	17♌
8	17♊	9♋	2♉	18♌
9	18♊	9♋	3♉	19♌
10	19♊	10♋	4♉	19♌
11	20♊	10♋	5♉	20♌
12	21♊	10♋	6♉	20♌
13	22♊	10♋	6♉	21♌
14	23♊	10♋	7♉	21♌
15	24♊	10♋	8♉	22♌
16	25♊	10♋	9♉	23♌
17	26♊	10♋	10♉	23♌
18	27♊	10♋	11♉	24♌
19	28♊	10♋	12♉	24♌
20	29♊	9♋	13♉	25♌
21	0♋	9♋	14♉	25♌
22	1♋	9♋	15♉	26♌
23	1♋	8♋	16♉	27♌
24	2♋	7♋	17♉	27♌
25	3♋	7♋	18♉	28♌
26	4♋	6♋	19♉	28♌
27	5♋	6♋	20♉	29♌
28	6♋	5♋	21♉	0♍
29	7♋	5♋	22♉	0♍
30	8♋	4♋	23♉	1♍

July

Day	☉	☿	♀	♂
1	9♋	3♋	24♉	1♍
2	10♋	3♋	25♉	2♍
3	11♋	3♋	26♉	2♍
4	12♋	2♋	27♉	3♍
5	13♋	2♋	28♉	4♍
6	14♋	2♋	29♉	4♍
7	15♋	1♋	0♊	5♍
8	16♋	1♋	1♊	5♍
9	17♋	1♋	2♊	6♍
10	18♋	1♋	3♊	7♍
11	19♋	2♋	4♊	7♍
12	20♋	2♋	5♊	8♍
13	21♋	2♋	6♊	8♍
14	22♋	3♋	7♊	9♍
15	22♋	3♋	9♊	10♍
16	23♋	4♋	10♊	10♍
17	24♋	4♋	11♊	11♍
18	25♋	5♋	12♊	11♍
19	26♋	6♋	13♊	12♍
20	27♋	7♋	14♊	13♍
21	28♋	8♋	15♊	13♍
22	29♋	9♋	16♊	14♍
23	0♌	10♋	17♊	15♍
24	1♌	12♋	18♊	15♍
25	2♌	13♋	19♊	16♍
26	3♌	14♋	21♊	16♍
27	4♌	16♋	22♊	17♍
28	5♌	18♋	23♊	18♍
29	6♌	19♋	24♊	18♍
30	7♌	21♋	25♊	19♍
31	8♌	23♋	26♊	19♍

August

Day	☉	☿	♀	♂
1	9♌	25♋	27♊	20♍
2	10♌	26♋	28♊	21♍
3	11♌	28♋	0♋	21♍
4	12♌	0♌	1♋	22♍
5	13♌	2♌	2♋	23♍
6	13♌	4♌	3♋	23♍
7	14♌	6♌	4♋	24♍
8	15♌	8♌	5♋	24♍
9	16♌	10♌	6♋	25♍
10	17♌	13♌	7♋	26♍
11	18♌	15♌	9♋	26♍
12	19♌	17♌	10♋	27♍
13	20♌	19♌	11♋	28♍
14	21♌	21♌	12♋	28♍
15	22♌	23♌	13♋	29♍
16	23♌	25♌	14♋	29♍
17	24♌	27♌	16♋	0♎
18	25♌	29♌	17♋	1♎
19	26♌	1♍	18♋	1♎
20	27♌	3♍	19♋	2♎
21	28♌	4♍	20♋	3♎
22	29♌	6♍	21♋	3♎
23	0♍	8♍	23♋	4♎
24	1♍	10♍	24♋	5♎
25	2♍	12♍	25♋	5♎
26	3♍	14♍	26♋	6♎
27	4♍	15♍	27♋	7♎
28	5♍	17♍	28♋	7♎
29	6♍	19♍	0♌	8♎
30	7♍	21♍	1♌	8♎
31	8♍	22♍	2♌	9♎

September

Day	☉	☿	♀	♂
1	9♍	24♍	3♌	10♎
2	9♍	26♍	4♌	10♎
3	10♍	27♍	5♌	11♎
4	11♍	29♍	7♌	12♎
5	12♍	0♎	8♌	12♎
6	13♍	2♎	9♌	13♎
7	14♍	4♎	10♌	14♎
8	15♍	5♎	11♌	14♎
9	16♍	7♎	13♌	15♎
10	17♍	8♎	14♌	16♎
11	18♍	9♎	15♌	16♎
12	19♍	11♎	16♌	17♎
13	20♍	12♎	17♌	18♎
14	21♍	14♎	19♌	18♎
15	22♍	15♎	20♌	19♎
16	23♍	16♎	21♌	20♎
17	24♍	18♎	22♌	20♎
18	25♍	19♎	23♌	21♎
19	26♍	20♎	25♌	22♎
20	27♍	22♎	26♌	22♎
21	28♍	23♎	27♌	23♎
22	29♍	24♎	28♌	24♎
23	0♎	25♎	29♌	24♎
24	1♎	26♎	1♍	25♎
25	2♎	28♎	2♍	26♎
26	3♎	29♎	3♍	26♎
27	4♎	0♏	4♍	27♎
28	5♎	1♏	6♍	28♎
29	6♎	2♏	7♍	28♎
30	7♎	3♏	8♍	29♎

October

Day	☉	☿	♀	♂
1	8♎	3♏	9♍	0♏
2	9♎	4♏	10♍	0♏
3	10♎	5♏	12♍	1♏
4	11♎	6♏	13♍	2♏
5	12♎	6♏	14♍	2♏
6	13♎	7♏	15♍	3♏
7	14♎	7♏	17♍	4♏
8	15♎	8♏	18♍	4♏
9	16♎	8♏	19♍	5♏
10	17♎	8♏	20♍	6♏
11	18♎	8♏	21♍	6♏
12	19♎	8♏	23♍	7♏
13	20♎	8♏	24♍	8♏
14	21♎	7♏	25♍	8♏
15	22♎	7♏	26♍	9♏
16	23♎	6♏	28♍	10♏
17	24♎	5♏	29♍	11♏
18	25♎	4♏	0♎	11♏
19	26♎	3♏	1♎	12♏
20	27♎	2♏	3♎	13♏
21	28♎	1♏	4♎	13♏
22	29♎	0♏	5♎	14♏
23	0♏	29♎	6♎	15♏
24	1♏	27♎	8♎	15♏
25	2♏	26♎	9♎	16♏
26	3♏	25♎	10♎	17♏
27	4♏	24♎	11♎	17♏
28	5♏	24♎	13♎	18♏
29	6♏	23♎	14♎	19♏
30	7♏	23♎	15♎	20♏
31	8♏	22♎	16♎	20♏

November

Day	☉	☿	♀	♂
1	9♏	22♎	17♎	21♏
2	10♏	23♎	19♎	22♏
3	11♏	23♎	20♎	22♏
4	12♏	23♎	21♎	23♏
5	13♏	24♎	22♎	24♏
6	14♏	25♎	24♎	25♏
7	15♏	26♎	25♎	25♏
8	16♏	27♎	26♎	26♏
9	17♏	28♎	27♎	27♏
10	18♏	29♎	29♎	27♏
11	19♏	0♏	0♏	28♏
12	20♏	2♏	1♏	29♏
13	21♏	3♏	2♏	29♏
14	22♏	4♏	4♏	0♐
15	23♏	6♏	5♏	1♐
16	24♏	7♏	6♏	2♐
17	25♏	9♏	7♏	2♐
18	26♏	10♏	9♏	3♐
19	27♏	12♏	10♏	4♐
20	28♏	13♏	11♏	5♐
21	29♏	15♏	12♏	5♐
22	0♐	16♏	14♏	6♐
23	1♐	18♏	15♏	7♐
24	2♐	19♏	16♏	7♐
25	3♐	21♏	18♏	8♐
26	4♐	23♏	19♏	9♐
27	5♐	24♏	20♏	10♐
28	6♐	26♏	21♏	10♐
29	7♐	27♏	23♏	11♐
30	8♐	29♏	24♏	12♐

December

Day	☉	☿	♀	♂
1	9♐	0♐	25♏	13♐
2	10♐	2♐	26♏	13♐
3	11♐	4♐	28♏	14♐
4	12♐	5♐	29♏	15♐
5	13♐	7♐	0♐	15♐
6	14♐	8♐	1♐	16♐
7	15♐	10♐	3♐	17♐
8	16♐	11♐	4♐	18♐
9	17♐	13♐	5♐	18♐
10	18♐	15♐	6♐	19♐
11	19♐	16♐	8♐	20♐
12	20♐	18♐	9♐	21♐
13	21♐	19♐	10♐	21♐
14	22♐	21♐	11♐	22♐
15	23♐	22♐	13♐	23♐
16	24♐	24♐	14♐	24♐
17	25♐	26♐	15♐	24♐
18	26♐	27♐	16♐	25♐
19	27♐	29♐	18♐	26♐
20	28♐	0♑	19♐	27♐
21	29♐	2♑	20♐	27♐
22	0♑	3♑	21♐	28♐
23	1♑	5♑	23♐	29♐
24	2♑	7♑	24♐	0♑
25	3♑	8♑	25♐	0♑
26	4♑	10♑	26♐	1♑
27	5♑	11♑	28♐	2♑
28	6♑	13♑	29♐	3♑
29	7♑	15♑	0♑	3♑
30	8♑	16♑	2♑	4♑
31	9♑	18♑	3♑	5♑

1962

Planetary Positions

♌ = Leo ♍ = Virgo ♎ = Libra ♏ = Scorpio ♐ = Sagittarius ♑ = Capricorn ♒ = Aquarius ♓ = Pisces

January

Day	☉	☿	♀	♂
1	10♑	20♑	4♑	6♑
2	11♑	21♑	5♑	6♑
3	12♑	23♑	7♑	7♑
4	13♑	24♑	8♑	8♑
5	14♑	26♑	9♑	9♑
6	15♑	28♑	10♑	9♑
7	16♑	29♑	12♑	10♑
8	17♑	1♒	13♑	11♑
9	18♑	3♒	14♑	12♑
10	19♑	4♒	15♑	12♑
11	20♑	6♒	17♑	13♑
12	22♑	7♒	18♑	14♑
13	23♑	9♒	19♑	15♑
14	24♑	10♒	20♑	16♑
15	25♑	12♒	22♑	16♑
16	26♑	13♒	23♑	17♑
17	27♑	15♒	24♑	18♑
18	28♑	16♒	25♑	19♑
19	29♑	17♒	27♑	19♑
20	0♒	18♒	28♑	20♑
21	1♒	19♒	29♑	21♑
22	2♒	20♒	0♒	22♑
23	3♒	21♒	2♒	22♑
24	4♒	22♒	3♒	23♑
25	5♒	22♒	4♒	24♑
26	6♒	23♒	5♒	25♑
27	7♒	23♒	7♒	26♑
28	8♒	23♒	8♒	26♑
29	9♒	23♒	9♒	27♑
30	10♒	22♒	10♒	28♑
31	11♒	22♒	12♒	29♑

February

Day	☉	☿	♀	♂
1	12♒	21♒	13♒	29♑
2	13♒	20♒	14♒	0♒
3	14♒	19♒	16♒	1♒
4	15♒	18♒	17♒	2♒
5	16♒	17♒	18♒	3♒
6	17♒	15♒	19♒	3♒
7	18♒	14♒	21♒	4♒
8	19♒	13♒	22♒	5♒
9	20♒	12♒	23♒	6♒
10	21♒	11♒	24♒	6♒
11	22♒	10♒	26♒	7♒
12	23♒	9♒	27♒	8♒
13	24♒	9♒	28♒	9♒
14	25♒	8♒	29♒	10♒
15	26♒	8♒	1♓	10♒
16	27♒	7♒	2♓	11♒
17	28♒	7♒	3♓	12♒
18	29♒	7♒	4♓	13♒
19	0♓	7♒	6♓	13♒
20	1♓	8♒	7♓	14♒
21	2♓	8♒	8♓	15♒
22	3♓	8♒	9♓	16♒
23	4♓	9♒	11♓	17♒
24	5♓	9♒	12♓	17♒
25	6♓	10♒	13♓	18♒
26	7♓	11♒	14♓	19♒
27	8♓	11♒	16♓	20♒
28	9♓	12♒	17♓	20♒

March

Day	☉	☿	♀	♂
1	10♓	13♒	18♓	21♒
2	11♓	14♒	19♓	22♒
3	12♓	15♒	21♓	23♒
4	13♓	16♒	22♓	24♒
5	14♓	17♒	23♓	24♒
6	15♓	18♒	24♓	25♒
7	16♓	19♒	26♓	26♒
8	17♓	21♒	27♓	27♒
9	18♓	22♒	28♓	28♒
10	19♓	23♒	29♓	28♒
11	20♓	24♒	1♈	29♒
12	21♓	26♒	2♈	0♓
13	22♓	27♒	3♈	1♓
14	23♓	28♒	4♈	1♓
15	24♓	0♓	6♈	2♓
16	25♓	1♓	7♈	3♓
17	26♓	2♓	8♈	4♓
18	27♓	4♓	9♈	5♓
19	28♓	5♓	10♈	5♓
20	29♓	7♓	12♈	6♓
21	0♈	8♓	13♈	7♓
22	1♈	10♓	14♈	8♓
23	2♈	11♓	15♈	9♓
24	3♈	13♓	17♈	9♓
25	4♈	15♓	18♈	10♓
26	5♈	16♓	19♈	11♓
27	6♈	18♓	20♈	12♓
28	7♈	20♓	22♈	12♓
29	8♈	21♓	23♈	13♓
30	9♈	23♓	24♈	14♓
31	10♈	25♓	25♈	15♓

April

Day	☉	☿	♀	♂
1	11♈	27♓	27♈	16♓
2	12♈	28♓	28♈	16♓
3	13♈	0♈	29♈	17♓
4	14♈	2♈	0♉	18♓
5	15♈	4♈	2♉	19♓
6	16♈	6♈	3♉	19♓
7	17♈	8♈	4♉	20♓
8	18♈	10♈	5♉	21♓
9	19♈	12♈	6♉	22♓
10	20♈	14♈	8♉	23♓
11	21♈	16♈	9♉	23♓
12	22♈	18♈	10♉	24♓
13	23♈	20♈	11♉	25♓
14	24♈	22♈	13♉	26♓
15	25♈	24♈	14♉	27♓
16	26♈	26♈	15♉	27♓
17	27♈	28♈	16♉	28♓
18	28♈	0♉	18♉	29♓
19	29♈	2♉	19♉	0♈
20	0♉	4♉	20♉	0♈
21	1♉	6♉	21♉	1♈
22	2♉	9♉	22♉	2♈
23	3♉	11♉	24♉	3♈
24	4♉	13♉	25♉	3♈
25	5♉	15♉	26♉	4♈
26	5♉	17♉	27♉	5♈
27	6♉	19♉	29♉	6♈
28	7♉	21♉	0♊	7♈
29	8♉	23♉	1♊	7♈
30	9♉	25♉	2♊	8♈

May

Day	☉	☿	♀	♂
1	10♉	26♉	3♊	9♈
2	11♉	28♉	5♊	10♈
3	12♉	0♊	6♊	10♈
4	13♉	2♊	7♊	11♈
5	14♉	3♊	8♊	12♈
6	15♉	5♊	10♊	13♈
7	16♉	6♊	11♊	13♈
8	17♉	8♊	12♊	14♈
9	18♉	9♊	13♊	15♈
10	19♉	10♊	14♊	16♈
11	20♉	11♊	16♊	17♈
12	21♉	13♊	17♊	17♈
13	22♉	14♊	18♊	18♈
14	23♉	15♊	19♊	19♈
15	24♉	15♊	20♊	20♈
16	25♉	16♊	22♊	20♈
17	26♉	17♊	23♊	21♈
18	27♉	18♊	24♊	22♈
19	28♉	18♊	25♊	23♈
20	29♉	19♊	26♊	23♈
21	0♊	19♊	28♊	24♈
22	1♊	20♊	29♊	25♈
23	2♊	20♊	0♋	26♈
24	3♊	20♊	1♋	26♈
25	4♊	20♊	3♋	27♈
26	4♊	20♊	4♋	28♈
27	5♊	20♊	5♋	29♈
28	6♊	20♊	6♋	29♈
29	7♊	20♊	7♋	0♉
30	8♊	20♊	9♋	1♉
31	9♊	20♊	10♋	2♉

June

Day	☉	☿	♀	♂
1	10♊	19♊	11♋	2♉
2	11♊	19♊	12♋	3♉
3	12♊	18♊	13♋	4♉
4	13♊	18♊	15♋	5♉
5	14♊	17♊	16♋	5♉
6	15♊	17♊	17♋	6♉
7	16♊	16♊	18♋	7♉
8	17♊	16♊	19♋	8♉
9	18♊	15♊	20♋	8♉
10	19♊	15♊	22♋	9♉
11	20♊	14♊	23♋	10♉
12	21♊	14♊	24♋	11♉
13	22♊	13♊	25♋	11♉
14	23♊	13♊	26♋	12♉
15	24♊	12♊	28♋	13♉
16	25♊	12♊	29♋	13♉
17	26♊	12♊	0♌	14♉
18	26♊	12♊	1♌	15♉
19	27♊	12♊	2♌	16♉
20	28♊	12♊	4♌	16♉
21	29♊	12♊	5♌	17♉
22	0♋	12♊	6♌	18♉
23	1♋	12♊	7♌	19♉
24	2♋	13♊	8♌	19♉
25	3♋	13♊	9♌	20♉
26	4♋	14♊	11♌	21♉
27	5♋	14♊	12♌	21♉
28	6♋	15♊	13♌	22♉
29	7♋	16♊	14♌	23♉
30	8♋	16♊	15♌	24♉

July

Day	☉	☿	♀	♂
1	9♋	17♊	16♌	24♉
2	10♋	18♊	18♌	25♉
3	11♋	19♊	19♌	26♉
4	12♋	20♊	20♌	26♉
5	13♋	22♊	21♌	27♉
6	14♋	23♊	22♌	28♉
7	15♋	24♊	23♌	29♉
8	16♋	25♊	25♌	29♉
9	17♋	27♊	26♌	0♊
10	17♋	28♊	27♌	1♊
11	18♋	0♋	28♌	1♊
12	19♋	1♋	29♌	2♊
13	20♋	3♋	0♍	3♊
14	21♋	5♋	1♍	4♊
15	22♋	7♋	3♍	4♊
16	23♋	8♋	4♍	5♊
17	24♋	10♋	5♍	6♊
18	25♋	12♋	6♍	6♊
19	26♋	14♋	7♍	7♊
20	27♋	16♋	8♍	8♊
21	28♋	18♋	9♍	8♊
22	29♋	20♋	11♍	9♊
23	0♌	22♋	12♍	10♊
24	1♌	25♋	13♍	10♊
25	2♌	27♋	14♍	11♊
26	3♌	29♋	15♍	12♊
27	4♌	1♌	16♍	13♊
28	5♌	3♌	17♍	13♊
29	6♌	5♌	18♍	14♊
30	7♌	7♌	20♍	15♊
31	8♌	9♌	21♍	15♊

August

Day	☉	☿	♀	♂
1	8♌	11♌	22♍	16♊
2	9♌	13♌	23♍	17♊
3	10♌	15♌	24♍	17♊
4	11♌	17♌	25♍	18♊
5	12♌	19♌	26♍	19♊
6	13♌	21♌	27♍	19♊
7	14♌	23♌	28♍	20♊
8	15♌	25♌	29♍	21♊
9	16♌	27♌	1♎	21♊
10	17♌	29♌	2♎	22♊
11	18♌	1♍	3♎	23♊
12	19♌	3♍	4♎	23♊
13	20♌	4♍	5♎	24♊
14	21♌	6♍	6♎	25♊
15	22♌	8♍	7♎	25♊
16	23♌	9♍	8♎	26♊
17	24♌	11♍	9♎	27♊
18	25♌	13♍	10♎	27♊
19	26♌	14♍	11♎	28♊
20	27♌	16♍	12♎	29♊
21	28♌	18♍	13♎	29♊
22	29♌	19♍	14♎	0♋
23	0♍	21♍	15♎	0♋
24	1♍	22♍	16♎	1♋
25	2♍	24♍	17♎	2♋
26	2♍	25♍	18♎	2♋
27	3♍	27♍	19♎	3♋
28	4♍	28♍	20♎	4♋
29	5♍	29♍	21♎	4♋
30	6♍	1♎	22♎	5♋
31	7♍	2♎	23♎	6♋

September

Day	☉	☿	♀	♂
1	8♍	3♎	24♎	6♋
2	9♍	5♎	25♎	7♋
3	10♍	6♎	26♎	7♋
4	11♍	7♎	27♎	8♋
5	12♍	8♎	28♎	9♋
6	13♍	10♎	29♎	9♋
7	14♍	11♎	0♏	10♋
8	15♍	12♎	1♏	11♋
9	16♍	13♎	2♏	11♋
10	17♍	14♎	3♏	12♋
11	18♍	15♎	4♏	12♋
12	19♍	16♎	5♏	13♋
13	20♍	17♎	6♏	14♋
14	21♍	17♎	7♏	14♋
15	22♍	18♎	7♏	15♋
16	23♍	19♎	8♏	15♋
17	24♍	20♎	9♏	16♋
18	25♍	20♎	10♏	17♋
19	26♍	21♎	11♏	17♋
20	27♍	21♎	12♏	18♋
21	28♍	21♎	12♏	18♋
22	29♍	22♎	13♏	19♋
23	0♎	22♎	14♏	20♋
24	1♎	22♎	15♏	20♋
25	2♎	22♎	16♏	21♋
26	3♎	22♎	16♏	21♋
27	4♎	21♎	17♏	22♋
28	5♎	21♎	18♏	22♋
29	6♎	20♎	18♏	23♋
30	7♎	20♎	19♏	24♋

October

Day	☉	☿	♀	♂
1	8♎	19♎	20♏	24♋
2	9♎	18♎	20♏	25♋
3	10♎	17♎	21♏	25♋
4	10♎	16♎	22♏	26♋
5	11♎	15♎	22♏	26♋
6	12♎	13♎	23♏	27♋
7	13♎	12♎	23♏	27♋
8	14♎	11♎	24♏	28♋
9	15♎	10♎	24♏	29♋
10	16♎	9♎	25♏	29♋
11	17♎	8♎	25♏	0♌
12	18♎	8♎	25♏	0♌
13	19♎	7♎	26♏	1♌
14	20♎	7♎	26♏	1♌
15	21♎	7♎	26♏	2♌
16	22♎	7♎	27♏	2♌
17	23♎	7♎	27♏	3♌
18	24♎	7♎	27♏	3♌
19	25♎	8♎	27♏	4♌
20	26♎	8♎	27♏	4♌
21	27♎	9♎	28♏	5♌
22	28♎	10♎	28♏	5♌
23	29♎	11♎	28♏	6♌
24	0♏	12♎	28♏	6♌
25	1♏	14♎	28♏	7♌
26	2♏	15♎	27♏	7♌
27	3♏	16♎	27♏	8♌
28	4♏	18♎	27♏	8♌
29	5♏	19♎	27♏	9♌
30	6♏	21♎	27♏	9♌
31	7♏	22♎	26♏	10♌

November

Day	☉	☿	♀	♂
1	8♏	24♎	26♏	10♌
2	9♏	25♎	26♏	10♌
3	10♏	27♎	25♏	11♌
4	11♏	29♎	25♏	11♌
5	12♏	0♏	24♏	12♌
6	13♏	2♏	24♏	12♌
7	14♏	3♏	23♏	13♌
8	15♏	5♏	23♏	13♌
9	16♏	7♏	22♏	14♌
10	17♏	8♏	22♏	14♌
11	18♏	10♏	21♏	14♌
12	19♏	12♏	20♏	15♌
13	20♏	13♏	20♏	15♌
14	21♏	15♏	19♏	16♌
15	22♏	16♏	19♏	16♌
16	23♏	18♏	18♏	16♌
17	24♏	20♏	17♏	17♌
18	25♏	21♏	17♏	17♌
19	26♏	23♏	16♏	17♌
20	27♏	24♏	16♏	18♌
21	28♏	26♏	15♏	18♌
22	29♏	28♏	15♏	18♌
23	0♐	29♏	14♏	19♌
24	1♐	1♐	14♏	19♌
25	2♐	2♐	14♏	19♌
26	3♐	4♐	13♏	20♌
27	4♐	5♐	13♏	20♌
28	5♐	7♐	13♏	20♌
29	6♐	9♐	13♏	21♌
30	8♐	10♐	12♏	21♌

December

Day	☉	☿	♀	♂
1	9♐	12♐	12♏	21♌
2	10♐	13♐	12♏	21♌
3	11♐	15♐	12♏	22♌
4	12♐	16♐	12♏	22♌
5	13♐	18♐	12♏	22♌
6	14♐	20♐	12♏	22♌
7	15♐	21♐	12♏	23♌
8	16♐	23♐	13♏	23♌
9	17♐	24♐	13♏	23♌
10	18♐	26♐	13♏	23♌
11	19♐	27♐	13♏	23♌
12	20♐	29♐	14♏	24♌
13	21♐	1♑	14♏	24♌
14	22♐	2♑	14♏	24♌
15	23♐	4♑	15♏	24♌
16	24♐	5♑	15♏	24♌
17	25♐	7♑	16♏	24♌
18	26♐	8♑	16♏	24♌
19	27♐	10♑	17♏	24♌
20	28♐	11♑	17♏	25♌
21	29♐	13♑	18♏	25♌
22	0♑	15♑	18♏	25♌
23	1♑	16♑	19♏	25♌
24	2♑	18♑	20♏	25♌
25	3♑	19♑	20♏	25♌
26	4♑	21♑	21♏	25♌
27	5♑	22♑	22♏	25♌
28	6♑	24♑	22♏	25♌
29	7♑	25♑	23♏	25♌
30	8♑	26♑	24♏	25♌
31	9♑	28♑	25♏	25♌

☉ =Sun ☿ = Mercury ♀ = Venus ♂ = Mars ♈ = Aries ♉ = Taurus ♊ = Gemini ♋ = Cancer

1963

January

Day	☉	☿	♀	♂
1	10♑	29♑	25♏	25♌
2	11♑	0♒	26♏	24♌
3	12♑	1♒	27♏	24♌
4	13♑	2♒	28♏	24♌
5	14♑	3♒	29♏	24♌
6	15♑	4♒	0♐	24♌
7	16♑	5♒	0♐	24♌
8	17♑	6♒	1♐	24♌
9	18♑	6♒	2♐	23♌
10	19♑	7♒	3♐	23♌
11	20♑	7♒	4♐	23♌
12	21♑	7♒	5♐	23♌
13	22♑	6♒	6♐	23♌
14	23♑	6♒	7♐	22♌
15	24♑	5♒	8♐	22♌
16	25♑	5♒	9♐	22♌
17	26♑	4♒	10♐	22♌
18	27♑	2♒	11♐	21♌
19	28♑	1♒	12♐	21♌
20	29♑	0♒	13♐	21♌
21	0♒	29♑	14♐	20♌
22	1♒	27♑	15♐	20♌
23	2♒	26♑	16♐	20♌
24	3♒	25♑	17♐	19♌
25	4♒	24♑	18♐	19♌
26	6♒	23♑	19♐	19♌
27	7♒	22♑	20♐	18♌
28	8♒	22♑	21♐	18♌
29	9♒	21♑	22♐	17♌
30	10♒	21♑	23♐	17♌
31	11♒	21♑	24♐	17♌

April

Day	☉	☿	♀	♂
1	11♈	12♈	3♓	7♌
2	12♈	14♈	4♓	7♌
3	13♈	16♈	5♓	7♌
4	14♈	18♈	6♓	7♌
5	15♈	20♈	7♓	7♌
6	16♈	22♈	9♓	8♌
7	17♈	24♈	10♓	8♌
8	18♈	27♈	11♓	8♌
9	19♈	29♈	12♓	8♌
10	20♈	1♉	13♓	9♌
11	21♈	3♉	14♓	9♌
12	22♈	5♉	16♓	9♌
13	23♈	6♉	17♓	9♌
14	24♈	8♉	18♓	10♌
15	25♈	10♉	19♓	10♌
16	25♈	12♉	20♓	10♌
17	26♈	14♉	22♓	10♌
18	27♈	15♉	23♓	11♌
19	28♈	17♉	24♓	11♌
20	29♈	18♉	25♓	11♌
21	0♉	20♉	26♓	12♌
22	1♉	21♉	28♓	12♌
23	2♉	22♉	29♓	12♌
24	3♉	23♉	0♈	13♌
25	4♉	24♉	1♈	13♌
26	5♉	25♉	2♈	13♌
27	6♉	26♉	4♈	14♌
28	7♉	27♉	5♈	14♌
29	8♉	28♉	6♈	15♌
30	9♉	29♉	7♈	15♌

July

Day	☉	☿	♀	♂
1	9♋	24♊	22♊	15♍
2	10♋	26♊	24♊	15♍
3	11♋	28♊	25♊	16♍
4	12♋	0♋	26♊	17♍
5	12♋	2♋	27♊	17♍
6	13♋	4♋	28♊	18♍
7	14♋	6♋	0♋	18♍
8	15♋	9♋	1♋	19♍
9	16♋	11♋	2♋	19♍
10	17♋	13♋	3♋	20♍
11	18♋	15♋	5♋	21♍
12	19♋	17♋	6♋	21♍
13	20♋	19♋	7♋	22♍
14	21♋	21♋	8♋	22♍
15	22♋	24♋	9♋	23♍
16	23♋	26♋	11♋	23♍
17	24♋	28♋	12♋	24♍
18	25♋	0♌	13♋	25♍
19	26♋	2♌	14♋	25♍
20	27♋	4♌	16♋	26♍
21	28♋	6♌	17♋	26♍
22	29♋	8♌	18♋	27♍
23	0♌	10♌	19♋	28♍
24	1♌	12♌	20♋	28♍
25	2♌	14♌	22♋	29♍
26	3♌	16♌	23♋	29♍
27	3♌	18♌	24♋	0♎
28	4♌	19♌	25♋	1♎
29	5♌	21♌	27♋	1♎
30	6♌	23♌	28♋	2♎
31	7♌	25♌	29♋	2♎

October

Day	☉	☿	♀	♂
1	7♎	21♍	16♎	13♏
2	8♎	21♍	17♎	13♏
3	9♎	22♍	18♎	14♏
4	10♎	23♍	20♎	15♏
5	11♎	23♍	21♎	16♏
6	12♎	24♍	22♎	16♏
7	13♎	25♍	23♎	17♏
8	14♎	27♍	25♎	18♏
9	15♎	28♍	26♎	18♏
10	16♎	29♍	27♎	19♏
11	17♎	1♎	28♎	20♏
12	18♎	2♎	0♏	20♏
13	19♎	4♎	1♏	21♏
14	20♎	5♎	2♏	22♏
15	21♎	7♎	3♏	23♏
16	22♎	9♎	5♏	23♏
17	23♎	10♎	6♏	24♏
18	24♎	12♎	7♏	25♏
19	25♎	14♎	8♏	25♏
20	26♎	15♎	10♏	26♏
21	27♎	17♎	11♏	27♏
22	28♎	19♎	12♏	27♏
23	29♎	20♎	13♏	28♏
24	0♏	22♎	15♏	29♏
25	1♏	24♎	16♏	0♐
26	2♏	26♎	17♏	0♐
27	3♏	27♎	18♏	1♐
28	4♏	29♎	20♏	2♐
29	5♏	1♏	21♏	3♐
30	6♏	2♏	22♏	3♐
31	7♏	4♏	23♏	4♐

February

Day	☉	☿	♀	♂
1	12♒	21♑	25♐	16♌
2	13♒	21♑	26♐	16♌
3	14♒	21♑	27♐	15♌
4	15♒	21♑	28♐	15♌
5	16♒	22♑	29♐	15♌
6	17♒	22♑	0♑	14♌
7	18♒	23♑	1♑	14♌
8	19♒	23♑	3♑	13♌
9	20♒	24♑	4♑	13♌
10	21♒	25♑	5♑	13♌
11	22♒	26♑	6♑	12♌
12	23♒	27♑	7♑	12♌
13	24♒	28♑	8♑	12♌
14	25♒	29♑	9♑	11♌
15	26♒	0♒	10♑	11♌
16	27♒	1♒	11♑	10♌
17	28♒	2♒	13♑	10♌
18	29♒	3♒	14♑	10♌
19	0♓	4♒	15♑	9♌
20	1♓	6♒	16♑	9♌
21	2♓	7♒	17♑	9♌
22	3♓	8♒	18♑	9♌
23	4♓	9♒	19♑	8♌
24	5♓	11♒	20♑	8♌
25	6♓	12♒	22♑	8♌
26	7♓	13♒	23♑	8♌
27	8♓	15♒	24♑	7♌
28	9♓	16♒	25♑	7♌

May

Day	☉	☿	♀	♂
1	10♉	29♉	8♈	15♌
2	11♉	0♊	10♈	16♌
3	12♉	0♊	11♈	16♌
4	13♉	0♊	12♈	16♌
5	14♉	0♊	13♈	17♌
6	15♉	1♊	15♈	17♌
7	16♉	1♊	16♈	18♌
8	17♉	1♊	17♈	18♌
9	18♉	0♊	18♈	18♌
10	19♉	0♊	19♈	19♌
11	20♉	0♊	21♈	19♌
12	21♉	0♊	22♈	20♌
13	22♉	29♉	23♈	20♌
14	23♉	29♉	24♈	21♌
15	24♉	28♉	25♈	21♌
16	25♉	28♉	27♈	21♌
17	26♉	27♉	28♈	22♌
18	27♉	26♉	29♈	22♌
19	28♉	26♉	0♉	23♌
20	28♉	25♉	1♉	23♌
21	29♉	25♉	3♉	24♌
22	0♊	24♉	4♉	24♌
23	1♊	24♉	5♉	25♌
24	2♊	23♉	6♉	25♌
25	3♊	23♉	7♉	26♌
26	4♊	22♉	9♉	26♌
27	5♊	22♉	10♉	27♌
28	6♊	22♉	11♉	27♌
29	7♊	22♉	12♉	28♌
30	8♊	22♉	13♉	28♌
31	9♊	22♉	15♉	28♌

August

Day	☉	☿	♀	♂
1	8♌	26♌	0♌	3♎
2	9♌	28♌	2♌	4♎
3	10♌	0♍	3♌	4♎
4	11♌	1♍	4♌	5♎
5	12♌	3♍	5♌	6♎
6	13♌	4♍	6♌	6♎
7	14♌	6♍	8♌	7♎
8	15♌	8♍	9♌	7♎
9	16♌	9♍	10♌	8♎
10	17♌	10♍	11♌	9♎
11	18♌	12♍	13♌	9♎
12	19♌	13♍	14♌	10♎
13	20♌	15♍	15♌	10♎
14	21♌	16♍	16♌	11♎
15	22♌	17♍	18♌	12♎
16	23♌	19♍	19♌	12♎
17	24♌	20♍	20♌	13♎
18	25♌	21♍	21♌	14♎
19	26♌	22♍	23♌	14♎
20	26♌	23♍	24♌	15♎
21	27♌	25♍	25♌	16♎
22	28♌	26♍	26♌	16♎
23	29♌	27♍	27♌	17♎
24	0♍	28♍	29♌	17♎
25	1♍	29♍	0♍	18♎
26	2♍	29♍	1♍	19♎
27	3♍	0♎	2♍	19♎
28	4♍	1♎	4♍	20♎
29	5♍	2♎	5♍	21♎
30	6♍	2♎	6♍	21♎
31	7♍	3♎	7♍	22♎

November

Day	☉	☿	♀	♂
1	8♏	6♏	25♏	5♐
2	9♏	7♏	26♏	5♐
3	10♏	9♏	27♏	6♐
4	11♏	11♏	28♏	7♐
5	12♏	12♏	0♐	8♐
6	13♏	14♏	1♐	8♐
7	14♏	15♏	2♐	9♐
8	15♏	17♏	3♐	10♐
9	16♏	19♏	5♐	10♐
10	17♏	20♏	6♐	11♐
11	18♏	22♏	7♐	12♐
12	19♏	23♏	8♐	13♐
13	20♏	25♏	10♐	13♐
14	21♏	26♏	11♐	14♐
15	22♏	28♏	12♐	15♐
16	23♏	0♐	13♐	16♐
17	24♏	1♐	15♐	16♐
18	25♏	3♐	16♐	17♐
19	26♏	4♐	17♐	18♐
20	27♏	6♐	18♐	19♐
21	28♏	7♐	20♐	19♐
22	29♏	9♐	21♐	20♐
23	0♐	10♐	22♐	21♐
24	1♐	12♐	23♐	22♐
25	2♐	13♐	24♐	22♐
26	3♐	15♐	26♐	23♐
27	4♐	17♐	27♐	24♐
28	5♐	18♐	28♐	25♐
29	6♐	20♐	29♐	25♐
30	7♐	21♐	1♑	26♐

March

Day	☉	☿	♀	♂
1	10♓	18♒	26♑	7♌
2	11♓	19♒	27♑	7♌
3	12♓	21♒	29♑	6♌
4	13♓	22♒	0♒	6♌
5	14♓	24♒	1♒	6♌
6	15♓	25♒	2♒	6♌
7	16♓	27♒	3♒	6♌
8	17♓	28♒	4♒	6♌
9	18♓	0♓	5♒	6♌
10	19♓	2♓	7♒	6♌
11	20♓	3♓	8♒	6♌
12	21♓	5♓	9♒	5♌
13	22♓	7♓	10♒	5♌
14	23♓	8♓	11♒	5♌
15	24♓	10♓	12♒	5♌
16	25♓	12♓	14♒	5♌
17	26♓	13♓	15♒	5♌
18	27♓	15♓	16♒	5♌
19	28♓	17♓	17♒	5♌
20	29♓	19♓	18♒	5♌
21	0♈	21♓	20♒	5♌
22	1♈	22♓	21♒	6♌
23	2♈	24♓	22♒	6♌
24	3♈	26♓	23♒	6♌
25	4♈	28♓	24♒	6♌
26	5♈	0♈	25♒	6♌
27	6♈	2♈	27♒	6♌
28	7♈	4♈	28♒	6♌
29	8♈	6♈	29♒	6♌
30	9♈	8♈	0♓	6♌
31	10♈	10♈	1♓	7♌

June

Day	☉	☿	♀	♂
1	10♊	22♉	16♉	29♌
2	11♊	22♉	17♉	29♌
3	12♊	22♉	18♉	0♍
4	13♊	22♉	20♉	0♍
5	14♊	23♉	21♉	1♍
6	15♊	23♉	22♉	1♍
7	16♊	24♉	23♉	2♍
8	17♊	24♉	24♉	2♍
9	18♊	25♉	26♉	3♍
10	19♊	26♉	27♉	4♍
11	20♊	26♉	28♉	4♍
12	21♊	27♉	29♉	5♍
13	21♊	28♉	0♊	5♍
14	22♊	29♉	2♊	6♍
15	23♊	0♊	3♊	6♍
16	24♊	1♊	4♊	7♍
17	25♊	2♊	5♊	7♍
18	26♊	4♊	7♊	8♍
19	27♊	5♊	8♊	9♍
20	28♊	6♊	9♊	9♍
21	29♊	8♊	10♊	9♍
22	0♋	9♊	11♊	10♍
23	1♋	11♊	13♊	10♍
24	2♋	12♊	14♊	11♍
25	3♋	14♊	15♊	12♍
26	4♋	15♊	16♊	12♍
27	5♋	17♊	17♊	13♍
28	6♋	19♊	19♊	13♍
29	7♋	21♊	20♊	14♍
30	8♋	22♊	21♊	14♍

September

Day	☉	☿	♀	♂
1	8♍	4♎	9♍	23♎
2	9♍	4♎	10♍	23♎
3	10♍	4♎	11♍	24♎
4	11♍	5♎	12♍	25♎
5	12♍	5♎	14♍	25♎
6	13♍	5♎	15♍	26♎
7	14♍	5♎	16♍	27♎
8	15♍	5♎	17♍	27♎
9	16♍	5♎	19♍	28♎
10	17♍	5♎	20♍	29♎
11	18♍	4♎	21♍	29♎
12	19♍	4♎	22♍	0♏
13	20♍	3♎	24♍	1♏
14	21♍	2♎	25♍	1♏
15	22♍	2♎	26♍	2♏
16	23♍	1♎	27♍	3♏
17	24♍	0♎	29♍	3♏
18	25♍	29♍	0♎	4♏
19	26♍	28♍	1♎	5♏
20	27♍	27♍	2♎	5♏
21	27♍	25♍	3♎	6♏
22	28♍	24♍	5♎	7♏
23	29♍	24♍	6♎	7♏
24	0♎	23♍	7♎	8♏
25	1♎	22♍	8♎	9♏
26	2♎	21♍	10♎	9♏
27	3♎	21♍	11♎	10♏
28	4♎	21♍	12♎	11♏
29	5♎	21♍	13♎	11♏
30	6♎	21♍	15♎	12♏

December

Day	☉	☿	♀	♂
1	8♐	23♐	2♑	27♐
2	9♐	24♐	3♑	28♐
3	10♐	26♐	4♑	28♐
4	11♐	27♐	6♑	29♐
5	12♐	29♐	7♑	0♑
6	13♐	0♑	8♑	1♑
7	14♐	1♑	9♑	1♑
8	15♐	3♑	11♑	2♑
9	16♐	4♑	12♑	3♑
10	17♐	6♑	13♑	4♑
11	18♐	7♑	14♑	4♑
12	19♐	8♑	16♑	5♑
13	20♐	10♑	17♑	6♑
14	21♐	11♑	18♑	7♑
15	22♐	12♑	19♑	7♑
16	24♐	14♑	21♑	8♑
17	25♐	15♑	22♑	9♑
18	26♐	16♑	23♑	10♑
19	27♐	17♑	24♑	11♑
20	28♐	18♑	26♑	11♑
21	29♐	19♑	27♑	12♑
22	0♑	19♑	28♑	13♑
23	1♑	20♑	29♑	14♑
24	2♑	20♑	1♒	14♑
25	3♑	21♑	2♒	15♑
26	4♑	21♑	3♒	16♑
27	5♑	21♑	4♒	17♑
28	6♑	20♑	5♒	17♑
29	7♑	20♑	7♒	18♑
30	8♑	19♑	8♒	19♑
31	9♑	19♑	9♒	20♑

Planetary Positions

♌ = Leo ♍ = Virgo ♎ = Libra ♏ = Scorpio ♐ = Sagittarius ♑ = Capricorn ♒ = Aquarius ♓ = Pisces

1964

January

Day	☉	☿	♀	♂
1	10♑	18♑	10♒	21♑
2	11♑	16♑	12♒	21♑
3	12♑	15♑	13♒	22♑
4	13♑	14♑	14♒	23♑
5	14♑	12♑	15♒	24♑
6	15♑	11♑	17♒	24♑
7	16♑	10♑	18♒	25♑
8	17♑	9♑	19♒	26♑
9	18♑	8♑	20♒	27♑
10	19♑	7♑	22♒	28♑
11	20♑	6♑	23♒	28♑
12	21♑	5♑	24♒	29♑
13	22♑	5♑	25♒	0♒
14	23♑	5♑	26♒	1♒
15	24♑	5♑	28♒	2♒
16	25♑	5♑	29♒	2♒
17	26♑	5♑	0♓	3♒
18	27♑	5♑	1♓	4♒
19	28♑	5♑	3♓	5♒
20	29♑	6♑	4♓	5♒
21	0♒	6♑	5♓	6♒
22	1♒	7♑	6♓	7♒
23	2♒	8♑	7♓	8♒
24	3♒	9♑	9♓	9♒
25	4♒	10♑	10♓	9♒
26	5♒	11♑	11♓	10♒
27	6♒	12♑	12♓	11♒
28	7♒	13♑	14♓	12♒
29	8♒	14♑	15♓	13♒
30	9♒	15♑	16♓	13♒
31	10♒	16♑	17♓	14♒

April

Day	☉	☿	♀	♂
1	11♈	29♈	27♉	2♈
2	12♈	0♉	28♉	3♈
3	13♈	2♉	29♉	4♈
4	14♈	3♉	0♊	4♈
5	15♈	4♉	1♊	5♈
6	16♈	5♉	2♊	6♈
7	17♈	7♉	3♊	7♈
8	18♈	8♉	4♊	8♈
9	19♈	8♉	5♊	8♈
10	20♈	9♉	6♊	9♈
11	21♈	10♉	7♊	10♈
12	22♈	10♉	8♊	11♈
13	23♈	11♉	9♊	11♈
14	24♈	11♉	10♊	12♈
15	25♈	11♉	11♊	13♈
16	26♈	11♉	12♊	14♈
17	27♈	12♉	13♊	14♈
18	28♈	11♉	14♊	15♈
19	29♈	11♉	15♊	16♈
20	0♉	11♉	15♊	17♈
21	1♉	11♉	16♊	18♈
22	2♉	10♉	17♊	18♈
23	3♉	10♉	18♊	19♈
24	4♉	9♉	19♊	20♈
25	5♉	9♉	20♊	21♈
26	6♉	8♉	21♊	21♈
27	7♉	7♉	21♊	22♈
28	8♉	7♉	22♊	23♈
29	9♉	6♉	23♊	24♈
30	10♉	5♉	24♊	24♈

July

Day	☉	☿	♀	♂
1	9♋	14♋	22♊	10♊
2	10♋	16♋	22♊	10♊
3	11♋	18♋	22♊	11♊
4	12♋	20♋	21♊	12♊
5	13♋	22♋	21♊	13♊
6	14♋	24♋	21♊	13♊
7	15♋	26♋	21♊	14♊
8	16♋	28♋	21♊	15♊
9	17♋	0♌	20♊	15♊
10	18♋	2♌	20♊	16♊
11	19♋	4♌	20♊	17♊
12	20♋	6♌	20♊	17♊
13	21♋	8♌	20♊	18♊
14	22♋	10♌	20♊	19♊
15	23♋	11♌	21♊	19♊
16	24♋	13♌	21♊	20♊
17	25♋	15♌	21♊	21♊
18	26♋	16♌	21♊	21♊
19	27♋	18♌	21♊	22♊
20	27♋	19♌	22♊	23♊
21	28♋	21♌	22♊	24♊
22	29♋	23♌	22♊	24♊
23	0♌	24♌	23♊	25♊
24	1♌	25♌	23♊	26♊
25	2♌	27♌	24♊	26♊
26	3♌	28♌	24♊	27♊
27	4♌	0♍	25♊	28♊
28	5♌	1♍	25♊	28♊
29	6♌	2♍	26♊	29♊
30	7♌	3♍	26♊	0♋
31	8♌	5♍	27♊	0♋

October

Day	☉	☿	♀	♂
1	8♎	27♍	25♌	10♌
2	9♎	29♍	26♌	10♌
3	10♎	0♎	27♌	11♌
4	11♎	2♎	28♌	11♌
5	12♎	4♎	29♌	12♌
6	13♎	6♎	1♍	13♌
7	14♎	8♎	2♍	13♌
8	15♎	9♎	3♍	14♌
9	16♎	11♎	4♍	14♌
10	17♎	13♎	5♍	15♌
11	18♎	15♎	6♍	16♌
12	19♎	16♎	7♍	16♌
13	20♎	18♎	9♍	17♌
14	21♎	20♎	10♍	17♌
15	22♎	21♎	11♍	18♌
16	23♎	23♎	12♍	18♌
17	24♎	25♎	13♍	19♌
18	25♎	27♎	14♍	20♌
19	26♎	28♎	16♍	20♌
20	27♎	0♏	17♍	21♌
21	28♎	1♏	18♍	21♌
22	29♎	3♏	19♍	22♌
23	0♏	5♏	20♍	22♌
24	1♏	6♏	21♍	23♌
25	2♏	8♏	23♍	24♌
26	3♏	10♏	24♍	24♌
27	4♏	11♏	25♍	25♌
28	5♏	13♏	26♍	25♌
29	6♏	14♏	27♍	26♌
30	7♏	16♏	29♍	26♌
31	8♏	17♏	0♎	27♌

February

Day	☉	☿	♀	♂
1	11♒	17♑	18♓	15♒
2	12♒	18♑	20♓	16♒
3	13♒	20♑	21♓	16♒
4	14♒	21♑	22♓	17♒
5	15♒	22♑	23♓	18♒
6	16♒	24♑	24♓	19♒
7	17♒	25♑	26♓	20♒
8	18♒	26♑	27♓	20♒
9	19♒	28♑	28♓	21♒
10	20♒	29♑	29♓	22♒
11	21♒	0♒	0♈	23♒
12	23♒	2♒	2♈	24♒
13	24♒	3♒	3♈	24♒
14	25♒	5♒	4♈	25♒
15	26♒	6♒	5♈	26♒
16	27♒	8♒	6♈	27♒
17	28♒	9♒	8♈	28♒
18	29♒	11♒	9♈	28♒
19	0♓	12♒	10♈	29♒
20	1♓	14♒	11♈	0♓
21	2♓	16♒	12♈	1♓
22	3♓	17♒	13♈	1♓
23	4♓	19♒	15♈	2♓
24	5♓	20♒	16♈	3♓
25	6♓	22♒	17♈	4♓
26	7♓	24♒	18♈	5♓
27	8♓	25♒	19♈	5♓
28	9♓	27♒	20♈	6♓
29	10♓	29♒	22♈	7♓

May

Day	☉	☿	♀	♂
1	11♉	5♉	25♊	25♈
2	12♉	4♉	25♊	26♈
3	13♉	4♉	26♊	27♈
4	14♉	3♉	27♊	27♈
5	15♉	3♉	27♊	28♈
6	16♉	2♉	28♊	29♈
7	17♉	2♉	29♊	0♉
8	18♉	2♉	29♊	0♉
9	19♉	2♉	0♋	1♉
10	20♉	2♉	1♋	2♉
11	21♉	2♉	1♋	3♉
12	21♉	2♉	2♋	3♉
13	22♉	2♉	2♋	4♉
14	23♉	2♉	3♋	5♉
15	24♉	2♉	3♋	6♉
16	25♉	3♉	4♋	6♉
17	26♉	3♉	4♋	7♉
18	27♉	4♉	5♋	8♉
19	28♉	4♉	5♋	9♉
20	29♉	5♉	5♋	9♉
21	0♊	6♉	6♋	10♉
22	1♊	6♉	6♋	11♉
23	2♊	7♉	6♋	12♉
24	3♊	8♉	6♋	12♉
25	4♊	9♉	7♋	13♉
26	5♊	10♉	7♋	14♉
27	6♊	11♉	7♋	15♉
28	7♊	12♉	7♋	15♉
29	8♊	13♉	7♋	16♉
30	9♊	15♉	7♋	17♉
31	10♊	16♉	7♋	18♉

August

Day	☉	☿	♀	♂
1	9♌	6♍	27♊	1♋
2	10♌	7♍	28♊	2♋
3	11♌	8♍	29♊	2♋
4	12♌	9♍	29♊	3♋
5	13♌	10♍	0♋	4♋
6	14♌	11♍	1♋	4♋
7	15♌	12♍	1♋	5♋
8	16♌	13♍	2♋	6♋
9	17♌	14♍	3♋	6♋
10	18♌	14♍	4♋	7♋
11	19♌	15♍	4♋	8♋
12	20♌	16♍	5♋	8♋
13	20♌	16♍	6♋	9♋
14	21♌	17♍	7♋	10♋
15	22♌	17♍	7♋	10♋
16	23♌	17♍	8♋	11♋
17	24♌	18♍	9♋	12♋
18	25♌	18♍	10♋	12♋
19	26♌	18♍	11♋	13♋
20	27♌	18♍	12♋	14♋
21	28♌	18♍	13♋	14♋
22	29♌	18♍	14♋	15♋
23	0♍	17♍	14♋	15♋
24	1♍	17♍	15♋	16♋
25	2♍	16♍	16♋	17♋
26	3♍	16♍	17♋	17♋
27	4♍	15♍	18♋	18♋
28	5♍	14♍	19♋	19♋
29	6♍	14♍	20♋	19♋
30	7♍	13♍	21♋	20♋
31	8♍	12♍	22♋	21♋

November

Day	☉	☿	♀	♂
1	9♏	19♏	1♎	27♌
2	10♏	21♏	2♎	28♌
3	11♏	22♏	3♎	28♌
4	12♏	24♏	5♎	29♌
5	13♏	25♏	6♎	0♍
6	14♏	27♏	7♎	0♍
7	15♏	28♏	8♎	1♍
8	16♏	0♐	9♎	1♍
9	17♏	1♐	11♎	2♍
10	18♏	3♐	12♎	2♍
11	19♏	4♐	13♎	3♍
12	20♏	6♐	14♎	3♍
13	21♏	7♐	16♎	4♍
14	22♏	8♐	17♎	4♍
15	23♏	10♐	18♎	5♍
16	24♏	11♐	19♎	5♍
17	25♏	13♐	20♎	6♍
18	26♏	14♐	22♎	6♍
19	27♏	16♐	23♎	7♍
20	28♏	17♐	24♎	7♍
21	29♏	18♐	25♎	8♍
22	0♐	20♐	26♎	8♍
23	1♐	21♐	28♎	9♍
24	2♐	22♐	29♎	9♍
25	3♐	24♐	0♏	10♍
26	4♐	25♐	1♏	10♍
27	5♐	26♐	3♏	10♍
28	6♐	27♐	4♏	11♍
29	7♐	28♐	5♏	11♍
30	8♐	29♐	6♏	12♍

March

Day	☉	☿	♀	♂
1	11♓	0♓	23♈	8♓
2	12♓	2♓	24♈	9♓
3	13♓	4♓	25♈	9♓
4	14♓	6♓	26♈	10♓
5	15♓	8♓	27♈	11♓
6	16♓	9♓	28♈	12♓
7	17♓	11♓	0♉	13♓
8	18♓	13♓	1♉	13♓
9	19♓	15♓	2♉	14♓
10	20♓	17♓	3♉	15♓
11	21♓	19♓	4♉	16♓
12	22♓	21♓	5♉	16♓
13	23♓	23♓	6♉	17♓
14	24♓	24♓	8♉	18♓
15	25♓	26♓	9♉	19♓
16	26♓	28♓	10♉	20♓
17	27♓	0♈	11♉	20♓
18	28♓	2♈	12♉	21♓
19	29♓	4♈	13♉	22♓
20	0♈	6♈	14♉	23♓
21	1♈	8♈	15♉	24♓
22	2♈	10♈	16♉	24♓
23	3♈	12♈	17♉	25♓
24	4♈	14♈	19♉	26♓
25	5♈	16♈	20♉	27♓
26	6♈	18♈	21♉	27♓
27	7♈	20♈	22♉	28♓
28	8♈	22♈	23♉	29♓
29	9♈	24♈	24♉	0♈
30	10♈	25♈	25♉	1♈
31	11♈	27♈	26♉	1♈

June

Day	☉	☿	♀	♂
1	11♊	17♉	7♋	18♉
2	12♊	19♉	7♋	19♉
3	13♊	20♉	6♋	20♉
4	14♊	21♉	6♋	20♉
5	15♊	23♉	6♋	21♉
6	16♊	24♉	6♋	22♉
7	16♊	26♉	5♋	23♉
8	17♊	28♉	5♋	23♉
9	18♊	29♉	5♋	24♉
10	19♊	1♊	4♋	25♉
11	20♊	3♊	4♋	25♉
12	21♊	4♊	3♋	26♉
13	22♊	6♊	3♋	27♉
14	23♊	8♊	2♋	28♉
15	24♊	10♊	2♋	28♉
16	25♊	12♊	1♋	29♉
17	26♊	14♊	0♋	0♊
18	27♊	16♊	0♋	1♊
19	28♊	18♊	29♊	1♊
20	29♊	20♊	28♊	2♊
21	0♋	22♊	28♊	3♊
22	1♋	25♊	27♊	3♊
23	2♋	27♊	27♊	4♊
24	3♋	29♊	26♊	5♊
25	4♋	1♋	25♊	5♊
26	5♋	3♋	25♊	6♊
27	6♋	5♋	24♊	7♊
28	7♋	8♋	24♊	8♊
29	7♋	10♋	23♊	8♊
30	8♋	12♋	23♊	9♊

September

Day	☉	☿	♀	♂
1	9♍	11♍	23♋	21♋
2	10♍	10♍	24♋	22♋
3	11♍	9♍	25♋	22♋
4	12♍	8♍	26♋	23♋
5	13♍	7♍	27♋	24♋
6	14♍	6♍	28♋	24♋
7	15♍	6♍	29♋	25♋
8	16♍	5♍	0♌	26♋
9	17♍	5♍	1♌	26♋
10	18♍	4♍	2♌	27♋
11	18♍	4♍	3♌	28♋
12	19♍	4♍	4♌	28♋
13	20♍	4♍	5♌	29♋
14	21♍	5♍	6♌	29♋
15	22♍	5♍	7♌	0♌
16	23♍	6♍	8♌	1♌
17	24♍	7♍	9♌	1♌
18	25♍	7♍	11♌	2♌
19	26♍	8♍	12♌	2♌
20	27♍	10♍	13♌	3♌
21	28♍	11♍	14♌	4♌
22	29♍	12♍	15♌	4♌
23	0♎	14♍	16♌	5♌
24	1♎	15♍	17♌	6♌
25	2♎	17♍	18♌	6♌
26	3♎	18♍	19♌	7♌
27	4♎	20♍	20♌	7♌
28	5♎	22♍	21♌	8♌
29	6♎	23♍	23♌	9♌
30	7♎	25♍	24♌	9♌

December

Day	☉	☿	♀	♂
1	9♐	0♑	8♏	12♍
2	10♐	1♑	9♏	13♍
3	11♐	2♑	10♏	13♍
4	12♐	3♑	11♏	14♍
5	13♐	4♑	13♏	14♍
6	14♐	4♑	14♏	15♍
7	15♐	5♑	15♏	15♍
8	16♐	5♑	16♏	15♍
9	17♐	5♑	17♏	16♍
10	18♐	5♑	19♏	16♍
11	19♐	5♑	20♏	17♍
12	20♐	4♑	21♏	17♍
13	21♐	3♑	22♏	17♍
14	22♐	3♑	24♏	18♍
15	23♐	2♑	25♏	18♍
16	24♐	0♑	26♏	19♍
17	25♐	29♐	27♏	19♍
18	26♐	28♐	29♏	19♍
19	27♐	26♐	0♐	20♍
20	28♐	25♐	1♐	20♍
21	29♐	24♐	2♐	20♍
22	0♑	23♐	4♐	21♍
23	1♑	22♐	5♐	21♍
24	2♑	21♐	6♐	21♍
25	3♑	20♐	7♐	22♍
26	4♑	19♐	9♐	22♍
27	5♑	19♐	10♐	22♍
28	7♑	19♐	11♐	23♍
29	8♑	19♐	12♐	23♍
30	9♑	19♐	14♐	23♍
31	10♑	19♐	15♐	24♍

1965

☉ =Sun ☿ = Mercury ♀ = Venus ♂ = Mars ♈ = Aries ♉ = Taurus ♊ = Gemini ♋ = Cancer

January

Day	☉	☿	♀	♂
1	11♑	19♐	16♐	24♍
2	12♑	20♐	17♐	24♍
3	13♑	20♐	19♐	24♍
4	14♑	21♐	20♐	25♍
5	15♑	22♐	21♐	25♍
6	16♑	23♐	22♐	25♍
7	17♑	24♐	24♐	25♍
8	18♑	25♐	25♐	26♍
9	19♑	26♐	26♐	26♍
10	20♑	27♐	27♐	26♍
11	21♑	28♐	29♐	26♍
12	22♑	29♐	0♑	26♍
13	23♑	0♑	1♑	27♍
14	24♑	1♑	2♑	27♍
15	25♑	3♑	4♑	27♍
16	26♑	4♑	5♑	27♍
17	27♑	5♑	6♑	27♍
18	28♑	6♑	7♑	27♍
19	29♑	8♑	9♑	27♍
20	0♒	9♑	10♑	28♍
21	1♒	11♑	11♑	28♍
22	2♒	12♑	12♑	28♍
23	3♒	13♑	14♑	28♍
24	4♒	15♑	15♑	28♍
25	5♒	16♑	16♑	28♍
26	6♒	18♑	17♑	28♍
27	7♒	19♑	19♑	28♍
28	8♒	21♑	20♑	28♍
29	9♒	22♑	21♑	28♍
30	10♒	24♑	22♑	28♍
31	11♒	25♑	24♑	28♍

February

Day	☉	☿	♀	♂
1	12♒	27♑	25♑	28♍
2	13♒	28♑	26♑	28♍
3	14♒	0♒	27♑	28♍
4	15♒	1♒	29♑	28♍
5	16♒	3♒	0♒	28♍
6	17♒	4♒	1♒	28♍
7	18♒	6♒	2♒	27♍
8	19♒	8♒	4♒	27♍
9	20♒	9♒	5♒	27♍
10	21♒	11♒	6♒	27♍
11	22♒	13♒	7♒	27♍
12	23♒	14♒	9♒	27♍
13	24♒	16♒	10♒	27♍
14	25♒	18♒	11♒	26♍
15	26♒	19♒	12♒	26♍
16	27♒	21♒	14♒	26♍
17	28♒	23♒	15♒	26♍
18	29♒	25♒	16♒	25♍
19	0♓	26♒	17♒	25♍
20	1♓	28♒	19♒	25♍
21	2♓	0♓	20♒	25♍
22	3♓	2♓	21♒	24♍
23	4♓	4♓	22♒	24♍
24	5♓	5♓	24♒	24♍
25	6♓	7♓	25♒	23♍
26	7♓	9♓	26♒	23♍
27	8♓	11♓	27♒	23♍
28	9♓	13♓	29♒	22♍

March

Day	☉	☿	♀	♂
1	10♓	15♓	0♓	22♍
2	11♓	17♓	1♓	22♍
3	12♓	19♓	2♓	21♍
4	13♓	21♓	4♓	21♍
5	14♓	23♓	5♓	20♍
6	15♓	25♓	6♓	20♍
7	16♓	26♓	7♓	20♍
8	17♓	28♓	9♓	19♍
9	18♓	0♈	10♓	19♍
10	19♓	2♈	11♓	18♍
11	20♓	4♈	12♓	18♍
12	21♓	6♈	14♓	18♍
13	22♓	7♈	15♓	17♍
14	23♓	9♈	16♓	17♍
15	24♓	11♈	17♓	16♍
16	25♓	12♈	19♓	16♍
17	26♓	14♈	20♓	16♍
18	27♓	15♈	21♓	15♍
19	28♓	17♈	22♓	15♍
20	29♓	18♈	24♓	15♍
21	0♈	19♈	25♓	14♍
22	1♈	20♈	26♓	14♍
23	2♈	21♈	27♓	14♍
24	3♈	21♈	29♓	13♍
25	4♈	22♈	0♈	13♍
26	5♈	23♈	1♈	13♍
27	6♈	23♈	2♈	12♍
28	7♈	23♈	3♈	12♍
29	8♈	23♈	5♈	12♍
30	9♈	23♈	6♈	11♍
31	10♈	23♈	7♈	11♍

April

Day	☉	☿	♀	♂
1	11♈	23♈	8♈	11♍
2	12♈	23♈	10♈	11♍
3	13♈	22♈	11♈	11♍
4	14♈	22♈	12♈	10♍
5	15♈	21♈	13♈	10♍
6	16♈	20♈	15♈	10♍
7	17♈	20♈	16♈	10♍
8	18♈	19♈	17♈	10♍
9	19♈	18♈	18♈	9♍
10	20♈	17♈	20♈	9♍
11	21♈	16♈	21♈	9♍
12	22♈	16♈	22♈	9♍
13	23♈	15♈	23♈	9♍
14	24♈	14♈	25♈	9♍
15	25♈	14♈	26♈	9♍
16	26♈	13♈	27♈	9♍
17	27♈	13♈	28♈	9♍
18	28♈	12♈	0♉	9♍
19	29♈	12♈	1♉	9♍
20	0♉	12♈	2♉	9♍
21	1♉	12♈	3♉	9♍
22	2♉	12♈	4♉	9♍
23	3♉	12♈	6♉	9♍
24	4♉	12♈	7♉	9♍
25	5♉	12♈	8♉	9♍
26	6♉	12♈	9♉	9♍
27	7♉	13♈	11♉	9♍
28	8♉	13♈	12♉	9♍
29	9♉	14♈	13♉	9♍
30	10♉	14♈	14♉	9♍

May

Day	☉	☿	♀	♂
1	11♉	15♈	16♉	9♍
2	12♉	16♈	17♉	10♍
3	13♉	16♈	18♉	10♍
4	14♉	17♈	19♉	10♍
5	14♉	18♈	21♉	10♍
6	15♉	19♈	22♉	10♍
7	16♉	20♈	23♉	10♍
8	17♉	21♈	24♉	11♍
9	18♉	22♈	25♉	11♍
10	19♉	23♈	27♉	11♍
11	20♉	24♈	28♉	11♍
12	21♉	26♈	29♉	11♍
13	22♉	27♈	0♊	12♍
14	23♉	28♈	2♊	12♍
15	24♉	0♉	3♊	12♍
16	25♉	1♉	4♊	13♍
17	26♉	2♉	5♊	13♍
18	27♉	4♉	7♊	13♍
19	28♉	5♉	8♊	13♍
20	29♉	7♉	9♊	14♍
21	0♊	8♉	10♊	14♍
22	1♊	10♉	11♊	14♍
23	2♊	12♉	13♊	15♍
24	3♊	13♉	14♊	15♍
25	4♊	15♉	15♊	15♍
26	5♊	17♉	16♊	16♍
27	6♊	19♉	18♊	16♍
28	7♊	20♉	19♊	16♍
29	8♊	22♉	20♊	17♍
30	9♊	24♉	21♊	17♍
31	10♊	26♉	22♊	17♍

June

Day	☉	☿	♀	♂
1	10♊	28♉	24♊	18♍
2	11♊	0♊	25♊	18♍
3	12♊	2♊	26♊	18♍
4	13♊	4♊	27♊	19♍
5	14♊	6♊	29♊	19♍
6	15♊	8♊	0♋	20♍
7	16♊	11♊	1♋	20♍
8	17♊	13♊	2♋	20♍
9	18♊	15♊	3♋	21♍
10	19♊	17♊	5♋	21♍
11	20♊	19♊	6♋	22♍
12	21♊	22♊	7♋	22♍
13	22♊	24♊	8♋	23♍
14	23♊	26♊	10♋	23♍
15	24♊	28♊	11♋	23♍
16	25♊	0♋	12♋	24♍
17	26♊	2♋	13♋	24♍
18	27♊	5♋	14♋	25♍
19	28♊	7♋	16♋	25♍
20	29♊	9♋	17♋	26♍
21	0♋	11♋	18♋	26♍
22	1♋	13♋	19♋	27♍
23	2♋	15♋	21♋	27♍
24	2♋	17♋	22♋	28♍
25	3♋	19♋	23♋	28♍
26	4♋	20♋	24♋	29♍
27	5♋	22♋	25♋	29♍
28	6♋	24♋	27♋	0♎
29	7♋	26♋	28♋	0♎
30	8♋	28♋	29♋	1♎

July

Day	☉	☿	♀	♂
1	9♋	29♋	0♌	1♎
2	10♋	1♌	2♌	2♎
3	11♋	3♌	3♌	2♎
4	12♋	4♌	4♌	3♎
5	13♋	6♌	5♌	3♎
6	14♋	7♌	6♌	4♎
7	15♋	9♌	8♌	4♎
8	16♋	10♌	9♌	5♎
9	17♋	11♌	10♌	5♎
10	18♋	13♌	11♌	6♎
11	19♋	14♌	13♌	6♎
12	20♋	15♌	14♌	7♎
13	21♋	17♌	15♌	7♎
14	22♋	18♌	16♌	8♎
15	22♋	19♌	17♌	8♎
16	23♋	20♌	19♌	9♎
17	24♋	21♌	20♌	10♎
18	25♋	22♌	21♌	10♎
19	26♋	23♌	22♌	11♎
20	27♋	24♌	23♌	11♎
21	28♋	25♌	25♌	12♎
22	29♋	26♌	26♌	12♎
23	0♌	26♌	27♌	13♎
24	1♌	27♌	28♌	14♎
25	2♌	28♌	0♍	14♎
26	3♌	28♌	1♍	15♎
27	4♌	29♌	2♍	15♎
28	5♌	29♌	3♍	16♎
29	6♌	0♍	4♍	16♎
30	7♌	0♍	6♍	17♎
31	8♌	0♍	7♍	18♎

August

Day	☉	☿	♀	♂
1	9♌	0♍	8♍	18♎
2	10♌	0♍	9♍	19♎
3	11♌	0♍	10♍	19♎
4	12♌	0♍	12♍	20♎
5	13♌	0♍	13♍	21♎
6	14♌	29♌	14♍	21♎
7	14♌	29♌	15♍	22♎
8	15♌	28♌	16♍	22♎
9	16♌	28♌	18♍	23♎
10	17♌	27♌	19♍	24♎
11	18♌	26♌	20♍	24♎
12	19♌	26♌	21♍	25♎
13	20♌	25♌	22♍	25♎
14	21♌	24♌	24♍	26♎
15	22♌	23♌	25♍	27♎
16	23♌	22♌	26♍	27♎
17	24♌	22♌	27♍	28♎
18	25♌	21♌	28♍	29♎
19	26♌	20♌	0♎	29♎
20	27♌	19♌	1♎	0♏
21	28♌	19♌	2♎	0♏
22	29♌	18♌	3♎	1♏
23	0♍	18♌	4♎	2♏
24	1♍	18♌	6♎	2♏
25	2♍	18♌	7♎	3♏
26	3♍	18♌	8♎	4♏
27	4♍	18♌	9♎	4♏
28	5♍	18♌	10♎	5♏
29	6♍	18♌	12♎	6♏
30	7♍	19♌	13♎	6♏
31	8♍	20♌	14♎	7♏

September

Day	☉	☿	♀	♂
1	9♍	20♌	15♎	8♏
2	10♍	21♌	16♎	8♏
3	10♍	22♌	17♎	9♏
4	11♍	24♌	19♎	9♏
5	12♍	25♌	20♎	10♏
6	13♍	26♌	21♎	11♏
7	14♍	28♌	22♎	11♏
8	15♍	29♌	23♎	12♏
9	16♍	1♍	25♎	13♏
10	17♍	2♍	26♎	13♏
11	18♍	4♍	27♎	14♏
12	19♍	6♍	28♎	15♏
13	20♍	8♍	29♎	15♏
14	21♍	10♍	0♏	16♏
15	22♍	11♍	2♏	17♏
16	23♍	13♍	3♏	17♏
17	24♍	15♍	4♏	18♏
18	25♍	17♍	5♏	19♏
19	26♍	19♍	6♏	20♏
20	27♍	21♍	7♏	20♏
21	28♍	23♍	9♏	21♏
22	29♍	24♍	10♏	22♏
23	0♎	26♍	11♏	22♏
24	1♎	28♍	12♏	23♏
25	2♎	0♎	13♏	24♏
26	3♎	2♎	14♏	24♏
27	4♎	4♎	16♏	25♏
28	5♎	5♎	17♏	26♏
29	6♎	7♎	18♏	26♏
30	7♎	9♎	19♏	27♏

October

Day	☉	☿	♀	♂
1	8♎	11♎	20♏	28♏
2	9♎	12♎	21♏	29♏
3	10♎	14♎	23♏	29♏
4	11♎	16♎	24♏	0♐
5	12♎	17♎	25♏	1♐
6	13♎	19♎	26♏	1♐
7	14♎	21♎	27♏	2♐
8	15♎	22♎	28♏	3♐
9	16♎	24♎	29♏	3♐
10	17♎	26♎	1♐	4♐
11	18♎	27♎	2♐	5♐
12	19♎	29♎	3♐	6♐
13	20♎	1♏	4♐	6♐
14	21♎	2♏	5♐	7♐
15	22♎	4♏	6♐	8♐
16	23♎	5♏	7♐	9♐
17	24♎	7♏	9♐	9♐
18	25♎	8♏	10♐	10♐
19	26♎	10♏	11♐	11♐
20	27♎	11♏	12♐	11♐
21	28♎	13♏	13♐	12♐
22	29♎	14♏	14♐	13♐
23	0♏	16♏	15♐	14♐
24	1♏	17♏	16♐	14♐
25	2♏	19♏	17♐	15♐
26	3♏	20♏	19♐	16♐
27	4♏	22♏	20♐	17♐
28	5♏	23♏	21♐	17♐
29	6♏	24♏	22♐	18♐
30	7♏	26♏	23♐	19♐
31	8♏	27♏	24♐	19♐

November

Day	☉	☿	♀	♂
1	9♏	29♏	25♐	20♐
2	10♏	0♐	26♐	21♐
3	11♏	1♐	27♐	22♐
4	12♏	3♐	28♐	22♐
5	13♏	4♐	29♐	23♐
6	14♏	5♐	0♑	24♐
7	15♏	6♐	1♑	25♐
8	16♏	8♐	3♑	25♐
9	17♏	9♐	4♑	26♐
10	18♏	10♐	5♑	27♐
11	19♏	11♐	6♑	28♐
12	20♏	12♐	7♑	28♐
13	21♏	13♐	8♑	29♐
14	22♏	14♐	9♑	0♑
15	23♏	15♐	10♑	1♑
16	24♏	16♐	11♑	1♑
17	25♏	17♐	12♑	2♑
18	26♏	17♐	13♑	3♑
19	27♏	18♐	14♑	4♑
20	28♏	18♐	15♑	4♑
21	29♏	19♐	16♑	5♑
22	0♐	19♐	17♑	6♑
23	1♐	19♐	18♑	7♑
24	2♐	19♐	19♑	8♑
25	3♐	19♐	20♑	8♑
26	4♐	18♐	20♑	9♑
27	5♐	18♐	21♑	10♑
28	6♐	17♐	22♑	11♑
29	7♐	16♐	23♑	11♑
30	8♐	15♐	24♑	12♑

December

Day	☉	☿	♀	♂
1	9♐	13♐	25♑	13♑
2	10♐	12♐	26♑	14♑
3	11♐	11♐	27♑	14♑
4	12♐	9♐	28♑	15♑
5	13♐	8♐	28♑	16♑
6	14♐	7♐	29♑	17♑
7	15♐	6♐	0♒	18♑
8	16♐	5♐	1♒	18♑
9	17♐	4♐	2♒	19♑
10	18♐	3♐	2♒	20♑
11	19♐	3♐	3♒	21♑
12	20♐	3♐	4♒	21♑
13	21♐	3♐	5♒	22♑
14	22♐	3♐	5♒	23♑
15	23♐	3♐	6♒	24♑
16	24♐	4♐	7♒	25♑
17	25♐	4♐	7♒	25♑
18	26♐	5♐	8♒	26♑
19	27♐	6♐	8♒	27♑
20	28♐	7♐	9♒	28♑
21	29♐	7♐	9♒	28♑
22	0♑	8♐	10♒	29♑
23	1♑	9♐	10♒	0♒
24	2♑	11♐	11♒	1♒
25	3♑	12♐	11♒	2♒
26	4♑	13♐	12♒	2♒
27	5♑	14♐	12♒	3♒
28	6♑	15♐	12♒	4♒
29	7♑	17♐	13♒	5♒
30	8♑	18♐	13♒	5♒
31	9♑	19♐	13♒	6♒

Planetary Positions

♌ = Leo ♍ = Virgo ♎ = Libra ♏ = Scorpio ♐ = Sagittarius ♑ = Capricorn ♒ = Aquarius ♓ = Pisces

1966

January

Day	☉	☿	♀	♂
1	10♑	21♐	13♒	7♒
2	11♑	22♐	14♒	8♒
3	12♑	23♐	14♒	9♒
4	13♑	25♐	14♒	9♒
5	14♑	26♐	14♒	10♒
6	15♑	28♐	14♒	11♒
7	16♑	29♐	14♒	12♒
8	17♑	1♑	14♒	13♒
9	18♑	2♑	14♒	13♒
10	20♑	4♑	13♒	14♒
11	21♑	5♑	13♒	15♒
12	22♑	7♑	13♒	16♒
13	23♑	8♑	13♒	17♒
14	24♑	10♑	12♒	17♒
15	25♑	11♑	12♒	18♒
16	26♑	13♑	12♒	19♒
17	27♑	14♑	11♒	20♒
18	28♑	16♑	11♒	20♒
19	29♑	17♑	10♒	21♒
20	0♒	19♑	10♒	22♒
21	1♒	20♑	9♒	23♒
22	2♒	22♑	8♒	24♒
23	3♒	24♑	8♒	24♒
24	4♒	25♑	7♒	25♒
25	5♒	27♑	7♒	26♒
26	6♒	28♑	6♒	27♒
27	7♒	0♒	5♒	28♒
28	8♒	2♒	5♒	28♒
29	9♒	3♒	4♒	29♒
30	10♒	5♒	4♒	0♓
31	11♒	7♒	3♒	1♓

February

Day	☉	☿	♀	♂
1	12♒	8♒	2♒	2♓
2	13♒	10♒	2♒	2♓
3	14♒	12♒	1♒	3♓
4	15♒	14♒	1♒	4♓
5	16♒	15♒	1♒	5♓
6	17♒	17♒	0♒	5♓
7	18♒	19♒	0♒	6♓
8	19♒	21♒	29♑	7♓
9	20♒	22♒	29♑	8♓
10	21♒	24♒	29♑	9♓
11	22♒	26♒	29♑	9♓
12	23♒	28♒	28♑	10♓
13	24♒	0♓	28♑	11♓
14	25♒	1♓	28♑	12♓
15	26♒	3♓	28♑	13♓
16	27♒	5♓	28♑	13♓
17	28♒	7♓	28♑	14♓
18	29♒	9♓	28♑	15♓
19	0♓	11♓	28♑	16♓
20	1♓	12♓	29♑	16♓
21	2♓	14♓	29♑	17♓
22	3♓	16♓	29♑	18♓
23	4♓	18♓	29♑	19♓
24	5♓	20♓	0♒	20♓
25	6♓	21♓	0♒	20♓
26	7♓	23♓	0♒	21♓
27	8♓	25♓	1♒	22♓
28	9♓	26♓	1♒	23♓

March

Day	☉	☿	♀	♂
1	10♓	27♓	2♒	24♓
2	11♓	29♓	2♒	24♓
3	12♓	0♈	2♒	25♓
4	13♓	1♈	3♒	26♓
5	14♓	2♈	4♒	27♓
6	15♓	3♈	4♒	27♓
7	16♓	4♈	5♒	28♓
8	17♓	5♈	5♒	29♓
9	18♓	5♈	6♒	0♈
10	19♓	5♈	7♒	1♈
11	20♓	6♈	7♒	1♈
12	21♓	6♈	8♒	2♈
13	22♓	6♈	9♒	3♈
14	23♓	5♈	9♒	4♈
15	24♓	5♈	10♒	4♈
16	25♓	5♈	11♒	5♈
17	26♓	4♈	12♒	6♈
18	27♓	3♈	12♒	7♈
19	28♓	3♈	13♒	7♈
20	29♓	2♈	14♒	8♈
21	0♈	1♈	15♒	9♈
22	1♈	0♈	16♒	10♈
23	2♈	29♓	17♒	11♈
24	3♈	28♓	17♒	11♈
25	4♈	27♓	18♒	12♈
26	5♈	26♓	19♒	13♈
27	6♈	26♓	20♒	14♈
28	7♈	25♓	21♒	14♈
29	8♈	24♓	22♒	15♈
30	9♈	24♓	23♒	16♈
31	10♈	23♓	24♒	17♈

April

Day	☉	☿	♀	♂
1	11♈	23♓	25♒	17♈
2	12♈	23♓	26♒	18♈
3	13♈	23♓	27♒	19♈
4	14♈	23♓	28♒	20♈
5	15♈	23♓	29♒	20♈
6	16♈	23♓	0♓	21♈
7	17♈	23♓	1♓	22♈
8	18♈	23♓	2♓	23♈
9	19♈	24♓	3♓	23♈
10	20♈	24♓	4♓	24♈
11	21♈	25♓	5♓	25♈
12	22♈	25♓	6♓	26♈
13	23♈	26♓	7♓	27♈
14	24♈	27♓	8♓	27♈
15	25♈	28♓	9♓	28♈
16	26♈	28♓	10♓	29♈
17	27♈	29♓	11♓	0♉
18	28♈	0♈	12♓	0♉
19	29♈	1♈	13♓	1♉
20	0♉	2♈	14♓	2♉
21	1♉	3♈	15♓	3♉
22	2♉	5♈	16♓	3♉
23	3♉	6♈	17♓	4♉
24	4♉	7♈	18♓	5♉
25	5♉	8♈	19♓	5♉
26	6♉	9♈	20♓	6♉
27	6♉	11♈	21♓	7♉
28	7♉	12♈	22♓	8♉
29	8♉	14♈	23♓	8♉
30	9♉	15♈	25♓	9♉

May

Day	☉	☿	♀	♂
1	10♉	16♈	26♓	10♉
2	11♉	18♈	27♓	11♉
3	12♉	19♈	28♓	11♉
4	13♉	21♈	29♓	12♉
5	14♉	23♈	0♈	13♉
6	15♉	24♈	1♈	14♉
7	16♉	26♈	2♈	14♉
8	17♉	28♈	3♈	15♉
9	18♉	29♈	4♈	16♉
10	19♉	1♉	6♈	17♉
11	20♉	3♉	7♈	17♉
12	21♉	5♉	8♈	18♉
13	22♉	6♉	9♈	19♉
14	23♉	8♉	10♈	19♉
15	24♉	10♉	11♈	20♉
16	25♉	12♉	12♈	21♉
17	26♉	14♉	13♈	22♉
18	27♉	16♉	15♈	22♉
19	28♉	18♉	16♈	23♉
20	29♉	20♉	17♈	24♉
21	0♊	22♉	18♈	24♉
22	1♊	25♉	19♈	25♉
23	2♊	27♉	20♈	26♉
24	3♊	29♉	21♈	27♉
25	4♊	1♊	23♈	27♉
26	5♊	3♊	24♈	28♉
27	5♊	5♊	25♈	29♉
28	6♊	8♊	26♈	29♉
29	7♊	10♊	27♈	0♊
30	8♊	12♊	28♈	1♊
31	9♊	14♊	29♈	2♊

June

Day	☉	☿	♀	♂
1	10♊	16♊	1♉	2♊
2	11♊	18♊	2♉	3♊
3	12♊	21♊	3♉	4♊
4	13♊	23♊	4♉	4♊
5	14♊	25♊	5♉	5♊
6	15♊	27♊	6♉	6♊
7	16♊	29♊	7♉	7♊
8	17♊	1♋	9♉	7♊
9	18♊	3♋	10♉	8♊
10	19♊	5♋	11♉	9♊
11	20♊	6♋	12♉	9♊
12	21♊	8♋	13♉	10♊
13	22♊	10♋	14♉	11♊
14	23♊	12♋	16♉	11♊
15	24♊	14♋	17♉	12♊
16	25♊	15♋	18♉	13♊
17	26♊	17♋	19♉	14♊
18	27♊	18♋	20♉	14♊
19	27♊	20♋	21♉	15♊
20	28♊	21♋	23♉	16♊
21	29♊	23♋	24♉	16♊
22	0♋	24♋	25♉	17♊
23	1♋	26♋	26♉	18♊
24	2♋	27♋	27♉	18♊
25	3♋	28♋	28♉	19♊
26	4♋	29♋	0♊	20♊
27	5♋	0♌	1♊	21♊
28	6♋	2♌	2♊	21♊
29	7♋	3♌	3♊	22♊
30	8♋	4♌	4♊	23♊

July

Day	☉	☿	♀	♂
1	9♋	5♌	6♊	23♊
2	10♋	6♌	7♊	24♊
3	11♋	6♌	8♊	25♊
4	12♋	7♌	9♊	25♊
5	13♋	8♌	10♊	26♊
6	14♋	9♌	11♊	27♊
7	15♋	9♌	13♊	27♊
8	16♋	10♌	14♊	28♊
9	17♋	10♌	15♊	29♊
10	17♋	11♌	16♊	29♊
11	18♋	11♌	17♊	0♋
12	19♋	11♌	19♊	1♋
13	20♋	11♌	20♊	1♋
14	21♋	11♌	21♊	2♋
15	22♋	11♌	22♊	3♋
16	23♋	11♌	23♊	3♋
17	24♋	11♌	25♊	4♋
18	25♋	11♌	26♊	5♋
19	26♋	11♌	27♊	5♋
20	27♋	10♌	28♊	6♋
21	28♋	10♌	29♊	7♋
22	29♋	9♌	1♋	7♋
23	0♌	9♌	2♋	8♋
24	1♌	8♌	3♋	9♋
25	2♌	7♌	4♋	9♋
26	3♌	7♌	5♋	10♋
27	4♌	6♌	7♋	11♋
28	5♌	5♌	8♋	11♋
29	6♌	5♌	9♋	12♋
30	7♌	4♌	10♋	13♋
31	8♌	3♌	11♋	13♋

August

Day	☉	☿	♀	♂
1	9♌	3♌	13♋	14♋
2	9♌	2♌	14♋	15♋
3	10♌	2♌	15♋	15♋
4	11♌	1♌	16♋	16♋
5	12♌	1♌	17♋	17♋
6	13♌	1♌	19♋	17♋
7	14♌	0♌	20♋	18♋
8	15♌	0♌	21♋	19♋
9	16♌	0♌	22♋	19♋
10	17♌	1♌	24♋	20♋
11	18♌	1♌	25♋	21♋
12	19♌	1♌	26♋	21♋
13	20♌	2♌	27♋	22♋
14	21♌	3♌	28♋	23♋
15	22♌	3♌	0♌	23♋
16	23♌	4♌	1♌	24♋
17	24♌	5♌	2♌	25♋
18	25♌	6♌	3♌	25♋
19	26♌	8♌	4♌	26♋
20	27♌	9♌	6♌	26♋
21	28♌	10♌	7♌	27♋
22	29♌	12♌	8♌	28♋
23	0♍	13♌	9♌	28♋
24	1♍	15♌	11♌	29♋
25	2♍	17♌	12♌	0♌
26	3♍	18♌	13♌	0♌
27	3♍	20♌	14♌	1♌
28	4♍	22♌	16♌	2♌
29	5♍	24♌	17♌	2♌
30	6♍	26♌	18♌	3♌
31	7♍	28♌	19♌	4♌

September

Day	☉	☿	♀	♂
1	8♍	0♍	20♌	4♌
2	9♍	1♍	22♌	5♌
3	10♍	3♍	23♌	5♌
4	11♍	5♍	24♌	6♌
5	12♍	7♍	25♌	7♌
6	13♍	9♍	27♌	7♌
7	14♍	11♍	28♌	8♌
8	15♍	13♍	29♌	9♌
9	16♍	15♍	0♍	9♌
10	17♍	17♍	2♍	10♌
11	18♍	19♍	3♍	11♌
12	19♍	21♍	4♍	11♌
13	20♍	23♍	5♍	12♌
14	21♍	24♍	6♍	12♌
15	22♍	26♍	8♍	13♌
16	23♍	28♍	9♍	14♌
17	24♍	0♎	10♍	14♌
18	25♍	2♎	11♍	15♌
19	26♍	3♎	13♍	16♌
20	27♍	5♎	14♍	16♌
21	28♍	7♎	15♍	17♌
22	29♍	8♎	16♍	17♌
23	0♎	10♎	18♍	18♌
24	1♎	12♎	19♍	19♌
25	2♎	13♎	20♍	19♌
26	3♎	15♎	21♍	20♌
27	4♎	17♎	23♍	20♌
28	5♎	18♎	24♍	21♌
29	6♎	20♎	25♍	22♌
30	7♎	21♎	26♍	22♌

October

Day	☉	☿	♀	♂
1	8♎	23♎	28♍	23♌
2	9♎	24♎	29♍	24♌
3	10♎	26♎	0♎	24♌
4	11♎	27♎	1♎	25♌
5	12♎	29♎	3♎	25♌
6	12♎	0♏	4♎	26♌
7	13♎	2♏	5♎	27♌
8	14♎	3♏	6♎	27♌
9	15♎	5♏	8♎	28♌
10	16♎	6♏	9♎	28♌
11	17♎	8♏	10♎	29♌
12	18♎	9♏	11♎	0♍
13	19♎	10♏	13♎	0♍
14	20♎	12♏	14♎	1♍
15	21♎	13♏	15♎	1♍
16	22♎	14♏	16♎	2♍
17	23♎	16♏	18♎	3♍
18	24♎	17♏	19♎	3♍
19	25♎	18♏	20♎	4♍
20	26♎	19♏	21♎	4♍
21	27♎	21♏	23♎	5♍
22	28♎	22♏	24♎	6♍
23	29♎	23♏	25♎	6♍
24	0♏	24♏	26♎	7♍
25	1♏	25♏	28♎	7♍
26	2♏	26♏	29♎	8♍
27	3♏	27♏	0♏	9♍
28	4♏	28♏	1♏	9♍
29	5♏	29♏	3♏	10♍
30	6♏	0♐	4♏	10♍
31	7♏	1♐	5♏	11♍

November

Day	☉	☿	♀	♂
1	8♏	1♐	6♏	12♍
2	9♏	2♐	8♏	12♍
3	10♏	2♐	9♏	13♍
4	11♏	3♐	10♏	13♍
5	12♏	3♐	11♏	14♍
6	13♏	3♐	13♏	14♍
7	14♏	3♐	14♏	15♍
8	15♏	3♐	15♏	16♍
9	16♏	3♐	16♏	16♍
10	17♏	2♐	18♏	17♍
11	18♏	2♐	19♏	17♍
12	19♏	1♐	20♏	18♍
13	20♏	0♐	21♏	18♍
14	21♏	29♏	23♏	19♍
15	22♏	28♏	24♏	20♍
16	23♏	26♏	25♏	20♍
17	24♏	25♏	26♏	21♍
18	25♏	24♏	28♏	21♍
19	26♏	22♏	29♏	22♍
20	27♏	21♏	0♐	22♍
21	28♏	20♏	1♐	23♍
22	29♏	19♏	3♐	24♍
23	0♐	18♏	4♐	24♍
24	1♐	18♏	5♐	25♍
25	2♐	17♏	6♐	25♍
26	3♐	17♏	8♐	26♍
27	4♐	17♏	9♐	26♍
28	6♐	17♏	10♐	27♍
29	7♐	18♏	12♐	27♍
30	8♐	18♏	13♐	28♍

December

Day	☉	☿	♀	♂
1	9♐	19♏	14♐	28♍
2	10♐	19♏	15♐	29♍
3	11♐	20♏	17♐	0♎
4	12♐	21♏	18♐	0♎
5	13♐	22♏	19♐	1♎
6	14♐	23♏	20♐	1♎
7	15♐	24♏	22♐	2♎
8	16♐	26♏	23♐	2♎
9	17♐	27♏	24♐	3♎
10	18♐	28♏	25♐	3♎
11	19♐	29♏	27♐	4♎
12	20♐	1♐	28♐	4♎
13	21♐	2♐	29♐	5♎
14	22♐	4♐	0♑	5♎
15	23♐	5♐	2♑	6♎
16	24♐	6♐	3♑	6♎
17	25♐	8♐	4♑	7♎
18	26♐	9♐	5♑	7♎
19	27♐	11♐	7♑	8♎
20	28♐	12♐	8♑	8♎
21	29♐	14♐	9♑	9♎
22	0♑	15♐	10♑	9♎
23	1♑	17♐	12♑	10♎
24	2♑	18♐	13♑	10♎
25	3♑	20♐	14♑	11♎
26	4♑	21♐	15♑	11♎
27	5♑	23♐	17♑	12♎
28	6♑	24♐	18♑	12♎
29	7♑	26♐	19♑	13♎
30	8♑	27♐	20♑	13♎
31	9♑	29♐	22♑	14♎

☉ =Sun ☿ = Mercury ♀ = Venus ♂ = Mars ♈ = Aries ♉ = Taurus ♊ = Gemini ♋ = Cancer

1967

January

Day	☉	☿	♀	♂
1	10♑	0♑	23♑	14♎
2	11♑	2♑	24♑	15♎
3	12♑	3♑	25♑	15♎
4	13♑	5♑	27♑	16♎
5	14♑	6♑	28♑	16♎
6	15♑	8♑	29♑	17♎
7	16♑	10♑	0♒	17♎
8	17♑	11♑	2♒	17♎
9	18♑	13♑	3♒	18♎
10	19♑	14♑	4♒	18♎
11	20♑	16♑	6♒	19♎
12	21♑	18♑	7♒	19♎
13	22♑	19♑	8♒	20♎
14	23♑	21♑	9♒	20♎
15	24♑	23♑	11♒	20♎
16	25♑	24♑	12♒	21♎
17	26♑	26♑	13♒	21♎
18	27♑	27♑	14♒	22♎
19	28♑	29♑	16♒	22♎
20	29♑	1♒	17♒	22♎
21	0♒	3♒	18♒	23♎
22	1♒	4♒	19♒	23♎
23	2♒	6♒	21♒	24♎
24	4♒	8♒	22♒	24♎
25	5♒	9♒	23♒	24♎
26	6♒	11♒	24♒	25♎
27	7♒	13♒	26♒	25♎
28	8♒	15♒	27♒	25♎
29	9♒	16♒	28♒	26♎
30	10♒	18♒	29♒	26♎
31	11♒	20♒	1♓	26♎

February

Day	☉	☿	♀	♂
1	12♒	22♒	2♓	27♎
2	13♒	23♒	3♓	27♎
3	14♒	25♒	4♓	27♎
4	15♒	27♒	6♓	28♎
5	16♒	29♒	7♓	28♎
6	17♒	0♓	8♓	28♎
7	18♒	2♓	9♓	29♎
8	19♒	4♓	10♓	29♎
9	20♒	5♓	12♓	29♎
10	21♒	7♓	13♓	29♎
11	22♒	8♓	14♓	0♏
12	23♒	10♓	15♓	0♏
13	24♒	11♓	17♓	0♏
14	25♒	13♓	18♓	0♏
15	26♒	14♓	19♓	1♏
16	27♒	15♓	20♓	1♏
17	28♒	16♓	22♓	1♏
18	29♒	17♓	23♓	1♏
19	0♓	18♓	24♓	1♏
20	1♓	18♓	25♓	2♏
21	2♓	18♓	27♓	2♏
22	3♓	19♓	28♓	2♏
23	4♓	19♓	29♓	2♏
24	5♓	19♓	0♈	2♏
25	6♓	18♓	2♈	2♏
26	7♓	18♓	3♈	3♏
27	8♓	18♓	4♈	3♏
28	9♓	17♓	5♈	3♏

March

Day	☉	☿	♀	♂
1	10♓	16♓	7♈	3♏
2	11♓	15♓	8♈	3♏
3	12♓	14♓	9♈	3♏
4	13♓	13♓	10♈	3♏
5	14♓	12♓	11♈	3♏
6	15♓	11♓	13♈	3♏
7	16♓	10♓	14♈	3♏
8	17♓	9♓	15♈	3♏
9	18♓	8♓	16♈	3♏
10	19♓	7♓	18♈	3♏
11	20♓	7♓	19♈	3♏
12	21♓	6♓	20♈	3♏
13	22♓	6♓	21♈	3♏
14	23♓	5♓	22♈	3♏
15	24♓	5♓	24♈	3♏
16	25♓	5♓	25♈	3♏
17	26♓	5♓	26♈	3♏
18	27♓	5♓	27♈	3♏
19	28♓	5♓	29♈	3♏
20	29♓	5♓	0♉	2♏
21	0♈	5♓	1♉	2♏
22	1♈	6♓	2♉	2♏
23	2♈	6♓	3♉	2♏
24	3♈	7♓	5♉	2♏
25	4♈	7♓	6♉	1♏
26	5♈	8♓	7♉	1♏
27	6♈	9♓	8♉	1♏
28	7♈	9♓	9♉	1♏
29	8♈	10♓	11♉	1♏
30	9♈	11♓	12♉	0♏
31	10♈	12♓	13♉	0♏

April

Day	☉	☿	♀	♂
1	11♈	13♓	14♉	0♏
2	12♈	14♓	15♉	29♎
3	13♈	15♓	17♉	29♎
4	14♈	16♓	18♉	29♎
5	15♈	17♓	19♉	28♎
6	16♈	19♓	20♉	28♎
7	17♈	20♓	21♉	28♎
8	18♈	21♓	23♉	27♎
9	19♈	22♓	24♉	27♎
10	20♈	24♓	25♉	27♎
11	21♈	25♓	26♉	26♎
12	22♈	27♓	27♉	26♎
13	23♈	28♓	29♉	26♎
14	24♈	29♓	0♊	25♎
15	25♈	1♈	1♊	25♎
16	26♈	2♈	2♊	25♎
17	27♈	4♈	3♊	24♎
18	27♈	6♈	4♊	24♎
19	28♈	7♈	6♊	23♎
20	29♈	9♈	7♊	23♎
21	0♉	10♈	8♊	23♎
22	1♉	12♈	9♊	22♎
23	2♉	14♈	10♊	22♎
24	3♉	16♈	12♊	22♎
25	4♉	17♈	13♊	21♎
26	5♉	19♈	14♊	21♎
27	6♉	21♈	15♊	20♎
28	7♉	23♈	16♊	20♎
29	8♉	25♈	17♊	20♎
30	9♉	27♈	18♊	19♎

May

Day	☉	☿	♀	♂
1	10♉	28♈	20♊	19♎
2	11♉	0♉	21♊	19♎
3	12♉	2♉	22♊	19♎
4	13♉	4♉	23♊	18♎
5	14♉	7♉	24♊	18♎
6	15♉	9♉	25♊	18♎
7	16♉	11♉	27♊	17♎
8	17♉	13♉	28♊	17♎
9	18♉	15♉	29♊	17♎
10	19♉	17♉	0♋	17♎
11	20♉	19♉	1♋	17♎
12	21♉	21♉	2♋	16♎
13	22♉	24♉	3♋	16♎
14	23♉	26♉	4♋	16♎
15	24♉	28♉	6♋	16♎
16	25♉	0♊	7♋	16♎
17	26♉	2♊	8♋	16♎
18	27♉	4♊	9♋	15♎
19	28♉	7♊	10♋	15♎
20	29♉	9♊	11♋	15♎
21	29♉	11♊	12♋	15♎
22	0♊	13♊	13♋	15♎
23	1♊	15♊	14♋	15♎
24	2♊	17♊	16♋	15♎
25	3♊	19♊	17♋	15♎
26	4♊	20♊	18♋	15♎
27	5♊	22♊	19♋	15♎
28	6♊	24♊	20♋	15♎
29	7♊	26♊	21♋	15♎
30	8♊	27♊	22♋	15♎
31	9♊	29♊	23♋	15♎

June

Day	☉	☿	♀	♂
1	10♊	1♋	24♋	15♎
2	11♊	2♋	25♋	15♎
3	12♊	4♋	26♋	15♎
4	13♊	5♋	27♋	15♎
5	14♊	7♋	28♋	16♎
6	15♊	8♋	29♋	16♎
7	16♊	9♋	1♌	16♎
8	17♊	10♋	2♌	16♎
9	18♊	12♋	3♌	16♎
10	19♊	13♋	4♌	16♎
11	20♊	14♋	5♌	17♎
12	21♊	15♋	6♌	17♎
13	22♊	16♋	7♌	17♎
14	22♊	17♋	8♌	17♎
15	23♊	17♋	9♌	17♎
16	24♊	18♋	10♌	18♎
17	25♊	19♋	11♌	18♎
18	26♊	20♋	12♌	18♎
19	27♊	20♋	13♌	18♎
20	28♊	21♋	14♌	19♎
21	29♊	21♋	15♌	19♎
22	0♋	21♋	15♌	19♎
23	1♋	22♋	16♌	19♎
24	2♋	22♋	17♌	20♎
25	3♋	22♋	18♌	20♎
26	4♋	22♋	19♌	20♎
27	5♋	22♋	20♌	21♎
28	6♋	22♋	21♌	21♎
29	7♋	22♋	22♌	21♎
30	8♋	21♋	23♌	22♎

July

Day	☉	☿	♀	♂
1	9♋	21♋	24♌	22♎
2	10♋	21♋	25♌	22♎
3	11♋	20♋	25♌	23♎
4	12♋	20♋	26♌	23♎
5	13♋	19♋	27♌	24♎
6	13♋	19♋	28♌	24♎
7	14♋	18♋	29♌	24♎
8	15♋	17♋	29♌	25♎
9	16♋	17♋	0♍	25♎
10	17♋	16♋	1♍	26♎
11	18♋	16♋	2♍	26♎
12	19♋	15♋	2♍	26♎
13	20♋	14♋	3♍	27♎
14	21♋	14♋	4♍	27♎
15	22♋	13♋	5♍	28♎
16	23♋	13♋	5♍	28♎
17	24♋	13♋	6♍	29♎
18	25♋	12♋	7♍	29♎
19	26♋	12♋	7♍	0♏
20	27♋	12♋	8♍	0♏
21	28♋	12♋	8♍	1♏
22	29♋	12♋	9♍	1♏
23	0♌	13♋	9♍	2♏
24	1♌	13♋	10♍	2♏
25	2♌	13♋	10♍	3♏
26	3♌	14♋	11♍	3♏
27	3♌	14♋	11♍	4♏
28	4♌	15♋	12♍	4♏
29	5♌	16♋	12♍	5♏
30	6♌	17♋	12♍	5♏
31	7♌	18♋	13♍	6♏

August

Day	☉	☿	♀	♂
1	8♌	19♋	13♍	6♏
2	9♌	20♋	13♍	7♏
3	10♌	21♋	13♍	7♏
4	11♌	23♋	14♍	8♏
5	12♌	24♋	14♍	8♏
6	13♌	26♋	14♍	9♏
7	14♌	27♋	14♍	9♏
8	15♌	29♋	14♍	10♏
9	16♌	0♌	14♍	11♏
10	17♌	2♌	14♍	11♏
11	18♌	4♌	14♍	12♏
12	19♌	6♌	14♍	12♏
13	20♌	8♌	13♍	13♏
14	21♌	10♌	13♍	13♏
15	22♌	12♌	13♍	14♏
16	23♌	14♌	13♍	15♏
17	24♌	16♌	12♍	15♏
18	25♌	18♌	12♍	16♏
19	26♌	20♌	12♍	16♏
20	27♌	22♌	11♍	17♏
21	27♌	24♌	11♍	18♏
22	28♌	26♌	10♍	18♏
23	29♌	28♌	10♍	19♏
24	0♍	0♍	9♍	19♏
25	1♍	2♍	9♍	20♏
26	2♍	4♍	8♍	21♏
27	3♍	6♍	8♍	21♏
28	4♍	8♍	7♍	22♏
29	5♍	10♍	6♍	22♏
30	6♍	11♍	6♍	23♏
31	7♍	13♍	5♍	24♏

September

Day	☉	☿	♀	♂
1	8♍	15♍	4♍	24♏
2	9♍	17♍	4♍	25♏
3	10♍	19♍	3♍	26♏
4	11♍	21♍	3♍	26♏
5	12♍	22♍	2♍	27♏
6	13♍	24♍	2♍	27♏
7	14♍	26♍	1♍	28♏
8	15♍	27♍	1♍	29♏
9	16♍	29♍	0♍	29♏
10	17♍	1♎	0♍	0♐
11	18♍	2♎	29♌	1♐
12	19♍	4♎	29♌	1♐
13	20♍	6♎	29♌	2♐
14	21♍	7♎	28♌	3♐
15	22♍	9♎	28♌	3♐
16	23♍	10♎	28♌	4♐
17	24♍	12♎	28♌	5♐
18	25♍	13♎	28♌	5♐
19	26♍	15♎	28♌	6♐
20	27♍	16♎	28♌	7♐
21	28♍	18♎	28♌	7♐
22	29♍	19♎	28♌	8♐
23	29♍	21♎	28♌	9♐
24	0♎	22♎	28♌	9♐
25	1♎	24♎	28♌	10♐
26	2♎	25♎	28♌	11♐
27	3♎	26♎	29♌	12♐
28	4♎	28♎	29♌	12♐
29	5♎	29♎	29♌	13♐
30	6♎	0♏	29♌	14♐

October

Day	☉	☿	♀	♂
1	7♎	1♏	0♍	14♐
2	8♎	3♏	0♍	15♐
3	9♎	4♏	1♍	16♐
4	10♎	5♏	1♍	16♐
5	11♎	6♏	2♍	17♐
6	12♎	7♏	2♍	18♐
7	13♎	8♏	3♍	19♐
8	14♎	9♏	3♍	19♐
9	15♎	10♏	4♍	20♐
10	16♎	11♏	4♍	21♐
11	17♎	12♏	5♍	21♐
12	18♎	13♏	6♍	22♐
13	19♎	14♏	6♍	23♐
14	20♎	15♏	7♍	24♐
15	21♎	15♏	8♍	24♐
16	22♎	16♏	8♍	25♐
17	23♎	16♏	9♍	26♐
18	24♎	17♏	10♍	26♐
19	25♎	17♏	11♍	27♐
20	26♎	17♏	11♍	28♐
21	27♎	17♏	12♍	29♐
22	28♎	17♏	13♍	29♐
23	29♎	17♏	14♍	0♑
24	0♏	17♏	15♍	1♑
25	1♏	16♏	15♍	2♑
26	2♏	16♏	16♍	2♑
27	3♏	15♏	17♍	3♑
28	4♏	14♏	18♍	4♑
29	5♏	13♏	19♍	5♑
30	6♏	12♏	20♍	5♑
31	7♏	10♏	21♍	6♑

November

Day	☉	☿	♀	♂
1	8♏	9♏	22♍	7♑
2	9♏	8♏	23♍	7♑
3	10♏	7♏	24♍	8♑
4	11♏	5♏	25♍	9♑
5	12♏	4♏	26♍	10♑
6	13♏	3♏	27♍	10♑
7	14♏	3♏	28♍	11♑
8	15♏	2♏	29♍	12♑
9	16♏	2♏	0♎	13♑
10	17♏	1♏	1♎	13♑
11	18♏	1♏	2♎	14♑
12	19♏	2♏	3♎	15♑
13	20♏	2♏	4♎	16♑
14	21♏	3♏	5♎	17♑
15	22♏	3♏	6♎	17♑
16	23♏	4♏	7♎	18♑
17	24♏	5♏	8♎	19♑
18	25♏	6♏	9♎	20♑
19	26♏	7♏	10♎	20♑
20	27♏	8♏	11♎	21♑
21	28♏	9♏	12♎	22♑
22	29♏	11♏	13♎	23♑
23	0♐	12♏	14♎	23♑
24	1♐	13♏	15♎	24♑
25	2♐	15♏	16♎	25♑
26	3♐	16♏	17♎	26♑
27	4♐	17♏	19♎	26♑
28	5♐	19♏	20♎	27♑
29	6♐	20♏	21♎	28♑
30	7♐	22♏	22♎	29♑

December

Day	☉	☿	♀	♂
1	8♐	23♏	23♎	0♒
2	9♐	25♏	24♎	0♒
3	10♐	26♏	25♎	1♒
4	11♐	28♏	26♎	2♒
5	12♐	29♏	28♎	3♒
6	13♐	1♐	29♎	3♒
7	14♐	3♐	0♏	4♒
8	15♐	4♐	1♏	5♒
9	16♐	6♐	2♏	6♒
10	17♐	7♐	3♏	6♒
11	18♐	9♐	4♏	7♒
12	19♐	10♐	6♏	8♒
13	20♐	12♐	7♏	9♒
14	22♐	13♐	8♏	10♒
15	23♐	15♐	9♏	10♒
16	24♐	16♐	10♏	11♒
17	25♐	18♐	11♏	12♒
18	26♐	20♐	13♏	13♒
19	27♐	21♐	14♏	13♒
20	28♐	23♐	15♏	14♒
21	29♐	24♐	16♏	15♒
22	0♑	26♐	17♏	16♒
23	1♑	27♐	18♏	17♒
24	2♑	29♐	20♏	17♒
25	3♑	1♑	21♏	18♒
26	4♑	2♑	22♏	19♒
27	5♑	4♑	23♏	20♒
28	6♑	5♑	24♏	20♒
29	7♑	7♑	26♏	21♒
30	8♑	9♑	27♏	22♒
31	9♑	10♑	28♏	23♒

Planetary Positions

♌ = Leo ♍ = Virgo ♎ = Libra ♏ = Scorpio ♐ = Sagittarius ♑ = Capricorn ♒ = Aquarius ♓ = Pisces

1968

January

Day	☉	☿	♀	♂
1	10♑	12♑	29♏	24♒
2	11♑	13♑	0♐	24♒
3	12♑	15♑	2♐	25♒
4	13♑	17♑	3♐	26♒
5	14♑	18♑	4♐	27♒
6	15♑	20♑	5♐	28♒
7	16♑	22♑	6♐	28♒
8	17♑	23♑	8♐	29♒
9	18♑	25♑	9♐	0♓
10	19♑	27♑	10♐	1♓
11	20♑	28♑	11♐	1♓
12	21♑	0♒	12♐	2♓
13	22♑	2♒	14♐	3♓
14	23♑	3♒	15♐	4♓
15	24♑	5♒	16♐	5♓
16	25♑	7♒	17♐	5♓
17	26♑	8♒	18♐	6♓
18	27♑	10♒	20♐	7♓
19	28♑	12♒	21♐	8♓
20	29♑	13♒	22♐	8♓
21	0♒	15♒	23♐	9♓
22	1♒	16♒	24♐	10♓
23	2♒	18♒	26♐	11♓
24	3♒	20♒	27♐	12♓
25	4♒	21♒	28♐	12♓
26	5♒	23♒	29♐	13♓
27	6♒	24♒	1♑	14♓
28	7♒	25♒	2♑	15♓
29	8♒	27♒	3♑	15♓
30	9♒	28♒	4♑	16♓
31	10♒	29♒	5♑	17♓

February

Day	☉	☿	♀	♂
1	11♒	0♓	7♑	18♓
2	12♒	1♓	8♑	19♓
3	13♒	1♓	9♑	19♓
4	14♒	2♓	10♑	20♓
5	15♒	2♓	12♑	21♓
6	16♒	2♓	13♑	22♓
7	17♒	2♓	14♑	22♓
8	18♒	2♓	15♑	23♓
9	20♒	2♓	16♑	24♓
10	21♒	1♓	18♑	25♓
11	22♒	0♓	19♑	25♓
12	23♒	0♓	20♑	26♓
13	24♒	29♒	21♑	27♓
14	25♒	28♒	23♑	28♓
15	26♒	26♒	24♑	29♓
16	27♒	25♒	25♑	29♓
17	28♒	24♒	26♑	0♈
18	29♒	23♒	28♑	1♈
19	0♓	22♒	29♑	2♈
20	1♓	21♒	0♒	2♈
21	2♓	20♒	1♒	3♈
22	3♓	19♒	2♒	4♈
23	4♓	19♒	4♒	5♈
24	5♓	18♒	5♒	5♈
25	6♓	18♒	6♒	6♈
26	7♓	17♒	7♒	7♈
27	8♓	17♒	9♒	8♈
28	9♓	17♒	10♒	8♈
29	10♓	17♒	11♒	9♈

March

Day	☉	☿	♀	♂
1	11♓	17♒	12♒	10♈
2	12♓	18♒	14♒	11♈
3	13♓	18♒	15♒	11♈
4	14♓	18♒	16♒	12♈
5	15♓	19♒	17♒	13♈
6	16♓	19♒	18♒	14♈
7	17♓	20♒	20♒	14♈
8	18♓	21♒	21♒	15♈
9	19♓	22♒	22♒	16♈
10	20♓	22♒	23♒	17♈
11	21♓	23♒	25♒	18♈
12	22♓	24♒	26♒	18♈
13	23♓	25♒	27♒	19♈
14	24♓	26♒	28♒	20♈
15	25♓	27♒	0♓	21♈
16	26♓	28♒	1♓	21♈
17	27♓	0♓	2♓	22♈
18	28♓	1♓	3♓	23♈
19	29♓	2♓	4♓	23♈
20	0♈	3♓	6♓	24♈
21	1♈	4♓	7♓	25♈
22	2♈	6♓	8♓	26♈
23	3♈	7♓	9♓	26♈
24	4♈	8♓	11♓	27♈
25	5♈	10♓	12♓	28♈
26	6♈	11♓	13♓	29♈
27	7♈	13♓	14♓	29♈
28	8♈	14♓	16♓	0♉
29	9♈	16♓	17♓	1♉
30	10♈	17♓	18♓	2♉
31	11♈	19♓	19♓	2♉

April

Day	☉	☿	♀	♂
1	12♈	20♓	21♓	3♉
2	13♈	22♓	22♓	4♉
3	14♈	24♓	23♓	5♉
4	14♈	25♓	24♓	5♉
5	15♈	27♓	25♓	6♉
6	16♈	29♓	27♓	7♉
7	17♈	0♈	28♓	8♉
8	18♈	2♈	29♓	8♉
9	19♈	4♈	0♈	9♉
10	20♈	6♈	2♈	10♉
11	21♈	7♈	3♈	10♉
12	22♈	9♈	4♈	11♉
13	23♈	11♈	5♈	12♉
14	24♈	13♈	7♈	13♉
15	25♈	15♈	8♈	13♉
16	26♈	17♈	9♈	14♉
17	27♈	19♈	10♈	15♉
18	28♈	21♈	11♈	15♉
19	29♈	23♈	13♈	16♉
20	0♉	25♈	14♈	17♉
21	1♉	27♈	15♈	18♉
22	2♉	29♈	16♈	18♉
23	3♉	1♉	18♈	19♉
24	4♉	3♉	19♈	20♉
25	5♉	5♉	20♈	21♉
26	6♉	7♉	21♈	21♉
27	7♉	10♉	23♈	22♉
28	8♉	12♉	24♈	23♉
29	9♉	14♉	25♈	23♉
30	10♉	16♉	26♈	24♉

May

Day	☉	☿	♀	♂
1	11♉	18♉	27♈	25♉
2	12♉	20♉	29♈	25♉
3	13♉	22♉	0♉	26♉
4	14♉	24♉	1♉	27♉
5	15♉	27♉	2♉	28♉
6	16♉	29♉	4♉	28♉
7	17♉	0♊	5♉	29♉
8	18♉	2♊	6♉	0♊
9	19♉	4♊	7♉	0♊
10	20♉	6♊	9♉	1♊
11	21♉	8♊	10♉	2♊
12	22♉	10♊	11♉	3♊
13	22♉	11♊	12♉	3♊
14	23♉	13♊	13♉	4♊
15	24♉	14♊	15♉	5♊
16	25♉	16♊	16♉	5♊
17	26♉	17♊	17♉	6♊
18	27♉	19♊	18♉	7♊
19	28♉	20♊	20♉	7♊
20	29♉	21♊	21♉	8♊
21	0♊	22♊	22♉	9♊
22	1♊	24♊	23♉	10♊
23	2♊	25♊	24♉	10♊
24	3♊	26♊	26♉	11♊
25	4♊	27♊	27♉	12♊
26	5♊	27♊	28♉	12♊
27	6♊	28♊	29♉	13♊
28	7♊	29♊	1♊	14♊
29	8♊	0♋	2♊	14♊
30	9♊	0♋	3♊	15♊
31	10♊	1♋	4♊	16♊

June

Day	☉	☿	♀	♂
1	11♊	1♋	6♊	16♊
2	12♊	1♋	7♊	17♊
3	13♊	2♋	8♊	18♊
4	14♊	2♋	9♊	18♊
5	15♊	2♋	10♊	19♊
6	16♊	2♋	12♊	20♊
7	17♊	2♋	13♊	21♊
8	17♊	2♋	14♊	21♊
9	18♊	2♋	15♊	22♊
10	19♊	1♋	17♊	23♊
11	20♊	1♋	18♊	23♊
12	21♊	1♋	19♊	24♊
13	22♊	0♋	20♊	25♊
14	23♊	0♋	21♊	25♊
15	24♊	29♊	23♊	26♊
16	25♊	29♊	24♊	27♊
17	26♊	28♊	25♊	27♊
18	27♊	28♊	26♊	28♊
19	28♊	27♊	28♊	29♊
20	29♊	27♊	29♊	29♊
21	0♋	26♊	0♋	0♋
22	1♋	25♊	1♋	1♋
23	2♋	25♊	3♋	1♋
24	3♋	25♊	4♋	2♋
25	4♋	24♊	5♋	3♋
26	5♋	24♊	6♋	3♋
27	6♋	24♊	7♋	4♋
28	7♋	23♊	9♋	5♋
29	8♋	23♊	10♋	5♋
30	8♋	23♊	11♋	6♋

July

Day	☉	☿	♀	♂
1	9♋	23♊	12♋	7♋
2	10♋	23♊	14♋	7♋
3	11♋	24♊	15♋	8♋
4	12♋	24♊	16♋	9♋
5	13♋	24♊	17♋	9♋
6	14♋	25♊	19♋	10♋
7	15♋	25♊	20♋	11♋
8	16♋	26♊	21♋	11♋
9	17♋	27♊	22♋	12♋
10	18♋	27♊	23♋	13♋
11	19♋	28♊	25♋	13♋
12	20♋	29♊	26♋	14♋
13	21♋	0♋	27♋	15♋
14	22♋	1♋	28♋	15♋
15	23♋	2♋	0♌	16♋
16	24♋	4♋	1♌	17♋
17	25♋	5♋	2♌	17♋
18	26♋	6♋	3♌	18♋
19	27♋	8♋	5♌	19♋
20	28♋	9♋	6♌	19♋
21	28♋	11♋	7♌	20♋
22	29♋	13♋	8♌	21♋
23	0♌	14♋	9♌	21♋
24	1♌	16♋	11♌	22♋
25	2♌	18♋	12♌	23♋
26	3♌	20♋	13♌	23♋
27	4♌	22♋	14♌	24♋
28	5♌	24♋	16♌	24♋
29	6♌	26♋	17♌	25♋
30	7♌	28♋	18♌	26♋
31	8♌	0♌	19♌	26♋

August

Day	☉	☿	♀	♂
1	9♌	2♌	21♌	27♋
2	10♌	4♌	22♌	28♋
3	11♌	6♌	23♌	28♋
4	12♌	8♌	24♌	29♋
5	13♌	10♌	25♌	0♌
6	14♌	12♌	27♌	0♌
7	15♌	14♌	28♌	1♌
8	16♌	17♌	29♌	2♌
9	17♌	19♌	0♍	2♌
10	18♌	21♌	2♍	3♌
11	19♌	23♌	3♍	4♌
12	20♌	25♌	4♍	4♌
13	20♌	26♌	5♍	5♌
14	21♌	28♌	7♍	5♌
15	22♌	0♍	8♍	6♌
16	23♌	2♍	9♍	7♌
17	24♌	4♍	10♍	7♌
18	25♌	6♍	11♍	8♌
19	26♌	8♍	13♍	9♌
20	27♌	10♍	14♍	9♌
21	28♌	11♍	15♍	10♌
22	29♌	13♍	16♍	11♌
23	0♍	15♍	18♍	11♌
24	1♍	16♍	19♍	12♌
25	2♍	18♍	20♍	13♌
26	3♍	20♍	21♍	13♌
27	4♍	21♍	23♍	14♌
28	5♍	23♍	24♍	14♌
29	6♍	25♍	25♍	15♌
30	7♍	26♍	26♍	16♌
31	8♍	28♍	27♍	16♌

September

Day	☉	☿	♀	♂
1	9♍	29♍	29♍	17♌
2	10♍	1♎	0♎	18♌
3	11♍	2♎	1♎	18♌
4	12♍	4♎	2♎	19♌
5	13♍	5♎	4♎	20♌
6	14♍	7♎	5♎	20♌
7	15♍	8♎	6♎	21♌
8	16♍	9♎	7♎	21♌
9	17♍	11♎	9♎	22♌
10	18♍	12♎	10♎	23♌
11	19♍	13♎	11♎	23♌
12	19♍	15♎	12♎	24♌
13	20♍	16♎	13♎	25♌
14	21♍	17♎	15♎	25♌
15	22♍	18♎	16♎	26♌
16	23♍	19♎	17♎	26♌
17	24♍	20♎	18♎	27♌
18	25♍	22♎	20♎	28♌
19	26♍	23♎	21♎	28♌
20	27♍	24♎	22♎	29♌
21	28♍	25♎	23♎	0♍
22	29♍	25♎	24♎	0♍
23	0♎	26♎	26♎	1♍
24	1♎	27♎	27♎	2♍
25	2♎	28♎	28♎	2♍
26	3♎	29♎	29♎	3♍
27	4♎	29♎	1♏	3♍
28	5♎	0♏	2♏	4♍
29	6♎	0♏	3♏	5♍
30	7♎	1♏	4♏	5♍

October

Day	☉	☿	♀	♂
1	8♎	1♏	6♏	6♍
2	9♎	1♏	7♏	7♍
3	10♎	1♏	8♏	7♍
4	11♎	1♏	9♏	8♍
5	12♎	1♏	10♏	8♍
6	13♎	1♏	12♏	9♍
7	14♎	0♏	13♏	10♍
8	15♎	0♏	14♏	10♍
9	16♎	29♎	15♏	11♍
10	17♎	28♎	17♏	12♍
11	18♎	27♎	18♏	12♍
12	19♎	26♎	19♏	13♍
13	20♎	25♎	20♏	13♍
14	21♎	24♎	21♏	14♍
15	22♎	23♎	23♏	15♍
16	23♎	22♎	24♏	15♍
17	24♎	20♎	25♏	16♍
18	25♎	19♎	26♏	16♍
19	26♎	18♎	28♏	17♍
20	27♎	18♎	29♏	18♍
21	28♎	17♎	0♐	18♍
22	29♎	16♎	1♐	19♍
23	0♏	16♎	2♐	20♍
24	1♏	16♎	4♐	20♍
25	2♏	16♎	5♐	21♍
26	3♏	16♎	6♐	21♍
27	4♏	16♎	7♐	22♍
28	5♏	17♎	9♐	23♍
29	6♏	18♎	10♐	23♍
30	7♏	18♎	11♐	24♍
31	8♏	19♎	12♐	24♍

November

Day	☉	☿	♀	♂
1	9♏	20♎	13♐	25♍
2	10♏	21♎	15♐	26♍
3	11♏	23♎	16♐	26♍
4	12♏	24♎	17♐	27♍
5	13♏	25♎	18♐	28♍
6	14♏	27♎	19♐	28♍
7	15♏	28♎	21♐	29♍
8	16♏	0♏	22♐	29♍
9	17♏	1♏	23♐	0♎
10	18♏	3♏	24♐	1♎
11	19♏	4♏	26♐	1♎
12	20♏	6♏	27♐	2♎
13	21♏	7♏	28♐	2♎
14	22♏	9♏	29♐	3♎
15	23♏	10♏	0♑	4♎
16	24♏	12♏	2♑	4♎
17	25♏	14♏	3♑	5♎
18	26♏	15♏	4♑	5♎
19	27♏	17♏	5♑	6♎
20	28♏	18♏	6♑	7♎
21	29♏	20♏	8♑	7♎
22	0♐	22♏	9♑	8♎
23	1♐	23♏	10♑	8♎
24	2♐	25♏	11♑	9♎
25	3♐	26♏	12♑	10♎
26	4♐	28♏	14♑	10♎
27	5♐	29♏	15♑	11♎
28	6♐	1♐	16♑	11♎
29	7♐	3♐	17♑	12♎
30	8♐	4♐	18♑	13♎

December

Day	☉	☿	♀	♂
1	9♐	6♐	20♑	13♎
2	10♐	7♐	21♑	14♎
3	11♐	9♐	22♑	14♎
4	12♐	11♐	23♑	15♎
5	13♐	12♐	24♑	16♎
6	14♐	14♐	26♑	16♎
7	15♐	15♐	27♑	17♎
8	16♐	17♐	28♑	17♎
9	17♐	18♐	29♑	18♎
10	18♐	20♐	0♒	19♎
11	19♐	22♐	1♒	19♎
12	20♐	23♐	3♒	20♎
13	21♐	25♐	4♒	20♎
14	22♐	26♐	5♒	21♎
15	23♐	28♐	6♒	21♎
16	24♐	29♐	7♒	22♎
17	25♐	1♑	9♒	23♎
18	26♐	3♑	10♒	23♎
19	27♐	4♑	11♒	24♎
20	28♐	6♑	12♒	24♎
21	29♐	7♑	13♒	25♎
22	0♑	9♑	14♒	26♎
23	1♑	11♑	16♒	26♎
24	2♑	12♑	17♒	27♎
25	3♑	14♑	18♒	27♎
26	5♑	15♑	19♒	28♎
27	6♑	17♑	20♒	28♎
28	7♑	19♑	21♒	29♎
29	8♑	20♑	22♒	0♏
30	9♑	22♑	24♒	0♏
31	10♑	23♑	25♒	1♏

1969

Your Starway to Love

☉ = Sun ☿ = Mercury ♀ = Venus ♂ = Mars ♈ = Aries ♉ = Taurus ♊ = Gemini ♋ = Cancer

January

Day	☉	☿	♀	♂
1	11♑	25♑	26♒	1♏
2	12♑	26♑	27♒	2♏
3	13♑	28♑	28♒	2♏
4	14♑	0♒	29♒	3♏
5	15♑	1♒	0♓	4♏
6	16♑	3♒	2♓	4♏
7	17♑	4♒	3♓	5♏
8	18♑	5♒	4♓	5♏
9	19♑	7♒	5♓	6♏
10	20♑	8♒	6♓	6♏
11	21♑	9♒	7♓	7♏
12	22♑	11♒	8♓	7♏
13	23♑	12♒	9♓	8♏
14	24♑	13♒	10♓	9♏
15	25♑	14♒	11♓	9♏
16	26♑	14♒	13♓	10♏
17	27♑	15♒	14♓	10♏
18	28♑	16♒	15♓	11♏
19	29♑	16♒	16♓	11♏
20	0♒	16♒	17♓	12♏
21	1♒	16♒	18♓	12♏
22	2♒	16♒	19♓	13♏
23	3♒	15♒	20♓	13♏
24	4♒	15♒	21♓	14♏
25	5♒	14♒	22♓	15♏
26	6♒	13♒	23♓	15♏
27	7♒	12♒	24♓	16♏
28	8♒	11♒	25♓	16♏
29	9♒	9♒	26♓	17♏
30	10♒	8♒	27♓	17♏
31	11♒	7♒	28♓	18♏

April

Day	☉	☿	♀	♂
1	11♈	3♈	23♈	13♐
2	12♈	5♈	22♈	13♐
3	13♈	7♈	22♈	14♐
4	14♈	9♈	21♈	14♐
5	15♈	11♈	21♈	14♐
6	16♈	13♈	20♈	14♐
7	17♈	15♈	20♈	14♐
8	18♈	17♈	19♈	15♐
9	19♈	19♈	18♈	15♐
10	20♈	22♈	18♈	15♐
11	21♈	24♈	17♈	15♐
12	22♈	26♈	16♈	15♐
13	23♈	28♈	16♈	16♐
14	24♈	0♉	15♈	16♐
15	25♈	2♉	15♈	16♐
16	26♈	4♉	14♈	16♐
17	27♈	6♉	14♈	16♐
18	28♈	8♉	13♈	16♐
19	29♈	10♉	13♈	16♐
20	0♉	12♉	12♈	16♐
21	1♉	14♉	12♈	17♐
22	2♉	16♉	12♈	17♐
23	3♉	18♉	11♈	17♐
24	4♉	20♉	11♈	17♐
25	5♉	22♉	11♈	17♐
26	6♉	23♉	11♈	17♐
27	7♉	25♉	11♈	17♐
28	8♉	26♉	11♈	17♐
29	9♉	28♉	11♈	17♐
30	10♉	29♉	10♈	17♐

July

Day	☉	☿	♀	♂
1	9♋	19♊	24♉	2♐
2	10♋	20♊	25♉	2♐
3	11♋	22♊	26♉	2♐
4	12♋	23♊	27♉	2♐
5	13♋	25♊	28♉	2♐
6	14♋	27♊	29♉	2♐
7	15♋	28♊	0♊	2♐
8	16♋	0♋	1♊	2♐
9	17♋	2♋	2♊	2♐
10	18♋	4♋	3♊	2♐
11	19♋	6♋	5♊	2♐
12	20♋	8♋	6♊	2♐
13	21♋	10♋	7♊	2♐
14	22♋	12♋	8♊	2♐
15	23♋	14♋	9♊	2♐
16	23♋	16♋	10♊	2♐
17	24♋	18♋	11♊	2♐
18	25♋	20♋	12♊	2♐
19	26♋	22♋	13♊	3♐
20	27♋	24♋	14♊	3♐
21	28♋	27♋	15♊	3♐
22	29♋	29♋	17♊	3♐
23	0♌	1♌	18♊	3♐
24	1♌	3♌	19♊	3♐
25	2♌	5♌	20♊	4♐
26	3♌	7♌	21♊	4♐
27	4♌	9♌	22♊	4♐
28	5♌	11♌	23♊	4♐
29	6♌	13♌	24♊	5♐
30	7♌	15♌	25♊	5♐
31	8♌	17♌	27♊	5♐

October

Day	☉	☿	♀	♂
1	8♎	4♎	10♍	6♑
2	9♎	3♎	11♍	7♑
3	10♎	2♎	12♍	8♑
4	11♎	1♎	14♍	8♑
5	12♎	1♎	15♍	9♑
6	13♎	0♎	16♍	10♑
7	14♎	0♎	17♍	10♑
8	15♎	0♎	18♍	11♑
9	16♎	0♎	20♍	12♑
10	17♎	0♎	21♍	12♑
11	18♎	1♎	22♍	13♑
12	19♎	1♎	23♍	14♑
13	20♎	2♎	25♍	14♑
14	21♎	3♎	26♍	15♑
15	22♎	4♎	27♍	16♑
16	23♎	5♎	28♍	16♑
17	24♎	6♎	0♎	17♑
18	25♎	7♎	1♎	18♑
19	26♎	9♎	2♎	18♑
20	27♎	10♎	3♎	19♑
21	28♎	11♎	4♎	20♑
22	29♎	13♎	6♎	20♑
23	0♏	14♎	7♎	21♑
24	1♏	16♎	8♎	22♑
25	2♏	18♎	9♎	22♑
26	3♏	19♎	11♎	23♑
27	4♏	21♎	12♎	24♑
28	5♏	23♎	13♎	25♑
29	6♏	24♎	14♎	25♑
30	7♏	26♎	16♎	26♑
31	8♏	28♎	17♎	27♑

February

Day	☉	☿	♀	♂
1	12♒	6♒	29♓	18♏
2	13♒	5♒	0♈	19♏
3	14♒	4♒	1♈	19♏
4	15♒	3♒	2♈	20♏
5	16♒	2♒	3♈	20♏
6	17♒	1♒	4♈	21♏
7	18♒	1♒	5♈	21♏
8	19♒	1♒	6♈	22♏
9	20♒	0♒	7♈	22♏
10	21♒	0♒	7♈	23♏
11	22♒	0♒	8♈	23♏
12	23♒	0♒	9♈	24♏
13	24♒	1♒	10♈	24♏
14	25♒	1♒	11♈	25♏
15	26♒	2♒	12♈	25♏
16	27♒	2♒	13♈	26♏
17	28♒	3♒	13♈	26♏
18	29♒	3♒	14♈	27♏
19	0♓	4♒	15♈	27♏
20	1♓	5♒	16♈	28♏
21	2♓	6♒	16♈	28♏
22	3♓	7♒	17♈	29♏
23	4♓	8♒	18♈	29♏
24	5♓	9♒	18♈	0♐
25	6♓	10♒	19♈	0♐
26	7♓	11♒	20♈	0♐
27	8♓	12♒	20♈	1♐
28	9♓	13♒	21♈	1♐

May

Day	☉	☿	♀	♂
1	11♉	1♊	11♈	17♐
2	12♉	2♊	11♈	17♐
3	13♉	3♊	11♈	17♐
4	14♉	4♊	11♈	16♐
5	15♉	5♊	11♈	16♐
6	15♉	6♊	11♈	16♐
7	16♉	7♊	12♈	16♐
8	17♉	8♊	12♈	16♐
9	18♉	9♊	12♈	16♐
10	19♉	10♊	12♈	16♐
11	20♉	10♊	13♈	16♐
12	21♉	11♊	13♈	15♐
13	22♉	11♊	14♈	15♐
14	23♉	11♊	14♈	15♐
15	24♉	12♊	15♈	15♐
16	25♉	12♊	15♈	15♐
17	26♉	12♊	16♈	14♐
18	27♉	12♊	16♈	14♐
19	28♉	12♊	17♈	14♐
20	29♉	12♊	17♈	14♐
21	0♊	12♊	18♈	13♐
22	1♊	11♊	19♈	13♐
23	2♊	11♊	19♈	13♐
24	3♊	11♊	20♈	12♐
25	4♊	10♊	21♈	12♐
26	5♊	10♊	21♈	12♐
27	6♊	9♊	22♈	11♐
28	7♊	9♊	23♈	11♐
29	8♊	8♊	24♈	11♐
30	9♊	7♊	24♈	10♐
31	10♊	7♊	25♈	10♐

August

Day	☉	☿	♀	♂
1	9♌	19♌	28♊	5♐
2	10♌	21♌	29♊	6♐
3	11♌	23♌	0♋	6♐
4	12♌	25♌	1♋	6♐
5	13♌	26♌	2♋	7♐
6	14♌	28♌	3♋	7♐
7	15♌	0♍	5♋	7♐
8	15♌	2♍	6♋	8♐
9	16♌	4♍	7♋	8♐
10	17♌	5♍	8♋	8♐
11	18♌	7♍	9♋	9♐
12	19♌	8♍	10♋	9♐
13	20♌	10♍	11♋	10♐
14	21♌	12♍	13♋	10♐
15	22♌	13♍	14♋	10♐
16	23♌	15♍	15♋	11♐
17	24♌	16♍	16♋	11♐
18	25♌	18♍	17♋	12♐
19	26♌	19♍	18♋	12♐
20	27♌	21♍	20♋	13♐
21	28♌	22♍	21♋	13♐
22	29♌	23♍	22♋	14♐
23	0♍	25♍	23♋	14♐
24	1♍	26♍	24♋	14♐
25	2♍	27♍	25♋	15♐
26	3♍	29♍	27♋	15♐
27	4♍	0♎	28♋	16♐
28	5♍	1♎	29♋	16♐
29	6♍	2♎	0♌	17♐
30	7♍	3♎	1♌	17♐
31	8♍	5♎	2♌	18♐

November

Day	☉	☿	♀	♂
1	9♏	29♎	18♎	27♑
2	10♏	1♏	19♎	28♑
3	11♏	2♏	21♎	29♑
4	12♏	4♏	22♎	0♒
5	13♏	6♏	23♎	0♒
6	14♏	7♏	24♎	1♒
7	15♏	9♏	26♎	2♒
8	16♏	11♏	27♎	2♒
9	17♏	12♏	28♎	3♒
10	18♏	14♏	29♎	4♒
11	19♏	16♏	1♏	5♒
12	20♏	17♏	2♏	5♒
13	21♏	19♏	3♏	6♒
14	22♏	20♏	4♏	7♒
15	23♏	22♏	6♏	8♒
16	24♏	24♏	7♏	8♒
17	25♏	25♏	8♏	9♒
18	26♏	27♏	9♏	10♒
19	27♏	28♏	11♏	10♒
20	28♏	0♐	12♏	11♒
21	29♏	2♐	13♏	12♒
22	0♐	3♐	14♏	13♒
23	1♐	5♐	16♏	13♒
24	2♐	6♐	17♏	14♒
25	3♐	8♐	18♏	15♒
26	4♐	9♐	19♏	16♒
27	5♐	11♐	21♏	16♒
28	6♐	12♐	22♏	17♒
29	7♐	14♐	23♏	18♒
30	8♐	16♐	24♏	19♒

March

Day	☉	☿	♀	♂
1	10♓	14♒	22♈	2♐
2	11♓	16♒	22♈	2♐
3	12♓	17♒	23♈	3♐
4	13♓	18♒	23♈	3♐
5	14♓	19♒	24♈	3♐
6	15♓	21♒	24♈	4♐
7	16♓	22♒	24♈	4♐
8	17♓	24♒	25♈	5♐
9	18♓	25♒	25♈	5♐
10	19♓	26♒	26♈	6♐
11	20♓	28♒	26♈	6♐
12	21♓	29♒	26♈	6♐
13	22♓	1♓	26♈	7♐
14	23♓	2♓	26♈	7♐
15	24♓	4♓	27♈	7♐
16	25♓	5♓	27♈	8♐
17	26♓	7♓	27♈	8♐
18	27♓	9♓	27♈	9♐
19	28♓	10♓	27♈	9♐
20	29♓	12♓	27♈	9♐
21	0♈	14♓	27♈	10♐
22	1♈	15♓	27♈	10♐
23	2♈	17♓	26♈	10♐
24	3♈	19♓	26♈	11♐
25	4♈	21♓	26♈	11♐
26	5♈	22♓	26♈	11♐
27	6♈	24♓	25♈	12♐
28	7♈	26♓	25♈	12♐
29	8♈	28♓	24♈	12♐
30	9♈	0♈	24♈	12♐
31	10♈	1♈	24♈	13♐

June

Day	☉	☿	♀	♂
1	11♊	6♊	26♈	10♐
2	11♊	6♊	27♈	9♐
3	12♊	5♊	28♈	9♐
4	13♊	5♊	28♈	9♐
5	14♊	4♊	29♈	8♐
6	15♊	4♊	0♉	8♐
7	16♊	4♊	1♉	8♐
8	17♊	4♊	2♉	7♐
9	18♊	4♊	3♉	7♐
10	19♊	3♊	4♉	7♐
11	20♊	3♊	5♉	6♐
12	21♊	4♊	5♉	6♐
13	22♊	4♊	6♉	6♐
14	23♊	4♊	7♉	6♐
15	24♊	4♊	8♉	5♐
16	25♊	5♊	9♉	5♐
17	26♊	5♊	10♉	5♐
18	27♊	6♊	11♉	4♐
19	28♊	6♊	12♉	4♐
20	29♊	7♊	13♉	4♐
21	0♋	8♊	14♉	4♐
22	1♋	8♊	15♉	3♐
23	2♋	9♊	16♉	3♐
24	3♋	10♊	17♉	3♐
25	3♋	11♊	18♉	3♐
26	4♋	12♊	19♉	3♐
27	5♋	13♊	20♉	3♐
28	6♋	15♊	21♉	2♐
29	7♋	16♊	22♉	2♐
30	8♋	17♊	23♉	2♐

September

Day	☉	☿	♀	♂
1	9♍	6♎	4♌	18♐
2	10♍	7♎	5♌	19♐
3	11♍	8♎	6♌	20♐
4	11♍	8♎	7♌	20♐
5	12♍	9♎	8♌	21♐
6	13♍	10♎	10♌	21♐
7	14♍	11♎	11♌	22♐
8	15♍	12♎	12♌	22♐
9	16♍	12♎	13♌	23♐
10	17♍	13♎	14♌	23♐
11	18♍	13♎	16♌	24♐
12	19♍	14♎	17♌	25♐
13	20♍	14♎	18♌	25♐
14	21♍	15♎	19♌	26♐
15	22♍	15♎	20♌	26♐
16	23♍	15♎	22♌	27♐
17	24♍	15♎	23♌	28♐
18	25♍	15♎	24♌	28♐
19	26♍	14♎	25♌	29♐
20	27♍	14♎	26♌	29♐
21	28♍	14♎	28♌	0♑
22	29♍	13♎	29♌	1♑
23	0♎	12♎	0♍	1♑
24	1♎	11♎	1♍	2♑
25	2♎	11♎	3♍	2♑
26	3♎	10♎	4♍	3♑
27	4♎	9♎	5♍	4♑
28	5♎	7♎	6♍	4♑
29	6♎	6♎	7♍	5♑
30	7♎	5♎	9♍	6♑

December

Day	☉	☿	♀	♂
1	9♐	17♐	26♏	19♒
2	10♐	19♐	27♏	20♒
3	11♐	20♐	28♏	21♒
4	12♐	22♐	29♏	22♒
5	13♐	23♐	1♐	22♒
6	14♐	25♐	2♐	23♒
7	15♐	26♐	3♐	24♒
8	16♐	28♐	5♐	24♒
9	17♐	29♐	6♐	25♒
10	18♐	1♑	7♐	26♒
11	19♐	3♑	8♐	27♒
12	20♐	4♑	10♐	27♒
13	21♐	6♑	11♐	28♒
14	22♐	7♑	12♐	29♒
15	23♐	9♑	13♐	0♓
16	24♐	10♑	15♐	0♓
17	25♐	12♑	16♐	1♓
18	26♐	13♑	17♐	2♓
19	27♐	15♑	18♐	3♓
20	28♐	16♑	20♐	3♓
21	29♐	17♑	21♐	4♓
22	0♑	19♑	22♐	5♓
23	1♑	20♑	23♐	6♓
24	2♑	21♑	25♐	6♓
25	3♑	23♑	26♐	7♓
26	4♑	24♑	27♐	8♓
27	5♑	25♑	28♐	9♓
28	6♑	26♑	0♑	9♓
29	7♑	27♑	1♑	10♓
30	8♑	28♑	2♑	11♓
31	9♑	29♑	3♑	12♓

Planetary Positions

♌ = Leo ♍ = Virgo ♎ = Libra ♏ = Scorpio ♐ = Sagittarius ♑ = Capricorn ♒ = Aquarius ♓ = Pisces

1970

January

Day	☉	☿	♀	♂
1	10♑	29♑	5♑	12♓
2	11♑	0♒	6♑	13♓
3	12♑	0♒	7♑	14♓
4	13♑	0♒	8♑	15♓
5	14♑	0♒	10♑	15♓
6	15♑	0♒	11♑	16♓
7	16♑	29♑	12♑	17♓
8	18♑	29♑	14♑	18♓
9	19♑	28♑	15♑	18♓
10	20♑	27♑	16♑	19♓
11	21♑	26♑	17♑	20♓
12	22♑	24♑	19♑	21♓
13	23♑	23♑	20♑	21♓
14	24♑	22♑	21♑	22♓
15	25♑	20♑	22♑	23♓
16	26♑	19♑	24♑	24♓
17	27♑	18♑	25♑	24♓
18	28♑	17♑	26♑	25♓
19	29♑	16♑	27♑	26♓
20	0♒	15♑	29♑	27♓
21	1♒	15♑	0♒	27♓
22	2♒	14♑	1♒	28♓
23	3♒	14♑	2♒	29♓
24	4♒	14♑	4♒	29♓
25	5♒	14♑	5♒	0♈
26	6♒	14♑	6♒	1♈
27	7♒	14♑	7♒	2♈
28	8♒	15♑	9♒	2♈
29	9♒	15♑	10♒	3♈
30	10♒	16♑	11♒	4♈
31	11♒	16♑	12♒	5♈

April

Day	☉	☿	♀	♂
1	11♈	20♈	27♈	18♉
2	12♈	22♈	29♈	19♉
3	13♈	24♈	0♉	19♉
4	14♈	26♈	1♉	20♉
5	15♈	28♈	2♉	21♉
6	16♈	0♉	3♉	21♉
7	17♈	2♉	5♉	22♉
8	18♈	3♉	6♉	23♉
9	19♈	5♉	7♉	23♉
10	20♈	7♉	8♉	24♉
11	21♈	8♉	10♉	25♉
12	22♈	10♉	11♉	25♉
13	23♈	11♉	12♉	26♉
14	24♈	13♉	13♉	27♉
15	25♈	14♉	15♉	28♉
16	26♈	15♉	16♉	28♉
17	27♈	16♉	17♉	29♉
18	28♈	17♉	18♉	0♊
19	29♈	18♉	19♉	0♊
20	0♉	19♉	21♉	1♊
21	1♉	20♉	22♉	2♊
22	2♉	21♉	23♉	2♊
23	3♉	21♉	24♉	3♊
24	4♉	22♉	26♉	4♊
25	5♉	22♉	27♉	4♊
26	6♉	22♉	28♉	5♊
27	7♉	22♉	29♉	6♊
28	7♉	22♉	0♊	6♊
29	8♉	22♉	2♊	7♊
30	9♉	22♉	3♊	8♊

July

Day	☉	☿	♀	♂
1	9♋	2♋	17♌	19♋
2	10♋	4♋	18♌	20♋
3	11♋	6♋	19♌	20♋
4	12♋	8♋	20♌	21♋
5	13♋	11♋	22♌	22♋
6	14♋	13♋	23♌	22♋
7	15♋	15♋	24♌	23♋
8	16♋	17♋	25♌	23♋
9	17♋	19♋	26♌	24♋
10	18♋	21♋	27♌	25♋
11	18♋	24♋	29♌	25♋
12	19♋	26♋	0♍	26♋
13	20♋	28♋	1♍	27♋
14	21♋	0♌	2♍	27♋
15	22♋	2♌	3♍	28♋
16	23♋	4♌	4♍	29♋
17	24♋	6♌	5♍	29♋
18	25♋	8♌	6♍	0♌
19	26♋	10♌	8♍	1♌
20	27♋	11♌	9♍	1♌
21	28♋	13♌	10♍	2♌
22	29♋	15♌	11♍	3♌
23	0♌	17♌	12♍	3♌
24	1♌	19♌	13♍	4♌
25	2♌	20♌	14♍	4♌
26	3♌	22♌	15♍	5♌
27	4♌	24♌	17♍	6♌
28	5♌	25♌	18♍	6♌
29	6♌	27♌	19♍	7♌
30	7♌	28♌	20♍	8♌
31	8♌	0♍	21♍	8♌

October

Day	☉	☿	♀	♂
1	8♎	20♍	19♏	18♍
2	9♎	21♍	19♏	18♍
3	10♎	23♍	20♏	19♍
4	11♎	24♍	21♏	20♍
5	12♎	26♍	21♏	20♍
6	13♎	27♍	22♏	21♍
7	14♎	29♍	22♏	22♍
8	15♎	1♎	22♏	22♍
9	15♎	2♎	23♏	23♍
10	16♎	4♎	23♏	23♍
11	17♎	6♎	24♏	24♍
12	18♎	8♎	24♏	25♍
13	19♎	9♎	24♏	25♍
14	20♎	11♎	24♏	26♍
15	21♎	13♎	25♏	27♍
16	22♎	15♎	25♏	27♍
17	23♎	16♎	25♏	28♍
18	24♎	18♎	25♏	29♍
19	25♎	20♎	25♏	29♍
20	26♎	21♎	25♏	0♎
21	27♎	23♎	25♏	0♎
22	28♎	25♎	25♏	1♎
23	29♎	27♎	25♏	2♎
24	0♏	28♎	25♏	2♎
25	1♏	0♏	25♏	3♎
26	2♏	2♏	25♏	4♎
27	3♏	3♏	24♏	4♎
28	4♏	5♏	24♏	5♎
29	5♏	7♏	24♏	6♎
30	6♏	8♏	23♏	6♎
31	7♏	10♏	23♏	7♎

February

Day	☉	☿	♀	♂
1	12♒	17♑	14♒	5♈
2	13♒	18♑	15♒	6♈
3	14♒	19♑	16♒	7♈
4	15♒	20♑	17♒	8♈
5	16♒	20♑	19♒	8♈
6	17♒	21♑	20♒	9♈
7	18♒	23♑	21♒	10♈
8	19♒	24♑	22♒	11♈
9	20♒	25♑	24♒	11♈
10	21♒	26♑	25♒	12♈
11	22♒	27♑	26♒	13♈
12	23♒	28♑	27♒	13♈
13	24♒	0♒	29♒	14♈
14	25♒	1♒	0♓	15♈
15	26♒	2♒	1♓	16♈
16	27♒	3♒	3♓	16♈
17	28♒	5♒	4♓	17♈
18	29♒	6♒	5♓	18♈
19	0♓	8♒	6♓	19♈
20	1♓	9♒	8♓	19♈
21	2♓	10♒	9♓	20♈
22	3♓	12♒	10♓	21♈
23	4♓	13♒	11♓	21♈
24	5♓	15♒	13♓	22♈
25	6♓	16♒	14♓	23♈
26	7♓	18♒	15♓	24♈
27	8♓	19♒	16♓	24♈
28	9♓	21♒	18♓	25♈

May

Day	☉	☿	♀	♂
1	10♉	22♉	4♊	8♊
2	11♉	22♉	5♊	9♊
3	12♉	22♉	7♊	10♊
4	13♉	21♉	8♊	11♊
5	14♉	21♉	9♊	11♊
6	15♉	20♉	10♊	12♊
7	16♉	20♉	11♊	13♊
8	17♉	19♉	13♊	13♊
9	18♉	18♉	14♊	14♊
10	19♉	18♉	15♊	15♊
11	20♉	17♉	16♊	15♊
12	21♉	17♉	17♊	16♊
13	22♉	16♉	19♊	17♊
14	23♉	15♉	20♊	17♊
15	24♉	15♉	21♊	18♊
16	25♉	15♉	22♊	19♊
17	26♉	14♉	24♊	19♊
18	27♉	14♉	25♊	20♊
19	28♉	14♉	26♊	21♊
20	29♉	13♉	27♊	21♊
21	0♊	13♉	28♊	22♊
22	1♊	13♉	0♋	23♊
23	2♊	13♉	1♋	23♊
24	3♊	13♉	2♋	24♊
25	4♊	14♉	3♋	25♊
26	5♊	14♉	4♋	25♊
27	5♊	14♉	6♋	26♊
28	6♊	15♉	7♋	27♊
29	7♊	15♉	8♋	27♊
30	8♊	16♉	9♋	28♊
31	9♊	16♉	10♋	29♊

August

Day	☉	☿	♀	♂
1	9♌	1♍	22♍	9♌
2	9♌	3♍	23♍	10♌
3	10♌	4♍	24♍	10♌
4	11♌	6♍	25♍	11♌
5	12♌	7♍	27♍	12♌
6	13♌	9♍	28♍	12♌
7	14♌	10♍	29♍	13♌
8	15♌	11♍	0♎	13♌
9	16♌	12♍	1♎	14♌
10	17♌	14♍	2♎	15♌
11	18♌	15♍	3♎	15♌
12	19♌	16♍	4♎	16♌
13	20♌	17♍	5♎	17♌
14	21♌	18♍	6♎	17♌
15	22♌	19♍	7♎	18♌
16	23♌	20♍	8♎	19♌
17	24♌	21♍	9♎	19♌
18	25♌	22♍	10♎	20♌
19	26♌	23♍	11♎	20♌
20	27♌	24♍	12♎	21♌
21	28♌	25♍	13♎	22♌
22	29♌	25♍	15♎	22♌
23	0♍	26♍	16♎	23♌
24	1♍	26♍	17♎	24♌
25	2♍	27♍	18♎	24♌
26	3♍	27♍	19♎	25♌
27	4♍	28♍	20♎	26♌
28	4♍	28♍	21♎	26♌
29	5♍	28♍	22♎	27♌
30	6♍	28♍	23♎	27♌
31	7♍	28♍	23♎	28♌

November

Day	☉	☿	♀	♂
1	8♏	11♏	23♏	7♎
2	9♏	13♏	22♏	8♎
3	10♏	15♏	22♏	9♎
4	11♏	16♏	21♏	9♎
5	12♏	18♏	21♏	10♎
6	13♏	19♏	20♏	11♎
7	14♏	21♏	19♏	11♎
8	15♏	22♏	19♏	12♎
9	16♏	24♏	18♏	13♎
10	17♏	26♏	18♏	13♎
11	18♏	27♏	17♏	14♎
12	19♏	29♏	16♏	14♎
13	20♏	0♐	16♏	15♎
14	21♏	2♐	15♏	16♎
15	22♏	3♐	15♏	16♎
16	23♏	5♐	14♏	17♎
17	24♏	6♐	14♏	18♎
18	25♏	8♐	13♏	18♎
19	26♏	9♐	13♏	19♎
20	27♏	11♐	12♏	20♎
21	28♏	12♐	12♏	20♎
22	29♏	14♐	11♏	21♎
23	0♐	15♐	11♏	21♎
24	1♐	17♐	11♏	22♎
25	3♐	18♐	10♏	23♎
26	4♐	20♐	10♏	23♎
27	5♐	21♐	10♏	24♎
28	6♐	23♐	10♏	25♎
29	7♐	24♐	10♏	25♎
30	8♐	26♐	10♏	26♎

March

Day	☉	☿	♀	♂
1	10♓	22♒	19♓	26♈
2	11♓	24♒	20♓	27♈
3	12♓	26♒	21♓	27♈
4	13♓	27♒	22♓	28♈
5	14♓	29♒	24♓	29♈
6	15♓	1♓	25♓	29♈
7	16♓	2♓	26♓	0♉
8	17♓	4♓	27♓	1♉
9	18♓	6♓	29♓	2♉
10	19♓	7♓	0♈	2♉
11	20♓	9♓	1♈	3♉
12	21♓	11♓	2♈	4♉
13	22♓	13♓	4♈	4♉
14	23♓	15♓	5♈	5♉
15	24♓	16♓	6♈	6♉
16	25♓	18♓	7♈	7♉
17	26♓	20♓	9♈	7♉
18	27♓	22♓	10♈	8♉
19	28♓	24♓	11♈	9♉
20	29♓	26♓	12♈	9♉
21	0♈	28♓	14♈	10♉
22	1♈	0♈	15♈	11♉
23	2♈	2♈	16♈	11♉
24	3♈	4♈	17♈	12♉
25	4♈	6♈	19♈	13♉
26	5♈	8♈	20♈	14♉
27	6♈	10♈	21♈	14♉
28	7♈	12♈	22♈	15♉
29	8♈	14♈	24♈	16♉
30	9♈	16♈	25♈	16♉
31	10♈	18♈	26♈	17♉

June

Day	☉	☿	♀	♂
1	10♊	17♉	12♋	29♊
2	11♊	18♉	13♋	0♋
3	12♊	18♉	14♋	1♋
4	13♊	19♉	15♋	1♋
5	14♊	20♉	16♋	2♋
6	15♊	21♉	18♋	3♋
7	16♊	22♉	19♋	3♋
8	17♊	23♉	20♋	4♋
9	18♊	24♉	21♋	5♋
10	19♊	26♉	22♋	5♋
11	20♊	27♉	23♋	6♋
12	21♊	28♉	25♋	7♋
13	22♊	0♊	26♋	7♋
14	23♊	1♊	27♋	8♋
15	24♊	2♊	28♋	9♋
16	25♊	4♊	29♋	9♋
17	26♊	5♊	1♌	10♋
18	27♊	7♊	2♌	10♋
19	28♊	9♊	3♌	11♋
20	28♊	10♊	4♌	12♋
21	29♊	12♊	5♌	12♋
22	0♋	14♊	6♌	13♋
23	1♋	16♊	8♌	14♋
24	2♋	18♊	9♌	14♋
25	3♋	20♊	10♌	15♋
26	4♋	22♊	11♌	16♋
27	5♋	24♊	12♌	16♋
28	6♋	26♊	13♌	17♋
29	7♋	28♊	15♌	18♋
30	8♋	0♋	16♌	18♋

September

Day	☉	☿	♀	♂
1	8♍	28♍	24♎	29♌
2	9♍	28♍	25♎	29♌
3	10♍	27♍	26♎	0♍
4	11♍	27♍	27♎	1♍
5	12♍	26♍	28♎	1♍
6	13♍	26♍	29♎	2♍
7	14♍	25♍	0♏	3♍
8	15♍	24♍	1♏	3♍
9	16♍	23♍	2♏	4♍
10	17♍	22♍	3♏	4♍
11	18♍	21♍	4♏	5♍
12	19♍	20♍	5♏	6♍
13	20♍	19♍	5♏	6♍
14	21♍	18♍	6♏	7♍
15	22♍	17♍	7♏	8♍
16	23♍	16♍	8♏	8♍
17	24♍	16♍	9♏	9♍
18	25♍	15♍	10♏	10♍
19	26♍	14♍	10♏	10♍
20	27♍	14♍	11♏	11♍
21	28♍	14♍	12♏	11♍
22	29♍	14♍	13♏	12♍
23	0♎	14♍	14♏	13♍
24	1♎	14♍	14♏	13♍
25	2♎	15♍	15♏	14♍
26	3♎	15♍	16♏	15♍
27	4♎	16♍	16♏	15♍
28	5♎	17♍	17♏	16♍
29	6♎	18♍	18♏	17♍
30	7♎	19♍	18♏	17♍

December

Day	☉	☿	♀	♂
1	9♐	27♐	10♏	27♎
2	10♐	28♐	10♏	27♎
3	11♐	0♑	10♏	28♎
4	12♐	1♑	10♏	28♎
5	13♐	2♑	10♏	29♎
6	14♐	4♑	10♏	0♏
7	15♐	5♑	11♏	0♏
8	16♐	6♑	11♏	1♏
9	17♐	7♑	11♏	2♏
10	18♐	8♑	11♏	2♏
11	19♐	9♑	12♏	3♏
12	20♐	10♑	12♏	4♏
13	21♐	11♑	13♏	4♏
14	22♐	12♑	13♏	5♏
15	23♐	13♑	13♏	5♏
16	24♐	13♑	14♏	6♏
17	25♐	14♑	15♏	7♏
18	26♐	14♑	15♏	7♏
19	27♐	14♑	16♏	8♏
20	28♐	14♑	16♏	9♏
21	29♐	14♑	17♏	9♏
22	0♑	13♑	18♏	10♏
23	1♑	13♑	18♏	10♏
24	2♑	12♑	19♏	11♏
25	3♑	11♑	20♏	12♏
26	4♑	10♑	20♏	12♏
27	5♑	8♑	21♏	13♏
28	6♑	7♑	22♏	14♏
29	7♑	6♑	23♏	14♏
30	8♑	4♑	23♏	15♏
31	9♑	3♑	24♏	16♏

☉ =Sun ☿ = Mercury ♀ = Venus ♂ = Mars ♈ = Aries ♉ = Taurus ♊ = Gemini ♋ = Cancer

1971

January

Day	☉	☿	♀	♂
1	10♑	2♑	25♏	16♏
2	11♑	1♑	26♏	17♏
3	12♑	0♑	27♏	17♏
4	13♑	29♐	28♏	18♏
5	14♑	29♐	28♏	19♏
6	15♑	28♐	29♏	19♏
7	16♑	28♐	0♐	20♏
8	17♑	28♐	1♐	21♏
9	18♑	28♐	2♐	21♏
10	19♑	28♐	3♐	22♏
11	20♑	28♐	4♐	23♏
12	21♑	29♐	5♐	23♏
13	22♑	29♐	6♐	24♏
14	23♑	0♑	7♐	24♏
15	24♑	1♑	8♐	25♏
16	25♑	2♑	9♐	26♏
17	26♑	2♑	10♐	26♏
18	27♑	3♑	11♐	27♏
19	28♑	4♑	12♐	28♏
20	29♑	5♑	13♐	28♏
21	0♒	7♑	14♐	29♏
22	2♒	8♑	15♐	29♏
23	3♒	9♑	16♐	0♐
24	4♒	10♑	17♐	1♐
25	5♒	11♑	18♐	1♐
26	6♒	12♑	19♐	2♐
27	7♒	14♑	20♐	3♐
28	8♒	15♑	21♐	3♐
29	9♒	16♑	22♐	4♐
30	10♒	18♑	23♐	4♐
31	11♒	19♑	24♐	5♐

February

Day	☉	☿	♀	♂
1	12♒	20♑	25♐	6♐
2	13♒	22♑	26♐	6♐
3	14♒	23♑	27♐	7♐
4	15♒	25♑	28♐	8♐
5	16♒	26♑	0♑	8♐
6	17♒	28♑	1♑	9♐
7	18♒	29♑	2♑	10♐
8	19♒	1♒	3♑	10♐
9	20♒	2♒	4♑	11♐
10	21♒	4♒	5♑	11♐
11	22♒	5♒	6♑	12♐
12	23♒	7♒	7♑	13♐
13	24♒	8♒	8♑	13♐
14	25♒	10♒	10♑	14♐
15	26♒	11♒	11♑	14♐
16	27♒	13♒	12♑	15♐
17	28♒	15♒	13♑	16♐
18	29♒	16♒	14♑	16♐
19	0♓	18♒	15♑	17♐
20	1♓	19♒	16♑	18♐
21	2♓	21♒	17♑	18♐
22	3♓	23♒	19♑	19♐
23	4♓	25♒	20♑	19♐
24	5♓	26♒	21♑	20♐
25	6♓	28♒	22♑	21♐
26	7♓	0♓	23♑	21♐
27	8♓	2♓	24♑	22♐
28	9♓	3♓	25♑	23♐

March

Day	☉	☿	♀	♂
1	10♓	5♓	27♑	23♐
2	11♓	7♓	28♑	24♐
3	12♓	9♓	29♑	24♐
4	13♓	11♓	0♒	25♐
5	14♓	13♓	1♒	26♐
6	15♓	14♓	2♒	26♐
7	16♓	16♓	4♒	27♐
8	17♓	18♓	5♒	27♐
9	18♓	20♓	6♒	28♐
10	19♓	22♓	7♒	29♐
11	20♓	24♓	8♒	29♐
12	21♓	26♓	9♒	0♑
13	22♓	28♓	11♒	0♑
14	23♓	0♈	12♒	1♑
15	24♓	2♈	13♒	2♑
16	25♓	4♈	14♒	2♑
17	26♓	6♈	15♒	3♑
18	27♓	8♈	17♒	3♑
19	28♓	10♈	18♒	4♑
20	29♓	12♈	19♒	5♑
21	0♈	14♈	20♒	5♑
22	1♈	15♈	21♒	6♑
23	2♈	17♈	22♒	6♑
24	3♈	19♈	24♒	7♑
25	4♈	20♈	25♒	8♑
26	5♈	22♈	26♒	8♑
27	6♈	24♈	27♒	9♑
28	7♈	25♈	28♒	9♑
29	8♈	26♈	0♓	10♑
30	9♈	27♈	1♓	11♑
31	10♈	29♈	2♓	11♑

April

Day	☉	☿	♀	♂
1	11♈	0♉	3♓	12♑
2	12♈	1♉	4♓	12♑
3	13♈	1♉	6♓	13♑
4	14♈	2♉	7♓	14♑
5	15♈	3♉	8♓	14♑
6	16♈	3♉	9♓	15♑
7	17♈	3♉	10♓	15♑
8	18♈	4♉	11♓	16♑
9	19♈	4♉	13♓	16♑
10	20♈	4♉	14♓	17♑
11	21♈	4♉	15♓	18♑
12	22♈	3♉	16♓	18♑
13	23♈	3♉	17♓	19♑
14	24♈	3♉	19♓	19♑
15	25♈	2♉	20♓	20♑
16	26♈	2♉	21♓	20♑
17	27♈	1♉	22♓	21♑
18	28♈	0♉	23♓	22♑
19	28♈	0♉	25♓	22♑
20	29♈	29♈	26♓	23♑
21	0♉	28♈	27♓	23♑
22	1♉	28♈	28♓	24♑
23	2♉	27♈	29♓	24♑
24	3♉	26♈	1♈	25♑
25	4♉	26♈	2♈	25♑
26	5♉	25♈	3♈	26♑
27	6♉	25♈	4♈	26♑
28	7♉	24♈	5♈	27♑
29	8♉	24♈	7♈	28♑
30	9♉	24♈	8♈	28♑

May

Day	☉	☿	♀	♂
1	10♉	23♈	9♈	29♑
2	11♉	23♈	10♈	29♑
3	12♉	23♈	12♈	0♒
4	13♉	23♈	13♈	0♒
5	14♉	23♈	14♈	1♒
6	15♉	23♈	15♈	1♒
7	16♉	24♈	16♈	2♒
8	17♉	24♈	18♈	2♒
9	18♉	24♈	19♈	3♒
10	19♉	25♈	20♈	3♒
11	20♉	25♈	21♈	4♒
12	21♉	26♈	22♈	4♒
13	22♉	27♈	24♈	5♒
14	23♉	27♈	25♈	5♒
15	24♉	28♈	26♈	6♒
16	25♉	29♈	27♈	6♒
17	26♉	0♉	28♈	7♒
18	27♉	1♉	0♉	7♒
19	28♉	2♉	1♉	8♒
20	29♉	3♉	2♉	8♒
21	0♊	4♉	3♉	8♒
22	0♊	5♉	4♉	9♒
23	1♊	7♉	6♉	9♒
24	2♊	8♉	7♉	10♒
25	3♊	9♉	8♉	10♒
26	4♊	10♉	9♉	11♒
27	5♊	12♉	10♉	11♒
28	6♊	13♉	12♉	12♒
29	7♊	15♉	13♉	12♒
30	8♊	16♉	14♉	12♒
31	9♊	18♉	15♉	13♒

June

Day	☉	☿	♀	♂
1	10♊	19♉	17♉	13♒
2	11♊	21♉	18♉	14♒
3	12♊	23♉	19♉	14♒
4	13♊	24♉	20♉	14♒
5	14♊	26♉	21♉	15♒
6	15♊	28♉	23♉	15♒
7	16♊	0♊	24♉	15♒
8	17♊	2♊	25♉	16♒
9	18♊	4♊	26♉	16♒
10	19♊	6♊	27♉	16♒
11	20♊	8♊	29♉	17♒
12	21♊	10♊	0♊	17♒
13	22♊	12♊	1♊	17♒
14	23♊	14♊	2♊	18♒
15	23♊	16♊	4♊	18♒
16	24♊	18♊	5♊	18♒
17	25♊	20♊	6♊	19♒
18	26♊	22♊	7♊	19♒
19	27♊	25♊	8♊	19♒
20	28♊	27♊	10♊	19♒
21	29♊	29♊	11♊	20♒
22	0♋	1♋	12♊	20♒
23	1♋	3♋	13♊	20♒
24	2♋	6♋	14♊	20♒
25	3♋	8♋	16♊	20♒
26	4♋	10♋	17♊	21♒
27	5♋	12♋	18♊	21♒
28	6♋	14♋	19♊	21♒
29	7♋	16♋	21♊	21♒
30	8♋	18♋	22♊	21♒

July

Day	☉	☿	♀	♂
1	9♋	20♋	23♊	21♒
2	10♋	22♋	24♊	21♒
3	11♋	24♋	25♊	22♒
4	12♋	26♋	27♊	22♒
5	13♋	28♋	28♊	22♒
6	13♋	0♌	29♊	22♒
7	14♋	2♌	0♋	22♒
8	15♋	3♌	2♋	22♒
9	16♋	5♌	3♋	22♒
10	17♋	7♌	4♋	22♒
11	18♋	8♌	5♋	22♒
12	19♋	10♌	6♋	22♒
13	20♋	12♌	8♋	22♒
14	21♋	13♌	9♋	22♒
15	22♋	15♌	10♋	22♒
16	23♋	16♌	11♋	22♒
17	24♋	18♌	13♋	22♒
18	25♋	19♌	14♋	22♒
19	26♋	21♌	15♋	22♒
20	27♋	22♌	16♋	21♒
21	28♋	23♌	17♋	21♒
22	29♋	25♌	19♋	21♒
23	0♌	26♌	20♋	21♒
24	1♌	27♌	21♋	21♒
25	2♌	28♌	22♋	21♒
26	3♌	29♌	24♋	21♒
27	4♌	1♍	25♋	20♒
28	4♌	2♍	26♋	20♒
29	5♌	3♍	27♋	20♒
30	6♌	4♍	29♋	20♒
31	7♌	4♍	0♌	20♒

August

Day	☉	☿	♀	♂
1	8♌	5♍	1♌	19♒
2	9♌	6♍	2♌	19♒
3	10♌	7♍	3♌	19♒
4	11♌	8♍	5♌	19♒
5	12♌	8♍	6♌	18♒
6	13♌	9♍	7♌	18♒
7	14♌	9♍	8♌	18♒
8	15♌	10♍	10♌	18♒
9	16♌	10♍	11♌	17♒
10	17♌	10♍	12♌	17♒
11	18♌	10♍	13♌	17♒
12	19♌	11♍	15♌	16♒
13	20♌	11♍	16♌	16♒
14	21♌	10♍	17♌	16♒
15	22♌	10♍	18♌	16♒
16	23♌	10♍	20♌	15♒
17	24♌	10♍	21♌	15♒
18	25♌	9♍	22♌	15♒
19	26♌	9♍	23♌	15♒
20	27♌	8♍	24♌	14♒
21	28♌	7♍	26♌	14♒
22	28♌	7♍	27♌	14♒
23	29♌	6♍	28♌	14♒
24	0♍	5♍	29♌	14♒
25	1♍	4♍	1♍	13♒
26	2♍	3♍	2♍	13♒
27	3♍	2♍	3♍	13♒
28	4♍	1♍	4♍	13♒
29	5♍	1♍	6♍	13♒
30	6♍	0♍	7♍	13♒
31	7♍	29♌	8♍	12♒

September

Day	☉	☿	♀	♂
1	8♍	28♌	9♍	12♒
2	9♍	28♌	11♍	12♒
3	10♍	28♌	12♍	12♒
4	11♍	27♌	13♍	12♒
5	12♍	27♌	14♍	12♒
6	13♍	27♌	16♍	12♒
7	14♍	28♌	17♍	12♒
8	15♍	28♌	18♍	12♒
9	16♍	29♌	19♍	12♒
10	17♍	29♌	20♍	12♒
11	18♍	0♍	22♍	12♒
12	19♍	1♍	23♍	12♒
13	20♍	2♍	24♍	12♒
14	21♍	3♍	25♍	12♒
15	22♍	4♍	27♍	12♒
16	23♍	6♍	28♍	12♒
17	24♍	7♍	29♍	12♒
18	25♍	9♍	0♎	12♒
19	26♍	10♍	2♎	13♒
20	27♍	12♍	3♎	13♒
21	28♍	14♍	4♎	13♒
22	29♍	15♍	5♎	13♒
23	0♎	17♍	7♎	13♒
24	0♎	19♍	8♎	13♒
25	1♎	21♍	9♎	13♒
26	2♎	22♍	10♎	14♒
27	3♎	24♍	12♎	14♒
28	4♎	26♍	13♎	14♒
29	5♎	28♍	14♎	14♒
30	6♎	0♎	15♎	15♒

October

Day	☉	☿	♀	♂
1	7♎	1♎	17♎	15♒
2	8♎	3♎	18♎	15♒
3	9♎	5♎	19♎	15♒
4	10♎	7♎	20♎	16♒
5	11♎	9♎	22♎	16♒
6	12♎	10♎	23♎	16♒
7	13♎	12♎	24♎	17♒
8	14♎	14♎	25♎	17♒
9	15♎	16♎	27♎	17♒
10	16♎	17♎	28♎	18♒
11	17♎	19♎	29♎	18♒
12	18♎	21♎	0♏	18♒
13	19♎	23♎	2♏	19♒
14	20♎	24♎	3♏	19♒
15	21♎	26♎	4♏	20♒
16	22♎	27♎	5♏	20♒
17	23♎	29♎	7♏	20♒
18	24♎	1♏	8♏	21♒
19	25♎	2♏	9♏	21♒
20	26♎	4♏	10♏	22♒
21	27♎	6♏	12♏	22♒
22	28♎	7♏	13♏	23♒
23	29♎	9♏	14♏	23♒
24	0♏	10♏	15♏	23♒
25	1♏	12♏	17♏	24♒
26	2♏	13♏	18♏	24♒
27	3♏	15♏	19♏	25♒
28	4♏	16♏	20♏	25♒
29	5♏	18♏	22♏	26♒
30	6♏	20♏	23♏	26♒
31	7♏	21♏	24♏	27♒

November

Day	☉	☿	♀	♂
1	8♏	23♏	25♏	27♒
2	9♏	24♏	26♏	28♒
3	10♏	25♏	28♏	28♒
4	11♏	27♏	29♏	29♒
5	12♏	28♏	0♐	29♒
6	13♏	0♐	1♐	0♓
7	14♏	1♐	3♐	0♓
8	15♏	3♐	4♐	1♓
9	16♏	4♐	5♐	1♓
10	17♏	6♐	6♐	2♓
11	18♏	7♐	8♐	3♓
12	19♏	8♐	9♐	3♓
13	20♏	10♐	10♐	4♓
14	21♏	11♐	11♐	4♓
15	22♏	12♐	13♐	5♓
16	23♏	14♐	14♐	5♓
17	24♏	15♐	15♐	6♓
18	25♏	16♐	16♐	6♓
19	26♏	18♐	18♐	7♓
20	27♏	19♐	19♐	8♓
21	28♏	20♐	20♐	8♓
22	29♏	21♐	21♐	9♓
23	0♐	22♐	23♐	9♓
24	1♐	23♐	24♐	10♓
25	2♐	24♐	25♐	10♓
26	3♐	25♐	26♐	11♓
27	4♐	26♐	28♐	12♓
28	5♐	27♐	29♐	12♓
29	6♐	27♐	0♑	13♓
30	7♐	28♐	1♑	13♓

December

Day	☉	☿	♀	♂
1	8♐	28♐	3♑	14♓
2	9♐	28♐	4♑	15♓
3	10♐	28♐	5♑	15♓
4	11♐	28♐	6♑	16♓
5	12♐	28♐	8♑	16♓
6	13♐	27♐	9♑	17♓
7	14♐	27♐	10♑	18♓
8	15♐	26♐	11♑	18♓
9	16♐	25♐	13♑	19♓
10	17♐	24♐	14♑	20♓
11	18♐	22♐	15♑	20♓
12	20♐	21♐	16♑	21♓
13	21♐	20♐	18♑	21♓
14	22♐	18♐	19♑	22♓
15	23♐	17♐	20♑	23♓
16	24♐	16♐	21♑	23♓
17	25♐	15♐	22♑	24♓
18	26♐	14♐	24♑	25♓
19	27♐	13♐	25♑	25♓
20	28♐	13♐	26♑	26♓
21	29♐	12♐	27♑	26♓
22	0♑	12♐	29♑	27♓
23	1♑	12♐	0♒	28♓
24	2♑	12♐	1♒	28♓
25	3♑	12♐	2♒	29♓
26	4♑	13♐	4♒	0♈
27	5♑	13♐	5♒	0♈
28	6♑	14♐	6♒	1♈
29	7♑	15♐	7♒	2♈
30	8♑	15♐	9♒	2♈
31	9♑	16♐	10♒	3♈

Planetary Positions

♌ = Leo ♍ = Virgo ♎ = Libra ♏ = Scorpio ♐ = Sagittarius ♑ = Capricorn ♒ = Aquarius ♓ = Pisces

1972

January

Day	☉	☿	♀	♂
1	10♑	17♐	11♒	4♈
2	11♑	18♐	12♒	4♈
3	12♑	19♐	14♒	5♈
4	13♑	21♐	15♒	5♈
5	14♑	22♐	16♒	6♈
6	15♑	23♐	17♒	7♈
7	16♑	24♐	18♒	7♈
8	17♑	25♐	20♒	8♈
9	18♑	27♐	21♒	9♈
10	19♑	28♐	22♒	9♈
11	20♑	29♐	23♒	10♈
12	21♑	1♑	25♒	11♈
13	22♑	2♑	26♒	11♈
14	23♑	3♑	27♒	12♈
15	24♑	5♑	28♒	13♈
16	25♑	6♑	29♒	13♈
17	26♑	8♑	1♓	14♈
18	27♑	9♑	2♓	15♈
19	28♑	10♑	3♓	15♈
20	29♑	12♑	4♓	16♈
21	0♒	13♑	6♓	17♈
22	1♒	15♑	7♓	17♈
23	2♒	16♑	8♓	18♈
24	3♒	18♑	9♓	19♈
25	4♒	19♑	10♓	19♈
26	5♒	21♑	12♓	20♈
27	6♒	22♑	13♓	21♈
28	7♒	24♑	14♓	21♈
29	8♒	26♑	15♓	22♈
30	9♒	27♑	17♓	22♈
31	10♒	29♑	18♓	23♈

February

Day	☉	☿	♀	♂
1	11♒	0♒	19♓	24♈
2	12♒	2♒	20♓	24♈
3	13♒	4♒	21♓	25♈
4	14♒	5♒	23♓	26♈
5	15♒	7♒	24♓	26♈
6	17♒	8♒	25♓	27♈
7	18♒	10♒	26♓	28♈
8	19♒	12♒	27♓	28♈
9	20♒	14♒	29♓	29♈
10	21♒	15♒	0♈	0♉
11	22♒	17♒	1♈	0♉
12	23♒	19♒	2♈	1♉
13	24♒	20♒	3♈	2♉
14	25♒	22♒	5♈	2♉
15	26♒	24♒	6♈	3♉
16	27♒	26♒	7♈	4♉
17	28♒	28♒	8♈	4♉
18	29♒	29♒	9♈	5♉
19	0♓	1♓	10♈	6♉
20	1♓	3♓	12♈	6♉
21	2♓	5♓	13♈	7♉
22	3♓	7♓	14♈	8♉
23	4♓	9♓	15♈	8♉
24	5♓	11♓	16♈	9♉
25	6♓	12♓	17♈	10♉
26	7♓	14♓	19♈	10♉
27	8♓	16♓	20♈	11♉
28	9♓	18♓	21♈	12♉
29	10♓	20♓	22♈	12♉

March

Day	☉	☿	♀	♂
1	11♓	22♓	23♈	13♉
2	12♓	24♓	24♈	14♉
3	13♓	26♓	26♈	14♉
4	14♓	27♓	27♈	15♉
5	15♓	29♓	28♈	16♉
6	16♓	1♈	29♈	16♉
7	17♓	3♈	0♉	17♉
8	18♓	4♈	1♉	18♉
9	19♓	6♈	2♉	18♉
10	20♓	7♈	3♉	19♉
11	21♓	8♈	5♉	20♉
12	22♓	10♈	6♉	20♉
13	23♓	11♈	7♉	21♉
14	24♓	12♈	8♉	21♉
15	25♓	13♈	9♉	22♉
16	26♓	14♈	10♉	23♉
17	27♓	14♈	11♉	23♉
18	28♓	15♈	12♉	24♉
19	29♓	15♈	13♉	25♉
20	0♈	16♈	15♉	25♉
21	1♈	16♈	16♉	26♉
22	2♈	16♈	17♉	27♉
23	3♈	16♈	18♉	27♉
24	4♈	15♈	19♉	28♉
25	5♈	15♈	20♉	29♉
26	6♈	15♈	21♉	29♉
27	7♈	14♈	22♉	0♊
28	8♈	13♈	23♉	1♊
29	9♈	13♈	24♉	1♊
30	10♈	12♈	25♉	2♊
31	11♈	11♈	26♉	3♊

April

Day	☉	☿	♀	♂
1	12♈	10♈	27♉	3♊
2	13♈	9♈	28♉	4♊
3	14♈	9♈	29♉	5♊
4	15♈	8♈	0♊	5♊
5	16♈	7♈	1♊	6♊
6	16♈	6♈	2♊	7♊
7	17♈	6♈	3♊	7♊
8	18♈	5♈	4♊	8♊
9	19♈	5♈	5♊	8♊
10	20♈	4♈	6♊	9♊
11	21♈	4♈	7♊	10♊
12	22♈	4♈	8♊	10♊
13	23♈	4♈	9♊	11♊
14	24♈	4♈	10♊	12♊
15	25♈	4♈	11♊	12♊
16	26♈	4♈	12♊	13♊
17	27♈	4♈	13♊	14♊
18	28♈	4♈	14♊	14♊
19	29♈	5♈	14♊	15♊
20	0♉	5♈	15♊	16♊
21	1♉	6♈	16♊	16♊
22	2♉	6♈	17♊	17♊
23	3♉	7♈	18♊	18♊
24	4♉	8♈	19♊	18♊
25	5♉	8♈	20♊	19♊
26	6♉	9♈	20♊	19♊
27	7♉	10♈	21♊	20♊
28	8♉	11♈	22♊	21♊
29	9♉	12♈	23♊	21♊
30	10♉	13♈	23♊	22♊

May

Day	☉	☿	♀	♂
1	11♉	14♈	24♊	23♊
2	12♉	15♈	25♊	23♊
3	13♉	16♈	26♊	24♊
4	14♉	18♈	26♊	25♊
5	15♉	19♈	27♊	25♊
6	16♉	20♈	27♊	26♊
7	17♉	22♈	28♊	27♊
8	18♉	23♈	29♊	27♊
9	19♉	24♈	29♊	28♊
10	20♉	26♈	0♋	28♊
11	21♉	27♈	0♋	29♊
12	22♉	29♈	1♋	0♋
13	23♉	0♉	1♋	0♋
14	23♉	2♉	2♋	1♋
15	24♉	4♉	2♋	2♋
16	25♉	5♉	3♋	2♋
17	26♉	7♉	3♋	3♋
18	27♉	9♉	3♋	4♋
19	28♉	10♉	4♋	4♋
20	29♉	12♉	4♋	5♋
21	0♊	14♉	4♋	6♋
22	1♊	16♉	4♋	6♋
23	2♊	18♉	4♋	7♋
24	3♊	20♉	5♋	7♋
25	4♊	22♉	5♋	8♋
26	5♊	24♉	5♋	9♋
27	6♊	26♉	5♋	9♋
28	7♊	28♉	5♋	10♋
29	8♊	0♊	5♋	11♋
30	9♊	2♊	5♋	11♋
31	10♊	4♊	4♋	12♋

June

Day	☉	☿	♀	♂
1	11♊	6♊	4♋	13♋
2	12♊	8♊	4♋	13♋
3	13♊	11♊	4♋	14♋
4	14♊	13♊	3♋	14♋
5	15♊	15♊	3♋	15♋
6	16♊	17♊	3♋	16♋
7	17♊	19♊	2♋	16♋
8	17♊	22♊	2♋	17♋
9	18♊	24♊	1♋	18♋
10	19♊	26♊	1♋	18♋
11	20♊	28♊	0♋	19♋
12	21♊	0♋	0♋	20♋
13	22♊	2♋	29♊	20♋
14	23♊	4♋	29♊	21♋
15	24♊	6♋	28♊	21♋
16	25♊	8♋	27♊	22♋
17	26♊	10♋	27♊	23♋
18	27♊	12♋	26♊	23♋
19	28♊	14♋	26♊	24♋
20	29♊	16♋	25♊	25♋
21	0♋	18♋	24♊	25♋
22	1♋	19♋	24♊	26♋
23	2♋	21♋	23♊	27♋
24	3♋	23♋	23♊	27♋
25	4♋	25♋	22♊	28♋
26	5♋	26♋	22♊	28♋
27	6♋	28♋	21♊	29♋
28	7♋	29♋	21♊	0♌
29	8♋	1♌	20♊	0♌
30	8♋	2♌	20♊	1♌

July

Day	☉	☿	♀	♂
1	9♋	4♌	19♊	2♌
2	10♋	5♌	19♊	2♌
3	11♋	6♌	19♊	3♌
4	12♋	8♌	19♊	4♌
5	13♋	9♌	19♊	4♌
6	14♋	10♌	18♊	5♌
7	15♋	11♌	18♊	5♌
8	16♋	12♌	18♊	6♌
9	17♋	13♌	18♊	7♌
10	18♋	14♌	18♊	7♌
11	19♋	15♌	18♊	8♌
12	20♋	16♌	18♊	9♌
13	21♋	17♌	19♊	9♌
14	22♋	18♌	19♊	10♌
15	23♋	19♌	19♊	10♌
16	24♋	19♌	19♊	11♌
17	25♋	20♌	19♊	12♌
18	26♋	21♌	20♊	12♌
19	27♋	21♌	20♊	13♌
20	28♋	21♌	20♊	14♌
21	29♋	22♌	21♊	14♌
22	29♋	22♌	21♊	15♌
23	0♌	22♌	22♊	16♌
24	1♌	22♌	22♊	16♌
25	2♌	22♌	23♊	17♌
26	3♌	22♌	23♊	17♌
27	4♌	22♌	24♊	18♌
28	5♌	22♌	24♊	19♌
29	6♌	22♌	25♊	19♌
30	7♌	21♌	25♊	20♌
31	8♌	21♌	26♊	21♌

August

Day	☉	☿	♀	♂
1	9♌	20♌	27♊	21♌
2	10♌	20♌	27♊	22♌
3	11♌	19♌	28♊	22♌
4	12♌	18♌	29♊	23♌
5	13♌	17♌	29♊	24♌
6	14♌	17♌	0♋	24♌
7	15♌	16♌	1♋	25♌
8	16♌	15♌	2♋	26♌
9	17♌	14♌	2♋	26♌
10	18♌	14♌	3♋	27♌
11	19♌	13♌	4♋	28♌
12	20♌	12♌	5♋	28♌
13	21♌	12♌	6♋	29♌
14	21♌	11♌	6♋	29♌
15	22♌	11♌	7♋	0♍
16	23♌	11♌	8♋	1♍
17	24♌	10♌	9♋	1♍
18	25♌	10♌	10♋	2♍
19	26♌	11♌	11♋	3♍
20	27♌	11♌	12♋	3♍
21	28♌	11♌	13♋	4♍
22	29♌	12♌	14♋	5♍
23	0♍	12♌	14♋	5♍
24	1♍	13♌	15♋	6♍
25	2♍	14♌	16♋	6♍
26	3♍	15♌	17♋	7♍
27	4♍	16♌	18♋	8♍
28	5♍	17♌	19♋	8♍
29	6♍	18♌	20♋	9♍
30	7♍	20♌	21♋	10♍
31	8♍	21♌	22♋	10♍

September

Day	☉	☿	♀	♂
1	9♍	23♌	23♋	11♍
2	10♍	24♌	24♋	12♍
3	11♍	26♌	25♋	12♍
4	12♍	28♌	26♋	13♍
5	13♍	0♍	27♋	13♍
6	14♍	1♍	28♋	14♍
7	15♍	3♍	29♋	15♍
8	16♍	5♍	0♌	15♍
9	17♍	7♍	1♌	16♍
10	18♍	9♍	2♌	17♍
11	19♍	11♍	3♌	17♍
12	20♍	13♍	4♌	18♍
13	21♍	15♍	5♌	19♍
14	21♍	16♍	7♌	19♍
15	22♍	18♍	8♌	20♍
16	23♍	20♍	9♌	21♍
17	24♍	22♍	10♌	21♍
18	25♍	24♍	11♌	22♍
19	26♍	26♍	12♌	22♍
20	27♍	28♍	13♌	23♍
21	28♍	29♍	14♌	24♍
22	29♍	1♎	15♌	24♍
23	0♎	3♎	16♌	25♍
24	1♎	5♎	17♌	26♍
25	2♎	7♎	19♌	26♍
26	3♎	8♎	20♌	27♍
27	4♎	10♎	21♌	28♍
28	5♎	12♎	22♌	28♍
29	6♎	13♎	23♌	29♍
30	7♎	15♎	24♌	0♎

October

Day	☉	☿	♀	♂
1	8♎	17♎	25♌	0♎
2	9♎	18♎	26♌	1♎
3	10♎	20♎	28♌	1♎
4	11♎	22♎	29♌	2♎
5	12♎	23♎	0♍	3♎
6	13♎	25♎	1♍	3♎
7	14♎	26♎	2♍	4♎
8	15♎	28♎	3♍	5♎
9	16♎	0♏	4♍	5♎
10	17♎	1♏	6♍	6♎
11	18♎	3♏	7♍	7♎
12	19♎	4♏	8♍	7♎
13	20♎	6♏	9♍	8♎
14	21♎	7♏	10♍	9♎
15	22♎	9♏	11♍	9♎
16	23♎	10♏	13♍	10♎
17	24♎	12♏	14♍	11♎
18	25♎	13♏	15♍	11♎
19	26♎	15♏	16♍	12♎
20	27♎	16♏	17♍	12♎
21	28♎	17♏	18♍	13♎
22	29♎	19♏	20♍	14♎
23	0♏	20♏	21♍	14♎
24	1♏	21♏	22♍	15♎
25	2♏	23♏	23♍	16♎
26	3♏	24♏	24♍	16♎
27	4♏	25♏	26♍	17♎
28	5♏	27♏	27♍	18♎
29	6♏	28♏	28♍	18♎
30	7♏	29♏	29♍	19♎
31	8♏	0♐	0♎	20♎

November

Day	☉	☿	♀	♂
1	9♏	2♐	2♎	20♎
2	10♏	3♐	3♎	21♎
3	11♏	4♐	4♎	22♎
4	12♏	5♐	5♎	22♎
5	13♏	6♐	6♎	23♎
6	14♏	7♐	8♎	24♎
7	15♏	8♐	9♎	24♎
8	16♏	9♐	10♎	25♎
9	17♏	10♐	11♎	26♎
10	18♏	10♐	12♎	26♎
11	19♏	11♐	14♎	27♎
12	20♏	12♐	15♎	28♎
13	21♏	12♐	16♎	28♎
14	22♏	12♐	17♎	29♎
15	23♏	12♐	19♎	0♏
16	24♏	12♐	20♎	0♏
17	25♏	12♐	21♎	1♏
18	26♏	12♐	22♎	2♏
19	27♏	12♐	23♎	2♏
20	28♏	11♐	25♎	3♏
21	29♏	10♐	26♎	3♏
22	0♐	9♐	27♎	4♏
23	1♐	8♐	28♎	5♏
24	2♐	7♐	0♏	5♏
25	3♐	5♐	1♏	6♏
26	4♐	4♐	2♏	7♏
27	5♐	3♐	3♏	7♏
28	6♐	1♐	4♏	8♏
29	7♐	0♐	6♏	9♏
30	8♐	29♏	7♏	9♏

December

Day	☉	☿	♀	♂
1	9♐	28♏	8♏	10♏
2	10♐	27♏	9♏	11♏
3	11♐	27♏	11♏	11♏
4	12♐	26♏	12♏	12♏
5	13♐	26♏	13♏	13♏
6	14♐	26♏	14♏	13♏
7	15♐	26♏	16♏	14♏
8	16♐	27♏	17♏	15♏
9	17♐	27♏	18♏	16♏
10	18♐	28♏	19♏	16♏
11	19♐	29♏	21♏	17♏
12	20♐	29♏	22♏	18♏
13	21♐	0♐	23♏	18♏
14	22♐	1♐	24♏	19♏
15	23♐	2♐	26♏	20♏
16	24♐	3♐	27♏	20♏
17	25♐	4♐	28♏	21♏
18	26♐	6♐	29♏	21♏
19	27♐	7♐	1♐	22♏
20	28♐	8♐	2♐	23♏
21	29♐	9♐	3♐	24♏
22	0♑	11♐	4♐	24♏
23	1♑	12♐	6♐	25♏
24	2♑	13♐	7♐	26♏
25	4♑	15♐	8♐	26♏
26	5♑	16♐	9♐	27♏
27	6♑	18♐	11♐	28♏
28	7♑	19♐	12♐	28♏
29	8♑	21♐	13♐	29♏
30	9♑	22♐	14♐	0♐
31	10♑	23♐	16♐	0♐

Your Starway to Love

☉ =Sun ☿ = Mercury ♀ = Venus ♂ = Mars ♈ = Aries ♉ = Taurus ♊ = Gemini ♋ = Cancer

January

Day	☉	☿	♀	♂
1	11♑	25♐	17♐	1♐
2	12♑	26♐	18♐	2♐
3	13♑	28♐	19♐	2♐
4	14♑	29♐	21♐	3♐
5	15♑	1♑	22♐	4♐
6	16♑	2♑	23♐	4♐
7	17♑	4♑	24♐	5♐
8	18♑	5♑	26♐	6♐
9	19♑	7♑	27♐	7♐
10	20♑	9♑	28♐	7♐
11	21♑	10♑	29♐	8♐
12	22♑	12♑	1♑	9♐
13	23♑	13♑	2♑	9♐
14	24♑	15♑	3♑	10♐
15	25♑	16♑	4♑	11♐
16	26♑	18♑	6♑	11♐
17	27♑	20♑	7♑	12♐
18	28♑	21♑	8♑	13♐
19	29♑	23♑	9♑	13♐
20	0♒	24♑	11♑	14♐
21	1♒	26♑	12♑	15♐
22	2♒	28♑	13♑	15♐
23	3♒	29♑	14♑	16♐
24	4♒	1♒	16♑	17♐
25	5♒	3♒	17♑	17♐
26	6♒	4♒	18♑	18♐
27	7♒	6♒	19♑	19♐
28	8♒	8♒	21♑	20♐
29	9♒	9♒	22♑	20♐
30	10♒	11♒	23♑	21♐
31	11♒	13♒	24♑	22♐

February

Day	☉	☿	♀	♂
1	12♒	15♒	26♑	22♐
2	13♒	16♒	27♑	23♐
3	14♒	18♒	28♑	24♐
4	15♒	20♒	29♑	24♐
5	16♒	22♒	1♒	25♐
6	17♒	23♒	2♒	26♐
7	18♒	25♒	3♒	26♐
8	19♒	27♒	4♒	27♐
9	20♒	29♒	6♒	28♐
10	21♒	1♓	7♒	29♐
11	22♒	3♓	8♒	29♐
12	23♒	4♓	9♒	0♑
13	24♒	6♓	11♒	1♑
14	25♒	8♓	12♒	1♑
15	26♒	10♓	13♒	2♑
16	27♒	11♓	14♒	3♑
17	28♒	13♓	16♒	3♑
18	29♒	15♓	17♒	4♑
19	0♓	16♓	18♒	5♑
20	1♓	18♓	19♒	6♑
21	2♓	19♓	21♒	6♑
22	3♓	21♓	22♒	7♑
23	4♓	22♓	23♒	8♑
24	5♓	23♓	24♒	8♑
25	6♓	25♓	26♒	9♑
26	7♓	26♓	27♒	10♑
27	8♓	26♓	28♒	10♑
28	9♓	27♓	29♒	11♑

March

Day	☉	☿	♀	♂
1	10♓	28♓	1♓	12♑
2	11♓	28♓	2♓	13♑
3	12♓	28♓	3♓	13♑
4	13♓	29♓	4♓	14♑
5	14♓	29♓	6♓	15♑
6	15♓	28♓	7♓	15♑
7	16♓	28♓	8♓	16♑
8	17♓	28♓	9♓	17♑
9	18♓	27♓	11♓	18♑
10	19♓	26♓	12♓	18♑
11	20♓	26♓	13♓	19♑
12	21♓	25♓	14♓	20♑
13	22♓	24♓	16♓	20♑
14	23♓	23♓	17♓	21♑
15	24♓	22♓	18♓	22♑
16	25♓	21♓	19♓	22♑
17	26♓	20♓	20♓	23♑
18	27♓	19♓	22♓	24♑
19	28♓	18♓	23♓	25♑
20	29♓	18♓	24♓	25♑
21	0♈	17♓	25♓	26♑
22	1♈	16♓	27♓	27♑
23	2♈	16♓	28♓	27♑
24	3♈	15♓	29♓	28♑
25	4♈	15♓	0♈	29♑
26	5♈	15♓	2♈	0♒
27	6♈	15♓	3♈	0♒
28	7♈	15♓	4♈	1♒
29	8♈	15♓	5♈	2♒
30	9♈	15♓	7♈	2♒
31	10♈	16♓	8♈	3♒

April

Day	☉	☿	♀	♂
1	11♈	16♓	9♈	4♒
2	12♈	17♓	10♈	4♒
3	13♈	17♓	12♈	5♒
4	14♈	18♓	13♈	6♒
5	15♈	18♓	14♈	7♒
6	16♈	19♓	15♈	7♒
7	17♈	20♓	17♈	8♒
8	18♈	21♓	18♈	9♒
9	19♈	22♓	19♈	9♒
10	20♈	23♓	20♈	10♒
11	21♈	24♓	22♈	11♒
12	22♈	25♓	23♈	12♒
13	23♈	26♓	24♈	12♒
14	24♈	27♓	25♈	13♒
15	25♈	28♓	26♈	14♒
16	26♈	29♓	28♈	14♒
17	27♈	0♈	29♈	15♒
18	28♈	2♈	0♉	16♒
19	29♈	3♈	1♉	17♒
20	0♉	4♈	3♉	17♒
21	1♉	6♈	4♉	18♒
22	2♉	7♈	5♉	19♒
23	3♉	9♈	6♉	19♒
24	4♉	10♈	8♉	20♒
25	5♉	12♈	9♉	21♒
26	6♉	13♈	10♉	22♒
27	7♉	15♈	11♉	22♒
28	8♉	16♈	13♉	23♒
29	9♉	18♈	14♉	24♒
30	10♉	20♈	15♉	24♒

May

Day	☉	☿	♀	♂
1	11♉	21♈	16♉	25♒
2	12♉	23♈	17♉	26♒
3	13♉	25♈	19♉	26♒
4	14♉	27♈	20♉	27♒
5	15♉	28♈	21♉	28♒
6	16♉	0♉	22♉	29♒
7	17♉	2♉	24♉	29♒
8	17♉	4♉	25♉	0♓
9	18♉	6♉	26♉	1♓
10	19♉	8♉	27♉	1♓
11	20♉	10♉	29♉	2♓
12	21♉	12♉	0♊	3♓
13	22♉	14♉	1♊	4♓
14	23♉	16♉	2♊	4♓
15	24♉	18♉	3♊	5♓
16	25♉	20♉	5♊	6♓
17	26♉	22♉	6♊	6♓
18	27♉	25♉	7♊	7♓
19	28♉	27♉	8♊	8♓
20	29♉	29♉	10♊	8♓
21	0♊	1♊	11♊	9♓
22	1♊	3♊	12♊	10♓
23	2♊	5♊	13♊	11♓
24	3♊	8♊	15♊	11♓
25	4♊	10♊	16♊	12♓
26	5♊	12♊	17♊	13♓
27	6♊	14♊	18♊	13♓
28	7♊	16♊	19♊	14♓
29	8♊	18♊	21♊	15♓
30	9♊	20♊	22♊	15♓
31	10♊	22♊	23♊	16♓

June

Day	☉	☿	♀	♂
1	11♊	24♊	24♊	17♓
2	12♊	26♊	26♊	17♓
3	12♊	28♊	27♊	18♓
4	13♊	0♋	28♊	19♓
5	14♊	2♋	29♊	20♓
6	15♊	4♋	0♋	20♓
7	16♊	5♋	2♋	21♓
8	17♊	7♋	3♋	22♓
9	18♊	9♋	4♋	22♓
10	19♊	10♋	5♋	23♓
11	20♊	12♋	7♋	24♓
12	21♊	13♋	8♋	24♓
13	22♊	15♋	9♋	25♓
14	23♊	16♋	10♋	26♓
15	24♊	18♋	12♋	26♓
16	25♊	19♋	13♋	27♓
17	26♊	20♋	14♋	28♓
18	27♊	21♋	15♋	28♓
19	28♊	23♋	16♋	29♓
20	29♊	24♋	18♋	0♈
21	0♋	25♋	19♋	0♈
22	1♋	26♋	20♋	1♈
23	2♋	27♋	21♋	2♈
24	3♋	28♋	22♋	2♈
25	3♋	28♋	24♋	3♈
26	4♋	29♋	25♋	3♈
27	5♋	0♌	26♋	4♈
28	6♋	1♌	27♋	5♈
29	7♋	1♌	29♋	5♈
30	8♋	2♌	0♌	6♈

July

Day	☉	☿	♀	♂
1	9♋	2♌	1♌	7♈
2	10♋	3♌	2♌	7♈
3	11♋	3♌	3♌	8♈
4	12♋	3♌	5♌	9♈
5	13♋	3♌	6♌	9♈
6	14♋	3♌	7♌	10♈
7	15♋	3♌	8♌	10♈
8	16♋	3♌	10♌	11♈
9	17♋	3♌	11♌	12♈
10	18♋	3♌	12♌	12♈
11	19♋	3♌	13♌	13♈
12	20♋	2♌	14♌	13♈
13	21♋	2♌	16♌	14♈
14	22♋	1♌	17♌	15♈
15	23♋	1♌	18♌	15♈
16	24♋	0♌	19♌	16♈
17	24♋	29♋	20♌	16♈
18	25♋	29♋	22♌	17♈
19	26♋	28♋	23♌	18♈
20	27♋	27♋	24♌	18♈
21	28♋	27♋	25♌	19♈
22	29♋	26♋	27♌	19♈
23	0♌	25♋	28♌	20♈
24	1♌	25♋	29♌	20♈
25	2♌	24♋	0♍	21♈
26	3♌	24♋	1♍	21♈
27	4♌	24♋	3♍	22♈
28	5♌	23♋	4♍	23♈
29	6♌	23♋	5♍	23♈
30	7♌	23♋	6♍	24♈
31	8♌	23♋	7♍	24♈

August

Day	☉	☿	♀	♂
1	9♌	23♋	9♍	25♈
2	10♌	23♋	10♍	25♈
3	11♌	23♋	11♍	26♈
4	12♌	24♋	12♍	26♈
5	13♌	24♋	13♍	27♈
6	14♌	25♋	15♍	27♈
7	15♌	26♋	16♍	28♈
8	16♌	27♋	17♍	28♈
9	16♌	27♋	18♍	28♈
10	17♌	28♋	19♍	29♈
11	18♌	0♌	21♍	29♈
12	19♌	1♌	22♍	0♉
13	20♌	2♌	23♍	0♉
14	21♌	4♌	24♍	1♉
15	22♌	5♌	25♍	1♉
16	23♌	7♌	27♍	2♉
17	24♌	8♌	28♍	2♉
18	25♌	10♌	29♍	2♉
19	26♌	12♌	0♎	3♉
20	27♌	14♌	1♎	3♉
21	28♌	15♌	3♎	3♉
22	29♌	17♌	4♎	4♉
23	0♍	19♌	5♎	4♉
24	1♍	21♌	6♎	4♉
25	2♍	23♌	7♎	5♉
26	3♍	25♌	9♎	5♉
27	4♍	27♌	10♎	5♉
28	5♍	29♌	11♎	6♉
29	6♍	1♍	12♎	6♉
30	7♍	3♍	13♎	6♉
31	8♍	5♍	14♎	7♉

September

Day	☉	☿	♀	♂
1	9♍	7♍	16♎	7♉
2	10♍	9♍	17♎	7♉
3	11♍	11♍	18♎	7♉
4	12♍	13♍	19♎	8♉
5	12♍	15♍	20♎	8♉
6	13♍	17♍	22♎	8♉
7	14♍	18♍	23♎	8♉
8	15♍	20♍	24♎	8♉
9	16♍	22♍	25♎	8♉
10	17♍	24♍	26♎	9♉
11	18♍	26♍	27♎	9♉
12	19♍	27♍	29♎	9♉
13	20♍	29♍	0♏	9♉
14	21♍	1♎	1♏	9♉
15	22♍	3♎	2♏	9♉
16	23♍	4♎	3♏	9♉
17	24♍	6♎	4♏	9♉
18	25♍	8♎	6♏	9♉
19	26♍	9♎	7♏	9♉
20	27♍	11♎	8♏	9♉
21	28♍	13♎	9♏	9♉
22	29♍	14♎	10♏	9♉
23	0♎	16♎	11♏	9♉
24	1♎	17♎	13♏	9♉
25	2♎	19♎	14♏	9♉
26	3♎	20♎	15♏	9♉
27	4♎	22♎	16♏	9♉
28	5♎	23♎	17♏	9♉
29	6♎	25♎	18♏	9♉
30	7♎	26♎	20♏	8♉

October

Day	☉	☿	♀	♂
1	8♎	28♎	21♏	8♉
2	9♎	29♎	22♏	8♉
3	10♎	1♏	23♏	8♉
4	11♎	2♏	24♏	8♉
5	12♎	3♏	25♏	8♉
6	13♎	5♏	26♏	7♉
7	14♎	6♏	28♏	7♉
8	15♎	7♏	29♏	7♉
9	16♎	9♏	0♐	7♉
10	17♎	10♏	1♐	6♉
11	18♎	11♏	2♐	6♉
12	19♎	12♏	3♐	6♉
13	20♎	14♏	4♐	5♉
14	21♎	15♏	5♐	5♉
15	22♎	16♏	7♐	5♉
16	23♎	17♏	8♐	5♉
17	24♎	18♏	9♐	4♉
18	25♎	19♏	10♐	4♉
19	26♎	20♏	11♐	4♉
20	27♎	21♏	12♐	3♉
21	28♎	22♏	13♐	3♉
22	29♎	23♏	14♐	3♉
23	0♏	24♏	16♐	2♉
24	1♏	24♏	17♐	2♉
25	2♏	25♏	18♐	2♉
26	3♏	25♏	19♐	1♉
27	4♏	26♏	20♐	1♉
28	5♏	26♏	21♐	1♉
29	6♏	27♏	22♐	0♉
30	7♏	27♏	23♐	0♉
31	8♏	27♏	24♐	0♉

November

Day	☉	☿	♀	♂
1	9♏	26♏	25♐	29♈
2	10♏	26♏	26♐	29♈
3	11♏	26♏	27♐	29♈
4	12♏	25♏	28♐	28♈
5	13♏	24♏	0♑	28♈
6	14♏	23♏	1♑	28♈
7	15♏	22♏	2♑	28♈
8	16♏	21♏	3♑	27♈
9	17♏	20♏	4♑	27♈
10	18♏	18♏	5♑	27♈
11	19♏	17♏	6♑	27♈
12	20♏	16♏	7♑	27♈
13	21♏	14♏	8♑	26♈
14	22♏	13♏	9♑	26♈
15	23♏	12♏	10♑	26♈
16	24♏	12♏	11♑	26♈
17	25♏	11♏	12♑	26♈
18	26♏	11♏	13♑	26♈
19	27♏	11♏	14♑	26♈
20	28♏	11♏	15♑	26♈
21	29♏	11♏	16♑	25♈
22	0♐	11♏	17♑	25♈
23	1♐	12♏	18♑	25♈
24	2♐	12♏	18♑	25♈
25	3♐	13♏	19♑	25♈
26	4♐	14♏	20♑	25♈
27	5♐	15♏	21♑	25♈
28	6♐	16♏	22♑	25♈
29	7♐	17♏	23♑	25♈
30	8♐	18♏	24♑	25♈

December

Day	☉	☿	♀	♂
1	9♐	19♏	25♑	25♈
2	10♐	21♏	25♑	26♈
3	11♐	22♏	26♑	26♈
4	12♐	23♏	27♑	26♈
5	13♐	25♏	28♑	26♈
6	14♐	26♏	29♑	26♈
7	15♐	28♏	29♑	26♈
8	16♐	29♏	0♒	26♈
9	17♐	0♐	1♒	26♈
10	18♐	2♐	2♒	27♈
11	19♐	3♐	2♒	27♈
12	20♐	5♐	3♒	27♈
13	21♐	6♐	4♒	27♈
14	22♐	8♐	4♒	27♈
15	23♐	9♐	5♒	28♈
16	24♐	11♐	6♒	28♈
17	25♐	12♐	6♒	28♈
18	26♐	14♐	7♒	28♈
19	27♐	15♐	7♒	29♈
20	28♐	17♐	8♒	29♈
21	29♐	18♐	8♒	29♈
22	0♑	20♐	9♒	29♈
23	1♑	22♐	9♒	0♉
24	2♑	23♐	9♒	0♉
25	3♑	25♐	10♒	0♉
26	4♑	26♐	10♒	1♉
27	5♑	28♐	10♒	1♉
28	6♑	29♐	11♒	1♉
29	7♑	1♑	11♒	2♉
30	8♑	2♑	11♒	2♉
31	9♑	4♑	11♒	2♉

Planetary Positions

♌ = Leo ♍ = Virgo ♎ = Libra ♏ = Scorpio ♐ = Sagittarius ♑ = Capricorn ♒ = Aquarius ♓ = Pisces

1974

January

Day	☉	☿	♀	♂
1	10♑	6♑	11♒	3♉
2	11♑	7♑	11♒	3♉
3	12♑	9♑	11♒	3♉
4	13♑	10♑	11♒	4♉
5	14♑	12♑	11♒	4♉
6	15♑	14♑	11♒	4♉
7	17♑	15♑	11♒	5♉
8	18♑	17♑	11♒	5♉
9	19♑	18♑	11♒	6♉
10	20♑	20♑	10♒	6♉
11	21♑	22♑	10♒	7♉
12	22♑	23♑	10♒	7♉
13	23♑	25♑	9♒	7♉
14	24♑	27♑	9♒	8♉
15	25♑	28♑	8♒	8♉
16	26♑	0♒	8♒	9♉
17	27♑	2♒	7♒	9♉
18	28♑	3♒	7♒	10♉
19	29♑	5♒	6♒	10♉
20	0♒	7♒	6♒	10♉
21	1♒	9♒	5♒	11♉
22	2♒	10♒	5♒	11♉
23	3♒	12♒	4♒	12♉
24	4♒	14♒	3♒	12♉
25	5♒	15♒	3♒	13♉
26	6♒	17♒	2♒	13♉
27	7♒	19♒	1♒	14♉
28	8♒	21♒	1♒	14♉
29	9♒	22♒	0♒	15♉
30	10♒	24♒	0♒	15♉
31	11♒	26♒	29♑	16♉

February

Day	☉	☿	♀	♂
1	12♒	27♒	29♑	16♉
2	13♒	29♒	28♑	17♉
3	14♒	0♓	28♑	17♉
4	15♒	2♓	28♑	18♉
5	16♒	3♓	27♑	18♉
6	17♒	5♓	27♑	19♉
7	18♒	6♓	27♑	19♉
8	19♒	7♓	26♑	20♉
9	20♒	8♓	26♑	20♉
10	21♒	9♓	26♑	21♉
11	22♒	10♓	26♑	21♉
12	23♒	11♓	26♑	22♉
13	24♒	11♓	26♑	22♉
14	25♒	12♓	26♑	23♉
15	26♒	12♓	26♑	23♉
16	27♒	12♓	26♑	24♉
17	28♒	12♓	26♑	24♉
18	29♒	11♓	26♑	25♉
19	0♓	11♓	26♑	26♉
20	1♓	10♓	27♑	26♉
21	2♓	9♓	27♑	27♉
22	3♓	9♓	27♑	27♉
23	4♓	8♓	28♑	28♉
24	5♓	7♓	28♑	28♉
25	6♓	5♓	28♑	29♉
26	7♓	4♓	29♑	29♉
27	8♓	3♓	29♑	0♊
28	9♓	2♓	0♒	0♊

March

Day	☉	☿	♀	♂
1	10♓	1♓	0♒	1♊
2	11♓	0♓	1♒	2♊
3	12♓	0♓	1♒	2♊
4	13♓	29♒	2♒	3♊
5	14♓	28♒	3♒	3♊
6	15♓	28♒	3♒	4♊
7	16♓	28♒	4♒	4♊
8	17♓	27♒	5♒	5♊
9	18♓	27♒	5♒	5♊
10	19♓	27♒	6♒	6♊
11	20♓	27♒	7♒	7♊
12	21♓	27♒	7♒	7♊
13	22♓	28♒	8♒	8♊
14	23♓	28♒	9♒	8♊
15	24♓	28♒	10♒	9♊
16	25♓	29♒	10♒	9♊
17	26♓	0♓	11♒	10♊
18	27♓	0♓	12♒	11♊
19	28♓	1♓	13♒	11♊
20	29♓	2♓	14♒	12♊
21	0♈	3♓	15♒	12♊
22	1♈	3♓	16♒	13♊
23	2♈	4♓	16♒	13♊
24	3♈	5♓	17♒	14♊
25	4♈	6♓	18♒	15♊
26	5♈	8♓	19♒	15♊
27	6♈	9♓	20♒	16♊
28	7♈	10♓	21♒	16♊
29	8♈	11♓	22♒	17♊
30	9♈	12♓	23♒	18♊
31	10♈	14♓	24♒	18♊

April

Day	☉	☿	♀	♂
1	11♈	15♓	25♒	19♊
2	12♈	16♓	26♒	19♊
3	13♈	17♓	27♒	20♊
4	14♈	19♓	28♒	20♊
5	15♈	20♓	29♒	21♊
6	16♈	22♓	0♓	22♊
7	17♈	23♓	1♓	22♊
8	18♈	25♓	2♓	23♊
9	19♈	26♓	3♓	23♊
10	20♈	28♓	4♓	24♊
11	21♈	29♓	5♓	25♊
12	22♈	1♈	6♓	25♊
13	23♈	3♈	7♓	26♊
14	24♈	4♈	8♓	26♊
15	25♈	6♈	9♓	27♊
16	26♈	8♈	10♓	28♊
17	27♈	9♈	11♓	28♊
18	28♈	11♈	12♓	29♊
19	29♈	13♈	13♓	29♊
20	0♉	15♈	14♓	0♋
21	1♉	17♈	15♓	1♋
22	2♉	18♈	16♓	1♋
23	3♉	20♈	17♓	2♋
24	4♉	22♈	18♓	2♋
25	5♉	24♈	19♓	3♋
26	6♉	26♈	21♓	3♋
27	7♉	28♈	22♓	4♋
28	8♉	0♉	23♓	5♋
29	9♉	2♉	24♓	5♋
30	9♉	4♉	25♓	6♋

May

Day	☉	☿	♀	♂
1	10♉	6♉	26♓	6♋
2	11♉	8♉	27♓	7♋
3	12♉	11♉	28♓	8♋
4	13♉	13♉	29♓	8♋
5	14♉	15♉	0♈	9♋
6	15♉	17♉	2♈	9♋
7	16♉	19♉	3♈	10♋
8	17♉	21♉	4♈	11♋
9	18♉	24♉	5♈	11♋
10	19♉	26♉	6♈	12♋
11	20♉	28♉	7♈	13♋
12	21♉	0♊	8♈	13♋
13	22♉	2♊	9♈	14♋
14	23♉	4♊	10♈	14♋
15	24♉	6♊	12♈	15♋
16	25♉	8♊	13♈	16♋
17	26♉	10♊	14♈	16♋
18	27♉	12♊	15♈	17♋
19	28♉	14♊	16♈	17♋
20	29♉	16♊	17♈	18♋
21	0♊	18♊	18♈	19♋
22	1♊	19♊	20♈	19♋
23	2♊	21♊	21♈	20♋
24	3♊	23♊	22♈	20♋
25	4♊	24♊	23♈	21♋
26	5♊	26♊	24♈	22♋
27	6♊	27♊	25♈	22♋
28	7♊	28♊	26♈	23♋
29	7♊	0♋	28♈	23♋
30	8♊	1♋	29♈	24♋
31	9♊	2♋	0♉	25♋

June

Day	☉	☿	♀	♂
1	10♊	4♋	1♉	25♋
2	11♊	5♋	2♉	26♋
3	12♊	6♋	3♉	26♋
4	13♊	7♋	5♉	27♋
5	14♊	8♋	6♉	28♋
6	15♊	9♋	7♉	28♋
7	16♊	9♋	8♉	29♋
8	17♊	10♋	9♉	29♋
9	18♊	11♋	10♉	0♌
10	19♊	11♋	11♉	1♌
11	20♊	12♋	13♉	1♌
12	21♊	12♋	14♉	2♌
13	22♊	13♋	15♉	3♌
14	23♊	13♋	16♉	3♌
15	24♊	13♋	17♉	4♌
16	25♊	14♋	18♉	4♌
17	26♊	14♋	20♉	5♌
18	27♊	14♋	21♉	6♌
19	28♊	14♋	22♉	6♌
20	29♊	13♋	23♉	7♌
21	29♊	13♋	24♉	7♌
22	0♋	13♋	26♉	8♌
23	1♋	13♋	27♉	9♌
24	2♋	12♋	28♉	9♌
25	3♋	12♋	29♉	10♌
26	4♋	11♋	0♊	11♌
27	5♋	11♋	1♊	11♌
28	6♋	10♋	3♊	12♌
29	7♋	10♋	4♊	12♌
30	8♋	9♋	5♊	13♌

July

Day	☉	☿	♀	♂
1	9♋	8♋	6♊	14♌
2	10♋	8♋	7♊	14♌
3	11♋	7♋	9♊	15♌
4	12♋	7♋	10♊	15♌
5	13♋	6♋	11♊	16♌
6	14♋	6♋	12♊	17♌
7	15♋	5♋	13♊	17♌
8	16♋	5♋	14♊	18♌
9	17♋	5♋	16♊	19♌
10	18♋	5♋	17♊	19♌
11	19♋	4♋	18♊	20♌
12	19♋	4♋	19♊	20♌
13	20♋	4♋	20♊	21♌
14	21♋	5♋	22♊	22♌
15	22♋	5♋	23♊	22♌
16	23♋	5♋	24♊	23♌
17	24♋	6♋	25♊	24♌
18	25♋	6♋	26♊	24♌
19	26♋	7♋	28♊	25♌
20	27♋	7♋	29♊	25♌
21	28♋	8♋	0♋	26♌
22	29♋	9♋	1♋	27♌
23	0♌	10♋	2♋	27♌
24	1♌	11♋	4♋	28♌
25	2♌	12♋	5♋	29♌
26	3♌	13♋	6♋	29♌
27	4♌	15♋	7♋	0♍
28	5♌	16♋	8♋	0♍
29	6♌	17♋	10♋	1♍
30	7♌	19♋	11♋	2♍
31	8♌	21♋	12♋	2♍

August

Day	☉	☿	♀	♂
1	9♌	22♋	13♋	3♍
2	10♌	24♋	14♋	4♍
3	10♌	26♋	16♋	4♍
4	11♌	28♋	17♋	5♍
5	12♌	29♋	18♋	5♍
6	13♌	1♌	19♋	6♍
7	14♌	3♌	21♋	7♍
8	15♌	5♌	22♋	7♍
9	16♌	7♌	23♋	8♍
10	17♌	9♌	24♋	9♍
11	18♌	11♌	25♋	9♍
12	19♌	13♌	27♋	10♍
13	20♌	16♌	28♋	10♍
14	21♌	18♌	29♋	11♍
15	22♌	20♌	0♌	12♍
16	23♌	22♌	1♌	12♍
17	24♌	24♌	3♌	13♍
18	25♌	26♌	4♌	14♍
19	26♌	28♌	5♌	14♍
20	27♌	0♍	6♌	15♍
21	28♌	2♍	8♌	16♍
22	29♌	4♍	9♌	16♍
23	0♍	5♍	10♌	17♍
24	1♍	7♍	11♌	17♍
25	2♍	9♍	12♌	18♍
26	3♍	11♍	14♌	19♍
27	4♍	13♍	15♌	19♍
28	5♍	15♍	16♌	20♍
29	5♍	16♍	17♌	21♍
30	6♍	18♍	19♌	21♍
31	7♍	20♍	20♌	22♍

September

Day	☉	☿	♀	♂
1	8♍	22♍	21♌	23♍
2	9♍	23♍	22♌	23♍
3	10♍	25♍	24♌	24♍
4	11♍	27♍	25♌	24♍
5	12♍	28♍	26♌	25♍
6	13♍	0♎	27♌	26♍
7	14♍	2♎	28♌	26♍
8	15♍	3♎	0♍	27♍
9	16♍	5♎	1♍	28♍
10	17♍	6♎	2♍	28♍
11	18♍	8♎	3♍	29♍
12	19♍	9♎	5♍	0♎
13	20♍	11♎	6♍	0♎
14	21♍	12♎	7♍	1♎
15	22♍	14♎	8♍	2♎
16	23♍	15♎	10♍	2♎
17	24♍	16♎	11♍	3♎
18	25♍	18♎	12♍	4♎
19	26♍	19♎	13♍	4♎
20	27♍	20♎	15♍	5♎
21	28♍	22♎	16♍	5♎
22	29♍	23♎	17♍	6♎
23	0♎	24♎	18♍	7♎
24	1♎	26♎	20♍	7♎
25	2♎	27♎	21♍	8♎
26	3♎	28♎	22♍	9♎
27	4♎	29♎	23♍	9♎
28	5♎	0♏	25♍	10♎
29	6♎	1♏	26♍	11♎
30	7♎	2♏	27♍	11♎

October

Day	☉	☿	♀	♂
1	8♎	3♏	28♍	12♎
2	9♎	4♏	0♎	13♎
3	10♎	5♏	1♎	13♎
4	11♎	6♏	2♎	14♎
5	12♎	7♏	3♎	15♎
6	13♎	8♏	4♎	15♎
7	14♎	8♏	6♎	16♎
8	15♎	9♏	7♎	17♎
9	16♎	9♏	8♎	17♎
10	17♎	10♏	9♎	18♎
11	18♎	10♏	11♎	19♎
12	18♎	10♏	12♎	19♎
13	19♎	11♏	13♎	20♎
14	20♎	11♏	14♎	21♎
15	21♎	11♏	16♎	21♎
16	22♎	10♏	17♎	22♎
17	23♎	10♏	18♎	23♎
18	24♎	9♏	19♎	23♎
19	25♎	9♏	21♎	24♎
20	26♎	8♏	22♎	25♎
21	27♎	7♏	23♎	25♎
22	28♎	6♏	25♎	26♎
23	29♎	5♏	26♎	27♎
24	0♏	3♏	27♎	27♎
25	1♏	2♏	28♎	28♎
26	2♏	1♏	0♏	29♎
27	3♏	0♏	1♏	29♎
28	4♏	29♎	2♏	0♏
29	5♏	28♎	3♏	1♏
30	6♏	27♎	5♏	1♏
31	7♏	26♎	6♏	2♏

November

Day	☉	☿	♀	♂
1	8♏	25♎	7♏	3♏
2	9♏	25♎	8♏	3♏
3	10♏	25♎	10♏	4♏
4	11♏	25♎	11♏	5♏
5	12♏	25♎	12♏	5♏
6	13♏	26♎	13♏	6♏
7	14♏	26♎	15♏	7♏
8	15♏	27♎	16♏	7♏
9	16♏	28♎	17♏	8♏
10	17♏	28♎	18♏	9♏
11	18♏	29♎	20♏	9♏
12	19♏	1♏	21♏	10♏
13	20♏	2♏	22♏	11♏
14	21♏	3♏	23♏	11♏
15	22♏	4♏	25♏	12♏
16	23♏	6♏	26♏	13♏
17	24♏	7♏	27♏	14♏
18	25♏	9♏	28♏	14♏
19	26♏	10♏	0♐	15♏
20	27♏	11♏	1♐	16♏
21	28♏	13♏	2♐	16♏
22	0♐	14♏	3♐	17♏
23	1♐	16♏	5♐	18♏
24	2♐	17♏	6♐	18♏
25	3♐	19♏	7♐	19♏
26	4♐	21♏	8♐	20♏
27	5♐	22♏	10♐	20♏
28	6♐	24♏	11♐	21♏
29	7♐	25♏	12♐	22♏
30	8♐	27♏	13♐	23♏

December

Day	☉	☿	♀	♂
1	9♐	28♏	15♐	23♏
2	10♐	0♐	16♐	24♏
3	11♐	1♐	17♐	25♏
4	12♐	3♐	18♐	25♏
5	13♐	5♐	20♐	26♏
6	14♐	6♐	21♐	27♏
7	15♐	8♐	22♐	27♏
8	16♐	9♐	24♐	28♏
9	17♐	11♐	25♐	29♏
10	18♐	12♐	26♐	29♏
11	19♐	14♐	27♐	0♐
12	20♐	16♐	29♐	1♐
13	21♐	17♐	0♑	2♐
14	22♐	19♐	1♑	2♐
15	23♐	20♐	2♑	3♐
16	24♐	22♐	4♑	4♐
17	25♐	23♐	5♑	4♐
18	26♐	25♐	6♑	5♐
19	27♐	27♐	7♑	6♐
20	28♐	28♐	9♑	7♐
21	29♐	0♑	10♑	7♐
22	0♑	1♑	11♑	8♐
23	1♑	3♑	12♑	9♐
24	2♑	4♑	14♑	9♐
25	3♑	6♑	15♑	10♐
26	4♑	8♑	16♑	11♐
27	5♑	9♑	17♑	12♐
28	6♑	11♑	19♑	12♐
29	7♑	13♑	20♑	13♐
30	8♑	14♑	21♑	14♐
31	9♑	16♑	22♑	14♐

1975

Your Starway to Love

☉ =Sun ☿ = Mercury ♀ = Venus ♂ = Mars ♈ = Aries ♉ = Taurus ♊ = Gemini ♋ = Cancer

January

Day	☉	☿	♀	♂
1	10♑	17♑	24♑	15♐
2	11♑	19♑	25♑	16♐
3	12♑	21♑	26♑	17♐
4	13♑	22♑	27♑	17♐
5	14♑	24♑	29♑	18♐
6	15♑	26♑	0♒	19♐
7	16♑	27♑	1♒	19♐
8	17♑	29♑	2♒	20♐
9	18♑	0♒	4♒	21♐
10	19♑	2♒	5♒	22♐
11	20♑	4♒	6♒	22♐
12	21♑	5♒	7♒	23♐
13	22♑	7♒	9♒	24♐
14	23♑	9♒	10♒	24♐
15	24♑	10♒	11♒	25♐
16	25♑	12♒	12♒	26♐
17	26♑	13♒	14♒	27♐
18	27♑	15♒	15♒	27♐
19	28♑	16♒	16♒	28♐
20	0♒	17♒	17♒	29♐
21	1♒	19♒	19♒	0♑
22	2♒	20♒	20♒	0♑
23	3♒	21♒	21♒	1♑
24	4♒	22♒	22♒	2♑
25	5♒	23♒	24♒	3♑
26	6♒	24♒	25♒	3♑
27	7♒	24♒	26♒	4♑
28	8♒	25♒	27♒	5♑
29	9♒	25♒	29♒	5♑
30	10♒	25♒	0♓	6♑
31	11♒	25♒	1♓	7♑

February

Day	☉	☿	♀	♂
1	12♒	25♒	2♓	8♑
2	13♒	25♒	4♓	8♑
3	14♒	24♒	5♓	9♑
4	15♒	23♒	6♓	10♑
5	16♒	22♒	7♓	11♑
6	17♒	21♒	9♓	11♑
7	18♒	20♒	10♓	12♑
8	19♒	19♒	11♓	13♑
9	20♒	18♒	12♓	14♑
10	21♒	17♒	14♓	14♑
11	22♒	16♒	15♓	15♑
12	23♒	15♒	16♓	16♑
13	24♒	14♒	17♓	17♑
14	25♒	13♒	19♓	17♑
15	26♒	12♒	20♓	18♑
16	27♒	11♒	21♓	19♑
17	28♒	11♒	22♓	20♑
18	29♒	10♒	24♓	20♑
19	0♓	10♒	25♓	21♑
20	1♓	10♒	26♓	22♑
21	2♓	10♒	27♓	22♑
22	3♓	10♒	29♓	23♑
23	4♓	10♒	0♈	24♑
24	5♓	11♒	1♈	25♑
25	6♓	11♒	2♈	25♑
26	7♓	11♒	3♈	26♑
27	8♓	12♒	5♈	27♑
28	9♓	13♒	6♈	28♑

March

Day	☉	☿	♀	♂
1	10♓	13♒	7♈	28♑
2	11♓	14♒	8♈	29♑
3	12♓	15♒	10♈	0♒
4	13♓	16♒	11♈	1♒
5	14♓	17♒	12♈	1♒
6	15♓	18♒	13♈	2♒
7	16♓	19♒	15♈	3♒
8	17♓	20♒	16♈	4♒
9	18♓	21♒	17♈	5♒
10	19♓	22♒	18♈	5♒
11	20♓	23♒	19♈	6♒
12	21♓	24♒	21♈	7♒
13	22♓	26♒	22♈	8♒
14	23♓	27♒	23♈	8♒
15	24♓	28♒	24♈	9♒
16	25♓	0♓	26♈	10♒
17	26♓	1♓	27♈	11♒
18	27♓	2♓	28♈	11♒
19	28♓	4♓	29♈	12♒
20	29♓	5♓	0♉	13♒
21	0♈	7♓	2♉	14♒
22	1♈	8♓	3♉	14♒
23	2♈	10♓	4♉	15♒
24	3♈	11♓	5♉	16♒
25	4♈	13♓	6♉	17♒
26	5♈	14♓	8♉	17♒
27	6♈	16♓	9♉	18♒
28	7♈	17♓	10♉	19♒
29	8♈	19♓	11♉	20♒
30	9♈	21♓	12♉	20♒
31	10♈	22♓	14♉	21♒

April

Day	☉	☿	♀	♂
1	11♈	24♓	15♉	22♒
2	12♈	26♓	16♉	23♒
3	13♈	28♓	17♉	23♒
4	14♈	29♓	18♉	24♒
5	15♈	1♈	20♉	25♒
6	16♈	3♈	21♉	26♒
7	17♈	5♈	22♉	27♒
8	18♈	7♈	23♉	27♒
9	19♈	9♈	24♉	28♒
10	20♈	11♈	26♉	29♒
11	21♈	13♈	27♉	0♓
12	22♈	15♈	28♉	0♓
13	23♈	17♈	29♉	1♓
14	24♈	19♈	0♊	2♓
15	25♈	21♈	2♊	3♓
16	26♈	23♈	3♊	3♓
17	27♈	25♈	4♊	4♓
18	28♈	27♈	5♊	5♓
19	29♈	29♈	6♊	6♓
20	0♉	1♉	7♊	6♓
21	0♉	3♉	9♊	7♓
22	1♉	5♉	10♊	8♓
23	2♉	7♉	11♊	9♓
24	3♉	10♉	12♊	9♓
25	4♉	12♉	13♊	10♓
26	5♉	14♉	14♊	11♓
27	6♉	16♉	16♊	12♓
28	7♉	18♉	17♊	12♓
29	8♉	20♉	18♊	13♓
30	9♉	22♉	19♊	14♓

May

Day	☉	☿	♀	♂
1	10♉	24♉	20♊	15♓
2	11♉	26♉	21♊	16♓
3	12♉	28♉	22♊	16♓
4	13♉	29♉	24♊	17♓
5	14♉	1♊	25♊	18♓
6	15♉	3♊	26♊	19♓
7	16♉	5♊	27♊	19♓
8	17♉	6♊	28♊	20♓
9	18♉	8♊	29♊	21♓
10	19♉	9♊	0♋	22♓
11	20♉	11♊	2♋	22♓
12	21♉	12♊	3♋	23♓
13	22♉	13♊	4♋	24♓
14	23♉	14♊	5♋	25♓
15	24♉	16♊	6♋	25♓
16	25♉	17♊	7♋	26♓
17	26♉	18♊	8♋	27♓
18	27♉	18♊	9♋	28♓
19	28♉	19♊	10♋	28♓
20	29♉	20♊	12♋	29♓
21	0♊	21♊	13♋	0♈
22	1♊	21♊	14♋	1♈
23	1♊	22♊	15♋	1♈
24	2♊	22♊	16♋	2♈
25	3♊	23♊	17♋	3♈
26	4♊	23♊	18♋	4♈
27	5♊	23♊	19♋	4♈
28	6♊	24♊	20♋	5♈
29	7♊	24♊	21♋	6♈
30	8♊	24♊	22♋	7♈
31	9♊	24♊	23♋	7♈

June

Day	☉	☿	♀	♂
1	10♊	23♊	25♋	8♈
2	11♊	23♊	26♋	9♈
3	12♊	23♊	27♋	10♈
4	13♊	23♊	28♋	10♈
5	14♊	22♊	29♋	11♈
6	15♊	22♊	0♌	12♈
7	16♊	21♊	1♌	13♈
8	17♊	21♊	2♌	13♈
9	18♊	20♊	3♌	14♈
10	19♊	20♊	4♌	15♈
11	20♊	19♊	5♌	16♈
12	21♊	18♊	6♌	16♈
13	22♊	18♊	7♌	17♈
14	23♊	17♊	8♌	18♈
15	23♊	17♊	9♌	18♈
16	24♊	16♊	10♌	19♈
17	25♊	16♊	11♌	20♈
18	26♊	16♊	12♌	21♈
19	27♊	15♊	13♌	21♈
20	28♊	15♊	14♌	22♈
21	29♊	15♊	15♌	23♈
22	0♋	15♊	16♌	24♈
23	1♋	15♊	16♌	24♈
24	2♋	15♊	17♌	25♈
25	3♋	15♊	18♌	26♈
26	4♋	16♊	19♌	26♈
27	5♋	16♊	20♌	27♈
28	6♋	16♊	21♌	28♈
29	7♋	17♊	22♌	29♈
30	8♋	17♊	23♌	29♈

July

Day	☉	☿	♀	♂
1	9♋	18♊	23♌	0♉
2	10♋	19♊	24♌	1♉
3	11♋	19♊	25♌	1♉
4	12♋	20♊	26♌	2♉
5	13♋	21♊	27♌	3♉
6	14♋	22♊	28♌	4♉
7	14♋	23♊	28♌	4♉
8	15♋	24♊	29♌	5♉
9	16♋	26♊	0♍	6♉
10	17♋	27♊	1♍	6♉
11	18♋	28♊	1♍	7♉
12	19♋	0♋	2♍	8♉
13	20♋	1♋	3♍	8♉
14	21♋	3♋	3♍	9♉
15	22♋	4♋	4♍	10♉
16	23♋	6♋	5♍	11♉
17	24♋	8♋	5♍	11♉
18	25♋	10♋	6♍	12♉
19	26♋	11♋	6♍	13♉
20	27♋	13♋	7♍	13♉
21	28♋	15♋	7♍	14♉
22	29♋	17♋	8♍	15♉
23	0♌	19♋	8♍	15♉
24	1♌	21♋	9♍	16♉
25	2♌	23♋	9♍	17♉
26	3♌	26♋	10♍	17♉
27	4♌	28♋	10♍	18♉
28	5♌	0♌	10♍	19♉
29	5♌	2♌	11♍	19♉
30	6♌	4♌	11♍	20♉
31	7♌	6♌	11♍	21♉

August

Day	☉	☿	♀	♂
1	8♌	8♌	11♍	21♉
2	9♌	10♌	11♍	22♉
3	10♌	12♌	12♍	23♉
4	11♌	14♌	12♍	23♉
5	12♌	16♌	12♍	24♉
6	13♌	18♌	12♍	25♉
7	14♌	20♌	12♍	25♉
8	15♌	22♌	12♍	26♉
9	16♌	24♌	12♍	26♉
10	17♌	26♌	11♍	27♉
11	18♌	28♌	11♍	28♉
12	19♌	0♍	11♍	28♉
13	20♌	2♍	11♍	29♉
14	21♌	4♍	10♍	0♊
15	22♌	5♍	10♍	0♊
16	23♌	7♍	10♍	1♊
17	24♌	9♍	9♍	1♊
18	25♌	11♍	9♍	2♊
19	26♌	12♍	8♍	3♊
20	27♌	14♍	8♍	3♊
21	28♌	16♍	7♍	4♊
22	28♌	17♍	7♍	4♊
23	29♌	19♍	6♍	5♊
24	0♍	20♍	6♍	6♊
25	1♍	22♍	5♍	6♊
26	2♍	23♍	4♍	7♊
27	3♍	25♍	4♍	7♊
28	4♍	26♍	3♍	8♊
29	5♍	28♍	3♍	9♊
30	6♍	29♍	2♍	9♊
31	7♍	1♎	1♍	10♊

September

Day	☉	☿	♀	♂
1	8♍	2♎	1♍	10♊
2	9♍	3♎	0♍	11♊
3	10♍	5♎	0♍	11♊
4	11♍	6♎	29♌	12♊
5	12♍	7♎	29♌	12♊
6	13♍	9♎	28♌	13♊
7	14♍	10♎	28♌	14♊
8	15♍	11♎	27♌	14♊
9	16♍	12♎	27♌	15♊
10	17♍	13♎	27♌	15♊
11	18♍	14♎	26♌	16♊
12	19♍	15♎	26♌	16♊
13	20♍	16♎	26♌	17♊
14	21♍	17♎	26♌	17♊
15	22♍	18♎	26♌	18♊
16	23♍	19♎	25♌	18♊
17	24♍	20♎	25♌	19♊
18	25♍	21♎	25♌	19♊
19	26♍	22♎	25♌	20♊
20	27♍	22♎	26♌	20♊
21	28♍	23♎	26♌	20♊
22	29♍	23♎	26♌	21♊
23	0♎	24♎	26♌	21♊
24	1♎	24♎	26♌	22♊
25	2♎	24♎	26♌	22♊
26	2♎	24♎	27♌	23♊
27	3♎	24♎	27♌	23♊
28	4♎	24♎	27♌	24♊
29	5♎	24♎	28♌	24♊
30	6♎	24♎	28♌	24♊

October

Day	☉	☿	♀	♂
1	7♎	23♎	29♌	25♊
2	8♎	23♎	29♌	25♊
3	9♎	22♎	29♌	26♊
4	10♎	21♎	0♍	26♊
5	11♎	20♎	1♍	26♊
6	12♎	19♎	1♍	27♊
7	13♎	18♎	2♍	27♊
8	14♎	17♎	2♍	27♊
9	15♎	16♎	3♍	28♊
10	16♎	15♎	4♍	28♊
11	17♎	14♎	4♍	28♊
12	18♎	12♎	5♍	29♊
13	19♎	12♎	6♍	29♊
14	20♎	11♎	6♍	29♊
15	21♎	10♎	7♍	29♊
16	22♎	10♎	8♍	0♋
17	23♎	9♎	9♍	0♋
18	24♎	9♎	9♍	0♋
19	25♎	9♎	10♍	0♋
20	26♎	9♎	11♍	1♋
21	27♎	10♎	12♍	1♋
22	28♎	10♎	13♍	1♋
23	29♎	11♎	14♍	1♋
24	0♏	12♎	14♍	1♋
25	1♏	13♎	15♍	2♋
26	2♏	14♎	16♍	2♋
27	3♏	15♎	17♍	2♋
28	4♏	16♎	18♍	2♋
29	5♏	18♎	19♍	2♋
30	6♏	19♎	20♍	2♋
31	7♏	21♎	21♍	2♋

November

Day	☉	☿	♀	♂
1	8♏	22♎	22♍	2♋
2	9♏	23♎	23♍	3♋
3	10♏	25♎	24♍	3♋
4	11♏	27♎	25♍	3♋
5	12♏	28♎	26♍	3♋
6	13♏	0♏	27♍	3♋
7	14♏	1♏	28♍	3♋
8	15♏	3♏	29♍	3♋
9	16♏	5♏	0♎	3♋
10	17♏	6♏	1♎	3♋
11	18♏	8♏	2♎	3♋
12	19♏	9♏	3♎	2♋
13	20♏	11♏	4♎	2♋
14	21♏	13♏	5♎	2♋
15	22♏	14♏	6♎	2♋
16	23♏	16♏	7♎	2♋
17	24♏	17♏	8♎	2♋
18	25♏	19♏	9♎	2♋
19	26♏	21♏	10♎	1♋
20	27♏	22♏	11♎	1♋
21	28♏	24♏	12♎	1♋
22	29♏	25♏	13♎	1♋
23	0♐	27♏	14♎	1♋
24	1♐	29♏	16♎	0♋
25	2♐	0♐	17♎	0♋
26	3♐	2♐	18♎	0♋
27	4♐	3♐	19♎	0♋
28	5♐	5♐	20♎	29♊
29	6♐	7♐	21♎	29♊
30	7♐	8♐	22♎	29♊

December

Day	☉	☿	♀	♂
1	8♐	10♐	23♎	28♊
2	9♐	11♐	25♎	28♊
3	10♐	13♐	26♎	28♊
4	11♐	14♐	27♎	27♊
5	12♐	16♐	28♎	27♊
6	13♐	18♐	29♎	27♊
7	14♐	19♐	0♏	26♊
8	15♐	21♐	1♏	26♊
9	16♐	22♐	3♏	25♊
10	18♐	24♐	4♏	25♊
11	19♐	25♐	5♏	25♊
12	20♐	27♐	6♏	24♊
13	21♐	28♐	7♏	24♊
14	22♐	0♑	8♏	24♊
15	23♐	2♑	9♏	23♊
16	24♐	3♑	11♏	23♊
17	25♐	5♑	12♏	22♊
18	26♐	6♑	13♏	22♊
19	27♐	8♑	14♏	22♊
20	28♐	9♑	15♏	21♊
21	29♐	11♑	17♏	21♊
22	0♑	13♑	18♏	20♊
23	1♑	14♑	19♏	20♊
24	2♑	16♑	20♏	20♊
25	3♑	17♑	21♏	19♊
26	4♑	19♑	22♏	19♊
27	5♑	20♑	24♏	19♊
28	6♑	22♑	25♏	18♊
29	7♑	23♑	26♏	18♊
30	8♑	25♑	27♏	18♊
31	9♑	26♑	28♏	18♊

Planetary Positions

♌ = Leo ♍ = Virgo ♎ = Libra ♏ = Scorpio ♐ = Sagittarius ♑ = Capricorn ♒ = Aquarius ♓ = Pisces

1976

January

Day	☉	☿	♀	♂
1	10♑	28♑	0♐	17♊
2	11♑	29♑	1♐	17♊
3	12♑	0♒	2♐	17♊
4	13♑	2♒	3♐	17♊
5	14♑	3♒	4♐	16♊
6	15♑	4♒	6♐	16♊
7	16♑	5♒	7♐	16♊
8	17♑	6♒	8♐	16♊
9	18♑	7♒	9♐	16♊
10	19♑	8♒	10♐	15♊
11	20♑	8♒	12♐	15♊
12	21♑	9♒	13♐	15♊
13	22♑	9♒	14♐	15♊
14	23♑	9♒	15♐	15♊
15	24♑	9♒	17♐	15♊
16	25♑	9♒	18♐	15♊
17	26♑	8♒	19♐	15♊
18	27♑	8♒	20♐	15♊
19	28♑	7♒	21♐	15♊
20	29♑	6♒	23♐	15♊
21	0♒	5♒	24♐	15♊
22	1♒	4♒	25♐	15♊
23	2♒	2♒	26♐	15♊
24	3♒	1♒	27♐	15♊
25	4♒	0♒	29♐	15♊
26	5♒	29♑	0♑	15♊
27	6♒	27♑	1♑	15♊
28	7♒	26♑	2♑	15♊
29	8♒	26♑	4♑	15♊
30	9♒	25♑	5♑	15♊
31	10♒	24♑	6♑	15♊

April

Day	☉	☿	♀	♂
1	12♈	11♈	21♓	6♋
2	13♈	13♈	22♓	7♋
3	14♈	15♈	24♓	7♋
4	15♈	17♈	25♓	8♋
5	16♈	19♈	26♓	8♋
6	17♈	21♈	27♓	9♋
7	18♈	23♈	29♓	9♋
8	18♈	25♈	0♈	10♋
9	19♈	28♈	1♈	10♋
10	20♈	0♉	2♈	11♋
11	21♈	2♉	3♈	11♋
12	22♈	4♉	5♈	12♋
13	23♈	6♉	6♈	12♋
14	24♈	8♉	7♈	13♋
15	25♈	9♉	8♈	13♋
16	26♈	11♉	10♈	14♋
17	27♈	13♉	11♈	14♋
18	28♈	15♉	12♈	15♋
19	29♈	17♉	13♈	15♋
20	0♉	18♉	15♈	16♋
21	1♉	20♉	16♈	16♋
22	2♉	21♉	17♈	17♋
23	3♉	23♉	18♈	17♋
24	4♉	24♉	19♈	18♋
25	5♉	25♉	21♈	18♋
26	6♉	26♉	22♈	19♋
27	7♉	27♉	23♈	19♋
28	8♉	28♉	24♈	20♋
29	9♉	29♉	26♈	21♋
30	10♉	0♊	27♈	21♋

July

Day	☉	☿	♀	♂
1	9♋	24♊	13♋	27♌
2	10♋	25♊	14♋	27♌
3	11♋	27♊	16♋	28♌
4	12♋	29♊	17♋	28♌
5	13♋	1♋	18♋	29♌
6	14♋	3♋	19♋	0♍
7	15♋	5♋	20♋	0♍
8	16♋	7♋	22♋	1♍
9	17♋	9♋	23♋	1♍
10	18♋	12♋	24♋	2♍
11	19♋	14♋	25♋	3♍
12	20♋	16♋	27♋	3♍
13	21♋	18♋	28♋	4♍
14	22♋	20♋	29♋	4♍
15	23♋	22♋	0♌	5♍
16	24♋	24♋	2♌	6♍
17	25♋	27♋	3♌	6♍
18	26♋	29♋	4♌	7♍
19	27♋	1♌	5♌	7♍
20	28♋	3♌	6♌	8♍
21	29♋	5♌	8♌	9♍
22	0♌	7♌	9♌	9♍
23	0♌	9♌	10♌	10♍
24	1♌	11♌	11♌	11♍
25	2♌	13♌	13♌	11♍
26	3♌	15♌	14♌	12♍
27	4♌	17♌	15♌	12♍
28	5♌	19♌	16♌	13♍
29	6♌	20♌	18♌	14♍
30	7♌	22♌	19♌	14♍
31	8♌	24♌	20♌	15♍

October

Day	☉	☿	♀	♂
1	8♎	23♍	6♏	25♎
2	9♎	23♍	7♏	26♎
3	10♎	24♍	9♏	26♎
4	11♎	24♍	10♏	27♎
5	12♎	25♍	11♏	28♎
6	13♎	25♍	12♏	28♎
7	14♎	26♍	14♏	29♎
8	15♎	27♍	15♏	0♏
9	16♎	28♍	16♏	0♏
10	17♎	29♍	17♏	1♏
11	18♎	1♎	18♏	2♏
12	19♎	2♎	20♏	2♏
13	20♎	4♎	21♏	3♏
14	21♎	5♎	22♏	4♏
15	22♎	7♎	23♏	4♏
16	23♎	8♎	24♏	5♏
17	24♎	10♎	26♏	6♏
18	25♎	11♎	27♏	6♏
19	26♎	13♎	28♏	7♏
20	27♎	15♎	29♏	8♏
21	28♎	17♎	1♐	8♏
22	29♎	18♎	2♐	9♏
23	0♏	20♎	3♐	10♏
24	1♏	22♎	4♐	10♏
25	2♏	23♎	5♐	11♏
26	3♏	25♎	7♐	12♏
27	4♏	27♎	8♐	13♏
28	5♏	28♎	9♐	13♏
29	6♏	0♏	10♐	14♏
30	7♏	2♏	12♐	15♏
31	8♏	3♏	13♐	15♏

February

Day	☉	☿	♀	♂
1	11♒	24♑	7♑	16♊
2	12♒	24♑	9♑	16♊
3	13♒	23♑	10♑	16♊
4	15♒	23♑	11♑	16♊
5	16♒	23♑	12♑	16♊
6	17♒	24♑	13♑	16♊
7	18♒	24♑	15♑	16♊
8	19♒	24♑	16♑	17♊
9	20♒	25♑	17♑	17♊
10	21♒	25♑	18♑	17♊
11	22♒	26♑	20♑	17♊
12	23♒	27♑	21♑	18♊
13	24♒	28♑	22♑	18♊
14	25♒	29♑	23♑	18♊
15	26♒	29♑	24♑	18♊
16	27♒	0♒	26♑	19♊
17	28♒	1♒	27♑	19♊
18	29♒	2♒	28♑	19♊
19	0♓	4♒	29♑	19♊
20	1♓	5♒	1♒	20♊
21	2♓	6♒	2♒	20♊
22	3♓	7♒	3♒	20♊
23	4♓	8♒	4♒	21♊
24	5♓	10♒	6♒	21♊
25	6♓	11♒	7♒	21♊
26	7♓	12♒	8♒	22♊
27	8♓	13♒	9♒	22♊
28	9♓	15♒	10♒	22♊
29	10♓	16♒	12♒	23♊

May

Day	☉	☿	♀	♂
1	11♉	1♊	28♈	22♋
2	12♉	2♊	29♈	22♋
3	13♉	2♊	1♉	23♋
4	14♉	3♊	2♉	23♋
5	15♉	3♊	3♉	24♋
6	16♉	3♊	4♉	24♋
7	17♉	4♊	5♉	25♋
8	18♉	4♊	7♉	25♋
9	19♉	4♊	8♉	26♋
10	20♉	4♊	9♉	27♋
11	21♉	4♊	10♉	27♋
12	22♉	3♊	12♉	28♋
13	23♉	3♊	13♉	28♋
14	24♉	3♊	14♉	29♋
15	24♉	2♊	15♉	29♋
16	25♉	2♊	17♉	0♌
17	26♉	1♊	18♉	0♌
18	27♉	1♊	19♉	1♌
19	28♉	0♊	20♉	2♌
20	29♉	0♊	21♉	2♌
21	0♊	29♉	23♉	3♌
22	1♊	29♉	24♉	3♌
23	2♊	28♉	25♉	4♌
24	3♊	28♉	26♉	4♌
25	4♊	27♉	28♉	5♌
26	5♊	27♉	29♉	5♌
27	6♊	26♉	0♊	6♌
28	7♊	26♉	1♊	7♌
29	8♊	25♉	3♊	7♌
30	9♊	25♉	4♊	8♌
31	10♊	25♉	5♊	8♌

August

Day	☉	☿	♀	♂
1	9♌	26♌	21♌	15♍
2	10♌	27♌	22♌	16♍
3	11♌	29♌	24♌	17♍
4	12♌	1♍	25♌	17♍
5	13♌	2♍	26♌	18♍
6	14♌	4♍	27♌	19♍
7	15♌	6♍	29♌	19♍
8	16♌	7♍	0♍	20♍
9	17♌	9♍	1♍	20♍
10	18♌	10♍	2♍	21♍
11	19♌	12♍	4♍	22♍
12	20♌	13♍	5♍	22♍
13	21♌	15♍	6♍	23♍
14	22♌	16♍	7♍	24♍
15	22♌	17♍	8♍	24♍
16	23♌	19♍	10♍	25♍
17	24♌	20♍	11♍	26♍
18	25♌	21♍	12♍	26♍
19	26♌	23♍	13♍	27♍
20	27♌	24♍	15♍	27♍
21	28♌	25♍	16♍	28♍
22	29♌	26♍	17♍	29♍
23	0♍	27♍	18♍	29♍
24	1♍	28♍	20♍	0♎
25	2♍	29♍	21♍	1♎
26	3♍	0♎	22♍	1♎
27	4♍	1♎	23♍	2♎
28	5♍	2♎	24♍	3♎
29	6♍	3♎	26♍	3♎
30	7♍	4♎	27♍	4♎
31	8♍	4♎	28♍	4♎

November

Day	☉	☿	♀	♂
1	9♏	5♏	14♐	16♏
2	10♏	7♏	15♐	17♏
3	11♏	8♏	16♐	17♏
4	12♏	10♏	18♐	18♏
5	13♏	12♏	19♐	19♏
6	14♏	13♏	20♐	20♏
7	15♏	15♏	21♐	20♏
8	16♏	16♏	22♐	21♏
9	17♏	18♏	24♐	22♏
10	18♏	20♏	25♐	22♏
11	19♏	21♏	26♐	23♏
12	20♏	23♏	27♐	24♏
13	21♏	24♏	29♐	24♏
14	22♏	26♏	0♑	25♏
15	23♏	28♏	1♑	26♏
16	24♏	29♏	2♑	27♏
17	25♏	1♐	3♑	27♏
18	26♏	2♐	5♑	28♏
19	27♏	4♐	6♑	29♏
20	28♏	5♐	7♑	29♏
21	29♏	7♐	8♑	0♐
22	0♐	8♐	9♑	1♐
23	1♐	10♐	11♑	2♐
24	2♐	11♐	12♑	2♐
25	3♐	13♐	13♑	3♐
26	4♐	15♐	14♑	4♐
27	5♐	16♐	15♑	4♐
28	6♐	18♐	17♑	5♐
29	7♐	19♐	18♑	6♐
30	8♐	21♐	19♑	7♐

March

Day	☉	☿	♀	♂
1	11♓	18♒	13♒	23♊
2	12♓	19♒	14♒	23♊
3	13♓	20♒	15♒	24♊
4	14♓	22♒	17♒	24♊
5	15♓	23♒	18♒	25♊
6	16♓	25♒	19♒	25♊
7	17♓	26♒	20♒	25♊
8	18♓	28♒	22♒	26♊
9	19♓	0♓	23♒	26♊
10	20♓	1♓	24♒	26♊
11	21♓	3♓	25♒	27♊
12	22♓	4♓	27♒	27♊
13	23♓	6♓	28♒	28♊
14	24♓	8♓	29♒	28♊
15	25♓	9♓	0♓	29♊
16	26♓	11♓	1♓	29♊
17	27♓	13♓	3♓	29♊
18	28♓	14♓	4♓	0♋
19	29♓	16♓	5♓	0♋
20	0♈	18♓	6♓	1♋
21	1♈	20♓	8♓	1♋
22	2♈	22♓	9♓	2♋
23	3♈	23♓	10♓	2♋
24	4♈	25♓	11♓	3♋
25	5♈	27♓	13♓	3♋
26	6♈	29♓	14♓	3♋
27	7♈	1♈	15♓	4♋
28	8♈	3♈	16♓	4♋
29	9♈	5♈	17♓	5♋
30	10♈	7♈	19♓	5♋
31	11♈	9♈	20♓	6♋

June

Day	☉	☿	♀	♂
1	11♊	25♉	6♊	9♌
2	12♊	25♉	7♊	9♌
3	13♊	25♉	9♊	10♌
4	14♊	25♉	10♊	11♌
5	15♊	25♉	11♊	11♌
6	16♊	26♉	12♊	12♌
7	17♊	26♉	14♊	12♌
8	18♊	26♉	15♊	13♌
9	18♊	27♉	16♊	14♌
10	19♊	27♉	17♊	14♌
11	20♊	28♉	18♊	15♌
12	21♊	29♉	20♊	15♌
13	22♊	0♊	21♊	16♌
14	23♊	0♊	22♊	16♌
15	24♊	1♊	23♊	17♌
16	25♊	2♊	25♊	18♌
17	26♊	3♊	26♊	18♌
18	27♊	4♊	27♊	19♌
19	28♊	5♊	28♊	19♌
20	29♊	7♊	0♋	20♌
21	0♋	8♊	1♋	21♌
22	1♋	9♊	2♋	21♌
23	2♋	11♊	3♋	22♌
24	3♋	12♊	4♋	22♌
25	4♋	14♊	6♋	23♌
26	5♋	15♊	7♋	24♌
27	6♋	17♊	8♋	24♌
28	7♋	18♊	9♋	25♌
29	8♋	20♊	11♋	25♌
30	9♋	22♊	12♋	26♌

September

Day	☉	☿	♀	♂
1	9♍	5♎	29♍	5♎
2	10♍	6♎	1♎	6♎
3	11♍	6♎	2♎	6♎
4	12♍	7♎	3♎	7♎
5	13♍	7♎	4♎	8♎
6	14♍	7♎	5♎	8♎
7	15♍	8♎	7♎	9♎
8	16♍	8♎	8♎	10♎
9	17♍	8♎	9♎	10♎
10	18♍	8♎	10♎	11♎
11	19♍	8♎	12♎	12♎
12	20♍	7♎	13♎	12♎
13	21♍	7♎	14♎	13♎
14	22♍	6♎	15♎	14♎
15	22♍	6♎	17♎	14♎
16	23♍	5♎	18♎	15♎
17	24♍	4♎	19♎	16♎
18	25♍	3♎	20♎	16♎
19	26♍	2♎	21♎	17♎
20	27♍	1♎	23♎	18♎
21	28♍	0♎	24♎	18♎
22	29♍	29♍	25♎	19♎
23	0♎	28♍	26♎	20♎
24	1♎	27♍	28♎	20♎
25	2♎	26♍	29♎	21♎
26	3♎	25♍	0♏	22♎
27	4♎	24♍	1♏	22♎
28	5♎	24♍	2♏	23♎
29	6♎	23♍	4♏	24♎
30	7♎	23♍	5♏	24♎

December

Day	☉	☿	♀	♂
1	9♐	22♐	20♑	7♐
2	10♐	24♐	21♑	8♐
3	11♐	25♐	23♑	9♐
4	12♐	27♐	24♑	10♐
5	13♐	28♐	25♑	10♐
6	14♐	0♑	26♑	11♐
7	15♐	1♑	27♑	12♐
8	16♐	3♑	28♑	12♐
9	17♐	4♑	0♒	13♐
10	18♐	6♑	1♒	14♐
11	19♐	7♑	2♒	15♐
12	20♐	8♑	3♒	15♐
13	21♐	10♑	4♒	16♐
14	22♐	11♑	5♒	17♐
15	23♐	13♑	7♒	18♐
16	24♐	14♑	8♒	18♐
17	25♐	15♑	9♒	19♐
18	26♐	16♑	10♒	20♐
19	27♐	17♑	11♒	20♐
20	28♐	19♑	12♒	21♐
21	29♐	20♑	14♒	22♐
22	0♑	20♑	15♒	23♐
23	2♑	21♑	16♒	23♐
24	3♑	22♑	17♒	24♐
25	4♑	23♑	18♒	25♐
26	5♑	23♑	19♒	26♐
27	6♑	23♑	21♒	26♐
28	7♑	23♑	22♒	27♐
29	8♑	23♑	23♒	28♐
30	9♑	23♑	24♒	29♐
31	10♑	22♑	25♒	29♐

☉ =Sun ☿ = Mercury ♀ = Venus ♂ = Mars ♈ = Aries ♉ = Taurus ♊ = Gemini ♋ = Cancer

1977

January

Day	☉	☿	♀	♂
1	11♑	22♑	26♒	0♑
2	12♑	21♑	27♒	1♑
3	13♑	20♑	29♒	2♑
4	14♑	19♑	0♓	2♑
5	15♑	17♑	1♓	3♑
6	16♑	16♑	2♓	4♑
7	17♑	15♑	3♓	5♑
8	18♑	13♑	4♓	5♑
9	19♑	12♑	5♓	6♑
10	20♑	11♑	6♓	7♑
11	21♑	10♑	7♓	8♑
12	22♑	9♑	8♓	8♑
13	23♑	8♑	10♓	9♑
14	24♑	8♑	11♓	10♑
15	25♑	7♑	12♓	11♑
16	26♑	7♑	13♓	11♑
17	27♑	7♑	14♓	12♑
18	28♑	7♑	15♓	13♑
19	29♑	7♑	16♓	14♑
20	0♒	8♑	17♓	14♑
21	1♒	8♑	18♓	15♑
22	2♒	9♑	19♓	16♑
23	3♒	9♑	20♓	17♑
24	4♒	10♑	21♓	18♑
25	5♒	11♑	22♓	18♑
26	6♒	11♑	23♓	19♑
27	7♒	12♑	24♓	20♑
28	8♒	13♑	25♓	21♑
29	9♒	14♑	26♓	21♑
30	10♒	15♑	27♓	22♑
31	11♒	16♑	28♓	23♑

April

Day	☉	☿	♀	♂
1	11♈	27♈	19♈	9♓
2	12♈	28♈	19♈	10♓
3	13♈	0♉	18♈	11♓
4	14♈	2♉	18♈	12♓
5	15♈	3♉	17♈	13♓
6	16♈	5♉	16♈	13♓
7	17♈	6♉	16♈	14♓
8	18♈	7♉	15♈	15♓
9	19♈	8♉	15♈	16♓
10	20♈	9♉	14♈	16♓
11	21♈	10♉	13♈	17♓
12	22♈	11♉	13♈	18♓
13	23♈	12♉	12♈	19♓
14	24♈	13♉	12♈	20♓
15	25♈	13♉	11♈	20♓
16	26♈	14♉	11♈	21♓
17	27♈	14♉	10♈	22♓
18	28♈	14♉	10♈	23♓
19	29♈	14♉	10♈	23♓
20	0♉	15♉	9♈	24♓
21	1♉	14♉	9♈	25♓
22	2♉	14♉	9♈	26♓
23	3♉	14♉	9♈	27♓
24	4♉	14♉	8♈	27♓
25	5♉	13♉	8♈	28♓
26	6♉	13♉	8♈	29♓
27	7♉	12♉	8♈	0♈
28	8♉	12♉	8♈	0♈
29	9♉	11♉	8♈	1♈
30	10♉	11♉	8♈	2♈

July

Day	☉	☿	♀	♂
1	9♋	11♋	24♉	18♉
2	10♋	13♋	25♉	19♉
3	11♋	15♋	26♉	20♉
4	12♋	17♋	27♉	21♉
5	13♋	19♋	28♉	21♉
6	14♋	21♋	0♊	22♉
7	15♋	23♋	1♊	23♉
8	16♋	25♋	2♊	23♉
9	17♋	27♋	3♊	24♉
10	18♋	29♋	4♊	25♉
11	19♋	1♌	5♊	25♉
12	20♋	3♌	6♊	26♉
13	21♋	5♌	7♊	27♉
14	22♋	7♌	8♊	28♉
15	23♋	9♌	9♊	28♉
16	24♋	11♌	10♊	29♉
17	25♋	12♌	11♊	0♊
18	25♋	14♌	13♊	0♊
19	26♋	16♌	14♊	1♊
20	27♋	17♌	15♊	2♊
21	28♋	19♌	16♊	2♊
22	29♋	21♌	17♊	3♊
23	0♌	22♌	18♊	4♊
24	1♌	24♌	19♊	5♊
25	2♌	25♌	20♊	5♊
26	3♌	27♌	21♊	6♊
27	4♌	28♌	23♊	7♊
28	5♌	0♍	24♊	7♊
29	6♌	1♍	25♊	8♊
30	7♌	2♍	26♊	9♊
31	8♌	4♍	27♊	9♊

October

Day	☉	☿	♀	♂
1	8♎	24♍	10♍	18♋
2	9♎	26♍	12♍	18♋
3	10♎	28♍	13♍	19♋
4	11♎	0♎	14♍	19♋
5	12♎	1♎	15♍	20♋
6	13♎	3♎	17♍	20♋
7	14♎	5♎	18♍	21♋
8	15♎	7♎	19♍	21♋
9	16♎	9♎	20♍	22♋
10	17♎	10♎	22♍	22♋
11	18♎	12♎	23♍	23♋
12	19♎	14♎	24♍	23♋
13	20♎	16♎	25♍	24♋
14	21♎	17♎	26♍	24♋
15	22♎	19♎	28♍	25♋
16	23♎	21♎	29♍	25♋
17	24♎	22♎	0♎	26♋
18	25♎	24♎	1♎	26♋
19	26♎	26♎	3♎	27♋
20	27♎	28♎	4♎	27♋
21	28♎	29♎	5♎	28♋
22	29♎	1♏	6♎	28♋
23	0♏	3♏	8♎	28♋
24	1♏	4♏	9♎	29♋
25	2♏	6♏	10♎	29♋
26	3♏	7♏	11♎	0♌
27	4♏	9♏	13♎	0♌
28	5♏	11♏	14♎	1♌
29	6♏	12♏	15♎	1♌
30	7♏	14♏	16♎	1♌
31	8♏	15♏	18♎	2♌

February

Day	☉	☿	♀	♂
1	12♒	18♑	29♓	24♑
2	13♒	19♑	0♈	24♑
3	14♒	20♑	1♈	25♑
4	15♒	21♑	2♈	26♑
5	16♒	22♑	3♈	27♑
6	17♒	24♑	4♈	27♑
7	18♒	25♑	5♈	28♑
8	19♒	26♑	5♈	29♑
9	20♒	28♑	6♈	0♒
10	21♒	29♑	7♈	1♒
11	22♒	0♒	8♈	1♒
12	23♒	2♒	9♈	2♒
13	24♒	3♒	10♈	3♒
14	25♒	5♒	11♈	4♒
15	26♒	6♒	11♈	4♒
16	27♒	7♒	12♈	5♒
17	28♒	9♒	13♈	6♒
18	29♒	10♒	14♈	7♒
19	0♓	12♒	14♈	8♒
20	1♓	14♒	15♈	8♒
21	2♓	15♒	16♈	9♒
22	3♓	17♒	16♈	10♒
23	4♓	18♒	17♈	11♒
24	5♓	20♒	18♈	11♒
25	6♓	21♒	18♈	12♒
26	7♓	23♒	19♈	13♒
27	8♓	25♒	19♈	14♒
28	9♓	26♒	20♈	14♒

May

Day	☉	☿	♀	♂
1	11♉	10♉	9♈	3♈
2	12♉	9♉	9♈	4♈
3	13♉	9♉	9♈	4♈
4	14♉	8♉	9♈	5♈
5	15♉	7♉	9♈	6♈
6	16♉	7♉	10♈	7♈
7	17♉	6♉	10♈	7♈
8	17♉	6♉	10♈	8♈
9	18♉	6♉	11♈	9♈
10	19♉	5♉	11♈	10♈
11	20♉	5♉	12♈	10♈
12	21♉	5♉	12♈	11♈
13	22♉	5♉	13♈	12♈
14	23♉	5♉	13♈	13♈
15	24♉	5♉	14♈	13♈
16	25♉	5♉	14♈	14♈
17	26♉	5♉	15♈	15♈
18	27♉	5♉	15♈	16♈
19	28♉	6♉	16♈	17♈
20	29♉	6♉	17♈	17♈
21	0♊	7♉	17♈	18♈
22	1♊	7♉	18♈	19♈
23	2♊	8♉	19♈	20♈
24	3♊	9♉	19♈	20♈
25	4♊	9♉	20♈	21♈
26	5♊	10♉	21♈	22♈
27	6♊	11♉	22♈	23♈
28	7♊	12♉	22♈	23♈
29	8♊	13♉	23♈	24♈
30	9♊	14♉	24♈	25♈
31	10♊	15♉	25♈	26♈

August

Day	☉	☿	♀	♂
1	9♌	5♍	28♊	10♊
2	10♌	6♍	29♊	11♊
3	11♌	7♍	0♋	11♊
4	12♌	9♍	2♋	12♊
5	13♌	10♍	3♋	13♊
6	14♌	11♍	4♋	13♊
7	15♌	12♍	5♋	14♊
8	16♌	13♍	6♋	15♊
9	16♌	14♍	7♋	15♊
10	17♌	15♍	8♋	16♊
11	18♌	16♍	10♋	17♊
12	19♌	16♍	11♋	17♊
13	20♌	17♍	12♋	18♊
14	21♌	18♍	13♋	19♊
15	22♌	18♍	14♋	19♊
16	23♌	19♍	15♋	20♊
17	24♌	20♍	17♋	21♊
18	25♌	20♍	18♋	21♊
19	26♌	20♍	19♋	22♊
20	27♌	21♍	20♋	23♊
21	28♌	21♍	21♋	23♊
22	29♌	21♍	22♋	24♊
23	0♍	21♍	24♋	24♊
24	1♍	21♍	25♋	25♊
25	2♍	20♍	26♋	26♊
26	3♍	20♍	27♋	26♊
27	4♍	20♍	28♋	27♊
28	5♍	19♍	29♋	28♊
29	6♍	19♍	1♌	28♊
30	7♍	18♍	2♌	29♊
31	8♍	17♍	3♌	0♋

November

Day	☉	☿	♀	♂
1	9♏	17♏	19♎	2♌
2	10♏	18♏	20♎	3♌
3	11♏	20♏	21♎	3♌
4	12♏	22♏	23♎	3♌
5	13♏	23♏	24♎	4♌
6	14♏	25♏	25♎	4♌
7	15♏	26♏	26♎	4♌
8	16♏	28♏	28♎	5♌
9	17♏	29♏	29♎	5♌
10	18♏	1♐	0♏	6♌
11	19♏	2♐	1♏	6♌
12	20♏	4♐	3♏	6♌
13	21♏	5♐	4♏	7♌
14	22♏	7♐	5♏	7♌
15	23♏	8♐	6♏	7♌
16	24♏	10♐	8♏	7♌
17	25♏	11♐	9♏	8♌
18	26♏	13♐	10♏	8♌
19	27♏	14♐	11♏	8♌
20	28♏	15♐	13♏	9♌
21	29♏	17♐	14♏	9♌
22	0♐	18♐	15♏	9♌
23	1♐	20♐	16♏	9♌
24	2♐	21♐	18♏	9♌
25	3♐	22♐	19♏	10♌
26	4♐	24♐	20♏	10♌
27	5♐	25♐	21♏	10♌
28	6♐	26♐	23♏	10♌
29	7♐	28♐	24♏	10♌
30	8♐	29♐	25♏	11♌

March

Day	☉	☿	♀	♂
1	11♓	28♒	21♈	15♒
2	12♓	0♓	21♈	16♒
3	13♓	1♓	21♈	17♒
4	14♓	3♓	22♈	18♒
5	15♓	5♓	22♈	18♒
6	16♓	7♓	23♈	19♒
7	17♓	9♓	23♈	20♒
8	18♓	10♓	23♈	21♒
9	19♓	12♓	24♈	22♒
10	20♓	14♓	24♈	22♒
11	21♓	16♓	24♈	23♒
12	22♓	18♓	24♈	24♒
13	23♓	20♓	24♈	25♒
14	24♓	22♓	24♈	25♒
15	24♓	24♓	25♈	26♒
16	25♓	25♓	25♈	27♒
17	26♓	27♓	25♈	28♒
18	27♓	29♓	24♈	29♒
19	28♓	1♈	24♈	29♒
20	29♓	3♈	24♈	0♓
21	0♈	5♈	24♈	1♓
22	1♈	7♈	24♈	2♓
23	2♈	9♈	24♈	2♓
24	3♈	11♈	23♈	3♓
25	4♈	13♈	23♈	4♓
26	5♈	15♈	22♈	5♓
27	6♈	17♈	22♈	6♓
28	7♈	19♈	22♈	6♓
29	8♈	21♈	21♈	7♓
30	9♈	23♈	21♈	8♓
31	10♈	25♈	20♈	9♓

June

Day	☉	☿	♀	♂
1	11♊	16♉	26♈	26♈
2	12♊	18♉	27♈	27♈
3	13♊	19♉	27♈	28♈
4	13♊	20♉	28♈	29♈
5	14♊	21♉	29♈	29♈
6	15♊	23♉	0♉	0♉
7	16♊	24♉	1♉	1♉
8	17♊	26♉	2♉	2♉
9	18♊	27♉	3♉	2♉
10	19♊	29♉	4♉	3♉
11	20♊	1♊	4♉	4♉
12	21♊	2♊	5♉	5♉
13	22♊	4♊	6♉	5♉
14	23♊	6♊	7♉	6♉
15	24♊	7♊	8♉	7♉
16	25♊	9♊	9♉	7♉
17	26♊	11♊	10♉	8♉
18	27♊	13♊	11♉	9♉
19	28♊	15♊	12♉	10♉
20	29♊	17♊	13♉	10♉
21	0♋	19♊	14♉	11♉
22	1♋	21♊	15♉	12♉
23	2♋	23♊	16♉	13♉
24	3♋	25♊	17♉	13♉
25	4♋	28♊	18♉	14♉
26	4♋	0♋	19♉	15♉
27	5♋	2♋	20♉	15♉
28	6♋	4♋	21♉	16♉
29	7♋	6♋	22♉	17♉
30	8♋	9♋	23♉	18♉

September

Day	☉	☿	♀	♂
1	9♍	16♍	4♌	0♋
2	10♍	15♍	5♌	1♋
3	11♍	15♍	7♌	1♋
4	12♍	14♍	8♌	2♋
5	13♍	13♍	9♌	3♋
6	13♍	12♍	10♌	3♋
7	14♍	11♍	11♌	4♋
8	15♍	10♍	13♌	4♋
9	16♍	9♍	14♌	5♋
10	17♍	8♍	15♌	6♋
11	18♍	8♍	16♌	6♋
12	19♍	7♍	17♌	7♋
13	20♍	7♍	19♌	7♋
14	21♍	7♍	20♌	8♋
15	22♍	7♍	21♌	9♋
16	23♍	7♍	22♌	9♋
17	24♍	7♍	23♌	10♋
18	25♍	8♍	25♌	10♋
19	26♍	9♍	26♌	11♋
20	27♍	9♍	27♌	11♋
21	28♍	10♍	28♌	12♋
22	29♍	11♍	29♌	13♋
23	0♎	12♍	1♍	13♋
24	1♎	14♍	2♍	14♋
25	2♎	15♍	3♍	14♋
26	3♎	16♍	4♍	15♋
27	4♎	18♍	6♍	15♋
28	5♎	20♍	7♍	16♋
29	6♎	21♍	8♍	16♋
30	7♎	23♍	9♍	17♋

December

Day	☉	☿	♀	♂
1	9♐	0♑	26♏	11♌
2	10♐	1♑	28♏	11♌
3	11♐	2♑	29♏	11♌
4	12♐	3♑	0♐	11♌
5	13♐	4♑	1♐	11♌
6	14♐	5♑	3♐	11♌
7	15♐	6♑	4♐	11♌
8	16♐	6♑	5♐	11♌
9	17♐	7♑	6♐	11♌
10	18♐	7♑	8♐	12♌
11	19♐	7♑	9♐	12♌
12	20♐	7♑	10♐	12♌
13	21♐	7♑	11♐	12♌
14	22♐	7♑	13♐	12♌
15	23♐	7♑	14♐	12♌
16	24♐	6♑	15♐	11♌
17	25♐	5♑	17♐	11♌
18	26♐	4♑	18♐	11♌
19	27♐	3♑	19♐	11♌
20	28♐	1♑	20♐	11♌
21	29♐	0♑	22♐	11♌
22	0♑	29♐	23♐	11♌
23	1♑	27♐	24♐	11♌
24	2♑	26♐	25♐	11♌
25	3♑	25♐	27♐	11♌
26	4♑	24♐	28♐	10♌
27	5♑	23♐	29♐	10♌
28	6♑	22♐	0♑	10♌
29	7♑	22♐	2♑	10♌
30	8♑	21♐	3♑	9♌
31	9♑	21♐	4♑	9♌

Planetary Positions

♌ = Leo ♍ = Virgo ♎ = Libra ♏ = Scorpio ♐ = Sagittarius ♑ = Capricorn ♒ = Aquarius ♓ = Pisces

1978

January

Day	☉	☿	♀	♂
1	10♑	21♐	5♑	9♌
2	11♑	21♐	7♑	9♌
3	12♑	22♐	8♑	8♌
4	13♑	22♐	9♑	8♌
5	15♑	22♐	10♑	8♌
6	16♑	23♐	12♑	8♌
7	17♑	24♐	13♑	7♌
8	18♑	24♐	14♑	7♌
9	19♑	25♐	15♑	7♌
10	20♑	26♐	17♑	6♌
11	21♑	27♐	18♑	6♌
12	22♑	28♐	19♑	5♌
13	23♑	29♐	20♑	5♌
14	24♑	0♑	22♑	5♌
15	25♑	2♑	23♑	4♌
16	26♑	3♑	24♑	4♌
17	27♑	4♑	26♑	4♌
18	28♑	5♑	27♑	3♌
19	29♑	6♑	28♑	3♌
20	0♒	8♑	29♑	2♌
21	1♒	9♑	1♒	2♌
22	2♒	10♑	2♒	2♌
23	3♒	12♑	3♒	1♌
24	4♒	13♑	4♒	1♌
25	5♒	15♑	6♒	0♌
26	6♒	16♑	7♒	0♌
27	7♒	17♑	8♒	0♌
28	8♒	19♑	9♒	29♋
29	9♒	20♑	11♒	29♋
30	10♒	22♑	12♒	28♋
31	11♒	23♑	13♒	28♋

April

Day	☉	☿	♀	♂
1	11♈	26♈	28♈	27♋
2	12♈	26♈	29♈	27♋
3	13♈	26♈	0♉	28♋
4	14♈	26♈	2♉	28♋
5	15♈	25♈	3♉	28♋
6	16♈	25♈	4♉	28♋
7	17♈	24♈	5♉	29♋
8	18♈	24♈	7♉	29♋
9	19♈	23♈	8♉	29♋
10	20♈	23♈	9♉	0♌
11	21♈	22♈	10♉	0♌
12	22♈	21♈	11♉	0♌
13	23♈	20♈	13♉	1♌
14	24♈	20♈	14♉	1♌
15	25♈	19♈	15♉	2♌
16	26♈	18♈	16♉	2♌
17	27♈	17♈	18♉	2♌
18	28♈	17♈	19♉	3♌
19	29♈	16♈	20♉	3♌
20	0♉	16♈	21♉	3♌
21	1♉	16♈	23♉	4♌
22	2♉	15♈	24♉	4♌
23	3♉	15♈	25♉	5♌
24	4♉	15♈	26♉	5♌
25	5♉	15♈	27♉	6♌
26	6♉	15♈	29♉	6♌
27	7♉	15♈	0♊	6♌
28	8♉	15♈	1♊	7♌
29	9♉	15♈	2♊	7♌
30	9♉	16♈	4♊	8♌

July

Day	☉	☿	♀	♂
1	9♋	27♋	17♌	10♍
2	10♋	29♋	19♌	10♍
3	11♋	0♌	20♌	11♍
4	12♋	2♌	21♌	11♍
5	13♋	4♌	22♌	12♍
6	14♋	5♌	23♌	12♍
7	15♋	7♌	24♌	13♍
8	16♋	9♌	26♌	14♍
9	17♋	10♌	27♌	14♍
10	18♋	11♌	28♌	15♍
11	19♋	13♌	29♌	15♍
12	20♋	14♌	0♍	16♍
13	20♋	16♌	1♍	17♍
14	21♋	17♌	2♍	17♍
15	22♋	18♌	4♍	18♍
16	23♋	19♌	5♍	18♍
17	24♋	21♌	6♍	19♍
18	25♋	22♌	7♍	20♍
19	26♋	23♌	8♍	20♍
20	27♋	24♌	9♍	21♍
21	28♋	25♌	10♍	21♍
22	29♋	26♌	11♍	22♍
23	0♌	27♌	13♍	23♍
24	1♌	28♌	14♍	23♍
25	2♌	29♌	15♍	24♍
26	3♌	29♌	16♍	24♍
27	4♌	0♍	17♍	25♍
28	5♌	1♍	18♍	26♍
29	6♌	1♍	19♍	26♍
30	7♌	2♍	20♍	27♍
31	8♌	2♍	21♍	27♍

October

Day	☉	☿	♀	♂
1	8♎	8♎	18♏	8♏
2	9♎	10♎	18♏	8♏
3	10♎	12♎	19♏	9♏
4	11♎	13♎	19♏	10♏
5	12♎	15♎	20♏	10♏
6	13♎	17♎	20♏	11♏
7	14♎	18♎	21♏	12♏
8	15♎	20♎	21♏	12♏
9	16♎	22♎	21♏	13♏
10	17♎	23♎	22♏	14♏
11	18♎	25♎	22♏	15♏
12	19♎	27♎	22♏	15♏
13	20♎	28♎	22♏	16♏
14	20♎	0♏	23♏	17♏
15	21♎	2♏	23♏	17♏
16	22♎	3♏	23♏	18♏
17	23♎	5♏	23♏	19♏
18	24♎	6♏	23♏	19♏
19	25♎	8♏	23♏	20♏
20	26♎	9♏	23♏	21♏
21	27♎	11♏	23♏	22♏
22	28♎	12♏	22♏	22♏
23	29♎	14♏	22♏	23♏
24	0♏	15♏	22♏	24♏
25	1♏	17♏	22♏	24♏
26	2♏	18♏	22♏	25♏
27	3♏	20♏	21♏	26♏
28	4♏	21♏	21♏	27♏
29	5♏	23♏	20♏	27♏
30	6♏	24♏	20♏	28♏
31	7♏	26♏	19♏	29♏

February

Day	☉	☿	♀	♂
1	12♒	25♑	14♒	28♋
2	13♒	26♑	16♒	27♋
3	14♒	28♑	17♒	27♋
4	15♒	29♑	18♒	27♋
5	16♒	1♒	19♒	26♋
6	17♒	2♒	21♒	26♋
7	18♒	4♒	22♒	26♋
8	19♒	6♒	23♒	25♋
9	20♒	7♒	24♒	25♋
10	21♒	9♒	26♒	25♋
11	22♒	10♒	27♒	25♋
12	23♒	12♒	28♒	24♋
13	24♒	14♒	29♒	24♋
14	25♒	15♒	1♓	24♋
15	26♒	17♒	2♓	24♋
16	27♒	19♒	3♓	24♋
17	28♒	20♒	4♓	23♋
18	29♒	22♒	6♓	23♋
19	0♓	24♒	7♓	23♋
20	1♓	26♒	8♓	23♋
21	2♓	27♒	9♓	23♋
22	3♓	29♒	11♓	23♋
23	4♓	1♓	12♓	23♋
24	5♓	3♓	13♓	23♋
25	6♓	5♓	14♓	22♋
26	7♓	6♓	16♓	22♋
27	8♓	8♓	17♓	22♋
28	9♓	10♓	18♓	22♋

May

Day	☉	☿	♀	♂
1	10♉	16♈	5♊	8♌
2	11♉	17♈	6♊	9♌
3	12♉	17♈	7♊	9♌
4	13♉	18♈	8♊	9♌
5	14♉	19♈	10♊	10♌
6	15♉	19♈	11♊	10♌
7	16♉	20♈	12♊	11♌
8	17♉	21♈	13♊	11♌
9	18♉	22♈	14♊	12♌
10	19♉	23♈	16♊	12♌
11	20♉	24♈	17♊	13♌
12	21♉	25♈	18♊	13♌
13	22♉	26♈	19♊	14♌
14	23♉	27♈	21♊	14♌
15	24♉	29♈	22♊	15♌
16	25♉	0♉	23♊	15♌
17	26♉	1♉	24♊	16♌
18	27♉	2♉	25♊	16♌
19	28♉	4♉	27♊	16♌
20	29♉	5♉	28♊	17♌
21	0♊	7♉	29♊	17♌
22	1♊	8♉	0♋	18♌
23	2♊	10♉	1♋	18♌
24	3♊	11♉	3♋	19♌
25	4♊	13♉	4♋	19♌
26	5♊	15♉	5♋	20♌
27	6♊	16♉	6♋	21♌
28	7♊	18♉	7♋	21♌
29	7♊	20♉	9♋	22♌
30	8♊	22♉	10♋	22♌
31	9♊	23♉	11♋	23♌

August

Day	☉	☿	♀	♂
1	9♌	2♍	23♍	28♍
2	10♌	3♍	24♍	29♍
3	11♌	3♍	25♍	29♍
4	11♌	3♍	26♍	0♎
5	12♌	3♍	27♍	1♎
6	13♌	3♍	28♍	1♎
7	14♌	3♍	29♍	2♎
8	15♌	3♍	0♎	2♎
9	16♌	2♍	1♎	3♎
10	17♌	2♍	2♎	4♎
11	18♌	1♍	3♎	4♎
12	19♌	1♍	4♎	5♎
13	20♌	0♍	5♎	6♎
14	21♌	29♌	6♎	6♎
15	22♌	29♌	7♎	7♎
16	23♌	28♌	9♎	7♎
17	24♌	27♌	10♎	8♎
18	25♌	26♌	11♎	9♎
19	26♌	25♌	12♎	9♎
20	27♌	24♌	13♎	10♎
21	28♌	24♌	14♎	11♎
22	29♌	23♌	15♎	11♎
23	0♍	22♌	16♎	12♎
24	1♍	22♌	17♎	12♎
25	2♍	21♌	18♎	13♎
26	3♍	21♌	19♎	14♎
27	4♍	20♌	20♎	14♎
28	5♍	20♌	21♎	15♎
29	6♍	20♌	22♎	16♎
30	6♍	21♌	23♎	16♎
31	7♍	21♌	24♎	17♎

November

Day	☉	☿	♀	♂
1	8♏	27♏	19♏	29♏
2	9♏	28♏	18♏	0♐
3	10♏	0♐	18♏	1♐
4	11♏	1♐	17♏	2♐
5	12♏	3♐	17♏	2♐
6	13♏	4♐	16♏	3♐
7	14♏	5♐	16♏	4♐
8	15♏	7♐	15♏	4♐
9	16♏	8♐	14♏	5♐
10	17♏	9♐	14♏	6♐
11	18♏	10♐	13♏	7♐
12	19♏	12♐	13♏	7♐
13	20♏	13♐	12♏	8♐
14	21♏	14♐	11♏	9♐
15	22♏	15♐	11♏	10♐
16	23♏	16♐	10♏	10♐
17	24♏	17♐	10♏	11♐
18	25♏	18♐	10♏	12♐
19	27♏	19♐	9♏	12♐
20	28♏	19♐	9♏	13♐
21	29♏	20♐	8♏	14♐
22	0♐	21♐	8♏	15♐
23	1♐	21♐	8♏	15♐
24	2♐	21♐	8♏	16♐
25	3♐	22♐	8♏	17♐
26	4♐	22♐	7♏	18♐
27	5♐	21♐	7♏	18♐
28	6♐	21♐	7♏	19♐
29	7♐	21♐	7♏	20♐
30	8♐	20♐	7♏	21♐

March

Day	☉	☿	♀	♂
1	10♓	12♓	19♓	22♋
2	11♓	14♓	21♓	22♋
3	12♓	16♓	22♓	22♋
4	13♓	18♓	23♓	22♋
5	14♓	20♓	24♓	22♋
6	15♓	22♓	26♓	22♋
7	16♓	24♓	27♓	22♋
8	17♓	26♓	28♓	22♋
9	18♓	28♓	29♓	23♋
10	19♓	29♓	1♈	23♋
11	20♓	1♈	2♈	23♋
12	21♓	3♈	3♈	23♋
13	22♓	5♈	4♈	23♋
14	23♓	7♈	6♈	23♋
15	24♓	9♈	7♈	23♋
16	25♓	10♈	8♈	23♋
17	26♓	12♈	9♈	24♋
18	27♓	14♈	11♈	24♋
19	28♓	15♈	12♈	24♋
20	29♓	17♈	13♈	24♋
21	0♈	18♈	14♈	24♋
22	1♈	19♈	16♈	24♋
23	2♈	21♈	17♈	25♋
24	3♈	22♈	18♈	25♋
25	4♈	23♈	19♈	25♋
26	5♈	24♈	21♈	25♋
27	6♈	24♈	22♈	26♋
28	7♈	25♈	23♈	26♋
29	8♈	25♈	24♈	26♋
30	9♈	26♈	25♈	26♋
31	10♈	26♈	27♈	27♋

June

Day	☉	☿	♀	♂
1	10♊	25♉	12♋	23♌
2	11♊	27♉	13♋	24♌
3	12♊	29♉	15♋	24♌
4	13♊	1♊	16♋	25♌
5	14♊	3♊	17♋	25♌
6	15♊	5♊	18♋	26♌
7	16♊	7♊	19♋	26♌
8	17♊	9♊	20♋	27♌
9	18♊	12♊	22♋	27♌
10	19♊	14♊	23♋	28♌
11	20♊	16♊	24♋	28♌
12	21♊	18♊	25♋	29♌
13	22♊	20♊	26♋	0♍
14	23♊	22♊	28♋	0♍
15	24♊	25♊	29♋	1♍
16	25♊	27♊	0♌	1♍
17	26♊	29♊	1♌	2♍
18	27♊	1♋	2♌	2♍
19	28♊	3♋	3♌	3♍
20	29♊	5♋	5♌	3♍
21	29♊	8♋	6♌	4♍
22	0♋	10♋	7♌	4♍
23	1♋	12♋	8♌	5♍
24	2♋	14♋	9♌	6♍
25	3♋	16♋	10♌	6♍
26	4♋	18♋	12♌	7♍
27	5♋	20♋	13♌	7♍
28	6♋	22♋	14♌	8♍
29	7♋	23♋	15♌	8♍
30	8♋	25♋	16♌	9♍

September

Day	☉	☿	♀	♂
1	8♍	21♌	24♎	18♎
2	9♍	22♌	25♎	18♎
3	10♍	22♌	26♎	19♎
4	11♍	23♌	27♎	20♎
5	12♍	24♌	28♎	20♎
6	13♍	25♌	29♎	21♎
7	14♍	26♌	0♏	22♎
8	15♍	28♌	1♏	22♎
9	16♍	29♌	2♏	23♎
10	17♍	1♍	3♏	24♎
11	18♍	2♍	4♏	24♎
12	19♍	4♍	4♏	25♎
13	20♍	5♍	5♏	26♎
14	21♍	7♍	6♏	26♎
15	22♍	9♍	7♏	27♎
16	23♍	11♍	8♏	28♎
17	24♍	12♍	8♏	28♎
18	25♍	14♍	9♏	29♎
19	26♍	16♍	10♏	0♏
20	27♍	18♍	11♏	0♏
21	28♍	20♍	11♏	1♏
22	29♍	22♍	12♏	2♏
23	0♎	24♍	13♏	2♏
24	1♎	25♍	14♏	3♏
25	2♎	27♍	14♏	4♏
26	3♎	29♍	15♏	4♏
27	4♎	1♎	16♏	5♏
28	5♎	3♎	16♏	6♏
29	6♎	5♎	17♏	6♏
30	7♎	6♎	17♏	7♏

December

Day	☉	☿	♀	♂
1	9♐	19♐	7♏	21♐
2	10♐	18♐	8♏	22♐
3	11♐	17♐	8♏	23♐
4	12♐	16♐	8♏	24♐
5	13♐	14♐	8♏	24♐
6	14♐	13♐	8♏	25♐
7	15♐	12♐	9♏	26♐
8	16♐	10♐	9♏	27♐
9	17♐	9♐	9♏	27♐
10	18♐	8♐	10♏	28♐
11	19♐	7♐	10♏	29♐
12	20♐	6♐	11♏	0♑
13	21♐	6♐	11♏	0♑
14	22♐	6♐	12♏	1♑
15	23♐	5♐	12♏	2♑
16	24♐	5♐	13♏	3♑
17	25♐	6♐	13♏	3♑
18	26♐	6♐	14♏	4♑
19	27♐	6♐	15♏	5♑
20	28♐	7♐	15♏	6♑
21	29♐	8♐	16♏	6♑
22	0♑	8♐	17♏	7♑
23	1♑	9♐	17♏	8♑
24	2♑	10♐	18♏	9♑
25	3♑	11♐	19♏	9♑
26	4♑	12♐	20♏	10♑
27	5♑	13♐	20♏	11♑
28	6♑	14♐	21♏	12♑
29	7♑	16♐	22♏	13♑
30	8♑	17♐	23♏	13♑
31	9♑	18♐	24♏	14♑

1979

Your Starway to Love

☉ =Sun ☿ = Mercury ♀ = Venus ♂ = Mars ♈ = Aries ♉ = Taurus ♊ = Gemini ♋ = Cancer

January

Day	☉	☿	♀	♂
1	10♑	19♐	25♏	15♑
2	11♑	21♐	25♏	16♑
3	12♑	22♐	26♏	16♑
4	13♑	23♐	27♏	17♑
5	14♑	25♐	28♏	18♑
6	15♑	26♐	29♏	19♑
7	16♑	28♐	0♐	19♑
8	17♑	29♐	1♐	20♑
9	18♑	0♑	2♐	21♑
10	19♑	2♑	3♐	22♑
11	20♑	3♑	4♐	23♑
12	21♑	5♑	5♐	23♑
13	22♑	6♑	6♐	24♑
14	23♑	8♑	7♐	25♑
15	24♑	9♑	8♐	26♑
16	25♑	11♑	9♐	26♑
17	26♑	12♑	10♐	27♑
18	27♑	14♑	11♐	28♑
19	29♑	15♑	12♐	29♑
20	0♒	17♑	13♐	0♒
21	1♒	18♑	14♐	0♒
22	2♒	20♑	15♐	1♒
23	3♒	21♑	16♐	2♒
24	4♒	23♑	17♐	3♒
25	5♒	25♑	18♐	4♒
26	6♒	26♑	19♐	4♒
27	7♒	28♑	20♐	5♒
28	8♒	29♑	21♐	6♒
29	9♒	1♒	22♐	7♒
30	10♒	3♒	23♐	7♒
31	11♒	4♒	24♐	8♒

April

Day	☉	☿	♀	♂
1	11♈	27♓	4♓	25♓
2	12♈	27♓	5♓	26♓
3	13♈	26♓	6♓	27♓
4	14♈	26♓	7♓	28♓
5	15♈	26♓	8♓	29♓
6	16♈	26♓	10♓	29♓
7	17♈	26♓	11♓	0♈
8	18♈	26♓	12♓	1♈
9	19♈	26♓	13♓	2♈
10	20♈	26♓	14♓	2♈
11	21♈	26♓	16♓	3♈
12	22♈	27♓	17♓	4♈
13	23♈	27♓	18♓	5♈
14	24♈	28♓	19♓	6♈
15	25♈	28♓	20♓	6♈
16	26♈	29♓	22♓	7♈
17	27♈	0♈	23♓	8♈
18	28♈	1♈	24♓	9♈
19	29♈	1♈	25♓	9♈
20	0♉	2♈	26♓	10♈
21	1♉	3♈	28♓	11♈
22	1♉	4♈	29♓	12♈
23	2♉	5♈	0♈	13♈
24	3♉	6♈	1♈	13♈
25	4♉	7♈	2♈	14♈
26	5♉	9♈	4♈	15♈
27	6♉	10♈	5♈	16♈
28	7♉	11♈	6♈	16♈
29	8♉	12♈	7♈	17♈
30	9♉	14♈	8♈	18♈

July

Day	☉	☿	♀	♂
1	9♋	4♌	24♊	4♊
2	10♋	6♌	25♊	4♊
3	11♋	7♌	26♊	5♊
4	12♋	8♌	27♊	6♊
5	13♋	8♌	29♊	6♊
6	14♋	9♌	0♋	7♊
7	15♋	10♌	1♋	8♊
8	15♋	11♌	2♋	9♊
9	16♋	12♌	3♋	9♊
10	17♋	12♌	5♋	10♊
11	18♋	13♌	6♋	11♊
12	19♋	13♌	7♋	11♊
13	20♋	14♌	8♋	12♊
14	21♋	14♌	10♋	13♊
15	22♋	14♌	11♋	13♊
16	23♋	14♌	12♋	14♊
17	24♋	14♌	13♋	15♊
18	25♋	14♌	14♋	16♊
19	26♋	14♌	16♋	16♊
20	27♋	14♌	17♋	17♊
21	28♋	14♌	18♋	18♊
22	29♋	14♌	19♋	18♊
23	0♌	13♌	21♋	19♊
24	1♌	13♌	22♋	20♊
25	2♌	12♌	23♋	20♊
26	3♌	12♌	24♋	21♊
27	4♌	11♌	26♋	22♊
28	5♌	10♌	27♋	22♊
29	6♌	10♌	28♋	23♊
30	6♌	9♌	29♋	24♊
31	7♌	8♌	0♌	24♊

October

Day	☉	☿	♀	♂
1	7♎	21♎	17♎	4♌
2	8♎	22♎	19♎	4♌
3	9♎	24♎	20♎	5♌
4	10♎	26♎	21♎	5♌
5	11♎	27♎	22♎	6♌
6	12♎	29♎	24♎	7♌
7	13♎	0♏	25♎	7♌
8	14♎	2♏	26♎	8♌
9	15♎	3♏	27♎	8♌
10	16♎	5♏	29♎	9♌
11	17♎	6♏	0♏	10♌
12	18♎	7♏	1♏	10♌
13	19♎	9♏	2♏	11♌
14	20♎	10♏	3♏	11♌
15	21♎	12♏	5♏	12♌
16	22♎	13♏	6♏	12♌
17	23♎	14♏	7♏	13♌
18	24♎	16♏	8♏	13♌
19	25♎	17♏	10♏	14♌
20	26♎	18♏	11♏	15♌
21	27♎	20♏	12♏	15♌
22	28♎	21♏	13♏	16♌
23	29♎	22♏	15♏	16♌
24	0♏	23♏	16♏	17♌
25	1♏	25♏	17♏	17♌
26	2♏	26♏	18♏	18♌
27	3♏	27♏	20♏	18♌
28	4♏	28♏	21♏	19♌
29	5♏	29♏	22♏	19♌
30	6♏	0♐	23♏	20♌
31	7♏	1♐	25♏	20♌

February

Day	☉	☿	♀	♂
1	12♒	6♒	25♐	9♒
2	13♒	8♒	27♐	10♒
3	14♒	9♒	28♐	11♒
4	15♒	11♒	29♐	11♒
5	16♒	13♒	0♑	12♒
6	17♒	15♒	1♑	13♒
7	18♒	16♒	2♑	14♒
8	19♒	18♒	3♑	15♒
9	20♒	20♒	4♑	15♒
10	21♒	22♒	5♑	16♒
11	22♒	23♒	6♑	17♒
12	23♒	25♒	8♑	18♒
13	24♒	27♒	9♑	18♒
14	25♒	29♒	10♑	19♒
15	26♒	1♓	11♑	20♒
16	27♒	2♓	12♑	21♒
17	28♒	4♓	13♑	22♒
18	29♒	6♓	14♑	22♒
19	0♓	8♓	16♑	23♒
20	1♓	10♓	17♑	24♒
21	2♓	12♓	18♑	25♒
22	3♓	14♓	19♑	26♒
23	4♓	15♓	20♑	26♒
24	5♓	17♓	21♑	27♒
25	6♓	19♓	22♑	28♒
26	7♓	21♓	24♑	29♒
27	8♓	23♓	25♑	29♒
28	9♓	24♓	26♑	0♓

May

Day	☉	☿	♀	♂
1	10♉	15♈	10♈	19♈
2	11♉	16♈	11♈	19♈
3	12♉	18♈	12♈	20♈
4	13♉	19♈	13♈	21♈
5	14♉	21♈	15♈	22♈
6	15♉	22♈	16♈	22♈
7	16♉	24♈	17♈	23♈
8	17♉	26♈	18♈	24♈
9	18♉	27♈	19♈	25♈
10	19♉	29♈	21♈	25♈
11	20♉	0♉	22♈	26♈
12	21♉	2♉	23♈	27♈
13	22♉	4♉	24♈	28♈
14	23♉	6♉	25♈	29♈
15	24♉	8♉	27♈	29♈
16	25♉	9♉	28♈	0♉
17	26♉	11♉	29♈	1♉
18	27♉	13♉	0♉	2♉
19	28♉	15♉	1♉	2♉
20	29♉	17♉	3♉	3♉
21	0♊	19♉	4♉	4♉
22	1♊	21♉	5♉	5♉
23	1♊	23♉	6♉	5♉
24	2♊	25♉	7♉	6♉
25	3♊	28♉	9♉	7♉
26	4♊	0♊	10♉	7♉
27	5♊	2♊	11♉	8♉
28	6♊	4♊	12♉	9♉
29	7♊	6♊	14♉	10♉
30	8♊	8♊	15♉	10♉
31	9♊	11♊	16♉	11♉

August

Day	☉	☿	♀	♂
1	8♌	8♌	2♌	25♊
2	9♌	7♌	3♌	26♊
3	10♌	6♌	4♌	26♊
4	11♌	6♌	5♌	27♊
5	12♌	5♌	7♌	28♊
6	13♌	4♌	8♌	28♊
7	14♌	4♌	9♌	29♊
8	15♌	4♌	10♌	0♋
9	16♌	3♌	12♌	0♋
10	17♌	3♌	13♌	1♋
11	18♌	3♌	14♌	2♋
12	19♌	3♌	15♌	2♋
13	20♌	3♌	16♌	3♋
14	21♌	4♌	18♌	4♋
15	22♌	4♌	19♌	4♋
16	23♌	5♌	20♌	5♋
17	24♌	5♌	21♌	6♋
18	25♌	6♌	23♌	6♋
19	26♌	7♌	24♌	7♋
20	27♌	8♌	25♌	8♋
21	28♌	9♌	26♌	8♋
22	29♌	10♌	28♌	9♋
23	29♌	12♌	29♌	10♋
24	0♍	13♌	0♍	10♋
25	1♍	15♌	1♍	11♋
26	2♍	16♌	3♍	12♋
27	3♍	18♌	4♍	12♋
28	4♍	20♌	5♍	13♋
29	5♍	21♌	6♍	13♋
30	6♍	23♌	8♍	14♋
31	7♍	25♌	9♍	15♋

November

Day	☉	☿	♀	♂
1	8♏	2♐	26♏	21♌
2	9♏	3♐	27♏	21♌
3	10♏	3♐	28♏	22♌
4	11♏	4♐	0♐	22♌
5	12♏	5♐	1♐	23♌
6	13♏	5♐	2♐	23♌
7	14♏	5♐	3♐	24♌
8	15♏	6♐	5♐	24♌
9	16♏	6♐	6♐	25♌
10	17♏	6♐	7♐	25♌
11	18♏	6♐	8♐	26♌
12	19♏	5♐	10♐	26♌
13	20♏	5♐	11♐	27♌
14	21♏	4♐	12♐	27♌
15	22♏	3♐	13♐	28♌
16	23♏	2♐	15♐	28♌
17	24♏	1♐	16♐	29♌
18	25♏	0♐	17♐	29♌
19	26♏	29♏	18♐	0♍
20	27♏	27♏	20♐	0♍
21	28♏	26♏	21♐	1♍
22	29♏	25♏	22♐	1♍
23	0♐	23♏	23♐	1♍
24	1♐	22♏	25♐	2♍
25	2♐	21♏	26♐	2♍
26	3♐	21♏	27♐	3♍
27	4♐	20♏	28♐	3♍
28	5♐	20♏	0♑	4♍
29	6♐	20♏	1♑	4♍
30	7♐	20♏	2♑	4♍

March

Day	☉	☿	♀	♂
1	10♓	26♓	27♑	1♓
2	11♓	27♓	28♑	2♓
3	12♓	29♓	29♑	3♓
4	13♓	0♈	1♒	3♓
5	14♓	2♈	2♒	4♓
6	15♓	3♈	3♒	5♓
7	16♓	4♈	4♒	6♓
8	17♓	5♈	5♒	7♓
9	18♓	6♈	6♒	7♓
10	19♓	7♈	8♒	8♓
11	20♓	7♈	9♒	9♓
12	21♓	8♈	10♒	10♓
13	22♓	8♈	11♒	11♓
14	23♓	8♈	12♒	11♓
15	24♓	9♈	13♒	12♓
16	25♓	8♈	15♒	13♓
17	26♓	8♈	16♒	14♓
18	27♓	8♈	17♒	14♓
19	28♓	7♈	18♒	15♓
20	29♓	7♈	19♒	16♓
21	0♈	6♈	21♒	17♓
22	1♈	5♈	22♒	18♓
23	2♈	5♈	23♒	18♓
24	3♈	4♈	24♒	19♓
25	4♈	3♈	25♒	20♓
26	5♈	2♈	27♒	21♓
27	6♈	1♈	28♒	22♓
28	7♈	0♈	29♒	22♓
29	8♈	29♓	0♓	23♓
30	9♈	29♓	1♓	24♓
31	10♈	28♓	2♓	25♓

June

Day	☉	☿	♀	♂
1	10♊	13♊	17♉	12♉
2	11♊	15♊	18♉	13♉
3	12♊	17♊	20♉	13♉
4	13♊	19♊	21♉	14♉
5	14♊	22♊	22♉	15♉
6	15♊	24♊	23♉	16♉
7	16♊	26♊	24♉	16♉
8	17♊	28♊	26♉	17♉
9	18♊	0♋	27♉	18♉
10	19♊	2♋	28♉	19♉
11	20♊	4♋	29♉	19♉
12	21♊	6♋	1♊	20♉
13	22♊	8♋	2♊	21♉
14	23♊	9♋	3♊	21♉
15	24♊	11♋	4♊	22♉
16	24♊	13♋	5♊	23♉
17	25♊	15♋	7♊	24♉
18	26♊	16♋	8♊	24♉
19	27♊	18♋	9♊	25♉
20	28♊	20♋	10♊	26♉
21	29♊	21♋	11♊	27♉
22	0♋	23♋	13♊	27♉
23	1♋	24♋	14♊	28♉
24	2♋	26♋	15♊	29♉
25	3♋	27♋	16♊	29♉
26	4♋	28♋	18♊	0♊
27	5♋	0♌	19♊	1♊
28	6♋	1♌	20♊	2♊
29	7♋	2♌	21♊	2♊
30	8♋	3♌	22♊	3♊

September

Day	☉	☿	♀	♂
1	8♍	27♌	10♍	15♋
2	9♍	29♌	11♍	16♋
3	10♍	1♍	12♍	17♋
4	11♍	3♍	14♍	17♋
5	12♍	4♍	15♍	18♋
6	13♍	6♍	16♍	19♋
7	14♍	8♍	17♍	19♋
8	15♍	10♍	19♍	20♋
9	16♍	12♍	20♍	20♋
10	17♍	14♍	21♍	21♋
11	18♍	16♍	22♍	22♋
12	19♍	18♍	24♍	22♋
13	20♍	20♍	25♍	23♋
14	21♍	22♍	26♍	24♋
15	22♍	24♍	27♍	24♋
16	23♍	25♍	29♍	25♋
17	24♍	27♍	0♎	25♋
18	25♍	29♍	1♎	26♋
19	26♍	1♎	2♎	27♋
20	27♍	3♎	4♎	27♋
21	28♍	4♎	5♎	28♋
22	29♍	6♎	6♎	28♋
23	0♎	8♎	7♎	29♋
24	1♎	9♎	9♎	0♌
25	2♎	11♎	10♎	0♌
26	3♎	13♎	11♎	1♌
27	4♎	14♎	12♎	1♌
28	4♎	16♎	14♎	2♌
29	5♎	18♎	15♎	3♌
30	6♎	19♎	16♎	3♌

December

Day	☉	☿	♀	♂
1	8♐	20♏	3♑	5♍
2	9♐	20♏	4♑	5♍
3	10♐	21♏	6♑	6♍
4	11♐	21♏	7♑	6♍
5	12♐	22♏	8♑	6♍
6	13♐	23♏	9♑	7♍
7	14♐	24♏	11♑	7♍
8	15♐	25♏	12♑	7♍
9	17♐	26♏	13♑	8♍
10	18♐	27♏	14♑	8♍
11	19♐	28♏	16♑	9♍
12	20♐	0♐	17♑	9♍
13	21♐	1♐	18♑	9♍
14	22♐	2♐	19♑	10♍
15	23♐	3♐	21♑	10♍
16	24♐	5♐	22♑	10♍
17	25♐	6♐	23♑	10♍
18	26♐	8♐	24♑	11♍
19	27♐	9♐	26♑	11♍
20	28♐	10♐	27♑	11♍
21	29♐	12♐	28♑	12♍
22	0♑	13♐	29♑	12♍
23	1♑	15♐	1♒	12♍
24	2♑	16♐	2♒	12♍
25	3♑	18♐	3♒	13♍
26	4♑	19♐	4♒	13♍
27	5♑	21♐	5♒	13♍
28	6♑	22♐	7♒	13♍
29	7♑	24♐	8♒	13♍
30	8♑	25♐	9♒	14♍
31	9♑	27♐	10♒	14♍

Planetary Positions

♌ = Leo ♍ = Virgo ♎ = Libra ♏ = Scorpio ♐ = Sagittarius ♑ = Capricorn ♒ = Aquarius ♓ = Pisces

1980

January

Day	⊙	☿	♀	♂
1	10♑	28♐	12♒	14♍
2	11♑	0♑	13♒	14♍
3	12♑	1♑	14♒	14♍
4	13♑	3♑	15♒	14♍
5	14♑	4♑	17♒	15♍
6	15♑	6♑	18♒	15♍
7	16♑	8♑	19♒	15♍
8	17♑	9♑	20♒	15♍
9	18♑	11♑	21♒	15♍
10	19♑	12♑	23♒	15♍
11	20♑	14♑	24♒	15♍
12	21♑	15♑	25♒	15♍
13	22♑	17♑	26♒	15♍
14	23♑	19♑	28♒	15♍
15	24♑	20♑	29♒	15♍
16	25♑	22♑	0♓	15♍
17	26♑	24♑	1♓	15♍
18	27♑	25♑	3♓	15♍
19	28♑	27♑	4♓	15♍
20	29♑	29♑	5♓	15♍
21	0♒	0♒	6♓	15♍
22	1♒	2♒	7♓	15♍
23	2♒	4♒	9♓	15♍
24	3♒	5♒	10♓	15♍
25	4♒	7♒	11♓	15♍
26	5♒	9♒	12♓	15♍
27	6♒	10♒	13♓	15♍
28	7♒	12♒	15♓	14♍
29	8♒	14♒	16♓	14♍
30	9♒	16♒	17♓	14♍
31	10♒	17♒	18♓	14♍

April

Day	⊙	☿	♀	♂
1	12♈	14♓	27♉	26♌
2	13♈	15♓	28♉	26♌
3	14♈	16♓	29♉	26♌
4	15♈	17♓	0♊	26♌
5	16♈	18♓	1♊	26♌
6	17♈	19♓	2♊	26♌
7	18♈	20♓	3♊	26♌
8	19♈	21♓	4♊	26♌
9	19♈	23♓	5♊	26♌
10	20♈	24♓	6♊	26♌
11	21♈	25♓	7♊	26♌
12	22♈	27♓	8♊	26♌
13	23♈	28♓	9♊	26♌
14	24♈	29♓	10♊	26♌
15	25♈	1♈	11♊	26♌
16	26♈	2♈	12♊	26♌
17	27♈	4♈	13♊	27♌
18	28♈	5♈	13♊	27♌
19	29♈	7♈	14♊	27♌
20	0♉	8♈	15♊	27♌
21	1♉	10♈	16♊	27♌
22	2♉	12♈	17♊	27♌
23	3♉	13♈	18♊	27♌
24	4♉	15♈	18♊	28♌
25	5♉	17♈	19♊	28♌
26	6♉	18♈	20♊	28♌
27	7♉	20♈	21♊	28♌
28	8♉	22♈	21♊	29♌
29	9♉	24♈	22♊	29♌
30	10♉	26♈	23♊	29♌

July

Day	⊙	☿	♀	♂
1	10♋	25♋	17♊	25♍
2	10♋	25♋	16♊	25♍
3	11♋	24♋	16♊	26♍
4	12♋	24♋	16♊	26♍
5	13♋	23♋	16♊	27♍
6	14♋	23♋	16♊	27♍
7	15♋	22♋	16♊	28♍
8	16♋	22♋	16♊	29♍
9	17♋	21♋	16♊	29♍
10	18♋	21♋	16♊	0♎
11	19♋	20♋	16♊	0♎
12	20♋	19♋	17♊	1♎
13	21♋	19♋	17♊	1♎
14	22♋	18♋	17♊	2♎
15	23♋	18♋	17♊	3♎
16	24♋	17♋	18♊	3♎
17	25♋	17♋	18♊	4♎
18	26♋	16♋	18♊	4♎
19	27♋	16♋	19♊	5♎
20	28♋	15♋	19♊	5♎
21	29♋	15♋	20♊	6♎
22	0♌	15♋	20♊	7♎
23	0♌	15♋	21♊	7♎
24	1♌	15♋	21♊	8♎
25	2♌	16♋	22♊	8♎
26	3♌	16♋	22♊	9♎
27	4♌	16♋	23♊	9♎
28	5♌	17♋	23♊	10♎
29	6♌	17♋	24♊	11♎
30	7♌	18♋	25♊	11♎
31	8♌	19♋	25♊	12♎

October

Day	⊙	☿	♀	♂
1	8♎	2♏	26♌	22♏
2	9♎	3♏	27♌	23♏
3	10♎	4♏	28♌	24♏
4	11♎	5♏	29♌	24♏
5	12♎	6♏	0♍	25♏
6	13♎	8♏	1♍	26♏
7	14♎	9♏	3♍	26♏
8	15♎	10♏	4♍	27♏
9	16♎	11♏	5♍	28♏
10	17♎	12♏	6♍	29♏
11	18♎	13♏	7♍	29♏
12	19♎	14♏	8♍	0♐
13	20♎	15♏	10♍	1♐
14	21♎	16♏	11♍	1♐
15	22♎	17♏	12♍	2♐
16	23♎	17♏	13♍	3♐
17	24♎	18♏	14♍	4♐
18	25♎	19♏	15♍	4♐
19	26♎	19♏	17♍	5♐
20	27♎	19♏	18♍	6♐
21	28♎	20♏	19♍	6♐
22	29♎	20♏	20♍	7♐
23	0♏	20♏	21♍	8♐
24	1♏	20♏	23♍	9♐
25	2♏	20♏	24♍	9♐
26	3♏	19♏	25♍	10♐
27	4♏	19♏	26♍	11♐
28	5♏	18♏	27♍	11♐
29	6♏	17♏	29♍	12♐
30	7♏	16♏	0♎	13♐
31	8♏	15♏	1♎	14♐

February

Day	⊙	☿	♀	♂
1	11♒	19♒	19♓	14♍
2	13♒	21♒	21♓	13♍
3	14♒	23♒	22♓	13♍
4	15♒	24♒	23♓	13♍
5	16♒	26♒	24♓	13♍
6	17♒	28♒	25♓	12♍
7	18♒	0♓	27♓	12♍
8	19♒	2♓	28♓	12♍
9	20♒	3♓	29♓	12♍
10	21♒	5♓	0♈	11♍
11	22♒	7♓	1♈	11♍
12	23♒	8♓	3♈	11♍
13	24♒	10♓	4♈	10♍
14	25♒	11♓	5♈	10♍
15	26♒	13♓	6♈	10♍
16	27♒	14♓	7♈	9♍
17	28♒	15♓	9♈	9♍
18	29♒	17♓	10♈	9♍
19	0♓	18♓	11♈	8♍
20	1♓	19♓	12♈	8♍
21	2♓	20♓	13♈	7♍
22	3♓	20♓	14♈	7♍
23	4♓	21♓	16♈	7♍
24	5♓	21♓	17♈	6♍
25	6♓	21♓	18♈	6♍
26	7♓	22♓	19♈	5♍
27	8♓	21♓	20♈	5♍
28	9♓	21♓	21♈	5♍
29	10♓	21♓	23♈	4♍

May

Day	⊙	☿	♀	♂
1	11♉	28♈	24♊	29♌
2	12♉	0♉	24♊	29♌
3	13♉	1♉	25♊	0♍
4	14♉	3♉	26♊	0♍
5	15♉	5♉	26♊	0♍
6	16♉	7♉	27♊	1♍
7	17♉	10♉	27♊	1♍
8	18♉	12♉	28♊	1♍
9	19♉	14♉	28♊	1♍
10	20♉	16♉	29♊	2♍
11	21♉	18♉	29♊	2♍
12	22♉	20♉	0♋	2♍
13	23♉	22♉	0♋	3♍
14	24♉	25♉	1♋	3♍
15	25♉	27♉	1♋	3♍
16	25♉	29♉	1♋	4♍
17	26♉	1♊	1♋	4♍
18	27♉	3♊	2♋	5♍
19	28♉	5♊	2♋	5♍
20	29♉	8♊	2♋	5♍
21	0♊	10♊	2♋	6♍
22	1♊	12♊	2♋	6♍
23	2♊	14♊	3♋	6♍
24	3♊	16♊	3♋	7♍
25	4♊	18♊	3♋	7♍
26	5♊	20♊	3♋	8♍
27	6♊	22♊	2♋	8♍
28	7♊	23♊	2♋	8♍
29	8♊	25♊	2♋	9♍
30	9♊	27♊	2♋	9♍
31	10♊	29♊	2♋	10♍

August

Day	⊙	☿	♀	♂
1	9♌	20♋	26♊	12♎
2	10♌	21♋	27♊	13♎
3	11♌	22♋	27♊	14♎
4	12♌	23♋	28♊	14♎
5	13♌	24♋	29♊	15♎
6	14♌	26♋	0♋	15♎
7	15♌	27♋	0♋	16♎
8	16♌	29♋	1♋	17♎
9	17♌	0♌	2♋	17♎
10	18♌	2♌	3♋	18♎
11	19♌	3♌	4♋	19♎
12	20♌	5♌	5♋	19♎
13	21♌	7♌	5♋	20♎
14	22♌	9♌	6♋	20♎
15	23♌	11♌	7♋	21♎
16	23♌	13♌	8♋	22♎
17	24♌	15♌	9♋	22♎
18	25♌	17♌	10♋	23♎
19	26♌	19♌	11♋	24♎
20	27♌	21♌	12♋	24♎
21	28♌	23♌	13♋	25♎
22	29♌	25♌	13♋	25♎
23	0♍	27♌	14♋	26♎
24	1♍	29♌	15♋	27♎
25	2♍	1♍	16♋	27♎
26	3♍	3♍	17♋	28♎
27	4♍	5♍	18♋	29♎
28	5♍	7♍	19♋	29♎
29	6♍	9♍	20♋	0♏
30	7♍	11♍	21♋	1♏
31	8♍	12♍	22♋	1♏

November

Day	⊙	☿	♀	♂
1	9♏	14♏	2♎	14♐
2	10♏	13♏	3♎	15♐
3	11♏	11♏	5♎	16♐
4	12♏	10♏	6♎	17♐
5	13♏	9♏	7♎	17♐
6	14♏	8♏	8♎	18♐
7	15♏	7♏	9♎	19♐
8	16♏	6♏	11♎	20♐
9	17♏	5♏	12♎	20♐
10	18♏	4♏	13♎	21♐
11	19♏	4♏	14♎	22♐
12	20♏	4♏	15♎	23♐
13	21♏	4♏	17♎	23♐
14	22♏	4♏	18♎	24♐
15	23♏	5♏	19♎	25♐
16	24♏	5♏	20♎	26♐
17	25♏	6♏	22♎	26♐
18	26♏	7♏	23♎	27♐
19	27♏	8♏	24♎	28♐
20	28♏	9♏	25♎	29♐
21	29♏	10♏	26♎	29♐
22	0♐	11♏	28♎	0♑
23	1♐	12♏	29♎	1♑
24	2♐	13♏	0♏	2♑
25	3♐	15♏	1♏	2♑
26	4♐	16♏	3♏	3♑
27	5♐	17♏	4♏	4♑
28	6♐	19♏	5♏	5♑
29	7♐	20♏	6♏	5♑
30	8♐	22♏	8♏	6♑

March

Day	⊙	☿	♀	♂
1	11♓	20♓	24♈	4♍
2	12♓	19♓	25♈	3♍
3	13♓	19♓	26♈	3♍
4	14♓	18♓	27♈	3♍
5	15♓	17♓	28♈	2♍
6	16♓	16♓	29♈	2♍
7	17♓	15♓	0♉	2♍
8	18♓	14♓	2♉	1♍
9	19♓	13♓	3♉	1♍
10	20♓	12♓	4♉	1♍
11	21♓	11♓	5♉	0♍
12	22♓	10♓	6♉	0♍
13	23♓	10♓	7♉	0♍
14	24♓	9♓	8♉	29♌
15	25♓	8♓	9♉	29♌
16	26♓	8♓	10♉	29♌
17	27♓	8♓	12♉	28♌
18	28♓	8♓	13♉	28♌
19	29♓	7♓	14♉	28♌
20	0♈	7♓	15♉	28♌
21	1♈	8♓	16♉	28♌
22	2♈	8♓	17♉	27♌
23	3♈	8♓	18♉	27♌
24	4♈	8♓	19♉	27♌
25	5♈	9♓	20♉	27♌
26	6♈	9♓	21♉	27♌
27	7♈	10♓	22♉	27♌
28	8♈	11♓	23♉	26♌
29	9♈	11♓	24♉	26♌
30	10♈	12♓	25♉	26♌
31	11♈	13♓	26♉	26♌

June

Day	⊙	☿	♀	♂
1	11♊	0♋	1♋	10♍
2	12♊	2♋	1♋	11♍
3	13♊	4♋	1♋	11♍
4	14♊	5♋	0♋	11♍
5	15♊	7♋	0♋	12♍
6	16♊	8♋	0♋	12♍
7	17♊	10♋	29♊	13♍
8	18♊	11♋	29♊	13♍
9	19♊	12♋	28♊	14♍
10	19♊	13♋	27♊	14♍
11	20♊	15♋	27♊	15♍
12	21♊	16♋	26♊	15♍
13	22♊	17♋	26♊	16♍
14	23♊	18♋	25♊	16♍
15	24♊	19♋	24♊	17♍
16	25♊	20♋	24♊	17♍
17	26♊	20♋	23♊	18♍
18	27♊	21♋	23♊	18♍
19	28♊	22♋	22♊	19♍
20	29♊	23♋	21♊	19♍
21	0♋	23♋	21♊	20♍
22	1♋	24♋	20♊	20♍
23	2♋	24♋	20♊	21♍
24	3♋	24♋	19♊	21♍
25	4♋	25♋	19♊	22♍
26	5♋	25♋	18♊	22♍
27	6♋	25♋	18♊	23♍
28	7♋	25♋	18♊	23♍
29	8♋	25♋	17♊	24♍
30	9♋	25♋	17♊	24♍

September

Day	⊙	☿	♀	♂
1	9♍	14♍	23♋	2♏
2	10♍	16♍	24♋	3♏
3	11♍	18♍	25♋	3♏
4	12♍	20♍	26♋	4♏
5	13♍	22♍	27♋	5♏
6	14♍	23♍	28♋	5♏
7	15♍	25♍	29♋	6♏
8	16♍	27♍	0♌	7♏
9	17♍	29♍	2♌	7♏
10	18♍	0♎	3♌	8♏
11	19♍	2♎	4♌	9♏
12	20♍	4♎	5♌	9♏
13	21♍	5♎	6♌	10♏
14	22♍	7♎	7♌	11♏
15	23♍	8♎	8♌	11♏
16	23♍	10♎	9♌	12♏
17	24♍	12♎	10♌	13♏
18	25♍	13♎	11♌	13♏
19	26♍	15♎	12♌	14♏
20	27♍	16♎	13♌	15♏
21	28♍	18♎	14♌	15♏
22	29♍	19♎	16♌	16♏
23	0♎	21♎	17♌	17♏
24	1♎	22♎	18♌	17♏
25	2♎	23♎	19♌	18♏
26	3♎	25♎	20♌	19♏
27	4♎	26♎	21♌	19♏
28	5♎	28♎	22♌	20♏
29	6♎	29♎	23♌	21♏
30	7♎	0♏	25♌	22♏

December

Day	⊙	☿	♀	♂
1	9♐	23♏	9♏	7♑
2	10♐	25♏	10♏	8♑
3	11♐	26♏	11♏	8♑
4	12♐	28♏	13♏	9♑
5	13♐	29♏	14♏	10♑
6	14♐	1♐	15♏	11♑
7	15♐	2♐	16♏	12♑
8	16♐	4♐	17♏	12♑
9	17♐	5♐	19♏	13♑
10	18♐	7♐	20♏	14♑
11	19♐	8♐	21♏	15♑
12	20♐	10♐	22♏	15♑
13	21♐	11♐	24♏	16♑
14	22♐	13♐	25♏	17♑
15	23♐	14♐	26♏	18♑
16	24♐	16♐	27♏	19♑
17	25♐	18♐	29♏	19♑
18	26♐	19♐	0♐	20♑
19	27♐	21♐	1♐	21♑
20	28♐	22♐	2♐	22♑
21	29♐	24♐	4♐	22♑
22	1♑	25♐	5♐	23♑
23	2♑	27♐	6♐	24♑
24	3♑	28♐	7♐	25♑
25	4♑	0♑	9♐	26♑
26	5♑	2♑	10♐	26♑
27	6♑	3♑	11♐	27♑
28	7♑	5♑	12♐	28♑
29	8♑	6♑	14♐	29♑
30	9♑	8♑	15♐	29♑
31	10♑	10♑	16♐	0♒

1981

Your Starway to Love

☉ =Sun ☿ = Mercury ♀ = Venus ♂ = Mars ♈ = Aries ♉ = Taurus ♊ = Gemini ♋ = Cancer

January

Day	☉	☿	♀	♂
1	11♑	11♑	17♐	1♒
2	12♑	13♑	19♐	2♒
3	13♑	14♑	20♐	3♒
4	14♑	16♑	21♐	3♒
5	15♑	18♑	22♐	4♒
6	16♑	19♑	24♐	5♒
7	17♑	21♑	25♐	6♒
8	18♑	23♑	26♐	6♒
9	19♑	24♑	27♐	7♒
10	20♑	26♑	29♐	8♒
11	21♑	28♑	0♑	9♒
12	22♑	29♑	1♑	10♒
13	23♑	1♒	2♑	10♒
14	24♑	3♒	4♑	11♒
15	25♑	4♒	5♑	12♒
16	26♑	6♒	6♑	13♒
17	27♑	8♒	7♑	14♒
18	28♑	9♒	9♑	14♒
19	29♑	11♒	10♑	15♒
20	0♒	13♒	11♑	16♒
21	1♒	14♒	12♑	17♒
22	2♒	16♒	14♑	18♒
23	3♒	18♒	15♑	18♒
24	4♒	19♒	16♑	19♒
25	5♒	21♒	17♑	20♒
26	6♒	22♒	19♑	21♒
27	7♒	24♒	20♑	22♒
28	8♒	25♒	21♑	22♒
29	9♒	27♒	22♑	23♒
30	10♒	28♒	24♑	24♒
31	11♒	29♒	25♑	25♒

April

Day	☉	☿	♀	♂
1	11♈	18♓	10♈	12♈
2	12♈	20♓	11♈	12♈
3	13♈	22♓	12♈	13♈
4	14♈	23♓	14♈	14♈
5	15♈	25♓	15♈	15♈
6	16♈	26♓	16♈	16♈
7	17♈	28♓	17♈	16♈
8	18♈	0♈	18♈	17♈
9	19♈	1♈	20♈	18♈
10	20♈	3♈	21♈	19♈
11	21♈	5♈	22♈	19♈
12	22♈	7♈	23♈	20♈
13	23♈	8♈	25♈	21♈
14	24♈	10♈	26♈	22♈
15	25♈	12♈	27♈	22♈
16	26♈	14♈	28♈	23♈
17	27♈	16♈	0♉	24♈
18	28♈	18♈	1♉	25♈
19	29♈	20♈	2♉	25♈
20	0♉	22♈	3♉	26♈
21	1♉	24♈	5♉	27♈
22	2♉	26♈	6♉	28♈
23	3♉	28♈	7♉	28♈
24	4♉	0♉	8♉	29♈
25	5♉	2♉	10♉	0♉
26	6♉	4♉	11♉	1♉
27	7♉	6♉	12♉	1♉
28	8♉	8♉	13♉	2♉
29	9♉	11♉	14♉	3♉
30	10♉	13♉	16♉	4♉

July

Day	☉	☿	♀	♂
1	9♋	27♊	2♌	18♊
2	10♋	26♊	3♌	19♊
3	11♋	26♊	4♌	20♊
4	12♋	26♊	5♌	20♊
5	13♋	26♊	7♌	21♊
6	14♋	27♊	8♌	22♊
7	15♋	27♊	9♌	22♊
8	16♋	27♊	10♌	23♊
9	17♋	28♊	11♌	24♊
10	18♋	28♊	13♌	24♊
11	19♋	29♊	14♌	25♊
12	20♋	29♊	15♌	26♊
13	21♋	0♋	16♌	26♊
14	22♋	1♋	17♌	27♊
15	23♋	2♋	19♌	28♊
16	24♋	3♋	20♌	29♊
17	25♋	4♋	21♌	29♊
18	25♋	5♋	22♌	0♋
19	26♋	7♋	24♌	1♋
20	27♋	8♋	25♌	1♋
21	28♋	9♋	26♌	2♋
22	29♋	11♋	27♌	3♋
23	0♌	12♋	28♌	3♋
24	1♌	14♋	0♍	4♋
25	2♌	16♋	1♍	5♋
26	3♌	17♋	2♍	5♋
27	4♌	19♋	3♍	6♋
28	5♌	21♋	4♍	7♋
29	6♌	23♋	6♍	7♋
30	7♌	25♋	7♍	8♋
31	8♌	27♋	8♍	9♋

October

Day	☉	☿	♀	♂
1	8♎	2♏	21♏	18♌
2	9♎	3♏	22♏	19♌
3	10♎	3♏	23♏	19♌
4	11♎	4♏	25♏	20♌
5	12♎	4♏	26♏	21♌
6	13♎	4♏	27♏	21♌
7	14♎	4♏	28♏	22♌
8	15♎	4♏	29♏	22♌
9	16♎	3♏	0♐	23♌
10	17♎	3♏	1♐	24♌
11	18♎	2♏	2♐	24♌
12	19♎	2♏	4♐	25♌
13	20♎	1♏	5♐	25♌
14	21♎	0♏	6♐	26♌
15	22♎	29♎	7♐	27♌
16	23♎	28♎	8♐	27♌
17	24♎	26♎	9♐	28♌
18	25♎	25♎	10♐	28♌
19	26♎	24♎	11♐	29♌
20	27♎	23♎	13♐	29♌
21	28♎	22♎	14♐	0♍
22	29♎	21♎	15♐	1♍
23	0♏	20♎	16♐	1♍
24	1♏	19♎	17♐	2♍
25	2♏	19♎	18♐	2♍
26	3♏	18♎	19♐	3♍
27	4♏	18♎	20♐	4♍
28	5♏	18♎	21♐	4♍
29	6♏	19♎	22♐	5♍
30	7♏	19♎	23♐	5♍
31	8♏	20♎	24♐	6♍

February

Day	☉	☿	♀	♂
1	12♒	1♓	26♑	25♒
2	13♒	2♓	27♑	26♒
3	14♒	3♓	29♑	27♒
4	15♒	3♓	0♒	28♒
5	16♒	4♓	1♒	29♒
6	17♒	4♓	2♒	29♒
7	18♒	5♓	4♒	0♓
8	19♒	5♓	5♒	1♓
9	20♒	5♓	6♒	2♓
10	21♒	5♓	7♒	3♓
11	22♒	4♓	9♒	3♓
12	23♒	4♓	10♒	4♓
13	24♒	3♓	11♒	5♓
14	25♒	2♓	12♒	6♓
15	26♒	1♓	14♒	7♓
16	27♒	0♓	15♒	7♓
17	28♒	29♒	16♒	8♓
18	29♒	28♒	17♒	9♓
19	0♓	27♒	19♒	10♓
20	1♓	26♒	20♒	10♓
21	2♓	25♒	21♒	11♓
22	3♓	24♒	22♒	12♓
23	4♓	23♒	24♒	13♓
24	6♓	22♒	25♒	14♓
25	7♓	21♒	26♒	14♓
26	8♓	21♒	27♒	15♓
27	9♓	20♒	29♒	16♓
28	10♓	20♒	0♓	17♓

May

Day	☉	☿	♀	♂
1	11♉	15♉	17♉	4♉
2	12♉	17♉	18♉	5♉
3	13♉	19♉	19♉	6♉
4	14♉	21♉	21♉	7♉
5	15♉	23♉	22♉	7♉
6	16♉	26♉	23♉	8♉
7	17♉	28♉	24♉	9♉
8	18♉	0♊	26♉	10♉
9	18♉	2♊	27♉	10♉
10	19♉	4♊	28♉	11♉
11	20♉	5♊	29♉	12♉
12	21♉	7♊	0♊	13♉
13	22♉	9♊	2♊	13♉
14	23♉	11♊	3♊	14♉
15	24♉	13♊	4♊	15♉
16	25♉	14♊	5♊	16♉
17	26♉	16♊	7♊	16♉
18	27♉	17♊	8♊	17♉
19	28♉	19♊	9♊	18♉
20	29♉	20♊	10♊	18♉
21	0♊	22♊	12♊	19♉
22	1♊	23♊	13♊	20♉
23	2♊	24♊	14♊	21♉
24	3♊	25♊	15♊	21♉
25	4♊	27♊	16♊	22♉
26	5♊	28♊	18♊	23♉
27	6♊	29♊	19♊	24♉
28	7♊	0♋	20♊	24♉
29	8♊	0♋	21♊	25♉
30	9♊	1♋	23♊	26♉
31	10♊	2♋	24♊	26♉

August

Day	☉	☿	♀	♂
1	9♌	29♋	9♍	9♋
2	10♌	1♌	10♍	10♋
3	11♌	3♌	12♍	11♋
4	12♌	5♌	13♍	11♋
5	13♌	7♌	14♍	12♋
6	14♌	9♌	15♍	13♋
7	15♌	11♌	16♍	13♋
8	16♌	13♌	18♍	14♋
9	17♌	15♌	19♍	15♋
10	17♌	17♌	20♍	15♋
11	18♌	19♌	21♍	16♋
12	19♌	21♌	22♍	17♋
13	20♌	23♌	24♍	17♋
14	21♌	25♌	25♍	18♋
15	22♌	27♌	26♍	18♋
16	23♌	29♌	27♍	19♋
17	24♌	1♍	28♍	20♋
18	25♌	3♍	0♎	20♋
19	26♌	5♍	1♎	21♋
20	27♌	7♍	2♎	22♋
21	28♌	9♍	3♎	22♋
22	29♌	11♍	4♎	23♋
23	0♍	12♍	6♎	24♋
24	1♍	14♍	7♎	24♋
25	2♍	16♍	8♎	25♋
26	3♍	18♍	9♎	26♋
27	4♍	19♍	10♎	26♋
28	5♍	21♍	11♎	27♋
29	6♍	23♍	13♎	28♋
30	7♍	24♍	14♎	28♋
31	8♍	26♍	15♎	29♋

November

Day	☉	☿	♀	♂
1	9♏	20♎	25♐	6♍
2	10♏	21♎	27♐	7♍
3	11♏	22♎	28♐	8♍
4	12♏	23♎	29♐	8♍
5	13♏	24♎	0♑	9♍
6	14♏	25♎	1♑	9♍
7	15♏	27♎	2♑	10♍
8	16♏	28♎	3♑	10♍
9	17♏	0♏	4♑	11♍
10	18♏	1♏	5♑	11♍
11	19♏	2♏	6♑	12♍
12	20♏	4♏	7♑	13♍
13	21♏	5♏	8♑	13♍
14	22♏	7♏	9♑	14♍
15	23♏	8♏	10♑	14♍
16	24♏	10♏	11♑	15♍
17	25♏	12♏	12♑	15♍
18	26♏	13♏	13♑	16♍
19	27♏	15♏	14♑	16♍
20	28♏	16♏	15♑	17♍
21	29♏	18♏	15♑	17♍
22	0♐	19♏	16♑	18♍
23	1♐	21♏	17♑	19♍
24	2♐	23♏	18♑	19♍
25	3♐	24♏	19♑	20♍
26	4♐	26♏	20♑	20♍
27	5♐	27♏	21♑	21♍
28	6♐	29♏	22♑	21♍
29	7♐	1♐	23♑	22♍
30	8♐	2♐	23♑	22♍

March

Day	☉	☿	♀	♂
1	11♓	20♒	1♓	18♓
2	12♓	20♒	2♓	18♓
3	13♓	20♒	4♓	19♓
4	14♓	20♒	5♓	20♓
5	15♓	20♒	6♓	21♓
6	16♓	21♒	7♓	21♓
7	17♓	21♒	9♓	22♓
8	18♓	22♒	10♓	23♓
9	19♓	22♒	11♓	24♓
10	20♓	23♒	12♓	25♓
11	21♓	23♒	14♓	25♓
12	22♓	24♒	15♓	26♓
13	23♓	25♒	16♓	27♓
14	24♓	26♒	17♓	28♓
15	25♓	27♒	19♓	29♓
16	26♓	28♒	20♓	29♓
17	27♓	29♒	21♓	0♈
18	28♓	0♓	22♓	1♈
19	29♓	1♓	24♓	2♈
20	0♈	2♓	25♓	2♈
21	0♈	3♓	26♓	3♈
22	1♈	5♓	27♓	4♈
23	2♈	6♓	29♓	5♈
24	3♈	7♓	0♈	6♈
25	4♈	9♓	1♈	6♈
26	5♈	10♓	2♈	7♈
27	6♈	11♓	4♈	8♈
28	7♈	13♓	5♈	9♈
29	8♈	14♓	6♈	9♈
30	9♈	16♓	7♈	10♈
31	10♈	17♓	9♈	11♈

June

Day	☉	☿	♀	♂
1	11♊	3♋	25♊	27♉
2	12♊	3♋	26♊	28♉
3	13♊	4♋	27♊	29♉
4	13♊	4♋	29♊	29♉
5	14♊	5♋	0♋	0♊
6	15♊	5♋	1♋	1♊
7	16♊	5♋	2♋	1♊
8	17♊	5♋	4♋	2♊
9	18♊	5♋	5♋	3♊
10	19♊	5♋	6♋	4♊
11	20♊	5♋	7♋	4♊
12	21♊	5♋	8♋	5♊
13	22♊	5♋	10♋	6♊
14	23♊	4♋	11♋	6♊
15	24♊	4♋	12♋	7♊
16	25♊	4♋	13♋	8♊
17	26♊	3♋	15♋	8♊
18	27♊	3♋	16♋	9♊
19	28♊	2♋	17♋	10♊
20	29♊	2♋	18♋	11♊
21	0♋	1♋	19♋	11♊
22	1♋	0♋	21♋	12♊
23	2♋	0♋	22♋	13♊
24	3♋	29♊	23♋	13♊
25	4♋	29♊	24♋	14♊
26	5♋	28♊	26♋	15♊
27	5♋	28♊	27♋	15♊
28	6♋	27♊	28♋	16♊
29	7♋	27♊	29♋	17♊
30	8♋	27♊	0♌	18♊

September

Day	☉	☿	♀	♂
1	9♍	27♍	16♎	29♋
2	10♍	29♍	17♎	0♌
3	11♍	0♎	19♎	1♌
4	12♍	2♎	20♎	1♌
5	13♍	3♎	21♎	2♌
6	14♍	5♎	22♎	3♌
7	14♍	6♎	23♎	3♌
8	15♍	8♎	24♎	4♌
9	16♍	9♎	26♎	5♌
10	17♍	11♎	27♎	5♌
11	18♍	12♎	28♎	6♌
12	19♍	13♎	29♎	6♌
13	20♍	15♎	0♏	7♌
14	21♍	16♎	1♏	8♌
15	22♍	17♎	3♏	8♌
16	23♍	18♎	4♏	9♌
17	24♍	20♎	5♏	10♌
18	25♍	21♎	6♏	10♌
19	26♍	22♎	7♏	11♌
20	27♍	23♎	8♏	11♌
21	28♍	24♎	10♏	12♌
22	29♍	25♎	11♏	13♌
23	0♎	26♎	12♏	13♌
24	1♎	27♎	13♏	14♌
25	2♎	28♎	14♏	14♌
26	3♎	29♎	15♏	15♌
27	4♎	0♏	17♏	16♌
28	5♎	1♏	18♏	16♌
29	6♎	1♏	19♏	17♌
30	7♎	2♏	20♏	18♌

December

Day	☉	☿	♀	♂
1	9♐	4♐	24♑	23♍
2	10♐	5♐	25♑	23♍
3	11♐	7♐	26♑	24♍
4	12♐	8♐	27♑	24♍
5	13♐	10♐	27♑	25♍
6	14♐	12♐	28♑	25♍
7	15♐	13♐	29♑	26♍
8	16♐	15♐	0♒	26♍
9	17♐	16♐	0♒	27♍
10	18♐	18♐	1♒	27♍
11	19♐	19♐	2♒	28♍
12	20♐	21♐	2♒	28♍
13	21♐	23♐	3♒	29♍
14	22♐	24♐	3♒	29♍
15	23♐	26♐	4♒	0♎
16	24♐	27♐	4♒	0♎
17	25♐	29♐	5♒	1♎
18	26♐	0♑	5♒	1♎
19	27♐	2♑	6♒	1♎
20	28♐	4♑	6♒	2♎
21	29♐	5♑	7♒	2♎
22	0♑	7♑	7♒	3♎
23	1♑	8♑	7♒	3♎
24	2♑	10♑	8♒	4♎
25	3♑	12♑	8♒	4♎
26	4♑	13♑	8♒	5♎
27	5♑	15♑	8♒	5♎
28	6♑	16♑	9♒	5♎
29	7♑	18♑	9♒	6♎
30	8♑	20♑	9♒	6♎
31	9♑	21♑	9♒	7♎

Planetary Positions

♌ = Leo ♍ = Virgo ♎ = Libra ♏ = Scorpio ♐ = Sagittarius ♑ = Capricorn ♒ = Aquarius ♓ = Pisces

1982

January

Day	☉	☿	♀	♂
1	10♑	23♑	9♒	7♎
2	11♑	24♑	9♒	8♎
3	12♑	26♑	9♒	8♎
4	14♑	28♑	9♒	8♎
5	15♑	29♑	8♒	9♎
6	16♑	1♒	8♒	9♎
7	17♑	2♒	8♒	10♎
8	18♑	4♒	8♒	10♎
9	19♑	5♒	7♒	10♎
10	20♑	7♒	7♒	11♎
11	21♑	8♒	7♒	11♎
12	22♑	10♒	6♒	11♎
13	23♑	11♒	6♒	12♎
14	24♑	12♒	5♒	12♎
15	25♑	13♒	5♒	12♎
16	26♑	15♒	4♒	13♎
17	27♑	16♒	4♒	13♎
18	28♑	16♒	3♒	13♎
19	29♑	17♒	2♒	14♎
20	0♒	18♒	2♒	14♎
21	1♒	18♒	1♒	14♎
22	2♒	19♒	1♒	15♎
23	3♒	19♒	0♒	15♎
24	4♒	19♒	29♑	15♎
25	5♒	18♒	29♑	15♎
26	6♒	18♒	28♑	16♎
27	7♒	17♒	28♑	16♎
28	8♒	16♒	27♑	16♎
29	9♒	15♒	27♑	16♎
30	10♒	14♒	26♑	17♎
31	11♒	13♒	26♑	17♎

February

Day	☉	☿	♀	♂
1	12♒	12♒	25♑	17♎
2	13♒	11♒	25♑	17♎
3	14♒	9♒	25♑	17♎
4	15♒	8♒	24♑	18♎
5	16♒	7♒	24♑	18♎
6	17♒	6♒	24♑	18♎
7	18♒	5♒	24♑	18♎
8	19♒	5♒	24♑	18♎
9	20♒	4♒	23♑	18♎
10	21♒	4♒	23♑	19♎
11	22♒	3♒	23♑	19♎
12	23♒	3♒	23♑	19♎
13	24♒	3♒	23♑	19♎
14	25♒	3♒	24♑	19♎
15	26♒	3♒	24♑	19♎
16	27♒	3♒	24♑	19♎
17	28♒	4♒	24♑	19♎
18	29♒	4♒	24♑	19♎
19	0♓	5♒	25♑	19♎
20	1♓	5♒	25♑	19♎
21	2♓	6♒	25♑	19♎
22	3♓	7♒	26♑	19♎
23	4♓	8♒	26♑	19♎
24	5♓	9♒	27♑	19♎
25	6♓	9♒	27♑	19♎
26	7♓	10♒	28♑	19♎
27	8♓	11♒	28♑	19♎
28	9♓	12♒	29♑	19♎

March

Day	☉	☿	♀	♂
1	10♓	14♒	29♑	19♎
2	11♓	15♒	0♒	19♎
3	12♓	16♒	0♒	18♎
4	13♓	17♒	1♒	18♎
5	14♓	18♒	2♒	18♎
6	15♓	20♒	2♒	18♎
7	16♓	21♒	3♒	18♎
8	17♓	22♒	4♒	18♎
9	18♓	24♒	5♒	17♎
10	19♓	25♒	5♒	17♎
11	20♓	26♒	6♒	17♎
12	21♓	28♒	7♒	17♎
13	22♓	29♒	8♒	17♎
14	23♓	1♓	8♒	16♎
15	24♓	2♓	9♒	16♎
16	25♓	4♓	10♒	16♎
17	26♓	5♓	11♒	15♎
18	27♓	7♓	12♒	15♎
19	28♓	8♓	13♒	15♎
20	29♓	10♓	13♒	14♎
21	0♈	11♓	14♒	14♎
22	1♈	13♓	15♒	14♎
23	2♈	15♓	16♒	13♎
24	3♈	16♓	17♒	13♎
25	4♈	18♓	18♒	13♎
26	5♈	20♓	19♒	12♎
27	6♈	22♓	20♒	12♎
28	7♈	23♓	21♒	12♎
29	8♈	25♓	22♒	11♎
30	9♈	27♓	23♒	11♎
31	10♈	29♓	24♒	10♎

April

Day	☉	☿	♀	♂
1	11♈	1♈	25♒	10♎
2	12♈	3♈	26♒	10♎
3	13♈	4♈	27♒	9♎
4	14♈	6♈	28♒	9♎
5	15♈	8♈	29♒	9♎
6	16♈	10♈	0♓	8♎
7	17♈	12♈	1♓	8♎
8	18♈	14♈	2♓	7♎
9	19♈	16♈	3♓	7♎
10	20♈	18♈	4♓	7♎
11	21♈	20♈	5♓	6♎
12	22♈	22♈	6♓	6♎
13	23♈	25♈	7♓	6♎
14	24♈	27♈	8♓	5♎
15	25♈	29♈	9♓	5♎
16	26♈	1♉	10♓	5♎
17	27♈	3♉	11♓	4♎
18	28♈	5♉	12♓	4♎
19	29♈	7♉	13♓	4♎
20	0♉	9♉	14♓	3♎
21	1♉	11♉	15♓	3♎
22	2♉	13♉	16♓	3♎
23	3♉	15♉	18♓	3♎
24	4♉	17♉	19♓	2♎
25	5♉	19♉	20♓	2♎
26	6♉	21♉	21♓	2♎
27	7♉	23♉	22♓	2♎
28	8♉	25♉	23♓	2♎
29	9♉	26♉	24♓	1♎
30	10♉	28♉	25♓	1♎

May

Day	☉	☿	♀	♂
1	11♉	29♉	26♓	1♎
2	11♉	1♊	27♓	1♎
3	12♉	2♊	29♓	1♎
4	13♉	4♊	0♈	1♎
5	14♉	5♊	1♈	1♎
6	15♉	6♊	2♈	1♎
7	16♉	7♊	3♈	1♎
8	17♉	8♊	4♈	0♎
9	18♉	9♊	5♈	0♎
10	19♉	10♊	6♈	0♎
11	20♉	11♊	8♈	0♎
12	21♉	12♊	9♈	0♎
13	22♉	13♊	10♈	0♎
14	23♉	13♊	11♈	0♎
15	24♉	14♊	12♈	0♎
16	25♉	14♊	13♈	1♎
17	26♉	15♊	14♈	1♎
18	27♉	15♊	15♈	1♎
19	28♉	15♊	17♈	1♎
20	29♉	15♊	18♈	1♎
21	0♊	15♊	19♈	1♎
22	1♊	15♊	20♈	1♎
23	2♊	15♊	21♈	1♎
24	3♊	15♊	22♈	1♎
25	4♊	15♊	23♈	1♎
26	5♊	14♊	25♈	2♎
27	6♊	14♊	26♈	2♎
28	7♊	13♊	27♈	2♎
29	8♊	13♊	28♈	2♎
30	8♊	12♊	29♈	2♎
31	9♊	12♊	0♉	3♎

June

Day	☉	☿	♀	♂
1	10♊	11♊	2♉	3♎
2	11♊	11♊	3♉	3♎
3	12♊	10♊	4♉	3♎
4	13♊	10♊	5♉	4♎
5	14♊	9♊	6♉	4♎
6	15♊	9♊	7♉	4♎
7	16♊	8♊	9♉	4♎
8	17♊	8♊	10♉	5♎
9	18♊	7♊	11♉	5♎
10	19♊	7♊	12♉	5♎
11	20♊	7♊	13♉	6♎
12	21♊	7♊	14♉	6♎
13	22♊	7♊	16♉	6♎
14	23♊	7♊	17♉	6♎
15	24♊	7♊	18♉	7♎
16	25♊	7♊	19♉	7♎
17	26♊	7♊	20♉	8♎
18	27♊	7♊	21♉	8♎
19	28♊	8♊	23♉	8♎
20	29♊	8♊	24♉	9♎
21	0♋	9♊	25♉	9♎
22	0♋	9♊	26♉	9♎
23	1♋	10♊	27♉	10♎
24	2♋	11♊	28♉	10♎
25	3♋	11♊	0♊	11♎
26	4♋	12♊	1♊	11♎
27	5♋	13♊	2♊	11♎
28	6♋	14♊	3♊	12♎
29	7♋	15♊	4♊	12♎
30	8♋	16♊	6♊	13♎

July

Day	☉	☿	♀	♂
1	9♋	18♊	7♊	13♎
2	10♋	19♊	8♊	13♎
3	11♋	20♊	9♊	14♎
4	12♋	22♊	10♊	14♎
5	13♋	23♊	12♊	15♎
6	14♋	25♊	13♊	15♎
7	15♋	26♊	14♊	16♎
8	16♋	28♊	15♊	16♎
9	17♋	0♋	16♊	17♎
10	18♋	1♋	17♊	17♎
11	19♋	3♋	19♊	18♎
12	20♋	5♋	20♊	18♎
13	20♋	7♋	21♊	19♎
14	21♋	9♋	22♊	19♎
15	22♋	11♋	23♊	20♎
16	23♋	13♋	25♊	20♎
17	24♋	15♋	26♊	21♎
18	25♋	17♋	27♊	21♎
19	26♋	19♋	28♊	22♎
20	27♋	21♋	29♊	22♎
21	28♋	23♋	1♋	23♎
22	29♋	25♋	2♋	23♎
23	0♌	28♋	3♋	24♎
24	1♌	0♌	4♋	24♎
25	2♌	2♌	5♋	25♎
26	3♌	4♌	7♋	25♎
27	4♌	6♌	8♋	26♎
28	5♌	8♌	9♋	26♎
29	6♌	10♌	10♋	27♎
30	7♌	12♌	11♋	28♎
31	8♌	14♌	13♋	28♎

August

Day	☉	☿	♀	♂
1	9♌	16♌	14♋	29♎
2	10♌	18♌	15♋	29♎
3	11♌	20♌	16♋	0♏
4	12♌	22♌	18♋	0♏
5	12♌	24♌	19♋	1♏
6	13♌	26♌	20♋	2♏
7	14♌	28♌	21♋	2♏
8	15♌	29♌	22♋	3♏
9	16♌	1♍	24♋	3♏
10	17♌	3♍	25♋	4♏
11	18♌	5♍	26♋	4♏
12	19♌	6♍	27♋	5♏
13	20♌	8♍	28♋	6♏
14	21♌	10♍	0♌	6♏
15	22♌	11♍	1♌	7♏
16	23♌	13♍	2♌	7♏
17	24♌	14♍	3♌	8♏
18	25♌	16♍	5♌	9♏
19	26♌	17♍	6♌	9♏
20	27♌	19♍	7♌	10♏
21	28♌	20♍	8♌	11♏
22	29♌	22♍	9♌	11♏
23	0♍	23♍	11♌	12♏
24	1♍	25♍	12♌	12♏
25	2♍	26♍	13♌	13♏
26	3♍	27♍	14♌	14♏
27	4♍	29♍	16♌	14♏
28	5♍	0♎	17♌	15♏
29	6♍	1♎	18♌	16♏
30	7♍	3♎	19♌	16♏
31	7♍	4♎	21♌	17♏

September

Day	☉	☿	♀	♂
1	8♍	5♎	22♌	17♏
2	9♍	6♎	23♌	18♏
3	10♍	7♎	24♌	19♏
4	11♍	8♎	25♌	19♏
5	12♍	9♎	27♌	20♏
6	13♍	10♎	28♌	21♏
7	14♍	11♎	29♌	21♏
8	15♍	12♎	0♍	22♏
9	16♍	13♎	2♍	23♏
10	17♍	14♎	3♍	23♏
11	18♍	14♎	4♍	24♏
12	19♍	15♎	5♍	25♏
13	20♍	16♎	7♍	25♏
14	21♍	16♎	8♍	26♏
15	22♍	17♎	9♍	27♏
16	23♍	17♎	10♍	27♏
17	24♍	17♎	12♍	28♏
18	25♍	17♎	13♍	29♏
19	26♍	18♎	14♍	29♏
20	27♍	17♎	15♍	0♐
21	28♍	17♎	16♍	1♐
22	29♍	17♎	18♍	1♐
23	0♎	17♎	19♍	2♐
24	1♎	16♎	20♍	3♐
25	2♎	16♎	21♍	4♐
26	3♎	15♎	23♍	4♐
27	4♎	14♎	24♍	5♐
28	5♎	13♎	25♍	6♐
29	6♎	12♎	26♍	6♐
30	7♎	11♎	28♍	7♐

October

Day	☉	☿	♀	♂
1	8♎	10♎	29♍	8♐
2	9♎	9♎	0♎	8♐
3	10♎	8♎	1♎	9♐
4	11♎	7♎	3♎	10♐
5	12♎	6♎	4♎	11♐
6	13♎	5♎	5♎	11♐
7	14♎	4♎	6♎	12♐
8	15♎	3♎	8♎	13♐
9	16♎	3♎	9♎	13♐
10	17♎	3♎	10♎	14♐
11	18♎	2♎	11♎	15♐
12	19♎	3♎	13♎	16♐
13	20♎	3♎	14♎	16♐
14	21♎	3♎	15♎	17♐
15	22♎	4♎	16♎	18♐
16	23♎	5♎	18♎	18♐
17	23♎	5♎	19♎	19♐
18	24♎	6♎	20♎	20♐
19	25♎	8♎	21♎	21♐
20	26♎	9♎	23♎	21♐
21	27♎	10♎	24♎	22♐
22	28♎	11♎	25♎	23♐
23	29♎	13♎	26♎	24♐
24	0♏	14♎	28♎	24♐
25	1♏	16♎	29♎	25♐
26	2♏	17♎	0♏	26♐
27	3♏	19♎	1♏	26♐
28	4♏	20♎	3♏	27♐
29	5♏	22♎	4♏	28♐
30	6♏	24♎	5♏	29♐
31	7♏	25♎	6♏	29♐

November

Day	☉	☿	♀	♂
1	8♏	27♎	8♏	0♑
2	9♏	29♎	9♏	1♑
3	10♏	0♏	10♏	2♑
4	11♏	2♏	11♏	2♑
5	12♏	4♏	13♏	3♑
6	13♏	5♏	14♏	4♑
7	14♏	7♏	15♏	5♑
8	15♏	8♏	16♏	5♑
9	16♏	10♏	18♏	6♑
10	17♏	12♏	19♏	7♑
11	18♏	13♏	20♏	8♑
12	19♏	15♏	22♏	8♑
13	20♏	17♏	23♏	9♑
14	21♏	18♏	24♏	10♑
15	22♏	20♏	25♏	11♑
16	24♏	21♏	27♏	11♑
17	25♏	23♏	28♏	12♑
18	26♏	25♏	29♏	13♑
19	27♏	26♏	0♐	14♑
20	28♏	28♏	2♐	15♑
21	29♏	29♏	3♐	15♑
22	0♐	1♐	4♐	16♑
23	1♐	3♐	5♐	17♑
24	2♐	4♐	7♐	18♑
25	3♐	6♐	8♐	18♑
26	4♐	7♐	9♐	19♑
27	5♐	9♐	10♐	20♑
28	6♐	10♐	12♐	21♑
29	7♐	12♐	13♐	21♑
30	8♐	13♐	14♐	22♑

December

Day	☉	☿	♀	♂
1	9♐	15♐	15♐	23♑
2	10♐	17♐	17♐	24♑
3	11♐	18♐	18♐	25♑
4	12♐	20♐	19♐	25♑
5	13♐	21♐	20♐	26♑
6	14♐	23♐	22♐	27♑
7	15♐	24♐	23♐	28♑
8	16♐	26♐	24♐	28♑
9	17♐	27♐	25♐	29♑
10	18♐	29♐	27♐	0♒
11	19♐	1♑	28♐	1♒
12	20♐	2♑	29♐	2♒
13	21♐	4♑	0♑	2♒
14	22♐	5♑	2♑	3♒
15	23♐	7♑	3♑	4♒
16	24♐	8♑	4♑	5♒
17	25♐	10♑	5♑	5♒
18	26♐	11♑	7♑	6♒
19	27♐	13♑	8♑	7♒
20	28♐	14♑	9♑	8♒
21	29♐	16♑	11♑	9♒
22	0♑	17♑	12♑	9♒
23	1♑	19♑	13♑	10♒
24	2♑	20♑	14♑	11♒
25	3♑	22♑	16♑	12♒
26	4♑	23♑	17♑	12♒
27	5♑	24♑	18♑	13♒
28	6♑	25♑	19♑	14♒
29	7♑	27♑	21♑	15♒
30	8♑	28♑	22♑	16♒
31	9♑	29♑	23♑	16♒

Your Starway to Love

☉ = Sun ☿ = Mercury ♀ = Venus ♂ = Mars ♈ = Aries ♉ = Taurus ♊ = Gemini ♋ = Cancer

1983

January

Day	☉	☿	♀	♂
1	10♑	0♒	24♑	17♒
2	11♑	1♒	26♑	18♒
3	12♑	1♒	27♑	19♒
4	13♑	2♒	28♑	20♒
5	14♑	2♒	29♑	20♒
6	15♑	2♒	1♒	21♒
7	16♑	3♒	2♒	22♒
8	17♑	2♒	3♒	23♒
9	18♑	2♒	4♒	23♒
10	19♑	2♒	6♒	24♒
11	20♑	1♒	7♒	25♒
12	21♑	0♒	8♒	26♒
13	22♑	29♑	9♒	27♒
14	23♑	28♑	11♒	27♒
15	24♑	27♑	12♒	28♒
16	25♑	25♑	13♒	29♒
17	27♑	24♑	14♒	0♓
18	28♑	23♑	16♒	1♓
19	29♑	22♑	17♒	1♓
20	0♒	20♑	18♒	2♓
21	1♒	19♑	19♒	3♓
22	2♒	19♑	21♒	4♓
23	3♒	18♑	22♒	4♓
24	4♒	17♑	23♒	5♓
25	5♒	17♑	24♒	6♓
26	6♒	17♑	26♒	7♓
27	7♒	16♑	27♒	8♓
28	8♒	17♑	28♒	8♓
29	9♒	17♑	29♒	9♓
30	10♒	17♑	1♓	10♓
31	11♒	17♑	2♓	11♓

February

Day	☉	☿	♀	♂
1	12♒	18♑	3♓	11♓
2	13♒	18♑	4♓	12♓
3	14♒	19♑	6♓	13♓
4	15♒	20♑	7♓	14♓
5	16♒	20♑	8♓	15♓
6	17♒	21♑	9♓	15♓
7	18♒	22♑	11♓	16♓
8	19♒	23♑	12♓	17♓
9	20♒	24♑	13♓	18♓
10	21♒	25♑	14♓	19♓
11	22♒	26♑	16♓	19♓
12	23♒	27♑	17♓	20♓
13	24♒	29♑	18♓	21♓
14	25♒	0♒	19♓	22♓
15	26♒	1♒	20♓	22♓
16	27♒	2♒	22♓	23♓
17	28♒	4♒	23♓	24♓
18	29♒	5♒	24♓	25♓
19	0♓	6♒	25♓	26♓
20	1♓	7♒	27♓	26♓
21	2♓	9♒	28♓	27♓
22	3♓	10♒	29♓	28♓
23	4♓	12♒	0♈	29♓
24	5♓	13♒	2♈	29♓
25	6♓	15♒	3♈	0♈
26	7♓	16♒	4♈	1♈
27	8♓	17♒	5♈	2♈
28	9♓	19♒	7♈	2♈

March

Day	☉	☿	♀	♂
1	10♓	21♒	8♈	3♈
2	11♓	22♒	9♈	4♈
3	12♓	24♒	10♈	5♈
4	13♓	25♒	11♈	6♈
5	14♓	27♒	13♈	6♈
6	15♓	28♒	14♈	7♈
7	16♓	0♓	15♈	8♈
8	17♓	2♓	16♈	9♈
9	18♓	3♓	18♈	9♈
10	19♓	5♓	19♈	10♈
11	20♓	7♓	20♈	11♈
12	21♓	8♓	21♈	12♈
13	22♓	10♓	22♈	12♈
14	23♓	12♓	24♈	13♈
15	24♓	14♓	25♈	14♈
16	25♓	16♓	26♈	15♈
17	26♓	17♓	27♈	15♈
18	27♓	19♓	29♈	16♈
19	28♓	21♓	0♉	17♈
20	29♓	23♓	1♉	18♈
21	0♈	25♓	2♉	18♈
22	1♈	27♓	3♉	19♈
23	2♈	29♓	5♉	20♈
24	3♈	1♈	6♉	21♈
25	4♈	3♈	7♉	21♈
26	5♈	5♈	8♉	22♈
27	6♈	7♈	9♉	23♈
28	7♈	9♈	11♉	24♈
29	8♈	11♈	12♉	24♈
30	9♈	13♈	13♉	25♈
31	10♈	15♈	14♉	26♈

April

Day	☉	☿	♀	♂
1	11♈	17♈	15♉	27♈
2	12♈	19♈	17♉	27♈
3	13♈	21♈	18♉	28♈
4	14♈	23♈	19♉	29♈
5	15♈	25♈	20♉	0♉
6	16♈	27♈	21♉	0♉
7	17♈	29♈	23♉	1♉
8	18♈	1♉	24♉	2♉
9	19♈	3♉	25♉	3♉
10	20♈	5♉	26♉	3♉
11	21♈	6♉	27♉	4♉
12	22♈	8♉	29♉	5♉
13	23♈	10♉	0♊	6♉
14	24♈	11♉	1♊	6♉
15	25♈	13♉	2♊	7♉
16	26♈	14♉	3♊	8♉
17	27♈	16♉	4♊	9♉
18	28♈	17♉	6♊	9♉
19	29♈	18♉	7♊	10♉
20	0♉	19♉	8♊	11♉
21	1♉	20♉	9♊	12♉
22	2♉	21♉	10♊	12♉
23	2♉	22♉	11♊	13♉
24	3♉	23♉	13♊	14♉
25	4♉	24♉	14♊	14♉
26	5♉	24♉	15♊	15♉
27	6♉	25♉	16♊	16♉
28	7♉	25♉	17♊	17♉
29	8♉	25♉	18♊	17♉
30	9♉	25♉	19♊	18♉

May

Day	☉	☿	♀	♂
1	10♉	26♉	21♊	19♉
2	11♉	26♉	22♊	19♉
3	12♉	25♉	23♊	20♉
4	13♉	25♉	24♊	21♉
5	14♉	25♉	25♊	22♉
6	15♉	25♉	26♊	22♉
7	16♉	24♉	27♊	23♉
8	17♉	24♉	29♊	24♉
9	18♉	23♉	0♋	25♉
10	19♉	23♉	1♋	25♉
11	20♉	22♉	2♋	26♉
12	21♉	22♉	3♋	27♉
13	22♉	21♉	4♋	27♉
14	23♉	20♉	5♋	28♉
15	24♉	20♉	6♋	29♉
16	25♉	19♉	8♋	0♊
17	26♉	19♉	9♋	0♊
18	27♉	18♉	10♋	1♊
19	28♉	18♉	11♋	2♊
20	29♉	17♉	12♋	2♊
21	0♊	17♉	13♋	3♊
22	1♊	17♉	14♋	4♊
23	2♊	17♉	15♋	4♊
24	2♊	16♉	16♋	5♊
25	3♊	16♉	17♋	6♊
26	4♊	16♉	18♋	7♊
27	5♊	17♉	20♋	7♊
28	6♊	17♉	21♋	8♊
29	7♊	17♉	22♋	9♊
30	8♊	17♉	23♋	9♊
31	9♊	18♉	24♋	10♊

June

Day	☉	☿	♀	♂
1	10♊	18♉	25♋	11♊
2	11♊	19♉	26♋	11♊
3	12♊	19♉	27♋	12♊
4	13♊	20♉	28♋	13♊
5	14♊	21♉	29♋	14♊
6	15♊	21♉	0♌	14♊
7	16♊	22♉	1♌	15♊
8	17♊	23♉	2♌	16♊
9	18♊	24♉	3♌	16♊
10	19♊	25♉	4♌	17♊
11	20♊	26♉	5♌	18♊
12	21♊	27♉	6♌	18♊
13	22♊	29♉	7♌	19♊
14	23♊	0♊	8♌	20♊
15	24♊	1♊	9♌	20♊
16	25♊	2♊	10♌	21♊
17	25♊	4♊	11♌	22♊
18	26♊	5♊	12♌	22♊
19	27♊	7♊	13♌	23♊
20	28♊	8♊	14♌	24♊
21	29♊	10♊	15♌	25♊
22	0♋	12♊	15♌	25♊
23	1♋	13♊	16♌	26♊
24	2♋	15♊	17♌	27♊
25	3♋	17♊	18♌	27♊
26	4♋	19♊	19♌	28♊
27	5♋	21♊	20♌	29♊
28	6♋	23♊	21♌	29♊
29	7♋	25♊	22♌	0♋
30	8♋	27♊	22♌	1♋

July

Day	☉	☿	♀	♂
1	9♋	29♊	23♌	1♋
2	10♋	1♋	24♌	2♋
3	11♋	3♋	25♌	3♋
4	12♋	5♋	26♌	3♋
5	13♋	7♋	26♌	4♋
6	14♋	9♋	27♌	5♋
7	15♋	12♋	28♌	5♋
8	15♋	14♋	29♌	6♋
9	16♋	16♋	29♌	7♋
10	17♋	18♋	0♍	7♋
11	18♋	20♋	1♍	8♋
12	19♋	22♋	1♍	9♋
13	20♋	24♋	2♍	9♋
14	21♋	27♋	3♍	10♋
15	22♋	29♋	3♍	11♋
16	23♋	1♌	4♍	11♋
17	24♋	3♌	4♍	12♋
18	25♋	5♌	5♍	13♋
19	26♋	7♌	5♍	13♋
20	27♋	9♌	6♍	14♋
21	28♋	11♌	6♍	15♋
22	29♋	12♌	7♍	15♋
23	0♌	14♌	7♍	16♋
24	1♌	16♌	7♍	17♋
25	2♌	18♌	8♍	17♋
26	3♌	20♌	8♍	18♋
27	4♌	21♌	8♍	19♋
28	5♌	23♌	9♍	19♋
29	6♌	25♌	9♍	20♋
30	6♌	26♌	9♍	21♋
31	7♌	28♌	9♍	21♋

August

Day	☉	☿	♀	♂
1	8♌	0♍	9♍	22♋
2	9♌	1♍	9♍	23♋
3	10♌	3♍	9♍	23♋
4	11♌	4♍	9♍	24♋
5	12♌	6♍	9♍	24♋
6	13♌	7♍	9♍	25♋
7	14♌	9♍	9♍	26♋
8	15♌	10♍	9♍	26♋
9	16♌	11♍	9♍	27♋
10	17♌	13♍	9♍	28♋
11	18♌	14♍	8♍	28♋
12	19♌	15♍	8♍	29♋
13	20♌	16♍	8♍	0♌
14	21♌	18♍	7♍	0♌
15	22♌	19♍	7♍	1♌
16	23♌	20♍	7♍	2♌
17	24♌	21♍	6♍	2♌
18	25♌	22♍	6♍	3♌
19	26♌	23♍	5♍	4♌
20	27♌	24♍	4♍	4♌
21	28♌	25♍	4♍	5♌
22	29♌	26♍	3♍	5♌
23	0♍	27♍	3♍	6♌
24	0♍	27♍	2♍	7♌
25	1♍	28♍	1♍	7♌
26	2♍	29♍	1♍	8♌
27	3♍	29♍	0♍	9♌
28	4♍	0♎	0♍	9♌
29	5♍	0♎	29♌	10♌
30	6♍	0♎	28♌	11♌
31	7♍	1♎	28♌	11♌

September

Day	☉	☿	♀	♂
1	8♍	1♎	27♌	12♌
2	9♍	1♎	27♌	13♌
3	10♍	1♎	26♌	13♌
4	11♍	1♎	26♌	14♌
5	12♍	0♎	25♌	14♌
6	13♍	0♎	25♌	15♌
7	14♍	29♍	25♌	16♌
8	15♍	29♍	24♌	16♌
9	16♍	28♍	24♌	17♌
10	17♍	28♍	24♌	18♌
11	18♍	27♍	24♌	18♌
12	19♍	26♍	23♌	19♌
13	20♍	25♍	23♌	19♌
14	21♍	24♍	23♌	20♌
15	22♍	23♍	23♌	21♌
16	23♍	22♍	23♌	21♌
17	24♍	21♍	23♌	22♌
18	25♍	20♍	23♌	23♌
19	26♍	19♍	23♌	23♌
20	27♍	18♍	24♌	24♌
21	28♍	17♍	24♌	25♌
22	29♍	17♍	24♌	25♌
23	0♎	17♍	24♌	26♌
24	1♎	16♍	25♌	26♌
25	2♎	16♍	25♌	27♌
26	3♎	17♍	25♌	28♌
27	4♎	17♍	26♌	28♌
28	5♎	17♍	26♌	29♌
29	5♎	18♍	26♌	0♍
30	6♎	19♍	27♌	0♍

October

Day	☉	☿	♀	♂
1	7♎	20♍	27♌	1♍
2	8♎	21♍	28♌	1♍
3	9♎	22♍	28♌	2♍
4	10♎	23♍	29♌	3♍
5	11♎	24♍	0♍	3♍
6	12♎	26♍	0♍	4♍
7	13♎	27♍	1♍	4♍
8	14♎	29♍	2♍	5♍
9	15♎	0♎	2♍	6♍
10	16♎	2♎	3♍	6♍
11	17♎	4♎	4♍	7♍
12	18♎	5♎	4♍	8♍
13	19♎	7♎	5♍	8♍
14	20♎	9♎	6♍	9♍
15	21♎	10♎	7♍	9♍
16	22♎	12♎	7♍	10♍
17	23♎	14♎	8♍	11♍
18	24♎	16♎	9♍	11♍
19	25♎	17♎	10♍	12♍
20	26♎	19♎	11♍	12♍
21	27♎	21♎	12♍	13♍
22	28♎	22♎	12♍	14♍
23	29♎	24♎	13♍	14♍
24	0♏	26♎	14♍	15♍
25	1♏	28♎	15♍	15♍
26	2♏	29♎	16♍	16♍
27	3♏	1♏	17♍	17♍
28	4♏	3♏	18♍	17♍
29	5♏	4♏	19♍	18♍
30	6♏	6♏	20♍	19♍
31	7♏	8♏	21♍	19♍

November

Day	☉	☿	♀	♂
1	8♏	9♏	22♍	20♍
2	9♏	11♏	23♍	20♍
3	10♏	12♏	24♍	21♍
4	11♏	14♏	25♍	22♍
5	12♏	16♏	26♍	22♍
6	13♏	17♏	27♍	23♍
7	14♏	19♏	28♍	23♍
8	15♏	20♏	29♍	24♍
9	16♏	22♏	0♎	25♍
10	17♏	24♏	1♎	25♍
11	18♏	25♏	2♎	26♍
12	19♏	27♏	3♎	26♍
13	20♏	28♏	4♎	27♍
14	21♏	0♐	5♎	28♍
15	22♏	1♐	6♎	28♍
16	23♏	3♐	7♎	29♍
17	24♏	4♐	8♎	29♍
18	25♏	6♐	9♎	0♎
19	26♏	7♐	10♎	0♎
20	27♏	9♐	11♎	1♎
21	28♏	10♐	13♎	2♎
22	29♏	12♐	14♎	2♎
23	0♐	13♐	15♎	3♎
24	1♐	15♐	16♎	3♎
25	2♐	16♐	17♎	4♎
26	3♐	18♐	18♎	5♎
27	4♐	19♐	19♎	5♎
28	5♐	21♐	20♎	6♎
29	6♐	22♐	21♎	6♎
30	7♐	24♐	23♎	7♎

December

Day	☉	☿	♀	♂
1	8♐	25♐	24♎	7♎
2	9♐	27♐	25♎	8♎
3	10♐	28♐	26♎	9♎
4	11♐	0♑	27♎	9♎
5	12♐	1♑	28♎	10♎
6	13♐	2♑	29♎	10♎
7	15♐	4♑	1♏	11♎
8	16♐	5♑	2♏	11♎
9	17♐	6♑	3♏	12♎
10	18♐	8♑	4♏	13♎
11	19♐	9♑	5♏	13♎
12	20♐	10♑	6♏	14♎
13	21♐	11♑	8♏	14♎
14	22♐	12♑	9♏	15♎
15	23♐	13♑	10♏	15♎
16	24♐	14♑	11♏	16♎
17	25♐	15♑	12♏	17♎
18	26♐	15♑	13♏	17♎
19	27♐	16♑	15♏	18♎
20	28♐	16♑	16♏	18♎
21	29♐	17♑	17♏	19♎
22	0♑	17♑	18♏	19♎
23	1♑	17♑	19♏	20♎
24	2♑	16♑	21♏	20♎
25	3♑	16♑	22♏	21♎
26	4♑	15♑	23♏	22♎
27	5♑	14♑	24♏	22♎
28	6♑	13♑	25♏	23♎
29	7♑	12♑	27♏	23♎
30	8♑	11♑	28♏	24♎
31	9♑	9♑	29♏	24♎

1984

Planetary Positions

♌ = Leo ♍ = Virgo ♎ = Libra ♏ = Scorpio ♐ = Sagittarius ♑ = Capricorn ♒ = Aquarius ♓ = Pisces

January

Day	☉	☿	♀	♂
1	10♑	8♑	0♐	25♎
2	11♑	7♑	1♐	25♎
3	12♑	5♑	3♐	26♎
4	13♑	4♑	4♐	26♎
5	14♑	3♑	5♐	27♎
6	15♑	2♑	6♐	27♎
7	16♑	2♑	7♐	28♎
8	17♑	1♑	9♐	28♎
9	18♑	1♑	10♐	29♎
10	19♑	0♑	11♐	0♏
11	20♑	0♑	12♐	0♏
12	21♑	0♑	13♐	1♏
13	22♑	1♑	15♐	1♏
14	23♑	1♑	16♐	2♏
15	24♑	2♑	17♐	2♏
16	25♑	2♑	18♐	3♏
17	26♑	3♑	20♐	3♏
18	27♑	3♑	21♐	4♏
19	28♑	4♑	22♐	4♏
20	29♑	5♑	23♐	5♏
21	0♒	6♑	24♐	5♏
22	1♒	7♑	26♐	6♏
23	2♒	8♑	27♐	6♏
24	3♒	9♑	28♐	7♏
25	4♒	10♑	29♐	7♏
26	5♒	11♑	1♑	8♏
27	6♒	13♑	2♑	8♏
28	7♒	14♑	3♑	8♏
29	8♒	15♑	4♑	9♏
30	9♒	16♑	5♑	9♏
31	11♒	18♑	7♑	10♏

February

Day	☉	☿	♀	♂
1	12♒	19♑	8♑	10♏
2	13♒	20♑	9♑	11♏
3	14♒	22♑	10♑	11♏
4	15♒	23♑	12♑	12♏
5	16♒	24♑	13♑	12♏
6	17♒	26♑	14♑	13♏
7	18♒	27♑	15♑	13♏
8	19♒	29♑	16♑	13♏
9	20♒	0♒	18♑	14♏
10	21♒	2♒	19♑	14♏
11	22♒	3♒	20♑	15♏
12	23♒	5♒	21♑	15♏
13	24♒	6♒	23♑	16♏
14	25♒	8♒	24♑	16♏
15	26♒	9♒	25♑	16♏
16	27♒	11♒	26♑	17♏
17	28♒	12♒	28♑	17♏
18	29♒	14♒	29♑	18♏
19	0♓	16♒	0♒	18♏
20	1♓	17♒	1♒	18♏
21	2♓	19♒	2♒	19♏
22	3♓	21♒	4♒	19♏
23	4♓	22♒	5♒	20♏
24	5♓	24♒	6♒	20♏
25	6♓	26♒	7♒	20♏
26	7♓	27♒	9♒	21♏
27	8♓	29♒	10♒	21♏
28	9♓	1♓	11♒	21♏
29	10♓	3♓	12♒	22♏

March

Day	☉	☿	♀	♂
1	11♓	4♓	14♒	22♏
2	12♓	6♓	15♒	22♏
3	13♓	8♓	16♒	23♏
4	14♓	10♓	17♒	23♏
5	15♓	12♓	19♒	23♏
6	16♓	14♓	20♒	23♏
7	17♓	15♓	21♒	24♏
8	18♓	17♓	22♒	24♏
9	19♓	19♓	23♒	24♏
10	20♓	21♓	25♒	25♏
11	21♓	23♓	26♒	25♏
12	22♓	25♓	27♒	25♏
13	23♓	27♓	28♒	25♏
14	24♓	29♓	0♓	26♏
15	25♓	1♈	1♓	26♏
16	26♓	3♈	2♓	26♏
17	27♓	5♈	3♓	26♏
18	28♓	7♈	5♓	26♏
19	29♓	9♈	6♓	27♏
20	0♈	11♈	7♓	27♏
21	1♈	13♈	8♓	27♏
22	2♈	15♈	9♓	27♏
23	3♈	17♈	11♓	27♏
24	4♈	18♈	12♓	27♏
25	5♈	20♈	13♓	28♏
26	6♈	22♈	14♓	28♏
27	7♈	23♈	16♓	28♏
28	8♈	25♈	17♓	28♏
29	9♈	27♈	18♓	28♏
30	10♈	28♈	19♓	28♏
31	11♈	29♈	21♓	28♏

April

Day	☉	☿	♀	♂
1	12♈	0♉	22♓	28♏
2	13♈	2♉	23♓	28♏
3	14♈	3♉	24♓	28♏
4	15♈	3♉	26♓	28♏
5	16♈	4♉	27♓	28♏
6	17♈	5♉	28♓	28♏
7	18♈	6♉	29♓	28♏
8	19♈	6♉	0♈	28♏
9	20♈	6♉	2♈	28♏
10	21♈	7♉	3♈	28♏
11	21♈	7♉	4♈	28♏
12	22♈	7♉	5♈	28♏
13	23♈	7♉	7♈	28♏
14	24♈	6♉	8♈	28♏
15	25♈	6♉	9♈	28♏
16	26♈	6♉	10♈	28♏
17	27♈	5♉	12♈	27♏
18	28♈	5♉	13♈	27♏
19	29♈	4♉	14♈	27♏
20	0♉	4♉	15♈	27♏
21	1♉	3♉	16♈	27♏
22	2♉	2♉	18♈	27♏
23	3♉	2♉	19♈	26♏
24	4♉	1♉	20♈	26♏
25	5♉	0♉	21♈	26♏
26	6♉	0♉	23♈	26♏
27	7♉	29♈	24♈	25♏
28	8♉	28♈	25♈	25♏
29	9♉	28♈	26♈	25♏
30	10♉	27♈	28♈	25♏

May

Day	☉	☿	♀	♂
1	11♉	27♈	29♈	24♏
2	12♉	27♈	0♉	24♏
3	13♉	27♈	1♉	24♏
4	14♉	26♈	2♉	23♏
5	15♉	26♈	4♉	23♏
6	16♉	26♈	5♉	23♏
7	17♉	26♈	6♉	22♏
8	18♉	27♈	7♉	22♏
9	19♉	27♈	9♉	22♏
10	20♉	27♈	10♉	21♏
11	21♉	28♈	11♉	21♏
12	22♉	28♈	12♉	21♏
13	23♉	29♈	14♉	20♏
14	24♉	29♈	15♉	20♏
15	25♉	0♉	16♉	19♏
16	26♉	1♉	17♉	19♏
17	26♉	1♉	18♉	19♏
18	27♉	2♉	20♉	18♏
19	28♉	3♉	21♉	18♏
20	29♉	4♉	22♉	18♏
21	0♊	5♉	23♉	17♏
22	1♊	6♉	25♉	17♏
23	2♊	7♉	26♉	17♏
24	3♊	8♉	27♉	16♏
25	4♊	10♉	28♉	16♏
26	5♊	11♉	0♊	16♏
27	6♊	12♉	1♊	15♏
28	7♊	13♉	2♊	15♏
29	8♊	15♉	3♊	15♏
30	9♊	16♉	4♊	15♏
31	10♊	18♉	6♊	14♏

June

Day	☉	☿	♀	♂
1	11♊	19♉	7♊	14♏
2	12♊	21♉	8♊	14♏
3	13♊	22♉	9♊	14♏
4	14♊	24♉	11♊	13♏
5	15♊	26♉	12♊	13♏
6	16♊	27♉	13♊	13♏
7	17♊	29♉	14♊	13♏
8	18♊	1♊	15♊	13♏
9	19♊	3♊	17♊	12♏
10	19♊	5♊	18♊	12♏
11	20♊	7♊	19♊	12♏
12	21♊	9♊	20♊	12♏
13	22♊	11♊	22♊	12♏
14	23♊	13♊	23♊	12♏
15	24♊	15♊	24♊	12♏
16	25♊	17♊	25♊	12♏
17	26♊	19♊	27♊	12♏
18	27♊	21♊	28♊	12♏
19	28♊	23♊	29♊	12♏
20	29♊	25♊	0♋	12♏
21	0♋	28♊	1♋	12♏
22	1♋	0♋	3♋	12♏
23	2♋	2♋	4♋	12♏
24	3♋	4♋	5♋	12♏
25	4♋	6♋	6♋	12♏
26	5♋	9♋	8♋	12♏
27	6♋	11♋	9♋	12♏
28	7♋	13♋	10♋	12♏
29	8♋	15♋	11♋	12♏
30	9♋	17♋	13♋	12♏

July

Day	☉	☿	♀	♂
1	10♋	19♋	14♋	13♏
2	10♋	21♋	15♋	13♏
3	11♋	23♋	16♋	13♏
4	12♋	25♋	17♋	13♏
5	13♋	27♋	19♋	13♏
6	14♋	29♋	20♋	13♏
7	15♋	1♌	21♋	14♏
8	16♋	3♌	22♋	14♏
9	17♋	4♌	24♋	14♏
10	18♋	6♌	25♋	14♏
11	19♋	8♌	26♋	15♏
12	20♋	10♌	27♋	15♏
13	21♋	11♌	28♋	15♏
14	22♋	13♌	0♌	15♏
15	23♋	15♌	1♌	16♏
16	24♋	16♌	2♌	16♏
17	25♋	18♌	3♌	16♏
18	26♋	19♌	5♌	17♏
19	27♋	21♌	6♌	17♏
20	28♋	22♌	7♌	17♏
21	29♋	23♌	8♌	18♏
22	0♌	25♌	10♌	18♏
23	1♌	26♌	11♌	18♏
24	1♌	27♌	12♌	19♏
25	2♌	29♌	13♌	19♏
26	3♌	0♍	14♌	20♏
27	4♌	1♍	16♌	20♏
28	5♌	2♍	17♌	20♏
29	6♌	3♍	18♌	21♏
30	7♌	4♍	19♌	21♏
31	8♌	5♍	21♌	22♏

August

Day	☉	☿	♀	♂
1	9♌	6♍	22♌	22♏
2	10♌	7♍	23♌	22♏
3	11♌	8♍	24♌	23♏
4	12♌	9♍	26♌	23♏
5	13♌	10♍	27♌	24♏
6	14♌	10♍	28♌	24♏
7	15♌	11♍	29♌	25♏
8	16♌	12♍	0♍	25♏
9	17♌	12♍	2♍	26♏
10	18♌	12♍	3♍	26♏
11	19♌	13♍	4♍	27♏
12	20♌	13♍	5♍	27♏
13	21♌	13♍	7♍	28♏
14	22♌	13♍	8♍	28♏
15	23♌	13♍	9♍	29♏
16	24♌	13♍	10♍	29♏
17	24♌	13♍	12♍	0♐
18	25♌	13♍	13♍	0♐
19	26♌	12♍	14♍	1♐
20	27♌	12♍	15♍	1♐
21	28♌	11♍	16♍	2♐
22	29♌	11♍	18♍	2♐
23	0♍	10♍	19♍	3♐
24	1♍	9♍	20♍	3♐
25	2♍	9♍	21♍	4♐
26	3♍	8♍	23♍	5♐
27	4♍	7♍	24♍	5♐
28	5♍	6♍	25♍	6♐
29	6♍	5♍	26♍	6♐
30	7♍	4♍	28♍	7♐
31	8♍	3♍	29♍	7♐

September

Day	☉	☿	♀	♂
1	9♍	2♍	0♎	8♐
2	10♍	2♍	1♎	9♐
3	11♍	1♍	2♎	9♐
4	12♍	1♍	4♎	10♐
5	13♍	0♍	5♎	10♐
6	14♍	0♍	6♎	11♐
7	15♍	0♍	7♎	12♐
8	16♍	0♍	9♎	12♐
9	17♍	0♍	10♎	13♐
10	18♍	1♍	11♎	14♐
11	19♍	1♍	12♎	14♐
12	20♍	2♍	14♎	15♐
13	21♍	3♍	15♎	15♐
14	22♍	4♍	16♎	16♐
15	23♍	5♍	17♎	17♐
16	24♍	6♍	18♎	17♐
17	24♍	7♍	20♎	18♐
18	25♍	9♍	21♎	19♐
19	26♍	10♍	22♎	19♐
20	27♍	12♍	23♎	20♐
21	28♍	13♍	25♎	21♐
22	29♍	15♍	26♎	21♐
23	0♎	16♍	27♎	22♐
24	1♎	18♍	28♎	23♐
25	2♎	20♍	29♎	23♐
26	3♎	22♍	1♏	24♐
27	4♎	23♍	2♏	25♐
28	5♎	25♍	3♏	25♐
29	6♎	27♍	4♏	26♐
30	7♎	29♍	6♏	27♐

October

Day	☉	☿	♀	♂
1	8♎	1♎	7♏	27♐
2	9♎	3♎	8♏	28♐
3	10♎	4♎	9♏	29♐
4	11♎	6♎	10♏	29♐
5	12♎	8♎	12♏	0♑
6	13♎	10♎	13♏	1♑
7	14♎	11♎	14♏	1♑
8	15♎	13♎	15♏	2♑
9	16♎	15♎	17♏	3♑
10	17♎	17♎	18♏	3♑
11	18♎	18♎	19♏	4♑
12	19♎	20♎	20♏	5♑
13	20♎	22♎	21♏	6♑
14	21♎	24♎	23♏	6♑
15	22♎	25♎	24♏	7♑
16	23♎	27♎	25♏	8♑
17	24♎	28♎	26♏	8♑
18	25♎	0♏	28♏	9♑
19	26♎	2♏	29♏	10♑
20	27♎	3♏	0♐	11♑
21	28♎	5♏	1♐	11♑
22	29♎	7♏	2♐	12♑
23	0♏	8♏	4♐	13♑
24	1♏	10♏	5♐	13♑
25	2♏	11♏	6♐	14♑
26	3♏	13♏	7♐	15♑
27	4♏	14♏	8♐	16♑
28	5♏	16♏	10♐	16♑
29	6♏	18♏	11♐	17♑
30	7♏	19♏	12♐	18♑
31	8♏	21♏	13♐	18♑

November

Day	☉	☿	♀	♂
1	9♏	22♏	15♐	19♑
2	10♏	24♏	16♐	20♑
3	11♏	25♏	17♐	21♑
4	12♏	27♏	18♐	21♑
5	13♏	28♏	19♐	22♑
6	14♏	0♐	21♐	23♑
7	15♏	1♐	22♐	24♑
8	16♏	2♐	23♐	24♑
9	17♏	4♐	24♐	25♑
10	18♏	5♐	25♐	26♑
11	19♏	7♐	27♐	27♑
12	20♏	8♐	28♐	27♑
13	21♏	10♐	29♐	28♑
14	22♏	11♐	0♑	29♑
15	23♏	12♐	1♑	0♒
16	24♏	14♐	3♑	0♒
17	25♏	15♐	4♑	1♒
18	26♏	16♐	5♑	2♒
19	27♏	18♐	6♑	3♒
20	28♏	19♐	7♑	3♒
21	29♏	20♐	9♑	4♒
22	0♐	21♐	10♑	5♒
23	1♐	23♐	11♑	6♒
24	2♐	24♐	12♑	6♒
25	3♐	25♐	13♑	7♒
26	4♐	26♐	15♑	8♒
27	5♐	27♐	16♑	9♒
28	6♐	28♐	17♑	9♒
29	7♐	28♐	18♑	10♒
30	8♐	29♐	19♑	11♒

December

Day	☉	☿	♀	♂
1	9♐	0♑	21♑	12♒
2	10♐	0♑	22♑	12♒
3	11♐	1♑	23♑	13♒
4	12♐	1♑	24♑	14♒
5	13♐	1♑	25♑	15♒
6	14♐	1♑	27♑	15♒
7	15♐	0♑	28♑	16♒
8	16♐	0♑	29♑	17♒
9	17♐	29♐	0♒	18♒
10	18♐	28♐	1♒	18♒
11	19♐	27♐	2♒	19♒
12	20♐	26♐	4♒	20♒
13	21♐	25♐	5♒	21♒
14	22♐	23♐	6♒	22♒
15	23♐	22♐	7♒	22♒
16	24♐	21♐	8♒	23♒
17	25♐	19♐	9♒	24♒
18	26♐	18♐	11♒	25♒
19	27♐	17♐	12♒	25♒
20	28♐	16♐	13♒	26♒
21	0♑	16♐	14♒	27♒
22	1♑	15♐	15♒	28♒
23	2♑	15♐	16♒	28♒
24	3♑	15♐	18♒	29♒
25	4♑	15♐	19♒	0♓
26	5♑	15♐	20♒	1♓
27	6♑	15♐	21♒	1♓
28	7♑	15♐	22♒	2♓
29	8♑	16♐	23♒	3♓
30	9♑	17♐	24♒	4♓
31	10♑	17♐	25♒	5♓

1985

Your Starway to Love

☉ =Sun ☿ = Mercury ♀ = Venus ♂ = Mars ♈ = Aries ♉ = Taurus ♊ = Gemini ♋ = Cancer

January

Day	☉	☿	♀	♂
1	11♑	18♐	27♒	5♓
2	12♑	19♐	28♒	6♓
3	13♑	20♐	29♒	7♓
4	14♑	21♐	0♓	8♓
5	15♑	22♐	1♓	8♓
6	16♑	23♐	2♓	9♓
7	17♑	24♐	3♓	10♓
8	18♑	26♐	4♓	11♓
9	19♑	27♐	5♓	11♓
10	20♑	28♐	7♓	12♓
11	21♑	29♐	8♓	13♓
12	22♑	1♑	9♓	14♓
13	23♑	2♑	10♓	14♓
14	24♑	3♑	11♓	15♓
15	25♑	5♑	12♓	16♓
16	26♑	6♑	13♓	17♓
17	27♑	7♑	14♓	17♓
18	28♑	9♑	15♓	18♓
19	29♑	10♑	16♓	19♓
20	0♒	12♑	17♓	20♓
21	1♒	13♑	18♓	21♓
22	2♒	15♑	19♓	21♓
23	3♒	16♑	20♓	22♓
24	4♒	18♑	21♓	23♓
25	5♒	19♑	22♓	24♓
26	6♒	21♑	23♓	24♓
27	7♒	22♑	24♓	25♓
28	8♒	24♑	25♓	26♓
29	9♒	25♑	26♓	27♓
30	10♒	27♑	27♓	27♓
31	11♒	28♑	28♓	28♓

February

Day	☉	☿	♀	♂
1	12♒	0♒	29♓	29♓
2	13♒	1♒	0♈	0♈
3	14♒	3♒	1♈	0♈
4	15♒	5♒	2♈	1♈
5	16♒	6♒	3♈	2♈
6	17♒	8♒	3♈	3♈
7	18♒	10♒	4♈	3♈
8	19♒	11♒	5♈	4♈
9	20♒	13♒	6♈	5♈
10	21♒	15♒	7♈	6♈
11	22♒	16♒	8♈	6♈
12	23♒	18♒	9♈	7♈
13	24♒	20♒	9♈	8♈
14	25♒	21♒	10♈	9♈
15	26♒	23♒	11♈	9♈
16	27♒	25♒	12♈	10♈
17	28♒	27♒	12♈	11♈
18	29♒	29♒	13♈	12♈
19	0♓	0♓	14♈	12♈
20	2♓	2♓	14♈	13♈
21	3♓	4♓	15♈	14♈
22	4♓	6♓	16♈	15♈
23	5♓	8♓	16♈	15♈
24	6♓	10♓	17♈	16♈
25	7♓	12♓	17♈	17♈
26	8♓	13♓	18♈	18♈
27	9♓	15♓	18♈	18♈
28	10♓	17♓	19♈	19♈

March

Day	☉	☿	♀	♂
1	11♓	19♓	19♈	20♈
2	12♓	21♓	20♈	20♈
3	13♓	23♓	20♈	21♈
4	14♓	25♓	21♈	22♈
5	15♓	27♓	21♈	23♈
6	16♓	29♓	21♈	23♈
7	17♓	0♈	21♈	24♈
8	18♓	2♈	22♈	25♈
9	19♓	4♈	22♈	26♈
10	20♓	6♈	22♈	26♈
11	21♓	7♈	22♈	27♈
12	22♓	9♈	22♈	28♈
13	23♓	10♈	22♈	29♈
14	24♓	11♈	22♈	29♈
15	25♓	13♈	22♈	0♉
16	26♓	14♈	22♈	1♉
17	27♓	15♈	22♈	1♉
18	28♓	16♈	22♈	2♉
19	29♓	17♈	22♈	3♉
20	0♈	17♈	21♈	4♉
21	1♈	18♈	21♈	4♉
22	2♈	18♈	21♈	5♉
23	3♈	18♈	20♈	6♉
24	4♈	19♈	20♈	7♉
25	4♈	19♈	20♈	7♉
26	5♈	19♈	19♈	8♉
27	6♈	18♈	19♈	9♉
28	7♈	18♈	18♈	9♉
29	8♈	17♈	18♈	10♉
30	9♈	17♈	17♈	11♉
31	10♈	16♈	16♈	12♉

April

Day	☉	☿	♀	♂
1	11♈	16♈	16♈	12♉
2	12♈	15♈	15♈	13♉
3	13♈	14♈	15♈	14♉
4	14♈	13♈	14♈	14♉
5	15♈	12♈	13♈	15♉
6	16♈	12♈	13♈	16♉
7	17♈	11♈	12♈	17♉
8	18♈	10♈	11♈	17♉
9	19♈	9♈	11♈	18♉
10	20♈	9♈	10♈	19♉
11	21♈	8♈	10♈	19♉
12	22♈	8♈	9♈	20♉
13	23♈	7♈	9♈	21♉
14	24♈	7♈	8♈	21♉
15	25♈	7♈	8♈	22♉
16	26♈	7♈	8♈	23♉
17	27♈	7♈	7♈	24♉
18	28♈	7♈	7♈	24♉
19	29♈	7♈	7♈	25♉
20	0♉	7♈	6♈	26♉
21	1♉	7♈	6♈	26♉
22	2♉	8♈	6♈	27♉
23	3♉	8♈	6♈	28♉
24	4♉	9♈	6♈	28♉
25	5♉	9♈	6♈	29♉
26	6♉	10♈	6♈	0♊
27	7♉	11♈	6♈	1♊
28	8♉	11♈	6♈	1♊
29	9♉	12♈	6♈	2♊
30	10♉	13♈	7♈	3♊

May

Day	☉	☿	♀	♂
1	11♉	14♈	7♈	3♊
2	12♉	15♈	7♈	4♊
3	13♉	16♈	7♈	5♊
4	14♉	17♈	8♈	5♊
5	15♉	18♈	8♈	6♊
6	16♉	19♈	8♈	7♊
7	17♉	21♈	9♈	7♊
8	18♉	22♈	9♈	8♊
9	19♉	23♈	10♈	9♊
10	19♉	24♈	10♈	10♊
11	20♉	26♈	11♈	10♊
12	21♉	27♈	11♈	11♊
13	22♉	29♈	12♈	12♊
14	23♉	0♉	12♈	12♊
15	24♉	2♉	13♈	13♊
16	25♉	3♉	13♈	14♊
17	26♉	5♉	14♈	14♊
18	27♉	6♉	15♈	15♊
19	28♉	8♉	15♈	16♊
20	29♉	10♉	16♈	16♊
21	0♊	12♉	17♈	17♊
22	1♊	13♉	17♈	18♊
23	2♊	15♉	18♈	18♊
24	3♊	17♉	19♈	19♊
25	4♊	19♉	20♈	20♊
26	5♊	21♉	21♈	20♊
27	6♊	23♉	21♈	21♊
28	7♊	25♉	22♈	22♊
29	8♊	27♉	23♈	22♊
30	9♊	29♉	24♈	23♊
31	10♊	1♊	25♈	24♊

June

Day	☉	☿	♀	♂
1	11♊	3♊	25♈	24♊
2	12♊	5♊	26♈	25♊
3	13♊	7♊	27♈	26♊
4	14♊	9♊	28♈	26♊
5	14♊	12♊	29♈	27♊
6	15♊	14♊	0♉	28♊
7	16♊	16♊	1♉	29♊
8	17♊	18♊	2♉	29♊
9	18♊	20♊	3♉	0♋
10	19♊	23♊	4♉	1♋
11	20♊	25♊	4♉	1♋
12	21♊	27♊	5♉	2♋
13	22♊	29♊	6♉	3♋
14	23♊	1♋	7♉	3♋
15	24♊	3♋	8♉	4♋
16	25♊	5♋	9♉	5♋
17	26♊	7♋	10♉	5♋
18	27♊	9♋	11♉	6♋
19	28♊	11♋	12♉	6♋
20	29♊	13♋	13♉	7♋
21	0♋	15♋	14♉	8♋
22	1♋	17♋	15♉	8♋
23	2♋	19♋	16♉	9♋
24	3♋	21♋	17♉	10♋
25	4♋	22♋	18♉	10♋
26	5♋	24♋	19♉	11♋
27	5♋	26♋	20♉	12♋
28	6♋	27♋	21♉	12♋
29	7♋	29♋	22♉	13♋
30	8♋	1♌	24♉	14♋

July

Day	☉	☿	♀	♂
1	9♋	2♌	25♉	14♋
2	10♋	4♌	26♉	15♋
3	11♋	5♌	27♉	16♋
4	12♋	6♌	28♉	16♋
5	13♋	8♌	29♉	17♋
6	14♋	9♌	0♊	18♋
7	15♋	10♌	1♊	18♋
8	16♋	12♌	2♊	19♋
9	17♋	13♌	3♊	20♋
10	18♋	14♌	4♊	20♋
11	19♋	15♌	5♊	21♋
12	20♋	16♌	6♊	22♋
13	21♋	17♌	7♊	22♋
14	22♋	18♌	9♊	23♋
15	23♋	19♌	10♊	24♋
16	24♋	20♌	11♊	24♋
17	25♋	21♌	12♊	25♋
18	26♋	22♌	13♊	25♋
19	26♋	22♌	14♊	26♋
20	27♋	23♌	15♊	27♋
21	28♋	23♌	16♊	27♋
22	29♋	24♌	17♊	28♋
23	0♌	24♌	19♊	29♋
24	1♌	25♌	20♊	29♋
25	2♌	25♌	21♊	0♌
26	3♌	25♌	22♊	1♌
27	4♌	25♌	23♊	1♌
28	5♌	25♌	24♊	2♌
29	6♌	25♌	25♊	3♌
30	7♌	25♌	26♊	3♌
31	8♌	25♌	28♊	4♌

August

Day	☉	☿	♀	♂
1	9♌	25♌	29♊	5♌
2	10♌	24♌	0♋	5♌
3	11♌	24♌	1♋	6♌
4	12♌	23♌	2♋	6♌
5	13♌	23♌	3♋	7♌
6	14♌	22♌	4♋	8♌
7	15♌	21♌	6♋	8♌
8	16♌	20♌	7♋	9♌
9	17♌	20♌	8♋	10♌
10	18♌	19♌	9♋	10♌
11	18♌	18♌	10♋	11♌
12	19♌	17♌	11♋	12♌
13	20♌	16♌	12♋	12♌
14	21♌	16♌	14♋	13♌
15	22♌	15♌	15♋	14♌
16	23♌	15♌	16♋	14♌
17	24♌	14♌	17♋	15♌
18	25♌	14♌	18♋	15♌
19	26♌	13♌	19♋	16♌
20	27♌	13♌	21♋	17♌
21	28♌	13♌	22♋	17♌
22	29♌	13♌	23♋	18♌
23	0♍	14♌	24♋	19♌
24	1♍	14♌	25♋	19♌
25	2♍	14♌	27♋	20♌
26	3♍	15♌	28♋	21♌
27	4♍	16♌	29♋	21♌
28	5♍	17♌	0♌	22♌
29	6♍	18♌	1♌	22♌
30	7♍	19♌	2♌	23♌
31	8♍	20♌	4♌	24♌

September

Day	☉	☿	♀	♂
1	9♍	21♌	5♌	24♌
2	10♍	23♌	6♌	25♌
3	11♍	24♌	7♌	26♌
4	12♍	26♌	8♌	26♌
5	13♍	27♌	10♌	27♌
6	14♍	29♌	11♌	28♌
7	15♍	1♍	12♌	28♌
8	15♍	2♍	13♌	29♌
9	16♍	4♍	14♌	29♌
10	17♍	6♍	16♌	0♍
11	18♍	8♍	17♌	1♍
12	19♍	10♍	18♌	1♍
13	20♍	12♍	19♌	2♍
14	21♍	14♍	20♌	3♍
15	22♍	16♍	22♌	3♍
16	23♍	17♍	23♌	4♍
17	24♍	19♍	24♌	5♍
18	25♍	21♍	25♌	5♍
19	26♍	23♍	26♌	6♍
20	27♍	25♍	28♌	6♍
21	28♍	27♍	29♌	7♍
22	29♍	29♍	0♍	8♍
23	0♎	0♎	1♍	8♍
24	1♎	2♎	3♍	9♍
25	2♎	4♎	4♍	10♍
26	3♎	6♎	5♍	10♍
27	4♎	8♎	6♍	11♍
28	5♎	9♎	7♍	11♍
29	6♎	11♎	9♍	12♍
30	7♎	13♎	10♍	13♍

October

Day	☉	☿	♀	♂
1	8♎	14♎	11♍	13♍
2	9♎	16♎	12♍	14♍
3	10♎	18♎	14♍	15♍
4	11♎	19♎	15♍	15♍
5	12♎	21♎	16♍	16♍
6	13♎	23♎	17♍	17♍
7	14♎	24♎	18♍	17♍
8	15♎	26♎	20♍	18♍
9	16♎	28♎	21♍	18♍
10	17♎	29♎	22♍	19♍
11	18♎	1♏	23♍	20♍
12	19♎	2♏	25♍	20♍
13	20♎	4♏	26♍	21♍
14	21♎	5♏	27♍	22♍
15	22♎	7♏	28♍	22♍
16	23♎	8♏	0♎	23♍
17	24♎	10♏	1♎	23♍
18	25♎	11♏	2♎	24♍
19	26♎	13♏	3♎	25♍
20	27♎	14♏	5♎	25♍
21	28♎	16♏	6♎	26♍
22	29♎	17♏	7♎	27♍
23	0♏	19♏	8♎	27♍
24	1♏	20♏	10♎	28♍
25	2♏	21♏	11♎	28♍
26	3♏	23♏	12♎	29♍
27	4♏	24♏	13♎	0♎
28	5♏	25♏	14♎	0♎
29	6♏	27♏	16♎	1♎
30	7♏	28♏	17♎	2♎
31	8♏	29♏	18♎	2♎

November

Day	☉	☿	♀	♂
1	9♏	1♐	19♎	3♎
2	10♏	2♐	21♎	3♎
3	11♏	3♐	22♎	4♎
4	12♏	4♐	23♎	5♎
5	13♏	5♐	24♎	5♎
6	14♏	7♐	26♎	6♎
7	15♏	8♐	27♎	7♎
8	16♏	9♐	28♎	7♎
9	17♏	10♐	29♎	8♎
10	18♏	11♐	1♏	8♎
11	19♏	12♐	2♏	9♎
12	20♏	12♐	3♏	10♎
13	21♏	13♐	4♏	10♎
14	22♏	14♐	6♏	11♎
15	23♏	14♐	7♏	12♎
16	24♏	15♐	8♏	12♎
17	25♏	15♐	9♏	13♎
18	26♏	15♐	11♏	13♎
19	27♏	15♐	12♏	14♎
20	28♏	15♐	13♏	15♎
21	29♏	14♐	15♏	15♎
22	0♐	14♐	16♏	16♎
23	1♐	13♐	17♏	17♎
24	2♐	12♐	18♏	17♎
25	3♐	11♐	20♏	18♎
26	4♐	10♐	21♏	18♎
27	5♐	9♐	22♏	19♎
28	6♐	8♐	23♏	20♎
29	7♐	6♐	25♏	20♎
30	8♐	5♐	26♏	21♎

December

Day	☉	☿	♀	♂
1	9♐	4♐	27♏	22♎
2	10♐	2♐	28♏	22♎
3	11♐	1♐	0♐	23♎
4	12♐	0♐	1♐	23♎
5	13♐	0♐	2♐	24♎
6	14♐	29♏	3♐	25♎
7	15♐	29♏	5♐	25♎
8	16♐	29♏	6♐	26♎
9	17♐	29♏	7♐	27♎
10	18♐	29♏	8♐	27♎
11	19♐	29♏	10♐	28♎
12	20♐	0♐	11♐	28♎
13	21♐	0♐	12♐	29♎
14	22♐	1♐	13♐	0♏
15	23♐	2♐	15♐	0♏
16	24♐	3♐	16♐	1♏
17	25♐	4♐	17♐	1♏
18	26♐	5♐	18♐	2♏
19	27♐	6♐	20♐	3♏
20	28♐	7♐	21♐	3♏
21	29♐	8♐	22♐	4♏
22	0♑	10♐	23♐	5♏
23	1♑	11♐	25♐	5♏
24	2♑	12♐	26♐	6♏
25	3♑	13♐	27♐	6♏
26	4♑	15♐	29♐	7♏
27	5♑	16♐	0♑	8♏
28	6♑	18♐	1♑	8♏
29	7♑	19♐	2♑	9♏
30	8♑	20♐	4♑	9♏
31	9♑	22♐	5♑	10♏

Planetary Positions

♌ = Leo ♍ = Virgo ♎ = Libra ♏ = Scorpio ♐ = Sagittarius ♑ = Capricorn ♒ = Aquarius ♓ = Pisces

1986

January

Day	☉	☿	♀	♂
1	10♑	23♐	6♑	11♏
2	11♑	25♐	7♑	11♏
3	13♑	26♐	9♑	12♏
4	14♑	28♐	10♑	13♏
5	15♑	29♐	11♑	13♏
6	16♑	1♑	12♑	14♏
7	17♑	2♑	14♑	14♏
8	18♑	4♑	15♑	15♏
9	19♑	5♑	16♑	16♏
10	20♑	7♑	17♑	16♏
11	21♑	8♑	19♑	17♏
12	22♑	10♑	20♑	17♏
13	23♑	11♑	21♑	18♏
14	24♑	13♑	22♑	19♏
15	25♑	14♑	24♑	19♏
16	26♑	16♑	25♑	20♏
17	27♑	17♑	26♑	20♏
18	28♑	19♑	27♑	21♏
19	29♑	21♑	29♑	22♏
20	0♒	22♑	0♒	22♏
21	1♒	24♑	1♒	23♏
22	2♒	25♑	2♒	23♏
23	3♒	27♑	4♒	24♏
24	4♒	29♑	5♒	25♏
25	5♒	0♒	6♒	25♏
26	6♒	2♒	8♒	26♏
27	7♒	4♒	9♒	26♏
28	8♒	5♒	10♒	27♏
29	9♒	7♒	11♒	28♏
30	10♒	9♒	13♒	28♏
31	11♒	10♒	14♒	29♏

April

Day	☉	☿	♀	♂
1	11♈	18♓	29♈	2♑
2	12♈	18♓	0♉	3♑
3	13♈	19♓	1♉	3♑
4	14♈	19♓	2♉	4♑
5	15♈	19♓	4♉	4♑
6	16♈	20♓	5♉	4♑
7	17♈	21♓	6♉	5♑
8	18♈	21♓	7♉	5♑
9	19♈	22♓	8♉	6♑
10	20♈	23♓	10♉	6♑
11	21♈	24♓	11♉	7♑
12	22♈	24♓	12♉	7♑
13	23♈	25♓	13♉	8♑
14	24♈	26♓	15♉	8♑
15	25♈	27♓	16♉	9♑
16	26♈	29♓	17♉	9♑
17	27♈	0♈	18♉	10♑
18	28♈	1♈	20♉	10♑
19	29♈	2♈	21♉	10♑
20	0♉	3♈	22♉	11♑
21	1♉	5♈	23♉	11♑
22	2♉	6♈	24♉	12♑
23	3♉	7♈	26♉	12♑
24	4♉	9♈	27♉	12♑
25	5♉	10♈	28♉	13♑
26	6♉	11♈	29♉	13♑
27	7♉	13♈	0♊	14♑
28	8♉	14♈	2♊	14♑
29	9♉	16♈	3♊	14♑
30	10♉	18♈	4♊	15♑

July

Day	☉	☿	♀	♂
1	9♋	4♌	18♌	20♑
2	10♋	4♌	19♌	20♑
3	11♋	5♌	20♌	20♑
4	12♋	5♌	21♌	19♑
5	13♋	6♌	23♌	19♑
6	14♋	6♌	24♌	19♑
7	15♋	6♌	25♌	19♑
8	16♋	6♌	26♌	18♑
9	17♋	6♌	27♌	18♑
10	18♋	6♌	28♌	18♑
11	19♋	6♌	29♌	17♑
12	20♋	6♌	1♍	17♑
13	21♋	6♌	2♍	17♑
14	21♋	6♌	3♍	17♑
15	22♋	5♌	4♍	16♑
16	23♋	5♌	5♍	16♑
17	24♋	4♌	6♍	16♑
18	25♋	4♌	7♍	15♑
19	26♋	3♌	8♍	15♑
20	27♋	3♌	10♍	15♑
21	28♋	2♌	11♍	15♑
22	29♋	1♌	12♍	14♑
23	0♌	0♌	13♍	14♑
24	1♌	0♌	14♍	14♑
25	2♌	29♋	15♍	14♑
26	3♌	28♋	16♍	13♑
27	4♌	28♋	17♍	13♑
28	5♌	27♋	18♍	13♑
29	6♌	27♋	20♍	13♑
30	7♌	26♋	21♍	13♑
31	8♌	26♋	22♍	12♑

October

Day	☉	☿	♀	♂
1	8♎	26♎	17♏	26♑
2	9♎	27♎	17♏	26♑
3	10♎	29♎	18♏	27♑
4	11♎	0♏	18♏	27♑
5	12♎	2♏	18♏	28♑
6	13♎	3♏	19♏	28♑
7	14♎	5♏	19♏	29♑
8	15♎	6♏	19♏	0♒
9	16♎	7♏	20♏	0♒
10	17♎	9♏	20♏	1♒
11	18♎	10♏	20♏	1♒
12	19♎	11♏	20♏	2♒
13	20♎	13♏	20♏	2♒
14	21♎	14♏	20♏	3♒
15	22♎	15♏	20♏	3♒
16	23♎	16♏	20♏	4♒
17	24♎	17♏	20♏	5♒
18	25♎	19♏	20♏	5♒
19	26♎	20♏	20♏	6♒
20	27♎	21♏	20♏	6♒
21	28♎	22♏	20♏	7♒
22	28♎	23♏	20♏	8♒
23	29♎	24♏	19♏	8♒
24	0♏	25♏	19♏	9♒
25	1♏	25♏	19♏	9♒
26	2♏	26♏	18♏	10♒
27	3♏	27♏	18♏	11♒
28	4♏	28♏	17♏	11♒
29	5♏	28♏	17♏	12♒
30	6♏	29♏	16♏	12♒
31	7♏	29♏	16♏	13♒

February

Day	☉	☿	♀	♂
1	12♒	12♒	15♒	29♏
2	13♒	14♒	16♒	0♐
3	14♒	16♒	18♒	1♐
4	15♒	17♒	19♒	1♐
5	16♒	19♒	20♒	2♐
6	17♒	21♒	21♒	2♐
7	18♒	23♒	23♒	3♐
8	19♒	25♒	24♒	3♐
9	20♒	26♒	25♒	4♐
10	21♒	28♒	26♒	5♐
11	22♒	0♓	28♒	5♐
12	23♒	2♓	29♒	6♐
13	24♒	4♓	0♓	6♐
14	25♒	5♓	1♓	7♐
15	26♒	7♓	3♓	8♐
16	27♒	9♓	4♓	8♐
17	28♒	11♓	5♓	9♐
18	29♒	13♓	6♓	9♐
19	0♓	14♓	8♓	10♐
20	1♓	16♓	9♓	10♐
21	2♓	18♓	10♓	11♐
22	3♓	19♓	11♓	12♐
23	4♓	21♓	13♓	12♐
24	5♓	22♓	14♓	13♐
25	6♓	24♓	15♓	13♐
26	7♓	25♓	16♓	14♐
27	8♓	26♓	18♓	14♐
28	9♓	27♓	19♓	15♐

May

Day	☉	☿	♀	♂
1	11♉	19♈	5♊	15♑
2	12♉	21♈	7♊	16♑
3	12♉	22♈	8♊	16♑
4	13♉	24♈	9♊	16♑
5	14♉	26♈	10♊	17♑
6	15♉	28♈	11♊	17♑
7	16♉	29♈	13♊	17♑
8	17♉	1♉	14♊	18♑
9	18♉	3♉	15♊	18♑
10	19♉	5♉	16♊	18♑
11	20♉	7♉	18♊	18♑
12	21♉	9♉	19♊	19♑
13	22♉	11♉	20♊	19♑
14	23♉	13♉	21♊	19♑
15	24♉	15♉	22♊	20♑
16	25♉	17♉	24♊	20♑
17	26♉	19♉	25♊	20♑
18	27♉	21♉	26♊	20♑
19	28♉	23♉	27♊	21♑
20	29♉	25♉	28♊	21♑
21	0♊	28♉	0♋	21♑
22	1♊	0♊	1♋	21♑
23	2♊	2♊	2♋	21♑
24	3♊	4♊	3♋	22♑
25	4♊	6♊	4♋	22♑
26	5♊	9♊	6♋	22♑
27	6♊	11♊	7♋	22♑
28	7♊	13♊	8♋	22♑
29	8♊	15♊	9♋	22♑
30	9♊	17♊	10♋	23♑
31	9♊	19♊	12♋	23♑

August

Day	☉	☿	♀	♂
1	9♌	26♋	23♍	12♑
2	10♌	26♋	24♍	12♑
3	11♌	26♋	25♍	12♑
4	12♌	26♋	26♍	12♑
5	12♌	26♋	27♍	12♑
6	13♌	26♋	28♍	12♑
7	14♌	27♋	29♍	12♑
8	15♌	27♋	0♎	12♑
9	16♌	28♋	1♎	11♑
10	17♌	29♋	2♎	11♑
11	18♌	29♋	4♎	11♑
12	19♌	0♌	5♎	11♑
13	20♌	1♌	6♎	11♑
14	21♌	3♌	7♎	11♑
15	22♌	4♌	8♎	11♑
16	23♌	5♌	9♎	12♑
17	24♌	7♌	10♎	12♑
18	25♌	8♌	11♎	12♑
19	26♌	10♌	12♎	12♑
20	27♌	11♌	13♎	12♑
21	28♌	13♌	14♎	12♑
22	29♌	15♌	15♎	12♑
23	0♍	17♌	16♎	12♑
24	1♍	18♌	17♎	12♑
25	2♍	20♌	18♎	13♑
26	3♍	22♌	19♎	13♑
27	4♍	24♌	20♎	13♑
28	5♍	26♌	21♎	13♑
29	6♍	28♌	22♎	13♑
30	7♍	0♍	23♎	14♑
31	8♍	2♍	23♎	14♑

November

Day	☉	☿	♀	♂
1	8♏	29♏	15♏	14♒
2	9♏	29♏	15♏	14♒
3	10♏	29♏	14♏	15♒
4	11♏	29♏	13♏	16♒
5	12♏	29♏	13♏	16♒
6	13♏	28♏	12♏	17♒
7	14♏	27♏	12♏	18♒
8	15♏	26♏	11♏	18♒
9	16♏	25♏	10♏	19♒
10	18♏	24♏	10♏	19♒
11	19♏	23♏	9♏	20♒
12	20♏	22♏	9♏	21♒
13	21♏	20♏	8♏	21♒
14	22♏	19♏	8♏	22♒
15	23♏	18♏	7♏	23♒
16	24♏	17♏	7♏	23♒
17	25♏	16♏	7♏	24♒
18	26♏	15♏	6♏	25♒
19	27♏	14♏	6♏	25♒
20	28♏	14♏	6♏	26♒
21	29♏	13♏	5♏	27♒
22	0♐	13♏	5♏	27♒
23	1♐	13♏	5♏	28♒
24	2♐	13♏	5♏	29♒
25	3♐	14♏	5♏	29♒
26	4♐	14♏	5♏	0♓
27	5♐	15♏	5♏	1♓
28	6♐	16♏	5♏	1♓
29	7♐	17♏	5♏	2♓
30	8♐	18♏	5♏	3♓

March

Day	☉	☿	♀	♂
1	10♓	28♓	20♓	16♐
2	11♓	29♓	21♓	16♐
3	12♓	0♈	23♓	17♐
4	13♓	1♈	24♓	17♐
5	14♓	1♈	25♓	18♐
6	15♓	1♈	26♓	18♐
7	16♓	1♈	28♓	19♐
8	17♓	1♈	29♓	19♐
9	18♓	1♈	0♈	20♐
10	19♓	1♈	1♈	21♐
11	20♓	0♈	3♈	21♐
12	21♓	0♈	4♈	22♐
13	22♓	29♓	5♈	22♐
14	23♓	28♓	6♈	23♐
15	24♓	27♓	8♈	23♐
16	25♓	26♓	9♈	24♐
17	26♓	26♓	10♈	24♐
18	27♓	25♓	11♈	25♐
19	28♓	24♓	13♈	25♐
20	29♓	23♓	14♈	26♐
21	0♈	22♓	15♈	26♐
22	1♈	21♓	16♈	27♐
23	2♈	20♓	17♈	27♐
24	3♈	20♓	19♈	28♐
25	4♈	19♓	20♈	28♐
26	5♈	19♓	21♈	29♐
27	6♈	18♓	22♈	0♑
28	7♈	18♓	24♈	0♑
29	8♈	18♓	25♈	1♑
30	9♈	18♓	26♈	1♑
31	10♈	18♓	27♈	2♑

June

Day	☉	☿	♀	♂
1	10♊	21♊	13♋	23♑
2	11♊	23♊	14♋	23♑
3	12♊	25♊	15♋	23♑
4	13♊	27♊	16♋	23♑
5	14♊	29♊	17♋	23♑
6	15♊	1♋	19♋	23♑
7	16♊	3♋	20♋	23♑
8	17♊	5♋	21♋	23♑
9	18♊	7♋	22♋	23♑
10	19♊	8♋	23♋	23♑
11	20♊	10♋	25♋	23♑
12	21♊	12♋	26♋	23♑
13	22♊	13♋	27♋	23♑
14	23♊	15♋	28♋	23♑
15	24♊	16♋	29♋	23♑
16	25♊	18♋	0♌	23♑
17	26♊	19♋	2♌	23♑
18	27♊	20♋	3♌	23♑
19	28♊	22♋	4♌	22♑
20	29♊	23♋	5♌	22♑
21	0♋	24♋	6♌	22♑
22	0♋	25♋	8♌	22♑
23	1♋	27♋	9♌	22♑
24	2♋	28♋	10♌	22♑
25	3♋	29♋	11♌	21♑
26	4♋	0♌	12♌	21♑
27	5♋	1♌	13♌	21♑
28	6♋	1♌	15♌	21♑
29	7♋	2♌	16♌	21♑
30	8♋	3♌	17♌	20♑

September

Day	☉	☿	♀	♂
1	8♍	4♍	24♎	14♑
2	9♍	6♍	25♎	14♑
3	10♍	8♍	26♎	15♑
4	11♍	10♍	27♎	15♑
5	12♍	12♍	28♎	15♑
6	13♍	14♍	29♎	15♑
7	14♍	16♍	0♏	16♑
8	15♍	18♍	1♏	16♑
9	16♍	19♍	2♏	16♑
10	17♍	21♍	2♏	17♑
11	18♍	23♍	3♏	17♑
12	19♍	25♍	4♏	18♑
13	20♍	27♍	5♏	18♑
14	21♍	28♍	6♏	18♑
15	22♍	0♎	6♏	19♑
16	23♍	2♎	7♏	19♑
17	24♍	4♎	8♏	19♑
18	25♍	5♎	9♏	20♑
19	26♍	7♎	9♏	20♑
20	27♍	9♎	10♏	21♑
21	28♍	10♎	11♏	21♑
22	29♍	12♎	12♏	22♑
23	0♎	14♎	12♏	22♑
24	1♎	15♎	13♏	22♑
25	2♎	17♎	13♏	23♑
26	3♎	18♎	14♏	23♑
27	4♎	20♎	15♏	24♑
28	5♎	21♎	15♏	24♑
29	6♎	23♎	16♏	25♑
30	7♎	24♎	16♏	25♑

December

Day	☉	☿	♀	♂
1	9♐	19♏	5♏	3♓
2	10♐	20♏	6♏	4♓
3	11♐	21♏	6♏	5♓
4	12♐	22♏	6♏	6♓
5	13♐	23♏	6♏	6♓
6	14♐	25♏	7♏	7♓
7	15♐	26♏	7♏	8♓
8	16♐	27♏	8♏	8♓
9	17♐	29♏	8♏	9♓
10	18♐	0♐	9♏	10♓
11	19♐	2♐	9♏	10♓
12	20♐	3♐	10♏	11♓
13	21♐	5♐	10♏	12♓
14	22♐	6♐	11♏	12♓
15	23♐	8♐	11♏	13♓
16	24♐	9♐	12♏	14♓
17	25♐	11♐	13♏	14♓
18	26♐	12♐	13♏	15♓
19	27♐	14♐	14♏	16♓
20	28♐	15♐	15♏	17♓
21	29♐	17♐	15♏	17♓
22	0♑	18♐	16♏	18♓
23	1♑	20♐	17♏	19♓
24	2♑	21♐	18♏	19♓
25	3♑	23♐	18♏	20♓
26	4♑	24♐	19♏	21♓
27	5♑	26♐	20♏	21♓
28	6♑	27♐	21♏	22♓
29	7♑	29♐	22♏	23♓
30	8♑	0♑	23♏	23♓
31	9♑	2♑	23♏	24♓

1987

Your Starway to Love

☉ =Sun ☿ = Mercury ♀ = Venus ♂ = Mars ♈ = Aries ♉ = Taurus ♊ = Gemini ♋ = Cancer

January

Day	☉	☿	♀	♂
1	10♑	4♑	24♏	25♓
2	11♑	5♑	25♏	26♓
3	12♑	7♑	26♏	26♓
4	13♑	8♑	27♏	27♓
5	14♑	10♑	28♏	28♓
6	15♑	11♑	29♏	28♓
7	16♑	13♑	0♐	29♓
8	17♑	15♑	1♐	0♈
9	18♑	16♑	2♐	0♈
10	19♑	18♑	3♐	1♈
11	20♑	19♑	4♐	2♈
12	21♑	21♑	5♐	3♈
13	22♑	23♑	6♐	3♈
14	23♑	24♑	7♐	4♈
15	24♑	26♑	8♐	5♈
16	26♑	28♑	9♐	5♈
17	27♑	29♑	10♐	6♈
18	28♑	1♒	11♐	7♈
19	29♑	3♒	12♐	7♈
20	0♒	5♒	13♐	8♈
21	1♒	6♒	14♐	9♈
22	2♒	8♒	15♐	10♈
23	3♒	10♒	16♐	10♈
24	4♒	11♒	17♐	11♈
25	5♒	13♒	18♐	12♈
26	6♒	15♒	19♐	12♈
27	7♒	17♒	20♐	13♈
28	8♒	18♒	21♐	14♈
29	9♒	20♒	22♐	14♈
30	10♒	22♒	23♐	15♈
31	11♒	23♒	25♐	16♈

April

Day	☉	☿	♀	♂
1	11♈	14♓	4♓	27♉
2	12♈	15♓	5♓	28♉
3	13♈	16♓	7♓	28♉
4	14♈	18♓	8♓	29♉
5	15♈	19♓	9♓	0♊
6	16♈	20♓	10♓	0♊
7	17♈	22♓	11♓	1♊
8	18♈	23♓	13♓	2♊
9	19♈	25♓	14♓	2♊
10	20♈	26♓	15♓	3♊
11	21♈	27♓	16♓	4♊
12	22♈	29♓	17♓	4♊
13	23♈	1♈	19♓	5♊
14	24♈	2♈	20♓	6♊
15	25♈	4♈	21♓	6♊
16	26♈	5♈	22♓	7♊
17	27♈	7♈	23♓	8♊
18	28♈	9♈	25♓	8♊
19	29♈	10♈	26♓	9♊
20	0♉	12♈	27♓	10♊
21	1♉	14♈	28♓	10♊
22	2♉	16♈	29♓	11♊
23	3♉	18♈	1♈	12♊
24	3♉	19♈	2♈	12♊
25	4♉	21♈	3♈	13♊
26	5♉	23♈	4♈	14♊
27	6♉	25♈	5♈	14♊
28	7♉	27♈	7♈	15♊
29	8♉	29♈	8♈	16♊
30	9♉	1♉	9♈	16♊

July

Day	☉	☿	♀	♂
1	9♋	13♋	24♊	26♋
2	10♋	13♋	26♊	27♋
3	11♋	12♋	27♊	28♋
4	12♋	12♋	28♊	28♋
5	13♋	11♋	29♊	29♋
6	14♋	10♋	0♋	0♌
7	15♋	10♋	2♋	0♌
8	16♋	9♋	3♋	1♌
9	16♋	9♋	4♋	2♌
10	17♋	8♋	5♋	2♌
11	18♋	8♋	7♋	3♌
12	19♋	8♋	8♋	4♌
13	20♋	8♋	9♋	4♌
14	21♋	7♋	10♋	5♌
15	22♋	7♋	11♋	5♌
16	23♋	7♋	13♋	6♌
17	24♋	8♋	14♋	7♌
18	25♋	8♋	15♋	7♌
19	26♋	8♋	16♋	8♌
20	27♋	8♋	18♋	9♌
21	28♋	9♋	19♋	9♌
22	29♋	10♋	20♋	10♌
23	0♌	10♋	21♋	11♌
24	1♌	11♋	23♋	11♌
25	2♌	12♋	24♋	12♌
26	3♌	13♋	25♋	12♌
27	4♌	14♋	26♋	13♌
28	5♌	15♋	27♋	14♌
29	6♌	16♋	29♋	14♌
30	7♌	18♋	0♌	15♌
31	7♌	19♋	1♌	16♌

October

Day	☉	☿	♀	♂
1	7♎	3♏	18♎	25♍
2	8♎	4♏	19♎	26♍
3	9♎	5♏	20♎	26♍
4	10♎	6♏	22♎	27♍
5	11♎	7♏	23♎	28♍
6	12♎	8♏	24♎	28♍
7	13♎	9♏	25♎	29♍
8	14♎	10♏	27♎	0♎
9	15♎	10♏	28♎	0♎
10	16♎	11♏	29♎	1♎
11	17♎	12♏	0♏	2♎
12	18♎	12♏	2♏	2♎
13	19♎	13♏	3♏	3♎
14	20♎	13♏	4♏	3♎
15	21♎	13♏	5♏	4♎
16	22♎	13♏	7♏	5♎
17	23♎	13♏	8♏	5♎
18	24♎	13♏	9♏	6♎
19	25♎	13♏	10♏	7♎
20	26♎	12♏	12♏	7♎
21	27♎	12♏	13♏	8♎
22	28♎	11♏	14♏	9♎
23	29♎	10♏	15♏	9♎
24	0♏	9♏	17♏	10♎
25	1♏	8♏	18♏	11♎
26	2♏	7♏	19♏	11♎
27	3♏	6♏	20♏	12♎
28	4♏	5♏	22♏	12♎
29	5♏	3♏	23♏	13♎
30	6♏	2♏	24♏	14♎
31	7♏	1♏	25♏	14♎

February

Day	☉	☿	♀	♂
1	12♒	25♒	26♐	17♈
2	13♒	27♒	27♐	17♈
3	14♒	29♒	28♐	18♈
4	15♒	0♓	29♐	19♈
5	16♒	2♓	0♑	19♈
6	17♒	3♓	1♑	20♈
7	18♒	5♓	2♑	21♈
8	19♒	6♓	3♑	21♈
9	20♒	8♓	5♑	22♈
10	21♒	9♓	6♑	23♈
11	22♒	10♓	7♑	23♈
12	23♒	11♓	8♑	24♈
13	24♒	12♓	9♑	25♈
14	25♒	13♓	10♑	26♈
15	26♒	13♓	11♑	26♈
16	27♒	14♓	12♑	27♈
17	28♒	14♓	14♑	28♈
18	29♒	14♓	15♑	28♈
19	0♓	14♓	16♑	29♈
20	1♓	14♓	17♑	0♉
21	2♓	14♓	18♑	0♉
22	3♓	13♓	19♑	1♉
23	4♓	13♓	21♑	2♉
24	5♓	12♓	22♑	2♉
25	6♓	11♓	23♑	3♉
26	7♓	10♓	24♑	4♉
27	8♓	9♓	25♑	5♉
28	9♓	8♓	26♑	5♉

May

Day	☉	☿	♀	♂
1	10♉	3♉	10♈	17♊
2	11♉	5♉	12♈	18♊
3	12♉	7♉	13♈	18♊
4	13♉	9♉	14♈	19♊
5	14♉	12♉	15♈	20♊
6	15♉	14♉	16♈	20♊
7	16♉	16♉	18♈	21♊
8	17♉	18♉	19♈	22♊
9	18♉	20♉	20♈	22♊
10	19♉	22♉	21♈	23♊
11	20♉	25♉	22♈	24♊
12	21♉	27♉	24♈	24♊
13	22♉	29♉	25♈	25♊
14	23♉	1♊	26♈	25♊
15	24♉	3♊	27♈	26♊
16	25♉	5♊	28♈	27♊
17	26♉	7♊	0♉	27♊
18	27♉	9♊	1♉	28♊
19	28♉	11♊	2♉	29♊
20	29♉	13♊	3♉	29♊
21	0♊	15♊	4♉	0♋
22	1♊	17♊	6♉	1♋
23	2♊	19♊	7♉	1♋
24	3♊	21♊	8♉	2♋
25	3♊	22♊	9♉	3♋
26	4♊	24♊	11♉	3♋
27	5♊	26♊	12♉	4♋
28	6♊	27♊	13♉	5♋
29	7♊	29♊	14♉	5♋
30	8♊	0♋	15♉	6♋
31	9♊	1♋	17♉	7♋

August

Day	☉	☿	♀	♂
1	8♌	20♋	2♌	16♌
2	9♌	22♋	4♌	17♌
3	10♌	24♋	5♌	18♌
4	11♌	25♋	6♌	18♌
5	12♌	27♋	7♌	19♌
6	13♌	29♋	9♌	19♌
7	14♌	1♌	10♌	20♌
8	15♌	2♌	11♌	21♌
9	16♌	4♌	12♌	21♌
10	17♌	6♌	13♌	22♌
11	18♌	8♌	15♌	23♌
12	19♌	10♌	16♌	23♌
13	20♌	12♌	17♌	24♌
14	21♌	14♌	18♌	25♌
15	22♌	16♌	20♌	25♌
16	23♌	19♌	21♌	26♌
17	24♌	21♌	22♌	26♌
18	25♌	23♌	23♌	27♌
19	26♌	25♌	25♌	28♌
20	27♌	27♌	26♌	28♌
21	28♌	29♌	27♌	29♌
22	29♌	1♍	28♌	0♍
23	0♍	3♍	0♍	0♍
24	1♍	5♍	1♍	1♍
25	1♍	6♍	2♍	2♍
26	2♍	8♍	3♍	2♍
27	3♍	10♍	4♍	3♍
28	4♍	12♍	6♍	3♍
29	5♍	14♍	7♍	4♍
30	6♍	16♍	8♍	5♍
31	7♍	17♍	9♍	5♍

November

Day	☉	☿	♀	♂
1	8♏	0♏	27♏	15♎
2	9♏	29♎	28♏	16♎
3	10♏	28♎	29♏	16♎
4	11♏	28♎	0♐	17♎
5	12♏	28♎	2♐	18♎
6	13♏	27♎	3♐	18♎
7	14♏	27♎	4♐	19♎
8	15♏	28♎	5♐	20♎
9	16♏	28♎	7♐	20♎
10	17♏	29♎	8♐	21♎
11	18♏	29♎	9♐	22♎
12	19♏	0♏	10♐	22♎
13	20♏	1♏	12♐	23♎
14	21♏	2♏	13♐	24♎
15	22♏	3♏	14♐	24♎
16	23♏	5♏	15♐	25♎
17	24♏	6♏	16♐	25♎
18	25♏	7♏	18♐	26♎
19	26♏	8♏	19♐	27♎
20	27♏	10♏	20♐	27♎
21	28♏	11♏	21♐	28♎
22	29♏	13♏	23♐	29♎
23	0♐	14♏	24♐	29♎
24	1♐	16♏	25♐	0♏
25	2♐	17♏	26♐	1♏
26	3♐	19♏	28♐	1♏
27	4♐	20♏	29♐	2♏
28	5♐	22♏	0♑	3♏
29	6♐	23♏	1♑	3♏
30	7♐	25♏	3♑	4♏

March

Day	☉	☿	♀	♂
1	10♓	7♓	28♑	6♉
2	11♓	6♓	29♑	7♉
3	12♓	5♓	0♒	7♉
4	13♓	4♓	1♒	8♉
5	14♓	3♓	2♒	9♉
6	15♓	2♓	3♒	9♉
7	16♓	2♓	5♒	10♉
8	17♓	1♓	6♒	11♉
9	18♓	1♓	7♒	11♉
10	19♓	0♓	8♒	12♉
11	20♓	0♓	9♒	13♉
12	21♓	0♓	10♒	13♉
13	22♓	0♓	12♒	14♉
14	23♓	0♓	13♒	15♉
15	24♓	0♓	14♒	15♉
16	25♓	0♓	15♒	16♉
17	26♓	1♓	16♒	17♉
18	27♓	1♓	18♒	18♉
19	28♓	2♓	19♒	18♉
20	29♓	2♓	20♒	19♉
21	0♈	3♓	21♒	20♉
22	1♈	4♓	22♒	20♉
23	2♈	5♓	23♒	21♉
24	3♈	5♓	25♒	22♉
25	4♈	6♓	26♒	22♉
26	5♈	7♓	27♒	23♉
27	6♈	8♓	28♒	24♉
28	7♈	9♓	29♒	24♉
29	8♈	10♓	1♓	25♉
30	9♈	11♓	2♓	26♉
31	10♈	13♓	3♓	26♉

June

Day	☉	☿	♀	♂
1	10♊	3♋	18♉	7♋
2	11♊	4♋	19♉	8♋
3	12♊	5♋	20♉	8♋
4	13♊	7♋	21♉	9♋
5	14♊	8♋	23♉	10♋
6	15♊	9♋	24♉	10♋
7	16♊	10♋	25♉	11♋
8	17♊	11♋	26♉	12♋
9	18♊	12♋	28♉	12♋
10	19♊	12♋	29♉	13♋
11	20♊	13♋	0♊	14♋
12	21♊	14♋	1♊	14♋
13	22♊	14♋	2♊	15♋
14	23♊	15♋	4♊	16♋
15	24♊	15♋	5♊	16♋
16	25♊	16♋	6♊	17♋
17	25♊	16♋	7♊	18♋
18	26♊	16♋	9♊	18♋
19	27♊	17♋	10♊	19♋
20	28♊	17♋	11♊	19♋
21	29♊	17♋	12♊	20♋
22	0♋	17♋	13♊	21♋
23	1♋	17♋	15♊	21♋
24	2♋	16♋	16♊	22♋
25	3♋	16♋	17♊	23♋
26	4♋	16♋	18♊	23♋
27	5♋	15♋	19♊	24♋
28	6♋	15♋	21♊	25♋
29	7♋	15♋	22♊	25♋
30	8♋	14♋	23♊	26♋

September

Day	☉	☿	♀	♂
1	8♍	19♍	11♍	6♍
2	9♍	21♍	12♍	7♍
3	10♍	23♍	13♍	7♍
4	11♍	24♍	14♍	8♍
5	12♍	26♍	16♍	9♍
6	13♍	28♍	17♍	9♍
7	14♍	29♍	18♍	10♍
8	15♍	1♎	19♍	10♍
9	16♍	3♎	21♍	11♍
10	17♍	4♎	22♍	12♍
11	18♍	6♎	23♍	12♍
12	19♍	7♎	24♍	13♍
13	20♍	9♎	26♍	14♍
14	21♍	10♎	27♍	14♍
15	22♍	12♎	28♍	15♍
16	23♍	13♎	29♍	16♍
17	24♍	15♎	1♎	16♍
18	25♍	16♎	2♎	17♍
19	26♍	18♎	3♎	17♍
20	27♍	19♎	4♎	18♍
21	28♍	20♎	6♎	19♍
22	29♍	22♎	7♎	19♍
23	0♎	23♎	8♎	20♍
24	1♎	24♎	9♎	21♍
25	2♎	26♎	11♎	21♍
26	3♎	27♎	12♎	22♍
27	4♎	28♎	13♎	23♍
28	5♎	29♎	14♎	23♍
29	6♎	1♏	15♎	24♍
30	7♎	2♏	17♎	24♍

December

Day	☉	☿	♀	♂
1	8♐	26♏	4♑	5♏
2	9♐	28♏	5♑	5♏
3	10♐	29♏	6♑	6♏
4	11♐	1♐	8♑	7♏
5	13♐	3♐	9♑	7♏
6	14♐	4♐	10♑	8♏
7	15♐	6♐	11♑	9♏
8	16♐	7♐	13♑	9♏
9	17♐	9♐	14♑	10♏
10	18♐	10♐	15♑	11♏
11	19♐	12♐	16♑	11♏
12	20♐	13♐	18♑	12♏
13	21♐	15♐	19♑	13♏
14	22♐	17♐	20♑	13♏
15	23♐	18♐	21♑	14♏
16	24♐	20♐	22♑	14♏
17	25♐	21♐	24♑	15♏
18	26♐	23♐	25♑	16♏
19	27♐	24♐	26♑	16♏
20	28♐	26♐	27♑	17♏
21	29♐	28♐	29♑	18♏
22	0♑	29♐	0♒	18♏
23	1♑	1♑	1♒	19♏
24	2♑	2♑	2♒	20♏
25	3♑	4♑	4♒	20♏
26	4♑	6♑	5♒	21♏
27	5♑	7♑	6♒	22♏
28	6♑	9♑	7♒	22♏
29	7♑	10♑	9♒	23♏
30	8♑	12♑	10♒	24♏
31	9♑	14♑	11♒	24♏

♌ = Leo ♍ = Virgo ♎ = Libra ♏ = Scorpio ♐ = Sagittarius ♑ = Capricorn ♒ = Aquarius ♓ = Pisces

January

Day	☉	☿	♀	♂
1	10♑	15♑	12♒	25♏
2	11♑	17♑	13♒	26♏
3	12♑	18♑	15♒	26♏
4	13♑	20♑	16♒	27♏
5	14♑	22♑	17♒	28♏
6	15♑	23♑	18♒	28♏
7	16♑	25♑	20♒	29♏
8	17♑	27♑	21♒	0♐
9	18♑	28♑	22♒	0♐
10	19♑	0♒	23♒	1♐
11	20♑	2♒	25♒	2♐
12	21♑	3♒	26♒	2♐
13	22♑	5♒	27♒	3♐
14	23♑	7♒	28♒	4♐
15	24♑	8♒	29♒	4♐
16	25♑	10♒	1♓	5♐
17	26♑	11♒	2♓	6♐
18	27♑	13♒	3♓	6♐
19	28♑	15♒	4♓	7♐
20	29♑	16♒	6♓	8♐
21	0♒	18♒	7♓	8♐
22	1♒	19♒	8♓	9♐
23	2♒	20♒	9♓	10♐
24	3♒	22♒	10♓	10♐
25	4♒	23♒	12♓	11♐
26	5♒	24♒	13♓	12♐
27	6♒	25♒	14♓	12♐
28	7♒	26♒	15♓	13♐
29	9♒	27♒	16♓	14♐
30	10♒	27♒	18♓	14♐
31	11♒	28♒	19♓	15♐

February

Day	☉	☿	♀	♂
1	12♒	28♒	20♓	16♐
2	13♒	28♒	21♓	16♐
3	14♒	28♒	22♓	17♐
4	15♒	28♒	24♓	18♐
5	16♒	27♒	25♓	18♐
6	17♒	27♒	26♓	19♐
7	18♒	26♒	27♓	20♐
8	19♒	25♒	28♓	20♐
9	20♒	24♒	0♈	21♐
10	21♒	23♒	1♈	22♐
11	22♒	22♒	2♈	22♐
12	23♒	20♒	3♈	23♐
13	24♒	19♒	4♈	24♐
14	25♒	18♒	6♈	24♐
15	26♒	17♒	7♈	25♐
16	27♒	16♒	8♈	26♐
17	28♒	15♒	9♈	26♐
18	29♒	15♒	10♈	27♐
19	0♓	14♒	11♈	28♐
20	1♓	13♒	13♈	29♐
21	2♓	13♒	14♈	29♐
22	3♓	13♒	15♈	0♑
23	4♓	13♒	16♈	1♑
24	5♓	13♒	17♈	1♑
25	6♓	13♒	18♈	2♑
26	7♓	13♒	20♈	3♑
27	8♓	13♒	21♈	3♑
28	9♓	14♒	22♈	4♑
29	10♓	14♒	23♈	5♑

March

Day	☉	☿	♀	♂
1	11♓	15♒	24♈	5♑
2	12♓	15♒	25♈	6♑
3	13♓	16♒	26♈	7♑
4	14♓	17♒	27♈	7♑
5	15♓	18♒	29♈	8♑
6	16♓	19♒	0♉	9♑
7	17♓	20♒	1♉	9♑
8	18♓	20♒	2♉	10♑
9	19♓	22♒	3♉	10♑
10	20♓	23♒	4♉	11♑
11	21♓	24♒	5♉	12♑
12	22♓	25♒	6♉	13♑
13	23♓	26♒	8♉	13♑
14	24♓	27♒	9♉	14♑
15	25♓	28♒	10♉	15♑
16	26♓	0♓	11♉	15♑
17	27♓	1♓	12♉	16♑
18	28♓	2♓	13♉	17♑
19	29♓	4♓	14♉	17♑
20	0♈	5♓	15♉	18♑
21	1♈	7♓	16♉	19♑
22	2♈	8♓	17♉	19♑
23	3♈	9♓	18♉	20♑
24	4♈	11♓	19♉	21♑
25	5♈	12♓	20♉	21♑
26	6♈	14♓	21♉	22♑
27	7♈	15♓	22♉	23♑
28	8♈	17♓	23♉	23♑
29	9♈	19♓	25♉	24♑
30	10♈	20♓	26♉	25♑
31	11♈	22♓	27♉	25♑

April

Day	☉	☿	♀	♂
1	12♈	24♓	28♉	26♑
2	13♈	25♓	29♉	27♑
3	14♈	27♓	0♊	28♑
4	15♈	29♓	0♊	28♑
5	16♈	1♈	1♊	29♑
6	17♈	2♈	2♊	0♒
7	18♈	4♈	3♊	0♒
8	19♈	6♈	4♊	1♒
9	20♈	8♈	5♊	2♒
10	21♈	10♈	6♊	2♒
11	22♈	12♈	7♊	3♒
12	23♈	14♈	8♊	4♒
13	23♈	16♈	9♊	4♒
14	24♈	17♈	10♊	5♒
15	25♈	20♈	11♊	6♒
16	26♈	22♈	12♊	6♒
17	27♈	24♈	12♊	7♒
18	28♈	26♈	13♊	8♒
19	29♈	28♈	14♊	8♒
20	0♉	0♉	15♊	9♒
21	1♉	2♉	16♊	10♒
22	2♉	4♉	17♊	10♒
23	3♉	6♉	17♊	11♒
24	4♉	8♉	18♊	12♒
25	5♉	11♉	19♊	12♒
26	6♉	13♉	20♊	13♒
27	7♉	15♉	20♊	14♒
28	8♉	17♉	21♊	14♒
29	9♉	19♉	22♊	15♒
30	10♉	21♉	22♊	16♒

May

Day	☉	☿	♀	♂
1	11♉	23♉	23♊	16♒
2	12♉	25♉	24♊	17♒
3	13♉	27♉	24♊	18♒
4	14♉	29♉	25♊	18♒
5	15♉	1♊	25♊	19♒
6	16♉	3♊	26♊	20♒
7	17♉	4♊	26♊	20♒
8	18♉	6♊	27♊	21♒
9	19♉	8♊	27♊	22♒
10	20♉	9♊	28♊	22♒
11	21♉	11♊	28♊	23♒
12	22♉	12♊	28♊	23♒
13	23♉	14♊	29♊	24♒
14	24♉	15♊	29♊	25♒
15	25♉	16♊	29♊	25♒
16	26♉	17♊	0♋	26♒
17	27♉	18♊	0♋	27♒
18	27♉	20♊	0♋	27♒
19	28♉	21♊	0♋	28♒
20	29♉	21♊	0♋	29♒
21	0♊	22♊	0♋	29♒
22	1♊	23♊	0♋	0♓
23	2♊	24♊	0♋	1♓
24	3♊	24♊	0♋	1♓
25	4♊	25♊	0♋	2♓
26	5♊	26♊	0♋	2♓
27	6♊	26♊	0♋	3♓
28	7♊	26♊	0♋	4♓
29	8♊	26♊	0♋	4♓
30	9♊	27♊	29♊	5♓
31	10♊	27♊	29♊	6♓

June

Day	☉	☿	♀	♂
1	11♊	27♊	29♊	6♓
2	12♊	27♊	28♊	7♓
3	13♊	27♊	28♊	7♓
4	14♊	26♊	27♊	8♓
5	15♊	26♊	27♊	9♓
6	16♊	26♊	26♊	9♓
7	17♊	25♊	26♊	10♓
8	18♊	25♊	25♊	11♓
9	19♊	25♊	25♊	11♓
10	20♊	24♊	24♊	12♓
11	20♊	23♊	23♊	12♓
12	21♊	23♊	23♊	13♓
13	22♊	22♊	22♊	14♓
14	23♊	22♊	21♊	14♓
15	24♊	21♊	21♊	15♓
16	25♊	21♊	20♊	15♓
17	26♊	20♊	20♊	16♓
18	27♊	20♊	19♊	16♓
19	28♊	19♊	18♊	17♓
20	29♊	19♊	18♊	18♓
21	0♋	19♊	17♊	18♓
22	1♋	18♊	17♊	19♓
23	2♋	18♊	16♊	19♓
24	3♋	18♊	16♊	20♓
25	4♋	18♊	16♊	20♓
26	5♋	18♊	15♊	21♓
27	6♋	18♊	15♊	22♓
28	7♋	19♊	15♊	22♓
29	8♋	19♊	14♊	23♓
30	9♋	19♊	14♊	23♓

July

Day	☉	☿	♀	♂
1	10♋	20♊	14♊	24♓
2	11♋	20♊	14♊	24♓
3	11♋	21♊	14♊	25♓
4	12♋	22♊	14♊	25♓
5	13♋	22♊	14♊	26♓
6	14♋	23♊	14♊	26♓
7	15♋	24♊	14♊	27♓
8	16♋	25♊	14♊	27♓
9	17♋	26♊	14♊	28♓
10	18♋	27♊	15♊	28♓
11	19♋	29♊	15♊	29♓
12	20♋	0♋	15♊	29♓
13	21♋	1♋	15♊	0♈
14	22♋	3♋	16♊	0♈
15	23♋	4♋	16♊	1♈
16	24♋	6♋	16♊	1♈
17	25♋	7♋	17♊	2♈
18	26♋	9♋	17♊	2♈
19	27♋	11♋	18♊	2♈
20	28♋	13♋	18♊	3♈
21	29♋	15♋	19♊	3♈
22	0♌	16♋	19♊	4♈
23	1♌	18♋	20♊	4♈
24	2♌	20♋	20♊	4♈
25	2♌	22♋	21♊	5♈
26	3♌	24♋	21♊	5♈
27	4♌	26♋	22♊	6♈
28	5♌	29♋	23♊	6♈
29	6♌	1♌	23♊	6♈
30	7♌	3♌	24♊	7♈
31	8♌	5♌	25♊	7♈

August

Day	☉	☿	♀	♂
1	9♌	7♌	26♊	7♈
2	10♌	9♌	26♊	8♈
3	11♌	11♌	27♊	8♈
4	12♌	13♌	28♊	8♈
5	13♌	15♌	29♊	8♈
6	14♌	17♌	29♊	9♈
7	15♌	19♌	0♋	9♈
8	16♌	21♌	1♋	9♈
9	17♌	23♌	2♋	9♈
10	18♌	25♌	3♋	10♈
11	19♌	27♌	4♋	10♈
12	20♌	29♌	4♋	10♈
13	21♌	1♍	5♋	10♈
14	22♌	3♍	6♋	10♈
15	23♌	5♍	7♋	11♈
16	24♌	6♍	8♋	11♈
17	25♌	8♍	9♋	11♈
18	25♌	10♍	10♋	11♈
19	26♌	12♍	11♋	11♈
20	27♌	13♍	12♋	11♈
21	28♌	15♍	13♋	11♈
22	29♌	17♍	14♋	11♈
23	0♍	18♍	15♋	11♈
24	1♍	20♍	15♋	11♈
25	2♍	21♍	16♋	11♈
26	3♍	23♍	17♋	11♈
27	4♍	25♍	18♋	11♈
28	5♍	26♍	19♋	11♈
29	6♍	28♍	20♋	11♈
30	7♍	29♍	21♋	11♈
31	8♍	1♎	22♋	11♈

September

Day	☉	☿	♀	♂
1	9♍	2♎	23♋	11♈
2	10♍	3♎	24♋	11♈
3	11♍	5♎	26♋	11♈
4	12♍	6♎	27♋	11♈
5	13♍	7♎	28♋	11♈
6	14♍	9♎	29♋	11♈
7	15♍	10♎	0♌	11♈
8	16♍	11♎	1♌	10♈
9	17♍	12♎	2♌	10♈
10	18♍	14♎	3♌	10♈
11	19♍	15♎	4♌	10♈
12	20♍	16♎	5♌	10♈
13	21♍	17♎	6♌	9♈
14	22♍	18♎	7♌	9♈
15	23♍	19♎	8♌	9♈
16	24♍	20♎	9♌	9♈
17	25♍	21♎	10♌	8♈
18	26♍	22♎	12♌	8♈
19	26♍	23♎	13♌	8♈
20	27♍	23♎	14♌	8♈
21	28♍	24♎	15♌	7♈
22	29♍	25♎	16♌	7♈
23	0♎	25♎	17♌	7♈
24	1♎	26♎	18♌	6♈
25	2♎	26♎	19♌	6♈
26	3♎	27♎	20♌	6♈
27	4♎	27♎	22♌	6♈
28	5♎	27♎	23♌	5♈
29	6♎	27♎	24♌	5♈
30	7♎	27♎	25♌	5♈

October

Day	☉	☿	♀	♂
1	8♎	27♎	26♌	4♈
2	9♎	26♎	27♌	4♈
3	10♎	26♎	28♌	4♈
4	11♎	25♎	0♍	3♈
5	12♎	25♎	1♍	3♈
6	13♎	24♎	2♍	3♈
7	14♎	23♎	3♍	3♈
8	15♎	22♎	4♍	2♈
9	16♎	21♎	5♍	2♈
10	17♎	19♎	7♍	2♈
11	18♎	18♎	8♍	2♈
12	19♎	17♎	9♍	2♈
13	20♎	16♎	10♍	1♈
14	21♎	15♎	11♍	1♈
15	22♎	14♎	12♍	1♈
16	23♎	13♎	14♍	1♈
17	24♎	12♎	15♍	1♈
18	25♎	12♎	16♍	1♈
19	26♎	12♎	17♍	0♈
20	27♎	12♎	18♍	0♈
21	28♎	12♎	20♍	0♈
22	29♎	12♎	21♍	0♈
23	0♏	12♎	22♍	0♈
24	1♏	13♎	23♍	0♈
25	2♏	14♎	24♍	0♈
26	3♏	15♎	25♍	0♈
27	4♏	16♎	27♍	0♈
28	5♏	17♎	28♍	0♈
29	6♏	18♎	29♍	0♈
30	7♏	19♎	0♎	0♈
31	8♏	20♎	1♎	0♈

November

Day	☉	☿	♀	♂
1	9♏	22♎	3♎	0♈
2	10♏	23♎	4♎	0♈
3	11♏	25♎	5♎	0♈
4	12♏	26♎	6♎	0♈
5	13♏	28♎	8♎	0♈
6	14♏	29♎	9♎	0♈
7	15♏	1♏	10♎	1♈
8	16♏	2♏	11♎	1♈
9	17♏	4♏	12♎	1♈
10	18♏	6♏	14♎	1♈
11	19♏	7♏	15♎	1♈
12	20♏	9♏	16♎	1♈
13	21♏	10♏	17♎	1♈
14	22♏	12♏	19♎	2♈
15	23♏	14♏	20♎	2♈
16	24♏	15♏	21♎	2♈
17	25♏	17♏	22♎	2♈
18	26♏	19♏	23♎	3♈
19	27♏	20♏	25♎	3♈
20	28♏	22♏	26♎	3♈
21	29♏	23♏	27♎	3♈
22	0♐	25♏	28♎	4♈
23	1♐	26♏	0♏	4♈
24	2♐	28♏	1♏	4♈
25	3♐	0♐	2♏	5♈
26	4♐	1♐	3♏	5♈
27	5♐	3♐	4♏	5♈
28	6♐	4♐	6♏	6♈
29	7♐	6♐	7♏	6♈
30	8♐	8♐	8♏	6♈

December

Day	☉	☿	♀	♂
1	9♐	9♐	9♏	7♈
2	10♐	11♐	11♏	7♈
3	11♐	12♐	12♏	7♈
4	12♐	14♐	13♏	8♈
5	13♐	15♐	14♏	8♈
6	14♐	17♐	16♏	8♈
7	15♐	19♐	17♏	9♈
8	16♐	20♐	18♏	9♈
9	17♐	22♐	19♏	10♈
10	18♐	23♐	21♏	10♈
11	19♐	25♐	22♏	10♈
12	20♐	26♐	23♏	11♈
13	21♐	28♐	24♏	11♈
14	22♐	0♑	26♏	12♈
15	23♐	1♑	27♏	12♈
16	24♐	3♑	28♏	13♈
17	25♐	4♑	29♏	13♈
18	27♐	6♑	1♐	14♈
19	28♐	7♑	2♐	14♈
20	29♐	9♑	3♐	14♈
21	0♑	11♑	4♐	15♈
22	1♑	12♑	6♐	15♈
23	2♑	14♑	7♐	16♈
24	3♑	15♑	8♐	16♈
25	4♑	17♑	9♐	17♈
26	5♑	18♑	11♐	17♈
27	6♑	20♑	12♐	18♈
28	7♑	22♑	13♐	18♈
29	8♑	23♑	14♐	19♈
30	9♑	25♑	16♐	19♈
31	10♑	26♑	17♐	20♈

1989

Your Starway to Love

☉ =Sun ☿ = Mercury ♀ = Venus ♂ = Mars ♈ = Aries ♉ = Taurus ♊ = Gemini ♋ = Cancer

January

Day	☉	☿	♀	♂
1	11♑	28♑	18♐	20♈
2	12♑	29♑	19♐	21♈
3	13♑	1♒	21♐	21♈
4	14♑	2♒	22♐	22♈
5	15♑	3♒	23♐	22♈
6	16♑	5♒	24♐	23♈
7	17♑	6♒	26♐	23♈
8	18♑	7♒	27♐	24♈
9	19♑	8♒	28♐	24♈
10	20♑	9♒	29♐	25♈
11	21♑	10♒	1♑	26♈
12	22♑	11♒	2♑	26♈
13	23♑	11♒	3♑	27♈
14	24♑	12♒	4♑	27♈
15	25♑	12♒	6♑	28♈
16	26♑	12♒	7♑	28♈
17	27♑	12♒	8♑	29♈
18	28♑	11♒	9♑	29♈
19	29♑	11♒	11♑	0♉
20	0♒	10♒	12♑	0♉
21	1♒	9♒	13♑	1♉
22	2♒	8♒	14♑	2♉
23	3♒	7♒	16♑	2♉
24	4♒	6♒	17♑	3♉
25	5♒	5♒	18♑	3♉
26	6♒	3♒	19♑	4♉
27	7♒	2♒	21♑	4♉
28	8♒	1♒	22♑	5♉
29	9♒	0♒	23♑	6♉
30	10♒	29♑	24♑	6♉
31	11♒	28♑	26♑	7♉

April

Day	☉	☿	♀	♂
1	11♈	8♈	10♈	13♊
2	12♈	10♈	12♈	13♊
3	13♈	12♈	13♈	14♊
4	14♈	14♈	14♈	15♊
5	15♈	16♈	15♈	15♊
6	16♈	18♈	17♈	16♊
7	17♈	20♈	18♈	16♊
8	18♈	22♈	19♈	17♊
9	19♈	24♈	20♈	18♊
10	20♈	26♈	22♈	18♊
11	21♈	29♈	23♈	19♊
12	22♈	1♉	24♈	20♊
13	23♈	3♉	25♈	20♊
14	24♈	5♉	27♈	21♊
15	25♈	7♉	28♈	21♊
16	26♈	9♉	29♈	22♊
17	27♈	11♉	0♉	23♊
18	28♈	13♉	2♉	23♊
19	29♈	14♉	3♉	24♊
20	0♉	16♉	4♉	24♊
21	1♉	18♉	5♉	25♊
22	2♉	20♉	6♉	26♊
23	3♉	21♉	8♉	26♊
24	4♉	23♉	9♉	27♊
25	5♉	24♉	10♉	28♊
26	6♉	26♉	11♉	28♊
27	7♉	27♉	13♉	29♊
28	8♉	28♉	14♉	29♊
29	9♉	29♉	15♉	0♋
30	10♉	0♊	16♉	1♋

July

Day	☉	☿	♀	♂
1	9♋	21♊	2♌	9♌
2	10♋	23♊	4♌	10♌
3	11♋	25♊	5♌	10♌
4	12♋	27♊	6♌	11♌
5	13♋	28♊	7♌	12♌
6	14♋	0♋	8♌	12♌
7	15♋	2♋	10♌	13♌
8	16♋	4♋	11♌	13♌
9	17♋	6♋	12♌	14♌
10	18♋	8♋	13♌	15♌
11	19♋	10♋	14♌	15♌
12	20♋	13♋	16♌	16♌
13	21♋	15♋	17♌	17♌
14	22♋	17♋	18♌	17♌
15	23♋	19♋	19♌	18♌
16	24♋	21♋	21♌	18♌
17	25♋	23♋	22♌	19♌
18	26♋	25♋	23♌	20♌
19	27♋	28♋	24♌	20♌
20	27♋	0♌	25♌	21♌
21	28♋	2♌	27♌	22♌
22	29♋	4♌	28♌	22♌
23	0♌	6♌	29♌	23♌
24	1♌	8♌	0♍	23♌
25	2♌	10♌	1♍	24♌
26	3♌	12♌	3♍	25♌
27	4♌	14♌	4♍	25♌
28	5♌	16♌	5♍	26♌
29	6♌	18♌	6♍	27♌
30	7♌	20♌	7♍	27♌
31	8♌	21♌	9♍	28♌

October

Day	☉	☿	♀	♂
1	8♎	26♍	22♏	8♎
2	9♎	26♍	23♏	8♎
3	10♎	26♍	24♏	9♎
4	11♎	26♍	25♏	9♎
5	12♎	26♍	26♏	10♎
6	13♎	26♍	27♏	11♎
7	14♎	27♍	28♏	11♎
8	15♎	27♍	29♏	12♎
9	16♎	28♍	1♐	13♎
10	17♎	29♍	2♐	13♎
11	18♎	0♎	3♐	14♎
12	19♎	1♎	4♐	15♎
13	20♎	2♎	5♐	15♎
14	21♎	4♎	6♐	16♎
15	22♎	5♎	7♐	17♎
16	23♎	6♎	8♐	17♎
17	24♎	8♎	10♐	18♎
18	25♎	10♎	11♐	19♎
19	26♎	11♎	12♐	19♎
20	27♎	13♎	13♐	20♎
21	28♎	14♎	14♐	21♎
22	29♎	16♎	15♐	21♎
23	0♏	18♎	16♐	22♎
24	1♏	19♎	17♐	23♎
25	2♏	21♎	18♐	23♎
26	3♏	23♎	19♐	24♎
27	4♏	24♎	20♐	25♎
28	5♏	26♎	21♐	25♎
29	6♏	28♎	22♐	26♎
30	7♏	29♎	24♐	27♎
31	8♏	1♏	25♐	27♎

February

Day	☉	☿	♀	♂
1	12♒	27♑	27♑	7♉
2	13♒	27♑	28♑	8♉
3	14♒	26♑	29♑	8♉
4	15♒	26♑	1♒	9♉
5	16♒	26♑	2♒	10♉
6	17♒	26♑	3♒	10♉
7	18♒	26♑	4♒	11♉
8	19♒	26♑	6♒	11♉
9	20♒	27♑	7♒	12♉
10	21♒	27♑	8♒	13♉
11	22♒	28♑	9♒	13♉
12	23♒	28♑	11♒	14♉
13	24♒	29♑	12♒	14♉
14	25♒	0♒	13♒	15♉
15	26♒	0♒	14♒	15♉
16	28♒	1♒	16♒	16♉
17	29♒	2♒	17♒	17♉
18	0♓	3♒	18♒	17♉
19	1♓	4♒	19♒	18♉
20	2♓	5♒	21♒	18♉
21	3♓	6♒	22♒	19♉
22	4♓	7♒	23♒	20♉
23	5♓	9♒	24♒	20♉
24	6♓	10♒	26♒	21♉
25	7♓	11♒	27♒	21♉
26	8♓	12♒	28♒	22♉
27	9♓	14♒	29♒	23♉
28	10♓	15♒	1♓	23♉

May

Day	☉	☿	♀	♂
1	11♉	1♊	18♉	1♋
2	12♉	2♊	19♉	2♋
3	13♉	3♊	20♉	2♋
4	14♉	4♊	21♉	3♋
5	15♉	5♊	23♉	4♋
6	16♉	5♊	24♉	4♋
7	17♉	6♊	25♉	5♋
8	18♉	6♊	26♉	6♋
9	19♉	6♊	27♉	6♋
10	20♉	7♊	29♉	7♋
11	20♉	7♊	0♊	7♋
12	21♉	7♊	1♊	8♋
13	22♉	7♊	2♊	9♋
14	23♉	7♊	4♊	9♋
15	24♉	7♊	5♊	10♋
16	25♉	6♊	6♊	11♋
17	26♉	6♊	7♊	11♋
18	27♉	6♊	9♊	12♋
19	28♉	5♊	10♊	12♋
20	29♉	5♊	11♊	13♋
21	0♊	4♊	12♊	14♋
22	1♊	4♊	13♊	14♋
23	2♊	3♊	15♊	15♋
24	3♊	3♊	16♊	15♋
25	4♊	2♊	17♊	16♋
26	5♊	1♊	18♊	17♋
27	6♊	1♊	20♊	17♋
28	7♊	0♊	21♊	18♋
29	8♊	0♊	22♊	19♋
30	9♊	29♉	23♊	19♋
31	10♊	29♉	24♊	20♋

August

Day	☉	☿	♀	♂
1	9♌	23♌	10♍	29♌
2	10♌	25♌	11♍	29♌
3	11♌	27♌	12♍	0♍
4	12♌	29♌	13♍	0♍
5	13♌	0♍	15♍	1♍
6	14♌	2♍	16♍	2♍
7	15♌	4♍	17♍	2♍
8	16♌	5♍	18♍	3♍
9	17♌	7♍	19♍	4♍
10	18♌	8♍	21♍	4♍
11	19♌	10♍	22♍	5♍
12	19♌	12♍	23♍	5♍
13	20♌	13♍	24♍	6♍
14	21♌	15♍	25♍	7♍
15	22♌	16♍	27♍	7♍
16	23♌	17♍	28♍	8♍
17	24♌	19♍	29♍	9♍
18	25♌	20♍	0♎	9♍
19	26♌	21♍	1♎	10♍
20	27♌	23♍	3♎	11♍
21	28♌	24♍	4♎	11♍
22	29♌	25♍	5♎	12♍
23	0♍	27♍	6♎	12♍
24	1♍	28♍	7♎	13♍
25	2♍	29♍	8♎	14♍
26	3♍	0♎	10♎	14♍
27	4♍	1♎	11♎	15♍
28	5♍	2♎	12♎	16♍
29	6♍	3♎	13♎	16♍
30	7♍	4♎	14♎	17♍
31	8♍	5♎	16♎	18♍

November

Day	☉	☿	♀	♂
1	9♏	3♏	26♐	28♎
2	10♏	4♏	27♐	29♎
3	11♏	6♏	28♐	29♎
4	12♏	8♏	29♐	0♏
5	13♏	9♏	0♑	1♏
6	14♏	11♏	1♑	1♏
7	15♏	13♏	2♑	2♏
8	16♏	14♏	3♑	3♏
9	17♏	16♏	4♑	3♏
10	18♏	17♏	5♑	4♏
11	19♏	19♏	6♑	5♏
12	20♏	21♏	7♑	5♏
13	21♏	22♏	8♑	6♏
14	22♏	24♏	9♑	7♏
15	23♏	25♏	10♑	7♏
16	24♏	27♏	11♑	8♏
17	25♏	29♏	12♑	9♏
18	26♏	0♐	13♑	9♏
19	27♏	2♐	13♑	10♏
20	28♏	3♐	14♑	11♏
21	29♏	5♐	15♑	11♏
22	0♐	6♐	16♑	12♏
23	1♐	8♐	17♑	13♏
24	2♐	9♐	18♑	13♏
25	3♐	11♐	19♑	14♏
26	4♐	13♐	20♑	15♏
27	5♐	14♐	20♑	16♏
28	6♐	16♐	21♑	16♏
29	7♐	17♐	22♑	17♏
30	8♐	19♐	23♑	18♏

March

Day	☉	☿	♀	♂
1	11♓	16♒	2♓	24♉
2	12♓	18♒	3♓	24♉
3	13♓	19♒	4♓	25♉
4	14♓	20♒	6♓	26♉
5	15♓	22♒	7♓	26♉
6	16♓	23♒	8♓	27♉
7	17♓	25♒	9♓	27♉
8	18♓	26♒	11♓	28♉
9	19♓	28♒	12♓	29♉
10	20♓	29♒	13♓	29♉
11	21♓	1♓	14♓	0♊
12	22♓	2♓	16♓	1♊
13	23♓	4♓	17♓	1♊
14	24♓	5♓	18♓	2♊
15	25♓	7♓	19♓	2♊
16	26♓	9♓	21♓	3♊
17	27♓	10♓	22♓	4♊
18	28♓	12♓	23♓	4♊
19	29♓	14♓	24♓	5♊
20	0♈	16♓	26♓	5♊
21	1♈	17♓	27♓	6♊
22	2♈	19♓	28♓	7♊
23	3♈	21♓	29♓	7♊
24	4♈	23♓	1♈	8♊
25	5♈	25♓	2♈	8♊
26	6♈	26♓	3♈	9♊
27	7♈	28♓	4♈	10♊
28	7♈	0♈	6♈	10♊
29	8♈	2♈	7♈	11♊
30	9♈	4♈	8♈	12♊
31	10♈	6♈	9♈	12♊

June

Day	☉	☿	♀	♂
1	11♊	29♉	26♊	20♋
2	12♊	29♉	27♊	21♋
3	13♊	28♉	28♊	22♋
4	14♊	28♉	29♊	22♋
5	15♊	28♉	1♋	23♋
6	15♊	28♉	2♋	24♋
7	16♊	28♉	3♋	24♋
8	17♊	28♉	4♋	25♋
9	18♊	29♉	5♋	25♋
10	19♊	29♉	7♋	26♋
11	20♊	29♉	8♋	27♋
12	21♊	0♊	9♋	27♋
13	22♊	0♊	10♋	28♋
14	23♊	1♊	12♋	29♋
15	24♊	2♊	13♋	29♋
16	25♊	3♊	14♋	0♌
17	26♊	3♊	15♋	0♌
18	27♊	4♊	16♋	1♌
19	28♊	5♊	18♋	2♌
20	29♊	6♊	19♋	2♌
21	0♋	7♊	20♋	3♌
22	1♋	8♊	21♋	3♌
23	2♋	10♊	23♋	4♌
24	3♋	11♊	24♋	5♌
25	4♋	12♊	25♋	5♌
26	5♋	14♊	26♋	6♌
27	6♋	15♊	27♋	7♌
28	6♋	16♊	29♋	7♌
29	7♋	18♊	0♌	8♌
30	8♋	20♊	1♌	8♌

September

Day	☉	☿	♀	♂
1	9♍	6♎	17♎	18♍
2	10♍	7♎	18♎	19♍
3	11♍	7♎	19♎	19♍
4	12♍	8♎	20♎	20♍
5	13♍	9♎	21♎	21♍
6	14♍	9♎	23♎	21♍
7	15♍	10♎	24♎	22♍
8	16♍	10♎	25♎	23♍
9	17♍	10♎	26♎	23♍
10	17♍	10♎	27♎	24♍
11	18♍	11♎	28♎	25♍
12	19♍	11♎	0♏	25♍
13	20♍	10♎	1♏	26♍
14	21♍	10♎	2♏	27♍
15	22♍	10♎	3♏	27♍
16	23♍	10♎	4♏	28♍
17	24♍	9♎	5♏	28♍
18	25♍	8♎	7♏	29♍
19	26♍	8♎	8♏	0♎
20	27♍	7♎	9♏	0♎
21	28♍	6♎	10♏	1♎
22	29♍	5♎	11♏	2♎
23	0♎	4♎	12♏	2♎
24	1♎	3♎	14♏	3♎
25	2♎	2♎	15♏	4♎
26	3♎	0♎	16♏	4♎
27	4♎	29♍	17♏	5♎
28	5♎	28♍	18♏	6♎
29	6♎	28♍	19♏	6♎
30	7♎	27♍	20♏	7♎

December

Day	☉	☿	♀	♂
1	9♐	20♐	24♑	18♏
2	10♐	22♐	24♑	19♏
3	11♐	23♐	25♑	20♏
4	12♐	25♐	26♑	20♏
5	13♐	26♐	27♑	21♏
6	14♐	28♐	27♑	22♏
7	15♐	29♐	28♑	22♏
8	16♐	1♑	29♑	23♏
9	17♐	2♑	29♑	24♏
10	18♐	4♑	0♒	24♏
11	19♐	5♑	1♒	25♏
12	20♐	7♑	1♒	26♏
13	21♐	8♑	2♒	27♏
14	22♐	10♑	2♒	27♏
15	23♐	11♑	3♒	28♏
16	24♐	13♑	3♒	29♏
17	25♐	14♑	4♒	29♏
18	26♐	15♑	4♒	0♐
19	27♐	17♑	4♒	1♐
20	28♐	18♑	5♒	1♐
21	29♐	19♑	5♒	2♐
22	0♑	20♑	5♒	3♐
23	1♑	21♑	6♒	3♐
24	2♑	22♑	6♒	4♐
25	3♑	23♑	6♒	5♐
26	4♑	24♑	6♒	6♐
27	5♑	25♑	6♒	6♐
28	6♑	25♑	6♒	7♐
29	7♑	26♑	6♒	8♐
30	8♑	26♑	6♒	8♐
31	9♑	26♑	6♒	9♐

Planetary Positions

♌ = Leo ♍ = Virgo ♎ = Libra ♏ = Scorpio ♐ = Sagittarius ♑ = Capricorn ♒ = Aquarius ♓ = Pisces

1990

January

Day	☉	☿	♀	♂
1	11♑	26♑	6♒	10♐
2	12♑	25♑	6♒	10♐
3	13♑	25♑	6♒	11♐
4	14♑	24♑	6♒	12♐
5	15♑	23♑	5♒	13♐
6	16♑	22♑	5♒	13♐
7	17♑	21♑	5♒	14♐
8	18♑	20♑	4♒	15♐
9	19♑	18♑	4♒	15♐
10	20♑	17♑	4♒	16♐
11	21♑	16♑	3♒	17♐
12	22♑	15♑	3♒	18♐
13	23♑	13♑	2♒	18♐
14	24♑	12♑	1♒	19♐
15	25♑	12♑	1♒	20♐
16	26♑	11♑	0♒	20♐
17	27♑	10♑	0♒	21♐
18	28♑	10♑	29♑	22♐
19	29♑	10♑	28♑	23♐
20	0♒	10♑	28♑	23♐
21	1♒	10♑	27♑	24♐
22	2♒	10♑	27♑	25♐
23	3♒	10♑	26♑	25♐
24	4♒	11♑	25♑	26♐
25	5♒	11♑	25♑	27♐
26	6♒	12♑	24♑	28♐
27	7♒	13♑	24♑	28♐
28	8♒	13♑	23♑	29♐
29	9♒	14♑	23♑	0♑
30	10♒	15♑	23♑	0♑
31	11♒	16♑	22♑	1♑

April

Day	☉	☿	♀	♂
1	11♈	24♈	25♒	15♒
2	12♈	26♈	26♒	16♒
3	13♈	28♈	27♒	17♒
4	14♈	0♉	28♒	18♒
5	15♈	2♉	29♒	18♒
6	16♈	3♉	0♓	19♒
7	17♈	5♉	1♓	20♒
8	18♈	6♉	2♓	20♒
9	19♈	8♉	3♓	21♒
10	20♈	9♉	4♓	22♒
11	21♈	10♉	5♓	23♒
12	22♈	11♉	6♓	23♒
13	23♈	12♉	7♓	24♒
14	24♈	13♉	8♓	25♒
15	25♈	14♉	9♓	26♒
16	26♈	15♉	10♓	26♒
17	27♈	16♉	11♓	27♒
18	28♈	16♉	12♓	28♒
19	29♈	17♉	14♓	29♒
20	0♉	17♉	15♓	29♒
21	1♉	17♉	16♓	0♓
22	2♉	17♉	17♓	1♓
23	3♉	18♉	18♓	2♓
24	4♉	17♉	19♓	2♓
25	5♉	17♉	20♓	3♓
26	6♉	17♉	21♓	4♓
27	7♉	17♉	22♓	5♓
28	8♉	16♉	23♓	5♓
29	9♉	16♉	24♓	6♓
30	10♉	16♉	26♓	7♓

July

Day	☉	☿	♀	♂
1	9♋	7♋	7♊	22♈
2	10♋	9♋	9♊	23♈
3	11♋	12♋	10♊	24♈
4	12♋	14♋	11♊	24♈
5	13♋	16♋	12♊	25♈
6	14♋	18♋	13♊	26♈
7	15♋	20♋	14♊	26♈
8	16♋	22♋	16♊	27♈
9	17♋	24♋	17♊	28♈
10	18♋	26♋	18♊	28♈
11	19♋	28♋	19♊	29♈
12	20♋	0♌	20♊	0♉
13	21♋	2♌	22♊	0♉
14	22♋	4♌	23♊	1♉
15	22♋	6♌	24♊	2♉
16	23♋	8♌	25♊	2♉
17	24♋	10♌	26♊	3♉
18	25♋	12♌	28♊	4♉
19	26♋	14♌	29♊	4♉
20	27♋	15♌	0♋	5♉
21	28♋	17♌	1♋	6♉
22	29♋	19♌	2♋	6♉
23	0♌	20♌	4♋	7♉
24	1♌	22♌	5♋	8♉
25	2♌	24♌	6♋	8♉
26	3♌	25♌	7♋	9♉
27	4♌	27♌	9♋	10♉
28	5♌	28♌	10♋	10♉
29	6♌	0♍	11♋	11♉
30	7♌	1♍	12♋	12♉
31	8♌	2♍	13♋	12♉

October

Day	☉	☿	♀	♂
1	8♎	22♍	0♎	12♊
2	9♎	24♍	1♎	12♊
3	10♎	26♍	2♎	12♊
4	11♎	27♍	3♎	13♊
5	12♎	29♍	5♎	13♊
6	13♎	1♎	6♎	13♊
7	14♎	3♎	7♎	13♊
8	15♎	4♎	8♎	13♊
9	16♎	6♎	10♎	14♊
10	17♎	8♎	11♎	14♊
11	18♎	10♎	12♎	14♊
12	19♎	11♎	13♎	14♊
13	20♎	13♎	15♎	14♊
14	21♎	15♎	16♎	14♊
15	22♎	17♎	17♎	14♊
16	23♎	18♎	18♎	14♊
17	24♎	20♎	20♎	14♊
18	25♎	22♎	21♎	15♊
19	26♎	23♎	22♎	15♊
20	27♎	25♎	23♎	15♊
21	28♎	27♎	25♎	15♊
22	29♎	29♎	26♎	15♊
23	0♏	0♏	27♎	15♊
24	1♏	2♏	28♎	14♊
25	2♏	4♏	0♏	14♊
26	3♏	5♏	1♏	14♊
27	4♏	7♏	2♏	14♊
28	5♏	8♏	3♏	14♊
29	6♏	10♏	5♏	14♊
30	7♏	12♏	6♏	14♊
31	8♏	13♏	7♏	14♊

February

Day	☉	☿	♀	♂
1	12♒	17♑	22♑	2♑
2	13♒	18♑	22♑	3♑
3	14♒	19♑	21♑	3♑
4	15♒	20♑	21♑	4♑
5	16♒	21♑	21♑	5♑
6	17♒	23♑	21♑	5♑
7	18♒	24♑	21♑	6♑
8	19♒	25♑	21♑	7♑
9	20♒	26♑	21♑	8♑
10	21♒	28♑	21♑	8♑
11	22♒	29♑	21♑	9♑
12	23♒	0♒	21♑	10♑
13	24♒	2♒	21♑	11♑
14	25♒	3♒	22♑	11♑
15	26♒	4♒	22♑	12♑
16	27♒	6♒	22♑	13♑
17	28♒	7♒	22♑	13♑
18	29♒	9♒	23♑	14♑
19	0♓	10♒	23♑	15♑
20	1♓	12♒	24♑	16♑
21	2♓	13♒	24♑	16♑
22	3♓	15♒	24♑	17♑
23	4♓	16♒	25♑	18♑
24	5♓	18♒	25♑	19♑
25	6♓	19♒	26♑	19♑
26	7♓	21♒	27♑	20♑
27	8♓	23♒	27♑	21♑
28	9♓	24♒	28♑	22♑

May

Day	☉	☿	♀	♂
1	11♉	15♉	27♓	8♓
2	12♉	14♉	28♓	8♓
3	13♉	14♉	29♓	9♓
4	13♉	13♉	0♈	10♓
5	14♉	13♉	1♈	11♓
6	15♉	12♉	2♈	11♓
7	16♉	11♉	3♈	12♓
8	17♉	11♉	5♈	13♓
9	18♉	10♉	6♈	14♓
10	19♉	10♉	7♈	14♓
11	20♉	9♉	8♈	15♓
12	21♉	9♉	9♈	16♓
13	22♉	8♉	10♈	17♓
14	23♉	8♉	11♈	17♓
15	24♉	8♉	12♈	18♓
16	25♉	8♉	14♈	19♓
17	26♉	8♉	15♈	20♓
18	27♉	8♉	16♈	20♓
19	28♉	8♉	17♈	21♓
20	29♉	8♉	18♈	22♓
21	0♊	9♉	19♈	23♓
22	1♊	9♉	21♈	23♓
23	2♊	9♉	22♈	24♓
24	3♊	10♉	23♈	25♓
25	4♊	10♉	24♈	26♓
26	5♊	11♉	25♈	26♓
27	6♊	12♉	26♈	27♓
28	7♊	12♉	27♈	28♓
29	8♊	13♉	29♈	28♓
30	9♊	14♉	0♉	29♓
31	10♊	15♉	1♉	0♈

August

Day	☉	☿	♀	♂
1	9♌	4♍	15♋	13♉
2	10♌	5♍	16♋	13♉
3	11♌	7♍	17♋	14♉
4	12♌	8♍	18♋	15♉
5	13♌	9♍	19♋	15♉
6	13♌	10♍	21♋	16♉
7	14♌	11♍	22♋	16♉
8	15♌	13♍	23♋	17♉
9	16♌	14♍	24♋	18♉
10	17♌	15♍	25♋	18♉
11	18♌	16♍	27♋	19♉
12	19♌	17♍	28♋	19♉
13	20♌	18♍	29♋	20♉
14	21♌	18♍	0♌	21♉
15	22♌	19♍	2♌	21♉
16	23♌	20♍	3♌	22♉
17	24♌	21♍	4♌	22♉
18	25♌	21♍	5♌	23♉
19	26♌	22♍	6♌	23♉
20	27♌	22♍	8♌	24♉
21	28♌	23♍	9♌	25♉
22	29♌	23♍	10♌	25♉
23	0♍	23♍	11♌	26♉
24	1♍	23♍	13♌	26♉
25	2♍	24♍	14♌	27♉
26	3♍	24♍	15♌	27♉
27	4♍	23♍	16♌	28♉
28	5♍	23♍	18♌	28♉
29	6♍	23♍	19♌	29♉
30	7♍	23♍	20♌	29♉
31	8♍	22♍	21♌	0♊

November

Day	☉	☿	♀	♂
1	9♏	15♏	8♏	14♊
2	10♏	16♏	10♏	13♊
3	11♏	18♏	11♏	13♊
4	12♏	20♏	12♏	13♊
5	13♏	21♏	13♏	13♊
6	14♏	23♏	15♏	13♊
7	15♏	24♏	16♏	12♊
8	16♏	26♏	17♏	12♊
9	17♏	27♏	18♏	12♊
10	18♏	29♏	20♏	12♊
11	19♏	0♐	21♏	11♊
12	20♏	2♐	22♏	11♊
13	21♏	3♐	23♏	11♊
14	22♏	5♐	25♏	10♊
15	23♏	6♐	26♏	10♊
16	24♏	8♐	27♏	10♊
17	25♏	9♐	28♏	9♊
18	26♏	11♐	0♐	9♊
19	27♏	12♐	1♐	9♊
20	28♏	14♐	2♐	8♊
21	29♏	15♐	4♐	8♊
22	0♐	17♐	5♐	7♊
23	1♐	18♐	6♐	7♊
24	2♐	20♐	7♐	7♊
25	3♐	21♐	9♐	6♊
26	4♐	22♐	10♐	6♊
27	5♐	24♐	11♐	6♊
28	6♐	25♐	12♐	5♊
29	7♐	26♐	14♐	5♊
30	8♐	28♐	15♐	4♊

March

Day	☉	☿	♀	♂
1	10♓	26♒	28♑	22♑
2	11♓	27♒	29♑	23♑
3	12♓	29♒	0♒	24♑
4	13♓	1♓	0♒	24♑
5	14♓	3♓	1♒	25♑
6	15♓	4♓	2♒	26♑
7	16♓	6♓	2♒	27♑
8	17♓	8♓	3♒	27♑
9	18♓	10♓	4♒	28♑
10	19♓	11♓	5♒	29♑
11	20♓	13♓	6♒	0♒
12	21♓	15♓	6♒	0♒
13	22♓	17♓	7♒	1♒
14	23♓	19♓	8♒	2♒
15	24♓	21♓	9♒	3♒
16	25♓	23♓	10♒	3♒
17	26♓	25♓	11♒	4♒
18	27♓	26♓	11♒	5♒
19	28♓	28♓	12♒	6♒
20	29♓	0♈	13♒	6♒
21	0♈	2♈	14♒	7♒
22	1♈	4♈	15♒	8♒
23	2♈	6♈	16♒	9♒
24	3♈	8♈	17♒	9♒
25	4♈	10♈	18♒	10♒
26	5♈	12♈	19♒	11♒
27	6♈	15♈	20♒	12♒
28	7♈	17♈	21♒	12♒
29	8♈	19♈	22♒	13♒
30	9♈	20♈	23♒	14♒
31	10♈	22♈	24♒	15♒

June

Day	☉	☿	♀	♂
1	10♊	16♉	2♉	1♈
2	11♊	17♉	3♉	1♈
3	12♊	18♉	4♉	2♈
4	13♊	19♉	6♉	3♈
5	14♊	21♉	7♉	4♈
6	15♊	22♉	8♉	4♈
7	16♊	23♉	9♉	5♈
8	17♊	24♉	10♉	6♈
9	18♊	26♉	11♉	6♈
10	19♊	27♉	13♉	7♈
11	20♊	29♉	14♉	8♈
12	21♊	0♊	15♉	9♈
13	22♊	2♊	16♉	9♈
14	23♊	4♊	17♉	10♈
15	24♊	5♊	18♉	11♈
16	25♊	7♊	20♉	12♈
17	26♊	9♊	21♉	12♈
18	27♊	11♊	22♉	13♈
19	28♊	12♊	23♉	14♈
20	29♊	14♊	24♉	14♈
21	0♋	16♊	26♉	15♈
22	1♋	18♊	27♉	16♈
23	1♋	20♊	28♉	17♈
24	2♋	22♊	29♉	17♈
25	3♋	24♊	0♊	18♈
26	4♋	26♊	1♊	19♈
27	5♋	29♊	3♊	19♈
28	6♋	1♋	4♊	20♈
29	7♋	3♋	5♊	21♈
30	8♋	5♋	6♊	21♈

September

Day	☉	☿	♀	♂
1	9♍	21♍	22♌	0♊
2	9♍	21♍	24♌	1♊
3	10♍	20♍	25♌	1♊
4	11♍	19♍	26♌	2♊
5	12♍	18♍	27♌	2♊
6	13♍	17♍	29♌	3♊
7	14♍	16♍	0♍	3♊
8	15♍	15♍	1♍	4♊
9	16♍	14♍	2♍	4♊
10	17♍	13♍	4♍	5♊
11	18♍	12♍	5♍	5♊
12	19♍	12♍	6♍	5♊
13	20♍	11♍	7♍	6♊
14	21♍	10♍	8♍	6♊
15	22♍	10♍	10♍	7♊
16	23♍	10♍	11♍	7♊
17	24♍	10♍	12♍	7♊
18	25♍	10♍	13♍	8♊
19	26♍	10♍	15♍	8♊
20	27♍	10♍	16♍	9♊
21	28♍	11♍	17♍	9♊
22	29♍	11♍	18♍	9♊
23	0♎	12♍	20♍	10♊
24	1♎	13♍	21♍	10♊
25	2♎	14♍	22♍	10♊
26	3♎	15♍	23♍	11♊
27	4♎	17♍	25♍	11♊
28	5♎	18♍	26♍	11♊
29	6♎	19♍	27♍	11♊
30	7♎	21♍	28♍	12♊

December

Day	☉	☿	♀	♂
1	9♐	29♐	16♐	4♊
2	10♐	0♑	17♐	4♊
3	11♐	1♑	19♐	3♊
4	12♐	3♑	20♐	3♊
5	13♐	4♑	21♐	3♊
6	14♐	5♑	22♐	2♊
7	15♐	6♑	24♐	2♊
8	16♐	7♑	25♐	2♊
9	17♐	8♑	26♐	1♊
10	18♐	8♑	27♐	1♊
11	19♐	9♑	29♐	1♊
12	20♐	9♑	0♑	1♊
13	21♐	10♑	1♑	0♊
14	22♐	10♑	2♑	0♊
15	23♐	10♑	4♑	0♊
16	24♐	10♑	5♑	0♊
17	25♐	10♑	6♑	29♉
18	26♐	9♑	7♑	29♉
19	27♐	8♑	9♑	29♉
20	28♐	7♑	10♑	29♉
21	29♐	6♑	11♑	29♉
22	0♑	5♑	12♑	28♉
23	1♑	4♑	14♑	28♉
24	2♑	2♑	15♑	28♉
25	3♑	1♑	16♑	28♉
26	4♑	0♑	17♑	28♉
27	5♑	28♐	19♑	28♉
28	6♑	27♐	20♑	28♉
29	7♑	26♐	21♑	28♉
30	8♑	25♐	22♑	28♉
31	9♑	25♐	24♑	28♉

1991

Your Starway to Love

☉ =Sun ☿ = Mercury ♀ = Venus ♂ = Mars ♈ = Aries ♉ = Taurus ♊ = Gemini ♋ = Cancer

January

Day	☉	☿	♀	♂
1	10♑	24♐	25♑	28♉
2	11♑	24♐	26♑	28♉
3	12♑	24♐	27♑	28♉
4	13♑	24♐	29♑	28♉
5	14♑	24♐	0♒	28♉
6	15♑	24♐	1♒	28♉
7	16♑	25♐	3♒	28♉
8	17♑	25♐	4♒	28♉
9	18♑	26♐	5♒	28♉
10	19♑	26♐	6♒	28♉
11	20♑	27♐	8♒	28♉
12	21♑	28♐	9♒	28♉
13	22♑	29♐	10♒	29♉
14	24♑	0♑	11♒	29♉
15	25♑	1♑	13♒	29♉
16	26♑	2♑	14♒	29♉
17	27♑	3♑	15♒	29♉
18	28♑	4♑	16♒	29♉
19	29♑	5♑	18♒	0♊
20	0♒	7♑	19♒	0♊
21	1♒	8♑	20♒	0♊
22	2♒	9♑	21♒	0♊
23	3♒	10♑	23♒	0♊
24	4♒	12♑	24♒	1♊
25	5♒	13♑	25♒	1♊
26	6♒	14♑	26♒	1♊
27	7♒	16♑	28♒	2♊
28	8♒	17♑	29♒	2♊
29	9♒	19♑	0♓	2♊
30	10♒	20♑	1♓	2♊
31	11♒	21♑	3♓	3♊

February

Day	☉	☿	♀	♂
1	12♒	23♑	4♓	3♊
2	13♒	24♑	5♓	3♊
3	14♒	26♑	6♓	4♊
4	15♒	27♑	7♓	4♊
5	16♒	29♑	9♓	4♊
6	17♒	0♒	10♓	5♊
7	18♒	2♒	11♓	5♊
8	19♒	4♒	12♓	5♊
9	20♒	5♒	14♓	6♊
10	21♒	7♒	15♓	6♊
11	22♒	8♒	16♓	6♊
12	23♒	10♒	17♓	7♊
13	24♒	11♒	19♓	7♊
14	25♒	13♒	20♓	7♊
15	26♒	15♒	21♓	8♊
16	27♒	16♒	22♓	8♊
17	28♒	18♒	24♓	9♊
18	29♒	20♒	25♓	9♊
19	0♓	21♒	26♓	9♊
20	1♓	23♒	27♓	10♊
21	2♓	25♒	29♓	10♊
22	3♓	27♒	0♈	11♊
23	4♓	28♒	1♈	11♊
24	5♓	0♓	2♈	12♊
25	6♓	2♓	3♈	12♊
26	7♓	4♓	5♈	12♊
27	8♓	6♓	6♈	13♊
28	9♓	7♓	7♈	13♊

March

Day	☉	☿	♀	♂
1	10♓	9♓	8♈	14♊
2	11♓	11♓	10♈	14♊
3	12♓	13♓	11♈	15♊
4	13♓	15♓	12♈	15♊
5	14♓	17♓	13♈	16♊
6	15♓	19♓	15♈	16♊
7	16♓	21♓	16♈	17♊
8	17♓	23♓	17♈	17♊
9	18♓	25♓	18♈	17♊
10	19♓	27♓	19♈	18♊
11	20♓	29♓	21♈	18♊
12	21♓	1♈	22♈	19♊
13	22♓	2♈	23♈	19♊
14	23♓	4♈	24♈	20♊
15	24♓	6♈	26♈	20♊
16	25♓	8♈	27♈	21♊
17	26♓	10♈	28♈	21♊
18	27♓	12♈	29♈	22♊
19	28♓	13♈	0♉	22♊
20	29♓	15♈	2♉	23♊
21	0♈	17♈	3♉	23♊
22	1♈	18♈	4♉	24♊
23	2♈	20♈	5♉	24♊
24	3♈	21♈	6♉	25♊
25	4♈	22♈	8♉	25♊
26	5♈	24♈	9♉	26♊
27	6♈	25♈	10♉	26♊
28	7♈	26♈	11♉	27♊
29	8♈	26♈	12♉	27♊
30	9♈	27♈	14♉	28♊
31	10♈	28♈	15♉	29♊

April

Day	☉	☿	♀	♂
1	11♈	28♈	16♉	29♊
2	12♈	29♈	17♉	0♋
3	13♈	29♈	18♉	0♋
4	14♈	29♈	20♉	1♋
5	15♈	29♈	21♉	1♋
6	16♈	29♈	22♉	2♋
7	17♈	29♈	23♉	2♋
8	18♈	28♈	24♉	3♋
9	19♈	28♈	26♉	3♋
10	20♈	27♈	27♉	4♋
11	21♈	27♈	28♉	4♋
12	22♈	26♈	29♉	5♋
13	23♈	26♈	0♊	5♋
14	24♈	25♈	1♊	6♋
15	25♈	24♈	3♊	7♋
16	26♈	23♈	4♊	7♋
17	27♈	23♈	5♊	8♋
18	28♈	22♈	6♊	8♋
19	29♈	21♈	7♊	9♋
20	0♉	21♈	8♊	9♋
21	1♉	20♈	10♊	10♋
22	2♉	20♈	11♊	10♋
23	3♉	19♈	12♊	11♋
24	4♉	19♈	13♊	12♋
25	5♉	18♈	14♊	12♋
26	5♉	18♈	15♊	13♋
27	6♉	18♈	17♊	13♋
28	7♉	18♈	18♊	14♋
29	8♉	18♈	19♊	14♋
30	9♉	18♈	20♊	15♋

May

Day	☉	☿	♀	♂
1	10♉	18♈	21♊	15♋
2	11♉	19♈	22♊	16♋
3	12♉	19♈	23♊	17♋
4	13♉	19♈	25♊	17♋
5	14♉	20♈	26♊	18♋
6	15♉	20♈	27♊	18♋
7	16♉	21♈	28♊	19♋
8	17♉	22♈	29♊	19♋
9	18♉	22♈	0♋	20♋
10	19♉	23♈	1♋	21♋
11	20♉	24♈	2♋	21♋
12	21♉	25♈	4♋	22♋
13	22♉	26♈	5♋	22♋
14	23♉	27♈	6♋	23♋
15	24♉	28♈	7♋	23♋
16	25♉	29♈	8♋	24♋
17	26♉	0♉	9♋	25♋
18	27♉	2♉	10♋	25♋
19	28♉	3♉	11♋	26♋
20	29♉	4♉	12♋	26♋
21	0♊	5♉	13♋	27♋
22	1♊	7♉	14♋	27♋
23	2♊	8♉	16♋	28♋
24	3♊	10♉	17♋	29♋
25	4♊	11♉	18♋	29♋
26	4♊	13♉	19♋	0♌
27	5♊	14♉	20♋	0♌
28	6♊	16♉	21♋	1♌
29	7♊	18♉	22♋	2♌
30	8♊	19♉	23♋	2♌
31	9♊	21♉	24♋	3♌

June

Day	☉	☿	♀	♂
1	10♊	23♉	25♋	3♌
2	11♊	25♉	26♋	4♌
3	12♊	26♉	27♋	5♌
4	13♊	28♉	28♋	5♌
5	14♊	0♊	29♋	6♌
6	15♊	2♊	0♌	6♌
7	16♊	4♊	1♌	7♌
8	17♊	6♊	2♌	7♌
9	18♊	8♊	3♌	8♌
10	19♊	10♊	4♌	9♌
11	20♊	12♊	5♌	9♌
12	21♊	15♊	6♌	10♌
13	22♊	17♊	7♌	10♌
14	23♊	19♊	8♌	11♌
15	24♊	21♊	9♌	12♌
16	25♊	23♊	10♌	12♌
17	26♊	26♊	11♌	13♌
18	26♊	28♊	12♌	13♌
19	27♊	0♋	13♌	14♌
20	28♊	2♋	14♌	15♌
21	29♊	4♋	15♌	15♌
22	0♋	6♋	15♌	16♌
23	1♋	9♋	16♌	16♌
24	2♋	11♋	17♌	17♌
25	3♋	13♋	18♌	18♌
26	4♋	15♋	19♌	18♌
27	5♋	17♋	20♌	19♌
28	6♋	19♋	21♌	19♌
29	7♋	21♋	21♌	20♌
30	8♋	23♋	22♌	21♌

July

Day	☉	☿	♀	♂
1	9♋	24♋	23♌	21♌
2	10♋	26♋	24♌	22♌
3	11♋	28♋	24♌	22♌
4	12♋	0♌	25♌	23♌
5	13♋	2♌	26♌	24♌
6	14♋	3♌	27♌	24♌
7	15♋	5♌	27♌	25♌
8	16♋	7♌	28♌	26♌
9	17♋	8♌	29♌	26♌
10	17♋	10♌	29♌	27♌
11	18♋	11♌	0♍	27♌
12	19♋	13♌	1♍	28♌
13	20♋	14♌	1♍	29♌
14	21♋	16♌	2♍	29♌
15	22♋	17♌	2♍	0♍
16	23♋	18♌	3♍	0♍
17	24♋	20♌	3♍	1♍
18	25♋	21♌	4♍	2♍
19	26♋	22♌	4♍	2♍
20	27♋	23♌	5♍	3♍
21	28♋	25♌	5♍	4♍
22	29♋	26♌	5♍	4♍
23	0♌	27♌	6♍	5♍
24	1♌	28♌	6♍	5♍
25	2♌	29♌	6♍	6♍
26	3♌	0♍	7♍	7♍
27	4♌	1♍	7♍	7♍
28	5♌	1♍	7♍	8♍
29	6♌	2♍	7♍	8♍
30	7♌	3♍	7♍	9♍
31	8♌	3♍	7♍	10♍

August

Day	☉	☿	♀	♂
1	8♌	4♍	7♍	10♍
2	9♌	5♍	7♍	11♍
3	10♌	5♍	7♍	12♍
4	11♌	5♍	7♍	12♍
5	12♌	6♍	7♍	13♍
6	13♌	6♍	7♍	13♍
7	14♌	6♍	7♍	14♍
8	15♌	6♍	6♍	15♍
9	16♌	6♍	6♍	15♍
10	17♌	6♍	6♍	16♍
11	18♌	5♍	5♍	17♍
12	19♌	5♍	5♍	17♍
13	20♌	5♍	5♍	18♍
14	21♌	4♍	4♍	18♍
15	22♌	4♍	4♍	19♍
16	23♌	3♍	3♍	20♍
17	24♌	2♍	3♍	20♍
18	25♌	1♍	2♍	21♍
19	26♌	1♍	1♍	22♍
20	27♌	0♍	1♍	22♍
21	28♌	29♌	0♍	23♍
22	29♌	28♌	0♍	24♍
23	0♍	27♌	29♌	24♍
24	1♍	26♌	28♌	25♍
25	2♍	26♌	28♌	25♍
26	2♍	25♌	27♌	26♍
27	3♍	24♌	27♌	27♍
28	4♍	24♌	26♌	27♍
29	5♍	23♌	25♌	28♍
30	6♍	23♌	25♌	29♍
31	7♍	23♌	24♌	29♍

September

Day	☉	☿	♀	♂
1	8♍	23♌	24♌	0♎
2	9♍	23♌	23♌	1♎
3	10♍	24♌	23♌	1♎
4	11♍	24♌	23♌	2♎
5	12♍	25♌	22♌	3♎
6	13♍	25♌	22♌	3♎
7	14♍	26♌	22♌	4♎
8	15♍	27♌	22♌	4♎
9	16♍	28♌	21♌	5♎
10	17♍	29♌	21♌	6♎
11	18♍	1♍	21♌	6♎
12	19♍	2♍	21♌	7♎
13	20♍	4♍	21♌	8♎
14	21♍	5♍	21♌	8♎
15	22♍	7♍	21♌	9♎
16	23♍	8♍	21♌	10♎
17	24♍	10♍	21♌	10♎
18	25♍	12♍	21♌	11♎
19	26♍	14♍	22♌	12♎
20	27♍	15♍	22♌	12♎
21	28♍	17♍	22♌	13♎
22	29♍	19♍	22♌	14♎
23	0♎	21♍	23♌	14♎
24	1♎	23♍	23♌	15♎
25	2♎	25♍	24♌	16♎
26	3♎	26♍	24♌	16♎
27	4♎	28♍	24♌	17♎
28	5♎	0♎	25♌	18♎
29	6♎	2♎	25♌	18♎
30	7♎	4♎	26♌	19♎

October

Day	☉	☿	♀	♂
1	8♎	6♎	26♌	20♎
2	9♎	7♎	27♌	20♎
3	9♎	9♎	28♌	21♎
4	10♎	11♎	28♌	22♎
5	11♎	13♎	29♌	22♎
6	12♎	14♎	0♍	23♎
7	13♎	16♎	0♍	24♎
8	14♎	18♎	1♍	24♎
9	15♎	19♎	2♍	25♎
10	16♎	21♎	2♍	26♎
11	17♎	23♎	3♍	26♎
12	18♎	24♎	4♍	27♎
13	19♎	26♎	5♍	28♎
14	20♎	28♎	5♍	28♎
15	21♎	29♎	6♍	29♎
16	22♎	1♏	7♍	0♏
17	23♎	3♏	8♍	0♏
18	24♎	4♏	9♍	1♏
19	25♎	6♏	10♍	2♏
20	26♎	7♏	10♍	2♏
21	27♎	9♏	11♍	3♏
22	28♎	10♏	12♍	4♏
23	29♎	12♏	13♍	4♏
24	0♏	13♏	14♍	5♏
25	1♏	15♏	15♍	6♏
26	2♏	17♏	16♍	6♏
27	3♏	18♏	17♍	7♏
28	4♏	20♏	18♍	8♏
29	5♏	21♏	19♍	8♏
30	6♏	22♏	20♍	9♏
31	7♏	24♏	21♍	10♏

November

Day	☉	☿	♀	♂
1	8♏	25♏	22♍	11♏
2	9♏	27♏	23♍	11♏
3	10♏	28♏	24♍	12♏
4	11♏	0♐	25♍	13♏
5	12♏	1♐	26♍	13♏
6	13♏	2♐	27♍	14♏
7	14♏	4♐	28♍	15♏
8	15♏	5♐	29♍	15♏
9	16♏	7♐	0♎	16♏
10	17♏	8♐	1♎	17♏
11	18♏	9♐	2♎	17♏
12	19♏	10♐	3♎	18♏
13	20♏	12♐	4♎	19♏
14	21♏	13♐	5♎	20♏
15	22♏	14♐	6♎	20♏
16	23♏	15♐	7♎	21♏
17	24♏	16♐	8♎	22♏
18	25♏	18♐	10♎	22♏
19	26♏	19♐	11♎	23♏
20	27♏	20♐	12♎	24♏
21	28♏	20♐	13♎	24♏
22	29♏	21♐	14♎	25♏
23	0♐	22♐	15♎	26♏
24	1♐	23♐	16♎	27♏
25	2♐	23♐	17♎	27♏
26	3♐	24♐	18♎	28♏
27	4♐	24♐	20♎	29♏
28	5♐	24♐	21♎	29♏
29	6♐	24♐	22♎	0♐
30	7♐	24♐	23♎	1♐

December

Day	☉	☿	♀	♂
1	8♐	24♐	24♎	2♐
2	10♐	23♐	25♎	2♐
3	11♐	22♐	26♎	3♐
4	12♐	22♐	28♎	4♐
5	13♐	20♐	29♎	4♐
6	14♐	19♐	0♏	5♐
7	15♐	18♐	1♏	6♐
8	16♐	17♐	2♏	7♐
9	17♐	15♐	3♏	7♐
10	18♐	14♐	5♏	8♐
11	19♐	13♐	6♏	9♐
12	20♐	11♐	7♏	9♐
13	21♐	10♐	8♏	10♐
14	22♐	10♐	9♏	11♐
15	23♐	9♐	10♏	12♐
16	24♐	8♐	12♏	12♐
17	25♐	8♐	13♏	13♐
18	26♐	8♐	14♏	14♐
19	27♐	8♐	15♏	14♐
20	28♐	8♐	16♏	15♐
21	29♐	8♐	18♏	16♐
22	0♑	9♐	19♏	17♐
23	1♑	10♐	20♏	17♐
24	2♑	10♐	21♏	18♐
25	3♑	11♐	22♏	19♐
26	4♑	12♐	23♏	20♐
27	5♑	13♐	25♏	20♐
28	6♑	14♐	26♏	21♐
29	7♑	15♐	27♏	22♐
30	8♑	16♐	28♏	22♐
31	9♑	17♐	29♏	23♐

Planetary Positions

♌ = Leo ♍ = Virgo ♎ = Libra ♏ = Scorpio ♐ = Sagittarius ♑ = Capricorn ♒ = Aquarius ♓ = Pisces

1992

January

Day	☉	☿	♀	♂
1	10♑	18♐	1♐	24♐
2	11♑	20♐	2♐	25♐
3	12♑	21♐	3♐	25♐
4	13♑	22♐	4♐	26♐
5	14♑	23♐	6♐	27♐
6	15♑	25♐	7♐	28♐
7	16♑	26♐	8♐	28♐
8	17♑	27♐	9♐	29♐
9	18♑	29♐	10♐	0♑
10	19♑	0♑	12♐	1♑
11	20♑	2♑	13♐	1♑
12	21♑	3♑	14♐	2♑
13	22♑	4♑	15♐	3♑
14	23♑	6♑	16♐	4♑
15	24♑	7♑	18♐	4♑
16	25♑	9♑	19♐	5♑
17	26♑	10♑	20♐	6♑
18	27♑	12♑	21♐	7♑
19	28♑	13♑	23♐	7♑
20	29♑	15♑	24♐	8♑
21	0♒	16♑	25♐	9♑
22	1♒	18♑	26♐	10♑
23	2♒	19♑	27♐	10♑
24	3♒	21♑	29♐	11♑
25	4♒	23♑	0♑	12♑
26	5♒	24♑	1♑	13♑
27	7♒	26♑	2♑	13♑
28	8♒	27♑	4♑	14♑
29	9♒	29♑	5♑	15♑
30	10♒	1♒	6♑	16♑
31	11♒	2♒	7♑	16♑

April

Day	☉	☿	♀	♂
1	12♈	2♈	22♓	3♓
2	13♈	1♈	24♓	4♓
3	14♈	0♈	25♓	5♓
4	15♈	0♈	26♓	6♓
5	16♈	29♓	27♓	6♓
6	17♈	29♓	29♓	7♓
7	18♈	29♓	0♈	8♓
8	19♈	29♓	1♈	9♓
9	20♈	29♓	2♈	9♓
10	21♈	29♓	4♈	10♓
11	22♈	29♓	5♈	11♓
12	23♈	29♓	6♈	12♓
13	24♈	29♓	7♈	12♓
14	25♈	0♈	9♈	13♓
15	25♈	0♈	10♈	14♓
16	26♈	1♈	11♈	15♓
17	27♈	1♈	12♈	16♓
18	28♈	2♈	13♈	16♓
19	29♈	3♈	15♈	17♓
20	0♉	3♈	16♈	18♓
21	1♉	4♈	17♈	19♓
22	2♉	5♈	18♈	19♓
23	3♉	6♈	20♈	20♓
24	4♉	7♈	21♈	21♓
25	5♉	8♈	22♈	22♓
26	6♉	9♈	23♈	23♓
27	7♉	10♈	25♈	23♓
28	8♉	12♈	26♈	24♓
29	9♉	13♈	27♈	25♓
30	10♉	14♈	28♈	26♓

July

Day	☉	☿	♀	♂
1	10♋	5♌	14♋	12♉
2	11♋	6♌	16♋	13♉
3	12♋	7♌	17♋	13♉
4	12♋	8♌	18♋	14♉
5	13♋	9♌	19♋	15♉
6	14♋	10♌	21♋	16♉
7	15♋	11♌	22♋	16♉
8	16♋	12♌	23♋	17♉
9	17♋	13♌	24♋	18♉
10	18♋	14♌	25♋	18♉
11	19♋	14♌	27♋	19♉
12	20♋	15♌	28♋	20♉
13	21♋	16♌	29♋	21♉
14	22♋	16♌	0♌	21♉
15	23♋	17♌	2♌	22♉
16	24♋	17♌	3♌	23♉
17	25♋	17♌	4♌	23♉
18	26♋	17♌	5♌	24♉
19	27♋	17♌	7♌	25♉
20	28♋	17♌	8♌	25♉
21	29♋	17♌	9♌	26♉
22	0♌	17♌	10♌	27♉
23	1♌	17♌	11♌	28♉
24	2♌	17♌	13♌	28♉
25	3♌	16♌	14♌	29♉
26	3♌	16♌	15♌	0♊
27	4♌	15♌	16♌	0♊
28	5♌	15♌	18♌	1♊
29	6♌	14♌	19♌	2♊
30	7♌	14♌	20♌	2♊
31	8♌	13♌	21♌	3♊

October

Day	☉	☿	♀	♂
1	8♎	20♎	7♏	10♋
2	9♎	22♎	9♏	11♋
3	10♎	23♎	10♏	11♋
4	11♎	25♎	11♏	12♋
5	12♎	27♎	12♏	12♋
6	13♎	28♎	14♏	13♋
7	14♎	0♏	15♏	13♋
8	15♎	1♏	16♏	14♋
9	16♎	3♏	17♏	14♋
10	17♎	4♏	18♏	14♋
11	18♎	6♏	20♏	15♋
12	19♎	7♏	21♏	15♋
13	20♎	9♏	22♏	16♋
14	21♎	10♏	23♏	16♋
15	22♎	11♏	24♏	17♋
16	23♎	13♏	26♏	17♋
17	24♎	14♏	27♏	18♋
18	25♎	16♏	28♏	18♋
19	26♎	17♏	29♏	18♋
20	27♎	18♏	1♐	19♋
21	28♎	20♏	2♐	19♋
22	29♎	21♏	3♐	20♋
23	0♏	22♏	4♐	20♋
24	1♏	24♏	5♐	20♋
25	2♏	25♏	7♐	21♋
26	3♏	26♏	8♐	21♋
27	4♏	27♏	9♐	21♋
28	5♏	28♏	10♐	22♋
29	6♏	29♏	11♐	22♋
30	7♏	1♐	13♐	22♋
31	8♏	2♐	14♐	23♋

February

Day	☉	☿	♀	♂
1	12♒	4♒	8♑	17♑
2	13♒	5♒	10♑	18♑
3	14♒	7♒	11♑	19♑
4	15♒	9♒	12♑	19♑
5	16♒	10♒	13♑	20♑
6	17♒	12♒	15♑	21♑
7	18♒	14♒	16♑	22♑
8	19♒	16♒	17♑	22♑
9	20♒	17♒	18♑	23♑
10	21♒	19♒	20♑	24♑
11	22♒	21♒	21♑	25♑
12	23♒	23♒	22♑	25♑
13	24♒	24♒	23♑	26♑
14	25♒	26♒	24♑	27♑
15	26♒	28♒	26♑	28♑
16	27♒	0♓	27♑	28♑
17	28♒	2♓	28♑	29♑
18	29♒	4♓	29♑	0♒
19	0♓	5♓	1♒	1♒
20	1♓	7♓	2♒	2♒
21	2♓	9♓	3♒	2♒
22	3♓	11♓	4♒	3♒
23	4♓	13♓	6♒	4♒
24	5♓	15♓	7♒	5♒
25	6♓	17♓	8♒	5♒
26	7♓	18♓	9♒	6♒
27	8♓	20♓	11♒	7♒
28	9♓	22♓	12♒	8♒
29	10♓	24♓	13♒	8♒

May

Day	☉	☿	♀	♂
1	11♉	15♈	29♈	26♓
2	12♉	17♈	1♉	27♓
3	13♉	18♈	2♉	28♓
4	14♉	19♈	3♉	29♓
5	15♉	21♈	4♉	29♓
6	16♉	22♈	6♉	0♈
7	17♉	24♈	7♉	1♈
8	18♉	25♈	8♉	2♈
9	19♉	27♈	9♉	3♈
10	20♉	28♈	11♉	3♈
11	21♉	0♉	12♉	4♈
12	22♉	2♉	13♉	5♈
13	23♉	3♉	14♉	6♈
14	24♉	5♉	15♉	6♈
15	25♉	7♉	17♉	7♈
16	26♉	9♉	18♉	8♈
17	27♉	11♉	19♉	9♈
18	28♉	12♉	20♉	9♈
19	28♉	14♉	22♉	10♈
20	29♉	16♉	23♉	11♈
21	0♊	18♉	24♉	12♈
22	1♊	20♉	25♉	12♈
23	2♊	22♉	27♉	13♈
24	3♊	24♉	28♉	14♈
25	4♊	26♉	29♉	15♈
26	5♊	29♉	0♊	15♈
27	6♊	1♊	1♊	16♈
28	7♊	3♊	3♊	17♈
29	8♊	5♊	4♊	18♈
30	9♊	7♊	5♊	18♈
31	10♊	9♊	6♊	19♈

August

Day	☉	☿	♀	♂
1	9♌	12♌	23♌	4♊
2	10♌	11♌	24♌	4♊
3	11♌	11♌	25♌	5♊
4	12♌	10♌	26♌	6♊
5	13♌	9♌	27♌	6♊
6	14♌	8♌	29♌	7♊
7	15♌	8♌	0♍	8♊
8	16♌	7♌	1♍	8♊
9	17♌	7♌	2♍	9♊
10	18♌	6♌	4♍	10♊
11	19♌	6♌	5♍	10♊
12	20♌	6♌	6♍	11♊
13	21♌	6♌	7♍	11♊
14	22♌	6♌	9♍	12♊
15	23♌	6♌	10♍	13♊
16	24♌	7♌	11♍	14♊
17	25♌	7♌	12♍	14♊
18	25♌	8♌	13♍	15♊
19	26♌	8♌	15♍	15♊
20	27♌	9♌	16♍	16♊
21	28♌	10♌	17♍	17♊
22	29♌	11♌	18♍	17♊
23	0♍	12♌	20♍	18♊
24	1♍	13♌	21♍	19♊
25	2♍	15♌	22♍	19♊
26	3♍	16♌	23♍	20♊
27	4♍	18♌	25♍	20♊
28	5♍	19♌	26♍	21♊
29	6♍	21♌	27♍	22♊
30	7♍	22♌	28♍	22♊
31	8♍	24♌	29♍	23♊

November

Day	☉	☿	♀	♂
1	9♏	3♐	15♐	23♋
2	10♏	4♐	16♐	23♋
3	11♏	4♐	18♐	24♋
4	12♏	5♐	19♐	24♋
5	13♏	6♐	20♐	24♋
6	14♏	7♐	21♐	24♋
7	15♏	7♐	22♐	25♋
8	16♏	8♐	24♐	25♋
9	17♏	8♐	25♐	25♋
10	18♏	8♐	26♐	25♋
11	19♏	8♐	27♐	26♋
12	20♏	8♐	28♐	26♋
13	21♏	8♐	0♑	26♋
14	22♏	8♐	1♑	26♋
15	23♏	7♐	2♑	26♋
16	24♏	7♐	3♑	27♋
17	25♏	6♐	4♑	27♋
18	26♏	5♐	6♑	27♋
19	27♏	3♐	7♑	27♋
20	28♏	2♐	8♑	27♋
21	29♏	1♐	9♑	27♋
22	0♐	29♏	10♑	27♋
23	1♐	28♏	12♑	27♋
24	2♐	27♏	13♑	27♋
25	3♐	26♏	14♑	28♋
26	4♐	25♏	15♑	28♋
27	5♐	24♏	16♑	28♋
28	6♐	23♏	18♑	28♋
29	7♐	23♏	19♑	28♋
30	8♐	22♏	20♑	28♋

March

Day	☉	☿	♀	♂
1	11♓	26♓	14♒	9♒
2	12♓	27♓	15♒	10♒
3	13♓	29♓	17♒	11♒
4	14♓	0♈	18♒	12♒
5	15♓	2♈	19♒	12♒
6	16♓	3♈	20♒	13♒
7	17♓	5♈	22♒	14♒
8	18♓	6♈	23♒	15♒
9	19♓	7♈	24♒	15♒
10	20♓	8♈	25♒	16♒
11	21♓	9♈	27♒	17♒
12	22♓	10♈	28♒	18♒
13	23♓	10♈	29♒	18♒
14	24♓	11♈	0♓	19♒
15	25♓	11♈	1♓	20♒
16	26♓	11♈	3♓	21♒
17	27♓	11♈	4♓	22♒
18	28♓	11♈	5♓	22♒
19	29♓	11♈	6♓	23♒
20	0♈	11♈	8♓	24♒
21	1♈	10♈	9♓	25♒
22	2♈	10♈	10♓	25♒
23	3♈	9♈	11♓	26♒
24	4♈	8♈	13♓	27♒
25	5♈	7♈	14♓	28♒
26	6♈	7♈	15♓	29♒
27	7♈	6♈	16♓	29♒
28	8♈	5♈	18♓	0♓
29	9♈	4♈	19♓	1♓
30	10♈	3♈	20♓	2♓
31	11♈	2♈	21♓	2♓

June

Day	☉	☿	♀	♂
1	11♊	12♊	8♊	20♈
2	12♊	14♊	9♊	21♈
3	13♊	16♊	10♊	21♈
4	14♊	18♊	11♊	22♈
5	15♊	20♊	12♊	23♈
6	16♊	23♊	14♊	24♈
7	17♊	25♊	15♊	24♈
8	18♊	27♊	16♊	25♈
9	19♊	29♊	17♊	26♈
10	20♊	1♋	19♊	27♈
11	21♊	3♋	20♊	27♈
12	21♊	5♋	21♊	28♈
13	22♊	7♋	22♊	29♈
14	23♊	9♋	24♊	0♉
15	24♊	11♋	25♊	0♉
16	25♊	12♋	26♊	1♉
17	26♊	14♋	27♊	2♉
18	27♊	16♋	28♊	3♉
19	28♊	18♋	0♋	3♉
20	29♊	19♋	1♋	4♉
21	0♋	21♋	2♋	5♉
22	1♋	23♋	3♋	6♉
23	2♋	24♋	5♋	6♉
24	3♋	26♋	6♋	7♉
25	4♋	27♋	7♋	8♉
26	5♋	29♋	8♋	8♉
27	6♋	0♌	10♋	9♉
28	7♋	1♌	11♋	10♉
29	8♋	3♌	12♋	11♉
30	9♋	4♌	13♋	11♉

September

Day	☉	☿	♀	♂
1	9♍	26♌	1♎	24♊
2	10♍	28♌	2♎	24♊
3	11♍	0♍	3♎	25♊
4	12♍	2♍	4♎	25♊
5	13♍	4♍	6♎	26♊
6	14♍	5♍	7♎	26♊
7	15♍	7♍	8♎	27♊
8	16♍	9♍	9♎	28♊
9	17♍	11♍	10♎	28♊
10	18♍	13♍	12♎	29♊
11	19♍	15♍	13♎	29♊
12	20♍	17♍	14♎	0♋
13	21♍	19♍	15♎	1♋
14	22♍	21♍	17♎	1♋
15	23♍	23♍	18♎	2♋
16	24♍	24♍	19♎	2♋
17	25♍	26♍	20♎	3♋
18	26♍	28♍	22♎	3♋
19	27♍	0♎	23♎	4♋
20	27♍	2♎	24♎	4♋
21	28♍	4♎	25♎	5♋
22	29♍	5♎	26♎	6♋
23	0♎	7♎	28♎	6♋
24	1♎	9♎	29♎	7♋
25	2♎	10♎	0♏	7♋
26	3♎	12♎	1♏	8♋
27	4♎	14♎	3♏	8♋
28	5♎	15♎	4♏	9♋
29	6♎	17♎	5♏	9♋
30	7♎	19♎	6♏	10♋

December

Day	☉	☿	♀	♂
1	9♐	22♏	21♑	28♋
2	10♐	22♏	22♑	28♋
3	11♐	23♏	23♑	27♋
4	12♐	23♏	25♑	27♋
5	13♐	23♏	26♑	27♋
6	14♐	24♏	27♑	27♋
7	15♐	25♏	28♑	27♋
8	16♐	26♏	29♑	27♋
9	17♐	27♏	1♒	27♋
10	18♐	28♏	2♒	27♋
11	19♐	29♏	3♒	27♋
12	20♐	0♐	4♒	26♋
13	21♐	1♐	5♒	26♋
14	22♐	2♐	6♒	26♋
15	23♐	4♐	8♒	26♋
16	24♐	5♐	9♒	26♋
17	26♐	6♐	10♒	25♋
18	27♐	8♐	11♒	25♋
19	28♐	9♐	12♒	25♋
20	29♐	10♐	13♒	24♋
21	0♑	12♐	14♒	24♋
22	1♑	13♐	16♒	24♋
23	2♑	15♐	17♒	24♋
24	3♑	16♐	18♒	23♋
25	4♑	17♐	19♒	23♋
26	5♑	19♐	20♒	23♋
27	6♑	20♐	21♒	22♋
28	7♑	22♐	22♒	22♋
29	8♑	23♐	24♒	21♋
30	9♑	25♐	25♒	21♋
31	10♑	26♐	26♒	21♋

1993

Your Starway to Love

⊙ =Sun ☿ = Mercury ♀ = Venus ♂ = Mars ♈ = Aries ♉ = Taurus ♊ = Gemini ♋ = Cancer

January

Day	⊙	☿	♀	♂
1	11♑	28♐	27♒	20♋
2	12♑	29♐	28♒	20♋
3	13♑	1♑	29♒	20♋
4	14♑	2♑	0♓	19♋
5	15♑	4♑	1♓	19♋
6	16♑	6♑	2♓	18♋
7	17♑	7♑	4♓	18♋
8	18♑	9♑	5♓	18♋
9	19♑	10♑	6♓	17♋
10	20♑	12♑	7♓	17♋
11	21♑	13♑	8♓	16♋
12	22♑	15♑	9♓	16♋
13	23♑	17♑	10♓	16♋
14	24♑	18♑	11♓	15♋
15	25♑	20♑	12♓	15♋
16	26♑	21♑	13♓	14♋
17	27♑	23♑	14♓	14♋
18	28♑	25♑	15♓	14♋
19	29♑	26♑	16♓	13♋
20	0♒	28♑	17♓	13♋
21	1♒	0♒	18♓	13♋
22	2♒	1♒	19♓	12♋
23	3♒	3♒	20♓	12♋
24	4♒	5♒	21♓	12♋
25	5♒	6♒	22♓	12♋
26	6♒	8♒	23♓	11♋
27	7♒	10♒	24♓	11♋
28	8♒	11♒	25♓	11♋
29	9♒	13♒	26♓	11♋
30	10♒	15♒	27♓	10♋
31	11♒	17♒	28♓	10♋

April

Day	⊙	☿	♀	♂
1	11♈	14♓	12♈	18♋
2	12♈	15♓	11♈	19♋
3	13♈	16♓	11♈	19♋
4	14♈	17♓	10♈	20♋
5	15♈	18♓	10♈	20♋
6	16♈	19♓	9♈	20♋
7	17♈	20♓	8♈	21♋
8	18♈	21♓	8♈	21♋
9	19♈	22♓	7♈	22♋
10	20♈	23♓	7♈	22♋
11	21♈	24♓	6♈	22♋
12	22♈	26♓	6♈	23♋
13	23♈	27♓	6♈	23♋
14	24♈	28♓	5♈	24♋
15	25♈	29♓	5♈	24♋
16	26♈	1♈	5♈	25♋
17	27♈	2♈	4♈	25♋
18	28♈	4♈	4♈	25♋
19	29♈	5♈	4♈	26♋
20	0♉	7♈	4♈	26♋
21	1♉	8♈	4♈	27♋
22	2♉	10♈	4♈	27♋
23	3♉	11♈	4♈	28♋
24	4♉	13♈	4♈	28♋
25	5♉	14♈	4♈	29♋
26	6♉	16♈	4♈	29♋
27	7♉	18♈	4♈	0♌
28	8♉	20♈	4♈	0♌
29	9♉	21♈	5♈	1♌
30	10♉	23♈	5♈	1♌

July

Day	⊙	☿	♀	♂
1	9♋	28♋	25♉	5♍
2	10♋	28♋	26♉	5♍
3	11♋	28♋	27♉	6♍
4	12♋	28♋	28♉	6♍
5	13♋	28♋	29♉	7♍
6	14♋	27♋	0♊	8♍
7	15♋	27♋	1♊	8♍
8	16♋	27♋	2♊	9♍
9	17♋	26♋	3♊	9♍
10	18♋	26♋	5♊	10♍
11	19♋	25♋	6♊	10♍
12	20♋	24♋	7♊	11♍
13	21♋	24♋	8♊	12♍
14	22♋	23♋	9♊	12♍
15	23♋	22♋	10♊	13♍
16	24♋	22♋	11♊	13♍
17	25♋	21♋	12♊	14♍
18	26♋	21♋	13♊	15♍
19	27♋	20♋	14♊	15♍
20	27♋	20♋	16♊	16♍
21	28♋	19♋	17♊	17♍
22	29♋	19♋	18♊	17♍
23	0♌	18♋	19♊	18♍
24	1♌	18♋	20♊	18♍
25	2♌	18♋	21♊	19♍
26	3♌	18♋	22♊	20♍
27	4♌	18♋	23♊	20♍
28	5♌	18♋	25♊	21♍
29	6♌	19♋	26♊	21♍
30	7♌	19♋	27♊	22♍
31	8♌	20♋	28♊	23♍

October

Day	⊙	☿	♀	♂
1	8♎	0♏	12♍	3♏
2	9♎	2♏	13♍	3♏
3	10♎	3♏	14♍	4♏
4	11♎	4♏	15♍	5♏
5	12♎	5♏	17♍	6♏
6	13♎	7♏	18♍	6♏
7	14♎	8♏	19♍	7♏
8	15♎	9♏	20♍	8♏
9	16♎	10♏	22♍	8♏
10	17♎	11♏	23♍	9♏
11	18♎	13♏	24♍	10♏
12	19♎	14♏	25♍	10♏
13	20♎	15♏	27♍	11♏
14	21♎	16♏	28♍	12♏
15	22♎	17♏	29♍	12♏
16	23♎	18♏	0♎	13♏
17	24♎	18♏	1♎	14♏
18	25♎	19♏	3♎	14♏
19	26♎	20♏	4♎	15♏
20	27♎	21♏	5♎	16♏
21	28♎	21♏	6♎	17♏
22	29♎	22♏	8♎	17♏
23	0♏	22♏	9♎	18♏
24	1♏	22♏	10♎	19♏
25	2♏	22♏	11♎	19♏
26	3♏	23♏	13♎	20♏
27	4♏	22♏	14♎	21♏
28	5♏	22♏	15♎	21♏
29	6♏	22♏	16♎	22♏
30	7♏	21♏	18♎	23♏
31	8♏	20♏	19♎	24♏

February

Day	⊙	☿	♀	♂
1	12♒	18♒	29♓	10♋
2	13♒	20♒	0♈	10♋
3	14♒	22♒	1♈	10♋
4	15♒	24♒	1♈	9♋
5	16♒	26♒	2♈	9♋
6	17♒	27♒	3♈	9♋
7	18♒	29♒	4♈	9♋
8	19♒	1♓	5♈	9♋
9	20♒	3♓	6♈	9♋
10	21♒	4♓	7♈	9♋
11	22♒	6♓	7♈	9♋
12	23♒	8♓	8♈	9♋
13	25♒	10♓	9♈	9♋
14	26♒	11♓	10♈	9♋
15	27♒	13♓	10♈	9♋
16	28♒	14♓	11♈	9♋
17	29♒	16♓	12♈	9♋
18	0♓	17♓	12♈	9♋
19	1♓	18♓	13♈	9♋
20	2♓	20♓	14♈	9♋
21	3♓	21♓	14♈	9♋
22	4♓	22♓	15♈	9♋
23	5♓	22♓	15♈	9♋
24	6♓	23♓	16♈	9♋
25	7♓	24♓	16♈	9♋
26	8♓	24♓	17♈	9♋
27	9♓	24♓	17♈	10♋
28	10♓	24♓	18♈	10♋

May

Day	⊙	☿	♀	♂
1	11♉	25♈	5♈	2♌
2	12♉	27♈	5♈	2♌
3	13♉	29♈	6♈	3♌
4	14♉	1♉	6♈	3♌
5	15♉	3♉	7♈	4♌
6	16♉	4♉	7♈	4♌
7	17♉	6♉	7♈	4♌
8	18♉	8♉	8♈	5♌
9	19♉	11♉	8♈	5♌
10	20♉	13♉	9♈	6♌
11	21♉	15♉	10♈	7♌
12	21♉	17♉	10♈	7♌
13	22♉	19♉	11♈	8♌
14	23♉	21♉	11♈	8♌
15	24♉	23♉	12♈	9♌
16	25♉	25♉	13♈	9♌
17	26♉	28♉	13♈	10♌
18	27♉	0♊	14♈	10♌
19	28♉	2♊	15♈	11♌
20	29♉	4♊	16♈	11♌
21	0♊	6♊	16♈	12♌
22	1♊	9♊	17♈	12♌
23	2♊	11♊	18♈	13♌
24	3♊	13♊	19♈	13♌
25	4♊	15♊	19♈	14♌
26	5♊	17♊	20♈	14♌
27	6♊	19♊	21♈	15♌
28	7♊	21♊	22♈	15♌
29	8♊	23♊	23♈	16♌
30	9♊	25♊	24♈	16♌
31	10♊	27♊	24♈	17♌

August

Day	⊙	☿	♀	♂
1	9♌	20♋	29♊	23♍
2	10♌	21♋	0♋	24♍
3	11♌	22♋	1♋	24♍
4	12♌	23♋	3♋	25♍
5	13♌	24♋	4♋	26♍
6	14♌	25♋	5♋	26♍
7	15♌	26♋	6♋	27♍
8	16♌	27♋	7♋	28♍
9	17♌	28♋	8♋	28♍
10	18♌	0♌	10♋	29♍
11	19♌	1♌	11♋	29♍
12	20♌	3♌	12♋	0♎
13	20♌	5♌	13♋	1♎
14	21♌	6♌	14♋	1♎
15	22♌	8♌	15♋	2♎
16	23♌	10♌	17♋	3♎
17	24♌	12♌	18♋	3♎
18	25♌	14♌	19♋	4♎
19	26♌	16♌	20♋	5♎
20	27♌	18♌	21♋	5♎
21	28♌	20♌	22♋	6♎
22	29♌	22♌	24♋	6♎
23	0♍	24♌	25♋	7♎
24	1♍	26♌	26♋	8♎
25	2♍	28♌	27♋	8♎
26	3♍	0♍	28♋	9♎
27	4♍	2♍	29♋	10♎
28	5♍	4♍	1♌	10♎
29	6♍	6♍	2♌	11♎
30	7♍	8♍	3♌	12♎
31	8♍	10♍	4♌	12♎

November

Day	⊙	☿	♀	♂
1	9♏	20♏	20♎	24♏
2	10♏	19♏	21♎	25♏
3	11♏	17♏	23♎	26♏
4	12♏	16♏	24♎	26♏
5	13♏	15♏	25♎	27♏
6	14♏	14♏	26♎	28♏
7	15♏	12♏	28♎	29♏
8	16♏	11♏	29♎	29♏
9	17♏	10♏	0♏	0♐
10	18♏	9♏	1♏	1♐
11	19♏	8♏	3♏	1♐
12	20♏	7♏	4♏	2♐
13	21♏	7♏	5♏	3♐
14	22♏	7♏	6♏	4♐
15	23♏	7♏	8♏	4♐
16	24♏	7♏	9♏	5♐
17	25♏	7♏	10♏	6♐
18	26♏	7♏	11♏	6♐
19	27♏	8♏	13♏	7♐
20	28♏	9♏	14♏	8♐
21	29♏	9♏	15♏	9♐
22	0♐	10♏	16♏	9♐
23	1♐	11♏	18♏	10♐
24	2♐	12♏	19♏	11♐
25	3♐	14♏	20♏	12♐
26	4♐	15♏	21♏	12♐
27	5♐	16♏	23♏	13♐
28	6♐	17♏	24♏	14♐
29	7♐	19♏	25♏	15♐
30	8♐	20♏	26♏	15♐

March

Day	⊙	☿	♀	♂
1	11♓	24♓	18♈	10♋
2	12♓	24♓	18♈	10♋
3	13♓	23♓	19♈	10♋
4	14♓	23♓	19♈	10♋
5	15♓	22♓	19♈	11♋
6	16♓	21♓	19♈	11♋
7	17♓	20♓	20♈	11♋
8	18♓	20♓	20♈	11♋
9	19♓	19♓	20♈	11♋
10	20♓	18♓	20♈	12♋
11	21♓	17♓	20♈	12♋
12	22♓	16♓	20♈	12♋
13	23♓	15♓	20♈	12♋
14	24♓	14♓	20♈	13♋
15	25♓	13♓	20♈	13♋
16	26♓	12♓	20♈	13♋
17	27♓	12♓	19♈	13♋
18	28♓	11♓	19♈	14♋
19	29♓	11♓	19♈	14♋
20	0♈	11♓	18♈	14♋
21	1♈	10♓	18♈	15♋
22	2♈	10♓	18♈	15♋
23	3♈	10♓	17♈	15♋
24	4♈	10♓	17♈	16♋
25	5♈	11♓	16♈	16♋
26	6♈	11♓	16♈	16♋
27	7♈	11♓	15♈	17♋
28	8♈	12♓	15♈	17♋
29	9♈	12♓	14♈	17♋
30	10♈	13♓	13♈	18♋
31	10♈	14♓	13♈	18♋

June

Day	⊙	☿	♀	♂
1	11♊	28♊	25♈	18♌
2	12♊	0♋	26♈	18♌
3	13♊	2♋	27♈	19♌
4	14♊	3♋	28♈	19♌
5	15♊	5♋	29♈	20♌
6	16♊	7♋	0♉	20♌
7	16♊	8♋	1♉	21♌
8	17♊	10♋	2♉	21♌
9	18♊	11♋	3♉	22♌
10	19♊	12♋	4♉	23♌
11	20♊	14♋	5♉	23♌
12	21♊	15♋	5♉	24♌
13	22♊	16♋	6♉	24♌
14	23♊	17♋	7♉	25♌
15	24♊	19♋	8♉	25♌
16	25♊	20♋	9♉	26♌
17	26♊	21♋	10♉	27♌
18	27♊	22♋	11♉	27♌
19	28♊	23♋	12♉	28♌
20	29♊	23♋	13♉	28♌
21	0♋	24♋	14♉	29♌
22	1♋	25♋	15♉	29♌
23	2♋	26♋	16♉	0♍
24	3♋	26♋	18♉	1♍
25	4♋	27♋	19♉	1♍
26	5♋	27♋	20♉	2♍
27	6♋	27♋	21♉	2♍
28	7♋	28♋	22♉	3♍
29	7♋	28♋	23♉	3♍
30	8♋	28♋	24♉	4♍

September

Day	⊙	☿	♀	♂
1	9♍	12♍	5♌	13♎
2	10♍	13♍	7♌	14♎
3	11♍	15♍	8♌	14♎
4	12♍	17♍	9♌	15♎
5	13♍	19♍	10♌	15♎
6	14♍	21♍	11♌	16♎
7	15♍	23♍	13♌	17♎
8	16♍	24♍	14♌	17♎
9	17♍	26♍	15♌	18♎
10	18♍	28♍	16♌	19♎
11	18♍	0♎	17♌	19♎
12	19♍	1♎	19♌	20♎
13	20♍	3♎	20♌	21♎
14	21♍	5♎	21♌	21♎
15	22♍	6♎	22♌	22♎
16	23♍	8♎	23♌	23♎
17	24♍	9♎	25♌	23♎
18	25♍	11♎	26♌	24♎
19	26♍	13♎	27♌	25♎
20	27♍	14♎	28♌	25♎
21	28♍	16♎	0♍	26♎
22	29♍	17♎	1♍	27♎
23	0♎	19♎	2♍	27♎
24	1♎	20♎	3♍	28♎
25	2♎	22♎	4♍	29♎
26	3♎	23♎	6♍	29♎
27	4♎	25♎	7♍	0♏
28	5♎	26♎	8♍	1♏
29	6♎	27♎	9♍	1♏
30	7♎	29♎	11♍	2♏

December

Day	⊙	☿	♀	♂
1	9♐	21♏	28♏	16♐
2	10♐	23♏	29♏	17♐
3	11♐	24♏	0♐	17♐
4	12♐	26♏	2♐	18♐
5	13♐	27♏	3♐	19♐
6	14♐	29♏	4♐	20♐
7	15♐	0♐	5♐	20♐
8	16♐	2♐	7♐	21♐
9	17♐	3♐	8♐	22♐
10	18♐	5♐	9♐	23♐
11	19♐	6♐	10♐	23♐
12	20♐	8♐	12♐	24♐
13	21♐	9♐	13♐	25♐
14	22♐	11♐	14♐	26♐
15	23♐	12♐	15♐	26♐
16	24♐	14♐	17♐	27♐
17	25♐	15♐	18♐	28♐
18	26♐	17♐	19♐	29♐
19	27♐	19♐	20♐	29♐
20	28♐	20♐	22♐	0♑
21	29♐	22♐	23♐	1♑
22	0♑	23♐	24♐	2♑
23	1♑	25♐	25♐	2♑
24	2♑	26♐	27♐	3♑
25	3♑	28♐	28♐	4♑
26	4♑	29♐	29♐	5♑
27	5♑	1♑	0♑	5♑
28	6♑	3♑	2♑	6♑
29	7♑	4♑	3♑	7♑
30	9♑	6♑	4♑	8♑
31	10♑	7♑	5♑	8♑

Planetary Positions

♌ = Leo ♍ = Virgo ♎ = Libra ♏ = Scorpio ♐ = Sagittarius ♑ = Capricorn ♒ = Aquarius ♓ = Pisces

1994

January

Day	☉	☿	♀	♂
1	11♑	9♑	7♑	9♑
2	12♑	11♑	8♑	10♑
3	13♑	12♑	9♑	11♑
4	14♑	14♑	11♑	12♑
5	15♑	15♑	12♑	12♑
6	16♑	17♑	13♑	13♑
7	17♑	19♑	14♑	14♑
8	18♑	20♑	16♑	15♑
9	19♑	22♑	17♑	15♑
10	20♑	24♑	18♑	16♑
11	21♑	25♑	19♑	17♑
12	22♑	27♑	21♑	18♑
13	23♑	29♑	22♑	18♑
14	24♑	0♒	23♑	19♑
15	25♑	2♒	24♑	20♑
16	26♑	4♒	26♑	21♑
17	27♑	5♒	27♑	22♑
18	28♑	7♒	28♑	22♑
19	29♑	9♒	29♑	23♑
20	0♒	10♒	1♒	24♑
21	1♒	12♒	2♒	25♑
22	2♒	14♒	3♒	25♑
23	3♒	16♒	4♒	26♑
24	4♒	17♒	6♒	27♑
25	5♒	19♒	7♒	28♑
26	6♒	21♒	8♒	28♑
27	7♒	22♒	9♒	29♑
28	8♒	24♒	11♒	0♒
29	9♒	25♒	12♒	1♒
30	10♒	27♒	13♒	2♒
31	11♒	28♒	14♒	2♒

February

Day	☉	☿	♀	♂
1	12♒	0♓	16♒	3♒
2	13♒	1♓	17♒	4♒
3	14♒	2♓	18♒	5♒
4	15♒	3♓	19♒	5♒
5	16♒	4♓	21♒	6♒
6	17♒	5♓	22♒	7♒
7	18♒	6♓	23♒	8♒
8	19♒	7♓	25♒	9♒
9	20♒	7♓	26♒	9♒
10	21♒	7♓	27♒	10♒
11	22♒	8♓	28♒	11♒
12	23♒	8♓	0♓	12♒
13	24♒	7♓	1♓	13♒
14	25♒	7♓	2♓	13♒
15	26♒	6♓	3♓	14♒
16	27♒	6♓	5♓	15♒
17	28♒	5♓	6♓	16♒
18	29♒	4♓	7♓	16♒
19	0♓	3♓	8♓	17♒
20	1♓	2♓	10♓	18♒
21	2♓	0♓	11♓	19♒
22	3♓	29♒	12♓	20♒
23	4♓	28♒	13♓	20♒
24	5♓	27♒	15♓	21♒
25	6♓	26♒	16♓	22♒
26	7♓	25♒	17♓	23♒
27	8♓	25♒	18♓	24♒
28	9♓	24♒	20♓	24♒

March

Day	☉	☿	♀	♂
1	10♓	24♒	21♓	25♒
2	11♓	23♒	22♓	26♒
3	12♓	23♒	23♓	27♒
4	13♓	23♒	25♓	27♒
5	14♓	23♒	26♓	28♒
6	15♓	23♒	27♓	29♒
7	16♓	23♒	28♓	0♓
8	17♓	23♒	0♈	1♓
9	18♓	23♒	1♈	1♓
10	19♓	24♒	2♈	2♓
11	20♓	24♒	3♈	3♓
12	21♓	25♒	4♈	4♓
13	22♓	26♒	6♈	5♓
14	23♓	26♒	7♈	5♓
15	24♓	27♒	8♈	6♓
16	25♓	28♒	9♈	7♓
17	26♓	29♒	11♈	8♓
18	27♓	0♓	12♈	8♓
19	28♓	1♓	13♈	9♓
20	29♓	2♓	14♈	10♓
21	0♈	3♓	16♈	11♓
22	1♈	4♓	17♈	12♓
23	2♈	5♓	18♈	12♓
24	3♈	6♓	19♈	13♓
25	4♈	7♓	21♈	14♓
26	5♈	9♓	22♈	15♓
27	6♈	10♓	23♈	16♓
28	7♈	11♓	24♈	16♓
29	8♈	13♓	26♈	17♓
30	9♈	14♓	27♈	18♓
31	10♈	15♓	28♈	19♓

April

Day	☉	☿	♀	♂
1	11♈	17♓	29♈	19♓
2	12♈	18♓	0♉	20♓
3	13♈	20♓	2♉	21♓
4	14♈	21♓	3♉	22♓
5	15♈	23♓	4♉	23♓
6	16♈	24♓	5♉	23♓
7	17♈	26♓	7♉	24♓
8	18♈	28♓	8♉	25♓
9	19♈	29♓	9♉	26♓
10	20♈	1♈	10♉	26♓
11	21♈	3♈	12♉	27♓
12	22♈	4♈	13♉	28♓
13	23♈	6♈	14♉	29♓
14	24♈	8♈	15♉	0♈
15	25♈	10♈	16♉	0♈
16	26♈	11♈	18♉	1♈
17	27♈	13♈	19♉	2♈
18	28♈	15♈	20♉	3♈
19	29♈	17♈	21♉	3♈
20	0♉	19♈	23♉	4♈
21	1♉	21♈	24♉	5♈
22	2♉	23♈	25♉	6♈
23	3♉	25♈	26♉	7♈
24	4♉	27♈	27♉	7♈
25	5♉	29♈	29♉	8♈
26	6♉	1♉	0♊	9♈
27	7♉	3♉	1♊	10♈
28	8♉	5♉	2♊	10♈
29	9♉	7♉	4♊	11♈
30	10♉	9♉	5♊	12♈

May

Day	☉	☿	♀	♂
1	11♉	12♉	6♊	13♈
2	12♉	14♉	7♊	13♈
3	13♉	16♉	8♊	14♈
4	14♉	18♉	10♊	15♈
5	14♉	20♉	11♊	16♈
6	15♉	22♉	12♊	17♈
7	16♉	24♉	13♊	17♈
8	17♉	27♉	15♊	18♈
9	18♉	29♉	16♊	19♈
10	19♉	1♊	17♊	20♈
11	20♉	3♊	18♊	20♈
12	21♉	5♊	19♊	21♈
13	22♉	7♊	21♊	22♈
14	23♉	9♊	22♊	23♈
15	24♉	10♊	23♊	23♈
16	25♉	12♊	24♊	24♈
17	26♉	14♊	25♊	25♈
18	27♉	16♊	27♊	26♈
19	28♉	17♊	28♊	26♈
20	29♉	19♊	29♊	27♈
21	0♊	20♊	0♋	28♈
22	1♊	22♊	1♋	29♈
23	2♊	23♊	3♋	29♈
24	3♊	25♊	4♋	0♉
25	4♊	26♊	5♋	1♉
26	5♊	27♊	6♋	2♉
27	6♊	28♊	7♋	2♉
28	7♊	0♋	9♋	3♉
29	8♊	1♋	10♋	4♉
30	9♊	2♋	11♋	5♉
31	10♊	3♋	12♋	5♉

June

Day	☉	☿	♀	♂
1	10♊	3♋	13♋	6♉
2	11♊	4♋	15♋	7♉
3	12♊	5♋	16♋	8♉
4	13♊	6♋	17♋	8♉
5	14♊	6♋	18♋	9♉
6	15♊	7♋	19♋	10♉
7	16♊	7♋	20♋	11♉
8	17♊	8♋	22♋	11♉
9	18♊	8♋	23♋	12♉
10	19♊	8♋	24♋	13♉
11	20♊	8♋	25♋	14♉
12	21♊	8♋	26♋	14♉
13	22♊	8♋	28♋	15♉
14	23♊	8♋	29♋	16♉
15	24♊	8♋	0♌	17♉
16	25♊	8♋	1♌	17♉
17	26♊	8♋	2♌	18♉
18	27♊	7♋	3♌	19♉
19	28♊	7♋	5♌	19♉
20	29♊	6♋	6♌	20♉
21	0♋	6♋	7♌	21♉
22	1♋	5♋	8♌	22♉
23	2♋	5♋	9♌	22♉
24	2♋	4♋	10♌	23♉
25	3♋	4♋	12♌	24♉
26	4♋	3♋	13♌	24♉
27	5♋	3♋	14♌	25♉
28	6♋	2♋	15♌	26♉
29	7♋	2♋	16♌	27♉
30	8♋	1♋	17♌	27♉

July

Day	☉	☿	♀	♂
1	9♋	1♋	18♌	28♉
2	10♋	0♋	20♌	29♉
3	11♋	0♋	21♌	29♉
4	12♋	0♋	22♌	0♊
5	13♋	0♋	23♌	1♊
6	14♋	29♊	24♌	2♊
7	15♋	29♊	25♌	2♊
8	16♋	29♊	27♌	3♊
9	17♋	0♋	28♌	4♊
10	18♋	0♋	29♌	4♊
11	19♋	0♋	0♍	5♊
12	20♋	1♋	1♍	6♊
13	21♋	1♋	2♍	7♊
14	22♋	2♋	3♍	7♊
15	22♋	2♋	4♍	8♊
16	23♋	3♋	6♍	9♊
17	24♋	4♋	7♍	9♊
18	25♋	5♋	8♍	10♊
19	26♋	6♋	9♍	11♊
20	27♋	7♋	10♍	11♊
21	28♋	8♋	11♍	12♊
22	29♋	10♋	12♍	13♊
23	0♌	11♋	13♍	13♊
24	1♌	12♋	14♍	14♊
25	2♌	14♋	16♍	15♊
26	3♌	15♋	17♍	16♊
27	4♌	17♋	18♍	16♊
28	5♌	19♋	19♍	17♊
29	6♌	20♋	20♍	18♊
30	7♌	22♋	21♍	18♊
31	8♌	24♋	22♍	19♊

August

Day	☉	☿	♀	♂
1	9♌	26♋	23♍	20♊
2	10♌	28♋	24♍	20♊
3	11♌	0♌	25♍	21♊
4	12♌	2♌	26♍	22♊
5	13♌	4♌	27♍	22♊
6	14♌	6♌	29♍	23♊
7	14♌	8♌	0♎	24♊
8	15♌	10♌	1♎	24♊
9	16♌	12♌	2♎	25♊
10	17♌	14♌	3♎	26♊
11	18♌	16♌	4♎	26♊
12	19♌	18♌	5♎	27♊
13	20♌	20♌	6♎	28♊
14	21♌	22♌	7♎	28♊
15	22♌	24♌	8♎	29♊
16	23♌	26♌	9♎	0♋
17	24♌	28♌	10♎	0♋
18	25♌	0♍	11♎	1♋
19	26♌	2♍	12♎	2♋
20	27♌	4♍	13♎	2♋
21	28♌	6♍	14♎	3♋
22	29♌	8♍	15♎	4♋
23	0♍	10♍	16♎	4♋
24	1♍	12♍	17♎	5♋
25	2♍	13♍	18♎	5♋
26	3♍	15♍	19♎	6♋
27	4♍	17♍	20♎	7♋
28	5♍	19♍	21♎	7♋
29	6♍	20♍	22♎	8♋
30	7♍	22♍	22♎	9♋
31	8♍	24♍	23♎	9♋

September

Day	☉	☿	♀	♂
1	9♍	25♍	24♎	10♋
2	10♍	27♍	25♎	11♋
3	10♍	28♍	26♎	11♋
4	11♍	0♎	27♎	12♋
5	12♍	2♎	28♎	12♋
6	13♍	3♎	29♎	13♋
7	14♍	5♎	0♏	14♋
8	15♍	6♎	0♏	14♋
9	16♍	8♎	1♏	15♋
10	17♍	9♎	2♏	16♋
11	18♍	10♎	3♏	16♋
12	19♍	12♎	4♏	17♋
13	20♍	13♎	4♏	17♋
14	21♍	15♎	5♏	18♋
15	22♍	16♎	6♏	19♋
16	23♍	17♎	7♏	19♋
17	24♍	19♎	7♏	20♋
18	25♍	20♎	8♏	20♋
19	26♍	21♎	9♏	21♋
20	27♍	22♎	9♏	22♋
21	28♍	23♎	10♏	22♋
22	29♍	25♎	11♏	23♋
23	0♎	26♎	11♏	23♋
24	1♎	27♎	12♏	24♋
25	2♎	28♎	12♏	25♋
26	3♎	29♎	13♏	25♋
27	4♎	0♏	14♏	26♋
28	5♎	1♏	14♏	26♋
29	6♎	2♏	15♏	27♋
30	7♎	2♏	15♏	27♋

October

Day	☉	☿	♀	♂
1	8♎	3♏	15♏	28♋
2	9♎	4♏	16♏	29♋
3	10♎	5♏	16♏	29♋
4	11♎	5♏	17♏	0♌
5	12♎	6♏	17♏	0♌
6	13♎	6♏	17♏	1♌
7	14♎	6♏	17♏	1♌
8	15♎	6♏	18♏	2♌
9	16♎	6♏	18♏	3♌
10	17♎	6♏	18♏	3♌
11	18♎	6♏	18♏	4♌
12	19♎	6♏	18♏	4♌
13	20♎	5♏	18♏	5♌
14	21♎	5♏	18♏	5♌
15	22♎	4♏	18♏	6♌
16	23♎	3♏	18♏	6♌
17	24♎	2♏	18♏	7♌
18	25♎	1♏	18♏	7♌
19	26♎	0♏	17♏	8♌
20	27♎	29♎	17♏	8♌
21	28♎	28♎	17♏	9♌
22	29♎	26♎	16♏	10♌
23	0♏	25♎	16♏	10♌
24	1♏	24♎	16♏	11♌
25	2♏	23♎	15♏	11♌
26	3♏	22♎	15♏	12♌
27	4♏	22♎	14♏	12♌
28	5♏	21♎	14♏	13♌
29	6♏	21♎	13♏	13♌
30	7♏	21♎	13♏	14♌
31	8♏	21♎	12♏	14♌

November

Day	☉	☿	♀	♂
1	9♏	21♎	11♏	15♌
2	10♏	22♎	11♏	15♌
3	11♏	22♎	10♏	15♌
4	12♏	23♎	10♏	16♌
5	13♏	24♎	9♏	16♌
6	14♏	25♎	8♏	17♌
7	15♏	26♎	8♏	17♌
8	16♏	27♎	7♏	18♌
9	17♏	28♎	7♏	18♌
10	18♏	0♏	6♏	19♌
11	19♏	1♏	6♏	19♌
12	20♏	2♏	5♏	20♌
13	21♏	4♏	5♏	20♌
14	22♏	5♏	4♏	20♌
15	23♏	7♏	4♏	21♌
16	24♏	8♏	4♏	21♌
17	25♏	10♏	3♏	22♌
18	26♏	11♏	3♏	22♌
19	27♏	13♏	3♏	22♌
20	28♏	14♏	3♏	23♌
21	29♏	16♏	3♏	23♌
22	0♐	17♏	3♏	24♌
23	1♐	19♏	2♏	24♌
24	2♐	21♏	2♏	24♌
25	3♐	22♏	3♏	25♌
26	4♐	24♏	3♏	25♌
27	5♐	25♏	3♏	25♌
28	6♐	27♏	3♏	26♌
29	7♐	28♏	3♏	26♌
30	8♐	0♐	3♏	27♌

December

Day	☉	☿	♀	♂
1	9♐	2♐	4♏	27♌
2	10♐	3♐	4♏	27♌
3	11♐	5♐	4♏	27♌
4	12♐	6♐	5♏	28♌
5	13♐	8♐	5♏	28♌
6	14♐	9♐	5♏	28♌
7	15♐	11♐	6♏	29♌
8	16♐	13♐	6♏	29♌
9	17♐	14♐	7♏	29♌
10	18♐	16♐	7♏	29♌
11	19♐	17♐	8♏	0♍
12	20♐	19♐	9♏	0♍
13	21♐	20♐	9♏	0♍
14	22♐	22♐	10♏	0♍
15	23♐	24♐	10♏	1♍
16	24♐	25♐	11♏	1♍
17	25♐	27♐	12♏	1♍
18	26♐	28♐	12♏	1♍
19	27♐	0♑	13♏	1♍
20	28♐	1♑	14♏	2♍
21	29♐	3♑	15♏	2♍
22	0♑	5♑	15♏	2♍
23	1♑	6♑	16♏	2♍
24	2♑	8♑	17♏	2♍
25	3♑	9♑	18♏	2♍
26	4♑	11♑	19♏	2♍
27	5♑	13♑	20♏	2♍
28	6♑	14♑	20♏	2♍
29	7♑	16♑	21♏	3♍
30	8♑	18♑	22♏	3♍
31	9♑	19♑	23♏	3♍

☉ =Sun ☿ = Mercury ♀ = Venus ♂ = Mars ♈ = Aries ♉ = Taurus ♊ = Gemini ♋ = Cancer

1995

January

Day	☉	☿	♀	♂
1	10♑	21♑	24♏	3♍
2	11♑	22♑	25♏	3♍
3	12♑	24♑	26♏	3♍
4	13♑	26♑	27♏	3♍
5	14♑	27♑	28♏	3♍
6	15♑	29♑	29♏	3♍
7	16♑	0♒	0♐	3♍
8	17♑	2♒	1♐	2♍
9	18♑	4♒	2♐	2♍
10	19♑	5♒	3♐	2♍
11	20♑	7♒	4♐	2♍
12	22♑	8♒	5♐	2♍
13	23♑	10♒	6♐	2♍
14	24♑	11♒	7♐	2♍
15	25♑	13♒	8♐	2♍
16	26♑	14♒	9♐	1♍
17	27♑	15♒	10♐	1♍
18	28♑	16♒	11♐	1♍
19	29♑	17♒	12♐	1♍
20	0♒	18♒	13♐	1♍
21	1♒	19♒	14♐	0♍
22	2♒	20♒	15♐	0♍
23	3♒	21♒	16♐	0♍
24	4♒	21♒	17♐	0♍
25	5♒	21♒	18♐	29♌
26	6♒	21♒	19♐	29♌
27	7♒	21♒	20♐	29♌
28	8♒	21♒	22♐	28♌
29	9♒	20♒	23♐	28♌
30	10♒	20♒	24♐	28♌
31	11♒	19♒	25♐	27♌

February

Day	☉	☿	♀	♂
1	12♒	18♒	26♐	27♌
2	13♒	17♒	27♐	27♌
3	14♒	16♒	28♐	26♌
4	15♒	14♒	29♐	26♌
5	16♒	13♒	0♑	26♌
6	17♒	12♒	2♑	25♌
7	18♒	11♒	3♑	25♌
8	19♒	10♒	4♑	24♌
9	20♒	9♒	5♑	24♌
10	21♒	8♒	6♑	24♌
11	22♒	7♒	7♑	23♌
12	23♒	7♒	8♑	23♌
13	24♒	6♒	9♑	22♌
14	25♒	6♒	11♑	22♌
15	26♒	6♒	12♑	22♌
16	27♒	6♒	13♑	21♌
17	28♒	6♒	14♑	21♌
18	29♒	6♒	15♑	20♌
19	0♓	6♒	16♑	20♌
20	1♓	6♒	18♑	20♌
21	2♓	7♒	19♑	19♌
22	3♓	7♒	20♑	19♌
23	4♓	8♒	21♑	19♌
24	5♓	9♒	22♑	18♌
25	6♓	10♒	23♑	18♌
26	7♓	10♒	24♑	18♌
27	8♓	11♒	26♑	17♌
28	9♓	12♒	27♑	17♌

March

Day	☉	☿	♀	♂
1	10♓	13♒	28♑	17♌
2	11♓	14♒	29♑	16♌
3	12♓	15♒	0♒	16♌
4	13♓	16♒	2♒	16♌
5	14♓	17♒	3♒	16♌
6	15♓	19♒	4♒	15♌
7	16♓	20♒	5♒	15♌
8	17♓	21♒	6♒	15♌
9	18♓	22♒	7♒	15♌
10	19♓	24♒	9♒	15♌
11	20♓	25♒	10♒	14♌
12	21♓	26♒	11♒	14♌
13	22♓	28♒	12♒	14♌
14	23♓	29♒	13♒	14♌
15	24♓	0♓	14♒	14♌
16	25♓	2♓	16♒	14♌
17	26♓	3♓	17♒	14♌
18	27♓	5♓	18♒	13♌
19	28♓	6♓	19♒	13♌
20	29♓	8♓	20♒	13♌
21	0♈	9♓	22♒	13♌
22	1♈	11♓	23♒	13♌
23	2♈	13♓	24♒	13♌
24	3♈	14♓	25♒	13♌
25	4♈	16♓	26♒	13♌
26	5♈	18♓	28♒	13♌
27	6♈	19♓	29♒	13♌
28	7♈	21♓	0♓	13♌
29	8♈	23♓	1♓	13♌
30	9♈	24♓	2♓	13♌
31	10♈	26♓	4♓	13♌

April

Day	☉	☿	♀	♂
1	11♈	28♓	5♓	13♌
2	12♈	0♈	6♓	14♌
3	13♈	2♈	7♓	14♌
4	14♈	4♈	8♓	14♌
5	15♈	5♈	10♓	14♌
6	16♈	7♈	11♓	14♌
7	17♈	9♈	12♓	14♌
8	18♈	11♈	13♓	14♌
9	19♈	13♈	14♓	15♌
10	20♈	15♈	16♓	15♌
11	21♈	17♈	17♓	15♌
12	22♈	19♈	18♓	15♌
13	23♈	21♈	19♓	15♌
14	24♈	23♈	20♓	15♌
15	25♈	26♈	22♓	16♌
16	26♈	28♈	23♓	16♌
17	27♈	0♉	24♓	16♌
18	28♈	2♉	25♓	16♌
19	29♈	4♉	26♓	17♌
20	0♉	6♉	28♓	17♌
21	1♉	8♉	29♓	17♌
22	2♉	10♉	0♈	17♌
23	3♉	12♉	1♈	18♌
24	4♉	14♉	2♈	18♌
25	5♉	16♉	4♈	18♌
26	6♉	18♉	5♈	19♌
27	6♉	20♉	6♈	19♌
28	7♉	22♉	7♈	19♌
29	8♉	24♉	8♈	20♌
30	9♉	26♉	10♈	20♌

May

Day	☉	☿	♀	♂
1	10♉	28♉	11♈	20♌
2	11♉	29♉	12♈	21♌
3	12♉	1♊	13♈	21♌
4	13♉	2♊	15♈	21♌
5	14♉	4♊	16♈	22♌
6	15♉	5♊	17♈	22♌
7	16♉	7♊	18♈	22♌
8	17♉	8♊	19♈	23♌
9	18♉	9♊	21♈	23♌
10	19♉	10♊	22♈	24♌
11	20♉	11♊	23♈	24♌
12	21♉	12♊	24♈	24♌
13	22♉	13♊	25♈	25♌
14	23♉	14♊	27♈	25♌
15	24♉	15♊	28♈	25♌
16	25♉	16♊	29♈	26♌
17	26♉	16♊	0♉	26♌
18	27♉	17♊	1♉	27♌
19	28♉	17♊	3♉	27♌
20	29♉	18♊	4♉	28♌
21	0♊	18♊	5♉	28♌
22	1♊	18♊	6♉	28♌
23	2♊	18♊	8♉	29♌
24	3♊	18♊	9♉	29♌
25	4♊	18♊	10♉	0♍
26	5♊	18♊	11♉	0♍
27	5♊	18♊	12♉	1♍
28	6♊	18♊	14♉	1♍
29	7♊	18♊	15♉	2♍
30	8♊	17♊	16♉	2♍
31	9♊	17♊	17♉	3♍

June

Day	☉	☿	♀	♂
1	10♊	16♊	18♉	3♍
2	11♊	16♊	20♉	3♍
3	12♊	15♊	21♉	4♍
4	13♊	15♊	22♉	4♍
5	14♊	14♊	23♉	5♍
6	15♊	14♊	25♉	5♍
7	16♊	13♊	26♉	6♍
8	17♊	12♊	27♉	6♍
9	18♊	12♊	28♉	7♍
10	19♊	12♊	29♉	7♍
11	20♊	11♊	1♊	8♍
12	21♊	11♊	2♊	8♍
13	22♊	10♊	3♊	9♍
14	23♊	10♊	4♊	9♍
15	24♊	10♊	6♊	10♍
16	25♊	10♊	7♊	10♍
17	26♊	10♊	8♊	11♍
18	27♊	10♊	9♊	12♍
19	27♊	10♊	10♊	12♍
20	28♊	10♊	12♊	13♍
21	29♊	10♊	13♊	13♍
22	0♋	11♊	14♊	14♍
23	1♋	11♊	15♊	14♍
24	2♋	12♊	16♊	15♍
25	3♋	12♊	18♊	15♍
26	4♋	13♊	19♊	16♍
27	5♋	14♊	20♊	16♍
28	6♋	14♊	21♊	17♍
29	7♋	15♊	23♊	17♍
30	8♋	16♊	24♊	18♍

July

Day	☉	☿	♀	♂
1	9♋	17♊	25♊	18♍
2	10♋	18♊	26♊	19♍
3	11♋	19♊	27♊	20♍
4	12♋	21♊	29♊	20♍
5	13♋	22♊	0♋	21♍
6	14♋	23♊	1♋	21♍
7	15♋	25♊	2♋	22♍
8	16♋	26♊	4♋	22♍
9	17♋	28♊	5♋	23♍
10	18♋	29♊	6♋	24♍
11	18♋	1♋	7♋	24♍
12	19♋	3♋	8♋	25♍
13	20♋	4♋	10♋	25♍
14	21♋	6♋	11♋	26♍
15	22♋	8♋	12♋	26♍
16	23♋	10♋	13♋	27♍
17	24♋	12♋	15♋	28♍
18	25♋	14♋	16♋	28♍
19	26♋	16♋	17♋	29♍
20	27♋	18♋	18♋	29♍
21	28♋	20♋	20♋	0♎
22	29♋	22♋	21♋	0♎
23	0♌	24♋	22♋	1♎
24	1♌	26♋	23♋	2♎
25	2♌	28♋	24♋	2♎
26	3♌	1♌	26♋	3♎
27	4♌	3♌	27♋	3♎
28	5♌	5♌	28♋	4♎
29	6♌	7♌	29♋	5♎
30	7♌	9♌	1♌	5♎
31	8♌	11♌	2♌	6♎

August

Day	☉	☿	♀	♂
1	9♌	13♌	3♌	6♎
2	9♌	15♌	4♌	7♎
3	10♌	17♌	6♌	8♎
4	11♌	19♌	7♌	8♎
5	12♌	21♌	8♌	9♎
6	13♌	23♌	9♌	10♎
7	14♌	25♌	10♌	10♎
8	15♌	27♌	12♌	11♎
9	16♌	29♌	13♌	11♎
10	17♌	0♍	14♌	12♎
11	18♌	2♍	15♌	13♎
12	19♌	4♍	17♌	13♎
13	20♌	6♍	18♌	14♎
14	21♌	7♍	19♌	14♎
15	22♌	9♍	20♌	15♎
16	23♌	11♍	22♌	16♎
17	24♌	12♍	23♌	16♎
18	25♌	14♍	24♌	17♎
19	26♌	16♍	25♌	18♎
20	27♌	17♍	27♌	18♎
21	28♌	19♍	28♌	19♎
22	29♌	20♍	29♌	20♎
23	0♍	22♍	0♍	20♎
24	1♍	23♍	1♍	21♎
25	2♍	25♍	3♍	21♎
26	3♍	26♍	4♍	22♎
27	3♍	27♍	5♍	23♎
28	4♍	29♍	6♍	23♎
29	5♍	0♎	8♍	24♎
30	6♍	1♎	9♍	25♎
31	7♍	3♎	10♍	25♎

September

Day	☉	☿	♀	♂
1	8♍	4♎	11♍	26♎
2	9♍	5♎	13♍	27♎
3	10♍	6♎	14♍	27♎
4	11♍	8♎	15♍	28♎
5	12♍	9♎	16♍	29♎
6	13♍	10♎	18♍	29♎
7	14♍	11♎	19♍	0♏
8	15♍	12♎	20♍	1♏
9	16♍	13♎	21♍	1♏
10	17♍	14♎	23♍	2♏
11	18♍	15♎	24♍	3♏
12	19♍	16♎	25♍	3♏
13	20♍	16♎	26♍	4♏
14	21♍	17♎	28♍	5♏
15	22♍	18♎	29♍	5♏
16	23♍	18♎	0♎	6♏
17	24♍	19♎	1♎	7♏
18	25♍	19♎	2♎	7♏
19	26♍	20♎	4♎	8♏
20	27♍	20♎	5♎	9♏
21	28♍	20♎	6♎	9♏
22	29♍	20♎	7♎	10♏
23	0♎	20♎	9♎	11♏
24	1♎	20♎	10♎	11♏
25	2♎	20♎	11♎	12♏
26	3♎	19♎	12♎	13♏
27	4♎	19♎	14♎	13♏
28	5♎	18♎	15♎	14♏
29	6♎	17♎	16♎	15♏
30	7♎	17♎	17♎	15♏

October

Day	☉	☿	♀	♂
1	8♎	16♎	19♎	16♏
2	9♎	15♎	20♎	17♏
3	10♎	13♎	21♎	18♏
4	11♎	12♎	22♎	18♏
5	11♎	11♎	24♎	19♏
6	12♎	10♎	25♎	20♏
7	13♎	9♎	26♎	20♏
8	14♎	8♎	27♎	21♏
9	15♎	7♎	29♎	22♏
10	16♎	6♎	0♏	22♏
11	17♎	6♎	1♏	23♏
12	18♎	5♎	2♏	24♏
13	19♎	5♎	4♏	25♏
14	20♎	5♎	5♏	25♏
15	21♎	5♎	6♏	26♏
16	22♎	5♎	7♏	27♏
17	23♎	6♎	9♏	27♏
18	24♎	7♎	10♏	28♏
19	25♎	7♎	11♏	29♏
20	26♎	8♎	12♏	0♐
21	27♎	9♎	14♏	0♐
22	28♎	10♎	15♏	1♐
23	29♎	12♎	16♏	2♐
24	0♏	13♎	17♏	2♐
25	1♏	14♎	19♏	3♐
26	2♏	16♎	20♏	4♐
27	3♏	17♎	21♏	5♐
28	4♏	19♎	22♏	5♐
29	5♏	20♎	24♏	6♐
30	6♏	22♎	25♏	7♐
31	7♏	23♎	26♏	7♐

November

Day	☉	☿	♀	♂
1	8♏	25♎	27♏	8♐
2	9♏	26♎	28♏	9♐
3	10♏	28♎	0♐	10♐
4	11♏	0♏	1♐	10♐
5	12♏	1♏	2♐	11♐
6	13♏	3♏	3♐	12♐
7	14♏	5♏	5♐	13♐
8	15♏	6♏	6♐	13♐
9	16♏	8♏	7♐	14♐
10	17♏	10♏	8♐	15♐
11	18♏	11♏	10♐	16♐
12	19♏	13♏	11♐	16♐
13	20♏	14♏	12♐	17♐
14	21♏	16♏	13♐	18♐
15	22♏	18♏	15♐	18♐
16	23♏	19♏	16♐	19♐
17	24♏	21♏	17♐	20♐
18	25♏	22♏	18♐	21♐
19	26♏	24♏	20♐	21♐
20	27♏	26♏	21♐	22♐
21	28♏	27♏	22♐	23♐
22	29♏	29♏	23♐	24♐
23	0♐	0♐	25♐	24♐
24	1♐	2♐	26♐	25♐
25	2♐	4♐	27♐	26♐
26	3♐	5♐	28♐	27♐
27	4♐	7♐	0♑	27♐
28	5♐	8♐	1♑	28♐
29	6♐	10♐	2♑	29♐
30	8♐	11♐	3♑	0♑

December

Day	☉	☿	♀	♂
1	9♐	13♐	5♑	0♑
2	10♐	15♐	6♑	1♑
3	11♐	16♐	7♑	2♑
4	12♐	18♐	8♑	3♑
5	13♐	19♐	9♑	4♑
6	14♐	21♐	11♑	4♑
7	15♐	22♐	12♑	5♑
8	16♐	24♐	13♑	6♑
9	17♐	25♐	14♑	7♑
10	18♐	27♐	16♑	7♑
11	19♐	29♐	17♑	8♑
12	20♐	0♑	18♑	9♑
13	21♐	2♑	19♑	10♑
14	22♐	3♑	21♑	10♑
15	23♐	5♑	22♑	11♑
16	24♐	6♑	23♑	12♑
17	25♐	8♑	24♑	13♑
18	26♐	9♑	26♑	13♑
19	27♐	11♑	27♑	14♑
20	28♐	13♑	28♑	15♑
21	29♐	14♑	29♑	16♑
22	0♑	16♑	1♒	17♑
23	1♑	17♑	2♒	17♑
24	2♑	19♑	3♒	18♑
25	3♑	20♑	4♒	19♑
26	4♑	21♑	5♒	20♑
27	5♑	23♑	7♒	20♑
28	6♑	24♑	8♒	21♑
29	7♑	26♑	9♒	22♑
30	8♑	27♑	10♒	23♑
31	9♑	28♑	12♒	24♑

Planetary Positions

♌ = Leo ♍ = Virgo ♎ = Libra ♏ = Scorpio ♐ = Sagittarius ♑ = Capricorn ♒ = Aquarius ♓ = Pisces

1996

January

Day	☉	☿	♀	♂
1	10♑	29♑	13♒	24♑
2	11♑	0♒	14♒	25♑
3	12♑	2♒	15♒	26♑
4	13♑	2♒	17♒	27♑
5	14♑	3♒	18♒	27♑
6	15♑	4♒	19♒	28♑
7	16♑	5♒	20♒	29♑
8	17♑	5♒	21♒	0♒
9	18♑	5♒	23♒	1♒
10	19♑	5♒	24♒	1♒
11	20♑	5♒	25♒	2♒
12	21♑	5♒	26♒	3♒
13	22♑	4♒	28♒	4♒
14	23♑	3♒	29♒	5♒
15	24♑	2♒	0♓	5♒
16	25♑	1♒	1♓	6♒
17	26♑	0♒	2♓	7♒
18	27♑	29♑	4♓	8♒
19	28♑	28♑	5♓	8♒
20	29♑	26♑	6♓	9♒
21	0♒	25♑	7♓	10♒
22	1♒	24♑	9♓	11♒
23	2♒	23♑	10♓	12♒
24	3♒	22♑	11♓	12♒
25	5♒	21♑	12♓	13♒
26	6♒	20♑	13♓	14♒
27	7♒	20♑	15♓	15♒
28	8♒	19♑	16♓	16♒
29	9♒	19♑	17♓	16♒
30	10♒	19♑	18♓	17♒
31	11♒	19♑	19♓	18♒

February

Day	☉	☿	♀	♂
1	12♒	19♑	21♓	19♒
2	13♒	20♑	22♓	19♒
3	14♒	20♑	23♓	20♒
4	15♒	20♑	24♓	21♒
5	16♒	21♑	25♓	22♒
6	17♒	22♑	27♓	23♒
7	18♒	22♑	28♓	23♒
8	19♒	23♑	29♓	24♒
9	20♒	24♑	0♈	25♒
10	21♒	25♑	1♈	26♒
11	22♒	26♑	2♈	27♒
12	23♒	27♑	4♈	27♒
13	24♒	28♑	5♈	28♒
14	25♒	29♑	6♈	29♒
15	26♒	0♒	7♈	0♓
16	27♒	1♒	8♈	1♓
17	28♒	2♒	10♈	1♓
18	29♒	4♒	11♈	2♓
19	0♓	5♒	12♈	3♓
20	1♓	6♒	13♈	4♓
21	2♓	8♒	14♈	5♓
22	3♓	9♒	15♈	5♓
23	4♓	10♒	17♈	6♓
24	5♓	12♒	18♈	7♓
25	6♓	13♒	19♈	8♓
26	7♓	14♒	20♈	8♓
27	8♓	16♒	21♈	9♓
28	9♓	17♒	22♈	10♓
29	10♓	19♒	23♈	11♓

March

Day	☉	☿	♀	♂
1	11♓	20♒	25♈	12♓
2	12♓	22♒	26♈	12♓
3	13♓	23♒	27♈	13♓
4	14♓	25♒	28♈	14♓
5	15♓	26♒	29♈	15♓
6	16♓	28♒	0♉	16♓
7	17♓	0♓	1♉	16♓
8	18♓	1♓	2♉	17♓
9	19♓	3♓	3♉	18♓
10	20♓	4♓	5♉	19♓
11	21♓	6♓	6♉	19♓
12	22♓	8♓	7♉	20♓
13	23♓	10♓	8♉	21♓
14	24♓	11♓	9♉	22♓
15	25♓	13♓	10♉	23♓
16	26♓	15♓	11♉	23♓
17	27♓	17♓	12♉	24♓
18	28♓	18♓	13♉	25♓
19	29♓	20♓	14♉	26♓
20	0♈	22♓	15♉	27♓
21	1♈	24♓	16♉	27♓
22	2♈	26♓	17♉	28♓
23	3♈	28♓	19♉	29♓
24	4♈	0♈	20♉	0♈
25	5♈	2♈	21♉	0♈
26	6♈	4♈	22♉	1♈
27	7♈	6♈	23♉	2♈
28	8♈	8♈	24♉	3♈
29	9♈	10♈	25♉	4♈
30	10♈	12♈	26♉	4♈
31	11♈	14♈	27♉	5♈

April

Day	☉	☿	♀	♂
1	12♈	16♈	28♉	6♈
2	13♈	18♈	29♉	7♈
3	14♈	20♈	0♊	7♈
4	15♈	22♈	1♊	8♈
5	16♈	24♈	1♊	9♈
6	17♈	26♈	2♊	10♈
7	18♈	28♈	3♊	11♈
8	19♈	0♉	4♊	11♈
9	20♈	2♉	5♊	12♈
10	21♈	4♉	6♊	13♈
11	22♈	6♉	7♊	14♈
12	23♈	8♉	8♊	14♈
13	24♈	10♉	9♊	15♈
14	25♈	11♉	10♊	16♈
15	26♈	13♉	11♊	17♈
16	26♈	14♉	11♊	17♈
17	27♈	16♉	12♊	18♈
18	28♈	17♉	13♊	19♈
19	29♈	19♉	14♊	20♈
20	0♉	20♉	15♊	20♈
21	1♉	21♉	15♊	21♈
22	2♉	22♉	16♊	22♈
23	3♉	23♉	17♊	23♈
24	4♉	24♉	18♊	24♈
25	5♉	25♉	18♊	24♈
26	6♉	26♉	19♊	25♈
27	7♉	27♉	20♊	26♈
28	8♉	27♉	20♊	27♈
29	9♉	28♉	21♊	27♈
30	10♉	28♉	22♊	28♈

May

Day	☉	☿	♀	♂
1	11♉	28♉	22♊	29♈
2	12♉	29♉	23♊	0♉
3	13♉	29♉	23♊	0♉
4	14♉	29♉	24♊	1♉
5	15♉	29♉	24♊	2♉
6	16♉	28♉	25♊	3♉
7	17♉	28♉	25♊	3♉
8	18♉	28♉	26♊	4♉
9	19♉	28♉	26♊	5♉
10	20♉	27♉	26♊	6♉
11	21♉	27♉	27♊	6♉
12	22♉	26♉	27♊	7♉
13	23♉	26♉	27♊	8♉
14	24♉	25♉	28♊	9♉
15	25♉	24♉	28♊	9♉
16	26♉	24♉	28♊	10♉
17	27♉	23♉	28♊	11♉
18	28♉	23♉	28♊	12♉
19	29♉	22♉	28♊	12♉
20	29♉	22♉	28♊	13♉
21	0♊	21♉	28♊	14♉
22	1♊	21♉	28♊	14♉
23	2♊	20♉	28♊	15♉
24	3♊	20♉	28♊	16♉
25	4♊	20♉	28♊	17♉
26	5♊	20♉	28♊	17♉
27	6♊	20♉	27♊	18♉
28	7♊	20♉	27♊	19♉
29	8♊	20♉	27♊	20♉
30	9♊	20♉	26♊	20♉
31	10♊	20♉	26♊	21♉

June

Day	☉	☿	♀	♂
1	11♊	20♉	25♊	22♉
2	12♊	21♉	25♊	23♉
3	13♊	21♉	24♊	23♉
4	14♊	22♉	24♊	24♉
5	15♊	22♉	23♊	25♉
6	16♊	23♉	23♊	25♉
7	17♊	24♉	22♊	26♉
8	18♊	24♉	22♊	27♉
9	19♊	25♉	21♊	28♉
10	20♊	26♉	20♊	28♉
11	21♊	27♉	20♊	29♉
12	22♊	28♉	19♊	0♊
13	22♊	29♉	18♊	0♊
14	23♊	0♊	18♊	1♊
15	24♊	2♊	17♊	2♊
16	25♊	3♊	17♊	3♊
17	26♊	4♊	16♊	3♊
18	27♊	5♊	16♊	4♊
19	28♊	7♊	15♊	5♊
20	29♊	8♊	15♊	5♊
21	0♋	10♊	14♊	6♊
22	1♋	11♊	14♊	7♊
23	2♋	13♊	13♊	8♊
24	3♋	15♊	13♊	9♊
25	4♋	16♊	13♊	9♊
26	5♋	18♊	13♊	10♊
27	6♋	20♊	12♊	10♊
28	7♋	22♊	12♊	11♊
29	8♋	24♊	12♊	12♊
30	9♋	26♊	12♊	12♊

July

Day	☉	☿	♀	♂
1	10♋	28♊	12♊	13♊
2	11♋	0♋	12♊	14♊
3	12♋	2♋	12♊	15♊
4	12♋	4♋	12♊	15♊
5	13♋	6♋	12♊	16♊
6	14♋	8♋	12♊	17♊
7	15♋	10♋	12♊	17♊
8	16♋	12♋	12♊	18♊
9	17♋	15♋	13♊	19♊
10	18♋	17♋	13♊	19♊
11	19♋	19♋	13♊	20♊
12	20♋	21♋	14♊	21♊
13	21♋	23♋	14♊	21♊
14	22♋	25♋	14♊	22♊
15	23♋	27♋	15♊	23♊
16	24♋	0♌	15♊	24♊
17	25♋	2♌	16♊	24♊
18	26♋	4♌	16♊	25♊
19	27♋	6♌	17♊	26♊
20	28♋	8♌	17♊	26♊
21	29♋	10♌	18♊	27♊
22	0♌	12♌	18♊	28♊
23	1♌	13♌	19♊	28♊
24	2♌	15♌	20♊	29♊
25	3♌	17♌	20♊	0♋
26	3♌	19♌	21♊	0♋
27	4♌	21♌	22♊	1♋
28	5♌	23♌	22♊	2♋
29	6♌	24♌	23♊	2♋
30	7♌	26♌	24♊	3♋
31	8♌	28♌	24♊	4♋

August

Day	☉	☿	♀	♂
1	9♌	29♌	25♊	4♋
2	10♌	1♍	26♊	5♋
3	11♌	2♍	27♊	6♋
4	12♌	4♍	27♊	6♋
5	13♌	6♍	28♊	7♋
6	14♌	7♍	29♊	8♋
7	15♌	8♍	0♋	8♋
8	16♌	10♍	1♋	9♋
9	17♌	11♍	2♋	10♋
10	18♌	13♍	3♋	10♋
11	19♌	14♍	3♋	11♋
12	20♌	15♍	4♋	12♋
13	21♌	17♍	5♋	12♋
14	22♌	18♍	6♋	13♋
15	23♌	19♍	7♋	14♋
16	24♌	20♍	8♋	14♋
17	25♌	22♍	9♋	15♋
18	26♌	23♍	10♋	16♋
19	26♌	24♍	11♋	16♋
20	27♌	25♍	12♋	17♋
21	28♌	26♍	13♋	17♋
22	29♌	27♍	14♋	18♋
23	0♍	28♍	15♋	19♋
24	1♍	28♍	16♋	19♋
25	2♍	29♍	17♋	20♋
26	3♍	0♎	18♋	21♋
27	4♍	1♎	19♋	21♋
28	5♍	1♎	20♋	22♋
29	6♍	2♎	21♋	23♋
30	7♍	2♎	22♋	23♋
31	8♍	3♎	23♋	24♋

September

Day	☉	☿	♀	♂
1	9♍	3♎	24♋	25♋
2	10♍	3♎	25♋	25♋
3	11♍	3♎	26♋	26♋
4	12♍	3♎	27♋	26♋
5	13♍	3♎	28♋	27♋
6	14♍	3♎	29♋	28♋
7	15♍	3♎	0♌	28♋
8	16♍	3♎	1♌	29♋
9	17♍	2♎	2♌	0♌
10	18♍	2♎	3♌	0♌
11	19♍	1♎	4♌	1♌
12	20♍	0♎	5♌	1♌
13	21♍	29♍	6♌	2♌
14	22♍	28♍	8♌	3♌
15	23♍	27♍	9♌	3♌
16	24♍	26♍	10♌	4♌
17	25♍	25♍	11♌	5♌
18	26♍	24♍	12♌	5♌
19	27♍	23♍	13♌	6♌
20	28♍	22♍	14♌	6♌
21	28♍	21♍	15♌	7♌
22	29♍	21♍	16♌	8♌
23	0♎	20♍	18♌	8♌
24	1♎	20♍	19♌	9♌
25	2♎	19♍	20♌	10♌
26	3♎	19♍	21♌	10♌
27	4♎	19♍	22♌	11♌
28	5♎	19♍	23♌	11♌
29	6♎	20♍	24♌	12♌
30	7♎	20♍	25♌	13♌

October

Day	☉	☿	♀	♂
1	8♎	21♍	27♌	13♌
2	9♎	21♍	28♌	14♌
3	10♎	22♍	29♌	14♌
4	11♎	23♍	0♍	15♌
5	12♎	25♍	1♍	16♌
6	13♎	26♍	2♍	16♌
7	14♎	27♍	4♍	17♌
8	15♎	29♍	5♍	17♌
9	16♎	0♎	6♍	18♌
10	17♎	2♎	7♍	18♌
11	18♎	3♎	8♍	19♌
12	19♎	5♎	9♍	20♌
13	20♎	6♎	11♍	20♌
14	21♎	8♎	12♍	21♌
15	22♎	10♎	13♍	21♌
16	23♎	12♎	14♍	22♌
17	24♎	13♎	15♍	23♌
18	25♎	15♎	16♍	23♌
19	26♎	17♎	18♍	24♌
20	27♎	18♎	19♍	24♌
21	28♎	20♎	20♍	25♌
22	29♎	22♎	21♍	25♌
23	0♏	24♎	22♍	26♌
24	1♏	25♎	24♍	27♌
25	2♏	27♎	25♍	27♌
26	3♏	29♎	26♍	28♌
27	4♏	0♏	27♍	28♌
28	5♏	2♏	28♍	29♌
29	6♏	4♏	0♎	29♌
30	7♏	5♏	1♎	0♍
31	8♏	7♏	2♎	1♍

November

Day	☉	☿	♀	♂
1	9♏	9♏	3♎	1♍
2	10♏	10♏	4♎	2♍
3	11♏	12♏	6♎	2♍
4	12♏	13♏	7♎	3♍
5	13♏	15♏	8♎	3♍
6	14♏	17♏	9♎	4♍
7	15♏	18♏	11♎	4♍
8	16♏	20♏	12♎	5♍
9	17♏	21♏	13♎	5♍
10	18♏	23♏	14♎	6♍
11	19♏	25♏	15♎	6♍
12	20♏	26♏	17♎	7♍
13	21♏	28♏	18♎	8♍
14	22♏	29♏	19♎	8♍
15	23♏	1♐	20♎	9♍
16	24♏	2♐	22♎	9♍
17	25♏	4♐	23♎	10♍
18	26♏	5♐	24♎	10♍
19	27♏	7♐	25♎	11♍
20	28♏	9♐	26♎	11♍
21	29♏	10♐	28♎	12♍
22	0♐	12♐	29♎	12♍
23	1♐	13♐	0♏	13♍
24	2♐	15♐	1♏	13♍
25	3♐	16♐	3♏	14♍
26	4♐	18♐	4♏	14♍
27	5♐	19♐	5♏	15♍
28	6♐	21♐	6♏	15♍
29	7♐	22♐	8♏	16♍
30	8♐	24♐	9♏	16♍

December

Day	☉	☿	♀	♂
1	9♐	25♐	10♏	17♍
2	10♐	27♐	11♏	17♍
3	11♐	28♐	13♏	18♍
4	12♐	29♐	14♏	18♍
5	13♐	1♑	15♏	18♍
6	14♐	2♑	16♏	19♍
7	15♐	4♑	18♏	19♍
8	16♐	5♑	19♏	20♍
9	17♐	6♑	20♏	20♍
10	18♐	8♑	21♏	21♍
11	19♐	9♑	22♏	21♍
12	20♐	10♑	24♏	22♍
13	21♐	12♑	25♏	22♍
14	22♐	13♑	26♏	22♍
15	24♐	14♑	27♏	23♍
16	25♐	15♑	29♏	23♍
17	26♐	16♑	0♐	24♍
18	27♐	17♑	1♐	24♍
19	28♐	17♑	2♐	25♍
20	29♐	18♑	4♐	25♍
21	0♑	19♑	5♐	25♍
22	1♑	19♑	6♐	26♍
23	2♑	19♑	7♐	26♍
24	3♑	19♑	9♐	26♍
25	4♑	19♑	10♐	27♍
26	5♑	19♑	11♐	27♍
27	6♑	18♑	12♐	28♍
28	7♑	17♑	14♐	28♍
29	8♑	16♑	15♐	28♍
30	9♑	15♑	16♐	29♍
31	10♑	14♑	17♐	29♍

1997

Your Starway to Love

☉ = Sun ☿ = Mercury ♀ = Venus ♂ = Mars ♈ = Aries ♉ = Taurus ♊ = Gemini ♋ = Cancer

January

Day	☉	☿	♀	♂
1	11♑	13♑	19♐	29♍
2	12♑	11♑	20♐	0♎
3	13♑	10♑	21♐	0♎
4	14♑	9♑	22♐	0♎
5	15♑	8♑	24♐	1♎
6	16♑	6♑	25♐	1♎
7	17♑	5♑	26♐	1♎
8	18♑	5♑	27♐	1♎
9	19♑	4♑	29♐	2♎
10	20♑	4♑	0♑	2♎
11	21♑	3♑	1♑	2♎
12	22♑	3♑	2♑	3♎
13	23♑	3♑	4♑	3♎
14	24♑	3♑	5♑	3♎
15	25♑	3♑	6♑	3♎
16	26♑	4♑	7♑	3♎
17	27♑	4♑	9♑	4♎
18	28♑	5♑	10♑	4♎
19	29♑	5♑	11♑	4♎
20	0♒	6♑	12♑	4♎
21	1♒	7♑	14♑	4♎
22	2♒	8♑	15♑	5♎
23	3♒	9♑	16♑	5♎
24	4♒	10♑	18♑	5♎
25	5♒	11♑	19♑	5♎
26	6♒	12♑	20♑	5♎
27	7♒	13♑	21♑	5♎
28	8♒	14♑	23♑	5♎
29	9♒	15♑	24♑	6♎
30	10♒	17♑	25♑	6♎
31	11♒	18♑	26♑	6♎

April

Day	☉	☿	♀	♂
1	12♈	29♈	11♈	21♍
2	12♈	1♉	12♈	21♍
3	13♈	2♉	14♈	21♍
4	14♈	3♉	15♈	20♍
5	15♈	4♉	16♈	20♍
6	16♈	5♉	17♈	20♍
7	17♈	6♉	19♈	19♍
8	18♈	7♉	20♈	19♍
9	19♈	8♉	21♈	19♍
10	20♈	8♉	22♈	19♍
11	21♈	9♉	24♈	19♍
12	22♈	9♉	25♈	18♍
13	23♈	9♉	26♈	18♍
14	24♈	10♉	27♈	18♍
15	25♈	10♉	29♈	18♍
16	26♈	10♉	0♉	18♍
17	27♈	9♉	1♉	17♍
18	28♈	9♉	2♉	17♍
19	29♈	9♉	3♉	17♍
20	0♉	8♉	5♉	17♍
21	1♉	8♉	6♉	17♍
22	2♉	7♉	7♉	17♍
23	3♉	7♉	8♉	17♍
24	4♉	6♉	10♉	17♍
25	5♉	5♉	11♉	17♍
26	6♉	5♉	12♉	17♍
27	7♉	4♉	13♉	17♍
28	8♉	3♉	15♉	17♍
29	9♉	3♉	16♉	17♍
30	10♉	2♉	17♉	17♍

July

Day	☉	☿	♀	♂
1	9♋	16♋	3♌	5♎
2	10♋	18♋	4♌	6♎
3	11♋	20♋	5♌	6♎
4	12♋	22♋	7♌	7♎
5	13♋	24♋	8♌	7♎
6	14♋	26♋	9♌	8♎
7	15♋	28♋	10♌	8♎
8	16♋	0♌	11♌	9♎
9	17♋	2♌	13♌	9♎
10	18♋	4♌	14♌	10♎
11	19♋	6♌	15♌	11♎
12	20♋	7♌	16♌	11♎
13	21♋	9♌	18♌	12♎
14	22♋	11♌	19♌	12♎
15	23♋	12♌	20♌	13♎
16	24♋	14♌	21♌	13♎
17	25♋	16♌	22♌	14♎
18	26♋	17♌	24♌	14♎
19	27♋	19♌	25♌	15♎
20	28♋	20♌	26♌	15♎
21	28♋	22♌	27♌	16♎
22	29♋	23♌	28♌	16♎
23	0♌	25♌	0♍	17♎
24	1♌	26♌	1♍	18♎
25	2♌	28♌	2♍	18♎
26	3♌	29♌	3♍	19♎
27	4♌	0♍	4♍	19♎
28	5♌	1♍	6♍	20♎
29	6♌	3♍	7♍	20♎
30	7♌	4♍	8♍	21♎
31	8♌	5♍	9♍	22♎

October

Day	☉	☿	♀	♂
1	8♎	28♍	22♏	2♐
2	9♎	0♎	23♏	2♐
3	10♎	2♎	24♏	3♐
4	11♎	4♎	25♏	4♐
5	12♎	5♎	26♏	4♐
6	13♎	7♎	28♏	5♐
7	14♎	9♎	29♏	6♐
8	15♎	11♎	0♐	7♐
9	16♎	12♎	1♐	7♐
10	17♎	14♎	2♐	8♐
11	18♎	16♎	3♐	9♐
12	19♎	18♎	4♐	9♐
13	20♎	19♎	5♐	10♐
14	21♎	21♎	7♐	11♐
15	22♎	23♎	8♐	12♐
16	23♎	25♎	9♐	12♐
17	24♎	26♎	10♐	13♐
18	25♎	28♎	11♐	14♐
19	26♎	0♏	12♐	14♐
20	27♎	1♏	13♐	15♐
21	28♎	3♏	14♐	16♐
22	29♎	4♏	15♐	17♐
23	0♏	6♏	16♐	17♐
24	1♏	8♏	17♐	18♐
25	2♏	9♏	18♐	19♐
26	3♏	11♏	19♐	20♐
27	4♏	12♏	21♐	20♐
28	5♏	14♏	22♐	21♐
29	6♏	16♏	23♐	22♐
30	7♏	17♏	24♐	23♐
31	8♏	19♏	25♐	23♐

February

Day	☉	☿	♀	♂
1	12♒	19♑	28♑	6♎
2	13♒	20♑	29♑	6♎
3	14♒	22♑	0♒	6♎
4	15♒	23♑	1♒	6♎
5	16♒	24♑	3♒	6♎
6	17♒	26♑	4♒	6♎
7	18♒	27♑	5♒	6♎
8	19♒	29♑	6♒	6♎
9	20♒	0♒	8♒	6♎
10	22♒	1♒	9♒	6♎
11	23♒	3♒	10♒	6♎
12	24♒	4♒	11♒	6♎
13	25♒	6♒	13♒	6♎
14	26♒	7♒	14♒	5♎
15	27♒	9♒	15♒	5♎
16	28♒	10♒	16♒	5♎
17	29♒	12♒	18♒	5♎
18	0♓	14♒	19♒	5♎
19	1♓	15♒	20♒	5♎
20	2♓	17♒	21♒	5♎
21	3♓	18♒	23♒	4♎
22	4♓	20♒	24♒	4♎
23	5♓	22♒	25♒	4♎
24	6♓	23♒	26♒	4♎
25	7♓	25♒	28♒	4♎
26	8♓	27♒	29♒	3♎
27	9♓	28♒	0♓	3♎
28	10♓	0♓	1♓	3♎

May

Day	☉	☿	♀	♂
1	11♉	2♉	18♉	17♍
2	12♉	1♉	20♉	17♍
3	13♉	1♉	21♉	17♍
4	14♉	0♉	22♉	17♍
5	15♉	0♉	23♉	17♍
6	16♉	0♉	24♉	17♍
7	17♉	0♉	26♉	17♍
8	18♉	29♈	27♉	17♍
9	19♉	29♈	28♉	18♍
10	20♉	0♉	29♉	18♍
11	21♉	0♉	1♊	18♍
12	22♉	0♉	2♊	18♍
13	22♉	0♉	3♊	18♍
14	23♉	1♉	4♊	18♍
15	24♉	1♉	6♊	18♍
16	25♉	2♉	7♊	19♍
17	26♉	2♉	8♊	19♍
18	27♉	3♉	9♊	19♍
19	28♉	4♉	10♊	19♍
20	29♉	4♉	12♊	20♍
21	0♊	5♉	13♊	20♍
22	1♊	6♉	14♊	20♍
23	2♊	7♉	15♊	20♍
24	3♊	8♉	17♊	21♍
25	4♊	9♉	18♊	21♍
26	5♊	10♉	19♊	21♍
27	6♊	11♉	20♊	21♍
28	7♊	12♉	21♊	22♍
29	8♊	14♉	23♊	22♍
30	9♊	15♉	24♊	22♍
31	10♊	16♉	25♊	23♍

August

Day	☉	☿	♀	♂
1	9♌	6♍	10♍	22♎
2	10♌	7♍	12♍	23♎
3	11♌	8♍	13♍	23♎
4	12♌	9♍	14♍	24♎
5	13♌	10♍	15♍	24♎
6	14♌	11♍	16♍	25♎
7	15♌	12♍	18♍	26♎
8	16♌	12♍	19♍	26♎
9	17♌	13♍	20♍	27♎
10	18♌	14♍	21♍	27♎
11	19♌	14♍	22♍	28♎
12	20♌	15♍	24♍	29♎
13	20♌	15♍	25♍	29♎
14	21♌	16♍	26♍	0♏
15	22♌	16♍	27♍	1♏
16	23♌	16♍	28♍	1♏
17	24♌	16♍	0♎	2♏
18	25♌	16♍	1♎	2♏
19	26♌	16♍	2♎	3♏
20	27♌	16♍	3♎	4♏
21	28♌	16♍	4♎	4♏
22	29♌	15♍	5♎	5♏
23	0♍	15♍	7♎	6♏
24	1♍	14♍	8♎	6♏
25	2♍	14♍	9♎	7♏
26	3♍	13♍	10♎	7♏
27	4♍	12♍	11♎	8♏
28	5♍	11♍	13♎	9♏
29	6♍	10♍	14♎	9♏
30	7♍	9♍	15♎	10♏
31	8♍	9♍	16♎	11♏

November

Day	☉	☿	♀	♂
1	9♏	20♏	26♐	24♐
2	10♏	22♏	27♐	25♐
3	11♏	23♏	28♐	25♐
4	12♏	25♏	29♐	26♐
5	13♏	26♏	0♑	27♐
6	14♏	28♏	1♑	28♐
7	15♏	29♏	2♑	28♐
8	16♏	1♐	3♑	29♐
9	17♏	2♐	4♑	0♑
10	18♏	4♐	5♑	1♑
11	19♏	5♐	6♑	1♑
12	20♏	7♐	7♑	2♑
13	21♏	8♐	8♑	3♑
14	22♏	9♐	9♑	4♑
15	23♏	11♐	10♑	5♑
16	24♏	12♐	11♑	5♑
17	25♏	14♐	11♑	6♑
18	26♏	15♐	12♑	7♑
19	27♏	16♐	13♑	8♑
20	28♏	18♐	14♑	8♑
21	29♏	19♐	15♑	9♑
22	0♐	20♐	16♑	10♑
23	1♐	22♐	17♑	11♑
24	2♐	23♐	18♑	11♑
25	3♐	24♐	18♑	12♑
26	4♐	25♐	19♑	13♑
27	5♐	26♐	20♑	14♑
28	6♐	28♐	21♑	14♑
29	7♐	29♐	22♑	15♑
30	8♐	29♐	22♑	16♑

March

Day	☉	☿	♀	♂
1	11♓	2♓	3♓	2♎
2	12♓	4♓	4♓	2♎
3	13♓	5♓	5♓	2♎
4	14♓	7♓	6♓	2♎
5	15♓	9♓	8♓	1♎
6	16♓	11♓	9♓	1♎
7	17♓	13♓	10♓	1♎
8	18♓	15♓	11♓	0♎
9	19♓	16♓	13♓	0♎
10	20♓	18♓	14♓	29♍
11	21♓	20♓	15♓	29♍
12	22♓	22♓	16♓	29♍
13	23♓	24♓	18♓	28♍
14	24♓	26♓	19♓	28♍
15	25♓	28♓	20♓	28♍
16	26♓	0♈	21♓	27♍
17	27♓	2♈	23♓	27♍
18	28♓	4♈	24♓	26♍
19	29♓	6♈	25♓	26♍
20	0♈	8♈	26♓	26♍
21	1♈	10♈	27♓	25♍
22	2♈	12♈	29♓	25♍
23	3♈	14♈	0♈	24♍
24	4♈	16♈	1♈	24♍
25	5♈	18♈	2♈	24♍
26	6♈	20♈	4♈	23♍
27	7♈	21♈	5♈	23♍
28	8♈	23♈	6♈	23♍
29	9♈	25♈	7♈	22♍
30	10♈	26♈	9♈	22♍
31	11♈	28♈	10♈	22♍

June

Day	☉	☿	♀	♂
1	11♊	18♉	26♊	23♍
2	12♊	19♉	28♊	23♍
3	13♊	21♉	29♊	24♍
4	14♊	22♉	0♋	24♍
5	15♊	24♉	1♋	24♍
6	16♊	25♉	2♋	25♍
7	16♊	27♉	4♋	25♍
8	17♊	29♉	5♋	25♍
9	18♊	0♊	6♋	26♍
10	19♊	2♊	7♋	26♍
11	20♊	4♊	9♋	27♍
12	21♊	6♊	10♋	27♍
13	22♊	8♊	11♋	27♍
14	23♊	10♊	12♋	28♍
15	24♊	12♊	13♋	28♍
16	25♊	14♊	15♋	29♍
17	26♊	16♊	16♋	29♍
18	27♊	18♊	17♋	0♎
19	28♊	20♊	18♋	0♎
20	29♊	22♊	20♋	0♎
21	0♋	24♊	21♋	1♎
22	1♋	26♊	22♋	1♎
23	2♋	29♊	23♋	2♎
24	3♋	1♋	24♋	2♎
25	4♋	3♋	26♋	3♎
26	5♋	5♋	27♋	3♎
27	6♋	7♋	28♋	4♎
28	7♋	9♋	29♋	4♎
29	7♋	12♋	1♌	4♎
30	8♋	14♋	2♌	5♎

September

Day	☉	☿	♀	♂
1	9♍	8♍	17♎	11♏
2	10♍	7♍	18♎	12♏
3	11♍	6♍	20♎	13♏
4	12♍	5♍	21♎	13♏
5	13♍	4♍	22♎	14♏
6	14♍	4♍	23♎	15♏
7	15♍	3♍	24♎	15♏
8	16♍	3♍	25♎	16♏
9	17♍	3♍	27♎	17♏
10	18♍	3♍	28♎	17♏
11	19♍	3♍	29♎	18♏
12	19♍	3♍	0♏	19♏
13	20♍	3♍	1♏	19♏
14	21♍	4♍	2♏	20♏
15	22♍	5♍	4♏	21♏
16	23♍	6♍	5♏	21♏
17	24♍	6♍	6♏	22♏
18	25♍	8♍	7♏	23♏
19	26♍	9♍	8♏	23♏
20	27♍	10♍	9♏	24♏
21	28♍	11♍	11♏	25♏
22	29♍	13♍	12♏	25♏
23	0♎	14♍	13♏	26♏
24	1♎	16♍	14♏	27♏
25	2♎	18♍	15♏	27♏
26	3♎	19♍	16♏	28♏
27	4♎	21♍	17♏	29♏
28	5♎	23♍	19♏	29♏
29	6♎	25♍	20♏	0♐
30	7♎	26♍	21♏	1♐

December

Day	☉	☿	♀	♂
1	9♐	0♑	23♑	17♑
2	10♐	1♑	24♑	18♑
3	11♐	2♑	25♑	18♑
4	12♐	2♑	25♑	19♑
5	13♐	3♑	26♑	20♑
6	14♐	3♑	27♑	21♑
7	15♐	3♑	27♑	21♑
8	16♐	3♑	28♑	22♑
9	17♐	3♑	28♑	23♑
10	18♐	3♑	29♑	24♑
11	19♐	2♑	29♑	24♑
12	20♐	2♑	0♒	25♑
13	21♐	1♑	0♒	26♑
14	22♐	29♐	1♒	27♑
15	23♐	28♐	1♒	28♑
16	24♐	27♐	2♒	28♑
17	25♐	26♐	2♒	29♑
18	26♐	24♐	2♒	0♒
19	27♐	23♐	3♒	1♒
20	28♐	22♐	3♒	2♒
21	29♐	20♐	3♒	2♒
22	0♑	19♐	4♒	3♒
23	1♑	19♐	4♒	4♒
24	2♑	18♐	4♒	5♒
25	3♑	17♐	4♒	5♒
26	4♑	17♐	4♒	6♒
27	5♑	17♐	4♒	7♒
28	6♑	17♐	4♒	8♒
29	8♑	17♐	4♒	9♒
30	9♑	18♐	4♒	9♒
31	10♑	18♐	4♒	10♒

Planetary Positions

♌ = Leo ♍ = Virgo ♎ = Libra ♏ = Scorpio ♐ = Sagittarius ♑ = Capricorn ♒ = Aquarius ♓ = Pisces

1998

January

Day	☉	☿	♀	♂
1	11♑	19♐	3♒	11♒
2	12♑	19♐	3♒	12♒
3	13♑	20♐	3♒	13♒
4	14♑	21♐	3♒	13♒
5	15♑	22♐	2♒	14♒
6	16♑	23♐	2♒	15♒
7	17♑	24♐	1♒	16♒
8	18♑	25♐	1♒	16♒
9	19♑	26♐	0♒	17♒
10	20♑	27♐	0♒	18♒
11	21♑	28♐	29♑	19♒
12	22♑	29♐	29♑	20♒
13	23♑	1♑	28♑	20♒
14	24♑	2♑	28♑	21♒
15	25♑	3♑	27♑	22♒
16	26♑	5♑	26♑	23♒
17	27♑	6♑	26♑	24♒
18	28♑	7♑	25♑	24♒
19	29♑	9♑	24♑	25♒
20	0♒	10♑	24♑	26♒
21	1♒	11♑	23♑	27♒
22	2♒	13♑	23♑	27♒
23	3♒	14♑	22♑	28♒
24	4♒	16♑	22♑	29♒
25	5♒	17♑	21♑	0♓
26	6♒	19♑	21♑	1♓
27	7♒	20♑	20♑	1♓
28	8♒	22♑	20♑	2♓
29	9♒	23♑	20♑	3♓
30	10♒	25♑	19♑	4♓
31	11♒	26♑	19♑	5♓

April

Day	☉	☿	♀	♂
1	11♈	20♈	25♒	21♈
2	12♈	20♈	26♒	22♈
3	13♈	19♈	27♒	23♈
4	14♈	19♈	28♒	23♈
5	15♈	18♈	29♒	24♈
6	16♈	17♈	0♓	25♈
7	17♈	16♈	1♓	26♈
8	18♈	15♈	2♓	26♈
9	19♈	15♈	3♓	27♈
10	20♈	14♈	4♓	28♈
11	21♈	13♈	5♓	29♈
12	22♈	13♈	6♓	29♈
13	23♈	12♈	7♓	0♉
14	24♈	11♈	8♓	1♉
15	25♈	11♈	9♓	2♉
16	26♈	11♈	11♓	2♉
17	27♈	10♈	12♓	3♉
18	28♈	10♈	13♓	4♉
19	29♈	10♈	14♓	5♉
20	0♉	10♈	15♓	5♉
21	1♉	10♈	16♓	6♉
22	2♉	10♈	17♓	7♉
23	3♉	10♈	18♓	8♉
24	4♉	10♈	19♓	8♉
25	5♉	11♈	20♓	9♉
26	6♉	11♈	22♓	10♉
27	7♉	12♈	23♓	10♉
28	8♉	12♈	24♓	11♉
29	9♉	13♈	25♓	12♉
30	10♉	14♈	26♓	13♉

July

Day	☉	☿	♀	♂
1	9♋	0♌	8♊	26♊
2	10♋	2♌	9♊	27♊
3	11♋	4♌	10♊	28♊
4	12♋	5♌	12♊	29♊
5	13♋	7♌	13♊	29♊
6	14♋	8♌	14♊	0♋
7	15♋	9♌	15♊	1♋
8	16♋	11♌	16♊	1♋
9	17♋	12♌	17♊	2♋
10	18♋	13♌	19♊	3♋
11	19♋	15♌	20♊	3♋
12	20♋	16♌	21♊	4♋
13	21♋	17♌	22♊	5♋
14	22♋	18♌	23♊	5♋
15	23♋	19♌	25♊	6♋
16	23♋	20♌	26♊	7♋
17	24♋	21♌	27♊	7♋
18	25♋	22♌	28♊	8♋
19	26♋	23♌	29♊	9♋
20	27♋	24♌	1♋	9♋
21	28♋	24♌	2♋	10♋
22	29♋	25♌	3♋	11♋
23	0♌	26♌	4♋	11♋
24	1♌	26♌	6♋	12♋
25	2♌	27♌	7♋	13♋
26	3♌	27♌	8♋	13♋
27	4♌	28♌	9♋	14♋
28	5♌	28♌	10♋	15♋
29	6♌	28♌	12♋	15♋
30	7♌	28♌	13♋	16♋
31	8♌	28♌	14♋	17♋

October

Day	☉	☿	♀	♂
1	8♎	12♎	0♎	26♌
2	9♎	14♎	2♎	27♌
3	10♎	15♎	3♎	27♌
4	11♎	17♎	4♎	28♌
5	12♎	19♎	5♎	29♌
6	13♎	20♎	7♎	29♌
7	14♎	22♎	8♎	0♍
8	15♎	24♎	9♎	0♍
9	16♎	25♎	10♎	1♍
10	17♎	27♎	12♎	2♍
11	18♎	29♎	13♎	2♍
12	19♎	0♏	14♎	3♍
13	20♎	2♏	15♎	3♍
14	21♎	3♏	17♎	4♍
15	22♎	5♏	18♎	5♍
16	23♎	6♏	19♎	5♍
17	24♎	8♏	20♎	6♍
18	25♎	9♏	22♎	6♍
19	26♎	11♏	23♎	7♍
20	27♎	12♏	24♎	8♍
21	28♎	14♏	25♎	8♍
22	29♎	15♏	27♎	9♍
23	0♏	17♏	28♎	10♍
24	1♏	18♏	29♎	10♍
25	2♏	20♏	0♏	11♍
26	3♏	21♏	2♏	11♍
27	4♏	23♏	3♏	12♍
28	5♏	24♏	4♏	12♍
29	6♏	25♏	5♏	13♍
30	7♏	27♏	7♏	14♍
31	8♏	28♏	8♏	14♍

February

Day	☉	☿	♀	♂
1	12♒	28♑	19♑	5♓
2	13♒	29♑	19♑	6♓
3	14♒	1♒	19♑	7♓
4	15♒	2♒	19♑	8♓
5	16♒	4♒	18♑	9♓
6	17♒	6♒	18♑	9♓
7	18♒	7♒	19♑	10♓
8	19♒	9♒	19♑	11♓
9	20♒	11♒	19♑	12♓
10	21♒	12♒	19♑	12♓
11	22♒	14♒	19♑	13♓
12	23♒	16♒	19♑	14♓
13	24♒	17♒	19♑	15♓
14	25♒	19♒	20♑	16♓
15	26♒	21♒	20♑	16♓
16	27♒	22♒	20♑	17♓
17	28♒	24♒	21♑	18♓
18	29♒	26♒	21♑	19♓
19	0♓	28♒	22♑	20♓
20	1♓	0♓	22♑	20♓
21	2♓	1♓	23♑	21♓
22	3♓	3♓	23♑	22♓
23	4♓	5♓	24♑	23♓
24	5♓	7♓	24♑	23♓
25	6♓	9♓	25♑	24♓
26	7♓	11♓	26♑	25♓
27	8♓	13♓	26♑	26♓
28	9♓	15♓	27♑	27♓

May

Day	☉	☿	♀	♂
1	11♉	14♈	27♓	13♉
2	12♉	15♈	28♓	14♉
3	13♉	16♈	29♓	15♉
4	14♉	17♈	0♈	16♉
5	15♉	18♈	2♈	16♉
6	15♉	19♈	3♈	17♉
7	16♉	20♈	4♈	18♉
8	17♉	21♈	5♈	19♉
9	18♉	22♈	6♈	19♉
10	19♉	24♈	7♈	20♉
11	20♉	25♈	8♈	21♉
12	21♉	26♈	10♈	21♉
13	22♉	27♈	11♈	22♉
14	23♉	29♈	12♈	23♉
15	24♉	0♉	13♈	24♉
16	25♉	2♉	14♈	24♉
17	26♉	3♉	15♈	25♉
18	27♉	5♉	16♈	26♉
19	28♉	6♉	18♈	26♉
20	29♉	8♉	19♈	27♉
21	0♊	9♉	20♈	28♉
22	1♊	11♉	21♈	29♉
23	2♊	13♉	22♈	29♉
24	3♊	15♉	23♈	0♊
25	4♊	16♉	24♈	1♊
26	5♊	18♉	26♈	1♊
27	6♊	20♉	27♈	2♊
28	7♊	22♉	28♈	3♊
29	8♊	24♉	29♈	4♊
30	9♊	26♉	0♉	4♊
31	10♊	28♉	1♉	5♊

August

Day	☉	☿	♀	♂
1	9♌	28♌	15♋	17♋
2	10♌	28♌	16♋	18♋
3	11♌	28♌	18♋	19♋
4	12♌	28♌	19♋	19♋
5	13♌	27♌	20♋	20♋
6	14♌	27♌	21♋	21♋
7	15♌	26♌	22♋	21♋
8	15♌	25♌	24♋	22♋
9	16♌	25♌	25♋	22♋
10	17♌	24♌	26♋	23♋
11	18♌	23♌	27♋	24♋
12	19♌	22♌	29♋	24♋
13	20♌	22♌	0♌	25♋
14	21♌	21♌	1♌	26♋
15	22♌	20♌	2♌	26♋
16	23♌	19♌	3♌	27♋
17	24♌	19♌	5♌	28♋
18	25♌	18♌	6♌	28♋
19	26♌	17♌	7♌	29♋
20	27♌	17♌	8♌	0♌
21	28♌	16♌	10♌	0♌
22	29♌	16♌	11♌	1♌
23	0♍	16♌	12♌	2♌
24	1♍	16♌	13♌	2♌
25	2♍	16♌	14♌	3♌
26	3♍	16♌	16♌	3♌
27	4♍	17♌	17♌	4♌
28	5♍	17♌	18♌	5♌
29	6♍	18♌	19♌	5♌
30	7♍	19♌	21♌	6♌
31	8♍	19♌	22♌	7♌

November

Day	☉	☿	♀	♂
1	9♏	29♏	9♏	15♍
2	10♏	1♐	10♏	15♍
3	11♏	2♐	12♏	16♍
4	12♏	3♐	13♏	17♍
5	13♏	5♐	14♏	17♍
6	14♏	6♐	15♏	18♍
7	15♏	7♐	17♏	18♍
8	16♏	8♐	18♏	19♍
9	17♏	9♐	19♏	20♍
10	18♏	10♐	20♏	20♍
11	19♏	11♐	22♏	21♍
12	20♏	12♐	23♏	21♍
13	21♏	13♐	24♏	22♍
14	22♏	14♐	25♏	22♍
15	23♏	15♐	27♏	23♍
16	24♏	16♐	28♏	24♍
17	25♏	16♐	29♏	24♍
18	26♏	17♐	0♐	25♍
19	27♏	17♐	2♐	25♍
20	28♏	17♐	3♐	26♍
21	29♏	18♐	4♐	26♍
22	0♐	18♐	5♐	27♍
23	1♐	17♐	7♐	28♍
24	2♐	17♐	8♐	28♍
25	3♐	16♐	9♐	29♍
26	4♐	16♐	10♐	29♍
27	5♐	15♐	12♐	0♎
28	6♐	14♐	13♐	0♎
29	7♐	12♐	14♐	1♎
30	8♐	11♐	15♐	2♎

March

Day	☉	☿	♀	♂
1	10♓	16♓	28♑	27♓
2	11♓	18♓	28♑	28♓
3	12♓	20♓	29♑	29♓
4	13♓	22♓	0♒	0♈
5	14♓	24♓	0♒	0♈
6	15♓	26♓	1♒	1♈
7	16♓	28♓	2♒	2♈
8	17♓	0♈	3♒	3♈
9	18♓	2♈	4♒	4♈
10	19♓	3♈	4♒	4♈
11	20♓	5♈	5♒	5♈
12	21♓	7♈	6♒	6♈
13	22♓	9♈	7♒	7♈
14	23♓	10♈	8♒	7♈
15	24♓	12♈	9♒	8♈
16	25♓	13♈	9♒	9♈
17	26♓	14♈	10♒	10♈
18	27♓	16♈	11♒	10♈
19	28♓	17♈	12♒	11♈
20	29♓	18♈	13♒	12♈
21	0♈	19♈	14♒	13♈
22	1♈	19♈	15♒	13♈
23	2♈	20♈	16♒	14♈
24	3♈	21♈	17♒	15♈
25	4♈	21♈	18♒	16♈
26	5♈	21♈	19♒	17♈
27	6♈	21♈	20♒	17♈
28	7♈	21♈	21♒	18♈
29	8♈	21♈	22♒	19♈
30	9♈	21♈	23♒	20♈
31	10♈	21♈	24♒	20♈

June

Day	☉	☿	♀	♂
1	11♊	0♊	3♉	6♊
2	11♊	2♊	4♉	6♊
3	12♊	4♊	5♉	7♊
4	13♊	6♊	6♉	8♊
5	14♊	8♊	7♉	9♊
6	15♊	10♊	8♉	9♊
7	16♊	12♊	10♉	10♊
8	17♊	15♊	11♉	11♊
9	18♊	17♊	12♉	11♊
10	19♊	19♊	13♉	12♊
11	20♊	21♊	14♉	13♊
12	21♊	23♊	15♉	13♊
13	22♊	26♊	17♉	14♊
14	23♊	28♊	18♉	15♊
15	24♊	0♋	19♉	15♊
16	25♊	2♋	20♉	16♊
17	26♊	4♋	21♉	17♊
18	27♊	6♋	23♉	18♊
19	28♊	8♋	24♉	18♊
20	29♊	10♋	25♉	19♊
21	0♋	12♋	26♉	20♊
22	1♋	14♋	27♉	20♊
23	2♋	16♋	28♉	21♊
24	3♋	18♋	0♊	22♊
25	3♋	20♋	1♊	22♊
26	4♋	22♋	2♊	23♊
27	5♋	24♋	3♊	24♊
28	6♋	25♋	4♊	24♊
29	7♋	27♋	6♊	25♊
30	8♋	29♋	7♊	26♊

September

Day	☉	☿	♀	♂
1	9♍	20♌	23♌	7♌
2	10♍	22♌	24♌	8♌
3	11♍	23♌	26♌	9♌
4	11♍	24♌	27♌	9♌
5	12♍	26♌	28♌	10♌
6	13♍	27♌	29♌	10♌
7	14♍	29♌	0♍	11♌
8	15♍	0♍	2♍	12♌
9	16♍	2♍	3♍	12♌
10	17♍	4♍	4♍	13♌
11	18♍	5♍	5♍	14♌
12	19♍	7♍	7♍	14♌
13	20♍	9♍	8♍	15♌
14	21♍	11♍	9♍	16♌
15	22♍	13♍	10♍	16♌
16	23♍	15♍	12♍	17♌
17	24♍	17♍	13♍	17♌
18	25♍	18♍	14♍	18♌
19	26♍	20♍	15♍	19♌
20	27♍	22♍	17♍	19♌
21	28♍	24♍	18♍	20♌
22	29♍	26♍	19♍	21♌
23	0♎	28♍	20♍	21♌
24	1♎	0♎	22♍	22♌
25	2♎	1♎	23♍	22♌
26	3♎	3♎	24♍	23♌
27	4♎	5♎	25♍	24♌
28	5♎	7♎	27♍	24♌
29	6♎	9♎	28♍	25♌
30	7♎	10♎	29♍	26♌

December

Day	☉	☿	♀	♂
1	9♐	10♐	17♐	2♎
2	10♐	8♐	18♐	3♎
3	11♐	7♐	19♐	3♎
4	12♐	6♐	21♐	4♎
5	13♐	5♐	22♐	4♎
6	14♐	4♐	23♐	5♎
7	15♐	3♐	24♐	5♎
8	16♐	2♐	26♐	6♎
9	17♐	2♐	27♐	7♎
10	18♐	1♐	28♐	7♎
11	19♐	1♐	29♐	8♎
12	20♐	1♐	1♑	8♎
13	21♐	2♐	2♑	9♎
14	22♐	2♐	3♑	9♎
15	23♐	2♐	4♑	10♎
16	24♐	3♐	6♑	10♎
17	25♐	4♐	7♑	11♎
18	26♐	5♐	8♑	11♎
19	27♐	6♐	9♑	12♎
20	28♐	7♐	11♑	12♎
21	29♐	8♐	12♑	13♎
22	0♑	9♐	13♑	13♎
23	1♑	10♐	14♑	14♎
24	2♑	11♐	16♑	14♎
25	3♑	12♐	17♑	15♎
26	4♑	14♐	18♑	15♎
27	5♑	15♐	19♑	16♎
28	6♑	16♐	21♑	16♎
29	7♑	17♐	22♑	17♎
30	8♑	19♐	23♑	17♎
31	9♑	20♐	24♑	18♎

1999

☉ = Sun ☿ = Mercury ♀ = Venus ♂ = Mars ♈ = Aries ♉ = Taurus ♊ = Gemini ♋ = Cancer

January

Day	☉	☿	♀	♂
1	10♑	22♐	26♑	18♎
2	11♑	23♐	27♑	19♎
3	12♑	24♐	28♑	19♎
4	13♑	26♐	29♑	20♎
5	14♑	27♐	1♒	20♎
6	15♑	29♐	2♒	21♎
7	16♑	0♑	3♒	21♎
8	17♑	2♑	4♒	22♎
9	18♑	3♑	6♒	22♎
10	19♑	5♑	7♒	23♎
11	21♑	6♑	8♒	23♎
12	22♑	8♑	9♒	24♎
13	23♑	9♑	11♒	24♎
14	24♑	11♑	12♒	25♎
15	25♑	12♑	13♒	25♎
16	26♑	14♑	14♒	26♎
17	27♑	15♑	16♒	26♎
18	28♑	17♑	17♒	26♎
19	29♑	18♑	18♒	27♎
20	0♒	20♑	19♒	27♎
21	1♒	22♑	21♒	28♎
22	2♒	23♑	22♒	28♎
23	3♒	25♑	23♒	29♎
24	4♒	26♑	24♒	29♎
25	5♒	28♑	26♒	29♎
26	6♒	0♒	27♒	0♏
27	7♒	1♒	28♒	0♏
28	8♒	3♒	29♒	1♏
29	9♒	5♒	1♓	1♏
30	10♒	6♒	2♓	1♏
31	11♒	8♒	3♓	2♏

April

Day	☉	☿	♀	♂
1	11♈	21♓	17♉	11♏
2	12♈	21♓	18♉	11♏
3	13♈	21♓	19♉	11♏
4	14♈	21♓	20♉	10♏
5	15♈	21♓	21♉	10♏
6	16♈	22♓	23♉	10♏
7	17♈	22♓	24♉	10♏
8	18♈	22♓	25♉	10♏
9	19♈	23♓	26♉	9♏
10	20♈	23♓	27♉	9♏
11	21♈	24♓	28♉	9♏
12	22♈	25♓	0♊	8♏
13	23♈	26♓	1♊	8♏
14	24♈	26♓	2♊	8♏
15	25♈	27♓	3♊	7♏
16	26♈	28♓	4♊	7♏
17	27♈	29♓	5♊	7♏
18	28♈	0♈	7♊	6♏
19	29♈	1♈	8♊	6♏
20	0♉	3♈	9♊	6♏
21	1♉	4♈	10♊	5♏
22	2♉	5♈	11♊	5♏
23	3♉	6♈	12♊	5♏
24	4♉	7♈	14♊	4♏
25	5♉	9♈	15♊	4♏
26	6♉	10♈	16♊	4♏
27	7♉	11♈	17♊	3♏
28	7♉	13♈	18♊	3♏
29	8♉	14♈	19♊	2♏
30	9♉	16♈	20♊	2♏

July

Day	☉	☿	♀	♂
1	9♋	4♌	23♌	29♎
2	10♋	5♌	23♌	29♎
3	11♋	6♌	24♌	29♎
4	12♋	7♌	25♌	0♏
5	13♋	7♌	25♌	0♏
6	14♋	8♌	26♌	0♏
7	15♋	8♌	27♌	1♏
8	16♋	9♌	27♌	1♏
9	17♋	9♌	28♌	1♏
10	18♋	9♌	29♌	2♏
11	18♋	9♌	29♌	2♏
12	19♋	9♌	0♍	3♏
13	20♋	9♌	0♍	3♏
14	21♋	9♌	1♍	3♏
15	22♋	9♌	1♍	4♏
16	23♋	9♌	2♍	4♏
17	24♋	9♌	2♍	5♏
18	25♋	8♌	3♍	5♏
19	26♋	8♌	3♍	5♏
20	27♋	7♌	3♍	6♏
21	28♋	7♌	4♍	6♏
22	29♋	6♌	4♍	7♏
23	0♌	6♌	4♍	7♏
24	1♌	5♌	4♍	8♏
25	2♌	4♌	5♍	8♏
26	3♌	4♌	5♍	9♏
27	4♌	3♌	5♍	9♏
28	5♌	2♌	5♍	9♏
29	6♌	1♌	5♍	10♏
30	7♌	1♌	5♍	10♏
31	8♌	0♌	5♍	11♏

October

Day	☉	☿	♀	♂
1	8♎	24♎	26♌	19♐
2	9♎	26♎	26♌	19♐
3	10♎	27♎	27♌	20♐
4	11♎	29♎	28♌	21♐
5	12♎	0♏	28♌	22♐
6	12♎	1♏	29♌	22♐
7	13♎	3♏	0♍	23♐
8	14♎	4♏	0♍	24♐
9	15♎	6♏	1♍	24♐
10	16♎	7♏	2♍	25♐
11	17♎	9♏	3♍	26♐
12	18♎	10♏	3♍	27♐
13	19♎	11♏	4♍	27♐
14	20♎	13♏	5♍	28♐
15	21♎	14♏	6♍	29♐
16	22♎	15♏	7♍	29♐
17	23♎	16♏	8♍	0♑
18	24♎	18♏	9♍	1♑
19	25♎	19♏	9♍	2♑
20	26♎	20♏	10♍	2♑
21	27♎	21♏	11♍	3♑
22	28♎	22♏	12♍	4♑
23	29♎	23♏	13♍	4♑
24	0♏	24♏	14♍	5♑
25	1♏	25♏	15♍	6♑
26	2♏	26♏	16♍	7♑
27	3♏	27♏	17♍	7♑
28	4♏	28♏	18♍	8♑
29	5♏	29♏	19♍	9♑
30	6♏	0♐	20♍	10♑
31	7♏	0♐	21♍	10♑

February

Day	☉	☿	♀	♂
1	12♒	10♒	4♓	2♏
2	13♒	11♒	6♓	3♏
3	14♒	13♒	7♓	3♏
4	15♒	15♒	8♓	3♏
5	16♒	17♒	9♓	4♏
6	17♒	18♒	11♓	4♏
7	18♒	20♒	12♓	4♏
8	19♒	22♒	13♓	5♏
9	20♒	24♒	14♓	5♏
10	21♒	26♒	16♓	5♏
11	22♒	27♒	17♓	6♏
12	23♒	29♒	18♓	6♏
13	24♒	1♓	19♓	6♏
14	25♒	3♓	21♓	7♏
15	26♒	5♓	22♓	7♏
16	27♒	7♓	23♓	7♏
17	28♒	8♓	24♓	8♏
18	29♒	10♓	25♓	8♏
19	0♓	12♓	27♓	8♏
20	1♓	14♓	28♓	8♏
21	2♓	16♓	29♓	9♏
22	3♓	17♓	0♈	9♏
23	4♓	19♓	2♈	9♏
24	5♓	21♓	3♈	9♏
25	6♓	22♓	4♈	10♏
26	7♓	24♓	5♈	10♏
27	8♓	25♓	7♈	10♏
28	9♓	27♓	8♈	10♏

May

Day	☉	☿	♀	♂
1	10♉	17♈	22♊	2♏
2	11♉	19♈	23♊	1♏
3	12♉	20♈	24♊	1♏
4	13♉	22♈	25♊	1♏
5	14♉	24♈	26♊	0♏
6	15♉	25♈	27♊	0♏
7	16♉	27♈	28♊	0♏
8	17♉	29♈	29♊	29♎
9	18♉	1♉	1♋	29♎
10	19♉	2♉	2♋	29♎
11	20♉	4♉	3♋	28♎
12	21♉	6♉	4♋	28♎
13	22♉	8♉	5♋	28♎
14	23♉	10♉	6♋	27♎
15	24♉	12♉	7♋	27♎
16	25♉	14♉	8♋	27♎
17	26♉	16♉	9♋	27♎
18	27♉	18♉	10♋	26♎
19	28♉	20♉	12♋	26♎
20	29♉	22♉	13♋	26♎
21	0♊	24♉	14♋	26♎
22	1♊	26♉	15♋	26♎
23	2♊	29♉	16♋	25♎
24	3♊	1♊	17♋	25♎
25	4♊	3♊	18♋	25♎
26	5♊	5♊	19♋	25♎
27	5♊	7♊	20♋	25♎
28	6♊	9♊	21♋	25♎
29	7♊	12♊	22♋	25♎
30	8♊	14♊	23♋	25♎
31	9♊	16♊	24♋	25♎

August

Day	☉	☿	♀	♂
1	9♌	0♌	5♍	11♏
2	9♌	29♋	5♍	12♏
3	10♌	29♋	5♍	12♏
4	11♌	29♋	5♍	13♏
5	12♌	29♋	4♍	14♏
6	13♌	29♋	4♍	14♏
7	14♌	29♋	4♍	15♏
8	15♌	29♋	3♍	15♏
9	16♌	29♋	3♍	16♏
10	17♌	0♌	3♍	16♏
11	18♌	0♌	2♍	17♏
12	19♌	1♌	2♍	17♏
13	20♌	1♌	1♍	18♏
14	21♌	2♌	1♍	18♏
15	22♌	3♌	0♍	19♏
16	23♌	4♌	0♍	19♏
17	24♌	5♌	29♌	20♏
18	25♌	7♌	28♌	21♏
19	26♌	8♌	28♌	21♏
20	27♌	9♌	27♌	22♏
21	28♌	11♌	27♌	22♏
22	29♌	13♌	26♌	23♏
23	0♍	14♌	25♌	24♏
24	1♍	16♌	25♌	24♏
25	2♍	18♌	24♌	25♏
26	3♍	20♌	24♌	25♏
27	4♍	21♌	23♌	26♏
28	4♍	23♌	23♌	27♏
29	5♍	25♌	22♌	27♏
30	6♍	27♌	22♌	28♏
31	7♍	29♌	21♌	28♏

November

Day	☉	☿	♀	♂
1	8♏	1♐	22♍	11♑
2	9♏	1♐	23♍	12♑
3	10♏	1♐	24♍	13♑
4	11♏	2♐	25♍	13♑
5	12♏	2♐	26♍	14♑
6	13♏	2♐	27♍	15♑
7	14♏	1♐	28♍	16♑
8	15♏	1♐	29♍	16♑
9	16♏	0♐	0♎	17♑
10	17♏	0♐	1♎	18♑
11	18♏	29♏	2♎	19♑
12	19♏	28♏	3♎	19♑
13	20♏	27♏	4♎	20♑
14	21♏	25♏	5♎	21♑
15	22♏	24♏	7♎	22♑
16	23♏	23♏	8♎	22♑
17	24♏	21♏	9♎	23♑
18	25♏	20♏	10♎	24♑
19	26♏	19♏	11♎	25♑
20	27♏	18♏	12♎	25♑
21	28♏	17♏	13♎	26♑
22	29♏	16♏	14♎	27♑
23	0♐	16♏	15♎	28♑
24	1♐	16♏	17♎	28♑
25	2♐	16♏	18♎	29♑
26	3♐	16♏	19♎	0♒
27	4♐	16♏	20♎	1♒
28	6♐	16♏	21♎	1♒
29	7♐	17♏	22♎	2♒
30	8♐	18♏	23♎	3♒

March

Day	☉	☿	♀	♂
1	10♓	28♓	9♈	10♏
2	11♓	29♓	10♈	11♏
3	12♓	0♈	11♈	11♏
4	13♓	1♈	13♈	11♏
5	14♓	2♈	14♈	11♏
6	15♓	3♈	15♈	11♏
7	16♓	3♈	16♈	11♏
8	17♓	4♈	18♈	12♏
9	18♓	4♈	19♈	12♏
10	19♓	4♈	20♈	12♏
11	20♓	4♈	21♈	12♏
12	21♓	4♈	22♈	12♏
13	22♓	3♈	24♈	12♏
14	23♓	3♈	25♈	12♏
15	24♓	2♈	26♈	12♏
16	25♓	2♈	27♈	12♏
17	26♓	1♈	29♈	12♏
18	27♓	0♈	0♉	12♏
19	28♓	29♓	1♉	12♏
20	29♓	28♓	2♉	12♏
21	0♈	27♓	3♉	12♏
22	1♈	27♓	5♉	12♏
23	2♈	26♓	6♉	12♏
24	3♈	25♓	7♉	12♏
25	4♈	24♓	8♉	12♏
26	5♈	23♓	9♉	12♏
27	6♈	23♓	11♉	12♏
28	7♈	22♓	12♉	12♏
29	8♈	22♓	13♉	11♏
30	9♈	21♓	14♉	11♏
31	10♈	21♓	15♉	11♏

June

Day	☉	☿	♀	♂
1	10♊	18♊	25♋	25♎
2	11♊	20♊	26♋	24♎
3	12♊	22♊	27♋	24♎
4	13♊	24♊	28♋	24♎
5	14♊	26♊	29♋	24♎
6	15♊	28♊	0♌	24♎
7	16♊	0♋	1♌	25♎
8	17♊	2♋	2♌	25♎
9	18♊	4♋	3♌	25♎
10	19♊	6♋	4♌	25♎
11	20♊	8♋	5♌	25♎
12	21♊	10♋	6♌	25♎
13	22♊	11♋	7♌	25♎
14	23♊	13♋	8♌	25♎
15	24♊	15♋	9♌	25♎
16	25♊	16♋	10♌	25♎
17	26♊	18♋	11♌	26♎
18	27♊	19♋	12♌	26♎
19	28♊	21♋	13♌	26♎
20	28♊	22♋	14♌	26♎
21	29♊	23♋	14♌	26♎
22	0♋	25♋	15♌	26♎
23	1♋	26♋	16♌	27♎
24	2♋	27♋	17♌	27♎
25	3♋	28♋	18♌	27♎
26	4♋	0♌	19♌	27♎
27	5♋	1♌	19♌	28♎
28	6♋	2♌	20♌	28♎
29	7♋	3♌	21♌	28♎
30	8♋	3♌	22♌	28♎

September

Day	☉	☿	♀	♂
1	8♍	1♍	21♌	29♏
2	9♍	3♍	20♌	0♐
3	10♍	5♍	20♌	0♐
4	11♍	7♍	20♌	1♐
5	12♍	9♍	19♌	2♐
6	13♍	11♍	19♌	2♐
7	14♍	13♍	19♌	3♐
8	15♍	15♍	19♌	3♐
9	16♍	17♍	19♌	4♐
10	17♍	19♍	19♌	5♐
11	18♍	20♍	19♌	5♐
12	19♍	22♍	19♌	6♐
13	20♍	24♍	19♌	7♐
14	21♍	26♍	19♌	7♐
15	22♍	28♍	19♌	8♐
16	23♍	29♍	19♌	9♐
17	24♍	1♎	20♌	9♐
18	25♍	3♎	20♌	10♐
19	26♍	5♎	20♌	11♐
20	27♍	6♎	20♌	11♐
21	28♍	8♎	21♌	12♐
22	29♍	10♎	21♌	13♐
23	0♎	11♎	21♌	13♐
24	1♎	13♎	22♌	14♐
25	2♎	15♎	22♌	15♐
26	3♎	16♎	23♌	15♐
27	4♎	18♎	23♌	16♐
28	5♎	19♎	24♌	17♐
29	6♎	21♎	24♌	17♐
30	7♎	22♎	25♌	18♐

December

Day	☉	☿	♀	♂
1	9♐	18♏	25♎	4♒
2	10♐	19♏	26♎	5♒
3	11♐	20♏	27♎	5♒
4	12♐	21♏	28♎	6♒
5	13♐	22♏	29♎	7♒
6	14♐	24♏	0♏	8♒
7	15♐	25♏	1♏	8♒
8	16♐	26♏	3♏	9♒
9	17♐	27♏	4♏	10♒
10	18♐	29♏	5♏	11♒
11	19♐	0♐	6♏	11♒
12	20♐	2♐	7♏	12♒
13	21♐	3♐	9♏	13♒
14	22♐	4♐	10♏	14♒
15	23♐	6♐	11♏	15♒
16	24♐	7♐	12♏	15♒
17	25♐	9♐	13♏	16♒
18	26♐	10♐	14♏	17♒
19	27♐	12♐	16♏	18♒
20	28♐	13♐	17♏	18♒
21	29♐	15♐	18♏	19♒
22	0♑	16♐	19♏	20♒
23	1♑	18♐	20♏	21♒
24	2♑	19♐	22♏	22♒
25	3♑	21♐	23♏	22♒
26	4♑	22♐	24♏	23♒
27	5♑	24♐	25♏	24♒
28	6♑	25♐	26♏	25♒
29	7♑	27♐	28♏	25♒
30	8♑	28♐	29♏	26♒
31	9♑	0♑	0♐	27♒

Planetary Positions

♌ = Leo ♍ = Virgo ♎ = Libra ♏ = Scorpio ♐ = Sagittarius ♑ = Capricorn ♒ = Aquarius ♓ = Pisces

2000

January

Day	☉	☿	♀	♂
1	10♑	1♑	1♐	28♒
2	11♑	3♑	2♐	29♒
3	12♑	5♑	4♐	29♒
4	13♑	6♑	5♐	0♓
5	14♑	8♑	6♐	1♓
6	15♑	9♑	7♐	2♓
7	16♑	11♑	8♐	2♓
8	17♑	12♑	10♐	3♓
9	18♑	14♑	11♐	4♓
10	19♑	16♑	12♐	5♓
11	20♑	17♑	13♐	5♓
12	21♑	19♑	15♐	6♓
13	22♑	21♑	16♐	7♓
14	23♑	22♑	17♐	8♓
15	24♑	24♑	18♐	9♓
16	25♑	25♑	19♐	9♓
17	26♑	27♑	21♐	10♓
18	27♑	29♑	22♐	11♓
19	28♑	0♒	23♐	12♓
20	29♑	2♒	24♐	12♓
21	0♒	4♒	26♐	13♓
22	1♒	6♒	27♐	14♓
23	2♒	7♒	28♐	15♓
24	4♒	9♒	29♐	16♓
25	5♒	11♒	0♑	16♓
26	6♒	12♒	2♑	17♓
27	7♒	14♒	3♑	18♓
28	8♒	16♒	4♑	19♓
29	9♒	18♒	5♑	19♓
30	10♒	19♒	7♑	20♓
31	11♒	21♒	8♑	21♓

April

Day	☉	☿	♀	♂
1	12♈	14♓	23♓	7♉
2	13♈	15♓	24♓	7♉
3	14♈	17♓	26♓	8♉
4	15♈	18♓	27♓	9♉
5	16♈	19♓	28♓	10♉
6	17♈	20♓	29♓	10♉
7	18♈	22♓	1♈	11♉
8	19♈	23♓	2♈	12♉
9	20♈	24♓	3♈	12♉
10	21♈	26♓	4♈	13♉
11	22♈	27♓	5♈	14♉
12	23♈	29♓	7♈	15♉
13	24♈	0♈	8♈	15♉
14	25♈	2♈	9♈	16♉
15	26♈	3♈	10♈	17♉
16	27♈	5♈	12♈	18♉
17	27♈	7♈	13♈	18♉
18	28♈	8♈	14♈	19♉
19	29♈	10♈	15♈	20♉
20	0♉	12♈	17♈	20♉
21	1♉	13♈	18♈	21♉
22	2♉	15♈	19♈	22♉
23	3♉	17♈	20♈	23♉
24	4♉	19♈	21♈	23♉
25	5♉	20♈	23♈	24♉
26	6♉	22♈	24♈	25♉
27	7♉	24♈	25♈	25♉
28	8♉	26♈	26♈	26♉
29	9♉	28♈	28♈	27♉
30	10♉	0♉	29♈	27♉

July

Day	☉	☿	♀	♂
1	10♋	18♋	15♋	10♋
2	11♋	17♋	16♋	10♋
3	12♋	17♋	18♋	11♋
4	13♋	16♋	19♋	12♋
5	13♋	15♋	20♋	12♋
6	14♋	15♋	21♋	13♋
7	15♋	14♋	22♋	14♋
8	16♋	14♋	24♋	14♋
9	17♋	13♋	25♋	15♋
10	18♋	13♋	26♋	16♋
11	19♋	12♋	27♋	16♋
12	20♋	12♋	29♋	17♋
13	21♋	11♋	0♌	18♋
14	22♋	11♋	1♌	18♋
15	23♋	11♋	2♌	19♋
16	24♋	10♋	4♌	20♋
17	25♋	10♋	5♌	20♋
18	26♋	10♋	6♌	21♋
19	27♋	11♋	7♌	22♋
20	28♋	11♋	8♌	22♋
21	29♋	11♋	10♌	23♋
22	0♌	11♋	11♌	24♋
23	1♌	12♋	12♌	24♋
24	2♌	12♋	13♌	25♋
25	3♌	13♋	15♌	26♋
26	4♌	14♋	16♌	26♋
27	4♌	15♋	17♌	27♋
28	5♌	16♋	18♌	28♋
29	6♌	17♋	20♌	28♋
30	7♌	18♋	21♌	29♋
31	8♌	19♋	22♌	29♋

October

Day	☉	☿	♀	♂
1	8♎	3♏	8♏	9♍
2	9♎	4♏	9♏	10♍
3	10♎	5♏	10♏	10♍
4	11♎	7♏	12♏	11♍
5	12♎	8♏	13♏	11♍
6	13♎	9♏	14♏	12♍
7	14♎	10♏	15♏	13♍
8	15♎	10♏	17♏	13♍
9	16♎	11♏	18♏	14♍
10	17♎	12♏	19♏	15♍
11	18♎	13♏	20♏	15♍
12	19♎	14♏	21♏	16♍
13	20♎	14♏	23♏	16♍
14	21♎	15♏	24♏	17♍
15	22♎	15♏	25♏	18♍
16	23♎	15♏	26♏	18♍
17	24♎	16♏	28♏	19♍
18	25♎	16♏	29♏	20♍
19	26♎	16♏	0♐	20♍
20	27♎	16♏	1♐	21♍
21	28♎	15♏	2♐	21♍
22	29♎	15♏	4♐	22♍
23	0♏	14♏	5♐	23♍
24	1♏	14♏	6♐	23♍
25	2♏	13♏	7♐	24♍
26	3♏	12♏	8♐	25♍
27	4♏	11♏	10♐	25♍
28	5♏	9♏	11♐	26♍
29	6♏	8♏	12♐	26♍
30	7♏	7♏	13♐	27♍
31	8♏	6♏	14♐	28♍

February

Day	☉	☿	♀	♂
1	12♒	23♒	9♑	22♓
2	13♒	25♒	10♑	22♓
3	14♒	26♒	12♑	23♓
4	15♒	28♒	13♑	24♓
5	16♒	0♓	14♑	25♓
6	17♒	1♓	15♑	26♓
7	18♒	3♓	16♑	26♓
8	19♒	5♓	18♑	27♓
9	20♒	6♓	19♑	28♓
10	21♒	8♓	20♑	29♓
11	22♒	9♓	21♑	29♓
12	23♒	10♓	23♑	0♈
13	24♒	12♓	24♑	1♈
14	25♒	13♓	25♑	2♈
15	26♒	14♓	26♑	2♈
16	27♒	15♓	28♑	3♈
17	28♒	16♓	29♑	4♈
18	29♒	16♓	0♒	5♈
19	0♓	17♓	1♒	5♈
20	1♓	17♓	2♒	6♈
21	2♓	17♓	4♒	7♈
22	3♓	17♓	5♒	8♈
23	4♓	17♓	6♒	8♈
24	5♓	17♓	7♒	9♈
25	6♓	16♓	9♒	10♈
26	7♓	15♓	10♒	11♈
27	8♓	15♓	11♒	11♈
28	9♓	14♓	12♒	12♈
29	10♓	13♓	14♒	13♈

May

Day	☉	☿	♀	♂
1	11♉	2♉	0♉	28♉
2	12♉	4♉	1♉	29♉
3	13♉	6♉	3♉	0♊
4	14♉	8♉	4♉	0♊
5	15♉	10♉	5♉	1♊
6	16♉	12♉	6♉	2♊
7	17♉	15♉	7♉	2♊
8	18♉	17♉	9♉	3♊
9	19♉	19♉	10♉	4♊
10	20♉	21♉	11♉	4♊
11	21♉	23♉	12♉	5♊
12	22♉	25♉	14♉	6♊
13	23♉	28♉	15♉	7♊
14	24♉	0♊	16♉	7♊
15	25♉	2♊	17♉	8♊
16	26♉	4♊	19♉	9♊
17	27♉	6♊	20♉	9♊
18	28♉	8♊	21♉	10♊
19	29♉	10♊	22♉	11♊
20	29♉	12♊	23♉	11♊
21	0♊	14♊	25♉	12♊
22	1♊	16♊	26♉	13♊
23	2♊	18♊	27♉	13♊
24	3♊	20♊	28♉	14♊
25	4♊	22♊	0♊	15♊
26	5♊	24♊	1♊	16♊
27	6♊	25♊	2♊	16♊
28	7♊	27♊	3♊	17♊
29	8♊	28♊	5♊	18♊
30	9♊	0♋	6♊	18♊
31	10♊	2♋	7♊	19♊

August

Day	☉	☿	♀	♂
1	9♌	20♋	23♌	0♌
2	10♌	22♋	24♌	1♌
3	11♌	23♋	26♌	1♌
4	12♌	25♋	27♌	2♌
5	13♌	27♋	28♌	3♌
6	14♌	28♋	29♌	3♌
7	15♌	0♌	1♍	4♌
8	16♌	2♌	2♍	5♌
9	17♌	4♌	3♍	5♌
10	18♌	6♌	4♍	6♌
11	19♌	7♌	6♍	7♌
12	20♌	9♌	7♍	7♌
13	21♌	11♌	8♍	8♌
14	22♌	13♌	9♍	8♌
15	23♌	15♌	10♍	9♌
16	24♌	17♌	12♍	10♌
17	25♌	19♌	13♍	10♌
18	26♌	22♌	14♍	11♌
19	27♌	24♌	15♍	12♌
20	27♌	26♌	17♍	12♌
21	28♌	28♌	18♍	13♌
22	29♌	0♍	19♍	14♌
23	0♍	2♍	20♍	14♌
24	1♍	4♍	21♍	15♌
25	2♍	5♍	23♍	16♌
26	3♍	7♍	24♍	16♌
27	4♍	9♍	25♍	17♌
28	5♍	11♍	26♍	17♌
29	6♍	13♍	28♍	18♌
30	7♍	15♍	29♍	19♌
31	8♍	17♍	0♎	19♌

November

Day	☉	☿	♀	♂
1	9♏	4♏	16♐	28♍
2	10♏	3♏	17♐	29♍
3	11♏	2♏	18♐	29♍
4	12♏	1♏	19♐	0♎
5	13♏	1♏	21♐	1♎
6	14♏	0♏	22♐	1♎
7	15♏	0♏	23♐	2♎
8	16♏	0♏	24♐	3♎
9	17♏	0♏	25♐	3♎
10	18♏	0♏	27♐	4♎
11	19♏	1♏	28♐	4♎
12	20♏	1♏	29♐	5♎
13	21♏	2♏	0♑	6♎
14	22♏	3♏	1♑	6♎
15	23♏	4♏	3♑	7♎
16	24♏	5♏	4♑	7♎
17	25♏	6♏	5♑	8♎
18	26♏	7♏	6♑	9♎
19	27♏	9♏	7♑	9♎
20	28♏	10♏	9♑	10♎
21	29♏	11♏	10♑	11♎
22	0♐	13♏	11♑	11♎
23	1♐	14♏	12♑	12♎
24	2♐	15♏	13♑	12♎
25	3♐	17♏	14♑	13♎
26	4♐	18♏	16♑	14♎
27	5♐	20♏	17♑	14♎
28	6♐	21♏	18♑	15♎
29	7♐	23♏	19♑	15♎
30	8♐	24♏	20♑	16♎

March

Day	☉	☿	♀	♂
1	11♓	12♓	15♒	14♈
2	12♓	11♓	16♒	15♈
3	13♓	10♓	17♒	15♈
4	14♓	9♓	19♒	16♈
5	15♓	8♓	20♒	17♈
6	16♓	7♓	21♒	18♈
7	17♓	6♓	22♒	18♈
8	18♓	5♓	23♒	19♈
9	19♓	4♓	25♒	20♈
10	20♓	4♓	26♒	20♈
11	21♓	3♓	27♒	21♈
12	22♓	3♓	28♒	22♈
13	23♓	3♓	0♓	23♈
14	24♓	3♓	1♓	23♈
15	25♓	3♓	2♓	24♈
16	26♓	3♓	3♓	25♈
17	27♓	3♓	5♓	26♈
18	28♓	3♓	6♓	26♈
19	29♓	4♓	7♓	27♈
20	0♈	4♓	8♓	28♈
21	1♈	5♓	10♓	29♈
22	2♈	5♓	11♓	29♈
23	3♈	6♓	12♓	0♉
24	4♈	7♓	13♓	1♉
25	5♈	7♓	14♓	2♉
26	6♈	8♓	16♓	2♉
27	7♈	9♓	17♓	3♉
28	8♈	10♓	18♓	4♉
29	9♈	11♓	19♓	5♉
30	10♈	12♓	21♓	5♉
31	11♈	13♓	22♓	6♉

June

Day	☉	☿	♀	♂
1	11♊	3♋	8♊	20♊
2	12♊	4♋	9♊	20♊
3	13♊	6♋	11♊	21♊
4	14♊	7♋	12♊	22♊
5	15♊	8♋	13♊	22♊
6	16♊	9♋	14♊	23♊
7	17♊	11♋	16♊	24♊
8	18♊	12♋	17♊	24♊
9	19♊	13♋	18♊	25♊
10	20♊	14♋	19♊	26♊
11	21♊	15♋	21♊	26♊
12	22♊	15♋	22♊	27♊
13	22♊	16♋	23♊	28♊
14	23♊	17♋	24♊	28♊
15	24♊	17♋	25♊	29♊
16	25♊	18♋	27♊	0♋
17	26♊	19♋	28♊	0♋
18	27♊	19♋	29♊	1♋
19	28♊	19♋	0♋	2♋
20	29♊	20♋	2♋	2♋
21	0♋	20♋	3♋	3♋
22	1♋	20♋	4♋	4♋
23	2♋	20♋	5♋	4♋
24	3♋	20♋	6♋	5♋
25	4♋	20♋	8♋	6♋
26	5♋	20♋	9♋	6♋
27	6♋	19♋	10♋	7♋
28	7♋	19♋	11♋	8♋
29	8♋	19♋	13♋	8♋
30	9♋	18♋	14♋	9♋

September

Day	☉	☿	♀	♂
1	9♍	18♍	1♎	20♌
2	10♍	20♍	3♎	21♌
3	11♍	22♍	4♎	21♌
4	12♍	24♍	5♎	22♌
5	13♍	25♍	6♎	23♌
6	14♍	27♍	7♎	23♌
7	15♍	29♍	9♎	24♌
8	16♍	0♎	10♎	24♌
9	17♍	2♎	11♎	25♌
10	18♍	4♎	12♎	26♌
11	19♍	5♎	14♎	26♌
12	20♍	7♎	15♎	27♌
13	21♍	8♎	16♎	28♌
14	22♍	10♎	17♎	28♌
15	23♍	12♎	18♎	29♌
16	24♍	13♎	20♎	29♌
17	25♍	14♎	21♎	0♍
18	26♍	16♎	22♎	1♍
19	27♍	17♎	23♎	1♍
20	28♍	19♎	25♎	2♍
21	29♍	20♎	26♎	3♍
22	29♍	22♎	27♎	3♍
23	0♎	23♎	28♎	4♍
24	1♎	24♎	29♎	5♍
25	2♎	26♎	1♏	5♍
26	3♎	27♎	2♏	6♍
27	4♎	28♎	3♏	6♍
28	5♎	0♏	4♏	7♍
29	6♎	1♏	6♏	8♍
30	7♎	2♏	7♏	8♍

December

Day	☉	☿	♀	♂
1	9♐	26♏	22♑	17♎
2	10♐	27♏	23♑	17♎
3	11♐	29♏	24♑	18♎
4	12♐	1♐	25♑	18♎
5	13♐	2♐	26♑	19♎
6	14♐	4♐	27♑	20♎
7	15♐	5♐	29♑	20♎
8	16♐	7♐	0♒	21♎
9	17♐	8♐	1♒	21♎
10	18♐	10♐	2♒	22♎
11	19♐	11♐	3♒	23♎
12	20♐	13♐	4♒	23♎
13	21♐	15♐	6♒	24♎
14	23♐	16♐	7♒	24♎
15	24♐	18♐	8♒	25♎
16	25♐	19♐	9♒	26♎
17	26♐	21♐	10♒	26♎
18	27♐	22♐	11♒	27♎
19	28♐	24♐	13♒	27♎
20	29♐	25♐	14♒	28♎
21	0♑	27♐	15♒	29♎
22	1♑	29♐	16♒	29♎
23	2♑	0♑	17♒	0♏
24	3♑	2♑	18♒	0♏
25	4♑	3♑	19♒	1♏
26	5♑	5♑	21♒	2♏
27	6♑	7♑	22♒	2♏
28	7♑	8♑	23♒	3♏
29	8♑	10♑	24♒	3♏
30	9♑	11♑	25♒	4♏
31	10♑	13♑	26♒	4♏

Moon Movements

1909

1. Turn to the page containing the year you were born.

2. Select the month you were born.

3. Find the day you were born. If two signs are shown, the time listed is when the Moon changed signs. This time is given in **Eastern Standard Time**. Please refer to the Ascendant Tables (pages 543-567) for conversion information. Note the sign of the Zodiac listed for your Moon on your worksheet.

4. Repeats steps 1, 2 and 3 for your partner's birthday.

January

Day	Moon	Time	New Sign
9	♌		
10	♌	12:34 am	♍
11	♍		
12	♍	1:11 pm	♎
13	♎		
26	♈		
27	♈	8:02 pm	
28	♉		
29	♉		
30	♉	1:22 am	♊
31	♊		

April

Day	Moon	Time	New Sign
9	♏	7:17 am	♐
10	♐		
11	♐	3:57 pm	♑
12	♑		
13	♑	9:44 pm	♒
26	♋	3:02 pm	♌
27	♌		
28	♌		
29	♌	2:33 am	♍
30	♍		

July

Day	Moon	Time	New Sign
9	♈		
10	♈	11:29 pm	♉
11	♉		
12	♉		
13	♉	3:30 am	♊
26	♏		
27	♏	2:00 pm	♐
28	♐		
29	♐	9:32 pm	♑
30	♑		
31	♑		

October

Day	Moon	Time	New Sign
1	♉		
2	♉	11:04 pm	♊
3	♊		
4	♊		
5	♊	3:09 am	♋
6	♋		
7	♋	10:58 am	♌
8	♌		
9	♌	9:42 pm	♍
10	♍		
11	♍		
12	♍	10:01 am	♎
13	♎		
14	♎	10:46 pm	♏
15	♏		
16	♏		
17	♏	11:02 am	♐
18	♐		
19	♐	9:37 pm	♑
20	♑		
21	♑		
22	♑	5:13 am	♒
23	♒		
24	♒	9:09 am	♓
25	♓		
26	♓	10:01 am	♈
27	♈		
28	♈	9:27 am	♉
29	♉		
30	♉	9:27 am	♊
31	♊		

February

Day	Moon	Time	New Sign
1	♊	9:32 am	♋
2	♋		
3	♋	7:50 pm	♌
4	♌		
5	♌		
6	♌	7:35 am	♍
7	♍		
8	♍	8:10 pm	♎
9	♎		
11	♎	8:30 am	♏
13	♏	6:48 pm	♐
14	♐		
15	♐		
16	♐	1:27 am	♑
23			
24			
25			
26			
27			
28			

May

Day	Moon	Time	New Sign
1	♍	3:11 pm	♎
2	♎		
3	♎		
4	♎	3:04 am	♏
5	♏		
6	♏	1:16 pm	♐
7	♐		
8	♐	9:26 pm	♑
9	♑		
10	♑		
11	♑	3:26 am	♒
12	♒		
13	♒	7:14 am	♓
14	♓		
15	♓	9:13 am	♈
16	♈		

August

Day	Moon	Time	New Sign
1	♑	1:22 am	♒
2	♒		
3	♒	2:42 am	♓
4	♓		
5	♓	3:22 am	♈
6	♈		
7	♈	5:05 am	♉
8	♉		
9	♉	8:55 am	♊
10	♊		
11	♊	3:08 pm	♋
12	♋		
13	♋	11:29 pm	♌
14	♌		
15	♌		
16	♌	9:42 am	♍

November

Day	Moon	Time	New Sign
1	♊	11:57 am	♋
2	♋		
3	♋	6:10 pm	♌
4	♌		
5	♌		
6	♌	4:04 am	♍
7	♍		
8	♍	4:19 pm	♎
9	♎		
10	♎		
11	♎	5:04 am	♏
12	♏		
13	♏	4:57 pm	♐
14	♐		
15	♐		
16	♐	3:09 am	♑
17	♑		
18	♑	11:05 am	♒
19	♒		
20	♒	4:20 pm	♓
21	♓		
22	♓	7:02 pm	♈
23	♈		
24	♈	7:57 pm	♉
25	♉		
26	♉	8:31 pm	♊
27	♊		
28	♊	10:26 pm	♋
29	♋		
30	♋		

March

Day	Moon	Time	New Sign
1	♋		
2	♋		
3	♋	1:41 am	♌
4	♌		
17	♑	2:09 pm	♒
18	♒		
19	♒	3:07 pm	♓
20	♓		
21	♓	2:17 pm	♈
22	♈		
23	♈	1:50 pm	♉
24	♉		
25	♉	3:55 pm	♊
26	♊		
27	♊	9:55 pm	♋
28	♋		
29	♋		
30	♋	7:43 am	♌
31	♌		

June

Day	Moon	Time	New Sign
1	♏		
2	♏	8:32 pm	♐
3	♐		
4	♐		
17	♊		
18	♊	1:28 am	♋
19	♋		
20	♋	8:32 am	♌
21	♌		
22	♌	6:29 pm	♍
23	♍		
24	♍		
25	♍	6:36 am	♎
26	♎		
27	♎	6:51 pm	♏
28	♏		
29	♏		
30	♏	5:03 am	♐

September

Day	Moon	Time	New Sign
1	♓	12:19 pm	♈
2	♈		
3	♈	12:27 pm	♉
4	♉		
17	♎	4:49 pm	♏
18	♏		
19	♏		
20	♏	5:11 am	♐
21	♐		
22	♐	3:13 pm	♑
23	♑		
24	♑	9:22 pm	♒
25	♒		
26	♒	11:32 pm	♓
27	♓		
28	♓	11:07 pm	♈
29	♈		
30	♈	10:14 pm	♉

December

Day	Moon	Time	New Sign
1	♋	3:17 am	♌
2	♌		
3	♌	11:50 am	♍
4	♍		
5	♍	11:30 pm	♎
6	♎		
7	♎		
8	♎	12:17 pm	♏
9	♏		
10	♏		
11	♏	12:01 am	♐
12	♐		
13	♐	9:31 am	♑
14	♑		
15	♑	4:39 pm	♒
16	♒		
17	♒	9:48 pm	♓
18	♓		
19	♓		
20	♓	1:25 am	♈
21	♈		
22	♈	3:57 am	♉
23	♉		
24	♉	6:04 am	♊
25	♊		
26	♊	8:45 am	♋
27	♋		
28	♋	1:17 pm	♌
29	♌		
30	♌	8:49 pm	♍
31	♍		

1900

Moon Movements

♎ = Libra ♏ = Scorpio ♐ = Sagittarius ♑ = Capricorn ♒ = Aquarius ♓ = Pisces

January

1	♑		
2	♑	4:26 pm	♒
3	♒		
4	♒	5:09 pm	♓
5	♓		
6	♓	6:46 pm	♈
7	♈		
8	♈	10:26 pm	♉
9	♉		
10	♉		
11	♉	4:37 am	♊
12	♊		
13	♊	1:06 pm	♋
14	♋		
15	♋	11:31 pm	♌
16	♌		
17	♌		
18	♌	11:27 am	♍
19	♍		
20	♍		
21	♍	12:07 pm	♎
22	♎		
23	♎	11:55 am	♏
24	♏		
25	♏	8:50 pm	♐
26	♐		
27	♐		
28	♐	1:48 am	♑
29	♑		
30	♑	3:13 am	♒
31	♒		

February

1	♒	2:48 am	♓
2	♓		
3	♓	2:38 am	♈
4	♈		
5	♈	4:42 am	♉
6	♉		
7	♉	10:08 am	♊
8	♊		
9	♊	6:50 pm	♋
10	♋		
11	♋		
12	♋	5:49 am	♌
13	♌		
14	♌	6:00 pm	♍
15	♍		
16	♍		
17	♍	6:37 am	♎
18	♎		
19	♎	6:45 pm	♏
20	♏		
21	♏		
22	♏	4:54 am	♐
23	♐		
24	♐	11:33 am	♑
25	♑		
26	♑	2:16 pm	♒
27	♒		
28	♒	2:05 pm	♓

March

1	♓		
2	♓	1:02 pm	♈
3	♈		
4	♈	1:25 pm	♉
5	♉		
6	♉	5:05 pm	♊
7	♊		
8	♊		
9	♊	12:46 am	♋
10	♋		
11	♋	11:39 am	♌
12	♌		
13	♌		
14	♌	12:04 pm	♍
15	♍		
16	♍	12:39 pm	♎
17	♎		
18	♎		
19	♎	12:35 am	♏
20	♏		
21	♏	11:03 am	♐
22	♐		
23	♐	6:57 pm	♑
24	♑		
25	♑	11:26 pm	♒
26	♒		
27	♒		
28	♒	12:42 am	♓
29	♓		
30	♓	12:13 am	♈
31	♈		

April

1	♈	12:01 am	♉
2	♉		
3	♉	2:14 am	♊
4	♊		
5	♊	8:17 am	♋
6	♋		
7	♋	6:11 pm	♌
8	♌		
9	♌		
10	♌	6:25 am	♍
11	♍		
12	♍	7:01 pm	♎
13	♎		
14	♎		
15	♎	6:38 pm	♏
16	♏		
17	♏	4:39 pm	♐
18	♐		
19	♐		
20	♐	12:37 am	♑
21	♑		
22	♑	6:06 am	♒
23	♒		
24	♒	8:59 am	♓
25	♓		
26	♓	10:00 am	♈
27	♈		
28	♈	10:34 am	♉
29	♉		
30	♉	12:30 pm	♊

May

1	♊		
2	♊	5:24 pm	♋
3	♋		
4	♋		
5	♋	2:01 am	♌
6	♌		
7	♌	1:36 pm	♍
8	♍		
9	♍		
10	♍	2:10 am	♎
11	♎		
12	♎	1:42 pm	♏
13	♏		
14	♏	11:08 pm	♐
15	♐		
16	♐		
17	♐	6:20 am	♑
18	♑		
19	♑	11:31 am	♒
20	♒		
21	♒	3:01 pm	♓
22	♓		
23	♓	5:22 pm	♈
24	♈		
25	♈	7:21 pm	♉
26	♉		
27	♉	10:06 pm	♊
28	♊		
29	♊		
30	♊	2:55 am	♋
31	♋		

June

1	♋	10:45 am	♌
2	♌		
3	♌	9:34 pm	♍
4	♍		
5	♍		
6	♍	10:00 am	♎
7	♎		
8	♎	9:46 pm	♏
9	♏		
10	♏		
11	♏	7:06 am	♐
12	♐		
13	♐	1:31 pm	♑
14	♑		
15	♑	5:38 pm	♒
16	♒		
17	♒	8:27 pm	♓
18	♓		
19	♓	10:57 pm	♈
20	♈		
21	♈		
22	♈	1:54 am	♉
23	♉		
24	♉	5:52 am	♊
25	♊		
26	♊	11:28 am	♋
27	♋		
28	♋	7:19 pm	♌
29	♌		
30	♌		

July

1	♌	5:43 am	♍
2	♍		
3	♍	5:59 pm	♎
4	♎		
5	♎		
6	♎	6:12 am	♏
7	♏		
8	♏	4:05 pm	♐
9	♐		
10	♐	10:27 pm	♑
11	♑		
12	♑		
13	♑	1:41 am	♒
14	♒		
15	♒	3:12 am	♓
16	♓		
17	♓	4:38 am	♈
18	♈		
19	♈	7:17 am	♉
20	♉		
21	♉	11:49 am	♊
22	♊		
23	♊	6:20 pm	♋
24	♋		
25	♋		
26	♋	2:49 am	♌
27	♌		
28	♌	1:18 pm	♍
29	♍		
30	♍		
31	♍	1:30 am	♎

August

1	♎		
2	♎	2:09 pm	♏
3	♏		
4	♏		
5	♏	1:01 am	♐
6	♐		
7	♐	8:14 am	♑
8	♑		
9	♑	11:32 am	♒
10	♒		
11	♒	12:10 pm	♓
12	♓		
13	♓	12:09 pm	♈
14	♈		
15	♈	1:25 pm	♉
16	♉		
17	♉	5:14 pm	♊
18	♊		
19	♊	11:56 pm	♋
20	♋		
21	♋		
22	♋	9:03 am	♌
23	♌		
24	♌	7:57 pm	♍
25	♍		
26	♍		
27	♍	8:13 am	♎
28	♎		
29	♎	9:03 pm	♏
30	♏		
31	♏		

September

1	♏	8:49 am	♐
2	♐		
3	♐	5:27 pm	♑
4	♑		
5	♑	9:53 pm	♒
6	♒		
7	♒	10:47 pm	♓
8	♓		
9	♓	10:00 pm	♈
10	♈		
11	♈	9:45 pm	♉
12	♉		
13	♉	11:58 pm	♊
14	♊		
15	♊		
16	♊	5:40 am	♋
17	♋		
18	♋	2:39 pm	♌
19	♌		
20	♌		
21	♌	1:53 am	♍
22	♍		
23	♍	2:19 pm	♎
24	♎		
25	♎		
26	♎	3:06 am	♏
27	♏		
28	♏	3:10 pm	♐
29	♐		
30	♐		

October

1	♐	12:57 am	♑
2	♑		
3	♑	7:04 am	♒
4	♒		
5	♒	9:22 am	♓
6	♓		
7	♓	9:06 am	♈
8	♈		
9	♈	8:17 am	♉
10	♉		
11	♉	9:02 am	♊
12	♊		
13	♊	1:02 pm	♋
14	♋		
15	♋	8:53 pm	♌
16	♌		
17	♌		
18	♌	7:52 am	♍
19	♍		
20	♍	8:25 pm	♎
21	♎		
22	♎		
23	♎	9:05 am	♏
24	♏		
25	♏	8:50 am	♐
26	♐		
27	♐		
28	♐	6:47 am	♑
29	♑		
30	♑	2:02 pm	♒
31	♒		

November

1	♒	6:06 pm	♓
2	♓		
3	♓	7:27 pm	♈
4	♈		
5	♈	7:25 pm	♉
6	♉		
7	♉	7:50 pm	♊
8	♊		
9	♊	10:32 pm	♋
10	♋		
11	♋		
12	♋	4:49 am	♌
13	♌		
14	♌	2:48 pm	♍
15	♍		
16	♍		
17	♍	3:09 am	♎
18	♎		
19	♎	3:48 pm	♏
20	♏		
21	♏		
22	♏	3:09 am	♐
23	♐		
24	♐	12:26 pm	♑
25	♑		
26	♑	7:30 pm	♒
27	♒		
28	♒		
29	♒	12:24 am	♓
30	♓		

December

1	♓	3:22 am	♈
2	♈		
3	♈	5:01 am	♉
4	♉		
5	♉	6:27 am	♊
6	♊		
7	♊	9:04 am	♋
8	♋		
9	♋	2:19 pm	♌
10	♌		
11	♌	11:04 pm	♍
12	♍		
13	♍		
14	♍	10:49 am	♎
15	♎		
16	♎	11:34 pm	♏
17	♏		
18	♏		
19	♏	10:54 am	♐
20	♐		
21	♐	7:33 pm	♑
22	♑		
23	♑		
24	♑	1:34 am	♒
25	♒		
26	♒	5:47 am	♓
27	♓		
28	♓	9:02 am	♈
29	♈		
30	♈	11:55 am	♉
31	♉		

Your Starway to Love

♈ = Aries ♉ = Taurus ♊ = Gemini ♋ = Cancer ♌ = Leo ♍ = Virgo

1901

January

Day	Sign	Time	Enters
1	♉	2:54 pm	♊
2	♊		
3	♊	6:36 pm	♋
4	♋		
5	♋	11:59 pm	♌
6	♌		
7	♌		
8	♌	8:04 am	♍
9	♍		
10	♍	7:07 pm	♎
11	♎		
12	♎		
13	♎	7:52 am	♏
14	♏		
15	♏	7:43 pm	♐
16	♐		
17	♐		
18	♐	4:30 am	♑
19	♑		
20	♑	9:48 am	♒
21	♒		
22	♒	12:41 pm	♓
23	♓		
24	♓	2:45 pm	♈
25	♈		
26	♈	5:16 pm	♉
27	♉		
28	♉	8:54 pm	♊
29	♊		
30	♊		
31	♊	1:50 am	♋

February

Day	Sign	Time	Enters
1	♋		
2	♋	8:12 am	♌
3	♌		
4	♌	4:33 pm	♍
5	♍		
6	♍		
7	♍	3:18 am	♎
8	♎		
9	♎	3:56 pm	♏
10	♏		
11	♏		
12	♏	4:26 am	♐
13	♐		
14	♐	2:10 pm	♑
15	♑		
16	♑	7:50 pm	♒
17	♒		
18	♒	10:06 pm	♓
19	♓		
20	♓	10:44 pm	♈
21	♈		
22	♈	11:41 pm	♉
23	♉		
24	♉		
25	♉	2:22 am	♊
26	♊		
27	♊	7:20 am	♋
28	♋		

March

Day	Sign	Time	Enters
1	♋	2:30 pm	♌
2	♌		
3	♌	11:37 pm	♍
4	♍		
5	♍		
6	♍	10:37 am	♎
7	♎		
8	♎	11:12 pm	♏
9	♏		
10	♏		
11	♏	12:04 pm	♐
12	♐		
13	♐	10:56 pm	♑
14	♑		
15	♑		
16	♑	5:56 am	♒
17	♒		
18	♒	8:52 am	♓
19	♓		
20	♓	9:06 am	♈
21	♈		
22	♈	8:41 am	♉
23	♉		
24	♉	9:37 am	♊
25	♊		
26	♊	1:15 pm	♋
27	♋		
28	♋	8:00 pm	♌
29	♌		
30	♌		
31	♌	5:29 am	♍

April

Day	Sign	Time	Enters
1	♍		
2	♍	4:57 pm	♎
3	♎		
4	♎		
5	♎	5:38 am	♏
6	♏		
7	♏	6:31 pm	♐
8	♐		
9	♐		
10	♐	6:02 am	♑
11	♑		
12	♑	2:27 pm	♒
13	♒		
14	♒	6:56 pm	♓
15	♓		
16	♓	8:06 pm	♈
17	♈		
18	♈	7:33 pm	♉
19	♉		
20	♉	7:18 pm	♊
21	♊		
22	♊	9:11 pm	♋
23	♋		
24	♋		
25	♋	2:28 am	♌
26	♌		
27	♌	11:20 am	♍
28	♍		
29	♍	10:54 pm	♎
30	♎		

May

Day	Sign	Time	Enters
1	♎		
2	♎	11:44 am	♏
3	♏		
4	♏		
5	♏	12:27 am	♐
6	♐		
7	♐	11:54 am	♑
8	♑		
9	♑	8:58 pm	♒
10	♒		
11	♒		
12	♒	2:55 am	♓
13	♓		
14	♓	5:43 am	♈
15	♈		
16	♈	6:16 am	♉
17	♉		
18	♉	6:07 am	♊
19	♊		
20	♊	7:03 am	♋
21	♋		
22	♋	10:47 am	♌
23	♌		
24	♌	6:18 pm	♍
25	♍		
26	♍		
27	♍	5:18 am	♎
28	♎		
29	♎	6:07 pm	♏
30	♏		
31	♏		

June

Day	Sign	Time	Enters
1	♏	6:44 am	♐
2	♐		
3	♐	5:43 pm	♑
4	♑		
5	♑		
6	♑	2:30 am	♒
7	♒		
8	♒	8:55 am	♓
9	♓		
10	♓	1:01 pm	♈
11	♈		
12	♈	3:10 pm	♉
13	♉		
14	♉	4:10 pm	♊
15	♊		
16	♊	5:22 pm	♋
17	♋		
18	♋	8:23 pm	♌
19	♌		
20	♌		
21	♌	2:40 am	♍
22	♍		
23	♍	12:42 pm	♎
24	♎		
25	♎		
26	♎	1:14 am	♏
27	♏		
28	♏	1:51 pm	♐
29	♐		
30	♐		

July

Day	Sign	Time	Enters
1	♐	12:31 am	♑
2	♑		
3	♑	8:34 am	♒
4	♒		
5	♒	2:22 pm	♓
6	♓		
7	♓	6:36 pm	♈
8	♈		
9	♈	9:45 pm	♉
10	♉		
11	♉		
12	♉	12:10 am	♊
13	♊		
14	♊	2:31 am	♋
15	♋		
16	♋	5:54 am	♌
17	♌		
18	♌	11:43 am	♍
19	♍		
20	♍	8:55 pm	♎
21	♎		
22	♎		
23	♎	9:00 am	♏
24	♏		
25	♏	9:45 pm	♐
26	♐		
27	♐		
28	♐	8:33 am	♑
29	♑		
30	♑	4:09 pm	♒
31	♒		

August

Day	Sign	Time	Enters
1	♒	8:59 pm	♓
2	♓		
3	♓		
4	♓	12:16 am	♈
5	♈		
6	♈	3:07 am	♉
7	♉		
8	♉	6:08 am	♊
9	♊		
10	♊	9:37 am	♋
11	♋		
12	♋	2:04 pm	♌
13	♌		
14	♌	8:17 pm	♍
15	♍		
16	♍		
17	♍	5:14 am	♎
18	♎		
19	♎	4:58 pm	♏
20	♏		
21	♏		
22	♏	5:54 am	♐
23	♐		
24	♐	5:18 pm	♑
25	♑		
26	♑		
27	♑	1:13 am	♒
28	♒		
29	♒	5:36 am	♓
30	♓		
31	♓	7:44 am	♈

September

Day	Sign	Time	Enters
1	♈		
2	♈	9:17 am	♉
3	♉		
4	♉	11:32 am	♊
5	♊		
6	♊	3:11 pm	♋
7	♋		
8	♋	8:26 pm	♌
9	♌		
10	♌		
11	♌	3:33 am	♍
12	♍		
13	♍	12:52 pm	♎
14	♎		
15	♎		
16	♎	12:31 am	♏
17	♏		
18	♏	1:33 pm	♐
19	♐		
20	♐		
21	♐	1:44 am	♑
22	♑		
23	♑	10:45 am	♒
24	♒		
25	♒	3:43 pm	♓
26	♓		
27	♓	5:29 pm	♈
28	♈		
29	♈	5:47 pm	♉
30	♉		

October

Day	Sign	Time	Enters
1	♉	6:28 pm	♊
2	♊		
3	♊	8:54 pm	♋
4	♋		
5	♋		
6	♋	1:52 am	♌
7	♌		
8	♌	9:28 am	♍
9	♍		
10	♍	7:26 pm	♎
11	♎		
12	♎		
13	♎	7:19 am	♏
14	♏		
15	♏	8:22 pm	♐
16	♐		
17	♐		
18	♐	9:01 am	♑
19	♑		
20	♑	7:18 pm	♒
21	♒		
22	♒		
23	♒	1:46 am	♓
24	♓		
25	♓	4:26 am	♈
26	♈		
27	♈	4:34 am	♉
28	♉		
29	♉	4:01 am	♊
30	♊		
31	♊	4:42 am	♋

November

Day	Sign	Time	Enters
1	♋		
2	♋	8:09 am	♌
3	♌		
4	♌	3:06 pm	♍
5	♍		
6	♍		
7	♍	1:15 am	♎
8	♎		
9	♎	1:30 pm	♏
10	♏		
11	♏		
12	♏	2:32 am	♐
13	♐		
14	♐	3:09 pm	♑
15	♑		
16	♑		
17	♑	2:04 am	♒
18	♒		
19	♒	10:04 am	♓
20	♓		
21	♓	2:31 pm	♈
22	♈		
23	♈	3:52 pm	♉
24	♉		
25	♉	3:24 pm	♊
26	♊		
27	♊	3:02 pm	♋
28	♋		
29	♋	4:44 pm	♌
30	♌		

December

Day	Sign	Time	Enters
1	♌	10:02 pm	♍
2	♍		
3	♍		
4	♍	7:24 am	♎
5	♎		
6	♎	7:38 pm	♏
7	♏		
8	♏		
9	♏	8:45 am	♐
10	♐		
11	♐	9:04 pm	♑
12	♑		
13	♑		
14	♑	7:42 am	♒
15	♒		
16	♒	4:12 pm	♓
17	♓		
18	♓	10:09 pm	♈
19	♈		
20	♈		
21	♈	1:23 am	♉
22	♉		
23	♉	2:22 am	♊
24	♉		
25	♊	2:23 am	♋
26	♊		
27	♋	3:18 am	♌
28	♋		
29	♌	7:04 am	♍
30	♍		
31	♍	2:56 pm	♎

Moon Movements

♎ = Libra ♏ = Scorpio ♐ = Sagittarius ♑ = Capricorn ♒ = Aquarius ♓ = Pisces

1902

January

Day	Moon	Time	Enters
1	♎		
2	♎		
3	♎	2:30 am	♏
4	♏		
5	♏	3:36 pm	♐
6	♐		
7	♐		
8	♐	3:47 am	♑
9	♑		
10	♑	1:48 pm	♒
11	♒		
12	♒	9:40 pm	♓
13	♓		
14	♓		
15	♓	3:44 am	♈
16	♈		
17	♈	8:06 am	♉
18	♉		
19	♉	10:49 am	♊
20	♊		
21	♊	12:21 pm	♋
22	♋		
23	♋	1:56 pm	♌
24	♌		
25	♌	5:16 pm	♍
26	♍		
27	♍	11:57 pm	♎
28	♎		
29	♎		
30	♎	10:28 am	♏
31	♏		

February

Day	Moon	Time	Enters
1	♏	11:17 pm	♐
2	♐		
3	♐		
4	♐	11:37 am	♑
5	♑		
6	♑	9:27 pm	♒
7	♒		
8	♒		
9	♒	4:29 am	♓
10	♓		
11	♓	9:31 am	♈
12	♈		
13	♈	1:26 pm	♉
14	♉		
15	♉	4:43 pm	♊
16	♊		
17	♊	7:37 pm	♋
18	♋		
19	♋	10:37 pm	♌
20	♌		
21	♌		
22	♌	2:44 am	♍
23	♍		
24	♍	9:18 am	♎
25	♎		
26	♎	7:05 pm	♏
27	♏		
28	♏		

March

Day	Moon	Time	Enters
1	♏	7:27 am	♐
2	♐		
3	♐	8:04 pm	♑
4	♑		
5	♑		
6	♑	6:22 am	♒
7	♒		
8	♒	1:16 pm	♓
9	♓		
10	♓	5:21 pm	♈
11	♈		
12	♈	7:55 pm	♉
13	♉		
14	♉	10:13 pm	♊
15	♊		
16	♊		
17	♊	1:04 am	♋
18	♋		
19	♋	4:54 am	♌
20	♌		
21	♌	10:12 am	♍
22	♍		
23	♍	5:31 pm	♎
24	♎		
25	♎		
26	♎	3:20 am	♏
27	♏		
28	♏	3:24 pm	♐
29	♐		
30	♐		
31	♐	4:12 am	♑

April

Day	Moon	Time	Enters
1	♑		
2	♑	3:20 pm	♒
3	♒		
4	♒	11:03 pm	♓
5	♓		
6	♓		
7	♓	3:11 am	♈
8	♈		
9	♈	4:50 am	♉
10	♉		
11	♉	5:37 am	♊
12	♊		
13	♊	7:04 am	♋
14	♋		
15	♋	10:18 am	♌
16	♌		
17	♌	3:57 pm	♍
18	♍		
19	♍		
20	♍	12:05 am	♎
21	♎		
22	♎	10:28 am	♏
23	♏		
24	♏	10:36 pm	♐
25	♐		
26	♐		
27	♐	11:26 am	♑
28	♑		
29	♑	11:16 pm	♒
30	♒		

May

Day	Moon	Time	Enters
1	♒		
2	♒	8:16 am	♓
3	♓		
4	♓	1:29 pm	♈
5	♈		
6	♈	3:23 pm	♉
7	♉		
8	♉	3:21 pm	♊
9	♊		
10	♊	3:15 pm	♋
11	♋		
12	♋	4:54 pm	♌
13	♌		
14	♌	9:36 pm	♍
15	♍		
16	♍		
17	♍	5:42 am	♎
18	♎		
19	♎	4:33 pm	♏
20	♏		
21	♏		
22	♏	4:58 am	♐
23	♐		
24	♐	5:47 pm	♑
25	♑		
26	♑		
27	♑	5:50 am	♒
28	♒		
29	♒	3:50 pm	♓
30	♓		
31	♓	10:35 pm	♈

June

Day	Moon	Time	Enters
1	♈		
2	♈		
3	♈	1:46 am	♉
4	♉		
5	♉	2:10 am	♊
6	♊		
7	♊	1:26 am	♋
8	♋		
9	♋	1:39 am	♌
10	♌		
11	♌	4:44 am	♍
12	♍		
13	♍	11:45 am	♎
14	♎		
15	♎	10:22 pm	♏
16	♏		
17	♏		
18	♏	10:58 am	♐
19	♐		
20	♐	11:46 pm	♑
21	♑		
22	♑		
23	♑	11:37 am	♒
24	♒		
25	♒	9:50 pm	♓
26	♓		
27	♓		
28	♓	5:39 am	♈
29	♈		
30	♈	10:26 am	♉

July

Day	Moon	Time	Enters
1	♉		
2	♉	12:14 pm	♊
3	♊		
4	♊	12:07 pm	♋
5	♋		
6	♋	11:54 am	♌
7	♌		
8	♌	1:44 pm	♍
9	♍		
10	♍	7:16 pm	♎
11	♎		
12	♎		
13	♎	4:56 am	♏
14	♏		
15	♏	5:17 pm	♐
16	♐		
17	♐		
18	♐	6:04 am	♑
19	♑		
20	♑	5:38 pm	♒
21	♒		
22	♒		
23	♒	3:24 am	♓
24	♓		
25	♓	11:15 am	♈
26	♈		
27	♈	4:57 pm	♉
28	♉		
29	♉	8:16 pm	♊
30	♊		
31	♊	9:34 pm	♋

August

Day	Moon	Time	Enters
1	♋		
2	♋	10:06 pm	♌
3	♌		
4	♌	11:43 pm	♍
5	♍		
6	♍		
7	♍	4:15 am	♎
8	♎		
9	♎	12:43 pm	♏
10	♏		
11	♏		
12	♏	12:26 am	♐
13	♐		
14	♐	1:10 pm	♑
15	♑		
16	♑		
17	♑	12:38 am	♒
18	♒		
19	♒	9:51 am	♓
20	♓		
21	♓	4:57 pm	♈
22	♈		
23	♈	10:20 pm	♉
24	♉		
25	♉		
26	♉	2:13 am	♊
27	♊		
28	♊	4:50 am	♋
29	♋		
30	♋	6:45 am	♌
31	♌		

September

Day	Moon	Time	Enters
1	♌	9:12 am	♍
2	♍		
3	♍	1:42 pm	♎
4	♎		
5	♎	9:26 pm	♏
6	♏		
7	♏		
8	♏	8:25 am	♐
9	♐		
10	♐	9:01 pm	♑
11	♑		
12	♑		
13	♑	8:44 am	♒
14	♒		
15	♒	5:53 pm	♓
16	♓		
17	♓		
18	♓	12:14 am	♈
19	♈		
20	♈	4:31 am	♉
21	♉		
22	♉	7:39 am	♊
23	♊		
24	♊	10:23 am	♋
25	♋		
26	♋	1:16 pm	♌
27	♌		
28	♌	4:58 pm	♍
29	♍		
30	♍	10:19 pm	♎

October

Day	Moon	Time	Enters
1	♎		
2	♎		
3	♎	6:07 am	♏
4	♏		
5	♏	4:40 pm	♐
6	♐		
7	♐		
8	♐	5:06 am	♑
9	♑		
10	♑	5:19 pm	♒
11	♒		
12	♒		
13	♒	3:07 am	♓
14	♓		
15	♓	9:30 am	♈
16	♈		
17	♈	12:56 pm	♉
18	♉		
19	♉	2:40 pm	♊
20	♊		
21	♊	4:10 pm	♋
22	♋		
23	♋	6:39 pm	♌
24	♌		
25	♌	10:53 pm	♍
26	♍		
27	♍		
28	♍	5:14 am	♎
29	♎		
30	♎	1:46 pm	♏
31	♏		

November

Day	Moon	Time	Enters
1	♏		
2	♏	12:26 am	♐
3	♐		
4	♐	12:44 pm	♑
5	♑		
6	♑		
7	♑	1:22 am	♒
8	♒		
9	♒	12:16 pm	♓
10	♓		
11	♓	7:44 pm	♈
12	♈		
13	♈	11:24 pm	♉
14	♉		
15	♉		
16	♉	12:19 am	♊
17	♊		
18	♊	12:14 am	♋
19	♋		
20	♋	1:05 am	♌
21	♌		
22	♌	4:24 am	♍
23	♍		
24	♍	10:49 am	♎
25	♎		
26	♎	8:01 pm	♏
27	♏		
28	♏		
29	♏	7:12 am	♐
30	♐		

December

Day	Moon	Time	Enters
1	♐	7:33 pm	♑
2	♑		
3	♑		
4	♑	8:16 am	♒
5	♒		
6	♒	8:01 pm	♓
7	♓		
8	♓		
9	♓	5:03 am	♈
10	♈		
11	♈	10:11 am	♉
12	♉		
13	♉	11:38 am	♊
14	♊		
15	♊	10:55 am	♋
16	♋		
17	♋	10:13 am	♌
18	♌		
19	♌	11:40 am	♍
20	♍		
21	♍	4:46 pm	♎
22	♎		
23	♎		
24	♎	1:39 am	♏
25	♏		
26	♏	1:09 pm	♐
27	♐		
28	♐		
29	♐	1:44 am	♑
30	♑		
31	♑	2:20 pm	♒

Your Starway to Love

♈ = Aries ♉ = Taurus ♊ = Gemini ♋ = Cancer ♌ = Leo ♍ = Virgo

1903

January			
1	♒		
2	♒		
3	♒	2:12 am	♓
4	♓		
5	♓	12:14 pm	♈
6	♈		
7	♈	7:09 pm	♉
8	♉		
9	♉	10:19 pm	♊
10	♊		
11	♊	10:28 pm	♋
12	♋		
13	♋	9:27 pm	♌
14	♌		
15	♌	9:32 pm	♍
16	♍		
17	♍		
18	♍	12:47 am	♎
19	♎		
20	♎	8:14 am	♏
21	♏		
22	♏	7:15 pm	♐
23	♐		
24	♐		
25	♐	7:55 am	♑
26	♑		
27	♑	8:27 pm	♒
28	♒		
29	♒		
30	♒	7:55 am	♓
31	♓		

February			
1	♓	5:52 pm	♈
2	♈		
3	♈		
4	♈	1:36 am	♉
5	♉		
6	♉	6:27 am	♊
7	♊		
8	♊	8:25 am	♋
9	♋		
10	♋	8:33 am	♌
11	♌		
12	♌	8:41 am	♍
13	♍		
14	♍	10:53 am	♎
15	♎		
16	♎	4:43 pm	♏
17	♏		
18	♏		
19	♏	2:29 am	♐
20	♐		
21	♐	2:46 pm	♑
22	♑		
23	♑		
24	♑	3:20 am	♒
25	♒		
26	♒	2:31 pm	♓
27	♓		
28	♓	11:45 pm	♈

March			
1	♈		
2	♈		
3	♈	7:00 am	♉
4	♉		
5	♉	12:16 pm	♊
6	♊		
7	♊	3:34 pm	♋
8	♋		
9	♋	5:23 pm	♌
10	♌		
11	♌	6:47 pm	♍
12	♍		
13	♍	9:18 pm	♎
14	♎		
15	♎		
16	♎	2:26 am	♏
17	♏		
18	♏	11:01 am	♐
19	♐		
20	♐	10:33 pm	♑
21	♑		
22	♑		
23	♑	11:06 am	♒
24	♒		
25	♒	10:24 pm	♓
26	♓		
27	♓		
28	♓	7:13 am	♈
29	♈		
30	♈	1:29 pm	♉
31	♉		

April			
1	♉	5:50 pm	♊
2	♊		
3	♊	9:00 pm	♋
4	♋		
5	♋	11:39 pm	♌
6	♌		
7	♌		
8	♌	2:27 am	♍
9	♍		
10	♍	6:11 am	♎
11	♎		
12	♎	11:45 am	♏
13	♏		
14	♏	7:56 pm	♐
15	♐		
16	♐		
17	♐	6:49 am	♑
18	♑		
19	♑	7:15 pm	♒
20	♒		
21	♒		
22	♒	7:01 am	♓
23	♓		
24	♓	4:07 pm	♈
25	♈		
26	♈	9:55 pm	♉
27	♉		
28	♉		
29	♉	1:07 am	♊
30	♊		

May			
1	♊	3:02 am	♋
2	♋		
3	♋	5:02 am	♌
4	♌		
5	♌	8:08 am	♍
6	♍		
7	♍	12:52 pm	♎
8	♎		
9	♎	7:26 pm	♏
10	♏		
11	♏		
12	♏	4:02 am	♐
13	♐		
14	♐	2:46 pm	♑
15	♑		
16	♑		
17	♑	3:05 am	♒
18	♒		
19	♒	3:21 pm	♓
20	♓		
21	♓		
22	♓	1:22 am	♈
23	♈		
24	♈	7:40 am	♉
25	♉		
26	♉	10:27 am	♊
27	♊		
28	♊	11:10 am	♋
29	♋		
30	♋	11:42 am	♌
31	♌		

June			
1	♌	1:45 pm	♍
2	♍		
3	♍	6:18 pm	♎
4	♎		
5	♎		
6	♎	1:28 am	♏
7	♏		
8	♏	10:46 am	♐
9	♐		
10	♐	9:47 pm	♑
11	♑		
12	♑		
13	♑	10:06 am	♒
14	♒		
15	♒	10:42 pm	♓
16	♓		
17	♓		
18	♓	9:43 am	♈
19	♈		
20	♈	5:17 pm	♉
21	♉		
22	♉	8:46 pm	♊
23	♊		
24	♊	9:12 pm	♋
25	♋		
26	♋	8:35 pm	♌
27	♌		
28	♌	9:04 pm	♍
29	♍		
30	♍		

July			
1	♍	12:19 am	♎
2	♎		
3	♎	6:58 am	♏
4	♏		
5	♏	4:31 pm	♐
6	♐		
7	♐		
8	♐	3:56 am	♑
9	♑		
10	♑	4:21 pm	♒
11	♒		
12	♒		
13	♒	4:59 am	♓
14	♓		
15	♓	4:36 pm	♈
16	♈		
17	♈		
18	♈	1:28 am	♉
19	♉		
20	♉	6:26 am	♊
21	♊		
22	♊	7:47 am	♋
23	♋		
24	♋	7:06 am	♌
25	♌		
26	♌	6:33 am	♍
27	♍		
28	♍	8:13 am	♎
29	♎		
30	♎	1:27 pm	♏
31	♏		

August			
1	♏	10:21 pm	♐
2	♐		
3	♐		
4	♐	9:49 am	♑
5	♑		
6	♑	10:21 pm	♒
7	♒		
8	♒		
9	♒	10:50 am	♓
10	♓		
11	♓	10:23 pm	♈
12	♈		
13	♈		
14	♈	7:52 am	♉
15	♉		
16	♉	2:15 pm	♊
17	♊		
18	♊	5:12 pm	♋
19	♋		
20	♋	5:37 pm	♌
21	♌		
22	♌	5:13 pm	♍
23	♍		
24	♍	6:01 pm	♎
25	♎		
26	♎	9:46 pm	♏
27	♏		
28	♏		
29	♏	5:21 am	♐
30	♐		
31	♐	4:14 pm	♑

September			
1	♑		
2	♑		
3	♑	4:45 am	♒
4	♒		
5	♒	5:07 pm	♓
6	♓		
7	♓		
8	♓	4:12 am	♈
9	♈		
10	♈	1:22 pm	♉
11	♉		
12	♉	8:11 pm	♊
13	♊		
14	♊		
15	♊	12:27 am	♋
16	♋		
17	♋	2:30 am	♌
18	♌		
19	♌	3:20 am	♍
20	♍		
21	♍	4:28 am	♎
22	♎		
23	♎	7:33 am	♏
24	♏		
25	♏	1:53 pm	♐
26	♐		
27	♐	11:45 pm	♑
28	♑		
29	♑		
30	♑	11:59 am	♒

October			
1	♒		
2	♒		
3	♒	12:24 am	♓
4	♓		
5	♓	11:11 am	♈
6	♈		
7	♈	7:34 pm	♉
8	♉		
9	♉		
10	♉	1:41 am	♊
11	♊		
12	♊	6:00 am	♋
13	♋		
14	♋	9:03 am	♌
15	♌		
16	♌	11:24 am	♍
17	♍		
18	♍	1:49 pm	♎
19	♎		
20	♎	5:23 pm	♏
21	♏		
22	♏	11:15 pm	♐
23	♐		
24	♐		
25	♐	8:14 am	♑
26	♑		
27	♑	7:58 pm	♒
28	♒		
29	♒		
30	♒	8:35 am	♓
31	♓		

November			
1	♓	7:36 pm	♈
2	♈		
3	♈		
4	♈	3:36 am	♉
5	♉		
6	♉	8:39 am	♊
7	♊		
8	♊	11:50 am	♋
9	♋		
10	♋	2:24 pm	♌
11	♌		
12	♌	5:16 pm	♍
13	♍		
14	♍	8:55 pm	♎
15	♎		
16	♎		
17	♎	1:41 am	♏
18	♏		
19	♏	8:06 am	♐
20	♐		
21	♐	4:50 pm	♑
22	♑		
23	♑		
24	♑	4:09 am	♒
25	♒		
26	♒	4:55 pm	♓
27	♓		
28	♓		
29	♓	4:42 am	♈
30	♈		

December			
1	♈	1:14 pm	♉
2	♉		
3	♉	5:56 pm	♊
4	♊		
5	♊	7:55 pm	♋
6	♋		
7	♋	8:58 pm	♌
8	♌		
9	♌	10:47 pm	♍
10	♍		
11	♍		
12	♍	2:21 am	♎
13	♎		
14	♎	7:55 am	♏
15	♏		
16	♏	3:19 pm	♐
17	♐		
18	♐		
19	♐	12:34 am	♑
20	♑		
21	♑	11:48 am	♒
22	♒		
23	♒		
24	♒	12:35 am	♓
25	♓		
26	♓	1:08 pm	♈
27	♈		
28	♈	10:57 pm	♉
29	♉		
30	♉		
31	♉	4:33 am	♊

Moon Movements

♎ = Libra ♏ = Scorpio ♐ = Sagittarius ♑ = Capricorn ♒ = Aquarius ♓ = Pisces

1904

January

1	♊		
2	♊	6:25 am	♋
3	♋		
4	♋	6:18 am	♌
5	♌		
6	♌	6:23 am	♍
7	♍		
8	♍	8:25 am	♎
9	♎		
10	♎	1:20 pm	♏
11	♏		
12	♏	9:03 pm	♐
13	♐		
14	♐		
15	♐	6:57 am	♑
16	♑		
17	♑	6:32 pm	♒
18	♒		
19	♒		
20	♒	7:18 am	♓
21	♓		
22	♓	8:10 pm	♈
23	♈		
24	♈		
25	♈	7:09 am	♉
26	♉		
27	♉	2:25 pm	♊
28	♊		
29	♊	5:32 pm	♋
30	♋		
31	♋	5:37 pm	♌

April

1	♎	4:04 pm	♏
2	♏		
3	♏	7:41 pm	♐
4	♐		
5	♐		
6	♐	2:57 am	♑
7	♑		
8	♑	1:49 pm	♒
9	♒		
10	♒		
11	♒	2:38 am	♓
12	♓		
13	♓	3:04 pm	♈
14	♈		
15	♈		
16	♈	1:31 am	♉
17	♉		
18	♉	9:31 am	♊
19	♊		
20	♊	3:22 pm	♋
21	♋		
22	♋	7:27 pm	♌
23	♌		
24	♌	10:10 pm	♍
25	♍		
26	♍		
27	♍	12:05 am	♎
28	♎		
29	♎	2:06 am	♏
30	♏		

July

1	♒		
2	♒	1:58 am	♓
3	♓		
4	♓	2:55 pm	♈
5	♈		
6	♈		
7	♈	2:29 am	♉
8	♉		
9	♉	10:32 am	♊
10	♊		
11	♊	2:41 pm	♋
12	♋		
13	♋	4:10 pm	♌
14	♌		
15	♌	4:48 pm	♍
16	♍		
17	♍	6:14 pm	♎
18	♎		
19	♎	9:34 pm	♏
20	♏		
21	♏		
22	♏	3:10 am	♐
23	♐		
24	♐	11:01 am	♑
25	♑		
26	♑	9:01 pm	♒
27	♒		
28	♒		
29	♒	8:58 am	♓
30	♓		
31	♓	9:59 pm	♈

October

1	♊	4:50 pm	♋
2	♋		
3	♋	9:38 pm	♌
4	♌		
5	♌	11:36 pm	♍
6	♍		
7	♍	11:45 pm	♎
8	♎		
9	♎	11:43 pm	♏
10	♏		
11	♏		
12	♏	1:25 am	♐
13	♐		
14	♐	6:31 am	♑
15	♑		
16	♑	3:39 pm	♒
17	♒		
18	♒		
19	♒	3:50 am	♓
20	♓		
21	♓	4:51 pm	♈
22	♈		
23	♈		
24	♈	4:44 am	♉
25	♉		
26	♉	2:38 pm	♊
27	♊		
28	♊	10:24 pm	♋
29	♋		
30	♋		
31	♋	4:04 am	♌

February

1	♌		
2	♌	4:45 pm	♍
3	♍		
4	♍	5:01 pm	♎
5	♎		
6	♎	8:08 pm	♏
7	♏		
8	♏		
9	♏	2:49 am	♐
10	♐		
11	♐	12:41 pm	♑
12	♑		
13	♑		
14	♑	12:36 am	♒
15	♒		
16	♒	1:27 pm	♓
17	♓		
18	♓		
19	♓	2:10 am	♈
20	♈		
21	♈	1:31 pm	♉
22	♉		
23	♉	10:05 pm	♊
24	♊		
25	♊		
26	♊	3:00 am	♋
27	♋		
28	♋	4:36 am	♌
29	♌		

May

1	♏	5:36 am	♐
2	♐		
3	♐	11:58 am	♑
4	♑		
5	♑	9:50 pm	♒
6	♒		
7	♒		
8	♒	10:17 am	♓
9	♓		
10	♓	10:51 pm	♈
11	♈		
12	♈		
13	♈	9:12 am	♉
14	♉		
15	♉	4:30 pm	♊
16	♊		
17	♊	9:21 pm	♋
18	♋		
19	♋		
20	♋	12:50 am	♌
21	♌		
22	♌	3:49 am	♍
23	♍		
24	♍	6:48 am	♎
25	♎		
26	♎	10:08 am	♏
27	♏		
28	♏	2:29 pm	♐
29	♐		
30	♐	8:53 pm	♑
31	♑		

August

1	♈		
2	♈		
3	♈	10:13 am	♉
4	♉		
5	♉	7:30 pm	♊
6	♊		
7	♊		
8	♊	12:44 am	♋
9	♋		
10	♋	2:30 am	♌
11	♌		
12	♌	2:25 am	♍
13	♍		
14	♍	2:25 am	♎
15	♎		
16	♎	4:12 am	♏
17	♏		
18	♏	8:51 am	♐
19	♐		
20	♐	4:37 pm	♑
21	♑		
22	♑		
23	♑	3:02 am	♒
24	♒		
25	♒	3:16 pm	♓
26	♓		
27	♓		
28	♓	4:17 am	♈
29	♈		
30	♈	4:44 pm	♉
31	♉		

November

1	♌		
2	♌	7:40 am	♍
3	♍		
4	♍	9:27 am	♎
5	♎		
6	♎	10:20 am	♏
7	♏		
8	♏	11:54 am	♐
9	♐		
10	♐	3:56 pm	♑
11	♑		
12	♑	11:47 pm	♒
13	♒		
14	♒		
15	♒	11:14 am	♓
16	♓		
17	♓		
18	♓	12:14 am	♈
19	♈		
20	♈	12:06 pm	♉
21	♉		
22	♉	9:25 pm	♊
23	♊		
24	♊		
25	♊	4:17 am	♋
26	♋		
27	♋	9:26 am	♌
28	♌		
29	♌	1:27 pm	♍
30	♍		

March

1	♌	4:16 am	♍
2	♍		
3	♍	3:53 am	♎
4	♎		
5	♎	5:24 am	♏
6	♏		
7	♏	10:18 am	♐
8	♐		
9	♐	7:03 pm	♑
10	♑		
11	♑		
12	♑	6:47 am	♒
13	♒		
14	♒	7:43 pm	♓
15	♓		
16	♓		
17	♓	8:13 am	♈
18	♈		
19	♈	7:09 pm	♉
20	♉		
21	♉		
22	♉	3:52 am	♊
23	♊		
24	♊	9:55 am	♋
25	♋		
26	♋	1:16 pm	♌
27	♌		
28	♌	2:31 pm	♍
29	♍		
30	♍	2:54 pm	♎
31	♎		

June

1	♑		
2	♑	6:13 am	♒
3	♒		
4	♒	6:15 pm	♓
5	♓		
6	♓		
7	♓	7:02 am	♈
8	♈		
9	♈	5:50 pm	♉
10	♉		
11	♉		
12	♉	1:06 am	♊
13	♊		
14	♊	5:10 am	♋
15	♋		
16	♋	7:26 am	♌
17	♌		
18	♌	9:26 am	♍
19	♍		
20	♍	12:11 pm	♎
21	♎		
22	♎	4:09 pm	♏
23	♏		
24	♏	9:31 pm	♐
25	♐		
26	♐		
27	♐	4:40 am	♑
28	♑		
29	♑	2:07 pm	♒
30	♒		

September

1	♉		
2	♉	2:59 am	♊
3	♊		
4	♊	9:46 am	♋
5	♋		
6	♋	12:53 pm	♌
7	♌		
8	♌	1:18 pm	♍
9	♍		
10	♍	12:44 pm	♎
11	♎		
12	♎	1:05 pm	♏
13	♏		
14	♏	4:05 pm	♐
15	♐		
16	♐	10:45 pm	♑
17	♑		
18	♑		
19	♑	8:55 am	♒
20	♒		
21	♒	9:20 pm	♓
22	♓		
23	♓		
24	♓	10:20 am	♈
25	♈		
26	♈	10:33 pm	♉
27	♉		
28	♉		
29	♉	8:59 am	♊
30	♊		

December

1	♍	4:33 pm	♎
2	♎		
3	♎	7:01 pm	♏
4	♏		
5	♏	9:38 pm	♐
6	♐		
7	♐		
8	♐	1:46 am	♑
9	♑		
10	♑	8:53 am	♒
11	♒		
12	♒	7:30 pm	♓
13	♓		
14	♓		
15	♓	8:19 am	♈
16	♈		
17	♈	8:33 pm	♉
18	♉		
19	♉		
20	♉	5:57 am	♊
21	♊		
22	♊	12:08 pm	♋
23	♋		
24	♋	4:04 pm	♌
25	♌		
26	♌	7:01 pm	♍
27	♍		
28	♍	9:56 pm	♎
29	♎		
30	♎		
31	♎	1:12 am	♏

Your Starway to Love

♈ = Aries ♉ = Taurus ♊ = Gemini ♋ = Cancer ♌ = Leo ♍ = Virgo

1905

January

1	♏		
2	♏	5:08 am	♐
3	♐		
4	♐	10:20 am	♑
5	♑		
6	♑	5:43 pm	♒
7	♒		
8	♒		
9	♒	3:57 am	♓
10	♓		
11	♓	4:29 pm	♈
12	♈		
13	♈		
14	♈	5:11 am	♉
15	♉		
16	♉	3:25 pm	♊
17	♊		
18	♊	9:56 pm	♋
19	♋		
20	♋		
21	♋	1:13 am	♌
22	♌		
23	♌	2:46 am	♍
24	♍		
25	♍	4:09 am	♎
26	♎		
27	♎	6:35 am	♏
28	♏		
29	♏	10:44 am	♐
30	♐		
31	♐	4:51 pm	♑

February

1	♑		
2	♑		
3	♑	1:08 am	♒
4	♒		
5	♒	11:39 am	♓
6	♓		
7	♓		
8	♓	12:03 am	♈
9	♈		
10	♈	1:00 pm	♉
11	♉		
12	♉		
13	♉	12:17 am	♊
14	♊		
15	♊	8:05 am	♋
16	♋		
17	♋	12:00 pm	♌
18	♌		
19	♌	1:05 pm	♍
20	♍		
21	♍	1:03 pm	♎
22	♎		
23	♎	1:42 pm	♏
24	♏		
25	♏	4:31 pm	♐
26	♐		
27	♐	10:19 pm	♑
28	♑		

March

1	♑		
2	♑	7:05 am	♒
3	♒		
4	♒	6:12 pm	♓
5	♓		
6	♓		
7	♓	6:46 am	♈
8	♈		
9	♈	7:42 pm	♉
10	♉		
11	♉		
12	♉	7:35 am	♊
13	♊		
14	♊	4:48 pm	♋
15	♋		
16	♋	10:19 pm	♌
17	♌		
18	♌		
19	♌	12:18 am	♍
20	♍		
21	♍	12:03 am	♎
22	♎	11:26 pm	♏
23	♏		
24	♏		
25	♏	12:25 am	♐
26	♐		
27	♐	4:40 am	♑
28	♑		
29	♑	12:47 pm	♒
30	♒		
31	♒		

April

1	♒	12:03 am	♓
2	♓		
3	♓	12:52 pm	♈
4	♈		
5	♈		
6	♈	1:44 am	♉
7	♉		
8	♉	1:35 pm	♊
9	♊		
10	♊	11:28 pm	♋
11	♋		
12	♋		
13	♋	6:30 am	♌
14	♌		
15	♌	10:13 am	♍
16	♍		
17	♍	11:04 am	♎
18	♎		
19	♎	10:30 am	♏
20	♏		
21	♏	10:28 am	♐
22	♐		
23	♐	1:04 pm	♑
24	♑		
25	♑	7:41 pm	♒
26	♒		
27	♒		
28	♒	6:15 am	♓
29	♓		
30	♓	7:03 pm	♈

May

1	♈		
2	♈		
3	♈	7:52 am	♉
4	♉		
5	♉	7:21 pm	♊
6	♊		
7	♊		
8	♊	5:01 am	♋
9	♋		
10	♋	12:34 pm	♌
11	♌		
12	♌	5:40 pm	♍
13	♍		
14	♍	8:12 pm	♎
15	♎		
16	♎	8:50 pm	♏
17	♏		
18	♏	9:05 pm	♐
19	♐		
20	♐	10:56 pm	♑
21	♑		
22	♑		
23	♑	4:12 am	♒
24	♒		
25	♒	1:34 pm	♓
26	♓		
27	♓		
28	♓	1:53 am	♈
29	♈		
30	♈	2:41 pm	♉
31	♉		

June

1	♉		
2	♉	1:55 am	♊
3	♊		
4	♊	10:57 am	♋
5	♋		
6	♋	5:59 pm	♌
7	♌		
8	♌	11:17 pm	♍
9	♍		
10	♍		
11	♍	2:53 am	♎
12	♎		
13	♎	5:00 am	♏
14	♏		
15	♏	6:29 am	♐
16	♐		
17	♐	8:46 am	♑
18	♑		
19	♑	1:33 pm	♒
20	♒		
21	♒	9:57 pm	♓
22	♓		
23	♓		
24	♓	9:33 am	♈
25	♈		
26	♈	10:16 pm	♉
27	♉		
28	♉		
29	♉	9:36 am	♊
30	♊		

July

1	♊	6:17 pm	♋
2	♋		
3	♋		
4	♋	12:27 am	♌
5	♌		
6	♌	4:53 am	♍
7	♍		
8	♍	8:16 am	♎
9	♎		
10	♎	11:04 am	♏
11	♏		
12	♏	1:46 pm	♐
13	♐		
14	♐	5:12 pm	♑
15	♑		
16	♑	10:29 pm	♒
17	♒		
18	♒		
19	♒	6:36 am	♓
20	♓		
21	♓	5:39 pm	♈
22	♈		
23	♈		
24	♈	6:16 am	♉
25	♉		
26	♉	6:01 pm	♊
27	♊		
28	♊		
29	♊	3:00 am	♋
30	♋		
31	♋	8:47 am	♌

August

1	♌		
2	♌	12:09 pm	♍
3	♍		
4	♍	2:20 pm	♎
5	♎		
6	♎	4:28 pm	♏
7	♏		
8	♏	7:24 pm	♐
9	♐		
10	♐	11:45 pm	♑
11	♑		
12	♑		
13	♑	6:00 am	♒
14	♒		
15	♒	2:34 pm	♓
16	♓		
17	♓		
18	♓	1:30 am	♈
19	♈		
20	♈	2:02 pm	♉
21	♉		
22	♉		
23	♉	2:18 am	♊
24	♊		
25	♊	12:12 pm	♋
26	♋		
27	♋	6:31 pm	♌
28	♌		
29	♌	9:32 pm	♍
30	♍		
31	♍	10:32 pm	♎

September

1	♎		
2	♎	11:12 pm	♏
3	♏		
4	♏		
5	♏	1:04 am	♐
6	♐		
7	♐	5:13 am	♑
8	♑		
9	♑	12:02 pm	♒
10	♒		
11	♒	9:20 pm	♓
12	♓		
13	♓		
14	♓	8:35 am	♈
15	♈		
16	♈	9:05 pm	♉
17	♉		
18	♉		
19	♉	9:40 am	♊
20	♊		
21	♊	8:37 pm	♋
22	♋		
23	♋		
24	♋	4:17 am	♌
25	♌		
26	♌	8:06 am	♍
27	♍		
28	♍	8:54 am	♎
29	♎		
30	♎	8:22 am	♏

October

1	♏		
2	♏	8:35 am	♐
3	♐		
4	♐	11:20 am	♑
5	♑		
6	♑	5:36 pm	♒
7	♒		
8	♒		
9	♒	3:09 am	♓
10	♓		
11	♓	2:49 pm	♈
12	♈		
13	♈		
14	♈	3:25 am	♉
15	♉		
16	♉	3:59 pm	♊
17	♊		
18	♊		
19	♊	3:29 am	♋
20	♋		
21	♋	12:33 pm	♌
22	♌		
23	♌	6:02 pm	♍
24	♍		
25	♍	7:55 pm	♎
26	♎		
27	♎	7:24 pm	♏
28	♏		
29	♏	6:34 pm	♐
30	♐		
31	♐	7:37 pm	♑

November

1	♑		
2	♑		
3	♑	12:19 am	♒
4	♒		
5	♒	9:05 am	♓
6	♓		
7	♓	8:48 pm	♈
8	♈		
9	♈		
10	♈	9:32 am	♉
11	♉		
12	♉	9:54 pm	♊
13	♊		
14	♊		
15	♊	9:14 am	♋
16	♋		
17	♋	6:50 pm	♌
18	♌		
19	♌		
20	♌	1:47 am	♍
21	♍		
22	♍	5:29 am	♎
23	♎		
24	♎	6:18 am	♏
25	♏		
26	♏	5:47 am	♐
27	♐		
28	♐	6:03 am	♑
29	♑		
30	♑	9:11 am	♒

December

1	♒		
2	♒	4:26 pm	♓
3	♓		
4	♓		
5	♓	3:24 am	♈
6	♈		
7	♈	4:06 pm	♉
8	♉		
9	♉		
10	♉	4:24 am	♊
11	♊		
12	♊	3:14 pm	♋
13	♋		
14	♋		
15	♋	12:19 am	♌
16	♌		
17	♌	7:30 am	♍
18	♍		
19	♍	12:25 pm	♎
20	♎		
21	♎	3:01 pm	♏
22	♏		
23	♏	4:00 pm	♐
24	♐		
25	♐	4:53 pm	♑
26	♑		
27	♑	7:32 pm	♒
28	♒		
29	♒		
30	♒	1:30 am	♓
31	♓		

Moon Movements

♎ = Libra ♏ = Scorpio ♐ = Sagittarius ♑ = Capricorn ♒ = Aquarius ♓ = Pisces

1906

January

1	♓	11:16 am	♈
2	♈		
3	♈	11:33 pm	♉
4	♉		
5	♉		
6	♉	11:58 am	♊
7	♊		
8	♊	10:38 pm	♋
9	♋		
10	♋		
11	♋	6:57 am	♌
12	♌		
13	♌	1:11 pm	♍
14	♍		
15	♍	5:48 pm	♎
16	♎		
17	♎	9:07 pm	♏
18	♏		
19	♏	11:36 pm	♐
20	♐		
21	♐		
22	♐	1:59 am	♑
23	♑		
24	♑	5:26 am	♒
25	♒		
26	♒	11:13 am	♓
27	♓		
28	♓	8:06 pm	♈
29	♈		
30	♈		
31	♈	7:44 am	♉

February

1	♉		
2	♉	8:17 pm	♊
3	♊		
4	♊		
5	♊	7:21 am	♋
6	♋		
7	♋	3:32 pm	♌
8	♌		
9	♌	8:50 pm	♍
10	♍		
11	♍		
12	♍	12:07 am	♎
13	♎		
14	♎	2:34 am	♏
15	♏		
16	♏	5:08 am	♐
17	♐		
18	♐	8:32 am	♑
19	♑		
20	♑	1:17 pm	♒
21	♒		
22	♒	7:52 pm	♓
23	♓		
24	♓		
25	♓	4:45 am	♈
26	♈		
27	♈	3:58 pm	♉
28	♉		

March

1	♉		
2	♉	4:31 am	♊
3	♊		
4	♊	4:19 pm	♋
5	♋		
6	♋		
7	♋	1:16 am	♌
8	♌		
9	♌	6:33 am	♍
10	♍		
11	♍	8:53 am	♎
12	♎		
13	♎	9:48 am	♏
14	♏		
15	♏	11:01 am	♐
16	♐		
17	♐	1:54 pm	♑
18	♑		
19	♑	7:06 pm	♒
20	♒		
21	♒		
22	♒	2:38 am	♓
23	♓		
24	♓	12:10 pm	♈
25	♈		
26	♈	11:27 pm	♉
27	♉		
28	♉		
29	♉	11:58 am	♊
30	♊		
31	♊		

April

1	♊	12:20 am	♋
2	♋		
3	♋	10:31 am	♌
4	♌		
5	♌	4:53 pm	♍
6	♍		
7	♍	7:25 pm	♎
8	♎		
9	♎	7:29 pm	♏
10	♏		
11	♏	7:08 pm	♐
12	♐		
13	♐	8:23 pm	♑
14	♑		
15	♑		
16	♑	12:39 am	♒
17	♒		
18	♒	8:10 am	♓
19	♓		
20	♓	6:15 pm	♈
21	♈		
22	♈		
23	♈	5:56 am	♉
24	♉		
25	♉	6:28 pm	♊
26	♊		
27	♊		
28	♊	7:02 am	♋
29	♋		
30	♋	6:09 pm	♌

May

1	♌		
2	♌		
3	♌	2:03 am	♍
4	♍		
5	♍	5:53 am	♎
6	♎		
7	♎	6:23 am	♏
8	♏		
9	♏	5:24 am	♐
10	♐		
11	♐	5:12 am	♑
12	♑		
13	♑	7:45 am	♒
14	♒		
15	♒	2:06 pm	♓
16	♓		
17	♓	11:54 pm	♈
18	♈		
19	♈		
20	♈	11:48 am	♉
21	♉		
22	♉		
23	♉	12:27 am	♊
24	♊		
25	♊	12:54 pm	♋
26	♋		
27	♋		
28	♋	12:14 pm	♌
29	♌		
30	♌	9:10 am	♍
31	♍		

June

1	♍	2:38 pm	♎
2	♎		
3	♎	4:35 pm	♏
4	♏		
5	♏	4:15 pm	♐
6	♐		
7	♐	3:40 pm	♑
8	♑		
9	♑	4:56 pm	♒
10	♒		
11	♒	9:40 pm	♓
12	♓		
13	♓		
14	♓	6:20 am	♈
15	♈		
16	♈	5:55 pm	♉
17	♉		
18	♉		
19	♉	6:35 am	♊
20	♊		
21	♊	6:51 pm	♋
22	♋		
23	♋		
24	♋	5:49 am	♌
25	♌		
26	♌	2:50 pm	♍
27	♍		
28	♍	9:13 pm	♎
29	♎		
30	♎		

July

1	♎	12:43 am	♏
2	♏		
3	♏	1:53 am	♐
4	♐		
5	♐	2:06 am	♑
6	♑		
7	♑	3:11 am	♒
8	♒		
9	♒	6:52 am	♓
10	♓		
11	♓	2:12 pm	♈
12	♈		
13	♈		
14	♈	12:55 am	♉
15	♉		
16	♉	1:25 pm	♊
17	♊		
18	♊		
19	♊	1:37 am	♋
20	♋		
21	♋	12:09 pm	♌
22	♌		
23	♌	8:29 pm	♍
24	♍		
25	♍		
26	♍	2:38 am	♎
27	♎		
28	♎	6:46 am	♏
29	♏		
30	♏	9:17 am	♐
31	♐		

August

1	♐	10:58 am	♑
2	♑		
3	♑	12:57 pm	♒
4	♒		
5	♒	4:36 pm	♓
6	♓		
7	♓	11:07 pm	♈
8	♈		
9	♈		
10	♈	8:55 am	♉
11	♉		
12	♉	9:03 pm	♊
13	♊		
14	♊		
15	♊	9:23 am	♋
16	♋		
17	♋	7:50 pm	♌
18	♌		
19	♌		
20	♌	3:31 am	♍
21	♍		
22	♍	8:40 am	♎
23	♎		
24	♎	12:10 pm	♏
25	♏		
26	♏	2:55 pm	♐
27	♐		
28	♐	5:38 pm	♑
29	♑		
30	♑	8:56 pm	♒
31	♒		

September

1	♒		
2	♒	1:28 am	♓
3	♓		
4	♓	8:04 am	♈
5	♈		
6	♈	5:21 pm	♉
7	♉		
8	♉		
9	♉	5:05 am	♊
10	♊		
11	♊	5:39 pm	♋
12	♋		
13	♋		
14	♋	4:37 am	♌
15	♌		
16	♌	12:18 pm	♍
17	♍		
18	♍	4:39 pm	♎
19	♎		
20	♎	6:53 pm	♏
21	♏		
22	♏	8:35 pm	♐
23	♐		
24	♐	11:02 pm	♑
25	♑		
26	♑		
27	♑	2:58 am	♒
28	♒		
29	♒	8:34 am	♓
30	♓		

October

1	♓	3:56 pm	♈
2	♈		
3	♈		
4	♈	1:20 am	♉
5	♉		
6	♉	12:52 pm	♊
7	♊		
8	♊		
9	♊	1:38 am	♋
10	♋		
11	♋	1:27 pm	♌
12	♌		
13	♌	10:02 pm	♍
14	♍		
15	♍		
16	♍	2:34 am	♎
17	♎		
18	♎	4:00 am	♏
19	♏		
20	♏	4:14 am	♐
21	♐		
22	♐	5:14 am	♑
23	♑		
24	♑	8:24 am	♒
25	♒		
26	♒	2:11 pm	♓
27	♓		
28	♓	10:18 pm	♈
29	♈		
30	♈		
31	♈	8:18 am	♉

November

1	♉		
2	♉	7:56 pm	♊
3	♊		
4	♊		
5	♊	8:43 am	♋
6	♋		
7	♋	9:13 pm	♌
8	♌		
9	♌		
10	♌	7:10 am	♍
11	♍		
12	♍	1:00 pm	♎
13	♎		
14	♎	2:53 pm	♏
15	♏		
16	♏	2:29 pm	♐
17	♐		
18	♐	1:58 pm	♑
19	♑		
20	♑	3:23 pm	♒
21	♒		
22	♒	7:59 pm	♓
23	♓		
24	♓		
25	♓	3:53 am	♈
26	♈		
27	♈	2:17 pm	♉
28	♉		
29	♉		
30	♉	2:15 am	♊

December

1	♊		
2	♊	3:01 pm	♋
3	♋		
4	♋		
5	♋	3:37 am	♌
6	♌		
7	♌	2:30 pm	♍
8	♍		
9	♍	10:00 pm	♎
10	♎		
11	♎		
12	♎	1:31 am	♏
13	♏		
14	♏	1:55 am	♐
15	♐		
16	♐	1:02 am	♑
17	♑		
18	♑	1:03 am	♒
19	♒		
20	♒	3:48 am	♓
21	♓		
22	♓	10:17 am	♈
23	♈		
24	♈	8:15 pm	♉
25	♉		
26	♉		
27	♉	8:23 am	♊
28	♊		
29	♊	9:11 pm	♋
30	♋		
31	♋		

Your Starway to Love

♈ = Aries ♉ = Taurus ♊ = Gemini ♋ = Cancer ♌ = Leo ♍ = Virgo

1907

January

1	♋	9:29 am	♌
2	♌		
3	♌	8:18 pm	♍
4	♍		
5	♍		
6	♍	4:41 am	♎
7	♎		
8	♎	9:55 am	♏
9	♏		
10	♏	12:07 pm	♐
11	♐		
12	♐	12:21 pm	♑
13	♑		
14	♑	12:20 pm	♒
15	♒		
16	♒	1:55 pm	♓
17	♓		
18	♓	6:42 pm	♈
19	♈		
20	♈		
21	♈	3:21 am	♉
22	♉		
23	♉	3:04 pm	♊
24	♊		
25	♊		
26	♊	3:56 am	♋
27	♋		
28	♋	4:00 pm	♌
29	♌		
30	♌		
31	♌	2:12 am	♍

February

1	♍		
2	♍	10:10 am	♎
3	♎		
4	♎	3:55 pm	♏
5	♏		
6	♏	7:34 pm	♐
7	♐		
8	♐	9:35 pm	♑
9	♑		
10	♑	10:50 pm	♒
11	♒		
12	♒		
13	♒	12:41 am	♓
14	♓		
15	♓	4:38 am	♈
16	♈		
17	♈	11:58 am	♉
18	♉		
19	♉	10:46 pm	♊
20	♊		
21	♊		
22	♊	11:30 am	♋
23	♋		
24	♋	11:41 pm	♌
25	♌		
26	♌		
27	♌	9:28 am	♍
28	♍		

March

1	♍	4:31 pm	♎
2	♎		
3	♎	9:26 pm	♏
4	♏		
5	♏		
6	♏	1:04 am	♐
7	♐		
8	♐	4:03 am	♑
9	♑		
10	♑	6:50 am	♒
11	♒		
12	♒	9:56 am	♓
13	♓		
14	♓	2:20 pm	♈
15	♈		
16	♈	9:10 pm	♉
17	♉		
18	♉		
19	♉	7:10 am	♊
20	♊		
21	♊	7:36 pm	♋
22	♋		
23	♋		
24	♋	8:07 am	♌
25	♌		
26	♌	6:10 pm	♍
27	♍		
28	♍		
29	♍	12:46 am	♎
30	♎		
31	♎	4:33 am	♏

April

1	♏		
2	♏	6:59 am	♐
3	♐		
4	♐	9:24 am	♑
5	♑		
6	♑	12:35 pm	♒
7	♒		
8	♒	4:47 pm	♓
9	♓		
10	♓	10:16 pm	♈
11	♈		
12	♈		
13	♈	5:36 am	♉
14	♉		
15	♉	3:24 pm	♊
16	♊		
17	♊		
18	♊	3:34 am	♋
19	♋		
20	♋	4:25 pm	♌
21	♌		
22	♌		
23	♌	3:17 am	♍
24	♍		
25	♍	10:22 am	♎
26	♎		
27	♎	1:47 pm	♏
28	♏		
29	♏	3:02 pm	♐
30	♐		

May

1	♐	3:59 pm	♑
2	♑		
3	♑	6:07 pm	♒
4	♒		
5	♒	10:12 pm	♓
6	♓		
7	♓		
8	♓	4:20 am	♈
9	♈		
10	♈	12:29 pm	♉
11	♉		
12	♉	10:41 pm	♊
13	♊		
14	♊		
15	♊	10:50 am	♋
16	♋		
17	♋	11:52 pm	♌
18	♌		
19	♌		
20	♌	11:37 am	♍
21	♍		
22	♍	7:54 pm	♎
23	♎		
24	♎		
25	♎	12:03 am	♏
26	♏		
27	♏	1:05 am	♐
28	♐		
29	♐	12:54 am	♑
30	♑		
31	♑	1:26 am	♒

June

1	♒		
2	♒	4:10 am	♓
3	♓		
4	♓	9:46 am	♈
5	♈		
6	♈	6:12 pm	♉
7	♉		
8	♉		
9	♉	4:55 am	♊
10	♊		
11	♊	5:16 pm	♋
12	♋		
13	♋		
14	♋	6:21 am	♌
15	♌		
16	♌	6:35 pm	♍
17	♍		
18	♍		
19	♍	4:05 am	♎
20	♎		
21	♎	9:42 am	♏
22	♏		
23	♏	11:42 am	♐
24	♐		
25	♐	11:30 am	♑
26	♑		
27	♑	11:00 am	♒
28	♒		
29	♒	12:07 pm	♓
30	♓		

July

1	♓	4:14 pm	♈
2	♈		
3	♈	11:56 pm	♉
4	♉		
5	♉		
6	♉	10:41 am	♊
7	♊		
8	♊	11:16 pm	♋
9	♋		
10	♋		
11	♋	12:18 pm	♌
12	♌		
13	♌		
14	♌	12:29 am	♍
15	♍		
16	♍	10:34 am	♎
17	♎		
18	♎	5:34 pm	♏
19	♏		
20	♏	9:11 pm	♐
21	♐		
22	♐	10:06 pm	♑
23	♑		
24	♑	9:46 pm	♒
25	♒		
26	♒	10:00 pm	♓
27	♓		
28	♓		
29	♓	12:37 am	♈
30	♈		
31	♈	6:53 am	♉

August

1	♉		
2	♉	4:56 pm	♊
3	♊		
4	♊		
5	♊	5:27 am	♋
6	♋		
7	♋	6:26 pm	♌
8	♌		
9	♌		
10	♌	6:16 am	♍
11	♍		
12	♍	4:07 pm	♎
13	♎		
14	♎	11:35 pm	♏
15	♏		
16	♏		
17	♏	4:31 am	♐
18	♐		
19	♐	7:05 am	♑
20	♑		
21	♑	8:00 am	♒
22	♒		
23	♒	8:33 am	♓
24	♓		
25	♓	10:28 am	♈
26	♈		
27	♈	3:26 pm	♉
28	♉		
29	♉		
30	♉	12:19 am	♊
31	♊		

September

1	♊	12:22 pm	♋
2	♋		
3	♋		
4	♋	1:20 am	♌
5	♌		
6	♌	12:56 pm	♍
7	♍		
8	♍	10:07 pm	♎
9	♎		
10	♎		
11	♎	5:01 am	♏
12	♏		
13	♏	10:07 am	♐
14	♐		
15	♐	1:46 pm	♑
16	♑		
17	♑	4:12 pm	♒
18	♒		
19	♒	6:02 pm	♓
20	♓		
21	♓	8:25 pm	♈
22	♈		
23	♈		
24	♈	12:55 am	♉
25	♉		
26	♉	8:49 am	♊
27	♊		
28	♊	8:09 pm	♋
29	♋		
30	♋		

October

1	♋	9:05 am	♌
2	♌		
3	♌	8:49 pm	♍
4	♍		
5	♍		
6	♍	5:39 am	♎
7	♎		
8	♎	11:38 am	♏
9	♏		
10	♏	3:47 pm	♐
11	♐		
12	♐	7:07 pm	♑
13	♑		
14	♑	10:13 pm	♒
15	♒		
16	♒		
17	♒	1:20 am	♓
18	♓		
19	♓	4:57 am	♈
20	♈		
21	♈	10:00 am	♉
22	♉		
23	♉	5:39 pm	♊
24	♊		
25	♊		
26	♊	4:25 am	♋
27	♋		
28	♋	5:14 pm	♌
29	♌		
30	♌		
31	♌	5:28 am	♍

November

1	♍		
2	♍	2:43 pm	♎
3	♎		
4	♎	8:23 pm	♏
5	♏		
6	♏	11:25 pm	♐
7	♐		
8	♐		
9	♐	1:24 am	♑
10	♑		
11	♑	3:38 am	♒
12	♒		
13	♒	6:52 am	♓
14	♓		
15	♓	11:24 am	♈
16	♈		
17	♈	5:31 pm	♉
18	♉		
19	♉		
20	♉	1:43 am	♊
21	♊		
22	♊	12:24 pm	♋
23	♋		
24	♋		
25	♋	1:04 am	♌
26	♌		
27	♌	1:50 pm	♍
28	♍		
29	♍		
30	♍	12:09 am	♎

December

1	♎		
2	♎	6:35 am	♏
3	♏		
4	♏	9:28 am	♐
5	♐		
6	♐	10:18 am	♑
7	♑		
8	♑	10:53 am	♒
9	♒		
10	♒	12:44 pm	♓
11	♓		
12	♓	4:48 pm	♈
13	♈		
14	♈	11:24 pm	♉
15	♉		
16	♉		
17	♉	8:25 am	♊
18	♊		
19	♊	7:31 pm	♋
20	♋		
21	♋		
22	♋	8:09 am	♌
23	♌		
24	♌	9:06 pm	♍
25	♍		
26	♍		
27	♍	8:27 am	♎
28	♎		
29	♎	4:26 pm	♏
30	♏		
31	♏	8:28 pm	♐

1908

Moon Movements

♎ = Libra ♏ = Scorpio ♐ = Sagittarius ♑ = Capricorn ♒ = Aquarius ♓ = Pisces

January

Day	Moon	Time	Enters
1	♐		
2	♐	9:25 pm	♑
3	♑		
4	♑	8:58 pm	♒
5	♒		
6	♒	9:03 pm	♓
7	♓		
8	♓	11:24 pm	♈
9	♈		
10	♈		
11	♈	5:05 am	♉
12	♉		
13	♉	2:10 pm	♊
14	♊		
15	♊		
16	♊	1:45 am	♋
17	♋		
18	♋	2:33 pm	♌
19	♌		
20	♌		
21	♌	3:23 am	♍
22	♍		
23	♍	3:03 pm	♎
24	♎		
25	♎		
26	♎	12:17 am	♏
27	♏		
28	♏	6:08 am	♐
29	♐		
30	♐	8:33 am	♑
31	♑		

February

Day	Moon	Time	Enters
1	♑	8:32 am	♒
2	♒		
3	♒	7:50 am	♓
4	♓		
5	♓	8:31 am	♈
6	♈		
7	♈	12:24 pm	♉
8	♉		
9	♉	8:23 pm	♊
10	♊		
11	♊		
12	♊	7:48 am	♋
13	♋		
14	♋	8:46 pm	♌
15	♌		
16	♌		
17	♌	9:28 am	♍
18	♍		
19	♍	8:48 pm	♎
20	♎		
21	♎		
22	♎	6:14 am	♏
23	♏		
24	♏	1:15 pm	♐
25	♐		
26	♐	5:28 pm	♑
27	♑		
28	♑	7:04 pm	♒
29	♒		

March

Day	Moon	Time	Enters
1	♒	7:05 pm	♓
2	♓		
3	♓	7:20 pm	♈
4	♈		
5	♈	9:50 pm	♉
6	♉		
7	♉		
8	♉	4:13 am	♊
9	♊		
10	♊	2:39 pm	♋
11	♋		
12	♋		
13	♋	3:28 am	♌
14	♌		
15	♌	4:09 pm	♍
16	♍		
17	♍		
18	♍	3:04 am	♎
19	♎		
20	♎	11:52 am	♏
21	♏		
22	♏	6:45 pm	♐
23	♐		
24	♐	11:48 pm	♑
25	♑		
26	♑		
27	♑	2:57 am	♒
28	♒		
29	♒	4:33 am	♓
30	♓		
31	♓	5:41 am	♈

April

Day	Moon	Time	Enters
1	♈		
2	♈	8:04 am	♉
3	♉		
4	♉	1:26 pm	♊
5	♊		
6	♊	10:43 pm	♋
7	♋		
8	♋		
9	♋	10:58 am	♌
10	♌		
11	♌	11:41 pm	♍
12	♍		
13	♍		
14	♍	10:33 am	♎
15	♎		
16	♎	6:44 pm	♏
17	♏		
18	♏		
19	♏	12:41 am	♐
20	♐		
21	♐	5:10 am	♑
22	♑		
23	♑	8:39 am	♒
24	♒		
25	♒	11:25 am	♓
26	♓		
27	♓	1:57 pm	♈
28	♈		
29	♈	5:16 pm	♉
30	♉		

May

Day	Moon	Time	Enters
1	♉	10:44 pm	♊
2	♊		
3	♊		
4	♊	7:23 am	♋
5	♋		
6	♋	7:01 pm	♌
7	♌		
8	♌		
9	♌	7:46 am	♍
10	♍		
11	♍	7:00 pm	♎
12	♎		
13	♎		
14	♎	3:12 am	♏
15	♏		
16	♏	8:26 am	♐
17	♐		
18	♐	11:44 am	♑
19	♑		
20	♑	2:14 pm	♒
21	♒		
22	♒	4:49 pm	♓
23	♓		
24	♓	8:03 pm	♈
25	♈		
26	♈		
27	♈	12:30 am	♉
28	♉		
29	♉	6:48 am	♊
30	♊		
31	♊	3:37 pm	♋

June

Day	Moon	Time	Enters
1	♋		
2	♋		
3	♋	2:59 am	♌
4	♌		
5	♌	3:42 pm	♍
6	♍		
7	♍		
8	♍	3:33 am	♎
9	♎		
10	♎	12:30 pm	♏
11	♏		
12	♏	5:52 pm	♐
13	♐		
14	♐	8:25 pm	♑
15	♑		
16	♑	9:35 pm	♒
17	♒		
18	♒	10:51 pm	♓
19	♓		
20	♓		
21	♓	1:27 am	♈
22	♈		
23	♈	6:09 am	♉
24	♉		
25	♉	1:16 pm	♊
26	♊		
27	♊	10:44 pm	♋
28	♋		
29	♋		
30	♋	10:14 am	♌

July

Day	Moon	Time	Enters
1	♌		
2	♌	10:58 pm	♍
3	♍		
4	♍		
5	♍	11:19 am	♎
6	♎		
7	♎	9:23 pm	♏
8	♏		
9	♏		
10	♏	3:49 am	♐
11	♐		
12	♐	6:40 am	♑
13	♑		
14	♑	7:07 am	♒
15	♒		
16	♒	6:58 am	♓
17	♓		
18	♓	8:02 am	♈
19	♈		
20	♈	11:46 am	♉
21	♉		
22	♉	6:48 pm	♊
23	♊		
24	♊		
25	♊	4:44 am	♋
26	♋		
27	♋	4:38 pm	♌
28	♌		
29	♌		
30	♌	5:24 am	♍
31	♍		

August

Day	Moon	Time	Enters
1	♍	5:56 pm	♎
2	♎		
3	♎		
4	♎	4:53 am	♏
5	♏		
6	♏	12:47 pm	♐
7	♐		
8	♐	4:56 pm	♑
9	♑		
10	♑	5:53 pm	♒
11	♒		
12	♒	5:09 pm	♓
13	♓		
14	♓	4:49 pm	♈
15	♈		
16	♈	6:55 pm	♉
17	♉		
18	♉		
19	♉	12:48 am	♊
20	♊		
21	♊	10:26 am	♋
22	♋		
23	♋	10:32 pm	♌
24	♌		
25	♌		
26	♌	11:23 am	♍
27	♍		
28	♍	11:47 pm	♎
29	♎		
30	♎		
31	♎	10:55 am	♏

September

Day	Moon	Time	Enters
1	♏		
2	♏	7:52 pm	♐
3	♐		
4	♐		
5	♐	1:40 am	♑
6	♑		
7	♑	4:06 am	♒
8	♒		
9	♒	4:04 am	♓
10	♓		
11	♓	3:21 am	♈
12	♈		
13	♈	4:11 am	♉
14	♉		
15	♉	8:27 am	♊
16	♊		
17	♊	4:57 pm	♋
18	♋		
19	♋		
20	♋	4:42 am	♌
21	♌		
22	♌	5:34 pm	♍
23	♍		
24	♍		
25	♍	5:46 am	♎
26	♎		
27	♎	4:30 pm	♏
28	♏		
29	♏		
30	♏	1:28 am	♐

October

Day	Moon	Time	Enters
1	♐		
2	♐	8:12 am	♑
3	♑		
4	♑	12:16 pm	♒
5	♒		
6	♒	1:49 pm	♓
7	♓		
8	♓	2:01 pm	♈
9	♈		
10	♈	2:43 pm	♉
11	♉		
12	♉	5:55 pm	♊
13	♊		
14	♊		
15	♊	1:00 am	♋
16	♋		
17	♋	11:51 am	♌
18	♌		
19	♌		
20	♌	12:32 am	♍
21	♍		
22	♍	12:43 pm	♎
23	♎		
24	♎	10:59 pm	♏
25	♏		
26	♏		
27	♏	7:12 am	♐
28	♐		
29	♐	1:34 pm	♑
30	♑		
31	♑	6:12 pm	♒

November

Day	Moon	Time	Enters
1	♒		
2	♒	9:10 pm	♓
3	♓		
4	♓	10:58 pm	♈
5	♈		
6	♈		
7	♈	12:43 am	♉
8	♉		
9	♉	4:00 am	♊
10	♊		
11	♊	10:18 am	♋
12	♋		
13	♋	8:07 pm	♌
14	♌		
15	♌		
16	♌	8:23 am	♍
17	♍		
18	♍	8:44 pm	♎
19	♎		
20	♎		
21	♎	7:04 am	♏
22	♏		
23	♏	2:39 pm	♐
24	♐		
25	♐	7:54 pm	♑
26	♑		
27	♑	11:40 pm	♒
28	♒		
29	♒		
30	♒	2:39 am	♓

December

Day	Moon	Time	Enters
1	♓		
2	♓	5:26 am	♈
3	♈		
4	♈	8:37 am	♉
5	♉		
6	♉	1:01 pm	♊
7	♊		
8	♊	7:33 pm	♋
9	♋		
10	♋		
11	♋	4:52 am	♌
12	♌		
13	♌	4:38 pm	♍
14	♍		
15	♍		
16	♍	5:12 am	♎
17	♎		
18	♎	4:12 pm	♏
19	♏		
20	♏		
21	♏	12:02 am	♐
22	♐		
23	♐	4:38 am	♑
24	♑		
25	♑	7:01 am	♒
26	♒		
27	♒	8:38 am	♓
28	♓		
29	♓	10:48 am	♈
30	♈		
31	♈	2:24 pm	♉

♈ = Aries ♉ = Taurus ♊ = Gemini ♋ = Cancer ♌ = Leo ♍ = Virgo

1909

January

1	♉		
2	♉	7:54 pm	♊
3	♊		
4	♊		
5	♊	3:24 am	♋
6	♋		
7	♋	1:01 pm	♌
8	♌		
9	♌		
10	♌	12:34 am	♍
11	♍		
12	♍	1:11 pm	♎
13	♎		
14	♎		
15	♎	1:02 am	♏
16	♏		
17	♏	10:01 am	♐
18	♐		
19	♐	3:09 pm	♑
20	♑		
21	♑	4:59 pm	♒
22	♒		
23	♒	5:09 pm	♓
24	♓		
25	♓	5:36 pm	♈
26	♈		
27	♈	8:02 pm	♉
28	♉		
29	♉		
30	♉	1:22 am	♊
31	♊		

April

1	♌	7:51 pm	♍
2	♍		
3	♍		
4	♍	8:31 am	♎
5	♎		
6	♎	8:33 pm	♏
7	♏		
8	♏		
9	♏	7:17 am	♐
10	♐		
11	♐	3:57 pm	♑
12	♑		
13	♑	9:44 pm	♒
14	♒		
15	♒		
16	♒	12:26 am	♓
17	♓		
18	♓	12:51 am	♈
19	♈		
20	♈	12:43 am	♉
21	♉		
22	♉	2:02 am	♊
23	♊		
24	♊	6:34 am	♋
25	♋		
26	♋	3:02 pm	♌
27	♌		
28	♌		
29	♌	2:33 am	♍
30	♍		

July

1	♐		
2	♐	12:04 pm	♑
3	♑		
4	♑	4:13 pm	♒
5	♒		
6	♒	6:41 pm	♓
7	♓		
8	♓	8:45 pm	♈
9	♈		
10	♈	11:29 pm	♉
11	♉		
12	♉		
13	♉	3:30 am	♊
14	♊		
15	♊	9:07 am	♋
16	♋		
17	♋	4:41 pm	♌
18	♌		
19	♌		
20	♌	2:32 am	♍
21	♍		
22	♍	2:26 pm	♎
23	♎		
24	♎		
25	♎	3:01 am	♏
26	♏		
27	♏	2:00 pm	♐
28	♐		
29	♐	9:32 pm	♑
30	♑		
31	♑		

October

1	♉		
2	♉	11:04 pm	♊
3	♊		
4	♊		
5	♊	3:09 am	♋
6	♋		
7	♋	10:58 am	♌
8	♌		
9	♌	9:42 pm	♍
10	♍		
11	♍		
12	♍	10:01 am	♎
13	♎		
14	♎	10:46 pm	♏
15	♏		
16	♏		
17	♏	11:02 am	♐
18	♐		
19	♐	9:37 pm	♑
20	♑		
21	♑		
22	♑	5:13 am	♒
23	♒		
24	♒	9:09 am	♓
25	♓		
26	♓	10:01 am	♈
27	♈		
28	♈	9:27 am	♉
29	♉		
30	♉	9:27 am	♊
31	♊		

February

1	♊	9:32 am	♋
2	♋		
3	♋	7:50 pm	♌
4	♌		
5	♌		
6	♌	7:35 am	♍
7	♍		
8	♍	8:10 pm	♎
9	♎		
10	♎		
11	♎	8:30 am	♏
12	♏		
13	♏	6:48 pm	♐
14	♐		
15	♐		
16	♐	1:27 am	♑
17	♑		
18	♑	4:08 am	♒
19	♒		
20	♒	4:00 am	♓
21	♓		
22	♓	3:08 am	♈
23	♈		
24	♈	3:44 am	♉
25	♉		
26	♉	7:33 am	♊
27	♊		
28	♊	3:08 pm	♋

May

1	♍	3:11 pm	♎
2	♎		
3	♎		
4	♎	3:04 am	♏
5	♏		
6	♏	1:16 pm	♐
7	♐		
8	♐	9:26 pm	♑
9	♑		
10	♑		
11	♑	3:26 am	♒
12	♒		
13	♒	7:14 am	♓
14	♓		
15	♓	9:13 am	♈
16	♈		
17	♈	10:24 am	♉
18	♉		
19	♉	12:13 pm	♊
20	♊		
21	♊	4:15 pm	♋
22	♋		
23	♋	11:36 pm	♌
24	♌		
25	♌		
26	♌	10:14 am	♍
27	♍		
28	♍	10:39 pm	♎
29	♎		
30	♎		
31	♎	10:37 am	♏

August

1	♑	1:22 am	♒
2	♒		
3	♒	2:42 am	♓
4	♓		
5	♓	3:22 am	♈
6	♈		
7	♈	5:05 am	♉
8	♉		
9	♉	8:55 am	♊
10	♊		
11	♊	3:08 pm	♋
12	♋		
13	♋	11:29 pm	♌
14	♌		
15	♌		
16	♌	9:42 am	♍
17	♍		
18	♍	9:36 pm	♎
19	♎		
20	♎		
21	♎	10:24 am	♏
22	♏		
23	♏	10:16 pm	♐
24	♐		
25	♐		
26	♐	7:01 am	♑
27	♑		
28	♑	11:36 am	♒
29	♒		
30	♒	12:45 pm	♓
31	♓		

November

1	♊	11:57 am	♋
2	♋		
3	♋	6:10 pm	♌
4	♌		
5	♌		
6	♌	4:04 am	♍
7	♍		
8	♍	4:19 pm	♎
9	♎		
10	♎		
11	♎	5:04 am	♏
12	♏		
13	♏	4:57 pm	♐
14	♐		
15	♐		
16	♐	3:09 am	♑
17	♑		
18	♑	11:05 am	♒
19	♒		
20	♒	4:20 pm	♓
21	♓		
22	♓	7:02 pm	♈
23	♈		
24	♈	7:57 pm	♉
25	♉		
26	♉	8:31 pm	♊
27	♊		
28	♊	10:26 pm	♋
29	♋		
30	♋		

March

1	♋		
2	♋		
3	♋	1:41 am	♌
4	♌		
5	♌	1:48 pm	♍
6	♍		
7	♍		
8	♍	2:23 am	♎
9	♎		
10	♎	2:40 pm	♏
11	♏		
12	♏		
13	♏	1:37 am	♐
14	♐		
15	♐	9:46 am	♑
16	♑		
17	♑	2:09 pm	♒
18	♒		
19	♒	3:07 pm	♓
20	♓		
21	♓	2:17 pm	♈
22	♈		
23	♈	1:50 pm	♉
24	♉		
25	♉	3:55 pm	♊
26	♊		
27	♊	9:55 pm	♋
28	♋		
29	♋		
30	♋	7:43 am	♌
31	♌		

June

1	♏		
2	♏	8:32 pm	♐
3	♐		
4	♐		
5	♐	3:54 am	♑
6	♑		
7	♑	9:03 am	♒
8	♒		
9	♒	12:40 pm	♓
10	♓		
11	♓	3:21 pm	♈
12	♈		
13	♈	5:50 pm	♉
14	♉		
15	♉	8:53 pm	♊
16	♊		
17	♊		
18	♊	1:28 am	♋
19	♋		
20	♋	8:32 am	♌
21	♌		
22	♌	6:29 pm	♍
23	♍		
24	♍		
25	♍	6:36 am	♎
26	♎		
27	♎	6:51 pm	♏
28	♏		
29	♏		
30	♏	5:03 am	♐

September

1	♓	12:19 pm	♈
2	♈		
3	♈	12:27 pm	♉
4	♉		
5	♉	2:55 pm	♊
6	♊		
7	♊	8:35 pm	♋
8	♋		
9	♋		
10	♋	5:11 am	♌
11	♌		
12	♌	3:54 pm	♍
13	♍		
14	♍		
15	♍	4:00 am	♎
16	♎		
17	♎	4:49 pm	♏
18	♏		
19	♏		
20	♏	5:11 am	♐
21	♐		
22	♐	3:13 pm	♑
23	♑		
24	♑	9:22 pm	♒
25	♒		
26	♒	11:32 pm	♓
27	♓		
28	♓	11:07 pm	♈
29	♈		
30	♈	10:14 pm	♉

December

1	♋	3:17 am	♌
2	♌		
3	♌	11:50 am	♍
4	♍		
5	♍	11:30 pm	♎
6	♎		
7	♎		
8	♎	12:17 pm	♏
9	♏		
10	♏		
11	♏	12:01 am	♐
12	♐		
13	♐	9:31 am	♑
14	♑		
15	♑	4:39 pm	♒
16	♒		
17	♒	9:48 pm	♓
18	♓		
19	♓		
20	♓	1:25 am	♈
21	♈		
22	♈	3:57 am	♉
23	♉		
24	♉	6:04 am	♊
25	♊		
26	♊	8:45 am	♋
27	♋		
28	♋	1:17 pm	♌
29	♌		
30	♌	8:49 pm	♍
31	♍		

Moon Movements

♎ = Libra ♏ = Scorpio ♐ = Sagittarius ♑ = Capricorn ♒ = Aquarius ♓ = Pisces

1910

January

1	♍		
2	♍	7:37 am	♎
3	♎		
4	♎	8:19 pm	♏
5	♏		
6	♏		
7	♏	8:20 am	♐
8	♐		
9	♐	5:40 pm	♑
10	♑		
11	♑	11:53 pm	♒
12	♒		
13	♒		
14	♒	3:50 am	♓
15	♓		
16	♓	6:46 am	♈
17	♈		
18	♈	9:38 am	♉
19	♉		
20	♉	12:58 pm	♊
21	♊		
22	♊	5:02 pm	♋
23	♋		
24	♋	10:24 pm	♌
25	♌		
26	♌		
27	♌	5:52 am	♍
28	♍		
29	♍	4:05 pm	♎
30	♎		
31	♎		

February

1	♎	4:33 am	♏
2	♏		
3	♏	5:05 pm	♐
4	♐		
5	♐		
6	♐	3:03 am	♑
7	♑		
8	♑	9:14 am	♒
9	♒		
10	♒	12:13 pm	♓
11	♓		
12	♓	1:41 pm	♈
13	♈		
14	♈	3:20 pm	♉
15	♉		
16	♉	6:19 pm	♊
17	♊		
18	♊	11:03 pm	♋
19	♋		
20	♋		
21	♋	5:28 am	♌
22	♌		
23	♌	1:41 pm	♍
24	♍		
25	♍	11:58 pm	♎
26	♎		
27	♎		
28	♎	12:16 pm	♏

March

1	♏		
2	♏		
3	♏	1:10 am	♐
4	♐		
5	♐	12:12 pm	♑
6	♑		
7	♑	7:23 pm	♒
8	♒		
9	♒	10:33 pm	♓
10	♓		
11	♓	11:10 pm	♈
12	♈		
13	♈	11:15 pm	♉
14	♉		
15	♉		
16	♉	12:39 am	♊
17	♊		
18	♊	4:31 am	♋
19	♋		
20	♋	11:03 am	♌
21	♌		
22	♌	7:57 pm	♍
23	♍		
24	♍		
25	♍	6:46 am	♎
26	♎		
27	♎	7:07 pm	♏
28	♏		
29	♏		
30	♏	8:06 am	♐
31	♐		

April

1	♐	7:56 pm	♑
2	♑		
3	♑		
4	♑	4:32 am	♒
5	♒		
6	♒	9:01 am	♓
7	♓		
8	♓	10:05 am	♈
9	♈		
10	♈	9:32 am	♉
11	♉		
12	♉	9:26 am	♊
13	♊		
14	♊	11:34 am	♋
15	♋		
16	♋	4:56 pm	♌
17	♌		
18	♌		
19	♌	1:35 am	♍
20	♍		
21	♍	12:44 pm	♎
22	♎		
23	♎		
24	♎	1:19 am	♏
25	♏		
26	♏	2:14 pm	♐
27	♐		
28	♐		
29	♐	2:12 am	♑
30	♑		

May

1	♑	11:46 am	♒
2	♒		
3	♒	5:50 pm	♓
4	♓		
5	♓	8:24 pm	♈
6	♈		
7	♈	8:33 pm	♉
8	♉		
9	♉	8:03 pm	♊
10	♊		
11	♊	8:50 pm	♋
12	♋		
13	♋		
14	♋	12:32 am	♌
15	♌		
16	♌	7:58 am	♍
17	♍		
18	♍	6:46 pm	♎
19	♎		
20	♎		
21	♎	7:27 am	♏
22	♏		
23	♏	8:17 pm	♐
24	♐		
25	♐		
26	♐	7:57 am	♑
27	♑		
28	♑	5:33 pm	♒
29	♒		
30	♒		
31	♒	12:31 am	♓

June

1	♓		
2	♓	4:37 am	♈
3	♈		
4	♈	6:19 am	♉
5	♉		
6	♉	6:40 am	♊
7	♊		
8	♊	7:16 am	♋
9	♋		
10	♋	9:51 am	♌
11	♌		
12	♌	3:52 pm	♍
13	♍		
14	♍		
15	♍	1:42 am	♎
16	♎		
17	♎	2:08 pm	♏
18	♏		
19	♏		
20	♏	2:56 am	♐
21	♐		
22	♐	2:14 pm	♑
23	♑		
24	♑	11:15 pm	♒
25	♒		
26	♒		
27	♒	5:59 am	♓
28	♓		
29	♓	10:44 am	♈
30	♈		

July

1	♈	1:48 pm	♉
2	♉		
3	♉	3:38 pm	♊
4	♊		
5	♊	5:09 pm	♋
6	♋		
7	♋	7:44 pm	♌
8	♌		
9	♌		
10	♌	12:54 am	♍
11	♍		
12	♍	9:41 am	♎
13	♎		
14	♎	9:35 pm	♏
15	♏		
16	♏		
17	♏	10:25 am	♐
18	♐		
19	♐	9:41 pm	♑
20	♑		
21	♑		
22	♑	6:06 am	♒
23	♒		
24	♒	11:57 am	♓
25	♓		
26	♓	4:08 pm	♈
27	♈		
28	♈	7:27 pm	♉
29	♉		
30	♉	10:20 pm	♊
31	♊		

August

1	♊		
2	♊	1:11 am	♋
3	♋		
4	♋	4:40 am	♌
5	♌		
6	♌	9:58 am	♍
7	♍		
8	♍	6:13 pm	♎
9	♎		
10	♎		
11	♎	5:34 am	♏
12	♏		
13	♏	6:27 pm	♐
14	♐		
15	♐		
16	♐	6:05 am	♑
17	♑		
18	♑	2:31 pm	♒
19	♒		
20	♒	7:40 pm	♓
21	♓		
22	♓	10:42 pm	♈
23	♈		
24	♈		
25	♈	1:02 am	♉
26	♉		
27	♉	3:43 am	♊
28	♊		
29	♊	7:14 am	♋
30	♋		
31	♋	11:48 am	♌

September

1	♌		
2	♌	5:57 pm	♍
3	♍		
4	♍		
5	♍	2:22 am	♎
6	♎		
7	♎	1:29 pm	♏
8	♏		
9	♏		
10	♏	2:22 am	♐
11	♐		
12	♐	2:39 pm	♑
13	♑		
14	♑	11:53 pm	♒
15	♒		
16	♒		
17	♒	5:12 am	♓
18	♓		
19	♓	7:30 am	♈
20	♈		
21	♈	8:29 am	♉
22	♉		
23	♉	9:49 am	♊
24	♊		
25	♊	12:37 pm	♋
26	♋		
27	♋	5:26 pm	♌
28	♌		
29	♌		
30	♌	12:22 am	♍

October

1	♍		
2	♍	9:28 am	♎
3	♎		
4	♎	8:45 pm	♏
5	♏		
6	♏		
7	♏	9:37 am	♐
8	♐		
9	♐	10:25 pm	♑
10	♑		
11	♑		
12	♑	8:51 am	♒
13	♒		
14	♒	3:22 pm	♓
15	♓		
16	♓	6:06 pm	♈
17	♈		
18	♈	6:27 pm	♉
19	♉		
20	♉	6:18 pm	♊
21	♊		
22	♊	7:26 pm	♋
23	♋		
24	♋	11:08 pm	♌
25	♌		
26	♌		
27	♌	5:54 am	♍
28	♍		
29	♍	3:30 pm	♎
30	♎		
31	♎		

November

1	♎	3:12 am	♏
2	♏		
3	♏	4:06 pm	♐
4	♐		
5	♐		
6	♐	5:01 am	♑
7	♑		
8	♑	4:19 pm	♒
9	♒		
10	♒		
11	♒	12:26 am	♓
12	♓		
13	♓	4:43 am	♈
14	♈		
15	♈	5:47 am	♉
16	♉		
17	♉	5:12 am	♊
18	♊		
19	♊	4:53 am	♋
20	♋		
21	♋	6:45 am	♌
22	♌		
23	♌	12:08 pm	♍
24	♍		
25	♍	9:17 pm	♎
26	♎		
27	♎		
28	♎	9:12 am	♏
29	♏		
30	♏	10:15 pm	♐

December

1	♐		
2	♐		
3	♐	10:57 am	♑
4	♑		
5	♑	10:17 pm	♒
6	♒		
7	♒		
8	♒	7:20 am	♓
9	♓		
10	♓	1:22 pm	♈
11	♈		
12	♈	4:13 pm	♉
13	♉		
14	♉	4:39 pm	♊
15	♊		
16	♊	4:11 pm	♋
17	♋		
18	♋	4:48 pm	♌
19	♌		
20	♌	8:25 pm	♍
21	♍		
22	♍		
23	♍	4:10 am	♎
24	♎		
25	♎	3:36 pm	♏
26	♏		
27	♏		
28	♏	4:41 am	♐
29	♐		
30	♐	5:14 pm	♑
31	♑		

Your Starway to Love

♈ = Aries ♉ = Taurus ♊ = Gemini ♋ = Cancer ♌ = Leo ♍ = Virgo

1911

January

1	♑		
2	♑	4:02 am	♒
3	♒		
4	♒	12:50 pm	♓
5	♓		
6	♓	7:33 pm	♈
7	♈		
8	♈		
9	♈	12:01 am	♉
10	♉		
11	♉	2:17 am	♊
12	♊		
13	♊	3:03 am	♋
14	♋		
15	♋	3:50 am	♌
16	♌		
17	♌	6:31 am	♍
18	♍		
19	♍	12:47 pm	♎
20	♎		
21	♎	11:06 pm	♏
22	♏		
23	♏		
24	♏	11:54 am	♐
25	♐		
26	♐		
27	♐	12:30 am	♑
28	♑		
29	♑	10:57 am	♒
30	♒		
31	♒	6:55 pm	♓

April

1	♉		
2	♉	8:49 pm	♊
3	♊		
4	♊	10:53 pm	♋
5	♋		
6	♋		
7	♋	2:15 am	♌
8	♌		
9	♌	7:23 am	♍
10	♍		
11	♍	2:36 pm	♎
12	♎		
13	♎		
14	♎	12:06 am	♏
15	♏		
16	♏	11:46 am	♐
17	♐		
18	♐		
19	♐	12:34 am	♑
20	♑		
21	♑	12:33 pm	♒
22	♒		
23	♒	9:41 pm	♓
24	♓		
25	♓		
26	♓	3:03 am	♈
27	♈		
28	♈	5:13 am	♉
29	♉		
30	♉	5:39 am	♊

July

1	♍		
2	♍	8:59 am	♎
3	♎		
4	♎	6:27 pm	♏
5	♏		
6	♏		
7	♏	6:39 am	♐
8	♐		
9	♐	7:32 pm	♑
10	♑		
11	♑		
12	♑	7:34 am	♒
13	♒		
14	♒	6:04 pm	♓
15	♓		
16	♓		
17	♓	2:35 am	♈
18	♈		
19	♈	8:33 am	♉
20	♉		
21	♉	11:42 am	♊
22	♊		
23	♊	12:30 pm	♋
24	♋		
25	♋	12:24 pm	♌
26	♌		
27	♌	1:26 pm	♍
28	♍		
29	♍	5:32 pm	♎
30	♎		
31	♎		

October

1	♑		
2	♑	5:56 am	♒
3	♒		
4	♒	3:59 pm	♓
5	♓		
6	♓	10:56 pm	♈
7	♈		
8	♈		
9	♈	3:12 am	♉
10	♉		
11	♉	5:55 am	♊
12	♊		
13	♊	8:12 am	♋
14	♋		
15	♋	10:54 am	♌
16	♌		
17	♌	2:41 pm	♍
18	♍		
19	♍	8:05 pm	♎
20	♎		
21	♎		
22	♏	3:36 am	♏
23	♏		
24	♏	1:34 pm	♐
25	♐		
26	♐		
27	♐	1:37 am	♑
28	♑		
29	♑	2:14 pm	♒
30	♒		
31	♒		

February

1	♓		
2	♓		
3	♓	12:57 am	♈
4	♈		
5	♈	5:36 am	♉
6	♉		
7	♉	9:03 am	♊
8	♊		
9	♊	11:28 am	♋
10	♋		
11	♋	1:33 pm	♌
12	♌		
13	♌	4:39 pm	♍
14	♍		
15	♍	10:22 pm	♎
16	♎		
17	♎		
18	♎	7:39 am	♏
19	♏		
20	♏	7:53 pm	♐
21	♐		
22	♐		
23	♐	8:37 am	♑
24	♑		
25	♑	7:17 pm	♒
26	♒		
27	♒		
28	♒	2:51 am	♓

May

1	♊		
2	♊	6:06 am	♋
3	♋		
4	♋	8:09 am	♌
5	♌		
6	♌	12:50 pm	♍
7	♍		
8	♍	8:26 pm	♎
9	♎		
10	♎		
11	♎	6:35 am	♏
12	♏		
13	♏	6:33 pm	♐
14	♐		
15	♐		
16	♐	7:20 am	♑
17	♑		
18	♑	7:40 pm	♒
19	♒		
20	♒		
21	♒	5:53 am	♓
22	♓		
23	♓	12:41 pm	♈
24	♈		
25	♈	3:48 pm	♉
26	♉		
27	♉	4:12 pm	♊
28	♊		
29	♊	3:37 pm	♋
30	♋		
31	♋	4:03 pm	♌

August

1	♎	1:44 am	♏
2	♏		
3	♏	1:21 pm	♐
4	♐		
5	♐		
6	♐	2:10 am	♑
7	♑		
8	♑	2:02 pm	♒
9	♒		
10	♒		
11	♒	12:00 am	♓
12	♓		
13	♓	8:02 am	♈
14	♈		
15	♈	2:12 pm	♉
16	♉		
17	♉	6:23 pm	♊
18	♊		
19	♊	8:42 pm	♋
20	♋		
21	♋	9:54 pm	♌
22	♌		
23	♌	11:26 pm	♍
24	♍		
25	♍		
26	♍	3:06 am	♎
27	♎		
28	♎	10:16 am	♏
29	♏		
30	♏	9:01 pm	♐
31	♐		

November

1	♒	1:12 am	♓
2	♓		
3	♓	8:49 am	♈
4	♈		
5	♈	12:54 pm	♉
6	♉		
7	♉	2:29 pm	♊
8	♊		
9	♊	3:11 pm	♋
10	♋		
11	♋	4:39 pm	♌
12	♌		
13	♌	8:05 pm	♍
14	♍		
15	♍		
16	♍	2:04 am	♎
17	♎		
18	♎	10:28 am	♏
19	♏		
20	♏	8:54 pm	♐
21	♐		
22	♐		
23	♐	8:55 am	♑
24	♑		
25	♑	9:40 pm	♒
26	♒		
27	♒		
28	♒	9:32 am	♓
29	♓		
30	♓	6:35 pm	♈

March

1	♓		
2	♓	7:49 am	♈
3	♈		
4	♈	11:21 am	♉
5	♉		
6	♉	2:23 pm	♊
7	♊		
8	♊	5:23 pm	♋
9	♋		
10	♋	8:45 pm	♌
11	♌		
12	♌		
13	♌	1:04 am	♍
14	♍		
15	♍	7:19 am	♎
16	♎		
17	♎	4:21 pm	♏
18	♏		
19	♏		
20	♏	4:05 am	♐
21	♐		
22	♐	4:53 pm	♑
23	♑		
24	♑		
25	♑	4:12 am	♒
26	♒		
27	♒	12:14 pm	♓
28	♓		
29	♓	4:52 pm	♈
30	♈		
31	♈	7:14 pm	♉

June

1	♌		
2	♌	7:14 pm	♍
3	♍		
4	♍		
5	♍	2:07 am	♎
6	♎		
7	♎	12:21 pm	♏
8	♏		
9	♏		
10	♏	12:37 am	♐
11	♐		
12	♐	1:27 pm	♑
13	♑		
14	♑		
15	♑	1:44 am	♒
16	♒		
17	♒	12:27 pm	♓
18	♓		
19	♓	8:32 pm	♈
20	♈		
21	♈		
22	♈	1:14 am	♉
23	♉		
24	♉	2:46 am	♊
25	♊		
26	♊	2:20 am	♋
27	♋		
28	♋	1:54 am	♌
29	♌		
30	♌	3:35 am	♍

September

1	♐		
2	♐	9:37 am	♑
3	♑		
4	♑	9:35 pm	♒
5	♒		
6	♒		
7	♒	7:17 am	♓
8	♓		
9	♓	2:31 pm	♈
10	♈		
11	♈	7:49 pm	♉
12	♉		
13	♉	11:47 pm	♊
14	♊		
15	♊		
16	♊	2:47 am	♋
17	♋		
18	♋	5:18 am	♌
19	♌		
20	♌	8:05 am	♍
21	♍		
22	♍	12:21 pm	♎
23	♎		
24	♎	7:17 pm	♏
25	♏		
26	♏		
27	♏	5:21 am	♐
28	♐		
29	♐	5:39 pm	♑
30	♑		

December

1	♈		
2	♈	11:43 pm	♉
3	♉		
4	♉		
5	♉	1:18 am	♊
6	♊		
7	♊	12:55 am	♋
8	♋		
9	♋	12:39 am	♌
10	♌		
11	♌	2:27 am	♍
12	♍		
13	♍	7:36 am	♎
14	♎		
15	♎	4:09 pm	♏
16	♏		
17	♏		
18	♏	3:08 am	♐
19	♐		
20	♐	3:24 pm	♑
21	♑		
22	♑		
23	♑	4:05 am	♒
24	♒		
25	♒	4:18 pm	♓
26	♓		
27	♓		
28	♓	2:36 am	♈
29	♈		
30	♈	9:30 am	♉
31	♉		

Moon Movements

♎ = Libra ♏ = Scorpio ♐ = Sagittarius ♑ = Capricorn ♒ = Aquarius ♓ = Pisces

1912

January

Day	Sign	Time	Enters
1	♉	12:28 pm	♊
2	♊		
3	♊	12:25 pm	♋
4	♋		
5	♋	11:17 am	♌
6	♌		
7	♌	11:23 am	♍
8	♍		
9	♍	2:42 pm	♎
10	♎		
11	♎	10:07 pm	♏
12	♏		
13	♏		
14	♏	8:57 am	♐
15	♐		
16	♐	9:28 pm	♑
17	♑		
18	♑		
19	♑	10:07 am	♒
20	♒		
21	♒	10:06 pm	♓
22	♓		
23	♓		
24	♓	8:41 am	♈
25	♈		
26	♈	4:52 pm	♉
27	♉		
28	♉	9:42 pm	♊
29	♊		
30	♊	11:15 pm	♋
31	♋		

April

Day	Sign	Time	Enters
1	♎		
2	♎		
3	♎	1:15 am	♏
4	♏		
5	♏	8:47 am	♐
6	♐		
7	♐	7:24 pm	♑
8	♑		
9	♑		
10	♑	7:47 am	♒
11	♒		
12	♒	7:42 pm	♓
13	♓		
14	♓		
15	♓	5:15 am	♈
16	♈		
17	♈	11:51 am	♉
18	♉		
19	♉	4:03 pm	♊
20	♊		
21	♊	6:53 pm	♋
22	♋		
23	♋	9:22 pm	♌
24	♌		
25	♌		
26	♌	12:18 am	♍
27	♍		
28	♍	4:15 am	♎
29	♎		
30	♎	9:47 am	♏

July

Day	Sign	Time	Enters
1	♑	5:57 am	♒
2	♒		
3	♒	6:40 pm	♓
4	♓		
5	♓		
6	♓	6:30 am	♈
7	♈		
8	♈	3:33 pm	♉
9	♉		
10	♉	8:34 pm	♊
11	♊		
12	♊	9:55 pm	♋
13	♋		
14	♋	9:16 pm	♌
15	♌		
16	♌	8:49 pm	♍
17	♍		
18	♍	10:37 pm	♎
19	♎		
20	♎		
21	♎	3:52 am	♏
22	♏		
23	♏	12:34 pm	♐
24	♐		
25	♐	11:41 pm	♑
26	♑		
27	♑		
28	♑	12:01 pm	♒
29	♒		
30	♒		
31	♒	12:40 am	♓

October

Day	Sign	Time	Enters
1	♊		
2	♊	10:09 pm	♋
3	♋		
4	♋		
5	♋	1:11 am	♌
6	♌		
7	♌	2:55 am	♍
8	♍		
9	♍	4:25 am	♎
10	♎		
11	♎	7:04 am	♏
12	♏		
13	♏	12:18 pm	♐
14	♐		
15	♐	8:56 pm	♑
16	♑		
17	♑		
18	♑	8:30 am	♒
19	♒		
20	♒	9:08 pm	♓
21	♓		
22	♓		
23	♓	8:29 am	♈
24	♈		
25	♈	5:15 pm	♉
26	♉		
27	♉	11:22 pm	♊
28	♊		
29	♊		
30	♊	3:36 am	♋
31	♋		

February

Day	Sign	Time	Enters
1	♋	10:47 pm	♌
2	♌		
3	♌	10:23 pm	♍
4	♍		
5	♍		
6	♍	12:12 am	♎
7	♎		
8	♎	5:53 am	♏
9	♏		
10	♏	3:35 pm	♐
11	♐		
12	♐		
13	♐	3:52 am	♑
14	♑		
15	♑	4:33 pm	♒
16	♒		
17	♒		
18	♒	4:13 am	♓
19	♓		
20	♓	2:17 pm	♈
21	♈		
22	♈	10:26 pm	♉
23	♉		
24	♉		
25	♉	4:15 am	♊
26	♊		
27	♊	7:30 am	♋
28	♋		
29	♋	8:42 am	♌

May

Day	Sign	Time	Enters
1	♏		
2	♏	5:30 pm	♐
3	♐		
4	♐		
5	♐	3:42 am	♑
6	♑		
7	♑	3:50 pm	♒
8	♒		
9	♒		
10	♒	4:08 am	♓
11	♓		
12	♓	2:20 pm	♈
13	♈		
14	♈	9:04 pm	♉
15	♉		
16	♉		
17	♉	12:33 am	♊
18	♊		
19	♊	2:04 am	♋
20	♋		
21	♋	3:18 am	♌
22	♌		
23	♌	5:40 am	♍
24	♍		
25	♍	10:00 am	♎
26	♎		
27	♎	4:27 pm	♏
28	♏		
29	♏		
30	♏	12:54 am	♐
31	♐		

August

Day	Sign	Time	Enters
1	♓		
2	♓	12:40 pm	♈
3	♈		
4	♈	10:37 pm	♉
5	♉		
6	♉		
7	♉	5:10 am	♊
8	♊		
9	♊	7:57 am	♋
10	♋		
11	♋	8:00 am	♌
12	♌		
13	♌	7:14 am	♍
14	♍		
15	♍	7:48 am	♎
16	♎		
17	♎	11:28 am	♏
18	♏		
19	♏	6:59 pm	♐
20	♐		
21	♐		
22	♐	5:43 am	♑
23	♑		
24	♑	6:07 pm	♒
25	♒		
26	♒		
27	♒	6:40 am	♓
28	♓		
29	♓	6:21 pm	♈
30	♈		
31	♈		

November

Day	Sign	Time	Enters
1	♋	6:46 am	♌
2	♌		
3	♌	9:34 am	♍
4	♍		
5	♍	12:32 pm	♎
6	♎		
7	♎	4:17 pm	♏
8	♏		
9	♏	9:44 pm	♐
10	♐		
11	♐		
12	♐	5:48 am	♑
13	♑		
14	♑	4:45 pm	♒
15	♒		
16	♒		
17	♒	5:24 am	♓
18	♓		
19	♓	5:17 pm	♈
20	♈		
21	♈		
22	♈	2:13 am	♉
23	♉		
24	♉	7:40 am	♊
25	♊		
26	♊	10:36 am	♋
27	♋		
28	♋	12:34 pm	♌
29	♌		
30	♌	2:55 pm	♍

March

Day	Sign	Time	Enters
1	♌		
2	♌	9:14 am	♍
3	♍		
4	♍	10:53 am	♎
5	♎		
6	♎	3:25 pm	♏
7	♏		
8	♏	11:43 pm	♐
9	♐		
10	♐		
11	♐	11:12 am	♑
12	♑		
13	♑	11:50 pm	♒
14	♒		
15	♒		
16	♒	11:28 am	♓
17	♓		
18	♓	8:59 pm	♈
19	♈		
20	♈		
21	♈	4:16 am	♉
22	♉		
23	♉	9:37 am	♊
24	♊		
25	♊	1:22 pm	♋
26	♋		
27	♋	3:54 pm	♌
28	♌		
29	♌	5:58 pm	♍
30	♍		
31	♍	8:40 pm	♎

June

Day	Sign	Time	Enters
1	♐	11:17 am	♑
2	♑		
3	♑	11:19 pm	♒
4	♒		
5	♒		
6	♒	11:55 am	♓
7	♓		
8	♓	11:03 pm	♈
9	♈		
10	♈		
11	♈	6:46 am	♉
12	♉		
13	♉	10:32 am	♊
14	♊		
15	♊	11:24 am	♋
16	♋		
17	♋	11:16 am	♌
18	♌		
19	♌	12:09 pm	♍
20	♍		
21	♍	3:33 pm	♎
22	♎		
23	♎	9:58 pm	♏
24	♏		
25	♏		
26	♏	6:58 am	♐
27	♐		
28	♐	5:49 pm	♑
29	♑		
30	♑		

September

Day	Sign	Time	Enters
1	♈	4:20 am	♉
2	♉		
3	♉	11:45 am	♊
4	♊		
5	♊	4:06 pm	♋
6	♋		
7	♋	5:43 pm	♌
8	♌		
9	♌	5:51 pm	♍
10	♍		
11	♍	6:18 pm	♎
12	♎		
13	♎	8:54 pm	♏
14	♏		
15	♏		
16	♏	2:58 am	♐
17	♐		
18	♐	12:42 pm	♑
19	♑		
20	♑		
21	♑	12:51 am	♒
22	♒		
23	♒	1:25 pm	♓
24	♓		
25	♓		
26	♓	12:44 am	♈
27	♈		
28	♈	10:04 am	♉
29	♉		
30	♉	5:12 pm	♊

December

Day	Sign	Time	Enters
1	♍		
2	♍	6:26 pm	♎
3	♎		
4	♎	11:22 pm	♏
5	♏		
6	♏		
7	♏	5:48 am	♐
8	♐		
9	♐	2:10 pm	♑
10	♑		
11	♑		
12	♑	12:51 am	♒
13	♒		
14	♒	1:26 pm	♓
15	♓		
16	♓		
17	♓	2:00 am	♈
18	♈		
19	♈	11:57 am	♉
20	♉		
21	♉	5:50 pm	♊
22	♊		
23	♊	8:11 pm	♋
24	♋		
25	♋	8:43 pm	♌
26	♌		
27	♌	9:27 pm	♍
28	♍		
29	♍	11:55 pm	♎
30	♎		
31	♎		

Your Starway to Love

♈ = Aries ♉ = Taurus ♊ = Gemini ♋ = Cancer ♌ = Leo ♍ = Virgo

1913

January

1	♎	4:49 am	♏
2	♏		
3	♏	12:01 pm	♐
4	♐		
5	♐	9:10 pm	♑
6	♑		
7	♑		
8	♑	8:07 am	♒
9	♒		
10	♒	8:38 pm	♓
11	♓		
12	♓		
13	♓	9:36 am	♈
14	♈		
15	♈	8:46 pm	♉
16	♉		
17	♉		
18	♉	4:07 am	♊
19	♊		
20	♊	7:14 am	♋
21	♋		
22	♋	7:26 am	♌
23	♌		
24	♌	6:48 am	♍
25	♍		
26	♍	7:26 am	♎
27	♎		
28	♎	10:50 am	♏
29	♏		
30	♏	5:30 pm	♐
31	♐		

February

1	♐		
2	♐	2:59 am	♑
3	♑		
4	♑	2:25 pm	♒
5	♒		
6	♒		
7	♒	3:03 am	♓
8	♓		
9	♓	3:59 pm	♈
10	♈		
11	♈		
12	♈	3:47 am	♉
13	♉		
14	♉	12:38 pm	♊
15	♊		
16	♊	5:29 pm	♋
17	♋		
18	♋	6:47 pm	♌
19	♌		
20	♌	6:08 pm	♍
21	♍		
22	♍	5:37 pm	♎
23	♎		
24	♎	7:11 pm	♏
25	♏		
26	♏		
27	♏	12:11 am	♐
28	♐		

March

1	♐	8:52 am	♑
2	♑		
3	♑	8:21 pm	♒
4	♒		
5	♒		
6	♒	9:10 am	♓
7	♓		
8	♓	9:57 pm	♈
9	♈		
10	♈		
11	♈	9:35 am	♉
12	♉		
13	♉	7:00 pm	♊
14	♊		
15	♊		
16	♊	1:21 am	♋
17	♋		
18	♋	4:27 am	♌
19	♌		
20	♌	5:08 am	♍
21	♍		
22	♍	4:54 am	♎
23	♎		
24	♎	5:37 am	♏
25	♏		
26	♏	8:59 am	♐
27	♐		
28	♐	4:09 pm	♑
29	♑		
30	♑		
31	♑	2:53 am	♒

April

1	♒		
2	♒	3:39 pm	♓
3	♓		
4	♓		
5	♓	4:22 am	♈
6	♈		
7	♈	3:32 pm	♉
8	♉		
9	♉		
10	♉	12:31 am	♊
11	♊		
12	♊	7:09 am	♋
13	♋		
14	♋	11:30 am	♌
15	♌		
16	♌	1:53 pm	♍
17	♍		
18	♍	3:02 pm	♎
19	♎		
20	♎	4:14 pm	♏
21	♏		
22	♏	7:03 pm	♐
23	♐		
24	♐		
25	♐	12:56 am	♑
26	♑		
27	♑	10:33 am	♒
28	♒		
29	♒	10:54 pm	♓
30	♓		

May

1	♓		
2	♓	11:39 am	♈
3	♈		
4	♈	10:35 pm	♉
5	♉		
6	♉		
7	♉	6:49 am	♊
8	♊		
9	♊	12:43 pm	♋
10	♋		
11	♋	4:57 pm	♌
12	♌		
13	♌	8:10 pm	♍
14	♍		
15	♍	10:44 pm	♎
16	♎		
17	♎		
18	♎	1:14 am	♏
19	♏		
20	♏	4:38 am	♐
21	♐		
22	♐	10:13 am	♑
23	♑		
24	♑	7:00 pm	♒
25	♒		
26	♒		
27	♒	6:47 am	♓
28	♓		
29	♓	7:36 pm	♈
30	♈		
31	♈		

June

1	♈	6:45 am	♉
2	♉		
3	♉	2:42 pm	♊
4	♊		
5	♊	7:40 pm	♋
6	♋		
7	♋	10:51 pm	♌
8	♌		
9	♌		
10	♌	1:31 am	♍
11	♍		
12	♍	4:27 am	♎
13	♎		
14	♎	8:00 am	♏
15	♏		
16	♏	12:31 pm	♐
17	♐		
18	♐	6:41 pm	♑
19	♑		
20	♑		
21	♑	3:21 am	♒
22	♒		
23	♒	2:45 pm	♓
24	♓		
25	♓		
26	♓	3:38 am	♈
27	♈		
28	♈	3:22 pm	♉
29	♉		
30	♉	11:47 pm	♊

July

1	♊		
2	♊		
3	♊	4:29 am	♋
4	♋		
5	♋	6:40 am	♌
6	♌		
7	♌	8:00 am	♍
8	♍		
9	♍	9:59 am	♎
10	♎		
11	♎	1:26 pm	♏
12	♏		
13	♏	6:37 pm	♐
14	♐		
15	♐		
16	♐	1:39 am	♑
17	♑		
18	♑	10:48 am	♒
19	♒		
20	♒	10:12 pm	♓
21	♓		
22	♓		
23	♓	11:07 am	♈
24	♈		
25	♈	11:29 pm	♉
26	♉		
27	♉		
28	♉	8:57 am	♊
29	♊		
30	♊	2:23 pm	♋
31	♋		

August

1	♋	4:25 pm	♌
2	♌		
3	♌	4:44 pm	♍
4	♍		
5	♍	5:13 pm	♎
6	♎		
7	♎	7:22 pm	♏
8	♏		
9	♏		
10	♏	12:03 am	♐
11	♐		
12	♐	7:24 am	♑
13	♑		
14	♑	5:09 pm	♒
15	♒		
16	♒		
17	♒	4:52 am	♓
18	♓		
19	♓	5:47 pm	♈
20	♈		
21	♈		
22	♈	6:30 am	♉
23	♉		
24	♉	5:03 pm	♊
25	♊		
26	♊	11:54 pm	♋
27	♋		
28	♋		
29	♋	2:55 am	♌
30	♌		
31	♌	3:16 am	♍

September

1	♍		
2	♍	2:47 am	♎
3	♎		
4	♎	3:21 am	♏
5	♏		
6	♏	6:32 am	♐
7	♐		
8	♐	1:07 pm	♑
9	♑		
10	♑	10:56 pm	♒
11	♒		
12	♒		
13	♒	10:57 am	♓
14	♓		
15	♓	11:55 pm	♈
16	♈		
17	♈		
18	♈	12:34 pm	♉
19	♉		
20	♉	11:35 pm	♊
21	♊		
22	♊		
23	♊	7:45 am	♋
24	♋		
25	♋	12:26 pm	♌
26	♌		
27	♌	2:02 pm	♍
28	♍		
29	♍	1:47 pm	♎
30	♎		

October

1	♎	1:31 pm	♏
2	♏		
3	♏	3:08 pm	♐
4	♐		
5	♐	8:10 pm	♑
6	♑		
7	♑		
8	♑	5:09 am	♒
9	♒		
10	♒	5:07 pm	♓
11	♓		
12	♓		
13	♓	6:08 am	♈
14	♈		
15	♈	6:30 pm	♉
16	♉		
17	♉		
18	♉	5:13 am	♊
19	♊		
20	♊	1:45 pm	♋
21	♋		
22	♋	7:45 pm	♌
23	♌		
24	♌	11:06 pm	♍
25	♍		
26	♍		
27	♍	12:17 am	♎
28	♎		
29	♎	12:30 am	♏
30	♏		
31	♏	1:29 am	♐

November

1	♐		
2	♐	5:08 am	♑
3	♑		
4	♑	12:44 pm	♒
5	♒		
6	♒		
7	♒	12:01 am	♓
8	♓		
9	♓	1:02 pm	♈
10	♈		
11	♈		
12	♈	1:17 am	♉
13	♉		
14	♉	11:24 am	♊
15	♊		
16	♊	7:17 pm	♋
17	♋		
18	♋		
19	♋	1:18 am	♌
20	♌		
21	♌	5:40 am	♍
22	♍		
23	♍	8:30 am	♎
24	♎		
25	♎	10:13 am	♏
26	♏		
27	♏	11:54 am	♐
28	♐		
29	♐	3:12 pm	♑
30	♑		

December

1	♑	9:42 pm	♒
2	♒		
3	♒		
4	♒	8:00 am	♓
5	♓		
6	♓	8:45 pm	♈
7	♈		
8	♈		
9	♈	9:12 am	♉
10	♉		
11	♉	7:09 pm	♊
12	♊		
13	♊		
14	♊	2:12 am	♋
15	♋		
16	♋	7:09 am	♌
17	♌		
18	♌	11:00 am	♍
19	♍		
20	♍	2:19 pm	♎
21	♎		
22	♎	5:21 pm	♏
23	♏		
24	♏	8:28 pm	♐
25	♐		
26	♐		
27	♐	12:36 am	♑
28	♑		
29	♑	7:01 am	♒
30	♒		
31	♒	4:38 pm	♓

Moon Movements

♎ = Libra ♏ = Scorpio ♐ = Sagittarius ♑ = Capricorn ♒ = Aquarius ♓ = Pisces

1914

January

Day	Sign	Time	Enters
1	♓		
2	♓		
3	♓	4:57 am	♈
4	♈		
5	♈	5:43 pm	♉
6	♉		
7	♉		
8	♉	4:13 am	♊
9	♊		
10	♊	11:12 am	♋
11	♋		
12	♋	3:13 pm	♌
13	♌		
14	♌	5:40 pm	♍
15	♍		
16	♍	7:53 pm	♎
17	♎		
18	♎	10:44 pm	♏
19	♏		
20	♏		
21	♏	2:40 am	♐
22	♐		
23	♐	7:59 am	♑
24	♑		
25	♑	3:13 pm	♒
26	♒		
27	♒		
28	♒	12:54 am	♓
29	♓		
30	♓	12:57 pm	♈
31	♈		

April

Day	Sign	Time	Enters
1	♊		
2	♊	1:59 pm	♋
3	♋		
4	♋	9:06 pm	♌
5	♌		
6	♌		
7	♌	12:37 am	♍
8	♍		
9	♍	1:12 am	♎
10	♎		
11	♎	12:27 am	♏
12	♏		
13	♏	12:23 am	♐
14	♐		
15	♐	2:59 am	♑
16	♑		
17	♑	9:31 am	♒
18	♒		
19	♒	7:52 pm	♓
20	♓		
21	♓		
22	♓	8:30 am	♈
23	♈		
24	♈	9:28 pm	♉
25	♉		
26	♉		
27	♉	9:29 am	♊
28	♊		
29	♊	7:50 pm	♋
30	♋		

July

Day	Sign	Time	Enters
1	♎		
2	♎	3:19 am	♏
3	♏		
4	♏	5:25 am	♐
5	♐		
6	♐	7:54 am	♑
7	♑		
8	♑	12:11 pm	♒
9	♒		
10	♒	7:33 pm	♓
11	♓		
12	♓		
13	♓	6:14 am	♈
14	♈		
15	♈	6:49 pm	♉
16	♉		
17	♉		
18	♉	6:47 am	♊
19	♊		
20	♊	4:12 pm	♋
21	♋		
22	♋	10:42 pm	♌
23	♌		
24	♌		
25	♌	3:00 am	♍
26	♍		
27	♍	6:05 am	♎
28	♎		
29	♎	8:45 am	♏
30	♏		
31	♏	11:35 am	♐

October

Day	Sign	Time	Enters
1	♓		
2	♓		
3	♓	4:38 am	♈
4	♈		
5	♈	4:58 pm	♉
6	♉		
7	♉		
8	♉	5:40 am	♊
9	♊		
10	♊	5:26 pm	♋
11	♋		
12	♋		
13	♋	2:36 am	♌
14	♌		
15	♌	8:02 am	♍
16	♍		
17	♍	9:49 am	♎
18	♎		
19	♎	9:21 am	♏
20	♏		
21	♏	8:40 am	♐
22	♐		
23	♐	9:55 am	♑
24	♑		
25	♑	2:39 pm	♒
26	♒		
27	♒	11:13 pm	♓
28	♓		
29	♓		
30	♓	10:34 am	♈
31	♈		

February

Day	Sign	Time	Enters
1	♈		
2	♈	1:54 am	♉
3	♉		
4	♉	1:20 pm	♊
5	♊		
6	♊	9:16 pm	♋
7	♋		
8	♋		
9	♋	1:26 am	♌
10	♌		
11	♌	3:00 am	♍
12	♍		
13	♍	3:37 am	♎
14	♎		
15	♎	4:55 am	♏
16	♏		
17	♏	8:03 am	♐
18	♐		
19	♐	1:38 pm	♑
20	♑		
21	♑	9:41 pm	♒
22	♒		
23	♒		
24	♒	8:01 am	♓
25	♓		
26	♓	8:09 pm	♈
27	♈		
28	♈		

May

Day	Sign	Time	Enters
1	♋		
2	♋	3:53 am	♌
3	♌		
4	♌	9:02 am	♍
5	♍		
6	♍	11:13 am	♎
7	♎		
8	♎	11:20 am	♏
9	♏		
10	♏	11:04 am	♐
11	♐		
12	♐	12:30 pm	♑
13	♑		
14	♑	5:29 pm	♒
15	♒		
16	♒		
17	♒	2:40 am	♓
18	♓		
19	♓	2:54 pm	♈
20	♈		
21	♈		
22	♈	3:51 am	♉
23	♉		
24	♉	3:37 pm	♊
25	♊		
26	♊		
27	♊	1:28 am	♋
28	♋		
29	♋	9:22 am	♌
30	♌		
31	♌	3:13 pm	♍

August

Day	Sign	Time	Enters
1	♐		
2	♐	3:14 pm	♑
3	♑		
4	♑	8:27 pm	♒
5	♒		
6	♒		
7	♒	4:03 am	♓
8	♓		
9	♓	2:25 pm	♈
10	♈		
11	♈		
12	♈	2:46 am	♉
13	♉		
14	♉	3:06 pm	♊
15	♊		
16	♊		
17	♊	1:11 am	♋
18	♋		
19	♋	7:52 am	♌
20	♌		
21	♌	11:30 am	♍
22	♍		
23	♍	1:18 pm	♎
24	♎		
25	♎	2:43 pm	♏
26	♏		
27	♏	4:59 pm	♐
28	♐		
29	♐	8:57 pm	♑
30	♑		
31	♑		

November

Day	Sign	Time	Enters
1	♈	11:08 pm	♉
2	♉		
3	♉		
4	♉	11:44 am	♊
5	♊		
6	♊	11:33 pm	♋
7	♋		
8	♋		
9	♋	9:36 am	♌
10	♌		
11	♌	4:42 pm	♍
12	♍		
13	♍	8:10 pm	♎
14	♎		
15	♎	8:36 pm	♏
16	♏		
17	♏	7:42 pm	♐
18	♐		
19	♐	7:42 pm	♑
20	♑		
21	♑	10:42 pm	♒
22	♒		
23	♒		
24	♒	5:53 am	♓
25	♓		
26	♓	4:44 pm	♈
27	♈		
28	♈		
29	♈	5:22 am	♉
30	♉		

March

Day	Sign	Time	Enters
1	♈	9:07 am	♉
2	♉		
3	♉	9:14 pm	♊
4	♊		
5	♊		
6	♊	6:34 am	♋
7	♋		
8	♋	12:03 pm	♌
9	♌		
10	♌	2:02 pm	♍
11	♍		
12	♍	1:57 pm	♎
13	♎		
14	♎	1:40 pm	♏
15	♏		
16	♏	3:01 pm	♐
17	♐		
18	♐	7:23 pm	♑
19	♑		
20	♑		
21	♑	3:15 am	♒
22	♒		
23	♒	2:01 pm	♓
24	♓		
25	♓		
26	♓	2:30 am	♈
27	♈		
28	♈	3:27 pm	♉
29	♉		
30	♉		
31	♉	3:42 am	♊

June

Day	Sign	Time	Enters
1	♍		
2	♍	6:51 pm	♎
3	♎		
4	♎	8:30 pm	♏
5	♏		
6	♏	9:12 pm	♐
7	♐		
8	♐	10:40 pm	♑
9	♑		
10	♑		
11	♑	2:46 am	♒
12	♒		
13	♒	10:44 am	♓
14	♓		
15	♓	10:11 pm	♈
16	♈		
17	♈		
18	♈	11:01 am	♉
19	♉		
20	♉	10:44 pm	♊
21	♊		
22	♊		
23	♊	8:07 am	♋
24	♋		
25	♋	3:14 pm	♌
26	♌		
27	♌	8:35 pm	♍
28	♍		
29	♍		
30	♍	12:32 am	♎

September

Day	Sign	Time	Enters
1	♑	3:03 am	♒
2	♒		
3	♒	11:26 am	♓
4	♓		
5	♓	10:00 pm	♈
6	♈		
7	♈		
8	♈	10:15 am	♉
9	♉		
10	♉	10:53 pm	♊
11	♊		
12	♊		
13	♊	9:56 am	♋
14	♋		
15	♋	5:41 pm	♌
16	♌		
17	♌	9:42 pm	♍
18	♍		
19	♍	10:52 pm	♎
20	♎		
21	♎	10:53 pm	♏
22	♏		
23	♏	11:36 pm	♐
24	♐		
25	♐		
26	♐	2:34 am	♑
27	♑		
28	♑	8:36 am	♒
29	♒		
30	♒	5:33 pm	♓

December

Day	Sign	Time	Enters
1	♉	5:53 pm	♊
2	♊		
3	♊		
4	♊	5:19 am	♋
5	♋		
6	♋	3:13 pm	♌
7	♌		
8	♌	11:03 pm	♍
9	♍		
10	♍		
11	♍	4:09 am	♎
12	♎		
13	♎	6:23 am	♏
14	♏		
15	♏	6:40 am	♐
16	♐		
17	♐	6:46 am	♑
18	♑		
19	♑	8:47 am	♒
20	♒		
21	♒	2:25 pm	♓
22	♓		
23	♓		
24	♓	12:02 am	♈
25	♈		
26	♈	12:19 pm	♉
27	♉		
28	♉		
29	♉	12:53 am	♊
30	♊		
31	♊	12:01 pm	♋

Your Starway to Love

♈ = Aries ♉ = Taurus ♊ = Gemini ♋ = Cancer ♌ = Leo ♍ = Virgo

1915

January

1	♋		
2	♋	9:12 pm	♌
3	♌		
4	♌		
5	♌	4:28 am	♍
6	♍		
7	♍	9:53 am	♎
8	♎		
9	♎	1:25 pm	♏
10	♏		
11	♏	3:25 pm	♐
12	♐		
13	♐	4:52 pm	♑
14	♑		
15	♑	7:17 pm	♒
16	♒		
17	♒		
18	♒	12:14 am	♓
19	♓		
20	♓	8:42 am	♈
21	♈		
22	♈	8:13 pm	♉
23	♉		
24	♉		
25	♉	8:48 am	♊
26	♊		
27	♊	8:08 pm	♋
28	♋		
29	♋		
30	♋	4:55 am	♌
31	♌		

February

1	♌	11:10 am	♍
2	♍		
3	♍	3:32 pm	♎
4	♎		
5	♎	6:48 pm	♏
6	♏		
7	♏	9:33 pm	♐
8	♐		
9	♐		
10	♐	12:25 am	♑
11	♑		
12	♑	4:09 am	♒
13	♒		
14	♒	9:40 am	♓
15	♓		
16	♓	5:46 pm	♈
17	♈		
18	♈		
19	♈	4:37 am	♉
20	♉		
21	♉	5:05 pm	♊
22	♊		
23	♊		
24	♊	4:57 am	♋
25	♋		
26	♋	2:11 pm	♌
27	♌		
28	♌	8:03 pm	♍

March

1	♍		
2	♍	11:15 pm	♎
3	♎		
4	♎		
5	♎	1:05 am	♏
6	♏		
7	♏	2:58 am	♐
8	♐		
9	♐	5:59 am	♑
10	♑		
11	♑	10:40 am	♒
12	♒		
13	♒	5:16 pm	♓
14	♓		
15	♓		
16	♓	1:55 am	♈
17	♈		
18	♈	12:38 pm	♉
19	♉		
20	♉		
21	♉	12:58 am	♊
22	♊		
23	♊	1:22 pm	♋
24	♋		
25	♋	11:38 pm	♌
26	♌		
27	♌		
28	♌	6:13 am	♍
29	♍		
30	♍	9:10 am	♎
31	♎		

April

1	♎	9:49 am	♏
2	♏		
3	♏	10:05 am	♐
4	♐		
5	♐	11:47 am	♑
6	♑		
7	♑	4:03 pm	♒
8	♒		
9	♒	11:08 pm	♓
10	♓		
11	♓		
12	♓	8:31 am	♈
13	♈		
14	♈	7:38 pm	♉
15	♉		
16	♉		
17	♉	7:57 am	♊
18	♊		
19	♊	8:36 pm	♋
20	♋		
21	♋		
22	♋	7:53 am	♌
23	♌		
24	♌	3:53 pm	♍
25	♍		
26	♍	7:47 pm	♎
27	♎		
28	♎	8:23 pm	♏
29	♏		
30	♏	7:37 pm	♐

May

1	♐		
2	♐	7:39 pm	♑
3	♑		
4	♑	10:23 pm	♒
5	♒		
6	♒		
7	♒	4:41 am	♓
8	♓		
9	♓	2:10 pm	♈
10	♈		
11	♈		
12	♈	1:40 am	♉
13	♉		
14	♉	2:09 pm	♊
15	♊		
16	♊		
17	♊	2:47 am	♋
18	♋		
19	♋	2:31 pm	♌
20	♌		
21	♌	11:47 pm	♍
22	♍		
23	♍		
24	♍	5:16 am	♎
25	♎		
26	♎	7:02 am	♏
27	♏		
28	♏	6:27 am	♐
29	♐		
30	♐	5:39 am	♑
31	♑		

June

1	♑	6:49 am	♒
2	♒		
3	♒	11:32 am	♓
4	♓		
5	♓	8:06 pm	♈
6	♈		
7	♈		
8	♈	7:30 am	♉
9	♉		
10	♉	8:06 pm	♊
11	♊		
12	♊		
13	♊	8:38 am	♋
14	♋		
15	♋	8:12 pm	♌
16	♌		
17	♌		
18	♌	5:53 am	♍
19	♍		
20	♍	12:39 pm	♎
21	♎		
22	♎	4:03 pm	♏
23	♏		
24	♏	4:45 pm	♐
25	♐		
26	♐	4:22 pm	♑
27	♑		
28	♑	4:54 pm	♒
29	♒		
30	♒	8:14 pm	♓

July

1	♓		
2	♓		
3	♓	3:24 am	♈
4	♈		
5	♈	2:01 pm	♉
6	♉		
7	♉		
8	♉	2:30 am	♊
9	♊		
10	♊	2:56 pm	♋
11	♋		
12	♋		
13	♋	2:06 am	♌
14	♌		
15	♌	11:22 am	♍
16	♍		
17	♍	6:21 pm	♎
18	♎		
19	♎	10:50 pm	♏
20	♏		
21	♏		
22	♏	1:06 am	♐
23	♐		
24	♐	2:03 am	♑
25	♑		
26	♑	3:10 am	♒
27	♒		
28	♒	6:04 am	♓
29	♓		
30	♓	12:06 pm	♈
31	♈		

August

1	♈	9:40 pm	♉
2	♉		
3	♉		
4	♉	9:43 am	♊
5	♊		
6	♊	10:11 pm	♋
7	♋		
8	♋		
9	♋	9:08 am	♌
10	♌		
11	♌	5:42 pm	♍
12	♍		
13	♍	11:55 pm	♎
14	♎		
15	♎		
16	♎	4:16 am	♏
17	♏		
18	♏	7:18 am	♐
19	♐		
20	♐	9:38 am	♑
21	♑		
22	♑	12:03 pm	♒
23	♒		
24	♒	3:35 pm	♓
25	♓		
26	♓	9:21 pm	♈
27	♈		
28	♈		
29	♈	6:08 am	♉
30	♉		
31	♉	5:38 pm	♊

September

1	♊		
2	♊		
3	♊	6:12 am	♋
4	♋		
5	♋	5:24 pm	♌
6	♌		
7	♌		
8	♌	1:42 am	♍
9	♍		
10	♍	7:00 am	♎
11	♎		
12	♎	10:14 am	♏
13	♏		
14	♏	12:41 pm	♐
15	♐		
16	♐	3:20 pm	♑
17	♑		
18	♑	6:49 pm	♒
19	♒		
20	♒	11:32 pm	♓
21	♓		
22	♓		
23	♓	5:55 am	♈
24	♈		
25	♈	2:35 pm	♉
26	♉		
27	♉		
28	♉	1:42 am	♊
29	♊		
30	♊	2:20 pm	♋

October

1	♋		
2	♋		
3	♋	2:13 am	♌
4	♌		
5	♌	11:04 am	♍
6	♍		
7	♍	4:09 pm	♎
8	♎		
9	♎	6:20 pm	♏
10	♏		
11	♏	7:21 pm	♐
12	♐		
13	♐	8:56 pm	♑
14	♑		
15	♑		
16	♑	12:15 am	♒
17	♒		
18	♒	5:38 am	♓
19	♓		
20	♓	12:57 pm	♈
21	♈		
22	♈	10:08 pm	♉
23	♉		
24	♉		
25	♉	9:15 am	♊
26	♊		
27	♊	9:53 pm	♋
28	♋		
29	♋		
30	♋	10:26 am	♌
31	♌		

November

1	♌	8:30 pm	♍
2	♍		
3	♍		
4	♍	2:29 am	♎
5	♎		
6	♎	4:37 am	♏
7	♏		
8	♏	4:36 am	♐
9	♐		
10	♐	4:33 am	♑
11	♑		
12	♑	6:22 am	♒
13	♒		
14	♒	11:05 am	♓
15	♓		
16	♓	6:40 pm	♈
17	♈		
18	♈		
19	♈	4:29 am	♉
20	♉		
21	♉	3:56 pm	♊
22	♊		
23	♊		
24	♊	4:34 am	♋
25	♋		
26	♋	5:23 pm	♌
27	♌		
28	♌		
29	♌	4:33 am	♍
30	♍		

December

1	♍	12:09 pm	♎
2	♎		
3	♎	3:33 pm	♏
4	♏		
5	♏	3:47 pm	♐
6	♐		
7	♐	2:53 pm	♑
8	♑		
9	♑	3:01 pm	♒
10	♒		
11	♒	5:57 pm	♓
12	♓		
13	♓		
14	♓	12:30 am	♈
15	♈		
16	♈	10:14 am	♉
17	♉		
18	♉	10:02 pm	♊
19	♊		
20	♊		
21	♊	10:44 am	♋
22	♋		
23	♋	11:23 pm	♌
24	♌		
25	♌		
26	♌	10:51 am	♍
27	♍		
28	♍	7:41 pm	♎
29	♎		
30	♎		
31	♎	12:55 am	♏

1916

Moon Movements

♎ = Libra ♏ = Scorpio ♐ = Sagittarius ♑ = Capricorn ♒ = Aquarius ♓ = Pisces

January

Day	Sign	Time	Enters
1	♏		
2	♏	2:43 am	♐
3	♐		
4	♐	2:25 am	♑
5	♑		
6	♑	1:58 am	♒
7	♒		
8	♒	3:21 am	♓
9	♓		
10	♓	8:07 am	♈
11	♈		
12	♈	4:43 pm	♉
13	♉		
14	♉		
15	♉	4:18 am	♊
16	♊		
17	♊	5:07 pm	♋
18	♋		
19	♋		
20	♋	5:33 am	♌
21	♌		
22	♌	4:32 pm	♍
23	♍		
24	♍		
25	♍	1:26 am	♎
26	♎		
27	♎	7:43 am	♏
28	♏		
29	♏	11:18 am	♐
30	♐		
31	♐	12:42 pm	♑

April

Day	Sign	Time	Enters
1	♓	12:48 pm	♈
2	♈		
3	♈	7:11 pm	♉
4	♉		
5	♉		
6	♉	4:19 am	♊
7	♊		
8	♊	4:11 pm	♋
9	♋		
10	♋		
11	♋	5:01 am	♌
12	♌		
13	♌	4:07 pm	♍
14	♍		
15	♍	11:40 pm	♎
16	♎		
17	♎		
18	♎	3:48 am	♏
19	♏		
20	♏	5:52 am	♐
21	♐		
22	♐	7:34 am	♑
23	♑		
24	♑	10:07 am	♒
25	♒		
26	♒	2:05 pm	♓
27	♓		
28	♓	7:35 pm	♈
29	♈		
30	♈		

July

Day	Sign	Time	Enters
1	♋		
2	♋	1:57 am	♌
3	♌		
4	♌	2:32 pm	♍
5	♍		
6	♍		
7	♍	1:06 am	♎
8	♎		
9	♎	8:16 am	♏
10	♏		
11	♏	11:43 am	♐
12	♐		
13	♐	12:20 pm	♑
14	♑		
15	♑	11:46 am	♒
16	♒		
17	♒	11:55 am	♓
18	♓		
19	♓	2:32 pm	♈
20	♈		
21	♈	8:46 pm	♉
22	♉		
23	♉		
24	♉	6:36 am	♊
25	♊		
26	♊	6:53 pm	♋
27	♋		
28	♋		
29	♋	7:56 am	♌
30	♌		
31	♌	8:18 pm	♍

October

Day	Sign	Time	Enters
1	♏	7:28 am	♐
2	♐		
3	♐	11:23 am	♑
4	♑		
5	♑	2:28 pm	♒
6	♒		
7	♒	5:00 pm	♓
8	♓		
9	♓	7:40 pm	♈
10	♈		
11	♈	11:45 pm	♉
12	♉		
13	♉		
14	♉	6:38 am	♊
15	♊		
16	♊	4:58 pm	♋
17	♋		
18	♋		
19	♋	5:40 am	♌
20	♌		
21	♌	6:03 pm	♍
22	♍		
23	♍		
24	♍	3:45 am	♎
25	♎		
26	♎	10:09 am	♏
27	♏		
28	♏	2:07 pm	♐
29	♐		
30	♐	5:00 pm	♑
31	♑		

February

Day	Sign	Time	Enters
1	♑		
2	♑	1:09 pm	♒
3	♒		
4	♒	2:16 pm	♓
5	♓		
6	♓	5:45 pm	♈
7	♈		
8	♈		
9	♈	12:50 am	♉
10	♉		
11	♉	11:30 am	♊
12	♊		
13	♊		
14	♊	12:13 pm	♋
15	♋		
16	♋	12:38 pm	♌
17	♌		
18	♌	11:08 pm	♍
19	♍		
20	♍		
21	♍	7:13 am	♎
22	♎		
23	♎	1:09 pm	♏
24	♏		
25	♏	5:20 pm	♐
26	♐		
27	♐	8:13 pm	♑
28	♑		
29	♑	10:18 pm	♒

May

Day	Sign	Time	Enters
1	♈	2:49 am	♉
2	♉		
3	♉	12:12 pm	♊
4	♊		
5	♊	11:53 pm	♋
6	♋		
7	♋		
8	♋	12:51 pm	♌
9	♌		
10	♌		
11	♌	12:45 am	♍
12	♍		
13	♍	9:15 am	♎
14	♎		
15	♎	1:42 pm	♏
16	♏		
17	♏	3:09 pm	♐
18	♐		
19	♐	3:30 pm	♑
20	♑		
21	♑	4:33 pm	♒
22	♒		
23	♒	7:35 pm	♓
24	♓		
25	♓		
26	♓	1:03 am	♈
27	♈		
28	♈	8:54 am	♉
29	♉		
30	♉	6:53 pm	♊
31	♊		

August

Day	Sign	Time	Enters
1	♍		
2	♍		
3	♍	6:54 am	♎
4	♎		
5	♎	2:56 pm	♏
6	♏		
7	♏	7:56 pm	♐
8	♐		
9	♐	10:08 pm	♑
10	♑		
11	♑	10:28 pm	♒
12	♒		
13	♒	10:29 pm	♓
14	♓		
15	♓		
16	♓	12:02 am	♈
17	♈		
18	♈	4:45 am	♉
19	♉		
20	♉	1:27 pm	♊
21	♊		
22	♊		
23	♊	1:21 am	♋
24	♋		
25	♋	2:24 pm	♌
26	♌		
27	♌		
28	♌	2:29 am	♍
29	♍		
30	♍	12:34 pm	♎
31	♎		

November

Day	Sign	Time	Enters
1	♑	7:50 pm	♒
2	♒		
3	♒	11:04 pm	♓
4	♓		
5	♓		
6	♓	2:59 am	♈
7	♈		
8	♈	8:07 am	♉
9	♉		
10	♉	3:19 pm	♊
11	♊		
12	♊		
13	♊	1:19 am	♋
14	♋		
15	♋	1:44 pm	♌
16	♌		
17	♌		
18	♌	2:33 pm	♍
19	♍		
20	♍	1:03 pm	♎
21	♎		
22	♎	7:48 pm	♏
23	♏		
24	♏	11:12 pm	♐
25	♐		
26	♐		
27	♐	12:45 am	♑
28	♑		
29	♑	2:06 am	♒
30	♒		

March

Day	Sign	Time	Enters
1	♒		
2	♒		
3	♒	12:27 am	♓
4	♓		
5	♓	3:56 am	♈
6	♈		
7	♈	10:08 am	♉
8	♉		
9	♉	7:46 pm	♊
10	♊		
11	♊		
12	♊	8:03 am	♋
13	♋		
14	♋	8:41 pm	♌
15	♌		
16	♌		
17	♌	7:12 am	♍
18	♍		
19	♍	2:37 pm	♎
20	♎		
21	♎	7:26 pm	♏
22	♏		
23	♏	10:48 pm	♐
24	♐		
25	♐		
26	♐	1:43 am	♑
27	♑		
28	♑	4:47 am	♒
29	♒		
30	♒	8:18 am	♓
31	♓		

June

Day	Sign	Time	Enters
1	♊		
2	♊	6:46 am	♋
3	♋		
4	♋	7:47 pm	♌
5	♋		
6	♌		
7	♌	8:15 am	♍
8	♍		
9	♍	5:59 pm	♎
10	♎		
11	♎	11:40 pm	♏
12	♏		
13	♏		
14	♏	1:40 am	♐
15	♐		
16	♐	1:33 am	♑
17	♑		
18	♑	1:16 am	♒
19	♒		
20	♒	2:39 am	♓
21	♓		
22	♓	6:55 am	♈
23	♈		
24	♈	2:26 pm	♉
25	♉		
26	♉		
27	♉	12:43 am	♊
28	♊		
29	♊	12:55 pm	♋
30	♋		

September

Day	Sign	Time	Enters
1	♎	8:24 pm	♏
2	♏		
3	♏		
4	♏	2:05 am	♐
5	♐		
6	♐	5:44 am	♑
7	♑		
8	♑	7:39 am	♒
9	♒		
10	♒	8:42 am	♓
11	♓		
12	♓	10:17 am	♈
13	♈		
14	♈	2:09 pm	♉
15	♉		
16	♉	9:38 pm	♊
17	♊		
18	♊		
19	♊	8:45 am	♋
20	♋		
21	♋	9:41 pm	♌
22	♌		
23	♌		
24	♌	9:46 am	♍
25	♍		
26	♍	7:22 pm	♎
27	♎		
28	♎		
29	♎	2:21 am	♏
30	♏		

December

Day	Sign	Time	Enters
1	♒	4:29 am	♓
2	♓		
3	♓	8:34 am	♈
4	♈		
5	♈	2:35 pm	♉
6	♉		
7	♉	10:40 pm	♊
8	♊		
9	♊		
10	♊	9:00 am	♋
11	♋		
12	♋	9:18 pm	♌
13	♌		
14	♌		
15	♌	10:19 am	♍
16	♍		
17	♍	9:50 pm	♎
18	♎		
19	♎		
20	♎	5:52 am	♏
21	♏		
22	♏	9:58 am	♐
23	♐		
24	♐	11:07 am	♑
25	♑		
26	♑	11:05 am	♒
27	♒		
28	♒	11:41 am	♓
29	♓		
30	♓	2:25 pm	♈
31	♈		

Your Starway to Love

♈ = Aries ♉ = Taurus ♊ = Gemini ♋ = Cancer ♌ = Leo ♍ = Virgo

1917

January

1	♈	8:04 pm	♉
2	♉		
3	♉		
4	♉	4:39 am	♊
5	♊		
6	♊	3:35 pm	♋
7	♋		
8	♋		
9	♋	4:03 am	♌
10	♌		
11	♌	5:01 pm	♍
12	♍		
13	♍		
14	♍	5:04 am	♎
15	♎		
16	♎	2:32 pm	♏
17	♏		
18	♏	8:17 pm	♐
19	♐		
20	♐	10:28 pm	♑
21	♑		
22	♑	10:19 pm	♒
23	♒		
24	♒	9:41 pm	♓
25	♓		
26	♓	10:33 pm	♈
27	♈		
28	♈		
29	♈	2:34 am	♉
30	♉		
31	♉	10:26 am	♊

February

1	♊		
2	♊	9:31 pm	♋
3	♋		
4	♋		
5	♋	10:16 am	♌
6	♌		
7	♌	11:09 pm	♍
8	♍		
9	♍		
10	♍	11:04 am	♎
11	♎		
12	♎	9:06 pm	♏
13	♏		
14	♏		
15	♏	4:23 am	♐
16	♐		
17	♐	8:24 am	♑
18	♑		
19	♑	9:32 am	♒
20	♒		
21	♒	9:06 am	♓
22	♓		
23	♓	9:00 am	♈
24	♈		
25	♈	11:19 am	♉
26	♉		
27	♉	5:34 pm	♊
28	♊		

March

1	♊		
2	♊	3:52 am	♋
3	♋		
4	♋	4:36 pm	♌
5	♌		
6	♌		
7	♌	5:29 am	♍
8	♍		
9	♍	5:01 pm	♎
10	♎		
11	♎		
12	♎	2:40 am	♏
13	♏		
14	♏	10:18 am	♐
15	♐		
16	♐	3:38 pm	♑
17	♑		
18	♑	6:32 pm	♒
19	♒		
20	♒	7:31 pm	♓
21	♓		
22	♓	7:53 pm	♈
23	♈		
24	♈	9:35 pm	♉
25	♉		
26	♉		
27	♉	2:28 am	♊
28	♊		
29	♊	11:28 am	♋
30	♋		
31	♋	11:39 pm	♌

April

1	♌		
2	♌		
3	♌	12:32 pm	♍
4	♍		
5	♍	11:54 pm	♎
6	♎		
7	♎		
8	♎	8:54 am	♏
9	♏		
10	♏	3:50 pm	♐
11	♐		
12	♐	9:08 pm	♑
13	♑		
14	♑		
15	♑	12:56 am	♒
16	♒		
17	♒	3:25 am	♓
18	♓		
19	♓	5:10 am	♈
20	♈		
21	♈	7:31 am	♉
22	♉		
23	♉	12:04 pm	♊
24	♊		
25	♊	8:07 pm	♋
26	♋		
27	♋		
28	♋	7:31 am	♌
29	♌		
30	♌	8:19 pm	♍

May

1	♍		
2	♍		
3	♍	7:52 am	♎
4	♎		
5	♎	4:39 pm	♏
6	♏		
7	♏	10:44 pm	♐
8	♐		
9	♐		
10	♐	3:00 am	♑
11	♑		
12	♑	6:18 am	♒
13	♒		
14	♒	9:11 am	♓
15	♓		
16	♓	12:04 pm	♈
17	♈		
18	♈	3:38 pm	♉
19	♉		
20	♉	8:53 pm	♊
21	♊		
22	♊		
23	♊	4:49 am	♋
24	♋		
25	♋	3:42 pm	♌
26	♌		
27	♌		
28	♌	4:21 am	♍
29	♍		
30	♍	4:20 pm	♎
31	♎		

June

1	♎		
2	♎	1:34 am	♏
3	♏		
4	♏	7:27 am	♐
5	♐		
6	♐	10:45 am	♑
7	♑		
8	♑	12:45 pm	♒
9	♒		
10	♒	2:42 pm	♓
11	♓		
12	♓	5:31 pm	♈
13	♈		
14	♈	9:48 pm	♉
15	♉		
16	♉		
17	♉	4:02 am	♊
18	♊		
19	♊	12:33 pm	♋
20	♋		
21	♋	11:27 pm	♌
22	♌		
23	♌		
24	♌	11:59 am	♍
25	♍		
26	♍		
27	♍	12:26 am	♎
28	♎		
29	♎	10:37 am	♏
30	♏		

July

1	♏	5:14 pm	♐
2	♐		
3	♐	8:25 pm	♑
4	♑		
5	♑	9:25 pm	♒
6	♒		
7	♒	9:53 pm	♓
8	♓		
9	♓	11:25 pm	♈
10	♈		
11	♈		
12	♈	3:13 am	♉
13	♉		
14	♉	9:47 am	♊
15	♊		
16	♊	7:00 pm	♋
17	♋		
18	♋		
19	♋	6:17 am	♌
20	♌		
21	♌	6:51 pm	♍
22	♍		
23	♍		
24	♍	7:33 am	♎
25	♎		
26	♎	6:40 pm	♏
27	♏		
28	♏		
29	♏	2:38 am	♐
30	♐		
31	♐	6:48 am	♑

August

1	♑		
2	♑	7:49 am	♒
3	♒		
4	♒	7:20 am	♓
5	♓		
6	♓	7:18 am	♈
7	♈		
8	♈	9:36 am	♉
9	♉		
10	♉	3:24 pm	♊
11	♊		
12	♊		
13	♊	12:39 am	♋
14	♋		
15	♋	12:19 pm	♌
16	♌		
17	♌		
18	♌	1:02 am	♍
19	♍		
20	♍	1:42 pm	♎
21	♎		
22	♎		
23	♎	1:16 am	♏
24	♏		
25	♏	10:28 am	♐
26	♐		
27	♐	4:15 pm	♑
28	♑		
29	♑	6:27 pm	♒
30	♒		
31	♒	6:11 pm	♓

September

1	♓		
2	♓	5:20 pm	♈
3	♈		
4	♈	6:06 pm	♉
5	♉		
6	♉	10:19 pm	♊
7	♊		
8	♊		
9	♊	6:40 am	♋
10	♋		
11	♋	6:13 pm	♌
12	♌		
13	♌		
14	♌	7:02 am	♍
15	♍		
16	♍	7:33 pm	♎
17	♎		
18	♎		
19	♎	6:55 am	♏
20	♏		
21	♏	4:32 pm	♐
22	♐		
23	♐	11:37 pm	♑
24	♑		
25	♑		
26	♑	3:33 am	♒
27	♒		
28	♒	4:39 am	♓
29	♓		
30	♓	4:15 am	♈

October

1	♈		
2	♈	4:25 am	♉
3	♉		
4	♉	7:14 am	♊
5	♊		
6	♊	2:06 pm	♋
7	♋		
8	♋		
9	♋	12:50 am	♌
10	♌		
11	♌	1:32 pm	♍
12	♍		
13	♍		
14	♍	1:58 am	♎
15	♎		
16	♎	12:53 pm	♏
17	♏		
18	♏	10:00 pm	♐
19	♐		
20	♐		
21	♐	5:14 am	♑
22	♑		
23	♑	10:16 am	♒
24	♒		
25	♒	1:03 pm	♓
26	♓		
27	♓	2:08 pm	♈
28	♈		
29	♈	2:59 pm	♉
30	♉		
31	♉	5:26 pm	♊

November

1	♊		
2	♊	11:09 pm	♋
3	♋		
4	♋		
5	♋	8:42 am	♌
6	♌		
7	♌	8:56 pm	♍
8	♍		
9	♍		
10	♍	9:26 am	♎
11	♎		
12	♎	8:13 pm	♏
13	♏		
14	♏		
15	♏	4:36 am	♐
16	♐		
17	♐	10:55 am	♑
18	♑		
19	♑	3:38 pm	♒
20	♒		
21	♒	7:04 pm	♓
22	♓		
23	♓	9:35 pm	♈
24	♈		
25	♈	11:55 pm	♉
26	♉		
27	♉		
28	♉	3:13 am	♊
29	♊		
30	♊	8:48 am	♋

December

1	♋		
2	♋	5:32 pm	♌
3	♌		
4	♌		
5	♌	5:07 am	♍
6	♍		
7	♍	5:42 pm	♎
8	♎		
9	♎		
10	♎	4:52 am	♏
11	♏		
12	♏	1:10 pm	♐
13	♐		
14	♐	6:35 pm	♑
15	♑		
16	♑	9:59 pm	♒
17	♒		
18	♒		
19	♒	12:31 am	♓
20	♓		
21	♓	3:06 am	♈
22	♈		
23	♈	6:26 am	♉
24	♉		
25	♉	11:03 am	♊
26	♊		
27	♊	5:29 pm	♋
28	♋		
29	♋		
30	♋	2:15 am	♌
31	♌		

Moon Movements

♎ = Libra ♏ = Scorpio ♐ = Sagittarius ♑ = Capricorn ♒ = Aquarius ♓ = Pisces

1918

January

1	♌	1:23 pm	♍
2	♍		
3	♍		
4	♍	1:56 am	♎
5	♎		
6	♎	1:50 pm	♏
7	♏		
8	♏	10:58 pm	♐
9	♐		
10	♐		
11	♐	4:27 am	♑
12	♑		
13	♑	6:55 am	♒
14	♒		
15	♒	7:54 am	♓
16	♓		
17	♓	9:03 am	♈
18	♈		
19	♈	11:48 am	♉
20	♉		
21	♉	4:52 pm	♊
22	♊		
23	♊		
24	♊	12:17 am	♋
25	♋		
26	♋	9:45 am	♌
27	♌		
28	♌	8:59 pm	♍
29	♍		
30	♍		
31	♍	9:26 am	♎

February

1	♎		
2	♎	9:52 pm	♏
3	♏		
4	♏		
5	♏	8:15 am	♐
6	♐		
7	♐	2:57 pm	♑
8	♑		
9	♑	5:46 pm	♒
10	♒		
11	♒	5:57 pm	♓
12	♓		
13	♓	5:31 pm	♈
14	♈		
15	♈	6:31 pm	♉
16	♉		
17	♉	10:29 pm	♊
18	♊		
19	♊		
20	♊	5:50 am	♋
21	♋		
22	♋	3:53 pm	♌
23	♌		
24	♌		
25	♌	3:33 am	♍
26	♍		
27	♍	4:01 pm	♎
28	♎		

March

1	♎		
2	♎	4:32 am	♏
3	♏		
4	♏	3:47 pm	♐
5	♐		
6	♐		
7	♐	12:05 am	♑
8	♑		
9	♑	4:23 am	♒
10	♒		
11	♒	5:12 am	♓
12	♓		
13	♓	4:15 am	♈
14	♈		
15	♈	3:48 am	♉
16	♉		
17	♉	5:57 am	♊
18	♊		
19	♊	11:58 am	♋
20	♋		
21	♋	9:37 pm	♌
22	♌		
23	♌		
24	♌	9:30 am	♍
25	♍		
26	♍	10:07 pm	♎
27	♎		
28	♎		
29	♎	10:28 am	♏
30	♏		
31	♏	9:47 pm	♐

April

1	♐		
2	♐		
3	♐	6:59 am	♑
4	♑		
5	♑	12:56 pm	♒
6	♒		
7	♒	3:22 pm	♓
8	♓		
9	♓	3:18 pm	♈
10	♈		
11	♈	2:40 pm	♉
12	♉		
13	♉	3:37 pm	♊
14	♊		
15	♊	7:57 pm	♋
16	♋		
17	♋		
18	♋	4:19 am	♌
19	♌		
20	♌	3:46 pm	♍
21	♍		
22	♍		
23	♍	4:25 am	♎
24	♎		
25	♎	4:37 pm	♏
26	♏		
27	♏		
28	♏	3:30 am	♐
29	♐		
30	♐	12:33 pm	♑

May

1	♑		
2	♑	7:12 pm	♒
3	♒		
4	♒	11:07 pm	♓
5	♓		
6	♓		
7	♓	12:41 am	♈
8	♈		
9	♈	1:05 am	♉
10	♉		
11	♉	2:06 am	♊
12	♊		
13	♊	5:31 am	♋
14	♋		
15	♋	12:31 pm	♌
16	♌		
17	♌	11:00 pm	♍
18	♍		
19	♍		
20	♍	11:25 am	♎
21	♎		
22	♎	11:38 pm	♏
23	♏		
24	♏		
25	♏	10:08 am	♐
26	♐		
27	♐	6:27 pm	♑
28	♑		
29	♑		
30	♑	12:38 am	♒
31	♒		

June

1	♒	4:53 am	♓
2	♓		
3	♓	7:37 am	♈
4	♈		
5	♈	9:30 am	♉
6	♉		
7	♉	11:36 am	♊
8	♊		
9	♊	3:14 pm	♋
10	♋		
11	♋	9:35 pm	♌
12	♌		
13	♌		
14	♌	7:10 am	♍
15	♍		
16	♍	7:10 pm	♎
17	♎		
18	♎		
19	♎	7:30 am	♏
20	♏		
21	♏	6:04 pm	♐
22	♐		
23	♐		
24	♐	1:51 am	♑
25	♑		
26	♑	7:01 am	♒
27	♒		
28	♒	10:26 am	♓
29	♓		
30	♓	1:04 pm	♈

July

1	♈		
2	♈	3:44 pm	♉
3	♉		
4	♉	7:04 pm	♊
5	♊		
6	♊	11:42 pm	♋
7	♋		
8	♋		
9	♋	6:20 am	♌
10	♌		
11	♌	3:33 pm	♍
12	♍		
13	♍		
14	♍	3:09 am	♎
15	♎		
16	♎	3:41 pm	♏
17	♏		
18	♏		
19	♏	2:49 am	♐
20	♐		
21	♐	10:46 am	♑
22	♑		
23	♑	3:19 pm	♒
24	♒		
25	♒	5:32 pm	♓
26	♓		
27	♓	6:59 pm	♈
28	♈		
29	♈	9:06 pm	♉
30	♉		
31	♉		

August

1	♉	12:48 am	♊
2	♊		
3	♊	6:21 am	♋
4	♋		
5	♋	1:49 pm	♌
6	♌		
7	♌	11:17 pm	♍
8	♍		
9	♍		
10	♍	10:45 am	♎
11	♎		
12	♎	11:27 pm	♏
13	♏		
14	♏		
15	♏	11:22 am	♐
16	♐		
17	♐	8:17 pm	♑
18	♑		
19	♑		
20	♑	1:11 am	♒
21	♒		
22	♒	2:48 am	♓
23	♓		
24	♓	2:56 am	♈
25	♈		
26	♈	3:35 am	♉
27	♉		
28	♉	6:19 am	♊
29	♊		
30	♊	11:50 am	♋
31	♋		

September

1	♋	7:53 pm	♌
2	♌		
3	♌		
4	♌	5:56 am	♍
5	♍		
6	♍	5:35 pm	♎
7	♎		
8	♎		
9	♎	6:19 am	♏
10	♏		
11	♏	6:50 pm	♐
12	♐		
13	♐		
14	♐	5:02 am	♑
15	♑		
16	♑	11:15 am	♒
17	♒		
18	♒	1:26 pm	♓
19	♓		
20	♓	1:07 pm	♈
21	♈		
22	♈	12:27 pm	♉
23	♉		
24	♉	1:31 pm	♊
25	♊		
26	♊	5:45 pm	♋
27	♋		
28	♋		
29	♋	1:25 am	♌
30	♌		

October

1	♌	11:46 am	♍
2	♍		
3	♍	11:43 pm	♎
4	♎		
5	♎		
6	♎	12:28 pm	♏
7	♏		
8	♏		
9	♏	1:04 am	♐
10	♐		
11	♐	12:06 pm	♑
12	♑		
13	♑	7:54 pm	♒
14	♒		
15	♒	11:42 pm	♓
16	♓		
17	♓		
18	♓	12:14 am	♈
19	♈	11:20 pm	♉
20	♉		
21	♉	11:10 pm	♊
22	♊		
23	♊		
24	♊	1:40 am	♋
25	♋		
26	♋	7:54 am	♌
27	♌		
28	♌	5:42 pm	♍
29	♍		
30	♍		
31	♍	5:45 am	♎

November

1	♎		
2	♎	6:31 pm	♏
3	♏		
4	♏		
5	♏	6:52 am	♐
6	♐		
7	♐	5:50 pm	♑
8	♑		
9	♑		
10	♑	2:25 am	♒
11	♒		
12	♒	7:52 am	♓
13	♓		
14	♓	10:11 am	♈
15	♈		
16	♈	10:26 am	♉
17	♉		
18	♉	10:20 am	♊
19	♊		
20	♊	11:46 am	♋
21	♋		
22	♋	4:23 pm	♌
23	♌		
24	♌		
25	♌	12:50 am	♍
26	♍		
27	♍	12:25 pm	♎
28	♎		
29	♎		
30	♎	1:13 am	♏

December

1	♏		
2	♏	1:20 pm	♐
3	♐		
4	♐	11:41 pm	♑
5	♑		
6	♑		
7	♑	7:52 am	♒
8	♒		
9	♒	1:47 pm	♓
10	♓		
11	♓	5:33 pm	♈
12	♈		
13	♈	7:35 pm	♉
14	♉		
15	♉	8:49 pm	♊
16	♊		
17	♊	10:35 pm	♋
18	♋		
19	♋		
20	♋	2:25 am	♌
21	♌		
22	♌	9:33 am	♍
23	♍		
24	♍	8:10 pm	♎
25	♎		
26	♎		
27	♎	8:49 am	♏
28	♏		
29	♏	9:03 pm	♐
30	♐		
31	♐		

1919

Your Starway to Love

♈ = Aries ♉ = Taurus ♊ = Gemini ♋ = Cancer ♌ = Leo ♍ = Virgo

January

1	♐	7:01 am	♑
2	♑		
3	♑	2:15 pm	♒
4	♒		
5	♒	7:18 pm	♓
6	♓		
7	♓	11:00 pm	♈
8	♈		
9	♈		
10	♈	2:01 am	♉
11	♉		
12	♉	4:49 am	♊
13	♊		
14	♊	7:56 am	♋
15	♋		
16	♋	12:16 pm	♌
17	♌		
18	♌	6:57 pm	♍
19	♍		
20	♍		
21	♍	4:43 am	♎
22	♎		
23	♎	5:00 pm	♏
24	♏		
25	♏		
26	♏	5:35 am	♐
27	♐		
28	♐	3:54 pm	♑
29	♑		
30	♑	10:44 pm	♒
31	♒		

April

1	♈	11:40 pm	♉
2	♉		
3	♉	11:56 pm	♊
4	♊		
5	♊		
6	♊	2:22 am	♋
7	♋		
8	♋	7:48 am	♌
9	♌		
10	♌	4:07 pm	♍
11	♍		
12	♍		
13	♍	2:43 am	♎
14	♎		
15	♎	2:54 pm	♏
16	♏		
17	♏		
18	♏	3:52 am	♐
19	♐		
20	♐	4:14 pm	♑
21	♑		
22	♑		
23	♑	2:09 am	♒
24	♒		
25	♒	8:17 am	♓
26	♓		
27	♓	10:40 am	♈
28	♈		
29	♈	10:36 am	♉
30	♉		

July

1	♌	2:06 pm	♍
2	♍		
3	♍	10:34 pm	♎
4	♎		
5	♎		
6	♎	10:18 am	♏
7	♏		
8	♏	11:13 pm	♐
9	♐		
10	♐		
11	♐	10:56 am	♑
12	♑		
13	♑	8:14 pm	♒
14	♒		
15	♒		
16	♒	3:06 am	♓
17	♓		
18	♓	8:06 am	♈
19	♈		
20	♈	11:43 am	♉
21	♉		
22	♉	2:19 pm	♊
23	♊		
24	♊	4:25 pm	♋
25	♋		
26	♋	7:00 pm	♌
27	♌		
28	♌	11:28 pm	♍
29	♍		
30	♍		
31	♍	7:06 am	♎

October

1	♐	11:28 am	♑
2	♑		
3	♑	10:03 pm	♒
4	♒		
5	♒		
6	♒	4:44 am	♓
7	♓		
8	♓	7:44 am	♈
9	♈		
10	♈	8:32 am	♉
11	♉		
12	♉	8:59 am	♊
13	♊		
14	♊	10:39 am	♋
15	♋		
16	♋	2:32 pm	♌
17	♌		
18	♌	8:58 pm	♍
19	♍		
20	♍		
21	♍	5:51 am	♎
22	♎		
23	♎	4:52 pm	♏
24	♏		
25	♏		
26	♏	5:31 am	♐
27	♐		
28	♐	6:34 pm	♑
29	♑		
30	♑		
31	♑	6:08 am	♒

February

1	♒		
2	♒	2:38 pm	♓
3	♓		
4	♓	5:02 am	♈
5	♈		
6	♈	7:22 am	♉
7	♉		
8	♉	10:31 am	♊
9	♊		
10	♊	2:46 pm	♋
11	♋		
12	♋	8:17 pm	♌
13	♌		
14	♌		
15	♌	3:32 am	♍
16	♍		
17	♍	1:07 pm	♎
18	♎		
19	♎		
20	♎	1:04 am	♏
21	♏		
22	♏	1:57 pm	♐
23	♐		
24	♐		
25	♐	1:08 am	♑
26	♑		
27	♑	8:36 am	♒
28	♒		

May

1	♉	10:00 am	♊
2	♊		
3	♊	10:51 am	♋
4	♋		
5	♋	2:38 pm	♌
6	♌		
7	♌	10:01 pm	♍
8	♍		
9	♍		
10	♍	8:32 am	♎
11	♎		
12	♎	8:57 pm	♏
13	♏		
14	♏		
15	♏	9:54 am	♐
16	♐		
17	♐	10:06 pm	♑
18	♑		
19	♑		
20	♑	8:23 am	♒
21	♒		
22	♒	3:45 pm	♓
23	♓		
24	♓	7:47 pm	♈
25	♈		
26	♈	9:02 pm	♉
27	♉		
28	♉	8:53 pm	♊
29	♊		
30	♊	9:05 pm	♋
31	♋		

August

1	♎		
2	♎	6:08 pm	♏
3	♏		
4	♏		
5	♏	6:57 am	♐
6	♐		
7	♐	6:52 pm	♑
8	♑		
9	♑		
10	♑	3:56 am	♒
11	♒		
12	♒	9:59 am	♓
13	♓		
14	♓	1:59 pm	♈
15	♈		
16	♈	5:05 pm	♉
17	♉		
18	♉	8:03 pm	♊
19	♊		
20	♊	11:14 pm	♋
21	♋		
22	♋		
23	♋	3:00 am	♌
24	♌		
25	♌	8:08 am	♍
26	♍		
27	♍	3:41 pm	♎
28	♎		
29	♎		
30	♎	2:15 am	♏
31	♏		

November

1	♒		
2	♒	2:19 pm	♓
3	♓		
4	♓	6:30 pm	♈
5	♈		
6	♈	7:31 pm	♉
7	♉		
8	♉	7:03 pm	♊
9	♊		
10	♊	7:03 pm	♋
11	♋		
12	♋	9:14 pm	♌
13	♌		
14	♌		
15	♌	2:41 am	♍
16	♍		
17	♍	11:32 am	♎
18	♎		
19	♎	10:58 pm	♏
20	♏		
21	♏		
22	♏	11:47 am	♐
23	♐		
24	♐		
25	♐	12:45 am	♑
26	♑		
27	♑	12:37 pm	♒
28	♒		
29	♒	10:03 pm	♓
30	♓		

March

1	♒	12:14 pm	♓
2	♓		
3	♓	1:28 pm	♈
4	♈		
5	♈	2:14 pm	♉
6	♉		
7	♉	4:10 pm	♊
8	♊		
9	♊	8:09 pm	♋
10	♋		
11	♋		
12	♋	2:18 am	♌
13	♌		
14	♌	10:26 am	♍
15	♍		
16	♍	8:29 pm	♎
17	♎		
18	♎		
19	♎	8:25 am	♏
20	♏		
21	♏	9:23 pm	♐
22	♐		
23	♐		
24	♐	9:25 am	♑
25	♑		
26	♑	6:11 pm	♒
27	♒		
28	♒	10:45 pm	♓
29	♓		
30	♓	11:57 pm	♈
31	♈		

June

1	♋	11:26 pm	♌
2	♌		
3	♌		
4	♌	5:18 am	♍
5	♍		
6	♍	2:58 pm	♎
7	♎		
8	♎		
9	♎	3:15 am	♏
10	♏		
11	♏	4:12 pm	♐
12	♐		
13	♐		
14	♐	4:04 am	♑
15	♑		
16	♑	1:58 pm	♒
17	♒		
18	♒	9:31 pm	♓
19	♓		
20	♓		
21	♓	2:38 am	♈
22	♈		
23	♈	5:29 am	♉
24	♉		
25	♉	6:42 am	♊
26	♊		
27	♊	7:28 am	♋
28	♋		
29	♋	9:24 am	♌
30	♌		

September

1	♏	2:58 pm	♐
2	♐		
3	♐		
4	♐	3:21 am	♑
5	♑		
6	♑	12:54 pm	♒
7	♒		
8	♒	6:45 pm	♓
9	♓		
10	♓	9:48 pm	♈
11	♈		
12	♈	11:35 pm	♉
13	♉		
14	♉		
15	♉	1:35 am	♊
16	♊		
17	♊	4:39 am	♋
18	♋		
19	♋	9:08 am	♌
20	♌		
21	♌	3:15 pm	♍
22	♍		
23	♍	11:24 pm	♎
24	♎		
25	♎		
26	♎	9:59 am	♏
27	♏		
28	♏	10:36 pm	♐
29	♐		
30	♐		

December

1	♓		
2	♓	4:02 am	♈
3	♈		
4	♈	6:33 am	♉
5	♉		
6	♉	6:36 am	♊
7	♊		
8	♊	5:54 am	♋
9	♋		
10	♋	6:28 am	♌
11	♌		
12	♌	10:06 am	♍
13	♍		
14	♍	5:47 pm	♎
15	♎		
16	♎		
17	♎	5:01 am	♏
18	♏		
19	♏	5:59 pm	♐
20	♐		
21	♐		
22	♐	6:49 am	♑
23	♑		
24	♑	6:20 pm	♒
25	♒		
26	♒		
27	♒	3:55 am	♓
28	♓		
29	♓	11:06 am	♈
30	♈		
31	♈	3:28 pm	♉

Moon Movements

♎ = Libra ♏ = Scorpio ♐ = Sagittarius ♑ = Capricorn ♒ = Aquarius ♓ = Pisces

1920

January

1	♉		
2	♉	5:13 pm	♊
3	♊		
4	♊	5:19 pm	♋
5	♋		
6	♋	5:30 pm	♌
7	♌		
8	♌	7:46 pm	♍
9	♍		
10	♍		
11	♍	1:47 am	♎
12	♎		
13	♎	11:57 am	♏
14	♏		
15	♏		
16	♏	12:43 am	♐
17	♐		
18	♐	1:34 pm	♑
19	♑		
20	♑		
21	♑	12:39 am	♒
22	♒		
23	♒	9:34 am	♓
24	♓		
25	♓	4:32 pm	♈
26	♈		
27	♈	9:43 pm	♉
28	♉		
29	♉		
30	♉	1:05 am	♊
31	♊		

February

1	♊	2:54 am	♋
2	♋		
3	♋	4:05 am	♌
4	♌		
5	♌	6:18 am	♍
6	♍		
7	♍	11:19 am	♎
8	♎		
9	♎	8:13 pm	♏
10	♏		
11	♏		
12	♏	8:21 am	♐
13	♐		
14	♐	9:14 pm	♑
15	♑		
16	♑		
17	♑	8:20 am	♒
18	♒		
19	♒	4:39 pm	♓
20	♓		
21	♓	10:36 pm	♈
22	♈		
23	♈		
24	♈	3:06 am	♉
25	♉		
26	♉	6:42 am	♊
27	♊		
28	♊	9:40 am	♋
29	♋		

March

1	♋	12:22 pm	♌
2	♌		
3	♌	3:40 pm	♍
4	♍		
5	♍	8:53 pm	♎
6	♎		
7	♎		
8	♎	5:10 am	♏
9	♏		
10	♏	4:35 pm	♐
11	♐		
12	♐		
13	♐	5:25 am	♑
14	♑		
15	♑	4:58 pm	♒
16	♒		
17	♒		
18	♒	1:25 am	♓
19	♓		
20	♓	6:43 am	♈
21	♈		
22	♈	9:58 am	♉
23	♉		
24	♉	12:25 pm	♊
25	♊		
26	♊	3:02 pm	♋
27	♋		
28	♋	6:20 pm	♌
29	♌		
30	♌	10:48 pm	♍
31	♍		

April

1	♍		
2	♍	4:59 am	♎
3	♎		
4	♎	1:34 pm	♏
5	♏		
6	♏		
7	♏	12:42 am	♐
8	♐		
9	♐	1:25 pm	♑
10	♑		
11	♑		
12	♑	1:32 am	♒
13	♒		
14	♒	10:50 am	♓
15	♓		
16	♓	4:29 pm	♈
17	♈		
18	♈	7:08 pm	♉
19	♉		
20	♉	8:14 pm	♊
21	♊		
22	♊	9:22 pm	♋
23	♋		
24	♋	11:48 pm	♌
25	♌		
26	♌		
27	♌	4:21 am	♍
28	♍		
29	♍	11:18 am	♎
30	♎		

May

1	♎	8:37 pm	♏
2	♏		
3	♏		
4	♏	7:59 am	♐
5	♐		
6	♐	8:39 pm	♑
7	♑		
8	♑		
9	♑	9:09 am	♒
10	♒		
11	♒	7:32 pm	♓
12	♓		
13	♓		
14	♓	2:23 am	♈
15	♈		
16	♈	5:35 am	♉
17	♉		
18	♉	6:13 am	♊
19	♊		
20	♊	6:01 am	♋
21	♋		
22	♋	6:49 am	♌
23	♌		
24	♌	10:10 am	♍
25	♍		
26	♍	4:50 pm	♎
27	♎		
28	♎		
29	♎	2:32 am	♏
30	♏		
31	♏	2:20 pm	♐

June

1	♐		
2	♐		
3	♐	3:05 am	♑
4	♑		
5	♑	3:38 pm	♒
6	♒		
7	♒		
8	♒	2:43 am	♓
9	♓		
10	♓	10:57 am	♈
11	♈		
12	♈	3:35 pm	♉
13	♉		
14	♉	4:57 pm	♊
15	♊		
16	♊	4:26 pm	♋
17	♋		
18	♋	4:01 pm	♌
19	♌		
20	♌	5:45 pm	♍
21	♍		
22	♍	11:05 pm	♎
23	♎		
24	♎		
25	♎	8:19 am	♏
26	♏		
27	♏	8:15 pm	♐
28	♐		
29	♐		
30	♐	9:06 am	♑

July

1	♑		
2	♑	9:30 pm	♒
3	♒		
4	♒		
5	♒	8:37 am	♓
6	♓		
7	♓	5:38 pm	♈
8	♈		
9	♈	11:45 pm	♉
10	♉		
11	♉		
12	♉	2:40 am	♊
13	♊		
14	♊	3:03 am	♋
15	♋		
16	♋	2:32 am	♌
17	♌		
18	♌	3:12 am	♍
19	♍		
20	♍	7:02 am	♎
21	♎		
22	♎	3:03 pm	♏
23	♏		
24	♏		
25	♏	2:31 am	♐
26	♐		
27	♐	3:22 pm	♑
28	♑		
29	♑		
30	♑	3:37 am	♒
31	♒		

August

1	♒	2:18 pm	♓
2	♓		
3	♓	11:10 pm	♈
4	♈		
5	♈		
6	♈	5:56 am	♉
7	♉		
8	♉	10:15 am	♊
9	♊		
10	♊	12:11 pm	♋
11	♋		
12	♋	12:41 pm	♌
13	♌		
14	♌	1:27 pm	♍
15	♍		
16	♍	4:28 pm	♎
17	♎		
18	♎	11:12 pm	♏
19	♏		
20	♏		
21	♏	9:45 am	♐
22	♐		
23	♐	10:22 pm	♑
24	♑		
25	♑		
26	♑	10:36 am	♒
27	♒		
28	♒	8:55 pm	♓
29	♓		
30	♓		
31	♓	5:03 am	♈

September

1	♈		
2	♈	11:19 am	♉
3	♉		
4	♉	3:58 pm	♊
5	♊		
6	♊	7:04 pm	♋
7	♋		
8	♋	9:02 pm	♌
9	♌		
10	♌	10:54 pm	♍
11	♍		
12	♍		
13	♍	2:10 am	♎
14	♎		
15	♎	8:19 am	♏
16	♏		
17	♏	5:58 pm	♐
18	♐		
19	♐		
20	♐	6:09 am	♑
21	♑		
22	♑	6:33 pm	♒
23	♒		
24	♒		
25	♒	4:57 am	♓
26	♓		
27	♓	12:35 pm	♈
28	♈		
29	♈	5:49 pm	♉
30	♉		

October

1	♉	9:32 pm	♊
2	♊		
3	♊		
4	♊	12:29 am	♋
5	♋		
6	♋	3:14 am	♌
7	♌		
8	♌	6:23 am	♍
9	♍		
10	♍	10:44 am	♎
11	♎		
12	♎	5:14 pm	♏
13	♏		
14	♏		
15	♏	2:30 am	♐
16	♐		
17	♐	2:16 pm	♑
18	♑		
19	♑		
20	♑	2:52 am	♒
21	♒		
22	♒	1:57 pm	♓
23	♓		
24	♓	9:52 pm	♈
25	♈		
26	♈		
27	♈	2:33 am	♉
28	♉		
29	♉	4:59 am	♊
30	♊		
31	♊	6:35 am	♋

November

1	♋		
2	♋	8:37 am	♌
3	♌		
4	♌	12:03 pm	♍
5	♍		
6	♍	5:23 pm	♎
7	♎		
8	♎		
9	♎	12:49 am	♏
10	♏		
11	♏	10:26 am	♐
12	♐		
13	♐	10:03 pm	♑
14	♑		
15	♑		
16	♑	10:44 am	♒
17	♒		
18	♒	10:39 pm	♓
19	♓		
20	♓		
21	♓	7:45 am	♈
22	♈		
23	♈	1:02 pm	♉
24	♉		
25	♉	3:00 pm	♊
26	♊		
27	♊	3:12 pm	♋
28	♋		
29	♋	3:33 pm	♌
30	♌		

December

1	♌	5:45 pm	♍
2	♍		
3	♍	10:50 pm	♎
4	♎		
5	♎		
6	♎	6:51 am	♏
7	♏		
8	♏	5:09 pm	♐
9	♐		
10	♐		
11	♐	4:59 am	♑
12	♑		
13	♑	5:39 pm	♒
14	♒		
15	♒		
16	♒	6:03 am	♓
17	♓		
18	♓	4:30 pm	♈
19	♈		
20	♈	11:22 pm	♉
21	♉		
22	♉		
23	♉	2:15 am	♊
24	♊		
25	♊	2:13 am	♋
26	♋		
27	♋	1:16 am	♌
28	♌		
29	♌	1:37 am	♍
30	♍		
31	♍	5:06 am	♎

Your Starway to Love

♈ = Aries ♉ = Taurus ♊ = Gemini ♋ = Cancer ♌ = Leo ♍ = Virgo

1921

January

1	♎		
2	♎	12:27 pm	♏
3	♏		
4	♏	10:58 pm	♐
5	♐		
6	♐		
7	♐	11:10 am	♑
8	♑		
9	♑	11:50 pm	♒
10	♒		
11	♒		
12	♒	12:10 pm	♓
13	♓		
14	♓	11:15 pm	♈
15	♈		
16	♈		
17	♈	7:40 am	♉
18	♉		
19	♉	12:23 pm	♊
20	♊		
21	♊	1:35 pm	♋
22	♋		
23	♋	12:45 pm	♌
24	♌		
25	♌	12:04 pm	♍
26	♍		
27	♍	1:46 pm	♎
28	♎		
29	♎	7:25 pm	♏
30	♏		
31	♏		

February

1	♏	5:04 am	♐
2	♐		
3	♐	5:14 pm	♑
4	♑		
5	♑		
6	♑	5:59 am	♒
7	♒		
8	♒	6:03 pm	♓
9	♓		
10	♓		
11	♓	4:51 am	♈
12	♈		
13	♈	1:45 pm	♉
14	♉		
15	♉	7:54 pm	♊
16	♊		
17	♊	10:58 pm	♋
18	♋		
19	♋	11:34 pm	♌
20	♌		
21	♌	11:20 pm	♍
22	♍		
23	♍		
24	♍	12:21 am	♎
25	♎		
26	♎	4:28 am	♏
27	♏		
28	♏	12:36 pm	♐

March

1	♐		
2	♐		
3	♐	12:03 am	♑
4	♑		
5	♑	12:46 pm	♒
6	♒		
7	♒		
8	♒	12:44 am	♓
9	♓		
10	♓	10:58 am	♈
11	♈		
12	♈	7:14 pm	♉
13	♉		
14	♉		
15	♉	1:29 am	♊
16	♊		
17	♊	5:36 am	♋
18	♋		
19	♋	7:52 am	♌
20	♌		
21	♌	9:07 am	♍
22	♍		
23	♍	10:49 am	♎
24	♎		
25	♎	2:33 pm	♏
26	♏		
27	♏	9:34 pm	♐
28	♐		
29	♐		
30	♐	7:58 am	♑
31	♑		

April

1	♑	8:22 pm	♒
2	♒		
3	♒		
4	♒	8:28 am	♓
5	♓		
6	♓	6:31 pm	♈
7	♈		
8	♈		
9	♈	2:00 am	♉
10	♉		
11	♉	7:16 am	♊
12	♊		
13	♊	10:58 am	♋
14	♋		
15	♋	1:47 pm	♌
16	♌		
17	♌	4:21 pm	♍
18	♍		
19	♍	7:24 pm	♎
20	♎		
21	♎	11:54 pm	♏
22	♏		
23	♏		
24	♏	6:45 am	♐
25	♐		
26	♐	4:27 pm	♑
27	♑		
28	♑		
29	♑	4:26 am	♒
30	♒		

May

1	♒	4:46 pm	♓
2	♓		
3	♓		
4	♓	3:14 am	♈
5	♈		
6	♈	10:31 am	♉
7	♉		
8	♉	2:51 pm	♊
9	♊		
10	♊	5:19 pm	♋
11	♋		
12	♋	7:16 pm	♌
13	♌		
14	♌	9:51 pm	♍
15	♍		
16	♍		
17	♍	1:46 am	♎
18	♎		
19	♎	7:21 am	♏
20	♏		
21	♏	2:53 pm	♐
22	♐		
23	♐		
24	♐	12:34 pm	♑
25	♑		
26	♑	12:17 pm	♒
27	♒		
28	♒		
29	♒	12:50 am	♓
30	♓		
31	♓	12:05 pm	♈

June

1	♈		
2	♈	8:03 pm	♉
3	♉		
4	♉		
5	♉	12:17 am	♊
6	♊		
7	♊	1:46 am	♋
8	♋		
9	♋	2:18 am	♌
10	♌		
11	♌	3:41 am	♍
12	♍		
13	♍	7:10 am	♎
14	♎		
15	♎	1:10 pm	♏
16	♏		
17	♏	9:28 pm	♐
18	♐		
19	♐		
20	♐	7:39 am	♑
21	♑		
22	♑	7:24 pm	♒
23	♒		
24	♒		
25	♒	8:04 am	♓
26	♓		
27	♓	8:02 pm	♈
28	♈		
29	♈		
30	♈	5:14 am	♉

July

1	♉		
2	♉	10:23 am	♊
3	♊		
4	♊	11:55 am	♋
5	♋		
6	♋	11:33 am	♌
7	♌		
8	♌	11:26 am	♍
9	♍		
10	♍	1:28 pm	♎
11	♎		
12	♎	6:43 pm	♏
13	♏		
14	♏		
15	♏	3:05 am	♐
16	♐		
17	♐	1:43 pm	♑
18	♑		
19	♑		
20	♑	1:43 am	♒
21	♒		
22	♒	2:23 pm	♓
23	♓		
24	♓		
25	♓	2:42 am	♈
26	♈		
27	♈	12:58 pm	♉
28	♉		
29	♉	7:37 pm	♊
30	♊		
31	♊	10:18 pm	♋

August

1	♋		
2	♋	10:11 pm	♌
3	♌		
4	♌	9:18 pm	♍
5	♍		
6	♍	9:51 pm	♎
7	♎		
8	♎		
9	♎	1:33 am	♏
10	♏		
11	♏	8:59 am	♐
12	♐		
13	♐	7:30 pm	♑
14	♑		
15	♑		
16	♑	7:42 am	♒
17	♒		
18	♒	8:20 pm	♓
19	♓		
20	♓		
21	♓	8:30 am	♈
22	♈		
23	♈	7:07 pm	♉
24	♉		
25	♉		
26	♉	2:58 am	♊
27	♊		
28	♊	7:17 am	♋
29	♋		
30	♋	8:30 am	♌
31	♌		

September

1	♌	8:06 am	♍
2	♍		
3	♍	8:05 am	♎
4	♎		
5	♎	10:24 am	♏
6	♏		
7	♏	4:20 pm	♐
8	♐		
9	♐		
10	♐	1:58 am	♑
11	♑		
12	♑	2:01 pm	♒
13	♒		
14	♒		
15	♒	2:39 am	♓
16	♓		
17	♓	2:29 pm	♈
18	♈		
19	♈		
20	♈	12:41 am	♉
21	♉		
22	♉	8:41 am	♊
23	♊		
24	♊	2:06 pm	♋
25	♋		
26	♋	4:57 pm	♌
27	♌		
28	♌	6:01 pm	♍
29	♍		
30	♍	6:41 pm	♎

October

1	♎		
2	♎	8:37 pm	♏
3	♏		
4	♏		
5	♏	1:22 am	♐
6	♐		
7	♐	9:45 am	♑
8	♑		
9	♑	9:12 pm	♒
10	♒		
11	♒		
12	♒	9:51 am	♓
13	♓		
14	♓	9:34 pm	♈
15	♈		
16	♈		
17	♈	7:08 am	♉
18	♉		
19	♉	2:21 pm	♊
20	♊		
21	♊	7:32 pm	♋
22	♋		
23	♋	11:08 pm	♌
24	♌		
25	♌		
26	♌	1:40 am	♍
27	♍		
28	♍	3:49 am	♎
29	♎		
30	♎	6:33 am	♏
31	♏		

November

1	♏	11:08 am	♐
2	♐		
3	♐	6:38 pm	♑
4	♑		
5	♑		
6	♑	5:17 am	♒
7	♒		
8	♒	5:51 pm	♓
9	♓		
10	♓		
11	♓	5:52 am	♈
12	♈		
13	♈	3:19 pm	♉
14	♉		
15	♉	9:41 pm	♊
16	♊		
17	♊		
18	♊	1:41 am	♋
19	♋		
20	♋	4:32 am	♌
21	♌		
22	♌	7:17 am	♍
23	♍		
24	♍	10:31 am	♎
25	♎		
26	♎	2:37 pm	♏
27	♏		
28	♏	8:03 pm	♐
29	♐		
30	♐		

December

1	♐	3:32 am	♑
2	♑		
3	♑	1:41 pm	♒
4	♒		
5	♒		
6	♒	2:03 am	♓
7	♓		
8	♓	2:37 pm	♈
9	♈		
10	♈		
11	♈	12:46 am	♉
12	♉		
13	♉	7:07 am	♊
14	♊		
15	♊	10:11 am	♋
16	♋		
17	♋	11:34 am	♌
18	♌		
19	♌	1:02 pm	♍
20	♍		
21	♍	3:52 pm	♎
22	♎		
23	♎	8:33 pm	♏
24	♏		
25	♏		
26	♏	3:01 am	♐
27	♐		
28	♐	11:16 am	♑
29	♑		
30	♑	9:31 pm	♒
31	♒		

Moon Movements

♎ = Libra ♏ = Scorpio ♐ = Sagittarius ♑ = Capricorn ♒ = Aquarius ♓ = Pisces

1922

January

1	♒		
2	♒	9:44 am	♓
3	♓		
4	♓	10:42 pm	♈
5	♈		
6	♈		
7	♈	9:58 am	♉
8	♉		
9	♉	5:27 pm	♊
10	♊		
11	♊	8:47 pm	♋
12	♋		
13	♋	9:21 pm	♌
14	♌		
15	♌	9:13 pm	♍
16	♍		
17	♍	10:21 pm	♎
18	♎		
19	♎		
20	♎	2:02 am	♏
21	♏		
22	♏	8:33 am	♐
23	♐		
24	♐	5:28 pm	♑
25	♑		
26	♑		
27	♑	4:16 am	♒
28	♒		
29	♒	4:34 pm	♓
30	♓		
31	♓		

February

1	♓	5:35 am	♈
2	♈		
3	♈	5:41 pm	♉
4	♉		
5	♉		
6	♉	2:42 am	♊
7	♊		
8	♊	7:30 am	♋
9	♋		
10	♋	8:39 am	♌
11	♌		
12	♌	7:58 am	♍
13	♍		
14	♍	7:34 am	♎
15	♎		
16	♎	9:23 am	♏
17	♏		
18	♏	2:32 pm	♐
19	♐		
20	♐	11:05 pm	♑
21	♑		
22	♑		
23	♑	10:12 am	♒
24	♒		
25	♒	10:45 pm	♓
26	♓		
27	♓		
28	♓	11:41 am	♈

March

1	♈		
2	♈	11:52 pm	♉
3	♉		
4	♉		
5	♉	9:49 am	♊
6	♊		
7	♊	4:19 pm	♋
8	♋		
9	♋	7:09 pm	♌
10	♌		
11	♌	7:22 pm	♍
12	♍		
13	♍	6:44 pm	♎
14	♎		
15	♎	7:13 pm	♏
16	♏		
17	♏	10:33 pm	♐
18	♐		
19	♐		
20	♐	5:41 am	♑
21	♑		
22	♑	4:18 pm	♒
23	♒		
24	♒		
25	♒	4:56 am	♓
26	♓		
27	♓	5:49 pm	♈
28	♈		
29	♈		
30	♈	5:38 am	♉
31	♉		

April

1	♉	3:29 pm	♊
2	♊		
3	♊	10:46 pm	♋
4	♋		
5	♋		
6	♋	3:13 am	♌
7	♌		
8	♌	5:09 am	♍
9	♍		
10	♍	5:36 am	♎
11	♎		
12	♎	6:07 am	♏
13	♏		
14	♏	8:25 am	♐
15	♐		
16	♐	2:01 pm	♑
17	♑		
18	♑	11:28 pm	♒
19	♒		
20	♒		
21	♒	11:44 am	♓
22	♓		
23	♓		
24	♓	12:37 am	♈
25	♈		
26	♈	12:08 pm	♉
27	♉		
28	♉	9:19 pm	♊
29	♊		
30	♊		

May

1	♊	4:12 am	♋
2	♋		
3	♋	9:05 am	♌
4	♌		
5	♌	12:19 pm	♍
6	♍		
7	♍	2:21 pm	♎
8	♎		
9	♎	4:00 pm	♏
10	♏		
11	♏	6:32 pm	♐
12	♐		
13	♐	11:25 pm	♑
14	♑		
15	♑		
16	♑	7:46 am	♒
17	♒		
18	♒	7:21 pm	♓
19	♓		
20	♓		
21	♓	8:13 am	♈
22	♈		
23	♈	7:46 pm	♉
24	♉		
25	♉		
26	♉	4:29 am	♊
27	♊		
28	♊	10:26 am	♋
29	♋		
30	♋	2:34 pm	♌
31	♌		

June

1	♌	5:48 pm	♍
2	♍		
3	♍	8:43 pm	♎
4	♎		
5	♎	11:42 pm	♏
6	♏		
7	♏		
8	♏	3:18 am	♐
9	♐		
10	♐	8:30 am	♑
11	♑		
12	♑	4:25 pm	♒
13	♒		
14	♒		
15	♒	3:25 am	♓
16	♓		
17	♓	4:12 pm	♈
18	♈		
19	♈		
20	♈	4:09 am	♉
21	♉		
22	♉	1:02 pm	♊
23	♊		
24	♊	6:27 pm	♋
25	♋		
26	♋	9:28 pm	♌
27	♌		
28	♌	11:36 pm	♍
29	♍		
30	♍		

July

1	♍	2:04 am	♎
2	♎		
3	♎	5:29 am	♏
4	♏		
5	♏	10:05 am	♐
6	♐		
7	♐	4:12 pm	♑
8	♑		
9	♑		
10	♑	12:27 am	♒
11	♒		
12	♒	11:16 am	♓
13	♓		
14	♓	11:59 pm	♈
15	♈		
16	♈		
17	♈	12:28 pm	♉
18	♉		
19	♉	10:10 pm	♊
20	♊		
21	♊		
22	♊	3:56 am	♋
23	♋		
24	♋	6:26 am	♌
25	♌		
26	♌	7:21 am	♍
27	♍		
28	♍	8:26 am	♎
29	♎		
30	♎	10:59 am	♏
31	♏		

August

1	♏	3:35 pm	♐
2	♐		
3	♐	10:22 pm	♑
4	♑		
5	♑		
6	♑	7:19 am	♒
7	♒		
8	♒	6:23 pm	♓
9	♓		
10	♓		
11	♓	7:05 am	♈
12	♈		
13	♈	7:57 pm	♉
14	♉		
15	♉		
16	♉	6:42 am	♊
17	♊		
18	♊	1:40 pm	♋
19	♋		
20	♋	4:45 pm	♌
21	♌		
22	♌	5:16 pm	♍
23	♍		
24	♍	5:05 pm	♎
25	♎		
26	♎	6:02 pm	♏
27	♏		
28	♏	9:26 pm	♐
29	♐		
30	♐		
31	♐	3:53 am	♑

September

1	♑		
2	♑	1:12 pm	♒
3	♒		
4	♒		
5	♒	12:41 am	♓
6	♓		
7	♓	1:29 pm	♈
8	♈		
9	♈		
10	♈	2:24 am	♉
11	♉		
12	♉	1:50 pm	♊
13	♊		
14	♊	10:13 pm	♋
15	♋		
16	♋		
17	♋	2:48 am	♌
18	♌		
19	♌	4:08 am	♍
20	♍		
21	♍	3:43 am	♎
22	♎		
23	♎	3:27 am	♏
24	♏		
25	♏	5:11 am	♐
26	♐		
27	♐	10:15 am	♑
28	♑		
29	♑	7:02 pm	♒
30	♒		

October

1	♒		
2	♒	6:40 am	♓
3	♓		
4	♓	7:36 pm	♈
5	♈		
6	♈		
7	♈	8:20 am	♉
8	♉		
9	♉	7:44 pm	♊
10	♊		
11	♊		
12	♊	4:52 am	♋
13	♋		
14	♋	11:01 am	♌
15	♌		
16	♌	2:04 pm	♍
17	♍		
18	♍	2:43 pm	♎
19	♎		
20	♎	2:26 pm	♏
21	♏		
22	♏	3:05 pm	♐
23	♐		
24	♐	6:33 pm	♑
25	♑		
26	♑		
27	♑	2:00 am	♒
28	♒		
29	♒	1:07 pm	♓
30	♓		
31	♓		

November

1	♓	2:04 am	♈
2	♈		
3	♈	2:40 pm	♉
4	♉		
5	♉		
6	♉	1:33 am	♊
7	♊		
8	♊	10:23 am	♋
9	♋		
10	♋	5:05 pm	♌
11	♌		
12	♌	9:36 pm	♍
13	♍		
14	♍		
15	♍	12:01 am	♎
16	♎		
17	♎	12:59 am	♏
18	♏		
19	♏	1:52 am	♐
20	♐		
21	♐	4:31 am	♑
22	♑		
23	♑	10:36 am	♒
24	♒		
25	♒	8:39 pm	♓
26	♓		
27	♓		
28	♓	9:20 am	♈
29	♈		
30	♈	10:00 pm	♉

December

1	♉		
2	♉		
3	♉	8:34 am	♊
4	♊		
5	♊	4:34 pm	♋
6	♋		
7	♋	10:33 pm	♌
8	♌		
9	♌		
10	♌	3:09 am	♍
11	♍		
12	♍	6:39 am	♎
13	♎		
14	♎	9:14 am	♏
15	♏		
16	♏	11:28 am	♐
17	♐		
18	♐	2:34 pm	♑
19	♑		
20	♑	8:08 pm	♒
21	♒		
22	♒		
23	♒	5:14 am	♓
24	♓		
25	♓	5:22 pm	♈
26	♈		
27	♈		
28	♈	6:13 am	♉
29	♉		
30	♉	5:02 pm	♊
31	♊		

Your Starway to Love

♈ = Aries ♉ = Taurus ♊ = Gemini ♋ = Cancer ♌ = Leo ♍ = Virgo

1923

January

1	♊		
2	♊	12:39 am	♋
3	♋		
4	♋	5:34 am	♌
5	♌		
6	♌	8:59 am	♍
7	♍		
8	♍	11:59 am	♎
9	♎		
10	♎	3:04 pm	♏
11	♏		
12	♏	6:34 pm	♐
13	♐		
14	♐	10:56 pm	♑
15	♑		
16	♑		
17	♑	5:05 am	♒
18	♒		
19	♒	1:57 pm	♓
20	♓		
21	♓		
22	♓	1:37 am	♈
23	♈		
24	♈	2:34 pm	♉
25	♉		
26	♉		
27	♉	2:07 am	♊
28	♊		
29	♊	10:19 am	♋
30	♋		
31	♋	2:57 pm	♌

February

1	♌		
2	♌	5:12 pm	♍
3	♍		
4	♍	6:38 pm	♎
5	♎		
6	♎	8:37 pm	♏
7	♏		
8	♏	11:59 pm	♐
9	♐		
10	♐		
11	♐	5:08 am	♑
12	♑		
13	♑	12:18 pm	♒
14	♒		
15	♒	9:43 pm	♓
16	♓		
17	♓		
18	♓	9:20 am	♈
19	♈		
20	♈	10:15 pm	♉
21	♉		
22	♉		
23	♉	10:31 am	♊
24	♊		
25	♊	7:57 pm	♋
26	♋		
27	♋		
28	♋	1:30 am	♌

March

1	♌		
2	♌	3:41 am	♍
3	♍		
4	♍	4:00 am	♎
5	♎		
6	♎	4:16 am	♏
7	♏		
8	♏	6:05 am	♐
9	♐		
10	♐	10:34 am	♑
11	♑		
12	♑	6:02 pm	♒
13	♒		
14	♒		
15	♒	4:08 am	♓
16	♓		
17	♓	4:06 pm	♈
18	♈		
19	♈		
20	♈	5:00 am	♉
21	♉		
22	♉	5:33 pm	♊
23	♊		
24	♊		
25	♊	4:05 am	♋
26	♋		
27	♋	11:13 am	♌
28	♌		
29	♌	2:36 pm	♍
30	♍		
31	♍	3:06 pm	♎

April

1	♎		
2	♎	2:26 pm	♏
3	♏		
4	♏	2:33 pm	♐
5	♐		
6	♐	5:19 pm	♑
7	♑		
8	♑	11:48 pm	♒
9	♒		
10	♒		
11	♒	9:51 am	♓
12	♓		
13	♓	10:08 pm	♈
14	♈		
15	♈		
16	♈	11:07 am	♉
17	♉		
18	♉	11:33 pm	♊
19	♊		
20	♊		
21	♊	10:28 am	♋
22	♋		
23	♋	6:50 pm	♌
24	♌		
25	♌	11:56 pm	♍
26	♍		
27	♍		
28	♍	1:48 am	♎
29	♎		
30	♎	1:32 am	♏

May

1	♏		
2	♏	12:59 am	♐
3	♐		
4	♐	2:14 am	♑
5	♑		
6	♑	7:05 am	♒
7	♒		
8	♒	4:06 pm	♓
9	♓		
10	♓		
11	♓	4:12 am	♈
12	♈		
13	♈	5:14 pm	♉
14	♉		
15	♉		
16	♉	5:27 am	♊
17	♊		
18	♊	4:03 pm	♋
19	♋		
20	♋		
21	♋	12:40 am	♌
22	♌		
23	♌	6:54 am	♍
24	♍		
25	♍	10:25 am	♎
26	♎		
27	♎	11:35 am	♏
28	♏		
29	♏	11:37 am	♐
30	♐		
31	♐	12:27 pm	♑

June

1	♑		
2	♑	4:04 pm	♒
3	♒		
4	♒	11:43 pm	♓
5	♓		
6	♓		
7	♓	11:02 am	♈
8	♈		
9	♈	11:56 pm	♉
10	♉		
11	♉		
12	♉	12:03 pm	♊
13	♊		
14	♊	10:10 pm	♋
15	♋		
16	♋		
17	♋	6:12 am	♌
18	♌		
19	♌	12:22 pm	♍
20	♍		
21	♍	4:44 pm	♎
22	♎		
23	♎	7:20 pm	♏
24	♏		
25	♏	8:46 pm	♐
26	♐		
27	♐	10:20 pm	♑
28	♑		
29	♑		
30	♑	1:44 am	♒

July

1	♒		
2	♒	8:28 am	♓
3	♓		
4	♓	6:51 pm	♈
5	♈		
6	♈		
7	♈	7:25 am	♉
8	♉		
9	♉	7:37 pm	♊
10	♊		
11	♊		
12	♊	5:34 am	♋
13	♋		
14	♋	12:53 pm	♌
15	♌		
16	♌	6:10 pm	♍
17	♍		
18	♍	10:05 pm	♎
19	♎		
20	♎		
21	♎	1:08 am	♏
22	♏		
23	♏	3:43 am	♐
24	♐		
25	♐	6:32 am	♑
26	♑		
27	♑	10:42 am	♒
28	♒		
29	♒	5:23 pm	♓
30	♓		
31	♓		

August

1	♓	3:11 am	♈
2	♈		
3	♈	3:22 pm	♉
4	♉		
5	♉		
6	♉	3:47 am	♊
7	♊		
8	♊	2:08 pm	♋
9	♋		
10	♋	9:19 pm	♌
11	♌		
12	♌		
13	♌	1:44 am	♍
14	♍		
15	♍	4:27 am	♎
16	♎		
17	♎	6:38 am	♏
18	♏		
19	♏	9:12 am	♐
20	♐		
21	♐	12:49 pm	♑
22	♑		
23	♑	6:03 pm	♒
24	♒		
25	♒		
26	♒	1:25 am	♓
27	♓		
28	♓	11:15 am	♈
29	♈		
30	♈	11:12 pm	♉
31	♉		

September

1	♉		
2	♉	11:50 am	♊
3	♊		
4	♊	10:59 pm	♋
5	♋		
6	♋		
7	♋	6:54 am	♌
8	♌		
9	♌	11:16 am	♍
10	♍		
11	♍	1:03 pm	♎
12	♎		
13	♎	1:47 pm	♏
14	♏		
15	♏	3:05 pm	♐
16	♐		
17	♐	6:14 pm	♑
18	♑		
19	♑	11:53 pm	♒
20	♒		
21	♒		
22	♒	8:03 am	♓
23	♓		
24	♓	6:23 pm	♈
25	♈		
26	♈		
27	♈	6:22 am	♉
28	♉		
29	♉	7:06 pm	♊
30	♊		

October

1	♊		
2	♊	7:00 am	♋
3	♋		
4	♋	4:14 pm	♌
5	♌		
6	♌	9:41 pm	♍
7	♍		
8	♍	11:35 pm	♎
9	♎		
10	♎	11:25 pm	♏
11	♏		
12	♏	11:08 pm	♐
13	♐		
14	♐		
15	♐	12:43 am	♑
16	♑		
17	♑	5:29 am	♒
18	♒		
19	♒	1:43 pm	♓
20	♓		
21	♓		
22	♓	12:33 am	♈
23	♈		
24	♈	12:48 pm	♉
25	♉		
26	♉		
27	♉	1:29 am	♊
28	♊		
29	♊	1:39 pm	♋
30	♋		
31	♋		

November

1	♋	12:00 am	♌
2	♌		
3	♌	7:07 am	♍
4	♍		
5	♍	10:24 am	♎
6	♎		
7	♎	10:37 am	♏
8	♏		
9	♏	9:37 am	♐
10	♐		
11	♐	9:37 am	♑
12	♑		
13	♑	12:40 pm	♒
14	♒		
15	♒	7:46 pm	♓
16	♓		
17	♓		
18	♓	6:25 am	♈
19	♈		
20	♈	6:53 pm	♉
21	♉		
22	♉		
23	♉	7:32 am	♊
24	♊		
25	♊	7:28 pm	♋
26	♋		
27	♋		
28	♋	6:01 am	♌
29	♌		
30	♌	2:19 pm	♍

December

1	♍		
2	♍	7:24 pm	♎
3	♎		
4	♎	9:14 pm	♏
5	♏		
6	♏	8:57 pm	♐
7	♐		
8	♐	8:31 pm	♑
9	♑		
10	♑	10:10 pm	♒
11	♒		
12	♒		
13	♒	3:35 am	♓
14	♓		
15	♓	1:08 pm	♈
16	♈		
17	♈		
18	♈	1:21 am	♉
19	♉		
20	♉	2:03 pm	♊
21	♊		
22	♊		
23	♊	1:40 am	♋
24	♋		
25	♋	11:40 am	♌
26	♌		
27	♌	7:51 pm	♍
28	♍		
29	♍		
30	♍	1:51 am	♎
31	♎		

Moon Movements

♎ = Libra ♏ = Scorpio ♐ = Sagittarius ♑ = Capricorn ♒ = Aquarius ♓ = Pisces

1924

January

1	♎	5:23 am	♏
2	♏		
3	♏	6:48 am	♐
4	♐		
5	♐	7:22 am	♑
6	♑		
7	♑	8:54 am	♒
8	♒		
9	♒	1:13 pm	♓
10	♓		
11	♓	9:22 pm	♈
12	♈		
13	♈		
14	♈	8:48 am	♉
15	♉		
16	♉	9:28 pm	♊
17	♊		
18	♊		
19	♊	9:05 am	♋
20	♋		
21	♋	6:33 pm	♌
22	♌		
23	♌		
24	♌	1:49 am	♍
25	♍		
26	♍	7:14 am	♎
27	♎		
28	♎	11:09 am	♏
29	♏		
30	♏	1:52 pm	♐
31	♐		

February

1	♐	4:03 pm	♑
2	♑		
3	♑	6:43 pm	♒
4	♒		
5	♒	11:12 pm	♓
6	♓		
7	♓		
8	♓	6:36 am	♈
9	♈		
10	♈	5:09 pm	♉
11	♉		
12	♉		
13	♉	5:35 am	♊
14	♊		
15	♊	5:34 pm	♋
16	♋		
17	♋		
18	♋	3:09 am	♌
19	♌		
20	♌	9:45 am	♍
21	♍		
22	♍	1:57 pm	♎
23	♎		
24	♎	4:47 pm	♏
25	♏		
26	♏	7:16 pm	♐
27	♐		
28	♐	10:12 pm	♑
29	♑		

March

1	♑		
2	♑	2:11 am	♒
3	♒		
4	♒	7:44 am	♓
5	♓		
6	♓	3:26 pm	♈
7	♈		
8	♈		
9	♈	1:35 am	♉
10	♉		
11	♉	1:44 pm	♊
12	♊		
13	♊		
14	♊	2:08 am	♋
15	♋		
16	♋	12:31 pm	♌
17	♌		
18	♌	7:27 pm	♍
19	♍		
20	♍	11:00 pm	♎
21	♎		
22	♎		
23	♎	12:27 am	♏
24	♏		
25	♏	1:29 am	♐
26	♐		
27	♐	3:37 am	♑
28	♑		
29	♑	7:47 am	♒
30	♒		
31	♒	2:13 pm	♓

April

1	♓		
2	♓	10:45 pm	♈
3	♈		
4	♈		
5	♈	9:11 am	♉
6	♉		
7	♉	9:13 pm	♊
8	♊		
9	♊		
10	♊	9:53 am	♋
11	♋		
12	♋	9:15 pm	♌
13	♌		
14	♌		
15	♌	5:21 am	♍
16	♍		
17	♍	9:27 am	♎
18	♎		
19	♎	10:24 am	♏
20	♏		
21	♏	10:04 am	♐
22	♐		
23	♐	10:33 am	♑
24	♑		
25	♑	1:30 pm	♒
26	♒		
27	♒	7:39 pm	♓
28	♓		
29	♓		
30	♓	4:39 am	♈

May

1	♈		
2	♈	3:37 pm	♉
3	♉		
4	♉		
5	♉	3:48 am	♊
6	♊		
7	♊	4:31 pm	♋
8	♋		
9	♋		
10	♋	4:30 am	♌
11	♌		
12	♌	1:57 pm	♍
13	♍		
14	♍	7:28 pm	♎
15	♎		
16	♎	9:10 pm	♏
17	♏		
18	♏	8:33 pm	♐
19	♐		
20	♐	7:49 pm	♑
21	♑		
22	♑	9:04 pm	♒
23	♒		
24	♒		
25	♒	1:49 am	♓
26	♓		
27	♓	10:16 am	♈
28	♈		
29	♈	9:23 pm	♉
30	♉		
31	♉		

June

1	♉	9:47 am	♊
2	♊		
3	♊	10:27 pm	♋
4	♋		
5	♋		
6	♋	10:29 am	♌
7	♌		
8	♌	8:41 pm	♍
9	♍		
10	♍		
11	♍	3:41 am	♎
12	♎		
13	♎	6:57 am	♏
14	♏		
15	♏	7:17 am	♐
16	♐		
17	♐	6:28 am	♑
18	♑		
19	♑	6:42 am	♒
20	♒		
21	♒	9:52 am	♓
22	♓		
23	♓	4:56 pm	♈
24	♈		
25	♈		
26	♈	3:27 am	♉
27	♉		
28	♉	3:51 pm	♊
29	♊		
30	♊		

July

1	♊	4:28 am	♋
2	♋		
3	♋	4:11 pm	♌
4	♌		
5	♌		
6	♌	2:15 am	♍
7	♍		
8	♍	9:55 am	♎
9	♎		
10	♎	2:36 pm	♏
11	♏		
12	♏	4:32 pm	♐
13	♐		
14	♐	4:49 pm	♑
15	♑		
16	♑	5:11 pm	♒
17	♒		
18	♒	7:30 pm	♓
19	♓		
20	♓		
21	♓	1:12 am	♈
22	♈		
23	♈	10:36 am	♉
24	♉		
25	♉	10:36 pm	♊
26	♊		
27	♊		
28	♊	11:11 am	♋
29	♋		
30	♋	10:38 pm	♌
31	♌		

August

1	♌		
2	♌	8:05 am	♍
3	♍		
4	♍	3:20 pm	♎
5	♎		
6	♎	8:24 pm	♏
7	♏		
8	♏	11:32 pm	♐
9	♐		
10	♐		
11	♐	1:20 am	♑
12	♑		
13	♑	2:52 am	♒
14	♒		
15	♒	5:28 am	♓
16	♓		
17	♓	10:32 am	♈
18	♈		
19	♈	6:54 pm	♉
20	♉		
21	♉		
22	♉	6:14 am	♊
23	♊		
24	♊	6:48 pm	♋
25	♋		
26	♋		
27	♋	6:19 am	♌
28	♌		
29	♌	3:19 pm	♍
30	♍		
31	♍	9:38 pm	♎

September

1	♎		
2	♎		
3	♎	1:54 am	♏
4	♏		
5	♏	5:00 am	♐
6	♐		
7	♐	7:41 am	♑
8	♑		
9	♑	10:33 am	♒
10	♒		
11	♒	2:17 pm	♓
12	♓		
13	♓	7:42 pm	♈
14	♈		
15	♈		
16	♈	3:39 am	♉
17	♉		
18	♉	2:24 pm	♊
19	♊		
20	♊		
21	♊	2:54 am	♋
22	♋		
23	♋	2:52 pm	♌
24	♌		
25	♌		
26	♌	12:06 am	♍
27	♍		
28	♍	5:53 am	♎
29	♎		
30	♎	9:00 am	♏

October

1	♏		
2	♏	10:54 am	♐
3	♐		
4	♐	1:02 pm	♑
5	♑		
6	♑	4:19 pm	♒
7	♒		
8	♒	9:06 pm	♓
9	♓		
10	♓		
11	♓	3:31 am	♈
12	♈		
13	♈	11:50 am	♉
14	♉		
15	♉	10:23 pm	♊
16	♊		
17	♊		
18	♊	10:48 am	♋
19	♋		
20	♋	11:21 pm	♌
21	♌		
22	♌		
23	♌	9:33 am	♍
24	♍		
25	♍	3:49 pm	♎
26	♎		
27	♎	6:26 pm	♏
28	♏		
29	♏	7:03 pm	♐
30	♐		
31	♐	7:39 pm	♑

November

1	♑		
2	♑	9:53 pm	♒
3	♒		
4	♒		
5	♒	2:34 am	♓
6	♓		
7	♓	9:39 am	♈
8	♈		
9	♈	6:44 pm	♉
10	♉		
11	♉		
12	♉	5:34 am	♊
13	♊		
14	♊	5:57 pm	♋
15	♋		
16	♋		
17	♋	6:51 am	♌
18	♌		
19	♌	6:11 pm	♍
20	♍		
21	♍		
22	♍	1:51 am	♎
23	♎		
24	♎	5:17 am	♏
25	♏		
26	♏	5:38 am	♐
27	♐		
28	♐	4:57 am	♑
29	♑		
30	♑	5:26 am	♒

December

1	♒		
2	♒	8:38 am	♓
3	♓		
4	♓	3:10 pm	♈
5	♈		
6	♈		
7	♈	12:33 am	♉
8	♉		
9	♉	11:52 am	♊
10	♊		
11	♊		
12	♊	12:21 am	♋
13	♋		
14	♋	1:13 pm	♌
15	♌		
16	♌		
17	♌	1:07 am	♍
18	♍		
19	♍	10:15 am	♎
20	♎		
21	♎	3:25 pm	♏
22	♏		
23	♏	4:55 pm	♐
24	♐		
25	♐	4:18 pm	♑
26	♑		
27	♑	3:41 pm	♒
28	♒		
29	♒	5:06 pm	♓
30	♓		
31	♓	9:57 pm	♈

Your Starway to Love

♈ = Aries ♉ = Taurus ♊ = Gemini ♋ = Cancer ♌ = Leo ♍ = Virgo

1925

January

1	♈		
2	♈		
3	♈	6:31 am	♉
4	♉		
5	♉	5:52 pm	♊
6	♊		
7	♊		
8	♊	6:32 am	♋
9	♋		
10	♋	7:14 pm	♌
11	♌		
12	♌		
13	♌	6:55 am	♍
14	♍		
15	♍	4:33 pm	♎
16	♎		
17	♎	11:11 pm	♏
18	♏		
19	♏		
20	♏	2:34 am	♐
21	♐		
22	♐	3:22 am	♑
23	♑		
24	♑	3:09 am	♒
25	♒		
26	♒	3:46 am	♓
27	♓		
28	♓	6:59 am	♈
29	♈		
30	♈	1:58 pm	♉
31	♉		

April

1	♋		
2	♋	5:32 pm	♌
3	♌		
4	♌		
5	♌	4:55 am	♍
6	♍		
7	♍	1:04 pm	♎
8	♎		
9	♎	6:04 pm	♏
10	♏		
11	♏	9:05 pm	♐
12	♐		
13	♐	11:32 pm	♑
14	♑		
15	♑		
16	♑	2:23 am	♒
17	♒		
18	♒	6:02 am	♓
19	♓		
20	♓	10:45 am	♈
21	♈		
22	♈	5:00 pm	♉
23	♉		
24	♉		
25	♉	1:33 am	♊
26	♊		
27	♊	12:45 pm	♋
28	♋		
29	♋		
30	♋	1:36 am	♌

July

1	♏		
2	♏		
3	♏	1:55 am	♐
4	♐		
5	♐	2:24 am	♑
6	♑		
7	♑	1:49 am	♒
8	♒		
9	♒	2:06 am	♓
10	♓		
11	♓	4:53 am	♈
12	♈		
13	♈	11:05 am	♉
14	♉		
15	♉	8:37 pm	♊
16	♊		
17	♊		
18	♊	8:33 am	♋
19	♋		
20	♋	9:32 pm	♌
21	♌		
22	♌		
23	♌	10:17 am	♍
24	♍		
25	♍	9:30 pm	♎
26	♎		
27	♎		
28	♎	5:56 am	♏
29	♏		
30	♏	10:56 am	♐
31	♐		

October

1	♓	10:06 am	♈
2	♈		
3	♈	1:20 pm	♉
4	♉		
5	♉	7:35 pm	♊
6	♊		
7	♊		
8	♊	5:33 am	♋
9	♋		
10	♋	6:09 pm	♌
11	♌		
12	♌		
13	♌	6:43 am	♍
14	♍		
15	♍	4:57 pm	♎
16	♎		
17	♎		
18	♎	12:12 am	♏
19	♏		
20	♏	5:11 am	♐
21	♐		
22	♐	8:57 am	♑
23	♑		
24	♑	12:12 pm	♒
25	♒		
26	♒	3:14 pm	♓
27	♓		
28	♓	6:24 pm	♈
29	♈		
30	♈	10:29 pm	♉
31	♉		

February

1	♉		
2	♉	12:32 am	♊
3	♊		
4	♊	1:11 pm	♋
5	♋		
6	♋		
7	♋	1:50 am	♌
8	♌		
9	♌	1:01 pm	♍
10	♍		
11	♍	10:06 pm	♎
12	♎		
13	♎		
14	♎	4:54 am	♏
15	♏		
16	♏	9:28 am	♐
17	♐		
18	♐	12:02 pm	♑
19	♑		
20	♑	1:21 pm	♒
21	♒		
22	♒	2:36 pm	♓
23	♓		
24	♓	5:21 pm	♈
25	♈		
26	♈	11:04 pm	♉
27	♉		
28	♉		

May

1	♌		
2	♌	1:38 pm	♍
3	♍		
4	♍	10:26 pm	♎
5	♎		
6	♎		
7	♎	3:22 am	♏
8	♏		
9	♏	5:27 am	♐
10	♐		
11	♐	6:30 am	♑
12	♑		
13	♑	8:08 am	♒
14	♒		
15	♒	11:23 am	♓
16	♓		
17	♓	4:34 pm	♈
18	♈		
19	♈	11:41 pm	♉
20	♉		
21	♉		
22	♉	8:50 am	♊
23	♊		
24	♊	8:08 pm	♋
25	♋		
26	♋		
27	♋	8:59 am	♌
28	♌		
29	♌	9:35 pm	♍
30	♍		
31	♍		

August

1	♐	12:46 pm	♑
2	♑		
3	♑	12:40 pm	♒
4	♒		
5	♒	12:23 pm	♓
6	♓		
7	♓	1:46 pm	♈
8	♈		
9	♈	6:24 pm	♉
10	♉		
11	♉		
12	♉	2:57 am	♊
13	♊		
14	♊	2:39 pm	♋
15	♋		
16	♋		
17	♋	3:41 am	♌
18	♌		
19	♌	4:13 pm	♍
20	♍		
21	♍		
22	♍	3:05 am	♎
23	♎		
24	♎	11:44 am	♏
25	♏		
26	♏	5:50 pm	♐
27	♐		
28	♐	9:19 pm	♑
29	♑		
30	♑	10:41 pm	♒
31	♒		

November

1	♉		
2	♉	4:44 am	♊
3	♊		
4	♊	2:06 pm	♋
5	♋		
6	♋		
7	♋	2:16 am	♌
8	♌		
9	♌	3:07 pm	♍
10	♍		
11	♍		
12	♍	1:52 am	♎
13	♎		
14	♎	9:05 am	♏
15	♏		
16	♏	1:13 pm	♐
17	♐		
18	♐	3:38 pm	♑
19	♑		
20	♑	5:48 pm	♒
21	♒		
22	♒	8:37 pm	♓
23	♓		
24	♓		
25	♓	12:31 am	♈
26	♈		
27	♈	5:46 am	♉
28	♉		
29	♉	12:50 pm	♊
30	♊		

March

1	♉	8:26 am	♊
2	♊		
3	♊	8:38 pm	♋
4	♋		
5	♋		
6	♋	9:22 am	♌
7	♌		
8	♌	8:24 pm	♍
9	♍		
10	♍		
11	♍	4:44 am	♎
12	♎		
13	♎	10:37 am	♏
14	♏		
15	♏	2:51 pm	♐
16	♐		
17	♐	6:07 pm	♑
18	♑		
19	♑	8:51 pm	♒
20	♒		
21	♒	11:33 pm	♓
22	♓		
23	♓		
24	♓	3:04 am	♈
25	♈		
26	♈	8:34 am	♉
27	♉		
28	♉	5:08 pm	♊
29	♊		
30	♊		
31	♊	4:42 am	♋

June

1	♍	7:30 am	♎
2	♎		
3	♎	1:21 pm	♏
4	♏		
5	♏	3:33 pm	♐
6	♐		
7	♐	3:45 pm	♑
8	♑		
9	♑	3:54 pm	♒
10	♒		
11	♒	5:40 pm	♓
12	♓		
13	♓	10:03 pm	♈
14	♈		
15	♈		
16	♈	5:15 am	♉
17	♉		
18	♉	2:57 pm	♊
19	♊		
20	♊		
21	♊	2:36 am	♋
22	♋		
23	♋	3:31 pm	♌
24	♌		
25	♌		
26	♌	4:21 am	♍
27	♍		
28	♍	3:15 pm	♎
29	♎		
30	♎	10:33 pm	♏

September

1	♒	11:02 pm	♓
2	♓		
3	♓		
4	♓	12:02 am	♈
5	♈		
6	♈	3:27 am	♉
7	♉		
8	♉	10:39 am	♊
9	♊		
10	♊	9:35 pm	♋
11	♋		
12	♋		
13	♋	10:30 am	♌
14	♌		
15	♌	10:56 pm	♍
16	♍		
17	♍		
18	♍	9:18 am	♎
19	♎		
20	♎	5:18 pm	♏
21	♏		
22	♏	11:17 pm	♐
23	♐		
24	♐		
25	♐	3:37 am	♑
26	♑		
27	♑	6:29 am	♒
28	♒		
29	♒	8:19 am	♓
30	♓		

December

1	♊	10:19 pm	♋
2	♋		
3	♋		
4	♋	10:13 am	♌
5	♌		
6	♌	11:13 pm	♍
7	♍		
8	♍		
9	♍	10:52 am	♎
10	♎		
11	♎	7:03 pm	♏
12	♏		
13	♏	11:23 pm	♐
14	♐		
15	♐		
16	♐	12:59 am	♑
17	♑		
18	♑	1:35 am	♒
19	♒		
20	♒	2:51 am	♓
21	♓		
22	♓	5:57 am	♈
23	♈		
24	♈	11:25 am	♉
25	♉		
26	♉	7:18 pm	♊
27	♊		
28	♊		
29	♊	5:26 am	♋
30	♋		
31	♋	5:26 pm	♌

Moon Movements

♎ = Libra ♏ = Scorpio ♐ = Sagittarius ♑ = Capricorn ♒ = Aquarius ♓ = Pisces

1926

January

Day	Sign	Time	Enters
1	♌		
2	♌		
3	♌	6:26 am	♍
4	♍		
5	♍	6:44 pm	♎
6	♎		
7	♎		
8	♎	4:19 am	♏
9	♏		
10	♏	10:01 am	♐
11	♐		
12	♐	12:09 pm	♑
13	♑		
14	♑	12:07 pm	♒
15	♒		
16	♒	11:48 am	♓
17	♓		
18	♓	1:03 pm	♈
19	♈		
20	♈	5:16 pm	♉
21	♉		
22	♉		
23	♉	12:55 am	♊
24	♊		
25	♊	11:30 am	♋
26	♋		
27	♋	11:52 pm	♌
28	♌		
29	♌		
30	♌	12:49 pm	♍
31	♍		

February

Day	Sign	Time	Enters
1	♍		
2	♍	1:11 am	♎
3	♎		
4	♎	11:39 am	♏
5	♏		
6	♏	7:02 pm	♐
7	♐		
8	♐	10:49 pm	♑
9	♑		
10	♑	11:37 pm	♒
11	♒		
12	♒	10:57 pm	♓
13	♓		
14	♓	10:47 pm	♈
15	♈		
16	♈		
17	♈	1:08 am	♉
18	♉		
19	♉	7:22 am	♊
20	♊		
21	♊	5:28 pm	♋
22	♋		
23	♋		
24	♋	6:00 am	♌
25	♌		
26	♌	6:59 pm	♍
27	♍		
28	♍		

March

Day	Sign	Time	Enters
1	♍	7:03 am	♎
2	♎		
3	♎	5:28 pm	♏
4	♏		
5	♏		
6	♏	1:40 am	♐
7	♐		
8	♐	7:06 am	♑
9	♑		
10	♑	9:40 am	♒
11	♒		
12	♒	10:03 am	♓
13	♓		
14	♓	9:52 am	♈
15	♈		
16	♈	11:06 am	♉
17	♉		
18	♉	3:42 pm	♊
19	♊		
20	♊		
21	♊	12:30 am	♋
22	♋		
23	♋	12:35 pm	♌
24	♌		
25	♌		
26	♌	1:36 am	♍
27	♍		
28	♍	1:27 pm	♎
29	♎		
30	♎	11:17 pm	♏
31	♏		

April

Day	Sign	Time	Enters
1	♏		
2	♏	7:08 am	♐
3	♐		
4	♐	1:04 pm	♑
5	♑		
6	♑	5:00 pm	♒
7	♒		
8	♒	7:03 pm	♓
9	♓		
10	♓	8:02 pm	♈
11	♈		
12	♈	9:31 pm	♉
13	♉		
14	♉		
15	♉	1:20 am	♊
16	♊		
17	♊	8:55 am	♋
18	♋		
19	♋	8:07 pm	♌
20	♌		
21	♌		
22	♌	8:59 am	♍
23	♍		
24	♍	8:52 pm	♎
25	♎		
26	♎		
27	♎	6:19 am	♏
28	♏		
29	♏	1:19 pm	♐
30	♐		

May

Day	Sign	Time	Enters
1	♐	6:32 pm	♑
2	♑		
3	♑	10:31 pm	♒
4	♒		
5	♒		
6	♒	1:32 am	♓
7	♓		
8	♓	3:55 am	♈
9	♈		
10	♈	6:33 am	♉
11	♉		
12	♉	10:46 am	♊
13	♊		
14	♊	5:53 pm	♋
15	♋		
16	♋		
17	♋	4:20 am	♌
18	♌		
19	♌	4:54 pm	♍
20	♍		
21	♍		
22	♍	5:04 am	♎
23	♎		
24	♎	2:41 pm	♏
25	♏		
26	♏	9:14 pm	♐
27	♐		
28	♐		
29	♐	1:24 am	♑
30	♑		
31	♑	4:19 am	♒

June

Day	Sign	Time	Enters
1	♒		
2	♒	6:53 am	♓
3	♓		
4	♓	9:45 am	♈
5	♈		
6	♈	1:28 pm	♉
7	♉		
8	♉	6:43 pm	♊
9	♊		
10	♊		
11	♊	2:15 am	♋
12	♋		
13	♋	12:29 pm	♌
14	♌		
15	♌		
16	♌	12:48 am	♍
17	♍		
18	♍	1:19 pm	♎
19	♎		
20	♎	11:40 pm	♏
21	♏		
22	♏		
23	♏	6:35 am	♐
24	♐		
25	♐	10:18 am	♑
26	♑		
27	♑	12:01 pm	♒
28	♒		
29	♒	1:13 pm	♓
30	♓		

July

Day	Sign	Time	Enters
1	♓	3:14 pm	♈
2	♈		
3	♈	6:59 pm	♉
4	♉		
5	♉		
6	♉	12:57 am	♊
7	♊		
8	♊	9:16 am	♋
9	♋		
10	♋	7:50 pm	♌
11	♌		
12	♌		
13	♌	8:07 am	♍
14	♍		
15	♍	8:52 pm	♎
16	♎		
17	♎		
18	♎	8:08 am	♏
19	♏		
20	♏	4:10 pm	♐
21	♐		
22	♐	8:28 pm	♑
23	♑		
24	♑	9:48 pm	♒
25	♒		
26	♒	9:46 pm	♓
27	♓		
28	♓	10:13 pm	♈
29	♈		
30	♈		
31	♈	12:46 am	♉

August

Day	Sign	Time	Enters
1	♉		
2	♉	6:24 am	♊
3	♊		
4	♊	3:08 pm	♋
5	♋		
6	♋		
7	♋	2:12 am	♌
8	♌		
9	♌	2:39 pm	♍
10	♍		
11	♍		
12	♍	3:26 am	♎
13	♎		
14	♎	3:18 pm	♏
15	♏		
16	♏		
17	♏	12:39 pm	♐
18	♐		
19	♐	6:23 am	♑
20	♑		
21	♑	8:31 am	♒
22	♒		
23	♒	8:14 am	♓
24	♓		
25	♓	7:30 am	♈
26	♈		
27	♈	8:24 am	♉
28	♉		
29	♉	12:39 pm	♊
30	♊		
31	♊	8:48 pm	♋

September

Day	Sign	Time	Enters
1	♋		
2	♋		
3	♋	8:01 am	♌
4	♌		
5	♌	8:40 pm	♍
6	♍		
7	♍		
8	♍	9:23 am	♎
9	♎		
10	♎	9:15 pm	♏
11	♏		
12	♏		
13	♏	7:22 am	♐
14	♐		
15	♐	2:37 pm	♑
16	♑		
17	♑	6:23 pm	♒
18	♒		
19	♒	7:06 pm	♓
20	♓		
21	♓	6:20 pm	♈
22	♈		
23	♈	6:12 pm	♉
24	♉		
25	♉	8:50 pm	♊
26	♊		
27	♊		
28	♊	3:35 am	♋
29	♋		
30	♋	2:10 pm	♌

October

Day	Sign	Time	Enters
1	♌		
2	♌		
3	♌	2:49 am	♍
4	♍		
5	♍	3:28 pm	♎
6	♎		
7	♎		
8	♎	2:59 am	♏
9	♏		
10	♏	12:54 pm	♐
11	♐		
12	♐	8:47 pm	♑
13	♑		
14	♑		
15	♑	2:02 am	♒
16	♒		
17	♒	4:29 am	♓
18	♓		
19	♓	4:56 am	♈
20	♈		
21	♈	5:01 am	♉
22	♉		
23	♉	6:50 am	♊
24	♊		
25	♊	12:08 pm	♋
26	♋		
27	♋	9:31 pm	♌
28	♌		
29	♌		
30	♌	9:43 am	♍
31	♍		

November

Day	Sign	Time	Enters
1	♍	10:22 pm	♎
2	♎		
3	♎		
4	♎	9:37 am	♏
5	♏		
6	♏	6:51 pm	♐
7	♐		
8	♐		
9	♐	2:11 am	♑
10	♑		
11	♑	7:42 am	♒
12	♒		
13	♒	11:22 am	♓
14	♓		
15	♓	1:28 pm	♈
16	♈		
17	♈	2:54 pm	♉
18	♉		
19	♉	5:10 pm	♊
20	♊		
21	♊	9:54 pm	♋
22	♋		
23	♋		
24	♋	6:10 am	♌
25	♌		
26	♌	5:36 pm	♍
27	♍		
28	♍		
29	♍	6:14 am	♎
30	♎		

December

Day	Sign	Time	Enters
1	♎	5:39 pm	♏
2	♏		
3	♏		
4	♏	2:32 am	♐
5	♐		
6	♐	8:52 am	♑
7	♑		
8	♑	1:22 pm	♒
9	♒		
10	♒	4:44 pm	♓
11	♓		
12	♓	7:33 pm	♈
13	♈		
14	♈	10:23 pm	♉
15	♉		
16	♉		
17	♉	1:59 am	♊
18	♊		
19	♊	7:20 am	♋
20	♋		
21	♋	3:17 pm	♌
22	♌		
23	♌		
24	♌	2:02 am	♍
25	♍		
26	♍	2:31 pm	♎
27	♎		
28	♎		
29	♎	2:28 am	♏
30	♏		
31	♏	11:50 am	♐

Your Starway to Love

♈ = Aries ♉ = Taurus ♊ = Gemini ♋ = Cancer ♌ = Leo ♍ = Virgo

1927

January

1	♐		
2	♐	5:51 pm	♑
3	♑		
4	♑	9:10 pm	♒
5	♒		
6	♒	11:05 pm	♓
7	♓		
8	♓		
9	♓	12:59 am	♈
10	♈		
11	♈	3:56 am	♉
12	♉		
13	♉	8:30 am	♊
14	♊		
15	♊	2:59 pm	♋
16	♋		
17	♋	11:31 pm	♌
18	♌		
19	♌		
20	♌	10:10 am	♍
21	♍		
22	♍	10:27 pm	♎
23	♎		
24	♎		
25	♎	10:54 am	♏
26	♏		
27	♏	9:21 pm	♐
28	♐		
29	♐		
30	♐	4:12 am	♑
31	♑		

April

1	♓	5:30 am	♈
2	♈		
3	♈	4:36 am	♉
4	♉		
5	♉	5:25 am	♊
6	♊		
7	♊	9:42 am	♋
8	♋		
9	♋	6:00 pm	♌
10	♌		
11	♌		
12	♌	5:19 am	♍
13	♍		
14	♍	5:53 pm	♎
15	♎		
16	♎		
17	♎	6:20 am	♏
18	♏		
19	♏	5:49 pm	♐
20	♐		
21	♐		
22	♐	3:35 am	♑
23	♑		
24	♑	10:43 am	♒
25	♒		
26	♒	2:37 pm	♓
27	♓		
28	♓	3:43 pm	♈
29	♈		
30	♈	3:28 pm	♉

July

1	♌		
2	♌		
3	♌	4:27 am	♍
4	♍		
5	♍	3:47 pm	♎
6	♎		
7	♎		
8	♎	4:17 am	♏
9	♏		
10	♏	3:37 pm	♐
11	♐		
12	♐		
13	♐	12:06 am	♑
14	♑		
15	♑	5:31 am	♒
16	♒		
17	♒	8:43 am	♓
18	♓		
19	♓	10:58 am	♈
20	♈		
21	♈	1:24 pm	♉
22	♉		
23	♉	4:46 pm	♊
24	♊		
25	♊	9:31 pm	♋
26	♋		
27	♋		
28	♋	4:00 am	♌
29	♌		
30	♌	12:42 pm	♍
31	♍		

October

1	♐		
2	♐		
3	♐	2:13 am	♑
4	♑		
5	♑	10:07 am	♒
6	♒		
7	♒	1:50 pm	♓
8	♓		
9	♓	2:14 pm	♈
10	♈		
11	♈	1:17 pm	♉
12	♉		
13	♉	1:12 pm	♊
14	♊		
15	♊	3:50 pm	♋
16	♋		
17	♋	10:07 pm	♌
18	♌		
19	♌		
20	♌	7:43 am	♍
21	♍		
22	♍	7:28 pm	♎
23	♎		
24	♎		
25	♎	8:08 am	♏
26	♏		
27	♏	8:48 pm	♐
28	♐		
29	♐		
30	♐	8:22 am	♑
31	♑		

February

1	♑	7:22 am	♒
2	♒		
3	♒	8:07 am	♓
4	♓		
5	♓	8:19 am	♈
6	♈		
7	♈	9:50 am	♉
8	♉		
9	♉	1:54 pm	♊
10	♊		
11	♊	8:51 pm	♋
12	♋		
13	♋		
14	♋	6:11 am	♌
15	♌		
16	♌	5:15 pm	♍
17	♍		
18	♍		
19	♍	5:31 am	♎
20	♎		
21	♎	6:08 pm	♏
22	♏		
23	♏		
24	♏	5:35 am	♐
25	♐		
26	♐	1:56 pm	♑
27	♑		
28	♑	6:14 pm	♒

May

1	♉		
2	♉	3:52 pm	♊
3	♊		
4	♊	6:51 pm	♋
5	♋		
6	♋		
7	♋	1:39 am	♌
8	♌		
9	♌	12:03 pm	♍
10	♍		
11	♍		
12	♍	12:27 am	♎
13	♎		
14	♎	12:52 pm	♏
15	♏		
16	♏	11:58 pm	♐
17	♐		
18	♐		
19	♐	9:11 am	♑
20	♑		
21	♑	4:16 pm	♒
22	♒		
23	♒	9:01 pm	♓
24	♓		
25	♓	11:37 pm	♈
26	♈		
27	♈		
28	♈	12:50 am	♉
29	♉		
30	♉	2:02 am	♊
31	♊		

August

1	♍	11:44 pm	♎
2	♎		
3	♎		
4	♎	12:16 pm	♏
5	♏		
6	♏		
7	♏	12:14 am	♐
8	♐		
9	♐	9:23 am	♑
10	♑		
11	♑	2:46 pm	♒
12	♒		
13	♒	5:04 pm	♓
14	♓		
15	♓	5:57 pm	♈
16	♈		
17	♈	7:12 pm	♉
18	♉		
19	♉	10:08 pm	♊
20	♊		
21	♊		
22	♊	3:19 am	♋
23	♋		
24	♋	10:39 am	♌
25	♌		
26	♌	7:55 pm	♍
27	♍		
28	♍		
29	♍	7:02 am	♎
30	♎		
31	♎	7:36 pm	♏

November

1	♑	5:26 pm	♒
2	♒		
3	♒	10:56 pm	♓
4	♓		
5	♓		
6	♓	12:53 am	♈
7	♈		
8	♈	12:37 am	♉
9	♉		
10	♉	12:03 am	♊
11	♊		
12	♊	1:15 am	♋
13	♋		
14	♋	5:48 am	♌
15	♌		
16	♌	2:14 pm	♍
17	♍		
18	♍		
19	♍	1:41 am	♎
20	♎		
21	♎	2:26 pm	♏
22	♏		
23	♏		
24	♏	2:53 am	♐
25	♐		
26	♐	2:01 pm	♑
27	♑		
28	♑	11:06 pm	♒
29	♒		
30	♒		

March

1	♒		
2	♒	7:05 pm	♓
3	♓		
4	♓	6:19 pm	♈
5	♈		
6	♈	6:07 pm	♉
7	♉		
8	♉	8:29 pm	♊
9	♊		
10	♊		
11	♊	2:29 am	♋
12	♋		
13	♋	11:52 am	♌
14	♌		
15	♌	11:22 pm	♍
16	♍		
17	♍		
18	♍	11:48 am	♎
19	♎		
20	♎		
21	♎	12:21 am	♏
22	♏		
23	♏	12:06 pm	♐
24	♐		
25	♐	9:39 pm	♑
26	♑		
27	♑		
28	♑	3:39 am	♒
29	♒		
30	♒	5:52 am	♓
31	♓		

June

1	♊	4:50 am	♋
2	♋		
3	♋	10:37 am	♌
4	♌		
5	♌	7:55 pm	♍
6	♍		
7	♍		
8	♍	7:49 am	♎
9	♎		
10	♎	8:16 pm	♏
11	♏		
12	♏		
13	♏	7:16 am	♐
14	♐		
15	♐	3:51 pm	♑
16	♑		
17	♑	10:05 pm	♒
18	♒		
19	♒		
20	♒	2:25 am	♓
21	♓		
22	♓	5:29 am	♈
23	♈		
24	♈	7:54 am	♉
25	♉		
26	♉	10:26 am	♊
27	♊		
28	♊	2:03 pm	♋
29	♋		
30	♋	7:48 pm	♌

September

1	♏		
2	♏		
3	♏	8:10 am	♐
4	♐		
5	♐	6:28 pm	♑
6	♑		
7	♑		
8	♑	12:50 am	♒
9	♒		
10	♒	3:16 am	♓
11	♓		
12	♓	3:18 am	♈
13	♈		
14	♈	3:03 am	♉
15	♉		
16	♉	4:29 am	♊
17	♊		
18	♊	8:49 am	♋
19	♋		
20	♋	4:13 pm	♌
21	♌		
22	♌		
23	♌	2:01 am	♍
24	♍		
25	♍	1:30 pm	♎
26	♎		
27	♎		
28	♎	2:05 am	♏
29	♏		
30	♏	2:54 pm	♐

December

1	♒	5:37 am	♓
2	♓		
3	♓	9:20 am	♈
4	♈		
5	♈	10:47 am	♉
6	♉		
7	♉	11:10 am	♊
8	♊		
9	♊	12:11 pm	♋
10	♋		
11	♋	3:31 pm	♌
12	♌		
13	♌	10:25 pm	♍
14	♍		
15	♍		
16	♍	8:55 am	♎
17	♎		
18	♎	9:31 pm	♏
19	♏		
20	♏		
21	♏	9:59 am	♐
22	♐		
23	♐	8:38 pm	♑
24	♑		
25	♑		
26	♑	4:54 am	♒
27	♒		
28	♒	11:00 am	♓
29	♓		
30	♓	3:19 pm	♈
31	♈		

Moon Movements

♎ = Libra ♏ = Scorpio ♐ = Sagittarius ♑ = Capricorn ♒ = Aquarius ♓ = Pisces

1928

January

1	♈	6:15 pm	♉
2	♉		
3	♉	8:20 pm	♊
4	♊		
5	♊	10:28 pm	♋
6	♋		
7	♋		
8	♋	1:52 am	♌
9	♌		
10	♌	7:53 am	♍
11	♍		
12	♍	5:18 pm	♎
13	♎		
14	♎		
15	♎	5:26 am	♏
16	♏		
17	♏	6:06 pm	♐
18	♐		
19	♐		
20	♐	4:49 am	♑
21	♑		
22	♑	12:27 pm	♒
23	♒		
24	♒	5:24 pm	♓
25	♓		
26	♓	8:48 pm	♈
27	♈		
28	♈	11:42 pm	♉
29	♉		
30	♉		
31	♉	2:47 am	♊

April

1	♌	6:53 am	♍
2	♍		
3	♍	4:47 pm	♎
4	♎		
5	♎		
6	♎	4:27 am	♏
7	♏		
8	♏	5:20 pm	♐
9	♐		
10	♐		
11	♐	5:56 am	♑
12	♑		
13	♑	4:07 pm	♒
14	♒		
15	♒	10:19 pm	♓
16	♓		
17	♓		
18	♓	12:40 am	♈
19	♈		
20	♈	12:36 am	♉
21	♉		
22	♉	12:09 am	♊
23	♊		
24	♊	1:14 am	♋
25	♋		
26	♋	5:11 am	♌
27	♌		
28	♌	12:28 pm	♍
29	♍		
30	♍	10:36 pm	♎

July

1	♐		
2	♐	12:23 am	♑
3	♑		
4	♑	10:32 am	♒
5	♒		
6	♒	6:23 pm	♓
7	♓		
8	♓		
9	♓	12:04 am	♈
10	♈		
11	♈	3:49 am	♉
12	♉		
13	♉	5:59 am	♊
14	♊		
15	♊	7:20 am	♋
16	♋		
17	♋	9:06 am	♌
18	♌		
19	♌	12:53 pm	♍
20	♍		
21	♍	8:02 pm	♎
22	♎		
23	♎		
24	♎	6:47 am	♏
25	♏		
26	♏	7:34 pm	♐
27	♐		
28	♐		
29	♐	7:47 am	♑
30	♑		
31	♑	5:33 pm	♒

October

1	♉		
2	♉		
3	♉	12:09 am	♊
4	♊		
5	♊	2:21 am	♋
6	♋		
7	♋	6:18 am	♌
8	♌		
9	♌	12:13 pm	♍
10	♍		
11	♍	8:14 pm	♎
12	♎		
13	♎		
14	♎	6:29 am	♏
15	♏		
16	♏	6:44 pm	♐
17	♐		
18	♐		
19	♐	7:50 am	♑
20	♑		
21	♑	7:33 pm	♒
22	♒		
23	♒		
24	♒	3:50 am	♓
25	♓		
26	♓	8:04 am	♈
27	♈		
28	♈	9:16 am	♉
29	♉		
30	♉	9:11 am	♊
31	♊		

February

1	♊		
2	♊	6:21 am	♋
3	♋		
4	♋	10:53 am	♌
5	♌		
6	♌	5:09 pm	♍
7	♍		
8	♍		
9	♍	2:03 am	♎
10	♎		
11	♎	1:41 pm	♏
12	♏		
13	♏		
14	♏	2:32 am	♐
15	♐		
16	♐	1:54 pm	♑
17	♑		
18	♑	9:47 pm	♒
19	♒		
20	♒		
21	♒	2:05 am	♓
22	♓		
23	♓	4:09 am	♈
24	♈		
25	♈	5:42 am	♉
26	♉		
27	♉	8:07 am	♊
28	♊		
29	♊	12:04 pm	♋

May

1	♎		
2	♎		
3	♎	10:38 am	♏
4	♏		
5	♏	11:32 pm	♐
6	♐		
7	♐		
8	♐	12:09 pm	♑
9	♑		
10	♑	10:58 pm	♒
11	♒		
12	♒		
13	♒	6:35 am	♓
14	♓		
15	♓	10:30 am	♈
16	♈		
17	♈	11:25 am	♉
18	♉		
19	♉	10:56 am	♊
20	♊		
21	♊	10:57 am	♋
22	♋		
23	♋	1:17 pm	♌
24	♌		
25	♌	7:07 pm	♍
26	♍		
27	♍		
28	♍	4:36 am	♎
29	♎		
30	♎	4:40 pm	♏
31	♏		

August

1	♒		
2	♒		
3	♒	12:35 am	♓
4	♓		
5	♓	5:33 am	♈
6	♈		
7	♈	9:18 am	♉
8	♉		
9	♉	12:22 pm	♊
10	♊		
11	♊	3:03 pm	♋
12	♋		
13	♋	5:57 pm	♌
14	♌		
15	♌	10:07 pm	♍
16	♍		
17	♍		
18	♍	4:53 am	♎
19	♎		
20	♎	2:57 pm	♏
21	♏		
22	♏		
23	♏	3:29 am	♐
24	♐		
25	♐	3:59 pm	♑
26	♑		
27	♑		
28	♑	1:57 am	♒
29	♒		
30	♒	8:31 am	♓
31	♓		

November

1	♊	9:40 am	♋
2	♋		
3	♋	12:14 pm	♌
4	♌		
5	♌	5:41 pm	♍
6	♍		
7	♍		
8	♍	2:05 am	♎
9	♎		
10	♎	12:53 pm	♏
11	♏		
12	♏		
13	♏	1:20 am	♐
14	♐		
15	♐	2:25 pm	♑
16	♑		
17	♑		
18	♑	2:40 am	♒
19	♒		
20	♒	12:19 pm	♓
21	♓		
22	♓	6:14 pm	♈
23	♈		
24	♈	8:30 pm	♉
25	♉		
26	♉	8:23 pm	♊
27	♊		
28	♊	7:43 pm	♋
29	♋		
30	♋	8:29 pm	♌

March

1	♋		
2	♋	5:38 pm	♌
3	♌		
4	♌		
5	♌	12:51 am	♍
6	♍		
7	♍	10:04 am	♎
8	♎		
9	♎	9:31 pm	♏
10	♏		
11	♏		
12	♏	10:24 am	♐
13	♐		
14	♐	10:33 pm	♑
15	♑		
16	♑		
17	♑	7:31 am	♒
18	♒		
19	♒	12:20 pm	♓
20	♓		
21	♓	1:54 pm	♈
22	♈		
23	♈	2:06 pm	♉
24	♉		
25	♉	2:53 pm	♊
26	♊		
27	♊	5:42 pm	♋
28	♋		
29	♋	11:04 pm	♌
30	♌		
31	♌		

June

1	♏		
2	♏	5:38 am	♐
3	♐		
4	♐	6:00 pm	♑
5	♑		
6	♑		
7	♑	4:41 am	♒
8	♒		
9	♒	12:54 pm	♓
10	♓		
11	♓	6:13 pm	♈
12	♈		
13	♈	8:46 pm	♉
14	♉		
15	♉	9:24 pm	♊
16	♊		
17	♊	9:34 pm	♋
18	♋		
19	♋	11:02 pm	♌
20	♌		
21	♌		
22	♌	3:27 am	♍
23	♍		
24	♍	11:43 am	♎
25	♎		
26	♎	11:17 pm	♏
27	♏		
28	♏		
29	♏	12:13 pm	♐
30	♐		

September

1	♓	12:26 pm	♈
2	♈		
3	♈	3:07 pm	♉
4	♉		
5	♉	5:43 pm	♊
6	♊		
7	♊	8:51 pm	♋
8	♋		
9	♋		
10	♋	12:49 am	♌
11	♌		
12	♌	6:01 am	♍
13	♍		
14	♍	1:12 pm	♎
15	♎		
16	♎	11:05 pm	♏
17	♏		
18	♏		
19	♏	11:23 am	♐
20	♐		
21	♐		
22	♐	12:16 am	♑
23	♑		
24	♑	11:01 am	♒
25	♒		
26	♒	6:01 pm	♓
27	♓		
28	♓	9:31 pm	♈
29	♈		
30	♈	10:59 pm	♉

December

1	♌		
2	♌		
3	♌	12:16 am	♍
4	♍		
5	♍	7:52 am	♎
6	♎		
7	♎	6:46 pm	♏
8	♏		
9	♏		
10	♏	7:29 am	♐
11	♐		
12	♐	8:29 pm	♑
13	♑		
14	♑		
15	♑	8:36 am	♒
16	♒		
17	♒	6:49 pm	♓
18	♓		
19	♓		
20	♓	2:15 am	♈
21	♈		
22	♈	6:25 am	♉
23	♉		
24	♉	7:40 am	♊
25	♊		
26	♊	7:17 am	♋
27	♋		
28	♋	7:07 am	♌
29	♌		
30	♌	9:12 am	♍
31	♍		

Your Starway to Love

♈ = Aries ♉ = Taurus ♊ = Gemini ♋ = Cancer ♌ = Leo ♍ = Virgo

1929

January

Day	Sign	Time	New Sign
1	♍	3:08 pm	♎
2	♎		
3	♎		
4	♎	1:10 am	♏
5	♏		
6	♏	1:50 pm	♐
7	♐		
8	♐		
9	♐	2:51 am	♑
10	♑		
11	♑	2:33 pm	♒
12	♒		
13	♒		
14	♒	12:21 am	♓
15	♓		
16	♓	8:07 am	♈
17	♈		
18	♈	1:37 pm	♉
19	♉		
20	♉	4:43 pm	♊
21	♊		
22	♊	5:52 pm	♋
23	♋		
24	♋	6:16 pm	♌
25	♌		
26	♌	7:47 pm	♍
27	♍		
28	♍		
29	♍	12:19 am	♎
30	♎		
31	♎	8:57 am	♏

April

Day	Sign	Time	New Sign
1	♐	2:03 am	♑
2	♑		
3	♑	2:18 pm	♒
4	♒		
5	♒	11:52 pm	♓
6	♓		
7	♓		
8	♓	5:57 am	♈
9	♈		
10	♈	9:17 am	♉
11	♉		
12	♉	11:13 am	♊
13	♊		
14	♊	1:04 pm	♋
15	♋		
16	♋	3:50 pm	♌
17	♌		
18	♌	8:05 pm	♍
19	♍		
20	♍		
21	♍	2:13 am	♎
22	♎		
23	♎	10:34 am	♏
24	♏		
25	♏	9:16 pm	♐
26	♐		
27	♐		
28	♐	9:43 am	♑
29	♑		
30	♑	10:19 pm	♒

July

Day	Sign	Time	New Sign
1	♈	2:31 pm	♉
2	♉		
3	♉	5:14 pm	♊
4	♊		
5	♊	5:21 pm	♋
6	♋		
7	♋	4:37 pm	♌
8	♌		
9	♌	5:10 pm	♍
10	♍		
11	♍	8:54 pm	♎
12	♎		
13	♎		
14	♎	4:44 am	♏
15	♏		
16	♏	4:00 pm	♐
17	♐		
18	♐		
19	♐	4:47 am	♑
20	♑		
21	♑	5:20 pm	♒
22	♒		
23	♒		
24	♒	4:39 am	♓
25	♓		
26	♓	2:13 pm	♈
27	♈		
28	♈	9:25 pm	♉
29	♉		
30	♉		
31	♉	1:43 am	♊

October

Day	Sign	Time	New Sign
1	♍		
2	♍	1:09 am	♎
3	♎		
4	♎	6:40 am	♏
5	♏		
6	♏	3:18 pm	♐
7	♐		
8	♐		
9	♐	2:49 am	♑
10	♑		
11	♑	3:25 pm	♒
12	♒		
13	♒		
14	♒	2:40 am	♓
15	♓		
16	♓	11:02 am	♈
17	♈		
18	♈	4:29 pm	♉
19	♉		
20	♉	7:54 pm	♊
21	♊		
22	♊	10:24 pm	♋
23	♋		
24	♋		
25	♋	12:55 am	♌
26	♌		
27	♌	4:08 am	♍
28	♍		
29	♍	8:39 am	♎
30	♎		
31	♎	3:02 pm	♏

February

Day	Sign	Time	New Sign
1	♏		
2	♏	8:59 pm	♐
3	♐		
4	♐		
5	♐	10:00 am	♑
6	♑		
7	♑	9:34 pm	♒
8	♒		
9	♒		
10	♒	6:43 am	♓
11	♓		
12	♓	1:41 pm	♈
13	♈		
14	♈	7:02 pm	♉
15	♉		
16	♉	11:01 pm	♊
17	♊		
18	♊		
19	♊	1:45 am	♋
20	♋		
21	♋	3:41 am	♌
22	♌		
23	♌	5:58 am	♍
24	♍		
25	♍	10:15 am	♎
26	♎		
27	♎	5:54 pm	♏
28	♏		

May

Day	Sign	Time	New Sign
1	♒		
2	♒		
3	♒	8:51 am	♓
4	♓		
5	♓	3:51 pm	♈
6	♈		
7	♈	7:18 pm	♉
8	♉		
9	♉	8:22 pm	♊
10	♊		
11	♊	8:44 pm	♋
12	♋		
13	♋	10:03 pm	♌
14	♌		
15	♌		
16	♌	1:33 am	♍
17	♍		
18	♍	7:52 am	♎
19	♎		
20	♎	4:54 pm	♏
21	♏		
22	♏		
23	♏	4:04 am	♐
24	♐		
25	♐	4:34 pm	♑
26	♑		
27	♑		
28	♑	5:17 am	♒
29	♒		
30	♒	4:37 pm	♓
31	♓		

August

Day	Sign	Time	New Sign
1	♊		
2	♊	3:15 am	♋
3	♋		
4	♋	3:11 am	♌
5	♌		
6	♌	3:23 am	♍
7	♍		
8	♍	5:56 am	♎
9	♎		
10	♎	12:22 pm	♏
11	♏		
12	♏	10:44 pm	♐
13	♐		
14	♐		
15	♐	11:21 am	♑
16	♑		
17	♑	11:50 pm	♒
18	♒		
19	♒		
20	♒	10:46 am	♓
21	♓		
22	♓	7:47 pm	♈
23	♈		
24	♈		
25	♈	2:55 am	♉
26	♉		
27	♉	8:03 am	♊
28	♊		
29	♊	11:04 am	♋
30	♋		
31	♋	12:26 pm	♌

November

Day	Sign	Time	New Sign
1	♏		
2	♏	11:47 pm	♐
3	♐		
4	♐		
5	♐	10:57 am	♑
6	♑		
7	♑	11:33 pm	♒
8	♒		
9	♒		
10	♒	11:30 am	♓
11	♓		
12	♓	8:43 pm	♈
13	♈		
14	♈		
15	♈	2:19 am	♉
16	♉		
17	♉	4:53 am	♊
18	♊		
19	♊	5:53 am	♋
20	♋		
21	♋	6:58 am	♌
22	♌		
23	♌	9:32 am	♍
24	♍		
25	♍	2:23 pm	♎
26	♎		
27	♎	9:40 pm	♏
28	♏		
29	♏		
30	♏	7:08 am	♐

March

Day	Sign	Time	New Sign
1	♏		
2	♏	5:03 am	♐
3	♐		
4	♐	5:55 pm	♑
5	♑		
6	♑		
7	♑	5:44 am	♒
8	♒		
9	♒	2:44 pm	♓
10	♓		
11	♓	8:51 pm	♈
12	♈		
13	♈		
14	♈	1:05 am	♉
15	♉		
16	♉	4:23 am	♊
17	♊		
18	♊	7:24 am	♋
19	♋		
20	♋	10:27 am	♌
21	♌		
22	♌	2:05 pm	♍
23	♍		
24	♍	7:11 pm	♎
25	♎		
26	♎		
27	♎	2:49 am	♏
28	♏		
29	♏	1:26 pm	♐
30	♐		
31	♐		

June

Day	Sign	Time	New Sign
1	♓		
2	♓	12:58 am	♈
3	♈		
4	♈	5:34 am	♉
5	♉		
6	♉	6:57 am	♊
7	♊		
8	♊	6:35 am	♋
9	♋		
10	♋	6:25 am	♌
11	♌		
12	♌	8:20 am	♍
13	♍		
14	♍	1:39 pm	♎
15	♎		
16	♎	10:32 pm	♏
17	♏		
18	♏		
19	♏	10:03 am	♐
20	♐		
21	♐	10:45 pm	♑
22	♑		
23	♑		
24	♑	11:24 am	♒
25	♒		
26	♒	10:59 pm	♓
27	♓		
28	♓		
29	♓	8:22 am	♈
30	♈		

September

Day	Sign	Time	New Sign
1	♌		
2	♌	1:27 pm	♍
3	♍		
4	♍	3:51 pm	♎
5	♎		
6	♎	9:20 pm	♏
7	♏		
8	♏		
9	♏	6:38 am	♐
10	♐		
11	♐	6:45 pm	♑
12	♑		
13	♑		
14	♑	7:17 am	♒
15	♒		
16	♒	6:07 pm	♓
17	♓		
18	♓		
19	♓	2:30 am	♈
20	♈		
21	♈	8:45 am	♉
22	♉		
23	♉	1:25 pm	♊
24	♊		
25	♊	4:52 pm	♋
26	♋		
27	♋	7:28 pm	♌
28	♌		
29	♌	9:52 pm	♍
30	♍		

December

Day	Sign	Time	New Sign
1	♐		
2	♐	6:25 pm	♑
3	♑		
4	♑		
5	♑	6:57 am	♒
6	♒		
7	♒	7:27 pm	♓
8	♓		
9	♓		
10	♓	5:57 am	♈
11	♈		
12	♈	12:50 pm	♉
13	♉		
14	♉	3:49 pm	♊
15	♊		
16	♊	4:05 pm	♋
17	♋		
18	♋	3:34 pm	♌
19	♌		
20	♌	4:22 pm	♍
21	♍		
22	♍	8:03 pm	♎
23	♎		
24	♎		
25	♎	3:12 am	♏
26	♏		
27	♏	1:12 pm	♐
28	♐		
29	♐		
30	♐	12:56 am	♑
31	♑		

Moon Movements

♎ = Libra ♏ = Scorpio ♐ = Sagittarius ♑ = Capricorn ♒ = Aquarius ♓ = Pisces

1930

January

Date	Moon	Time	Enters
1	♑	1:29 pm	♒
2	♒		
3	♒		
4	♒	2:04 am	♓
5	♓		
6	♓	1:27 pm	♈
7	♈		
8	♈	9:59 pm	♉
9	♉		
10	♉		
11	♉	2:35 am	♊
12	♊		
13	♊	3:35 am	♋
14	♋		
15	♋	2:37 am	♌
16	♌		
17	♌	1:56 am	♍
18	♍		
19	♍	3:44 am	♎
20	♎		
21	♎	9:25 am	♏
22	♏		
23	♏	6:56 pm	♐
24	♐		
25	♐		
26	♐	6:53 am	♑
27	♑		
28	♑	7:35 pm	♒
29	♒		
30	♒		
31	♒	7:59 am	♓

February

Date	Moon	Time	Enters
1	♓		
2	♓	7:23 pm	♈
3	♈		
4	♈		
5	♈	4:49 am	♉
6	♉		
7	♉	11:08 am	♊
8	♊		
9	♊	1:55 pm	♋
10	♋		
11	♋	2:00 pm	♌
12	♌		
13	♌	1:14 pm	♍
14	♍		
15	♍	1:50 pm	♎
16	♎		
17	♎	5:45 pm	♏
18	♏		
19	♏		
20	♏	1:49 am	♐
21	♐		
22	♐	1:13 pm	♑
23	♑		
24	♑		
25	♑	1:57 am	♒
26	♒		
27	♒	2:13 pm	♓
28	♓		

March

Date	Moon	Time	Enters
1	♓		
2	♓	1:08 am	♈
3	♈		
4	♈	10:19 am	♉
5	♉		
6	♉	5:16 pm	♊
7	♊		
8	♊	9:34 pm	♋
9	♋		
10	♋	11:25 pm	♌
11	♌		
12	♌	11:54 pm	♍
13	♍		
14	♍		
15	♍	12:43 am	♎
16	♎		
17	♎	3:46 am	♏
18	♏		
19	♏	10:23 am	♐
20	♐		
21	♐	8:40 pm	♑
22	♑		
23	♑		
24	♑	9:05 am	♒
25	♒		
26	♒	9:24 pm	♓
27	♓		
28	♓		
29	♓	8:00 am	♈
30	♈		
31	♈	4:24 pm	♉

April

Date	Moon	Time	Enters
1	♉		
2	♉	10:42 pm	♊
3	♊		
4	♊		
5	♊	3:11 am	♋
6	♋		
7	♋	6:09 am	♌
8	♌		
9	♌	8:11 am	♍
10	♍		
11	♍	10:17 am	♎
12	♎		
13	♎	1:45 pm	♏
14	♏		
15	♏	7:49 pm	♐
16	♐		
17	♐		
18	♐	5:07 am	♑
19	♑		
20	♑	4:58 pm	♒
21	♒		
22	♒		
23	♒	5:23 am	♓
24	♓		
25	♓	4:10 pm	♈
26	♈		
27	♈		
28	♈	12:08 am	♉
29	♉		
30	♉	5:26 am	♊

May

Date	Moon	Time	Enters
1	♊		
2	♊	8:54 am	♋
3	♋		
4	♋	11:32 am	♌
5	♌		
6	♌	2:11 pm	♍
7	♍		
8	♍	5:30 pm	♎
9	♎		
10	♎	10:06 pm	♏
11	♏		
12	♏		
13	♏	4:39 am	♐
14	♐		
15	♐	1:39 pm	♑
16	♑		
17	♑		
18	♑	1:03 am	♒
19	♒		
20	♒	1:34 pm	♓
21	♓		
22	♓		
23	♓	12:56 am	♈
24	♈		
25	♈	9:15 am	♉
26	♉		
27	♉	2:07 pm	♊
28	♊		
29	♊	4:26 pm	♋
30	♋		
31	♋	5:45 pm	♌

June

Date	Moon	Time	Enters
1	♌		
2	♌	7:37 pm	♍
3	♍		
4	♍	11:04 pm	♎
5	♎		
6	♎		
7	♎	4:30 am	♏
8	♏		
9	♏	11:56 am	♐
10	♐		
11	♐	9:20 pm	♑
12	♑		
13	♑		
14	♑	8:39 am	♒
15	♒		
16	♒	9:12 pm	♓
17	♓		
18	♓		
19	♓	9:15 am	♈
20	♈		
21	♈	6:35 pm	♉
22	♉		
23	♉		
24	♉	12:00 am	♊
25	♊		
26	♊	1:57 am	♋
27	♋		
28	♋	2:06 am	♌
29	♌		
30	♌	2:28 am	♍

July

Date	Moon	Time	Enters
1	♍		
2	♍	4:47 am	♎
3	♎		
4	♎	9:56 am	♏
5	♏		
6	♏	5:49 pm	♐
7	♐		
8	♐		
9	♐	3:49 am	♑
10	♑		
11	♑	3:23 pm	♒
12	♒		
13	♒		
14	♒	3:57 am	♓
15	♓		
16	♓	4:26 pm	♈
17	♈		
18	♈		
19	♈	2:54 am	♉
20	♉		
21	♉	9:39 am	♊
22	♊		
23	♊	12:22 pm	♋
24	♋		
25	♋	12:19 pm	♌
26	♌		
27	♌	11:34 am	♍
28	♍		
29	♍	12:18 pm	♎
30	♎		
31	♎	4:05 pm	♏

August

Date	Moon	Time	Enters
1	♏		
2	♏	11:24 pm	♐
3	♐		
4	♐		
5	♐	9:34 am	♑
6	♑		
7	♑	9:26 pm	♒
8	♒		
9	♒		
10	♒	10:03 am	♓
11	♓		
12	♓	10:32 pm	♈
13	♈		
14	♈		
15	♈	9:38 am	♉
16	♉		
17	♉	5:46 pm	♊
18	♊		
19	♊	10:02 pm	♋
20	♋		
21	♋	10:58 pm	♌
22	♌		
23	♌	10:13 pm	♍
24	♍		
25	♍	9:58 pm	♎
26	♎		
27	♎		
28	♎	12:11 am	♏
29	♏		
30	♏	6:04 am	♐
31	♐		

September

Date	Moon	Time	Enters
1	♐	3:35 pm	♑
2	♑		
3	♑		
4	♑	3:27 am	♒
5	♒		
6	♒	4:06 pm	♓
7	♓		
8	♓		
9	♓	4:21 am	♈
10	♈		
11	♈	3:18 pm	♉
12	♉		
13	♉		
14	♉	12:01 am	♊
15	♊		
16	♊	5:42 am	♋
17	♋		
18	♋	8:18 am	♌
19	♌		
20	♌	8:45 am	♍
21	♍		
22	♍	8:43 am	♎
23	♎		
24	♎	10:07 am	♏
25	♏		
26	♏	2:34 pm	♐
27	♐		
28	♐	10:48 pm	♑
29	♑		
30	♑		

October

Date	Moon	Time	Enters
1	♑	10:09 am	♒
2	♒		
3	♒	10:48 pm	♓
4	♓		
5	♓		
6	♓	10:52 am	♈
7	♈		
8	♈	9:14 pm	♉
9	♉		
10	♉		
11	♉	5:29 am	♊
12	♊		
13	♊	11:29 am	♋
14	♋		
15	♋	3:19 pm	♌
16	♌		
17	♌	5:26 pm	♍
18	♍		
19	♍	6:43 pm	♎
20	♎		
21	♎	8:32 pm	♏
22	♏		
23	♏		
24	♏	12:23 am	♐
25	♐		
26	♐	7:27 am	♑
27	♑		
28	♑	5:54 pm	♒
29	♒		
30	♒		
31	♒	6:23 am	♓

November

Date	Moon	Time	Enters
1	♓		
2	♓	6:34 pm	♈
3	♈		
4	♈		
5	♈	4:37 am	♉
6	♉		
7	♉	11:58 am	♊
8	♊		
9	♊	5:05 pm	♋
10	♋		
11	♋	8:45 pm	♌
12	♌		
13	♌	11:42 pm	♍
14	♍		
15	♍		
16	♍	2:27 am	♎
17	♎		
18	♎	5:36 am	♏
19	♏		
20	♏	10:00 am	♐
21	♐		
22	♐	4:42 pm	♑
23	♑		
24	♑		
25	♑	2:23 am	♒
26	♒		
27	♒	2:33 pm	♓
28	♓		
29	♓		
30	♓	3:06 am	♈

December

Date	Moon	Time	Enters
1	♈		
2	♈	1:32 pm	♉
3	♉		
4	♉	8:32 pm	♊
5	♊		
6	♊		
7	♊	12:31 am	♋
8	♋		
9	♋	2:53 am	♌
10	♌		
11	♌	5:04 am	♍
12	♍		
13	♍	8:05 am	♎
14	♎		
15	♎	12:19 pm	♏
16	♏		
17	♏	5:54 pm	♐
18	♐		
19	♐		
20	♐	1:11 am	♑
21	♑		
22	♑	10:44 am	♒
23	♒		
24	♒	10:35 pm	♓
25	♓		
26	♓		
27	♓	11:29 am	♈
28	♈		
29	♈	10:52 pm	♉
30	♉		
31	♉		

Your Starway to Love

♈ = Aries ♉ = Taurus ♊ = Gemini ♋ = Cancer ♌ = Leo ♍ = Virgo

1931

January

1	♉	6:34 am	♊
2	♊		
3	♊	10:21 am	♋
4	♋		
5	♋	11:32 am	♌
6	♌		
7	♌	12:06 pm	♍
8	♍		
9	♍	1:48 pm	♎
10	♎		
11	♎	5:40 pm	♏
12	♏		
13	♏	11:51 pm	♐
14	♐		
15	♐		
16	♐	8:02 am	♑
17	♑		
18	♑	6:04 pm	♒
19	♒		
20	♒		
21	♒	5:55 am	♓
22	♓		
23	♓	6:55 pm	♈
24	♈		
25	♈		
26	♈	7:10 am	♉
27	♉		
28	♉	4:18 pm	♊
29	♊		
30	♊	9:09 pm	♋
31	♋		

April

1	♍	7:49 pm	♎
2	♎		
3	♎	7:50 pm	♏
4	♏		
5	♏	9:52 pm	♐
6	♐		
7	♐		
8	♐	3:20 am	♑
9	♑		
10	♑	12:40 pm	♒
11	♒		
12	♒		
13	♒	12:49 am	♓
14	♓		
15	♓	1:48 pm	♈
16	♈		
17	♈		
18	♈	1:50 am	♉
19	♉		
20	♉	11:56 am	♊
21	♊		
22	♊	7:42 pm	♋
23	♋		
24	♋		
25	♋	1:04 am	♌
26	♌		
27	♌	4:10 am	♍
28	♍		
29	♍	5:35 am	♎
30	♎		

July

1	♑	1:56 pm	♒
2	♒		
3	♒		
4	♒	12:09 am	♓
5	♓		
6	♓	12:40 pm	♈
7	♈		
8	♈		
9	♈	1:14 am	♉
10	♉		
11	♉	11:14 am	♊
12	♊		
13	♊	5:30 pm	♋
14	♋		
15	♋	8:41 pm	♌
16	♌		
17	♌	10:22 pm	♍
18	♍		
19	♍		
20	♍	12:06 am	♎
21	♎		
22	♎	2:56 am	♏
23	♏		
24	♏	7:18 am	♐
25	♐		
26	♐	1:22 pm	♑
27	♑		
28	♑	9:24 pm	♒
29	♒		
30	♒		
31	♒	7:45 am	♓

October

1	♉	10:03 am	♊
2	♊		
3	♊	7:38 pm	♋
4	♋		
5	♋		
6	♋	1:49 am	♌
7	♌		
8	♌	4:34 am	♍
9	♍		
10	♍	4:50 am	♎
11	♎		
12	♎	4:17 am	♏
13	♏		
14	♏	4:51 am	♐
15	♐		
16	♐	8:18 am	♑
17	♑		
18	♑	3:39 pm	♒
19	♒		
20	♒		
21	♒	2:32 am	♓
22	♓		
23	♓	3:21 pm	♈
24	♈		
25	♈		
26	♈	4:12 am	♉
27	♉		
28	♉	3:48 pm	♊
29	♊		
30	♊		
31	♊	1:26 am	♋

February

1	♋	10:24 pm	♌
2	♌		
3	♌	9:56 pm	♍
4	♍		
5	♍	9:54 pm	♎
6	♎		
7	♎		
8	♎	12:04 am	♏
9	♏		
10	♏	5:21 am	♐
11	♐		
12	♐	1:39 pm	♑
13	♑		
14	♑		
15	♑	12:14 am	♒
16	♒		
17	♒	12:23 pm	♓
18	♓		
19	♓		
20	♓	1:21 am	♈
21	♈		
22	♈	1:54 pm	♉
23	♉		
24	♉		
25	♉	12:13 am	♊
26	♊		
27	♊	6:47 am	♋
28	♋		

May

1	♎	6:26 am	♏
2	♏		
3	♏	8:14 am	♐
4	♐		
5	♐	12:35 pm	♑
6	♑		
7	♑	8:37 pm	♒
8	♒		
9	♒		
10	♒	8:02 am	♓
11	♓		
12	♓	8:57 pm	♈
13	♈		
14	♈		
15	♈	8:54 am	♉
16	♉		
17	♉	6:26 pm	♊
18	♊		
19	♊		
20	♊	1:26 am	♋
21	♋		
22	♋	6:27 am	♌
23	♌		
24	♌	10:07 am	♍
25	♍		
26	♍	12:51 pm	♎
27	♎		
28	♎	3:08 pm	♏
29	♏		
30	♏	5:48 pm	♐
31	♐		

August

1	♓		
2	♓	8:10 pm	♈
3	♈		
4	♈		
5	♈	9:05 am	♉
6	♉		
7	♉	8:01 pm	♊
8	♊		
9	♊		
10	♊	3:10 am	♋
11	♋		
12	♋	6:31 am	♌
13	♌		
14	♌	7:25 am	♍
15	♍		
16	♍	7:45 am	♎
17	♎		
18	♎	9:10 am	♏
19	♏		
20	♏	12:47 pm	♐
21	♐		
22	♐	6:58 pm	♑
23	♑		
24	♑		
25	♑	3:38 am	♒
26	♒		
27	♒	2:27 pm	♓
28	♓		
29	♓		
30	♓	2:56 am	♈
31	♈		

November

1	♋		
2	♋	8:39 am	♌
3	♌		
4	♌	1:08 pm	♍
5	♍		
6	♍	3:03 pm	♎
7	♎		
8	♎	3:21 pm	♏
9	♏		
10	♏	3:39 pm	♐
11	♐		
12	♐	5:52 pm	♑
13	♑		
14	♑	11:40 pm	♒
15	♒		
16	♒		
17	♒	9:32 am	♓
18	♓		
19	♓	10:08 pm	♈
20	♈		
21	♈		
22	♈	11:00 am	♉
23	♉		
24	♉	10:12 pm	♊
25	♊		
26	♊		
27	♊	7:09 am	♋
28	♋		
29	♋	2:06 pm	♌
30	♌		

March

1	♋	9:25 am	♌
2	♌		
3	♌	9:21 am	♍
4	♍		
5	♍	8:32 am	♎
6	♎		
7	♎	9:03 am	♏
8	♏		
9	♏	12:30 pm	♐
10	♐		
11	♐	7:39 pm	♑
12	♑		
13	♑		
14	♑	6:03 am	♒
15	♒		
16	♒	6:26 pm	♓
17	♓		
18	♓		
19	♓	7:24 am	♈
20	♈		
21	♈	7:44 pm	♉
22	♉		
23	♉		
24	♉	6:19 am	♊
25	♊		
26	♊	2:04 pm	♋
27	♋		
28	♋	6:29 pm	♌
29	♌		
30	♌	7:58 pm	♍
31	♍		

June

1	♐	10:07 pm	♑
2	♑		
3	♑		
4	♑	5:23 am	♒
5	♒		
6	♒	4:01 pm	♓
7	♓		
8	♓		
9	♓	4:44 am	♈
10	♈		
11	♈	4:54 pm	♉
12	♉		
13	♉		
14	♉	2:22 am	♊
15	♊		
16	♊	8:38 am	♋
17	♋		
18	♋	12:36 pm	♌
19	♌		
20	♌	3:32 pm	♍
21	♍		
22	♍	6:23 pm	♎
23	♎		
24	♎	9:34 pm	♏
25	♏		
26	♏		
27	♏	1:26 am	♐
28	♐		
29	♐	6:35 am	♑
30	♑		

September

1	♈	3:59 pm	♉
2	♉		
3	♉		
4	♉	3:43 am	♊
5	♊		
6	♊	12:15 pm	♋
7	♋		
8	♋	4:47 pm	♌
9	♌		
10	♌	6:04 pm	♍
11	♍		
12	♍	5:43 pm	♎
13	♎		
14	♎	5:40 pm	♏
15	♏		
16	♏	7:39 pm	♐
17	♐		
18	♐		
19	♐	12:48 am	♑
20	♑		
21	♑	9:18 am	♒
22	♒		
23	♒	8:28 pm	♓
24	♓		
25	♓		
26	♓	9:09 am	♈
27	♈		
28	♈	10:07 pm	♉
29	♉		
30	♉		

December

1	♌	7:16 pm	♍
2	♍		
3	♍	10:44 pm	♎
4	♎		
5	♎		
6	♎	12:43 am	♏
7	♏		
8	♏	2:04 am	♐
9	♐		
10	♐	4:18 am	♑
11	♑		
12	♑	9:10 am	♒
13	♒		
14	♒	5:50 pm	♓
15	♓		
16	♓		
17	♓	5:49 am	♈
18	♈		
19	♈	6:45 pm	♉
20	♉		
21	♉		
22	♉	5:59 am	♊
23	♊		
24	♊	2:22 pm	♋
25	♋		
26	♋	8:16 pm	♌
27	♌		
28	♌		
29	♌	12:41 am	♍
30	♍		
31	♍	4:17 am	♎

Moon Movements

♎ = Libra ♏ = Scorpio ♐ = Sagittarius ♑ = Capricorn ♒ = Aquarius ♓ = Pisces

1932

January

1	♎		
2	♎	7:24 am	♏
3	♏		
4	♏	10:15 am	♐
5	♐		
6	♐	1:37 pm	♑
7	♑		
8	♑	6:44 pm	♒
9	♒		
10	♒		
11	♒	2:49 am	♓
12	♓		
13	♓	2:07 pm	♈
14	♈		
15	♈		
16	♈	3:02 am	♉
17	♉		
18	♉	2:47 pm	♊
19	♊		
20	♊	11:22 pm	♋
21	♋		
22	♋		
23	♋	4:39 am	♌
24	♌		
25	♌	7:47 am	♍
26	♍		
27	♍	10:07 am	♎
28	♎		
29	♎	12:43 pm	♏
30	♏		
31	♏	4:07 pm	♐

February

1	♐		
2	♐	8:39 pm	♑
3	♑		
4	♑		
5	♑	2:48 am	♒
6	♒		
7	♒	11:15 am	♓
8	♓		
9	♓	10:17 pm	♈
10	♈		
11	♈		
12	♈	11:05 am	♉
13	♉		
14	♉	11:28 pm	♊
15	♊		
16	♊		
17	♊	9:02 am	♋
18	♋		
19	♋	2:49 pm	♌
20	♌		
21	♌	5:25 pm	♍
22	♍		
23	♍	6:22 pm	♎
24	♎		
25	♎	7:20 pm	♏
26	♏		
27	♏	9:39 pm	♐
28	♐		
29	♐		

March

1	♐	2:06 am	♑
2	♑		
3	♑	9:00 am	♒
4	♒		
5	♒	6:15 pm	♓
6	♓		
7	♓		
8	♓	5:35 am	♈
9	♈		
10	♈	6:19 pm	♉
11	♉		
12	♉		
13	♉	7:03 am	♊
14	♊		
15	♊	5:46 pm	♋
16	♋		
17	♋		
18	♋	12:56 am	♌
19	♌		
20	♌	4:18 am	♍
21	♍		
22	♍	4:56 am	♎
23	♎		
24	♎	4:35 am	♏
25	♏		
26	♏	5:07 am	♐
27	♐		
28	♐	8:08 am	♑
29	♑		
30	♑	2:30 pm	♒
31	♒		

April

1	♒		
2	♒	12:05 am	♓
3	♓		
4	♓	11:53 am	♈
5	♈		
6	♈		
7	♈	12:44 am	♉
8	♉		
9	♉	1:27 pm	♊
10	♊		
11	♊		
12	♊	12:47 am	♋
13	♋		
14	♋	9:22 am	♌
15	♌		
16	♌	2:21 pm	♍
17	♍		
18	♍	4:00 pm	♎
19	♎		
20	♎	3:33 pm	♏
21	♏		
22	♏	2:57 pm	♐
23	♐		
24	♐	4:15 pm	♑
25	♑		
26	♑	9:04 pm	♒
27	♒		
28	♒		
29	♒	5:55 am	♓
30	♓		

May

1	♓	5:46 pm	♈
2	♈		
3	♈		
4	♈	6:46 am	♉
5	♉		
6	♉	7:20 pm	♊
7	♊		
8	♊		
9	♊	6:34 am	♋
10	♋		
11	♋	3:47 pm	♌
12	♌		
13	♌	10:13 pm	♍
14	♍		
15	♍		
16	♍	1:32 am	♎
17	♎		
18	♎	2:15 am	♏
19	♏		
20	♏	1:48 am	♐
21	♐		
22	♐	2:12 am	♑
23	♑		
24	♑	5:31 am	♒
25	♒		
26	♒	12:57 pm	♓
27	♓		
28	♓		
29	♓	12:09 am	♈
30	♈		
31	♈	1:05 pm	♉

June

1	♉		
2	♉		
3	♉	1:32 am	♊
4	♊		
5	♊	12:21 pm	♋
6	♋		
7	♋	9:14 pm	♌
8	♌		
9	♌		
10	♌	4:06 am	♍
11	♍		
12	♍	8:41 am	♎
13	♎		
14	♎	11:00 am	♏
15	♏		
16	♏	11:45 am	♐
17	♐		
18	♐	12:31 pm	♑
19	♑		
20	♑	3:12 pm	♒
21	♒		
22	♒	9:25 pm	♓
23	♓		
24	♓		
25	♓	7:34 am	♈
26	♈		
27	♈	8:08 pm	♉
28	♉		
29	♉		
30	♉	8:35 am	♊

July

1	♊		
2	♊	7:07 pm	♋
3	♋		
4	♋		
5	♋	3:18 am	♌
6	♌		
7	♌	9:33 am	♍
8	♍		
9	♍	2:12 pm	♎
10	♎		
11	♎	5:27 pm	♏
12	♏		
13	♏	7:38 pm	♐
14	♐		
15	♐	9:35 pm	♑
16	♑		
17	♑		
18	♑	12:44 am	♒
19	♒		
20	♒	6:34 am	♓
21	♓		
22	♓	3:52 pm	♈
23	♈		
24	♈		
25	♈	3:54 am	♉
26	♉		
27	♉	4:26 pm	♊
28	♊		
29	♊		
30	♊	3:07 am	♋
31	♋		

August

1	♋	10:57 am	♌
2	♌		
3	♌	4:15 pm	♍
4	♍		
5	♍	7:56 pm	♎
6	♎		
7	♎	10:49 pm	♏
8	♏		
9	♏		
10	♏	1:32 am	♐
11	♐		
12	♐	4:38 am	♑
13	♑		
14	♑	8:54 am	♒
15	♒		
16	♒	3:13 pm	♓
17	♓		
18	♓		
19	♓	12:18 am	♈
20	♈		
21	♈	11:56 am	♉
22	♉		
23	♉		
24	♉	12:33 am	♊
25	♊		
26	♊	11:50 am	♋
27	♋		
28	♋	8:03 pm	♌
29	♌		
30	♌		
31	♌	12:58 am	♍

September

1	♍		
2	♍	3:32 am	♎
3	♎		
4	♎	5:06 am	♏
5	♏		
6	♏	7:00 am	♐
7	♐		
8	♐	10:11 am	♑
9	♑		
10	♑	3:16 pm	♒
11	♒		
12	♒	10:31 pm	♓
13	♓		
14	♓		
15	♓	8:01 am	♈
16	♈		
17	♈	7:34 pm	♉
18	♉		
19	♉		
20	♉	8:14 am	♊
21	♊		
22	♊	8:13 pm	♋
23	♋		
24	♋		
25	♋	5:32 am	♌
26	♌		
27	♌	11:07 am	♍
28	♍		
29	♍	1:22 pm	♎
30	♎		

October

1	♎	1:44 pm	♏
2	♏		
3	♏	2:02 pm	♐
4	♐		
5	♐	4:00 pm	♑
6	♑		
7	♑	8:44 pm	♒
8	♒		
9	♒		
10	♒	4:26 am	♓
11	♓		
12	♓	2:36 pm	♈
13	♈		
14	♈		
15	♈	2:24 am	♉
16	♉		
17	♉	3:03 pm	♊
18	♊		
19	♊		
20	♊	3:26 am	♋
21	♋		
22	♋	1:57 pm	♌
23	♌		
24	♌	9:03 pm	♍
25	♍		
26	♍		
27	♍	12:15 am	♎
28	♎		
29	♎	12:30 am	♏
30	♏	11:40 pm	♐
31	♐		

November

1	♐	11:54 pm	♑
2	♑		
3	♑		
4	♑	3:06 am	♒
5	♒		
6	♒	10:06 am	♓
7	♓		
8	♓	8:24 pm	♈
9	♈		
10	♈		
11	♈	8:33 am	♉
12	♉		
13	♉	9:13 pm	♊
14	♊		
15	♊		
16	♊	9:32 am	♋
17	♋		
18	♋	8:35 pm	♌
19	♌		
20	♌		
21	♌	5:08 am	♍
22	♍		
23	♍	10:08 am	♎
24	♎		
25	♎	11:38 am	♏
26	♏		
27	♏	10:58 am	♐
28	♐		
29	♐	10:16 am	♑
30	♑		

December

1	♑	11:46 am	♒
2	♒		
3	♒	5:08 pm	♓
4	♓		
5	♓		
6	♓	2:35 am	♈
7	♈		
8	♈	2:41 pm	♉
9	♉		
10	♉		
11	♉	3:26 am	♊
12	♊		
13	♊	3:28 pm	♋
14	♋		
15	♋		
16	♋	2:13 am	♌
17	♌		
18	♌	11:09 am	♍
19	♍		
20	♍	5:32 pm	♎
21	♎		
22	♎	8:53 pm	♏
23	♏		
24	♏	9:42 pm	♐
25	♐		
26	♐	9:31 pm	♑
27	♑		
28	♑	10:23 pm	♒
29	♒		
30	♒		
31	♒	2:16 am	♓

1933

Your Starway to Love

♈ = Aries ♉ = Taurus ♊ = Gemini ♋ = Cancer ♌ = Leo ♍ = Virgo

January

1	♓		
2	♓	10:13 am	♈
3	♈		
4	♈	9:36 pm	♉
5	♉		
6	♉		
7	♉	10:19 am	♊
8	♊		
9	♊	10:16 pm	♋
10	♋		
11	♋		
12	♋	8:27 am	♌
13	♌		
14	♌	4:42 pm	♍
15	♍		
16	♍	11:03 pm	♎
17	♎		
18	♎		
19	♎	3:24 am	♏
20	♏		
21	♏	5:54 am	♐
22	♐		
23	♐	7:18 am	♑
24	♑		
25	♑	8:57 am	♒
26	♒		
27	♒	12:31 pm	♓
28	♓		
29	♓	7:21 pm	♈
30	♈		
31	♈		

February

1	♈	5:40 am	♉
2	♉		
3	♉	6:05 pm	♊
4	♊		
5	♊		
6	♊	6:13 am	♋
7	♋		
8	♋	4:16 pm	♌
9	♌		
10	♌	11:43 pm	♍
11	♍		
12	♍		
13	♍	4:59 am	♎
14	♎		
15	♎	8:46 am	♏
16	♏		
17	♏	11:42 am	♐
18	♐		
19	♐	2:22 pm	♑
20	♑		
21	♑	5:29 pm	♒
22	♒		
23	♒	9:56 pm	♓
24	♓		
25	♓		
26	♓	4:42 am	♈
27	♈		
28	♈	2:20 pm	♉

March

1	♉		
2	♉		
3	♉	2:18 am	♊
4	♊		
5	♊	2:43 pm	♋
6	♋		
7	♋		
8	♋	1:18 am	♌
9	♌		
10	♌	8:42 am	♍
11	♍		
12	♍	1:03 pm	♎
13	♎		
14	♎	3:27 pm	♏
15	♏		
16	♏	5:18 pm	♐
17	♐		
18	♐	7:47 pm	♑
19	♑		
20	♑	11:39 pm	♒
21	♒		
22	♒		
23	♒	5:16 am	♓
24	♓		
25	♓	12:49 pm	♈
26	♈		
27	♈	10:32 pm	♉
28	♉		
29	♉		
30	♉	10:13 am	♊
31	♊		

April

1	♊	10:50 pm	♋
2	♋		
3	♋		
4	♋	10:16 am	♌
5	♌		
6	♌	6:33 pm	♍
7	♍		
8	♍	11:00 pm	♎
9	♎		
10	♎		
11	♎	12:32 am	♏
12	♏		
13	♏	12:52 am	♐
14	♐		
15	♐	1:53 am	♑
16	♑		
17	♑	5:02 am	♒
18	♒		
19	♒	10:54 am	♓
20	♓		
21	♓	7:14 pm	♈
22	♈		
23	♈		
24	♈	5:31 am	♉
25	♉		
26	♉	5:18 pm	♊
27	♊		
28	♊		
29	♊	5:58 am	♋
30	♋		

May

1	♋	6:06 pm	♌
2	♌		
3	♌		
4	♌	3:41 am	♍
5	♍		
6	♍	9:17 am	♎
7	♎		
8	♎	11:07 am	♏
9	♏		
10	♏	10:43 am	♐
11	♐		
12	♐	10:15 am	♑
13	♑		
14	♑	11:46 am	♒
15	♒		
16	♒	4:34 pm	♓
17	♓		
18	♓		
19	♓	12:45 am	♈
20	♈		
21	♈	11:26 am	♉
22	♉		
23	♉	11:31 pm	♊
24	♊		
25	♊		
26	♊	12:12 pm	♋
27	♋		
28	♋		
29	♋	12:33 am	♌
30	♌		
31	♌	11:06 am	♍

June

1	♍		
2	♍	6:15 pm	♎
3	♎		
4	♎	9:25 pm	♏
5	♏		
6	♏	9:32 pm	♐
7	♐		
8	♐	8:33 pm	♑
9	♑		
10	♑	8:41 pm	♒
11	♒		
12	♒	11:50 pm	♓
13	♓		
14	♓		
15	♓	6:50 am	♈
16	♈		
17	♈	5:12 pm	♉
18	♉		
19	♉		
20	♉	5:25 am	♊
21	♊		
22	♊	6:07 pm	♋
23	♋		
24	♋		
25	♋	6:17 am	♌
26	♌		
27	♌	5:01 pm	♍
28	♍		
29	♍		
30	♍	1:11 am	♎

July

1	♎		
2	♎	5:57 am	♏
3	♏		
4	♏	7:32 am	♐
5	♐		
6	♐	7:15 am	♑
7	♑		
8	♑	7:05 am	♒
9	♒		
10	♒	9:01 am	♓
11	♓		
12	♓	2:31 pm	♈
13	♈		
14	♈	11:49 pm	♉
15	♉		
16	♉		
17	♉	11:44 am	♊
18	♊		
19	♊		
20	♊	12:25 am	♋
21	♋		
22	♋	12:19 pm	♌
23	♌		
24	♌	10:36 pm	♍
25	♍		
26	♍		
27	♍	6:44 am	♎
28	♎		
29	♎	12:21 pm	♏
30	♏		
31	♏	3:27 pm	♐

August

1	♐		
2	♐	4:40 pm	♑
3	♑		
4	♑	5:22 pm	♒
5	♒		
6	♒	7:11 pm	♓
7	♓		
8	♓	11:40 pm	♈
9	♈		
10	♈		
11	♈	7:45 am	♉
12	♉		
13	♉	6:57 pm	♊
14	♊		
15	♊		
16	♊	7:32 am	♋
17	♋		
18	♋	7:22 pm	♌
19	♌		
20	♌		
21	♌	5:07 am	♍
22	♍		
23	♍	12:29 pm	♎
24	♎		
25	♎	5:44 pm	♏
26	♏		
27	♏	9:21 pm	♐
28	♐		
29	♐	11:52 pm	♑
30	♑		
31	♑		

September

1	♑	2:00 am	♒
2	♒		
3	♒	4:44 am	♓
4	♓		
5	♓	9:15 am	♈
6	♈		
7	♈	4:35 pm	♉
8	♉		
9	♉		
10	♉	3:01 am	♊
11	♊		
12	♊	3:25 pm	♋
13	♋		
14	♋		
15	♋	3:31 am	♌
16	♌		
17	♌	1:13 pm	♍
18	♍		
19	♍	7:51 pm	♎
20	♎		
21	♎	12:00 pm	♏
22	♏		
23	♏		
24	♏	2:49 am	♐
25	♐		
26	♐	5:23 am	♑
27	♑		
28	♑	8:27 am	♒
29	♒		
30	♒	12:27 pm	♓

October

1	♓		
2	♓	5:51 pm	♈
3	♈		
4	♈		
5	♈	1:18 am	♉
6	♉		
7	♉	11:18 am	♊
8	♊		
9	♊	11:29 pm	♋
10	♋		
11	♋		
12	♋	12:02 pm	♌
13	♌		
14	♌	10:24 pm	♍
15	♍		
16	♍		
17	♍	5:07 am	♎
18	♎		
19	♎	8:27 am	♏
20	♏		
21	♏	9:54 am	♐
22	♐		
23	♐	11:13 am	♑
24	♑		
25	♑	1:48 pm	♒
26	♒		
27	♒	6:17 pm	♓
28	♓		
29	♓		
30	♓	12:40 am	♈
31	♈		

November

1	♈	8:53 am	♉
2	♉		
3	♉	7:02 pm	♊
4	♊		
5	♊		
6	♊	7:05 am	♋
7	♋		
8	♋	7:58 pm	♌
9	♌		
10	♌		
11	♌	7:24 am	♍
12	♍		
13	♍	3:12 pm	♎
14	♎		
15	♎	6:52 pm	♏
16	♏		
17	♏	7:34 pm	♐
18	♐		
19	♐	7:24 pm	♑
20	♑		
21	♑	8:21 pm	♒
22	♒		
23	♒	11:50 pm	♓
24	♓		
25	♓		
26	♓	6:13 am	♈
27	♈		
28	♈	3:03 pm	♉
29	♉		
30	♉		

December

1	♉	1:45 am	♊
2	♊		
3	♊	1:53 pm	♋
4	♋		
5	♋		
6	♋	2:49 am	♌
7	♌		
8	♌	3:00 pm	♍
9	♍		
10	♍		
11	♍	12:19 am	♎
12	♎		
13	♎	5:27 am	♏
14	♏		
15	♏	6:49 am	♐
16	♐		
17	♐	6:08 am	♑
18	♑		
19	♑	5:37 am	♒
20	♒		
21	♒	7:15 am	♓
22	♓		
23	♓	12:15 pm	♈
24	♈		
25	♈	8:43 pm	♉
26	♉		
27	♉		
28	♉	7:43 am	♊
29	♊		
30	♊	8:07 pm	♋
31	♋		

Moon Movements

♎ = Libra ♏ = Scorpio ♐ = Sagittarius ♑ = Capricorn ♒ = Aquarius ♓ = Pisces

1934

January

Day	Moon	Time	Enters
1	♋		
2	♋	8:56 am	♌
3	♌		
4	♌	9:09 pm	♍
5	♍		
6	♍		
7	♍	7:20 am	♎
8	♎		
9	♎	2:11 pm	♏
10	♏		
11	♏	5:18 pm	♐
12	♐		
13	♐	5:37 pm	♑
14	♑		
15	♑	4:56 pm	♒
16	♒		
17	♒	5:17 pm	♓
18	♓		
19	♓	8:28 pm	♈
20	♈		
21	♈		
22	♈	3:26 am	♉
23	♉		
24	♉	1:54 pm	♊
25	♊		
26	♊		
27	♊	2:24 am	♋
28	♋		
29	♋	3:12 pm	♌
30	♌		
31	♌		

April

Day	Moon	Time	Enters
1	♎	8:35 am	♏
2	♏		
3	♏	12:37 pm	♐
4	♐		
5	♐	3:45 pm	♑
6	♑		
7	♑	6:43 pm	♒
8	♒		
9	♒	9:52 pm	♓
10	♓		
11	♓		
12	♓	1:40 am	♈
13	♈		
14	♈	6:56 am	♉
15	♉		
16	♉	2:41 pm	♊
17	♊		
18	♊		
19	♊	1:26 am	♋
20	♋		
21	♋	2:10 pm	♌
22	♌		
23	♌		
24	♌	2:20 am	♍
25	♍		
26	♍	11:32 am	♎
27	♎		
28	♎	5:07 pm	♏
29	♏		
30	♏	8:02 pm	♐

July

Day	Moon	Time	Enters
1	♓		
2	♓	7:39 pm	♈
3	♈		
4	♈		
5	♈	1:47 am	♉
6	♉		
7	♉	10:55 am	♊
8	♊		
9	♊	10:20 pm	♋
10	♋		
11	♋		
12	♋	11:07 am	♌
13	♌		
14	♌		
15	♌	12:07 am	♍
16	♍		
17	♍	11:47 am	♎
18	♎		
19	♎	8:31 pm	♏
20	♏		
21	♏		
22	♏	1:28 am	♐
23	♐		
24	♐	3:03 am	♑
25	♑		
26	♑	2:43 am	♒
27	♒		
28	♒	2:20 am	♓
29	♓		
30	♓	3:45 am	♈
31	♈		

October

Day	Moon	Time	Enters
1	♋		
2	♋	6:44 am	♌
3	♌		
4	♌	7:31 pm	♍
5	♍		
6	♍		
7	♍	6:20 am	♎
8	♎		
9	♎	2:31 pm	♏
10	♏		
11	♏	8:32 pm	♐
12	♐		
13	♐		
14	♐	1:04 am	♑
15	♑		
16	♑	4:32 am	♒
17	♒		
18	♒	7:10 am	♓
19	♓		
20	♓	9:28 am	♈
21	♈		
22	♈	12:34 pm	♉
23	♉		
24	♉	5:58 pm	♊
25	♊		
26	♊		
27	♊	2:46 am	♋
28	♋		
29	♋	2:42 pm	♌
30	♌		
31	♌		

February

Day	Moon	Time	Enters
1	♌	3:00 am	♍
2	♍		
3	♍	1:00 pm	♎
4	♎		
5	♎	8:31 pm	♏
6	♏		
7	♏		
8	♏	1:14 am	♐
9	♐		
10	♐	3:23 am	♑
11	♑		
12	♑	3:57 am	♒
13	♒		
14	♒	4:27 am	♓
15	♓		
16	♓	6:39 am	♈
17	♈		
18	♈	12:03 pm	♉
19	♉		
20	♉	9:16 pm	♊
21	♊		
22	♊		
23	♊	9:22 am	♋
24	♋		
25	♋	10:13 pm	♌
26	♌		
27	♌		
28	♌	9:46 am	♍

May

Day	Moon	Time	Enters
1	♐		
2	♐	9:53 pm	♑
3	♑		
4	♑		
5	♑	12:06 am	♒
6	♒		
7	♒	3:26 am	♓
8	♓		
9	♓	8:09 am	♈
10	♈		
11	♈	2:24 pm	♉
12	♉		
13	♉	10:38 pm	♊
14	♊		
15	♊		
16	♊	9:17 am	♋
17	♋		
18	♋	9:55 pm	♌
19	♌		
20	♌		
21	♌	10:35 am	♍
22	♍		
23	♍	8:43 pm	♎
24	♎		
25	♎		
26	♎	2:52 am	♏
27	♏		
28	♏	5:28 am	♐
29	♐		
30	♐	6:12 am	♑
31	♑		

August

Day	Moon	Time	Enters
1	♈	8:25 am	♉
2	♉		
3	♉	4:48 pm	♊
4	♊		
5	♊		
6	♊	4:13 am	♋
7	♋		
8	♋	5:08 pm	♌
9	♌		
10	♌		
11	♌	5:59 am	♍
12	♍		
13	♍	5:33 pm	♎
14	♎		
15	♎		
16	♎	2:51 am	♏
17	♏		
18	♏	9:12 am	♐
19	♐		
20	♐	12:27 pm	♑
21	♑		
22	♑	1:18 pm	♒
23	♒		
24	♒	1:08 pm	♓
25	♓		
26	♓	1:44 pm	♈
27	♈		
28	♈	4:55 pm	♉
29	♉		
30	♉	11:55 pm	♊
31	♊		

November

Day	Moon	Time	Enters
1	♌	3:36 am	♍
2	♍		
3	♍	2:41 pm	♎
4	♎		
5	♎	10:32 pm	♏
6	♏		
7	♏		
8	♏	3:33 am	♐
9	♐		
10	♐	6:57 am	♑
11	♑		
12	♑	9:52 am	♒
13	♒		
14	♒	12:56 pm	♓
15	♓		
16	♓	4:26 pm	♈
17	♈		
18	♈	8:46 pm	♉
19	♉		
20	♉		
21	♉	2:47 am	♊
22	♊		
23	♊	11:25 am	♋
24	♋		
25	♋	10:54 pm	♌
26	♌		
27	♌		
28	♌	11:52 am	♍
29	♍		
30	♍	11:39 pm	♎

March

Day	Moon	Time	Enters
1	♍		
2	♍	7:02 pm	♎
3	♎		
4	♎		
5	♎	1:59 am	♏
6	♏		
7	♏	6:58 am	♐
8	♐		
9	♐	10:22 am	♑
10	♑		
11	♑	12:36 pm	♒
12	♒		
13	♒	2:25 pm	♓
14	♓		
15	♓	5:00 pm	♈
16	♈		
17	♈	9:46 pm	♉
18	♉		
19	♉		
20	♉	5:51 am	♊
21	♊		
22	♊	5:13 pm	♋
23	♋		
24	♋		
25	♋	6:03 am	♌
26	♌		
27	♌	5:44 pm	♍
28	♍		
29	♍		
30	♍	2:37 am	♎
31	♎		

June

Day	Moon	Time	Enters
1	♑	6:55 am	♒
2	♒		
3	♒	9:06 am	♓
4	♓		
5	♓	1:31 pm	♈
6	♈		
7	♈	8:17 pm	♉
8	♉		
9	♉		
10	♉	5:14 am	♊
11	♊		
12	♊	4:14 pm	♋
13	♋		
14	♋		
15	♋	4:53 am	♌
16	♌		
17	♌	5:51 pm	♍
18	♍		
19	♍		
20	♍	4:59 am	♎
21	♎		
22	♎	12:25 pm	♏
23	♏		
24	♏	3:49 pm	♐
25	♐		
26	♐	4:24 pm	♑
27	♑		
28	♑	4:02 pm	♒
29	♒		
30	♒	4:38 pm	♓

September

Day	Moon	Time	Enters
1	♊		
2	♊	10:40 am	♋
3	♋		
4	♋	11:32 pm	♌
5	♌		
6	♌		
7	♌	12:16 pm	♍
8	♍		
9	♍	11:23 pm	♎
10	♎		
11	♎		
12	♎	8:19 am	♏
13	♏		
14	♏	3:03 pm	♐
15	♐		
16	♐	7:36 pm	♑
17	♑		
18	♑	10:06 pm	♒
19	♒		
20	♒	11:14 pm	♓
21	♓		
22	♓		
23	♓	12:13 am	♈
24	♈		
25	♈	2:47 am	♉
26	♉		
27	♉	8:33 am	♊
28	♊		
29	♊	6:14 pm	♋
30	♋		

December

Day	Moon	Time	Enters
1	♎		
2	♎		
3	♎	8:06 am	♏
4	♏		
5	♏	12:52 pm	♐
6	♐		
7	♐	3:09 pm	♑
8	♑		
9	♑	4:34 pm	♒
10	♒		
11	♒	6:31 pm	♓
12	♓		
13	♓	9:51 pm	♈
14	♈		
15	♈		
16	♈	2:56 am	♉
17	♉		
18	♉	9:58 am	♊
19	♊		
20	♊	7:11 pm	♋
21	♋		
22	♋		
23	♋	6:37 am	♌
24	♌		
25	♌	7:32 pm	♍
26	♍		
27	♍		
28	♍	7:59 am	♎
29	♎		
30	♎	5:41 pm	♏
31	♏		

♈ = Aries ♉ = Taurus ♊ = Gemini ♋ = Cancer ♌ = Leo ♍ = Virgo

1935

January

1	♏	11:27 pm	♐
2	♐		
3	♐		
4	♐	1:44 am	♑
5	♑		
6	♑	2:04 am	♒
7	♒		
8	♒	2:17 am	♓
9	♓		
10	♓	4:03 am	♈
11	♈		
12	♈	8:25 am	♉
13	♉		
14	♉	3:43 pm	♊
15	♊		
16	♊		
17	♊	1:37 am	♋
18	♋		
19	♋	1:27 pm	♌
20	♌		
21	♌		
22	♌	2:19 am	♍
23	♍		
24	♍	2:59 pm	♎
25	♎		
26	♎		
27	♎	1:46 am	♏
28	♏		
29	♏	9:11 am	♐
30	♐		
31	♐	12:47 pm	♑

February

1	♑		
2	♑	1:26 pm	♒
3	♒		
4	♒	12:47 pm	♓
5	♓		
6	♓	12:49 pm	♈
7	♈		
8	♈	3:22 pm	♉
9	♉		
10	♉	9:35 pm	♊
11	♊		
12	♊		
13	♊	7:24 am	♋
14	♋		
15	♋	7:35 pm	♌
16	♌		
17	♌		
18	♌	8:33 am	♍
19	♍		
20	♍	9:02 pm	♎
21	♎		
22	♎		
23	♎	8:04 am	♏
24	♏		
25	♏	4:40 pm	♐
26	♐		
27	♐	10:05 pm	♑
28	♑		

March

1	♑		
2	♑	12:16 am	♒
3	♒		
4	♒	12:13 am	♓
5	♓	11:40 pm	♈
6	♈		
7	♈		
8	♈	12:43 am	♉
9	♉		
10	♉	5:11 am	♊
11	♊		
12	♊	1:52 pm	♋
13	♋		
14	♋		
15	♋	1:48 am	♌
16	♌		
17	♌	2:51 pm	♍
18	♍		
19	♍		
20	♍	3:08 am	♎
21	♎		
22	♎	1:44 pm	♏
23	♏		
24	♏	10:24 pm	♐
25	♐		
26	♐		
27	♐	4:49 am	♑
28	♑		
29	♑	8:41 am	♒
30	♒		
31	♒	10:14 am	♓

April

1	♓		
2	♓	10:31 am	♈
3	♈		
4	♈	11:18 am	♉
5	♉		
6	♉	2:35 pm	♊
7	♊		
8	♊	9:49 pm	♋
9	♋		
10	♋		
11	♋	8:52 am	♌
12	♌		
13	♌	9:47 pm	♍
14	♍		
15	♍		
16	♍	10:01 am	♎
17	♎		
18	♎	8:09 pm	♏
19	♏		
20	♏		
21	♏	4:06 am	♐
22	♐		
23	♐	10:13 am	♑
24	♑		
25	♑	2:43 pm	♒
26	♒		
27	♒	5:40 pm	♓
28	♓		
29	♓	7:26 pm	♈
30	♈		

May

1	♈	9:09 pm	♉
2	♉		
3	♉		
4	♉	12:26 am	♊
5	♊		
6	♊	6:50 am	♋
7	♋		
8	♋	4:55 pm	♌
9	♌		
10	♌		
11	♌	5:26 am	♍
12	♍		
13	♍	5:48 pm	♎
14	♎		
15	♎		
16	♎	3:54 am	♏
17	♏		
18	♏	11:13 am	♐
19	♐		
20	♐	4:20 pm	♑
21	♑		
22	♑	8:08 pm	♒
23	♒		
24	♒	11:13 pm	♓
25	♓		
26	♓		
27	♓	1:59 am	♈
28	♈		
29	♈	4:59 am	♉
30	♉		
31	♉	9:11 am	♊

June

1	♊		
2	♊	3:44 pm	♋
3	♋		
4	♋		
5	♋	1:19 am	♌
6	♌		
7	♌	1:26 pm	♍
8	♍		
9	♍		
10	♍	2:00 am	♎
11	♎		
12	♎	12:35 pm	♏
13	♏		
14	♏	7:57 pm	♐
15	♐		
16	♐		
17	♐	12:21 am	♑
18	♑		
19	♑	2:56 am	♒
20	♒		
21	♒	4:56 am	♓
22	♓		
23	♓	7:21 am	♈
24	♈		
25	♈	10:54 am	♉
26	♉		
27	♉	4:06 pm	♊
28	♊		
29	♊	11:26 pm	♋
30	♋		

July

1	♋		
2	♋	9:13 am	♌
3	♌		
4	♌	9:08 pm	♍
5	♍		
6	♍		
7	♍	9:52 am	♎
8	♎		
9	♎	9:15 pm	♏
10	♏		
11	♏		
12	♏	5:27 am	♐
13	♐		
14	♐	10:03 am	♑
15	♑		
16	♑	11:53 am	♒
17	♒		
18	♒	12:30 pm	♓
19	♓		
20	♓	1:33 pm	♈
21	♈		
22	♈	4:21 pm	♉
23	♉		
24	♉	9:42 pm	♊
25	♊		
26	♊		
27	♊	5:43 am	♋
28	♋		
29	♋	4:04 pm	♌
30	♌		
31	♌		

August

1	♌	4:07 am	♍
2	♍		
3	♍	4:55 pm	♎
4	♎		
5	♎		
6	♎	4:57 am	♏
7	♏		
8	♏	2:25 pm	♐
9	♐		
10	♐	8:10 pm	♑
11	♑		
12	♑	10:22 pm	♒
13	♒		
14	♒	10:19 pm	♓
15	♓		
16	♓	9:55 pm	♈
17	♈		
18	♈	11:07 pm	♉
19	♉		
20	♉		
21	♉	3:25 am	♊
22	♊		
23	♊	11:17 am	♋
24	♋		
25	♋	10:00 pm	♌
26	♌		
27	♌		
28	♌	10:20 am	♍
29	♍		
30	♍	11:08 pm	♎
31	♎		

September

1	♎		
2	♎	11:22 am	♏
3	♏		
4	♏	9:48 pm	♐
5	♐		
6	♐		
7	♐	5:08 am	♑
8	♑		
9	♑	8:44 am	♒
10	♒		
11	♒	9:15 am	♓
12	♓		
13	♓	8:20 am	♈
14	♈		
15	♈	8:10 am	♉
16	♉		
17	♉	10:48 am	♊
18	♊		
19	♊	5:27 pm	♋
20	♋		
21	♋		
22	♋	3:50 am	♌
23	♌		
24	♌	4:18 pm	♍
25	♍		
26	♍		
27	♍	5:05 am	♎
28	♎		
29	♎	5:06 pm	♏
30	♏		

October

1	♏		
2	♏	3:41 am	♐
3	♐		
4	♐	12:02 pm	♑
5	♑		
6	♑	5:20 pm	♒
7	♒		
8	♒	7:27 pm	♓
9	♓		
10	♓	7:20 pm	♈
11	♈		
12	♈	6:53 pm	♉
13	♉		
14	♉	8:17 pm	♊
15	♊		
16	♊		
17	♊	1:21 am	♋
18	♋		
19	♋	10:35 am	♌
20	♌		
21	♌	10:44 pm	♍
22	♍		
23	♍		
24	♍	11:31 am	♎
25	♎		
26	♎	11:15 pm	♏
27	♏		
28	♏		
29	♏	9:17 am	♐
30	♐		
31	♐	5:31 pm	♑

November

1	♑		
2	♑	11:38 pm	♒
3	♒		
4	♒		
5	♒	3:20 am	♓
6	♓		
7	♓	4:54 am	♈
8	♈		
9	♈	5:29 am	♉
10	♉		
11	♉	6:52 am	♊
12	♊		
13	♊	10:56 am	♋
14	♋		
15	♋	6:51 pm	♌
16	♌		
17	♌		
18	♌	6:10 am	♍
19	♍		
20	♍	6:52 pm	♎
21	♎		
22	♎		
23	♎	6:36 am	♏
24	♏		
25	♏	4:08 pm	♐
26	♐		
27	♐	11:28 pm	♑
28	♑		
29	♑		
30	♑	5:00 am	♒

December

1	♒		
2	♒	9:03 am	♓
3	♓		
4	♓	11:53 am	♈
5	♈		
6	♈	2:03 pm	♉
7	♉		
8	♉	4:37 pm	♊
9	♊		
10	♊	8:54 pm	♋
11	♋		
12	♋		
13	♋	4:07 am	♌
14	♌		
15	♌	2:33 pm	♍
16	♍		
17	♍		
18	♍	2:58 am	♎
19	♎		
20	♎	3:03 pm	♏
21	♏		
22	♏		
23	♏	12:45 am	♐
24	♐		
25	♐	7:27 am	♑
26	♑		
27	♑	11:46 am	♒
28	♒		
29	♒	2:42 pm	♓
30	♓		
31	♓	5:15 pm	♈

Moon Movements

♎ = Libra ♏ = Scorpio ♐ = Sagittarius ♑ = Capricorn ♒ = Aquarius ♓ = Pisces

1936

January

Day	Sign	Time	Enters
1	♈		
2	♈	8:11 pm	♉
3	♉		
4	♉		
5	♉	12:04 am	♊
6	♊		
7	♊	5:29 am	♋
8	♋		
9	♋	1:02 pm	♌
10	♌		
11	♌	11:05 pm	♍
12	♍		
13	♍		
14	♍	11:10 am	♎
15	♎		
16	♎	11:38 pm	♏
17	♏		
18	♏		
19	♏	10:11 am	♐
20	♐		
21	♐	5:18 pm	♑
22	♑		
23	♑	9:02 pm	♒
24	♒		
25	♒	10:35 pm	♓
26	♓		
27	♓	11:36 pm	♈
28	♈		
29	♈		
30	♈	1:37 am	♉
31	♉		

February

Day	Sign	Time	Enters
1	♉	5:39 am	♊
2	♊		
3	♊	11:58 am	♋
4	♋		
5	♋	8:26 pm	♌
6	♌		
7	♌		
8	♌	6:48 am	♍
9	♍		
10	♍	6:45 pm	♎
11	♎		
12	♎		
13	♎	7:24 am	♏
14	♏		
15	♏	6:56 pm	♐
16	♐		
17	♐		
18	♐	3:21 am	♑
19	♑		
20	♑	7:46 am	♒
21	♒		
22	♒	8:55 am	♓
23	♓		
24	♓	8:35 am	♈
25	♈		
26	♈	8:51 am	♉
27	♉		
28	♉	11:30 am	♊
29	♊		

March

Day	Sign	Time	Enters
1	♊	5:25 pm	♋
2	♋		
3	♋		
4	♋	2:20 am	♌
5	♌		
6	♌	1:18 pm	♍
7	♍		
8	♍		
9	♍	1:26 am	♎
10	♎		
11	♎	2:03 pm	♏
12	♏		
13	♏		
14	♏	2:06 am	♐
15	♐		
16	♐	11:51 am	♑
17	♑		
18	♑	5:52 pm	♒
19	♒		
20	♒	7:59 pm	♓
21	♓		
22	♓	7:31 pm	♈
23	♈		
24	♈	6:37 pm	♉
25	♉		
26	♉	7:31 pm	♊
27	♊		
28	♊	11:52 pm	♋
29	♋		
30	♋		
31	♋	8:04 am	♌

April

Day	Sign	Time	Enters
1	♌		
2	♌	7:07 pm	♍
3	♍		
4	♍		
5	♍	7:31 am	♎
6	♎		
7	♎	8:05 pm	♏
8	♏		
9	♏		
10	♏	8:03 am	♐
11	♐		
12	♐	6:23 pm	♑
13	♑		
14	♑		
15	♑	1:49 am	♒
16	♒		
17	♒	5:37 am	♓
18	♓		
19	♓	6:20 am	♈
20	♈		
21	♈	5:37 am	♉
22	♉		
23	♉	5:37 am	♊
24	♊		
25	♊	8:22 am	♋
26	♋		
27	♋	3:03 pm	♌
28	♌		
29	♌		
30	♌	1:22 am	♍

May

Day	Sign	Time	Enters
1	♍		
2	♍	1:43 pm	♎
3	♎		
4	♎		
5	♎	2:16 am	♏
6	♏		
7	♏	1:54 pm	♐
8	♐		
9	♐	11:57 pm	♑
10	♑		
11	♑		
12	♑	7:47 am	♒
13	♒		
14	♒	12:52 pm	♓
15	♓		
16	♓	3:14 pm	♈
17	♈		
18	♈	3:47 pm	♉
19	♉		
20	♉	4:12 pm	♊
21	♊		
22	♊	6:19 pm	♋
23	♋		
24	♋	11:41 pm	♌
25	♌		
26	♌		
27	♌	8:48 am	♍
28	♍		
29	♍	8:38 pm	♎
30	♎		
31	♎		

June

Day	Sign	Time	Enters
1	♎	9:11 am	♏
2	♏		
3	♏	8:37 pm	♐
4	♐		
5	♐		
6	♐	6:03 am	♑
7	♑		
8	♑	1:17 pm	♒
9	♒		
10	♒	6:27 pm	♓
11	♓		
12	♓	9:46 pm	♈
13	♈		
14	♈	11:48 pm	♉
15	♉		
16	♉		
17	♉	1:29 am	♊
18	♊		
19	♊	4:08 am	♋
20	♋		
21	♋	9:06 am	♌
22	♌		
23	♌	5:15 pm	♍
24	♍		
25	♍		
26	♍	4:23 am	♎
27	♎		
28	♎	4:53 pm	♏
29	♏		
30	♏		

July

Day	Sign	Time	Enters
1	♏	4:27 am	♐
2	♐		
3	♐	1:34 pm	♑
4	♑		
5	♑	7:56 pm	♒
6	♒		
7	♒		
8	♒	12:10 am	♓
9	♓		
10	♓	3:10 am	♈
11	♈		
12	♈	5:46 am	♉
13	♉		
14	♉	8:38 am	♊
15	♊		
16	♊	12:28 pm	♋
17	♋		
18	♋	5:58 pm	♌
19	♌		
20	♌		
21	♌	1:54 am	♍
22	♍		
23	♍	12:31 pm	♎
24	♎		
25	♎		
26	♎	12:54 am	♏
27	♏		
28	♏	12:56 pm	♐
29	♐		
30	♐	10:24 pm	♑
31	♑		

August

Day	Sign	Time	Enters
1	♑		
2	♑	4:25 am	♒
3	♒		
4	♒	7:36 am	♓
5	♓		
6	♓	9:21 am	♈
7	♈		
8	♈	11:11 am	♉
9	♉		
10	♉	2:12 pm	♊
11	♊		
12	♊	6:52 pm	♋
13	♋		
14	♋		
15	♋	1:20 am	♌
16	♌		
17	♌	9:44 am	♍
18	♍		
19	♍	8:17 pm	♎
20	♎		
21	♎		
22	♎	8:36 am	♏
23	♏		
24	♏	9:09 pm	♐
25	♐		
26	♐		
27	♐	7:35 am	♑
28	♑		
29	♑	2:12 pm	♒
30	♒		
31	♒	5:05 pm	♓

September

Day	Sign	Time	Enters
1	♓		
2	♓	5:43 pm	♈
3	♈		
4	♈	6:04 pm	♉
5	♉		
6	♉	7:54 pm	♊
7	♊		
8	♊		
9	♊	12:16 am	♋
10	♋		
11	♋	7:13 am	♌
12	♌		
13	♌	4:20 pm	♍
14	♍		
15	♍		
16	♍	3:12 am	♎
17	♎		
18	♎	3:32 pm	♏
19	♏		
20	♏		
21	♏	4:24 am	♐
22	♐		
23	♐	3:53 pm	♑
24	♑		
25	♑	11:53 pm	♒
26	♒		
27	♒		
28	♒	3:39 am	♓
29	♓		
30	♓	4:10 am	♈

October

Day	Sign	Time	Enters
1	♈		
2	♈	3:25 am	♉
3	♉		
4	♉	3:37 am	♊
5	♊		
6	♊	6:29 am	♋
7	♋		
8	♋	12:45 pm	♌
9	♌		
10	♌	10:01 pm	♍
11	♍		
12	♍		
13	♍	9:19 am	♎
14	♎		
15	♎	9:47 pm	♏
16	♏		
17	♏		
18	♏	10:38 am	♐
19	♐		
20	♐	10:37 pm	♑
21	♑		
22	♑		
23	♑	8:00 am	♒
24	♒		
25	♒	1:28 pm	♓
26	♓		
27	♓	3:09 pm	♈
28	♈		
29	♈	2:34 pm	♉
30	♉		
31	♉	1:49 pm	♊

November

Day	Sign	Time	Enters
1	♊		
2	♊	3:00 pm	♋
3	♋		
4	♋	7:37 pm	♌
5	♌		
6	♌		
7	♌	4:00 am	♍
8	♍		
9	♍	3:15 pm	♎
10	♎		
11	♎		
12	♎	3:52 am	♏
13	♏		
14	♏	4:33 pm	♐
15	♐		
16	♐		
17	♐	4:20 am	♑
18	♑		
19	♑	2:11 pm	♒
20	♒		
21	♒	9:04 pm	♓
22	♓		
23	♓		
24	♓	12:37 am	♈
25	♈		
26	♈	1:29 am	♉
27	♉		
28	♉	1:11 am	♊
29	♊		
30	♊	1:40 am	♋

December

Day	Sign	Time	Enters
1	♋		
2	♋	4:43 am	♌
3	♌		
4	♌	11:31 am	♍
5	♍		
6	♍	9:55 pm	♎
7	♎		
8	♎		
9	♎	10:28 am	♏
10	♏		
11	♏	11:07 pm	♐
12	♐		
13	♐		
14	♐	10:25 am	♑
15	♑		
16	♑	7:42 pm	♒
17	♒		
18	♒		
19	♒	2:43 am	♓
20	♓		
21	♓	7:26 am	♈
22	♈		
23	♈	10:05 am	♉
24	♉		
25	♉	11:24 am	♊
26	♊		
27	♊	12:36 pm	♋
28	♋		
29	♋	3:14 pm	♌
30	♌		
31	♌	8:45 pm	♍

Your Starway to Love

♈ = Aries ♉ = Taurus ♊ = Gemini ♋ = Cancer ♌ = Leo ♍ = Virgo

1937

January

1	♍		
2	♍		
3	♍	5:55 am	♎
4	♎		
5	♎	5:58 pm	♏
6	♏		
7	♏		
8	♏	6:43 am	♐
9	♐		
10	♐	5:53 pm	♑
11	♑		
12	♑		
13	♑	2:25 am	♒
14	♒		
15	♒	8:28 am	♓
16	♓		
17	♓	12:48 pm	♈
18	♈		
19	♈	4:07 pm	♉
20	♉		
21	♉	6:54 pm	♊
22	♊		
23	♊	9:38 pm	♋
24	♋		
25	♋		
26	♋	1:08 am	♌
27	♌		
28	♌	6:30 am	♍
29	♍		
30	♍	2:49 pm	♎
31	♎		

February

1	♎		
2	♎	2:10 am	♏
3	♏		
4	♏	2:59 pm	♐
5	♐		
6	♐		
7	♐	2:34 am	♑
8	♑		
9	♑	11:00 am	♒
10	♒		
11	♒	4:10 pm	♓
12	♓		
13	♓	7:12 pm	♈
14	♈		
15	♈	9:34 pm	♉
16	♉		
17	♉		
18	♉	12:22 am	♊
19	♊		
20	♊	4:04 am	♋
21	♋		
22	♋	8:51 am	♌
23	♌		
24	♌	3:04 pm	♍
25	♍		
26	♍	11:26 pm	♎
27	♎		
28	♎		

March

1	♎	10:23 am	♏
2	♏		
3	♏	11:08 pm	♐
4	♐		
5	♐		
6	♐	11:23 am	♑
7	♑		
8	♑	8:36 pm	♒
9	♒		
10	♒		
11	♒	1:50 am	♓
12	♓		
13	♓	4:00 am	♈
14	♈		
15	♈	4:54 am	♉
16	♉		
17	♉	6:19 am	♊
18	♊		
19	♊	9:25 am	♋
20	♋		
21	♋	2:35 pm	♌
22	♌		
23	♌	9:44 pm	♍
24	♍		
25	♍		
26	♍	6:47 am	♎
27	♎		
28	♎	5:51 pm	♏
29	♏		
30	♏		
31	♏	6:32 am	♐

April

1	♐		
2	♐	7:16 pm	♑
3	♑		
4	♑		
5	♑	5:39 am	♒
6	♒		
7	♒	11:59 am	♓
8	♓		
9	♓	2:28 pm	♈
10	♈		
11	♈	2:39 pm	♉
12	♉		
13	♉	2:34 pm	♊
14	♊		
15	♊	4:03 pm	♋
16	♋		
17	♋	8:11 pm	♌
18	♌		
19	♌		
20	♌	3:16 am	♍
21	♍		
22	♍	12:51 pm	♎
23	♎		
24	♎		
25	♎	12:21 am	♏
26	♏		
27	♏	1:05 pm	♐
28	♐		
29	♐		
30	♐	1:56 am	♑

May

1	♑		
2	♑	1:08 pm	♒
3	♒		
4	♒	8:57 pm	♓
5	♓		
6	♓		
7	♓	12:47 am	♈
8	♈		
9	♈	1:32 am	♉
10	♉		
11	♉	12:56 am	♊
12	♊		
13	♊	1:00 am	♋
14	♋		
15	♋	3:27 am	♌
16	♌		
17	♌	9:19 am	♍
18	♍		
19	♍	6:34 pm	♎
20	♎		
21	♎		
22	♎	6:18 am	♏
23	♏		
24	♏	7:10 pm	♐
25	♐		
26	♐		
27	♐	7:53 am	♑
28	♑		
29	♑	7:13 pm	♒
30	♒		
31	♒		

June

1	♒	3:58 am	♓
2	♓		
3	♓	9:22 am	♈
4	♈		
5	♈	11:36 am	♉
6	♉		
7	♉	11:46 am	♊
8	♊		
9	♊	11:31 am	♋
10	♋		
11	♋	12:44 pm	♌
12	♌		
13	♌	5:01 pm	♍
14	♍		
15	♍		
16	♍	1:08 am	♎
17	♎		
18	♎	12:31 pm	♏
19	♏		
20	♏		
21	♏	1:25 am	♐
22	♐		
23	♐	1:58 pm	♑
24	♑		
25	♑		
26	♑	12:54 am	♒
27	♒		
28	♒	9:37 am	♓
29	♓		
30	♓	3:50 pm	♈

July

1	♈		
2	♈	7:34 pm	♉
3	♉		
4	♉	9:15 pm	♊
5	♊		
6	♊	9:53 pm	♋
7	♋		
8	♋	10:59 pm	♌
9	♌		
10	♌		
11	♌	2:15 am	♍
12	♍		
13	♍	9:04 am	♎
14	♎		
15	♎	7:36 pm	♏
16	♏		
17	♏		
18	♏	8:20 am	♐
19	♐		
20	♐	8:50 pm	♑
21	♑		
22	♑		
23	♑	7:20 am	♒
24	♒		
25	♒	3:21 pm	♓
26	♓		
27	♓	9:15 pm	♈
28	♈		
29	♈		
30	♈	1:31 am	♉
31	♉		

August

1	♉	4:29 am	♊
2	♊		
3	♊	6:34 am	♋
4	♋		
5	♋	8:35 am	♌
6	♌		
7	♌	11:54 am	♍
8	♍		
9	♍	5:58 pm	♎
10	♎		
11	♎		
12	♎	3:37 am	♏
13	♏		
14	♏	3:59 pm	♐
15	♐		
16	♐		
17	♐	4:37 am	♑
18	♑		
19	♑	3:05 pm	♒
20	♒		
21	♒	10:28 pm	♓
22	♓		
23	♓		
24	♓	3:23 am	♈
25	♈		
26	♈	6:57 am	♉
27	♉		
28	♉	10:01 am	♊
29	♊		
30	♊	1:03 pm	♋
31	♋		

September

1	♋	4:21 pm	♌
2	♌		
3	♌	8:34 pm	♍
4	♍		
5	♍		
6	♍	2:48 am	♎
7	♎		
8	♎	11:59 am	♏
9	♏		
10	♏	11:59 pm	♐
11	♐		
12	♐		
13	♐	12:52 pm	♑
14	♑		
15	♑	11:51 pm	♒
16	♒		
17	♒		
18	♒	7:19 am	♓
19	♓		
20	♓	11:31 am	♈
21	♈		
22	♈	1:49 pm	♉
23	♉		
24	♉	3:46 pm	♊
25	♊		
26	♊	6:24 pm	♋
27	♋		
28	♋	10:14 pm	♌
29	♌		
30	♌		

October

1	♌	3:29 am	♍
2	♍		
3	♍	10:31 am	♎
4	♎		
5	♎	7:55 pm	♏
6	♏		
7	♏		
8	♏	7:44 am	♐
9	♐		
10	♐	8:47 pm	♑
11	♑		
12	♑		
13	♑	8:37 am	♒
14	♒		
15	♒	5:03 pm	♓
16	♓		
17	♓	9:32 pm	♈
18	♈		
19	♈	11:09 pm	♉
20	♉		
21	♉	11:40 pm	♊
22	♊		
23	♊		
24	♊	12:47 am	♋
25	♋		
26	♋	3:42 am	♌
27	♌		
28	♌	9:01 am	♍
29	♍		
30	♍	4:47 pm	♎
31	♎		

November

1	♎		
2	♎	2:48 am	♏
3	♏		
4	♏	2:46 pm	♐
5	♐		
6	♐		
7	♐	3:50 am	♑
8	♑		
9	♑	4:19 pm	♒
10	♒		
11	♒		
12	♒	2:07 am	♓
13	♓		
14	♓	7:59 am	♈
15	♈		
16	♈	10:12 am	♉
17	♉		
18	♉	10:10 am	♊
19	♊		
20	♊	9:47 am	♋
21	♋		
22	♋	10:55 am	♌
23	♌		
24	♌	2:56 pm	♍
25	♍		
26	♍	10:22 pm	♎
27	♎		
28	♎		
29	♎	8:46 am	♏
30	♏		

December

1	♏	9:05 pm	♐
2	♐		
3	♐		
4	♐	10:07 am	♑
5	♑		
6	♑	10:40 pm	♒
7	♒		
8	♒		
9	♒	9:21 am	♓
10	♓		
11	♓	4:55 pm	♈
12	♈		
13	♈	8:50 pm	♉
14	♉		
15	♉	9:42 pm	♊
16	♊		
17	♊	9:03 pm	♋
18	♋		
19	♋	8:48 pm	♌
20	♌		
21	♌	10:57 pm	♍
22	♍		
23	♍		
24	♍	4:53 am	♎
25	♎		
26	♎	2:45 pm	♏
27	♏		
28	♏		
29	♏	3:12 am	♐
30	♐		
31	♐	4:17 pm	♑

Moon Movements

♎ = Libra ♏ = Scorpio ♐ = Sagittarius ♑ = Capricorn ♒ = Aquarius ♓ = Pisces

1938

January

1	♑		
2	♑		
3	♑	4:31 am	♒
4	♒		
5	♒	3:07 pm	♓
6	♓		
7	♓	11:29 pm	♈
8	♈		
9	♈		
10	♈	5:06 am	♉
11	♉		
12	♉	7:50 am	♊
13	♊		
14	♊	8:21 am	♋
15	♋		
16	♋	8:09 am	♌
17	♌		
18	♌	9:13 am	♍
19	♍		
20	♍	1:27 pm	♎
21	♎		
22	♎	9:55 pm	♏
23	♏		
24	♏		
25	♏	9:51 am	♐
26	♐		
27	♐	10:58 pm	♑
28	♑		
29	♑		
30	♑	11:00 am	♒
31	♒		

February

1	♒	8:58 pm	♓
2	♓		
3	♓		
4	♓	4:54 am	♈
5	♈		
6	♈	10:58 am	♉
7	♉		
8	♉	3:08 pm	♊
9	♊		
10	♊	5:26 pm	♋
11	♋		
12	♋	6:33 pm	♌
13	♌		
14	♌	7:57 pm	♍
15	♍		
16	♍	11:28 pm	♎
17	♎		
18	♎		
19	♎	6:37 am	♏
20	♏		
21	♏	5:33 pm	♐
22	♐		
23	♐		
24	♐	6:28 am	♑
25	♑		
26	♑	6:36 pm	♒
27	♒		
28	♒		

March

1	♒	4:13 am	♓
2	♓		
3	♓	11:16 am	♈
4	♈		
5	♈	4:29 pm	♉
6	♉		
7	♉	8:33 pm	♊
8	♊		
9	♊	11:46 pm	♋
10	♋		
11	♋		
12	♋	2:23 am	♌
13	♌		
14	♌	5:05 am	♍
15	♍		
16	♍	9:08 am	♎
17	♎		
18	♎	3:54 pm	♏
19	♏		
20	♏		
21	♏	2:01 am	♐
22	♐		
23	♐	2:32 pm	♑
24	♑		
25	♑		
26	♑	2:56 am	♒
27	♒		
28	♒	12:52 pm	♓
29	♓		
30	♓	7:33 pm	♈
31	♈		

April

1	♈	11:43 pm	♉
2	♉		
3	♉		
4	♉	2:33 am	♊
5	♊		
6	♊	5:07 am	♋
7	♋		
8	♋	8:04 am	♌
9	♌		
10	♌	11:51 am	♍
11	♍		
12	♍	5:02 pm	♎
13	♎		
14	♎		
15	♎	12:21 am	♏
16	♏		
17	♏	10:19 am	♐
18	♐		
19	♐	10:31 pm	♑
20	♑		
21	♑		
22	♑	11:11 am	♒
23	♒		
24	♒	9:53 pm	♓
25	♓		
26	♓		
27	♓	5:08 am	♈
28	♈		
29	♈	9:02 am	♉
30	♉		

May

1	♉	10:45 am	♊
2	♊		
3	♊	11:51 am	♋
4	♋		
5	♋	1:42 pm	♌
6	♌		
7	♌	5:17 pm	♍
8	♍		
9	♍	11:06 pm	♎
10	♎		
11	♎		
12	♎	7:16 am	♏
13	♏		
14	♏	5:40 pm	♐
15	♐		
16	♐		
17	♐	5:51 am	♑
18	♑		
19	♑	6:37 pm	♒
20	♒		
21	♒		
22	♒	6:08 am	♓
23	♓		
24	♓	2:35 pm	♈
25	♈		
26	♈	7:17 pm	♉
27	♉		
28	♉	8:52 pm	♊
29	♊		
30	♊	8:52 pm	♋
31	♋		

June

1	♋	9:09 pm	♌
2	♌		
3	♌	11:21 pm	♍
4	♍		
5	♍		
6	♍	4:35 am	♎
7	♎		
8	♎	1:01 pm	♏
9	♏		
10	♏	11:57 pm	♐
11	♐		
12	♐		
13	♐	12:21 pm	♑
14	♑		
15	♑		
16	♑	1:07 am	♒
17	♒		
18	♒	1:02 pm	♓
19	♓		
20	♓	10:40 pm	♈
21	♈		
22	♈		
23	♈	4:50 am	♉
24	♉		
25	♉	7:25 am	♊
26	♊		
27	♊	7:27 am	♋
28	♋		
29	♋	6:45 am	♌
30	♌		

July

1	♌	7:24 am	♍
2	♍		
3	♍	11:09 am	♎
4	♎		
5	♎	6:49 pm	♏
6	♏		
7	♏		
8	♏	5:45 am	♐
9	♐		
10	♐	6:22 pm	♑
11	♑		
12	♑		
13	♑	7:05 am	♒
14	♒		
15	♒	6:55 pm	♓
16	♓		
17	♓		
18	♓	5:02 am	♈
19	♈		
20	♈	12:31 pm	♉
21	♉		
22	♉	4:43 pm	♊
23	♊		
24	♊	5:54 pm	♋
25	♋		
26	♋	5:26 pm	♌
27	♌		
28	♌	5:17 pm	♍
29	♍		
30	♍	7:35 pm	♎
31	♎		

August

1	♎		
2	♎	1:49 am	♏
3	♏		
4	♏	12:02 pm	♐
5	♐		
6	♐		
7	♐	12:33 am	♑
8	♑		
9	♑	1:15 pm	♒
10	♒		
11	♒		
12	♒	12:45 am	♓
13	♓		
14	♓	10:34 am	♈
15	♈		
16	♈	6:25 pm	♉
17	♉		
18	♉	11:51 pm	♊
19	♊		
20	♊		
21	♊	2:39 am	♋
22	♋		
23	♋	3:27 am	♌
24	♌		
25	♌	3:43 am	♍
26	♍		
27	♍	5:26 am	♎
28	♎		
29	♎	10:26 am	♏
30	♏		
31	♏	7:28 pm	♐

September

1	♐		
2	♐		
3	♐	7:30 am	♑
4	♑		
5	♑	8:10 pm	♒
6	♒		
7	♒		
8	♒	7:28 am	♓
9	♓		
10	♓	4:40 pm	♈
11	♈		
12	♈	11:54 pm	♉
13	♉		
14	♉		
15	♉	5:23 am	♊
16	♊		
17	♊	9:09 am	♋
18	♋		
19	♋	11:26 am	♌
20	♌		
21	♌	1:01 pm	♍
22	♍		
23	♍	3:19 pm	♎
24	♎		
25	♎	7:57 pm	♏
26	♏		
27	♏		
28	♏	4:02 am	♐
29	♐		
30	♐	3:20 pm	♑

October

1	♑		
2	♑		
3	♑	3:58 am	♒
4	♒		
5	♒	3:27 pm	♓
6	♓		
7	♓		
8	♓	12:22 am	♈
9	♈		
10	♈	6:43 am	♉
11	♉		
12	♉	11:10 am	♊
13	♊		
14	♊	2:31 pm	♋
15	♋		
16	♋	5:19 pm	♌
17	♌		
18	♌	8:09 pm	♍
19	♍		
20	♍	11:43 pm	♎
21	♎		
22	♎		
23	♎	5:00 am	♏
24	♏		
25	♏	12:54 pm	♐
26	♐		
27	♐	11:39 pm	♑
28	♑		
29	♑		
30	♑	12:08 pm	♒
31	♒		

November

1	♒		
2	♒	12:09 am	♓
3	♓		
4	♓	9:35 am	♈
5	♈		
6	♈	3:41 pm	♉
7	♉		
8	♉	7:03 pm	♊
9	♊		
10	♊	8:59 pm	♋
11	♋		
12	♋	10:50 pm	♌
13	♌		
14	♌		
15	♌	1:38 am	♍
16	♍		
17	♍	6:03 am	♎
18	♎		
19	♎	12:26 pm	♏
20	♏		
21	♏	8:56 pm	♐
22	♐		
23	♐		
24	♐	7:38 am	♑
25	♑		
26	♑	7:58 pm	♒
27	♒		
28	♒		
29	♒	8:30 am	♓
30	♓		

December

1	♓	7:02 pm	♈
2	♈		
3	♈		
4	♈	2:01 am	♉
5	♉		
6	♉	5:18 am	♊
7	♊		
8	♊	6:08 am	♋
9	♋		
10	♋	6:17 am	♌
11	♌		
12	♌	7:37 am	♍
13	♍		
14	♍	11:27 am	♎
15	♎		
16	♎	6:13 pm	♏
17	♏		
18	♏		
19	♏	3:31 am	♐
20	♐		
21	♐	2:39 pm	♑
22	♑		
23	♑		
24	♑	2:59 am	♒
25	♒		
26	♒	3:41 pm	♓
27	♓		
28	♓		
29	♓	3:14 am	♈
30	♈		
31	♈	11:47 am	♉

Your Starway to Love

♈ = Aries ♉ = Taurus ♊ = Gemini ♋ = Cancer ♌ = Leo ♍ = Virgo

1939

January

Day	Moon	Time	Enters
1	♉		
2	♉	4:19 pm	♊
3	♊		
4	♊	5:20 pm	♋
5	♋		
6	♋	4:32 pm	♌
7	♌		
8	♌	4:08 pm	♍
9	♍		
10	♍	6:11 pm	♎
11	♎		
12	♎	11:54 pm	♏
13	♏		
14	♏		
15	♏	9:10 am	♐
16	♐		
17	♐	8:44 pm	♑
18	♑		
19	♑		
20	♑	9:15 am	♒
21	♒		
22	♒	9:51 pm	♓
23	♓		
24	♓		
25	♓	9:42 am	♈
26	♈		
27	♈	7:29 pm	♉
28	♉		
29	♉		
30	♉	1:50 am	♊
31	♊		

April

Day	Moon	Time	Enters
1	♍		
2	♍		
3	♍	12:48 am	♎
4	♎		
5	♎	3:21 am	♏
6	♏		
7	♏	8:47 am	♐
8	♐		
9	♐	5:47 pm	♑
10	♑		
11	♑		
12	♑	5:33 am	♒
13	♒		
14	♒	6:04 pm	♓
15	♓		
16	♓		
17	♓	5:13 am	♈
18	♈		
19	♈	1:57 pm	♉
20	♉		
21	♉	8:16 pm	♊
22	♊		
23	♊		
24	♊	12:43 am	♋
25	♋		
26	♋	3:55 am	♌
27	♌		
28	♌	6:26 am	♍
29	♍		
30	♍	9:02 am	♎

July

Day	Moon	Time	Enters
1	♑		
2	♑		
3	♑	4:54 am	♒
4	♒		
5	♒	5:17 pm	♓
6	♓		
7	♓		
8	♓	5:50 am	♈
9	♈		
10	♈	4:27 pm	♉
11	♉		
12	♉	11:21 pm	♊
13	♊		
14	♊		
15	♊	2:16 am	♋
16	♋		
17	♋	2:30 am	♌
18	♌		
19	♌	2:07 am	♍
20	♍		
21	♍	3:10 am	♎
22	♎		
23	♎	7:04 am	♏
24	♏		
25	♏	2:10 pm	♐
26	♐		
27	♐	11:51 pm	♑
28	♑		
29	♑		
30	♑	11:15 am	♒
31	♒		

October

Day	Moon	Time	Enters
1	♉		
2	♉	8:38 pm	♊
3	♊		
4	♊		
5	♊	3:16 am	♋
6	♋		
7	♋	7:10 am	♌
8	♌		
9	♌	8:46 am	♍
10	♍		
11	♍	9:15 am	♎
12	♎		
13	♎	10:18 am	♏
14	♏		
15	♏	1:36 pm	♐
16	♐		
17	♐	8:22 pm	♑
18	♑		
19	♑		
20	♑	6:40 am	♒
21	♒		
22	♒	7:05 pm	♓
23	♓		
24	♓		
25	♓	7:28 am	♈
26	♈		
27	♈	6:09 pm	♉
28	♉		
29	♉		
30	♉	2:31 am	♊
31	♊		

February

Day	Moon	Time	Enters
1	♊	4:22 am	♋
2	♋		
3	♋	4:06 am	♌
4	♌		
5	♌	3:02 am	♍
6	♍		
7	♍	3:29 am	♎
8	♎		
9	♎	7:22 am	♏
10	♏		
11	♏	3:24 pm	♐
12	♐		
13	♐		
14	♐	2:41 am	♑
15	♑		
16	♑	3:22 pm	♒
17	♒		
18	♒		
19	♒	3:52 am	♓
20	♓		
21	♓	3:23 pm	♈
22	♈		
23	♈		
24	♈	1:19 am	♉
25	♉		
26	♉	8:47 am	♊
27	♊		
28	♊	1:06 pm	♋

May

Day	Moon	Time	Enters
1	♎		
2	♎	12:36 pm	♏
3	♏		
4	♏	6:11 pm	♐
5	♐		
6	♐		
7	♐	2:34 am	♑
8	♑		
9	♑	1:41 pm	♒
10	♒		
11	♒		
12	♒	2:09 am	♓
13	♓		
14	♓	1:41 pm	♈
15	♈		
16	♈	10:28 pm	♉
17	♉		
18	♉		
19	♉	4:06 am	♊
20	♊		
21	♊	7:23 am	♋
22	♋		
23	♋	9:33 am	♌
24	♌		
25	♌	11:51 am	♍
26	♍		
27	♍	3:06 pm	♎
28	♎		
29	♎	7:47 pm	♏
30	♏		
31	♏		

August

Day	Moon	Time	Enters
1	♒	11:41 pm	♓
2	♓		
3	♓		
4	♓	12:22 pm	♈
5	♈		
6	♈	11:47 pm	♉
7	♉		
8	♉		
9	♉	8:06 am	♊
10	♊		
11	♊	12:21 pm	♋
12	♋		
13	♋	1:09 pm	♌
14	♌		
15	♌	12:19 pm	♍
16	♍		
17	♍	12:04 pm	♎
18	♎		
19	♎	2:20 pm	♏
20	♏		
21	♏	8:14 pm	♐
22	♐		
23	♐		
24	♐	5:33 am	♑
25	♑		
26	♑	5:09 pm	♒
27	♒		
28	♒		
29	♒	5:42 am	♓
30	♓		
31	♓	6:15 pm	♈

November

Day	Moon	Time	Enters
1	♊	8:41 am	♋
2	♋		
3	♋	1:01 pm	♌
4	♌		
5	♌	3:57 pm	♍
6	♍		
7	♍	6:03 pm	♎
8	♎		
9	♎	8:14 pm	♏
10	♏		
11	♏	11:41 pm	♐
12	♐		
13	♐		
14	♐	5:42 am	♑
15	♑		
16	♑	3:00 pm	♒
17	♒		
18	♒		
19	♒	3:00 am	♓
20	♓		
21	♓	3:36 pm	♈
22	♈		
23	♈		
24	♈	2:23 am	♉
25	♉		
26	♉	10:09 am	♊
27	♊		
28	♊	3:11 pm	♋
29	♋		
30	♋	6:34 pm	♌

March

Day	Moon	Time	Enters
1	♋		
2	♋	2:30 pm	♌
3	♌		
4	♌	2:17 pm	♍
5	♍		
6	♍	2:26 pm	♎
7	♎		
8	♎	5:00 pm	♏
9	♏		
10	♏	11:23 pm	♐
11	♐		
12	♐		
13	♐	9:35 am	♑
14	♑		
15	♑	10:01 pm	♒
16	♒		
17	♒		
18	♒	10:31 am	♓
19	♓		
20	♓	9:41 pm	♈
21	♈		
22	♈		
23	♈	6:58 am	♉
24	♉		
25	♉	2:15 pm	♊
26	♊		
27	♊	7:19 pm	♋
28	♋		
29	♋	10:15 pm	♌
30	♌		
31	♌	11:39 pm	♍

June

Day	Moon	Time	Enters
1	♏	2:15 am	♐
2	♐		
3	♐	10:50 am	♑
4	♑		
5	♑	9:40 pm	♒
6	♒		
7	♒		
8	♒	10:04 am	♓
9	♓		
10	♓	10:10 pm	♈
11	♈		
12	♈		
13	♈	7:43 am	♉
14	♉		
15	♉	1:32 pm	♊
16	♊		
17	♊	4:06 pm	♋
18	♋		
19	♋	4:58 pm	♌
20	♌		
21	♌	5:56 pm	♍
22	♍		
23	♍	8:30 pm	♎
24	♎		
25	♎		
26	♎	1:25 am	♏
27	♏		
28	♏	8:39 am	♐
29	♐		
30	♐	5:53 pm	♑

September

Day	Moon	Time	Enters
1	♈		
2	♈		
3	♈	5:47 am	♉
4	♉		
5	♉	3:02 pm	♊
6	♊		
7	♊	8:52 pm	♋
8	♋		
9	♋	11:12 pm	♌
10	♌		
11	♌	11:09 pm	♍
12	♍		
13	♍	10:39 pm	♎
14	♎		
15	♎	11:43 pm	♏
16	♏		
17	♏		
18	♏	4:02 am	♐
19	♐		
20	♐	12:11 pm	♑
21	♑		
22	♑	11:24 pm	♒
23	♒		
24	♒		
25	♒	12:00 pm	♓
26	♓		
27	♓		
28	♓	12:22 am	♈
29	♈		
30	♈	11:29 am	♉

December

Day	Moon	Time	Enters
1	♌		
2	♌	9:23 pm	♍
3	♍		
4	♍		
5	♍	12:22 am	♎
6	♎		
7	♎	3:57 am	♏
8	♏		
9	♏	8:32 am	♐
10	♐		
11	♐	2:51 pm	♑
12	♑		
13	♑	11:42 pm	♒
14	♒		
15	♒		
16	♒	11:14 am	♓
17	♓		
18	♓		
19	♓	12:03 am	♈
20	♈		
21	♈	11:32 am	♉
22	♉		
23	♉	7:37 pm	♊
24	♊		
25	♊		
26	♊	12:03 am	♋
27	♋		
28	♋	2:05 am	♌
29	♌		
30	♌	3:29 am	♍
31	♍		

Moon Movements

♎ = Libra ♏ = Scorpio ♐ = Sagittarius ♑ = Capricorn ♒ = Aquarius ♓ = Pisces

1940

January

1	♍	5:43 am	♎
2	♎		
3	♎	9:36 am	♏
4	♏		
5	♏	3:12 pm	♐
6	♐		
7	♐	10:30 pm	♑
8	♑		
9	♑		
10	♑	7:42 am	♒
11	♒		
12	♒	7:03 pm	♓
13	♓		
14	♓		
15	♓	7:56 am	♈
16	♈		
17	♈	8:15 pm	♉
18	♉		
19	♉		
20	♉	5:32 am	♊
21	♊		
22	♊	10:35 am	♋
23	♋		
24	♋	12:10 pm	♌
25	♌		
26	♌	12:12 pm	♍
27	♍		
28	♍	12:43 pm	♎
29	♎		
30	♎	3:17 pm	♏
31	♏		

April

1	♑	2:13 am	♒
2	♒		
3	♒	2:11 pm	♓
4	♓		
5	♓		
6	♓	3:10 am	♈
7	♈		
8	♈	3:39 pm	♉
9	♉		
10	♉		
11	♉	2:32 am	♊
12	♊		
13	♊	11:04 am	♋
14	♋		
15	♋	4:44 pm	♌
16	♌		
17	♌	7:34 pm	♍
18	♍		
19	♍	8:23 pm	♎
20	♎		
21	♎	8:33 pm	♏
22	♏		
23	♏	9:48 pm	♐
24	♐		
25	♐		
26	♐	1:50 am	♑
27	♑		
28	♑	9:39 am	♒
29	♒		
30	♒	8:56 pm	♓

July

1	♉		
2	♉	12:15 am	♊
3	♊		
4	♊	7:10 am	♋
5	♋		
6	♋	11:12 am	♌
7	♌		
8	♌	1:44 pm	♍
9	♍		
10	♍	4:07 pm	♎
11	♎		
12	♎	7:07 pm	♏
13	♏		
14	♏	11:05 pm	♐
15	♐		
16	♐		
17	♐	4:17 am	♑
18	♑		
19	♑	11:22 am	♒
20	♒		
21	♒	8:58 pm	♓
22	♓		
23	♓		
24	♓	9:01 am	♈
25	♈		
26	♈	9:56 pm	♉
27	♉		
28	♉		
29	♉	9:04 am	♊
30	♊		
31	♊	4:32 pm	♋

October

1	♎		
2	♎	6:12 pm	♏
3	♏		
4	♏	6:54 pm	♐
5	♐		
6	♐	10:28 pm	♑
7	♑		
8	♑		
9	♑	5:44 am	♒
10	♒		
11	♒	4:18 pm	♓
12	♓		
13	♓		
14	♓	4:50 am	♈
15	♈		
16	♈	5:49 pm	♉
17	♉		
18	♉		
19	♉	5:59 am	♊
20	♊		
21	♊	4:18 pm	♋
22	♋		
23	♋	11:51 pm	♌
24	♌		
25	♌		
26	♌	4:10 am	♍
27	♍		
28	♍	5:37 am	♎
29	♎		
30	♎	5:25 am	♏
31	♏		

February

1	♏	8:36 pm	♐
2	♐		
3	♐		
4	♐	4:27 am	♑
5	♑		
6	♑	2:21 pm	♒
7	♒		
8	♒		
9	♒	1:58 am	♓
10	♓		
11	♓	2:49 pm	♈
12	♈		
13	♈		
14	♈	3:36 am	♉
15	♉		
16	♉	2:10 pm	♊
17	♊		
18	♊	8:46 pm	♋
19	♋		
20	♋	11:19 pm	♌
21	♌		
22	♌	11:11 pm	♍
23	♍		
24	♍	10:29 pm	♎
25	♎		
26	♎	11:13 pm	♏
27	♏		
28	♏		
29	♏	2:54 am	♐

May

1	♓		
2	♓		
3	♓	9:52 am	♈
4	♈		
5	♈	10:12 pm	♉
6	♉		
7	♉		
8	♉	8:34 am	♊
9	♊		
10	♊	4:33 pm	♋
11	♋		
12	♋	10:22 pm	♌
13	♌		
14	♌		
15	♌	2:18 am	♍
16	♍		
17	♍	4:40 am	♎
18	♎		
19	♎	6:12 am	♏
20	♏		
21	♏	8:00 am	♐
22	♐		
23	♐	11:35 am	♑
24	♑		
25	♑	6:19 pm	♒
26	♒		
27	♒		
28	♒	4:39 am	♓
29	♓		
30	♓	5:18 pm	♈
31	♈		

August

1	♋		
2	♋	8:20 pm	♌
3	♌		
4	♌	9:50 pm	♍
5	♍		
6	♍	10:50 pm	♎
7	♎		
8	♎		
9	♎	12:46 am	♏
10	♏		
11	♏	4:29 am	♐
12	♐		
13	♐	10:15 am	♑
14	♑		
15	♑	6:07 pm	♒
16	♒		
17	♒		
18	♒	4:10 am	♓
19	♓		
20	♓	4:14 pm	♈
21	♈		
22	♈		
23	♈	5:17 am	♉
24	♉		
25	♉	5:13 pm	♊
26	♊		
27	♊		
28	♊	1:53 am	♋
29	♋		
30	♋	6:31 am	♌
31	♌		

November

1	♏	5:21 am	♐
2	♐		
3	♐	7:22 am	♑
4	♑		
5	♑	1:03 pm	♒
6	♒		
7	♒	10:46 pm	♓
8	♓		
9	♓		
10	♓	11:13 am	♈
11	♈		
12	♈		
13	♈	12:13 am	♉
14	♉		
15	♉	12:00 pm	♊
16	♊		
17	♊	9:52 pm	♋
18	♋		
19	♋		
20	♋	5:38 am	♌
21	♌		
22	♌	11:11 am	♍
23	♍		
24	♍	2:25 pm	♎
25	♎		
26	♎	3:44 pm	♏
27	♏		
28	♏	4:18 pm	♐
29	♐		
30	♐	5:50 pm	♑

March

1	♐		
2	♐	10:02 am	♑
3	♑		
4	♑	8:07 pm	♒
5	♒		
6	♒		
7	♒	8:07 am	♓
8	♓		
9	♓	9:01 pm	♈
10	♈		
11	♈		
12	♈	9:44 am	♉
13	♉		
14	♉	8:53 pm	♊
15	♊		
16	♊		
17	♊	4:57 am	♋
18	♋		
19	♋	9:15 am	♌
20	♌		
21	♌	10:20 am	♍
22	♍		
23	♍	9:47 am	♎
24	♎		
25	♎	9:33 am	♏
26	♏		
27	♏	11:31 am	♐
28	♐		
29	♐	5:00 pm	♑
30	♑		
31	♑		

June

1	♈		
2	♈	5:44 am	♉
3	♉		
4	♉	3:49 pm	♊
5	♊		
6	♊	11:02 pm	♋
7	♋		
8	♋		
9	♋	4:00 am	♌
10	♌		
11	♌	7:41 am	♍
12	♍		
13	♍	10:43 am	♎
14	♎		
15	♎	1:31 pm	♏
16	♏		
17	♏	4:34 pm	♐
18	♐		
19	♐	8:44 pm	♑
20	♑		
21	♑		
22	♒	3:15 am	♒
23	♒		
24	♒	12:55 pm	♓
25	♓		
26	♓		
27	♈	1:13 am	♈
28	♈		
29	♈	1:52 pm	♉
30	♉		

September

1	♌	7:57 am	♍
2	♍		
3	♍	7:54 am	♎
4	♎		
5	♎	8:16 am	♏
6	♏		
7	♏	10:36 am	♐
8	♐		
9	♐	3:45 pm	♑
10	♑		
11	♑	11:51 pm	♒
12	♒		
13	♒		
14	♒	10:25 am	♓
15	♓		
16	♓	10:43 pm	♈
17	♈		
18	♈		
19	♈	11:45 am	♉
20	♉		
21	♉		
22	♉	12:05 am	♊
23	♊		
24	♊	9:57 am	♋
25	♋		
26	♋	4:09 pm	♌
27	♌		
28	♌	6:41 pm	♍
29	♍		
30	♍	6:46 pm	♎

December

1	♑		
2	♑	10:12 pm	♒
3	♒		
4	♒		
5	♒	6:35 am	♓
6	♓		
7	♓	6:26 pm	♈
8	♈		
9	♈		
10	♈	7:27 am	♉
11	♉		
12	♉	7:08 pm	♊
13	♊		
14	♊		
15	♊	4:20 am	♋
16	♋		
17	♋	11:16 am	♌
18	♌		
19	♌	4:35 pm	♍
20	♍		
21	♍	8:37 pm	♎
22	♎		
23	♎	11:30 pm	♏
24	♏		
25	♏		
26	♏	1:36 am	♐
27	♐		
28	♐	3:58 am	♑
29	♑		
30	♑	8:09 am	♒
31	♒		

Your Starway to Love

♈ = Aries ♉ = Taurus ♊ = Gemini ♋ = Cancer ♌ = Leo ♍ = Virgo

1941

January			
1	♒	3:35 pm	♓
2	♓		
3	♓		
4	♓	2:34 am	♈
5	♈		
6	♈	3:28 pm	♉
7	♉		
8	♉		
9	♉	3:27 am	♊
10	♊		
11	♊	12:33 pm	♋
12	♋		
13	♋	6:39 pm	♌
14	♌		
15	♌	10:45 pm	♍
16	♍		
17	♍		
18	♍	2:00 am	♎
19	♎		
20	♎	5:04 am	♏
21	♏		
22	♏	8:16 am	♐
23	♐		
24	♐	12:01 pm	♑
25	♑		
26	♑	5:06 pm	♒
27	♒		
28	♒		
29	♒	12:34 am	♓
30	♓		
31	♓	11:02 am	♈

April			
1	♉	3:06 am	♊
2	♊		
3	♊	2:44 pm	♋
4	♋		
5	♋	11:26 pm	♌
6	♌		
7	♌		
8	♌	4:21 am	♍
9	♍		
10	♍	5:54 am	♎
11	♎		
12	♎	5:31 am	♏
13	♏		
14	♏	5:07 am	♐
15	♐		
16	♐	6:38 am	♑
17	♑		
18	♑	11:31 am	♒
19	♒		
20	♒	8:07 pm	♓
21	♓		
22	♓		
23	♓	7:34 am	♈
24	♈		
25	♈	8:23 pm	♉
26	♉		
27	♉		
28	♉	9:11 am	♊
29	♊		
30	♊	8:56 pm	♋

July			
1	♍	6:17 am	♎
2	♎		
3	♎	9:33 am	♏
4	♏		
5	♏	11:13 am	♐
6	♐		
7	♐	12:21 pm	♑
8	♑		
9	♑	2:36 pm	♒
10	♒		
11	♒	7:42 pm	♓
12	♓		
13	♓		
14	♓	4:35 am	♈
15	♈		
16	♈	4:30 pm	♉
17	♉		
18	♉		
19	♉	5:10 am	♊
20	♊		
21	♊	4:15 pm	♋
22	♋		
23	♋		
24	♋	12:48 am	♌
25	♌		
26	♌	7:03 am	♍
27	♍		
28	♍	11:41 am	♎
29	♎		
30	♎	3:09 pm	♏
31	♏		

October			
1	♒	7:18 pm	♓
2	♓		
3	♓		
4	♓	4:37 am	♈
5	♈		
6	♈	3:52 pm	♉
7	♉		
8	♉		
9	♉	4:23 am	♊
10	♊		
11	♊	4:53 pm	♋
12	♋		
13	♋		
14	♋	3:29 am	♌
15	♌		
16	♌	10:36 am	♍
17	♍		
18	♍	1:54 pm	♎
19	♎		
20	♎	2:25 pm	♏
21	♏		
22	♏	2:00 pm	♐
23	♐		
24	♐	2:40 pm	♑
25	♑		
26	♑	6:02 pm	♒
27	♒		
28	♒		
29	♒	12:51 am	♓
30	♓		
31	♓	10:38 am	♈

February			
1	♈		
2	♈	11:41 pm	♉
3	♉		
4	♉		
5	♉	12:09 pm	♊
6	♊		
7	♊	9:57 pm	♋
8	♋		
9	♋		
10	♋	4:07 am	♌
11	♌		
12	♌	7:21 am	♍
13	♍		
14	♍	9:07 am	♎
15	♎		
16	♎	10:52 am	♏
17	♏		
18	♏	1:37 pm	♐
19	♐		
20	♐	5:54 pm	♑
21	♑		
22	♑		
23	♑	12:02 am	♒
24	♒		
25	♒	8:18 am	♓
26	♓		
27	♓	6:54 pm	♈
28	♈		

May			
1	♋		
2	♋		
3	♋	6:34 am	♌
4	♌		
5	♌	1:06 pm	♍
6	♍		
7	♍	4:11 pm	♎
8	♎		
9	♎	4:34 pm	♏
10	♏		
11	♏	3:49 pm	♐
12	♐		
13	♐	4:04 pm	♑
14	♑		
15	♑	7:15 pm	♒
16	♒		
17	♒		
18	♒	2:33 am	♓
19	♓		
20	♓	1:34 pm	♈
21	♈		
22	♈		
23	♈	2:26 am	♉
24	♉		
25	♉	3:10 pm	♊
26	♊		
27	♊		
28	♊	2:36 am	♋
29	♋		
30	♋	12:15 pm	♌
31	♌		

August			
1	♏	5:49 pm	♐
2	♐		
3	♐	8:17 pm	♑
4	♑		
5	♑	11:32 pm	♒
6	♒		
7	♒		
8	♒	4:51 am	♓
9	♓		
10	♓	1:13 pm	♈
11	♈		
12	♈		
13	♈	12:32 am	♉
14	♉		
15	♉	1:09 pm	♊
16	♊		
17	♊		
18	♊	12:37 am	♋
19	♋		
20	♋	9:15 am	♌
21	♌		
22	♌	2:53 pm	♍
23	♍		
24	♍	6:21 pm	♎
25	♎		
26	♎	8:49 pm	♏
27	♏		
28	♏	11:13 pm	♐
29	♐		
30	♐		
31	♐	2:18 am	♑

November			
1	♈		
2	♈	10:19 pm	♉
3	♉		
4	♉		
5	♉	10:52 am	♊
6	♊		
7	♊	11:26 pm	♋
8	♋		
9	♋		
10	♋	10:49 am	♌
11	♌		
12	♌	7:29 pm	♍
13	♍		
14	♍		
15	♍	12:22 am	♎
16	♎		
17	♎	1:40 am	♏
18	♏		
19	♏	12:53 am	♐
20	♐		
21	♐	12:11 am	♑
22	♑		
23	♑	1:46 am	♒
24	♒		
25	♒	7:09 am	♓
26	♓		
27	♓	4:26 pm	♈
28	♈		
29	♈		
30	♈	4:18 am	♉

March			
1	♈		
2	♈	7:23 am	♉
3	♉		
4	♉	8:12 pm	♊
5	♊		
6	♊		
7	♊	7:04 am	♋
8	♋		
9	♋	2:19 pm	♌
10	♌		
11	♌	5:51 pm	♍
12	♍		
13	♍	6:51 pm	♎
14	♎		
15	♎	7:03 pm	♏
16	♏		
17	♏	8:08 pm	♐
18	♐		
19	♐	11:25 pm	♑
20	♑		
21	♑		
22	♑	5:34 am	♒
23	♒		
24	♒	2:30 pm	♓
25	♓		
26	♓		
27	♓	1:39 am	♈
28	♈		
29	♈	2:14 pm	♉
30	♉		
31	♉		

June			
1	♌	7:38 pm	♍
2	♍		
3	♍		
4	♍	12:17 am	♎
5	♎		
6	♎	2:13 am	♏
7	♏		
8	♏	2:24 am	♐
9	♐		
10	♐	2:31 am	♑
11	♑		
12	♑	4:41 am	♒
13	♒		
14	♒	10:33 am	♓
15	♓		
16	♓	8:30 pm	♈
17	♈		
18	♈		
19	♈	9:03 am	♉
20	♉		
21	♉	9:44 pm	♊
22	♊		
23	♊		
24	♊	8:51 am	♋
25	♋		
26	♋	5:55 pm	♌
27	♌		
28	♌		
29	♌	1:03 am	♍
30	♍		

September			
1	♑		
2	♑	6:39 am	♒
3	♒		
4	♒	12:52 pm	♓
5	♓		
6	♓	9:28 pm	♈
7	♈		
8	♈		
9	♈	8:32 am	♉
10	♉		
11	♉	9:06 pm	♊
12	♊		
13	♊		
14	♊	9:09 am	♋
15	♋		
16	♋	6:36 pm	♌
17	♌		
18	♌		
19	♌	12:29 am	♍
20	♍		
21	♍	3:17 am	♎
22	♎		
23	♎	4:24 am	♏
24	♏		
25	♏	5:24 am	♐
26	♐		
27	♐	7:44 am	♑
28	♑		
29	♑	12:17 pm	♒
30	♒		

December			
1	♉		
2	♉	5:00 pm	♊
3	♊		
4	♊		
5	♊	5:22 am	♋
6	♋		
7	♋	4:43 pm	♌
8	♌		
9	♌		
10	♌	2:12 am	♍
11	♍		
12	♍	8:46 am	♎
13	♎		
14	♎	11:51 am	♏
15	♏		
16	♏	12:10 pm	♐
17	♐		
18	♐	11:26 am	♑
19	♑		
20	♑	11:53 am	♒
21	♒		
22	♒	3:33 pm	♓
23	♓		
24	♓	11:24 pm	♈
25	♈		
26	♈		
27	♈	10:43 am	♉
28	♉		
29	♉	11:27 pm	♊
30	♊		
31	♊		

Moon Movements

♎ = Libra ♏ = Scorpio ♐ = Sagittarius ♑ = Capricorn ♒ = Aquarius ♓ = Pisces

1942

January

1	♊	11:42 am	♋
2	♋		
3	♋	10:32 pm	♌
4	♌		
5	♌		
6	♌	7:42 am	♍
7	♍		
8	♍	2:48 pm	♎
9	♎		
10	♎	7:24 pm	♏
11	♏		
12	♏	9:31 pm	♐
13	♐		
14	♐	10:07 pm	♑
15	♑		
16	♑	10:52 pm	♒
17	♒		
18	♒		
19	♒	1:43 am	♓
20	♓		
21	♓	8:08 am	♈
22	♈		
23	♈	6:18 pm	♉
24	♉		
25	♉		
26	♉	6:44 am	♊
27	♊		
28	♊	7:03 pm	♋
29	♋		
30	♋		
31	♋	5:37 am	♌

February

1	♌		
2	♌	1:57 pm	♍
3	♍		
4	♍	8:18 pm	♎
5	♎		
6	♎		
7	♎	12:56 am	♏
8	♏		
9	♏	4:06 am	♐
10	♐		
11	♐	6:19 am	♑
12	♑		
13	♑	8:27 am	♒
14	♒		
15	♒	11:51 am	♓
16	♓		
17	♓	5:46 pm	♈
18	♈		
19	♈		
20	♈	2:57 am	♉
21	♉		
22	♉	2:47 pm	♊
23	♊		
24	♊		
25	♊	3:15 am	♋
26	♋		
27	♋	2:06 pm	♌
28	♌		

March

1	♌	10:06 pm	♍
2	♍		
3	♍		
4	♍	3:23 am	♎
5	♎		
6	♎	6:50 am	♏
7	♏		
8	♏	9:28 am	♐
9	♐		
10	♐	12:08 pm	♑
11	♑		
12	♑	3:30 pm	♒
13	♒		
14	♒	8:09 pm	♓
15	♓		
16	♓		
17	♓	2:41 am	♈
18	♈		
19	♈	11:39 am	♉
20	♉		
21	♉	11:00 pm	♊
22	♊		
23	♊		
24	♊	11:33 am	♋
25	♋		
26	♋	11:04 pm	♌
27	♌		
28	♌		
29	♌	7:36 am	♍
30	♍		
31	♍	12:36 pm	♎

April

1	♎		
2	♎	2:54 pm	♏
3	♏		
4	♏	4:04 pm	♐
5	♐		
6	♐	5:42 pm	♑
7	♑		
8	♑	8:56 pm	♒
9	♒		
10	♒		
11	♒	2:19 am	♓
12	♓		
13	♓	9:49 am	♈
14	♈		
15	♈	7:18 pm	♉
16	♉		
17	♉		
18	♉	6:37 am	♊
19	♊		
20	♊	7:10 pm	♋
21	♋		
22	♋		
23	♋	7:21 am	♌
24	♌		
25	♌	5:02 pm	♍
26	♍		
27	♍	10:50 pm	♎
28	♎		
29	♎		
30	♎	12:59 am	♏

May

1	♏		
2	♏	1:03 am	♐
3	♐		
4	♐	1:04 am	♑
5	♑		
6	♑	2:56 am	♒
7	♒		
8	♒	7:44 am	♓
9	♓		
10	♓	3:31 pm	♈
11	♈		
12	♈		
13	♈	1:37 am	♉
14	♉		
15	♉	1:15 pm	♊
16	♊		
17	♊		
18	♊	1:49 am	♋
19	♋		
20	♋	2:21 pm	♌
21	♌		
22	♌		
23	♌	1:07 am	♍
24	♍		
25	♍	8:22 am	♎
26	♎		
27	♎	11:32 am	♏
28	♏		
29	♏	11:39 am	♐
30	♐		
31	♐	10:43 am	♑

June

1	♑		
2	♑	10:59 am	♒
3	♒		
4	♒	2:14 pm	♓
5	♓		
6	♓	9:11 pm	♈
7	♈		
8	♈		
9	♈	7:16 am	♉
10	♉		
11	♉	7:11 pm	♊
12	♊		
13	♊		
14	♊	7:50 am	♋
15	♋		
16	♋	8:19 pm	♌
17	♌		
18	♌		
19	♌	7:33 am	♍
20	♍		
21	♍	4:04 pm	♎
22	♎		
23	♎	8:50 pm	♏
24	♏		
25	♏	10:09 pm	♐
26	♐		
27	♐	9:30 pm	♑
28	♑		
29	♑	9:00 pm	♒
30	♒		

July

1	♒	10:46 pm	♓
2	♓		
3	♓		
4	♓	4:10 am	♈
5	♈		
6	♈	1:22 pm	♉
7	♉		
8	♉		
9	♉	1:10 am	♊
10	♊		
11	♊	1:51 pm	♋
12	♋		
13	♋		
14	♋	2:08 am	♌
15	♌		
16	♌	1:08 pm	♍
17	♍		
18	♍	10:02 pm	♎
19	♎		
20	♎		
21	♎	4:02 am	♏
22	♏		
23	♏	6:58 am	♐
24	♐		
25	♐	7:38 am	♑
26	♑		
27	♑	7:37 am	♒
28	♒		
29	♒	8:49 am	♓
30	♓		
31	♓	12:55 pm	♈

August

1	♈		
2	♈	8:47 pm	♉
3	♉		
4	♉		
5	♉	7:54 am	♊
6	♊		
7	♊	8:30 pm	♋
8	♋		
9	♋		
10	♋	8:39 am	♌
11	♌		
12	♌	7:09 pm	♍
13	♍		
14	♍		
15	♍	3:31 am	♎
16	♎		
17	♎	9:38 am	♏
18	♏		
19	♏	1:35 pm	♐
20	♐		
21	♐	3:46 pm	♑
22	♑		
23	♑	5:07 pm	♒
24	♒		
25	♒	6:55 pm	♓
26	♓		
27	♓	10:39 pm	♈
28	♈		
29	♈		
30	♈	5:29 am	♉
31	♉		

September

1	♉	3:40 pm	♊
2	♊		
3	♊		
4	♊	4:00 am	♋
5	♋		
6	♋	4:15 pm	♌
7	♌		
8	♌		
9	♌	2:31 am	♍
10	♍		
11	♍	10:05 am	♎
12	♎		
13	♎	3:19 pm	♏
14	♏		
15	♏	6:58 pm	♐
16	♐		
17	♐	9:48 pm	♑
18	♑		
19	♑		
20	♑	12:27 am	♒
21	♒		
22	♒	3:34 am	♓
23	♓		
24	♓	7:57 am	♈
25	♈		
26	♈	2:35 pm	♉
27	♉		
28	♉		
29	♉	12:05 am	♊
30	♊		

October

1	♊	12:03 pm	♋
2	♋		
3	♋		
4	♋	12:35 am	♌
5	♌		
6	♌	11:13 am	♍
7	♍		
8	♍	6:33 pm	♎
9	♎		
10	♎	10:46 pm	♏
11	♏		
12	♏		
13	♏	1:10 am	♐
14	♐		
15	♐	3:13 am	♑
16	♑		
17	♑	6:01 am	♒
18	♒		
19	♒	10:05 am	♓
20	♓		
21	♓	3:37 pm	♈
22	♈		
23	♈	10:52 pm	♉
24	♉		
25	♉		
26	♉	8:18 am	♊
27	♊		
28	♊	8:00 pm	♋
29	♋		
30	♋		
31	♋	8:48 am	♌

November

1	♌		
2	♌	8:19 pm	♍
3	♍		
4	♍		
5	♍	4:21 am	♎
6	♎		
7	♎	8:27 am	♏
8	♏		
9	♏	9:47 am	♐
10	♐		
11	♐	10:18 am	♑
12	♑		
13	♑	11:48 am	♒
14	♒		
15	♒	3:28 pm	♓
16	♓		
17	♓	9:30 pm	♈
18	♈		
19	♈		
20	♈	5:38 am	♉
21	♉		
22	♉	3:35 pm	♊
23	♊		
24	♊		
25	♊	3:17 am	♋
26	♋		
27	♋	4:09 pm	♌
28	♌		
29	♌		
30	♌	4:29 am	♍

December

1	♍		
2	♍	1:55 pm	♎
3	♎		
4	♎	7:06 pm	♏
5	♏		
6	♏	8:34 pm	♐
7	♐		
8	♐	8:07 pm	♑
9	♑		
10	♑	7:57 pm	♒
11	♒		
12	♒	9:56 pm	♓
13	♓		
14	♓		
15	♓	3:04 am	♈
16	♈		
17	♈	11:16 am	♉
18	♉		
19	♉	9:46 pm	♊
20	♊		
21	♊		
22	♊	9:46 am	♋
23	♋		
24	♋	10:35 pm	♌
25	♌		
26	♌		
27	♌	11:10 am	♍
28	♍		
29	♍	9:44 pm	♎
30	♎		
31	♎		

Your Starway to Love

♈ = Aries ♉ = Taurus ♊ = Gemini ♋ = Cancer ♌ = Leo ♍ = Virgo

1943

January

1	♎	4:40 am	♏
2	♏		
3	♏	7:34 am	♐
4	♐		
5	♐	7:35 am	♑
6	♑		
7	♑	6:42 am	♒
8	♒		
9	♒	7:03 am	♓
10	♓		
11	♓	10:21 am	♈
12	♈		
13	♈	5:22 pm	♉
14	♉		
15	♉		
16	♉	3:39 am	♊
17	♊		
18	♊	3:53 pm	♋
19	♋		
20	♋		
21	♋	4:44 am	♌
22	♌		
23	♌	5:03 pm	♍
24	♍		
25	♍		
26	♍	3:47 am	♎
27	♎		
28	♎	11:51 am	♏
29	♏		
30	♏	4:34 pm	♐
31	♐		

April

1	♒	1:27 pm	♓
2	♓		
3	♓	4:17 pm	♈
4	♈		
5	♈	8:37 pm	♉
6	♉		
7	♉		
8	♉	3:41 am	♊
9	♊		
10	♊	2:03 pm	♋
11	♋		
12	♋		
13	♋	2:39 am	♌
14	♌		
15	♌	2:59 pm	♍
16	♍		
17	♍		
18	♍	12:41 am	♎
19	♎		
20	♎	7:04 am	♏
21	♏		
22	♏	10:56 am	♐
23	♐		
24	♐	1:40 pm	♑
25	♑		
26	♑	4:21 pm	♒
27	♒		
28	♒	7:36 pm	♓
29	♓		
30	♓	11:39 pm	♈

July

1	♊	12:13 pm	♋
2	♋		
3	♋		
4	♋	12:39 am	♌
5	♌		
6	♌	1:45 pm	♍
7	♍		
8	♍		
9	♍	1:44 am	♎
10	♎		
11	♎	10:40 am	♏
12	♏		
13	♏	3:37 pm	♐
14	♐		
15	♐	5:06 pm	♑
16	♑		
17	♑	4:46 pm	♒
18	♒		
19	♒	4:30 pm	♓
20	♓		
21	♓	6:08 pm	♈
22	♈		
23	♈	10:53 pm	♉
24	♉		
25	♉		
26	♉	7:04 am	♊
27	♊		
28	♊	6:04 pm	♋
29	♋		
30	♋		
31	♋	6:43 am	♌

October

1	♎	5:04 am	♏
2	♏		
3	♏	12:03 pm	♐
4	♐		
5	♐	5:11 pm	♑
6	♑		
7	♑	8:39 pm	♒
8	♒		
9	♒	10:44 pm	♓
10	♓		
11	♓		
12	♓	12:12 am	♈
13	♈		
14	♈	2:26 am	♉
15	♉		
16	♉	7:07 am	♊
17	♊		
18	♊	3:28 pm	♋
19	♋		
20	♋		
21	♋	3:12 am	♌
22	♌		
23	♌	4:10 pm	♍
24	♍		
25	♍		
26	♍	3:38 am	♎
27	♎		
28	♎	12:14 pm	♏
29	♏		
30	♏	6:14 pm	♐
31	♐		

February

1	♐	6:15 pm	♑
2	♑		
3	♑	6:10 pm	♒
4	♒		
5	♒	6:08 pm	♓
6	♓		
7	♓	8:00 pm	♈
8	♈		
9	♈		
10	♈	1:17 am	♉
11	♉		
12	♉	10:25 am	♊
13	♊		
14	♊	10:24 pm	♋
15	♋		
16	♋		
17	♋	11:18 am	♌
18	♌		
19	♌	11:20 pm	♍
20	♍		
21	♍		
22	♍	9:30 am	♎
23	♎		
24	♎	5:25 pm	♏
25	♏		
26	♏	10:59 pm	♐
27	♐		
28	♐		

May

1	♈		
2	♈		
3	♈	4:57 am	♉
4	♉		
5	♉	12:16 pm	♊
6	♊		
7	♊	10:17 pm	♋
8	♋		
9	♋		
10	♋	10:39 am	♌
11	♌		
12	♌	11:21 pm	♍
13	♍		
14	♍		
15	♍	9:44 am	♎
16	♎		
17	♎	4:19 pm	♏
18	♏		
19	♏	7:33 pm	♐
20	♐		
21	♐	9:00 pm	♑
22	♑		
23	♑	10:23 pm	♒
24	♒		
25	♒		
26	♒	12:58 am	♓
27	♓		
28	♓	5:16 am	♈
29	♈		
30	♈	11:25 am	♉
31	♉		

August

1	♌		
2	♌	7:45 pm	♍
3	♍		
4	♍		
5	♍	7:51 am	♎
6	♎		
7	♎	5:40 pm	♏
8	♏		
9	♏		
10	♏	12:08 am	♐
11	♐		
12	♐	3:09 am	♑
13	♑		
14	♑	3:36 am	♒
15	♒		
16	♒	3:06 am	♓
17	♓		
18	♓	3:32 am	♈
19	♈		
20	♈	6:39 am	♉
21	♉		
22	♉	1:34 pm	♊
23	♊		
24	♊		
25	♊	12:07 am	♋
26	♋		
27	♋	12:49 pm	♌
28	♌		
29	♌		
30	♌	1:47 am	♍
31	♍		

November

1	♐	10:37 pm	♑
2	♑		
3	♑		
4	♑	2:10 am	♒
5	♒		
6	♒	5:16 am	♓
7	♓		
8	♓	8:10 am	♈
9	♈		
10	♈	11:32 am	♉
11	♉		
12	♉	4:31 pm	♊
13	♊		
14	♊		
15	♊	12:22 am	♋
16	♋		
17	♋	11:27 am	♌
18	♌		
19	♌		
20	♌	12:21 am	♍
21	♍		
22	♍	12:19 pm	♎
23	♎		
24	♎	9:09 pm	♏
25	♏		
26	♏		
27	♏	2:35 am	♐
28	♐		
29	♐	5:43 am	♑
30	♑		

March

1	♐	2:19 am	♑
2	♑		
3	♑	3:56 am	♒
4	♒		
5	♒	4:54 am	♓
6	♓		
7	♓	6:41 am	♈
8	♈		
9	♈	10:53 am	♉
10	♉		
11	♉	6:39 pm	♊
12	♊		
13	♊		
14	♊	5:51 am	♋
15	♋		
16	♋	6:41 pm	♌
17	♌		
18	♌		
19	♌	6:43 am	♍
20	♍		
21	♍	4:21 pm	♎
22	♎		
23	♎	11:23 pm	♏
24	♏		
25	♏		
26	♏	4:23 am	♐
27	♐		
28	♐	8:05 am	♑
29	♑		
30	♑	10:57 am	♒
31	♒		

June

1	♉	7:29 pm	♊
2	♊		
3	♊		
4	♊	5:45 am	♋
5	♋		
6	♋	6:03 pm	♌
7	♌		
8	♌		
9	♌	7:03 am	♍
10	♍		
11	♍	6:22 pm	♎
12	♎		
13	♎		
14	♎	1:59 am	♏
15	♏		
16	♏	5:36 am	♐
17	♐		
18	♐	6:30 am	♑
19	♑		
20	♑	6:33 am	♒
21	♒		
22	♒	7:36 am	♓
23	♓		
24	♓	10:52 am	♈
25	♈		
26	♈	4:52 pm	♉
27	♉		
28	♉		
29	♉	1:27 am	♊
30	♊		

September

1	♍	1:33 pm	♎
2	♎		
3	♎	11:20 pm	♏
4	♏		
5	♏		
6	♏	6:38 am	♐
7	♐		
8	♐	11:13 am	♑
9	♑		
10	♑	1:18 pm	♒
11	♒		
12	♒	1:46 pm	♓
13	♓		
14	♓	2:09 pm	♈
15	♈		
16	♈	4:14 pm	♉
17	♉		
18	♉	9:42 pm	♊
19	♊		
20	♊		
21	♊	7:10 am	♋
22	♋		
23	♋	7:34 pm	♌
24	♌		
25	♌		
26	♌	8:30 am	♍
27	♍		
28	♍	7:56 pm	♎
29	♎		
30	♎		

December

1	♑	8:01 am	♒
2	♒		
3	♒	10:36 am	♓
4	♓		
5	♓	2:00 pm	♈
6	♈		
7	♈	6:30 pm	♉
8	♉		
9	♉		
10	♉	12:32 am	♊
11	♊		
12	♊	8:46 am	♋
13	♋		
14	♋	7:37 pm	♌
15	♌		
16	♌		
17	♌	8:22 am	♍
18	♍		
19	♍	8:55 pm	♎
20	♎		
21	♎		
22	♎	6:46 am	♏
23	♏		
24	♏	12:44 pm	♐
25	♐		
26	♐	3:24 pm	♑
27	♑		
28	♑	4:21 pm	♒
29	♒		
30	♒	5:17 pm	♓
31	♓		

Moon Movements

♎ = Libra ♏ = Scorpio ♐ = Sagittarius ♑ = Capricorn ♒ = Aquarius ♓ = Pisces

1944

January

1	♓	7:34 pm	♈
2	♈		
3	♈	11:58 pm	♉
4	♉		
5	♉		
6	♉	6:44 am	♊
7	♊		
8	♊	3:48 pm	♋
9	♋		
10	♋		
11	♋	2:58 am	♌
12	♌		
13	♌	3:38 pm	♍
14	♍		
15	♍		
16	♍	4:29 am	♎
17	♎		
18	♎	3:27 pm	♏
19	♏		
20	♏	10:53 pm	♐
21	♐		
22	♐		
23	♐	2:26 am	♑
24	♑		
25	♑	3:09 am	♒
26	♒		
27	♒	2:48 am	♓
28	♓		
29	♓	3:15 am	♈
30	♈		
31	♈	6:07 am	♉

February

1	♉		
2	♉	12:17 pm	♊
3	♊		
4	♊	9:40 pm	♋
5	♋		
6	♋		
7	♋	9:20 am	♌
8	♌		
9	♌	10:08 pm	♍
10	♍		
11	♍		
12	♍	10:54 am	♎
13	♎		
14	♎	10:24 pm	♏
15	♏		
16	♏		
17	♏	7:15 am	♐
18	♐		
19	♐	12:33 pm	♑
20	♑		
21	♑	2:27 pm	♒
22	♒		
23	♒	2:09 pm	♓
24	♓		
25	♓	1:31 pm	♈
26	♈		
27	♈	2:36 pm	♉
28	♉		
29	♉	7:06 pm	♊

March

1	♊		
2	♊		
3	♊	3:38 am	♋
4	♋		
5	♋	3:19 pm	♌
6	♌		
7	♌		
8	♌	4:18 am	♍
9	♍		
10	♍	4:55 pm	♎
11	♎		
12	♎		
13	♎	4:12 am	♏
14	♏		
15	♏	1:31 pm	♐
16	♐		
17	♐	8:13 pm	♑
18	♑		
19	♑	11:55 pm	♒
20	♒		
21	♒		
22	♒	12:59 am	♓
23	♓		
24	♓	12:42 am	♈
25	♈		
26	♈	1:01 am	♉
27	♉		
28	♉	3:58 am	♊
29	♊		
30	♊	10:59 am	♋
31	♋		

April

1	♋	9:54 pm	♌
2	♌		
3	♌		
4	♌	10:49 am	♍
5	♍		
6	♍	11:22 pm	♎
7	♎		
8	♎		
9	♎	10:12 am	♏
10	♏		
11	♏	7:02 pm	♐
12	♐		
13	♐		
14	♐	1:56 am	♑
15	♑		
16	♑	6:46 am	♒
17	♒		
18	♒	9:28 am	♓
19	♓		
20	♓	10:35 am	♈
21	♈		
22	♈	11:29 am	♉
23	♉		
24	♉	1:59 pm	♊
25	♊		
26	♊	7:49 pm	♋
27	♋		
28	♋		
29	♋	5:36 am	♌
30	♌		

May

1	♌	6:04 pm	♍
2	♍		
3	♍		
4	♍	6:40 am	♎
5	♎		
6	♎	5:18 pm	♏
7	♏		
8	♏		
9	♏	1:27 am	♐
10	♐		
11	♐	7:33 am	♑
12	♑		
13	♑	12:10 pm	♒
14	♒		
15	♒	3:35 pm	♓
16	♓		
17	♓	6:03 pm	♈
18	♈		
19	♈	8:15 pm	♉
20	♉		
21	♉	11:26 pm	♊
22	♊		
23	♊		
24	♊	5:04 am	♋
25	♋		
26	♋	2:04 pm	♌
27	♌		
28	♌		
29	♌	1:58 am	♍
30	♍		
31	♍	2:37 pm	♎

June

1	♎		
2	♎		
3	♎	1:32 am	♏
4	♏		
5	♏	9:27 am	♐
6	♐		
7	♐	2:41 pm	♑
8	♑		
9	♑	6:12 pm	♒
10	♒		
11	♒	8:58 pm	♓
12	♓		
13	♓	11:41 pm	♈
14	♈		
15	♈		
16	♈	2:52 am	♉
17	♉		
18	♉	7:11 am	♊
19	♊		
20	♊	1:28 pm	♋
21	♋		
22	♋	10:25 pm	♌
23	♌		
24	♌		
25	♌	9:58 am	♍
26	♍		
27	♍	10:40 pm	♎
28	♎		
29	♎		
30	♎	10:10 am	♏

July

1	♏		
2	♏	6:38 pm	♐
3	♐		
4	♐	11:42 pm	♑
5	♑		
6	♑		
7	♑	2:14 am	♒
8	♒		
9	♒	3:39 am	♓
10	♓		
11	♓	5:18 am	♈
12	♈		
13	♈	8:16 am	♉
14	♉		
15	♉	1:11 pm	♊
16	♊		
17	♊	8:21 pm	♋
18	♋		
19	♋		
20	♋	5:51 am	♌
21	♌		
22	♌	5:24 pm	♍
23	♍		
24	♍		
25	♍	6:08 am	♎
26	♎		
27	♎	6:16 pm	♏
28	♏		
29	♏		
30	♏	3:50 am	♐
31	♐		

August

1	♐	9:42 am	♑
2	♑		
3	♑	12:10 pm	♒
4	♒		
5	♒	12:35 pm	♓
6	♓		
7	♓	12:43 pm	♈
8	♈		
9	♈	2:20 pm	♉
10	♉		
11	♉	6:38 pm	♊
12	♊		
13	♊		
14	♊	2:03 am	♋
15	♋		
16	♋	12:08 pm	♌
17	♌		
18	♌		
19	♌	12:01 am	♍
20	♍		
21	♍	12:45 pm	♎
22	♎		
23	♎		
24	♎	1:13 am	♏
25	♏		
26	♏	11:52 am	♐
27	♐		
28	♐	7:12 pm	♑
29	♑		
30	♑	10:44 pm	♒
31	♒		

September

1	♒	11:14 pm	♓
2	♓		
3	♓	10:27 pm	♈
4	♈		
5	♈	10:28 pm	♉
6	♉		
7	♉		
8	♉	1:14 am	♊
9	♊		
10	♊	7:47 am	♋
11	♋		
12	♋	5:50 pm	♌
13	♌		
14	♌		
15	♌	6:00 am	♍
16	♍		
17	♍	6:48 pm	♎
18	♎		
19	♎		
20	♎	7:11 am	♏
21	♏		
22	♏	6:16 pm	♐
23	♐		
24	♐		
25	♐	2:55 am	♑
26	♑		
27	♑	8:10 am	♒
28	♒		
29	♒	9:58 am	♓
30	♓		

October

1	♓	9:30 am	♈
2	♈		
3	♈	8:46 am	♉
4	♉		
5	♉	9:59 am	♊
6	♊		
7	♊	2:56 pm	♋
8	♋		
9	♋		
10	♋	12:03 am	♌
11	♌		
12	♌	12:04 pm	♍
13	♍		
14	♍		
15	♍	12:55 am	♎
16	♎		
17	♎	1:03 pm	♏
18	♏		
19	♏	11:50 pm	♐
20	♐		
21	♐		
22	♐	8:48 am	♑
23	♑		
24	♑	3:19 pm	♒
25	♒		
26	♒	6:53 pm	♓
27	♓		
28	♓	7:54 pm	♈
29	♈		
30	♈	7:45 pm	♉
31	♉		

November

1	♉	8:28 pm	♊
2	♊		
3	♊		
4	♊	12:04 am	♋
5	♋		
6	♋	7:44 am	♌
7	♌		
8	♌	6:59 pm	♍
9	♍		
10	♍		
11	♍	7:45 am	♎
12	♎		
13	♎	7:48 pm	♏
14	♏		
15	♏		
16	♏	6:02 am	♐
17	♐		
18	♐	2:20 pm	♑
19	♑		
20	♑	8:47 pm	♒
21	♒		
22	♒		
23	♒	1:18 am	♓
24	♓		
25	♓	3:57 am	♈
26	♈		
27	♈	5:22 am	♉
28	♉		
29	♉	6:55 am	♊
30	♊		

December

1	♊	10:17 am	♋
2	♋		
3	♋	4:53 pm	♌
4	♌		
5	♌		
6	♌	3:04 am	♍
7	♍		
8	♍	3:28 pm	♎
9	♎		
10	♎		
11	♎	3:42 am	♏
12	♏		
13	♏	1:50 pm	♐
14	♐		
15	♐	9:22 pm	♑
16	♑		
17	♑		
18	♑	2:44 am	♒
19	♒		
20	♒	6:39 am	♓
21	♓		
22	♓	9:42 am	♈
23	♈		
24	♈	12:24 pm	♉
25	♉		
26	♉	3:26 pm	♊
27	♊		
28	♊	7:44 pm	♋
29	♋		
30	♋		
31	♋	2:19 am	♌

1945

Your Starway to Love

♈ = Aries ♉ = Taurus ♊ = Gemini ♋ = Cancer ♌ = Leo ♍ = Virgo

January

Day	Sign	Time	Enters
1	♌		
2	♌	11:49 am	♍
3	♍		
4	♍	11:44 pm	♎
5	♎		
6	♎		
7	♎	12:13 pm	♏
8	♏		
9	♏	10:55 pm	♐
10	♐		
11	♐		
12	♐	6:28 am	♑
13	♑		
14	♑	10:57 am	♒
15	♒		
16	♒	1:27 pm	♓
17	♓		
18	♓	3:21 pm	♈
19	♈		
20	♈	5:48 pm	♉
21	♉		
22	♉	9:35 pm	♊
23	♊		
24	♊		
25	♊	3:05 am	♋
26	♋		
27	♋	10:33 am	♌
28	♌		
29	♌	8:09 pm	♍
30	♍		
31	♍		

February

Day	Sign	Time	Enters
1	♍	7:46 am	♎
2	♎		
3	♎	8:22 pm	♏
4	♏		
5	♏		
6	♏	7:57 am	♐
7	♐		
8	♐	4:29 pm	♑
9	♑		
10	♑	9:12 pm	♒
11	♒		
12	♒	10:52 pm	♓
13	♓		
14	♓	11:12 pm	♈
15	♈		
16	♈		
17	♈	12:05 am	♉
18	♉		
19	♉	3:01 am	♊
20	♊		
21	♊	8:42 am	♋
22	♋		
23	♋	4:58 pm	♌
24	♌		
25	♌		
26	♌	3:13 am	♍
27	♍		
28	♍	2:57 pm	♎

March

Day	Sign	Time	Enters
1	♎		
2	♎		
3	♎	3:32 am	♏
4	♏		
5	♏	3:45 pm	♐
6	♐		
7	♐		
8	♐	1:37 am	♑
9	♑		
10	♑	7:40 am	♒
11	♒		
12	♒	9:50 am	♓
13	♓		
14	♓	9:32 am	♈
15	♈		
16	♈	8:54 am	♉
17	♉		
18	♉	10:04 am	♊
19	♊		
20	♊	2:31 pm	♋
21	♋		
22	♋	10:32 pm	♌
23	♌		
24	♌		
25	♌	9:11 am	♍
26	♍		
27	♍	9:15 pm	♎
28	♎		
29	♎		
30	♎	9:50 am	♏
31	♏		

April

Day	Sign	Time	Enters
1	♏	10:08 pm	♐
2	♐		
3	♐		
4	♐	8:51 am	♑
5	♑		
6	♑	4:28 pm	♒
7	♒		
8	♒	8:10 pm	♓
9	♓		
10	♓	8:38 pm	♈
11	♈		
12	♈	7:40 pm	♉
13	♉		
14	♉	7:31 pm	♊
15	♊		
16	♊	10:14 pm	♋
17	♋		
18	♋		
19	♋	4:52 am	♌
20	♌		
21	♌	3:03 pm	♍
22	♍		
23	♍		
24	♍	3:15 am	♎
25	♎		
26	♎	3:52 pm	♏
27	♏		
28	♏		
29	♏	3:56 am	♐
30	♐		

May

Day	Sign	Time	Enters
1	♐	2:40 pm	♑
2	♑		
3	♑	11:06 pm	♒
4	♒		
5	♒		
6	♒	4:21 am	♓
7	♓		
8	♓	6:25 am	♈
9	♈		
10	♈	6:24 am	♉
11	♉		
12	♉	6:12 am	♊
13	♊		
14	♊	7:51 am	♋
15	♋		
16	♋	12:57 pm	♌
17	♌		
18	♌	9:56 pm	♍
19	♍		
20	♍		
21	♍	9:43 am	♎
22	♎		
23	♎	10:21 pm	♏
24	♏		
25	♏		
26	♏	10:11 am	♐
27	♐		
28	♐	8:24 pm	♑
29	♑		
30	♑		
31	♑	4:35 am	♒

June

Day	Sign	Time	Enters
1	♒		
2	♒	10:25 am	♓
3	♓		
4	♓	1:51 pm	♈
5	♈		
6	♈	3:23 pm	♉
7	♉		
8	♉	4:15 pm	♊
9	♊		
10	♊	6:02 pm	♋
11	♋		
12	♋	10:20 pm	♌
13	♌		
14	♌		
15	♌	6:07 am	♍
16	♍		
17	♍	5:06 pm	♎
18	♎		
19	♎		
20	♎	5:36 am	♏
21	♏		
22	♏	5:27 pm	♐
23	♐		
24	♐		
25	♐	3:14 am	♑
26	♑		
27	♑	10:36 am	♒
28	♒		
29	♒	3:51 pm	♓
30	♓		

July

Day	Sign	Time	Enters
1	♓	7:29 pm	♈
2	♈		
3	♈	10:04 pm	♉
4	♉		
5	♉		
6	♉	12:20 am	♊
7	♊		
8	♊	3:10 am	♋
9	♋		
10	♋	7:43 am	♌
11	♌		
12	♌	2:58 pm	♍
13	♍		
14	♍		
15	♍	1:13 am	♎
16	♎		
17	♎	1:29 pm	♏
18	♏		
19	♏		
20	♏	1:36 am	♐
21	♐		
22	♐	11:29 am	♑
23	♑		
24	♑	6:16 pm	♒
25	♒		
26	♒	10:26 pm	♓
27	♓		
28	♓		
29	♓	1:07 am	♈
30	♈		
31	♈	3:29 am	♉

August

Day	Sign	Time	Enters
1	♉		
2	♉	6:23 am	♊
3	♊		
4	♊	10:23 am	♋
5	♋		
6	♋	3:53 pm	♌
7	♌		
8	♌	11:24 pm	♍
9	♍		
10	♍		
11	♍	9:21 am	♎
12	♎		
13	♎	9:24 pm	♏
14	♏		
15	♏		
16	♏	9:56 am	♐
17	♐		
18	♐	8:31 pm	♑
19	♑		
20	♑		
21	♑	3:32 am	♒
22	♒		
23	♒	7:05 am	♓
24	♓		
25	♓	8:30 am	♈
26	♈		
27	♈	9:34 am	♉
28	♉		
29	♉	11:47 am	♊
30	♊		
31	♊	4:00 pm	♋

September

Day	Sign	Time	Enters
1	♋		
2	♋	10:20 pm	♌
3	♌		
4	♌		
5	♌	6:36 am	♍
6	♍		
7	♍	4:48 pm	♎
8	♎		
9	♎		
10	♎	4:48 am	♏
11	♏		
12	♏	5:37 pm	♐
13	♐		
14	♐		
15	♐	5:11 am	♑
16	♑		
17	♑	1:19 pm	♒
18	♒		
19	♒	5:19 pm	♓
20	♓		
21	♓	6:10 pm	♈
22	♈		
23	♈	5:53 pm	♉
24	♉		
25	♉	6:32 pm	♊
26	♊		
27	♊	9:38 pm	♋
28	♋		
29	♋		
30	♋	3:47 am	♌

October

Day	Sign	Time	Enters
1	♌		
2	♌	12:34 pm	♍
3	♍		
4	♍	11:17 pm	♎
5	♎		
6	♎		
7	♎	11:24 am	♏
8	♏		
9	♏		
10	♏	12:17 am	♐
11	♐		
12	♐	12:33 pm	♑
13	♑		
14	♑	10:07 pm	♒
15	♒		
16	♒		
17	♒	3:34 am	♓
18	♓		
19	♓	5:09 am	♈
20	♈		
21	♈	4:30 am	♉
22	♉		
23	♉	3:49 am	♊
24	♊		
25	♊	5:11 am	♋
26	♋		
27	♋	9:55 am	♌
28	♌		
29	♌	6:12 pm	♍
30	♍		
31	♍		

November

Day	Sign	Time	Enters
1	♍	5:08 am	♎
2	♎		
3	♎	5:29 pm	♏
4	♏		
5	♏		
6	♏	6:18 am	♐
7	♐		
8	♐	6:35 pm	♑
9	♑		
10	♑		
11	♑	4:59 am	♒
12	♒		
13	♒	12:05 pm	♓
14	♓		
15	♓	3:24 pm	♈
16	♈		
17	♈	3:48 pm	♉
18	♉		
19	♉	3:02 pm	♊
20	♊		
21	♊	3:14 pm	♋
22	♋		
23	♋	6:12 pm	♌
24	♌		
25	♌		
26	♌	12:59 am	♍
27	♍		
28	♍	11:18 am	♎
29	♎		
30	♎	11:43 pm	♏

December

Day	Sign	Time	Enters
1	♏		
2	♏		
3	♏	12:30 pm	♐
4	♐		
5	♐		
6	♐	12:23 am	♑
7	♑		
8	♑	10:34 am	♒
9	♒		
10	♒	6:20 pm	♓
11	♓		
12	♓	11:15 pm	♈
13	♈		
14	♈		
15	♈	1:30 am	♉
16	♉		
17	♉	2:03 am	♊
18	♊		
19	♊	2:27 am	♋
20	♋		
21	♋	4:30 am	♌
22	♌		
23	♌	9:44 am	♍
24	♍		
25	♍	6:45 pm	♎
26	♎		
27	♎		
28	♎	6:43 am	♏
29	♏		
30	♏	7:32 pm	♐
31	♐		

Moon Movements

♎ = Libra ♏ = Scorpio ♐ = Sagittarius ♑ = Capricorn ♒ = Aquarius ♓ = Pisces

1946

January

Day	Moon	Time	Enters
1	♐		
2	♐	7:11 am	♑
3	♑		
4	♑	4:38 pm	♒
5	♒		
6	♒	11:47 pm	♓
7	♓		
8	♓		
9	♓	4:56 am	♈
10	♈		
11	♈	8:25 am	♉
12	♉		
13	♉	10:42 am	♊
14	♊		
15	♊	12:32 pm	♋
16	♋		
17	♋	3:04 pm	♌
18	♌		
19	♌	7:40 pm	♍
20	♍		
21	♍		
22	♍	3:31 am	♎
23	♎		
24	♎	2:40 pm	♏
25	♏		
26	♏		
27	♏	3:27 am	♐
28	♐		
29	♐	3:18 pm	♑
30	♑		
31	♑		

April

Day	Moon	Time	Enters
1	♓	4:16 am	♈
2	♈		
3	♈	4:56 am	♉
4	♉		
5	♉	5:25 am	♊
6	♊		
7	♊	7:21 am	♋
8	♋		
9	♋	11:37 am	♌
10	♌		
11	♌	6:20 pm	♍
12	♍		
13	♍		
14	♍	3:13 am	♎
15	♎		
16	♎	2:03 pm	♏
17	♏		
18	♏		
19	♏	2:30 am	♐
20	♐		
21	♐	3:28 pm	♑
22	♑		
23	♑		
24	♑	2:56 am	♒
25	♒		
26	♒	10:54 am	♓
27	♓		
28	♓	2:45 pm	♈
29	♈		
30	♈	3:31 pm	♉

July

Day	Moon	Time	Enters
1	♌		
2	♌	3:45 pm	♍
3	♍		
4	♍	10:21 pm	♎
5	♎		
6	♎		
7	♎	8:41 am	♏
8	♏		
9	♏	9:20 pm	♐
10	♐		
11	♐		
12	♐	10:05 am	♑
13	♑		
14	♑	9:17 pm	♒
15	♒		
16	♒		
17	♒	6:15 am	♓
18	♓		
19	♓	12:59 pm	♈
20	♈		
21	♈	5:35 pm	♉
22	♉		
23	♉	8:18 pm	♊
24	♊		
25	♊	9:44 pm	♋
26	♋		
27	♋	10:57 pm	♌
28	♌		
29	♌		
30	♌	1:32 am	♍
31	♍		

October

Day	Moon	Time	Enters
1	♐		
2	♐	9:29 am	♑
3	♑		
4	♑	9:27 pm	♒
5	♒		
6	♒		
7	♒	6:09 am	♓
8	♓		
9	♓	11:05 am	♈
10	♈		
11	♈	1:20 pm	♉
12	♉		
13	♉	2:37 pm	♊
14	♊		
15	♊	4:23 pm	♋
16	♋		
17	♋	7:35 pm	♌
18	♌		
19	♌		
20	♌	12:35 am	♍
21	♍		
22	♍	7:33 am	♎
23	♎		
24	♎	4:41 pm	♏
25	♏		
26	♏		
27	♏	4:03 am	♐
28	♐		
29	♐	4:59 pm	♑
30	♑		
31	♑		

February

Day	Moon	Time	Enters
1	♑	12:23 am	♒
2	♒		
3	♒	6:32 am	♓
4	♓		
5	♓	10:38 am	♈
6	♈		
7	♈	1:47 pm	♉
8	♉		
9	♉	4:45 pm	♊
10	♊		
11	♊	7:59 pm	♋
12	♋		
13	♋	11:50 pm	♌
14	♌		
15	♌		
16	♌	5:03 am	♍
17	♍		
18	♍	12:36 pm	♎
19	♎		
20	♎	11:05 pm	♏
21	♏		
22	♏		
23	♏	11:41 am	♐
24	♐		
25	♐		
26	♐	12:01 am	♑
27	♑		
28	♑	9:34 am	♒

May

Day	Moon	Time	Enters
1	♉		
2	♉	3:03 pm	♊
3	♊		
4	♊	3:23 pm	♋
5	♋		
6	♋	6:04 pm	♌
7	♌		
8	♌	11:57 pm	♍
9	♍		
10	♍		
11	♍	8:53 am	♎
12	♎		
13	♎	8:08 pm	♏
14	♏		
15	♏		
16	♏	8:46 am	♐
17	♐		
18	♐	9:42 pm	♑
19	♑		
20	♑		
21	♑	9:31 am	♒
22	♒		
23	♒	6:39 pm	♓
24	♓		
25	♓		
26	♓	12:05 am	♈
27	♈		
28	♈	2:04 am	♉
29	♉		
30	♉	1:54 am	♊
31	♊		

August

Day	Moon	Time	Enters
1	♍	7:05 am	♎
2	♎		
3	♎	4:23 pm	♏
4	♏		
5	♏		
6	♏	4:36 am	♐
7	♐		
8	♐	5:23 pm	♑
9	♑		
10	♑		
11	♑	4:23 am	♒
12	♒		
13	♒	12:41 pm	♓
14	♓		
15	♓	6:37 pm	♈
16	♈		
17	♈	10:59 pm	♉
18	♉		
19	♉		
20	♉	2:22 am	♊
21	♊		
22	♊	5:06 am	♋
23	♋		
24	♋	7:38 am	♌
25	♌		
26	♌	10:54 am	♍
27	♍		
28	♍	4:15 pm	♎
29	♎		
30	♎		
31	♎	12:49 am	♏

November

Day	Moon	Time	Enters
1	♑	5:36 am	♒
2	♒		
3	♒	3:32 pm	♓
4	♓		
5	♓	9:28 pm	♈
6	♈		
7	♈	11:49 pm	♉
8	♉		
9	♉		
10	♉	12:07 am	♊
11	♊		
12	♊	12:15 am	♋
13	♋		
14	♋	1:53 am	♌
15	♌		
16	♌	6:05 am	♍
17	♍		
18	♍	1:12 pm	♎
19	♎		
20	♎	10:58 pm	♏
21	♏		
22	♏		
23	♏	10:44 am	♐
24	♐		
25	♐	11:40 pm	♑
26	♑		
27	♑		
28	♑	12:30 pm	♒
29	♒		
30	♒	11:30 pm	♓

March

Day	Moon	Time	Enters
1	♒		
2	♒	3:25 pm	♓
3	♓		
4	♓	6:23 pm	♈
5	♈		
6	♈	8:08 pm	♉
7	♉		
8	♉	10:12 pm	♊
9	♊		
10	♊		
11	♊	1:29 am	♋
12	♋		
13	♋	6:14 am	♌
14	♌		
15	♌	12:32 pm	♍
16	♍		
17	♍	8:40 pm	♎
18	♎		
19	♎		
20	♎	7:04 am	♏
21	♏		
22	♏	7:30 pm	♐
23	♐		
24	♐		
25	♐	8:18 am	♑
26	♑		
27	♑	6:51 pm	♒
28	♒		
29	♒		
30	♒	1:26 am	♓
31	♓		

June

Day	Moon	Time	Enters
1	♊	1:28 am	♋
2	♋		
3	♋	2:39 am	♌
4	♌		
5	♌	6:57 am	♍
6	♍		
7	♍	2:57 pm	♎
8	♎		
9	♎		
10	♎	2:04 am	♏
11	♏		
12	♏	2:50 pm	♐
13	♐		
14	♐		
15	♐	3:39 am	♑
16	♑		
17	♑	3:16 pm	♒
18	♒		
19	♒		
20	♒	12:43 am	♓
21	♓		
22	♓	7:19 am	♈
23	♈		
24	♈	10:56 am	♉
25	♉		
26	♉	12:07 pm	♊
27	♊		
28	♊	12:10 pm	♋
29	♋		
30	♋	12:47 pm	♌

September

Day	Moon	Time	Enters
1	♏		
2	♏	12:31 pm	♐
3	♐		
4	♐		
5	♐	1:24 am	♑
6	♑		
7	♑	12:41 pm	♒
8	♒		
9	♒	8:46 pm	♓
10	♓		
11	♓		
12	♓	1:49 am	♈
13	♈		
14	♈	5:03 am	♉
15	♉		
16	♉	7:45 am	♊
17	♊		
18	♊	10:42 am	♋
19	♋		
20	♋	2:13 pm	♌
21	♌		
22	♌	6:38 pm	♍
23	♍		
24	♍		
25	♍	12:40 am	♎
26	♎		
27	♎	9:12 am	♏
28	♏		
29	♏	8:32 pm	♐
30	♐		

December

Day	Moon	Time	Enters
1	♓		
2	♓		
3	♓	7:05 am	♈
4	♈		
5	♈	10:48 am	♉
6	♉		
7	♉	11:30 am	♊
8	♊		
9	♊	10:50 am	♋
10	♋		
11	♋	10:46 am	♌
12	♌		
13	♌	1:09 pm	♍
14	♍		
15	♍	7:07 pm	♎
16	♎		
17	♎		
18	♎	4:43 am	♏
19	♏		
20	♏	4:48 pm	♐
21	♐		
22	♐		
23	♐	5:50 am	♑
24	♑		
25	♑	6:29 pm	♒
26	♒		
27	♒		
28	♒	5:43 am	♓
29	♓		
30	♓	2:31 pm	♈
31	♈		

Your Starway to Love

♈ = Aries ♉ = Taurus ♊ = Gemini ♋ = Cancer ♌ = Leo ♍ = Virgo

1947

January

1	♈	8:06 pm	♉
2	♉		
3	♉	10:26 pm	♊
4	♊		
5	♊	10:28 pm	♋
6	♋		
7	♋	9:53 pm	♌
8	♌		
9	♌	10:45 pm	♍
10	♍		
11	♍		
12	♍	2:54 am	♎
13	♎		
14	♎	11:15 am	♏
15	♏		
16	♏	11:03 pm	♐
17	♐		
18	♐		
19	♐	12:10 pm	♑
20	♑		
21	♑		
22	♑	12:37 am	♒
23	♒		
24	♒	11:23 am	♓
25	♓		
26	♓	8:10 pm	♈
27	♈		
28	♈		
29	♈	2:45 am	♉
30	♉		
31	♉	6:52 am	♊

April

1	♌		
2	♌	3:30 am	♍
3	♍		
4	♍	7:39 am	♎
5	♎		
6	♎	1:57 pm	♏
7	♏		
8	♏	11:12 pm	♐
9	♐		
10	♐		
11	♐	11:08 am	♑
12	♑		
13	♑	11:51 pm	♒
14	♒		
15	♒		
16	♒	10:47 am	♓
17	♓		
18	♓	6:25 pm	♈
19	♈		
20	♈	10:56 pm	♉
21	♉		
22	♉		
23	♉	1:27 am	♊
24	♊		
25	♊	3:22 am	♋
26	♋		
27	♋	5:44 am	♌
28	♌		
29	♌	9:15 am	♍
30	♍		

July

1	♐		
2	♐	8:03 am	♑
3	♑		
4	♑	8:50 pm	♒
5	♒		
6	♒		
7	♒	9:03 am	♓
8	♓		
9	♓	7:34 pm	♈
10	♈		
11	♈		
12	♈	3:12 am	♉
13	♉		
14	♉	7:17 am	♊
15	♊		
16	♊	8:14 am	♋
17	♋		
18	♋	7:34 am	♌
19	♌		
20	♌	7:19 am	♍
21	♍		
22	♍	9:33 am	♎
23	♎		
24	♎	3:41 pm	♏
25	♏		
26	♏		
27	♏	1:40 am	♐
28	♐		
29	♐	2:01 pm	♑
30	♑		
31	♑		

October

1	♈	9:15 pm	♉
2	♉		
3	♉		
4	♉	2:44 am	♊
5	♊		
6	♊	6:47 am	♋
7	♋		
8	♋	9:41 am	♌
9	♌		
10	♌	11:57 am	♍
11	♍		
12	♍	2:31 pm	♎
13	♎		
14	♎	6:45 pm	♏
15	♏		
16	♏		
17	♏	1:53 am	♐
18	♐		
19	♐	12:14 pm	♑
20	♑		
21	♑		
22	♑	12:39 am	♒
23	♒		
24	♒	12:45 pm	♓
25	♓		
26	♓	10:31 pm	♈
27	♈		
28	♈		
29	♈	5:16 am	♉
30	♉		
31	♉	9:36 am	♊

February

1	♊		
2	♊	8:38 pm	♋
3	♋		
4	♋	9:01 am	♌
5	♌		
6	♌	9:42 am	♍
7	♍		
8	♍	12:39 pm	♎
9	♎		
10	♎	7:28 pm	♏
11	♏		
12	♏		
13	♏	6:15 am	♐
14	♐		
15	♐	7:12 pm	♑
16	♑		
17	♑		
18	♑	7:38 am	♒
19	♒		
20	♒	5:57 pm	♓
21	♓		
22	♓		
23	♓	1:58 am	♈
24	♈		
25	♈	8:08 am	♉
26	♉		
27	♉	12:47 pm	♊
28	♊		

May

1	♍	2:24 pm	♎
2	♎		
3	♎	9:35 pm	♏
4	♏		
5	♏		
6	♏	7:09 am	♐
7	♐		
8	♐	6:55 pm	♑
9	♑		
10	♑		
11	♑	7:41 am	♒
12	♒		
13	♒	7:20 pm	♓
14	♓		
15	♓		
16	♓	3:56 am	♈
17	♈		
18	♈	8:51 am	♉
19	♉		
20	♉	10:51 am	♊
21	♊		
22	♊	11:27 am	♋
23	♋		
24	♋	12:18 pm	♌
25	♌		
26	♌	2:50 pm	♍
27	♍		
28	♍	7:54 pm	♎
29	♎		
30	♎		
31	♎	3:42 am	♏

August

1	♑	2:50 am	♒
2	♒		
3	♒	2:49 pm	♓
4	♓		
5	♓		
6	♓	1:20 am	♈
7	♈		
8	♈	9:43 am	♉
9	♉		
10	♉	3:17 pm	♊
11	♊		
12	♊	5:49 pm	♋
13	♋		
14	♋	6:06 pm	♌
15	♌		
16	♌	5:49 pm	♍
17	♍		
18	♍	7:04 pm	♎
19	♎		
20	♎	11:44 pm	♏
21	♏		
22	♏		
23	♏	8:34 am	♐
24	♐		
25	♐	8:31 pm	♑
26	♑		
27	♑		
28	♑	9:18 am	♒
29	♒		
30	♒	9:03 pm	♓
31	♓		

November

1	♊		
2	♊	12:32 pm	♋
3	♋		
4	♋	3:03 pm	♌
5	♌		
6	♌	5:55 pm	♍
7	♍		
8	♍	9:42 pm	♎
9	♎		
10	♎		
11	♎	3:03 am	♏
12	♏		
13	♏	10:33 am	♐
14	♐		
15	♐	8:37 pm	♑
16	♑		
17	♑		
18	♑	8:45 am	♒
19	♒		
20	♒	9:16 pm	♓
21	♓		
22	♓		
23	♓	7:53 am	♈
24	♈		
25	♈	3:06 pm	♉
26	♉		
27	♉	6:55 pm	♊
28	♊		
29	♊	8:31 pm	♋
30	♋		

March

1	♊	3:59 pm	♋
2	♋		
3	♋	6:00 pm	♌
4	♌		
5	♌	7:46 pm	♍
6	♍		
7	♍	10:51 pm	♎
8	♎		
9	♎		
10	♎	4:51 am	♏
11	♏		
12	♏	2:34 pm	♐
13	♐		
14	♐		
15	♐	3:00 am	♑
16	♑		
17	♑	3:35 pm	♒
18	♒		
19	♒		
20	♒	1:57 am	♓
21	♓		
22	♓	9:23 am	♈
23	♈		
24	♈	2:29 pm	♉
25	♉		
26	♉	6:16 pm	♊
27	♊		
28	♊	9:26 pm	♋
29	♋		
30	♋		
31	♋	12:22 am	♌

June

1	♏		
2	♏	1:54 pm	♐
3	♐		
4	♐		
5	♐	1:51 am	♑
6	♑		
7	♑	2:38 pm	♒
8	♒		
9	♒		
10	♒	2:47 am	♓
11	♓		
12	♓	12:34 pm	♈
13	♈		
14	♈	6:45 pm	♉
15	♉		
16	♉	9:21 pm	♊
17	♊		
18	♊	9:32 pm	♋
19	♋		
20	♋	9:06 pm	♌
21	♌		
22	♌	10:01 pm	♍
23	♍		
24	♍		
25	♍	1:51 am	♎
26	♎		
27	♎	9:17 am	♏
28	♏		
29	♏	7:46 pm	♐
30	♐		

September

1	♓		
2	♓	7:03 am	♈
3	♈		
4	♈	3:10 pm	♉
5	♉		
6	♉	9:18 pm	♊
7	♊		
8	♊		
9	♊	1:12 am	♋
10	♋		
11	♋	3:03 am	♌
12	♌		
13	♌	3:51 am	♍
14	♍		
15	♍	5:16 am	♎
16	♎		
17	♎	9:11 am	♏
18	♏		
19	♏	4:49 pm	♐
20	♐		
21	♐		
22	♐	3:58 am	♑
23	♑		
24	♑	4:38 pm	♒
25	♒		
26	♒		
27	♒	4:24 am	♓
28	♓		
29	♓	1:58 pm	♈
30	♈		

December

1	♋	9:30 pm	♌
2	♌		
3	♌	11:23 pm	♍
4	♍		
5	♍		
6	♍	3:14 am	♎
7	♎		
8	♎	9:24 am	♏
9	♏		
10	♏	5:49 pm	♐
11	♐		
12	♐		
13	♐	4:14 am	♑
14	♑		
15	♑	4:16 pm	♒
16	♒		
17	♒		
18	♒	4:59 am	♓
19	♓		
20	♓	4:37 pm	♈
21	♈		
22	♈		
23	♈	1:11 am	♉
24	♉		
25	♉	5:47 am	♊
26	♊		
27	♊	7:03 am	♋
28	♋		
29	♋	6:41 am	♌
30	♌		
31	♌	6:47 am	♍

Moon Movements

♎ = Libra ♏ = Scorpio ♐ = Sagittarius ♑ = Capricorn ♒ = Aquarius ♓ = Pisces

1948

January

1	♍		
2	♍	9:10 am	♎
3	♎		
4	♎	2:51 pm	♏
5	♏		
6	♏	11:41 pm	♐
7	♐		
8	♐		
9	♐	10:41 am	♑
10	♑		
11	♑	10:54 pm	♒
12	♒		
13	♒		
14	♒	11:35 am	♓
15	♓		
16	♓	11:44 pm	♈
17	♈		
18	♈		
19	♈	9:42 am	♉
20	♉		
21	♉	4:01 pm	♊
22	♊		
23	♊	6:23 pm	♋
24	♋		
25	♋	6:00 pm	♌
26	♌		
27	♌	4:56 pm	♍
28	♍		
29	♍	5:29 pm	♎
30	♎		
31	♎	9:27 pm	♏

February

1	♏		
2	♏		
3	♏	5:26 am	♐
4	♐		
5	♐	4:30 pm	♑
6	♑		
7	♑		
8	♑	4:59 am	♒
9	♒		
10	♒	5:37 pm	♓
11	♓		
12	♓		
13	♓	5:37 am	♈
14	♈		
15	♈	4:08 pm	♉
16	♉		
17	♉	11:56 pm	♊
18	♊		
19	♊		
20	♊	4:09 am	♋
21	♋		
22	♋	5:07 am	♌
23	♌		
24	♌	4:22 am	♍
25	♍		
26	♍	4:05 am	♎
27	♎		
28	♎	6:24 am	♏
29	♏		

March

1	♏	12:41 pm	♐
2	♐		
3	♐	10:50 pm	♑
4	♑		
5	♑		
6	♑	11:14 am	♒
7	♒		
8	♒	11:53 pm	♓
9	♓		
10	♓		
11	♓	11:33 am	♈
12	♈		
13	♈	9:40 pm	♉
14	♉		
15	♉		
16	♉	5:45 am	♊
17	♊		
18	♊	11:14 am	♋
19	♋		
20	♋	1:58 pm	♌
21	♌		
22	♌	2:42 pm	♍
23	♍		
24	♍	3:01 pm	♎
25	♎		
26	♎	4:50 pm	♏
27	♏		
28	♏	9:46 pm	♐
29	♐		
30	♐		
31	♐	6:34 am	♑

April

1	♑		
2	♑	6:18 pm	♒
3	♒		
4	♒		
5	♒	6:56 am	♓
6	♓		
7	♓	6:28 pm	♈
8	♈		
9	♈		
10	♈	3:58 am	♉
11	♉		
12	♉	11:20 am	♊
13	♊		
14	♊	4:41 pm	♋
15	♋		
16	♋	8:16 pm	♌
17	♌		
18	♌	10:30 pm	♍
19	♍		
20	♍		
21	♍	12:16 am	♎
22	♎		
23	♎	2:49 am	♏
24	♏		
25	♏	7:31 am	♐
26	♐		
27	♐	3:22 pm	♑
28	♑		
29	♑		
30	♑	2:16 am	♒

May

1	♒		
2	♒	2:44 pm	♓
3	♓		
4	♓		
5	♓	2:28 am	♈
6	♈		
7	♈	11:48 am	♉
8	♉		
9	♉	6:20 pm	♊
10	♊		
11	♊	10:38 pm	♋
12	♋		
13	♋		
14	♋	1:39 am	♌
15	♌		
16	♌	4:14 am	♍
17	♍		
18	♍	7:07 am	♎
19	♎		
20	♎	10:56 am	♏
21	♏		
22	♏	4:22 pm	♐
23	♐		
24	♐		
25	♐	12:08 am	♑
26	♑		
27	♑	10:31 am	♒
28	♒		
29	♒	10:46 pm	♓
30	♓		
31	♓		

June

1	♓	10:55 am	♈
2	♈		
3	♈	8:43 pm	♉
4	♉		
5	♉		
6	♉	3:06 am	♊
7	♊		
8	♊	6:28 am	♋
9	♋		
10	♋	8:11 am	♌
11	♌		
12	♌	9:49 am	♍
13	♍		
14	♍	12:33 pm	♎
15	♎		
16	♎	5:03 pm	♏
17	♏		
18	♏	11:28 pm	♐
19	♐		
20	♐		
21	♐	7:51 am	♑
22	♑		
23	♑	6:15 pm	♒
24	♒		
25	♒		
26	♒	6:23 am	♓
27	♓		
28	♓	6:56 pm	♈
29	♈		
30	♈		

July

1	♈	5:40 am	♉
2	♉		
3	♉	12:48 pm	♊
4	♊		
5	♊	4:07 pm	♋
6	♋		
7	♋	4:53 pm	♌
8	♌		
9	♌	5:04 pm	♍
10	♍		
11	♍	6:31 pm	♎
12	♎		
13	♎	10:28 pm	♏
14	♏		
15	♏		
16	♏	5:11 am	♐
17	♐		
18	♐	2:13 pm	♑
19	♑		
20	♑		
21	♑	1:02 am	♒
22	♒		
23	♒	1:13 pm	♓
24	♓		
25	♓		
26	♓	1:57 am	♈
27	♈		
28	♈	1:34 pm	♉
29	♉		
30	♉	10:01 pm	♊
31	♊		

August

1	♊		
2	♊	2:20 am	♋
3	♋		
4	♋	3:13 am	♌
5	♌		
6	♌	2:32 am	♍
7	♍		
8	♍	2:30 am	♎
9	♎		
10	♎	4:56 am	♏
11	♏		
12	♏	10:49 am	♐
13	♐		
14	♐	7:51 pm	♑
15	♑		
16	♑		
17	♑	7:02 am	♒
18	♒		
19	♒	7:23 pm	♓
20	♓		
21	♓		
22	♓	8:05 am	♈
23	♈		
24	♈	8:03 pm	♉
25	♉		
26	♉		
27	♉	5:40 am	♊
28	♊		
29	♊	11:34 am	♋
30	♋		
31	♋	1:41 pm	♌

September

1	♌		
2	♌	1:20 pm	♍
3	♍		
4	♍	12:35 pm	♎
5	♎		
6	♎	1:34 pm	♏
7	♏		
8	♏	5:52 pm	♐
9	♐		
10	♐		
11	♐	1:56 am	♑
12	♑		
13	♑	12:58 pm	♒
14	♒		
15	♒		
16	♒	1:27 am	♓
17	♓		
18	♓	2:02 pm	♈
19	♈		
20	♈		
21	♈	1:45 am	♉
22	♉		
23	♉	11:40 am	♊
24	♊		
25	♊	6:46 pm	♋
26	♋		
27	♋	10:35 pm	♌
28	♌		
29	♌	11:40 pm	♍
30	♍		

October

1	♍	11:30 pm	♎
2	♎		
3	♎	11:58 pm	♏
4	♏		
5	♏		
6	♏	2:55 am	♐
7	♐		
8	♐	9:31 am	♑
9	♑		
10	♑	7:42 pm	♒
11	♒		
12	♒		
13	♒	8:03 am	♓
14	♓		
15	♓	8:36 pm	♈
16	♈		
17	♈		
18	♈	7:54 am	♉
19	♉		
20	♉	5:15 pm	♊
21	♊		
22	♊		
23	♊	12:21 am	♋
24	♋		
25	♋	5:10 am	♌
26	♌		
27	♌	7:53 am	♍
28	♍		
29	♍	9:16 am	♎
30	♎		
31	♎	10:31 am	♏

November

1	♏		
2	♏	1:10 pm	♐
3	♐		
4	♐	6:40 pm	♑
5	♑		
6	♑		
7	♑	3:41 am	♒
8	♒		
9	♒	3:34 pm	♓
10	♓		
11	♓		
12	♓	4:12 am	♈
13	♈		
14	♈	3:24 pm	♉
15	♉		
16	♉		
17	♉	12:02 am	♊
18	♊		
19	♊	6:11 am	♋
20	♋		
21	♋	10:32 am	♌
22	♌		
23	♌	1:48 pm	♍
24	♍		
25	♍	4:33 pm	♎
26	♎		
27	♎	7:19 pm	♏
28	♏		
29	♏	10:52 pm	♐
30	♐		

December

1	♐		
2	♐	4:16 am	♑
3	♑		
4	♑	12:32 pm	♒
5	♒		
6	♒	11:46 pm	♓
7	♓		
8	♓		
9	♓	12:30 pm	♈
10	♈		
11	♈		
12	♈	12:09 am	♉
13	♉		
14	♉	8:44 am	♊
15	♊		
16	♊	2:01 pm	♋
17	♋		
18	♋	5:03 pm	♌
19	♌		
20	♌	7:19 pm	♍
21	♍		
22	♍	9:59 pm	♎
23	♎		
24	♎		
25	♎	1:39 am	♏
26	♏		
27	♏	6:29 am	♐
28	♐		
29	♐	12:47 pm	♑
30	♑		
31	♑	9:07 pm	♒

Your Starway to Love

♈ = Aries ♉ = Taurus ♊ = Gemini ♋ = Cancer ♌ = Leo ♍ = Virgo

1949

January

1	♒		
2	♒		
3	♒	7:58 am	♓
4	♓		
5	♓	8:40 pm	♈
6	♈		
7	♈		
8	♈	9:03 am	♉
9	♉		
10	♉	6:31 pm	♊
11	♊		
12	♊	11:57 pm	♋
13	♋		
14	♋		
15	♋	2:08 am	♌
16	♌		
17	♌	2:52 am	♍
18	♍		
19	♍	4:03 am	♎
20	♎		
21	♎	6:59 am	♏
22	♏		
23	♏	12:09 pm	♐
24	♐		
25	♐	7:22 pm	♑
26	♑		
27	♑		
28	♑	4:26 am	♒
29	♒		
30	♒	3:26 pm	♓
31	♓		

February

1	♓		
2	♓	4:04 am	♈
3	♈		
4	♈	4:57 pm	♉
5	♉		
6	♉		
7	♉	3:40 am	♊
8	♊		
9	♊	10:22 am	♋
10	♋		
11	♋	1:00 pm	♌
12	♌		
13	♌	1:05 pm	♍
14	♍		
15	♍	12:44 pm	♎
16	♎		
17	♎	1:53 pm	♏
18	♏		
19	♏	5:49 pm	♐
20	♐		
21	♐		
22	♐	12:50 am	♑
23	♑		
24	♑	10:26 am	♒
25	♒		
26	♒	9:54 pm	♓
27	♓		
28	♓		

March

1	♓	10:36 am	♈
2	♈		
3	♈	11:33 pm	♉
4	♉		
5	♉		
6	♉	11:05 am	♊
7	♊		
8	♊	7:21 pm	♋
9	♋		
10	♋	11:33 pm	♌
11	♌		
12	♌		
13	♌	12:24 am	♍
14	♍	11:40 pm	♎
15	♎		
16	♎	11:25 pm	♏
17	♏		
18	♏		
19	♏	1:30 am	♐
20	♐		
21	♐	7:04 am	♑
22	♑		
23	♑	4:10 pm	♒
24	♒		
25	♒		
26	♒	3:50 am	♓
27	♓		
28	♓	4:41 pm	♈
29	♈		
30	♈		
31	♈	5:29 am	♉

April

1	♉		
2	♉	5:03 pm	♊
3	♊		
4	♊		
5	♊	2:10 am	♋
6	♋		
7	♋	7:59 am	♌
8	♌		
9	♌	10:32 am	♍
10	♍		
11	♍	10:48 am	♎
12	♎		
13	♎	10:27 am	♏
14	♏		
15	♏	11:23 am	♐
16	♐		
17	♐	3:16 pm	♑
18	♑		
19	♑	10:59 pm	♒
20	♒		
21	♒		
22	♒	10:08 am	♓
23	♓		
24	♓	11:01 pm	♈
25	♈		
26	♈		
27	♈	11:41 am	♉
28	♉		
29	♉	10:48 pm	♊
30	♊		

May

1	♊		
2	♊	7:43 am	♋
3	♋		
4	♋	2:11 pm	♌
5	♌		
6	♌	6:11 pm	♍
7	♍		
8	♍	8:07 pm	♎
9	♎		
10	♎	8:54 pm	♏
11	♏		
12	♏	9:57 pm	♐
13	♐		
14	♐		
15	♐	12:57 am	♑
16	♑		
17	♑	7:19 am	♒
18	♒		
19	♒	5:26 pm	♓
20	♓		
21	♓		
22	♓	6:02 am	♈
23	♈		
24	♈	6:42 pm	♉
25	♉		
26	♉		
27	♉	5:27 am	♊
28	♊		
29	♊	1:39 pm	♋
30	♋		
31	♋	7:36 pm	♌

June

1	♌		
2	♌	11:53 pm	♍
3	♍		
4	♍		
5	♍	2:58 am	♎
6	♎		
7	♎	5:13 am	♏
8	♏		
9	♏	7:24 am	♐
10	♐		
11	♐	10:40 am	♑
12	♑		
13	♑	4:26 pm	♒
14	♒		
15	♒		
16	♒	1:38 am	♓
17	♓		
18	♓	1:45 pm	♈
19	♈		
20	♈		
21	♈	2:30 am	♉
22	♉		
23	♉	1:20 pm	♊
24	♊		
25	♊	9:01 pm	♋
26	♋		
27	♋		
28	♋	2:01 am	♌
29	♌		
30	♌	5:27 am	♍

July

1	♍		
2	♍	8:22 am	♎
3	♎		
4	♎	11:22 am	♏
5	♏		
6	♏	2:45 pm	♐
7	♐		
8	♐	7:02 pm	♑
9	♑		
10	♑		
11	♑	1:09 am	♒
12	♒		
13	♒	10:01 am	♓
14	♓		
15	♓	9:43 pm	♈
16	♈		
17	♈		
18	♈	10:36 am	♉
19	♉		
20	♉	9:57 pm	♊
21	♊		
22	♊		
23	♊	5:52 am	♋
24	♋		
25	♋	10:19 am	♌
26	♌		
27	♌	12:36 pm	♍
28	♍		
29	♍	2:20 pm	♎
30	♎		
31	♎	4:44 pm	♏

August

1	♏		
2	♏	8:25 pm	♐
3	♐		
4	♐		
5	♐	1:36 am	♑
6	♑		
7	♑	8:34 am	♒
8	♒		
9	♒	5:45 pm	♓
10	♓		
11	♓		
12	♓	5:20 am	♈
13	♈		
14	♈	6:18 pm	♉
15	♉		
16	♉		
17	♉	6:23 am	♊
18	♊		
19	♊	3:15 pm	♋
20	♋		
21	♋	8:07 pm	♌
22	♌		
23	♌	9:56 pm	♍
24	♍		
25	♍	10:24 pm	♎
26	♎		
27	♎	11:19 pm	♏
28	♏		
29	♏		
30	♏	2:00 am	♐
31	♐		

September

1	♐	7:05 am	♑
2	♑		
3	♑	2:37 pm	♒
4	♒		
5	♒		
6	♒	12:26 am	♓
7	♓		
8	♓	12:13 pm	♈
9	♈		
10	♈		
11	♈	1:12 am	♉
12	♉		
13	♉	1:47 pm	♊
14	♊		
15	♊	11:52 pm	♋
16	♋		
17	♋		
18	♋	6:04 am	♌
19	♌		
20	♌	8:34 am	♍
21	♍		
22	♍	8:41 am	♎
23	♎		
24	♎	8:20 am	♏
25	♏		
26	♏	9:21 am	♐
27	♐		
28	♐	1:07 pm	♑
29	♑		
30	♑	8:13 pm	♒

October

1	♒		
2	♒		
3	♒	6:19 am	♓
4	♓		
5	♓	6:27 pm	♈
6	♈		
7	♈		
8	♈	7:26 am	♉
9	♉		
10	♉	8:02 pm	♊
11	♊		
12	♊		
13	♊	6:51 am	♋
14	♋		
15	♋	2:35 pm	♌
16	♌		
17	♌	6:42 pm	♍
18	♍		
19	♍	7:48 pm	♎
20	♎		
21	♎	7:18 pm	♏
22	♏		
23	♏	7:08 pm	♐
24	♐		
25	♐	9:10 pm	♑
26	♑		
27	♑		
28	♑	2:50 am	♒
29	♒		
30	♒	12:21 pm	♓
31	♓		

November

1	♓		
2	♓	12:34 am	♈
3	♈		
4	♈	1:37 pm	♉
5	♉		
6	♉		
7	♉	1:55 am	♊
8	♊		
9	♊	12:35 pm	♋
10	♋		
11	♋	9:00 pm	♌
12	♌		
13	♌		
14	♌	2:42 am	♍
15	♍		
16	♍	5:36 am	♎
17	♎		
18	♎	6:18 am	♏
19	♏		
20	♏	6:15 am	♐
21	♐		
22	♐	7:19 am	♑
23	♑		
24	♑	11:24 am	♒
25	♒		
26	♒	7:35 pm	♓
27	♓		
28	♓		
29	♓	7:18 am	♈
30	♈		

December

1	♈	8:22 pm	♉
2	♉		
3	♉		
4	♉	8:28 am	♊
5	♊		
6	♊	6:31 pm	♋
7	♋		
8	♋		
9	♋	2:28 am	♌
10	♌		
11	♌	8:31 am	♍
12	♍		
13	♍	12:45 pm	♎
14	♎		
15	♎	3:13 pm	♏
16	♏		
17	♏	4:32 pm	♐
18	♐		
19	♐	6:00 pm	♑
20	♑		
21	♑	9:24 pm	♒
22	♒		
23	♒		
24	♒	4:20 am	♓
25	♓		
26	♓	3:05 pm	♈
27	♈		
28	♈		
29	♈	3:58 am	♉
30	♉		
31	♉	4:13 pm	♊

Moon Movements

♎ = Libra ♏ = Scorpio ♐ = Sagittarius ♑ = Capricorn ♒ = Aquarius ♓ = Pisces

1950

January

1	♊		
2	♊		
3	♊	1:56 am	♋
4	♋		
5	♋	8:58 am	♌
6	♌		
7	♌	2:06 pm	♍
8	♍		
9	♍	6:08 pm	♎
10	♎		
11	♎	9:28 pm	♏
12	♏		
13	♏		
14	♏	12:16 am	♐
15	♐		
16	♐	3:06 am	♑
17	♑		
18	♑	7:07 am	♒
19	♒		
20	♒	1:41 pm	♓
21	♓		
22	♓	11:37 pm	♈
23	♈		
24	♈		
25	♈	12:08 pm	♉
26	♉		
27	♉		
28	♉	12:43 am	♊
29	♊		
30	♊	10:50 am	♋
31	♋		

February

1	♋	5:34 pm	♌
2	♌		
3	♌	9:37 pm	♍
4	♍		
5	♍		
6	♍	12:19 am	♎
7	♎		
8	♎	2:50 am	♏
9	♏		
10	♏	5:51 am	♐
11	♐		
12	♐	9:45 am	♑
13	♑		
14	♑	2:57 pm	♒
15	♒		
16	♒	10:11 pm	♓
17	♓		
18	♓		
19	♓	8:01 am	♈
20	♈		
21	♈	8:12 pm	♉
22	♉		
23	♉		
24	♉	9:03 am	♊
25	♊		
26	♊	8:03 pm	♋
27	♋		
28	♋		

March

1	♋	3:30 am	♌
2	♌		
3	♌	7:24 am	♍
4	♍		
5	♍	9:00 am	♎
6	♎		
7	♎	9:55 am	♏
8	♏		
9	♏	11:37 am	♐
10	♐		
11	♐	3:07 pm	♑
12	♑		
13	♑	8:52 pm	♒
14	♒		
15	♒		
16	♒	4:59 am	♓
17	♓		
18	♓	3:21 pm	♈
19	♈		
20	♈		
21	♈	3:32 am	♉
22	♉		
23	♉	4:28 pm	♊
24	♊		
25	♊		
26	♊	4:17 am	♋
27	♋		
28	♋	1:04 pm	♌
29	♌		
30	♌	6:01 pm	♍
31	♍		

April

1	♍	7:40 pm	♎
2	♎		
3	♎	7:35 pm	♏
4	♏		
5	♏	7:37 pm	♐
6	♐		
7	♐	9:29 pm	♑
8	♑		
9	♑		
10	♑	2:24 am	♒
11	♒		
12	♒	10:38 am	♓
13	♓		
14	♓	9:32 pm	♈
15	♈		
16	♈		
17	♈	10:00 am	♉
18	♉		
19	♉	10:54 pm	♊
20	♊		
21	♊		
22	♊	11:02 am	♋
23	♋		
24	♋	8:57 pm	♌
25	♌		
26	♌		
27	♌	3:30 am	♍
28	♍		
29	♍	6:25 am	♎
30	♎		

May

1	♎	6:37 am	♏
2	♏		
3	♏	5:50 am	♐
4	♐		
5	♐	6:08 am	♑
6	♑		
7	♑	9:22 am	♒
8	♒		
9	♒	4:34 pm	♓
10	♓		
11	♓		
12	♓	3:18 am	♈
13	♈		
14	♈	3:59 pm	♉
15	♉		
16	♉		
17	♉	4:52 am	♊
18	♊		
19	♊	4:51 pm	♋
20	♋		
21	♋		
22	♋	3:06 am	♌
23	♌		
24	♌	10:50 am	♍
25	♍		
26	♍	3:26 pm	♎
27	♎		
28	♎	5:01 pm	♏
29	♏		
30	♏	4:43 pm	♐
31	♐		

June

1	♐	4:27 pm	♑
2	♑		
3	♑	6:18 pm	♒
4	♒		
5	♒	11:57 pm	♓
6	♓		
7	♓		
8	♓	9:44 am	♈
9	♈		
10	♈	10:12 pm	♉
11	♉		
12	♉		
13	♉	11:05 am	♊
14	♊		
15	♊	10:45 pm	♋
16	♋		
17	♋		
18	♋	8:37 am	♌
19	♌		
20	♌	4:31 pm	♍
21	♍		
22	♍	10:09 pm	♎
23	♎		
24	♎		
25	♎	1:19 am	♏
26	♏		
27	♏	2:26 am	♐
28	♐		
29	♐	2:48 am	♑
30	♑		

July

1	♑	4:19 am	♒
2	♒		
3	♒	8:51 am	♓
4	♓		
5	♓	5:24 pm	♈
6	♈		
7	♈		
8	♈	5:13 am	♉
9	♉		
10	♉	6:02 pm	♊
11	♊		
12	♊		
13	♊	5:34 am	♋
14	♋		
15	♋	2:52 pm	♌
16	♌		
17	♌	10:05 pm	♍
18	♍		
19	♍		
20	♍	3:34 am	♎
21	♎		
22	♎	7:27 am	♏
23	♏		
24	♏	9:55 am	♐
25	♐		
26	♐	11:39 am	♑
27	♑		
28	♑	1:55 pm	♒
29	♒		
30	♒	6:19 pm	♓
31	♓		

August

1	♓		
2	♓	2:03 am	♈
3	♈		
4	♈	1:06 pm	♉
5	♉		
6	♉		
7	♉	1:44 am	♊
8	♊		
9	♊	1:27 pm	♋
10	♋		
11	♋	10:36 pm	♌
12	♌		
13	♌		
14	♌	5:03 am	♍
15	♍		
16	♍	9:31 am	♎
17	♎		
18	♎	12:49 pm	♏
19	♏		
20	♏	3:36 pm	♐
21	♐		
22	♐	6:23 pm	♑
23	♑		
24	♑	9:53 pm	♒
25	♒		
26	♒		
27	♒	3:02 am	♓
28	♓		
29	♓	10:45 am	♈
30	♈		
31	♈	9:19 pm	♉

September

1	♉		
2	♉		
3	♉	9:45 am	♊
4	♊		
5	♊	9:54 pm	♋
6	♋		
7	♋		
8	♋	7:34 am	♌
9	♌		
10	♌	1:55 pm	♍
11	♍		
12	♍	5:28 pm	♎
13	♎		
14	♎	7:27 pm	♏
15	♏		
16	♏	9:12 pm	♐
17	♐		
18	♐	11:49 pm	♑
19	♑		
20	♑		
21	♑	3:59 am	♒
22	♒		
23	♒	10:09 am	♓
24	♓		
25	♓	6:32 pm	♈
26	♈		
27	♈		
28	♈	5:08 am	♉
29	♉		
30	♉	5:26 pm	♊

October

1	♊		
2	♊		
3	♊	5:59 am	♋
4	♋		
5	♋	4:40 pm	♌
6	♌		
7	♌	11:54 pm	♍
8	♍		
9	♍		
10	♍	3:29 am	♎
11	♎		
12	♎	4:31 am	♏
13	♏		
14	♏	4:44 am	♐
15	♐		
16	♐	5:55 am	♑
17	♑		
18	♑	9:27 am	♒
19	♒		
20	♒	3:53 pm	♓
21	♓		
22	♓		
23	♓	12:59 am	♈
24	♈		
25	♈	12:03 pm	♉
26	♉		
27	♉		
28	♉	12:22 am	♊
29	♊		
30	♊	1:03 pm	♋
31	♋		

November

1	♋		
2	♋	12:38 am	♌
3	♌		
4	♌	9:21 am	♍
5	♍		
6	♍	2:10 pm	♎
7	♎		
8	♎	3:28 pm	♏
9	♏		
10	♏	2:51 pm	♐
11	♐		
12	♐	2:25 pm	♑
13	♑		
14	♑	4:14 pm	♒
15	♒		
16	♒	9:38 pm	♓
17	♓		
18	♓		
19	♓	6:39 am	♈
20	♈		
21	♈	6:08 pm	♉
22	♉		
23	♉		
24	♉	6:38 am	♊
25	♊		
26	♊	7:13 pm	♋
27	♋		
28	♋		
29	♋	7:02 am	♌
30	♌		

December

1	♌	4:53 pm	♍
2	♍		
3	♍	11:29 pm	♎
4	♎		
5	♎		
6	♎	2:19 am	♏
7	♏		
8	♏	2:17 am	♐
9	♐		
10	♐	1:16 am	♑
11	♑		
12	♑	1:34 am	♒
13	♒		
14	♒	5:10 am	♓
15	♓		
16	♓	12:58 pm	♈
17	♈		
18	♈		
19	♈	12:10 am	♉
20	♉		
21	♉	12:49 pm	♊
22	♊		
23	♊		
24	♊	1:18 am	♋
25	♋		
26	♋	12:45 pm	♌
27	♌		
28	♌	10:41 pm	♍
29	♍		
30	♍		
31	♍	6:20 am	♎

Your Starway to Love

♈ = Aries ♉ = Taurus ♊ = Gemini ♋ = Cancer ♌ = Leo ♍ = Virgo

1951

January

1	♎		
2	♎	10:58 am	♏
3	♏		
4	♏	12:38 pm	♐
5	♐		
6	♐	12:32 pm	♑
7	♑		
8	♑	12:35 pm	♒
9	♒		
10	♒	2:56 pm	♓
11	♓		
12	♓	9:05 pm	♈
13	♈		
14	♈		
15	♈	7:10 am	♉
16	♉		
17	♉	7:36 pm	♊
18	♊		
19	♊		
20	♊	8:06 am	♋
21	♋		
22	♋	7:12 pm	♌
23	♌		
24	♌		
25	♌	4:26 am	♍
26	♍		
27	♍	11:46 am	♎
28	♎		
29	♎	5:04 pm	♏
30	♏		
31	♏	8:16 pm	♐

April

1	♒		
2	♒	5:44 pm	♓
3	♓		
4	♓		
5	♓	12:16 am	♈
6	♈		
7	♈	8:52 am	♉
8	♉		
9	♉	7:41 pm	♊
10	♊		
11	♊		
12	♊	8:04 am	♋
13	♋		
14	♋	8:18 pm	♌
15	♌		
16	♌		
17	♌	6:07 am	♍
18	♍		
19	♍	12:13 pm	♎
20	♎		
21	♎	2:55 pm	♏
22	♏		
23	♏	3:40 pm	♐
24	♐		
25	♐	4:20 pm	♑
26	♑		
27	♑	6:32 pm	♒
28	♒		
29	♒	11:13 pm	♓
30	♓		

July

1	♊		
2	♊		
3	♊	3:27 am	♋
4	♋		
5	♋	4:00 pm	♌
6	♌		
7	♌		
8	♌	3:36 am	♍
9	♍		
10	♍	1:04 pm	♎
11	♎		
12	♎	7:19 pm	♏
13	♏		
14	♏	10:03 pm	♐
15	♐		
16	♐	10:14 pm	♑
17	♑		
18	♑	9:41 pm	♒
19	♒		
20	♒	10:29 pm	♓
21	♓		
22	♓		
23	♓	2:21 am	♈
24	♈		
25	♈	10:07 am	♉
26	♉		
27	♉	9:08 pm	♊
28	♊		
29	♊		
30	♊	9:42 am	♋
31	♋		

October

1	♎		
2	♎	1:23 pm	♏
3	♏		
4	♏	4:48 pm	♐
5	♐		
6	♐	7:30 pm	♑
7	♑		
8	♑	10:19 pm	♒
9	♒		
10	♒		
11	♒	1:46 am	♓
12	♓		
13	♓	6:19 am	♈
14	♈		
15	♈	12:37 pm	♉
16	♉		
17	♉	9:22 pm	♊
18	♊		
19	♊		
20	♊	8:43 am	♋
21	♋		
22	♋	9:25 pm	♌
23	♌		
24	♌		
25	♌	9:01 am	♍
26	♍		
27	♍	5:25 pm	♎
28	♎		
29	♎	10:09 pm	♏
30	♏		
31	♏		

February

1	♐		
2	♐	9:52 pm	♑
3	♑		
4	♑	11:04 pm	♒
5	♒		
6	♒		
7	♒	1:29 am	♓
8	♓		
9	♓	6:43 am	♈
10	♈		
11	♈	3:33 pm	♉
12	♉		
13	♉		
14	♉	3:18 am	♊
15	♊		
16	♊	3:51 pm	♋
17	♋		
18	♋		
19	♋	3:01 am	♌
20	♌		
21	♌	11:43 am	♍
22	♍		
23	♍	6:01 pm	♎
24	♎		
25	♎	10:31 pm	♏
26	♏		
27	♏		
28	♏	1:49 am	♐

May

1	♓		
2	♓	6:26 am	♈
3	♈		
4	♈	3:46 pm	♉
5	♉		
6	♉		
7	♉	2:51 am	♊
8	♊		
9	♊	3:13 pm	♋
10	♋		
11	♋		
12	♋	3:49 am	♌
13	♌		
14	♌	2:44 pm	♍
15	♍		
16	♍	10:05 pm	♎
17	♎		
18	♎		
19	♎	1:23 am	♏
20	♏		
21	♏	1:44 am	♐
22	♐		
23	♐	1:07 am	♑
24	♑		
25	♑	1:41 am	♒
26	♒		
27	♒	5:05 am	♓
28	♓		
29	♓	11:53 am	♈
30	♈		
31	♈	9:33 pm	♉

August

1	♋	10:08 pm	♌
2	♌		
3	♌		
4	♌	9:18 am	♍
5	♍		
6	♍	6:34 pm	♎
7	♎		
8	♎		
9	♎	1:24 am	♏
10	♏		
11	♏	5:31 am	♐
12	♐		
13	♐	7:18 am	♑
14	♑		
15	♑	7:53 am	♒
16	♒		
17	♒	8:52 am	♓
18	♓		
19	♓	11:58 am	♈
20	♈		
21	♈	6:26 pm	♉
22	♉		
23	♉		
24	♉	4:27 am	♊
25	♊		
26	♊	4:44 pm	♋
27	♋		
28	♋		
29	♋	5:10 am	♌
30	♌		
31	♌	4:00 pm	♍

November

1	♏	12:20 am	♐
2	♐		
3	♐	1:40 am	♑
4	♑		
5	♑	3:43 am	♒
6	♒		
7	♒	7:23 am	♓
8	♓		
9	♓	12:52 pm	♈
10	♈		
11	♈	8:07 pm	♉
12	♉		
13	♉		
14	♉	5:15 am	♊
15	♊		
16	♊	4:28 pm	♋
17	♋		
18	♋		
19	♋	5:12 am	♌
20	♌		
21	♌	5:35 pm	♍
22	♍		
23	♍		
24	♍	3:09 am	♎
25	♎		
26	♎	8:32 am	♏
27	♏		
28	♏	10:20 am	♐
29	♐		
30	♐	10:22 am	♑

March

1	♐		
2	♐	4:29 am	♑
3	♑		
4	♑	7:11 am	♒
5	♒		
6	♒	10:45 am	♓
7	♓		
8	♓	4:16 pm	♈
9	♈		
10	♈		
11	♈	12:33 am	♉
12	♉		
13	♉	11:36 am	♊
14	♊		
15	♊		
16	♊	12:06 am	♋
17	♋		
18	♋	11:44 am	♌
19	♌		
20	♌	8:39 pm	♍
21	♍		
22	♍		
23	♍	2:21 am	♎
24	♎		
25	♎	5:36 am	♏
26	♏		
27	♏	7:40 am	♐
28	♐		
29	♐	9:51 am	♑
30	♑		
31	♑	1:02 pm	♒

June

1	♉		
2	♉		
3	♉	9:03 am	♊
4	♊		
5	♊	9:31 pm	♋
6	♋		
7	♋		
8	♋	10:12 am	♌
9	♌		
10	♌	9:47 pm	♍
11	♍		
12	♍		
13	♍	6:31 am	♎
14	♎		
15	♎	11:17 am	♏
16	♏		
17	♏	12:26 pm	♐
18	♐		
19	♐	11:38 am	♑
20	♑		
21	♑	11:04 am	♒
22	♒		
23	♒	12:49 pm	♓
24	♓		
25	♓	6:13 pm	♈
26	♈		
27	♈		
28	♈	3:17 am	♉
29	♉		
30	♉	2:51 pm	♊

September

1	♍		
2	♍		
3	♍	12:32 am	♎
4	♎		
5	♎	6:49 am	♏
6	♏		
7	♏	11:11 am	♐
8	♐		
9	♐	2:06 pm	♑
10	♑		
11	♑	4:11 pm	♒
12	♒		
13	♒	6:21 pm	♓
14	♓		
15	♓	9:47 pm	♈
16	♈		
17	♈		
18	♈	3:41 am	♉
19	♉		
20	♉	12:47 pm	♊
21	♊		
22	♊		
23	♊	12:34 am	♋
24	♋		
25	♋	1:08 pm	♌
26	♌		
27	♌		
28	♌	12:05 am	♍
29	♍		
30	♍	8:08 am	♎

December

1	♑		
2	♑	10:45 am	♒
3	♒		
4	♒	1:08 pm	♓
5	♓		
6	♓	6:18 pm	♈
7	♈		
8	♈		
9	♈	2:04 am	♉
10	♉		
11	♉	11:54 am	♊
12	♊		
13	♊	11:22 pm	♋
14	♋		
15	♋		
16	♋	12:05 pm	♌
17	♌		
18	♌		
19	♌	12:52 am	♍
20	♍		
21	♍	11:41 am	♎
22	♎		
23	♎	6:38 pm	♏
24	♏		
25	♏	9:27 pm	♐
26	♐		
27	♐	9:24 pm	♑
28	♑		
29	♑	8:36 pm	♒
30	♒		
31	♒	9:10 pm	♓

Moon Movements

♎ = Libra ♏ = Scorpio ♐ = Sagittarius ♑ = Capricorn ♒ = Aquarius ♓ = Pisces

1952

January

Day	Sign	Time	Enters
1	♓		
2	♓		
3	♓	12:42 am	♈
4	♈		
5	♈	7:43 am	♉
6	♉		
7	♉	5:42 pm	♊
8	♊		
9	♊		
10	♊	5:34 am	♋
11	♋		
12	♋	6:19 pm	♌
13	♌		
14	♌		
15	♌	7:00 am	♍
16	♍		
17	♍	6:19 pm	♎
18	♎		
19	♎		
20	♎	2:44 am	♏
21	♏		
22	♏	7:22 am	♐
23	♐		
24	♐	8:39 am	♑
25	♑		
26	♑	8:06 am	♒
27	♒		
28	♒	7:45 am	♓
29	♓		
30	♓	9:33 am	♈
31	♈		

February

Day	Sign	Time	Enters
1	♈	2:51 pm	♉
2	♉		
3	♉	11:55 pm	♊
4	♊		
5	♊		
6	♊	11:44 am	♋
7	♋		
8	♋		
9	♋	12:36 am	♌
10	♌		
11	♌	1:02 pm	♍
12	♍		
13	♍		
14	♍	12:00 am	♎
15	♎		
16	♎	8:45 am	♏
17	♏		
18	♏	2:42 pm	♐
19	♐		
20	♐	5:49 pm	♑
21	♑		
22	♑	6:48 pm	♒
23	♒		
24	♒	7:01 pm	♓
25	♓		
26	♓	8:12 pm	♈
27	♈		
28	♈		
29	♈	12:02 am	♉

March

Day	Sign	Time	Enters
1	♉		
2	♉	7:36 am	♊
3	♊		
4	♊	6:40 pm	♋
5	♋		
6	♋		
7	♋	7:30 am	♌
8	♌		
9	♌	7:51 pm	♍
10	♍		
11	♍		
12	♍	6:16 am	♎
13	♎		
14	♎	2:20 pm	♏
15	♏		
16	♏	8:15 pm	♐
17	♐		
18	♐		
19	♐	12:19 am	♑
20	♑		
21	♑	2:55 am	♒
22	♒		
23	♒	4:39 am	♓
24	♓		
25	♓	6:34 am	♈
26	♈		
27	♈	10:05 am	♉
28	♉		
29	♉	4:36 pm	♊
30	♊		
31	♊		

April

Day	Sign	Time	Enters
1	♊	2:39 am	♋
2	♋		
3	♋	3:10 pm	♌
4	♌		
5	♌		
6	♌	3:40 am	♍
7	♍		
8	♍	1:56 pm	♎
9	♎		
10	♎	9:13 pm	♏
11	♏		
12	♏		
13	♏	2:08 am	♐
14	♐		
15	♐	5:41 am	♑
16	♑		
17	♑	8:43 am	♒
18	♒		
19	♒	11:40 am	♓
20	♓		
21	♓	2:56 pm	♈
22	♈		
23	♈	7:15 pm	♉
24	♉		
25	♉		
26	♉	1:40 am	♊
27	♊		
28	♊	11:06 am	♋
29	♋		
30	♋	11:12 pm	♌

May

Day	Sign	Time	Enters
1	♌		
2	♌		
3	♌	11:57 am	♍
4	♍		
5	♍	10:39 pm	♎
6	♎		
7	♎		
8	♎	5:49 am	♏
9	♏		
10	♏	9:50 am	♐
11	♐		
12	♐	12:09 pm	♑
13	♑		
14	♑	2:14 pm	♒
15	♒		
16	♒	5:05 pm	♓
17	♓		
18	♓	9:07 pm	♈
19	♈		
20	♈		
21	♈	2:29 am	♉
22	♉		
23	♉	9:37 am	♊
24	♊		
25	♊	7:06 pm	♋
26	♋		
27	♋		
28	♋	6:59 am	♌
29	♌		
30	♌	7:57 pm	♍
31	♍		

June

Day	Sign	Time	Enters
1	♍		
2	♍	7:26 am	♎
3	♎		
4	♎	3:19 pm	♏
5	♏		
6	♏	7:21 pm	♐
7	♐		
8	♐	8:46 pm	♑
9	♑		
10	♑	9:27 pm	♒
11	♒		
12	♒	11:00 pm	♓
13	♓		
14	♓		
15	♓	2:29 am	♈
16	♈		
17	♈	8:11 am	♉
18	♉		
19	♉	4:03 pm	♊
20	♊		
21	♊		
22	♊	2:04 am	♋
23	♋		
24	♋	2:02 pm	♌
25	♌		
26	♌		
27	♌	3:06 am	♍
28	♍		
29	♍	3:18 pm	♎
30	♎		

July

Day	Sign	Time	Enters
1	♎		
2	♎	12:25 am	♏
3	♏		
4	♏	5:27 am	♐
5	♐		
6	♐	7:02 am	♑
7	♑		
8	♑	6:54 am	♒
9	♒		
10	♒	6:59 am	♓
11	♓		
12	♓	8:56 am	♈
13	♈		
14	♈	1:45 pm	♉
15	♉		
16	♉	9:37 pm	♊
17	♊		
18	♊		
19	♊	8:05 am	♋
20	♋		
21	♋	8:20 pm	♌
22	♌		
23	♌		
24	♌	9:25 am	♍
25	♍		
26	♍	9:54 pm	♎
27	♎		
28	♎		
29	♎	8:04 am	♏
30	♏		
31	♏	2:37 pm	♐

August

Day	Sign	Time	Enters
1	♐		
2	♐	5:27 pm	♑
3	♑		
4	♑	5:41 pm	♒
5	♒		
6	♒	5:05 pm	♓
7	♓		
8	♓	5:33 pm	♈
9	♈		
10	♈	8:46 pm	♉
11	♉		
12	♉		
13	♉	3:36 am	♊
14	♊		
15	♊	1:52 pm	♋
16	♋		
17	♋		
18	♋	2:19 am	♌
19	♌		
20	♌	3:22 pm	♍
21	♍		
22	♍		
23	♍	3:42 am	♎
24	♎		
25	♎	2:10 pm	♏
26	♏		
27	♏	9:53 pm	♐
28	♐		
29	♐		
30	♐	2:24 am	♑
31	♑		

September

Day	Sign	Time	Enters
1	♑	4:03 am	♒
2	♒		
3	♒	4:00 am	♓
4	♓		
5	♓	3:57 am	♈
6	♈		
7	♈	5:48 am	♉
8	♉		
9	♉	11:06 am	♊
10	♊		
11	♊	8:24 pm	♋
12	♋		
13	♋		
14	♋	8:38 am	♌
15	♌		
16	♌	9:42 pm	♍
17	♍		
18	♍		
19	♍	9:41 am	♎
20	♎		
21	♎	7:43 pm	♏
22	♏		
23	♏		
24	♏	3:33 am	♐
25	♐		
26	♐	9:06 am	♑
27	♑		
28	♑	12:24 pm	♒
29	♒		
30	♒	1:52 pm	♓

October

Day	Sign	Time	Enters
1	♓		
2	♓	2:34 pm	♈
3	♈		
4	♈	4:05 pm	♉
5	♉		
6	♉	8:15 pm	♊
7	♊		
8	♊		
9	♊	4:16 am	♋
10	♋		
11	♋	3:50 pm	♌
12	♌		
13	♌		
14	♌	4:51 am	♍
15	♍		
16	♍	4:44 pm	♎
17	♎		
18	♎		
19	♎	2:10 am	♏
20	♏		
21	♏	9:12 am	♐
22	♐		
23	♐	2:28 pm	♑
24	♑		
25	♑	6:28 pm	♒
26	♒		
27	♒	9:23 pm	♓
28	♓		
29	♓	11:34 pm	♈
30	♈		
31	♈		

November

Day	Sign	Time	Enters
1	♈	1:58 am	♉
2	♉		
3	♉	6:02 am	♊
4	♊		
5	♊	1:12 pm	♋
6	♋		
7	♋	11:56 pm	♌
8	♌		
9	♌		
10	♌	12:47 pm	♍
11	♍		
12	♍		
13	♍	12:57 am	♎
14	♎		
15	♎	10:18 am	♏
16	♏		
17	♏	4:33 pm	♐
18	♐		
19	♐	8:40 pm	♑
20	♑		
21	♑	11:52 pm	♒
22	♒		
23	♒		
24	♒	2:55 am	♓
25	♓		
26	♓	6:09 am	♈
27	♈		
28	♈	9:54 am	♉
29	♉		
30	♉	2:53 pm	♊

December

Day	Sign	Time	Enters
1	♊		
2	♊	10:09 pm	♋
3	♋		
4	♋		
5	♋	8:23 am	♌
6	♌		
7	♌	8:57 pm	♍
8	♍		
9	♍		
10	♍	9:35 am	♎
11	♎		
12	♎	7:39 pm	♏
13	♏		
14	♏		
15	♏	2:00 am	♐
16	♐		
17	♐	5:17 am	♑
18	♑		
19	♑	7:02 am	♒
20	♒		
21	♒	8:45 am	♓
22	♓		
23	♓	11:30 am	♈
24	♈		
25	♈	3:46 pm	♉
26	♉		
27	♉	9:48 pm	♊
28	♊		
29	♊		
30	♊	5:53 am	♋
31	♋		

♈ = Aries ♉ = Taurus ♊ = Gemini ♋ = Cancer ♌ = Leo ♍ = Virgo

1953

January

1	♋	4:17 pm	♌
2	♌		
3	♌		
4	♌	4:41 am	♍
5	♍		
6	♍	5:36 pm	♎
7	♎		
8	♎		
9	♎	4:44 am	♏
10	♏		
11	♏	12:14 pm	♐
12	♐		
13	♐	3:55 pm	♑
14	♑		
15	♑	4:57 pm	♒
16	♒		
17	♒	5:07 pm	♓
18	♓		
19	♓	6:08 pm	♈
20	♈		
21	♈	9:20 pm	♉
22	♉		
23	♉		
24	♉	3:21 am	♊
25	♊		
26	♊	12:07 pm	♋
27	♋		
28	♋	11:06 pm	♌
29	♌		
30	♌		
31	♌	11:35 am	♍

February

1	♍		
2	♍		
3	♍	12:31 am	♎
4	♎		
5	♎	12:21 pm	♏
6	♏		
7	♏	9:20 pm	♐
8	♐		
9	♐		
10	♐	2:32 am	♑
11	♑		
12	♑	4:17 am	♒
13	♒		
14	♒	3:58 am	♓
15	♓		
16	♓	3:30 am	♈
17	♈		
18	♈	4:51 am	♉
19	♉		
20	♉	9:27 am	♊
21	♊		
22	♊	5:48 pm	♋
23	♋		
24	♋		
25	♋	5:05 am	♌
26	♌		
27	♌	5:51 pm	♍
28	♍		

March

1	♍		
2	♍	6:41 am	♎
3	♎		
4	♎	6:31 pm	♏
5	♏		
6	♏		
7	♏	4:20 am	♐
8	♐		
9	♐	11:10 am	♑
10	♑		
11	♑	2:37 pm	♒
12	♒		
13	♒	3:17 pm	♓
14	♓		
15	♓	2:39 pm	♈
16	♈		
17	♈	2:44 pm	♉
18	♉		
19	♉	5:35 pm	♊
20	♊		
21	♊		
22	♊	12:29 am	♋
23	♋		
24	♋	11:14 am	♌
25	♌		
26	♌		
27	♌	12:04 am	♍
28	♍		
29	♍	12:51 pm	♎
30	♎		
31	♎		

April

1	♎	12:19 am	♏
2	♏		
3	♏	9:58 am	♐
4	♐		
5	♐	5:29 pm	♑
6	♑		
7	♑	10:27 pm	♒
8	♒		
9	♒		
10	♒	12:49 am	♓
11	♓		
12	♓	1:19 am	♈
13	♈		
14	♈	1:31 am	♉
15	♉		
16	♉	3:27 am	♊
17	♊		
18	♊	8:53 am	♋
19	♋		
20	♋	6:27 pm	♌
21	♌		
22	♌		
23	♌	6:53 am	♍
24	♍		
25	♍	7:40 pm	♎
26	♎		
27	♎		
28	♎	6:52 am	♏
29	♏		
30	♏	3:52 pm	♐

May

1	♐		
2	♐	10:55 pm	♑
3	♑		
4	♑		
5	♑	4:12 am	♒
6	♒		
7	♒	7:46 am	♓
8	♓		
9	♓	9:49 am	♈
10	♈		
11	♈	11:12 am	♉
12	♉		
13	♉	1:27 pm	♊
14	♊		
15	♊	6:16 pm	♋
16	♋		
17	♋		
18	♋	2:47 am	♌
19	♌		
20	♌	2:31 pm	♍
21	♍		
22	♍		
23	♍	3:16 am	♎
24	♎		
25	♎	2:32 pm	♏
26	♏		
27	♏	11:08 pm	♐
28	♐		
29	♐		
30	♐	5:17 am	♑
31	♑		

June

1	♑	9:45 am	♒
2	♒		
3	♒	1:12 pm	♓
4	♓		
5	♓	4:01 pm	♈
6	♈		
7	♈	6:41 pm	♉
8	♉		
9	♉	10:03 pm	♊
10	♊		
11	♊		
12	♊	3:17 am	♋
13	♋		
14	♋	11:27 am	♌
15	♌		
16	♌	10:37 pm	♍
17	♍		
18	♍		
19	♍	11:16 am	♎
20	♎		
21	♎	10:57 pm	♏
22	♏		
23	♏		
24	♏	7:48 am	♐
25	♐		
26	♐	1:29 pm	♑
27	♑		
28	♑	4:51 pm	♒
29	♒		
30	♒	7:08 pm	♓

July

1	♓		
2	♓	9:23 pm	♈
3	♈		
4	♈		
5	♈	12:23 am	♉
6	♉		
7	♉	4:42 am	♊
8	♊		
9	♊	10:54 am	♋
10	♋		
11	♋	7:28 pm	♌
12	♌		
13	♌		
14	♌	6:28 am	♍
15	♍		
16	♍	7:04 pm	♎
17	♎		
18	♎		
19	♎	7:17 am	♏
20	♏		
21	♏	4:59 pm	♐
22	♐		
23	♐	11:07 pm	♑
24	♑		
25	♑		
26	♑	2:03 am	♒
27	♒		
28	♒	3:07 am	♓
29	♓		
30	♓	3:56 am	♈
31	♈		

August

1	♈	5:57 am	♉
2	♉		
3	♉	10:10 am	♊
4	♊		
5	♊	4:59 pm	♋
6	♋		
7	♋		
8	♋	2:16 am	♌
9	♌		
10	♌	1:33 pm	♍
11	♍		
12	♍		
13	♍	2:08 am	♎
14	♎		
15	♎	2:43 pm	♏
16	♏		
17	♏		
18	♏	1:30 am	♐
19	♐		
20	♐	8:53 am	♑
21	♑		
22	♑	12:29 pm	♒
23	♒		
24	♒	1:12 pm	♓
25	♓		
26	♓	12:46 pm	♈
27	♈		
28	♈	1:10 pm	♉
29	♉		
30	♉	4:07 pm	♊
31	♊		

September

1	♊	10:30 pm	♋
2	♋		
3	♋		
4	♋	8:05 am	♌
5	♌		
6	♌	7:47 pm	♍
7	♍		
8	♍		
9	♍	8:27 am	♎
10	♎		
11	♎	9:05 pm	♏
12	♏		
13	♏		
14	♏	8:32 am	♐
15	♐		
16	♐	5:21 pm	♑
17	♑		
18	♑	10:30 pm	♒
19	♒		
20	♒		
21	♒	12:06 am 11:30 pm	♓ ♈
22	♓		
23	♈		
24	♈	10:45 pm	♉
25	♉		
26	♉		
27	♉	12:01 am	♊
28	♊		
29	♊	4:56 am	♋
30	♋		

October

1	♋	1:53 pm	♌
2	♌		
3	♌		
4	♌	1:40 am	♍
5	♍		
6	♍	2:28 pm	♎
7	♎		
8	♎		
9	♎	2:56 am	♏
10	♏		
11	♏	2:19 pm	♐
12	♐		
13	♐	11:51 pm	♑
14	♑		
15	♑		
16	♑	6:34 am	♒
17	♒		
18	♒	9:55 am	♓
19	♓		
20	♓	10:27 am	♈
21	♈		
22	♈	9:47 am	♉
23	♉		
24	♉	10:04 am	♊
25	♊		
26	♊	1:24 pm	♋
27	♋		
28	♋	8:55 pm	♌
29	♌		
30	♌		
31	♌	8:04 am	♍

November

1	♍		
2	♍	8:51 pm	♎
3	♎		
4	♎		
5	♎	9:12 am	♏
6	♏		
7	♏	8:06 pm	♐
8	♐		
9	♐		
10	♐	5:18 am	♑
11	♑		
12	♑	12:31 pm	♒
13	♒		
14	♒	5:17 pm	♓
15	♓		
16	♓	7:35 pm	♈
17	♈		
18	♈	8:15 pm	♉
19	♉		
20	♉	8:55 pm	♊
21	♊		
22	♊	11:31 pm	♋
23	♋		
24	♋		
25	♋	5:40 am	♌
26	♌		
27	♌	3:41 pm	♍
28	♍		
29	♍		
30	♍	4:06 am	♎

December

1	♎		
2	♎	4:30 pm	♏
3	♏		
4	♏		
5	♏	3:09 am	♐
6	♐		
7	♐	11:33 am	♑
8	♑		
9	♑	5:59 pm	♒
10	♒		
11	♒	10:46 pm	♓
12	♓		
13	♓		
14	♓	2:06 am	♈
15	♈		
16	♈	4:22 am	♉
17	♉		
18	♉	6:27 am	♊
19	♊		
20	♊	9:40 am	♋
21	♋		
22	♋	3:23 pm	♌
23	♌		
24	♌		
25	♌	12:24 am	♍
26	♍		
27	♍	12:11 pm	♎
28	♎		
29	♎		
30	♎	12:43 am	♏
31	♏		

Moon Movements

♎ = Libra ♏ = Scorpio ♐ = Sagittarius ♑ = Capricorn ♒ = Aquarius ♓ = Pisces

1954

January

1	♏	11:39 am	♐
2	♐		
3	♐	7:45 pm	♑
4	♑		
5	♑		
6	♑	1:09 am	♒
7	♒		
8	♒	4:43 am	♓
9	♓		
10	♓	7:27 am	♈
11	♈		
12	♈	10:10 am	♉
13	♉		
14	♉	1:29 pm	♊
15	♊		
16	♊	6:01 pm	♋
17	♋		
18	♋		
19	♋	12:24 am	♌
20	♌		
21	♌	9:14 am	♍
22	♍		
23	♍	8:30 pm	♎
24	♎		
25	♎		
26	♎	9:03 am	♏
27	♏		
28	♏	8:42 pm	♐
29	♐		
30	♐		
31	♐	5:27 am	♑

February

1	♑		
2	♑	10:38 am	♒
3	♒		
4	♒	1:03 pm	♓
5	♓		
6	♓	2:14 pm	♈
7	♈		
8	♈	3:47 pm	♉
9	♉		
10	♉	6:54 pm	♊
11	♊		
12	♊		
13	♊	12:10 am	♋
14	♋		
15	♋	7:35 am	♌
16	♌		
17	♌	5:00 pm	♍
18	♍		
19	♍		
20	♍	4:14 am	♎
21	♎		
22	♎	4:43 pm	♏
23	♏		
24	♏		
25	♏	5:00 am	♐
26	♐		
27	♐	2:58 pm	♑
28	♑		

March

1	♑	9:07 pm	♒
2	♒		
3	♒	11:32 pm	♓
4	♓		
5	♓	11:40 pm	♈
6	♈		
7	♈	11:32 pm	♉
8	♉		
9	♉		
10	♉	1:06 am	♊
11	♊		
12	♊	5:37 am	♋
13	♋		
14	♋	1:17 pm	♌
15	♌		
16	♌	11:21 pm	♍
17	♍		
18	♍		
19	♍	10:57 am	♎
20	♎		
21	♎	11:26 pm	♏
22	♏		
23	♏		
24	♏	11:56 am	♐
25	♐		
26	♐	10:55 pm	♑
27	♑		
28	♑		
29	♑	6:37 am	♒
30	♒		
31	♒	10:16 am	♓

April

1	♓		
2	♓	10:40 am	♈
3	♈		
4	♈	9:43 am	♉
5	♉		
6	♉	9:40 am	♊
7	♊		
8	♊	12:29 pm	♋
9	♋		
10	♋	7:05 pm	♌
11	♌		
12	♌		
13	♌	5:03 am	♍
14	♍		
15	♍	4:58 pm	♎
16	♎		
17	♎		
18	♎	5:32 am	♏
19	♏		
20	♏	5:55 pm	♐
21	♐		
22	♐		
23	♐	5:11 am	♑
24	♑		
25	♑	2:02 pm	♒
26	♒		
27	♒	7:21 pm	♓
28	♓		
29	♓	9:08 pm	♈
30	♈		

May

1	♈	8:42 pm	♉
2	♉		
3	♉	8:06 pm	♊
4	♊		
5	♊	9:30 pm	♋
6	♋		
7	♋		
8	♋	2:29 am	♌
9	♌		
10	♌	11:23 am	♍
11	♍		
12	♍	11:03 pm	♎
13	♎		
14	♎		
15	♎	11:42 am	♏
16	♏		
17	♏	11:53 pm	♐
18	♐		
19	♐		
20	♐	10:49 am	♑
21	♑		
22	♑	7:48 pm	♒
23	♒		
24	♒		
25	♒	2:08 am	♓
26	♓		
27	♓	5:32 am	♈
28	♈		
29	♈	6:33 am	♉
30	♉		
31	♉	6:41 am	♊

June

1	♊		
2	♊	7:46 am	♋
3	♋		
4	♋	11:34 am	♌
5	♌		
6	♌	7:06 pm	♍
7	♍		
8	♍		
9	♍	5:59 am	♎
10	♎		
11	♎	6:30 pm	♏
12	♏		
13	♏		
14	♏	6:37 am	♐
15	♐		
16	♐	5:05 pm	♑
17	♑		
18	♑		
19	♑	1:26 am	♒
20	♒		
21	♒	7:37 am	♓
22	♓		
23	♓	11:43 am	♈
24	♈		
25	♈	2:09 pm	♉
26	♉		
27	♉	3:41 pm	♊
28	♊		
29	♊	5:35 pm	♋
30	♋		

July

1	♋	9:16 pm	♌
2	♌		
3	♌		
4	♌	3:56 am	♍
5	♍		
6	♍	1:53 pm	♎
7	♎		
8	♎		
9	♎	2:04 am	♏
10	♏		
11	♏	2:19 pm	♐
12	♐		
13	♐		
14	♐	12:40 am	♑
15	♑		
16	♑	8:19 am	♒
17	♒		
18	♒	1:33 pm	♓
19	♓		
20	♓	5:07 pm	♈
21	♈		
22	♈	7:52 pm	♉
23	♉		
24	♉	10:30 pm	♊
25	♊		
26	♊		
27	♊	1:41 am	♋
28	♋		
29	♋	6:10 am	♌
30	♌		
31	♌	12:50 pm	♍

August

1	♍		
2	♍	10:14 pm	♎
3	♎		
4	♎		
5	♎	10:03 am	♏
6	♏		
7	♏	10:32 pm	♐
8	♐		
9	♐		
10	♐	9:20 am	♑
11	♑		
12	♑	4:54 pm	♒
13	♒		
14	♒	9:17 pm	♓
15	♓		
16	♓	11:37 pm	♈
17	♈		
18	♈		
19	♈	1:26 am	♉
20	♉		
21	♉	3:56 am	♊
22	♊		
23	♊	7:50 am	♋
24	♋		
25	♋	1:22 pm	♌
26	♌		
27	♌	8:44 pm	♍
28	♍		
29	♍		
30	♍	6:12 am	♎
31	♎		

September

1	♎	5:49 pm	♏
2	♏		
3	♏		
4	♏	6:32 am	♐
5	♐		
6	♐	6:10 pm	♑
7	♑		
8	♑		
9	♑	2:31 am	♒
10	♒		
11	♒	6:55 am	♓
12	♓		
13	♓	8:22 am	♈
14	♈		
15	♈	8:44 am	♉
16	♉		
17	♉	9:55 am	♊
18	♊		
19	♊	1:13 pm	♋
20	♋		
21	♋	7:04 pm	♌
22	♌		
23	♌		
24	♌	3:11 am	♍
25	♍		
26	♍	1:11 pm	♎
27	♎		
28	♎		
29	♎	12:52 am	♏
30	♏		

October

1	♏	1:41 pm	♐
2	♐		
3	♐		
4	♐	2:04 am	♑
5	♑		
6	♑	11:45 am	♒
7	♒		
8	♒	5:17 pm	♓
9	♓		
10	♓	6:58 pm	♈
11	♈		
12	♈	6:32 pm	♉
13	♉		
14	♉	6:10 pm	♊
15	♊		
16	♊	7:50 pm	♋
17	♋		
18	♋		
19	♋	12:41 am	♌
20	♌		
21	♌	8:44 am	♍
22	♍		
23	♍	7:12 pm	♎
24	♎		
25	♎		
26	♎	7:11 am	♏
27	♏		
28	♏	7:59 pm	♐
29	♐		
30	♐		
31	♐	8:36 am	♑

November

1	♑		
2	♑	7:22 pm	♒
3	♒		
4	♒		
5	♒	2:34 am	♓
6	♓		
7	♓	5:42 am	♈
8	♈		
9	♈	5:48 am	♉
10	♉		
11	♉	4:50 am	♊
12	♊		
13	♊	4:59 am	♋
14	♋		
15	♋	8:03 am	♌
16	♌		
17	♌	2:52 pm	♍
18	♍		
19	♍		
20	♍	1:02 am	♎
21	♎		
22	♎	1:13 pm	♏
23	♏		
24	♏		
25	♏	2:01 am	♐
26	♐		
27	♐	2:24 pm	♑
28	♑		
29	♑		
30	♑	1:19 am	♒

December

1	♒		
2	♒	9:38 am	♓
3	♓		
4	♓	2:35 pm	♈
5	♈		
6	♈	4:23 pm	♉
7	♉		
8	♉	4:16 pm	♊
9	♊		
10	♊	4:06 pm	♋
11	♋		
12	♋	5:48 pm	♌
13	♌		
14	♌	10:54 pm	♍
15	♍		
16	♍		
17	♍	7:51 am	♎
18	♎		
19	♎	7:43 pm	♏
20	♏		
21	♏		
22	♏	8:35 am	♐
23	♐		
24	♐	8:40 pm	♑
25	♑		
26	♑		
27	♑	7:00 am	♒
28	♒		
29	♒	3:09 pm	♓
30	♓		
31	♓	8:56 pm	♈

Your Starway to Love

♈ = Aries ♉ = Taurus ♊ = Gemini ♋ = Cancer ♌ = Leo ♍ = Virgo

1955

January

1	♈		
2	♈		
3	♈	12:24 am	♉
4	♉		
5	♉	2:04 am	♊
6	♊		
7	♊	3:00 am	♋
8	♋		
9	♋	4:41 am	♌
10	♌		
11	♌	8:43 am	♍
12	♍		
13	♍	4:15 pm	♎
14	♎		
15	♎		
16	♎	3:15 am	♏
17	♏		
18	♏	4:01 pm	♐
19	♐		
20	♐		
21	♐	4:09 am	♑
22	♑		
23	♑	1:58 pm	♒
24	♒		
25	♒	9:11 pm	♓
26	♓		
27	♓		
28	♓	2:19 am	♈
29	♈		
30	♈	6:06 am	♉
31	♉		

April

1	♋	3:20 am	♌
2	♌		
3	♌	9:31 am	♍
4	♍		
5	♍	5:34 pm	♎
6	♎		
7	♎		
8	♎	3:38 am	♏
9	♏		
10	♏	3:41 pm	♐
11	♐		
12	♐		
13	♐	4:40 am	♑
14	♑		
15	♑	4:20 pm	♒
16	♒		
17	♒		
18	♒	12:28 am	♓
19	♓		
20	♓	4:29 am	♈
21	♈		
22	♈	5:29 am	♉
23	♉		
24	♉	5:24 am	♊
25	♊		
26	♊	6:09 am	♋
27	♋		
28	♋	9:09 am	♌
29	♌		
30	♌	2:58 pm	♍

July

1	♏	10:34 am	♐
2	♐		
3	♐	11:29 pm	♑
4	♑		
5	♑		
6	♑	11:18 am	♒
7	♒		
8	♒	9:09 pm	♓
9	♓		
10	♓		
11	♓	4:33 am	♈
12	♈		
13	♈	9:20 am	♉
14	♉		
15	♉	11:43 am	♊
16	♊		
17	♊	12:30 pm	♋
18	♋		
19	♋	1:03 pm	♌
20	♌		
21	♌	3:06 pm	♍
22	♍		
23	♍	8:16 pm	♎
24	♎		
25	♎		
26	♎	5:19 am	♏
27	♏		
28	♏	5:24 pm	♐
29	♐		
30	♐		
31	♐	6:18 am	♑

October

1	♓	12:46 am	♈
2	♈		
3	♈	3:52 am	♉
4	♉		
5	♉	5:59 am	♊
6	♊		
7	♊	8:23 am	♋
8	♋		
9	♋	11:41 am	♌
10	♌		
11	♌	4:11 pm	♍
12	♍		
13	♍	10:13 pm	♎
14	♎		
15	♎		
16	♎	6:23 am	♏
17	♏		
18	♏	5:07 pm	♐
19	♐		
20	♐		
21	♐	5:52 am	♑
22	♑		
23	♑	6:33 pm	♒
24	♒		
25	♒		
26	♒	4:37 am	♓
27	♓		
28	♓	10:46 am	♈
29	♈		
30	♈	1:30 pm	♉
31	♉		

February

1	♉	9:02 am	♊
2	♊		
3	♊	11:36 am	♋
4	♋		
5	♋	2:28 pm	♌
6	♌		
7	♌	6:43 pm	♍
8	♍		
9	♍		
10	♍	1:33 am	♎
11	♎		
12	♎	11:38 am	♏
13	♏		
14	♏		
15	♏	12:07 am	♐
16	♐		
17	♐	12:34 pm	♑
18	♑		
19	♑	10:33 pm	♒
20	♒		
21	♒		
22	♒	5:09 am	♓
23	♓		
24	♓	9:06 am	♈
25	♈		
26	♈	11:46 am	♉
27	♉		
28	♉	2:24 pm	♊

May

1	♍		
2	♍	11:26 pm	♎
3	♎		
4	♎		
5	♎	10:04 am	♏
6	♏		
7	♏	10:19 pm	♐
8	♐		
9	♐		
10	♐	11:19 am	♑
11	♑		
12	♑	11:29 pm	♒
13	♒		
14	♒		
15	♒	8:53 am	♓
16	♓		
17	♓	2:21 pm	♈
18	♈		
19	♈	4:12 pm	♉
20	♉		
21	♉	3:56 pm	♊
22	♊		
23	♊	3:33 pm	♋
24	♋		
25	♋	4:53 pm	♌
26	♌		
27	♌	9:16 pm	♍
28	♍		
29	♍		
30	♍	5:08 am	♎
31	♎		

August

1	♑		
2	♑	5:52 pm	♒
3	♒		
4	♒		
5	♒	3:04 am	♓
6	♓		
7	♓	10:00 am	♈
8	♈		
9	♈	3:03 pm	♉
10	♉		
11	♉	6:33 pm	♊
12	♊		
13	♊	8:50 pm	♋
14	♋		
15	♋	10:34 pm	♌
16	♌		
17	♌		
18	♌	12:57 am	♍
19	♍		
20	♍	5:34 am	♎
21	♎		
22	♎	1:37 pm	♏
23	♏		
24	♏		
25	♏	1:03 am	♐
26	♐		
27	♐	1:57 pm	♑
28	♑		
29	♑		
30	♑	1:35 am	♒
31	♒		

November

1	♉	2:23 pm	♊
2	♊		
3	♊	3:11 pm	♋
4	♋		
5	♋	5:20 pm	♌
6	♌		
7	♌	9:36 pm	♍
8	♍		
9	♍		
10	♍	4:15 am	♎
11	♎		
12	♎	1:12 pm	♏
13	♏		
14	♏		
15	♏	12:17 am	♐
16	♐		
17	♐	12:59 pm	♑
18	♑		
19	♑		
20	♑	1:58 am	♒
21	♒		
22	♒	1:10 pm	♓
23	♓		
24	♓	8:47 pm	♈
25	♈		
26	♈		
27	♈	12:27 am	♉
28	♉		
29	♉	1:11 am	♊
30	♊		

March

1	♊		
2	♊	5:40 pm	♋
3	♋		
4	♋	9:48 pm	♌
5	♌		
6	♌		
7	♌	3:09 am	♍
8	♍		
9	♍	10:20 am	♎
10	♎		
11	♎	8:04 pm	♏
12	♏		
13	♏		
14	♏	8:13 am	♐
15	♐		
16	♐	9:01 pm	♑
17	♑		
18	♑		
19	♑	7:47 am	♒
20	♒		
21	♒	2:45 pm	♓
22	♓		
23	♓	6:09 pm	♈
24	♈		
25	♈	7:31 pm	♉
26	♉		
27	♉	8:42 pm	♊
28	♊		
29	♊	11:05 pm	♋
30	♋		
31	♋		

June

1	♎	3:54 pm	♏
2	♏		
3	♏		
4	♏	4:24 am	♐
5	♐		
6	♐	5:21 pm	♑
7	♑		
8	♑		
9	♑	5:30 am	♒
10	♒		
11	♒	3:32 pm	♓
12	♓		
13	♓	10:24 pm	♈
14	♈		
15	♈		
16	♈	1:50 am	♉
17	♉		
18	♉	2:36 am	♊
19	♊		
20	♊	2:15 am	♋
21	♋		
22	♋	2:36 am	♌
23	♌		
24	♌	5:26 am	♍
25	♍		
26	♍	11:55 am	♎
27	♎		
28	♎	10:04 pm	♏
29	♏		
30	♏		

September

1	♒	10:23 am	♓
2	♓		
3	♓	4:24 pm	♈
4	♈		
5	♈	8:36 pm	♉
6	♉		
7	♉	11:58 pm	♊
8	♊		
9	♊		
10	♊	3:01 am	♋
11	♋		
12	♋	6:02 am	♌
13	♌		
14	♌	9:33 am	♍
15	♍		
16	♍	2:35 pm	♎
17	♎		
18	♎	10:18 pm	♏
19	♏		
20	♏		
21	♏	9:11 am	♐
22	♐		
23	♐	10:01 pm	♑
24	♑		
25	♑		
26	♑	10:07 am	♒
27	♒		
28	♒	7:12 pm	♓
29	♓		
30	♓		

December

1	♊	12:46 am	♋
2	♋		
3	♋	1:07 am	♌
4	♌		
5	♌	3:50 am	♍
6	♍		
7	♍	9:48 am	♎
8	♎		
9	♎	6:59 pm	♏
10	♏		
11	♏		
12	♏	6:34 am	♐
13	♐		
14	♐	7:23 pm	♑
15	♑		
16	♑		
17	♑	8:19 am	♒
18	♒		
19	♒	8:02 pm	♓
20	♓		
21	♓		
22	♓	5:05 am	♈
23	♈		
24	♈	10:33 am	♉
25	♉		
26	♉	12:33 pm	♊
27	♊		
28	♊	12:17 pm	♋
29	♋		
30	♋	11:36 am	♌
31	♌		

Moon Movements

♎ = Libra ♏ = Scorpio ♐ = Sagittarius ♑ = Capricorn ♒ = Aquarius ♓ = Pisces

January

Day	Moon	Time	Enters
1	♌	12:31 pm	♍
2	♍		
3	♍	4:44 pm	♎
4	♎		
5	♎		
6	♎	1:00 am	♏
7	♏		
8	♏	12:32 pm	♐
9	♐		
10	♐		
11	♐	1:33 am	♑
12	♑		
13	♑	2:19 pm	♒
14	♒		
15	♒		
16	♒	1:47 am	♓
17	♓		
18	♓	11:17 am	♈
19	♈		
20	♈	6:11 pm	♉
21	♉		
22	♉	10:06 pm	♊
23	♊		
24	♊	11:20 pm	♋
25	♋		
26	♋	11:06 pm	♌
27	♌		
28	♌	11:17 pm	♍
29	♍		
30	♍		
31	♍	1:56 am	♎

February

Day	Moon	Time	Enters
1	♎		
2	♎	8:33 am	♏
3	♏		
4	♏	7:13 pm	♐
5	♐		
6	♐		
7	♐	8:08 am	♑
8	♑		
9	♑	8:52 pm	♒
10	♒		
11	♒		
12	♒	7:52 am	♓
13	♓		
14	♓	4:48 pm	♈
15	♈		
16	♈	11:48 pm	♉
17	♉		
18	♉		
19	♉	4:50 am	♊
20	♊		
21	♊	7:50 am	♋
22	♋		
23	♋	9:10 am	♌
24	♌		
25	♌	10:05 am	♍
26	♍		
27	♍	12:20 pm	♎
28	♎		
29	♎	5:45 pm	♏

March

Day	Moon	Time	Enters
1	♏		
2	♏		
3	♏	3:09 am	♐
4	♐		
5	♐	3:32 pm	♑
6	♑		
7	♑		
8	♑	4:19 am	♒
9	♒		
10	♒	3:11 pm	♓
11	♓		
12	♓	11:26 pm	♈
13	♈		
14	♈		
15	♈	5:32 am	♉
16	♉		
17	♉	10:12 am	♊
18	♊		
19	♊	1:47 pm	♋
20	♋		
21	♋	4:31 pm	♌
22	♌		
23	♌	6:53 pm	♍
24	♍		
25	♍	10:00 pm	♎
26	♎		
27	♎		
28	♎	3:18 am	♏
29	♏		
30	♏	11:56 am	♐
31	♐		

April

Day	Moon	Time	Enters
1	♐	11:37 pm	♑
2	♑		
3	♑		
4	♑	12:24 pm	♒
5	♒		
6	♒	11:37 pm	♓
7	♓		
8	♓		
9	♓	7:46 am	♈
10	♈		
11	♈	1:03 pm	♉
12	♉		
13	♉	4:31 pm	♊
14	♊		
15	♊	7:15 pm	♋
16	♋		
17	♋	10:00 pm	♌
18	♌		
19	♌		
20	♌	1:17 am	♍
21	♍		
22	♍	5:36 am	♎
23	♎		
24	♎	11:44 am	♏
25	♏		
26	♏	8:25 pm	♐
27	♐		
28	♐		
29	♐	7:44 am	♑
30	♑		

May

Day	Moon	Time	Enters
1	♑	8:27 pm	♒
2	♒		
3	♒		
4	♒	8:15 am	♓
5	♓		
6	♓	5:05 pm	♈
7	♈		
8	♈	10:24 pm	♉
9	♉		
10	♉		
11	♉	1:00 am	♊
12	♊		
13	♊	2:21 am	♋
14	♋		
15	♋	3:52 am	♌
16	♌		
17	♌	6:40 am	♍
18	♍		
19	♍	11:25 am	♎
20	♎		
21	♎	6:26 pm	♏
22	♏		
23	♏		
24	♏	3:46 am	♐
25	♐		
26	♐	3:11 pm	♑
27	♑		
28	♑		
29	♑	3:52 am	♒
30	♒		
31	♒	4:09 pm	♓

June

Day	Moon	Time	Enters
1	♓		
2	♓		
3	♓	2:04 am	♈
4	♈		
5	♈	8:22 am	♉
6	♉		
7	♉	11:09 am	♊
8	♊		
9	♊	11:42 am	♋
10	♋		
11	♋	11:45 am	♌
12	♌		
13	♌	1:03 pm	♍
14	♍		
15	♍	4:58 pm	♎
16	♎		
17	♎		
18	♎	12:03 am	♏
19	♏		
20	♏	9:55 am	♐
21	♐		
22	♐	9:43 pm	♑
23	♑		
24	♑		
25	♑	10:26 am	♒
26	♒		
27	♒	10:54 pm	♓
28	♓		
29	♓		
30	♓	9:43 am	♈

July

Day	Moon	Time	Enters
1	♈		
2	♈	5:26 pm	♉
3	♉		
4	♉	9:26 pm	♊
5	♊		
6	♊	10:20 pm	♋
7	♋		
8	♋	9:42 pm	♌
9	♌		
10	♌	9:34 pm	♍
11	♍		
12	♍	11:54 pm	♎
13	♎		
14	♎		
15	♎	5:56 am	♏
16	♏		
17	♏	3:38 pm	♐
18	♐		
19	♐		
20	♐	3:40 am	♑
21	♑		
22	♑	4:28 pm	♒
23	♒		
24	♒		
25	♒	4:50 am	♓
26	♓		
27	♓	3:54 pm	♈
28	♈		
29	♈		
30	♈	12:40 am	♉
31	♉		

August

Day	Moon	Time	Enters
1	♉	6:16 am	♊
2	♊		
3	♊	8:32 am	♋
4	♋		
5	♋	8:27 am	♌
6	♌		
7	♌	7:50 am	♍
8	♍		
9	♍	8:50 am	♎
10	♎		
11	♎	1:20 pm	♏
12	♏		
13	♏	10:00 pm	♐
14	♐		
15	♐		
16	♐	9:47 am	♑
17	♑		
18	♑	10:38 pm	♒
19	♒		
20	♒		
21	♒	10:47 am	♓
22	♓		
23	♓	9:30 pm	♈
24	♈		
25	♈		
26	♈	6:23 am	♉
27	♉		
28	♉	12:59 pm	♊
29	♊		
30	♊	4:51 pm	♋
31	♋		

September

Day	Moon	Time	Enters
1	♋	6:14 pm	♌
2	♌		
3	♌	6:20 pm	♍
4	♍		
5	♍	7:04 pm	♎
6	♎		
7	♎	10:27 pm	♏
8	♏		
9	♏		
10	♏	5:46 am	♐
11	♐		
12	♐	4:46 pm	♑
13	♑		
14	♑		
15	♑	5:28 am	♒
16	♒		
17	♒	5:34 pm	♓
18	♓		
19	♓		
20	♓	3:47 am	♈
21	♈		
22	♈	12:01 pm	♉
23	♉		
24	♉	6:25 pm	♊
25	♊		
26	♊	11:00 pm	♋
27	♋		
28	♋		
29	♋	1:49 am	♌
30	♌		

October

Day	Moon	Time	Enters
1	♌	3:24 am	♍
2	♍		
3	♍	5:01 am	♎
4	♎		
5	♎	8:19 am	♏
6	♏		
7	♏	2:46 pm	♐
8	♐		
9	♐		
10	♐	12:48 am	♑
11	♑		
12	♑	1:09 pm	♒
13	♒		
14	♒		
15	♒	1:25 am	♓
16	♓		
17	♓	11:35 am	♈
18	♈		
19	♈	7:07 pm	♉
20	♉		
21	♉		
22	♉	12:29 am	♊
23	♊		
24	♊	4:23 am	♋
25	♋		
26	♋	7:27 am	♌
27	♌		
28	♌	10:09 am	♍
29	♍		
30	♍	1:10 pm	♎
31	♎		

November

Day	Moon	Time	Enters
1	♎	5:24 pm	♏
2	♏		
3	♏	11:56 pm	♐
4	♐		
5	♐		
6	♐	9:24 am	♑
7	♑		
8	♑	9:19 pm	♒
9	♒		
10	♒		
11	♒	9:51 am	♓
12	♓		
13	♓	8:36 pm	♈
14	♈		
15	♈		
16	♈	4:12 am	♉
17	♉		
18	♉	8:45 am	♊
19	♊		
20	♊	11:18 am	♋
21	♋		
22	♋	1:10 pm	♌
23	♌		
24	♌	3:32 pm	♍
25	♍		
26	♍	7:11 pm	♎
27	♎		
28	♎		
29	♎	12:34 am	♏
30	♏		

December

Day	Moon	Time	Enters
1	♏	7:59 am	♐
2	♐		
3	♐	5:36 pm	♑
4	♑		
5	♑		
6	♑	5:16 am	♒
7	♒		
8	♒	5:57 pm	♓
9	♓		
10	♓		
11	♓	5:37 am	♈
12	♈		
13	♈	2:15 pm	♉
14	♉		
15	♉	7:06 pm	♊
16	♊		
17	♊	8:52 pm	♋
18	♋		
19	♋	9:11 pm	♌
20	♌		
21	♌	9:56 pm	♍
22	♍		
23	♍		
24	♍	12:39 am	♎
25	♎		
26	♎	6:09 am	♏
27	♏		
28	♏	2:20 pm	♐
29	♐		
30	♐		
31	♐	12:37 am	♑

Your Starway to Love

♈ = Aries ♉ = Taurus ♊ = Gemini ♋ = Cancer ♌ = Leo ♍ = Virgo

1957

January

1	♑		
2	♑	12:25 pm	♒
3	♒		
4	♒		
5	♒	1:04 am	♓
6	♓		
7	♓	1:23 pm	♈
8	♈		
9	♈	11:27 pm	♉
10	♉		
11	♉		
12	♉	5:44 am	♊
13	♊		
14	♊	8:05 am	♋
15	♋		
16	♋	7:50 am	♌
17	♌		
18	♌	7:03 am	♍
19	♍		
20	♍	7:55 am	♎
21	♎		
22	♎	12:02 pm	♏
23	♏		
24	♏	7:52 pm	♐
25	♐		
26	♐		
27	♐	6:32 am	♑
28	♑		
29	♑	6:42 pm	♒
30	♒		
31	♒		

April

1	♈	6:11 pm	♉
2	♉		
3	♉		
4	♉	2:30 am	♊
5	♊		
6	♊	8:37 am	♋
7	♋		
8	♋	12:24 pm	♌
9	♌		
10	♌	2:13 pm	♍
11	♍		
12	♍	3:08 pm	♎
13	♎		
14	♎	4:45 pm	♏
15	♏		
16	♏	8:43 pm	♐
17	♐		
18	♐		
19	♐	4:08 am	♑
20	♑		
21	♑	2:53 pm	♒
22	♒		
23	♒		
24	♒	3:23 am	♓
25	♓		
26	♓	3:22 pm	♈
27	♈		
28	♈		
29	♈	1:18 am	♉
30	♉		

July

1	♌	8:23 am	♍
2	♍		
3	♍	10:16 am	♎
4	♎		
5	♎	2:10 pm	♏
6	♏		
7	♏	8:20 pm	♐
8	♐		
9	♐		
10	♐	4:35 am	♑
11	♑		
12	♑	2:43 pm	♒
13	♒		
14	♒		
15	♒	2:32 am	♓
16	♓		
17	♓	3:14 pm	♈
18	♈		
19	♈		
20	♈	2:58 am	♉
21	♉		
22	♉	11:34 am	♊
23	♊		
24	♊	4:05 pm	♋
25	♋		
26	♋	5:16 pm	♌
27	♌		
28	♌	4:59 pm	♍
29	♍		
30	♍	5:20 pm	♎
31	♎		

October

1	♑		
2	♑	9:04 am	♒
3	♒		
4	♒	9:17 pm	♓
5	♓		
6	♓		
7	♓	9:57 am	♈
8	♈		
9	♈	9:48 pm	♉
10	♉		
11	♉		
12	♉	8:01 am	♊
13	♊		
14	♊	3:54 pm	♋
15	♋		
16	♋	8:59 pm	♌
17	♌		
18	♌	11:23 pm	♍
19	♍		
20	♍		
21	♍	12:03 am	♎
22	♎		
23	♎	12:31 am	♏
24	♏		
25	♏	2:33 am	♐
26	♐		
27	♐	7:41 am	♑
28	♑		
29	♑	4:32 pm	♒
30	♒		
31	♒		

February

1	♒	7:20 am	♓
2	♓		
3	♓	7:42 pm	♈
4	♈		
5	♈		
6	♈	6:37 am	♉
7	♉		
8	♉	2:34 pm	♊
9	♊		
10	♊	6:39 pm	♋
11	♋		
12	♋	7:18 pm	♌
13	♌		
14	♌	6:17 pm	♍
15	♍		
16	♍	5:50 pm	♎
17	♎		
18	♎	8:06 pm	♏
19	♏		
20	♏		
21	♏	2:23 am	♐
22	♐		
23	♐	12:27 pm	♑
24	♑		
25	♑		
26	♑	12:42 am	♒
27	♒		
28	♒	1:25 pm	♓

May

1	♉	8:47 am	♊
2	♊		
3	♊	2:08 pm	♋
4	♋		
5	♋	5:54 pm	♌
6	♌		
7	♌	8:37 pm	♍
8	♍		
9	♍	10:57 pm	♎
10	♎		
11	♎		
12	♎	1:48 am	♏
13	♏		
14	♏	6:13 am	♐
15	♐		
16	♐	1:13 pm	♑
17	♑		
18	♑	11:12 pm	♒
19	♒		
20	♒		
21	♒	11:20 am	♓
22	♓		
23	♓	11:34 pm	♈
24	♈		
25	♈		
26	♈	9:43 am	♉
27	♉		
28	♉	4:47 pm	♊
29	♊		
30	♊	9:05 pm	♋
31	♋		

August

1	♎	8:01 pm	♏
2	♏		
3	♏		
4	♏	1:47 am	♐
5	♐		
6	♐	10:23 am	♑
7	♑		
8	♑	9:01 pm	♒
9	♒		
10	♒		
11	♒	9:02 am	♓
12	♓		
13	♓	9:46 pm	♈
14	♈		
15	♈		
16	♈	10:00 am	♉
17	♉		
18	♉	7:51 pm	♊
19	♊		
20	♊		
21	♊	1:48 am	♋
22	♋		
23	♋	3:51 am	♌
24	♌		
25	♌	3:26 am	♍
26	♍		
27	♍	2:41 am	♎
28	♎		
29	♎	3:45 am	♏
30	♏		
31	♏	8:07 am	♐

November

1	♒	4:18 am	♓
2	♓		
3	♓	5:00 pm	♈
4	♈		
5	♈		
6	♈	4:38 am	♉
7	♉		
8	♉	2:09 pm	♊
9	♊		
10	♊	9:24 pm	♋
11	♋		
12	♋		
13	♋	2:36 am	♌
14	♌		
15	♌	6:07 am	♍
16	♍		
17	♍	8:25 am	♎
18	♎		
19	♎	10:17 am	♏
20	♏		
21	♏	12:52 pm	♐
22	♐		
23	♐	5:29 pm	♑
24	♑		
25	♑		
26	♑	1:16 am	♒
27	♒		
28	♒	12:16 pm	♓
29	♓		
30	♓		

March

1	♓		
2	♓		
3	♓	1:31 am	♈
4	♈		
5	♈	12:20 pm	♉
6	♉		
7	♉	9:03 pm	♊
8	♊		
9	♊		
10	♊	2:45 am	♋
11	♋		
12	♋	5:12 am	♌
13	♌		
14	♌	5:20 am	♍
15	♍		
16	♍	4:59 am	♎
17	♎		
18	♎	6:15 am	♏
19	♏		
20	♏	10:54 am	♐
21	♐		
22	♐	7:34 pm	♑
23	♑		
24	♑		
25	♑	7:17 am	♒
26	♒		
27	♒	8:00 pm	♓
28	♓		
29	♓		
30	♓	7:55 am	♈
31	♈		

June

1	♋	11:45 pm	♌
2	♌		
3	♌		
4	♌	1:59 am	♍
5	♍		
6	♍	4:45 am	♎
7	♎		
8	♎	8:41 am	♏
9	♏		
10	♏	2:09 pm	♐
11	♐		
12	♐	9:36 pm	♑
13	♑		
14	♑		
15	♑	7:23 am	♒
16	♒		
17	♒	7:15 pm	♓
18	♓		
19	♓		
20	♓	7:46 am	♈
21	♈		
22	♈	6:38 pm	♉
23	♉		
24	♉		
25	♉	2:07 am	♊
26	♊		
27	♊	6:01 am	♋
28	♋		
29	♋	7:31 am	♌
30	♌		

September

1	♐		
2	♐	4:05 pm	♑
3	♑		
4	♑		
5	♑	2:50 am	♒
6	♒		
7	♒	3:04 pm	♓
8	♓		
9	♓		
10	♓	3:45 am	♈
11	♈		
12	♈	3:57 pm	♉
13	♉		
14	♉		
15	♉	2:26 am	♊
16	♊		
17	♊	9:49 am	♋
18	♋		
19	♋	1:31 pm	♌
20	♌		
21	♌	2:11 pm	♍
22	♍		
23	♍	1:33 pm	♎
24	♎		
25	♎	1:40 pm	♏
26	♏		
27	♏	4:27 pm	♐
28	♐		
29	♐	10:59 pm	♑
30	♑		

December

1	♓	12:56 am	♈
2	♈		
3	♈	12:48 pm	♉
4	♉		
5	♉	10:00 pm	♊
6	♊		
7	♊		
8	♊	4:16 am	♋
9	♋		
10	♋	8:23 am	♌
11	♌		
12	♌	11:28 am	♍
13	♍		
14	♍	2:23 pm	♎
15	♎		
16	♎	5:35 pm	♏
17	♏		
18	♏	9:30 pm	♐
19	♐		
20	♐		
21	♐	2:47 am	♑
22	♑		
23	♑	10:19 am	♒
24	♒		
25	♒	8:41 pm	♓
26	♓		
27	♓		
28	♓	9:13 am	♈
29	♈		
30	♈	9:37 pm	♉
31	♉		

1958

Moon Movements

♎ = Libra ♏ = Scorpio ♐ = Sagittarius ♑ = Capricorn ♒ = Aquarius ♓ = Pisces

January

1	♉		
2	♉	7:21 am	♊
3	♊		
4	♊	1:22 pm	♋
5	♋		
6	♋	4:21 pm	♌
7	♌		
8	♌	5:59 pm	♍
9	♍		
10	♍	7:52 pm	♎
11	♎		
12	♎	11:02 pm	♏
13	♏		
14	♏		
15	♏	3:49 am	♐
16	♐		
17	♐	10:13 am	♑
18	♑		
19	♑	6:22 pm	♒
20	♒		
21	♒		
22	♒	4:42 am	♓
23	♓		
24	♓	5:03 pm	♈
25	♈		
26	♈		
27	♈	5:56 am	♉
28	♉		
29	♉	4:47 pm	♊
30	♊		
31	♊	11:41 pm	♋

February

1	♋		
2	♋		
3	♋	2:37 am	♌
4	♌		
5	♌	3:11 am	♍
6	♍		
7	♍	3:23 am	♎
8	♎		
9	♎	5:03 am	♏
10	♏		
11	♏	9:11 am	♐
12	♐		
13	♐	3:55 pm	♑
14	♑		
15	♑		
16	♑	12:51 am	♒
17	♒		
18	♒	11:39 am	♓
19	♓		
20	♓		
21	♓	12:02 am	♈
22	♈		
23	♈	1:05 pm	♉
24	♉		
25	♉		
26	♉	12:52 am	♊
27	♊		
28	♊	9:17 am	♋

March

1	♋		
2	♋	1:27 pm	♌
3	♌		
4	♌	2:15 pm	♍
5	♍		
6	♍	1:35 pm	♎
7	♎		
8	♎	1:34 pm	♏
9	♏		
10	♏	3:56 pm	♐
11	♐		
12	♐	9:36 pm	♑
13	♑		
14	♑		
15	♑	6:28 am	♒
16	♒		
17	♒	5:41 pm	♓
18	♓		
19	♓		
20	♓	6:17 am	♈
21	♈		
22	♈	7:16 pm	♉
23	♉		
24	♉		
25	♉	7:20 am	♊
26	♊		
27	♊	4:53 pm	♋
28	♋		
29	♋	10:45 pm	♌
30	♌		
31	♌		

April

1	♌	1:01 am	♍
2	♍		
3	♍	12:54 am	♎
4	♎		
5	♎	12:16 am	♏
6	♏		
7	♏	1:07 am	♐
8	♐		
9	♐	5:01 am	♑
10	♑		
11	♑	12:41 pm	♒
12	♒		
13	♒	11:38 pm	♓
14	♓		
15	♓		
16	♓	12:23 pm	♈
17	♈		
18	♈		
19	♈	1:16 am	♉
20	♉		
21	♉	1:03 pm	♊
22	♊		
23	♊	10:46 pm	♋
24	♋		
25	♋		
26	♋	5:44 am	♌
27	♌		
28	♌	9:40 am	♍
29	♍		
30	♍	11:06 am	♎

May

1	♎		
2	♎	11:14 am	♏
3	♏		
4	♏	11:43 am	♐
5	♐		
6	♐	2:21 pm	♑
7	♑		
8	♑	8:29 pm	♒
9	♒		
10	♒		
11	♒	6:27 am	♓
12	♓		
13	♓	6:58 pm	♈
14	♈		
15	♈		
16	♈	7:50 am	♉
17	♉		
18	♉	7:14 pm	♊
19	♊		
20	♊		
21	♊	4:23 am	♋
22	♋		
23	♋	11:14 am	♌
24	♌		
25	♌	4:00 pm	♍
26	♍		
27	♍	6:55 pm	♎
28	♎		
29	♎	8:33 pm	♏
30	♏		
31	♏	9:54 pm	♐

June

1	♐		
2	♐		
3	♐	12:23 am	♑
4	♑		
5	♑	5:34 am	♒
6	♒		
7	♒	2:24 pm	♓
8	♓		
9	♓		
10	♓	2:20 am	♈
11	♈		
12	♈	3:12 pm	♉
13	♉		
14	♉		
15	♉	2:31 am	♊
16	♊		
17	♊	11:04 am	♋
18	♋		
19	♋	5:04 pm	♌
20	♌		
21	♌	9:22 pm	♍
22	♍		
23	♍		
24	♍	12:42 am	♎
25	♎		
26	♎	3:30 am	♏
27	♏		
28	♏	6:11 am	♐
29	♐		
30	♐	9:32 am	♑

July

1	♑		
2	♑	2:44 pm	♒
3	♒		
4	♒	10:57 pm	♓
5	♓		
6	♓		
7	♓	10:18 am	♈
8	♈		
9	♈	11:09 pm	♉
10	♉		
11	♉		
12	♉	10:46 am	♊
13	♊		
14	♊	7:15 pm	♋
15	♋		
16	♋		
17	♋	12:31 am	♌
18	♌		
19	♌	3:42 am	♍
20	♍		
21	♍	6:11 am	♎
22	♎		
23	♎	8:57 am	♏
24	♏		
25	♏	12:25 pm	♐
26	♐		
27	♐	4:53 pm	♑
28	♑		
29	♑	10:52 pm	♒
30	♒		
31	♒		

August

1	♒	7:11 am	♓
2	♓		
3	♓	6:14 pm	♈
4	♈		
5	♈		
6	♈	7:04 am	♉
7	♉		
8	♉	7:16 pm	♊
9	♊		
10	♊		
11	♊	4:25 am	♋
12	♋		
13	♋	9:43 am	♌
14	♌		
15	♌	12:07 pm	♍
16	♍		
17	♍	1:17 pm	♎
18	♎		
19	♎	2:50 pm	♏
20	♏		
21	♏	5:48 pm	♐
22	♐		
23	♐	10:38 pm	♑
24	♑		
25	♑		
26	♑	5:28 am	♒
27	♒		
28	♒	2:25 pm	♓
29	♓		
30	♓		
31	♓	1:35 am	♈

September

1	♈		
2	♈	2:24 pm	♉
3	♉		
4	♉		
5	♉	3:07 am	♊
6	♊		
7	♊	1:22 pm	♋
8	♋		
9	♋	7:42 pm	♌
10	♌		
11	♌	10:19 pm	♍
12	♍		
13	♍	10:44 pm	♎
14	♎		
15	♎	10:49 pm	♏
16	♏		
17	♏		
18	♏	12:16 am	♐
19	♐		
20	♐	4:13 am	♑
21	♑		
22	♑	11:03 am	♒
23	♒		
24	♒	8:33 pm	♓
25	♓		
26	♓		
27	♓	8:07 am	♈
28	♈		
29	♈	8:58 pm	♉
30	♉		

October

1	♉		
2	♉	9:50 am	♊
3	♊		
4	♊	9:00 pm	♋
5	♋		
6	♋		
7	♋	4:51 am	♌
8	♌		
9	♌	8:49 am	♍
10	♍		
11	♍	9:44 am	♎
12	♎		
13	♎	9:11 am	♏
14	♏		
15	♏	9:09 am	♐
16	♐		
17	♐	11:23 am	♑
18	♑		
19	♑	5:04 pm	♒
20	♒		
21	♒		
22	♒	2:19 am	♓
23	♓		
24	♓	2:10 pm	♈
25	♈		
26	♈		
27	♈	3:07 am	♉
28	♉		
29	♉	3:49 pm	♊
30	♊		
31	♊		

November

1	♊	3:09 am	♋
2	♋		
3	♋	12:02 pm	♌
4	♌		
5	♌	5:45 pm	♍
6	♍		
7	♍	8:16 pm	♎
8	♎		
9	♎	8:30 pm	♏
10	♏		
11	♏	8:03 pm	♐
12	♐		
13	♐	8:54 pm	♑
14	♑		
15	♑		
16	♑	12:53 am	♒
17	♒		
18	♒	8:56 am	♓
19	♓		
20	♓	8:28 pm	♈
21	♈		
22	♈		
23	♈	9:30 am	♉
24	♉		
25	♉	10:00 pm	♊
26	♊		
27	♊		
28	♊	8:51 am	♋
29	♋		
30	♋	5:41 pm	♌

December

1	♌		
2	♌		
3	♌	12:18 am	♍
4	♍		
5	♍	4:31 am	♎
6	♎		
7	♎	6:28 am	♏
8	♏		
9	♏	7:02 am	♐
10	♐		
11	♐	7:46 am	♑
12	♑		
13	♑	10:38 am	♒
14	♒		
15	♒	5:12 pm	♓
16	♓		
17	♓		
18	♓	3:45 am	♈
19	♈		
20	♈	4:38 pm	♉
21	♉		
22	♉		
23	♉	5:09 am	♊
24	♊		
25	♊	3:33 pm	♋
26	♋		
27	♋	11:33 pm	♌
28	♌		
29	♌		
30	♌	5:41 am	♍
31	♍		

Your Starway to Love

♈ = Aries ♉ = Taurus ♊ = Gemini ♋ = Cancer ♌ = Leo ♍ = Virgo

1959

January

1	♍	10:21 am	♎
2	♎		
3	♎	1:42 pm	♏
4	♏		
5	♏	3:55 pm	♐
6	♐		
7	♐	5:50 pm	♑
8	♑		
9	♑	8:52 pm	♒
10	♒		
11	♒		
12	♒	2:39 am	♓
13	♓		
14	♓	12:10 pm	♈
15	♈		
16	♈		
17	♈	12:33 am	♉
18	♉		
19	♉	1:16 pm	♊
20	♊		
21	♊	11:47 pm	♋
22	♋		
23	♋		
24	♋	7:13 am	♌
25	♌		
26	♌	12:13 pm	♍
27	♍		
28	♍	3:54 pm	♎
29	♎		
30	♎	7:05 pm	♏
31	♏		

April

1	♑	5:41 pm	♒
2	♒		
3	♒		
4	♒	1:23 am	♓
5	♓		
6	♓	11:33 am	♈
7	♈		
8	♈	11:32 pm	♉
9	♉		
10	♉		
11	♉	12:25 pm	♊
12	♊		
13	♊		
14	♊	12:48 am	♋
15	♋		
16	♋	10:55 am	♌
17	♌		
18	♌	5:27 pm	♍
19	♍		
20	♍	8:19 pm	♎
21	♎		
22	♎	8:34 pm	♏
23	♏		
24	♏	7:59 pm	♐
25	♐		
26	♐	8:32 pm	♑
27	♑		
28	♑	11:55 pm	♒
29	♒		
30	♒		

July

1	♉		
2	♉	7:05 am	♊
3	♊		
4	♊	7:03 pm	♋
5	♋		
6	♋		
7	♋	5:08 am	♌
8	♌		
9	♌	1:15 pm	♍
10	♍		
11	♍	7:26 pm	♎
12	♎		
13	♎	11:33 pm	♏
14	♏		
15	♏		
16	♏	1:42 am	♐
17	♐		
18	♐	2:42 am	♑
19	♑		
20	♑	4:05 am	♒
21	♒		
22	♒	7:41 am	♓
23	♓		
24	♓	2:53 pm	♈
25	♈		
26	♈		
27	♈	1:43 am	♉
28	♉		
29	♉	2:23 pm	♊
30	♊		
31	♊		

October

1	♍	5:08 pm	♎
2	♎		
3	♎	6:54 pm	♏
4	♏		
5	♏	7:54 pm	♐
6	♐		
7	♐	9:38 pm	♑
8	♑		
9	♑		
10	♑	1:12 am	♒
11	♒		
12	♒	7:06 am	♓
13	♓		
14	♓	3:20 pm	♈
15	♈		
16	♈		
17	♈	1:40 am	♉
18	♉		
19	♉	1:40 pm	♊
20	♊		
21	♊		
22	♊	2:22 am	♋
23	♋		
24	♋	2:03 pm	♌
25	♌		
26	♌	10:48 pm	♍
27	♍		
28	♍		
29	♍	3:41 am	♎
30	♎		
31	♎	5:14 am	♏

February

1	♏	10:11 pm	♐
2	♐		
3	♐		
4	♐	1:29 am	♑
5	♑		
6	♑	5:40 am	♒
7	♒		
8	♒	11:50 am	♓
9	♓		
10	♓	8:55 pm	♈
11	♈		
12	♈		
13	♈	8:47 am	♉
14	♉		
15	♉	9:39 pm	♊
16	♊		
17	♊		
18	♊	8:50 am	♋
19	♋		
20	♋	4:38 pm	♌
21	♌		
22	♌	9:06 pm	♍
23	♍		
24	♍	11:29 pm	♎
25	♎		
26	♎		
27	♎	1:14 am	♏
28	♏		

May

1	♒	6:58 am	♓
2	♓		
3	♓	5:19 pm	♈
4	♈		
5	♈		
6	♈	5:39 am	♉
7	♉		
8	♉	6:34 pm	♊
9	♊		
10	♊		
11	♊	6:57 am	♋
12	♋		
13	♋	5:40 pm	♌
14	♌		
15	♌		
16	♌	1:38 am	♍
17	♍		
18	♍	6:06 am	♎
19	♎		
20	♎	7:24 am	♏
21	♏		
22	♏	6:51 am	♐
23	♐		
24	♐	6:24 am	♑
25	♑		
26	♑	8:09 am	♒
27	♒		
28	♒	1:42 pm	♓
29	♓		
30	♓	11:18 pm	♈
31	♈		

August

1	♊	2:24 am	♋
2	♋		
3	♋	12:09 pm	♌
4	♌		
5	♌	7:29 pm	♍
6	♍		
7	♍		
8	♍	12:56 am	♎
9	♎		
10	♎	5:00 am	♏
11	♏		
12	♏	7:58 am	♐
13	♐		
14	♐	10:18 am	♑
15	♑		
16	♑	12:53 pm	♒
17	♒		
18	♒	4:59 pm	♓
19	♓		
20	♓	11:51 pm	♈
21	♈		
22	♈		
23	♈	9:58 am	♉
24	♉		
25	♉	10:18 pm	♊
26	♊		
27	♊		
28	♊	10:33 am	♋
29	♋		
30	♋	8:33 pm	♌
31	♌		

November

1	♏		
2	♏	5:02 am	♐
3	♐		
4	♐	5:05 am	♑
5	♑		
6	♑	7:14 am	♒
7	♒		
8	♒	12:35 pm	♓
9	♓		
10	♓	9:10 pm	♈
11	♈		
12	♈		
13	♈	8:04 am	♉
14	♉		
15	♉	8:16 pm	♊
16	♊		
17	♊		
18	♊	8:56 am	♋
19	♋		
20	♋	9:04 pm	♌
21	♌		
22	♌		
23	♌	7:08 am	♍
24	♍		
25	♍	1:41 pm	♎
26	♎		
27	♎	4:21 pm	♏
28	♏		
29	♏	4:12 pm	♐
30	♐		

March

1	♏	3:33 am	♐
2	♐		
3	♐	7:05 am	♑
4	♑		
5	♑	12:16 pm	♒
6	♒		
7	♒	7:25 pm	♓
8	♓		
9	♓		
10	♓	4:54 am	♈
11	♈		
12	♈	4:37 pm	♉
13	♉		
14	♉		
15	♉	5:31 am	♊
16	♊		
17	♊	5:28 pm	♋
18	♋		
19	♋		
20	♋	2:22 am	♌
21	♌		
22	♌	7:28 am	♍
23	♍		
24	♍	9:27 am	♎
25	♎		
26	♎	9:54 am	♏
27	♏		
28	♏	10:31 am	♐
29	♐		
30	♐	12:49 pm	♑
31	♑		

June

1	♈		
2	♈	11:37 am	♉
3	♉		
4	♉		
5	♉	12:35 am	♊
6	♊		
7	♊	12:44 pm	♋
8	♋		
9	♋	11:19 pm	♌
10	♌		
11	♌		
12	♌	7:50 am	♍
13	♍		
14	♍	1:42 pm	♎
15	♎		
16	♎	4:38 pm	♏
17	♏		
18	♏	5:14 pm	♐
19	♐		
20	♐	5:01 pm	♑
21	♑		
22	♑	6:00 pm	♒
23	♒		
24	♒	10:09 pm	♓
25	♓		
26	♓		
27	♓	6:28 am	♈
28	♈		
29	♈	6:11 pm	♉
30	♉		

September

1	♌		
2	♌	3:31 am	♍
3	♍		
4	♍	7:56 am	♎
5	♎		
6	♎	10:53 am	♏
7	♏		
8	♏	1:20 pm	♐
9	♐		
10	♐	4:04 pm	♑
11	♑		
12	♑	7:43 pm	♒
13	♒		
14	♒		
15	♒	12:54 am	♓
16	♓		
17	♓	8:16 am	♈
18	♈		
19	♈	6:12 pm	♉
20	♉		
21	♉		
22	♉	6:16 am	♊
23	♊		
24	♊	6:49 pm	♋
25	♋		
26	♋		
27	♋	5:36 am	♌
28	♌		
29	♌	1:04 pm	♍
30	♍		

December

1	♐	3:11 pm	♑
2	♑		
3	♑	3:35 pm	♒
4	♒		
5	♒	7:16 pm	♓
6	♓		
7	♓		
8	♓	2:59 am	♈
9	♈		
10	♈	1:56 pm	♉
11	♉		
12	♉		
13	♉	2:24 am	♊
14	♊		
15	♊	3:00 pm	♋
16	♋		
17	♋		
18	♋	2:58 am	♌
19	♌		
20	♌	1:29 pm	♍
21	♍		
22	♍	9:29 pm	♎
23	♎		
24	♎		
25	♎	2:01 am	♏
26	♏		
27	♏	3:16 am	♐
28	♐		
29	♐	2:38 am	♑
30	♑		
31	♑	2:15 am	♒

Moon Movements

♎ = Libra ♏ = Scorpio ♐ = Sagittarius ♑ = Capricorn ♒ = Aquarius ♓ = Pisces

1960

January

1	♒		
2	♒	4:19 am	♓
3	♓		
4	♓	10:21 am	♈
5	♈		
6	♈	8:22 pm	♉
7	♉		
8	♉		
9	♉	8:45 am	♊
10	♊		
11	♊	9:23 pm	♋
12	♋		
13	♋		
14	♋	8:59 am	♌
15	♌		
16	♌	7:03 pm	♍
17	♍		
18	♍		
19	♍	3:14 am	♎
20	♎		
21	♎	8:59 am	♏
22	♏		
23	♏	12:02 pm	♐
24	♐		
25	♐	12:59 pm	♑
26	♑		
27	♑	1:19 pm	♒
28	♒		
29	♒	2:56 pm	♓
30	♓		
31	♓	7:39 pm	♈

April

1	♊		
2	♊	8:46 pm	♋
3	♋		
4	♋		
5	♋	9:01 am	♌
6	♌		
7	♌	7:02 pm	♍
8	♍		
9	♍		
10	♍	1:35 am	♎
11	♎		
12	♎	5:01 am	♏
13	♏		
14	♏	6:37 am	♐
15	♐		
16	♐	8:01 am	♑
17	♑		
18	♑	10:32 am	♒
19	♒		
20	♒	2:55 pm	♓
21	♓		
22	♓	9:23 pm	♈
23	♈		
24	♈		
25	♈	5:50 am	♉
26	♉		
27	♉	4:16 pm	♊
28	♊		
29	♊		
30	♊	4:22 am	♋

July

1	♍	3:46 am	♎
2	♎		
3	♎	10:08 am	♏
4	♏		
5	♏	12:42 pm	♐
6	♐		
7	♐	12:34 pm	♑
8	♑		
9	♑	11:43 am	♒
10	♒		
11	♒	12:19 pm	♓
12	♓		
13	♓	4:07 pm	♈
14	♈		
15	♈	11:48 pm	♉
16	♉		
17	♉		
18	♉	10:40 am	♊
19	♊		
20	♊	11:09 pm	♋
21	♋		
22	♋		
23	♋	11:46 am	♌
24	♌		
25	♌	11:31 pm	♍
26	♍		
27	♍		
28	♍	9:33 am	♎
29	♎		
30	♎	4:55 pm	♏
31	♏		

October

1	♒	5:14 pm	♓
2	♓		
3	♓	8:46 pm	♈
4	♈		
5	♈		
6	♈	2:09 am	♉
7	♉		
8	♉	10:16 am	♊
9	♊		
10	♊	9:18 pm	♋
11	♋		
12	♋		
13	♋	9:55 am	♌
14	♌		
15	♌	9:40 pm	♍
16	♍		
17	♍		
18	♍	6:32 am	♎
19	♎		
20	♎	12:06 pm	♏
21	♏		
22	♏	3:16 pm	♐
23	♐		
24	♐	5:28 pm	♑
25	♑		
26	♑	7:57 pm	♒
27	♒		
28	♒	11:26 pm	♓
29	♓		
30	♓		
31	♓	4:11 am	♈

February

1	♈		
2	♈		
3	♈	4:16 am	♉
4	♉		
5	♉	3:58 pm	♊
6	♊		
7	♊		
8	♊	4:37 am	♋
9	♋		
10	♋	4:08 pm	♌
11	♌		
12	♌		
13	♌	1:35 am	♍
14	♍		
15	♍	8:55 am	♎
16	♎		
17	♎	2:24 pm	♏
18	♏		
19	♏	6:12 pm	♐
20	♐		
21	♐	8:39 pm	♑
22	♑		
23	♑	10:32 pm	♒
24	♒		
25	♒		
26	♒	1:04 am	♓
27	♓		
28	♓	5:38 am	♈
29	♈		

May

1	♋		
2	♋	4:59 pm	♌
3	♌		
4	♌		
5	♌	3:59 am	♍
6	♍		
7	♍	11:30 am	♎
8	♎		
9	♎	3:06 pm	♏
10	♏		
11	♏	3:55 pm	♐
12	♐		
13	♐	3:50 pm	♑
14	♑		
15	♑	4:51 pm	♒
16	♒		
17	♒	8:23 pm	♓
18	♓		
19	♓		
20	♓	2:55 am	♈
21	♈		
22	♈	12:00 pm	♉
23	♉		
24	♉	10:55 pm	♊
25	♊		
26	♊		
27	♊	11:06 am	♋
28	♋		
29	♋	11:50 pm	♌
30	♌		
31	♌		

August

1	♏	9:04 pm	♐
2	♐		
3	♐	10:25 pm	♑
4	♑		
5	♑	10:21 pm	♒
6	♒		
7	♒	10:42 pm	♓
8	♓		
9	♓		
10	♓	1:21 am	♈
11	♈		
12	♈	7:36 am	♉
13	♉		
14	♉	5:29 pm	♊
15	♊		
16	♊		
17	♊	5:43 am	♋
18	♋		
19	♋	6:18 pm	♌
20	♌		
21	♌		
22	♌	5:41 am	♍
23	♍		
24	♍	3:09 pm	♎
25	♎		
26	♎	10:24 pm	♏
27	♏		
28	♏		
29	♏	3:19 am	♐
30	♐		
31	♐	6:09 am	♑

November

1	♈		
2	♈	10:27 am	♉
3	♉		
4	♉	6:44 pm	♊
5	♊		
6	♊		
7	♊	5:26 am	♋
8	♋		
9	♋	5:59 pm	♌
10	♌		
11	♌		
12	♌	6:24 am	♍
13	♍		
14	♍	4:07 pm	♎
15	♎		
16	♎	9:53 pm	♏
17	♏		
18	♏		
19	♏	12:17 am	♐
20	♐		
21	♐	1:02 am	♑
22	♑		
23	♑	2:04 am	♒
24	♒		
25	♒	4:49 am	♓
26	♓		
27	♓	9:51 am	♈
28	♈		
29	♈	5:00 pm	♉
30	♉		

March

1	♈	1:18 pm	♉
2	♉		
3	♉		
4	♉	12:08 am	♊
5	♊		
6	♊	12:37 pm	♋
7	♋		
8	♋		
9	♋	12:25 am	♌
10	♌		
11	♌	9:47 am	♍
12	♍		
13	♍	4:19 pm	♎
14	♎		
15	♎	8:37 pm	♏
16	♏		
17	♏	11:37 pm	♐
18	♐		
19	♐		
20	♐	2:14 am	♑
21	♑		
22	♑	5:10 am	♒
23	♒		
24	♒	9:02 am	♓
25	♓		
26	♓	2:29 pm	♈
27	♈		
28	♈	10:13 pm	♉
29	♉		
30	♉		
31	♉	8:32 am	♊

June

1	♌	11:38 am	♍
2	♍		
3	♍	8:31 pm	♎
4	♎		
5	♎		
6	♎	1:20 am	♏
7	♏		
8	♏	2:31 am	♐
9	♐		
10	♐	1:48 am	♑
11	♑		
12	♑	1:23 am	♒
13	♒		
14	♒	3:17 am	♓
15	♓		
16	♓	8:42 am	♈
17	♈		
18	♈	5:33 pm	♉
19	♉		
20	♉		
21	♉	4:46 am	♊
22	♊		
23	♊	5:10 pm	♋
24	♋		
25	♋		
26	♋	5:51 am	♌
27	♌		
28	♌	5:53 pm	♍
29	♍		
30	♍		

September

1	♑		
2	♑	7:35 am	♒
3	♒		
4	♒	8:51 am	♓
5	♓		
6	♓	11:26 am	♈
7	♈		
8	♈	4:44 pm	♉
9	♉		
10	♉		
11	♉	1:31 am	♊
12	♊		
13	♊	1:10 pm	♋
14	♋		
15	♋		
16	♋	1:46 am	♌
17	♌		
18	♌	1:07 pm	♍
19	♍		
20	♍	9:58 pm	♎
21	♎		
22	♎		
23	♎	4:18 am	♏
24	♏		
25	♏	8:42 am	♐
26	♐		
27	♐	11:54 am	♑
28	♑		
29	♑	2:32 pm	♒
30	♒		

December

1	♉		
2	♉	2:01 am	♊
3	♊		
4	♊	12:52 pm	♋
5	♋		
6	♋		
7	♋	1:21 am	♌
8	♌		
9	♌	2:13 pm	♍
10	♍		
11	♍		
12	♍	1:10 am	♎
13	♎		
14	♎	8:13 am	♏
15	♏		
16	♏	11:07 am	♐
17	♐		
18	♐	11:16 am	♑
19	♑		
20	♑	10:49 am	♒
21	♒		
22	♒	11:47 am	♓
23	♓		
24	♓	3:34 pm	♈
25	♈		
26	♈	10:30 pm	♉
27	♉		
28	♉		
29	♉	8:01 am	♊
30	♊		
31	♊	7:22 pm	♋

1961

Your Starway to Love

♈ = Aries ♉ = Taurus ♊ = Gemini ♋ = Cancer ♌ = Leo ♍ = Virgo

January

1	♋		
2	♋		
3	♋	7:54 am	♌
4	♌		
5	♌	8:48 pm	♍
6	♍		
7	♍		
8	♍	8:31 am	♎
9	♎		
10	♎	5:09 pm	♏
11	♏		
12	♏	9:40 pm	♐
13	♐		
14	♐	10:41 pm	♑
15	♑		
16	♑	9:55 pm	♒
17	♒		
18	♒	9:32 pm	♓
19	♓		
20	♓	11:26 pm	♈
21	♈		
22	♈		
23	♈	4:51 am	♉
24	♉		
25	♉	1:50 pm	♊
26	♊		
27	♊		
28	♊	1:22 am	♋
29	♋		
30	♋	2:05 pm	♌
31	♌		

February

1	♌		
2	♌	2:48 am	♍
3	♍		
4	♍	2:27 pm	♎
5	♎		
6	♎	11:51 pm	♏
7	♏		
8	♏		
9	♏	6:01 am	♐
10	♐		
11	♐	8:50 am	♑
12	♑		
13	♑	9:14 am	♒
14	♒		
15	♒	8:53 am	♓
16	♓		
17	♓	9:41 am	♈
18	♈		
19	♈	1:21 pm	♉
20	♉		
21	♉	8:51 pm	♊
22	♊		
23	♊		
24	♊	7:49 am	♋
25	♋		
26	♋	8:34 pm	♌
27	♌		
28	♌		

March

1	♌	9:12 am	♍
2	♍		
3	♍	8:21 pm	♎
4	♎		
5	♎		
6	♎	5:24 am	♏
7	♏		
8	♏	12:04 pm	♐
9	♐		
10	♐	4:19 pm	♑
11	♑		
12	♑	6:29 pm	♒
13	♒		
14	♒	7:26 pm	♓
15	♓		
16	♓	8:32 pm	♈
17	♈		
18	♈	11:25 pm	♉
19	♉		
20	♉		
21	♉	5:32 am	♊
22	♊		
23	♊	3:22 pm	♋
24	♋		
25	♋		
26	♋	3:48 am	♌
27	♌		
28	♌	4:30 pm	♍
29	♍		
30	♍		
31	♍	3:21 am	♎

April

1	♎		
2	♎	11:36 am	♏
3	♏		
4	♏	5:34 pm	♐
5	♐		
6	♐	9:52 pm	♑
7	♑		
8	♑		
9	♑	1:03 am	♒
10	♒		
11	♒	3:31 am	♓
12	♓		
13	♓	5:55 am	♈
14	♈		
15	♈	9:16 am	♉
16	♉		
17	♉	2:55 pm	♊
18	♊		
19	♊	11:50 pm	♋
20	♋		
21	♋		
22	♋	11:43 am	♌
23	♌		
24	♌		
25	♌	12:31 am	♍
26	♍		
27	♍	11:34 am	♎
28	♎		
29	♎	7:27 pm	♏
30	♏		

May

1	♏		
2	♏	12:25 am	♐
3	♐		
4	♐	3:40 am	♑
5	♑		
6	♑	6:24 am	♒
7	♒		
8	♒	9:23 am	♓
9	♓		
10	♓	12:56 pm	♈
11	♈		
12	♈	5:25 pm	♉
13	♉		
14	♉	11:34 pm	♊
15	♊		
16	♊		
17	♊	8:17 am	♋
18	♋		
19	♋	7:45 pm	♌
20	♌		
21	♌		
22	♌	8:38 am	♍
23	♍		
24	♍	8:18 pm	♎
25	♎		
26	♎		
27	♎	4:34 am	♏
28	♏		
29	♏	9:11 am	♐
30	♐		
31	♐	11:20 am	♑

June

1	♑		
2	♑	12:45 pm	♒
3	♒		
4	♒	2:50 pm	♓
5	♓		
6	♓	6:23 pm	♈
7	♈		
8	♈	11:38 pm	♉
9	♉		
10	♉		
11	♉	6:40 am	♊
12	♊		
13	♊	3:50 pm	♋
14	♋		
15	♋		
16	♋	3:16 am	♌
17	♌		
18	♌	4:12 pm	♍
19	♍		
20	♍		
21	♍	4:32 am	♎
22	♎		
23	♎	1:51 pm	♏
24	♏		
25	♏	7:05 pm	♐
26	♐		
27	♐	9:00 pm	♑
28	♑		
29	♑	9:18 pm	♒
30	♒		

July

1	♒	9:52 pm	♓
2	♓		
3	♓		
4	♓	12:12 am	♈
5	♈		
6	♈	5:01 am	♉
7	♉		
8	♉	12:27 pm	♊
9	♊		
10	♊	10:13 pm	♋
11	♋		
12	♋		
13	♋	9:56 am	♌
14	♌		
15	♌	10:55 pm	♍
16	♍		
17	♍		
18	♍	11:39 am	♎
19	♎		
20	♎	10:05 pm	♏
21	♏		
22	♏		
23	♏	4:42 am	♐
24	♐		
25	♐	7:28 am	♑
26	♑		
27	♑	7:41 am	♒
28	♒		
29	♒	7:13 am	♓
30	♓		
31	♓	7:56 am	♈

August

1	♈		
2	♈	11:19 am	♉
3	♉		
4	♉	6:04 pm	♊
5	♊		
6	♊		
7	♊	3:56 am	♋
8	♋		
9	♋	3:59 pm	♌
10	♌		
11	♌		
12	♌	5:00 am	♍
13	♍		
14	♍	5:44 pm	♎
15	♎		
16	♎		
17	♎	4:44 am	♏
18	♏		
19	♏	12:44 pm	♐
20	♐		
21	♐	5:07 pm	♑
22	♑		
23	♑	6:25 pm	♒
24	♒		
25	♒	6:02 pm	♓
26	♓		
27	♓	5:49 pm	♈
28	♈		
29	♈	7:37 pm	♉
30	♉		
31	♉		

September

1	♉	12:52 am	♊
2	♊		
3	♊	10:00 am	♋
4	♋		
5	♋	10:01 pm	♌
6	♌		
7	♌		
8	♌	11:05 am	♍
9	♍		
10	♍	11:33 pm	♎
11	♎		
12	♎		
13	♎	10:23 am	♏
14	♏		
15	♏	6:54 pm	♐
16	♐		
17	♐		
18	♐	12:42 am	♑
19	♑		
20	♑	3:43 am	♒
21	♒		
22	♒	4:36 am	♓
23	♓		
24	♓	4:40 am	♈
25	♈		
26	♈	5:42 am	♉
27	♉		
28	♉	9:31 am	♊
29	♊		
30	♊	5:19 pm	♋

October

1	♋		
2	♋		
3	♋	4:43 am	♌
4	♌		
5	♌	5:45 pm	♍
6	♍		
7	♍		
8	♍	6:04 am	♎
9	♎		
10	♎	4:19 pm	♏
11	♏		
12	♏		
13	♏	12:21 am	♐
14	♐		
15	♐	6:24 am	♑
16	♑		
17	♑	10:37 am	♒
18	♒		
19	♒	1:10 pm	♓
20	♓		
21	♓	2:35 pm	♈
22	♈		
23	♈	4:07 pm	♉
24	♉		
25	♉	7:24 pm	♊
26	♊		
27	♊		
28	♊	2:03 am	♋
29	♋		
30	♋	12:30 pm	♌
31	♌		

November

1	♌		
2	♌	1:17 am	♍
3	♍		
4	♍	1:42 pm	♎
5	♎		
6	♎	11:40 pm	♏
7	♏		
8	♏		
9	♏	6:51 am	♐
10	♐		
11	♐	11:59 am	♑
12	♑		
13	♑	3:59 pm	♒
14	♒		
15	♒	7:18 pm	♓
16	♓		
17	♓	10:10 pm	♈
18	♈		
19	♈		
20	♈	1:03 am	♉
21	♉		
22	♉	4:59 am	♊
23	♊		
24	♊	11:20 am	♋
25	♋		
26	♋	9:01 pm	♌
27	♌		
28	♌		
29	♌	9:25 am	♍
30	♍		

December

1	♍	10:08 pm	♎
2	♎		
3	♎		
4	♎	8:30 am	♏
5	♏		
6	♏	3:24 pm	♐
7	♐		
8	♐	7:31 pm	♑
9	♑		
10	♑	10:11 pm	♒
11	♒		
12	♒		
13	♒	12:41 am	♓
14	♓		
15	♓	3:44 am	♈
16	♈		
17	♈	7:39 am	♉
18	♉		
19	♉	12:47 pm	♊
20	♊		
21	♊	7:50 pm	♋
22	♋		
23	♋		
24	♋	5:26 am	♌
25	♌		
26	♌	5:29 pm	♍
27	♍		
28	♍		
29	♍	6:26 am	♎
30	♎		
31	♎	5:42 pm	♏

Moon Movements

♎ = Libra ♏ = Scorpio ♐ = Sagittarius ♑ = Capricorn ♒ = Aquarius ♓ = Pisces

1962

January

Day	Moon	Time	Enters
1	♏		
2	♏		
3	♏	1:23 am	♐
4	♐		
5	♐	5:24 am	♑
6	♑		
7	♑	7:00 am	♒
8	♒		
9	♒	7:53 am	♓
10	♓		
11	♓	9:34 am	♈
12	♈		
13	♈	1:01 pm	♉
14	♉		
15	♉	6:42 pm	♊
16	♊		
17	♊		
18	♊	2:39 am	♋
19	♋		
20	♋	12:50 pm	♌
21	♌		
22	♌		
23	♌	12:53 am	♍
24	♍		
25	♍	1:52 pm	♎
26	♎		
27	♎		
28	♎	1:54 am	♏
29	♏		
30	♏	10:59 am	♐
31	♐		

April

Day	Moon	Time	Enters
1	♒	3:42 pm	♓
2	♓		
3	♓	3:41 pm	♈
4	♈		
5	♈	3:25 pm	♉
6	♉		
7	♉	5:00 pm	♊
8	♊		
9	♊	10:12 pm	♋
10	♋		
11	♋		
12	♋	7:36 am	♌
13	♌		
14	♌	7:57 pm	♍
15	♍		
16	♍		
17	♍	8:54 am	♎
18	♎		
19	♎	8:37 pm	♏
20	♏		
21	♏		
22	♏	6:27 am	♐
23	♐		
24	♐	2:20 pm	♑
25	♑		
26	♑	8:08 pm	♒
27	♒		
28	♒	11:40 pm	♓
29	♓		
30	♓		

July

Day	Moon	Time	Enters
1	♊	1:19 am	♋
2	♋		
3	♋	8:55 am	♌
4	♌		
5	♌	7:22 pm	♍
6	♍		
7	♍		
8	♍	7:48 am	♎
9	♎		
10	♎	8:05 pm	♏
11	♏		
12	♏		
13	♏	6:00 am	♐
14	♐		
15	♐	12:32 pm	♑
16	♑		
17	♑	4:07 pm	♒
18	♒		
19	♒	6:00 pm	♓
20	♓		
21	♓	7:34 pm	♈
22	♈		
23	♈	9:57 pm	♉
24	♉		
25	♉		
26	♉	1:57 am	♊
27	♊		
28	♊	8:00 am	♋
29	♋		
30	♋	4:21 pm	♌
31	♌		

October

Day	Moon	Time	Enters
1	♏		
2	♏		
3	♏	4:40 am	♐
4	♐		
5	♐	2:35 pm	♑
6	♑		
7	♑	9:22 pm	♒
8	♒		
9	♒		
10	♒	12:29 am	♓
11	♓		
12	♓	12:41 am	♈
13	♈	11:43 pm	♉
14	♉		
15	♉	11:50 pm	♊
16	♊		
17	♊		
18	♊	3:05 am	♋
19	♋		
20	♋	10:30 am	♌
21	♌		
22	♌	9:31 pm	♍
23	♍		
24	♍		
25	♍	10:13 am	♎
26	♎		
27	♎	10:49 pm	♏
28	♏		
29	♏		
30	♏	10:19 am	♐
31	♐		

February

Day	Moon	Time	Enters
1	♐	4:09 pm	♑
2	♑		
3	♑	5:57 pm	♒
4	♒		
5	♒	5:53 pm	♓
6	♓		
7	♓	5:50 pm	♈
8	♈		
9	♈	7:35 pm	♉
10	♉		
11	♉		
12	♉	12:18 am	♊
13	♊		
14	♊	8:20 am	♋
15	♋		
16	♋	7:04 pm	♌
17	♌		
18	♌		
19	♌	7:27 am	♍
20	♍		
21	♍	8:22 pm	♎
22	♎		
23	♎		
24	♎	8:36 am	♏
25	♏		
26	♏	6:46 pm	♐
27	♐		
28	♐		

May

Day	Moon	Time	Enters
1	♓	1:12 am	♈
2	♈		
3	♈	1:49 am	♉
4	♉		
5	♉	3:16 am	♊
6	♊		
7	♊	7:28 am	♋
8	♋		
9	♋	3:35 pm	♌
10	♌		
11	♌		
12	♌	3:11 am	♍
13	♍		
14	♍	4:03 pm	♎
15	♎		
16	♎		
17	♎	3:43 am	♏
18	♏		
19	♏	1:02 pm	♐
20	♐		
21	♐	8:08 pm	♑
22	♑		
23	♑		
24	♑	1:31 am	♒
25	♒		
26	♒	5:29 am	♓
27	♓		
28	♓	8:15 am	♈
29	♈		
30	♈	10:17 am	♉
31	♉		

August

Day	Moon	Time	Enters
1	♌		
2	♌	2:57 am	♍
3	♍		
4	♍	3:17 pm	♎
5	♎		
6	♎		
7	♎	3:56 am	♏
8	♏		
9	♏	2:48 pm	♐
10	♐		
11	♐	10:18 pm	♑
12	♑		
13	♑		
14	♑	2:07 am	♒
15	♒		
16	♒	3:17 am	♓
17	♓		
18	♓	3:25 am	♈
19	♈		
20	♈	4:20 am	♉
21	♉		
22	♉	7:28 am	♊
23	♊		
24	♊	1:34 pm	♋
25	♋		
26	♋	10:30 pm	♌
27	♌		
28	♌		
29	♌	9:36 am	♍
30	♍		
31	♍	10:01 pm	♎

November

Day	Moon	Time	Enters
1	♐	8:17 pm	♑
2	♑		
3	♑		
4	♑	4:02 am	♒
5	♒		
6	♒	8:52 am	♓
7	♓		
8	♓	10:45 am	♈
9	♈		
10	♈	10:45 am	♉
11	♉		
12	♉	10:43 am	♊
13	♊		
14	♊	12:49 pm	♋
15	♋		
16	♋	6:40 pm	♌
17	♌		
18	♌		
19	♌	4:33 am	♍
20	♍		
21	♍	4:58 pm	♎
22	♎		
23	♎		
24	♎	5:33 am	♏
25	♏		
26	♏	4:43 pm	♐
27	♐		
28	♐		
29	♐	2:00 am	♑
30	♑		

March

Day	Moon	Time	Enters
1	♐	1:38 am	♑
2	♑		
3	♑	4:52 am	♒
4	♒		
5	♒	5:16 am	♓
6	♓		
7	♓	4:32 am	♈
8	♈		
9	♈	4:40 am	♉
10	♉		
11	♉	7:35 am	♊
12	♊		
13	♊	2:25 pm	♋
14	♋		
15	♋		
16	♋	12:56 am	♌
17	♌		
18	♌	1:33 pm	♍
19	♍		
20	♍		
21	♍	2:28 am	♎
22	♎		
23	♎	2:29 pm	♏
24	♏		
25	♏		
26	♏	12:49 am	♐
27	♐		
28	♐	8:46 am	♑
29	♑		
30	♑	1:43 pm	♒
31	♒		

June

Day	Moon	Time	Enters
1	♉	12:40 pm	♊
2	♊		
3	♊	4:56 pm	♋
4	♋		
5	♋		
6	♋	12:23 am	♌
7	♌		
8	♌	11:12 am	♍
9	♍		
10	♍	11:51 pm	♎
11	♎		
12	♎		
13	♎	11:45 am	♏
14	♏		
15	♏	9:03 pm	♐
16	♐		
17	♐		
18	♐	3:30 am	♑
19	♑		
20	♑	7:49 am	♒
21	♒		
22	♒	10:59 am	♓
23	♓		
24	♓	1:43 pm	♈
25	♈		
26	♈	4:34 pm	♉
27	♉		
28	♉	8:09 pm	♊
29	♊		
30	♊		

September

Day	Moon	Time	Enters
1	♎		
2	♎		
3	♎	10:46 am	♏
4	♏		
5	♏	10:26 pm	♐
6	♐		
7	♐		
8	♐	7:20 am	♑
9	♑		
10	♑	12:26 pm	♒
11	♒		
12	♒	2:02 pm	♓
13	♓		
14	♓	1:33 pm	♈
15	♈		
16	♈	1:01 pm	♉
17	♉		
18	♉	2:29 pm	♊
19	♊		
20	♊	7:26 pm	♋
21	♋		
22	♋		
23	♋	4:07 am	♌
24	♌		
25	♌	3:31 pm	♍
26	♍		
27	♍		
28	♍	4:08 am	♎
29	♎		
30	♎	4:49 pm	♏

December

Day	Moon	Time	Enters
1	♑	9:26 am	♒
2	♒		
3	♒	2:53 pm	♓
4	♓		
5	♓	6:17 pm	♈
6	♈		
7	♈	7:59 pm	♉
8	♉		
9	♉	9:07 pm	♊
10	♊		
11	♊	11:21 pm	♋
12	♋		
13	♋		
14	♋	4:20 am	♌
15	♌		
16	♌	12:59 pm	♍
17	♍		
18	♍		
19	♍	12:41 am	♎
20	♎		
21	♎	1:18 pm	♏
22	♏		
23	♏		
24	♏	12:33 am	♐
25	♐		
26	♐	9:19 am	♑
27	♑		
28	♑	3:42 pm	♒
29	♒		
30	♒	8:20 pm	♓
31	♓		

Your Starway to Love

♈ = Aries ♉ = Taurus ♊ = Gemini ♋ = Cancer ♌ = Leo ♍ = Virgo

1963

January

1	♓	11:48 pm	♈
2	♈		
3	♈		
4	♈	2:33 am	♉
5	♉		
6	♉	5:14 am	♊
7	♊		
8	♊	8:41 am	♋
9	♋		
10	♋	2:01 pm	♌
11	♌		
12	♌	10:07 pm	♍
13	♍		
14	♍		
15	♍	9:05 am	♎
16	♎		
17	♎	9:35 pm	♏
18	♏		
19	♏		
20	♏	9:20 am	♐
21	♐		
22	♐	6:23 pm	♑
23	♑		
24	♑		
25	♑	12:14 am	♒
26	♒		
27	♒	3:35 am	♓
28	♓		
29	♓	5:44 am	♈
30	♈		
31	♈	7:55 am	♉

February

1	♉		
2	♉	11:03 am	♊
3	♊		
4	♊	3:40 pm	♋
5	♋		
6	♋	10:06 pm	♌
7	♌		
8	♌		
9	♌	6:36 am	♍
10	♍		
11	♍	5:18 pm	♎
12	♎		
13	♎		
14	♎	5:38 am	♏
15	♏		
16	♏	5:57 pm	♐
17	♐		
18	♐		
19	♐	4:00 am	♑
20	♑		
21	♑	10:23 am	♒
22	♒		
23	♒	1:17 pm	♓
24	♓		
25	♓	2:05 pm	♈
26	♈		
27	♈	2:38 pm	♉
28	♉		

March

1	♉	4:39 pm	♊
2	♊		
3	♊	9:08 pm	♋
4	♋		
5	♋		
6	♋	4:15 am	♌
7	♌		
8	♌	1:34 pm	♍
9	♍		
10	♍		
11	♍	12:35 am	♎
12	♎		
13	♎	12:51 pm	♏
14	♏		
15	♏		
16	♏	1:27 am	♐
17	♐		
18	♐	12:35 pm	♑
19	♑		
20	♑	8:21 pm	♒
21	♒		
22	♒		
23	♒	12:04 am	♓
24	♓		
25	♓	12:38 am	♈
26	♈	11:57 pm	♉
27	♉		
28	♉		
29	♉	12:13 am	♊
30	♊		
31	♊	3:14 am	♋

April

1	♋		
2	♋	9:45 am	♌
3	♌		
4	♌	7:20 pm	♍
5	♍		
6	♍		
7	♍	6:49 am	♎
8	♎		
9	♎	7:14 pm	♏
10	♏		
11	♏		
12	♏	7:48 am	♐
13	♐		
14	♐	7:27 pm	♑
15	♑		
16	♑		
17	♑	4:34 am	♒
18	♒		
19	♒	9:53 am	♓
20	♓		
21	♓	11:30 am	♈
22	♈		
23	♈	10:51 am	♉
24	♉		
25	♉	10:06 am	♊
26	♊		
27	♊	11:27 am	♋
28	♋		
29	♋	4:25 pm	♌
30	♌		

May

1	♌		
2	♌	1:13 am	♍
3	♍		
4	♍	12:42 pm	♎
5	♎		
6	♎		
7	♎	1:16 am	♏
8	♏		
9	♏	1:42 pm	♐
10	♐		
11	♐		
12	♐	1:13 am	♑
13	♑		
14	♑	10:51 am	♒
15	♒		
16	♒	5:32 pm	♓
17	♓		
18	♓	8:48 pm	♈
19	♈		
20	♈	9:21 pm	♉
21	♉		
22	♉	8:53 pm	♊
23	♊		
24	♊	9:29 pm	♋
25	♋		
26	♋		
27	♋	12:58 am	♌
28	♌		
29	♌	8:22 am	♍
30	♍		
31	♍	7:09 pm	♎

June

1	♎		
2	♎		
3	♎	7:38 am	♏
4	♏		
5	♏	8:01 pm	♐
6	♐		
7	♐		
8	♐	7:07 am	♑
9	♑		
10	♑	4:22 pm	♒
11	♒		
12	♒	11:21 pm	♓
13	♓		
14	♓		
15	♓	3:46 am	♈
16	♈		
17	♈	5:54 am	♉
18	♉		
19	♉	6:44 am	♊
20	♊		
21	♊	7:46 am	♋
22	♋		
23	♋	10:44 am	♌
24	♌		
25	♌	4:56 pm	♍
26	♍		
27	♍		
28	♍	2:41 am	♎
29	♎		
30	♎	2:48 pm	♏

July

1	♏		
2	♏		
3	♏	3:11 am	♐
4	♐		
5	♐	2:03 pm	♑
6	♑		
7	♑	10:36 pm	♒
8	♒		
9	♒		
10	♒	4:53 am	♓
11	♓		
12	♓	9:16 am	♈
13	♈		
14	♈	12:15 pm	♉
15	♉		
16	♉	2:27 pm	♊
17	♊		
18	♊	4:45 pm	♋
19	♋		
20	♋	8:15 pm	♌
21	♌		
22	♌		
23	♌	2:06 am	♍
24	♍		
25	♍	11:02 am	♎
26	♎		
27	♎	10:38 pm	♏
28	♏		
29	♏		
30	♏	11:08 am	♐
31	♐		

August

1	♐	10:12 pm	♑
2	♑		
3	♑		
4	♑	6:25 am	♒
5	♒		
6	♒	11:46 am	♓
7	♓		
8	♓	3:07 pm	♈
9	♈		
10	♈	5:37 pm	♉
11	♉		
12	♉	8:16 pm	♊
13	♊		
14	♊	11:39 pm	♋
15	♋		
16	♋		
17	♋	4:17 am	♌
18	♌		
19	♌	10:40 am	♍
20	♍		
21	♍	7:25 pm	♎
22	♎		
23	♎		
24	♎	6:39 am	♏
25	♏		
26	♏	7:15 pm	♐
27	♐		
28	♐		
29	♐	6:57 am	♑
30	♑		
31	♑	3:37 pm	♒

September

1	♒		
2	♒	8:37 pm	♓
3	♓		
4	♓	10:52 pm	♈
5	♈		
6	♈		
7	♈	12:02 am	♉
8	♉		
9	♉	1:45 am	♊
10	♊		
11	♊	5:08 am	♋
12	♋		
13	♋	10:30 am	♌
14	♌		
15	♌	5:47 pm	♍
16	♍		
17	♍		
18	♍	3:00 am	♎
19	♎		
20	♎	2:10 pm	♏
21	♏		
22	♏		
23	♏	2:50 am	♐
24	♐		
25	♐	3:15 pm	♑
26	♑		
27	♑		
28	♑	1:03 am	♒
29	♒		
30	♒	6:46 am	♓

October

1	♓		
2	♓	8:48 am	♈
3	♈		
4	♈	8:50 am	♉
5	♉		
6	♉	8:58 am	♊
7	♊		
8	♊	11:01 am	♋
9	♋		
10	♋	3:54 pm	♌
11	♌		
12	♌	11:34 pm	♍
13	♍		
14	♍		
15	♍	9:24 am	♎
16	♎		
17	♎	8:53 pm	♏
18	♏		
19	♏		
20	♏	9:32 am	♐
21	♐		
22	♐	10:21 pm	♑
23	♑		
24	♑		
25	♑	9:20 am	♒
26	♒		
27	♒	4:36 pm	♓
28	♓		
29	♓	7:40 pm	♈
30	♈		
31	♈	7:42 pm	♉

November

1	♉		
2	♉	6:48 pm	♊
3	♊		
4	♊	7:08 pm	♋
5	♋		
6	♋	10:24 pm	♌
7	♌		
8	♌		
9	♌	5:14 am	♍
10	♍		
11	♍	3:07 pm	♎
12	♎		
13	♎		
14	♎	2:57 am	♏
15	♏		
16	♏	3:40 pm	♐
17	♐		
18	♐		
19	♐	4:23 am	♑
20	♑		
21	♑	3:51 pm	♒
22	♒		
23	♒		
24	♒	12:32 am	♓
25	♓		
26	♓	5:25 am	♈
27	♈		
28	♈	6:49 am	♉
29	♉		
30	♉	6:14 am	♊

December

1	♊		
2	♊	5:45 am	♋
3	♋		
4	♋	7:20 am	♌
5	♌		
6	♌	12:26 pm	♍
7	♍		
8	♍	9:21 pm	♎
9	♎		
10	♎		
11	♎	9:04 am	♏
12	♏		
13	♏	9:53 pm	♐
14	♐		
15	♐		
16	♐	10:21 am	♑
17	♑		
18	♑	9:29 pm	♒
19	♒		
20	♒		
21	♒	6:28 am	♓
22	♓		
23	♓	12:41 pm	♈
24	♈		
25	♈	3:57 pm	♉
26	♉		
27	♉	4:58 pm	♊
28	♊		
29	♊	5:07 pm	♋
30	♋		
31	♋	6:09 pm	♌

Moon Movements

♎ = Libra ♏ = Scorpio ♐ = Sagittarius ♑ = Capricorn ♒ = Aquarius ♓ = Pisces

1964

January

1	♌		
2	♌	9:48 pm	♍
3	♍		
4	♍		
5	♍	5:10 am	♎
6	♎		
7	♎	4:04 pm	♏
8	♏		
9	♏		
10	♏	4:49 am	♐
11	♐		
12	♐	5:14 pm	♑
13	♑		
14	♑		
15	♑	3:48 am	♒
16	♒		
17	♒	12:04 pm	♓
18	♓		
19	♓	6:10 pm	♈
20	♈		
21	♈	10:23 pm	♉
22	♉		
23	♉		
24	♉	1:05 am	♊
25	♊		
26	♊	2:51 am	♋
27	♋		
28	♋	4:45 am	♌
29	♌		
30	♌	8:09 am	♍
31	♍		

April

1	♏	4:41 am	♐
2	♐		
3	♐	5:36 pm	♑
4	♑		
5	♑		
6	♑	5:24 am	♒
7	♒		
8	♒	1:47 pm	♓
9	♓		
10	♓	6:08 pm	♈
11	♈		
12	♈	7:37 pm	♉
13	♉		
14	♉	8:06 pm	♊
15	♊		
16	♊	9:23 pm	♋
17	♋		
18	♋		
19	♋	12:40 am	♌
20	♌		
21	♌	6:17 am	♍
22	♍		
23	♍	2:08 pm	♎
24	♎		
25	♎		
26	♎	12:01 am	♏
27	♏		
28	♏	11:46 am	♐
29	♐		
30	♐		

July

1	♓	7:52 pm	♈
2	♈		
3	♈		
4	♈	12:42 am	♉
5	♉		
6	♉	2:43 am	♊
7	♊		
8	♊	2:57 am	♋
9	♋		
10	♋	3:01 am	♌
11	♌		
12	♌	4:44 am	♍
13	♍		
14	♍	9:41 am	♎
15	♎		
16	♎	6:32 pm	♏
17	♏		
18	♏		
19	♏	6:28 am	♐
20	♐		
21	♐	7:27 pm	♑
22	♑		
23	♑		
24	♑	7:30 am	♒
25	♒		
26	♒	5:36 pm	♓
27	♓		
28	♓		
29	♓	1:25 am	♈
30	♈		
31	♈	7:00 am	♉

October

1	♌		
2	♌	7:42 am	♍
3	♍		
4	♍	12:44 pm	♎
5	♎		
6	♎	7:57 pm	♏
7	♏		
8	♏		
9	♏	6:02 am	♐
10	♐		
11	♐	6:32 pm	♑
12	♑		
13	♑		
14	♑	7:15 am	♒
15	♒		
16	♒	5:33 pm	♓
17	♓		
18	♓		
19	♓	12:05 am	♈
20	♈		
21	♈	3:24 am	♉
22	♉		
23	♉	5:03 am	♊
24	♊		
25	♊	6:37 am	♋
26	♋		
27	♋	9:14 am	♌
28	♌		
29	♌	1:25 pm	♍
30	♍		
31	♍	7:24 pm	♎

February

1	♍	2:25 pm	♎
2	♎		
3	♎		
4	♎	12:12 am	♏
5	♏		
6	♏	12:35 pm	♐
7	♐		
8	♐		
9	♐	1:11 am	♑
10	♑		
11	♑	11:39 am	♒
12	♒		
13	♒	7:09 pm	♓
14	♓		
15	♓		
16	♓	12:10 am	♈
17	♈		
18	♈	3:45 am	♉
19	♉		
20	♉	6:48 am	♊
21	♊		
22	♊	9:49 am	♋
23	♋		
24	♋	1:11 pm	♌
25	♌		
26	♌	5:30 pm	♍
27	♍		
28	♍	11:46 pm	♎
29	♎		

May

1	♐	12:42 am	♑
2	♑		
3	♑	1:06 pm	♒
4	♒		
5	♒	10:43 pm	♓
6	♓		
7	♓		
8	♓	4:16 am	♈
9	♈		
10	♈	6:09 am	♉
11	♉		
12	♉	6:01 am	♊
13	♊		
14	♊	5:53 am	♋
15	♋		
16	♋	7:31 am	♌
17	♌		
18	♌	12:02 pm	♍
19	♍		
20	♍	7:41 pm	♎
21	♎		
22	♎		
23	♎	5:58 am	♏
24	♏		
25	♏	6:03 pm	♐
26	♐		
27	♐		
28	♐	7:00 am	♑
29	♑		
30	♑	7:32 pm	♒
31	♒		

August

1	♉		
2	♉	10:28 am	♊
3	♊		
4	♊	12:13 pm	♋
5	♋		
6	♋	1:11 pm	♌
7	♌		
8	♌	2:50 pm	♍
9	♍		
10	♍	6:51 pm	♎
11	♎		
12	♎		
13	♎	2:31 am	♏
14	♏		
15	♏	1:44 pm	♐
16	♐		
17	♐		
18	♐	2:38 am	♑
19	♑		
20	♑	2:39 pm	♒
21	♒		
22	♒		
23	♒	12:13 am	♓
24	♓		
25	♓	7:15 am	♈
26	♈		
27	♈	12:24 pm	♉
28	♉		
29	♉	4:16 pm	♊
30	♊		
31	♊	7:13 pm	♋

November

1	♎		
2	♎		
3	♎	3:25 am	♏
4	♏		
5	♏	1:43 pm	♐
6	♐		
7	♐		
8	♐	2:06 am	♑
9	♑		
10	♑	3:08 pm	♒
11	♒		
12	♒		
13	♒	2:28 am	♓
14	♓		
15	♓	10:10 am	♈
16	♈		
17	♈	1:57 pm	♉
18	♉		
19	♉	2:58 pm	♊
20	♊		
21	♊	3:04 pm	♋
22	♋		
23	♋	3:59 pm	♌
24	♌		
25	♌	7:03 pm	♍
26	♍		
27	♍		
28	♍	12:54 am	♎
29	♎		
30	♎	9:31 am	♏

March

1	♎		
2	♎	8:54 am	♏
3	♏		
4	♏	8:47 pm	♐
5	♐		
6	♐		
7	♐	9:35 am	♑
8	♑		
9	♑	8:35 pm	♒
10	♒		
11	♒		
12	♒	4:05 am	♓
13	♓		
14	♓	8:15 am	♈
15	♈		
16	♈	10:30 am	♉
17	♉		
18	♉	12:26 pm	♊
19	♊		
20	♊	3:11 pm	♋
21	♋		
22	♋	7:15 pm	♌
23	♌		
24	♌		
25	♌	12:42 am	♍
26	♍		
27	♍	7:48 am	♎
28	♎		
29	♎	5:03 pm	♏
30	♏		
31	♏		

June

1	♒		
2	♒	6:01 am	♓
3	♓		
4	♓	1:03 pm	♈
5	♈		
6	♈	4:20 pm	♉
7	♉		
8	♉	4:50 pm	♊
9	♊		
10	♊	4:16 pm	♋
11	♋		
12	♋	4:35 pm	♌
13	♌		
14	♌	7:27 pm	♍
15	♍		
16	♍		
17	♍	1:54 am	♎
18	♎		
19	♎	11:49 am	♏
20	♏		
21	♏		
22	♏	12:03 am	♐
23	♐		
24	♐	1:02 pm	♑
25	♑		
26	♑		
27	♑	1:22 am	♒
28	♒		
29	♒	11:56 am	♓
30	♓		

September

1	♋		
2	♋	9:36 pm	♌
3	♌		
4	♌		
5	♌	12:12 am	♍
6	♍		
7	♍	4:19 am	♎
8	♎		
9	♎	11:20 am	♏
10	♏		
11	♏	9:47 pm	♐
12	♐		
13	♐		
14	♐	10:30 am	♑
15	♑		
16	♑	10:47 pm	♒
17	♒		
18	♒		
19	♒	8:22 am	♓
20	♓		
21	♓	2:44 pm	♈
22	♈		
23	♈	6:46 pm	♉
24	♉		
25	♉	9:46 pm	♊
26	♊		
27	♊		
28	♊	12:39 am	♋
29	♋		
30	♋	3:52 am	♌

December

1	♏		
2	♏	8:24 pm	♐
3	♐		
4	♐		
5	♐	8:53 am	♑
6	♑		
7	♑	9:57 pm	♒
8	♒		
9	♒		
10	♒	10:00 am	♓
11	♓		
12	♓	7:12 pm	♈
13	♈		
14	♈		
15	♈	12:33 am	♉
16	♉		
17	♉	2:21 am	♊
18	♊		
19	♊	2:02 am	♋
20	♋		
21	♋	1:31 am	♌
22	♌		
23	♌	2:41 am	♍
24	♍		
25	♍	7:04 am	♎
26	♎		
27	♎	3:11 pm	♏
28	♏		
29	♏		
30	♏	2:20 am	♐
31	♐		

Your Starway to Love

♈ = Aries ♉ = Taurus ♊ = Gemini ♋ = Cancer ♌ = Leo ♍ = Virgo

1965

January

1	♐	3:06 pm	♑
2	♑		
3	♑		
4	♑	4:04 am	♒
5	♒		
6	♒	4:06 pm	♓
7	♓		
8	♓		
9	♓	2:08 am	♈
10	♈		
11	♈	9:10 am	♉
12	♉		
13	♉	12:48 pm	♊
14	♊		
15	♊	1:35 pm	♋
16	♋		
17	♋	12:57 pm	♌
18	♌		
19	♌	12:55 pm	♍
20	♍		
21	♍	3:28 pm	♎
22	♎		
23	♎	10:01 pm	♏
24	♏		
25	♏		
26	♏	8:32 am	♐
27	♐		
28	♐	9:21 pm	♑
29	♑		
30	♑		
31	♑	10:17 am	♒

February

1	♒		
2	♒	9:56 pm	♓
3	♓		
4	♓		
5	♓	7:43 am	♈
6	♈		
7	♈	3:24 pm	♉
8	♉		
9	♉	8:36 pm	♊
10	♊		
11	♊	11:14 pm	♋
12	♋		
13	♋	11:54 pm	♌
14	♌		
15	♌		
16	♌	12:05 am	♍
17	♍		
18	♍	1:45 am	♎
19	♎		
20	♎	6:45 am	♏
21	♏		
22	♏	3:57 pm	♐
23	♐		
24	♐		
25	♐	4:17 am	♑
26	♑		
27	♑	5:14 pm	♒
28	♒		

March

1	♒		
2	♒	4:38 am	♓
3	♓		
4	♓	1:45 pm	♈
5	♈		
6	♈	8:49 pm	♉
7	♉		
8	♉		
9	♉	2:14 am	♊
10	♊		
11	♊	6:03 am	♋
12	♋		
13	♋	8:23 am	♌
14	♌		
15	♌	9:55 am	♍
16	♍		
17	♍	12:04 pm	♎
18	♎		
19	♎	4:32 pm	♏
20	♏		
21	♏		
22	♏	12:37 am	♐
23	♐		
24	♐	12:07 pm	♑
25	♑		
26	♑		
27	♑	12:59 am	♒
28	♒		
29	♒	12:32 pm	♓
30	♓		
31	♓	9:19 pm	♈

April

1	♈		
2	♈		
3	♈	3:29 am	♉
4	♉		
5	♉	7:55 am	♊
6	♊		
7	♊	11:24 am	♋
8	♋		
9	♋	2:23 pm	♌
10	♌		
11	♌	5:14 pm	♍
12	♍		
13	♍	8:38 pm	♎
14	♎		
15	♎		
16	♎	1:42 am	♏
17	♏		
18	♏	9:31 am	♐
19	♐		
20	♐	8:24 pm	♑
21	♑		
22	♑		
23	♑	9:04 am	♒
24	♒		
25	♒	9:02 pm	♓
26	♓		
27	♓		
28	♓	6:12 am	♈
29	♈		
30	♈	12:03 pm	♉

May

1	♉		
2	♉	3:26 pm	♊
3	♊		
4	♊	5:39 pm	♋
5	♋		
6	♋	7:50 pm	♌
7	♌		
8	♌	10:47 pm	♍
9	♍		
10	♍		
11	♍	3:04 am	♎
12	♎		
13	♎	9:10 am	♏
14	♏		
15	♏	5:32 pm	♐
16	♐		
17	♐		
18	♐	4:20 am	♑
19	♑		
20	♑	4:50 pm	♒
21	♒		
22	♒		
23	♒	5:14 am	♓
24	♓		
25	♓	3:18 pm	♈
26	♈		
27	♈	9:48 pm	♉
28	♉		
29	♉		
30	♉	12:58 am	♊
31	♊		

June

1	♊	2:05 am	♋
2	♋		
3	♋	2:46 am	♌
4	♌		
5	♌	4:33 am	♍
6	♍		
7	♍	8:29 am	♎
8	♎		
9	♎	3:04 pm	♏
10	♏		
11	♏		
12	♏	12:10 am	♐
13	♐		
14	♐	11:20 am	♑
15	♑		
16	♑	11:51 pm	♒
17	♒		
18	♒		
19	♒	12:29 pm	♓
20	♓		
21	♓	11:29 pm	♈
22	♈		
23	♈		
24	♈	7:16 am	♉
25	♉		
26	♉	11:18 am	♊
27	♊		
28	♊	12:20 pm	♋
29	♋		
30	♋	11:59 am	♌

July

1	♌		
2	♌	12:11 pm	♍
3	♍		
4	♍	2:43 pm	♎
5	♎		
6	♎	8:38 pm	♏
7	♏		
8	♏		
9	♏	5:53 am	♐
10	♐		
11	♐	5:29 pm	♑
12	♑		
13	♑		
14	♑	6:08 am	♒
15	♒		
16	♒	6:45 pm	♓
17	♓		
18	♓		
19	♓	6:13 am	♈
20	♈		
21	♈	3:14 pm	♉
22	♉		
23	♉	8:48 pm	♊
24	♊		
25	♊	10:53 pm	♋
26	♋		
27	♋	10:37 pm	♌
28	♌		
29	♌	9:55 pm	♍
30	♍		
31	♍	10:54 pm	♎

August

1	♎		
2	♎		
3	♎	3:20 am	♏
4	♏		
5	♏	11:49 am	♐
6	♐		
7	♐	11:22 pm	♑
8	♑		
9	♑		
10	♑	12:09 pm	♒
11	♒		
12	♒		
13	♒	12:37 am	♓
14	♓		
15	♓	11:57 am	♈
16	♈		
17	♈	9:27 pm	♉
18	♉		
19	♉		
20	♉	4:20 am	♊
21	♊		
22	♊	8:04 am	♋
23	♋		
24	♋	9:01 am	♌
25	♌		
26	♌	8:36 am	♍
27	♍		
28	♍	8:52 am	♎
29	♎		
30	♎	11:54 am	♏
31	♏		

September

1	♏	7:00 pm	♐
2	♐		
3	♐		
4	♐	5:51 am	♑
5	♑		
6	♑	6:34 pm	♒
7	♒		
8	♒		
9	♒	6:56 am	♓
10	♓		
11	♓	5:50 pm	♈
12	♈		
13	♈		
14	♈	2:56 am	♉
15	♉		
16	♉	10:06 am	♊
17	♊		
18	♊	3:01 pm	♋
19	♋		
20	♋	5:35 pm	♌
21	♌		
22	♌	6:30 pm	♍
23	♍		
24	♍	7:15 pm	♎
25	♎		
26	♎	9:47 pm	♏
27	♏		
28	♏		
29	♏	3:42 am	♐
30	♐		

October

1	♐	1:29 pm	♑
2	♑		
3	♑		
4	♑	1:48 am	♒
5	♒		
6	♒	2:14 pm	♓
7	♓		
8	♓		
9	♓	12:54 am	♈
10	♈		
11	♈	9:16 am	♉
12	♉		
13	♉	3:40 pm	♊
14	♊		
15	♊	8:27 pm	♋
16	♋		
17	♋	11:51 pm	♌
18	♌		
19	♌		
20	♌	2:13 am	♍
21	♍		
22	♍	4:21 am	♎
23	♎		
24	♎	7:31 am	♏
25	♏		
26	♏	1:09 pm	♐
27	♐		
28	♐	10:05 pm	♑
29	♑		
30	♑		
31	♑	9:49 am	♒

November

1	♒		
2	♒	10:23 pm	♓
3	♓		
4	♓		
5	♓	9:21 am	♈
6	♈		
7	♈	5:29 pm	♉
8	♉		
9	♉	10:54 pm	♊
10	♊		
11	♊		
12	♊	2:29 am	♋
13	♋		
14	♋	5:13 am	♌
15	♌		
16	♌	7:55 am	♍
17	♍		
18	♍	11:10 am	♎
19	♎		
20	♎	3:37 pm	♏
21	♏		
22	♏	9:57 pm	♐
23	♐		
24	♐		
25	♐	6:45 am	♑
26	♑		
27	♑	6:03 pm	♒
28	♒		
29	♒		
30	♒	6:40 am	♓

December

1	♓		
2	♓	6:22 pm	♈
3	♈		
4	♈		
5	♈	3:11 am	♉
6	♉		
7	♉	8:27 am	♊
8	♊		
9	♊	10:57 am	♋
10	♋		
11	♋	12:08 pm	♌
12	♌		
13	♌	1:35 pm	♍
14	♍		
15	♍	4:33 pm	♎
16	♎		
17	♎	9:40 pm	♏
18	♏		
19	♏		
20	♏	5:01 am	♐
21	♐		
22	♐	2:27 pm	♑
23	♑		
24	♑		
25	♑	1:44 am	♒
26	♒		
27	♒	2:17 pm	♓
28	♓		
29	♓		
30	♓	2:40 am	♈
31	♈		

Moon Movements

♎ = Libra ♏ = Scorpio ♐ = Sagittarius ♑ = Capricorn ♒ = Aquarius ♓ = Pisces

1966

January

1	♈	12:46 pm	♉
2	♉		
3	♉	7:06 pm	♊
4	♊		
5	♊	9:40 pm	♋
6	♋		
7	♋	9:50 pm	♌
8	♌		
9	♌	9:34 pm	♍
10	♍		
11	♍	10:53 pm	♎
12	♎		
13	♎		
14	♎	3:08 am	♏
15	♏		
16	♏	10:39 am	♐
17	♐		
18	♐	8:45 pm	♑
19	♑		
20	♑		
21	♑	8:26 am	♒
22	♒		
23	♒	8:58 pm	♓
24	♓		
25	♓		
26	♓	9:33 am	♈
27	♈		
28	♈	8:43 pm	♉
29	♉		
30	♉		
31	♉	4:43 am	♊

April

1	♌		
2	♌	5:31 am	♍
3	♍		
4	♍	5:40 am	♎
5	♎		
6	♎	6:30 am	♏
7	♏		
8	♏	9:54 am	♐
9	♐		
10	♐	5:02 pm	♑
11	♑		
12	♑		
13	♑	3:42 am	♒
14	♒		
15	♒	4:13 pm	♓
16	♓		
17	♓		
18	♓	4:27 am	♈
19	♈		
20	♈	3:00 pm	♉
21	♉		
22	♉	11:27 pm	♊
23	♊		
24	♊		
25	♊	5:48 am	♋
26	♋		
27	♋	10:09 am	♌
28	♌		
29	♌	12:50 pm	♍
30	♍		

July

1	♐	6:51 pm	♑
2	♑		
3	♑		
4	♑	4:14 am	♒
5	♒		
6	♒	3:39 pm	♓
7	♓		
8	♓		
9	♓	4:16 am	♈
10	♈		
11	♈	4:03 pm	♉
12	♉		
13	♉		
14	♉	12:51 am	♊
15	♊		
16	♊	5:44 am	♋
17	♋		
18	♋	7:27 am	♌
19	♌		
20	♌	7:47 am	♍
21	♍		
22	♍	8:38 am	♎
23	♎		
24	♎	11:32 am	♏
25	♏		
26	♏	5:04 pm	♐
27	♐		
28	♐		
29	♐	1:04 am	♑
30	♑		
31	♑	11:02 am	♒

October

1	♈	11:47 am	♉
2	♉		
3	♉	10:43 pm	♊
4	♊		
5	♊		
6	♊	7:12 am	♋
7	♋		
8	♋	12:25 pm	♌
9	♌		
10	♌	2:27 pm	♍
11	♍		
12	♍	2:29 pm	♎
13	♎		
14	♎	2:21 pm	♏
15	♏		
16	♏	3:59 pm	♐
17	♐		
18	♐	8:55 pm	♑
19	♑		
20	♑		
21	♑	5:41 am	♒
22	♒		
23	♒	5:20 pm	♓
24	♓		
25	♓		
26	♓	6:03 am	♈
27	♈		
28	♈	6:05 pm	♉
29	♉		
30	♉		
31	♉	4:28 am	♊

February

1	♊		
2	♊	8:41 am	♋
3	♋		
4	♋	9:14 am	♌
5	♌		
6	♌	8:11 am	♍
7	♍		
8	♍	7:50 am	♎
9	♎		
10	♎	10:15 am	♏
11	♏		
12	♏	4:33 pm	♐
13	♐		
14	♐		
15	♐	2:26 am	♑
16	♑		
17	♑	2:25 pm	♒
18	♒		
19	♒		
20	♒	3:05 am	♓
21	♓		
22	♓	3:30 pm	♈
23	♈		
24	♈		
25	♈	2:53 am	♉
26	♉		
27	♉	12:03 pm	♊
28	♊		

May

1	♍	2:31 pm	♎
2	♎		
3	♎	4:23 pm	♏
4	♏		
5	♏	7:52 pm	♐
6	♐		
7	♐		
8	♐	2:12 am	♑
9	♑		
10	♑	11:52 am	♒
11	♒		
12	♒	11:55 pm	♓
13	♓		
14	♓		
15	♓	12:15 pm	♈
16	♈		
17	♈	10:49 pm	♉
18	♉		
19	♉		
20	♉	6:40 am	♊
21	♊		
22	♊	12:00 pm	♋
23	♋		
24	♋	3:37 pm	♌
25	♌		
26	♌	6:22 pm	♍
27	♍		
28	♍	9:00 pm	♎
29	♎		
30	♎		
31	♎	12:11 am	♏

August

1	♒		
2	♒	10:36 pm	♓
3	♓		
4	♓		
5	♓	11:15 am	♈
6	♈		
7	♈	11:38 pm	♉
8	♉		
9	♉		
10	♉	9:38 am	♊
11	♊		
12	♊	3:41 pm	♋
13	♋		
14	♋	5:50 pm	♌
15	♌		
16	♌	5:35 pm	♍
17	♍		
18	♍	5:05 pm	♎
19	♎		
20	♎	6:24 pm	♏
21	♏		
22	♏	10:51 pm	♐
23	♐		
24	♐		
25	♐	6:37 am	♑
26	♑		
27	♑	4:56 pm	♒
28	♒		
29	♒		
30	♒	4:48 am	♓
31	♓		

November

1	♊		
2	♊	12:43 pm	♋
3	♋		
4	♋	6:36 pm	♌
5	♌		
6	♌	10:10 pm	♍
7	♍		
8	♍	11:54 pm	♎
9	♎		
10	♎		
11	♎	12:53 am	♏
12	♏		
13	♏	2:36 am	♐
14	♐		
15	♐	6:37 am	♑
16	♑		
17	♑	2:03 pm	♒
18	♒		
19	♒		
20	♒	12:53 am	♓
21	♓		
22	♓	1:31 pm	♈
23	♈		
24	♈		
25	♈	1:37 am	♉
26	♉		
27	♉	11:31 am	♊
28	♊		
29	♊	6:50 pm	♋
30	♋		

March

1	♊	5:48 pm	♋
2	♋		
3	♋	7:56 pm	♌
4	♌		
5	♌	7:36 pm	♍
6	♍		
7	♍	6:49 pm	♎
8	♎		
9	♎	7:47 pm	♏
10	♏		
11	♏		
12	♏	12:18 am	♐
13	♐		
14	♐	8:55 am	♑
15	♑		
16	♑	8:35 pm	♒
17	♒		
18	♒		
19	♒	9:19 am	♓
20	♓		
21	♓	9:33 pm	♈
22	♈		
23	♈		
24	♈	8:32 am	♉
25	♉		
26	♉	5:41 pm	♊
27	♊		
28	♊		
29	♊	12:23 am	♋
30	♋		
31	♋	4:12 am	♌

June

1	♏		
2	♏	4:38 am	♐
3	♐		
4	♐	11:10 am	♑
5	♑		
6	♑	8:21 pm	♒
7	♒		
8	♒		
9	♒	7:57 am	♓
10	♓		
11	♓	8:26 pm	♈
12	♈		
13	♈		
14	♈	7:30 am	♉
15	♉		
16	♉	3:26 pm	♊
17	♊		
18	♊	8:05 pm	♋
19	♋		
20	♋	10:29 pm	♌
21	♌		
22	♌		
23	♌	12:08 am	♍
24	♍		
25	♍	2:23 am	♎
26	♎		
27	♎	6:04 am	♏
28	♏		
29	♏	11:31 am	♐
30	♐		

September

1	♓	5:27 pm	♈
2	♈		
3	♈		
4	♈	5:59 am	♉
5	♉		
6	♉	4:52 pm	♊
7	♊		
8	♊		
9	♊	12:26 am	♋
10	♋		
11	♋	4:01 am	♌
12	♌		
13	♌	4:26 am	♍
14	♍		
15	♍	3:33 am	♎
16	♎		
17	♎	3:34 am	♏
18	♏		
19	♏	6:21 am	♐
20	♐		
21	♐	12:52 pm	♑
22	♑		
23	♑	10:48 pm	♒
24	♒		
25	♒		
26	♒	10:48 am	♓
27	♓		
28	♓	11:29 pm	♈
29	♈		
30	♈		

December

1	♋		
2	♋	12:02 am	♌
3	♌		
4	♌	3:48 am	♍
5	♍		
6	♍	6:43 am	♎
7	♎		
8	♎	9:18 am	♏
9	♏		
10	♏	12:13 pm	♐
11	♐		
12	♐	4:30 pm	♑
13	♑		
14	♑	11:19 pm	♒
15	♒		
16	♒		
17	♒	9:17 am	♓
18	♓		
19	♓	9:39 pm	♈
20	♈		
21	♈		
22	♈	10:07 am	♉
23	♉		
24	♉	8:14 pm	♊
25	♊		
26	♊		
27	♊	2:58 am	♋
28	♋		
29	♋	6:57 am	♌
30	♌		
31	♌	9:33 am	♍

1967

Your Starway to Love

♈ = Aries ♉ = Taurus ♊ = Gemini ♋ = Cancer ♌ = Leo ♍ = Virgo

January

1	♍		
2	♍	12:04 pm	♎
3	♎		
4	♎	3:16 pm	♏
5	♏		
6	♏	7:28 pm	♐
7	♐		
8	♐		
9	♐	12:53 am	♑
10	♑		
11	♑	8:05 am	♒
12	♒		
13	♒	5:45 pm	♓
14	♓		
15	♓		
16	♓	5:48 am	♈
17	♈		
18	♈	6:39 pm	♉
19	♉		
20	♉		
21	♉	5:38 am	♊
22	♊		
23	♊	12:51 pm	♋
24	♋		
25	♋	4:20 pm	♌
26	♌		
27	♌	5:36 pm	♍
28	♍		
29	♍	6:33 pm	♎
30	♎		
31	♎	8:44 pm	♏

February

1	♏		
2	♏		
3	♏	12:55 am	♐
4	♐		
5	♐	7:10 am	♑
6	♑		
7	♑	3:17 pm	♒
8	♒		
9	♒		
10	♒	1:19 am	♓
11	♓		
12	♓	1:17 pm	♈
13	♈		
14	♈		
15	♈	2:19 am	♉
16	♉		
17	♉	2:15 pm	♊
18	♊		
19	♊	10:48 pm	♋
20	♋		
21	♋		
22	♋	3:04 am	♌
23	♌		
24	♌	4:04 am	♍
25	♍		
26	♍	3:44 am	♎
27	♎		
28	♎	4:09 am	♏

March

1	♏		
2	♏	6:53 am	♐
3	♐		
4	♐	12:35 pm	♑
5	♑		
6	♑	9:03 pm	♒
7	♒		
8	♒		
9	♒	7:41 am	♓
10	♓		
11	♓	7:53 pm	♈
12	♈		
13	♈		
14	♈	8:54 am	♉
15	♉		
16	♉	9:19 pm	♊
17	♊		
18	♊		
19	♊	7:10 am	♋
20	♋		
21	♋	1:04 pm	♌
22	♌		
23	♌	3:08 pm	♍
24	♍		
25	♍	2:50 pm	♎
26	♎		
27	♎	2:10 pm	♏
28	♏		
29	♏	3:08 pm	♐
30	♐		
31	♐	7:11 pm	♑

April

1	♑		
2	♑		
3	♑	2:49 am	♒
4	♒		
5	♒	1:29 pm	♓
6	♓		
7	♓		
8	♓	1:57 am	♈
9	♈		
10	♈	2:56 pm	♉
11	♉		
12	♉		
13	♉	3:15 am	♊
14	♊		
15	♊	1:37 pm	♋
16	♋		
17	♋	8:54 pm	♌
18	♌		
19	♌		
20	♌	12:43 am	♍
21	♍		
22	♍	1:41 am	♎
23	♎		
24	♎	1:19 am	♏
25	♏		
26	♏	1:27 am	♐
27	♐		
28	♐	3:54 am	♑
29	♑		
30	♑	9:57 am	♒

May

1	♒		
2	♒	7:47 pm	♓
3	♓		
4	♓		
5	♓	8:10 am	♈
6	♈		
7	♈	9:09 pm	♉
8	♉		
9	♉		
10	♉	9:08 am	♊
11	♊		
12	♊	7:11 pm	♋
13	♋		
14	♋		
15	♋	2:49 am	♌
16	♌		
17	♌	7:52 am	♍
18	♍		
19	♍	10:31 am	♎
20	♎		
21	♎	11:30 am	♏
22	♏		
23	♏	12:06 pm	♐
24	♐		
25	♐	1:58 pm	♑
26	♑		
27	♑	6:44 pm	♒
28	♒		
29	♒		
30	♒	3:18 am	♓
31	♓		

June

1	♓	3:07 pm	♈
2	♈		
3	♈		
4	♈	4:04 am	♉
5	♉		
6	♉	3:52 pm	♊
7	♊		
8	♊		
9	♊	1:18 am	♋
10	♋		
11	♋	8:19 am	♌
12	♌		
13	♌	1:24 pm	♍
14	♍		
15	♍	4:58 pm	♎
16	♎		
17	♎	7:25 pm	♏
18	♏		
19	♏	9:20 pm	♐
20	♐		
21	♐	11:46 pm	♑
22	♑		
23	♑		
24	♑	4:11 am	♒
25	♒		
26	♒	11:49 am	♓
27	♓		
28	♓	10:53 pm	♈
29	♈		
30	♈		

July

1	♈	11:43 am	♉
2	♉		
3	♉	11:39 pm	♊
4	♊		
5	♊		
6	♊	8:47 am	♋
7	♋		
8	♋	2:58 pm	♌
9	♌		
10	♌	7:07 pm	♍
11	♍		
12	♍	10:20 pm	♎
13	♎		
14	♎		
15	♎	1:17 am	♏
16	♏		
17	♏	4:22 am	♐
18	♐		
19	♐	7:59 am	♑
20	♑		
21	♑	12:59 pm	♒
22	♒		
23	♒	8:28 pm	♓
24	♓		
25	♓		
26	♓	7:00 am	♈
27	♈		
28	♈	7:40 pm	♉
29	♉		
30	♉		
31	♉	8:00 am	♊

August

1	♊		
2	♊	5:32 pm	♋
3	♋		
4	♋	11:26 pm	♌
5	♌		
6	♌		
7	♌	2:36 am	♍
8	♍		
9	♍	4:34 am	♎
10	♎		
11	♎	6:44 am	♏
12	♏		
13	♏	9:52 am	♐
14	♐		
15	♐	2:18 pm	♑
16	♑		
17	♑	8:17 pm	♒
18	♒		
19	♒		
20	♒	4:18 am	♓
21	♓		
22	♓	2:47 pm	♈
23	♈		
24	♈		
25	♈	3:21 am	♉
26	♉		
27	♉	4:08 pm	♊
28	♊		
29	♊		
30	♊	2:34 am	♋
31	♋		

September

1	♋	9:08 am	♌
2	♌		
3	♌	12:07 pm	♍
4	♍		
5	♍	1:03 pm	♎
6	♎		
7	♎	1:44 pm	♏
8	♏		
9	♏	3:40 pm	♐
10	♐		
11	♐	7:43 pm	♑
12	♑		
13	♑		
14	♑	2:08 am	♒
15	♒		
16	♒	10:53 am	♓
17	♓		
18	♓	9:46 pm	♈
19	♈		
20	♈		
21	♈	10:20 am	♉
22	♉		
23	♉	11:21 pm	♊
24	♊		
25	♊		
26	♊	10:45 am	♋
27	♋		
28	♋	6:41 pm	♌
29	♌		
30	♌	10:38 pm	♍

October

1	♍		
2	♍	11:34 pm	♎
3	♎		
4	♎	11:14 pm	♏
5	♏		
6	♏	11:32 pm	♐
7	♐		
8	♐		
9	♐	2:04 am	♑
10	♑		
11	♑	7:45 am	♒
12	♒		
13	♒	4:38 pm	♓
14	♓		
15	♓		
16	♓	3:58 am	♈
17	♈		
18	♈	4:41 pm	♉
19	♉		
20	♉		
21	♉	5:38 am	♊
22	♊		
23	♊	5:27 pm	♋
24	♋		
25	♋		
26	♋	2:40 am	♌
27	♌		
28	♌	8:19 am	♍
29	♍		
30	♍	10:31 am	♎
31	♎		

November

1	♎	10:26 am	♏
2	♏		
3	♏	9:51 am	♐
4	♐		
5	♐	10:44 am	♑
6	♑		
7	♑	2:45 pm	♒
8	♒		
9	♒	10:42 pm	♓
10	♓		
11	♓		
12	♓	9:58 am	♈
13	♈		
14	♈	10:52 pm	♉
15	♉		
16	♉		
17	♉	11:40 am	♊
18	♊		
19	♊	11:13 pm	♋
20	♋		
21	♋		
22	♋	8:47 am	♌
23	♌		
24	♌	3:46 pm	♍
25	♍		
26	♍	7:48 pm	♎
27	♎		
28	♎	9:13 pm	♏
29	♏		
30	♏	9:10 pm	♐

December

1	♐		
2	♐	9:25 pm	♑
3	♑		
4	♑	11:57 pm	♒
5	♒		
6	♒		
7	♒	6:19 am	♓
8	♓		
9	♓	4:43 pm	♈
10	♈		
11	♈		
12	♈	5:32 am	♉
13	♉		
14	♉	6:18 pm	♊
15	♊		
16	♊		
17	♊	5:23 am	♋
18	♋		
19	♋	2:21 pm	♌
20	♌		
21	♌	9:21 pm	♍
22	♍		
23	♍		
24	♍	2:27 am	♎
25	♎		
26	♎	5:36 am	♏
27	♏		
28	♏	7:09 am	♐
29	♐		
30	♐	8:11 am	♑
31	♑		

Moon Movements

♎ = Libra ♏ = Scorpio ♐ = Sagittarius ♑ = Capricorn ♒ = Aquarius ♓ = Pisces

1968

January

Day	Sign	Time	Enters
1	♑	10:24 am	♒
2	♒		
3	♒	3:35 pm	♓
4	♓		
5	♓		
6	♓	12:45 am	♈
7	♈		
8	♈	1:02 pm	♉
9	♉		
10	♉		
11	♉	1:54 am	♊
12	♊		
13	♊	12:54 pm	♋
14	♋		
15	♋	9:09 pm	♌
16	♌		
17	♌		
18	♌	3:11 am	♍
19	♍		
20	♍	7:47 am	♎
21	♎		
22	♎	11:28 am	♏
23	♏		
24	♏	2:23 pm	♐
25	♐		
26	♐	4:57 pm	♑
27	♑		
28	♑	8:06 pm	♒
29	♒		
30	♒		
31	♒	1:16 am	♓

April

Day	Sign	Time	Enters
1	♉		
2	♉	1:40 am	♊
3	♊		
4	♊	2:13 pm	♋
5	♋		
6	♋		
7	♋	12:28 am	♌
8	♌		
9	♌	7:04 am	♍
10	♍		
11	♍	10:01 am	♎
12	♎		
13	♎	10:32 am	♏
14	♏		
15	♏	10:23 am	♐
16	♐		
17	♐	11:23 am	♑
18	♑		
19	♑	2:57 pm	♒
20	♒		
21	♒	9:46 pm	♓
22	♓		
23	♓		
24	♓	7:32 am	♈
25	♈		
26	♈	7:22 pm	♉
27	♉		
28	♉		
29	♉	8:11 am	♊
30	♊		

July

Day	Sign	Time	Enters
1	♍		
2	♍	11:10 am	♎
3	♎		
4	♎	3:20 pm	♏
5	♏		
6	♏	5:04 pm	♐
7	♐		
8	♐	5:24 pm	♑
9	♑		
10	♑	6:03 pm	♒
11	♒		
12	♒	9:03 pm	♓
13	♓		
14	♓		
15	♓	3:51 am	♈
16	♈		
17	♈	2:30 pm	♉
18	♉		
19	♉		
20	♉	3:13 am	♊
21	♊		
22	♊	3:31 pm	♋
23	♋		
24	♋		
25	♋	1:55 am	♌
26	♌		
27	♌	10:10 am	♍
28	♍		
29	♍	4:32 pm	♎
30	♎		
31	♎	9:11 pm	♏

October

Day	Sign	Time	Enters
1	♒		
2	♒	10:21 pm	♓
3	♓		
4	♓		
5	♓	5:35 am	♈
6	♈		
7	♈	3:07 pm	♉
8	♉		
9	♉		
10	♉	2:43 am	♊
11	♊		
12	♊	3:23 pm	♋
13	♋		
14	♋		
15	♋	3:08 am	♌
16	♌		
17	♌	11:58 am	♍
18	♍		
19	♍	5:05 pm	♎
20	♎		
21	♎	7:05 pm	♏
22	♏		
23	♏	7:32 pm	♐
24	♐		
25	♐	8:13 pm	♑
26	♑		
27	♑	10:43 pm	♒
28	♒		
29	♒		
30	♒	3:54 am	♓
31	♓		

February

Day	Sign	Time	Enters
1	♓		
2	♓	9:39 am	♈
3	♈		
4	♈	9:15 pm	♉
5	♉		
6	♉		
7	♉	10:09 am	♊
8	♊		
9	♊	9:34 pm	♋
10	♋		
11	♋		
12	♋	5:50 am	♌
13	♌		
14	♌	11:02 am	♍
15	♍		
16	♍	2:21 pm	♎
17	♎		
18	♎	5:00 pm	♏
19	♏		
20	♏	7:48 pm	♐
21	♐		
22	♐	11:12 pm	♑
23	♑		
24	♑		
25	♑	3:37 am	♒
26	♒		
27	♒	9:42 am	♓
28	♓		
29	♓	6:14 pm	♈

May

Day	Sign	Time	Enters
1	♊	8:50 pm	♋
2	♋		
3	♋		
4	♋	7:54 am	♌
5	♌		
6	♌	3:58 pm	♍
7	♍		
8	♍	8:21 pm	♎
9	♎		
10	♎	9:30 pm	♏
11	♏		
12	♏	8:53 pm	♐
13	♐		
14	♐	8:31 pm	♑
15	♑		
16	♑	10:22 pm	♒
17	♒		
18	♒		
19	♒	3:53 am	♓
20	♓		
21	♓	1:14 pm	♈
22	♈		
23	♈		
24	♈	1:15 am	♉
25	♉		
26	♉	2:12 pm	♊
27	♊		
28	♊		
29	♊	2:43 am	♋
30	♋		
31	♋	1:53 pm	♌

August

Day	Sign	Time	Enters
1	♏		
2	♏		
3	♏	12:11 am	♐
4	♐		
5	♐	1:57 am	♑
6	♑		
7	♑	3:37 am	♒
8	♒		
9	♒	6:45 am	♓
10	♓		
11	♓	12:53 pm	♈
12	♈		
13	♈	10:36 pm	♉
14	♉		
15	♉		
16	♉	10:51 am	♊
17	♊		
18	♊	11:15 pm	♋
19	♋		
20	♋		
21	♋	9:40 am	♌
22	♌		
23	♌	5:21 pm	♍
24	♍		
25	♍	10:45 pm	♎
26	♎		
27	♎		
28	♎	2:38 am	♏
29	♏		
30	♏	5:40 am	♐
31	♐		

November

Day	Sign	Time	Enters
1	♓	11:51 am	♈
2	♈		
3	♈	10:01 pm	♉
4	♉		
5	♉		
6	♉	9:48 am	♊
7	♊		
8	♊	10:26 pm	♋
9	♋		
10	♋		
11	♋	10:45 am	♌
12	♌		
13	♌	8:55 pm	♍
14	♍		
15	♍		
16	♍	3:26 am	♎
17	♎		
18	♎	6:06 am	♏
19	♏		
20	♏	6:04 am	♐
21	♐		
22	♐	5:20 am	♑
23	♑		
24	♑	6:02 am	♒
25	♒		
26	♒	9:52 am	♓
27	♓		
28	♓	5:26 pm	♈
29	♈		
30	♈		

March

Day	Sign	Time	Enters
1	♈		
2	♈		
3	♈	5:27 am	♉
4	♉		
5	♉	6:17 pm	♊
6	♊		
7	♊		
8	♊	6:21 am	♋
9	♋		
10	♋	3:27 pm	♌
11	♌		
12	♌	8:51 pm	♍
13	♍		
14	♍	11:23 pm	♎
15	♎		
16	♎		
17	♎	12:33 am	♏
18	♏		
19	♏	1:54 am	♐
20	♐		
21	♐	4:34 am	♑
22	♑		
23	♑	9:16 am	♒
24	♒		
25	♒	4:15 pm	♓
26	♓		
27	♓		
28	♓	1:32 am	♈
29	♈		
30	♈	12:55 pm	♉
31	♉		

June

Day	Sign	Time	Enters
1	♌		
2	♌	10:52 pm	♍
3	♍		
4	♍		
5	♍	4:49 am	♎
6	♎		
7	♎	7:30 am	♏
8	♏		
9	♏	7:42 am	♐
10	♐		
11	♐	7:05 am	♑
12	♑		
13	♑	7:46 am	♒
14	♒		
15	♒	11:42 am	♓
16	♓		
17	♓	7:50 pm	♈
18	♈		
19	♈		
20	♈	7:25 am	♉
21	♉		
22	♉	8:22 pm	♊
23	♊		
24	♊		
25	♊	8:43 am	♋
26	♋		
27	♋	7:30 pm	♌
28	♌		
29	♌		
30	♌	4:26 am	♍

September

Day	Sign	Time	Enters
1	♐	8:22 am	♑
2	♑		
3	♑	11:19 am	♒
4	♒		
5	♒	3:27 pm	♓
6	♓		
7	♓	9:49 pm	♈
8	♈		
9	♈		
10	♈	7:06 am	♉
11	♉		
12	♉	6:54 pm	♊
13	♊		
14	♊		
15	♊	7:28 am	♋
16	♋		
17	♋	6:25 pm	♌
18	♌		
19	♌		
20	♌	2:15 am	♍
21	♍		
22	♍	7:00 am	♎
23	♎		
24	♎	9:39 am	♏
25	♏		
26	♏	11:30 am	♐
27	♐		
28	♐	1:44 pm	♑
29	♑		
30	♑	5:11 pm	♒

December

Day	Sign	Time	Enters
1	♈	3:58 am	♉
2	♉		
3	♉	4:06 pm	♊
4	♊		
5	♊		
6	♊	4:43 am	♋
7	♋		
8	♋	5:02 pm	♌
9	♌		
10	♌		
11	♌	3:59 am	♍
12	♍		
13	♍	12:08 pm	♎
14	♎		
15	♎	4:31 pm	♏
16	♏		
17	♏	5:27 pm	♐
18	♐		
19	♐	4:32 pm	♑
20	♑		
21	♑	3:59 pm	♒
22	♒		
23	♒	6:01 pm	♓
24	♓		
25	♓		
26	♓	12:02 am	♈
27	♈		
28	♈	9:57 am	♉
29	♉		
30	♉	10:11 pm	♊
31	♊		

Your Starway to Love

♈ = Aries ♉ = Taurus ♊ = Gemini ♋ = Cancer ♌ = Leo ♍ = Virgo

1969

January			
1	♊		
2	♊	10:53 am	♋
3	♋		
4	♋	10:55 pm	♌
5	♌		
6	♌		
7	♌	9:42 am	♍
8	♍		
9	♍	6:32 pm	♎
10	♎		
11	♎		
12	♎	12:32 am	♏
13	♏		
14	♏	3:19 am	♐
15	♐		
16	♐	3:39 pm	♑
17	♑		
18	♑	3:17 am	♒
19	♒		
20	♒	4:20 am	♓
21	♓		
22	♓	8:43 am	♈
23	♈		
24	♈	5:13 pm	♉
25	♉		
26	♉		
27	♉	4:53 am	♊
28	♊		
29	♊	5:36 pm	♋
30	♋		
31	♋		

April			
1	♍	3:03 pm	♎
2	♎		
3	♎	7:22 pm	♏
4	♏		
5	♏	9:57 pm	♐
6	♐		
7	♐		
8	♐	12:04 am	♑
9	♑		
10	♑	2:46 am	♒
11	♒		
12	♒	6:41 am	♓
13	♓		
14	♓	12:13 pm	♈
15	♈		
16	♈	7:43 pm	♉
17	♉		
18	♉		
19	♉	5:28 am	♊
20	♊		
21	♊	5:17 pm	♋
22	♋		
23	♋		
24	♋	5:51 am	♌
25	♌		
26	♌	4:57 pm	♍
27	♍		
28	♍		
29	♍	12:44 am	♎
30	♎		

July			
1	♑	1:49 am	♒
2	♒		
3	♒	2:26 am	♓
4	♓		
5	♓	6:16 am	♈
6	♈		
7	♈	1:53 pm	♉
8	♉		
9	♉		
10	♉	12:31 am	♊
11	♊		
12	♊	12:47 pm	♋
13	♋		
14	♋		
15	♋	1:29 am	♌
16	♌		
17	♌	1:42 pm	♍
18	♍		
19	♍		
20	♍	12:20 am	♎
21	♎		
22	♎	8:04 am	♏
23	♏		
24	♏	12:10 pm	♐
25	♐		
26	♐	1:09 pm	♑
27	♑		
28	♑	12:35 pm	♒
29	♒		
30	♒	12:30 pm	♓
31	♓		

October			
1	♊		
2	♊	9:52 am	♋
3	♋		
4	♋	10:25 pm	♌
5	♌		
6	♌		
7	♌	10:21 am	♍
8	♍		
9	♍	7:48 pm	♎
10	♎		
11	♎		
12	♎	2:19 am	♏
13	♏		
14	♏	6:33 am	♐
15	♐		
16	♐	9:35 am	♑
17	♑		
18	♑	12:21 pm	♒
19	♒		
20	♒	3:26 pm	♓
21	♓		
22	♓	7:17 pm	♈
23	♈		
24	♈		
25	♈	12:32 am	♉
26	♉		
27	♉	8:00 am	♊
28	♊		
29	♊	6:13 pm	♋
30	♋		
31	♋		

February			
1	♋	5:29 am	♌
2	♌		
3	♌	3:40 pm	♍
4	♍		
5	♍		
6	♍	12:00 am	♎
7	♎		
8	♎	6:18 am	♏
9	♏		
10	♏	10:23 am	♐
11	♐		
12	♐	12:28 pm	♑
13	♑		
14	♑	1:30 pm	♒
15	♒		
16	♒	3:03 pm	♓
17	♓		
18	♓	6:49 pm	♈
19	♈		
20	♈		
21	♈	2:02 am	♉
22	♉		
23	♉	12:41 pm	♊
24	♊		
25	♊		
26	♊	1:11 am	♋
27	♋		
28	♋	1:12 pm	♌

May			
1	♎	4:49 am	♏
2	♏		
3	♏	6:19 am	♐
4	♐		
5	♐	6:57 am	♑
6	♑		
7	♑	8:28 am	♒
8	♒		
9	♒	12:04 pm	♓
10	♓		
11	♓	6:09 pm	♈
12	♈		
13	♈		
14	♈	2:28 am	♉
15	♉		
16	♉	12:41 pm	♊
17	♊		
18	♊		
19	♊	12:30 am	♋
20	♋		
21	♋	1:12 pm	♌
22	♌		
23	♌		
24	♌	1:07 am	♍
25	♍		
26	♍	10:07 am	♎
27	♎		
28	♎	3:05 pm	♏
29	♏		
30	♏	4:30 pm	♐
31	♐		

August			
1	♓	2:55 pm	♈
2	♈		
3	♈	9:02 pm	♉
4	♉		
5	♉		
6	♉	6:49 am	♊
7	♊		
8	♊	6:57 pm	♋
9	♋		
10	♋		
11	♋	7:38 am	♌
12	♌		
13	♌	7:32 pm	♍
14	♍		
15	♍		
16	♍	5:51 am	♎
17	♎		
18	♎	1:54 pm	♏
19	♏		
20	♏	7:12 pm	♐
21	♐		
22	♐	9:49 pm	♑
23	♑		
24	♑	10:36 pm	♒
25	♒		
26	♒	11:03 pm	♓
27	♓		
28	♓		
29	♓	12:57 am	♈
30	♈		
31	♈	5:50 am	♉

November			
1	♋	6:35 am	♌
2	♌		
3	♌	7:00 pm	♍
4	♍		
5	♍		
6	♍	4:59 am	♎
7	♎		
8	♎	11:18 am	♏
9	♏		
10	♏	2:30 pm	♐
11	♐		
12	♐	4:08 pm	♑
13	♑		
14	♑	5:53 pm	♒
15	♒		
16	♒	8:52 pm	♓
17	♓		
18	♓		
19	♓	1:32 am	♈
20	♈		
21	♈	7:52 am	♉
22	♉		
23	♉	3:59 pm	♊
24	♊		
25	♊		
26	♊	2:10 am	♋
27	♋		
28	♋	2:22 pm	♌
29	♌		
30	♌		

March			
1	♌		
2	♌	11:07 pm	♍
3	♍		
4	♍		
5	♍	6:34 am	♎
6	♎		
7	♎	11:56 am	♏
8	♏		
9	♏	3:48 pm	♐
10	♐		
11	♐	6:40 pm	♑
12	♑		
13	♑	9:09 pm	♒
14	♒		
15	♒		
16	♒	12:04 am	♓
17	♓		
18	♓	4:27 am	♈
19	♈		
20	♈	11:20 am	♉
21	♉		
22	♉	9:12 pm	♊
23	♊		
24	♊		
25	♊	9:18 am	♋
26	♋		
27	♋	9:37 pm	♌
28	♌		
29	♌		
30	♌	7:54 am	♍
31	♍		

June			
1	♐	4:07 pm	♑
2	♑		
3	♑	4:04 pm	♒
4	♒		
5	♒	6:13 pm	♓
6	♓		
7	♓	11:36 pm	♈
8	♈		
9	♈		
10	♈	8:06 am	♉
11	♉		
12	♉	6:48 pm	♊
13	♊		
14	♊		
15	♊	6:52 am	♋
16	♋		
17	♋	7:35 pm	♌
18	♌		
19	♌		
20	♌	7:53 am	♍
21	♍		
22	♍	6:03 pm	♎
23	♎		
24	♎		
25	♎	12:31 am	♏
26	♏		
27	♏	3:00 am	♐
28	♐		
29	♐	2:44 am	♑
30	♑		

September			
1	♉		
2	♉	2:23 pm	♊
3	♊		
4	♊		
5	♊	1:57 am	♋
6	♋		
7	♋	2:36 pm	♌
8	♌		
9	♌		
10	♌	2:20 am	♍
11	♍		
12	♍	12:01 pm	♎
13	♎		
14	♎	7:25 pm	♏
15	♏		
16	♏		
17	♏	12:42 am	♐
18	♐		
19	♐	4:14 am	♑
20	♑		
21	♑	6:31 am	♒
22	♒		
23	♒	8:22 am	♓
24	♓		
25	♓	10:55 am	♈
26	♈		
27	♈	3:29 pm	♉
28	♉		
29	♉	11:05 pm	♊
30	♊		

December			
1	♌	3:14 am	♍
2	♍		
3	♍	2:17 pm	♎
4	♎		
5	♎	9:30 pm	♏
6	♏		
7	♏		
8	♏	12:43 am	♐
9	♐		
10	♐	1:20 am	♑
11	♑		
12	♑	1:27 am	♒
13	♒		
14	♒	2:56 am	♓
15	♓		
16	♓	6:56 am	♈
17	♈		
18	♈	1:35 pm	♉
19	♉		
20	♉	10:28 pm	♊
21	♊		
22	♊		
23	♊	9:09 am	♋
24	♋		
25	♋	9:21 pm	♌
26	♌		
27	♌		
28	♌	10:20 am	♍
29	♍		
30	♍	10:18 pm	♎
31	♎		

Moon Movements

♎ = Libra ♏ = Scorpio ♐ = Sagittarius ♑ = Capricorn ♒ = Aquarius ♓ = Pisces

January

1	♎		
2	♎	7:03 am	♏
3	♏		
4	♏	11:33 am	♐
5	♐		
6	♐	12:30 pm	♑
7	♑		
8	♑	11:47 am	♒
9	♒		
10	♒	11:37 am	♓
11	♓		
12	♓	1:48 pm	♈
13	♈		
14	♈	7:20 pm	♉
15	♉		
16	♉		
17	♉	4:07 am	♊
18	♊		
19	♊	3:13 pm	♋
20	♋		
21	♋		
22	♋	3:40 am	♌
23	♌		
24	♌	4:33 pm	♍
25	♍		
26	♍		
27	♍	4:42 am	♎
28	♎		
29	♎	2:34 pm	♏
30	♏		
31	♏	8:50 pm	♐

February

1	♐		
2	♐	11:22 pm	♑
3	♑		
4	♑	11:19 pm	♒
5	♒		
6	♒	10:37 pm	♓
7	♓		
8	♓	11:17 pm	♈
9	♈		
10	♈		
11	♈	2:59 am	♉
12	♉		
13	♉	10:29 am	♊
14	♊		
15	♊	9:17 pm	♋
16	♋		
17	♋		
18	♋	9:53 am	♌
19	♌		
20	♌	10:42 pm	♍
21	♍		
22	♍		
23	♍	10:30 am	♎
24	♎		
25	♎	8:23 pm	♏
26	♏		
27	♏		
28	♏	3:38 am	♐

March

1	♐		
2	♐	7:54 am	♑
3	♑		
4	♑	9:34 am	♒
5	♒		
6	♒	9:49 am	♓
7	♓		
8	♓	10:16 am	♈
9	♈		
10	♈	12:43 pm	♉
11	♉		
12	♉	6:37 pm	♊
13	♊		
14	♊		
15	♊	4:18 am	♋
16	♋		
17	♋	4:39 pm	♌
18	♌		
19	♌		
20	♌	5:30 am	♍
21	♍		
22	♍	4:56 pm	♎
23	♎		
24	♎		
25	♎	2:10 am	♏
26	♏		
27	♏	9:07 am	♐
28	♐		
29	♐	2:00 pm	♑
30	♑		
31	♑	5:08 pm	♒

April

1	♒		
2	♒	7:01 pm	♓
3	♓		
4	♓	8:32 pm	♈
5	♈		
6	♈	11:02 pm	♉
7	♉		
8	♉		
9	♉	4:02 am	♊
10	♊		
11	♊	12:33 pm	♋
12	♋		
13	♋		
14	♋	12:16 pm	♌
15	♌		
16	♌	1:07 pm	♍
17	♍		
18	♍		
19	♍	12:35 am	♎
20	♎		
21	♎	9:15 am	♏
22	♏		
23	♏	3:15 pm	♐
24	♐		
25	♐	7:26 pm	♑
26	♑		
27	♑	10:43 pm	♒
28	♒		
29	♒		
30	♒	1:37 am	♓

May

1	♓		
2	♓	4:32 am	♈
3	♈		
4	♈	8:05 am	♉
5	♉		
6	♉	1:17 pm	♊
7	♊		
8	♊	9:17 pm	♋
9	♋		
10	♋		
11	♋	8:22 am	♌
12	♌		
13	♌	9:10 pm	♍
14	♍		
15	♍		
16	♍	9:02 am	♎
17	♎		
18	♎	5:49 pm	♏
19	♏		
20	♏	11:11 pm	♐
21	♐		
22	♐		
23	♐	2:13 am	♑
24	♑		
25	♑	4:25 am	♒
26	♒		
27	♒	6:59 am	♓
28	♓		
29	♓	10:27 am	♈
30	♈		
31	♈	3:03 pm	♉

June

1	♉		
2	♉	9:10 pm	♊
3	♊		
4	♊		
5	♊	5:25 am	♋
6	♋		
7	♋	4:17 pm	♌
8	♌		
9	♌		
10	♌	5:02 am	♍
11	♍		
12	♍	5:28 pm	♎
13	♎		
14	♎		
15	♎	3:01 am	♏
16	♏		
17	♏	8:39 am	♐
18	♐		
19	♐	11:04 am	♑
20	♑		
21	♑	12:00 pm	♒
22	♒		
23	♒	1:12 pm	♓
24	♓		
25	♓	3:52 pm	♈
26	♈		
27	♈	8:35 pm	♉
28	♉		
29	♉		
30	♉	3:24 am	♊

July

1	♊		
2	♊	12:21 pm	♋
3	♋		
4	♋	11:26 pm	♌
5	♌		
6	♌		
7	♌	12:11 pm	♍
8	♍		
9	♍		
10	♍	1:02 am	♎
11	♎		
12	♎	11:41 am	♏
13	♏		
14	♏	6:26 pm	♐
15	♐		
16	♐	9:19 pm	♑
17	♑		
18	♑	9:44 pm	♒
19	♒		
20	♒	9:36 pm	♓
21	♓		
22	♓	10:42 pm	♈
23	♈		
24	♈		
25	♈	2:18 am	♉
26	♉		
27	♉	8:53 am	♊
28	♊		
29	♊	6:14 pm	♋
30	♋		
31	♋		

August

1	♋	5:44 am	♌
2	♌		
3	♌	6:34 pm	♍
4	♍		
5	♍		
6	♍	7:33 am	♎
7	♎		
8	♎	6:57 pm	♏
9	♏		
10	♏		
11	♏	3:07 am	♐
12	♐		
13	♐	7:25 am	♑
14	♑		
15	♑	8:31 am	♒
16	♒		
17	♒	8:01 am	♓
18	♓		
19	♓	7:50 am	♈
20	♈		
21	♈	9:46 am	♉
22	♉		
23	♉	3:03 pm	♊
24	♊		
25	♊	11:58 pm	♋
26	♋		
27	♋		
28	♋	11:38 am	♌
29	♌		
30	♌		
31	♌	12:36 pm	♍

September

1	♍		
2	♍	1:25 pm	♎
3	♎		
4	♎		
5	♎	12:54 am	♏
6	♏		
7	♏	9:58 am	♐
8	♐		
9	♐	3:51 pm	♑
10	♑		
11	♑	6:33 pm	♒
12	♒		
13	♒	6:57 pm	♓
14	♓		
15	♓	6:35 pm	♈
16	♈		
17	♈	7:21 pm	♉
18	♉		
19	♉	11:02 pm	♊
20	♊		
21	♊		
22	♊	6:41 am	♋
23	♋		
24	♋	5:54 pm	♌
25	♌		
26	♌		
27	♌	6:53 am	♍
28	♍		
29	♍	7:33 pm	♎
30	♎		

October

1	♎		
2	♎	6:35 am	♏
3	♏		
4	♏	3:31 pm	♐
5	♐		
6	♐	10:10 pm	♑
7	♑		
8	♑		
9	♑	2:26 am	♒
10	♒		
11	♒	4:30 am	♓
12	♓		
13	♓	5:12 am	♈
14	♈		
15	♈	6:00 am	♉
16	♉		
17	♉	8:43 am	♊
18	♊		
19	♊	2:59 pm	♋
20	♋		
21	♋		
22	♋	1:12 am	♌
23	♌		
24	♌	1:57 pm	♍
25	♍		
26	♍		
27	♍	2:37 am	♎
28	♎		
29	♎	1:15 pm	♏
30	♏		
31	♏	9:24 pm	♐

November

1	♐		
2	♐		
3	♐	3:32 am	♑
4	♑		
5	♑	8:11 am	♒
6	♒		
7	♒	11:33 am	♓
8	♓		
9	♓	1:52 pm	♈
10	♈		
11	♈	3:50 pm	♉
12	♉		
13	♉	6:48 pm	♊
14	♊		
15	♊		
16	♊	12:23 am	♋
17	♋		
18	♋	9:36 am	♌
19	♌		
20	♌	9:50 pm	♍
21	♍		
22	♍		
23	♍	10:39 am	♎
24	♎		
25	♎	9:25 pm	♏
26	♏		
27	♏		
28	♏	5:02 am	♐
29	♐		
30	♐	10:06 am	♑

December

1	♑		
2	♑	1:45 pm	♒
3	♒		
4	♒	4:55 pm	♓
5	♓		
6	♓	8:03 pm	♈
7	♈		
8	♈	11:24 pm	♉
9	♉		
10	♉		
11	♉	3:33 am	♊
12	♊		
13	♊	9:32 am	♋
14	♋		
15	♋	6:21 pm	♌
16	♌		
17	♌		
18	♌	6:04 am	♍
19	♍		
20	♍	7:01 pm	♎
21	♎		
22	♎		
23	♎	6:27 am	♏
24	♏		
25	♏	2:27 pm	♐
26	♐		
27	♐	7:01 pm	♑
28	♑		
29	♑	9:24 pm	♒
30	♒		
31	♒	11:08 pm	♓

Your Starway to Love

♈ = Aries ♉ = Taurus ♊ = Gemini ♋ = Cancer ♌ = Leo ♍ = Virgo

1971

January

1	♓		
2	♓		
3	♓	1:26 am	♈
4	♈		
5	♈	5:00 am	♉
6	♉		
7	♉	10:08 am	♊
8	♊		
9	♊	5:09 pm	♋
10	♋		
11	♋		
12	♋	2:24 am	♌
13	♌		
14	♌	1:57 pm	♍
15	♍		
16	♍		
17	♍	2:53 am	♎
18	♎		
19	♎	3:04 pm	♏
20	♏		
21	♏		
22	♏	12:16 am	♐
23	♐		
24	♐	5:32 am	♑
25	♑		
26	♑	7:36 am	♒
27	♒		
28	♒	8:02 am	♓
29	♓		
30	♓	8:36 am	♈
31	♈		

April

1	♊	11:51 am	♋
2	♋		
3	♋	9:05 pm	♌
4	♌		
5	♌		
6	♌	9:16 am	♍
7	♍		
8	♍	10:17 pm	♎
9	♎		
10	♎		
11	♎	10:28 am	♏
12	♏		
13	♏	9:03 pm	♐
14	♐		
15	♐		
16	♐	5:38 am	♑
17	♑		
18	♑	11:46 am	♒
19	♒		
20	♒	3:07 pm	♓
21	♓		
22	♓	4:08 pm	♈
23	♈		
24	♈	4:06 pm	♉
25	♉		
26	♉	4:58 pm	♊
27	♊		
28	♊	8:43 pm	♋
29	♋		
30	♋		

July

1	♎		
2	♎	8:46 am	♏
3	♏		
4	♏	6:59 pm	♐
5	♐		
6	♐		
7	♐	2:03 am	♑
8	♑		
9	♑	6:26 am	♒
10	♒		
11	♒	9:14 am	♓
12	♓		
13	♓	11:32 am	♈
14	♈		
15	♈	2:10 pm	♉
16	♉		
17	♉	5:47 pm	♊
18	♊		
19	♊	10:56 pm	♋
20	♋		
21	♋		
22	♋	6:16 am	♌
23	♌		
24	♌	4:09 pm	♍
25	♍		
26	♍		
27	♍	4:12 am	♎
28	♎		
29	♎	4:50 pm	♏
30	♏		
31	♏		

October

1	♒	2:36 pm	♓
2	♓		
3	♓	2:40 pm	♈
4	♈		
5	♈	1:42 pm	♉
6	♉		
7	♉	1:53 pm	♊
8	♊		
9	♊	5:11 pm	♋
10	♋		
11	♋		
12	♋	12:30 am	♌
13	♌		
14	♌	11:16 am	♍
15	♍		
16	♍	11:47 pm	♎
17	♎		
18	♎		
19	♎	12:31 pm	♏
20	♏		
21	♏		
22	♏	12:31 am	♐
23	♐		
24	♐	11:05 am	♑
25	♑		
26	♑	7:11 pm	♒
27	♒		
28	♒	11:57 pm	♓
29	♓		
30	♓		
31	♓	1:26 am	♈

February

1	♈	10:49 am	♉
2	♉		
3	♉	3:34 pm	♊
4	♊		
5	♊	11:07 pm	♋
6	♋		
7	♋		
8	♋	9:06 am	♌
9	♌		
10	♌	8:58 pm	♍
11	♍		
12	♍		
13	♍	9:50 am	♎
14	♎		
15	♎	10:22 pm	♏
16	♏		
17	♏		
18	♏	8:45 am	♐
19	♐		
20	♐	3:37 pm	♑
21	♑		
22	♑	6:43 pm	♒
23	♒		
24	♒	7:05 pm	♓
25	♓		
26	♓	6:30 pm	♈
27	♈		
28	♈	6:54 pm	♉

May

1	♋	4:34 am	♌
2	♌		
3	♌	4:03 pm	♍
4	♍		
5	♍		
6	♍	4:59 am	♎
7	♎		
8	♎	5:03 pm	♏
9	♏		
10	♏		
11	♏	3:08 am	♐
12	♐		
13	♐	11:09 am	♑
14	♑		
15	♑	5:19 pm	♒
16	♒		
17	♒	9:39 pm	♓
18	♓		
19	♓		
20	♓	12:11 am	♈
21	♈		
22	♈	1:31 am	♉
23	♉		
24	♉	3:01 am	♊
25	♊		
26	♊	6:26 am	♋
27	♋		
28	♋	1:16 pm	♌
29	♌		
30	♌	11:48 pm	♍
31	♍		

August

1	♏	3:49 am	♐
2	♐		
3	♐	11:32 am	♑
4	♑		
5	♑	3:46 pm	♒
6	♒		
7	♒	5:34 pm	♓
8	♓		
9	♓	6:27 pm	♈
10	♈		
11	♈	7:55 pm	♉
12	♉		
13	♉	11:10 pm	♊
14	♊		
15	♊		
16	♋	4:50 am	♋
17	♋		
18	♋	12:57 pm	♌
19	♌		
20	♌	11:19 pm	♍
21	♍		
22	♍		
23	♍	11:22 am	♎
24	♎		
25	♎		
26	♏	12:09 am	♏
27	♏		
28	♏	11:56 am	♐
29	♐		
30	♐	8:54 pm	♑
31	♑		

November

1	♈		
2	♈	12:55 am	♉
3	♉		
4	♉	12:27 am	♊
5	♊		
6	♊	2:15 am	♋
7	♋		
8	♋	7:56 am	♌
9	♌		
10	♌	5:44 pm	♍
11	♍		
12	♍		
13	♍	6:05 am	♎
14	♎		
15	♎	6:49 pm	♏
16	♏		
17	♏		
18	♏	6:30 am	♐
19	♐		
20	♐	4:36 pm	♑
21	♑		
22	♑		
23	♑	12:52 am	♒
24	♒		
25	♒	6:48 am	♓
26	♓		
27	♓	10:03 am	♈
28	♈		
29	♈	11:08 am	♉
30	♉		

March

1	♉		
2	♉	10:01 pm	♊
3	♊		
4	♊		
5	♊	4:47 am	♋
6	♋		
7	♋	2:55 pm	♌
8	♌		
9	♌		
10	♌	3:10 am	♍
11	♍		
12	♍	4:06 pm	♎
13	♎		
14	♎		
15	♎	4:31 am	♏
16	♏		
17	♏	3:23 pm	♐
18	♐		
19	♐	11:37 pm	♑
20	♑		
21	♑		
22	♑	4:29 am	♒
23	♒		
24	♒	6:07 am	♓
25	♓		
26	♓	5:45 am	♈
27	♈		
28	♈	5:16 am	♉
29	♉		
30	♉	6:43 am	♊
31	♊		

June

1	♍		
2	♍	12:26 pm	♎
3	♎		
4	♎		
5	♎	12:36 am	♏
6	♏		
7	♏	10:28 am	♐
8	♐		
9	♐	5:45 pm	♑
10	♑		
11	♑	11:03 pm	♒
12	♒		
13	♒		
14	♒	3:01 am	♓
15	♓		
16	♓	6:06 am	♈
17	♈		
18	♈	8:39 am	♉
19	♉		
20	♉	11:24 am	♊
21	♊		
22	♊	3:30 pm	♋
23	♋		
24	♋	10:12 pm	♌
25	♌		
26	♌		
27	♌	8:06 am	♍
28	♍		
29	♍	8:22 pm	♎
30	♎		

September

1	♑		
2	♑	2:04 am	♒
3	♒		
4	♒	3:51 am	♓
5	♓		
6	♓	3:43 am	♈
7	♈		
8	♈	3:37 am	♉
9	♉		
10	♉	5:25 am	♊
11	♊		
12	♊	10:21 am	♋
13	♋		
14	♋	6:38 pm	♌
15	♌		
16	♌		
17	♌	5:29 am	♍
18	♍		
19	♍	5:47 pm	♎
20	♎		
21	♎		
22	♎	6:33 am	♏
23	♏		
24	♏	6:43 pm	♐
25	♐		
26	♐		
27	♐	4:53 am	♑
28	♑		
29	♑	11:39 am	♒
30	♒		

December

1	♉	11:25 am	♊
2	♊		
3	♊	12:51 pm	♋
4	♋		
5	♋	5:17 pm	♌
6	♌		
7	♌		
8	♌	1:40 am	♍
9	♍		
10	♍	1:19 pm	♎
11	♎		
12	♎		
13	♎	2:01 am	♏
14	♏		
15	♏	1:37 pm	♐
16	♐		
17	♐	11:07 pm	♑
18	♑		
19	♑		
20	♑	6:32 am	♒
21	♒		
22	♒	12:10 pm	♓
23	♓		
24	♓	4:09 pm	♈
25	♈		
26	♈	6:45 pm	♉
27	♉		
28	♉	8:38 pm	♊
29	♊		
30	♊	11:01 pm	♋
31	♋		

Moon Movements

♎ = Libra ♏ = Scorpio ♐ = Sagittarius ♑ = Capricorn ♒ = Aquarius ♓ = Pisces

1972

January

Day	Moon	Time	Enters
1	♋		
2	♋	3:22 am	♌
3	♌		
4	♌	10:50 am	♍
5	♍		
6	♍	9:33 pm	♎
7	♎		
8	♎		
9	♎	10:03 am	♏
10	♏		
11	♏	9:57 pm	♐
12	♐		
13	♐		
14	♐	7:26 am	♑
15	♑		
16	♑	2:04 pm	♒
17	♒		
18	♒	6:28 pm	♓
19	♓		
20	♓	9:35 pm	♈
21	♈		
22	♈		
23	♈	12:17 am	♉
24	♉		
25	♉	3:14 am	♊
26	♊		
27	♊	7:01 am	♋
28	♋		
29	♋	12:21 pm	♌
30	♌		
31	♌	7:56 pm	♍

February

Day	Moon	Time	Enters
1	♍		
2	♍		
3	♍	6:06 am	♎
4	♎		
5	♎	6:18 pm	♏
6	♏		
7	♏		
8	♏	6:38 am	♐
9	♐		
10	♐	4:50 pm	♑
11	♑		
12	♑	11:36 pm	♒
13	♒		
14	♒		
15	♒	3:11 am	♓
16	♓		
17	♓	4:51 am	♈
18	♈		
19	♈	6:11 am	♉
20	♉		
21	♉	8:35 am	♊
22	♊		
23	♊	12:52 pm	♋
24	♋		
25	♋	7:15 pm	♌
26	♌		
27	♌		
28	♌	3:39 am	♍
29	♍		

March

Day	Moon	Time	Enters
1	♍	2:00 pm	♎
2	♎		
3	♎		
4	♎	2:00 am	♏
5	♏		
6	♏	2:36 pm	♐
7	♐		
8	♐		
9	♐	1:49 am	♑
10	♑		
11	♑	9:42 am	♒
12	♒		
13	♒	1:39 pm	♓
14	♓		
15	♓	2:37 pm	♈
16	♈		
17	♈	2:27 pm	♉
18	♉		
19	♉	3:12 pm	♊
20	♊		
21	♊	6:26 pm	♋
22	♋		
23	♋		
24	♋	12:46 am	♌
25	♌		
26	♌	9:48 am	♍
27	♍		
28	♍	8:42 pm	♎
29	♎		
30	♎		
31	♎	8:48 am	♏

April

Day	Moon	Time	Enters
1	♏		
2	♏	9:27 pm	♐
3	♐		
4	♐		
5	♐	9:20 am	♑
6	♑		
7	♑	6:37 pm	♒
8	♒		
9	♒	11:58 pm	♓
10	♓		
11	♓		
12	♓	1:32 am	♈
13	♈		
14	♈	12:54 am	♉
15	♉		
16	♉	12:16 am	♊
17	♊		
18	♊	1:46 am	♋
19	♋		
20	♋	6:47 am	♌
21	♌		
22	♌	3:24 pm	♍
23	♍		
24	♍		
25	♍	2:34 am	♎
26	♎		
27	♎	2:56 pm	♏
28	♏		
29	♏		
30	♏	3:31 am	♐

May

Day	Moon	Time	Enters
1	♐		
2	♐	3:29 pm	♑
3	♑		
4	♑		
5	♑	1:35 am	♒
6	♒		
7	♒	8:28 am	♓
8	♓		
9	♓	11:35 am	♈
10	♈		
11	♈	11:47 am	♉
12	♉		
13	♉	10:57 am	♊
14	♊		
15	♊	11:16 am	♋
16	♋		
17	♋	2:38 pm	♌
18	♌		
19	♌	9:56 pm	♍
20	♍		
21	♍		
22	♍	8:36 am	♎
23	♎		
24	♎	9:01 pm	♏
25	♏		
26	♏		
27	♏	9:33 am	♐
28	♐		
29	♐	9:13 pm	♑
30	♑		
31	♑		

June

Day	Moon	Time	Enters
1	♑	7:15 am	♒
2	♒		
3	♒	2:52 pm	♓
4	♓		
5	♓	7:27 pm	♈
6	♈		
7	♈	9:14 pm	♉
8	♉		
9	♉	9:24 pm	♊
10	♊		
11	♊	9:45 pm	♋
12	♋		
13	♋		
14	♋	12:10 am	♌
15	♌		
16	♌	6:03 am	♍
17	♍		
18	♍	3:39 pm	♎
19	♎		
20	♎		
21	♎	3:43 am	♏
22	♏		
23	♏	4:14 pm	♐
24	♐		
25	♐		
26	♐	3:36 am	♑
27	♑		
28	♑	1:02 pm	♒
29	♒		
30	♒	8:18 pm	♓

July

Day	Moon	Time	Enters
1	♓		
2	♓		
3	♓	1:22 am	♈
4	♈		
5	♈	4:25 am	♉
6	♉		
7	♉	6:05 am	♊
8	♊		
9	♊	7:29 am	♋
10	♋		
11	♋	10:05 am	♌
12	♌		
13	♌	3:16 pm	♍
14	♍		
15	♍	11:49 pm	♎
16	♎		
17	♎		
18	♎	11:15 am	♏
19	♏		
20	♏	11:46 pm	♐
21	♐		
22	♐		
23	♐	11:10 am	♑
24	♑		
25	♑	8:07 pm	♒
26	♒		
27	♒		
28	♒	2:29 am	♓
29	♓		
30	♓	6:50 am	♈
31	♈		

August

Day	Moon	Time	Enters
1	♈	9:57 am	♉
2	♉		
3	♉	12:33 pm	♊
4	♊		
5	♊	3:18 pm	♋
6	♋		
7	♋	6:56 pm	♌
8	♌		
9	♌		
10	♌	12:23 am	♍
11	♍		
12	♍	8:27 am	♎
13	♎		
14	♎	7:19 pm	♏
15	♏		
16	♏		
17	♏	7:49 am	♐
18	♐		
19	♐	7:38 pm	♑
20	♑		
21	♑		
22	♑	4:43 am	♒
23	♒		
24	♒	10:28 am	♓
25	♓		
26	♓	1:40 pm	♈
27	♈		
28	♈	3:43 pm	♉
29	♉		
30	♉	5:56 pm	♊
31	♊		

September

Day	Moon	Time	Enters
1	♊	9:11 pm	♋
2	♋		
3	♋		
4	♋	1:54 am	♌
5	♌		
6	♌	8:15 am	♍
7	♍		
8	♍	4:36 pm	♎
9	♎		
10	♎		
11	♎	3:15 am	♏
12	♏		
13	♏	3:42 pm	♐
14	♐		
15	♐		
16	♐	4:07 am	♑
17	♑		
18	♑	2:04 pm	♒
19	♒		
20	♒	8:09 pm	♓
21	♓		
22	♓	10:44 pm	♈
23	♈		
24	♈	11:27 pm	♉
25	♉		
26	♉		
27	♉	12:14 am	♊
28	♊		
29	♊	2:39 am	♋
30	♋		

October

Day	Moon	Time	Enters
1	♋	7:25 am	♌
2	♌		
3	♌	2:31 pm	♍
4	♍		
5	♍	11:35 pm	♎
6	♎		
7	♎		
8	♎	10:27 am	♏
9	♏		
10	♏	10:52 pm	♐
11	♐		
12	♐		
13	♐	11:44 am	♑
14	♑		
15	♑	10:51 pm	♒
16	♒		
17	♒		
18	♒	6:12 am	♓
19	♓		
20	♓	9:22 am	♈
21	♈		
22	♈	9:37 am	♉
23	♉		
24	♉	9:02 am	♊
25	♊		
26	♊	9:44 am	♋
27	♋		
28	♋	1:14 pm	♌
29	♌		
30	♌	7:59 pm	♍
31	♍		

November

Day	Moon	Time	Enters
1	♍		
2	♍	5:27 am	♎
3	♎		
4	♎	4:46 pm	♏
5	♏		
6	♏		
7	♏	5:16 am	♐
8	♐		
9	♐	6:11 pm	♑
10	♑		
11	♑		
12	♑	6:02 am	♒
13	♒		
14	♒	2:56 pm	♓
15	♓		
16	♓	7:44 pm	♈
17	♈		
18	♈	8:53 pm	♉
19	♉		
20	♉	8:05 pm	♊
21	♊		
22	♊	7:31 pm	♋
23	♋		
24	♋	9:12 pm	♌
25	♌		
26	♌		
27	♌	2:24 am	♍
28	♍		
29	♍	11:15 am	♎
30	♎		

December

Day	Moon	Time	Enters
1	♎	10:42 pm	♏
2	♏		
3	♏		
4	♏	11:22 am	♐
5	♐		
6	♐		
7	♐	12:06 am	♑
8	♑		
9	♑	11:53 am	♒
10	♒		
11	♒	9:33 pm	♓
12	♓		
13	♓		
14	♓	3:59 am	♈
15	♈		
16	♈	6:59 am	♉
17	♉		
18	♉	7:24 am	♊
19	♊		
20	♊	6:57 am	♋
21	♋		
22	♋	7:34 am	♌
23	♌		
24	♌	11:03 am	♍
25	♍		
26	♍	6:21 pm	♎
27	♎		
28	♎		
29	♎	5:10 am	♏
30	♏		
31	♏	5:51 pm	♐

Your Starway to Love

♈ = Aries ♉ = Taurus ♊ = Gemini ♋ = Cancer ♌ = Leo ♍ = Virgo

1973

January

Day	Sign	Time	Enters
1	♐		
2	♐		
3	♐	6:30 am	♑
4	♑		
5	♑	5:47 pm	♒
6	♒		
7	♒		
8	♒	3:03 am	♓
9	♓		
10	♓	9:57 am	♈
11	♈		
12	♈	2:24 pm	♉
13	♉		
14	♉	4:41 pm	♊
15	♊		
16	♊	5:39 pm	♋
17	♋		
18	♋	6:40 pm	♌
19	♌		
20	♌	9:24 pm	♍
21	♍		
22	♍		
23	♍	3:16 am	♎
24	♎		
25	♎	12:52 pm	♏
26	♏		
27	♏		
28	♏	1:10 am	♐
29	♐		
30	♐	1:54 pm	♑
31	♑		

April

Day	Sign	Time	Enters
1	♓		
2	♓	7:48 am	♈
3	♈		
4	♈	9:58 am	♉
5	♉		
6	♉	11:12 am	♊
7	♊		
8	♊	1:04 pm	♋
9	♋		
10	♋	4:31 pm	♌
11	♌		
12	♌	9:47 pm	♍
13	♍		
14	♍		
15	♍	4:50 am	♎
16	♎		
17	♎	1:51 pm	♏
18	♏		
19	♏		
20	♏	1:02 am	♐
21	♐		
22	♐	1:49 pm	♑
23	♑		
24	♑		
25	♑	2:21 am	♒
26	♒		
27	♒	12:09 pm	♓
28	♓		
29	♓	5:53 pm	♈
30	♈		

July

Day	Sign	Time	Enters
1	♋	4:55 pm	♌
2	♌		
3	♌	6:31 pm	♍
4	♍		
5	♍	11:23 pm	♎
6	♎		
7	♎		
8	♎	8:05 am	♏
9	♏		
10	♏	7:48 pm	♐
11	♐		
12	♐		
13	♐	8:45 am	♑
14	♑		
15	♑	9:15 pm	♒
16	♒		
17	♒		
18	♒	8:07 am	♓
19	♓		
20	♓	4:43 pm	♈
21	♈		
22	♈	10:41 pm	♉
23	♉		
24	♉		
25	♉	1:58 am	♊
26	♊		
27	♊	3:10 am	♋
28	♋		
29	♋	3:29 am	♌
30	♌		
31	♌	4:34 am	♍

October

Day	Sign	Time	Enters
1	♐		
2	♐		
3	♐	7:02 am	♑
4	♑		
5	♑	7:49 pm	♒
6	♒		
7	♒		
8	♒	6:23 am	♓
9	♓		
10	♓	1:29 pm	♈
11	♈		
12	♈	5:36 pm	♉
13	♉		
14	♉	8:09 pm	♊
15	♊		
16	♊	10:28 pm	♋
17	♋		
18	♋		
19	♋	1:25 am	♌
20	♌		
21	♌	5:19 am	♍
22	♍		
23	♍	10:28 am	♎
24	♎		
25	♎	5:28 pm	♏
26	♏		
27	♏		
28	♏	2:57 am	♐
29	♐		
30	♐	2:57 pm	♑
31	♑		

February

Day	Sign	Time	Enters
1	♑		
2	♑	12:55 am	♒
3	♒		
4	♒	9:22 am	♓
5	♓		
6	♓	3:29 pm	♈
7	♈		
8	♈	7:53 pm	♉
9	♉		
10	♉	11:10 pm	♊
11	♊		
12	♊		
13	♊	1:44 am	♋
14	♋		
15	♋	4:12 am	♌
16	♌		
17	♌	7:31 am	♍
18	♍		
19	♍	12:58 pm	♎
20	♎		
21	♎	9:35 pm	♏
22	♏		
23	♏		
24	♏	9:14 am	♐
25	♐		
26	♐	10:04 pm	♑
27	♑		
28	♑		

May

Day	Sign	Time	Enters
1	♈	8:01 pm	♉
2	♉		
3	♉	8:16 pm	♊
4	♊		
5	♊	8:35 pm	♋
6	♋		
7	♋	10:36 pm	♌
8	♌		
9	♌		
10	♌	3:13 am	♍
11	♍		
12	♍	10:31 am	♎
13	♎		
14	♎	8:09 pm	♏
15	♏		
16	♏		
17	♏	7:41 am	♐
18	♐		
19	♐	8:30 pm	♑
20	♑		
21	♑		
22	♑	9:17 am	♒
23	♒		
24	♒	8:05 pm	♓
25	♓		
26	♓		
27	♓	3:14 am	♈
28	♈		
29	♈	6:28 am	♉
30	♉		
31	♉	6:53 am	♊

August

Day	Sign	Time	Enters
1	♍		
2	♍	8:12 am	♎
3	♎		
4	♎	3:35 pm	♏
5	♏		
6	♏		
7	♏	2:37 am	♐
8	♐		
9	♐	3:30 pm	♑
10	♑		
11	♑		
12	♑	3:52 am	♒
13	♒		
14	♒	2:14 pm	♓
15	♓		
16	♓	10:16 pm	♈
17	♈		
18	♈		
19	♈	4:14 am	♉
20	♉		
21	♉	8:26 am	♊
22	♊		
23	♊	11:08 am	♋
24	♋		
25	♋	12:49 pm	♌
26	♌		
27	♌	2:33 pm	♍
28	♍		
29	♍	5:52 pm	♎
30	♎		
31	♎		

November

Day	Sign	Time	Enters
1	♑		
2	♑	3:58 am	♒
3	♒		
4	♒	3:26 pm	♓
5	♓		
6	♓	11:19 pm	♈
7	♈		
8	♈		
9	♈	3:25 am	♉
10	♉		
11	♉	4:59 am	♊
12	♊		
13	♊	5:46 am	♋
14	♋		
15	♋	7:20 am	♌
16	♌		
17	♌	10:41 am	♍
18	♍		
19	♍	4:15 pm	♎
20	♎		
21	♎		
22	♎	12:06 am	♏
23	♏		
24	♏	10:11 am	♐
25	♐		
26	♐	10:13 pm	♑
27	♑		
28	♑		
29	♑	11:17 am	♒
30	♒		

March

Day	Sign	Time	Enters
1	♑	9:22 am	♒
2	♒		
3	♒	5:31 pm	♓
4	♓		
5	♓	10:37 pm	♈
6	♈		
7	♈		
8	♈	1:51 am	♉
9	♉		
10	♉	4:31 am	♊
11	♊		
12	♊	7:29 am	♋
13	♋		
14	♋	11:07 am	♌
15	♌		
16	♌	3:42 pm	♍
17	♍		
18	♍	9:48 pm	♎
19	♎		
20	♎		
21	♎	6:15 am	♏
22	♏		
23	♏	5:26 pm	♐
24	♐		
25	♐		
26	♐	6:16 am	♑
27	♑		
28	♑	6:12 pm	♒
29	♒		
30	♒		
31	♒	2:55 am	♓

June

Day	Sign	Time	Enters
1	♊		
2	♊	6:21 am	♋
3	♋		
4	♋	6:49 am	♌
5	♌		
6	♌	9:51 am	♍
7	♍		
8	♍	4:16 pm	♎
9	♎		
10	♎		
11	♎	1:52 am	♏
12	♏		
13	♏	1:43 pm	♐
14	♐		
15	♐		
16	♐	2:37 am	♑
17	♑		
18	♑	3:19 pm	♒
19	♒		
20	♒		
21	♒	2:29 am	♓
22	♓		
23	♓	10:48 am	♈
24	♈		
25	♈	3:37 pm	♉
26	♉		
27	♉	5:18 pm	♊
28	♊		
29	♊	5:08 pm	♋
30	♋		

September

Day	Sign	Time	Enters
1	♎	12:17 am	♏
2	♏		
3	♏	10:24 am	♐
4	♐		
5	♐	11:01 pm	♑
6	♑		
7	♑		
8	♑	11:30 am	♒
9	♒		
10	♒	9:40 pm	♓
11	♓		
12	♓		
13	♓	4:56 am	♈
14	♈		
15	♈	9:59 am	♉
16	♉		
17	♉	1:48 pm	♊
18	♊		
19	♊	5:01 pm	♋
20	♋		
21	♋	7:56 pm	♌
22	♌		
23	♌	10:58 pm	♍
24	♍		
25	♍		
26	♍	3:00 am	♎
27	♎		
28	♎	9:18 am	♏
29	♏		
30	♏	6:47 pm	♐

December

Day	Sign	Time	Enters
1	♒	11:32 pm	♓
2	♓		
3	♓		
4	♓	8:50 am	♈
5	♈		
6	♈	2:08 pm	♉
7	♉		
8	♉	3:58 pm	♊
9	♊		
10	♊	3:52 pm	♋
11	♋		
12	♋	3:44 pm	♌
13	♌		
14	♌	5:20 pm	♍
15	♍		
16	♍	9:53 pm	♎
17	♎		
18	♎		
19	♎	5:44 am	♏
20	♏		
21	♏	4:20 pm	♐
22	♐		
23	♐		
24	♐	4:41 am	♑
25	♑		
26	♑	5:43 pm	♒
27	♒		
28	♒		
29	♒	6:10 am	♓
30	♓		
31	♓	4:34 pm	♈

Moon Movements

♎ = Libra ♏ = Scorpio ♐ = Sagittarius ♑ = Capricorn ♒ = Aquarius ♓ = Pisces

1974

January

1	♈		
2	♈	11:38 pm	♉
3	♉		
4	♉		
5	♉	3:00 am	♊
6	♊		
7	♊	3:28 am	♋
8	♋		
9	♋	2:42 am	♌
10	♌		
11	♌	2:41 am	♍
12	♍		
13	♍	5:21 am	♎
14	♎		
15	♎	11:54 am	♏
16	♏		
17	♏	10:12 pm	♐
18	♐		
19	♐		
20	♐	10:47 am	♑
21	♑		
22	♑	11:50 pm	♒
23	♒		
24	♒		
25	♒	12:00 pm	♓
26	♓		
27	♓	10:32 pm	♈
28	♈		
29	♈		
30	♈	6:41 am	♉
31	♉		

February

1	♉	11:53 am	♊
2	♊		
3	♊	2:05 pm	♋
4	♋		
5	♋	2:11 pm	♌
6	♌		
7	♌	1:52 pm	♍
8	♍		
9	♍	3:10 pm	♎
10	♎		
11	♎	7:58 pm	♏
12	♏		
13	♏		
14	♏	5:01 am	♐
15	♐		
16	♐	5:16 pm	♑
17	♑		
18	♑		
19	♑	6:21 am	♒
20	♒		
21	♒	6:15 pm	♓
22	♓		
23	♓		
24	♓	4:12 am	♈
25	♈		
26	♈	12:11 pm	♉
27	♉		
28	♉	6:10 pm	♊

March

1	♊		
2	♊	9:59 pm	♋
3	♋		
4	♋	11:49 pm	♌
5	♌		
6	♌		
7	♌	12:33 am	♍
8	♍		
9	♍	1:52 am	♎
10	♎		
11	♎	5:40 am	♏
12	♏		
13	♏	1:20 pm	♐
14	♐		
15	♐		
16	♐	12:41 am	♑
17	♑		
18	♑	1:38 pm	♒
19	♒		
20	♒		
21	♒	1:33 am	♓
22	♓		
23	♓	11:02 am	♈
24	♈		
25	♈	6:09 pm	♉
26	♉		
27	♉	11:33 pm	♊
28	♊		
29	♊		
30	♊	3:40 am	♋
31	♋		

April

1	♋	6:40 am	♌
2	♌		
3	♌	8:56 am	♍
4	♍		
5	♍	11:22 am	♎
6	♎		
7	♎	3:25 pm	♏
8	♏		
9	♏	10:27 pm	♐
10	♐		
11	♐		
12	♐	8:56 am	♑
13	♑		
14	♑	9:34 pm	♒
15	♒		
16	♒		
17	♒	9:44 am	♓
18	♓		
19	♓	7:20 pm	♈
20	♈		
21	♈		
22	♈	1:53 am	♉
23	♉		
24	♉	6:11 am	♊
25	♊		
26	♊	9:17 am	♋
27	♋		
28	♋	12:03 pm	♌
29	♌		
30	♌	3:00 pm	♍

May

1	♍		
2	♍	6:39 pm	♎
3	♎		
4	♎	11:43 pm	♏
5	♏		
6	♏		
7	♏	7:05 am	♐
8	♐		
9	♐	5:15 pm	♑
10	♑		
11	♑		
12	♑	5:34 am	♒
13	♒		
14	♒	6:03 pm	♓
15	♓		
16	♓		
17	♓	4:20 am	♈
18	♈		
19	♈	11:10 am	♉
20	♉		
21	♉	2:54 pm	♊
22	♊		
23	♊	4:46 pm	♋
24	♋		
25	♋	6:12 pm	♌
26	♌		
27	♌	8:25 pm	♍
28	♍		
29	♍		
30	♍	12:16 am	♎
31	♎		

June

1	♎	6:10 am	♏
2	♏		
3	♏	2:21 pm	♐
4	♐		
5	♐		
6	♐	12:48 am	♑
7	♑		
8	♑	1:02 pm	♒
9	♒		
10	♒		
11	♒	1:43 am	♓
12	♓		
13	♓	12:52 pm	♈
14	♈		
15	♈	8:46 pm	♉
16	♉		
17	♉		
18	♉	12:59 am	♊
19	♊		
20	♊	2:21 am	♋
21	♋		
22	♋	2:30 am	♌
23	♌		
24	♌	3:11 am	♍
25	♍		
26	♍	5:57 am	♎
27	♎		
28	♎	11:40 am	♏
29	♏		
30	♏	8:20 pm	♐

July

1	♐		
2	♐		
3	♐	7:19 am	♑
4	♑		
5	♑	7:41 pm	♒
6	♒		
7	♒		
8	♒	8:25 am	♓
9	♓		
10	♓	8:10 pm	♈
11	♈		
12	♈		
13	♈	5:21 am	♉
14	♉		
15	♉	10:54 am	♊
16	♊		
17	♊	12:56 pm	♋
18	♋		
19	♋	12:43 pm	♌
20	♌		
21	♌	12:10 pm	♍
22	♍		
23	♍	1:19 pm	♎
24	♎		
25	♎	5:45 pm	♏
26	♏		
27	♏		
28	♏	2:00 am	♐
29	♐		
30	♐	1:11 pm	♑
31	♑		

August

1	♑		
2	♑	1:46 am	♒
3	♒		
4	♒	2:26 pm	♓
5	♓		
6	♓		
7	♓	2:15 am	♈
8	♈		
9	♈	12:13 pm	♉
10	♉		
11	♉	7:15 pm	♊
12	♊		
13	♊	10:49 pm	♋
14	♋		
15	♋	11:26 pm	♌
16	♌		
17	♌	10:42 pm	♍
18	♍		
19	♍	10:45 pm	♎
20	♎		
21	♎		
22	♎	1:37 am	♏
23	♏		
24	♏	8:34 am	♐
25	♐		
26	♐	7:15 pm	♑
27	♑		
28	♑		
29	♑	7:52 am	♒
30	♒		
31	♒	8:29 pm	♓

September

1	♓		
2	♓		
3	♓	7:58 am	♈
4	♈		
5	♈	5:50 pm	♉
6	♉		
7	♉		
8	♉	1:36 am	♊
9	♊		
10	♊	6:39 am	♋
11	♋		
12	♋	8:54 am	♌
13	♌		
14	♌	9:12 am	♍
15	♍		
16	♍	9:17 am	♎
17	♎		
18	♎	11:14 am	♏
19	♏		
20	♏	4:46 pm	♐
21	♐		
22	♐		
23	♐	2:22 am	♑
24	♑		
25	♑	2:38 pm	♒
26	♒		
27	♒		
28	♒	3:14 am	♓
29	♓		
30	♓	2:25 pm	♈

October

1	♈		
2	♈	11:39 pm	♉
3	♉		
4	♉		
5	♉	7:00 am	♊
6	♊		
7	♊	12:30 pm	♋
8	♋		
9	♋	4:02 pm	♌
10	♌		
11	♌	5:56 pm	♍
12	♍		
13	♍	7:11 pm	♎
14	♎		
15	♎	9:23 pm	♏
16	♏		
17	♏		
18	♏	2:14 am	♐
19	♐		
20	♐	10:44 am	♑
21	♑		
22	♑	10:20 pm	♒
23	♒		
24	♒		
25	♒	10:57 am	♓
26	♓		
27	♓	10:13 pm	♈
28	♈		
29	♈		
30	♈	7:00 am	♉
31	♉		

November

1	♉	1:23 pm	♊
2	♊		
3	♊	6:01 pm	♋
4	♋		
5	♋	9:30 pm	♌
6	♌		
7	♌		
8	♌	12:18 am	♍
9	♍		
10	♍	2:58 am	♎
11	♎		
12	♎	6:23 am	♏
13	♏		
14	♏	11:39 am	♐
15	♐		
16	♐	7:42 pm	♑
17	♑		
18	♑		
19	♑	6:39 am	♒
20	♒		
21	♒	7:11 pm	♓
22	♓		
23	♓		
24	♓	6:59 am	♈
25	♈		
26	♈	4:05 pm	♉
27	♉		
28	♉	9:58 pm	♊
29	♊		
30	♊		

December

1	♊	1:22 am	♋
2	♋		
3	♋	3:31 am	♌
4	♌		
5	♌	5:40 am	♍
6	♍		
7	♍	8:42 am	♎
8	♎		
9	♎	1:13 pm	♏
10	♏		
11	♏	7:34 pm	♐
12	♐		
13	♐		
14	♐	4:04 am	♑
15	♑		
16	♑	2:48 pm	♒
17	♒		
18	♒		
19	♒	3:12 am	♓
20	♓		
21	♓	3:35 pm	♈
22	♈		
23	♈		
24	♈	1:45 am	♉
25	♉		
26	♉	8:15 am	♊
27	♊		
28	♊	11:15 am	♋
29	♋		
30	♋	12:05 pm	♌
31	♌		

Your Starway to Love

♈ = Aries ♉ = Taurus ♊ = Gemini ♋ = Cancer ♌ = Leo ♍ = Virgo

1975

January

1	♌	12:33 pm	♍
2	♍		
3	♍	2:21 pm	♎
4	♎		
5	♎	6:39 pm	♏
6	♏		
7	♏		
8	♏	1:39 am	♐
9	♐		
10	♐	10:58 am	♑
11	♑		
12	♑	10:03 pm	♒
13	♒		
14	♒		
15	♒	10:23 am	♓
16	♓		
17	♓	11:03 pm	♈
18	♈		
19	♈		
20	♈	10:21 am	♉
21	♉		
22	♉	6:23 pm	♊
23	♊		
24	♊	10:20 pm	♋
25	♋		
26	♋	11:00 pm	♌
27	♌		
28	♌	10:14 pm	♍
29	♍		
30	♍	10:13 pm	♎
31	♎		

February

1	♎		
2	♎	12:53 am	♏
3	♏		
4	♏	7:10 am	♐
5	♐		
6	♐	4:42 pm	♑
7	♑		
8	♑		
9	♑	4:16 am	♒
10	♒		
11	♒	4:45 pm	♓
12	♓		
13	♓		
14	♓	5:22 am	♈
15	♈		
16	♈	5:09 pm	♉
17	♉		
18	♉		
19	♉	2:35 am	♊
20	♊		
21	♊	8:18 am	♋
22	♋		
23	♋	10:13 am	♌
24	♌		
25	♌	9:37 am	♍
26	♍		
27	♍	8:38 am	♎
28	♎		

March

1	♎	9:33 am	♏
2	♏		
3	♏	2:05 pm	♐
4	♐		
5	♐	10:39 pm	♑
6	♑		
7	♑		
8	♑	10:09 am	♒
9	♒		
10	♒	10:49 pm	♓
11	♓		
12	♓		
13	♓	11:18 am	♈
14	♈		
15	♈	10:52 pm	♉
16	♉		
17	♉		
18	♉	8:43 am	♊
19	♊		
20	♊	3:48 pm	♋
21	♋		
22	♋	7:31 pm	♌
23	♌		
24	♌	8:21 pm	♍
25	♍		
26	♍	7:51 pm	♎
27	♎		
28	♎	8:08 pm	♏
29	♏		
30	♏	11:10 pm	♐
31	♐		

April

1	♐		
2	♐	6:08 am	♑
3	♑		
4	♑	4:45 pm	♒
5	♒		
6	♒		
7	♒	5:17 am	♓
8	♓		
9	♓	5:44 pm	♈
10	♈		
11	♈		
12	♈	4:53 am	♉
13	♉		
14	♉	2:14 pm	♊
15	♊		
16	♊	9:27 pm	♋
17	♋		
18	♋		
19	♋	2:14 am	♌
20	♌		
21	♌	4:42 am	♍
22	♍		
23	♍	5:41 am	♎
24	♎		
25	♎	6:39 am	♏
26	♏		
27	♏	9:20 am	♐
28	♐		
29	♐	3:08 pm	♑
30	♑		

May

1	♑		
2	♑	12:34 am	♒
3	♒		
4	♒	12:34 pm	♓
5	♓		
6	♓		
7	♓	1:03 am	♈
8	♈		
9	♈	12:03 pm	♉
10	♉		
11	♉	8:44 pm	♊
12	♊		
13	♊		
14	♊	3:08 am	♋
15	♋		
16	♋	7:38 am	♌
17	♌		
18	♌	10:45 am	♍
19	♍		
20	♍	1:05 pm	♎
21	♎		
22	♎	3:25 pm	♏
23	♏		
24	♏	6:51 pm	♐
25	♐		
26	♐		
27	♐	12:31 am	♑
28	♑		
29	♑	9:09 am	♒
30	♒		
31	♒	8:32 pm	♓

June

1	♓		
2	♓		
3	♓	9:01 am	♈
4	♈		
5	♈	8:19 pm	♉
6	♉		
7	♉		
8	♉	4:49 am	♊
9	♊		
10	♊	10:21 am	♋
11	♋		
12	♋	1:45 pm	♌
13	♌		
14	♌	4:11 pm	♍
15	♍		
16	♍	6:41 pm	♎
17	♎		
18	♎	9:59 pm	♏
19	♏		
20	♏		
21	♏	2:34 am	♐
22	♐		
23	♐	8:56 am	♑
24	♑		
25	♑	5:33 pm	♒
26	♒		
27	♒		
28	♒	4:33 am	♓
29	♓		
30	♓	5:02 pm	♈

July

1	♈		
2	♈		
3	♈	4:54 am	♉
4	♉		
5	♉	1:58 pm	♊
6	♊		
7	♊	7:23 pm	♋
8	♋		
9	♋	9:50 pm	♌
10	♌		
11	♌	10:55 pm	♍
12	♍		
13	♍		
14	♍	12:21 am	♎
15	♎		
16	♎	3:23 am	♏
17	♏		
18	♏	8:32 am	♐
19	♐		
20	♐	3:46 pm	♑
21	♑		
22	♑		
23	♑	12:56 am	♒
24	♒		
25	♒	11:58 am	♓
26	♓		
27	♓		
28	♓	12:27 am	♈
29	♈		
30	♈	12:53 pm	♉
31	♉		

August

1	♉	11:02 pm	♊
2	♊		
3	♊		
4	♊	5:17 am	♋
5	♋		
6	♋	7:44 am	♌
7	♌		
8	♌	7:53 am	♍
9	♍		
10	♍	7:51 am	♎
11	♎		
12	♎	9:30 am	♏
13	♏		
14	♏	1:59 pm	♐
15	♐		
16	♐	9:25 pm	♑
17	♑		
18	♑		
19	♑	7:09 am	♒
20	♒		
21	♒	6:32 pm	♓
22	♓		
23	♓		
24	♓	7:02 am	♈
25	♈		
26	♈	7:45 pm	♉
27	♉		
28	♉		
29	♉	6:53 am	♊
30	♊		
31	♊	2:35 pm	♋

September

1	♋		
2	♋	6:08 pm	♌
3	♌		
4	♌	6:29 pm	♍
5	♍		
6	♍	5:38 pm	♎
7	♎		
8	♎	5:46 pm	♏
9	♏		
10	♏	8:41 pm	♐
11	♐		
12	♐		
13	♐	3:11 am	♑
14	♑		
15	♑	12:51 pm	♒
16	♒		
17	♒		
18	♒	12:32 am	♓
19	♓		
20	♓	1:07 pm	♈
21	♈		
22	♈		
23	♈	1:43 am	♉
24	♉		
25	♉	1:13 pm	♊
26	♊		
27	♊	10:07 pm	♋
28	♋		
29	♋		
30	♋	3:20 am	♌

October

1	♌		
2	♌	5:03 am	♍
3	♍		
4	♍	4:39 am	♎
5	♎		
6	♎	4:09 am	♏
7	♏		
8	♏	5:35 am	♐
9	♐		
10	♐	10:29 am	♑
11	♑		
12	♑	7:10 pm	♒
13	♒		
14	♒		
15	♒	6:40 am	♓
16	♓		
17	♓	7:20 pm	♈
18	♈		
19	♈		
20	♈	7:43 am	♉
21	♉		
22	♉	6:51 pm	♊
23	♊		
24	♊		
25	♊	3:57 am	♋
26	♋		
27	♋	10:20 am	♌
28	♌		
29	♌	1:47 pm	♍
30	♍		
31	♍	2:55 pm	♎

November

1	♎		
2	♎	3:07 pm	♏
3	♏		
4	♏	4:10 pm	♐
5	♐		
6	♐	7:45 pm	♑
7	♑		
8	♑		
9	♑	2:59 am	♒
10	♒		
11	♒	1:42 pm	♓
12	♓		
13	♓		
14	♓	2:17 am	♈
15	♈		
16	♈	2:38 pm	♉
17	♉		
18	♉		
19	♉	1:14 am	♊
20	♊		
21	♊	9:36 am	♋
22	♋		
23	♋	3:48 pm	♌
24	♌		
25	♌	8:04 pm	♍
26	♍		
27	♍	10:48 pm	♎
28	♎		
29	♎		
30	♎	12:37 am	♏

December

1	♏		
2	♏	2:33 am	♐
3	♐		
4	♐	5:58 am	♑
5	♑		
6	♑	12:12 pm	♒
7	♒		
8	♒	9:52 pm	♓
9	♓		
10	♓		
11	♓	10:06 am	♈
12	♈		
13	♈	10:39 pm	♉
14	♉		
15	♉		
16	♉	9:12 am	♊
17	♊		
18	♊	4:49 pm	♋
19	♋		
20	♋	9:54 pm	♌
21	♌		
22	♌		
23	♌	1:28 am	♍
24	♍		
25	♍	4:27 am	♎
26	♎		
27	♎	7:28 am	♏
28	♏		
29	♏	10:53 am	♐
30	♐		
31	♐	3:16 pm	♑

Moon Movements

♎ = Libra ♏ = Scorpio ♐ = Sagittarius ♑ = Capricorn ♒ = Aquarius ♓ = Pisces

January

Day	Sign	Time	Enters
1	♑		
2	♑	9:33 pm	♒
3	♒		
4	♒		
5	♒	6:35 am	♓
6	♓		
7	♓	6:21 pm	♈
8	♈		
9	♈		
10	♈	7:10 am	♉
11	♉		
12	♉	6:19 pm	♊
13	♊		
14	♊		
15	♊	2:00 am	♋
16	♋		
17	♋	6:15 am	♌
18	♌		
19	♌	8:25 am	♍
20	♍		
21	♍	10:11 am	♎
22	♎		
23	♎	12:48 pm	♏
24	♏		
25	♏	4:51 pm	♐
26	♐		
27	♐	10:24 pm	♑
28	♑		
29	♑		
30	♑	5:34 am	♒
31	♒		

April

Day	Sign	Time	Enters
1	♈	4:34 am	♉
2	♉		
3	♉	5:15 pm	♊
4	♊		
5	♊		
6	♊	4:06 am	♋
7	♋		
8	♋	11:36 am	♌
9	♌		
10	♌	3:16 pm	♍
11	♍		
12	♍	3:54 pm	♎
13	♎		
14	♎	3:14 pm	♏
15	♏		
16	♏	3:15 pm	♐
17	♐		
18	♐	5:43 pm	♑
19	♑		
20	♑	11:47 pm	♒
21	♒		
22	♒		
23	♒	9:28 am	♓
24	♓		
25	♓	9:37 pm	♈
26	♈		
27	♈		
28	♈	10:37 am	♉
29	♉		
30	♉	11:05 pm	♊

July

Day	Sign	Time	Enters
1	♌	10:46 am	♍
2	♍		
3	♍	2:34 pm	♎
4	♎		
5	♎	5:33 pm	♏
6	♏		
7	♏	8:05 pm	♐
8	♐		
9	♐	10:49 pm	♑
10	♑		
11	♑		
12	♑	2:53 am	♒
13	♒		
14	♒	9:36 am	♓
15	♓		
16	♓	7:40 pm	♈
17	♈		
18	♈		
19	♈	8:11 am	♉
20	♉		
21	♉	8:40 pm	♊
22	♊		
23	♊		
24	♊	6:39 am	♋
25	♋		
26	♋	1:18 pm	♌
27	♌		
28	♌	5:23 pm	♍
29	♍		
30	♍	8:13 pm	♎
31	♎		

October

Day	Sign	Time	Enters
1	♑	10:49 pm	♒
2	♒		
3	♒		
4	♒	7:10 am	♓
5	♓		
6	♓	5:50 pm	♈
7	♈		
8	♈		
9	♈	6:11 am	♉
10	♉		
11	♉	7:14 pm	♊
12	♊		
13	♊		
14	♊	7:24 am	♋
15	♋		
16	♋	4:49 pm	♌
17	♌		
18	♌	10:25 pm	♍
19	♍		
20	♍		
21	♍	12:26 am	♎
22	♎		
23	♎	12:17 am	♏
24	♏	11:49 pm	♐
25	♐		
26	♐		
27	♐	12:55 am	♑
28	♑		
29	♑	5:05 am	♒
30	♒		
31	♒	12:53 pm	♓

February

Day	Sign	Time	Enters
1	♒	2:47 pm	♓
2	♓		
3	♓		
4	♓	2:17 am	♈
5	♈		
6	♈	3:13 pm	♉
7	♉		
8	♉		
9	♉	3:16 pm	♊
10	♊		
11	♊	11:59 am	♋
12	♋		
13	♋	4:32 pm	♌
14	♌		
15	♌	5:59 pm	♍
16	♍		
17	♍	6:14 pm	♎
18	♎		
19	♎	7:14 pm	♏
20	♏		
21	♏	10:18 pm	♐
22	♐		
23	♐		
24	♐	3:54 am	♑
25	♑		
26	♑	11:48 am	♒
27	♒		
28	♒	9:42 pm	♓
29	♓		

May

Day	Sign	Time	Enters
1	♊		
2	♊		
3	♊	9:53 am	♋
4	♋		
5	♋	6:09 pm	♌
6	♌		
7	♌	11:21 pm	♍
8	♍		
9	♍		
10	♍	1:39 am	♎
11	♎		
12	♎	2:03 am	♏
13	♏		
14	♏	2:04 am	♐
15	♐		
16	♐	3:31 am	♑
17	♑		
18	♑	8:02 am	♒
19	♒		
20	♒	4:27 pm	♓
21	♓		
22	♓		
23	♓	4:07 am	♈
24	♈		
25	♈	5:07 pm	♉
26	♉		
27	♉		
28	♉	5:22 am	♊
29	♊		
30	♊	3:39 pm	♋
31	♋		

August

Day	Sign	Time	Enters
1	♎	10:55 pm	♏
2	♏		
3	♏		
4	♏	2:03 am	♐
5	♐		
6	♐	5:54 am	♑
7	♑		
8	♑	10:57 am	♒
9	♒		
10	♒	6:00 pm	♓
11	♓		
12	♓		
13	♓	3:49 am	♈
14	♈		
15	♈	4:05 pm	♉
16	♉		
17	♉		
18	♉	4:54 am	♊
19	♊		
20	♊	3:34 pm	♋
21	♋		
22	♋	10:31 pm	♌
23	♌		
24	♌		
25	♌	2:04 am	♍
26	♍		
27	♍	3:42 am	♎
28	♎		
29	♎	5:05 am	♏
30	♏		
31	♏	7:28 am	♐

November

Day	Sign	Time	Enters
1	♓		
2	♓	11:46 pm	♈
3	♈		
4	♈		
5	♈	12:23 pm	♉
6	♉		
7	♉		
8	♉	1:21 am	♊
9	♊		
10	♊	1:28 pm	♋
11	♋		
12	♋	11:36 pm	♌
13	♌		
14	♌		
15	♌	6:46 am	♍
16	♍		
17	♍	10:34 am	♎
18	♎		
19	♎	11:31 am	♏
20	♏		
21	♏	11:03 am	♐
22	♐		
23	♐	11:03 am	♑
24	♑		
25	♑	1:30 pm	♒
26	♒		
27	♒	7:47 pm	♓
28	♓		
29	♓		
30	♓	6:01 am	♈

March

Day	Sign	Time	Enters
1	♓		
2	♓	9:22 am	♈
3	♈		
4	♈	10:18 pm	♉
5	♉		
6	♉		
7	♉	10:56 am	♊
8	♊		
9	♊	8:59 pm	♋
10	♋		
11	♋		
12	♋	2:55 am	♌
13	♌		
14	♌	4:59 am	♍
15	♍		
16	♍	4:44 am	♎
17	♎		
18	♎	4:18 am	♏
19	♏		
20	♏	5:34 am	♐
21	♐		
22	♐	9:48 am	♑
23	♑		
24	♑	5:19 pm	♒
25	♒		
26	♒		
27	♒	3:34 am	♓
28	♓		
29	♓	3:37 pm	♈
30	♈		
31	♈		

June

Day	Sign	Time	Enters
1	♋	11:37 pm	♌
2	♌		
3	♌		
4	♌	5:21 am	♍
5	♍		
6	♍	9:00 am	♎
7	♎		
8	♎	10:58 am	♏
9	♏		
10	♏	12:07 pm	♐
11	♐		
12	♐	1:45 pm	♑
13	♑		
14	♑	5:31 pm	♒
15	♒		
16	♒		
17	♒	12:43 am	♓
18	♓		
19	♓	11:32 am	♈
20	♈		
21	♈		
22	♈	12:21 am	♉
23	♉		
24	♉	12:37 pm	♊
25	♊		
26	♊	10:29 pm	♋
27	♋		
28	♋		
29	♋	5:39 am	♌
30	♌		

September

Day	Sign	Time	Enters
1	♐		
2	♐	11:29 am	♑
3	♑		
4	♑	5:20 pm	♒
5	♒		
6	♒		
7	♒	1:11 am	♓
8	♓		
9	♓	11:18 am	♈
10	♈		
11	♈	11:30 pm	♉
12	♉		
13	♉		
14	♉	12:32 pm	♊
15	♊		
16	♊		
17	♊	12:07 am	♋
18	♋		
19	♋	8:10 am	♌
20	♌		
21	♌	12:16 pm	♍
22	♍		
23	♍	1:28 pm	♎
24	♎		
25	♎	1:34 pm	♏
26	♏		
27	♏	2:22 pm	♐
28	♐		
29	♐	5:13 pm	♑
30	♑		

December

Day	Sign	Time	Enters
1	♈		
2	♈	6:41 pm	♉
3	♉		
4	♉		
5	♉	7:38 am	♊
6	♊		
7	♊	7:21 pm	♋
8	♋		
9	♋		
10	♋	5:12 am	♌
11	♌		
12	♌	12:55 pm	♍
13	♍		
14	♍	6:13 pm	♎
15	♎		
16	♎	9:01 pm	♏
17	♏		
18	♏	9:54 pm	♐
19	♐		
20	♐	10:12 pm	♑
21	♑		
22	♑	11:48 pm	♒
23	♒		
24	♒		
25	♒	4:36 am	♓
26	♓		
27	♓	1:32 pm	♈
28	♈		
29	♈		
30	♈	1:43 am	♉
31	♉		

1977

Your Starway to Love

♈ = Aries ♉ = Taurus ♊ = Gemini ♋ = Cancer ♌ = Leo ♍ = Virgo

January

1	♉	2:43 pm	♊
2	♊		
3	♊		
4	♊	2:12 am	♋
5	♋		
6	♋	11:20 am	♌
7	♌		
8	♌	6:23 pm	♍
9	♍		
10	♍	11:48 pm	♎
11	♎		
12	♎		
13	♎	3:44 am	♏
14	♏		
15	♏	6:18 am	♐
16	♐		
17	♐	8:02 am	♑
18	♑		
19	♑	10:12 am	♒
20	♒		
21	♒	2:30 pm	♓
22	♓		
23	♓	10:20 pm	♈
24	♈		
25	♈		
26	♈	9:41 am	♉
27	♉		
28	♉	10:37 pm	♊
29	♊		
30	♊		
31	♊	10:20 am	♋

February

1	♋		
2	♋	7:11 pm	♌
3	♌		
4	♌		
5	♌	1:17 am	♍
6	♍		
7	♍	5:36 am	♎
8	♎		
9	♎	9:04 am	♏
10	♏		
11	♏	12:11 pm	♐
12	♐		
13	♐	3:14 pm	♑
14	♑		
15	♑	6:45 pm	♒
16	♒		
17	♒	11:45 pm	♓
18	♓		
19	♓		
20	♓	7:22 am	♈
21	♈		
22	♈	6:06 pm	♉
23	♉		
24	♉		
25	♉	6:50 am	♊
26	♊		
27	♊	7:02 pm	♋
28	♋		

March

1	♋		
2	♋	4:25 am	♌
3	♌		
4	♌	10:19 am	♍
5	♍		
6	♍	1:34 pm	♎
7	♎		
8	♎	3:37 pm	♏
9	♏		
10	♏	5:42 pm	♐
11	♐		
12	♐	8:40 pm	♑
13	♑		
14	♑		
15	♑	1:00 am	♒
16	♒		
17	♒	7:06 am	♓
18	♓		
19	♓	3:23 pm	♈
20	♈		
21	♈		
22	♈	2:05 am	♉
23	♉		
24	♉	2:39 pm	♊
25	♊		
26	♊		
27	♊	3:16 am	♋
28	♋		
29	♋	1:40 pm	♌
30	♌		
31	♌	8:25 pm	♍

April

1	♍		
2	♍	11:39 pm	♎
3	♎		
4	♎		
5	♎	12:40 am	♏
6	♏		
7	♏	1:09 am	♐
8	♐		
9	♐	2:40 am	♑
10	♑		
11	♑	6:24 am	♒
12	♒		
13	♒	12:49 pm	♓
14	♓		
15	♓	9:52 pm	♈
16	♈		
17	♈		
18	♈	9:02 am	♉
19	♉		
20	♉	9:37 pm	♊
21	♊		
22	♊		
23	♊	10:25 am	♋
24	♋		
25	♋	9:43 pm	♌
26	♌		
27	♌		
28	♌	5:52 am	♍
29	♍		
30	♍	10:12 am	♎

May

1	♎		
2	♎	11:23 am	♏
3	♏		
4	♏	10:59 am	♐
5	♐		
6	♐	10:54 am	♑
7	♑		
8	♑	1:00 pm	♒
9	♒		
10	♒	6:29 pm	♓
11	♓		
12	♓		
13	♓	3:29 am	♈
14	♈		
15	♈	3:04 pm	♉
16	♉		
17	♉		
18	♉	3:50 am	♊
19	♊		
20	♊	4:35 pm	♋
21	♋		
22	♋		
23	♋	4:13 am	♌
24	♌		
25	♌	1:31 pm	♍
26	♍		
27	♍	7:28 pm	♎
28	♎		
29	♎	9:57 pm	♏
30	♏		
31	♏	9:54 pm	♐

June

1	♐		
2	♐	9:07 pm	♑
3	♑		
4	♑	9:44 pm	♒
5	♒		
6	♒		
7	♒	1:35 am	♓
8	♓		
9	♓	9:34 am	♈
10	♈		
11	♈	8:56 pm	♉
12	♉		
13	♉		
14	♉	9:50 am	♊
15	♊		
16	♊	10:28 pm	♋
17	♋		
18	♋		
19	♋	9:53 am	♌
20	♌		
21	♌	7:29 pm	♍
22	♍		
23	♍		
24	♍	2:35 am	♎
25	♎		
26	♎	6:42 am	♏
27	♏		
28	♏	8:02 am	♐
29	♐		
30	♐	7:48 am	♑

July

1	♑		
2	♑	7:56 am	♒
3	♒		
4	♒	10:31 am	♓
5	♓		
6	♓	5:03 pm	♈
7	♈		
8	♈		
9	♈	3:33 am	♉
10	♉		
11	♉	4:15 pm	♊
12	♊		
13	♊		
14	♊	4:50 am	♋
15	♋		
16	♋	3:51 pm	♌
17	♌		
18	♌		
19	♌	12:58 pm	♍
20	♍		
21	♍	8:09 am	♎
22	♎		
23	♎	1:13 pm	♏
24	♏		
25	♏	4:04 pm	♐
26	♐		
27	♐	5:15 pm	♑
28	♑		
29	♑	6:04 pm	♒
30	♒		
31	♒	8:23 pm	♓

August

1	♓		
2	♓		
3	♓	1:54 am	♈
4	♈		
5	♈	11:18 am	♉
6	♉		
7	♉	11:29 pm	♊
8	♊		
9	♊		
10	♊	12:04 pm	♋
11	♋		
12	♋	10:57 pm	♌
13	♌		
14	♌		
15	♌	7:26 am	♍
16	♍		
17	♍	1:49 pm	♎
18	♎		
19	♎	6:35 pm	♏
20	♏		
21	♏	10:03 pm	♐
22	♐		
23	♐		
24	♐	12:30 am	♑
25	♑		
26	♑	2:41 am	♒
27	♒		
28	♒	5:46 am	♓
29	♓		
30	♓	11:11 am	♈
31	♈		

September

1	♈	7:52 pm	♉
2	♉		
3	♉		
4	♉	7:27 am	♊
5	♊		
6	♊	8:03 pm	♋
7	♋		
8	♋		
9	♋	7:14 am	♌
10	♌		
11	♌	3:34 pm	♍
12	♍		
13	♍	9:07 pm	♎
14	♎		
15	♎		
16	♎	12:45 am	♏
17	♏		
18	♏	3:28 am	♐
19	♐		
20	♐	6:04 am	♑
21	♑		
22	♑	9:12 am	♒
23	♒		
24	♒	1:30 pm	♓
25	♓		
26	♓	7:40 pm	♈
27	♈		
28	♈		
29	♈	4:21 am	♉
30	♉		

October

1	♉	3:33 pm	♊
2	♊		
3	♊		
4	♊	4:09 am	♋
5	♋		
6	♋	3:58 pm	♌
7	♌		
8	♌		
9	♌	12:59 am	♍
10	♍		
11	♍	6:29 am	♎
12	♎		
13	♎	9:11 am	♏
14	♏		
15	♏	10:27 am	♐
16	♐		
17	♐	11:51 am	♑
18	♑		
19	♑	2:36 pm	♒
20	♒		
21	♒	7:26 pm	♓
22	♓		
23	♓		
24	♓	2:34 am	♈
25	♈		
26	♈	11:53 am	♉
27	♉		
28	♉	11:08 pm	♊
29	♊		
30	♊		
31	♊	11:40 am	♋

November

1	♋		
2	♋		
3	♋	12:03 am	♌
4	♌		
5	♌	10:17 am	♍
6	♍		
7	♍	4:51 pm	♎
8	♎		
9	♎	7:42 pm	♏
10	♏		
11	♏	8:03 pm	♐
12	♐		
13	♐	7:50 pm	♑
14	♑		
15	♑	9:00 pm	♒
16	♒		
17	♒		
18	♒	12:58 am	♓
19	♓		
20	♓	8:13 am	♈
21	♈		
22	♈	6:09 pm	♉
23	♉		
24	♉		
25	♉	5:48 am	♊
26	♊		
27	♊	6:20 pm	♋
28	♋		
29	♋		
30	♋	6:53 am	♌

December

1	♌		
2	♌	6:05 pm	♍
3	♍		
4	♍		
5	♍	2:18 am	♎
6	♎		
7	♎	6:33 am	♏
8	♏		
9	♏	7:22 am	♐
10	♐		
11	♐	6:26 am	♑
12	♑		
13	♑	5:59 am	♒
14	♒		
15	♒	8:09 am	♓
16	♓		
17	♓	2:11 pm	♈
18	♈		
19	♈	11:54 pm	♉
20	♉		
21	♉		
22	♉	11:51 am	♊
23	♊		
24	♊		
25	♊	12:30 am	♋
26	♋		
27	♋	12:52 pm	♌
28	♌		
29	♌		
30	♌	12:13 am	♍
31	♍		

Moon Movements

♎ = Libra ♏ = Scorpio ♐ = Sagittarius ♑ = Capricorn ♒ = Aquarius ♓ = Pisces

1978

January

Day	Moon	Time	Enters
1	♍	9:31 am	♎
2	♎		
3	♎	3:35 pm	♏
4	♏		
5	♏	6:03 pm	♐
6	♐		
7	♐	5:55 pm	♑
8	♑		
9	♑	5:05 pm	♒
10	♒		
11	♒	5:50 pm	♓
12	♓		
13	♓	10:05 pm	♈
14	♈		
15	♈		
16	♈	6:30 am	♉
17	♉		
18	♉	6:06 pm	♊
19	♊		
20	♊		
21	♊	6:50 am	♋
22	♋		
23	♋	7:02 pm	♌
24	♌		
25	♌		
26	♌	5:56 am	♍
27	♍		
28	♍	3:08 pm	♎
29	♎		
30	♎	10:04 pm	♏
31	♏		

February

Day	Moon	Time	Enters
1	♏		
2	♏	2:13 am	♐
3	♐		
4	♐	3:50 am	♑
5	♑		
6	♑	4:04 am	♒
7	♒		
8	♒	4:47 am	♓
9	♓		
10	♓	7:56 am	♈
11	♈		
12	♈	2:50 pm	♉
13	♉		
14	♉		
15	♉	1:24 am	♊
16	♊		
17	♊	1:56 pm	♋
18	♋		
19	♋		
20	♋	2:09 am	♌
21	♌		
22	♌	12:39 pm	♍
23	♍		
24	♍	9:03 pm	♎
25	♎		
26	♎		
27	♎	3:28 am	♏
28	♏		

March

Day	Moon	Time	Enters
1	♏	8:02 am	♐
2	♐		
3	♐	10:58 am	♑
4	♑		
5	♑	12:51 pm	♒
6	♒		
7	♒	2:46 pm	♓
8	♓		
9	♓	6:08 pm	♈
10	♈		
11	♈		
12	♈	12:18 am	♉
13	♉		
14	♉	9:48 am	♊
15	♊		
16	♊	9:49 pm	♋
17	♋		
18	♋		
19	♋	10:12 am	♌
20	♌		
21	♌	8:49 pm	♍
22	♍		
23	♍		
24	♍	4:41 am	♎
25	♎		
26	♎	10:01 am	♏
27	♏		
28	♏	1:37 pm	♐
29	♐		
30	♐	4:23 pm	♑
31	♑		

April

Day	Moon	Time	Enters
1	♑	7:05 pm	♒
2	♒		
3	♒	10:20 pm	♓
4	♓		
5	♓		
6	♓	2:51 am	♈
7	♈		
8	♈	9:21 am	♉
9	♉		
10	♉	6:27 pm	♊
11	♊		
12	♊		
13	♊	5:59 am	♋
14	♋		
15	♋	6:30 pm	♌
16	♌		
17	♌		
18	♌	5:44 am	♍
19	♍		
20	♍	1:53 pm	♎
21	♎		
22	♎	6:39 pm	♏
23	♏		
24	♏	9:00 pm	♐
25	♐		
26	♐	10:27 pm	♑
27	♑		
28	♑		
29	♑	12:28 am	♒
30	♒		

May

Day	Moon	Time	Enters
1	♒	4:00 am	♓
2	♓		
3	♓	9:27 am	♈
4	♈		
5	♈	4:52 pm	♉
6	♉		
7	♉		
8	♉	2:18 am	♊
9	♊		
10	♊	1:41 pm	♋
11	♋		
12	♋		
13	♋	2:17 am	♌
14	♌		
15	♌	2:15 pm	♍
16	♍		
17	♍	11:24 pm	♎
18	♎		
19	♎		
20	♎	4:39 am	♏
21	♏		
22	♏	6:31 am	♐
23	♐		
24	♐	6:41 am	♑
25	♑		
26	♑	7:10 am	♒
27	♒		
28	♒	9:36 am	♓
29	♓		
30	♓	2:52 pm	♈
31	♈		

June

Day	Moon	Time	Enters
1	♈	10:50 pm	♉
2	♉		
3	♉		
4	♉	8:53 am	♊
5	♊		
6	♊	8:30 pm	♋
7	♋		
8	♋		
9	♋	9:07 am	♌
10	♌		
11	♌	9:35 pm	♍
12	♍		
13	♍		
14	♍	7:55 am	♎
15	♎		
16	♎	2:28 pm	♏
17	♏		
18	♏	5:01 pm	♐
19	♐		
20	♐	4:52 pm	♑
21	♑		
22	♑	4:07 pm	♒
23	♒		
24	♒	4:57 pm	♓
25	♓		
26	♓	8:53 pm	♈
27	♈		
28	♈		
29	♈	4:21 am	♉
30	♉		

July

Day	Moon	Time	Enters
1	♉	2:37 pm	♊
2	♊		
3	♊		
4	♊	2:33 am	♋
5	♋		
6	♋	3:13 pm	♌
7	♌		
8	♌		
9	♌	3:44 am	♍
10	♍		
11	♍	2:48 pm	♎
12	♎		
13	♎	10:47 pm	♏
14	♏		
15	♏		
16	♏	2:50 am	♐
17	♐		
18	♐	3:33 am	♑
19	♑		
20	♑	2:41 am	♒
21	♒		
22	♒	2:26 am	♓
23	♓		
24	♓	4:46 am	♈
25	♈		
26	♈	10:50 am	♉
27	♉		
28	♉	8:31 pm	♊
29	♊		
30	♊		
31	♊	8:28 am	♋

August

Day	Moon	Time	Enters
1	♋		
2	♋	9:10 pm	♌
3	♌		
4	♌		
5	♌	9:29 am	♍
6	♍		
7	♍	8:30 pm	♎
8	♎		
9	♎		
10	♎	5:11 am	♏
11	♏		
12	♏	10:43 am	♐
13	♐		
14	♐	1:03 pm	♑
15	♑		
16	♑	1:15 pm	♒
17	♒		
18	♒	1:04 pm	♓
19	♓		
20	♓	2:29 pm	♈
21	♈		
22	♈	7:06 pm	♉
23	♉		
24	♉		
25	♉	3:31 am	♊
26	♊		
27	♊	2:59 pm	♋
28	♋		
29	♋		
30	♋	3:40 am	♌
31	♌		

September

Day	Moon	Time	Enters
1	♌	3:46 pm	♍
2	♍		
3	♍		
4	♍	2:15 am	♎
5	♎		
6	♎	10:38 am	♏
7	♏		
8	♏	4:39 pm	♐
9	♐		
10	♐	8:20 pm	♑
11	♑		
12	♑	10:09 pm	♒
13	♒		
14	♒	11:09 pm	♓
15	♓		
16	♓		
17	♓	12:50 am	♈
18	♈		
19	♈	4:43 am	♉
20	♉		
21	♉	11:56 am	♊
22	♊		
23	♊	10:31 pm	♋
24	♋		
25	♋		
26	♋	11:01 am	♌
27	♌		
28	♌	11:11 pm	♍
29	♍		
30	♍		

October

Day	Moon	Time	Enters
1	♍	9:17 am	♎
2	♎		
3	♎	4:48 pm	♏
4	♏		
5	♏	10:07 pm	♐
6	♐		
7	♐		
8	♐	1:52 am	♑
9	♑		
10	♑	4:42 am	♒
11	♒		
12	♒	7:12 am	♓
13	♓		
14	♓	10:06 am	♈
15	♈		
16	♈	2:22 pm	♉
17	♉		
18	♉	9:05 pm	♊
19	♊		
20	♊		
21	♊	6:52 am	♋
22	♋		
23	♋	7:04 pm	♌
24	♌		
25	♌		
26	♌	7:32 am	♍
27	♍		
28	♍	5:51 pm	♎
29	♎		
30	♎		
31	♎	12:53 am	♏

November

Day	Moon	Time	Enters
1	♏		
2	♏	5:03 am	♐
3	♐		
4	♐	7:40 am	♑
5	♑		
6	♑	10:04 am	♒
7	♒		
8	♒	1:06 pm	♓
9	♓		
10	♓	5:11 pm	♈
11	♈		
12	♈	10:35 pm	♉
13	♉		
14	♉		
15	♉	5:45 am	♊
16	♊		
17	♊	3:16 pm	♋
18	♋		
19	♋		
20	♋	3:09 am	♌
21	♌		
22	♌	3:57 pm	♍
23	♍		
24	♍		
25	♍	3:07 am	♎
26	♎		
27	♎	10:38 am	♏
28	♏		
29	♏	2:23 pm	♐
30	♐		

December

Day	Moon	Time	Enters
1	♐	3:44 pm	♑
2	♑		
3	♑	4:35 pm	♒
4	♒		
5	♒	6:36 pm	♓
6	♓		
7	♓	10:40 pm	♈
8	♈		
9	♈		
10	♈	4:50 am	♉
11	♉		
12	♉	12:54 pm	♊
13	♊		
14	♊	10:50 pm	♋
15	♋		
16	♋		
17	♋	10:37 am	♌
18	♌		
19	♌	11:34 pm	♍
20	♍		
21	♍		
22	♍	11:40 am	♎
23	♎		
24	♎	8:32 pm	♏
25	♏		
26	♏		
27	♏	1:07 am	♐
28	♐		
29	♐	2:15 am	♑
30	♑		
31	♑	1:53 am	♒

Your Starway to Love

♈ = Aries ♉ = Taurus ♊ = Gemini ♋ = Cancer ♌ = Leo ♍ = Virgo

1979

January

1	♒		
2	♒	2:08 am	♓
3	♓		
4	♓	4:41 am	♈
5	♈		
6	♈	10:17 am	♉
7	♉		
8	♉	6:42 pm	♊
9	♊		
10	♊		
11	♊	5:14 am	♋
12	♋		
13	♋	5:16 pm	♌
14	♌		
15	♌		
16	♌	6:10 am	♍
17	♍		
18	♍	6:40 pm	♎
19	♎		
20	♎		
21	♎	4:51 am	♏
22	♏		
23	♏	11:08 am	♐
24	♐		
25	♐	1:27 pm	♑
26	♑		
27	♑	1:12 pm	♒
28	♒		
29	♒	12:25 pm	♓
30	♓		
31	♓	1:11 pm	♈

February

1	♈		
2	♈	5:03 pm	♉
3	♉		
4	♉		
5	♉	12:33 am	♊
6	♊		
7	♊	11:06 am	♋
8	♋		
9	♋	11:25 pm	♌
10	♌		
11	♌		
12	♌	12:18 pm	♍
13	♍		
14	♍		
15	♍	12:37 am	♎
16	♎		
17	♎	11:12 am	♏
18	♏		
19	♏	6:51 pm	♐
20	♐		
21	♐	11:00 pm	♑
22	♑		
23	♑		
24	♑	12:12 am	♒
25	♒	11:52 pm	♓
26	♓		
27	♓	11:54 pm	♈
28	♈		

March

1	♈		
2	♈	2:09 am	♉
3	♉		
4	♉	7:58 am	♊
5	♊		
6	♊	5:34 pm	♋
7	♋		
8	♋		
9	♋	5:47 am	♌
10	♌		
11	♌	6:42 pm	♍
12	♍		
13	♍		
14	♍	6:42 am	♎
15	♎		
16	♎	4:49 pm	♏
17	♏		
18	♏		
19	♏	12:38 am	♐
20	♐		
21	♐	5:56 am	♑
22	♑		
23	♑	8:52 am	♒
24	♒		
25	♒	10:04 am	♓
26	♓		
27	♓	10:47 am	♈
28	♈		
29	♈	12:36 pm	♉
30	♉		
31	♉	5:08 pm	♊

April

1	♊		
2	♊		
3	♊	1:24 am	♋
4	♋		
5	♋	12:58 pm	♌
6	♌		
7	♌		
8	♌	1:52 am	♍
9	♍		
10	♍	1:45 pm	♎
11	♎		
12	♎	11:16 pm	♏
13	♏		
14	♏		
15	♏	6:18 am	♐
16	♐		
17	♐	11:23 am	♑
18	♑		
19	♑	3:02 pm	♒
20	♒		
21	♒	5:41 pm	♓
22	♓		
23	♓	7:51 pm	♈
24	♈		
25	♈	10:27 pm	♉
26	♉		
27	♉		
28	♉	2:49 am	♊
29	♊		
30	♊	10:11 am	♋

May

1	♋		
2	♋	8:56 pm	♌
3	♌		
4	♌		
5	♌	9:41 am	♍
6	♍		
7	♍	9:47 pm	♎
8	♎		
9	♎		
10	♎	7:10 am	♏
11	♏		
12	♏	1:25 pm	♐
13	♐		
14	♐	5:25 pm	♑
15	♑		
16	♑	8:26 pm	♒
17	♒		
18	♒	11:18 pm	♓
19	♓		
20	♓		
21	♓	2:30 am	♈
22	♈		
23	♈	6:20 am	♉
24	♉		
25	♉	11:28 am	♊
26	♊		
27	♊	6:51 pm	♋
28	♋		
29	♋		
30	♋	5:08 am	♌
31	♌		

June

1	♌	5:41 pm	♍
2	♍		
3	♍		
4	♍	6:12 am	♎
5	♎		
6	♎	4:05 pm	♏
7	♏		
8	♏	10:15 pm	♐
9	♐		
10	♐		
11	♐	1:23 am	♑
12	♑		
13	♑	3:06 am	♒
14	♒		
15	♒	4:56 am	♓
16	♓		
17	♓	7:52 am	♈
18	♈		
19	♈	12:18 pm	♉
20	♉		
21	♉	6:23 pm	♊
22	♊		
23	♊		
24	♊	2:24 am	♋
25	♋		
26	♋	12:47 pm	♌
27	♌		
28	♌		
29	♌	1:14 am	♍
30	♍		

July

1	♍	2:08 pm	♎
2	♎		
3	♎		
4	♎	12:57 am	♏
5	♏		
6	♏	7:55 am	♐
7	♐		
8	♐	11:07 am	♑
9	♑		
10	♑	11:59 am	♒
11	♒		
12	♒	12:23 pm	♓
13	♓		
14	♓	1:57 pm	♈
15	♈		
16	♈	5:43 pm	♉
17	♉		
18	♉	12:00 pm	♊
19	♊		
20	♊		
21	♊	8:40 am	♋
22	♋		
23	♋	7:30 pm	♌
24	♌		
25	♌		
26	♌	8:01 am	♍
27	♍		
28	♍	9:06 pm	♎
29	♎		
30	♎		
31	♎	8:46 am	♏

August

1	♏		
2	♏	5:05 pm	♐
3	♐		
4	♐	9:23 pm	♑
5	♑		
6	♑	10:28 pm	♒
7	♒		
8	♒	10:05 pm	♓
9	♓		
10	♓	10:10 pm	♈
11	♈		
12	♈		
13	♈	12:21 am	♉
14	♉		
15	♉	5:41 am	♊
16	♊		
17	♊	2:17 pm	♋
18	♋		
19	♋		
20	♋	1:28 am	♌
21	♌		
22	♌	2:11 pm	♍
23	♍		
24	♍		
25	♍	3:13 am	♎
26	♎		
27	♎	3:12 pm	♏
28	♏		
29	♏		
30	♏	12:39 am	♐
31	♐		

September

1	♐	6:33 am	♑
2	♑		
3	♑	8:59 am	♒
4	♒		
5	♒	9:03 am	♓
6	♓		
7	♓	8:29 am	♈
8	♈		
9	♈	9:12 am	♉
10	♉		
11	♉	12:54 pm	♊
12	♊		
13	♊	8:27 pm	♋
14	♋		
15	♋		
16	♋	7:25 am	♌
17	♌		
18	♌	8:15 pm	♍
19	♍		
20	♍		
21	♍	9:11 am	♎
22	♎		
23	♎	8:54 pm	♏
24	♏		
25	♏		
26	♏	6:36 am	♐
27	♐		
28	♐	1:40 pm	♑
29	♑		
30	♑	5:49 pm	♒

October

1	♒		
2	♒	7:23 pm	♓
3	♓		
4	♓	7:28 pm	♈
5	♈		
6	♈	7:45 pm	♉
7	♉		
8	♉	10:07 pm	♊
9	♊		
10	♊		
11	♊	4:09 am	♋
12	♋		
13	♋	2:12 pm	♌
14	♌		
15	♌		
16	♌	2:51 am	♍
17	♍		
18	♍	3:44 pm	♎
19	♎		
20	♎		
21	♎	3:02 am	♏
22	♏		
23	♏	12:09 pm	♐
24	♐		
25	♐	7:11 pm	♑
26	♑		
27	♑		
28	♑	12:16 am	♒
29	♒		
30	♒	3:29 am	♓
31	♓		

November

1	♓	5:09 am	♈
2	♈		
3	♈	6:16 am	♉
4	♉		
5	♉	8:26 am	♊
6	♊		
7	♊	1:24 pm	♋
8	♋		
9	♋	10:14 pm	♌
10	♌		
11	♌		
12	♌	10:20 am	♍
13	♍		
14	♍	11:16 pm	♎
15	♎		
16	♎		
17	♎	10:29 am	♏
18	♏		
19	♏	6:56 pm	♐
20	♐		
21	♐		
22	♐	1:01 am	♑
23	♑		
24	♑	5:37 am	♒
25	♒		
26	♒	9:17 am	♓
27	♓		
28	♓	12:17 pm	♈
29	♈		
30	♈	2:54 pm	♉

December

1	♉		
2	♉	6:02 pm	♊
3	♊		
4	♊	11:01 pm	♋
5	♋		
6	♋		
7	♋	7:09 am	♌
8	♌		
9	♌	6:33 pm	♍
10	♍		
11	♍		
12	♍	7:29 am	♎
13	♎		
14	♎	7:08 pm	♏
15	♏		
16	♏		
17	♏	3:36 am	♐
18	♐		
19	♐	8:55 am	♑
20	♑		
21	♑	12:13 pm	♒
22	♒		
23	♒	2:50 pm	♓
24	♓		
25	♓	5:40 pm	♈
26	♈		
27	♈	9:08 pm	♉
28	♉		
29	♉		
30	♉	1:32 am	♊
31	♊		

1980

Moon Movements

♎ = Libra ♏ = Scorpio ♐ = Sagittarius ♑ = Capricorn ♒ = Aquarius ♓ = Pisces

January

1	♊	7:29 am	♋
2	♋		
3	♋	3:47 pm	♌
4	♌		
5	♌		
6	♌	2:48 am	♍
7	♍		
8	♍	3:38 pm	♎
9	♎		
10	♎		
11	♎	3:55 am	♏
12	♏		
13	♏	1:17 pm	♐
14	♐		
15	♐	6:51 pm	♑
16	♑		
17	♑	9:25 pm	♒
18	♒		
19	♒	10:33 pm	♓
20	♓		
21	♓	11:52 pm	♈
22	♈		
23	♈		
24	♈	2:31 am	♉
25	♉		
26	♉	7:11 am	♊
27	♊		
28	♊	2:02 pm	♋
29	♋		
30	♋	11:08 pm	♌
31	♌		

April

1	♎		
2	♎	12:21 am	♏
3	♏		
4	♏	11:35 am	♐
5	♐		
6	♐	8:43 pm	♑
7	♑		
8	♑		
9	♑	3:00 am	♒
10	♒		
11	♒	6:07 am	♓
12	♓		
13	♓	6:40 am	♈
14	♈		
15	♈	6:11 am	♉
16	♉		
17	♉	6:41 am	♊
18	♊		
19	♊	10:11 am	♋
20	♋		
21	♋	5:52 pm	♌
22	♌		
23	♌		
24	♌	5:12 am	♍
25	♍		
26	♍	6:09 pm	♎
27	♎		
28	♎		
29	♎	6:35 am	♏
30	♏		

July

1	♒		
2	♒	12:48 am	♓
3	♓		
4	♓	3:46 am	♈
5	♈		
6	♈	6:30 am	♉
7	♉		
8	♉	9:33 am	♊
9	♊		
10	♊	1:44 pm	♋
11	♋		
12	♋	8:03 pm	♌
13	♌		
14	♌		
15	♌	5:11 am	♍
16	♍		
17	♍	4:55 pm	♎
18	♎		
19	♎		
20	♎	5:33 am	♏
21	♏		
22	♏	4:42 pm	♐
23	♐		
24	♐		
25	♐	12:45 am	♑
26	♑		
27	♑	5:34 am	♒
28	♒		
29	♒	8:11 am	♓
30	♓		
31	♓	9:53 am	♈

October

1	♋		
2	♋	2:57 pm	♌
3	♌		
4	♌		
5	♌	1:19 am	♍
6	♍		
7	♍	1:30 pm	♎
8	♎		
9	♎		
10	♎	2:15 am	♏
11	♏		
12	♏	2:37 pm	♐
13	♐		
14	♐		
15	♐	1:37 am	♑
16	♑		
17	♑	9:54 am	♒
18	♒		
19	♒	2:31 pm	♓
20	♓		
21	♓	3:43 pm	♈
22	♈		
23	♈	2:55 pm	♉
24	♉		
25	♉	2:17 pm	♊
26	♊		
27	♊	4:00 pm	♋
28	♋		
29	♋	9:38 pm	♌
30	♌		
31	♌		

February

1	♌		
2	♌	10:21 am	♍
3	♍		
4	♍	11:04 pm	♎
5	♎		
6	♎		
7	♎	11:46 am	♏
8	♏		
9	♏	10:19 pm	♐
10	♐		
11	♐		
12	♐	5:12 am	♑
13	♑		
14	♑	8:19 am	♒
15	♒		
16	♒	8:54 am	♓
17	♓		
18	♓	8:43 am	♈
19	♈		
20	♈	9:35 am	♉
21	♉		
22	♉	12:58 pm	♊
23	♊		
24	♊	7:34 pm	♋
25	♋		
26	♋		
27	♋	5:10 am	♌
28	♌		
29	♌	4:53 pm	♍

May

1	♏	5:22 pm	♐
2	♐		
3	♐		
4	♐	2:14 am	♑
5	♑		
6	♑	9:03 am	♒
7	♒		
8	♒	1:33 pm	♓
9	♓		
10	♓	3:44 pm	♈
11	♈		
12	♈	4:24 pm	♉
13	♉		
14	♉	5:07 pm	♊
15	♊		
16	♊	7:52 pm	♋
17	♋		
18	♋		
19	♋	2:14 am	♌
20	♌		
21	♌	12:32 pm	♍
22	♍		
23	♍		
24	♍	1:11 am	♎
25	♎		
26	♎	1:37 pm	♏
27	♏		
28	♏		
29	♏	12:05 am	♐
30	♐		
31	♐	8:14 am	♑

August

1	♈		
2	♈	11:55 am	♉
3	♉		
4	♉	3:10 pm	♊
5	♊		
6	♊	8:12 pm	♋
7	♋		
8	♋		
9	♋	3:23 am	♌
10	♌		
11	♌	12:54 pm	♍
12	♍		
13	♍		
14	♍	12:32 am	♎
15	♎		
16	♎	1:15 pm	♏
17	♏		
18	♏		
19	♏	1:08 am	♐
20	♐		
21	♐	10:11 am	♑
22	♑		
23	♑	3:32 pm	♒
24	♒		
25	♒	5:43 pm	♓
26	♓		
27	♓	6:11 pm	♈
28	♈		
29	♈	6:41 pm	♉
30	♉		
31	♉	8:50 pm	♊

November

1	♌	7:18 am	♍
2	♍		
3	♍	7:31 pm	♎
4	♎		
5	♎		
6	♎	8:19 am	♏
7	♏		
8	♏	8:25 pm	♐
9	♐		
10	♐		
11	♐	7:15 am	♑
12	♑		
13	♑	4:10 pm	♒
14	♒		
15	♒	10:21 pm	♓
16	♓		
17	♓		
18	♓	1:22 am	♈
19	♈		
20	♈	1:51 am	♉
21	♉		
22	♉	1:27 am	♊
23	♊		
24	♊	2:18 am	♋
25	♋		
26	♋	6:23 am	♌
27	♌		
28	♌	2:37 pm	♍
29	♍		
30	♍		

March

1	♍		
2	♍		
3	♍	5:40 am	♎
4	♎		
5	♎	6:23 pm	♏
6	♏		
7	♏		
8	♏	5:38 am	♐
9	♐		
10	♐	2:02 pm	♑
11	♑		
12	♑	6:45 pm	♒
13	♒		
14	♒	8:10 pm	♓
15	♓		
16	♓	7:41 pm	♈
17	♈		
18	♈	7:13 pm	♉
19	♉		
20	♉	8:47 pm	♊
21	♊		
22	♊		
23	♊	1:55 am	♋
24	♋		
25	♋	10:58 am	♌
26	♌		
27	♌	10:52 pm	♍
28	♍		
29	♍		
30	♍	11:49 am	♎
31	♎		

June

1	♑		
2	♑	2:29 pm	♒
3	♒		
4	♒	7:10 pm	♓
5	♓		
6	♓	10:23 pm	♈
7	♈		
8	♈		
9	♈	12:29 am	♉
10	♉		
11	♉	2:22 am	♊
12	♊		
13	♊	5:29 am	♋
14	♋		
15	♋	11:22 am	♌
16	♌		
17	♌	8:47 pm	♍
18	♍		
19	♍		
20	♍	8:55 am	♎
21	♎		
22	♎	9:26 pm	♏
23	♏		
24	♏		
25	♏	8:02 am	♐
26	♐		
27	♐	3:46 pm	♑
28	♑		
29	♑	9:04 pm	♒
30	♒		

September

1	♊		
2	♊		
3	♊	1:39 am	♋
4	♋		
5	♋	9:22 am	♌
6	♌		
7	♌	7:31 pm	♍
8	♍		
9	♍		
10	♍	7:22 am	♎
11	♎		
12	♎	8:06 pm	♏
13	♏		
14	♏		
15	♏	8:28 am	♐
16	♐		
17	♐	6:45 pm	♑
18	♑		
19	♑		
20	♑	1:31 am	♒
21	♒		
22	♒	4:27 am	♓
23	♓		
24	♓	4:37 am	♈
25	♈		
26	♈	3:53 am	♉
27	♉		
28	♉	4:21 am	♊
29	♊		
30	♊	7:46 am	♋

December

1	♍	2:13 am	♎
2	♎		
3	♎	3:00 pm	♏
4	♏		
5	♏		
6	♏	2:57 am	♐
7	♐		
8	♐	1:12 pm	♑
9	♑		
10	♑	9:36 pm	♒
11	♒		
12	♒		
13	♒	4:03 am	♓
14	♓		
15	♓	8:21 am	♈
16	♈		
17	♈	10:36 am	♉
18	♉		
19	♉	11:39 am	♊
20	♊		
21	♊	1:03 pm	♋
22	♋		
23	♋	4:34 pm	♌
24	♌		
25	♌	11:32 pm	♍
26	♍		
27	♍		
28	♍	10:05 am	♎
29	♎		
30	♎	10:36 pm	♏
31	♏		

♈ = Aries ♉ = Taurus ♊ = Gemini ♋ = Cancer ♌ = Leo ♍ = Virgo

1981

January

Day	Sign	Time	Enters
1	♏		
2	♏	10:42 am	♐
3	♐		
4	♐	8:41 pm	♑
5	♑		
6	♑		
7	♑	4:12 am	♒
8	♒		
9	♒	9:42 am	♓
10	♓		
11	♓	1:43 pm	♈
12	♈		
13	♈	4:45 pm	♉
14	♉		
15	♉	7:17 pm	♊
16	♊		
17	♊	10:08 pm	♋
18	♋		
19	♋		
20	♋	2:21 am	♌
21	♌		
22	♌	9:02 am	♍
23	♍		
24	♍	6:45 pm	♎
25	♎		
26	♎		
27	♎	6:49 am	♏
28	♏		
29	♏	7:12 pm	♐
30	♐		
31	♐		

April

Day	Sign	Time	Enters
1	♒	1:41 pm	♓
2	♓		
3	♓	3:25 pm	♈
4	♈		
5	♈	3:04 pm	♉
6	♉		
7	♉	2:47 pm	♊
8	♊		
9	♊	4:34 pm	♋
10	♋		
11	♋	9:36 pm	♌
12	♌		
13	♌		
14	♌	5:56 am	♍
15	♍		
16	♍	4:38 pm	♎
17	♎		
18	♎		
19	♎	4:39 am	♏
20	♏		
21	♏	5:15 pm	♐
22	♐		
23	♐		
24	♐	5:31 am	♑
25	♑		
26	♑	3:57 pm	♒
27	♒		
28	♒	10:56 pm	♓
29	♓		
30	♓		

July

Day	Sign	Time	Enters
1	♋		
2	♋	11:47 pm	♌
3	♌		
4	♌		
5	♌	4:26 am	♍
6	♍		
7	♍	12:42 pm	♎
8	♎		
9	♎		
10	♎	12:02 am	♏
11	♏		
12	♏	12:35 pm	♐
13	♐		
14	♐		
15	♐	12:19 am	♑
16	♑		
17	♑	10:02 am	♒
18	♒		
19	♒	5:26 pm	♓
20	♓		
21	♓	10:43 pm	♈
22	♈		
23	♈		
24	♈	2:18 am	♉
25	♉		
26	♉	4:42 am	♊
27	♊		
28	♊	6:41 am	♋
29	♋		
30	♋	9:20 am	♌
31	♌		

October

Day	Sign	Time	Enters
1	♏		
2	♏	12:00 pm	♐
3	♐		
4	♐		
5	♐	12:49 am	♑
6	♑		
7	♑	12:01 pm	♒
8	♒		
9	♒	7:32 pm	♓
10	♓		
11	♓	11:01 pm	♈
12	♈		
13	♈	11:43 pm	♉
14	♉		
15	♉	11:41 pm	♊
16	♊		
17	♊		
18	♊	12:52 am	♋
19	♋		
20	♋	4:34 pm	♌
21	♌		
22	♌	11:05 am	♍
23	♍		
24	♍	7:56 pm	♎
25	♎		
26	♎		
27	♎	6:38 am	♏
28	♏		
29	♏	6:48 pm	♐
30	♐		
31	♐		

February

Day	Sign	Time	Enters
1	♐	5:37 am	♑
2	♑		
3	♑	12:55 pm	♒
4	♒		
5	♒	5:21 pm	♓
6	♓		
7	♓	8:01 pm	♈
8	♈		
9	♈	10:11 pm	♉
10	♉		
11	♉		
12	♉	12:51 am	♊
13	♊		
14	♊	4:43 am	♋
15	♋		
16	♋	10:10 am	♌
17	♌		
18	♌	5:34 pm	♍
19	♍		
20	♍		
21	♍	3:12 am	♎
22	♎		
23	♎	2:54 pm	♏
24	♏		
25	♏		
26	♏	3:29 am	♐
27	♐		
28	♐	2:46 pm	♑

May

Day	Sign	Time	Enters
1	♓	1:57 am	♈
2	♈		
3	♈	1:59 am	♉
4	♉		
5	♉	1:01 am	♊
6	♊		
7	♊	1:18 am	♋
8	♋		
9	♋	4:40 am	♌
10	♌		
11	♌	11:55 am	♍
12	♍		
13	♍	10:24 pm	♎
14	♎		
15	♎		
16	♎	10:37 am	♏
17	♏		
18	♏	11:14 pm	♐
19	♐		
20	♐		
21	♐	11:20 am	♑
22	♑		
23	♑	10:01 pm	♒
24	♒		
25	♒		
26	♒	6:05 am	♓
27	♓		
28	♓	10:44 am	♈
29	♈		
30	♈	12:10 pm	♉
31	♉		

August

Day	Sign	Time	Enters
1	♌	1:54 pm	♍
2	♍		
3	♍	9:24 pm	♎
4	♎		
5	♎		
6	♎	7:58 am	♏
7	♏		
8	♏	8:22 pm	♐
9	♐		
10	♐		
11	♐	8:20 am	♑
12	♑		
13	♑	5:56 pm	♒
14	♒		
15	♒		
16	♒	12:34 am	♓
17	♓		
18	♓	4:49 am	♈
19	♈		
20	♈	7:43 am	♉
21	♉		
22	♉	10:18 am	♊
23	♊		
24	♊	1:17 pm	♋
25	♋		
26	♋	5:10 pm	♌
27	♌		
28	♌	10:32 pm	♍
29	♍		
30	♍		
31	♍	6:02 am	♎

November

Day	Sign	Time	Enters
1	♐	7:46 am	♑
2	♑		
3	♑	7:51 pm	♒
4	♒		
5	♒		
6	♒	4:52 am	♓
7	♓		
8	♓	9:38 am	♈
9	♈		
10	♈	10:44 am	♉
11	♉		
12	♉	9:59 am	♊
13	♊		
14	♊	9:37 am	♋
15	♋		
16	♋	11:33 am	♌
17	♌		
18	♌	4:53 pm	♍
19	♍		
20	♍		
21	♍	1:33 am	♎
22	♎		
23	♎	12:36 pm	♏
24	♏		
25	♏		
26	♏	1:00 am	♐
27	♐		
28	♐	1:53 pm	♑
29	♑		
30	♑		

March

Day	Sign	Time	Enters
1	♑		
2	♑	10:51 pm	♒
3	♒		
4	♒		
5	♒	3:12 am	♓
6	♓		
7	♓	4:48 am	♈
8	♈		
9	♈	5:22 am	♉
10	♉		
11	♉	6:42 am	♊
12	♊		
13	♊	10:06 am	♋
14	♋		
15	♋	4:02 pm	♌
16	♌		
17	♌		
18	♌	12:20 am	♍
19	♍		
20	♍	10:31 am	♎
21	♎		
22	♎	10:14 pm	♏
23	♏		
24	♏		
25	♏	10:51 am	♐
26	♐		
27	♐	10:52 pm	♑
28	♑		
29	♑		
30	♑	8:15 am	♒
31	♒		

June

Day	Sign	Time	Enters
1	♉	11:48 am	♊
2	♊		
3	♊	11:38 am	♋
4	♋		
5	♋	1:43 pm	♌
6	♌		
7	♌	7:25 pm	♍
8	♍		
9	♍		
10	♍	4:55 am	♎
11	♎		
12	♎	4:54 pm	♏
13	♏		
14	♏		
15	♏	5:31 am	♐
16	♐		
17	♐	5:21 pm	♑
18	♑		
19	♑		
20	♑	3:36 am	♒
21	♒		
22	♒	11:44 am	♓
23	♓		
24	♓	5:18 pm	♈
25	♈		
26	♈	8:16 pm	♉
27	♉		
28	♉	9:21 pm	♊
29	♊		
30	♊	9:57 pm	♋

September

Day	Sign	Time	Enters
1	♎		
2	♎	4:10 pm	♏
3	♏		
4	♏		
5	♏	4:24 am	♐
6	♐		
7	♐	4:48 pm	♑
8	♑		
9	♑		
10	♑	2:59 am	♒
11	♒		
12	♒	9:34 am	♓
13	♓		
14	♓	12:55 pm	♈
15	♈		
16	♈	2:30 pm	♉
17	♉		
18	♉	3:59 pm	♊
19	♊		
20	♊	6:39 pm	♋
21	♋		
22	♋	11:08 pm	♌
23	♌		
24	♌		
25	♌	5:29 am	♍
26	♍		
27	♍	1:40 pm	♎
28	♎		
29	♎	11:53 pm	♏
30	♏		

December

Day	Sign	Time	Enters
1	♑	2:09 am	♒
2	♒		
3	♒	12:16 pm	♓
4	♓		
5	♓	6:49 pm	♈
6	♈		
7	♈	9:31 pm	♉
8	♉		
9	♉	9:30 pm	♊
10	♊		
11	♊	8:40 pm	♋
12	♋		
13	♋	9:08 pm	♌
14	♌		
15	♌		
16	♌	12:38 am	♍
17	♍		
18	♍	7:58 am	♎
19	♎		
20	♎	6:39 pm	♏
21	♏		
22	♏		
23	♏	7:11 am	♐
24	♐		
25	♐	7:59 pm	♑
26	♑		
27	♑		
28	♑	7:54 am	♒
29	♒		
30	♒	6:01 pm	♓
31	♓		

Moon Movements

♎ = Libra ♏ = Scorpio ♐ = Sagittarius ♑ = Capricorn ♒ = Aquarius ♓ = Pisces

January

Day	Sign	Time	Enters
1	♓		
2	♓	1:33 am	♈
3	♈		
4	♈	6:02 am	♉
5	♉		
6	♉	7:48 am	♊
7	♊		
8	♊	8:01 am	♋
9	♋		
10	♋	8:21 am	♌
11	♌		
12	♌	10:37 am	♍
13	♍		
14	♍	4:17 pm	♎
15	♎		
16	♎		
17	♎	1:46 am	♏
18	♏		
19	♏	2:00 pm	♐
20	♐		
21	♐		
22	♐	2:51 am	♑
23	♑		
24	♑	2:25 pm	♒
25	♒		
26	♒	11:49 pm	♓
27	♓		
28	♓		
29	♓	6:58 am	♈
30	♈		
31	♈	12:03 pm	♉

February

Day	Sign	Time	Enters
1	♉		
2	♉	3:20 pm	♊
3	♊		
4	♊	5:18 pm	♋
5	♋		
6	♋	6:50 pm	♌
7	♌		
8	♌	9:15 pm	♍
9	♍		
10	♍		
11	♍	2:02 am	♎
12	♎		
13	♎	10:16 am	♏
14	♏		
15	♏	9:45 pm	♐
16	♐		
17	♐		
18	♐	10:36 am	♑
19	♑		
20	♑	10:15 pm	♒
21	♒		
22	♒		
23	♒	7:09 am	♓
24	♓		
25	♓	1:17 pm	♈
26	♈		
27	♈	5:32 pm	♉
28	♉		

March

Day	Sign	Time	Enters
1	♉	8:50 pm	♊
2	♊		
3	♊	11:48 pm	♋
4	♋		
5	♋		
6	♋	2:50 am	♌
7	♌		
8	♌	6:27 am	♍
9	♍		
10	♍	11:34 am	♎
11	♎		
12	♎	7:17 pm	♏
13	♏		
14	♏		
15	♏	6:03 am	♐
16	♐		
17	♐	6:47 pm	♑
18	♑		
19	♑		
20	♑	6:53 am	♒
21	♒		
22	♒	4:01 pm	♓
23	♓		
24	♓	9:37 pm	♈
25	♈		
26	♈		
27	♈	12:39 am	♉
28	♉		
29	♉	2:44 am	♊
30	♊		
31	♊	5:09 am	♋

April

Day	Sign	Time	Enters
1	♋		
2	♋	8:36 am	♌
3	♌		
4	♌	1:18 pm	♍
5	♍		
6	♍	7:26 pm	♎
7	♎		
8	♎		
9	♎	3:33 am	♏
10	♏		
11	♏	2:07 pm	♐
12	♐		
13	♐		
14	♐	2:41 am	♑
15	♑		
16	♑	3:18 pm	♒
17	♒		
18	♒		
19	♒	1:20 am	♓
20	♓		
21	♓	7:23 am	♈
22	♈		
23	♈	9:59 am	♉
24	♉		
25	♉	10:48 am	♊
26	♊		
27	♊	11:43 am	♋
28	♋		
29	♋	2:09 pm	♌
30	♌		

May

Day	Sign	Time	Enters
1	♌	6:45 pm	♍
2	♍		
3	♍		
4	♍	1:32 am	♎
5	♎		
6	♎	10:24 am	♏
7	♏		
8	♏	9:17 pm	♐
9	♐		
10	♐		
11	♐	9:50 am	♑
12	♑		
13	♑	10:44 pm	♒
14	♒		
15	♒		
16	♒	9:46 am	♓
17	♓		
18	♓	5:04 pm	♈
19	♈		
20	♈	8:22 pm	♉
21	♉		
22	♉	8:54 pm	♊
23	♊		
24	♊	8:38 pm	♋
25	♋		
26	♋	9:27 pm	♌
27	♌		
28	♌		
29	♌	12:43 am	♍
30	♍		
31	♍	7:02 am	♎

June

Day	Sign	Time	Enters
1	♎		
2	♎	4:12 pm	♏
3	♏		
4	♏		
5	♏	3:31 am	♐
6	♐		
7	♐	4:12 pm	♑
8	♑		
9	♑		
10	♑	5:08 am	♒
11	♒		
12	♒	4:44 pm	♓
13	♓		
14	♓		
15	♓	1:20 am	♈
16	♈		
17	♈	6:07 am	♉
18	♉		
19	♉	7:34 am	♊
20	♊		
21	♊	7:13 am	♋
22	♋		
23	♋	6:57 am	♌
24	♌		
25	♌	8:36 am	♍
26	♍		
27	♍	1:30 pm	♎
28	♎		
29	♎	10:02 pm	♏
30	♏		

July

Day	Sign	Time	Enters
1	♏		
2	♏	9:25 am	♐
3	♐		
4	♐	10:15 pm	♑
5	♑		
6	♑		
7	♑	11:03 am	♒
8	♒		
9	♒	10:35 pm	♓
10	♓		
11	♓		
12	♓	7:49 am	♈
13	♈		
14	♈	2:00 pm	♉
15	♉		
16	♉	5:03 pm	♊
17	♊		
18	♊	5:46 pm	♋
19	♋		
20	♋	5:35 pm	♌
21	♌		
22	♌	6:20 pm	♍
23	♍		
24	♍	9:45 pm	♎
25	♎		
26	♎		
27	♎	4:58 am	♏
28	♏		
29	♏	3:48 pm	♐
30	♐		
31	♐		

August

Day	Sign	Time	Enters
1	♐	4:36 am	♑
2	♑		
3	♑	5:17 pm	♒
4	♒		
5	♒		
6	♒	4:23 am	♓
7	♓		
8	♓	1:21 pm	♈
9	♈		
10	♈	8:00 pm	♉
11	♉		
12	♉		
13	♉	12:22 am	♊
14	♊		
15	♊	2:40 am	♋
16	♋		
17	♋	3:40 am	♌
18	♌		
19	♌	4:40 am	♍
20	♍		
21	♍	7:22 am	♎
22	♎		
23	♎	1:21 pm	♏
24	♏		
25	♏	11:11 pm	♐
26	♐		
27	♐		
28	♐	11:42 am	♑
29	♑		
30	♑		
31	♑	12:23 am	♒

September

Day	Sign	Time	Enters
1	♒		
2	♒	11:11 am	♓
3	♓		
4	♓	7:24 pm	♈
5	♈		
6	♈		
7	♈	1:27 am	♉
8	♉		
9	♉	5:57 am	♊
10	♊		
11	♊	9:18 am	♋
12	♋		
13	♋	11:46 am	♌
14	♌		
15	♌	1:57 pm	♍
16	♍		
17	♍	5:03 pm	♎
18	♎		
19	♎	10:32 pm	♏
20	♏		
21	♏		
22	♏	7:30 am	♐
23	♐		
24	♐	7:31 pm	♑
25	♑		
26	♑		
27	♑	8:21 am	♒
28	♒		
29	♒	7:18 pm	♓
30	♓		

October

Day	Sign	Time	Enters
1	♓		
2	♓	3:06 am	♈
3	♈		
4	♈	8:09 am	♉
5	♉		
6	♉	11:39 am	♊
7	♊		
8	♊	2:39 pm	♋
9	♋		
10	♋	5:44 pm	♌
11	♌		
12	♌	9:09 pm	♍
13	♍		
14	♍		
15	♍	1:23 am	♎
16	♎		
17	♎	7:21 am	♏
18	♏		
19	♏	4:02 pm	♐
20	♐		
21	♐		
22	♐	3:38 am	♑
23	♑		
24	♑	4:36 pm	♒
25	♒		
26	♒		
27	♒	4:12 am	♓
28	♓		
29	♓	12:25 pm	♈
30	♈		
31	♈	5:04 pm	♉

November

Day	Sign	Time	Enters
1	♉		
2	♉	7:23 pm	♊
3	♊		
4	♊	8:59 pm	♋
5	♋		
6	♋	11:10 pm	♌
7	♌		
8	♌		
9	♌	2:40 am	♍
10	♍		
11	♍	7:46 am	♎
12	♎		
13	♎	2:42 pm	♏
14	♏		
15	♏	11:52 pm	♐
16	♐		
17	♐		
18	♐	11:21 am	♑
19	♑		
20	♑		
21	♑	12:20 am	♒
22	♒		
23	♒	12:43 pm	♓
24	♓		
25	♓	10:07 pm	♈
26	♈		
27	♈		
28	♈	3:31 am	♉
29	♉		
30	♉	5:36 am	♊

December

Day	Sign	Time	Enters
1	♊		
2	♊	5:58 am	♋
3	♋		
4	♋	6:26 am	♌
5	♌		
6	♌	8:32 am	♍
7	♍		
8	♍	1:11 pm	♎
9	♎		
10	♎	8:34 pm	♏
11	♏		
12	♏		
13	♏	6:27 am	♐
14	♐		
15	♐	6:15 pm	♑
16	♑		
17	♑		
18	♑	7:12 am	♒
19	♒		
20	♒	7:56 pm	♓
21	♓		
22	♓		
23	♓	6:34 am	♈
24	♈		
25	♈	1:37 pm	♉
26	♉		
27	♉	4:48 pm	♊
28	♊		
29	♊	5:12 pm	♋
30	♋		
31	♋	4:33 pm	♌

1983

Your Starway to Love

♈ = Aries ♉ = Taurus ♊ = Gemini ♋ = Cancer ♌ = Leo ♍ = Virgo

January

1	♌		
2	♌	4:49 pm	♍
3	♍		
4	♍	7:44 pm	♎
5	♎		
6	♎		
7	♎	2:16 am	♏
8	♏		
9	♏	12:14 pm	♐
10	♐		
11	♐		
12	♐	12:26 am	♑
13	♑		
14	♑	1:26 pm	♒
15	♒		
16	♒		
17	♒	2:02 am	♓
18	♓		
19	♓	1:08 pm	♈
20	♈		
21	♈	9:36 pm	♉
22	♉		
23	♉		
24	♉	2:40 am	♊
25	♊		
26	♊	4:28 am	♋
27	♋		
28	♋	4:10 am	♌
29	♌		
30	♌	3:35 am	♍
31	♍		

February

1	♍	4:47 am	♎
2	♎		
3	♎	9:32 am	♏
4	♏		
5	♏	6:28 pm	♐
6	♐		
7	♐		
8	♐	6:33 am	♑
9	♑		
10	♑	7:40 pm	♒
11	♒		
12	♒		
13	♒	8:02 am	♓
14	♓		
15	♓	6:46 pm	♈
16	♈		
17	♈		
18	♈	3:30 am	♉
19	♉		
20	♉	9:52 am	♊
21	♊		
22	♊	1:31 pm	♋
23	♋		
24	♋	2:46 pm	♌
25	♌		
26	♌	2:49 pm	♍
27	♍		
28	♍	3:30 pm	♎

March

1	♎		
2	♎	6:51 pm	♏
3	♏		
4	♏		
5	♏	2:15 am	♐
6	♐		
7	♐	1:29 pm	♑
8	♑		
9	♑		
10	♑	2:30 am	♒
11	♒		
12	♒	2:47 pm	♓
13	♓		
14	♓		
15	♓	1:00 am	♈
16	♈		
17	♈	9:04 am	♉
18	♉		
19	♉	3:20 pm	♊
20	♊		
21	♊	7:52 pm	♋
22	♋		
23	♋	10:43 pm	♌
24	♌		
25	♌		
26	♌	12:18 am	♍
27	♍		
28	♍	1:48 am	♎
29	♎		
30	♎	4:57 am	♏
31	♏		

April

1	♏	11:20 am	♐
2	♐		
3	♐	9:30 pm	♑
4	♑		
5	♑		
6	♑	10:06 am	♒
7	♒		
8	♒	10:30 pm	♓
9	♓		
10	♓		
11	♓	8:37 am	♈
12	♈		
13	♈	3:59 pm	♉
14	♉		
15	♉	9:15 pm	♊
16	♊		
17	♊		
18	♊	1:14 am	♋
19	♋		
20	♋	4:26 am	♌
21	♌		
22	♌	7:12 am	♍
23	♍		
24	♍	10:04 am	♎
25	♎		
26	♎	2:04 pm	♏
27	♏		
28	♏	8:28 pm	♐
29	♐		
30	♐		

May

1	♐	6:01 am	♑
2	♑		
3	♑	6:09 pm	♒
4	♒		
5	♒		
6	♒	6:43 am	♓
7	♓		
8	♓	5:16 pm	♈
9	♈		
10	♈		
11	♈	12:36 am	♉
12	♉		
13	♉	5:03 am	♊
14	♊		
15	♊	7:48 am	♋
16	♋		
17	♋	10:01 am	♌
18	♌		
19	♌	12:37 pm	♍
20	♍		
21	♍	4:11 pm	♎
22	♎		
23	♎	9:17 pm	♏
24	♏		
25	♏		
26	♏	4:27 am	♐
27	♐		
28	♐	2:07 pm	♑
29	♑		
30	♑		
31	♑	2:00 am	♒

June

1	♒		
2	♒	2:42 pm	♓
3	♓		
4	♓		
5	♓	1:59 am	♈
6	♈		
7	♈	10:05 am	♉
8	♉		
9	♉	2:37 pm	♊
10	♊		
11	♊	4:32 pm	♋
12	♋		
13	♋	5:21 pm	♌
14	♌		
15	♌	6:38 pm	♍
16	♍		
17	♍	9:36 pm	♎
18	♎		
19	♎		
20	♎	2:59 am	♏
21	♏		
22	♏	10:55 am	♐
23	♐		
24	♐	9:08 pm	♑
25	♑		
26	♑		
27	♑	9:07 am	♒
28	♒		
29	♒	9:52 pm	♓
30	♓		

July

1	♓		
2	♓	9:47 am	♈
3	♈		
4	♈	7:05 pm	♉
5	♉		
6	♉		
7	♉	12:41 am	♊
8	♊		
9	♊	2:50 am	♋
10	♋		
11	♋	2:54 am	♌
12	♌		
13	♌	2:43 am	♍
14	♍		
15	♍	4:10 am	♎
16	♎		
17	♎	8:38 am	♏
18	♏		
19	♏	4:31 pm	♐
20	♐		
21	♐		
22	♐	3:11 am	♑
23	♑		
24	♑	3:26 pm	♒
25	♒		
26	♒		
27	♒	4:11 am	♓
28	♓		
29	♓	4:21 pm	♈
30	♈		
31	♈		

August

1	♈	2:37 am	♉
2	♉		
3	♉	9:43 am	♊
4	♊		
5	♊	1:09 pm	♋
6	♋		
7	♋	1:37 pm	♌
8	♌		
9	♌	12:49 pm	♍
10	♍		
11	♍	12:51 pm	♎
12	♎		
13	♎	3:44 pm	♏
14	♏		
15	♏	10:33 pm	♐
16	♐		
17	♐		
18	♐	8:59 am	♑
19	♑		
20	♑	9:25 pm	♒
21	♒		
22	♒		
23	♒	10:10 am	♓
24	♓		
25	♓	10:08 pm	♈
26	♈		
27	♈		
28	♈	8:38 am	♉
29	♉		
30	♉	4:49 pm	♊
31	♊		

September

1	♊	9:53 pm	♋
2	♋		
3	♋	11:47 pm	♌
4	♌		
5	♌	11:36 pm	♍
6	♍		
7	♍	11:13 pm	♎
8	♎		
9	♎		
10	♎	12:49 am	♏
11	♏		
12	♏	6:08 am	♐
13	♐		
14	♐	3:34 pm	♑
15	♑		
16	♑		
17	♑	3:45 am	♒
18	♒		
19	♒	4:30 pm	♓
20	♓		
21	♓		
22	♓	4:10 am	♈
23	♈		
24	♈	2:12 pm	♉
25	♉		
26	♉	10:24 pm	♊
27	♊		
28	♊		
29	♊	4:24 am	♋
30	♋		

October

1	♋	7:54 am	♌
2	♌		
3	♌	9:15 am	♍
4	♍		
5	♍	9:42 am	♎
6	♎		
7	♎	11:06 am	♏
8	♏		
9	♏	3:21 pm	♐
10	♐		
11	♐	11:30 pm	♑
12	♑		
13	♑		
14	♑	11:00 am	♒
15	♒		
16	♒	11:41 pm	♓
17	♓		
18	♓		
19	♓	11:18 am	♈
20	♈		
21	♈	8:47 pm	♉
22	♉		
23	♉		
24	♉	4:10 am	♊
25	♊		
26	♊	9:47 am	♋
27	♋		
28	♋	1:50 pm	♌
29	♌		
30	♌	4:33 pm	♍
31	♍		

November

1	♍	6:31 pm	♎
2	♎		
3	♎	8:53 pm	♏
4	♏		
5	♏		
6	♏	1:09 am	♐
7	♐		
8	♐	8:31 am	♑
9	♑		
10	♑	7:10 pm	♒
11	♒		
12	♒		
13	♒	7:41 am	♓
14	♓		
15	♓	7:36 pm	♈
16	♈		
17	♈		
18	♈	5:06 am	♉
19	♉		
20	♉	11:45 am	♊
21	♊		
22	♊	4:10 pm	♋
23	♋		
24	♋	7:19 pm	♌
25	♌		
26	♌	10:02 pm	♍
27	♍		
28	♍		
29	♍	12:57 am	♎
30	♎		

December

1	♎	4:41 am	♏
2	♏		
3	♏	9:56 am	♐
4	♐		
5	♐	5:28 pm	♑
6	♑		
7	♑		
8	♑	3:39 am	♒
9	♒		
10	♒	3:53 pm	♓
11	♓		
12	♓		
13	♓	4:17 am	♈
14	♈		
15	♈	2:33 pm	♉
16	♉		
17	♉	9:23 pm	♊
18	♊		
19	♊		
20	♊	1:02 am	♋
21	♋		
22	♋	2:44 am	♌
23	♌		
24	♌	4:01 am	♍
25	♍		
26	♍	6:18 am	♎
27	♎		
28	♎	10:27 am	♏
29	♏		
30	♏	4:44 pm	♐
31	♐		

Moon Movements

♎ = Libra ♏ = Scorpio ♐ = Sagittarius ♑ = Capricorn ♒ = Aquarius ♓ = Pisces

1984

January

1	♐		
2	♐	1:07 am	♑
3	♑		
4	♑	11:31 am	♒
5	♒		
6	♒	11:34 pm	♓
7	♓		
8	♓		
9	♓	12:15 pm	♈
10	♈		
11	♈	11:36 pm	♉
12	♉		
13	♉		
14	♉	7:40 am	♊
15	♊		
16	♊	11:47 am	♋
17	♋		
18	♋	12:49 pm	♌
19	♌		
20	♌	12:35 pm	♍
21	♍		
22	♍	1:07 pm	♎
23	♎		
24	♎	4:04 pm	♏
25	♏		
26	♏	10:12 pm	♐
27	♐		
28	♐		
29	♐	7:12 am	♑
30	♑		
31	♑	6:11 pm	♒

April

1	♈		
2	♈	6:55 pm	♉
3	♉		
4	♉		
5	♉	5:04 am	♊
6	♊		
7	♊	12:59 pm	♋
8	♋		
9	♋	6:01 pm	♌
10	♌		
11	♌	8:11 pm	♍
12	♍		
13	♍	8:29 pm	♎
14	♎		
15	♎	8:41 pm	♏
16	♏		
17	♏	10:44 pm	♐
18	♐		
19	♐		
20	♐	4:10 am	♑
21	♑		
22	♑	1:27 pm	♒
23	♒		
24	♒		
25	♒	1:26 am	♓
26	♓		
27	♓	2:02 pm	♈
28	♈		
29	♈		
30	♈	1:30 am	♉

July

1	♌		
2	♌	2:28 pm	♍
3	♍		
4	♍	4:27 pm	♎
5	♎		
6	♎	7:28 pm	♏
7	♏		
8	♏		
9	♏	12:03 am	♐
10	♐		
11	♐	6:23 am	♑
12	♑		
13	♑	2:41 pm	♒
14	♒		
15	♒		
16	♒	1:10 am	♓
17	♓		
18	♓	1:26 pm	♈
19	♈		
20	♈		
21	♈	1:52 am	♉
22	♉		
23	♉	12:10 pm	♊
24	♊		
25	♊	6:44 pm	♋
26	♋		
27	♋	9:41 pm	♌
28	♌		
29	♌	10:29 pm	♍
30	♍		
31	♍	11:03 pm	♎

October

1	♐	12:28 am	♑
2	♑		
3	♑	9:03 am	♒
4	♒		
5	♒	8:19 pm	♓
6	♓		
7	♓		
8	♓	8:51 am	♈
9	♈		
10	♈	9:28 pm	♉
11	♉		
12	♉		
13	♉	9:14 am	♊
14	♊		
15	♊	7:00 pm	♋
16	♋		
17	♋		
18	♋	1:41 am	♌
19	♌		
20	♌	4:56 am	♍
21	♍		
22	♍	5:32 am	♎
23	♎		
24	♎	5:08 am	♏
25	♏		
26	♏	5:43 am	♐
27	♐		
28	♐	9:05 am	♑
29	♑		
30	♑	4:13 pm	♒
31	♒		

February

1	♒		
2	♒		
3	♒	6:22 am	♓
4	♓		
5	♓	7:04 pm	♈
6	♈		
7	♈		
8	♈	7:05 am	♉
9	♉		
10	♉	4:39 pm	♊
11	♊		
12	♊	10:20 pm	♋
13	♋		
14	♋		
15	♋	12:09 am	♌
16	♌	11:32 pm	♍
17	♍		
18	♍	10:39 pm	♎
19	♎		
20	♎	11:44 pm	♏
21	♏		
22	♏		
23	♏	4:22 am	♐
24	♐		
25	♐	12:49 pm	♑
26	♑		
27	♑		
28	♑	12:02 am	♒
29	♒		

May

1	♉		
2	♉	11:02 am	♊
3	♊		
4	♊	6:26 pm	♋
5	♋		
6	♋	11:43 pm	♌
7	♌		
8	♌		
9	♌	3:02 am	♍
10	♍		
11	♍	4:54 am	♎
12	♎		
13	♎	6:22 am	♏
14	♏		
15	♏	8:50 am	♐
16	♐		
17	♐	1:43 pm	♑
18	♑		
19	♑	9:55 pm	♒
20	♒		
21	♒		
22	♒	9:09 am	♓
23	♓		
24	♓	9:39 pm	♈
25	♈		
26	♈		
27	♈	9:13 am	♉
28	♉		
29	♉	6:23 pm	♊
30	♊		
31	♊		

August

1	♎		
2	♎		
3	♎	1:04 am	♏
4	♏		
5	♏	5:30 am	♐
6	♐		
7	♐	12:24 pm	♑
8	♑		
9	♑	9:25 pm	♒
10	♒		
11	♒		
12	♒	8:13 am	♓
13	♓		
14	♓	8:28 pm	♈
15	♈		
16	♈		
17	♈	9:13 am	♉
18	♉		
19	♉	8:31 pm	♊
20	♊		
21	♊		
22	♊	4:20 am	♋
23	♋		
24	♋	8:00 am	♌
25	♌		
26	♌	8:32 am	♍
27	♍		
28	♍	7:57 am	♎
29	♎		
30	♎	8:23 am	♏
31	♏		

November

1	♒		
2	♒	2:50 am	♓
3	♓		
4	♓	3:20 pm	♈
5	♈		
6	♈		
7	♈	3:53 am	♉
8	♉		
9	♉	3:10 pm	♊
10	♊		
11	♊		
12	♊	12:31 am	♋
13	♋		
14	♋	7:34 am	♌
15	♌		
16	♌	12:08 pm	♍
17	♍		
18	♍	2:29 pm	♎
19	♎		
20	♎	3:30 pm	♏
21	♏		
22	♏	4:34 pm	♐
23	♐		
24	♐	7:17 pm	♑
25	♑		
26	♑		
27	♑	1:06 am	♒
28	♒		
29	♒	10:33 am	♓
30	♓		

March

1	♒	12:29 pm	♓
2	♓		
3	♓		
4	♓	1:07 am	♈
5	♈		
6	♈	1:09 pm	♉
7	♉		
8	♉	11:30 pm	♊
9	♊		
10	♊		
11	♊	6:48 am	♋
12	♋		
13	♋	10:21 am	♌
14	♌		
15	♌	10:47 am	♍
16	♍		
17	♍	9:52 am	♎
18	♎		
19	♎	9:49 am	♏
20	♏		
21	♏	12:41 pm	♐
22	♐		
23	♐	7:36 pm	♑
24	♑		
25	♑		
26	♑	6:09 am	♒
27	♒		
28	♒	6:37 pm	♓
29	♓		
30	♓		
31	♓	7:14 am	♈

June

1	♊	12:54 am	♋
2	♋		
3	♋	5:19 am	♌
4	♌		
5	♌	8:27 am	♍
6	♍		
7	♍	11:03 am	♎
8	♎		
9	♎	1:48 pm	♏
10	♏		
11	♏	5:26 pm	♐
12	♐		
13	♐	10:48 pm	♑
14	♑		
15	♑		
16	♑	6:41 am	♒
17	♒		
18	♒	5:18 pm	♓
19	♓		
20	♓		
21	♓	5:40 am	♈
22	♈		
23	♈	5:38 pm	♉
24	♉		
25	♉		
26	♉	3:04 am	♊
27	♊		
28	♊	9:09 am	♋
29	♋		
30	♋	12:30 pm	♌

September

1	♏	11:30 am	♐
2	♐		
3	♐	5:55 pm	♑
4	♑		
5	♑		
6	♑	3:11 am	♒
7	♒		
8	♒	2:24 pm	♓
9	♓		
10	♓		
11	♓	2:47 am	♈
12	♈		
13	♈	3:33 pm	♉
14	♉		
15	♉		
16	♉	3:26 am	♊
17	♊		
18	♊	12:36 pm	♋
19	♋		
20	♋	5:49 pm	♌
21	♌		
22	♌	7:19 pm	♍
23	♍		
24	♍	6:41 pm	♎
25	♎		
26	♎	6:04 pm	♏
27	♏		
28	♏	7:32 pm	♐
29	♐		
30	♐		

December

1	♓	10:42 pm	♈
2	♈		
3	♈		
4	♈	11:20 am	♉
5	♉		
6	♉	10:24 pm	♊
7	♊		
8	♊		
9	♊	6:56 am	♋
10	♋		
11	♋	1:08 pm	♌
12	♌		
13	♌	5:35 pm	♍
14	♍		
15	♍	8:52 pm	♎
16	♎		
17	♎	11:27 pm	♏
18	♏		
19	♏		
20	♏	1:58 am	♐
21	♐		
22	♐	5:21 am	♑
23	♑		
24	♑	10:47 am	♒
25	♒		
26	♒	7:18 pm	♓
27	♓		
28	♓		
29	♓	6:49 am	♈
30	♈		
31	♈	7:36 pm	♉

Your Starway to Love

♈ = Aries ♉ = Taurus ♊ = Gemini ♋ = Cancer ♌ = Leo ♍ = Virgo

1985

January

Day	Sign	Time	Enters
1	♉		
2	♉		
3	♉	7:00 am	♊
4	♊		
5	♊	3:18 pm	♋
6	♋		
7	♋	8:28 pm	♌
8	♌		
9	♌	11:40 pm	♍
10	♍		
11	♍		
12	♍	2:13 am	♎
13	♎		
14	♎	5:07 am	♏
15	♏		
16	♏	8:48 am	♐
17	♐		
18	♐	1:29 pm	♑
19	♑		
20	♑	7:38 pm	♒
21	♒		
22	♒		
23	♒	4:02 am	♓
24	♓		
25	♓	3:05 pm	♈
26	♈		
27	♈		
28	♈	3:53 am	♉
29	♉		
30	♉	4:01 pm	♊
31	♊		

February

Day	Sign	Time	Enters
1	♊		
2	♊	12:59 am	♋
3	♋		
4	♋	6:02 am	♌
5	♌		
6	♌	8:09 am	♍
7	♍		
8	♍	9:10 am	♎
9	♎		
10	♎	10:49 am	♏
11	♏		
12	♏	2:09 pm	♐
13	♐		
14	♐	7:27 pm	♑
15	♑		
16	♑		
17	♑	2:36 am	♒
18	♒		
19	♒	11:38 am	♓
20	♓		
21	♓	10:43 pm	♈
22	♈		
23	♈		
24	♈	11:27 am	♉
25	♉		
26	♉		
27	♉	12:11 am	♊
28	♊		

March

Day	Sign	Time	Enters
1	♊	10:23 am	♋
2	♋		
3	♋	4:28 pm	♌
4	♌		
5	♌	6:43 pm	♍
6	♍		
7	♍	6:47 pm	♎
8	♎		
9	♎	6:47 pm	♏
10	♏		
11	♏	8:29 pm	♐
12	♐		
13	♐		
14	♐	12:55 am	♑
15	♑		
16	♑	8:11 am	♒
17	♒		
18	♒	5:50 pm	♓
19	♓		
20	♓		
21	♓	5:20 am	♈
22	♈		
23	♈	6:06 pm	♉
24	♉		
25	♉		
26	♉	7:02 am	♊
27	♊		
28	♊	6:13 pm	♋
29	♋		
30	♋		
31	♋	1:51 am	♌

April

Day	Sign	Time	Enters
1	♌		
2	♌	5:25 am	♍
3	♍		
4	♍	5:54 am	♎
5	♎		
6	♎	5:10 am	♏
7	♏		
8	♏	5:18 am	♐
9	♐		
10	♐	7:57 am	♑
11	♑		
12	♑	2:04 pm	♒
13	♒		
14	♒	11:30 pm	♓
15	♓		
16	♓		
17	♓	11:18 am	♈
18	♈		
19	♈		
20	♈	12:12 am	♉
21	♉		
22	♉	1:01 pm	♊
23	♊		
24	♊		
25	♊	12:26 am	♋
26	♋		
27	♋	9:10 am	♌
28	♌		
29	♌	2:24 pm	♍
30	♍		

May

Day	Sign	Time	Enters
1	♍	4:22 pm	♎
2	♎		
3	♎	4:17 pm	♏
4	♏		
5	♏	3:56 pm	♐
6	♐		
7	♐	5:11 pm	♑
8	♑		
9	♑	9:38 pm	♒
10	♒		
11	♒		
12	♒	5:56 am	♓
13	♓		
14	♓	5:25 pm	♈
15	♈		
16	♈		
17	♈	6:23 am	♉
18	♉		
19	♉	7:01 pm	♊
20	♊		
21	♊		
22	♊	6:05 am	♋
23	♋		
24	♋	2:54 pm	♌
25	♌		
26	♌	9:06 pm	♍
27	♍		
28	♍		
29	♍	12:41 am	♎
30	♎		
31	♎	2:07 am	♏

June

Day	Sign	Time	Enters
1	♏		
2	♏	2:33 am	♐
3	♐		
4	♐	3:34 am	♑
5	♑		
6	♑	6:52 am	♒
7	♒		
8	♒	1:46 pm	♓
9	♓		
10	♓		
11	♓	12:24 am	♈
12	♈		
13	♈	1:11 pm	♉
14	♉		
15	♉		
16	♉	1:45 am	♊
17	♊		
18	♊	12:22 pm	♋
19	♋		
20	♋	8:32 pm	♌
21	♌		
22	♌		
23	♌	2:32 pm	♍
24	♍		
25	♍	6:48 am	♎
26	♎		
27	♎	9:37 am	♏
28	♏		
29	♏	11:30 am	♐
30	♐		

July

Day	Sign	Time	Enters
1	♐	1:22 pm	♑
2	♑		
3	♑	4:36 pm	♒
4	♒		
5	♒	10:40 pm	♓
6	♓		
7	♓		
8	♓	8:20 am	♈
9	♈		
10	♈	8:44 pm	♉
11	♉		
12	♉		
13	♉	9:23 am	♊
14	♊		
15	♊	7:54 pm	♋
16	♋		
17	♋		
18	♋	3:25 am	♌
19	♌		
20	♌	8:29 am	♍
21	♍		
22	♍	12:10 pm	♎
23	♎		
24	♎	3:16 pm	♏
25	♏		
26	♏	6:12 pm	♐
27	♐		
28	♐	9:21 pm	♑
29	♑		
30	♑		
31	♑	1:25 am	♒

August

Day	Sign	Time	Enters
1	♒		
2	♒	7:33 am	♓
3	♓		
4	♓	4:43 pm	♈
5	♈		
6	♈		
7	♈	4:41 am	♉
8	♉		
9	♉	5:31 pm	♊
10	♊		
11	♊		
12	♊	4:28 am	♋
13	♋		
14	♋	11:57 am	♌
15	♌		
16	♌	4:15 pm	♍
17	♍		
18	♍	6:44 pm	♎
19	♎		
20	♎	8:51 pm	♏
21	♏		
22	♏	11:36 pm	♐
23	♐		
24	♐		
25	♐	3:24 am	♑
26	♑		
27	♑	8:31 am	♒
28	♒		
29	♒	3:25 pm	♓
30	♓		
31	♓		

September

Day	Sign	Time	Enters
1	♓	12:42 am	♈
2	♈		
3	♈	12:28 pm	♉
4	♉		
5	♉		
6	♉	1:27 am	♊
7	♊		
8	♊	1:10 pm	♋
9	♋		
10	♋	9:27 pm	♌
11	♌		
12	♌		
13	♌	1:52 am	♍
14	♍		
15	♍	3:34 am	♎
16	♎		
17	♎	4:17 am	♏
18	♏		
19	♏	5:40 am	♐
20	♐		
21	♐	8:49 am	♑
22	♑		
23	♑	2:11 pm	♒
24	♒		
25	♒	9:50 pm	♓
26	♓		
27	♓		
28	♓	7:43 am	♈
29	♈		
30	♈	7:35 pm	♉

October

Day	Sign	Time	Enters
1	♉		
2	♉		
3	♉	8:36 am	♊
4	♊		
5	♊	8:59 pm	♋
6	♋		
7	♋		
8	♋	6:33 am	♌
9	♌		
10	♌	12:09 pm	♍
11	♍		
12	♍	2:12 pm	♎
13	♎		
14	♎	2:13 pm	♏
15	♏		
16	♏	2:06 pm	♐
17	♐		
18	♐	3:35 pm	♑
19	♑		
20	♑	7:54 pm	♒
21	♒		
22	♒		
23	♒	3:27 am	♓
24	♓		
25	♓	1:47 pm	♈
26	♈		
27	♈		
28	♈	1:59 am	♉
29	♉		
30	♉	2:59 pm	♊
31	♊		

November

Day	Sign	Time	Enters
1	♊		
2	♊	3:31 am	♋
3	♋		
4	♋	2:04 pm	♌
5	♌		
6	♌	9:18 pm	♍
7	♍		
8	♍		
9	♍	12:52 am	♎
10	♎		
11	♎	1:31 am	♏
12	♏		
13	♏	12:52 am	♐
14	♐		
15	♐	12:53 am	♑
16	♑		
17	♑	3:25 am	♒
18	♒		
19	♒	9:42 am	♓
20	♓		
21	♓	7:42 pm	♈
22	♈		
23	♈		
24	♈	8:07 am	♉
25	♉		
26	♉	9:08 pm	♊
27	♊		
28	♊		
29	♊	9:23 am	♋
30	♋		

December

Day	Sign	Time	Enters
1	♋	7:59 pm	♌
2	♌		
3	♌		
4	♌	4:14 am	♍
5	♍		
6	♍	9:33 am	♎
7	♎		
8	♎	11:56 am	♏
9	♏		
10	♏	12:13 pm	♐
11	♐		
12	♐	11:59 am	♑
13	♑		
14	♑	1:15 pm	♒
15	♒		
16	♒	5:50 pm	♓
17	♓		
18	♓		
19	♓	2:37 am	♈
20	♈		
21	♈	2:41 pm	♉
22	♉		
23	♉		
24	♉	3:45 am	♊
25	♊		
26	♊	3:44 pm	♋
27	♋		
28	♋		
29	♋	1:44 am	♌
30	♌		
31	♌	9:43 am	♍

Moon Movements

♎ = Libra ♏ = Scorpio ♐ = Sagittarius ♑ = Capricorn ♒ = Aquarius ♓ = Pisces

January

Day	Moon	Time	Enters
1	♍		
2	♍	3:45 pm	♎
3	♎		
4	♎	7:44 pm	♏
5	♏		
6	♏	9:47 pm	♐
7	♐		
8	♐	10:42 pm	♑
9	♑		
10	♑		
11	♑	12:01 am	♒
12	♒		
13	♒	3:39 am	♓
14	♓		
15	♓	11:03 am	♈
16	♈		
17	♈	10:14 pm	♉
18	♉		
19	♉		
20	♉	11:12 am	♊
21	♊		
22	♊	11:15 pm	♋
23	♋		
24	♋		
25	♋	8:47 am	♌
26	♌		
27	♌	3:51 pm	♍
28	♍		
29	♍	9:10 pm	♎
30	♎		
31	♎		

April

Day	Moon	Time	Enters
1	♑		
2	♑	10:11 pm	♒
3	♒		
4	♒		
5	♒	4:03 am	♓
6	♓		
7	♓	12:12 pm	♈
8	♈		
9	♈	10:36 pm	♉
10	♉		
11	♉		
12	♉	10:51 am	♊
13	♊		
14	♊	11:42 pm	♋
15	♋		
16	♋		
17	♋	11:10 am	♌
18	♌		
19	♌	7:24 pm	♍
20	♍		
21	♍	11:50 pm	♎
22	♎		
23	♎		
24	♎	1:15 am	♏
25	♏		
26	♏	1:16 am	♐
27	♐		
28	♐	1:41 am	♑
29	♑		
30	♑	4:06 am	♒

July

Day	Moon	Time	Enters
1	♉		
2	♉		
3	♉	5:32 am	♊
4	♊		
5	♊	6:19 pm	♋
6	♋		
7	♋		
8	♋	5:56 am	♌
9	♌		
10	♌	3:50 pm	♍
11	♍		
12	♍	11:40 pm	♎
13	♎		
14	♎		
15	♎	4:58 am	♏
16	♏		
17	♏	7:34 am	♐
18	♐		
19	♐	8:10 am	♑
20	♑		
21	♑	8:17 am	♒
22	♒		
23	♒	9:59 am	♓
24	♓		
25	♓	3:02 pm	♈
26	♈		
27	♈		
28	♈	12:11 am	♉
29	♉		
30	♉	12:19 pm	♊
31	♊		

October

Day	Moon	Time	Enters
1	♍		
2	♍	8:03 pm	♎
3	♎		
4	♎	11:35 pm	♏
5	♏		
6	♏		
7	♏	1:48 am	♐
8	♐		
9	♐	3:52 am	♑
10	♑		
11	♑	6:45 am	♒
12	♒		
13	♒	11:03 am	♓
14	♓		
15	♓	5:13 pm	♈
16	♈		
17	♈		
18	♈	1:35 am	♉
19	♉		
20	♉	12:15 pm	♊
21	♊		
22	♊		
23	♊	12:37 am	♋
24	♋		
25	♋	1:02 pm	♌
26	♌		
27	♌	11:20 pm	♍
28	♍		
29	♍		
30	♍	6:04 am	♎
31	♎		

February

Day	Moon	Time	Enters
1	♎	1:19 am	♏
2	♏		
3	♏	4:31 am	♐
4	♐		
5	♐	7:02 am	♑
6	♑		
7	♑	9:35 am	♒
8	♒		
9	♒	1:32 pm	♓
10	♓		
11	♓	8:21 pm	♈
12	♈		
13	♈		
14	♈	6:38 am	♉
15	♉		
16	♉	7:17 pm	♊
17	♊		
18	♊		
19	♊	7:39 am	♋
20	♋		
21	♋	5:25 pm	♌
22	♌		
23	♌	11:58 pm	♍
24	♍		
25	♍		
26	♍	4:07 am	♎
27	♎		
28	♎	7:06 am	♏

May

Day	Moon	Time	Enters
1	♒		
2	♒	9:30 am	♓
3	♓		
4	♓	6:01 pm	♈
5	♈		
6	♈		
7	♈	4:59 am	♉
8	♉		
9	♉	5:26 pm	♊
10	♊		
11	♊		
12	♊	6:18 am	♋
13	♋		
14	♋	6:15 pm	♌
15	♌		
16	♌		
17	♌	3:45 am	♍
18	♍		
19	♍	9:41 am	♎
20	♎		
21	♎	12:02 pm	♏
22	♏		
23	♏	11:57 am	♐
24	♐		
25	♐	11:15 am	♑
26	♑		
27	♑	12:00 pm	♒
28	♒		
29	♒	3:54 pm	♓
30	♓		
31	♓	11:43 pm	♈

August

Day	Moon	Time	Enters
1	♊		
2	♊	1:04 am	♋
3	♋		
4	♋	12:26 pm	♌
5	♌		
6	♌	9:44 pm	♍
7	♍		
8	♍		
9	♍	5:05 am	♎
10	♎		
11	♎	10:36 am	♏
12	♏		
13	♏	2:17 pm	♐
14	♐		
15	♐	4:22 pm	♑
16	♑		
17	♑	5:44 pm	♒
18	♒		
19	♒	7:52 pm	♓
20	♓		
21	♓		
22	♓	12:27 am	♈
23	♈		
24	♈	8:36 am	♉
25	♉		
26	♉	8:00 pm	♊
27	♊		
28	♊		
29	♊	8:40 am	♋
30	♋		
31	♋	8:08 pm	♌

November

Day	Moon	Time	Enters
1	♎	9:19 am	♏
2	♏		
3	♏	10:19 am	♐
4	♐		
5	♐	10:49 am	♑
6	♑		
7	♑	12:29 pm	♒
8	♒		
9	♒	4:30 pm	♓
10	♓		
11	♓	11:14 pm	♈
12	♈		
13	♈		
14	♈	8:24 am	♉
15	♉		
16	♉	7:26 pm	♊
17	♊		
18	♊		
19	♊	7:46 am	♋
20	♋		
21	♋	8:25 pm	♌
22	♌		
23	♌		
24	♌	7:46 am	♍
25	♍		
26	♍	3:59 pm	♎
27	♎		
28	♎	8:13 pm	♏
29	♏		
30	♏	9:08 pm	♐

March

Day	Moon	Time	Enters
1	♏		
2	♏	9:51 am	♐
3	♐		
4	♐	12:56 pm	♑
5	♑		
6	♑	4:42 pm	♒
7	♒		
8	♒	9:48 pm	♓
9	♓		
10	♓		
11	♓	5:03 am	♈
12	♈		
13	♈	3:04 pm	♉
14	♉		
15	♉		
16	♉	3:23 am	♊
17	♊		
18	♊	4:04 pm	♋
19	♋		
20	♋		
21	♋	2:38 am	♌
22	♌		
23	♌	9:39 am	♍
24	♍		
25	♍	1:22 pm	♎
26	♎		
27	♎	3:05 pm	♏
28	♏		
29	♏	4:20 pm	♐
30	♐		
31	♐	6:25 pm	♑

June

Day	Moon	Time	Enters
1	♈		
2	♈		
3	♈	10:45 am	♉
4	♉		
5	♉	11:26 pm	♊
6	♊		
7	♊		
8	♊	12:16 pm	♋
9	♋		
10	♋		
11	♋	12:11 am	♌
12	♌		
13	♌	10:18 am	♍
14	♍		
15	♍	5:38 pm	♎
16	♎		
17	♎	9:36 pm	♏
18	♏		
19	♏	10:36 pm	♐
20	♐		
21	♐	10:00 pm	♑
22	♑		
23	♑	9:50 pm	♒
24	♒		
25	♒		
26	♒	12:12 am	♓
27	♓		
28	♓	6:35 am	♈
29	♈		
30	♈	4:54 pm	♉

September

Day	Moon	Time	Enters
1	♌		
2	♌		
3	♌	5:06 am	♍
4	♍		
5	♍	11:33 am	♎
6	♎		
7	♎	4:12 pm	♏
8	♏		
9	♏	7:40 pm	♐
10	♐		
11	♐	10:28 pm	♑
12	♑		
13	♑		
14	♑	1:07 am	♒
15	♒		
16	♒	4:27 am	♓
17	♓		
18	♓	9:33 am	♈
19	♈		
20	♈	5:25 pm	♉
21	♉		
22	♉		
23	♉	4:13 am	♊
24	♊		
25	♊	4:44 pm	♋
26	♋		
27	♋		
28	♋	4:39 am	♌
29	♌		
30	♌	1:57 pm	♍

December

Day	Moon	Time	Enters
1	♐		
2	♐	8:28 pm	♑
3	♑		
4	♑	8:23 pm	♒
5	♒		
6	♒	10:48 pm	♓
7	♓		
8	♓		
9	♓	4:49 am	♈
10	♈		
11	♈	2:10 pm	♉
12	♉		
13	♉		
14	♉	1:41 am	♊
15	♊		
16	♊	2:09 pm	♋
17	♋		
18	♋		
19	♋	2:44 am	♌
20	♌		
21	♌	2:30 pm	♍
22	♍		
23	♍		
24	♍	12:05 am	♎
25	♎		
26	♎	6:06 am	♏
27	♏		
28	♏	8:19 am	♐
29	♐		
30	♐	7:54 am	♑
31	♑		

Your Starway to Love

♈ = Aries ♉ = Taurus ♊ = Gemini ♋ = Cancer ♌ = Leo ♍ = Virgo

1987

January

1	♑	6:54 am	♒
2	♒		
3	♒	7:36 am	♓
4	♓		
5	♓	11:51 am	♈
6	♈		
7	♈	8:13 pm	♉
8	♉		
9	♉		
10	♉	7:39 am	♊
11	♊		
12	♊	8:18 pm	♋
13	♋		
14	♋		
15	♋	8:45 am	♌
16	♌		
17	♌	8:15 pm	♍
18	♍		
19	♍		
20	♍	6:09 am	♎
21	♎		
22	♎	1:30 pm	♏
23	♏		
24	♏	5:35 pm	♐
25	♐		
26	♐	6:42 pm	♑
27	♑		
28	♑	6:17 pm	♒
29	♒		
30	♒	6:24 pm	♓
31	♓		

February

1	♓	9:09 pm	♈
2	♈		
3	♈		
4	♈	3:53 am	♉
5	♉		
6	♉	2:23 pm	♊
7	♊		
8	♊		
9	♊	2:55 am	♋
10	♋		
11	♋	3:21 pm	♌
12	♌		
13	♌		
14	♌	2:26 am	♍
15	♍		
16	♍	11:44 am	♎
17	♎		
18	♎	7:04 pm	♏
19	♏		
20	♏		
21	♏	12:09 am	♐
22	♐		
23	♐	2:57 am	♑
24	♑		
25	♑	4:08 am	♒
26	♒		
27	♒	5:07 am	♓
28	♓		

March

1	♓	7:37 am	♈
2	♈		
3	♈	1:11 pm	♉
4	♉		
5	♉	10:26 pm	♊
6	♊		
7	♊		
8	♊	10:24 am	♋
9	♋		
10	♋	10:54 pm	♌
11	♌		
12	♌		
13	♌	9:55 am	♍
14	♍		
15	♍	6:34 pm	♎
16	♎		
17	♎		
18	♎	12:57 am	♏
19	♏		
20	♏	5:32 am	♐
21	♐		
22	♐	8:48 am	♑
23	♑		
24	♑	11:18 am	♒
25	♒		
26	♒	1:46 pm	♓
27	♓		
28	♓	5:12 pm	♈
29	♈		
30	♈	10:46 pm	♉
31	♉		

April

1	♉		
2	♉	7:16 am	♊
3	♊		
4	♊	6:33 pm	♋
5	♋		
6	♋		
7	♋	7:04 am	♌
8	♌		
9	♌	6:28 pm	♍
10	♍		
11	♍		
12	♍	3:06 am	♎
13	♎		
14	♎	8:41 am	♏
15	♏		
16	♏	12:02 pm	♐
17	♐		
18	♐	2:21 pm	♑
19	♑		
20	♑	4:45 pm	♒
21	♒		
22	♒	8:02 pm	♓
23	♓		
24	♓		
25	♓	12:41 am	♈
26	♈		
27	♈	7:06 am	♉
28	♉		
29	♉	3:43 pm	♊
30	♊		

May

1	♊		
2	♊	2:39 am	♋
3	♋		
4	♋	3:06 pm	♌
5	♌		
6	♌		
7	♌	3:07 am	♍
8	♍		
9	♍	12:29 pm	♎
10	♎		
11	♎	6:09 pm	♏
12	♏		
13	♏	8:41 pm	♐
14	♐		
15	♐	9:37 pm	♑
16	♑		
17	♑	10:42 pm	♒
18	♒		
19	♒		
20	♒	1:24 am	♓
21	♓		
22	♓	6:23 am	♈
23	♈		
24	♈	1:39 pm	♉
25	♉		
26	♉	10:55 pm	♊
27	♊		
28	♊		
29	♊	9:59 am	♋
30	♋		
31	♋	10:25 pm	♌

June

1	♌		
2	♌		
3	♌	10:56 am	♍
4	♍		
5	♍	9:24 pm	♎
6	♎		
7	♎		
8	♎	4:06 am	♏
9	♏		
10	♏	6:53 am	♐
11	♐		
12	♐	7:05 am	♑
13	♑		
14	♑	6:45 am	♒
15	♒		
16	♒	7:54 am	♓
17	♓		
18	♓	11:56 am	♈
19	♈		
20	♈	7:09 pm	♉
21	♉		
22	♉		
23	♉	4:54 am	♊
24	♊		
25	♊	4:22 pm	♋
26	♋		
27	♋		
28	♋	4:52 am	♌
29	♌		
30	♌	5:34 pm	♍

July

1	♍		
2	♍		
3	♍	4:55 am	♎
4	♎		
5	♎	1:03 pm	♏
6	♏		
7	♏	5:05 pm	♐
8	♐		
9	♐	5:43 pm	♑
10	♑		
11	♑	4:49 pm	♒
12	♒		
13	♒	4:36 pm	♓
14	♓		
15	♓	7:00 pm	♈
16	♈		
17	♈		
18	♈	1:04 am	♉
19	♉		
20	♉	10:33 am	♊
21	♊		
22	♊	10:13 pm	♋
23	♋		
24	♋		
25	♋	10:50 am	♌
26	♌		
27	♌	11:26 pm	♍
28	♍		
29	♍		
30	♍	10:59 am	♎
31	♎		

August

1	♎	8:09 pm	♏
2	♏		
3	♏		
4	♏	1:47 am	♐
5	♐		
6	♐	3:51 am	♑
7	♑		
8	♑	3:37 am	♒
9	♒		
10	♒	3:01 am	♓
11	♓		
12	♓	4:09 am	♈
13	♈		
14	♈	8:38 am	♉
15	♉		
16	♉	4:59 pm	♊
17	♊		
18	♊		
19	♊	4:19 am	♋
20	♋		
21	♋	4:58 pm	♌
22	♌		
23	♌		
24	♌	5:23 am	♍
25	♍		
26	♍	4:35 pm	♎
27	♎		
28	♎		
29	♎	1:49 am	♏
30	♏		
31	♏	8:24 am	♐

September

1	♐		
2	♐	12:04 pm	♑
3	♑		
4	♑	1:22 pm	♒
5	♒		
6	♒	1:37 pm	♓
7	♓		
8	♓	2:34 pm	♈
9	♈		
10	♈	5:57 pm	♉
11	♉		
12	♉		
13	♉	12:54 am	♊
14	♊		
15	♊	11:22 am	♋
16	♋		
17	♋	11:50 pm	♌
18	♌		
19	♌		
20	♌	12:13 pm	♍
21	♍		
22	♍	10:58 pm	♎
23	♎		
24	♎		
25	♎	7:30 am	♏
26	♏		
27	♏	1:49 pm	♐
28	♐		
29	♐	6:08 pm	♑
30	♑		

October

1	♑	8:51 pm	♒
2	♒		
3	♒	10:39 pm	♓
4	♓		
5	♓		
6	♓	12:35 am	♈
7	♈		
8	♈	3:57 am	♉
9	♉		
10	♉	10:03 am	♊
11	♊		
12	♊	7:31 pm	♋
13	♋		
14	♋		
15	♋	7:34 am	♌
16	♌		
17	♌	8:06 pm	♍
18	♍		
19	♍		
20	♍	6:50 am	♎
21	♎		
22	♎	2:41 pm	♏
23	♏		
24	♏	7:57 pm	♐
25	♐		
26	♐	11:33 pm	♑
27	♑		
28	♑		
29	♑	2:27 am	♒
30	♒		
31	♒	5:19 am	♓

November

1	♓		
2	♓	8:40 am	♈
3	♈		
4	♈	1:02 pm	♉
5	♉		
6	♉	7:16 pm	♊
7	♊		
8	♊		
9	♊	4:10 am	♋
10	♋		
11	♋	3:45 pm	♌
12	♌		
13	♌		
14	♌	4:29 am	♍
15	♍		
16	♍	3:48 pm	♎
17	♎		
18	♎	11:47 pm	♏
19	♏		
20	♏		
21	♏	4:16 am	♐
22	♐		
23	♐	6:32 am	♑
24	♑		
25	♑	8:13 am	♒
26	♒		
27	♒	10:40 am	♓
28	♓		
29	♓	2:36 pm	♈
30	♈		

December

1	♈	8:05 pm	♉
2	♉		
3	♉		
4	♉	3:13 am	♊
5	♊		
6	♊	12:20 pm	♋
7	♋		
8	♋	11:40 pm	♌
9	♌		
10	♌		
11	♌	12:30 pm	♍
12	♍		
13	♍		
14	♍	12:40 am	♎
15	♎		
16	♎	9:41 am	♏
17	♏		
18	♏	2:33 pm	♐
19	♐		
20	♐	4:07 pm	♑
21	♑		
22	♑	4:20 pm	♒
23	♒		
24	♒	5:10 pm	♓
25	♓		
26	♓	8:05 pm	♈
27	♈		
28	♈		
29	♈	1:37 am	♉
30	♉		
31	♉	9:29 am	♊

Moon Movements

♎ = Libra ♏ = Scorpio ♐ = Sagittarius ♑ = Capricorn ♒ = Aquarius ♓ = Pisces

1988

January

1	♊		
2	♊	7:17 pm	♋
3	♋		
4	♋		
5	♋	6:47 am	♌
6	♌		
7	♌	7:35 pm	♍
8	♍		
9	♍		
10	♍	8:17 am	♎
11	♎		
12	♎	6:39 pm	♏
13	♏		
14	♏		
15	♏	12:58 am	♐
16	♐		
17	♐	3:15 am	♑
18	♑		
19	♑	3:02 am	♒
20	♒		
21	♒	2:27 am	♓
22	♓		
23	♓	3:31 am	♈
24	♈		
25	♈	7:36 am	♉
26	♉		
27	♉	3:02 pm	♊
28	♊		
29	♊		
30	♊	1:11 am	♋
31	♋		

February

1	♋	1:06 pm	♌
2	♌		
3	♌		
4	♌	1:54 am	♍
5	♍		
6	♍	2:36 pm	♎
7	♎		
8	♎		
9	♎	1:42 am	♏
10	♏		
11	♏	9:36 am	♐
12	♐		
13	♐	1:36 pm	♑
14	♑		
15	♑	2:25 pm	♒
16	♒		
17	♒	1:44 pm	♓
18	♓		
19	♓	1:35 pm	♈
20	♈		
21	♈	3:50 pm	♉
22	♉		
23	♉	9:42 pm	♊
24	♊		
25	♊		
26	♊	7:12 am	♋
27	♋		
28	♋	7:12 pm	♌
29	♌		

March

1	♌		
2	♌	8:06 am	♍
3	♍		
4	♍	8:32 pm	♎
5	♎		
6	♎		
7	♎	7:27 am	♏
8	♏		
9	♏	3:59 pm	♐
10	♐		
11	♐	9:31 pm	♑
12	♑		
13	♑		
14	♑	12:08 am	♒
15	♒		
16	♒	12:42 am	♓
17	♓		
18	♓	12:45 am	♈
19	♈		
20	♈	2:05 am	♉
21	♉		
22	♉	6:21 am	♊
23	♊		
24	♊	2:27 pm	♋
25	♋		
26	♋		
27	♋	1:54 am	♌
28	♌		
29	♌	2:49 pm	♍
30	♍		
31	♍		

April

1	♍	3:05 am	♎
2	♎		
3	♎	1:26 pm	♏
4	♏		
5	♏	9:29 pm	♐
6	♐		
7	♐		
8	♐	3:19 am	♑
9	♑		
10	♑	7:10 am	♒
11	♒		
12	♒	9:24 am	♓
13	♓		
14	♓	10:47 am	♈
15	♈		
16	♈	12:31 pm	♉
17	♉		
18	♉	4:10 pm	♊
19	♊		
20	♊	11:04 pm	♋
21	♋		
22	♋		
23	♋	9:34 am	♌
24	♌		
25	♌	10:16 pm	♍
26	♍		
27	♍		
28	♍	10:37 am	♎
29	♎		
30	♎	8:39 pm	♏

May

1	♏		
2	♏		
3	♏	3:52 am	♐
4	♐		
5	♐	8:54 am	♑
6	♑		
7	♑	12:37 pm	♒
8	♒		
9	♒	3:39 pm	♓
10	♓		
11	♓	6:23 pm	♈
12	♈		
13	♈	9:22 pm	♉
14	♉		
15	♉		
16	♉	1:31 am	♊
17	♊		
18	♊	8:05 am	♋
19	♋		
20	♋	5:51 pm	♌
21	♌		
22	♌		
23	♌	6:12 am	♍
24	♍		
25	♍	6:49 pm	♎
26	♎		
27	♎		
28	♎	5:06 am	♏
29	♏		
30	♏	11:57 am	♐
31	♐		

June

1	♐	3:58 pm	♑
2	♑		
3	♑	6:34 pm	♒
4	♒		
5	♒	9:00 pm	♓
6	♓		
7	♓		
8	♓	12:04 am	♈
9	♈		
10	♈	4:02 am	♉
11	♉		
12	♉	9:14 am	♊
13	♊		
14	♊	4:19 pm	♋
15	♋		
16	♋		
17	♋	1:57 am	♌
18	♌		
19	♌	2:03 pm	♍
20	♍		
21	♍		
22	♍	2:57 am	♎
23	♎		
24	♎	1:58 pm	♏
25	♏		
26	♏	9:18 pm	♐
27	♐		
28	♐		
29	♐	1:00 am	♑
30	♑		

July

1	♑	2:30 am	♒
2	♒		
3	♒	3:33 am	♓
4	♓		
5	♓	5:37 am	♈
6	♈		
7	♈	9:27 am	♉
8	♉		
9	♉	3:16 pm	♊
10	♊		
11	♊	11:08 pm	♋
12	♋		
13	♋		
14	♋	9:11 am	♌
15	♌		
16	♌	9:17 pm	♍
17	♍		
18	♍		
19	♍	10:22 am	♎
20	♎		
21	♎	10:13 pm	♏
22	♏		
23	♏		
24	♏	6:42 am	♐
25	♐		
26	♐	11:07 am	♑
27	♑		
28	♑	12:25 pm	♒
29	♒		
30	♒	12:23 pm	♓
31	♓		

August

1	♓	12:53 pm	♈
2	♈		
3	♈	3:24 pm	♉
4	♉		
5	♉	8:43 pm	♊
6	♊		
7	♊		
8	♊	4:52 am	♋
9	♋		
10	♋	3:26 pm	♌
11	♌		
12	♌		
13	♌	3:46 am	♍
14	♍		
15	♍	4:52 pm	♎
16	♎		
17	♎		
18	♎	5:12 am	♏
19	♏		
20	♏	2:55 pm	♐
21	♐		
22	♐	8:49 pm	♑
23	♑		
24	♑	11:05 pm	♒
25	♒		
26	♒	11:01 pm	♓
27	♓		
28	♓	10:29 pm	♈
29	♈		
30	♈	11:22 pm	♉
31	♉		

September

1	♉		
2	♉	3:11 am	♊
3	♊		
4	♊	10:37 am	♋
5	♋		
6	♋	9:14 pm	♌
7	♌		
8	♌		
9	♌	9:48 am	♍
10	♍		
11	♍	10:51 pm	♎
12	♎		
13	♎		
14	♎	11:07 am	♏
15	♏		
16	♏	9:25 pm	♐
17	♐		
18	♐		
19	♐	4:45 am	♑
20	♑		
21	♑	8:43 am	♒
22	♒		
23	♒	9:51 am	♓
24	♓		
25	♓	9:29 am	♈
26	♈		
27	♈	9:29 am	♉
28	♉		
29	♉	11:43 am	♊
30	♊		

October

1	♊	5:39 pm	♋
2	♋		
3	♋		
4	♋	3:31 am	♌
5	♌		
6	♌	4:01 pm	♍
7	♍		
8	♍		
9	♍	5:03 am	♎
10	♎		
11	♎	4:58 pm	♏
12	♏		
13	♏		
14	♏	2:58 am	♐
15	♐		
16	♐	10:44 am	♑
17	♑		
18	♑	4:05 pm	♒
19	♒		
20	♒	6:58 pm	♓
21	♓		
22	♓	7:59 pm	♈
23	♈		
24	♈	8:22 pm	♉
25	♉		
26	♉	9:55 pm	♊
27	♊		
28	♊		
29	♊	2:28 am	♋
30	♋		
31	♋	11:03 am	♌

November

1	♌		
2	♌	11:02 pm	♍
3	♍		
4	♍		
5	♍	12:04 pm	♎
6	♎		
7	♎	11:46 pm	♏
8	♏		
9	♏		
10	♏	9:06 am	♐
11	♐		
12	♐	4:12 pm	♑
13	♑		
14	♑	9:36 pm	♒
15	♒		
16	♒		
17	♒	1:34 am	♓
18	♓		
19	♓	4:12 am	♈
20	♈		
21	♈	6:02 am	♉
22	♉		
23	♉	8:12 am	♊
24	♊		
25	♊	12:20 pm	♋
26	♋		
27	♋	7:52 pm	♌
28	♌		
29	♌		
30	♌	7:00 am	♍

December

1	♍		
2	♍	7:56 pm	♎
3	♎		
4	♎		
5	♎	7:51 am	♏
6	♏		
7	♏	4:55 pm	♐
8	♐		
9	♐	11:07 pm	♑
10	♑		
11	♑		
12	♑	3:25 am	♒
13	♒		
14	♒	6:53 am	♓
15	♓		
16	♓	10:03 am	♈
17	♈		
18	♈	1:11 pm	♉
19	♉		
20	♉	4:43 pm	♊
21	♊		
22	♊	9:35 pm	♋
23	♋		
24	♋		
25	♋	4:57 am	♌
26	♌		
27	♌	3:27 pm	♍
28	♍		
29	♍		
30	♍	4:09 am	♎
31	♎		

Your Starway to Love

♈ = Aries ♉ = Taurus ♊ = Gemini ♋ = Cancer ♌ = Leo ♍ = Virgo

1989

January

1	♎	4:34 pm	♏
2	♏		
3	♏		
4	♏	2:12 am	♐
5	♐		
6	♐	8:14 am	♑
7	♑		
8	♑	11:31 am	♒
9	♒		
10	♒	1:31 pm	♓
11	♓		
12	♓	3:36 pm	♈
13	♈		
14	♈	6:36 pm	♉
15	♉		
16	♉	10:57 pm	♊
17	♊		
18	♊		
19	♊	4:57 am	♋
20	♋		
21	♋	1:02 pm	♌
22	♌		
23	♌	11:32 pm	♍
24	♍		
25	♍		
26	♍	12:01 pm	♎
27	♎		
28	♎		
29	♎	12:49 am	♏
30	♏		
31	♏	11:30 am	♐

April

1	♒		
2	♒	8:37 pm	♓
3	♓		
4	♓	8:51 pm	♈
5	♈		
6	♈	8:07 pm	♉
7	♉		
8	♉	8:31 pm	♊
9	♊		
10	♊	11:58 pm	♋
11	♋		
12	♋		
13	♋	7:31 am	♌
14	♌		
15	♌	6:39 pm	♍
16	♍		
17	♍		
18	♍	7:31 am	♎
19	♎		
20	♎	8:13 pm	♏
21	♏		
22	♏		
23	♏	7:38 am	♐
24	♐		
25	♐	5:15 pm	♑
26	♑		
27	♑		
28	♑	12:33 am	♒
29	♒		
30	♒	5:03 am	♓

July

1	♊		
2	♊	4:19 am	♋
3	♋		
4	♋	9:37 am	♌
5	♌		
6	♌	6:04 pm	♍
7	♍		
8	♍		
9	♍	5:30 am	♎
10	♎		
11	♎	6:09 pm	♏
12	♏		
13	♏		
14	♏	5:31 am	♐
15	♐		
16	♐	2:01 pm	♑
17	♑		
18	♑	7:35 pm	♒
19	♒		
20	♒	11:07 pm	♓
21	♓		
22	♓		
23	♓	1:41 am	♈
24	♈		
25	♈	4:10 am	♉
26	♉		
27	♉	7:15 am	♊
28	♊		
29	♊	11:32 am	♋
30	♋		
31	♋	5:41 pm	♌

October

1	♎	3:53 pm	♏
2	♏		
3	♏		
4	♏	4:29 am	♐
5	♐		
6	♐	3:45 pm	♑
7	♑		
8	♑		
9	♑	12:07 am	♒
10	♒		
11	♒	4:37 am	♓
12	♓		
13	♓	5:41 am	♈
14	♈		
15	♈	4:52 am	♉
16	♉		
17	♉	4:19 am	♊
18	♊		
19	♊	6:09 am	♋
20	♋		
21	♋	11:47 am	♌
22	♌		
23	♌	9:15 pm	♍
24	♍		
25	♍		
26	♍	9:11 am	♎
27	♎		
28	♎	9:56 pm	♏
29	♏		
30	♏		
31	♏	10:23 am	♐

February

1	♐		
2	♐	6:30 pm	♑
3	♑		
4	♑	9:51 pm	♒
5	♒		
6	♒	10:52 pm	♓
7	♓		
8	♓	11:18 pm	♈
9	♈		
10	♈		
11	♈	12:45 am	♉
12	♉		
13	♉	4:22 am	♊
14	♊		
15	♊	10:40 am	♋
16	♋		
17	♋	7:33 pm	♌
18	♌		
19	♌		
20	♌	6:34 am	♍
21	♍		
22	♍	7:05 pm	♎
23	♎		
24	♎		
25	♎	7:57 am	♏
26	♏		
27	♏	7:29 pm	♐
28	♐		

May

1	♓		
2	♓	6:50 am	♈
3	♈		
4	♈	6:55 am	♉
5	♉		
6	♉	7:03 am	♊
7	♊		
8	♊	9:19 am	♋
9	♋		
10	♋	3:23 pm	♌
11	♌		
12	♌		
13	♌	1:30 am	♍
14	♍		
15	♍	2:07 pm	♎
16	♎		
17	♎		
18	♎	2:48 am	♏
19	♏		
20	♏	1:52 pm	♐
21	♐		
22	♐	10:54 pm	♑
23	♑		
24	♑		
25	♑	6:01 am	♒
26	♒		
27	♒	11:13 am	♓
28	♓		
29	♓	2:25 pm	♈
30	♈		
31	♈	3:59 pm	♉

August

1	♌		
2	♌		
3	♌	2:19 am	♍
4	♍		
5	♍	1:28 pm	♎
6	♎		
7	♎		
8	♎	2:05 am	♏
9	♏		
10	♏	2:02 pm	♐
11	♐		
12	♐	11:16 pm	♑
13	♑		
14	♑		
15	♑	4:59 am	♒
16	♒		
17	♒	7:46 am	♓
18	♓		
19	♓	8:59 am	♈
20	♈		
21	♈	10:10 am	♉
22	♉		
23	♉	12:39 pm	♊
24	♊		
25	♊	5:13 pm	♋
26	♋		
27	♋		
28	♋	12:12 am	♌
29	♌		
30	♌	9:29 am	♍
31	♍		

November

1	♐		
2	♐	9:46 pm	♑
3	♑		
4	♑		
5	♑	7:09 am	♒
6	♒		
7	♒	1:25 pm	♓
8	♓		
9	♓	4:08 pm	♈
10	♈		
11	♈	4:09 pm	♉
12	♉		
13	♉	3:19 pm	♊
14	♊		
15	♊	3:51 pm	♋
16	♋		
17	♋	7:46 pm	♌
18	♌		
19	♌		
20	♌	3:54 am	♍
21	♍		
22	♍	3:25 pm	♎
23	♎		
24	♎		
25	♎	4:13 am	♏
26	♏		
27	♏	4:30 pm	♐
28	♐		
29	♐		
30	♐	3:26 am	♑

March

1	♐		
2	♐	3:58 am	♑
3	♑		
4	♑	8:36 am	♒
5	♒		
6	♒	9:59 am	♓
7	♓		
8	♓	9:36 am	♈
9	♈		
10	♈	9:25 am	♉
11	♉		
12	♉	11:16 am	♊
13	♊		
14	♊	4:27 pm	♋
15	♋		
16	♋		
17	♋	1:13 am	♌
18	♌		
19	♌	12:39 pm	♍
20	♍		
21	♍		
22	♍	1:24 am	♎
23	♎		
24	♎	2:10 pm	♏
25	♏		
26	♏		
27	♏	1:54 am	♐
28	♐		
29	♐	11:25 am	♑
30	♑		
31	♑	5:45 pm	♒

June

1	♉		
2	♉	5:02 pm	♊
3	♊		
4	♊	7:17 pm	♋
5	♋		
6	♋		
7	♋	12:28 am	♌
8	♌		
9	♌	9:29 am	♍
10	♍		
11	♍	9:31 pm	♎
12	♎		
13	♎		
14	♎	10:11 am	♏
15	♏		
16	♏	9:12 pm	♐
17	♐		
18	♐		
19	♐	5:41 am	♑
20	♑		
21	♑	11:57 am	♒
22	♒		
23	♒	4:36 pm	♓
24	♓		
25	♓	8:06 pm	♈
26	♈		
27	♈	10:45 pm	♉
28	♉		
29	♉		
30	♉	1:08 am	♊

September

1	♍	8:47 pm	♎
2	♎		
3	♎		
4	♎	9:23 am	♏
5	♏		
6	♏	9:51 pm	♐
7	♐		
8	♐		
9	♐	8:13 am	♑
10	♑		
11	♑	3:02 pm	♒
12	♒		
13	♒	6:07 pm	♓
14	♓		
15	♓	6:38 pm	♈
16	♈		
17	♈	6:22 pm	♉
18	♉		
19	♉	7:16 pm	♊
20	♊		
21	♊	10:50 pm	♋
22	♋		
23	♋		
24	♋	5:44 am	♌
25	♌		
26	♌	3:32 pm	♍
27	♍		
28	♍		
29	♍	3:15 am	♎
30	♎		

December

1	♑		
2	♑	12:42 pm	♒
3	♒		
4	♒	7:48 pm	♓
5	♓		
6	♓		
7	♓	12:11 am	♈
8	♈		
9	♈	1:59 am	♉
10	♉		
11	♉	2:15 am	♊
12	♊		
13	♊	2:49 am	♋
14	♋		
15	♋	5:41 am	♌
16	♌		
17	♌	12:19 pm	♍
18	♍		
19	♍	10:45 pm	♎
20	♎		
21	♎		
22	♎	11:18 am	♏
23	♏		
24	♏	11:37 pm	♐
25	♐		
26	♐		
27	♐	10:10 am	♑
28	♑		
29	♑	6:38 pm	♒
30	♒		
31	♒		

Moon Movements

♎ = Libra ♏ = Scorpio ♐ = Sagittarius ♑ = Capricorn ♒ = Aquarius ♓ = Pisces

1990

January

1	♒	1:10 am	♓
2	♓		
3	♓	5:56 am	♈
4	♈		
5	♈	9:04 am	♉
6	♉		
7	♉	11:02 am	♊
8	♊		
9	♊	12:52 pm	♋
10	♋		
11	♋	4:02 pm	♌
12	♌		
13	♌	9:57 pm	♍
14	♍		
15	♍		
16	♍	7:17 am	♎
17	♎		
18	♎	7:16 pm	♏
19	♏		
20	♏		
21	♏	7:44 am	♐
22	♐		
23	♐	6:27 pm	♑
24	♑		
25	♑		
26	♑	2:25 am	♒
27	♒		
28	♒	7:51 am	♓
29	♓		
30	♓	11:34 am	♈
31	♈		

February

1	♈	2:27 pm	♉
2	♉		
3	♉	5:12 pm	♊
4	♊		
5	♊	8:27 pm	♋
6	♋		
7	♋		
8	♋	12:51 am	♌
9	♌		
10	♌	7:13 am	♍
11	♍		
12	♍	4:09 pm	♎
13	♎		
14	♎		
15	♎	3:34 am	♏
16	♏		
17	♏	4:07 pm	♐
18	♐		
19	♐		
20	♐	3:30 am	♑
21	♑		
22	♑	11:52 am	♒
23	♒		
24	♒	4:49 pm	♓
25	♓		
26	♓	7:16 pm	♈
27	♈		
28	♈	8:43 pm	♉

March

1	♉		
2	♉	10:37 pm	♊
3	♊		
4	♊		
5	♊	2:02 am	♋
6	♋		
7	♋	7:24 am	♌
8	♌		
9	♌	2:47 pm	♍
10	♍		
11	♍		
12	♍	12:09 am	♎
13	♎		
14	♎	11:25 am	♏
15	♏		
16	♏	11:56 pm	♐
17	♐		
18	♐		
19	♐	12:01 pm	♑
20	♑		
21	♑	9:31 pm	♒
22	♒		
23	♒		
24	♒	3:08 am	♓
25	♓		
26	♓	5:15 am	♈
27	♈		
28	♈	5:26 am	♉
29	♉		
30	♉	5:42 am	♊
31	♊		

April

1	♊	7:50 am	♋
2	♋		
3	♋	12:50 pm	♌
4	♌		
5	♌	8:42 pm	♍
6	♍		
7	♍		
8	♍	6:44 am	♎
9	♎		
10	♎	6:18 pm	♏
11	♏		
12	♏		
13	♏	6:48 am	♐
14	♐		
15	♐	7:15 pm	♑
16	♑		
17	♑		
18	♑	5:53 am	♒
19	♒		
20	♒	12:57 pm	♓
21	♓		
22	♓	3:58 pm	♈
23	♈		
24	♈	4:03 pm	♉
25	♉		
26	♉	3:12 pm	♊
27	♊		
28	♊	3:39 pm	♋
29	♋		
30	♋	7:08 pm	♌

May

1	♌		
2	♌		
3	♌	2:18 am	♍
4	♍		
5	♍	12:28 pm	♎
6	♎		
7	♎		
8	♎	12:22 am	♏
9	♏		
10	♏	12:56 pm	♐
11	♐		
12	♐		
13	♐	1:21 am	♑
14	♑		
15	♑	12:30 pm	♒
16	♒		
17	♒	8:54 pm	♓
18	♓		
19	♓		
20	♓	1:31 am	♈
21	♈		
22	♈	2:42 am	♉
23	♉		
24	♉	2:00 am	♊
25	♊		
26	♊	1:34 am	♋
27	♋		
28	♋	3:29 am	♌
29	♌		
30	♌	9:08 am	♍
31	♍		

June

1	♍	6:31 pm	♎
2	♎		
3	♎		
4	♎	6:21 am	♏
5	♏		
6	♏	6:59 pm	♐
7	♐		
8	♐		
9	♐	7:12 am	♑
10	♑		
11	♑	6:09 pm	♒
12	♒		
13	♒		
14	♒	3:00 am	♓
15	♓		
16	♓	8:55 am	♈
17	♈		
18	♈	11:43 am	♉
19	♉		
20	♉	12:14 pm	♊
21	♊		
22	♊	12:10 pm	♋
23	♋		
24	♋	1:25 pm	♌
25	♌		
26	♌	5:42 pm	♍
27	♍		
28	♍		
29	♍	1:47 am	♎
30	♎		

July

1	♎	1:01 pm	♏
2	♏		
3	♏		
4	♏	1:35 am	♐
5	♐		
6	♐	1:39 pm	♑
7	♑		
8	♑		
9	♑	12:07 am	♒
10	♒		
11	♒	8:29 am	♓
12	♓		
13	♓	2:36 pm	♈
14	♈		
15	♈	6:29 pm	♉
16	♉		
17	♉	8:32 pm	♊
18	♊		
19	♊	9:44 pm	♋
20	♋		
21	♋	11:29 pm	♌
22	♌		
23	♌		
24	♌	3:17 am	♍
25	♍		
26	♍	10:19 am	♎
27	♎		
28	♎	8:39 pm	♏
29	♏		
30	♏		
31	♏	9:00 am	♐

August

1	♐		
2	♐	9:08 pm	♑
3	♑		
4	♑		
5	♑	7:19 am	♒
6	♒		
7	♒	2:54 pm	♓
8	♓		
9	♓	8:13 pm	♈
10	♈		
11	♈	11:55 pm	♉
12	♉		
13	♉		
14	♉	2:41 am	♊
15	♊		
16	♊	5:12 am	♋
17	♋		
18	♋	8:11 am	♌
19	♌		
20	♌	12:33 pm	♍
21	♍		
22	♍	7:17 pm	♎
23	♎		
24	♎		
25	♎	4:56 am	♏
26	♏		
27	♏	4:57 pm	♐
28	♐		
29	♐		
30	♐	5:23 am	♑
31	♑		

September

1	♑	3:51 pm	♒
2	♒		
3	♒	11:06 pm	♓
4	♓		
5	♓		
6	♓	3:23 am	♈
7	♈		
8	♈	5:55 am	♉
9	♉		
10	♉	8:05 am	♊
11	♊		
12	♊	10:53 am	♋
13	♋		
14	♋	2:52 pm	♌
15	♌		
16	♌	8:19 pm	♍
17	♍		
18	♍		
19	♍	3:34 am	♎
20	♎		
21	♎	1:06 pm	♏
22	♏		
23	♏		
24	♏	12:52 am	♐
25	♐		
26	♐	1:36 pm	♑
27	♑		
28	♑		
29	♑	12:54 am	♒
30	♒		

October

1	♒	8:42 am	♓
2	♓		
3	♓	12:42 pm	♈
4	♈		
5	♈	2:06 pm	♉
6	♉		
7	♉	2:47 pm	♊
8	♊		
9	♊	4:29 pm	♋
10	♋		
11	♋	8:16 pm	♌
12	♌		
13	♌		
14	♌	2:21 am	♍
15	♍		
16	♍	10:26 am	♎
17	♎		
18	♎	8:24 pm	♏
19	♏		
20	♏		
21	♏	8:09 am	♐
22	♐		
23	♐	9:03 pm	♑
24	♑		
25	♑		
26	♑	9:14 am	♒
27	♒		
28	♒	6:22 pm	♓
29	♓		
30	♓	11:14 pm	♈
31	♈		

November

1	♈		
2	♈	12:31 am	♉
3	♉		
4	♉	12:06 am	♊
5	♊		
6	♊	12:07 am	♋
7	♋		
8	♋	2:24 am	♌
9	♌		
10	♌	7:48 am	♍
11	♍		
12	♍	4:08 pm	♎
13	♎		
14	♎		
15	♎	2:39 am	♏
16	♏		
17	♏	2:39 pm	♐
18	♐		
19	♐		
20	♐	3:31 am	♑
21	♑		
22	♑	4:07 pm	♒
23	♒		
24	♒		
25	♒	2:32 am	♓
26	♓		
27	♓	9:06 am	♈
28	♈		
29	♈	11:37 am	♉
30	♉		

December

1	♉	11:22 am	♊
2	♊		
3	♊	10:27 am	♋
4	♋		
5	♋	11:00 am	♌
6	♌		
7	♌	2:39 pm	♍
8	♍		
9	♍	10:00 pm	♎
10	♎		
11	♎		
12	♎	8:28 am	♏
13	♏		
14	♏	8:44 pm	♐
15	♐		
16	♐		
17	♐	9:35 am	♑
18	♑		
19	♑	9:59 pm	♒
20	♒		
21	♒		
22	♒	8:48 am	♓
23	♓		
24	♓	4:45 pm	♈
25	♈		
26	♈	9:09 pm	♉
27	♉		
28	♉	10:26 pm	♊
29	♊		
30	♊	10:02 pm	♋
31	♋		

Your Starway to Love

♈ = Aries ♉ = Taurus ♊ = Gemini ♋ = Cancer ♌ = Leo ♍ = Virgo

1991

January

1	♋	9:54 pm	♌
2	♌		
3	♌	11:57 pm	♍
4	♍		
5	♍		
6	♍	5:33 am	♎
7	♎		
8	♎	2:59 pm	♏
9	♏		
10	♏		
11	♏	3:06 am	♐
12	♐		
13	♐	4:00 pm	♑
14	♑		
15	♑		
16	♑	4:04 am	♒
17	♒		
18	♒	2:23 pm	♓
19	♓		
20	♓	10:28 pm	♈
21	♈		
22	♈		
23	♈	4:01 am	♉
24	♉		
25	♉	7:06 am	♊
26	♊		
27	♊	8:23 am	♋
28	♋		
29	♋	9:03 am	♌
30	♌		
31	♌	10:44 am	♍

February

1	♍		
2	♍	3:02 pm	♎
3	♎		
4	♎	11:01 pm	♏
5	♏		
6	♏		
7	♏	10:23 am	♐
8	♐		
9	♐	11:16 pm	♑
10	♑		
11	♑		
12	♑	11:16 am	♒
13	♒		
14	♒	8:59 pm	♓
15	♓		
16	♓		
17	♓	4:11 am	♈
18	♈		
19	♈	9:24 am	♉
20	♉		
21	♉	1:10 pm	♊
22	♊		
23	♊	3:56 pm	♋
24	♋		
25	♋	6:13 pm	♌
26	♌		
27	♌	8:50 pm	♍
28	♍		

March

1	♍		
2	♍	1:03 am	♎
3	♎		
4	♎	8:08 am	♏
5	♏		
6	♏	6:35 pm	♐
7	♐		
8	♐		
9	♐	7:14 am	♑
10	♑		
11	♑	7:31 pm	♒
12	♒		
13	♒		
14	♒	5:11 am	♓
15	♓		
16	♓	11:37 am	♈
17	♈		
18	♈	3:40 pm	♉
19	♉		
20	♉	6:37 pm	♊
21	♊		
22	♊	9:27 pm	♋
23	♋		
24	♋		
25	♋	12:43 am	♌
26	♌		
27	♌	4:41 am	♍
28	♍		
29	♍	9:49 am	♎
30	♎		
31	♎	5:01 pm	♏

April

1	♏		
2	♏		
3	♏	2:59 am	♐
4	♐		
5	♐	3:20 pm	♑
6	♑		
7	♑		
8	♑	4:00 am	♒
9	♒		
10	♒	2:17 pm	♓
11	♓		
12	♓	8:49 pm	♈
13	♈		
14	♈		
15	♈	12:06 am	♉
16	♉		
17	♉	1:41 am	♊
18	♊		
19	♊	3:17 am	♋
20	♋		
21	♋	6:04 am	♌
22	♌		
23	♌	10:29 am	♍
24	♍		
25	♍	4:36 pm	♎
26	♎		
27	♎		
28	♎	12:34 am	♏
29	♏		
30	♏	10:42 am	♐

May

1	♐		
2	♐	10:55 pm	♑
3	♑		
4	♑		
5	♑	11:51 am	♒
6	♒		
7	♒	11:04 pm	♓
8	♓		
9	♓		
10	♓	6:34 am	♈
11	♈		
12	♈	10:07 am	♉
13	♉		
14	♉	11:02 am	♊
15	♊		
16	♊	11:14 am	♋
17	♋		
18	♋	12:30 pm	♌
19	♌		
20	♌	4:00 pm	♍
21	♍		
22	♍	10:08 pm	♎
23	♎		
24	♎		
25	♎	6:41 am	♏
26	♏		
27	♏	5:21 pm	♐
28	♐		
29	♐		
30	♐	5:40 am	♑
31	♑		

June

1	♑	6:42 pm	♒
2	♒		
3	♒		
4	♒	6:36 am	♓
5	♓		
6	♓	3:25 pm	♈
7	♈		
8	♈	8:13 pm	♉
9	♉		
10	♉	9:36 pm	♊
11	♊		
12	♊	9:16 pm	♋
13	♋		
14	♋	9:10 pm	♌
15	♌		
16	♌	11:03 pm	♍
17	♍		
18	♍		
19	♍	4:01 am	♎
20	♎		
21	♎	12:18 pm	♏
22	♏		
23	♏	11:16 pm	♐
24	♐		
25	♐		
26	♐	11:49 am	♑
27	♑		
28	♑		
29	♑	12:47 am	♒
30	♒		

July

1	♒	12:51 pm	♓
2	♓		
3	♓	10:33 pm	♈
4	♈		
5	♈		
6	♈	4:52 am	♉
7	♉		
8	♉	7:42 am	♊
9	♊		
10	♊	8:03 am	♋
11	♋		
12	♋	7:35 am	♌
13	♌		
14	♌	8:12 am	♍
15	♍		
16	♍	11:34 am	♎
17	♎		
18	♎	6:41 pm	♏
19	♏		
20	♏		
21	♏	5:16 am	♐
22	♐		
23	♐	5:55 pm	♑
24	♑		
25	♑		
26	♑	6:49 am	♒
27	♒		
28	♒	6:35 pm	♓
29	♓		
30	♓		
31	♓	4:20 am	♈

August

1	♈		
2	♈	11:32 am	♉
3	♉		
4	♉	3:54 pm	♊
5	♊		
6	♊	5:47 pm	♋
7	♋		
8	♋	6:09 pm	♌
9	♌		
10	♌	6:35 pm	♍
11	♍		
12	♍	8:52 pm	♎
13	♎		
14	♎		
15	♎	2:34 am	♏
16	♏		
17	♏	12:11 pm	♐
18	♐		
19	♐		
20	♐	12:34 am	♑
21	♑		
22	♑	1:27 pm	♒
23	♒		
24	♒		
25	♒	12:51 am	♓
26	♓		
27	♓	10:01 am	♈
28	♈		
29	♈	5:00 pm	♉
30	♉		
31	♉	10:02 pm	♊

September

1	♊		
2	♊		
3	♊	1:19 am	♋
4	♋		
5	♋	3:13 am	♌
6	♌		
7	♌	4:35 am	♍
8	♍		
9	♍	6:52 am	♎
10	♎		
11	♎	11:42 am	♏
12	♏		
13	♏	8:14 pm	♐
14	♐		
15	♐		
16	♐	8:04 am	♑
17	♑		
18	♑	8:58 pm	♒
19	♒		
20	♒		
21	♒	8:20 am	♓
22	♓		
23	♓	4:56 pm	♈
24	♈		
25	♈	10:59 pm	♉
26	♉		
27	♉		
28	♉	3:25 am	♊
29	♊		
30	♊	6:58 am	♋

October

1	♋		
2	♋	9:58 am	♌
3	♌		
4	♌	12:45 pm	♍
5	♍		
6	♍	4:00 pm	♎
7	♎		
8	♎	9:00 pm	♏
9	♏		
10	♏		
11	♏	4:58 am	♐
12	♐		
13	♐	4:10 pm	♑
14	♑		
15	♑		
16	♑	5:04 am	♒
17	♒		
18	♒	4:53 pm	♓
19	♓		
20	♓		
21	♓	1:33 am	♈
22	♈		
23	♈	6:55 am	♉
24	♉		
25	♉	10:09 am	♊
26	♊		
27	♊	12:37 pm	♋
28	♋		
29	♋	3:20 pm	♌
30	♌		
31	♌	6:47 pm	♍

November

1	♍		
2	♍	11:13 pm	♎
3	♎		
4	♎		
5	♎	5:09 am	♏
6	♏		
7	♏	1:21 pm	♐
8	♐		
9	♐		
10	♐	12:16 am	♑
11	♑		
12	♑	1:06 pm	♒
13	♒		
14	♒		
15	♒	1:33 am	♓
16	♓		
17	♓	11:08 am	♈
18	♈		
19	♈	4:49 pm	♉
20	♉		
21	♉	7:22 pm	♊
22	♊		
23	♊	8:25 pm	♋
24	♋		
25	♋	9:37 pm	♌
26	♌		
27	♌		
28	♌	12:12 am	♍
29	♍		
30	♍	4:47 am	♎

December

1	♎		
2	♎	11:33 am	♏
3	♏		
4	♏	8:32 pm	♐
5	♐		
6	♐		
7	♐	7:41 am	♑
8	♑		
9	♑	8:27 pm	♒
10	♒		
11	♒		
12	♒	9:19 am	♓
13	♓		
14	♓	8:06 pm	♈
15	♈		
16	♈		
17	♈	3:10 am	♉
18	♉		
19	♉	6:21 am	♊
20	♊		
21	♊	6:55 am	♋
22	♋		
23	♋	6:38 am	♌
24	♌		
25	♌	7:24 am	♍
26	♍		
27	♍	10:37 am	♎
28	♎		
29	♎	5:03 pm	♏
30	♏		
31	♏		

Moon Movements

♎ = Libra ♏ = Scorpio ♐ = Sagittarius ♑ = Capricorn ♒ = Aquarius ♓ = Pisces

1992

January

1	♏	2:30 am	♐
2	♐		
3	♐	2:09 pm	♑
4	♑		
5	♑		
6	♑	2:59 am	♒
7	♒		
8	♒	3:52 pm	♓
9	♓		
10	♓		
11	♓	3:22 am	♈
12	♈		
13	♈	12:00 pm	♉
14	♉		
15	♉	4:54 pm	♊
16	♊		
17	♊	6:26 pm	♋
18	♋		
19	♋	5:57 pm	♌
20	♌		
21	♌	5:22 pm	♍
22	♍		
23	♍	6:42 pm	♎
24	♎		
25	♎	11:32 pm	♏
26	♏		
27	♏		
28	♏	8:20 am	♐
29	♐		
30	♐	8:07 pm	♑
31	♑		

February

1	♑		
2	♑	9:09 am	♒
3	♒		
4	♒	9:51 pm	♓
5	♓		
6	♓		
7	♓	9:15 am	♈
8	♈		
9	♈	6:36 pm	♉
10	♉		
11	♉		
12	♉	1:08 am	♊
13	♊		
14	♊	4:31 am	♋
15	♋		
16	♋	5:15 am	♌
17	♌		
18	♌	4:47 am	♍
19	♍		
20	♍	5:05 am	♎
21	♎		
22	♎	8:11 am	♏
23	♏		
24	♏	3:26 pm	♐
25	♐		
26	♐		
27	♐	2:33 am	♑
28	♑		
29	♑	3:34 pm	♒

March

1	♒		
2	♒		
3	♒	4:11 am	♓
4	♓		
5	♓	3:07 pm	♈
6	♈		
7	♈		
8	♈	12:05 am	♉
9	♉		
10	♉	7:03 am	♊
11	♊		
12	♊	11:50 am	♋
13	♋		
14	♋	2:20 pm	♌
15	♌		
16	♌	3:13 pm	♍
17	♍		
18	♍	3:55 pm	♎
19	♎		
20	♎	6:20 pm	♏
21	♏		
22	♏		
23	♏	12:13 am	♐
24	♐		
25	♐	10:08 am	♑
26	♑		
27	♑	10:44 pm	♒
28	♒		
29	♒		
30	♒	11:23 am	♓
31	♓		

April

1	♓	10:04 pm	♈
2	♈		
3	♈		
4	♈	6:18 am	♉
5	♉		
6	♉	12:33 pm	♊
7	♊		
8	♊	5:18 pm	♋
9	♋		
10	♋	8:46 pm	♌
11	♌		
12	♌	11:09 pm	♍
13	♍		
14	♍		
15	♍	1:10 am	♎
16	♎		
17	♎	4:10 am	♏
18	♏		
19	♏	9:40 am	♐
20	♐		
21	♐	6:41 pm	♑
22	♑		
23	♑		
24	♑	6:38 am	♒
25	♒		
26	♒	7:20 pm	♓
27	♓		
28	♓		
29	♓	6:13 am	♈
30	♈		

May

1	♈	2:09 pm	♉
2	♉		
3	♉	7:28 pm	♊
4	♊		
5	♊	11:09 pm	♋
6	♋		
7	♋		
8	♋	2:07 am	♌
9	♌		
10	♌	4:56 am	♍
11	♍		
12	♍	8:05 am	♎
13	♎		
14	♎	12:15 pm	♏
15	♏		
16	♏	6:22 pm	♐
17	♐		
18	♐		
19	♐	3:13 am	♑
20	♑		
21	♑	2:43 pm	♒
22	♒		
23	♒		
24	♒	3:25 am	♓
25	♓		
26	♓	2:52 pm	♈
27	♈		
28	♈	11:16 pm	♉
29	♉		
30	♉		
31	♉	4:19 am	♊

June

1	♊		
2	♊	6:58 am	♋
3	♋		
4	♋	8:35 am	♌
5	♌		
6	♌	10:28 am	♍
7	♍		
8	♍	1:33 pm	♎
9	♎		
10	♎	6:27 pm	♏
11	♏		
12	♏		
13	♏	1:29 am	♐
14	♐		
15	♐	10:50 am	♑
16	♑		
17	♑	10:19 pm	♒
18	♒		
19	♒		
20	♒	11:00 am	♓
21	♓		
22	♓	11:03 pm	♈
23	♈		
24	♈		
25	♈	8:28 am	♉
26	♉		
27	♉	2:14 pm	♊
28	♊		
29	♊	4:42 pm	♋
30	♋		

July

1	♋	5:15 pm	♌
2	♌		
3	♌	5:37 pm	♍
4	♍		
5	♍	7:27 pm	♎
6	♎		
7	♎	11:53 pm	♏
8	♏		
9	♏		
10	♏	7:17 am	♐
11	♐		
12	♐	5:16 pm	♑
13	♑		
14	♑		
15	♑	5:03 am	♒
16	♒		
17	♒	5:44 pm	♓
18	♓		
19	♓		
20	♓	6:07 am	♈
21	♈		
22	♈	4:36 pm	♉
23	♉		
24	♉	11:44 pm	♊
25	♊		
26	♊		
27	♊	3:08 am	♋
28	♋		
29	♋	3:39 am	♌
30	♌		
31	♌	3:01 am	♍

August

1	♍		
2	♍	3:17 am	♎
3	♎		
4	♎	6:16 am	♏
5	♏		
6	♏	12:57 pm	♐
7	♐		
8	♐	11:00 pm	♑
9	♑		
10	♑		
11	♑	11:06 am	♒
12	♒		
13	♒	11:51 pm	♓
14	♓		
15	♓		
16	♓	12:11 pm	♈
17	♈		
18	♈	11:10 pm	♉
19	♉		
20	♉		
21	♉	7:36 am	♊
22	♊		
23	♊	12:36 pm	♋
24	♋		
25	♋	2:15 pm	♌
26	♌		
27	♌	1:46 pm	♍
28	♍		
29	♍	1:11 pm	♎
30	♎		
31	♎	2:38 pm	♏

September

1	♏		
2	♏	7:50 pm	♐
3	♐		
4	♐		
5	♐	5:06 am	♑
6	♑		
7	♑	5:08 pm	♒
8	♒		
9	♒		
10	♒	5:56 am	♓
11	♓		
12	♓	6:02 pm	♈
13	♈		
14	♈		
15	♈	4:47 am	♉
16	♉		
17	♉	1:40 pm	♊
18	♊		
19	♊	7:59 pm	♋
20	♋		
21	♋	11:19 pm	♌
22	♌		
23	♌		
24	♌	12:08 am	♍
25	♍	11:55 pm	♎
26	♎		
27	♎		
28	♎	12:44 am	♏
29	♏		
30	♏	4:33 am	♐

October

1	♐		
2	♐	12:29 pm	♑
3	♑		
4	♑	11:53 pm	♒
5	♒		
6	♒		
7	♒	12:38 pm	♓
8	♓		
9	♓		
10	♓	12:36 am	♈
11	♈		
12	♈	10:48 am	♉
13	♉		
14	♉	7:08 pm	♊
15	♊		
16	♊		
17	♊	1:36 am	♋
18	♋		
19	♋	6:01 am	♌
20	♌		
21	♌	8:27 am	♍
22	♍		
23	♍	9:39 am	♎
24	♎		
25	♎	11:04 am	♏
26	♏		
27	♏	2:29 pm	♐
28	♐		
29	♐	9:18 pm	♑
30	♑		
31	♑		

November

1	♑	7:43 am	♒
2	♒		
3	♒	8:13 pm	♓
4	♓		
5	♓		
6	♓	8:19 am	♈
7	♈		
8	♈	6:19 pm	♉
9	♉		
10	♉		
11	♉	1:49 am	♊
12	♊		
13	♊	7:19 am	♋
14	♋		
15	♋	11:23 am	♌
16	♌		
17	♌	2:28 pm	♍
18	♍		
19	♍	5:03 pm	♎
20	♎		
21	♎	7:52 pm	♏
22	♏		
23	♏		
24	♏	12:01 am	♐
25	♐		
26	♐	6:38 am	♑
27	♑		
28	♑	4:19 pm	♒
29	♒		
30	♒		

December

1	♒	4:23 am	♓
2	♓		
3	♓	4:49 pm	♈
4	♈		
5	♈		
6	♈	3:16 am	♉
7	♉		
8	♉	10:37 am	♊
9	♊		
10	♊	3:05 pm	♋
11	♋		
12	♋	5:47 pm	♌
13	♌		
14	♌	7:56 pm	♍
15	♍		
16	♍	10:33 pm	♎
17	♎		
18	♎		
19	♎	2:20 am	♏
20	♏		
21	♏	7:42 am	♐
22	♐		
23	♐	3:04 pm	♑
24	♑		
25	♑		
26	♑	12:43 am	♒
27	♒		
28	♒	12:28 pm	♓
29	♓		
30	♓		
31	♓	1:07 am	♈

1993

Your Starway to Love

♈ = Aries ♉ = Taurus ♊ = Gemini ♋ = Cancer ♌ = Leo ♍ = Virgo

January

1	♈		
2	♈	12:30 pm	♉
3	♉		
4	♉	8:42 pm	♊
5	♊		
6	♊		
7	♊	1:10 am	♋
8	♋		
9	♋	2:49 am	♌
10	♌		
11	♌	3:20 am	♍
12	♍		
13	♍	4:30 am	♎
14	♎		
15	♎	7:42 am	♏
16	♏		
17	♏	1:30 pm	♐
18	♐		
19	♐	9:46 pm	♑
20	♑		
21	♑		
22	♑	8:00 am	♒
23	♒		
24	♒	7:47 pm	♓
25	♓		
26	♓		
27	♓	8:28 am	♈
28	♈		
29	♈	8:37 pm	♉
30	♉		
31	♉		

April

1	♋	9:21 am	♌
2	♌		
3	♌	11:10 am	♍
4	♍		
5	♍	10:54 am	♎
6	♎		
7	♎	10:32 am	♏
8	♏		
9	♏	12:10 pm	♐
10	♐		
11	♐	5:24 pm	♑
12	♑		
13	♑		
14	♑	2:36 am	♒
15	♒		
16	♒	2:32 pm	♓
17	♓		
18	♓		
19	♓	3:14 am	♈
20	♈		
21	♈	3:08 pm	♉
22	♉		
23	♉		
24	♉	1:27 am	♊
25	♊		
26	♊	9:45 am	♋
27	♋		
28	♋	3:39 pm	♌
29	♌		
30	♌	7:00 pm	♍

July

1	♐		
2	♐	8:49 pm	♑
3	♑		
4	♑		
5	♑	4:14 am	♒
6	♒		
7	♒	2:10 pm	♓
8	♓		
9	♓		
10	♓	2:11 am	♈
11	♈		
12	♈	2:37 pm	♉
13	♉		
14	♉		
15	♉	1:07 am	♊
16	♊		
17	♊	8:08 am	♋
18	♋		
19	♋	11:47 am	♌
20	♌		
21	♌	1:24 pm	♍
22	♍		
23	♍	2:39 pm	♎
24	♎		
25	♎	5:00 pm	♏
26	♏		
27	♏	9:13 pm	♐
28	♐		
29	♐		
30	♐	3:27 am	♑
31	♑		

October

1	♈		
2	♈	11:13 am	♉
3	♉		
4	♉	11:27 pm	♊
5	♊		
6	♊		
7	♊	9:42 am	♋
8	♋		
9	♋	4:34 pm	♌
10	♌		
11	♌	7:36 pm	♍
12	♍		
13	♍	7:47 pm	♎
14	♎		
15	♎	7:01 pm	♏
16	♏		
17	♏	7:23 pm	♐
18	♐		
19	♐	10:42 pm	♑
20	♑		
21	♑		
22	♑	5:49 am	♒
23	♒		
24	♒	4:17 pm	♓
25	♓		
26	♓		
27	♓	4:39 am	♈
28	♈		
29	♈	5:20 pm	♉
30	♉		
31	♉		

February

1	♉	6:15 am	♊
2	♊		
3	♊	11:56 am	♋
4	♋		
5	♋	1:51 pm	♌
6	♌		
7	♌	1:29 pm	♍
8	♍		
9	♍	12:58 pm	♎
10	♎		
11	♎	2:24 pm	♏
12	♏		
13	♏	7:08 pm	♐
14	♐		
15	♐		
16	♐	3:20 am	♑
17	♑		
18	♑	2:05 pm	♒
19	♒		
20	♒		
21	♒	2:12 am	♓
22	♓		
23	♓	2:50 pm	♈
24	♈		
25	♈		
26	♈	3:11 am	♉
27	♉		
28	♉	1:52 pm	♊

May

1	♍		
2	♍	8:20 pm	♎
3	♎		
4	♎	8:57 pm	♏
5	♏		
6	♏	10:34 pm	♐
7	♐		
8	♐		
9	♐	2:51 am	♑
10	♑		
11	♑	10:44 am	♒
12	♒		
13	♒	9:51 pm	♓
14	♓		
15	♓		
16	♓	10:24 am	♈
17	♈		
18	♈	10:16 pm	♉
19	♉		
20	♉		
21	♉	8:07 am	♊
22	♊		
23	♊	3:38 pm	♋
24	♋		
25	♋	9:03 pm	♌
26	♌		
27	♌		
28	♌	12:46 am	♍
29	♍		
30	♍	3:18 am	♎
31	♎		

August

1	♑	11:36 am	♒
2	♒		
3	♒	9:44 pm	♓
4	♓		
5	♓		
6	♓	9:39 am	♈
7	♈		
8	♈	10:22 pm	♉
9	♉		
10	♉		
11	♉	9:47 am	♊
12	♊		
13	♊	5:46 pm	♋
14	♋		
15	♋	9:43 pm	♌
16	♌		
17	♌	10:41 pm	♍
18	♍		
19	♍	10:35 pm	♎
20	♎		
21	♎	11:27 pm	♏
22	♏		
23	♏		
24	♏	2:45 am	♐
25	♐		
26	♐	8:58 am	♑
27	♑		
28	♑	5:42 pm	♒
29	♒		
30	♒		
31	♒	4:19 am	♓

November

1	♉	5:13 am	♊
2	♊		
3	♊	3:25 pm	♋
4	♋		
5	♋	11:06 pm	♌
6	♌		
7	♌		
8	♌	3:47 am	♍
9	♍		
10	♍	5:42 am	♎
11	♎		
12	♎	6:00 am	♏
13	♏		
14	♏	6:20 am	♐
15	♐		
16	♐	8:34 am	♑
17	♑		
18	♑	2:08 pm	♒
19	♒		
20	♒	11:27 pm	♓
21	♓		
22	♓		
23	♓	11:30 am	♈
24	♈		
25	♈		
26	♈	12:14 am	♉
27	♉		
28	♉	11:48 am	♊
29	♊		
30	♊	9:17 pm	♋

March

1	♊		
2	♊	9:16 pm	♋
3	♋		
4	♋		
5	♋	12:40 am	♌
6	♌		
7	♌	12:52 am	♍
8	♍	11:46 pm	♎
9	♎		
10	♎	11:40 pm	♏
11	♏		
12	♏		
13	♏	2:33 am	♐
14	♐		
15	♐	9:28 am	♑
16	♑		
17	♑	7:52 pm	♒
18	♒		
19	♒		
20	♒	8:11 am	♓
21	♓		
22	♓	8:51 pm	♈
23	♈		
24	♈		
25	♈	8:59 am	♉
26	♉		
27	♉	7:48 pm	♊
28	♊		
29	♊		
30	♊	4:14 am	♋
31	♋		

June

1	♎	5:22 am	♏
2	♏		
3	♏	8:01 am	♐
4	♐		
5	♐	12:26 pm	♑
6	♑		
7	♑	7:39 pm	♒
8	♒		
9	♒		
10	♒	5:57 am	♓
11	♓		
12	♓	6:14 pm	♈
13	♈		
14	♈		
15	♈	6:19 am	♉
16	♉		
17	♉	4:12 pm	♊
18	♊		
19	♊	11:05 pm	♋
20	♋		
21	♋		
22	♋	3:26 am	♌
23	♌		
24	♌	6:18 am	♍
25	♍		
26	♍	8:45 am	♎
27	♎		
28	♎	11:37 am	♏
29	♏		
30	♏	3:28 pm	♐

September

1	♓		
2	♓	4:21 pm	♈
3	♈		
4	♈		
5	♈	5:09 am	♉
6	♉		
7	♉	5:16 pm	♊
8	♊		
9	♊		
10	♊	2:37 am	♋
11	♋		
12	♋	7:51 am	♌
13	♌		
14	♌	9:20 am	♍
15	♍		
16	♍	8:44 am	♎
17	♎		
18	♎	8:15 am	♏
19	♏		
20	♏	9:53 am	♐
21	♐		
22	♐	2:54 pm	♑
23	♑		
24	♑	11:19 pm	♒
25	♒		
26	♒		
27	♒	10:13 am	♓
28	♓		
29	♓	10:29 pm	♈
30	♈		

December

1	♋		
2	♋		
3	♋	4:33 am	♌
4	♌		
5	♌	9:43 am	♍
6	♍		
7	♍	1:03 pm	♎
8	♎		
9	♎	3:04 pm	♏
10	♏		
11	♏	4:39 pm	♐
12	♐		
13	♐	7:06 pm	♑
14	♑		
15	♑	11:51 pm	♒
16	♒		
17	♒		
18	♒	7:59 am	♓
19	♓		
20	♓	7:19 pm	♈
21	♈		
22	♈		
23	♈	8:05 am	♉
24	♉		
25	♉	7:46 pm	♊
26	♊		
27	♊		
28	♊	4:46 am	♋
29	♋		
30	♋	10:59 am	♌
31	♌		

Moon Movements

♎ = Libra ♏ = Scorpio ♐ = Sagittarius ♑ = Capricorn ♒ = Aquarius ♓ = Pisces

January

1	♌	3:15 pm	♍
2	♍		
3	♍	6:31 pm	♎
4	♎		
5	♎	9:29 pm	♏
6	♏		
7	♏		
8	♏	12:34 am	♐
9	♐		
10	♐	4:16 am	♑
11	♑		
12	♑	9:25 am	♒
13	♒		
14	♒	5:04 pm	♓
15	♓		
16	♓		
17	♓	3:42 am	♈
18	♈		
19	♈	4:22 pm	♉
20	♉		
21	♉		
22	♉	4:35 am	♊
23	♊		
24	♊	1:55 pm	♋
25	♋		
26	♋	7:38 pm	♌
27	♌		
28	♌	10:39 pm	♍
29	♍		
30	♍		
31	♍	12:34 am	♎

February

1	♎		
2	♎	2:49 am	♏
3	♏		
4	♏	6:14 am	♐
5	♐		
6	♐	11:02 am	♑
7	♑		
8	♑	5:16 pm	♒
9	♒		
10	♒		
11	♒	1:23 am	♓
12	♓		
13	♓	11:49 am	♈
14	♈		
15	♈		
16	♈	12:20 am	♉
17	♉		
18	♉	1:05 pm	♊
19	♊		
20	♊	11:27 pm	♋
21	♋		
22	♋		
23	♋	5:48 am	♌
24	♌		
25	♌	8:27 am	♍
26	♍		
27	♍	9:06 am	♎
28	♎		

March

1	♎	9:43 am	♏
2	♏		
3	♏	11:54 am	♐
4	♐		
5	♐	4:24 pm	♑
6	♑		
7	♑	11:15 pm	♒
8	♒		
9	♒		
10	♒	8:09 am	♓
11	♓		
12	♓	6:59 pm	♈
13	♈		
14	♈		
15	♈	7:27 am	♉
16	♉		
17	♉	8:29 pm	♊
18	♊		
19	♊		
20	♊	7:54 am	♋
21	♋		
22	♋	3:39 pm	♌
23	♌		
24	♌	7:14 pm	♍
25	♍		
26	♍	7:46 pm	♎
27	♎		
28	♎	7:15 pm	♏
29	♏		
30	♏	7:41 pm	♐
31	♐		

April

1	♐	10:38 pm	♑
2	♑		
3	♑		
4	♑	4:45 am	♒
5	♒		
6	♒	1:51 pm	♓
7	♓		
8	♓		
9	♓	1:09 am	♈
10	♈		
11	♈	1:48 pm	♉
12	♉		
13	♉		
14	♉	2:48 am	♊
15	♊		
16	♊	2:41 pm	♋
17	♋		
18	♋	11:45 pm	♌
19	♌		
20	♌		
21	♌	4:58 am	♍
22	♍		
23	♍	6:40 am	♎
24	♎		
25	♎	6:18 am	♏
26	♏		
27	♏	5:48 am	♐
28	♐		
29	♐	7:05 am	♑
30	♑		

May

1	♑	11:34 am	♒
2	♒		
3	♒	7:47 pm	♓
4	♓		
5	♓		
6	♓	7:01 am	♈
7	♈		
8	♈	7:50 pm	♉
9	♉		
10	♉		
11	♉	8:43 am	♊
12	♊		
13	♊	8:27 pm	♋
14	♋		
15	♋		
16	♋	5:58 am	♌
17	♌		
18	♌	12:31 pm	♍
19	♍		
20	♍	3:54 pm	♎
21	♎		
22	♎	4:51 pm	♏
23	♏		
24	♏	4:43 pm	♐
25	♐		
26	♐	5:17 pm	♑
27	♑		
28	♑	8:19 pm	♒
29	♒		
30	♒		
31	♒	3:03 am	♓

June

1	♓		
2	♓	1:31 pm	♈
3	♈		
4	♈		
5	♈	2:14 pm	♉
6	♉		
7	♉	3:03 pm	♊
8	♊		
9	♊		
10	♊	2:22 am	♋
11	♋		
12	♋	11:29 am	♌
13	♌		
14	♌	6:16 pm	♍
15	♍		
16	♍	10:48 pm	♎
17	♎		
18	♎		
19	♎	1:20 am	♏
20	♏		
21	♏	2:32 am	♐
22	♐		
23	♐	3:37 am	♑
24	♑		
25	♑	6:10 am	♒
26	♒		
27	♒	11:44 am	♓
28	♓		
29	♓	9:07 pm	♈
30	♈		

July

1	♈		
2	♈	9:23 am	♉
3	♉		
4	♉	10:12 pm	♊
5	♊		
6	♊		
7	♊	9:17 am	♋
8	♋		
9	♋	5:43 pm	♌
10	♌		
11	♌	11:48 pm	♍
12	♍		
13	♍		
14	♍	4:15 am	♎
15	♎		
16	♎	7:35 am	♏
17	♏		
18	♏	10:09 am	♐
19	♐		
20	♐	12:30 pm	♑
21	♑		
22	♑	3:38 pm	♒
23	♒		
24	♒	8:56 pm	♓
25	♓		
26	♓		
27	♓	5:31 am	♈
28	♈		
29	♈	5:13 pm	♉
30	♉		
31	♉		

August

1	♉	6:05 am	♊
2	♊		
3	♊	5:22 pm	♋
4	♋		
5	♋		
6	♋	1:31 am	♌
7	♌		
8	♌	6:42 am	♍
9	♍		
10	♍	10:07 am	♎
11	♎		
12	♎	12:56 pm	♏
13	♏		
14	♏	3:53 pm	♐
15	♐		
16	♐	7:18 pm	♑
17	♑		
18	♑	11:34 pm	♒
19	♒		
20	♒		
21	♒	5:27 am	♓
22	♓		
23	♓	1:55 pm	♈
24	♈		
25	♈		
26	♈	1:13 am	♉
27	♉		
28	♉	2:07 pm	♊
29	♊		
30	♊		
31	♊	2:00 am	♋

September

1	♋		
2	♋	10:37 am	♌
3	♌		
4	♌	3:33 pm	♍
5	♍		
6	♍	5:57 pm	♎
7	♎		
8	♎	7:26 pm	♏
9	♏		
10	♏	9:25 pm	♐
11	♐		
12	♐		
13	♐	12:44 am	♑
14	♑		
15	♑	5:42 am	♒
16	♒		
17	♒	12:31 pm	♓
18	♓		
19	♓	9:30 pm	♈
20	♈		
21	♈		
22	♈	8:47 am	♉
23	♉		
24	♉	9:41 pm	♊
25	♊		
26	♊		
27	♊	10:12 am	♋
28	♋		
29	♋	7:55 pm	♌
30	♌		

October

1	♌		
2	♌	1:39 am	♍
3	♍		
4	♍	3:56 am	♎
5	♎		
6	♎	4:22 am	♏
7	♏		
8	♏	4:47 am	♐
9	♐		
10	♐	6:44 am	♑
11	♑		
12	♑	11:09 am	♒
13	♒		
14	♒	6:18 pm	♓
15	♓		
16	♓		
17	♓	3:56 am	♈
18	♈		
19	♈	3:34 pm	♉
20	♉		
21	♉		
22	♉	4:28 am	♊
23	♊		
24	♊	5:15 pm	♋
25	♋		
26	♋		
27	♋	4:05 am	♌
28	♌		
29	♌	11:21 am	♍
30	♍		
31	♍	2:46 pm	♎

November

1	♎		
2	♎	3:19 pm	♏
3	♏		
4	♏	2:46 pm	♐
5	♐		
6	♐	3:02 pm	♑
7	♑		
8	♑	5:48 pm	♒
9	♒		
10	♒		
11	♒	12:04 am	♓
12	♓		
13	♓	9:44 am	♈
14	♈		
15	♈	9:44 pm	♉
16	♉		
17	♉		
18	♉	10:41 am	♊
19	♊		
20	♊	11:21 pm	♋
21	♋		
22	♋		
23	♋	10:33 am	♌
24	♌		
25	♌	7:09 pm	♍
26	♍		
27	♍		
28	♍	12:22 am	♎
29	♎		
30	♎	2:21 am	♏

December

1	♏		
2	♏	2:13 am	♐
3	♐		
4	♐	1:42 am	♑
5	♑		
6	♑	2:51 am	♒
7	♒		
8	♒	7:24 am	♓
9	♓		
10	♓	4:03 pm	♈
11	♈		
12	♈		
13	♈	3:56 am	♉
14	♉		
15	♉	5:00 pm	♊
16	♊		
17	♊		
18	♊	5:25 am	♋
19	♋		
20	♋	4:13 pm	♌
21	♌		
22	♌		
23	♌	1:01 am	♍
24	♍		
25	♍	7:27 am	♎
26	♎		
27	♎	11:17 am	♏
28	♏		
29	♏	12:45 pm	♐
30	♐		
31	♐	12:57 pm	♑

1995

Your Starway to Love

♈ = Aries ♉ = Taurus ♊ = Gemini ♋ = Cancer ♌ = Leo ♍ = Virgo

January

Day	Sign	Time	Enters
1	♑		
2	♑	1:39 pm	♒
3	♒		
4	♒	4:49 pm	♓
5	♓		
6	♓	11:56 pm	♈
7	♈		
8	♈		
9	♈	10:58 am	♉
10	♉		
11	♉	11:57 pm	♊
12	♊		
13	♊		
14	♊	12:20 pm	♋
15	♋		
16	♋	10:36 pm	♌
17	♌		
18	♌		
19	♌	6:39 am	♍
20	♍		
21	♍	12:54 pm	♎
22	♎		
23	♎	5:32 pm	♏
24	♏		
25	♏	8:37 pm	♐
26	♐		
27	♐	10:26 pm	♑
28	♑		
29	♑		
30	♑	12:03 am	♒
31	♒		

April

Day	Sign	Time	Enters
1	♈	11:59 am	♉
2	♉		
3	♉	11:49 pm	♊
4	♊		
5	♊		
6	♊	12:40 pm	♋
7	♋		
8	♋		
9	♋	12:16 am	♌
10	♌		
11	♌	8:39 am	♍
12	♍		
13	♍	1:20 pm	♎
14	♎		
15	♎	3:13 pm	♏
16	♏		
17	♏	3:52 pm	♐
18	♐		
19	♐	4:54 pm	♑
20	♑		
21	♑	7:38 pm	♒
22	♒		
23	♒		
24	♒	12:51 am	♓
25	♓		
26	♓	8:41 am	♈
27	♈		
28	♈	6:53 pm	♉
29	♉		
30	♉		

July

Day	Sign	Time	Enters
1	♌		
2	♌	6:35 am	♍
3	♍		
4	♍	2:55 pm	♎
5	♎		
6	♎	8:19 pm	♏
7	♏		
8	♏	10:37 pm	♐
9	♐		
10	♐	10:43 pm	♑
11	♑		
12	♑	10:21 pm	♒
13	♒		
14	♒	11:37 pm	♓
15	♓		
16	♓		
17	♓	4:23 am	♈
18	♈		
19	♈	1:20 pm	♉
20	♉		
21	♉		
22	♉	1:23 am	♊
23	♊		
24	♊	2:16 pm	♋
25	♋		
26	♋		
27	♋	2:07 am	♌
28	♌		
29	♌	12:12 pm	♍
30	♍		
31	♍	8:23 pm	♎

October

Day	Sign	Time	Enters
1	♑		
2	♑	10:59 pm	♒
3	♒		
4	♒		
5	♒	2:35 am	♓
6	♓		
7	♓	7:42 am	♈
8	♈		
9	♈	3:05 pm	♉
10	♉		
11	♉		
12	♉	1:10 am	♊
13	♊		
14	♊	1:20 pm	♋
15	♋		
16	♋		
17	♋	1:46 am	♌
18	♌		
19	♌	12:11 pm	♍
20	♍		
21	♍	7:15 pm	♎
22	♎		
23	♎	11:06 pm	♏
24	♏		
25	♏		
26	♏	12:56 am	♐
27	♐		
28	♐	2:15 am	♑
29	♑		
30	♑	4:23 am	♒
31	♒		

February

Day	Sign	Time	Enters
1	♒	3:05 am	♓
2	♓		
3	♓	9:12 am	♈
4	♈		
5	♈	7:09 pm	♉
6	♉		
7	♉		
8	♉	7:44 am	♊
9	♊		
10	♊	8:17 pm	♋
11	♋		
12	♋		
13	♋	6:31 am	♌
14	♌		
15	♌	1:52 pm	♍
16	♍		
17	♍	7:00 pm	♎
18	♎		
19	♎	10:55 pm	♏
20	♏		
21	♏		
22	♏	2:13 am	♐
23	♐		
24	♐	5:11 am	♑
25	♑		
26	♑	8:14 am	♒
27	♒		
28	♒	12:16 pm	♓

May

Day	Sign	Time	Enters
1	♉	6:53 am	♊
2	♊		
3	♊	7:45 pm	♋
4	♋		
5	♋		
6	♋	7:55 am	♌
7	♌		
8	♌	5:33 pm	♍
9	♍		
10	♍	11:30 pm	♎
11	♎		
12	♎		
13	♎	1:53 am	♏
14	♏		
15	♏	1:58 am	♐
16	♐		
17	♐	1:36 am	♑
18	♑		
19	♑	2:39 am	♒
20	♒		
21	♒	6:40 am	♓
22	♓		
23	♓	2:13 pm	♈
24	♈		
25	♈		
26	♈	12:46 am	♉
27	♉		
28	♉	1:07 pm	♊
29	♊		
30	♊		
31	♊	1:59 am	♋

August

Day	Sign	Time	Enters
1	♎		
2	♎		
3	♎	2:29 am	♏
4	♏		
5	♏	6:14 am	♐
6	♐		
7	♐	7:52 am	♑
8	♑		
9	♑	8:28 am	♒
10	♒		
11	♒	9:46 am	♓
12	♓		
13	♓	1:41 pm	♈
14	♈		
15	♈	9:25 pm	♉
16	♉		
17	♉		
18	♉	8:40 am	♊
19	♊		
20	♊	9:24 pm	♋
21	♋		
22	♋		
23	♋	9:13 am	♌
24	♌		
25	♌	6:50 pm	♍
26	♍		
27	♍		
28	♍	2:15 am	♎
29	♎		
30	♎	7:51 am	♏
31	♏		

November

Day	Sign	Time	Enters
1	♒	8:17 am	♓
2	♓		
3	♓	2:21 pm	♈
4	♈		
5	♈	10:35 pm	♉
6	♉		
7	♉		
8	♉	8:55 am	♊
9	♊		
10	♊	8:57 pm	♋
11	♋		
12	♋		
13	♋	9:37 am	♌
14	♌		
15	♌	9:02 pm	♍
16	♍		
17	♍		
18	♍	5:18 am	♎
19	♎		
20	♎	9:40 am	♏
21	♏		
22	♏	10:56 am	♐
23	♐		
24	♐	10:48 am	♑
25	♑		
26	♑	11:15 am	♒
27	♒		
28	♒	1:59 pm	♓
29	♓		
30	♓	7:51 pm	♈

March

Day	Sign	Time	Enters
1	♓		
2	♓	6:30 pm	♈
3	♈		
4	♈		
5	♈	3:50 am	♉
6	♉		
7	♉	3:55 pm	♊
8	♊		
9	♊		
10	♊	4:40 am	♋
11	♋		
12	♋	3:28 pm	♌
13	♌		
14	♌	10:54 pm	♍
15	♍		
16	♍		
17	♍	3:18 am	♎
18	♎		
19	♎	5:52 am	♏
20	♏		
21	♏	7:57 am	♐
22	♐		
23	♐	10:31 am	♑
24	♑		
25	♑	2:10 pm	♒
26	♒		
27	♒	7:18 pm	♓
28	♓		
29	♓		
30	♓	2:26 am	♈
31	♈		

June

Day	Sign	Time	Enters
1	♋		
2	♋	2:17 pm	♌
3	♌		
4	♌		
5	♌	12:46 am	♍
6	♍		
7	♍	8:13 am	♎
8	♎		
9	♎	12:03 pm	♏
10	♏		
11	♏	12:50 pm	♐
12	♐		
13	♐	12:05 pm	♑
14	♑		
15	♑	11:52 am	♒
16	♒		
17	♒	2:13 pm	♓
18	♓		
19	♓	8:29 pm	♈
20	♈		
21	♈		
22	♈	6:35 am	♉
23	♉		
24	♉	7:02 pm	♊
25	♊		
26	♊		
27	♊	7:56 am	♋
28	♋		
29	♋	8:02 pm	♌
30	♌		

September

Day	Sign	Time	Enters
1	♏	11:57 am	♐
2	♐		
3	♐	2:45 pm	♑
4	♑		
5	♑	4:47 pm	♒
6	♒		
7	♒	7:08 pm	♓
8	♓		
9	♓	11:14 pm	♈
10	♈		
11	♈		
12	♈	6:21 am	♉
13	♉		
14	♉	4:48 pm	♊
15	♊		
16	♊		
17	♊	5:16 am	♋
18	♋		
19	♋	5:19 pm	♌
20	♌		
21	♌		
22	♌	3:01 am	♍
23	♍		
24	♍	9:50 am	♎
25	♎		
26	♎	2:20 pm	♏
27	♏		
28	♏	5:30 pm	♐
29	♐		
30	♐	8:10 pm	♑

December

Day	Sign	Time	Enters
1	♈		
2	♈		
3	♈	4:40 am	♉
4	♉		
5	♉	3:35 pm	♊
6	♊		
7	♊		
8	♊	3:44 am	♋
9	♋		
10	♋	4:24 pm	♌
11	♌		
12	♌		
13	♌	4:26 am	♍
14	♍		
15	♍	2:09 pm	♎
16	♎		
17	♎	8:07 pm	♏
18	♏		
19	♏	10:13 pm	♐
20	♐		
21	♐	9:46 pm	♑
22	♑		
23	♑	8:52 pm	♒
24	♒		
25	♒	9:45 pm	♓
26	♓		
27	♓		
28	♓	2:06 am	♈
29	♈		
30	♈	10:21 am	♉
31	♉		

Moon Movements

♎ = Libra ♏ = Scorpio ♐ = Sagittarius ♑ = Capricorn ♒ = Aquarius ♓ = Pisces

January

Day	Sign	Time	Enters
1	♉	9:29 pm	♊
2	♊		
3	♊		
4	♊	9:56 am	♋
5	♋		
6	♋	10:30 pm	♌
7	♌		
8	♌		
9	♌	10:29 am	♍
10	♍		
11	♍	8:55 pm	♎
12	♎		
13	♎		
14	♎	4:30 am	♏
15	♏		
16	♏	8:25 am	♐
17	♐		
18	♐	9:07 am	♑
19	♑		
20	♑	8:15 am	♒
21	♒		
22	♒	8:02 am	♓
23	♓		
24	♓	10:37 am	♈
25	♈		
26	♈	5:16 pm	♉
27	♉		
28	♉		
29	♉	3:42 am	♊
30	♊		
31	♊	4:11 pm	♋

April

Day	Sign	Time	Enters
1	♍		
2	♍	4:26 pm	♎
3	♎		
4	♎	10:57 pm	♏
5	♏		
6	♏		
7	♏	3:21 am	♐
8	♐		
9	♐	6:30 am	♑
10	♑		
11	♑	9:09 am	♒
12	♒		
13	♒	12:00 pm	♓
14	♓		
15	♓	3:43 pm	♈
16	♈		
17	♈	9:05 pm	♉
18	♉		
19	♉		
20	♉	4:54 am	♊
21	♊		
22	♊	3:25 pm	♋
23	♋		
24	♋		
25	♋	3:44 am	♌
26	♌		
27	♌	3:49 pm	♍
28	♍		
29	♍		
30	♍	1:27 am	♎

July

Day	Sign	Time	Enters
1	♑		
2	♑	7:05 am	♒
3	♒		
4	♒	7:07 am	♓
5	♓		
6	♓	9:42 am	♈
7	♈		
8	♈	3:43 pm	♉
9	♉		
10	♉		
11	♉	12:52 am	♊
12	♊		
13	♊	12:08 pm	♋
14	♋		
15	♋		
16	♋	12:31 am	♌
17	♌		
18	♌	1:16 pm	♍
19	♍		
20	♍		
21	♍	1:14 am	♎
22	♎		
23	♎	10:43 am	♏
24	♏		
25	♏	4:24 pm	♐
26	♐		
27	♐	6:17 pm	♑
28	♑		
29	♑	5:47 pm	♒
30	♒		
31	♒	5:01 pm	♓

October

Day	Sign	Time	Enters
1	♊		
2	♊		
3	♊	8:14 am	♋
4	♋		
5	♋	8:12 pm	♌
6	♌		
7	♌		
8	♌	8:49 am	♍
9	♍		
10	♍	8:00 pm	♎
11	♎		
12	♎		
13	♎	4:46 am	♏
14	♏		
15	♏	11:07 am	♐
16	♐		
17	♐	3:37 pm	♑
18	♑		
19	♑	6:51 pm	♒
20	♒		
21	♒	9:22 pm	♓
22	♓		
23	♓	11:50 pm	♈
24	♈		
25	♈		
26	♈	3:11 am	♉
27	♉		
28	♉	8:35 am	♊
29	♊		
30	♊	4:56 pm	♋
31	♋		

February

Day	Sign	Time	Enters
1	♋		
2	♋		
3	♋	4:46 am	♌
4	♌		
5	♌	4:22 pm	♍
6	♍		
7	♍		
8	♍	2:30 am	♎
9	♎		
10	♎	10:35 am	♏
11	♏		
12	♏	3:58 pm	♐
13	♐		
14	♐	6:29 pm	♑
15	♑		
16	♑	7:00 pm	♒
17	♒		
18	♒	7:09 pm	♓
19	♓		
20	♓	8:58 pm	♈
21	♈		
22	♈		
23	♈	2:08 am	♉
24	♉		
25	♉	11:14 am	♊
26	♊		
27	♊	11:10 pm	♋
28	♋		
29	♋		

May

Day	Sign	Time	Enters
1	♎		
2	♎	7:42 am	♏
3	♏		
4	♏	11:05 am	♐
5	♐		
6	♐	12:54 pm	♑
7	♑		
8	♑	2:39 pm	♒
9	♒		
10	♒	5:29 pm	♓
11	♓		
12	♓	10:00 pm	♈
13	♈		
14	♈		
15	♈	4:25 am	♉
16	♉		
17	♉	12:48 pm	♊
18	♊		
19	♊	11:16 pm	♋
20	♋		
21	♋		
22	♋	11:28 am	♌
23	♌		
24	♌	11:58 pm	♍
25	♍		
26	♍		
27	♍	10:33 am	♎
28	♎		
29	♎	5:30 pm	♏
30	♏		
31	♏	8:43 pm	♐

August

Day	Sign	Time	Enters
1	♓		
2	♓	6:05 pm	♈
3	♈		
4	♈	10:33 pm	♉
5	♉		
6	♉		
7	♉	6:49 am	♊
8	♊		
9	♊	5:57 pm	♋
10	♋		
11	♋		
12	♋	6:29 am	♌
13	♌		
14	♌	7:07 pm	♍
15	♍		
16	♍		
17	♍	6:55 am	♎
18	♎		
19	♎	4:50 pm	♏
20	♏		
21	♏	11:48 pm	♐
22	♐		
23	♐		
24	♐	3:22 am	♑
25	♑		
26	♑	4:10 am	♒
27	♒		
28	♒	3:49 am	♓
29	♓		
30	♓	4:15 am	♈
31	♈		

November

Day	Sign	Time	Enters
1	♋		
2	♋	4:16 am	♌
3	♌		
4	♌	4:57 pm	♍
5	♍		
6	♍		
7	♍	4:29 am	♎
8	♎		
9	♎	1:02 pm	♏
10	♏		
11	♏	6:26 pm	♐
12	♐		
13	♐	9:44 pm	♑
14	♑		
15	♑		
16	♑	12:14 am	♒
17	♒		
18	♒	3:00 am	♓
19	♓		
20	♓	6:34 am	♈
21	♈		
22	♈	11:12 am	♉
23	♉		
24	♉	5:20 pm	♊
25	♊		
26	♊		
27	♊	1:37 am	♋
28	♋		
29	♋	12:30 pm	♌
30	♌		

March

Day	Sign	Time	Enters
1	♋	11:47 am	♌
2	♌		
3	♌	11:13 pm	♍
4	♍		
5	♍		
6	♍	8:40 am	♎
7	♎		
8	♎	4:05 pm	♏
9	♏		
10	♏	9:32 pm	♐
11	♐		
12	♐		
13	♐	1:08 am	♑
14	♑		
15	♑	3:15 am	♒
16	♒		
17	♒	4:50 am	♓
18	♓		
19	♓	7:15 am	♈
20	♈		
21	♈	11:59 am	♉
22	♉		
23	♉	7:59 pm	♊
24	♊		
25	♊		
26	♊	7:06 am	♋
27	♋		
28	♋	7:37 pm	♌
29	♌		
30	♌		
31	♌	7:15 am	♍

June

Day	Sign	Time	Enters
1	♐		
2	♐	9:29 pm	♑
3	♑		
4	♑	9:45 pm	♒
5	♒		
6	♒	11:19 pm	♓
7	♓		
8	♓		
9	♓	3:23 am	♈
10	♈		
11	♈	10:11 am	♉
12	♉		
13	♉	7:16 pm	♊
14	♊		
15	♊		
16	♊	6:08 am	♋
17	♋		
18	♋	6:22 pm	♌
19	♌		
20	♌		
21	♌	7:07 am	♍
22	♍		
23	♍	6:37 pm	♎
24	♎		
25	♎		
26	♎	2:53 am	♏
27	♏		
28	♏	7:01 am	♐
29	♐		
30	♐	7:47 am	♑

September

Day	Sign	Time	Enters
1	♈	7:19 am	♉
2	♉		
3	♉	2:08 pm	♊
4	♊		
5	♊		
6	♊	12:29 am	♋
7	♋		
8	♋	12:54 pm	♌
9	♌		
10	♌		
11	♌	1:28 am	♍
12	♍		
13	♍	12:51 pm	♎
14	♎		
15	♎	10:20 pm	♏
16	♏		
17	♏		
18	♏	5:31 am	♐
19	♐		
20	♐	10:12 am	♑
21	♑		
22	♑	12:39 pm	♒
23	♒		
24	♒	1:43 pm	♓
25	♓		
26	♓	2:46 pm	♈
27	♈		
28	♈	5:24 pm	♉
29	♉		
30	♉	11:01 pm	♊

December

Day	Sign	Time	Enters
1	♌		
2	♌	1:11 am	♍
3	♍		
4	♍	1:23 pm	♎
5	♎		
6	♎	10:39 pm	♏
7	♏		
8	♏		
9	♏	3:58 am	♐
10	♐		
11	♐	6:15 am	♑
12	♑		
13	♑	7:14 am	♒
14	♒		
15	♒	8:44 am	♓
16	♓		
17	♓	11:55 am	♈
18	♈		
19	♈	5:10 pm	♉
20	♉		
21	♉		
22	♉	12:17 am	♊
23	♊		
24	♊	9:14 am	♋
25	♋		
26	♋	8:09 pm	♌
27	♌		
28	♌		
29	♌	8:45 am	♍
30	♍		
31	♍	9:32 pm	♎

1996

Your Starway to Love

♈ = Aries ♉ = Taurus ♊ = Gemini ♋ = Cancer ♌ = Leo ♍ = Virgo

1997

January

1	♎		
2	♎		
3	♎	8:02 am	♏
4	♏		
5	♏	2:27 pm	♐
6	♐		
7	♐	4:55 pm	♑
8	♑		
9	♑	5:00 pm	♒
10	♒		
11	♒	4:51 pm	♓
12	♓		
13	♓	6:22 pm	♈
14	♈		
15	♈	10:40 pm	♉
16	♉		
17	♉		
18	♉	5:53 am	♊
19	♊		
20	♊	3:29 pm	♋
21	♋		
22	♋		
23	♋	2:50 am	♌
24	♌		
25	♌	3:26 pm	♍
26	♍		
27	♍		
28	♍	4:21 am	♎
29	♎		
30	♎	3:48 pm	♏
31	♏		

February

1	♏	11:51 pm	♐
2	♐		
3	♐		
4	♐	3:44 am	♑
5	♑		
6	♑	4:21 am	♒
7	♒		
8	♒	3:34 am	♓
9	♓		
10	♓	3:29 am	♈
11	♈		
12	♈	5:56 am	♉
13	♉		
14	♉	11:53 am	♊
15	♊		
16	♊	9:13 pm	♋
17	♋		
18	♋		
19	♋	8:52 am	♌
20	♌		
21	♌	9:38 pm	♍
22	♍		
23	♍		
24	♍	10:23 am	♎
25	♎		
26	♎	9:57 pm	♏
27	♏		
28	♏		

March

1	♏	7:01 am	♐
2	♐		
3	♐	12:38 pm	♑
4	♑		
5	♑	2:54 pm	♒
6	♒		
7	♒	2:57 pm	♓
8	♓		
9	♓	2:33 pm	♈
10	♈		
11	♈	3:37 pm	♉
12	♉		
13	♉	7:48 pm	♊
14	♊		
15	♊		
16	♊	3:51 am	♋
17	♋		
18	♋	3:08 pm	♌
19	♌		
20	♌		
21	♌	3:59 am	♍
22	♍		
23	♍	4:35 pm	♎
24	♎		
25	♎		
26	♎	3:42 am	♏
27	♏		
28	♏	12:40 pm	♐
29	♐		
30	♐	7:07 pm	♑
31	♑		

April

1	♑	10:59 pm	♒
2	♒		
3	♒		
4	♒	12:42 am	♓
5	♓		
6	♓	1:19 am	♈
7	♈		
8	♈	2:20 am	♉
9	♉		
10	♉	5:28 am	♊
11	♊		
12	♊	12:03 pm	♋
13	♋		
14	♋	10:22 pm	♌
15	♌		
16	♌		
17	♌	11:00 am	♍
18	♍		
19	♍	11:36 pm	♎
20	♎		
21	♎		
22	♎	10:19 am	♏
23	♏		
24	♏	6:32 pm	♐
25	♐		
26	♐		
27	♐	12:32 am	♑
28	♑		
29	♑	4:50 am	♒
30	♒		

May

1	♒	7:50 am	♓
2	♓		
3	♓	9:59 am	♈
4	♈		
5	♈	12:04 pm	♉
6	♉		
7	♉	3:21 pm	♊
8	♊		
9	♊	9:13 pm	♋
10	♋		
11	♋		
12	♋	6:33 am	♌
13	♌		
14	♌	6:43 pm	♍
15	♍		
16	♍		
17	♍	7:27 am	♎
18	♎		
19	♎	6:11 pm	♏
20	♏		
21	♏		
22	♏	1:51 am	♐
23	♐		
24	♐	6:51 am	♑
25	♑		
26	♑	10:20 am	♒
27	♒		
28	♒	1:18 pm	♓
29	♓		
30	♓	4:18 pm	♈
31	♈		

June

1	♈	7:39 pm	♉
2	♉		
3	♉	11:55 pm	♊
4	♊		
5	♊		
6	♊	6:02 am	♋
7	♋		
8	♋	2:58 pm	♌
9	♌		
10	♌		
11	♌	2:43 am	♍
12	♍		
13	♍	3:35 pm	♎
14	♎		
15	♎		
16	♎	2:51 am	♏
17	♏		
18	♏	10:39 am	♐
19	♐		
20	♐	3:02 pm	♑
21	♑		
22	♑	5:20 pm	♒
23	♒		
24	♒	7:09 pm	♓
25	♓		
26	♓	9:38 pm	♈
27	♈		
28	♈		
29	♈	1:23 am	♉
30	♉		

July

1	♉	6:35 am	♊
2	♊		
3	♊	1:33 pm	♋
4	♋		
5	♋	10:45 pm	♌
6	♌		
7	♌		
8	♌	10:22 am	♍
9	♍		
10	♍	11:21 pm	♎
11	♎		
12	♎		
13	♎	11:20 am	♏
14	♏		
15	♏	8:02 pm	♐
16	♐		
17	♐		
18	♐	12:45 am	♑
19	♑		
20	♑	2:29 am	♒
21	♒		
22	♒	3:00 am	♓
23	♓		
24	♓	4:03 am	♈
25	♈		
26	♈	6:53 am	♉
27	♉		
28	♉	12:04 pm	♊
29	♊		
30	♊	7:38 pm	♋
31	♋		

August

1	♋		
2	♋	5:27 am	♌
3	♌		
4	♌	5:15 pm	♍
5	♍		
6	♍		
7	♍	6:17 am	♎
8	♎		
9	♎	6:50 pm	♏
10	♏		
11	♏		
12	♏	4:45 am	♐
13	♐		
14	♐	10:42 am	♑
15	♑		
16	♑	12:58 pm	♒
17	♒		
18	♒	1:01 pm	♓
19	♓		
20	♓	12:45 pm	♈
21	♈		
22	♈	1:57 pm	♉
23	♉		
24	♉	5:56 pm	♊
25	♊		
26	♊		
27	♊	1:11 am	♋
28	♋		
29	♋	11:19 am	♌
30	♌		
31	♌	11:27 pm	♍

September

1	♍		
2	♍		
3	♍	12:30 pm	♎
4	♎		
5	♎		
6	♎	1:10 am	♏
7	♏		
8	♏	11:54 am	♐
9	♐		
10	♐	7:23 pm	♑
11	♑		
12	♑	11:10 pm	♒
13	♒		
14	♒	11:59 pm	♓
15	♓		
16	♓	11:25 pm	♈
17	♈		
18	♈	11:21 pm	♉
19	♉		
20	♉		
21	♉	1:38 am	♊
22	♊		
23	♊	7:33 am	♋
24	♋		
25	♋	5:12 pm	♌
26	♌		
27	♌		
28	♌	5:27 am	♍
29	♍		
30	♍	6:32 pm	♎

October

1	♎		
2	♎		
3	♎	6:57 am	♏
4	♏		
5	♏	5:43 pm	♐
6	♐		
7	♐		
8	♐	2:04 am	♑
9	♑		
10	♑	7:29 am	♒
11	♒		
12	♒	9:59 am	♓
13	♓		
14	♓	10:25 am	♈
15	♈		
16	♈	10:16 am	♉
17	♉		
18	♉	11:26 am	♊
19	♊		
20	♊	3:45 pm	♋
21	♋		
22	♋		
23	♋	12:10 am	♌
24	♌		
25	♌	11:59 am	♍
26	♍		
27	♍		
28	♍	1:05 am	♎
29	♎		
30	♎	1:15 pm	♏
31	♏		

November

1	♏	11:27 pm	♐
2	♐		
3	♐		
4	♐	7:31 am	♑
5	♑		
6	♑	1:33 pm	♒
7	♒		
8	♒	5:34 pm	♓
9	♓		
10	♓	7:44 pm	♈
11	♈		
12	♈	8:45 pm	♉
13	♉		
14	♉	10:05 pm	♊
15	♊		
16	♊		
17	♊	1:32 am	♋
18	♋		
19	♋	8:38 am	♌
20	♌		
21	♌	7:33 pm	♍
22	♍		
23	♍		
24	♍	8:29 am	♎
25	♎		
26	♎	8:43 pm	♏
27	♏		
28	♏		
29	♏	6:28 am	♐
30	♐		

December

1	♐	1:38 pm	♑
2	♑		
3	♑	6:58 pm	♒
4	♒		
5	♒	11:07 pm	♓
6	♓		
7	♓		
8	♓	2:24 am	♈
9	♈		
10	♈	5:00 am	♉
11	♉		
12	♉	7:35 am	♊
13	♊		
14	♊	11:25 am	♋
15	♋		
16	♋	5:58 pm	♌
17	♌		
18	♌		
19	♌	4:00 am	♍
20	♍		
21	♍	4:35 pm	♎
22	♎		
23	♎		
24	♎	5:07 am	♏
25	♏		
26	♏	3:07 pm	♐
27	♐		
28	♐	9:48 pm	♑
29	♑		
30	♑		
31	♑	1:58 am	♒

Moon Movements

♎ = Libra ♏ = Scorpio ♐ = Sagittarius ♑ = Capricorn ♒ = Aquarius ♓ = Pisces

1998

January

1	♒		
2	♒	4:56 am	♓
3	♓		
4	♓	7:43 am	♈
5	♈		
6	♈	10:52 am	♉
7	♉		
8	♉	2:42 pm	♊
9	♊		
10	♊	7:43 pm	♋
11	♋		
12	♋		
13	♋	2:45 am	♌
14	♌		
15	♌	12:31 pm	♍
16	♍		
17	♍		
18	♍	12:44 am	♎
19	♎		
20	♎	1:34 pm	♏
21	♏		
22	♏		
23	♏	12:25 am	♐
24	♐		
25	♐	7:39 am	♑
26	♑		
27	♑	11:27 am	♒
28	♒		
29	♒	1:08 pm	♓
30	♓		
31	♓	2:21 pm	♈

April

1	♊		
2	♊	2:10 pm	♋
3	♋		
4	♋	9:36 pm	♌
5	♌		
6	♌		
7	♌	8:25 am	♍
8	♍		
9	♍	9:04 pm	♎
10	♎		
11	♎		
12	♎	9:56 am	♏
13	♏		
14	♏	9:52 pm	♐
15	♐		
16	♐		
17	♐	8:05 am	♑
18	♑		
19	♑	3:41 pm	♒
20	♒		
21	♒	8:06 pm	♓
22	♓		
23	♓	9:30 pm	♈
24	♈		
25	♈	9:09 pm	♉
26	♉		
27	♉	8:55 pm	♊
28	♊		
29	♊	10:57 pm	♋
30	♋		

July

1	♎		
2	♎		
3	♎	6:45 am	♏
4	♏		
5	♏	6:24 pm	♐
6	♐		
7	♐		
8	♐	3:27 am	♑
9	♑		
10	♑	9:52 am	♒
11	♒		
12	♒	2:22 pm	♓
13	♓		
14	♓	5:45 pm	♈
15	♈		
16	♈	8:33 pm	♉
17	♉		
18	♉	11:18 pm	♊
19	♊		
20	♊		
21	♊	2:43 am	♋
22	♋		
23	♋	7:48 am	♌
24	♌		
25	♌	3:34 pm	♍
26	♍		
27	♍		
28	♍	2:14 am	♎
29	♎		
30	♎	2:44 pm	♏
31	♏		

October

1	♒		
2	♒	6:23 pm	♓
3	♓		
4	♓	7:32 pm	♈
5	♈		
6	♈	6:57 pm	♉
7	♉		
8	♉	6:44 pm	♊
9	♊		
10	♊	8:48 pm	♋
11	♋		
12	♋		
13	♋	2:25 am	♌
14	♌		
15	♌	11:32 am	♍
16	♍		
17	♍	11:02 pm	♎
18	♎		
19	♎		
20	♎	11:36 am	♏
21	♏		
22	♏		
23	♏	12:16 am	♐
24	♐		
25	♐	12:05 pm	♑
26	♑		
27	♑	9:44 pm	♒
28	♒		
29	♒		
30	♒	3:58 am	♓
31	♓		

February

1	♈		
2	♈	4:25 pm	♉
3	♉		
4	♉	8:09 pm	♊
5	♊		
6	♊		
7	♊	1:57 am	♋
8	♋		
9	♋	9:57 am	♌
10	♌		
11	♌	8:09 pm	♍
12	♍		
13	♍		
14	♍	8:17 am	♎
15	♎		
16	♎	9:13 pm	♏
17	♏		
18	♏		
19	♏	8:56 am	♐
20	♐		
21	♐	5:29 pm	♑
22	♑		
23	♑	10:10 pm	♒
24	♒		
25	♒	11:42 pm	♓
26	♓		
27	♓	11:42 pm	♈
28	♈		

May

1	♋		
2	♋	4:49 am	♌
3	♌		
4	♌	2:47 pm	♍
5	♍		
6	♍		
7	♍	3:19 am	♎
8	♎		
9	♎	4:10 pm	♏
10	♏		
11	♏		
12	♏	3:48 am	♐
13	♐		
14	♐	1:39 pm	♑
15	♑		
16	♑	9:30 pm	♒
17	♒		
18	♒		
19	♒	3:03 am	♓
20	♓		
21	♓	6:06 am	♈
22	♈		
23	♈	7:06 am	♉
24	♉		
25	♉	7:25 am	♊
26	♊		
27	♊	8:58 am	♋
28	♋		
29	♋	1:38 pm	♌
30	♌		
31	♌	10:21 pm	♍

August

1	♏		
2	♏	2:48 am	♐
3	♐		
4	♐	12:18 pm	♑
5	♑		
6	♑	6:31 pm	♒
7	♒		
8	♒	10:04 pm	♓
9	♓		
10	♓		
11	♓	12:10 am	♈
12	♈		
13	♈	2:04 am	♉
14	♉		
15	♉	4:46 am	♊
16	♊		
17	♊	8:55 am	♋
18	♋		
19	♋	3:01 pm	♌
20	♌		
21	♌	11:21 pm	♍
22	♍		
23	♍		
24	♍	10:02 am	♎
25	♎		
26	♎	10:25 pm	♏
27	♏		
28	♏		
29	♏	10:55 am	♐
30	♐		
31	♐	9:23 pm	♑

November

1	♓	6:27 am	♈
2	♈		
3	♈	6:12 am	♉
4	♉		
5	♉	5:11 am	♊
6	♊		
7	♊	5:39 am	♋
8	♋		
9	♋	9:33 am	♌
10	♌		
11	♌	5:37 pm	♍
12	♍		
13	♍		
14	♍	4:58 am	♎
15	♎		
16	♎	5:41 pm	♏
17	♏		
18	♏		
19	♏	6:13 am	♐
20	♐		
21	♐	5:45 pm	♑
22	♑		
23	♑		
24	♑	3:43 am	♒
25	♒		
26	♒	11:14 am	♓
27	♓		
28	♓	3:34 pm	♈
29	♈		
30	♈	4:52 pm	♉

March

1	♈		
2	♈	12:00 am	♉
3	♉		
4	♉	2:15 am	♊
5	♊		
6	♊	7:27 am	♋
7	♋		
8	♋	3:46 pm	♌
9	♌		
10	♌		
11	♌	2:35 am	♍
12	♍		
13	♍	2:58 pm	♎
14	♎		
15	♎		
16	♎	3:51 am	♏
17	♏		
18	♏	3:56 pm	♐
19	♐		
20	♐		
21	♐	1:43 am	♑
22	♑		
23	♑	8:01 am	♒
24	♒		
25	♒	10:43 am	♓
26	♓		
27	♓	10:49 am	♈
28	♈		
29	♈	10:06 am	♉
30	♉		
31	♉	10:38 am	♊

June

1	♍		
2	♍		
3	♍	10:17 am	♎
4	♎		
5	♎	11:06 pm	♏
6	♏		
7	♏		
8	♏	10:34 am	♐
9	♐		
10	♐	7:50 pm	♑
11	♑		
12	♑		
13	♑	3:03 am	♒
14	♒		
15	♒	8:31 am	♓
16	♓		
17	♓	12:23 pm	♈
18	♈		
19	♈	2:47 pm	♉
20	♉		
21	♉	4:26 pm	♊
22	♊		
23	♊	6:39 pm	♋
24	♋		
25	♋	11:04 pm	♌
26	♌		
27	♌		
28	♌	6:54 am	♍
29	♍		
30	♍	6:05 pm	♎

September

1	♑		
2	♑		
3	♑	4:21 am	♒
4	♒		
5	♒	7:48 am	♓
6	♓		
7	♓	8:52 am	♈
8	♈		
9	♈	9:16 am	♉
10	♉		
11	♉	10:40 am	♊
12	♊		
13	♊	2:20 pm	♋
14	♋		
15	♋	8:48 pm	♌
16	♌		
17	♌		
18	♌	5:52 am	♍
19	♍		
20	♍	4:57 pm	♎
21	♎		
22	♎		
23	♎	5:22 am	♏
24	♏		
25	♏	6:05 pm	♐
26	♐		
27	♐		
28	♐	5:30 am	♑
29	♑		
30	♑	1:53 pm	♒

December

1	♉		
2	♉	4:30 pm	♊
3	♊		
4	♊	4:28 pm	♋
5	♋		
6	♋	6:55 pm	♌
7	♌		
8	♌		
9	♌	1:21 am	♍
10	♍		
11	♍	11:43 am	♎
12	♎		
13	♎		
14	♎	12:16 am	♏
15	♏		
16	♏	12:47 pm	♐
17	♐		
18	♐	11:55 pm	♑
19	♑		
20	♑		
21	♑	9:17 am	♒
22	♒		
23	♒	4:45 pm	♓
24	♓		
25	♓	10:04 pm	♈
26	♈		
27	♈		
28	♈	1:05 am	♉
29	♉		
30	♉	2:22 am	♊
31	♊		

Your Starway to Love

♈ = Aries ♉ = Taurus ♊ = Gemini ♋ = Cancer ♌ = Leo ♍ = Virgo

1999

January

1	♊	3:15 am	♋
2	♋		
3	♋	5:31 am	♌
4	♌		
5	♌	10:49 am	♍
6	♍		
7	♍	7:53 pm	♎
8	♎		
9	♎		
10	♎	7:49 am	♏
11	♏		
12	♏	8:23 pm	♐
13	♐		
14	♐		
15	♐	7:28 am	♑
16	♑		
17	♑	4:11 pm	♒
18	♒		
19	♒	10:40 pm	♓
20	♓		
21	♓		
22	♓	3:25 am	♈
23	♈		
24	♈	6:52 am	♉
25	♉		
26	♉	9:29 am	♊
27	♊		
28	♊	11:57 am	♋
29	♋		
30	♋	3:16 pm	♌
31	♌		

February

1	♌	8:37 pm	♍
2	♍		
3	♍		
4	♍	4:56 am	♎
5	♎		
6	♎	4:06 pm	♏
7	♏		
8	♏		
9	♏	4:38 am	♐
10	♐		
11	♐	4:10 pm	♑
12	♑		
13	♑		
14	♑	12:57 am	♒
15	♒		
16	♒	6:40 am	♓
17	♓		
18	♓	10:06 am	♈
19	♈		
20	♈	12:29 pm	♉
21	♉		
22	♉	2:54 pm	♊
23	♊		
24	♊	6:09 pm	♋
25	♋		
26	♋	10:44 pm	♌
27	♌		
28	♌		

March

1	♌	5:05 am	♍
2	♍		
3	♍	1:34 pm	♎
4	♎		
5	♎		
6	♎	12:22 am	♏
7	♏		
8	♏	12:46 pm	♐
9	♐		
10	♐		
11	♐	12:54 am	♑
12	♑		
13	♑	10:32 am	♒
14	♒		
15	♒	4:30 pm	♓
16	♓		
17	♓	7:13 pm	♈
18	♈		
19	♈	8:09 pm	♉
20	♉		
21	♉	9:05 pm	♊
22	♊		
23	♊	11:33 pm	♋
24	♋		
25	♋		
26	♋	4:22 am	♌
27	♌		
28	♌	11:34 am	♍
29	♍		
30	♍	8:49 pm	♎
31	♎		

April

1	♎		
2	♎	7:49 am	♏
3	♏		
4	♏	8:07 pm	♐
5	♐		
6	♐		
7	♐	8:39 am	♑
8	♑		
9	♑	7:24 pm	♒
10	♒		
11	♒		
12	♒	2:35 am	♓
13	♓		
14	♓	5:46 am	♈
15	♈		
16	♈	6:07 am	♉
17	♉		
18	♉	5:39 am	♊
19	♊		
20	♊	6:27 am	♋
21	♋		
22	♋	10:06 am	♌
23	♌		
24	♌	5:04 pm	♍
25	♍		
26	♍		
27	♍	2:46 am	♎
28	♎		
29	♎	2:12 pm	♏
30	♏		

May

1	♏		
2	♏	2:36 am	♐
3	♐		
4	♐	3:12 pm	♑
5	♑		
6	♑		
7	♑	2:40 am	♒
8	♒		
9	♒	11:16 am	♓
10	♓		
11	♓	3:53 pm	♈
12	♈		
13	♈	4:56 pm	♉
14	♉		
15	♉	4:07 pm	♊
16	♊		
17	♊	3:39 pm	♋
18	♋		
19	♋	5:37 pm	♌
20	♌		
21	♌	11:15 pm	♍
22	♍		
23	♍		
24	♍	8:29 am	♎
25	♎		
26	♎	8:05 pm	♏
27	♏		
28	♏		
29	♏	8:37 am	♐
30	♐		
31	♐	9:06 pm	♑

June

1	♑		
2	♑		
3	♑	8:37 am	♒
4	♒		
5	♒	6:00 pm	♓
6	♓		
7	♓		
8	♓	12:08 am	♈
9	♈		
10	♈	2:44 am	♉
11	♉		
12	♉	2:48 am	♊
13	♊		
14	♊	2:14 am	♋
15	♋		
16	♋	3:07 am	♌
17	♌		
18	♌	7:12 am	♍
19	♍		
20	♍	3:10 pm	♎
21	♎		
22	♎		
23	♎	2:18 am	♏
24	♏		
25	♏	2:51 pm	♐
26	♐		
27	♐		
28	♐	3:12 am	♑
29	♑		
30	♑	2:19 pm	♒

July

1	♒		
2	♒	11:34 pm	♓
3	♓		
4	♓		
5	♓	6:21 am	♈
6	♈		
7	♈	10:22 am	♉
8	♉		
9	♉	12:00 pm	♊
10	♊		
11	♊	12:27 pm	♋
12	♋		
13	♋	1:26 pm	♌
14	♌		
15	♌	4:39 pm	♍
16	♍		
17	♍	11:19 pm	♎
18	♎		
19	♎		
20	♎	9:30 am	♏
21	♏		
22	♏	9:48 pm	♐
23	♐		
24	♐		
25	♐	10:08 am	♑
26	♑		
27	♑	8:54 pm	♒
28	♒		
29	♒		
30	♒	5:27 am	♓
31	♓		

August

1	♓	11:47 am	♈
2	♈		
3	♈	4:09 pm	♉
4	♉		
5	♉	6:57 am	♊
6	♊		
7	♊	8:52 pm	♋
8	♋		
9	♋	10:55 pm	♌
10	♌		
11	♌		
12	♌	2:22 am	♍
13	♍		
14	♍	8:24 am	♎
15	♎		
16	♎	5:40 pm	♏
17	♏		
18	♏		
19	♏	5:32 am	♐
20	♐		
21	♐	5:59 pm	♑
22	♑		
23	♑		
24	♑	4:49 am	♒
25	♒		
26	♒	12:50 pm	♓
27	♓		
28	♓	6:09 pm	♈
29	♈		
30	♈	9:41 pm	♉
31	♉		

September

1	♉		
2	♉	12:25 am	♊
3	♊		
4	♊	3:10 am	♋
5	♋		
6	♋	6:29 am	♌
7	♌		
8	♌	10:57 am	♍
9	♍		
10	♍	5:16 pm	♎
11	♎		
12	♎		
13	♎	2:08 am	♏
14	♏		
15	♏	1:35 pm	♐
16	♐		
17	♐		
18	♐	2:13 am	♑
19	♑		
20	♑	1:38 pm	♒
21	♒		
22	♒	9:51 pm	♓
23	♓		
24	♓		
25	♓	2:34 am	♈
26	♈		
27	♈	4:51 am	♉
28	♉		
29	♉	6:21 am	♊
30	♊		

October

1	♊	8:31 am	♋
2	♋		
3	♋	12:13 pm	♌
4	♌		
5	♌	5:40 pm	♍
6	♍		
7	♍		
8	♍	12:52 am	♎
9	♎		
10	♎	10:01 am	♏
11	♏		
12	♏	9:18 pm	♐
13	♐		
14	♐		
15	♐	10:04 am	♑
16	♑		
17	♑	10:17 pm	♒
18	♒		
19	♒		
20	♒	7:33 am	♓
21	♓		
22	♓	12:41 pm	♈
23	♈		
24	♈	2:25 pm	♉
25	♉		
26	♉	2:33 pm	♊
27	♊		
28	♊	3:09 pm	♋
29	♋		
30	♋	5:47 pm	♌
31	♌		

November

1	♌	11:07 pm	♍
2	♍		
3	♍		
4	♍	6:57 am	♎
5	♎		
6	♎	4:46 pm	♏
7	♏		
8	♏		
9	♏	4:15 am	♐
10	♐		
11	♐	5:00 pm	♑
12	♑		
13	♑		
14	♑	5:46 am	♒
15	♒		
16	♒	4:21 pm	♓
17	♓		
18	♓	10:57 pm	♈
19	♈		
20	♈		
21	♈	1:26 am	♉
22	♉		
23	♉	1:14 am	♊
24	♊		
25	♊	12:29 am	♋
26	♋		
27	♋	1:19 am	♌
28	♌		
29	♌	5:11 am	♍
30	♍		

December

1	♍	12:29 pm	♎
2	♎		
3	♎	10:35 pm	♏
4	♏		
5	♏		
6	♏	10:27 am	♐
7	♐		
8	♐	11:14 pm	♑
9	♑		
10	♑		
11	♑	11:59 am	♒
12	♒		
13	♒	11:18 pm	♓
14	♓		
15	♓		
16	♓	7:30 am	♈
17	♈		
18	♈	11:45 am	♉
19	♉		
20	♉	12:39 pm	♊
21	♊		
22	♊	11:52 am	♋
23	♋		
24	♋	11:32 am	♌
25	♌		
26	♌	1:34 pm	♍
27	♍		
28	♍	7:14 pm	♎
29	♎		
30	♎		
31	♎	4:36 am	♏

Moon Movements

♎ = Libra ♏ = Scorpio ♐ = Sagittarius ♑ = Capricorn ♒ = Aquarius ♓ = Pisces

2000

January

1	♏		
2	♏	4:32 pm	♐
3	♐		
4	♐		
5	♐	5:24 am	♑
6	♑		
7	♑	5:53 pm	♒
8	♒		
9	♒		
10	♒	4:59 am	♓
11	♓		
12	♓	1:48 pm	♈
13	♈		
14	♈	7:38 pm	♉
15	♉		
16	♉	10:25 pm	♊
17	♊		
18	♊	11:01 pm	♋
19	♋		
20	♋	10:58 pm	♌
21	♌		
22	♌		
23	♌	12:07 am	♍
24	♍		
25	♍	4:09 am	♎
26	♎		
27	♎	12:01 pm	♏
28	♏		
29	♏	11:17 pm	♐
30	♐		
31	♐		

April

1	♒	3:12 am	♓
2	♓		
3	♓	10:22 am	♈
4	♈		
5	♈	2:29 pm	♉
6	♉		
7	♉	4:58 pm	♊
8	♊		
9	♊	7:16 pm	♋
10	♋		
11	♋	10:16 pm	♌
12	♌		
13	♌		
14	♌	2:19 am	♍
15	♍		
16	♍	7:36 am	♎
17	♎		
18	♎	2:35 pm	♏
19	♏		
20	♏	11:58 pm	♐
21	♐		
22	♐		
23	♐	11:47 am	♑
24	♑		
25	♑		
26	♑	12:42 am	♒
27	♒		
28	♒	12:06 pm	♓
29	♓		
30	♓	7:55 pm	♈

July

1	♋		
2	♋	9:38 pm	♌
3	♌		
4	♌	10:19 pm	♍
5	♍		
6	♍		
7	♍	1:47 am	♎
8	♎		
9	♎	8:48 am	♏
10	♏		
11	♏	7:06 pm	♐
12	♐		
13	♐		
14	♐	7:28 am	♑
15	♑		
16	♑	8:27 pm	♒
17	♒		
18	♒		
19	♒	8:44 am	♓
20	♓		
21	♓	7:09 pm	♈
22	♈		
23	♈		
24	♈	2:44 am	♉
25	♉		
26	♉	7:01 am	♊
27	♊		
28	♊	8:30 am	♋
29	♋		
30	♋	8:24 am	♌
31	♌		

October

1	♏	5:50 pm	♐
2	♐		
3	♐		
4	♐	4:42 am	♑
5	♑		
6	♑	5:33 pm	♒
7	♒		
8	♒		
9	♒	5:36 am	♓
10	♓		
11	♓	2:51 pm	♈
12	♈		
13	♈	9:06 pm	♉
14	♉		
15	♉		
16	♉	1:19 am	♊
17	♊		
18	♊	4:37 am	♋
19	♋		
20	♋	7:42 am	♌
21	♌		
22	♌	10:52 am	♍
23	♍		
24	♍	2:30 pm	♎
25	♎		
26	♎	7:23 pm	♏
27	♏		
28	♏		
29	♏	2:40 am	♐
30	♐		
31	♐	1:02 pm	♑

February

1	♐	12:10 pm	♑
2	♑		
3	♑		
4	♑	12:31 am	♒
5	♒		
6	♒	11:02 am	♓
7	♓		
8	♓	7:17 pm	♈
9	♈		
10	♈		
11	♈	1:21 am	♉
12	♉		
13	♉	5:23 am	♊
14	♊		
15	♊	7:45 am	♋
16	♋		
17	♋	9:11 am	♌
18	♌		
19	♌	10:53 am	♍
20	♍		
21	♍	2:21 pm	♎
22	♎		
23	♎	8:58 pm	♏
24	♏		
25	♏		
26	♏	7:10 am	♐
27	♐		
28	♐	7:45 pm	♑
29	♑		

May

1	♈		
2	♈	11:54 pm	♉
3	♉		
4	♉		
5	♉	1:23 am	♊
6	♊		
7	♊	2:14 am	♋
8	♋		
9	♋	4:01 am	♌
10	♌		
11	♌	7:41 am	♍
12	♍		
13	♍	1:27 pm	♎
14	♎		
15	♎	9:16 pm	♏
16	♏		
17	♏		
18	♏	7:09 am	♐
19	♐		
20	♐	7:01 pm	♑
21	♑		
22	♑		
23	♑	8:00 am	♒
24	♒		
25	♒	8:07 pm	♓
26	♓		
27	♓		
28	♓	5:08 am	♈
29	♈		
30	♈	10:02 am	♉
31	♉		

August

1	♌	8:27 am	♍
2	♍		
3	♍	10:31 am	♎
4	♎		
5	♎	4:04 pm	♏
6	♏		
7	♏		
8	♏	1:30 am	♐
9	♐		
10	♐	1:44 pm	♑
11	♑		
12	♑		
13	♑	2:43 am	♒
14	♒		
15	♒	2:41 pm	♓
16	♓		
17	♓		
18	♓	12:44 am	♈
19	♈		
20	♈	8:31 am	♉
21	♉		
22	♉	1:55 pm	♊
23	♊		
24	♊	5:00 pm	♋
25	♋		
26	♋	6:17 pm	♌
27	♌		
28	♌	6:55 pm	♍
29	♍		
30	♍	8:33 pm	♎
31	♎		

November

1	♑		
2	♑		
3	♑	1:41 am	♒
4	♒		
5	♒	2:13 pm	♓
6	♓		
7	♓		
8	♓	12:02 am	♈
9	♈		
10	♈	6:12 am	♉
11	♉		
12	♉	9:27 am	♊
13	♊		
14	♊	11:21 am	♋
15	♋		
16	♋	1:19 pm	♌
17	♌		
18	♌	4:15 pm	♍
19	♍		
20	♍	8:35 pm	♎
21	♎		
22	♎		
23	♎	2:33 am	♏
24	♏		
25	♏	10:33 am	♐
26	♐		
27	♐	8:57 pm	♑
28	♑		
29	♑		
30	♑	9:26 am	♒

March

1	♑		
2	♑	8:14 am	♒
3	♒		
4	♒	6:30 pm	♓
5	♓		
6	♓		
7	♓	1:54 am	♈
8	♈		
9	♈	7:01 am	♉
10	♉		
11	♉	10:46 am	♊
12	♊		
13	♊	1:51 pm	♋
14	♋		
15	♋	4:43 pm	♌
16	♌		
17	♌	7:48 pm	♍
18	♍		
19	♍	11:57 pm	♎
20	♎		
21	♎		
22	♎	6:17 am	♏
23	♏		
24	♏	3:43 pm	♐
25	♐		
26	♐		
27	♐	3:51 am	♑
28	♑		
29	♑	4:34 pm	♒
30	♒		
31	♒		

June

1	♉	11:34 am	♊
2	♊		
3	♊	11:30 am	♋
4	♋		
5	♋	11:46 am	♌
6	♌		
7	♌	1:57 pm	♍
8	♍		
9	♍	6:59 pm	♎
10	♎		
11	♎		
12	♎	2:55 am	♏
13	♏		
14	♏	1:18 pm	♐
15	♐		
16	♐		
17	♐	1:26 am	♑
18	♑		
19	♑	2:26 pm	♒
20	♒		
21	♒		
22	♒	2:52 am	♓
23	♓		
24	♓	12:55 pm	♈
25	♈		
26	♈	7:19 pm	♉
27	♉		
28	♉	9:59 pm	♊
29	♊		
30	♊	10:09 pm	♋

September

1	♎		
2	♎	12:55 am	♏
3	♏		
4	♏	9:08 am	♐
5	♐		
6	♐	8:47 pm	♑
7	♑		
8	♑		
9	♑	9:44 am	♒
10	♒		
11	♒	9:34 pm	♓
12	♓		
13	♓		
14	♓	7:00 am	♈
15	♈		
16	♈	2:05 pm	♉
17	♉		
18	♉	7:22 pm	♊
19	♊		
20	♊	11:16 pm	♋
21	♋		
22	♋		
23	♋	2:00 am	♌
24	♌		
25	♌	4:02 am	♍
26	♍		
27	♍	6:22 am	♎
28	♎		
29	♎	10:30 am	♏
30	♏		

December

1	♒		
2	♒	10:23 pm	♓
3	♓		
4	♓		
5	♓	9:17 am	♈
6	♈		
7	♈	4:27 pm	♉
8	♉		
9	♉	7:50 pm	♊
10	♊		
11	♊	8:48 pm	♋
12	♋		
13	♋	9:09 pm	♌
14	♌		
15	♌	10:30 pm	♍
16	♍		
17	♍		
18	♍	2:01 am	♎
19	♎		
20	♎	8:12 am	♏
21	♏		
22	♏	4:57 pm	♐
23	♐		
24	♐		
25	♐	3:54 am	♑
26	♑		
27	♑	4:25 pm	♒
28	♒		
29	♒		
30	♒	5:27 am	♓
31	♓		

What Was Rising?

Sidereal Time Tables

1909	Jan	Feb	Mar	Apr	May	Jun	Jul	Aug	Sep	Oct	Nov	Dec
1	6:40	8:42	10:33	12:35	14:33	16:35	18:34	20:36	22:38	0:36	2:39	4:37
2	6:44	8:46	10:37	12:39	14:37	16:39	18:38	20:40	22:42	0:40	2:43	4:41
3	6:48	8:50	10:41	12:43	14:41	16:43	18:42	20:44	22:46	0:44	2:46	4:45
4	6:52	8:54	10:44	12:47	14:45	16:47	18:45	20:48	22:50	0:48	2:50	4:49
5	6:56	8:58	10:48	12:51	14:49	16:51	18:49	20:52	22:54	0:52	2:54	4:53
									22:58	0:56	2:58	4:57
									23:02	1:00	3:02	5:01
									23:06	1:04	3:06	5:04
									23:10	1:08	3:10	5:08
									23:14	1:12	3:14	5:12
									23:18	1:16	3:18	5:16
									23:21	1:20	3:22	5:20
									23:25	1:24	3:26	5:24
									23:29	1:28	3:30	5:28
									23:33	1:32	3:34	5:32
									23:37	1:35	3:38	5:36
17	7:43	9:45	11:36	13:38	15:36	17:38	19:37	21:39	23:41	1:39	3:42	5:40
18	7:47	9:49	11:40	13:42	15:40	17:42	19:41	21:43	23:45	1:43	3:46	5:44
19	7:51	9:53	11:44	13:46	15:44	17:46	19:45	21:47	23:49	1:47	3:50	5:48
20	7:55	9:57	11:48	13:50	15:48	17:50	19:49	21:51	23:53	1:51	3:53	5:52
21	7:59	10:01	11:51	13:54	15:52	17:54	19:52	21:55	23:57	1:55	3:57	5:56
22	8:03	10:05	11:55	13:58	15:56	17:58	19:56	21:59	0:01	1:59	4:01	6:00
23	8:07	10:09	11:59	14:02	16:00	18:02	20:00	22:03	0:05	2:03	4:05	6:04
24	8:11	10:13	12:03	14:06	16:04	18:06	20:04	22:07	0:09	2:07	4:09	6:08
25	8:15	10:17	12:07	14:09	16:08	18:10	20:08	22:10	0:13	2:11	4:13	6:11
26	8:19	10:21	12:11	14:13	16:12	18:14	20:12	22:14	0:17	2:15	4:17	6:15
27	8:23	10:25	12:15	14:17	16:16	18:18	20:16	22:18	0:21	2:19	4:21	6:19
28	8:26	10:29	12:19	14:21	16:20	18:22	20:20	22:22	0:25	2:23	4:25	6:23
29	8:30		12:23	14:25	16:24	18:26	20:24	22:26	0:28	2:27	4:29	6:27
30	8:34		12:27	14:29	16:27	18:30	20:28	22:30	0:32	2:31	4:33	6:31
31	8:38		12:31		16:31		20:32	22:34		2:35		6:35

1 Turn to the page containing the year you were born.

1910	Jan	Feb	Mar	Apr	May	Jun	Jul	Aug	Sep	Oct	Nov	Dec
1	6:39	8:41			14:32	16:34	18:33	20:35	22:37	0:35	2:38	4:36
2	6:43	8:45			14:36	16:38	18:37	20:39	22:41	0:39	2:42	4:40
3	6:47	8:49	10:40	12:42	14:40	16:42	18:41	20:43	22:45	0:43	2:46	4:44
4	6:51	8:53	10:44									4:48
5	6:55	8:57	10:47									4:52
6	6:59	9:01	10:51									4:56
7	7:03	9:05	10:55									5:00
8	7:07	9:09	10:59									5:03
9	7:11	9:13	11:03									5:07
			11:07									5:11
11	7:18	9:21	11:11									5:15
			11:15									5:19
13	7:26	9:29	11:19									5:23
14	7:30	9:33	11:23									5:27
15	7:34	9:36	11:27									5:31
16	:38	9:40	11:31	13:33	15:31	17:34	19:32	21:34	23:36	1:35	3:37	5:35
17		9:44	11:35	13:37	15:35	17:37	19:36	21:38	23:40	1:38	3:41	5:39
18										1:42	3:45	5:43
19										:46	3:49	5:47
20										:50	3:53	5:51
21										:54	3:56	5:55
22										:58	4:00	5:59
23										:02	4:04	6:03
24										:06	4:08	6:07
25	8:14									:10	4:12	6:11
26	8:18									:14	4:16	6:14
27	8:22									:18	4:20	6:18
28	8:26									:22	4:24	6:22
29	8:29									:26	4:28	6:26
30	8:33									:30	4:32	6:30
31	8:37		12:30		16:30		20:31	22:33		2:34		6:34

2 Select the year and month you were born.

3 Find the day you were born.
The time listed is the **Sidereal Time** for that day.
Add this to your birth time to get your **Star Time**.
Your **Star Time** will be used in the Ascendant Tables section.

1911	Jan	Feb	Mar	Apr	May	Jun	Jul	Aug	Sep	Oct	Nov	Dec
1	6:38	8:40	10:31	12:33	14:31	16:33	18:32	20:34	22:36	0:34	2:37	4:35
2	6:42	8:44	10:35	12:37	14:35	16:37	18:36	20:38	22:40	0:38	2:41	4:39
3	6:46	8:48	10:39	12:41	14:39	16:41	18:40	20:42	22:44	0:42	2:45	4:43
4	6:50	8:52	10:43	12:45	14:43	16:45	18:44	20:46	22:48	0:46	2:48	4:47
5	6:54	8:56	10:46	12:49	14:47	16:49	18:47	20:50	22:52	0:50	2:52	4:51
6	6:58	9:00	10:50	12:53	14:51	16:53	18:51	20:54	22:56	0:54	2:56	4:55
7	7:02	9:04	10:54									4:59
8	7:06	9:08	10:58									:03
9	7:10	9:12	11:02									:06
10	7:14	9:16	11:06									:10
11	7:18	9:20	11:10									:14
12	7:21	9:24	11:14									:18
13	7:25	9:28	11:18									:22
14	7:29	9:32	11:22									:26
15	7:33	9:36	11:26									:30
16	7:37	9:39	11:30									:34
17	7:41	9:43	11:34									:38
18	7:45	9:47	11:38	13:40	15:38	17:40	19:39	21:41	23:43	1:41	3:44	5:42
19	7:49	9:51	11:42	13:44	15:42	17:44	19:43	21:45	23:47	1:45	3:48	5:46
20	7:53	9:55	11:46	13:48	15:46	17:48	19:47	21:49	23:51	1:49	3:52	5:50
21	7:57	9:59	11:50	13:52	15:50	17:52	19:51	21:53	23:55	1:53	3:56	5:54
22	8:01	10:03	11:54	13:56	15:54	17:56	19:55	21:57	23:59	1:57	3:59	5:58
23	8:05	10:07	11:57	14:00	15:58	18:00	19:58	22:01	0:03	2:01	4:03	6:02
24	8:09	10:11	12:01	14:04	16:02	18:04	20:02	22:05	0:07	2:05	4:07	6:06
25	8:13	10:15	12:05	14:08	16:06	18:08	20:06	22:09	0:11	2:09	4:11	6:10
26	8:17	10:19	12:09	14:12	16:10	18:12	20:10	22:13	0:15	2:13	4:15	6:14
27	8:21	10:23	12:13	14:15	16:14	18:16	20:14	22:16	0:19	2:17	4:19	6:17
28	8:25	10:27	12:17	14:19	16:18	18:20	20:18	22:20	0:23	2:21	4:23	6:21
29	8:29		12:21	14:23	16:22	18:24	20:22	22:24	0:27	2:25	4:27	6:25
30	8:32		12:25	14:27	16:26	18:28	20:26	22:28	0:31	2:29	4:31	6:29
31	8:36		12:29		16:30		20:30	22:32		2:33		6:33

4 Repeats steps 1, 2 and 3 for your partner's birthday.

1900	Jan	Feb	Mar	Apr	May	Jun	Jul	Aug	Sep	Oct	Nov	Dec
1	6:41	8:43	10:33	12:36	14:34	16:36	18:34	20:37	22:39	0:37	2:39	4:38
2	6:45	8:47	10:37	12:40	14:38	16:40	18:38	20:41	22:43	0:41	2:43	4:42
3	6:49	8:51	10:41	12:43	14:42	16:44	18:42	20:44	22:47	0:45	2:47	4:45
4	6:53	8:55	10:45	12:47	14:46	16:48	18:46	20:48	22:51	0:49	2:51	4:49
5	6:57	8:59	10:49	12:51	14:50	16:52	18:50	20:52	22:55	0:53	2:55	4:53
6	7:00	9:03	10:53	12:55	14:54	16:56	18:54	20:56	22:58	0:57	2:59	4:57
7	7:04	9:07	10:57	12:59	14:58	17:00	18:58	21:00	23:02	1:01	3:03	5:01
8	7:08	9:11	11:01	13:03	15:01	17:04	19:02	21:04	23:06	1:05	3:07	5:05
9	7:12	9:14	11:05	13:07	15:05	17:08	19:06	21:08	23:10	1:09	3:11	5:09
10	7:16	9:18	11:09	13:11	15:09	17:12	19:10	21:12	23:14	1:13	3:15	5:13
11	7:20	9:22	11:13	13:15	15:13	17:15	19:14	21:16	23:18	1:16	3:19	5:17
12	7:24	9:26	11:17	13:19	15:17	17:19	19:18	21:20	23:22	1:20	3:23	5:21
13	7:28	9:30	11:21	13:23	15:21	17:23	19:22	21:24	23:26	1:24	3:27	5:25
14	7:32	9:34	11:25	13:27	15:25	17:27	19:26	21:28	23:30	1:28	3:31	5:29
15	7:36	9:38	11:29	13:31	15:29	17:31	19:30	21:32	23:34	1:32	3:34	5:33
16	7:40	9:42	11:32	13:35	15:33	17:35	19:33	21:36	23:38	1:36	3:38	5:37
17	7:44	9:46	11:36	13:39	15:37	17:39	19:37	21:40	23:42	1:40	3:42	5:41
18	7:48	9:50	11:40	13:43	15:41	17:43	19:41	21:44	23:46	1:44	3:46	5:45
19	7:52	9:54	11:44	13:47	15:45	17:47	19:45	21:48	23:50	1:48	3:50	5:49
20	7:56	9:58	11:48	13:50	15:49	17:51	19:49	21:51	23:54	1:52	3:54	5:52
21	8:00	10:02	11:52	13:54	15:53	17:55	19:53	21:55	23:58	1:56	3:58	5:56
22	8:04	10:06	11:56	13:58	15:57	17:59	19:57	21:59	0:02	2:00	4:02	6:00
23	8:07	10:10	12:00	14:02	16:01	18:03	20:01	22:03	0:06	2:04	4:06	6:04
24	8:11	10:14	12:04	14:06	16:05	18:07	20:05	22:07	0:09	2:08	4:10	6:08
25	8:15	10:18	12:08	14:10	16:08	18:11	20:09	22:11	0:13	2:12	4:14	6:12
26	8:19	10:22	12:12	14:14	16:12	18:15	20:13	22:15	0:17	2:16	4:18	6:16
27	8:23	10:25	12:16	14:18	16:16	18:19	20:17	22:19	0:21	2:20	4:22	6:20
28	8:27	10:29	12:20	14:22	16:20	18:23	20:21	22:23	0:25	2:24	4:26	6:24
29	8:31		12:24	14:26	16:24	18:26	20:25	22:27	0:29	2:27	4:30	6:28
30	8:35		12:28	14:30	16:28	18:30	20:29	22:31	0:33	2:31	4:34	6:32
31	8:39		12:32		16:32		20:33	22:35		2:35		6:36

1901	Jan	Feb	Mar	Apr	May	Jun	Jul	Aug	Sep	Oct	Nov	Dec
1	6:40	8:42	10:32	12:35	14:33	16:35	18:33	20:36	22:38	0:36	2:38	4:37
2	6:44	8:46	10:36	12:39	14:37	16:39	18:37	20:40	22:42	0:40	2:42	4:41
3	6:48	8:50	10:40	12:42	14:41	16:43	18:41	20:43	22:46	0:44	2:46	4:44
4	6:52	8:54	10:44	12:46	14:45	16:47	18:45	20:47	22:50	0:48	2:50	4:48
5	6:56	8:58	10:48	12:50	14:49	16:51	18:49	20:51	22:54	0:52	2:54	4:52
6	6:59	9:02	10:52	12:54	14:53	16:55	18:53	20:55	22:58	0:56	2:58	4:56
7	7:03	9:06	10:56	12:58	14:57	16:59	18:57	20:59	23:01	1:00	3:02	5:00
8	7:07	9:10	11:00	13:02	15:00	17:03	19:01	21:03	23:05	1:04	3:06	5:04
9	7:11	9:14	11:04	13:06	15:04	17:07	19:05	21:07	23:09	1:08	3:10	5:08
10	7:15	9:17	11:08	13:10	15:08	17:11	19:09	21:11	23:13	1:12	3:14	5:12
11	7:19	9:21	11:12	13:14	15:12	17:15	19:13	21:15	23:17	1:16	3:18	5:16
12	7:23	9:25	11:16	13:18	15:16	17:18	19:17	21:19	23:21	1:19	3:22	5:20
13	7:27	9:29	11:20	13:22	15:20	17:22	19:21	21:23	23:25	1:23	3:26	5:24
14	7:31	9:33	11:24	13:26	15:24	17:26	19:25	21:27	23:29	1:27	3:30	5:28
15	7:35	9:37	11:28	13:30	15:28	17:30	19:29	21:31	23:33	1:31	3:34	5:32
16	7:39	9:41	11:32	13:34	15:32	17:34	19:33	21:35	23:37	1:35	3:37	5:36
17	7:43	9:45	11:35	13:38	15:36	17:38	19:36	21:39	23:41	1:39	3:41	5:40
18	7:47	9:49	11:39	13:42	15:40	17:42	19:40	21:43	23:45	1:43	3:45	5:44
19	7:51	9:53	11:43	13:46	15:44	17:46	19:44	21:47	23:49	1:47	3:49	5:48
20	7:55	9:57	11:47	13:50	15:48	17:50	19:48	21:51	23:53	1:51	3:53	5:52
21	7:59	10:01	11:51	13:53	15:52	17:54	19:52	21:54	23:57	1:55	3:57	5:55
22	8:03	10:05	11:55	13:57	15:56	17:58	19:56	21:58	0:01	1:59	4:01	5:59
23	8:07	10:09	11:59	14:01	16:00	18:02	20:00	22:02	0:05	2:03	4:05	6:03
24	8:10	10:13	12:03	14:05	16:04	18:06	20:04	22:06	0:09	2:07	4:09	6:07
25	8:14	10:17	12:07	14:09	16:08	18:10	20:08	22:10	0:12	2:11	4:13	6:11
26	8:18	10:21	12:11	14:13	16:11	18:14	20:12	22:14	0:16	2:15	4:17	6:15
27	8:22	10:25	12:15	14:17	16:15	18:18	20:16	22:18	0:20	2:19	4:21	6:19
28	8:26	10:28	12:19	14:21	16:19	18:22	20:20	22:22	0:24	2:23	4:25	6:23
29	8:30		12:23	14:25	16:23	18:26	20:24	22:26	0:28	2:26	4:29	6:27
30	8:34		12:27	14:29	16:27	18:29	20:28	22:30	0:32	2:30	4:33	6:31
31	8:38		12:31		16:31		20:32	22:34		2:34		6:35

1902	Jan	Feb	Mar	Apr	May	Jun	Jul	Aug	Sep	Oct	Nov	Dec
1	6:39	8:41	10:31	12:34	14:32	16:34	18:32	20:35	22:37	0:35	2:37	4:36
2	6:43	8:45	10:35	12:38	14:36	16:38	18:36	20:39	22:41	0:39	2:41	4:40
3	6:47	8:49	10:39	12:42	14:40	16:42	18:40	20:43	22:45	0:43	2:45	4:44
4	6:51	8:53	10:43	12:45	14:44	16:46	18:44	20:46	22:49	0:47	2:49	4:47
5	6:55	8:57	10:47	12:49	14:48	16:50	18:48	20:50	22:53	0:51	2:53	4:51
6	6:59	9:01	10:51	12:53	14:52	16:54	18:52	20:54	22:57	0:55	2:57	4:55
7	7:02	9:05	10:55	12:57	14:56	16:58	18:56	20:58	23:01	0:59	3:01	4:59
8	7:06	9:09	10:59	13:01	15:00	17:02	19:00	21:02	23:04	1:03	3:05	5:03
9	7:10	9:13	11:03	13:05	15:03	17:06	19:04	21:06	23:08	1:07	3:09	5:07
10	7:14	9:17	11:07	13:09	15:07	17:10	19:08	21:10	23:12	1:11	3:13	5:11
11	7:18	9:20	11:11	13:13	15:11	17:14	19:12	21:14	23:16	1:15	3:17	5:15
12	7:22	9:24	11:15	13:17	15:15	17:18	19:16	21:18	23:20	1:19	3:21	5:19
13	7:26	9:28	11:19	13:21	15:19	17:21	19:20	21:22	23:24	1:22	3:25	5:23
14	7:30	9:32	11:23	13:25	15:23	17:25	19:24	21:26	23:28	1:26	3:29	5:27
15	7:34	9:36	11:27	13:29	15:27	17:29	19:28	21:30	23:32	1:30	3:33	5:31
16	7:38	9:40	11:31	13:33	15:31	17:33	19:32	21:34	23:36	1:34	3:37	5:35
17	7:42	9:44	11:35	13:37	15:35	17:37	19:36	21:38	23:40	1:38	3:40	5:39
18	7:46	9:48	11:38	13:41	15:39	17:41	19:39	21:42	23:44	1:42	3:44	5:43
19	7:50	9:52	11:42	13:45	15:43	17:45	19:43	21:46	23:48	1:46	3:48	5:47
20	7:54	9:56	11:46	13:49	15:47	17:49	19:47	21:50	23:52	1:50	3:52	5:51
21	7:58	10:00	11:50	13:53	15:51	17:53	19:51	21:54	23:56	1:54	3:56	5:55
22	8:02	10:04	11:54	13:56	15:55	17:57	19:55	21:57	0:00	1:58	4:00	5:58
23	8:06	10:08	11:58	14:00	15:59	18:01	19:59	22:01	0:04	2:02	4:04	6:02
24	8:10	10:12	12:02	14:04	16:03	18:05	20:03	22:05	0:08	2:06	4:08	6:06
25	8:13	10:16	12:06	14:08	16:07	18:09	20:07	22:09	0:11	2:10	4:12	6:10
26	8:17	10:20	12:10	14:12	16:11	18:13	20:11	22:13	0:15	2:14	4:16	6:14
27	8:21	10:24	12:14	14:16	16:14	18:17	20:15	22:17	0:19	2:18	4:20	6:18
28	8:25	10:27	12:18	14:20	16:18	18:21	20:19	22:21	0:23	2:22	4:24	6:22
29	8:29		12:22	14:24	16:22	18:25	20:23	22:25	0:27	2:26	4:28	6:26
30	8:33		12:26	14:28	16:26	18:28	20:27	22:29	0:31	2:29	4:32	6:30
31	8:37		12:30		16:30		20:31	22:33		2:33		6:34

1903	Jan	Feb	Mar	Apr	May	Jun	Jul	Aug	Sep	Oct	Nov	Dec
1	6:38	8:40	10:30	12:33	14:31	16:33	18:31	20:34	22:36	0:34	2:36	4:35
2	6:42	8:44	10:34	12:37	14:35	16:37	18:35	20:38	22:40	0:38	2:40	4:39
3	6:46	8:48	10:38	12:41	14:39	16:41	18:39	20:42	22:44	0:42	2:44	4:43
4	6:50	8:52	10:42	12:45	14:43	16:45	18:43	20:46	22:48	0:46	2:48	4:47
5	6:54	8:56	10:46	12:48	14:47	16:49	18:47	20:49	22:52	0:50	2:52	4:50
6	6:58	9:00	10:50	12:52	14:51	16:53	18:51	20:53	22:56	0:54	2:56	4:54
7	7:02	9:04	10:54	12:56	14:55	16:57	18:55	20:57	23:00	0:58	3:00	4:58
8	7:05	9:08	10:58	13:00	14:59	17:01	18:59	21:01	23:04	1:02	3:04	5:02
9	7:09	9:12	11:02	13:04	15:03	17:05	19:03	21:05	23:07	1:06	3:08	5:06
10	7:13	9:16	11:06	13:08	15:06	17:09	19:07	21:09	23:11	1:10	3:12	5:10
11	7:17	9:20	11:10	13:12	15:10	17:13	19:11	21:13	23:15	1:14	3:16	5:14
12	7:21	9:23	11:14	13:16	15:14	17:17	19:15	21:17	23:19	1:18	3:20	5:18
13	7:25	9:27	11:18	13:20	15:18	17:21	19:19	21:21	23:23	1:22	3:24	5:22
14	7:29	9:31	11:22	13:24	15:22	17:24	19:23	21:25	23:27	1:25	3:28	5:26
15	7:33	9:35	11:26	13:28	15:26	17:28	19:27	21:29	23:31	1:29	3:32	5:30
16	7:37	9:39	11:30	13:32	15:30	17:32	19:31	21:33	23:35	1:33	3:36	5:34
17	7:41	9:43	11:34	13:36	15:34	17:36	19:35	21:37	23:39	1:37	3:39	5:38
18	7:45	9:47	11:38	13:40	15:38	17:40	19:39	21:41	23:43	1:41	3:43	5:42
19	7:49	9:51	11:41	13:44	15:42	17:44	19:42	21:45	23:47	1:45	3:47	5:46
20	7:53	9:55	11:45	13:48	15:46	17:48	19:46	21:49	23:51	1:49	3:51	5:50
21	7:57	9:59	11:49	13:52	15:50	17:52	19:50	21:53	23:55	1:53	3:55	5:54
22	8:01	10:03	11:53	13:55	15:54	17:56	19:54	21:56	23:59	1:57	3:59	5:57
23	8:05	10:07	11:57	13:59	15:58	18:00	19:58	22:00	0:03	2:01	4:03	6:01
24	8:09	10:11	12:01	14:03	16:02	18:04	20:02	22:04	0:07	2:05	4:07	6:05
25	8:12	10:15	12:05	14:07	16:06	18:08	20:06	22:08	0:11	2:09	4:11	6:09
26	8:16	10:19	12:09	14:11	16:10	18:12	20:10	22:12	0:14	2:13	4:15	6:13
27	8:20	10:23	12:13	14:15	16:13	18:16	20:14	22:16	0:18	2:17	4:19	6:17
28	8:24	10:27	12:17	14:19	16:17	18:20	20:18	22:20	0:22	2:21	4:23	6:21
29	8:28		12:21	14:23	16:21	18:24	20:22	22:24	0:26	2:25	4:27	6:25
30	8:32		12:25	14:27	16:25	18:28	20:26	22:28	0:30	2:29	4:31	6:29
31	8:36		12:29		16:29		20:30	22:32		2:32		6:33

1904	Jan	Feb	Mar	Apr	May	Jun	Jul	Aug	Sep	Oct	Nov	Dec
1	6:37	8:39	10:33	12:36	14:34	16:36	18:34	20:37	22:39	0:37	2:39	4:38
2	6:41	8:43	10:37	12:40	14:38	16:40	18:38	20:41	22:43	0:41	2:43	4:42
3	6:45	8:47	10:41	12:44	14:42	16:44	18:42	20:45	22:47	0:45	2:47	4:46
4	6:49	8:51	10:45	12:48	14:46	16:48	18:46	20:49	22:51	0:49	2:51	4:50
5	6:53	8:55	10:49	12:51	14:50	16:52	18:50	20:52	22:55	0:53	2:55	4:53
6	6:57	8:59	10:53	12:55	14:54	16:56	18:54	20:56	22:59	0:57	2:59	4:57
7	7:01	9:03	10:57	12:59	14:58	17:00	18:58	21:00	23:03	1:01	3:03	5:01
8	7:05	9:07	11:01	13:03	15:02	17:04	19:02	21:04	23:07	1:05	3:07	5:05
9	7:08	9:11	11:05	13:07	15:06	17:08	19:06	21:08	23:10	1:09	3:11	5:09
10	7:12	9:15	11:09	13:11	15:09	17:12	19:10	21:12	23:14	1:13	3:15	5:13
11	7:16	9:19	11:13	13:15	15:13	17:16	19:14	21:16	23:18	1:17	3:19	5:17
12	7:20	9:23	11:17	13:19	15:17	17:20	19:18	21:20	23:22	1:21	3:23	5:21
13	7:24	9:26	11:21	13:23	15:21	17:24	19:22	21:24	23:26	1:24	3:27	5:25
14	7:28	9:30	11:25	13:27	15:25	17:27	19:26	21:28	23:30	1:28	3:31	5:29
15	7:32	9:34	11:29	13:31	15:29	17:31	19:30	21:32	23:34	1:32	3:35	5:33
16	7:36	9:38	11:33	13:35	15:33	17:35	19:34	21:36	23:38	1:36	3:39	5:37
17	7:40	9:42	11:37	13:39	15:37	17:39	19:38	21:40	23:42	1:40	3:42	5:41
18	7:44	9:46	11:40	13:43	15:41	17:43	19:41	21:44	23:46	1:44	3:46	5:45
19	7:48	9:50	11:44	13:47	15:45	17:47	19:45	21:48	23:50	1:48	3:50	5:49
20	7:52	9:54	11:48	13:51	15:49	17:51	19:49	21:52	23:54	1:52	3:54	5:53
21	7:56	9:58	11:52	13:55	15:53	17:55	19:53	21:56	23:58	1:56	3:58	5:57
22	8:00	10:02	11:56	13:58	15:57	17:59	19:57	21:59	0:02	2:00	4:02	6:00
23	8:04	10:06	12:00	14:02	16:01	18:03	20:01	22:03	0:06	2:04	4:06	6:04
24	8:08	10:10	12:04	14:06	16:05	18:07	20:05	22:07	0:10	2:08	4:10	6:08
25	8:12	10:14	12:08	14:10	16:09	18:11	20:09	22:11	0:14	2:12	4:14	6:12
26	8:15	10:18	12:12	14:14	16:13	18:15	20:13	22:15	0:17	2:16	4:18	6:16
27	8:19	10:22	12:16	14:18	16:16	18:19	20:17	22:19	0:21	2:20	4:22	6:20
28	8:23	10:26	12:20	14:22	16:20	18:23	20:21	22:23	0:25	2:24	4:26	6:24
29	8:27	10:30	12:24	14:26	16:24	18:27	20:25	22:27	0:29	2:28	4:30	6:28
30	8:31		12:28	14:30	16:28	18:31	20:29	22:31	0:33	2:32	4:34	6:32
31	8:35		12:32		16:32		20:33	22:35		2:35		6:36

1905	Jan	Feb	Mar	Apr	May	Jun	Jul	Aug	Sep	Oct	Nov	Dec
1	6:40	8:42	10:33	12:35	14:33	16:35	18:34	20:36	22:38	0:36	2:38	4:37
2	6:44	8:46	10:36	12:39	14:37	16:39	18:37	20:40	22:42	0:40	2:42	4:41
3	6:48	8:50	10:40	12:43	14:41	16:43	18:41	20:44	22:46	0:44	2:46	4:45
4	6:52	8:54	10:44	12:47	14:45	16:47	18:45	20:48	22:50	0:48	2:50	4:49
5	6:56	8:58	10:48	12:51	14:49	16:51	18:49	20:52	22:54	0:52	2:54	4:52
6	7:00	9:02	10:52	12:54	14:53	16:55	18:53	20:55	22:58	0:56	2:58	4:56
7	7:04	9:06	10:56	12:58	14:57	16:59	18:57	20:59	23:02	1:00	3:02	5:00
8	7:08	9:10	11:00	13:02	15:01	17:03	19:01	21:03	23:06	1:04	3:06	5:04
9	7:11	9:14	11:04	13:06	15:05	17:07	19:05	21:07	23:09	1:08	3:10	5:08
10	7:15	9:18	11:08	13:10	15:08	17:11	19:09	21:11	23:13	1:12	3:14	5:12
11	7:19	9:22	11:12	13:14	15:12	17:15	19:13	21:15	23:17	1:16	3:18	5:16
12	7:23	9:25	11:16	13:18	15:16	17:19	19:17	21:19	23:21	1:20	3:22	5:20
13	7:27	9:29	11:20	13:22	15:20	17:23	19:21	21:23	23:25	1:24	3:26	5:24
14	7:31	9:33	11:24	13:26	15:24	17:26	19:25	21:27	23:29	1:27	3:30	5:28
15	7:35	9:37	11:28	13:30	15:28	17:30	19:29	21:31	23:33	1:31	3:34	5:32
16	7:39	9:41	11:32	13:34	15:32	17:34	19:33	21:35	23:37	1:35	3:38	5:36
17	7:43	9:45	11:36	13:38	15:36	17:38	19:37	21:39	23:41	1:39	3:42	5:40
18	7:47	9:49	11:40	13:42	15:40	17:42	19:41	21:43	23:45	1:43	3:45	5:44
19	7:51	9:53	11:43	13:46	15:44	17:46	19:44	21:47	23:49	1:47	3:49	5:48
20	7:55	9:57	11:47	13:50	15:48	17:50	19:48	21:51	23:53	1:51	3:53	5:52
21	7:59	10:01	11:51	13:54	15:52	17:54	19:52	21:55	23:57	1:55	3:57	5:56
22	8:03	10:05	11:55	13:58	15:56	17:58	19:56	21:59	0:01	1:59	4:01	6:00
23	8:07	10:09	11:59	14:01	16:00	18:02	20:00	22:02	0:05	2:03	4:05	6:03
24	8:11	10:13	12:03	14:05	16:04	18:06	20:04	22:06	0:09	2:07	4:09	6:07
25	8:15	10:17	12:07	14:09	16:08	18:10	20:08	22:10	0:13	2:11	4:13	6:11
26	8:18	10:21	12:11	14:13	16:12	18:14	20:12	22:14	0:17	2:15	4:17	6:15
27	8:22	10:25	12:15	14:17	16:16	18:18	20:16	22:18	0:20	2:19	4:21	6:19
28	8:26	10:29	12:19	14:21	16:19	18:22	20:20	22:22	0:24	2:23	4:25	6:23
29	8:30		12:23	14:25	16:23	18:26	20:24	22:26	0:28	2:27	4:29	6:27
30	8:34		12:27	14:29	16:27	18:30	20:28	22:30	0:32	2:31	4:33	6:31
31	8:38		12:31		16:31		20:32	22:34		2:35		6:35

1906	Jan	Feb	Mar	Apr	May	Jun	Jul	Aug	Sep	Oct	Nov	Dec
1	6:39	8:41	10:32	12:34	14:32	16:34	18:33	20:35	22:37	0:35	2:37	4:36
2	6:43	8:45	10:36	12:38	14:36	16:38	18:36	20:39	22:41	0:39	2:41	4:40
3	6:47	8:49	10:39	12:42	14:40	16:42	18:40	20:43	22:45	0:43	2:45	4:44
4	6:51	8:53	10:43	12:46	14:44	16:46	18:44	20:47	22:49	0:47	2:49	4:48
5	6:55	8:57	10:47	12:50	14:48	16:50	18:48	20:51	22:53	0:51	2:53	4:52
6	6:59	9:01	10:51	12:53	14:52	16:54	18:52	20:54	22:57	0:55	2:57	4:55
7	7:03	9:05	10:55	12:57	14:56	16:58	18:56	20:58	23:01	0:59	3:01	4:59
8	7:07	9:09	10:59	13:01	15:00	17:02	19:00	21:02	23:05	1:03	3:05	5:03
9	7:10	9:13	11:03	13:05	15:04	17:06	19:04	21:06	23:09	1:07	3:09	5:07
10	7:14	9:17	11:07	13:09	15:08	17:10	19:08	21:10	23:12	1:11	3:13	5:11
11	7:18	9:21	11:11	13:13	15:11	17:14	19:12	21:14	23:16	1:15	3:17	5:15
12	7:22	9:25	11:15	13:17	15:15	17:18	19:16	21:18	23:20	1:19	3:21	5:19
13	7:26	9:28	11:19	13:21	15:19	17:22	19:20	21:22	23:24	1:23	3:25	5:23
14	7:30	9:32	11:23	13:25	15:23	17:26	19:24	21:26	23:28	1:27	3:29	5:27
15	7:34	9:36	11:27	13:29	15:27	17:29	19:28	21:30	23:32	1:30	3:33	5:31
16	7:38	9:40	11:31	13:33	15:31	17:33	19:32	21:34	23:36	1:34	3:37	5:35
17	7:42	9:44	11:35	13:37	15:35	17:37	19:36	21:38	23:40	1:38	3:41	5:39
18	7:46	9:48	11:39	13:41	15:39	17:41	19:40	21:42	23:44	1:42	3:45	5:43
19	7:50	9:52	11:43	13:45	15:43	17:45	19:44	21:46	23:48	1:46	3:48	5:47
20	7:54	9:56	11:46	13:49	15:47	17:49	19:47	21:50	23:52	1:50	3:52	5:51
21	7:58	10:00	11:50	13:53	15:51	17:53	19:51	21:54	23:56	1:54	3:56	5:55
22	8:02	10:04	11:54	13:57	15:55	17:57	19:55	21:58	0:00	1:58	4:00	5:59
23	8:06	10:08	11:58	14:01	15:59	18:01	19:59	22:02	0:04	2:02	4:04	6:03
24	8:10	10:12	12:02	14:04	16:03	18:05	20:03	22:05	0:08	2:06	4:08	6:06
25	8:14	10:16	12:06	14:08	16:07	18:09	20:07	22:09	0:12	2:10	4:12	6:10
26	8:18	10:20	12:10	14:12	16:11	18:13	20:11	22:13	0:16	2:14	4:16	6:14
27	8:21	10:24	12:14	14:16	16:15	18:17	20:15	22:17	0:20	2:18	4:20	6:18
28	8:25	10:28	12:18	14:20	16:19	18:21	20:19	22:21	0:23	2:22	4:24	6:22
29	8:29		12:22	14:24	16:22	18:25	20:23	22:25	0:27	2:26	4:28	6:26
30	8:33		12:26	14:28	16:26	18:29	20:27	22:29	0:31	2:30	4:32	6:30
31	8:37		12:30		16:30		20:31	22:33		2:34		6:34

1907	Jan	Feb	Mar	Apr	May	Jun	Jul	Aug	Sep	Oct	Nov	Dec
1	6:38	8:40	10:31	12:33	14:31	16:33	18:32	20:34	22:36	0:34	2:37	4:35
2	6:42	8:44	10:35	12:37	14:35	16:37	18:36	20:38	22:40	0:38	2:40	4:39
3	6:46	8:48	10:38	12:41	14:39	16:41	18:39	20:42	22:44	0:42	2:44	4:43
4	6:50	8:52	10:42	12:45	14:43	16:45	18:43	20:46	22:48	0:46	2:48	4:47
5	6:54	8:56	10:46	12:49	14:47	16:49	18:47	20:50	22:52	0:50	2:52	4:51
6	6:58	9:00	10:50	12:53	14:51	16:53	18:51	20:54	22:56	0:54	2:56	4:55
7	7:02	9:04	10:54	12:56	14:55	16:57	18:55	20:57	23:00	0:58	3:00	4:58
8	7:06	9:08	10:58	13:00	14:59	17:01	18:59	21:01	23:04	1:02	3:04	5:02
9	7:10	9:12	11:02	13:04	15:03	17:05	19:03	21:05	23:08	1:06	3:08	5:06
10	7:13	9:16	11:06	13:08	15:07	17:09	19:07	21:09	23:12	1:10	3:12	5:10
11	7:17	9:20	11:10	13:12	15:11	17:13	19:11	21:13	23:15	1:14	3:16	5:14
12	7:21	9:24	11:14	13:16	15:14	17:17	19:15	21:17	23:19	1:18	3:20	5:18
13	7:25	9:28	11:18	13:20	15:18	17:21	19:19	21:21	23:23	1:22	3:24	5:22
14	7:29	9:31	11:22	13:24	15:22	17:25	19:23	21:25	23:27	1:26	3:28	5:26
15	7:33	9:35	11:26	13:28	15:26	17:29	19:27	21:29	23:31	1:30	3:32	5:30
16	7:37	9:39	11:30	13:32	15:30	17:32	19:31	21:33	23:35	1:33	3:36	5:34
17	7:41	9:43	11:34	13:36	15:34	17:36	19:35	21:37	23:39	1:37	3:40	5:38
18	7:45	9:47	11:38	13:40	15:38	17:40	19:39	21:41	23:43	1:41	3:44	5:42
19	7:49	9:51	11:42	13:44	15:42	17:44	19:43	21:45	23:47	1:45	3:48	5:46
20	7:53	9:55	11:46	13:48	15:46	17:48	19:47	21:49	23:51	1:49	3:51	5:50
21	7:57	9:59	11:49	13:52	15:50	17:52	19:50	21:53	23:55	1:53	3:55	5:54
22	8:01	10:03	11:53	13:56	15:54	17:56	19:54	21:57	23:59	1:57	3:59	5:58
23	8:05	10:07	11:57	14:00	15:58	18:00	19:58	22:01	0:03	2:01	4:03	6:02
24	8:09	10:11	12:01	14:04	16:02	18:04	20:02	22:05	0:07	2:05	4:07	6:05
25	8:13	10:15	12:05	14:07	16:06	18:08	20:06	22:08	0:11	2:09	4:11	6:09
26	8:17	10:19	12:09	14:11	16:10	18:12	20:10	22:12	0:15	2:13	4:15	6:13
27	8:21	10:23	12:13	14:15	16:14	18:16	20:14	22:16	0:19	2:17	4:19	6:17
28	8:24	10:27	12:17	14:19	16:18	18:20	20:18	22:20	0:22	2:21	4:23	6:21
29	8:28		12:21	14:23	16:21	18:24	20:22	22:24	0:26	2:25	4:27	6:25
30	8:32		12:25	14:27	16:25	18:28	20:26	22:28	0:30	2:29	4:31	6:29
31	8:36		12:29		16:29		20:30	22:32		2:33		6:33

1908	Jan	Feb	Mar	Apr	May	Jun	Jul	Aug	Sep	Oct	Nov	Dec
1	6:37	8:39	10:34	12:36	14:34	16:36	18:35	20:37	22:39	0:37	2:40	4:38
2	6:41	8:43	10:38	12:40	14:38	16:40	18:39	20:41	22:43	0:41	2:43	4:42
3	6:45	8:47	10:41	12:44	14:42	16:44	18:42	20:45	22:47	0:45	2:47	4:46
4	6:49	8:51	10:45	12:48	14:46	16:48	18:46	20:49	22:51	0:49	2:51	4:50
5	6:53	8:55	10:49	12:52	14:50	16:52	18:50	20:53	22:55	0:53	2:55	4:54
6	6:57	8:59	10:53	12:56	14:54	16:56	18:54	20:57	22:59	0:57	2:59	4:58
7	7:01	9:03	10:57	12:59	14:58	17:00	18:58	21:00	23:03	1:01	3:03	5:01
8	7:05	9:07	11:01	13:03	15:02	17:04	19:02	21:04	23:07	1:05	3:07	5:05
9	7:09	9:11	11:05	13:07	15:06	17:08	19:06	21:08	23:11	1:09	3:11	5:09
10	7:13	9:15	11:09	13:11	15:10	17:12	19:10	21:12	23:15	1:13	3:15	5:13
11	7:16	9:19	11:13	13:15	15:14	17:16	19:14	21:16	23:18	1:17	3:19	5:17
12	7:20	9:23	11:17	13:19	15:17	17:20	19:18	21:20	23:22	1:21	3:23	5:21
13	7:24	9:27	11:21	13:23	15:21	17:24	19:22	21:24	23:26	1:25	3:27	5:25
14	7:28	9:31	11:25	13:27	15:25	17:28	19:26	21:28	23:30	1:29	3:31	5:29
15	7:32	9:34	11:29	13:31	15:29	17:32	19:30	21:32	23:34	1:33	3:35	5:33
16	7:36	9:38	11:33	13:35	15:33	17:35	19:34	21:36	23:38	1:36	3:39	5:37
17	7:40	9:42	11:37	13:39	15:37	17:39	19:38	21:40	23:42	1:40	3:43	5:41
18	7:44	9:46	11:41	13:43	15:41	17:43	19:42	21:44	23:46	1:44	3:47	5:45
19	7:48	9:50	11:45	13:47	15:45	17:47	19:46	21:48	23:50	1:48	3:50	5:49
20	7:52	9:54	11:49	13:51	15:49	17:51	19:49	21:52	23:54	1:52	3:54	5:53
21	7:56	9:58	11:52	13:55	15:53	17:55	19:53	21:56	23:58	1:56	3:58	5:57
22	8:00	10:02	11:56	13:59	15:57	17:59	19:57	22:00	0:02	2:00	4:02	6:01
23	8:04	10:06	12:00	14:03	16:01	18:03	20:01	22:04	0:06	2:04	4:06	6:05
24	8:08	10:10	12:04	14:06	16:05	18:07	20:05	22:07	0:10	2:08	4:10	6:08
25	8:12	10:14	12:08	14:10	16:09	18:11	20:09	22:11	0:14	2:12	4:14	6:12
26	8:16	10:18	12:12	14:14	16:13	18:15	20:13	22:15	0:18	2:16	4:18	6:16
27	8:20	10:22	12:16	14:18	16:17	18:19	20:17	22:19	0:22	2:20	4:22	6:20
28	8:23	10:26	12:20	14:22	16:21	18:23	20:21	22:23	0:25	2:24	4:26	6:24
29	8:27	10:30	12:24	14:26	16:24	18:27	20:25	22:27	0:29	2:28	4:30	6:28
30	8:31		12:28	14:30	16:28	18:31	20:29	22:31	0:33	2:32	4:34	6:32
31	8:35		12:32		16:32		20:33	22:35		2:36		6:36

1909	Jan	Feb	Mar	Apr	May	Jun	Jul	Aug	Sep	Oct	Nov	Dec
1	6:40	8:42	10:33	12:35	14:33	16:35	18:34	20:36	22:38	0:36	2:39	4:37
2	6:44	8:46	10:37	12:39	14:37	16:39	18:38	20:40	22:42	0:40	2:43	4:41
3	6:48	8:50	10:41	12:43	14:41	16:43	18:42	20:44	22:46	0:44	2:46	4:45
4	6:52	8:54	10:44	12:47	14:45	16:47	18:45	20:48	22:50	0:48	2:50	4:49
5	6:56	8:58	10:48	12:51	14:49	16:51	18:49	20:52	22:54	0:52	2:54	4:53
6	7:00	9:02	10:52	12:55	14:53	16:55	18:53	20:56	22:58	0:56	2:58	4:57
7	7:04	9:06	10:56	12:59	14:57	16:59	18:57	21:00	23:02	1:00	3:02	5:01
8	7:08	9:10	11:00	13:02	15:01	17:03	19:01	21:03	23:06	1:04	3:06	5:04
9	7:12	9:14	11:04	13:06	15:05	17:07	19:05	21:07	23:10	1:08	3:10	5:08
10	7:16	9:18	11:08	13:10	15:09	17:11	19:09	21:11	23:14	1:12	3:14	5:12
11	7:19	9:22	11:12	13:14	15:13	17:15	19:13	21:15	23:18	1:16	3:18	5:16
12	7:23	9:26	11:16	13:18	15:17	17:19	19:17	21:19	23:21	1:20	3:22	5:20
13	7:27	9:30	11:20	13:22	15:20	17:23	19:21	21:23	23:25	1:24	3:26	5:24
14	7:31	9:34	11:24	13:26	15:24	17:27	19:25	21:27	23:29	1:28	3:30	5:28
15	7:35	9:37	11:28	13:30	15:28	17:31	19:29	21:31	23:33	1:32	3:34	5:32
16	7:39	9:41	11:32	13:34	15:32	17:34	19:33	21:35	23:37	1:35	3:38	5:36
17	7:43	9:45	11:36	13:38	15:36	17:38	19:37	21:39	23:41	1:39	3:42	5:40
18	7:47	9:49	11:40	13:42	15:40	17:42	19:41	21:43	23:45	1:43	3:46	5:44
19	7:51	9:53	11:44	13:46	15:44	17:46	19:45	21:47	23:49	1:47	3:50	5:48
20	7:55	9:57	11:48	13:50	15:48	17:50	19:49	21:51	23:53	1:51	3:53	5:52
21	7:59	10:01	11:51	13:54	15:52	17:54	19:52	21:55	23:57	1:55	3:57	5:56
22	8:03	10:05	11:55	13:58	15:56	17:58	19:56	21:59	0:01	1:59	4:01	6:00
23	8:07	10:09	11:59	14:02	16:00	18:02	20:00	22:03	0:05	2:03	4:05	6:04
24	8:11	10:13	12:03	14:06	16:04	18:06	20:04	22:07	0:09	2:07	4:09	6:08
25	8:15	10:17	12:07	14:09	16:08	18:10	20:08	22:10	0:13	2:11	4:13	6:11
26	8:19	10:21	12:11	14:13	16:12	18:14	20:12	22:14	0:17	2:15	4:17	6:15
27	8:23	10:25	12:15	14:17	16:16	18:18	20:16	22:18	0:21	2:19	4:21	6:19
28	8:26	10:29	12:19	14:21	16:20	18:22	20:20	22:22	0:25	2:23	4:25	6:23
29	8:30		12:23	14:25	16:24	18:26	20:24	22:26	0:28	2:27	4:29	6:27
30	8:34		12:27	14:29	16:27	18:30	20:28	22:30	0:32	2:31	4:33	6:31
31	8:38		12:31		16:31		20:32	22:34		2:35		6:35

1910	Jan	Feb	Mar	Apr	May	Jun	Jul	Aug	Sep	Oct	Nov	Dec
1	6:39	8:41	10:32	12:34	14:32	16:34	18:33	20:35	22:37	0:35	2:38	4:36
2	6:43	8:45	10:36	12:38	14:36	16:38	18:37	20:39	22:41	0:39	2:42	4:40
3	6:47	8:49	10:40	12:42	14:40	16:42	18:41	20:43	22:45	0:43	2:46	4:44
4	6:51	8:53	10:44	12:46	14:44	16:46	18:45	20:47	22:49	0:47	2:49	4:48
5	6:55	8:57	10:47	12:50	14:48	16:50	18:48	20:51	22:53	0:51	2:53	4:52
6	6:59	9:01	10:51	12:54	14:52	16:54	18:52	20:55	22:57	0:55	2:57	4:56
7	7:03	9:05	10:55	12:58	14:56	16:58	18:56	20:59	23:01	0:59	3:01	5:00
8	7:07	9:09	10:59	13:02	15:00	17:02	19:00	21:02	23:05	1:03	3:05	5:03
9	7:11	9:13	11:03	13:05	15:04	17:06	19:04	21:06	23:09	1:07	3:09	5:07
10	7:15	9:17	11:07	13:09	15:08	17:10	19:08	21:10	23:13	1:11	3:13	5:11
11	7:18	9:21	11:11	13:13	15:12	17:14	19:12	21:14	23:17	1:15	3:17	5:15
12	7:22	9:25	11:15	13:17	15:16	17:18	19:16	21:18	23:20	1:19	3:21	5:19
13	7:26	9:29	11:19	13:21	15:19	17:22	19:20	21:22	23:24	1:23	3:25	5:23
14	7:30	9:33	11:23	13:25	15:23	17:26	19:24	21:26	23:28	1:27	3:29	5:27
15	7:34	9:36	11:27	13:29	15:27	17:30	19:28	21:30	23:32	1:31	3:33	5:31
16	7:38	9:40	11:31	13:33	15:31	17:34	19:32	21:34	23:36	1:35	3:37	5:35
17	7:42	9:44	11:35	13:37	15:35	17:37	19:36	21:38	23:40	1:38	3:41	5:39
18	7:46	9:48	11:39	13:41	15:39	17:41	19:40	21:42	23:44	1:42	3:45	5:43
19	7:50	9:52	11:43	13:45	15:43	17:45	19:44	21:46	23:48	1:46	3:49	5:47
20	7:54	9:56	11:47	13:49	15:47	17:49	19:48	21:50	23:52	1:50	3:53	5:51
21	7:58	10:00	11:51	13:53	15:51	17:53	19:52	21:54	23:56	1:54	3:56	5:55
22	8:02	10:04	11:54	13:57	15:55	17:57	19:55	21:58	0:00	1:58	4:00	5:59
23	8:06	10:08	11:58	14:01	15:59	18:01	19:59	22:02	0:04	2:02	4:04	6:03
24	8:10	10:12	12:02	14:05	16:03	18:05	20:03	22:06	0:08	2:06	4:08	6:07
25	8:14	10:16	12:06	14:09	16:07	18:09	20:07	22:10	0:12	2:10	4:12	6:11
26	8:18	10:20	12:10	14:12	16:11	18:13	20:11	22:13	0:16	2:14	4:16	6:14
27	8:22	10:24	12:14	14:16	16:15	18:17	20:15	22:17	0:20	2:18	4:20	6:18
28	8:26	10:28	12:18	14:20	16:19	18:21	20:19	22:21	0:24	2:22	4:24	6:22
29	8:29		12:22	14:24	16:23	18:25	20:23	22:25	0:28	2:26	4:28	6:26
30	8:33		12:26	14:28	16:27	18:29	20:27	22:29	0:31	2:30	4:32	6:30
31	8:37		12:30		16:30		20:31	22:33		2:34		6:34

1911	Jan	Feb	Mar	Apr	May	Jun	Jul	Aug	Sep	Oct	Nov	Dec
1	6:38	8:40	10:31	12:33	14:31	16:33	18:32	20:34	22:36	0:34	2:37	4:35
2	6:42	8:44	10:35	12:37	14:35	16:37	18:36	20:38	22:40	0:38	2:41	4:39
3	6:46	8:48	10:39	12:41	14:39	16:41	18:40	20:42	22:44	0:42	2:45	4:43
4	6:50	8:52	10:43	12:45	14:43	16:45	18:44	20:46	22:48	0:46	2:48	4:47
5	6:54	8:56	10:46	12:49	14:47	16:49	18:47	20:50	22:52	0:50	2:52	4:51
6	6:58	9:00	10:50	12:53	14:51	16:53	18:51	20:54	22:56	0:54	2:56	4:55
7	7:02	9:04	10:54	12:57	14:55	16:57	18:55	20:58	23:00	0:58	3:00	4:59
8	7:06	9:08	10:58	13:01	14:59	17:01	18:59	21:02	23:04	1:02	3:04	5:03
9	7:10	9:12	11:02	13:04	15:03	17:05	19:03	21:05	23:08	1:06	3:08	5:06
10	7:14	9:16	11:06	13:08	15:07	17:09	19:07	21:09	23:12	1:10	3:12	5:10
11	7:18	9:20	11:10	13:12	15:11	17:13	19:11	21:13	23:16	1:14	3:16	5:14
12	7:21	9:24	11:14	13:16	15:15	17:17	19:15	21:17	23:20	1:18	3:20	5:18
13	7:25	9:28	11:18	13:20	15:19	17:21	19:19	21:21	23:23	1:22	3:24	5:22
14	7:29	9:32	11:22	13:24	15:22	17:25	19:23	21:25	23:27	1:26	3:28	5:26
15	7:33	9:36	11:26	13:28	15:26	17:29	19:27	21:29	23:31	1:30	3:32	5:30
16	7:37	9:39	11:30	13:32	15:30	17:33	19:31	21:33	23:35	1:34	3:36	5:34
17	7:41	9:43	11:34	13:36	15:34	17:37	19:35	21:37	23:39	1:38	3:40	5:38
18	7:45	9:47	11:38	13:40	15:38	17:40	19:39	21:41	23:43	1:41	3:44	5:42
19	7:49	9:51	11:42	13:44	15:42	17:44	19:43	21:45	23:47	1:45	3:48	5:46
20	7:53	9:55	11:46	13:48	15:46	17:48	19:47	21:49	23:51	1:49	3:52	5:50
21	7:57	9:59	11:50	13:52	15:50	17:52	19:51	21:53	23:55	1:53	3:56	5:54
22	8:01	10:03	11:54	13:56	15:54	17:56	19:55	21:57	23:59	1:57	3:59	5:58
23	8:05	10:07	11:57	14:00	15:58	18:00	19:58	22:01	0:03	2:01	4:03	6:02
24	8:09	10:11	12:01	14:04	16:02	18:04	20:02	22:05	0:07	2:05	4:07	6:06
25	8:13	10:15	12:05	14:08	16:06	18:08	20:06	22:09	0:11	2:09	4:11	6:10
26	8:17	10:19	12:09	14:12	16:10	18:12	20:10	22:13	0:15	2:13	4:15	6:14
27	8:21	10:23	12:13	14:15	16:14	18:16	20:14	22:16	0:19	2:17	4:19	6:17
28	8:25	10:27	12:17	14:19	16:18	18:20	20:18	22:20	0:23	2:21	4:23	6:21
29	8:29		12:21	14:23	16:22	18:24	20:22	22:24	0:27	2:25	4:27	6:25
30	8:32		12:25	14:27	16:26	18:28	20:26	22:28	0:31	2:29	4:31	6:29
31	8:36		12:29		16:30		20:30	22:32		2:33		6:33

1912	Jan	Feb	Mar	Apr	May	Jun	Jul	Aug	Sep	Oct	Nov	Dec
1	6:37	8:39	10:34	12:36	14:34	16:36	18:35	20:37	22:39	0:37	2:40	4:38
2	6:41	8:43	10:38	12:40	14:38	16:40	18:39	20:41	22:43	0:41	2:44	4:42
3	6:45	8:47	10:42	12:44	14:42	16:44	18:43	20:45	22:47	0:45	2:48	4:46
4	6:49	8:51	10:46	12:48	14:46	16:48	18:47	20:49	22:51	0:49	2:51	4:50
5	6:53	8:55	10:49	12:52	14:50	16:52	18:50	20:53	22:55	0:53	2:55	4:54
6	6:57	8:59	10:53	12:56	14:54	16:56	18:54	20:57	22:59	0:57	2:59	4:58
7	7:01	9:03	10:57	13:00	14:58	17:00	18:58	21:01	23:03	1:01	3:03	5:02
8	7:05	9:07	11:01	13:04	15:02	17:04	19:02	21:05	23:07	1:05	3:07	5:06
9	7:09	9:11	11:05	13:07	15:06	17:08	19:06	21:08	23:11	1:09	3:11	5:09
10	7:13	9:15	11:09	13:11	15:10	17:12	19:10	21:12	23:15	1:13	3:15	5:13
11	7:17	9:19	11:13	13:15	15:14	17:16	19:14	21:16	23:19	1:17	3:19	5:17
12	7:21	9:23	11:17	13:19	15:18	17:20	19:18	21:20	23:23	1:21	3:23	5:21
13	7:24	9:27	11:21	13:23	15:22	17:24	19:22	21:24	23:26	1:25	3:27	5:25
14	7:28	9:31	11:25	13:27	15:25	17:28	19:26	21:28	23:30	1:29	3:31	5:29
15	7:32	9:35	11:29	13:31	15:29	17:32	19:30	21:32	23:34	1:33	3:35	5:33
16	7:36	9:39	11:33	13:35	15:33	17:36	19:34	21:36	23:38	1:37	3:39	5:37
17	7:40	9:42	11:37	13:39	15:37	17:40	19:38	21:40	23:42	1:41	3:43	5:41
18	7:44	9:46	11:41	13:43	15:41	17:43	19:42	21:44	23:46	1:44	3:47	5:45
19	7:48	9:50	11:45	13:47	15:45	17:47	19:46	21:48	23:50	1:48	3:51	5:49
20	7:52	9:54	11:49	13:51	15:49	17:51	19:50	21:52	23:54	1:52	3:55	5:53
21	7:56	9:58	11:53	13:55	15:53	17:55	19:54	21:56	23:58	1:56	3:59	5:57
22	8:00	10:02	11:57	13:59	15:57	17:59	19:58	22:00	0:02	2:00	4:02	6:01
23	8:04	10:06	12:00	14:03	16:01	18:03	20:01	22:04	0:06	2:04	4:06	6:05
24	8:08	10:10	12:04	14:07	16:05	18:07	20:05	22:08	0:10	2:08	4:10	6:09
25	8:12	10:14	12:08	14:11	16:09	18:11	20:09	22:12	0:14	2:12	4:14	6:13
26	8:16	10:18	12:12	14:15	16:13	18:15	20:13	22:15	0:18	2:16	4:18	6:16
27	8:20	10:22	12:16	14:18	16:17	18:19	20:17	22:19	0:22	2:20	4:22	6:20
28	8:24	10:26	12:20	14:22	16:21	18:23	20:21	22:23	0:26	2:24	4:26	6:24
29	8:28	10:30	12:24	14:26	16:25	18:27	20:25	22:27	0:30	2:28	4:30	6:28
30	8:31		12:28	14:30	16:29	18:31	20:29	22:31	0:33	2:32	4:34	6:32
31	8:35		12:32		16:32		20:33	22:35		2:36		6:36

1913	Jan	Feb	Mar	Apr	May	Jun	Jul	Aug	Sep	Oct	Nov	Dec
1	6:40	8:42	10:33	12:35	14:33	16:35	18:34	20:36	22:38	0:36	2:39	4:37
2	6:44	8:46	10:37	12:39	14:37	16:39	18:38	20:40	22:42	0:40	2:43	4:41
3	6:48	8:50	10:41	12:43	14:41	16:43	18:42	20:44	22:46	0:44	2:47	4:45
4	6:52	8:54	10:45	12:47	14:45	16:47	18:46	20:48	22:50	0:48	2:51	4:49
5	6:56	8:58	10:49	12:51	14:49	16:51	18:50	20:52	22:54	0:52	2:54	4:53
6	7:00	9:02	10:52	12:55	14:53	16:55	18:53	20:56	22:58	0:56	2:58	4:57
7	7:04	9:06	10:56	12:59	14:57	16:59	18:57	21:00	23:02	1:00	3:02	5:01
8	7:08	9:10	11:00	13:03	15:01	17:03	19:01	21:04	23:06	1:04	3:06	5:05
9	7:12	9:14	11:04	13:07	15:05	17:07	19:05	21:08	23:10	1:08	3:10	5:09
10	7:16	9:18	11:08	13:10	15:09	17:11	19:09	21:11	23:14	1:12	3:14	5:12
11	7:20	9:22	11:12	13:14	15:13	17:15	19:13	21:15	23:18	1:16	3:18	5:16
12	7:24	9:26	11:16	13:18	15:17	17:19	19:17	21:19	23:22	1:20	3:22	5:20
13	7:27	9:30	11:20	13:22	15:21	17:23	19:21	21:23	23:26	1:24	3:26	5:24
14	7:31	9:34	11:24	13:26	15:25	17:27	19:25	21:27	23:29	1:28	3:30	5:28
15	7:35	9:38	11:28	13:30	15:28	17:31	19:29	21:31	23:33	1:32	3:34	5:32
16	7:39	9:42	11:32	13:34	15:32	17:35	19:33	21:35	23:37	1:36	3:38	5:36
17	7:43	9:45	11:36	13:38	15:36	17:39	19:37	21:39	23:41	1:40	3:42	5:40
18	7:47	9:49	11:40	13:42	15:40	17:43	19:41	21:43	23:45	1:44	3:46	5:44
19	7:51	9:53	11:44	13:46	15:44	17:46	19:45	21:47	23:49	1:47	3:50	5:48
20	7:55	9:57	11:48	13:50	15:48	17:50	19:49	21:51	23:53	1:51	3:54	5:52
21	7:59	10:01	11:52	13:54	15:52	17:54	19:53	21:55	23:57	1:55	3:58	5:56
22	8:03	10:05	11:56	13:58	15:56	17:58	19:57	21:59	0:01	1:59	4:01	6:00
23	8:07	10:09	11:59	14:02	16:00	18:02	20:00	22:03	0:05	2:03	4:05	6:04
24	8:11	10:13	12:03	14:06	16:04	18:06	20:04	22:07	0:09	2:07	4:09	6:08
25	8:15	10:17	12:07	14:10	16:08	18:10	20:08	22:11	0:13	2:11	4:13	6:12
26	8:19	10:21	12:11	14:14	16:12	18:14	20:12	22:15	0:17	2:15	4:17	6:16
27	8:23	10:25	12:15	14:17	16:16	18:18	20:16	22:18	0:21	2:19	4:21	6:19
28	8:27	10:29	12:19	14:21	16:20	18:22	20:20	22:22	0:25	2:23	4:25	6:23
29	8:31		12:23	14:25	16:24	18:26	20:24	22:26	0:29	2:27	4:29	6:27
30	8:34		12:27	14:29	16:28	18:30	20:28	22:30	0:33	2:31	4:33	6:31
31	8:38		12:31		16:32		20:32	22:34		2:35		6:35

1914	Jan	Feb	Mar	Apr	May	Jun	Jul	Aug	Sep	Oct	Nov	Dec
1	6:39	8:41	10:32	12:34	14:32	16:35	18:33	20:35	22:37	0:36	2:38	4:36
2	6:43	8:45	10:36	12:38	14:36	16:38	18:37	20:39	22:41	0:39	2:42	4:40
3	6:47	8:49	10:40	12:42	14:40	16:42	18:41	20:43	22:45	0:43	2:46	4:44
4	6:51	8:53	10:44	12:46	14:44	16:46	18:45	20:47	22:49	0:47	2:50	4:48
5	6:55	8:57	10:48	12:50	14:48	16:50	18:49	20:51	22:53	0:51	2:54	4:52
6	6:59	9:01	10:52	12:54	14:52	16:54	18:53	20:55	22:57	0:55	2:57	4:56
7	7:03	9:05	10:55	12:58	14:56	16:58	18:56	20:59	23:01	0:59	3:01	5:00
8	7:07	9:09	10:59	13:02	15:00	17:02	19:00	21:03	23:05	1:03	3:05	5:04
9	7:11	9:13	11:03	13:06	15:04	17:06	19:04	21:07	23:09	1:07	3:09	5:08
10	7:15	9:17	11:07	13:10	15:08	17:10	19:08	21:11	23:13	1:11	3:13	5:12
11	7:19	9:21	11:11	13:13	15:12	17:14	19:12	21:14	23:17	1:15	3:17	5:15
12	7:23	9:25	11:15	13:17	15:16	17:18	19:16	21:18	23:21	1:19	3:21	5:19
13	7:27	9:29	11:19	13:21	15:20	17:22	19:20	21:22	23:25	1:23	3:25	5:23
14	7:30	9:33	11:23	13:25	15:24	17:26	19:24	21:26	23:28	1:27	3:29	5:27
15	7:34	9:37	11:27	13:29	15:28	17:30	19:28	21:30	23:32	1:31	3:33	5:31
16	7:38	9:41	11:31	13:33	15:31	17:34	19:32	21:34	23:36	1:35	3:37	5:35
17	7:42	9:44	11:35	13:37	15:35	17:38	19:36	21:38	23:40	1:39	3:41	5:39
18	7:46	9:48	11:39	13:41	15:39	17:42	19:40	21:42	23:44	1:43	3:45	5:43
19	7:50	9:52	11:43	13:45	15:43	17:45	19:44	21:46	23:48	1:46	3:49	5:47
20	7:54	9:56	11:47	13:49	15:47	17:49	19:48	21:50	23:52	1:50	3:53	5:51
21	7:58	10:00	11:51	13:53	15:51	17:53	19:52	21:54	23:56	1:54	3:57	5:55
22	8:02	10:04	11:55	13:57	15:55	17:57	19:56	21:58	0:00	1:58	4:01	5:59
23	8:06	10:08	11:59	14:01	15:59	18:01	20:00	22:02	0:04	2:02	4:04	6:03
24	8:10	10:12	12:02	14:05	16:03	18:05	20:03	22:06	0:08	2:06	4:08	6:07
25	8:14	10:16	12:06	14:09	16:07	18:09	20:07	22:10	0:12	2:10	4:12	6:11
26	8:18	10:20	12:10	14:13	16:11	18:13	20:11	22:14	0:16	2:14	4:16	6:15
27	8:22	10:24	12:14	14:17	16:15	18:17	20:15	22:18	0:20	2:18	4:20	6:19
28	8:26	10:28	12:18	14:20	16:19	18:21	20:19	22:21	0:24	2:22	4:24	6:22
29	8:30		12:22	14:24	16:23	18:25	20:23	22:25	0:28	2:26	4:28	6:26
30	8:34		12:26	14:28	16:27	18:29	20:27	22:29	0:32	2:30	4:32	6:30
31	8:37		12:30		16:31		20:31	22:33		2:34		6:34

1915	Jan	Feb	Mar	Apr	May	Jun	Jul	Aug	Sep	Oct	Nov	Dec
1	6:38	8:40	10:31	12:33	14:31	16:34	18:32	20:34	22:36	0:35	2:37	4:35
2	6:42	8:44	10:35	12:37	14:35	16:38	18:36	20:38	22:40	0:39	2:41	4:39
3	6:46	8:48	10:39	12:41	14:39	16:41	18:40	20:42	22:44	0:42	2:45	4:43
4	6:50	8:52	10:43	12:45	14:43	16:45	18:44	20:46	22:48	0:46	2:49	4:47
5	6:54	8:56	10:47	12:49	14:47	16:49	18:48	20:50	22:52	0:50	2:53	4:51
6	6:58	9:00	10:51	12:53	14:51	16:53	18:52	20:54	22:56	0:54	2:56	4:55
7	7:02	9:04	10:55	12:57	14:55	16:57	18:56	20:58	23:00	0:58	3:00	4:59
8	7:06	9:08	10:58	13:01	14:59	17:01	18:59	21:02	23:04	1:02	3:04	5:03
9	7:10	9:12	11:02	13:05	15:03	17:05	19:03	21:06	23:08	1:06	3:08	5:07
10	7:14	9:16	11:06	13:09	15:07	17:09	19:07	21:10	23:12	1:10	3:12	5:11
11	7:18	9:20	11:10	13:12	15:11	17:13	19:11	21:13	23:16	1:14	3:16	5:14
12	7:22	9:24	11:14	13:16	15:15	17:17	19:15	21:17	23:20	1:18	3:20	5:18
13	7:26	9:28	11:18	13:20	15:19	17:21	19:19	21:21	23:24	1:22	3:24	5:22
14	7:29	9:32	11:22	13:24	15:23	17:25	19:23	21:25	23:28	1:26	3:28	5:26
15	7:33	9:36	11:26	13:28	15:27	17:29	19:27	21:29	23:31	1:30	3:32	5:30
16	7:37	9:40	11:30	13:32	15:30	17:33	19:31	21:33	23:35	1:34	3:36	5:34
17	7:41	9:44	11:34	13:36	15:34	17:37	19:35	21:37	23:39	1:38	3:40	5:38
18	7:45	9:47	11:38	13:40	15:38	17:41	19:39	21:41	23:43	1:42	3:44	5:42
19	7:49	9:51	11:42	13:44	15:42	17:45	19:43	21:45	23:47	1:46	3:48	5:46
20	7:53	9:55	11:46	13:48	15:46	17:48	19:47	21:49	23:51	1:49	3:52	5:50
21	7:57	9:59	11:50	13:52	15:50	17:52	19:51	21:53	23:55	1:53	3:56	5:54
22	8:01	10:03	11:54	13:56	15:54	17:56	19:55	21:57	23:59	1:57	4:00	5:58
23	8:05	10:07	11:58	14:00	15:58	18:00	19:59	22:01	0:03	2:01	4:04	6:02
24	8:09	10:11	12:02	14:04	16:02	18:04	20:03	22:05	0:07	2:05	4:07	6:06
25	8:13	10:15	12:05	14:08	16:06	18:08	20:06	22:09	0:11	2:09	4:11	6:10
26	8:17	10:19	12:09	14:12	16:10	18:12	20:10	22:13	0:15	2:13	4:15	6:14
27	8:21	10:23	12:13	14:16	16:14	18:16	20:14	22:17	0:19	2:17	4:19	6:18
28	8:25	10:27	12:17	14:20	16:18	18:20	20:18	22:21	0:23	2:21	4:23	6:22
29	8:29		12:21	14:23	16:22	18:24	20:22	22:24	0:27	2:25	4:27	6:25
30	8:33		12:25	14:27	16:26	18:28	20:26	22:28	0:31	2:29	4:31	6:29
31	8:37		12:29		16:30		20:30	22:32		2:33		6:33

1916	Jan	Feb	Mar	Apr	May	Jun	Jul	Aug	Sep	Oct	Nov	Dec
1	6:37	8:40	10:34	12:36	14:34	16:37	18:35	20:37	22:39	0:38	2:40	4:38
2	6:41	8:43	10:38	12:40	14:38	16:41	18:39	20:41	22:43	0:41	2:44	4:42
3	6:45	8:47	10:42	12:44	14:42	16:44	18:43	20:45	22:47	0:45	2:48	4:46
4	6:49	8:51	10:46	12:48	14:46	16:48	18:47	20:49	22:51	0:49	2:52	4:50
5	6:53	8:55	10:50	12:52	14:50	16:52	18:51	20:53	22:55	0:53	2:56	4:54
6	6:57	8:59	10:54	12:56	14:54	16:56	18:55	20:57	22:59	0:57	2:59	4:58
7	7:01	9:03	10:57	13:00	14:58	17:00	18:58	21:01	23:03	1:01	3:03	5:02
8	7:05	9:07	11:01	13:04	15:02	17:04	19:02	21:05	23:07	1:05	3:07	5:06
9	7:09	9:11	11:05	13:08	15:06	17:08	19:06	21:09	23:11	1:09	3:11	5:10
10	7:13	9:15	11:09	13:12	15:10	17:12	19:10	21:13	23:15	1:13	3:15	5:14
11	7:17	9:19	11:13	13:15	15:14	17:16	19:14	21:16	23:19	1:17	3:19	5:17
12	7:21	9:23	11:17	13:19	15:18	17:20	19:18	21:20	23:23	1:21	3:23	5:21
13	7:25	9:27	11:21	13:23	15:22	17:24	19:22	21:24	23:27	1:25	3:27	5:25
14	7:29	9:31	11:25	13:27	15:26	17:28	19:26	21:28	23:31	1:29	3:31	5:29
15	7:32	9:35	11:29	13:31	15:30	17:32	19:30	21:32	23:34	1:33	3:35	5:33
16	7:36	9:39	11:33	13:35	15:33	17:36	19:34	21:36	23:38	1:37	3:39	5:37
17	7:40	9:43	11:37	13:39	15:37	17:40	19:38	21:40	23:42	1:41	3:43	5:41
18	7:44	9:47	11:41	13:43	15:41	17:44	19:42	21:44	23:46	1:45	3:47	5:45
19	7:48	9:50	11:45	13:47	15:45	17:48	19:46	21:48	23:50	1:49	3:51	5:49
20	7:52	9:54	11:49	13:51	15:49	17:51	19:50	21:52	23:54	1:52	3:55	5:53
21	7:56	9:58	11:53	13:55	15:53	17:55	19:54	21:56	23:58	1:56	3:59	5:57
22	8:00	10:02	11:57	13:59	15:57	17:59	19:58	22:00	0:02	2:00	4:03	6:01
23	8:04	10:06	12:01	14:03	16:01	18:03	20:02	22:04	0:06	2:04	4:07	6:05
24	8:08	10:10	12:05	14:07	16:05	18:07	20:06	22:08	0:10	2:08	4:10	6:09
25	8:12	10:14	12:08	14:11	16:09	18:11	20:09	22:12	0:14	2:12	4:14	6:13
26	8:16	10:18	12:12	14:15	16:13	18:15	20:13	22:16	0:18	2:16	4:18	6:17
27	8:20	10:22	12:16	14:19	16:17	18:19	20:17	22:20	0:22	2:20	4:22	6:21
28	8:24	10:26	12:20	14:23	16:21	18:23	20:21	22:24	0:26	2:24	4:26	6:25
29	8:28	10:30	12:24	14:26	16:25	18:27	20:25	22:27	0:30	2:28	4:30	6:28
30	8:32		12:28	14:30	16:29	18:31	20:29	22:31	0:34	2:32	4:34	6:32
31	8:36		12:32		16:33		20:33	22:35		2:36		6:36

1917	Jan	Feb	Mar	Apr	May	Jun	Jul	Aug	Sep	Oct	Nov	Dec
1	6:40	8:42	10:33	12:35	14:33	16:36	18:34	20:36	22:38	0:37	2:39	4:37
2	6:44	8:46	10:37	12:39	14:37	16:40	18:38	20:40	22:42	0:41	2:43	4:41
3	6:48	8:50	10:41	12:43	14:41	16:43	18:42	20:44	22:46	0:44	2:47	4:45
4	6:52	8:54	10:45	12:47	14:45	16:47	18:46	20:48	22:50	0:48	2:51	4:49
5	6:56	8:58	10:49	12:51	14:49	16:51	18:50	20:52	22:54	0:52	2:55	4:53
6	7:00	9:02	10:53	12:55	14:53	16:55	18:54	20:56	22:58	0:56	2:59	4:57
7	7:04	9:06	10:57	12:59	14:57	16:59	18:58	21:00	23:02	1:00	3:02	5:01
8	7:08	9:10	11:00	13:03	15:01	17:03	19:01	21:04	23:06	1:04	3:06	5:05
9	7:12	9:14	11:04	13:07	15:05	17:07	19:05	21:08	23:10	1:08	3:10	5:09
10	7:16	9:18	11:08	13:11	15:09	17:11	19:09	21:12	23:14	1:12	3:14	5:13
11	7:20	9:22	11:12	13:15	15:13	17:15	19:13	21:16	23:18	1:16	3:18	5:17
12	7:24	9:26	11:16	13:18	15:17	17:19	19:17	21:19	23:22	1:20	3:22	5:20
13	7:28	9:30	11:20	13:22	15:21	17:23	19:21	21:23	23:26	1:24	3:26	5:24
14	7:32	9:34	11:24	13:26	15:25	17:27	19:25	21:27	23:30	1:28	3:30	5:28
15	7:35	9:38	11:28	13:30	15:29	17:31	19:29	21:31	23:34	1:32	3:34	5:32
16	7:39	9:42	11:32	13:34	15:33	17:35	19:33	21:35	23:37	1:36	3:38	5:36
17	7:43	9:46	11:36	13:38	15:36	17:39	19:37	21:39	23:41	1:40	3:42	5:40
18	7:47	9:50	11:40	13:42	15:40	17:43	19:41	21:43	23:45	1:44	3:46	5:44
19	7:51	9:53	11:44	13:46	15:44	17:47	19:45	21:47	23:49	1:48	3:50	5:48
20	7:55	9:57	11:48	13:50	15:48	17:51	19:49	21:51	23:53	1:52	3:54	5:52
21	7:59	10:01	11:52	13:54	15:52	17:54	19:53	21:55	23:57	1:55	3:58	5:56
22	8:03	10:05	11:56	13:58	15:56	17:58	19:57	21:59	0:01	1:59	4:02	6:00
23	8:07	10:09	12:00	14:02	16:00	18:02	20:01	22:03	0:05	2:03	4:06	6:04
24	8:11	10:13	12:04	14:06	16:04	18:06	20:05	22:07	0:09	2:07	4:09	6:08
25	8:15	10:17	12:08	14:10	16:08	18:10	20:09	22:11	0:13	2:11	4:13	6:12
26	8:19	10:21	12:11	14:14	16:12	18:14	20:12	22:15	0:17	2:15	4:17	6:16
27	8:23	10:25	12:15	14:18	16:16	18:18	20:16	22:19	0:21	2:19	4:21	6:20
28	8:27	10:29	12:19	14:22	16:20	18:22	20:20	22:23	0:25	2:23	4:25	6:24
29	8:31		12:23	14:25	16:24	18:26	20:24	22:26	0:29	2:27	4:29	6:27
30	8:35		12:27	14:29	16:28	18:30	20:28	22:30	0:33	2:31	4:33	6:31
31	8:39		12:31		16:32		20:32	22:34		2:35		6:35

1918	Jan	Feb	Mar	Apr	May	Jun	Jul	Aug	Sep	Oct	Nov	Dec
1	6:39	8:42	10:32	12:34	14:32	16:35	18:33	20:35	22:37	0:36	2:38	4:36
2	6:43	8:45	10:36	12:38	14:36	16:39	18:37	20:39	22:41	0:40	2:42	4:40
3	6:47	8:49	10:40	12:42	14:40	16:43	18:41	20:43	22:45	0:44	2:46	4:44
4	6:51	8:53	10:44	12:46	14:44	16:46	18:45	20:47	22:49	0:47	2:50	4:48
5	6:55	8:57	10:48	12:50	14:48	16:50	18:49	20:51	22:53	0:51	2:54	4:52
6	6:59	9:01	10:52	12:54	14:52	16:54	18:53	20:55	22:57	0:55	2:58	4:56
7	7:03	9:05	10:56	12:58	14:56	16:58	18:57	20:59	23:01	0:59	3:02	5:00
8	7:07	9:09	11:00	13:02	15:00	17:02	19:01	21:03	23:05	1:03	3:05	5:04
9	7:11	9:13	11:03	13:06	15:04	17:06	19:04	21:07	23:09	1:07	3:09	5:08
10	7:15	9:17	11:07	13:10	15:08	17:10	19:08	21:11	23:13	1:11	3:13	5:12
11	7:19	9:21	11:11	13:14	15:12	17:14	19:12	21:15	23:17	1:15	3:17	5:16
12	7:23	9:25	11:15	13:18	15:16	17:18	19:16	21:19	23:21	1:19	3:21	5:20
13	7:27	9:29	11:19	13:21	15:20	17:22	19:20	21:22	23:25	1:23	3:25	5:23
14	7:31	9:33	11:23	13:25	15:24	17:26	19:24	21:26	23:29	1:27	3:29	5:27
15	7:35	9:37	11:27	13:29	15:28	17:30	19:28	21:30	23:33	1:31	3:33	5:31
16	7:38	9:41	11:31	13:33	15:32	17:34	19:32	21:34	23:37	1:35	3:37	5:35
17	7:42	9:45	11:35	13:37	15:36	17:38	19:36	21:38	23:40	1:39	3:41	5:39
18	7:46	9:49	11:39	13:41	15:39	17:42	19:40	21:42	23:44	1:43	3:45	5:43
19	7:50	9:53	11:43	13:45	15:43	17:46	19:44	21:46	23:48	1:47	3:49	5:47
20	7:54	9:56	11:47	13:49	15:47	17:50	19:48	21:50	23:52	1:51	3:53	5:51
21	7:58	10:00	11:51	13:53	15:51	17:54	19:52	21:54	23:56	1:54	3:57	5:55
22	8:02	10:04	11:55	13:57	15:55	17:57	19:56	21:58	0:00	1:58	4:01	5:59
23	8:06	10:08	11:59	14:01	15:59	18:01	20:00	22:02	0:04	2:02	4:05	6:03
24	8:10	10:12	12:03	14:05	16:03	18:05	20:04	22:06	0:08	2:06	4:09	6:07
25	8:14	10:16	12:07	14:09	16:07	18:09	20:08	22:10	0:12	2:10	4:12	6:11
26	8:18	10:20	12:10	14:13	16:11	18:13	20:11	22:14	0:16	2:14	4:16	6:15
27	8:22	10:24	12:14	14:17	16:15	18:17	20:15	22:18	0:20	2:18	4:20	6:19
28	8:26	10:28	12:18	14:21	16:19	18:21	20:19	22:22	0:24	2:22	4:24	6:23
29	8:30		12:22	14:25	16:23	18:25	20:23	22:26	0:28	2:26	4:28	6:27
30	8:34		12:26	14:28	16:27	18:29	20:27	22:29	0:32	2:30	4:32	6:30
31	8:38		12:30		16:31		20:31	22:33		2:34		6:34

1919	Jan	Feb	Mar	Apr	May	Jun	Jul	Aug	Sep	Oct	Nov	Dec
1	6:38	8:41	10:31	12:33	14:31	16:34	18:32	20:34	22:36	0:35	2:37	4:35
2	6:42	8:45	10:35	12:37	14:35	16:38	18:36	20:38	22:40	0:39	2:41	4:39
3	6:46	8:48	10:39	12:41	14:39	16:42	18:40	20:42	22:44	0:43	2:45	4:43
4	6:50	8:52	10:43	12:45	14:43	16:46	18:44	20:46	22:48	0:47	2:49	4:47
5	6:54	8:56	10:47	12:49	14:47	16:49	18:48	20:50	22:52	0:50	2:53	4:51
6	6:58	9:00	10:51	12:53	14:51	16:53	18:52	20:54	22:56	0:54	2:57	4:55
7	7:02	9:04	10:55	12:57	14:55	16:57	18:56	20:58	23:00	0:58	3:01	4:59
8	7:06	9:08	10:59	13:01	14:59	17:01	19:00	21:02	23:04	1:02	3:05	5:03
9	7:10	9:12	11:03	13:05	15:03	17:05	19:04	21:06	23:08	1:06	3:08	5:07
10	7:14	9:16	11:06	13:09	15:07	17:09	19:07	21:10	23:12	1:10	3:12	5:11
11	7:18	9:20	11:10	13:13	15:11	17:13	19:11	21:14	23:16	1:14	3:16	5:15
12	7:22	9:24	11:14	13:17	15:15	17:17	19:15	21:18	23:20	1:18	3:20	5:19
13	7:26	9:28	11:18	13:21	15:19	17:21	19:19	21:22	23:24	1:22	3:24	5:22
14	7:30	9:32	11:22	13:24	15:23	17:25	19:23	21:25	23:28	1:26	3:28	5:26
15	7:34	9:36	11:26	13:28	15:27	17:29	19:27	21:29	23:32	1:30	3:32	5:30
16	7:38	9:40	11:30	13:32	15:31	17:33	19:31	21:33	23:36	1:34	3:36	5:34
17	7:41	9:44	11:34	13:36	15:35	17:37	19:35	21:37	23:39	1:38	3:40	5:38
18	7:45	9:48	11:38	13:40	15:38	17:41	19:39	21:41	23:43	1:42	3:44	5:42
19	7:49	9:52	11:42	13:44	15:42	17:45	19:43	21:45	23:47	1:46	3:48	5:46
20	7:53	9:55	11:46	13:48	15:46	17:49	19:47	21:49	23:51	1:50	3:52	5:50
21	7:57	9:59	11:50	13:52	15:50	17:53	19:51	21:53	23:55	1:54	3:56	5:54
22	8:01	10:03	11:54	13:56	15:54	17:56	19:55	21:57	23:59	1:57	4:00	5:58
23	8:05	10:07	11:58	14:00	15:58	18:00	19:59	22:01	0:03	2:01	4:04	6:02
24	8:09	10:11	12:02	14:04	16:02	18:04	20:03	22:05	0:07	2:05	4:08	6:06
25	8:13	10:15	12:06	14:08	16:06	18:08	20:07	22:09	0:11	2:09	4:12	6:10
26	8:17	10:19	12:10	14:12	16:10	18:12	20:11	22:13	0:15	2:13	4:15	6:14
27	8:21	10:23	12:13	14:16	16:14	18:16	20:14	22:17	0:19	2:17	4:19	6:18
28	8:25	10:27	12:17	14:20	16:18	18:20	20:18	22:21	0:23	2:21	4:23	6:22
29	8:29		12:21	14:24	16:22	18:24	20:22	22:25	0:27	2:25	4:27	6:26
30	8:33		12:25	14:28	16:26	18:28	20:26	22:29	0:31	2:29	4:31	6:30
31	8:37		12:29		16:30		20:30	22:32		2:33		6:33

1920	Jan	Feb	Mar	Apr	May	Jun	Jul	Aug	Sep	Oct	Nov	Dec
1	6:37	8:40	10:34	12:36	14:34	16:37	18:35	20:37	22:39	0:38	2:40	4:38
2	6:41	8:44	10:38	12:40	14:38	16:41	18:39	20:41	22:43	0:42	2:44	4:42
3	6:45	8:48	10:42	12:44	14:42	16:45	18:43	20:45	22:47	0:46	2:48	4:46
4	6:49	8:51	10:46	12:48	14:46	16:49	18:47	20:49	22:51	0:50	2:52	4:50
5	6:53	8:55	10:50	12:52	14:50	16:52	18:51	20:53	22:55	0:53	2:56	4:54
6	6:57	8:59	10:54	12:56	14:54	16:56	18:55	20:57	22:59	0:57	3:00	4:58
7	7:01	9:03	10:58	13:00	14:58	17:00	18:59	21:01	23:03	1:01	3:04	5:02
8	7:05	9:07	11:02	13:04	15:02	17:04	19:03	21:05	23:07	1:05	3:07	5:06
9	7:09	9:11	11:06	13:08	15:06	17:08	19:06	21:09	23:11	1:09	3:11	5:10
10	7:13	9:15	11:09	13:12	15:10	17:12	19:10	21:13	23:15	1:13	3:15	5:14
11	7:17	9:19	11:13	13:16	15:14	17:16	19:14	21:17	23:19	1:17	3:19	5:18
12	7:21	9:23	11:17	13:20	15:18	17:20	19:18	21:21	23:23	1:21	3:23	5:22
13	7:25	9:27	11:21	13:23	15:22	17:24	19:22	21:24	23:27	1:25	3:27	5:25
14	7:29	9:31	11:25	13:27	15:26	17:28	19:26	21:28	23:31	1:29	3:31	5:29
15	7:33	9:35	11:29	13:31	15:30	17:32	19:30	21:32	23:35	1:33	3:35	5:33
16	7:37	9:39	11:33	13:35	15:34	17:36	19:34	21:36	23:39	1:37	3:39	5:37
17	7:40	9:43	11:37	13:39	15:38	17:40	19:38	21:40	23:42	1:41	3:43	5:41
18	7:44	9:47	11:41	13:43	15:41	17:44	19:42	21:44	23:46	1:45	3:47	5:45
19	7:48	9:51	11:45	13:47	15:45	17:48	19:46	21:48	23:50	1:49	3:51	5:49
20	7:52	9:55	11:49	13:51	15:49	17:52	19:50	21:52	23:54	1:53	3:55	5:53
21	7:56	9:58	11:53	13:55	15:53	17:56	19:54	21:56	23:58	1:57	3:59	5:57
22	8:00	10:02	11:57	13:59	15:57	17:59	19:58	22:00	0:02	2:00	4:03	6:01
23	8:04	10:06	12:01	14:03	16:01	18:03	20:02	22:04	0:06	2:04	4:07	6:05
24	8:08	10:10	12:05	14:07	16:05	18:07	20:06	22:08	0:10	2:08	4:11	6:09
25	8:12	10:14	12:09	14:11	16:09	18:11	20:10	22:12	0:14	2:12	4:15	6:13
26	8:16	10:18	12:13	14:15	16:13	18:15	20:14	22:16	0:18	2:16	4:18	6:17
27	8:20	10:22	12:16	14:19	16:17	18:19	20:17	22:20	0:22	2:20	4:22	6:21
28	8:24	10:26	12:20	14:23	16:21	18:23	20:21	22:24	0:26	2:24	4:26	6:25
29	8:28	10:30	12:24	14:27	16:25	18:27	20:25	22:28	0:30	2:28	4:30	6:29
30	8:32		12:28	14:31	16:29	18:31	20:29	22:32	0:34	2:32	4:34	6:33
31	8:36		12:32		16:33		20:33	22:35		2:36		6:36

1921	Jan	Feb	Mar	Apr	May	Jun	Jul	Aug	Sep	Oct	Nov	Dec
1	6:40	8:43	10:33	12:35	14:34	16:36	18:34	20:36	22:38	0:37	2:39	4:37
2	6:44	8:47	10:37	12:39	14:37	16:40	18:38	20:40	22:42	0:41	2:43	4:41
3	6:48	8:51	10:41	12:43	14:41	16:44	18:42	20:44	22:46	0:45	2:47	4:45
4	6:52	8:54	10:45	12:47	14:45	16:48	18:46	20:48	22:50	0:49	2:51	4:49
5	6:56	8:58	10:49	12:51	14:49	16:51	18:50	20:52	22:54	0:52	2:55	4:53
6	7:00	9:02	10:53	12:55	14:53	16:55	18:54	20:56	22:58	0:56	2:59	4:57
7	7:04	9:06	10:57	12:59	14:57	16:59	18:58	21:00	23:02	1:00	3:03	5:01
8	7:08	9:10	11:01	13:03	15:01	17:03	19:02	21:04	23:06	1:04	3:07	5:05
9	7:12	9:14	11:05	13:07	15:05	17:07	19:06	21:08	23:10	1:08	3:10	5:09
10	7:16	9:18	11:08	13:11	15:09	17:11	19:09	21:12	23:14	1:12	3:14	5:13
11	7:20	9:22	11:12	13:15	15:13	17:15	19:13	21:16	23:18	1:16	3:18	5:17
12	7:24	9:26	11:16	13:19	15:17	17:19	19:17	21:20	23:22	1:20	3:22	5:21
13	7:28	9:30	11:20	13:23	15:21	17:23	19:21	21:24	23:26	1:24	3:26	5:25
14	7:32	9:34	11:24	13:26	15:25	17:27	19:25	21:27	23:30	1:28	3:30	5:28
15	7:36	9:38	11:28	13:30	15:29	17:31	19:29	21:31	23:34	1:32	3:34	5:32
16	7:40	9:42	11:32	13:34	15:33	17:35	19:33	21:35	23:38	1:36	3:38	5:36
17	7:43	9:46	11:36	13:38	15:37	17:39	19:37	21:39	23:42	1:40	3:42	5:40
18	7:47	9:50	11:40	13:42	15:41	17:43	19:41	21:43	23:45	1:44	3:46	5:44
19	7:51	9:54	11:44	13:46	15:44	17:47	19:45	21:47	23:49	1:48	3:50	5:48
20	7:55	9:58	11:48	13:50	15:48	17:51	19:49	21:51	23:53	1:52	3:54	5:52
21	7:59	10:01	11:52	13:54	15:52	17:55	19:53	21:55	23:57	1:56	3:58	5:56
22	8:03	10:05	11:56	13:58	15:56	17:59	19:57	21:59	0:01	2:00	4:02	6:00
23	8:07	10:09	12:00	14:02	16:00	18:02	20:01	22:03	0:05	2:03	4:06	6:04
24	8:11	10:13	12:04	14:06	16:04	18:06	20:05	22:07	0:09	2:07	4:10	6:08
25	8:15	10:17	12:08	14:10	16:08	18:10	20:09	22:11	0:13	2:11	4:14	6:12
26	8:19	10:21	12:12	14:14	16:12	18:14	20:13	22:15	0:17	2:15	4:18	6:16
27	8:23	10:25	12:16	14:18	16:16	18:18	20:17	22:19	0:21	2:19	4:21	6:20
28	8:27	10:29	12:19	14:22	16:20	18:22	20:20	22:23	0:25	2:23	4:25	6:24
29	8:31		12:23	14:26	16:24	18:26	20:24	22:27	0:29	2:27	4:29	6:28
30	8:35		12:27	14:30	16:28	18:30	20:28	22:31	0:33	2:31	4:33	6:32
31	8:39		12:31		16:32		20:32	22:35		2:35		6:35

1922	Jan	Feb	Mar	Apr	May	Jun	Jul	Aug	Sep	Oct	Nov	Dec
1	6:39	8:42	10:32	12:34	14:33	16:35	18:33	20:35	22:37	0:36	2:38	4:36
2	6:43	8:46	10:36	12:38	14:36	16:39	18:37	20:39	22:41	0:40	2:42	4:40
3	6:47	8:50	10:40	12:42	14:40	16:43	18:41	20:43	22:45	0:44	2:46	4:44
4	6:51	8:53	10:44	12:46	14:44	16:47	18:45	20:47	22:49	0:48	2:50	4:48
5	6:55	8:57	10:48	12:50	14:48	16:51	18:49	20:51	22:53	0:52	2:54	4:52
6	6:59	9:01	10:52	12:54	14:52	16:54	18:53	20:55	22:57	0:55	2:58	4:56
7	7:03	9:05	10:56	12:58	14:56	16:58	18:57	20:59	23:01	0:59	3:02	5:00
8	7:07	9:09	11:00	13:02	15:00	17:02	19:01	21:03	23:05	1:03	3:06	5:04
9	7:11	9:13	11:04	13:06	15:04	17:06	19:05	21:07	23:09	1:07	3:10	5:08
10	7:15	9:17	11:08	13:10	15:08	17:10	19:09	21:11	23:13	1:11	3:13	5:12
11	7:19	9:21	11:11	13:14	15:12	17:14	19:12	21:15	23:17	1:15	3:17	5:16
12	7:23	9:25	11:15	13:18	15:16	17:18	19:16	21:19	23:21	1:19	3:21	5:20
13	7:27	9:29	11:19	13:22	15:20	17:22	19:20	21:23	23:25	1:23	3:25	5:24
14	7:31	9:33	11:23	13:26	15:24	17:26	19:24	21:27	23:29	1:27	3:29	5:28
15	7:35	9:37	11:27	13:29	15:28	17:30	19:28	21:30	23:33	1:31	3:33	5:31
16	7:39	9:41	11:31	13:33	15:32	17:34	19:32	21:34	23:37	1:35	3:37	5:35
17	7:43	9:45	11:35	13:37	15:36	17:38	19:36	21:38	23:41	1:39	3:41	5:39
18	7:46	9:49	11:39	13:41	15:40	17:42	19:40	21:42	23:45	1:43	3:45	5:43
19	7:50	9:53	11:43	13:45	15:44	17:46	19:44	21:46	23:48	1:47	3:49	5:47
20	7:54	9:57	11:47	13:49	15:47	17:50	19:48	21:50	23:52	1:51	3:53	5:51
21	7:58	10:01	11:51	13:53	15:51	17:54	19:52	21:54	23:56	1:55	3:57	5:55
22	8:02	10:04	11:55	13:57	15:55	17:58	19:56	21:58	0:00	1:59	4:01	5:59
23	8:06	10:08	11:59	14:01	15:59	18:02	20:00	22:02	0:04	2:03	4:05	6:03
24	8:10	10:12	12:03	14:05	16:03	18:05	20:04	22:06	0:08	2:06	4:09	6:07
25	8:14	10:16	12:07	14:09	16:07	18:09	20:08	22:10	0:12	2:10	4:13	6:11
26	8:18	10:20	12:11	14:13	16:11	18:13	20:12	22:14	0:16	2:14	4:17	6:15
27	8:22	10:24	12:15	14:17	16:15	18:17	20:16	22:18	0:20	2:18	4:20	6:19
28	8:26	10:28	12:19	14:21	16:19	18:21	20:19	22:22	0:24	2:22	4:24	6:23
29	8:30		12:22	14:25	16:23	18:25	20:23	22:26	0:28	2:26	4:28	6:27
30	8:34		12:26	14:29	16:27	18:29	20:27	22:30	0:32	2:30	4:32	6:31
31	8:38		12:30		16:31		20:31	22:34		2:34		6:35

1923	Jan	Feb	Mar	Apr	May	Jun	Jul	Aug	Sep	Oct	Nov	Dec
1	6:38	8:41	10:31	12:33	14:32	16:34	18:32	20:34	22:37	0:35	2:37	4:35
2	6:42	8:45	10:35	12:37	14:36	16:38	18:36	20:38	22:40	0:39	2:41	4:39
3	6:46	8:49	10:39	12:41	14:39	16:42	18:40	20:42	22:44	0:43	2:45	4:43
4	6:50	8:53	10:43	12:45	14:43	16:46	18:44	20:46	22:48	0:47	2:49	4:47
5	6:54	8:56	10:47	12:49	14:47	16:50	18:48	20:50	22:52	0:51	2:53	4:51
6	6:58	9:00	10:51	12:53	14:51	16:54	18:52	20:54	22:56	0:55	2:57	4:55
7	7:02	9:04	10:55	12:57	14:55	16:57	18:56	20:58	23:00	0:58	3:01	4:59
8	7:06	9:08	10:59	13:01	14:59	17:01	19:00	21:02	23:04	1:02	3:05	5:03
9	7:10	9:12	11:03	13:05	15:03	17:05	19:04	21:06	23:08	1:06	3:09	5:07
10	7:14	9:16	11:07	13:09	15:07	17:09	19:08	21:10	23:12	1:10	3:13	5:11
11	7:18	9:20	11:11	13:13	15:11	17:13	19:12	21:14	23:16	1:14	3:16	5:15
12	7:22	9:24	11:14	13:17	15:15	17:17	19:15	21:18	23:20	1:18	3:20	5:19
13	7:26	9:28	11:18	13:21	15:19	17:21	19:19	21:22	23:24	1:22	3:24	5:23
14	7:30	9:32	11:22	13:25	15:23	17:25	19:23	21:26	23:28	1:26	3:28	5:27
15	7:34	9:36	11:26	13:29	15:27	17:29	19:27	21:30	23:32	1:30	3:32	5:31
16	7:38	9:40	11:30	13:32	15:31	17:33	19:31	21:33	23:36	1:34	3:36	5:34
17	7:42	9:44	11:34	13:36	15:35	17:37	19:35	21:37	23:40	1:38	3:40	5:38
18	7:46	9:48	11:38	13:40	15:39	17:41	19:39	21:41	23:44	1:42	3:44	5:42
19	7:49	9:52	11:42	13:44	15:43	17:45	19:43	21:45	23:48	1:46	3:48	5:46
20	7:53	9:56	11:46	13:48	15:47	17:49	19:47	21:49	23:51	1:50	3:52	5:50
21	7:57	10:00	11:50	13:52	15:50	17:53	19:51	21:53	23:55	1:54	3:56	5:54
22	8:01	10:04	11:54	13:56	15:54	17:57	19:55	21:57	23:59	1:58	4:00	5:58
23	8:05	10:07	11:58	14:00	15:58	18:01	19:59	22:01	0:03	2:02	4:04	6:02
24	8:09	10:11	12:02	14:04	16:02	18:04	20:03	22:05	0:07	2:05	4:08	6:06
25	8:13	10:15	12:06	14:08	16:06	18:08	20:07	22:09	0:11	2:09	4:12	6:10
26	8:17	10:19	12:10	14:12	16:10	18:12	20:11	22:13	0:15	2:13	4:16	6:14
27	8:21	10:23	12:14	14:16	16:14	18:16	20:15	22:17	0:19	2:17	4:20	6:18
28	8:25	10:27	12:18	14:20	16:18	18:20	20:19	22:21	0:23	2:21	4:23	6:22
29	8:29		12:21	14:24	16:22	18:24	20:22	22:25	0:27	2:25	4:27	6:26
30	8:33		12:25	14:28	16:26	18:28	20:26	22:29	0:31	2:29	4:31	6:30
31	8:37		12:29		16:30		20:30	22:33		2:33		6:34

1924	Jan	Feb	Mar	Apr	May	Jun	Jul	Aug	Sep	Oct	Nov	Dec
1	6:38	8:40	10:34	12:36	14:35	16:37	18:35	20:37	22:40	0:38	2:40	4:38
2	6:41	8:44	10:38	12:40	14:39	16:41	18:39	20:41	22:43	0:42	2:44	4:42
3	6:45	8:48	10:42	12:44	14:42	16:45	18:43	20:45	22:47	0:46	2:48	4:46
4	6:49	8:52	10:46	12:48	14:46	16:49	18:47	20:49	22:51	0:50	2:52	4:50
5	6:53	8:56	10:50	12:52	14:50	16:53	18:51	20:53	22:55	0:54	2:56	4:54
6	6:57	8:59	10:54	12:56	14:54	16:57	18:55	20:57	22:59	0:58	3:00	4:58
7	7:01	9:03	10:58	13:00	14:58	17:00	18:59	21:01	23:03	1:01	3:04	5:02
8	7:05	9:07	11:02	13:04	15:02	17:04	19:03	21:05	23:07	1:05	3:08	5:06
9	7:09	9:11	11:06	13:08	15:06	17:08	19:07	21:09	23:11	1:09	3:12	5:10
10	7:13	9:15	11:10	13:12	15:10	17:12	19:11	21:13	23:15	1:13	3:16	5:14
11	7:17	9:19	11:14	13:16	15:14	17:16	19:15	21:17	23:19	1:17	3:19	5:18
12	7:21	9:23	11:17	13:20	15:18	17:20	19:18	21:21	23:23	1:21	3:23	5:22
13	7:25	9:27	11:21	13:24	15:22	17:24	19:22	21:25	23:27	1:25	3:27	5:26
14	7:29	9:31	11:25	13:28	15:26	17:28	19:26	21:29	23:31	1:29	3:31	5:30
15	7:33	9:35	11:29	13:32	15:30	17:32	19:30	21:32	23:35	1:33	3:35	5:33
16	7:37	9:39	11:33	13:35	15:34	17:36	19:34	21:36	23:39	1:37	3:39	5:37
17	7:41	9:43	11:37	13:39	15:38	17:40	19:38	21:40	23:43	1:41	3:43	5:41
18	7:45	9:47	11:41	13:43	15:42	17:44	19:42	21:44	23:47	1:45	3:47	5:45
19	7:48	9:51	11:45	13:47	15:46	17:48	19:46	21:48	23:50	1:49	3:51	5:49
20	7:52	9:55	11:49	13:51	15:49	17:52	19:50	21:52	23:54	1:53	3:55	5:53
21	7:56	9:59	11:53	13:55	15:53	17:56	19:54	21:56	23:58	1:57	3:59	5:57
22	8:00	10:03	11:57	13:59	15:57	18:00	19:58	22:00	0:02	2:01	4:03	6:01
23	8:04	10:06	12:01	14:03	16:01	18:04	20:02	22:04	0:06	2:05	4:07	6:05
24	8:08	10:10	12:05	14:07	16:05	18:07	20:06	22:08	0:10	2:08	4:11	6:09
25	8:12	10:14	12:09	14:11	16:09	18:11	20:10	22:12	0:14	2:12	4:15	6:13
26	8:16	10:18	12:13	14:15	16:13	18:15	20:14	22:16	0:18	2:16	4:19	6:17
27	8:20	10:22	12:17	14:19	16:17	18:19	20:18	22:20	0:22	2:20	4:23	6:21
28	8:24	10:26	12:21	14:23	16:21	18:23	20:22	22:24	0:26	2:24	4:26	6:25
29	8:28	10:30	12:24	14:27	16:25	18:27	20:25	22:28	0:30	2:28	4:30	6:29
30	8:32		12:28	14:31	16:29	18:31	20:29	22:32	0:34	2:32	4:34	6:33
31	8:36		12:32		16:33		20:33	22:36		2:36		6:37

1925	Jan	Feb	Mar	Apr	May	Jun	Jul	Aug	Sep	Oct	Nov	Dec
1	6:41	8:43	10:33	12:35	14:34	16:36	18:34	20:36	22:39	0:37	2:39	4:37
2	6:44	8:47	10:37	12:39	14:38	16:40	18:38	20:40	22:43	0:41	2:43	4:41
3	6:48	8:51	10:41	12:43	14:42	16:44	18:42	20:44	22:46	0:45	2:47	4:45
4	6:52	8:55	10:45	12:47	14:45	16:48	18:46	20:48	22:50	0:49	2:51	4:49
5	6:56	8:59	10:49	12:51	14:49	16:52	18:50	20:52	22:54	0:53	2:55	4:53
6	7:00	9:02	10:53	12:55	14:53	16:56	18:54	20:56	22:58	0:57	2:59	4:57
7	7:04	9:06	10:57	12:59	14:57	17:00	18:58	21:00	23:02	1:01	3:03	5:01
8	7:08	9:10	11:01	13:03	15:01	17:03	19:02	21:04	23:06	1:04	3:07	5:05
9	7:12	9:14	11:05	13:07	15:05	17:07	19:06	21:08	23:10	1:08	3:11	5:09
10	7:16	9:18	11:09	13:11	15:09	17:11	19:10	21:12	23:14	1:12	3:15	5:13
11	7:20	9:22	11:13	13:15	15:13	17:15	19:14	21:16	23:18	1:16	3:18	5:17
12	7:24	9:26	11:16	13:19	15:17	17:19	19:17	21:20	23:22	1:20	3:22	5:21
13	7:28	9:30	11:20	13:23	15:21	17:23	19:21	21:24	23:26	1:24	3:26	5:25
14	7:32	9:34	11:24	13:27	15:25	17:27	19:25	21:28	23:30	1:28	3:30	5:29
15	7:36	9:38	11:28	13:31	15:29	17:31	19:29	21:32	23:34	1:32	3:34	5:33
16	7:40	9:42	11:32	13:34	15:33	17:35	19:33	21:35	23:38	1:36	3:38	5:36
17	7:44	9:46	11:36	13:38	15:37	17:39	19:37	21:39	23:42	1:40	3:42	5:40
18	7:48	9:50	11:40	13:42	15:41	17:43	19:41	21:43	23:46	1:44	3:46	5:44
19	7:51	9:54	11:44	13:46	15:45	17:47	19:45	21:47	23:50	1:48	3:50	5:48
20	7:55	9:58	11:48	13:50	15:49	17:51	19:49	21:51	23:53	1:52	3:54	5:52
21	7:59	10:02	11:52	13:54	15:52	17:55	19:53	21:55	23:57	1:56	3:58	5:56
22	8:03	10:06	11:56	13:58	15:56	17:59	19:57	21:59	0:01	2:00	4:02	6:00
23	8:07	10:09	12:00	14:02	16:00	18:03	20:01	22:03	0:05	2:04	4:06	6:04
24	8:11	10:13	12:04	14:06	16:04	18:07	20:05	22:07	0:09	2:08	4:10	6:08
25	8:15	10:17	12:08	14:10	16:08	18:10	20:09	22:11	0:13	2:11	4:14	6:12
26	8:19	10:21	12:12	14:14	16:12	18:14	20:13	22:15	0:17	2:15	4:18	6:16
27	8:23	10:25	12:16	14:18	16:16	18:18	20:17	22:19	0:21	2:19	4:22	6:20
28	8:27	10:29	12:20	14:22	16:20	18:22	20:21	22:23	0:25	2:23	4:26	6:24
29	8:31		12:24	14:26	16:24	18:26	20:25	22:27	0:29	2:27	4:29	6:28
30	8:35		12:27	14:30	16:28	18:30	20:28	22:31	0:33	2:31	4:33	6:32
31	8:39		12:31		16:32		20:32	22:35		2:35		6:36

1926	Jan	Feb	Mar	Apr	May	Jun	Jul	Aug	Sep	Oct	Nov	Dec
1	6:40	8:42	10:32	12:34	14:33	16:35	18:33	20:35	22:38	0:36	2:38	4:36
2	6:44	8:46	10:36	12:38	14:37	16:39	18:37	20:39	22:42	0:40	2:42	4:40
3	6:47	8:50	10:40	12:42	14:41	16:43	18:41	20:43	22:45	0:44	2:46	4:44
4	6:51	8:54	10:44	12:46	14:45	16:47	18:45	20:47	22:49	0:48	2:50	4:48
5	6:55	8:58	10:48	12:50	14:48	16:51	18:49	20:51	22:53	0:52	2:54	4:52
6	6:59	9:01	10:52	12:54	14:52	16:55	18:53	20:55	22:57	0:56	2:58	4:56
7	7:03	9:05	10:56	12:58	14:56	16:59	18:57	20:59	23:01	1:00	3:02	5:00
8	7:07	9:09	11:00	13:02	15:00	17:02	19:01	21:03	23:05	1:03	3:06	5:04
9	7:11	9:13	11:04	13:06	15:04	17:06	19:05	21:07	23:09	1:07	3:10	5:08
10	7:15	9:17	11:08	13:10	15:08	17:10	19:09	21:11	23:13	1:11	3:14	5:12
11	7:19	9:21	11:12	13:14	15:12	17:14	19:13	21:15	23:17	1:15	3:18	5:16
12	7:23	9:25	11:16	13:18	15:16	17:18	19:17	21:19	23:21	1:19	3:21	5:20
13	7:27	9:29	11:19	13:22	15:20	17:22	19:20	21:23	23:25	1:23	3:25	5:24
14	7:31	9:33	11:23	13:26	15:24	17:26	19:24	21:27	23:29	1:27	3:29	5:28
15	7:35	9:37	11:27	13:30	15:28	17:30	19:28	21:31	23:33	1:31	3:33	5:32
16	7:39	9:41	11:31	13:34	15:32	17:34	19:32	21:35	23:37	1:35	3:37	5:36
17	7:43	9:45	11:35	13:37	15:36	17:38	19:36	21:38	23:41	1:39	3:41	5:39
18	7:47	9:49	11:39	13:41	15:40	17:42	19:40	21:42	23:45	1:43	3:45	5:43
19	7:51	9:53	11:43	13:45	15:44	17:46	19:44	21:46	23:49	1:47	3:49	5:47
20	7:54	9:57	11:47	13:49	15:48	17:50	19:48	21:50	23:53	1:51	3:53	5:51
21	7:58	10:01	11:51	13:53	15:52	17:54	19:52	21:54	23:56	1:55	3:57	5:55
22	8:02	10:05	11:55	13:57	15:55	17:58	19:56	21:58	0:00	1:59	4:01	5:59
23	8:06	10:09	11:59	14:01	15:59	18:02	20:00	22:02	0:04	2:03	4:05	6:03
24	8:10	10:12	12:03	14:05	16:03	18:06	20:04	22:06	0:08	2:07	4:09	6:07
25	8:14	10:16	12:07	14:09	16:07	18:10	20:08	22:10	0:12	2:11	4:13	6:11
26	8:18	10:20	12:11	14:13	16:11	18:13	20:12	22:14	0:16	2:14	4:17	6:15
27	8:22	10:24	12:15	14:17	16:15	18:17	20:16	22:18	0:20	2:18	4:21	6:19
28	8:26	10:28	12:19	14:21	16:19	18:21	20:20	22:22	0:24	2:22	4:25	6:23
29	8:30		12:23	14:25	16:23	18:25	20:24	22:26	0:28	2:26	4:29	6:27
30	8:34		12:27	14:29	16:27	18:29	20:28	22:30	0:32	2:30	4:32	6:31
31	8:38		12:30		16:31		20:31	22:34		2:34		6:35

1927	Jan	Feb	Mar	Apr	May	Jun	Jul	Aug	Sep	Oct	Nov	Dec
1	6:39	8:41	10:31	12:33	14:32	16:34	18:32	20:34	22:37	0:35	2:37	4:35
2	6:43	8:45	10:35	12:37	14:36	16:38	18:36	20:38	22:41	0:39	2:41	4:39
3	6:46	8:49	10:39	12:41	14:40	16:42	18:40	20:42	22:45	0:43	2:45	4:43
4	6:50	8:53	10:43	12:45	14:44	16:46	18:44	20:46	22:48	0:47	2:49	4:47
5	6:54	8:57	10:47	12:49	14:47	16:50	18:48	20:50	22:52	0:51	2:53	4:51
6	6:58	9:01	10:51	12:53	14:51	16:54	18:52	20:54	22:56	0:55	2:57	4:55
7	7:02	9:04	10:55	12:57	14:55	16:58	18:56	20:58	23:00	0:59	3:01	4:59
8	7:06	9:08	10:59	13:01	14:59	17:02	19:00	21:02	23:04	1:03	3:05	5:03
9	7:10	9:12	11:03	13:05	15:03	17:05	19:04	21:06	23:08	1:06	3:09	5:07
10	7:14	9:16	11:07	13:09	15:07	17:09	19:08	21:10	23:12	1:10	3:13	5:11
11	7:18	9:20	11:11	13:13	15:11	17:13	19:12	21:14	23:16	1:14	3:17	5:15
12	7:22	9:24	11:15	13:17	15:15	17:17	19:16	21:18	23:20	1:18	3:21	5:19
13	7:26	9:28	11:19	13:21	15:19	17:21	19:20	21:22	23:24	1:22	3:24	5:23
14	7:30	9:32	11:22	13:25	15:23	17:25	19:23	21:26	23:28	1:26	3:28	5:27
15	7:34	9:36	11:26	13:29	15:27	17:29	19:27	21:30	23:32	1:30	3:32	5:31
16	7:38	9:40	11:30	13:33	15:31	17:33	19:31	21:34	23:36	1:34	3:36	5:35
17	7:42	9:44	11:34	13:37	15:35	17:37	19:35	21:38	23:40	1:38	3:40	5:39
18	7:46	9:48	11:38	13:40	15:39	17:41	19:39	21:41	23:44	1:42	3:44	5:42
19	7:50	9:52	11:42	13:44	15:43	17:45	19:43	21:45	23:48	1:46	3:48	5:46
20	7:54	9:56	11:46	13:48	15:47	17:49	19:47	21:49	23:52	1:50	3:52	5:50
21	7:57	10:00	11:50	13:52	15:51	17:53	19:51	21:53	23:56	1:54	3:56	5:54
22	8:01	10:04	11:54	13:56	15:55	17:57	19:55	21:57	23:59	1:58	4:00	5:58
23	8:05	10:08	11:58	14:00	15:58	18:01	19:59	22:01	0:03	2:02	4:04	6:02
24	8:09	10:12	12:02	14:04	16:02	18:05	20:03	22:05	0:07	2:06	4:08	6:06
25	8:13	10:15	12:06	14:08	16:06	18:09	20:07	22:09	0:11	2:10	4:12	6:10
26	8:17	10:19	12:10	14:12	16:10	18:13	20:11	22:13	0:15	2:14	4:16	6:14
27	8:21	10:23	12:14	14:16	16:14	18:16	20:15	22:17	0:19	2:17	4:20	6:18
28	8:25	10:27	12:18	14:20	16:18	18:20	20:19	22:21	0:23	2:21	4:24	6:22
29	8:29		12:22	14:24	16:22	18:24	20:23	22:25	0:27	2:25	4:28	6:26
30	8:33		12:26	14:28	16:26	18:28	20:27	22:29	0:31	2:29	4:31	6:30
31	8:37		12:29		16:30		20:30	22:33		2:33		6:34

1928	Jan	Feb	Dec	Apr	May	Jun	Jul	Aug	Sep	Oct	Nov	Dec
1	6:38	8:40	10:34	12:36	14:35	16:37	18:35	20:37	22:40	0:38	2:40	4:38
2	6:42	8:44	10:38	12:40	14:39	16:41	18:39	20:41	22:44	0:42	2:44	4:42
3	6:46	8:48	10:42	12:44	14:43	16:45	18:43	20:45	22:48	0:46	2:48	4:46
4	6:49	8:52	10:46	12:48	14:47	16:49	18:47	20:49	22:51	0:50	2:52	4:50
5	6:53	8:56	10:50	12:52	14:50	16:53	18:51	20:53	22:55	0:54	2:56	4:54
6	6:57	9:00	10:54	12:56	14:54	16:57	18:55	20:57	22:59	0:58	3:00	4:58
7	7:01	9:04	10:58	13:00	14:58	17:01	18:59	21:01	23:03	1:02	3:04	5:02
8	7:05	9:07	11:02	13:04	15:02	17:05	19:03	21:05	23:07	1:06	3:08	5:06
9	7:09	9:11	11:06	13:08	15:06	17:08	19:07	21:09	23:11	1:09	3:12	5:10
10	7:13	9:15	11:10	13:12	15:10	17:12	19:11	21:13	23:15	1:13	3:16	5:14
11	7:17	9:19	11:14	13:16	15:14	17:16	19:15	21:17	23:19	1:17	3:20	5:18
12	7:21	9:23	11:18	13:20	15:18	17:20	19:19	21:21	23:23	1:21	3:24	5:22
13	7:25	9:27	11:22	13:24	15:22	17:24	19:23	21:25	23:27	1:25	3:27	5:26
14	7:29	9:31	11:25	13:28	15:26	17:28	19:26	21:29	23:31	1:29	3:31	5:30
15	7:33	9:35	11:29	13:32	15:30	17:32	19:30	21:33	23:35	1:33	3:35	5:34
16	7:37	9:39	11:33	13:36	15:34	17:36	19:34	21:37	23:39	1:37	3:39	5:38
17	7:41	9:43	11:37	13:40	15:38	17:40	19:38	21:41	23:43	1:41	3:43	5:42
18	7:45	9:47	11:41	13:43	15:42	17:44	19:42	21:44	23:47	1:45	3:47	5:45
19	7:49	9:51	11:45	13:47	15:46	17:48	19:46	21:48	23:51	1:49	3:51	5:49
20	7:53	9:55	11:49	13:51	15:50	17:52	19:50	21:52	23:55	1:53	3:55	5:53
21	7:57	9:59	11:53	13:55	15:54	17:56	19:54	21:56	23:58	1:57	3:59	5:57
22	8:00	10:03	11:57	13:59	15:58	18:00	19:58	22:00	0:02	2:01	4:03	6:01
23	8:04	10:07	12:01	14:03	16:01	18:04	20:02	22:04	0:06	2:05	4:07	6:05
24	8:08	10:11	12:05	14:07	16:05	18:08	20:06	22:08	0:10	2:09	4:11	6:09
25	8:12	10:14	12:09	14:11	16:09	18:12	20:10	22:12	0:14	2:13	4:15	6:13
26	8:16	10:18	12:13	14:15	16:13	18:15	20:14	22:16	0:18	2:16	4:19	6:17
27	8:20	10:22	12:17	14:19	16:17	18:19	20:18	22:20	0:22	2:20	4:23	6:21
28	8:24	10:26	12:21	14:23	16:21	18:23	20:22	22:24	0:26	2:24	4:27	6:25
29	8:28	10:30	12:25	14:27	16:25	18:27	20:26	22:28	0:30	2:28	4:31	6:29
30	8:32		12:29	14:31	16:29	18:31	20:30	22:32	0:34	2:32	4:34	6:33
31	8:36		12:32		16:33		20:33	22:36		2:36		6:37

1929	Jan	Feb	Mar	Apr	May	Jun	Jul	Aug	Sep	Oct	Nov	Dec
1	6:41	8:43	10:33	12:35	14:34	16:36	18:34	20:36	22:39	0:37	2:39	4:37
2	6:45	8:47	10:37	12:39	14:38	16:40	18:38	20:40	22:43	0:41	2:43	4:41
3	6:49	8:51	10:41	12:43	14:42	16:44	18:42	20:44	22:47	0:45	2:47	4:45
4	6:52	8:55	10:45	12:47	14:46	16:48	18:46	20:48	22:51	0:49	2:51	4:49
5	6:56	8:59	10:49	12:51	14:50	16:52	18:50	20:52	22:54	0:53	2:55	4:53
6	7:00	9:03	10:53	12:55	14:53	16:56	18:54	20:56	22:58	0:57	2:59	4:57
7	7:04	9:07	10:57	12:59	14:57	17:00	18:58	21:00	23:02	1:01	3:03	5:01
8	7:08	9:10	11:01	13:03	15:01	17:04	19:02	21:04	23:06	1:05	3:07	5:05
9	7:12	9:14	11:05	13:07	15:05	17:08	19:06	21:08	23:10	1:09	3:11	5:09
10	7:16	9:18	11:09	13:11	15:09	17:11	19:10	21:12	23:14	1:12	3:15	5:13
11	7:20	9:22	11:13	13:15	15:13	17:15	19:14	21:16	23:18	1:16	3:19	5:17
12	7:24	9:26	11:17	13:19	15:17	17:19	19:18	21:20	23:22	1:20	3:23	5:21
13	7:28	9:30	11:21	13:23	15:21	17:23	19:22	21:24	23:26	1:24	3:26	5:25
14	7:32	9:34	11:25	13:27	15:25	17:27	19:26	21:28	23:30	1:28	3:30	5:29
15	7:36	9:38	11:28	13:31	15:29	17:31	19:29	21:32	23:34	1:32	3:34	5:33
16	7:40	9:42	11:32	13:35	15:33	17:35	19:33	21:36	23:38	1:36	3:38	5:37
17	7:44	9:46	11:36	13:39	15:37	17:39	19:37	21:40	23:42	1:40	3:42	5:41
18	7:48	9:50	11:40	13:42	15:41	17:43	19:41	21:43	23:46	1:44	3:46	5:44
19	7:52	9:54	11:44	13:46	15:45	17:47	19:45	21:47	23:50	1:48	3:50	5:48
20	7:56	9:58	11:48	13:50	15:49	17:51	19:49	21:51	23:54	1:52	3:54	5:52
21	7:59	10:02	11:52	13:54	15:53	17:55	19:53	21:55	23:58	1:56	3:58	5:56
22	8:03	10:06	11:56	13:58	15:57	17:59	19:57	21:59	0:01	2:00	4:02	6:00
23	8:07	10:10	12:00	14:02	16:00	18:03	20:01	22:03	0:05	2:04	4:06	6:04
24	8:11	10:14	12:04	14:06	16:04	18:07	20:05	22:07	0:09	2:08	4:10	6:08
25	8:15	10:17	12:08	14:10	16:08	18:11	20:09	22:11	0:13	2:12	4:14	6:12
26	8:19	10:21	12:12	14:14	16:12	18:15	20:13	22:15	0:17	2:16	4:18	6:16
27	8:23	10:25	12:16	14:18	16:16	18:18	20:17	22:19	0:21	2:19	4:22	6:20
28	8:27	10:29	12:20	14:22	16:20	18:22	20:21	22:23	0:25	2:23	4:26	6:24
29	8:31		12:24	14:26	16:24	18:26	20:25	22:27	0:29	2:27	4:30	6:28
30	8:35		12:28	14:30	16:28	18:30	20:29	22:31	0:33	2:31	4:34	6:32
31	8:39		12:32		16:32		20:33	22:35		2:35		6:36

1930	Jan	Feb	Mar	Apr	May	Jun	Jul	Aug	Sep	Oct	Nov	Dec
1	6:40	8:42	10:32	12:35	14:33	16:35	18:33	20:36	22:38	0:36	2:38	4:37
2	6:44	8:46	10:36	12:38	14:37	16:39	18:37	20:39	22:42	0:40	2:42	4:40
3	6:48	8:50	10:40	12:42	14:41	16:43	18:41	20:43	22:46	0:44	2:46	4:44
4	6:52	8:54	10:44	12:46	14:45	16:47	18:45	20:47	22:50	0:48	2:50	4:48
5	6:55	8:58	10:48	12:50	14:49	16:51	18:49	20:51	22:54	0:52	2:54	4:52
6	6:59	9:02	10:52	12:54	14:53	16:55	18:53	20:55	22:57	0:56	2:58	4:56
7	7:03	9:06	10:56	12:58	14:56	16:59	18:57	20:59	23:01	1:00	3:02	5:00
8	7:07	9:10	11:00	13:02	15:00	17:03	19:01	21:03	23:05	1:04	3:06	5:04
9	7:11	9:13	11:04	13:06	15:04	17:07	19:05	21:07	23:09	1:08	3:10	5:08
10	7:15	9:17	11:08	13:10	15:08	17:11	19:09	21:11	23:13	1:11	3:14	5:12
11	7:19	9:21	11:12	13:14	15:12	17:14	19:13	21:15	23:17	1:15	3:18	5:16
12	7:23	9:25	11:16	13:18	15:16	17:18	19:17	21:19	23:21	1:19	3:22	5:20
13	7:27	9:29	11:20	13:22	15:20	17:22	19:21	21:23	23:25	1:23	3:26	5:24
14	7:31	9:33	11:24	13:26	15:24	17:26	19:25	21:27	23:29	1:27	3:29	5:28
15	7:35	9:37	11:27	13:30	15:28	17:30	19:28	21:31	23:33	1:31	3:33	5:32
16	7:39	9:41	11:31	13:34	15:32	17:34	19:32	21:35	23:37	1:35	3:37	5:36
17	7:43	9:45	11:35	13:38	15:36	17:38	19:36	21:39	23:41	1:39	3:41	5:40
18	7:47	9:49	11:39	13:42	15:40	17:42	19:40	21:43	23:45	1:43	3:45	5:44
19	7:51	9:53	11:43	13:45	15:44	17:46	19:44	21:46	23:49	1:47	3:49	5:47
20	7:55	9:57	11:47	13:49	15:48	17:50	19:48	21:50	23:53	1:51	3:53	5:51
21	7:59	10:01	11:51	13:53	15:52	17:54	19:52	21:54	23:57	1:55	3:57	5:55
22	8:02	10:05	11:55	13:57	15:56	17:58	19:56	21:58	0:01	1:59	4:01	5:59
23	8:06	10:09	11:59	14:01	16:00	18:02	20:00	22:02	0:04	2:03	4:05	6:03
24	8:10	10:13	12:03	14:05	16:03	18:06	20:04	22:06	0:08	2:07	4:09	6:07
25	8:14	10:17	12:07	14:09	16:07	18:10	20:08	22:10	0:12	2:11	4:13	6:11
26	8:18	10:20	12:11	14:13	16:11	18:14	20:12	22:14	0:16	2:15	4:17	6:15
27	8:22	10:24	12:15	14:17	16:15	18:18	20:16	22:18	0:20	2:19	4:21	6:19
28	8:26	10:28	12:19	14:21	16:19	18:21	20:20	22:22	0:24	2:22	4:25	6:23
29	8:30		12:23	14:25	16:23	18:25	20:24	22:26	0:28	2:26	4:29	6:27
30	8:34		12:27	14:29	16:27	18:29	20:28	22:30	0:32	2:30	4:33	6:31
31	8:38		12:31		16:31		20:32	22:34		2:34		6:35

1931	Jan	Feb	Mar	Apr	May	Jun	Jul	Aug	Sep	Oct	Nov	Dec
1	6:39	8:41	10:31	12:34	14:32	16:34	18:32	20:35	22:37	0:35	2:37	4:36
2	6:43	8:45	10:35	12:38	14:36	16:38	18:36	20:39	22:41	0:39	2:41	4:39
3	6:47	8:49	10:39	12:41	14:40	16:42	18:40	20:42	22:45	0:43	2:45	4:43
4	6:51	8:53	10:43	12:45	14:44	16:46	18:44	20:46	22:49	0:47	2:49	4:47
5	6:55	8:57	10:47	12:49	14:48	16:50	18:48	20:50	22:53	0:51	2:53	4:51
6	6:58	9:01	10:51	12:53	14:52	16:54	18:52	20:54	22:56	0:55	2:57	4:55
7	7:02	9:05	10:55	12:57	14:55	16:58	18:56	20:58	23:00	0:59	3:01	4:59
8	7:06	9:09	10:59	13:01	14:59	17:02	19:00	21:02	23:04	1:03	3:05	5:03
9	7:10	9:12	11:03	13:05	15:03	17:06	19:04	21:06	23:08	1:07	3:09	5:07
10	7:14	9:16	11:07	13:09	15:07	17:10	19:08	21:10	23:12	1:11	3:13	5:11
11	7:18	9:20	11:11	13:13	15:11	17:13	19:12	21:14	23:16	1:14	3:17	5:15
12	7:22	9:24	11:15	13:17	15:15	17:17	19:16	21:18	23:20	1:18	3:21	5:19
13	7:26	9:28	11:19	13:21	15:19	17:21	19:20	21:22	23:24	1:22	3:25	5:23
14	7:30	9:32	11:23	13:25	15:23	17:25	19:24	21:26	23:28	1:26	3:29	5:27
15	7:34	9:36	11:27	13:29	15:27	17:29	19:28	21:30	23:32	1:30	3:32	5:31
16	7:38	9:40	11:30	13:33	15:31	17:33	19:31	21:34	23:36	1:34	3:36	5:35
17	7:42	9:44	11:34	13:37	15:35	17:37	19:35	21:38	23:40	1:38	3:40	5:39
18	7:46	9:48	11:38	13:41	15:39	17:41	19:39	21:42	23:44	1:42	3:44	5:43
19	7:50	9:52	11:42	13:45	15:43	17:45	19:43	21:46	23:48	1:46	3:48	5:47
20	7:54	9:56	11:46	13:48	15:47	17:49	19:47	21:49	23:52	1:50	3:52	5:50
21	7:58	10:00	11:50	13:52	15:51	17:53	19:51	21:53	23:56	1:54	3:56	5:54
22	8:02	10:04	11:54	13:56	15:55	17:57	19:55	21:57	0:00	1:58	4:00	5:58
23	8:05	10:08	11:58	14:00	15:59	18:01	19:59	22:01	0:04	2:02	4:04	6:02
24	8:09	10:12	12:02	14:04	16:03	18:05	20:03	22:05	0:07	2:06	4:08	6:06
25	8:13	10:16	12:06	14:08	16:06	18:09	20:07	22:09	0:11	2:10	4:12	6:10
26	8:17	10:20	12:10	14:12	16:10	18:13	20:11	22:13	0:15	2:14	4:16	6:14
27	8:21	10:23	12:14	14:16	16:14	18:17	20:15	22:17	0:19	2:18	4:20	6:18
28	8:25	10:27	12:18	14:20	16:18	18:21	20:19	22:21	0:23	2:22	4:24	6:22
29	8:29		12:22	14:24	16:22	18:24	20:23	22:25	0:27	2:25	4:28	6:26
30	8:33		12:26	14:28	16:26	18:28	20:27	22:29	0:31	2:29	4:32	6:30
31	8:37		12:30		16:30		20:31	22:33		2:33		6:34

1932	Jan	Feb	Dec	Apr	May	Jun	Jul	Aug	Sep	Oct	Nov	Dec
1	6:38	8:40	10:34	12:37	14:35	16:37	18:35	20:38	22:40	0:38	2:40	4:39
2	6:42	8:44	10:38	12:40	14:39	16:41	18:39	20:41	22:44	0:42	2:44	4:42
3	6:46	8:48	10:42	12:44	14:43	16:45	18:43	20:45	22:48	0:46	2:48	4:46
4	6:50	8:52	10:46	12:48	14:47	16:49	18:47	20:49	22:52	0:50	2:52	4:50
5	6:54	8:56	10:50	12:52	14:51	16:53	18:51	20:53	22:56	0:54	2:56	4:54
6	6:57	9:00	10:54	12:56	14:55	16:57	18:55	20:57	22:59	0:58	3:00	4:58
7	7:01	9:04	10:58	13:00	14:58	17:01	18:59	21:01	23:03	1:02	3:04	5:02
8	7:05	9:08	11:02	13:04	15:02	17:05	19:03	21:05	23:07	1:06	3:08	5:06
9	7:09	9:12	11:06	13:08	15:06	17:09	19:07	21:09	23:11	1:10	3:12	5:10
10	7:13	9:15	11:10	13:12	15:10	17:13	19:11	21:13	23:15	1:14	3:16	5:14
11	7:17	9:19	11:14	13:16	15:14	17:16	19:15	21:17	23:19	1:17	3:20	5:18
12	7:21	9:23	11:18	13:20	15:18	17:20	19:19	21:21	23:23	1:21	3:24	5:22
13	7:25	9:27	11:22	13:24	15:22	17:24	19:23	21:25	23:27	1:25	3:28	5:26
14	7:29	9:31	11:26	13:28	15:26	17:28	19:27	21:29	23:31	1:29	3:32	5:30
15	7:33	9:35	11:30	13:32	15:30	17:32	19:31	21:33	23:35	1:33	3:35	5:34
16	7:37	9:39	11:33	13:36	15:34	17:36	19:34	21:37	23:39	1:37	3:39	5:38
17	7:41	9:43	11:37	13:40	15:38	17:40	19:38	21:41	23:43	1:41	3:43	5:42
18	7:45	9:47	11:41	13:44	15:42	17:44	19:42	21:45	23:47	1:45	3:47	5:46
19	7:49	9:51	11:45	13:48	15:46	17:48	19:46	21:49	23:51	1:49	3:51	5:50
20	7:53	9:55	11:49	13:51	15:50	17:52	19:50	21:52	23:55	1:53	3:55	5:53
21	7:57	9:59	11:53	13:55	15:54	17:56	19:54	21:56	23:59	1:57	3:59	5:57
22	8:01	10:03	11:57	13:59	15:58	18:00	19:58	22:00	0:03	2:01	4:03	6:01
23	8:05	10:07	12:01	14:03	16:02	18:04	20:02	22:04	0:07	2:05	4:07	6:05
24	8:08	10:11	12:05	14:07	16:06	18:08	20:06	22:08	0:10	2:09	4:11	6:09
25	8:12	10:15	12:09	14:11	16:09	18:12	20:10	22:12	0:14	2:13	4:15	6:13
26	8:16	10:19	12:13	14:15	16:13	18:16	20:14	22:16	0:18	2:17	4:19	6:17
27	8:20	10:23	12:17	14:19	16:17	18:20	20:18	22:20	0:22	2:21	4:23	6:21
28	8:24	10:26	12:21	14:23	16:21	18:24	20:22	22:24	0:26	2:24	4:27	6:25
29	8:28	10:30	12:25	14:27	16:25	18:27	20:26	22:28	0:30	2:28	4:31	6:29
30	8:32		12:29	14:31	16:29	18:31	20:30	22:32	0:34	2:32	4:35	6:33
31	8:36		12:33		16:33		20:34	22:36		2:36		6:37

1933	Jan	Feb	Mar	Apr	May	Jun	Jul	Aug	Sep	Oct	Nov	Dec
1	6:41	8:43	10:33	12:36	14:34	16:36	18:34	20:37	22:39	0:37	2:39	4:38
2	6:45	8:47	10:37	12:40	14:38	16:40	18:38	20:41	22:43	0:41	2:43	4:42
3	6:49	8:51	10:41	12:43	14:42	16:44	18:42	20:44	22:47	0:45	2:47	4:45
4	6:53	8:55	10:45	12:47	14:46	16:48	18:46	20:48	22:51	0:49	2:51	4:49
5	6:57	8:59	10:49	12:51	14:50	16:52	18:50	20:52	22:55	0:53	2:55	4:53
6	7:00	9:03	10:53	12:55	14:54	16:56	18:54	20:56	22:59	0:57	2:59	4:57
7	7:04	9:07	10:57	12:59	14:58	17:00	18:58	21:00	23:02	1:01	3:03	5:01
8	7:08	9:11	11:01	13:03	15:01	17:04	19:02	21:04	23:06	1:05	3:07	5:05
9	7:12	9:15	11:05	13:07	15:05	17:08	19:06	21:08	23:10	1:09	3:11	5:09
10	7:16	9:18	11:09	13:11	15:09	17:12	19:10	21:12	23:14	1:13	3:15	5:13
11	7:20	9:22	11:13	13:15	15:13	17:16	19:14	21:16	23:18	1:17	3:19	5:17
12	7:24	9:26	11:17	13:19	15:17	17:19	19:18	21:20	23:22	1:20	3:23	5:21
13	7:28	9:30	11:21	13:23	15:21	17:23	19:22	21:24	23:26	1:24	3:27	5:25
14	7:32	9:34	11:25	13:27	15:25	17:27	19:26	21:28	23:30	1:28	3:31	5:29
15	7:36	9:38	11:29	13:31	15:29	17:31	19:30	21:32	23:34	1:32	3:35	5:33
16	7:40	9:42	11:33	13:35	15:33	17:35	19:34	21:36	23:38	1:36	3:38	5:37
17	7:44	9:46	11:36	13:39	15:37	17:39	19:37	21:40	23:42	1:40	3:42	5:41
18	7:48	9:50	11:40	13:43	15:41	17:43	19:41	21:44	23:46	1:44	3:46	5:45
19	7:52	9:54	11:44	13:47	15:45	17:47	19:45	21:48	23:50	1:48	3:50	5:49
20	7:56	9:58	11:48	13:51	15:49	17:51	19:49	21:52	23:54	1:52	3:54	5:52
21	8:00	10:02	11:52	13:54	15:53	17:55	19:53	21:55	23:58	1:56	3:58	5:56
22	8:04	10:06	11:56	13:58	15:57	17:59	19:57	21:59	0:02	2:00	4:02	6:00
23	8:08	10:10	12:00	14:02	16:01	18:03	20:01	22:03	0:06	2:04	4:06	6:04
24	8:11	10:14	12:04	14:06	16:05	18:07	20:05	22:07	0:09	2:08	4:10	6:08
25	8:15	10:18	12:08	14:10	16:08	18:11	20:09	22:11	0:13	2:12	4:14	6:12
26	8:19	10:22	12:12	14:14	16:12	18:15	20:13	22:15	0:17	2:16	4:18	6:16
27	8:23	10:25	12:16	14:18	16:16	18:19	20:17	22:19	0:21	2:20	4:22	6:20
28	8:27	10:29	12:20	14:22	16:20	18:23	20:21	22:23	0:25	2:24	4:26	6:24
29	8:31		12:24	14:26	16:24	18:26	20:25	22:27	0:29	2:27	4:30	6:28
30	8:35		12:28	14:30	16:28	18:30	20:29	22:31	0:33	2:31	4:34	6:32
31	8:39		12:32		16:32		20:33	22:35		2:35		6:36

1934	Jan	Feb	Mar	Apr	May	Jun	Jul	Aug	Sep	Oct	Nov	Dec
1	6:40	8:42	10:32	12:35	14:33	16:35	18:33	20:36	22:38	0:36	2:38	4:37
2	6:44	8:46	10:36	12:39	14:37	16:39	18:37	20:40	22:42	0:40	2:42	4:41
3	6:48	8:50	10:40	12:43	14:41	16:43	18:41	20:44	22:46	0:44	2:46	4:45
4	6:52	8:54	10:44	12:46	14:45	16:47	18:45	20:47	22:50	0:48	2:50	4:48
5	6:56	8:58	10:48	12:50	14:49	16:51	18:49	20:51	22:54	0:52	2:54	4:52
6	7:00	9:02	10:52	12:54	14:53	16:55	18:53	20:55	22:58	0:56	2:58	4:56
7	7:03	9:06	10:56	12:58	14:57	16:59	18:57	20:59	23:02	1:00	3:02	5:00
8	7:07	9:10	11:00	13:02	15:01	17:03	19:01	21:03	23:05	1:04	3:06	5:04
9	7:11	9:14	11:04	13:06	15:04	17:07	19:05	21:07	23:09	1:08	3:10	5:08
10	7:15	9:18	11:08	13:10	15:08	17:11	19:09	21:11	23:13	1:12	3:14	5:12
11	7:19	9:21	11:12	13:14	15:12	17:15	19:13	21:15	23:17	1:16	3:18	5:16
12	7:23	9:25	11:16	13:18	15:16	17:19	19:17	21:19	23:21	1:20	3:22	5:20
13	7:27	9:29	11:20	13:22	15:20	17:22	19:21	21:23	23:25	1:23	3:26	5:24
14	7:31	9:33	11:24	13:26	15:24	17:26	19:25	21:27	23:29	1:27	3:30	5:28
15	7:35	9:37	11:28	13:30	15:28	17:30	19:29	21:31	23:33	1:31	3:34	5:32
16	7:39	9:41	11:32	13:34	15:32	17:34	19:33	21:35	23:37	1:35	3:37	5:36
17	7:43	9:45	11:36	13:38	15:36	17:38	19:36	21:39	23:41	1:39	3:41	5:40
18	7:47	9:49	11:39	13:42	15:40	17:42	19:40	21:43	23:45	1:43	3:45	5:44
19	7:51	9:53	11:43	13:46	15:44	17:46	19:44	21:47	23:49	1:47	3:49	5:48
20	7:55	9:57	11:47	13:50	15:48	17:50	19:48	21:51	23:53	1:51	3:53	5:52
21	7:59	10:01	11:51	13:53	15:52	17:54	19:52	21:54	23:57	1:55	3:57	5:55
22	8:03	10:05	11:55	13:57	15:56	17:58	19:56	21:58	0:01	1:59	4:01	5:59
23	8:07	10:09	11:59	14:01	16:00	18:02	20:00	22:02	0:05	2:03	4:05	6:03
24	8:10	10:13	12:03	14:05	16:04	18:06	20:04	22:06	0:09	2:07	4:09	6:07
25	8:14	10:17	12:07	14:09	16:08	18:10	20:08	22:10	0:12	2:11	4:13	6:11
26	8:18	10:21	12:11	14:13	16:11	18:14	20:12	22:14	0:16	2:15	4:17	6:15
27	8:22	10:25	12:15	14:17	16:15	18:18	20:16	22:18	0:20	2:19	4:21	6:19
28	8:26	10:28	12:19	14:21	16:19	18:22	20:20	22:22	0:24	2:23	4:25	6:23
29	8:30		12:23	14:25	16:23	18:26	20:24	22:26	0:28	2:27	4:29	6:27
30	8:34		12:27	14:29	16:27	18:29	20:28	22:30	0:32	2:30	4:33	6:31
31	8:38		12:31		16:31		20:32	22:34		2:34		6:35

1935	Jan	Feb	Mar	Apr	May	Jun	Jul	Aug	Sep	Oct	Nov	Dec
1	6:39	8:41	10:31	12:34	14:32	16:34	18:32	20:35	22:37	0:35	2:37	4:36
2	6:43	8:45	10:35	12:38	14:36	16:38	18:36	20:39	22:41	0:39	2:41	4:40
3	6:47	8:49	10:39	12:42	14:40	16:42	18:40	20:43	22:45	0:43	2:45	4:44
4	6:51	8:53	10:43	12:46	14:44	16:46	18:44	20:47	22:49	0:47	2:49	4:48
5	6:55	8:57	10:47	12:49	14:48	16:50	18:48	20:50	22:53	0:51	2:53	4:51
6	6:59	9:01	10:51	12:53	14:52	16:54	18:52	20:54	22:57	0:55	2:57	4:55
7	7:03	9:05	10:55	12:57	14:56	16:58	18:56	20:58	23:01	0:59	3:01	4:59
8	7:06	9:09	10:59	13:01	15:00	17:02	19:00	21:02	23:05	1:03	3:05	5:03
9	7:10	9:13	11:03	13:05	15:04	17:06	19:04	21:06	23:08	1:07	3:09	5:07
10	7:14	9:17	11:07	13:09	15:07	17:10	19:08	21:10	23:12	1:11	3:13	5:11
11	7:18	9:21	11:11	13:13	15:11	17:14	19:12	21:14	23:16	1:15	3:17	5:15
12	7:22	9:24	11:15	13:17	15:15	17:18	19:16	21:18	23:20	1:19	3:21	5:19
13	7:26	9:28	11:19	13:21	15:19	17:21	19:20	21:22	23:24	1:22	3:25	5:23
14	7:30	9:32	11:23	13:25	15:23	17:25	19:24	21:26	23:28	1:26	3:29	5:27
15	7:34	9:36	11:27	13:29	15:27	17:29	19:28	21:30	23:32	1:30	3:33	5:31
16	7:38	9:40	11:31	13:33	15:31	17:33	19:32	21:34	23:36	1:34	3:37	5:35
17	7:42	9:44	11:35	13:37	15:35	17:37	19:36	21:38	23:40	1:38	3:40	5:39
18	7:46	9:48	11:38	13:41	15:39	17:41	19:39	21:42	23:44	1:42	3:44	5:43
19	7:50	9:52	11:42	13:45	15:43	17:45	19:43	21:46	23:48	1:46	3:48	5:47
20	7:54	9:56	11:46	13:49	15:47	17:49	19:47	21:50	23:52	1:50	3:52	5:51
21	7:58	10:00	11:50	13:53	15:51	17:53	19:51	21:54	23:56	1:54	3:56	5:55
22	8:02	10:04	11:54	13:56	15:55	17:57	19:55	21:57	0:00	1:58	4:00	5:58
23	8:06	10:08	11:58	14:00	15:59	18:01	19:59	22:01	0:04	2:02	4:04	6:02
24	8:10	10:12	12:02	14:04	16:03	18:05	20:03	22:05	0:08	2:06	4:08	6:06
25	8:13	10:16	12:06	14:08	16:07	18:09	20:07	22:09	0:12	2:10	4:12	6:10
26	8:17	10:20	12:10	14:12	16:11	18:13	20:11	22:13	0:15	2:14	4:16	6:14
27	8:21	10:24	12:14	14:16	16:14	18:17	20:15	22:17	0:19	2:18	4:20	6:18
28	8:25	10:28	12:18	14:20	16:18	18:21	20:19	22:21	0:23	2:22	4:24	6:22
29	8:29		12:22	14:24	16:22	18:25	20:23	22:25	0:27	2:26	4:28	6:26
30	8:33		12:26	14:28	16:26	18:29	20:27	22:29	0:31	2:30	4:32	6:30
31	8:37		12:30		16:30		20:31	22:33		2:33		6:34

1936	Jan	Feb	Dec	Apr	May	Jun	Jul	Aug	Sep	Oct	Nov	Dec
1	6:38	8:40	10:34	12:37	14:35	16:37	18:35	20:38	22:40	0:38	2:40	4:39
2	6:42	8:44	10:38	12:41	14:39	16:41	18:39	20:42	22:44	0:42	2:44	4:43
3	6:46	8:48	10:42	12:45	14:43	16:45	18:43	20:46	22:48	0:46	2:48	4:47
4	6:50	8:52	10:46	12:49	14:47	16:49	18:47	20:49	22:52	0:50	2:52	4:50
5	6:54	8:56	10:50	12:52	14:51	16:53	18:51	20:53	22:56	0:54	2:56	4:54
6	6:58	9:00	10:54	12:56	14:55	16:57	18:55	20:57	23:00	0:58	3:00	4:58
7	7:02	9:04	10:58	13:00	14:59	17:01	18:59	21:01	23:04	1:02	3:04	5:02
8	7:05	9:08	11:02	13:04	15:03	17:05	19:03	21:05	23:07	1:06	3:08	5:06
9	7:09	9:12	11:06	13:08	15:06	17:09	19:07	21:09	23:11	1:10	3:12	5:10
10	7:13	9:16	11:10	13:12	15:10	17:13	19:11	21:13	23:15	1:14	3:16	5:14
11	7:17	9:20	11:14	13:16	15:14	17:17	19:15	21:17	23:19	1:18	3:20	5:18
12	7:21	9:23	11:18	13:20	15:18	17:21	19:19	21:21	23:23	1:22	3:24	5:22
13	7:25	9:27	11:22	13:24	15:22	17:24	19:23	21:25	23:27	1:25	3:28	5:26
14	7:29	9:31	11:26	13:28	15:26	17:28	19:27	21:29	23:31	1:29	3:32	5:30
15	7:33	9:35	11:30	13:32	15:30	17:32	19:31	21:33	23:35	1:33	3:36	5:34
16	7:37	9:39	11:34	13:36	15:34	17:36	19:35	21:37	23:39	1:37	3:40	5:38
17	7:41	9:43	11:38	13:40	15:38	17:40	19:39	21:41	23:43	1:41	3:43	5:42
18	7:45	9:47	11:41	13:44	15:42	17:44	19:42	21:45	23:47	1:45	3:47	5:46
19	7:49	9:51	11:45	13:48	15:46	17:48	19:46	21:49	23:51	1:49	3:51	5:50
20	7:53	9:55	11:49	13:52	15:50	17:52	19:50	21:53	23:55	1:53	3:55	5:54
21	7:57	9:59	11:53	13:56	15:54	17:56	19:54	21:57	23:59	1:57	3:59	5:58
22	8:01	10:03	11:57	13:59	15:58	18:00	19:58	22:00	0:03	2:01	4:03	6:01
23	8:05	10:07	12:01	14:03	16:02	18:04	20:02	22:04	0:07	2:05	4:07	6:05
24	8:09	10:11	12:05	14:07	16:06	18:08	20:06	22:08	0:11	2:09	4:11	6:09
25	8:13	10:15	12:09	14:11	16:10	18:12	20:10	22:12	0:15	2:13	4:15	6:13
26	8:16	10:19	12:13	14:15	16:14	18:16	20:14	22:16	0:18	2:17	4:19	6:17
27	8:20	10:23	12:17	14:19	16:17	18:20	20:18	22:20	0:22	2:21	4:23	6:21
28	8:24	10:27	12:21	14:23	16:21	18:24	20:22	22:24	0:26	2:25	4:27	6:25
29	8:28	10:31	12:25	14:27	16:25	18:28	20:26	22:28	0:30	2:29	4:31	6:29
30	8:32		12:29	14:31	16:29	18:32	20:30	22:32	0:34	2:33	4:35	6:33
31	8:36		12:33		16:33		20:34	22:36		2:36		6:37

1937	Jan	Feb	Mar	Apr	May	Jun	Jul	Aug	Sep	Oct	Nov	Dec
1	6:41	8:43	10:34	12:36	14:34	16:36	18:34	20:37	22:39	0:37	2:39	4:38
2	6:45	8:47	10:37	12:40	14:38	16:40	18:38	20:41	22:43	0:41	2:43	4:42
3	6:49	8:51	10:41	12:44	14:42	16:44	18:42	20:45	22:47	0:45	2:47	4:46
4	6:53	8:55	10:45	12:48	14:46	16:48	18:46	20:49	22:51	0:49	2:51	4:50
5	6:57	8:59	10:49	12:51	14:50	16:52	18:50	20:52	22:55	0:53	2:55	4:53
6	7:01	9:03	10:53	12:55	14:54	16:56	18:54	20:56	22:59	0:57	2:59	4:57
7	7:05	9:07	10:57	12:59	14:58	17:00	18:58	21:00	23:03	1:01	3:03	5:01
8	7:08	9:11	11:01	13:03	15:02	17:04	19:02	21:04	23:07	1:05	3:07	5:05
9	7:12	9:15	11:05	13:07	15:06	17:08	19:06	21:08	23:10	1:09	3:11	5:09
10	7:16	9:19	11:09	13:11	15:09	17:12	19:10	21:12	23:14	1:13	3:15	5:13
11	7:20	9:23	11:13	13:15	15:13	17:16	19:14	21:16	23:18	1:17	3:19	5:17
12	7:24	9:26	11:17	13:19	15:17	17:20	19:18	21:20	23:22	1:21	3:23	5:21
13	7:28	9:30	11:21	13:23	15:21	17:24	19:22	21:24	23:26	1:25	3:27	5:25
14	7:32	9:34	11:25	13:27	15:25	17:27	19:26	21:28	23:30	1:28	3:31	5:29
15	7:36	9:38	11:29	13:31	15:29	17:31	19:30	21:32	23:34	1:32	3:35	5:33
16	7:40	9:42	11:33	13:35	15:33	17:35	19:34	21:36	23:38	1:36	3:39	5:37
17	7:44	9:46	11:37	13:39	15:37	17:39	19:38	21:40	23:42	1:40	3:43	5:41
18	7:48	9:50	11:41	13:43	15:41	17:43	19:42	21:44	23:46	1:44	3:46	5:45
19	7:52	9:54	11:44	13:47	15:45	17:47	19:45	21:48	23:50	1:48	3:50	5:49
20	7:56	9:58	11:48	13:51	15:49	17:51	19:49	21:52	23:54	1:52	3:54	5:53
21	8:00	10:02	11:52	13:55	15:53	17:55	19:53	21:56	23:58	1:56	3:58	5:57
22	8:04	10:06	11:56	13:59	15:57	17:59	19:57	22:00	0:02	2:00	4:02	6:01
23	8:08	10:10	12:00	14:02	16:01	18:03	20:01	22:03	0:06	2:04	4:06	6:04
24	8:12	10:14	12:04	14:06	16:05	18:07	20:05	22:07	0:10	2:08	4:10	6:08
25	8:16	10:18	12:08	14:10	16:09	18:11	20:09	22:11	0:14	2:12	4:14	6:12
26	8:19	10:22	12:12	14:14	16:13	18:15	20:13	22:15	0:18	2:16	4:18	6:16
27	8:23	10:26	12:16	14:18	16:17	18:19	20:17	22:19	0:21	2:20	4:22	6:20
28	8:27	10:30	12:20	14:22	16:20	18:23	20:21	22:23	0:25	2:24	4:26	6:24
29	8:31		12:24	14:26	16:24	18:27	20:25	22:27	0:29	2:28	4:30	6:28
30	8:35		12:28	14:30	16:28	18:31	20:29	22:31	0:33	2:32	4:34	6:32
31	8:39		12:32		16:32		20:33	22:35		2:35		6:36

1938	Jan	Feb	Mar	Apr	May	Jun	Jul	Aug	Sep	Oct	Nov	Dec
1	6:40	8:42	10:33	12:35	14:33	16:35	18:34	20:36	22:38	0:36	2:38	4:37
2	6:44	8:46	10:36	12:39	14:37	16:39	18:37	20:40	22:42	0:40	2:42	4:41
3	6:48	8:50	10:40	12:43	14:41	16:43	18:41	20:44	22:46	0:44	2:46	4:45
4	6:52	8:54	10:44	12:47	14:45	16:47	18:45	20:48	22:50	0:48	2:50	4:49
5	6:56	8:58	10:48	12:51	14:49	16:51	18:49	20:52	22:54	0:52	2:54	4:53
6	7:00	9:02	10:52	12:54	14:53	16:55	18:53	20:55	22:58	0:56	2:58	4:56
7	7:04	9:06	10:56	12:58	14:57	16:59	18:57	20:59	23:02	1:00	3:02	5:00
8	7:08	9:10	11:00	13:02	15:01	17:03	19:01	21:03	23:06	1:04	3:06	5:04
9	7:11	9:14	11:04	13:06	15:05	17:07	19:05	21:07	23:10	1:08	3:10	5:08
10	7:15	9:18	11:08	13:10	15:09	17:11	19:09	21:11	23:13	1:12	3:14	5:12
11	7:19	9:22	11:12	13:14	15:12	17:15	19:13	21:15	23:17	1:16	3:18	5:16
12	7:23	9:26	11:16	13:18	15:16	17:19	19:17	21:19	23:21	1:20	3:22	5:20
13	7:27	9:29	11:20	13:22	15:20	17:23	19:21	21:23	23:25	1:24	3:26	5:24
14	7:31	9:33	11:24	13:26	15:24	17:27	19:25	21:27	23:29	1:28	3:30	5:28
15	7:35	9:37	11:28	13:30	15:28	17:30	19:29	21:31	23:33	1:31	3:34	5:32
16	7:39	9:41	11:32	13:34	15:32	17:34	19:33	21:35	23:37	1:35	3:38	5:36
17	7:43	9:45	11:36	13:38	15:36	17:38	19:37	21:39	23:41	1:39	3:42	5:40
18	7:47	9:49	11:40	13:42	15:40	17:42	19:41	21:43	23:45	1:43	3:46	5:44
19	7:51	9:53	11:44	13:46	15:44	17:46	19:45	21:47	23:49	1:47	3:49	5:48
20	7:55	9:57	11:47	13:50	15:48	17:50	19:48	21:51	23:53	1:51	3:53	5:52
21	7:59	10:01	11:51	13:54	15:52	17:54	19:52	21:55	23:57	1:55	3:57	5:56
22	8:03	10:05	11:55	13:58	15:56	17:58	19:56	21:59	0:01	1:59	4:01	6:00
23	8:07	10:09	11:59	14:02	16:00	18:02	20:00	22:02	0:05	2:03	4:05	6:03
24	8:11	10:13	12:03	14:05	16:04	18:06	20:04	22:06	0:09	2:07	4:09	6:07
25	8:15	10:17	12:07	14:09	16:08	18:10	20:08	22:10	0:13	2:11	4:13	6:11
26	8:18	10:21	12:11	14:13	16:12	18:14	20:12	22:14	0:17	2:15	4:17	6:15
27	8:22	10:25	12:15	14:17	16:16	18:18	20:16	22:18	0:20	2:19	4:21	6:19
28	8:26	10:29	12:19	14:21	16:19	18:22	20:20	22:22	0:24	2:23	4:25	6:23
29	8:30		12:23	14:25	16:23	18:26	20:24	22:26	0:28	2:27	4:29	6:27
30	8:34		12:27	14:29	16:27	18:30	20:28	22:30	0:32	2:31	4:33	6:31
31	8:38		12:31		16:31		20:32	22:34		2:35		6:35

1939	Jan	Feb	Mar	Apr	May	Jun	Jul	Aug	Sep	Oct	Nov	Dec
1	6:39	8:41	10:32	12:34	14:32	16:34	18:33	20:35	22:37	0:35	2:38	4:36
2	6:43	8:45	10:36	12:38	14:36	16:38	18:37	20:39	22:41	0:39	2:41	4:40
3	6:47	8:49	10:39	12:42	14:40	16:42	18:40	20:43	22:45	0:43	2:45	4:44
4	6:51	8:53	10:43	12:46	14:44	16:46	18:44	20:47	22:49	0:47	2:49	4:48
5	6:55	8:57	10:47	12:50	14:48	16:50	18:48	20:51	22:53	0:51	2:53	4:52
6	6:59	9:01	10:51	12:54	14:52	16:54	18:52	20:55	22:57	0:55	2:57	4:56
7	7:03	9:05	10:55	12:57	14:56	16:58	18:56	20:58	23:01	0:59	3:01	4:59
8	7:07	9:09	10:59	13:01	15:00	17:02	19:00	21:02	23:05	1:03	3:05	5:03
9	7:11	9:13	11:03	13:05	15:04	17:06	19:04	21:06	23:09	1:07	3:09	5:07
10	7:14	9:17	11:07	13:09	15:08	17:10	19:08	21:10	23:13	1:11	3:13	5:11
11	7:18	9:21	11:11	13:13	15:12	17:14	19:12	21:14	23:16	1:15	3:17	5:15
12	7:22	9:25	11:15	13:17	15:15	17:18	19:16	21:18	23:20	1:19	3:21	5:19
13	7:26	9:29	11:19	13:21	15:19	17:22	19:20	21:22	23:24	1:23	3:25	5:23
14	7:30	9:32	11:23	13:25	15:23	17:26	19:24	21:26	23:28	1:27	3:29	5:27
15	7:34	9:36	11:27	13:29	15:27	17:30	19:28	21:30	23:32	1:31	3:33	5:31
16	7:38	9:40	11:31	13:33	15:31	17:33	19:32	21:34	23:36	1:34	3:37	5:35
17	7:42	9:44	11:35	13:37	15:35	17:37	19:36	21:38	23:40	1:38	3:41	5:39
18	7:46	9:48	11:39	13:41	15:39	17:41	19:40	21:42	23:44	1:42	3:45	5:43
19	7:50	9:52	11:43	13:45	15:43	17:45	19:44	21:46	23:48	1:46	3:48	5:47
20	7:54	9:56	11:47	13:49	15:47	17:49	19:47	21:50	23:52	1:50	3:52	5:51
21	7:58	10:00	11:50	13:53	15:51	17:53	19:51	21:54	23:56	1:54	3:56	5:55
22	8:02	10:04	11:54	13:57	15:55	17:57	19:55	21:58	0:00	1:58	4:00	5:59
23	8:06	10:08	11:58	14:01	15:59	18:01	19:59	22:02	0:04	2:02	4:04	6:03
24	8:10	10:12	12:02	14:04	16:03	18:05	20:03	22:05	0:08	2:06	4:08	6:06
25	8:14	10:16	12:06	14:08	16:07	18:09	20:07	22:09	0:12	2:10	4:12	6:10
26	8:18	10:20	12:10	14:12	16:11	18:13	20:11	22:13	0:16	2:14	4:16	6:14
27	8:21	10:24	12:14	14:16	16:15	18:17	20:15	22:17	0:20	2:18	4:20	6:18
28	8:25	10:28	12:18	14:20	16:19	18:21	20:19	22:21	0:23	2:22	4:24	6:22
29	8:29		12:22	14:24	16:22	18:25	20:23	22:25	0:27	2:26	4:28	6:26
30	8:33		12:26	14:28	16:26	18:29	20:27	22:29	0:31	2:30	4:32	6:30
31	8:37		12:30		16:30		20:31	22:33		2:34		6:34

1940	Jan	Feb	Dec	Apr	May	Jun	Jul	Aug	Sep	Oct	Nov	Dec
1	6:38	8:40	10:35	12:37	14:35	16:37	18:36	20:38	22:40	0:38	2:41	4:39
2	6:42	8:44	10:39	12:41	14:39	16:41	18:40	20:42	22:44	0:42	2:44	4:43
3	6:46	8:48	10:42	12:45	14:43	16:45	18:43	20:46	22:48	0:46	2:48	4:47
4	6:50	8:52	10:46	12:49	14:47	16:49	18:47	20:50	22:52	0:50	2:52	4:51
5	6:54	8:56	10:50	12:53	14:51	16:53	18:51	20:54	22:56	0:54	2:56	4:55
6	6:58	9:00	10:54	12:57	14:55	16:57	18:55	20:58	23:00	0:58	3:00	4:59
7	7:02	9:04	10:58	13:00	14:59	17:01	18:59	21:01	23:04	1:02	3:04	5:02
8	7:06	9:08	11:02	13:04	15:03	17:05	19:03	21:05	23:08	1:06	3:08	5:06
9	7:10	9:12	11:06	13:08	15:07	17:09	19:07	21:09	23:12	1:10	3:12	5:10
10	7:14	9:16	11:10	13:12	15:11	17:13	19:11	21:13	23:15	1:14	3:16	5:14
11	7:17	9:20	11:14	13:16	15:15	17:17	19:15	21:17	23:19	1:18	3:20	5:18
12	7:21	9:24	11:18	13:20	15:18	17:21	19:19	21:21	23:23	1:22	3:24	5:22
13	7:25	9:28	11:22	13:24	15:22	17:25	19:23	21:25	23:27	1:26	3:28	5:26
14	7:29	9:31	11:26	13:28	15:26	17:29	19:27	21:29	23:31	1:30	3:32	5:30
15	7:33	9:35	11:30	13:32	15:30	17:32	19:31	21:33	23:35	1:33	3:36	5:34
16	7:37	9:39	11:34	13:36	15:34	17:36	19:35	21:37	23:39	1:37	3:40	5:38
17	7:41	9:43	11:38	13:40	15:38	17:40	19:39	21:41	23:43	1:41	3:44	5:42
18	7:45	9:47	11:42	13:44	15:42	17:44	19:43	21:45	23:47	1:45	3:48	5:46
19	7:49	9:51	11:46	13:48	15:46	17:48	19:47	21:49	23:51	1:49	3:51	5:50
20	7:53	9:55	11:49	13:52	15:50	17:52	19:50	21:53	23:55	1:53	3:55	5:54
21	7:57	9:59	11:53	13:56	15:54	17:56	19:54	21:57	23:59	1:57	3:59	5:58
22	8:01	10:03	11:57	14:00	15:58	18:00	19:58	22:01	0:03	2:01	4:03	6:02
23	8:05	10:07	12:01	14:04	16:02	18:04	20:02	22:05	0:07	2:05	4:07	6:06
24	8:09	10:11	12:05	14:07	16:06	18:08	20:06	22:08	0:11	2:09	4:11	6:09
25	8:13	10:15	12:09	14:11	16:10	18:12	20:10	22:12	0:15	2:13	4:15	6:13
26	8:17	10:19	12:13	14:15	16:14	18:16	20:14	22:16	0:19	2:17	4:19	6:17
27	8:21	10:23	12:17	14:19	16:18	18:20	20:18	22:20	0:23	2:21	4:23	6:21
28	8:24	10:27	12:21	14:23	16:22	18:24	20:22	22:24	0:26	2:25	4:27	6:25
29	8:28	10:31	12:25	14:27	16:25	18:28	20:26	22:28	0:30	2:29	4:31	6:29
30	8:32		12:29	14:31	16:29	18:32	20:30	22:32	0:34	2:33	4:35	6:33
31	8:36		12:33		16:33		20:34	22:36		2:37		6:37

1941	Jan	Feb	Mar	Apr	May	Jun	Jul	Aug	Sep	Oct	Nov	Dec
1	6:41	8:43	10:34	12:36	14:34	16:36	18:35	20:37	22:39	0:37	2:40	4:38
2	6:45	8:47	10:38	12:40	14:38	16:40	18:39	20:41	22:43	0:41	2:44	4:42
3	6:49	8:51	10:42	12:44	14:42	16:44	18:43	20:45	22:47	0:45	2:47	4:46
4	6:53	8:55	10:45	12:48	14:46	16:48	18:46	20:49	22:51	0:49	2:51	4:50
5	6:57	8:59	10:49	12:52	14:50	16:52	18:50	20:53	22:55	0:53	2:55	4:54
6	7:01	9:03	10:53	12:56	14:54	16:56	18:54	20:57	22:59	0:57	2:59	4:58
7	7:05	9:07	10:57	12:59	14:58	17:00	18:58	21:00	23:03	1:01	3:03	5:01
8	7:09	9:11	11:01	13:03	15:02	17:04	19:02	21:04	23:07	1:05	3:07	5:05
9	7:13	9:15	11:05	13:07	15:06	17:08	19:06	21:08	23:11	1:09	3:11	5:09
10	7:16	9:19	11:09	13:11	15:10	17:12	19:10	21:12	23:15	1:13	3:15	5:13
11	7:20	9:23	11:13	13:15	15:14	17:16	19:14	21:16	23:18	1:17	3:19	5:17
12	7:24	9:27	11:17	13:19	15:17	17:20	19:18	21:20	23:22	1:21	3:23	5:21
13	7:28	9:31	11:21	13:23	15:21	17:24	19:22	21:24	23:26	1:25	3:27	5:25
14	7:32	9:34	11:25	13:27	15:25	17:28	19:26	21:28	23:30	1:29	3:31	5:29
15	7:36	9:38	11:29	13:31	15:29	17:32	19:30	21:32	23:34	1:33	3:35	5:33
16	7:40	9:42	11:33	13:35	15:33	17:35	19:34	21:36	23:38	1:36	3:39	5:37
17	7:44	9:46	11:37	13:39	15:37	17:39	19:38	21:40	23:42	1:40	3:43	5:41
18	7:48	9:50	11:41	13:43	15:41	17:43	19:42	21:44	23:46	1:44	3:47	5:45
19	7:52	9:54	11:45	13:47	15:45	17:47	19:46	21:48	23:50	1:48	3:51	5:49
20	7:56	9:58	11:49	13:51	15:49	17:51	19:50	21:52	23:54	1:52	3:54	5:53
21	8:00	10:02	11:52	13:55	15:53	17:55	19:53	21:56	23:58	1:56	3:58	5:57
22	8:04	10:06	11:56	13:59	15:57	17:59	19:57	22:00	0:02	2:00	4:02	6:01
23	8:08	10:10	12:00	14:03	16:01	18:03	20:01	22:04	0:06	2:04	4:06	6:05
24	8:12	10:14	12:04	14:07	16:05	18:07	20:05	22:08	0:10	2:08	4:10	6:09
25	8:16	10:18	12:08	14:10	16:09	18:11	20:09	22:11	0:14	2:12	4:14	6:12
26	8:20	10:22	12:12	14:14	16:13	18:15	20:13	22:15	0:18	2:16	4:18	6:16
27	8:24	10:26	12:16	14:18	16:17	18:19	20:17	22:19	0:22	2:20	4:22	6:20
28	8:27	10:30	12:20	14:22	16:21	18:23	20:21	22:23	0:26	2:24	4:26	6:24
29	8:31		12:24	14:26	16:25	18:27	20:25	22:27	0:29	2:28	4:30	6:28
30	8:35		12:28	14:30	16:28	18:31	20:29	22:31	0:33	2:32	4:34	6:32
31	8:39		12:32		16:32		20:33	22:35		2:36		6:36

1942	Jan	Feb	Mar	Apr	May	Jun	Jul	Aug	Sep	Oct	Nov	Dec
1	6:40	8:42	10:33	12:35	14:33	16:35	18:34	20:36	22:38	0:36	2:39	4:37
2	6:44	8:46	10:37	12:39	14:37	16:39	18:38	20:40	22:42	0:40	2:43	4:41
3	6:48	8:50	10:41	12:43	14:41	16:43	18:42	20:44	22:46	0:44	2:46	4:45
4	6:52	8:54	10:44	12:47	14:45	16:47	18:45	20:48	22:50	0:48	2:50	4:49
5	6:56	8:58	10:48	12:51	14:49	16:51	18:49	20:52	22:54	0:52	2:54	4:53
6	7:00	9:02	10:52	12:55	14:53	16:55	18:53	20:56	22:58	0:56	2:58	4:57
7	7:04	9:06	10:56	12:59	14:57	16:59	18:57	21:00	23:02	1:00	3:02	5:01
8	7:08	9:10	11:00	13:02	15:01	17:03	19:01	21:03	23:06	1:04	3:06	5:04
9	7:12	9:14	11:04	13:06	15:05	17:07	19:05	21:07	23:10	1:08	3:10	5:08
10	7:16	9:18	11:08	13:10	15:09	17:11	19:09	21:11	23:14	1:12	3:14	5:12
11	7:19	9:22	11:12	13:14	15:13	17:15	19:13	21:15	23:18	1:16	3:18	5:16
12	7:23	9:26	11:16	13:18	15:17	17:19	19:17	21:19	23:21	1:20	3:22	5:20
13	7:27	9:30	11:20	13:22	15:20	17:23	19:21	21:23	23:25	1:24	3:26	5:24
14	7:31	9:34	11:24	13:26	15:24	17:27	19:25	21:27	23:29	1:28	3:30	5:28
15	7:35	9:37	11:28	13:30	15:28	17:31	19:29	21:31	23:33	1:32	3:34	5:32
16	7:39	9:41	11:32	13:34	15:32	17:35	19:33	21:35	23:37	1:36	3:38	5:36
17	7:43	9:45	11:36	13:38	15:36	17:38	19:37	21:39	23:41	1:39	3:42	5:40
18	7:47	9:49	11:40	13:42	15:40	17:42	19:41	21:43	23:45	1:43	3:46	5:44
19	7:51	9:53	11:44	13:46	15:44	17:46	19:45	21:47	23:49	1:47	3:50	5:48
20	7:55	9:57	11:48	13:50	15:48	17:50	19:49	21:51	23:53	1:51	3:54	5:52
21	7:59	10:01	11:52	13:54	15:52	17:54	19:53	21:55	23:57	1:55	3:57	5:56
22	8:03	10:05	11:55	13:58	15:56	17:58	19:56	21:59	0:01	1:59	4:01	6:00
23	8:07	10:09	11:59	14:02	16:00	18:02	20:00	22:03	0:05	2:03	4:05	6:04
24	8:11	10:13	12:03	14:06	16:04	18:06	20:04	22:07	0:09	2:07	4:09	6:08
25	8:15	10:17	12:07	14:10	16:08	18:10	20:08	22:11	0:13	2:11	4:13	6:12
26	8:19	10:21	12:11	14:13	16:12	18:14	20:12	22:14	0:17	2:15	4:17	6:15
27	8:23	10:25	12:15	14:17	16:16	18:18	20:16	22:18	0:21	2:19	4:21	6:19
28	8:27	10:29	12:19	14:21	16:20	18:22	20:20	22:22	0:25	2:23	4:25	6:23
29	8:30		12:23	14:25	16:24	18:26	20:24	22:26	0:28	2:27	4:29	6:27
30	8:34		12:27	14:29	16:28	18:30	20:28	22:30	0:32	2:31	4:33	6:31
31	8:38		12:31		16:31		20:32	22:34		2:35		6:35

1943	Jan	Feb	Mar	Apr	May	Jun	Jul	Aug	Sep	Oct	Nov	Dec
1	6:39	8:41	10:32	12:34	14:32	16:34	18:33	20:35	22:37	0:35	2:38	4:36
2	6:43	8:45	10:36	12:38	14:36	16:38	18:37	20:39	22:41	0:39	2:42	4:40
3	6:47	8:49	10:40	12:42	14:40	16:42	18:41	20:43	22:45	0:43	2:46	4:44
4	6:51	8:53	10:44	12:46	14:44	16:46	18:45	20:47	22:49	0:47	2:49	4:48
5	6:55	8:57	10:47	12:50	14:48	16:50	18:48	20:51	22:53	0:51	2:53	4:52
6	6:59	9:01	10:51	12:54	14:52	16:54	18:52	20:55	22:57	0:55	2:57	4:56
7	7:03	9:05	10:55	12:58	14:56	16:58	18:56	20:59	23:01	0:59	3:01	5:00
8	7:07	9:09	10:59	13:02	15:00	17:02	19:00	21:03	23:05	1:03	3:05	5:04
9	7:11	9:13	11:03	13:05	15:04	17:06	19:04	21:06	23:09	1:07	3:09	5:07
10	7:15	9:17	11:07	13:09	15:08	17:10	19:08	21:10	23:13	1:11	3:13	5:11
11	7:19	9:21	11:11	13:13	15:12	17:14	19:12	21:14	23:17	1:15	3:17	5:15
12	7:22	9:25	11:15	13:17	15:16	17:18	19:16	21:18	23:21	1:19	3:21	5:19
13	7:26	9:29	11:19	13:21	15:20	17:22	19:20	21:22	23:24	1:23	3:25	5:23
14	7:30	9:33	11:23	13:25	15:23	17:26	19:24	21:26	23:28	1:27	3:29	5:27
15	7:34	9:37	11:27	13:29	15:27	17:30	19:28	21:30	23:32	1:31	3:33	5:31
16	7:38	9:40	11:31	13:33	15:31	17:34	19:32	21:34	23:36	1:35	3:37	5:35
17	7:42	9:44	11:35	13:37	15:35	17:38	19:36	21:38	23:40	1:39	3:41	5:39
18	7:46	9:48	11:39	13:41	15:39	17:41	19:40	21:42	23:44	1:42	3:45	5:43
19	7:50	9:52	11:43	13:45	15:43	17:45	19:44	21:46	23:48	1:46	3:49	5:47
20	7:54	9:56	11:47	13:49	15:47	17:49	19:48	21:50	23:52	1:50	3:53	5:51
21	7:58	10:00	11:51	13:53	15:51	17:53	19:52	21:54	23:56	1:54	3:57	5:55
22	8:02	10:04	11:55	13:57	15:55	17:57	19:56	21:58	0:00	1:58	4:00	5:59
23	8:06	10:08	11:58	14:01	15:59	18:01	19:59	22:02	0:04	2:02	4:04	6:03
24	8:10	10:12	12:02	14:05	16:03	18:05	20:03	22:06	0:08	2:06	4:08	6:07
25	8:14	10:16	12:06	14:09	16:07	18:09	20:07	22:10	0:12	2:10	4:12	6:11
26	8:18	10:20	12:10	14:12	16:11	18:13	20:11	22:13	0:16	2:14	4:16	6:14
27	8:22	10:24	12:14	14:16	16:15	18:17	20:15	22:17	0:20	2:18	4:20	6:18
28	8:26	10:28	12:18	14:20	16:19	18:21	20:19	22:21	0:24	2:22	4:24	6:22
29	8:29		12:22	14:24	16:23	18:25	20:23	22:25	0:28	2:26	4:28	6:26
30	8:33		12:26	14:28	16:27	18:29	20:27	22:29	0:31	2:30	4:32	6:30
31	8:37		12:30		16:30		20:31	22:33		2:34		6:34

1944	Jan	Feb	Dec	Apr	May	Jun	Jul	Aug	Sep	Oct	Nov	Dec
1	6:38	8:40	10:35	12:37	14:35	16:37	18:36	20:38	22:40	0:38	2:41	4:39
2	6:42	8:44	10:39	12:41	14:39	16:41	18:40	20:42	22:44	0:42	2:45	4:43
3	6:46	8:48	10:43	12:45	14:43	16:45	18:44	20:46	22:48	0:46	2:49	4:47
4	6:50	8:52	10:47	12:49	14:47	16:49	18:48	20:50	22:52	0:50	2:52	4:51
5	6:54	8:56	10:50	12:53	14:51	16:53	18:51	20:54	22:56	0:54	2:56	4:55
6	6:58	9:00	10:54	12:57	14:55	16:57	18:55	20:58	23:00	0:58	3:00	4:59
7	7:02	9:04	10:58	13:01	14:59	17:01	18:59	21:02	23:04	1:02	3:04	5:03
8	7:06	9:08	11:02	13:05	15:03	17:05	19:03	21:06	23:08	1:06	3:08	5:07
9	7:10	9:12	11:06	13:08	15:07	17:09	19:07	21:09	23:12	1:10	3:12	5:10
10	7:14	9:16	11:10	13:12	15:11	17:13	19:11	21:13	23:16	1:14	3:16	5:14
11	7:18	9:20	11:14	13:16	15:15	17:17	19:15	21:17	23:20	1:18	3:20	5:18
12	7:22	9:24	11:18	13:20	15:19	17:21	19:19	21:21	23:24	1:22	3:24	5:22
13	7:25	9:28	11:22	13:24	15:23	17:25	19:23	21:25	23:27	1:26	3:28	5:26
14	7:29	9:32	11:26	13:28	15:26	17:29	19:27	21:29	23:31	1:30	3:32	5:30
15	7:33	9:36	11:30	13:32	15:30	17:33	19:31	21:33	23:35	1:34	3:36	5:34
16	7:37	9:40	11:34	13:36	15:34	17:37	19:35	21:37	23:39	1:38	3:40	5:38
17	7:41	9:43	11:38	13:40	15:38	17:41	19:39	21:41	23:43	1:41	3:44	5:42
18	7:45	9:47	11:42	13:44	15:42	17:44	19:43	21:45	23:47	1:45	3:48	5:46
19	7:49	9:51	11:46	13:48	15:46	17:48	19:47	21:49	23:51	1:49	3:52	5:50
20	7:53	9:55	11:50	13:52	15:50	17:52	19:51	21:53	23:55	1:53	3:56	5:54
21	7:57	9:59	11:54	13:56	15:54	17:56	19:55	21:57	23:59	1:57	3:59	5:58
22	8:01	10:03	11:57	14:00	15:58	18:00	19:58	22:01	0:03	2:01	4:03	6:02
23	8:05	10:07	12:01	14:04	16:02	18:04	20:02	22:05	0:07	2:05	4:07	6:06
24	8:09	10:11	12:05	14:08	16:06	18:08	20:06	22:09	0:11	2:09	4:11	6:10
25	8:13	10:15	12:09	14:12	16:10	18:12	20:10	22:13	0:15	2:13	4:15	6:14
26	8:17	10:19	12:13	14:15	16:14	18:16	20:14	22:16	0:19	2:17	4:19	6:17
27	8:21	10:23	12:17	14:19	16:18	18:20	20:18	22:20	0:23	2:21	4:23	6:21
28	8:25	10:27	12:21	14:23	16:22	18:24	20:22	22:24	0:27	2:25	4:27	6:25
29	8:29	10:31	12:25	14:27	16:26	18:28	20:26	22:28	0:31	2:29	4:31	6:29
30	8:32		12:29	14:31	16:30	18:32	20:30	22:32	0:34	2:33	4:35	6:33
31	8:36		12:33		16:33		20:34	22:36		2:37		6:37

1945	Jan	Feb	Mar	Apr	May	Jun	Jul	Aug	Sep	Oct	Nov	Dec
1	6:41	8:43	10:34	12:36	14:34	16:36	18:35	20:37	22:39	0:37	2:40	4:38
2	6:45	8:47	10:38	12:40	14:38	16:40	18:39	20:41	22:43	0:41	2:44	4:42
3	6:49	8:51	10:42	12:44	14:42	16:44	18:43	20:45	22:47	0:45	2:48	4:46
4	6:53	8:55	10:46	12:48	14:46	16:48	18:47	20:49	22:51	0:49	2:52	4:50
5	6:57	8:59	10:50	12:52	14:50	16:52	18:51	20:53	22:55	0:53	2:55	4:54
6	7:01	9:03	10:53	12:56	14:54	16:56	18:54	20:57	22:59	0:57	2:59	4:58
7	7:05	9:07	10:57	13:00	14:58	17:00	18:58	21:01	23:03	1:01	3:03	5:02
8	7:09	9:11	11:01	13:04	15:02	17:04	19:02	21:05	23:07	1:05	3:07	5:06
9	7:13	9:15	11:05	13:08	15:06	17:08	19:06	21:09	23:11	1:09	3:11	5:09
10	7:17	9:19	11:09	13:11	15:10	17:12	19:10	21:12	23:15	1:13	3:15	5:13
11	7:21	9:23	11:13	13:15	15:14	17:16	19:14	21:16	23:19	1:17	3:19	5:17
12	7:25	9:27	11:17	13:19	15:18	17:20	19:18	21:20	23:23	1:21	3:23	5:21
13	7:28	9:31	11:21	13:23	15:22	17:24	19:22	21:24	23:26	1:25	3:27	5:25
14	7:32	9:35	11:25	13:27	15:25	17:28	19:26	21:28	23:30	1:29	3:31	5:29
15	7:36	9:39	11:29	13:31	15:29	17:32	19:30	21:32	23:34	1:33	3:35	5:33
16	7:40	9:42	11:33	13:35	15:33	17:36	19:34	21:36	23:38	1:37	3:39	5:37
17	7:44	9:46	11:37	13:39	15:37	17:40	19:38	21:40	23:42	1:41	3:43	5:41
18	7:48	9:50	11:41	13:43	15:41	17:43	19:42	21:44	23:46	1:44	3:47	5:45
19	7:52	9:54	11:45	13:47	15:45	17:47	19:46	21:48	23:50	1:48	3:51	5:49
20	7:56	9:58	11:49	13:51	15:49	17:51	19:50	21:52	23:54	1:52	3:55	5:53
21	8:00	10:02	11:53	13:55	15:53	17:55	19:54	21:56	23:58	1:56	3:59	5:57
22	8:04	10:06	11:57	13:59	15:57	17:59	19:58	22:00	0:02	2:00	4:02	6:01
23	8:08	10:10	12:00	14:03	16:01	18:03	20:01	22:04	0:06	2:04	4:06	6:05
24	8:12	10:14	12:04	14:07	16:05	18:07	20:05	22:08	0:10	2:08	4:10	6:09
25	8:16	10:18	12:08	14:11	16:09	18:11	20:09	22:12	0:14	2:12	4:14	6:13
26	8:20	10:22	12:12	14:15	16:13	18:15	20:13	22:16	0:18	2:16	4:18	6:17
27	8:24	10:26	12:16	14:18	16:17	18:19	20:17	22:19	0:22	2:20	4:22	6:20
28	8:28	10:30	12:20	14:22	16:21	18:23	20:21	22:23	0:26	2:24	4:26	6:24
29	8:32		12:24	14:26	16:25	18:27	20:25	22:27	0:30	2:28	4:30	6:28
30	8:35		12:28	14:30	16:29	18:31	20:29	22:31	0:34	2:32	4:34	6:32
31	8:39		12:32		16:33		20:33	22:35		2:36		6:36

1946	Jan	Feb	Mar	Apr	May	Jun	Jul	Aug	Sep	Oct	Nov	Dec
1	6:40	8:42	10:33	12:35	14:33	16:36	18:34	20:36	22:38	0:37	2:39	4:37
2	6:44	8:46	10:37	12:39	14:37	16:39	18:38	20:40	22:42	0:40	2:43	4:41
3	6:48	8:50	10:41	12:43	14:41	16:43	18:42	20:44	22:46	0:44	2:47	4:45
4	6:52	8:54	10:45	12:47	14:45	16:47	18:46	20:48	22:50	0:48	2:51	4:49
5	6:56	8:58	10:49	12:51	14:49	16:51	18:50	20:52	22:54	0:52	2:54	4:53
6	7:00	9:02	10:53	12:55	14:53	16:55	18:54	20:56	22:58	0:56	2:58	4:57
7	7:04	9:06	10:56	12:59	14:57	16:59	18:57	21:00	23:02	1:00	3:02	5:01
8	7:08	9:10	11:00	13:03	15:01	17:03	19:01	21:04	23:06	1:04	3:06	5:05
9	7:12	9:14	11:04	13:07	15:05	17:07	19:05	21:08	23:10	1:08	3:10	5:09
10	7:16	9:18	11:08	13:10	15:09	17:11	19:09	21:11	23:14	1:12	3:14	5:12
11	7:20	9:22	11:12	13:14	15:13	17:15	19:13	21:15	23:18	1:16	3:18	5:16
12	7:24	9:26	11:16	13:18	15:17	17:19	19:17	21:19	23:22	1:20	3:22	5:20
13	7:27	9:30	11:20	13:22	15:21	17:23	19:21	21:23	23:26	1:24	3:26	5:24
14	7:31	9:34	11:24	13:26	15:25	17:27	19:25	21:27	23:29	1:28	3:30	5:28
15	7:35	9:38	11:28	13:30	15:28	17:31	19:29	21:31	23:33	1:32	3:34	5:32
16	7:39	9:42	11:32	13:34	15:32	17:35	19:33	21:35	23:37	1:36	3:38	5:36
17	7:43	9:45	11:36	13:38	15:36	17:39	19:37	21:39	23:41	1:40	3:42	5:40
18	7:47	9:49	11:40	13:42	15:40	17:43	19:41	21:43	23:45	1:44	3:46	5:44
19	7:51	9:53	11:44	13:46	15:44	17:46	19:45	21:47	23:49	1:47	3:50	5:48
20	7:55	9:57	11:48	13:50	15:48	17:50	19:49	21:51	23:53	1:51	3:54	5:52
21	7:59	10:01	11:52	13:54	15:52	17:54	19:53	21:55	23:57	1:55	3:58	5:56
22	8:03	10:05	11:56	13:58	15:56	17:58	19:57	21:59	0:01	1:59	4:02	6:00
23	8:07	10:09	12:00	14:02	16:00	18:02	20:01	22:03	0:05	2:03	4:05	6:04
24	8:11	10:13	12:03	14:06	16:04	18:06	20:04	22:07	0:09	2:07	4:09	6:08
25	8:15	10:17	12:07	14:10	16:08	18:10	20:08	22:11	0:13	2:11	4:13	6:12
26	8:19	10:21	12:11	14:14	16:12	18:14	20:12	22:15	0:17	2:15	4:17	6:16
27	8:23	10:25	12:15	14:18	16:16	18:18	20:16	22:19	0:21	2:19	4:21	6:20
28	8:27	10:29	12:19	14:21	16:20	18:22	20:20	22:22	0:25	2:23	4:25	6:23
29	8:31		12:23	14:25	16:24	18:26	20:24	22:26	0:29	2:27	4:29	6:27
30	8:35		12:27	14:29	16:28	18:30	20:28	22:30	0:33	2:31	4:33	6:31
31	8:38		12:31		16:32		20:32	22:34		2:35		6:35

1947	Jan	Feb	Mar	Apr	May	Jun	Jul	Aug	Sep	Oct	Nov	Dec
1	6:39	8:41	10:32	12:34	14:32	16:35	18:33	20:35	22:37	0:36	2:38	4:36
2	6:43	8:45	10:36	12:38	14:36	16:38	18:37	20:39	22:41	0:39	2:42	4:40
3	6:47	8:49	10:40	12:42	14:40	16:42	18:41	20:43	22:45	0:43	2:46	4:44
4	6:51	8:53	10:44	12:46	14:44	16:46	18:45	20:47	22:49	0:47	2:50	4:48
5	6:55	8:57	10:48	12:50	14:48	16:50	18:49	20:51	22:53	0:51	2:54	4:52
6	6:59	9:01	10:52	12:54	14:52	16:54	18:53	20:55	22:57	0:55	2:57	4:56
7	7:03	9:05	10:55	12:58	14:56	16:58	18:56	20:59	23:01	0:59	3:01	5:00
8	7:07	9:09	10:59	13:02	15:00	17:02	19:00	21:03	23:05	1:03	3:05	5:04
9	7:11	9:13	11:03	13:06	15:04	17:06	19:04	21:07	23:09	1:07	3:09	5:08
10	7:15	9:17	11:07	13:10	15:08	17:10	19:08	21:11	23:13	1:11	3:13	5:12
11	7:19	9:21	11:11	13:13	15:12	17:14	19:12	21:14	23:17	1:15	3:17	5:15
12	7:23	9:25	11:15	13:17	15:16	17:18	19:16	21:18	23:21	1:19	3:21	5:19
13	7:27	9:29	11:19	13:21	15:20	17:22	19:20	21:22	23:25	1:23	3:25	5:23
14	7:30	9:33	11:23	13:25	15:24	17:26	19:24	21:26	23:29	1:27	3:29	5:27
15	7:34	9:37	11:27	13:29	15:28	17:30	19:28	21:30	23:32	1:31	3:33	5:31
16	7:38	9:41	11:31	13:33	15:31	17:34	19:32	21:34	23:36	1:35	3:37	5:35
17	7:42	9:45	11:35	13:37	15:35	17:38	19:36	21:38	23:40	1:39	3:41	5:39
18	7:46	9:48	11:39	13:41	15:39	17:42	19:40	21:42	23:44	1:43	3:45	5:43
19	7:50	9:52	11:43	13:45	15:43	17:46	19:44	21:46	23:48	1:47	3:49	5:47
20	7:54	9:56	11:47	13:49	15:47	17:49	19:48	21:50	23:52	1:50	3:53	5:51
21	7:58	10:00	11:51	13:53	15:51	17:53	19:52	21:54	23:56	1:54	3:57	5:55
22	8:02	10:04	11:55	13:57	15:55	17:57	19:56	21:58	0:00	1:58	4:01	5:59
23	8:06	10:08	11:59	14:01	15:59	18:01	20:00	22:02	0:04	2:02	4:05	6:03
24	8:10	10:12	12:03	14:05	16:03	18:05	20:04	22:06	0:08	2:06	4:08	6:07
25	8:14	10:16	12:06	14:09	16:07	18:09	20:07	22:10	0:12	2:10	4:12	6:11
26	8:18	10:20	12:10	14:13	16:11	18:13	20:11	22:14	0:16	2:14	4:16	6:15
27	8:22	10:24	12:14	14:17	16:15	18:17	20:15	22:18	0:20	2:18	4:20	6:19
28	8:26	10:28	12:18	14:21	16:19	18:21	20:19	22:22	0:24	2:22	4:24	6:22
29	8:30		12:22	14:24	16:23	18:25	20:23	22:25	0:28	2:26	4:28	6:26
30	8:34		12:26	14:28	16:27	18:29	20:27	22:29	0:32	2:30	4:32	6:30
31	8:38		12:30		16:31		20:31	22:33		2:34		6:34

1948	Jan	Feb	Dec	Apr	May	Jun	Jul	Aug	Sep	Oct	Nov	Dec
1	6:38	8:40	10:35	12:37	14:35	16:38	18:36	20:38	22:40	0:39	2:41	4:39
2	6:42	8:44	10:39	12:41	14:39	16:41	18:40	20:42	22:44	0:42	2:45	4:43
3	6:46	8:48	10:43	12:45	14:43	16:45	18:44	20:46	22:48	0:46	2:49	4:47
4	6:50	8:52	10:47	12:49	14:47	16:49	18:48	20:50	22:52	0:50	2:53	4:51
5	6:54	8:56	10:51	12:53	14:51	16:53	18:52	20:54	22:56	0:54	2:57	4:55
6	6:58	9:00	10:55	12:57	14:55	16:57	18:56	20:58	23:00	0:58	3:00	4:59
7	7:02	9:04	10:58	13:01	14:59	17:01	18:59	21:02	23:04	1:02	3:04	5:03
8	7:06	9:08	11:02	13:05	15:03	17:05	19:03	21:06	23:08	1:06	3:08	5:07
9	7:10	9:12	11:06	13:09	15:07	17:09	19:07	21:10	23:12	1:10	3:12	5:11
10	7:14	9:16	11:10	13:13	15:11	17:13	19:11	21:14	23:16	1:14	3:16	5:15
11	7:18	9:20	11:14	13:16	15:15	17:17	19:15	21:17	23:20	1:18	3:20	5:18
12	7:22	9:24	11:18	13:20	15:19	17:21	19:19	21:21	23:24	1:22	3:24	5:22
13	7:26	9:28	11:22	13:24	15:23	17:25	19:23	21:25	23:28	1:26	3:28	5:26
14	7:30	9:32	11:26	13:28	15:27	17:29	19:27	21:29	23:32	1:30	3:32	5:30
15	7:33	9:36	11:30	13:32	15:31	17:33	19:31	21:33	23:35	1:34	3:36	5:34
16	7:37	9:40	11:34	13:36	15:34	17:37	19:35	21:37	23:39	1:38	3:40	5:38
17	7:41	9:44	11:38	13:40	15:38	17:41	19:39	21:41	23:43	1:42	3:44	5:42
18	7:45	9:48	11:42	13:44	15:42	17:45	19:43	21:45	23:47	1:46	3:48	5:46
19	7:49	9:51	11:46	13:48	15:46	17:49	19:47	21:49	23:51	1:50	3:52	5:50
20	7:53	9:55	11:50	13:52	15:50	17:52	19:51	21:53	23:55	1:53	3:56	5:54
21	7:57	9:59	11:54	13:56	15:54	17:56	19:55	21:57	23:59	1:57	4:00	5:58
22	8:01	10:03	11:58	14:00	15:58	18:00	19:59	22:01	0:03	2:01	4:04	6:02
23	8:05	10:07	12:02	14:04	16:02	18:04	20:03	22:05	0:07	2:05	4:07	6:06
24	8:09	10:11	12:06	14:08	16:06	18:08	20:07	22:09	0:11	2:09	4:11	6:10
25	8:13	10:15	12:09	14:12	16:10	18:12	20:10	22:13	0:15	2:13	4:15	6:14
26	8:17	10:19	12:13	14:16	16:14	18:16	20:14	22:17	0:19	2:17	4:19	6:18
27	8:21	10:23	12:17	14:20	16:18	18:20	20:18	22:21	0:23	2:21	4:23	6:22
28	8:25	10:27	12:21	14:23	16:22	18:24	20:22	22:24	0:27	2:25	4:27	6:25
29	8:29	10:31	12:25	14:27	16:26	18:28	20:26	22:28	0:31	2:29	4:31	6:29
30	8:33		12:29	14:31	16:30	18:32	20:30	22:32	0:35	2:33	4:35	6:33
31	8:37		12:33		16:34		20:34	22:36		2:37		6:37

1949	Jan	Feb	Mar	Apr	May	Jun	Jul	Aug	Sep	Oct	Nov	Dec
1	6:41	8:43	10:34	12:36	14:34	16:37	18:35	20:37	22:39	0:38	2:40	4:38
2	6:45	8:47	10:38	12:40	14:38	16:41	18:39	20:41	22:43	0:42	2:44	4:42
3	6:49	8:51	10:42	12:44	14:42	16:44	18:43	20:45	22:47	0:45	2:48	4:46
4	6:53	8:55	10:46	12:48	14:46	16:48	18:47	20:49	22:51	0:49	2:52	4:50
5	6:57	8:59	10:50	12:52	14:50	16:52	18:51	20:53	22:55	0:53	2:56	4:54
6	7:01	9:03	10:54	12:56	14:54	16:56	18:55	20:57	22:59	0:57	3:00	4:58
7	7:05	9:07	10:58	13:00	14:58	17:00	18:59	21:01	23:03	1:01	3:03	5:02
8	7:09	9:11	11:01	13:04	15:02	17:04	19:02	21:05	23:07	1:05	3:07	5:06
9	7:13	9:15	11:05	13:08	15:06	17:08	19:06	21:09	23:11	1:09	3:11	5:10
10	7:17	9:19	11:09	13:12	15:10	17:12	19:10	21:13	23:15	1:13	3:15	5:14
11	7:21	9:23	11:13	13:16	15:14	17:16	19:14	21:17	23:19	1:17	3:19	5:18
12	7:25	9:27	11:17	13:19	15:18	17:20	19:18	21:20	23:23	1:21	3:23	5:21
13	7:29	9:31	11:21	13:23	15:22	17:24	19:22	21:24	23:27	1:25	3:27	5:25
14	7:33	9:35	11:25	13:27	15:26	17:28	19:26	21:28	23:31	1:29	3:31	5:29
15	7:36	9:39	11:29	13:31	15:30	17:32	19:30	21:32	23:35	1:33	3:35	5:33
16	7:40	9:43	11:33	13:35	15:34	17:36	19:34	21:36	23:38	1:37	3:39	5:37
17	7:44	9:47	11:37	13:39	15:37	17:40	19:38	21:40	23:42	1:41	3:43	5:41
18	7:48	9:51	11:41	13:43	15:41	17:44	19:42	21:44	23:46	1:45	3:47	5:45
19	7:52	9:54	11:45	13:47	15:45	17:48	19:46	21:48	23:50	1:49	3:51	5:49
20	7:56	9:58	11:49	13:51	15:49	17:51	19:50	21:52	23:54	1:52	3:55	5:53
21	8:00	10:02	11:53	13:55	15:53	17:55	19:54	21:56	23:58	1:56	3:59	5:57
22	8:04	10:06	11:57	13:59	15:57	17:59	19:58	22:00	0:02	2:00	4:03	6:01
23	8:08	10:10	12:01	14:03	16:01	18:03	20:02	22:04	0:06	2:04	4:07	6:05
24	8:12	10:14	12:05	14:07	16:05	18:07	20:06	22:08	0:10	2:08	4:10	6:09
25	8:16	10:18	12:08	14:11	16:09	18:11	20:09	22:12	0:14	2:12	4:14	6:13
26	8:20	10:22	12:12	14:15	16:13	18:15	20:13	22:16	0:18	2:16	4:18	6:17
27	8:24	10:26	12:16	14:19	16:17	18:19	20:17	22:20	0:22	2:20	4:22	6:21
28	8:28	10:30	12:20	14:23	16:21	18:23	20:21	22:24	0:26	2:24	4:26	6:25
29	8:32		12:24	14:26	16:25	18:27	20:25	22:27	0:30	2:28	4:30	6:28
30	8:36		12:28	14:30	16:29	18:31	20:29	22:31	0:34	2:32	4:34	6:32
31	8:40		12:32		16:33		20:33	22:35		2:36		6:36

1950	Jan	Feb	Mar	Apr	May	Jun	Jul	Aug	Sep	Oct	Nov	Dec
1	6:40	8:43	10:33	12:35	14:33	16:36	18:34	20:36	22:38	0:37	2:39	4:37
2	6:44	8:46	10:37	12:39	14:37	16:40	18:38	20:40	22:42	0:41	2:43	4:41
3	6:48	8:50	10:41	12:43	14:41	16:44	18:42	20:44	22:46	0:45	2:47	4:45
4	6:52	8:54	10:45	12:47	14:45	16:47	18:46	20:48	22:50	0:48	2:51	4:49
5	6:56	8:58	10:49	12:51	14:49	16:51	18:50	20:52	22:54	0:52	2:55	4:53
6	7:00	9:02	10:53	12:55	14:53	16:55	18:54	20:56	22:58	0:56	2:59	4:57
7	7:04	9:06	10:57	12:59	14:57	16:59	18:58	21:00	23:02	1:00	3:03	5:01
8	7:08	9:10	11:01	13:03	15:01	17:03	19:02	21:04	23:06	1:04	3:06	5:05
9	7:12	9:14	11:04	13:07	15:05	17:07	19:05	21:08	23:10	1:08	3:10	5:09
10	7:16	9:18	11:08	13:11	15:09	17:11	19:09	21:12	23:14	1:12	3:14	5:13
11	7:20	9:22	11:12	13:15	15:13	17:15	19:13	21:16	23:18	1:16	3:18	5:17
12	7:24	9:26	11:16	13:19	15:17	17:19	19:17	21:19	23:22	1:20	3:22	5:20
13	7:28	9:30	11:20	13:22	15:21	17:23	19:21	21:23	23:26	1:24	3:26	5:24
14	7:32	9:34	11:24	13:26	15:25	17:27	19:25	21:27	23:30	1:28	3:30	5:28
15	7:35	9:38	11:28	13:30	15:29	17:31	19:29	21:31	23:34	1:32	3:34	5:32
16	7:39	9:42	11:32	13:34	15:33	17:35	19:33	21:35	23:37	1:36	3:38	5:36
17	7:43	9:46	11:36	13:38	15:36	17:39	19:37	21:39	23:41	1:40	3:42	5:40
18	7:47	9:50	11:40	13:42	15:40	17:43	19:41	21:43	23:45	1:44	3:46	5:44
19	7:51	9:53	11:44	13:46	15:44	17:47	19:45	21:47	23:49	1:48	3:50	5:48
20	7:55	9:57	11:48	13:50	15:48	17:51	19:49	21:51	23:53	1:52	3:54	5:52
21	7:59	10:01	11:52	13:54	15:52	17:54	19:53	21:55	23:57	1:55	3:58	5:56
22	8:03	10:05	11:56	13:58	15:56	17:58	19:57	21:59	0:01	1:59	4:02	6:00
23	8:07	10:09	12:00	14:02	16:00	18:02	20:01	22:03	0:05	2:03	4:06	6:04
24	8:11	10:13	12:04	14:06	16:04	18:06	20:05	22:07	0:09	2:07	4:10	6:08
25	8:15	10:17	12:08	14:10	16:08	18:10	20:09	22:11	0:13	2:11	4:13	6:12
26	8:19	10:21	12:11	14:14	16:12	18:14	20:12	22:15	0:17	2:15	4:17	6:16
27	8:23	10:25	12:15	14:18	16:16	18:18	20:16	22:19	0:21	2:19	4:21	6:20
28	8:27	10:29	12:19	14:22	16:20	18:22	20:20	22:23	0:25	2:23	4:25	6:24
29	8:31		12:23	14:26	16:24	18:26	20:24	22:27	0:29	2:27	4:29	6:28
30	8:35		12:27	14:29	16:28	18:30	20:28	22:30	0:33	2:31	4:33	6:31
31	8:39		12:31		16:32		20:32	22:34		2:35		6:35

1951	Jan	Feb	Mar	Apr	May	Jun	Jul	Aug	Sep	Oct	Nov	Dec
1	6:39	8:42	10:32	12:34	14:32	16:35	18:33	20:35	22:37	0:36	2:38	4:36
2	6:43	8:46	10:36	12:38	14:36	16:39	18:37	20:39	22:41	0:40	2:42	4:40
3	6:47	8:49	10:40	12:42	14:40	16:43	18:41	20:43	22:45	0:44	2:46	4:44
4	6:51	8:53	10:44	12:46	14:44	16:47	18:45	20:47	22:49	0:48	2:50	4:48
5	6:55	8:57	10:48	12:50	14:48	16:50	18:49	20:51	22:53	0:51	2:54	4:52
6	6:59	9:01	10:52	12:54	14:52	16:54	18:53	20:55	22:57	0:55	2:58	4:56
7	7:03	9:05	10:56	12:58	14:56	16:58	18:57	20:59	23:01	0:59	3:02	5:00
8	7:07	9:09	11:00	13:02	15:00	17:02	19:01	21:03	23:05	1:03	3:05	5:04
9	7:11	9:13	11:04	13:06	15:04	17:06	19:04	21:07	23:09	1:07	3:09	5:08
10	7:15	9:17	11:07	13:10	15:08	17:10	19:08	21:11	23:13	1:11	3:13	5:12
11	7:19	9:21	11:11	13:14	15:12	17:14	19:12	21:15	23:17	1:15	3:17	5:16
12	7:23	9:25	11:15	13:18	15:16	17:18	19:16	21:19	23:21	1:19	3:21	5:20
13	7:27	9:29	11:19	13:21	15:20	17:22	19:20	21:22	23:25	1:23	3:25	5:23
14	7:31	9:33	11:23	13:25	15:24	17:26	19:24	21:26	23:29	1:27	3:29	5:27
15	7:35	9:37	11:27	13:29	15:28	17:30	19:28	21:30	23:33	1:31	3:33	5:31
16	7:38	9:41	11:31	13:33	15:32	17:34	19:32	21:34	23:37	1:35	3:37	5:35
17	7:42	9:45	11:35	13:37	15:36	17:38	19:36	21:38	23:40	1:39	3:41	5:39
18	7:46	9:49	11:39	13:41	15:39	17:42	19:40	21:42	23:44	1:43	3:45	5:43
19	7:50	9:53	11:43	13:45	15:43	17:46	19:44	21:46	23:48	1:47	3:49	5:47
20	7:54	9:56	11:47	13:49	15:47	17:50	19:48	21:50	23:52	1:51	3:53	5:51
21	7:58	10:00	11:51	13:53	15:51	17:54	19:52	21:54	23:56	1:55	3:57	5:55
22	8:02	10:04	11:55	13:57	15:55	17:57	19:56	21:58	0:00	1:58	4:01	5:59
23	8:06	10:08	11:59	14:01	15:59	18:01	20:00	22:02	0:04	2:02	4:05	6:03
24	8:10	10:12	12:03	14:05	16:03	18:05	20:04	22:06	0:08	2:06	4:09	6:07
25	8:14	10:16	12:07	14:09	16:07	18:09	20:08	22:10	0:12	2:10	4:13	6:11
26	8:18	10:20	12:11	14:13	16:11	18:13	20:12	22:14	0:16	2:14	4:16	6:15
27	8:22	10:24	12:14	14:17	16:15	18:17	20:15	22:18	0:20	2:18	4:20	6:19
28	8:26	10:28	12:18	14:21	16:19	18:21	20:19	22:22	0:24	2:22	4:24	6:23
29	8:30		12:22	14:25	16:23	18:25	20:23	22:26	0:28	2:26	4:28	6:27
30	8:34		12:26	14:29	16:27	18:29	20:27	22:30	0:32	2:30	4:32	6:31
31	8:38		12:30		16:31		20:31	22:33		2:34		6:34

1952	Jan	Feb	Mar	Apr	May	Jun	Jul	Aug	Sep	Oct	Nov	Dec
1	6:38	8:41	10:35	12:37	14:35	16:38	18:36	20:38	22:40	0:39	2:41	4:39
2	6:42	8:45	10:39	12:41	14:39	16:42	18:40	20:42	22:44	0:43	2:45	4:43
3	6:46	8:48	10:43	12:45	14:43	16:46	18:44	20:46	22:48	0:47	2:49	4:47
4	6:50	8:52	10:47	12:49	14:47	16:49	18:48	20:50	22:52	0:50	2:53	4:51
5	6:54	8:56	10:51	12:53	14:51	16:53	18:52	20:54	22:56	0:54	2:57	4:55
6	6:58	9:00	10:55	12:57	14:55	16:57	18:56	20:58	23:00	0:58	3:01	4:59
7	7:02	9:04	10:59	13:01	14:59	17:01	19:00	21:02	23:04	1:02	3:05	5:03
8	7:06	9:08	11:03	13:05	15:03	17:05	19:04	21:06	23:08	1:06	3:08	5:07
9	7:10	9:12	11:06	13:09	15:07	17:09	19:07	21:10	23:12	1:10	3:12	5:11
10	7:14	9:16	11:10	13:13	15:11	17:13	19:11	21:14	23:16	1:14	3:16	5:15
11	7:18	9:20	11:14	13:17	15:15	17:17	19:15	21:18	23:20	1:18	3:20	5:19
12	7:22	9:24	11:18	13:21	15:19	17:21	19:19	21:22	23:24	1:22	3:24	5:23
13	7:26	9:28	11:22	13:24	15:23	17:25	19:23	21:25	23:28	1:26	3:28	5:26
14	7:30	9:32	11:26	13:28	15:27	17:29	19:27	21:29	23:32	1:30	3:32	5:30
15	7:34	9:36	11:30	13:32	15:31	17:33	19:31	21:33	23:36	1:34	3:36	5:34
16	7:38	9:40	11:34	13:36	15:35	17:37	19:35	21:37	23:40	1:38	3:40	5:38
17	7:41	9:44	11:38	13:40	15:39	17:41	19:39	21:41	23:43	1:42	3:44	5:42
18	7:45	9:48	11:42	13:44	15:42	17:45	19:43	21:45	23:47	1:46	3:48	5:46
19	7:49	9:52	11:46	13:48	15:46	17:49	19:47	21:49	23:51	1:50	3:52	5:50
20	7:53	9:56	11:50	13:52	15:50	17:53	19:51	21:53	23:55	1:54	3:56	5:54
21	7:57	9:59	11:54	13:56	15:54	17:57	19:55	21:57	23:59	1:58	4:00	5:58
22	8:01	10:03	11:58	14:00	15:58	18:00	19:59	22:01	0:03	2:01	4:04	6:02
23	8:05	10:07	12:02	14:04	16:02	18:04	20:03	22:05	0:07	2:05	4:08	6:06
24	8:09	10:11	12:06	14:08	16:06	18:08	20:07	22:09	0:11	2:09	4:12	6:10
25	8:13	10:15	12:10	14:12	16:10	18:12	20:11	22:13	0:15	2:13	4:16	6:14
26	8:17	10:19	12:14	14:16	16:14	18:16	20:15	22:17	0:19	2:17	4:19	6:18
27	8:21	10:23	12:17	14:20	16:18	18:20	20:18	22:21	0:23	2:21	4:23	6:22
28	8:25	10:27	12:21	14:24	16:22	18:24	20:22	22:25	0:27	2:25	4:27	6:26
29	8:29	10:31	12:25	14:28	16:26	18:28	20:26	22:29	0:31	2:29	4:31	6:30
30	8:33		12:29	14:32	16:30	18:32	20:30	22:32	0:35	2:33	4:35	6:33
31	8:37		12:33		16:34		20:34	22:36		2:37		6:37

1953	Jan	Feb	Mar	Apr	May	Jun	Jul	Aug	Sep	Oct	Nov	Dec
1	6:41	8:44	10:34	12:36	14:34	16:37	18:35	20:37	22:39	0:38	2:40	4:38
2	6:45	8:48	10:38	12:40	14:38	16:41	18:39	20:41	22:43	0:42	2:44	4:42
3	6:49	8:51	10:42	12:44	14:42	16:45	18:43	20:45	22:47	0:46	2:48	4:46
4	6:53	8:55	10:46	12:48	14:46	16:49	18:47	20:49	22:51	0:50	2:52	4:50
5	6:57	8:59	10:50	12:52	14:50	16:52	18:51	20:53	22:55	0:53	2:56	4:54
6	7:01	9:03	10:54	12:56	14:54	16:56	18:55	20:57	22:59	0:57	3:00	4:58
7	7:05	9:07	10:58	13:00	14:58	17:00	18:59	21:01	23:03	1:01	3:04	5:02
8	7:09	9:11	11:02	13:04	15:02	17:04	19:03	21:05	23:07	1:05	3:08	5:06
9	7:13	9:15	11:06	13:08	15:06	17:08	19:07	21:09	23:11	1:09	3:11	5:10
10	7:17	9:19	11:09	13:12	15:10	17:12	19:10	21:13	23:15	1:13	3:15	5:14
11	7:21	9:23	11:13	13:16	15:14	17:16	19:14	21:17	23:19	1:17	3:19	5:18
12	7:25	9:27	11:17	13:20	15:18	17:20	19:18	21:21	23:23	1:21	3:23	5:22
13	7:29	9:31	11:21	13:24	15:22	17:24	19:22	21:25	23:27	1:25	3:27	5:26
14	7:33	9:35	11:25	13:27	15:26	17:28	19:26	21:28	23:31	1:29	3:31	5:29
15	7:37	9:39	11:29	13:31	15:30	17:32	19:30	21:32	23:35	1:33	3:35	5:33
16	7:41	9:43	11:33	13:35	15:34	17:36	19:34	21:36	23:39	1:37	3:39	5:37
17	7:44	9:47	11:37	13:39	15:38	17:40	19:38	21:40	23:43	1:41	3:43	5:41
18	7:48	9:51	11:41	13:43	15:42	17:44	19:42	21:44	23:46	1:45	3:47	5:45
19	7:52	9:55	11:45	13:47	15:45	17:48	19:46	21:48	23:50	1:49	3:51	5:49
20	7:56	9:59	11:49	13:51	15:49	17:52	19:50	21:52	23:54	1:53	3:55	5:53
21	8:00	10:02	11:53	13:55	15:53	17:56	19:54	21:56	23:58	1:57	3:59	5:57
22	8:04	10:06	11:57	13:59	15:57	18:00	19:58	22:00	0:02	2:01	4:03	6:01
23	8:08	10:10	12:01	14:03	16:01	18:03	20:02	22:04	0:06	2:04	4:07	6:05
24	8:12	10:14	12:05	14:07	16:05	18:07	20:06	22:08	0:10	2:08	4:11	6:09
25	8:16	10:18	12:09	14:11	16:09	18:11	20:10	22:12	0:14	2:12	4:15	6:13
26	8:20	10:22	12:13	14:15	16:13	18:15	20:14	22:16	0:18	2:16	4:18	6:17
27	8:24	10:26	12:17	14:19	16:17	18:19	20:17	22:20	0:22	2:20	4:22	6:21
28	8:28	10:30	12:20	14:23	16:21	18:23	20:21	22:24	0:26	2:24	4:26	6:25
29	8:32		12:24	14:27	16:25	18:27	20:25	22:28	0:30	2:28	4:30	6:29
30	8:36		12:28	14:31	16:29	18:31	20:29	22:32	0:34	2:32	4:34	6:33
31	8:40		12:32		16:33		20:33	22:35		2:36		6:36

1954	Jan	Feb	Mar	Apr	May	Jun	Jul	Aug	Sep	Oct	Nov	Dec
1	6:40	8:43	10:33	12:35	14:34	16:36	18:34	20:36	22:38	0:37	2:39	4:37
2	6:44	8:47	10:37	12:39	14:37	16:40	18:38	20:40	22:42	0:41	2:43	4:41
3	6:48	8:51	10:41	12:43	14:41	16:44	18:42	20:44	22:46	0:45	2:47	4:45
4	6:52	8:54	10:45	12:47	14:45	16:48	18:46	20:48	22:50	0:49	2:51	4:49
5	6:56	8:58	10:49	12:51	14:49	16:52	18:50	20:52	22:54	0:53	2:55	4:53
6	7:00	9:02	10:53	12:55	14:53	16:55	18:54	20:56	22:58	0:56	2:59	4:57
7	7:04	9:06	10:57	12:59	14:57	16:59	18:58	21:00	23:02	1:00	3:03	5:01
8	7:08	9:10	11:01	13:03	15:01	17:03	19:02	21:04	23:06	1:04	3:07	5:05
9	7:12	9:14	11:05	13:07	15:05	17:07	19:06	21:08	23:10	1:08	3:11	5:09
10	7:16	9:18	11:09	13:11	15:09	17:11	19:10	21:12	23:14	1:12	3:14	5:13
11	7:20	9:22	11:12	13:15	15:13	17:15	19:13	21:16	23:18	1:16	3:18	5:17
12	7:24	9:26	11:16	13:19	15:17	17:19	19:17	21:20	23:22	1:20	3:22	5:21
13	7:28	9:30	11:20	13:23	15:21	17:23	19:21	21:24	23:26	1:24	3:26	5:25
14	7:32	9:34	11:24	13:27	15:25	17:27	19:25	21:28	23:30	1:28	3:30	5:29
15	7:36	9:38	11:28	13:30	15:29	17:31	19:29	21:31	23:34	1:32	3:34	5:32
16	7:40	9:42	11:32	13:34	15:33	17:35	19:33	21:35	23:38	1:36	3:38	5:36
17	7:44	9:46	11:36	13:38	15:37	17:39	19:37	21:39	23:42	1:40	3:42	5:40
18	7:47	9:50	11:40	13:42	15:41	17:43	19:41	21:43	23:45	1:44	3:46	5:44
19	7:51	9:54	11:44	13:46	15:45	17:47	19:45	21:47	23:49	1:48	3:50	5:48
20	7:55	9:58	11:48	13:50	15:48	17:51	19:49	21:51	23:53	1:52	3:54	5:52
21	7:59	10:01	11:52	13:54	15:52	17:55	19:53	21:55	23:57	1:56	3:58	5:56
22	8:03	10:05	11:56	13:58	15:56	17:59	19:57	21:59	0:01	2:00	4:02	6:00
23	8:07	10:09	12:00	14:02	16:00	18:02	20:01	22:03	0:05	2:03	4:06	6:04
24	8:11	10:13	12:04	14:06	16:04	18:06	20:05	22:07	0:09	2:07	4:10	6:08
25	8:15	10:17	12:08	14:10	16:08	18:10	20:09	22:11	0:13	2:11	4:14	6:12
26	8:19	10:21	12:12	14:14	16:12	18:14	20:13	22:15	0:17	2:15	4:18	6:16
27	8:23	10:25	12:16	14:18	16:16	18:18	20:17	22:19	0:21	2:19	4:21	6:20
28	8:27	10:29	12:19	14:22	16:20	18:22	20:20	22:23	0:25	2:23	4:25	6:24
29	8:31		12:23	14:26	16:24	18:26	20:24	22:27	0:29	2:27	4:29	6:28
30	8:35		12:27	14:30	16:28	18:30	20:28	22:31	0:33	2:31	4:33	6:32
31	8:39		12:31		16:32		20:32	22:35		2:35		6:36

1955	Jan	Feb	Mar	Apr	May	Jun	Jul	Aug	Sep	Oct	Nov	Dec
1	6:39	8:42	10:32	12:34	14:33	16:35	18:33	20:35	22:38	0:36	2:38	4:36
2	6:43	8:46	10:36	12:38	14:37	16:39	18:37	20:39	22:41	0:40	2:42	4:40
3	6:47	8:50	10:40	12:42	14:40	16:43	18:41	20:43	22:45	0:44	2:46	4:44
4	6:51	8:54	10:44	12:46	14:44	16:47	18:45	20:47	22:49	0:48	2:50	4:48
5	6:55	8:57	10:48	12:50	14:48	16:51	18:49	20:51	22:53	0:52	2:54	4:52
6	6:59	9:01	10:52	12:54	14:52	16:55	18:53	20:55	22:57	0:56	2:58	4:56
7	7:03	9:05	10:56	12:58	14:56	16:58	18:57	20:59	23:01	0:59	3:02	5:00
8	7:07	9:09	11:00	13:02	15:00	17:02	19:01	21:03	23:05	1:03	3:06	5:04
9	7:11	9:13	11:04	13:06	15:04	17:06	19:05	21:07	23:09	1:07	3:10	5:08
10	7:15	9:17	11:08	13:10	15:08	17:10	19:09	21:11	23:13	1:11	3:14	5:12
11	7:19	9:21	11:12	13:14	15:12	17:14	19:13	21:15	23:17	1:15	3:17	5:16
12	7:23	9:25	11:15	13:18	15:16	17:18	19:16	21:19	23:21	1:19	3:21	5:20
13	7:27	9:29	11:19	13:22	15:20	17:22	19:20	21:23	23:25	1:23	3:25	5:24
14	7:31	9:33	11:23	13:26	15:24	17:26	19:24	21:27	23:29	1:27	3:29	5:28
15	7:35	9:37	11:27	13:29	15:28	17:30	19:28	21:30	23:33	1:31	3:33	5:31
16	7:39	9:41	11:31	13:33	15:32	17:34	19:32	21:34	23:37	1:35	3:37	5:35
17	7:43	9:45	11:35	13:37	15:36	17:38	19:36	21:38	23:41	1:39	3:41	5:39
18	7:46	9:49	11:39	13:41	15:40	17:42	19:40	21:42	23:45	1:43	3:45	5:43
19	7:50	9:53	11:43	13:45	15:44	17:46	19:44	21:46	23:48	1:47	3:49	5:47
20	7:54	9:57	11:47	13:49	15:47	17:50	19:48	21:50	23:52	1:51	3:53	5:51
21	7:58	10:01	11:51	13:53	15:51	17:54	19:52	21:54	23:56	1:55	3:57	5:55
22	8:02	10:04	11:55	13:57	15:55	17:58	19:56	21:58	0:00	1:59	4:01	5:59
23	8:06	10:08	11:59	14:01	15:59	18:02	20:00	22:02	0:04	2:03	4:05	6:03
24	8:10	10:12	12:03	14:05	16:03	18:05	20:04	22:06	0:08	2:06	4:09	6:07
25	8:14	10:16	12:07	14:09	16:07	18:09	20:08	22:10	0:12	2:10	4:13	6:11
26	8:18	10:20	12:11	14:13	16:11	18:13	20:12	22:14	0:16	2:14	4:17	6:15
27	8:22	10:24	12:15	14:17	16:15	18:17	20:16	22:18	0:20	2:18	4:21	6:19
28	8:26	10:28	12:19	14:21	16:19	18:21	20:20	22:22	0:24	2:22	4:24	6:23
29	8:30		12:22	14:25	16:23	18:25	20:23	22:26	0:28	2:26	4:28	6:27
30	8:34		12:26	14:29	16:27	18:29	20:27	22:30	0:32	2:30	4:32	6:31
31	8:38		12:30		16:31		20:31	22:34		2:34		6:35

1956	Jan	Feb	Mar	Apr	May	Jun	Jul	Aug	Sep	Oct	Nov	Dec
1	6:39	8:41	10:35	12:37	14:36	16:38	18:36	20:38	22:41	0:39	2:41	4:39
2	6:42	8:45	10:39	12:41	14:40	16:42	18:40	20:42	22:44	0:43	2:45	4:43
3	6:46	8:49	10:43	12:45	14:43	16:46	18:44	20:46	22:48	0:47	2:49	4:47
4	6:50	8:53	10:47	12:49	14:47	16:50	18:48	20:50	22:52	0:51	2:53	4:51
5	6:54	8:57	10:51	12:53	14:51	16:54	18:52	20:54	22:56	0:55	2:57	4:55
6	6:58	9:00	10:55	12:57	14:55	16:58	18:56	20:58	23:00	0:58	3:01	4:59
7	7:02	9:04	10:59	13:01	14:59	17:01	19:00	21:02	23:04	1:02	3:05	5:03
8	7:06	9:08	11:03	13:05	15:03	17:05	19:04	21:06	23:08	1:06	3:09	5:07
9	7:10	9:12	11:07	13:09	15:07	17:09	19:08	21:10	23:12	1:10	3:13	5:11
10	7:14	9:16	11:11	13:13	15:11	17:13	19:12	21:14	23:16	1:14	3:16	5:15
11	7:18	9:20	11:14	13:17	15:15	17:17	19:15	21:18	23:20	1:18	3:20	5:19
12	7:22	9:24	11:18	13:21	15:19	17:21	19:19	21:22	23:24	1:22	3:24	5:23
13	7:26	9:28	11:22	13:25	15:23	17:25	19:23	21:26	23:28	1:26	3:28	5:27
14	7:30	9:32	11:26	13:29	15:27	17:29	19:27	21:30	23:32	1:30	3:32	5:31
15	7:34	9:36	11:30	13:32	15:31	17:33	19:31	21:33	23:36	1:34	3:36	5:34
16	7:38	9:40	11:34	13:36	15:35	17:37	19:35	21:37	23:40	1:38	3:40	5:38
17	7:42	9:44	11:38	13:40	15:39	17:41	19:39	21:41	23:44	1:42	3:44	5:42
18	7:46	9:48	11:42	13:44	15:43	17:45	19:43	21:45	23:48	1:46	3:48	5:46
19	7:49	9:52	11:46	13:48	15:47	17:49	19:47	21:49	23:51	1:50	3:52	5:50
20	7:53	9:56	11:50	13:52	15:50	17:53	19:51	21:53	23:55	1:54	3:56	5:54
21	7:57	10:00	11:54	13:56	15:54	17:57	19:55	21:57	23:59	1:58	4:00	5:58
22	8:01	10:04	11:58	14:00	15:58	18:01	19:59	22:01	0:03	2:02	4:04	6:02
23	8:05	10:07	12:02	14:04	16:02	18:05	20:03	22:05	0:07	2:06	4:08	6:06
24	8:09	10:11	12:06	14:08	16:06	18:08	20:07	22:09	0:11	2:09	4:12	6:10
25	8:13	10:15	12:10	14:12	16:10	18:12	20:11	22:13	0:15	2:13	4:16	6:14
26	8:17	10:19	12:14	14:16	16:14	18:16	20:15	22:17	0:19	2:17	4:20	6:18
27	8:21	10:23	12:18	14:20	16:18	18:20	20:19	22:21	0:23	2:21	4:24	6:22
28	8:25	10:27	12:22	14:24	16:22	18:24	20:23	22:25	0:27	2:25	4:27	6:26
29	8:29	10:31	12:25	14:28	16:26	18:28	20:26	22:29	0:31	2:29	4:31	6:30
30	8:33		12:29	14:32	16:30	18:32	20:30	22:33	0:35	2:33	4:35	6:34
31	8:37		12:33		16:34		20:34	22:37		2:37		6:38

1957	Jan	Feb	Mar	Apr	May	Jun	Jul	Aug	Sep	Oct	Nov	Dec
1	6:42	8:44	10:34	12:36	14:35	16:37	18:35	20:37	22:40	0:38	2:40	4:38
2	6:45	8:48	10:38	12:40	14:39	16:41	18:39	20:41	22:43	0:42	2:44	4:42
3	6:49	8:52	10:42	12:44	14:42	16:45	18:43	20:45	22:47	0:46	2:48	4:46
4	6:53	8:56	10:46	12:48	14:46	16:49	18:47	20:49	22:51	0:50	2:52	4:50
5	6:57	8:59	10:50	12:52	14:50	16:53	18:51	20:53	22:55	0:54	2:56	4:54
6	7:01	9:03	10:54	12:56	14:54	16:57	18:55	20:57	22:59	0:58	3:00	4:58
7	7:05	9:07	10:58	13:00	14:58	17:00	18:59	21:01	23:03	1:01	3:04	5:02
8	7:09	9:11	11:02	13:04	15:02	17:04	19:03	21:05	23:07	1:05	3:08	5:06
9	7:13	9:15	11:06	13:08	15:06	17:08	19:07	21:09	23:11	1:09	3:12	5:10
10	7:17	9:19	11:10	13:12	15:10	17:12	19:11	21:13	23:15	1:13	3:16	5:14
11	7:21	9:23	11:14	13:16	15:14	17:16	19:15	21:17	23:19	1:17	3:19	5:18
12	7:25	9:27	11:17	13:20	15:18	17:20	19:18	21:21	23:23	1:21	3:23	5:22
13	7:29	9:31	11:21	13:24	15:22	17:24	19:22	21:25	23:27	1:25	3:27	5:26
14	7:33	9:35	11:25	13:28	15:26	17:28	19:26	21:29	23:31	1:29	3:31	5:30
15	7:37	9:39	11:29	13:32	15:30	17:32	19:30	21:33	23:35	1:33	3:35	5:34
16	7:41	9:43	11:33	13:35	15:34	17:36	19:34	21:36	23:39	1:37	3:39	5:37
17	7:45	9:47	11:37	13:39	15:38	17:40	19:38	21:40	23:43	1:41	3:43	5:41
18	7:49	9:51	11:41	13:43	15:42	17:44	19:42	21:44	23:47	1:45	3:47	5:45
19	7:52	9:55	11:45	13:47	15:46	17:48	19:46	21:48	23:51	1:49	3:51	5:49
20	7:56	9:59	11:49	13:51	15:50	17:52	19:50	21:52	23:54	1:53	3:55	5:53
21	8:00	10:03	11:53	13:55	15:53	17:56	19:54	21:56	23:58	1:57	3:59	5:57
22	8:04	10:07	11:57	13:59	15:57	18:00	19:58	22:00	0:02	2:01	4:03	6:01
23	8:08	10:10	12:01	14:03	16:01	18:04	20:02	22:04	0:06	2:05	4:07	6:05
24	8:12	10:14	12:05	14:07	16:05	18:08	20:06	22:08	0:10	2:09	4:11	6:09
25	8:16	10:18	12:09	14:11	16:09	18:11	20:10	22:12	0:14	2:12	4:15	6:13
26	8:20	10:22	12:13	14:15	16:13	18:15	20:14	22:16	0:18	2:16	4:19	6:17
27	8:24	10:26	12:17	14:19	16:17	18:19	20:18	22:20	0:22	2:20	4:23	6:21
28	8:28	10:30	12:21	14:23	16:21	18:23	20:22	22:24	0:26	2:24	4:27	6:25
29	8:32		12:25	14:27	16:25	18:27	20:26	22:28	0:30	2:28	4:30	6:29
30	8:36		12:28	14:31	16:29	18:31	20:29	22:32	0:34	2:32	4:34	6:33
31	8:40		12:32		16:33		20:33	22:36		2:36		6:37

1958	Jan	Feb	Mar	Apr	May	Jun	Jul	Aug	Sep	Oct	Nov	Dec
1	6:41	8:43	10:33	12:35	14:34	16:36	18:34	20:36	22:39	0:37	2:39	4:37
2	6:44	8:47	10:37	12:39	14:38	16:40	18:38	20:40	22:43	0:41	2:43	4:41
3	6:48	8:51	10:41	12:43	14:42	16:44	18:42	20:44	22:46	0:45	2:47	4:45
4	6:52	8:55	10:45	12:47	14:45	16:48	18:46	20:48	22:50	0:49	2:51	4:49
5	6:56	8:59	10:49	12:51	14:49	16:52	18:50	20:52	22:54	0:53	2:55	4:53
6	7:00	9:02	10:53	12:55	14:53	16:56	18:54	20:56	22:58	0:57	2:59	4:57
7	7:04	9:06	10:57	12:59	14:57	17:00	18:58	21:00	23:02	1:01	3:03	5:01
8	7:08	9:10	11:01	13:03	15:01	17:03	19:02	21:04	23:06	1:04	3:07	5:05
9	7:12	9:14	11:05	13:07	15:05	17:07	19:06	21:08	23:10	1:08	3:11	5:09
10	7:16	9:18	11:09	13:11	15:09	17:11	19:10	21:12	23:14	1:12	3:15	5:13
11	7:20	9:22	11:13	13:15	15:13	17:15	19:14	21:16	23:18	1:16	3:19	5:17
12	7:24	9:26	11:17	13:19	15:17	17:19	19:18	21:20	23:22	1:20	3:22	5:21
13	7:28	9:30	11:20	13:23	15:21	17:23	19:21	21:24	23:26	1:24	3:26	5:25
14	7:32	9:34	11:24	13:27	15:25	17:27	19:25	21:28	23:30	1:28	3:30	5:29
15	7:36	9:38	11:28	13:31	15:29	17:31	19:29	21:32	23:34	1:32	3:34	5:33
16	7:40	9:42	11:32	13:35	15:33	17:35	19:33	21:36	23:38	1:36	3:38	5:37
17	7:44	9:46	11:36	13:38	15:37	17:39	19:37	21:39	23:42	1:40	3:42	5:40
18	7:48	9:50	11:40	13:42	15:41	17:43	19:41	21:43	23:46	1:44	3:46	5:44
19	7:52	9:54	11:44	13:46	15:45	17:47	19:45	21:47	23:50	1:48	3:50	5:48
20	7:55	9:58	11:48	13:50	15:49	17:51	19:49	21:51	23:54	1:52	3:54	5:52
21	7:59	10:02	11:52	13:54	15:53	17:55	19:53	21:55	23:57	1:56	3:58	5:56
22	8:03	10:06	11:56	13:58	15:56	17:59	19:57	21:59	0:01	2:00	4:02	6:00
23	8:07	10:10	12:00	14:02	16:00	18:03	20:01	22:03	0:05	2:04	4:06	6:04
24	8:11	10:13	12:04	14:06	16:04	18:07	20:05	22:07	0:09	2:08	4:10	6:08
25	8:15	10:17	12:08	14:10	16:08	18:11	20:09	22:11	0:13	2:11	4:14	6:12
26	8:19	10:21	12:12	14:14	16:12	18:14	20:13	22:15	0:17	2:15	4:18	6:16
27	8:23	10:25	12:16	14:18	16:16	18:18	20:17	22:19	0:21	2:19	4:22	6:20
28	8:27	10:29	12:20	14:22	16:20	18:22	20:21	22:23	0:25	2:23	4:26	6:24
29	8:31		12:24	14:26	16:24	18:26	20:25	22:27	0:29	2:27	4:29	6:28
30	8:35		12:27	14:30	16:28	18:30	20:28	22:31	0:33	2:31	4:33	6:32
31	8:39		12:31		16:32		20:32	22:35		2:35		6:36

1959	Jan	Feb	Mar	Apr	May	Jun	Jul	Aug	Sep	Oct	Nov	Dec
1	6:40	8:42	10:32	12:34	14:33	16:35	18:33	20:35	22:38	0:36	2:38	4:36
2	6:44	8:46	10:36	12:38	14:37	16:39	18:37	20:39	22:42	0:40	2:42	4:40
3	6:47	8:50	10:40	12:42	14:41	16:43	18:41	20:43	22:46	0:44	2:46	4:44
4	6:51	8:54	10:44	12:46	14:45	16:47	18:45	20:47	22:49	0:48	2:50	4:48
5	6:55	8:58	10:48	12:50	14:48	16:51	18:49	20:51	22:53	0:52	2:54	4:52
6	6:59	9:02	10:52	12:54	14:52	16:55	18:53	20:55	22:57	0:56	2:58	4:56
7	7:03	9:05	10:56	12:58	14:56	16:59	18:57	20:59	23:01	1:00	3:02	5:00
8	7:07	9:09	11:00	13:02	15:00	17:03	19:01	21:03	23:05	1:04	3:06	5:04
9	7:11	9:13	11:04	13:06	15:04	17:06	19:05	21:07	23:09	1:07	3:10	5:08
10	7:15	9:17	11:08	13:10	15:08	17:10	19:09	21:11	23:13	1:11	3:14	5:12
11	7:19	9:21	11:12	13:14	15:12	17:14	19:13	21:15	23:17	1:15	3:18	5:16
12	7:23	9:25	11:16	13:18	15:16	17:18	19:17	21:19	23:21	1:19	3:22	5:20
13	7:27	9:29	11:20	13:22	15:20	17:22	19:21	21:23	23:25	1:23	3:25	5:24
14	7:31	9:33	11:23	13:26	15:24	17:26	19:24	21:27	23:29	1:27	3:29	5:28
15	7:35	9:37	11:27	13:30	15:28	17:30	19:28	21:31	23:33	1:31	3:33	5:32
16	7:39	9:41	11:31	13:34	15:32	17:34	19:32	21:35	23:37	1:35	3:37	5:36
17	7:43	9:45	11:35	13:38	15:36	17:38	19:36	21:39	23:41	1:39	3:41	5:39
18	7:47	9:49	11:39	13:41	15:40	17:42	19:40	21:42	23:45	1:43	3:45	5:43
19	7:51	9:53	11:43	13:45	15:44	17:46	19:44	21:46	23:49	1:47	3:49	5:47
20	7:55	9:57	11:47	13:49	15:48	17:50	19:48	21:50	23:53	1:51	3:53	5:51
21	7:58	10:01	11:51	13:53	15:52	17:54	19:52	21:54	23:56	1:55	3:57	5:55
22	8:02	10:05	11:55	13:57	15:55	17:58	19:56	21:58	0:00	1:59	4:01	5:59
23	8:06	10:09	11:59	14:01	15:59	18:02	20:00	22:02	0:04	2:03	4:05	6:03
24	8:10	10:12	12:03	14:05	16:03	18:06	20:04	22:06	0:08	2:07	4:09	6:07
25	8:14	10:16	12:07	14:09	16:07	18:10	20:08	22:10	0:12	2:11	4:13	6:11
26	8:18	10:20	12:11	14:13	16:11	18:13	20:12	22:14	0:16	2:14	4:17	6:15
27	8:22	10:24	12:15	14:17	16:15	18:17	20:16	22:18	0:20	2:18	4:21	6:19
28	8:26	10:28	12:19	14:21	16:19	18:21	20:20	22:22	0:24	2:22	4:25	6:23
29	8:30		12:23	14:25	16:23	18:25	20:24	22:26	0:28	2:26	4:29	6:27
30	8:34		12:27	14:29	16:27	18:29	20:28	22:30	0:32	2:30	4:32	6:31
31	8:38		12:30		16:31		20:31	22:34		2:34		6:35

1960	Jan	Feb	Mar	Apr	May	Jun	Jul	Aug	Sep	Oct	Nov	Dec
1	6:39	8:41	10:35	12:37	14:36	16:38	18:36	20:38	22:41	0:39	2:41	4:39
2	6:43	8:45	10:39	12:41	14:40	16:42	18:40	20:42	22:45	0:43	2:45	4:43
3	6:47	8:49	10:43	12:45	14:44	16:46	18:44	20:46	22:49	0:47	2:49	4:47
4	6:50	8:53	10:47	12:49	14:48	16:50	18:48	20:50	22:52	0:51	2:53	4:51
5	6:54	8:57	10:51	12:53	14:51	16:54	18:52	20:54	22:56	0:55	2:57	4:55
6	6:58	9:01	10:55	12:57	14:55	16:58	18:56	20:58	23:00	0:59	3:01	4:59
7	7:02	9:05	10:59	13:01	14:59	17:02	19:00	21:02	23:04	1:03	3:05	5:03
8	7:06	9:08	11:03	13:05	15:03	17:06	19:04	21:06	23:08	1:07	3:09	5:07
9	7:10	9:12	11:07	13:09	15:07	17:09	19:08	21:10	23:12	1:10	3:13	5:11
10	7:14	9:16	11:11	13:13	15:11	17:13	19:12	21:14	23:16	1:14	3:17	5:15
11	7:18	9:20	11:15	13:17	15:15	17:17	19:16	21:18	23:20	1:18	3:21	5:19
12	7:22	9:24	11:19	13:21	15:19	17:21	19:20	21:22	23:24	1:22	3:24	5:23
13	7:26	9:28	11:23	13:25	15:23	17:25	19:24	21:26	23:28	1:26	3:28	5:27
14	7:30	9:32	11:26	13:29	15:27	17:29	19:27	21:30	23:32	1:30	3:32	5:31
15	7:34	9:36	11:30	13:33	15:31	17:33	19:31	21:34	23:36	1:34	3:36	5:35
16	7:38	9:40	11:34	13:37	15:35	17:37	19:35	21:38	23:40	1:38	3:40	5:39
17	7:42	9:44	11:38	13:40	15:39	17:41	19:39	21:41	23:44	1:42	3:44	5:42
18	7:46	9:48	11:42	13:44	15:43	17:45	19:43	21:45	23:48	1:46	3:48	5:46
19	7:50	9:52	11:46	13:48	15:47	17:49	19:47	21:49	23:52	1:50	3:52	5:50
20	7:54	9:56	11:50	13:52	15:51	17:53	19:51	21:53	23:56	1:54	3:56	5:54
21	7:57	10:00	11:54	13:56	15:55	17:57	19:55	21:57	23:59	1:58	4:00	5:58
22	8:01	10:04	11:58	14:00	15:58	18:01	19:59	22:01	0:03	2:02	4:04	6:02
23	8:05	10:08	12:02	14:04	16:02	18:05	20:03	22:05	0:07	2:06	4:08	6:06
24	8:09	10:12	12:06	14:08	16:06	18:09	20:07	22:09	0:11	2:10	4:12	6:10
25	8:13	10:15	12:10	14:12	16:10	18:13	20:11	22:13	0:15	2:14	4:16	6:14
26	8:17	10:19	12:14	14:16	16:14	18:16	20:15	22:17	0:19	2:17	4:20	6:18
27	8:21	10:23	12:18	14:20	16:18	18:20	20:19	22:21	0:23	2:21	4:24	6:22
28	8:25	10:27	12:22	14:24	16:22	18:24	20:23	22:25	0:27	2:25	4:28	6:26
29	8:29	10:31	12:26	14:28	16:26	18:28	20:27	22:29	0:31	2:29	4:32	6:30
30	8:33		12:30	14:32	16:30	18:32	20:31	22:33	0:35	2:33	4:35	6:34
31	8:37		12:33		16:34		20:34	22:37		2:37		6:38

1961	Jan	Feb	Mar	Apr	May	Jun	Jul	Aug	Sep	Oct	Nov	Dec
1	6:42	8:44	10:34	12:36	14:35	16:37	18:35	20:37	22:40	0:38	2:40	4:38
2	6:46	8:48	10:38	12:40	14:39	16:41	18:39	20:41	22:44	0:42	2:44	4:42
3	6:50	8:52	10:42	12:44	14:43	16:45	18:43	20:45	22:48	0:46	2:48	4:46
4	6:53	8:56	10:46	12:48	14:47	16:49	18:47	20:49	22:52	0:50	2:52	4:50
5	6:57	9:00	10:50	12:52	14:51	16:53	18:51	20:53	22:55	0:54	2:56	4:54
6	7:01	9:04	10:54	12:56	14:54	16:57	18:55	20:57	22:59	0:58	3:00	4:58
7	7:05	9:08	10:58	13:00	14:58	17:01	18:59	21:01	23:03	1:02	3:04	5:02
8	7:09	9:11	11:02	13:04	15:02	17:05	19:03	21:05	23:07	1:06	3:08	5:06
9	7:13	9:15	11:06	13:08	15:06	17:08	19:07	21:09	23:11	1:09	3:12	5:10
10	7:17	9:19	11:10	13:12	15:10	17:12	19:11	21:13	23:15	1:13	3:16	5:14
11	7:21	9:23	11:14	13:16	15:14	17:16	19:15	21:17	23:19	1:17	3:20	5:18
12	7:25	9:27	11:18	13:20	15:18	17:20	19:19	21:21	23:23	1:21	3:24	5:22
13	7:29	9:31	11:22	13:24	15:22	17:24	19:23	21:25	23:27	1:25	3:27	5:26
14	7:33	9:35	11:25	13:28	15:26	17:28	19:26	21:29	23:31	1:29	3:31	5:30
15	7:37	9:39	11:29	13:32	15:30	17:32	19:30	21:33	23:35	1:33	3:35	5:34
16	7:41	9:43	11:33	13:36	15:34	17:36	19:34	21:37	23:39	1:37	3:39	5:38
17	7:45	9:47	11:37	13:40	15:38	17:40	19:38	21:41	23:43	1:41	3:43	5:42
18	7:49	9:51	11:41	13:43	15:42	17:44	19:42	21:44	23:47	1:45	3:47	5:45
19	7:53	9:55	11:45	13:47	15:46	17:48	19:46	21:48	23:51	1:49	3:51	5:49
20	7:57	9:59	11:49	13:51	15:50	17:52	19:50	21:52	23:55	1:53	3:55	5:53
21	8:00	10:03	11:53	13:55	15:54	17:56	19:54	21:56	23:59	1:57	3:59	5:57
22	8:04	10:07	11:57	13:59	15:58	18:00	19:58	22:00	0:02	2:01	4:03	6:01
23	8:08	10:11	12:01	14:03	16:01	18:04	20:02	22:04	0:06	2:05	4:07	6:05
24	8:12	10:15	12:05	14:07	16:05	18:08	20:06	22:08	0:10	2:09	4:11	6:09
25	8:16	10:18	12:09	14:11	16:09	18:12	20:10	22:12	0:14	2:13	4:15	6:13
26	8:20	10:22	12:13	14:15	16:13	18:16	20:14	22:16	0:18	2:17	4:19	6:17
27	8:24	10:26	12:17	14:19	16:17	18:19	20:18	22:20	0:22	2:20	4:23	6:21
28	8:28	10:30	12:21	14:23	16:21	18:23	20:22	22:24	0:26	2:24	4:27	6:25
29	8:32		12:25	14:27	16:25	18:27	20:26	22:28	0:30	2:28	4:31	6:29
30	8:36		12:29	14:31	16:29	18:31	20:30	22:32	0:34	2:32	4:35	6:33
31	8:40		12:33		16:33		20:34	22:36		2:36		6:37

1962	Jan	Feb	Mar	Apr	May	Jun	Jul	Aug	Sep	Oct	Nov	Dec
1	6:41	8:43	10:33	12:36	14:34	16:36	18:34	20:37	22:39	0:37	2:39	4:37
2	6:45	8:47	10:37	12:39	14:38	16:40	18:38	20:40	22:43	0:41	2:43	4:41
3	6:49	8:51	10:41	12:43	14:42	16:44	18:42	20:44	22:47	0:45	2:47	4:45
4	6:52	8:55	10:45	12:47	14:46	16:48	18:46	20:48	22:51	0:49	2:51	4:49
5	6:56	8:59	10:49	12:51	14:50	16:52	18:50	20:52	22:54	0:53	2:55	4:53
6	7:00	9:03	10:53	12:55	14:53	16:56	18:54	20:56	22:58	0:57	2:59	4:57
7	7:04	9:07	10:57	12:59	14:57	17:00	18:58	21:00	23:02	1:01	3:03	5:01
8	7:08	9:10	11:01	13:03	15:01	17:04	19:02	21:04	23:06	1:05	3:07	5:05
9	7:12	9:14	11:05	13:07	15:05	17:08	19:06	21:08	23:10	1:09	3:11	5:09
10	7:16	9:18	11:09	13:11	15:09	17:11	19:10	21:12	23:14	1:12	3:15	5:13
11	7:20	9:22	11:13	13:15	15:13	17:15	19:14	21:16	23:18	1:16	3:19	5:17
12	7:24	9:26	11:17	13:19	15:17	17:19	19:18	21:20	23:22	1:20	3:23	5:21
13	7:28	9:30	11:21	13:23	15:21	17:23	19:22	21:24	23:26	1:24	3:27	5:25
14	7:32	9:34	11:25	13:27	15:25	17:27	19:26	21:28	23:30	1:28	3:30	5:29
15	7:36	9:38	11:28	13:31	15:29	17:31	19:29	21:32	23:34	1:32	3:34	5:33
16	7:40	9:42	11:32	13:35	15:33	17:35	19:33	21:36	23:38	1:36	3:38	5:37
17	7:44	9:46	11:36	13:39	15:37	17:39	19:37	21:40	23:42	1:40	3:42	5:41
18	7:48	9:50	11:40	13:43	15:41	17:43	19:41	21:44	23:46	1:44	3:46	5:45
19	7:52	9:54	11:44	13:46	15:45	17:47	19:45	21:47	23:50	1:48	3:50	5:48
20	7:56	9:58	11:48	13:50	15:49	17:51	19:49	21:51	23:54	1:52	3:54	5:52
21	8:00	10:02	11:52	13:54	15:53	17:55	19:53	21:55	23:58	1:56	3:58	5:56
22	8:03	10:06	11:56	13:58	15:57	17:59	19:57	21:59	0:02	2:00	4:02	6:00
23	8:07	10:10	12:00	14:02	16:01	18:03	20:01	22:03	0:05	2:04	4:06	6:04
24	8:11	10:14	12:04	14:06	16:04	18:07	20:05	22:07	0:09	2:08	4:10	6:08
25	8:15	10:18	12:08	14:10	16:08	18:11	20:09	22:11	0:13	2:12	4:14	6:12
26	8:19	10:21	12:12	14:14	16:12	18:15	20:13	22:15	0:17	2:16	4:18	6:16
27	8:23	10:25	12:16	14:18	16:16	18:19	20:17	22:19	0:21	2:20	4:22	6:20
28	8:27	10:29	12:20	14:22	16:20	18:22	20:21	22:23	0:25	2:23	4:26	6:24
29	8:31		12:24	14:26	16:24	18:26	20:25	22:27	0:29	2:27	4:30	6:28
30	8:35		12:28	14:30	16:28	18:30	20:29	22:31	0:33	2:31	4:34	6:32
31	8:39		12:32		16:32		20:33	22:35		2:35		6:36

1963	Jan	Feb	Mar	Apr	May	Jun	Jul	Aug	Sep	Oct	Nov	Dec
1	6:40	8:42	10:32	12:35	14:33	16:35	18:33	20:36	22:38	0:36	2:38	4:37
2	6:44	8:46	10:36	12:38	14:37	16:39	18:37	20:39	22:42	0:40	2:42	4:40
3	6:48	8:50	10:40	12:42	14:41	16:43	18:41	20:43	22:46	0:44	2:46	4:44
4	6:52	8:54	10:44	12:46	14:45	16:47	18:45	20:47	22:50	0:48	2:50	4:48
5	6:55	8:58	10:48	12:50	14:49	16:51	18:49	20:51	22:54	0:52	2:54	4:52
6	6:59	9:02	10:52	12:54	14:53	16:55	18:53	20:55	22:57	0:56	2:58	4:56
7	7:03	9:06	10:56	12:58	14:56	16:59	18:57	20:59	23:01	1:00	3:02	5:00
8	7:07	9:10	11:00	13:02	15:00	17:03	19:01	21:03	23:05	1:04	3:06	5:04
9	7:11	9:13	11:04	13:06	15:04	17:07	19:05	21:07	23:09	1:08	3:10	5:08
10	7:15	9:17	11:08	13:10	15:08	17:11	19:09	21:11	23:13	1:12	3:14	5:12
11	7:19	9:21	11:12	13:14	15:12	17:14	19:13	21:15	23:17	1:15	3:18	5:16
12	7:23	9:25	11:16	13:18	15:16	17:18	19:17	21:19	23:21	1:19	3:22	5:20
13	7:27	9:29	11:20	13:22	15:20	17:22	19:21	21:23	23:25	1:23	3:26	5:24
14	7:31	9:33	11:24	13:26	15:24	17:26	19:25	21:27	23:29	1:27	3:30	5:28
15	7:35	9:37	11:28	13:30	15:28	17:30	19:29	21:31	23:33	1:31	3:33	5:32
16	7:39	9:41	11:31	13:34	15:32	17:34	19:32	21:35	23:37	1:35	3:37	5:36
17	7:43	9:45	11:35	13:38	15:36	17:38	19:36	21:39	23:41	1:39	3:41	5:40
18	7:47	9:49	11:39	13:42	15:40	17:42	19:40	21:43	23:45	1:43	3:45	5:44
19	7:51	9:53	11:43	13:46	15:44	17:46	19:44	21:47	23:49	1:47	3:49	5:48
20	7:55	9:57	11:47	13:49	15:48	17:50	19:48	21:50	23:53	1:51	3:53	5:51
21	7:59	10:01	11:51	13:53	15:52	17:54	19:52	21:54	23:57	1:55	3:57	5:55
22	8:03	10:05	11:55	13:57	15:56	17:58	19:56	21:58	0:01	1:59	4:01	5:59
23	8:06	10:09	11:59	14:01	16:00	18:02	20:00	22:02	0:05	2:03	4:05	6:03
24	8:10	10:13	12:03	14:05	16:04	18:06	20:04	22:06	0:08	2:07	4:09	6:07
25	8:14	10:17	12:07	14:09	16:07	18:10	20:08	22:10	0:12	2:11	4:13	6:11
26	8:18	10:21	12:11	14:13	16:11	18:14	20:12	22:14	0:16	2:15	4:17	6:15
27	8:22	10:24	12:15	14:17	16:15	18:18	20:16	22:18	0:20	2:19	4:21	6:19
28	8:26	10:28	12:19	14:21	16:19	18:21	20:20	22:22	0:24	2:22	4:25	6:23
29	8:30		12:23	14:25	16:23	18:25	20:24	22:26	0:28	2:26	4:29	6:27
30	8:34		12:27	14:29	16:27	18:29	20:28	22:30	0:32	2:30	4:33	6:31
31	8:38		12:31		16:31		20:32	22:34		2:34		6:35

1964	Jan	Feb	Mar	Apr	May	Jun	Jul	Aug	Sep	Oct	Nov	Dec
1	6:39	8:41	10:35	12:38	14:36	16:38	18:36	20:39	22:41	0:39	2:41	4:40
2	6:43	8:45	10:39	12:41	14:40	16:42	18:40	20:42	22:45	0:43	2:45	4:43
3	6:47	8:49	10:43	12:45	14:44	16:46	18:44	20:46	22:49	0:47	2:49	4:47
4	6:51	8:53	10:47	12:49	14:48	16:50	18:48	20:50	22:53	0:51	2:53	4:51
5	6:55	8:57	10:51	12:53	14:52	16:54	18:52	20:54	22:57	0:55	2:57	4:55
6	6:58	9:01	10:55	12:57	14:56	16:58	18:56	20:58	23:00	0:59	3:01	4:59
7	7:02	9:05	10:59	13:01	14:59	17:02	19:00	21:02	23:04	1:03	3:05	5:03
8	7:06	9:09	11:03	13:05	15:03	17:06	19:04	21:06	23:08	1:07	3:09	5:07
9	7:10	9:13	11:07	13:09	15:07	17:10	19:08	21:10	23:12	1:11	3:13	5:11
10	7:14	9:16	11:11	13:13	15:11	17:14	19:12	21:14	23:16	1:15	3:17	5:15
11	7:18	9:20	11:15	13:17	15:15	17:17	19:16	21:18	23:20	1:18	3:21	5:19
12	7:22	9:24	11:19	13:21	15:19	17:21	19:20	21:22	23:24	1:22	3:25	5:23
13	7:26	9:28	11:23	13:25	15:23	17:25	19:24	21:26	23:28	1:26	3:29	5:27
14	7:30	9:32	11:27	13:29	15:27	17:29	19:28	21:30	23:32	1:30	3:33	5:31
15	7:34	9:36	11:31	13:33	15:31	17:33	19:32	21:34	23:36	1:34	3:36	5:35
16	7:38	9:40	11:34	13:37	15:35	17:37	19:35	21:38	23:40	1:38	3:40	5:39
17	7:42	9:44	11:38	13:41	15:39	17:41	19:39	21:42	23:44	1:42	3:44	5:43
18	7:46	9:48	11:42	13:45	15:43	17:45	19:43	21:46	23:48	1:46	3:48	5:47
19	7:50	9:52	11:46	13:49	15:47	17:49	19:47	21:49	23:52	1:50	3:52	5:50
20	7:54	9:56	11:50	13:52	15:51	17:53	19:51	21:53	23:56	1:54	3:56	5:54
21	7:58	10:00	11:54	13:56	15:55	17:57	19:55	21:57	0:00	1:58	4:00	5:58
22	8:02	10:04	11:58	14:00	15:59	18:01	19:59	22:01	0:04	2:02	4:04	6:02
23	8:05	10:08	12:02	14:04	16:03	18:05	20:03	22:05	0:07	2:06	4:08	6:06
24	8:09	10:12	12:06	14:08	16:06	18:09	20:07	22:09	0:11	2:10	4:12	6:10
25	8:13	10:16	12:10	14:12	16:10	18:13	20:11	22:13	0:15	2:14	4:16	6:14
26	8:17	10:20	12:14	14:16	16:14	18:17	20:15	22:17	0:19	2:18	4:20	6:18
27	8:21	10:23	12:18	14:20	16:18	18:21	20:19	22:21	0:23	2:22	4:24	6:22
28	8:25	10:27	12:22	14:24	16:22	18:24	20:23	22:25	0:27	2:25	4:28	6:26
29	8:29	10:31	12:26	14:28	16:26	18:28	20:27	22:29	0:31	2:29	4:32	6:30
30	8:33		12:30	14:32	16:30	18:32	20:31	22:33	0:35	2:33	4:36	6:34
31	8:37		12:34		16:34		20:35	22:37		2:37		6:38

1965	Jan	Feb	Mar	Apr	May	Jun	Jul	Aug	Sep	Oct	Nov	Dec
1	6:42	8:44	10:34	12:37	14:35	16:37	18:35	20:38	22:40	0:38	2:40	4:39
2	6:46	8:48	10:38	12:41	14:39	16:41	18:39	20:42	22:44	0:42	2:44	4:43
3	6:50	8:52	10:42	12:44	14:43	16:45	18:43	20:45	22:48	0:46	2:48	4:46
4	6:54	8:56	10:46	12:48	14:47	16:49	18:47	20:49	22:52	0:50	2:52	4:50
5	6:58	9:00	10:50	12:52	14:51	16:53	18:51	20:53	22:56	0:54	2:56	4:54
6	7:01	9:04	10:54	12:56	14:55	16:57	18:55	20:57	23:00	0:58	3:00	4:58
7	7:05	9:08	10:58	13:00	14:59	17:01	18:59	21:01	23:03	1:02	3:04	5:02
8	7:09	9:12	11:02	13:04	15:02	17:05	19:03	21:05	23:07	1:06	3:08	5:06
9	7:13	9:16	11:06	13:08	15:06	17:09	19:07	21:09	23:11	1:10	3:12	5:10
10	7:17	9:19	11:10	13:12	15:10	17:13	19:11	21:13	23:15	1:14	3:16	5:14
11	7:21	9:23	11:14	13:16	15:14	17:17	19:15	21:17	23:19	1:18	3:20	5:18
12	7:25	9:27	11:18	13:20	15:18	17:20	19:19	21:21	23:23	1:21	3:24	5:22
13	7:29	9:31	11:22	13:24	15:22	17:24	19:23	21:25	23:27	1:25	3:28	5:26
14	7:33	9:35	11:26	13:28	15:26	17:28	19:27	21:29	23:31	1:29	3:32	5:30
15	7:37	9:39	11:30	13:32	15:30	17:32	19:31	21:33	23:35	1:33	3:35	5:34
16	7:41	9:43	11:34	13:36	15:34	17:36	19:34	21:37	23:39	1:37	3:39	5:38
17	7:45	9:47	11:37	13:40	15:38	17:40	19:38	21:41	23:43	1:41	3:43	5:42
18	7:49	9:51	11:41	13:44	15:42	17:44	19:42	21:45	23:47	1:45	3:47	5:46
19	7:53	9:55	11:45	13:48	15:46	17:48	19:46	21:49	23:51	1:49	3:51	5:50
20	7:57	9:59	11:49	13:51	15:50	17:52	19:50	21:52	23:55	1:53	3:55	5:53
21	8:01	10:03	11:53	13:55	15:54	17:56	19:54	21:56	23:59	1:57	3:59	5:57
22	8:05	10:07	11:57	13:59	15:58	18:00	19:58	22:00	0:03	2:01	4:03	6:01
23	8:08	10:11	12:01	14:03	16:02	18:04	20:02	22:04	0:07	2:05	4:07	6:05
24	8:12	10:15	12:05	14:07	16:06	18:08	20:06	22:08	0:10	2:09	4:11	6:09
25	8:16	10:19	12:09	14:11	16:09	18:12	20:10	22:12	0:14	2:13	4:15	6:13
26	8:20	10:23	12:13	14:15	16:13	18:16	20:14	22:16	0:18	2:17	4:19	6:17
27	8:24	10:26	12:17	14:19	16:17	18:20	20:18	22:20	0:22	2:21	4:23	6:21
28	8:28	10:30	12:21	14:23	16:21	18:24	20:22	22:24	0:26	2:25	4:27	6:25
29	8:32		12:25	14:27	16:25	18:27	20:26	22:28	0:30	2:28	4:31	6:29
30	8:36		12:29	14:31	16:29	18:31	20:30	22:32	0:34	2:32	4:35	6:33
31	8:40		12:33		16:33		20:34	22:36		2:36		6:37

1966	Jan	Feb	Mar	Apr	May	Jun	Jul	Aug	Sep	Oct	Nov	Dec
1	6:41	8:43	10:33	12:36	14:34	16:36	18:34	20:37	22:39	0:37	2:39	4:38
2	6:45	8:47	10:37	12:40	14:38	16:40	18:38	20:41	22:43	0:41	2:43	4:42
3	6:49	8:51	10:41	12:44	14:42	16:44	18:42	20:45	22:47	0:45	2:47	4:46
4	6:53	8:55	10:45	12:47	14:46	16:48	18:46	20:48	22:51	0:49	2:51	4:49
5	6:57	8:59	10:49	12:51	14:50	16:52	18:50	20:52	22:55	0:53	2:55	4:53
6	7:01	9:03	10:53	12:55	14:54	16:56	18:54	20:56	22:59	0:57	2:59	4:57
7	7:04	9:07	10:57	12:59	14:58	17:00	18:58	21:00	23:02	1:01	3:03	5:01
8	7:08	9:11	11:01	13:03	15:02	17:04	19:02	21:04	23:06	1:05	3:07	5:05
9	7:12	9:15	11:05	13:07	15:05	17:08	19:06	21:08	23:10	1:09	3:11	5:09
10	7:16	9:18	11:09	13:11	15:09	17:12	19:10	21:12	23:14	1:13	3:15	5:13
11	7:20	9:22	11:13	13:15	15:13	17:16	19:14	21:16	23:18	1:17	3:19	5:17
12	7:24	9:26	11:17	13:19	15:17	17:19	19:18	21:20	23:22	1:20	3:23	5:21
13	7:28	9:30	11:21	13:23	15:21	17:23	19:22	21:24	23:26	1:24	3:27	5:25
14	7:32	9:34	11:25	13:27	15:25	17:27	19:26	21:28	23:30	1:28	3:31	5:29
15	7:36	9:38	11:29	13:31	15:29	17:31	19:30	21:32	23:34	1:32	3:35	5:33
16	7:40	9:42	11:33	13:35	15:33	17:35	19:34	21:36	23:38	1:36	3:38	5:37
17	7:44	9:46	11:36	13:39	15:37	17:39	19:37	21:40	23:42	1:40	3:42	5:41
18	7:48	9:50	11:40	13:43	15:41	17:43	19:41	21:44	23:46	1:44	3:46	5:45
19	7:52	9:54	11:44	13:47	15:45	17:47	19:45	21:48	23:50	1:48	3:50	5:49
20	7:56	9:58	11:48	13:51	15:49	17:51	19:49	21:52	23:54	1:52	3:54	5:53
21	8:00	10:02	11:52	13:54	15:53	17:55	19:53	21:55	23:58	1:56	3:58	5:56
22	8:04	10:06	11:56	13:58	15:57	17:59	19:57	21:59	0:02	2:00	4:02	6:00
23	8:08	10:10	12:00	14:02	16:01	18:03	20:01	22:03	0:06	2:04	4:06	6:04
24	8:11	10:14	12:04	14:06	16:05	18:07	20:05	22:07	0:10	2:08	4:10	6:08
25	8:15	10:18	12:08	14:10	16:09	18:11	20:09	22:11	0:13	2:12	4:14	6:12
26	8:19	10:22	12:12	14:14	16:12	18:15	20:13	22:15	0:17	2:16	4:18	6:16
27	8:23	10:26	12:16	14:18	16:16	18:19	20:17	22:19	0:21	2:20	4:22	6:20
28	8:27	10:29	12:20	14:22	16:20	18:23	20:21	22:23	0:25	2:24	4:26	6:24
29	8:31		12:24	14:26	16:24	18:27	20:25	22:27	0:29	2:28	4:30	6:28
30	8:35		12:28	14:30	16:28	18:30	20:29	22:31	0:33	2:31	4:34	6:32
31	8:39		12:32		16:32		20:33	22:35		2:35		6:36

1967	Jan	Feb	Mar	Apr	May	Jun	Jul	Aug	Sep	Oct	Nov	Dec
1	6:40	8:42	10:32	12:35	14:33	16:35	18:33	20:36	22:38	0:36	2:38	4:37
2	6:44	8:46	10:36	12:39	14:37	16:39	18:37	20:40	22:42	0:40	2:42	4:41
3	6:48	8:50	10:40	12:43	14:41	16:43	18:41	20:44	22:46	0:44	2:46	4:45
4	6:52	8:54	10:44	12:47	14:45	16:47	18:45	20:47	22:50	0:48	2:50	4:48
5	6:56	8:58	10:48	12:50	14:49	16:51	18:49	20:51	22:54	0:52	2:54	4:52
6	7:00	9:02	10:52	12:54	14:53	16:55	18:53	20:55	22:58	0:56	2:58	4:56
7	7:03	9:06	10:56	12:58	14:57	16:59	18:57	20:59	23:02	1:00	3:02	5:00
8	7:07	9:10	11:00	13:02	15:01	17:03	19:01	21:03	23:05	1:04	3:06	5:04
9	7:11	9:14	11:04	13:06	15:04	17:07	19:05	21:07	23:09	1:08	3:10	5:08
10	7:15	9:18	11:08	13:10	15:08	17:11	19:09	21:11	23:13	1:12	3:14	5:12
11	7:19	9:21	11:12	13:14	15:12	17:15	19:13	21:15	23:17	1:16	3:18	5:16
12	7:23	9:25	11:16	13:18	15:16	17:19	19:17	21:19	23:21	1:20	3:22	5:20
13	7:27	9:29	11:20	13:22	15:20	17:22	19:21	21:23	23:25	1:23	3:26	5:24
14	7:31	9:33	11:24	13:26	15:24	17:26	19:25	21:27	23:29	1:27	3:30	5:28
15	7:35	9:37	11:28	13:30	15:28	17:30	19:29	21:31	23:33	1:31	3:34	5:32
16	7:39	9:41	11:32	13:34	15:32	17:34	19:33	21:35	23:37	1:35	3:38	5:36
17	7:43	9:45	11:36	13:38	15:36	17:38	19:37	21:39	23:41	1:39	3:41	5:40
18	7:47	9:49	11:39	13:42	15:40	17:42	19:40	21:43	23:45	1:43	3:45	5:44
19	7:51	9:53	11:43	13:46	15:44	17:46	19:44	21:47	23:49	1:47	3:49	5:48
20	7:55	9:57	11:47	13:50	15:48	17:50	19:48	21:51	23:53	1:51	3:53	5:52
21	7:59	10:01	11:51	13:54	15:52	17:54	19:52	21:55	23:57	1:55	3:57	5:56
22	8:03	10:05	11:55	13:57	15:56	17:58	19:56	21:58	0:01	1:59	4:01	5:59
23	8:07	10:09	11:59	14:01	16:00	18:02	20:00	22:02	0:05	2:03	4:05	6:03
24	8:11	10:13	12:03	14:05	16:04	18:06	20:04	22:06	0:09	2:07	4:09	6:07
25	8:14	10:17	12:07	14:09	16:08	18:10	20:08	22:10	0:13	2:11	4:13	6:11
26	8:18	10:21	12:11	14:13	16:12	18:14	20:12	22:14	0:16	2:15	4:17	6:15
27	8:22	10:25	12:15	14:17	16:15	18:18	20:16	22:18	0:20	2:19	4:21	6:19
28	8:26	10:29	12:19	14:21	16:19	18:22	20:20	22:22	0:24	2:23	4:25	6:23
29	8:30		12:23	14:25	16:23	18:26	20:24	22:26	0:28	2:27	4:29	6:27
30	8:34		12:27	14:29	16:27	18:30	20:28	22:30	0:32	2:31	4:33	6:31
31	8:38		12:31		16:31		20:32	22:34		2:34		6:35

1968	Jan	Feb	Mar	Apr	May	Jun	Jul	Aug	Sep	Oct	Nov	Dec
1	6:39	8:41	10:35	12:38	14:36	16:38	18:36	20:39	22:41	0:39	2:41	4:40
2	6:43	8:45	10:39	12:42	14:40	16:42	18:40	20:43	22:45	0:43	2:45	4:44
3	6:47	8:49	10:43	12:46	14:44	16:46	18:44	20:47	22:49	0:47	2:49	4:48
4	6:51	8:53	10:47	12:49	14:48	16:50	18:48	20:50	22:53	0:51	2:53	4:51
5	6:55	8:57	10:51	12:53	14:52	16:54	18:52	20:54	22:57	0:55	2:57	4:55
6	6:59	9:01	10:55	12:57	14:56	16:58	18:56	20:58	23:01	0:59	3:01	4:59
7	7:03	9:05	10:59	13:01	15:00	17:02	19:00	21:02	23:05	1:03	3:05	5:03
8	7:06	9:09	11:03	13:05	15:04	17:06	19:04	21:06	23:08	1:07	3:09	5:07
9	7:10	9:13	11:07	13:09	15:07	17:10	19:08	21:10	23:12	1:11	3:13	5:11
10	7:14	9:17	11:11	13:13	15:11	17:14	19:12	21:14	23:16	1:15	3:17	5:15
11	7:18	9:21	11:15	13:17	15:15	17:18	19:16	21:18	23:20	1:19	3:21	5:19
12	7:22	9:24	11:19	13:21	15:19	17:22	19:20	21:22	23:24	1:23	3:25	5:23
13	7:26	9:28	11:23	13:25	15:23	17:25	19:24	21:26	23:28	1:26	3:29	5:27
14	7:30	9:32	11:27	13:29	15:27	17:29	19:28	21:30	23:32	1:30	3:33	5:31
15	7:34	9:36	11:31	13:33	15:31	17:33	19:32	21:34	23:36	1:34	3:37	5:35
16	7:38	9:40	11:35	13:37	15:35	17:37	19:36	21:38	23:40	1:38	3:41	5:39
17	7:42	9:44	11:39	13:41	15:39	17:41	19:40	21:42	23:44	1:42	3:44	5:43
18	7:46	9:48	11:42	13:45	15:43	17:45	19:43	21:46	23:48	1:46	3:48	5:47
19	7:50	9:52	11:46	13:49	15:47	17:49	19:47	21:50	23:52	1:50	3:52	5:51
20	7:54	9:56	11:50	13:53	15:51	17:53	19:51	21:54	23:56	1:54	3:56	5:55
21	7:58	10:00	11:54	13:57	15:55	17:57	19:55	21:58	0:00	1:58	4:00	5:59
22	8:02	10:04	11:58	14:00	15:59	18:01	19:59	22:01	0:04	2:02	4:04	6:02
23	8:06	10:08	12:02	14:04	16:03	18:05	20:03	22:05	0:08	2:06	4:08	6:06
24	8:10	10:12	12:06	14:08	16:07	18:09	20:07	22:09	0:12	2:10	4:12	6:10
25	8:14	10:16	12:10	14:12	16:11	18:13	20:11	22:13	0:15	2:14	4:16	6:14
26	8:17	10:20	12:14	14:16	16:15	18:17	20:15	22:17	0:19	2:18	4:20	6:18
27	8:21	10:24	12:18	14:20	16:18	18:21	20:19	22:21	0:23	2:22	4:24	6:22
28	8:25	10:28	12:22	14:24	16:22	18:25	20:23	22:25	0:27	2:26	4:28	6:26
29	8:29	10:31	12:26	14:28	16:26	18:29	20:27	22:29	0:31	2:30	4:32	6:30
30	8:33		12:30	14:32	16:30	18:32	20:31	22:33	0:35	2:33	4:36	6:34
31	8:37		12:34		16:34		20:35	22:37		2:37		6:38

1969	Jan	Feb	Mar	Apr	May	Jun	Jul	Aug	Sep	Oct	Nov	Dec
1	6:42	8:44	10:34	12:37	14:35	16:37	18:35	20:38	22:40	0:38	2:40	4:39
2	6:46	8:48	10:38	12:41	14:39	16:41	18:39	20:42	22:44	0:42	2:44	4:43
3	6:50	8:52	10:42	12:45	14:43	16:45	18:43	20:46	22:48	0:46	2:48	4:47
4	6:54	8:56	10:46	12:49	14:47	16:49	18:47	20:50	22:52	0:50	2:52	4:51
5	6:58	9:00	10:50	12:52	14:51	16:53	18:51	20:53	22:56	0:54	2:56	4:54
6	7:02	9:04	10:54	12:56	14:55	16:57	18:55	20:57	23:00	0:58	3:00	4:58
7	7:06	9:08	10:58	13:00	14:59	17:01	18:59	21:01	23:04	1:02	3:04	5:02
8	7:09	9:12	11:02	13:04	15:03	17:05	19:03	21:05	23:08	1:06	3:08	5:06
9	7:13	9:16	11:06	13:08	15:07	17:09	19:07	21:09	23:11	1:10	3:12	5:10
10	7:17	9:20	11:10	13:12	15:10	17:13	19:11	21:13	23:15	1:14	3:16	5:14
11	7:21	9:24	11:14	13:16	15:14	17:17	19:15	21:17	23:19	1:18	3:20	5:18
12	7:25	9:27	11:18	13:20	15:18	17:21	19:19	21:21	23:23	1:22	3:24	5:22
13	7:29	9:31	11:22	13:24	15:22	17:25	19:23	21:25	23:27	1:26	3:28	5:26
14	7:33	9:35	11:26	13:28	15:26	17:28	19:27	21:29	23:31	1:29	3:32	5:30
15	7:37	9:39	11:30	13:32	15:30	17:32	19:31	21:33	23:35	1:33	3:36	5:34
16	7:41	9:43	11:34	13:36	15:34	17:36	19:35	21:37	23:39	1:37	3:40	5:38
17	7:45	9:47	11:38	13:40	15:38	17:40	19:39	21:41	23:43	1:41	3:44	5:42
18	7:49	9:51	11:42	13:44	15:42	17:44	19:43	21:45	23:47	1:45	3:47	5:46
19	7:53	9:55	11:45	13:48	15:46	17:48	19:46	21:49	23:51	1:49	3:51	5:50
20	7:57	9:59	11:49	13:52	15:50	17:52	19:50	21:53	23:55	1:53	3:55	5:54
21	8:01	10:03	11:53	13:56	15:54	17:56	19:54	21:57	23:59	1:57	3:59	5:58
22	8:05	10:07	11:57	13:59	15:58	18:00	19:58	22:00	0:03	2:01	4:03	6:01
23	8:09	10:11	12:01	14:03	16:02	18:04	20:02	22:04	0:07	2:05	4:07	6:05
24	8:13	10:15	12:05	14:07	16:06	18:08	20:06	22:08	0:11	2:09	4:11	6:09
25	8:16	10:19	12:09	14:11	16:10	18:12	20:10	22:12	0:15	2:13	4:15	6:13
26	8:20	10:23	12:13	14:15	16:14	18:16	20:14	22:16	0:18	2:17	4:19	6:17
27	8:24	10:27	12:17	14:19	16:17	18:20	20:18	22:20	0:22	2:21	4:23	6:21
28	8:28	10:31	12:21	14:23	16:21	18:24	20:22	22:24	0:26	2:25	4:27	6:25
29	8:32		12:25	14:27	16:25	18:28	20:26	22:28	0:30	2:29	4:31	6:29
30	8:36		12:29	14:31	16:29	18:32	20:30	22:32	0:34	2:33	4:35	6:33
31	8:40		12:33		16:33		20:34	22:36		2:36		6:37

1970	Jan	Feb	Mar	Apr	May	Jun	Jul	Aug	Sep	Oct	Nov	Dec
1	6:41	8:43	10:34	12:36	14:34	16:36	18:35	20:37	22:39	0:37	2:39	4:38
2	6:45	8:47	10:37	12:40	14:38	16:40	18:38	20:41	22:43	0:41	2:43	4:42
3	6:49	8:51	10:41	12:44	14:42	16:44	18:42	20:45	22:47	0:45	2:47	4:46
4	6:53	8:55	10:45	12:48	14:46	16:48	18:46	20:49	22:51	0:49	2:51	4:50
5	6:57	8:59	10:49	12:52	14:50	16:52	18:50	20:53	22:55	0:53	2:55	4:54
6	7:01	9:03	10:53	12:55	14:54	16:56	18:54	20:56	22:59	0:57	2:59	4:57
7	7:05	9:07	10:57	12:59	14:58	17:00	18:58	21:00	23:03	1:01	3:03	5:01
8	7:09	9:11	11:01	13:03	15:02	17:04	19:02	21:04	23:07	1:05	3:07	5:05
9	7:12	9:15	11:05	13:07	15:06	17:08	19:06	21:08	23:11	1:09	3:11	5:09
10	7:16	9:19	11:09	13:11	15:10	17:12	19:10	21:12	23:14	1:13	3:15	5:13
11	7:20	9:23	11:13	13:15	15:13	17:16	19:14	21:16	23:18	1:17	3:19	5:17
12	7:24	9:27	11:17	13:19	15:17	17:20	19:18	21:20	23:22	1:21	3:23	5:21
13	7:28	9:30	11:21	13:23	15:21	17:24	19:22	21:24	23:26	1:25	3:27	5:25
14	7:32	9:34	11:25	13:27	15:25	17:28	19:26	21:28	23:30	1:28	3:31	5:29
15	7:36	9:38	11:29	13:31	15:29	17:31	19:30	21:32	23:34	1:32	3:35	5:33
16	7:40	9:42	11:33	13:35	15:33	17:35	19:34	21:36	23:38	1:36	3:39	5:37
17	7:44	9:46	11:37	13:39	15:37	17:39	19:38	21:40	23:42	1:40	3:43	5:41
18	7:48	9:50	11:41	13:43	15:41	17:43	19:42	21:44	23:46	1:44	3:46	5:45
19	7:52	9:54	11:44	13:47	15:45	17:47	19:45	21:48	23:50	1:48	3:50	5:49
20	7:56	9:58	11:48	13:51	15:49	17:51	19:49	21:52	23:54	1:52	3:54	5:53
21	8:00	10:02	11:52	13:55	15:53	17:55	19:53	21:56	23:58	1:56	3:58	5:57
22	8:04	10:06	11:56	13:59	15:57	17:59	19:57	22:00	0:02	2:00	4:02	6:01
23	8:08	10:10	12:00	14:02	16:01	18:03	20:01	22:03	0:06	2:04	4:06	6:04
24	8:12	10:14	12:04	14:06	16:05	18:07	20:05	22:07	0:10	2:08	4:10	6:08
25	8:16	10:18	12:08	14:10	16:09	18:11	20:09	22:11	0:14	2:12	4:14	6:12
26	8:19	10:22	12:12	14:14	16:13	18:15	20:13	22:15	0:18	2:16	4:18	6:16
27	8:23	10:26	12:16	14:18	16:17	18:19	20:17	22:19	0:21	2:20	4:22	6:20
28	8:27	10:30	12:20	14:22	16:20	18:23	20:21	22:23	0:25	2:24	4:26	6:24
29	8:31		12:24	14:26	16:24	18:27	20:25	22:27	0:29	2:28	4:30	6:28
30	8:35		12:28	14:30	16:28	18:31	20:29	22:31	0:33	2:32	4:34	6:32
31	8:39		12:32		16:32		20:33	22:35		2:36		6:36

1971	Jan	Feb	Mar	Apr	May	Jun	Jul	Aug	Sep	Oct	Nov	Dec
1	6:40	8:42	10:33	12:35	14:33	16:35	18:34	20:36	22:38	0:36	2:39	4:37
2	6:44	8:46	10:37	12:39	14:37	16:39	18:38	20:40	22:42	0:40	2:42	4:41
3	6:48	8:50	10:40	12:43	14:41	16:43	18:41	20:44	22:46	0:44	2:46	4:45
4	6:52	8:54	10:44	12:47	14:45	16:47	18:45	20:48	22:50	0:48	2:50	4:49
5	6:56	8:58	10:48	12:51	14:49	16:51	18:49	20:52	22:54	0:52	2:54	4:53
6	7:00	9:02	10:52	12:55	14:53	16:55	18:53	20:56	22:58	0:56	2:58	4:57
7	7:04	9:06	10:56	12:58	14:57	16:59	18:57	20:59	23:02	1:00	3:02	5:00
8	7:08	9:10	11:00	13:02	15:01	17:03	19:01	21:03	23:06	1:04	3:06	5:04
9	7:12	9:14	11:04	13:06	15:05	17:07	19:05	21:07	23:10	1:08	3:10	5:08
10	7:15	9:18	11:08	13:10	15:09	17:11	19:09	21:11	23:13	1:12	3:14	5:12
11	7:19	9:22	11:12	13:14	15:12	17:15	19:13	21:15	23:17	1:16	3:18	5:16
12	7:23	9:26	11:16	13:18	15:16	17:19	19:17	21:19	23:21	1:20	3:22	5:20
13	7:27	9:29	11:20	13:22	15:20	17:23	19:21	21:23	23:25	1:24	3:26	5:24
14	7:31	9:33	11:24	13:26	15:24	17:27	19:25	21:27	23:29	1:28	3:30	5:28
15	7:35	9:37	11:28	13:30	15:28	17:30	19:29	21:31	23:33	1:31	3:34	5:32
16	7:39	9:41	11:32	13:34	15:32	17:34	19:33	21:35	23:37	1:35	3:38	5:36
17	7:43	9:45	11:36	13:38	15:36	17:38	19:37	21:39	23:41	1:39	3:42	5:40
18	7:47	9:49	11:40	13:42	15:40	17:42	19:41	21:43	23:45	1:43	3:46	5:44
19	7:51	9:53	11:44	13:46	15:44	17:46	19:45	21:47	23:49	1:47	3:49	5:48
20	7:55	9:57	11:47	13:50	15:48	17:50	19:48	21:51	23:53	1:51	3:53	5:52
21	7:59	10:01	11:51	13:54	15:52	17:54	19:52	21:55	23:57	1:55	3:57	5:56
22	8:03	10:05	11:55	13:58	15:56	17:58	19:56	21:59	0:01	1:59	4:01	6:00
23	8:07	10:09	11:59	14:02	16:00	18:02	20:00	22:03	0:05	2:03	4:05	6:04
24	8:11	10:13	12:03	14:05	16:04	18:06	20:04	22:06	0:09	2:07	4:09	6:07
25	8:15	10:17	12:07	14:09	16:08	18:10	20:08	22:10	0:13	2:11	4:13	6:11
26	8:19	10:21	12:11	14:13	16:12	18:14	20:12	22:14	0:17	2:15	4:17	6:15
27	8:22	10:25	12:15	14:17	16:16	18:18	20:16	22:18	0:21	2:19	4:21	6:19
28	8:26	10:29	12:19	14:21	16:20	18:22	20:20	22:22	0:24	2:23	4:25	6:23
29	8:30		12:23	14:25	16:23	18:26	20:24	22:26	0:28	2:27	4:29	6:27
30	8:34		12:27	14:29	16:27	18:30	20:28	22:30	0:32	2:31	4:33	6:31
31	8:38		12:31		16:31		20:32	22:34		2:35		6:35

1972	Jan	Feb	Mar	Apr	May	Jun	Jul	Aug	Sep	Oct	Nov	Dec
1	6:39	8:41	10:36	12:38	14:36	16:38	18:37	20:39	22:41	0:39	2:41	4:40
2	6:43	8:45	10:40	12:42	14:40	16:42	18:41	20:43	22:45	0:43	2:45	4:44
3	6:47	8:49	10:43	12:46	14:44	16:46	18:44	20:47	22:49	0:47	2:49	4:48
4	6:51	8:53	10:47	12:50	14:48	16:50	18:48	20:51	22:53	0:51	2:53	4:52
5	6:55	8:57	10:51	12:54	14:52	16:54	18:52	20:55	22:57	0:55	2:57	4:56
6	6:59	9:01	10:55	12:57	14:56	16:58	18:56	20:58	23:01	0:59	3:01	4:59
7	7:03	9:05	10:59	13:01	15:00	17:02	19:00	21:02	23:05	1:03	3:05	5:03
8	7:07	9:09	11:03	13:05	15:04	17:06	19:04	21:06	23:09	1:07	3:09	5:07
9	7:11	9:13	11:07	13:09	15:08	17:10	19:08	21:10	23:13	1:11	3:13	5:11
10	7:14	9:17	11:11	13:13	15:12	17:14	19:12	21:14	23:16	1:15	3:17	5:15
11	7:18	9:21	11:15	13:17	15:15	17:18	19:16	21:18	23:20	1:19	3:21	5:19
12	7:22	9:25	11:19	13:21	15:19	17:22	19:20	21:22	23:24	1:23	3:25	5:23
13	7:26	9:29	11:23	13:25	15:23	17:26	19:24	21:26	23:28	1:27	3:29	5:27
14	7:30	9:32	11:27	13:29	15:27	17:30	19:28	21:30	23:32	1:31	3:33	5:31
15	7:34	9:36	11:31	13:33	15:31	17:33	19:32	21:34	23:36	1:34	3:37	5:35
16	7:38	9:40	11:35	13:37	15:35	17:37	19:36	21:38	23:40	1:38	3:41	5:39
17	7:42	9:44	11:39	13:41	15:39	17:41	19:40	21:42	23:44	1:42	3:45	5:43
18	7:46	9:48	11:43	13:45	15:43	17:45	19:44	21:46	23:48	1:46	3:49	5:47
19	7:50	9:52	11:47	13:49	15:47	17:49	19:48	21:50	23:52	1:50	3:52	5:51
20	7:54	9:56	11:50	13:53	15:51	17:53	19:51	21:54	23:56	1:54	3:56	5:55
21	7:58	10:00	11:54	13:57	15:55	17:57	19:55	21:58	0:00	1:58	4:00	5:59
22	8:02	10:04	11:58	14:01	15:59	18:01	19:59	22:02	0:04	2:02	4:04	6:03
23	8:06	10:08	12:02	14:05	16:03	18:05	20:03	22:06	0:08	2:06	4:08	6:07
24	8:10	10:12	12:06	14:08	16:07	18:09	20:07	22:09	0:12	2:10	4:12	6:10
25	8:14	10:16	12:10	14:12	16:11	18:13	20:11	22:13	0:16	2:14	4:16	6:14
26	8:18	10:20	12:14	14:16	16:15	18:17	20:15	22:17	0:20	2:18	4:20	6:18
27	8:22	10:24	12:18	14:20	16:19	18:21	20:19	22:21	0:24	2:22	4:24	6:22
28	8:25	10:28	12:22	14:24	16:23	18:25	20:23	22:25	0:27	2:26	4:28	6:26
29	8:29	10:32	12:26	14:28	16:26	18:29	20:27	22:29	0:31	2:30	4:32	6:30
30	8:33		12:30	14:32	16:30	18:33	20:31	22:33	0:35	2:34	4:36	6:34
31	8:37		12:34		16:34		20:35	22:37		2:38		6:38

1973	Jan	Feb	Mar	Apr	May	Jun	Jul	Aug	Sep	Oct	Nov	Dec
1	6:42	8:44	10:35	12:37	14:35	16:37	18:36	20:38	22:40	0:38	2:41	4:39
2	6:46	8:48	10:39	12:41	14:39	16:41	18:40	20:42	22:44	0:42	2:44	4:43
3	6:50	8:52	10:42	12:45	14:43	16:45	18:43	20:46	22:48	0:46	2:48	4:47
4	6:54	8:56	10:46	12:49	14:47	16:49	18:47	20:50	22:52	0:50	2:52	4:51
5	6:58	9:00	10:50	12:53	14:51	16:53	18:51	20:54	22:56	0:54	2:56	4:55
6	7:02	9:04	10:54	12:57	14:55	16:57	18:55	20:58	23:00	0:58	3:00	4:59
7	7:06	9:08	10:58	13:00	14:59	17:01	18:59	21:01	23:04	1:02	3:04	5:02
8	7:10	9:12	11:02	13:04	15:03	17:05	19:03	21:05	23:08	1:06	3:08	5:06
9	7:14	9:16	11:06	13:08	15:07	17:09	19:07	21:09	23:12	1:10	3:12	5:10
10	7:17	9:20	11:10	13:12	15:11	17:13	19:11	21:13	23:16	1:14	3:16	5:14
11	7:21	9:24	11:14	13:16	15:15	17:17	19:15	21:17	23:19	1:18	3:20	5:18
12	7:25	9:28	11:18	13:20	15:18	17:21	19:19	21:21	23:23	1:22	3:24	5:22
13	7:29	9:32	11:22	13:24	15:22	17:25	19:23	21:25	23:27	1:26	3:28	5:26
14	7:33	9:35	11:26	13:28	15:26	17:29	19:27	21:29	23:31	1:30	3:32	5:30
15	7:37	9:39	11:30	13:32	15:30	17:33	19:31	21:33	23:35	1:34	3:36	5:34
16	7:41	9:43	11:34	13:36	15:34	17:36	19:35	21:37	23:39	1:37	3:40	5:38
17	7:45	9:47	11:38	13:40	15:38	17:40	19:39	21:41	23:43	1:41	3:44	5:42
18	7:49	9:51	11:42	13:44	15:42	17:44	19:43	21:45	23:47	1:45	3:48	5:46
19	7:53	9:55	11:46	13:48	15:46	17:48	19:47	21:49	23:51	1:49	3:52	5:50
20	7:57	9:59	11:50	13:52	15:50	17:52	19:51	21:53	23:55	1:53	3:55	5:54
21	8:01	10:03	11:53	13:56	15:54	17:56	19:54	21:57	23:59	1:57	3:59	5:58
22	8:05	10:07	11:57	14:00	15:58	18:00	19:58	22:01	0:03	2:01	4:03	6:02
23	8:09	10:11	12:01	14:04	16:02	18:04	20:02	22:05	0:07	2:05	4:07	6:06
24	8:13	10:15	12:05	14:08	16:06	18:08	20:06	22:09	0:11	2:09	4:11	6:10
25	8:17	10:19	12:09	14:11	16:10	18:12	20:10	22:12	0:15	2:13	4:15	6:13
26	8:21	10:23	12:13	14:15	16:14	18:16	20:14	22:16	0:19	2:17	4:19	6:17
27	8:25	10:27	12:17	14:19	16:18	18:20	20:18	22:20	0:23	2:21	4:23	6:21
28	8:28	10:31	12:21	14:23	16:22	18:24	20:22	22:24	0:26	2:25	4:27	6:25
29	8:32		12:25	14:27	16:25	18:28	20:26	22:28	0:30	2:29	4:31	6:29
30	8:36		12:29	14:31	16:29	18:32	20:30	22:32	0:34	2:33	4:35	6:33
31	8:40		12:33		16:33		20:34	22:36		2:37		6:37

1974	Jan	Feb	Mar	Apr	May	Jun	Jul	Aug	Sep	Oct	Nov	Dec
1	6:41	8:43	10:34	12:36	14:34	16:36	18:35	20:37	22:39	0:37	2:40	4:38
2	6:45	8:47	10:38	12:40	14:38	16:40	18:39	20:41	22:43	0:41	2:44	4:42
3	6:49	8:51	10:42	12:44	14:42	16:44	18:43	20:45	22:47	0:45	2:47	4:46
4	6:53	8:55	10:45	12:48	14:46	16:48	18:46	20:49	22:51	0:49	2:51	4:50
5	6:57	8:59	10:49	12:52	14:50	16:52	18:50	20:53	22:55	0:53	2:55	4:54
6	7:01	9:03	10:53	12:56	14:54	16:56	18:54	20:57	22:59	0:57	2:59	4:58
7	7:05	9:07	10:57	13:00	14:58	17:00	18:58	21:01	23:03	1:01	3:03	5:02
8	7:09	9:11	11:01	13:03	15:02	17:04	19:02	21:04	23:07	1:05	3:07	5:05
9	7:13	9:15	11:05	13:07	15:06	17:08	19:06	21:08	23:11	1:09	3:11	5:09
10	7:17	9:19	11:09	13:11	15:10	17:12	19:10	21:12	23:15	1:13	3:15	5:13
11	7:20	9:23	11:13	13:15	15:14	17:16	19:14	21:16	23:19	1:17	3:19	5:17
12	7:24	9:27	11:17	13:19	15:18	17:20	19:18	21:20	23:22	1:21	3:23	5:21
13	7:28	9:31	11:21	13:23	15:21	17:24	19:22	21:24	23:26	1:25	3:27	5:25
14	7:32	9:35	11:25	13:27	15:25	17:28	19:26	21:28	23:30	1:29	3:31	5:29
15	7:36	9:38	11:29	13:31	15:29	17:32	19:30	21:32	23:34	1:33	3:35	5:33
16	7:40	9:42	11:33	13:35	15:33	17:36	19:34	21:36	23:38	1:37	3:39	5:37
17	7:44	9:46	11:37	13:39	15:37	17:39	19:38	21:40	23:42	1:40	3:43	5:41
18	7:48	9:50	11:41	13:43	15:41	17:43	19:42	21:44	23:46	1:44	3:47	5:45
19	7:52	9:54	11:45	13:47	15:45	17:47	19:46	21:48	23:50	1:48	3:51	5:49
20	7:56	9:58	11:49	13:51	15:49	17:51	19:50	21:52	23:54	1:52	3:54	5:53
21	8:00	10:02	11:53	13:55	15:53	17:55	19:54	21:56	23:58	1:56	3:58	5:57
22	8:04	10:06	11:56	13:59	15:57	17:59	19:57	22:00	0:02	2:00	4:02	6:01
23	8:08	10:10	12:00	14:03	16:01	18:03	20:01	22:04	0:06	2:04	4:06	6:05
24	8:12	10:14	12:04	14:07	16:05	18:07	20:05	22:08	0:10	2:08	4:10	6:09
25	8:16	10:18	12:08	14:10	16:09	18:11	20:09	22:11	0:14	2:12	4:14	6:12
26	8:20	10:22	12:12	14:14	16:13	18:15	20:13	22:15	0:18	2:16	4:18	6:16
27	8:24	10:26	12:16	14:18	16:17	18:19	20:17	22:19	0:22	2:20	4:22	6:20
28	8:27	10:30	12:20	14:22	16:21	18:23	20:21	22:23	0:26	2:24	4:26	6:24
29	8:31		12:24	14:26	16:25	18:27	20:25	22:27	0:29	2:28	4:30	6:28
30	8:35		12:28	14:30	16:28	18:31	20:29	22:31	0:33	2:32	4:34	6:32
31	8:39		12:32		16:32		20:33	22:35		2:36		6:36

1975	Jan	Feb	Mar	Apr	May	Jun	Jul	Aug	Sep	Oct	Nov	Dec
1	6:40	8:42	10:33	12:35	14:33	16:35	18:34	20:36	22:38	0:36	2:39	4:37
2	6:44	8:46	10:37	12:39	14:37	16:39	18:38	20:40	22:42	0:40	2:43	4:41
3	6:48	8:50	10:41	12:43	14:41	16:43	18:42	20:44	22:46	0:44	2:47	4:45
4	6:52	8:54	10:45	12:47	14:45	16:47	18:46	20:48	22:50	0:48	2:50	4:49
5	6:56	8:58	10:48	12:51	14:49	16:51	18:49	20:52	22:54	0:52	2:54	4:53
6	7:00	9:02	10:52	12:55	14:53	16:55	18:53	20:56	22:58	0:56	2:58	4:57
7	7:04	9:06	10:56	12:59	14:57	16:59	18:57	21:00	23:02	1:00	3:02	5:01
8	7:08	9:10	11:00	13:03	15:01	17:03	19:01	21:04	23:06	1:04	3:06	5:05
9	7:12	9:14	11:04	13:06	15:05	17:07	19:05	21:07	23:10	1:08	3:10	5:08
10	7:16	9:18	11:08	13:10	15:09	17:11	19:09	21:11	23:14	1:12	3:14	5:12
11	7:20	9:22	11:12	13:14	15:13	17:15	19:13	21:15	23:18	1:16	3:18	5:16
12	7:23	9:26	11:16	13:18	15:17	17:19	19:17	21:19	23:22	1:20	3:22	5:20
13	7:27	9:30	11:20	13:22	15:21	17:23	19:21	21:23	23:25	1:24	3:26	5:24
14	7:31	9:34	11:24	13:26	15:24	17:27	19:25	21:27	23:29	1:28	3:30	5:28
15	7:35	9:38	11:28	13:30	15:28	17:31	19:29	21:31	23:33	1:32	3:34	5:32
16	7:39	9:41	11:32	13:34	15:32	17:35	19:33	21:35	23:37	1:36	3:38	5:36
17	7:43	9:45	11:36	13:38	15:36	17:38	19:37	21:39	23:41	1:39	3:42	5:40
18	7:47	9:49	11:40	13:42	15:40	17:42	19:41	21:43	23:45	1:43	3:46	5:44
19	7:51	9:53	11:44	13:46	15:44	17:46	19:45	21:47	23:49	1:47	3:50	5:48
20	7:55	9:57	11:48	13:50	15:48	17:50	19:49	21:51	23:53	1:51	3:54	5:52
21	7:59	10:01	11:52	13:54	15:52	17:54	19:53	21:55	23:57	1:55	3:57	5:56
22	8:03	10:05	11:55	13:58	15:56	17:58	19:56	21:59	0:01	1:59	4:01	6:00
23	8:07	10:09	11:59	14:02	16:00	18:02	20:00	22:03	0:05	2:03	4:05	6:04
24	8:11	10:13	12:03	14:06	16:04	18:06	20:04	22:07	0:09	2:07	4:09	6:08
25	8:15	10:17	12:07	14:10	16:08	18:10	20:08	22:11	0:13	2:11	4:13	6:12
26	8:19	10:21	12:11	14:13	16:12	18:14	20:12	22:14	0:17	2:15	4:17	6:15
27	8:23	10:25	12:15	14:17	16:16	18:18	20:16	22:18	0:21	2:19	4:21	6:19
28	8:27	10:29	12:19	14:21	16:20	18:22	20:20	22:22	0:25	2:23	4:25	6:23
29	8:30		12:23	14:25	16:24	18:26	20:24	22:26	0:29	2:27	4:29	6:27
30	8:34		12:27	14:29	16:28	18:30	20:28	22:30	0:32	2:31	4:33	6:31
31	8:38		12:31		16:31		20:32	22:34		2:35		6:35

1976	Jan	Feb	Mar	Apr	May	Jun	Jul	Aug	Sep	Oct	Nov	Dec
1	6:39	8:41	10:36	12:38	14:36	16:38	18:37	20:39	22:41	0:39	2:42	4:40
2	6:43	8:45	10:40	12:42	14:40	16:42	18:41	20:43	22:45	0:43	2:46	4:44
3	6:47	8:49	10:44	12:46	14:44	16:46	18:45	20:47	22:49	0:47	2:50	4:48
4	6:51	8:53	10:48	12:50	14:48	16:50	18:49	20:51	22:53	0:51	2:53	4:52
5	6:55	8:57	10:51	12:54	14:52	16:54	18:52	20:55	22:57	0:55	2:57	4:56
6	6:59	9:01	10:55	12:58	14:56	16:58	18:56	20:59	23:01	0:59	3:01	5:00
7	7:03	9:05	10:59	13:02	15:00	17:02	19:00	21:03	23:05	1:03	3:05	5:04
8	7:07	9:09	11:03	13:06	15:04	17:06	19:04	21:07	23:09	1:07	3:09	5:07
9	7:11	9:13	11:07	13:09	15:08	17:10	19:08	21:10	23:13	1:11	3:13	5:11
10	7:15	9:17	11:11	13:13	15:12	17:14	19:12	21:14	23:17	1:15	3:17	5:15
11	7:19	9:21	11:15	13:17	15:16	17:18	19:16	21:18	23:21	1:19	3:21	5:19
12	7:22	9:25	11:19	13:21	15:20	17:22	19:20	21:22	23:24	1:23	3:25	5:23
13	7:26	9:29	11:23	13:25	15:23	17:26	19:24	21:26	23:28	1:27	3:29	5:27
14	7:30	9:33	11:27	13:29	15:27	17:30	19:28	21:30	23:32	1:31	3:33	5:31
15	7:34	9:37	11:31	13:33	15:31	17:34	19:32	21:34	23:36	1:35	3:37	5:35
16	7:38	9:40	11:35	13:37	15:35	17:38	19:36	21:38	23:40	1:39	3:41	5:39
17	7:42	9:44	11:39	13:41	15:39	17:41	19:40	21:42	23:44	1:42	3:45	5:43
18	7:46	9:48	11:43	13:45	15:43	17:45	19:44	21:46	23:48	1:46	3:49	5:47
19	7:50	9:52	11:47	13:49	15:47	17:49	19:48	21:50	23:52	1:50	3:53	5:51
20	7:54	9:56	11:51	13:53	15:51	17:53	19:52	21:54	23:56	1:54	3:57	5:55
21	7:58	10:00	11:55	13:57	15:55	17:57	19:56	21:58	0:00	1:58	4:00	5:59
22	8:02	10:04	11:58	14:01	15:59	18:01	19:59	22:02	0:04	2:02	4:04	6:03
23	8:06	10:08	12:02	14:05	16:03	18:05	20:03	22:06	0:08	2:06	4:08	6:07
24	8:10	10:12	12:06	14:09	16:07	18:09	20:07	22:10	0:12	2:10	4:12	6:11
25	8:14	10:16	12:10	14:13	16:11	18:13	20:11	22:14	0:16	2:14	4:16	6:15
26	8:18	10:20	12:14	14:16	16:15	18:17	20:15	22:17	0:20	2:18	4:20	6:18
27	8:22	10:24	12:18	14:20	16:19	18:21	20:19	22:21	0:24	2:22	4:24	6:22
28	8:26	10:28	12:22	14:24	16:23	18:25	20:23	22:25	0:28	2:26	4:28	6:26
29	8:30	10:32	12:26	14:28	16:27	18:29	20:27	22:29	0:32	2:30	4:32	6:30
30	8:33		12:30	14:32	16:31	18:33	20:31	22:33	0:35	2:34	4:36	6:34
31	8:37		12:34		16:34		20:35	22:37		2:38		6:38

1977	Jan	Feb	Mar	Apr	May	Jun	Jul	Aug	Sep	Oct	Nov	Dec
1	6:42	8:44	10:35	12:37	14:35	16:37	18:36	20:38	22:40	0:38	2:41	4:39
2	6:46	8:48	10:39	12:41	14:39	16:41	18:40	20:42	22:44	0:42	2:45	4:43
3	6:50	8:52	10:43	12:45	14:43	16:45	18:44	20:46	22:48	0:46	2:49	4:47
4	6:54	8:56	10:47	12:49	14:47	16:49	18:48	20:50	22:52	0:50	2:52	4:51
5	6:58	9:00	10:51	12:53	14:51	16:53	18:51	20:54	22:56	0:54	2:56	4:55
6	7:02	9:04	10:54	12:57	14:55	16:57	18:55	20:58	23:00	0:58	3:00	4:59
7	7:06	9:08	10:58	13:01	14:59	17:01	18:59	21:02	23:04	1:02	3:04	5:03
8	7:10	9:12	11:02	13:05	15:03	17:05	19:03	21:06	23:08	1:06	3:08	5:07
9	7:14	9:16	11:06	13:08	15:07	17:09	19:07	21:09	23:12	1:10	3:12	5:10
10	7:18	9:20	11:10	13:12	15:11	17:13	19:11	21:13	23:16	1:14	3:16	5:14
11	7:22	9:24	11:14	13:16	15:15	17:17	19:15	21:17	23:20	1:18	3:20	5:18
12	7:25	9:28	11:18	13:20	15:19	17:21	19:19	21:21	23:24	1:22	3:24	5:22
13	7:29	9:32	11:22	13:24	15:23	17:25	19:23	21:25	23:27	1:26	3:28	5:26
14	7:33	9:36	11:26	13:28	15:26	17:29	19:27	21:29	23:31	1:30	3:32	5:30
15	7:37	9:40	11:30	13:32	15:30	17:33	19:31	21:33	23:35	1:34	3:36	5:34
16	7:41	9:43	11:34	13:36	15:34	17:37	19:35	21:37	23:39	1:38	3:40	5:38
17	7:45	9:47	11:38	13:40	15:38	17:41	19:39	21:41	23:43	1:42	3:44	5:42
18	7:49	9:51	11:42	13:44	15:42	17:44	19:43	21:45	23:47	1:45	3:48	5:46
19	7:53	9:55	11:46	13:48	15:46	17:48	19:47	21:49	23:51	1:49	3:52	5:50
20	7:57	9:59	11:50	13:52	15:50	17:52	19:51	21:53	23:55	1:53	3:56	5:54
21	8:01	10:03	11:54	13:56	15:54	17:56	19:55	21:57	23:59	1:57	4:00	5:58
22	8:05	10:07	11:58	14:00	15:58	18:00	19:59	22:01	0:03	2:01	4:03	6:02
23	8:09	10:11	12:01	14:04	16:02	18:04	20:02	22:05	0:07	2:05	4:07	6:06
24	8:13	10:15	12:05	14:08	16:06	18:08	20:06	22:09	0:11	2:09	4:11	6:10
25	8:17	10:19	12:09	14:12	16:10	18:12	20:10	22:13	0:15	2:13	4:15	6:14
26	8:21	10:23	12:13	14:16	16:14	18:16	20:14	22:17	0:19	2:17	4:19	6:18
27	8:25	10:27	12:17	14:19	16:18	18:20	20:18	22:20	0:23	2:21	4:23	6:21
28	8:29	10:31	12:21	14:23	16:22	18:24	20:22	22:24	0:27	2:25	4:27	6:25
29	8:33		12:25	14:27	16:26	18:28	20:26	22:28	0:31	2:29	4:31	6:29
30	8:36		12:29	14:31	16:30	18:32	20:30	22:32	0:35	2:33	4:35	6:33
31	8:40		12:33		16:34		20:34	22:36		2:37		6:37

1978	Jan	Feb	Mar	Apr	May	Jun	Jul	Aug	Sep	Oct	Nov	Dec
1	6:41	8:43	10:34	12:36	14:34	16:36	18:35	20:37	22:39	0:37	2:40	4:38
2	6:45	8:47	10:38	12:40	14:38	16:40	18:39	20:41	22:43	0:41	2:44	4:42
3	6:49	8:51	10:42	12:44	14:42	16:44	18:43	20:45	22:47	0:45	2:48	4:46
4	6:53	8:55	10:46	12:48	14:46	16:48	18:47	20:49	22:51	0:49	2:52	4:50
5	6:57	8:59	10:50	12:52	14:50	16:52	18:51	20:53	22:55	0:53	2:55	4:54
6	7:01	9:03	10:53	12:56	14:54	16:56	18:54	20:57	22:59	0:57	2:59	4:58
7	7:05	9:07	10:57	13:00	14:58	17:00	18:58	21:01	23:03	1:01	3:03	5:02
8	7:09	9:11	11:01	13:04	15:02	17:04	19:02	21:05	23:07	1:05	3:07	5:06
9	7:13	9:15	11:05	13:08	15:06	17:08	19:06	21:09	23:11	1:09	3:11	5:10
10	7:17	9:19	11:09	13:11	15:10	17:12	19:10	21:12	23:15	1:13	3:15	5:13
11	7:21	9:23	11:13	13:15	15:14	17:16	19:14	21:16	23:19	1:17	3:19	5:17
12	7:25	9:27	11:17	13:19	15:18	17:20	19:18	21:20	23:23	1:21	3:23	5:21
13	7:28	9:31	11:21	13:23	15:22	17:24	19:22	21:24	23:27	1:25	3:27	5:25
14	7:32	9:35	11:25	13:27	15:26	17:28	19:26	21:28	23:30	1:29	3:31	5:29
15	7:36	9:39	11:29	13:31	15:29	17:32	19:30	21:32	23:34	1:33	3:35	5:33
16	7:40	9:43	11:33	13:35	15:33	17:36	19:34	21:36	23:38	1:37	3:39	5:37
17	7:44	9:46	11:37	13:39	15:37	17:40	19:38	21:40	23:42	1:41	3:43	5:41
18	7:48	9:50	11:41	13:43	15:41	17:44	19:42	21:44	23:46	1:45	3:47	5:45
19	7:52	9:54	11:45	13:47	15:45	17:47	19:46	21:48	23:50	1:48	3:51	5:49
20	7:56	9:58	11:49	13:51	15:49	17:51	19:50	21:52	23:54	1:52	3:55	5:53
21	8:00	10:02	11:53	13:55	15:53	17:55	19:54	21:56	23:58	1:56	3:59	5:57
22	8:04	10:06	11:57	13:59	15:57	17:59	19:58	22:00	0:02	2:00	4:03	6:01
23	8:08	10:10	12:01	14:03	16:01	18:03	20:02	22:04	0:06	2:04	4:06	6:05
24	8:12	10:14	12:04	14:07	16:05	18:07	20:05	22:08	0:10	2:08	4:10	6:09
25	8:16	10:18	12:08	14:11	16:09	18:11	20:09	22:12	0:14	2:12	4:14	6:13
26	8:20	10:22	12:12	14:15	16:13	18:15	20:13	22:16	0:18	2:16	4:18	6:17
27	8:24	10:26	12:16	14:19	16:17	18:19	20:17	22:20	0:22	2:20	4:22	6:20
28	8:28	10:30	12:20	14:22	16:21	18:23	20:21	22:23	0:26	2:24	4:26	6:24
29	8:32		12:24	14:26	16:25	18:27	20:25	22:27	0:30	2:28	4:30	6:28
30	8:35		12:28	14:30	16:29	18:31	20:29	22:31	0:34	2:32	4:34	6:32
31	8:39		12:32		16:33		20:33	22:35		2:36		6:36

1979	Jan	Feb	Mar	Apr	May	Jun	Jul	Aug	Sep	Oct	Nov	Dec
1	6:40	8:42	10:33	12:35	14:33	16:36	18:34	20:36	22:38	0:37	2:39	4:37
2	6:44	8:46	10:37	12:39	14:37	16:39	18:38	20:40	22:42	0:40	2:43	4:41
3	6:48	8:50	10:41	12:43	14:41	16:43	18:42	20:44	22:46	0:44	2:47	4:45
4	6:52	8:54	10:45	12:47	14:45	16:47	18:46	20:48	22:50	0:48	2:51	4:49
5	6:56	8:58	10:49	12:51	14:49	16:51	18:50	20:52	22:54	0:52	2:55	4:53
6	7:00	9:02	10:53	12:55	14:53	16:55	18:54	20:56	22:58	0:56	2:58	4:57
7	7:04	9:06	10:56	12:59	14:57	16:59	18:57	21:00	23:02	1:00	3:02	5:01
8	7:08	9:10	11:00	13:03	15:01	17:03	19:01	21:04	23:06	1:04	3:06	5:05
9	7:12	9:14	11:04	13:07	15:05	17:07	19:05	21:08	23:10	1:08	3:10	5:09
10	7:16	9:18	11:08	13:11	15:09	17:11	19:09	21:12	23:14	1:12	3:14	5:13
11	7:20	9:22	11:12	13:14	15:13	17:15	19:13	21:15	23:18	1:16	3:18	5:16
12	7:24	9:26	11:16	13:18	15:17	17:19	19:17	21:19	23:22	1:20	3:22	5:20
13	7:28	9:30	11:20	13:22	15:21	17:23	19:21	21:23	23:26	1:24	3:26	5:24
14	7:31	9:34	11:24	13:26	15:25	17:27	19:25	21:27	23:30	1:28	3:30	5:28
15	7:35	9:38	11:28	13:30	15:29	17:31	19:29	21:31	23:33	1:32	3:34	5:32
16	7:39	9:42	11:32	13:34	15:32	17:35	19:33	21:35	23:37	1:36	3:38	5:36
17	7:43	9:46	11:36	13:38	15:36	17:39	19:37	21:39	23:41	1:40	3:42	5:40
18	7:47	9:49	11:40	13:42	15:40	17:43	19:41	21:43	23:45	1:44	3:46	5:44
19	7:51	9:53	11:44	13:46	15:44	17:47	19:45	21:47	23:49	1:48	3:50	5:48
20	7:55	9:57	11:48	13:50	15:48	17:50	19:49	21:51	23:53	1:51	3:54	5:52
21	7:59	10:01	11:52	13:54	15:52	17:54	19:53	21:55	23:57	1:55	3:58	5:56
22	8:03	10:05	11:56	13:58	15:56	17:58	19:57	21:59	0:01	1:59	4:02	6:00
23	8:07	10:09	12:00	14:02	16:00	18:02	20:01	22:03	0:05	2:03	4:05	6:04
24	8:11	10:13	12:04	14:06	16:04	18:06	20:04	22:07	0:09	2:07	4:09	6:08
25	8:15	10:17	12:07	14:10	16:08	18:10	20:08	22:11	0:13	2:11	4:13	6:12
26	8:19	10:21	12:11	14:14	16:12	18:14	20:12	22:15	0:17	2:15	4:17	6:16
27	8:23	10:25	12:15	14:18	16:16	18:18	20:16	22:19	0:21	2:19	4:21	6:20
28	8:27	10:29	12:19	14:21	16:20	18:22	20:20	22:22	0:25	2:23	4:25	6:23
29	8:31		12:23	14:25	16:24	18:26	20:24	22:26	0:29	2:27	4:29	6:27
30	8:35		12:27	14:29	16:28	18:30	20:28	22:30	0:33	2:31	4:33	6:31
31	8:38		12:31		16:32		20:32	22:34		2:35		6:35

1980	Jan	Feb	Mar	Apr	May	Jun	Jul	Aug	Sep	Oct	Nov	Dec
1	6:39	8:41	10:36	12:38	14:36	16:39	18:37	20:39	22:41	0:40	2:42	4:40
2	6:43	8:45	10:40	12:42	14:40	16:42	18:41	20:43	22:45	0:43	2:46	4:44
3	6:47	8:49	10:44	12:46	14:44	16:46	18:45	20:47	22:49	0:47	2:50	4:48
4	6:51	8:53	10:48	12:50	14:48	16:50	18:49	20:51	22:53	0:51	2:54	4:52
5	6:55	8:57	10:52	12:54	14:52	16:54	18:53	20:55	22:57	0:55	2:58	4:56
6	6:59	9:01	10:56	12:58	14:56	16:58	18:57	20:59	23:01	0:59	3:01	5:00
7	7:03	9:05	10:59	13:02	15:00	17:02	19:00	21:03	23:05	1:03	3:05	5:04
8	7:07	9:09	11:03	13:06	15:04	17:06	19:04	21:07	23:09	1:07	3:09	5:08
9	7:11	9:13	11:07	13:10	15:08	17:10	19:08	21:11	23:13	1:11	3:13	5:12
10	7:15	9:17	11:11	13:14	15:12	17:14	19:12	21:15	23:17	1:15	3:17	5:16
11	7:19	9:21	11:15	13:17	15:16	17:18	19:16	21:18	23:21	1:19	3:21	5:19
12	7:23	9:25	11:19	13:21	15:20	17:22	19:20	21:22	23:25	1:23	3:25	5:23
13	7:27	9:29	11:23	13:25	15:24	17:26	19:24	21:26	23:29	1:27	3:29	5:27
14	7:31	9:33	11:27	13:29	15:28	17:30	19:28	21:30	23:32	1:31	3:33	5:31
15	7:34	9:37	11:31	13:33	15:32	17:34	19:32	21:34	23:36	1:35	3:37	5:35
16	7:38	9:41	11:35	13:37	15:35	17:38	19:36	21:38	23:40	1:39	3:41	5:39
17	7:42	9:45	11:39	13:41	15:39	17:42	19:40	21:42	23:44	1:43	3:45	5:43
18	7:46	9:48	11:43	13:45	15:43	17:46	19:44	21:46	23:48	1:47	3:49	5:47
19	7:50	9:52	11:47	13:49	15:47	17:49	19:48	21:50	23:52	1:50	3:53	5:51
20	7:54	9:56	11:51	13:53	15:51	17:53	19:52	21:54	23:56	1:54	3:57	5:55
21	7:58	10:00	11:55	13:57	15:55	17:57	19:56	21:58	0:00	1:58	4:01	5:59
22	8:02	10:04	11:59	14:01	15:59	18:01	20:00	22:02	0:04	2:02	4:05	6:03
23	8:06	10:08	12:03	14:05	16:03	18:05	20:04	22:06	0:08	2:06	4:08	6:07
24	8:10	10:12	12:06	14:09	16:07	18:09	20:07	22:10	0:12	2:10	4:12	6:11
25	8:14	10:16	12:10	14:13	16:11	18:13	20:11	22:14	0:16	2:14	4:16	6:15
26	8:18	10:20	12:14	14:17	16:15	18:17	20:15	22:18	0:20	2:18	4:20	6:19
27	8:22	10:24	12:18	14:21	16:19	18:21	20:19	22:22	0:24	2:22	4:24	6:23
28	8:26	10:28	12:22	14:24	16:23	18:25	20:23	22:25	0:28	2:26	4:28	6:26
29	8:30	10:32	12:26	14:28	16:27	18:29	20:27	22:29	0:32	2:30	4:32	6:30
30	8:34		12:30	14:32	16:31	18:33	20:31	22:33	0:36	2:34	4:36	6:34
31	8:38		12:34		16:35		20:35	22:37		2:38		6:38

1981	Jan	Feb	Mar	Apr	May	Jun	Jul	Aug	Sep	Oct	Nov	Dec
1	6:42	8:44	10:35	12:37	14:35	16:38	18:36	20:38	22:40	0:39	2:41	4:39
2	6:46	8:48	10:39	12:41	14:39	16:42	18:40	20:42	22:44	0:43	2:45	4:43
3	6:50	8:52	10:43	12:45	14:43	16:45	18:44	20:46	22:48	0:46	2:49	4:47
4	6:54	8:56	10:47	12:49	14:47	16:49	18:48	20:50	22:52	0:50	2:53	4:51
5	6:58	9:00	10:51	12:53	14:51	16:53	18:52	20:54	22:56	0:54	2:57	4:55
6	7:02	9:04	10:55	12:57	14:55	16:57	18:56	20:58	23:00	0:58	3:01	4:59
7	7:06	9:08	10:59	13:01	14:59	17:01	19:00	21:02	23:04	1:02	3:04	5:03
8	7:10	9:12	11:02	13:05	15:03	17:05	19:03	21:06	23:08	1:06	3:08	5:07
9	7:14	9:16	11:06	13:09	15:07	17:09	19:07	21:10	23:12	1:10	3:12	5:11
10	7:18	9:20	11:10	13:13	15:11	17:13	19:11	21:14	23:16	1:14	3:16	5:15
11	7:22	9:24	11:14	13:17	15:15	17:17	19:15	21:17	23:20	1:18	3:20	5:18
12	7:26	9:28	11:18	13:20	15:19	17:21	19:19	21:21	23:24	1:22	3:24	5:22
13	7:30	9:32	11:22	13:24	15:23	17:25	19:23	21:25	23:28	1:26	3:28	5:26
14	7:33	9:36	11:26	13:28	15:27	17:29	19:27	21:29	23:32	1:30	3:32	5:30
15	7:37	9:40	11:30	13:32	15:31	17:33	19:31	21:33	23:35	1:34	3:36	5:34
16	7:41	9:44	11:34	13:36	15:34	17:37	19:35	21:37	23:39	1:38	3:40	5:38
17	7:45	9:48	11:38	13:40	15:38	17:41	19:39	21:41	23:43	1:42	3:44	5:42
18	7:49	9:51	11:42	13:44	15:42	17:45	19:43	21:45	23:47	1:46	3:48	5:46
19	7:53	9:55	11:46	13:48	15:46	17:49	19:47	21:49	23:51	1:50	3:52	5:50
20	7:57	9:59	11:50	13:52	15:50	17:52	19:51	21:53	23:55	1:53	3:56	5:54
21	8:01	10:03	11:54	13:56	15:54	17:56	19:55	21:57	23:59	1:57	4:00	5:58
22	8:05	10:07	11:58	14:00	15:58	18:00	19:59	22:01	0:03	2:01	4:04	6:02
23	8:09	10:11	12:02	14:04	16:02	18:04	20:03	22:05	0:07	2:05	4:08	6:06
24	8:13	10:15	12:06	14:08	16:06	18:08	20:07	22:09	0:11	2:09	4:11	6:10
25	8:17	10:19	12:09	14:12	16:10	18:12	20:10	22:13	0:15	2:13	4:15	6:14
26	8:21	10:23	12:13	14:16	16:14	18:16	20:14	22:17	0:19	2:17	4:19	6:18
27	8:25	10:27	12:17	14:20	16:18	18:20	20:18	22:21	0:23	2:21	4:23	6:22
28	8:29	10:31	12:21	14:24	16:22	18:24	20:22	22:25	0:27	2:25	4:27	6:26
29	8:33		12:25	14:27	16:26	18:28	20:26	22:28	0:31	2:29	4:31	6:29
30	8:37		12:29	14:31	16:30	18:32	20:30	22:32	0:35	2:33	4:35	6:33
31	8:41		12:33		16:34		20:34	22:36		2:37		6:37

1982	Jan	Feb	Mar	Apr	May	Jun	Jul	Aug	Sep	Oct	Nov	Dec
1	6:41	8:44	10:34	12:36	14:34	16:37	18:35	20:37	22:39	0:38	2:40	4:38
2	6:45	8:47	10:38	12:40	14:38	16:41	18:39	20:41	22:43	0:42	2:44	4:42
3	6:49	8:51	10:42	12:44	14:42	16:45	18:43	20:45	22:47	0:45	2:48	4:46
4	6:53	8:55	10:46	12:48	14:46	16:48	18:47	20:49	22:51	0:49	2:52	4:50
5	6:57	8:59	10:50	12:52	14:50	16:52	18:51	20:53	22:55	0:53	2:56	4:54
6	7:01	9:03	10:54	12:56	14:54	16:56	18:55	20:57	22:59	0:57	3:00	4:58
7	7:05	9:07	10:58	13:00	14:58	17:00	18:59	21:01	23:03	1:01	3:03	5:02
8	7:09	9:11	11:01	13:04	15:02	17:04	19:02	21:05	23:07	1:05	3:07	5:06
9	7:13	9:15	11:05	13:08	15:06	17:08	19:06	21:09	23:11	1:09	3:11	5:10
10	7:17	9:19	11:09	13:12	15:10	17:12	19:10	21:13	23:15	1:13	3:15	5:14
11	7:21	9:23	11:13	13:16	15:14	17:16	19:14	21:17	23:19	1:17	3:19	5:18
12	7:25	9:27	11:17	13:19	15:18	17:20	19:18	21:20	23:23	1:21	3:23	5:21
13	7:29	9:31	11:21	13:23	15:22	17:24	19:22	21:24	23:27	1:25	3:27	5:25
14	7:33	9:35	11:25	13:27	15:26	17:28	19:26	21:28	23:31	1:29	3:31	5:29
15	7:36	9:39	11:29	13:31	15:30	17:32	19:30	21:32	23:35	1:33	3:35	5:33
16	7:40	9:43	11:33	13:35	15:34	17:36	19:34	21:36	23:38	1:37	3:39	5:37
17	7:44	9:47	11:37	13:39	15:37	17:40	19:38	21:40	23:42	1:41	3:43	5:41
18	7:48	9:51	11:41	13:43	15:41	17:44	19:42	21:44	23:46	1:45	3:47	5:45
19	7:52	9:54	11:45	13:47	15:45	17:48	19:46	21:48	23:50	1:49	3:51	5:49
20	7:56	9:58	11:49	13:51	15:49	17:52	19:50	21:52	23:54	1:53	3:55	5:53
21	8:00	10:02	11:53	13:55	15:53	17:55	19:54	21:56	23:58	1:56	3:59	5:57
22	8:04	10:06	11:57	13:59	15:57	17:59	19:58	22:00	0:02	2:00	4:03	6:01
23	8:08	10:10	12:01	14:03	16:01	18:03	20:02	22:04	0:06	2:04	4:07	6:05
24	8:12	10:14	12:05	14:07	16:05	18:07	20:06	22:08	0:10	2:08	4:11	6:09
25	8:16	10:18	12:09	14:11	16:09	18:11	20:10	22:12	0:14	2:12	4:14	6:13
26	8:20	10:22	12:12	14:15	16:13	18:15	20:13	22:16	0:18	2:16	4:18	6:17
27	8:24	10:26	12:16	14:19	16:17	18:19	20:17	22:20	0:22	2:20	4:22	6:21
28	8:28	10:30	12:20	14:23	16:21	18:23	20:21	22:24	0:26	2:24	4:26	6:25
29	8:32		12:24	14:27	16:25	18:27	20:25	22:28	0:30	2:28	4:30	6:29
30	8:36		12:28	14:30	16:29	18:31	20:29	22:31	0:34	2:32	4:34	6:32
31	8:40		12:32		16:33		20:33	22:35		2:36		6:36

1983	Jan	Feb	Mar	Apr	May	Jun	Jul	Aug	Sep	Oct	Nov	Dec
1	6:40	8:43	10:33	12:35	14:33	16:36	18:34	20:36	22:38	0:37	2:39	4:37
2	6:44	8:46	10:37	12:39	14:37	16:40	18:38	20:40	22:42	0:41	2:43	4:41
3	6:48	8:50	10:41	12:43	14:41	16:44	18:42	20:44	22:46	0:45	2:47	4:45
4	6:52	8:54	10:45	12:47	14:45	16:47	18:46	20:48	22:50	0:48	2:51	4:49
5	6:56	8:58	10:49	12:51	14:49	16:51	18:50	20:52	22:54	0:52	2:55	4:53
6	7:00	9:02	10:53	12:55	14:53	16:55	18:54	20:56	22:58	0:56	2:59	4:57
7	7:04	9:06	10:57	12:59	14:57	16:59	18:58	21:00	23:02	1:00	3:03	5:01
8	7:08	9:10	11:01	13:03	15:01	17:03	19:02	21:04	23:06	1:04	3:06	5:05
9	7:12	9:14	11:04	13:07	15:05	17:07	19:05	21:08	23:10	1:08	3:10	5:09
10	7:16	9:18	11:08	13:11	15:09	17:11	19:09	21:12	23:14	1:12	3:14	5:13
11	7:20	9:22	11:12	13:15	15:13	17:15	19:13	21:16	23:18	1:16	3:18	5:17
12	7:24	9:26	11:16	13:19	15:17	17:19	19:17	21:20	23:22	1:20	3:22	5:21
13	7:28	9:30	11:20	13:22	15:21	17:23	19:21	21:23	23:26	1:24	3:26	5:24
14	7:32	9:34	11:24	13:26	15:25	17:27	19:25	21:27	23:30	1:28	3:30	5:28
15	7:36	9:38	11:28	13:30	15:29	17:31	19:29	21:31	23:34	1:32	3:34	5:32
16	7:39	9:42	11:32	13:34	15:33	17:35	19:33	21:35	23:38	1:36	3:38	5:36
17	7:43	9:46	11:36	13:38	15:37	17:39	19:37	21:39	23:41	1:40	3:42	5:40
18	7:47	9:50	11:40	13:42	15:40	17:43	19:41	21:43	23:45	1:44	3:46	5:44
19	7:51	9:54	11:44	13:46	15:44	17:47	19:45	21:47	23:49	1:48	3:50	5:48
20	7:55	9:57	11:48	13:50	15:48	17:51	19:49	21:51	23:53	1:52	3:54	5:52
21	7:59	10:01	11:52	13:54	15:52	17:55	19:53	21:55	23:57	1:56	3:58	5:56
22	8:03	10:05	11:56	13:58	15:56	17:58	19:57	21:59	0:01	1:59	4:02	6:00
23	8:07	10:09	12:00	14:02	16:00	18:02	20:01	22:03	0:05	2:03	4:06	6:04
24	8:11	10:13	12:04	14:06	16:04	18:06	20:05	22:07	0:09	2:07	4:10	6:08
25	8:15	10:17	12:08	14:10	16:08	18:10	20:09	22:11	0:13	2:11	4:14	6:12
26	8:19	10:21	12:12	14:14	16:12	18:14	20:13	22:15	0:17	2:15	4:17	6:16
27	8:23	10:25	12:15	14:18	16:16	18:18	20:16	22:19	0:21	2:19	4:21	6:20
28	8:27	10:29	12:19	14:22	16:20	18:22	20:20	22:23	0:25	2:23	4:25	6:24
29	8:31		12:23	14:26	16:24	18:26	20:24	22:27	0:29	2:27	4:29	6:28
30	8:35		12:27	14:30	16:28	18:30	20:28	22:30	0:33	2:31	4:33	6:31
31	8:39		12:31		16:32		20:32	22:34		2:35		6:35

1984	Jan	Feb	Mar	Apr	May	Jun	Jul	Aug	Sep	Oct	Nov	Dec
1	6:39	8:42	10:36	12:38	14:36	16:39	18:37	20:39	22:41	0:40	2:42	4:40
2	6:43	8:46	10:40	12:42	14:40	16:43	18:41	20:43	22:45	0:44	2:46	4:44
3	6:47	8:49	10:44	12:46	14:44	16:47	18:45	20:47	22:49	0:48	2:50	4:48
4	6:51	8:53	10:48	12:50	14:48	16:50	18:49	20:51	22:53	0:51	2:54	4:52
5	6:55	8:57	10:52	12:54	14:52	16:54	18:53	20:55	22:57	0:55	2:58	4:56
6	6:59	9:01	10:56	12:58	14:56	16:58	18:57	20:59	23:01	0:59	3:02	5:00
7	7:03	9:05	11:00	13:02	15:00	17:02	19:01	21:03	23:05	1:03	3:06	5:04
8	7:07	9:09	11:04	13:06	15:04	17:06	19:05	21:07	23:09	1:07	3:09	5:08
9	7:11	9:13	11:07	13:10	15:08	17:10	19:08	21:11	23:13	1:11	3:13	5:12
10	7:15	9:17	11:11	13:14	15:12	17:14	19:12	21:15	23:17	1:15	3:17	5:16
11	7:19	9:21	11:15	13:18	15:16	17:18	19:16	21:19	23:21	1:19	3:21	5:20
12	7:23	9:25	11:19	13:22	15:20	17:22	19:20	21:23	23:25	1:23	3:25	5:24
13	7:27	9:29	11:23	13:25	15:24	17:26	19:24	21:26	23:29	1:27	3:29	5:27
14	7:31	9:33	11:27	13:29	15:28	17:30	19:28	21:30	23:33	1:31	3:33	5:31
15	7:35	9:37	11:31	13:33	15:32	17:34	19:32	21:34	23:37	1:35	3:37	5:35
16	7:39	9:41	11:35	13:37	15:36	17:38	19:36	21:38	23:41	1:39	3:41	5:39
17	7:42	9:45	11:39	13:41	15:40	17:42	19:40	21:42	23:44	1:43	3:45	5:43
18	7:46	9:49	11:43	13:45	15:43	17:46	19:44	21:46	23:48	1:47	3:49	5:47
19	7:50	9:53	11:47	13:49	15:47	17:50	19:48	21:50	23:52	1:51	3:53	5:51
20	7:54	9:57	11:51	13:53	15:51	17:54	19:52	21:54	23:56	1:55	3:57	5:55
21	7:58	10:00	11:55	13:57	15:55	17:58	19:56	21:58	0:00	1:58	4:01	5:59
22	8:02	10:04	11:59	14:01	15:59	18:01	20:00	22:02	0:04	2:02	4:05	6:03
23	8:06	10:08	12:03	14:05	16:03	18:05	20:04	22:06	0:08	2:06	4:09	6:07
24	8:10	10:12	12:07	14:09	16:07	18:09	20:08	22:10	0:12	2:10	4:13	6:11
25	8:14	10:16	12:11	14:13	16:11	18:13	20:12	22:14	0:16	2:14	4:16	6:15
26	8:18	10:20	12:14	14:17	16:15	18:17	20:15	22:18	0:20	2:18	4:20	6:19
27	8:22	10:24	12:18	14:21	16:19	18:21	20:19	22:22	0:24	2:22	4:24	6:23
28	8:26	10:28	12:22	14:25	16:23	18:25	20:23	22:26	0:28	2:26	4:28	6:27
29	8:30	10:32	12:26	14:29	16:27	18:29	20:27	22:30	0:32	2:30	4:32	6:31
30	8:34		12:30	14:32	16:31	18:33	20:31	22:33	0:36	2:34	4:36	6:34
31	8:38		12:34		16:35		20:35	22:37		2:38		6:38

1985	Jan	Feb	Mar	Apr	May	Jun	Jul	Aug	Sep	Oct	Nov	Dec
1	6:42	8:45	10:35	12:37	14:35	16:38	18:36	20:38	22:40	0:39	2:41	4:39
2	6:46	8:49	10:39	12:41	14:39	16:42	18:40	20:42	22:44	0:43	2:45	4:43
3	6:50	8:52	10:43	12:45	14:43	16:46	18:44	20:46	22:48	0:47	2:49	4:47
4	6:54	8:56	10:47	12:49	14:47	16:50	18:48	20:50	22:52	0:51	2:53	4:51
5	6:58	9:00	10:51	12:53	14:51	16:53	18:52	20:54	22:56	0:54	2:57	4:55
6	7:02	9:04	10:55	12:57	14:55	16:57	18:56	20:58	23:00	0:58	3:01	4:59
7	7:06	9:08	10:59	13:01	14:59	17:01	19:00	21:02	23:04	1:02	3:05	5:03
8	7:10	9:12	11:03	13:05	15:03	17:05	19:04	21:06	23:08	1:06	3:09	5:07
9	7:14	9:16	11:07	13:09	15:07	17:09	19:08	21:10	23:12	1:10	3:12	5:11
10	7:18	9:20	11:10	13:13	15:11	17:13	19:11	21:14	23:16	1:14	3:16	5:15
11	7:22	9:24	11:14	13:17	15:15	17:17	19:15	21:18	23:20	1:18	3:20	5:19
12	7:26	9:28	11:18	13:21	15:19	17:21	19:19	21:22	23:24	1:22	3:24	5:23
13	7:30	9:32	11:22	13:25	15:23	17:25	19:23	21:26	23:28	1:26	3:28	5:27
14	7:34	9:36	11:26	13:28	15:27	17:29	19:27	21:29	23:32	1:30	3:32	5:30
15	7:38	9:40	11:30	13:32	15:31	17:33	19:31	21:33	23:36	1:34	3:36	5:34
16	7:42	9:44	11:34	13:36	15:35	17:37	19:35	21:37	23:40	1:38	3:40	5:38
17	7:45	9:48	11:38	13:40	15:39	17:41	19:39	21:41	23:43	1:42	3:44	5:42
18	7:49	9:52	11:42	13:44	15:42	17:45	19:43	21:45	23:47	1:46	3:48	5:46
19	7:53	9:56	11:46	13:48	15:46	17:49	19:47	21:49	23:51	1:50	3:52	5:50
20	7:57	9:59	11:50	13:52	15:50	17:53	19:51	21:53	23:55	1:54	3:56	5:54
21	8:01	10:03	11:54	13:56	15:54	17:57	19:55	21:57	23:59	1:58	4:00	5:58
22	8:05	10:07	11:58	14:00	15:58	18:00	19:59	22:01	0:03	2:01	4:04	6:02
23	8:09	10:11	12:02	14:04	16:02	18:04	20:03	22:05	0:07	2:05	4:08	6:06
24	8:13	10:15	12:06	14:08	16:06	18:08	20:07	22:09	0:11	2:09	4:12	6:10
25	8:17	10:19	12:10	14:12	16:10	18:12	20:11	22:13	0:15	2:13	4:16	6:14
26	8:21	10:23	12:14	14:16	16:14	18:16	20:15	22:17	0:19	2:17	4:19	6:18
27	8:25	10:27	12:17	14:20	16:18	18:20	20:18	22:21	0:23	2:21	4:23	6:22
28	8:29	10:31	12:21	14:24	16:22	18:24	20:22	22:25	0:27	2:25	4:27	6:26
29	8:33		12:25	14:28	16:26	18:28	20:26	22:29	0:31	2:29	4:31	6:30
30	8:37		12:29	14:32	16:30	18:32	20:30	22:33	0:35	2:33	4:35	6:34
31	8:41		12:33		16:34		20:34	22:36		2:37		6:37

1986	Jan	Feb	Mar	Apr	May	Jun	Jul	Aug	Sep	Oct	Nov	Dec
1	6:41	8:44	10:34	12:36	14:35	16:37	18:35	20:37	22:39	0:38	2:40	4:38
2	6:45	8:48	10:38	12:40	14:38	16:41	18:39	20:41	22:43	0:42	2:44	4:42
3	6:49	8:52	10:42	12:44	14:42	16:45	18:43	20:45	22:47	0:46	2:48	4:46
4	6:53	8:55	10:46	12:48	14:46	16:49	18:47	20:49	22:51	0:50	2:52	4:50
5	6:57	8:59	10:50	12:52	14:50	16:53	18:51	20:53	22:55	0:54	2:56	4:54
6	7:01	9:03	10:54	12:56	14:54	16:56	18:55	20:57	22:59	0:57	3:00	4:58
7	7:05	9:07	10:58	13:00	14:58	17:00	18:59	21:01	23:03	1:01	3:04	5:02
8	7:09	9:11	11:02	13:04	15:02	17:04	19:03	21:05	23:07	1:05	3:08	5:06
9	7:13	9:15	11:06	13:08	15:06	17:08	19:07	21:09	23:11	1:09	3:11	5:10
10	7:17	9:19	11:10	13:12	15:10	17:12	19:11	21:13	23:15	1:13	3:15	5:14
11	7:21	9:23	11:13	13:16	15:14	17:16	19:14	21:17	23:19	1:17	3:19	5:18
12	7:25	9:27	11:17	13:20	15:18	17:20	19:18	21:21	23:23	1:21	3:23	5:22
13	7:29	9:31	11:21	13:24	15:22	17:24	19:22	21:25	23:27	1:25	3:27	5:26
14	7:33	9:35	11:25	13:27	15:26	17:28	19:26	21:28	23:31	1:29	3:31	5:29
15	7:37	9:39	11:29	13:31	15:30	17:32	19:30	21:32	23:35	1:33	3:35	5:33
16	7:41	9:43	11:33	13:35	15:34	17:36	19:34	21:36	23:39	1:37	3:39	5:37
17	7:44	9:47	11:37	13:39	15:38	17:40	19:38	21:40	23:43	1:41	3:43	5:41
18	7:48	9:51	11:41	13:43	15:42	17:44	19:42	21:44	23:46	1:45	3:47	5:45
19	7:52	9:55	11:45	13:47	15:45	17:48	19:46	21:48	23:50	1:49	3:51	5:49
20	7:56	9:59	11:49	13:51	15:49	17:52	19:50	21:52	23:54	1:53	3:55	5:53
21	8:00	10:02	11:53	13:55	15:53	17:56	19:54	21:56	23:58	1:57	3:59	5:57
22	8:04	10:06	11:57	13:59	15:57	18:00	19:58	22:00	0:02	2:01	4:03	6:01
23	8:08	10:10	12:01	14:03	16:01	18:03	20:02	22:04	0:06	2:04	4:07	6:05
24	8:12	10:14	12:05	14:07	16:05	18:07	20:06	22:08	0:10	2:08	4:11	6:09
25	8:16	10:18	12:09	14:11	16:09	18:11	20:10	22:12	0:14	2:12	4:15	6:13
26	8:20	10:22	12:13	14:15	16:13	18:15	20:14	22:16	0:18	2:16	4:19	6:17
27	8:24	10:26	12:17	14:19	16:17	18:19	20:18	22:20	0:22	2:20	4:22	6:21
28	8:28	10:30	12:20	14:23	16:21	18:23	20:21	22:24	0:26	2:24	4:26	6:25
29	8:32		12:24	14:27	16:25	18:27	20:25	22:28	0:30	2:28	4:30	6:29
30	8:36		12:28	14:31	16:29	18:31	20:29	22:32	0:34	2:32	4:34	6:33
31	8:40		12:32		16:33		20:33	22:36		2:36		6:37

1987	Jan	Feb	Mar	Apr	May	Jun	Jul	Aug	Sep	Oct	Nov	Dec
1	6:40	8:43	10:33	12:35	14:34	16:36	18:34	20:36	22:39	0:37	2:39	4:37
2	6:44	8:47	10:37	12:39	14:38	16:40	18:38	20:40	22:42	0:41	2:43	4:41
3	6:48	8:51	10:41	12:43	14:41	16:44	18:42	20:44	22:46	0:45	2:47	4:45
4	6:52	8:55	10:45	12:47	14:45	16:48	18:46	20:48	22:50	0:49	2:51	4:49
5	6:56	8:58	10:49	12:51	14:49	16:52	18:50	20:52	22:54	0:53	2:55	4:53
6	7:00	9:02	10:53	12:55	14:53	16:55	18:54	20:56	22:58	0:56	2:59	4:57
7	7:04	9:06	10:57	12:59	14:57	16:59	18:58	21:00	23:02	1:00	3:03	5:01
8	7:08	9:10	11:01	13:03	15:01	17:03	19:02	21:04	23:06	1:04	3:07	5:05
9	7:12	9:14	11:05	13:07	15:05	17:07	19:06	21:08	23:10	1:08	3:11	5:09
10	7:16	9:18	11:09	13:11	15:09	17:11	19:10	21:12	23:14	1:12	3:14	5:13
11	7:20	9:22	11:12	13:15	15:13	17:15	19:13	21:16	23:18	1:16	3:18	5:17
12	7:24	9:26	11:16	13:19	15:17	17:19	19:17	21:20	23:22	1:20	3:22	5:21
13	7:28	9:30	11:20	13:23	15:21	17:23	19:21	21:24	23:26	1:24	3:26	5:25
14	7:32	9:34	11:24	13:27	15:25	17:27	19:25	21:28	23:30	1:28	3:30	5:29
15	7:36	9:38	11:28	13:30	15:29	17:31	19:29	21:31	23:34	1:32	3:34	5:32
16	7:40	9:42	11:32	13:34	15:33	17:35	19:33	21:35	23:38	1:36	3:38	5:36
17	7:44	9:46	11:36	13:38	15:37	17:39	19:37	21:39	23:42	1:40	3:42	5:40
18	7:47	9:50	11:40	13:42	15:41	17:43	19:41	21:43	23:46	1:44	3:46	5:44
19	7:51	9:54	11:44	13:46	15:45	17:47	19:45	21:47	23:49	1:48	3:50	5:48
20	7:55	9:58	11:48	13:50	15:48	17:51	19:49	21:51	23:53	1:52	3:54	5:52
21	7:59	10:02	11:52	13:54	15:52	17:55	19:53	21:55	23:57	1:56	3:58	5:56
22	8:03	10:05	11:56	13:58	15:56	17:59	19:57	21:59	0:01	2:00	4:02	6:00
23	8:07	10:09	12:00	14:02	16:00	18:03	20:01	22:03	0:05	2:04	4:06	6:04
24	8:11	10:13	12:04	14:06	16:04	18:06	20:05	22:07	0:09	2:07	4:10	6:08
25	8:15	10:17	12:08	14:10	16:08	18:10	20:09	22:11	0:13	2:11	4:14	6:12
26	8:19	10:21	12:12	14:14	16:12	18:14	20:13	22:15	0:17	2:15	4:18	6:16
27	8:23	10:25	12:16	14:18	16:16	18:18	20:17	22:19	0:21	2:19	4:22	6:20
28	8:27	10:29	12:20	14:22	16:20	18:22	20:21	22:23	0:25	2:23	4:25	6:24
29	8:31		12:23	14:26	16:24	18:26	20:24	22:27	0:29	2:27	4:29	6:28
30	8:35		12:27	14:30	16:28	18:30	20:28	22:31	0:33	2:31	4:33	6:32
31	8:39		12:31		16:32		20:32	22:35		2:35		6:36

1988	Jan	Feb	Mar	Apr	May	Jun	Jul	Aug	Sep	Oct	Nov	Dec
1	6:40	8:42	10:36	12:38	14:37	16:39	18:37	20:39	22:41	0:40	2:42	4:40
2	6:43	8:46	10:40	12:42	14:40	16:43	18:41	20:43	22:45	0:44	2:46	4:44
3	6:47	8:50	10:44	12:46	14:44	16:47	18:45	20:47	22:49	0:48	2:50	4:48
4	6:51	8:54	10:48	12:50	14:48	16:51	18:49	20:51	22:53	0:52	2:54	4:52
5	6:55	8:57	10:52	12:54	14:52	16:55	18:53	20:55	22:57	0:56	2:58	4:56
6	6:59	9:01	10:56	12:58	14:56	16:58	18:57	20:59	23:01	0:59	3:02	5:00
7	7:03	9:05	11:00	13:02	15:00	17:02	19:01	21:03	23:05	1:03	3:06	5:04
8	7:07	9:09	11:04	13:06	15:04	17:06	19:05	21:07	23:09	1:07	3:10	5:08
9	7:11	9:13	11:08	13:10	15:08	17:10	19:09	21:11	23:13	1:11	3:14	5:12
10	7:15	9:17	11:12	13:14	15:12	17:14	19:13	21:15	23:17	1:15	3:17	5:16
11	7:19	9:21	11:15	13:18	15:16	17:18	19:16	21:19	23:21	1:19	3:21	5:20
12	7:23	9:25	11:19	13:22	15:20	17:22	19:20	21:23	23:25	1:23	3:25	5:24
13	7:27	9:29	11:23	13:26	15:24	17:26	19:24	21:27	23:29	1:27	3:29	5:28
14	7:31	9:33	11:27	13:30	15:28	17:30	19:28	21:31	23:33	1:31	3:33	5:32
15	7:35	9:37	11:31	13:33	15:32	17:34	19:32	21:34	23:37	1:35	3:37	5:35
16	7:39	9:41	11:35	13:37	15:36	17:38	19:36	21:38	23:41	1:39	3:41	5:39
17	7:43	9:45	11:39	13:41	15:40	17:42	19:40	21:42	23:45	1:43	3:45	5:43
18	7:47	9:49	11:43	13:45	15:44	17:46	19:44	21:46	23:49	1:47	3:49	5:47
19	7:50	9:53	11:47	13:49	15:48	17:50	19:48	21:50	23:52	1:51	3:53	5:51
20	7:54	9:57	11:51	13:53	15:51	17:54	19:52	21:54	23:56	1:55	3:57	5:55
21	7:58	10:01	11:55	13:57	15:55	17:58	19:56	21:58	0:00	1:59	4:01	5:59
22	8:02	10:05	11:59	14:01	15:59	18:02	20:00	22:02	0:04	2:03	4:05	6:03
23	8:06	10:08	12:03	14:05	16:03	18:06	20:04	22:06	0:08	2:07	4:09	6:07
24	8:10	10:12	12:07	14:09	16:07	18:09	20:08	22:10	0:12	2:10	4:13	6:11
25	8:14	10:16	12:11	14:13	16:11	18:13	20:12	22:14	0:16	2:14	4:17	6:15
26	8:18	10:20	12:15	14:17	16:15	18:17	20:16	22:18	0:20	2:18	4:21	6:19
27	8:22	10:24	12:19	14:21	16:19	18:21	20:20	22:22	0:24	2:22	4:24	6:23
28	8:26	10:28	12:23	14:25	16:23	18:25	20:24	22:26	0:28	2:26	4:28	6:27
29	8:30	10:32	12:26	14:29	16:27	18:29	20:27	22:30	0:32	2:30	4:32	6:31
30	8:34		12:30	14:33	16:31	18:33	20:31	22:34	0:36	2:34	4:36	6:35
31	8:38		12:34		16:35		20:35	22:38		2:38		6:39

1989	Jan	Feb	Mar	Apr	May	Jun	Jul	Aug	Sep	Oct	Nov	Dec
1	6:42	8:45	10:35	12:37	14:36	16:38	18:36	20:38	22:41	0:39	2:41	4:39
2	6:46	8:49	10:39	12:41	14:40	16:42	18:40	20:42	22:44	0:43	2:45	4:43
3	6:50	8:53	10:43	12:45	14:43	16:46	18:44	20:46	22:48	0:47	2:49	4:47
4	6:54	8:57	10:47	12:49	14:47	16:50	18:48	20:50	22:52	0:51	2:53	4:51
5	6:58	9:00	10:51	12:53	14:51	16:54	18:52	20:54	22:56	0:55	2:57	4:55
6	7:02	9:04	10:55	12:57	14:55	16:58	18:56	20:58	23:00	0:59	3:01	4:59
7	7:06	9:08	10:59	13:01	14:59	17:01	19:00	21:02	23:04	1:02	3:05	5:03
8	7:10	9:12	11:03	13:05	15:03	17:05	19:04	21:06	23:08	1:06	3:09	5:07
9	7:14	9:16	11:07	13:09	15:07	17:09	19:08	21:10	23:12	1:10	3:13	5:11
10	7:18	9:20	11:11	13:13	15:11	17:13	19:12	21:14	23:16	1:14	3:17	5:15
11	7:22	9:24	11:15	13:17	15:15	17:17	19:16	21:18	23:20	1:18	3:20	5:19
12	7:26	9:28	11:18	13:21	15:19	17:21	19:19	21:22	23:24	1:22	3:24	5:23
13	7:30	9:32	11:22	13:25	15:23	17:25	19:23	21:26	23:28	1:26	3:28	5:27
14	7:34	9:36	11:26	13:29	15:27	17:29	19:27	21:30	23:32	1:30	3:32	5:31
15	7:38	9:40	11:30	13:33	15:31	17:33	19:31	21:34	23:36	1:34	3:36	5:35
16	7:42	9:44	11:34	13:36	15:35	17:37	19:35	21:37	23:40	1:38	3:40	5:38
17	7:46	9:48	11:38	13:40	15:39	17:41	19:39	21:41	23:44	1:42	3:44	5:42
18	7:50	9:52	11:42	13:44	15:43	17:45	19:43	21:45	23:48	1:46	3:48	5:46
19	7:53	9:56	11:46	13:48	15:47	17:49	19:47	21:49	23:52	1:50	3:52	5:50
20	7:57	10:00	11:50	13:52	15:51	17:53	19:51	21:53	23:55	1:54	3:56	5:54
21	8:01	10:04	11:54	13:56	15:54	17:57	19:55	21:57	23:59	1:58	4:00	5:58
22	8:05	10:08	11:58	14:00	15:58	18:01	19:59	22:01	0:03	2:02	4:04	6:02
23	8:09	10:11	12:02	14:04	16:02	18:05	20:03	22:05	0:07	2:06	4:08	6:06
24	8:13	10:15	12:06	14:08	16:06	18:08	20:07	22:09	0:11	2:09	4:12	6:10
25	8:17	10:19	12:10	14:12	16:10	18:12	20:11	22:13	0:15	2:13	4:16	6:14
26	8:21	10:23	12:14	14:16	16:14	18:16	20:15	22:17	0:19	2:17	4:20	6:18
27	8:25	10:27	12:18	14:20	16:18	18:20	20:19	22:21	0:23	2:21	4:24	6:22
28	8:29	10:31	12:22	14:24	16:22	18:24	20:23	22:25	0:27	2:25	4:27	6:26
29	8:33		12:25	14:28	16:26	18:28	20:26	22:29	0:31	2:29	4:31	6:30
30	8:37		12:29	14:32	16:30	18:32	20:30	22:33	0:35	2:33	4:35	6:34
31	8:41		12:33		16:34		20:34	22:37		2:37		6:38

1990	Jan	Feb	Mar	Apr	May	Jun	Jul	Aug	Sep	Oct	Nov	Dec
1	6:42	8:44	10:34	12:36	14:35	16:37	18:35	20:37	22:40	0:38	2:40	4:38
2	6:45	8:48	10:38	12:40	14:39	16:41	18:39	20:41	22:44	0:42	2:44	4:42
3	6:49	8:52	10:42	12:44	14:43	16:45	18:43	20:45	22:47	0:46	2:48	4:46
4	6:53	8:56	10:46	12:48	14:46	16:49	18:47	20:49	22:51	0:50	2:52	4:50
5	6:57	9:00	10:50	12:52	14:50	16:53	18:51	20:53	22:55	0:54	2:56	4:54
6	7:01	9:03	10:54	12:56	14:54	16:57	18:55	20:57	22:59	0:58	3:00	4:58
7	7:05	9:07	10:58	13:00	14:58	17:01	18:59	21:01	23:03	1:02	3:04	5:02
8	7:09	9:11	11:02	13:04	15:02	17:04	19:03	21:05	23:07	1:05	3:08	5:06
9	7:13	9:15	11:06	13:08	15:06	17:08	19:07	21:09	23:11	1:09	3:12	5:10
10	7:17	9:19	11:10	13:12	15:10	17:12	19:11	21:13	23:15	1:13	3:16	5:14
11	7:21	9:23	11:14	13:16	15:14	17:16	19:15	21:17	23:19	1:17	3:20	5:18
12	7:25	9:27	11:18	13:20	15:18	17:20	19:19	21:21	23:23	1:21	3:23	5:22
13	7:29	9:31	11:21	13:24	15:22	17:24	19:22	21:25	23:27	1:25	3:27	5:26
14	7:33	9:35	11:25	13:28	15:26	17:28	19:26	21:29	23:31	1:29	3:31	5:30
15	7:37	9:39	11:29	13:32	15:30	17:32	19:30	21:33	23:35	1:33	3:35	5:34
16	7:41	9:43	11:33	13:36	15:34	17:36	19:34	21:37	23:39	1:37	3:39	5:37
17	7:45	9:47	11:37	13:39	15:38	17:40	19:38	21:40	23:43	1:41	3:43	5:41
18	7:49	9:51	11:41	13:43	15:42	17:44	19:42	21:44	23:47	1:45	3:47	5:45
19	7:52	9:55	11:45	13:47	15:46	17:48	19:46	21:48	23:51	1:49	3:51	5:49
20	7:56	9:59	11:49	13:51	15:50	17:52	19:50	21:52	23:54	1:53	3:55	5:53
21	8:00	10:03	11:53	13:55	15:53	17:56	19:54	21:56	23:58	1:57	3:59	5:57
22	8:04	10:07	11:57	13:59	15:57	18:00	19:58	22:00	0:02	2:01	4:03	6:01
23	8:08	10:10	12:01	14:03	16:01	18:04	20:02	22:04	0:06	2:05	4:07	6:05
24	8:12	10:14	12:05	14:07	16:05	18:08	20:06	22:08	0:10	2:09	4:11	6:09
25	8:16	10:18	12:09	14:11	16:09	18:11	20:10	22:12	0:14	2:12	4:15	6:13
26	8:20	10:22	12:13	14:15	16:13	18:15	20:14	22:16	0:18	2:16	4:19	6:17
27	8:24	10:26	12:17	14:19	16:17	18:19	20:18	22:20	0:22	2:20	4:23	6:21
28	8:28	10:30	12:21	14:23	16:21	18:23	20:22	22:24	0:26	2:24	4:27	6:25
29	8:32		12:25	14:27	16:25	18:27	20:26	22:28	0:30	2:28	4:30	6:29
30	8:36		12:28	14:31	16:29	18:31	20:29	22:32	0:34	2:32	4:34	6:33
31	8:40		12:32		16:33		20:33	22:36		2:36		6:37

1991	Jan	Feb	Mar	Apr	May	Jun	Jul	Aug	Sep	Oct	Nov	Dec
1	6:41	8:43	10:33	12:35	14:34	16:36	18:34	20:36	22:39	0:37	2:39	4:37
2	6:45	8:47	10:37	12:39	14:38	16:40	18:38	20:40	22:43	0:41	2:43	4:41
3	6:48	8:51	10:41	12:43	14:42	16:44	18:42	20:44	22:47	0:45	2:47	4:45
4	6:52	8:55	10:45	12:47	14:46	16:48	18:46	20:48	22:50	0:49	2:51	4:49
5	6:56	8:59	10:49	12:51	14:49	16:52	18:50	20:52	22:54	0:53	2:55	4:53
6	7:00	9:03	10:53	12:55	14:53	16:56	18:54	20:56	22:58	0:57	2:59	4:57
7	7:04	9:06	10:57	12:59	14:57	17:00	18:58	21:00	23:02	1:01	3:03	5:01
8	7:08	9:10	11:01	13:03	15:01	17:04	19:02	21:04	23:06	1:05	3:07	5:05
9	7:12	9:14	11:05	13:07	15:05	17:07	19:06	21:08	23:10	1:08	3:11	5:09
10	7:16	9:18	11:09	13:11	15:09	17:11	19:10	21:12	23:14	1:12	3:15	5:13
11	7:20	9:22	11:13	13:15	15:13	17:15	19:14	21:16	23:18	1:16	3:19	5:17
12	7:24	9:26	11:17	13:19	15:17	17:19	19:18	21:20	23:22	1:20	3:22	5:21
13	7:28	9:30	11:21	13:23	15:21	17:23	19:21	21:24	23:26	1:24	3:26	5:25
14	7:32	9:34	11:24	13:27	15:25	17:27	19:25	21:28	23:30	1:28	3:30	5:29
15	7:36	9:38	11:28	13:31	15:29	17:31	19:29	21:32	23:34	1:32	3:34	5:33
16	7:40	9:42	11:32	13:35	15:33	17:35	19:33	21:36	23:38	1:36	3:38	5:37
17	7:44	9:46	11:36	13:38	15:37	17:39	19:37	21:39	23:42	1:40	3:42	5:40
18	7:48	9:50	11:40	13:42	15:41	17:43	19:41	21:43	23:46	1:44	3:46	5:44
19	7:52	9:54	11:44	13:46	15:45	17:47	19:45	21:47	23:50	1:48	3:50	5:48
20	7:55	9:58	11:48	13:50	15:49	17:51	19:49	21:51	23:54	1:52	3:54	5:52
21	7:59	10:02	11:52	13:54	15:53	17:55	19:53	21:55	23:57	1:56	3:58	5:56
22	8:03	10:06	11:56	13:58	15:56	17:59	19:57	21:59	0:01	2:00	4:02	6:00
23	8:07	10:10	12:00	14:02	16:00	18:03	20:01	22:03	0:05	2:04	4:06	6:04
24	8:11	10:13	12:04	14:06	16:04	18:07	20:05	22:07	0:09	2:08	4:10	6:08
25	8:15	10:17	12:08	14:10	16:08	18:11	20:09	22:11	0:13	2:12	4:14	6:12
26	8:19	10:21	12:12	14:14	16:12	18:14	20:13	22:15	0:17	2:15	4:18	6:16
27	8:23	10:25	12:16	14:18	16:16	18:18	20:17	22:19	0:21	2:19	4:22	6:20
28	8:27	10:29	12:20	14:22	16:20	18:22	20:21	22:23	0:25	2:23	4:26	6:24
29	8:31		12:24	14:26	16:24	18:26	20:25	22:27	0:29	2:27	4:30	6:28
30	8:35		12:28	14:30	16:28	18:30	20:29	22:31	0:33	2:31	4:33	6:32
31	8:39		12:31		16:32		20:32	22:35		2:35		6:36

1992	Jan	Feb	Mar	Apr	May	Jun	Jul	Aug	Sep	Oct	Nov	Dec
1	6:40	8:42	10:36	12:38	14:37	16:39	18:37	20:39	22:42	0:40	2:42	4:40
2	6:44	8:46	10:40	12:42	14:41	16:43	18:41	20:43	22:46	0:44	2:46	4:44
3	6:48	8:50	10:44	12:46	14:45	16:47	18:45	20:47	22:50	0:48	2:50	4:48
4	6:51	8:54	10:48	12:50	14:49	16:51	18:49	20:51	22:53	0:52	2:54	4:52
5	6:55	8:58	10:52	12:54	14:52	16:55	18:53	20:55	22:57	0:56	2:58	4:56
6	6:59	9:02	10:56	12:58	14:56	16:59	18:57	20:59	23:01	1:00	3:02	5:00
7	7:03	9:05	11:00	13:02	15:00	17:03	19:01	21:03	23:05	1:04	3:06	5:04
8	7:07	9:09	11:04	13:06	15:04	17:06	19:05	21:07	23:09	1:07	3:10	5:08
9	7:11	9:13	11:08	13:10	15:08	17:10	19:09	21:11	23:13	1:11	3:14	5:12
10	7:15	9:17	11:12	13:14	15:12	17:14	19:13	21:15	23:17	1:15	3:18	5:16
11	7:19	9:21	11:16	13:18	15:16	17:18	19:17	21:19	23:21	1:19	3:22	5:20
12	7:23	9:25	11:20	13:22	15:20	17:22	19:21	21:23	23:25	1:23	3:25	5:24
13	7:27	9:29	11:23	13:26	15:24	17:26	19:24	21:27	23:29	1:27	3:29	5:28
14	7:31	9:33	11:27	13:30	15:28	17:30	19:28	21:31	23:33	1:31	3:33	5:32
15	7:35	9:37	11:31	13:34	15:32	17:34	19:32	21:35	23:37	1:35	3:37	5:36
16	7:39	9:41	11:35	13:38	15:36	17:38	19:36	21:39	23:41	1:39	3:41	5:40
17	7:43	9:45	11:39	13:41	15:40	17:42	19:40	21:42	23:45	1:43	3:45	5:43
18	7:47	9:49	11:43	13:45	15:44	17:46	19:44	21:46	23:49	1:47	3:49	5:47
19	7:51	9:53	11:47	13:49	15:48	17:50	19:48	21:50	23:53	1:51	3:53	5:51
20	7:55	9:57	11:51	13:53	15:52	17:54	19:52	21:54	23:57	1:55	3:57	5:55
21	7:58	10:01	11:55	13:57	15:56	17:58	19:56	21:58	0:00	1:59	4:01	5:59
22	8:02	10:05	11:59	14:01	15:59	18:02	20:00	22:02	0:04	2:03	4:05	6:03
23	8:06	10:09	12:03	14:05	16:03	18:06	20:04	22:06	0:08	2:07	4:09	6:07
24	8:10	10:13	12:07	14:09	16:07	18:10	20:08	22:10	0:12	2:11	4:13	6:11
25	8:14	10:16	12:11	14:13	16:11	18:14	20:12	22:14	0:16	2:15	4:17	6:15
26	8:18	10:20	12:15	14:17	16:15	18:17	20:16	22:18	0:20	2:18	4:21	6:19
27	8:22	10:24	12:19	14:21	16:19	18:21	20:20	22:22	0:24	2:22	4:25	6:23
28	8:26	10:28	12:23	14:25	16:23	18:25	20:24	22:26	0:28	2:26	4:29	6:27
29	8:30	10:32	12:27	14:29	16:27	18:29	20:28	22:30	0:32	2:30	4:33	6:31
30	8:34		12:31	14:33	16:31	18:33	20:32	22:34	0:36	2:34	4:36	6:35
31	8:38		12:34		16:35		20:35	22:38		2:38		6:39

1993	Jan	Feb	Mar	Apr	May	Jun	Jul	Aug	Sep	Oct	Nov	Dec
1	6:43	8:45	10:35	12:37	14:36	16:38	18:36	20:38	22:41	0:39	2:41	4:39
2	6:47	8:49	10:39	12:41	14:40	16:42	18:40	20:42	22:45	0:43	2:45	4:43
3	6:50	8:53	10:43	12:45	14:44	16:46	18:44	20:46	22:49	0:47	2:49	4:47
4	6:54	8:57	10:47	12:49	14:48	16:50	18:48	20:50	22:52	0:51	2:53	4:51
5	6:58	9:01	10:51	12:53	14:51	16:54	18:52	20:54	22:56	0:55	2:57	4:55
6	7:02	9:05	10:55	12:57	14:55	16:58	18:56	20:58	23:00	0:59	3:01	4:59
7	7:06	9:08	10:59	13:01	14:59	17:02	19:00	21:02	23:04	1:03	3:05	5:03
8	7:10	9:12	11:03	13:05	15:03	17:06	19:04	21:06	23:08	1:07	3:09	5:07
9	7:14	9:16	11:07	13:09	15:07	17:09	19:08	21:10	23:12	1:10	3:13	5:11
10	7:18	9:20	11:11	13:13	15:11	17:13	19:12	21:14	23:16	1:14	3:17	5:15
11	7:22	9:24	11:15	13:17	15:15	17:17	19:16	21:18	23:20	1:18	3:21	5:19
12	7:26	9:28	11:19	13:21	15:19	17:21	19:20	21:22	23:24	1:22	3:25	5:23
13	7:30	9:32	11:23	13:25	15:23	17:25	19:24	21:26	23:28	1:26	3:28	5:27
14	7:34	9:36	11:26	13:29	15:27	17:29	19:27	21:30	23:32	1:30	3:32	5:31
15	7:38	9:40	11:30	13:33	15:31	17:33	19:31	21:34	23:36	1:34	3:36	5:35
16	7:42	9:44	11:34	13:37	15:35	17:37	19:35	21:38	23:40	1:38	3:40	5:39
17	7:46	9:48	11:38	13:41	15:39	17:41	19:39	21:42	23:44	1:42	3:44	5:43
18	7:50	9:52	11:42	13:44	15:43	17:45	19:43	21:45	23:48	1:46	3:48	5:46
19	7:54	9:56	11:46	13:48	15:47	17:49	19:47	21:49	23:52	1:50	3:52	5:50
20	7:58	10:00	11:50	13:52	15:51	17:53	19:51	21:53	23:56	1:54	3:56	5:54
21	8:01	10:04	11:54	13:56	15:55	17:57	19:55	21:57	0:00	1:58	4:00	5:58
22	8:05	10:08	11:58	14:00	15:59	18:01	19:59	22:01	0:03	2:02	4:04	6:02
23	8:09	10:12	12:02	14:04	16:02	18:05	20:03	22:05	0:07	2:06	4:08	6:06
24	8:13	10:16	12:06	14:08	16:06	18:09	20:07	22:09	0:11	2:10	4:12	6:10
25	8:17	10:19	12:10	14:12	16:10	18:13	20:11	22:13	0:15	2:14	4:16	6:14
26	8:21	10:23	12:14	14:16	16:14	18:17	20:15	22:17	0:19	2:18	4:20	6:18
27	8:25	10:27	12:18	14:20	16:18	18:20	20:19	22:21	0:23	2:21	4:24	6:22
28	8:29	10:31	12:22	14:24	16:22	18:24	20:23	22:25	0:27	2:25	4:28	6:26
29	8:33		12:26	14:28	16:26	18:28	20:27	22:29	0:31	2:29	4:32	6:30
30	8:37		12:30	14:32	16:30	18:32	20:31	22:33	0:35	2:33	4:35	6:34
31	8:41		12:34		16:34		20:34	22:37		2:37		6:38

1994	Jan	Feb	Mar	Apr	May	Jun	Jul	Aug	Sep	Oct	Nov	Dec
1	6:42	8:44	10:34	12:36	14:35	16:37	18:35	20:37	22:40	0:38	2:40	4:38
2	6:46	8:48	10:38	12:40	14:39	16:41	18:39	20:41	22:44	0:42	2:44	4:42
3	6:50	8:52	10:42	12:44	14:43	16:45	18:43	20:45	22:48	0:46	2:48	4:46
4	6:53	8:56	10:46	12:48	14:47	16:49	18:47	20:49	22:52	0:50	2:52	4:50
5	6:57	9:00	10:50	12:52	14:51	16:53	18:51	20:53	22:55	0:54	2:56	4:54
6	7:01	9:04	10:54	12:56	14:54	16:57	18:55	20:57	22:59	0:58	3:00	4:58
7	7:05	9:08	10:58	13:00	14:58	17:01	18:59	21:01	23:03	1:02	3:04	5:02
8	7:09	9:11	11:02	13:04	15:02	17:05	19:03	21:05	23:07	1:06	3:08	5:06
9	7:13	9:15	11:06	13:08	15:06	17:09	19:07	21:09	23:11	1:10	3:12	5:10
10	7:17	9:19	11:10	13:12	15:10	17:12	19:11	21:13	23:15	1:13	3:16	5:14
11	7:21	9:23	11:14	13:16	15:14	17:16	19:15	21:17	23:19	1:17	3:20	5:18
12	7:25	9:27	11:18	13:20	15:18	17:20	19:19	21:21	23:23	1:21	3:24	5:22
13	7:29	9:31	11:22	13:24	15:22	17:24	19:23	21:25	23:27	1:25	3:28	5:26
14	7:33	9:35	11:26	13:28	15:26	17:28	19:27	21:29	23:31	1:29	3:31	5:30
15	7:37	9:39	11:29	13:32	15:30	17:32	19:30	21:33	23:35	1:33	3:35	5:34
16	7:41	9:43	11:33	13:36	15:34	17:36	19:34	21:37	23:39	1:37	3:39	5:38
17	7:45	9:47	11:37	13:40	15:38	17:40	19:38	21:41	23:43	1:41	3:43	5:42
18	7:49	9:51	11:41	13:44	15:42	17:44	19:42	21:45	23:47	1:45	3:47	5:46
19	7:53	9:55	11:45	13:47	15:46	17:48	19:46	21:48	23:51	1:49	3:51	5:49
20	7:57	9:59	11:49	13:51	15:50	17:52	19:50	21:52	23:55	1:53	3:55	5:53
21	8:01	10:03	11:53	13:55	15:54	17:56	19:54	21:56	23:59	1:57	3:59	5:57
22	8:04	10:07	11:57	13:59	15:58	18:00	19:58	22:00	0:03	2:01	4:03	6:01
23	8:08	10:11	12:01	14:03	16:02	18:04	20:02	22:04	0:06	2:05	4:07	6:05
24	8:12	10:15	12:05	14:07	16:05	18:08	20:06	22:08	0:10	2:09	4:11	6:09
25	8:16	10:18	12:09	14:11	16:09	18:12	20:10	22:12	0:14	2:13	4:15	6:13
26	8:20	10:22	12:13	14:15	16:13	18:16	20:14	22:16	0:18	2:17	4:19	6:17
27	8:24	10:26	12:17	14:19	16:17	18:19	20:18	22:20	0:22	2:20	4:23	6:21
28	8:28	10:30	12:21	14:23	16:21	18:23	20:22	22:24	0:26	2:24	4:27	6:25
29	8:32		12:25	14:27	16:25	18:27	20:26	22:28	0:30	2:28	4:31	6:29
30	8:36		12:29	14:31	16:29	18:31	20:30	22:32	0:34	2:32	4:35	6:33
31	8:40		12:33		16:33		20:34	22:36		2:36		6:37

1995	Jan	Feb	Mar	Apr	May	Jun	Jul	Aug	Sep	Oct	Nov	Dec
1	6:41	8:43	10:33	12:36	14:34	16:36	18:34	20:37	22:39	0:37	2:39	4:38
2	6:45	8:47	10:37	12:39	14:38	16:40	18:38	20:40	22:43	0:41	2:43	4:41
3	6:49	8:51	10:41	12:43	14:42	16:44	18:42	20:44	22:47	0:45	2:47	4:45
4	6:53	8:55	10:45	12:47	14:46	16:48	18:46	20:48	22:51	0:49	2:51	4:49
5	6:56	8:59	10:49	12:51	14:50	16:52	18:50	20:52	22:55	0:53	2:55	4:53
6	7:00	9:03	10:53	12:55	14:54	16:56	18:54	20:56	22:58	0:57	2:59	4:57
7	7:04	9:07	10:57	12:59	14:57	17:00	18:58	21:00	23:02	1:01	3:03	5:01
8	7:08	9:11	11:01	13:03	15:01	17:04	19:02	21:04	23:06	1:05	3:07	5:05
9	7:12	9:14	11:05	13:07	15:05	17:08	19:06	21:08	23:10	1:09	3:11	5:09
10	7:16	9:18	11:09	13:11	15:09	17:12	19:10	21:12	23:14	1:13	3:15	5:13
11	7:20	9:22	11:13	13:15	15:13	17:15	19:14	21:16	23:18	1:16	3:19	5:17
12	7:24	9:26	11:17	13:19	15:17	17:19	19:18	21:20	23:22	1:20	3:23	5:21
13	7:28	9:30	11:21	13:23	15:21	17:23	19:22	21:24	23:26	1:24	3:27	5:25
14	7:32	9:34	11:25	13:27	15:25	17:27	19:26	21:28	23:30	1:28	3:31	5:29
15	7:36	9:38	11:29	13:31	15:29	17:31	19:30	21:32	23:34	1:32	3:34	5:33
16	7:40	9:42	11:32	13:35	15:33	17:35	19:33	21:36	23:38	1:36	3:38	5:37
17	7:44	9:46	11:36	13:39	15:37	17:39	19:37	21:40	23:42	1:40	3:42	5:41
18	7:48	9:50	11:40	13:43	15:41	17:43	19:41	21:44	23:46	1:44	3:46	5:45
19	7:52	9:54	11:44	13:47	15:45	17:47	19:45	21:47	23:50	1:48	3:50	5:48
20	7:56	9:58	11:48	13:50	15:49	17:51	19:49	21:51	23:54	1:52	3:54	5:52
21	8:00	10:02	11:52	13:54	15:53	17:55	19:53	21:55	23:58	1:56	3:58	5:56
22	8:03	10:06	11:56	13:58	15:57	17:59	19:57	21:59	0:02	2:00	4:02	6:00
23	8:07	10:10	12:00	14:02	16:01	18:03	20:01	22:03	0:05	2:04	4:06	6:04
24	8:11	10:14	12:04	14:06	16:04	18:07	20:05	22:07	0:09	2:08	4:10	6:08
25	8:15	10:18	12:08	14:10	16:08	18:11	20:09	22:11	0:13	2:12	4:14	6:12
26	8:19	10:21	12:12	14:14	16:12	18:15	20:13	22:15	0:17	2:16	4:18	6:16
27	8:23	10:25	12:16	14:18	16:16	18:19	20:17	22:19	0:21	2:20	4:22	6:20
28	8:27	10:29	12:20	14:22	16:20	18:22	20:21	22:23	0:25	2:23	4:26	6:24
29	8:31		12:24	14:26	16:24	18:26	20:25	22:27	0:29	2:27	4:30	6:28
30	8:35		12:28	14:30	16:28	18:30	20:29	22:31	0:33	2:31	4:34	6:32
31	8:39		12:32		16:32		20:33	22:35		2:35		6:36

1996	Jan	Feb	Mar	Apr	May	Jun	Jul	Aug	Sep	Oct	Nov	Dec
1	6:40	8:42	10:36	12:39	14:37	16:39	18:37	20:40	22:42	0:40	2:42	4:41
2	6:44	8:46	10:40	12:42	14:41	16:43	18:41	20:43	22:46	0:44	2:46	4:44
3	6:48	8:50	10:44	12:46	14:45	16:47	18:45	20:47	22:50	0:48	2:50	4:48
4	6:52	8:54	10:48	12:50	14:49	16:51	18:49	20:51	22:54	0:52	2:54	4:52
5	6:56	8:58	10:52	12:54	14:53	16:55	18:53	20:55	22:58	0:56	2:58	4:56
6	6:59	9:02	10:56	12:58	14:57	16:59	18:57	20:59	23:01	1:00	3:02	5:00
7	7:03	9:06	11:00	13:02	15:00	17:03	19:01	21:03	23:05	1:04	3:06	5:04
8	7:07	9:10	11:04	13:06	15:04	17:07	19:05	21:07	23:09	1:08	3:10	5:08
9	7:11	9:14	11:08	13:10	15:08	17:11	19:09	21:11	23:13	1:12	3:14	5:12
10	7:15	9:17	11:12	13:14	15:12	17:15	19:13	21:15	23:17	1:15	3:18	5:16
11	7:19	9:21	11:16	13:18	15:16	17:18	19:17	21:19	23:21	1:19	3:22	5:20
12	7:23	9:25	11:20	13:22	15:20	17:22	19:21	21:23	23:25	1:23	3:26	5:24
13	7:27	9:29	11:24	13:26	15:24	17:26	19:25	21:27	23:29	1:27	3:30	5:28
14	7:31	9:33	11:28	13:30	15:28	17:30	19:29	21:31	23:33	1:31	3:33	5:32
15	7:35	9:37	11:31	13:34	15:32	17:34	19:32	21:35	23:37	1:35	3:37	5:36
16	7:39	9:41	11:35	13:38	15:36	17:38	19:36	21:39	23:41	1:39	3:41	5:40
17	7:43	9:45	11:39	13:42	15:40	17:42	19:40	21:43	23:45	1:43	3:45	5:44
18	7:47	9:49	11:43	13:46	15:44	17:46	19:44	21:47	23:49	1:47	3:49	5:48
19	7:51	9:53	11:47	13:49	15:48	17:50	19:48	21:50	23:53	1:51	3:53	5:51
20	7:55	9:57	11:51	13:53	15:52	17:54	19:52	21:54	23:57	1:55	3:57	5:55
21	7:59	10:01	11:55	13:57	15:56	17:58	19:56	21:58	0:01	1:59	4:01	5:59
22	8:03	10:05	11:59	14:01	16:00	18:02	20:00	22:02	0:05	2:03	4:05	6:03
23	8:06	10:09	12:03	14:05	16:04	18:06	20:04	22:06	0:08	2:07	4:09	6:07
24	8:10	10:13	12:07	14:09	16:07	18:10	20:08	22:10	0:12	2:11	4:13	6:11
25	8:14	10:17	12:11	14:13	16:11	18:14	20:12	22:14	0:16	2:15	4:17	6:15
26	8:18	10:21	12:15	14:17	16:15	18:18	20:16	22:18	0:20	2:19	4:21	6:19
27	8:22	10:24	12:19	14:21	16:19	18:22	20:20	22:22	0:24	2:23	4:25	6:23
28	8:26	10:28	12:23	14:25	16:23	18:25	20:24	22:26	0:28	2:26	4:29	6:27
29	8:30	10:32	12:27	14:29	16:27	18:29	20:28	22:30	0:32	2:30	4:33	6:31
30	8:34		12:31	14:33	16:31	18:33	20:32	22:34	0:36	2:34	4:37	6:35
31	8:38		12:35		16:35		20:36	22:38		2:38		6:39

1997	Jan	Feb	Mar	Apr	May	Jun	Jul	Aug	Sep	Oct	Nov	Dec
1	6:43	8:45	10:35	12:38	14:36	16:38	18:36	20:39	22:41	0:39	2:41	4:40
2	6:47	8:49	10:39	12:42	14:40	16:42	18:40	20:43	22:45	0:43	2:45	4:44
3	6:51	8:53	10:43	12:45	14:44	16:46	18:44	20:46	22:49	0:47	2:49	4:47
4	6:55	8:57	10:47	12:49	14:48	16:50	18:48	20:50	22:53	0:51	2:53	4:51
5	6:59	9:01	10:51	12:53	14:52	16:54	18:52	20:54	22:57	0:55	2:57	4:55
6	7:02	9:05	10:55	12:57	14:56	16:58	18:56	20:58	23:00	0:59	3:01	4:59
7	7:06	9:09	10:59	13:01	15:00	17:02	19:00	21:02	23:04	1:03	3:05	5:03
8	7:10	9:13	11:03	13:05	15:03	17:06	19:04	21:06	23:08	1:07	3:09	5:07
9	7:14	9:16	11:07	13:09	15:07	17:10	19:08	21:10	23:12	1:11	3:13	5:11
10	7:18	9:20	11:11	13:13	15:11	17:14	19:12	21:14	23:16	1:15	3:17	5:15
11	7:22	9:24	11:15	13:17	15:15	17:17	19:16	21:18	23:20	1:18	3:21	5:19
12	7:26	9:28	11:19	13:21	15:19	17:21	19:20	21:22	23:24	1:22	3:25	5:23
13	7:30	9:32	11:23	13:25	15:23	17:25	19:24	21:26	23:28	1:26	3:29	5:27
14	7:34	9:36	11:27	13:29	15:27	17:29	19:28	21:30	23:32	1:30	3:33	5:31
15	7:38	9:40	11:31	13:33	15:31	17:33	19:32	21:34	23:36	1:34	3:36	5:35
16	7:42	9:44	11:34	13:37	15:35	17:37	19:35	21:38	23:40	1:38	3:40	5:39
17	7:46	9:48	11:38	13:41	15:39	17:41	19:39	21:42	23:44	1:42	3:44	5:43
18	7:50	9:52	11:42	13:45	15:43	17:45	19:43	21:46	23:48	1:46	3:48	5:47
19	7:54	9:56	11:46	13:49	15:47	17:49	19:47	21:50	23:52	1:50	3:52	5:51
20	7:58	10:00	11:50	13:52	15:51	17:53	19:51	21:53	23:56	1:54	3:56	5:54
21	8:02	10:04	11:54	13:56	15:55	17:57	19:55	21:57	0:00	1:58	4:00	5:58
22	8:06	10:08	11:58	14:00	15:59	18:01	19:59	22:01	0:04	2:02	4:04	6:02
23	8:09	10:12	12:02	14:04	16:03	18:05	20:03	22:05	0:08	2:06	4:08	6:06
24	8:13	10:16	12:06	14:08	16:07	18:09	20:07	22:09	0:11	2:10	4:12	6:10
25	8:17	10:20	12:10	14:12	16:10	18:13	20:11	22:13	0:15	2:14	4:16	6:14
26	8:21	10:24	12:14	14:16	16:14	18:17	20:15	22:17	0:19	2:18	4:20	6:18
27	8:25	10:27	12:18	14:20	16:18	18:21	20:19	22:21	0:23	2:22	4:24	6:22
28	8:29	10:31	12:22	14:24	16:22	18:25	20:23	22:25	0:27	2:26	4:28	6:26
29	8:33		12:26	14:28	16:26	18:28	20:27	22:29	0:31	2:29	4:32	6:30
30	8:37		12:30	14:32	16:30	18:32	20:31	22:33	0:35	2:33	4:36	6:34
31	8:41		12:34		16:34		20:35	22:37		2:37		6:38

1998	Jan	Feb	Mar	Apr	May	Jun	Jul	Aug	Sep	Oct	Nov	Dec
1	6:42	8:44	10:34	12:37	14:35	16:37	18:35	20:38	22:40	0:38	2:40	4:39
2	6:46	8:48	10:38	12:41	14:39	16:41	18:39	20:42	22:44	0:42	2:44	4:43
3	6:50	8:52	10:42	12:44	14:43	16:45	18:43	20:45	22:48	0:46	2:48	4:46
4	6:54	8:56	10:46	12:48	14:47	16:49	18:47	20:49	22:52	0:50	2:52	4:50
5	6:58	9:00	10:50	12:52	14:51	16:53	18:51	20:53	22:56	0:54	2:56	4:54
6	7:01	9:04	10:54	12:56	14:55	16:57	18:55	20:57	23:00	0:58	3:00	4:58
7	7:05	9:08	10:58	13:00	14:59	17:01	18:59	21:01	23:03	1:02	3:04	5:02
8	7:09	9:12	11:02	13:04	15:02	17:05	19:03	21:05	23:07	1:06	3:08	5:06
9	7:13	9:16	11:06	13:08	15:06	17:09	19:07	21:09	23:11	1:10	3:12	5:10
10	7:17	9:19	11:10	13:12	15:10	17:13	19:11	21:13	23:15	1:14	3:16	5:14
11	7:21	9:23	11:14	13:16	15:14	17:17	19:15	21:17	23:19	1:18	3:20	5:18
12	7:25	9:27	11:18	13:20	15:18	17:20	19:19	21:21	23:23	1:21	3:24	5:22
13	7:29	9:31	11:22	13:24	15:22	17:24	19:23	21:25	23:27	1:25	3:28	5:26
14	7:33	9:35	11:26	13:28	15:26	17:28	19:27	21:29	23:31	1:29	3:32	5:30
15	7:37	9:39	11:30	13:32	15:30	17:32	19:31	21:33	23:35	1:33	3:36	5:34
16	7:41	9:43	11:34	13:36	15:34	17:36	19:35	21:37	23:39	1:37	3:39	5:38
17	7:45	9:47	11:37	13:40	15:38	17:40	19:38	21:41	23:43	1:41	3:43	5:42
18	7:49	9:51	11:41	13:44	15:42	17:44	19:42	21:45	23:47	1:45	3:47	5:46
19	7:53	9:55	11:45	13:48	15:46	17:48	19:46	21:49	23:51	1:49	3:51	5:50
20	7:57	9:59	11:49	13:52	15:50	17:52	19:50	21:53	23:55	1:53	3:55	5:54
21	8:01	10:03	11:53	13:55	15:54	17:56	19:54	21:56	23:59	1:57	3:59	5:57
22	8:05	10:07	11:57	13:59	15:58	18:00	19:58	22:00	0:03	2:01	4:03	6:01
23	8:09	10:11	12:01	14:03	16:02	18:04	20:02	22:04	0:07	2:05	4:07	6:05
24	8:12	10:15	12:05	14:07	16:06	18:08	20:06	22:08	0:11	2:09	4:11	6:09
25	8:16	10:19	12:09	14:11	16:10	18:12	20:10	22:12	0:14	2:13	4:15	6:13
26	8:20	10:23	12:13	14:15	16:13	18:16	20:14	22:16	0:18	2:17	4:19	6:17
27	8:24	10:27	12:17	14:19	16:17	18:20	20:18	22:20	0:22	2:21	4:23	6:21
28	8:28	10:30	12:21	14:23	16:21	18:24	20:22	22:24	0:26	2:25	4:27	6:25
29	8:32		12:25	14:27	16:25	18:28	20:26	22:28	0:30	2:28	4:31	6:29
30	8:36		12:29	14:31	16:29	18:31	20:30	22:32	0:34	2:32	4:35	6:33
31	8:40		12:33		16:33		20:34	22:36		2:36		6:37

1999	Jan	Feb	Mar	Apr	May	Jun	Jul	Aug	Sep	Oct	Nov	Dec
1	6:41	8:43	10:33	12:36	14:34	16:36	18:34	20:37	22:39	0:37	2:39	4:38
2	6:45	8:47	10:37	12:40	14:38	16:40	18:38	20:41	22:43	0:41	2:43	4:42
3	6:49	8:51	10:41	12:44	14:42	16:44	18:42	20:45	22:47	0:45	2:47	4:46
4	6:53	8:55	10:45	12:47	14:46	16:48	18:46	20:48	22:51	0:49	2:51	4:49
5	6:57	8:59	10:49	12:51	14:50	16:52	18:50	20:52	22:55	0:53	2:55	4:53
6	7:01	9:03	10:53	12:55	14:54	16:56	18:54	20:56	22:59	0:57	2:59	4:57
7	7:04	9:07	10:57	12:59	14:58	17:00	18:58	21:00	23:03	1:01	3:03	5:01
8	7:08	9:11	11:01	13:03	15:02	17:04	19:02	21:04	23:06	1:05	3:07	5:05
9	7:12	9:15	11:05	13:07	15:05	17:08	19:06	21:08	23:10	1:09	3:11	5:09
10	7:16	9:19	11:09	13:11	15:09	17:12	19:10	21:12	23:14	1:13	3:15	5:13
11	7:20	9:22	11:13	13:15	15:13	17:16	19:14	21:16	23:18	1:17	3:19	5:17
12	7:24	9:26	11:17	13:19	15:17	17:20	19:18	21:20	23:22	1:21	3:23	5:21
13	7:28	9:30	11:21	13:23	15:21	17:23	19:22	21:24	23:26	1:24	3:27	5:25
14	7:32	9:34	11:25	13:27	15:25	17:27	19:26	21:28	23:30	1:28	3:31	5:29
15	7:36	9:38	11:29	13:31	15:29	17:31	19:30	21:32	23:34	1:32	3:35	5:33
16	7:40	9:42	11:33	13:35	15:33	17:35	19:34	21:36	23:38	1:36	3:39	5:37
17	7:44	9:46	11:37	13:39	15:37	17:39	19:38	21:40	23:42	1:40	3:42	5:41
18	7:48	9:50	11:40	13:43	15:41	17:43	19:41	21:44	23:46	1:44	3:46	5:45
19	7:52	9:54	11:44	13:47	15:45	17:47	19:45	21:48	23:50	1:48	3:50	5:49
20	7:56	9:58	11:48	13:51	15:49	17:51	19:49	21:52	23:54	1:52	3:54	5:53
21	8:00	10:02	11:52	13:55	15:53	17:55	19:53	21:56	23:58	1:56	3:58	5:57
22	8:04	10:06	11:56	13:58	15:57	17:59	19:57	21:59	0:02	2:00	4:02	6:00
23	8:08	10:10	12:00	14:02	16:01	18:03	20:01	22:03	0:06	2:04	4:06	6:04
24	8:12	10:14	12:04	14:06	16:05	18:07	20:05	22:07	0:10	2:08	4:10	6:08
25	8:15	10:18	12:08	14:10	16:09	18:11	20:09	22:11	0:13	2:12	4:14	6:12
26	8:19	10:22	12:12	14:14	16:13	18:15	20:13	22:15	0:17	2:16	4:18	6:16
27	8:23	10:26	12:16	14:18	16:16	18:19	20:17	22:19	0:21	2:20	4:22	6:20
28	8:27	10:29	12:20	14:22	16:20	18:23	20:21	22:23	0:25	2:24	4:26	6:24
29	8:31		12:24	14:26	16:24	18:27	20:25	22:27	0:29	2:28	4:30	6:28
30	8:35		12:28	14:30	16:28	18:30	20:29	22:31	0:33	2:31	4:34	6:32
31	8:39		12:32		16:32		20:33	22:35		2:35		6:36

2000	Jan	Feb	Mar	Apr	May	Jun	Jul	Aug	Sep	Oct	Nov	Dec
1	6:40	8:42	10:36	12:39	14:37	16:39	18:37	20:40	22:42	0:40	2:42	4:41
2	6:44	8:46	10:40	12:43	14:41	16:43	18:41	20:44	22:46	0:44	2:46	4:45
3	6:48	8:50	10:44	12:47	14:45	16:47	18:45	20:48	22:50	0:48	2:50	4:49
4	6:52	8:54	10:48	12:50	14:49	16:51	18:49	20:51	22:54	0:52	2:54	4:52
5	6:56	8:58	10:52	12:54	14:53	16:55	18:53	20:55	22:58	0:56	2:58	4:56
6	7:00	9:02	10:56	12:58	14:57	16:59	18:57	20:59	23:02	1:00	3:02	5:00
7	7:04	9:06	11:00	13:02	15:01	17:03	19:01	21:03	23:06	1:04	3:06	5:04
8	7:07	9:10	11:04	13:06	15:05	17:07	19:05	21:07	23:09	1:08	3:10	5:08
9	7:11	9:14	11:08	13:10	15:08	17:11	19:09	21:11	23:13	1:12	3:14	5:12
10	7:15	9:18	11:12	13:14	15:12	17:15	19:13	21:15	23:17	1:16	3:18	5:16
11	7:19	9:22	11:16	13:18	15:16	17:19	19:17	21:19	23:21	1:20	3:22	5:20
12	7:23	9:25	11:20	13:22	15:20	17:23	19:21	21:23	23:25	1:24	3:26	5:24
13	7:27	9:29	11:24	13:26	15:24	17:26	19:25	21:27	23:29	1:27	3:30	5:28
14	7:31	9:33	11:28	13:30	15:28	17:30	19:29	21:31	23:33	1:31	3:34	5:32
15	7:35	9:37	11:32	13:34	15:32	17:34	19:33	21:35	23:37	1:35	3:38	5:36
16	7:39	9:41	11:36	13:38	15:36	17:38	19:37	21:39	23:41	1:39	3:41	5:40
17	7:43	9:45	11:40	13:42	15:40	17:42	19:41	21:43	23:45	1:43	3:45	5:44
18	7:47	9:49	11:43	13:46	15:44	17:46	19:44	21:47	23:49	1:47	3:49	5:48
19	7:51	9:53	11:47	13:50	15:48	17:50	19:48	21:51	23:53	1:51	3:53	5:52
20	7:55	9:57	11:51	13:54	15:52	17:54	19:52	21:55	23:57	1:55	3:57	5:56
21	7:59	10:01	11:55	13:57	15:56	17:58	19:56	21:58	0:01	1:59	4:01	5:59
22	8:03	10:05	11:59	14:01	16:00	18:02	20:00	22:02	0:05	2:03	4:05	6:03
23	8:07	10:09	12:03	14:05	16:04	18:06	20:04	22:06	0:09	2:07	4:09	6:07
24	8:11	10:13	12:07	14:09	16:08	18:10	20:08	22:10	0:13	2:11	4:13	6:11
25	8:14	10:17	12:11	14:13	16:12	18:14	20:12	22:14	0:16	2:15	4:17	6:15
26	8:18	10:21	12:15	14:17	16:15	18:18	20:16	22:18	0:20	2:19	4:21	6:19
27	8:22	10:25	12:19	14:21	16:19	18:22	20:20	22:22	0:24	2:23	4:25	6:23
28	8:26	10:29	12:23	14:25	16:23	18:26	20:24	22:26	0:28	2:27	4:29	6:27
29	8:30	10:32	12:27	14:29	16:27	18:30	20:28	22:30	0:32	2:31	4:33	6:31
30	8:34		12:31	14:33	16:31	18:33	20:32	22:34	0:36	2:34	4:37	6:35
31	8:38		12:35		16:35		20:36	22:38		2:38		6:39

United States Ascendant Tables

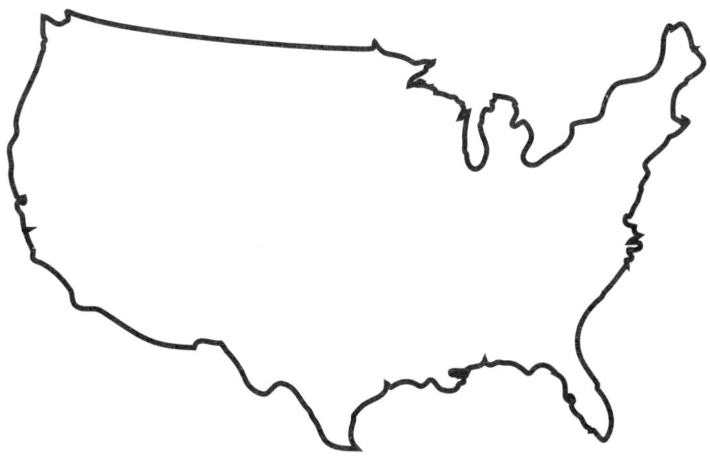

♈ = Aries ♉ = Taurus ♊ = Gemini ♋ = Cancer ♌ = Leo ♍ = Virgo

IN – LA

1 Turn to the page containing the state in which you were born.

2 Select the state in which you were born.

3 Locate the city in which (or near which) you were born.
Find the time that is just before your **Star Time**. Note the sign of the zodiac listed at the top of that column on your worksheet.

4 Repeats steps 1, 2 and 3 for your partner's birthday.

City										♏	♐	♑	♒	♓
India														
Koko										9:16	11:49	14:11	16:06	17:33
Lafa										9:19	11:52	14:14	16:09	17:36
Munc										9:13	11:45	14:08	16:03	17:29
New										9:12	11:42	14:03	15:59	17:29
Sout										9:18	11:53	14:16	16:10	17:35
Terre Haute										9:20	11:51	14:13	16:09	17:37
Versailles	EST	0.00	18:41	19:55	21:23	23:19	1:40	4:11	6:41	9:11	11:42	14:03	15:59	17:27
Be	CST	1.00	18:19	19:30	20:57	22:51	1:14	3:47	6:19	8:51	11:24	13:46	15:41	17:07
Carroll	CST	1.00	18:19	19:29	20:53	22:47	1:11	3:46	6:19	8:53	11:28	13:52	15:46	17:10
Ceda										8:40	11:15	13:39	15:33	16:57
Coun										8:56	11:30	13:53	15:47	17:13
Dave										8:35	11:09	13:33	15:27	16:52
Deco										8:43	11:19	13:44	15:37	17:00
Des										8:48	11:22	13:45	15:39	17:04
Dubu										8:37	11:13	13:36	15:30	16:54
Ft. D										8:51	11:27	13:50	15:44	17:08
Maso										8:48	11:25	13:49	15:42	17:05
Ottumwa		1.00	18:09	19:20	20:46	22:41	1:04	3:37	6:09	8:42	11:15	13:38	15:33	16:58
Sioux City		1.00	18:26	19:34	20:58	22:52	1:16	3:51	6:26	9:00	11:35	13:59	15:53	17:17
Spencer		1.00	18:21	19:28	20:51	22:45	1:09	3:45	6:21	8:56	11:32	13:57	15:50	17:13
Waterloo	CST	1.00	18:09	19:18	20:42	22:36	1:00	3:35	6:09	8:44	11:19	13:43	15:37	17:01
Kansas														
Colby	CST	1.00	18:44	19:57	21:25	23:21	1:43	4:14	6:44	9:14	11:46	14:08	16:03	17:31
Dodge City	CST	1.00	18:40	19:56	21:25	23:22	1:43	4:12	6:40	9:08	11:37	13:59	15:55	17:25
Emporia	CST	1.00	18:25	19:39	21:08	23:04	1:26	3:56	6:25	8:53	11:24	13:45	15:41	17:10
Garden City	CST	1.00	18:43	19:59	21:28	23:24	1:46	4:15	6:43	9:12	11:41	14:03	15:59	17:28
Girard	CST	1.00	18:19	19:35	21:05	23:02	1:23	3:52	6:19	8:47	11:16	13:37	15:34	17:04
Hays	**CST**	**1.00**	**18:37**	**19:51**	**21:20**	**23:15**	**1:37**	**4:08**	**6:37**	**9:07**	**11:37**	**13:59**	**15:55**	**17:23**
Independence														
Kansas City	CST	1.00	18:19	19:32	21:00	22:56	1:18	3:49	6:19	8:48	11:19	13:41	15:37	17:05
Liberal	CST	1.00	18:44	20:00	21:31	23:27	1:48	4:17	6:44	9:11	11:39	14:00	15:57	17:27
Manhattan	CST	1.00	18:26	19:40	21:08	23:03	1:25	3:57	6:26	8:56	11:27	13:49	15:45	17:13
Philli										9:08	11:40	14:02	15:57	17:25
Salin										9:00	11:30	13:52	15:48	17:16
Tope										8:52	11:23	13:45	15:41	17:09
Tribu										8:16	10:46	13:08	15:04	16:32
Wich										8:57	11:27	13:48	15:44	17:14
Kent														
Bowl										8:13	10:41	13:02	14:59	16:29
Catlett										8:59	11:29	13:51	15:47	17:16
Elizabethtown	EST	0.00	18:43	19:59	21:29	23:25	1:46	4:16	6:43	9:11	11:41	14:02	15:58	17:28
Hazard	EST	0.00	18:33	19:49	21:19	23:16	1:37	4:06	6:33	9:00	11:29	13:50	15:46	17:17
Henderson	CST	1.00	17:50	19:06	20:35	22:32	0:53	3:22	5:50	8:18	10:48	13:09	15:05	16:35
Independence	EST	0.00	18:38	19:52	21:20	23:16	1:38	4:09	6:38	9:08	11:39	14:00	15:56	17:24
Lexington	EST	0.00	18:38	19:53	21:22	23:19	1:40	4:10	6:38	9:06	11:36	13:57	15:54	17:23
Louisville	EST	0.00	18:43	19:58	21:27	23:23	1:45	4:15	6:43	9:12	11:42	14:03	15:59	17:28
Madis										8:17	10:46	13:07	15:04	16:34
More										9:02	11:32	13:54	15:50	17:19
Pikev										8:58	11:27	13:48	15:44	17:14
Pinev										9:01	11:30	13:50	15:47	17:18
Richm										9:05	11:35	13:56	15:52	17:22
Some										9:05	11:34	13:55	15:52	17:22
Louis														
Alexan										8:30	10:53	13:11	15:10	16:47
Baton Rouge	CST	1.00	18:05	19:29	21:06	23:06	1:24	3:46	6:05	8:24	10:46	13:04	15:03	16:41
Franklinton	CST	1.00	18:01	19:24	21:01	23:01	1:19	3:41	6:01	8:20	10:43	13:01	15:00	16:37
Houma	CST	1.00	18:03	19:28	21:06	23:06	1:23	3:45	6:03	8:21	10:42	13:00	15:00	16:38
Jonesboro	CST	1.00	18:11	19:33	21:09	23:07	1:26	3:50	6:11	8:32	10:56	13:14	15:13	16:49
Lafayette	CST	1.00	18:08	19:33	21:10	23:10	1:27	3:49	6:08	8:27	10:49	13:07	15:06	16:44
Lake Charles	CST	1.00	18:13	19:37	21:15	23:14	1:32	3:54	6:13	8:32	10:54	13:11	15:11	16:48
Many	CST	1.00	18:14	19:37	21:13	23:12	1:31	3:54	6:14	8:34	10:57	13:16	15:15	16:51
Monroe	CST	1.00	18:08	19:30	21:06	23:04	1:23	3:47	6:08	8:30	10:54	13:13	15:11	16:47
Natchez	CST	1.00	18:12	19:35	21:11	23:10	1:29	3:52	6:12	8:33	10:56	13:14	15:13	16:49
New Orleans	CST	1.00	18:00	19:25	21:03	23:02	1:20	3:42	6:00	8:19	10:40	12:58	14:58	16:36
Shreveport	CST	1.00	18:15	19:37	21:12	23:11	1:30	3:54	6:15	8:36	11:00	13:19	15:18	16:53

United States Ascendant Tables

♎ = Libra ♏ = Scorpio ♐ = Sagittarius ♑ = Capricorn ♒ = Aquarius ♓ = Pisces

City	Zone	—>EST	♈	♉	♊	♋	♌	♍	♎	♏	♐	♑	♒	♓
Alabama														
Birmingham	CST	1.00	17:47	19:08	20:42	22:40	1:00	3:25	5:47	8:10	10:35	12:54	14:52	16:26
Gadsden	CST	1.00	17:44	19:04	20:38	22:36	0:55	3:21	5:44	8:07	10:33	12:52	14:50	16:24
Greensboro	CST	1.00	17:50	19:12	20:47	22:46	1:05	3:29	5:50	8:12	10:36	12:55	14:54	16:29
Huntsville	CST	1.00	17:46	19:06	20:39	22:36	0:56	3:22	5:46	8:10	10:37	12:56	14:54	16:27
Mobile	CST	1.00	17:52	19:16	20:53	22:53	1:11	3:33	5:52	8:12	10:34	12:52	14:51	16:28
Monroeville	CST	1.00	17:49	19:12	20:48	22:48	1:06	3:29	5:49	8:10	10:33	12:51	14:50	16:26
Montgomery	CST	1.00	17:45	19:07	20:43	22:41	1:00	3:24	5:45	8:06	10:30	12:49	14:48	16:23
Ozark	CST	1.00	17:43	19:06	20:42	22:41	0:59	3:22	5:43	8:03	10:26	12:44	14:43	16:19
Phenix City	EST	0.00	18:40	20:02	21:37	23:36	1:55	4:19	6:40	9:01	11:25	13:44	15:43	17:18
Russellville	CST	1.00	17:51	19:10	20:44	22:42	1:01	3:27	5:51	8:15	10:41	13:00	14:58	16:31
Tuscaloosa	CST	1.00	17:50	19:11	20:46	22:44	1:03	3:28	5:50	8:12	10:37	12:56	14:55	16:29
Alaska														
Anchorage	YST	4.00	19:00	19:24	20:03	21:31	0:21	3:41	7:00	10:18	13:39	16:28	17:56	18:35
Bethel	YST	4.00	19:47	20:13	20:54	22:23	1:11	4:30	7:47	11:04	14:23	17:11	18:40	19:21
Fairbanks	YST	4.00	18:51	19:00	19:17	20:21	23:34	3:17	6:51	10:25	14:08	17:20	18:25	18:42
Galena	YST	4.00	19:28	19:37	19:55	21:01	0:12	3:54	7:28	11:01	14:43	17:55	19:01	19:18
Juneau	YST	4.00	17:58	18:33	19:23	20:59	23:41	2:49	5:58	9:06	12:15	14:56	16:32	17:23
King Cove	YST	4.00	19:49	20:33	21:34	23:16	1:51	4:50	7:49	10:48	13:47	16:23	18:05	19:05
Kodiak	YST	4.00	19:10	19:46	20:38	22:16	0:56	4:03	7:10	10:16	13:23	16:04	17:41	18:33
Nome	YST	4.00	20:02	20:12	20:32	21:40	0:49	4:29	8:02	11:34	15:14	18:23	19:32	19:51
Arizona														
Bisbee	MST	2.00	18:20	19:43	21:19	23:18	1:37	4:00	6:20	8:40	11:03	13:21	15:20	16:57
Casa Grande	MST	2.00	18:27	19:48	21:23	23:22	1:41	4:05	6:27	8:49	11:13	13:32	15:31	17:06
Chinle	MST	2.00	18:18	19:36	21:07	23:04	1:25	3:52	6:18	8:44	11:12	13:32	15:29	17:01
Clifton	MST	2.00	18:17	19:38	21:13	23:12	1:31	3:55	6:17	8:39	11:04	13:23	15:21	16:56
Flagstaff	MST	2.00	18:27	19:45	21:18	23:15	1:35	4:02	6:27	8:51	11:18	13:38	15:35	17:08
Fredonia	MST	2.00	18:30	19:47	21:17	23:14	1:35	4:03	6:30	8:57	11:26	13:46	15:43	17:14
Holbrook	MST	2.00	18:21	19:40	21:13	23:10	1:30	3:56	6:21	8:45	11:11	13:31	15:29	17:02
Kingman	MST	2.00	18:36	19:55	21:27	23:25	1:45	4:12	6:36	9:01	11:27	13:47	15:45	17:17
Lake Havasu City	MST	2.00	18:37	19:57	21:30	23:28	1:48	4:14	6:37	9:01	11:27	13:47	15:44	17:18
Phoenix	MST	2.00	18:28	19:49	21:23	23:22	1:41	4:06	6:28	8:51	11:16	13:35	15:33	17:07
Tucson	MST	2.00	18:24	19:46	21:22	23:20	1:39	4:03	6:24	8:45	11:09	13:27	15:26	17:02
Yuma	MST	2.00	18:38	20:00	21:35	23:34	1:53	4:17	6:38	9:00	11:24	13:43	15:42	17:17
Arkansas														
Batesville	CST	1.00	18:07	19:25	20:56	22:54	1:14	3:41	6:07	8:32	10:59	13:19	15:17	16:49
DeWitt	CST	1.00	18:05	19:25	20:59	22:56	1:16	3:42	6:05	8:29	10:55	13:14	15:12	16:46
Fayetteville	CST	1.00	18:17	19:34	21:06	23:03	1:23	3:51	6:17	8:42	11:10	13:30	15:27	16:59
Forrest City	CST	1.00	18:03	19:22	20:55	22:52	1:12	3:39	6:03	8:27	10:54	13:14	15:11	16:44
Ft. Smith	CST	1.00	18:18	19:36	21:08	23:06	1:26	3:53	6:18	8:42	11:09	13:29	15:27	16:59
Harrison	CST	1.00	18:12	19:30	21:01	22:58	1:19	3:47	6:12	8:38	11:06	13:27	15:24	16:55
Hope	CST	1.00	18:14	19:35	21:09	23:07	1:26	3:52	6:14	8:37	11:02	13:22	15:20	16:54
Hot Springs	CST	1.00	18:12	19:32	21:05	23:03	1:22	3:48	6:12	8:36	11:02	13:22	15:19	16:53
Jonesboro	CST	1.00	18:03	19:21	20:53	22:50	1:10	3:37	6:03	8:28	10:56	13:16	15:13	16:45
Little Rock	CST	1.00	18:09	19:28	21:01	22:59	1:19	3:45	6:09	8:33	10:59	13:19	15:17	16:50
Russellville	CST	1.00	18:13	19:31	21:04	23:01	1:21	3:48	6:13	8:37	11:04	13:24	15:21	16:54
Warren	CST	1.00	18:08	19:29	21:03	23:01	1:20	3:46	6:08	8:31	10:56	13:15	15:14	16:48
California														
Alturas	PST	3.00	18:02	19:12	20:38	22:32	0:55	3:29	6:02	8:35	11:09	13:32	15:27	16:52
Bakersfield	PST	3.00	17:56	19:15	20:47	22:44	1:04	3:31	5:56	8:21	10:48	13:08	15:05	16:38
Barstow	PST	3.00	17:48	19:07	20:40	22:38	0:57	3:24	5:48	8:12	10:39	12:59	14:56	16:29
Bridgeport	PST	3.00	17:57	19:12	20:41	22:37	0:58	3:28	5:57	8:25	10:55	13:17	15:13	16:42
Crescent City	PST	3.00	18:17	19:27	20:52	22:46	1:09	3:43	6:17	8:50	11:25	13:48	15:42	17:07
El Centro	PST	3.00	17:42	19:04	20:39	22:37	0:56	3:21	5:42	8:04	10:28	12:47	14:46	16:21
Essex	PST	3.00	17:41	19:00	20:33	22:31	0:51	3:17	5:41	8:05	10:31	12:51	14:49	16:22
Eureka	PST	3.00	18:17	19:28	20:54	22:49	1:12	3:45	6:17	8:49	11:22	13:45	15:39	17:05
Fresno	PST	3.00	17:59	19:16	20:47	22:43	1:04	3:33	5:59	8:26	10:54	13:15	15:11	16:42
Independence	PST	3.00	17:53	19:09	20:40	22:37	0:58	3:26	5:53	8:19	10:48	13:09	15:05	16:36
Irvine	PST	3.00	17:51	19:12	20:46	22:44	1:03	3:29	5:51	8:14	10:39	12:58	14:57	16:31
Lodi	PST	3.00	18:05	19:20	20:49	22:45	1:07	3:37	6:05	8:33	11:03	13:25	15:21	16:50
Long Beach	PST	3.00	17:53	19:13	20:47	22:45	1:05	3:30	5:53	8:16	10:41	13:00	14:58	16:32
Los Angeles	PST	3.00	17:53	19:13	20:47	22:45	1:04	3:30	5:53	8:16	10:42	13:01	14:59	16:33
Modesto	PST	3.00	18:04	19:20	20:50	22:46	1:07	3:36	6:04	8:32	11:01	13:22	15:18	16:48
Monterey	PST	3.00	18:08	19:25	20:56	22:52	1:13	3:41	6:08	8:34	11:02	13:23	15:20	16:51
Nevada City	PST	3.00	18:04	19:17	20:45	22:41	1:03	3:34	6:04	8:34	11:05	13:27	15:23	16:51
Oakland	PST	3.00	18:09	19:24	20:54	22:50	1:12	3:41	6:09	8:37	11:07	13:28	15:24	16:54
Oceanside	PST	3.00	17:50	19:11	20:45	22:44	1:03	3:27	5:50	8:12	10:36	12:55	14:54	16:28

Your Starway to Love

♈ = Aries ♉ = Taurus ♊ = Gemini ♋ = Cancer ♌ = Leo ♍ = Virgo

City	Zone	->EST	♈	♉	♊	♋	♌	♍	♎	♏	♐	♑	♒	♓
California, continued														
Palm Springs	PST	3.00	17:46	19:07	20:40	22:39	0:58	3:23	5:46	8:09	10:34	12:54	14:52	16:26
Redding	PST	3.00	18:10	19:21	20:47	22:42	1:05	3:38	6:10	8:41	11:14	13:37	15:32	16:58
Ridgecrest	PST	3.00	17:51	19:09	20:41	22:38	0:58	3:26	5:51	8:16	10:43	13:03	15:00	16:32
Riverside	PST	3.00	17:50	19:10	20:44	22:42	1:01	3:27	5:50	8:13	10:38	12:58	14:56	16:29
Sacramento	PST	3.00	18:06	19:20	20:49	22:45	1:07	3:37	6:06	8:35	11:05	13:27	15:23	16:52
Salinas	PST	3.00	18:07	19:23	20:54	22:51	1:12	3:40	6:07	8:33	11:01	13:22	15:19	16:50
San Bernardino	PST	3.00	17:49	19:09	20:43	22:41	1:00	3:26	5:49	8:12	10:38	12:58	14:56	16:29
San Diego	PST	3.00	17:49	19:10	20:45	22:44	1:03	3:27	5:49	8:10	10:34	12:53	14:52	16:27
San Francisco	PST	3.00	18:10	19:25	20:55	22:51	1:12	3:42	6:10	8:38	11:07	13:28	15:25	16:54
San Jose	PST	3.00	18:08	19:24	20:54	22:50	1:11	3:40	6:08	8:35	11:04	13:25	15:21	16:52
San Luis Obispo	PST	3.00	18:03	19:21	20:54	22:51	1:11	3:38	6:03	8:27	10:54	13:14	15:12	16:44
Santa Barbara	PST	3.00	17:59	19:18	20:52	22:50	1:09	3:35	5:59	8:22	10:48	13:08	15:06	16:39
Santa Rosa	PST	3.00	18:11	19:25	20:54	22:50	1:12	3:42	6:11	8:40	11:10	13:31	15:27	16:56
Susanville	PST	3.00	18:03	19:14	20:41	22:36	0:58	3:31	6:03	8:34	11:07	13:29	15:24	16:51
Yreka	PST	3.00	18:11	19:20	20:45	22:39	1:03	3:37	6:11	8:44	11:18	13:42	15:36	17:01
Colorado														
Alamosa	MST	2.00	18:03	19:19	20:49	22:46	1:07	3:36	6:03	8:31	11:00	13:21	15:18	16:48
Aspen	MST	2.00	18:07	19:21	20:49	22:44	1:06	3:38	6:07	8:37	11:08	13:30	15:26	16:54
Boulder	MST	2.00	18:01	19:13	20:41	22:36	0:58	3:30	6:01	8:32	11:04	13:26	15:22	16:49
Burlington	MST	2.00	17:49	19:02	20:30	22:26	0:48	3:19	5:49	8:19	10:50	13:12	15:08	16:36
Colorado Springs	MST	2.00	17:59	19:13	20:42	22:38	0:59	3:30	5:59	8:29	10:59	13:21	15:17	16:45
Denver	MST	2.00	18:00	19:13	20:40	22:35	0:58	3:29	6:00	8:30	11:02	13:24	15:20	16:47
Dove Creek	MST	2.00	18:16	19:31	21:01	22:57	1:18	3:48	6:16	8:43	11:13	13:34	15:30	17:00
Durango	MST	2.00	18:12	19:28	20:58	22:54	1:15	3:44	6:12	8:39	11:08	13:29	15:25	16:55
Ft. Collins	MST	2.00	18:00	19:12	20:38	22:33	0:56	3:29	6:00	8:32	11:05	13:28	15:22	16:49
Ft. Morgan	MST	2.00	17:55	19:07	20:34	22:29	0:52	3:24	5:55	8:26	10:59	13:21	15:16	16:43
Grand Junction	MST	2.00	18:14	19:28	20:56	22:52	1:14	3:45	6:14	8:44	11:15	13:37	15:32	17:01
Hugo	MST	2.00	17:54	19:07	20:36	22:31	0:53	3:24	5:54	8:24	10:55	13:17	15:12	16:40
La Junta	MST	2.00	17:54	19:09	20:39	22:35	0:56	3:26	5:54	8:22	10:52	13:13	15:10	16:39
Meeker	MST	2.00	18:12	19:24	20:51	22:46	1:09	3:41	6:12	8:43	11:15	13:37	15:32	16:59
Montrose	MST	2.00	18:12	19:26	20:55	22:51	1:12	3:43	6:12	8:40	11:11	13:32	15:28	16:57
Pueblo	MST	2.00	17:58	19:13	20:42	22:38	1:00	3:30	5:58	8:27	10:57	13:18	15:14	16:44
Salida	MST	2.00	18:04	19:18	20:47	22:43	1:05	3:35	6:04	8:33	11:03	13:25	15:21	16:50
Steamboat Springs	MST	2.00	18:07	19:19	20:46	22:40	1:03	3:36	6:07	8:39	11:12	13:34	15:29	16:56
Trinidad	MST	2.00	17:58	19:14	20:45	22:41	1:02	3:31	5:58	8:25	10:54	13:15	15:11	16:42
Wray	MST	2.00	17:49	19:01	20:28	22:23	0:46	3:18	5:49	8:20	10:52	13:15	15:10	16:37
Connecticut														
Bunker Hill	EST	0.00	17:52	19:02	20:28	22:22	0:45	3:19	5:52	8:25	11:00	13:23	15:17	16:42
Hartford	EST	0.00	17:51	19:01	20:25	22:20	0:43	3:17	5:51	8:24	10:59	13:22	15:16	16:41
New Haven	EST	0.00	17:52	19:02	20:28	22:22	0:45	3:19	5:52	8:24	10:58	13:21	15:16	16:41
New London	EST	0.00	17:48	18:59	20:24	22:19	0:42	3:16	5:48	8:21	10:55	13:18	15:13	16:38
Stamford	EST	0.00	17:54	19:05	20:31	22:25	0:48	3:22	5:54	8:27	11:00	13:23	15:17	16:43
Waterbury	EST	0.00	17:52	19:02	20:28	22:22	0:45	3:19	5:52	8:25	10:59	13:23	15:17	16:42
District of Columbia														
Washington	EST	0.00	18:08	19:22	20:50	22:46	1:08	3:39	6:08	8:37	11:08	13:30	15:26	16:54
Delaware														
Dover	EST	0.00	18:02	19:16	20:44	22:39	1:01	3:32	6:02	8:32	11:03	13:25	15:20	16:48
Lewes	EST	0.00	18:01	19:15	20:43	22:39	1:01	3:31	6:01	8:30	11:00	13:22	15:18	16:46
Wilmington	EST	0.00	18:02	19:15	20:42	22:38	1:00	3:32	6:02	8:33	11:05	13:27	15:22	16:49
Florida														
Daytona Beach	EST	0.00	18:24	19:50	21:28	23:28	1:45	4:06	6:24	8:42	11:03	13:20	15:20	16:59
Ft. Pierce	EST	0.00	18:21	19:49	21:29	23:29	1:46	4:05	6:21	8:37	10:57	13:13	15:14	16:54
Gainesville	EST	0.00	18:29	19:54	21:32	23:32	1:50	4:11	6:29	8:48	11:09	13:27	15:26	17:04
Jacksonville	EST	0.00	18:27	19:51	21:28	23:28	1:46	4:08	6:27	8:46	11:07	13:25	15:25	17:02
Jasper	EST	0.00	18:32	19:56	21:33	23:33	1:51	4:13	6:32	8:51	11:13	13:31	15:31	17:08
Key West	EST	0.00	18:27	19:57	21:40	23:41	1:57	4:14	6:27	8:40	10:57	13:13	15:14	16:57
Miami	EST	0.00	18:21	19:50	21:31	23:32	1:49	4:07	6:21	8:35	10:53	13:09	15:10	16:52
Naples	EST	0.00	18:27	19:56	21:37	23:38	1:54	4:13	6:27	8:42	11:00	13:16	15:17	16:58
Orlando	EST	0.00	18:26	19:52	21:31	23:31	1:48	4:09	6:26	8:43	11:03	13:20	15:20	16:59
Pensacola	CST	1.00	17:49	19:13	20:50	22:50	1:08	3:30	5:49	8:08	10:30	12:48	14:47	16:25
St. Petersburg	EST	0.00	18:31	19:58	21:37	23:38	1:55	4:14	6:31	8:47	11:06	13:23	15:24	17:04
Sarasota	EST	0.00	18:30	19:58	21:38	23:38	1:55	4:14	6:30	8:46	11:05	13:22	15:23	17:03
Sebring	EST	0.00	18:26	19:53	21:33	23:34	1:50	4:10	6:26	8:42	11:01	13:18	15:19	16:58
Tallahassee	EST	0.00	18:37	20:01	21:39	23:38	1:56	4:18	6:37	8:56	11:18	13:36	15:36	17:13
Tampa	EST	0.00	18:30	19:57	21:36	23:37	1:54	4:13	6:30	8:46	11:06	13:23	15:24	17:03
West Palm Beach	EST	0.00	18:20	19:48	21:29	23:30	1:46	4:05	6:20	8:35	10:54	13:11	15:12	16:52

♎ = Libra ♏ = Scorpio ♐ = Sagittarius ♑ = Capricorn ♒ = Aquarius ♓ = Pisces

City	Zone	->EST	♈	♉	♊	♋	♌	♍	♎	♏	♐	♑	♒	♓
Georgia														
Americus	EST	0.00	18:37	19:59	21:35	23:34	1:52	4:16	6:37	8:58	11:21	13:40	15:39	17:15
Athens	EST	0.00	18:34	19:54	21:28	23:26	1:45	4:10	6:34	8:57	11:22	13:41	15:40	17:13
Atlanta	EST	0.00	18:38	19:58	21:32	23:30	1:49	4:15	6:38	9:00	11:26	13:45	15:43	17:17
Augusta	EST	0.00	18:28	19:49	21:23	23:21	1:40	4:05	6:28	8:50	11:15	13:35	15:33	17:07
Bainbridge	EST	0.00	18:38	20:02	21:39	23:38	1:56	4:19	6:38	8:58	11:20	13:39	15:38	17:15
Brunswick	EST	0.00	18:26	19:49	21:26	23:25	1:43	4:06	6:26	8:46	11:09	13:27	15:26	17:03
Columbus	EST	0.00	18:40	20:02	21:37	23:36	1:55	4:19	6:40	9:01	11:25	13:44	15:43	17:18
Dalton	EST	0.00	18:40	19:59	21:32	23:30	1:50	4:16	6:40	9:04	11:30	13:50	15:48	17:21
Douglas	EST	0.00	18:31	19:54	21:31	23:30	1:48	4:11	6:31	8:52	11:15	13:33	15:32	17:08
Dublin	EST	0.00	18:32	19:53	21:29	23:27	1:46	4:10	6:32	8:53	11:17	13:36	15:35	17:10
Macon	EST	0.00	18:35	19:56	21:31	23:30	1:48	4:13	6:35	8:56	11:21	13:40	15:38	17:13
Savannah	EST	0.00	18:24	19:47	21:22	23:21	1:40	4:04	6:24	8:45	11:09	13:28	15:26	17:02
Statesboro	EST	0.00	18:27	19:49	21:24	23:23	1:42	4:06	6:27	8:48	11:12	13:31	15:30	17:05
Valdosta	EST	0.00	18:33	19:57	21:34	23:33	1:51	4:14	6:33	8:53	11:15	13:33	15:32	17:09
Hawaii														
Hana	AHST	5.00	18:24	19:58	21:43	23:46	2:01	4:15	6:24	8:33	10:47	13:02	15:05	16:50
Hanalei	AHST	5.00	18:38	20:11	21:55	23:57	2:12	4:27	6:38	8:49	11:04	13:19	15:21	17:05
Hilo	AHST	5.00	18:20	19:55	21:41	23:45	1:59	4:12	6:20	8:29	10:42	12:56	14:59	16:45
Honolulu	AHST	5.00	18:31	20:05	21:50	23:53	2:07	4:22	6:31	8:41	10:56	13:10	15:13	16:58
Kalaupapa	AHST	5.00	18:28	20:02	21:46	23:49	2:04	4:18	6:28	8:38	10:52	13:07	15:09	16:54
Kawaihae	AHST	5.00	18:23	19:58	21:44	23:47	2:01	4:15	6:23	8:32	10:45	13:00	15:03	16:49
Lanai City	AHST	5.00	18:28	20:02	21:47	23:50	2:04	4:18	6:28	8:37	10:51	13:06	15:09	16:54
Lihue	AHST	5.00	18:37	20:10	21:55	23:57	2:12	4:27	6:37	8:48	11:03	13:18	15:20	17:05
Pahala	AHST	5.00	18:22	19:57	21:44	23:47	2:01	4:14	6:22	8:30	10:43	12:57	15:00	16:47
Wahiawa	AHST	5.00	18:32	20:05	21:50	23:53	2:08	4:22	6:32	8:42	10:57	13:11	15:14	16:59
Wailuku	AHST	5.00	18:26	20:00	21:45	23:48	2:03	4:17	6:26	8:35	10:49	13:04	15:07	16:52
Idaho														
Boise	MST	2.00	18:45	19:52	21:14	23:07	1:32	4:09	6:45	9:21	11:58	14:22	16:15	17:38
Bonners Ferry	PST	3.00	17:45	18:43	19:58	21:47	0:15	3:00	5:45	8:30	11:15	13:44	15:33	16:47
Cascade	MST	2.00	18:44	19:50	21:11	23:03	1:28	4:06	6:44	9:22	12:00	14:25	16:17	17:39
Coeur d'Alene	PST	3.00	17:47	18:47	20:03	21:53	0:21	3:04	5:47	8:30	11:13	13:41	15:31	16:47
Dubois	MST	2.00	18:29	19:35	20:57	22:49	1:14	3:52	6:29	9:06	11:44	14:09	16:01	17:23
Grangeville	PST	3.00	17:44	18:48	20:07	21:58	0:24	3:04	5:44	8:25	11:05	13:31	15:22	16:41
Hailey	MST	2.00	18:37	19:44	21:07	23:00	1:24	4:01	6:37	9:13	11:50	14:15	16:08	17:30
Idaho Falls	MST	2.00	18:28	19:35	20:58	22:51	1:15	3:52	6:28	9:04	11:41	14:05	15:58	17:21
Lewiston	PST	3.00	17:48	18:50	20:09	22:00	0:26	3:07	5:48	8:29	11:10	13:37	15:28	16:46
Pocatello	MST	2.00	18:30	19:38	21:01	22:55	1:19	3:55	6:30	9:05	11:41	14:05	15:58	17:22
Riddle	MST	2.00	18:44	19:54	21:18	23:12	1:35	4:10	6:44	9:19	11:53	14:17	16:11	17:35
Salmon	MST	2.00	18:36	19:40	21:00	22:52	1:18	3:57	6:36	9:14	11:54	14:19	16:11	17:31
Twin Falls	MST	2.00	18:38	19:47	21:10	23:04	1:28	4:03	6:38	9:12	11:48	14:12	16:05	17:29
Wallace	PST	3.00	17:44	18:44	20:01	21:51	0:18	3:01	5:44	8:27	11:09	13:37	15:27	16:43
Illinois														
Chester	CST	1.00	17:59	19:15	20:44	22:40	1:02	3:31	5:59	8:27	10:57	13:18	15:14	16:44
Chicago	CST	1.00	17:51	19:00	20:25	22:19	0:43	3:17	5:51	8:24	10:59	13:22	15:16	16:41
Decatur	CST	1.00	17:56	19:08	20:36	22:31	0:53	3:25	5:56	8:26	10:58	13:21	15:16	16:43
Edwardsville	CST	1.00	18:00	19:14	20:42	22:38	1:00	3:31	6:00	8:29	11:00	13:21	15:17	16:46
Kankakee	CST	1.00	17:51	19:02	20:28	22:22	0:45	3:19	5:51	8:24	10:57	13:20	15:15	16:41
Lawrenceville	CST	1.00	17:51	19:05	20:34	22:29	0:51	3:22	5:51	8:20	10:50	13:12	15:08	16:37
Marion	CST	1.00	17:56	19:11	20:41	22:37	0:58	3:28	5:56	8:24	10:53	13:14	15:10	16:40
Peoria	CST	1.00	17:58	19:10	20:36	22:31	0:53	3:26	5:58	8:30	11:03	13:26	15:21	16:47
Quincy	CST	1.00	18:06	19:18	20:45	22:41	1:03	3:35	6:06	8:36	11:09	13:31	15:26	16:53
Rantoul	CST	1.00	17:53	19:05	20:31	22:26	0:49	3:21	5:53	8:24	10:56	13:19	15:14	16:41
Rockford	CST	1.00	17:56	19:06	20:30	22:24	0:47	3:22	5:56	8:31	11:06	13:29	15:23	16:47
Rock Island	CST	1.00	18:02	19:13	20:38	22:32	0:55	3:29	6:02	8:35	11:09	13:33	15:27	16:52
Salem	CST	1.00	17:56	19:10	20:39	22:35	0:56	3:27	5:56	8:25	10:55	13:17	15:13	16:42
Springfield	CST	1.00	17:59	19:11	20:39	22:34	0:56	3:28	5:59	8:29	11:01	13:23	15:19	16:46
Urbana	CST	1.00	17:53	19:05	20:32	22:27	0:49	3:22	5:53	8:24	10:56	13:19	15:14	16:41
Indiana														
Bloomington	EST	0.00	18:46	20:00	21:28	23:23	1:45	4:16	6:46	9:16	11:47	14:09	16:04	17:33
Dubois	EST	0.00	18:47	20:02	21:31	23:27	1:48	4:18	6:47	9:16	11:46	14:08	16:04	17:33
Evansville	CST	1.00	17:50	19:06	20:35	22:31	0:52	3:22	5:50	8:18	10:48	13:09	15:06	16:35
Ft. Wayne	EST	0.00	18:41	19:51	21:17	23:12	1:35	4:08	6:41	9:13	11:46	14:09	16:04	17:30
French Lick	EST	0.00	18:46	20:01	21:30	23:26	1:47	4:18	6:46	9:15	11:46	14:07	16:03	17:32
Gary	CST	1.00	17:49	18:59	20:25	22:19	0:42	3:16	5:49	8:23	10:57	13:20	15:14	16:39
Indianapolis	EST	0.00	18:45	19:57	21:25	23:20	1:42	4:14	6:45	9:15	11:47	14:09	16:04	17:32
Knox	CST	1.00	17:47	18:57	20:23	22:17	0:40	3:14	5:47	8:19	10:53	13:16	15:11	16:36

Your Starway to Love

♈ = Aries ♉ = Taurus ♊ = Gemini ♋ = Cancer ♌ = Leo ♍ = Virgo

City	Zone	—>EST	♈	♉	♊	♋	♌	♍	♎	♏	♐	♑	♒	♓
Indiana, continued														
Kokomo	EST	0.00	18:45	19:56	21:23	23:18	1:40	4:13	6:45	9:16	11:49	14:11	16:06	17:33
Lafayette	EST	0.00	18:48	19:59	21:26	23:21	1:43	4:16	6:48	9:19	11:52	14:14	16:09	17:36
Muncie	EST	0.00	18:42	19:54	21:21	23:16	1:38	4:10	6:42	9:13	11:45	14:08	16:03	17:29
New Albany	EST	0.00	18:43	19:58	21:27	23:23	1:45	4:15	6:43	9:12	11:42	14:03	15:59	17:29
South Bend	EST	0.00	18:45	19:55	21:20	23:14	1:37	4:12	6:45	9:18	11:53	14:16	16:10	17:35
Terre Haute	EST	0.00	18:50	20:03	21:31	23:26	1:48	4:20	6:50	9:20	11:51	14:13	16:09	17:37
Versailles	EST	0.00	18:41	19:55	21:23	23:19	1:40	4:11	6:41	9:11	11:42	14:03	15:59	17:27
Iowa														
Bedford	CST	1.00	18:19	19:30	20:57	22:51	1:14	3:47	6:19	8:51	11:24	13:46	15:41	17:07
Carroll	CST	1.00	18:19	19:29	20:53	22:47	1:11	3:46	6:19	8:53	11:28	13:52	15:46	17:10
Cedar Rapids	CST	1.00	18:07	19:16	20:41	22:35	0:58	3:33	6:07	8:40	11:15	13:39	15:33	16:57
Council Bluffs	CST	1.00	18:23	19:34	21:00	22:54	1:17	3:51	6:23	8:56	11:30	13:53	15:47	17:13
Davenport	CST	1.00	18:02	19:13	20:38	22:32	0:55	3:29	6:02	8:35	11:09	13:33	15:27	16:52
Decorah	CST	1.00	18:07	19:15	20:37	22:31	0:55	3:31	6:07	8:43	11:19	13:44	15:37	17:00
Des Moines	CST	1.00	18:14	19:25	20:50	22:44	1:07	3:41	6:14	8:48	11:22	13:45	15:39	17:04
Dubuque	CST	1.00	18:03	19:11	20:35	22:29	0:53	3:28	6:03	8:37	11:13	13:36	15:30	16:54
Ft. Dodge	CST	1.00	18:17	19:25	20:49	22:43	1:07	3:42	6:17	8:51	11:27	13:50	15:44	17:08
Mason City	CST	1.00	18:13	19:21	20:44	22:37	1:01	3:37	6:13	8:48	11:25	13:49	15:42	17:05
Ottumwa	CST	1.00	18:09	19:20	20:46	22:41	1:04	3:37	6:09	8:42	11:15	13:38	15:33	16:58
Sioux City	CST	1.00	18:26	19:34	20:58	22:52	1:16	3:51	6:26	9:00	11:35	13:59	15:53	17:17
Spencer	CST	1.00	18:21	19:28	20:51	22:45	1:09	3:45	6:21	8:56	11:32	13:57	15:50	17:13
Waterloo	CST	1.00	18:09	19:18	20:42	22:36	1:00	3:35	6:09	8:44	11:19	13:43	15:37	17:01
Kansas														
Colby	CST	1.00	18:44	19:57	21:25	23:21	1:43	4:14	6:44	9:14	11:46	14:08	16:03	17:31
Dodge City	CST	1.00	18:40	19:56	21:25	23:22	1:43	4:12	6:40	9:08	11:37	13:59	15:55	17:25
Emporia	CST	1.00	18:25	19:39	21:08	23:04	1:26	3:56	6:25	8:53	11:24	13:45	15:41	17:10
Garden City	CST	1.00	18:43	19:59	21:28	23:24	1:46	4:15	6:43	9:12	11:41	14:03	15:59	17:28
Girard	CST	1.00	18:19	19:35	21:05	23:02	1:23	3:52	6:19	8:47	11:16	13:37	15:34	17:04
Hays	CST	1.00	18:37	19:51	21:20	23:15	1:37	4:08	6:37	9:07	11:37	13:59	15:55	17:23
Independence	CST	1.00	18:23	19:39	21:09	23:06	1:27	3:56	6:23	8:50	11:19	13:40	15:36	17:07
Kansas City	CST	1.00	18:19	19:32	21:00	22:56	1:18	3:49	6:19	8:48	11:19	13:41	15:37	17:05
Liberal	CST	1.00	18:44	20:00	21:31	23:27	1:48	4:17	6:44	9:11	11:39	14:00	15:57	17:27
Manhattan	CST	1.00	18:26	19:40	21:08	23:03	1:25	3:57	6:26	8:56	11:27	13:49	15:45	17:13
Phillipsburg	CST	1.00	18:37	19:50	21:17	23:13	1:35	4:07	6:37	9:08	11:40	14:02	15:57	17:25
Salina	CST	1.00	18:30	19:44	21:13	23:09	1:30	4:01	6:30	9:00	11:30	13:52	15:48	17:16
Topeka	CST	1.00	18:23	19:36	21:05	23:00	1:22	3:53	6:23	8:52	11:23	13:45	15:41	17:09
Tribune	MST	2.00	17:47	19:02	20:30	22:26	0:48	3:18	5:47	8:16	10:46	13:08	15:04	16:32
Wichita	CST	1.00	18:29	19:45	21:15	23:11	1:32	4:02	6:29	8:57	11:27	13:48	15:44	17:14
Kentucky														
Bowling Green	CST	1.00	17:46	19:02	20:33	22:30	0:50	3:19	5:46	8:13	10:41	13:02	14:59	16:29
Catlettsburg	EST	0.00	18:30	19:45	21:14	23:10	1:31	4:02	6:30	8:59	11:29	13:51	15:47	17:16
Elizabethtown	EST	0.00	18:43	19:59	21:29	23:25	1:46	4:16	6:43	9:11	11:41	14:02	15:58	17:28
Hazard	EST	0.00	18:33	19:49	21:19	23:16	1:37	4:06	6:33	9:00	11:29	13:50	15:46	17:17
Henderson	CST	1.00	17:50	19:06	20:35	22:32	0:53	3:22	5:50	8:18	10:48	13:09	15:05	16:35
Independence	EST	0.00	18:38	19:52	21:20	23:16	1:38	4:09	6:38	9:08	11:39	14:00	15:56	17:24
Lexington	EST	0.00	18:38	19:53	21:22	23:19	1:40	4:10	6:38	9:06	11:36	13:57	15:54	17:23
Louisville	EST	0.00	18:43	19:58	21:27	23:23	1:45	4:15	6:43	9:12	11:42	14:03	15:59	17:28
Madisonville	CST	1.00	17:50	19:06	20:36	22:33	0:54	3:23	5:50	8:17	10:46	13:07	15:04	16:34
Morehead	EST	0.00	18:34	19:49	21:18	23:14	1:35	4:05	6:34	9:02	11:32	13:54	15:50	17:19
Pikeville	EST	0.00	18:30	19:46	21:16	23:12	1:33	4:03	6:30	8:58	11:27	13:48	15:44	17:14
Pineville	EST	0.00	18:35	19:52	21:22	23:19	1:40	4:08	6:35	9:01	11:30	13:50	15:47	17:18
Richmond	EST	0.00	18:37	19:53	21:22	23:19	1:40	4:09	6:37	9:05	11:35	13:56	15:52	17:22
Somerset	EST	0.00	18:38	19:55	21:25	23:22	1:43	4:11	6:38	9:05	11:34	13:55	15:52	17:22
Louisiana														
Alexandria	CST	1.00	18:10	19:33	21:09	23:09	1:27	3:50	6:10	8:30	10:53	13:11	15:10	16:47
Baton Rouge	CST	1.00	18:05	19:29	21:06	23:06	1:24	3:46	6:05	8:24	10:46	13:04	15:03	16:41
Franklinton	CST	1.00	18:01	19:24	21:01	23:01	1:19	3:41	6:01	8:20	10:43	13:01	15:00	16:37
Houma	CST	1.00	18:03	19:28	21:06	23:06	1:23	3:45	6:03	8:21	10:42	13:00	15:00	16:38
Jonesboro	CST	1.00	18:11	19:33	21:09	23:07	1:26	3:50	6:11	8:32	10:56	13:14	15:13	16:49
Lafayette	CST	1.00	18:08	19:33	21:10	23:10	1:27	3:49	6:08	8:27	10:49	13:07	15:06	16:44
Lake Charles	CST	1.00	18:13	19:37	21:15	23:14	1:32	3:54	6:13	8:32	10:54	13:11	15:11	16:48
Many	CST	1.00	18:14	19:37	21:13	23:12	1:31	3:54	6:14	8:34	10:57	13:16	15:15	16:51
Monroe	CST	1.00	18:08	19:30	21:06	23:04	1:23	3:47	6:08	8:30	10:54	13:13	15:11	16:47
Natchez	CST	1.00	18:12	19:35	21:11	23:10	1:29	3:52	6:12	8:33	10:56	13:14	15:13	16:49
New Orleans	CST	1.00	18:00	19:25	21:03	23:02	1:20	3:42	6:00	8:19	10:40	12:58	14:58	16:36
Shreveport	CST	1.00	18:15	19:37	21:12	23:11	1:30	3:54	6:15	8:36	11:00	13:19	15:18	16:53

City	Zone —>EST		♈	♉	♊	♋	♌	♍	♎	♏	♐	♑	♒	♓
Louisiana, continued														
Tallulah	CST	1.00	18:05	19:27	21:02	23:01	1:20	3:43	6:05	8:26	10:50	13:09	15:07	16:43
Maine														
Augusta	EST	0.00	17:39	18:45	20:06	21:59	0:24	3:02	5:39	8:17	10:54	13:19	15:12	16:33
Bangor	EST	0.00	17:35	18:40	20:01	21:53	0:18	2:57	5:35	8:13	10:52	13:17	15:09	16:30
Caribou	EST	0.00	17:32	18:34	19:51	21:42	0:09	2:50	5:32	8:14	10:56	13:22	15:13	16:30
Dover-Foxcroft	EST	0.00	17:37	18:41	20:01	21:53	0:19	2:58	5:37	8:16	10:55	13:20	15:12	16:32
Frenchville	EST	0.00	17:33	18:35	19:53	21:44	0:10	2:52	5:33	8:15	10:56	13:23	15:14	16:31
Houlton	EST	0.00	17:31	18:34	19:53	21:44	0:10	2:51	5:31	8:12	10:52	13:19	15:10	16:28
Lewiston	EST	0.00	17:41	18:47	20:09	22:01	0:26	3:04	5:41	8:18	10:55	13:20	15:13	16:35
Machias	EST	0.00	17:30	18:35	19:56	21:48	0:13	2:52	5:30	8:08	10:46	13:12	15:04	16:25
Millinocket	EST	0.00	17:35	18:39	19:58	21:50	0:15	2:55	5:35	8:14	10:54	13:20	15:12	16:31
Portland	EST	0.00	17:41	18:48	20:10	22:03	0:28	3:05	5:41	8:17	10:54	13:19	15:12	16:34
Stratton	EST	0.00	17:42	18:46	20:06	21:58	0:24	3:03	5:42	8:20	11:00	13:25	15:17	16:37
Maryland														
Annapolis	EST	0.00	18:06	19:20	20:48	22:44	1:06	3:37	6:06	8:35	11:06	13:28	15:24	16:52
Baltimore	EST	0.00	18:06	19:20	20:48	22:43	1:05	3:37	6:06	8:36	11:08	13:30	15:25	16:53
Frederick	EST	0.00	18:10	19:23	20:51	22:46	1:08	3:40	6:10	8:40	11:11	13:33	15:29	16:56
Glen Burnie	EST	0.00	18:07	19:20	20:48	22:44	1:06	3:37	6:07	8:36	11:07	13:29	15:25	16:53
LaPlata	EST	0.00	18:08	19:22	20:51	22:47	1:09	3:39	6:08	8:37	11:07	13:29	15:25	16:54
Oakland	EST	0.00	18:18	19:31	20:59	22:54	1:16	3:48	6:18	8:48	11:19	13:41	15:37	17:04
Ocean City	EST	0.00	18:00	19:15	20:44	22:40	1:02	3:32	6:00	8:29	10:59	13:21	15:17	16:46
Princess Anne	EST	0.00	18:03	19:18	20:47	22:43	1:04	3:34	6:03	8:31	11:01	13:23	15:19	16:48
Massachussetts														
Barnstable	EST	0.00	17:41	18:51	20:16	22:10	0:34	3:08	5:41	8:15	10:49	13:12	15:06	16:31
Boston	EST	0.00	17:44	18:53	20:17	22:11	0:35	3:10	5:44	8:19	10:54	13:17	15:11	16:35
Fall River	EST	0.00	17:45	18:55	20:20	22:14	0:37	3:11	5:45	8:18	10:52	13:16	15:10	16:35
Lawrence	EST	0.00	17:45	18:53	20:17	22:10	0:34	3:10	5:45	8:19	10:55	13:19	15:13	16:36
Milton	EST	0.00	17:44	18:53	20:18	22:11	0:35	3:10	5:44	8:18	10:53	13:17	15:11	16:35
Pittsfield	EST	0.00	17:53	19:02	20:26	22:19	0:43	3:19	5:53	8:27	11:03	13:27	15:20	16:44
Plymouth	EST	0.00	17:43	18:52	20:17	22:11	0:34	3:09	5:43	8:16	10:51	13:15	15:09	16:33
Springfield	EST	0.00	17:50	19:00	20:24	22:18	0:42	3:16	5:50	8:24	10:59	13:23	15:17	16:41
Tewksbury	EST	0.00	17:45	18:54	20:17	22:11	0:35	3:10	5:45	8:20	10:55	13:19	15:13	16:36
Worcester	EST	0.00	17:47	18:56	20:21	22:14	0:38	3:13	5:47	8:21	10:56	13:20	15:14	16:38
Michigan														
Adrian	EST	0.00	18:36	19:46	21:10	23:05	1:28	4:03	6:36	9:10	11:44	14:08	16:02	17:26
Alpena	EST	0.00	18:34	19:38	20:59	22:51	1:16	3:55	6:34	9:12	11:51	14:17	16:09	17:29
Bad Axe	EST	0.00	18:32	19:39	21:01	22:54	1:18	3:55	6:32	9:09	11:46	14:10	16:03	17:25
Big Rapids	EST	0.00	18:42	19:49	21:11	23:04	1:29	4:06	6:42	9:18	11:55	14:20	16:13	17:35
Cheboygan	EST	0.00	18:38	19:42	21:01	22:53	1:18	3:58	6:38	9:17	11:57	14:23	16:15	17:34
Dearborn	EST	0.00	18:33	19:42	21:06	23:00	1:23	3:58	6:33	9:07	11:42	14:06	16:00	17:24
Detroit	EST	0.00	18:32	19:41	21:05	22:59	1:23	3:58	6:32	9:06	11:42	14:05	15:59	17:23
Escanaba	EST	0.00	18:48	19:52	21:11	23:03	1:28	4:09	6:48	9:28	12:08	14:34	16:26	17:45
Flint	EST	0.00	18:35	19:43	21:06	22:59	1:23	3:59	6:35	9:10	11:46	14:10	16:04	17:27
Grand Rapids	EST	0.00	18:43	19:51	21:14	23:07	1:31	4:07	6:43	9:18	11:54	14:18	16:11	17:35
Houghton	EST	0.00	18:54	19:55	21:12	23:03	1:30	4:12	6:54	9:36	12:19	14:46	16:36	17:53
Kalamazoo	EST	0.00	18:42	19:51	21:16	23:09	1:33	4:08	6:42	9:17	11:52	14:15	16:09	17:33
Lansing	EST	0.00	18:38	19:47	21:10	23:04	1:28	4:03	6:38	9:13	11:49	14:13	16:06	17:30
Marquette	EST	0.00	18:50	19:52	21:10	23:01	1:27	4:08	6:50	9:31	12:12	14:39	16:30	17:47
McMillan	EST	0.00	18:43	19:45	21:04	22:55	1:21	4:02	6:43	9:23	12:04	14:31	16:22	17:40
Midland	EST	0.00	18:37	19:44	21:06	22:59	1:24	4:01	6:37	9:13	11:50	14:15	16:08	17:30
Port Huron	EST	0.00	18:30	19:38	21:01	22:54	1:18	3:54	6:30	9:05	11:41	14:05	15:58	17:22
Roscommon	EST	0.00	18:38	19:44	21:05	22:57	1:23	4:01	6:38	9:16	11:54	14:19	16:12	17:33
Sault Ste. Marie	EST	0.00	18:37	19:40	20:58	22:49	1:15	3:56	6:37	9:18	12:00	14:26	16:17	17:35
Traverse City	EST	0.00	18:42	19:48	21:08	23:01	1:26	4:04	6:42	9:21	11:59	14:24	16:17	17:37
Minnesota														
Albert Lea	CST	1.00	18:13	19:20	20:43	22:36	1:00	3:37	6:13	8:50	11:27	13:51	15:44	17:06
Baudette	CST	1.00	18:18	19:17	20:31	22:20	0:48	3:33	6:18	9:04	11:49	14:17	16:06	17:20
Bemidji	CST	1.00	18:20	19:20	20:36	22:27	0:54	3:37	6:20	9:02	11:45	14:12	16:03	17:19
Brainerd	CST	1.00	18:17	19:19	20:38	22:29	0:55	3:36	6:17	8:58	11:39	14:05	15:56	17:14
Crookston	CST	1.00	18:26	19:26	20:42	22:32	1:00	3:43	6:26	9:10	11:53	14:21	16:11	17:26
Duluth	CST	1.00	18:08	19:10	20:28	22:18	0:45	3:27	6:08	8:50	11:32	13:58	15:49	17:07
Fergus Falls	CST	1.00	18:24	19:27	20:45	22:36	1:03	3:44	6:24	9:05	11:46	14:12	16:03	17:22
Grand Marais	CST	1.00	18:01	19:01	20:17	22:07	0:35	3:18	6:01	8:45	11:28	13:55	15:45	17:01
Grand Rapids	CST	1.00	18:14	19:15	20:32	22:22	0:49	3:32	6:14	8:56	11:39	14:06	15:56	17:13
Hibbing	CST	1.00	18:12	19:12	20:29	22:19	0:46	3:29	6:12	8:54	11:37	14:04	15:55	17:11
International Falls	CST	1.00	18:14	19:12	20:27	22:16	0:44	3:29	6:14	8:59	11:43	14:12	16:01	17:15

♈ = Aries ♉ = Taurus ♊ = Gemini ♋ = Cancer ♌ = Leo ♍ = Virgo

City	Zone —>EST		♈	♉	♊	♋	♌	♍	♎	♏	♐	♑	♒	♓
Minnesota, continued														
Mahnomen	CST	1.00	18:24	19:25	20:41	22:32	0:59	3:41	6:24	9:06	11:49	14:16	16:06	17:23
Mankato	CST	1.00	18:16	19:22	20:44	22:36	1:01	3:39	6:16	8:53	11:31	13:56	15:48	17:10
Marshall	CST	1.00	18:23	19:29	20:50	22:42	1:07	3:46	6:23	9:01	11:39	14:04	15:56	17:17
Minneapolis	CST	1.00	18:13	19:18	20:38	22:30	0:56	3:35	6:13	8:52	11:30	13:56	15:48	17:08
Moorhead	CST	1.00	18:27	19:29	20:46	22:37	1:04	3:45	6:27	9:09	11:51	14:17	16:08	17:25
Ortonville	CST	1.00	18:26	19:30	20:50	22:42	1:07	3:47	6:26	9:05	11:44	14:10	16:02	17:22
Pine City	CST	1.00	18:12	19:15	20:34	22:26	0:52	3:32	6:12	8:52	11:32	13:58	15:49	17:08
Rochester	CST	1.00	18:10	19:16	20:38	22:31	0:55	3:33	6:10	8:47	11:24	13:49	15:42	17:03
Roseau	CST	1.00	18:23	19:21	20:35	22:24	0:52	3:38	6:23	9:08	11:54	14:22	16:11	17:25
St. Cloud	CST	1.00	18:17	19:20	20:40	22:32	0:57	3:37	6:17	8:56	11:36	14:02	15:53	17:13
St. Paul	CST	1.00	18:12	19:17	20:38	22:30	0:55	3:34	6:12	8:51	11:30	13:55	15:47	17:08
Silver Bay	CST	1.00	18:05	19:06	20:23	22:13	0:40	3:23	6:05	8:47	11:30	13:57	15:47	17:04
Willmar	CST	1.00	18:20	19:25	20:45	22:37	1:02	3:42	6:20	8:59	11:38	14:03	15:55	17:16
Winona	CST	1.00	18:07	19:13	20:35	22:27	0:52	3:30	6:07	8:43	11:21	13:46	15:38	17:00
Worthington	CST	1.00	18:22	19:29	20:52	22:45	1:09	3:46	6:22	8:59	11:36	14:00	15:53	17:15
Mississippi														
Biloxi	CST	1.00	17:56	19:20	20:57	22:57	1:15	3:37	5:56	8:15	10:37	12:55	14:54	16:31
Brookhaven	CST	1.00	18:02	19:25	21:01	23:00	1:18	3:41	6:02	8:22	10:45	13:04	15:03	16:39
Cleveland	CST	1.00	18:03	19:23	20:57	22:55	1:15	3:40	6:03	8:26	10:51	13:10	15:08	16:42
Columbus	CST	1.00	17:54	19:14	20:49	22:47	1:06	3:31	5:54	8:16	10:41	13:00	14:59	16:33
Corinth	CST	1.00	17:54	19:13	20:46	22:44	1:03	3:30	5:54	8:18	10:45	13:05	15:02	16:35
Greenville	CST	1.00	18:04	19:25	20:59	22:58	1:17	3:42	6:04	8:27	10:52	13:11	15:09	16:43
Grenada	CST	1.00	17:59	19:20	20:54	22:52	1:11	3:36	5:59	8:22	10:47	13:07	15:05	16:39
Gulfport	CST	1.00	17:56	19:21	20:58	22:58	1:15	3:37	5:56	8:15	10:37	12:55	14:55	16:32
Hattiesburg	CST	1.00	17:57	19:20	20:57	22:56	1:14	3:37	5:57	8:17	10:40	12:58	14:58	16:34
Hernando	CST	1.00	18:00	19:19	20:52	22:50	1:10	3:36	6:00	8:24	10:50	13:10	15:08	16:41
Jackson	CST	1.00	18:01	19:23	20:58	22:57	1:16	3:40	6:01	8:22	10:46	13:04	15:03	16:39
Kosciusko	CST	1.00	17:58	19:20	20:54	22:53	1:12	3:36	5:58	8:20	10:45	13:04	15:02	16:37
Laurel	CST	1.00	17:57	19:19	20:55	22:54	1:13	3:36	5:57	8:17	10:40	12:59	14:58	16:34
Meridian	CST	1.00	17:55	19:17	20:52	22:51	1:10	3:34	5:55	8:16	10:40	12:59	14:57	16:33
Natchez	CST	1.00	18:06	19:29	21:05	23:04	1:22	3:45	6:06	8:26	10:49	13:07	15:06	16:43
Pascagoula	CST	1.00	17:54	19:19	20:56	22:55	1:13	3:35	5:54	8:13	10:35	12:53	14:53	16:30
Tupelo	CST	1.00	17:55	19:15	20:48	22:46	1:06	3:31	5:55	8:18	10:44	13:04	15:01	16:35
Vicksburg	CST	1.00	18:04	19:26	21:01	23:00	1:18	3:42	6:04	8:25	10:49	13:07	15:06	16:41
Yazoo City	CST	1.00	18:02	19:23	20:58	22:57	1:15	3:40	6:02	8:23	10:48	13:07	15:05	16:40
Missouri														
Butler	CST	1.00	18:17	19:32	21:01	22:57	1:19	3:49	6:17	8:46	11:16	13:37	15:33	17:03
Cape Girardeau	CST	1.00	17:58	19:14	20:44	22:41	1:02	3:31	5:58	8:25	10:54	13:15	15:12	16:42
Chillicothe	CST	1.00	18:14	19:27	20:54	22:49	1:12	3:44	6:14	8:45	11:17	13:39	15:34	17:02
Columbia	CST	1.00	18:09	19:23	20:52	22:47	1:09	3:40	6:09	8:39	11:10	13:31	15:27	16:55
Hannibal	CST	1.00	18:05	19:18	20:46	22:41	1:03	3:35	6:05	8:36	11:08	13:30	15:25	16:53
Ironton	CST	1.00	18:03	19:18	20:48	22:44	1:06	3:35	6:03	8:30	10:59	13:21	15:17	16:47
Jefferson City	CST	1.00	18:09	19:23	20:52	22:48	1:09	3:40	6:09	8:38	11:08	13:30	15:26	16:54
Joplin	CST	1.00	18:18	19:34	21:05	23:02	1:22	3:51	6:18	8:45	11:14	13:35	15:31	17:02
Kansas City	CST	1.00	18:18	19:32	21:00	22:56	1:18	3:49	6:18	8:48	11:19	13:41	15:36	17:05
Kennett	CST	1.00	18:00	19:18	20:49	22:46	1:07	3:34	6:00	8:26	10:54	13:14	15:11	16:43
Kirksville	CST	1.00	18:10	19:22	20:49	22:44	1:07	3:39	6:10	8:41	11:14	13:36	15:31	16:58
Maryville	CST	1.00	18:19	19:31	20:58	22:53	1:16	3:48	6:19	8:51	11:23	13:46	15:41	17:08
Saint Joseph	CST	1.00	18:19	19:32	21:00	22:55	1:17	3:49	6:19	8:50	11:22	13:44	15:39	17:07
Sedalia	CST	1.00	18:13	19:27	20:56	22:52	1:13	3:44	6:13	8:42	11:13	13:34	15:30	16:59
Springfield	CST	1.00	18:13	19:29	21:00	22:56	1:17	3:46	6:13	8:40	11:09	13:30	15:27	16:57
St. Louis	CST	1.00	18:01	19:15	20:44	22:40	1:01	3:32	6:01	8:30	11:00	13:22	15:18	16:47
Union	CST	1.00	18:04	19:19	20:47	22:43	1:05	3:35	6:04	8:33	11:03	13:25	15:21	16:49
Waynesville	CST	1.00	18:09	19:24	20:54	22:50	1:11	3:41	6:09	8:37	11:06	13:28	15:24	16:53
West Plains	CST	1.00	18:07	19:24	20:55	22:52	1:13	3:41	6:07	8:34	11:02	13:23	15:20	16:51
Montana														
Billings	MST	2.00	18:14	19:17	20:37	22:28	0:54	3:34	6:14	8:54	11:34	14:00	15:51	17:11
Bozeman	MST	2.00	18:24	19:28	20:47	22:39	1:05	3:44	6:24	9:04	11:44	14:10	16:01	17:20
Broadus	MST	2.00	18:02	19:06	20:25	22:17	0:43	3:22	6:02	8:41	11:20	13:46	15:38	16:58
Butte	MST	2.00	18:30	19:33	20:52	22:43	1:09	3:50	6:30	9:10	11:51	14:17	16:08	17:27
Dillon	MST	2.00	18:31	19:35	20:55	22:47	1:12	3:52	6:31	9:09	11:49	14:14	16:06	17:26
Forsyth	MST	2.00	18:07	19:09	20:28	22:19	0:45	3:26	6:07	8:47	11:28	13:55	15:46	17:04
Great Falls	MST	2.00	18:25	19:26	20:42	22:32	0:59	3:42	6:25	9:08	11:51	14:18	16:08	17:25
Hamilton	MST	2.00	18:37	19:39	20:58	22:49	1:15	3:56	6:37	9:17	11:58	14:24	16:16	17:34
Havre	MST	2.00	18:19	19:17	20:32	22:21	0:49	3:34	6:19	9:04	11:48	14:16	16:06	17:20
Helena	MST	2.00	18:28	19:30	20:48	22:39	1:05	3:47	6:28	9:09	11:51	14:17	16:08	17:26

United States Ascendant Tables

♎ = Libra ♏ = Scorpio ♐ = Sagittarius ♑ = Capricorn ♒ = Aquarius ♓ = Pisces

City	Zone	–>EST	♈	♉	♊	♋	♌	♍	♎	♏	♐	♑	♒	♓
Montana, continued														
Jordan	MST	2.00	18:08	19:08	20:25	22:15	0:43	3:25	6:08	8:50	11:33	14:00	15:50	17:07
Kalispell	MST	2.00	18:37	19:36	20:52	22:41	1:09	3:53	6:37	9:21	12:05	14:33	16:23	17:38
Lewistown	MST	2.00	18:18	19:19	20:36	22:27	0:54	3:36	6:18	9:00	11:42	14:09	15:59	17:17
Libby	MST	2.00	18:42	19:41	20:56	22:45	1:13	3:58	6:42	9:27	12:11	14:39	16:29	17:43
Malta	MST	2.00	18:11	19:10	20:25	22:15	0:43	3:27	6:11	8:56	11:40	14:08	15:58	17:13
Miles City	MST	2.00	18:03	19:06	20:24	22:15	0:41	3:22	6:03	8:44	11:25	13:52	15:43	17:01
Missoula	MST	2.00	18:36	19:38	20:55	22:46	1:12	3:54	6:36	9:18	12:00	14:26	16:17	17:34
Plentywood	MST	2.00	17:58	18:56	20:10	22:00	0:28	3:13	5:58	8:43	11:29	13:57	15:46	17:00
Red Lodge	MST	2.00	18:17	19:21	20:42	22:33	0:59	3:38	6:17	8:56	11:35	14:01	15:52	17:13
Shelby	MST	2.00	18:27	19:26	20:41	22:30	0:58	3:43	6:27	9:12	11:57	14:25	16:14	17:29
Sidney	MST	2.00	17:57	18:57	20:13	22:03	0:30	3:13	5:57	8:40	11:23	13:51	15:41	16:57
White Sulphur Springs	MST	2.00	18:24	19:26	20:44	22:35	1:01	3:42	6:24	9:05	11:46	14:13	16:04	17:21
Wolf Point	MST	2.00	18:03	19:02	20:17	22:07	0:35	3:19	6:03	8:46	11:30	13:58	15:48	17:03
Nebraska														
Bartlett	CST	1.00	18:34	19:44	21:09	23:03	1:26	4:01	6:34	9:08	11:42	14:06	16:00	17:25
Bassett	CST	1.00	18:38	19:47	21:11	23:04	1:28	4:03	6:38	9:13	11:48	14:12	16:06	17:30
Broken Bow	CST	1.00	18:39	19:49	21:14	23:09	1:32	4:06	6:39	9:11	11:45	14:08	16:03	17:28
Center	CST	1.00	18:32	19:40	21:04	22:57	1:21	3:57	6:32	9:06	11:42	14:06	15:59	17:23
Chadron	MST	2.00	17:52	19:00	20:24	22:17	0:41	3:17	5:52	8:27	11:03	13:27	15:20	16:44
Dakota City	CST	1.00	18:26	19:35	20:59	22:52	1:16	3:51	6:26	9:00	11:35	13:59	15:53	17:17
Fairbury	CST	1.00	18:29	19:41	21:08	23:03	1:25	3:58	6:29	9:00	11:32	13:55	15:50	17:17
Falls City	CST	1.00	18:22	19:35	21:02	22:57	1:19	3:51	6:22	8:53	11:26	13:48	15:43	17:10
Grand Island	CST	1.00	18:33	19:44	21:10	23:05	1:28	4:01	6:33	9:06	11:39	14:02	15:56	17:22
Hyannis	MST	2.00	17:47	18:57	20:21	22:15	0:39	3:13	5:47	8:21	10:56	13:19	15:13	16:38
Kearney	CST	1.00	18:36	19:48	21:14	23:09	1:31	4:04	6:36	9:08	11:41	14:04	15:59	17:25
Lincoln	CST	1.00	18:27	19:38	21:04	22:59	1:22	3:55	6:27	8:59	11:32	13:55	15:49	17:15
McCook	CST	1.00	18:43	19:55	21:22	23:17	1:39	4:11	6:43	9:14	11:46	14:09	16:04	17:30
North Platte	CST	1.00	18:43	19:54	21:20	23:14	1:37	4:11	6:43	9:16	11:49	14:12	16:07	17:32
Ogallala	MST	2.00	17:47	18:58	20:23	22:18	0:41	3:14	5:47	8:19	10:53	13:16	15:10	16:36
Omaha	CST	1.00	18:24	19:35	21:00	22:55	1:18	3:51	6:24	8:57	11:31	13:54	15:48	17:14
Scottsbluff	MST	2.00	17:55	19:04	20:29	22:23	0:47	3:21	5:55	8:28	11:03	13:26	15:20	16:45
Sidney	MST	2.00	17:52	19:03	20:28	22:23	0:46	3:19	5:52	8:24	10:58	13:21	15:16	16:41
Valentine	CST	1.00	18:42	19:50	21:14	23:07	1:31	4:07	6:42	9:17	11:53	14:17	16:11	17:34
Nevada														
Austin	PST	3.00	17:48	19:01	20:29	22:24	0:47	3:18	5:48	8:18	10:50	13:12	15:07	16:35
Carson City	PST	3.00	17:59	19:13	20:41	22:36	0:58	3:29	5:59	8:29	11:00	13:22	15:17	16:46
Contact	MST	2.00	18:39	19:49	21:14	23:08	1:31	4:06	6:39	9:12	11:47	14:10	16:04	17:29
Elko	PST	3.00	17:43	18:54	20:20	22:15	0:38	3:11	5:43	8:15	10:48	13:11	15:06	16:32
Ely	PST	3.00	17:40	18:53	20:21	22:17	0:38	3:10	5:40	8:09	10:41	13:03	14:58	16:26
Goldfield	PST	3.00	17:49	19:04	20:34	22:31	0:52	3:21	5:49	8:17	10:46	13:07	15:04	16:33
Hawthorne	PST	3.00	17:54	19:09	20:38	22:34	0:55	3:26	5:54	8:23	10:54	13:15	15:11	16:40
Lake Tahoe	PST	3.00	18:00	19:14	20:42	22:37	0:59	3:30	6:00	8:29	11:00	13:22	15:18	16:46
Las Vegas	PST	3.00	17:41	18:58	20:29	22:27	0:47	3:15	5:41	8:06	10:34	12:55	14:52	16:23
Pioche	PST	3.00	17:38	18:53	20:23	22:19	0:40	3:10	5:38	8:06	10:36	12:57	14:53	16:23
Reno	PST	3.00	17:59	19:12	20:40	22:35	0:57	3:29	5:59	8:29	11:01	13:23	15:19	16:46
Vya	PST	3.00	17:59	19:10	20:35	22:29	0:52	3:26	5:59	8:33	11:07	13:30	15:24	16:49
Winnemucca	PST	3.00	17:51	19:02	20:28	22:22	0:45	3:19	5:51	8:23	10:57	13:19	15:14	16:40
New Hampshire														
Concord	EST	0.00	17:46	18:54	20:17	22:10	0:34	3:11	5:46	8:22	10:58	13:22	15:16	16:38
Conway	EST	0.00	17:44	18:51	20:13	22:05	0:30	3:08	5:44	8:21	10:59	13:23	15:16	16:38
Exeter	EST	0.00	17:44	18:52	20:15	22:08	0:33	3:09	5:44	8:19	10:55	13:19	15:13	16:36
Keene	EST	0.00	17:49	18:57	20:21	22:14	0:38	3:14	5:49	8:24	11:00	13:24	15:18	16:41
Laconia	EST	0.00	17:46	18:53	20:15	22:09	0:33	3:10	5:46	8:22	10:59	13:23	15:16	16:39
Lancaster	EST	0.00	17:46	18:52	20:13	22:05	0:30	3:09	5:46	8:24	11:02	13:27	15:20	16:41
Lebanon	EST	0.00	17:49	18:56	20:18	22:11	0:36	3:13	5:49	8:25	11:02	13:27	15:20	16:42
Manchester	EST	0.00	17:46	18:54	20:17	22:10	0:34	3:11	5:46	8:21	10:57	13:21	15:15	16:38
West Stewartstown	EST	0.00	17:46	18:51	20:11	22:03	0:29	3:08	5:46	8:25	11:04	13:29	15:21	16:41
Woodsville	EST	0.00	17:48	18:54	20:16	22:09	0:33	3:11	5:48	8:25	11:03	13:28	15:20	16:42
New Jersey														
Atlantic City	EST	0.00	17:58	19:11	20:39	22:34	0:56	3:28	5:58	8:28	10:59	13:21	15:17	16:44
Bridgeton	EST	0.00	18:01	19:14	20:42	22:37	0:59	3:31	6:01	8:31	11:02	13:25	15:20	16:48
Camden	EST	0.00	18:00	19:13	20:40	22:35	0:58	3:30	6:00	8:31	11:03	13:26	15:21	16:48
Cape May	EST	0.00	18:00	19:13	20:42	22:38	0:59	3:30	6:00	8:29	11:00	13:22	15:17	16:46
Jersey City	EST	0.00	17:56	19:08	20:34	22:29	0:51	3:24	5:56	8:28	11:01	13:24	15:19	16:45
Newark	EST	0.00	17:57	19:08	20:34	22:29	0:52	3:25	5:57	8:29	11:02	13:24	15:19	16:45
New Brunswick	EST	0.00	17:58	19:10	20:36	22:31	0:53	3:26	5:58	8:29	11:02	13:25	15:20	16:46

Your Starway to Love

♈ = Aries ♉ = Taurus ♊ = Gemini ♋ = Cancer ♌ = Leo ♍ = Virgo

City	Zone	—>EST	♈	♉	♊	♋	♌	♍	♎	♏	♐	♑	♒	♓
New Jersey, continued														
Newton	EST	0.00	17:59	19:10	20:36	22:30	0:53	3:27	5:59	8:31	11:05	13:28	15:22	16:48
Paterson	EST	0.00	17:57	19:08	20:34	22:28	0:51	3:24	5:57	8:29	11:02	13:25	15:20	16:46
Phillipsburg	EST	0.00	18:01	19:12	20:38	22:33	0:56	3:29	6:01	8:33	11:06	13:28	15:23	16:49
Toms River	EST	0.00	17:57	19:09	20:36	22:32	0:54	3:26	5:57	8:28	11:00	13:22	15:17	16:44
Trenton	EST	0.00	17:59	19:11	20:38	22:33	0:55	3:28	5:59	8:30	11:03	13:25	15:20	16:47
New Mexico														
Alamogordo	MST	2.00	18:04	19:25	21:00	22:59	1:18	3:42	6:04	8:26	10:50	13:09	15:08	16:42
Albuquerque	MST	2.00	18:07	19:25	20:58	22:56	1:16	3:42	6:07	8:31	10:58	13:18	15:15	16:48
Carlsbad	MST	2.00	17:57	19:19	20:54	22:53	1:12	3:36	5:57	8:18	10:42	13:01	15:00	16:35
Clayton	MST	2.00	17:53	19:10	20:41	22:38	0:59	3:27	5:53	8:19	10:47	13:07	15:04	16:36
Clovis	MST	2.00	17:53	19:12	20:46	22:44	1:03	3:29	5:53	8:16	10:42	13:02	15:00	16:33
Farmington	MST	2.00	18:13	19:30	21:01	22:57	1:18	3:46	6:13	8:39	11:08	13:28	15:25	16:56
Gallup	MST	2.00	18:15	19:33	21:05	23:03	1:23	3:50	6:15	8:40	11:07	13:27	15:25	16:57
Las Cruces	MST	2.00	18:07	19:29	21:05	23:03	1:22	3:46	6:07	8:28	10:52	13:11	15:10	16:45
Lovington	MST	2.00	17:53	19:15	20:50	22:48	1:07	3:32	5:53	8:15	10:40	12:59	14:57	16:32
Raton	MST	2.00	17:58	19:14	20:45	22:42	1:02	3:31	5:58	8:24	10:53	13:14	15:10	16:41
Reserve	MST	2.00	18:15	19:35	21:10	23:08	1:27	3:52	6:15	8:38	11:03	13:22	15:20	16:55
Roswell	MST	2.00	17:58	19:19	20:53	22:52	1:11	3:36	5:58	8:20	10:45	13:05	15:03	16:37
Santa Fe	MST	2.00	18:04	19:22	20:54	22:51	1:11	3:39	6:04	8:29	10:56	13:16	15:14	16:46
Santa Rosa	MST	2.00	17:59	19:18	20:51	22:48	1:08	3:34	5:59	8:23	10:49	13:09	15:07	16:40
Silver City	MST	2.00	18:13	19:35	21:10	23:08	1:27	3:51	6:13	8:35	10:59	13:18	15:17	16:52
Socorro	MST	2.00	18:08	19:28	21:01	22:59	1:19	3:44	6:08	8:31	10:56	13:16	15:14	16:47
Tucumcari	MST	2.00	17:55	19:14	20:46	22:44	1:04	3:30	5:55	8:19	10:46	13:06	15:04	16:36
New York														
Albany	EST	0.00	17:55	19:04	20:27	22:21	0:45	3:20	5:55	8:30	11:05	13:29	15:23	16:46
Belmont	EST	0.00	18:12	19:21	20:46	22:39	1:03	3:38	6:12	8:46	11:21	13:45	15:39	17:03
Buffalo	EST	0.00	18:16	19:24	20:47	22:41	1:05	3:40	6:16	8:51	11:27	13:51	15:44	17:07
Corning	EST	0.00	18:08	19:17	20:42	22:36	0:59	3:34	6:08	8:42	11:17	13:41	15:35	16:59
Delhi	EST	0.00	18:00	19:09	20:33	22:27	0:50	3:25	6:00	8:34	11:09	13:33	15:26	16:51
Glens Falls	EST	0.00	17:55	19:02	20:25	22:18	0:42	3:19	5:55	8:30	11:07	13:31	15:24	16:47
Jamestown	EST	0.00	18:17	19:26	20:51	22:45	1:08	3:43	6:17	8:51	11:26	13:49	15:43	17:08
Kingston	EST	0.00	17:56	19:06	20:30	22:24	0:48	3:22	5:56	8:30	11:04	13:28	15:22	16:46
Lake Placid	EST	0.00	17:56	19:02	20:23	22:16	0:41	3:19	5:56	8:33	11:11	13:36	15:29	16:50
New York	EST	0.00	17:56	19:07	20:33	22:28	0:51	3:24	5:56	8:28	11:01	13:24	15:18	16:44
Niagara Falls	EST	0.00	18:16	19:24	20:47	22:40	1:05	3:41	6:16	8:52	11:28	13:52	15:45	17:08
Rochester	EST	0.00	18:10	19:18	20:41	22:35	0:59	3:35	6:10	8:46	11:22	13:46	15:40	17:03
Schenectady	EST	0.00	17:56	19:04	20:27	22:21	0:45	3:21	5:56	8:31	11:07	13:31	15:24	16:47
Syracuse	EST	0.00	18:05	19:13	20:36	22:29	0:53	3:29	6:05	8:40	11:16	13:40	15:34	16:57
Utica	EST	0.00	18:01	19:09	20:32	22:25	0:49	3:25	6:01	8:36	11:13	13:37	15:30	16:53
Watertown	EST	0.00	18:04	19:10	20:32	22:25	0:49	3:27	6:04	8:40	11:18	13:43	15:35	16:57
North Carolina														
Albemarle	EST	0.00	18:21	19:39	21:12	23:09	1:29	3:56	6:21	8:46	11:12	13:32	15:30	17:02
Charlotte	EST	0.00	18:23	19:42	21:15	23:12	1:32	3:59	6:23	8:48	11:15	13:35	15:32	17:05
Durham	EST	0.00	18:16	19:33	21:05	23:02	1:22	3:50	6:16	8:41	11:09	13:29	15:26	16:58
Elizabeth City	EST	0.00	18:05	19:22	20:54	22:51	1:11	3:39	6:05	8:31	10:59	13:19	15:16	16:48
Goldsboro	EST	0.00	18:12	19:30	21:03	23:00	1:20	3:47	6:12	8:37	11:04	13:24	15:21	16:54
Greensboro	EST	0.00	18:19	19:37	21:08	23:06	1:26	3:54	6:19	8:45	11:12	13:33	15:30	17:02
Jacksonville	EST	0.00	18:10	19:29	21:02	23:00	1:19	3:46	6:10	8:34	11:00	13:20	15:17	16:50
Lumberton	EST	0.00	18:16	19:35	21:09	23:06	1:26	3:52	6:16	8:40	11:06	13:26	15:24	16:57
Morganton	EST	0.00	18:27	19:45	21:17	23:14	1:34	4:01	6:27	8:52	11:19	13:40	15:37	17:09
Murphy	EST	0.00	18:36	19:55	21:28	23:25	1:45	4:12	6:36	9:01	11:27	13:47	15:45	17:17
Raleigh	EST	0.00	18:15	19:33	21:04	23:02	1:22	3:49	6:15	8:40	11:07	13:27	15:25	16:57
Roanoke Rapids	EST	0.00	18:11	19:28	20:59	22:56	1:16	3:44	6:11	8:37	11:05	13:25	15:22	16:53
Rocky Mount	EST	0.00	18:11	19:29	21:01	22:58	1:18	3:46	6:11	8:37	11:04	13:24	15:22	16:53
Rutherfordton	EST	0.00	18:28	19:46	21:19	23:16	1:36	4:03	6:28	8:53	11:19	13:40	15:37	17:09
Sparta	EST	0.00	18:24	19:42	21:13	23:10	1:30	3:58	6:24	8:51	11:19	13:39	15:36	17:07
Washington	EST	0.00	18:08	19:26	20:59	22:56	1:16	3:43	6:08	8:33	11:00	13:20	15:18	16:50
Waynesville	EST	0.00	18:32	19:50	21:23	23:20	1:40	4:07	6:32	8:57	11:24	13:44	15:41	17:14
Wilmington	EST	0.00	18:12	19:32	21:05	23:03	1:23	3:48	6:12	8:35	11:01	13:20	15:18	16:52
Winston-Salem	EST	0.00	18:21	19:39	21:10	23:07	1:28	3:55	6:21	8:47	11:14	13:35	15:32	17:03
North Dakota														
Ashley	CST	1.00	18:38	19:41	20:59	22:51	1:17	3:57	6:38	9:18	11:58	14:24	16:16	17:34
Bismarck	CST	1.00	18:43	19:45	21:02	22:53	1:20	4:02	6:43	9:25	12:07	14:33	16:24	17:41
Bottineau	CST	1.00	18:42	19:40	20:54	22:43	1:11	3:56	6:42	9:27	12:12	14:41	16:30	17:44
Bowbells	CST	1.00	18:49	19:47	21:01	22:50	1:19	4:04	6:49	9:34	12:19	14:48	16:37	17:51
Bowman	MST	2.00	17:54	18:56	20:15	22:06	0:32	3:13	5:54	8:34	11:15	13:41	15:32	16:51

♎ = Libra ♏ = Scorpio ♐ = Sagittarius ♑ = Capricorn ♒ = Aquarius ♓ = Pisces

City	Zone	–>EST	♈	♉	♊	♋	♌	♍	♎	♏	♐	♑	♒	♓
North Dakota, continued														
Carrington	CST	1.00	18:37	19:37	20:54	22:44	1:11	3:54	6:37	9:19	12:02	14:29	16:20	17:36
Carson	MST	2.00	17:46	18:49	20:07	21:58	0:24	3:05	5:46	8:27	11:08	13:35	15:26	16:44
Crosby	CST	1.00	18:53	19:51	21:05	22:54	1:22	4:08	6:53	9:39	12:24	14:53	16:42	17:55
Dickinson	MST	2.00	17:51	18:53	20:10	22:01	0:28	3:09	5:51	8:33	11:15	13:42	15:32	16:50
Fargo	CST	1.00	18:27	19:29	20:46	22:37	1:04	3:45	6:27	9:09	11:51	14:18	16:08	17:26
Grafton	CST	1.00	18:30	19:28	20:43	22:33	1:01	3:45	6:30	9:14	11:59	14:27	16:16	17:31
Grand Forks	CST	1.00	18:28	19:28	20:43	22:33	1:01	3:44	6:28	9:12	11:55	14:23	16:13	17:28
Jamestown	CST	1.00	18:35	19:36	20:54	22:44	1:11	3:53	6:35	9:17	11:59	14:25	16:16	17:33
Langdon	CST	1.00	18:33	19:32	20:46	22:35	1:03	3:48	6:33	9:19	12:04	14:32	16:21	17:35
Minot	CST	1.00	18:45	19:44	20:59	22:49	1:17	4:01	6:45	9:29	12:14	14:41	16:31	17:46
Rugby	CST	1.00	18:40	19:39	20:54	22:43	1:11	3:56	6:40	9:24	12:09	14:37	16:26	17:41
Wahpeton	CST	1.00	18:26	19:29	20:47	22:39	1:05	3:46	6:26	9:07	11:48	14:14	16:05	17:24
Williston	CST	1.00	18:55	19:54	21:09	22:59	1:27	4:11	6:55	9:39	12:23	14:50	16:40	17:55
Ohio														
Akron	EST	0.00	18:26	19:37	21:03	22:57	1:20	3:54	6:26	8:58	11:32	13:55	15:49	17:15
Athens	EST	0.00	18:28	19:42	21:10	23:05	1:27	3:58	6:28	8:58	11:30	13:52	15:47	17:15
Canton	EST	0.00	18:26	19:37	21:03	22:58	1:20	3:54	6:26	8:58	11:31	13:53	15:48	17:14
Cincinnati	EST	0.00	18:38	19:52	21:20	23:16	1:37	4:08	6:38	9:08	11:39	14:01	15:56	17:24
Cleveland	EST	0.00	18:27	19:37	21:02	22:57	1:20	3:54	6:27	9:00	11:34	13:57	15:51	17:17
Columbus	EST	0.00	18:32	19:44	21:12	23:07	1:29	4:01	6:32	9:03	11:35	13:57	15:52	17:20
Dayton	EST	0.00	18:37	19:50	21:17	23:12	1:34	4:06	6:37	9:07	11:39	14:01	15:57	17:24
Lima	EST	0.00	18:36	19:48	21:14	23:09	1:31	4:04	6:36	9:08	11:41	14:04	15:59	17:25
Marion	EST	0.00	18:33	19:44	21:10	23:05	1:28	4:01	6:33	9:04	11:37	14:00	15:55	17:21
Portsmouth	EST	0.00	18:32	19:46	21:15	23:11	1:32	4:03	6:32	9:01	11:32	13:53	15:49	17:18
Sandusky	EST	0.00	18:31	19:41	21:06	23:01	1:24	3:58	6:31	9:04	11:38	14:01	15:55	17:20
Toledo	EST	0.00	18:34	19:44	21:09	23:03	1:27	4:01	6:34	9:07	11:42	14:05	15:59	17:24
Woodsfield	EST	0.00	18:24	19:37	21:05	23:00	1:22	3:54	6:24	8:55	11:27	13:49	15:44	17:12
Youngstown	EST	0.00	18:23	19:33	20:59	22:54	1:17	3:50	6:23	8:55	11:29	13:52	15:46	17:12
Zanesville	EST	0.00	18:28	19:41	21:08	23:03	1:25	3:57	6:28	8:59	11:31	13:53	15:48	17:16
Oklahoma														
Altus	CST	1.00	18:37	19:57	21:30	23:28	1:47	4:13	6:37	9:01	11:27	13:47	15:45	17:18
Ardmore	CST	1.00	18:29	19:49	21:22	23:20	1:40	4:05	6:29	8:52	11:18	13:37	15:35	17:09
Beaver	CST	1.00	18:42	19:59	21:30	23:26	1:47	4:15	6:42	9:09	11:37	13:58	15:55	17:25
Boise City	CST	1.00	18:50	20:07	21:38	23:35	1:55	4:24	6:50	9:17	11:45	14:06	16:02	17:33
Clinton	CST	1.00	18:36	19:54	21:26	23:24	1:44	4:11	6:36	9:01	11:28	13:48	15:45	17:18
Edmond	CST	1.00	18:30	19:48	21:20	23:17	1:38	4:05	6:30	8:55	11:22	13:42	15:40	17:12
Enid	CST	1.00	18:32	19:49	21:20	23:17	1:37	4:05	6:32	8:58	11:26	13:46	15:43	17:14
Guymon	CST	1.00	18:46	20:03	21:34	23:31	1:51	4:20	6:46	9:12	11:41	14:01	15:58	17:29
Lawton	CST	1.00	18:34	19:53	21:26	23:24	1:44	4:10	6:34	8:57	11:24	13:43	15:41	17:14
McAlester	CST	1.00	18:23	19:42	21:15	23:13	1:32	3:59	6:23	8:47	11:14	13:34	15:31	17:04
Miami	CST	1.00	18:20	19:36	21:07	23:04	1:24	3:53	6:20	8:46	11:15	13:35	15:32	17:03
Muskogee	CST	1.00	18:21	19:39	21:11	23:09	1:29	3:56	6:21	8:47	11:14	13:34	15:31	17:03
Norman	CST	1.00	18:30	19:48	21:21	23:18	1:38	4:05	6:30	8:54	11:21	13:41	15:39	17:11
Oklahoma City	CST	1.00	18:30	19:48	21:21	23:18	1:38	4:05	6:30	8:55	11:22	13:42	15:39	17:12
Shawnee	CST	1.00	18:28	19:46	21:19	23:16	1:36	4:03	6:28	8:52	11:19	13:39	15:37	17:09
Stillwater	CST	1.00	18:28	19:46	21:17	23:14	1:35	4:02	6:28	8:54	11:22	13:42	15:39	17:11
Tulsa	CST	1.00	18:24	19:41	21:13	23:10	1:30	3:58	6:24	8:49	11:17	13:38	15:35	17:06
Woodward	CST	1.00	18:38	19:55	21:26	23:23	1:43	4:11	6:38	9:04	11:32	13:52	15:49	17:20
Oregon														
Baker	PST	3.00	17:51	18:56	20:17	22:09	0:35	3:13	5:51	8:29	11:08	13:33	15:26	16:46
Bend	PST	3.00	18:05	19:12	20:33	22:26	0:51	3:28	6:05	8:42	11:20	13:45	15:37	16:59
Burns	PST	3.00	17:56	19:03	20:26	22:19	0:43	3:20	5:56	8:32	11:09	13:34	15:27	16:49
Eugene	PST	3.00	18:12	19:19	20:40	22:33	0:58	3:35	6:12	8:49	11:27	13:52	15:44	17:06
Fossil	PST	3.00	18:01	19:06	20:26	22:18	0:43	3:22	6:01	8:39	11:18	13:44	15:36	16:56
Grant's Pass	PST	3.00	18:13	19:22	20:46	22:40	1:04	3:39	6:13	8:48	11:23	13:47	15:40	17:04
Klamath Falls	PST	3.00	18:07	19:16	20:41	22:34	0:58	3:33	6:07	8:41	11:16	13:40	15:34	16:58
Lakeview	PST	3.00	18:01	19:11	20:35	22:29	0:52	3:27	6:01	8:35	11:10	13:34	15:28	16:52
Medford	PST	3.00	18:11	19:20	20:45	22:38	1:02	3:37	6:11	8:46	11:21	13:45	15:38	17:02
Pendleton	PST	3.00	17:55	18:59	20:18	22:10	0:36	3:16	5:55	8:35	11:15	13:41	15:32	16:51
Portland	PST	3.00	18:10	19:14	20:34	22:26	0:51	3:31	6:10	8:50	11:30	13:55	15:47	17:07
Salem	PST	3.00	18:12	19:17	20:37	22:30	0:55	3:34	6:12	8:51	11:29	13:55	15:47	17:07
The Dalles	PST	3.00	18:05	19:09	20:28	22:20	0:45	3:25	6:05	8:44	11:24	13:50	15:42	17:01
Vale	MST	2.00	18:49	19:55	21:17	23:10	1:35	4:12	6:49	9:26	12:03	14:28	16:21	17:42
Pennsylvania														
Allentown	EST	0.00	18:02	19:13	20:40	22:35	0:57	3:30	6:02	8:34	11:07	13:29	15:24	16:50
Altoona	EST	0.00	18:14	19:25	20:52	22:47	1:09	3:42	6:14	8:45	11:18	13:41	15:35	17:02

Your Starway to Love

♈ = Aries ♉ = Taurus ♊ = Gemini ♋ = Cancer ♌ = Leo ♍ = Virgo

City	Zone	->EST	♈	♉	♊	♋	♌	♍	♎	♏	♐	♑	♒	♓
Pennsylvania, continued														
Chambersburg	EST	0.00	18:11	19:23	20:50	22:46	1:08	3:40	6:11	8:41	11:14	13:36	15:31	16:58
Du Bois	EST	0.00	18:15	19:26	20:52	22:46	1:09	3:43	6:15	8:48	11:21	13:44	15:39	17:04
Erie	EST	0.00	18:20	19:30	20:54	22:48	1:11	3:46	6:20	8:54	11:29	13:53	15:47	17:11
Harrisburg	EST	0.00	18:08	19:20	20:46	22:41	1:04	3:36	6:08	8:39	11:11	13:34	15:29	16:56
New Castle	EST	0.00	18:21	19:32	20:58	22:53	1:16	3:49	6:21	8:54	11:27	13:50	15:45	17:10
Philadelphia	EST	0.00	18:01	19:13	20:40	22:35	0:58	3:30	6:01	8:31	11:04	13:26	15:21	16:48
Pittsburgh	EST	0.00	18:20	19:32	20:58	22:53	1:16	3:49	6:20	8:51	11:24	13:47	15:42	17:08
Reading	EST	0.00	18:04	19:16	20:42	22:37	1:00	3:32	6:04	8:35	11:08	13:30	15:25	16:52
Scranton	EST	0.00	18:03	19:13	20:38	22:33	0:56	3:30	6:03	8:36	11:10	13:33	15:27	16:52
Uniontown	EST	0.00	18:19	19:31	20:59	22:54	1:16	3:48	6:19	8:50	11:22	13:44	15:39	17:06
Warren	EST	0.00	18:17	19:26	20:51	22:45	1:09	3:43	6:17	8:50	11:25	13:48	15:42	17:07
Wilkes-Barre	EST	0.00	18:04	19:14	20:40	22:34	0:57	3:31	6:04	8:36	11:10	13:33	15:27	16:53
Williamsport	EST	0.00	18:08	19:19	20:44	22:39	1:02	3:35	6:08	8:41	11:14	13:37	15:32	16:57
Rhode Island														
Newport	EST	0.00	17:45	18:56	20:21	22:15	0:38	3:12	5:45	8:18	10:52	13:15	15:10	16:35
Providence	EST	0.00	17:46	18:55	20:20	22:14	0:38	3:12	5:46	8:19	10:54	13:17	15:11	16:36
Westerly	EST	0.00	17:47	18:58	20:23	22:17	0:41	3:14	5:47	8:20	10:54	13:17	15:12	16:37
Woonsocket	EST	0.00	17:46	18:56	20:20	22:14	0:38	3:12	5:46	8:20	10:55	13:18	15:12	16:37
South Carolina														
Aiken	EST	0.00	18:27	19:48	21:22	23:20	1:39	4:04	6:27	8:49	11:15	13:34	15:32	17:06
Anderson	EST	0.00	18:31	19:50	21:23	23:21	1:41	4:07	6:31	8:54	11:20	13:40	15:38	17:11
Bennettsville	EST	0.00	18:19	19:38	21:11	23:09	1:29	3:55	6:19	8:43	11:09	13:28	15:26	16:59
Charleston	EST	0.00	18:20	19:41	21:16	23:15	1:34	3:58	6:20	8:41	11:06	13:25	15:23	16:58
Columbia	EST	0.00	18:24	19:44	21:18	23:16	1:36	4:01	6:24	8:47	11:13	13:32	15:30	17:04
Conway	EST	0.00	18:16	19:37	21:10	23:09	1:28	3:53	6:16	8:39	11:04	13:24	15:22	16:56
Greenville	EST	0.00	18:30	19:49	21:22	23:19	1:39	4:05	6:30	8:54	11:20	13:40	15:38	17:10
Lancaster	EST	0.00	18:23	19:42	21:15	23:13	1:33	3:59	6:23	8:47	11:13	13:33	15:31	17:04
Newberry	EST	0.00	18:26	19:46	21:20	23:18	1:37	4:03	6:26	8:50	11:16	13:35	15:33	17:07
Port Royal	EST	0.00	18:23	19:45	21:20	23:19	1:38	4:02	6:23	8:44	11:08	13:27	15:25	17:01
Spartanburg	EST	0.00	18:28	19:47	21:20	23:17	1:37	4:03	6:28	8:52	11:18	13:38	15:36	17:09
Sumter	EST	0.00	18:21	19:42	21:16	23:14	1:33	3:58	6:21	8:44	11:10	13:29	15:27	17:01
South Dakota														
Aberdeen	CST	1.00	18:34	19:38	20:58	22:49	1:15	3:55	6:34	9:13	11:53	14:19	16:10	17:30
Belle Fourche	MST	2.00	17:55	19:01	20:22	22:14	0:39	3:17	5:55	8:33	11:12	13:37	15:29	16:50
Bison	MST	2.00	17:50	18:54	20:13	22:05	0:31	3:11	5:50	8:29	11:09	13:35	15:26	16:46
Brookings	CST	1.00	18:27	19:33	20:54	22:47	1:12	3:50	6:27	9:05	11:42	14:07	16:00	17:21
Buffalo	MST	2.00	17:54	18:58	20:17	22:09	0:35	3:15	5:54	8:34	11:13	13:39	15:31	16:50
Chamberlain	CST	1.00	18:37	19:44	21:06	22:59	1:24	4:01	6:37	9:14	11:51	14:16	16:09	17:31
Dupree	MST	2.00	17:46	18:51	20:11	22:03	0:29	3:08	5:46	8:25	11:04	13:29	15:21	16:42
Hot Springs	MST	2.00	17:54	19:01	20:24	22:17	0:41	3:18	5:54	8:30	11:06	13:31	15:24	16:47
Huron	CST	1.00	18:33	19:39	21:00	22:52	1:17	3:55	6:33	9:10	11:48	14:13	16:06	17:27
Mitchell	CST	1.00	18:32	19:39	21:01	22:54	1:19	3:56	6:32	9:09	11:46	14:10	16:03	17:25
Mobridge	CST	1.00	18:42	19:46	21:05	22:57	1:23	4:02	6:42	9:21	12:01	14:27	16:18	17:38
Pierre	CST	1.00	18:41	19:47	21:08	23:01	1:26	4:04	6:41	9:19	11:57	14:22	16:14	17:36
Rapid City	MST	2.00	17:53	18:59	20:21	22:14	0:38	3:16	5:53	8:30	11:08	13:32	15:25	16:47
Sioux Falls	CST	1.00	18:27	19:34	20:57	22:50	1:14	3:51	6:27	9:03	11:40	14:04	15:57	17:20
Sisseton	CST	1.00	18:28	19:32	20:51	22:43	1:09	3:49	6:28	9:08	11:48	14:14	16:05	17:25
Vermillion	CST	1.00	18:28	19:36	21:00	22:53	1:17	3:53	6:28	9:03	11:38	14:02	15:56	17:19
Watertown	CST	1.00	18:28	19:33	20:54	22:46	1:11	3:50	6:28	9:07	11:46	14:11	16:03	17:24
White River	MST	2.00	17:43	18:50	20:13	22:06	0:30	3:07	5:43	8:19	10:56	13:20	15:13	16:36
Tennessee														
Athens	EST	0.00	18:38	19:57	21:29	23:26	1:47	4:14	6:38	9:03	11:30	13:50	15:48	17:20
Chattanooga	EST	0.00	18:41	20:00	21:33	23:30	1:50	4:17	6:41	9:06	11:32	13:52	15:50	17:22
Cookeville	CST	1.00	17:42	18:59	20:31	22:28	0:48	3:16	5:42	8:08	10:36	12:56	14:53	16:25
Dyersburg	CST	1.00	17:58	19:15	20:47	22:44	1:04	3:32	5:58	8:23	10:51	13:11	15:08	16:40
Henderson	CST	1.00	17:55	19:13	20:45	22:43	1:03	3:30	5:55	8:19	10:46	13:06	15:04	16:36
Jamestown	CST	1.00	17:40	18:57	20:28	22:25	0:46	3:14	5:40	8:06	10:34	12:54	14:51	16:23
Kingsport	EST	0.00	18:30	19:47	21:18	23:15	1:36	4:04	6:30	8:57	11:25	13:45	15:42	17:13
Knoxville	EST	0.00	18:36	19:53	21:25	23:22	1:43	4:10	6:36	9:01	11:29	13:49	15:46	17:18
Lawrenceburg	CST	1.00	17:49	19:08	20:40	22:38	0:58	3:25	5:49	8:14	10:41	13:01	14:58	16:31
Memphis	CST	1.00	18:00	19:19	20:52	22:49	1:09	3:36	6:00	8:25	10:51	13:11	15:09	16:41
Morristown	EST	0.00	18:33	19:51	21:22	23:19	1:40	4:07	6:33	8:59	11:27	13:47	15:44	17:16
Nashville	CST	1.00	17:47	19:05	20:36	22:33	0:54	3:21	5:47	8:13	10:41	13:01	14:58	16:30
Paris	CST	1.00	17:53	19:11	20:42	22:39	0:59	3:27	5:53	8:19	10:47	13:08	15:05	16:36
Shelbyville	CST	1.00	17:46	19:04	20:36	22:34	0:54	3:21	5:46	8:11	10:38	12:58	14:55	16:28

♎ = Libra ♏ = Scorpio ♐ = Sagittarius ♑ = Capricorn ♒ = Aquarius ♓ = Pisces

City	Zone	->EST	♈	♉	♊	♋	♌	♍	♎	♏	♐	♑	♒	♓
Texas														
Abilene	CST	1.00	18:39	20:01	21:36	23:35	1:54	4:18	6:39	9:00	11:24	13:43	15:42	17:17
Amarillo	CST	1.00	18:47	20:06	21:39	23:36	1:56	4:23	6:47	9:12	11:39	13:59	15:56	17:29
Austin	CST	1.00	18:31	19:55	21:33	23:32	1:50	4:12	6:31	8:50	11:12	13:30	15:29	17:07
Beaumont	CST	1.00	18:16	19:41	21:19	23:18	1:36	3:58	6:16	8:35	10:57	13:15	15:14	16:52
Brownsville	CST	1.00	18:30	19:59	21:40	23:41	1:58	4:16	6:30	8:44	11:02	13:19	15:20	17:01
Corpus Christi	CST	1.00	18:30	19:57	21:36	23:37	1:54	4:13	6:30	8:46	11:06	13:22	15:23	17:03
Dallas	CST	1.00	18:27	19:49	21:24	23:22	1:41	4:06	6:27	8:49	11:13	13:32	15:31	17:06
Del Rio	CST	1.00	18:44	20:09	21:47	23:47	2:05	4:26	6:44	9:01	11:23	13:40	15:40	17:18
El Paso	MST	2.00	18:06	19:29	21:05	23:04	1:22	3:45	6:06	8:26	10:50	13:08	15:07	16:43
Ft. Worth	CST	1.00	18:29	19:51	21:26	23:25	1:43	4:08	6:29	8:51	11:15	13:34	15:33	17:08
Houston	CST	1.00	18:21	19:46	21:24	23:24	1:42	4:03	6:21	8:40	11:01	13:19	15:19	16:57
Laredo	CST	1.00	18:38	20:05	21:45	23:46	2:03	4:22	6:38	8:54	11:13	13:30	15:31	17:11
Lubbock	CST	1.00	18:47	20:08	21:42	23:40	2:00	4:25	6:47	9:10	11:35	13:54	15:53	17:27
Marfa	CST	1.00	18:56	20:20	21:58	23:57	2:15	4:37	6:56	9:15	11:37	13:55	15:54	17:32
Midland	CST	1.00	18:48	20:11	21:47	23:45	2:04	4:28	6:48	9:09	11:33	13:51	15:50	17:26
Nacogdoches	CST	1.00	18:19	19:42	21:18	23:17	1:35	3:58	6:19	8:39	11:02	13:21	15:20	16:56
Odessa	CST	1.00	18:49	20:12	21:48	23:47	2:05	4:29	6:49	9:10	11:33	13:52	15:51	17:27
Paris	CST	1.00	18:22	19:43	21:17	23:15	1:34	3:59	6:22	8:45	11:10	13:29	15:28	17:02
San Angelo	CST	1.00	18:42	20:05	21:41	23:40	1:59	4:22	6:42	9:02	11:25	13:43	15:42	17:19
San Antonio	CST	1.00	18:34	19:59	21:37	23:37	1:55	4:16	6:34	8:52	11:13	13:31	15:31	17:09
Sonora	CST	1.00	18:43	20:07	21:44	23:43	2:01	4:23	6:43	9:02	11:24	13:42	15:41	17:19
Tyler	CST	1.00	18:21	19:43	21:19	23:17	1:36	4:00	6:21	8:42	11:06	13:25	15:24	16:59
Waco	CST	1.00	18:29	19:52	21:28	23:27	1:45	4:08	6:29	8:49	11:12	13:30	15:29	17:06
Wichita Falls	CST	1.00	18:34	19:54	21:28	23:26	1:46	4:11	6:34	8:57	11:22	13:42	15:40	17:14
Utah														
Brigham City	MST	2.00	18:28	19:38	21:03	22:58	1:21	3:55	6:28	9:01	11:35	13:58	15:53	17:18
Dugway	MST	2.00	18:31	19:43	21:10	23:05	1:27	4:00	6:31	9:02	11:35	13:57	15:52	17:19
Junction	MST	2.00	18:29	19:44	21:13	23:09	1:30	4:00	6:29	8:57	11:27	13:49	15:45	17:14
Manti	MST	2.00	18:27	19:40	21:08	23:03	1:25	3:57	6:27	8:56	11:28	13:50	15:45	17:13
Mexican Hat	MST	2.00	18:19	19:36	21:06	23:03	1:24	3:52	6:19	8:46	11:15	13:36	15:33	17:03
Moab	MST	2.00	18:18	19:33	21:01	22:57	1:19	3:49	6:18	8:47	11:18	13:39	15:35	17:04
Monticello	MST	2.00	18:17	19:33	21:02	22:59	1:20	3:49	6:17	8:45	11:15	13:36	15:32	17:02
Ogden	MST	2.00	18:28	19:39	21:04	22:59	1:22	3:55	6:28	9:00	11:34	13:57	15:52	17:17
Price	MST	2.00	18:23	19:36	21:04	22:59	1:21	3:53	6:23	8:54	11:25	13:47	15:43	17:10
Provo	MST	2.00	18:27	19:39	21:05	23:00	1:23	3:55	6:27	8:58	11:30	13:53	15:48	17:15
St. George	MST	2.00	18:34	19:51	21:21	23:18	1:39	4:07	6:34	9:01	11:30	13:51	15:48	17:18
Salt Lake City	MST	2.00	18:28	19:39	21:05	23:00	1:22	3:56	6:28	8:59	11:33	13:55	15:50	17:16
Vernal	MST	2.00	18:18	19:30	20:56	22:51	1:14	3:47	6:18	8:50	11:22	13:45	15:40	17:06
Wendover	MST	2.00	18:36	19:47	21:14	23:08	1:31	4:04	6:36	9:08	11:41	14:04	15:59	17:25
Vermont														
Bennington	EST	0.00	17:53	19:01	20:24	22:18	0:42	3:18	5:53	8:28	11:04	13:28	15:21	16:45
Burlington	EST	0.00	17:53	18:58	20:20	22:12	0:37	3:15	5:53	8:31	11:09	13:34	15:26	16:47
Montpelier	EST	0.00	17:50	18:56	20:18	22:10	0:35	3:13	5:50	8:28	11:05	13:30	15:23	16:44
Newport	EST	0.00	17:49	18:54	20:14	22:06	0:32	3:10	5:49	8:27	11:06	13:31	15:23	16:44
Rutland	EST	0.00	17:52	18:59	20:21	22:14	0:39	3:16	5:52	8:28	11:05	13:30	15:22	16:45
St. Albans	EST	0.00	17:52	18:57	20:18	22:10	0:35	3:14	5:52	8:31	11:09	13:34	15:27	16:47
Springfield	EST	0.00	17:50	18:57	20:20	22:13	0:38	3:14	5:50	8:26	11:02	13:26	15:20	16:42
Virginia														
Bristol	EST	0.00	18:29	19:46	21:17	23:14	1:34	4:02	6:29	8:55	11:23	13:44	15:41	17:12
Charlottesville	EST	0.00	18:14	19:29	20:58	22:55	1:16	3:46	6:14	8:42	11:12	13:33	15:29	16:59
Danville	EST	0.00	18:18	19:35	21:06	23:02	1:23	3:51	6:18	8:44	11:12	13:33	15:30	17:01
Fredericksburg	EST	0.00	18:10	19:25	20:54	22:50	1:11	3:41	6:10	8:38	11:09	13:30	15:26	16:55
Jamestown	EST	0.00	18:07	19:23	20:54	22:50	1:11	3:40	6:07	8:34	11:03	13:24	15:21	16:51
Lynchburg	EST	0.00	18:17	19:32	21:03	22:59	1:20	3:49	6:17	8:44	11:13	13:34	15:31	17:01
Marion	EST	0.00	18:26	19:43	21:13	23:10	1:31	3:59	6:26	8:53	11:21	13:42	15:39	17:09
Norfolk	EST	0.00	18:05	19:22	20:53	22:49	1:10	3:38	6:05	8:32	11:00	13:21	15:18	16:49
Petersburg	EST	0.00	18:10	19:26	20:56	22:53	1:14	3:42	6:10	8:37	11:06	13:27	15:23	16:53
Richmond	EST	0.00	18:10	19:26	20:56	22:52	1:13	3:42	6:10	8:37	11:07	13:28	15:24	16:54
Roanoke	EST	0.00	18:20	19:36	21:06	23:03	1:24	3:53	6:20	8:47	11:16	13:37	15:33	17:04
Staunton	EST	0.00	18:16	19:31	21:00	22:57	1:18	3:48	6:16	8:45	11:15	13:36	15:32	17:01
Winchester	EST	0.00	18:13	19:26	20:54	22:50	1:12	3:43	6:13	8:42	11:14	13:35	15:31	16:59
Virginia Beach	EST	0.00	18:04	19:21	20:51	22:48	1:09	3:37	6:04	8:31	10:59	13:20	15:17	16:47
Washington														
Asotin	PST	3.00	17:48	18:51	20:09	22:00	0:26	3:07	5:48	8:29	11:10	13:36	15:27	16:46
Bellingham	PST	3.00	18:10	19:08	20:22	22:11	0:40	3:25	6:10	8:55	11:40	14:09	15:58	17:12
Bremerton	PST	3.00	18:11	19:11	20:27	22:17	0:45	3:28	6:11	8:53	11:37	14:04	15:54	17:10

Your Starway to Love

♈ = Aries ♉ = Taurus ♊ = Gemini ♋ = Cancer ♌ = Leo ♍ = Virgo

City	Zone	->EST	♈	♉	♊	♋	♌	♍	♎	♏	♐	♑	♒	♓
Washington, continued														
Colville	PST	3.00	17:52	18:50	20:05	21:54	0:22	3:07	5:52	8:36	11:21	13:49	15:39	16:53
Everett	PST	3.00	18:09	19:08	20:24	22:14	0:41	3:25	6:09	8:53	11:36	14:04	15:54	17:09
Goldendale	PST	3.00	18:03	19:07	20:26	22:17	0:43	3:23	6:03	8:43	11:23	13:49	15:41	17:00
Kelso	PST	3.00	18:12	19:14	20:33	22:24	0:50	3:31	6:12	8:52	11:33	13:59	15:50	17:09
Moses Lake	PST	3.00	17:57	18:58	20:15	22:06	0:33	3:15	5:57	8:39	11:22	13:49	15:39	16:56
Pasco	PST	3.00	17:56	18:59	20:18	22:09	0:35	3:16	5:56	8:37	11:18	13:44	15:35	16:54
Seattle	PST	3.00	18:09	19:10	20:26	22:16	0:43	3:26	6:09	8:52	11:35	14:03	15:53	17:09
Spokane	PST	3.00	17:50	18:50	20:06	21:56	0:23	3:06	5:50	8:33	11:16	13:43	15:33	16:49
Tacoma	PST	3.00	18:10	19:11	20:27	22:18	0:45	3:27	6:10	8:52	11:35	14:02	15:52	17:09
Vancouver	PST	3.00	18:11	19:14	20:34	22:25	0:51	3:31	6:11	8:50	11:30	13:56	15:48	17:07
Walla Walla	PST	3.00	17:53	18:56	20:15	22:06	0:33	3:13	5:53	8:34	11:14	13:40	15:32	16:50
Waterville	PST	3.00	18:00	19:00	20:17	22:07	0:34	3:17	6:00	8:43	11:27	13:54	15:44	17:00
Yakima	PST	3.00	18:02	19:04	20:22	22:13	0:39	3:21	6:02	8:43	11:25	13:51	15:42	17:00
West Virginia														
Beckley	EST	0.00	18:25	19:40	21:10	23:06	1:27	3:57	6:25	8:53	11:22	13:43	15:40	17:09
Charleston	EST	0.00	18:27	19:41	21:10	23:06	1:28	3:58	6:27	8:55	11:25	13:47	15:43	17:12
Clarksburg	EST	0.00	18:21	19:35	21:03	22:58	1:20	3:52	6:21	8:51	11:23	13:45	15:40	17:08
Elkins	EST	0.00	18:19	19:33	21:02	22:57	1:19	3:50	6:19	8:49	11:20	13:41	15:37	17:06
Fairmont	EST	0.00	18:21	19:34	21:01	22:57	1:19	3:50	6:21	8:51	11:22	13:44	15:40	17:07
Huntington	EST	0.00	18:30	19:44	21:13	23:09	1:31	4:01	6:30	8:58	11:29	13:50	15:46	17:15
Keyser	EST	0.00	18:16	19:29	20:57	22:52	1:14	3:46	6:16	8:46	11:17	13:39	15:35	17:03
Martinsburg	EST	0.00	18:12	19:25	20:53	22:48	1:10	3:42	6:12	8:42	11:13	13:36	15:31	16:59
Parkersburg	EST	0.00	18:26	19:40	21:08	23:03	1:25	3:56	6:26	8:56	11:27	13:49	15:45	17:13
Webster Springs	EST	0.00	18:22	19:36	21:05	23:01	1:23	3:53	6:22	8:50	11:21	13:42	15:38	17:07
Wheeling	EST	0.00	18:23	19:35	21:02	22:57	1:20	3:52	6:23	8:54	11:26	13:48	15:44	17:11
Williamson	EST	0.00	18:29	19:45	21:15	23:11	1:32	4:01	6:29	8:57	11:26	13:47	15:44	17:14
Wisconsin														
Ashland	CST	1.00	18:04	19:06	20:23	22:14	0:41	3:22	6:04	8:45	11:26	13:53	15:44	17:01
Balsam Lake	CST	1.00	18:10	19:14	20:33	22:25	0:51	3:31	6:10	8:49	11:29	13:54	15:46	17:06
Eagle River	CST	1.00	17:57	19:00	20:19	22:11	0:37	3:17	5:57	8:37	11:17	13:43	15:35	16:54
Eau Claire	CST	1.00	18:06	19:11	20:32	22:24	0:49	3:28	6:06	8:44	11:23	13:48	15:40	17:01
Green Bay	CST	1.00	17:52	18:58	20:19	22:11	0:36	3:14	5:52	8:30	11:08	13:33	15:25	16:46
La Crosse	CST	1.00	18:05	19:12	20:34	22:27	0:51	3:28	6:05	8:41	11:19	13:43	15:36	16:58
Lancaster	CST	1.00	18:03	19:11	20:34	22:28	0:52	3:28	6:03	8:38	11:14	13:38	15:31	16:55
Madison	CST	1.00	17:58	19:05	20:29	22:22	0:46	3:22	5:58	8:33	11:09	13:33	15:27	16:50
Milwaukee	CST	1.00	17:52	19:00	20:23	22:16	0:40	3:16	5:52	8:27	11:03	13:27	15:21	16:44
Oshkosh	CST	1.00	17:54	19:01	20:22	22:15	0:40	3:17	5:54	8:31	11:09	13:33	15:26	16:48
Racine	CST	1.00	17:51	19:00	20:23	22:17	0:41	3:16	5:51	8:26	11:02	13:26	15:19	16:43
Sheboygan	CST	1.00	17:51	18:58	20:20	22:13	0:37	3:14	5:51	8:27	11:04	13:29	15:22	16:44
Wausau	CST	1.00	17:59	19:03	20:24	22:16	0:41	3:20	5:59	8:37	11:16	13:41	15:33	16:54
Wisconsin Rapids	CST	1.00	17:59	19:05	20:26	22:19	0:44	3:22	5:59	8:37	11:15	13:40	15:32	16:53
Wyoming														
Casper	MST	2.00	18:05	19:13	20:37	22:30	0:54	3:30	6:05	8:40	11:16	13:40	15:34	16:57
Cheyenne	MST	2.00	17:59	19:10	20:36	22:30	0:53	3:27	5:59	8:32	11:05	13:28	15:23	16:48
Cody	MST	2.00	18:16	19:22	20:43	22:35	1:00	3:38	6:16	8:54	11:32	13:57	15:50	17:11
Evanston	MST	2.00	18:24	19:34	21:00	22:54	1:17	3:51	6:24	8:57	11:30	13:53	15:48	17:13
Gillette	MST	2.00	18:02	19:08	20:29	22:22	0:47	3:25	6:02	8:39	11:17	13:42	15:35	16:56
Jackson	MST	2.00	18:23	19:30	20:53	22:46	1:10	3:47	6:23	8:59	11:36	14:00	15:53	17:16
Lander	MST	2.00	18:15	19:23	20:47	22:40	1:04	3:40	6:15	8:50	11:26	13:50	15:43	17:07
Laramie	MST	2.00	18:02	19:13	20:38	22:33	0:56	3:30	6:02	8:35	11:09	13:32	15:26	16:52
Medicine Bow	MST	2.00	18:05	19:14	20:39	22:33	0:57	3:31	6:05	8:38	11:13	13:36	15:30	16:55
Newcastle	MST	2.00	17:57	19:03	20:25	22:18	0:43	3:20	5:57	8:33	11:11	13:35	15:28	16:50
Rawlins	MST	2.00	18:09	19:19	20:44	22:38	1:01	3:35	6:09	8:42	11:17	13:40	15:34	16:59
Rock Springs	MST	2.00	18:17	19:27	20:52	22:46	1:10	3:44	6:17	8:50	11:24	13:47	15:42	17:07
Sheridan	MST	2.00	18:08	19:13	20:34	22:26	0:51	3:30	6:08	8:46	11:25	13:50	15:42	17:03
Thermopolis	MST	2.00	18:13	19:20	20:42	22:35	1:00	3:37	6:13	8:49	11:26	13:51	15:44	17:06
Torrington	MST	2.00	17:57	19:06	20:31	22:25	0:48	3:23	5:57	8:31	11:05	13:29	15:23	16:47

International Ascendant Tables

I – L

Your Starway to Love

♈ = Aries ♉ = Taurus ♊ = Gemini ♋ = Cancer ♌ = Leo ♍ = Virgo

City	Zone	->EST	♈	♉	♊	♋	♌	♍	♎	♏	♐	♑	♒	♓
Indonesia, continued														
Pakanbaru	SST	-12.00	18:14	20:05	22:05	0:13	2:22	4:22	6:14	8:06	10:06	12:15	14:24	16:23
Palembang	SST	-12.00	18:01	19:55	21:57	0:06	2:14	4:12	6:01	7:50	9:48	11:56	14:05	16:07
Pema										8:18	10:19	12:29	14:37	16:35
Ponti										8:34	10:34	12:43	14:51	16:51
Sama										8:03	10:02	12:11	14:19	16:19
Sema										7:24	9:19	11:26	13:37	15:41
Surab										7:15	9:10	11:16	13:27	15:31
Surak										7:22	9:17	11:23	13:34	15:39
Teluk										7:46	9:42	11:49	14:00	16:03
Ujung Pandang										7:50	9:46	11:53	14:04	16:07
Yogyakarta	SST	-12.00	17:39	19:37	21:41	23:52	1:59	3:53	5:39	7:24	9:18	11:25	13:36	15:41
Iran														
Abadan	-3.5	-8.50	18:17	19:41	21:19	23:18	1:36	3:58	6:17	8:36	10:58	13:16	15:15	16:53
Esfahan	-3.5	-8.50	18:03	19:25	21:00	22:59	1:18	3:42	6:03	8:25	10:49	13:08	15:07	16:42
Mashhad	-3.5	-8.50	17:32	18:49	20:20	22:17	0:38	3:06	5:32	7:58	10:25	12:46	14:43	16:14
Tabri										8:53	11:23	13:44	15:40	17:10
Tehra										8:29	10:57	13:17	15:14	16:46
Iraq														
Bagh										8:25	10:50	13:09	15:07	16:41
Irela														
Belfa										9:22	12:19	14:54	16:37	17:38
Cork										9:26	12:17	14:48	16:34	17:42
Dublin										9:20	12:14	14:48	16:32	17:37
Israel														
Jerusalem		-7.00	17:39	19:02	20:38	22:37	0:55	3:19	5:39	8:00	10:23	12:41	14:40	16:16
TelAviv	EET	-7.00	17:41	19:03	20:39	22:38	0:56	3:20	5:41	8:02	10:25	12:44	14:43	16:19
Italy														
	MET	-6.00	17:53	19:03	20:29	22:24	0:47	3:20	5:53	8:25	10:59	13:22	15:16	16:42
Bologna	MET	-6.00	18:15	19:20	20:41	22:34	0:59	3:37	6:15	8:52	11:30	13:56	15:48	17:09
Catania	MET	-6.00	18:00	19:15	20:45	22:42	1:03	3:32	6:00	8:27	10:56	13:17	15:14	16:44
Florence	MET	-6.00	18:15	19:22	20:44	22:37	1:01	3:39	6:15	8:51	11:29	13:53	15:46	17:08
Milan	MET	-6.00	18:23	19:27	20:47	22:39	1:04	3:44	6:23	9:02	11:42	14:08	16:00	17:19
Naples	**MET**	**-6.00**	**18:03**	**19:14**	**20:40**	**22:35**	**0:58**	**3:31**	**6:03**	**8:35**	**11:08**	**13:31**	**15:26**	**16:52**
Palermo														
Rome	MET	-6.00	18:10	19:20	20:44	22:38	1:02	3:36	6:10	8:44	11:18	13:42	15:36	17:00
Torino	MET	-6.00	18:29	19:34	20:54	22:46	1:12	3:51	6:29	9:08	11:47	14:12	16:04	17:25
Trieste	MET	-6.00	18:05	19:09	20:28	22:20	0:45	3:25	6:05	8:45	11:24	13:50	15:42	17:01
Venic										8:50	11:29	13:55	15:47	17:07
Ivory														
Abidj										8:12	10:15	12:25	14:33	16:29
Boua										8:18	10:23	12:34	14:40	16:35
Jama														
Kings										8:14	10:26	12:40	14:43	16:31
Japa														
Fukuoka	JST	-14.00	18:18	19:39	21:13	23:11	1:31	3:56	6:18	8:41	11:06	13:25	15:24	16:58
Kawasaki	JST	-14.00	18:17	19:37	21:12	23:10	1:29	3:54	6:17	8:39	11:04	13:24	15:22	16:56
Kyoto	JST	-14.00	17:57	19:16	20:49	22:46	1:06	3:33	5:57	8:21	10:48	13:08	15:05	16:38
Naha	JST	-14.00	18:29	19:58	21:39	23:40	1:56	4:15	6:29	8:44	11:02	13:19	15:20	17:01
Niigata	JST	-14.00	17:44	18:59	20:29	22:25	0:46	3:16	5:44	8:12	10:42	13:03	14:59	16:29
Osaka	JST	-14.00	17:58	19:17	20:50	22:48	1:08	3:34	5:58	8:22	10:48	13:08	15:06	16:39
Sapporo	JST	-14.00	17:35	18:43	20:06	21:59	0:23	2:59	5:35					
Toky														
Jord														
Amm														
Kamp														
Phno														
Keny														
Momb														
Nairobi	BT	-8.00	18:33	20:25	22:26	0:35	2:43	4:42	6:33					
Laos														
Vientiane	SST	-12.00	18:10	19:46	21:34	23:37	1:51	4:03	6:10					
Latvia														
Riga	BT	-8.00	19:24	20:03	20:57	22:36	1:15	4:19	7:24					

1 Turn to the page containing the country in which you were born.

2 Select the country in which you were born.

3 Locate the city in which (or near which) you were born.
Find the time that is just before your **Star Time**. Note the sign of the zodiac listed at the top of that column on your worksheet.

4 Repeats steps 1, 2 and 3 for your partner's birthday.

***** Cities in the former U.S.S.R. are still listed under U.S.S.R. as a country, as most readers would have been born in what was known as the Union of Soviet Socialist Republics.

International Ascendant Tables

♎ = Libra ♏ = Scorpio ♐ = Sagittarius ♑ = Capricorn ♒ = Aquarius ♓ = Pisces

City	Zone	->EST	♈	♉	♊	♋	♌	♍	♎	♏	♐	♑	♒	♓
Afghanistan														
Herat	-4.5	-9.50	18:21	19:41	21:14	23:12	1:32	3:58	6:21	8:45	11:11	13:30	15:28	17:01
Kabul	-4.5	-9.50	17:53	19:13	20:46	22:44	1:03	3:29	5:53	8:17	10:43	13:03	15:00	16:34
Albania														
Tirane	MET	-6.00	17:41	18:51	20:17	22:11	0:34	3:08	5:41	8:13	10:47	13:10	15:05	16:30
Algeria														
Algiers	MET	-6.00	18:48	20:05	21:35	23:32	1:53	4:21	6:48	9:14	11:43	14:03	16:00	17:31
Oran	MET	-6.00	19:03	20:21	21:53	23:50	2:10	4:38	7:03	9:28	11:55	14:16	16:13	17:45
Qacentina	MET	-6.00	18:34	19:51	21:22	23:19	1:40	4:08	6:34	9:00	11:28	13:48	15:45	17:16
Angola														
Huambo	MET	-6.00	17:57	19:59	22:07	0:19	2:25	4:16	5:57	7:38	9:29	11:34	13:47	15:55
Lobito	MET	-6.00	18:06	20:08	22:15	0:28	2:33	4:24	6:06	7:47	9:39	11:44	13:56	16:04
Luanda	MET	-6.00	18:07	20:06	22:11	0:22	2:29	4:23	6:07	7:51	9:45	11:52	14:03	16:08
Argentina														
Bahia Blanca	BZ2	-2.00	19:09	21:38	0:09	2:31	4:26	5:55	7:09	8:23	9:52	11:48	14:09	16:40
Buenos Aires	BZ2	-2.00	18:54	21:18	23:44	2:03	4:01	5:34	6:54	8:13	9:46	11:44	14:04	16:30
Comodoro Rivadavia	BZ2	-2.00	19:30	22:10	0:50	3:16	5:08	6:27	7:30	8:33	9:52	11:44	14:10	16:50
Cordoba	BZ2	-2.00	19:17	21:37	0:00	2:18	4:17	5:54	7:17	8:40	10:16	12:15	14:34	16:57
Corrientes	BZ2	-2.00	18:55	21:11	23:31	1:47	3:48	5:28	6:55	8:23	10:03	12:03	14:20	16:39
Mardel Plata	BZ2	-2.00	18:50	21:18	23:48	2:09	4:06	5:35	6:50	8:05	9:35	11:31	13:52	16:22
Mendoza	BZ2	-2.00	19:35	21:57	0:21	2:40	4:39	6:14	7:35	8:57	10:32	12:30	14:49	17:13
Rio Cuarto	BZ2	-2.00	19:17	21:39	0:04	2:23	4:22	5:56	7:17	8:39	10:13	12:12	14:31	16:55
Rosario	BZ2	-2.00	19:03	21:25	23:49	2:08	4:06	5:41	7:03	8:24	9:59	11:57	14:16	16:41
San Miguel de Tucuman	BZ2	-2.00	19:21	21:36	23:55	2:12	4:12	5:53	7:21	8:49	10:29	12:30	14:47	17:06
Santa Fe	BZ2	-2.00	19:03	21:23	23:46	2:05	4:04	5:40	7:03	8:26	10:02	12:01	14:19	16:42
Australia														
Albury	EST	-15.00	18:12	20:38	23:06	1:26	3:23	4:55	6:12	7:30	9:02	10:59	13:19	15:47
Brisbane	EST	-15.00	17:48	20:04	22:23	0:40	2:41	4:20	5:48	7:15	8:55	10:56	13:13	15:32
Bunbury	WST	-13.00	18:17	20:40	23:05	1:24	3:22	4:57	6:17	7:38	9:13	11:11	13:30	15:55
Cairns	EST	-15.00	18:17	20:23	22:34	0:47	2:51	4:39	6:17	7:54	9:43	11:47	14:00	16:11
Canberra	EST	-15.00	18:03	20:28	22:55	1:15	3:12	4:45	6:03	7:22	8:55	10:52	13:12	15:39
Darwin	CST	-14.50	18:47	20:49	22:57	1:09	3:14	5:05	6:47	8:28	10:19	12:25	14:37	16:45
Geraldton	WST	-13.00	18:22	20:39	22:59	1:17	3:17	4:56	6:22	7:48	9:26	11:26	13:44	16:04
Hobart	EST	-15.00	18:11	20:46	23:22	1:46	3:39	5:03	6:11	7:19	8:42	10:36	13:00	15:36
Ipswich	EST	-15.00	17:49	20:05	22:24	0:41	2:42	4:22	5:49	7:16	8:56	10:57	13:13	15:33
Kalgoorlie	WST	-13.00	17:54	20:14	22:36	0:54	2:53	4:30	5:54	7:18	8:55	10:54	13:12	15:35
Katherine	CST	-14.50	18:41	20:45	22:54	1:07	3:11	5:01	6:41	8:21	10:10	12:15	14:28	16:37
Launceston	EST	-15.00	18:11	20:44	23:18	1:42	3:36	5:01	6:11	7:22	8:47	10:41	13:05	15:39
Melbourne	EST	-15.00	18:20	20:48	23:18	1:39	3:35	5:05	6:20	7:36	9:05	11:01	13:23	15:52
Newcastle	EST	-15.00	17:53	20:15	22:39	0:58	2:57	4:32	5:53	7:14	8:49	10:48	13:07	15:31
Parramatta	EST	-15.00	17:56	20:19	22:44	1:04	3:02	4:36	5:56	7:16	8:50	10:48	13:08	15:33
Perth	WST	-13.00	18:17	20:37	23:01	1:19	3:18	4:54	6:17	7:39	9:15	11:14	13:32	15:56
Rockhampton	EST	-15.00	17:58	20:10	22:26	0:41	2:43	4:26	5:58	7:29	9:13	11:15	13:30	15:46
Southport	EST	-15.00	17:46	20:03	22:23	0:40	2:40	4:19	5:46	7:13	8:53	10:53	13:10	15:30
Sydney	EST	-15.00	17:55	20:18	22:43	1:03	3:01	4:35	5:55	7:15	8:49	10:47	13:07	15:32
Toowoomba	EST	-15.00	17:52	20:08	22:28	0:45	2:45	4:25	5:52	7:20	8:59	11:00	13:17	15:36
Townsville	EST	-15.00	18:13	20:21	22:34	0:48	2:51	4:37	6:13	7:48	9:35	11:38	13:52	16:05
Wollongong	EST	-15.00	17:56	20:20	22:46	1:06	3:03	4:37	5:56	7:16	8:49	10:47	13:07	15:33
Austria														
Vienna	MET	-6.00	17:55	18:54	20:09	21:59	0:26	3:11	5:55	8:39	11:23	13:51	15:40	16:56
Bangladesh														
Chittagong	90E	-11.00	17:53	19:25	21:09	23:12	1:27	3:42	5:53	8:03	10:19	12:34	14:36	16:20
Dacca	90E	-11.00	17:58	19:30	21:12	23:14	1:30	3:46	5:58	8:10	10:27	12:42	14:44	16:27
Belgium														
Antwerp	MET	-6.00	18:42	19:35	20:45	22:32	1:02	3:52	6:42	9:33	12:22	14:53	16:40	17:49
Brussels	MET	-6.00	18:43	19:37	20:47	22:34	1:04	3:53	6:43	9:32	12:21	14:51	16:39	17:49
Liege	MET	-6.00	18:38	19:32	20:43	22:30	1:00	3:49	6:38	9:27	12:15	14:45	16:33	17:43
Belize														
Belize City	CST	1.00	17:53	19:30	21:17	23:21	1:35	3:46	5:53	7:59	10:11	12:24	14:28	16:16
Benin														
Porto-Novo	MET	-6.00	18:50	20:36	22:31	0:38	2:49	4:53	6:50	8:46	10:50	13:01	15:08	17:03
Bolivia														
Cochabamba	AST	-1.00	18:25	20:31	22:42	0:56	3:00	4:48	6:25	8:02	9:49	11:53	14:07	16:18
La Paz	AST	-1.00	18:33	20:38	22:49	1:02	3:06	4:55	6:33	8:10	9:59	12:03	14:16	16:27
Oruro	AST	-1.00	18:29	20:35	22:47	1:01	3:05	4:52	6:29	8:05	9:52	11:56	14:10	16:22

♈ = Aries ♉ = Taurus ♊ = Gemini ♋ = Cancer ♌ = Leo ♍ = Virgo

City	Zone	->EST	♈	♉	♊	♋	♌	♍	♎	♏	♐	♑	♒	♓
Bolivia, continued														
Potosi	AST	-1.00	18:23	20:31	22:44	0:59	3:02	4:48	6:23	7:58	9:44	11:47	14:02	16:15
Santa Cruz	AST	-1.00	18:13	20:19	22:31	0:45	2:48	4:36	6:13	7:49	9:37	11:41	13:54	16:06
Sucre	AST	-1.00	18:21	20:29	22:42	0:56	2:59	4:46	6:21	7:57	9:43	11:47	14:01	16:13
Bophuthatswana														
Mmabatho	EET	-7.00	18:18	20:32	22:50	1:06	3:07	4:49	6:18	7:47	9:28	11:29	13:46	16:04
Botswana														
Gaborone	EET	-7.00	18:16	20:29	22:47	1:02	3:04	4:46	6:16	7:46	9:29	11:30	13:46	16:03
Lobatse	EET	-7.00	18:17	20:31	22:48	1:04	3:06	4:48	6:17	7:47	9:29	11:30	13:46	16:04
Serowe	EET	-7.00	18:13	20:24	22:39	0:54	2:57	4:41	6:13	7:45	9:29	11:32	13:47	16:02
Brazil														
Belem	BZ2	-2.00	18:14	20:07	22:07	0:16	2:25	4:23	6:14	8:04	10:03	12:11	14:21	16:21
Belo Horizonte	BZ2	-2.00	17:56	20:04	22:18	0:32	2:35	4:21	5:56	7:30	9:16	11:20	13:34	15:47
Brasilia	BZ2	-2.00	18:12	20:16	22:27	0:40	2:44	4:33	6:12	7:50	9:39	11:43	13:57	16:07
Campo Grande	AST	-1.00	17:38	19:47	22:01	0:16	2:19	4:04	5:38	7:13	8:58	11:01	13:16	15:29
Corumba	AST	-1.00	17:51	19:58	22:11	0:25	2:28	4:15	5:51	7:26	9:13	11:16	13:30	15:43
Cuiaba	AST	-1.00	17:44	19:49	21:59	0:12	2:17	4:06	5:44	7:23	9:12	11:17	13:30	15:40
Curitiba	BZ2	-2.00	18:17	20:31	22:48	1:05	3:06	4:48	6:17	7:46	9:28	11:29	13:46	16:03
Fortaleza	BZ2	-2.00	17:34	19:29	21:31	23:40	1:48	3:45	5:34	7:23	9:20	11:28	13:37	15:39
Imperatriz	BZ2	-2.00	18:10	20:06	22:09	0:20	2:27	4:23	6:10	7:57	9:53	12:00	14:11	16:14
Maceio	BZ2	-2.00	17:23	19:22	21:28	23:40	1:46	3:39	5:23	7:07	9:00	11:06	13:17	15:23
Manaus	AST	-1.00	18:00	19:54	21:56	0:06	2:13	4:11	6:00	7:49	9:47	11:55	14:04	16:06
Porto Alegre	BZ2	-2.00	18:25	20:43	23:05	1:23	3:23	5:00	6:25	7:49	9:27	11:27	13:44	16:06
Porto Velho	AST	-1.00	18:16	20:14	22:20	0:31	2:37	4:31	6:16	8:00	9:54	12:00	14:11	16:17
Recife	BZ2	-2.00	17:20	19:18	21:23	23:34	1:40	3:35	5:20	7:05	8:59	11:06	13:16	15:21
Rio de Janeiro	BZ2	-2.00	17:53	20:04	22:20	0:35	2:37	4:21	5:53	7:25	9:09	11:11	13:26	15:42
Salvador	BZ2	-2.00	17:34	19:36	21:45	23:57	2:02	3:53	5:34	7:15	9:06	11:11	13:23	15:32
Santanado Livramento	AST	-1.00	17:42	20:02	22:24	0:42	2:42	4:18	5:42	7:06	8:43	10:42	13:00	15:23
Santarem	AST	-1.00	17:39	19:32	21:34	23:43	1:51	3:49	5:39	7:28	9:26	11:35	13:44	15:45
Santos	BZ2	-2.00	18:05	20:18	22:34	0:50	2:52	4:34	6:05	7:36	9:19	11:21	13:37	15:53
Sao Paulo	BZ2	-2.00	18:06	20:18	22:35	0:50	2:52	4:35	6:06	7:38	9:21	11:23	13:38	15:55
Teresina	BZ2	-2.00	17:51	19:47	21:50	0:00	2:07	4:04	5:51	7:39	9:35	11:42	13:53	15:55
Vitoria	BZ2	-2.00	17:41	19:50	22:04	0:18	2:21	4:07	5:41	7:16	9:01	11:04	13:19	15:33
Brunei														
Bandar Seri Begawan	WST	-13.00	18:20	20:08	22:04	0:12	2:22	4:25	6:20	8:16	10:19	12:29	14:36	16:33
Bulgaria														
Plovdiv	EET	-7.00	18:21	19:30	20:55	22:49	1:12	3:47	6:21	8:55	11:30	13:53	15:47	17:12
Sofia	EET	-7.00	18:27	19:35	20:59	22:52	1:16	3:52	6:27	9:02	11:37	14:01	15:55	17:18
Varna	EET	-7.00	18:08	19:16	20:39	22:32	0:56	3:33	6:08	8:44	11:20	13:45	15:38	17:01
Burkina Faso														
Bobo Dioulasso	GMT	-5.00	18:17	20:00	21:52	23:57	2:09	4:16	6:17	8:18	10:25	12:37	14:43	16:35
Ouagadougou	GMT	-5.00	18:06	19:47	21:39	23:44	1:56	4:04	6:06	8:08	10:16	12:28	14:33	16:25
Burma														
Mandalay	NST	-11.50	18:06	19:38	21:23	23:25	1:40	3:55	6:06	8:16	10:31	12:46	14:49	16:33
Rangoon	NST	-11.50	18:05	19:43	21:31	23:35	1:49	4:00	6:05	8:11	10:22	12:35	14:39	16:28
Burundi														
Bujumbura	EET	-7.00	18:03	19:57	21:59	0:08	2:16	4:14	6:03	7:51	9:49	11:57	14:06	16:08
Cameroon														
Bafoussam	MET	-6.00	18:18	20:06	22:02	0:09	2:19	4:22	6:18	8:15	10:18	12:28	14:35	16:31
Douala	MET	-6.00	18:21	20:10	22:07	0:14	2:24	4:26	6:21	8:16	10:18	12:28	14:36	16:33
Yaounde	MET	-6.00	18:14	20:02	22:00	0:07	2:17	4:19	6:14	8:09	10:11	12:21	14:28	16:25
Canada														
Brandon, MB	CST	1.00	18:40	19:36	20:48	22:36	1:05	3:52	6:40	9:27	12:14	14:43	16:32	17:44
Calgary, AB	MST	2.00	18:36	19:30	20:40	22:27	0:57	3:47	6:36	9:26	12:16	14:46	16:33	17:43
Chicoutimi, QU	EST	0.00	17:44	18:43	19:58	21:47	0:15	3:00	5:44	8:29	11:13	13:41	15:31	16:46
Corner Brook,NF	NST	-1.50	18:22	19:20	20:33	22:22	0:51	3:36	6:22	9:07	11:53	14:21	16:10	17:24
Edmonton, AB	MST	2.00	18:34	19:22	20:26	22:10	0:43	3:38	6:34	9:29	12:24	14:58	16:42	17:46
Fredericton, NB	AST	-1.00	18:27	19:30	20:49	22:40	1:06	3:46	6:27	9:07	11:47	14:13	16:05	17:23
Halifax, NS	AST	-1.00	18:14	19:20	20:41	22:33	0:58	3:36	6:14	8:52	11:31	13:56	15:48	17:09
Hamilton, ON	EST	0.00	18:19	19:27	20:50	22:43	1:07	3:44	6:19	8:55	11:31	13:56	15:49	17:12
Kelowna, BC	PST	3.00	17:58	18:54	20:06	21:54	0:23	3:11	5:58	8:45	11:33	14:02	15:50	17:02
Kenora, ON	CST	1.00	18:18	19:14	20:26	22:14	0:44	3:31	6:18	9:05	11:52	14:21	16:10	17:22
London, ON	EST	0.00	18:25	19:33	20:56	22:50	1:14	3:50	6:25	9:00	11:36	14:00	15:54	17:17
Medicine Hat, AB	MST	2.00	18:23	19:18	20:30	22:18	0:47	3:35	6:23	9:10	11:58	14:27	16:15	17:27
Moncton, NB	AST	-1.00	18:19	19:22	20:41	22:32	0:58	3:39	6:19	8:59	11:40	14:06	15:58	17:16

♎ = Libra ♏ = Scorpio ♐ = Sagittarius ♑ = Capricorn ♒ = Aquarius ♓ = Pisces

City	Zone	->EST	♈	♉	♊	♋	♌	♍	♎	♏	♐	♑	♒	♓
Canada, continued														
Montreal, QU	EST	0.00	17:54	18:58	20:18	22:09	0:35	3:15	5:54	8:34	11:13	13:39	15:31	16:50
Moose Jaw, SK	MST	2.00	18:02	18:57	20:08	21:56	0:26	3:14	6:02	8:51	11:39	14:09	15:56	17:07
Ottawa, ON	EST	0.00	18:03	19:07	20:27	22:18	0:44	3:24	6:03	8:42	11:22	13:47	15:39	16:59
Prince George, BC	PST	3.00	18:11	18:58	20:01	21:45	0:19	3:15	6:11	9:07	12:03	14:37	16:21	17:24
Prince Rupert, BC	PST	3.00	18:41	19:27	20:30	22:13	0:47	3:44	6:41	9:39	12:36	15:10	16:53	17:55
Quebec, QU	EST	0.00	17:45	18:47	20:04	21:55	0:22	3:03	5:45	8:27	11:08	13:35	15:26	16:43
Regina, SK	MST	2.00	17:59	18:53	20:04	21:52	0:22	3:10	5:59	8:47	11:35	14:05	15:53	17:04
Saskatoon, SK	MST	2.00	18:07	18:58	20:05	21:51	0:23	3:14	6:07	8:59	11:50	14:22	16:08	17:15
St. John, NB	AST	-1.00	18:24	19:29	20:48	22:40	1:06	3:45	6:24	9:03	11:42	14:08	16:00	17:20
Sudbury, ON	EST	0.00	18:24	19:26	20:44	22:35	1:02	3:43	6:24	9:05	11:46	14:13	16:04	17:22
Sydney, NS	AST	-1.00	18:01	19:04	20:22	22:13	0:40	3:20	6:01	8:41	11:22	13:48	15:39	16:58
Thunder Bay, ON	EST	0.00	18:57	19:56	21:11	23:00	1:28	4:13	6:57	9:41	12:26	14:54	16:43	17:58
Toronto, ON	EST	0.00	18:18	19:25	20:47	22:40	1:04	3:41	6:18	8:54	11:31	13:55	15:48	17:11
Vancouver, BC	PST	3.00	18:12	19:10	20:23	22:11	0:40	3:26	6:12	8:59	11:45	14:13	16:02	17:15
Victoria, BC	PST	3.00	18:13	19:12	20:27	22:16	0:44	3:29	6:13	8:58	11:42	14:11	16:00	17:15
Winnipeg, MB	CST	1.00	18:29	19:24	20:37	22:25	0:54	3:41	6:29	9:16	12:03	14:33	16:21	17:33
Central African Republic														
Bangui	MET	-6.00	17:46	19:34	21:31	23:38	1:48	3:50	5:46	7:41	9:43	11:53	14:01	15:58
Chad														
N'Djamena	MET	-6.00	18:00	19:41	21:33	23:38	1:50	3:58	6:00	8:01	10:09	12:21	14:27	16:18
Chile														
Antofagasta	AST	-1.00	18:42	20:54	23:10	1:25	3:27	5:10	6:42	8:13	9:56	11:58	14:13	16:30
Arica	AST	-1.00	18:41	20:49	23:01	1:15	3:18	5:05	6:41	8:17	10:04	12:08	14:22	16:34
Concepcion	AST	-1.00	18:52	21:19	23:47	2:08	4:05	5:36	6:52	8:09	9:40	11:36	13:57	16:26
Iquique	AST	-1.00	18:41	20:49	23:03	1:17	3:20	5:06	6:41	8:15	10:01	12:04	14:18	16:32
Puerto Montt	AST	-1.00	18:52	21:25	23:59	2:22	4:16	5:42	6:52	8:02	9:27	11:22	13:45	16:19
Santiago	AST	-1.00	18:43	21:05	23:30	1:49	3:48	5:22	6:43	8:03	9:38	11:36	13:55	16:20
Temuco	AST	-1.00	18:50	21:20	23:50	2:12	4:08	5:36	6:50	8:05	9:33	11:29	13:51	16:21
Valparaiso	AST	-1.00	18:47	21:09	23:33	1:52	3:51	5:25	6:47	8:08	9:43	11:41	14:00	16:25
China														
Beijing	WST	-13.00	18:14	19:27	20:54	22:49	1:12	3:44	6:14	8:45	11:17	13:39	15:35	17:02
Canton	WST	-13.00	18:27	19:59	21:42	23:44	2:00	4:15	6:27	8:38	10:54	13:10	15:12	16:55
Chengdu	WST	-13.00	19:04	20:28	22:05	0:04	2:22	4:44	7:04	9:23	11:45	14:03	16:03	17:40
Chungking	WST	-13.00	18:54	20:19	21:57	23:57	2:14	4:36	6:54	9:12	11:33	13:51	15:50	17:28
Harbin	WST	-13.00	17:33	18:37	19:56	21:48	0:13	2:54	5:33	8:13	10:53	13:19	15:11	16:30
Kunming	WST	-13.00	19:09	20:39	22:21	0:22	2:38	4:56	7:09	9:23	11:40	13:56	15:58	17:40
Lhasa	WST	-13.00	19:55	21:20	22:58	0:58	3:16	5:37	7:55	10:14	12:35	14:53	16:52	18:30
Nanking	WST	-13.00	18:05	19:27	21:03	23:02	1:20	3:44	6:05	8:26	10:49	13:08	15:07	16:42
Shanghai	WST	-13.00	17:54	19:17	20:54	22:53	1:11	3:34	5:54	8:14	10:37	12:55	14:54	16:31
Shenyang	WST	-13.00	17:46	18:56	20:21	22:15	0:38	3:13	5:46	8:20	10:54	13:17	15:12	16:36
Tientsin	WST	-13.00	18:11	19:25	20:53	22:49	1:10	3:42	6:11	8:41	11:12	13:34	15:29	16:58
Wuhan	WST	-13.00	18:23	19:47	21:24	23:23	1:41	4:04	6:23	8:42	11:04	13:22	15:22	16:59
Xi'an	WST	-13.00	18:45	20:04	21:38	23:36	1:55	4:21	6:45	9:08	11:34	13:53	15:51	17:25
Ciskei														
Bisho	EET	-7.00	18:11	20:32	22:57	1:16	3:14	4:49	6:11	7:32	9:07	11:06	13:25	15:49
Colombia														
Barranquilla	EST	0.00	17:59	19:42	21:34	23:40	1:52	3:59	5:59	8:00	10:07	12:19	14:24	16:17
Bogota	EST	0.00	17:56	19:44	21:41	23:48	1:58	4:01	5:56	7:52	9:54	12:04	14:12	16:08
Buenaventura	EST	0.00	18:08	19:57	21:54	0:02	2:11	4:13	6:08	8:03	10:05	12:15	14:23	16:20
Cali	EST	0.00	18:06	19:55	21:52	0:00	2:10	4:12	6:06	8:01	10:02	12:12	14:20	16:17
Cartagena	EST	0.00	18:02	19:45	21:38	23:44	1:55	4:02	6:02	8:02	10:09	12:20	14:26	16:19
Cucuta	EST	0.00	17:50	19:35	21:30	23:36	1:47	3:52	5:50	7:48	9:53	12:04	14:10	16:05
Medellin	EST	0.00	18:02	19:49	21:44	23:51	2:02	4:06	6:02	7:59	10:03	12:13	14:20	16:16
Pasto	EST	0.00	18:09	20:00	21:59	0:07	2:16	4:17	6:09	8:02	10:02	12:11	14:20	16:18
Congo														
Brazzaville	MET	-6.00	17:59	19:54	21:56	0:06	2:14	4:11	5:59	7:47	9:44	11:51	14:01	16:04
Pointe-Noire	MET	-6.00	18:13	20:08	22:11	0:21	2:28	4:25	6:13	8:00	9:57	12:04	14:14	16:17
Costa Rica														
SanJose	CST	1.00	17:36	19:20	21:13	23:19	1:30	3:37	5:36	7:36	9:42	11:54	14:00	15:53
Cuba														
Havana	EST	0.00	18:29	20:01	21:45	23:47	2:02	4:18	6:29	8:41	10:57	13:12	15:14	16:58
Czechoslovakia														
Bratislava	MET	-6.00	17:52	18:51	20:06	21:56	0:23	3:07	5:52	8:36	11:20	13:47	15:37	16:52
Brno	MET	-6.00	17:54	18:51	20:04	21:53	0:22	3:07	5:54	8:40	11:25	13:54	15:43	16:56

♈ = Aries ♉ = Taurus ♊ = Gemini ♋ = Cancer ♌ = Leo ♍ = Virgo

City	Zone	—>EST	♈	♉	♊	♋	♌	♍	♎	♏	♐	♑	♒	♓
Czechoslovakia, continued														
Kosice	MET	-6.00	17:35	18:33	19:47	21:37	0:05	2:50	5:35	8:20	11:05	13:33	15:23	16:37
Ostrava	MET	-6.00	17:47	18:43	19:55	21:43	0:12	3:00	5:47	8:34	11:21	13:51	15:39	16:51
Prague	MET	-6.00	18:02	18:58	20:09	21:57	0:27	3:14	6:02	8:50	11:38	14:07	15:55	17:07
Denmark														
Arhus	MET	-6.00	18:19	19:00	19:58	21:38	0:15	3:17	6:19	9:21	12:23	15:00	16:41	17:38
Copenhagen	MET	-6.00	18:10	18:52	19:51	21:32	0:08	3:09	6:10	9:10	12:11	14:47	16:28	17:27
Djibouti														
Djibouti	BT	-8.00	18:07	19:49	21:41	23:47	1:59	4:06	6:07	8:09	10:16	12:28	14:33	16:25
Dominican Republic														
Santo Domingo	AST	-1.00	18:40	20:16	22:03	0:06	2:20	4:32	6:40	8:47	10:59	13:13	15:16	17:04
Ecuador														
Cuenca	EST	0.00	18:16	20:10	22:11	0:21	2:29	4:27	6:16	8:05	10:03	12:11	14:20	16:22
Guayaquil	EST	0.00	18:19	20:13	22:14	0:23	2:31	4:29	6:19	8:09	10:07	12:16	14:25	16:26
Quito	EST	0.00	18:14	20:06	22:06	0:14	2:23	4:23	6:14	8:05	10:05	12:14	14:22	16:22
Egypt														
Alexandria	EET	-7.00	18:00	19:24	21:00	22:59	1:18	3:41	6:00	8:20	10:43	13:01	15:01	16:37
Cairo	EET	-7.00	17:55	19:20	20:57	22:57	1:15	3:36	5:55	8:14	10:35	12:53	14:53	16:30
Port Said	EET	-7.00	17:51	19:14	20:51	22:50	1:08	3:31	5:51	8:11	10:34	12:52	14:51	16:27
Suez	EET	-7.00	17:50	19:15	20:52	22:52	1:10	3:31	5:50	8:08	10:30	12:48	14:47	16:25
El Salvador														
San Salvador	CST	1.00	17:57	19:37	21:28	23:33	1:45	3:54	5:57	8:00	10:09	12:21	14:26	16:17
England														
Birmingham	GMT	-5.00	18:07	18:58	20:04	21:50	0:22	3:14	6:07	9:00	11:53	14:25	16:10	17:17
Liverpool	GMT	-5.00	18:12	19:00	20:04	21:49	0:22	3:17	6:12	9:07	12:02	14:35	16:19	17:24
London	GMT	-5.00	18:01	18:53	20:02	21:48	0:19	3:10	6:01	8:51	11:42	14:13	15:59	17:08
Manchester	GMT	-5.00	18:09	18:57	20:01	21:45	0:19	3:14	6:09	9:04	11:59	14:33	16:17	17:21
Ethiopia														
Addis Ababa	BT	-8.00	18:25	20:09	22:03	0:09	2:21	4:26	6:25	8:24	10:30	12:41	14:47	16:41
Asmera	BT	-8.00	18:24	20:03	21:53	23:57	2:10	4:20	6:24	8:29	10:39	12:52	14:56	16:46
Gonder	BT	-8.00	18:30	20:11	22:02	0:08	2:20	4:28	6:30	8:32	10:40	12:52	14:58	16:49
Jima	BT	-8.00	18:33	20:18	22:13	0:19	2:30	4:35	6:33	8:31	10:35	12:46	14:53	16:47
Falkland Islands														
Stanley	AST	-1.00	17:51	20:43	23:33	2:05	3:51	4:59	5:51	6:43	7:52	9:38	12:09	15:00
Fiji														
Lautoka	NZT	-17.00	18:10	20:17	22:28	0:42	2:46	4:33	6:10	7:47	9:35	11:39	13:52	16:04
Suva	NZT	-17.00	18:06	20:13	22:25	0:39	2:43	4:30	6:06	7:43	9:30	11:34	13:47	15:59
Finland														
Helsinki	EET	-7.00	18:20	18:49	19:32	21:04	23:50	3:06	6:20	9:35	12:51	15:37	17:08	17:51
Oulu	EET	-7.00	18:18	18:26	18:41	19:44	22:59	2:43	6:18	9:53	13:37	16:52	17:55	18:10
France														
Bordeaux	MET	-6.00	19:02	20:07	21:28	23:20	1:45	4:24	7:02	9:40	12:19	14:44	16:37	17:57
Lille	MET	-6.00	18:48	19:42	20:53	22:40	1:10	3:59	6:48	9:37	12:25	14:55	16:43	17:53
Lyon	MET	-6.00	18:41	19:44	21:03	22:55	1:21	4:01	6:41	9:20	12:00	14:26	16:18	17:37
Marseille	MET	-6.00	18:38	19:46	21:09	23:02	1:26	4:03	6:38	9:14	11:51	14:15	16:08	17:31
Nantes	MET	-6.00	19:06	20:07	21:24	23:14	1:41	4:24	7:06	9:49	12:31	14:58	16:48	18:05
Paris	MET	-6.00	18:51	19:49	21:03	22:52	1:20	4:05	6:51	9:36	12:21	14:50	16:39	17:53
Rouen	MET	-6.00	18:56	19:52	21:05	22:54	1:23	4:09	6:56	9:42	12:28	14:57	16:46	17:59
Strasbourg	MET	-6.00	18:29	19:27	20:42	22:31	0:59	3:44	6:29	9:14	11:59	14:27	16:16	17:31
Toulouse	MET	-6.00	18:54	20:01	21:24	23:17	1:41	4:18	6:54	9:30	12:07	14:32	16:25	17:47
French Guyana														
Cayenne	BZ2	-2.00	18:29	20:17	22:13	0:21	2:31	4:34	6:29	8:25	10:28	12:38	14:45	16:42
Gabon														
Libreville	MET	-6.00	18:22	20:14	22:13	0:22	2:30	4:30	6:22	8:14	10:14	12:23	14:31	16:31
Gambia														
Banjul	GMT	-5.00	19:07	20:47	22:38	0:43	2:55	5:04	7:07	9:09	11:18	13:30	15:36	17:26
Germany														
Berlin	MET	-6.00	18:07	18:57	20:03	21:49	0:21	3:14	6:07	9:00	11:52	14:24	16:10	17:16
Bonn	MET	-6.00	18:32	19:26	20:36	22:23	0:54	3:43	6:32	9:21	12:10	14:40	16:27	17:38
Bremen	MET	-6.00	18:25	19:14	20:19	22:04	0:37	3:30	6:25	9:19	12:13	14:46	16:30	17:36
Cologne	MET	-6.00	18:32	19:26	20:36	22:23	0:53	3:42	6:32	9:22	12:11	14:41	16:28	17:38
Dusseldorf	MET	-6.00	18:33	19:26	20:35	22:22	0:53	3:43	6:33	9:23	12:13	14:43	16:30	17:40
Essen	MET	-6.00	18:32	19:24	20:33	22:20	0:51	3:41	6:32	9:23	12:13	14:44	16:30	17:39
Frankfurt	MET	-6.00	18:25	19:21	20:32	22:20	0:50	3:37	6:25	9:13	12:01	14:30	16:18	17:30

♎ = Libra ♏ = Scorpio ♐ = Sagittarius ♑ = Capricorn ♒ = Aquarius ♓ = Pisces

City	Zone	->EST	♈	♉	♊	♋	♌	♍	♎	♏	♐	♑	♒	♓
Germany, continued														
Hamburg	MET	-6.00	18:20	19:08	20:12	21:56	0:30	3:25	6:20	9:16	12:11	14:44	16:28	17:32
Hannover	MET	-6.00	18:21	19:12	20:18	22:04	0:36	3:28	6:21	9:14	12:06	14:38	16:24	17:31
Leipzig	MET	-6.00	18:11	19:04	20:13	21:59	0:30	3:20	6:11	9:01	11:51	14:22	16:09	17:18
Munich	MET	-6.00	18:14	19:13	20:28	22:18	0:46	3:30	6:14	8:58	11:42	14:10	15:59	17:14
Nurnberg	MET	-6.00	18:16	19:12	20:25	22:14	0:43	3:29	6:16	9:02	11:49	14:18	16:06	17:19
Stuttgart	MET	-6.00	18:23	19:21	20:35	22:25	0:53	3:38	6:23	9:08	11:54	14:22	16:11	17:25
Ghana														
Accra	GMT	-5.00	18:01	19:48	21:44	23:51	2:01	4:05	6:01	7:57	10:00	12:11	14:18	16:14
Kumasi	GMT	-5.00	18:06	19:53	21:48	23:55	2:05	4:09	6:06	8:03	10:07	12:18	14:25	16:20
Sekondi-Takoradi	GMT	-5.00	18:07	19:54	21:51	23:58	2:08	4:11	6:07	8:03	10:05	12:16	14:23	16:19
Tamale	GMT	-5.00	18:03	19:47	21:41	23:47	1:58	4:04	6:03	8:03	10:09	12:20	14:26	16:19
Great Britain														
Gibraltar	MET	-6.00	19:21	20:39	22:10	0:08	2:28	4:56	7:21	9:47	12:15	14:35	16:32	18:04
Greece														
Athens	EET	-7.00	18:25	19:40	21:10	23:06	1:27	3:57	6:25	8:53	11:23	13:44	15:40	17:10
Patrai	EET	-7.00	18:33	19:48	21:17	23:13	1:35	4:05	6:33	9:02	11:32	13:53	15:49	17:18
Thessalonika	EET	-7.00	18:28	19:40	21:06	23:01	1:24	3:56	6:28	9:00	11:33	13:56	15:50	17:17
Guatemala														
Guatemala	CST	1.00	18:02	19:42	21:31	23:36	1:49	3:58	6:02	8:06	10:15	12:28	14:33	16:23
Guinea														
Conakry	GMT	-5.00	18:55	20:39	22:32	0:38	2:49	4:55	6:55	8:54	11:00	13:12	15:18	17:11
Kankan	GMT	-5.00	18:37	20:20	22:13	0:19	2:31	4:37	6:37	8:37	10:44	12:55	15:01	16:54
Guinea-Bissau														
Bissau	GMT	-5.00	19:02	20:44	22:36	0:41	2:53	5:01	7:02	9:04	11:11	13:23	15:29	17:20
Guyana														
Georgetown	BZ2	-2.00	18:53	20:39	22:34	0:41	2:51	4:55	6:53	8:50	10:54	13:05	15:11	17:07
New Amsterdam	BZ2	-2.00	18:50	20:37	22:32	0:39	2:50	4:53	6:50	8:47	10:51	13:01	15:08	17:04
Haiti														
Port-au-Prince	EST	0.00	17:49	19:25	21:12	23:16	1:30	3:42	5:49	7:57	10:09	12:23	14:26	16:13
Honduras														
San Pedro Sula	CST	1.00	17:52	19:31	21:20	23:25	1:38	3:48	5:52	7:57	10:07	12:20	14:24	16:13
Tegucigalpa	CST	1.00	17:49	19:29	21:19	23:24	1:36	3:46	5:49	7:52	10:01	12:14	14:19	16:09
Hong Kong														
Victoria	WST	-13.00	18:23	19:56	21:40	23:42	1:58	4:13	6:23	8:34	10:49	13:04	15:07	16:51
Hungary														
Budapest	MET	-6.00	17:44	18:44	20:00	21:51	0:18	3:01	5:44	8:27	11:09	13:37	15:27	16:43
Iceland														
Reykjavik	GMT	-5.00	19:27	19:40	20:02	21:13	0:19	3:57	7:27	10:58	14:36	17:42	18:53	19:15
India														
Agra	IST	-10.50	18:18	19:46	21:26	23:26	1:43	4:02	6:18	8:34	10:53	13:09	15:10	16:50
Ahmadabad	IST	-10.50	18:40	20:11	21:55	23:57	2:12	4:28	6:40	8:51	11:07	13:22	15:24	17:08
Bangalore	IST	-10.50	18:20	20:01	21:52	23:57	2:09	4:17	6:20	8:22	10:30	12:43	14:48	16:39
Bombay	IST	-10.50	18:39	20:14	22:01	0:04	2:18	4:31	6:39	8:46	10:59	13:13	15:16	17:03
Calcutta	IST	-10.50	17:37	19:09	20:53	22:55	1:10	3:26	5:37	7:47	10:03	12:18	14:20	16:04
Delhi	IST	-10.50	18:21	19:47	21:26	23:26	1:44	4:04	6:21	8:38	10:59	13:16	15:16	16:55
Hyderabad	IST	-10.50	18:16	19:53	21:41	23:45	1:58	4:10	6:16	8:22	10:34	12:47	14:51	16:39
Jaipur	IST	-10.50	18:27	19:55	21:35	23:36	1:53	4:11	6:27	8:42	11:01	13:18	15:18	16:59
Kanpur	IST	-10.50	18:09	19:37	21:18	23:19	1:35	3:54	6:09	8:23	10:42	12:58	14:59	16:40
Madras	IST	-10.50	18:09	19:50	21:41	23:46	1:58	4:06	6:09	8:11	10:20	12:32	14:37	16:28
Nagpur	IST	-10.50	18:14	19:47	21:32	23:35	1:50	4:04	6:14	8:23	10:38	12:52	14:55	16:40
Indonesia														
Balikpapan	WST	-13.00	18:13	20:05	22:06	0:15	2:23	4:22	6:13	8:03	10:02	12:10	14:20	16:20
Bandung	SST	-12.00	17:50	19:47	21:51	0:02	2:09	4:04	5:50	7:36	9:31	11:38	13:48	15:52
Banjarmasin	WST	-13.00	18:22	20:16	22:18	0:27	2:35	4:33	6:22	8:11	10:08	12:16	14:25	16:27
Cirebon	SST	-12.00	17:46	19:43	21:47	23:57	2:04	4:00	5:46	7:32	9:27	11:34	13:45	15:49
Jakarta	SST	-12.00	17:53	19:49	21:53	0:04	2:11	4:06	5:53	7:39	9:35	11:42	13:52	15:56
Jambi	SST	-12.00	18:06	19:59	21:59	0:09	2:17	4:15	6:06	7:56	9:55	12:03	14:12	16:13
Jayapura	JST	-14.00	17:37	19:31	21:32	23:42	1:50	3:48	5:37	7:27	9:25	11:33	13:42	15:44
Kupang	WST	-13.00	17:46	19:46	21:52	0:04	2:09	4:02	5:46	7:29	9:22	11:28	13:39	15:46
Malang	SST	-12.00	17:30	19:28	21:33	23:43	1:50	3:44	5:30	7:15	9:09	11:16	13:26	15:31
Manado	WST	-13.00	17:41	19:31	21:30	23:38	1:47	3:48	5:41	7:33	9:34	11:43	13:52	15:50
Medan	SST	-12.00	18:25	20:14	22:11	0:19	2:29	4:31	6:25	8:20	10:22	12:32	14:39	16:37
Padang	WST	-13.00	19:19	21:11	23:11	1:20	3:29	5:28	7:19	9:09	11:08	13:17	15:26	17:26

City	Zone	->EST	♈	♉	♊	♋	♌	♍	♎	♏	♐	♑	♒	♓
Indonesia, continued														
Pakanbaru	SST	-12.00	18:14	20:05	22:05	0:13	2:22	4:22	6:14	8:06	10:06	12:15	14:24	16:23
Palembang	SST	-12.00	18:01	19:55	21:57	0:06	2:14	4:12	6:01	7:50	9:48	11:56	14:05	16:07
Pematangsiantar	SST	-12.00	18:24	20:13	22:11	0:19	2:28	4:30	6:24	8:18	10:19	12:29	14:37	16:35
Pontianak	WST	-13.00	18:43	20:34	22:34	0:43	2:51	4:51	6:43	8:34	10:34	12:43	14:51	16:51
Samarinda	WST	-13.00	18:11	20:03	22:03	0:12	2:21	4:20	6:11	8:03	10:02	12:11	14:19	16:19
Semarang	SST	-12.00	17:38	19:36	21:40	23:50	1:57	3:52	5:38	7:24	9:19	11:26	13:37	15:41
Surabaya	SST	-12.00	17:29	19:27	21:31	23:42	1:48	3:43	5:29	7:15	9:10	11:16	13:27	15:31
Surakarta	SST	-12.00	17:37	19:34	21:39	23:50	1:57	3:51	5:37	7:22	9:17	11:23	13:34	15:39
Telukbetung	SST	-12.00	17:59	19:55	21:58	0:08	2:16	4:12	5:59	7:46	9:42	11:49	14:00	16:03
Ujung Pandang	WST	-13.00	18:02	19:58	22:01	0:11	2:19	4:15	6:02	7:50	9:46	11:53	14:04	16:07
Yogyakarta	SST	-12.00	17:39	19:37	21:41	23:52	1:59	3:53	5:39	7:24	9:18	11:25	13:36	15:41
Iran														
Abadan	-3.5	-8.50	18:17	19:41	21:19	23:18	1:36	3:58	6:17	8:36	10:58	13:16	15:15	16:53
Esfahan	-3.5	-8.50	18:03	19:25	21:00	22:59	1:18	3:42	6:03	8:25	10:49	13:08	15:07	16:42
Mashhad	-3.5	-8.50	17:32	18:49	20:20	22:17	0:38	3:06	5:32	7:58	10:25	12:46	14:43	16:14
Tabriz	-3.5	-8.50	18:25	19:40	21:09	23:05	1:27	3:57	6:25	8:53	11:23	13:44	15:40	17:10
Tehran	-3.5	-8.50	18:04	19:22	20:54	22:52	1:12	3:39	6:04	8:29	10:57	13:17	15:14	16:46
Iraq														
Baghdad	BT	-8.00	18:02	19:23	20:58	22:56	1:15	3:40	6:02	8:25	10:50	13:09	15:07	16:41
Ireland														
Belfast	GMT	-5.00	18:24	19:09	20:11	21:53	0:28	3:26	6:24	9:22	12:19	14:54	16:37	17:38
Cork	GMT	-5.00	18:34	19:25	20:33	22:20	0:51	3:42	6:34	9:26	12:17	14:48	16:34	17:42
Dublin	GMT	-5.00	18:25	19:13	20:18	22:02	0:36	3:30	6:25	9:20	12:14	14:48	16:32	17:37
Israel														
Jerusalem	EET	-7.00	17:39	19:02	20:38	22:37	0:55	3:19	5:39	8:00	10:23	12:41	14:40	16:16
Tel Aviv	EET	-7.00	17:41	19:03	20:39	22:38	0:56	3:20	5:41	8:02	10:25	12:44	14:43	16:19
Italy														
Bari	MET	-6.00	17:53	19:03	20:29	22:24	0:47	3:20	5:53	8:25	10:59	13:22	15:16	16:42
Bologna	MET	-6.00	18:15	19:20	20:41	22:34	0:59	3:37	6:15	8:52	11:30	13:56	15:48	17:09
Catania	MET	-6.00	18:00	19:15	20:45	22:42	1:03	3:32	6:00	8:27	10:56	13:17	15:14	16:44
Florence	MET	-6.00	18:15	19:22	20:44	22:37	1:01	3:39	6:15	8:51	11:29	13:53	15:46	17:08
Milan	MET	-6.00	18:23	19:27	20:47	22:39	1:04	3:44	6:23	9:02	11:42	14:08	16:00	17:19
Naples	MET	-6.00	18:03	19:14	20:40	22:35	0:58	3:31	6:03	8:35	11:08	13:31	15:26	16:52
Palermo	MET	-6.00	18:07	19:22	20:51	22:47	1:08	3:38	6:07	8:35	11:05	13:26	15:22	16:52
Rome	MET	-6.00	18:10	19:20	20:44	22:38	1:02	3:36	6:10	8:44	11:18	13:42	15:36	17:00
Torino	MET	-6.00	18:29	19:34	20:54	22:46	1:12	3:51	6:29	9:08	11:47	14:12	16:04	17:25
Trieste	MET	-6.00	18:05	19:09	20:28	22:20	0:45	3:25	6:05	8:45	11:24	13:50	15:42	17:01
Venice	MET	-6.00	18:11	19:15	20:34	22:26	0:52	3:31	6:11	8:50	11:29	13:55	15:47	17:07
Ivory Coast														
Abidjan	GMT	-5.00	18:16	20:03	22:00	0:07	2:17	4:20	6:16	8:12	10:15	12:25	14:33	16:29
Bouake	GMT	-5.00	18:20	20:05	22:00	0:07	2:18	4:22	6:20	8:18	10:23	12:34	14:40	16:35
Jamaica														
Kingston	EST	0.00	18:07	19:44	21:31	23:35	1:49	4:00	6:07	8:14	10:26	12:40	14:43	16:31
Japan														
Fukuoka	JST	-14.00	18:18	19:39	21:13	23:11	1:31	3:56	6:18	8:41	11:06	13:25	15:24	16:58
Kawasaki	JST	-14.00	18:17	19:37	21:12	23:10	1:29	3:54	6:17	8:39	11:04	13:24	15:22	16:56
Kyoto	JST	-14.00	17:57	19:16	20:49	22:46	1:06	3:33	5:57	8:21	10:48	13:08	15:05	16:38
Naha	JST	-14.00	18:29	19:58	21:39	23:40	1:56	4:15	6:29	8:44	11:02	13:19	15:20	17:01
Niigata	JST	-14.00	17:44	18:59	20:29	22:25	0:46	3:16	5:44	8:12	10:42	13:03	14:59	16:29
Osaka	JST	-14.00	17:58	19:17	20:50	22:48	1:08	3:34	5:58	8:22	10:48	13:08	15:06	16:39
Sapporo	JST	-14.00	17:35	18:43	20:06	21:59	0:23	2:59	5:35	8:10	10:46	13:10	15:04	16:27
Tokyo	JST	-14.00	17:41	18:59	20:31	22:28	0:49	3:16	5:41	8:06	10:33	12:54	14:51	16:23
Jordan														
Amman	EET	-7.00	17:36	18:59	20:35	22:33	0:52	3:16	5:36	7:57	10:20	12:39	14:38	16:14
Kampuchea														
Phnom Penh	SST	-12.00	18:00	19:42	21:34	23:40	1:52	3:59	6:00	8:01	10:09	12:21	14:26	16:18
Kenya														
Mombasa	BT	-8.00	18:21	20:16	22:19	0:28	2:36	4:33	6:21	8:10	10:07	12:14	14:24	16:26
Nairobi	BT	-8.00	18:33	20:25	22:26	0:35	2:43	4:42	6:33	8:23	10:22	12:31	14:40	16:40
Laos														
Vientiane	SST	-12.00	18:10	19:46	21:34	23:37	1:51	4:03	6:10	8:16	10:28	12:42	14:46	16:33
Latvia														
Riga	BT	-8.00	19:24	20:03	20:57	22:36	1:15	4:19	7:24	10:28	13:32	16:11	17:50	18:45

♎ = Libra ♏ = Scorpio ♐ = Sagittarius ♑ = Capricorn ♒ = Aquarius ♓ = Pisces

City	Zone	->EST	♈	♉	♊	♋	♌	♍	♎	♏	♐	♑	♒	♓
Lebanon														
Beirut	EET	-7.00	17:38	18:58	20:32	22:30	0:50	3:15	5:38	8:01	10:26	12:46	14:44	16:18
Lesotho														
Maseru	EET	-7.00	18:10	20:28	22:49	1:07	3:07	4:45	6:10	7:35	9:13	11:13	13:31	15:52
Liberia														
Monrovia	GMT	-5.00	18:43	20:30	22:25	0:32	2:43	4:46	6:43	8:40	10:44	12:54	15:01	16:57
Libya														
Banghazi	MET	-6.00	17:40	19:02	20:38	22:37	0:55	3:19	5:40	8:01	10:24	12:43	14:42	16:17
Tripoli	MET	-6.00	18:07	19:29	21:04	23:02	1:21	3:45	6:07	8:29	10:53	13:12	15:11	16:46
Lithuania														
Vilna	BT	-8.00	19:19	20:04	21:05	22:48	1:23	4:20	7:19	10:17	13:15	15:50	17:32	18:34
Luxembourg														
Luxembourg	MET	-6.00	18:35	19:32	20:44	22:33	1:02	3:49	6:35	9:22	12:09	14:38	16:26	17:39
Macau														
Macau	WST	-13.00	18:26	19:58	21:42	23:45	2:00	4:15	6:26	8:36	10:51	13:07	15:09	16:53
Madagascar														
Antananarivo	BT	-8.00	17:50	19:58	22:10	0:24	2:28	4:14	5:50	7:26	9:12	11:16	13:30	15:42
Antsiranana	BT	-8.00	17:43	19:45	21:52	0:05	2:10	4:01	5:43	7:24	9:16	11:21	13:33	15:41
Mahajanga	BT	-8.00	17:55	19:59	22:10	0:23	2:27	4:16	5:55	7:33	9:22	11:27	13:40	15:50
Toamasina	BT	-8.00	17:42	19:49	22:01	0:15	2:19	4:06	5:42	7:19	9:06	11:10	13:24	15:36
Toliara	BT	-8.00	18:05	20:17	22:33	0:49	2:51	4:34	6:05	7:37	9:20	11:22	13:38	15:54
Malawi														
Blantyre	EET	-7.00	17:40	19:45	21:55	0:08	2:13	4:02	5:40	7:18	9:07	11:12	13:25	15:35
Malaysia														
George Town	WST	-13.00	19:19	21:06	23:02	1:09	3:19	5:23	7:19	9:15	11:18	13:28	15:35	17:31
Kota Baharu	WST	-13.00	19:11	20:58	22:53	1:00	3:11	5:14	7:11	9:08	11:11	13:22	15:29	17:24
Kuala Lumpur	WST	-13.00	19:13	21:02	23:00	1:08	3:17	5:19	7:13	9:07	11:09	13:19	15:27	17:24
Mali														
Bamako	GMT	-5.00	18:32	20:13	22:04	0:10	2:22	4:30	6:32	8:34	10:42	12:54	15:00	16:51
Mauritania														
Nouakchott	GMT	-5.00	19:04	20:40	22:28	0:31	2:45	4:57	7:04	9:11	11:23	13:36	15:40	17:27
Mexico														
Acapulco	CST	1.00	18:40	20:17	22:05	0:10	2:23	4:34	6:40	8:45	10:57	13:10	15:14	17:02
Chihuahua	CST	1.00	19:04	20:31	22:09	0:10	2:27	4:47	7:04	9:21	11:42	13:59	15:59	17:38
Ensenada	PST	3.00	17:46	19:09	20:45	22:44	1:02	3:26	5:46	8:07	10:30	12:49	14:48	16:24
Guadalajara	CST	1.00	18:53	20:27	22:13	0:16	2:30	4:44	6:53	9:03	11:16	13:31	15:34	17:19
Hermosillo	MST	2.00	18:24	19:50	21:28	23:28	1:46	4:06	6:24	8:41	11:02	13:20	15:20	16:58
La Paz	MST	2.00	18:21	19:52	21:35	23:36	1:52	4:09	6:21	8:34	10:50	13:06	15:08	16:50
Mazatlan	MST	2.00	18:06	19:37	21:21	23:23	1:38	3:54	6:06	8:17	10:33	12:49	14:51	16:34
Merida	CST	1.00	17:58	19:32	21:17	23:20	1:35	3:49	5:58	8:08	10:22	12:37	14:40	16:25
Mexicali	PST	3.00	17:42	19:04	20:39	22:37	0:56	3:20	5:42	8:03	10:28	12:47	14:45	16:20
Mexico City	CST	1.00	18:37	20:12	21:58	0:01	2:16	4:29	6:37	8:45	10:58	13:12	15:15	17:01
Monterrey	CST	1.00	18:41	20:11	21:52	23:53	2:09	4:27	6:41	8:55	11:13	13:29	15:31	17:12
Oaxaca	CST	1.00	18:27	20:04	21:52	23:56	2:10	4:21	6:27	8:33	10:44	12:57	15:01	16:50
Orizaba	CST	1.00	18:28	20:04	21:51	23:54	2:08	4:21	6:28	8:36	10:48	13:02	15:06	16:53
Puebla	CST	1.00	18:33	20:08	21:55	23:58	2:12	4:25	6:33	8:41	10:53	13:07	15:11	16:57
San Luis Potosi	CST	1.00	18:44	20:17	22:01	0:03	2:18	4:33	6:44	8:55	11:10	13:25	15:27	17:11
Tijuana	PST	3.00	17:48	19:10	20:45	22:44	1:03	3:27	5:48	8:09	10:34	12:52	14:51	16:26
Torreon	CST	1.00	18:54	20:23	22:05	0:06	2:22	4:40	6:54	9:08	11:25	13:42	15:43	17:24
Tuxtla Gutierrez	CST	1.00	18:12	19:50	21:38	23:42	1:56	4:07	6:12	8:18	10:29	12:42	14:47	16:35
Veracruz	PST	3.00	16:25	18:00	19:46	21:50	0:04	2:17	4:25	6:32	8:45	10:59	13:03	14:49
Villahermosa	CST	1.00	18:12	19:48	21:36	23:39	1:53	4:05	6:12	8:18	10:30	12:44	14:48	16:35
Morocco														
Casablanca	GMT	-5.00	18:30	19:51	21:25	23:23	1:42	4:08	6:30	8:53	11:18	13:37	15:36	17:10
Fes	GMT	-5.00	18:20	19:40	21:14	23:12	1:31	3:57	6:20	8:43	11:09	13:28	15:26	17:00
Marrakech	GMT	-5.00	18:32	19:55	21:31	23:30	1:48	4:12	6:32	8:52	11:16	13:34	15:33	17:09
Meknes	GMT	-5.00	18:22	19:43	21:17	23:15	1:34	3:59	6:22	8:45	11:11	13:30	15:28	17:02
Rabat	GMT	-5.00	18:27	19:48	21:21	23:19	1:39	4:04	6:27	8:51	11:16	13:36	15:34	17:07
Mozambique														
Beira	EET	-7.00	17:41	19:49	22:02	0:17	2:20	4:06	5:41	7:15	9:01	11:05	13:19	15:32
Maputo	EET	-7.00	17:50	20:04	22:22	0:38	2:40	4:21	5:50	7:19	9:00	11:01	13:17	15:35
Namibia														
Luderitz	EET	-7.00	18:59	21:14	23:33	1:50	3:50	5:31	6:59	8:28	10:08	12:09	14:26	16:44
Windhoek	EET	-7.00	18:52	21:03	23:18	1:33	3:35	5:19	6:52	8:24	10:08	12:10	14:25	16:41

City	Zone	—>EST	♈	♉	♊	♋	♌	♍	♎	♏	♐	♑	♒	♓
Nepal														
Kathmandu	-5.8	-10.75	18:04	19:31	21:11	23:11	1:28	3:48	6:04	8:20	10:39	12:56	14:57	16:37
Netherlands														
Amsterdam	MET	-6.00	18:40	19:31	20:38	22:23	0:55	3:48	6:40	9:33	12:25	14:57	16:43	17:50
Rotterdam	MET	-6.00	18:42	19:34	20:42	22:28	0:59	3:50	6:42	9:34	12:25	14:57	16:43	17:51
New Caledonia														
Noumea	165E	-16.00	17:54	20:05	22:20	0:35	2:38	4:22	5:54	7:27	9:11	11:13	13:28	15:43
New Zealand														
Auckland	NZT	-17.00	18:21	20:48	23:16	1:37	3:34	5:04	6:21	7:38	9:08	11:05	13:26	15:54
Christchurch	NZT	-17.00	18:29	21:06	23:42	2:07	4:00	5:22	6:29	7:37	8:59	10:52	13:17	15:53
Invercargill	NZT	-17.00	18:47	21:27	0:09	2:35	4:26	5:44	6:47	7:49	9:07	10:58	13:25	16:06
Nelson	NZT	-17.00	18:27	21:00	23:33	1:56	3:51	5:16	6:27	7:37	9:03	10:57	13:20	15:54
New Plymouth	NZT	-17.00	18:24	20:53	23:24	1:46	3:42	5:10	6:24	7:37	9:06	11:01	13:23	15:54
Palmerston	NZT	-17.00	18:18	20:49	23:21	1:44	3:39	5:06	6:18	7:29	8:56	10:51	13:14	15:46
Timaru	NZT	-17.00	18:35	21:13	23:51	2:16	4:08	5:29	6:35	7:41	9:02	10:54	13:19	15:57
Wellington	NZT	-17.00	18:21	20:54	23:27	1:50	3:45	5:10	6:21	7:31	8:57	10:51	13:14	15:48
Whangarei	NZT	-17.00	18:23	20:48	23:15	1:35	3:33	5:05	6:23	7:41	9:13	11:10	13:30	15:58
Nicaragua														
Managua	CST	1.00	17:45	19:27	21:18	23:24	1:36	3:43	5:45	7:47	9:55	12:07	14:12	16:04
Niger														
Niamey	MET	-6.00	18:52	20:32	22:23	0:28	2:40	4:49	6:52	8:54	11:03	13:15	15:21	17:11
Nigeria														
Abeokuta	MET	-6.00	18:46	20:32	22:27	0:34	2:44	4:49	6:46	8:44	10:48	12:59	15:06	17:00
Enugu	MET	-6.00	18:30	20:17	22:12	0:19	2:29	4:33	6:30	8:27	10:31	12:41	14:48	16:44
Ibadan	MET	-6.00	18:46	20:32	22:27	0:33	2:44	4:48	6:46	8:44	10:48	12:59	15:05	17:00
Kaduna	MET	-6.00	18:30	20:13	22:06	0:12	2:23	4:30	6:30	8:31	10:37	12:49	14:55	16:47
Kano	MET	-6.00	18:26	20:08	21:59	0:05	2:17	4:24	6:26	8:28	10:35	12:47	14:53	16:44
Lagos	MET	-6.00	18:46	20:33	22:28	0:35	2:46	4:50	6:46	8:43	10:47	12:58	15:05	17:00
Maiduguri	MET	-6.00	18:07	19:49	21:41	23:46	1:58	4:06	6:07	8:09	10:16	12:28	14:34	16:25
Onitsha	MET	-6.00	18:33	20:19	22:15	0:22	2:33	4:36	6:33	8:30	10:33	12:44	14:51	16:46
Port Harcourt	MET	-6.00	18:32	20:19	22:16	0:23	2:33	4:36	6:32	8:27	10:30	12:40	14:47	16:44
Zaria	MET	-6.00	18:29	20:12	22:04	0:10	2:21	4:28	6:29	8:30	10:37	12:49	14:54	16:47
North Korea														
Pyongyang	JST	-14.00	18:37	19:51	21:19	23:15	1:37	4:07	6:37	9:07	11:37	13:59	15:55	17:23
Norway														
Bergen	MET	-6.00	18:39	19:07	19:49	21:20	0:07	3:23	6:39	9:54	13:11	15:58	17:28	18:11
Oslo	MET	-6.00	18:17	18:47	19:31	21:03	23:48	3:03	6:17	9:31	12:46	15:31	17:03	17:47
Pakistan														
Faisalabad	75E	-10.00	18:08	19:31	21:07	23:06	1:25	3:48	6:08	8:28	10:51	13:09	15:08	16:45
Hyderabad	75E	-10.00	18:27	19:56	21:38	23:39	1:55	4:13	6:27	8:40	10:58	13:14	15:15	16:57
Karachi	75E	-10.00	18:32	20:02	21:44	23:45	2:01	4:19	6:32	8:45	11:02	13:18	15:20	17:02
Lahore	75E	-10.00	18:03	19:26	21:02	23:01	1:19	3:42	6:03	8:23	10:46	13:05	15:04	16:40
Multan	75E	-10.00	18:14	19:39	21:16	23:16	1:33	3:55	6:14	8:33	10:55	13:13	15:12	16:50
Rawalpindi	75E	-10.00	18:08	19:28	21:03	23:01	1:20	3:45	6:08	8:30	10:55	13:15	15:13	16:47
Panama														
Panama	EST	0.00	18:18	20:02	21:56	0:02	2:14	4:19	6:18	8:17	10:23	12:34	14:40	16:34
Papua New Guinea														
Lae	EST	-15.00	18:12	20:09	22:13	0:24	2:31	4:26	6:12	7:58	9:53	12:00	14:11	16:15
Popondetta	EST	-15.00	18:07	20:06	22:11	0:22	2:29	4:23	6:07	7:52	9:45	11:52	14:03	16:08
Port Moresby	EST	-15.00	18:11	20:11	22:17	0:28	2:34	4:27	6:11	7:55	9:49	11:55	14:06	16:12
Wewak	EST	-15.00	18:25	20:20	22:22	0:32	2:39	4:37	6:25	8:14	10:11	12:19	14:29	16:31
Paraguay														
Asuncion	AST	-1.00	17:51	20:04	22:22	0:38	2:39	4:21	5:51	7:20	9:02	11:03	13:19	15:37
Peru														
Arequipa	EST	0.00	17:46	19:52	22:02	0:16	2:20	4:08	5:46	7:24	9:13	11:17	13:30	15:41
Chimbote	EST	0.00	18:14	20:13	22:19	0:30	2:37	4:30	6:14	7:59	9:52	11:58	14:10	16:15
Cuzco	EST	0.00	17:48	19:51	21:59	0:12	2:17	4:07	5:48	7:28	9:19	11:24	13:36	15:45
Iquitos	EST	0.00	17:53	19:48	21:50	0:00	2:07	4:04	5:53	7:42	9:39	11:46	13:56	15:58
Lima	EST	0.00	18:08	20:10	22:17	0:29	2:35	4:26	6:08	7:50	9:41	11:47	13:59	16:07
Piura	EST	0.00	18:23	20:18	22:21	0:32	2:39	4:35	6:23	8:10	10:06	12:13	14:24	16:27
Trujillo	EST	0.00	18:16	20:14	22:19	0:30	2:37	4:31	6:16	8:01	9:55	12:02	14:13	16:18
Philippines														
Cebu	WST	-13.00	17:44	19:28	21:20	23:26	1:38	3:44	5:44	7:44	9:51	12:02	14:08	16:01
Davao	WST	-13.00	17:38	19:23	21:18	23:25	1:36	3:40	5:38	7:35	9:39	11:50	13:57	15:52

♎ = Libra ♏ = Scorpio ♐ = Sagittarius ♑ = Capricorn ♒ = Aquarius ♓ = Pisces

City	Zone	->EST	♈	♉	♊	♋	♌	♍	♎	♏	♐	♑	♒	♓
Philippines, continued														
Manila	WST	-13.00	17:56	19:36	21:25	23:30	1:43	3:52	5:56	8:00	10:09	12:22	14:27	16:16
Poland														
Gdansk	MET	-6.00	17:45	18:31	19:33	21:16	23:51	2:48	5:45	8:43	11:40	14:14	15:57	17:00
Katowice	MET	-6.00	17:44	18:39	19:50	21:38	0:08	2:56	5:44	8:32	11:20	13:50	15:38	16:49
Krakow	MET	-6.00	17:40	18:36	19:47	21:35	0:05	2:52	5:40	8:28	11:15	13:45	15:33	16:45
Poznan	MET	-6.00	17:52	18:43	19:50	21:35	0:07	3:00	5:52	8:45	11:38	14:10	15:55	17:02
Warsaw	MET	-6.00	17:36	18:27	19:34	21:20	23:52	2:44	5:36	8:28	11:20	13:52	15:38	16:45
Wroclaw	MET	-6.00	17:52	18:45	19:55	21:42	0:12	3:02	5:52	8:42	11:32	14:02	15:49	16:59
Portugal														
Lisbon	GMT	-5.00	18:37	19:51	21:19	23:15	1:37	4:07	6:37	9:06	11:36	13:58	15:54	17:22
Portugalo	GMT	-5.00	18:34	19:45	21:11	23:05	1:28	4:02	6:34	9:07	11:41	14:04	15:58	17:24
Puerto Rico														
San Juan	AST	-1.00	18:24	20:00	21:48	23:51	2:05	4:17	6:24	8:32	10:44	12:58	15:01	16:48
Romania														
Bucharest	EET	-7.00	18:16	19:21	20:42	22:35	1:00	3:38	6:16	8:53	11:31	13:56	15:49	17:10
Cluj	EET	-7.00	18:26	19:27	20:45	22:36	1:02	3:44	6:26	9:07	11:49	14:16	16:06	17:24
Craiova	EET	-7.00	18:25	19:31	20:52	22:45	1:10	3:47	6:25	9:02	11:40	14:05	15:58	17:19
Rwanda														
Kigali	EET	-7.00	18:00	19:53	21:54	0:03	2:11	4:10	6:00	7:50	9:48	11:56	14:06	16:07
Saudi Arabia														
Mecca	BT	-8.00	18:21	19:54	21:39	23:41	1:56	4:11	6:21	8:31	10:45	13:00	15:03	16:47
Medina	BT	-8.00	18:22	19:52	21:34	23:36	1:52	4:09	6:22	8:34	10:51	13:07	15:09	16:51
Riyadh	BT	-8.00	17:53	19:23	21:06	23:07	1:23	3:40	5:53	8:06	10:23	12:39	14:41	16:23
Scotland														
Edinburgh	GMT	-5.00	18:13	18:55	19:53	21:33	0:10	3:11	6:13	9:14	12:16	14:53	16:33	17:31
Glasgow	GMT	-5.00	18:17	18:59	19:57	21:38	0:14	3:16	6:17	9:18	12:20	14:56	16:37	17:35
Senegal														
Dakar	GMT	-5.00	19:10	20:49	22:39	0:44	2:56	5:06	7:10	9:14	11:23	13:36	15:41	17:30
Sierra Leone														
Freetown	GMT	-5.00	18:53	20:38	22:32	0:38	2:49	4:54	6:53	8:52	10:57	13:08	15:14	17:08
Singapore														
Singapore	WST	-13.00	19:05	20:55	22:54	1:02	3:11	5:12	7:05	8:57	10:58	13:07	15:15	17:14
Solomon Islands														
Honiara	165E	-16.00	18:20	20:20	22:25	0:37	2:43	4:36	6:20	8:04	9:57	12:04	14:15	16:21
Somalia														
Hargeysa	BT	-8.00	18:04	19:48	21:41	23:47	1:58	4:04	6:04	8:03	10:09	12:21	14:27	16:20
Mogadishu	BT	-8.00	17:59	19:48	21:47	23:55	2:04	4:05	5:59	7:52	9:53	12:02	14:10	16:09
South Africa														
Bloemfontein	EET	-7.00	18:16	20:33	22:54	1:12	3:12	4:50	6:16	7:41	9:19	11:19	13:37	15:58
Cape Town	EET	-7.00	18:47	21:10	23:35	1:54	3:52	5:26	6:47	8:07	9:41	11:39	13:58	16:24
Durban	EET	-7.00	17:56	20:15	22:36	0:54	2:54	4:31	5:56	7:21	8:59	10:58	13:16	15:38
Johannesburg	EET	-7.00	18:08	20:23	22:41	0:57	2:58	4:39	6:08	7:37	9:18	11:19	13:35	15:53
Klerksdorp	EET	-7.00	18:13	20:29	22:48	1:04	3:05	4:45	6:13	7:41	9:22	11:22	13:39	15:58
Oos-Londen	EET	-7.00	18:08	20:30	22:55	1:14	3:12	4:47	6:08	7:30	9:04	11:03	13:22	15:46
Pietermaritzburg	EET	-7.00	17:59	20:17	22:38	0:56	2:56	4:34	5:59	7:24	9:02	11:02	13:19	15:41
Port Elizabeth	EET	-7.00	18:17	20:40	23:06	1:25	3:23	4:57	6:17	7:38	9:11	11:09	13:29	15:54
Pretoria	EET	-7.00	18:07	20:21	22:39	0:56	2:57	4:38	6:07	7:36	9:18	11:19	13:35	15:53
Walvis Bay	EET	-7.00	19:02	21:13	23:29	1:44	3:46	5:30	7:02	8:34	10:17	12:20	14:35	16:51
Welkom	EET	-7.00	18:13	20:29	22:49	1:06	3:07	4:46	6:13	7:40	9:19	11:20	13:37	15:57
South Korea														
Pusan	JST	-14.00	18:24	19:43	21:15	23:13	1:33	3:59	6:24	8:48	11:15	13:35	15:32	17:05
Seoul	JST	-14.00	18:32	19:48	21:18	23:14	1:35	4:05	6:32	9:00	11:29	13:50	15:46	17:16
Spain														
Barcelona	MET	-6.00	18:51	20:02	21:27	23:21	1:45	4:18	6:51	9:24	11:58	14:21	16:15	17:41
Bilbao	MET	-6.00	19:12	20:19	21:42	23:36	2:00	4:36	7:12	9:48	12:24	14:48	16:41	18:04
La Coruna	MET	-6.00	19:34	20:41	22:04	23:57	2:21	4:58	7:34	10:09	12:46	15:10	17:03	18:26
Madrid	MET	-6.00	19:15	20:27	21:53	23:48	2:11	4:43	7:15	9:46	12:19	14:41	16:36	18:03
Malaga	MET	-6.00	19:18	20:34	22:05	0:02	2:23	4:51	7:18	9:44	12:12	14:33	16:30	18:01
Seville	MET	-6.00	19:24	20:40	22:10	0:07	2:28	4:57	7:24	9:51	12:20	14:41	16:38	18:08
Valencia	MET	-6.00	19:01	20:15	21:42	23:38	2:00	4:31	7:01	9:32	12:03	14:25	16:21	17:48
Zaragoza	MET	-6.00	19:04	20:14	21:39	23:33	1:56	4:30	7:04	9:37	12:11	14:34	16:28	17:53
Sri Lanka														
Colombo	IST	-10.50	18:11	19:57	21:52	23:59	2:09	4:13	6:11	8:08	10:12	12:23	14:30	16:25

♈ = Aries ♉ = Taurus ♊ = Gemini ♋ = Cancer ♌ = Leo ♍ = Virgo

City	Zone	->EST	♈	♉	♊	♋	♌	♍	♎	♏	♐	♑	♒	♓
Sudan														
Al-Ubayyid	EET	-7.00	17:59	19:40	21:31	23:36	1:48	3:57	5:59	8:02	10:10	12:22	14:28	16:18
Khartoum	EET	-7.00	17:50	19:29	21:18	23:22	1:35	3:45	5:50	7:55	10:05	12:18	14:22	16:11
Port Sudan	EET	-7.00	17:31	19:06	20:52	22:55	1:10	3:23	5:31	7:39	9:52	12:07	14:10	15:56
Surinam														
Paramaribo	BZ2	-2.00	18:41	20:28	22:23	0:31	2:41	4:44	6:41	8:37	10:41	12:51	14:58	16:54
Swaziland														
Mbabane	EET	-7.00	17:56	20:10	22:29	0:45	2:46	4:27	5:56	7:24	9:05	11:06	13:23	15:41
Sweden														
Goteborg	MET	-6.00	18:12	18:49	19:41	21:19	23:59	3:06	6:12	9:19	12:26	15:06	16:43	17:35
Malmo	MET	-6.00	18:08	18:51	19:50	21:31	0:07	3:07	6:08	9:09	12:09	14:45	16:26	17:25
Stockholm	MET	-6.00	17:48	18:19	19:06	20:40	23:24	2:36	5:48	9:00	12:12	14:56	16:30	17:16
Switzerland														
Basel	MET	-6.00	18:30	19:30	20:46	22:36	1:04	3:47	6:30	9:13	11:56	14:23	16:13	17:29
Bern	MET	-6.00	18:30	19:32	20:49	22:40	1:06	3:48	6:30	9:12	11:54	14:21	16:12	17:29
Geneva	MET	-6.00	18:35	19:38	20:57	22:48	1:14	3:55	6:35	9:16	11:57	14:23	16:14	17:33
Zurich	MET	-6.00	18:26	19:27	20:43	22:33	1:01	3:43	6:26	9:08	11:51	14:18	16:09	17:25
Syria														
Damascus	EET	-7.00	17:35	18:56	20:30	22:28	0:47	3:12	5:35	7:57	10:22	12:42	14:40	16:14
Taiwan														
Taipei	WST	-13.00	17:54	19:24	21:06	23:07	1:23	3:41	5:54	8:07	10:25	12:41	14:42	16:24
Tanzania														
Dar Es Salaam	BT	-8.00	18:23	20:20	22:24	0:35	2:42	4:37	6:23	8:09	10:04	12:11	14:22	16:26
Morogoro	BT	-8.00	18:29	20:27	22:31	0:41	2:48	4:43	6:29	8:15	10:11	12:17	14:28	16:32
Mwanza	BT	-8.00	18:48	20:42	22:43	0:53	3:01	4:59	6:48	8:38	10:36	12:44	14:53	16:55
Tanga	BT	-8.00	18:24	20:19	22:22	0:32	2:40	4:36	6:24	8:11	10:07	12:15	14:25	16:28
Thailand														
Bangkok	SST	-12.00	18:18	19:58	21:49	23:54	2:06	4:15	6:18	8:21	10:30	12:42	14:47	16:38
Togo														
Lome	GMT	-5.00	17:55	19:42	21:37	23:44	1:55	3:58	5:55	7:52	9:55	12:06	14:13	16:08
Transkei														
Umtata	EET	-7.00	18:05	20:25	22:48	1:07	3:06	4:42	6:05	7:28	9:04	11:03	13:21	15:45
Trinidad & Tobago														
Port Of Spain	AST	-1.00	18:06	19:49	21:42	23:47	1:59	4:06	6:06	8:06	10:13	12:25	14:31	16:23
Tunisia														
Tunis	MET	-6.00	18:19	19:36	21:07	23:04	1:24	3:53	6:19	8:46	11:14	13:35	15:32	17:03
Turkey														
Ankara	EET	-7.00	17:49	19:01	20:28	22:23	0:46	3:18	5:49	8:19	10:51	13:14	15:09	16:36
Istanbul	EET	-7.00	18:04	19:15	20:41	22:35	0:58	3:32	6:04	8:36	11:10	13:33	15:27	16:53
USSR (former)														
Alma-Ata	90E	-11.00	18:52	20:00	21:23	23:16	1:40	4:17	6:52	9:28	12:04	14:29	16:22	17:45
Archangelsk	BT	-8.00	18:18	18:28	18:47	19:55	23:04	2:45	6:18	9:51	13:31	16:41	17:49	18:07
Astrakhan	60E	-9.00	18:48	19:50	21:09	23:00	1:26	4:07	6:48	9:29	12:10	14:36	16:27	17:45
Baku	60E	-9.00	18:41	19:52	21:19	23:14	1:37	4:09	6:41	9:12	11:45	14:07	16:02	17:29
Celabinsk	75E	-10.00	18:54	19:38	20:38	22:20	0:56	3:55	6:54	9:54	12:53	15:29	17:10	18:11
Dnepropetrovsk	BT	-8.00	18:40	19:39	20:53	22:43	1:11	3:55	6:40	9:25	12:09	14:37	16:27	17:41
Doneck	BT	-8.00	18:29	19:28	20:44	22:34	1:01	3:45	6:29	9:13	11:56	14:24	16:14	17:29
Gorky	BT	-8.00	18:04	18:45	19:41	21:21	23:59	3:01	6:04	9:07	12:09	14:47	16:27	17:23
Irkutsk	WST	-13.00	19:03	19:53	21:01	22:46	1:18	4:10	7:03	9:55	12:47	15:19	17:05	18:12
Kaliningrad	BT	-8.00	19:38	20:23	21:24	23:07	1:42	4:40	7:38	10:36	13:34	16:09	17:52	18:53
Kharkov	BT	-8.00	18:35	19:31	20:42	22:30	1:00	3:47	6:35	9:23	12:10	14:39	16:28	17:39
Kiev	BT	-8.00	18:58	19:53	21:04	22:51	1:21	4:09	6:58	9:46	12:35	15:05	16:52	18:03
Kisinov	BT	-8.00	19:05	20:06	21:23	23:14	1:41	4:23	7:05	9:47	12:29	14:56	16:46	18:03
Krasnojarsk	SST	-12.00	18:49	19:30	20:28	22:08	0:45	3:47	6:49	9:50	12:52	15:29	17:09	18:07
Kujbyschev	SST	-12.00	21:39	22:28	23:33	1:18	3:51	6:45	9:39	12:34	15:28	18:01	19:46	20:51
Leningrad	BT	-8.00	18:59	19:29	20:13	21:45	0:30	3:45	6:59	10:13	13:28	16:13	17:45	18:29
Lvov	BT	-8.00	19:24	20:20	21:32	23:20	1:50	4:37	7:24	10:11	12:58	15:28	17:16	18:28
Minsk	BT	-8.00	19:10	19:57	21:00	22:44	1:18	4:13	7:10	10:06	13:02	15:36	17:19	18:23
Moscow	BT	-8.00	18:30	19:12	20:10	21:51	0:28	3:29	6:30	9:31	12:31	15:08	16:49	17:47
Novokuzneck	SST	-12.00	19:12	19:59	21:03	22:47	1:20	4:16	7:12	10:08	13:03	15:37	17:21	18:24
Novosibirsk	SST	-12.00	19:28	20:12	21:13	22:55	1:30	4:29	7:28	10:27	13:26	16:02	17:44	18:44
Odessa	BT	-8.00	18:57	19:59	21:17	23:08	1:35	4:16	6:57	9:38	12:19	14:46	16:37	17:55
Omsk	90E	-11.00	19:06	19:51	20:51	22:33	1:09	4:07	7:06	10:05	13:04	15:40	17:22	18:22
Rostov Na Donu	BT	-8.00	18:21	19:22	20:39	22:29	0:56	3:39	6:21	9:04	11:46	14:13	16:03	17:20

♎ = Libra ♏ = Scorpio ♐ = Sagittarius ♑ = Capricorn ♒ = Aquarius ♓ = Pisces

City	Zone	—>EST	♈	♉	♊	♋	♌	♍	♎	♏	♐	♑	♒	♓
USSR, continued														
Saratov	60E	-9.00	18:56	19:48	20:57	22:43	1:14	4:05	6:56	9:47	12:37	15:08	16:55	18:04
Sverdlovsk	75E	-10.00	18:58	19:37	20:32	22:11	0:50	3:54	6:58	10:02	13:06	15:44	17:23	18:18
Tallinn	BT	-8.00	19:21	19:52	20:39	22:12	0:56	4:09	7:21	10:33	13:46	16:30	18:03	18:50
Tashkent	90E	-11.00	19:23	20:33	21:59	23:53	2:16	4:50	7:23	9:56	12:29	14:53	16:47	18:12
Tbilisi	60E	-9.00	19:01	20:11	21:36	23:30	1:53	4:27	7:01	9:34	12:08	14:32	16:26	17:51
Vladivostok	EST	-15.00	19:12	20:20	21:43	23:36	2:00	4:37	7:12	9:48	12:24	14:48	16:42	18:05
Volgograd	60E	-9.00	19:02	20:00	21:15	23:04	1:32	4:17	7:02	9:47	12:33	15:01	16:50	18:04
Uganda														
Kampala	BT	-8.00	18:50	20:42	22:41	0:50	2:59	4:58	6:50	8:42	10:42	12:51	15:00	16:59
Uruguay														
Montevideo	BZ2	-2.00	18:45	21:09	23:35	1:55	3:53	5:26	6:45	8:04	9:37	11:34	13:54	16:21
Paysandu	BZ2	-2.00	18:52	21:13	23:37	1:56	3:55	5:30	6:52	8:14	9:50	11:49	14:07	16:31
Salto	BZ2	-2.00	18:52	21:12	23:35	1:53	3:52	5:29	6:52	8:15	9:51	11:50	14:09	16:32
Vanuatu														
Port-Vila	165E	-16.00	17:47	19:53	22:05	0:19	2:22	4:10	5:47	7:23	9:11	11:15	13:28	15:40
Venda														
Thohoyandou	EET	-7.00	17:58	20:09	22:25	0:41	2:43	4:26	5:58	7:30	9:13	11:16	13:31	15:47
Venezuela														
Barquisimeto	AST	-1.00	18:37	20:21	22:14	0:20	2:31	4:37	6:37	8:37	10:43	12:55	15:01	16:54
Caracas	AST	-1.00	18:28	20:11	22:03	0:09	2:21	4:27	6:28	8:28	10:35	12:46	14:52	16:45
Ciudad Guayana	AST	-1.00	18:11	19:55	21:50	23:56	2:07	4:12	6:11	8:09	10:14	12:25	14:32	16:26
Maracaibo	AST	-1.00	18:46	20:29	22:22	0:28	2:39	4:46	6:46	8:47	10:54	13:05	15:11	17:04
Valencia	AST	-1.00	18:32	20:15	22:08	0:14	2:26	4:32	6:32	8:32	10:38	12:50	14:56	16:49
Yemen														
Aden	BT	-8.00	17:59	19:40	21:31	23:37	1:49	3:57	5:59	8:01	10:10	12:22	14:27	16:18
Yugoslavia														
Belgrade	MET	-6.00	17:38	18:43	20:04	21:56	0:21	3:00	5:38	8:16	10:55	13:20	15:12	16:33
Zagreb	MET	-6.00	17:56	19:00	20:19	22:10	0:36	3:16	5:56	8:36	11:16	13:42	15:34	16:53
Zaire														
Kananga	EET	-7.00	18:30	20:27	22:30	0:41	2:48	4:44	6:30	8:17	10:13	12:20	14:30	16:34
Kinshasa	MET	-6.00	17:59	19:54	21:56	0:06	2:14	4:11	5:59	7:47	9:44	11:51	14:01	16:04
Kisangani	EET	-7.00	18:19	20:11	22:11	0:20	2:29	4:28	6:19	8:10	10:10	12:18	14:27	16:27
Likasi	EET	-7.00	18:13	20:14	22:21	0:32	2:38	4:30	6:13	7:56	9:48	11:54	14:05	16:12
Lubumbashi	EET	-7.00	18:10	20:11	22:19	0:31	2:36	4:28	6:10	7:52	9:44	11:50	14:01	16:09
Matadi	MET	-6.00	18:06	20:03	22:06	0:16	2:24	4:19	6:06	7:53	9:49	11:56	14:06	16:10
Mbandaka	MET	-6.00	17:47	19:39	21:38	23:47	1:56	3:55	5:47	7:39	9:38	11:47	13:56	15:55
Mbuji-Mayi	EET	-7.00	18:25	20:22	22:26	0:36	2:43	4:39	6:25	8:12	10:08	12:15	14:25	16:29
Zambia														
Kitwe	EET	-7.00	18:07	20:09	22:18	0:30	2:35	4:26	6:07	7:48	9:39	11:44	13:57	16:05
Lusaka	EET	-7.00	18:07	20:11	22:21	0:34	2:39	4:28	6:07	7:46	9:35	11:39	13:52	16:02
Ndola	EET	-7.00	18:05	20:08	22:16	0:28	2:34	4:25	6:05	7:46	9:37	11:43	13:55	16:03
Zimbabwe														
Bulawayo	EET	-7.00	18:06	20:14	22:28	0:42	2:45	4:31	6:06	7:40	9:26	11:29	13:43	15:57
Harare	EET	-7.00	17:56	20:02	22:14	0:28	2:32	4:19	5:56	7:32	9:20	11:24	13:37	15:49

APPENDIX

ASTROLOGICAL FUNDAMENTALS

This section will cover many astrological terms and principles. It is excerpted from Maritha Pottenger's book *Astro Essentials* (published by Astro Communications Services).

Planets

Planets are one of the four basic building blocks of astrology. When astrologers say "planets," they usually refer to the eight known planets of our solar system other than Earth, which is our platform for viewing the rest of the system. The planets include Mercury, Venus, Mars, Jupiter, Saturn, Uranus, Neptune and Pluto, plus the Sun and the Moon. We know that the Sun is actually a star and the Moon is actually a satellite of Earth, but for convenience they are included with the planets when describing the heavenly bodies as distinct from other factors in astrology such as houses and signs.

Astrologically, each of the planets represents a drive or need within you. A planet is like the verb in a sentence; it indicates where the action is. Planets comprise the most significant building block of astrology. Following is a brief description of each of the planets. Each planet has its own glyph (symbol) used to represent it in the horoscope. Glyphs follow (in parens) the name of each planet. Each planet occupies a house in the horoscope (to be defined later) and a sign in the zodiac (definitions to follow).

Just as the **Sun** (☉) is the center of our solar system, so is it the center of the horoscope. Our Sun in the solar system provides light and makes life possible. The Sun in the horoscope is a key to vitality, life force, and our central, creative urge. The Sun represents our need to shine, our desire for recognition, our self-esteem, and pride/shame issues.

Wherever our Sun (☉) is (occupying one of 12 houses, and one of 12 signs), we want to be admired, noticed, loved, or applauded by the world. We feel most vital and alive when expressing the themes of our Sun's house and sign. Since it is a key to vitality and zest, we naturally pour energy into the activities represented by our Sun's house and sign.

The **Moon** (☽), which shines by reflected light, is a key to our emotions, particularly our need for emotional security and safety. It symbolizes our dependency needs and our desire to nurture and care for others. It represents the people we depend on, the parent who was a nurturing figure (usually mother), and our capacity to be an assisting, helpful, caring individual. It also is a key to our home, our roots (ancestry), and our sensitivities.

Wherever the Moon (☽) is (by house and sign), we want to nurture or be nurtured, to make warm, emotional connections with others. Family feelings may be sought or explored and emotions are the focus. It shows our hunger for a nest, and is connected to the unconscious side of the mind and to habits.

Mercury (☿) represents our need to communicate. It is a key to the conscious side of the mind, to our verbal ability, our logic, our capacity to be objective and detached. Mercury symbolizes the reasoning mind that observes the world, gathers information, learns, teaches, and disseminates knowledge.

Wherever Mercury (☿) is in our horoscope (by house and sign), we are curious, interested, and want to know. We may learn and/or teach in that area. Our Mercury placements help to describe our verbal styles and the way we use our minds.

Venus (♀) represents our need to enjoy the physical world and the pleasure principle. We may seek pleasure through money, possessions, tangible beauty, or sensual gratification. We may also seek pleasure through relationships, through sharing, through partnerships with others. Venus is a key to affection, love, our need for balance, our appreciation of beauty, and our orientation toward ease, comfort, and personal enjoyment.

Wherever Venus (♀) is in our horoscope (by house and sign), we want to enjoy! We seek pleasure, comfort, ease, beauty, teamwork, grace, and goodness in the areas inhabited by Venus.

Mars (♂) represents our need to assert ourselves, to defend our own rights, to identify and go after what we want in the world. Mars can be a key to healthy self-expression and personal power, but it can also represent aggression, fights, arguments, and negative forms of assertion. Mars is an indicator of our basic physical energy and health, sexual drive, anger, where we seek freedom, our desire to do things on our own, and our sense of basic identity.

Wherever Mars (♂) is in our horoscope (by house and sign), we want to express ourselves, be free and be active. If the personal energy symbolized by Mars is blocked, we might experience physical or interpersonal problems as a result of not defending our own needs. If we carry Martian themes too far, (assert our own rights too strongly), we may be rash, impulsive or self-centered in the areas where Mars lies. If we balance our Martian side with other drives, we can be assertive in a healthy fashion, meeting our own needs and drives in a constructive manner.

Jupiter (♃) represents our need to believe and to aspire. It indicates our ideals, what we tend to value and where we want more in life. It is also a key to where we can exaggerate or overdo, and indicates opportunities (which we may or may not take advantage of) plus the confidence to pursue our visions.

Wherever Jupiter (♃) is in our horoscope (by house and sign), we tend to place our faith. We are likely to seek more in that area, and may overdo. (If we see something as good, more is better.) Jupiter's placement may indicate that an individual trusts and values money, or a partner, or power, or personal creativity, or a religion, etc. Where Jupiter is a key, we may idealize and put a part of life (e.g., a marriage, a child, a job) on a pedestal. We may expect more than is possible, that a fragment of life (rather than the whole process) should give us total fulfillment, should make our life meaningful. (If, for instance, we idealize a marital partner, we may believe that individual gives our life meaning. If so, we are apt to be emotionally destroyed if the individual dies or leaves. Alternately, if we expect our profession to provide our total meaning in life, we are likely to be chronically dissatisfied because it will never be enough. There could always be something more.)

Our ultimate goals in life depend on our beliefs about what is true, desirable, possible, and morally correct. Jupiter symbolizes our optimistic spirit, where we tend to look on the bright side, have hope, and see the highest potentials.

Saturn (♄) represents our need to structure life, to test and cope with material reality. Saturn is a key to the limits of life in this physical world: what we can do, cannot do, and have to do. It is also symbolic of authority figures in our lives: from the rulemaker parent (traditionally Dad) to police officers and presidents.

Wherever Saturn (♄) is in our horoscope (by house and sign), we learn to face reality and what is possible. We often deal with consequences (cause and effect). Saturn represents the principle of learning through experience (sometimes the "school of hard knocks"). Where Saturn's rules (the power of the external world to limit us) are given too much weight, people may feel blocked, inhibited, incapable, incompetent, or unable to do anything. Where Saturn's rules are ignored, people may be overly responsible, trying to carry the whole world (the "Atlas Syndrome"). Or, individuals might push the world (or others) until they discover certain principles (including the laws of the land) that are bigger than they are. Individuals in the latter case may be irresponsible (ignoring limits, rules, duties) or even outright criminals (fighting the laws of the land). Eventually we reap the consequences of what we have sown. We learn to drive on the right side of the road in the U.S. and on the left side of the road in England. To stay healthy, we have to eat, sleep, move our bodies, etc. People who are handling the Saturn principle properly understand the rules and live within them voluntarily. They are practical achievers who do not attempt the impossible but do what is necessary and possible within the structures of society and natural law.

Uranus (♅) represents our urge to go beyond Saturn, to resist limits, to change and alter. It is a key to our drive for individuality and uniqueness, our capacity to rebel; the lure of the unusual and the unknown. Uranus symbolizes our need for the freedom to be different, to explore alternatives, and to look toward the future and progress.

Wherever Uranus (♅) is in our horoscope (by house and sign), we need to be independent. We need to come from our own unique essence. Uranus shows where we seek space, where we can innovate and be inventive, and where we can be surprised. Uranus mirrors our urge to consider alternatives, to be open and equalitarian, and to expand knowledge which connects it to modern technology.

Neptune (♆) represents our need to merge and seek transcendence. Neptune is a key to our search for the beautiful dream. That vision may be sought through art, through healing or helping activities, or through escapist means. Neptune indicates our drive to experience Oneness, to be attuned with something Higher or ecstatic in life. We may seek transcendence through spiritual or religious paths, be "swept away" in nature worship, look to drugs for ecstasy, live in a "perfect" fantasy world, or find inspiration in philanthropy and compassionate assistance of humanity, or in artistic expressions.

Wherever Neptune (♆) is in our horoscope (by house and sign), we want to be inspired and must be wary of rose-colored glasses. We need to feel uplifted where our Neptune is placed, and may fool ourselves into viewing matters through a romantic haze. But Neptune can point to inadequate as well as excessive faith. Jupiter symbolizes our more conscious search for faith—a world view we can put into words, a set of moral, religious or ethical principles. With Neptune, the search for the Absolute is partly unconscious—whether we are seeking personal "salvation" or trying to "save" others. Neptune represents an intense emotional need to be inspired, swept away, united and unified with something Higher. We seek transcendent experiences in the areas connected to Neptune in our horoscope, and need to be able to do our share and then trust a Higher Power.

For those who lack the (partly unconscious) faith in a Higher Power, who think they have to do it all themselves (the Atlas side of Saturn), Neptune can be associated with anxiety which is simply a lack of faith. In such cases, it is important to find ways to encourage faith, whether by reading inspirational literature, associating with people who have a strong faith, or looking for times in our lives or in the lives of others when faith brought help and healing. People who are overdoing the Neptunian themes may be passive, escapist victims who expect God to balance the checkbook, provide the ideal partner, drop the "perfect" job in their laps, etc. People need enough (but not too much) of the faith and trust that Neptune symbolizes.

Pluto (♇) represents our need to relate intimately with another person and with our own psyche. Pluto, like Mars, can be a key to sexuality. It symbolizes our drive to share the world (especially sensually and financially) with another person—and learning about ourselves through interacting with someone else. Pluto also indicates our inner drive for self-understanding and self-mastery, including mastery of our emotions and of our appetites. Pluto themes have to do with depth analysis, tearing things down to open the way for something better, regeneration and transformation.

Wherever Pluto (♇) is in our horoscope (by house and sign), we tend to probe beneath the surface. We are apt to pick at, and painstakingly examine those areas, looking for hidden meanings and deeper layers. We may tear down and then build up, analyze carefully, and then rework and transform. Pluto also symbolizes our approach to shared resources, money, and sexuality. Pluto represents our deepest, most intense feelings and our capacity to share power, pleasure and possessions with another person. With Pluto, we may give in to others, struggle with them, run from them, but eventually we have to learn to share with them for mutual pleasure. We have to learn what is ours and what belongs to others; when we have done, said, or had enough; and how to let go.

Following are some key words for each of the planets. These are based on astrological traditions (and trial-and-error observations of people and horoscopes). Notice that each set of key words for a planet revolves around a few central, psychological drives, such as a need to shine, to do more than one has done before in life associated with the Sun; a need to nurture, protect, be emotionally attached with the Moon; a need to learn and communicate with Mercury, etc.

Sun: self-esteem, life force, vitality, creativity, risk-taking instincts, pride, star quality, fun-loving spirit, inner child, drive for excitement, need for recreation, speculative side, romantic passion, need to shine.

Moon: emotions, security needs, caretaking instincts, dependency needs, drive to nurture, vulnerabilities, homing instincts, receptivity, moods, habit patterns, women (including mother).

Mercury: urge to communicate, thinking, listening/talking, capacity to learn cognitively, adaptability/flexibility, information-gathering skills, casual contacts, logic, conscious awareness, dexterity, intellectual perception.

Venus: desire for pleasure, sensuality, urge for comfort/ease, need for tangible beauty, drive for stability/predictability, sweetness, affection, relating needs, instincts for teamwork, partnership, material assets.

Mars: assertion, self-expression, independence, personal power, desires, spontaneous instincts, immediate needs, anger, sexual drive, men in general, early identity, doing one's thing, need to be first, energy level.

Jupiter: ideals and goals, beliefs, values, morality/ethics, faith, optimism, quest for the truth, philosophy/religion, drive for expanded horizons, high expectations, seeking the best/highest, expansiveness.

Saturn: reality quotient, response to and desire for authority, authority figures (usually including father), attitudes toward the orthodox and what society deems appropriate, the personal conscience and guilt, practicality, capacity to deal with limits, career drives, sense of responsibility, discipline/effort, status ambitions, urge to solidify/contract, wisdom of experience.

Uranus: individuality, freedom drives, inventiveness, originality, humanitarian instincts, equalitarian principles, detachment, pull toward the future, eccentricity, innovation, sudden changes, interest in technology, the new or "cutting edge."

Neptune: quest for Oneness/Union/transcendence, idealism, seeking of infinite love and beauty, intuition, savior/victim potentials, compassion, imagination/ fantasy, mysticism, escapism, psychic openness.

Pluto: intensity, drive for self-knowledge and self-mastery, intimacy instincts, sexual needs, drive for transformation, elimination or completion urges, resentment and forgiveness, probing, complicated motives, compulsions, addictions, ability to know when "enough is enough" and how to let go, ability to share possessions, pleasures and power with an intimate other.

Houses of the Horoscope

Your time of birth is required in order to calculate which houses are occupied by the planets. Houses are a division of space based on the Earth's 24-hour rotation. The Earth turns completely on its axis in one 24-hour period, creating our day and night. The space around earth is divided into 12 areas called houses which are shown as pie-shaped wedges in a circular horoscope. (Think of these wedges as three-dimensional, extending out from one's birthplace into space.)

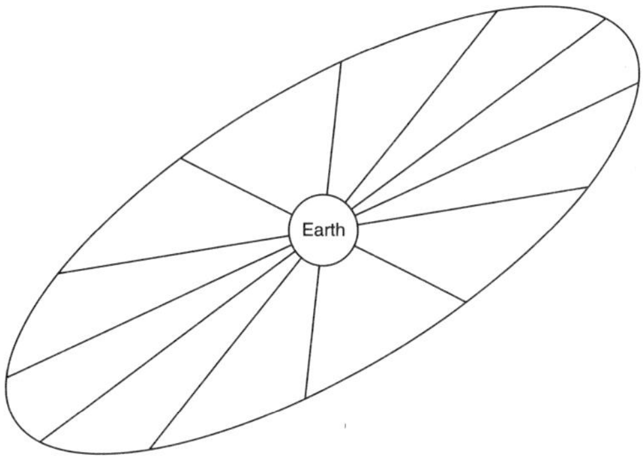

If you had looked out from your place of birth at your moment of birth, each planet would have been in one of these areas of space which are numbered from one to twelve in a counter-clockwise direction starting at the eastern horizon. Although houses are represented most commonly by 12 equally-sized wedges, they are actually of **unequal** size. One house might be only 18° wide, while another might be 45°.

When a house is more than 30° wide, an entire sign is inside that house, with no cusp of its own. Such a sign is called "intercepted" and its opposite sign will also be intercepted. In Bruce Springsteen's chart (page 579), Virgo is intercepted in the 4th and Pisces in the 10th. When a pair of signs is intercepted, another pair must do double duty, appearing on two cusps. (That occurs in Springsteen's chart with Leo and Aquarius.) Clearly houses with intercepted signs are always larger (have more degrees in them) than houses with no interceptions.

Most astrological texts portray equal-sized "apple pie" houses

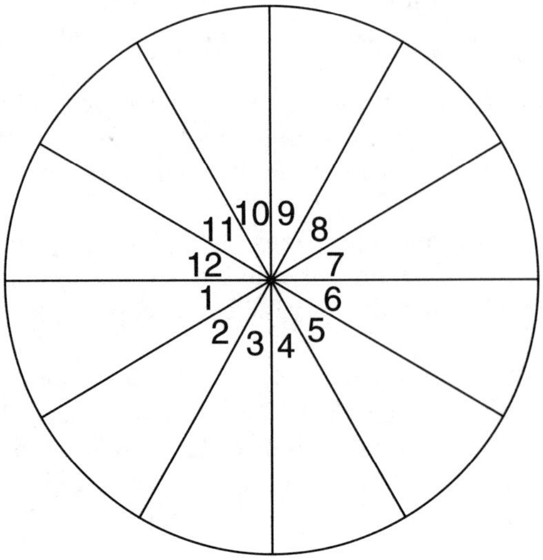

Each sign is 30° (so 12 make up the 360° circle), but houses are of different sizes (although all 12 will total 360°).

It would be more visually accurate to show houses of unequal sizes (and some astrologers do so).

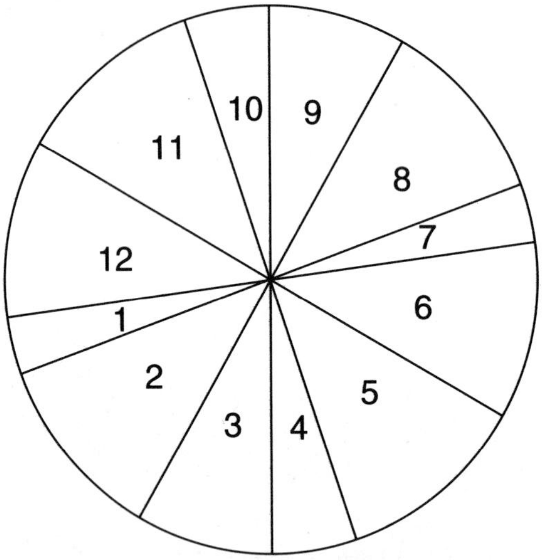

The line which separates one house from the next is called a cusp. Certain house cusps are considered to have extra significance in astrology. Many years of observation have led to traditions as to their importance and meanings. One of the most important is the cusp of the first house which points to the eastern horizon and which is called the Ascendant in the horoscope. Planets which will soon rise above the horizon will be in the first house. If you were born around sunrise, the Sun will be near the cusp of your first house. Astrologers consider the sign on the Ascendant (the "rising sign") an important key to personal identity and action. Similarly the sign on the cusp of the tenth house (the Midheaven) is considered significant in matters of career and status. The 7th cusp (Descendant) is important in regard to relationships, while the 4th cusp (IC) reveals home and family issues. Think of the Ascendant as similar to Mars; the IC to the Moon; the Descendant to Venus; and the Midheaven to Saturn.

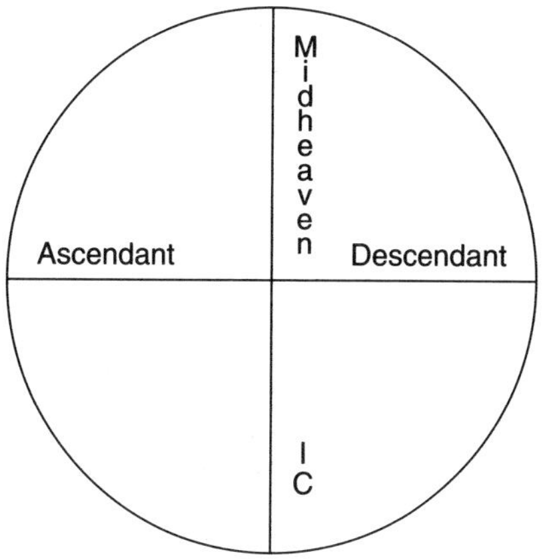

Cusps are the boundary lines in a horoscope (the fence posts). They show where each house begins and ends. In Bruce Springsteen's horoscope, for example (page 579), the Ascendant (1st house cusp) is 22 degrees Gemini 49 minutes. The cusp of the 2nd house is 13° Cancer 32'. Thus, any planets which are later in the zodiac than 22° Gemini 49' and earlier than 13° Cancer 32' fall in the 1st house of Bruce Springsteen's horoscope.

Houses (like planets and signs) represent inner drives and needs to experience certain areas of life. The tools of astrology represent both inner psychological desires and other people and conditions in our lives to which we are drawn to play out our inner urges. For example, the 3rd house represents our capacity to learn, our logic and objectivity, and our communication skills. The 3rd house also symbolizes the people with whom we first practice learning and communicating: brothers, sisters, neighbors and other people near-at-hand. It also represents the near-at-hand (short) trips we make to satisfy our curiosity, and the short periodicals (newspapers and magazines rather than books) which we read for the same purpose. As with each house (and planet and sign), a central thread links the various associations. For the 3rd house, the central issue is learning and communication. The people, objects and needs associated with the 3rd house all derive from the basic human drive to learn and to communicate.

No matter where they are on Earth, people born at the same moment will have their planets in the same degree of their zodiacal signs. Because the outer planets (Jupiter through Pluto) take so long to orbit the Sun, they occupy each sign of the zodiac for a rather long time. A whole generation may have Pluto in the same sign of the zodiac. But all twelve houses turn past the planets as the Earth rotates each day, and houses also shift with the individual's location on Earth. So the house a planet occupies in a horoscope is a much more personal statement than the sign it occupies.

Following is a list of keywords for the houses. Notice again that the associations of each house cluster around a central thread of related drives and the people or objects connected to those drives.

1st house: personal action, identity, self-expression, spontaneous instincts, physical body, the beginning of life, appearance, what you do instinctively and automatically.

2nd house: possessions and pleasures, sensuality, money, comfort, stability, capacity to earn a living, tangible beauty, physical security, your material base.

3rd house: communication, relatives, learning capacity, lightheartedness, short trips, transportation, media, early schooling, immediate environment, conscious mind.

4th house: home, family, emotional vulnerabilities, nurturing instincts, roots, real estate, parent who was main nurturer, heredity and ancestry, emotional needs.

5th house: procreation, creativity, onstage activities, lovers, children, romance, speculation, hobbies, recreation, risk-taking, love given and received, pride and power.

6th house: competence, efficiency, work, health, handling of details, colleagues and co-workers, tenants, service and servants, employees, routines, nutrition, hygiene.

7th house: partners and partnership, need for balance, fair play, harmony, aesthetics, especially the graphic arts and design, contracts, lawsuits, competitors, attitude toward marriage, grandparent(s), spouse.

8th house: depth investigations, shared money, resources, pleasures, and power, intimacy instincts, sexuality, debts, taxes, inheritance, hidden matters, surgery, endings, therapy.

9th house: aspirations, beliefs, values, world view (religion or philosophy), optimism, law, science, ideals, higher education, books, distant travel/cultures, grandchildren, spiritual consciousness, the judicial branch of the government.

10th house: sense of responsibility, career, authorities, and your own authority in the world, reality principle, status, employer, how the world sees you, rulemaker parent, achievements, the executive branch of the government.

11th house: drive for individuation, originality, resistance to limits, equalitarian principles, friends, networking, hopes for the future, foster and stepchildren, voluntary organizations such as clubs, the legislative branch of the government.

12th house: desire for infinite love and beauty, union, mysticism, imagination, intuition, savior/victim issues including institutions such as hospitals where victims are helped, and jails where people are prevented from victimizing people outside but often victimize fellow inmates, protective retreats (e.g., ashrams) as well as escapist withdrawals (e.g., into fantasy, illness), the unconscious mind, especially unconscious faith or fear, charity, hidden weaknesses and strengths.

If you look over the the descriptions of the planets, and blend them with the house descriptions provided here, you may be able to identify some possible interpretations.

Signs of the Zodiac

Your "sky map" (horoscope) places planets in any of 12 signs and any of 12 houses. (There are 1,440 different possible planet/house/sign combinations and the variations rise even more if you include aspects as well.) Each planet has a different meaning, depending upon the house and the sign of the zodiac which it occupies.

The zodiac is an imaginary circle out in space. The Earth's path around the Sun (the ecliptic) is projected against infinity and is divided into twelve equal sections.

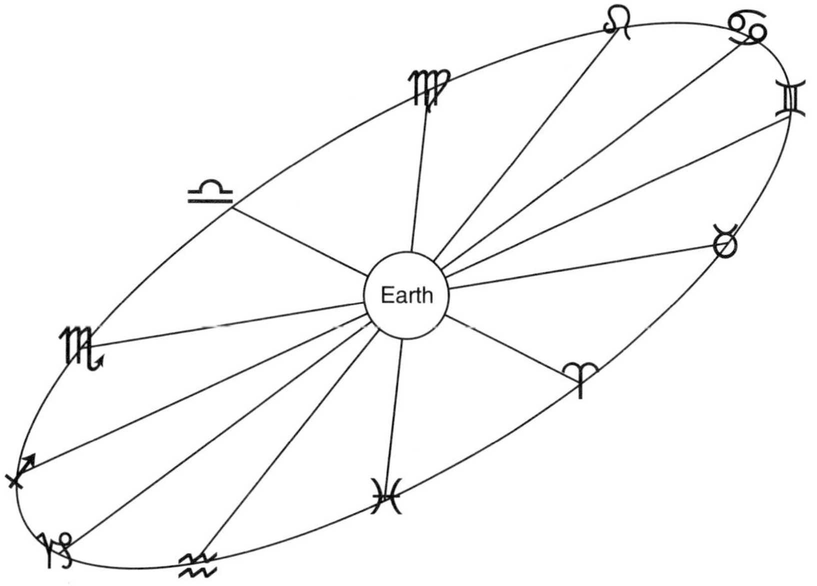

These twelve sections of the sky are not the same as the constellations or groups of stars which have the same names as the zodiac signs. Constellations do not exist in neat, 30° packages. Some constellations sprawl over 45°; others are only about 18° wide. The stars in some constellations overlap, while other constellations have empty spaces between them. Some of the constellations bearing the same names as our zodiac signs are not even located on the ecliptic; they reside above or below the plane of our Earth's orbit.

The position of the Sun at the vernal equinox (spring in the Northern Hemisphere) defines 0 degrees of the sign Aries—the beginning of the zodiac. Looking out from the Earth, we see each planet in front of a certain part of the zodiac circle and the planet is said to be "in" that sign. Around 200 AD, the seasonal zodiac which we use (also called the **tropical** zodiac) was roughly equivalent to the positions of many constellations bearing the same names. However, nothing in the universe is static. Due to the (slow) movement of the so-called "fixed" stars and the precession of the equinoxes (a slow westward motion of the equinoxes along the ecliptic), the seasonal or tropical zodiac has been diverging more and more from the constellations. They are almost one sign apart at this point. Thus, where an astrologer would define a planet as in the (tropical zodiac) sign of Aries, to an astronomer that planet would probably appear to be in the constellation of Pisces.

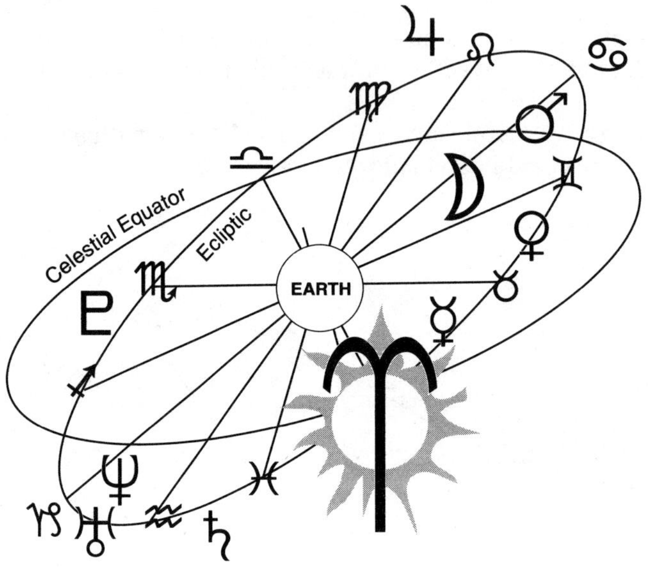

Some astrologers have assigned meaning to the movement of the zero Aries point (which defines our seasonal zodiac) against the backdrop of the constellations and "fixed" stars. The phrase "The Age of Aquarius" made famous by the musical *Hair* refers to a future time when the zero Aries point of our seasonal zodiac will move in front of the constellation named Aquarius.

One way to envision the interweaving of planets, houses and signs is to think of the horoscope as similar to a complicated clock with two dials and many hands. The zodiac circle is the "stationary" dial. (Actually nothing in the cosmos is really standing still). The planets move in front of the zodiac signs, each at its own respective speed. The house dial turns past the planets and signs as the Earth rotates every day, so every day, the planets and signs "appear" to move through the houses.

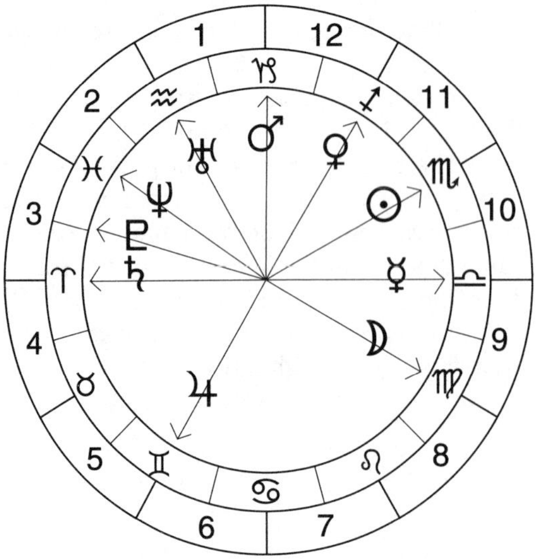

Outer (house) dial rotates.
Hands (planets) move.
Inner (sign) dial is
[relatively] stationary

Your **day of birth** determines the sign of the zodiac occupied by the Sun. That is your "Sun sign" which many popular newspaper and magazine columns abbreviate to just "your sign." The signs occupied by the other planets are determined by both your **year** of birth and your **day** of birth.

Your **time of birth** may be needed to know your Moon sign, because the Moon changes signs about every 2½ days. Also, if you were born on a day when the Sun or a planet was changing signs (near one of twelve boundary points in the zodiacal circle), you will need to know your time of birth to determine which sign that planet is in. (Remember, astrologers call the Sun and Moon "planets" for convenience, even though the Sun is a star and the Moon is a satellite of Earth.)

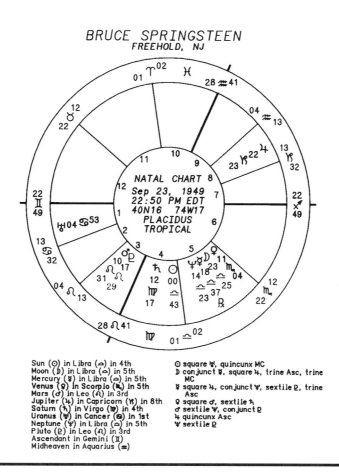

Each planet occupies a position (a number of degrees) within a sign. Each sign is made up of 30 degrees (and 12 signs comprise the 360° circle of the zodiac). Furthermore, each degree of the zodiac has 60 minutes within it. These minutes are **not** the same as minutes of time. Zodiacal minutes are positions in space. In this chart of Bruce Springsteen, for example, the positions are as follows:

Sun	—	00 degrees of Libra and 43 minutes or 0♎43
Moon	—	23 degrees of Libra and 25 minutes or 23♎25
Mercury	—	18 degrees of Libra and 37 minutes or 18♎37
Venus	—	11 degrees of Scorpio and 4 minutes or 11♏4
Mars	—	10 degrees of Leo and 31 minutes or 10♌31
Jupiter	—	22 degrees of Capricorn and 23 minutes or 22♑23
Saturn	—	12 degrees of Virgo and 17 minutes or 12♍17
Uranus	—	04 degrees of Cancer and 53 minutes or 4♋53
Neptune	—	14 degrees of Libra and 23 minutes or 14♎23
Pluto	—	17 degrees of Leo and 29 minutes or 17♌29

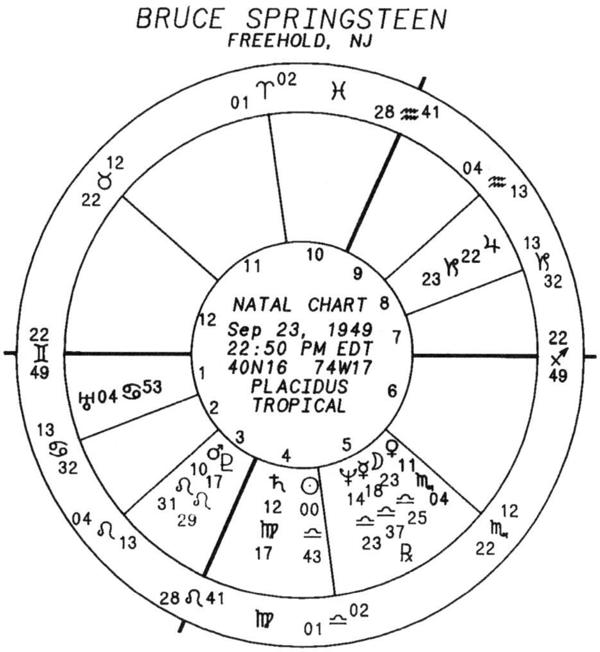

Sun (☉) in Libra (♎) in 4th
Moon (☽) in Libra (♎) in 5th
Mercury (☿) in Libra (♎) in 5th
Venus (♀) in Scorpio (♏) in 5th
Mars (♂) in Leo (♌) in 3rd
Jupiter (♃) in Capricorn (♑) in 8th
Saturn (♄) in Virgo (♍) in 4th
Uranus (♅) in Cancer (♋) in 1st
Neptune (♆) in Libra (♎) in 5th
Pluto (♇) in Leo (♌) in 3rd
Ascendant in Gemini (♊)
Midheaven in Aquarius (♒)

☉ square ♅, quincunx MC
☽ conjunct ☿, square ♃, trine Asc, trine MC
☿ square ♃, conjunct ♆, sextile ♇, trine Asc
♀ square ♂, sextile ♄
♂ sextile ♆, conjunct ♇
♃ quincunx Asc
♆ sextile ♇

The house cusps (boundary lines) determine in which house each of those planets falls. A planet's position in the zodiac (degree and minute of a sign) is always after the cusp which marks the beginning of the house that planet is in, but before the cusp of the next house. Bruce Springsteen's Sun, for example, (at 0° Libra 43') is after 28♌41 (the cusp of the 4th house) and before 1♎02 (the cusp of the 5th house) so his Sun is in the 4th house.

The signs modify the planets, like adjectives modify verbs in English. You tend to express the drive symbolized by the planet in a manner described by the sign it occupies. Here are a few traditional key words (based on centuries of observation) for the signs. The glyph (symbol) for each sign follows its name. As with planets and houses, note that each sign has a central, connected thread of shared drives and psychological principles. The central core of Aries radiates around forceful initiative; the central core of Taurus revolves around physical pleasures and comfort; the central core of Gemini emphasizes hunger for knowledge, etc.

Aries ♈: assertive, brave, first, impetuous, energetic, self-oriented, pioneering, rash, competitive, rapid, eager, likes to be on one's own, lives in the present.

Taurus ♉: comfortable, deliberate, dependable, placid, possessive, sensual, patient, loyal, thorough, stubborn, stable, money-oriented, practical, artistic.

Gemini ♊: fluent, versatile, curious, intermittent, clever, nimble, quick-witted, adaptable, scattered, gossipy, dexterous, superficial, flexible, lighthearted, articulate.

Cancer ♋: nurturing, warm, dependent, sympathetic, protective, security-oriented, maternal, patriotic, retentive, helpful, moody, domestic, touchy (easily hurt), focused on home and family.

Leo ♌: creative, risk-taking, charismatic, fun-loving, generous, exciting, dramatic, proud, self-confident, childish, ambitious, arrogant, self-conscious (fears ridicule unless self-esteem is very high), enthusiastic, magnetic.

Virgo ♍: work-oriented, painstaking, efficient, pragmatic, exacting, discreet, industrious, thorough, critical, finds flaws, pedantic, methodical, careful, detail-oriented, concerned with health/cleanliness.

Libra ♎: cooperative and/or competitive, seeing both sides and concerned with fair play which can lead to fence-sitting, diplomatic, aesthetic, charming, easily deterred, refined, sociable, seeks a partner/companion, placates, equalitarian.

Scorpio ♏: penetrating, emotionally intense, resourceful, powerful, compulsive, determined, jealous, passionate, secretive, probing, suspicious, controlling, fascinated by the hidden or taboo.

Sagittarius ♐: benevolent, optimistic, extravagant, athletic, enthusiastic, idealistic, philosophical, freedom-loving, exaggerative, blunt, overindulgent, broad-minded, truth-seeking and truth-telling, just.

Capricorn ♑: responsible, formal, traditional, authoritative, career-oriented, cautious, inhibited, hardworking, scrupulous, conventional, status-seeking, economical, businesslike, thorough, conscientious, organized, ambitious.

Aquarius ♒: unique, rebellious, futuristic, independent, inventive, objective, intellectual, unpredictable, tolerant, eccentric, aloof, progressive, has a wide perspective.

Pisces ♓: compassionate, mystical, illusory, sensitive, spiritual, dreamy, artistic, passive, sacrificial, intuitive, charitable, impractical, escapist, visionary, inspirational.

As you can see, each sign has a number of different possibilities. The symbols of astrology work on many levels. Everything has **more than one** meaning when you deal with the details of life. Each principle in astrology has both "up" and "down" sides—both positive and negative possibilities. An emphasis in the chart on a particular planet, house or sign simply means that the individual has to deal often with the issues associated with that planet, house or sign. They may overdo certain drives or have trouble expressing them. Astrology only mirrors our potentials. When we express the life principles which astrology reflects, we have the power to manifest either positive or painful details in our lives, and with awareness and effort, we can change from one to the other.

You could extrapolate planet in sign interpretations by combining the key words given here for signs with the descriptions provided of the planets.

Astrological Alphabet

You can think of the astrological model of life as an alphabet. An alphabet can be printed with capital letters, small case letters, script, etc., but we recognize an "A" as the same principle as an "a." Similarly in astrology, the same twelve basic drives or "sides of life" are symbolized by the planets, the houses, and the signs.

Each sign of the zodiac is associated with a house of the horoscope: the first sign (Aries) with the 1st house; the second sign (Taurus) with the 2nd house, and so on. These house/sign pairs share common themes, drives and issues. Similarly, each planet is said to "rule" a certain sign and house. That ruling planet symbolizes the same basic principles as the house/sign pair—but in a more active, significant and powerful sense. (Planets are like the verbs in a sentence; houses and signs qualify planets as adverbs qualify verbs.)

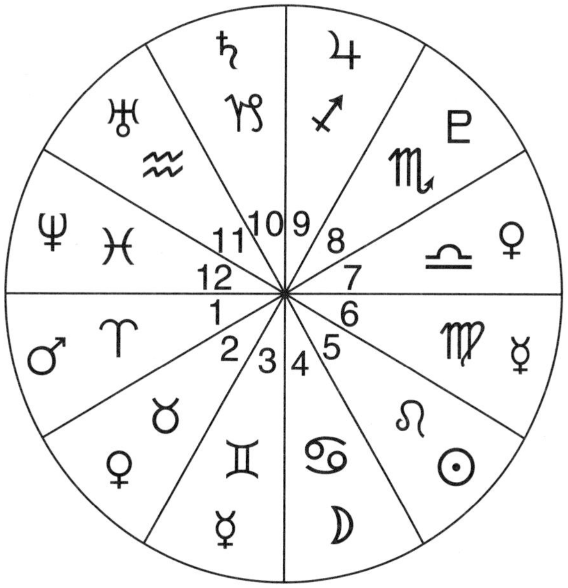

Because there are twelve signs and twelve houses, but only ten planets, some planets must do "double duty"—ruling two signs and houses. Mercury rules both Gemini/3rd house and Virgo/6th house and thus indicates principles associated with both house/sign pairs. Venus rules both Taurus/2nd house and Libra/7th house and is a key to principles associated with both of those pairs.

Astrology is inherently repetitive. What is most significant in the psyche and in one's life will be repeated in the horoscope. Recognizing the astrological alphabet helps us to see those reiterated messages. Following is a list of the planet/house/sign triplets that make up the astrological alphabet and the psychological issues and drives connected with each "letter" of the alphabet.

KEY PHRASES FOR HOUSE-PLANET-SIGN COMBINATIONS
by Zipporah Pottenger Dobyns, Ph.D.

1. Free self-expression; self-will in spontaneous action; initiative, impulse, courage, pioneering spirit, vitality, skilled coordination, enthusiasm for the new, ready to fight against any limits on personal freedom. "**I do my thing.**" ♂ ♈ 1st House

2. Pleasure in manipulating the physical sense world; comfort, security, contentment, love of beauty in tangible possessions; deliberate, persisting determination, slow to become angry or to forget. "**I enjoy the sense world.**" ♀ ♉ 2nd House

3. Consciousness; capacity to learn and communicate; thought, language, contact with nearby equals, dexterity, curiosity, versatility, multiple interests, flexibility, cheerful, witty, flippant. "**I see, conceptualize and talk.**" ☿ ♊ 3rd House

4. Memory, nurturance-dependence; absorption, protection, preservation, sensitivity, empathy, need for warmth and emotional closeness and rootedness. "**I save, protect, nourish and assimilate.**" ☽ ♋ 4th House

5. Creativity and self-expression; capacity to transcend the past; joy, love, drama, need for admiration, the limelight, power; increase through children, speculation; intensifying emotions through stage, screen, etc.; pride, generosity, magnetic vitality. "**I rejoice in expansion.**" ☉ ♌ 5th House

6. Service; productive work; analysis, discrimination, pragmatism, quiet efficiency, attention to detail, self-restraint, humility, interest in health and healing. "**I work competently.**" ☿ ♍ 6th House

7. Partnership; cooperation or competition with equals; justice, both sides in balance; harmony, arbitration, pleasure from grace, line, form, a feeling for space and from interaction with peers; need for "equal others" to feel complete. "**I enjoy balance.**" ♀ ♎ 7th House

8. Insight and self-control for regeneration; intensity, passion, no surrender to death; where we learn the boundary of self-will by accepting what comes, using what is of value, purifying or eliminating waste for optimal functioning; search for hidden knowledge. "**I penetrate, control, absorb or eliminate according to my desire.**" ♇ ♏ 8th House

9. Faith and values; philosophical, religious, and ethical belief systems; what is considered true and morally good, ultimate knowledge and trust; optimism, humor, generosity, expansiveness, love of sports, nature, travel, based on faith in life and the urge to reach farther. "**I trust, value and direct my life according to my understanding.**" ♃ ♐ 9th House

10. Law—Karmic, natural, human-made; power above self-will; bureaucracy; puritan virtues—duty, responsibility, thrift, practicality, realism; ambition for reassurance of self-worth, security or to avoid guilt; sense of pressure from forces beyond personal control; crystallized structures from social institutions to bones and teeth. "**I carry out the Law.**" ♄ ♑ 10th House

11. New opportunity for all people; rebellion against the old, constriction and control and for humanitarian principles; sudden, unexpected change to permit growth; explosive, individualistic, open, equalitarian; chaos or voluntary community. "**I seek new knowledge and brotherhood (sisterhood) for all mankind.**" ♅ ♒ 11th House

12. Oneness with the whole; hunger for infinite love and beauty; creative imagination, fantasy; selflessness or escapism including drugs, alcohol and psychosis; the artist or savior-martyr; sensitive, compassionate, or passive-submissive. "**I dream of love and beauty and am absorbed in the whole.**" ♆ ♓ 12th House

If you compare the listing on page 582 to the key words supplied earlier for planets, houses, and signs, you will note that the alphabet principles include the major themes associated with all the planets, houses and signs. Rather than learning twelve different signs, twelve different houses, and ten different planets, many people find it easier to learn the astrological alphabet. Each of the twelve sides of life is represented by a planet, a house, and a sign.

Aspects

The fourth building block of astrology is aspects. Aspects refer to the relationships between the planets or between planets and points in the chart such as the Ascendant (or 1st house cusp). The relationships or aspects between the planets indicate the relationships between various drives and needs in our nature which are symbolized by the planets.

Every circle has 360 degrees and the circle of the zodiac is no exception. Thus each planet (or point in the horoscope) is separated from other planets (and points) by a specific number of degrees. Certain degree segments (0, 60, 90, 120, 150, 180) have—with time and trial-and-error observation of correspondences—been assigned meanings in astrology. (Some astrologers suggest that **any** number of degrees between two planets is significant. Historically, only certain degree segments were observed as offering useful information.) Most modern astrologers find that the six degree segments listed previously (0, 60, 90, 120, 150, 180) do "work" astrologically.

The aspect which is easiest to "see" in a horoscope is the conjunction, an aspect of zero degrees so the planets are seen together in the chart. (If, for example, a horoscope has the Sun at 13° Gemini 35' and Mercury is at 13° Gemini 55', we would say that the Sun is conjunct Mercury. We could also say that Mercury is conjunct the Sun.)

The meaning of a conjunction is that the drives of the two planets are mixed. It is as if these planets are married or living together. In your horoscope, you do not get one without the other. They symbolize desires which are melded in your personality. The blending may be comfortable or not so comfortable—depending on the nature of the drives involved.

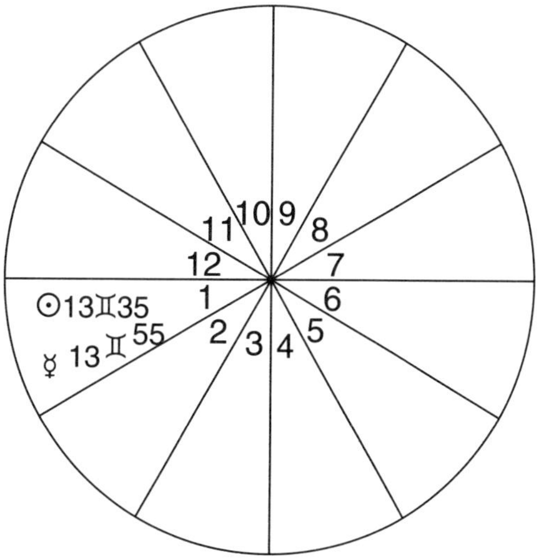

Someone with the Sun (where we need to shine and be recognized) conjunct Mercury (the mind, communication skills, need to learn), for example, might be very ego-invested in his or her mind. Positive attention for knowledge would be vital to that person. Appearing "smart" would be an ego need. Conversely, someone with the Sun conjunct Venus could be very ego-involved in either relationships (needing much admiration and attention from partners) or material possessions (measuring self-worth by what they own). People who do not have the Sun conjunct either of those planets are less likely to have intense ego investments in being admired and applauded for intellect, sharing, or possessions.

Remember, however, that Venus is associated with Taurus and the 2nd house in the natural zodiac and also with Libra and the 7th house. So, a Sun in the 2nd house or in Taurus, like a Sun conjunct Venus, could denote someone ego-invested in ownership or pleasure. A Sun in the 7th house, like a Sun conjunct Venus, might symbolize an individual who is ego-vulnerable in relationships. A Sun in the 3rd or 6th houses (or in Gemini or Virgo) probably identifies someone wishing to shine through the mind, as does the Sun conjunct Mercury. The major distinction is that planets [which are like verbs] point to more central, intense issues. Houses and signs are a less powerful statement of a similar principle. A Sun/Venus conjunction would represent more intense gratification and ego involvement through possessions and pleasures or relationships, than just the Sun in the 2nd or only the Sun in Taurus.

☉ ☌ ♀
(Sun conjunct Venus)

↙	↘
☉ in 2nd house ☉ in ♉ (Taurus) Ego on line with possessions and pleasures.	☉ in 7th house ☉ in ♎ (Libra) Ego on line in relationships.

☉ ☌ ☿
(Sun conjunct Mercury)

↙	↘
☉ in 3rd house ☉ in ♊ (Gemini) Wants to shine through mind, communication.	☉ in 6th house ☉ in ♍ (Virgo) Wants to shine for precision, competence.

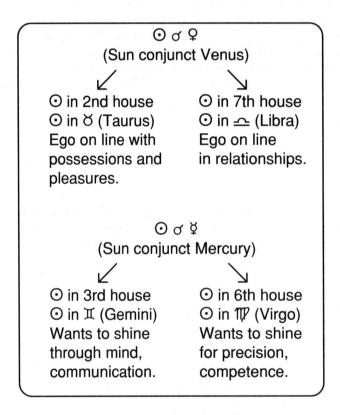

Interpreting a conjunction is not very different from putting together the meanings of a planet in a house or a planet in a sign. You are combining two of the twelve basic drives, two of the twelve sides of life (or two letters of the astrological alphabet). Consider both sides: how might these two planets reinforce and support one another's themes and how might their basic drives conflict and compete with one other?

In terms of the meaning of a conjunction, look to the nature of the planets (or points) involved to determine likely positive or negative manifestations. Certain planets stand for drives which "get along" easily, that is they tend to want the same sort of things, and tend to pull in the same direction. When such planets conjunct each other, they suggest inner agreement, reinforcement and harmony. (Examples would include conjunctions between the Sun, Jupiter, and/or Mars.)

Other planets represent drives which are contradictory or at odds with one another. Where such planets conjunct each other, the individual must strive to somehow "make peace" between possibly warring factions. Integration takes more effort. (An example would include the Moon with Uranus.)

There are few hard and fast rules. Venus as ruler of Libra tends to conflict with Saturn as ruler of Capricorn, but Venus also rules Taurus which usually harmonizes with Capricorn. A Venus conjunction with Saturn can therefore show a good ability to be successful in the material world, whether in business or in a field of the arts. More attention is needed to maintain a comfortable, equalitarian relationship which Venus (as ruler of Libra) symbolizes while Saturn shows a desire to be in control. When Saturn aspects the planet of peer relationships (Venus), there is the danger in that individual's relationships that one partner might try to control the other, or neglect the relationship because of the importance of the career, or direct the work attitude (looking for flaws in order to correct them) into the relationship instead of keeping the critical focus for one's job.

The principles will be illustrated more fully later. At this point, it is important to realize that the picture is complex and that you will meet a variety of opinions in different astrology texts. There are writers who consider all aspects to Jupiter to be "good" and all aspects to Saturn to be "bad." It is true that Saturn calls for realism and effort while Jupiter encourages faith that we can have what we want without effort, but in the well-known parable of the grasshopper and the ant, the worker came out better than the one who trusted his luck. Of course, for fuller information, you would also consider the nature of the sign(s) and house(s) involved in your conjunction (and all other aspects that you analyze). Anything which is truly central in your nature will be repeated in the horoscope by different aspects or planet in house or planet in sign combinations. Notice what comes up again and again in astrological interpretations. Repetition reveals significance. (Familiarity with the astrological alphabet will help you to quickly and easily spot many repetitive themes.)

Ideally, conjuncting planets are separated by zero degrees. Few aspects, however, are exact to the degree. Astrology uses a concept called "orb" to handle that. The orb of an aspect refers to how many degrees **away** from exact the aspect can be, and still be considered relevant. (If, for example, an individual's Sun is at 5° Capricorn and the Moon is at 10° Capricorn, are the Sun and Moon conjunct? What if the Moon is at 15° or 20° or Capricorn? Is that still a conjunction?) Astrologers have differing opinions in regard to orb, but all agree that the tighter (closer to exact) an aspect is, the more important it is! So closer aspects are given more weight in any analysis. (A table of suggested orbs is provided later.)

As has already been indicated, a conjunction is not the only aspect which exists, but the conjunction is the most significant of all aspects. Other aspects (angular separations between the planets) provide additional information regarding the drives represented by the planets. Subject to the complications discussed briefly above, aspects other than the conjunction fall into two groups: (1) **harmonious** (indicating parts of our nature which tend to combine easily, support and reinforce one another, where we may overdo) and (2) **challenging** (indicating parts of our nature which tend to be at odds with one another; where we have to work to make room for differing drives, for ambivalent needs). With **any** aspect, the nature of the two planets involved is **most** significant, but some additional subtle shadings are implied, depending upon the aspect involved.

One can consider the conjunction the fundamental aspect. Even if two planets make an aspect other than a conjunction, it is worthwhile to read text interpreting a conjunction between them, as it will usually delineate the major issues and themes involved. Actually, it is a good idea to read descriptions of all of the planet-pairs which are aspecting each other in your chart. (See *Astro Essentials* for interpretations of every possible conjunction, harmony and conflict aspect in your horoscope.) Even with a harmony aspect, there may still be some issues you are working on, and you may have resolved the tension suggested by a conflict aspect so that you are handling the two sides of life quite successfully.

Five aspects other than the conjunction are considered important by many astrologers. Most are a division of the 360° circle by a whole number (e.g., division by 2, 3, 4, and 6). Following is a list of the six major aspects plus a few key words indicating the meaning of each aspect. Also listed is the symbol astrologers use for each aspect and the fraction of the circle which each aspect represents. Illustrations follow to graphically show the angular relationships between planets. (Other aspects exist besides those listed here, but these are the basics.)

0°: conjunction—blending, combining, living together, role models, intensification, concentration, focus ☌.

60° (one-sixth of the circle): sextile—mild harmony; compatibility; may be opportunity, attraction or support ⚹.

90° (one-fourth of the circle): square—conflict, competition, challenges, inner and/or outer tension, may point to turning points □.

120° (one-third of the circle): trine—harmony, mutual reinforcement which could lead to excesses, easy flow, natural talents △.

150° (five-twelfths of the circle): quincunx—difficult to combine, very different desires, seeming incompatibility, may feel like a forced choice is necessary, tendency to pull apart, may need to improve/adjust or to figure out what to keep and what to throw away ⚻.

180° (one-half of the circle): opposition—polarities, natural partners, seesaw tendencies, potential for awareness (and projection—attracting other people who express disowned parts of one's own nature), could flip from one extreme to the other until synthesis is reached ☍.

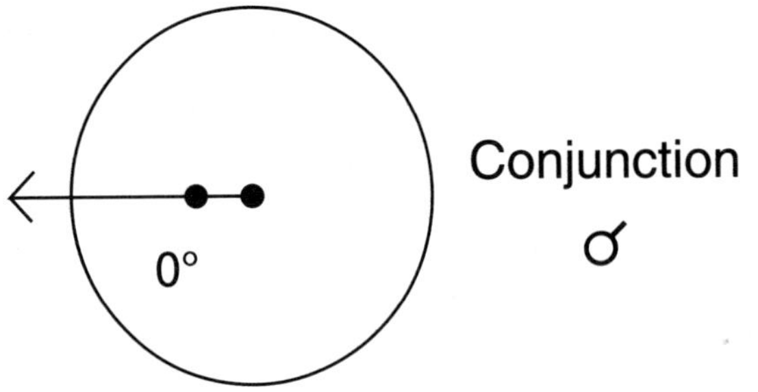

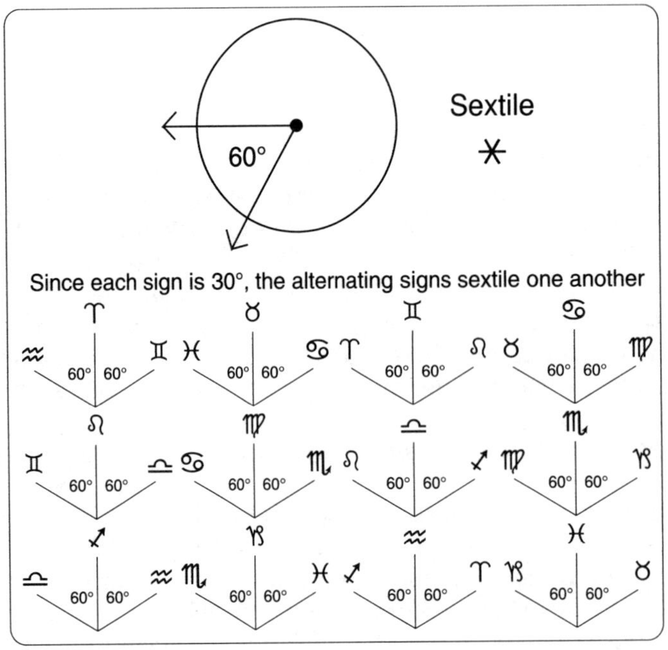

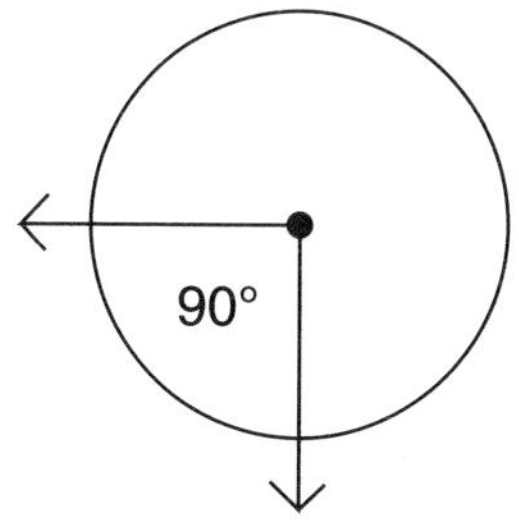

Square

□

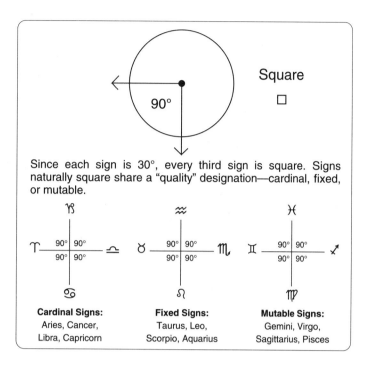

Since each sign is 30°, every third sign is square. Signs naturally square share a "quality" designation—cardinal, fixed, or mutable.

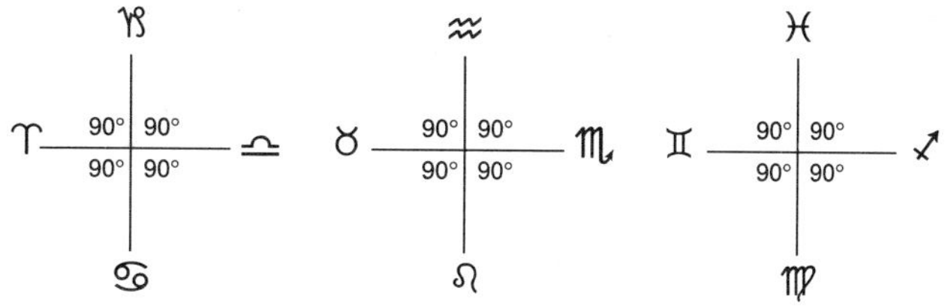

Cardinal Signs:
Aries, Cancer,
Libra, Capricorn

Fixed Signs:
Taurus, Leo,
Scorpio, Aquarius

Mutable Signs:
Gemini, Virgo,
Sagittarius, Pisces

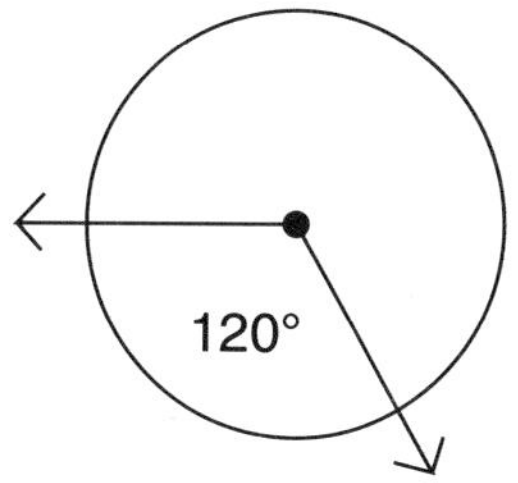

Trine

△

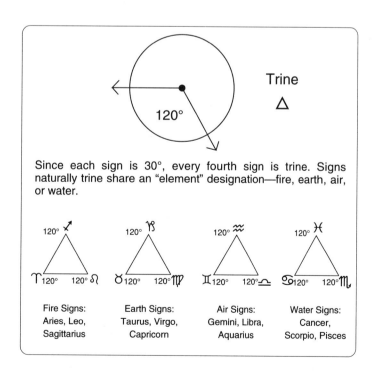

Since each sign is 30°, every fourth sign is trine. Signs naturally trine share an "element" designation—fire, earth, air, or water.

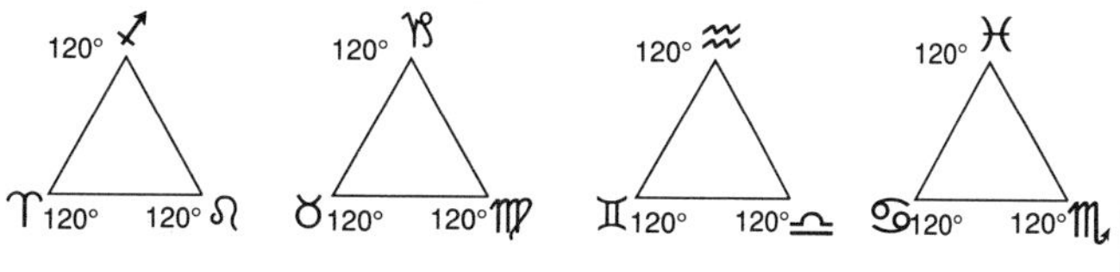

Fire Signs:
Aries, Leo,
Sagittarius

Earth Signs:
Taurus, Virgo,
Capricorn

Air Signs:
Gemini, Libra,
Aquarius

Water Signs:
Cancer,
Scorpio, Pisces

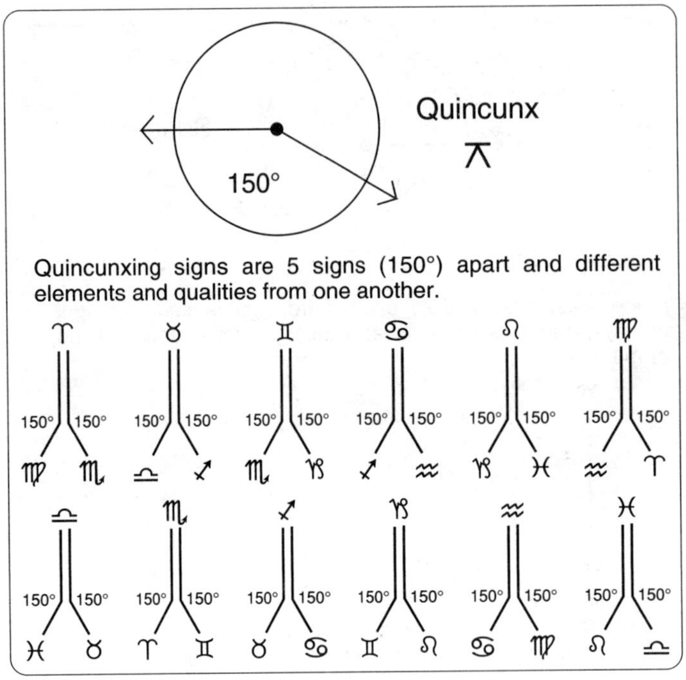

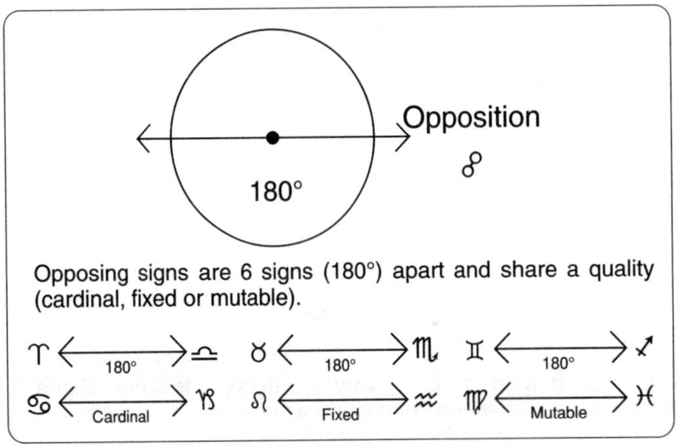

Below, is a table of suggested orbs.

0°	conjunction	☌	8° orb (or 8 degrees + or -)
60°	sextile	⚹	3° orb (or 57° to 63 °)
90°	square	□	6° orb (or 84° to 96 °)
120°	trine	△	6° orb (or 114° to 126 °)
150°	quincunx	⚻	3° orb (or 147° to 153 °)
180°	opposition	☍	6° orb (or 174° to 186 °)

You can experiment with simple key word combinations for your aspects. Some sentences might sound a bit awkward. If so, a little thought will clarify matters. If, for example, the Sun conjuncts Venus, you might say: "Your life force is tied to your drive for pleasure." This suggests the person feels most vital and alive when indulging the physical senses, exercising aesthetic talents or engaged in activity with partners.

It is important to remember that all aspects can be reversed. Think in terms of an automatic "and vice versa" at the end of all your sentences. Thus, a Sun conjunct Mercury could be interpreted as: "Your self-esteem is tied to your ability to communicate." (Reverse: "Your ability to communicate is tied to your self-esteem.") This gets across the idea that the person gains pride and feels best about him/herself when communicating effectively. It also implies that the individual will not communicate well when feeling low in self-esteem.

In addition to the many psychological principles which aspects symbolize, they can point to issues in different life areas in the outer world which are associated with each planet. Aspects can be keys to how you might (or might not) get along with other people in your life. Following is a list of the people/objects in your life who can be represented by the planets.

Sun:	loved ones (especially children/lovers); husband; leader; father; seller/promoter.
Moon:	home; family; mother (figure); women; wife; the public; immovable resources; land; food; commodities.
Mercury:	relatives; neighbors; short trips; brothers and sisters; means of transportation; trade/commerce.
Venus:	self-earned money; possessions; the arts; partners.
Mars:	personal action; men; competition; accidents; energy; physical body, mechanical objects, metal tools and weapons.
Jupiter:	in-laws; grandchildren; long trips; higher education; sports; churches, libraries, law courts, publishing.
Saturn:	authority figures; boss; older people; time; rules and roles; father (figure); societal structures, heights and falls.
Uranus:	friends; groups; causes; science; technology; the new; progress; revolutions; astrology; sudden changes.
Neptune:	mystical activities; drugs; glamor industries; film; secrets; illusions; psychic insights; inspired arts, healing arts.
Pluto:	mates; hidden matters; occult studies; research; debts; pollution; obsessions; death/endings; unconscious complexes.

Harmony (sextiles, trines) and conflict (squares, quincunxes and oppositions) aspects tend to be manifested more literally when other people are involved. Someone with a Moon-Mars square, quincunx or opposition, for example, is more likely to experience tension between men and women in his/her life (or at least be sensitive to such tension) than someone with a Moon-Mars trine or sextile.

Defense Mechanisms

People can and sometimes do attract outer conflicts as an unconscious mechanism for dealing with inner tension. Facing outer challenges may seem easier than dealing with inner ambivalences. If, however, we balance internally, outer relationships tend to flow more smoothly as well. Anyone with a Moon-Mars aspect (whether a conjunction, sextile, trine, square, quincunx or opposition) is facing inner issues around the integration of dependency and independence, separation and attachment, being alone and being together, spontaneous expression versus cautious holding in, and anger versus tenderness. The individual with a harmony aspect is likely to find it somewhat easier to balance these different needs, than the individual with a conflict aspect, but both must face the Moon-Mars issues.

The three major defense mechanisms used by individuals to deal with inner conflict are **repression** (or denial), **projection**, and **displacement**. **Repression** means simply burying something in the unconscious and forgetting that we buried it. If we push something underground long enough, the most likely outcome is psychic stress and then (potentially) physical illness. Usually the illness is connected to whatever drive we are repressing. If we deny the Martian side of our nature, we may be subject to frequent headaches or colds; if we deny the Moon side of our nature, we may be subject to stomach problems. (Each planet is associated with different parts of the body, beginning with Mars and Aries for the head and ending with Pisces and Neptune at the feet. That, however, is a topic for another book. See, for example, the chapter on repression in *Healing with the Horoscope*.) If we find certain kinds of ailments recurring, however, it is worthwhile to query whether the issue might be related to unresolved needs and drives and not purely physical in manifestation.

Projection (like the projector of movies on a screen) refers to "projecting" our unrecognized needs or drives onto other people. Generally, however, this is not a matter of imagination, but rather a matter of unconsciously being attracted to people who manifest qualities we deny in ourselves. The psyche appears to abhor a vacuum and draws into our lives people who bring us face to face with what we have not developed within. The only problem is, the other person (living out our unrealized drive) is usually doing the expression to excess. As an example, the individual who totally denies his/her own Martian drive for assertion and self-expression may attract others who carry it to excess, perhaps in violence, perhaps in cutthroat competition, perhaps in extreme self-centeredness.

Projection offers us an opportunity to recognize what we have been denying and make a **moderate** place for it in our lives and psyches. The goal is not to become like the other person (who is usually overdoing what we have been underdoing), but to recognize the validity of that inner need and find a constructive outlet for it.

Displacement refers to doing the right thing in the wrong place. At times we may express our different drives and needs, but perhaps in circumstances which are inappropriate. That does not mean those drives or needs are "bad"—only that we need to find the "right" time and place to express them. As an example, the degree of assertion and aggression which would be appropriate on a football field is not appropriate for a quiet evening at home with friends or family. Each of us has a Martian side and must choose when, where, and how to express it constructively.

Aspect Review

When first learning aspects, mixing and matching key words can be instructive. You might say, for example, with a Jupiter-Saturn conjunction that your career (Saturn) is tied to (conjunct) travel, education or philosophy (Jupiter). You could also say that your world view (Jupiter) is likely to be (conjunct) realistic (Saturn). Another choice would be that father or authority figures (Saturn) are (conjunct) jovial, extraverted, confident, extravagant or optimistic (Jupiter). Or you might idealize (Jupiter) your father (Saturn) or be disillusioned by his failure (Saturn) to live up to your ideals (Jupiter). And there are many other combinations available! By mixing and matching aspect key words and planetary key words you can come up with additional possibilities. Be open to seeing the variety of potentials that astrology pictures.

Practice Example

Check what you've learned about spotting aspects with the horoscope on the next page. Remember that each sign has 30 degrees and each degree has 60 minutes.

First, we consider **conjunctions**. Are there any planets occupying the same degree of the same sign? No. Are there any planets within 8 degrees (our allowable orb) of each other? No. There are, however, planets within 8 degrees of our horoscope angles. Mercury is 1° 28' away from the 7th house cusp (also called the Descendant). [The Descendant is 25 Pisces 32 and Mercury is 24 Pisces 04. That is a difference of 1° 28'.] The Moon is 2° 10' from the 10th house cusp (Midheaven). Saturn is 8° 0' from the 1st house cusp (Ascendant). Mars is 5° 48' from the 4th house cusp (also called I.C.).

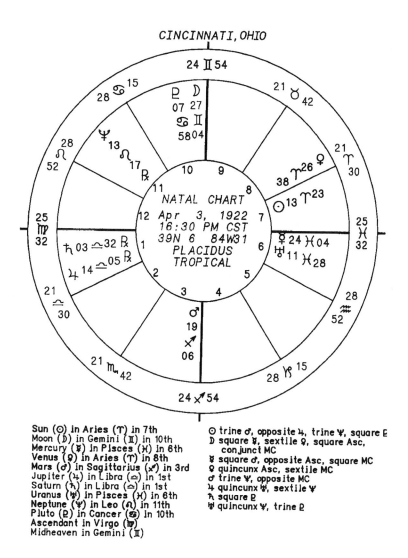

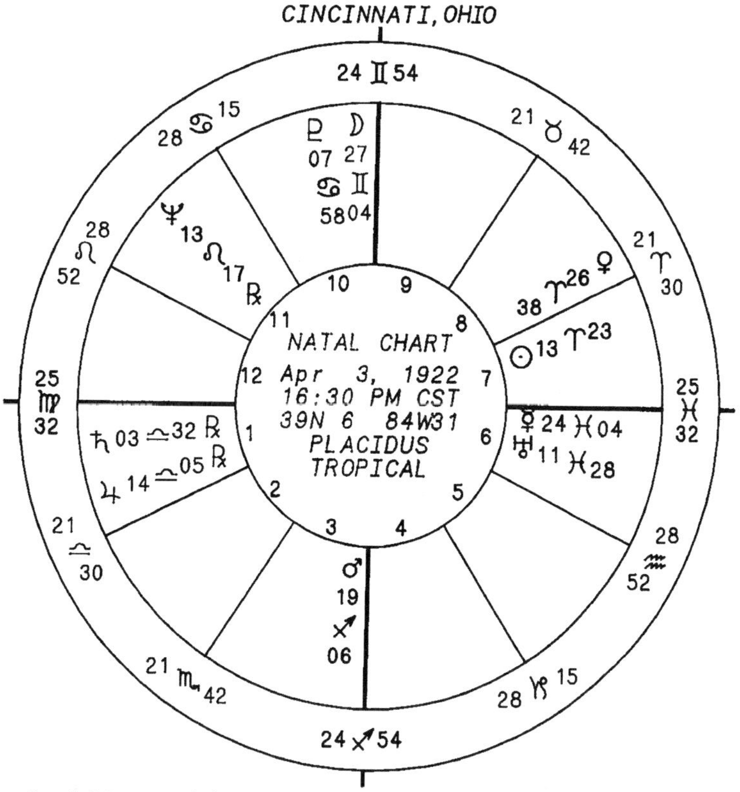

Sun (☉) in Aries (♈) in 7th
Moon (☽) in Gemini (♊) in 10th
Mercury (☿) in Pisces (♓) in 6th
Venus (♀) in Aries (♈) in 8th
Mars (♂) in Sagittarius (♐) in 3rd
Jupiter (♃) in Libra (♎) in 1st
Saturn (♄) in Libra (♎) in 1st
Uranus (♅) in Pisces (♓) in 6th
Neptune (♆) in Leo (♌) in 11th
Pluto (♇) in Cancer (♋) in 10th
Ascendant in Virgo (♍)
Midheaven in Gemini (♊)

☉ trine ♂, opposite ♃, trine ♆, square ♇
☽ square ☿, sextile ♀, square Asc, conjunct MC
☿ square ♂, opposite Asc, square MC
♀ quincunx Asc, sextile MC
♂ trine ♆, opposite MC
♃ quincunx ♅, sextile ♆
♄ square ♇
♅ quincunx ♆, trine ♇

We might expect, then, Saturnian themes (responsible, hardworking, career-oriented) in terms of identity and self-expression (the Ascendant). We would expect Martian themes (active, restless, assertive, independent) in terms of the home and family (4th cusp). We would suspect Mercurial issues (communication, thinking, and work, health, competence) to be significant in relationships. We would look for a lunar (Moon) focus (family, nurturing, emotional closeness, caring, protection) within the career (Midheaven).

Sextiles are 60° aspects. In this chart we have the Sun and Moon in signs naturally sextile each other, but the Sun and Moon are farther apart than the 3° orb we are allowing for sextiles. Venus and the Moon are not too far apart, however. The Moon is 60° 26' away from Venus—well within our orb (57° - 63°). Also, Jupiter is 60° 48' ahead of Neptune—again an allowable sextile.

The Venus/Moon harmony suggests friendliness, sociability, charm, grace and attractiveness. The feminine is highlighted in that combination as both planets can signify women. The Jupiter/Neptune harmony suggests idealism, quest for something more, desire to rescue, save, or uplift in some fashion.

Squares (90°) are next. We note that the Sun barely makes a square to Pluto (with an orb of 5°25'). The Moon squares the Ascendant/Descendant axis (with an orb of 1° 32'). The Moon also squares Mercury (orb of 3° 0'). This individual may feel tension between thinking (Mercury) and feeling (Moon) and may be torn between nurturing and protecting (Moon), versus defending her own rights and needs (Ascendant) versus sharing the world with another person (Descendant). Pluto squares Saturn and the orb is 4° 26'. The Pluto squares to Sun and Saturn can be indicators of power struggles, especially with authority figures. It is usually helpful to channel the drive into competitive sports, business, or politics where we fight for causes in a constructive manner. Mars squares Mercury with an orb of 4° 58'. This suggests a quick mind, a quick tongue and possibly the ability to use words as weapons (debate, sarcasm, extemporaneous speaking, etc.).

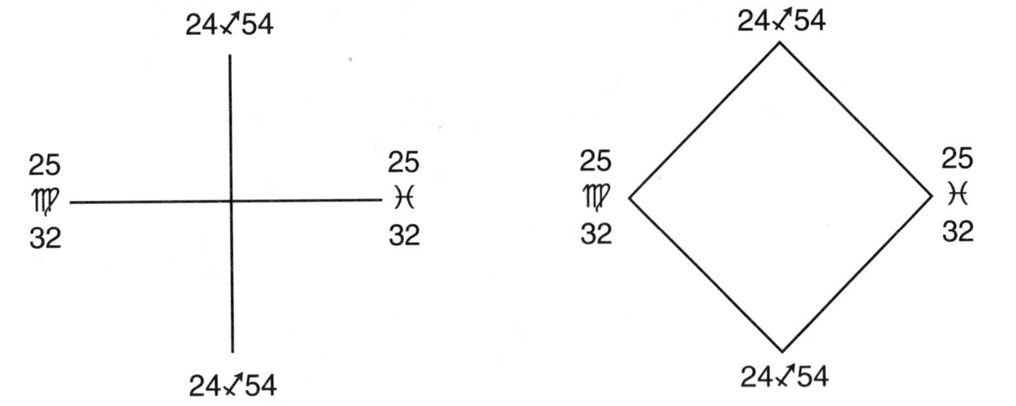

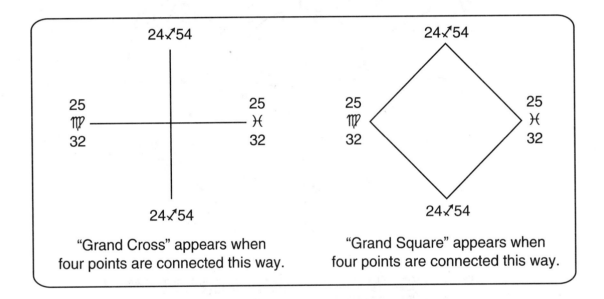

"Grand Cross" appears when four points are connected this way.

"Grand Square" appears when four points are connected this way.

Notice that all of the angles of this horoscope are closely square one another: the Ascendant (and the Descendant) square the IC (and the Midheaven) with an orb of 0° 38'. This configuration, of four planets or points each 90° from the next, is called a **grand cross** or **grand square**. It indicates more inner conflict and challenge than four, unrelated squares. Since the angles occupy mutable signs, we would expect the issues to particularly revolve around issues of thinking, communication, and idealism. A mutable challenge includes tension between the real and the ideal—the necessities of getting along in the world, making a living and understanding others—versus our dreams and visions of utopia, something more, and something ecstatic or inspirational. A common manifestation is wanting more than is possible, never being satisfied. A more positive potential is a marriage of practicality and idealism so that the person works hard (and sensibly) to achieve his/her dreams over time.

The Sun **trines** (120°) Neptune very closely; the orb is zero degrees and only 6 minutes! (The Sun is just within the 6° [5°43'] orb of a trine to Mars.) Neptune trines Mars (orb of 5° 49'). Both Neptune aspects point to strong, personal idealism, romanticism, urge to rescue, compassion and potential grace in action or beauty in motion. Mars trine Sun suggests high energy, enthusiasm, courage and fighting spirit. We also note that Uranus trines Pluto (with an orb of 3° 30'). This can suggest the political reformer, the person who puts passion into humanitarian instincts, the individual who can balance their needs for independence and for emotional commitment.

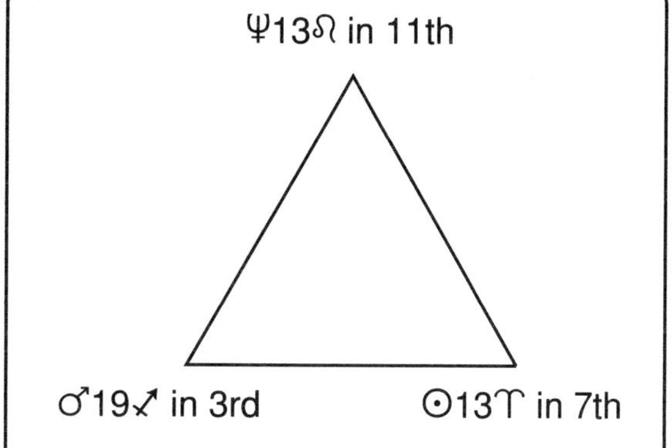

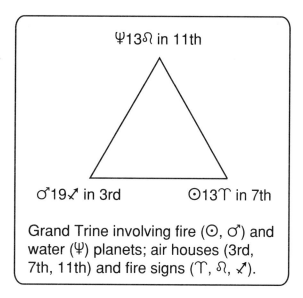

Grand Trine involving fire (☉, ♂) and water (♆) planets; air houses (3rd, 7th, 11th) and fire signs (♈, ♌, ♐).

This chart has a **grand trine**—three planets, each 120° [give or take our 6° orb] from the next (Sun, Neptune, Mars). Grand trines indicate strong inner harmony, talents and abilities (but also potential excess) more emphatically than three, unrelated trines.

Trines in fire signs (or involving Sun, Mars, Jupiter or 1st, 5th, 9th houses) point to confidence, extraversion, expression, faith, movement and initiation. Trines in earth signs (or involving Venus, Mercury, Saturn or 2nd, 6th, 10th houses) point to practicality, a literal focus, concern with tangible results, ability in the material plane. Trines in air signs (or involving Mercury, Venus or Uranus or 3rd, 7th, 11th houses) point to communication skills, capacity to detach and be objective, a focus on ideas and people. Trines in water signs (or involving Moon, Pluto, Neptune or 4th, 8th, 12th houses) point to sensitivity, intuition, inward tendencies, merging instincts, emotional depth.

Quincunxes are next (150°). Uranus forms two quincunxes. One is to Neptune (1° 49' orb) and the other is to Jupiter (2° 37' orb). You will recall that Jupiter and Neptune are sextile one another. This aspect configuration of two planets sextile each other and both quincunx a third is called a "yod" or double quincunx. It carries even more restlessness and instability than two unrelated quincunxes.

The yod of Uranus to Neptune and Jupiter suggests a challenge integrating idealism with independence, or compassion with detachment. Restlessness and constant activity are likely in the transpersonal realm (dealing with large issues and the wider reach of humanity).

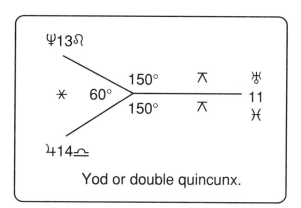

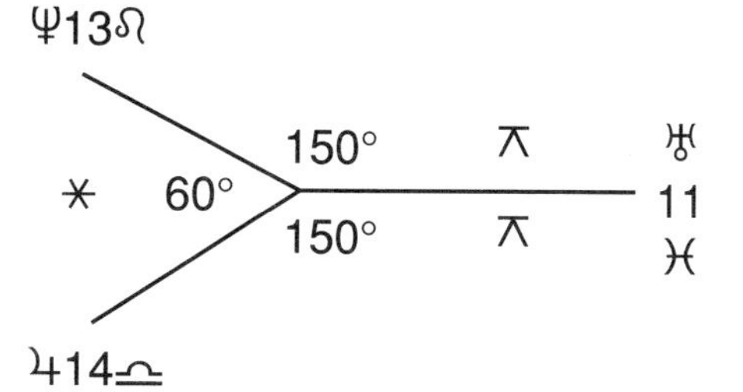

Yod or double quincunx.

Finally, we consider **oppositions** (180°). The Sun is closely opposite Jupiter (with an orb of 0° 42'). This opposition highlights emotional idealism, the importance of beliefs and values, the capacity to be swept away in "grand" projects, a need for excitement, expansion and a tendency to seek the best. Although they occupy opposing signs (Aries/Libra), the Sun is too far from an exact opposition to Saturn to count it (past a 6° orb). The Moon and Mars are naturally opposite in terms of their signs, but are outside our allowable orb. Similarly, the Sun to Saturn, and Venus to Saturn and to Jupiter, although in opposite signs, are not within the 6° orb we are using.

For the curious reader, these aspects and the horoscope above belong to Doris Day—an actress noted for her family-oriented movies in which she played very feminine, charming roles. She is now a political activist on behalf of animals (founder of the Doris Day Animal League, which campaigns against testing and abuses of animals).

The pages which follow offer tools to further explore the ancient wisdom of Astrology.
Enjoy your journey of discovery!

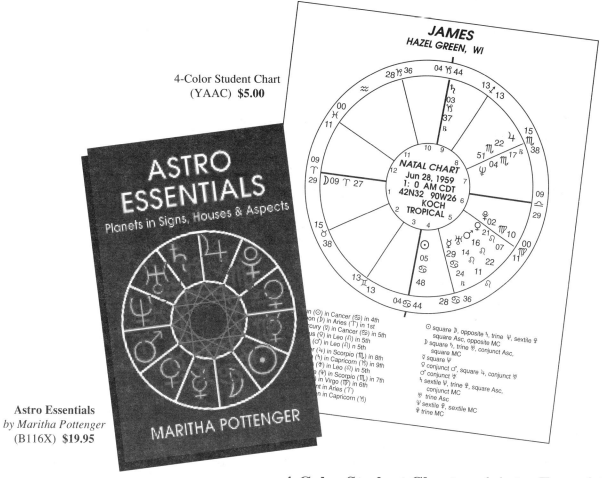

Also by ACS Publications

Your Starway to Love

Comprehensive Compatibility Worksheet

Your Name: ______________________________

Your Partner's Name: ______________________________

♥ Love Line	☉	☽	☿	♀	♂	ASC	Totals
☉	♥	✻		✚			
☽	✻	♥		★			
☿			♥				
♀	✚	★		♥	❢		
♂				❢	♥		
ASC						♥	
Totals							Shared Strengths

Grid of Gratification

Shared Strengths: ☐ **Bonus Bonds:** ☐

Positive Planets (check any):

Yours		Your Partner's	
☉ ☐	♀ ☐	☉ ☐	♀ ☐
☽ ☐	♂ ☐	☽ ☐	♂ ☐
☿ ☐	ASC ☐	☿ ☐	ASC ☐

Love Line: ♥ ☐

Togetherness: ✻ ☐

Sexual Sizzle: ❢ ☐

Attraction & Affection: ✚ ☐

Close Comfort: ★ ☐

Your Starway to Love

Quick Compatibility Worksheet

(Also for No Birth Time)

Your Name:________________________________

Your Partner's Name:________________________________

♥ Love Line	☉	☽	☿	♀	♂
☉	♥				
☽		♥			
☿			♥		
♀				♥	
♂					♥